Roget's Thesaurus

Roget's Thesaurus
of English words and phrases

New edition prepared by
***Susan M. Lloyd** BA MPhil*

ACADEMIC PRESS CANADA
TORONTO

Longman Group Limited
Longman House,
Burnt Mill,
Harlow, Essex

First Edition by Peter Mark Roget 1852

New and Enlarged Edition by John Lewis Roget 1879

New Edition Revised and Enlarged
by Samuel Romilly Roget 1936

New Edition revised and modernized
by Robert A. Dutch O B E 1962

New Edition prepared
by Susan M. Lloyd 1982
Fifth impression 1984

ISBN 7747 0137 4

Printed in Great Britain

Contents

Acknowledgments	vi
Editor's Preface, 1982:	
What is a thesaurus?	vii
The present edition	ix
Dr Peter Mark Roget and his Thesaurus	xiii
Roget's Preface to the original edition, 1852	xix
Roget's Introduction	xxi
Instructions: the Text	xxxiii
the Index	xxxiv
Plan of Classification	xxxvi
Tabular Synopsis of Categories	xxxviii
Text	1
Index	629

Acknowledgments

This revision has been undertaken under the aegis of the Longman Dictionary and Reference Book Department (Paul Procter, John Ayto, Janet Whitcut, Ruth Swan, Beverley Britton, Catharine Freer, Elaine Roberts, Ursula Lawrence and Linda O'Donnell), and with the help and expert advice of the following past and present members of the Lexicographic Unit: Tim Burton, Roger Cohen, Norman Gill, Ellayne Parker, Paul Surzyn and Kathy Seed, and in particular Faye Carney, Robin Mann and Penny Stock, who also proofread the text and made valuable suggestions at every stage. Thanks are also due to Clive McKeough (production), Ken Moore (data processing), Chris Kirby (marketing) and to Paul Price-Smith and Randall Harris for designing the layout and jacket; also to Robert Fairchild and his colleagues at CDS Ltd., for coming to grips with the not inconsiderable computer technology involved.

The editor would also like to thank all those readers who have taken the trouble to write in with criticisms and suggestions, and hopes they will continue to do so. Finally, I must express my gratitude to friends and relations who have taken a constructive interest in the work of revision, and especially to Geoff, Ruth and Stephen Lloyd, without whose patient understanding and support it could not have been completed.

S.M.L.

Preface

to the 1982 edition

What is a thesaurus?

Roget's Thesaurus is well-known to word-lovers and word-users as a collection of words and phrases arranged according to ideas rather than alphabetically—a 'treasure house' of language as its name, taken from the Greek, implies. Generations have found it invaluable in finding the most apt, the most accurate, the most telling or the most elegant expression for their thoughts. Roget began to compile a simple wordlist for his own use when quite a young man, and during his long and active life, which included much writing and lecturing (see pp xiii–xv), he continued to improve and add to it. Finally he spent some years of his retirement preparing it for publication, considering that others might find such a compilation as helpful as he himself had. The immediate and continuing popularity of the *Thesaurus* showed that he was right.

The originality of the *Thesaurus*

It could be argued that the success of the *Thesaurus* is due to its combination of the philosophical and the practical. There had been practical wordlists arranged according to topics before, but these were mainly simple vocabularies intended for students of a foreign language, and consequently the topics were listed in no logical order and often seemed arbitrarily chosen. Roget arranged his far more extensive material into a comprehensive framework with a clearly visible structure, in which each topic, or concept, had its own logical place. In this, he was following in the steps of the seventeenth-century philosophers such as Leibniz, who had attempted the classification of concepts as a preliminary to inventing a Universal Language (this was a language of symbols rather than words which could be universally understood, as each symbol would represent a particular concept). Roget was a particular admirer of Bishop Wilkins, whose influential work "An Essay towards a Real Character and Philosophical Language" had appeared in 1668 (see *Roget's Introduction to the 1852 edition*, p xxxi). Wilkins's system of classification finds many echoes in the *Thesaurus,* but his project of inventing symbols to represent individual concepts was too cumbersome for use either for communication or as a tool for analytical and scientific thought. While Roget approved of Wilkins's aims, and expressed the wish that his own classification might be instrumental in preparing the way for further investigations into a Universal Language, his primary intention in compiling the *Thesaurus* was more practical: to offer the reader a choice of expressions from which he or she could choose the most suitable or the most effective in a given context. His task, then, was twofold. First, like the philosophers, he had to create a hierarchy of concepts which would provide the framework for his book; then he had to discover and classify the language which would express these concepts. While the philosophers sought to simplify, in order to discover what they hoped were the limited number of concepts basic to any language, Roget had to recognize and come to grips with the protean ambiguity of language itself, with all its interrelationships and its infinite capacity for expressing shades of meaning. This was the Herculean labour which Roget undertook, and as his *Introduction* makes clear, he fully realised its difficulties and pitfalls. The result was an entirely new tool for the word-user: the *Thesaurus.*

Dictionaries, synonym dictionaries and the *Thesaurus*

As Roget pointed out in his *Introduction,* a thesaurus is just the opposite of a dictionary in that a dictionary offers meanings for a given word, while a thesaurus offers words to express a given meaning. An unknown or alternative word cannot be found from a dictionary, as without knowing how it is spelt there is no way to look it up. To fulfil this need, synonym dictionaries have been compiled – several were already in print by 1852, when *Roget's Thesaurus* was published. The purpose of these, however, was different from that of the *Thesaurus,* as by discriminating between several words close in meaning, they narrowed the choice for their readers. Roget, on the contrary, aimed to enlarge the scope for the reader, offering a wide range of expressions from which he or she could make their own choice. These might include synonyms or near synonyms, but this was coincidental. His main purpose was to illustrate every aspect of the topic under consideration. Ironically, the success of *Roget's Thesaurus* was not without its effect on synonym dictionaries, which began to interpret the term 'synonym' far more loosely, to include words which coincided in only part of their meaning. Such works have often dropped the practice of discriminating between the expressions they offer, and some claim to be a 'thesaurus in dictionary form'. The two, however, synonym dictionary and thesaurus, remain distinct forms, as they have different functions. The synonym dictionary provides alternatives for a given word, whether it distinguishes between them or not, while a thesaurus offers a variety of ways to express a given idea. The range of a thesaurus, too, is far more comprehensive, as it includes concepts represented by only one term, while a synonym dictionary concerns itself with those concepts for which several terms are available. It is the classification of words according to ideas which makes the scope of a thesaurus possible, while it also ensures that related expressions are found together. The alphabetical arrangement of synonym dictionaries means that analogous terms are separated from each other by differences in spelling, even if they are only different forms of the same word. 'Pride' and 'proud', for example, may be several entries apart. Sometimes, too, as in this case, where there is no verbal form, there will be no list of verbal synonyms.

The advantages of a thesaurus

By contrast, in the *Thesaurus*, all the words dealing with the same idea are grouped together in one place, regardless of their spelling and grammatical function. Every topic is followed by its negative, if there is one, and sometimes by a correlative topic, so that every aspect of each is represented. Closely related topics follow each other in the text, or are indicated by cross-references. The reader can therefore inspect all the ways of expressing a given concept, and choose the most suitable. If a noun, say, cannot be found to convey the exact shade of meaning required, a verb may be substituted. Rephrasing the sentence in the negative may prove more effective or add variety to the writer's style. Not only new words, but new ideas may result from consulting the *Thesaurus.* A cross-reference may suggest a new train of thought, or a metaphor a new image. The reader may recognize the word lurking at the back of his or her mind, or discover a new one to add to his or her own wordstock. The range of vocabulary offered in a thesaurus is wider than that in a synonym dictionary: metaphors, euphemisms, catchphrases, slang, poetic and literary expressions, archaisms, illustrations from history, literature and everyday life – all are grist to the mill of a thesaurus as long as they illustrate the topic in question.

Who will find a thesaurus useful?

The special arrangement and wide range of the *Thesaurus* make it an invaluable tool for *anyone* concerned with language, whether they are writing a speech, a novel or a letter. Not only does it offer expressions for every occasion, it encourages the formation of a better style, by obviating repetition and suggesting alternative ways of structuring sentences. It is conducive to clarity of thought and expression by making the user more aware of what he or she wishes to say, by offering a choice between several alternatives representing every shade of meaning.

Creative writers such as poets, playwrights, novelists and above all, translators, naturally give *Roget's Thesaurus* a special place on their bookshelves, not only for the quantity of its vocabulary but for its variety of register, from the everyday to the poetic; the possibilities of finding a suitable rhyme or a striking simile, too, are greatly enhanced by following up the cross-references. But students of English will also find the work helpful, especially in writing essays, as the grouping of words under topics provides them with a ready source of suitable expressions and reminds them of the ideas connected with the subject under consideration. Linguists will find ready-made semantic fields, with cross-references to suggest the links between them. Roget, as we have noted above, had linguists very much in mind when he constructed the *Thesaurus.* In view of the renewed interest in the possibility of reducing language to its basic concepts, it is to be hoped that Roget's aspirations for the *Thesaurus* in this connection may at last be realized.

The present edition

Since Longman (then known as Longman, Brown, Green and Longmans) first published Roget's *Thesaurus of English words and Phrases* in 1852, it has been revised many times. (The history of the *Thesaurus* is traced in "Dr Peter Mark Roget and his Thesaurus", pp xvi–xviii). The most recent revision was undertaken in 1962 by Robert A. Dutch OBE, who gave the *Thesaurus* its present form, reducing the number of Heads to 990, and printing them consecutively rather than in contrasting pairs. He also introduced the idea of keywords. Roget's system of classification has, however, survived all revisions virtually unchanged, as it has proved capable of absorbing new concepts and new vocabulary. The present edition, like its predecessors, should therefore be seen rather as an overhaul of an efficient and valuable machine, than as an attempt to completely rebuild it. New refinements have been added, worn parts replaced, and advantage taken of modern computer technology to ensure reliability and smooth working.

* * * *

The main task has been to incorporate the huge number of new expressions generated by twenty years of rapid technological change, and the corresponding changes in our lifestyle. A modern man or woman may work as a *Eurocrat*, an *ombudsman*, a *troubleshooter*, a *psephologist*, a *spokesperson*, an *anchorman*, a *gogo dancer* or a *DJ.* Their children may be *yobs*, *punks*, *skinheads*, *groupies*, or *Hell's Angels*, learn *modern maths* at the local *poly* or *sixthform college*, attend a *playgroup* or study *structuralism* with the *Open University.* They pay *VAT* and *PAYE*, but do not practise *tax evasion* as they disapprove of the *black economy.* Instead they *bulk-buy* at the *cash and carry* with their *credit cards.* They may live in a *tower block*, a *mobile home*, a *listed building* or *condemned housing*, while their mother has a *granny flat.* Their home has *solar panels* and a *heat exchanger*, and is *sound-proofed* against *sonic boom.* They eat *junk food* from a *takeaway*, though some are *vegans* eating *wholefood*, or *dropouts* into *self-sufficiency.* They wear *kagoules*, *caftans*, *bodystockings*, *jumpsuits*, *homeknits*, or *unisex hipsters*, which they buy *off-the-peg* at a *boutique* or in a *bargain basement.* They speak *Basic English*, *franglais* and *Strine*, but sometimes they *fudge* with *weasel words* and *buzz words.* To get to work, they travel along a *ring road*, *bus lane*, *cycleway* or *pedestrian precinct*, driving a *hatchback*, *minicab*, *gas guzzler* or a *juggernaut.* They might take the *high speed train* or the *intercity*, but the *jet set* prefer to go by *jumbo jet*, *chopper* or *airbus*, in spite of *hijackings* and *jetlag*, and may plan to take off in a *space shuttle* to look for *UFOs.*

To amuse themselves, they go *hang-gliding*, *wind-surfing*, *sky-diving*, *backpacking*, or *orienteering*, visit a *safari park*, or play *bingo* at the *community centre. Discos* attract those who are *with it*, others feel more *laidback* listening to *reggae* or *country-and-western* on the *hifi*; they might read some *sci-fi*, dip into a *coffee-table book*, or watch a *telethon*, *sitcom*, *dramadocumentary* or *soap opera* on the *box* or the *video*. Some get their *kicks* from *jogging*, others from *yoga* or *TM*. If they go to a *shrink* with their *hang-ups*, he will set them *role-playing* in an *encounter group*, or is this just an *ego trip*? If they consult a *naturopath*, a *barefoot doctor* or a *paramedic* with a *bleeper*, he or she may study their *biorhythms*, and prescribe *hormone therapy*, *pep pills* or *EST*. If they become unconscious, they may be put on a *life support system* or given the *kiss of life*.

The neighbours include a *mole*, a *lookalike* and a *talking head*. One is a *cowboy* who *rips off* his customers with *downmarket double glazing*. Another is a *groovy trendy* who has good *vibes* – when he is *psyched up*. In a *squat* nearby live a *dissident*, a *single parent family*, a couple of *gays* and a *captain of industry* given a *golden handshake* by his *multinational*.

In their own *nuclear family*, the brother is an *ex-directory supergrass* who *keeps a low profile* since he *got on the gravy train* with *leaks* to the *colour supplements*. The sister, a *conservationist* who *recycles* whatever is not *biodegradable*, is a *militant* who does a lot of *legwork* for *civil rights* and *women's lib*. Her husband is a *Male Chauvinist Pig* and not *supportive* as a *house-husband*, but they have a *meaningful* relationship and go to *sit-ins* together. All of them would like to see the *neutron bomb* put down a *black hole* or lost in a *time warp*.

* * * *

We live in a technological age, and this accounts for a large proportion of the vocabulary which is new to the *Thesaurus*. New paragraphs have been added to deal with *data processing*, *microelectronics*, *space travel* and *sources of energy*, while existing paragraphs on *nucleonics*, *bombs*, *spaceships* and *satellites*, to name but a few, have been expanded. The danger here is to betray Roget's intention of catering primarily for the layman. But most of us have become familiar with *strobes*, *lasers*, *aerosols*, *silicon chips*, *word processors* and *PWRs*, and at least the names of sciences such as *robotics*, *cybernetics*, *computer programming* and *advanced technology*. Many of these terms are also found in commerce and industry, which adds *ergonomics*, *market research*, *cost-benefit analysis* and *operational research*. (A new paragraph has been added for statistical terms.) We also have *factory farming* and *agribusiness*, *privatization* and *hiving off*, *fringe benefits* and *bridging loans*, *monetarism* and the *Common Market*, and unfortunately also *soft sell*, *hard sell* and *hype*. Telecommunications has seen the new science of *informatics*, technological developments such as *Viewdata*, *ENG* and *quadraphonic sound*, and terms such as *feedback*, *multimedia* and *bugging*.

The increasing part played by technology in our lives has led to a reaction against it by many people, who question whether the benefits it brings may not be outweighed by the problems it causes. *Ecology* and *conservation* are areas of increasing public awareness, and concepts such as *intermediate technology*, *renewable energy sources*, *recycling*, *post-industrial* and *greenhouse effect* are becoming familiar. Sociology and politics have also seen an explosion of terms: *The Third World*, *superpowers*, *multinationals* and the *global village*, for example. Modern warfare gives us *theatre nuclear weapons*, *cruise missiles*, *defoliation*, *overkill* and *fallout shelter*. Politics offers *grass roots*, *slush fund*, *quango* and *cover-up*, the *National Front* and the *Ecology Party*. The *Swinging Sixties* and the *permissive society* have contributed *doing your own thing*, *letting it all hang out* and the *open marriage*, but also *flashing*, *streaking*, *mugging* and *hard-core porn*. (A new paragraph has been devoted to *drug-taking*.) On the other hand, there is a growing awareness of the *civil rights* of every human being, seen in movements such as *feminism*, *Negritude*, *black power*, *women's liberation* and *gay lib*, and opposed to *sexism*, *ageism* and *machismo*. Linked with these are *positive discrimination*, *networking* and *civil disobedience*.

Advances in science and medicine have led to many new treatments, including *transplants*, *dialysis*, *immunotherapy*, *AID* and *fertility drugs*. (*Family planning* has been given a new paragraph.) We now have the *cyborg*, the *bionic man* and the *test-tube baby*, along with *fringe medicine*, *genetic engineering*, *clones* and *interferon*.

Living longer and healthier lives, we can spend more time and energy on leisure activities. Broadcasting, which provides much of our entertainment, has three new paragraphs, and film has one. Many new terms have also been added to relevant paragraphs such as those on literature, art forms and the drama, while ballet now has a paragraph to itself. In the field of philosophy and religion, we have *lateral thinking*, *transcendental meditation*, the *Baha'i faith*, new sects such as the *Moonies* and the *Rastafarians*, the *Hare Krishna* sect and *Black Muslims*. Names and places which have become familiarly associated with a particular idea include *Rachmanism*, *Leavisite*, the *Berlin Wall*, *Watergate*, *Heath Robinson*, *Carnaby Street*, *McCarthyism*, the *Peter principle* and the perhaps mythical *Murphy's Law*, while literature and film contribute *Catch-22*, *Pinteresque*, *Big Brother*, *King Kong*, *Lolita*, *hobbits* and *orcs*. Though not all of these appeared after 1962, they have become more familiar to us since then.

Finally the past decades have given us a ragbag of slang and jargon words which we may deplore, but which are now part of the language. These include *track record*, *hatchet job*, *disaster area*, *interface*, *infrastructure*, *ongoing*, *knock-on effect*, *freewheeling*, *on the ball*, *double think* and *walkabout*. All the terms given as examples represent just a fraction of those added during this revision.

Besides words representing new concepts, many old ones have been added to make the vocabulary of the *Thesaurus* more representative, or to give better coverage to ideas previously underrepresented. Words whose meanings have changed since 1962 also had to be reallocated to a more suitable position. It has also been our aim to include as many as possible of the idioms and colloquialisms which give liveliness and colour to the language. Many of these originated in American English, but only those which have become naturalized have been included. In listing nouns denoting people, we have borne in mind the fact that according to recent research the particle 'man', in such words as 'mankind', is not always taken, as formerly, to include men *and* women. Care has therefore been taken to include female terms as well, or general terms such as 'chairperson', where these exist.

Inevitably, the number of additions has meant that some deletions have had to be made. Bearing in mind the range of vocabulary which should be available in a thesaurus, this has not meant simply deleting obsolete words and archaisms. Only when such a word is both obsolete *and* forgotten can it be safely omitted. But there are other obvious candidates for deletion: yesterday's catchphrases, forgotten neologisms, unidiomatic expressions or explanatory phrases no longer needed. Less familiar words are not repeated under different Heads, as long as these can be found by using the cross-references. Latinisms that have dropped out of sight except in learned journals, and some abstruse classical or mythological allusions have also been removed. A few paragraphs felt to be of little interest to modern users, such as *theosophy* and *theomancy*, have been taken out, and any worthwhile material they contained incorporated into other paragraphs.

The lists (of animals, plants and so on), which Roget himself included rather apologetically (see his *Introduction*, p xxviii) have been retained, both for their usefulness to crossword puzzle enthusiasts, and because it is often helpful to be able to look up the name of something, such as a particular kind of tool or aircraft, which cannot be found from a dictionary. No attempt has been made to make these lists complete, but they have been brought up to date and expanded where necessary.

Changes to the actual layout of the *Thesaurus* have been few, and are designed to make the book more accessible to readers. The Heads are numbered as in the 1962 edition, with the following changes: *Propagation* has been separated from *Production* (164) and given a Head of its own, 167. *Producer*, formerly at 167 is now a paragraph within 164. The colours have been rearranged into the order of the spectrum, so that 432 becomes *Orange*,

434 *Greenness* and 436 *Purple.* The paragraphs *Messenger* and *Courier* have been moved to 529 *News* to leave room for *Broadcasting* in 531 *Communications.* Headwords and *keywords* play an important part in finding one's way around the *Thesaurus,* so they should be easily understandable and unambiguous. It has therefore been necessary to change many of them, but as they are still in their original position former users of the *Thesaurus* should quickly become accustomed to the replacements.

Roget's original layout contrasted positive and negative aspects of the same idea by printing the Heads opposite one another. This proved too space-consuming and later editions of the *Thesaurus* have printed the Heads consecutively. To remind readers of the ideas behind the *Thesaurus,* and to make more clear the relationship of one Head to another, we have set out the *Tabular Synopsis of Categories* to show pairs and opposites, as it did originally, and kept Roget's subtitles. It is hoped that this will enable the reader to understand the classification and find his or her own way around the text. A few titles have been changed or simplified: Division Two of Class Five is now called *Social volition*, while Class Six becomes *Emotion, religion and morality.* The Sections in Class Six have been renamed *General*, *Personal emotion*, *Interpersonal emotion*, *Morality* and *Religion.*

Still with the aim of keeping Roget's system in the reader's mind, we have added catchwords at the top of each page. Those on the left give the Class title, those on the right the Section title. The text itself has been divided into the six Classes, with each Class beginning a new facing page. To guide the reader to connected Heads, many more cross-references have been added, and in the lists at the end of each Head, those references most likely to be helpful are now printed in bold type. Within the actual cross-references, the part of speech label has been omitted, as the reference is always to the same part of speech. This saves space, and enables the *keyword* to be more easily seen as part of the vocabulary within the Head.

Accuracy is essential in a book of this kind, and the resources of modern technology have been drawn on to eliminate human error where possible. All cross-references have been checked by computer, and the lists of cross-references at the end of Heads have been computer-generated. Above all the Index, now much expanded, is based on a computer-listing of all the items in the text. The use of a computer, and the resources of the Lexicographic Unit of Longman's Dictionary and Reference Book Department should make this edition accurate, comprehensive and a worthy successor to earlier editions. But improvements are also due in no small measure to the efforts of readers themselves, who have kindly written to point out errors and omissions and suggest modifications. It has been encouraging to discover in what great affection *Roget's Thesaurus* is held by its users, and the editor hopes that readers will continue to offer suggestions and criticisms.

S. M. Lloyd
Harleston, Norfolk
January 1982.

Dr Peter Mark Roget and his Thesaurus

The name of Roget has become synonymous with the *Thesaurus*, yet Dr Roget himself is a shadowy figure. This is rather surprising as he played an active part in the intellectual, scientific and social life of his time, besides achieving some eminence in his own profession of medicine. It is also ironic that one who made such an important contribution to the study and practice of the English language should have so little English blood in his veins. His father, Jean Roget, was a Genevan pastor only recently come to Britain, while his mother's grandfather was a French Huguenot who had fled to London after the revocation of the Edict of Nantes. Roget's early years were spent in the French Protestant community, where he absorbed liberal ideas and a belief in the perfectibility of man, which was soon shaken, however, by the aftermath of the French Revolution.

Jean Roget died when his son was only four, so the young Roget was brought up by his mother Catherine, with some financial and moral support from her brother, the famous law reformer Sir Samuel Romilly. Catherine was strongly influenced by the ideas on education of Jean Roget's countryman Jean Jacques Rousseau, and went to great lengths to try to find the ideal environment for her son, even moving to Edinburgh when he was fourteen so that he could complete his education at the university there, considered superior to Oxford and Cambridge, and especially so for mathematics and science. These were Roget's absorbing interests, and remained so throughout his life. However, science was not yet a safe or lucrative career for a young man, and Roget finally took his degree in medicine and became a doctor.

In later life, Roget appears to us as rather a staid, unimaginative figure, but as a young man he found himself in some far from staid situations. He spent some time at Bristol observing Dr Beddoes's and Humphrey Davy's experiments with laughing gas at the famous Clifton 'Pneumatic Institution'. He also worked for a while for Jeremy Bentham on a project for a 'Frigidarium'. The unconventionality of the Bentham household soon led him to leave, but he was influenced all his life by Bentham's ideas of Utilitarianism and the happiness of the greatest number. Perhaps his most exciting adventure was when he took two young boys from Manchester on their 'Grand Tour' of Europe. This was during 1802–3, and when the fragile entente between Britain and France broke with the collapse of the Peace of Amiens, Roget and his charges were trapped in Geneva. He showed great ingenuity and persistence in getting them safely away, and only just in time: his friend Edgeworth did not succeed in escaping, and was imprisoned for eleven years.

On his return to England, Roget began to practise as a doctor, gaining experience in Manchester before settling in London, where he had a house in Barnard Street, Bloomsbury. His lively mind, his eagerness to become part of the ferment of scientific life of the capital, and his willingness to work hard quickly made him acceptable in intellectual circles. Only five years after his arrival, he was elected a Fellow of the prestigious Royal Society, of which he was later Secretary for twenty years. This was just the beginning of a long and energetic working life, both as a doctor and a scientist. Roget's medical skills were soon being called upon by people he knew socially and he quickly built up a considerable practice. He was also instrumental in setting up a charity clinic, the Northern Dispensary, where he treated needy patients free of charge. He added to his medical reputation by giving lectures to medical students and writing papers for the Medical and Chirurgical Society, of which he soon became Secretary. This involved him in editing their Transactions and classifying the library. Roget's reputation as a doctor was such that in 1823 he was one of the doctors appointed to investigate the Millbank prison epidemic. Later, he was called in to head a Commission to investigate London's water supply. One of his recommendations, that of sand filtration, is still in use today.

The crowning point of Roget's medical career came in 1831, with his election as Fellow *speciali grata* to the Royal College of Physicians. For many men such a distinguished career would have been enough. But simultaneously with his work as a doctor, Roget was also strenuously pursuing his other love, science. Besides his work for the Royal Society, he was a member, and frequently an active member, of many of the learned societies then proliferating in London. It was an exciting time, a time of discoveries, experiments and inventions, a time when the flood of new knowledge was leading inevitably to the specialization that is even more marked today. Societies were therefore formed to deal with separate branches of science, the Zoological Society, the Royal Geographical Society, the Royal Astronomical Society and so on. Roget, a polymath, like many of his generation, belonged to a number of them, writing papers on every aspect of knowledge, from insects to electricity. He also conducted his own experiments, and enjoyed inventing mathematical and optical devices. This was not mere amateur tinkering: Roget's reputation as a scientist was as high as his reputation as a doctor. Some of Roget's inventions indeed, still affect us today. It was Roget who invented the log-log scale still used on modern slide rules. It was this which secured his entry to the Royal Society. Always busy with new ideas, he left it to others to explore the possibilities of his inventions or observations. It was the same with his paper on the effects of seeing a moving object through slats—in this case a carriage wheel seen through the venetian blinds in his basement. Roget had noticed that an image appeared to be retained on the retina for a fraction of time after it had disappeared from sight. This discovery was taken up by other scientists, notably Faraday. and eventually led to the making of moving pictures and the cinema industry.

With all this activity, Roget still found time to read voraciously, including works in French, Latin, German and Italian, and to amuse himself by the setting and solving of chess problems. Moreover, he was no recluse. He enjoyed dining with friends, going to the theatre and, especially after his marriage in 1824, strolling or driving round the London parks and squares, noting the new buildings and other improvements. He was an affectionate father to his two children, Kate and John, and with his wife Mary took great pleasure in their education.

Writing and lecturing took up a good deal of Roget's time. He was eager to communicate knowledge to as wide a public as possible, and took a professional pride in his lectures, which were very popular, especially in an age of self-improvement. He lectured for thirty years at the Russell Institution, where he was appointed Fullerian Professor of Physiology, and also gave courses at the Royal Institution, a signal honour. But it was typical of Roget that he should also be one of the founders of the Society for the Diffusion of Useful Knowledge, which issued sixpenny treatises in simple English on such subjects as electricity and magnetism. Of Roget's involvement with his Society, its publisher wrote:

> "Amongst the founders of the Society, Dr Roget was, from his accepted high reputation, the most eminent of its men of science. . . . He was a diligent attendant on its committees; a vigilant corrector of its proofs. Of most winning manners, he was as beloved as he was respected . . ."[1]

Less ephemeral than such treatises, but also with a lay audience in mind, were Roget's articles for the Encyclopedia Britannica. These included a major piece on his speciality, physiology, and shorter ones on subjects ranging from ants and bees to phrenology (on

[1] D. L. Emblen, *Peter Mark Roget* (London 1970), p. 187

which he poured scorn), and from the education of the deaf and dumb to the kaleidoscope. These, with several brief biographies of European scientists, were first published in the Supplement to the 4th, 5th and 6th Editions, but were often reprinted in a shortened form in later editions, though without acknowledgment. Roget's other major publication (apart from the *Thesaurus*), was much praised by his contemporaries, who thought it would carry his name to posterity. This was *Animal and Vegetable Physiology considered with reference to Natural Theology,* one of eight similar works commissioned by the Earl of Bridgewater to propound 'the power, wisdom and goodness of God, as manifested in the creation'. The world view it expressed, however, was already being challenged when it was published in 1834, and though it went through several editions, Roget's monumental work is no longer remembered.

Ironically, the work which did make him known to later generations, the *Thesaurus of English Words and Phrases,* was a product of Roget's retirement. Ousted from his Secretaryship of the Royal Society by a younger and more adventurous group of scientists, he found himself with unwonted leisure, and promptly began to devote himself to the conclusion of a project he had nursed for many years: the classification and organization of the English language. This may seem a strange preoccupation for a scientist and mathematician, but it was in many ways a task which Roget was uniquely equipped to carry out. All his life he had been concerned with order, with marshalling a mass of facts or observations into a meaningful form which both expressed their special qualities and reaffirmed their unity. He had done this, in particular, in his Bridgewater Treatise, where he had set out Natural History in all its variety, while showing the close links between the parts, and claiming that the whole revealed the design of the Creator. His involvement with the classification of the libraries of the Medical and Chirurgical Society, and of the Royal Society, had also been valuable experience. As a doctor, his preference had been for anatomy and physiology, subjects which by their very nature involved dissection and classification. It was the organization of knowledge (rather than the making of profound discoveries, for which he lacked the imagination), that was Roget's forte, and which he was able to put to good use in compiling the *Thesaurus*. Then again, his lifelong belief in progress and utilitarianism were served by the book, which he hoped would enable people to communicate with each other more easily and effectively. Roget had always been concerned with communicating knowledge and was more concerned with this aspect of language than with beauties of style. Though a Renaissance man in the variety of his interests, literature for its own sake seems to have held little attraction for him: he was more concerned with facts and ideas. Though the *Thesaurus* is often used nowadays to achieve a polished style, Roget's intention for it was chiefly utilitarian and philosophical, as he made plain in his Introduction.

The *Thesaurus* began as a notebook Roget had carried round with him from his earliest lecturing days. In it he made lists of related words and phrases in various orders to help him express himself in the best possible way. Now, in his seventies, he was able to draw on a lifetime's experience of lecturing, writing and editing to make these lists into a coherent system available for others to use. It took him four years, longer than he had thought, and required all his organizational skills and the meticulous attention to detail that had characterized his editing work. Not only did the *Thesaurus* utilize all Roget's competences, it also fulfilled a need for him: the need, in a society changing with frightening speed, where the old moral and religious order was increasingly in question, to reaffirm order, stability and unity, and through them the purpose of a universal, supernatural authority.

Even with the publication of his *Thesaurus* when he was seventy-one, Roget did not cease from his labours. He continued to note improvements and prepare new editions as well as pursuing many other projects. He died in his ninety-first year at West Malvern secure in the knowledge that the work which summed up all his achievements in a long and productive life had gained public acceptance and proved its worth.[1]

[1] My thanks are due to John Herkless, who is preparing a new biography of Roget, for some of the above information. I have also drawn on D. L. Emblen's biography (see p xiv).

The Thesaurus

Roget's *Thesaurus of English words and phrases* was first published by Longman, Brown, Green, and Longmans in May 1852, selling at 14 shillings. It was a handsome volume, a generous octavo, printed on good quality paper, with the text well spaced-out. The Heads numbered exactly one thousand, and were printed in two columns, positive Heads facing their negatives or correlatives. This layout, which Roget explained in his *Introduction* (see p. xxiii), was retained in the copyright edition until 1962. The text was divided into the six Classes, each Class beginning a new page, with double column headings. Within each Head, the words given were sorted into parts of speech, and grouped according to ideas. Roget made a point of including phrases and idioms (see his *Introduction*, pp xxiv), though these were not included in the Index. The vocabulary reflected Roget's wide knowledge, and the many classical and literary allusions, with some examples from the theatre of the day, could be expected to be familiar to all educated men and women. The work still bears some signs of being adapted from a private compilation to one for public use: explanatory subtitles were subjoined to the Class and Section titles, and sometimes to the Head titles as well, while footnotes frequently drew the reader's attention to points of interest or usage.

The success of the first edition (of only one thousand copies) led to a second in March 1853 and a third, described as "a cheaper edition, enlarged and improved"[1], which sold for half a guinea, in February 1855. This edition was stereotyped, and used as the basis for the frequent subsequent printings until the plates were worn out. For the 1855 edition, Roget rewrote parts of the text, added "many thousand" new expressions, and introduced a number of subsidiary Heads, labelled (a), to fill gaps which he had noticed in his scheme. Though the new duodecimo volume necessitated smaller type and a less spacious-looking format, Roget welcomed it in his *Advertisement to the third edition* as "more portable and convenient". The fame of the *Thesaurus* appears to have crossed the Atlantic, as he notes with some asperity that "in the course of last summer, an imperfect edition of this work was published at Boston, in the United States of America, in which the editor, among other mutilations, has altogether omitted the Phrases . . . and has removed from the body of the work all the words and expressions borrowed from a foreign language, throwing them into an Appendix, where . . . they are completely lost to the inquirer . . ." The American edition[2] was the first of many imitations of Roget's work, both at home and abroad.

Roget continued to collect new words and expressions for his *Thesaurus* until his death in 1869. He noted them in the margins of his copy, planning to use them in a new enlarged edition. This duly appeared ten years later, thanks to the labours of his son, John Lewis Roget, MA. A lawyer, who was active in art circles as a critic and watercolourist, and later wrote the history of the Old Water-Colour Society (1891), John Roget modestly disclaimed in his Preface any special qualifications for his task, claiming that it was "almost entirely of a practical nature, demanding industry and attention, rather than philosophic culture or the learning of a philologist". Without changing Roget's system of classification in any way, he nevertheless made a distinctive contribution of his own to the evolution of the *Thesaurus*. Discovering that the sheer number of additions, both his father's and his own, threatened to overload the different Heads and blur the distinctions made between them, he extended the system of cross-references already present in embryo, and gave this policy a sound linguistic basis by observing that "the fabric of our language has become a texture woven into one by the interlacing of countless branches, springing from separate stems". To place each word in only one of its possible locations would be to lose much of the richness of the language, but to insert it under every suitable Head would lead to ideas being lost in a welter of words. The system of cross-references

[1]Samuel R. Roget, in the Preface to the 1933 edition
[2]Probably that by Rev. B. Sears (Boston 1854)

was the ideal compromise between too much or too little repetition, and has been adopted and extended by successive editors.

John Roget's other major contribution to the development of the *Thesaurus* was his recognition of the importance of the Index. Roget himself had thought of it only as a last resort – his original notebook had not had one. John Roget, however, noted in his Preface to the 1879 edition: "I believe that almost everyone who uses the book finds it more convenient to have recourse to the Index first." He accordingly expanded it to include for the first time not only all the words in the text, but also most of the phrases. The index, now in four columns rather than three, took up very nearly half of the new edition, which had also expanded from the original 418 pages to 646 of smaller, close-set print, in a rather smaller octavo size.

Frequent reprints of the *Thesaurus*, revised by John Roget, continued to be issued by the publishers, now known as Longmans & Co., until the former's death in 1908. New words added to the text were listed in a supplementary index, bringing the book up to 670 pages. These additions reflect the topics of the day – 'veldt', 'outspan' and 'Afrikander' from Southern Africa, weapons such as 'Lee-Metford rifle' and 'Gatling gun', with the appearance of 'electrolier', 'lorry' and 'motor car'.

Samuel Romilly Roget, John's son, now took on the editorship. He was an electrical engineer who had something of his grandfather's gift for popularizing, publishing among other works a *Dictionary of Electrical Terms*[1] which was still in print twenty years later. He greatly expanded the vocabulary of the book, and extended the system of cross-references, but made no changes to the layout. His energetic promotion of the *Thesaurus* in papers such as The Times kept it in the public eye and helped to consolidate it as an English institution. The great crossword-puzzle boom soon generated a new class of Roget-user, and editions followed each other with great rapidity. From a printing about every other year, between 1890 and 1908, there was at least one a year from 1911 to 1929, and five printings in 1925, when Samuel Roget brought out his own new enlarged version. A New York edition was published in 1933, containing many expressions "in commoner use in America than in England". This seems to have been the same edition to appear in 1936 at home. The importance of the Index was now well-established: Roget noted in his Preface that it had been checked line by line for the 1936 edition. New plates were made, and used for frequent reprints, even during the war years. In 1953, a Penguin paperback *Thesaurus* appeared.

Samuel Roget sold the family rights to Longmans, Green & Co., in 1952, and with his death in 1953, the family connection with the *Thesaurus* came to an end. The publishers commissioned Robert A. Dutch OBE, sometime Senior Scholar of Christ's College, Cambridge, to prepare a new edition, bringing *Roget's Thesaurus*, still much in the form the author had left it, up to date.

The new editor had to adapt the *Thesaurus* to users whose needs and background were rather different to those of the first generation of Roget readers a hundred years or so earlier. The philosophical interest in classification and analysis of words and their relationships, which had played an important part in Roget's conception of his book, already relegated to second place by his son John's extension of the Index, was now thought to be of negligible interest to most modern readers, who looked on the work as a purely practical aid in communication. The system of classification, therefore, though still the basis of the book, became latent rather than apparent in the text. While keeping the two-column layout, Heads were now printed consecutively instead of opposite each other, without any visual reminder of their relationship other than their consecutiveness. Classes and Sections were not labelled or separated in any way, the Heads following each other without a break. The original titles and subtitles were listed in the Tabular Synopsis for reference, and this too was printed consecutively, rather than in columns showing Roget's three categories of positive, negative and intermediate.

[1]London 1924

Robert Dutch's revision resulted in the *Thesaurus* familiar to us today. He rewrote the whole text, within Roget's Heads, aiming to make each group of related words follow each other in a logical sequence, so that "the mind is led by easy transitions from one nuance to another without distraction" (Preface, p. xii in the 1962 edition). Heads which had shown their superfluity by wasting away in successive revisions were absorbed elsewhere, thus reducing the number of Heads to 990. Other Heads whose titles had become obscure were renamed. A useful innovation for linguists and others was the appending at the end of each Head a list of cross-references used. But perhaps Robert Dutch's happiest idea was the invention of *keywords.* The *keyword,* the word in italics at the beginning of each paragraph, whose use is explained on page xxxiii, showed readers where to begin their search for the right word within the Head. Its use to identify paragraphs in cross-references and in the Index at once standardized references and enabled readers to pick out the most suitable of several locations for the meaning they sought.

After almost twenty years of rapid social and technological change, and more than two hundred years after Roget was born, the *Thesaurus* has now been revised yet again. (See the Preface, pp ix–xii for the changes made by the present editor). There can be little doubt that revisions will continue to be called for, as the never-ending task of inserting new vocabulary and reassessing the existing word-stock continues, so that *Roget's Thesaurus* may continue to serve future generations as well as it has done past ones. With the dawn of the electronic age, however, the possibilities become very exciting. All editors of *Roget* have had in the past to exclude many items for lack of space. The data bank of a computer knows no such limitations. Every new use of every word could be fed in, thus creating a thesaurus that was continually updated. When every home has its own computer terminal, the *Roget* user would have the resources of such a thesaurus at his or her fingertips. Every item, moreover, could be listed in the Index. Even this, however, does not exhaust the possibilities. Roget's original dream could be fulfilled: since a thesaurus consists of concepts first, then words, any language in the world can be analyzed according to Roget's Classification and thus added to the data bank. Such a multilingual thesaurus would have more than merely practical applications: it would greatly assist international understanding. It might even be the imperfect forerunner of that Universal Language to which Roget and his fellow reformists aspired, which would help to bring about a golden age of union and harmony.[1]

[1] See the Introduction to the original edition, p. (xxxi).

Preface

to the first edition, 1852

It is now nearly fifty years since I first projected a system of verbal classification similar to that on which the present Work is founded. Conceiving that such a compilation might help to supply my own deficiencies, I had, in the year 1805, completed a classed catalogue of words on a small scale, but on the same principle, and nearly in the same form, as the Thesaurus now published. I had often during that long interval found this little collection, scanty and imperfect as it was, of much use to me in literary composition, and often contemplated its extension and improvement; but a sense of the magnitude of the task, amidst a multitude of other avocations, deterred me from the attempt. Since my retirement from the duties of Secretary of the Royal Society, however, finding myself possessed of more leisure, and believing that a repertory of which I had myself experienced the advantage might, when amplified, prove useful to others, I resolved to embark in an undertaking which, for the last three or four years, has given me incessant occupation, and has, indeed, imposed upon me an amount of labour very much greater than I had anticipated. Notwithstanding all the pains I have bestowed on its execution, I am fully aware of its numerous deficiencies and imperfections, and of its falling far short of the degree of excellence that might be attained. But, in a Work of this nature, where perfection is placed at so great a distance, I have thought it best to limit my ambition to that moderate share of merit which it may claim in its present form; trusting to the indulgence of those for whose benefit it is intended, and to the candour of critics who, while they find it easy to detect faults, can at the same time duly appreciate difficulties.

P. M. Roget
29 April, 1852

Introduction

to the original edition, 1852

Unbracketed footnotes are by Peter Mark Roget. Footnotes within brackets are attributed as follows: [JLR] – John Lewis Roget; [SRR] – Samuel Romilly Roget; [RAD] – Robert A. Dutch; [SML] – Susan M. Lloyd. Not all later footnotes have been retained.

The present Work is intended to supply, with respect to the English language, a desideratum hitherto unsupplied in any language; namely, a collection of the words it contains and of the idiomatic combinations peculiar to it, arranged, not in alphabetical order as they are in a Dictionary, but according to the ideas which they express. The purpose of an ordinary dictionary is simply to explain the meaning of the words; and the problem of which it professes to furnish the solution may be stated thus:– The word being given, to find its signification, or the idea it is intended to convey. The object aimed at in the present undertaking is exactly the converse of this: namely,– The idea being given, to find the word, or words, by which that idea may be most fitly and aptly expressed. For this purpose, the words and phrases of the language are here classed, not according to their sound or their orthography, but strictly according to their *signification*.

The communication of our thoughts by means of language, whether spoken or written, like every other object of mental exertion, constitutes a peculiar art, which, like other arts, cannot be acquired in any perfection but by long and continued practice. Some, indeed, there are more highly gifted than others with a facility of expression, and naturally endowed with the power of eloquence; but to none is it at all times an easy process to embody, in exact and appropriate language, the various trains of ideas that are passing through the mind, or to depict in their true colours and proportions, the diversified and nicer shades of feeling which accompany them. To those who are unpractised in the art of composition, or unused to extempore speaking, these difficulties present themselves in their most formidable aspect. However distinct may be our views, however vivid our conceptions, or however fervent our emotions, we cannot but be often conscious that the phraseology we have at our command is inadequate to do them justice. We seek in vain the words we need, and strive ineffectually to devise forms of expression which shall faithfully portray our thoughts and sentiments. The appropriate terms, notwithstanding our utmost efforts, cannot be conjured up at will. Like 'spirits from the vasty deep', they come not when we call; and we are driven to the employment of a set of words and phrases either too general or too limited, too strong or too feeble, which suit not the occasion, which hit not the mark we aim at; and the result of our prolonged exertion is a style at once laboured and obscure, vapid and redundant, or vitiated by the still graver faults of affectation or ambiguity.

It is to those who are thus painfully groping their way and struggling with the difficulties of composition, that this Work professes to hold out a helping hand. The assistance it gives is that of furnishing on every topic a copious store of words and phrases, adapted to express all the recognizable shades and modifications of the general idea under which those words and phrases are arranged. The inquirer can readily select, out of the ample collection spread out before his eyes in the following pages, those expressions which are best suited to his purpose, and which might not have occurred to him without such assist-

Introduction

to the original edition, 1852

Unbracketed footnotes are by Peter Mark Roget. Footnotes within brackets are attributed as follows: [JLR] – John Lewis Roget; [SRR] – Samuel Romilly Roget; [RAD] – Robert A. Dutch; [SML] – Susan M. Lloyd. Not all later footnotes have been retained.

The present Work is intended to supply, with respect to the English language, a desideratum hitherto unsupplied in any language; namely, a collection of the words it contains and of the idiomatic combinations peculiar to it, arranged, not in alphabetical order as they are in a Dictionary, but according to the *ideas* which they express. The purpose of an ordinary dictionary is simply to explain the meaning of the words; and the problem of which it professes to furnish the solution may be stated thus:—The word being given, to find its signification, or the idea it is intended to convey. The object aimed at in the present undertaking is exactly the converse of this: namely,—The idea being given, to find the word, or words, by which that idea may be most fitly and aptly expressed. For this purpose, the words and phrases of the language are here classed, not according to their sound or their orthography, but strictly according to their *signification.*

The communication of our thoughts by means of language, whether spoken or written, like every other object of mental exertion, constitutes a peculiar art, which, like other arts, cannot be acquired in any perfection but by long and continued practice. Some, indeed, there are more highly gifted than others with a facility of expression, and naturally endowed with the power of eloquence; but to none is it at all times an easy process to embody, in exact and appropriate language, the various trains of ideas that are passing through the mind, or to depict in their true colours and proportions, the diversified and nicer shades of feeling which accompany them. To those who are unpractised in the art of composition, or unused to extempore speaking, these difficulties present themselves in their most formidable aspect. However distinct may be our views, however vivid our conceptions, or however fervent our emotions, we cannot but be often conscious that the phraseology we have at our command is inadequate to do them justice. We seek in vain the words we need, and strive ineffectually to devise forms of expression which shall faithfully portray our thoughts and sentiments. The appropriate terms, notwithstanding our utmost efforts, cannot be conjured up at will. Like 'spirits from the vasty deep', they come not when we call; and we are driven to the employment of a set of words and phrases either too general or too limited, too strong or too feeble, which suit not the occasion, which hit not the mark we aim at; and the result of our prolonged exertion is a style at once laboured and obscure, vapid and redundant, or vitiated by the still graver faults of affectation or ambiguity.

It is to those who are thus painfully groping their way and struggling with the difficulties of composition, that this Work professes to hold out a helping hand. The assistance it gives is that of furnishing on every topic a copious store of words and phrases, adapted to express all the recognizable shades and modifications of the general idea under which those words and phrases are arranged. The inquirer can readily select, out of the ample collection spread out before his eyes in the following pages, those expressions which are best suited to his purpose, and which might not have occurred to him without such assistance. In order to make this selection, he scarcely ever need engage in any critical or elaborate study of the subtle distinction existing between synonymous terms; for if the materials set before him be sufficiently abundant, an instinctive tact will rarely fail to lead him to the proper choice. Even while glancing over the columns of this Work, his eye may chance to light upon a particular term, which may save the cost of a clumsy paraphrase, or spare the labour of a tortuous circumlocution. Some felicitous turn of expression thus introduced will frequently open to the mind of the reader a whole vista of collateral ideas, which could not, without an extended and obtrusive episode, have been unfolded to his view; and often will the judicious insertion of a happy epithet, like a beam of sunshine in a landscape, illumine and adorn the subject which it touches, imparting new grace and giving life and spirit to the picture.

Every workman in the exercise of his art should be provided with proper implements. For the fabrication of complicated and curious pieces of mechanism, the artisan requires a corresponding assortment of various tools and instruments. For giving proper effect to the fictions of the drama, the actor should have at his disposal a well-furnished wardrobe, supplying the costumes best suited to the personages he is to represent. For the perfect delineation of the beauties of nature, the painter should have within reach of his pencil every variety and combination of hues and tints. Now, the writer, as well as the orator, employs for the accomplishment of his purposes the instrumentality of words; it is in words that he clothes his thoughts; it is by means of words that he depicts his feelings. It is therefore essential to his success that he be provided with a copious vocabulary, and that he possess an entire command of all the resources and appliances of his language. To the acquisition of this power no procedure appears more directly conducive than the study of a methodized system such as that now offered to his use.

The utility of the present Work will be appreciated more especially by those who are engaged in the arduous process of translating into English a Work written in another language. Simple as the operation may appear, on a superficial view, of rendering into English each of its sentences, the task of transfusing, with perfect exactness, the sense of the original, preserving at the same time the style and character of its composition, and reflecting with fidelity the mind and the spirit of the author, is a task of extreme difficulty. The cultivation of this useful department of literature was in ancient times strongly recommended both by Cicero and by Quintilian, as essential to the formation of a good writer and accomplished orator. Regarded simply as a mental exercise, the practice of translation is the best training for the attainment of that mastery of language and felicity of diction, which are the sources of the highest oratory, and are requisite for the possession of a graceful and persuasive eloquence. By rendering ourselves the faithful interpreters of the thoughts and feelings of others, we are rewarded with the acquisition of greater readiness and facility in correctly expressing our own; as he who has best learned to execute the orders of a commander, becomes himself best qualified to command.

In the earliest periods of civilization, translators have been the agents for propagating knowledge from nation to nation, and the value of their labours has been inestimable; but, in the present age, when so many different languages have become the depositories of the vast treasures of literature and of science which have been accumulating for centuries, the utility of accurate translations has greatly increased, and it has become a more important object to attain perfection in the art.

The use of language is not confined to its being the medium through which we communicate our ideas to one another; it fulfils a no less important function as an *instrument of thought*; not being merely its vehicle, but giving it wings for flight. Metaphysicians are agreed that scarcely any of our intellectual operations could be carried on to any considerable extent, without the agency of words. None but those who are conversant with the philosophy of mental phenomena, can be aware of the immense influence that is exercised by language in promoting the development of our ideas, in fixing them in the mind, and in detaining them for steady contemplation. Into every process of reasoning, language enters as an essential element. Words are the instruments by which we form all our abstractions, by which we fashion and embody our ideas, and by which we are enabled to glide along a series of premises and conclusions with a rapidity so great as to leave in the memory no trace of the successive steps of the process; and we remain unconscious how much we owe to this potent auxiliary of the reasoning faculty. It is on this ground, also, that the present Work founds a claim to utility. The review of a catalogue of words of analogous signification, will often suggest by association other trains of thought, which, presenting the subject under new and varied aspects, will vastly expand the sphere of our mental vision. Amidst the many objects thus brought within the range of our contemplation, some striking similitude or appropriate image, some excursive flight or brilliant conception, may flash on the mind, giving point and force to our arguments, awakening a responsive chord in the imagination or sensibility of the reader, and procuring for our reasonings a more ready access both to his understanding and to his heart.

It is of the utmost consequence that strict accuracy should regulate our use of language, and that every one should acquire the power and the habit of expressing his thoughts with perspicuity and correctness. Few, indeed, can appreciate the real extent and importance of that influence which language has always exercised on human affairs, or can be aware how often these are determined by causes much slighter than are apparent to a superficial observer. False logic, disguised under specious phraseology, too often gains the assent of the unthinking multitude, disseminating far and wide the seeds of prejudice and error. Truisms pass current, and wear the semblance of profound wisdom, when dressed up in the tinsel garb of antithetical phrases, or set off by an imposing pomp of paradox. By a confused jargon of involved and mystical sentences, the imagination is easily inveigled into a transcendental region of clouds, and the understanding beguiled into the belief that it is acquiring knowledge and approaching truth. A misapplied or misapprehended term is sufficient to give rise to fierce and interminable disputes; a misnomer has turned the tide of popular opinion; a verbal sophism has decided a party question; an artful watchword, thrown among combustible materials, has kindled the flame of deadly warfare, and changed the destiny of an empire.

In constructing the following system of classification of the ideas which are expressible by language, my chief aim has been to obtain the greatest amount of practical utility. I have accordingly adopted such principles of arrangement as appeared to me to be the simplest and most natural, and which would not require, either for their comprehension or application, any disciplined acumen, or depth of metaphysical or antiquarian lore. Eschewing all needless refinements and subtleties, I have taken as my guide the more obvious characters of the ideas for which expressions were to be tabulated, arranging them under such classes and categories as reflection and experience had taught me would conduct the inquirer most readily and quickly to the object of his search. Commencing with the ideas expressing abstract relations, I proceeded to those which relate to space and to the phenomena of the material world, and lastly to those in which the mind is concerned, and which comprehend intellect, volition, and feeling; thus establishing six primary Classes or Categories.

1. The first of these classes comprehends ideas derived from the more general and ABSTRACT RELATIONS among things, such as *Existence, Resemblance, Quantity, Order, Number, Time, Power.*

2. The second class refers to SPACE and its various relations, including *Motion,* or change of place.

3. The third class includes all ideas that relate to the MATERIAL WORLD; namely, the *Properties of Matter,* such as *Solidity, Fluidity, Heat, Sound, Light,* and the *Phenomena* they present, as well as the simple *Perceptions* to which they give rise.

4. The fourth class embraces all ideas of phenomena relating to the INTELLECT and its operations; comprising the *Acquisition,* the *Retention,* and the *Communication of Ideas.*

5. The fifth class includes the ideas derived from the exercise of VOLITION; embracing the phenomena and results of our *Voluntary and Active Powers;* such as *Choice, Intention, Utility, Action, Antagonism, Authority, Compact, Property,* &c.

6. The sixth and last class comprehends all ideas derived from the operation of our SENTIENT AND MORAL POWERS; including our *Feelings, Emotions, Passions,* and

Moral and Religious Sentiments.[1]

The further subdivisions and minuter details will be best understood from an inspection of the Tabular Synopsis of Categories prefixed to the Work, in which are specified the several *topics* or *heads of signification*, under which the words have been arranged. By the aid of this table the reader will, with a little practice, readily discover the place which the particular topic he is in search of occupies in the series; and on turning to the page in the body of the Work which contains it, he will find the group of expressions he requires, out of which he may cull those that are most appropriate to his purpose. For the convenience of reference, I have designated each separate group or heading by a particular number; so that if, during the search, any doubt or difficulty should occur, recourse may be had to the copious alphabetical Index of Words at the end of the volume, which will at once indicate the number of the required group.[2]

The object I have proposed to myself in this Work would have been but imperfectly attained if I had confined myself to a mere catalogue of words, and had omitted the numerous phrases and forms of expression composed of several words, which are of such frequent use as to entitle them to rank among the constituent parts of the language.[3] Very few of these verbal combinations, so essential to the knowledge of our native tongue, and so profusely abounding in its daily use, are to be met with in ordinary dictionaries. These phrases and forms of expression I have endeavoured diligently to collect and to insert in their proper places, under the general ideas that they are designed to convey. Some of these conventional forms, indeed, partake of the nature of proverbial expressions; but actual proverbs, as such, being wholly of a didactic character, do not come within the scope of the present Work; and the reader must therefore not expect to find them here inserted.[4].

For the purpose of exhibiting with greater distinctness the relations between words expressing opposite and correlative ideas, I have, whenever the subject admitted of such an arrangement, placed them in two parallel columns in the same page, so that each group of expressions may be readily contrasted with those which occupy the adjacent column, and constitute their antithesis.[5] By carrying the eye from the one to the other, the inquirer may often discover forms of expression, of which he may avail himself advantageously, to diversify and infuse vigour into his phraseology. Rhetoricians, indeed, are well aware of the power derived from the skilful introduction of antithesis in giving point to an

[1] It must necessarily happen in every system of classification framed with this view, that ideas and expressions arranged under one class must include also ideas relating to another class; for the operations of the *Intellect* generally involve also those of the *Will*, and *vice versa*; and our *Affections* and *Emotions*, in like manner, generally imply the agency both of the *Intellect* and of the *Will*. All that can be effected, therefore, is to arrange the words according to the principal or dominant idea they convey. *Teaching*, for example, although a Voluntary act, relates primarily to the Communication of Ideas, and is accordingly placed at No. 537, under Class IV Division (II). On the other hand, *Choice*, *Conduct*, *Skill*, &c., although implying the co-operation of Voluntary with Intellectual acts, relate principally to the former, and are therefore arranged under Class V.

[2] It often happens that the same word admits of various applications, or may be used in different senses. In consulting the Index the reader will be guided to the number of the heading under which that word, in each particular acceptation, will be found, by means of *supplementary words* printed in Italics; which words, however, are not to be understood as explaining the meaning of the word to which they are annexed, but only as assisting in the required reference. I have also, for shortness' sake, generally omitted words immediately derived from the primary one inserted, which sufficiently represents the whole group of correlative words referable to the same heading. Thus the number affixed to *Beauty* applies to all its derivatives, such as *Beautiful*, *Beauteous*, *Beautifulness*, *Beautifully*, &c., the insertion of which was therefore needless.

[3] For example:—To take time by the forelock;—to turn over a new leaf;—to show the white feather;—to have a finger in the pie;—to let the cat out of the bag;—to take care of number one;—to kill two birds with one stone, &c., &c.

[4] See Trench, *On the Lessons In Proverbs*.

[5] [This arrangement has been modified.] [RAD].

argument, and imparting force and brilliancy to the diction. A too frequent and indiscreet employment of this figure of rhetoric may, it is true, give rise to a vicious and affected style; but is unreasonable to condemn indiscriminately the occasional and moderate use of a practice on account of its possible abuse.

The study of correlative terms existing in a particular language, may often throw valuable light on the manners and customs of the nations using it. Thus, Hume has drawn important inferences with regard to the state of society among the ancient Romans, from certain deficiencies which he remarked in the Latin language.[1]

In many cases, two ideas which are completely opposed to each other, admit of an intermediate or neutral idea, equidistant from both; all these being expressible by corresponding definite terms. Thus, in the following examples, the words in the first and third columns, which express opposite ideas, admit of the intermediate terms contained in the middle column, having a neutral sense with reference to the former.

Identity	*Difference*	*Contrariety*
Beginning	*Middle*	*End*
Past	*Present*	*Future*

In other cases, the intermediate word is simply the negative to each of two opposite positions; as, for example—

Convexity	*Flatness*	*Concavity*
Desire	*Indifference*	*Aversion*

Sometimes the intermediate word is properly the standard with which each of the extremes is compared; as in the case of

Insufficiency	*Sufficiency*	*Redundance*

for here the middle term, *Sufficiency,* is equally opposed, on the one hand to *Insufficiency,* and on the other to *Redundance.*[2]

These forms of correlative expressions would suggest the use of triple, instead of double, columns, for tabulating this threefold order of words; but the practical inconvenience attending such an arrangement would probably overbalance its advantages.

[1] 'It is an universal observation', he remarks, 'which we may form upon language, that where two related parts of a whole bear any proportion to each other, in numbers, ranks, or consideration, there are always correlative terms invented which answer to both the parts, and express their mutual relation. If they bear no proportion to each other, the term is only invented for the less, and marks its distinction from the whole. Thus, *man* and *woman*, *master* and *servant*, *father* and *son*, *prince* and *subject*, *stranger* and *citizen*, are correlative terms. But the words *seaman*, *carpenter*, *smith*, *tailor*, &c., have no correspondent terms, which express those who are no seamen, no carpenters, &c. Languages differ very much with regard to the particular words where this distinction obtains; and may thence afford very strong inferences concerning the manners and customs of different nations. The military government of the Roman emperors had exalted the soldiery so high that they balanced all the other orders of the state: hence *miles* and *paganus* became relative terms; a thing, till then, unknown to ancient, and still so to modern languages.'—'The term for a slave, born and bred in the family, was *verna.* As *servus* was the name of the genus, and *verna* of the species without any correlative, this forms a strong presumption that the latter were by far the least numerous: and from the same principles I infer that if the number of slaves brought by the Romans from foreign countries had not extremely exceeded those which were bred at home, *verna* would have had a correlative, which would have expressed the former species of slaves. But these, it would seem, composed the main body of the ancient slaves, and the latter were but a few exceptions.'—HUME, *Essay on the Populousness of Ancient Nations.*

The warlike propensity of the same nation may, in like manner, be inferred from the use of the word *hostis* to denote both a *foreigner* and *an enemy.*

[2] [In the following cases, the intermediate word signifies an imperfect degree of each of the qualities set in opposition—

Light	*Dimness*	*Darkness*
Transparency	*Semitransparency*	*Opacity*
Vision	*Dimsightedness*	*Blindness*] [JLR]

If often happens that the same word has several correlative terms, according to the different relations in which it is considered. Thus, to the word *Giving* are opposed both *Receiving* and *Taking*; the former correlation having reference to the *persons* concerned in the transfer, while the latter relates to the *mode* of transfer. *Old* has for opposite both *New* and *Young*, according as it is applied to *things* or to *living things*. *Attack* and *Defence* are correlative terms; as are also *Attack* and *Resistance. Resistance*, again, has for its other correlative *Submission. Truth in the abstract* is opposed to *Error*; but the opposite of *Truth communicated* is *Falsehood. Acquisition* is contrasted both with *Deprivation* and with *Loss. Refusal* is the counterpart both of *Offer* and of *Consent. Disuse* and *Misuse* may either of them be considered as the correlative of *Use. Teaching* with reference to what is taught, is opposed to *Misteaching*; but with reference to the act itself, its proper reciprocal is *Learning*.

Words contrasted in form do not always bear the same contrast in their meaning. The word *Malefactor*, for example, would, from its derivation, appear to be exactly the opposite of *Benefactor*: but the ideas attached to these two words are far from being directly opposed; for while the latter expresses one who confers a benefit, the former denotes one who has violated the laws.

Independently of the immediate practical uses derivable from the arrangement of words in double columns, many considerations, interesting in a philosophical point of view, are presented by the study of correlative expressions. It will be found, on strict examination, that there seldom exists an exact opposition between two words which may at first sight appear to be the counterparts of one another; for in general, the one will be found to possess in reality more force or extent of meaning than the other with which it is contrasted. The correlative term sometimes assumes the form of a mere negative, although it is really endowed with a considerable positive form. Thus *Disrespect* is not merely the absence of *Respect*: its signification trenches on the opposite idea, namely, *Contempt*. In like manner, *Untruth* is not merely the negative of *Truth*; it involves a degree of *Falsehood. Irreligion,* which is properly *the want of Religion,* is understood as being nearly synonymous with *Impiety*. For these reasons, the reader must not expect that all the words which stand side by side in the two columns shall be the precise correlatives of each other; for the nature of the subject, as well as the imperfections of language, renders it impossible always to preserve such an exactness of correlation.

There exist comparatively few words of a general character to which no correlative term, either of negation or of opposition, can be assigned, and which therefore require no corresponding second column. The correlative idea, especially that which constitutes a sense negative to the primary one, may, indeed, be formed or conceived; but, from its occurring rarely, no word has been framed to represent it; for, in language, as in other matters, the supply fails when there is no probability of a demand. Occasionally we find this deficiency provided for by the contrivance of prefixing the syllable *non*; as, for instance, the negatives of *existence*, *performance*, *payment*, &c. are expressed by the compound words, *non-existence*, *non-performance*, *non-payment*, &c. Functions of a similar kind are performed by the prefixes *dis-*,[1] *anti-*, *contra-*, *mis-*, *in-*, and *un-*.[2] With respect to all these, and especially the last, great latitude is allowed according to the necessities of the case; a latitude which is limited only by the taste and discretion of the writer.

On the other hand, it is hardly possible to find two words having in all respects the same meaning, and being therefore interchangeable; that is, admitting of being employed indiscriminately, the one or the other, in all their applications. The investigation of the

[1] The words *disannul* and *dissever*, however, have the same meaning as *annul* and *sever*; *to unloose* is the same as *to loose*, and *inebriety* is synonymous with *ebriety*.

[2] In the case of adjectives, the addition to a substantive of the terminal syllable *less*, gives it a negative meaning: as *taste, tasteless*; *care, careless*; *hope, hopeless*; *friend, friendless*; *fault, faultless*; &c.

distinctions to be drawn between words apparently synonymous, forms a separate branch of inquiry, which I have not presumed here to enter upon; for the subject has already occupied the attention of much abler critics than myself, and its complete exhaustion would require the devotion of a whole life. The purpose of this Work, it must be borne in mind, is, not to explain the signification of words, but simply to classify and arrange them according to the sense in which they are now used, and which I presume to be already known to the reader. I enter into no inquiry into the changes of meaning they may have undergone in the course of time.[1] I am content to accept them at the value of their present currency, and have no concern with their etymologies, or with the history of their transformations; far less do I venture to thrid the mazes of the vast labyrinth into which I should be led by any attempt at a general discrimination of synonyms. The difficulties I have had to contend with have already been sufficiently great, without this addition to my labours.

The most cursory glance over the pages of a Dictionary will show that a great number of words are used in various senses, sometimes distinguished by slight shades of difference, but often diverging widely from their primary signification, and even, in some cases, bearing to it no perceptible relation. It may even happen that the very same word has two significations quite opposite to one another. This is the case with the verb to *cleave*, which means *to adhere tenaciously,* and also *to separate by a blow. To propugn* sometimes expressed *to attack*; at other times *to defend. To let* is *to hinder*, as well as *to permit. To ravel* means both *to entangle* and *to disentangle. Shameful* and *shameless* are nearly synonymous. *Priceless* may either mean *invaluable* or *of no value. Nervous* is used sometimes for *strong*, at other times for *weak*. The alphabetical Index at the end of this Work sufficiently shows the multiplicity of uses to which, by the elasticity of language, the meaning of words has been stretched, so as to adapt them to a great variety of modified significations in subservience to the nicer shades of thought, which, under peculiarity of circumstances, require corresponding expression. Words thus admitting of different meanings have therefore to be arranged under each of the respective heads corresponding to these various acceptations. There are many words, again, which express ideas compounded of two elementary ideas belonging to different classes. It is therefore necessary to place these words respectively under each of the generic heads to which they relate. The necessity of these repetitions is increased by the circumstance, that ideas included under one class are often connected by relations of the same kind as the ideas which belong to another class. Thus we find the same relations of *order* and of *quantity* existing among the ideas of *Time* as well as those of *Space*. Sequence in the one is denoted by the same terms as sequence in the other; and the measures of time also express the measures of space. The cause and the effect are often designated by the same word. The word *Sound*, for instance, denotes both the impression made upon the ear by sonorous vibrations, and also the vibrations themselves, which are the cause or source of that impression. *Mixture* is used for the act of mixing, as well as for the product of that operation. *Taste* and *Smell* express both the sensations and the qualities of material bodies giving rise to them. *Thought* is the act of thinking; but the same word denotes also the idea resulting from the act. *Judgment* is the act of deciding, and also the decision come to. *Purchase* is that acquisition of a thing by payment, as well as the thing itself so acquired. *Speech* is both the act of speaking and the words spoken; and so on with regard to an endless multiplicity of words. Mind is essentially distinct from Matter; and yet, in all languages, the attributes of the one are metaphorically transferred to those of the other. Matter, in all its forms, is

[1] Such changes are innumerable: for instance, the words *tyrant*, *parasite*, *sophist*, *churl*, *knave*, *villain*, anciently conveyed no opprobrious meaning. *Impertinent* merely expressed *irrelative*, and implied neither *rudeness* nor *intrusion*, as it does at present. *Indifferent* originally meant *impartial*; *extravagant* was simply *digressive*; and *to prevent* was properly *to precede* and *assist*. The old translations of the Scriptures furnish many striking examples of the alterations which time has brought in the signification of words. Much curious information on this subject is contained in Trench's *Lectures on the Study of Words*.

endowed by the figurative genius of every language with the functions which pertain to intellect; and we perpetually talk of its phenomena and of its powers, as if they resulted from the voluntary influence of one body on another, acting and reacting, impelling and being impelled, controlling and being controlled, as if animated by spontaneous energies and guided by specific intentions. On the other hand, expressions, of which the primary signification refers exclusively to the properties and actions of matter, are metaphorically applied to the phenomena of thought and volition, and even to the feelings and passions of the soul; and in speaking of a *ray of hope*, a *shade of doubt*, a *flight of fancy*, a *flash of wit*, the *warmth of emotion*, or the *ebullitions of anger*, we are scarcely conscious that we are employing metaphors which have this material origin.

As a general rule, I have deemed it incumbent on me to place words and phrases which appertain more especially to one head, also under the other heads to which they have a relation, whenever it appeared to me that this repetition would suit the convenience of the inquirer, and spare him the trouble of turning to other parts of the work; for I have always preferred to subject myself to the imputation of redundance, rather than incur the reproach of insufficiency.[1] When, however, the divergence of the associated from the primary idea is sufficiently marked, I have contented myself with making a reference to the place where the modified signification will be found.[2] But in order to prevent needless extension, I have, in general, omitted *conjugate words*,[3] which are so obviously derivable from those that are given in the same place, that the reader may safely be left to form them for himself. This is the case with adverbs derived from adjectives by the simple addition of the terminal syllable *-ly*; such as *closely*, *carefully*, *safely*, &c., from *close*, *careful*, *safe*, &c., and also with adjectives or participles immediately derived from the verbs which are already given. In all such cases, an '&c.' indicates that reference is understood to be made to these roots. I have observed the same rule in compiling the Index; retaining only the primary or more simple word, and omitting the conjugate words obviously derived from them. Thus I assume the word *short* as the representative of its immediate derivatives *shortness*, *shorten*, *shortening*, *shortened*, *shorter*, *shortly*, which would have had the same references, and which the reader can readily supply.

The same verb is frequently used indiscriminately either in the active or transitive, or in the neuter or intransitive sense. In these cases, I have generally not thought it worth while to increase the bulk of the Work by the needless repetition of that word; for the reader, whom I suppose to understand the use of the words, must also be presumed to be competent to apply them correctly.

There are a multitude of words of a specific character which, although they properly occupy places in the columns of a dictionary, yet, having no relation to general ideas, do not come within the scope of this compilation, and are consequently omitted.[4] The names

[1] Frequent repetitions of the same series of expressions, accordingly, will be met with under various headings. For example, the word *Relinquishment* with its synonyms, occurs as a heading at No. 624, where it applies to *intention*, and also at No. 782, where it refers to *property*. The word *Chance* has two significations, distinct from one another: the one implying the *absence of an assignable cause;* in which case it comes under the category of the relation of Causation, and occupies the No. 156: the other, the *absence of design*, in which latter sense it ranks under the operations of the Will, and has assigned to it the place No. 621. I have, in like manner, distinguished *Sensibility*, *Pleasure*, *Pain*, *Taste*, &c., according as they relate to *Physical*, or to *Moral Affections*; the former being found at Nos. 375, 377, 378, 390, &c., and the latter at Nos. 822, 827, 828, 850, &c.

[2] [Successive editors have developed this system of cross-references.] [SML]

[3] By '*conjugate* or *paronymous* words is meant, correctly speaking, different parts of speech from the same root, which exactly corresponds in point of meaning'.—*A Selection of English Synonyms*, edited by Archbishop Whately.

[4] [The author did not in all cases rigidly adhere to this rule; and the editors have thought themselves justified both in retaining and in adding some words of the specific character here mentioned, which may be occasionally in request by general writers [JLR], although in categories of this nature no attempt at completeness has been made. [SRR] See 1982 Preface, p xi] [SML]

of objects in Natural History, and technical terms belonging exclusively to Science or to Art, or relating to particular operations, and of which the signification is restricted to those specific objects, come under this category. Exceptions must, however, be made in favour of such words as admit of metaphorical application to general subjects, with which custom has associated them, and of which they may be cited as being typical or illustrative. Thus, the word *Lion* will find a place under the head of *Courage*, of which it is regarded as the type. *Anchor*, being emblematic of *Hope*, is introduced among the words expressing that emotion; and in like manner, *butterfly* and *weathercock*, which are suggestive of fickleness, are included in the category of *Irresolution*.

With regard to the admission of many words and expressions, which the classical reader might be disposed to condemn as vulgarisms, or which he, perhaps, might stigmatize as pertaining rather to the slang than to the legitimate language of the day, I would beg to observe, that, having due regard to the uses to which this Work was to be adapted, I did not feel myself justified in excluding them solely on that ground, if they possessed an acknowledged currency in general intercourse. It is obvious that, with respect to degrees of conventionality, I could not have attempted to draw any strict lines of demarcation; and far less could I have presumed to erect any absolute standard of purity. My object, be it remembered, is not to regulate the use of words, but simply to supply and to suggest such as may be wanted on occasion, leaving the proper selection entirely to the discretion and taste of the employer.[1] If a novelist or a dramatist, for example, proposed to delineate some vulgar personage, he would wish to have the power of putting into the mouth of the speaker expressions that would accord with his character; just as the actor, to revert to a former comparison, who had to personate a peasant, would choose for his attire the most homely garb, and would have just reason to complain if the theatrical wardrobe furnished him with no suitable costume.

Words which have, in process of time, become obsolete, are of course rejected from this collection.[2] On the other hand, I have admitted a considerable number of words and phrases borrowed from other languages, chiefly the French and Latin, some of which may be considered as already naturalized; while others, though avowedly foreign, are frequently employed in English composition, particularly in familiar style, on account of their being peculiarly expressive, and because we have no corresponding words of equal force in our own language.[3] The rapid advances which are being made in scientific knowledge, and consequent improvement in all the arts of life, and the extension of those arts and sciences to so many new purposes and objects, create a continual demand for the formation of new terms to express new agencies, new wants, and new combinations. Such terms, from being at first merely technical, are rendered, by more general use, familiar to the multitude, and having a well-defined acceptation, are eventually incorporated into the language, which they contribute to enlarge and to enrich. *Neologies* of this kind are perfectly legitimate, and highly advantageous; and they necessarily introduce those gradual and progressive changes which every language is destined to undergo.[4]

[1] [It may be added that the Thesaurus is an aid not only in the choice of appropriate forms of expression, but in the rejection of those which are unfit; and that a vulgar phrase may often furnish a convenient clue to the group of classic synonyms among which it is placed. Moreover, the slang expressions admitted into the work bear a small proportion to those in constant use by English writers and speakers.] [JLR]

[2] [A few apparently obsolete words have nevertheless found their way into the Thesaurus. In justification of their admission, it may be contended that well-known words, though no longer current, give occasional point by an archaic form of expression, and are of value to the novelist or dramatist who has to depict a bygone age.] [JLR]

[3] All these words and phrases are printed in Italics. [A few of these expressions, although widely used by writers of English, are of a form which is really incorrect or unusual in their own language; in some more extreme cases of this kind, the more widely used or incorrect form has been given.] [SRR]

[4] Thus, in framing the present classification, I have frequently felt the want of substantive terms corresponding to abstract qualities or ideas denoted by certain adjectives, and have been often tempted to invent words that might express these abstractions; but I have yielded to this temptation

Some modern writers, however, have indulged in a habit of arbitrarily fabricating new words and a new-fangled phraseology, without any necessity, and with manifest injury to the purity of the language. This vicious practice, the offspring of indolence or conceit, implies an ignorance or neglect of the riches in which the English language already abounds, and which would have supplied them with words of recognized legitimacy, conveying precisely the same meaning as those they so recklessly coin in the illegal mint of their own fancy.

A work constructed on the plan of classification I have proposed might, if ably executed, be of great value, in tending to limit the fluctuations to which language has always been subject, by establishing an authoritative standard for its regulation. Future historians, philologists, and lexicographers, when investigating the period when new words were introduced, or discussing the import given at the present time to the old, might find their labours lightened by being enabled to appeal to such a standard, instead of having to search for data among the scattered writings of the age. Nor would its utility be confined to a single language; for the principles of its construction are universally applicable to all languages, whether living or dead. On the same plan of classification there might be formed a French, a German, a Latin, or a Greek Thesaurus, possessing, in their respective spheres, the same advantages as those of the English model.[1] Still more useful would be a conjunction of these methodized compilations in two languages, the French and English, for instance; the columns of each being placed in parallel juxtaposition. No means yet devised would so greatly facilitate the acquisition of the one language, by those who are acquainted with the other: none would afford such ample assistance to the translator in either language; and none would supply such ready and effectual means of instituting an accurate comparison between them, and of fairly appreciating their respective merits and defects. In a still higher degree would all those advantages be combined and multiplied in a *Polyglot Lexicon* constructed on this system.

Metaphysicians engaged in the more profound investigation of the Philosophy of Language will be materially assisted by having the ground thus prepared for them, in a previous analysis and classification of our ideas; for such classification of ideas is the true basis on which words, which are their symbols, should be classified.[2] It is by such analysis alone that we can arrive at a clear perception of the relation which these symbols bear to their corresponding ideas, or can obtain a correct knowledge of the elements which enter into the formation of compound ideas, and of the exclusions by which we arrive at the abstractions so perpetually resorted to in the process of reasoning, and in the communication of our thoughts.

only in the four following instances, having framed from the adjectives *irrelative*, *amorphous*, *sinistral*, and *gaseous*, the abstract nouns *irrelation*, *amorphism*, *sinistrality*, and *gaseity*. I have ventured also to introduce the adjective *intersocial* to express the active voluntary relations between man and man. [Not all these coinages have been retained.] [SML]

[1] [This suggestion has been followed, in French, in a '*Dictionnaire Idéologique*' by T. Robertson (Paris, 1859); and, in German, in a '*Deutscher Sprachschatz*' by D. Sanders (Hamburg, 1878), and '*Deutscher Wortschatz oder Der passende Ausdruck*' by A. Schelling (Stuttgart, 1892).] [JLR]

[2] The principle by which I have been guided in framing my verbal classification is the same as that which is employed in the various departments of Natural History. Thus the sectional divisions I have formed, correspond to Natural Families in Botany and Zoology, and the filiation of words presents a network analogous to the natural filiation of plants or animals.

The following are the only publications that have come to my knowledge in which any attempt has been made to construct a systematic arrangement of ideas with a view to their expression. The earliest of these, supposed to be at least nine hundred years old, is the AMERA CÓSHA, or *Vocabulary of the Sanscrit Language,* by Amera Sinha, of which an English translation, by the late Henry T. Colebrooke, was printed at Serampoor, in the year 1808. The classification of words is there, as might be expected, exceedingly imperfect and confused, especially in all that relates to abstract ideas or mental operations. This will be apparent from the very title of the first section, which comprehends '*Heaven, Gods, Demons, Fire, Air, Velocity, Eternity, Much*': while *Sin, Virtue, Happiness, Destiny, Cause, Nature, Intellect, Reasoning, Knowledge, Senses, Tastes, Odours,*

Lastly, such analysis alone can determine the principles on which a strictly *Philosophical Language* might be constructed. The probable result of the construction of such a language would be its eventual adoption by every civilized nation; thus realizing that splendid aspiration of philanthropists—the establishment of a Universal Language. However utopian such a project may appear to the present generation, and however abortive may have been the former endeavours of Bishop Wilkins and others to realize it,[1] its accomplishment is surely not beset with greater difficulties than have impeded the progress to many other beneficial objects, which in former times appeared to be no less visionary, and which yet were successfully achieved, in later ages, by the continued and persevering exertions of the human intellect. Is there at the present day, then, any ground for despair, that at some future stage of that higher civilization to which we trust the world is gradually tending, some new and bolder effort of genius towards the solution of this great problem may be crowned with success, and compass an object of such vast and paramount utility? Nothing, indeed, would conduce more directly to bring about a golden age of union and harmony among the several nations and races of mankind than the removal of that barrier to the interchange of thought and mutual good understanding between man and man, which is now interposed by the diversity of their respective languages.

Colours, are all included and jumbled together in the fourth section. A more logical order, however, pervades the sections relating to natural objects, such as *Seas*, *Earth*, *Towns*, *Plants*, and *Animals*, which form separate classes; exhibiting a remarkable effort at analysis at so remote a period of Indian literature.

The well-known work of Bishop Wilkins entitled '*An Essay towards a Real Character and a Philosophical Language*', published in 1668, had for its object the formation of a system of symbols which might serve as a universal language. It professed to be founded on a 'scheme of analysis of the things or notions to which names were to be assigned'; but notwithstanding the immense labour and ingenuity expended in the construction of this system, it was soon found to be far too abstruse and recondite for practical application.

In the year 1797, there appeared in Paris an anonymous work, entitled 'PASIGRAPHIE, *ou Premiers Eléments du nouvel Art-Science d'écrire et d'imprimer une langue de manière à être lu et entendu dans toute autre langue sans traduction*', of which an edition in German was also published. It contains a great number of tabular schemes of categories; all of which appear to be excessively arbitrary and artificial, and extremely difficult of application, as well as of apprehension. [Systems of grouping with relation to ideas are also adopted in an '*Analytical Dictionary of the English Language*' by David Booth (London, 1835), a '*Dictionnaire Analogique de la Langue Française*' by P. Boissière (Paris), and a '*Dictionnaire Logique de la Langue Française*' by L'Abbé Elie Blanc (Paris, 1882).] [JLR]

[1] 'The Languages', observes Horne Tooke, 'which are commonly used throughout the world, are much more simple and easy, convenient and philosophical, than Wilkins' scheme for a *real character*; or than any other scheme that has been at any other time imagined or proposed for the purpose.'—'Επεα Πτερόεντα, p. 125.

Instructions

The Text

The *Thesaurus* is divided into six *Classes*. The first three Classes cover the external world: Class One, *Abstract Relations*, deals with such ideas as number, order and time; Class Two, *Space*, is concerned with movement, shapes and sizes, while Class Three, *Matter*, covers the physical world and humankind's perception of it by means of the five senses. The last three Classes deal with the internal world of human beings: the human mind (Class Four, *Intellect*), the human will (Class Five, *Volition*) and the human heart and soul (Class Six, *Emotion, Religion and Morality*). There is a logical progression from abstract concepts, through the material universe, to mankind itself, culminating in what Roget saw as mankind's highest achievements: morality and religion.

Roget borrowed his scheme from natural history, with its hierarchy of Phyla, Classes, Orders and Families. His system has also been compared to a tree, with ever smaller ramifications diverging from the main branches. This is a workable way of dividing up human experience, as can be seen from the way Roget's system has survived intact through numerous revisions. But life, as Roget himself points out (see his *Introduction* p xxiv), is not easily compartmentalized. 'Choice', for example, involves both the will (Class Five) and the intellect (Class Four). The language which reflects our experience is equally complex, more like a web than a tree, for it interconnects at all points. Also one word may have many meanings depending on its context. Roget was aware of this problem. His solution was to use copious cross-references to link related groups of words, a method which succeeded in both reflecting the complexity of language and coming to terms with it.

To see at a glance how Roget's system works, look up the *Plan of Classification* on pp xxxvi–xxxvii. This shows the six Classes, further subdivided into *Sections*. Each Section deals with a particular aspect of the Class within which it is found. So under Class One, *Abstract Relations*, we find Sections for *Quantity*, *Order*, *Time* and so on. The Sections themselves are further subdivided into *Heads*. Within Class One Section Six, *Time*, for instance, there are 35 Heads dealing with, among others, the ideas of *Present Time*, *Past Time*, *Transience*, and *Age*. Each Head is numbered. There are 990 in the present edition, a slight reduction from Roget's original 1,000. It is the Heads which form the basic units of the book, and they follow each other in a logical progression, as can be seen in the *Tabular Synopsis of Categories* which follows the *Plan of Classification*. It is a sign of Roget's skill in compiling the *Thesaurus* that this basic framework has remained virtually intact through edition after edition of the copyright version, of which this is the most recent.

The Heads themselves are divided into paragraphs, grouped together according to their part of speech. Head 852, *Hope*, for example, has three paragraphs of nouns (marked N.), two of adjectives (Adj.), two of verbs (Vb.), one of adverbs (Adv.) and one of interjections (Int.). Not all Heads have a full complement of parts of speech, nor are the labels themselves applied too strictly, words and phrases being allocated to the part of speech which most closely describes their function. Each paragraph begins with a word in italics known as the *Keyword*. This is both a clue to the kind of words found in that paragraph and also itself part of the vocabulary. It is *not* a synonym of the words which follow. It was Roget's intention to offer words which express every aspect of an idea, rather than to list

Instructions

The Text

The *Thesaurus* is divided into six *Classes.* The first three Classes cover the external world: Class One, *Abstract Relations*, deals with such ideas as number, order and time; Class Two, *Space*, is concerned with movement, shapes and sizes, while Class Three, *Matter*, covers the physical world and humankind's perception of it by means of the five senses. The last three Classes deal with the internal world of human beings: the human mind (Class Four, *Intellect*), the human will (Class Five, *Volition*), and the human heart and soul (Class Six, *Emotion, Religion and Morality*). There is a logical progression from abstract concepts, through the material universe, to mankind itself, culminating in what Roget saw as mankind's highest achievements: morality and religion.

Roget borrowed his scheme from natural history, with its hierarchy of Phyla, Classes, Orders and Families. His system has also been compared to a tree, with ever smaller ramifications diverging from the main branches. This is a workable way of dividing up human experience, as can be seen from the way Roget's system has survived intact through numerous revisions. But life, as Roget himself points out (see his *Introduction* p xxiv), is not easily compartmentalized. 'Choice', for example, involves both the will (Class Five) and the intellect (Class Four). The language which reflects our experience is equally complex, more like a web than a tree, for it interconnects at all points. Also one word may have many meanings depending on its context. Roget was aware of this problem. His solution was to use copious cross-references to link related groups of words, a method which succeeded in both reflecting the complexity of language and coming to terms with it.

To see at a glance how Roget's system works, look up the *Plan of Classification* on pp xxxvi–xxxvii. This shows the Six Classes, further subdivided into *Sections.* Each Section deals with a particular aspect of the Class within which it is found. So under Class One, *Abstract Relations*, we find Sections for *Quantity*, *Order*, *Time* and so on. The Sections themselves are further subdivided into *Heads.* Within Class One Section Six, *Time*, for instance, there are 35 Heads dealing with, among others, the ideas of *Present Time*, *Past Time*, *Transience*, and *Age.* Each Head is numbered. There are 990 in the present edition, a slight reduction from Roget's original 1,000. It is the Heads which form the basic units of the book, and they follow each other in a logical progression, as can be seen in the *Tabular Synopsis of Categories* which follows the *Plan of Classification.* It is a sign of Roget's skill in compiling the *Thesaurus* that this basic framework has remained virtually intact through edition after edition of the copyright version, of which this is the most recent.

The Heads themselves are divided into paragraphs, grouped together according to their part of speech. Head **852**, *Hope,* for example, has three paragraphs of nouns (marked **N.**), two of adjectives (**Adj.**), two of verbs (**Vb.**), one of adverbs (**Adv.**) and one of interjections (**Int.**). Not all Heads have a full complement of parts of speech, nor are the labels themselves applied too strictly, words and phrases being allocated to the part of speech which most closely describes their function. Each paragraph begins with a word in italics known as the *keyword.* This is both a clue to the kind of words found in that paragraph, and also itself part of the vocabulary. It is *not* a synonym of the words which follow: it was Roget's intention to offer words which express every aspect of an idea, rather than to list the synonyms. It is called the *keyword* because it is both the 'key' to the rest of the paragraph, and the 'open sesame' to the whole book, being used to identify the position of other words in the index and cross-references.

Within the paragraphs, words are grouped between semicolons according to their meaning, context or level of usage (i.e. colloquial, formal, etc.). These groups follow one another in a logical sequence, exploring every aspect of the idea under consideration. By comparing, whether consciously or not, the words and phrases offered, you can now select the most appropriate. It was Roget's expectation that his readers would "recognize" the word they wanted, guided by "an instinctive tact".[1] On this assumption, words having more than one meaning or context are not usually repeated within paragraphs, nor are transitive and intransitive verbs listed separately. Where the right word is not immediately apparent, but an unfamiliar one seems from the context as if it might answer, it is advisable, especially for non-English speakers, to check with a dictionary. Yet more ideas can be obtained by looking up the cross-references. These are found at the end of some groups of words and consist of a Head number and a word in italics. The latter, besides being an item of vocabulary in its own right, is also the *keyword* of a paragraph in the given Head. It is also worth consulting the Heads before and after the one originally looked up. Most Heads are in pairs, representing the positive and negative aspects of an idea, e.g. **852** *Hope*, **853** *Hopelessness*. Sometimes several Heads between them cover an idea – 'education' is dealt with in **534** *Teaching*, **535** *Misteaching*, **536** *Learning*, **537** *Teacher*, **538** *Learner* and **539** *School*. The *Tabular Synopsis of Categories* shows how the Heads are related to one another.

A few conventions should be explained. These have mainly been designed to avoid repetition and save space. Conjugate forms are often indicated by the use of 'etc.' For instance, 'be content, – satisfied etc. adj.' suggests that readers can form further verbs for themselves on the same pattern. In the same way, 'darkness etc. adj.' suggests how more nouns may be formed from the adjectives already given. Where consecutive expressions use the same word, two means are used to avoid repeating it. The phrases may be linked by '*or*', as in 'drop a brick *or* a clanger', 'countryman *or* -woman'. Alternatively, the repeated word is simply indicated by its first letter, followed by a full stop: 'weasel word, loan w., nonce w.,' and so on. Brackets within the text are occasionally used to clarify the context of a word, as in 'dissolve (a marriage)'. 'Tdmk' in brackets following a noun indicates a registered trade mark. An 'e' in brackets added to the end of a word means that it is of French origin and requires a final 'e' if applied to a woman. '**See** . . .' is used to refer the reader to another paragraph within the same Head, where the idea under consideration is dealt with more thoroughly. This often happens where a general paragraph, such as '*killing*' in Head **362**, is followed by more specific paragraphs, in this case '*homicide*' and '*slaughter*'.

Spelling and hyphenation is uniform with Longman dictionaries. It should be borne in mind, however, that a living language takes many shapes, and these are not the only correct or permitted orthographies. For the benefit of crossword puzzle enthusiasts and others, alternative current spellings are given in the Index.

The Index

Once familiar with Roget's *Plan of Classification*, readers will be able to find their own way round the book, and this is certainly the most rewarding method of using the *Thesaurus*. However, new readers, and those in a hurry, will probably prefer to use the Index at the back of this book.

The Index is based on a complete computer-listing of all the items in the book. It is intended as a guide to the text rather than as a catalogue of its contents, and the reader

[1] Introduction to the 1852 edition, p. xxii

should not assume that a word is missing from the book simply because it is not in the Index. Nor is the list of references at each entry intended to be exhaustive. The reader should bear in mind that the Heads offer words to express a given idea or ideas; it really does not matter whether you look up a noun, a verb or an adjective, as once you have found the right Head, all the parts of speech conveying that idea will be available to you.

The Index consists of a list of items, each of which is followed by one or more references to the text. These references consist of: a Head number; a *keyword* in italics, and a part of speech label (n. for nouns, adj. for adjectives, vb. for verbs, adv. for adverbs, and int. for interjections). The *keyword* is given to identify the paragraph which contains the word you have looked up; it also gives an indication of the ideas contained in that paragraph, so it can be used as a clue where a word has several meanings and therefore several references. To use the Index, look up your word, turn to the Head number given in your chosen reference, and under the relevant part of speech you will find a paragraph beginning with the *keyword* given in the Index.

Where several references are given choose the most appropriate *keyword*. For instance, suppose you need another expression for 'feeling happy'. Look up 'happy' in the Index, and you will find a list of references. The *keywords* given include 'apt', 'willing' and 'drunk', which refer to other uses of the word 'happy'. But the *keywords* 'cheerful' and 'happy' are obviously relevant, and looking up **833** *cheerful* and **824** *happy* will offer you an abundance of suitable terms.

Some points to note

1) *Items are listed in alphabetical order*, whether they are words or phrases. For example: "hall, halleluja, halliard, hallmark, hall of residence, halloo, hallow, hallowed, hallowed by custom, Hallowe'en". 'The', 'a', and 'be' are disregarded for this purpose. The only exception to this rule is (2).

2) *Phrases beginning with a verb* are listed immediately under that verb, which is replaced by a dash. For example: "hang, – about, – back, – by a thread" etc. A glance at this list will often help the reader to find the most apposite reference more quickly.

3) *References to the same Head* are not usually repeated under different grammatical forms of the same word. For example: "abundance" has references to Heads **32, 171, 632, 625** and **637**, while "abundant" has references to none of these, but lists **104, 800** and **813**. This means that the adjective is found in three Heads which do not list the noun form: the idea of "abundance", however, is present in all the Heads listed. It is a good idea to check other forms of the word you are looking up, to obtain the fullest list of references to suitable Heads. Forms that do not follow each other immediately are linked by the direction '*See* . . .'.

Obvious derivatives of words, such as nouns ending in '-ness', adjectives in '-ing' or '-ed' and adverbs in '-ly', are not usually given an entry of their own unless they have a different meaning from the parent word.

4) *Objects* should be looked up in their simplest form, e.g. "ship" rather than "clipper", "dog" rather than "wolfhound" and "flag" rather than "banneret". An object with a compound name, such as "money box" may be dealt with under either or both of its constituent parts.

5) *Phrases* are listed in alphabetical order as noted above. In idioms where the first word is variable, such as "have (*or* know) by heart", the phrase will be indexed under both, or under the next word in the phrase.

6) *General expressions* such as "good example", "bad health", "no meaning" and "not mind" have been retained in the Index as useful guides for the reader.

7) *(s) after a word* indicates that references may apply to either the singular or the plural form.

8) *Alternative spellings* are given after the main form.

Plan of classification

Class	*Section*	*Heads*
1 Abstract relations	***1 Existence***	**1–8**
	2 Relation	**9–25**
	3 Quantity	**26–59**
	4 Order	**60–84**
	5 Number	**85–107**
	6 Time	**108–142**
	7 Change	**143–155**
	8 Causation	**156–182**
2 Space	***1 Space in general***	**183–194**
	2 Dimensions	**195–242**
	3 Form	**243–264**
	4 Motion	**265–318**
3 Matter	***1 Matter in general***	**319–323**
	2 Inorganic matter	**324–357**
	3 Organic matter	**358–446**
4 Intellect: the exercise of the mind		
Division one: Formation of ideas	***1 General***	**447–452**
	2 Precursory conditions and operations	**453–465**
	3 Materials for reasoning	**466–474**
	4 Reasoning processes	**475–479**
	5 Results of reasoning	**480–504**
	6 Extension of thought	**505–511**
	7 Creative thought	**512–513**
Division two: Communication of ideas	***1 Nature of ideas communicated***	**514–521**
	2 Modes of communication	**522–546**
	3 Means of communicating ideas	**547–594**

Class	*Section*	*Heads*
5 Volition: the exercise of the will		
Division one*: *Individual volition	***1 Volition in general***	595–616
	2 Prospective volition	617–675
	3 Voluntary action	676–699
	4 Antagonism	700–724
	5 Results of action	725–732
Division two*: *Social volition	***1 General social volition***	733–755
	2 Special social volition	756–763
	3 Conditional social volition	764–770
	4 Possessive relations	771–816
6 Emotion, religion and morality	***1 General***	817–823
	2 Personal emotion	824–879
	3 Interpersonal emotion	880–912
	4 Morality	913–964
	5 Religion	965–990

Tabular synopsis of categories

Class one: Abstract relations

1 Existence

Abstract:	1 Existence	2 Nonexistence
Concrete:	3 Substantiality	4 Insubstantiality
Formal: (internal/external)	5 Intrinsicality	6 Extrinsicality
Modal: (absolute/relative)	7 State	8 Circumstance

2 Relation

Absolute:	9 Relation	10 Unrelatedness
	11 Consanguinity	
	12 Correlation	
	13 Identity	14 Contrariety
	15 Difference	
Continuous:	16 Uniformity	17 Nonuniformity
Partial:	18 Similarity	19 Dissimilarity
	20 Imitation	21 Originality
	22 Copy	23 Prototype
General:	24 Agreement	25 Disagreement

3 Quantity

Simple: (absolute/relative)	26 Quantity	27 Degree
	28 Equality	29 Inequality
Comparative:	30 Mean	
	31 Compensation	
(by comparison with a standard)	32 Greatness	33 Smallness
(by comparison with an object)	34 Superiority	35 Inferiority
(changes in quantity)	36 Increase	37 Decrease
Conjunctive:	38 Addition	39 Subtraction
	40 Adjunct	41 Remainder
		42 Decrement
	43 Mixture	44 Simpleness
	45 Union	46 Disunion
	47 Bond	
	48 Coherence	49 Noncoherence
	50 Combination	51 Decomposition
Concrete:	52 Whole	53 Part
	54 Completeness	55 Incompleteness
	56 Composition	57 Exclusion
	58 Component	59 Extraneousness

4 Order

General:	60 Order	61 Disorder
	62 Arrangement	63 Derangement
Consecutive:	64 Precedence	65 Sequence
	66 Precursor	67 Sequel
	68 Beginning	69 End
	70 Middle	
	71 Continuity	72 Discontinuity
	73 Term	
Collective:	74 Assemblage	75 Nonassembly
	76 Focus	
Distributive:	77 Class	
	78 Inclusion	
	79 Generality	80 Speciality
Categorical:	81 Rule	82 Multiformity
	83 Conformity	84 Nonconformity

5 Number

Abstract:	85 Number	
	86 Numeration	
	87 List	
Determinate:	88 Unity	89 Accompaniment
	90 Duality	
	91 Duplication	92 Bisection
	93 Triality	
	94 Triplication	95 Trisection
	96 Quaternity	
	97 Quadruplication	98 Quadrisection
	99 Five and over	100 Multisection
Indeterminate:	101 Plurality	102 Fraction
		103 Zero
	104 Multitude	105 Fewness
	106 Repetition	
	107 Infinity	

6 Time

Absolute:	108 Time	109 Neverness
(definite/indefinite)	110 Period	111 Course
	112 Contingent duration	
	113 Long duration	114 Transience
	115 Perpetuity	116 Instantaneity
	117 Chronometry	118 Anachronism
Relative: (to succession)	119 Priority	120 Posteriority
	121 Present time	122 Different time
	123 Synchronism	
(to a period)	124 Futurity	125 Past time
	126 Newness	127 Oldness
	128 Morning	129 Evening
	130 Youth	131 Age
	132 Young person	133 Old person
	134 Adultness	

(to an effect or purpose)	135 Earliness	136 Lateness
	137 Occasion	138 Untimeliness
Recurrent:	139 Frequency	140 Infrequency
	141 Periodicity	142 Fitfulness

7 Change

Simple:	143 Change	144 Permanence
	145 Cessation	146 Continuance
	147 Conversion	148 Reversion
	149 Revolution	
	150 Substitution	151 Interchange
Complex:	152 Changeableness	153 Stability
(present/future)	154 Event	155 Destiny

8 Causation

Constancy of sequence:	156 Cause	157 Effect
	158 Attribution	159 Chance
Connection between cause and effect:	160 Power	161 Impotence
	162 Strength	163 Weakness
Power in operation:	164 Production	165 Destruction
	166 Reproduction	
	167 Propagation	168 Destroyer
	169 Parentage	170 Posterity
	171 Productiveness	172 Unproductiveness
	173 Agency	
	174 Vigorousnes	175 Inertness
	176 Violence	177 Moderation
Indirect power:	178 Influence	
	179 Tendency	
	180 Liability	
Combination of causes:	181 Concurrence	182 Counteraction

Class two: Space

1 Space in general

Abstract space: (indefinite)	183 Space	
(definite)		184 Region
(limited)		185 Place
Relative space:	186 Situation	
	187 Location	188 Displacement
Existence in space:	189 Presence	190 Absence
	191 Inhabitant	192 Abode
	193 Contents	194 Receptacle

2 Dimensions

General:	195 Size	196 Littleness
	197 Expansion	198 Contraction
	199 Distance	200 Nearness
	201 Interval	202 Contiguity
Linear:	203 Length	204 Shortness
	205 Breadth	206 Narrowness
	207 Layer	208 Filament
	209 Height	210 Lowness
	211 Depth	212 Shallowness
	213 Summit	214 Base
	215 Verticality	216 Horizontality
	217 Pendency	218 Support
	219 Parallelism	220 Obliquity
	221 Inversion	
	222 Crossing	
Centrical: (general)	223 Exteriority	224 Interiority
		225 Centrality
	226 Covering	227 Lining
	228 Dressing	229 Undressing
	230 Surroundings	231 Interjacency
	232 Circumscription	
	233 Outline	
	234 Edge	
	235 Enclosure	
	236 Limit	
(special)	237 Front	238 Rear
	239 Laterality	240 Contraposition
	241 Dextrality	242 Sinistrality

3 Form

General:	243 Form	244 Amorphism
	245 Symmetry	246 Distortion
Special:	247 Angularity	
	248 Curvature	249 Straightness
	250 Circularity	251 Convolution
	252 Rotundity	
Superficial:	253 Convexity	
	254 Prominence	255 Concavity
	256 Sharpness	257 Bluntness
	258 Smoothness	259 Roughness
	260 Notch	261 Fold
	262 Furrow	
	263 Opening	264 Closure

4 Motion

General:	265 Motion	266 Quiescence
	267 Land travel	268 Traveller
	269 Water travel	270 Mariner
	271 Aeronautics	
	272 Transference	273 Carrier
	274 Vehicle	275 Ship

		276 Aircraft
Degrees of motion:	277 Velocity	278 Slowness
Conjoined with force:	279 Impulse	280 Recoil
With reference to direction:	281 Direction	282 Deviation
	283 Preceding	284 Following
	285 Progression	286 Regression
	287 Propulsion	288 Traction
	289 Approach	290 Recession
	291 Attraction	292 Repulsion
	293 Convergence	294 Divergence
	295 Arrival	296 Departure
	297 Ingress	298 Egress
	299 Reception	300 Ejection
	301 Food	302 Excretion
	303 Insertion	304 Extraction
	305 Passage	
	306 Overstepping	307 Shortfall
	308 Ascent	309 Descent
	310 Elevation	311 Lowering
	312 Leap	313 Plunge
	314 Circuition	315 Rotator
	316 Evolution	
	317 Oscillation	
	318 Agitation	

Class three: Matter

1 Matter in general

	319 Materiality	320 Immateriality
	321 Universe	
	322 Gravity	323 Lightness

2 Inorganic matter

Solids:	324 Density	325 Rarity
	326 Hardness	327 Softness
	328 Elasticity	
	329 Toughness	330 Brittleness
	331 Structure	332 Powderiness
	333 Friction	334 Lubrication
Fluids: (in general)	335 Fluidity	336 Gaseousness
	337 Liquefaction	338 Vaporization
(specific)	339 Water	340 Air
	341 Moisture	342 Dryness
	343 Ocean	344 Land
	345 Gulf	
	346 Lake	347 Marsh
		348 Plain

		349 Island
(in motion)	350 Stream	
	351 Conduit	352 Wind
		353 Air-pipe
	354 Semiliquidity	355 Bubble. Cloud
	356 Pulpiness	357 Unctuousness

3 Organic matter

Vitality: (general)	358 Organisms	359 Mineral
	360 Life	361 Death
		362 Killing
		363 Corpse
		364 Internment
(special)	365 Animality	366 Vegetable life
	367 Zoology	368 Biology
	369 Animal husbandry	370 Agriculture
	371 Humankind	
	372 Male	373 Female
Sensation: (general)	374 Physical sensibility	375 Physical insensibility
	376 Pleasure	377 Pain
(touch)	378 Touch	
(heat)	379 Heat	380 Cold
	381 Heating	382 Refrigeration
	383 Furnace	384 Refrigerator
	385 Fuel	
(taste)	386 Taste	387 Insipidity
	388 Pungency	
	389 Condiment	
	390 Savouriness	391 Unsavouriness
	392 Sweetness	393 Sourness
(odour)	394 Odour	395 Inodorousness
	396 Fragrance	397 Stench
(sound: general)	398 Sound	399 Silence
	400 Loudness	401 Faintness
(specific sounds)	402 Bang	403 Roll
	404 Resonance	405 Nonresonance
	406 Sibilation	407 Stridor
	408 Human cry	409 Ululation
(musical sounds)	410 Melody	411 Discord
	412 Music	
	413 Musician	414 Musical instrument
(perception of sound)	415 Hearing	416 Deafness
(light: general)	417 Light	418 Darkness
	419 Dimness	
	420 Luminary	421 Screen
	422 Transparency	423 Opacity
	424 Semitransparency	
(specific light)	425 Colour	426 Achromatism
	427 Whiteness	428 Blackness
	429 Grey	430 Brownness
	431 Redness	432 Orange
	433 Yellowness	434 Greenness
	435 Blueness	436 Purple

	437 Variegation	
(perception of light)	438 Vision	439 Blindness
	440 Dimsightedness	
	441 Spectator	442 Optical instrument
	443 Visibility	444 Invisibility
	445 Appearance	446 Disappearance

Class four: Intellect: the exercise of the mind

Division one: Formation of ideas

1 Intellectual operations in general

	447 Intellect	448 Absence of intellect
	449 Thought	450 Absence of thought
	451 Idea	
	452 Topic	

2 Precursory conditions and operations

	453 Curiosity	454 Incuriosity
	455 Attention	456 Inattention
	457 Carefulness	458 Negligence
	459 Enquiry	460 Answer
	461 Experiment	
	462 Comparison	
	463 Discrimination	464 Indiscrimination
	465 Measurement	

3 Materials for reasoning

	466 Evidence	467 Counterevidence
	468 Qualification	
(degrees of evidence)	469 Possibility	470 Impossibility
	471 Probability	472 Improbability
	473 Certainty	474 Uncertainty

4 Reasoning processes

	475 Reasoning	476 Intuition
		477 Sophistry
	478 Demonstration	479 Confutation

5 Results of reasoning

	480 Judgment	481 Misjudgment
	482 Overestimation	483 Underestimation
	484 Discovery	
	485 Belief	486 Unbelief
	487 Credulity	

	488 Assent	489 Dissent
	490 Knowledge	491 Ignorance
	492 Scholar	493 Ignoramus
	494 Truth	495 Error
	496 Maxim	497 Absurdity
(faculties)	498 Intelligence	499 Unintelligence
	500 Sage	501 Fool
	502 Sanity	503 Insanity
		504 Madman

6 Extension of thought

(to the past)	505 Memory	506 Oblivion
(to the future)	507 Expectation	508 Lack of expectation
		509 Disappointment
	510 Foresight	
	511 Prediction	

7 Creative thought

	512 Supposition	
	513 Imagination	

Division two: Communication of ideas

1 Nature of ideas communicated

	514 Meaning	515 Lack of meaning
	516 Intelligibility	517 Unintelligibility
	518 Equivocalness	
	519 Metaphor	
	520 Interpretation	521 Misinterpretation

2 Modes of communication

	522 Manifestation	523 Latency
	524 Information	525 Concealment
	526 Disclosure	527 Hiding
	528 Publication	
	529 News	530 Secret
	531 Communications	
	532 Affirmation	533 Negation
	534 Teaching	535 Misteaching
		536 Learning
	537 Teacher	538 Learner
	539 School	
	540 Veracity	541 Falsehood
		542 Deception
		543 Untruth
	544 Dupe	545 Deceiver
		546 Exaggeration

3 Means of communicating ideas

(natural means)	547 Indication	
	548 Record	
	549 Recorder	550 Obliteration
	551 Representation	552 Misrepresentation
	553 Painting	
	554 Sculpture	
	555 Engraving	
	556 Artist	
(conventional means: language)	557 Language	
	558 Letter	
	559 Word	560 Neology
	561 Nomenclature	562 Misnomer
	563 Phrase	
	564 Grammar	565 Solecism
	566 Style	
(qualities of style)	567 Perspicuity	568 Imperspicuity
	569 Conciseness	570 Diffuseness
	571 Vigour	572 Feebleness
	573 Plainness	574 Ornament
	575 Elegance	576 Inelegance
(spoken language)	577 Voice	578 Voicelessness
	579 Speech	580 Speech defect
	581 Loquacity	582 Taciturnity
	583 Allocution	
	584 Interlocution	585 Soliloquy
(written language)	586 Writing	
	587 Print	
	588 Correspondence	
	589 Book	
	590 Description	
	591 Dissertation	
	592 Compendium	
	593 Poetry. Prose	
	594 Drama	

Class five: Volition: the exercise of the will

Division one: Individual volition

1 Volition in general

Acts:	595 Will	596 Necessity
	597 Willingness	598 Unwillingness
	599 Resolution	
	600 Perseverance	601 Irresolution
	602 Obstinacy	603 Tergiversation
		604 Caprice

	605 Choice	606 Absence of choice
		607 Rejection
	608 Predetermination	609 Spontaneity
	610 Habit	611 Desuetude
Causes:	612 Motive	613 Dissuasion
	614 Pretext	
Objects:	615 Good	616 Evil

2 Prospective volition

Conceptional:	617 Intention	618 Nondesign
	619 Pursuit	620 Avoidance
		621 Relinquishment
	622 Business	
	623 Plan	
	624 Way	
	625 Middle way	626 Circuit
	627 Requirement	
Subservience to ends:	628 Instrumentality	
	629 Means	
	630 Tool	
	631 Materials	
	632 Store	
	633 Provision	634 Waste
	635 Sufficiency	
	636 Insufficiency	637 Redundance
(degrees of subservience)	638 Importance	639 Unimportance
	640 Utility	641 Inutility
	642 Good policy	643 Inexpedience
	644 Goodness	645 Badness
	646 Perfection	647 Imperfection
	648 Cleanness	649 Uncleanness
	650 Health	651 Ill health
	652 Salubrity	653 Insalubrity
	654 Improvement	655 Deterioration
	656 Restoration	657 Relapse
	658 Remedy	659 Bane
(contingent subservience)	660 Safety	661 Danger
	662 Refuge	663 Pitfall
	664 Warning	665 Danger signal
	666 Preservation	
	667 Escape	
	668 Deliverance	
Precursory measures:	669 Preparation	670 Nonpreparation
	671 Attempt	
	672 Undertaking	
	673 Use	674 Nonuse
		675 Misuse

3 Voluntary action

Simple:	676 Action	677 Inaction
	678 Activity	679 Inactivity
	680 Haste	681 Leisure
	682 Exertion	683 Repose
	684 Fatigue	685 Refreshment

	686 Agent	
	687 Workshop	
Complex:	688 Conduct	
	689 Management	
	690 Director	
	691 Advice	
	692 Council	
	693 Precept	
	694 Skill	695 Unskilfulness
	696 Proficient person	697 Bungler
	698 Cunning	699 Artlessness

4 Antagonism

Conditional:	700 Difficulty	701 Facility
Active:	702 Hindrance	703 Aid
	704 Opposition	705 Cooperation
	706 Opponent	707 Auxiliary
	708 Party	
	709 Dissension	710 Concord
	711 Defiance	
	712 Attack	713 Defence
	714 Retaliation	715 Resistance
	716 Contention	717 Peace
	718 War	719 Pacification
	720 Mediation	
	721 Submission	
	722 Combatant	
	723 Arms	
	724 Arena	

5 Results of action

	725 Completion	726 Noncompletion
	727 Success	728 Failure
	729 Trophy	
	730 Prosperity	731 Adversity
	732 Averageness	

Division two: Social volition

1 General social volition

	733 Authority	734 Laxity
	735 Severity	736 Leniency
	737 Command	
	738 Disobedience	739 Obedience
	740 Compulsion	
	741 Master	742 Servant
	743 Badge of rule	
	744 Freedom	745 Subjection
	746 Liberation	747 Restraint

	748 Prison
749 Keeper	750 Prisoner
751 Commission	752 Abrogation
	753 Resignation
754 Consignee	
755 Deputy	

2 Special social volition

756 Permission	757 Prohibition
758 Consent	
759 Offer	760 Refusal
761 Request	762 Deprecation
763 Petitioner	

3 Conditional social volition

764 Promise	
765 Compact	
766 Conditions	
767 Security	
768 Observance	769 Nonobservance
770 Compromise	

4 Possessive Relations

Property in general:	771 Acquisition	772 Loss
	773 Possession	774 Nonownership
	775 Joint possession	
	776 Possessor	
	777 Property	
	778 Retention	779 Nonretention
Transfer of property:	780 Transfer	
	781 Giving	782 Receiving
	783 Apportionment	
	784 Lending	785 Borrowing
	786 Taking	787 Restitution
	788 Stealing	
	789 Thief	
	790 Booty	
Interchange of property:	791 Barter	
	792 Purchase	793 Sale
	794 Merchant	
	795 Merchandise	
	796 Market	
Monetary relations:	797 Money	
	798 Treasury	
	799 Treasurer	
	800 Wealth	801 Poverty
	802 Credit	803 Debt
	804 Payment	805 Nonpayment
	806 Expenditure	807 Receipt
	808 Accounts	
	809 Price	810 Discount
	811 Dearness	812 Cheapness

	813 Liberality	814 Economy
	815 Prodigality	816 Parsimony

Class six: Emotion, religion and morality

1 General

	817 Affections	
	818 Feeling	
	819 Sensibility	820 Insensibility
	821 Excitation	
	822 Excitability	823 Inexcitability

2 Personal emotion

Passive:	824 Joy	825 Suffering
	826 Pleasurableness	827 Painfulness
	828 Content	829 Discontent
		830 Regret
	831 Relief	832 Aggravation
	833 Cheerfulness	834 Dejection
	835 Rejoicing	836 Lamentation
	837 Amusement	838 Tedium
	839 Wit	840 Dullness
Discriminative:	841 Beauty	842 Ugliness
	843 Beautification	
	844 Ornamentation	845 Blemish
	846 Good taste	847 Bad taste
	848 Fashion	849 Ridiculousness
		850 Affectation
		851 Ridicule
Prospective:	852 Hope	853 Hopelessness
		854 Fear
	855 Courage	856 Cowardice
	857 Rashness	858 Caution
	859 Desire	860 Indifference
		861 Dislike
		862 Fastidiousness
		863 Satiety
Contemplative:	864 Wonder	865 Lack of wonder
Extrinsic:	866 Repute	867 Disrepute
	868 Nobility	869 Commonalty
	870 Title	
	871 Pride	872 Humility
	873 Vanity	874 Modesty
	875 Ostentation	
	876 Celebration	
	877 Boasting	
	878 Insolence	879 Servility

3 Interpersonal emotion

Social:	880 Friendship	881 Enmity
	882 Sociality	883 Unsociability
	884 Courtesy	885 Discourtesy
	886 Congratulation	
	887 Love	888 Hatred
	889 Endearment	
	890 Darling	891 Resentment
		892 Irascibility
		893 Sullenness
	894 Marriage	895 Celibacy
		896 Divorce
Diffusive:	897 Benevolence	898 Malevolence
		899 Malediction
		900 Threat
	901 Philanthropy	902 Misanthropy
	903 Benefactor	904 Evildoer
Special:	905 Pity	906 Pitilessness
Retrospective:	907 Gratitude	908 Ingratitude
	909 Forgiveness	910 Revenge
		911 Jealousy
		912 Envy

4 Morality

Obligation:	913 Right	914 Wrong
	915 Dueness	916 Undueness
	917 Duty	918 Undutifulness
		919 Nonliability
Sentiments:	920 Respect	921 Disrespect
		922 Contempt
	923 Approbation	924 Disapprobation
	925 Flattery	926 Detraction
	927 Vindication	928 Accusation
Conditions:	929 Probity	930 Improbity
	931 Disinterestedness	932 Selfishness
	933 Virtue	934 Wickedness
	935 Innocence	936 Guilt
	937 Good person	938 Bad person
	939 Penitence	940 Impenitence
	941 Atonement	
Practice:	942 Temperance	943 Intemperance
		944 Sensualism
	945 Asceticism	
	946 Fasting	947 Gluttony
	948 Sobriety	949 Drunkenness
	950 Purity	951 Impurity
		952 Libertine
Institutions:	953 Legality	954 Illegality
	955 Jurisdiction	
	956 Tribunal	
	957 Judge	
	958 Lawyer	
	959 Litigation	

	960 Acquittal	961 Condemnation
	962 Reward	963 Punishment
		964 Means of punishment

5 Religion

Superhuman beings and regions:	965 Divineness	
	966 Deities in general	
	967 Pantheon	
	968 Angel	969 Devil
	970 Fairy	
	971 Heaven	972 Hell
Doctrines:	973 Religion	974 Irreligion
	975 Revelation	
	976 Orthodoxy	977 Heterodoxy
		978 Sectarianism
Sentiments:	979 Piety	980 Impiety
Acts:	981 Worship	982 Idolatry
		983 Sorcery
		984 Occultism
Institutions:	985 The church	
	986 Clergy	987 Laity
	988 Ritual	
	989 Canonicals	
	990 Temple	

Class one

Abstract relations

Section one: Existence

1 Existence

N. *existence*, being, entity; absolute being, the absolute 965 *divineness*; aseity, self-existence; monad, a being, an entity, ens, essence; Platonic idea, universal; subsistence 360 *life*; survival, eternity 115 *perpetuity*; preexistence 119 *priority*; this life 121 *present time*; existence in space, prevalence 189 *presence*; entelechy, realization, becoming, evolution 147 *conversion*; creation 164 *production*; potentiality 469 *possibility*; ontology, metaphysics; realism, materialism, idealism, existentialism 449 *philosophy*.

reality, realness, actuality, entelechy, Dasein; actual existence, material e. 319 *materiality*; thatness 80 *speciality*; positiveness; historicity, factuality, factualness 494 *truth*; fact, fact of life, positive f., stubborn f., matter of f., fait accompli 154 *event*; real thing, not a dream, no joke; realities, basics, fundamentals, bedrock, brass tacks 638 *important matter*.

essence, nature, very n., essential n., quiddity, hypostasis 3 *substance*; constitutive principle, inner being, sum and substance 5 *essential part*; prime constituent, soul, heart, core, centre 224 *interiority*.

Adj. *existing*, existent, in esse, ontic; existential; essential 5 *intrinsic*; absolute, given, self-existent, uncreated; being, in existence, under the sun, living 360 *alive*; preexistent 119 *prior*; coexistent 121 *present*; undying, immortal, eternal, enduring 115 *perpetual*; extant, standing, surviving, indestructible 113 *lasting*; rife, prevalent, afloat, afoot 189 *ubiquitous*; ontological, metaphysical.

real, essential, substantive 3 *substantial*; not imagined, uninvented, actual, positive, factual, historical, grounded, well-g. 494 *true*; natural, of nature, physical, flesh and blood 319 *material*; concrete, solid, tangible 324 *dense*.

Vb. *be*, exist, have being; be so and not otherwise; be the case 494 *be true*; consist in, inhere in, reside in 5 *be intrinsic*; preexist 119 *be before*; coexist, coincide, subsist 121 *be now*; abide, continue 146 *go on*; endure 113 *last*; vegetate, pass the time, live out one's life; be alive, breathe, live, move, have one's being, draw breath 360 *live*; exist in space, be found, be met with, stand, lie 186 *be situated*; be here, be there, meet one 189 *be present*; obtain, prevail, reign, be rife 189 *pervade*; take place, come about, occur 154 *happen*; hold, hold good 494 *be true*; represent, stand for, stand as 13 *be identical*.

become, come to be, come into existence, first see the light of day, take flesh 360 *be born*; arise, spring up 68 *begin*; unfold, develop, grow, take form, take shape 316 *evolve*; turn out, change into 147 *be turned to*.

Adv. *actually*, really, substantively; essentially, substantially, inherently, intrinsically; ipso facto; in essence, virtually, to all intents and purposes; potentially 469 *possibly*; positively, factually, in fact, in point of f. 494 *truly*.

See: 3, 5, 13, 68, 80, 113, 115, 119, 121, 146, 147, 154, 164, 186, 189, 224, 316, **319**, 324, **360**, 449, 469, **494**, 638, 965.

2 Nonexistence

N. *nonexistence*, inexistence, non-being, non-entity, nothingness, nullity; nonexistence in time 109 *neverness*; nonexistence in space 190 *absence*; blank, vacuum 190 *emptiness*; nothing, nil, cipher 103 *zero*; a nothing, nonentity 4 *insubstantial thing*; no such thing, no one 190 *nobody*; nihilism, negativeness.

extinction, oblivion, nirvana; no life 361 *death*; dying out, obsolescence 51 *decay*; annihilation, nihilism 165 *destruction*; abeyance, suspension 752 *abrogation*; amnesty 506 *oblivion*; cancellation, erasure, clean slate 550 *obliteration*.

Adj. *nonexistent*, inexistent, unexisting, without being; null, minus; nowhere, missing, omitted 190 *absent*; negatived, null and void 752 *abrogated*; cancelled, wiped out 550 *obliterated*.

unreal, without reality, baseless, groundless, unfounded, false 495 *erroneous*; fictitious, fabulous, visionary 513 *imaginary*; without substance, intangible 4 *insubstantial*; unrealized, undeveloped 670 *immature*; potential, in posse, only possible 469 *possible*; only supposed 512 *suppositional*.

unborn, uncreated, unmade; unbegotten, unconceived; undiscovered, uninvented, unimagined; yet to come, in the womb of time 124 *future*.

extinct, died out, vanished, lost and gone forever; no more, dead and gone, defunct 361 *dead*; obsolescent, vanishing 361 *dying*; obsolete, dead as the dodo; finished, over and done with 125 *past*.

Vb. *not be*, have no existence, have no life; lack reality, exist only in the imagination; be null and void; not happen, never happen, fail to materialize, not come off; be yet unborn.

pass away, cease to exist, become extinct, die out, vanish from the face of the earth; be no more 361 *die*; lose one's life 361 *perish*; come to nothing 728 *miscarry*; sink into oblivion 506 *be forgotten*; go, vanish, leave no trace; dematerialize, melt into thin air, sink into the earth 446 *disappear*; evaporate 338 *vaporize*; melt, dissolve 337 *liquefy*.

nullify, reduce to nothing, annihilate, extinguish, snuff out, blow o.; render null and void, suspend 752 *abrogate*; neutralize, negative 533 *negate*; cancel 550 *obliterate*; abolish, wipe out 165 *destroy*.

Adv. *negatively*; not really, by courtesy only.

See: **4**, 51, 103, 109, 124, 125, 165, 190, 337, 338, **361**, 446, 469, 495, 506, 512, **513**, 533, 550, 670, 728, 752.

3 Substantiality

N. *substantiality*, essentiality 1 *reality*; personality, personal existence; substantivity, objectivity; corporeality, corporeity; visibility, tangibility, palpability, concreteness, solidity 319 *materiality*; ponderability, weight 322 *gravity*; pithiness, meatiness; stuff, material 319 *matter*; totality of existence, plenum, world, world of nature 321 *universe*.

substance, hypostasis; substratum, core 5 *essential part*; entity, thing, something, somebody 319 *object*; person, creature; body, flesh and blood, living matter 360 *life*; solid, concretion 324 *solid body*; pith, marrow, meat 224 *interiority*; gist 514 *meaning*.

Adj. *substantial*, hypostatic, personal 5 *intrinsic*; real, objective, natural, corporeal, phenomenal, physical 319 *material*; concrete, solid, tangible, palpable 324 *dense*; considerable 638 *important*; bulky 195 *large*; heavy 322 *weighty*; pithy, meaty, full of substance.

Adv. *substantially*, corporeally, bodily, physically; personally, in person; really 1 *actually*; essentially 5 *intrinsically*; largely, mainly, in the main 32 *greatly*.

See: 1, 5, 32, 195, 224, 319, 321, 322, 324, 360, 514, 638.

4 Insubstantiality

N. *insubstantiality*, unsubstantiality, nothingness 2 *nonexistence*; naught, nothing, nothing at all, not a whit, not a jot, not a scrap 103 *zero*; no one, not a soul 190 *nobody*; abstraction, incorporeity, incorporeality 320 *immateriality*; lack of substance, imponderability 323 *lightness*; meagreness, tenuity 206 *thinness*; sparseness 325 *rarity*; lack of depth, superficiality 212 *shallowness*; intangibility, invisibility; vacuity, vacancy, void, hollowness 190 *emptiness*; inanity, vanity, fatuity 497 *absurdity*; pointlessness 10 *irrelevance*; hallucination, self-delusion 542 *deception*; fantasy 513 *ideality*; maya, unreality.

insubstantial thing, emblem, token, symbol 547 *indication*; mind, soul 447 *spirit*; abstraction, shadow without substance, shadow, shade, ghost, phantom, vision, dream, mirage, optical illusion 440 *visual fallacy*; air, thin a., wind, breath, vapour, mist; bubble, gossamer, snowflake, snowman 163 *weak thing*; wisp, straw 639 *trifle*; vain thing, bauble; vanity, vanity of vanities, inanity, fatuity, fool's paradise 499 *folly*; flight of fancy, figment of the imagination, myth, pipe dream 513 *fan-*

tasy; all talk, moonshine, cock and bull story; hot air, idle talk, gossip, rumour 515 *empty talk*; tall talk 546 *exaggeration*; cry of 'wolf' 665 *false alarm*; mockery, pretence 875 *ostentation*; chimera, figment, courtesy title; nine days' wonder, flash in the pan; cipher, figurehead, man of straw 639 *nonentity*; pompous ass, stuffed shirt 873 *vain person*; fictitious person, invented character; Pope Joan 970 *mythical being*; pseudonym 562 *no name*.

Adj. *insubstantial*, unsubstantial, abstract, metaphysical, ideal, noumenal; inessential, not intrinsic; nonphysical, nonmaterial 320 *immaterial*; bodiless, bloodless, incorporeal; lightweight, light as air, airy, ethereal 323 *light*; thin, tenuous, gauzy, gossamer 422 *transparent*; pale 426 *colourless*; vaporous, misty 336 *gaseous*; fragile, delicate, brittle, unsound 163 *flimsy*; ghostly, spectral 970 *spooky*; fleeting, shadowy, vague 419 *dim*, 446 *disappearing*; vacuous, vacant, hollow, void 190 *empty*; vain, inane; honorary, nominal, paper, fictitious, mythical; emblematic, symbolic, token 547 *indicating*; without substance, groundless, unfounded; visionary, dreamy, chimerical, fantastical 513 *imaginary*; pointless, senseless 515 *meaningless*; blank, characterless, featureless, null; without depth, superficial 212 *shallow*.

Vb. 2 *not be, pass away, nullify*.

Adv. *unsubstantially*, unreally; nominally, by courtesy; in a vacuum; sic transit gloria mundi.

See: 2, 10, 103, 163, 190, 206, 212, **320**, 323, 325, 336, 419, 422, 426, 440, 446, 447, 497, 499, 513, 515, 542, 546, 547, 562, 639, 665, 873, 875, 970.

5 Intrinsicality

N. *intrinsicality*, inherence, inhesion, immanence; essentialness, essentiality; virtuality, potentiality 160 *ability*; inwardness, introversion, autism; subjectiveness, subjectivity; ego, personality 80 *self*; subjectivism.

essential part, important part, sine qua non; prime ingredient, prime constituent 1 *essence*; principle, property, mark, attribute 89 *concomitant*; virtue, capacity; quintessence, flower, distillation, inscape; stuff, quiddity 3 *substance*; incarnation, embodiment; life, lifeblood, heart's blood, sap; jugular vein, artery; heart, soul, inner man 447 *spirit*; backbone, marrow, pith, fibre; core, kernel 225 *centre*; focus, gist, nub, nucleus 638 *chief thing*.

character, nature, quality; make-up, personality, type, make, stamp, breed 77 *sort*; constitution, characteristics, ethos; cast, colour, hue, complexion; aspects, features; diagnosis, diagnostics.

temperament, temper, humour, disposition, mood, spirit 817 *affections*; grain, vein, streak, strain, trait 179 *tendency*; idiosyncrasy, foible, habit, peculiarity 80 *speciality*.

heredity, endowment; DNA, chromosome, gene, allelomorph, inherited characteristic; inborn capacity *or* tendency, original sin; ancestry 169 *genealogy*; telegony, atavism 106 *recurrence*; hereditariness, heritability; Galton's law, Mendel's law, Mendelism; genetics 358 *biology*.

Adj. *intrinsic*, immanent, deep down, deep-seated, deep-rooted, ingrained; inherent, integral 58 *component*; inward, internal, indwelling 224 *interior*; inwrought, inwoven, implicit, part and parcel of, built-in 78 *included*; indispensable, unalienable, inseparable 13 *identical*; autistic, subjective, introversive, reflexive, inward-looking, introverted; characteristic, personal; indigenous, native; natural, instinctive; basic, structural, radical, central, organic 156 *fundamental*; a priori, original, primary, elemental, cardinal, normal; essential, constitutional; virtual, potential, capable.

genetic, inherited, hereditary, atavistic, heritable; native, inborn, innate, connate, congenital, connatural; inbred, bred in the bone.

characteristic 80 *special*; characterizing, qualitative; diagnostic, idiomorphic, proper; ineradicable, incurable, invariable; constant, unchanging 153 *established*.

Vb. *be intrinsic*, - immanent etc. adj.; inhere, indwell 773 *belong*; be born like it; inherit, take after, run in the blood, run in the family; be marked with, be stamped with, be characterized by; involve, mean, boil down to 523 *imply*.

Adv. *intrinsically*, implicitly etc. adj.; at bottom, fundamentally, essentially, substantially, virtually; per se, as such; in effect, in the main.

See: 1, 3, 13, 58, 77, 78, 80, 89, 106, 153,

156, 160, 169, 179, **224**, 225, 358, 447, 523, 638, 773, 817.

6 Extrinsicality

N. *extrinsicality*, objectiveness, objectivity; transcendence 34 *superiority*; otherness, the other, non-ego, not-self 59 *extraneousness*; externality, outwardness, outer darkness, outer space 223 *exteriority*; objectification, externalization; projection, extrapolation, extroversion, extrovert; accidence 7 *modality*; accident, contingency 159 *chance*; accrual, accessory, acquired characteristic 40 *adjunct*.

Adj. *extrinsic*, alien, foreign 59 *extraneous*; transcendent 34 *superior*; outward, external, extramural 223 *exterior*; outward-looking, extroverted; derived from without, acquired, engrafted, implanted, inbred, instilled, inculcated; supervenient, accessory, adventitious, adscititious; superadded, annexed, appended 38 *additional*; incidental, accidental, contingent, fortuitous 159 *casual*; nonessential, inessential; subsidiary, subordinate 35 *inferior*.

Vb. *be extrinsic*, lie without, not belong; transcend 34 *be superior*; come from without, supervene 38 *accrue*.

make extrinsic, objectify, realize, project 223 *externalize*; body forth 551 *represent*.

Adv. *extrinsically*, superficially, outwardly; from outside.

See: 7, 34, 35, 38, **40**, **59**, 159, **223**, 551.

7 State: absolute condition

N. *state*, modal existence, state of being, condition; estate, lot, walk, walk of life; case, way, plight, pickle 8 *circumstance*; position, category, status, footing, standing, rank; habitude, habit, disposition, complexion 5 *temperament*; attitude, frame of mind, vein, temper, mood 817 *affections*; state of mind, spirits, morale; state of health, physical condition; trim, fettle, fig.

modality, mode, manner, fashion, style; stamp, set, fit, mould 243 *form*; shape, frame, fabric 331 *structure*; aspect, phase, light, complexion, character, guise 445 *appearance*; tenor, tone 179 *tendency*.

Adj. *such*; modal, conditional, formal 243 *formative*; organic 331 *structural*; in a state of; in condition, in form, in good f. 694 *skilful*; in bad form 695 *clumsy*.

Vb. *be in a state of*, be such, be so; be on a footing; stand, lie, labour under; do, fare.

Adv. *conditionally*, it being so, as it is, as things are, as the matter stands, provisionally.

See: 5, **8**, 179, 243, 331, 445, 694, 695, 817.

8 Circumstance: relative condition

N. *circumstance*, situation, circumstances, conditions, factors, the times; total situation, personal world, life space; environment, milieu 230 *surroundings*; context 9 *relation*; status quo, state of affairs, how things stand; regime, set-up 7 *state*; posture, attitude; aspect, look of things, appearances 445 *appearance*; lie of the land, how the land lies 186 *situation*; sphere, background, footing, standing, status, relative position 73 *serial place*, 9 *relativeness*; awkward situation, plight, pickle, pass, pinch, corner, hole, jam, dilemma 700 *predicament*.

juncture, conjuncture, stage, point 154 *event*; contingency, eventuality; crossroads, turning point, match point, point of no return; moment, hour, right time, opportunity 137 *occasion*; critical moment, crucial m., hour of decision, emergency, exigency 137 *crisis*.

Adj. *circumstantial*, given, modal 7 *such*; situated, placed, circumstanced; surrounding, environmental, situational, contextual 230 *circumjacent*; circumscribing, limiting 232 *circumscribed*; modifying 468 *qualifying*; provisional, temporary 114 *transient*; variable 152 *changeful*; dependent on circumstances, relative, contingent, incidental, adventitious 154 *eventual*; emergent, critical, crucial; auspicious, favourable 137 *opportune*; fitting the circumstances, suitable, seemly 24 *agreeing*; appropriate, convenient 642 *advisable*.

Adv. *thus*, so; like this, in this way; from that angle.

accordingly, and so, according as, depending on; according to circumstances, as the wind blows, as it turns out, as the case may be.

if, if so be, should it so happen, should it be that; in the event of, in the case of, in case; provisionally, provided that 7 *conditionally*; supposing, assuming, granting, allowing, taking it that; if not, unless, except, without.

See: 7, 9, 24, 73, 114, 137, 152, 154, 186, 230, 232, 445, 468, 642, 700.

Section two: Relation

9 Relation

N. *relation*, relatedness, connectedness, rapport, reference, respect, regard; bearing, direction; concern, concernment, interest, import 638 *importance*; involvement, implication 5 *intrinsicality*; appetency 291 *attraction*; relationship, homogeneity, affinity; filiation, kinship 11 *consanguinity*; classification, classifiability 62 *arrangement*; affiliation, alliance 706 *association*; relations, amicable r., friendly terms, intimacy 880 *friendship*; liaison, linkage, connection, link, tie-up 47 *bond*; commercial relations 622 *business*; something in common, common reference, common source, common denominator; interdependence, ecology; context, milieu, environment 8 *circumstance*; import, intention 514 *meaning*.

relativeness, relativity, interconnection, mutual relation 12 *correlation*; same relation, homology, correspondence 13 *identity*, 28 *equality*; similar relation, analogy 18 *similarity*; comparability 462 *comparison*; close relation, apposition, approximation 289 *approach*, 200 *nearness*, 202 *contiguity*, 89 *accompaniment*; parallel relation, collaterality 219 *parallelism*, 245 *symmetry*; proportionality, perspective, proportion, ratio, scale; causal relation, causality, cause and effect 156 *cause*; dependence 157 *effect*; governing relation 178 *influence*; subordinate relation 35 *inferiority*; logical relation (**see** *relevance*); relative position, stage, status, rank 27 *degree*; serial order 65 *sequence*; relativism, relationism; relativist, relationist.

relevance, logical relation, logicality, logical argument 475 *reasoning*; chain of reasoning 475 *argumentation*; just relation, due proportion 24 *conformance*; suitability, point, application, applicability, appositeness, pertinence, propriety, comparability 24 *fitness*; case in point, good example, poor e., palmary instance 83 *example*.

referral, making reference, reference, cross-r.; application, allusion, mention; citation, quotation; frame of reference, object of reference, referent; referee.

Adj. *relative*, not absolute 8 *circumstantial*; relational, referential, respective; relativist, relativistic; referable; related, connected, associated, en rapport, linked, entwined; bearing upon, concerning, in aid of; of concern, of interest, of import 638 *important*; belonging, appertaining, appurtenant 78 *included*; in common 775 *sharing*; mutual, reciprocal, corresponding, answering to 12 *correlative*; classifiable, in the same category 62 *arranged*; serial, consecutive 65 *sequential*; affinitive, congenial, affiliated, cognate, kindred 11 *akin*; homologous, analogous, like 18 *similar*; comparative, comparable 462 *compared*; approximative, approximating, approaching 200 *near*; collateral 219 *parallel*; proportional, proportionate, varying as, in ratio, to scale; in due proportion, proportionable, commensurate 245 *symmetrical*; perspectival, in perspective; contextual, environmental, ecological.

relevant, logical, in context; apposite, pertinent, applicable; pointed, to the point, to the purpose, well-directed 475 *rational*; proper, appropriate, suitable, fitting 24 *apt*; alluding, allusive; quotable, worth mentioning.

Vb. *be related*, have a relationship, stand in relation to; have reference to, refer to, regard, respect, have to do with; bear upon, be a factor 178 *influence*; touch, concern, deal with, interest, affect; be a relation 11 *be akin*; belong, pertain, appertain; approximate to 289 *approach*; answer to, correspond, reciprocate 12 *correlate*; have a connection, tie in with; be congruent 24 *accord*; be proportionate, vary as; be relevant, have some point, support an analogy, serve as an example; come to the point, get down to brass tacks.

relate, bring into relation, put in perspective, get into proportion; connect with, gear to, gear with; apply, bring to bear upon; link, connect, bracket together, entwine, tie up with 45 *tie*; put in its context, provide a background; compare 18 *liken*; proportion, symmetrize, parallel; balance 28 *equalize*; establish a connection, draw a parallel, find an example 475 *reason*; make a reference to, refer to, touch on, allude to, mention; index, supply or furnish with references 547 *indi-*

cate.

Adv. *relatively*, not absolutely, in a context; in relation to, contextually; in some degree, comparatively, in comparison; proportionally, in ratio, to scale, in perspective; conditionally, circumstantially; appropriately 24 *pertinently*.

concerning, touching, regarding; as to, as regards, with regard to, with respect to; relative to, relating to, vis-à-vis, with reference to, about, re, anent, on, under; in connection with; in relation to, bearing on; speaking of, apropos, by the way, by the bye, on the subject of; on the point of, as far as concerns; in the matter of, in re; under the head of; on the part of, on the score of; whereas; forasmuch, inasmuch; concerning which, whereto, whereunder; thereto, thereunder; hereto, hereunder; whereof, thereof, hereof.

See: 5, 8, 11, 12, 13, 18, 24, 27, 28, 35, 45, 47, 62, 65, 78, 83, 89, 156, 157, 178, 200, 202, 219, 245, 289, 291, 462, 475, 514, 547, 622, 638, 706, 775, 880.

10 Unrelatedness: absence of relation

N. *unrelatedness*, absoluteness; noninvolvement, independence 744 *freedom*; arbitrariness; unilaterality; separateness, insularity, isolation 46 *separation*; singularity, individuality 80 *speciality*; rootlessness, homelessness; lack of connection, unconnectedness, no context; unclassifiability; randomness 61 *disorder*; inconsequence (**see** *irrelevance*); disconnection, disconnectedness, dissociation 46 *disunion*, 72 *discontinuity*; misconnection, wrong association 495 *error*; disproportion, asymmetry 246 *distortion*; incommensurability, disparity 29 *inequality*; diversity, heterogeneity, multifariousness 15 *difference*, 17 *nonuniformity*, 19 *dissimilarity*, 82 *multiformity*; incongruence 84 *nonconformity*; irreconcilability 14 *contrariety*; intrusion, intrusiveness 138 *untimeliness*; no concern of, no business of, nobody's b.; square peg in a round hole 25 *misfit*; exotic, alien element, intruder, cuckoo in the nest 59 *extraneousness*.

irrelevance, irrelevancy; illogicality 477 *sophism*; pointlessness, inapplicability, bad example; ineptitude, inconsequence, non sequitur; parenthesis, obiter dictum 231 *interjection*; diversion, red herring 282 *deviation*; episode, incidental 154 *event*; inessential, nonessential 639 *unimportance*.

Adj. *unrelated*, irrelative, absolute, self-existent; independent 744 *unconfined*; owing nothing to 21 *original*; irrespective, regardless, unilateral, arbitrary; unclassified, unidentified; unclassifiable, rootless, homeless; adrift, wandering, astray 282 *deviating*; kinless, isolated, insular 88 *alone*; unconcerned, uninvolved 860 *indifferent*; detached, unconnected, without context, disconnected, unallied 46 *disunited*; digressive, parenthetic, anecdotal; episodic, incidental 72 *discontinuous*; separate, singular, individual 80 *special*; private, of no concern, without interest, nothing to do with; inessential 6 *extrinsic*; exotic, foreign, alien, strange, outlandish 59 *extraneous*; intrusive, untimely 138 *ill-timed*; uncongenial, ungermane, inappropriate, incompatible 25 *disagreeing*; not comparable, incommensurable, disparate 29 *unequal*; disproportionate, out of proportion, asymmetrical 246 *distorted*; incongruent, discordant 84 *unconformable*; irreconcilable 14 *contrary*; heterogeneous 17 *nonuniform*; multifarious 82 *multiform*.

irrelevant, illogical; inapposite, inapplicable, pointless; impertinent, inept 25 *unapt*; out of order, misapplied 188 *misplaced*; misdirected 495 *erroneous*; off-target, off the beam, off-centre, peripheral; rambling, wandering 570 *diffuse*; adrift, beside the point, beside the mark, beside the purpose, off the point, neither here nor there; trivial, inessential 639 *unimportant*; inconsequent, inconsequential; incidental 159 *casual*; remote, far-fetched, forced, strained; academic, impractical, immaterial.

Vb. *be unrelated*, have no concern with, have nothing to do w., have no bearing on; owe nothing to, disown; have no right to be there, have no place in; not be one's business, be nobody's b.; not concern, not touch, not interest; be irrelevant, be off the point, avoid the issue, cloud the i., draw a red herring; force, strain; drag in by the heels; ramble, wander, lose the thread 570 *be diffuse*.

Adv. *unrelatedly*, irrespective, regardless; without regard, without respect, without reference, without relation to; irrelevantly, illogically, inappropriately; parenthetically, incidentally, episodically, coincidentally, by the way.

See: 6, 14, 15, 17, 19, 21, 25, 29, 46, 59, 61, 72, 80, 82, 84, 88, 138, 154, 159, 188, 231, 246, 282, 477, 495, 570, 639, 744, 860.

11 Consanguinity: relations of kindred

N. *consanguinity*, kinship, kindred, blood 169 *parentage*; filiation, affiliation, relationship, affinity, propinquity; blood relationship, agnation, cognation; ancestry, lineage, descent 169 *genealogy*; connection, alliance, family, family connection; ties of family, ties of blood, ties of race, tribalism, nationality 371 *nation*; nepotism; atavism 5 *heredity*.

kinsman, kinswoman, sib; kin, kindred, kith and kin, kinsfolk, relations; near relative, next of kin; distant relation, blood r., kissing cousin; one of the family, relation by marriage, in-law, step-relation; grandparents, father, mother 169 *parentage*; children, offspring, issue, one's flesh and blood 170 *posterity*; agnate, cognate, collateral; twin, identical t., fraternal t.; sibling, sib; sister, brother, uterine b. *or* s., blood b. *or* s., brother *or* sister german, half-b. *or* -s.; stepbrother; cousin, cousin german, first c., second c., cousin once removed; uncle, aunt, auntie, great-uncle, great-aunt; nephew, niece, grand-nephew, grand-niece; clansman, tribesman, compatriot.

family, matriarchy, patriarchy; motherhood, fatherhood, brotherhood, sisterhood, cousinhood; fraternity, sorority; adopted son *or* daughter, foster child, godchild, stepchild, adopted c.; relations by marriage, in-laws; one's people, one's folks; family circle, home c. 882 *sociality*; the old folks at home, household, hearth and home 192 *home*; nuclear family, extended f.; tribe, horde.

race, stock, stem, stirps, breed, strain, line, side, spear s., distaff s.; house, tribe, clan, moiety, phratry, sept; ethnic group; nation, people; nationalism, racialism 481 *prejudice*; inbreeding, interbreeding.

Adj. *akin*, sib, kindred, kin, consanguineous, twin-born; matrilineal, out of; patrilineal, by; maternal, paternal 169 *parental*; sibling, fraternal, brotherly, sisterly, cousinly; avuncular; novercal; family, familial, collateral, allied, affined; connatural, congenerous; agnate, cognate, german, uterine; near, related, intimately r. 9 *relative*; once removed, twice r.; next-of-kin; step-.

ethnic, racial, tribal, clannish 371 *national*; interracial, intertribal; interbred, inbred 43 *mixed*; Caucasian, Mongolian, Negroid.

Vb. *be akin*, share the blood of; claim relationship etc. n.; own a connection 9 *be related*; marry into 894 *wed*; father, sire 167 *generate*; be brother *or* sister to, brother, sister; affiliate, adopt, foster, bring into the family.

See: 5, **9**, 43, 167, **169**, **170**, 192, **371**, 481, 882, 894.

12 Correlation: double or reciprocal relation

N. *correlation*, correlativity, mutual relation, functionality 9 *relation*; proportionment, proportionality, proportion 245 *symmetry*; texture, design, pattern 62 *arrangement*; grid 222 *network*; correspondence 18 *similarity*; opposite number 13 *identity*; mutuality, interrelation, interconnection; interdependence, mutual dependence; mutualism, mutualist; interaction, interplay, mutual influence; alternation, turn and turn about, seesaw 317 *oscillation*; reciprocity, reciprocation 151 *interchange*; each, each other, one another; give and take 770 *compromise*; exchange, change, payment in kind 791 *barter*; tit for tat 714 *retaliation*.

Adj. *correlative*, reciprocal, functional 9 *relative*; corresponding, opposite, answering to, analogous, parallel 18 *similar*; proportioned, proportional, proportionate 245 *symmetrical*; complementary, complemental, interdependent; interconnecting, interlocking; mutual, requited; reciprocating 714 *retaliatory*; reacting 280 *recoiling*; alternating, alternate, seesaw 317 *oscillating*; balancing 28 *equivalent*; interlocking, geared, interacting; patterned, woven; interchangeable, exchangeable 151 *interchanged*; inter-, intertribal, interracial, international, interstate; two-way, bilateral.

Vb. *correlate*, interrelate, interconnect, interlock, interplay, interact; interdepend; vary as, be a function of; proportion, symmetrize; correspond, answer to, reflect 18 *resemble*; react 280 *recoil*; alternate 317 *oscillate*; counterchange 151 *interchange*; reciprocate 714 *retaliate*; exchange, swap, barter 791 *trade*; balance 28 *equalize*; set off 31 *compensate*.

Adv. *correlatively*, proportionately, as...

so...; mutually, reciprocally, each to each, each other, one another; equivalently 28 *equally*; interchangeably, in mutual exchange 151 *in exchange*; in kind 791 *in trade*; alternately, by turns, turn and turn about, first one and then the other; contrariwise, vice versa 14 *contrarily*; inter, between, shuttlewise 317 *to and fro.*

See: 9, 13, 14, 18, 28, 31, 62, **151**, 222, 245, 280, 317, 714, 770, 791.

13 Identity

N. *identity*, identicalness, sameness, oneness 88 *unity*; the same, no other, the very same, the very one; genuineness 494 *authenticity*; the real thing, it, absolutely it 21 *no imitation*; the very words, ipsissima verba, ditto, tautology 106 *repetition*; other self, alter ego, ka, ba, genius, double; oneness with, identification, coincidence, congruence 24 *agreement*; coalescence, mergence, absorption 299 *reception*; convertibility, interchangeability, equivalence 28 *equality*; no difference, distinction without a difference, indistinguishability; synonymity, synonymy 514 *meaning*; same kind, homogeneity, consubstantiality 16 *uniformity*; no change, invariability, invariant, constant 153 *fixture*; counterpart, duplicate 22 *copy*; fellow, pair, match, twin, Tweedledum and Tweedledee 18 *analogue*; homonym, homophone, synonym 559 *word*.

Adj. *identical*, same, self, selfsame, of that ilk; one and the same, one and only 88 *one*; coalescent, merging, absorbed; identified with, indistinguishable, interchangeable, confusable, unisex, convertible, equivalent 28 *equal*; homonymous, synonymous, synonymic; coincident, congruent 24 *agreeing*; always the same, invariable, invariant, constant, unchanging, unaltered 153 *unchangeable*; monotonous 838 *tedious*; homogeneous, monolithic 16 *uniform*; tautologous, repetitive, repetitional 106 *repeated*.

Vb. *be identical*, show no difference, ditto 106 *repeat*; coincide, coalesce, merge, be one with, sink one's identity; be congruent, register, agree in all respects 24 *accord*; phase 123 *synchronize*.

identify, make as one, treat as o., unify, consubstantiate; treat as the same, not distinguish, recognize no distinction 464 *not discriminate*; equate, tar with the same brush 28 *equalize*; assimilate, match, pair 18 *liken*.

Adv. *identically*, interchangeably, without distinction; in phase, on all fours; ibidem; ditto; in like case, same here.

See: 16, 18, 21, **22**, 24, 28, 88, 106, 123, 153, 299, 464, 494, 514, 559, 838.

14 Contrariety

N. *contrariety*, nonidentity, absolute difference, world of d. 15 *difference*; exclusiveness, mutual e., irreconcilability 10 *unrelatedness*; antipathy, repugnance, hostility 888 *hatred*; adverseness, contrariness, antagonism 704 *opposition*; antidote 182 *counteraction*; conflict, clash 279 *collision*; discord 25 *disagreement*; contradistinction, contrast, relief, light r., variation, undertone, counterpoint 15 *differentiation*; contradiction, flat c. 533 *negation*; contraindication 467 *counterevidence*; countersense, antonym 514 *meaning*; antinomy, antilogy; inconsistency, two voices 17 *nonuniformity*; paradox, ambivalence 518 *equivocalness*; oppositeness, antithesis, direct opposite, antipodes, antipole, opposite pole; other extreme, opposite e., quite the contrary, quite the reverse; other side, opposite s. 240 *contraposition*; reverse, wrong side 238 *rear*; inverse 221 *inversion*; converse, reverse image, mirror, mirror symmetry 417 *reflection*; opposite direction, headwind, undertow, countercurrent 182 *counteraction*.

polarity, contraries 704 *opposites*; positive and negative; north and south; east and west; day and night; light and darkness; hot and cold; fire and water; black and white; good and evil; yin and yang, male and female; Hyperion to a satyr 19 *dissimilarity*.

Adj. *contrary*, nonidentical, as different as chalk from cheese, anything but 15 *different*; contrasting, contrasted, incompatible, clashing, conflicting, discordant 25 *disagreeing*; inconsistent, not uniform 17 *nonuniform*; ambivalent, bittersweet, love-hate, sweet and sour; contradictory, antithetic, adversative 533 *negative*; antithetical, antonymous; diametrically opposite, poles asunder, antipodal, antipodean 240 *opposite*; reverse, converse, inverse; antipathetic, inimical, hostile 888 *hating*; adverse, untoward, antagonistic 704 *opposing*; counteractive, antidotal 182 *counteracting*; counter-, contra-, anti-.

Vb. *be contrary*, have nothing in common 10 *be unrelated*, 15 *differ*; contrast, stand out 25 *disagree*; clash, conflict with; run counter to 240 *be opposite*; speak with two voices 518 *be equivocal*; contravene, fly in the face of 704 *oppose*, 738 *disobey*; exclude, deny, contradict, contraindicate 533 *negate*; cancel out 182 *counteract*; turn the tables 221 *invert*.

Adv. *contrarily*, per contra, on the other hand, conversely, contrariwise; vice versa, topsy-turvy, upside down; invertedly, inversely; on the contrary; otherwise, quite the other way; in contrast, in opposition to; by contraries, by opposites.

See: 10, **15**, 17, 19, 25, 182, 221, 238, 240, 279, 417, 467, 514, 518, 533, **704**, 738, 888.

15 Difference

N. *difference*, unlikeness 19 *dissimilarity*; disparity, odds 29 *inequality*; margin, differential, minus, plus 41 *remainder*; wide margin 199 *distance*; narrow margin 200 *nearness*; heterogeneity, variety, diverseness, diversity 17 *nonuniformity*; divergence, departure from 282 *deviation*; otherness, differentia, distinctness 10 *unrelatedness*, 21 *originality*; discrepancy, incongruity 25 *disagreement*; incompatibility, antipathy 861 *dislike*; disharmony, discord, variance 709 *dissension*; contrast 14 *contrariety*; opposite, antithesis 240 *contraposition*; variation, modification, alteration 143 *change*, 147 *conversion*.

differentiation 463 *discrimination*; specification 80 *speciality*; contradistinction, distinction, nice d., delicate d., subtle d.; nuance, nicety, shade of difference, fine shade of meaning 514 *meaning*; distinction without a difference 13 *identity*; conjugation, declension 564 *grammar*.

variant, different thing, another t., something else; this, that or the other; quite another matter, different kettle of fish; another story, another version, horse of another colour, another light on, the other side of the coin; special case 80 *speciality*; freak, sport 84 *nonconformist*; new version, new edition 589 *edition*.

Adj. *different*, differing, unlike 19 *dissimilar*; original, fresh 126 *new*; various, variform, diverse, diversified, heterogeneous 17 *nonuniform*; multifarious 82 *multiform*; assorted, of all sorts, all manner of, divers 43 *mixed*; distinct, distinguished, differentiated, discriminated, divided 46 *separate*; divergent, departing from 282 *deviating*; odd 84 *unusual*; discrepant, discordant, clashing, incongruent, incongruous 25 *disagreeing*; disparate 29 *unequal*; contrasting, contradistinctive; contrasted, far from it, wide apart, poles asunder, anything but 14 *contrary*; other, another, not the same, peculiar 80 *special*; in a different class 34 *superior*, 35 *inferior*; somehow different, the same yet not the same, changed, altered 147 *converted*.

distinctive, diagnostic 5 *characteristic*; differentiating, distinguishing, marking out; comparative, superlative, augmentative.

Vb. *differ*, be different etc. adj.; show variety; vary from, diverge f., depart f. 282 *deviate*; contrast, clash, jar, conflict 25 *disagree*; be at variance 709 *quarrel*; change one's tune, modify, vary, make alterations 143 *change*.

differentiate, distinguish, mark out, single o., severalize 463 *discriminate*; shade, refine, make a distinction, sharpen a d.; particularize 80 *specify*; widen the gap 46 *set apart*.

Adv. *differently*, variously, as modified, after alteration; otherwise, not so, some other way, in a different fashion, with a difference; in different ways, in many w., multifariously.

See: 5, 10, 13, 14, **17**, **19**, 21, 25, 29, 34, 35, 41, 43, 46, 80, 82, 84, 126, 143, 147, 199, 200, 240, 282, 463, 514, 564, 589, 709, 861.

16 Uniformity

N. *uniformity*, uniformness, consistency, constancy, steadiness 153 *stability*; persistence 71 *continuity*, 146 *continuance*; unfailing regularity 141 *periodicity*; order, regularity, method, centralization 60 *order*; homogeneity, homology 18 *similarity*; monolithic quality; unity, unison, correspondence, accordance 24 *agreement*; evenness, levelness, flushness 258 *smoothness*; roundness 245 *symmetry*; sameness 13 *identity*; invariableness, invariability, monotony, even tenor; mixture as before, same old story; even pace, jog trot, rhythm; round, daily r., routine, drill, treadmill 610 *habit*; monotone, greyness; droning, drone, sing-song, monologue; monolith; pattern, same p., mould; type, stereotype 22 *copy*; stamp, common s., same s., same mint; set, assortment;

suit, flush; standard dress 228 *uniform*; assimilation, standardization, mass production 83 *conformity*; cliché 106 *repetition*; regimentation, totalitarianism, intolerance, closed shop 740 *compulsion*.
uniformist, regimenter, sergeant major; leveller, equalitarian, egalitarian.

Adj. *uniform*, all of a piece, one-piece; same all through, solid, monolithic; of one kind, connatural, homogenetic; homogeneous, of a piece, of a pattern 18 *similar*; same, consistent, self-c., constant, steady, stable 153 *fixed*; undeviating, unchanging, unvarying, invariable 144 *permanent*; equable 823 *inexcitable*; rhythmic, measured, even-paced 258 *smooth*; undiversified, undifferentiated, unrelieved, unbroken 573 *plain*; uncontrasting, without contrast, lacking variety, in uniform, uniformed, liveried; characterless, featureless, faceless, blank; monotonous, droning, sing-song, monotone; monochrome, drab, grey; repetitive, running through 106 *repeated*; standard, normal 83 *typical*; patterned, standardized, stereotyped, mass-produced, unisex; sorted, assorted, sized; drilled, aligned, in line; orderly, regular 245 *symmetrical*; straight, even, flush, level, dead l. 216 *flat*.

Vb. *be uniform*, - homogeneous etc. adj.; follow routine 610 *be wont*; sing in unison, sing the same song, chorus 24 *accord*; typify 83 *conform*; fall in, dress; wear uniform, be in u.
make uniform, homogenize; stamp, characterize, run through 547 *mark*; level, level up *or* down, abolish differentials 28 *equalize*; assimilate 18 *liken*; size, assort, grade; drill, align; regiment, institutionalize; standardize, stereotype, pattern; mass-produce; put into uniform; normalize, regularize, conventionalize 83 *make conform*.

Adv. *uniformly*, solidly etc. adj.; like clockwork, methodically, habitually, invariably, eternally, endlessly; without exception, in a rut, in a groove.

See: 13, **18**, 22, 24, **28**, 60, 71, 83, 106, 141, 144, 146, 153, 216, 228, 245, 258, 547, 573, 610, 740, 823.

17 Nonuniformity

N. *nonuniformity*, variability, patchiness 72 *discontinuity*; unpredictability 152 *changeableness*; inconstancy, inconsistency, capriciousness 604 *caprice*; irregularity, no system, no pattern 61 *disorder*; asymmetry 244 *amorphism*; ruggedness, raggedness, unevenness, jerkiness 259 *roughness*; heterogeneity, heteromorphism 15 *difference*; contrast 14 *contrariety*, 19 *dissimilarity*; decentralization, divarication, divergence 282 *deviation*; diversity, variety, variousness, multifariousness 82 *multiformity*; all sorts and conditions, all shapes and sizes, mixed bag, lucky dip, odds and ends 43 *medley*; patchwork, motley, crazy paving, mosaic 437 *variegation*; abnormality, exception, special case, sport, mutation 84 *nonconformity*; odd man out, lone wolf, rogue elephant 59 *extraneousness*; uniqueness, individuality 80 *speciality*; every man in his humour; quot homines tot sententiae.

Adj. *nonuniform*, variable, unpredictable, changeable, never the same 152 *changeful*; spasmodic, sporadic 142 *fitful*; inconstant, inconsistent 604 *capricious*; temperamental 822 *excitable*; patchy 29 *unequal*; random, irregular, unsystematic; asymmetrical 244 *amorphous*; untidy, out of order 61 *orderless*; uneven, bumpy, lumpy, choppy, jerky 259 *rough*; erratic, out of step, out of time, gaining, losing; contrasting, contrasted 14 *contrary*; heterogeneous, various, diverse 15 *different*, 19 *dissimilar*; multifarious, miscellaneous, of many kinds, of all sorts 82 *multiform*; multicoloured, decorated 844 *ornamental*; divergent, diversified 282 *deviating*; dissenting 25 *disagreeing*; aberrant, atypical 84 *unconformable*; exceptional, unusual, unconventional 84 *abnormal*; unique, lone 80 *special*; individual, handmade; out of uniform, in mufti.

Adv. *nonuniformly*, irregularly, erratically, unsystematically; unevenly, bumpily, jerkily; confusedly, chaotically; all anyhow, all over the place; here, there and everywhere.

See: 14, **15**, **19**, 25, 29, 43, 59, 61, 72, 80, 82, 84, 142, 152, 244, 259, 282, 437, 604, 822, 844.

18 Similarity

N. *similarity*, resemblance, likeness, similitude; semblance, seeming, look 445 *appearance*; fashion, style 243 *form*; common feature, point in common, point of resemblance 9 *relation*; congruity 24 *agreement*; affinity, kinship 11 *consanguinity*; homogeneity, homomorphism, connaturality; comparability, analogousness, analogy, correspondence, parallelism 12 *correlation*; equivalence, parity 28 *equality*; proportionality 245 *symmetry*; no difference 13 *identity*; general resemblance, family likeness; close resemblance, good likeness, perfect l.; striking likeness, faithful l., photographic l. 551 *representation*; lifelikeness 494 *accuracy*; approximation 200 *nearness*; partial likeness, distant l., faint resemblance, simulacrum; adumbration, suggestion, hint; fair comparison, sufficient resemblance, about the size of it.

assimilation, likening 462 *comparison*; reduction to, identification 13 *identity*; simulation, camouflage, mimicry 20 *imitation*; parable, allegory; portrayal 590 *description*; portraiture 553 *picture*; alliteration, assonance, rhyme 593 *prosody*; pun, play on words 518 *equivocalness*.

analogue, congener, the like, suchlike, the likes of; type, good example, perfect e. 83 *example*; correlate, correlative 12 *correlation*; simile, parallel, metaphor; equivalent 150 *substitute*; brother, sister, twin; match, fellow, mate, companion, pendant; complement, counterpart, other half 89 *concomitant*; alter ego, other self, genius, ka, ba; fetch, doppelgänger; double, ringer, lookalike; likeness, reflection, shadow, the picture of 551 *image*; another edition of, dead spit of, spitting image, living image, chip off the old block; twins, two peas, couple, pair 90 *duality*; two of a kind, Arcades ambo, birds of a feather; reproduction, copy, clone 22 *duplicate*.

Adj. *similar*, resembling, like, much l.; alike, ridiculously a., twin, matching, like as two peas, cast in the same mould; tarred with the same brush; much of a muchness, nothing to choose between 13 *identical*; of a piece 16 *uniform*; analogical; analogous, parallel 28 *equivalent*; corresponding, bracketed with; consubstantial, homogeneous, connatural, congeneric 11 *akin*; close, approximate 200 *near*; typical, representative 551 *representing*; reproducing, reflecting; after the fashion of, in the style of, à la; much the same, something like, such as, quasi; rhyming, alliterative, assonant 106 *repeated*; punning 518 *equivocal*.

lifelike, realistic, photographic, exact, faithful, natural, typical; good of one, true to life, true to nature, true to type; graphic, vivid, eidetic 443 *visible*.

simulating 20 *imitative*; seeming, deceptive, camouflaged 542 *deceiving*; mock, pseudo 542 *spurious*; making a show of 875 *ostentatious*; synthetic, artificial, ersatz 150 *substituted*.

Vb. *resemble*, be similar to, pass for, bear a resemblance; mirror, reflect 20 *imitate*; seem, seem like, sound l., look as if; look like, take after, put one in mind of, have the look of; savour of, smack of; compare with, approximate to, come near to 289 *approach*; match, correspond to, answer to 24 *accord*; assonate, rhyme; run in pairs; typify 551 *represent*.

liken, assimilate to, approximate 462 *compare*; reduce to 13 *identify*; pair, twin, bracket with 28 *equalize*; allegorize, use a simile; portray 20 *imitate*; alliterate, rhyme 106 *repeat*; pun 518 *be equivocal*.

Adv. *similarly*, as, like, as if, quasi, so to speak, as it were; allegorically 519 *metaphorically*; likewise, so, correspondingly, by the same token; just as, in a way; as in a mirror; like father like son.

See: 9, 11, 12, 13, 16, **20**, 22, 24, **28**, 83, 89, 90, 106, 150, 200, 243, 245, 289, 443, 445, **462**, 494, 518, 519, 542, 551, 553, 590, 593, 875.

19 Dissimilarity

N. *dissimilarity*, dissimilitude, unlikeness; incomparability 10 *unrelatedness*; disparity 29 *inequality*; diversity, divergence 15 *difference*; variation, variance, variety 17 *nonuniformity*, 82 *multiformity*; contrast 14 *contrariety*; little in common, nothing in c., no match, not a pair 25 *disagreement*; novelty, uniqueness 21 *originality*; dissemblance, dissimilation, camouflage, make-up 525 *concealment*, 527 *disguise*; caricature, bad likeness 552 *misrepresentation*; foreign body, alien element 59 *extraneousness*; odd man out 25 *misfit*.

Adj. *dissimilar*, unlike, distinct, diverse 15 *different*; various 82 *multiform*; disparate 29 *unequal*; unalike, not comparable 10 *unrelated*; far above 34 *superior*; far below 35 *inferior*; unrelated, unmatched, unpaired 17 *nonuniform*; unique, peerless, one and only, original 21 *inimitable*; incongruent 25 *disagreeing*; untypical, atypical, exotic 84 *unconformable*; unprecedented, new and strange, novel 126 *new*; a far cry from 199 *distant*; bad of, not true to life, unrealistic.

Vb. *be unlike*, - dissimilar etc. adj.; bear no resemblance, have nothing in common 15 *differ*; stand out 34 *be superior*, 35 *be inferior*.

make unlike, discriminate, distinguish 15 *differentiate*; innovate, modify, modulate 143 *change*, 147 *convert*; caricature 552 *misrepresent*, 246 *distort*; dissemble 542 *deceive*; disguise 525 *conceal*; camouflage 18 *liken*, 541 *fake*.

Adv. *dissimilarly*, discordantly, contrastingly, variously 15 *differently*.

See: 10, 14, **15**, **17**, 18, 21, 25, 29, 34, 35, 59, 82, 84, 126, 143, 147, 199, 246, 525, 527, 541, 542, 552.

20 Imitation

N. *imitation*, copying etc. vb; sincerest form of flattery; rivalry, emulation 716 *contention*; conventionality, doing as Rome does 83 *conformity*; want of originality, following, literalism, slavishness, slavish imitation; imitativeness, parrotry (**see** *mimicry*); affectedness 850 *affectation*; mimesis 551 *representation*; reflection, mirror, echo, shadow 18 *assimilation*; paraphrase, translation 520 *interpretation*; borrowing, cribbing, plagiary, plagiarism, literary theft 788 *stealing*; forgery, falsification, counterfeit, fake 541 *falsehood*; copying, transcribing, transcription, transliteration, tracing 22 *copy*; duplication, reduplication, multiplication 166 *reproduction*, 551 *photography*.

mimicry, mimesis 551 *representation*; onomatopoeia; noises off 594 *dramaturgy*; mime, pantomime, sign language, gesticulation 547 *gesture*; ventriloquism 579 *speech*; portrayal, portraiture 553 *painting*, 590 *description*; realism 494 *accuracy*; mockery, caricature, parody, spoof, burlesque 851 *satire*; travesty 552 *misrepresentation*, 246 *distortion*; imitativeness, mimicking, apery, apishness, parrotry 106 *repetition*, 850 *affectation*; conjuring, illusionism; simulator, simulation exercise 534 *teaching*; simulation, semblance, disguise, protective colouring, camouflage, dissimulation 18 *similarity*, 19 *dissimilarity*; pretence, mockery, simulacrum, pale shadow 542 *sham*, 4 *insubstantiality*.

imitator, copycat, ape, sedulous a., monkey; mockingbird, parrot, echo; sheep 83 *conformist*, 284 *follower*; poseur 850 *affecter*; echoer, yes-man 925 *flatterer*; mocker, burlesquer, parodist, caricaturist 839 *humorist*, 926 *detractor*; mime, ventriloquist, mimic, impersonator, female i., drag artiste, illusionist 594 *entertainer*; actor, portrayer, portraitist 556 *artist*; copyist, printer, tracer 586 *calligrapher*; translator, paraphraser 520 *interpreter*; transcriber of life, realist, naturalist; simulator, shammer, hypocrite 545 *impostor*; borrower, plagiarist; counterfeiter, forger, faker; duplicator, spirit d., copier, photocopier, mimeograph, pantograph, stencil.

Adj. *imitative*, mimetic; onomatopoeic, echoic; apish, aping, parroting, parrotlike; following; echoing, flattering; posing 850 *affected*; disguised, camouflaged; mock, mimic; simulating, shamming 541 *hypocritical*; pseudo, sham, imitation, phoney, counterfeit 541 *false*; ersatz, synthetic 150 *substituted*; unoriginal, uninventive, hackneyed 610 *usual*; unimaginative, derivative, imitated, secondhand 106 *repeated*; conventional 83 *conformable*; paraphrastic, modelled, moulded on; taken from nature, copied, slavish, literal; caricatured, parodied, travestied, burlesque; transcribed, transliterated; easy to copy, imitable.

Vb. *imitate*, ape, parrot, flatter, echo, mirror, reflect 18 *resemble*; make a show of, pose 850 *be affected*; pretend, masquerade, make-believe, make as if; act, mimic, mime, portray, paint 551 *represent*; parody, take off, caricature, burlesque, travesty 851 *ridicule*; sham, simulate, put on, feign, play the hypocrite 541 *dissemble*; disguise, camouflage 525 *conceal*; ventriloquize 542 *deceive*.

copy, draw, trace; copy faithfully, catch; set up 587 *print*; reprint, duplicate, mimeograph, cyclostyle, photocopy; make copies, reduplicate, multiply, reel off 166 *reproduce*; copy out, transcribe, transliterate, type, type out; paraphrase, translate 520 *interpret*; copy from, crib, plagiarize, borrow 788 *steal*; counterfeit, forge 541 *fake*.

do likewise, do as the Romans do, mould oneself on, pattern oneself on, take as a model; take a leaf out of another's book; follow, follow suit, follow my leader 284 *follow*; echo, ditto, reecho, chorus 106 *repeat*; follow precedent, follow another's example, join in the cry, hunt with the hounds, jump on the bandwagon 83 *conform*; emulate, rival 716 *contend*.

Adv. *imitatively*, emulously, in rivalry; parrot-fashion; 'en travesti', in drag; literally, to the letter, word for word, verbatim, literatim 494 *truly*.

See: 4, **18**, 19, 22, 83, **106**, 150, 166, 246, 284, 494, 520, 525, 534, **541**, 542, 545, 547, **551**, 552, 553, 556, 579, 586, 587, 590, 594, 610, 716, 788, 839, 850, 851, 925, 926.

21 Originality

N. *originality*, creativeness, inventiveness 513 *imagination*; creation, invention, all my own work 164 *production*; originality 119 *priority*, 10 *unrelatedness*; uniqueness, the one and only 88 *unity*; inimitability, transcendence 34 *superiority*; independence, defiance of precedent, line of one's own 744 *freedom*; precedent, example 23 *prototype*; new departure 68 *beginning*; something new, novelty, innovation, freshness 126 *newness*; eccentricity, individuality 84 *nonconformity*; unlikeness 19 *dissimilarity*.

no imitation, genuineness, sincerity 494 *authenticity*; real thing, the very thing, the real McCoy, the genuine article; it, absolutely it 13 *identity*, 80 *self*; autograph, holograph, manuscript, one's own hand, usual signature.

Adj. *original*, creative, inventive 513 *imaginative*; unimitated, underived, not derivative; prototypal, archetypal; primordial, primary; first, first-hand, first in the field 119 *prior*; unprecedented, fresh, novel 126 *new*; individual, personal 80 *special*; independent 744 *free*; eccentric 84 *unconformable*.

inimitable, transcendent, unmatched, incomparable, out of reach 34 *superior*; not imitated, uncopied, unhackneyed; atypical 15 *different*; unique, one and only 88 *one*; authentic, real, true 494 *genuine*; natural 5 *intrinsic*; sincere, unadulterated 44 *unmixed*.

See: 5, **10**, 13, 15, **19**, 23, 34, 44, 68, 80, 84, 88, 119, 126, 164, 494, 513, 744.

22 Copy

N. *copy*, exact c.; clone 166 *reproduction*; replica, replication, facsimile, tracing; fair copy, transcript, transcription, counterpart 18 *analogue*; cast, death mask; ectype, stamp, seal, impress, impression, imprint; mechanical copy, stereotype, electrotype, collotype, lithograph, print, offprint, printed matter 587 *letterpress*, 555 *engraving*; photocopy, Xerox (tdmk), photograph, photogravure, Photostat (tdmk), positive, negative, contact print 551 *photography*; microfilm, microfiche 548 *record*; an imitation, dummy, pastiche; forgery, counterfeit, fake 542 *sham*; plagiarism, crib 20 *imitation*; a likeness, resemblance, semblance 18 *similarity*; study, portrait, drawing 553 *picture*; icon, image 551 *representation*; model, effigy, statue 554 *sculpture*; faithful copy, servile imitation, reflex, echo, mirror 106 *repetition*, 417 *reflection*; bad copy, apology for, mockery of 552 *misrepresentation*; malicious copy, distorted image, caricature, cartoon, travesty, parody 851 *ridicule*; hint, adumbration, shadow; silhouette, outline, sketch, diagram, first copy, draft; metaphrase, paraphrase 520 *translation*.

duplicate, flimsy, carbon copy, carbon; stencil, master copy; transfer, rubbing; photograph 551 *photography*; reprint, reissue 589 *edition*; model, specimen, inspection copy 83 *example*.

See: **18**, **20**, 83, 106, 166, 417, 520, 542, 548, **551**, 552, 553, 554, 555, 587, 589, 851.

23 Prototype

N. *prototype*, archetype, antitype; type, biotype, common type, norm, everyman 30 *average*; primitive form, protoplasm 358 *organism*; original, protoplast 68 *origin*; first occurrence, precedent, test case 119 *priority*; guide, rule, maxim 693 *precept*; standard, criterion, touchstone, standard of comparison, frame of reference 9 *referral*; ideal 646 *perfection*; cynosure 646 *paragon*; keynote, tuning fork, metronome 465 *gauge*; module, unit; specimen, sample 83 *example*; model, subject; exemplar, pattern, paradigm; dummy, mock-up; copybook, copy, printer's c., text, manuscript; blueprint, design, master plan, scheme 623 *plan*; rough plan, outline, draft, sketch.

living model, model, artist's m., poser, sitter, subject; fashion model, mannequin; stroke, pacer, pacemaker; bandleader, conductor, fugleman, drum major 690 *leader*.

mould, matrix, mint; plate, shell; stencil, template; frame 243 *form*; wax figure, lay f., tailor's dummy; last; die, stamp, punch, seal, intaglio 555 *printing*.

Adj. *prototypal*, paradigmatic, exemplary, model, standard, classic, copybook.

Vb. *be an example*, set an e., serve as e., stand as e.; serve as a model, model, sit for, pose.

See: 9, 30, 68, **83**, 119, 243, 358, 465, 555, 623, 646, 690, 693.

24 Agreement

N. *agreement*, consentaneity 181 *concurrence*; consentience, consent 488 *assent*; accord, accordance, chorus, unison 16 *uniformity*; harmony 410 *melody*; consonance, concinnity, concordance; concert, understanding, mutual understanding, entente, entente cordiale; concordat, convention, pact 765 *compact*; unity, solidarity, unanimity 488 *consensus*; consortium 706 *cooperation*; union 50 *combination*; peace 710 *concord*.

conformance 83 *conformity*; congruence, coincidence 13 *identity*; consistency, congruity 16 *uniformity*; coherence, consequentiality, consequence, logic, logical conclusion 475 *reasoning*; correspondence, parallelism 18 *similarity*.

fitness, aptness, qualification, capability 694 *aptitude*; suitability, propriety 642 *good policy*; the right man in the right place, perfect candidate, the very thing 13 *identity*; relevancy, pertinence, admissibility, appositeness, case in point, good example 9 *relevance*; commensurability, proportion 9 *relation*; timeliness, right moment, fit occasion 137 *occasion*.

adaptation, conformation, harmonization, synchronization, matching 18 *assimilation*; reconciliation, reconcilement 719 *pacification*; accommodation, negotiation 770 *compromise*; attunement, adjustment 62 *arrangement*; compatibility, congeniality, naturalness; fitting, suiting, good fit, perfect f., close f., tight f.

Adj. *agreeing*, right, accordant, in accord, in accordance with, in keeping with; corresponding, correspondent, answering; proportional, proportionate, commensurate, according to 12 *correlative*; coincident, coinciding, congruent, congruous 28 *equal*; squared with, consistent w., conforming 83 *conformable*; in conformity, in step, in phase, in tune, synchronized 123 *synchronous*; of a piece with, consistent, self-c. 16 *uniform*; consonant, concordant, harmonized 410 *harmonious*; combining, mixing; suiting, matching 18 *similar*; becoming 846 *tasteful*; natural, congenial, sympathetic; reconcilable, compatible, coexistent, coexisting, symbiotic; consentaneous, consensual, consentient, agreeable, acquiescent 488 *assenting*; concurrent, agreed, all a., at one, in unison, in chorus, unanimous; united, concerted; like-minded, of like mind, bipartisan 706 *cooperative*; treating, treaty-making, in treaty, negotiating 765 *contractual*.

apt, applicable, admissible, germane, appropriate, pertinent, in point, to the point, pointed, well-aimed 9 *relevant*; to the purpose, bearing upon; in loco, pat, in place, apropos; right, happy, felicitous, idiomatic 575 *elegant*; at home, in one's element; seasonable, opportune 137 *timely*.

fit, fitting, befitting, seemly, decorous; suited, well-adapted, adaptable; capable, qualified, cut out for 694 *skilful*; suitable, up one's street 642 *advisable*; meet, proper 913 *right*.

adjusted, well-a. 60 *orderly*, 494 *accurate*; timed, synchronized; focused, tuned, fine-t.; strung, pitched, attuned 412 *musical*; trimmed, balanced 28 *equal*; well-cut, fitting, well-fitting, close-fitting, tight-fitting, tight; made to measure, tailored, tailor-made, snug, comfortable.

Vb. *accord*, be accordant etc. adj.; agree, concur 488 *assent*, 758 *consent*; respond, echo, chorus, chime in, ditto 106 *repeat*; coincide, square with, quadrate w., mesh w., gear w., dovetail 45 *join*; fit, fit like a glove, fit to a T; tally, correspond, match 18 *resemble*; go with, comport with, tone in w., harmonize; come naturally to; take to like a duck to water; fit in, belong, feel at home; answer, do, meet, suit, suit down to the ground 642 *be expedient*; fall pat, come apropos, prove timely, fit the occasion; beseem, befit; keep together, pull t. 706 *cooperate*; be consistent, be logical, hang together, hold t. 475 *be reasonable*; seek accord, treat, negotiate, come to terms 766 *make terms*; get on with, be on the same wavelength, hit it off, fraternize, make friends 880 *befriend*; be natural, behave naturally, be oneself.

adjust, make adjustments 654 *rectify*; render accordant etc. adj.; readjust, repair 656 *restore*; fit, suit, adapt, accommodate, conform; attune, tune, tune up, pitch, string 410 *harmonize*; modulate, tune in; regulate 60 *order*; graduate, proportion 12 *correlate*; dress, align 62 *arrange*; balance 28 *equalize*; cut, trim 31 *compensate*; tailor, make to measure; concert; focus, synchronize.

Adv. *pertinently*, aptly etc. adj.; apropos of; in the right context.

See: 9, 12, 13, **16**, 18, 28, 31, 45, 50, 60, 62, **83**, 106, 123, 137, 181, 410, 412, 475, **488**, 494, 575, 642, 654, 656, 694, 706, 710, 719, 758, 765, 766, 770, 846, 880, 913.

25 Disagreement

N. *disagreement*, disaccord; nonagreement, failure to agree, agreement to disagree 489 *dissent*; divergent opinions, conflict of opinion, controversy, argumentation 475 *argument*; wrangle, wrangling, bickering 709 *quarrel*; disunion, disunity, faction 709 *dissension*; dissidence 978 *schism*; jarring, clash 279 *collision*; challenge, defiance, rupture, breach 718 *war*; variance, divergence, discrepancy 15 *difference*; two voices, ambiguity, ambivalence 518 *equivocalness*; inconsistency, credibility gap; variety, inconsistency 17 *nonuniformity*; opposition, contradiction, conflict 14 *contrariety*; dissonance, discordance, disharmony, inharmoniousness 411 *discord*; noncoincidence, incongruence, incongruity 10 *unrelatedness*; disparity 29 *inequality*; disproportion, asymmetry 246 *distortion*; incompatibility, irreconcilability, hostility 881 *enmity*.

inaptitude, unfitness, incapacity, incompetence 695 *unskilfulness*; unfittingness, unsuitability, undecorousness; impropriety 643 *inexpedience*, 847 *bad taste*; inconcinnity 576 *inelegance*; inapplicability, inadmissibility, irrelevancy 10 *irrelevance*; intrusiveness, intrusion, interruption 138 *untimeliness*; maladjustment, incompatibility, unconformability 84 *nonconformity*.

misfit, maladjustment, bad fit; bad match, misalliance, mésalliance 894 *marriage*; oxymoron; paradox; incongruity, false note, jar 411 *discord*; fish out of water, square peg in a round hole; outsider, foreigner, foreign body 59 *intruder*; dissident, dissenter 84 *nonconformist*; joker, odd man out, freak, sport 84 *abnormality*; eccentric, oddity 851 *laughingstock*; ass in a lion's skin, mutton dressed up as lamb 501 *fool*; wolf in sheep's clothing 542 *sham*.

Adj. *disagreeing*, dissenting, unagreed, not unanimous 489 *dissenting*; challenging 711 *defiant*; at odds, at cross purposes, at variance; at loggerheads, at war 718 *warring*; bickering, snapping 709 *quarrelling*; hostile, antagonistic 881 *inimical*; uncongenial, antipathetic 861 *disliked*; conflicting, clashing, contradictory 14 *contrary*; unnatural, against one's nature, out of character; inconsistent 17 *nonuniform*; inconsonant, incompatible; unadaptable 84 *unconformable*; odd, foreign 59 *extraneous*; not combining, not mixing; incommensurable 10 *unrelated*; disproportionate, out of proportion, unsymmetrical 246 *distorted*; inharmonious, grating 411 *discordant*; mismatched, misallied; ill-matching, badly matched, ill-assorted, discrepant 15 *different*; incongruous 497 *absurd*.

unapt, unfitted, unsuited, incapable, incompetent 695 *unskilful*; inept, maladjusted 695 *clumsy*; wrong, unfitting, unsuitable, unfortunate, unbecoming, not for one, improper, undue, inappropriate 643 *inexpedient*; impracticable 470 *impossible*; unfit for, ineligible 607 *rejected*; intrusive, ill-timed, unseasonable 138 *inopportune*; malapropos, inapplicable, inadmissible 10 *irrelevant*; unidiomatic 576 *inelegant*; out of character, out of keeping; misplaced, out of place, out of joint, out of tune, out of time, out of step, out of phase.

Vb. *disagree* 489 *dissent*; differ, dispute 475 *argue*; fall out 709 *quarrel*, *bicker*; clash, conflict, collide, contradict 14 *be contrary*; be discrepant, - unapt etc. adj.; vary, diverge 15 *differ*; not play, noncooperate 702 *be obstructive*; have nothing to do with 10 *be unrelated*; come amiss, interfere, intrude; be incongruous, stick out like a sore thumb, strike a false note, jar.

mismatch, misalign, misfit, fit badly; miscast, misplace, mistime.

Adv. *in defiance of*, in contempt of, despite, in spite of; discordantly etc. adj.

See: **10**, 14, 15, 17, 29, 59, **84**, 138, 246, 279, 411, 470, 475, **489**, 497, 501, 518, 542, 576, 607, 643, 695, 702, 709, 711, 718,

847, 851, 861, 881, 894, 978.

Section three: Quantity

26 Quantity

N. *quantity*, amount, sum 38 *addition*; total 52 *whole*; magnitude, amplitude, extent 465 *measurement*; mass, substance, body, bulk 195 *size*; dimension, dimensions, longitude 203 *length*; width, thickness 205 *breadth*; altitude 209 *height*; deepness 211 *depth*; area, volume, extension 183 *space*; weight 322 *gravity*, 323 *lightness*; strength, force, flow, potential, pressure, tension, stress, strain, torque 160 *energy*; numbers 104 *multitude*; quotient, fraction, multiple, function, quantic, vector 85 *number*, 86 *mathematics*, 101 *plurality*, 102 *fraction*, 103 *zero*, 107 *infinity*; mean, median 30 *average*.

finite quantity, matter of, limited amount, definite figure; lower limit, upper l., ceiling 236 *limit*; definite amount, quantum, quota, quorum; measured quantity, measure, dose, dosage 465 *measurement*; avoirdupois 322 *weighing*; ration, whack 783 *portion*; pittance, driblet, spoonful, thimbleful, cupful; capful, bagful, sackful; whole amount, lot, batch; load, lorryload 193 *contents*; lock, stock and barrel 52 *whole*; large amount, masses, heaps 32 *great quantity*; small amount, bit 33 *small quantity*; greater amount, more, most, majority 36 *increase*, 104 *greater number*; smaller amount, less, not so much 37 *decrease*, 39 *subtraction*, 105 *fewness*; stint, piece, task 682 *labour*.

Adj. *quantitative*, some, certain, any, more or less; so many, so much; quantified, measured.

Vb. *quantify*, express the quantity; allot, rate, ration 783 *apportion*.

Adv. *to the amount of*; to the sum of, to the tune of; to such an extent.

See: 30, 32, 33, 36, 37, 38, 39, 52, 85, 86, 101, 102, 103, 104, 105, 107, 160, 183, 193, 195, 203, 205, 209, 211, 236, 322, 323, **465**, 682, 783.

27 Degree: relative quantity

N. *degree*, relative quantity, proportion, ratio, scale 9 *relativeness*, 462 *comparison*; ration, stint 783 *portion*, 53 *part*; amplitude, extent, intensity, frequency, magnitude, size 26 *quantity*; level, pitch, altitude 209 *height*, 211 *depth*; key, register 410 *musical note*; reach, compass, scope 183 *range*; rate, tenor, way, speed 265 *motion*; gradation, graduation, calibration 15 *differentiation*; differential, shade, nuance; grade, remove, stepping-stone; step, rung, tread, stair 308 *ascent*; point, stage, milestone, turning point, crisis 8 *juncture*; mark, peg, notch, score 547 *indicator*; bar, line, interval 410 *notation*; valuation, value 465 *measurement*; ranking, grading 77 *classification*; class, kind 77 *sort*; standard, rank, grade 73 *serial place*; military rank, lieutenancy, captaincy, majority, colonelcy; ecclesiastical rank 985 *church office*; hierarchy 733 *authority*; sphere, station, status, standing, footing 8 *circumstance*; gradualism, gradualness 278 *slowness*.

Adj. *gradational*, hierarchical, graduated, scalar, calibrated, graded, scaled; gradual, shading off, tapering; fading, fading out.

comparative, relative, proportional, in scale 9 *relative*; within the bounds of 236 *limited*; measured by.

Vb. *graduate*, rate, class, rank 73 *grade*; scale, calibrate; compare, measure.

shade off, taper, die away, pass into, melt into, change gradually, dissolve, fade, fade out; raise by degrees 36 *augment*; lower by degrees 37 *abate*; whittle down, pare, trim 204 *shorten*.

Adv. *by degrees*, gradually, little by little, step by step, drop by drop, bit by bit, inch by inch; by inches, by slow degrees; in some degree, in slight measure; to some extent, just a bit; however little, however much.

See: 8, **9**, 15, **26**, 36, 37, 53, 73, 77, 183, 204, 209, 211, 236, 265, 278, 308, 410, 462, 465, 547, 733, 783, 985.

28 Equality: sameness of quantity or degree

N. *equality*, same quantity, same degree; parity, coequality, coextension, coincidence 24 *agreement*; symmetry, balance, poise; evenness, level 258 *smoothness*, 216 *horizontality*; equability, monotony 16 *uniformity*; roundness 250 *circularity*; impartiality 913 *justice*.

equivalence, likeness 18 *similarity*; sameness 13 *identity*, 219 *parallelism*; equation; interchangeability 151 *interchange*; equipollence, isotropy; synonymity, synonym;

reciprocation, exchange, fair e. 791 *barter*; par, quits; equivalent, value, fair v., just price 809 *price*; not a pin to choose, six of one and half a dozen of the other; level bet, even money.

equilibrium, equipoise, equiponderance, stable equilibrium, balance, poise; even keel, steadiness, uprightness; state of equilibrium, balance of forces, balance of nature, balance of power, balance of trade, balance of payments; deadlock, stalemate 145 *stop*; status quo, stable state, equilibration, homoeostasis; road-holding ability 153 *stability*; sea legs, seat; fin, aileron 153 *stabilizer*; balance, equilibrant; equilibrist, tightrope walker, acrobat 162 *athlete*.

equalization, equation, equilibration; balancing 322 *weighing*; coordination, adjustment, readjustment, levelling up *or* down 656 *restoration*, 31 *compensation*; equal division, going halves 92 *bisection*, 775 *participation*; reciprocity 12 *correlation*; tit for tat 714 *retaliation*, 151 *interchange*; equalizer, counterpoise 31 *offset*; equator 92 *dividing line*; equalization fund; standardizer, bed of Procrustes; return match, second chance.

draw, drawn game, drawn battle; level-pegging; tie, dead heat; no decision, stalemate, deadlock; neck and neck race, photo finish; love all, deuce; near thing, narrow margin 200 *short distance*.

compeer, peer, equal, coequal, match, mate, twin; fellow, brother 18 *analogue*; equivalent, parallel, opposite number, counterpart, shadow; rival, corrival, competitor 716 *contender*.

Adj. *equal*, equi-, iso-, co-; same 13 *identical*; like 18 *similar*; neither more nor less, coequal, coordinate, coextensive, coincident, congruent, homologous 24 *agreeing*; equiponderant; equipollent; equidistant; isotropic; balanced, poised, in equilibrium; homoeostatic, steady, stable 153 *fixed*; even, level, round, square, flush 258 *smooth*; even-sided, equilateral, regular 16 *uniform*, 245 *symmetrical*; equable, unvarying, monotonous 153 *unchangeable*; competitive, rival 716 *contending*; dingdong, Greek meeting Greek, matched, drawn, tied; parallel, level-pegging, running level, abreast, neck-and-neck; equalized, bracketed; sharing, cosharing; equally divided, half-and-half, fifty-fifty; impartial, democratic, equitable 913 *just*; on equal terms, on the same footing, on a par, on a level; par, quits, upsides with.

equivalent, comparable, parallel, interchangeable, synonymous, virtual, convertible; corresponding, reciprocal 12 *correlative*; as good as, no better, no worse; tantamount, virtually the same, indistinguishable; much the same, all the s., all one, as broad as it is long, pot calling the kettle black 18 *similar*; worth, valued at, priced at, standing at 809 *priced*.

Vb. *be equal*, equal, countervail, counterbalance, counterpoise, compensate 31 *set off*; add nothing, detract n., make no difference, come to the same thing, coincide with, agree w. 24 *accord*; be equal to, measure up to, reach, touch; cope with 160 *be able*; make the grade, pass muster 635 *suffice*; hold one's own, keep up with, keep pace w., run abreast, be level; parallel 219 *be parallel*; match, twin 18 *resemble*; tie, draw, halve the match; break even; make it all square; leave no remainder; go halves, go shares 775 *participate*.

equalize, equate; bracket, match; parallel 462 *compare*; balance, strike a b., poise; trim, dress, square, round off, make flush, level 258 *smooth*, 16 *make uniform*; fit, accommodate, readjust 24 *adjust*; add a makeweight, counterpoise, even up 31 *set off*; redress the balance, give points to, handicap 31 *compensate*; set on an even keel, equilibrate, restore to equilibrium 153 *stabilize*; right oneself, keep one's balance, hold the road.

Adv. *equally*, evenly etc. adj.; pari passu, ceteris paribus; at the same rate; to all intents and purposes, as good as; on equal terms; in equilibrium; on an even keel.

See: 12, 13, **16**, **18**, 24, **31**, 92, 145, 151, 153, 160, 162, 200, 216, 219, 245, 250, 258, 322, 462, 635, 656, 714, 716, 775, 791, 809, 913.

29 Inequality: difference of quantity or degree

N. *inequality*, difference of degree 34 *superiority*, 35 *inferiority*; irregularity, variability, patchiness 17 *nonuniformity*; unevenness 259 *roughness*; disproportion, asymmetry 246 *distortion*, 25 *disagreement*; oddness, skewness, lopsidedness 220 *obliquity*; imparity, disparity 15 *difference*; unlikeness 19 *dissimilarity*;

disequilibrium, unstable equilibrium, imbalance, unbalance; dizziness, the staggers; tilting of the scales, preponderance, overweight, top-hamper 322 *gravity*; underweight, short weight 323 *lightness*; defect, shortcoming, inadequacy 636 *insufficiency*; odds 15 *difference*; makeweight, counterpoise 31 *offset*; bonus 40 *extra*; casting vote; partiality, discrimination 481 *bias*, 914 *injustice*.

Adj. *unequal*, disparate, incongruent 15 *different*, 25 *disagreeing*, 19 *dissimilar*; unique, unequalled, at an advantage 34 *superior*, 644 *excellent*; at a disadvantage, below par 35 *inferior*; disproportionate, disproportioned, asymmetrical 246 *distorted*; irregular, scalene, lopsided 17 *nonuniform*; askew, awry 220 *oblique*; odd, uneven; unequable, variable, patchy 437 *variegated*; deficient, defective, falling short, inadequate 636 *insufficient*; underweight 323 *light*; overweight 322 *weighty*; in disequilibrium, unbalanced, swinging, swaying, rocking 152 *unstable*; untrimmed, unballasted, uncompensated; overloaded, top-heavy, unwieldy 695 *clumsy*; listing, leaning, canting, heeling 220 *oblique*; off balance, overbalanced, losing balance, dizzy, toppling, falling 309 *descending*; unequitable, partial, unfair, undemocratic 914 *unjust*, 481 *biased*.

Vb. *be unequal*, be mismatched 25 *disagree*; not balance, not equate, leave a remainder 15 *differ*; fall short 35 *be inferior*; preponderate, have the advantage, give points to, overtop, outclass, outrank 34 *be superior*; outstrip 306 *outdo*; be deficient 636 *not suffice*; overcompensate, overweight, tip the scales 322 *weigh*; be underweight, need a makeweight 323 *be light*; throw the casting vote; unbalance, throw off balance; overbalance, capsize; list, tilt, lean 220 *be oblique*; rock, swing, sway 317 *fluctuate*; vary 143 *change*.

Adv. *unevenly*, unequally etc. adj.

See: **15**, **17**, **19**, 25, 31, 34, 35, 40, 143, 152, 220, 246, 259, 306, 309, 317, 322, 323, 437, 481, 636, 644, 695, 914.

30 Mean

N. *average*, medium, mean, median 86 *statistics*; intermedium, middle term 73 *serial place*; balance; happy medium, golden mean 177 *moderation*; standard product 79 *generality*; ruck, ordinary run 732 *averageness*; norm, par; the normal 610 *habit*.

middle point, midpoint, middle distance, half way 70 *middle*; middle years 131 *middle age*; middle class 869 *middle classes*; middle of the road, midway, middle course 625 *middle way*; splitting the difference 770 *compromise*; neutrality 606 *no choice*; central position 225 *centre*.

common man 869 *commoner*; everywoman, man *or* woman in the street, man on the Clapham omnibus, ordinary m. *or* w., plain m. *or* w. 79 *everyman*; typical individual, average specimen 732 *averageness*.

Adj. *median*, mean, average, medial 70 *middle*, 225 *central*; neither hot nor cold, lukewarm; intermediate, grey; normal, standard, par, ordinary, commonplace, run-of-the-mill, mediocre 732 *middling*; moderate, middle-of-the-road 625 *neutral*; middle class, middlebrow.

Vb. *average out*, average, take the mean; split the difference, go halfway 770 *compromise*; strike a balance 28 *equalize*.

Adv. *on an average*, in the long run 79 *generally*; on the whole, all in all; taking one thing with another, taking all things together; in round numbers.

See: 28, **70**, 73, **79**, 86, 131, 177, 225, 606, 610, **625**, **732**, 770, 869.

31 Compensation

N. *compensation*, weighting 28 *equalization*; rectification 654 *amendment*; reaction, neutralization, nullification 182 *counteraction*; commutation 151 *interchange*, 150 *substitution*; redemption, recoupment, recovery; retrieval 771 *acquisition*; indemnification, reparation, redress 787 *restitution*, 656 *restoration*; amends, expiation 941 *atonement*; recompense, repayment 962 *reward*, 910 *revenge*, 714 *retaliation*; reciprocity, measure for measure 12 *correlation*.

offset, set-off, allowance, makeweight, balance, weighting, counterweight, counterpoise, counterbalance, ballast 28 *equalization*; indemnity, reparations, compensation, costs, damages 787 *restitution*; refund, one's money back; amends, penance 941 *atonement*; equivalent, quid pro quo 150 *substitute*; swings and roundabouts 151 *interchange*; cover, collateral, hostage 767 *security*; counterclaim 627 *requirement*; counter-blow 713 *defence*;

counterattraction 291 *attraction*; concession, cession 770 *compromise*; bribe, sweetener, hush money, tribute 804 *payment*, 962 *reward*.

Adj. *compensatory*, compensating, redeeming, countervailing, balancing 28 *equivalent*; self-correcting, self-cancelling; indemnificatory, in damages, restitutory 787 *restoring*; amendatory, expiatory 941 *atoning*; in the opposite scale, weighed against 462 *compared*.

Vb. *compensate*, offer compensation, make amends, make compensation etc. n.; do penance 941 *atone*; indemnify, restore, pay back 787 *restitute*; make good, make up, make up for, do instead 150 *substitute*; add a makeweight, ballast; pay, repay 714 *retaliate*; bribe, square 962 *reward*; reimburse, pay overtime 804 *pay*; redeem, outweigh; overcompensate, lean over backwards.

set off, offset, allow for; counterpoise, countervail, balance 28 *equalize*; neutralize, cancel, nullify 182 *counteract*; cover, hedge 858 *be cautious*; give and take, concede, cede 770 *compromise*.

recoup, recover 656 *retrieve*; make up leeway, take up the slack; indemnify oneself, take back, get back 786 *take*; make a comeback 656 *be restored*.

Adv. *in return*, in consideration, in compensation, in lieu; though, although; at the same time, on the other hand; nevertheless, regardless of; despite, for all that, notwithstanding; but, still, even so, be that as it may; after all, allowing for; when all is said and done, taking one thing with another; at least, at all events, at any rate.

See: 12, **28**, 150, 151, 182, 291, 462, 627, 654, 656, 713, 714, 767, 770, 771, 786, 787, 804, 858, 910, 941, 962.

32 Greatness

N. *greatness*, largeness, bigness, girth 195 *size*; large scale, generous proportions, outsize dimensions, vastness, enormousness, gigantism 195 *hugeness*; muchness, abundance 635 *plenty*; amplitude, ampleness, fullness, maximum 54 *completeness*, *plenitude*; superabundance, superfluity, more than enough 637 *redundance*; immoderation 815 *prodigality*; exorbitance, excessiveness, excess 546 *exaggeration*; enormity, immensity, boundlessness 107 *infinity*; numerousness, countlessness 104 *multitude*; dimensions, magnitude 26 *quantity*, 27 *degree*; extension, extent 203 *length*, 205 *breadth*, 209 *height*, 211 *depth*; expanse, area, volume, capacity 183 *space*; spaciousness, roominess 183 *room*; mightiness, might, strength, intensity 160 *power*, 178 *influence*; intensification, magnification, multiplication 197 *expansion*; aggrandizement 36 *increase*; seriousness, significance 638 *importance*; eminence 34 *superiority*; grandeur, grandness 868 *nobility*, 871 *pride*; majesty 733 *authority*; fame, renown 866 *repute, prestige*; noise, din 400 *loudness*.

great quantity, muchness, galore 635 *plenty*; crop, harvest, profusion, abundance, productivity 171 *productiveness*; superfluity, superabundance, shower, flood, spate, torrent 637 *redundance*, 350 *stream*; expanse, sheet, lake, sea, ocean, world, universe, sight of, world of, mort of, power of; much, lot, whole l., fat l., deal, good d., great d.; not a little, not peanuts; too much, more than one bargained for; stock, mint, mine 632 *store*; quantity, peck, bushel, pints, gallons; lump, heap, mass, stack, mountain 74 *accumulation*; packet (of), pack (of), load (of), full l., cargo, shipload, boatload, trainload, carload, lorryload, truckload, sackload 193 *contents*; quantities, lots, lashings, oodles, scads, wads, pots, bags; heaps, loads, masses, stacks; oceans, seas, floods, streams; volumes, reams, sheets; numbers, not a few, quite a f., crowds, masses, hosts, swarms, multitudes 104 *multitude*; all, entirety, corpus 52 *whole*.

main part, almost all, principal part, best p., essential p. 52 *chief part*; greater part, major p., majority 104 *greater number*; body, bulk, mass, substance; soul 1 *essence*.

Adj. *great*, greater, main, most, major 34 *superior*; maximum, greatest 34 *supreme*; grand, big, mickle 195 *large*; fair-sized, largish, biggish, pretty big; substantial, considerable, respectable; sizable, of size, large-s., full-s., man-s., life-s.; bulky, massy, massive, heavy 322 *weighty*; prolonged, lengthy 203 *long*; wide, thick 205 *broad*; puffed up, swollen 197 *expanded*; ample, generous, voluminous, capacious 183 *spacious*; profound 211 *deep*; great in stature, tall, lofty 209 *high*; great in strength, Herculean 162 *strong*; mighty

160 *powerful,* 178 *influential*; intense, violent 174 *vigorous*; noisy 400 *loud*; soaring, mounting, climbing 308 *ascending*; culminating, at the maximum, at the peak, at the top, at its height, in the zenith, at the limit, at the summit 213 *topmost*; great in quantity, plentiful, abundant, overflowing 635 *plenteous*; superabundant 637 *redundant*; great in number, many, swarming, teeming 104 *multitudinous*; great in age, antique, ancient, venerable, immemorial 127 *olden,* 131 *ageing*; great in honour, imperial, august, goodly, precious, of value 644 *valuable,* 868 *noble*; sublime, exalted 821 *impressive*; glorious, famed, famous 866 *renowned, worshipful*; grave, solemn, serious 638 *important*; excelling, excellent 306 *surpassing,* 644 *best.*

extensive, ranging, wide-ranging, far-flying, far-flung, far-reaching, far-stretching 183 *spacious*; widespread, prevalent, epidemic; worldwide, universal, cosmic; mass, indiscriminate, wholesale, whole-hogging, full-scale, all-embracing, sweeping, comprehensive 78 *inclusive.*

enormous, immense, vast, colossal, giant, gigantic, monumental 195 *huge*; towering, sky-high 209 *high*; record, record-breaking, record-smashing, excelling 306 *surpassing.*

prodigious, marvellous, astounding, amazing, astonishing 864 *wonderful*; fantastic, fabulous, incredible, unbelievable, passing belief 486 *unbelieved,* 472 *improbable,* 470 *impossible*; stupendous, tremendous, terrific; dreadful, frightful 854 *frightening*; breathtaking, overwhelming, out of this world 821 *impressive.*

remarkable, signal, noticeable, worth looking at 866 *noteworthy*; outstanding, extraordinary, exceptional, uncommon 84 *unusual*; eminent, distinguished, marked, of mark 638 *notable.*

whopping, walloping, whacking, spanking, thumping, thundering, socking, rattling, howling, father and mother of; hefty, husky, hulking, strapping, overgrown, clumsy 195 *unwieldy.*

flagrant, blatant, flaring, glaring, stark, staring; signal, shocking 867 *discreditable.*

unspeakable, unutterable, indescribable, indefinable, ineffable; beyond expression, past speaking 517 *inexpressible.*

exorbitant, extortionate, harsh, stringent, severe 735 *oppressive*; excessive, exceeding, passing, extreme, utmost 306 *surpassing*; monstrous, outrageous, swingeing, unconscionable; unbearable 827 *intolerable*; inordinate, unwarranted, preposterous, extravagant, astronomical 546 *exaggerated*; beyond the limit, going too far.

consummate 54 *complete*; finished, flawless 646 *perfect*; entire, sound 52 *whole*; thorough, thoroughpaced, thoroughgoing; utter, total, out and out, dyed in the wool, double-dyed, arch, crass, gross, arrant, rank, regular, downright, desperate, unmitigated; far gone.

absolute, the veriest; essential, positive, unequivocal; stark, pure, sheer, mere 44 *unmixed*; unlimited, unrestricted 107 *infinite*; undiminished, unabated, unreduced.

Vb. *be great* - large, etc. adj.; bulk, bulk large, loom, loom up; stretch 183 *extend*; tower, soar, mount 308 *ascend*; scale, transcend 34 *be superior*; clear, overtop; exceed, know no bounds, run to extremes, go off the deep end 306 *overstep*; enlarge 36 *augment,* 197 *expand*; swamp, overwhelm 54 *fill.*

Adv. *positively,* verily, veritably, actually, indeed, in fact 494 *truly*; seriously, indubitably, in all conscience 473 *certainly*; decidedly, absolutely, definitely, finally, unequivocally, without equivocation; directly, specifically, unreservedly; essentially, fundamentally, radically; downright, plumb.

greatly, much, well; very, right, so; very much, mighty, ever so; fully, quite, entirely, utterly, without reservation 52 *wholly,* 54 *completely*; thoroughly, wholesale; widely, extensively, universally 79 *generally*; largely, mainly, mostly, to a large extent; something, considerably, fairly, pretty, pretty well; a sight, a deal, a great d., ever so much; materially, substantially; increasingly, more than ever, doubly, trebly; specially, particularly; dearly, deeply; vitally; exceptionally; on a large scale, in a big way; vastly, hugely, enormously, gigantically, colossally; heavily, strongly, powerfully, mightily 178 *influentially*; actively, strenuously, vigorously, heartily, intensely; closely, narrowly, intensively, zealously, fanatically, hotly, bitterly, fiercely; acutely, sharply, shrewdly, exquisitely; enough, more than e., abundantly, profusely, prodigiously; generously, richly, worthily, magnificently, splendidly, nobly; supremely, preeminently, superlatively; rarely, unusually, wonderfully, incomparably, strangely; indefinitely, immeasurably, incalculably, infinitely, unspeakably, ineffably.

extremely, ultra-, to extremes, to the limit, to the nth degree; no end of; beyond measure, beyond all bounds; beyond comparison, beyond compare; overly, unduly, improperly, to a fault; out of all proportion; bitterly, harshly, drastically, rigorously, unconscionably, with a vengeance 735 *severely*; immoderately, uncontrollably, desperately, madly, frantically, furiously, fanatically, bitterly 176 *violently*; exceedingly, excessively, exorbitantly, inordinately, outrageously, prohibitively, preposterously; foully, abominably, grossly, beastly, monstrously, horribly; confoundedly, deucedly, devilishly, damnably, hellishly; tremendously, terribly, fearfully, dreadfully, awfully, frightfully, horribly; finally, irretrievably; unforgivably, mortally.

remarkably, noticeably, sensibly, markedly, pointedly; notably, strikingly, conspicuously, signally, emphatically, prominently, glaringly, flagrantly, blatantly; publicly 400 *loudly*; preeminently 34 *eminently*; outstandingly, unco; singularly, peculiarly, curiously, oddly, queerly, strangely, uncommonly, unusually 84 *unconformably*; surprisingly, astonishingly, amazingly, impressively, incredibly, marvellously, magically 864 *wonderfully*.

painfully, unsparingly, till it hurts; badly, bitterly, hard; seriously, sorely, grievously; sadly, miserably, wretchedly; distressingly, pitiably, piteously, woefully, lamentably; shrewdly, cruelly; savagely; unbearably, intolerably; exquisitely, excruciatingly, shockingly, frighteningly, terrifyingly; balefully, mortally.

See: 1, 26, 27, **34**, 36, 44, 52, 54, 74, 78, 79, 84, **104**, 107, 127, 131, 160, 162, 171, 174, 176, 178, 183, 193, **195**, 197, 203, 205, 209, 211, 213, 306, 308, 322, 350, 400, 470, 472, 473, 486, 494, 517, 546, 632, 635, 637, 638, 644, 646, 733, 735, 815, 821, 827, 854, 864, 866, 867, 868, 871.

33 Smallness

N. *smallness*, small size, diminutiveness, minuteness 196 *littleness*; brevity 204 *shortness*; leanness, meagreness 206 *thinness*; rarefaction 325 *rarity*; briefness, momentariness 114 *transience*; paucity 105 *fewness*; rareness, sparseness, sparsity 140 *infrequency*; scarceness, scarcity, inadequacy 636 *insufficiency*, 307 *shortfall*; exiguousness, exiguity, scantiness; moderateness, moderation; intermediate technology, applied t.; small means 801 *poverty*; pettiness, insignificance, meanness 639 *unimportance*, 35 *inferiority*; mediocrity 30 *average*, 732 *averageness*; no depth 212 *shallowness*; tenuity 4 *insubstantiality*; compression, abbreviation, abridgment 198 *contraction*; diminution 37 *decrease*; vanishing point, nothingness 2 *nonexistence*, 103 *zero*, 444 *invisibility*.

small quantity, fraction, modicum, minimum 26 *finite quantity*; minutiae, trivia; peanuts 639 *trifle*; detail, petty detail 80 *particulars*; nutshell 592 *compendium*; drop in the bucket, drop in the ocean; homoeopathic dose, trifling amount; thimbleful, spoonful, mouthful, cupful; trickle, dribble, sprinkling, sprinkle, dash, splash, squirt, squeeze; tinge, tincture, trace, spice, smack, lick, smell, breath, whisper, suspicion, vestige, soupçon, thought, suggestion, nuance, shade, shadow, touch, cast; vein, strain, streak; spark, scintilla, gleam, flash, flicker, ray; pinch, snatch, handful; snack, sip, bite, mite, scrap, morsel, sop; dole, pittance, iron ration; fragment 53 *piece*; whit, bit, mite; iota, jot, tittle; ounce, gram, pennyweight, scruple, minim 322 *weighing*; inch, micron, millimetre 200 *short distance*; second, moment, nanosecond 116 *instant*; vanishing point, next to nothing, hardly anything; the shadow of a shade 4 *insubstantial thing*.

small thing 196 *miniature*; particle, atom; dot, point, pinpoint; dab, spot, fleck, speck, mote, smut; grain, granule, seed, crumb 332 *powder*; drop, droplet, driblet; thread, wisp, shred, rag, tatter, fragment 53 *piece*; flinders, smithereens, confetti; flake, snip, snippet, gobbet, small slice, finger; splinter, chip, clipping, paring, shaving; shiver, sliver, slip; pinprick, snick, prick, nick; hair 208 *filament*.

small coin, groat, farthing, halfpenny, mite, widow's m.; cent, nickel, dime; sou, centime, stiver, bean, small change 797 *coinage*.

small animal, amoeba 196 *microorganism*; gnat, flea, ant; minnow, shrimp, sprat; sparrow, wren; mouse, shrew, bantam, toy dog; homunculus, manikin, midget, Tom Thumb 196 *dwarf*.

Adj. *small*, exiguous, not much, moderate, modest, homoeopathic, minimal, infinitesimal; microscopic, ultramicroscopic 444 *invisible*; tiny, weeny, wee, minute, diminutive, miniature 196 *little*; smaller 35 *lesser*; least, minimum; small-sized, small-framed, small-boned, undersized 196 *dwarfish*; slim, slender, lean, meagre, thin 206 *narrow*; slight, feeble, puny, frail 163 *weak*; delicate, dainty, minikin, fragile 330 *brittle*; flimsy, weightless 323 *light*; fine, subtle, rarefied 325 *rare*; quiet, not loud, soft, low, faint, hushed 401 *muted*; not tall, squat 210 *low*; not long, brief, skimpy, abbreviated 204 *short*; shortened, abridged, cut, compact, compendious, thumbnail 198 *contracted*; scanty, scant, scarce 307 *deficient*; dribbling, trickling 636 *insufficient*; reduced, limited, restricted 747 *restrained*; declining, ebbing, at low ebb, less 37 *decreasing*.

inconsiderable, minor, lightweight, trifling, trivial, petty, paltry, insignificant 639 *unimportant*; not many, soon counted 105 *few*; inappreciable, imperceptible, unnoticeable 444 *invisible*; shadowy, tenuous, evanescent 446 *disappearing*, 114 *transient*; marginal, negligible, remote, slight; superficial, cursory 4 *insubstantial*; skin-deep 212 *shallow*; average, middling, fair, fairish, so-so 30 *median*; moderate, modest, humble, tolerable, passable 732 *middling*; not much of a, no great shakes, second-rate 35 *inferior*; no more than, just, only, mere, bare; plain, simple 44 *unmixed*.

Vb. *be small*, fit into a nutshell; stay small, not grow 196 *be little*; have no height 210 *be low*; have no depth; have no weight 323 *be light*; make no sound 401 *sound faint*; be less 307 *fall short*; get less 37 *decrease*; shrink 198 *become small*.

Adv. *slightly*, exiguously, to a small degree, little; lightly, softly, faintly, feebly; superficially, cursorily, grazingly; gradually, imperceptibly, insensibly, invisibly; on a small scale, in a small way, modestly, humbly; fairly, moderately, tolerably, quite; comparatively, relatively, rather, enough, well e.; indifferently, poorly, badly, miserably, wretchedly, dismally; hardly, scarcely, barely, only just; narrowly, by the skin of one's teeth; hardly at all, no more than; only, merely, purely, simply; at least, at the very least.

partially, to some degree, in some measure, to a certain extent; somehow, after a fashion, sort of, in a manner of speaking; some, somewhat, a little, a bit, just a bit, ever so little, as little as maybe; not fully, restrictedly, limitedly, within bounds 55 *incompletely*; not wholly, in part, partly; not perfectly 647 *imperfectly*.

almost, all but, within an ace of, within an inch of, on the brink of, on the verge of, within sight of, in a fair way to 200 *near*; near upon, close u., approximately 200 *nearly*; pretty near, just short of, not quite, virtually.

about, somewhere, somewhere about, in the region of, thereabouts; on an average, more or less; near enough, a little more, a little less; at a guess, say.

in no way, no way, in no wise, by no means, not by any manner of means, in no respect, not at all, not in the least, not a bit, not the least bit, not in the slightest; not a whit, not a jot, not by a long chalk.

See: 2, 4, 26, 30, 35, 37, 44, **53**, 55, 80, 103, 105, 114, 116, 140, 163, **196**, 198, 200, 204, 206, 208, 210, 212, 307, 322, 323, 325, 330, 332, 401, 444, 446, 592, 636, 639, 647, 732, 747, 797, 801.

34 Superiority

N. *superiority*, superior elevation, higher position; altitude, loftiness, sublimity 209 *height*; transcendence 32 *greatness*, 306 *overstepping*; top 213 *summit*; quality, excellence 644 *goodness*; ne plus ultra 646 *perfection*; preferability 605 *choice*; primacy, pride of place, seniority 64 *precedence*, 119 *priority*; eminence, preeminence 866 *prestige*; higher rank, higher degree 27 *degree*, 868 *nobility*, *aristocracy*; overlordship, paramountcy, supremacy, sovereignty, majesty, imperium 733 *authority*; ascendancy, domination, predominance, hegemony 178 *influence*; directorship, leadership 689 *management*; preponderance, prevalence 29 *inequality*; win, championship 727 *victory*; prominence 638 *importance*; one-upmanship 698 *cunning*, 727 *success*; excess, surplus

637 *superfluity*; climax, zenith, culmination 725 *completion*; maximum, top, peak, pinnacle, crest, crest of the wave; record, high, new h. 213 *summit*.

advantage, privilege, prerogative, handicap, favour 615 *benefit*; start, head s., flying s., lead, commanding l., winning position, pole p., inside track; odds, points, vantage, pull, edge; command, upper hand, whip h.; one up, something in hand, reserves; trump card, ace up one's sleeve, ace in the hole; majority, the big battalions 104 *greater number*; lion's share; leverage, scope 183 *room*; vantage ground, coign of vantage.

superior, superior person 644 *exceller*; superman, wonderwoman 864 *prodigy*; better man *or* woman, first choice 890 *favourite*; select few 644 *elite*; high-ups, one's betters, top people, best p. 638 *bigwig*; nobility, aristocracy 868 *upper class*; overlord, lord, sovereign 741 *master*; commander, chief, prophet, guide 690 *leader*; boss, foreman 690 *manager*; primate, president, prime minister, primus inter pares 690 *director*; model 646 *paragon*; star, virtuoso 696 *proficient person*; specialist 696 *expert*; mastermind 500 *sage*; world-beater, record-breaker; winner, prizewinner, champion, cup-holder, record-h. 727 *victor*; prima donna, first lady, head boy *or* girl; firstborn, elder, senior; Triton among the minnows, big fish in a small pool.

Adj. *superior*, more so; comparative, superlative; major, greater 32 *great*; upper, higher, senior, over-, super-, supra-, hyper-; supernormal, above average, in a different class 15 *different*; better, a cut above, head and shoulders above 644 *excellent*; competitive, more than a match for; one up, ahead, far a., streets a. 64 *preceding*; prior, preferable, preferred, favourite 605 *chosen*; record, a record for, exceeding, overtopping, vaulting, outclassing 306 *surpassing*; on top, winning, victorious 727 *successful*; outstanding, marked, distinguished 866 *noteworthy*; rare, not like the rest, not as others are 84 *unusual*; top-level, high-l., high-powered 689 *directing*, 638 *important*; commanding, in authority 733 *ruling*; revised, reformed, bettered, all the better for 654 *improved*; enlarged, enhanced 197 *expanded*.

supreme, arch-, greatest 32 *great*; highest, uppermost 213 *topmost*; first, chief, foremost 64 *preceding*; main, principal, leading, overruling, overriding, cardinal, capital 638 *important*; excellent, classic, superlative, super, champion, tip-top, top-notch, first-rate, first-class, A1, 5-star, front-rank, world-beating 644 *best*; facile princeps, on top, top of the class, nulli secundus, second to none, none such; dominant, paramount, preeminent, sovereign, royal, every inch a king *or* queen; incomparable, unrivalled, unparagoned, matchless, peerless, unparalleled, unequalled, unsurpassable, unapproached, unapproachable 21 *inimitable*; unsurpassed, ultimate, the last word in 306 *surpassing*; without comparison, beyond compare, beyond criticism 646 *perfect*; transcendent, transcendental, out of this world.

crowning, capping, culminating 725 *completive*; climactic, maximal, maximum; record, record-breaking, best ever 644 *best*.

Vb. *be superior*, transcend, rise above, surmount, overtop, tower over, overlook, command 209 *be high*; go beyond, outrange, outreach 306 *overstep*; exceed, out-Herod Herod, beat the limit, take the cake, take the biscuit; carry off the laurels, bear the palm, wear the crown; pass, surpass, beat the record, reach a new high; improve on, better, go one b., cap, trump, overtrump; show quality, shine, excel 644 *be good*; assert one's superiority, be too much for; steal the show, outshine, eclipse, overshadow, throw into the shade; put another's nose out of joint, take the shine out of; score off, have the laugh on 851 *ridicule*; best, outrival, outclass, outrank 306 *outdo*; outplay, outpoint, outmanoeuvre, outwit 542 *befool*; overtake, leave behind, lap 277 *outstrip*, get the better of, worst, sit on, beat, beat hollow, knock into a cocked hat, beat all comers 727 *defeat*; rise to the occasion.

predominate, preponderate, overbalance, overweigh, tip the scale, turn the s.; change the balance 29 *be unequal*; override, sit on 178 *prevail*; have the advantage, have the start of, have the whip hand, have the upper h., have the edge on; hold all the aces; lead, hold the l., be up on, be one up.

come first, stand f., head the list 64 *come before*; take precedence, play first fiddle

638 *be important*; take the lead, lead the dance, be in the van 237 *be in front*; lead, play the l., star; head, captain 689 *direct*.

culminate, come to a head; cap, crown all 213 *crown*; rise to a peak; set a new record, reach a new high 725 *climax*.

Adv.*beyond*, more, over; over the mark, above the m., above par, over the average; upwards of, in advance of; over and above; at the top of the scale, on the crest, at its height, at the peak, at an advantage.

eminently, preeminently, outstandingly, surpassingly, prominently, superlatively, supremely; above all, of all things; the most, to crown it all, to cap it all; par excellence; principally, especially, particularly, peculiarly; a fortiori, even more, all the m.; still more, ever more, far and away, by far 32 *extremely*.

See:1, 5, 15, 21, 27, 29, **32**, 64, 84, 104, 119, 178, 183, 197, 209, **213**, 237, 277, 306, 500, 542, 605, 615, 637, 638, **644**, **646**, 654, 689, 690, 696, 698, 725, 727, 733, 741, 851, 864, 866, 868, 890.

35 Inferiority

N.*inferiority*, minority, inferior numbers 105 *fewness*; littleness 33 *smallness*; subordinacy, subordination, dependence 745 *subjection*; secondariness, supporting role, second fiddle 639 *unimportance*; lowliness, humbleness 872 *humility*; second rank, back seat, obscurity, commonness 869 *commonalty*; disadvantage, handicap 702 *hindrance*; faultiness, blemish, defect 647 *imperfection*; deficiency, inadequateness 307 *shortfall*, 636 *insufficiency*; failure 728 *defeat*; poor quality, second best 645 *badness*, 812 *cheapness*; vulgarity 847 *bad taste*; beggarliness, shabbiness 801 *poverty*; worsening, decline 655 *deterioration*; record low, low, minimum, lowest point, nadir, the bottom, rock b. 214 *base*; depression, trough 210 *lowness*; flatness, level, plain 216 *horizontality*; mediocrity 732 *averageness*.

inferior, subordinate, subaltern, sub, underling, assistant, subsidiary 707 *auxiliary*; agent 755 *deputy*, 150 *substitute*; tool, pawn 628 *instrument*; follower, retainer 742 *dependant*; menial, hireling 742 *servant*; poor relation, small fry 639 *nonentity*; subject, underdog 742 *slave*; backbencher, private, other ranks, lower classes 869 *commonalty*; second, runner-up; second best, second string, second fiddle, second-rater; bad second, poor s., also-ran; failure, reject, dregs 607 *rejection*; lesser creation, beast, worm; younger, junior, minor.

Adj.*lesser*, less, minor, small-time, one-horse 639 *unimportant*; small 33 *inconsiderable*; smaller, diminished 37 *decreasing*; reduced 198 *contracted*; least, smallest, minimal, minimum; lowest, bottommost 214 *undermost*; minus 307 *deficient*.

inferior, lower, junior, under-, sub-; subordinate, subaltern 742 *serving*; unfree, dependent, parasitical 745 *subjected, subject*; secondary, tributary, ancillary, subsidiary, auxiliary 703 *aiding*, 639 *unimportant*; second, second-best, second-class, second-rate, mediocre; third-rate 922 *contemptible*; humble, lowly, low-level, menial; low-ranking, unclassified; subnormal, substandard, low-grade, not up to snuff 607 *rejected*; slight, underweight 307 *deficient*; spoilt, marred, shop-soiled 655 *deteriorated*; unsound, defective, patchy, unequal 647 *imperfect*; failing 636 *insufficient*; shoddy, crummy 645 *bad*, 812 *cheap*, 847 *vulgar*; low, common, low-caste 869 *plebeian*; scratch, makeshift 670 *unprepared*; temporary, provisional 114 *ephemeral*; feeble 163 *weak*; in a lower class, outclassed, outshone, thrown into the shade, worsted, beaten 728 *defeated*; humiliated 872 *humbled*; unworthy, not fit, not fit to hold a candle to, not a patch on; nothing special, nothing to shout about, nothing to write home about.

Vb.*be inferior*, fall short, come short of, not come up to, fall below 307 *fall short*; lag, fall behind; trail 284 *follow*; want, lack 636 *not suffice*; not make the grade, not pass 728 *fail*; bow to 739 *obey*; concede the victory; yield, cede, yield the palm, hand it to, knuckle under 721 *submit*; play second fiddle, play a supporting role 742 *serve*; take a back seat, retire into the shade; sink into obscurity; lose face, lose caste 867 *lose repute*; get worse 655 *deteriorate*; slump, sink, sink low, touch rock bottom, reach one's nadir 309 *descend*, 313 *plunge*.

Adv.*less*, minus, short of; beneath 210 *under*; below average, below par, below the mark; at the bottom, in the lowest place, at low ebb; inferiorly, poorly, basely.

See: **33**, 37, 105, 114, 150, 163, 198, 210, **214**, 216, 284, 307, 309, 313, 607, 628, 636, 639, **645**, **647**, 655, 670, 702, 703, 707, 721, 728, 732, 739, 742, 745, 755, 801, 812, 847, 867, 869, 872, 922.

36 Increase

N. *increase*, increment, augmentation, waxing, crescendo; advance, progress 285 *progression*; growth, growth area, boom town; buildup, development 164 *production*; growing pains 68 *beginning*; extension, prolongation, protraction 203 *lengthening*; widening, broadening; spread, escalation, amplification, inflation, dilation 197 *expansion*; proliferation, swarming 171 *productiveness, abundance*; multiplication, squaring, cubing 86 *numerical operation*; adding 38 *addition*; enlargement, magnification, aggrandizement 32 *greatness*; overenlargement, excess 546 *exaggeration*; enhancement, appreciation, heightening, raising 310 *elevation*; concentration 324 *condensation*; recruitment 162 *strengthening*; intensification, stepping up, doubling, redoubling, trebling 91 *duplication*, 94 *triplication*; acceleration, speeding 277 *spurt*; hotting up 381 *heating*; excitation 174 *stimulation*; exacerbation 832 *aggravation*; advancement, boost 654 *improvement*; rise, spiral, upward curve, upward trend, upswing 308 *ascent*; uprush, upsurge, flood, tide, rising t., swell, surge 350 *wave*; progressiveness, cumulativeness, cumulative effect, synergistic e., snowball 74 *accumulation*; ascending order 71 *series*.

increment, augmentation, bulge; accretion, accrual, accession, contribution 38 *addition*; supplement, pay rise 40 *extra*; padding, stuffing 303 *insertion*; percentage, commission, rake-off 771 *earnings*; interest, profit 771 *gain*; plunder, prey 790 *booty*; prize 962 *reward*; produce, harvest 164 *product*; takings, receipts, proceeds 782 *receiving*.

Adj. *increasing*, spreading, progressive, escalating; greater than ever 32 *great*; growing, waxing, filling, crescent, on the increase; supplementary 38 *additional*; ever-increasing, snowballing, cumulative 71 *continuous*; augmentative, intensive; productive, fruitful 171 *prolific*; increased, stretched, enlarged, swollen, bloated 197 *expanded*.

Vb. *grow*, increase, gain, develop, escalate; dilate, swell, bulge, wax, fill 197 *expand*; fill out, fatten, thicken 205 *be broad*; put on weight 322 *weigh*; sprout, bud, burgeon, flower, blossom 167 *reproduce itself*; breed, spread, swarm, proliferate, mushroom, multiply 104 *be many*, 171 *be fruitful*; grow up 669 *mature*; spring up, shoot up, grow taller 209 *be high*; spiral, climb, mount, rise, rocket, skyrocket, take off 308 *ascend*; flare up, shine out 379 *be hot*, 417 *shine*; gain strength 656 *be restored*, 162 *be strong*; improve 654 *get better*; flourish, thrive, prosper; gain ground, advance, snowball, accumulate 285 *progress*; earn interest 771 *be profitable*; gain in value, appreciate, rise in price 811 *be dear*; boom, surge, exceed, overflow 637 *superabound*, 32 *be great*; rise to a maximum 34 *culminate*.

augment, increase, bump up, double, triple 94 *treble*, 97 *quadruple*; redouble, square, cube; duplicate 106 *repeat*; multiply 166 *reproduce*; grow, breed, raise, rear 369 *breed stock*, 370 *cultivate*, 669 *mature*; enlarge, magnify, distend, inflate, blow up 197 *expand*; amplify, develop, build up, fill out, fill in, pad out 54 *make complete*; condense, concentrate 324 *be dense*; supplement, enrich, superadd, repay with interest; bring to, contribute to; increase the numbers, accrue 38 *add*; extend, prolong, stretch 203 *lengthen*; broaden, widen, thicken, deepen; heighten, enhance, send up 209 *make higher*; raise, exalt 310 *elevate*; advance, aggrandize 285 *promote*; aim higher, raise the sights; speed up 277 *accelerate*; intensify, redouble, step up, stimulate, energize 174 *invigorate*; recruit, reinforce, boost 685 *refresh*, 656 *restore*, 162 *strengthen*; glorify 546 *exaggerate*, 482 *overrate*; stoke, add fuel to the flames, exacerbate 832 *aggravate*; maximize, bring to the boil, bring to a head 725 *climax*.

Adv. *crescendo*, increasingly etc. adj.; more so, with a vengeance, with knobs on; on the increase, on the up and up, more and more, all the m.

See: 32, 34, **38**, **40**, 54, 68, 71, 74, 86, 91, 94, 97, 104, 106, 162, 164, 166, 167, 171, 174, 197, 203, 205, 209, 277, 285, 303, 308, 310, 322, 324, 350, 369, 370, 379, 381, 417, 482, 546, 637, 654, 656, 669, 685, 725, 771, 782, 790, 811, 832, 962.

37 Decrease: no increase

N. *decrease,* getting less, lessening, dwindling, falling off; waning, fading; fadeout, dimming 419 *dimness*; wane 198 *contraction*; shrinking 206 *narrowing*; ebb, reflux, retreat, withdrawal 286 *regression*; ebb tide, neap 210 *lowness*; descending order 71 *series*; subsidence, sinking, decline, declension, downward curve, downward trend, fall, drop, plunge 309 *descent,* 165 *ruin*; deflation, recession, slump 655 *deterioration*; loss of value, depreciation 812 *cheapness*; loss of reputation 867 *disrepute*; weakening, enfeeblement 163 *weakness*; impoverishment 801 *poverty*; shortage 636 *scarcity*; diminishing returns, exhaustion 190 *emptiness*; shrinkage, evaporation, deliquescence, erosion, attrition, decay, crumbling 655 *dilapidation*; spoilage, leakage, wastage, damage, loss, wear and tear 42 *decrement*; using up, consumption 634 *waste*; limits to growth; no increase, anticlimax 14 *contrariety*; underproduction 175 *inertness*; slackness, slackening 679 *inactivity*; forfeit, levy 963 *penalty,* 772 *loss.*

diminution, making less; deduction 39 *subtraction*; exception 57 *exclusion*; abatement, reduction, restriction 747 *restraint*; slowing down, deceleration 278 *slowness*; retrenchment, cut, economization 814 *economy*; cutting back, pruning, paring, shaving, clipping, docking, curtailment, abridgment, abbreviation 204 *shortening*; compression, squeeze 198 *contraction*; abrasion, erosion 333 *friction*; melting, dissolution 337 *liquefaction*; scattering, dispersal 75 *dispersion*; weeding out, elimination 62 *sorting,* 300 *ejection*; extenuation, alleviation, mitigation, minimization 177 *moderation*; belittlement, undervaluation 483 *underestimation,* 926 *detraction*; demotion, degradation 872 *humiliation.*

Adj. *decreasing,* dwindling; decrescent, waning, fading; deliquescent, melting, evaporating 337 *liquefied*; abated, decreased, diminished etc. vb.; unexpanded, unincreased, unstretched; declining, going down, sinking, ebbing; decaying, ruinous 655 *dilapidated.*

Vb. *abate,* make less, diminish, decrease, lessen, minify; take away, detract from, deduct 39 *subtract*; except 57 *exclude*; reduce, attenuate, scale down, whittle, pare, scrape 206 *make thin*; clip, trim, slash 46 *cut*; shrink, abridge, abbreviate, boil down 204 *shorten*; squeeze, compress, contract 198 *make smaller*; limit, curtail 747 *restrain*; cut down, cut back, retrench 814 *economize*; reduce speed, slow down, decelerate 278 *retard*; depress, send down 311 *lower*; tone down, minimize, mitigate, extenuate 177 *moderate*; allay, alleviate 831 *relieve*; deflate, puncture; disparage, decry, belittle, depreciate, undervalue 483 *underestimate,* 812 *cheapen,* 926 *detract*; dwarf, overshadow 34 *be superior*; put in the shade, obscure 419 *bedim*; degrade, demote 872 *humiliate*; loosen, ease, relax 701 *disencumber*; remit, pardon 909 *forgive*; unload, throw overboard 323 *lighten*; run down, drain, exhaust 300 *empty*; use up, consume, fritter away 634 *waste*; let escape, let evaporate, boil away 338 *vaporize*; melt down 337 *liquefy*; grind, crumble 332 *pulverize*; rub away, abrade, file 333 *rub*; gnaw, nibble at, eat away 301 *eat*; erode, rust 655 *impair*; strip, peel, denude 229 *uncover*; pillage, plunder, dispossess 786 *deprive,* 801 *impoverish*; emasculate, unman 161 *disable*; dilute, water down 163 *weaken,* 43 *mix*; thin, thin out, weed o., depopulate 105 *render few*; eliminate, expel 300 *eject*; decimate, slaughter, kill off, wipe out 165 *destroy,* 362 *kill*; reduce to nothing, annihilate 2 *nullify*; hush, quiet 399 *silence,* 578 *make mute*; damp down, cool 382 *extinguish*; quell, subdue, tame 745 *subjugate.*

decrease, grow less, lessen, suffer loss; abate, slacken, ease, moderate, subside, die down; dwindle, shrink, shrivel up, contract 198 *become small*; wane, waste, decay, wear away, wither away, degenerate 655 *deteriorate*; fade, die away, grow dim 419 *be dim*; retreat, withdraw, ebb 286 *regress,* 290 *recede*; run low, run down, ebb away, drain away, dry up, fail 636 *not suffice*; tail off, taper off, peter out 206 *be narrow,* 293 *converge*; subside, sink 313 *plunge*; come down, decline, fall, drop, spiral, slump, collapse 309 *descend*; not grow, level off, lag 278 *decelerate*; melt away 446 *disappear*; evaporate 338 *vaporize*; thin, thin out, become scarce 105 *be few,* 75 *disperse*; die out, become extinct 2 *pass away*; lose weight, reduce 323 *be light,* 946 *starve*; lose one's voice, stop one's noise, pipe down, dry up 578 *be mute*; lose, shed, rid oneself of; cast off 229 *doff*; forfeit, sacrifice 772 *lose.*

Adv. *diminuendo*, decrescendo, decreasingly; less and less, ever l.; in decline, on the wane, at low ebb.

See: 2, 14, 34, **39**, **42**, 43, 46, 57, 62, 71, 75, 105, 161, 163, 165, 175, 177, 190, **198**, 204, 206, 210, 229, 278, 286, 290, 293, 300, 301, 309, 311, 313, 323, 332, 333, 337, 338, 362, 382, 399, 419, 446, 483, 578, 634, 636, 655, 679, 701, 745, 747, 772, 786, 801, 812, 814, 831, 867, 872, 909, 926, 946, 963.

38 Addition

N. *addition*, adding to, annexation, fixture, agglutination 45 *union*; superimposing, superposition 187 *location*; prefixion 64 *precedence*; suffixion, affixture 65 *sequence*; supplementation, suppletion 725 *completion*; contribution 703 *aid*; superaddition, imposition, load 702 *encumbrance*; accession, accretion, accrual, supervention; interposition, interjection, epenthesis 303 *insertion*, 78 *inclusion*; reinforcement 36 *increase*; increment, supplement, addendum, appendage, appendix 40 *adjunct*; extra time, overtime 113 *protraction*; appurtenance 89 *accompaniment*; summation, adding up, total, toll 86 *numeration*.

Adj. *additional*, additive; added, included etc. vb.; adjunctive, adventitious, supervenient, adopted, adscititious, occasional 59 *extraneous*, 6 *extrinsic*; supplementary, supplemental, suppletory 725 *completive*; conjunctive 45 *joined*; subsidiary, auxiliary, contributory 703 *aiding*; supernumerary, supererogatory; another, further, more; extra, spare 637 *superfluous*; interjected, interposed, epenthetic 303 *inserted*, 231 *interjacent*; prefixed 64 *preceding*.

Vb. *add*, add up, sum, total, do the addition 86 *do sums*; carry over 272 *transfer*; add to, annex, append, subjoin; attach, pin to, clip to, tag on, tack on; conjoin, hitch to, yoke to, unite to 45 *join, tie*; stick on, glue on 48 *agglutinate*; add on, preface, prefix, affix, suffix, infix; introduce 231 *put between*; interpose, interject; engraft, let in 303 *insert*; bring to, contribute to, make one's contribution, add one's share 36 *augment*; swell, extend, expand 197 *enlarge*; supplement, crown 54 *make complete*; lay on, place on, impose, clap on, saddle with, burden w., load w. 187 *stow*, 702 *hinder*; superadd, superimpose, pile on, heap on 74 *bring together*; ornament, add frills, embellish 844 *decorate*; plaster, paint over, coat 226 *overlay*; mix with, mix in 43 *mix*; take to oneself, annex 786 *take*; encompass 78 *number with*; absorb, take in, include, receive 299 *admit*.

accrue, be added 78 *be included*; supervene 295 *arrive*, 189 *be present*; adhere, join 708 *join a party*; mix with, combine w. 50 *combine*; make an extra, make an addition to, make one more; reinforce, recruit 162 *strengthen*; swell the ranks, fill the gap.

Adv. *in addition*, additionally, more, plus, extra; with interest, with a vengeance, with knobs on; and, too, also, item, furthermore, further; likewise, and also, to boot; else, besides; et cetera; and so on, and so forth, moreover, into the bargain, over and above, including, inclusive of, with, as well as, not to mention, let alone, not forgetting; together with, along w., coupled w., in conjunction w.; conjointly, jointly; even with, despite, for all that.

See: 6, **36**, **40**, 43, 45, 48, 50, 54, 59, 64, 65, 74, 78, 86, 89, 113, 162, 187, 189, 197, 226, 231, 272, 295, 299, 303, 637, 702, 703, 708, 725, 786, 844.

39 Subtraction

N. *subtraction*, deduction 86 *numerical operation*; diminution 37 *decrease*; abstraction, removal, withdrawal 786 *taking*; elimination 62 *sorting*; expulsion, clearance 300 *ejection*; unloading, unpacking 188 *displacement*, 304 *extraction*; precipitation, sedimentation, ablation, abrasion, erosion, detrition 333 *friction*; retrenchment, curtailment 204 *shortening*; severance, detruncation, amputation, excision, abscission, circumcision 46 *scission*; castration, mutilation 655 *impairment*; expurgation, bowdlerization 648 *cleansing*; deletion 550 *obliteration*; minuend 85 *numerical element*; subtrahend, discount 42 *decrement*.

Adj. *subtracted*, subtractive, deducted; mutilated etc. vb.; curtailed, docked, tailless; beheaded, headless, decapitated; minus, without 307 *deficient*.

Vb. *subtract*, take away, deduct, do subtraction; detract from, diminish, decrease 37 *abate*; cut 810 *discount*; take off, knock o., allow 31 *set off*; except, take out, keep o., leave o. 57 *exclude*; expel 300 *eject*; abstract 786 *take*, 788 *steal*; withdraw, remove; unload, unpack 188 *displace*;

shift 272 *transfer*; draw off 300 *empty*; abrade, scrape away, file down, erode 333 *rub*; eradicate, uproot, pull up, pull out 304 *extract*; pick, pick out, put on one side 605 *select*; cross out, blot o., delete, blue-pencil, censor 550 *obliterate*; expurgate, bowdlerize, garble, mutilate 655 *impair*; sever, separate, amputate, excise; shear, shave off, clip 46 *cut*; retrench, cut back, cut down, lop, prune, pare, decapitate, behead, dock, curtail, abridge, abbreviate 204 *shorten*; geld, castrate, caponize, spay, emasculate 161 *unman*; peel, skin, strip, divest, denude 229 *uncover*.

Adv. *in deduction*, by subtraction etc. n.; at a discount; less; short of; minus, without, except, excepting, with the exception of, barring, bar, save, exclusive of, save and except, with reservations.

See: 31, **37**, **42**, **46**, 57, 62, 85, 86, 161, 188, 204, 229, 272, 300, 304, 307, 333, 550, 605, 648, 655, 786, 788, 810.

40 Adjunct: thing added

N. *adjunct*, addition, something added, contribution 38 *addition*; additament, addendum, carry-over; supplement, annex; attachment, fixture; inflection, affix, suffix, prefix, infix; adjective, adverb 564 *part of speech*; ticket, tab,tag 547 *label*; appendage, tail, train, following 67 *sequel*; wake, trail 65 *sequence*; appendix, postscript, P.S., envoi, coda, ending 69 *extremity*;codicil, rider 468 *qualification*; marginalia, footnotes; corollary, complement 725 *completion*; appurtenance, appanage, accessory 89 *concomitant*; pendant, companion piece, fellow 18 *analogue*; extension, prolongation, continuation, second part; annexe, wing (of a house), offices, outhouse 164 *edifice*; offshoot 53 *branch*; arm, extremity 53 *limb*; accretion 59 *extraneousness*; increment 36 *increase*; patch, reinforcement 656 *repair*; padding, stuffing 227 *lining*; interpolation, interlineation 303 *insertion*; interlude, intermezzo 231 *interjacency*; insertion, gusset, gore 228 *garment*; flap, lappet, lapel; admixture, ingredient 58 *component*; fringe, border, frill, edging 234 *edge*; embroidery 844 *ornamentation*; garnish, garnishing, seasoning 389 *sauce*; frills, trimmings, all that goes with it; trappings 228 *dressing*, 226 *covering*; equipment, furnishing 633 *provision*.

extra, additive, addendum, increment, superaddition, something over and above, by-product; percentage, interest 771 *gain*; bonus, tip, perk, perquisite, something on the side 962 *reward*; free gift, gratuity, golden handshake 781 *gift*; windfall, find, lucky f.; allowance 31 *offset*; oddment, item, odd i.;supernumerary, extra; reserves, spare parts, spares 633 *provision*; extra help, reinforcement 707 *auxiliary*; surplus 637 *superfluity*; extra time, overtime 113 *protraction*.

See: 18, 31, **36**, **38**, 53, 58, 59, 65, 67, 69, 89, 113, 164, 226, 227, 228, 231, 234, 303, 389, 468, 547, 564, 633, 637, 656, 707, 725, 771, 781, 844, 962.

41 Remainder: thing remaining

N. *remainder*, residue, residuum; residual, result, resultant 157 *effect*, 164 *product*; margin 15 *difference*; outstanding, balance, net b. 31 *offset*; surplus, carry-over 36 *increment*; excess 637 *superfluity*; relic, rest, remnant 105 *fewness*; rump, stump, stub, scrag end, fag e., butt e. 69 *extremity*; frustum, torso, trunk 53 *piece*; fossil, skeleton, bones 363 *corpse*; husk, empty h., shell; wreck, wreckage, debris 165 *ruin*; ashes 332 *powder*; track, fingerprint 548 *record, trace*; wake, afterglow 67 *sequel*; all that is left, memories 505 *remembrance*; survival 113 *durability*; vestige, remains.

leavings, leftovers; precipitate, deposit, sediment; alluvium, silt 344 *soil*; drift, loess, moraine, detritus 272 *thing transferred*; grounds, lees, heeltaps, dregs; scum, skimmings, dross, scoria, slag, sludge; bilge, dottle; scrapings, shavings, filings, sawdust, crumbs 332 *powder*; husks, bran, chaff, stubble; peel, peelings; skin, slough, scurf; combings, trimmings, clippings, remnants; scraps, candle-ends, odds and ends, lumber 641 *rubbish*; rejects 779 *derelict*; sweepings, scourings, offscourings; waste, sewage 302 *excrement*; refuse, litter 649 *dirt*.

survivor, finisher; inheritor, heir, successor 776 *beneficiary*; widower, widow 896 *widowhood*; orphan 779 *derelict*; descendant 170 *posterity*.

Adj. *remaining*, surviving, left, vestigial, resting, resultant; residual, residuary; left behind, deposited, sedimentary, precipitated 187 *located*; abandoned, discarded 779 *not retained*; on the shelf 860 *unwanted*; over, left over, odd; net, surplus; unspent, unexpended, unexpired, unconsumed; outstanding, carried over; spare, to s., superfluous 637 *redundant*; cast-off, outcast 607 *rejected*; orphaned, orphan, widowed.

Vb. *be left*, remain, rest, result, survive.

leave over, leave out 57 *exclude*; leave, leave behind, discard, abandon 607 *reject*.

See: 15, 31, 36, 53, 57, 67, 69, 105, 113, 157, 164, 165, 170, 187, 272, 302, 332, 344, 363, 505, 548, 607, 637, 641, 649, 776, **779**, 860, 896.

42 Decrement: thing deducted

N. *decrement*, deduction, depreciation, cut 37 *diminution*; allowance; remission; tare, drawback, rebate 810 *discount*; refund, shortage, defect 307 *shortfall*, 636 *insufficiency*; loss, sacrifice, forfeit 963 *penalty*; leak, leakage, escape 298 *outflow*; shrinkage 204 *shortening*; spoilage, wastage, consumption 634 *waste*; subtrahend, rake-off 786 *taking*; toll 809 *tax*.

See: **37**, 204, 298, 307, 634, 636, 786, 809, **810**, 963.

43 Mixture

N. *mixture*, mingling, mixing, stirring; blending, harmonization; admixture 38 *addition*; commixture 45 *union*; immixture 303 *insertion*; intermixture, interlarding, interpolation 231 *interjacency*; interweaving, interlacing 222 *crossing*; amalgamation, integration 50 *combination*; merger 706 *association*; syncretism, eclecticism; fusion, interfusion, infusion, suffusion, transfusion, instillation, impregnation 341 *moistening*; adulteration, watering down, sophistication 655 *impairment*; contamination, infection 653 *insalubrity*; infiltration, penetration, pervasion, permeation 297 *ingress*; interbreeding, miscegenation, intermarriage 894 *marriage*; syngamy, allogamy 167 *propagation*; cross-fertilization, hybridism, hybridization, mongrelism; miscibility, solubility 337 *liquefaction*; crucible, melting pot; mixer, beater, shaker, blender; churn 315 *rotator*.

tincture, admixture; ingredient 58 *component*; strain, streak; sprinkling, infusion; tinge, touch, drop, dash, soupçon 33 *small quantity*; smack, hint, flavour 386 *taste*; seasoning, spice 389 *condiment*; colour, dye 425 *hue*; stain, blot 845 *blemish*.

a mixture, mélange; blend, harmony 710 *concord*; composition 331 *structure*; amalgam, fusion, compound, confection, concoction 50 *combination*; cento, pastiche, pasticcio; alloy, bronze, brass, billon, electrum, pewter, steel; magma, paste; soup, stew, hash, ragout, olla podrida, salmagundi 301 *dish*; cocktail, brew, witches' b.; solution, infusion; medicinal compound, the mixture 658 *remedy*.

medley, heterogeneity, complexity, variety 17 *nonuniformity*, 82 *multiformity*; motley, patchwork, mosaic 437 *variegation*; assortment, miscellany, miscellanea, mixed bag, job lot, ragbag, lucky dip; farrago, gallimaufry, hotchpotch, hodgepodge, mishmash, linsey-woolsey, potpourri; jumble, hash, mess; conglomeration 74 *accumulation*; tangle, entanglement, imbroglio 61 *confusion*; phantasmagoria, kaleidoscope; clatter 411 *discord*; omnium gatherum, motley crew 74 *crowd*; menagerie, circus 369 *zoo*; variety show 594 *stage show*; all sorts, odds and ends, bits and pieces, paraphernalia, oddments.

hybrid, cross, cross-breed, mongrel; mule, hinny; half-blood, half-breed, half-caste; mestizo, métis; Eurasian, Cape Coloured, Creole, mulatto; quadroon, octaroon.

Adj. *mixed*, in the melting pot, mixed up, stirred; mixed up in, involved in; well-integrated, blended, harmonized; syncretic, eclectic; fused, alloyed 50 *combined*; tempered, qualified, adulterated, sophisticated, watered down 163 *weakened*; merged, amalgamated 45 *joined*; composite, half-and-half, fifty-fifty; complex, complicated, involved 251 *intricate*; tangled, confused, jumbled; unclassified, unsorted, out of order 61 *orderless*; heterogeneous 17 *nonuniform*; kaleidoscopic, phantasmagoric 82 *multiform*; patched, patchy, dappled, motley 437 *variegated*; shot 437 *iridescent*; miscellaneous, random 464 *indiscriminate*; miscible, soluble 337 *liquefied*; pervasive, spreading 653 *infectious*; hybrid, mongrel; cross-bred, crossed; half-blooded, half-caste; of mixed blood, interbred; intermixed, multiracial.

Vb. *mix*, make a mixture, mix up, stir, shake; shuffle, scramble 63 *jumble*; knead, pound together, mash 332 *pulverize*; brew, compound 56 *compose*; fuse, alloy, merge, amalgamate 45 *join*; interfuse, blend, harmonize 50 *combine*; mingle, intermingle, commingle, intersperse 437 *variegate*; immix, intermix, interlard, interleave 303 *insert*; intertwine, interlace, interweave 222 *weave*; tinge, dye 425 *colour*; imbue, instil, impregnate 303 *infuse*; dash, sprinkle, besprinkle 341 *moisten*; water, adulterate, sophisticate 163 *weaken*; temper, doctor, tamper with 143 *modify*; season, spice, fortify, lace, spike; hybridize, mongrelize, cross, cross-fertilize, crossbreed 167 *generate*.

be mixed, be entangled with, be involved, be mixed up in; pervade, permeate, run through 297 *infiltrate*; infect, contaminate; stain 425 *colour*; intermarry, interbreed, cross with 167 *reproduce itself*.

Adv. *among*, amongst, amid, amidst, with; in the midst of, in the crowd; amongst many, inter alia.

See: 17, 33, **38**, **45**, **50**, 56, 58, 61, 63, 74, 82, 143, 163, 167, 222, 231, 251, 297, 301, 303, 315, 331, 332, 337, 341, 369, 386, 389, 411, 425, **437**, 464, 594, 653, 655, 658, 706, 710, 845, 894.

44 Simpleness: freedom from mixture

N. *simpleness*, homogeneity 16 *uniformity*; purity 648 *cleanness*; oneness 88 *unity*; absoluteness, sheerness; fundamentality, bedrock 1 *essence*; indivisibility, insolubility, asexuality; lack of complication, simplicity 516 *intelligibility*, 573 *plainness*, 699 *artlessness*; freedom from mixture, not a trace of, not a hint of 190 *absence*.

simplification, purification, distillation 648 *cleansing*; reduction 51 *decomposition*; unification, assimilation 13 *identity*.

elimination, riddance, clearance 300 *ejection*; sifting, straining 62 *sorting*; expulsion 57 *exclusion*.

Adj. *simple*, homogeneous, monolithic, all of a piece 16 *uniform*; sheer, mere, utter, nothing but; undifferentiated, asexual; single, unified 88 *one*; elemental, indivisible, entire 52 *whole*; primary, irreducible, fundamental, basic 5 *intrinsic*; elementary, uncomplicated, unravelled, disentangled, simplified 516 *intelligible*; direct, unmediated 249 *straight*; unsophisticated, homespun 573 *plain*, 699 *artless*; single-minded, whole-hearted, sincere, downright, unaffected 540 *veracious*, 929 *honourable*; bare, naked 522 *undisguised*.

unmixed, pure and simple, without alloy; clear, pure, undefiled, unpolluted, clarified, purified, cleansed 648 *clean*; pure-bred, thoroughbred 868 *noble*; free from, exempt f., excluding; unblemished, untarnished 646 *perfect*; unmingled, unblended, unalloyed, uncompounded, uncombined; undiluted, unadulterated, neat 162 *strong*; unqualified, unmodified; unmedicated, unfortified, unstrengthened; unflavoured, unspiced, unseasoned 387 *tasteless*; untinged, undyed, uncoloured 427 *white*.

Vb. *simplify*, render simple 16 *make uniform*; narrow down, break d., factorize, reduce, reduce to its elements 51 *decompose*; disentangle, unscramble 62 *unravel*; unify, make one, unite.

eliminate, sift 62 *class*; winnow, sieve, pan; purge 648 *purify*; clear, clarify, cleanse, distil; get rid of, weed out 57 *exclude*; expel 300 *eject*.

Adv. *simply*, purely etc. adj.; simply and solely; only, merely, exclusively.

See: 1, 5, 13, **16**, 51, 52, 57, 62, **88**, 162, 190, 249, 300, 387, 427, 516, 522, 540, 573, 646, 648, 699, 868, 929.

45 Union

N. *union*, junction, joining etc. vb.; coming together, meeting, concurrence, conjunction 293 *convergence*; clash 279 *collision*; contact 202 *contiguity*, 378 *touch*; congress, concourse, forgathering, reunion 74 *assembly*; confluence, meeting-point, meeting-place 76 *focus*; concrescence, coalescence, fusion, merger 43 *mixture*; unification, synthesis 50 *combination*; cohesion, tenacity, inextricability, agglutination 48 *coherence*; concretion, consolidation, solidification, coagulation 324 *condensation*; closeness, tightness, compactness, impaction; coalition, alliance, symbiosis 706 *association*; connection, linkage, tieup, hookup, linkup 47 *bond*; syngamy, wedlock 894 *marriage*; interconnection, cross-connection, anastomosis, inosculation; interlocking 222 *crossing*; communication 305 *passage*; intercommunication, intercourse 882 *sociability*; trade, traffic, exchange 151 *interchange*, 791 *trade*; involvement 9 *relation*; arrival, latecomer 297 *incomer*; partner, sharer 775 *participator*; companion 89 *concomitant*.

joining together, bringing together 74 *assemblage*; unification 50 *combination*; jointing, articulation 56 *composition*, 331 *structure*; joining, stringing together, threading t., linking t., concatenation; suture, stitching, knitting, sewing, weaving 222 *crossing*; tightening, astriction, drawing together, contraction 198 *compression*, 264 *closure*; knotting, tying, binding, bandaging, ligation; fastening, pinning, infibulation; attaching, attachment, annexing, annexation 38 *addition*; connecting, earthing; affixture, suffixation, prefixion; grafting, planting; inoculation, injection 303 *insertion*; sticking on, fixture 48 *coherence*; coupling, yoking, pairing, matching 18 *assimilation*, 462 *comparison*; bracketing 28 *equalization*; hyphenization 547 *punctuation*; joiner, coupler, riveter, welder; go-between 231 *intermediary*, 894 *matchmaker*.

coition, coitus, copulation, sexual intercourse, sex, intimacy, carnal knowledge; generation 167 *propagation*; pairing, mating, coupling; union 894 *marriage*; enjoyment, consummation; violation, ravishment 951 *rape*.

joint, joining, juncture, commissure; crease 261 *fold*; suture, seam, stitching 47 *bond*; bonding, English bond, Flemish b., rattrap b.; weld, welded joint; splice, spliced joint; mitre, mitre joint; dovetail, dovetail and mortise joint; ball and socket j.; hasp, latch, catch 218 *pivot*; hinge-joint, ginglymus 247 *angularity*; finger, wrist, ankle, knuckle, knee, elbow; node; junction, point of j., intersection, crossroads 222 *crossing*; decussation, figure X 222 *cross*.

Adj. *joined*, united etc. vb.; connected, earthed; coupled, matched, paired 28 *equal*; conjoined, conjoint, partnered, participant 775 *sharing*; rolled into one, merged; conjunct, joint, allied, incorporated, associated, symbiotic 706 *cooperative*, 708 *corporate*; betrothed, wedded 894 *married*; holding hands, hand in hand, arm in arm; intimate, involved 5 *intrinsic*; coalescent, concretive, adhesive 48 *cohesive*; composite 50 *combined*; put together 74 *assembled*; articulated, jointed 331 *structural, textural*; stitched, patched; stitched up.

conjunctive, adjunctive, copulative, adhesive 48 *cohesive*; coagulating, astringent 324 *solidifying*; coincident 181 *concurrent*; copulatory, coital, venereal.

firm, close, fast, secure, sound 153 *fixed*; solid, set, solidified 324 *dense*; glued, cemented 48 *cohesive*; put, pat; planted, rooted; ingrown, impacted; close-set, crowded, tight, tight-fitting, wedged, jammed, stuck; inextricable, inseparable, immovable, unshakable; packed, jam-p. 54 *full*.

tied, bound, knotted, roped, lashed, belayed, spliced; stitched, sewn, gathered; attached, fastened, adhering 48 *cohesive*; well-tied, tight, taut, tense, fast, secure; intricate, involved, tangled, inextricable, indissoluble.

Vb. *join*, conjoin, couple, yoke, hyphenate, harness together; pair, match 18 *liken*, 462 *compare*, 894 *marry*; bracket 28 *equalize*; put together, lay t., clap t., fit t., piece t., assemble, unite 50 *combine*; collect, gather, mobilize, mass 74 *bring together*; add to, amass, accumulate 38 *add*, 632 *store*; associate, ally, twin (town); merge 43 *mix*; incorporate, consolidate, make one, unify 88 *be one*, 16 *make uniform*; lump together, roll into one 464 *not discriminate*; include, embrace 78 *comprise*; grip, grapple 778 *retain*; make a joint, hinge, articulate, dovetail, mortise, mitre, rabbet; fit, set, interlock, engage, gear to; wedge, jam 303 *insert*; weld, solder, braze, fuse, cement 48 *agglutinate*; draw together, lace, knit, sew, stitch; pin, buckle; infibulate; do up, fasten, button up, zip up 264 *close*; lock, latch; close a gap, seal up; darn, patch, mend, heal over, scab over 656 *repair*.

connect, attach, annex (**see** *affix*); staple, clip, pin together; thread t., string t., rope t., link t., chain t., concatenate; contact 378 *touch*; make contact, plug in, earth 202 *juxtapose*; interconnect, inosculate, open into; link, bridge, span, straddle, bestride 305 *pass*; communicate, intercommunicate, establish communication; put through to, put in touch; hook up with, tie up w. 9 *relate*; link closely, entwine.

affix, attach, fix, fasten; fix on, yoke, leash, harness, saddle, bridle; tie up, moor, anchor; tie to, tether, picket; pin on, hang on, hook on, screw on, nail on; stick on, gum on 48 *agglutinate*; suffix, prefix 38 *add*; infix, splice, engraft, implant 303 *insert*; impact, set, frame 235 *enclose*; drive in, knock in, hammer in 279 *strike*; wedge, jam; screw, nail, rivet, bolt, clamp, clinch; thread, pass through, weave t.

tie, knot, hitch, lash, belay; knit, sew, stitch,

suture; tack, baste; braid, plait, crochet, twine, twist, intertwine, lace, interlace, interweave 222 *weave*; truss, string, rope, strap; lace up, lash up; tether, picket, moor; pinion, manacle, handcuff; hobble, shackle 747 *fetter*; bind, splice, gird, girdle; bandage, swathe, swaddle, wrap; enfold, embrace, grip, grapple 235 *enclose*, 778 *retain*.

tighten, jam, impact; constrict, compress, narrow; fasten, screw up, make firm, make fast, secure; tauten, draw tight, pull t., lace t.; frap, brace, trice up, brail.

unite with, be joined, linked etc. vb.; join, meet 293 *converge*; fit tight, hold t., fit closely, adhere, hang together, hold t., stick t. 48 *cohere*; mesh, interlock, engage, grip, grapple, clinch; embrace, entwine; link up with, hold hands; associate with, partner, mix w. 882 *be sociable*; league together 708 *join a party*; marry, get hitched 894 *wed*; live with, cohabit; go to bed with, lie with, sleep w., make love, have sex with; have intercourse, have carnal knowledge; consummate a marriage *or* a union; know, enjoy, possess, have, do; lay, bed, tumble; knock off, have it off *or* away with; deflower, rape, ravish, violate, take by force 951 *debauch*; copulate, couple, mate, pair 167 *generate*; mount, tup, cover, serve; cross with, breed w.

Adv. *conjointly*, jointly, with, in conjunction, in partnership 708 *in league*; all together, as one.

inseparably, inextricably, intimately; securely, firmly, fast, tight.

See: 5, 9, 16, 18, 28, 38, 43, 47, **48**, **50**, 54, 56, 74, 76, 78, 88, 89, 151, 153, 167, 181, 198, 202, 218, 222, 231, 235, 247, 261, 264, 279, 293, 297, 303, 305, 324, 331, 378, 462, 464, 547, 632, 656, 706, 708, 747, 775, 778, 791, 882, 894, 951.

46 Disunion

N. *disunion*, disjunction, being separated; disconnection, disconnectedness, incoherence, break 72 *discontinuity*; looseness, separability, fissility 49 *noncoherence*; dissilience, diffusion, dispersal, scattering 75 *dispersion*; breakup, disintegration, dissolution, decay 51 *decomposition*, 655 *dilapidation*; abstraction, absentmindedness 456 *abstractedness*; dissociation, withdrawal, disengagement, retirement 621 *relinquishment*, 753 *resignation*; surrender, sacrifice 779 *nonretention*, 37 *decrease*; moving apart, broadening, widening 294 *divergence*, 282 *deviation*; split, schism (**see** *separation*); detachment, nonattachment, neutrality 860 *indifference*; isolation, loneliness, quarantine, segregation 883 *seclusion*; zone, compartment, box, cage 748 *prison*; insularity 620 *avoidance*; lack of unity 709 *dissension*; immiscibility, separateness, severalty 80 *speciality*; isolationism, separatism 80 *particularism*; no connection 10 *unrelatedness*; distance apart 199 *farness*; dichotomy 15 *difference*; interval, space, opening, hole, breach, break, rent, rift, tear, split; fissure, crack, cleft, chasm; cleavage, slit, slot, cut, incision 201 *gap*.

separation, disjoining, severance, parting; uncoupling, divorcement 896 *divorce*; untying, undoing, unthreading, unravelling, laddering; loosening, loosing, freeing 746 *liberation*; setting apart, segregation, apartheid 883 *seclusion*; exception, exemption 57 *exclusion*; boycott 620 *avoidance*; expulsion 300 *ejection*; picking out, selection 605 *choice*; putting aside, keeping a. 632 *storage*; conservation 666 *preservation*; taking away 39 *subtraction*; abstraction, deprivation, expropriation 786 *taking*; detaching, detachment, withdrawal, removal, transfer 188 *displacement*, 272 *transference*; denudation, stripping, peeling, plucking 229 *uncovering*; disjointing, dislocation, luxation; scattering, dispersal 75 *dispersion*; dissolution, resolution, disintegration 51 *decomposition*; dissection, analysis, breakdown; disruption, shattering, fragmentation 165 *destruction*; splitting, fission, nuclear f. 160 *nucleonics*; breaking, cracking, rupture, fracture 330 *brittleness*; dividing line, caesura; wall, hedge 231 *partition*; curtain 421 *screen*; boundary 236 *limit*.

scission, section, cleavage, cutting, tearing; division, dichotomy 92 *bisection*; subdivision, segmentation; partition 783 *apportionment*; abscission, cutting off, decapitation, curtailment 204 *shortening*, 37 *diminution*; cutting away, resection, circumcision; cutting open, incision, opening 658 *surgery*; dissection; rending, clawing, laceration, dilaceration, divulsion; tearing off, avulsion; nipping, pinching, biting etc. vb.

Adj. *disunited*, disjunct, disjoined, divorced; separated, disconnected, unplugged, unstuck; unseated, dismounted; broken, interrupted 72 *discontinuous*; divided, subdivided, partitioned, bipartite, multipartite; in pieces, quartered, dismembered; severed, cut; torn, rent, riven, cleft, cloven; digitate 201 *spaced*; radiating, divergent 282 *deviating*; scattered, dispersed, fugitive, uncollected 75 *unassembled*; untied, loosened, loose, free 746 *liberated*.

separate, apart, asunder; adrift, lost; unjoined, unfixed, unfastened; unattached, unannexed, unassociated; distinct, discrete, differentiated, separable, distinguishable 15 *different*; exempt, excepted 57 *excluded*; hived off, abstracted 304 *extracted*; immiscible, unassimilable, unassimilated 44 *unmixed*; alien, foreign 59 *extraneous*; external 6 *extrinsic*, 223 *exterior*; insular, self-sufficient, lonely, isolated 88 *alone*, 883 *friendless*; shunned, dropped, avoided, boycotted 620 *avoiding*; cast-off 607 *rejected*; picked out, set apart 605 *chosen*; abandoned, left 41 *remaining*; hostile, opposed, antipathetic 881 *inimical*, 14 *contrary*, 240 *opposite*; disjunctive, separative; dichotomous, dividing; selective, diagnostic 15 *distinctive*.

severable, separable, detachable; partible, divisible, fissionable, fissile, scissile, tearable; dissoluble, dissolvable; biodegradable 51 *decomposable*; distinguishable, not belonging 10 *unrelated*.

Vb. *separate*, stand apart, not mix 620 *avoid*; go, go away 296 *depart*; go apart, go different ways, radiate 294 *diverge*; go another way 282 *deviate*; part, part company, cut adrift, cut loose, divorce; split off, hive off; get free, get loose 667 *escape*; disengage, unclinch, free oneself, break away 746 *achieve liberty*; cast off, unmoor, let go 779 *not retain*; leave, quit, fall away 621 *relinquish*; scatter, break up 75 *disperse*; spring apart 280 *recoil*; come apart, fall a., break, come to bits, disintegrate 51 *decompose*; come undone, unravel, ladder, run; fall off 49 *come unstuck*; split, crack 263 *open*.

disunite, disjoin, dissociate, divorce; part, separate, sunder, sever, dissever; uncouple, unhitch, disconnect, unplug; disengage, throw out of gear; disjoint, dislocate, wrench; detach, unseat, dismount 49 *unstick*; remove, detract, deduct 39 *subtract*, 272 *transfer*; skin, denude, strip, flay, peel, pluck 229 *uncover*; unfasten, undo, unbutton, unhook, unzip, unclasp, unlock, unlatch 263 *open*; untie, cut the knot, disentangle 62 *unravel*; unstitch, unpick; loosen, relax, slacken, unstring 177 *moderate*; unbind, unchain, unfetter, unloose, loose, free, release 746 *liberate*; expel 300 *eject*; dispel, scatter, break up, disband, demobilize 75 *disperse*; disintegrate, break down 51 *decompose*, 332 *pulverize*, 165 *destroy*.

set apart, put aside 632 *store*; conserve 666 *preserve*; mark out, tick off, distinguish 15 *differentiate*, 463 *discriminate*; single out, pick o. 605 *select*; except, exempt, leave out 57 *exclude*; boycott, send to Coventry 620 *avoid*; taboo, black, blacklist 757 *prohibit*; insulate, isolate, cut off 235 *enclose*; zone, compartmentalize, screen off 232 *circumscribe*; segregate, sequester, quarantine, maroon 883 *seclude*; keep apart, hold a., drive a.; drive a wedge between, estrange, alienate, set against 881 *make enemies*, 888 *excite hate*.

sunder (**see** *disunite*); divide, keep apart, flow between, stand b.; subdivide, fragment, fractionate, segment, sectionalize, fractionalize, fractionize; reduce, factorize, analyse; dissect, anatomize 51 *decompose*; dichotomize, halve 92 *bisect*; divide up, split, partition, parcel out 783 *apportion*; dismember, disbranch, quarter, carve (**see** *cut*); behead, decapitate, curtail, dock, amputate 204 *shorten*; take apart, take to pieces, cannibalize, dismantle, break up, dismount; force open, force apart, wedge a. 263 *open*; slit, split, rive; cleave 263 *pierce*. **See** *break*.

cut, hew, hack, slash, gash 655 *wound*; prick, stab, knife 263 *pierce*; cut through, cleave, rive, saw, chop; cut open, slit 263 *open*; cut into, make an incision, incise 555 *engrave*; cut deep, cut to the bone, carve, slice; cut round, pare, whittle, chisel, chip, trim, bevel, skive; clip, snick, snip; cut short, shave 204 *shorten*; cut down, fell, scythe, mow; cut off, lop, prune, dock, curtail (**see** *sunder*); cut up, chop up, quarter, dismember; dice, shred, mince, make mincemeat of 332 *pulverize*; bite, bite into, bite through 301 *chew*; scratch, scarify, score, plough 262 *groove*; nick 260 *notch*.

rend, rive (**see** *sunder*); tear, scratch, claw; gnaw, fret, fray, make ragged; rip, slash, slit (**see** *cut*); lacerate, dilacerate, dismember; tear limb from limb, tear to pieces, tear to shreds, tear to tatters 165 *destroy*; pluck to pieces; mince, grind, crunch, scrunch 301 *chew*, 332 *pulverize*; explode, blow up, blow to pieces, burst.

break, fracture, rupture, bust; split, burst, blow up, explode; break in pieces, smash, shatter, splinter, shiver 165 *demolish*; fragment, comminute, crumble, grind, triturate 332 *pulverize*; disintegrate, cave in 51 *decompose*; break up, dismantle (**see** *sunder*); chip, crack, damage 655 *impair*; bend, buckle, warp 246 *distort*; break in two, snap, knap; cleave, force apart, wedge a. 263 *open*.

Adv.*separately*, severally, singly, one by one, bit by bit, piecemeal, in bits, in pieces, in halves, in twain; discontinuously, unconnectedly, disjointedly, interruptedly.

apart, open, asunder, adrift; to pieces, to bits, to tatters, to shreds; limb from limb.

See:6, 10, 14, 15, 37, 39, 41, 44, **49**, **51**, 57, 59, 62, 72, 75, 80, 88, 92, 160, 165, 177, 188, 199, 201, 204, 223, 229, 231, 232, 235, 236, 240, 246, 260, 262, 263, 272, 280, 282, 294, 296, 300, 301, 304, 330, 332, 421, 456, 463, 555, 605, 607, 620, 621, 632, 655, 658, 666, 667, 709, 746, 748, 753, 757, 779, 783, 786, 860, 881, 883, 888, 896.

47 Bond: connecting medium

N.*bond*, connecting medium, vinculum, chain, shackle, fetter, tie, band, hoop, yoke; bond of union, sympathy, fellow feeling 905 *pity*; obligation 917 *duty*; nexus, connection, link, liaison 9 *relation*; junction, hinge 45 *joint*; ramification 53 *branch*; connective, copula; hyphen, dash, bracket 547 *punctuation*; intermedium, cement (**see** *adhesive*); bondstone, binder; tie-beam, stretcher, girder 218 *beam*; strut, stay 218 *prop*; interconnection, intercommunication, channel, passage, corridor 624 *access*; stepping-stone, causeway 624 *bridge*; span, arch; isthmus, neck; col, ridge; stair, ladder 308 *ascent*; lifeline; umbilical cord.

cable, line, guy, hawser, painter, moorings; guest-rope, towline, towrope, ripcord, lanyard, communication cord; rope, cord, whipcord, string, tape, twine 208 *fibre*; chain, wire, earth.

tackling, tackle, cordage; rig, rigging, running r., standing r., shroud, ratline; sheets, guy, stay; clewline, garnet, halliard, bowline, lanyard; harness.

ligature, ligament, tendon, muscle; tendril, withe, withy, osier, bast, bass, raffia 208 *fibre*; lashing, binding; string, cord, thread, tape, band, fillet, ribbon, ribband; bandage, roller b., roller, tourniquet 198 *compressor*; drawstring, thong, lace, bootlace, tag; braid, plait 222 *network*; tie, stock, cravat 228 *neckwear*; knot, hitch, clinch, bend; running k., slip k., granny k., reef k.; half hitch, clove h.; sheepshank, Turk's head; true-love knot, Gordian k.

fastening 45 *joining together*; fastener, snap f., press-stud, popper, zip fastener, zip; drawstring, ripcord; stitch, basting; button, buttonhole, eyelet, loop, frog; hook and eye; stud, cufflink; garter, suspender, braces; tiepin, brooch 844 *jewellery*; clip, grip, slide, curlers; hairpin, hatpin; skewer, spit, brochette; pin, drawing p., safety p., toggle p., cotter p., linch p., king p.; peg, dowel, treenail, trenail, nail, brad, tack, tintack 256 *sharp point*; holdfast, staple, clamp, brace, batten, cramp 778 *nippers*; nut, bolt, screw, rivet; buckle, clasp, morse; hasp, hinge 45 *joint*; catch, safety c., spring c., pawl, click, detent; latch, bolt; lock, lock and key 264 *closure*; combination lock, yale l., mortise l.; padlock, handcuffs, bracelets 748 *fetter*; ring, cleat; hold, bar, post, pile, pale, stake, bollard.

coupling, yoke; coupler, drawbar, traces; grappling iron, hook, claw; anchor, sheet a. 662 *safeguard*.

girdle, band, strap 228 *belt*; waistband, bellyband, girth, cinch, surcingle; sash, shoulder belt, bandolier, Sam Browne; collar, neckband 228 *neckwear*; bandeau, fillet.

halter, collar, noose; tether, lead, leash, jess, reins, ribbons; lasso, lariat 250 *loop*; shackle 748 *fetter*.

adhesive, glue, fish glue, lime, birdlime, gum, epoxy resin; fixative, hair lacquer, hair spray, brilliantine, grease; solder; paste, size, lute, clay, cement, putty, mortar, stucco, plaster, grout 226 *facing*; wafer, sealing wax; sticker, stamp, adhesive tape, sticky t., sellotape (tdmk); flypaper 542 *trap*; sticking plaster 48 *coherence*.

See:9, **45**, **48**, 53, 198, 208, 218, 222, 226, 228, 250, 256, 264, 308, 542, 547, 624,

662, 748, 778, 844, 905, 917.

48 Coherence

N. *coherence*, connection, connectedness 71 *continuity*; chain 71 *series*; holding together, cohesion, cohesiveness; holding on, tenacity, tenaciousness 778 *retention*; adherence, adhesion, adhesiveness; stickiness 354 *viscidity*; cementation, cementing, sticking, soldering, agglutination, conglutination 45 *union*; compaction, conglomeration, agglomeration, consolidation, congealment, set 324 *condensation*; inseparability, indivisibility, union 88 *unity*; indigestibility 329 *toughness*; phalanx, serried ranks, unbroken front; monolith, agglomerate, concrete 324 *solid body*; bur, leech, remora, limpet, barnacle, parasite, clinging vine; gum, plaster, sticking p. 47 *adhesive*; toffee.

Adj. *cohesive*, coherent, adhesive, adherent; sessile, clinging, tenacious; indigestible 329 *tough*; sticky, tacky, gummy, gluey, viscous 354 *viscid*; compact, well-knit, solid, coagulated, concrete, frozen 324 *dense*; shoulder to shoulder, phalanxed, serried; monolithic 16 *uniform*; united, infrangible, indivisible, inseparable, inextricable; close, tight, close-fitting, skintight, figure-hugging, clinging, moulding.

Vb. *cohere*, hang together, grow together 50 *combine*; hold, stick close, hold fast; bunch, close the ranks, stand shoulder to shoulder, rally 74 *congregate*; grip, take hold of 778 *retain*; hug, clasp, embrace, twine round; close with, clinch; fit, fit tight, mould the figure; adhere, cling, stick; stick to, cleave to, come off on, rub off on; stick on to, freeze on to; stick like a leech, stick like a bur, stick like a limpet, cling like a shadow, cling like ivy; cake, coagulate, agglomerate, conglomerate, solidify, consolidate, freeze 324 *be dense*.

agglutinate, conglutinate, glue, gum, paste, lute, cement, weld, braze 45 *join*; stick to, affix 38 *add*.

Adv. *cohesively*, indivisibly, unitedly, solidly, compactly.

See: 16, 38, **45**, **47**, 50, 71, 74, 88, 324, 329, 354, **778**.

49 Noncoherence

N. *noncoherence*, incoherence 72 *discontinuity*; uncombined state, noncombination, chaos 51 *decomposition*; scattering 75 *dispersion*; separability, immiscibility; looseness, bagginess; loosening, relaxation, laxity, freedom 46 *separation*; wateriness, runniness 335 *fluidity*; slipperiness 258 *smoothness*; frangibility, friability, rope of sand 330 *brittleness*; nonadhesion, aloofness; individualist, lone wolf, separatist 84 *nonconformist*.

Adj. *nonadhesive*, nonadhering, slippery 258 *smooth*; not sticky, dry; detached, semidetached 46 *separate*; noncohesive, incoherent, unconsolidated, loose, like grains of sand; unconfined, free, at large 746 *liberated*; relaxed, lax, slack, baggy, loose-fitting, flopping, floppy, flapping, flying, streaming; watery, liquid, runny 335 *fluid*; pendulous, dangling 217 *hanging*; uncombined 51 *decomposed*; immiscible, unassimilated 59 *extraneous*; aloof 620 *avoiding*.

Vb. *unstick*, unglue, peel off; detach, unpin, unfasten; free, loosen, loose, slacken 46 *disunite*; shake off, unseat, dismount; shed, slough 229 *doff*.

come unstuck, peel off, melt, thaw, run 337 *liquefy*; totter, slip 309 *tumble*; dangle, flap 217 *hang*; rattle, shake, flap.

See: **46**, **51**, 59, 72, 75, 84, 217, 229, 258, 309, 330, 335, 337, 620, 746.

50 Combination

N. *combination*, composition 45 *joining together*; growing together, coalescence, symphysis 45 *union*; fusion, blending, conflation, synthesis, syncretism 43 *mixture*; amalgamation, merger, assimilation, digestion, absorption 299 *reception*; uniting, unification, integration, centralization 88 *unity*; incorporation, embodiment; synchronization 706 *cooperation*; coagency 181 *concurrence*; marriage, union, league, alliance, federation, confederation 706 *association*; conspiracy, cabal 623 *plot*; chord, counterpoint 412 *music*; chorus 24 *agreement*; harmony, orchestration 710 *concord*; aggregation, assembly 74 *assemblage*; synopsis, conspectus, bird's-eye view 592 *compendium*; mosaic, jigsaw, collage.

compound, alloy, amalgam, blend, composite 43 *a mixture*; portmanteau word; make-up 56 *composition*.

Adj. *combined*, united, unified 88 *one*; integrated, centralized; incorporate, embodied; inbred, ingrained, absorbed 5 *intrinsic*; fused, impregnated 43 *mixed*; blended, harmonized, adapted 24 *adjusted*; connected, yoked, linked, conjugate, conjoint 45 *joined*; aggregated, congregated 74 *assembled*; coalescent, symphystic; synchronized 123 *synchronous*; in harmony, in partnership, in league; associated, leagued, allied 706 *cooperative*; conspiratorial; coagent 181 *concurrent*.

Vb. *combine*, put together, fit t.; make up 56 *compose*; intertwine, interweave 222 *weave*; harmonize, synchronize 24 *accord*; bind, tie 45 *join*; unite, unify, centralize; incorporate, embody, integrate, absorb, assimilate; merge, amalgamate, pool; blend, fuse, compound 43 *mix*; impregnate, imbue, instil, inoculate 303 *infuse*; lump together 38 *add*; group, regroup, rally 74 *bring together*; band together, brigade, associate; federate, ally, league with; partner, join hands, team up with 706 *cooperate*; fraternize, make friends 880 *be friendly*; cement a union, marry 894 *wed*; mate, couple 90 *pair*; put heads together, conspire 623 *plot*; coalesce, grow together, run t.; have an affinity, combine with; combine with water, hydrate 339 *add water*.

See: 5, 24, 38, **43**, **45**, **56**, 74, 88, 90, 123, 181, 222, 299, 303, 339, 412, 592, 623, 706, 710, 880, 894.

51 Decomposition

N. *decomposition* 46 *disunion*; division, partition, compartmentation 46 *separation*; dissection, dismemberment; anatomization, analysis, breakdown; factorization 44 *simplification*; syllabification, parsing 564 *grammar*; resolution, electrolysis, hydrolysis, photolysis, catalysis; atomization; dissolving, dissolution 337 *liquefaction*; fission 160 *nucleonics*; decentralization, devolution, delegation; regionalism; collapse, breakup, disintegration, entropy 165 *destruction*; chaos 17 *nonuniformity*.

decay 655 *dilapidation*; erosion, wear and tear 37 *diminution*; disintegration 361 *death*; corruption, mouldering, rotting, putridness, putrefaction, adipocere, mortification, necrosis, gangrene, caries 649 *uncleanness*; rot, rust, mould 659 *blight*; carrion 363 *corpse*.

Adj. *decomposed*, resolved, reduced, disintegrated, uncombined, chaotic 46 *disunited*; corrupted, mouldering 655 *dilapidated*; putrid, gangrenous, rotten, bad, off, high, rancid, sour.

decomposable, disposable, biodegradable, compostable, recyclable 656 *restored*.

Vb. *decompose*, decompound, unscramble; resolve, reduce, factorize 44 *simplify*; separate, separate out, parse, dissect; break down, analyse, take to pieces 46 *sunder*; electrolyse, catalyse; split, fission 46 *disunite*; atomize 165 *demolish*; disband, break up 75 *disperse*; decentralize, regionalize 783 *apportion*; unsettle, disorder, disturb, cause chaos 63 *derange*; dissolve, melt 337 *liquefy*; erode 37 *abate*; rot, rust, moulder, decay, consume, waste away, crumble, wear, perish 655 *deteriorate*; corrupt, putrefy, mortify, gangrene 649 *be unclean*; disintegrate, go to pieces 165 *be destroyed*.

Adv. *analytically*, partitively; on analysis, by a.

See: 17, 37, 44, **46**, 63, 75, 160, **165**, 337, 361, 363, 564, 649, **655**, 656, 659, 783.

52 Whole. Principal part

N. *whole*, wholeness, integrality, omneity, fullness 54 *completeness*; integration, indivisibility, indiscerptibility, integrity, oneness 88 *unity*; a whole, whole number, integer, entity 88 *unit*; entirety, ensemble, corpus, complex, four corners of; totality, summation, sum 38 *addition*; holism, holistic approach, universalization, generalization 79 *generality*; comprehensiveness, inclusiveness 78 *inclusion*; collectivity, system, world, cosmos 321 *universe*; idioverse, life space, total situation 7 *state*; grand view, bird's-eye v., panorama, conspectus, synopsis 438 *view*; whole course, round, circuit 314 *circuition*.

all, no omissions, one and all, the quick and the dead, everybody, everyone 79 *everyman*; the world, all the w. 74 *crowd*; the whole, total, aggregate, gross amount, sum, sum total; ensemble, tout e., length and breadth, rough with the smooth; Alpha and Omega, 'be-all and end-all', lock, stock and barrel; hook, line and sinker; unit, family; set, complete s. 71 *series*; outfit, pack, kit; complete list, inventory 87 *list*; lot, whole l., the whole caboodle, the whole kit and caboodle, the whole bang shoot, the works.

chief part, best part, principal p., major p., essential p. 638 *chief thing*; ninety-nine per cent, bulk, mass, substance; heap, lump 32 *great quantity*; tissue, staple, stuff; body, torso, trunk, bole, stem, stalk; hull, hulk, skeleton; lion's share, biggest slice of the cake; gist, sum and substance, the long and the short of it; almost all, nearly all, everything but the kitchen sink; all but a few, majority 104 *greater number*.

Adj. *whole*, total, universal, holistic; integral, pure, unadulterated 44 *unmixed*; entire, sound 646 *perfect*; grand, gross, full 54 *complete*; individual, single, integrated 88 *one*; in one piece, seamless; fully restored 656 *restored*.

intact, untouched, unaffected; unspoiled, virgin 126 *new*; undivided, unsevered, undiminished, unclipped, uncropped, unshorn; undissolved, unabolished, still there; unbroken, undestroyed, unbruised, unmangled, unimpaired, without a scratch 646 *undamaged*; uncut, unabridged, unedited, uncensored, unexpurgated.

indivisible, impartible 324 *indissoluble*; undissolvable, indiscerptible; inseparable 45 *joined*; monolithic 16 *uniform*.

comprehensive, omnibus, all-embracing, all-encompassing, full-length 78 *inclusive*; wholesale, sweeping 32 *extensive*; widespread, epidemic 79 *general*; international, world, world-wide, cosmic 79 *universal*, 189 *ubiquitous*.

Adv. *wholly*, integrally, body and soul, as a whole; entirely, totally, fully, every inch, in toto 54 *completely*; without deduction, one hundred per cent.

on the whole, by and large, altogether, all in all, all things considered, in the long run; substantially, essentially, in substance, in essence; virtually, to all intents and purposes, effectually, in effect; as good as; mainly, in the main 32 *greatly*; almost, all but 200 *nearly*.

collectively, one and all, all together; comprehensively, and all; in bulk, in the mass; in sum, in the aggregate; bodily, en masse, en bloc.

See: 7, 16, **32**, 38, 44, 45, **54**, 71, 74, 78, 79, 87, **88**, 104, 126, 189, 200, 314, 321, 324, 438, 638, 646, 656.

53 Part

N. *part*, not the whole, portion; proportion, certain p.; majority 32 *main part*, 104 *greater number*; minority 105 *fewness*, 33 *small quantity*; fraction, half, moiety, quarter, tithe, percentage; factor, aliquot, aliquant 85 *number*; balance, surplus 41 *remainder*; quota, contingent; dividend, share, whack 783 *portion*; item, particular, detail 80 *particulars*; sentence, paragraph 563 *phrase*; ingredient, member, constituent, element 58 *component*; dissident element, schism, faction 708 *party*; leg, lap, round 110 *period*; side 239 *laterality*; group, species (**see** *subdivision*); detachment 42 *decrement*; attachment, fixture, wing 40 *adjunct*; page, leaf, folio, sheet 589 *book*; excerpt, extract, gobbet, passage, quotation 605 *choice*; text, pericope; segment, sector, section 46 *scission*; arc 248 *curve*; hemisphere 252 *sphere*; part payment, instalment, advance, deposit, earnest 804 *payment*; sample, foretaste 83 *example*; fragment (**see** *piece*).

limb, member, organ, appendage; hind limb 267 *leg*; forelimb 271 *wing*; flipper, fin 269 *propeller*; arm, forearm, hand 378 *feeler*; elbow, funny bone 247 *angularity*.

subdivision, segment, sector, section 46 *scission*; division, compartment; group, subgroup, species, subspecies, family 74 *group*; classification 62 *arrangement*; ward, parish, department 184 *district*; chapter, paragraph, clause, subordinate clause, phrase, verse; part, number, issue, instalment, volume 589 *edition*, *reading matter*; canto 593 *poem*.

branch, sub-b., ramification, offshoot 40 *adjunct*; bough, limb, spur, twig, tendril, leaf, leaflet; switch, shoot, scion, sucker, slip, sprig, spray 366 *foliage*.

piece, torso, trunk, stump 41 *remainder*; limb, segment, section (**see** *part*); patch, insertion 40 *adjunct*; length, roll 222 *textile*; strip, swatch; fragment, unfinished symphony 55 *incompleteness*; bit, scrap, shred, wisp, rag 33 *small thing*; morsel, bite, crust, crumb 33 *small quantity*; splinter, sliver, chip, snip, snippet; cut, wedge, finger, slice, rasher; collop, cutlet, chop, steak; hunk, chunk, wad, wodge, slab, lump, mass 195 *bulk*; clod, turf, divot, sod 344 *soil*; sherd, shard, potsherd, flake, scale 207 *lamina*; dollop, dose 783 *portion*; bits and pieces, odds and ends, miscellanea, disjecta membra, flotsam and jetsam 43 *medley*; clippings, shavings, parings, brash, rubble, scree, detritus, moraine, debris 41 *leavings*, 641 *rubbish*; rags, tatters 801 *poverty*; piece of land, parcel, plot, allotment.

Adj. *fragmentary*, broken, brashy, crumbly

330 *brittle*; in bits, in pieces 46 *disunited*; not whole, limbless, armless, legless 647 *imperfect*; partial, bitty, scrappy 636 *insufficient*; half-finished 55 *unfinished*; fractional, half, semi-, hemi-, aliquot; segmental, sectional, divided, multifid; departmentalized, compartmentalized, in compartments 46 *separate*; shredded, wispy, sliced, minced 33 *small*.

brachial, cubital; membered, brachiate; with branches, branched, branchy.

Vb. *part*, divide, partition, segment; compartmentalize 46 *sunder*; share out 783 *apportion*; fragment 46 *disunite*.

Adv. *partly*, in part, scrappily, partially; in a sense 55 *incompletely*.

piecemeal, part by part, limb from limb; by instalments, by snatches, by inches, in dribs and drabs; bit by bit, inch by inch, foot by foot, drop by drop, a little at a time, by degrees; in detail, in lots.

See: 32, **33**, 40, 41, 42, 43, 46, 55, 58, 62, 74, 80, 83, 85, 104, 105, 110, 184, 195, 207, 222, 239, 247, 248, 252, 267, 269, 271, 330, 344, 366, 378, 563, 589, 593, 605, 636, 641, 647, 708, 783, 801, 804.

54 Completeness

N. *completeness*, nothing lacking, nothing to add, entireness, wholeness 52 *whole*; integration, integrality 88 *unity*; solidity, solidarity 706 *cooperation*; harmony, balance 710 *concord*; self-sufficiency 635 *sufficiency*; entirety, totality 52 *all*; universality, comprehensiveness 79 *generality*; the ideal 646 *perfection*; ne plus ultra, the limit 236 *limit*; peak, culmination, crown 213 *summit*; finish 69 *end*; last touch 725 *completion*; fulfilment, consummation 69 *finality*; whole hog; nothing less than, the utmost 69 *extremity*.

plenitude, fullness, amplitude, capacity, maximum, one's fill, saturation 635 *sufficiency*; saturation point 863 *satiety*; completion, filling, replenishment, refill; filling up, brimming, overfilling, swamping, drowning; overfulfilment 637 *redundance*; full house, complement, full c., full crew, full load; full measure, brimmer, bumper; bellyful, skinful, repletion; full size, full length, full extent, full volume; complement, supplement, makeweight 31 *compensation*.

Adj. *complete*, plenary, full; utter, total; integral, integrated 52 *whole*; entire, with all its parts, with nothing missing, with supplement 52 *intact*, 646 *perfect*; full-blown, full-grown, full-fledged 669 *matured*; unbroken, undivided, solid 324 *dense*; self-contained, self-sufficient, self-sufficing 635 *sufficient*; fully furnished 633 *provisioning*; comprehensive, full-scale 78 *inclusive*; exhaustive, circumstantial, detailed 570 *diffuse*; absolute, extreme, radical; thorough, thoroughgoing, whole-hogging, sweeping, wholesale, regular 32 *consummate*; unmitigated, downright, plumb, plain 44 *unmixed*; crowning, completing, culminating, consummating, supplementary, complementary 725 *completive*, 38 *additional*; unconfined, unqualified 744 *unconditional*.

full, replete 635 *filled*; replenished, refilled, topped up 633 *provisioning*; well-filled, well-lined, bulging; brimful, brimming, level with, flush; overfull, overflowing, running over, slopping, swamped, drowned; saturated, oozing, leaking 637 *redundant*; coming out at the ears, bursting at the seams; crop-full, gorged, fit to burst, full to bursting, sickened with 863 *sated*; chock-full, chock-a-block, not an inch to spare; cram-full, crammed, stuffed, packed, full-p., jam-p., packed like sardines, jammed, tight 45 *firm*; laden, heavy-l., freighted, fraught, fully charged, full to the hatches; all seats taken, standing room only; infested, overrun, crawling with, lousy w., stiff w.; full of, rolling in; soaked in, dripping with 341 *drenched*; ever-full, inexhaustible 146 *unceasing*.

Vb. *be complete*, be integrated, make a whole; reach *or* touch perfection, have everything; culminate, come to a head 725 *climax*; reach an end, come to a close, be all over 69 *end*; be self-sufficient 635 *have enough*; want nothing, lack n. 828 *be content*; become complete, fill out, attain full growth, reach maturity 669 *mature*; be filled, fill, fill up, brim, hold no more, run over, slop o., overflow 637 *superabound*; gorge, eat *or* drink one's fill 947 *gluttonize*, 949 *get drunk*.

make complete, complete, complement, integrate, make into a whole 45 *join*; make whole 656 *restore*; build up, make up, piece together 56 *compose*; eke out, supplement, supply, fill a gap 38 *add*; make good 31 *compensate*; do thoroughly, leave nothing to add, carry out 725 *carry through*; overfulfil 637 *be superfluous*; put the finishing touch, round off 69 *terminate*.

fill, fill up, brim, top; soak, saturate 341 *drench*; overfill, swamp, drown, overwhelm; top up, replenish 633 *provide*; satisfy 635 *suffice*, 828 *content*, 863 *sate*; fill to capacity, cram, pack, stuff, line, bulge out, pack in, pile in, squeeze in, ram in, jam in 303 *insert*; load, charge, ram down; lade, freight 187 *stow*; fill space, occupy 226 *cover*; reach to, extend to 183 *extend*; spread over, sprawl o., overrun 189 *pervade*; leave no corner, fit tight, be chock-a-block 45 *tighten*; fill in, put in, write in, enter 38 *add*.

Adv. *completely*, fully, wholly, totally, entirely, utterly, extremely 32 *greatly*; all told, in all, in toto; effectually, virtually, as good as; to all intents, to all intents and purposes; on all counts, in all respects, in every way; quite, all of, altogether; outright, downright; to the heart, to the core, to the marrow, through and through; thoroughly, clean, stark, hollow; to one's fill, to the top of one's bent, to the utmost, to the end, to the full; out and out, all out, heart and soul, through thick and thin; head and shoulders, head over heels, neck and crop; to the brim, up to the hilt, up to the neck, up to the ears, up to the eyes; hook, line and sinker; root and branch; down to the ground; with a vengeance, with all the trimmings, and then some; to the last man, to the last breath; every whit, every inch; at full length, full out, in full; as ... as can be; as far as possible; to capacity, not an inch to spare.

throughout, all the way, all round, from first to last, from beginning to end, from end to end, from one end to the other, the length and breadth of, from coast to coast, from Land's End to John o' Groats 183 *widely*; from north and south and east and west; fore and aft; high and low; from top to bottom, de fond en comble; from top to toe, from head to foot, cap-à-pie; to the bitter end, to the end of the chapter, for good and all.

See: 31, 32, 38, 44, 45, **52**, 56, 69, 78, 79, 88, 146, 183, 187, 189, 213, 226, 236, 303, 324, 341, 570, 633, 635, 637, **646**, 656, 669, 706, 710, 725, 744, 828, 863, 947, 949.

55 Incompleteness

N. *incompleteness*, defectiveness; unfinished state 647 *imperfection*; unreadiness 670 *nonpreparation*; underdevelopment, immaturity 670 *undevelopment*; first beginnings 68 *debut*; sketch, outline, first draft, rough d. 623 *plan*; torso, trunk 53 *piece*; half measures, sketchiness, scrappiness, a lick and a promise 726 *noncompletion*; perfunctoriness, superficiality, hollowness 4 *insubstantiality*, 458 *negligence*; nonfulfilment, deficiency, falling short 307 *shortfall*, 636 *insufficiency*; nonsatisfaction, dissatisfaction 829 *discontent*; mutilation, impairment 655 *deterioration*; omission, break, gap, missing link 72 *discontinuity*, 201 *interval*; semi-, half, quarter; instalment, part payment 53 *part*.

deficit, part wanting, screw loose, missing link, omission 647 *defect*; shortfall, ullage 42 *decrement*, 772 *loss*; default, defalcation 930 *improbity*; want, lack, need 627 *requirement*.

Adj. *incomplete*, inadequate, defective 307 *deficient*; short, scant, unsatisfactory 636 *insufficient*; like Hamlet without the Prince 641 *useless*; omitting, wanting, lacking, needing, requiring 627 *demanding*; short of, shy of; maimed, lame, limping, mangled, marred, mutilated; without, -less; limbless, armless, legless, one-armed, one-legged, one-eyed 163 *crippled*; garbled, impaired 655 *deteriorated*; cropped, lopped, docked, truncated, shortened 204 *short*; blemished, flawed 647 *imperfect*; half, semi-, partial 53 *fragmentary*; left unfinished, half-finished, neglected 726 *uncompleted*; not ready, unready 670 *unprepared*; undeveloped, underdeveloped, unripe 670 *immature*; raw, crude, rough-hewn 244 *amorphous*; sketchy, scrappy, bitty, hollow, superficial, meagre, thin, poor 4 *insubstantial*; perfunctory, half-hearted, half-done, undone 458 *neglected*; left in the air, left hanging; omitted, missing, lost 190 *absent*; interrupted 72 *discontinuous*; in default, in arrears, defaulting.

unfinished, in progress, in hand, going on; in embryo, begun 68 *beginning*; in preparation, on the stocks.

Vb. *be incomplete*, miss, lack, need 627 *require*, 307 *fall short*; be wanting 190 *be absent*; default, leave undone 458 *neglect*; omit, miss out 57 *exclude*; break off, interrupt 72 *discontinue*; leave in the air, leave hanging 726 *not complete*;

Adv. *incompletely*, partially, by halves, in instalments; inadequately, insufficiently; in arrears, in default.

See: 4, 42, **53**, 57, 68, 72, 163, 190, 201, 204, 244, 307, 458, 623, 627, **636**, 641, **647**, 655, 670, 726, 772, 829, 930.

56 Composition

N. *composition*, constitution, setup, make-up; make, conformation, formation, construction, build-up, build 331 *structure*; organization 62 *arrangement*; temper, habit, nature, character, condition, syndrome 5 *temperament*; embodiment, incorporation 78 *inclusion*; compound 43 *mixture*, 50 *combination*, 358 *organism*; syntax, sentence, period 563 *phrase*; artistic composition 412 *music*, 551 *art*, 553 *painting*, 554 *sculpture*; architecture 164 *edifice*; authorship 586 *writing*, 593 *poetry*; dramatic art 594 *drama*; composing, setting-up, printing, typography 587 *print*; compilation 74 *assemblage*; work, construction 164 *production*; choreography 594 *ballet*; orchestration, instrumentation, score 412 *musical piece*; work of art, picture, sculpture, model; literary work 589 *book*, 593 *poem*, 591 *dissertation*, 592 *anthology*; play 594 *stage play*; ballet 837 *dance*; pattern, design 12 *correlation*.

Adj. *composing*, constituting, making; composed of, made of; containing, having 78 *inclusive*.

Vb. *constitute*, compose, be the whole of, form, make; make up, build up to; inhere, belong to, go to the making of, enter into 58 *be one of*.

contain, subsume, include, consist of 78 *comprise*; hold, have, take in, absorb 299 *admit*; comprehend, embrace, embody 235 *enclose*; involve, imply 5 *be intrinsic*; hide 525 *conceal*.

compose, compound 43 *mix*, 50 *combine*; organize, set in order 62 *arrange*; synthesize, put together, make up 45 *join*; compile, assemble 74 *bring together*; compose, set up 587 *print*; draft, draw up, indite 586 *write*; orchestrate, score 413 *compose music*; draw 553 *paint*; construct, build, make, fabricate 164 *produce*; knit, interweave 222 *weave*; pattern, design 12 *correlate*.

See: 5, 12, 43, 45, 50, **58**, 62, 74, **78**, 164, 222, 235, 299, 331, 358, 412, 413, 525, 551, 553, 554, 563, 586, 587, 589, 591, 592, 593, 594, 837.

57 Exclusion

N. *exclusion*, preclusion, preoccupation, preemption; anticipation, forestalling 702 *hindrance*; exclusiveness, monopoly, closed shop, dog-in-the-manger policy; possessiveness 932 *selfishness*; noninclusion, exception; an exception, special case; exception in favour of, exemption, dispensation 746 *liberation*; leaving out, omission, deliberate o. 607 *rejection*; non-admission, blackball; no entry, no admission; closed door, lockout; picket line; embargo, ban, bar, taboo 757 *prohibition*; ostracism, boycott 620 *avoidance*; segregation, quarantine, caste system, colour bar, apartheid 883 *seclusion*; intolerance, repression, suppression 481 *prejudice*; expulsion, eviction; disbarment, dismissal, suspension, excommunication; deportation, exile, expatriation; removal, elimination, eradication 188 *displacement*; cancellation, blotting out 550 *obliteration*; dam, coffer d., wall, barricade, screen, partition, pale, curtain, Iron C., Bamboo C. 235 *barrier*; Great Wall of China, Hadrian's Wall 713 *defence*; customs' barrier, tariff, tariff wall 809 *tax*; place of exile, place of segregation, ghetto, outer darkness 223 *exteriority*.

Adj. *excluding*, exclusive, exclusionary, exemptive; restrictive, cliquish 708 *sectional*; preventive, interdictory, prohibitive 757 *prohibiting*; preclusive, preemptive; silent about 582 *taciturn*.

excluded, barred, excepted etc. vb.; extra-, not included, not admitted; peripheral, hardly in, half in, half out; included out, counted o.; not told, unrecounted, suppressed, stifled; not allowed, disallowed, banned 757 *prohibited*; disbarred, struck off 550 *obliterated*; shut out, outcast 607 *rejected*; inadmissible, beyond the pale 470 *impossible*; foreign 59 *extraneous*, 84 *unconformable*; removable, exemptile.

Vb. *be excluded*, not belong, stay outside, not gain admission; suffer exile, go into e. 296 *depart*, 190 *be absent*.

exclude, preclude 470 *make impossible*; preempt, forestall 64 *come before*; keep out, warn off 747 *restrain*; blackball, deny entry, shut out, debar, shut the door on, spurn 607 *reject*; bar, ban, taboo, black, disallow 757 *prohibit*; ostracize, cold-shoulder, boycott, send to Coventry 620 *avoid*, 883 *make unwelcome*; not include, leave out, count o.; exempt, dispense, excuse 746 *liberate*; except, make an exception, treat as a special case 19 *make unlike*; omit, miss out, pass over, disregard 458 *neglect*; lay aside, put a., relegate 46 *set apart*; take out, strike o., cancel 550 *obliterate*; disbar, strike off, remove, disqualify 188 *displace*, 963 *punish*; rule out, draw the line; wall off, curtain off, quarantine 232 *circumscribe*, 235 *enclose*; excommunicate, segregate, sequester 883 *seclude*; thrust out, dismiss, deport, extradite, exile, banish, outlaw, expatriate; weed, sift, sort out 44 *eliminate*; eradicate, uproot 300 *eject*; expurgate, censor 648 *purify*; deny 760 *refuse*; abandon 779 *not retain*.

Adv. *exclusive of*, excepting, barring, bar, not counting, except, with the exception of, save; outside of, short of; let alone, apart from; outside of, extra-.

See: 19, 44, 46, 59, 64, 84, 188, 190, 223, 232, 235, 296, 300, 458, 470, 481, 550, 582, **607**, 620, 648, 702, 708, 713, 746, 747, 757, 760, 779, 809, **883**, 932, 963.

58 Component

N. *component*, component part, integral p., integrant p., element, item; unit, module; piece, bit, segment; link, stitch; word, letter; constituent, part and parcel 53 *part*; factor, leaven 178 *influence*; additive, appurtenance, feature 40 *adjunct*; one of, member, one of us; staff, crew, men, company, complement 686 *personnel*; ingredient 193 *contents*, 43 *tincture*; works, insides, interior 224 *interiority*; nuts and bolts, machinery 630 *machine*; spare part 40 *extra*; components, set, outfit 88 *unit*.

Adj. *component*, constituent, ingredient, integrant 56 *composing*; entering into, belonging, proper, native, inherent 5 *intrinsic*; built-in, appurtenant 45 *joined*; admitted, entered, made a member, part of, one of, on the staff; involved, implicated, mixed up in 43 *mixed*.

Vb. *be one of*, make part of, be a member etc. n.; inhere, belong 5 *be intrinsic*; enter into, enter into the composition of 56 *constitute*; become involved with, be implicated in, share 775 *participate*; merge in, be merged in 43 *be mixed*; belong to, appertain to 9 *be related*.

See: 5, 9, 40, 43, 45, **53**, **56**, 88, 178, 193, 224, 630, 686, 775.

59 Extraneousness

N. *extraneousness*, foreignness 6 *extrinsicality*, 223 *exteriority*; foreign parts 199 *farness*; foreign body, foreign substance, accretion 38 *addition*; alien element 84 *nonconformity*; exotica.

foreigner, person from foreign parts 268 *traveller*; alien, stranger, unco, emmet, Uitlander, outlander; continental, tramontane, ultramontane; Southerner, Northerner, Easterner, Westerner; Martian, Venusian, little green men; Celtic fringe; Sassenach, pommie, limey, rooineck; Yank, Yankee, Aussie, Kiwi; gringo, paleface; colonial, Creole 191 *settler*; resident alien, expatriate; migrant, migrant worker, guest w., Gastarbeiter, emigrant, émigré, exile; immigrant, declarant 297 *incomer*; refugee, déraciné(e) 268 *wanderer*; Diaspora, ten lost tribes.

intruder, interloper, trespasser, cuckoo in the nest, squatter; uninvited guest, gatecrasher, stowaway; outsider, novus homo 126 *upstart*; not one of us, stranger in our midst; arrival, new a., new face, newcomer, new boy, tenderfoot 297 *incomer*; invader 712 *attacker*.

Adj. *extraneous*, of external origin, ulterior, outside 223 *exterior*, 6 *extrinsic*; ultramundane, extragalactic 199 *distant*; not indigenous, imported, foreign-made; foreign, alien, unearthly; strange, outlandish, barbarian; overseas, ultramarine, transatlantic; continental, tramontane, ultramontane; extraterrestrial; exotic, hothouse, unacclimatized; gipsy, nomad, wandering 267 *travelling*; unassimilated, undigested, unintegrated 46 *separate*; immigrant 297 *incoming*; intrusive, interloping, trespassing; infringing, invading 712 *attacking*; exceptional 84 *unusual*; un-British, un-American 15 *different*; not of this world, unnatural, supernatural 983 *magical*; inadmissible 57 *excluded*.

Adv. *abroad*, in foreign parts, in foreign lands; beyond seas, overseas; from outer space.

See: **6**, 15, 38, 46, 57, 84, 126, 191, 199, **223**, 267, 268, 297, 712, 983.

Section four: Order

60 Order

N. *order,* state of order, orderliness, tidiness, neatness 648 *cleanness,* 258 *smoothness;* proportion 245 *symmetry;* peace, quiet 266 *quietude;* harmony, music of the spheres 710 *concord;* good order, economy, system, method, methodicalness, methodology, systematization; fixed order, pattern, rule 81 *regularity,* 16 *uniformity;* custom, routine 610 *habit;* rite 988 *ritual;* strict order, discipline 739 *obedience;* due order, hierarchy, gradation, subordination, rank, place, position 73 *serial place;* unbroken order, course, even tenor, progression, series 71 *continuity;* logical order, serial o., alphabetical o. 65 *sequence,* 12 *correlation;* organization, putting in order, disposition, array 62 *arrangement,* 56 *composition;* a place for everything and e. in its place.

Adj. *orderly,* harmonious 710 *concordant,* 245 *symmetrical;* well-behaved, decorous 848 *well-bred;* well-drilled, disciplined 739 *obedient;* well-regulated, under control, according to rule 81 *regular;* ordered, classified, schematic 62 *arranged;* methodical, systematic, businesslike; strict, invariable 16 *uniform;* routine, steady 610 *habitual;* correct, shipshape, Bristol fashion, trim, neat, tidy, dinky, neat and tidy, neat as a pin, out of a bandbox; spick and span, spruce, dapper, well-groomed 648 *clean;* in good trim, well-kept, uncluttered, in apple-pie order, in perfect o., in its proper place, unconfused 62 *arranged;* unruffled, unrumpled 258 *smooth;* direct 249 *straight;* clear, lucid 516 *intelligible.*

Vb. *order,* reduce to order, dispose 62 *arrange;* schematize, systematize, organize 62 *regularize;* harmonize, synchronize, regulate 24 *adjust;* normalize, standardize 16 *make uniform;* keep order, call to order, police, control, govern 733 *rule,* 737 *command.*

be in order, harmonize, synchronize 24 *accord;* fall in, range oneself, draw up, line up; fall into place, find one's level; take one's place, station oneself, take up one's station; take up one's position 187 *place oneself;* keep one's place; rally, rally round 74 *congregate;* follow routine 610 *be wont.*

Adv. *in order,* strictly, just so, by the book, by the card 81 *to rule;* by order, as directed; in turn, in its t., seriatim; step by step, by regular steps, by regular gradations, by regular stages, at regular intervals 141 *periodically;* orderly, in orderly fashion, methodically, systematically, schematically; all correct, OK.

See: 12, 16, 24, 56, **62**, 65, 71, 73, 74, 81, 141, 187, 245, 249, 258, 266, 516, 610, **648**, 710, 733, 737, 739, 848, 988.

61 Disorder

N. *disorder,* random order, nonarrangement, nonclassification; incoordination, muddle, no plan, no order, no method, no system (**see** *confusion*); chaotic state, chaos, mayhem 734 *anarchy;* irregularity, anomalousness, anomaly 17 *nonuniformity;* disunion, disaccord 25 *disagreement;* disharmony 411 *discord;* disorderliness, unruliness, no discipline 738 *disobedience;* violent behaviour, outbreak (**see** *turmoil*); nihilism 738 *sedition;* untidiness, littering, sluttishness, slovenliness 649 *uncleanness;* neglect 458 *negligence;* discomposure, disarray, dishevelment 63 *derangement;* dissolution, scattering 75 *dispersion,* 51 *decomposition;* upheaval, convulsion 149 *revolution;* subversion 221 *overturning;* destruction 165 *havoc.*

confusion (**see** *disorder*); welter, jumble, shambles, hugger-mugger, mix-up, medley, embroilment, imbroglio 43 *mixture;* wilderness, jungle; chaos, fortuitous concourse of atoms; swarm, seething mass, scramble 74 *crowd;* muddle, litter, clutter, lumber 641 *rubbish;* farrago, mess, mishmash, hash, hotchpotch, witches' brew, jumble sale, lucky dip 43 *medley;* Babel, bedlam, madhouse (**see** *turmoil*).

complexity, complication, snarl-up 700 *difficulty,* 702 *hindrance;* implication, involvement, imbroglio, embroilment; intricacy, interlocking, involution, kink 251 *convolution;* maze, labyrinth, warren; web, spider's w. 222 *network;* coil, tangle, twist, tangled skein, snarl, ravel; knot, Gordian k. 47 *ligature;* wheels within wheels, clockwork, machinery; puzzle 517 *unintelligibility;* awkward situation, pretty kettle of fish, pickle 700 *predicament.*

turmoil, turbulence, tumult, frenzy, ferment, storm, convulsion 176 *violence;* pandemonium, inferno; hullabaloo, hubbub, racket, row, riot, uproar 400 *loudness;* affray, fracas, dustup, brawl, mêlée

716 *fight*; hurly-burly, to-do, rumpus, ructions, shemozzle, pother, trouble, disturbance 318 *commotion*; whirlwind, tornado, hurricane 352 *gale*; beargarden, shambles, madhouse, bedlam; Saturnalia, Bacchanalia; shindy, Donnybrook, breach of the peace; roughhouse, rough and tumble, free for all, all hell broken loose, bull in a china shop; street fighting, gang warfare 709 *quarrel*; fat in the fire, devil to pay.

slut, sloven, slattern, draggletail, litterer, litterlout 649 *dirty person*; ragamuffin, tatterdemalion 801 *poor person*.

anarchist, nihilist; lord of misrule, sons of Belial 738 *rioter*.

Adj. *orderless*, in disorder, in disarray, disordered, deranged, disorganized, jumbled, shuffled 63 *disarranged*; unclassified, ungraded, unsorted; out of order, not in working order, not working 641 *useless*; out of joint, out of gear, dislocated 46 *disunited*; out of sorts 651 *sick*; out of place, misplaced 188 *displaced*; askew, awry, snafu; topsy-turvy, upside down 221 *inverted*; wandering, straggling, dispersed 75 *unassembled*; random, unarranged, unorganized, uncoordinated, unschematic, planless 244 *amorphous*; incoherent, rambling; irregular, anomalous 17 *nonuniform*; unsystematic, unmethodical, desultory, aimless, casual; confused, muddled, chaotic, in chaos, in a mess, messy, all anyhow, haywire; unkempt, uncombed, dishevelled, tumbled, windswept, windblown, tousled, discomposed, pulled through a hedge backwards; littering, untidy, slovenly, sluttish, slatternly, bedraggled, messy 649 *dirty*; sloppy, slipshod, slack, careless 456 *inattentive*.

complex, intricate, involved, elaborate, sophisticated, complicated, over-c., overinvolved 251 *coiled*, 517 *puzzling*; mazy, winding, inextricable 251 *labyrinthine*; entangled, balled up, snarled 702 *hindered*; knotted 45 *tied*.

disorderly, undisciplined, unruly; out of step, out of line; tumultuous, rumbustious 738 *riotous*; frantic 503 *frenzied*; orgiastic, Saturnalian, Bacchic, Dionysiac 949 *drunken*; rough, tempestuous, turbulent 176 *violent*, 318 *agitated*; anarchical, lawless 954 *lawbreaking*; wild, harum-scarum, rantipole, tomboyish, boisterous, scatterbrained 456 *light-minded*.

Vb. *be disordered*, fall into disarray, scatter, break up 75 *disperse*; get in a mess, fall into confusion, lose cohesion 49 *come unstuck*; get out of hand, throw off discipline, riot 738 *disobey*; not keep one's place, jump the queue 64 *come before*; disorder 63 *derange*.

rampage, storm 176 *be violent*; rush, mob, break the cordon; roister, riot 738 *revolt*; romp 837 *amuse oneself*; play the fool 497 *be absurd*; fete, give a riotous welcome 876 *celebrate*.

Adv. *confusedly*, in confusion, in disorder, without order, anyhow, all a., all over the place, all over the shop; irregularly, without rhyme or reason; by fits and snatches, by fits and starts; chaotically, pell-mell, higgledy-piggledy, helter-skelter, harum-scarum; in turmoil, in a ferment; on the rampage; at sixes and sevens, at cross purposes; topsy-turvy, upside down 221 *inversely*; inextricably.

See: 17, 25, 43, 45, 46, 47, 49, 51, **63**, 64, 74, 75, 149, 165, 176, 188, 221, 222, 244, 251, 318, 352, 400, 411, 456, 458, 497, 503, 517, 641, 649, 651, 700, 702, 709, 716, 734, 738, 801, 837, 876, 949, 954.

62 Arrangement: reduction to order

N. *arrangement*, reduction to order; ordering, disposal, disposition, marshalling, arraying, placing 187 *location*; collocation, grouping 45 *joining together*, 74 *assemblage*; division, distribution, allocation, allotment 783 *apportionment*; method, systematization, organization, reorganization; rationalization 44 *simplification*; streamlining 654 *improvement*; centralization 48 *coherence*; decentralization 49 *noncoherence*; administration, staff-work 689 *management*; planning, making arrangements 623 *contrivance*, 669 *preparation*; taxonomy, categorization, classification 561 *nomenclature*; analysis 51 *decomposition*; codification, digestion, consolidation; syntax, conjugation 564 *grammar*; grading, gradation, subordination, graduation, calibration 465 *measurement*, 71 *series*; continuation, serialization 71 *continuity*; timing, synchronization 123 *synchronism*; formulation, construction 56 *composition*; result of arrangement, array, system, form 60 *order*; cosmos 321 *universe*; organic creature 358 *organism*; orchestration, score 412 *music*; layout, pattern, architecture

331 *structure*; weave 222 *crossing*; choreography 837 *dance*; collection, assortment 74 *accumulation*; schematic arrangement, schematism; computer program; register, file 548 *record*; inventory, catalogue, table 87 *list*; syntagma, code, digest, synopsis 592 *compendium*; treatise, essay, article 591 *dissertation*, 589 *book*; atlas 551 *map*; scheme 623 *plan*; composition 770 *compromise*, 765 *compact*, 766 *conditions*; class, group, sub-g. 77 *classification*.

sorting, grading, seeding; reference system, cross-reference 12 *correlation*; file, folder, filing system, card index, pigeonhole, slot; sieve, strainer 263 *porosity*.

Adj. *arranged*, disposed, marshalled, arrayed etc. vb.; ordered, schematic, tabulated, tabular; methodical, systematic, organizational; precise, definite, cut and dried; analysed, classified, assorted; unravelled, disentangled, unscrambled, straightened out; regulated 81 *regular*; unconfused 60 *orderly*; sorted, seeded, graded, streamed, banded.

Vb. *arrange*, set, dispose, set up, set out, lay out; formulate, form, put into shape, orchestrate, score 56 *compose*; range, rank, align, line up, form up; position 187 *place*; marshal, array; bring back to order, rally 74 *bring together*; place in order, put in order, set in order; grade, size, group, space; collocate, thread together 45 *connect*; settle, fix, determine, define; allot, allocate, assign, distribute, deal, parcel out 783 *apportion*; rearrange, trim, neaten, tidy, tidy up (**see** *unravel*); arrange for, make arrangements 669 *prepare*, 623 *plan*, 689 *manage*.

regularize, reduce to order, bring order into, straighten out, put to rights 654 *rectify*, 24 *adjust*; regulate, coordinate, phase; organize, systematize, methodize, schematize; standardize, normalize, centralize 16 *make uniform*.

class, classify, subsume, group; specify 561 *name*; process, process the data; analyse, anatomize, divide; dissect 51 *decompose*; rate, rank, grade, evaluate 480 *estimate*; sort, sift, seed; sift out 44 *eliminate*; docket, label 547 *mark*; file, pigeonhole; index, reference, cross-r.; tabulate, alphabetize; catalogue, inventory 87 *list*; register 548 *record*; codify, program, digest.

unravel, untangle, disentangle, disembroil, ravel, card, comb out, unweave, uncoil, unsnarl, untwist, untwine 316 *evolve*; iron, press, uncrease, iron out 258 *smooth*; debug 654 *make better*; unscramble; straighten out, tidy up, clean up, neaten 648 *clean*; clear the air, remove misunderstanding, explain 520 *interpret*.

See: 12, 16, 24, 44, 45, 48, 49, 51, 56, **60**, 71, 74, 77, 81, 87, 123, 187, 222, 258, 263, 316, 321, 331, 358, 412, 465, 480, 520, 547, 548, 551, 561, 564, 589, 591, 592, 623, 648, 654, 669, 689, 765, 766, 770, 783, 837.

63 Derangement

N. *derangement*, subversion of order; shuffling 151 *interchange*; translocation, displacement 272 *transference*; sabotage, obstruction 702 *hindrance*; disarrangement, disorganization, discomposure, dishevelment; dislocation 46 *separation*; disturbance, interruption 138 *untimeliness*; timeslip 108 *time*; creasing, corrugation 261 *fold*; madness 503 *insanity*; upsetting 221 *inversion*; convulsion 176 *violence*, 318 *agitation*; state of disorder 61 *disorder*.

Adj. *disarranged*, deranged, disordered 61 *orderless*; demented 503 *insane*; sabotaged 702 *hindered*.

Vb. *derange*, disarrange, disorder, put out of gear, get out of order; disturb, touch 265 *move*; meddle, interfere 702 *hinder*; mislay, lose 188 *misplace*; disorganize, muddle, confound, confuse, convulse, throw into confusion, make havoc, scramble; tamper, spoil, mar, damage, sabotage 655 *impair*; strain, bend, twist 176 *force*; unhinge, dislocate, sprain, rick 188 *displace*; unseat, dislodge, derail, throw off the rails; unbalance, upset, overturn, capsize 221 *invert*, 149 *revolutionize*; declassify, detribalize, denationalize; shake, jiggle, toss 318 *agitate*; trouble, perturb, unsettle, discompose, disconcert, ruffle, rattle, flurry, fluster 456 *distract*; interrupt, break in on 138 *mistime*; misdirect, disorientate, throw one off his bearings 495 *mislead*, 655 *pervert*; unhinge, dement, drive mad 503 *make mad*, 891 *enrage*.

jumble, shuffle, get out of order 151 *interchange*, 272 *transpose*; mix up 43 *mix*; toss, tumble 318 *agitate*; ruffle, dishevel, tousle, fluff up; rumple, crumple, crease, crush 261 *fold*; untidy, mess, muck up; muddle, mess up, litter, clutter; scatter, fling about 75 *disperse*; play havoc with, play merry hell with 702 *hinder*.

bedevil, confuse, make a mess *or* hash of; confound, complicate, perplex, involve, ravel, ball up, entangle, tangle, embroil; turn topsy-turvy, turn upside down 221 *invert*; send haywire.

See: 43, 46, **61**, 75, 108, 138, 149, 151, 176, 188, 221, 261, 265, 272, 318, 456, 495, 503, 655, 702, 891.

64 Precedence

N. *precedence*, antecedence, going before, coming b., queue-jumping 283 *preceding*; anteriority 119 *priority*; front position, anteposition, prefixion, prosthesis 237 *front*; higher position, pride of place 34 *superiority*; preference 605 *choice*; preeminence, excellence 638 *importance*; captaincy, leadership, hegemony 733 *authority*; the lead, the pas; leading, guiding, pioneering; precedent 66 *precursor*; past history 125 *past time*.

Adj. *preceding*, going first etc. vb.; precedent, antecedent, foregoing, outgoing; anterior, former, previous 119 *prior*; before-mentioned, above-m.; aforesaid, said; precursory, precursive, prevenient, anticipatory; leading, guiding, pioneering, avant-garde; forewarning, premonitory, prodromal; preliminary, prelusive, proemial, prefatory, preparatory, introductory; prepositive, prosthetic, prefixed, prepositional 237 *frontal*; first come, first served.

Vb. *come before*, be first to arrive 283 *precede*; go first, run ahead, jump the queue; lead, guide, conduct, show the way, point the way 547 *indicate*; forerun, pioneer, clear the way, blaze the trail 484 *discover*; head, take the lead 237 *be in front*; have precedence, take p., outrank 34 *be superior*; lead the dance, set the fashion, set the example 178 *influence*; open, lead off, kick off 68 *begin*; preamble, prelude, preface, prologize; introduce, usher in, ring in 68 *auspicate*; have the start, get ahead 119 *be before*; antedate 125 *be past*.

put in front, lead with, head w.; advance, send ahead, station before 187 *place*; prefix 38 *add*; front, face, tip, top 237 *be in front*; presuppose 512 *suppose*, 475 *premise*; preface, prelude 68 *initiate*.

Adv. *before*, in advance 283 *ahead*; preparatory to, as a preliminary; earlier 119 *before* (in time); ante, supra, above 237 *in front*.

See: 34, 38, **66**, **68**, **119**, 125, 178, 187, 237, **283**, 475, 484, 512, 547, 605, 638, 733.

65 Sequence

N. *sequence*, coming after, subsequence, descent, line, lineage 120 *posteriority*; going after 284 *following*; consecution, inference 475 *reasoning*; postposition, suffixion 38 *addition*, 45 *joining together*; sonship 170 *posterity*; succession, successorship, Elijah's mantle 780 *transfer*; rota, Buggins's turn; series 71 *continuity*; successiveness, alternation, serialization; continuation, prolongation 113 *protraction*, 146 *continuance*; pursuance 619 *pursuit*; overtaking 306 *overstepping*, 727 *success*; subordination, second place, proxime accessit 35 *inferiority*; last place 238 *rear*; no priority 639 *unimportance*; consequence 67 *sequel*, 157 *effect*; conclusion 69 *end*.

Adj. *sequential*, sequent, following, succeeding, successional; incoming, ensuing; proximate, next 200 *near*; posterior, latter, later 120 *subsequent*; another, second, third 38 *additional*; successive, consecutive 71 *continuous*; alternating, antiphonal 12 *correlative*; alternate, every second, every other; postpositive, postpositional 238 *back*; consequent, resulting 157 *caused*.

Vb. *come after*, have one's turn, come next, ensue 284 *follow*; follow close, tread on the heels 200 *be near*; succeed, inherit, step into the shoes of, supplant 150 *substitute*; alternate, take turn and turn about 141 *be periodic*; relieve, take over.

place after, suffix, append; subscribe, subjoin 38 *add*.

Adv. *after*, following; afterwards 120 *subsequently*, 238 *rearward*; at the end, in relays, in waves, successively; as follows, consequentially 157 *consequently*; in the end 69 *finally*; next, later; infra, below.

See: 12, 35, 38, 45, 67, **69**, 71, 113, **120**, 141, 146, 150, 157, 170, 200, 238, **284**, 306, 475, 619, 639, 727, 780.

66 Precursor

N. *precursor*, predecessor, ancestor, forebears, patriarch 169 *parentage*; Adam and Eve, early man 371 *humankind*; the ancients, Deucalion and Pyrrha 125 *antiquity*; eldest, firstborn; protomartyr;

discoverer, inventor 461 *experimenter*; pioneer, Voortrekker, pathfinder, explorer 268 *traveller*; guide, pilot 690 *leader*; scout, skirmisher; vanguard, avant-garde, innovator, trail-blazer; trend-setter; forerunner, outrider; herald, harbinger, announcer 529 *messenger*; dawn, false d.; anticipation, prefigurement, foretaste, prognostic, preview, premonition, forewarning 664 *warning*, 511 *omen*; prodrome, trailer; precedent 83 *example*; antecedent, prefix, preposition 40 *adjunct*; eve, vigil, day before 119 *priority*.

prelude, preliminary, prolusion, preamble, preface, prologue, foreword, avant-propos; proem, opening, exordium, prolegomena, introduction 68 *beginning*; lead, heading, frontispiece 237 *front*; groundwork, foundation 218 *basis*, 669 *preparation*; aperitif, appetizer; overture, voluntary 412 *musical piece*; premises, presupposition 512 *supposition*, 475 *premise*.

Adj. *precursory*, preliminary, exploratory 669 *preparatory*; prelusory, proemial, introductory, prefatory 68 *beginning*; inaugural, foundational; precedent 64 *preceding*.

See: 40, **64**, 68, 83, **119**, 125, 169, 218, 237, 268, 371, 412, 461, 475, 511, 512, 529, 664, 669, 690.

67 Sequel

N. *sequel*, consequence, result, aftermath, by-product, spin-off 157 *effect*; conclusion 69 *end*; sequela, aftereffect; hangover, morning after 949 *crapulence*; aftertaste; afterglow, fallout; afterbirth, placenta, afterpains 167 *obstetrics*; inheritance, legacy 777 *dower*; surprise, afterclap 508 *lack of expectation*; afterthought, second thoughts, better t., esprit de l'escalier; double take, second try; afterword, postlude, epilogue, postscript; peroration, envoi, last words; follow-through, follow-up 725 *completion*; continuation, sequel 589 *book*; tag, tailpiece, colophon, coda 238 *rear*; appendage, appendix, codicil, supplement 40 *adjunct*; suffix, affix, inflection 564 *grammar*; afterpart, tail; queue, pigtail, ponytail 259 *hair*; afters, dessert 301 *dish*; survival, afterlife, afterworld, hereafter 124 *future state*.

retinue, following, followers 284 *follower*; queue 71 *series*; suite, train, cortège 71 *procession*; tail, tailback, wake 89 *concomitant*; trailer 274 *vehicle*.

successor, descendant, later generations, future g., the unborn 170 *posterity*; heir, inheritor 776 *beneficiary*; next man in; replacement, supplanter 150 *substitute*; fresh blood, new broom 126 *modernist*, *upstart*; latecomer, newcomer 297 *incomer*; gleaner 370 *farmer*; satellite, hanger-on 742 *dependant*; last man in, finalist, finisher 41 *survivor*.

See: 40, 41, 69, 71, 89, 124, 126, 150, 157, 167, 170, **238**, 259, 274, **284**, 297, 301, 370, 508, 564, 589, 725, 742, 776, 777, 949.

68 Beginning

N. *beginning*, birth, rise (**see** *origin*); infancy, babyhood 130 *youth*, 126 *newness*; primitiveness 127 *oldness*; commencement; onset 295 *arrival*; emergence 445 *appearance*; incipience, inception, inchoation, institution, constitution, foundation, establishment 156 *causation*; origination, invention 484 *discovery*; creation 164 *production*; innovation 21 *originality*; initiative, démarche; exordium, introduction, curtain-raiser 66 *prelude*; alpha, first letter, initial; head, heading, headline, caption 547 *label*; title page, prelims; van, front, forefront 237 *front*; dawn 128 *morning*; running in, teething troubles, growing pains; first blush, first glance, first sight, first impression, first lap, first round, first stage; early stages, early days, incunabula; primer, outline; rudiments, elements, first principles, alphabet, ABC; leading up to 289 *approach*; outbreak, onset 712 *attack*; debutante, starter 538 *beginner*; precedent 66 *precursor*; preliminaries 669 *preparation*.

debut, coming out, presentation, initiation, launching; inauguration, opening, unveiling; first night, premiere, first appearance, first offence; premier pas, first step, first move, move, gambit; maiden voyage, maiden speech; baptism of fire.

start, outset; starting point, point of departure, zero hour, D-day; send-off, setting out, embarkation, countdown 296 *departure*; rising of the curtain; starting pistol, kick-off; house-warming, honeymoon; fresh start, new beginning, resumption, reopening 148 *reversion*; new departure, thin end of the wedge, precedent; standing

start, flying s.; starter, self-s.
origin, origination, derivation, conception, genesis, birth, nativity; provenance, ancestry 169 *parentage*; fount, fons et origo; rise 156 *source*; nest, womb 156 *seedbed*; bud, germ, seed; egg, protoplasm, primordial soup 358 *organism*; first beginnings, cradle 192 *home*.
entrance 297 *way in*; inlet 345 *gulf*; mouth, opening 263 *orifice*; threshold 624 *access*; porch 194 *lobby*; gateway 263 *doorway*; frontier, border 236 *limit*; outskirts, skirts, environs, suburbs 230 *surroundings*; foothills, outlier; pass, corridor 289 *approach*, 305 *passage*.
Adj. *beginning*, initiatory, initiative, inceptive; introductory, prefatory, proemial 66 *precursory*; inaugural, foundational; elemental, rudimental 156 *fundamental*; aboriginal, primeval, primordial 127 *primal*; rudimentary, elementary, crude 670 *immature*; embryonic, germinal, nascent, budding, incipient, inchoate, raw, begun, in preparation 726 *uncompleted*; early, infant 126 *new*; just begun, newly opened, launched.
first, initial, primary, maiden, starting, natal; pioneering 21 *original*; unprecedented 126 *new*; foremost, front 237 *frontal*; leading, principal, head, chief 34 *supreme*.
Vb. *begin*, make a beginning, commence, inchoate; set in, open, dawn, break out, burst forth, spring up, crop up; arise, emerge, appear; rise, take one's r., take one's birth; spring from; sprout, germinate; come into existence, come into the world, see the light of day 360 *be born*; make one's debut, come out; start, enter upon, embark on 296 *start out*; fire away, kick off, strike up; start work, clock in; roll up one's sleeves, limber up 669 *prepare*; run in; begin at the beginning, start from scratch, begin ab ovo; resume, begin again, go back to square one, make a fresh start 148 *revert*; start afresh, shuffle the cards, reshuffle, resume, recommence, reopen; put one's hand to the plough, set to, set about, set to work, get cracking; attack, wade into, tackle, face, address oneself; go to it 672 *undertake*.
initiate, found, launch; originate, invent, think of 484 *discover*; call into being 167 *generate*; usher in, ring in, open the door to, introduce; start, start up, switch on, ring up the curtain; prompt, promote, set going, set in motion, get under way; raise, set on foot; put to work 622 *employ*; handsel, run in; take the initiative, lead, lead off, lead the way, take the lead, pioneer, open up, break new ground 64 *come before*; broach, open, raise the subject, ventilate, air; open the ball, break the ice, set the ball rolling; throw the first stone, open fire; take the first step, take the plunge, cross the Rubicon, burn one's boats; apply the match, trigger off, touch off, spark off, set off.
auspicate, inaugurate, open; institute, install, induct 751 *commission*; found, set up, establish 156 *cause*; be a founder member, be in on the ground floor; baptize, christen, launch 561 *name*; initiate, blood, flesh; lay the foundations, lay the foundation stone, cut the first turf 669 *prepare*.
Adv. *initially*, originally, at the beginning, in the b., in the bud, in embryo, in its infancy, from its birth; from the beginning, from the word go; ab initio, ab ovo; de novo, de nouveau; first, firstly, in the first place, imprimis, primo; primarily, first of all, before everything, first and foremost; as a start, for starters, for a beginning; from scratch.
See: 21, 34, 64, 66, **126**, 127, 128, 130, 148, **156**, 164, 167, 169, 192, 194, 230, 236, 237, 263, 289, 295, 296, 297, 305, 345, 358, 360, 445, 484, **538**, 547, 561, 622, 624, 669, 670, 672, 712, 726, 751.

69 End

N. *end*, close, conclusion, consummation 725 *completion*; payoff, result, end r. 157 *effect*; expiration, lapse; termination, determination, closure, guillotine; finishing stroke, death blow, quietus, coup de grace; knockout, finisher, clincher 279 *knock*; catastrophe, denouement; ending, finish, finale, curtain; term, period, stop, halt 145 *cessation*; final stage, latter end 129 *evening*; beginning of the end, peroration, last words, swansong, envoi, coda 67 *sequel*; last stage, last round, last lap, home stretch; last ball, last over; last breath, last gasp, extremities 361 *decease*; final examination, finals 459 *exam*. **See** *finality*.
extremity, final point, omega; ultimate point, extreme, pole, antipodes; extreme case, ne plus ultra; farthest point, world's end, ultima Thule, where the rainbow

ends 199 *farness*; fringe, verge, brink 234 *edge*; frontier, boundary 236 *limit*; end of the line, terminal point, terminus, terminal 295 *goal*, 617 *objective*; dregs, last d.; foot, toe, bottom, nadir 214 *base*; bottom dollar, last penny 801 *poverty*; tip, cusp, point 256 *sharp point*; vertex, peak, head, top 213 *summit*; tail, tail end 67 *sequel*; arm, stump 53 *limb*; shirt-tail, coat-t. 217 *hanging object*; end, butt end, gable e., fag e. 238 *rear*; tag, epilogue, postscript, appendix 40 *adjunct*; desinence, inflection, suffix 564 *grammar*.

finality, bitter end; time, time up, deadline; curtains, conclusion, end of the matter 54 *completeness*; drop of the curtain, breakup, wind-up 145 *cessation*; dissolution 165 *destruction*; eschatology, last things, doom, destiny 596 *fate*; last trump, crack of doom, Götterdämmerung; resurrection day, Day of Judgment, end of the world, end of time, end of all things 124 *future state*.

Adj. *ending*, final, terminal, last, ultimate, supreme, closing; extreme, polar; definitive, conclusive, crowning, completing 725 *completive*; conterminal, conterminous, coterminous; ended, at an end; settled, terminated, finalized, decided, set at rest; over, over and done with; off, all off, cancelled; played out, finished; eschatological; penultimate, last but one; antepenultimate, last but two; hindmost, rear 238 *back*; caudal.

Vb. *end*, come to an end, expire, run out 111 *elapse*; close, finish, conclude, be all over; become extinct, die out 361 *die*, 2 *pass away*; come to a close, draw to a c., have run its course; fade away, peter out, tail off; stop, clock out, go home 145 *cease*.

terminate, conclude, close, determine, decide, settle; apply the closure, bring to an end, put an end to, put a term to, put a stop to, make an end of, put paid to; discontinue, drop, pursue no further; finish, achieve, consummate, get through, play out, act o., see it o. 725 *carry through*; ring down the curtain, draw stumps, put up the shutters, shut up shop, wind up, close down, call it a day; switch off, ring off, hang up, stop 145 *halt*.

Adv. *finally*, in conclusion, in fine; at last, at long last; once for all, for good, for good and all; never again, nevermore; to the bitter end, to the utterance, to the last gasp, to the end of the chapter; in the end, in the long run, in the final analysis, when all's said and done.

See: 2, 40, 53, 54, **67**, 111, 124, 129, 145, **157**, 165, 199, 213, 214, 217, 234, 236, 238, 256, 279, 295, 361, 459, 564, 596, 617, **725**, 801.

70 Middle

N. *middle*, midst, midpoint; mean 30 *average*; medium, middle term; thick, thick of things; heart, body, kernel; nave, hub, navel 225 *centre*; nucleus, nucleolus 224 *interiority*; midweek, midwinter, half tide; midstream 625 *middle way*; bisection, midline, equator, the Line 28 *equalization*; midrib, midriff, diaphragm 231 *partition*; half distance, middle d., equidistance, halfway house; intermediate technology; mixed economy 43 *mixture*.

Adj. *middle*, medial, mesial, mean, mezzo, mid 30 *median*; mediate, middlemost, midmost 225 *central*; intermediate, betwixt and between 231 *interjacent*; equidistant; mediterranean, equatorial.

Adv. *midway*, in the middle, in the thick, in medias res; at the midpoint, halfway; midships.

See: 28, **30**, 43, 224, **225**, 231, 625.

71 Continuity: uninterrupted sequence

N. *continuity*, continuousness, uninterruptedness, unbrokenness, monotony 16 *uniformity*; continuation, consecution, overlap; immediacy, directness; consecutiveness, successiveness, succession; line, lineage, descent, dynasty; one thing after another, serialization 65 *sequence*; natural sequence, sere; continuous time, continuum 115 *perpetuity*; continuous motion, assembly line, conveyor belt 146 *continuance*; endless band 315 *rotation*; repetitiveness, alternation, recurrence, cycle 106 *repetition*, 141 *periodicity*, 139 *frequency*; cumulativeness, snowball 36 *increase*; gradualism 278 *slowness*; course, run, career, flow, steady f., trend, steady t. 179 *tendency*; progressiveness 285 *progression*; circuit, round 314 *circuition*; daily round, routine, practice, custom 610 *habit*; track, trail, wake 67 *sequel*; catenation, concatenation, catena, chain, food c.; chain reaction, knock-on effect, domino theory; Möbius strip, circle, vicious c. 250 *circularity*.

series, seriation, gradation 27 *degree*; succession, run, rally, break; progression, arithmetical p., geometrical p.; ascending order 36 *increase*; descending order 37 *decrease*; pedigree, family tree, lineage 169 *genealogy*; chain, line, string, thread; unbroken line, line of battle, line ahead, line abreast; rank, file, echelon; array 62 *arrangement*; row, windrow; range, ridge; colonnade, peristyle, portico; ladder, steps, stairs, staircase 308 *ascent*; range, tier, storey 207 *layer*; keyboard, manual; set, suite, suit (of cards); assortment 77 *classification*; spectrum, rainbow; gamut, scale 410 *musical note*; stepping stones 624 *bridge*; hierarchy, pyramid.

procession 267 *marching*; crocodile, queue, traffic jam; tail, train, suite 67 *retinue*; caravan, file, single f., Indian f.; cortège, funeral procession 364 *obsequies*; triumph, Lord Mayor's Show 876 *celebration*; cavalcade 875 *pageant*.

Adj. *continuous*, continued, run-on 45 *joined*; consecutive, running, successive 65 *sequential*; serial, serialized; seriate, catenary; progressive, gradual 179 *tending*; overlapping, unbroken, solid, smooth, uninterrupted, circular; direct, immediate, unmediated; continuing, ongoing; continual, incessant, ceaseless, unremitting, unintermitted, nonstop, constant 115 *perpetual*; rhythmic 110 *periodic*; repetitive, recurrent, monotonous 106 *repeated*, 16 *uniform*; linear, lineal, rectilinear 249 *straight*.

Vb. *run on*, continue, follow in a series; line up, fall in, queue up, join the queue; succeed, overlap 65 *come after*; file, defile, keep in single file; circle 626 *circuit*.

continue, run on, extend, prolong 113 *spin out*, 203 *lengthen*; serialize, arrange in succession, catenate, thread, string 45 *connect*; size, grade 27 *graduate*; file, tabulate 87 *list*; maintain continuity, keep the kettle boiling 600 *persevere*; keep the succession, provide an heir.

Adv. *continuously*, consecutively etc. adj.; serially, seriatim; successively, in succession, in turn; one after another; at a stretch, together, running; without stopping, on the trot; around the clock, night and day 115 *for ever*; cumulatively, progressively; gradually, step by step, hand over hand 27 *by degrees*; in procession, in file, in single f., in Indian f., in column, in line ahead, nose to tail.

See: 16, 27, 36, 37, 45, 62, **65**, **67**, 77, 87, 106, 110, 113, 115, 139, 141, **146**, 169, 179, 203, 207, 249, 250, 267, 278, 285, 308, 314, 315, 364, 410, 600, 610, 624, 626, 875, 876.

72 Discontinuity: interrupted sequence

N. *discontinuity*, lack of continuity, intermittence; discontinuation, discontinuance 145 *cessation*; interval, hiatus, pause, time lag 145 *lull*; disconnection, disconnectedness, randomness 61 *disorder*; unevenness, joltiness, jerkiness 17 *nonuniformity*, 259 *roughness*; dotted line; broken ranks; ladder, run 46 *disunion*; disruption, interruption, intervention, interposition; parenthesis, episode 231 *interjection*; caesura, division 46 *separation*, 547 *punctuation*; break, fracture, flaw, fault, split, crack, cut 201 *gap*; missing link, lost connection; broken thread, anacoluthon, non sequitur; illogicality, sophism 477 *sophistry*; patchwork, crazy paving 437 *variegation*; incoherence, purple patch 568 *imperspicuity*, 25 *misfit*; alternation 141 *periodicity*; irregularity, ragged volley 142 *fitfulness*.

Adj. *discontinuous*, unsuccessive, nonrecurrent, unrepeated; discontinued; interrupted, broken, stopping; disconnected 46 *disunited*; discrete 46 *separate*; few and far between 140 *infrequent*; patchy, bitty 437 *variegated*; desultory, irregular, intermittent, intermitting 142 *fitful*; alternate, alternating, stop-go, on-off 141 *periodical*; spasmodic, snatchy 17 *nonuniform*; jerky, jolty, bumpy, uneven 259 *rough*; incoherent, anacoluthic 477 *illogical*; parenthetic, episodic, not belonging 303 *inserted*, 59 *extraneous*.

Vb. *be discontinuous*, halt, rest 145 *pause*; alternate, intermit.

discontinue, suspend, break off, desist; interrupt, intervene, chip in, break, break in upon 231 *interfere*; interpose, interject, punctuate 231 *put between*; disconnect, break the connection, snap the thread 46 *disunite*.

Adv. *discontinuously*, at intervals, occasionally, infrequently, irregularly, in jerks and snatches, in fits and starts; skippingly, desultorily; now and then, here and there, passim.

See: 17, 25, 46, 59, **61**, 140, 141, 142, **145**, 201, 231, 259, 303, 437, 477, 547, 568.

73 Term: serial position

N. *serial place*, term, order, remove 27 *degree*; rank, ranking, grade, gradation; station, place, position, slot; status, standing, footing; point, mark, pitch, level, storey; step, tread, round, rung; stage, milestone, climacteric, climax 213 *summit*; bottom rung, nadir 214 *base*.

Vb. *grade*, rank, rate, place; put one in his *or* her place; bring down a peg; stagger, space out 201 *space*, 27 *graduate*.

have rank, hold r., hold a place, occupy a position 186 *be situated*; fall into place, drop into p., find a niche 187 *place oneself*.

See: 27, 186, 187, 201, 213, 214.

74 Assemblage

N. *assemblage*, bringing together, collection 50 *combination*, 62 *arrangement*; collocation, juxtaposition 202 *contiguity*; colligation 45 *joining together*; compilation, corpus, anthology 56 *composition*; gathering, ingathering, reaping, harvest, vintage 370 *agriculture*, 771 *acquisition*; harvest home 632 *storage*, 876 *celebration*; consolidation, concentration; centring, focusing; rallying point 76 *focus*; mobilization, muster, levy, call-up 718 *war measures*; review, parade 875 *pageant*; march, demonstration, rally; whipping in, roundup, lineup; herding, shepherding 369 *animal husbandry*; collectivization, collective, kolkhoz 740 *compulsion*, 370 *farm*; conspiracy, caucus 708 *party*; collective noun, syntax 564 *grammar*.

assembly, mutual attraction 291 *attraction*; getting together, ganging up; forgathering, congregation, concourse, conflux, concurrence 293 *convergence*; gathering, meeting, mass m., meet; coven; conventicle; business meeting, board m.; convention, convocation 985 *synod*; gemot, shire moot, legislature, conclave 692 *council*; eisteddfod, festival 876 *celebration*; reunion, get-together, gathering of the clans 882 *social gathering*; company, at home, party 882 *sociality*; circle, sewing-bee, knit-in; encounter group 658 *therapy*; discussion group, symposium 584 *conference*.

group, constellation, galaxy, cluster 321 *star*; pride (lions), leap (leopards), troop, bevy, swarm, flock, herd; drove, team; pack, kennel; stable, string; nest, eyrie; brood, hatch, litter, kindle (kittens); gaggle, flight, skein, covey, wing (plovers), charm (goldfinches), exaltation (larks); shoal, school; unit, brigade 722 *formation*; batch, lot, clutch; brace, pair, span 90 *duality*; leash, four-in-hand 96 *quaternity*; set, class, genus, species, sub-s. 77 *sort*; breed, tribe, clan, household 11 *family*; brotherhood, sisterhood, fellowship, guild, union 706 *association*; club 708 *society*; sphere, quarter, circle 524 *informant*; charmed circle, coterie 644 *elite*; social group, the classes 868 *nobility*, 869 *commonalty*; in-group, out-group, us and them, they 80 *self*; age group, year g., stream 538 *class*; hand (at cards), set 71 *series*.

band, company, troupe; cast 594 *actor*; brass band, dance b., pop group 413 *orchestra*; team, string, fifteen, eleven, eight; knot, bunch; set, coterie, clique, ring; gang, squad, party, work p., fatigue p.; ship's company, crew, complement, manpower, staff 686 *personnel*; following 67 *retinue*; squadron, troop, platoon; unit, regiment, corps 722 *formation*; squad, posse; force, body, host 722 *armed force*, 104 *multitude*; Boy Scouts, Girl Guides 708 *society*; band of brothers, sisters, merry men 880 *friendship*; committee, commission 754 *consignee*; panel 87 *list*; establishment, cadre 331 *structure*.

crowd, throng 104 *multitude*; huddle, cluster, swarm, colony; small crowd, knot, bunch; the masses, mass, mob, ruck 869 *rabble*; sea of faces, full house, houseful 54 *completeness*; congestion, press, squash, squeeze, jam, scrum, rush, crush; rush hour, crush h. 680 *haste*; flood, spate, deluge, stream, streams of 32 *great quantity*; volley, shower, hail, storm; populousness, overpopulation 36 *increase*; infestation, invasion 297 *ingress*; herd instinct, crowd psychology, mass hysteria 818 *feeling*.

bunch, assortment, lot, mixed l. 43 *medley*; clump, tuft, wisp, handful; pencil (of rays), fan; bag 194 *receptacle*; hand (tobacco), bundle, packet, wad; batch, pack, package, parcel; portfolio, file, dossier 548 *record*; bale, roll, bolt; load, pack 193 *contents*; fascine, faggot; fascicle; tussock, shock, sheaf, stook, truss, heap; swath, rick, stack 632 *storage*; thicket, copse 366 *wood*; bouquet, nosegay, posy, spray; skein, hank.

accumulation, heaping up, cumulation;

agglomeration, conglomeration, conglobation, aggregation; massing, amassment; concentration, collectivization, centralization; pileup 279 *collision*; masonry, mass, pile, pyramid 164 *edifice*, 209 *high structure*; congeries, heap; drift, snowdrift; snowball 36 *increment*; debris, detritus 41 *leavings*; dustheap, dump 641 *rubbish*; cumulus, storm cloud 355 *cloud*; store, storage 633 *provision*, 799 *treasury*; magazine, battery, armoury, quiver 723 *arsenal*; bus garage, car park; set, lot 71 *series*; mixed lot, mixed bag 43 *medley*; kit, stock; range, selection, assortment 795 *merchandise*; shop window, display 522 *exhibit*; museum 632 *collection*; menagerie, aquarium 369 *zoo*; literary collection 589 *library*; miscellanea, miscellany, collectanea, compilation 56 *composition*; symposium, Festschrift 591 *dissertation*.

accumulator, hoarder, squirrel, miser 816 *niggard*, 798 *treasurer*; connoisseur 492 *collector*; gatherer, reaper, harvester, picker, gleaner 370 *farmer*; convener, assembler; whip, whipper-in; shepherd, sheep dog 369 *herdsman*.

Adj. *assembled*, met, well-met, ill-m.; convened, summoned; mobilized, called-up; banded 62 *arranged*; collectivized; crowded, packed, huddled, serried, high-density 324 *dense*; close-printed, tight; populated, over-p., overcrowded, humming with, lousy with, stiff with 54 *full*; populous, teeming, swarming, thick on the ground, thick as flies 104 *multitudinous*; in a crowd, seething, milling; in formation, ranked, in order 62 *arranged*.

Vb. *congregate*, meet, forgather, rendezvous; assemble, reassemble, rejoin; associate, come together, get t., join t., flock t., make a crowd, gather, gather round, collect, troop, rally, roll up, swell the ranks; resort to, centre on, focus on, make for 293 *converge*; band together, gang up; mass, concentrate, mobilize; conglomerate, huddle, cluster, bunch, crowd; throng, swarm, seethe, mill around; surge, stream, flood 36 *grow*; swarm in, infest, invade 297 *burst in*.

bring together, assemble, put together, draw t. 45 *join*; draw, pack them in 291 *attract*; gather, collect, rally, muster, call up, mobilize; concentrate, consolidate; collocate, lump together, group, brigade, unite; compile 56 *compose*; bring into focus, focus, centre; convene, convoke, convocate, summon, hold a meeting; herd, shepherd, get in, whip in, call in, round up, corral 235 *enclose*; mass, aggregate, rake up, dredge up; accumulate, conglomerate, heap, pile, amass; catch, take, rake in, net 771 *acquire*; scrape together, garner 632 *store*; truss, bundle, parcel, package; bunch, bind, colligate 45 *tie*; pack, cram, stuff 54 *fill*; build up, pile up, stack 310 *elevate*.

Adv. *together*, unitedly, as one; collectively, all together, en masse, in a mass, in a body.

See: 11, 32, 36, 41, 43, **45**, **50**, 54, 56, 62, 67, 71, 76, 77, 80, 87, 90, 96, 104, 164, 193, 194, 202, 209, 235, 279, 291, 293, 297, 310, 321, 324, 331, 355, 366, 369, 370, 413, 492, 522, 524, 538, 548, 564, 584, 589, 591, 594, 632, 633, 641, 644, 658, 680, 686, 692, 706, **708**, 718, 722, 723, 740, 754, 771, 795, 798, 799, 816, 818, 868, 869, 875, 876, 880, 882, 985.

75 Nonassembly. Dispersion

N. *dispersion*, scattering, diffraction, breakup 46 *separation*; branching out, fanning o., spread, scatter, radiation 294 *divergence*; sprawl, suburbia; distribution 783 *apportionment*; delegation, decentralization; disintegration 51 *decomposition*; evaporation, boiling away 338 *vaporization*, 337 *liquefaction*; dissipation 634 *waste*; circulation, diffusion; dissemination, broadcasting; interspersion; spraying, sprinkling, circumfusion 341 *moistening*; dispersal, going home; disbandment, demobilization; flotsam and jetsam, sea drift, driftwood 272 *thing transferred*; disjecta membra; waifs and strays, dispersed population, Diaspora.

Adj. *unassembled*, dispersed, disbanded, demobilized etc. vb.; scattered, dotted about, strung out, sporadic, sparse, few and far between 140 *infrequent*; broadcast, diffused; spreading, widespread, far-flung 183 *spacious*; epidemic 79 *universal*; spread, separated, in open order 46 *separate*; dishevelled, streaming, trailing, sprawling 61 *orderless*; decentralized; branching, radiating, centrifugal 294 *divergent*; off-centre, adrift, astray; straggling, wandering 267 *travelling*.

Vb. *be dispersed*, disperse, scatter, spread, spread out, fan o., thin o. 325 *rarefy*;

spread fast, spread like wildfire, flood; radiate, branch, branch out 294 *diverge*; break up, break ranks, fall out 46 *separate*; lose coherence, break away 49 *come unstuck*; hive off, go off on one's own, go each their own ways 267 *wander*; drift away, drift apart; straggle, trail, fall behind 282 *stray*; spread over, sprawl over, cover, litter 226 *overlie*; explode, blow up, burst, fly apart, fly in all directions 176 *be violent*; evaporate, melt 338 *vaporize*, 337 *liquefy*; disintegrate, dissolve, decay 51 *decompose*.

disperse, scatter, diffract; spread out, splay 294 *diverge*; separate 46 *sunder*; thin out, string o.; disseminate, diffuse, broadcast, sow, strew, bestrew, spread; dissipate, dispel, disintegrate 51 *decompose*; scatter to the winds 634 *waste*; dispense, deal, deal out, allot 783 *apportion*; decentralize; break up, disband, disembody, demobilize, dismiss, send home 46 *disunite*; draft, draft off, detach 272 *send*; sprinkle, besprinkle, splash, spray, spatter, bespatter 341 *moisten*; circulate, put into circulation; throw into confusion, disorder 63 *derange*; rout 727 *defeat*.

Adv. *sporadically*, here and there, sparsely, in twos and threes; passim, everywhere, in all quarters.

See: **46**, 49, **51**, 61, 63, 79, 140, 176, 183, 226, 267, 272, 282, **294**, 325, 337, 338, 341, 634, 727, 783.

76 Focus: place of meeting

N. *focus*, focal point, point of convergence, junction, town centre 293 *convergence*, 225 *centre*; crossways, crossroads; switchboard, exchange, nerve centre; hub, nub, core, heart, kernel 70 *middle*; hall, civic centre, community c., village hall, village green; campus, quad; market place 796 *market*; resort, retreat, haunt, stamping ground; club, pub, local 192 *tavern*; headquarters, depot; rallying point, standard; venue, rendezvous, trysting place 192 *meeting place*; nest, home ground 192 *home*; fireside, campfire; cynosure, centre of attraction, honeypot 291 *attraction*; place of pilgrimage, Mecca, Rome, Zion, promised land 295 *goal*, 617 *objective*.

Vb. *focus*, centre on 293 *converge*; centralize, concentrate, focus upon; bring to a point, point to, focus attention on.

See: 70, **192**, **225**, 291, **293**, 295, 617, 796.

77 Class

N. *classification*, categorization 62 *arrangement*; biosystematics, taxonomy; diagnosis, specification, designation; category, class, bracket; set, subset; head, heading, subhead, section, subsection 53 *subdivision*; division, branch, department, faculty; pocket, pigeonhole 194 *compartment*; tier, rank, caste, status, standing 27 *degree*; province, domain, sphere, range; sex, gender; blood group, age g., stream 74 *group*; coterie, clique 74 *band*; persuasion, school of thought, denomination 978 *sect*.

sort, order, type, version, variety, kind, species; manner, genre, style; nature, quality, grade, calibre 5 *character*; mark, brand 547 *label*; ilk, stripe, kidney, feather, colour; stamp, mould, shape, frame, make 243 *form*; assortment, kit, set, suit, lot 71 *series*.

breed, strain, blood, family, kin, tribe, clan, sept, caste, line 11 *race*, 169 *genealogy*; kingdom, phylum, class, order, genus, species, subspecies; genotype, monotype.

Adj. *generic*, typical; sexual, masculine, feminine, neuter.

classificatory, classificational, taxonomic; sectional, denominational 978 *sectarian*.

See: 5, 11, 27, **53**, 62, 71, **74**, 169, 194, 243, 547, 978.

78 Inclusion

N. *inclusion*, comprising; incorporation, embodiment, assimilation, encapsulation; comprehension, admission, integration 299 *reception*; admissibility, eligibility; membership 775 *participation*; inclusiveness, coverage, full c. 79 *generality*; all-roundness, versatility 694 *skill*; comprehensiveness, no exception, no omission, nothing omitted; set, complete s., complement, package 52 *whole*; package deal 765 *compact*; constitution 56 *composition*; capacity, volume, measure 183 *space*, 465 *measurement*; accommodation 183 *room*.

Adj. *inclusive*, including, comprising, counting, containing, having; holding, consisting of 56 *composing*; incorporative, incorporating; fully-furnished, all-inclusive, all-in; nonexclusive, nondiscriminatory, accommodating; overall, all-embracing 52 *comprehensive*; wholesale, blanket, sweeping 32 *extensive*; without omission, without exception, total, global, worldwide, universal 52 *whole*; encyclopedic, expansive, broad-based 79 *general*.

included, admitted, counted; admissible, eligible; integrated, unsegregated; constituent, making up 56 *composing*; inherent 58 *component*, 5 *intrinsic*; belonging, pertinent 9 *relative*; classified with, of the same class 18 *similar*; congenerous, congeneric 11 *akin*; entered, recorded, on the list 87 *listed*; merged 38 *additional*, 45 *joined*; inner 224 *interior*.

Vb. *be included*, be contained, be comprised, make one of 58 *be one of*; enlist, enrol oneself, swell the ranks, join, obtain membership 708 *join a party*; come under, fall u. 58 *be one of*; merge in 43 *be mixed*; appertain to, pertain, refer to 9 *be related*; come in, go in, enter into 297 *enter*; constitute 56 *compose*; overlap, inhere, belong 5 *be intrinsic*.

comprise, include, involve, imply, consist of, hold, have, count, boast 56 *contain*; take, measure 28 *be equal*; receive, take in 299 *admit*; accommodate, find room for; comprehend, encapsulate, cover; embody, incorporate; encompass, embrace, encircle, envelop 235 *enclose*; have everything, exhaust the possibilities 54 *be complete*.

number with, count w., reckon among, enumerate with; subsume, place under, classify as; put in, arrange in 62 *class*; not omit, take into account.

Adv. *including*, inclusively; from A to Z; et cetera.

See: 5, 9, 11, 18, 28, 32, 38, 43, 45, **52**, 54, **56**, 58, 62, **79**, 87, 183, 224, 235, 297, 299, 465, 694, 708, 765, 775.

79 Generality

N. *generality*, universality, general applicability; catholicity, catholicism; ecumenicity, ecumenicalism 976 *orthodoxy*; universalism; generalization, universal; macrocosm 321 *universe*; globalization, world-view; panorama, synopsis, conspectus, bird's eye view 52 *whole*; inclusiveness, comprehensivity, something for everybody, open house, dragnet 78 *inclusion*; currency, prevalence, custom 610 *habit*, 848 *fashion*; pervasiveness, rifeness, ubiquity 189 *presence*; pandemic, epidemic 651 *disease*; broadness, looseness, imprecision 495 *inexactness*, 464 *indiscrimination*; open letter, circular 528 *publicity*; commonness, ruck, run, general r., run of the mill 30 *average*; ordinariness 732 *averageness*; internationalism, cosmopolitanism 901 *philanthropy*; impersonality; categorization 77 *classification*.

everyman, everywoman; man *or* woman in the street, man on the Clapham omnibus, little man; common type 30 *common man*; everybody, every one, each one, one and all, the long and the short and the tall, all and sundry, every mother's son, every man Jack, all hands 52 *all*; all the world and his wife, Tom, Dick and Harry, the masses 869 *commonalty*; all sorts, anyone, whosoever, N or M; anything, whatsoever, what have you, what you will 562 *no name*.

Adj. *general*, generic, typical, representative, standard; encyclopedic, broad-based; collective, all-embracing, pan-, blanket, across-the-board 52 *comprehensive*; broad, sweeping, panoramic, synoptic; current, prevalent 189 *ubiquitous*; usual, normal, unexceptional, customary 610 *habitual*; vague, loose, indefinite 495 *inexact*; undetermined, unspecified, undenominational, unsectarian, impersonal 10 *unrelated*; common, ordinary, average 30 *median*; commonplace 83 *typical*; popular, mass, vulgar 869 *plebeian*; for everybody, for every occasion, multipurpose.

universal, catholic, ecumenical; national, international, cosmopolitan, global, worldwide, nationwide, widespread 32 *extensive*; pervasive, penetrating, besetting, rampant, prevalent, epidemic, pandemic 189 *ubiquitous*; every, each, any, all, all without exception 52 *whole*.

Vb. *be general*, cover all cases 78 *comprise*; prevail, obtain, be the rule, have currency 610 *be wont*; penetrate 189 *pervade*.

generalize, render general etc. adj.; broaden, widen, universalize, globalize; spread, broadcast, diffuse 75 *disperse*.

Adv. *generally*, without exception, universally etc. adj.; mainly 52 *wholly*; to a man, to the last m.; always, for better for worse; generally speaking, in the long run, by and large 30 *on an average*; loosely, vaguely.

See: 10, **30**, 32, **52**, 75, 77, **78**, 83, 189, 321, 464, 495, 528, 562, 610, 651, 732, 848, 869, 901, 976.

80 Speciality

N. *speciality*, specific quality, specificity, personality, uniqueness; singularity 88 *unity*; originality, individuality, particularity; personality, make-up 5 *character*; characteristic, personal c., recessive c., dominant c., one's middle name; idiosyncrasy, eccentricity, peculiarity, distinctive feature, trademark, mannerism, quirk, foible; trait, mark, feature, attribute; sine qua non 89 *accompaniment*; distinction, point of difference, differentiae 15 *difference*; idiom, peculiar i.; jargon, brogue, patois 560 *dialect*; technical language, private l., idiolect 557 *language*; variant reading, version, lection 15 *variant*; exception, isolated instance, special case 84 *nonconformity*; specialty, special skill, special study, specialization 694 *skill*.

particulars, details, minutiae, items, counts, special points, specification; circumstances; the ins and outs of.

particularism, chosen race, chosen few, the elect; exclusiveness, class consciousness, caste; chauvinism, nationality, nationalism, individualism, egoism.

self, ego, id, identity, selfhood, personality 320 *subjectivity*; atman, psyche, soul 447 *spirit*; I, myself, number one; we, ourselves; yourself, himself, herself, itself, themselves; us, in-group 74 *group*; real self, inner s.; outward s.; a person, a character, individual, being 371 *person*.

Adj. *special*, specific, respective, particular; sui generis, peculiar, singular, unique 88 *one*; individual, idiosyncratic, characteristic, idiomatic, original 21 *inimitable*; native, proper, personal, private; appropriate 24 *apt*; typical, diagnostic 5 *characteristic*; distinctive, uncommon, marked, noteworthy, out of the ordinary 84 *unusual*; several 15 *different*.

definite, definitive, defining; determinate, quantified, specified; distinct, concrete, express, explicit, clear-cut, clean-c., cut and dried; certain, exact, precise 494 *accurate*; itemized, detailed, circumstantial; bespoke, made to order, made to measure, personalized.

private, intimate, esoteric, personal, exclusive; patented; extra-professional; off the record, for one's private ear, secret 523 *latent*.

Vb. *specify*, be specific, express in figures, enumerate, quantify 86 *number*; particularize, itemize, detail, inventorize 87 *list*; cite, mention, name names 561 *name*; descend to particulars, enter into detail, spell out 570 *be diffuse*; define, determine 236 *limit*, 463 *discriminate*; pinpoint, locate 187 *place*; come to the point, explain 520 *interpret*; signify, denote 514 *mean*; designate, point out 547 *indicate*; realize, translate into fact, substantiate 156 *cause*; individualize, personalize 15 *differentiate*; specialize 455 *be attentive*, 536 *study*.

Adv. *specially*, especially, in particular; personally, for one's own part; specifically, ad hoc, ad hominem, to order; with respect to.

severally, each, apiece, one by one; respectively, in turn, seriatim; in detail, bit by bit.

namely, that is to say, videlicet, viz., to wit, i.e., e.g.

See: **5**, **15**, 21, 24, 74, 84, 86, 87, 88, 89, 156, 187, 236, 320, 371, 447, 455, 463, 494, 514, 520, 523, 536, 547, 557, 560, 561, 570, 694.

81 Rule

N. *rule*, norm, formula, canon, code; maxim, principle 693 *precept*; law, law of nature, universal principle; firm principle, hard and fast rule; strict law, law of the Medes and Persians; statute, by-law 953 *law*; regulation, order, standing o., party line; guide, precedent, model, pattern 23 *prototype*; form, standard, keynote 83 *example*.

regularity, consistency, constancy 16 *uniformity*; order, natural o., established o. 60 *order*; normality, normalcy, normal state, natural condition; form, set f., routine, drill, practice, custom 610 *habit*; fixed ways, rut, groove, tramlines; methodicalness, method, system 62 *arrangement*; convention 83 *conformity*.

Adj. *regular*, constant, steady 141 *periodical*; even 258 *smooth*; circular, square 245 *symmetrical*; standardized 16 *uniform*; regulated, according to rule, methodical, systematic 60 *orderly*; regulative, normative; legal, technical; normal, unexceptional 83 *typical*; customary 610 *usual*; conforming, conventional 83 *conformable*.

Adv. *to rule*, by the book, by the clock; regularly.

See: 16, 23, **60**, **62**, 83, 141, 245, 258, 610,

693, 953.

82 Multiformity

N. *multiformity*, multiplicity, omnifariousness; heterogeneity, variety, diversity 17 *nonuniformity*; multifariousness, many-sidedness, many-headedness, polymorphism 101 *plurality*; schizophrenia, split personality, multiple p. 503 *psychopathy*; metamorphism, metamorphosis; variability, changeability 152 *changeableness*, 437 *variegation*; capriciousness 604 *caprice*; all-rounder; Proteus, Jekyll and Hyde; kaleidoscope.

Adj. *multiform*, multifarious, polymorphous, polymorphic; multifid; multiple, multiplex, multiplicate, manifold, many-headed, many-sided, hydra-headed, omnigenous, omnifarious; metamorphic; protean, versatile, all-round; variform, heterogeneous, diverse 17 *nonuniform*; motley, mosaic, kaleidoscopic 43 *mixed*; epicene; indiscriminate, irregular, diversified, many-coloured, polychrome 437 *variegated*; divers, sundry; all manner of, of every description, of all sorts and kinds 15 *different*; variable, changeable 152 *changeful*; whimsical 604 *capricious*; polypsychical; schizophrenic.

See: 15, **17**, 43, 101, 152, **437**, 503, 604.

83 Conformity

N. *conformity*, conformation 24 *conformance*; faithfulness 768 *observance*; accommodation, adjustment, reconcilement, reconciliation 24 *agreement*, *adaptation*; self-adaptation, pliancy, malleability 327 *softness*; acquiescence 721 *submission*; assimilation, acclimatization, naturalization 147 *conversion*, 18 *similarity*; conventionality, conventionalism, bourgeois ethic 848 *etiquette*; traditionalism; orthodoxness 976 *orthodoxy*; formalism, strictness 735 *severity*; convention, form 848 *fashion*, 610 *practice*; Babbittry 850 *affectation*; parrotry, emulation 106 *repetition*, 925 *flattery*, 20 *imitation*; ordinariness 79 *generality*.

example, exemplar, type, pattern, model 23 *prototype*; exemplification, stock example, locus classicus; case, case in point, instance, palmary i.; illustration, practical demonstration, object lesson; sample, random s., cross-section; representative, specimen, specimen page, representative selection; trailer, foretaste 66 *precursor*; precedent.

conformist, conventionalist, traditionalist; philistine, Babbitt; organization man; formalist, pedant, precisian; copycat, yes-man 20 *imitator*, 925 *flatterer*; follower, loyalist 976 *the orthodox*.

Adj. *conformable*, adaptable, adjustable, consistent with; malleable, pliant 327 *flexible*; agreeable, complaisant, accommodating 24 *agreeing*; conforming, following, faithful, loyal, true-blue 768 *observant*; conventional, traditional 976 *orthodox*; slavish, servile 20 *imitative*, 925 *flattering*; adjusted, adapted, acclimatized 610 *habituated*; absorbed, digested, assimilated, naturalized 78 *included*.

typical, normal, natural, of daily occurrence, everyday, ordinary, common, common or garden 79 *general*; average 30 *median*, 732 *middling*; true to type; commonplace, prosaic; conventional; heterosexual, straight; habitual 610 *usual*; representative, stock, standard; normative, exemplary, illustrative; in point 9 *relevant*.

regulated, according to the book, according to rule, regular; shipshape, copybook 60 *orderly*; correct, sound, proper, canonical 976 *orthodox*; precise, scrupulous, meticulous 875 *formal*; rigid, strict, unbending, uncompromising, Procrustean 735 *severe*.

Vb. *conform*, correspond, conform to 24 *accord*; adapt oneself, accommodate o., adjust o., mould o.; fit in, know one's place; pass, pass muster 635 *suffice*; bend, yield, take the shape of 327 *soften*; fall into line, toe the l., fall in with 721 *submit*; comply with 768 *observe*; tally with, fit in with 24 *accord*; rubberstamp, echo 106 *repeat*; stick to the rules, obey regulations, follow precedent 739 *obey*; keep in step, follow the fashion, follow the crowd, do as others do, do as the Romans do; join in the cry, jump on the bandwagon, keep up with the Joneses 848 *be in fashion*; emulate, follow suit 20 *imitate*, *copy*; have no will of one's own, drift with the tide, swim with the stream 601 *be irresolute*; follow in the steps of, keep to the beaten track, run on tramlines, run in a groove, stick in a rut 610 *be wont*.

make conform, conform, assimilate, naturalize 18 *liken*; acclimatize 610 *habituate*; bring under rule, systematize 62 *regularize*; normalize, conventionalize, standardize; put in uniform, drill 16 *make uniform*; shape, press 243 *form*; stamp, imprint 547 *mark*; train, lead 689 *direct*; bend, twist, force 740 *compel*; accommodate, fit, fit in, square, trim, cut down to size 24 *adjust*; rub off the corners 258 *smooth*.

exemplify, illustrate, cite, quote, instance; produce an example, give an instance.

Adv. *conformably*, conventionally etc. adj.; to rule; by the book; in conformity, in line with, in accordance, in keeping; according to; according to plan; consistently with; as usual, of course, as a matter of c.; for form's sake; for the look of it; for example, for instance.

See: 9, 16, 18, 20, 23, **24**, 30, 60, 62, 66, 78, **79**, 106, 147, 243, 258, 327, 547, 601, **610**, 635, 689, 721, 732, 735, 739, 740, 768, 848, 850, 875, 925, 976.

84 Nonconformity

N. *nonconformity*, nonconformance, unconformity, inconsistency 25 *disagreement*, 17 *nonuniformity*; contrast, oasis 14 *contrariety*; exceptionality, strangeness 59 *extraneousness*; nonconformism, unorthodoxy 977 *heterodoxy*; disconformity, dissidence 489 *dissent*, 769 *nonobservance*; deviationism, Titoism 744 *independence*; anomalousness, eccentricity, irregularity 282 *deviation*; informality, unconventionality, angularity, awkwardness 893 *sullenness*; bizarrerie, piquancy, freakishness, oddity; rarity 140 *infrequency*; infringement, infraction, infraction of the rules, violation of the law 954 *illegality*; breach of practice, defiance of custom, departure from usage; wonder, miracle 864 *prodigy*; anomaly, exception 57 *exclusion*; exemption, escape clause 919 *nonliability*; special case, isolated instance 80 *speciality*; individuality, idiosyncrasy, quirk, kink, peculiarity, singularity, mannerism; uniqueness 21 *originality*.

abnormality, aberration 282 *deviation*; mutation 15 *variant*; abortion, monstrous birth, terata, teratogenesis, monstrosity, monster; sexual abnormality, bisexuality; sexual inversion, homosexuality, lesbianism, Sapphism; necrophilia, sadism, masochism; transvestism; virilism, gynandry 372 *male*; androgyny 373 *female*; hermaphroditism 161 *impotence*.

nonconformist, dissident, deviationist, dissenter, maverick 489 *dissentient*, 977 *heretic*, 978 *sectarian*; nonstriker, blackleg, scab 938 *cad*; unconventionalist, Bohemian, hippie, dropout, longhaired weirdie; rebel, angry young man, punk, handful, recalcitrant 738 *revolter*; fanatic 504 *crank*; outsider, outlaw, criminal 904 *offender*; pariah 883 *outcast*; hermit, loner 883 *solitary*; gipsy, nomad, tramp 268 *wanderer*; odd man out, joker, ugly duckling; square peg in a round hole, fish out of water 25 *misfit*; heteroclite, deviant, odd type, albino, sport, freak, f. of nature, lusus naturae; oddity, original, character, card, caution, odd customer, oddball, weirdo 504 *crank*; queer fish 851 *laughingstock*; curiosity, rarity, rare example, one in a million; neither fish, flesh, fowl nor good red herring, neither one thing nor the other; transsexual, hermaphrodite, gynander, androgyne 161 *eunuch*; invert, homosexual, lesbian, gay; pansy, fairy, nancy, poof, poofter, queen, queer; transvestite 143 *transformation*; pervert; sadist, masochist; mongrel, half-breed, half-blood 43 *hybrid*.

rara avis, mythical beast, unicorn, phoenix, griffin, simurg, roc; sphinx, hippogriff, manticore, chimera, centaur, Minotaur; dragon, wyvern, firedrake, cockatrice, basilisk, salamander, hydra; sea serpent, leviathan, kraken, Loch Ness monster; merman, mermaid, siren, Lorelei; gorgon, cyclops 970 *mythical being*; snark, Jabberwocky 513 *fantasy*.

Adj. *unconformable*, inadjustable 25 *unapt*; antipathetic 14 *contrary*; unmalleable, stiff 326 *rigid*, 602 *obstinate*; recalcitrant 711 *defiant*; crotchety, prickly, awkward, eccentric, whimsical 604 *capricious*, 893 *sullen*; arbitrary, a law unto oneself 744 *independent*; freakish, outlandish; original, sui generis, unique 80 *special*; solitary, standoffish 883 *unsociable*; blacklegging 603 *tergiversating*; nonconformist, dissident 489 *dissenting*, 978 *sectarian*; unorthodox, heretical 977 *heterodox*; unconverted, nonpractising 769 *nonobservant*; unconventional, offbeat, Bohemian, informal, unfashionable; irregular, against the rules, not done 924 *disapproved*; infringing, lawless, criminal 954 *illegal*; aberrant, astray, off the beam, off the rails 282 *deviating*; misplaced, out of one's element, out of place, ectopic, out of order 188 *displaced*, 61 *orderless*; incongruous, out of step, out of line, out of tune, out of keeping 25 *disagreeing*; alien, exotic 59 *extraneous*; unidentifiable, unclassifiable, hard to place, nondescript, nameless 491 *unknown*; stray, nomadic, wandering 267 *travelling*; amphibious, ambiguous 518 *equivocal*; exempted, exempt 919 *nonliable*.

unusual, uncustomary, unwonted 611 *unhabituated*; unfamiliar 491 *unknown*; newfangled 126 *new*; out of the way, exotic 59 *extraneous*; out of the ordinary, extraordinary, way-out; phenomenal, supernormal; unparalleled, unexampled; singular, unique 80 *special*, 140 *infrequent*; rare, choice, recherché 644 *excellent*; strange, bizarre, curious, odd, queer, rum, unco; funny, peculiar, fantastic, grotesque 849 *ridiculous*; noteworthy, remarkable, surprising, astonishing, miraculous 864 *wonderful*; mysterious, inexplicable, unaccountable 523 *occult*; unimaginable, incredible 470 *impossible*, 472 *improbable*; monstrous, miscreated; unnatural, preternatural, supernatural; outsize 32 *enormous*; outré 546 *exaggerated*; shocking, scandalizing 924 *disapproved*; mind-boggling, indescribable 517 *inexpressible*.

abnormal, unnatural, supernatural, preternatural (**see** *unusual*); aberrant, freakish; uncharacteristic, untypical, atypical, unrepresentative, exceptional; anomalous, anomalistic 17 *nonuniform*; morbid, kinky, deviant; homosexual, lesbian, gay, bent, queer; bisexual, AC/DC; epicene, androgynous, gynandrous; mongrel, hybrid 43 *mixed*; irregular, heteroclite; unidiomatic, solecistic 565 *ungrammatical*; nonstandard, substandard, subnormal; supernormal 32 *great*; asymmetrical, deformed, amorphous, shapeless 246 *distorted*.

Vb. *be unconformable*, - unconventional etc. adj.; not fit in, have no business there; be the exception that proves the rule; infringe a law, infringe usage, infringe custom; break a law, break a habit, break with custom; violate a law, violate custom; drop out, freak o., do one's own thing 744 *be free*; be ahead of one's time 135 *be early*; put the clock back 125 *look back*; get round, drive a coach and six through; stretch a point; leave the beaten track; baffle all description, beggar all d.

Adv. *unconformably*, unusually etc. adj.; except, unless, save, barring, beside, without, save and except, let alone; however, yet, but.

See: 14, 15, 17, 21, 25, 32, 43, 57, 59, 61, 80, 125, 126, 135, 140, 143, 161, 188, 246, 267, 268, 282, 326, 372, 373, 470, 472, 489, 491, 504, 513, 517, 518, 523, 546, 565, 602, 603, 604, 611, 644, 711, 738, 744, 769, 849, 851, 864, 883, 893, 904, 919, 924, 938, 954, 970, 977, 978.

Section five: Number

85 Number

N. *number*, any n., real number, imaginary n.; natural n., cardinal n., ordinal n.; round n., complex n.; prime number, odd n., even n., whole n., integer; irrational n., transcendental n.; numeral, cipher, digit, figure, character; numerals, Arabic n., Roman n., algorism; decimal system, binary s.; quantity, unknown q., X, symbol, constant; mapping; operator, sign; function, variable, argument; vector, matrix, tensor, quaternion; surd; expression, quadratics; formula, series.

numerical element, minuend, subtrahend; multiplicand, multiplier; coefficient, multiple, dividend, divisor, aliquant, aliquot; quotient, factor, submultiple, fraction, proper f., improper f.; mixed number; numerator, denominator; decimal, recurring d., repetend; common factor, common denominator; reciprocal, complement; parameter; power, root, square r., cube r.; exponent, index, logarithm, natural l., mantissa, antilogarithm; modulus, differential, derivative, integral, integrand, determinant, fluxion.

ratio, proportion; progression, arithmetical progression, geometrical p., harmonic p.; trigonometrical ratio, sine, tangent, secant; cosine, cotangent, cosecant; pi; percentage, per cent, percentile.

numerical result, answer, product, equation; sum, total, aggregate 52 *whole*; difference, residual 41 *remainder*; bill, score, tally 38 *addition*.

Adj. *numerical*, numerary, numeral, digital; arithmetical; cardinal, ordinal; round, whole; even, odd; prime; figurate; positive, negative, surd, radical; divisible, aliquot; multiple; reciprocal, complementary; fractional, decimal;

incommensurable; commensurable, proportional; exponential, logarithmic, differential, fluxional, integral; algebraic, transcendental; rational, irrational.
See: 38, 41, 52.

86 Numeration

N. *numeration*, numbering, enumeration, census, counting, ciphering, figuring, reckoning, dead r.; sum, tally, score, runs, points; count, recount, countdown; figure-work, summation, calculation, computation 465 *measurement*; page-numbering, pagination; algorithm, decimal system; accountancy 808 *accounts*; counting heads, poll, capitation; head-count, hand-c.; numeracy.

numerical operation, figure-work, notation; addition, subtraction, multiplication, division, proportion, rule of three, practice, equations, analysis, extraction of roots, reduction, involution, evolution, convolution, approximation, extrapolation, interpolation; differentiation, integration, permutation, combination, variation.

mathematics, pure m., applied m., arithmetic, algebra; quadratic equations; set theory, modern maths; differential calculus, integral c., infinitesimal c., vector c.; fluxions; calculus of variations; topology; geometry, trigonometry; graphs, logarithms; algorithm, systems analysis (**see** *data processing*); operational research, critical path analysis, linear programming 623 *policy*; axiomatics 475 *reasoning*.

statistics, figures, tables, averages; mode, mean 30 *average*; significance, deviation, normal d., standard d., standard error; distribution curve, skew; regression; correlation, rank c. test, chi-squared t.; statistical enquiry, poll, Gallup p. (tdmk) 605 *vote*; census, capitation; roll call, muster, muster roll, account 87 *list*; demography, birth rate, death r.; vital statistics; price index, cost of living 809 *price*; bar graph, histogram, scatter diagram, pie chart, flow c. 623 *plan*; cartogram 551 *map*.

data processing, electronic d.p., EDP, computing, computation; computer technology, cybernetics 630 *mechanics*; software, program, computer p.; input, output, throughput, feedback; storage, retrieval; batch processing, time-sharing, multiprogramming; machine code, computer language, BASIC, Fortran, Algol, Cobol; hardware (**see** *counting instrument*); card punch, keypunch, keyboard; data, bit, byte; punched cards, magnetic tape, floppy disk; processor, word processor; central processing unit; data bank, memory 632 *store*; visual display unit, VDU 445 *appearance*; hard copy, printout; viewdata 524 *information*.

counting instrument, abacus, suanpan, quipu; ready reckoner, multiplication table; tape measure, yardstick 465 *gauge*; sliding rule, slide r.; tallies, counters, Cuisenaire rods, Napier's bones; (tdmk) comptometer, calculating machine, calculator, pocket c.; cash register, totalizator, tote; computer, digital c., analogue c; mainframe; microcomputer, minicomputer, microprocessor 196 *microelectronics*.

enumerator, numberer, computer, census-taker; calculator, counter, teller, pollster; mathematician, wrangler; arithmetician, geometrician, geometer, algebraist; programmer, computer p., computernik, systems analyst 623 *planner*; statistician, actuary, bookkeeper 808 *accountant*; geodesist 465 *surveyor*.

Adj. *numerable*, numberable, countable; calculable, computable, measurable, mensurable 465 *metrical*; commensurable, commensurate 28 *equal*; proportionate 9 *relative*; incommensurable, incommensurate 29 *unequal*, 10 *unrelated*; eligible, admissible 78 *included*.

statistical, expressed in numbers, digital, ciphered, numbered, figured out; mathematical, arithmetical, algebraical; geometrical, trigonometrical; in ratio, in proportion, percentile, quartile.

computerized, automatic, on-line, off-line; programmable, processable; real-time, random-access; analogue, digital, binary, alphanumeric.

Vb. *number*, cast, count, tell; score, keep the s., keep a count, notch up; tell off, tick off, count down; affix numbers, foliate, paginate; enumerate, poll, count heads, count hands; take the number, take a poll, take a census; muster, call over, call the roll, take roll call; take stock, inventory 87 *list*; recount, go over 106 *repeat*; check, audit, balance, keep accounts 808 *account*; aggregate, amount to, add up to, total, tot up to, come to.

do sums, cast up, count up, carry over, totalize, tot up 38 *add*; take away 39 *subtract*; multiply 36 *augment*; divide 46 *sunder*; square, cube, extract roots; integrate, differentiate; figure, cipher; work out, reduce; map; compute, calculate, reckon, reckon up 465 *measure*; estimate 465 *appraise*.

computerize, automate 160 *empower*; digitize, digitalize; program, process; debug; compute 173 *operate*.

See: 9, 10, 28, 29, 30, 36, 38, 39, 46, 78, 87, 106, 160, 173, 196, 445, **465**, 475, 524, 551, 605, 623, 630, 632, **808**, 809.

87 List

N. *list*, enumeration, items; list of items, inventory, stock list; chart, table, catalogue, listing; portfolio 767 *security*; statement, tabular s., schedule, manifest, bill of lading; checklist; invoice; numerical list, score; price list, tariff, bill, account, itemized a. 809 *price*; registry, cartulary; cadastre, terrier, Domesday Book; file, register, death r., birth r. 548 *record*; ticket, docket, tally 547 *label*; ledger, books 808 *account book*; table of contents, index, card i. 547 *indication*; bill of fare, menu, calorie table 301 *eating*; playbill, programme, prospectus, synopsis, syllabus 592 *compendium*; roll, electoral r., voting list 605 *electorate*; muster roll, payroll; Army List, Navy L., active l., retired l. 686 *personnel*; statistical list, census 86 *numeration*; book list, bibliography, catalogue raisonnée 589 *reading matter*; discography, filmography; list of names, rota, roster, panel; waiting list, short l.; string of names, visitors' book; dramatis personae; family tree, pedigree 169 *genealogy*; scroll, roll of honour, honours' board, martyrology, beadroll, diptych; blacklist 928 *accused person*, 924 *censure*; sick list 651 *sick person*; list of dates, calendar, engagement book 505 *reminder*; question paper, questionnaire; alphabetical list, alphabet 60 *order*, 558 *letter*; repertory, repertoire.

word list, vocabulary, glossary, lexicon, thesaurus, gradus 559 *dictionary*.

directory, gazetteer, atlas; almanac, calendar, timetable 117 *chronology*; Bradshaw, ABC 524 *guidebook*; Army List, Navy L., Crockford, Debrett, Burke's Peerage, Who's Who 589 *reference book*.

Adj. *listed*, entered, catalogued, tabulated, indexed; cadastral.

Vb. *list*, make a l., enumerate; itemize, inventory, catalogue, calendar, index, tabulate; file, docket, schedule, enter, book, post 548 *register*; enlist, matriculate, enrol, empanel, inscribe; score, keep the s., keep count 86 *number*.

See: 60, 86, 117, 169, 301, 505, **524**, 547, **548**, 558, 559, **589**, 592, 605, 651, 686, 767, 808, 809, 924, 928.

88 Unity

N. *unity*, oneness, absoluteness 44 *simpleness*; consubstantiality 13 *identity*; integrality, integration, wholeness 52 *whole*; uniqueness, singularity, individuality 80 *speciality*; monotheism; monism; singleness 895 *celibacy*; isolation, solitude, loneliness 883 *seclusion*; isolability 46 *separation*; union, undividedness, indivisibility, solidarity 48 *coherence*, 706 *association*; unification 50 *combination*.

unit, integer, one, ace, item, piece; individual, atom, monad, entity 371 *person*; single piece, monolith; singleton, nonce word; none else, no other, naught beside; single instance, isolated i., only exception; solo, monologue; single person, bachelor 895 *celibate*; single parent 896 *divorce, widowhood*; hermit 883 *solitary*; set, outfit, package 78 *inclusion*; package deal.

Adj. *one*, not plural, singular, sole, single, solitary; unique, only, lone, one and only; one and the same 13 *identical*; unrepeated, only-begotten; without a second, first and last; once only, one-off; a, an, a certain 562 *anonymous*; individual 80 *special*; absolute, universal 79 *general*; unitary, unific, univocal, unicameral, unilateral, unicellular; mono-; all of a piece, monolithic 16 *uniform*; unified, rolled into one, compact, solid 45 *joined*; 324 *dense*, 48 *cohesive*; indivisible, indissoluble.

alone, lonely, homeless, orphaned, deserted, forsaken 883 *friendless*; lonesome, solitary, lone 883 *unsociable*; isolable, isolated 46 *disunited*; insular, enisled 199 *distant*; single-handed, on one's own; by oneself, on one's tod; unaccompanied, unescorted, unchaperoned; unpaired, fellowless, azygous; monadic, monatomic; celibate 895 *unwedded*.

Vb. *be one*, stand alone, stew in one's own juice; unite 50 *combine*; isolate 46 *set apart*.

Adv. *singly*, one by one, one at a time; once, once only, for the nonce, just this once, never again, only, solely, simply; alone, on one's own, by oneself, per se; in the singular.

See: 13, 16, 44, 45, 46, 48, **50**, **52**, 78, 79, 80, 199, 324, 371, 562, 706, **883**, 895, 896.

89 Accompaniment

N. *accompaniment*, concomitance 71 *continuity*, 45 *union*, 5 *intrinsicality*; inseparability, permanent attribute; society 882 *sociability*; companionship, togetherness 880 *friendship*; partnership 706 *association*; coexistence, coagency 181 *concurrence*; coincidence, contemporaneity, simultaneity 123 *synchronism*; attendance, company; parallel course 219 *parallelism*.

concomitant, attribute, sine qua non 5 *essential part*; complement 54 *completeness*; accessory, appendage, appurtenance, fixture 40 *adjunct*; by-product, corollary; epiphenomenon, symptom 547 *indication*; coincidence 159 *chance*; context, circumstance 7 *state*; background, noises off; accompaniment, obbligato; accompanist 413 *musician*; entourage, court 742 *retainer*; attendant, following, suite 67 *retinue*; convoy, escort, guide 690 *leader*; chaperon, bodyguard 660 *protector*, 749 *keeper*; suitor, wooer 887 *lover*; tracker 619 *hunter*; inseparable, shadow, Mary's little lamb 284 *follower*; consort 894 *spouse*; comrade, companion, boon c. 880 *friend*; stable companion, yokefellow, mate, co-worker, partner, associate 707 *colleague*; accomplice 707 *collaborator*; twin, fellow 18 *analogue*; satellite, parasite, hanger-on 742 *dependant*.

Adj. *accompanying*, with, concomitant, attendant, background; always with, inseparable, built-in 45 *joined*; partnering, associated, coupled, paired; hand-in-glove 706 *cooperative*, 181 *concurrent*; obbligato 410 *harmonious*; accessory, belonging 78 *included*, 58 *component*; satellite, satellitic 745 *subject*; parallel, collateral; incidental, coincidental 159 *casual*; coexistent, contemporaneous, contemporary, simultaneous.

Vb. *accompany*, be found with, be seen w.; coexist; cohabit, live with, walk w., keep company w., consort w., walk out w.; string along with; attend, wait on, come to heel, dance attendance on 284 *follow*; bear one company, squire, chaperon, protect 660 *safeguard*; convoy, escort, guide, conduct, lead, usher, bring in tow 64 *come before*; track, dog, shadow 619 *pursue*; associate with, partner 706 *cooperate*; gang up with, chum up w. 880 *befriend*; coincide, keep time with 123 *synchronize*, 181 *concur*; imply 5 *be intrinsic*; carry with, bring in its train 156 *cause*; be inseparable, go hand in hand with, follow as night follows day 157 *depend*; belong, go with, go together 9 *be related*.

Adv. *with*, herewith 38 *in addition*; together with, along w., in company w.; in the same boat; in convoy, hand in hand, arm in arm, side by side; cheek by jowl; jointly, all together, in a body, collectively, inseparably, unitedly.

See: 5, 7, 9, 18, 38, **40**, 45, 54, 58, 64, 67, 71, **78**, 123, 156, 157, 159, **181**, 219, 284, 410, 413, 547, 619, 660, 690, 706, 707, 742, 745, 749, 880, 882, 887, 894.

90 Duality

N. *duality*, dualism; double-sidedness; double life, dual personality, Jekyll and Hyde; positive and negative, yin and yang 14 *polarity*; dyad, two, deuce, duo, twain, couple, Darby and Joan, Jack and Jill; brace, pair; doublets, twins, Castor and Pollux, Gemini, Siamese twins, identical t., Tweedledum and Tweedledee 18 *analogue*; yoke, span, double file; couplet, distich; double harness, twosome, two-hander; duel; duet; tandem, two-seater; biped; bivalve; Janus.

Adj. *dual*, dualistic; dyadic, binary, binomial; bilateral, bicameral; twin, biparous; double-barrelled, duplex 91 *double*; paired, coupled etc. vb.; conjugate, binate; two abreast, two by two; in twos, both; tête-à-tête, à deux; double-sided, bipartisan; amphibious; ambidextrous 91 *double*; bifocal; biform, two-dimensional, two-faced; dihedral; di-, bi-.

Vb. *pair*, couple, match, bracket, yoke; mate, pair off.

See: 14, 18, **91**.

91 Duplication

N. *duplication*, doubleness; doubling 261 *fold*; gemination, reduplication, encore, repeat, repeat performance; iteration, echo 106 *repetition*; renewal 656 *restoration*; copy, carbon c., photocopy 22 *duplicate*; double exposure; living image 18 *analogue*.

Adj. *double*, doubled, twice; duplex, bifarious; biform; twofold, two-sided, two-headed, two-edged; bifacial, double-faced; amphibious, ambidextrous; dual-purpose, two-way; of double meaning 518 *equivocal*; bisexual, hermaphrodite; twin, duplicate, geminate; second; dualistic 90 *dual*.

Vb. *double*, multiply by two; redouble, square; geminate, encore, echo, second 106 *repeat*; renew 656 *restore*; duplicate, twin; reduplicate, stencil 20 *copy*.

Adv. *twice*, two times, once more; over again 106 *again*; as much again, twofold; secondly, in the second place, again; twice as much, twice over; doubly.

See: 18, 20, **22**, **90**, **106**, 261, 518, 656.

92 Bisection

N. *bisection*, bipartition, dichotomy; dividing by two, halving etc. vb.; hendiadys; half, moiety, fifty per cent 53 *part*; hemistich; hemisphere 252 *sphere*.

bifurcation, forking, branching, furcation 294 *divergence*; swallowtail, fork, prong 222 *cross*.

dividing line, diameter, diagonal, equator; parting, seam; date line; party wall 231 *partition*.

Adj. *bisected*, halved etc. vb.; dimidiate, bifid, bipartite; bicuspid; bifurcate, bifurcated, forked; dichotomic, dichotomous; semi-, demi-, hemi-; split, cloven, cleft 46 *disunited*.

Vb. *bisect*, transect; divide, split, cleave 46 *sunder*; cut in two, dimidiate, dichotomize; share, go halves, go fifty-fifty 783 *apportion*; halve, divide by two.

bifurcate, separate, fork; branch off, ramify 294 *diverge*.

See: 46, 53, 222, 231, 252, **294**, 783.

93 Triality

N. *triality*, trinity, trimurti; triunity; trimorphism; triplicity 94 *triplication*.

three, triad, trine; Fates, Furies, Graces; Faith, Hope and Charity; threesome, triumvirate, leash; troika; triplet, trey, trio, tern, trigon; trimester, triennium; trefoil, shamrock, triangle, trident, tripod, trivet, triskelion; three-wheeler, tricycle; three-decker, three-hander; three-headed monster, Cerberus; triphthong, triptych, trilogy, triolet, trimeter; third power, cube; third person, gooseberry; tertium quid.

Adj. *three*, trinal, triadic, triform, trinomial; three in one, triune, tripartite; triphibious; tricolour; three-dimensional, tridimensional; three-sided, triangular, deltoid, trigonal, trilateral; three-pointed; three-pronged, three-cornered; tricorn, tricuspid, tridentate; three-monthly, trimestrial, quarterly; tri-.

Adv. *in threes*, three by three; three times, thrice.

See: 94.

94 Triplication

N. *triplication*, triplicity; trebleness; hat trick; tercentenary.

Adj. *treble*, triple; trine, trinal, ternary; triplex, triplicate, threefold, three-ply; third, tertiary; trihedral; trilateral.

Vb. *treble*, triple, triplicate, cube.

Adv. *trebly*, triply, threefold; three times, thrice; in the third place, thirdly, in trine.

95 Trisection

N. *trisection*, tripartition, trichotomy; third, third part; tierce.

Adj. *trifid*, trisected; tripartite, trichotomous, trifurcate, trifoliate.

Vb. *trisect*, divide into three parts, divide by three; trifurcate.

96 Quaternity

N. *quaternity*, four, tetrad, tetrarchy; square, tetragon, quadrilateral, quadrangle, quad; tetrahedron; quadrature, quarter; fylfot, swastika 222 *cross*; tetrapod; tetrameter, quatrain; tetragram, Tetragrammaton; tetramorph; quaternion, quartet, foursome; four winds, four gospel-writers; four-in-hand, quadriga; quatrefoil; quadruplet, quad; quadruped, tetrapod; quadrennium; four corners of 52 *whole*.

Adj. *four*, quaternary, quadratic; quadrate, square, quadrilateral, tetrahedral, four-square; four-footed, quadrupedal; quadrennial; quadri-, tetra-.

See: 52, 222.

97 Quadruplication

N. *quadruplication*, quadruplicity; squaring; quatercentenary.

Adj. *fourfold*, quadruple, quadruplicate, quadruplex; squared; quadrable.

Vb. *quadruple*, quadruplicate, multiply by four; square, quadrate.

Adv. *four times*; fourthly, in the fourth place; in square.

98 Quadrisection

N. *quadrisection*, quadripartition; quartering, fourth, fourth part; quarterly; quart, quarter; farthing, quarto.

Adj. *quartered*; quadrifid, quadripartite.

Vb. *quadrisect*, quarter, divide into four parts, divide by four.

99 Five and over

N. *five*, cinque, quint, quintuplet, quin; quintet; lustrum; pentad; quincunx; pentagon, pentacle, pentagram, pentahedron; pentameter; Pentateuch; pentarchy; pentathlon; cinquefoil; quinquereme; five senses, Five Towns.

over five, six, half-a-dozen, sextet, hexad, sixer; hexagon, hexagram; Hexateuch; hexameter; seven, heptad, week, sabbatical year; septennium; septenary, septet; Pleiad; Heptateuch; Seven Deadly Sins, Seven Wonders of the World; eight, octave, octet, octad; octagon; nine, three times three; ennead, nonary; novena; nine Muses; ten, tenner, decade; decagon, decahedron, Decalogue; decury, decemvirate; Ten Commandments; eleven, hendecasyllable; twelve, dozen; dodecahedron; twelve apostles, twelve tribes; thirteen, baker's dozen, long d.; double figures, teens.

twenty and over, twenty, a score; icosahedron; four and twenty, two dozen; twenty-five, pony; forty, two score; fifty, half a hundred, jubilee; sixty, three score; sexagenarian; seventy, three score and ten, septuagenarian; eighty, four score, octogenarian; ninety, nonagenarian.

hundred, century, centenary; hundredweight; centurion; centenarian; centipede; the hundred days; Old Hundredth; hundred per cent; treble figures.

over one hundred, a gross; thousand, chiliad, grand; millennium; ten thousand, myriad; hundred thousand, lakh; million; ten million, crore; thousand million, milliard; billion; million million; trillion, quadrillion, centillion, multimillion; zillion; millionaire, billionaire, milliardaire.

Adj. *fifth and over*, five, fifth; quinquennial, quinary, quintuple, fivefold; sixfold etc. n.; senary, sextuple; sixth; septuple; seventh; octuple; eighth; nonary; ninth; tenfold, decimal, denary, decuple, tenth; eleventh; twelfth; duodenary, duodecimal; thirteenth etc. n., in one's teens; vigesimal, vicenary, twentieth; vicennial; centesimal, centuple, centuplicate, centennial, centenary, centenarian, centurial; secular, hundredth; sesquicentenary, bicentenary, quincentenary; thousandth, millenary; bimillenary; millionth, billionth.

100 Multisection

N. *multisection*, decimation.

Adj. *multifid*, multifoil, multipartite, quinquepartite; octifid; decimal, tenth, tithe; duodecimal, twelfth; sexagesimal, sexagenary; hundredth, centesimal; millesimal.

Vb. *multisect*, decimate, decimalize.

101 Plurality

N. *plurality*, the plural; multiplicity 104 *multitude*; many-sidedness 82 *multiformity*; polygon, polyhedron; polytheism; a number, a certain number; some, one or two, two or three; a few, several; majority 104 *greater number*.

Adj. *plural*, in the p., not singular; composite, multiple; polydactyl, polypod; multiparous; polymorphic, multiform; many-sided; multilateral, multipurpose, multirole; multi-, poly-; more than one, some, certain; not alone, accompanied, in company 45 *joined*; upwards of, more, in the majority 104 *many*.

Adv. *et cetera*.

See: 45, 82, 104.

102 Fraction: less than one

N. *fraction*, decimal f. 85 *numerical element*; fractional part, fragment 53 *part*, 783 *portion*; shred 33 *small quantity*.

Adj. *fractional*, partial 53 *fragmentary*, 33 *small*.

See: 33, 53, 85, 783.

103 Zero

N. *zero*, nil, zilch, nothing, simply n., next to nothing, infinitely little; naught, nought, nix; no score, love, duck; blank; figure nought, cipher; nullity, nothingness 2 *nonexistence*, 4 *insubstantiality*; none, nobody, not a soul 190 *absence*; zero level, nadir.

Adj. *not one*, not any, zero; invisible, infinitely little, null 4 *insubstantial*, 2 *nonex-*

istent.
See: 2, 4, 190.

104 Multitude

N. *multitude*, numerousness, multiplicity; large number, round n., enormous n., million 99 *over one hundred*; a quantity, lots, loads, heaps 32 *great quantity*; numbers, scores, myriads, millions, trillions, zillions; a sea of, a world of, a sight of; forest, thicket; host, array, fleet, battalions 722 *army*; throng, mob, high turnout, all the world and his wife 74 *crowd*; tribe, horde.
certain quantity, peck, bushel, pinch; galaxy, bevy, cloud, flock, flight, covey; shoal, school; flock, herd, drove; coachload, trainload; swarm, hive, colony 74 *group*; nest, clutch, litter, brood 132 *young creature*.
greater number, weight of numbers, majority, great m., mass, bulk, mainstream 32 *main part*; multiplication, multiple 101 *plurality*.
Adj. *many*, myriad, several, sundry, divers, various, a thousand and one; quite a few, not a f., a good f.; considerable, numerous, very many, a good many, ever so m., many more, no end of, umpteen, n; untold, unnumbered, uncounted 107 *infinite*; multifarious, manifold 82 *multiform*; everrecurring 139 *frequent*, 106 *repeated*; much, ample, multiple, multiplied; profuse, in profusion, abundant, superabundant, generous, lavish, overflowing, galore 635 *plenteous*, 32 *great*.
multitudinous, massed, crowded, thronged, studded with 54 *full*; populous, peopled, populated, over-p., high-density 324 *dense*; teeming, crawling, humming, lousy with, alive with 171 *prolific*; thick, thick on the ground, thick as hail, thick as flies; coming thick and fast 139 *frequent*; incalculable, innumerable, inexhaustible, countless, endless 107 *infinite*; countless as the stars, as the sands on the seashore, as the hairs on one's head; heaven knows how many.
Vb. *be many*, - various etc. adj.; swarm with, crawl w., hum w., bristle w., teem w. 54 *fill*; pullulate, multiply 171 *be fruitful*; clutter, crowd, throng, swarm, mass, flock, troop 74 *congregate*; swarm like ants, swarm like locusts; flood, overflow, snow under, swamp, overwhelm 637 *superabound*; infest, overrun 297 *burst in*; add to the number, swell the ranks 36 *augment*; overweigh, outnumber, make a majority 32 *be great*.
See: **32**, 36, 54, **74**, 82, 99, 101, 106, 107, 132, 139, 171, 297, 324, 635, 637, 722.

105 Fewness

N. *fewness*, paucity, underpopulation; exiguity, thinness, sparsity, sparseness, rarity 140 *infrequency*; scantiness 636 *scarcity*; a few, a handful; wisps, tuft; thin audience, low turnout; small number, trickle, mere t. 33 *small quantity*; almost none; limited number, too few, no quorum; minority, one or two, two or three, half a dozen, not enough to matter; remnant, sole survivor 41 *remainder*.
Adj. *few*, precious few, weak in numbers, scant, scanty, light, little 636 *scarce*; thin, thin on the ground, sparse, rare, scattered, low-density, few and far between 140 *infrequent*; not many, hardly any; soon counted, to be counted on one's fingers; fewer, reduced, diminishing 37 *decreasing*; too few, in a minority, without a quorum.
Vb. *be few*, be weak in numbers, be underpopulated; straggle; seldom occur.
render few, reduce, diminish, pare 198 *make smaller*; scale down, decimate, thin the ranks; eliminate, weed, thin, sort out 300 *eject*; defect, desert; underman, understaff.
Adv. *here and there*, in dribs and drabs, in twos and threes, in a trickle; sparsely, rarely, infrequently.
See: **33**, 37, 41, **140**, 198, 300, **636**.

106 Repetition

N. *repetition*, doing again, iteration, reiteration; doubling, ditto, reduplication 20 *imitation*, 91 *duplication*; going over, recital, recapitulation; practice, practising, rehearsal; beginning again, renewal, resumption, reprise 68 *beginning*; saying again, anaphora 574 *ornament*; harping, tautology 570 *diffuseness*; stammering 580 *speech defect*; a repetition, repeat, repeat performance, encore; second helping; playback, replay, return match, revenge; chorus, refrain, ritornello 412 *vocal music*; echo, repercussion, reverberation 404 *resonance*; cliché, quotation, citation, plagiarism; hardy annual (**see** *recurrence*); twice-told tale, old story, chestnut 838 *tedium*; parrot-cry, gramophone record; new edition, reprint, reissue 589 *edition*; rifacimento, remake, rehash, recast, revival 656 *restoration*; repeater, cuckoo, parrot; creature of habit.

recurrence, repetitiveness 139 *frequency*; cycle, round, return, rebirth, reincarnation 141 *regular return*; succession, run, series, serial 71 *continuity*; recurring decimal, repetend; throwback, atavism 5 *heredity*; reappearance, curtain call; rhythm, drumming, hammering 141 *periodicity*; alliteration, assonance, rhyme 18 *assimilation*, 593 *prosody*; stale repetition, monotony 16 *uniformity*, 838 *tedium*; same old round, mixture as before, busman's holiday, routine 610 *habit*.

Adj. *repeated*, repetitional; recurrent, recurring, ever-r. 141 *periodical*; haunting 505 *remembered*; tautological, repetitive, repetitious, harping, iterative; stuck in a groove; stale, cliché-ridden 572 *feeble*; echoing, rhyming, chiming, alliterative, assonant 18 *similar*; monotonous, singsong, dingdong 16 *uniform*, 838 *tedious*; rhythmical, drumming, hammering; incessant, habitual 139 *frequent*; retold, twice-told, said before, quoted, cited; above-mentioned, aforesaid 66 *precursory*; plagiarized 20 *imitative*.

Vb. *repeat*, do again, iterate, cut and come again; duplicate, reduplicate, redouble 91 *double*; multiply 166 *reproduce*; reiterate, ingeminate, say again, recapitulate, go over, ring the changes on; retell, restate, reword, rephrase; always say, trot out; say one's piece, recite, say over, say after; echo, ditto, parrot, plagiarize 20 *copy*, 925 *flatter*; quote, cite 505 *remember*; go over the same ground, practise, rehearse; play back, rerun, rewind; recycle, reprocess; begin again, restart, resume 68 *begin*; replay, give an encore; reprint, reissue, republish; rehash, remake, renew, revive 656 *restore*.

repeat oneself, give an encore; reverberate, reecho 404 *resound*; chant, chorus 16 *be uniform*; quote oneself, tautologize 570 *be diffuse*; stutter 580 *stammer*; trot out, plug, labour, harp on, harp on the same string; din into one's ears, go on at, hammer at; recur to, revert to, return to 505 *remember*; go back, retrace one's steps 286 *regress*; stick in a groove, be a creature of habit 610 *be wont*.

reoccur, recur, return, revert, happen again; reappear, pop up, show up again; never hear the last of; turn up like a bad penny; haunt, obsess 505 *be remembered*.

Adv. *repeatedly*, recurrently, frequently 139 *often*; by rote, parrot fashion; again and again, over and over, many times o., times without number, time and again; time after time, day after day, year after year; day by day, year in year out; morning, noon and night; ad nauseam.

again, afresh, anew, over again, for the second time, once more; ditto; encore, bis; de novo, da capo; re-.

See: 5, 16, 18, **20**, 66, 68, **71**, 91, **139**, **141**, 166, 286, 404, 412, 505, 570, 572, 574, 580, 589, 593, 610, 656, 838, 925.

107 Infinity

N. *infinity*, infinitude, infiniteness, boundlessness, limitlessness, illimitability; infinite space, outer s. 183 *space*; eternity 115 *perpetuity*.

Adj. *infinite*, indefinite; immense, measureless; eternal 115 *perpetual*; numberless, countless, innumerable, immeasurable, illimitable, interminable; incalculable, unfathomable, incomprehensible, unapproachable, beyond reckoning, beyond comprehension; inexhaustible, without number, without limit, without end, no end of; without measure, limitless, endless, boundless, termless; untold, unnumbered 104 *many*; unmeasured, unbounded, unlimited.

Adv. *infinitely*, to infinity, ad infinitum; without end, indefinitely; boundlessly, illimitably; immeasurably 32 *greatly*.

See: 32, 104, **115**, 183.

Section six: Time

108 Time

N. *time*, tide; tense 564 *grammar*; duration, extent 113 *long duration*; limited time, season, term, semester, tenancy, tenure; tour, shift, spell, stint; span, space 110 *period*; a bit, a while; the whole time, the entire period, life, lifetime; eternity 115 *perpetuity*; passage of time, lapse, course 111 *course of time*; years, days; Time, Father Time, Time's scythe, Time's hourglass,sands of time, ravages of t., whirligig of t., t. the enemy, t. the healer; fourth dimension, space-time; timeslip, timewarp; aorist, indefinite time; past time, past tense, retrospective time 125 *past time,* 119 *priority*; prospective time 124 *futurity*; contemporaneity 121 *present time*; recent time 126 *newness*; antiquity, distant time 127 *oldness.*

interim, intermediate time, meantime, pendency, while; interval, interlude, break, pause 145 *lull*; vacation 681 *leisure*; time-lag, intermittence, interregnum, interlude, episode 72 *discontinuity*; close season, respite, adjournment 136 *delay*; midweek 70 *middle.*

date, day, age, day and a., reign 110 *era*; vintage, year, regnal y., time of life 117 *chronology*; birthday, saint's day 141 *anniversary*; day of the week, calends, ides, nones; time of day 117 *clock time*; moment 116 *instant*; target date, zero hour, D-day; term, fixed day, quarter day, payday.

Adj. *continuing,* permanent 115 *perpetual,* 146 *unceasing*; on foot, in process of, pending; repetitive, recurrent 106 *repeated*; temporal 141 *periodical.*

intermediate, interglacial, interlunar, interwar; midweek; intercalary, intercalated, inter-.

dated, calendared; pre-Christian 119 *prior*; post-Christian, postwar 120 *subsequent.*

Vb. *continue,* endure, drag on 113 *last*; roll on, intervene, pass 111 *elapse*; take time, take up t., fill t., occupy t. 183 *extend*; live through, sustain; stay, remain, abide, outlive, survive 113 *outlast*; take its time, wait 136 *be pending.*

pass time, vegetate, breathe, subsist 360 *live*; age 131 *grow old*; spend time, consume t., use t., employ t. 678 *be busy*; while away time, kill t., summer, winter, weekend 681 *have leisure*; waste time, fritter away t. 679 *be inactive*; mark time, tide over 136 *wait*; choose the right time, seize an opportunity 137 *profit by*; enjoy a spell of, have one's day.

fix the time, calendar, date, put a date to 117 *time.*

Adv. *while,* whilst, during, pending; day by day 113 *all along*; in the course of, so long as; for the time being, meantime, meanwhile; between whiles, in the meantime, in the interim; from day to day, from hour to hour; hourly 139 *often*; for a time, for a season; till, until, up to, yet; always, the whole time, all the time 139 *perpetually*; all along 54 *throughout*; for good 113 *for a long time.*

when, what time; one day, once upon a time, one fine morning; in the days of, in the time of, in the year of.

anno domini, AD; ante Christum, AC; before Christ, BC; anno urbis conditae, ab urbe condita, AUC; anno hegirae; anno regni, AR, in the year of his *or* her reign.

See: 54, 70, 72, 106, **110**, 111, 113, 115, 116, **117**, 119, 120, 121, 124, 125, 126, 127, 131, 136, 137, 139, 141, 145, 146, 183, 360, 564, 678, 679, 681.

109 Neverness

N. *neverness,* Greek Calends; month of Sundays, blue moon; jam tomorrow, mañana; dies non; no time, datelessness, eternity 115 *perpetuity.*

Adv. *never,* not ever, at no time, at no period, on no occasion; not in donkey's years; nevermore, never again; over one's dead body; never before, never in one's born days; without date, sine die; before the beginning of time; out of time.

See: 115.

110 Period

N. *period,* matter of time; long period, long run 113 *long duration*; short period, short run 114 *transience*; season; close season 145 *lull*; time of day, morning, evening; time of year, spring, summer, autumn, winter 128 *morning,* 129 *evening*; one's time, fixed t., term; notice, warning, ultimatum 766 *conditions*; time up 69 *finality*; measured time, spell, tour, stint, shift, span, stretch, sentence; innings, turn; round, bout, lap; vigil, watch, nightwatch, dogwatch; length of time, second, minute, hour; particular time, rush hour; pause, interval 108 *interim*; day, weekday, working day; week, sennight, octave, novena; fortnight, month, calendar m., lunar m., moon, lunation; quarter, trimester; half year, semester; twelvemonth, year, solar y., sidereal y., light y., leap y.; Olympiad, lustrum, quinquennium; decade, decennium, Gay Nineties, Hungry Thirties, Swinging Sixties; golden wedding, jubilee 141 *anniversary*; century, millennium; annus mirabilis; time up to now, one's born days; life, lifetime, life sentence.

era, time, period, generation, age, days; epoch; aeon; cycle, Sothic c., Metonic c.; Platonic year, Great Year, Yuga, Kalpa; geological period, Ice Age; Stone A., Iron

A., Dark Ages, Middle A. 125 *antiquity*; Renaissance, Age of Enlightenment, A. of Reason, belle époque, fin de siècle; modern times, Machine Age, Space A.; Golden A., A. of Aquarius.

Adj. *periodic* 141 *seasonal*; hourly, horary; annual, biennial, quinquennial, decennial, centennial; period 127 *olden*.

secular, epochal, millennial; Pre-Cambrian, Palaeozoic, Mesozoic, Cainozoic, Quaternary; Pleistocene, Holocene; neolithic 127 *primal*.

Adv. *man and boy*, in a lifetime; periodically, seasonally; for a term, for the term of one's natural life, for a lifetime.

See: 69, 108, 113, 114, 125, 127, 128, 129, 141, 145, 766.

111 Course: indefinite duration

N. *course of time*, matter of t., progress of t., process of t., lapse of t., flow of t., flux of t., stream of time, tide of t., march of t., heavy tread of t., flight of t.; duration 108 *time*, 146 *continuance*; continuous tense, imperfect t. 564 *grammar*; indefinite time, infinite t. 113 *long duration*.

Adj. *elapsing*, wearing, passing, rolling 285 *progressive*, 146 *unceasing*; consuming 114 *transient*; getting older 131 *ageing*.

Vb. *elapse*, pass, lapse, flow, run, roll, proceed, advance, press on 285 *progress*; wear on, drag on, crawl 278 *move slowly*; flit, fly, slip, slide, glide 277 *move fast*; run its course, run out, expire 69 *end*; go by, pass by, slip by 125 *be past*; have one's day, spend time 108 *pass time*.

Adv. *in time*, in due time, in due season; in the course of time, in the process of t., in the fullness of t., with the years.

See: 69, 108, 113, 114, 125, 131, 146, 277, 278, 285, 564.

112 Contingent Duration

Adv. *provisionally*, precariously, by favour; at the pleasure of; for the present; so long as it lasts; as *or* so long as.

113 Long Duration

N. *long duration*, length of time, a long t., unconscionable t.; a month of Sundays, years, donkey's years, years on end, yonks; a lifetime, life sentence; generations, a century, an age, ages, aeons 115 *perpetuity*; length of days, cat's nine lives, longevity 131 *old age*; distance of time, corridor of t., antiquity 125 *past time*.

durability, lasting quality, endurance, defiance of time; stamina, staying power 162 *strength*; survival 146 *continuance*; permanence 153 *stability*; inveteracy, long standing, good age 127 *oldness*; long run, long innings.

protraction, prolongation, extension 203 *lengthening*; dragging out, spinning o., filibustering, stonewalling 702 *hindrance*, 715 *resistance*; interminability, wait, long w., long haul 136 *delay*, 278 *slowness*; extra time, overtime 38 *addition*.

Adj. *lasting*, abiding 146 *unceasing*; secular, agelong, lifelong, livelong; longtime, longstanding, inveterate, deep-seated, deeprooted; of long duration, long-term, long-service, marathon 203 *long*; too long, unconscionable; durable, perdurable, enduring 162 *strong*; longeval, long-lived 127 *immemorial*; evergreen, unfading, fresh 126 *new*; eternal, perennial 115 *perpetual*; persistent, chronic 602 *obstinate*; nonbiodegradable 162 *unyielding*; constant, stable, permanent 153 *unchangeable*.

protracted, prolonged, lengthened, extended, stretched, spun out, drawn o. 197 *expanded*; lingering, delayed, tarrying 278 *slow*; long-pending, long-awaited 136 *late*; interminable, longwinded, timewasting 570 *prolix*.

Vb. *last*, endure, stand, stay, remain, abide, continue 146 *go on*; brave the years, defy time, never end 115 *be eternal*; carry one's years 131 *grow old*; wear, wear well 162 *be strong*.

outlast, outlive, outwear, outstay, survive; remain 41 *be left*; live to fight another day; have nine lives.

spin out, draw o., drag o.; protract, prolong 203 *lengthen*; temporize, gain time, procrastinate 136 *put off*; talk out, filibuster 702 *obstruct*.

drag on, be interminable, never end; inch, creep, linger, dawdle 278 *move slowly*; tarry, delay, waste time, wait 136 *be late*.

Adv. *for a long time*, long, for long, for ages, for years, many a long day; for good, for all time, for better for worse; all one's life, from the cradle to the grave; till blue in the face; till the cows come home.

all along, all day, all day long, the livelong day, as the day is long; all the year round, round the clock, hour by hour, day by day; day in day out, year in year out;

before and since; ever since.
long ago, long since, in the distant past, long long ago; in ancient days, in bygone times 125 *formerly*.
at last, at long last, in the long run, after many days, not before it was time.
See: 38, 41, **115**, 125, 126, 127, 131, 136, 146, 153, 162, 197, **203**, 278, 570, 602, 702, 715.

114 Transience

N. *transience*, transientness, transitoriness 4 *insubstantiality*; ephemerality, impermanence; evanescence 446 *disappearance*; volatility 338 *vaporization*; fugacity 277 *velocity*; caducity, fragility 330 *brittleness*; mortality, perishability 361 *death*; frailty 163 *weakness*; mutability 152 *changeableness*; capriciousness, fickleness 604 *caprice*; suddenness 116 *instantaneity*; temporariness, provisionality; temporary arrangement, makeshift 150 *substitute*; interregnum 108 *interim*.
brief span, short space of time, short while; briefness, momentariness, brevity 204 *shortness*; mortal span, short life and a merry one; summer lightning, shooting star, meteor, flash in the pan, nine days' wonder; ephemera, bubble, mayfly, snows of yesteryear, smoke in the wind; April shower, summer cloud 4 *insubstantial thing*; bird of passage, ship that passes in the night; brief encounter; short run 110 *period*, 277 *spurt*; spasm, moment 116 *instant*.
Adj. *transient*, time-bound, temporal, impermanent, transitory, fading, passing 4 *insubstantial*; fair-weather, summer; cursory, flying, fleeting, flitting, fugitive, fugacious 277 *speedy*; shifting, slipping; precarious, volatile, written in water; evanescent 446 *disappearing*; unsettled, rootless; flickering, mutable, changeable 152 *changeful*; fickle, flighty 604 *capricious*.
ephemeral, of a day, short-lived, nondurable; throwaway, disposable, biodegradable 51 *decomposable*; perishable, mortal 361 *dying*; annual, deciduous, frail 163 *weak*, 330 *brittle*; impermanent, temporary, acting, provisional, for the time being; doomed, under sentence.
brief, short-term, short-service 204 *short*; summary, short and sweet 569 *concise*; quick, fleet, brisk 277 *speedy*; sudden, momentary, meteoric, like a flash 116 *instantaneous*; hurried, pressed for time, in a hurry 680 *hasty*; at short notice, extemporaneous, offhand 609 *spontaneous*.
Vb. *be transient*, - transitory etc. adj.; not stay, not last; flit, fleet, fly, gallop 277 *move fast*; fade, flicker, vanish, evanesce, melt, evaporate 446 *disappear*; fade like a dream, flit like a shadow, pass like a summer cloud, burst like a bubble, have no roots 2 *pass away*.
Adv. *transiently*, briefly, momentarily; awhile, in passing; temporarily, provisionally; for the present, for the moment, for a time, for the time being, not for long; instantly 116 *instantaneously*; easy come, easy go; here today and gone tomorrow.
See: 2, 4, 51, 108, 110, **116**, 150, **152**, 163, 204, 277, 330, 338, 361, 446, 569, 604, 609, 680.

115 Perpetuity: endless duration

N. *perpetuity*, endless time, infinite duration 107 *infinity*; sempiternity, everlastingness; eternity, timelessness; neverendingness, interminability 113 *long duration*; endurance 144 *permanence*, 71 *continuity*; immortality, athanasia, deathlessness, incorruption 146 *continuance*; perpetuation, immortalization; lasting monument 505 *reminder*.
Adj. *perpetual*, perennial, longlasting, enduring, durable, perdurable 113 *lasting*; aeonian, agelong 127 *immemorial*; nonstop, constant, continual, ceaseless, incessant 146 *unceasing*; flowing, everflowing, uninterrupted 71 *continuous*; dateless, ageless, unageing, unchanging, immutable 144 *permanent*; evergreen, unfading, amaranthine, everlasting, incorruptible; imperishable, undying, deathless, immortal; unending, neverending, interminable; endless, without end, timeless, eternal, coeternal.
Vb. *perpetuate*, make permanent, establish; immortalize, eternalize.
be eternal, - perpetual etc. adj.; last for ever, endure for e., live for e.; go on for e., have no end, never cease.
Adv. *for ever*, in perpetuity, on and on; ever and always, for aye, evermore, for ever and ever, for ever and a day; time without end, world without e.; for keeps, for good and all, for better for worse; to the end of time, till doomsday, to the crack of doom; to infinity 107 *infinitely*; from age to age,

from generation to generation; unchangeably, constantly, nonstop 71 *continuously*.

See: 71, **107**, **113**, 127, 144, 146, 505.

116 Instantaneity: point of time

N. *instantaneity*, instantaneousness, immediateness, immediacy; simultaneity 121 *present time*; suddenness, abruptness 508 *lack of expectation*; precise time 135 *punctuality*; momentariness 114 *transience*.

instant, moment, point, point of time; second, split s., half a s., tick, trice, jiffy, half a j.; breath; burst, crack; stroke, coup; flash, lightning f.; twinkle, twinkling, the twinkling of an eye; two shakes; the very moment, the very hour, the stroke of.

Adj. *instantaneous*, simultaneous, immediate, instant, sudden, abrupt, snap; flickering, flashing; quick as thought, quick as lightning, with the speed of light, like a flash 277 *speedy*; on time, punctual 135 *early*.

Adv. *instantaneously*, instantly, instanter, on the instant, at once, immediately, directly; punctually, without delay, forthwith; in half a mo, soon; in no time at all, in less than no time; promptly, readily, presto, pronto; without warning, without notice, out of hand, abruptly; overnight, all at once, all of a sudden 135 *suddenly*; plump, slap, slap-bang, in one's tracks; in the same breath, at the same instant, at a stroke, at one jump, at one fell swoop; in a trice, in a moment, in a wink, in the twinkling of an eye; in two ticks, in a brace of shakes, in two shakes of a lamb's tail; at the drop of a hat, on the spot, on the dot; extempore, impromptu, on the spur of the moment, off the cuff; before you could say Jack Robinson, before you could say knife; like a flash, like a shot, like greased lightning 277 *swiftly*; no sooner said than done.

See: 114, 121, 135, **277**, 508.

117 Chronometry

N. *chronometry*, chronoscopy, horometry, horology; watch-making; calendar-making, timetabling; timing, dating; time-keeping 108 *time*.

clock time, right time, exact t., correct t., BBC t., true t., astronomer's t., solar t., sidereal t., Greenwich Mean T., G.M.T., British Standard T., B.S.T., local t., continental t.; date, date line; the time now, the hour, time of day, time of night; bedtime; summer time, double summer t., daylight saving.

timekeeper, chronometer, timepiece, horologe; clock, dial, face; hand; bob, pendulum 317 *oscillation*; electric clock, grandfather c., calendar c., carriage c., cuckoo c., alarm c., alarum; Big Ben; water-clock, clepsydra; watch, ticker; turnip, fob-watch, hunter, repeater; wrist-watch, digital watch, dial w.; sundial, gnomon; hourglass, sand-glass, egg timer; chronograph, chronoscope, chronopher; time signal, pip, siren, hooter; gong, bell, five-minute b., minute-gun, time-ball; time-clock, timer, stopwatch; parking meter, traffic light 305 *traffic control*; time fuse, time switch, time bomb; metronome, conductor, bandleader; watchmaker, clockmaker, horologist.

chronology, dendrochronology; radiocarbon dating, thermoluminescence; dating, chronogram; date, age, epoch, style 110 *era*; old style, O.S., new style, N.S.; almanac, calendar, perpetual c., fixed c., Gregorian c., Julian c.; ephemeris, astronomical almanac; menology, chronicle, annals, fasti, diary, journal, log-book 548 *record*; date list, time-chart 87 *list*; tide-table, timetable 87 *directory*.

chronologist, chronographer, chronologer, calendar-maker, calendarist; chronicler, annalist, diarist 549 *recorder*.

Adj. *chronological*, chronometrical, horological, timekeeping; chronographic; annalistic, diaristic 548 *recording*; calendrical, chronogrammatic, datal, temporal; isochronous, isochronal 123 *synchronous*; in time 137 *timely*.

Vb. *time*, clock; fix the time, fix the date; timetable; match times 123 *synchronize*; phase 24 *adjust*; adjust the hands, put the clock forward 135 *be early*; put the clock back 136 *be late*; wind the clock, set the alarm 669 *make ready*; calendar, chronologize, chronicle, diarize 548 *record*; date, be dated, bear a date; measure time, mark t., beat t., keep t.; count the minutes, watch the clock; clock in 68 *begin*; clock out 145 *cease*; ring in 68 *initiate*; ring out 69 *terminate*.

Adv. *o'clock*, a.m., p.m.

See: 24, 68, 69, 87, 108, 110, 123, 135, 136, 137, 145, 305, 317, 548, 549, 669.

118 Anachronism

N. *anachronism*, parachronism, prochronism; wrong date, wrong day, chronological error; mistiming, previousness, prolepsis 135 *anticipation*; disregard of time, unpunctuality 136 *lateness*; neglect of time, oblivion of t. 506 *oblivion*; wrong moment 138 *untimeliness*.

Adj. *anachronistic*, misdated, undated; antedated, foredated, previous, before time, too early 135 *early*; parachronistic, post-dated 136 *late*; overdue, unpunctual, behind time; slow, losing; fast, gaining; out of due time, out of season, out of date, behind the times, old-fashioned 127 *antiquated*.

Vb. *misdate*, mistake the date 138 *mistime*; antedate, foredate, anticipate 135 *be early*; be overdue, be behind time, postdate 136 *be late*; be fast, gain; be slow, lose; be unpunctual, take no note of time.

See: 127, 135, 136, 138, 506.

119 Priority

N. *priority*, antecedence, anteriority, previousness, preexistence; primogeniture, birthright; eldest, firstborn, son and heir; flying start 64 *precedence*; leading 283 *preceding*; the past, yesteryear, yesterday 125 *past time*; eve, vigil, day before; precedent, antecedent; foretaste, preview, prerelease; premonition, presentiment 510 *foresight*; herald 66 *precursor*.

Adj. *prior*, pre-, fore; earliest, first, first in the field, precedent 64 *preceding*; previous, earlier, anterior, antecedent; antediluvian, prehistoric; pre-Christian, BC; prewar, antebellum; preexisting, preexistent; prenatal, antenatal; elder, eldest, firstborn; former, ci-devant, onetime, whilom, erstwhile, sometime, ex-, retired; foregoing, aforementioned, abovementioned; aforesaid, said; introductory, prefatory, preliminary, preluding 66 *precursory*; premised, given, presupposed 512 *supposed*.

Vb. *be before* 135 *be early*; come before, go b. 283 *precede*; forerun, foreshadow, antecede; preexist.

do before, premise, presuppose 512 *suppose*; predecease, prefabricate, prearrange, precontract, preempt, prejudge, precondemn, prenotify, preview; be previous, anticipate, forestall, be beforehand with, jump the gun, jump the queue; steal a march on, have a start on 277 *outstrip*; lead 283 *precede*, 64 *come before*.

Adv. *before*, pre-, prior to, beforehand, by; just before, on the eve of; earlier, previously, formerly; ultimo, ult.; afore, ere; aforetime, ere now, before n.; ere then, before t., already, yet; in anticipation; until now.

See: **64**, **66**, 125, 135, 277, **283**, 510, 512.

120 Posteriority

N. *posteriority*, subsequence, supervention; ultimogeniture, succession 65 *sequence*, 284 *following*; days to come 124 *futurity*; line, lineage, descent, successor, descendant 170 *posterity*; cadet; latecomer, new arrival; remainder, inheritance; aftermath 67 *sequel*.

Adj. *subsequent*, post-, posterior, following, next, after, later; last in date, junior, cadet, younger, youngest 130 *young*; succeeding, designate, to be 124 *future*; postnatal; postdiluvian, postglacial; posthumous, post-obit; postindustrial, postwar; after Christ, AD; postprandial, afterdinner 65 *sequential*.

Vb. *ensue*, supervene, follow after 65 *come after*; go after 284 *follow*, 157 *result*; succeed, step into the shoes of 771 *inherit*.

Adv. *subsequently*, later, in the process of time; after, afterwards; at a later date; next, next time; thereafter, thereupon; since, from that time, from that moment; from the start, from the word 'go'; after a while, after a time; soon after, close upon; next month, proximo.

See: **65**, **67**, 124, 130, 157, 170, **284**, 771.

121 The Present Time

N. *present time*, contemporaneity, contemporaneousness, topicality 126 *modernism*; time being, the present, present time, present day, present moment; this hour, this moment, this instant 116 *instantaneity*; juncture, opportunity, crisis 137 *occasion*; ongoing situation 146 *continuance*; this time, the nonce; the times, modern t., current t., these days, this day and age; today, twentieth century, nowadays; this date, current d.; one's age, one's present a., mental a., physical a.; present generation, one's contemporaries 123 *contemporary*.

Adj. *present*, actual, instant, current, extant 1 *existing*; of this date, of today's d.; topical, contemporary, contemporaneous; present-day, latter-day, latest, up-to-the-minute, up-to-date 126 *modern*; for the occasion, occasional.

Vb. *be now*, exist 1 *be*; live in the present, live for the day, live from hand to mouth; be modern 126 *modernize*; be one's age, admit one's a. 123 *synchronize*.

Adv. *at present*, now, right now, at this time, at this moment; live; at the present time, contemporaneously, contemporarily; today, nowadays; at this time of day, even now; already, but now, just now; this time, on the present occasion; for the time being, for the nonce; on the nail, on the spot 116 *instantaneously*; on the spur of the moment 609 *extempore*; now or never; now as always.

until now, to this day, to the present day, up to now, to date; including today, through; from the start, from the word 'go' 113 *all along*.

See: 1, 113, **116**, 123, **126**, 137, 146, 609.

122 Different Time

N. *different time*, other times, better t. 124 *futurity*, 125 *past time*; another time, some other t., not now, not today, any time but this; jam yesterday, and jam tomorrow, but never jam today 109 *neverness*; parachronism 118 *anachronism*.

Adj. *not contemporary*, unmodern 84 *unconformable*; behind the times 127 *antiquated*; before the times 126 *new*; misdated 118 *anachronistic*.

Adv. *not now*, ago, earlier, later, then; sometimes; once, once upon a time; one day, one fine morning, one of these days; someday, sometime, some time or other, sooner or later; any time, any old t.; any time now; soon; whenever you will, as soon as you like.

See: 84, 109, 118, 124, 125, 126, 127.

123 Synchronism

N. *synchronism*, synchrony; coexistence, coincidence, concurrence, concomitance 89 *accompaniment*; simultaneity, simultaneousness, same time 116 *instantaneity*; contemporaneity, contemporaneousness, same date, same day 121 *present time*; coevality, same age, twin birth 28 *equality*; level-pegging, level time, dead heat 28 *draw*; synchronization, sync, phasing, isochronism.

contemporary, coeval, twin 28 *compeer*; one's contemporaries, one's own generation; age group, peer g., class, year 74 *group*.

Adj. *synchronous*, synchronal; synchronic; contemporary, contemporaneous 121 *present*, 126 *modern*; simultaneous, coinstantaneous, coincident, coexistent, coeternal, conterminous, concomitant 24 *agreeing*, 89 *accompanying*; level, neck and neck 28 *equal*; matched in age, coeval, coetaneous, twin; of the same age, of the same year, of the same vintage; synchronized, timed, phased, isochronous, on the beat, punctual.

Vb. *synchronize*, sync, contemporize; concur, coexist 89 *accompany*; encounter, coincide 295 *meet*; keep time 410 *harmonize*; say together, chorus; tune, phase 24 *adjust*; run neck and neck, run a dead heat 28 *be equal*; pace, keep in step with; isochronize.

Adv. *synchronously*, concurrently, at the same time, isochronously, for the same time, along with, pari passu; in time, on the beat, simultaneously; in concert, in chorus, with one voice; as soon as, just as, at the moment of, in the same breath 116 *instantaneously*; while, whilst, concomitantly 89 *with*.

See: **24**, 28, 74, **89**, 116, 121, 126, 295, 410.

124 Futurity: prospective time

N. *futurity*, future tense; womb of time, time to come, days and years to come; morrow 120 *posteriority*; future, time ahead, prospect, outlook 507 *expectation*; coming events, fate 154 *event*, 155 *destiny*; near future, tomorrow, mañana, next week, next year 121 *present time*, 200 *nearness*; advent 289 *approach*; long run, distant future, remote f., after ages 199 *distance*; future generations, descendants, heirs, heritage 170 *posterity*; successorship, shadow cabinet 65 *sequence*, 669 *preparation*.

future state, what fate holds in store 155 *destiny*, 596 *fate*; latter days, postindustrial age; doomsday, crack of doom 69 *finality*; post-existence, afterlife, life to come, hereafter, kingdom come 971 *heaven*; damnation 972 *hell*; good time coming, millennium 730 *prosperity*; rebirth, reincarnation 106 *repetition*.

looking ahead, anticipation 669 *preparation*; procrastination 136 *delay*; prospect, prospects, outlook 507 *expectation*; great expectations, expectancy 852 *hope*; horoscope, forecast 511 *prediction*.

Adj. *future*, to be, to come; coming, nearing 289 *approaching*; nigh, close at hand 200 *near*; on the horizon, in the wind; due, destined, fated, threatening, imminent, overhanging 155 *impending*; in the future, ahead, yet to come, waiting, millennial 154 *eventual*; in embryo 669 *preparatory*; prospective, designate, earmarked 605 *chosen*; promised, looked for 507 *expected*, 471 *probable*; predicted, predictable, foreseeable, sure 473 *certain*; ready to, rising, getting on for; potential, promising 469 *possible*; later, ulterior, posterior 120 *subsequent*.

Vb. *be to come*, lie ahead, lie in the future, be for tomorrow; be destined, threaten, overhang 155 *impend*; near, draw nigh 289 *approach*; be imminent, be just round the corner, cast its shadow before, stare one in the face 200 *be near*; shall, will.

look ahead, look forward, see it coming, await 507 *expect*, 852 *hope*; foresee 511 *predict*; anticipate, forestall 135 *be early*; take the long view 669 *prepare oneself*.

Adv. *prospectively*, eventually, ultimately, later; in the fullness of time, in due course, in the long run, by and by; tomorrow, soon, sooner or later, some day 122 *not now*; hereafter; on the eve of, on the point of, about to; in the wings, in the offing.

henceforth, in future, from this time forth, from now on.

See: 65, 69, 106, **120**, 121, 122, 135, 136, **154**, 155, 170, 199, 200, 289, 469, 471, 473, **507**, 511, 596, 605, 669, 730, 852, 971, 972.

125 Past Time: retrospective time

N. *past time* 119 *priority*; retrospection, looking back 505 *remembrance*; past tense, historic t., preterite, perfect, pluperfect 564 *grammar*; the past, recent p., only yesterday 126 *newness*; distant past, history, antiquity; old story, ancient history 127 *oldness*; past times, days of yore, olden days, good old d., bygone d.; auld lang syne, yesterday, yesteryear, former times; ancien régime; Victorian Age, Elizabethan A., Renaissance 110 *era*.

antiquity, high a., rust of a., eld; creation, when time began, time immemorial, distance of time, remote ages; prehistory, protohistory, ancient world, medieval times; geological times, Stone Age, prehistoric a., heroic a., Classical A.; Dark Ages, Middle A. 110 *era*; the ancients; antiquities, relics, eolith, neolith, microlith 41 *remainder*, 127 *archaism*; ruin, ancient monument, megalith, Stonehenge 548 *monument*, 253 *earthwork*; excavation, dig 484 *discovery*; museum 632 *collection*; ancient lineage 169 *genealogy*.

fossil, fossilized remains *or* relics, petrified forest, trilobite, ammonite; trace fossil, fossil footprint 548 *record*; coal forest 385 *fuel*; sponge, coral 358 *organism*; mammoth, dinosaur 365 *animal*; fossilization, petrification.

palaeology, palaeontology, palaeozoology, palaeography; palaeoanthropology 371 *humankind*; archaeology, digging up the past; antiquarianism; medievalism; industrial archaeology.

antiquarian, palaeontologist, archaeologist; palaeologist, palaeographer; antiquary, Dryasdust 492 *scholar*; historian, prehistorian; medievalist 549 *chronicler*; Egyptologist, Assyriologist, Hebraist, Arabist, Sanskritist, classicist 557 *linguist*; revivalist; archaist, Pre-Raphaelite.

Adj. *past*, in the p., historical; ancient, prehistoric 127 *olden*; early, primitive, proto- 127 *primal*; recently past 126 *new*; wholly past, gone, bygone, lost, irrecoverable, dead and buried 506 *forgotten*; passed away, no more, died out, dead as the Dodo 2 *extinct*, 361 *dead*; passé, has-been, obsolete 674 *disused*, 127 *antiquated*; fossilized 326 *hard*; over, blown o., done, over and done with, behind one; elapsed, lapsed, expired, run out, ended, finished 69 *ending*; unrenewed, unrevived.

former, late, quondam, sometime, ex- 119 *prior*; retired, outgoing 753 *resigning*; ancestral, ancient, prehistoric 127 *immemorial*; not within living memory.

preterite, grammatically past, in the past tense; simple past, past continuous, perfect, imperfect, pluperfect.

foregoing, last, latter 64 *preceding*; recent, overnight 126 *new*.

retrospective, looking back, backward-looking; archaizing 505 *remembering*; diachronic, historical; retroactive, going back; with hindsight.

Vb. *be past*, have elapsed, have expired; have run its course, have had its day; pass, elapse, blow over, be o. 69 *end*; be a dead letter.

look back, trace back, cast the eyes b.; antiquarianize, archaeologize, dig up the past, exhume; put the clock back, go back to the past, archaize, hark back 505 *retrospect*.

Adv. *formerly*, aforetime, of old, of yore; time was, ago, in olden times; long ago, long since; a long while, a long time ago; once upon a time; years ago, ages a. 127 *anciently*; lately, some time ago, some time back; yesterday, the day before yesterday; yestreen, yestereve, yesteryear; last year, last season, last month.

retrospectively, retroactively; historically speaking; before now, hitherto; no longer; from time immemorial, time out of mind; already, yet; till now, up to this time 121 *until now*; ex post facto.

See: 2, 41, 64, 69, **110**, **119**, 121, 126, **127**, 169, 253, 326, 358, 361, 365, 371, 385, 484, 492, 505, 506, 548, 549, 557, 564, 632, 674, 753.

126 Newness

N. *newness*, recency, recentness; recent date, recent occurrence, recent past 125 *past time*, 121 *present time*; innovation, neoterism 560 *neology*, 21 *originality*; novelty, gloss of n.; freshness, dewiness 648 *cleanness*; greenness, immaturity, rawness 130 *youth*; renovation, restoration, renewal, resurrection 656 *revival*; new leaf, new broom.

modernism, modernity, modernness, modernization; up-to-dateness, topicality, contemporaneity 121 *present time*; the latest, the latest thing, latest fashion; the last word, dernier cri; new look, contemporary style 848 *fashion*.

modernist, neologist, neologian, neoteric, futurist; advanced thinker, avant-garde; bright young thing, trendy 848 *beau monde*; modern generation, younger g.

upstart, novus homo, parvenu, nouveau riche 847 *vulgarian*; Johnny-come-lately 297 *incomer*.

Adj. *new*, newish, recent, of recent date, of recent occurrence, overnight; upstart, mushroom; novel, unhackneyed, unprecedented, unheard of 21 *original*; brand-new, spick and span, like new, in mint condition 648 *clean*; green, evergreen, dewy, juicy, sappy 128 *vernal*; fresh, fresh as a daisy, fresh as paint; maiden, virgin, virginal; newborn 130 *young*; raw, unfledged 670 *immature*; just out, just published, hot from the press; new-made, new-laid; straight from the oven, factory-fresh; unused, first-hand; untried, untrodden, unbeaten, unexplored 491 *unknown*; untested 461 *experimental*; not broken in, not yet run in; budding, fledgling 68 *beginning*.

modern, late, latter-day; contemporary, topical 121 *present*; up-to-the-minute, up-to-date, with it; à la mode, in the latest fashion, trendy 848 *fashionable*; ultramodern, modernistic, advanced, avant-garde, futuristic, untraditional, nontraditional, revolutionary; innovating, neoteric, newfangled, new-fashioned 560 *neological*.

modernized, renewed, renovated, rejuvenated, refurbished, repainted 656 *restored*; given a new look, brought up to date, revised; looking like new, freshened up 648 *clean*.

Vb. *modernize*, do up; update, bring up to date; have the new look, go modern, go contemporary, get with it; move with the times 285 *progress*.

Adv. *newly*, freshly, afresh, anew, like new; fresh-, new-; recently, overnight, just now, only yesterday; not long ago, a short time a.; lately, latterly, of late.

See: 21, 68, **121**, 125, **128**, **130**, 285, 297, 461, 491, 560, 648, 656, 670, 847, 848.

127 Oldness

N. *oldness*, primitiveness 68 *beginning*; olden times 110 *era*; age, hoary a., eld; cobwebs of antiquity, dust of ages, ruins 125 *antiquity*; maturity, mellowness 129 *autumn*; decline, rust 51 *decay*; senility 131 *old age*; eldership 131 *seniority*.

archaism, antiquities 125 *antiquity*; ancien régime; thing of the past, relic of the p.; listed building; museum piece, antique, heirloom, bygone, Victoriana; dodo, dinosaur 125 *fossil*; oldie, golden o.; old fogy, old fossil, fuddy-duddy; archaist, square, old-timer, has-been, back number.

tradition, lore, folklore, mythology; inveteracy, custom, prescription, immemorial usage 610 *habit*; common law, smriti, Sunna, Hadith; ancient wisdom, the way of our forefathers; word of mouth 579 *speech*.

Adj. *olden*, old, ancient, antique, antiquarian, of historical interest; veteran, vintage; venerable, patriarchal; archaic, ancient; time-worn, ruined; prehistoric, mythological, heroic, classic, Hellenic, Byzantine, feudal, medieval, Saxon, Norman, Romanesque, Gothic, Tudor, Elizabethan, Jacobean, Georgian, Regency, Victorian; historical 125 *past*, 866 *renowned*.

primal, prime, primitive, primeval, primordial, aboriginal 68 *beginning*; geological, preglacial, fossil, palaeozoic 110 *secular*; eolithic, palaeolithic, mesolithic, neolithic; early, proto-, dawn-, eo-; antemundane, pre-adamite, antediluvian.

immemorial, ancestral, traditional, time-honoured 610 *habitual*; venerable 866 *worshipful*; inveterate, rooted, established, long-standing 153 *fixed*; Ogygian, old as the hills, old as Adam, old as Methuselah, old as history, old as time, age-old 113 *lasting*.

antiquated, of other times, archaic; old-world, old-time; olde worlde, ye olde; pre-war, interwar 119 *prior*; anachronistic, archaistic, archaizing 125 *retrospective*; fossilized, ossified, static 144 *permanent*; behind the times, out of date, out of fashion, dated, antediluvian, out of the ark, horse-and-buggy, silent-screen; conservative, Victorian, old-fashioned, old-school, square, not with it; outworn, outdated, outmoded; passé, démodé, vieux jeu, old hat; gone by 125 *past*; decayed, perished 655 *dilapidated*; rusty, moth-eaten, crumbling; mildewed, moss-grown, mouldering 51 *decomposed*; fusty, stale, secondhand; obsolete, obsolescent; superseded, superannuated 674 *disused*; old 131 *ageing*.

Vb. *be old*, - antiquated etc. adj.; go back in time, belong to the past, have had its day 69 *end*; age 131 *grow old*; fade, wither 655 *deteriorate*; fossilize; moulder, rot, rust, decay 51 *decompose*.

Adv. *anciently*, since the world was made, since the year dot, since the days of Methuselah, before the Flood 125 *formerly*.

See: 51, 68, 69, 110, 113, 119, **125**, 129, **131**, 144, 153, 579, 610, 655, 674, 866.

128 Morning. Spring. Summer

N. *morning*, morn, forenoon, a.m.; small hours 135 *earliness*; matins, prime, tierce; dawn, false d., dawning, morning twilight, cockcrow, dawn chorus 66 *precursor*; sunrise, sun-up, daybreak, dayspring 417 *light*; peep of day, break of d.; first blush of day; daylight, daytime; full day, prime of the morning; Aurora, Eos, rosy-fingered Dawn; daystar, orb of day 321 *sun*.

noon, high noon, meridian, midday, noonday, noontide; eight bells, twelve o'clock.

spring, springtime, springtide, Eastertide, vernal season, spring s., seed-time, blossom-time, maying; first cuckoo; vernal equinox, first point of Aries.

summer 379 *heat*; summertime, summertide, Whitsuntide; midsummer, summer solstice, Midsummer's Day, high summer, dog days; haymaking; aestivation; Indian summer, St Luke's s., St Martin's s.

Adj. *matinal*, matutinal, morning; diurnal, daytime; auroral, dawning, fresh, dewy 135 *early*; antemeridian; noon, meridian.

vernal, equinoctial, spring; springlike, sappy, juicy, flowering, florescent 130 *young*.

summery, summer, aestival 379 *warm*.

Adv. *at sunrise*, at dawn of day, at first light, at crack of dawn; with the lark; past midnight, in the small hours; a.m.

See: 66, 130, 135, 321, **379**, **417**.

129 Evening. Autumn. Winter

N. *evening*, eventide, even, eve, dewy e.; evensong, vespers, afternoon, p.m.; matinée; afternoon tea, five o'clock; sundowner, soirée; dog-watches; sunset, sundown, setting sun, going down of the sun; evening star, Hesperus, Vesper; dusk, crepuscule, twilight, gloaming 419 *half-light*; candlelight, cockshut, dewfall; moonrise, moonset 321 *moon*; close of day, nightfall, dark, blind man's holiday, nighttime, night-owl 418 *darkness*; bedtime 679 *sleep*; curfew, last post 136 *lateness*, 69 *finality*.

midnight, dead of night, witching time; night-watch, small hours.

autumn, back-end, fall, fall of the leaf; harvest, harvest-time; harvest moon, hunter's m.; Michaelmas; Indian summer; autumnal equinox; 'season of mists and mellow fruitfulness'.

winter 380 *wintriness*; wintertime, wintertide; yuletide, Christmas; midwinter, winter solstice; hibernation.

Adj. *vespertine*, afternoon, postmeridian; vesperal, evening; dusky, crepuscular 418 *dark*, 419 *dim*; nightly, nocturnal, noctivagant; benighted, late; bedtime.

autumnal, equinoctial.
wintry, winter, brumal, brumous, snow-bound 380 *cold*; leafless, stark, bleak.
Adv. *post meridiem*, late, late at night; at night, by n.; all through the night.
See: 69, 136, 321, **380**, **418**, 419, 679.

130 Youth

N. *youth*, freshness, juiciness, sappiness 126 *newness*, 174 *vigorousness*; young blood, youthfulness, youngness, juvenility, juvenescence; juniority 35 *inferiority*; babyhood, infancy, childhood, childish years, tender age 68 *beginning*; puppyhood, puppy fat; boyhood, girlhood; one's teens, adolescence, pubescence, age of puberty, boyishness, girlishness, awkward age, growing pains; younger generation, rising g., young idea 132 *youngster*; growing boy *or* girl, minor, ward; Peter Pan.
nonage, tender age, immaturity, minority, infancy, pupillage, wardship, leading strings; cradle, nursery, kindergarten.
salad days, school d., student d., happiest days of one's life; heyday, heyday of the blood, springtime of youth; prime of life, flower of l., bloom, florescence.
Adj. *young*, youthful, boyish, girlish; virginal, maidenly, sweet-sixteen; adolescent, pubescent; teenage, subteenage, juvenile; maturing, developing, growing; budding, burgeoning, blooming, flowering 128 *vernal*; beardless, unripe, green, callow, awkward, raw, unfledged 670 *immature*; school-age, under-age, minor, infant, pre-school; younger, minor, junior, puisné, cadet; youngest; childish 132 *infantine*; juvenescent; young at heart, ever-young, evergreen, ageless.
See: 35, 68, 126, **128**, **132**, 174, 670.

131 Age

N. *age*, one's age, time of life, years, lifespan 113 *long duration*.
middle age, middle years, middle life; riper years, years of discretion 134 *adultness*; maturity, prime of life; a certain age, climacteric, change of life, menopause, male m., mid-life crisis; middle-aged spread.
old age, anno domini; pensionable age, retirement age; advanced years, three-score years and ten, grey hairs, white hairs 133 *old person*; senescence, declining years, vale of years, evening of one's days, autumn *or* winter of life; infirmity, debility 163 *weakness*; second childhood, dotage, anecdotage, caducity, anility, senility 655 *deterioration*; longevity, green old age, ripe old age.
seniority, old man's privilege 64 *precedence*; primogeniture 119 *priority*; higher rank 34 *superiority*; eldership, deanship; doyen; gerontocracy, elders, presbytery, senate 692 *council*.
gerontology, nostology, geriatrics, care of the aged 658 *therapy*.
Adj. *ageing*, aged, old, elderly, matronly; middle-aged, ripe, mature, mellow 669 *matured*; overblown, overripe, run to seed; of a certain age, not so young as one was, no chicken; past one's prime, getting on, getting old, going grey, greying; white-haired, grey-h., hoary, hoary-headed, long in the tooth; senescent, waning, declining, moribund 361 *dying*; wrinkled, lined, marked with crow's feet, rheumy-eyed, toothless, shrivelled, wizened, decrepit, rickety 655 *deteriorated*; drivelling, doddering, gaga 499 *foolish*; senile, anile, failing, with softening of the brain; full of years, advanced in y., stricken in y., living on borrowed time, with one foot in the grave; longeval, old as Methuselah, old as Adam; well-preserved 650 *healthy*; venerable, patriarchal 920 *respected*; so many years old, turned, rising; too old, past it; retired 681 *leisurely*; superannuated, passé(e) 127 *antiquated*; gerontologic, geriatric.
older, major; elder, senior 34 *superior*; first-born, eldest, primogenital 119 *prior*; eldest, maximus.
Vb. *grow old*, age; show one's years, have seen better days, go grey, turn white; pass three-score years and ten, have one foot in the grave.
See: 34, 64, 113, 119, **127**, 133, 134, 163, 361, 499, 650, 655, 658, 669, 681, 692, 920.

132 Young person. Young animal. Young plant

N. *child*, children, small fry; babe, baby, bundle of joy; infant, nursling, suckling, weanling, fosterling; bairn, little one, tot, tiny tot, little chap, mite, moppet, toddler; brat, kid, kiddie; papoose, bambino; little darling, little angel, little monkey, little imp, imp of mischief; cherub, young innocent; changeling. **See** *young creature*.
youngster, juvenile, young person, young adult, young hopeful, young'un; young

people 130 *youth*; boy, schoolboy, stripling, adolescent; youth, young man, lad, laddie, sonny; urchin, nipper, cub, young shaver, whippersnapper; hobbledehoy, yob, yoblet; Ted, mod, rocker, punk, skinhead; girl, young woman; schoolgirl, lass, lassie, missie, wench, maid, maiden, virgin; chit, slip, chick, puss, miss; teenager, teenybopper, groupie; tomboy, hoyden; little minx, baggage; colleen, mademoiselle, damsel, nymph, nymphet. **See** *young creature*.

young creature, young animal, yearling, lamb, lambkin, kid, calf, heifer; pigling, piglet; fawn, colt, foal, filly; kitten; puppy, pup, whelp, cub; chick, chicken, pullet; duckling, gosling, cygnet 365 *animal, bird*; fledgling, nestling, eyas, squab; fry, litter, farrow, clutch, spawn, brood; larva, pupa, nymph; caterpillar, grub; chrysalis, cocoon; tadpole, polliwog; embryo, foetus 156 *source*.

young plant, seedling, set; sucker, shoot, sprout, slip; twig, sprig, scion, sapling 366 *plant*.

Adj. *infantine*, baby, infantile, babyish, childish, childlike; juvenile, boyish, girlish 130 *young*; kittenish, coltish, hoydenish; newborn, new-fledged, unfledged 126 *new*; in the cradle, in arms, in nappies, at the breast; small, knee-high, half-grown 196 *little*.

See: 126, **130**, 156, 196, 365, 366.

133 Old person

N. *old person*, retired p., pensioner, senior citizen; old dear, old body; sexagenarian, septuagenarian, octogenarian, nonagenarian, centenarian; Methuselah.

old man, old gentleman, elderly g., patriarch, elder statesman, Nestor 500 *sage*; grandsire, grandfather, grandad 169 *paternity*; veteran, old soldier, old hand, old stager, old-timer 696 *expert*; oldster, old'un, old boy, gaffer, greybeard; old geezer, o. codger, o. buffer, dotard; old fogy, fossil 127 *archaism*.

old woman, old lady, elderly l., dowager; grandmother, grandma, gran, granny; old girl, old trout; old dutch 894 *spouse*; no spring chicken; gammer, crone, hag, beldam, witch.

old couple, Darby and Joan, Philemon and Baucis, the old folks.

See: 127, 169, 500, 696, 894.

134 Adultness

N. *adultness*, adulthood, grown-upness, maturation, development 669 *preparedness*; riper years, years of discretion, matureness; legal age, voting a., majority, full age, man's *or* woman's estate; manhood, womanhood, virility, nubility 372 *male*, 373 *female*; badge of manhood, beard, toga virilis, key of the door; maturity, prime, prime of life 131 *middle age*; bloom, florescence; meridian of life, floruit.

adult, grown-up, big boy, big girl; man 372 *male*; woman, matron 373 *female*; youth, stripling.

Adj. *grown-up*, adult, post-pubescent, out of one's teens; major, of age, responsible; mature, fully-developed, full-grown 669 *matured*; nubile 894 *marriageable*; virile, manly 372 *male*; womanly, matronly 373 *female*; blooming, florescent, full-blown, in full bloom, full-fledged; in one's prime 130 *young*.

Vb. *come of age*, grow up, mature 36 *grow*; be grown up, reach man's *or* woman's estate, attain one's majority, have a vote, have the key of the door; grow a beard, put one's hair up; leave home, fly the nest; fend for oneself, earn one's living.

See: 36, 130, **131**, 372, 373, 669, 894.

135 Earliness

N. *earliness*, early hour, prime 128 *morning*; beginnings, early stage, primitiveness 68 *beginning*; early riser, early bird; early comer, first arrival 66 *precursor*; primitive, aborigine, earliest inhabitant 191 *native*.

punctuality, timeliness 137 *occasion*; dispatch, promptitude 678 *activity*; immediacy 116 *instantaneity*.

anticipation, prevenience, a stitch in time 510 *foresight*, 669 *preparation*; prematurity, early maturity, precocity; forestalling 64 *precedence*.

Adj. *early*, bright and e., in the small hours; prevenient, previous 119 *prior*; timely, in time, on t., in good t., punctual, prompt; forward, advance, in advance; advanced, precocious, ahead of its time 126 *new*; summary, sudden, immediate 116 *instantaneous*, 508 *unexpected*; expected soon, next on the list, forthcoming, ready 669 *prepared*; impending, imminent, at hand 200 *near*; too early, premature 670 *immature*.

Vb. *be early*, - premature etc. adj.; be betimes, be beforehand etc. adv.; anticipate, nip in the bud; forestall, get there first 64 *come before*; seize the occasion, take time by the forelock; gain the start, corner the market, steal a march on 306 *outdo*; engage, book, preempt, reserve, pay in advance; secure, order, bespeak; expedite 277 *accelerate*; lose no time 680 *hasten*; be precocious, ripen early; start too soon, jump the gun; put the clock forward, gain time, gain, go fast.

Adv. *betimes*, early, soon, anon; before long; first thing, at the first opportunity; with time to spare; punctually, to the minute, in time, in good time, in due time; time enough.

beforehand, in advance, in anticipation; without waiting, precipitately 680 *hastily*; precociously, prematurely, too soon, before one's time.

suddenly, without notice 508 *unexpectedly*; without delay 116 *instantaneously*; at the sight of; before the ink was dry; forthwith, shortly, directly; at short notice, at the drop of a hat.

See: 64, 66, 68, 116, 119, 126, 128, 137, 191, 200, 277, 306, 508, 510, 669, 670, 678, 680.

136 Lateness

N. *lateness*, late hour, small hours 129 *midnight*; high time, eleventh hour, last minute; unreadiness, backwardness, slow development 670 *nonpreparation*, 499 *unintelligence*; tardiness, lagging 278 *slowness*; afterthought, delayed reaction, esprit de l'escalier 67 *sequel*; latecomer, last arrival; late developer 538 *learner*; slow starter, late riser 278 *slowcoach*; lie-abed, laggard 679 *idler*; Fabius Cunctator.

delay, cunctation, Fabian policy, 'wait and see' 858 *caution*; delaying tactics, prolongation, gaining time, dragging out, obstruction, filibustering, filibuster 113 *protraction*, 702 *hindrance*; deceleration, retardation, check 278 *slowness*; detention, holdup 747 *restraint*; postponement, adjournment, cooling-off period; prorogation, remand, pause, truce, time lag, jet lag 145 *lull*; deferment, moratorium, respite, days of grace; suspension, stay, stay of execution; suspension of penalty, reprieve 752 *abrogation*; putting off, procrastination, mañana 679 *sluggishness*; dilatoriness, law's delays, red tape, form-filling 678 *overactivity*; shelving, pigeonholing, cold storage 679 *inactivity*.

Adj. *late*, late in the day, eleventh-hour, last-minute, deathbed; too late, time up; overdue, delayed, belated, benighted; held up, bogged down 702 *hindered*; behindhand, lagging, after time, behind t., behind schedule; sluggish, tardy; backward 278 *slow*; Fabian 858 *cautious*; unready, unpunctual, never on time; procrastinating, dilatory 679 *inactive*; delayed-action; deferred etc. vb.; posthumous 120 *subsequent*.

Vb. *be late*, sit up late, rise late, keep late hours, burn the midnight oil; lag, lag behind 284 *follow*; stay, tarry, take one's time, be long about it, linger, dawdle, saunter, loiter 278 *move slowly*; hang about, hang around, hang back 679 *be inactive*; dally, dilly-dally; miss a chance, lose an opportunity, let the moment pass, oversleep 138 *lose a chance*; be behindhand, have leeway to make up; put the clock back, not move with the times 125 *look back*; be losing, lose, stop (clock).

wait 507 *await*; bide, stay, bide one's time, hold one's horses, take one's time, wait and see 145 *pause*; sleep on it, consult one's pillow 677 *not act*; hang on, hold on, hold the line; stand about, sit a.; be kept waiting, wait impatiently, cool one's heels.

be pending, drag 113 *drag on*; hang fire, hang in the balance, tremble in the b. 474 *be uncertain*; stand, stand over, stay put 266 *be quiescent*; play a waiting game.

put off, defer, postpone, adjourn; keep, reserve, hold over; keep pending, file, pigeonhole; table, lay on the t.; shelve, put in cold storage, keep on ice; remand, send back; suspend, hold in abeyance; grant respite, reprieve 909 *forgive*; procrastinate, protract, delay, retard, set back, hold up, gain time, filibuster 113 *spin out*; temporize, tide over; stall, keep one waiting, withhold 760 *refuse*.

Adv. *late*, after time, behind t.; late in the day, at sunset, at the eleventh hour, last thing; at length, at last, at long l., ultimately; till all hours; too late, too late for 138 *inopportunely*.

tardily, slowly, leisurely, deliberately, at one's leisure.

See: 67, 113, 120, 125, 129, 138, 145, 266, **278**, 284, 474, 499, 507, 538, 670, 677,

678, 679, 702, 747, 752, 760, 858, 909.

137 Occasion: timeliness

N. *occasion*, happy chance 154 *event*; meeting of events, juncture, conjuncture 181 *concurrence*; timeliness, opportuneness, readiness, ripeness; fittingness 24 *fitness*, 642 *good policy*; just the time, just the moment; right time, proper t., suitable season; auspicious hour, moment, well-chosen m., well-timed initiative; high time, nick of t., eleventh hour 136 *lateness*.

opportunity, given time, borrowed t. 759 *offer*; favourable opportunity, fine o., golden o. 469 *possibility*; one's chance, break, lucky moment, piece of luck 159 *chance*; best chance 605 *choice*; only chance 606 *no choice*; opening, look-in, room, elbow r., field 744 *scope*; liberty, independence, freedom of choice 744 *freedom*; convenience, spare time 681 *leisure*; no obstacle, clear field, clear stage 159 *fair chance*; handle, lever, instrument 630 *tool*, 629 *means*; stepping-stone 624 *bridge*.

crisis, critical time, key point, key moment; turning point, psychological moment, crucial m., emergency, extremity, pressure, pinch, push 700 *predicament*; eleventh hour, last minute 136 *lateness*.

Adj. *timely*, in time, within the time limit; on time, to the minute, punctual 135 *early*; seasonable, welcome, well-timed; just in time, not before time, in the nick of t., at the eleventh hour.

opportune, favourable, providential, heaven-sent, auspicious, propitious; fortunate, lucky, happy 730 *prosperous*; for the occasion, fitting 24 *apt*, 642 *advisable*; as occasion requires, occasional 140 *infrequent*.

crucial, critical, key, momentous, decisive 638 *important*.

Vb. *profit by*, improve the occasion; seize the chance, take the opportunity, make an opening, create an o.; take time by the forelock, carpe diem, strike while the iron is hot, make hay while the sun shines; spare the time for; cash in on, capitalize, exploit, turn to good account 673 *use*.

Adv. *opportunely*, seasonably, in proper time, in due time, in proper course, in due c., in the fullness of time; in due season; at the right time, all in good time; in the nick of time, just in time, at the eleventh hour, now or never.

incidentally, by the way, by the bye; en passant, apropos; parenthetically, by way of parenthesis; while speaking of, while on this subject; on the spur of the moment, for this occasion.

See: 24, 135, 136, 140, 154, 159, 181, 469, 605, 606, 624, 629, 630, 638, **642**, 673, 681, 700, 730, 744, 759.

138 Untimeliness

N. *untimeliness*, wrong time, unsuitable t., improper t., inopportuneness, unseasonableness 643 *inexpedience*; mishap, contretemps; evil hour 731 *misfortune*; off day; intrusion, interruption, disturbance 72 *discontinuity*; mistiming 118 *anachronism*.

Adj. *ill-timed*, mistimed, misjudged, ill-judged, ill-advised 481 *misjudging*; out of turn, untimely, untoward; interrupting, intrusive; malapropos, inconvenient, unsuited 25 *unapt*, 643 *inexpedient*; unseasonable, off-season; unpunctual, not in time 136 *late*; premature, too soon for 135 *early*; wise after the event 118 *anachronistic*.

inopportune, untoward, inauspicious, unpropitious, unfavourable, ill-omened, ill-starred, unlucky, unhappy 731 *adverse*.

Vb. *mistime*, time it badly 481 *misjudge*; intrude, disturb, break in upon, find engaged.

be engaged, be too busy, be occupied, be not at home; be otherwise engaged, have other fish to fry 678 *be busy*.

lose a chance, waste time, miss the bus, miss the boat, miss the train 728 *fail*; drop a sitter, bungle 695 *be unskilful*; oversleep, lose the opportunity, let the opportunity slip, let the occasion pass 136 *be late*; allow to lapse, let slip through one's fingers 458 *neglect*; spoil a good chance, stand in one's own light, shut the stable door after the horse has bolted 695 *act foolishly*.

Adv. *inopportunely*, amiss; as ill luck would have it, in an evil hour; a day after the fair.

See: 25, 72, 118, **135**, **136**, 458, 481, **643**, 678, 695, 728, 731.

139 Frequency

N. *frequency*, rapid succession, rapid fire 71 *continuity*; oftenness, unfailing regularity 141 *periodicity*; doubling, redoubling 106 *repetition*; frequenting, haunting, regular visits, assiduous attendance.

Adj. *frequent*, recurrent 106 *repeated*; common, of common occurrence, not rare 104 *many*; thick on the ground 104 *multitudinous*; incessant, perpetual, continual, non-stop, constant, sustained, steady 146 *unceasing*; regular, hourly 141 *periodical*; haunting, frequenting, assiduous 610 *habitual*.

Vb. *recur* 106 *reoccur*; do nothing but; keep, keep on, fire away 146 *go on*, 106 *repeat oneself*; frequent, haunt 882 *visit*; obsess; plague, pester 827 *trouble*.

Adv. *often*, oft, many a time, time and time again, times out of number; a thousand t.; frequently, commonly, generally; more often than not; not seldom, not infrequently, again and again 106 *repeatedly*; in quick succession, in rapid succession; thick and fast; regularly, daily, hourly, every hour, every minute; in innumerable cases, in many instances; as often as you like, ad libitum.

perpetually, continually, constantly, incessantly, steadily, without ceasing 71 *continuously*; at all times, daily and hourly, night and day, day and night, day after day, morning, noon and night; ever and anon.

sometimes, occasionally, every so often, once in a while; at times, now and then, now and again; from time to time, often enough, more often than not.

See: 71, **104**, **106**, 141, 146, 610, 827, 882.

140 Infrequency

N. *infrequency*, rareness, rarity 105 *fewness*; seldomness, uncommonness; intermittence 72 *discontinuity*; phoenix 84 *rara avis*.

Adj. *infrequent*, uncommon, sporadic, occasional; intermittent, few and far between 72 *discontinuous*; scarce, rare, scarce as hen's teeth, rare as a blue diamond 105 *few*; almost unobtainable, like gold dust 811 *of price*; almost unheard of, unprecedented 84 *unusual*; not to be repeated; single 88 *one*.

Adv. *seldom*, little, once in a way; rarely, scarcely, hardly, only sometimes, only occasionally; not often, infrequently; scarcely ever, hardly e., once in a blue moon; once, once for all, just this once, once only; like angel's visits, few and far between.

See: 72, 84, 88, **105**, 811.

141 Periodicity: regularity of recurrence

N. *periodicity*, regularity, punctuality, regularity of recurrence, rhythm, steadiness, evenness 16 *uniformity*; timing, phasing, serialization 71 *continuity*; alternation, turn and turn about; reciprocity 12 *correlation*; tidal flow, ebb and f., alternating current, AC, wave movement, tidal m. 317 *fluctuation*; to-and-fro movement, pendulum m., piston m., shuttle m.; shuttle service; pulsation, pulse, tick, beat, throb, rhythm, swing 317 *oscillation*; chorus, refrain 106 *recurrence*; drumbeat 403 *roll*; tide 350 *wave*; rate of pulsation, frequency, wave f.; turn, round, circuit, lap; shift, relay 110 *period*.

regular return, rota, cycle, circuit, revolution, life cycle, wheel of life 314 *circuition*, 315 *rotation*; biorhythm; menstrual cycle, menses; yearly cycle, seasons 128 *morning*, 129 *evening*; fixed interval, stated time 110 *period*; routine, daily round 60 *order*, 610 *habit*; days of the week, months of the year; leap year.

anniversary, birthday, jubilee, diamond j., silver j., silver wedding, ruby w., golden w.; centenary, bicentenary, tercentenary, quatercentenary, quincentenary; St George's Day, St Andrew's D., St Patrick's D., St David's D. 988 *holy day*; Sovereign's Birthday, Fourth of July, 14 Juillet 876 *special day*.

Adj. *periodical*, periodic, cyclic, circling, revolving 315 *rotary*; tidal, fluctuating 317 *oscillating*; measured, rhythmical, steady, even, regular, constant, punctual, like clockwork 81 *regular*; breathing, pulsating, pulsatory, pulsatile; throbbing, beating 318 *agitated*; recurrent, recurring, intermittent, remittent 106 *repeated*; reciprocal, alternate, alternating 12 *correlative*; serial, successive, serialized 65 *sequential*, 71 *continuous*.

seasonal, anniversary; paschal, Lenten; at fixed intervals, hourly, daily, nightly, diurnal, semi-diurnal, quotidian, tertian, biweekly, weekly, hebdomadal, hebdomadary, fortnightly, monthly; menstrual; yearly, annual, biennial, triennial, quadrennial, quinquennial, decennial; bissextile, centennial, secular.

Vb. *be periodic*, recur 106 *reoccur*; serialize, recur in regular order, recur in constant succession 60 *be in order*, 71 *run on*, 65 *come after*; turn, revolve, circle 315 *rotate*; return, come round again; take its turn, alternate; be intermittent, intermit; reciprocate 12 *correlate*; fluctuate, undulate 317 *oscillate*; beat, pulse, pulsate, throb 318 *be agitated*; heave, pant 352 *breathe*; swing, sway 217 *hang*; ply, go and return, commute 610 *be wont*.

Adv. *periodically*, rhythmically etc. adj.; regularly, at regular intervals, at stated times; at fixed periods, at established p.; punctually etc. adj.; seasonally, hourly, daily, weekly, monthly, yearly; per diem, per annum; at intervals, intermittently, every now and then, every so often, ever and anon.

by turns, in turn, in rotation, turn and turn about, alternately, every other day, off and on; round and round, to and fro, up and down, from side to side.

See: 12, 14, 16, 60, 65, 71, **81**, **106**, **110**, 128, 129, 217, 314, 315, 317, 318, 350, 352, 403, 610, 876, 988.

142 Fitfulness: irregularity of recurrence

N. *fitfulness*, irregularity, randomness of recurrence 61 *disorder*; jerkiness, fits and starts 17 *nonuniformity*, 318 *spasm*; remission 114 *transience*, 72 *discontinuity*; unsteadiness, inconstancy, variability 152 *changeableness*, 143 *change*; whimsicality, capriciousness, April weather, unpredictability 604 *caprice*; eccentricity; wobbling, staggering, lurching 317 *oscillation*.

Adj. *fitful*, periodic, remittent, intermittent, on-off, stop-go 72 *discontinuous*; irregular 84 *unconformable*; uneven 29 *unequal*; occasional 140 *infrequent*; unrhythmical, unsteady, fluttering 17 *nonuniform*; inconstant, uncertain, unpunctual; variable, veering 152 *changeful*; spasmodic, jerky 318 *agitated*; wobbling, halting, wavering, flickering, guttering, desultory, unsystematic 61 *orderless*; erratic, eccentric, moody 604 *capricious*.

Adv. *fitfully*, irregularly etc. adj.; unevenly, by fits and starts, now and then 72 *discontinuously*.

See: 17, 29, 61, **72**, 84, 114, 140, 143, 152, **317**, 318, 604.

Section seven: Change

143 Change: difference at different times

N. *change*, alteration, variation 15 *difference*; mutation, permutation, modulation, inflection, declension; frequent change, mutability, variability 152 *changeableness*; partial change, modification, adjustment, process, treatment 468 *qualification*; total change 147 *conversion*; sudden change, violent c. 149 *revolution*; break, break with the past, innovation 126 *newness*; winds of change; change for the better, reformation 654 *improvement*; change for the worse 655 *deterioration*; change of direction, diversion, shift, turn 282 *deviation*, 286 *regression*; change of position, transition 305 *passage*; translation, transposition 272 *transference*, 151 *interchange*; alternation 141 *periodicity*; eversion, overthrow 221 *inversion*; catalysis, leavening; change of mind, c. of heart 603 *tergiversation*.

transformation, transfiguration, transfigurement; unrecognizability, transmogrification; metamorphosis, geological m., metasomatism; metabolism, anabolism, catabolism; transmutation, transubstantiation 147 *conversion*; metempsychosis, transmigration of souls; reincarnation, avatar; version, adaptation, transcription, translation 520 *interpretation*, 521 *misinterpretation*.

alterer, alterant, alterative; activator, converter, transformer; catalytic agent, catalyst, enzyme, ferment, leaven; adapter, modifier, reviser, editor; censor, bowdlerizer; alchemist, chemist; decorator, dyer; changer; magician 983 *sorcerer*; kaleidoscope 437 *variegation*; weathercock, renegade 603 *tergiversator*; improver, new broom 654 *reformer*; bad influence, bad apple 612 *motivator*.

Adj. *changeable*, variable, mutable; fickle 604 *capricious*; affected, changed etc. vb.; newfangled 126 *new*; transitional, provisional, modifiable, qualifiable; alternative, transmutative; chequered, kaleidoscopic 437 *variegated*.

Vb. *change*, be changed, alter 152 *vary*; wax and wane 36 *grow*, 37 *decrease*; change colour, change countenance 426 *lose colour*; change one's tune 603 *tergiversate*; vacillate, wobble 474 *be uncertain*; blow hot and cold, chop and change 604 *be capricious*; turn, shift, veer, change course

282 *deviate*; make a transition, pass to 305 *pass*; take a turn, turn the corner 656 *be restored*; turn over a new leaf, be converted 654 *get better*; submit to change 83 *conform*; move with the times 126 *modernize*.

modify, alter, vary, modulate, diversify, shift the scene 437 *variegate*; superimpose 38 *add*; make a change, introduce changes, innovate, bring in new blood 126 *modernize*; turn upside down, subvert, evert 149 *revolutionize*, 221 *invert*; reverse, turn back 148 *revert*; make changes, rearrange, reorder, reset 62 *arrange*; adapt 24 *adjust*; conform 83 *make conform*; recast, remould, reshape 243 *form*; process, treat; revise, edit, correct 654 *rectify*; reform 654 *make better*; vamp up, revamp, patch, darn 656 *restore*; change for the worse 655 *pervert*; tamper with, fiddle w., mar, spoil 655 *impair*; warp, bend, strain, twist, deform 246 *distort*; stain, dye, discolour 425 *colour*, 426 *decolorize*; adulterate, denature, doctor, qualify 43 *mix*, 163 *weaken*; cover, mask, disguise 525 *conceal*; change round, ring the changes, shuffle the cards 151 *interchange*, 272 *transpose*; try a change, spin the wheel 461 *experiment*; effect a change, work a c., leaven 156 *cause*; affect, turn the scale 178 *influence*; transform, transfigure, metamorphose, transmute, transubstantiate, alchemize 147 *convert*; metabolize, digest; conjure, juggle 542 *deceive*.

Adv. *mutatis mutandis*.

See: 15, 24, 36, 37, 38, 43, 62, 83, 126, 141, **147**, 148, **149**, **151**, **152**, 156, 163, 178, 221, 243, 246, 272, 282, 286, 305, 425, 426, 437, 461, 468, 474, 520, 521, 525, 542, 603, 604, 612, 654, 655, 656, 983.

144 Permanence: absence of change

N. *permanence*, permanency, no change, status quo; invariability, unchangeability, immutability 153 *stability*; lasting quality, persistence 600 *perseverance*; endurance, duration 113 *durability*, 115 *perpetuity*; fixity, fixity of purpose, immobility, immovableness 602 *obstinacy*; firmness, rock, bedrock, foundation, solidity 324 *density*; sustenance, maintenance, conservation 666 *preservation*, 146 *continuance*; law, rule 81 *regularity*; fixed law, entrenched clause 153 *fixture*; standing, long s., inveteracy 127 *oldness*; tradition, custom, practice 610 *habit*; fixed attitude, conservatism; routine, fixed r. 60 *order*; unprogressiveness, static condition 266 *quiescence*; traditionalist, conservative, reactionary, true blue, stick-in-the-mud, die-hard 602 *obstinate person*.

Adj. *permanent*, enduring, durable 113 *lasting*; persisting, persistent, continuing, unfailing, sustained, maintained 146 *unceasing*, 115 *perpetual*; inveterate, long-standing 127 *immemorial*; perpetuated, standing, well-established, entrenched, fixed, unchangeable, immutable, unmodifiable, unrepealable 153 *established*; intact, inviolate, undestroyed, unchanged, unsuppressed; living, well-preserved 666 *preserved*; unchanging, conservative, reactionary, dyed in the wool, diehard 602 *obstinate*; unprogressive, stationary, static, immobile 266 *quiescent*; unaltered, uninfluenced, unaffected, still the same 13 *identical*.

Vb. *stay*, come to stay, set in 153 *be stable*; abide, endure, subsist, outlive, survive, outlast 113 *last*; persist, hold, hold good; hold on, hold it, maintain, sustain, keep up, keep on 146 *go on*; rest, remain, tarry, live 192 *dwell*; stand fast, dig one's toes in 600 *persevere*; stand pat, stand one's ground, hold one's ground, keep one's footing 599 *stand firm*; stand still, resist change 266 *be quiescent*; grow moss 127 *be old*; remain the same, not change one's spots; allow to stand, let be, let alone, live and let live, let sleeping dogs lie 756 *permit*.

Adv. *as before*, in statu quo; at a standstill; permanently, for good.

See: 13, 60, 81, 113, 115, 127, **146**, **153**, 192, 266, 324, 599, 600, 602, 610, 666, 756.

145 Cessation: change from action to rest

N. *cessation*, ceasing; desistance, discontinuance, discontinuation 72 *discontinuity*; arrest 747 *restraint*; withdrawal 753 *resignation*, 621 *relinquishment*.

stop, halt, dead stop; standstill, deadlock, stalemate 28 *draw*; checkmate 728 *defeat*; breakdown 728 *failure*; discontinuance, stoppage, stall; shutdown, closing down, nonresumption 69 *end*; hitch, check 702 *hindrance*; stasis, stopping-up, blockage 264 *closure*; interruption 72 *discontinuity*; breaking-off, walkout 709 *dissension*; closure of debate, guillotine 399 *silence*.

strike, stopping work 679 *inactivity*, 715 *resistance*; general strike, 'national holiday', hartal; slow down, work to rule; stoppage, walkout, sit-down strike, lightning s.; unofficial strike, wildcat s., mutiny 738 *disobedience*; lockout 57 *exclusion*.

lull, interval, pause, remission, letup; break, breather, rest 685 *refreshment*; holiday, day off, time o. 681 *leisure*; interlude, cooling-off period, breathing space 108 *interim*; abeyance, suspension; close season, respite, moratorium, truce, armistice, cease-fire, standstill 136 *delay*.

stopping place, port of call, port, harbour; stop, halt, pull-up, whistle-stop, station; bus stop, request s.; terminus, terminal, air t. 271 *air travel*; dead end, blind alley, cul-de-sac; billet, destination, the grave 266 *resting place*, 295 *goal*.

Vb. *cease*, stay, desist, refrain, hold, hold one's hand; stop, halt, pull up, draw up; stand, rest, rest on one's oars, repose on one's laurels 683 *repose*; have done with, see the last of, end, finish 69 *terminate*; interrupt, leave off, knock o.; break o., let up 72 *discontinue*; ring off, hang up 578 *be mute*; withhold one's labour, cease work, stop w., down tools, strike, come out 715 *resist*; lock out 57 *exclude*; pipe down 399 *be silent*; come to an end, dry up, peter out, run o., run down 636 *not suffice*; slacken off, fade out, fade away 446 *disappear*; come off, end its run, be taken off; fold up, collapse 728 *fail*; die away, blow over, clear up 125 *be past*; stand down, withdraw, retire 753 *resign*; leave, leave off; give up, give over 621 *relinquish*; shut up, shut down, close; shut up shop, put up the shutters, go out of business, wind up; shut off steam, switch off; cease fire 719 *make peace*; sound the last post, ring down the curtain, call it a day 266 *be quiescent*, 679 *sleep*.

halt, stop, put a stop to; arrest, check, stem 702 *obstruct*; hold up, call off; pull up, cut short, call a halt, interrupt 747 *restrain*; cause a stoppage, call out, stage a strike; bring to a standstill, freeze; checkmate, stalemate, thwart 702 *hinder*; check oneself, stop short, stop in one's tracks, stop dead; grind to a halt, seize, seize up, stall, jam, stick, catch; brake, put on the b. 278 *retard*.

pause, halt for a moment, stop for breath; hold back, hang fire 278 *move slowly*; stay one's hand, hold one's horses, hesitate 679 *be inactive*; wait awhile, suspend, adjourn, intermit, remit, put on ice 136 *wait*; rest 683 *repose*.

Int. halt! hold! stop! enough! whoa! belay there! refrain! leave off! shut up! give over! cut it out! chuck it! drop it! knock it off! come off it! stow it!

See: 28, 57, 69, **72**, 108, 125, 136, 264, **266**, 271, 278, 295, 399, 446, 578, 621, 636, 679, 681, 683, 685, 702, 709, 715, 719, 728, 738, 747, 753.

146 Continuance in action

N. *continuance*, continuation 71 *continuity*, 144 *permanence*; flow 179 *tendency*; extension, prolongation 113 *protraction*; maintenance, perpetuation 115 *perpetuity*; sustained action, persistence 600 *perseverance*; progress 285 *progression*; uninterrupted course, break, run, rally 71 *series*; recurrence 106 *repetition*.

Adj. *unceasing*, continuing etc. vb.; continual, steady, sustained; nonstop, uninterrupted, unremitting, incessant 71 *continuous*; unvarying, unshifting 81 *regular*; standing, unreversed, unrevoked, unvaried 153 *fixed*; undying 115 *perpetual*; unfailing, ever-running, inexhaustible 635 *plenteous*; invariable, inconvertible 153 *unchangeable*; not out, still in, in play 113 *lasting*; unstoppable, persistent, persisting 600 *persevering*; haunting, obsessive, recurrent, ongoing 106 *repeated*.

Vb. *go on*, wag; keep going, march on, drive on, proceed, advance 285 *progress*; run on, never end 115 *be eternal*; - and - (e.g. rain and rain, pour and pour); roll on, pursue its course, take its c., trend 179 *tend*; endure, stick, hold, abide, rest, remain, linger 144 *stay*; obsess, haunt, frequent 139 *recur*; keep at it, persist, hold on, carry on, jog on, plod on, peg away 600 *persevere*; sit it out, wait, wait till the end, see the end of, hang on 725 *carry through*; be not out, carry one's bat; see one's days out, live out one's time 69 *end*.

sustain, maintain, uphold, keep on foot 218 *support*; follow up, follow through 71 *continue*; keep up, keep alive 666 *preserve*; keep on, harp on 106 *repeat*; keep it up, prolong, protract 113 *spin out*, 115 *perpetuate*; keep the pot boiling, keep the ball rolling; not interfere, let be, let alone, let things take their course, laisser faire 744 *give scope*, 734 *be lax*.

Int. carry on! drive on! never say die! not out!

See: 69, **71**, 81, 106, **113**, **115**, 139, **144**, 153, 179, 218, 285, 600, 635, 666, 725, 734, 744.

147 Conversion: change to something different

N. *conversion*, converting, turning into, making i.; processing 164 *production*; reduction, resolution, crystallization; fermentation, ferment, leaven 143 *alterer*; chemistry, alchemy; mutation, transmutation, transfiguration 143 *transformation*; bewitchment, enchantment 983 *sorcery*; progress 285 *progression*, 157 *growth*; course, lapse, flux 111 *course of time*; development 36 *increase*; evolution 358 *biology*; degeneration, perversion 655 *deterioration*; regeneration, reformation 654 *improvement*; rebirth 656 *restoration*; assimilation, naturalization 78 *inclusion*; alienization, denaturalization 916 *loss of right*; brainwashing 178 *influence*; evangelization, proselytization 534 *teaching*, 612 *inducement*; convertibility 469 *possibility*.

transition, transit 305 *passage*; movement, shift, translation, transfer 272 *transference*; alteration 143 *change*; life cycle.

crucible, melting pot, alembic, cauldron, retort, test tube 461 *testing agent*; laboratory, foundry 687 *workshop*.

changed person, new man *or* woman; convert, neophyte, catechumen, proselyte 538 *learner*; renegade, deserter, apostate, turncoat 603 *tergiversator*; pervert, degenerate 938 *bad person*.

Adj. *converted*, influenced, affected; turned into, made i. etc. vb.; assimilated, naturalized; reborn, regenerate 656 *restored*; proselytized, brainwashed; becoming, transitional; evolving, developing, growing into; transformed, transfigured, bewitched, unrecognizable 15 *different*; convertible, impressionable 143 *changeable*.

Vb. *be turned to*, be converted into, become, get; come to, turn to, ferment, develop into, evolve i., ripen i. 316 *evolve*; fall into, pass i., slide i., shift i. 305 *pass*; melt into, merge i. 43 *be mixed*; settle into, sink i.; mellow 669 *mature*; wax 36 *grow*; degenerate 655 *deteriorate*; take the shape of, take the nature of, assume the character of; be transformed, not know oneself; suffer a sea change, turn over a new leaf 143 *change*; enter a phase, enter a stage.

convert, reduce, process, ferment, leaven; make into, reduce to, resolve into, turn i., conjure i., enchant 983 *bewitch*; transmute, alchemize; render, make, mould, shape, hew into shape 243 *form*; brainwash 178 *influence*; proselytize, evangelize 534 *teach*; win over 485 *convince*; regenerate 656 *revive*; paganize 655 *pervert*.

transform, transfigure; landscape 844 *decorate*; camouflage, disguise 525 *conceal*; render 520 *translate*; traduce 521 *misinterpret*; reshape, deform 246 *distort*; change the face of, change out of recognition 149 *revolutionize*; metamorphose 143 *modify*; reform, make something of 654 *make better*; remodel, reorganize, redress 656 *restore*; assimilate, naturalize, Americanize, Anglicize, Frenchify, Europeanize, Africanize, westernize, orientalize; internationalize; detribalize, denaturalize, alienize 916 *disentitle*, 57 *exclude*.

Adv. *convertibly*, evolvingly; on the way to, in transit.

See: 15, 36, 43, 57, 78, 111, **143**, 149, 157, 164, 178, 243, 246, 272, 285, 305, 316, 358, 461, 469, 485, 520, 521, 525, 534, 538, 603, 612, 654, **655**, **656**, 669, 687, 844, 916, 938, 983.

148 Reversion

N. *reversion*, reverting, going back, return, regress, retrogression, retreat, withdrawal, ebb 286 *regression*; tracing back, derivation 156 *source*; return to the past, harking back 127 *archaism*; atavism, throwback 5 *heredity*; looking back, retrospection 505 *remembrance*; retrospective action, retroaction; reaction 182 *counteraction*, 31 *compensation*; repercussion, backlash, backfire 280 *recoil*; revulsion, revulsion of feeling, disenchantment 830 *regret*; counter-revolution, reversal 149 *revolution*; retraction, backdown 603 *tergiversation*; volte face, about-turn, U-t., right-about t. 240 *contraposition*; backsliding, recidivism 657 *relapse*; reconversion 656 *restoration*; retroversion, retroflexion, retortion 248 *curvature*, 246 *distortion*; giving back, cession, replacement, reinstatement 787 *restitution*; getting back, recovery, retrieval 771 *acquisition*; taking back, escheat 786 *taking*;

reply, feedback 460 *answer*; retort, tu quoque 479 *confutation*; turn, turning point, turn of the tide, calm before the storm 137 *crisis*; alternation, swing, swing of the pendulum 141 *periodicity*, 106 *recurrence*, 317 *oscillation*; to-and-fro movement, coming and going, commuting; round trip, there and back, out and home; return journey, return ticket; back where one started, status quo; resumption, recommencement 68 *start*.

Adj. *reverted*, reversed, reversionary, retrograde, retrogressive, recessive, reflexive 286 *regressive*; reactive 280 *recoiling*; reactionary, retroactive 125 *retrospective*; atavistic 5 *genetic*; recycled, returned; recovered, disenchanted 656 *restored*.

Vb. *revert*, go back, turn b., turn, return, retrace 286 *regress*; reverse, face about, turn a. 221 *invert*; ebb, retreat, withdraw 290 *recede*; kick back, rebound 280 *recoil*; slip back, slide b., backslide 657 *relapse*; backdown, retract 603 *recant*; hark back, archaize; start again, restart, go back to the beginning, undo, unmake 68 *begin*; restore the status quo, revive 656 *restore*; derestrict, decontrol, deration 746 *liberate*; reconvert, disenchant, remove the spell 613 *dissuade*; take back, recover 656 *retrieve*; resume 771 *acquire*; get one's own back 714 *retaliate*; give back, make restitution, reinstate, replace 787 *restitute*.

Adv. *reversibly*, invertedly, wrong side out; back to the beginning, as you were.

See: 5, 31, 68, 106, 125, 127, 137, 141, 149, 156, 182, 221, 240, 246, 248, **280**, **286**, 290, 317, 460, 479, 505, **603**, 613, 656, 657, 714, 746, 771, 786, 787, 830.

149 Revolution: sudden or violent change

N. *revolution*, full circle, circuit 315 *rotation*; radical change, organic c.; tabula rasa, clean slate, clean sweep 550 *obliteration*; sudden change, catastrophe, peripeteia, surprise, coup d'état 508 *lack of expectation*; transilience, leap, plunge, jerk, start, throe 318 *spasm*; shift, swing, switch, switch over, landslide; violent change, bouleversement, upset, overthrow, subversion, inversion 221 *overturning*; convulsion, shake-up, upheaval, eruption, explosion, cataclysm 176 *outbreak*; avalanche, landslip, crash, debacle 309 *descent*, 165 *havoc*; revulsion, rebellion, counter-revolution 148 *reversion*, 738 *revolt*; total change, abolition, nullification 752 *abrogation, deposal*.

revolutionist, abolitionist, radical, revolutionary, Marxist, Red 738 *revolter*; seditionist 738 *agitator*; anarchist 168 *destroyer*; idealist 654 *reformer*.

Adj. *revolutionary* 126 *new*; innovating, radical, thoroughgoing, root and branch 54 *complete*; cataclysmic, catastrophic, seismic, world-shaking 176 *violent*; seditious, subversive, Marxist, red 738 *disobedient*; anarchistic 165 *destructive*.

Vb. *revolutionize*, subvert, overturn 221 *invert*; switch over 603 *tergiversate*; uproot, eradicate, make a clean sweep 550 *obliterate*, 165 *demolish*; break with the past, remodel, refashion 126 *modernize*; change the face of, change beyond recognition 147 *transform*.

See: 54, 126, **147**, 148, 165, 168, 176, 221, 309, 315, 318, 508, 550, 603, 654, **738**, 752.

150 Substitution: change of one thing for another.

N. *substitution*, subrogation, surrogation; by-election 605 *vote*; commutation, exchange, switch, shuffle 151 *interchange*; supplanting, supersession, replacement, transfer 272 *transference*; vicariousness, self-sacrifice 931 *disinterestedness*; expiation, compensation 941 *atonement*.

substitute, sub, succedaneum; proxy, alternate, agent, representative 755 *deputy*; dual representative, twofer; understudy, stand-in 594 *actor*; ghost, ghost-writer 589 *author*; locum tenens, locum 658 *doctor*; reserve, reservist, twelfth man 707 *auxiliary*; supply, replacement, remount; relief, supplanter 67 *successor*; double, ringer, changeling 545 *impostor*; mother figure, father f., foster parent; synonym, doublet 559 *word*; metaphor, symbol 551 *representation*; prosthesis, artificial limb, pacemaker; transplant; alternative, second best, pis aller, ersatz 35 *inferiority*; whipping boy, chopping block, scapegoat, guilt-offering, sacrifice 981 *oblation*; makeshift, stopgap; sticking plaster 177 *moderator*; expedient, temporary e., modus vivendi 770 *compromise*, 642 *good policy*.

quid pro quo, equivalent 28 *compeer*; consideration, purchase money; value, worth 809 *price*; redemption, compensation 31 *offset*; something in exchange, new lamps for old, replacement; change 797 *money*.

Adj. *substituted*, substitutive, substitutionary, substitutional; vicarious 931 *disinterested*; substitutable, interchangeable, commutable 28 *equivalent*; dummy, imitation, plastic, mock, ersatz, counterfeit 542 *spurious*; makeshift, stopgap, provisional, acting, temporary 114 *ephemeral*.

Vb. *substitute*, change for, commute; exchange, switch 151 *interchange*; take *or* offer in exchange, compound 770 *compromise*; palm off with, fob off w. 542 *deceive*; make do with, put up w., make shift w.; put in the place of, replace with; count as, treat as, regard as; replace, step into the shoes of, succeed 65 *come after*; supersede, supplant, displace, oust 300 *eject*; replace, take the place of, be substitute for, do duty f., count f., stand in f., act f., understudy f. 755 *deputize*; act the part of, ghost for; hold the fort; shoulder the blame for, take the rap f., cover up f.; rob Peter to pay Paul.

Adv. *instead*, in place, in lieu; in favour of; in loco parentis; by proxy; alternatively, as an alternative; in default of, for want of better, faute de mieux.

See: 28, 31, 35, 65, 67, 114, **151**, 177, 272, 300, 542, 545, 551, 559, 589, 594, 605, 642, 658, 707, 755, 770, 797, 809, 931, 941, 981.

151 Interchange: double or mutual change

N. *interchange*, interchangeability, reciprocality; swap, exchange 791 *barter*; commutation, permutation, anagram; transposal, transposition, mutual transfer; all change, general post; castling (chess), shuffle, shuffling 272 *transference*; reciprocity, mutuality; interplay, two-way traffic, reciprocation 12 *correlation*; quid pro quo; rally (tennis), give and take; retort, repartee 460 *rejoinder*; tit for tat, eye for an eye, tooth for a tooth 714 *retaliation*; logrolling 706 *cooperation*.

Adj. *interchanged*, switched, exchanged, counter-changed etc. vb.; bartered, swapped; in exchange, au pair; reciprocating, mutual, two-way 12 *correlative*; reciprocal, requited 714 *retaliatory*; inter-, intercontinental, interdepartmental; interchangeable, substitutable, convertible, commutable 28 *equivalent*.

Vb. *interchange*, exchange, counterchange; change money, convert; swap, barter 791 *trade*; permute, commute; switch, shuffle, castle (chess) 272 *transpose*; give and take 770 *compromise*; reciprocate 12 *correlate*; requite, give as good as one gets 714 *retaliate*; bandy words, answer back, return the compliment, rejoin 460 *answer*; take in each other's washing, scratch each other's back 706 *cooperate*.

Adv. *in exchange*, vice versa, mutatis mutandis; backwards and forwards, to and fro, by turns, turn and turn about; each in his turn; in kind; au pair; interchangeably, conversely.

See: **12**, 28, 272, 460, 706, **714**, 770, 791.

152 Changeableness

N. *changeableness*, changeability, mutability, modifiability, changefulness 143 *change*; variability, variety 17 *nonuniformity*, 437 *variegation*; inconsistency, inconstancy, irregularity; instability, imbalance, disequilibrium, unstable equilibrium 29 *inequality*; weak foundation, unsteadiness, rockiness, wobbliness; plasticity, pliancy 327 *softness*; fluidness 335 *fluidity*; lubricity, slipperiness 258 *smoothness*; mobility, restlessness, darting, starting, fidgeting, inquietude, disquiet 318 *agitation*; fluctuation, alternation 317 *oscillation*; turning, veering, chopping and changing 142 *fitfulness*; impermanence, flicker, flash 114 *transience*; vacillation, hesitation, wavering 601 *irresolution*; yea and nay 603 *tergiversation*; fickleness, capriciousness 604 *caprice*; flightiness, light-mindedness 456 *inattention*; versatility 694 *aptitude*.

changeable thing, moon, Proteus, chameleon; changing scene, kaleidoscope; shifting sands; wax, clay; mercury, quicksilver 335 *fluid*; wind, weathercock, weathervane; eddy; April showers; wheel, whirligig; mobile 265 *motion*; fortune, wheel of Fortune; vicissitude, luck 159 *chance*; variable, variable quantity 85 *numerical element*; play of expression, mobile features 445 *appearance*; grasshopper mind 456 *inattention*; floating voter 603 *tergiversator*.

Adj. *changeful*, changing, mutable, alterable, phased 143 *changeable*; shifting, vicissitudinous; varying, variant, variable 17 *nonuniform*; kaleidoscopic 437 *iridescent*; protean 82 *multiform*; quick-change, versatile 694 *skilful*; uncertain, unreliable, vacillating, wavering 601 *irresolute*; unpredictable, unaccountable 508 *unexpected*; never the same, volatile, mercurial 15 *different*; wayward, fickle, whimsical 604 *capricious*; giddy, dizzy, flighty, wanton, irresponsible 456 *light-minded*; shifty, inconstant, unfaithful, disloyal 603 *tergiversating*.

unstable, unsteady, unsound, built on sand; wavering, wobbling, rocky, tottering, staggery, reeling, rolling 317 *oscillating*; mobile, unquiet, restless, fidgety 318 *agitated*; desultory, spasmodic, flickering 142 *fitful*; touch and go 114 *transient*; shifting, veering, turning, chopping and changing 282 *deviating*; whiffling, gusty 352 *windy*; unsettled, unfixed, loose, unattached, floating; erratic, mercurial; rootless, homeless 59 *extraneous*; vagrant, rambling, roving, wandering 267 *travelling*; vibrating, vibratory, alternating, fluctuating, tidal 141 *periodical*; yielding, impressionable, malleable, alterable, plastic 327 *soft*; flowing, running, melting 335 *fluid*.

Vb. *vary*, be changeful, show variety 437 *variegate*; ring the changes, go through phases, show p., have as many phases as the moon 143 *change*; chop and change, change and change about; dodge, double 620 *avoid*; shuffle, be shifty 518 *be equivocal*; writhe 251 *wriggle*; dart, flit, flitter 265 *be in motion*; leap, dance, flicker, gutter 417 *shine*; twinkle, flash; wave, wave in the wind, flutter, flap 217 *hang*; shake, tremble 318 *be agitated*; wobble, stagger, rock, reel, sway, swing, vibrate 317 *oscillate*; alternate, ebb and flow, wax and wane 317 *fluctuate*; veer, tack, yaw 282 *deviate*, 269 *navigate*; whiffle, puff 352 *blow*; vacillate, waver, hesitate, float, drift, change one's mind 601 *be irresolute*; hover, hover between two extremes, blow hot and cold, play fast and loose 603 *tergiversate*; be inconstant, change one's fancy 604 *be capricious*.

Adv. *changeably*, variably; fitfully, off and on, now this now that.

See: 15, 17, 29, 59, 82, 85, 114, 141, **142**, **143**, 159, 217, 251, 258, 265, 267, 269, 282, **317**, **318**, 327, 335, 352, 417, 437, 445, 456, 508, 518, 601, 603, 604, 620, 694.

153 Stability

N. *stability*, immutability; unchangeableness, unchangeability; irreversibility, invariability, constancy 16 *uniformity*; firmness, fixity, rootedness 144 *permanence*; rest, immobility, immovability 266 *quiescence*; stableness, stabilization, steadiness, steady state, stable equilibrium, homoeostasis, balance 28 *equality*; nerve, unshaken n., iron n., aplomb 599 *resolution*; stiffness, inflexibility 326 *hardness*, 602 *obstinacy*; solidarity, solidity 324 *density*; stiffening, ankylosis 326 *hardening*.

fixture, establishment, firm foundation; foundations, rock, bedrock, pillar, tower, pyramid; invariant, constant; fast colour, indelible ink; leopard's spots; law, law of the Medes and Persians, the Twelve Tables, the Ten Commandments, written constitution, entrenched clause, prescriptive right 953 *legality*.

stabilizer, fin, centreboard, keel; counterweight, ballast 31 *offset*; buttress 218 *prop*.

Adj. *unchangeable*, unsusceptible of change; stiff, inflexible 602 *obstinate*; unwavering 599 *resolute*; predictable, reliable 473 *certain*; immutable, intransmutable, incommutable; unalterable, inconvertible; irreducible, indissoluble; changeless, unchanging, unchanged, unaltered, inalterable, irreversible; unshrinkable, shrinkproof; indeclinable; stereotyped, unvarying, invariable, constant 16 *uniform*; steady, undeviating 81 *regular*; durable, as the hills 113 *lasting*, 144 *permanent*; undying, perennial, evergreen 115 *perpetual*; imperishable, indestructible, inextinguishable 660 *invulnerable*. **See** *fixed*.

established, well-e., entrenched, vested, settled; inveterate, prescriptive 113 *lasting*; irrevocable, irreversible; incontrovertible, indefeasible, of right; valid, confirmed, ratified 473 *undisputed*, 488 *assented*.

fixed, steadfast, firm, secure, immovable, irremovable; unassailable, unshakable, steady as a rock; steady, stable, balanced, homoeostatic; fast, ingrained, indelible; engraved; ineradicable, rooted, well-r., deep-r.; deep-seated, foursquare, well-founded, built on a rock; standing, pat; tethered, moored, anchored 45 *tied*; at rest, at anchor, riding at a.; run aground, stuck fast, stranded, grounded, high and dry; pinned down, transfixed; immobile, frozen, like a statue, still as a stone 266 *still*.

Vb. *be stable*, - fixed etc. adj.; stand, stick fast, hold 599 *stand firm*; show aplomb, show self-assurance, not bat an eyelid; weather the storm 113 *outlast*; set in, come to stay 144 *stay*; settle, settle down 192 *dwell*; strike root, take r., strike deep, have long roots.

stabilize, root, entrench, found, establish, build on a rock 115 *perpetuate*; erect, set up, set on its feet 218 *support*; float, set afloat; fix, set, stereotype, grave on granite; make valid, validate, confirm, ratify 488 *endorse*; retain, stet; bind, make sure, make fast 45 *tie*; keep steady, hold the road, retain equilibrium, balance 28 *equalize*.

See: 16, 28, 31, 45, 81, **113**, **115**, **144**, 192, 218, 266, 324, 326, 473, 488, 599, 602, 660, 953.

154 Present Events

N. *event*, phenomenon; fact, matter of f., actual f. 1 *reality*; case, circumstance, state of affairs 7 *state*; occurrence, eventuality, incidence, realization, happening, turn of events; incident, episode, adventure 137 *occasion*; milestone 8 *juncture*; fortune, accident, casualty, contingency 159 *chance*; misadventure, mishap 731 *misfortune*; emergency, pass 137 *crisis*; coincidence 181 *concurrence*; advent 289 *approach*; encounter, meeting; transaction, proceeding, affairs 676 *action*; result, product, consequence, issue, outcome, upshot 157 *effect*; denouement, solution, unravelling 316 *evolution*; peripeteia, catastrophe 69 *end*.

affairs, matters, doings, transactions 676 *deed*; agenda, order of the day; involvement, concern, concerns, interests, irons in the fire, axes to grind 622 *business*; world, life, situation 8 *circumstance*; current affairs, affairs in general, state of affairs; course of events, march of e., stream of e., tide of e. 111 *course of time*; run of affairs, chapter of accidents, ups and downs of life, vicissitudes 730 *prosperity*, 731 *adversity*.

Adj. *eventual*, consequential, resulting, resultant, eventuating, issuing in 157 *caused*; circumstantial, contingent.

happening, incidental, accidental, occasional; doing, current, on foot, afloat, in the wind, on the agenda; on the stocks, in preparation.

eventful, stirring, bustling, busy, full of incident, crowded with i. 678 *active*; momentous, critical 638 *important*.

Vb. *happen*, become, come into existence 360 *be born*; materialize, be realized, come off 727 *succeed*; take place, occur, come about, come to pass, fulfil expectations; befall, betide 159 *chance*; turn up, pop up, crop up, start up, spring up, arise 295 *arrive*; present itself, announce i. 189 *be present*; supervene 284 *follow*; eventuate, issue, transpire, emanate 157 *result*; turn out, fall o., work o., pan o.; be on foot, take its course, hold its c., advance 285 *progress*; continue 146 *go on*; go off, pass o. 125 *be past*; fall to one's lot, be one's great chance; be so, prove, prove to be; bring about, occasion 156 *cause*.

meet with, incur, encounter 295 *meet*; realize, find 484 *discover*; experience, pass through, go t.; have been through 490 *know*, 818 *feel*; have adventures, endure, undergo 825 *suffer*.

Adv. *eventually*, ultimately, in the event of, in case; in the course of things, in the natural course of t., in the ordinary course of t.; as things go, as times go; as the world goes, as the world wags; as the cookie crumbles; as the cat jumps; as it may turn out, as it may happen.

See: 1, 7, 8, 69, 111, 125, **137**, 146, 156, **157**, **159**, 181, 189, 284, 285, 289, 295, 316, 360, 484, 490, 622, 638, 676, 678, 727, 730, 731, 818, 825.

155 Destiny: future events

N. *destiny*, what's to come, one's stars 596 *fate*; horoscope, forecast 511 *prediction*; prospect, outlook 507 *expectation*; coming events, future plans, intentions 124 *futurity*, 617 *intention*; trouble in store, danger 900 *threat*; imminence, impendence, proximity 200 *nearness*, 289 *approach*; post-existence, future existence, hereafter 124 *future state*; next world, afterworld, world to come 971 *heaven*; foredoom, predestination 596 *necessity*, 473 *certainty*.

Adj. *impending*, overhanging, hanging over, louring, hovering, imminent 900 *threatening*; preparing, brewing, cooking 669 *preparatory*; destined, predestined, in the stars, in the lap of the gods 596 *fated*;

predicted, forthcoming, forecast 511 *predicting*; inescapable, inevitable, going to be, bound to happen 473 *certain*; due, owing 596 *necessary*; in the wind, on the cards 471 *probable*; on the agenda, intended, decided on 608 *predetermined*; in prospect, in view, in the offing, on the horizon, looming on the h., in the distance 443 *visible*; in the future, to come, in the womb of time 124 *future*; at hand, close 200 *near*, 289 *approaching*; instant, immediate, about to be, on the point of 116 *instantaneous*; pregnant with, heavy w. 511 *presageful*; in store, in reserve, in pickle, ready, kept r. 669 *prepared*; in embryo 68 *beginning*.

Vb. *impend* 124 *be to come*; hang over, lie o., hover, lour, loom 900 *threaten*; come on, draw nigh 289 *approach*; front, face, stare one in the f. 237 *be in front*; breathe down one's neck 200 *be near*; ripen 669 *mature*.

predestine, destine, doom, foredoom, preordain, foreordain 596 *necessitate*; foreshadow, adumbrate, presage 511 *predict*; have ready, get r., have in store, have in pickle 669 *make ready*; plan, intend 608 *predetermine*.

Adv. *in the future*, in time, in the long run; all in good time; in the event 154 *eventually*; whatever may happen; expectedly 471 *probably*; soon, at any moment.

See: 68, 116, **124**, 154, 200, 237, 289, 443, 471, 473, 507, 511, **596**, 608, 617, 669, 900, 971.

Section eight: Causation

156 Cause: constant antecedent

N. *causation*, causality, cause and effect, ground and consequent; aetiology 158 *attribution*; authorship; origination, creation 21 *originality*; invention 484 *discovery*; inspiration 178 *influence*; generation, evocation, provocation 164 *production*; impulsion, stimulation, fomentation, encouragement, motivation 612 *motive*; planting, watering, cultivation 370 *agriculture*; abetment 706 *cooperation*; temptation 612 *inducement*; opportunity 137 *occasion*.

cause, formal c., efficient c., material c., first c., final c.; prime mover, primum mobile, God 965 *the Deity*; sui causa 1 *existence*; creator, maker 164 *producer*; begetter, father 169 *parentage*; causer, effecter, occasioner; author, inventor, originator, founder; agent, leaven; stimulus 174 *stimulant*; contributor, factor, decisive f., moment, determinant; inspirer, tempter, mainspring 612 *motivator*; fomenter, aider, abettor; hidden hand, undercurrents 178 *influence*; planetary influence, stars 155 *destiny*; fate 596 *necessity*; force 740 *compulsion*.

source, fountain, fount, fons et origo 68 *origin*; headwaters, spring, wellhead, fountainhead, wellspring; mine, quarry 632 *store*; birthplace, roots 192 *home*; genesis, ancestry, lineage, descent 169 *parentage*; parent, ancestor, progenitor; loins 167 *genitalia*; rudiment, element, principle, first p., first thing; nucleus, germ, seed, sperm, spore; egg, foetus, embryo; chrysalis, cocoon 132 *young creature*; bud, stem, stock, rootstock; taproot, root, bulb 366 *plant*; radix, radical, etymon, derivation, etymology 557 *linguistics*; foundation, bedrock 214 *base*; groundwork, spadework, beginnings 68 *beginning*; raw material, ore 631 *materials*.

seedbed, hotbed, nidus 192 *nest*; cradle, nursery 68 *origin*; fertile soil, breeding ground, incubator, womb 167 *propagation*; hothouse, conservatory, propagator 370 *garden*.

causal means, appliance 629 *means*; pivot, hinge, lever, instrument 630 *tool*; dynamo, generator, battery, spark 160 *energy*; motor, engine, turbine 630 *machine*; last straw that breaks the camel's back.

reason why, reason, cause, the why and wherefore; explanation, key 460 *answer*, 520 *interpretation*; excuse 614 *pretext*; ground, basis, rationale, motive, idea, occasion, causa causans, raison d'être.

Adj. *causal*, causative, formative, effective, effectual 727 *successful*; pivotal, determinant, decisive, final 69 *ending*; seminal, germinal 164 *productive*; inceptive, embryonic 68 *beginning*; suggestive, inspiring 178 *influential*; impelling 740 *compelling*; answerable, responsible; at the bottom of, original; aetiological, explanatory 158 *attributed*; creative, inventive 21 *inimitable*.

fundamental, primary, elemental, ultimate; foundational, radical, basic 5 *intrinsic*; crucial, central 638 *important*; original, aboriginal 68 *first*; primitive, primordial

127 *primal*.

Vb. *cause*, originate, create, make 164 *produce*; beget, be the author of 167 *generate*; invent 484 *discover*; be the reason 158 *account for*; underlie, be *or* lie at the bottom of, be at the root of; sow the seeds of, be answerable, be responsible, have a hand in, be to blame; institute, found, lay the foundations, inaugurate 68 *auspicate*; set up, erect 310 *elevate*; launch, set afloat, set afoot, set going, trigger off, spark off, touch o. 68 *begin*; open, open up, broach 68 *initiate*; seed, sow, plant, water 370 *cultivate*; contrive, effect, effectuate, bring about, bring off, bring to pass 727 *succeed*; procure, provide the means 629 *find means*; stage-manage, engineer 623 *plan*; bring on, induce, precipitate 680 *hasten*; bring out, draw o., evoke, elicit 291 *attract*; provoke, arouse, awaken 821 *excite*; stimulate 174 *invigorate*; kindle, inspire, incite, tempt 612 *induce*; occasion, give occasion for 612 *motivate*; have an effect, show its result, make or mar 178 *influence*; be the agent, do the deed 676 *do*; determine, decide, give the decision 480 *judge*; decide the result, turn the scale, give the casting vote 178 *prevail*, 34 *predominate*.

conduce, tend to 179 *tend*; lead to 64 *come before*; contribute to, operate to 628 *be instrumental*; involve, imply 5 *be intrinsic*; have the effect, entail, draw down, give rise to, open the door to 68 *initiate*; promote, advance, encourage, foster, foment, abet 703 *aid*.

Adv. *causally*, because, by reason of, behind the scenes 178 *influentially*.

See: 1, 5, 21, 34, 64, **68**, 69, 127, 132, 137, 155, **158**, 160, 164, 167, 169, 174, **178**, 179, 192, 214, 291, 310, 366, 370, 460, 480, 484, 520, 557, 596, **612**, 614, 623, 628, 629, 630, 631, 632, 638, 676, 680, 703, 706, 727, 740, 821, 965.

157 Effect: constant sequel

N. *effect*, consequent, consequence, corollary 65 *sequence*; result, resultance; derivation, derivative, precipitate 41 *remainder*; upshot, outcome, issue, denouement 154 *event*; final result, termination 725 *completion*; visible effect, mark, print, impress 548 *trace*; by-product, side effect, spin-off; aftermath, legacy, backwash, wake, repercussion 67 *sequel*; resultant action, response 460 *answer*; performance 676 *deed*; reaction, backlash 182 *counteraction*; offspring 170 *posterity*; handiwork 164 *product*; karma 596 *fate*; moral effect 178 *influence*.

growth, outgrowth, development 36 *increase*; bud, blossom, florescence, fruit; ear, spike; produce, crop, harvest; profit 771 *gain*.

Adj. *caused*, owing to, due to, attributed to; consequential, resulting from, consequent upon 65 *sequential*; contingent, depending, dependent on 745 *subject*; resultant, derivable, derivative, descended; unoriginal, secondary 20 *imitative*; arising, emergent, emanating, developed from, evolved f.; born of, out of, by; ending in, issuing in 154 *eventual*; effected, done.

inherited, heritable, hereditary, Mendelian 5 *genetic*.

Vb. *result*, be the r., come of; follow on, wait on, accrue 284 *follow*; be owing to, be due to; owe everything to, borrow from 785 *borrow*; have a common origin 9 *be related*; take its source, derive from, descend f., originate f. *or* in, come from *or* out of; issue, proceed, emanate 298 *emerge*; begin from, grow f., spring f., arise f., flow f.; develop, unfold 316 *evolve*; bud, sprout, germinate 36 *grow*; show a trace, show an effect, receive an impression, bear the stamp 522 *be plain*; bear the consequences 154 *meet with*, 963 *be punished*; turn out, pan o., work o., eventuate 154 *happen*; result in 164 *produce*.

depend, hang upon, hinge on, pivot on, turn on 12 *correlate*, 745 *be subject*.

Adv. *consequently*, as a consequence, in consequence; because of, as a result; of course, naturally, necessarily; it follows that, and so 158 *hence*.

See: 5, 9, 12, 20, 36, 41, **65**, 67, **154**, 158, **164**, 170, 178, 182, 284, 298, 316, 460, 522, 548, 596, 676, 725, 745, 771, 785, 963.

158 Attribution: assignment of cause

N. *attribution*, assignment of cause; reference to, imputation, ascription; theory, hypothesis, model, assumption, conjecture 512 *supposition*; explanation 520 *interpretation*; finding reasons, accounting for; aetiology, palaetiology 459 *enquiry*; rationale 156 *reason why*; filiation, affiliation 169 *parentage*; derivation 156 *source*; attribute 89 *concomitant*;

credit, credit title, acknowledgment 915 *dueness.*

Adj. *attributed*, assigned etc. vb.; attributable, assignable, imputable, referable, referrible; assigned to, referred to 9 *relative*; credited, imputed, putative 512 *supposed*; inferred, inferable, derivable, traceable; owing to, explained by 157 *caused.*

Vb. *attribute*, ascribe, impute; say of, assert of, predicate 532 *affirm*; accord, grant, allow 781 *give*; put down to, set down to; assign to, refer to, point to, trace to, connect with, derive from 9 *relate*; lay at the door of, affiliate, father upon; charge with, charge on, saddle with *or* on; found upon, ground u.; make responsible, scapegoat, blame for 928 *accuse*; bring home to 478 *demonstrate*; credit, credit with, acknowledge 915 *grant claims.*

account for, explain, say how it happens 520 *interpret*; theorize, hypothesize, assume 512 *suppose*; infer the cause, derive the reason.

Adv. *hence*, thence, therefore; whence, wherefore; for, since, on account of, because, owing to, thanks to, on that account, from this cause, from that cause, propter hoc, ergo, thus, so; that's why.

why? wherefore? whence? how? how come? cui bono?

somehow, in some way, in some such way; somehow or other.

See: 9, 89, **156**, 157, 169, 459, 478, 512, 520, 532, 781, 915, 928.

159 Chance: no assignable cause

N. *chance*, blind c., fortuity, indeterminacy; randomness; indetermination, fortuitousness; uncertainty principle, unpredictability 474 *uncertainty*; unaccountability, inexplicability 517 *unintelligibility*; lot, fortune, wheel of f. 596 *fate*; whatever comes, potluck, luck of the draw; good fortune, luck, good l., run of l. 730 *prosperity*; bad luck, rotten l. 731 *misfortune*; hap, hazard, accident, casualty, contingency, coincidence, chapter of accidents 154 *event*; nonintention, chance hit, lucky shot, fluke 618 *nondesign*; rare chance, chance in a million 140 *infrequency*; chance meeting, chance encounter 508 *lack of expectation*; chance discovery, serendipity 484 *discovery.*

equal chance, even c., fifty-fifty 28 *equality*; toss-up, spin of the coin, heads or tails, throw of the dice, turn of the card; lucky dip, random sample; lottery, raffle, tombola, sweepstake, premium bond 618 *gambling*; sortes Biblicae 511 *divination.*

fair chance, sporting c., fighting c., gambling c. 469 *possibility*; half a chance, small c. 472 *improbability*; good chance, main c., best c., favourable c. 137 *opportunity*; long odds, odds on, odds 34 *advantage*; small risk, safe bet, the probabilities 471 *probability.*

calculation of chance, theory of probabilities, doctrine of chance, actuarial calculation, mathematical probability; risk-taking, assurance, insurance, underwriting 672 *undertaking*; speculation 461 *experiment*; bookmaking 618 *gambling.*

Adj. *casual*, fortuitous, aleatory, chance, haphazard, random, stray, out of a hat 618 *designless*; adventitious, accidental, incidental, contingent 154 *happening*; noncausal, epiphenomenal, coincidental 89 *accompanying*, 10 *unrelated*; chancy, fluky, dicey, incalculable, stochastic 474 *uncertain.*

causeless, groundless, uncaused, unforeseeable, unpredictable, undetermined, indeterminate 474 *uncertain*; unmotivated, unintended, undesigned, unplanned, unmeant 618 *unintentional*; unaccountable, inexplicable 517 *puzzling.*

Vb. *chance*, hap, turn up, crop up, fall to one's lot, so happen 154 *happen*; chance upon, light u., hit u., stumble u., blunder u. 154 *meet with*, 484 *discover*; risk it, chance it, leave it to chance 618 *gamble*; have small chance 472 *be unlikely.*

Adv. *by chance*, by accident; accidentally, casually, unintentionally, fortuitously, randomly 618 *at random*; perchance, perhaps; for all one knows 469 *possibly*; luckily, as good luck would have it; unluckily, as ill luck would have it; according to chance, as it may be, as it may chance, as it may turn up, as it may happen, as the case may be, whatever happens, in any event; unpredictably 508 *unexpectedly*; unaccountably, inexplicably.

See: 10, 28, 34, 89, 137, 140, 154, 461, 469, 471, 472, **474**, 484, 508, 511, 517, 596, **618**, 672, 730, 731.

160 Power

N. *power*, potency, mightiness 32 *greatness*; prepotency, prevalence, predominance 34 *superiority*; omnipotence, almightiness

733 *authority*; control, sway 733 *governance*; moral power, ascendancy 178 *influence*; spiritual power, charisma, mana; witchcraft 983 *sorcery*; staying power, endurance 153 *stability*; driving force 612 *motive*; physical power, might, muscle, right arm, right hand 162 *strength*; dint, might and main, effort, endeavour 682 *exertion*; force 740 *compulsion*; stress, strain, shear; weight 322 *gravity*; weight of numbers 104 *greater number*; manpower 686 *personnel*; position of power, vantage ground 34 *advantage*; validity 494 *truth*; cogency, emphasis 532 *affirmation*; extra power, overdrive.

ability, ableness, capability, potentiality, virtuality 469 *possibility*; competence, efficiency, efficacy, effectuality 694 *skill*; capacity, faculty, virtue, property 5 *intrinsicality*; qualification 24 *fitness*; attribute 89 *concomitant*; endowment, gift 694 *aptitude*; compass, reach, grasp 183 *range*; susceptibility, affectibility 180 *liability*; trend 179 *tendency*; empowering, enablement, authorization 756 *permission*.

energy, liveliness, vigour, drive, dynamism 174 *vigorousness*; internal energy, thermal e., chemical e., potential e.; work, binding energy, kinetic e., mass *or* rest e., radiant e., electrical e., atomic e., nuclear e.; mechanical energy, pedal power, engine power, horsepower; inertia, vis inertiae 175 *inertness*; resistance 333 *friction*; force, field of f. 162 *science of forces*; force of gravity 322 *gravity*; buoyancy 323 *lightness*; compression, spring 328 *elasticity*; pressure, head, charge, steam; full pressure, steam up; tension, high t.; motive power, electromotive force; pulling power 288 *traction*; pushing power, thrust, jet, jet propulsion 287 *propulsion*; momentum, impetus 279 *impulse*; magnetism, magnetic field 291 *attraction*; negative magnetism 292 *repulsion*; suction 299 *reception*; expulsion 300 *ejection*; potential function, potential; unit of work, erg, joule; unit of force, newton; foot-pound, poundal; calorie.

sources of energy, coal, gas, oil 385 *fuel*; nuclear power (**see** *nucleonics*); renewable energy sources, wind power, wave p., geothermal p., solar energy, hydroelectricity; powerhouse, power station, generating s., pumped storage scheme, hydroelectric station 350 *waterfall*; tidal barrage, tide mill 317 *fluctuation*; windmill 315 *rotator*; solar panel, solar battery, heat exchanger 383 *heater*; generator, turbine, motor 630 *machine*.

electricity, induced electricity, thermoelectricity, photoelectricity, piezoelectricity; voltaic electricity, galvanic e.; static e.; lightning; electrodynamics, electrostatics, electromagnetism; induction, inductance, capacitance; resistance, conduction; oscillation, pulsation, frequency; electric charge, pulse, shock; electric current, direct c., alternating c.; circuit, short c., closed c.; electrode, anode, cathode; positive, negative; conductor, semiconductor, nonconductor, insulator; lightning conductor, earth 662 *safeguard*; electrification, live wire 661 *danger*.

electronics, electron physics, optics 417 *optics*; lasers 417 *radiation*; integrated circuit, microprocessor 196 *microelectronics*; computer electronics 86 *data processing*; automation 630 *machine*; telegraph, telephone, television, radio 531 *telecommunication*; electrical engineering, electricity supply; power line, lead, flex 47 *cable*; distributor; pylon, grid, national g.; generator, magneto, dynamo; oscillator, alternator; transformer, commutator, power pack; battery, storage b., accumulator; cell, wet c., dry c., fuel c., photo c., photoelectric c.; valve, tube, transistor; voltage, volt, watt, kilowatt, megawatt; ohm; amperage, ampere, amp.

nucleonics, nuclear physics; fission, fusion, thermonuclear reaction; atom-smasher, particle accelerator, linear a., cyclotron, synchrotron; Zeta, Jet, Tokamek; atomic pile, nuclear reactor, fast breeder r., waste-reprocessing plant; Magnox reactor, AGR, LWR, PWR, SGHWR; fuel rods, moderator, coolant; radioactivity, fallout 417 *radiation*; radioactive waste 659 *poison*; atomic bomb 723 *bomb*.

Adj. *powerful*, potent 162 *strong*; puissant, mighty 32 *great*; ascendant, rising, in the ascendant 36 *increasing*; prepotent, prevalent, prevailing, predominant 178 *influential*; almighty, omnipotent, irresistible 34 *supreme*; with full powers, empowered, plenipotentiary 733 *authoritative*; virtual, potential 469 *possible*; competent, capable, able, adequate, equal to, up to 635 *sufficient*; with resources 800 *rich*; omnicompetent 694 *expert*; efficacious, effectual, effective 727 *successful*; of power, of might, operative, workable, having teeth; in force, valid, unrepealed, unrepealable 153 *established*; cogent, compulsive 740 *compelling*; forcible 176 *violent*; bellicose 718 *warlike*.

dynamic, energetic 174 *vigorous*; high-potential, high-tension, supercharged, souped-up; magnetic 291 *attracting*; tractive 288 *drawing*; propelling 287 *propulsive*, 279 *impelling*; locomotive, kinetic 265 *moving*; powered, engined, driven; automated 630 *mechanical*; electric, electrical, electromagnetic, electronic; solid-state; live, charged; on stream; atomic, nuclear, thermonuclear; hydroelectric, geothermal, wave-powered, solar-p., wind-driven, water-d., steam-operated.

Vb. *be able*, - powerful etc. adj.; can, have it in one's power, have it in one; be capable of, have the virtue, have the property; compass, manage 676 *do*; measure up to 635 *suffice*; have power, exercise p., control 733 *dominate*; force 740 *compel*; gain power, come to p. 178 *prevail*.

empower, enable, endow, authorize; endow with power, invest with p.; put teeth into, arm 162 *strengthen*; electrify, charge, magnetize; plug in, switch on, transistorize, automate; power, drive.

Adv. *powerfully*, mightily etc. adj.; by virtue of, by dint of, with might and main.

See: 5, 24, 32, 34, 36, 47, 86, 89, 104, 153, **162**, **174**, 175, 176, 178, 179, 180, 183, 196, 265, 279, 287, 288, 291, 292, 299, 300, 315, 317, 322, 323, 328, 333, 350, 383, 385, 417, 469, 494, 531, 532, 612, 630, 635, 659, 661, 662, 676, 682, 686, 694, 718, 723, 727, 733, 740, 756, 800, 983.

161 Impotence

N. *impotence*, lack of power, no authority, power vacuum; invalidity, impuissance 163 *weakness*; inability, incapacity; incapability, incompetence, inefficiency 728 *failure*, 695 *unskilfulness*; ineptitude, unfitness 25 *inaptitude*; decrepitude 131 *age*; frailness 114 *transience*; invalidation, disqualification 752 *abrogation*; sterility, sterilization 172 *unproductiveness*, *contraception*; disarmament, demilitarization 719 *pacification*; demobilization 75 *dispersion*.

helplessness, defencelessness 661 *vulnerability*; harmlessness 935 *innocence*; powerlessness 745 *subjection*, 747 *restraint*; impotent fury, gnashing of teeth 891 *anger*; prostration, exhaustion, inanition 684 *fatigue*; collapse, breakdown 728 *failure*; unconsciousness, faint, swoon, coma; numbness, narcosis 375 *insensibility*; stroke, apoplexy, paralysis, hemiplegia, paraplegia 651 *disease*; torpor 677 *inaction*; atrophy 655 *deterioration*; senility, old age 131 *age*; ataxia, locomotor a.; loss of control, incontinence; mental decay, softening of the brain 503 *insanity*; mental weakness, imbecility 499 *unintelligence*; mutism, deaf mutism 578 *voicelessness*; legal incapacity, pupillage, minority 130 *nonage*; babyhood, infancy 130 *youth*; invalid 651 *sick person*, 163 *weakling*.

eunuch, castrato; gelding, capon, bullock, steer, neuter; freemartin, hermaphrodite.

ineffectuality, ineffectiveness, futility 497 *absurdity*; vanity 4 *insubstantiality*; uselessness 641 *inutility*; flash in the pan 114 *transience*; dead letter, scrap of paper 752 *abrogation*; figurehead, dummy, man of straw, broken reed 4 *insubstantial thing*; empty threats, bluster 515 *empty talk*.

Adj. *powerless*, impotent, not able, unable; not enabled, unempowered, unauthorized, without authority; nominal, figurehead, constitutional 4 *insubstantial*; nugatory, invalid, null and void; unconstitutional 954 *illegal*; without a leg to stand on 163 *weak*; inoperative, not working, unexercised, unemployed 677 *nonactive*; suspended, in abeyance, cancelled, withdrawn 752 *abrogated*; abolished, swept away, gone by the board 165 *destroyed*; obsolete, on the shelf 674 *disused*; laid up, out of circulation, kaput; disqualified, deposed; unqualified, unfit, unfitted, inept 25 *unapt*; unworkable, dud, good for nothing 641 *useless*; inadequate 636 *insufficient*; ineffective, inefficacious, ineffectual, feeble 728 *unsuccessful*; incapable, incompetent, inefficient 695 *unskilful*; mechanically powerless, unpowered, unengined; unequipped 670 *unprepared*.

defenceless, helpless, without resource; bereaved, bereft 772 *losing*; kithless, kinless, orphan, unfriended 883 *friendless*; weak, harmless 935 *innocent*; weaponless, unarmed, disarmed 670 *unequipped*; unfortified, exposed, indefensible, untenable, pregnable 661 *vulnerable*.

impotent, powerless, feeble 163 *weak*; emasculated, castrated, caponized, gelded, unsexed, unmanned, sterilized; sexless, neuter; sterile, barren, infertile 172 *unproductive*; worn out, exhausted, used up, effete; senile 131 *ageing*; paralytic, arthritic, stiff 326 *rigid*; unconscious, comatose, drugged, hypnotized 375 *insensible*; incapacitated, disabled, paralysed 163 *crippled*; without self-control, incontinent; done up, dead-beat, clapped out 684 *fatigued*; prostrated 216 *supine*; nerveless, spineless, boneless 601 *irresolute*; shattered, unhinged, unnerved, demoralized, shell-shocked 854 *nervous*; hors de combat, out of the running 728 *defeated*; helpless, rudderless, drifting 282 *deviating*; waterlogged, swamped; on one's beam ends, laid on one's back 728 *grounded*; baffled, thwarted, gnashing one's teeth 702 *hindered*.

Vb. *be impotent*, - defenceless etc. adj.; be unable, cannot, not work, not do, not alter things; not help, have no help to offer 641 *be useless*; strive in vain, avail nothing 728 *fail*; not make the grade 307 *fall short*; have no power 745 *be subject*; have no say, cut no ice 639 *be unimportant*; lose the power of resistance 721 *submit*; feel helpless, shrug, wring one's hands; gnash one's teeth 830 *regret*; do nothing, look on, stand by 441 *watch*; have a hopeless case, not have a leg to stand on; go by the board 446 *disappear*; lose consciousness, faint, swoon, pass out 375 *be insensible*; drop, collapse 163 *be weak*.

disable, incapacitate, unfit 641 *make useless*; disqualify 916 *disentitle*; deprive of power, invalidate 752 *abrogate*; disarm, demilitarize 163 *weaken*; neutralize 182 *counteract*; undermine, sap 255 *make concave*; exhaust, use up, consume 634 *waste*; wind, prostrate, bowl over, knock out 279 *strike*; double up, benumb, paralyse 679 *make inactive*; sprain, rick, wrench, twist, dislocate; cripple, lame, maim, hobble, nobble, hamstring 702 *hinder*, 655 *impair*; stifle, throttle, suffocate, strangle, garrotte 362 *kill*; muzzle, deaden 399 *silence*; spike the guns, draw the teeth, clip the wings, tie one's hands, cramp one's style; sabotage, put a spoke in one's wheel, throw a spanner in the works; deflate, take the wind out of one's sails; put out of gear, unhinge, unstring 46 *disunite*; put out of action, put out of commission 674 *stop using*.

unman, unnerve, enervate, paralyse 854 *frighten*; devitalize 163 *weaken*; emasculate, castrate, neuter, spay, geld, caponize, effeminize 172 *make sterile*.

See: 4, 25, 46, 75, 114, 130, 131, **163**, 165, 172, 182, 216, 255, 279, 282, 307, 326, 362, 375, 399, 441, 446, 497, 499, 503, 515, 578, 601, 634, 636, 639, 641, 651, **655**, 661, 670, 674, 677, 679, 684, 695, 702, 719, 721, 728, 745, 747, 752, 772, 830, 854, 883, 891, 916, 935, 954.

162 Strength

N. *strength*, might, potency, horsepower, HP 160 *power*; energy 174 *vigorousness*; force, physical f., main f. 735 *brute force*; resilience, spring 328 *elasticity*; tone, tonicity, temper; load-bearing capacity, tensile strength; iron, steel 326 *hardness*; oak, heart of oak 329 *toughness*; staying power, endurance, grit 600 *stamina*.

vitality, healthiness 650 *health*; vim, vigour, liveliness 360 *life*; animal spirits 833 *cheerfulness*; virility, red-bloodedness 855 *manliness*; guts, nerve, backbone 599 *resolution*; aggressiveness 718 *bellicosity*; physique, muscularity, muscle, biceps, sinews, thews and sinews; beefiness, brawn 195 *size*; grip, iron g., vicelike g. 778 *retention*; titanic strength, strength of Hercules.

athletics 837 *sport*, 716 *contest*; athleticism, gymnastics, acrobatics, feats of strength, callisthenics 682 *exercise*; stadium, gymnasium 724 *arena*.

athlete, gymnast, tumbler, acrobat, funambulist, contortionist, trapeze artist, circus rider, bareback r., stunt man 594 *entertainer*; Blue, all-rounder 716 *contender*; wrestler 716 *wrestling*; heavyweight 722 *pugilist*; weight-lifter, strong man; champion 644 *exceller*; he-man, muscle man 372 *male*; strongarm man, bully, bruiser, tough guy 857 *desperado*; chucker-out, bouncer 300 *ejector*; amazon, virago 373 *woman*; matador, picador, toreador 362 *killer*; Tarzan, Hercules; Samson, Goliath, Atlas, Titan 195 *giant*; tower of strength 707 *auxiliary*.

strengthening, fortifying etc. vb.; reinforcement 703 *aid*; stiffening, toughening, tempering 326 *hardening*; invigoration, tonic effect 174 *stimulation*; reanimation 685 *refreshment*; revival 656 *restoration*; emphasis, stress 532 *affirmation*.

science of forces, dynamics, statics, hydrodynamics, hydrostatics, electrodynamics, electrostatics; thermodynamics; triangle of forces.

Adj. *strong*, lusty, vigorous, youthful 130 *young*; mighty, puissant, potent, armed 160 *powerful*; high-powered, high-geared, high-tension; all-powerful, omnipotent, overpowering, overwhelming 34 *superior*; incontestable, irresistible, more than a match for, victorious 727 *unbeaten*; sovereign, supreme 733 *ruling*; valid, in full force; in full swing 146 *unceasing*; in the plenitude of power, undiminished 32 *great*; like a giant refreshed 685 *refreshed*; in high feather, in fine mettle, fit as a fiddle, sound as a bell 650 *healthy*; heavy 322 *weighty*; strongarm, forceful, forcible 735 *severe*; urgent, pressing, compulsive 740 *compelling*; emphatic, emphasized 532 *assertive*; tempered, iron-hard, hard as iron, steely, adamantine 326 *hard*; case-hardened, reinforced, toughened 329 *tough*; deep-rooted 45 *firm*; solid, substantial, stable 153 *fixed*; thick-ribbed, well-built, stout; strong as a horse, strong as a lion, strong as an ox; strong as brandy, heady, alcoholic 949 *intoxicating*; undiluted, neat, undiminished 52 *whole*; strengthened, fortified, double-strength; entrenched, defended, inviolable, unassailable 660 *invulnerable*.

unyielding, staunch 599 *resolute*; stubborn 602 *obstinate*; persistent 600 *persevering*; unstretchable, inelastic 326 *rigid*; shatterproof, unbreakable, infrangible, solid 324 *dense*; impregnable 660 *invulnerable*; of iron nerve, indomitable, unconquerable, invincible, unbeatable 727 *unbeaten*; inextinguishable, unquenchable, unallayed 146 *unceasing*; unflagging, tireless, unexhausted 678 *industrious*; unweakened, unwithered, unworn; indestructible, nonbiodegradable 113 *lasting*; proof, sound; waterproof, weatherproof, rustproof, damp-proof, impermeable, gasproof, leakproof 264 *sealed off*; fireproof, bulletproof, bombproof.

stalwart, stout, sturdy, hardy, rugged, robust, doughty 174 *vigorous*; of good physique, able-bodied, muscular, brawny; sinewy, wiry 678 *active*; strapping, well-knit, well set-up, broad-shouldered, barrel-chested, thickset, stocky, mesomorphic, burly, beefy, husky, hefty 195 *large*; gigantic, colossal, titanic, Herculean 195 *huge*.

athletic, gymnastic, acrobatic 837 *amusing*, 716 *contending*; exercised, fit, fighting f., in training, in condition 650 *healthy*; amazonian.

manly, masculine 372 *male*; amazonian; virile, red-blooded, manful 855 *courageous*; in the prime of manhood 134 *grown-up*.

Vb. *be strong*, - mighty etc. adj.; have what it takes; pack a punch; gird up one's loins 669 *prepare*; come in force; be stronger, overpower, overmatch, overwhelm 727 *overmaster*; get stronger, rally, recover, revive 656 *be restored*, 685 *be refreshed*; get up, freshen (wind), blow hard, blow great guns 352 *blow*.

strengthen, confirm, give strength to, lend force to 36 *augment*; underline, stress 532 *emphasize*; reinforce, fortify, entrench; stuff, pad 227 *line*; buttress, prop, sustain 218 *support*; nerve, brace, steel 855 *give courage*; stiffen, toughen, temper, caseharden 326 *harden*; energize, act like a tonic, put beef into 174 *invigorate*; beef up, tone up, animate, enliven, quicken 821 *excite*; vivify, revivify 656 *revive*; reinvigorate 685 *refresh*; set one on his legs 656 *cure*; set up, build up 310 *elevate*; screw up 45 *tighten*; power, engine, motor 160 *empower*.

Adv. *strongly*, powerfully etc. adj.; by force etc. n.; by main force, by compulsion, with might and main; in force.

See: 32, 34, 36, 45, 52, 113, 130, 134, 146, 153, **160**, **174**, 195, 218, 227, 264, 300, 310, 322, 324, 326, 328, 329, 352, 360, 362, 372, 373, 532, 594, 599, 600, 602, 644, 650, 656, 660, 669, 678, 682, 685, 703, 707, 716, 718, 722, 724, 727, 733, 735, 740, 778, 821, 833, 837, 855, 857, 949.

163 Weakness

N. *weakness*, lack of strength, feebleness, puniness; helplessness 161 *impotence*; slightness 323 *lightness*; flimsiness, wispiness, fragility, frailness 330 *brittleness*; delicacy, tenderness 374 *sensibility*; effeminacy, womanishness; unfirmness, unsteadiness, shakiness, wobbliness, giddiness, disequilibrium 29 *inequality*; weak foundation, feet of clay, instability 152 *changeableness*; ineffectiveness 161 *ineffectuality*; moral weakness, frailty, infirmity of purpose 601 *irresolution*; bodily weakness, weakliness, debility, infirmity, decrepitude, caducity, senility 131 *old age*; invalidism, delicate health 651 *ill* *health*; atony, no tone, no toughness, flaccidity, flabbiness, floppiness 327 *softness*; fleshiness, corpulence 195 *bulk*; weak state, asthenia, cachexia; anaemia, bloodlessness; loss of strength, enervation, inanition, faintness, languor, torpor, inactivity 679 *sluggishness*; exhaustion, prostration, collapse 684 *fatigue*; unconsciousness, swoon 375 *insensibility*; decline, declension 655 *deterioration*; weakening, softening, mitigation 177 *moderation*; relaxation 734 *laxity*; loosening 46 *disunion*; adulteration, watering, dilution 43 *mixture*; enfeeblement, debilitation, devitalization 655 *impairment*; emasculation, evisceration; invalidation 752 *abrogation*; effect of weakness, crack, fault 201 *gap*; flaw 845 *blemish*; strain, sprain, dislocation 63 *derangement*; inadequacy 636 *insufficiency*; weak point, Achilles' heel 647 *defect*.

weakling, effeminate, pansy; lightweight 639 *nonentity*; softy, sissy, milksop, mollycoddle, namby-pamby; old woman, invalid, hypochondriac 651 *sick person*; lame dog, lame duck 731 *unlucky person*; infant, babe-in-arms, kitten 132 *young creature*; baby, crybaby 856 *coward*; mummy's boy, mother's darling, teacher's pet 890 *favourite*; doormat, jellyfish, drip, weed, wet; victim 825 *sufferer*; gull 544 *dupe*.

weak thing, flimsy article, reed, broken r., thread, rope of sand; sandcastle, mud pie, house built on sand, house of cards, house of bricks, cobweb, gossamer 4 *insubstantial thing*; matchwood, matchstick, eggshell, paper, tissue p.; glass, china 330 *brittleness*; water, dishwater, slops, milk and water, thin gruel.

Adj. *weak*, powerless, strengthless 161 *impotent*; without force, invalid, unconfirmed 161 *powerless*; understrength, underproof; unfortified, unstrengthened, unaided, helpless 161 *defenceless*; harmless 935 *innocent*; namby-pamby, babyish 132 *infantine*; effeminate, limp-wristed, pansy, womanish 373 *female*; poor, feeble, slight, puny 33 *small*; lightweight 323 *light*; slightly built, of poor physique 196 *little*; thin 206 *lean*; feeble-minded, imbecile 499 *foolish*; sheepish, gutless, weak-willed, half-hearted 601 *irresolute*; nerveless, unnerved 854 *nervous*; spineless, weak-kneed, submissive, yielding 721 *submitting*; marrowless, pithless 4 *insubstantial*; sapless 342 *dry*; bloodless, anaemic, pale 426 *colourless*; untempered, unhardened, limp, flaccid, flabby, floppy 327 *soft*; drooping, sagging, giving 217 *hanging*; untaut, unstrung, slack, loose, relaxed 734 *lax*, 46 *disunited*; watery, washy, wishy-washy, milk-and-water, insipid 387 *tasteless*; low, quiet, faint, hardly heard 401 *muted*; palsied, doddering, tottering, decrepit, old 131 *ageing*; too weak, past it, weak as a child, weak as a baby, weak as a kitten; wavering, unreliable 604 *capricious*; rickety, tottery, shaky, wobbly 152 *unstable*; torpid 679 *inactive*, 266 *quiescent*; in its beginnings, only beginning, infant 68 *beginning*, 126 *new*, 130 *young*. **See** *flimsy*.

weakened, debilitated, diminished, deflated 37 *decreasing*; tapped, drained, wasted, dissipated, spent, effete, used up, burnt out 673 *used*; misused, abused; sapped, undermined, disarmed, disabled, laid low 161 *defenceless*; stripped, denuded, exposed, bare 229 *uncovered*; flagging, failing, exhausted, wearied, weary 684 *fatigued*; strained, overstrained 246 *distorted*; weatherbeaten, worn, broken, crumbling, tumbledown 655 *dilapidated*; the worse for wear, not what it was, on its last legs; rotten, rusting, withered, decaying, in decay 51 *decomposed*; deactivated, neutralized 175 *inert*; diluted, adulterated, watered, watered down 43 *mixed*. **See** *crippled*.

weakly, infirm, asthenic, delicate, sickly 651 *unhealthy*; groggy, rocky; run down, seedy, poorly; underweight, skinny 206 *lean*; languid, languishing, listless; faint, fainting, faintish; sallow, wan, lacklustre 426 *colourless*.

crippled, disabled 161 *impotent*; halt, lame, game, limping, hobbling; hamstrung, hobbled; knock-kneed 246 *deformed*; stiff in the joints, arthritic, rheumatic, gouty; legless, armless, handless, eyeless 647 *imperfect*.

flimsy, gossamer, sleazy, wispy, tenuous 4 *insubstantial*; delicate, dainty, lacy 331 *textural*; frail, tearable, fragile, frangible, friable 330 *brittle*; gimcrack, jerry-built, shoddy 641 *useless*; rickety, ramshackle, shaky, tottery, teetering, wobbly, wonky, creaky, crazy, tumbledown 655 *dilapidated*.

Vb. *be weak*, grow w., weaken; sicken 651 *be ill*; faint, fail, languish, flag 684 *be* *fatigued*; drop, fall 309 *tumble*; dwindle 37 *decrease*; decline 655 *deteriorate*; droop, wilt, fade 131 *grow old*; wear thin, crumble; yield, give way, sag 327 *soften*; split 263 *open*; dodder, totter, teeter, sway, reel 317 *oscillate*; tremble, shake 318 *be agitated*; halt, limp, go lame 278 *move slowly*; have one foot in the grave 127 *be old*.

weaken, enfeeble, debilitate, enervate; unnerve, rattle 854 *frighten*; relax, slacken, unbrace, loosen 46 *disunite*; shake, soften up 327 *soften*; strain, sprain, cripple, lame 161 *disable*; hurt, injure 655 *wound*; cramp 702 *obstruct*; effeminate 161 *unman*; disarm, take the edge off, cushion 257 *blunt*; impoverish, starve; deprive, rob 786 *take away*; reduce, extenuate, thin, lessen 37 *abate*; dilute, water, water down, adulterate 43 *mix*; denature, devitalize, eviscerate; deactivate, neutralize 182 *counteract*; reduce in number, decimate 105 *render few*; muffle 401 *mute*; invalidate 752 *abrogate*; damage, spoil 655 *impair*; sap, undermine; dismantle 165 *demolish*.

See: 4, 29, 33, 37, 43, 46, 51, 63, 68, 105, 126, 127, 130, 131, 132, 152, **161**, 165, 175, 177, 182, 195, 196, 201, 206, 217, 229, 246, 257, 263, 266, 278, 309, 317, 318, 323, 327, 330, 331, 342, 373, 374, 375, 387, 401, 426, 499, 544, 601, 604, 636, 639, 641, 647, 651, **655**, 673, 679, 684, 702, 721, 731, 734, 752, 786, 825, 845, 854, 856, 890, 935.

164 Production

N. *production*, producing, creation; mental creation, cerebration 449 *thought*; origination, invention, original work 21 *originality*, 484 *discovery*; creative urge, productivity 171 *productiveness*; effort, endeavour 671 *attempt*, 672 *undertaking*; artistic effort, composition, authorship 551 *art*, 553 *painting*, 554 *sculpture*, 586 *writing*; musicianship 413 *musical skill*; doing, performance, output, throughput, turnout 676 *action*; execution, accomplishment, achievement 725 *effectuation*; concoction, brewing 669 *preparation*; shaping, forming, conformation, workmanship, craftsmanship 243 *formation*; planning, design 623 *plan*; organization 331 *structure*, 62 *arrangement*; tectonics, engineering, civil e., building, architecture; construction, establishment, erection 310 *elevation*; making, fabrication, manufacture, industry 622 *business*; processing, process 147 *conversion*; machining, assembly; assembly line, production l. 71 *continuity*, 630 *machine*; factory 687 *workshop*; technology, intermediate t., ecodevelopment; industrialization, increased output, mass production, automation; productivity deal 706 *cooperation*; development, growth 36 *increase*, 171 *abundance*; limits to growth 636 *scarcity*; farming, growing, factory farming 370 *agriculture*; breeding 369 *animal husbandry*; procreation 167 *propagation*.

product, creature, creation, result 157 *effect*; output, turnout; printout; end product, by-p.; waste, slag 41 *leavings*; extract, essence; confection, compound 43 *a mixture*; work of one's hands, handiwork, artifact; manufacture, article, finished a., thing 319 *object*; goods, wares 795 *merchandise*; goods and services, gross national product, GNP; earthenware 381 *pottery*; stoneware, hardware, ironware; fabric, cloth 222 *textile*; production, work, opus, oeuvre, piece 56 *composition*; chef d'oeuvre, crowning achievement 694 *masterpiece*; fruit, flower, blossom, berry; produce, yield, harvest, crop, vintage 157 *growth*; interest, increase, return 771 *gain*; mental product, brainchild, conception 451 *idea*; figment, fiction 513 *ideality*; offspring, young, egg, spawn, seed 132 *young creature*.

edifice, piece of architecture, building, structure, erection, pile, dome, tower, skyscraper 209 *high structure*; pyramid 548 *monument*; church 990 *temple*; mausoleum 364 *tomb*; habitation, mansion, hall 192 *house*; college 539 *school*; fortress 713 *fort*; stonework, timbering, brickwork, bricks and mortar 631 *building material*.

producer, creator, maker, Nature; the Creator 965 *the Deity*; originator, inventor, discoverer, mover, instigator 612 *motivator*; founding father, founder, establisher 156 *cause*; begetter 169 *parentage*; creative worker, writer 589 *author*; composer 413 *musician*; painter, sculptor 556 *artist*; deviser, designer 623 *planner*; developer, constructor, builder, architect, engineer; manufacturer, industrialist 686 *agent*; executive 676 *doer*; labourer 686 *worker*; artificer, craftsman *or* - woman 686 *arti-*

san; grower, planter, cultivator, agriculturalist, gardener 370 *farmer*; stock farmer, stock breeder, sheep farmer 369 *breeder*; miner, extractor; play-producer 594 *stage manager*.

Adj. *productive*, creative, inventive 513 *imaginative*; shaping, constructive, architectonic 331 *structural*; manufacturing, industrial 243 *formative*; developed, industrialized; mechanized, automated; paying 640 *profitable*; fruitful 171 *prolific*; life-giving 167 *generative*.

produced, made, made-up, cobbled together; created, creaturely; artificial, man-made, synthetic, cultivated; manufactured, processed; handmade, done by hand; homemade, homespun; architect-designed, craftsman-built; ready-made 243 *formed*; untouched by hand, machine-made, mass-produced; multiplied 166 *reproduced*; begotten 360 *born*; bred, hatched; sown, grown; thought of, invented.

Vb. *produce*, create, originate, make; invent 484 *discover*; think up, conceive 513 *imagine*; write, design 56 *compose*; operate 676 *do*; frame, fashion, shape 243 *form*; knit, spin 222 *weave*; sew, run up 45 *tie*; forge, chisel, carve, sculpture, cast; coin 797 *mint*; manufacture, fabricate, prefabricate, process, turn out, mill, machine; mass-produce, churn out, multiply 166 *reproduce*; construct, build, raise, rear, erect, set up, run up 310 *elevate*; put together, make up, assemble, compose, cobble together 45 *join*; synthesize, blend 50 *combine*; mine, quarry 304 *extract*; establish, found, constitute, institute 68 *initiate*; organize, get up 62 *arrange*; develop, exploit; industrialize, mechanize, automate; engineer, contrive 623 *plan*; perform, implement, execute, achieve, accomplish 725 *carry out*; bring about, yield results, effect 156 *cause*; unfold, develop 316 *evolve*; breed, hatch, rear 369 *breed stock*; sow, grow, farm 370 *cultivate*; bear young 167 *reproduce itself*; bring up, educate 534 *train*.

See: 21, 36, 41, 43, 45, 50, 56, 62, 68, 71, 132, 147, 156, 157, 166, **167**, 169, **171**, 192, 209, 222, **243**, 304, 310, 316, 319, 331, 360, 364, 369, 370, 381, 413, 449, 451, 484, 513, 534, 539, 548, 551, 553, 554, 556, 586, 589, 594, 612, **622**, 623, 630, 631, 636, 640, 669, 671, 672, 676, 686, 687, 694, 706, 713, 725, 771, 795, 797, 965, 990.

165 Destruction

N. *destruction*, unmaking, undoing 148 *reversion*; blotting out 550 *obliteration*; blowing out, snuffing o., annihilation, nullification 2 *extinction*; abolition, suppression, supersession 752 *abrogation*; suffocation, stifling, silencing 399 *silence*; subversion 221 *overturning*, 149 *revolution*; prostration, precipitation, overthrow 311 *lowering*; levelling, razing, flattening 216 *horizontality*; dissolving, dissolution 51 *decomposition*; breaking up, tearing down, demolition, demolishment 655 *dilapidation*, 46 *disunion*; disruption 46 *separation*; crushing, grinding, pulverization 332 *powderiness*; incineration 381 *burning*; liquidation, elimination, extermination; extirpation, eradication, deracination, uprooting 300 *ejection*; wiping out, mopping up 725 *completion*; decimation, mass murder, massacre, genocide 362 *slaughter*; hatchet job; destructiveness, wanton d., mischief, vandalism, iconoclasm 176 *violence*; sabotage 702 *hindrance*; fire-raising, arson 381 *incendiarism*.

havoc, scene of destruction, disaster area, chaos 61 *confusion*, *turmoil*; desolation, wilderness, scorched earth 172 *desert*; carnage, shambles 362 *slaughterhouse*; upheaval, cataclysm, inundation, storm 176 *outbreak*; devastation, laying waste, ravages; depredation, raid 788 *spoliation*; blitz, explosion, nuclear blast 712 *bombardment*; holocaust, hecatomb 981 *oblation*.

ruin, downfall, ruination, perdition, one's undoing; crushing blow 731 *adversity*; catastrophe, disaster, act of God 731 *misfortune*; collapse, débâcle, landslide 149 *revolution*; breakdown, meltdown, break-up, crack-up 728 *failure*; crash, smash, smash-up 279 *collision*; wreck, shipwreck, wreckage, wrack; sinking, loss, total l.; Waterloo 728 *defeat*; knockout blow, KO 279 *knock*; beginning of the end, slippery slope, road to ruin 655 *deterioration*; coup de grace 725 *completion*; apocalypse, doom, crack of doom, knell, end 69 *finality*, 961 *condemnation*; ruins 127 *oldness*.

Adj. *destructive*, destroying, internecine, annihilating etc. vb.; root and branch 54 *complete*; consuming, ruinous 634 *waste-*

ful; sacrificial, costly 811 *dear*; exhausting, crushing 684 *fatiguing*; apocalyptic, cataclysmic, overwhelming 176 *violent*; raging 176 *furious*; merciless 906 *pitiless*; mortal, suicidal, cutthroat 362 *deadly*; subversive, subversionary 149 *revolutionary*; incendiary, mischievous, pernicious 645 *harmful*; poisonous 653 *toxic*.

destroyed, undone, ruined, fallen; wiped out etc. vb.; crushed, ground; pulped, broken up; suppressed, squashed, quashed 752 *abrogated*; lost, foundered, torpedoed, sunk, sunk without trace; dished, done for, had it, kaput; falling, crumbling, in ruins 655 *dilapidated*; doomed, marked out for destruction; in course of demolition, in the breaker's hands, on the scrapheap 69 *ending*.

Vb. *destroy*, undo, unmake 148 *revert*; destruct, self-d.; abolish, annihilate, liquidate, exterminate, axe 2 *nullify*; devour, consume 634 *waste*; swallow up, engulf 299 *absorb*; swamp, overwhelm, drown 341 *drench*; incinerate, burn up, gut 381 *burn*; wreck, shipwreck, sink (**see** *suppress*); end, put an end to 69 *terminate*; do for, do in, put down, put away, do away with, make away w., get rid of 362 *kill*; poison 362 *murder*; decimate 105 *render few*; exterminate, spare none, leave no survivor 362 *slaughter*, 906 *be pitiless*; remove, extirpate, eradicate, deracinate, uproot, root up 300 *eject*; wipe out, wipe off the map, expunge, efface, erase, delete, blot out, strike out, cancel 550 *obliterate*; annul, revoke, tear up 752 *abrogate*; dispel, scatter, dissipate 75 *disperse*; dissolve 337 *liquefy*; evaporate 338 *vaporize*; mutilate, deface 244 *deform*; knock out, flatten out; put the kibosh on, put the skids under, make short work of, mop up; spifflicate, trounce 726 *defeat*; dish, cook one's goose, sabotage 702 *obstruct*; play hell with, play the deuce with 63 *bedevil*, 634 *waste*; ruin, be the ruin of, be one's undoing.

demolish, unbuild, dismantle, break down, knock d., pull d., tear d. 46 *disunite*; level, raze, raze to the ground, lay in the dust 216 *flatten*; throw down, steamroller, bulldoze 311 *fell*; blow down, blow away, carry a.; cut down, mow d. 362 *slaughter*; knock over, kick o.; subvert, overthrow, overturn, overset, upset 221 *invert*; sap, sap the foundations 163 *weaken*; undermine, mine, dynamite, explode, blow up, blow sky-high; bombard, bomb, blitz, blow to bits 712 *fire at*; wreck, break up, smash up; smash, shatter, shiver, smash to smithereens 46 *break*; pulp, crush, grind 332 *pulverize*; crush to pieces, atomize, grind to bits, make mincemeat of; rend, tear up, rend to pieces, tear to bits, tear to shreds, tear to rags, pull to pieces, pluck to p., pick to p. 46 *sunder*; shake to pieces 318 *agitate*; beat down, batter, ram 279 *strike*; gut, strip bare 229 *uncover*.

suppress, quench, blow out, put o., snuff o. 382 *extinguish*; nip in the bud, cut short, cut off, abort 72 *discontinue*; quell, put down, stamp out, trample out, trample under foot, stamp on, sit on 735 *oppress*; squelch, squash 216 *flatten*; quash, revoke 752 *abrogate*; blanket, stifle, smother, suffocate, strangle 161 *disable*; keep down, repress 745 *subjugate*; cover 525 *conceal*; drown, submerge, sink, scuttle, scupper, torpedo, sink without trace 313 *plunge*, 311 *lower*.

lay waste, desolate, devastate, depopulate 300 *empty*; despoil, depredate, raid, ransack 788 *rob*; damage, spoil, mar, ruin 655 *impair*; ravage, deal destruction, run amok, make havoc, make a shambles 176 *be violent*; lay waste with fire and the sword 634 *waste*; lay in ruins 311 *abase*; lay in ashes 381 *burn*; deforest, defoliate 172 *make sterile*; make a wilderness and call it peace.

consume, devour, eat up, lick up, gobble up; swallow up, engulf 299 *absorb*; squander, run through, fling to the winds, play ducks and drakes with 634 *waste*; throw to the dogs, cast before swine 675 *misuse*.

be destroyed, go west, go under, be lost 361 *perish*; sink, go down 313 *plunge*; have had it, be all over with, be all up with 69 *end*; fall, fall to the ground, bite the dust 309 *tumble*; go on the rocks, break up, split, go to pieces, crumple up; fall into ruin, go to rack and ruin, crumble, crumble to dust 655 *deteriorate*; go to the wall, succumb; go to pot, go to the dogs, go to hell, go to blazes.

Adv. *destructively*, crushingly, with crushing effect, with a sledge hammer.

See: 2, 46, 51, 54, 61, 63, 69, 72, 75, 105, 127, 148, 149, 161, 163, 172, **176**, 216, 221, 229, 244, 279, 299, 300, 309, 311, 313, 318, 332, 337, 338, 341, 361, **362**, 381, 382, 399, 525, 550, **634**, 645, 653, **655**, 675, 684, 702, 712, 725, 726, 728,

731, 735, 745, 752, 788, 811, 906, 961, 981.

166 Reproduction

N.*reproduction*, procreation 167 *propagation*; remaking, refashioning, reshaping, reconstruction 164 *production*; rediscovery 484 *discovery*; redoing 106 *repetition*; reduplication, mass production 171 *productiveness*; multiplication, duplication, printing 587 *print*; renovation, renewal 656 *restoration*; regeneration, resuscitation, reanimation 656 *revival*; resurrection, resurgence; reappearance 106 *recurrence*; atavism 5 *heredity*; reincarnation, palingenesis 124 *future state*; new edition, reprint 589 *edition*; copy 22 *duplicate*; phoenix.

Adj.*reproduced*, renewed, renewing; reproductive 167 *generative*; resurrectional, resurrectionary; renascent, resurgent, reappearing; hydra-headed, phoenix-like.

Vb.*reproduce*, remake, refashion, recoin, reconstruct; rebuild, refound, reestablish, rediscover; duplicate, clone 20 *copy*, 106 *repeat*; take after, inherit 18 *resemble*, 148 *revert*; renovate, renew 656 *restore*; regenerate, revivify, resuscitate, reanimate 656 *revive*; reappear 106 *reoccur*; resurrect, stir up the embers; mass-produce, multiply; print off, reel o. 587 *print*; crop up, spring up like mushrooms, breed 167 *reproduce itself*, 104 *be many*.

See:5, 18, 20, 22, 104, **106**, 124, 148, 164, **167**, 171, 484, 587, 589, 656.

167 Propagation

N.*propagation* 166 *reproduction*; fertility, fecundity 171 *productiveness*; proliferation, multiplication 36 *increase*; breeding, hatching, incubation 369 *animal husbandry*; eugenics 358 *biology*; sex, facts of life, birds and the bees; copulation 45 *coition*; generation, procreation, genesis 156 *source*; biogenesis; parthenogenesis, virgin birth; abiogenesis, autogenesis, spontaneous generation; fertilization, pollination, fecundation, superfecundation, superfetation, impregnation, insemination, artificial i., AID; test-tube baby; fertility drug 171 *fertilizer*; conception, pregnancy, germination, gestation (**see** *obstetrics*); birth, nativity, happy event 68 *origin*; stillbirth 728 *failure*; birth rate, natality; development 157 *growth*; fructification, fruition, florescence, efflorescence, flowering 669 *maturation*; puberty 134 *adultness*: parenthood, maternity, paternity 169 *parentage*; procreator, begetter; inseminator, donor; fertilizer, pollinator; propagator, cultivator 370 *gardener*.

obstetrics, midwifery; parturition, birth, childbirth, childbed, confinement, lying in, accouchement; epidural 375 *anaesthetic*; labour, labour pains, contractions; travail, birth-throes, birth pangs; delivery, breech delivery, forceps d., Caesarian section, Caesarian; amniotic fluid, waters, bag of w., caul, umbilical cord; placenta, afterbirth; gynaecologist, obstetrician, maternity specialist, midwife 658 *nurse*; stork, gooseberry bush.

genitalia, loins, womb 156 *source*; genitals, reproductive organs; pudenda, private parts, privates; intromittent organ, male member, penis; testicles, scrotum; prostate, p. gland; vas deferens; vulva, clitoris, vagina, uterus, ovary, Fallopian tubes; ovum, egg; semen, seminal fluid, sperm, spermatozoa; seed, pollen.

Adj.*generative*, potent, virile; productive, reproductive, procreative, procreant; philoprogenitive, multiparous, fertile, fecund 171 *prolific*; life-giving, originative, germinal, seminal, spermatic, genetic 156 *fundamental*; sexual, bisexual, unisexual; genital, vulvar, clitoral, vaginal, penile, phallic.

fertilized, fecundated, impregnated; breeding, broody, pregnant, enceinte, gravid; in an interesting *or* delicate condition; heavy with, big with; expecting, carrying, with child, in the family way; up the spout, in the club, fallen, preggers; parturient, brought to bed of, in labour; obstetric, obstetrical 658 *medical*; puerperal, childbed, maternity; antenatal, perinatal, postnatal; viviparous, oviparous; parthenogenetic.

Vb.*reproduce itself*, yield, give increase 171 *be fruitful*; hatch, breed, spawn, multiply, teem, breed like rabbits 104 *be many*; germinate, sprout, burgeon 36 *grow*; bloom, flower, fruit, bear fruit, fructify 669 *mature*; seed, seed itself; conceive, get pregnant, fall; carry, bear; be brought to bed of, bring forth, give birth, have a baby; abort, lose the baby 728 *miscarry*; have children, have young, have offspring, have progeny; lay (eggs), drop, farrow, lamb, foal, calve, cub, pup, whelp, kitten, litter; have one's birth 360 *be*

born.
generate, evolve 164 *produce*; bring into being, bring into the world, usher into the world; give life to, bring into existence, call into being; beget, get, engender, spawn, father, sire; copulate 45 *unite with*; fecundate, impregnate, inseminate, pollinate; procreate, propagate; breed, hatch, incubate, raise, rear 369 *breed stock*; raise from seed, take cuttings, bud, graft, layer 370 *cultivate.*
See: 36, 45, 68, 104, 134, **156**, 157, 164, 166, **169**, **171**, 358, 360, 369, 370, 375, 658, 669, 728.

168 Destroyer

N. *destroyer*, demolisher, leveller; Luddite, iconoclast, destructionist, annihilationist, nihilist, anarchist 149 *revolutionist*; wrecker, vandal, arsonist, pyromaniac 381 *incendiarism*; spoiler, despoiler, ravager, raider 712 *attacker*, 789 *robber*; saboteur 702 *hinderer*; defacer, eraser, extinguisher 550 *obliteration*; hatchet man, killer, assassin 362 *murderer*; executioner 963 *punisher*; barbarian, Vandal, Hun; time, hand of t., time's scythe 111 *course of time*; angel of death 361 *death*; destructive agency, locust 947 *glutton*; moth, woodworm, rust, erosion 51 *decay*; corrosive, acid, mildew, blight, poison 659 *bane*; earthquake, fire, flood 165 *havoc*; grim-visaged war 718 *war*; instrument of destruction, sword 723 *weapon*; gunpowder, dynamite, blasting powder 723 *explosive*; blockbuster 723 *bomb*; juggernaut, bulldozer 216 *flattener*; Four Horsemen of the Apocalypse, Exterminating Angel.
See: 51, 111, 149, **165**, 216, 361, 362, 381, 550, 659, 702, 712, 718, 723, 789, 947, 963.

169 Parentage

N. *parentage*, paternity, maternity; parenthood, fatherhood, motherhood; loins, womb 156 *source*; kinship 11 *family*; adoption, fostering, guardianship 660 *protection*; parent, first parents, Adam and Eve 371 *humankind*; single parent 896 *divorce, widowhood*; godparent, guardian 660 *protection* .
genealogy, family tree, lineage, kin 11 *consanguinity*; race history, pedigree, heredity; line, blood-l., blood, strain; blue blood 868 *nobility*; stock, stem, tribe, house, clan 11 *race*; descent, extraction, birth, ancestry 68 *origin.*
paternity, fatherhood; dad, daddy, pop, papa, pater, governor, the old man; head of the family, paterfamilias; procreator, begetter, author of one's existence; grandfather, grandsire, grandad, grandpa, great-grandfather 133 *old man*; founder of the family, ancestor, progenitor, forefather, forebear, patriarch, predecessor 66 *precursor*; father figure; adoptive father, foster-f., stepfather, father-in-law; fatherland.
maternity, motherhood; maternal instinct 887 *love*; expectant mother, mother-to-be 167 *propagation*; mother, dam; mamma, mummy, mum, mater; grandmother, grandma, granny, gran, nan; materfamilias, matron, matriarch; ancestress, progenitrix; grandam 133 *old woman*; mother substitute; foster-mother, stepmother, mother-in-law; Mother Church, mother country.
Adj. *parental*, paternal; maternal, matronly; fatherly, fatherlike; motherly, stepmotherly; family, lineal, patrilineal, matrilineal; ancestral; hereditary 5 *genetic*; patriarchal 127 *immemorial*; racial, phyletic 11 *ethnic*.
See: 5, **11**, 66, 68, 127, 133, **156**, 167, 371, 660, 868, 887, 896.

170 Posterity

N. *posterity*, progeny, issue, offspring, young, little ones 132 *child*; breed 11 *race*; brood, seed, litter, farrow, spawn 132 *young creature*; fruit of the womb, children; grandchildren 11 *family*; aftercomers, succession, heirs, inheritance, heritage 120 *posteriority*; rising generation 130 *youth.*
descendant, son, daughter; chip off the old block, infant 132 *child*; scion, shoot, sprout 132 *young plant*; heir, heiress, heir of the body 776 *beneficiary*; love child 954 *bastardy*; branch, ramification, daughter-house, daughter-nation, colony; graft, offshoot, offset.
sonship, filiation, line, direct l., lineage, descent, male d.; agnation 11 *consanguinity*; indirect descent, collaterality, ramification; irregular descent, illegitimacy 954 *bastardy*; succession, heredity, heirship; primogeniture 119 *priority*.
Adj. *filial*, daughterly; descended, lineal; collateral; primogenital 119 *prior*;

adopted, adoptive; step-; hereditary, inherited, Mendelian 5 *genetic*.
See: 5, 11, 119, 120, 130, **132**, 776, 954.

171 Productiveness

N. *productiveness*, productivity, mass production 164 *production*; boom, booming economy 730 *prosperity*; overproductivity, superabundance, glut 637 *redundance*; fecundity, fertility, luxuriance, lushness, exuberance, richness, Green Revolution 635 *plenty*; high birthrate, baby boom, population explosion; productive capacity, biotic potential; procreation, multiplication 167 *propagation*; fructification 669 *maturation*; fecundation, fertilization, pollination; inventiveness, resourcefulness 513 *imagination*.

fertilizer, organic f., manure, dung, guano, compost, bonemeal; phosphates, nitrates, potash, lime; top-dressing, mulch 370 *agriculture*; semen, sperm, seed; fertility drug 167 *propagation*; fertility cult, f. rite, f. symbol, phallic s., phallus; linga, yoni; Earth Mother, Ceres, Demeter.

abundance, wealth, riot, profusion, harvest 32 *great quantity*; teeming womb, mother earth, rich soil; hotbed, nursery 156 *seedbed*; cornucopia, horn of plenty, land flowing with milk and honey; milch cow; second crop, aftergrowth, aftermath 67 *sequel*; rabbit warren, ant heap 104 *multitude*.

Adj. *prolific*, fertile, fecund; teeming, multiparous, spawning 167 *generative*; fruitful, fruitbearing, fructiferous; pregnant, heavy with, parturient; exuberant, lush, leafy, verdant, luxuriant, rich, fat 635 *plenteous*; copious, streaming, pouring; paying 640 *profitable*; creative, inventive, resourceful.

Vb. *make fruitful*, make productive etc. adj.; make the desert bloom; plant, fertilize, water, irrigate, manure, compost, top-dress 370 *cultivate*; impregnate, fecundate, inseminate; procreate, produce, propagate 167 *generate*.

be fruitful, - prolific etc. adj.; fructify, flourish; burgeon, bloom, blossom; germinate; conceive, bear, give birth, have children 167 *reproduce itself*; teem, proliferate, pullulate, swarm, multiply, mushroom 104 *be many*; send up the birthrate 36 *augment*; populate.

See: 32, 36, 67, 104, 156, **164**, **167**, 370, 513, 635, 637, 640, 669, 730.

172 Unproductiveness

N. *unproductiveness*, unproductivity, dearth, famine 636 *scarcity*; sterility, barrenness, infertility, infecundity 161 *impotence*; overfishing, overgrazing; deforestation, erosion; defoliation; scorched earth policy, desertification; dying race, falling birthrate, zero population growth 37 *decrease*; virginity 895 *celibacy*; change of life, menopause; unprofitableness, poor return, losing business 772 *loss*; unprofitability, fruitlessness 641 *inutility*; stagnation, waste of time 641 *lost labour*; slump, slack market, idleness 679 *inactivity*.

contraception, birth control, planned parenthood, family planning; contraceptive, the pill; coil, loop, intrauterine device, IUD; diaphragm, Dutch cap, French letter, condom, sheath; spermicide; rhythm method, chastity 747 *restraint*; sterilization, vasectomy.

desert, dryness, aridity 342 *dryness*; desolation, waste, barren w., wastelands, lunar landscape; heath, moor, bush, wild, wilderness, howling w.; desert sands, sand dunes, Sahara; dustbowl 634 *waste*; salt flat 347 *marsh*; Artic wastes 380 *ice*; waste of waters 343 *ocean*.

Adj. *unproductive*, dried up, exhausted 634 *wasted*; sparse, scarce 636 *insufficient*; waste, desert, desolate; treeless, bleak, gaunt, bare 190 *empty*; poor, stony, shallow, eroded; barren, infertile, sour, sterile; withered, shrivelled, blasted; unprolific, unfruitful, infecund; rootless, seedless, ungerminating; arid, unwatered, unirrigated 342 *dry*; fallow, stagnating 674 *disused*; unsown, unmanured, unploughed, untilled, uncultivated, unharvested; impotent, sterilized, on the pill; childless, issueless, without issue; celibate 895 *unwedded*; otiose 679 *inactive*; fruitless, unprofitable 641 *profitless*; inoperative, null and void, of no effect 161 *impotent*; ineffective 728 *unsuccessful*; addled, abortive 670 *unprepared*.

Vb. *be unproductive*, - unprolific etc. adj.; rust, stagnate, lie fallow 679 *be inactive*; cease work 145 *cease*; bury one's talent 674 *not use*; hang fire, come to nothing, come to naught 728 *fail*; abort 728 *miscarry*; take precautions, practise birth control; have no issue, lower the birthrate.

make sterile, make unproductive 634 *waste*; sterilize, vasectomize, castrate, geld 161 *unman*; deforest, overgraze 165 *lay waste*; addle 51 *decompose*; pasteurize, disinfect 648 *purify*.

See: 37, 51, 145, **161**, 165, 190, 342, 343, 347, 380, **634**, 636, **641**, 648, 670, 674, 679, 728, 747, 772, 895.

173 Agency

N. *agency*, operation, work, working, doing 676 *action*; job, office 622 *function*; exercise 673 *use*; force, strain, stress, play, swing 160 *power*; interaction, interworking 178 *influence*; procuration, procurement 689 *management*; service 628 *instrumentality*; effectiveness, efficiency 156 *causation*; quickening power 174 *stimulation*; maintenance, support 703 *aid*; co-agency 706 *cooperation*; implementation, execution 725 *effectuation*; process, processing, treatment, handling.

Adj. *operative*, effectual, efficient, efficacious 727 *successful*; drastic 735 *severe*; executive, operational, functional; acting, working, in action, in operation, in force, in play, being exercised, at work 676 *doing*, 673 *used*; on foot, on the active list, up and doing 678 *active*; live, potent 160 *dynamic*, 174 *vigorous*; practical, workable, applicable 642 *advisable*; serviceable 640 *useful*; worked upon, acted u., wrought u.

Vb. *operate*, be in action, be in play, play; act, work, go, run 676 *do*; start up, tick over, idle; serve, execute, perform 622 *function*; do its job 727 *be successful*; take effect 156 *cause*; have effect, act upon, bear u., work u., play u. 178 *influence*; take action, strike 678 *be active*; maintain, sustain 218 *support*; crew, man; make operate, bring into play, wind up, turn on, plug in, switch on, flick *or* flip the switch, press the button; actuate, power, drive 265 *move*; process, treat; manipulate, handle, wield 378 *touch*, 673 *use*; stimulate, excite 174 *invigorate*.

See: 156, **160**, 174, 178, 218, 265, 378, 622, 628, 640, 642, 673, **676**, 678, 689, 703, 706, 725, 727, 735.

174 Vigour: physical energy

N. *vigorousness*, lustiness, energy, vigour, life 678 *activity*; dynamism, physical energy, dynamic e., pressure, force, impetus 160 *energy*; intensity, high pressure 162 *strength*; dash, élan, impetuosity 680 *haste*; exertion, effort 682 *labour*; fervour, enthusiasm 571 *vigour*; gusto, relish, zest, zestfulness 824 *joy*; liveliness, spirit, vim, zip, éclat; fire, mettle, blood 855 *courage*; ginger, fizz, verve, snap, pep, drive, go, get up and go; enterprise, initiative 672 *undertaking*; vehemence 176 *violence*; aggressiveness, oomph, thrust, push, kick, punch 712 *attack*; grip, bite, teeth, backbone, spunk 599 *resolution*; guts, grit 600 *stamina*; virility 162 *vitality*; live wire, spark, dynamo, dynamite, quicksilver; rocket, jet; display of energy 277 *spurt*; show of force, demonstration 854 *intimidation*.

stimulation, activation, tonic effect; intensification, boost, stepping up, bumping up 36 *increase*; excitement 821 *excitation*; stir, bustle 678 *activity*; perturbation 318 *agitation*; ferment, fermentation, leavening; ebullience, ebullition 318 *commotion*; froth, effervescence 355 *bubble*; steam 381 *heating*.

keenness, acridity, acrimony, mordancy, causticity, virulence 388 *pungency*; poignancy, point, edge 256 *sharpness*; zeal 597 *willingness*.

stimulant, energizer, activator, booster; yeast, leaven, catalyst; stimulus, fillip, shot, shot in the arm; crack of the whip, spur, prick, prod, goad, lash 612 *incentive*; restorative, tonic, pep pill 658 *tonic*; bracer, pick-me-up, aperitif, appetizer 390 *savouriness*; seasoning, spice 389 *sauce*; liquor, alcohol 301 *alcoholic drink*; aphrodisiac, philtre, love p.; cantharides, Spanish fly; pep talk, rousing cheer 821 *excitant*.

Adj. *vigorous*, energetic 678 *active*; radioactive 362 *deadly*; forcible, forceful, vehement 176 *violent*; vivid, vibrant 160 *dynamic*; high-pressure, intense, strenuous 678 *industrious*; enterprising, go-getting, go-ahead 285 *progressive*; aggressive, pushful, thrustful 712 *attacking*; keen, alacritous 597 *willing*; double-edged, double-distilled, potent 160 *powerful*; hearty, virile, full-blooded 162 *strong*; full of beans, full of punch, full of pep, zestful, lusty, mettlesome 819 *lively*; blooming, bouncing 650 *healthy*; brisk, nippy, snappy; fizzy, heady, racy; tonic, bracing, rousing, invigorating, stimulating 821 *exciting*; drastic, stringent, harsh, punishing 735 *severe*; intensified, stepped up; gingered up, souped up 160 *powerful*; revived 685 *refreshed*, 656 *restored*; thriving, lush 171 *prolific*.

keen, acute, sharp, incisive, trenchant 571 *forceful*; mordant, biting, poignant, pointed, sarcastic 851 *derisive*; virulent, corrosive, caustic 388 *pungent*; acrid, acid 393 *sour*.

Vb. *be vigorous*, thrive, have zest, enjoy life 650 *be healthy*; burst with energy, overflow with e. 162 *be strong*; show energy 678 *be active*; steam away, be up and doing 682 *exert oneself*; exert energy, drive, push 279 *impel*; bang, slam, wrench, cut right through 176 *force*; raise the pressure, get up steam, put on a spurt 277 *accelerate*; be thorough, strike home 725 *carry through*; strike hard, hammer, dint, dent 279 *strike*; show one's power, tell upon, make an impression 178 *influence*, 821 *impress*; throw one's weight about 678 *meddle*; show fight, take the offensive 712 *attack*.

invigorate, energize, activate; galvanize, electrify, intensify, double, redouble; wind up, step up, bump up, pep up, ginger up, boost 162 *strengthen*; rouse, kindle, inflame, stimulate, enliven, quicken 821 *excite*; act like a tonic, hearten, animate 833 *cheer*; go to one's head, intoxicate 949 *inebriate*; freshen, revive 685 *refresh*; give an edge to 256 *sharpen*; fertilize, irrigate 370 *cultivate*.

Adv. *vigorously*, forcibly, hard, straight from the shoulder, with telling effect; zestfully, lustily, con brio, with a will; at full tilt, full steam ahead.

See: 36, **160**, **162**, 171, 176, 178, 256, 277, 279, 285, 301, 318, 355, 362, 370, 381, 388, 389, 390, 393, **571**, 597, 599, 600, 612, 650, 656, 658, 672, 678, 680, 682, 685, 712, 725, 735, 819, **821**, 824, 833, 851, 854, 855, 949.

175 Inertness

N. *inertness*, inertia, accidie 677 *inaction*; lifelessness, languor, paralysis, torpor, torpidity 375 *insensibility*; rest, vegetation, stagnation, stasis, passivity 266 *quiescence*; dormancy 523 *latency*; mental inertness, apathy, dullness, sloth 679 *sluggishness*; immobility, passive resistance 602 *obstinacy*; impassiveness, stolidity 823 *inexcitability*; gutlessness 601 *irresolution*; vegetable, cabbage; extinct volcano.

Adj. *inert*, unactivated, unaroused, passive, dead 677 *nonactive*; lifeless, languid, torpid, numb 375 *insensible*; heavy, lumpish, sluggish 278 *slow*, 679 *inactive*; hibernating 679 *sleepy*; quiet, vegetating, stagnant 266 *quiescent*; fallow 172 *unproductive*; slack, low-pressure, untensed 734 *lax*; limp, flaccid 163 *weak*; apathetic, neutral 860 *indifferent*, 820 *impassive*; pacific, unwarlike, unaggressive 717 *peaceful*, 823 *inexcitable*; uninfluential 161 *powerless*; deactivated, unexerted, suspended, in abeyance 752 *abrogated*; smouldering, dormant 523 *latent*.

Vb. *be inert*, be inactive etc. adj.; slumber 679 *sleep*; hang fire, not catch; smoulder 523 *lurk*; lie, stagnate, vegetate 266 *be quiescent*; just sit there 677 *not act*.

Adv. *inactively*, passively etc. adj.; at rest; in suspense, in abeyance, in reserve.

See: 161, 163, 172, 266, 278, 375, 523, 601, 602, **677**, **679**, 717, 734, 752, 820, 823, 860.

176 Violence

N. *violence*, vehemence, frenzy, ferment, impetuosity 174 *vigorousness*; destructiveness, vandalism 165 *destruction*; boisterousness, turbulence, storminess 318 *commotion*; bluster, uproar, riot, row, roughhouse, rumpus, furore 61 *turmoil*; roughness, ungentleness, rough handling 735 *severity*; force, hammer blows, high hand, coup de main, strong-arm tactics, thuggery, terrorism 735 *brute force*; atrocity, outrage, torture 898 *cruel act*; barbarity, brutality, savagery, blood lust 898 *inhumanity*; fierceness, ferocity, malignity, mercilessness 906 *pitilessness*; rage, hysterics 822 *excitable state*; fit, throes, paroxysm 318 *spasm*; shock, clash 279 *collision*; wrench, twist, dislocation 63 *derangement*, 246 *distortion*.

outbreak, outburst, ebullition, effervescence 318 *agitation*; flood, tidal wave 350 *wave*; cataclysm, convulsion, earthquake, quake, tremor 149 *revolution*; eruption, volcano 383 *furnace*; explosion, blow-up, burst, blast 165 *destruction*; bursting open, dissilience 46 *disunion*; detonation 400 *loudness*; rush, onrush, assault, sortie 712 *attack*; gush, spurt, jet, torrent 350 *stream*.

storm, turmoil, turbulence, war of the elements; weather, dirty w., rough w., inclement w., inclemency; squall, tempest, typhoon, hurricane, cyclone 352 *gale*; thunder, thunder and lightning, fulguration; rainstorm, cloudburst 350 *rain*;

hailstorm, snowstorm, blizzard 380 *wintriness*; sandstorm, duststorm 352 *gale*; magnetic storm.

violent creature, brute, beast, wild b.; dragon, tiger, wolf, she w., mad dog; demon, devil, hellhound, hellcat 938 *monster*; savage, barbarian, vandal, iconoclast 168 *destroyer*; he-man, cave m. 372 *male*; man of blood, assassin, executioner, butcher, Herod 362 *murderer*; berserker, homicidal maniac 504 *madman*; rough, tough, rowdy, thug, mugger 904 *ruffian*; hooligan, bully, bully boy, terror, holy t. 735 *tyrant*; thunderer, fire-eater, bravo 877 *boaster*; firebrand, incendiary 738 *agitator*; revolutionary, anarchist, nihilist, terrorist 149 *revolutionist*; hotspur, madcap 857 *desperado*; virago, termagant, Amazon; spitfire, fury, scold 892 *shrew*.

Adj. *violent*, vehement, forcible 162 *strong*; acute 256 *sharp*; unmitigated; excessive, outrageous, extravagant 32 *exorbitant*; rude, ungentle, abrupt, brusque, bluff 885 *discourteous*; extreme, severe, tyrannical, heavy-handed 735 *oppressive*; primitive, barbarous, savage, brutal, bloody 898 *cruel*; hot-blooded 892 *irascible*; aggressive, bellicose 718 *warlike*; rampant, charging 712 *attacking*; struggling, kicking, thrashing about 61 *disorderly*; rough, wild, furious, raging, blustery, tempestuous, stormy, gale force 352 *windy*; drenching, torrential 350 *rainy*; uproarious, obstreperous 400 *loud*; rowdy, turbulent, tumultuous, boisterous 738 *riotous*; incendiary, anarchistic, nihilistic 149 *revolutionary*; intemperate, immoderate, unbridled, unrestrained; ungovernable, unruly, uncontrollable 738 *disobedient*; irrepressible, inextinguishable 174 *vigorous*; ebullient, hot, red-hot, inflamed 381 *heated*; inflammatory, scorching, flaming 379 *fiery*; eruptive, cataclysmic, overwhelming, volcanic, seismic 165 *destructive*; detonating, explosive, bursting; convulsive, spasmodic 318 *agitated*; full of violence, disturbed, troublous 61 *orderless*.

furious, fuming, boiling, towering; infuriated, mad, maddened 891 *angry*; impetuous, rampant, gnashing; roaring, howling; headstrong 680 *hasty*; desperate 857 *rash*; savage, tameless, wild; blustering, threatening 899 *cursing*; vicious, fierce, ferocious 898 *cruel*; bloodthirsty, ravening, rabid, berserk 362 *murderous*; waspish, tigerish; frantic, hysterical, in hysterics 503 *frenzied*.

Vb. *be violent*, break bounds, run wild, run riot, run amok 165 *lay waste*; tear, rush, dash, hurtle, hurl oneself, rush headlong 277 *move fast*; crash in 297 *burst in*; surge forward, stampede, mob 712 *charge*; break the peace, raise a storm, riot, roughhouse, kick up a row, kick up a shindy, raise the dust, go on the rampage 61 *rampage*; resort to violence, take to arms 718 *go to war*, 738 *revolt*; see red, go berserk 891 *be angry*; storm, rage, roar, bluster, come in like a lion 352 *blow*; ferment, foam, fume, run high, boil over 318 *effervesce*; burst its banks, flood, overwhelm 350 *flow*; explode, go off, blow up, detonate, burst, fly, flash, flare; let fly, let off, fulminate; erupt, break out, fly o., burst o.; struggle, strain, scratch, bite, kick, lash out 715 *resist*; savage, maul 655 *wound*; bear down, bear hard on, ride roughshod, tyrannize, out-Herod Herod 735 *oppress*.

force, use f., smash 46 *break*; tear, rend 46 *sunder*; bruise, crush 332 *pulverize*; blow up 165 *demolish*; strain, wrench, pull, dislocate, sprain; twist, warp, deform 246 *distort*; force open, prize o., pry o., jimmy 263 *open*; blow open, burst o.; shock, shake 318 *agitate*; do violence to, abuse 675 *misuse*; violate, ravish, rape 951 *debauch*; torture 645 *ill-treat*.

make violent, stir, quicken, stimulate 821 *excite*; urge, goad, lash, whip 612 *incite*; stir up, inflame 381 *kindle*; add fuel to the flames, blow on the embers 381 *heat*; foment, exacerbate, exasperate 832 *aggravate*; whet 256 *sharpen*; irritate, infuriate, lash into fury 891 *enrage*; madden 503 *make mad*.

Adv. *violently*, forcibly, by storm, by force, by main force, amain; with might and main; tooth and nail, hammer and tongs, vi et armis, at the point of a sword, at the end of a gun; tyrannously, high-handedly; bodily, neck and crop; at one fell swoop; with a vengeance, like mad; precipitately, headlong, slap bang, wham; head foremost, head first; like a bull at a gate, like Gadarene swine.

See: 32, 46, 61, 63, 149, 162, **165**, 168, **174**, 246, 256, 263, 277, 279, 297, 318, 332, 350, 352, 362, 372, 379, 380, 381, 383, 400, 503, 504, 612, 645, 655, 675, 680, 712, 715, 718, 735, 738, 821, 822, 832,

857, 877, 885, 891, 892, 898, 899, 904, 906, 938, 951.

177 Moderation

N._moderation_, nonviolence; mildness, gentleness 736 _leniency_; harmlessness, innocuousness 935 _innocence_; moderateness, reasonableness 502 _sanity_; measure, golden mean 732 _averageness_; temperateness, restraint, self-control 942 _temperance_; soberness 948 _sobriety_, 874 _modesty_; impassivity, mental calmness 823 _inexcitability_; impartiality, neutrality 625 _middle way_; correction, adjustment, modulation; mutual concession 770 _compromise_; mitigation 831 _relief_; relaxation, remission 734 _laxity_; easing, alleviation; mollification, appeasement, assuagement, détente 719 _pacification_; tranquillization, sedation; quiet, calm, dead c. 266 _quietude_; control, check 747 _restraint_.

moderator, palliative 658 _remedy_; lenitive, alleviative, demulcent 658 _balm_; rose water, soothing syrup, milk, oil on troubled waters; calmative, sedative, tranquillizer, lullaby; nightcap, bromide, barbiturate 679 _soporific_; anodyne, opiate, opium, laudanum 375 _anaesthetic_; dummy 264 _stopper_; wet blanket, damper 613 _dissuasion_; cooler, cold water, cold shower 382 _extinguisher_; brake 747 _restraint_; neutralizer; anaphrodisiac 658 _antidote_; cushion, shock absorber 327 _softness_; third force, mollifier, peacemaker 720 _mediator_; controller, restraining hand, rein.

Adj._moderate_, unextreme, nonviolent, reasonable, judicious 913 _just_; tame, gentle, gentle as a lamb, harmless, mild, mild as milk 736 _lenient_; milk and water, innocuous 935 _innocent_, 163 _weak_; measured, restricted, limited, low-key 747 _restrained_; chastened, subdued, self-controlled, tempered 942 _temperate_, 948 _sober_; cool, calm, composed 823 _inexcitable_; still, quiet, untroubled 266 _tranquil_; peaceable, pacific 717 _peaceful_; leftish, pink, nonextreme, middle-of-the-road 625 _neutral_, 860 _indifferent_.

lenitive, unexciting, unirritating, nonirritant 658 _remedial_; alleviative, assuaging, pain-killing, anodyne, calmative, sedative, hypnotic, narcotic 679 _soporific_; smooth 327 _soft_; soothing, bland, demulcent; emollient; oily 334 _lubricated_; comforting 685 _refreshing_; disarming 719 _pacificatory_.

Vb._be moderate_, - gentle etc. adj.; not go to extremes 625 _be halfway_; go easy, keep within bounds, keep within reason 942 _be temperate_; sober down, settle 266 _be quiescent_; disarm, keep the peace 717 _be at peace_; remit, relent 905 _show mercy_; show consideration, not press 736 _be lenient_; not resist, go quietly, go out like a lamb; ease off 278 _decelerate_.

moderate, mitigate, temper; correct 24 _adjust_; tame, check, curb, control, chasten, govern, limit, keep within limits 747 _restrain_; lessen, diminish, slacken 37 _abate_; palliate, extenuate, qualify 163 _weaken_; obtund, take the edge off 257 _blunt_; break the fall, cushion 218 _support_; play down, soft-pedal, moderate language, tone down, blue-pencil, euphemize 648 _purify_; sober, sober down, dampen, damp, cool, chill, throw cold water on 382 _refrigerate_, 613 _dissuade_; reduce the temperature, bank down the fires; blanket, smother, subdue, quell 382 _extinguish_.

assuage, ease, pour balm, mollify 327 _soften_; alleviate, lighten 831 _relieve_; deactivate, neutralize, take the sting out 182 _counteract_; allay, dull, deaden 375 _render insensible_; soothe, calm, tranquillize, comfort, still, quiet, hush, lull, rock, cradle, rock to sleep 266 _bring to rest_; dulcify 392 _sweeten_; disarm, appease, smooth over, pour oil on troubled waters 719 _pacify_; assuage one's thirst, slake 301 _drink_.

Adv._moderately_, in moderation, within bounds, within limits, within compass, within reason; at half speed, gingerly, half-heartedly, nervously, softly softly 278 _gradatim_.

See:24, 37, 163, 182, 218, 257, 264, 266, 278, 301, 327, 334, 375, 382, 392, 502, 613, 625, 648, 658, 679, 685, 717, 719, 720, 732, 734, **736**, 747, 770, **823**, 831, 860, 874, 905, 913, 935, **942**, 948.

178 Influence

N._influence_, capability, power, potentiality 160 _ability_; prevalence, predominance 34 _superiority_; mightiness, magnitude 32 _greatness_, 638 _importance_; upper hand, whip h., casting vote; vantage ground, footing, hold, grip; leverage, play 744 _scope_; purchase 218 _pivot_; clout, weight, pressure; pull, drag, magnetism 291 _attraction_; counterattraction 292 _repul-_

sion, 182 *counteraction*; thrust, drive 287 *propulsion*; impact 279 *impulse*; leaven, contagion, infection; atmosphere, climate 8 *circumstance*; atavism, telegony 5 *heredity*; occult influence, mana, magic, spell 983 *sorcery*; stars, heavens, destiny 596 *fate*; fascination, hypnotism, mesmerism; malign influence, curse, ruin 659 *bane*; emotion, impulse, impression, feeling 817 *affections*; suasion, persuasion, insinuation, suggestion, impulsion, inspiration 612 *motive*; personality, charisma, leadership, credit, repute 866 *prestige*; hegemony, ascendancy, domination, tyranny 733 *authority*; sway, control, dominance, reign 733 *governance*; sphere of influence, orbit; factor, contributing f., vital role, leading part 156 *cause*; indirect influence, patronage, interest, favour, pull, friend at court, wire-pulling 703 *aid*; strings, lever 630 *tool*; secret influence, hidden hand, hand that rocks the cradle, power behind the throne, Grey Eminence 523 *latency*; force, f. to be reckoned with; lobby, pressure group 612 *inducement*; manipulator, mover, manoeuvrer 612 *motivator*; person of influence, uncrowned king *or* queen, a host in oneself, big noise, big shot 638 *bigwig*; multinational company, superpower; powers that be, the Establishment 733 *government*.

Adj. *influential*, dominant, predominant, prevalent, prevailing, monopolistic 34 *supreme*; in power, ruling, regnant, reigning, commanding, listened to, obeyed; recognized, with authority, of a., in a. 733 *authoritative*; rising, ascendant, in the ascendant 36 *increasing*; strong, potent, mighty, multinational 32 *great*, 160 *powerful*; leading, guiding, hegemonic 689 *directing*; activating, inspiring, encouraging; active in, busy, meddling 678 *active*; contributing, effective 156 *causal*; weighty, key, momentous, decisive, world-shattering, earth-shaking 638 *important*; telling, moving, emotional 821 *impressive*; appealing, attractive 291 *attracting*; gripping, fascinating, charismatic; irresistible, hypnotic, mesmeric 740 *compelling*; persuasive, suggestive, insinuating, tempting 612 *inducing*; habit-forming; educative, instructive 534 *educational*; spreading, catching, contagious 653 *infectious*; pervasive 189 *ubiquitous*.

Vb. *influence*, have i., command i., have a pull, carry weight, cut ice 638 *be important*; be well-connected, know the right people; have a hold on, have in one's power; have the ear of, be listened to, be recognized, be obeyed 737 *command*; dominate, tower over, bestride; lead by the nose, have under one's thumb, wind round one's little finger, wear the trousers 34 *be superior*; exert influence, make oneself felt, assert oneself; pull one's weight, throw one's weight into the scale, weigh in; put pressure on, lobby, pull strings, pull the s. 612 *motivate*; make one's voice heard, gain a hearing 455 *attract notice*; have a voice, have a say in; affect, tell, turn the scale; bear upon, work u., tell u. 821 *impress*; soften up, work on 925 *flatter*; urge, prompt, tempt, incite, inspire, dispose, persuade, prevail upon, convince, carry with one 612 *induce*; force 740 *compel*; sway, tyrannize; predispose, brainwash, prejudice 481 *bias*; appeal, allure, fascinate, hypnotize, mesmerize 291 *attract*; disgust, put off 292 *repel*; militate against, counterbalance 182 *counteract*; make, be the making of 654 *make better*; make or mar, change 147 *transform*; infect, leaven, colour 143 *modify*; contaminate, mar 655 *impair*; actuate, work 173 *operate*; play a part, play a leading p., guide 689 *direct*; lead the dance, set the fashion, be the model for 23 *be an example*.

prevail, establish one's influence, outweigh, overweigh, override, overbear, turn the scale 34 *predominate*; overawe, overcome, subdue, subjugate; hold the whip hand, gain the upper hand, gain full play, master 727 *overmaster*; control, rule, monopolize 733 *dominate*; take a hold on, take a grip on, hold 778 *retain*; gain a footing, take root, take hold, strike root in, settle 144 *stay*; permeate, run through, colour 189 *pervade*; catch on, spread, rage, be rife, spread like wildfire.

Adv. *influentially*, to good effect, with telling e.; within one's orbit.

See: 5, 8, 23, 32, **34**, 36, 143, 144, 147, 156, 160, 173, 182, 189, 218, 279, 287, 291, 292, 455, 481, 523, 534, 596, **612**, 630, **638**, 653, 654, 655, 659, 678, 689, 703, 727, **733**, 737, 740, 744, 778, 817, 821, 866, 925, 983.

179 Tendency

N. *tendency*, trend, tenor; tempo, rhythm, set, drift 281 *direction*; course, stream, main current, mainstream, Zeitgeist, spirit of the times, spirit of the age; climate 178 *influence*; gravitation, affinity 291 *attraction*; polarity 240 *contraposition*; aptness 24 *fitness*; gift, instinct for 694 *aptitude*; proneness, proclivity, propensity, predisposition, readiness, inclination, penchant, predilection, liking, leaning, bias, prejudice; weakness 180 *liability*; cast, bent, turn, grain; a strain of 43 *tincture*; vein, humour, mood; tone, quality, nature, characteristic 5 *temperament*; special gift, idiosyncrasy 80 *speciality*.

Adj. *tending*, trending, conducive, leading to, pointing to; tendentious, working towards, aiming at 617 *intending*; in a fair way to, calculated to 471 *probable*; centrifugal 620 *avoiding*; subservient 180 *liable*; apt to, prone to; ready to, about to 669 *prepared*.

Vb. *tend*, trend, verge, lean, incline; set in, set, set towards, gravitate t. 289 *approach*; affect, dispose, carry, bias, bend to, warp, turn 178 *influence*; point to, lead to 156 *conduce*; bid fair to, be calculated to 471 *be likely*; redound to, contribute to 285 *promote*.

See: 5, 24, 43, 80, 156, 178, **180**, 240, 281, 285, 289, 291, 471, 617, 620, 669, 694.

180 Liability

N. *liability*, liableness, weakness 179 *tendency*; exposure 661 *vulnerability*; susceptibility, susceptivity, impressibility 374 *sensibility*; potentiality 469 *possibility*; likelihood 471 *probability*; obligation, responsibility, accountability, amenability 917 *duty*.

Adj. *liable*, apt to 179 *tending*; subject to, prey to, at the mercy of 745 *subject*; open to, exposed to, in danger of 661 *vulnerable*; dependent on, contingent 157 *caused*; incident to, incidental; possible, on the cards, within the range of 469 *possible*; incurring, unexempt from; susceptible 819 *impressible*; answerable, responsible, amenable, accountable 917 *obliged*.

Vb. *be liable*, - subject to etc. adj.; be responsible, answer for 917 *incur a duty*; incur, lay oneself open to, run the chance of, stand the chance of; stand to gain, stand to lose; run the risk of 661 *be in danger*; lie under 745 *be subject*; open a door to 156 *conduce*.

See: 156, 157, **179**, 374, 469, 471, 661, 745, 819, 917.

181 Concurrence: combination of causes

N. *concurrence*, combined operation, joint effort, collaboration, coagency, synergy, synergism 706 *cooperation*; coincidence 24 *conformance*, 83 *conformity*; concord, harmony 24 *agreement*; compliance 758 *consent*; concurrent opinion, consensus 488 *assent*; acquiescence, nonresistance 721 *submission*; concert, joint planning, collusion, conspiracy 623 *plot*; league, alliance, partnership 706 *association*; conjunction, liaison 45 *union*.

Adj. *concurrent*, concurring etc. vb.; coactive, synergic 706 *cooperative*; coincident, concomitant, parallel 89 *accompanying*; in alliance, banded together 708 *corporate*; of one mind, at one with 488 *assenting*; joint, combined 45 *joined*; conforming 24 *agreeing*; colluding, conniving, abetting, contributing, involved 703 *aiding*.

Vb. *concur*, acquiesce 488 *assent*; collude, connive, conspire 623 *plot*; agree, harmonize 24 *accord*; hang together, pull t. 706 *cooperate*; contribute, help, aid, abet, serve 703 *minister to*; promote, subserve 156 *conduce*; go with, go along w., go hand in hand w., keep pace w., keep abreast of, run parallel to 89 *accompany*; unite, stand together 48 *cohere*.

Adv. *concurrently*, with one consent, with one accord, in harmony, hand in hand, hand in glove.

See: **24**, 45, 48, 83, 89, 156, 488, 623, 703, **706**, 708, 721, 758.

182 Counteraction

N. *counteraction*, opposing causes, action and reaction; polarity 240 *contraposition*; antagonism, antipathy, clash, conflict, mutual c. 14 *contrariety*, 279 *collision*; return action, reaction, retroaction, repercussion, backfire, backlash 280 *recoil*; renitency, recalcitrance, kicking back 715 *resistance*, 704 *opposition*; inertia, vis inertiae, friction, drag, check 702 *hindrance*; interference, counterpressure, repression, suppression 747 *restraint*; intolerance, persecution 735 *severity*; neutralization, deactivation 177 *moderation*; nullification, cancellation 165 *destruction*; cross-current, headwind 702 *obstacle*; counterspell, countercharm, counterirritant, neutralizer 658 *antidote*; counterbalance, counterweight 31 *offset*; counterblast, countermove 688 *tactics*; defensive measures, deterrent 713 *defence*; prevention, preventive, preventative, inhibitor 757 *prohibition*.

Adj. *counteracting*, counter, counteractive; conflicting 14 *contrary*; antipathetic, antagonistic, hostile 881 *inimical*; resistant, recalcitrant, renitent 715 *resisting*; reactionary, reactive 280 *recoiling*; frictional, retarding, checking 747 *restraining*; preventive, preventative, contraceptive; antidotal, corrective 658 *remedial*; balancing, offsetting 31 *compensatory*.

Vb. *counteract*, counter, run c., cross, traverse, work against, go a., militate a.; not conduce to 702 *hinder*; react 280 *recoil*; agitate against, persecute 881 *be inimical*; resist, withstand, defend oneself 704 *oppose*; antagonize, conflict with 14 *be contrary*; clash 279 *collide*; interfere 678 *meddle*; countervail, cancel out, counterpoise, counterbalance 31 *set off*; repress 165 *suppress*; undo, cancel 752 *abrogate*; neutralize, deactivate, demagnetize, degauss; find a remedy, cure 658 *remedy*; recover 656 *retrieve*; obviate, prevent, inhibit 757 *prohibit*.

Adv. *although*, in spite of, despite, notwithstanding; against, contrary to 704 *in opposition*.

See: **14**, 31, 165, 177, 240, 279, 280, 656, 658, 678, 688, 702, **704**, 713, 715, 735, 747, 752, 757, 881.

Class two

Space

Section one: Space in general

183 Space: indefinite space

N.*space*, expanse, expansion; extension, spatial e., extent, superficial e., surface, area; volume, cubic content; continuum, stretch 71 *continuity*; space-time 108 *time*; empty space 190 *emptiness*; depth of space, abyss 211 *depth*; unlimited space, infinite s. 107 *infinity*; sky, outer space, interstellar s. 321 *heavens*; world, wide w., length and breadth of the land; vastness, immensity, vastitude; geographical space, terrain, open space, open country; lung, green belt, wide horizons, wide open spaces 348 *plain*; upland, moorland, campagna, veld, prairie, steppe 348 *grassland*; outback, hinterland 184 *region*; wild, wilderness, waste 172 *desert*; everywhere, ubiquity 189 *presence*.

measure, proportions, dimension 203 *length*, 205 *breadth*, 209 *height*, 211 *depth*; area, surface a.; square measure, acreage, acres, rods, poles and perches; square inch, square yard, square metre, hectare, hide; volume, cubic content 195 *size*.

range, reach, carry, compass, coverage; stretch, grasp, span; radius, latitude, amplitude; sweep, spread, ramification; play, swing 744 *scope*; sphere, field, arena 184 *region*; purview, prospect 438 *view*; perspective, focal distance 199 *distance*; telescopic range, light-grasp; magnifying power 417 *optics*.

room, space, accommodation; capacity, internal c., stowage, storage space 632 *storage*; seating capacity, seating; standing room; margin, clearance, windage; room to spare, r. to manoeuvre, elbowroom, legroom, room to swing a cat; room overhead, headroom, headway; sea room, seaway, leeway; opening, way 263 *open space*; living space, Lebensraum.

Adj.*spatial*, space; spatio-temporal, space-time, fourth-dimensional; volumetric, cubic, three-dimensional; flat, superficial, two-dimensional.

spacious 32 *extensive*; expansive, roomy, commodious; ample, vast, vasty, cavernous, capacious, broad, deep, wide; voluminous, baggy 195 *large*; broad-based 79 *general*; far-reaching, far-flung, widespread, worldwide, global, world 52 *whole*; uncircumscribed, boundless, spaceless 107 *infinite*; shoreless, trackless, pathless; extending, spreading, branching, ramified.

Vb.*extend*, spread, spread out, range, cover; span, straddle, bestride 226 *overlie*; extend to, reach to 202 *be contiguous*; branch, ramify.

Adv.*widely*, extensively, everywhere, wherever; far and near, far and wide, all over, the whole world over, throughout the world; under the sun, on the face of the earth, in every quarter, in all quarters, in all lands; from end to end, from pole to pole, from coast to coast, from China to Peru, from Dan to Beersheba, from Land's End to John o' Groats 54 *throughout*; from all the points of the compass, from the furthest corners of the earth; to the four winds, to the uttermost parts of the earth; from here to the back of beyond; at every turn, here, there and everywhere, right and left, high and low, inside and out.

See:32, 52, 54, 71, 79, 107, 108, 172, 184, 189, 190, **195**, 199, 202, 203, 205, 209, 211, 226, 263, 321, 348, 417, 438, 632, 744.

184 Region: definite space

N.*region*, locality, parts 185 *place*; sphere, orb, hemisphere; zone, belt; latitude, parallel, meridian; clime, climate; tract, terrain, country, ground, soil 344 *land*; geographical unit, island, peninsula, continent, landmass; sea 343 *ocean*; global village 321 *world*; Old World, New W.; East and West, North and South; Third World 733 *political organization*; compass, circumference, circle, circuit 233 *outline*; boundaries, bounds, shore, confines, marches 236 *limit*; pale, precincts, close, enclave, exclave, salient 235 *enclosure*; corridor 624 *access*; area, field, theatre 724 *arena*; exclusive area, charmed circle. **See** *territory*.

territory, sphere, zone; catchment area; beat, pitch, ground; lot, holding, claim 235 *enclosure*; grounds, park 777 *estate*; national boundaries, domain, territorial waters, three-mile limit; continental shelf, airspace, defensible space; possession, dependency, protectorate, dominion; colony, settlement; motherland, fatherland, homeland 192 *home*; commonwealth, republic, kingdom, realm, state, empire 733 *political organization*; debatable territory, no-man's-land, Tom Tiddler's ground 774 *nonownership*.

district, purlieus, haunt 187 *locality*; subregion, quarter, division 53 *subdivision*; state, province, county, shire, bailiwick, riding, lathe, wapentake, hundred, soke, rape, tithing; diocese, bishopric, archbishopric; parish, ward, constituency; borough, township, municipality; county, district, metropolitan area; canton, department, arrondissement, commune; hamlet, village, town, market t., county t. 192 *abode*; built-up area 192 *housing*; garden city, new town; suburb, suburbia, subtopia, dormitory suburb, stockbroker belt; green belt 183 *space*; Home Counties, golden circle; north of Potters Bar, provinces, back of beyond, the sticks, Marches, Borders; Highlands, Lowlands, Wild West; outback, backwoods, bush, brush, bundu; woods and fields, countryside 344 *land*; hinterland, heartland.

city, capital c., cathedral c., metropolis, megalopolis, conurbation; Greater London, the Big City, the big smoke, the great wen, Cockaigne; Gotham, the Big Apple; West End, W. Side, East End, E. side, City, Wall Street, Manhattan; uptown, downtown.

Adj.*regional*, territorial, continental, peninsular, insular; national, state; subdivisional, local, municipal, parochial, redbrick 192 *provincial*; suburban, urban, rural, up-country; district, town, country.

See:53, 183, **185**, **187**, 192, 233, 235, 236, 321, 343, 344, 624, 724, 733, 774, 777.

185 Place: limited space

N.*place*, emplacement, site, location, position 186 *situation*; station, substation; quarter, locality 184 *district*; assigned place, pitch, beat, billet, socket, groove; centre, meeting place 76 *focus*; birthplace, dwelling place, fireside 192 *home*; place of residence, address, habitat 187 *locality*, 192 *quarters*; premises, building, mansion 192 *house*; spot, plot; point, dot, pinpoint; niche, nook, corner, hole, pigeonhole, pocket 194 *compartment*; confines, bounds, baseline, crease (cricket) 236 *limit*; confined place, prison, coffin, grave; precinct, bailey, garth, paddock, compound, pen 235 *enclosure*; close, quadrangle, quad, square; yard, area, backyard, courtyard, court 263 *open space*; farmyard, field 370 *farm*; sheepwalk, sheeprun 369 *stock farm*; highways and byways, ins and outs, every nook and corner.

Adv.*somewhere*, some place, wherever it may be, here and there, in various places, passim; locally 200 *near*.

See:76, 184, **186**, **187**, **192**, 194, 200, **235**, 236, 263, 369, 370.

186 Situation

N.*situation*, position, setting; scene, locale; time and place, when and where; location, address, whereabouts; point, stage, milestone 27 *degree*; site, seat, emplacement, base 185 *place*; habitat, biotype, range 184 *region*; post, station; standpoint, standing, ground, footing 7 *state*; side, aspect, attitude, posture; frontage, orientation 239 *laterality*, 240 *contraposition*; geography, topography, chorography, cosmography 321 *earth sciences*; chart 551 *map*.

bearings, compass direction, latitude and longitude, declination, right ascension, easting, westing, northing, southing 281 *direction*; radiolocation 187 *location*.

Adj.*situated*, situate, located at, living at, to be found at; settled, set; stationed, posted; occupying 187 *located*; local, topical; topographical, geographical.

Vb.*be situated*, be situate, centre on; be found at, have one's address at, have one's seat in; have its centre in; be, lie, stand; be stationed, be posted; live, live at 192 *dwell*; touch 200 *be near*.

Adv. *in place*, in situ, in loco, here, there; in, on, over, under; hereabouts, thereabouts; whereabouts; here and there, passim; at the sign of.

See: 7, 27, 184, **185**, **187**, 192, 200, 239, 240, 281, 321, 551.

187 Location

N. *location*, placing, placement, emplacement, collocation, disposition; posting, stationing; finding the place, locating, pinpointing; radiolocation, radar; centring, localization 200 *nearness*; domestication, naturalization; settling, colonization, population; settlement, resettlement, lodgment, establishment, fixation, installation; putting down, deposition, putting back, reposition 62 *arrangement*; putting in 303 *insertion*; packing, stowage, loading, lading 632 *storage*.

locality, quarters, purlieus, environs, environment, surroundings, milieu, neighbourhood, parts, neck of the woods 184 *district*; vicinity 200 *near place*; address, street, place of residence, habitat 192 *abode*; seat, site 185 *place*; meeting place, venue, haunt 76 *focus*; genius loci, spirit of place.

station, seat, site, emplacement, position 186 *situation*; depot, base, military b., naval b., air b.; colony, settlement; anchorage, roadstead, mooring 662 *shelter*; cantonment, lines, police l., civil l.; camp, encampment, laager, bivouac, campsite, temporary abode; hostel 192 *abode*; halting place, lay-by, parking place 145 *stopping place*.

Adj. *located*, placed etc. vb.; positioned, stationed, posted 186 *situated*; ensconced, embedded, cradled, nestled 232 *circumscribed*; rooted, settled, domesticated 153 *fixed*; encamped, camping, lodged 192 *residing*; moored, anchored, at anchor 266 *quiescent*; vested in, in the hands of, in the possession of 773 *possessed*; reposed in, transferred to 780 *transferred*; well-placed, favourably situated.

Vb. *place*, collocate, assign a place 62 *arrange*; situate, position, site, locate; base, centre, localize; narrow down, pinpoint, pin down; find the place, put one's finger on; place right, aim well, hit, hit the mark 281 *aim*; put, lay, set, seat; station, post, park; install, ensconce, set up, establish, fix 153 *stabilize*; fix in, root, plant, implant, embed, graft, slot in 303 *insert*; bed, bed down, put to bed, tuck in, tuck up, cradle; accommodate, find a place for, find room for, lodge, house, quarter, billet; quarter upon, billet on; impose, saddle on; moor, tether, picket, anchor 45 *tie*; dock, berth 266 *bring to rest*; deposit, lay down, put d., set d.; stand, put up, erect 310 *elevate*; place with, transfer, bestow, invest 780 *assign*; array, deploy.

replace, put back, sheathe, put up (a sword), bring back, reinstate 656 *restore*; repatriate, resettle 272 *transpose*; redeposit, reinvest, replant, reset.

stow, put away, put by; imburse, pocket, pouch, pack, bale, store, lade, freight, put on board 193 *load*; squeeze in, cram in 54 *fill*.

place oneself, stand, take one's place, take one's stand, anchor, drop a., cast a. 266 *come to rest*; settle, strike root, take r., gain a footing, entrench oneself, dig in 144 *stay*; perch, alight, sit on, sit, squat, park; pitch on, pitch one's tent, encamp, camp, bivouac; stop at, lodge, put up; hive, burrow; ensconce oneself, locate oneself, establish o., find a home, move in, put down roots; settle, colonize, populate, people 192 *dwell*; get naturalized, become a citizen.

See: 45, 54, 62, 76, 144, 145, 153, **184**, **185**, **186**, **192**, 193, 200, 232, 266, 272, 281, 303, 310, 632, 656, 662, 773, 780.

188 Displacement

N. *displacement*, dislocation, derailment 63 *derangement*; misplacement, wrong place, ectopia 84 *abnormality*; shift, move 265 *motion*; red shift, Doppler effect; parallax; aberration, perturbation (astronomy) 282 *deviation*; translocation, transposition, transhipment, transfer 272 *transference*; mutual transfer 151 *interchange*; relief, replacement 150 *substitution*; removal, taking away 304 *extraction*; unloading, unpacking, unshipping; expulsion 300 *ejection*; weeding, eradication 300 *voidance*; exile, banishment 883 *seclusion*; refugee 268 *wanderer*; fish out of water, square peg in a round hole 25 *misfit*; docker, stevedore, removal man.

Adj. *displaced*, disturbed etc. vb.; removed, transported 272 *transferable*; aberrant 282 *deviating*; unplaced, unhoused, unharboured; unestablished, rootless, unsettled, déraciné(e); roofless, houseless, homeless; out of a job, out of the picture, out of touch, out in the cold 57 *excluded*.

misplaced, ectopic 84 *abnormal*; out of one's element, like a fish out of water; out of place, inappropriate 10 *irrelevant*; mislaid, lost, missing 190 *absent*.

Vb. *displace*, disturb, disorientate, derail, dislocate; dislodge, unseat, unfix, unstick 46 *disunite*; dispel, scatter, send flying 75 *disperse*; shift, remove 265 *move*; cart away, transport 272 *transfer*; alter the position, change round; transpose 151 *interchange*; dispatch, post 272 *send*; relegate, banish, exile 300 *dismiss*; set aside, supersede 150 *substitute*, 752 *depose*; turn out, evict, unhouse 300 *eject*; eradicate, uproot 165 *destroy*; discharge, unload, offload, unship, tranship; clear away, rake, sweep, sweep up 648 *clean*; take away, take off, cart off; lift, raise, uplift 310 *elevate*; draw, draw out, pull o. 304 *extract*.

misplace, mislay, lose, lose touch with, lose track of.

See: 10, 25, 46, 57, **63**, 75, 84, 150, 151, 165, 190, 265, 268, **272**, 282, **300**, 304, 310, 648, 752, 883.

189 Presence

N. *presence*, being there, existence, whereness; whereabouts 186 *situation*; being somewhere, ubiety; being everywhere, ubiquity, ubiquitousness, omnipresence; permeation, pervasion, diffusion; availability, bird in the hand; physical presence, bodily p., personal p.; attendance, personal a.; residence, occupancy, occupation, sit-in 773 *possession*; visit, descent, stay; nowness, present moment 121 *present time*; man on the spot; spectator, bystander 441 *onlookers*.

Adj. *on the spot*, present, existent, in being 1 *existing*; occupying, in occupation; inhabiting, resident, residentiary, domiciled 192 *residing*; attendant, waiting, still there, not gone, hanging on; ready, on tap, available, on the menu, on 669 *prepared*; at home, at hand, within reach, on call; under one's nose, before one's eyes 443 *obvious*; looking on, standing by.

ubiquitous, omnipresent, permeating, pervading, pervasive 79 *universal*.

Vb. *be present*, exist, be; take up space, occupy; colonize, inhabit 192 *dwell*; hold 773 *possess*; stand, lie 186 *be situated*; look on, stand by, witness 441 *watch*; resort to, frequent, haunt, meet one at every turn; occur 154 *happen*; stay, sojourn, summer, winter, revisit 882 *visit*; attend, assist at, grace the occasion, honour with one's presence; take part, make one at, make one of; show up, turn up, present oneself, announce o. 295 *arrive*; be in evidence, show one's face, put in an appearance, look in on; face, confront 711 *defy*.

pervade, permeate, fill 54 *make complete*; be diffused through, be disseminated, imbue, impregnate, soak, run through; overrun, swarm over, spread, meet one at every turn 297 *infiltrate*; make one's presence felt 178 *influence*.

Adv. *here*, there, where, everywhere, all over the place; in situ, in place; on location; aboard, on board, at home; on the spot; in the presence of, before, under the eyes of, under the nose of, in the face of; personally, in person, in propria persona.

See: **1**, 54, 79, 121, 154, 178, 186, 192, 295, 297, 441, 443, 669, 711, 773, 882.

190 Absence

N. *absence*, nonpresence, disappearing trick 446 *disappearance*; lack 636 *scarcity*; deprivation 772 *loss*; being nowhere, Utopia 513 *fantasy*; inexistence 2 *nonexistence*; being elsewhere, alibi; nonresidence, living out; leave of absence, furlough; nonattendance, nonappearance, truancy, absenteeism, French leave 620 *avoidance*; absentee, truant 620 *avoider*; absentee landlord; backwoodsman, nonvoter, postal voter.

emptiness, bareness, empty space, void, vacuity, inanity, vacancy; blank 201 *gap*; nothing inside, hollowness, shell; vacuum, air pocket; empties, dead men (empty bottles); blank cartridge, blank paper, clean sheet; virgin territory, no-man's-land; waste, desolation 172 *desert*; vacant lot, bomb site 183 *room*.

nobody, no one, nobody present, nobody on earth; not a soul, not a living thing; empty seats, nonexistent audience.

Adj. *absent*, not present, not found, unrepresented; away, not resident; gone from home, on tour, on location; out, not at home; gone, flown, disappeared 446 *disappearing*; lacking, wanting, missing, wanted; absent without leave, AWOL; truant, absentee 667 *escaped*; unavailable, unprocurable, off the menu, off 636 *unprovided*; lost, mislaid, nowhere to be found; inexistent 2 *nonexistent*; exempt from, spared, exempted; on leave, on furlough; omitted, left out 57 *excluded*.

empty, vacant, vacuous, inane; void, devoid, bare; blank, clean; characterless, featureless; without content, hollow; vacant, unoccupied, uninhabited, untenanted, tenantless; unstaffed, crewless; depopulated; desert, deserted 621 *relinquished*; unpeopled, unsettled, uncolonized; godforsaken, lonely; bleak, desolate 172 *unproductive*; uninhabitable.

Vb. *be absent*, have no place in, take no part in; absent oneself, not show up, stay away, keep away, keep out of the way, cut, skip, play truant *or* hookey, take French leave 620 *avoid*; be missed, leave a gap, be conspicuous by one's absence; leave empty, evacuate, vacate; exhaust 300 *empty*.

go away, withdraw, leave 296 *depart*; make oneself scarce, slip out, slip away, be off, retreat 296 *decamp*, 667 *escape*; vanish 446 *disappear*; move over, make room, vacate.

Adv. *without*, minus, sans; in default of, for want of; in vacuo.

not here, not there; neither here nor there; elsewhere, somewhere else; nowhere, no place; in one's absence, behind one's back, in absentia.

See: **2**, 57, 172, 183, 201, 296, 300, 446, 513, 620, 621, 636, 667, 772.

191 Inhabitant

N. *dweller*, inhabitant, habitant, denizen, indweller; sojourner, transient, visitant; migrant, expatriate 59 *foreigner*; mainlander, continental; insular, islander; boat-dweller, water gipsy; landsman *or* -woman, hill-dweller, dalesman, dales-woman, highlander, lowlander, plains-dweller, fenman, fenwoman, forest-dweller, bush-d.; frontiersman *or* -woman, borderer; city-dweller, town-d., suburbanite, commuter; metropolitan, provincial; country-dweller, ruralist, villager; peasant 370 *farmer*; desert-dweller, tent-d., bedouin; cave-dweller, troglodyte; slum-dweller 801 *poor person*. **See** *native*.

resident, householder, ratepayer; housewife, hausfrau, chatelaine, housekeeper; cottager, crofter; addressee, occupier, occupant, incumbent, residentiary 776 *possessor*; locum tenens 150 *substitute*; tenant, sitting t., protected t., renter, lessee, lease-holder; inmate, in-patient; house surgeon 658 *doctor*; garrison, crew 686 *personnel*; lodger, boarder, au pair, paying guest, p.g.; guest, visitor, inquiline, commensal; uninvited guest, cuckoo, squatter 59 *intruder*; parasite 659 *bane*.

native, aboriginal, aborigines, autochthones, earliest inhabitants, first-comers 66 *precursor*; people, tribe 371 *nation*; local, local inhabitant; parishioner, villager, townsperson, townee, city person, urbanite, city slicker, cockney, suburbanite, weekender; yokel, rustic 869 *country-dweller*; fellow countryman *or* -woman, fellow citizen; national, patrial, citizen, burgher, burgess, voter; John Bull, Uncle Sam; Briton, Britisher; Celt, Gael, Scot, North Briton, Caledonian, Welshman *or* -woman, Irishman *or* -woman, Hibernian; Jock, Taffy, Paddy; Englishman *or* -woman, Northerner, Southerner, Midlander, East Anglian, Westcountryman *or* -woman; Londoner, Brummie, Bristolian, Mancunian, Liverpudlian, Scouse, Geordie, Glaswegian; New Yorker, Parisian, Muscovite 59 *foreigner*; earth-dweller, terrestrial, tellurian; space-dweller, Martian, Venusian.

settler, pioneer, Pilgrim Fathers 66 *precursor*; immigrant, colonist, colonial, Creole; planter 370 *farmer*; resident alien 59 *foreigner*.

inhabitants, population, urban p., rural p., townspeople, country folk; populace, people, people at large, citizenry, tenantry, yeomanry; villadom, suburbia 192 *housing*; city-full, houseful; household, ménage 11 *family*; settlement, stronghold; colony, commune, community, village c.

Adj. *native*, vernacular, popular, national, ethnic; indigenous, autochthonous, aboriginal; enchorial; earthbound, terrestrial, tellurian; home, home-made; domestic, domiciliary, domesticated; settled, domiciled, naturalized; resident 192 *residing*.

occupied, occupied by, indwelt; inhabited, lived in, tenanted, populated; garrisoned by, manned, staffed.

See: 11, **59**, 66, 150, **192**, 370, 371, 658, 659, 686, 776, 801, 869.

192 Abode: place of habitation or resort

N. *abode*, habitat, haunt, station 186 *situation*; place of residence 187 *locality*; habitation, street, house, home, second h.; address, house number, number; domicile, residence, residency; town, city 184 *district*; headquarters, base, seat 76 *focus*; temporary abode, hangout, camp, pad, pied-à-terre; weekend cottage, country seat, holiday home, seaside resort, watering place, hill station 837 *pleasure ground*; spa, sanatorium 658 *hospital*; cantonment, lines 187 *station*; bivouac, encampment; camp, refugee c.; campsite, caravan park; rus in urbe, home from home.

quarters, living q., married q., accommodation, lodging, billet, berth, squat; barracks, casern; lodgings, rooms, chambers, digs; residential hotel, guest house, boarding h., lodging h., pension; boarding school, hostel, dormitory, dorm; hall of residence; convent 986 *monastery*.

dwelling, roof over one's head 226 *roof*; prehistoric dwelling, lake d., crannog; tower, keep; cave, hut, kraal, igloo; wigwam, tepee, wickiup, tent 226 *canopy*; lair, den, hole, form, burrow, warren, earth, sett 662 *shelter*.

nest, nidus; drey; branch 366 *tree*; eyrie, perch, roost; covert, heronry, rookery, swannery, hatchery, aviary, apiary, beehive, skep; wasp's nest, antheap, anthill.

home, home-sweet-home, hearth, fireside, chimney corner, inglenook, rooftree, roof, paternal r., ancestral halls; homestead, toft, household; cradle, birthplace, 'house where I was born' 68 *origin*; native land, la patrie, motherland, fatherland, homeland, one's country, God's own country, the Old Country, Blighty, Albion; native soil, native sod, native ground, native heath, home ground, home town, own backyard; haunt, stamping ground; familiar territory, second home; household gods, Lares and Penates; Hestia, Vesta.

house, building 164 *edifice*; house of God 990 *temple*; home, residence, dwelling, dwelling house, messuage; country house, town h.; villa, detached house, semi-detached h., semi, terraced house; Queen Anne house, Georgian h., Regency h.; council h., prefab; ranch house, chalet, bungalow, chalet-b.; seat, place, mansion, hall, stately home; palace, dome, alcazar; château, castle, keep, tower, peel; manor house, dower h., manor, grange, lodge, priory, abbey; vicarage 986 *parsonage*; farmhouse, farmstead, croft, toft and croft, hacienda 370 *farm*; official residence, Buckingham Palace, Chequers, Mansion House, White House, embassy, consulate.

small house, bijou residence; two-up two-down, back-to-back; chalet, lodge, cottage, cruck c., thatched c., cot, but and ben; cabin, log c., hut, Nissen h., shanty, bothy; hovel, dump, hole, slum dwelling; box, hunting-box *or* -lodge; shed, shack, lean-to, outhouse, outbuilding; shelter, tent 226 *canopy*; kiosk, booth, stall, shieling; houseboat 275 *boat*; mobile home, caravan, trailer 274 *vehicle*. **See** *flat*.

housing, high-density h.; bricks and mortar 631 *building material*; built-up area, urban sprawl; asphalt jungle, concrete j., urban blight; urbanization, conurbation; town, satellite t., burgh, suburb 184 *city*; housing estate, overspill e., residential area 184 *district*; villadom, suburbia, subtopia; crescent, close, terrace, circus, square, avenue, street 624 *road*; block, court, row, mansions, villas, buildings; houses, tenements; inner city, ghetto, slum, condemned building; shanty town, hutments, bustee, barrio; hamlet, village, thorp, dorp; scattered settlement, isolated s.

flat, flatlet, granny flat, furnished f., service f., mews f., penthouse; apartment, suite, chambers; bedsitting room, bed-sitter, bed-sit 194 *chamber*; maisonette, duplex, walkup; block of flats, apartment block, tower b.; mews, tenements.

stable, byre, cowshed, shippen; kennel, doghouse; sty, pigpen, fold, sheepfold 235 *enclosure*; dovecote, pigeon loft; stall, cage, coop, hencoop, hutch, battery; stabling, mews, coach-house, garage, carport, hangar; boathouse; marina, dock, dry d., graving d., floating d.; basin, wharf, roads, roadstead, port 662 *shelter*; berth, quay, jetty, pier 266 *resting place*.

inn, hotel, hostelry, roadhouse, motel, bed and breakfast (**see** *quarters*); dosshouse, bunkhouse, kip, flophouse; hospice, night shelter; youth hostel; auberge, trattoria, posada, caravanserai, khan; dak bungalow, rest house.

tavern, alehouse, pothouse, beerhouse, boozer; public house, pub, local; free house, tied h.; gin palace, saloon; speakeasy, dive, joint, honky-tonk; shebeen;

wine cellar, wine bar, bodega; beer cellar, beer hall, beer garden; bar, public b., saloon b.; taproom.

cafe, restaurant, self-service r., cafeteria; eating-house, steakhouse, diner, brasserie, bistro, grill room, rotisserie; coffee bar, milk b., ice-cream parlour, soda fountain; lunch counter, fast-food c., snack bar, sandwich bar; teahouse, teashop, tearoom; refreshment room, buffet, canteen, Naafi; fish and chip shop, chippy, takeaway; coffee stall, pull-in, transport café.

meeting place, conventicle, meeting house 990 *church*; day centre, community c., village hall; assembly rooms, pump r.; club, clubhouse, night club, working men's c., holiday camp 837 *place of amusement*; football ground, racecourse, dog track 724 *arena*; theatre, concert hall, stadium, stand 441 *onlookers*; sports centre, gymnasium, drill hall, parade ground; piazza, quadrangle, quad, campus, village green 76 *focus*; shopping centre 796 *market*.

pleasance, park, grounds, pleasure g., gardens, green; walk, mall, avenue, parade, promenade, boulevard; national park, safari p.; parkland, chase 837 *pleasure ground*.

pavilion, kiosk, bandstand, rotunda, folly, bower, grotto 194 *arbour*; stoa, colonnade, arcade, peristyle; tent, marquee 226 *canopy*.

retreat, sanctuary, refuge, asylum, ark 662 *shelter*; priesthole 527 *hiding-place*; cubbyhole, den, snuggery, sanctum, study 194 *chamber*; cell, hermitage 883 *seclusion*; cloister 986 *monastery*; ashram; almshouse, grace and favour house; workhouse, poorhouse; orphanage, home, rest h., hospice, halfway house, sheltered housing.

Adj. *residing*, abiding, dwelling, living, domiciled; at home, in residence; residential, fit for habitation; parasitical; inquiline, commensal.

urban, towny, metropolitan, cosmopolitan, inner-city, suburban; built-up, citified, urbanized, suburbanized; bungaloid.

provincial, parochial, local, domestic, vernacular; up-country, countrified, rural, rustic 184 *regional*.

architectural, architectonic, edificial; designed, architect-d. 243 *formed*; Gothic 990 *churchlike*; classical, neoclassical, Palladian, Tudor 127 *olden*; brick, concrete, cob, timber-framed, half-timbered; thatched, tiled 226 *covered*; modest, substantial, palatial, grand; detached, semi-d.; back-to-back, jerry-built; single-storey, multistorey, high-rise; double-fronted.

Vb. *dwell*, dwell in, inhabit, populate, people 189 *be present*; settle, colonize 786 *appropriate*; frequent, haunt 882 *visit*; take up one's abode, take up residence, hang up one's hat, move in; reside, remain, abide, sojourn, live 186 *be situated*; take rooms, put up at, stay, keep, lodge, lie, sleep at; live in, board out, be in digs; have an address, hang out at; tenant, occupy, squat 773 *possess*; nestle, perch, roost, nest, hive, burrow, stable; camp, encamp, bivouac, doss down, pitch one's tent, make one's quarters 187 *place oneself*; tent, shelter 662 *seek refuge*; berth, dock, anchor 266 *come to rest*.

urbanize, citify, suburbanize, develop, build up.

See: 68, 76, 127, 164, 184, **186**, **187**, 189, 194, 226, 235, 243, 266, 274, 275, 366, 370, 441, 527, 624, 631, 658, 662, 724, 773, 786, 796, 837, 882, 883, 986, 990.

193 Contents: things contained

N. *contents*, ingredients, items, components, constituents, parts 58 *component*; inventory 87 *list*; furnishings, equipment 633 *provision*; load, payload, cargo, lading, freight, shipment, cartload, shipload 272 *thing transferred*; enclosure, inside 224 *insides*; stuffing, filling, stopping, wadding 227 *lining*; fistful, handful, cupful, quiverful 33 *small quantity*, 32 *great quantity*.

Vb. *load*, lade, freight, charge, burden 187 *stow*; palletize, containerize; take in, take on board, ship; overburden, break one's back 322 *weigh*; pack, pack in, fit in, tuck in 303 *insert*; pack tight, squeeze in, cram, stuff 54 *fill*; pad, wad 227 *line*; hide, conceal 226 *cover*.

See: 32, 33, 54, **58**, 87, 187, 224, 226, 227, 272, 303, 322, 633.

194 Receptacle

N. *receptacle*, container, holder; frame 218 *prop*; hutch, cage 748 *prison*; folder, wrapper, envelope, cover, file 235 *enclosure*; net, safety n., fishing n. 222 *network*; sheath, chrysalis, cocoon; packaging 226 *wrapping*; capsule, ampoule; pod, calyx, boll; mould 243 *form*; socket, mortise 255 *cavity*; groove, slot 262 *furrow*; hole, cave, cavity 263 *opening*; bosom, lap 261 *fold*; slot-machine; pin cushion; catch-all, trap; well, reservoir, hold, repository 632 *store*; drain, cesspit, sump 649 *sink*; crockery, chinaware, glassware 381 *pottery*.

bladder, airbladder, inflatable; inner tube; football; balloon, gasbag; sac, cyst, vesicle, utricle, blister, bubble 253 *swelling*; udder, teat 253 *bosom*.

maw, stomach, tummy, breadbasket, little Mary; abdomen, belly, corporation, pot belly, venter, paunch 253 *swelling*; gizzard, gullet, crop, craw, jaws, mouth, oesophagus 263 *orifice*.

compartment, cell, cellule, loculus, follicle, ventricle; tray, in t., out t.; cage, iron lung; cubicle, carrel, booth, stall; sentry box; box 594 *theatre*; pew, choirstall 990 *church interior*; niche, nook, cranny, recess, bay, oriel, mihrab; pigeonhole, cubbyhole; drawer, locker; shelving, rack 218 *shelf*; storey, floor, deck 207 *layer*.

cabinet, closet, commode, wardrobe, press, chest of drawers, chiffonier, tallboy; cupboard, corner c., built-in c., unit; whatnot, dresser, Welsh d., china cabinet; buffet, sideboard 218 *stand*; freezer 384 *refrigerator*; cellaret, cocktail cabinet, dumbwaiter; secretaire, escritoire, davenport, bureau, desk, writing d.; console; bookcase.

basket, creel; hamper, picnic basket; pannier; trug, punnet, pottle, rush basket, frail; crib, cradle, bassinet; clothesbasket, laundry basket; workbasket, workbox; wastepaper basket; wickerwork, basketwork; framework, crate 218 *frame*; gabion 713 *fortification*.

box, chest, ark; coffer, locker; case, canteen; safe, till, moneybox 799 *treasury*; coffin, sarcophagus 364 *tomb*; packing case, tea chest; tuckbox; attaché case, dispatch box; suitcase, expanding s.; trunk, valise, portmanteau; sea chest, ditty-box; bandbox, hat box; ammunition chest, canister, caisson 723 *ammunition*; boxes, luggage, baggage, impedimenta; boot, luggage van.

small box, pill b., snuff b., cigar b., pencil b., matchbox; cardboard box, carton, packet; plastic box, airtight container; metal box, can, tin, caddy, tea caddy, canister; casket, pyx 988 *ritual object*; salt cellar, pepper mill; castor; nest of boxes.

bag, sack, poke; handbag, vanity case, reticule, clutch bag, Dorothy b., shoulder b., tote b.; shopping bag, carrier b., polythene b., plastic b., paper b.; cornet, twist, satchet; Gladstone bag, carpet b., travelling bag, overnight b., flight b., sponge b.; sleeping bag, survival bag; bedding-roll; holdall, grip; haversack, knapsack, rucksack, backpack; kitbag, ditty bag, duffel b.; pouch, sling; pannier, saddlebag, nosebag; school bag, satchel, sabretache, bundle, swag.

case, étui, housewife; wallet, pocket book, notecase; spectacle case, cigarette c., compact; vasculum; briefcase, portfolio; file, box f.; scabbard, sheath; pistol case, holster; arrow case, quiver 632 *store*.

pocket, waistcoat p., side p., hip p., trouser p., breast p.; fob, pouch; purse, sporran.

vat, butt, water b., cask, barrel, tun, tub, keg, breaker; drum 252 *cylinder*; wine cask, puncheon, pipe, hogshead, firkin, kilderkin 465 *metrology*; hopper, cistern, tank 632 *store*.

vessel, vase, urn, jar, amphora, ampulla, cruse, crock, pot, water p.; pipkin, pitcher, ewer, jug, toby jug; gourd, calabash 366 *plant*; carafe, decanter, bottle; leather bottle, blackjack, wineskin; wine bottle, demijohn, magnum, jeroboam; flask, hip f., flagon, vial, phial; honeypot, jamjar; gallipot, carboy, crucible, retort, pipette, test tube, cupel 461 *testing agent*; chamber pot, bedpan 649 *latrine*; pail, bucket, wooden b., piggin; churn, can, watering c.; flowerpot, jardinière; bin, litter b., rubbish b., dustbin 649 *sink*; scuttle, coal s., hod; skip, kibble; bath, tin b., tub.

cauldron 383 *heater*; boiler, copper, kettle, skillet, pan, saucepan, stewpan, steamer, double-boiler; frying pan, grill p., girdle; casserole, Dutch oven, bain-marie; mess tin, dixie, billycan; tea urn, teapot, samovar, coffeepot, percolator; vacuum flask, thermos f. (tdmk); hot-water bottle, warming pan.

cup, eggcup, coffee cup, teacup, breakfast cup; tea service, tea set; chalice, goblet, beaker; drinking cup, loving c.; quaich; horn, drinking h., tankard, stoup, can, cannikin, pannikin, mug, stein, toby, noggin, rummer, schooner, tassie; tumbler, glass, liqueur g., wineglass, brandy balloon, pony.

bowl, finger b., basin, hand b., wash b.;

pudding basin, mixing bowl, punch bowl, drinking b., jorum; porringer, ramekin; manger, trough; colander, vegetable dish, tureen, terrine, gravy boat; rose bowl, vase 844 *ornamentation*.

plate, salver, tray, paten; platter, trencher, charger, dish; palette; saucer; pan, scale 322 *scales*; pallet; mortarboard, hod.

ladle, skimmer, dipper, baler, scoop, cupped hands; spoon, tablespoon, dessertspoon, teaspoon, eggspoon, soupspoon; spade, trowel, spatula, slice, shovel.

chamber, room, apartment 192 *flat*; cockpit, cubicle, cab; cabin, stateroom; audience chamber, presence c., throne room; cabinet, closet, study, den, sanctum, adytum 192 *retreat*; library, studio, atelier, workroom, office 687 *workshop*; playroom, nursery; reception room, drawing room, front r., sitting r., living r., lounge, parlour, salon, boudoir; bedroom, dormitory; dressing room; bathroom, washroom; dining room, breakfast r., dinette; messroom, mess, hall, refectory, canteen 192 *cafe*; gunroom, wardroom; smoking room, billiard r.; bar, snug 192 *tavern*; cookhouse, galley, kitchen; scullery, pantry, larder, stillroom; dairy, laundry, utility room, offices, outhouse; coachhouse, garage 192 *stable*; storeroom, box room, lumber r., glory hole 632 *storage*; cloakroom, smallest room, lavatory 649 *latrine*. **See** *compartment*.

lobby, vestibule, foyer, anteroom, waiting room; corridor, passage, hall; gallery, verandah, patio, piazza, loggia, balcony, portico, porch 263 *doorway*; extension, lean-to.

cellar, cellarage, vault, crypt, basement 214 *base*; coalhole, bunker 632 *storage*; hold, dungeon 748 *prison*.

attic, loft, hayloft; penthouse, garret 213 *summit*.

arbour, alcove, bower, grotto, grot, summerhouse, gazebo, folly, pergola 192 *pavilion*; sun lounge, conservatory, orangery, greenhouse, glasshouse 370 *garden*.

Adj. *recipient*, capacious, voluminous 183 *spacious*; containing, hiding, framing, enclosing; pouchy, baggy.

cellular, multicellular, honeycombed 255 *concave*; camerate, compartmentalized; multilocular, locular; marsupial, polygastric, ventricular; abdominal, gastral, ventral, stomachic, ventricose, bellied 253 *convex*.

capsular, sacculate, cystic; vascular, vesicular.

See: 183, 192, 207, 213, 214, 218, 222, 226, 235, 243, 252, 253, 255, 261, 262, 263, 322, 364, 366, 370, 381, 383, 384, 461, 465, 594, 632, 649, 687, 713, 723, 748, 799, 844, 988, 990.

Section two: Dimensions

195 Size

N. *size*, magnitude, order of m.; proportions, dimensions, measurements 183 *measure*; extent, expanse, area 183 *space*; extension 203 *length*, 209 *height*, 211 *depth*; width, amplitude 205 *breadth*; volume, cubature; girth, circumference 233 *outline*; bulk, mass, weight 322 *gravity*; capacity, intake, tonnage; measured size, scantling, calibre 465 *measurement*; real size, true dimensions 494 *accuracy*; greatest size, maximum 32 *greatness*; full size, life size 54 *plenitude*; large size, king s., magnum; largest portion 52 *chief part*; excessive size, hypertrophy, giantism, gigantism.

hugeness, largeness, bigness, grandiosity 32 *greatness*; enormity, enormousness, immensity, vastness; towering proportions, monstrosity, gigantism 209 *height*.

bulk, mass, weight, heaviness, avoirdupois 322 *gravity*; lump, block, clod, boulder 324 *solid body*; hunk, chunk 53 *piece*; mound, heap 32 *great quantity*; mountain, pyramid 209 *high structure*; massiveness, bulkiness; turgidity 197 *dilation*; obesity, corpulence, fatness, stoutness, chubbiness, plumpness, embonpoint, chunkiness, fleshiness, meatiness; flesh and blood, folds of flesh, double chin, rotund figure, spare tyre, corporation 253 *swelling*; muscle man 162 *athlete*; fat person, tub, dumpling, mound of flesh, tub of lard, lard-lump, hulk; Billy Bunter, Bessie B., Falstaff.

giant, giantess, colossus 209 *tall creature*; mountain of a man *or* woman, young giant, strapper; ogre, monster, King Kong; leviathan, behemoth, Triton among the minnows; whale, hippopotamus, elephant, jumbo; mammoth, dinosaur; giantry, Titan, Titaness, Gargantua, Brobdingnagian, Gog and

Magog, Typhon, Cyclops, Goliath.

whopper, spanker, walloper, whacker, humdinger; a mountain of a, a father and mother of a, a ... and a half.

Adj. *large*, of size, big 32 *great*; large size, economy s., king s., jumbo; pretty large, fair-sized, considerable, sizable, good-sized; bulky, massive, massy 322 *weighty*; ample, capacious, voluminous, baggy; amplitudinous, comprehensive 205 *broad*; vast, extensive 183 *spacious*; monumental, towering, mountainous 209 *tall*; fine, magnificent, spanking, thumping, thundering, whacking 32 *whopping*; man-size, life-s., large as life; well-grown, large-limbed, elephantine; macroscopic, large-scale, megalithic; big for one's age, lusty, healthy 162 *strong*; so big, of that order.

huge, immense, enormous, vast, mighty, grandiose, stupendous, monstrous 32 *prodigious*; biggest ever, record size; colossal, mammoth, dinosaurian, gigantic, gigantean, gigantesque, giant, giant-like, mountainous; Brobdingnagian, titanic, Herculean, gargantuan; Cyclopean, megalithic; outsize, oversize, overlarge 32 *exorbitant*; limitless 107 *infinite*.

fleshy, meaty, fat, stout, obese, overweight; well-covered, well-upholstered, Falstaffian; plump, ample, plumpish, chubby, podgy, pudgy 205 *thick*; squat, squab, square, dumpy, chunky, stocky 205 *broad*; tubby, portly, corpulent, paunchy, pot-bellied 253 *convex*; puffy, pursy, bloated, bosomy 197 *expanded*; round, rotund, roly-poly, full, full-faced, chubby-f.; double-chinned, dimpled, dimply, buxom, jolly, on the plump side; in condition, in good c., well-fed, well-grown, strapping, lusty, burly, beefy, brawny 162 *stalwart*; plump as a dumpling, plump as a partridge, fat as butter, fat as bacon, fat as a pig.

unwieldy, cumbersome, hulking, lumbering, gangling, lolloping; hulky, lumpy, lumpish, lubberly; too big, elephantine, overweight; awkward, muscle-bound 695 *clumsy*.

Vb. *be large*, - big etc. adj.; become large 197 *expand*; have size, loom large, bulk l., bulk, fill space 183 *extend*; tower, soar 209 *be high*.

See: 32, 52, 53, 54, 107, 162, 183, **197**, 203, **205**, 209, 211, 233, 253, 322, 324, 465, 494, 695.

196 Littleness

N. *littleness*, daintiness etc. adj.; small size, miniature quality 33 *smallness*; lack of height 204 *shortness*; diminutiveness, dwarfishness, stuntedness; scantiness, paucity, exiguity 105 *fewness*; meagreness 206 *thinness*; - kin, - let.

minuteness, point, mathematical p., vanishing p.; pinpoint, pinhead; crystal; atom, molecule, particle, electron, neutron, proton, quark; nucleus, cell; corpuscle; drop, droplet, dust, grain, g. of sand; seed, mustard s. 33 *small thing*; bubble, button, molehill 639 *trifle*.

miniature 553 *picture*; microphotograph, microdot, microfilm, microfiche 551 *photography*; pocket edition, Elzevir e., duodecimo 589 *edition*; thumbnail sketch, epitome 592 *compendium*; model, microcosm; bubble car, minicar 274 *automobile*.

dwarf, midget, minikin, pigmy, lilliputian, halfling, hobbit; little people 970 *elf*; chit, slip, titch; mite, tot, tiddler 132 *child*; dapperling, dandiprat, cocksparrow, bantam 33 *small animal*; pipsqueak, squit, squirt 639 *nonentity*; manikin, doll, puppet; Tom Thumb, Hop-o'-my-thumb, homunculus; shrimp, runt, miserable specimen.

microorganism, protozoan, plankton, microfauna, animalcule, amoeba; bacillus, bacteria, microbe, germ, virus, bug; microphyte, zoophyte; algae 366 *plant*.

microscopy, micrography, microphotography; microscope, electron m., microspectroscope, micrometer, vernier scale; microtechnique.

microelectronics, microminiaturization 160 *electronics*; integrated circuit, microcircuit; microchip, chip, silicon c.; microprocessor 86 *data processing*.

Adj. *little* 33 *small*; petite, dainty, dinky, dolly, elfin; diminutive, pigmy, lilliputian; no bigger than; wee, titchy, tiny, teeny, teeny-weeny, itsy-bitsy; toy, baby, pocket, pocket-size, pocket-handkerchief, pint-size, duodecimo, mini-; miniature, model; portable, handy, compact, bijou; snug, cosy, poky, cramped, no room to swing a cat 206 *narrow*; runty, puny 163 *weak*; petty 33 *inconsiderable*; one-horse 639 *unimportant*.

dwarfish, dwarf, dwarfed, pigmy, undersized, stunted, weazen, wizened, shrunk 198 *contracted*; squat, dumpy 204 *short*; knee-high, knee-high to a grasshopper.

exiguous, minimal, slight, scant, scanty, homoeopathic 33 *small*; thin, skinny, scraggy 206 *lean*; rudimentary, embryonic 68 *beginning*; bitty 53 *fragmentary*.

minute, micro-, microscopic, ultramicroscopic, infinitesimal; atomic, molecular, corpuscular; granular 332 *powdery*; inappreciable, imperceptible, intangible, impalpable 444 *invisible*.

Vb. *be little*, - petite etc. adj.; contract 198 *become small*; dwindle 37 *decrease*; require little space, take up no room, lie in a nutshell, fit in a small compass, fit on the head of a pin.

Adv. *in small compass*, in a nutshell; on a small scale, in miniature.

See: 33, 37, 53, 68, 86, 105, 132, 160, 163, **198**, 204, 206, 274, 332, 366, 444, 551, 553, 589, 592, 639, 970.

197 Expansion

N. *expansion*, increase of size, ascending order, crescendo; enlargement, augmentation, aggrandizement 36 *increase*; amplification, supplementation, reinforcement 38 *addition*; hypertrophy, giantism, gigantism; overenlargement, hyperbole 546 *exaggeration*; stretching, extension, spread, deployment, fanning out 75 *dispersion*; ribbon development, urban sprawl 192 *housing*; increment, accretion 40 *adjunct*; upgrowth, overgrowth, pullulation, development 157 *growth*, 171 *productiveness*; overstaffing, Parkinson's law 637 *superfluity*; extensibility, expansibility, dilatability 328 *elasticity*.

dilation, dilatation, distension, diastole; inflation, reflation, puffing, puff 352 *blowing*; swelling up, turgescence, turgidity, tumescence, intumescence, tumefaction; puffiness, dropsy, tumour 253 *swelling*.

Adj. *expanded*, blown up etc. vb.; larger, bigger, bigger than before, bigger than ever; expanding 36 *increasing*; stuffed, padded out, supplemented; spreading, widespread, deployed; expansive 183 *spacious*; fan-shaped, flabellate, flabelliform, flared 205 *broad*; wide open, patulous, gaping 263 *open*; tumescent, budding, bursting, florescent, flowering, out; full-blown, full-grown, fully-formed 669 *matured*; overblown, overgrown, hypertrophied 546 *exaggerated*; obese, puffy, pot-bellied, bloated, fat 195 *fleshy*; swollen, turgescent, turgid; distended, stretched, tight; tumid, dropsical, varicose, bulbous 253 *convex*; bladder-like; ampullaceous, pouchy.

Vb. *expand*, wax, grow larger, increase, snowball 36 *grow*; widen, broaden, flare, splay 205 *be broad*; spread, extend, sprawl; fan out, deploy, take open order 75 *be dispersed*; spread over, spread like wildfire, overrun, mantle, straddle 226 *cover*; rise, prove (e.g. dough); gather, swell, distend, dilate, fill out; mushroom, balloon, belly 253 *be convex*; get fat, gain flesh, put on weight; burst at the seams; grow up, spring up, bud, burgeon, shoot, sprout, open, put forth, burst f., blossom, flower, blow, bloom, be out 171 *be fruitful*.

enlarge, aggrandize; make larger, expand; rarefy (by expansion); leaven 310 *elevate*; bore, ream; widen, broaden, let out; open, pull out; stretch, extend 203 *lengthen*; intensify, heighten, deepen, draw out; amplify, supplement, reinforce 38 *add*; double, redouble; develop, build up 36 *augment*; distend, inflate, reflate, pump up, blow up, puff, puff up, puff out 352 *blow*; bulk, thicken; stuff, pad 227 *line*; cram, fill to bursting 54 *fill*; feed up, fatten, plump up, bloat 301 *feed*; enlarge, blow up 551 *photograph*; magnify, overenlarge, overdevelop 546 *exaggerate*.

See: 36, 38, 40, 54, 75, 157, 171, 183, 192, 195, 203, 205, 226, 227, **253**, 263, 301, 310, 328, 352, 546, 551, 637, 669.

198 Contraction

N. *contraction*, reduction, abatement, lessening, deflation 37 *diminution*; decrease, shrinkage, descending order, diminuendo 42 *decrement*; curtailment, abbreviation, syncope, elision 204 *shortening*; consolidation 324 *condensation*; freezing 382 *refrigeration*; pulling together, drawing t. 45 *joining together*, 264 *closure*; contracting, systole; contractions, labour pains 167 *obstetrics*; attenuation, emaciation, consumption, marasmus, withering, atrophy; decline, retreat, recession, slump 655 *deterioration*; neck, isthmus, bottleneck, hourglass, wasp-waist 206 *narrowness*; epitome 592 *compendium*.

compression, pressure, compressure, compaction, squeeze, squeezing, stenosis, strangulation; constriction, constringency, astriction, astringency; contractility, contractibility, compressibility.

compressor, squeezer, mangle, roller 258 *smoother*; tightener, constrictor, astringent; bandage, binder, tourniquet 658 *surgical dressing*; belt, band, garter 47 *girdle*; whalebone, stays, corset 228 *underwear*; straitjacket, iron boot, thumbscrew 964 *instrument of torture*; bear, python, boa constrictor.

Adj. *contracted*, shrunk, shrunken, smaller 33 *small*; waning 37 *decreasing*; constricted, strangled, strangulated; unexpanded, deflated, condensed 324 *dense*; compact, compacted, compressed; pinched, nipped, tightened, drawn tight 206 *narrow*, 264 *closed*; compressible, contractile, systaltic; stunted, shrivelled, wizened 196 *dwarfish*; tabid, tabescent, marasmic, wasting, consumptive 655 *deteriorated*.

compressive, contractional, astringent, binding, constipating.

Vb. *become small*, grow less, lessen, dwindle, wane, ebb, fall away 37 *decrease*; shrivel, wither, waste away 51 *decompose*; lose weight, lose flesh 323 *be light*; stop growing, level off; contract, shrink, narrow, taper, taper off, draw in 206 *be narrow*; condense 324 *be dense*; evaporate 338 *vaporize*; draw together, close up 264 *close*; pucker, purse, corrugate, wrinkle 261 *fold*.

make smaller, lessen, reduce 37 *abate*; contract, shrink, abridge, take in, cut down to life size, dwarf, stunt 204 *shorten*; diet, slim, take off weight 323 *lighten*; taper, narrow, attenuate, thin, emaciate 206 *make thin*; puncture, deflate, rarefy, pump out, exhaust, drain 300 *empty*; boil down, evaporate 338 *vaporize*; dehydrate 342 *dry*; cramp, constrict, constringe, pinch, nip, squeeze, bind, bandage, corset; draw in, draw tight, strain, tauten 45 *tighten*; draw together, clench 264 *close*, 45 *join*; hug, crush, strangle, strangulate; compress, compact, constipate, condense, nucleate 324 *be dense*; huddle, crowd together; squeeze in, pack tight, cram, jam 54 *fill*; squash 216 *flatten*; cramp, restrict 747 *restrain*; limit 232 *circumscribe*; chip away, whittle away, shave, shear, clip, trim, prune, pollard 46 *cut*; scrape, file, grind 332 *pulverize*; fold up, crumple 261 *fold*; roll, press, flatten 258 *smooth*.

See: 33, **37**, 42, 45, 46, 47, 51, 54, 167, 196, 204, **206**, 216, 228, 232, 258, 261, 264, 300, 323, 324, 332, 338, 342, 382, 592, 655, 658, 747, 964.

199 Distance

N. *distance*, astronomical d., light years, depths of space 183 *space*; measured distance, mileage, footage 203 *length*; focal distance; elongation, greatest e., aphelion, apogee; far distance, horizon, false h., skyline, offing; background 238 *rear*; periphery, circumference 233 *outline*; drift, dispersion 282 *deviation*; reach, grasp, compass, span, stride, giant's s. 183 *range*; far cry, long way, fair w., tidy step, day's march, long long trail, marathon.

farness, far distance, remoteness, aloofness; removal 46 *separation*; antipodes, pole 240 *contraposition*; world's end, ultima Thule, Pillars of Hercules; ne plus ultra, back of beyond; Far West, Far East; foreign parts 59 *extraneousness*; outpost 883 *seclusion*; purlieus, outskirts 223 *exteriority*; outer edge, frontier 236 *limit*; unavailability 190 *absence*.

Adj. *distant*, distal, peripheral, terminal; far, farther; ulterior; ultimate, farthest, furthest, furthermost; long-distance, long-range; yon, yonder; not local, away; outlying, peripheral; off-shore, on the horizon; remote, aloof, far-flung, godforsaken; hyperborean, antipodean; out of range, telescopic; lost to sight, lost to view, out of sight 444 *invisible*; off-centre, wide, wide of the mark.

removed, separated, inaccessible, unapproachable, unget-at-able, out of touch, out of the way; beyond, over the horizon; overseas, transmarine, transpontine, transoceanic, transatlantic, trans-Pacific, transpolar, transalpine, ultramontane; ultramundane, out of this world.

Vb. *be distant*, stretch to, reach to, extend to, spread to, go to, get to, stretch away to, carry to, carry on to 183 *extend*; carry, range; outdistance, outrange, outreach 306 *outdo*; keep one's distance, remain at a d., keep off, hold off, stand off, lie off; keep clear of, stand aloof, stand clear of, keep a safe distance, give a wide berth 620 *avoid*.

Adv. *afar*, away, not locally; far, far away, far afield, far off, way o., way behind, way in front; uptown, downtown; yonder, in the distance, in the offing, on the horizon, as far as the eye can see; at a distance, a great way off, a long way away, a far cry from; out of sight; nobody knows where, out of the way; to the ends of the earth, to the back of beyond, to the uttermost end; east of the sun and west of the moon; far and wide 183 *widely*; asunder, apart, far a., abroad, afield; at arm's length.

beyond, further, farther; further on, ahead, in front; clear of, wide of, wide of the mark; below the horizon, hull down; up over, down under, over the border, over the hills and far away.

too far, out of reach, out of range, out of sight, out of hearing, out of earshot, out of the sphere of, out of bounds.

See: 46, 59, **183**, 190, **203**, 223, 233, 236, 238, 240, 282, 306, 444, 620, 883.

200 Nearness

N. *nearness*, proximity, propinquity, closeness, near distance, foreground 237 *front*; vicinage, vicinity, neighbourhood 230 *surroundings*; brink, verge 234 *edge*; adjacency 202 *contiguity*; collision course 293 *convergence*; approximation 289 *approach*; localization 187 *location*.

short distance, no d., shortest d., beeline, short cut; step, short s., no distance, walking d.; striking distance, close quarters, close grips; close range, earshot, gunshot, pistolshot, bowshot, arrowshot, stone's throw, spitting distance; short span, inch, millimetre, finger's breadth, hair's breadth 201 *gap*; close-up, near approach; nearest approach, perigee, perihelion; close finish, photo f., near thing 716 *contest*.

near place, vicinage, vicinity, neighbourhood, purlieus, environs, suburbs, confines 187 *locality*; approaches, marches, borderlands; ringside seat, next door 202 *contiguity*; second place, proxime accessit 65 *sequence*.

Adj. *near*, proximate, proximal; very near, approximate; approximating, getting warm, warm 289 *approaching*; about to meet 293 *convergent*; nearby, wayside, roadside 289 *accessible*; not far, hard by, inshore; near at hand, at hand, handy, present 189 *on the spot*; near the surface 212 *shallow*; home, local, vicinal, in the neighbourhood; close to, next to, neighbouring, limitrophe, bordering on, verging on, adjacent, adjoining, jostling, rubbing shoulders 202 *contiguous*; fronting, facing 237 *frontal*; close, intimate, inseparable 45 *joined*; at close quarters, at close grips; close-run, neck-and-neck, with nothing between, level 716 *contending*; near in blood, related 11 *akin*.

Vb. *be near*, be around, be about 189 *be present*; hang around, hang about; approximate, draw near, get warm 289 *approach*; meet 293 *converge*; neighbour, stand next to, abut, adjoin, border, verge upon 202 *be contiguous*; trench upon 306 *encroach*; hug the shore; come close, skirt, graze, shave, brush, skim, hedge-hop, hover over; jostle, buzz, get in the way 702 *obstruct*; sit on one's tail, follow close, shadow; come to heel, tread on the heels of 284 *follow*; clasp, cling to, hug, cuddle 889 *caress*; huddle, crowd, close up, close the ranks 74 *congregate*.

bring near, approach, approximate; move up, place side by side 202 *juxtapose*.

Adv. *near*, not far, locally; nigh, hard by, fast by, close to, close up to, close upon, in the way, at close range, at close quarters; close behind, right b.; within call, within hearing, within earshot, within a stone's throw, only a step, at no great distance, not far from; on one's doorstep, in one's own backyard; at one's door, at one's feet, at one's elbow, at one's side, under one's nose, at one's fingertips, within reach, close at hand; in the presence of, face to face, eyeball to eyeball; in juxtaposition, next door, side by side, cheek by jowl, tête-à-tête, arm in arm, beside, alongside; on the circumference, on the periphery, on *or* in the confines of, on the skirts of, on the outskirts, at the threshold; brinking on, verging on, on the brink of, on the verge of, on the tip of one's tongue.

nearly, practically, almost, all but; more or less, near enough, roughly, around, somewhere around; in the region of; about, much a., hereabouts, thereabouts, nearabouts, circa; closely, approximately, hard on, close on; well-nigh, as good as, on the way to; within an ace of, just about to.

See: 11, 45, 65, 74, **187**, 189, 201, **202**, 212, 230, 234, 237, 284, 289, 293, 306, 702, 716, 889.

201 Interval

N. *interval*, distance between, space; narrow interval, half-space, hairspace 200 *short distance*; interspace, daylight, head, length; clearance, margin, freeboard 183 *room*; interval of time, timelag 108 *interim*; pause, break, truce 145 *lull*; hiatus 72 *discontinuity*; interruption, incompleteness, jump, leap; musical interval, tone, semitone, third, fourth, fifth 410 *musical note*.

gap, interstice, mesh 222 *network*; lacuna, cavity, hole 263 *orifice*; pass, defile, ghat, wind-gap 305 *passage*; firebreak 662 *safeguard*; ditch, dike, trench 351 *drain*; water jump, ha-ha, sunk fence 231 *partition*; ravine, gorge, gully, couloir, chimney, crevasse, canyon 255 *valley*; cleft, crevice, chink, crack, rift, cut, gash, tear, rent, slit 46 *scission*; flaw, fault, breach, break, split, fracture, rupture, fissure, chap 46 *separation*; slot, groove 262 *furrow*; indentation 260 *notch*; seam, join 45 *joint*; leak 298 *outlet*; abyss, chasm 211 *depth*; yawning gulf, void 190 *emptiness*; inlet, creek, gulch 345 *gulf*.

Adj. *spaced*, spaced out, intervallic, with an interval; gappy, gapped; split, cloven, cleft, cracked, rimous, rimose 46 *disunited*; dehiscent, gaping 263 *open*; far between; latticed, meshed, reticulated.

Vb. *space*, interval, space out 46 *set apart*; crack, split, start, gape, dehisce 263 *open*; win by a head, win by a length; clear, show daylight between; lattice, mesh, reticulate.

Adv. *at intervals* 72 *discontinuously*; now and then, now and again, every so often, off and on; with an interval, by a head, by a length.

See: 45, 46, **72**, 108, **145**, 183, 190, 200, 211, 222, 231, 255, 260, 262, 263, 298, 305, 345, 351, 410, 662.

202 Contiguity

N. *contiguity*, juxtaposition, apposition, proximity, close p. 200 *nearness*; touching 378 *touch*; no interval 71 *continuity*; contact, tangency; abuttal, abutment; intercommunication, osculation; meeting, encounter, interface 293 *convergence*; conjunction, syzygy (astronomy) 45 *union*; close contact, adhesion, cohesion 48 *coherence*; coexistence, coincidence, concomitance 89 *accompaniment*; grazing contact, tangent; border, fringe 234 *edge*; borderland, frontier 236 *limit*; buffer state 231 *interjacency*.

Adj. *contiguous*, touching, in contact; osculatory, intercommunicating; tangential, grazing, brushing, abutting, end to end, bumper-to-bumper; conterminous, adjacent, with no interval 71 *continuous*; adjoining, close, to, jostling, rubbing shoulders 200 *near*.

Vb. *be contiguous*, overlap 378 *touch*; make contact, come in c., brush, rub, skim, scrape, graze, kiss; join, meet 293 *converge*; stick, adhere 48 *cohere*; lie end to end, abut; abut on, adjoin, reach to, extend to 183 *extend*; sit next to, rub shoulders with, crowd, jostle 200 *be near*; border with, march w., skirt 234 *hem*; coexist, coincide 89 *accompany*; osculate, intercommunicate 45 *connect*; get in touch, contact.

juxtapose, set side by side, range together, bring into contact, knock persons' heads together.

Adv. *contiguously*, tangentially; in contact, in close c.; next, close; end to end; cheek by jowl; hand in hand, arm in arm; from hand to hand.

See: 45, 48, **71**, 89, 183, **200**, 231, 234, 236, 293, 378.

203 Length

N. *length*, longitude; extent, extension; reach, long arm; full length, overall l.; stretch, span, mileage, footage 199 *distance*; perspective 211 *depth*.

lengthening, extending etc. vb.; prolongation, extension, production, spinning out 113 *protraction*; stretching, tension; spreading out, stringing o.

line, bar, rule, tape, strip, stripe, streak; spoke, radius; single file, line ahead, crocodile, queue 65 *sequence*; straight line, right l. 249 *straightness*; bent line 248 *curvature*.

long measure, linear m., measurement of length, micrometry 465 *measurement*; unit of length, finger, hand, hand's breadth, palm, span, cubit; arm's length, fathom; head, length; pace, step; inch, foot, yard; rod, pole, perch; chain, furlong; mile, statute m., geographical m., nautical m., knot, league; millimetre, centimetre, metre, kilometre; degree of latitude, degree of longitude; micro-inch, micron, wavelength; astronomical unit, light year, parsec.

Adj. *long*, lengthy, extensive, a mile long, measured in miles; long-drawn out 113 *protracted*; lengthened, elongated, outstretched, extended, strung out 75 *unas-*

sembled; shoulder-length, ankle-length, down to ...; wire-drawn, lank 206 *lean*; lanky, long-legged 209 *tall*; as long as my arm, long as a wet week; interminable, no end to 838 *tedious*; polysyllabic; sesquipedalian 570 *diffuse*; unshortened, unabridged, full-length 54 *complete*.

longitudinal, oblong, linear; one-dimensional.

Vb. *be long*, - lengthy etc. adj.; stretch, outstretch, stretch out; make a long arm; reach, stretch to 183 *extend*; drag, trail, drag its slow length along 113 *drag on*.

lengthen, stretch, elongate, draw out, wiredraw 206 *make thin*; pull out, stretch o., spreadeagle 197 *expand*; spread oneself out, sprawl 216 *be horizontal*; spread out, string o., deploy 75 *disperse*; extend, pay out, uncoil, unfurl, unroll, unfold 316 *evolve*; let out, drop the hem; produce, continue; prolong, protract 113 *spin out*; drawl 580 *stammer*.

look along, view in perspective; have a clear view, see from end to end 438 *scan*; enfilade.

Adv. *longwise*, longways, lengthwise; along, longitudinally, radially, in line ahead, in single file; one in front and one behind, in tandem; in a line, in perspective; at full length, end to end, overall; fore and aft; head to foot, head to tail, stem to stern, top to toe, head to heels, from the crown of the head to the sole of the foot.

See: 54, 65, 75, 113, 183, 197, **199**, 206, 209, 211, 216, 248, 249, 316, 438, **465**, 570, 580, 838.

204 Shortness

N. *shortness*, squatness etc. adj.; brevity, briefness; transience 114 *brief span*; inch, centimetre 200 *short distance*; low stature, dwarfishness, short legs, duck's disease 196 *littleness*; no height 210 *lowness*; shrinkage 42 *decrement*; scantiness, exiguity; scarceness 636 *insufficiency*; concision 569 *conciseness*; short hair, bob, crew cut; shorts, miniskirt.

shortening, abridgment, abbreviation; précis 592 *compendium*; curtailment, cutback, cut, reduction 37 *diminution*; contraction 198 *compression*; aphaeresis, apocope, syncope.

shortener, cutter, abridger, abstracter 592 *epitomizer*.

Adj. *short*, brief 114 *transient*; not big, dwarfish, stunted 196 *little*; not tall, squab, squabby, squat, dumpy, stumpy, stocky, thickset, stubby 195 *fleshy*, 205 *thick*; not high 210 *low*; pug-nosed, snub-n.; snub, retroussé, blunt 257 *unsharpened*; not long, inch-long; skimpy, scanty 636 *insufficient*; foreshortened 246 *distorted*; abbreviated, abridged; shortened, sawn-off; cut, curtailed, docked, beheaded, truncated, topless, headless; shaven, shorn, mown; sparing of words, terse 569 *concise*; elliptic (of style); half-finished 55 *unfinished*; epitomized, potted, compact 592 *compendious*; compacted, compressed 198 *contracted*.

Vb. *be short*, - brief etc. adj.; not reach 307 *fall short*.

shorten, abridge, abbreviate; pot, epitomize, boil down 592 *abstract*; sum up, recapitulate 569 *be concise*; compress, contract, telescope 198 *make smaller*; reduce, diminish 37 *abate*; foreshorten 246 *distort*; take up, put a tuck in, raise the hem, turn up, tuck up, kilt; behead, obtruncate, guillotine, axe, chop up 46 *sunder*; cut short, dock, curtail, truncate; cut back, cut down, slash, lop, prune; shear, shave, trim, crop, clip, bob, shingle 46 *cut*; mow, scythe; nip in the bud, stunt, check the growth of 278 *retard*; scrimp, skimp 636 *make insufficient*.

Adv. *shortly*, briefly etc. adj.; in short 592 *in sum*.

See: 37, 42, 46, 55, 114, 195, **196**, 198, 200, 205, 210, 246, 257, 278, 307, 569, **592**, 636.

205 Breadth. Thickness

N. *breadth*, width, latitude; width across, span, wingspan, wingspread; diameter, radius, semidiameter; gauge, broad g., bore, calibre; broadness, expanse, superficial extent, amplitude 183 *range*; wideness, fullness, bagginess.

thickness, crassitude, stoutness, corpulence 195 *bulk*; widening, dilatation 197 *dilation*.

Adj. *broad*, wide, expansive, unspanned 183 *spacious*; wide-cut, full, flared, ample, baggy; fan-like, flabelliform, umbelliferous; outspread, outstretched, splayed out 197 *expanded*; bell-bottomed, broad-b., broad-based; callipygian, wide-hipped; broad in the beam, beamy, wide-bodied; wide as a church door; broad-brimmed, wide-awake (hat); wide-angle (lens); wide-mouthed 263 *open*; broad-shouldered, broad-chested 162 *stalwart*; wide-ranging 79 *general*.

thick, stout, dumpy, squat 204 *short*; thickset, tubby, stubby 195 *fleshy*; thick-lipped, blubber-l., full-l.; thick-necked, bull-n.; thick-skinned, pachydermatous; thick-ribbed, barrel-chested, stout-timbered 162 *strong*; thick as a rope; pyknic, endomorphic; solidly built 324 *dense*; semiliquid, ropy, lumpy, to be cut with a knife 354 *viscid*.

Vb. *be broad*, - thick etc. adj.; get broad, broaden, widen, fatten, thicken; fan out, flare, splay 197 *expand*; straddle, bestride, span 226 *overlie*.

Adv. *broadways*, broadwise, breadthways, breadthwise; widthways, widthwise; broadways on 239 *sideways*.

See: 79, 162, 183, **195**, **197**, 204, 226, 239, 263, 324, 354.

206 Narrowness. Thinness

N. *narrowness*, tightness etc. adj.; narrow interval, closeness, tight squeeze, crack, chink, hair's breadth, finger's b. 200 *short distance*; lack of breadth, length without b., line, strip, stripe, streak; vein, capillary 208 *filament*; knife-edge, razor's edge, tightrope, wire; narrow gauge; bottleneck, narrows, strait 345 *gulf*; ridge, col, saddle 209 *high land*; ravine, gully 255 *valley*; pass, defile 305 *passage*; neck, isthmus, land-bridge 624 *bridge*.

thinness, tenuity, fineness 325 *rarity*; slenderness, gracility; emaciation, consumption; scrag, skin and bone, skeleton; miserable specimen, scarecrow, rake, beanpole, broomstick, shadow, spindleshanks, barebones; haggardness, lantern jaws, hatchet face, sunken cheeks; thread, paper, tissue 422 *transparency*; shaving, splinter 33 *small thing*; slip, wisp 208 *filament*.

narrowing, compression 198 *contraction*; taper, tapering 293 *convergence*; neck, isthmus; stricture, constriction; waistline, waist, wasp-w., hourglass.

Adj. *narrow*, not wide, single track; strait, tight, close; compressed, coarctate, pinched, unexpanded 198 *contracted*; not thick, fine, thin, wafer-thin 422 *transparent*; tight-drawn, attenuated, spun, fine-s., wire-drawn 203 *long*; thread-like, capillary 208 *fibrous*; tapering 293 *convergent*; slight, slightly-built, wispy, delicate 163 *weak*; gracile, attenuate, slender, slim, svelte, slinky, sylph-like; willowy, rangy; long-legged, leggy, lanky, gangling; narrow-waisted, wasp-w.; isthmian; bottlenecked.

lean, thin, ectomorphic, spare, wiry; meagre, skinny, bony; cadaverous, fleshless, skin-and-bone, skeletal, raw-boned, haggard, gaunt, drawn, lantern-jawed, hatchet-faced; twiggy, spindly, spindleshanked, spidery; undersized, weedy, scrawny, scrubby, scraggy 196 *exiguous*; consumptive, emaciated, wasted, withered, wizened, pinched, peaky 651 *sick*; sere, shrivelled 131 *ageing*; starved, starveling 636 *underfed*; wraith-like, worn to a shadow, thin as a rake, thin as a lath, thin as a pencil, without an ounce of flesh to spare.

Vb. *be narrow*, - thin etc. adj.; narrow, taper 293 *converge*; taper off 198 *become small*.

make thin, contract, compress, pinch, nip 198 *make smaller*; make oneself thin, starve, underfeed, reduce, lose weight; improve one's figure, slenderize, slim; draw, wiredraw, spin, spin fine 203 *lengthen*; attenuate 325 *rarefy*.

See: 33, 131, 163, 196, **198**, 200, 203, 208, 209, 255, 293, 305, 325, 345, 422, 624, 636, 651.

207 Layer

N. *layer*, stratum, substratum, underlay, floor 214 *base*; outcrop, basset 254 *projection*; bed, course, string c., range, row; zone, vein, seam, lode; thickness, ply; storey, tier, floor, mezzanine f., entresol, landing; stage, planking, platform 218 *frame*; deck, top d., lower d., upper d., orlop d., quarterdeck, bridge 275 *ship*; film 423 *opacity*; bloom, dross, scum; patina, coating, coat, veneer, top layer 226 *covering*; scale, scab, membrane, peel, pellicle, sheath, bark, integument 226 *skin*; level, water l., water table 216 *horizontality*; atmospheric layer 340 *atmosphere*.

lamina, sheet, slab, foil, strip; plate glass, plate, tinplate, latten, sheet iron, sheet steel; plank, board, weatherboard, fascia; laminate, formica (tdmk), plywood; slat, lath, leaf, tabletop; tablet, plaque, panel, pane; slab, flag, flagstone, slate; shingle, tile; lamella, slide, wafer, shaving, flake, slice, rasher; cardboard, sheet of paper 631 *paper*; card, playing c.; platter, disc

250 *circle*.

stratification, stratigraphy; bedding, layering, lamination; laminability, flakiness, schistosity, scaliness, squamation; overlapping, overlap; nest of boxes, Chinese b., Russian doll; onion skin, exfoliation dome; layer cake, sandwich, double-decker; layer on layer, level upon level 231 *interjacency*.

Adj. *layered*, lamellar, lamelliform, lamellate; laminated, laminar, laminose; laminable, flaky; schistose, micaceous, slaty, shaly; foliated, foliaceous; foliate, leaf-like; bedded, stratified, stratiform; zoned, seamed; overlapping, clinker-built 226 *overlying*; tabular, decked, storeyed, in storeys, in layers; scaly, squamose, squamous; membranous, filmy 226 *covered*.

Vb. *laminate*, lay, deck, layer, shingle, overlap 226 *overlay*; zone, stratify, sandwich; plate, veneer 226 *coat*; exfoliate, delaminate, split; flake off, whittle, skive, pare, peel, strip 229 *uncover*; shave, slice 206 *make thin*.

See: 206, 214, 216, 218, **226**, 229, **231**, 250, 254, 275, 340, 423, 631.

208 Filament

N. *filament*, flagellum, cilium, lash, eyelash, beard, down 259 *hair*; barb, harl 259 *plumage*; flock, lock, shred of wool, lock of hair, wisp, curl; fringe 234 *edging*; fibril, rootlet, stalk, tendril 366 *plant*; whisker, antenna, antennule 378 *feeler*; gossamer, cobweb, web 222 *network*; capillary, vein, venule, veinlet 351 *conduit*; ramification, branch; wire, element, wick 420 *torch*.

fibre, natural f., animal f., hair, camel h., rabbit h.; Angora, goat's hair, mohair, cashmere; llama hair, alpaca, vicuna; wool, Shetland w., botany w., merino; mungo, shoddy; silk, real s., wild silk, tussore, floss; vegetable fibre, cotton, cotton wool, silk cotton, kapok; linen, flax; manila, hemp; jute, sisal, coir; hards; tow, oakum; bast, raffia; worsted, yarn; spun yarn, continuous filament y.; thread, twine, twist, strand, cord, string, line, rope 47 *cable*; artificial fibre, man-made f., acrylic f., rayon, nylon 222 *textile*; staple, denier 331 *texture*.

strip, fascia, band, bandage; braid, tape, strap, ribbon, ribband; fillet 47 *girdle*; lath, slat, batten, stave, spline 207 *lamina*; shaving, wafer; splinter, shiver, shred 53 *piece*; streak, strake 203 *line*.

Adj. *fibrous*, fibrillose, fibrillar, fibrilliform; woolly, cottony, silky; filamentous, filiform; whiskery, downy, fleecy 259 *hairy*; wiry, threadlike; capillary, capillaceous; fine-spun, wire-drawn 206 *narrow*; stringy, ropy 205 *thick*; flagelliform, lash-like; ligulate, strap-shaped; antenniform, antennary, antennal.

See: **47**, 53, 203, 205, 206, 207, **222**, 234, **259**, 331, 351, 366, 378, 420.

209 Height

N. *height*, perpendicular length, vertical range, long way to fall; altitude, elevation, ceiling, pitch 213 *summit*; loftiness, steepness, dizzy height; tallness, stature; eminence, sublimity; sky, stratosphere 340 *atmosphere*.

high land, height, highlands, heights, steeps, uplands, wold, moor, moorland, downs, rolling country; rising ground, rise, bank, ben, brae, slope, climb 220 *incline*; knap, hill, eminence, mount, mountain; fell, scar, tor, alp, Mont Blanc, Everest; mountain range, chain, sierra, cordillera, massif, Alps, Himalayas, Andes, Rockies; ridge, hog's back, col, saddle, spur, headland, foothill 254 *projection*; crest, peak, pike, hilltop 213 *summit*; steepness, precipice, cliff, white cliffs of Dover; crag, scar, bluff, steep, escarpment; gorge, canyon, ravine 255 *valley*; summit level, mesa; plateau, tableland 216 *horizontality*.

small hill, monticle, knoll, hillock, kopje, butte; roche moutonée, drumlin, hummock, hump, tump, dune, sand d., esker, moraine; barrow, long b., round b. 364 *tomb*; mound, heap 253 *earthwork*; cairn, tell 548 *monument*; anthill, molehill, tussock 253 *swelling*.

high structure, column, pillar, turret, tower, 'cloud-capped towers'; pile, noble p., skyscraper 164 *edifice*; steeple, spire, flèche, belfry, campanile 990 *church exterior*; minaret, muezzin's tower; obelisk, Cleopatra's Needle; dome, cupola 226 *roof*; colossus 554 *sculpture*; mausoleum, pyramid 364 *tomb*; pagoda 990 *temple*; ziggurat, Tower of Babel; Eiffel Tower; mast, topmast, topgallant mast; flagstaff, pike - staff;pole, maypole; lamppost, standard; pylon, radio mast; masthead 213 *summit*; watchtower, lookout, crow's nest, eyrie

438 *view*; column of smoke, mushroom cloud.
tall creature, giraffe, elephant, mammoth, longlegs, lamppost, beanpole, six-footer, seven-f., grenadier, colossus 195 *giant*; poplar, pine, sequoia, Californian redwood 366 *tree*.
high water, high tide, flood t., spring t. 350 *current*; billow, tidal wave 350 *wave*; cataract 350 *waterfall*; flood, flood level.
altimetry, altimeter, height-finder, hypsometer, barograph 465 *meter, gauge*.
Adj. *high*, high-up, sky-high; eminent, uplifted, exalted, lofty, sublime, supernal 310 *elevated*; highest 213 *topmost*; perching, hanging (gardens); aerial, midair, airborne, flying; soaring, aspiring 308 *ascending*; spiry, towering, cloud-capp'd, cloud-topped, sky-scraping; steep, dizzy, vertiginous; knee-high, breast-h., shoulder-h.; altitudinal.
tall, lanky, rangy, slab-sided 206 *narrow*; long-legged, long-necked, giraffelike; statuesque, Junoesque; colossal, gigantic, monumental 195 *huge*; tall as a maypole, high as a steeple.
alpine, subalpine, alpestrine, Himalayan; mountainous, hilly, moorland, upland, highland; not flat, rolling, hillocky, hummocky; orogenetic, orological.
overhanging, beetling, superimposed, overlying; towering over, overshadowing, dominating; incumbent, superincumbent; hovering, floating over; over one's head, aloft; jettied, prominent 254 *projecting*.
Vb. *be high*, - tall etc. adj.; tower, soar; surmount, clear, overtop, overlook, dominate, command 34 *be superior*; overhang, overshadow 226 *cover*; beetle, impend 254 *jut*; hover, hang over 217 *hang*; culminate, be at the zenith 725 *climax*; mount, bestride, bestraddle; grow taller, add to one's inches; rise 308 *ascend*; stand on tiptoe, stand on another's shoulders 310 *lift oneself*.
make higher, heighten, build up, raise, hold aloft 310 *elevate*.
Adv. *aloft*, up, on high, high up, in the clouds; atop, on top, on the crest; above, overhead, up over; above stairs, upstairs; upwards, skyward, heavenward; straight up, steeply 215 *vertically*; on tiptoe, on stilts, on the shoulders of; breast high, up to the neck, over head and ears; from top to bottom 54 *throughout*.
See: 34, 54, 164, 195, 206, **213**, 215, 216, 217, 220, 226, 253, 254, 255, 308, **310**, 340, 350, 364, 366, 438, 465, 548, 554, 725, 990.

210 Lowness

N. *lowness*, debasement 311 *lowering*; prostration 216 *recumbency*; nonelevation, no height, sea level, flatness 216 *horizontality*; flats, levels 347 *marsh*; levelness, steppe 348 *plain*; low elevation, lowlands, molehill, pimple 196 *littleness*; gentle slope, slight gradient 220 *incline*; subjacency, lower level, foothill 35 *inferiority*; bottom, hollow, depression 255 *valley*; sea-bottom, sea-floor 343 *ocean*; subterraneity, depths, cellar, well, mine 211 *depth*; floor, foot 214 *base*; underside, undersurface, underbelly 240 *contraposition*; nadir, lowest point; low water, low ebb, low tide, ebb t., neap t. 350 *current*; low ball, daisy-cutter.
Adj. *low*, not high, squat 204 *short*; unerect, not upright, crouched, crouching, stooping, bending 220 *oblique*; recumbent, laid low, prostrate 216 *supine*; low-lying, flat, level with the ground, at sea level 216 *flat*; low-level, single-storey; subjacent, lower, under, nether 35 *inferior*; sunken, lowered 255 *concave*; flattened, rounded, blunt 257 *unsharpened*; subterranean, subterraneous, underground, below the surface, submarine 523 *latent*, 211 *deep*; underfoot 745 *subjected*.
Vb. *be low*, - flat etc. adj.; lie low, lie flat 216 *be horizontal*; be beneath, underlie 523 *lurk*; slouch, crouch 311 *stoop*; crawl, wallow, grovel 721 *knuckle under*; depress 311 *lower*.
Adv. *under*, beneath, underneath, neath; below, at the foot of; downwards; adown, down, face-down; underfoot, underground, downstairs, below stairs; at a low ebb; below par.
See: 35, 196, 204, **211**, **214**, 216, 220, 240, 255, 257, **311**, 343, 347, 348, 350, 523, 721, 745.

211 Depth

N. *depth*, drop, fall; deepness etc. adj.; perspective 203 *length*; vertical range, profundity, lowest depth, lowest point, nadir; deeps, deep water 343 *ocean*; unknown depths 663 *pitfall*; depression, bottom 255 *valley*; hollow, pit, shaft, mine, well 255 *cavity*; abyss, abysm, chasm, yawning depths 201 *gap*; vault, crypt, dungeon 194 *cellar*; cave, catacomb, hypogeum, bowels of the earth 210 *lowness*; pot-holing 309 *descent*; underworld, bottomless pit 972 *hell*; fathoming, soundings, sounding line, sound, probe, plummet, lead, lead line; sonar 484 *detector*; diving bell, bathysphere, bathyscaphe; submarine, submariner, frogman 313 *diver*; depth required, draught, displacement, sinkage; bathometer, bathometry 465 *measurement*.

Adj. *deep*, steep, plunging, profound; abysmal, yawning, cavernous; abyssal, deep-sea; deep-seated, deep-rooted 153 *fixed*; unplumbed, bottomless, soundless, fathomless; unsounded, unfathomed, unsoundable, unfathomable; subjacent, subterranean, underground, hypogeal; underwater, undersea, subaqueous, submarine; buried, deep in, immersed, submerged 311 *lowered*; sunk, foundered, drowned; navigable; knee-deep, ankle-d.; deep as a well; infernal, deep as hell; depth-haunting, bathypelagic, benthic; depth-measuring, bathymetric.

Vb. *be deep*, - profound etc. adj.; gape, yawn; deepen, hollow, dig 255 *make concave*; fathom, sound, take soundings, plumb, heave the lead; drop, lower 311 *let fall*; go deep, plumb the depths, touch bottom, reach one's nadir; sink to the bottom, plunge 313 *founder*.

Adv. *deeply*, profoundly; deep down, beyond one's depth, out of one's depth, deep in, over one's head, over head and ears, up to the eyes.

See: 153, 194, 201, 203, 210, 255, 309, **311**, 313, **343**, 465, 484, 663, 972.

212 Shallowness

N. *shallowness*, no depth, superficiality 4 *insubstantiality*; thin surface 223 *exteriority*; veneer, thin coat 226 *skin*; surface injury, scratch, mere s., pinprick, graze 639 *trifle*; shoal water, shoals, shallows; ford 305 *passage*; pond, puddle 346 *lake*; ripple, catspaw 350 *wave*; light soil, stony ground 344 *soil*.

Adj. *shallow*, slight, superficial 4 *insubstantial*; surface, skin-deep; near the surface, not deep; ankle-deep, knee-d.; shoal, shoaly, unnavigable; just enough to wet one's feet; light, thin, thinly spread 206 *narrow*.

See: 4, 206, 223, 226, 305, 344, 346, 350, 639.

213 Summit

N. *summit*, sky, heaven, seventh h.; pole, North P., South P.; highest point, top, peak, crest, apex, pinnacle, crown; maximum height, utmost h., pitch; zenith, meridian, high noon, culmination, apogee; culminating point, crowning p.; acme, ne plus ultra 646 *perfection*; crest of the wave, top of the tree 730 *prosperity*; top of the curve, highwater mark 236 *limit*; climax, turning point, turn of the tide 137 *crisis*; dividing line, divide, watershed, water-parting, Great Divide 231 *partition*; coping, copingstone, capstone, keystone; lintel, pediment, entablature, architrave, epistyle; tympanum, capital, cornice; battlements, parapet 713 *fortification*.

vertex, apex, crown, cap, brow, head; tip, cusp, spike, nib, end 69 *extremity*; spire, finial 990 *church exterior*; stairhead, landing 308 *ascent*; acropolis 713 *fort*; summit level, hilltop, mountaintop, plateau, tableland 209 *high land*; treetop, housetop, rooftop; gable, gable-end; leads, ceiling 226 *roof*; upper chamber, garret 194 *attic*; top storey; topside, upper deck, quarterdeck, hurricane deck, boat d., bridge 275 *ship*; topmast, topgallant mast; masthead, crow's nest 209 *high structure*.

head, headpiece, pate, poll, sconce; noddle, nob, nut, noggin, coco, conk, bonce, crumpet, bean, block, chump; upper storey, belfry; brow, dome, temple, forehead; loaf, brain, grey matter 498 *intelligence*; epicranium, pericranium; scalp, crown, double c.; skull, cranium, brainpan 255 *cavity*; occiput, sinciput; fontanelle; craniology, craniometry; phrenology.

Adj. *topmost*, top, highest 209 *high*; uppermost, upmost 34 *supreme*; polar, apical, crowning; capital, head; cephalic, dolicocephalic, brachycephalic; cranial, occipital, sincipital; culminating, zenithal, meridian, meridional; tiptop, super 644 *best*.

Vb. *crown*, cap, head, top, tip, surmount, crest, overtop 209 *be high*; culminate, consummate 725 *climax*; go up top, take top place 34 *be superior*; top out 54 *make complete*.

Adv. *atop*, on top, at the top, at the top of the tree, at the top of the ladder; on the crest, on the crest of the wave; tiptoe, on tiptoe.

See: 34, 54, 69, 137, 194, **209**, 226, 231, 236,

255, 275, 308, 498, 644, 646, 713, 725, 730, 990.

214 Base

N. *base*, foot, toe, skirt 210 *lowness*; bottom, fundus, root; lowest point, rock bottom, nadir, low water; footing, foundation 218 *basis*; fundamental 68 *origin*; groundwork, substructure, infrastructure, chassis 218 *frame*; baseboard, plinth, pedestal 218 *stand*; substratum, floor, underlayer, bed, bedrock; subsoil, hardpan; ground, earth, foundations; footing, sill; damp course; basement, ground floor 194 *cellar*; flooring, pavement, pavingstone, hard standing 226 *paving*; carpet 226 *floor-cover*; skirting board, wainscot, plinth, dado; keel, keelson; hold, bilge; sump, drain 649 *sink*.

foot, feet, tootsies, pedal extremities; beetle-crusher; forefoot, hindfoot; sole, heel, instep, arch; toe, toenail, big toe, hallux; trotter, hoof, cloven h.; paw, pad; claw, talon 778 *nippers*; ankle, ankle-bone, fetlock, pastern.

Adj. *undermost*, lowermost, nethermost, bottom, rock-b. 210 *low*; basic, basal, fundamental; grounded, on the bottom, touching b.; based on, founded on, grounded on, built on, underlying 218 *supporting*.

footed, pedal; plantigrade, digitigrade; hoofed, cloven-h., ungulate, clawed, taloned; web-footed; soled, heeled, shod, shoed; toed, five-t.; club-footed, flat-f., hammer-toed 845 *blemished*.

Adv. *in the trough*, at the bottom 210 *under*; basically, fundamentally.

See: 68, 194, **210**, **218**, 226, 649, 778, 845.

215 Verticality

N. *verticality*, the vertical, erectness, uprightness, upright carriage; steepness, sheerness, precipitousness 209 *height*; perpendicularity, right angle, square; elevation, azimuth circle; vertical line, plumb-line, plummet; vertical structure, hoist, upright, pole, stalagmite 218 *pillar*; sheer face, precipice, cliff, bluff, scarp, steep 209 *high land*; perpendicular drop, straight d., vertical height, rise.

Adj. *vertical*, upright, erect, standing; perpendicular, rectangular, orthogonal; sheer, abrupt, steep, precipitous 209 *high*; straight, plumb; straight up, straight down; upstanding, standing up, on one's feet, on one's legs; bolt upright, stiff as a ramrod, unbowed, head-up; rampant, rearing; on end.

Vb. *be vertical*, stick up, cock up, bristle, stand on end; stand erect, stand upright, hold oneself straight; sit up, stand up, straighten up; rise, stand, rise to one's feet, ramp, rear; keep standing, have no seat, sit on one's thumb.

make vertical, erect, rear, raise, pitch 310 *elevate*; raise on its legs, up-end; stand, set up, stick up, raise up, cock up.

Adv. *vertically*, abruptly etc. adj.; palewise (heraldry); upright, head-up; on end, up on end, endwise, up; on one's legs, on one's hind legs, standing, all standing; at right angles, perpendicularly; down, straight-d., plumb.

See: **209**, 218, **310**.

216 Horizontality

N. *horizontality*, horizontalness; horizontal angle, azimuth; horizontal line, ruled line, ruler, rule; horizontal course, strike; flatness 258 *smoothness*; level, plane, dead level, dead flat, level plane; sea level, water l., water table; stratum; slab, tablet, table 207 *layer*; level stretch, steppe 348 *plain*; flats 347 *marsh*; platform, ledge 254 *projection*; terrace, esplanade; plateau, tableland 209 *high land*; billiard table, bowling green, cricket ground, croquet lawn 724 *arena*; gridiron, platter 194 *plate*; spirit level, T square 465 *gauge*; horizon, false h., horizon line 236 *limit*.

recumbency, lying down etc. vb.; supination; prostration; proneness, supineness.

flattener, iron, flatiron, mangle, press, trouser p.; rolling pin, roller, garden r., steamroller 258 *smoother*; bulldozer, juggernaut 168 *destroyer*.

Adj. *flat*, horizontal, two-dimensional, level, plane, even, flush 258 *smooth*; trodden, trodden flat, beaten f.; flat as a pancake, flat as a board, flat as my hand; unwrinkled, smooth, smooth as glass, calm, calm as a millpond.

supine, resupine, flat on one's back; prone, face down, prostrate; recumbent, decumbent, procumbent; lying down, couchant; abed, laid out; stretched out, sprawling, lolling.

Vb. *be horizontal*, lie, lie down, lie flat, lie prostrate, lie on one's back; measure one's length, recline, couch, sprawl, loll 311 *sit* *down*; grovel 311 *stoop*; become horizontal, straighten out, level out.

flatten, lay out, roll o., lay down, spread; lay flat, beat f., tread f., stamp down, trample d., squash; make flush, align, level, even, grade, plane 28 *equalize*; iron, iron out, roll out 258 *smooth*; pat down, smooth d., plaster d.; prostrate, knock down, floor, ground 311 *fell*.

Adv. *horizontally*, flat, on one's back; fessewise, fesse-ways (heraldry); at full length.

See: 28, 168, 194, 207, 209, 236, 254, **258**, 311, 347, 348, 465, 724.

217 Pendency

N. *pendency*, pensility, pensileness; suspension, hanging, dangle; set, hang, drape.

hanging object, hanging ornament, pendant, dangler, drop, eardrop, earring 844 *jewellery*; tassel, bobble, tag 844 *trimming*; hangings, draperies, drapes, curtains, arras, tapestry 226 *covering*; train, skirt, coat-tails; flap, lappet, tippet 228 *headgear*; pigtail, tail 67 *sequel*, 259 *hair*; dewlap, lobe, appendix 40 *adjunct*; pendulum, bob, swing, hammock 317 *oscillation*; chandelier 420 *lamp*; icicle, stalactite.

hanger, coat h., curtain rod, curtain ring, runner, rack; hook, peg, knob, nail 218 *prop*; suspender, braces, suspender belt 228 *underwear*; clothesline 47 *cable*; clotheshorse, airer, Scotch a. 218 *frame*; davit, crane 310 *lifter*; spar, mast 218 *pillar*; gallows, gibbet 964 *pillory*.

Adj. *hanging*, pendent, pendulous, pensile; hanging from, dependent, suspended, penduline, dangling etc.vb.; hanging the head, nodding, drooping, weeping; lowering, overhanging; beetling 254 *projecting*; open-ended, loose 46 *disunited*; baggy, flowing; floating (in the wind), waving, streaming, rippling; pedunculate, tailed, caudate; lop-eared.

Vb. *hang*, be pendent, drape, set; hang down, draggle, trail, flow; hang on to, swing from; swing, sway, dangle, bob; hang the head, nod, weep, loll, droop, sag, swag; hang in the wind, stream, wave, float, ripple, flap; hang over, hover; overhang, lour 226 *overlie*; suspend, hang up, sling, hook up, hitch, fasten to, append 45 *join*; curtain 226 *cover*.

See: 40, 45, 46, 47, 67, **218**, 226, 228, 254, 259, 310, 317, 420, 844, 964.

218 Support

N. *support*, underpinning 703 *aid*; leg to stand on, point d'appui, footing, ground, terra firma; hold, foothold, handhold, toehold 778 *retention*; life jacket, lifebelt 662 *safeguard*.

prop, support, mounting, bearing; carriage, carrier, underframe, chassis; buttress, flying b., arc boutant; abutment, bulwark, embankment, wall, retaining w.; underpinning, shore, jack; flagstaff, jackstaff, stanchion, rod, bar, transom, steadier, brace, strut; stay, mainstay, guy, shrouds, rigging 47 *tackling*; sprit, boom, spar, mast, yard, yardarm, crosstree 254 *projection*; trunk, stem, stalk, caudex, pedicle, pedicel, peduncle 366 *plant*; arch, Gothic a., Romanesque a., Moorish a., ogive 248 *curve*; keystone, headstone, cornerstone, springer; cantilever; pier (**see** *pillar*); bandage, jockstrap, truss, splint; stiffener, whalebone; corset 228 *underwear*; yoke 217 *hanger*; rest, headrest, backrest, footrest, stirrup; handrail (**see** *handle*); skid, chock, sprag, wedge 702 *obstacle*; staff, baton, stick, shooting s., walking s., cane, alpenstock, crutch, crook; leg support, irons; bracket (**see** *shelf*); trivet, hob (**see** *stand*); arm, back, shoulder, broad shoulders; shoulder blade, clavicle, collarbone, backbone (**see** *pillar*); worldbearer, Atlas; supporter, helper, patron 707 *auxiliary*.

handle, holder, pen h., cigarette h. 194 *receptacle*; hold, grip, hilt, pommel, haft; knob, doorhandle; lug, ear, loop; railing, handrail, rail, poop r., taffrail, banisters, balustrade; shaft, spear s., oar s., loom; handlebar, tiller; winder, crank, crankhandle; lever, trigger 630 *tool*.

basis, foundation, solid f., concrete f., footings, deck; raft, pallet, sleeper; stereobate, substratum 207 *layer*; ground, groundwork, floor, bed, bedrock, rock bottom 214 *base*; sill *or* cill; flooring, pavement 226 *paving*; terra firma 344 *land*; perch, footing, foothold.

stand, tripod, trivet, hob; table mat, coaster; anvil, block, bench; teapoy, trolley; table, console t., coffee t., card t., gateleg t., drop-leaf t., refectory t., board; sideboard, dresser 194 *cabinet*; work table, desk, counter; pedestal, plinth, socle; stylobate, podium; platform, staddle, gantry; emplacement, banquette; footplate; landing, half l.; landing stage, pier; dais, pulpit, stage 539 *rostrum*; doorstep, threshold; altar step, predella 990 *altar*; step, stair, tread, rung, round 308 *ascent*; stilt 310 *lifter*; shank 267 *leg*.

seat, throne, woolsack; bank, bench, form, settle; bucket seat, box s., rumble s., dicky; pew, choirstall, misericord 990 *church interior*; stall, fauteuil 594 *theatre*; chair, armchair, easy chair, wing c., rocking c., basket c., Windsor c., high c., deck c., lounger; chaise longue; sofa, settee, divan, couch, studio c., ottoman, chesterfield, sociable, loveseat; tabouret, pouffe, stool, footstool, campstool, faldstool; prie-dieu, hassock; saddle, side s., pillion, pad, howdah; stocks, ducking-stool 964 *pillory*; electric chair, hot seat; lap, knees; mat 226 *floor-cover*.

bed, cot, crib, cradle, bassinet; marriage bed, bridal b., double b., single b., bunk b., bunk; daybed, couch; tester, four-poster; charpoy, truckle bed, trundle b., camp b., pallet, airbed, bedroll, shakedown; hammock 217 *hanging object*; sick bed, litter, hurdle, stretcher 658 *hospital*; bier 364 *funeral*; bedding 226 *coverlet*; bedstead, divan.

cushion, pillow; bolster, Dutch wife; mattress, palliasse; squab, hassock, kneeler.

beam, balk, joist, girder, box g., rafter, purlin, tie beam, truss 47 *bond*; summer, bressummer; wall-plate 226 *roof*; crossbeam, transom, crossbar, traverse; architrave, lintel.

pillar, shaft, pier, pile, pole, stake, stud 331 *structure*; post, king post, queen p., crown p.; jamb, door j., doorpost; stanchion, puncheon; newelpost, banister, baluster; mullion; pilaster, column, Doric c., Ionic c., Corinthian c., Tuscan c.; caryatid, telamon, atlantes; spinal column, spine, backbone, vertebrae; neck, cervix.

pivot, fulcrum, lever, purchase; hinge 45 *joint*; pole, axis; axle, swivel, spindle, arbor, pintle 315 *rotator*; bearing, gudgeon, trunnion; rowlock, tholepin; centreboard, keel.

shelf, ledge, offset 254 *projection*; corbel, bracket, console, ancon; retable, niche 194 *compartment*; sill, windowsill, mantelpiece, mantelshelf, rack, dresser 194 *cabinet*; counter, plank, board, table, leaf, slab 207 *lamina*.

frame, bony f., skeleton, ribs; framework, staging, scaffolding 331 *structure*; trellis, espalier; chassis, fuselage, body (of a car), undercarriage; trestle; easel, clotheshorse; housing 235 *enclosure*; picture frame, window f., sash 233 *outline*.

Adj. *supporting*, sustaining; fundamental, basal; columnar; cervical, spinal; structural, skeletal; framing, holding.

Vb. *support*, sustain, bear, carry, hold, shoulder; uphold, hold up, bear up, buoy up; prop, shore up, underprop, underpin, jack up 310 *elevate*; buttress, bolster, bolster up, cushion; reinforce, underset 162 *strengthen*; bandage, brace, truss 45 *tighten*; steady, stay; cradle, pillow, cup, cup one's chin; maintain 633 *provide*; back up, give support, lend s., furnish s., afford s., supply s. 703 *aid*; frame, set, mount 235 *enclose*; give foundations, bottom, ground, found, base, embed 153 *stabilize*; stand, endure, stand up to, stand the strain, take the s. 635 *suffice*.

be supported, stand on, recline on, lie on, sit on, loll on, repose on, rest on; bear on, press, press on, step on, lean on, abut on; rely on, ground oneself on, be based on; command support, have at one's back, have behind one.

Adv. *astride*, astraddle, pick-a-back, piggyback.

See: 45, 47, 153, 162, 194, 207, 214, 217, 226, 228, 233, 235, 248, 254, 267, 308, 310, 315, 331, 344, 364, 366, 539, 594, 630, 633, 635, 658, 662, 702, 703, 707, 778, 964, 990.

219 Parallelism

N. *parallelism*, nonconvergence, nondivergence, equidistance, coextension, collimation, concentricity; parallel, correspondence 28 *equality*; parallel lines, lines of latitude; tramlines, rails, railway lines; parallel bars; parallelogram, parallelepiped.

Adj. *parallel*, coextensive, collateral, concurrent, concentric; equidistant 28 *equal*; corresponding, correspondent 18 *similar*.

Vb. *be parallel*, run together, run abreast, lie parallel; correspond, concur; collimate, parallel, draw a p.

Adv. *in parallel*, alongside, collaterally; side by side, abreast.

See: 18, 28.

220 Obliquity

N. *obliquity*, obliqueness, skewness; oblique line, diagonal; oblique figure, rhomboid 247 *angular figure*; oblique angle, inclination 247 *angularity*; indirection, indirectness, squint; curvature, camber, bend, humpback 248 *curve*; changing direction, crookedness, zigzag, chevron; switchback 251 *meandering*; oblique motion, divagation, digression, swerve, lurch, stagger 282 *deviation*; splay, bias, twist, warp 246 *distortion*; leaning, list, tip, cant; slope, slant, tilt, pitch, rake, rakish angle; sloping face, batter; sloping edge, bevel, bezel; inclined plane, ramp, chute, slide; Tower of Pisa, leaning tower; measurement of inclination 247 *angular measure*.

incline, rise, ascent; ramp, acclivity, gradient; hill, rising ground 209 *small hill*; hillside, versant 239 *laterality*; declivity, fall. dip, downhill 309 *descent*; easy ascent, easy descent, gentle slope, dip s.; scarp s., escarpment, steepness, cliff, precipice 215 *verticality*; scarp, counterscarp, glacis 713 *fortification*; talus, bank, scree, landslip, landslide.

Adj. *oblique*, inclined, bevel; tipsy, tilted, rakish; biased, askew, skew, slant, aslant, out of true; out of the perpendicular, battered, leaning; recumbent, stooping; catercornered, rhomboidal 247 *angular*; wry, awry, wonky, skew-whiff, crooked, squinting, cock-eyed, knock-kneed 246 *distorted*; diagonal, transverse, transversal; athwart, across 222 *crossed*; indirect, zigzag, herringbone, bent 248 *curved*; stepped, in echelon; divergent, nonparallel 282 *deviating*.

sloping, acclivous, uphill, rising 308 *ascending*; downhill, falling, declining, dipping 309 *descending*; anticlinal, synclinal; declivitous, steep, abrupt, sheer, precipitous, vertiginous, breakneck 215 *vertical*; easy, gentle, shelving, rounded.

Vb. *be oblique*, - tilted etc. adj.; incline, lean, tilt; pitch, slope, slant, shelve, dip, decline 309 *descend*; rise, climb 308 *ascend*; cut, cut across, transect 222 *cross*; lean, list, tip, lean over, bank, heel, careen, cant; bend, sag, give; bend over 311 *stoop*; walk sideways, edge, sidle, sidestep; look sideways, squint; zigzag; jink, dodge, swerve; diverge, converge.

make oblique, incline, lean, slant, slope, cant, tilt, tip, rake; splay 282 *deviate*; bend, crook, twist, warp, skew 246 *distort*; chamfer, bevel; sway, bias, divert 282 *deflect*; curve, camber 248 *make curved*.

Adv. *obliquely*, diagonally, crosswise 222 *across*; catercorner, cornerwise; on the cross, on the bias; askew, rakishly, tipsily; aslant, slantwise, on the slant; askance, askant, asquint; edgewise, crabwise, sidelong, sideways; aslope, off the vertical, off plumb, out of true, at an angle, at a rakish a.; on one side, all on one s.

See: 209, 215, 222, 239, **246**, **247**, **248**, 251, 282, 308, 309, 311, 713.

221 Inversion

N. *inversion*, turning back to front, palindrome, hysteron proteron; turning inside out, eversion, evagination; turning backwards, retroversion, reversal 148 *reversion*; turning inward, introversion, invagination; turning over, capsizal (**see** *overturning*); turn of the tide, return 286 *regression*; oppositeness 14 *contrariety*, 240 *contraposition*; transposition, metathesis 151 *interchange*; inverted order, chiasmus, anastrophe, hyperbaton 519 *trope*; confused order, spoonerism.

overturning, capsizal, upset, spill; somersault, summerset, cartwheel, handspring; subversion, undermining 149 *revolution*; pronation 216 *recumbency*.

Adj. *inverted*, invaginated etc. vb.; inverse, back-to-front; upside down, inside out, wrong side out; capsized, bottom up, keel upwards; capsizing, topheavy; topsy-turvy, head over heels, on one's head; flat, prone 216 *supine*; reverse, reversed 14 *contrary*; antipodean, antipodal 240 *opposite*; chiastic, palindromic.

Vb. *be inverted*, turn round, go r., wheel r., turn about, face a., right about turn 286 *turn back*; turn over, heel o., keel o., capsize, turn turtle; tilt over 220 *be oblique*; go over, topple o. 309 *tumble*; do a handstand, stand on one's head; loop the loop; reverse, back, back away, go backwards 286 *regress*.

invert, transpose, put the cart before the horse 151 *interchange*; reverse, turn the tables; retrovert, turn back; turn down 261 *fold*; introvert, invaginate; turn inside out, evaginate; upend, upturn, overturn, tip over, spill, upset, overset, capsize; turn topsy-turvy.

Adv. *inversely*, vice versa; contrariwise, other way round; back to front, upside down; arsy-versy, topsy-turvy, head over heels, heels in the air; face down, face downwards, bottom side up.

See: **14**, 148, 149, **151**, 216, 220, 240, 261,

286, 309, 519.

222 Crossing: intertexture

N. *crossing*, crossing over and under, plain weaving; crisscross, transection, intersection; decussation, X-shape; quincunx; intertexture, interlacement, interdigitation, intertwinement, interweaving, arabesque 844 *pattern*; anastomosis, inosculation; braid, wreath, plait 251 *convolution*; entanglement, intricacy, skein, cat's cradle 61 *complexity*; crossroads, intersection, road junction 624 *road*; level crossing 624 *railway*; viaduct, flyover 624 *bridge*, 305 *traffic control*.

cross, crux, rood, crucifix 988 *ritual object*; pectoral 989 *vestments*; ankh, ansate cross, tau c., Latin c., c. of Lorraine, Greek c., Maltese c., Celtic c., St Anthony's C., St Andrew's C.; saltire, crosslet 547 *heraldry*; gammadion, swastika, fylfot; crossbones, skull and c. 547 *flag*; crossbar, transom 218 *beam*; scissors, nutcrackers 778 *nippers*.

network, reticulation, meshwork, netting, wire n., chicken wire; webbing, matting, wickerwork, basketwork, trellis, wattle; honeycomb, lattice, grating, grid, grille, gridiron; craquelure; tracery, fretwork, filigree 844 *ornamental art*; lace, crochet, knitting, tatting, macramé 844 *needlework*; web, cobweb; net, fishnet, seine, purse-s., drag-net, trawl, beam t. 235 *enclosure*; plexus, mesh, reticle.

textile, weave, web, loom; woven stuff, piece goods, dry g.; bolt, roll, length, piece, cloth, stuff, material; broadcloth, fabric, tissue, suiting; batik 844 *ornamental art*; jute, hessian, gunny, sacking, hopsack, canvas, sailcloth, duck; ticking, crash, huckaback, towelling, terry t., candlewick; chintz, cretonne, damask, brocade, brocatelle, grosgrain, rep, chenille, tapestry 226 *covering*; mohair, cashmere; alpaca, vicuna, angora 208 *fibre*; wool, worsted, grosgram; frieze, felt, baize; homespun, khadar, duffel, kersey, tweed, serge, shalloon, bombazine, gabardine, doeskin; flannel, swanskin, swansdown; paisley, jacquard 844 *pattern*; stockinette, jersey, tricot, nainsook, flannelette, winceyette; velvet, velveteen, velour; corduroy, needlecord; cotton, denim, drill, nankeen, calvalry twill, khaki; fustian, moleskin, sharkskin; poplin, calico, dimity, gingham, madras, seersucker, piqué; batiste, organdie, organza; silesia, cheesecloth, muslin, mull, voile, percale; cambric, lawn, toile, holland, linen; silk, surah, foulard, georgette, crêpe de chine, chiffon, mousseline; satin, sateen, taffeta, moire; tussore *or* tussah, shantung, pongee; ninon; tulle, net, gauze; lace, guipure; rayon, nylon, Terylene (tdmk), crimplene (tdmk), polyester, Courtelle (tdmk), fibreglass 208 *fibre*.

weaving, texture; web, warp, weft, woof, selvage; nap, pile 259 *hair*; frame, loom, shuttle; weaver, knitter; knitting machine, sewing m.; spinning wheel, distaff, whorl; spinner, spider, weaverbird; Arachne, Penelope.

Adj. *crossed*, crossing, cross, crisscross; quadrivial; diagonal, transverse, cross-eyed, squinting 220 *oblique*; decussate, X-shaped, quincunxial; cross-legged, cruciform, crucial, cruciate, forked, furcate 247 *angular*; plexiform; knotted, matted, balled-up, ravelled 61 *complex*; pleached, plashed, plaited, interlaced, interfretted, interwoven; textile, loomed, woven, handwoven, tweedy; twill, herringbone; trellised, latticed, honeycombed, mullioned, barred; corded, ribbed, streaked, striped 437 *variegated*.

reticular, reticulated, retiform, webbed, webby, lacy; netted, meshed, micromesh 201 *spaced*.

Vb. *cross*, cross over, cross under 305 *pass*; intersect, cut 220 *be oblique*; decussate, inosculate, interdigitate; splice, dovetail, link 45 *join*; reticulate, mesh, net, knot; fork, bifurcate 247 *make angular*.

weave, loom; pleach, plash, plait, braid; felt, twill, knit, crochet; spin, slub.

enlace, interlace, interlink, interlock, interdigitate, intertwine, intertwist, interweave, enmesh, engage gear; twine, entwine, wattle, twist, raddle, wreathe, pleach; mat, ravel, snarl, tangle, entangle, dishevel 63 *derange*.

Adv. *across*, athwart, transversely; crosswise, saltire-wise; with folded arms, arm in arm.

See: 45, 61, 63, 201, 208, 218, **220**, 226, 235, 247, 251, 259, 305, 437, 547, 624, 778, **844**, 988, 989.

223 Exteriority

N. *exteriority*, the external; outwardness, externality 230 *surroundings*; periphery, circumference, sidelines 233 *outline*;

exterior, outward appearance 445 *appearance*; surface, superficies, superstratum, crust, cortex, shell 226 *skin*; outer side, face, facet, facade 237 *front*; other side 240 *contraposition*; externalism, regard for externals 982 *idolatry*; externalization, extroversion, extrovert 6 *extrinsicality*; outside, out of doors, open air; outer space 199 *distance*; extraterritoriality 57 *exclusion*; foreignness 59 *extraneousness*; eccentricity 84 *nonconformity*; outsider 84 *nonconformist*.

Adj. *exterior*, exoteric, outward, extra-; external 10 *unrelated*; roundabout, peripheral 230 *circumjacent*; outer, outermost, outlying, extraterrestrial 199 *distant*; outside, outboard; outdoor, extramural; foreign 59 *extraneous*; extraterritorial 57 *excluding*; extrovert, outward-looking 6 *extrinsic*; centrifugal 620 *avoiding*; exogenous; eccentric 282 *deviating*; surface, superficial, epidermal, cortical; skin-deep 212 *shallow*; facial 237 *frontal*.

Vb. *be exterior*, lie beyond, lie outside etc. adv.; frame, enclose 230 *surround*; look outward 6 *be extrinsic*.

externalize, body forth, objectify 6 *make extrinsic*; project, extrapolate; expel 300 *eject*.

Adv. *externally*, outwardly, outwards, superficially, on the surface; on the face of it, to the outsider; outside, extra muros; out, out of doors, in the cold, in the sun, in the open, in the open air, alfresco.

See: 6, 10, **57**, **59**, 84, 199, 212, **226**, 230, 233, 237, 240, 282, 300, 445, 620, 982.

224 Interiority

N. *interiority*, interior, inside, indoors; inner surface, undersurface; endoderm 226 *skin*; sapwood, heartwood 366 *wood*; inmost being, heart's blood, soul; heart, centre, breast, bosom 225 *centrality*; inland, Midlands, heartland, hinterland, up-country; pith, marrow 3 *substance*; subsoil, substratum 214 *base*; permeation, pervasion 189 *presence*, 231 *interjacency*; interspace 201 *interval*; deepness, cave, pit, penetralia, recesses, innermost r. 211 *depth*; endogamy 894 *marriage*; introversion 5 *intrinsicality*; self-absorption, egoism, egotism, egocentrism 932 *selfishness*; introvert, egoist 932 *egotist*; inmate, indweller 191 *dweller*; internee 750 *prisoner*.

insides 193 *contents*; inner man, interior man; internal organs, viscera, vitals; heart, ticker; lungs, lights; liver, kidneys, spleen; offal 301 *meat*; bowels, entrails, innards, guts, pluck, tripe; intestines, colon, rectum; abdomen, belly, paunch, underbelly; womb, uterus; stomach, tummy 194 *maw*; chest, solar plexus; gland; endocrine; cell 358 *organism*.

Adj. *interior*, internal, inward 5 *intrinsic*; inside, inner, innermost, midmost 225 *central*; inland, up-country 199 *removed*; domestic, home, vernacular; intimate, familiar 490 *known*; indoor, intramural, shut in, enclosed; inboard, built-in, inwrought; endemic 192 *residing*; deep-seated, ingrown 153 *fixed*; intestinal, visceral; intravenous, subcutaneous; interstitial 231 *interjacent*; inward-looking, introvert 5 *intrinsic*; endo-, endogamous; endogenous.

Vb. *be inside*, - internal etc. adj.; be within etc. adv.; lie within, lie beneath, be at the bottom of; show through 443 *be visible*.

hold within, hold 78 *comprise*; place within, embed 303 *insert*; keep inside, intern 747 *imprison*; enfold, embay 235 *enclose*; internalize 299 *absorb*.

Adv. *inside*, within, in, deep in, deep down; inly, inwardly, intimately; deeply, profoundly, at heart; withinside, within doors, indoors, at home, en famille, chez, at the sign of.

See: 3, **5**, 78, 153, 189, 191, 192, 193, 194, 199, 201, 211, 214, **225**, 226, 231, 235, 299, 301, 303, 358, 366, 443, 490, 747, 750, 894, 932.

225 Centrality

N. *centrality*, centricity, centralness; concentricity; centralization, focalization, concentration 324 *condensation*; central position, mid p. 231 *interjacency*; midriff, waistline, centreline, parting 231 *partition*; Ptolemaic system, Copernican s.

centre, dead c.; centroid, centre of mass, centre of gravity, centre of pressure, centre of percussion, centre of buoyancy, metacentre; nerve centre, ganglion; centre of activity 76 *focus*; epicentre; storm centre, hotbed; heart, core, kernel 5 *essential part*; omphalos, nub, hub; nucleus, nucleolus; navel, umbilicus; spine, backbone, chine, midrib; marrow, pith 224 *interiority*; pole, axis, fulcrum, centreboard 218 *pivot*; centre point, mid p. 70

middle; fess-point 547 *heraldry*; eye, pupil; bull's-eye, target 617 *objective*.

Adj. *central*, centro-, centric, centrical; nuclear, nucleolar; centremost, midmost 70 *middle*; axial, focal, pivotal; umbilical; homocentric, concentric; geocentric; heliocentric; spinal, vertebral; centripetal; metropolitan, chief, head 34 *supreme*.

Vb. *centralize*, centre, focus, bring to a f., centre upon; concentrate, nucleate, consolidate 324 *be dense*.

Adv. *centrally*, at the heart of, at the core, middle, midst, amongst; in the midst, in the middle.

See: 5, 34, **70**, 76, 218, **224**, 231, 324, 547, 617.

226 Covering

N. *covering*, capping etc. vb.; superposition, superimposition, overlaying; overlap, overlapping, imbrication; coating, stratification 207 *layer*; top layer, top dressing, mulch, topsoil 344 *soil*; topping, icing, frosting 844 *ornamentation*; cover, lid; gravestone, ledger 364 *tomb*; hatch, trapdoor; flap, shutter, operculum; film 423 *opacity*; glass, glass front, watch glass, crystal 422 *transparency*; cap, top, plug, bung, cork 264 *stopper*; pledget, plaster 658 *surgical dressing*; carapace, shell, snail s., tortoiseshell 326 *hardness*; mail, plate, armour p. 713 *armour*; shield, cowl, cowling, bonnet, hood (of a car); scab 207 *lamina*; crust, fur 649 *dirt*; capsule, ferrule, sheath, involucre, envelope 194 *receptacle*; pillowcase, pillowslip; table cloth, tray c.; chair cover, antimacassar; soft furnishings, loose covers; hangings, curtains 217 *hanging object*; wallpaper 227 *lining*; mask, domino 527 *disguise*.

roof, cupola 253 *dome*; mansard roof, hipped r., pitched r., gable r., flat r., catslide; housetop, rooftop, rooftree 213 *vertex*; leads, slates, slating, tiles, tiling, pantile, shingle, thatch, thatching, corrugated iron 631 *building material*; eaves 234 *edge*; ceiling, deck; vaulting, vault, barrel v., groin v.; rafters, hammerbeam roof 218 *beam*.

canopy, ciborium, baldachin; velarium, tilt, awning, sunblind 421 *screen*; marquee, pavilion, big top; tent, bell tent, ridge t., frame t.; tepee 192 *dwelling*; tentcloth, canvas, tarpaulin, fly sheet; mosquito net 222 *network*.

shade, hood, eyelid, eyelash; blind, venetian b., jalousie, persiennes, shutters, slats; curtain, veil; umbrella, gamp, brolly; parasol, sunshade; sun hat, sun helmet, topee 228 *headgear*; visor, eye shade 421 *screen*; peak (of a cap); dark glasses 442 *eyeglass*.

wrapping, wrapper, paper, cellophane, polythene; polystyrene 227 *lining*; packaging, blister pack 194 *receptacle*; bandage, roller 47 *girdle*; plaster cast 658 *surgical dressing*; book cover, binding, boards, dust jacket *or* cover 589 *bookbinding*; tunic, coat 228 *jacket*; mantle 228 *cloak*; comforter, scarf 228 *neckwear*; life belt, life jacket 662 *safeguard*; lagging; cocoon, chrysalis; shroud, winding sheet 364 *grave clothes*.

skin, epithelium; outer skin, scarf s., epidermis, cuticle; true skin, cutis, dermis, derma, corium; tegument 223 *exteriority*; integument, peel, bark, crust, rind, coat, cortex; pericarp, husk, hull, shell, pod, jacket; pellicle, membrane, film; scalp 213 *head*; scale 207 *lamina*; pelt, peltry, fleece, fell, fur; leather, hide, rawhide, imitation leather, leatheroid; shagreen, patent leather; crocodile, alligator; pigskin, morocco, calf, kid, chamois, suede, buff, buckskin, doeskin; rabbitskin, moleskin, sealskin; sheepskin, lamb, Persian l., astrakhan; mink, sable, ermine, vair, miniver, cony; chinchilla 208 *fibre*; feathers, coverts 259 *plumage*.

paving, flooring, floor, parquet, quarry tiles; deck, floorboards, duckboards; pavement, pavé; flags, paving stone, crazy paving; sett, cobble, cobblestone; gravel, chippings, asphalt, tarmac 624 *road*.

coverlet, bedspread, counterpane, bedding, bedclothes, bed linen; sheet, quilt, eiderdown, duvet; blanket, rug; caparison, housings, trappings; saddlecloth, horsecloth; pall.

floor-cover, carpeting, carpet, fitted c.; broadloom, pile carpet, Persian c.; mat, doormat, bath mat, prayer m.; rug, hearth r.; drugget, numdah; linoleum, lino, vinyl, tiles; matting, coconut m.; red carpet 875 *formality*.

facing, revetment, cladding 162 *strengthening*; veneer, coating, varnish, japan, lacquer, enamel, glaze; incrustation, roughcast, pebbledash; ashlar, weatherboarding 631 *building material*; stucco, compo, plaster, pargeting, rendering; wash, whitewash, distemper, emulsion, paint;

stain, polish, smearing, anointment; coat of paint 425 *pigment*.

Adj. *overlying*, overlaying, overarching; overlapping, tegular, imbricated; cloaking etc. vb.

covered, roofed, roofed in, vaulted, ceiled, wallpapered, carpeted; tented, garaged, under cover, under canvas; under shelter 660 *safe*; cloaked, cowled, veiled, hooded 525 *concealed*; loricate, armour-plated, iron-clad; metalled, paved; built over; snow-capped, ice-covered; inundated, flooded; smothered, plastered, coated etc. vb.

dermal, cutaneous, cortical, cuticular; tegumentary; scaly, squamous; epidermic, epidermal, epidermoid.

Vb. *cover*, superpose, superimpose; roof, roof in, put the lid on, cap, tip; ice, frost, decorate (a cake); spread, lay (a table); overlay, smother; insulate, lag 227 *line*; lap, enwrap, enfold, envelop 235 *enclose*; blanket, shroud, mantle, muffle; hood, veil 525 *conceal*; case, bind, cover (books); box, pack, vacuum-pack; wrap, shrink-w.; bandage, swathe, wrap round, dress 658 *doctor*; sheathe, encapsulate, encase 303 *insert*; wall in, wall up; keep under cover, garage.

overlie, overarch, overhang, overlap; overshadow 419 *bedim*; span, bestride, straddle, bestraddle 205 *be broad*; flood, inundate 341 *drench*; skin over, crust, scab.

overlay, pave, floor, cement; ceil, roof, dome, vault, overarch, deck; tile, thatch; paper, wallpaper 227 *line*; overspread, topdress, mulch; spread, smear, besmear; butter, anoint; powder, dust, sand; gravel, tarmac, metal.

coat, revet, face, front, do over; grout, roughcast, encrust, shingle; stucco, plaster, render, parget 844 *decorate*; veneer, varnish, lacquer, japan, enamel, glaze, size; paint, whitewash, colourwash, distemper, emulsion, stain 425 *colour*; creosote; tar, pitch, pay; daub, bedaub, scumble, overpaint, grease, lay it on thick; gild, plate, silver, besilver; electroplate, silverplate; waterproof, fireproof 660 *safeguard*.

See: 47, 162, 192, 194, 205, **207**, 208, 213, 217, 218, 222, 223, 227, **228**, 234, 235, 253, 259, 264, 303, 326, 341, 344, 364, 419, **421**, 422, 423, 425, 442, 525, 527, 589, 624, 631, 649, 658, 660, 662, 713, 844, 875.

227 Lining

N. *lining*, liner, interlining 231 *interjacency*; coating, inner c.; stuffing, wadding, padding, batting, quilting; kapok, foam 631 *materials*; lagging, insulation, double-glazing, soundproofing; backing, facing; doublure 589 *bookbinding*; upholstery; papering, wallpaper; wainscotting, panelling, wainscot, skirting board, brattice; metal lining, bush; brake lining; packing, dunnage; packaging 226 *wrapping*; filling, stopping (dentistry); washer, shim.

Vb. *line*, encrust 226 *coat*; insulate 226 *cover*; interlard, inlay; back, face, paper, wallpaper; upholster, cushion; stuff, pad, wad; fill, pack; bush 303 *insert*.

See: 226, 231, 303, 589, 631.

228 Dressing

N. *dressing*, investment, investiture; clothing, covering, dressing up, toilet, toilette; overdressing, foppishness 848 *fashion*; vesture, dress, garb, attire, rig; panoply, array; garniture, trim, accoutrements, caparison, harness, housing, trappings; traps, paraphernalia, accessories; rig-out, turn-out; tailoring, dressmaking, millinery; haute couture; the rag trade.

clothing, wear, apparel, raiment, linen; clothes, garments, vestments, habiliments; togs, gear, kit, clobber; outfit, wardrobe, trousseau; maternity wear; layette, baby clothes, swaddling c.; old clothes, duds, reach-me-downs, cast-offs, rags, tatters; working clothes, slops; leisure wear, casual clothes; best c., fine raiment; Sunday best, Sunday go-to-meeting, best bib and tucker; party dress, glad rags; pearlies, ostrich feathers, frippery 844 *finery*; fancy dress, masquerade; motley; silks, colours; national costume.

garment, article of clothing; neck, collar (**see** *neckwear*, *neckline*); top, bodice, bosom; corsage, bib, stomacher; shirt-front, dicky; waistline (**see** *belt*); peplum, bustle, train; crutch, codpiece; arms (**see** *sleeve*); flaps, coat tails 217 *hanging object*; placket, fly 263 *opening*; patch pocket 194 *pocket*; gusset, gore, pleat, kick pleat; lapel, turn-up 261 *fold*; cuff, hemline 234 *edging*.

formal dress, correct d., court d., full d. 875 *formality*; grande toilette, evening dress, tails, white tie and tails; morning dress;

academic dress, cap and gown, subfusc; mourning, black, widow's weeds.

uniform, regimentals 547 *livery*; dress uniform, undress, mess kit; battledress, fatigues, khaki; school uniform; robes, vestments, clerical dress 989 *canonicals*.

informal dress, undress, mufti, civvies; casual clothes, slacks, jeans; déshabillé, dishabille; dressing gown, peignoir, bathrobe, wrapper, housecoat; smoking jacket, slippers.

robe, gown, robes, drapery; sari; kimono, caftan; jubbah, burka; chiton, himation; toga, t. virilis; peplos, pallium (**see** *cloak*); cassock 989 *canonicals*; winding sheet, shroud 364 *grave clothes*.

dress, frock, gown; creation, number, cocktail dress; sheath d., cheongsam, chemise, shift, sack; shirtwaister, coatdress, overdress, pinafore dress, gymslip; sundress.

suit, outfit, ensemble; coordinates, separates; lounge suit, zoot s., drape s., pinstripe s.; costume, tweeds, trouser suit; jumpsuit, catsuit, leotard, body stocking; overalls, boiler suit, siren s., tracksuit, wetsuit; G-suit, spacesuit.

jacket, coat, tail c., dinner jacket, tuxedo; monkey jacket, mess j., pea j., Eton j.; blazer, reefer, sports jacket, Norfolk j., hacking j., riding habit, hunting pink; donkey jacket, lumber j. (**see** *overcoat*); parka, windcheater, anorak, kagoule; bomber jacket, blouson; jerkin, doublet, tunic, tabard, surcoat, waistcoat, gilet, spencer; bolero, coatee, matinée jacket.

jersey, pullover, woolly, homeknit, jumper, sweater, polo neck, sloppy joe, guernsey, Fair Isle, cardigan, tank top, twin set.

trousers, trews, breeks; cords, flannels, pinstripes; hipsters, drainpipes, bell-bottoms; slacks, bags, Oxford b., plus fours; galligaskins, breeches, jodhpurs, knickerbockers, pedal-pushers; chaps, dungarees, denims, jeans, blue j., Levi's (tdmk); shorts, Bermuda s.; lederhosen; bloomers, pantaloons, rompers.

skirt, maxi s., midi s., miniskirt; pleated s., flared s., full s., dirndl, kilt, kirtle, filibeg; sarong; straight skirt, slit s., hobble s.; divided s., culottes; ballet skirt, tutu; crinoline, farthingale, hoop, pannier.

loincloth, lungi, dhoti, sarong; fig leaf, G-string, jockstrap; nappy *or* diaper.

apron, bib, pinafore, pinny, overall.

shirt, smock, angel top; dashiki, caftan; polo neck, T-shirt, sweatshirt; blouse, choli, camisole, top, sun top.

underwear, underclothes, undies, linen; lingerie, smalls, unmentionables; underpants, pants, Y-fronts, boxer shorts; briefs, panties, scanties, French knickers, camiknickers, knickers, bloomers, drawers, pantalets; combinations, long johns, thermal underwear; singlet, vest, string v.; chemise, slip, half-slip, petticoat; foundation garment, corset, stays, girdle, pantie-g., roll-on; brassiere, bra; suspender belt, braces.

nightwear, nightclothes, sleeping suit; nightgown, nightdress, nightie, negligee; nightshirt, pyjamas; bedsocks, bed jacket, nightcap.

beachwear, sunsuit, bikini, monokini; swimming costume, swimsuit, bathing suit, trunks.

overcoat, coat (**see** *jacket*); fur coat, mink c. 226 *skin*; topcoat, greatcoat, frock coat; redingote, raglan, ulster; car coat, duffel c.; waterproof, oilskins; mac, mackintosh, raincoat, gabardine; Burberry (tdmk), trench coat; light coat, duster.

cloak, mantle; cape, cycling c.; pelisse, pelerine, dolman; domino 527 *disguise*; jellaba, burnous (**see** *robe*); shawl, plaid, poncho, Afghan.

neckwear, scarf, fichu; stole, boa, tippet; comforter, muffler; neckerchief, stock, jabot, cravat, tie, bow t.; necklace 844 *jewellery*; ruff, collar, dog c. 989 *canonicals*; Eton collar, mandarin c., Peter Pan c., Vandyke c., Bertha, sailor c., shawl c. **See** *neckline*.

headgear, millinery; hat, cap, lid, titfer; headdress, mantilla; plumes, ribbons 844 *finery*; coronet, tiara 743 *regalia*; fillet, snood; juliet cap, skull c., coif; headscarf, kerchief, bandanna, headband, sweatband; turban, puggaree; hood, cowl, wimple; veil, yashmak 421 *screen*; fez, tarboosh; shako, kepi, busby, bearskin, helmet 713 *armour*; tin hat, hard h., crash helmet, skidlid 662 *safeguard*; woolly hat, bobble h.; rainhat, sou'wester; cap, cloth c., beret, tam-o'-shanter; Balmoral, glengarry, deerstalker; Homburg, trilby, porkpie hat, billycock, fedora, beaver, bowler, derby; slouch hat, stetson, ten-gallon hat, sombrero, shovel hat, picture h., Dolly Varden, straw h., boater, panama, coolie hat, bush h., sunhat, pith helmet 226 *shade*; bonnet, poke b., mob cap, toque, cloche, pillbox; top hat, topper, silk hat, stovepipe h.; cocked h., tricorne, mortarboard; biretta 989 *canonicals*; witch's hat, dunce's cap.

wig, peruke, periwig; full-bottomed wig, bagwig, tie-wig; false hair, hairpiece, toupee; coiffure 259 *hair*.

neckline, boat neck, crew n., cowl n., turtle n., roll n., polo n., halter n., V-n.; low n. 229 *bareness*.

belt, waistband; cummerbund, sash, obi; armlet, armband; bandolier, baldric 47 *girdle*.

sleeve, arm, armhole; leg-of-mutton sleeve, raglan s., dolman s., batwing s., magyar s., puff s., cap s.; wristband, cuff.

glove, gauntlet, long gloves; mitten, mitt, muff.

legwear, hosiery; stockings, nylons, tights, fleshings; trunks, hose; half-hose, socks, ankle s., bootees; leggings, gaiters, spats, puttees; greaves 713 *armour*; garter, suspender 47 *fastening*.

footwear, footgear, buskin, cothurnus, sock; slipper, mule; patten, clog, sabot; flip-flops, sandals, Jesus boots, chappals; rope-soled shoes, espadrilles, rubber-soled shoes, crepe-soled s., creepers, sneakers, plimsolls, gym shoes, tennis s.; pumps, ballet shoes; moccasins, slip-ons, casuals; brothel creepers, winklepickers, beetle-crushers, clodhoppers; shoe, court s., high heels, stiletto h., platform h., Cuban h., wedge h.; square-toed shoes, peep-toed s., slingbacks, lace-ups, buckled shoes; Oxfords, brogues; boots, high b., cowboy b.; thigh b., waders, wellingtons, wellies, gumboots; skiboots 274 *sledge*; running shoes, spikes.

clothier, outfitter, costumier; tailor, couturier, couturière; fashion designer 848 *fashion*; dressmaker, sempstress, seamstress, modiste; shoemaker, bootmaker; cobbler, cordwainer, souter 686 *artisan*; hosier, hatter, milliner, draper, haberdasher; Savile Row, Carnaby Street; boutique; valet 742 *domestic*; dresser, mistress of the wardrobe 594 *stagehand*.

Adj. *dressed*, clothed, clad, dight, bedight; attired etc. adj.; rigged out, turned o., got up like a dog's dinner 844 *bedecked*; uniformed, liveried; shod, gloved, hatted; well-dressed, soigné(e), en grande toilette, en grande tenue.

tailored, tailor-made, bespoke, made-to-measure; ready-to-wear, off-the-peg; single-breasted, double-b.; one-piece, two-p.; unisex; well-cut, fully fashioned; classic, princess-line, Empire-line, A-line; ballerina-length; step-in, pull-on, button-through, zip-up; skintight, slinky 24 *adjusted*; gathered 261 *folded*; bloused, bouffant 205 *broad*; sartorial.

Vb. *dress*, clothe, array, apparel, garment, dight, garb, attire; robe, enrobe, drape, sheet, mantle; invest, accoutre, uniform, put in u., equip, rig out, fit o., harness, caparison 669 *make ready*; dress up, bedizen, deck, prink 843 *primp*; envelop, wrap, lap, enfold, wrap up, fold up, muffle up, roll up in, swaddle, swathe, shroud, sheathe 226 *cover*.

wear, put on, try on, assume, don, slip on, slip into, get i., huddle i.; clothe oneself, attire o., get dressed, get one's clothes on; button up, zip up, lace up 45 *tie*; change, get changed; have on, dress in, carry, sport; dress up 875 *be ostentatious*.

See: 24, 45, 47, 194, 205, 217, **226**, 229, 234, 259, 261, 263, 274, 364, 421, 527, 547, 594, 662, 669, 686, 713, 742, 743, 843, **844**, 848, 875, 989.

229 Uncovering

N. *uncovering*, divestment, undressing etc. vb.; exposure 526 *disclosure*; nudism, naturism; striptease 594 *stage show*; undress, dishabille, déshabillé 228 *informal dress*; moult, moulting, shedding; decortication, exfoliation, excoriation, peeling, desquamation; depilation, shaving; denudation, devastation 165 *havoc*.

bareness, décolleté, décolletage, bare neck, low n., plunging neckline; nudity, nakedness, state of nature, birthday suit, nu intégral, the altogether, the buff, the raw, not a stitch on; baldness, hairlessness, falling hair, alopecia; tonsure; baldpate, baldhead.

stripper, ecdysiast, striptease artiste; flasher, streaker; nudist, naturist; skinner, furrier, flayer, peeler; hair-remover, depilatory; nude figure, nude.

Adj. *uncovered*, bared; exposed, unveiled, showing 522 *manifest*; divested, forcibly d., debagged; stripped, peeled; without one's clothes, unclad, unclothed, undressed, unattired, unapparelled; décolleté(e), bare-necked, low-n., off-the-shoulder, topless; bare-backed, bare-armed, barelegged; barefoot, unshod, discalced; hatless, bareheaded; en déshabillé, in one's shirt-sleeves; miniskirted, bikini-clad; underclothed, underdressed, indecently dressed; bare, naked, nude, raw; in a state of nature, in nature's garb, mother naked, in the buff, au naturel, in one's birthday suit, with nothing on, without a stitch on; stark, stark naked, starkers; leafless; plucked, moulting, unfeathered, unfledged; poorly dressed, threadbare, out-at-elbows, ragged 801 *poor*; drawn, unsheathed 304 *extracted*.

hairless, bald, baldheaded, smooth, beardless, shaved, shaven, clean-s., tonsured; bald as a coot, bald as an egg, bald as a billiard ball, bare as the back of one's hand; napless, threadbare; mangy 651 *diseased*; thin, thin on top.

Vb. *uncover*, unveil, undrape, unrobe, uncloak, undress, unclothe; divest, debag; strip, skin, scalp, flay, tear off; pluck, deplume, peel, bark, decorticate, excoriate; hull, pod, shell, stone; bone, fillet 300 *empty*; denude, denudate 165 *lay waste*; expose, bare, lay open 526 *disclose*; unsheathe, draw (a sword) 304 *extract*; unwrap, unfold, unpack; unroof, uncap, take the lid off 263 *open*; scrape off, abrade 333 *rub*.

doff, uncap, uncover, raise one's hat; take off, strip off, peel off, slip off, slip out of, step out of, drop; change, change one's clothes; shed, cast, cast a clout; moult, slough, exuviate, cast its skin; desquamate, exfoliate; flake off, scale; divest oneself, undress, disrobe, peel, strip; undo, unbutton, unlace, untie 46 *disunite*.

See: 46, 165, 228, 263, 300, 304, 333, **522**, **526**, 594, 651, 801.

230 Surroundings

N. *surroundings* 223 *exteriority*; circumambience, circumjacence; ambience, atmosphere, aura; medium, matrix; encompassment, containment, surrounding 235 *enclosure*; compass, circuit, circumference, periphery, perimeter 233 *outline*; circumjacencies, milieu, environment, entourage; background, setting, scene 186 *situation*; neighbourhood, vicinity 200 *near place*; outskirts, environs, boulevards, suburbs, faubourgs, banlieue; green belt; purlieus, precincts 192 *housing*; outpost, border 236 *limit*; wall, fortification 235 *fence*; cordon 47 *girdle*.

Adj. *circumjacent*, circum-; circumambient, circumfluent, circumfluous, ambient, atmospheric; surrounding etc. vb.; framing, circumferential, peripheral; shutting in, claustrophobic; roundabout 314 *circuitous*; suburban 200 *near*.

Vb. *surround*, lie around, compass, encompass, environ, lap; encircle 314 *circle*; girdle, begird, engird, cincture 235 *enclose*; wreathe around, twine a.; embrace, hug 889 *caress*; contain, keep in, cloister, shut in, hem in 232 *circumscribe*; beset, invest, blockade 712 *besiege*.

Adv. *around*, about, on every side, round about, all round; on all sides, right and left; without, outside, in the neighbourhood, in the outskirts.

See: 47, 186, 192, 200, 223, 232, **233**, **235**, 236, 314, 712, 889.

231 Interjacency

N. *interjacency*, intermediacy, intervention, penetration, interpenetration, permeation, infiltration 189 *presence*; interdigitation 222 *crossing*; dovetailing 45 *union*; middle position 70 *middle*.

partition, curtain, Iron C. 421 *screen*; Great Wall of China 713 *defences*; Berlin Wall 57 *exclusion*; wall, party w., brattice, bulkhead 235 *fence*; divide, watershed, parting 46 *separation*; division, panel 53 *subdivision*; interface, septum, diaphragm, midriff 225 *centre*; field boundary, balk, hedge, ditch 201 *gap*; common frontier 236 *limit*.

intermediary, medium, intermedium, link 47 *bond*; negotiator, go-between, broker, usual channels 720 *mediator*; marriage broker 894 *matchmaker*; agent 755 *deputy*; middleman, retailer 794 *merchant*; intercessor, pleader, advocate 707 *patron*; buffer, bumper, fender, cushion 662 *safeguard*; air lock, buffer state, no-man's-land, halfway house 70 *middle*.

interjection, putting between, interposition, sandwiching; interpolation, intercalation, interlineation, interspersion 303 *insertion*; embolism 264 *closure*; interruption, intrusion, butting in 72 *discontinuity*; interference, meddling 702 *hindrance*; thing inserted, episode, parenthesis, obiter dictum 40 *adjunct*; infix, insert, fly leaf; wedge, washer, shim 227 *lining*; thin end of the wedge.

interjector, interpolator; intruder, interloper 702 *hinderer*.

Adj. *interjacent*, interposed, sandwiched; episodic, parenthetical, in brackets; intercurrent, intermediary, intervenient, intervening etc. vb.; intercessory, mediating 720 *mediatory*; intercalary 303 *inserted*; intrusive 59 *extraneous*; inter-, interstitial, intercostal, intermural; interplanetary, interstellar; intermediate, thematic 303 *inserted*; median, medium, mean, mediterranean 70 *middle*; partitioning, dividing, septal.

Vb. *lie between*, come b., stand b.; intervene 625 *be halfway*; slide in, interpenetrate, permeate, soak in 189 *pervade*.

introduce, let in 299 *admit*; sheathe, invaginate; throw in, foist in, plough in, work in, wedge in, edge in, jam in, force in 303 *insert*; ingrain 303 *infuse*; splice, dovetail, mortise 45 *join*; smuggle in, slide in, worm in, insinuate 297 *infiltrate*.

put between, sandwich; cushion 227 *line*; interpose, interject; spatchcock, interpolate, intercalate, interline; interleave, interlard, intersperse; interweave, interdigitate 222 *enlace*; bracket, put between brackets, parenthesize.

interfere, come between, get b., intercept 702 *hinder*; step in, intervene, intercede 720 *mediate*; interrupt, put in, chip in, get a word in; obtrude, thrust in, poke one's nose in, butt in 297 *intrude*; invade, trespass 306 *encroach*; put one's oar in; have a finger in the pie 678 *meddle*.

Adv. *between*, betwixt, 'twixt, betwixt and between; among, amongst, amid, amidst, mid, midst; in the middle of; in the thick of; parenthetically; in the meanwhile, in the meantime 108 *while*.

See: 40, 45, 46, 47, 53, 57, 59, **70**, 72, 108, 189, 201, 222, 225, 227, 235, 236, 264, 297, 299, **303**, 306, 421, 625, 662, 678, 702, 707, 713, 720, 755, 794, 894.

232 Circumscription

N. *circumscription*, enclosing 235 *enclosure*; drawing round, circle, balloon; ringing round, hedging r., fencing r.; surrounding, framing, girdling, cincture; investment, siege, blockade 712 *attack*; envelopment, encirclement, containment, confinement, limitation 747 *restriction*; ring 235 *fence*.

Adj. *circumscribed*, encircled, encompassed, enveloped; surrounded, begirt; lapped, enfolded, embosomed, embayed, landlocked; framed 233 *outlined*; boxed, boxed up, encysted; walled in, mewed up, cloistered, immured 747 *imprisoned*; invested, beleaguered, besieged; held in, contained, confined 747 *restrained*; limited, restricted, finite.

Vb. *circumscribe*, describe a circle, ring round, encircle, encompass; envelop, close in, cut off, cordon off, invest, beleaguer, blockade, picket 712 *besiege*; beset, hem in, corral; enclose, rail in, hedge in, fence in; box, cage, wall in, immure, cloister 747 *imprison*; frame 230 *surround*; encase, enfold, enshrine, embosom, embay; edge, border 236 *limit*; clasp, hug, embrace 889 *caress*.

See: **230**, 233, **235**, 236, 712, 747, 889.

233 Outline

N. *outline*, circumference, perimeter, periphery; surround, frame, rim 234 *edge*; ambit, compass, circuit 250 *circle*; delineation, lines, lineaments, features 445 *feature*; profile, relief 239 *laterality*; silhouette, skyline 553 *picture*; sketch, rough s. 623 *plan*; figure, diagram; trace, tracing; skeleton, framework 331 *structure*; contour, contour line, shape 243 *form*; isogonic line, coastline, bounds 236 *limit*; circlet, band 250 *loop*; balloon, circle 232 *circumscription*; ring, cordon 235 *barrier*.

Adj. *outlined*, framed etc. vb.; in outline, etched; peripheral, perimetric, circumferential.

Vb. *outline*, describe a circle, construct a figure 232 *circumscribe*; frame 230 *surround*; delineate, draw, silhouette, profile, trace 551 *represent*; etch 555 *engrave*; map, block out, sketch o., sketch; diagrammatize, not fill in.

See: **230**, **232**, 234, 235, 236, 239, 243, **250**, 331, 445, 551, 553, 555, 623.

234 Edge

N. *edge*, verge, brim; outer edge, fly (of a flag); tip, brink, skirt, fringe, margin 69 *extremity*; inner edge, hoist (of a flag); confines, bounds, boundary, frontier, border 236 *limit*; littoral, coast, coastline, beach, strand, seaside, seashore, waterline, waterside, water's edge, front, waterfront 344 *shore*; wharf, quay, dock 192 *stable*; sideline, side, brim, kerb, kerbside, wayside, roadside, riverside, bank 239 *laterality*; hedge, railing 235 *fence*; felloe, tyre 250 *wheel*; projecting edge, lip, ledge, eaves, cornice, rim, welt, flange, gunwale 254 *projection*; raised edge, coaming; horizon, ends of the earth, skyline 199 *farness*.

threshold, sill, doorstep, door, portal, porch 263 *doorway*; mouth, jaws, chops, chaps, fauces 194 *maw*.

edging, frame 233 *outline*; thrum, list, selvage; hem, hemline, border; purfling 844 *pattern*; binding, piping; basque, fringe, frill, ruffle, flounce, furbelow, valance 844 *trimming*; crenation, milling 260 *notch*; deckle edge, wavy edge, scallop, picot, purl 251 *coil*.

Adj. *marginal*, border, skirting, marginated; riverine, riparian, coastal; riverside, roadside, wayside; labial, labiated; edged, trimmed, bordered.

Vb. *hem*, edge, border, trim, fringe, purl; mill, crenellate 260 *notch*; bound, confine 236 *limit*.

See: **69**, 192, 194, 199, 233, 235, **236**, 239, 250, 251, 254, 260, 263, 344, 844.

235 Enclosure

N. *enclosure*, envelope, case 194 *receptacle*; wrapper 226 *wrapping*; girdle, ring, perimeter, circumference, periphery 233 *outline*; surround, frame, picture-f.; enceinte, precinct, close; cloister, courtyard 185 *place*; reserve 883 *seclusion*; lot, holding, claim 184 *territory*; fold, pen, pinfold, sheepfold, shippen, sty 369 *cattle pen*; stockyard, croft 370 *farm*; garth, park 370 *garden*; compound, yard, pound, paddock, field; car park 192 *stable*; corral, kraal, stockade, zareba, boma, circumvallation, lines 713 *defences*; net, trawl 222 *network*; lobster pot 542 *trap*; cell, box, cage 748 *prison*.

fence, ring f., barbed-wire f., electric f., chain-link f. 222 *network*; hurdle, wooden fence, picket f., sunk f., ha-ha, hedge, privet h., quickset h., hedgerow, espalier; rails, balustrade, banisters, paling, railing, taffrail; pale, wall, boundary w.; moat, dike, ditch, fosse, trench, vallum, curtain wall 713 *defences*.

barrier, wall, cavity w., brick w., dry-stone w. 231 *partition*; soundproofing, double-glazing 660 *protection*; barricade, cordon, pale; balustrade, parapet; turnstile 702 *obstacle*; palisade, stockade 713 *fort*; portcullis, gate, door, bolt, bar 264 *closure*.

Vb. *enclose*, fence in, cordon, cordon off, surround, wall; pen, hem, ring 232 *circumscribe*; cloister, immure, cage 747 *imprison*; wrap, lap, enwrap, enfold, fold up 261 *fold*; fold in one's arms, hug, embrace 889 *caress*; frame, set, mount, box.

See: 184, 185, 192, **194**, 222, **226**, 231, **232**, **233**, 261, 264, 369, 370, 542, 660, 702, 713, 747, 748, 883, 889.

236 Limit

N. *limit*, limitation 747 *restriction*, 468 *qualification*; definition, delimitation, demarcation 783 *apportionment*; limiting factor, upper limit, ceiling, high-water mark 213 *summit*; lower limit, threshold, low-water mark 214 *base*; legal limit, Plimsoll line; saturation point 54 *completeness*; utmost, uttermost, extreme, furthest point, farthest reach, ne plus ultra, pole 69 *extremity*; ends of the earth, Ultima Thule, Pillars of Hercules 199 *farness*; terminus, terminal 69 *end*; goal, target, winning post, touch, touchline, home, base 617 *objective*; turning point 137 *crisis*; point of no return, Rubicon 599 *resolution*; limit of endurance, tolerance, capacity, end of one's tether; physical limit, outside edge, perimeter, periphery, circumference 233 *outline*; tidemark, sea line 344 *shore*; landmark, boundary stone; milestone 27 *degree*; kerb, kerbstone 624 *road*; metes and bounds, bourne, boundary, verge; frontier, border, marches 234 *edge*; national frontier, state boundary; three-mile limit; line, demarcation l., international date l., divide, parting 231 *partition*; horizon, equator, terminator; deadline, time limit, term 110 *period*; ultimatum 900 *threat*; speed limit 278 *slowness*; sound barrier.

Adj. *limited*, definite, conterminous, conterminal; limitable, finite; limitative, limitary, terminal; frontier, border, borderline, bordering, boundary.

Vb. *limit*, bound, border, edge 234 *hem*; top 213 *crown*; define, confine, condition 468 *qualify*; restrict, stint 747 *restrain*; encompass, beat the bounds 232 *circumscribe*; draw the line, delimit, demarcate, stake out; mark out, chalk o. 547 *mark*.

Adv. *thus far*, so far, thus far and no further; between the tidemarks, on the borderline.

See: 27, 54, **69**, 110, 137, 199, 213, 214, 231, 232, **233**, **234**, 278, 344, 468, 547, 599, 617, 624, 747, 783, 900.

237 Front

N. *front*, fore, forefront 64 *precedence*; forepart; prefix, frontispiece; forelock 259 *hair*; forecourt, anteroom, entrance 263 *doorway*; foreground, proscenium 200 *nearness*; anteriority 119 *priority*; front rank, first line, front l., firing l.; forward line, centre forward; avant-garde, vanguard, van, advance guard; spearhead, bridgehead 712 *attacker*; outpost, scout; forerunner, pioneer 66 *precursor*.

face, frontage, façade, fascia; face of a coin, obverse, head; right side, outer s., recto; front view, front elevation; sinciput 213 *head*; brow, forehead, glabella; chin, physiognomy, metoposcopy, features, visage, countenance, phiz, phizog, mug, mush, kisser, dial, clock 445 *feature*; prominent feature, nose, snout, conk 254 *protuberance*.

prow, nose, beak, rostrum, figurehead; bow, bows; bowsprit; jib, foremast, forecastle, fo'c'sle, forestay, forepeak 275 *ship*.

Adj. *frontal*, fore, forward, front, obverse; full frontal, head-on, oncoming, facing 240 *opposite*; anterior, prefixed 64 *preceding*.

Vb. *be in front*, stand in front etc. adv.; front, confront, face, face up to 240 *be opposite*; breast, stem, brave; bend forwards, lean f. 220 *be oblique*; come to the front, come to the fore, forge ahead, take the lead, head 283 *precede*.

Adv. *in front*, before, in advance, in the lead, in the van, vanward; ahead, right a., infra, further on 199 *beyond*; far ahead, coastward, landward; before one's face, before one's eyes; face to face, vis-à-vis; in the foreground, in the forefront; head first, head foremost; feet first, feet foremost.

See: 3, **64**, **66**, 119, 199, 200, 213, 220, 240, 254, 259, 263, 275, 283, 445, 712.

238 Rear

N. *rear*, rearward, afterpart, back end, tail end, stern 69 *extremity*; tailpiece, heel, colophon; coda 412 *musical piece*; tail, brush, scut, pigtail 67 *sequel*; wake, train 67 *retinue*; last place, rear rank, back seat 35 *inferiority*; rearguard 67 *successor*; subsequence 120 *posteriority*; background, backdrop 594 *stage set*; hinterland, depths, far corner 199 *distance*; behind, backstage, back side; reverse side, wrong s., verso 240 *contraposition*; reverse, other side, flip side; back door, back entrance, postern 263 *doorway*; back (of the body), dorsum, chine; backbone, spine, rachis 218 *prop*; back of the neck, scruff of the n., nape, scruff, short hairs; back of the head, occiput 213 *head*.

buttocks, backside, behind, derrière, posterior, posteriors, cheeks; bottom, seat, sit-me-down; bum, arse, ass, fanny; rear, stern, tail; hindquarters, croup, crupper; hips, haunches, hams, hunkers; rump, loin; dorsal region, lumbar r., small of the back, lower back, coccyx; fundament, anus.

poop, stern, stern-sheets, afterpart, quarter, counter, rudderpost, rudder, rearmast, mizzenmast 275 *ship*.

Adj. *back*, rear, postern; posterior, after, hind, hinder, hindermost, rearmost, tail-end; bent back, backswept 253 *convex*; reverse 240 *opposite*; placed last 35 *inferior*; spinal, vertebral, retral, dorsal, lumbar; anal; caudal, caudate.

Vb. *be behind*, stand b.; back on, back; back up 703 *aid*; follow, bring up the rear 65 *come after*; lag, trail, drop behind, fall astern 278 *move slowly*; tail, shadow, dog 619 *pursue*; follow at heel 284 *follow*; bend backwards, lean b. 220 *be oblique*.

Adv. *rearward*, behind, back of; in the rear, in the ruck; at the back, in the background; behind one's back; behind the scenes; after, aftermost, sternmost; aft, abaft, astern, aback; to the rear, hindward, backward, retro-; supra, above; overleaf; on the heels of, at the tail of, at the back of, close behind; one behind the other, in tandem; back to back.

See: 35, 65, **67**, **69**, 120, 199, 213, 218, 220, 240, 253, 263, 275, 278, **284**, 412, 594, 619, 703.

239 Laterality

N. *laterality*, sidedness; side movement 317 *oscillation*; sidestep 282 *deviation*; sideline, side, bank 234 *edge*; coast 344 *shore*; siding, side entrance, side door; gable, gable-end; broadside; beam; quarter 238 *poop*; flank, ribs, pleura; wing, fin, hand; cheek, jowl, chops, chaps, gills; side whiskers 259 *hair*; temples, side-face, half-face; profile, side elevation; lee, lee side, leeward; weatherside, windward 281 *direction*; orientation, east, Orient, Levant; west, Occident 281 *compass point*; off side, on s., near s. 241 *dextrality*, 242 *sinistrality.*

Adj. *lateral*, laparo-; side 234 *marginal*; sidelong, glancing; parietal, buccal; costal, pleural, winglike, aliform; flanking, skirting; flanked, sided; manysided, multilateral, bilateral, trilateral, quadrilateral; collateral 219 *parallel*; moving sideways, edging, sidling; eastern, eastward, easterly, orient, oriental, auroral, Levantine; west, western, westerly, westward, occidental, Hesperian 281 *directed*.

Vb. *flank*, side, edge, skirt, border 234 *hem*; coast, move sideways, passage, sidle; sideslip, sidestep 282 *deviate*; extend sideways, deploy, outflank 306 *overstep*.

Adv. *sideways*, crabwise, laterally; askance, asquint 220 *obliquely*; half-face, in profile; sidelong, broadside on; on one side, abreast, abeam, alongside; aside, beside; by the side of, side by side, cheek by jowl 200 *near*; to windward, to leeward, alee; coastwise; right and left; on her beam ends.

See: 200, 219, 220, 234, 238, 241, 242, 259, 281, 282, 306, 317, 344.

240 Contraposition

N. *contraposition*, antithesis, opposition, antipodes 14 *contrariety*; frontage 281 *direction*; opposite side, other s.; reverse, back 238 *rear*; polarity, polarization; opposite poles, North and South; crosscurrent, headwind 704 *opposition*; reversal, inverse 221 *inversion*.

Adj. *opposite*, contrapositive, reverse, inverse 221 *inverted*; contrary, subcontrary 14 *contrary*; facing, fronting, confronting, oncoming 237 *frontal*; diametrically opposite, antipodal, antipodean; polarized, polar; antarctic, arctic, northern, septentrional, Boreal, southern, austral 281 *directed*.

Vb. *be opposite*, - facing etc. adj.; stand opposite, lie o.; subtend; face, confront 237 *be in front*; run counter 182 *counteract*; oppose, contrapose.

Adv. *against*, over the way, over against; poles asunder; facing, face to face, vis-à-vis; back to back; on the other side, overleaf; contrariwise, vice versa.

See: 14, 182, **221**, 237, 238, 281, 704.

241 Dextrality

N. *dextrality*, right hand, right-handedness; ambidexterity, ambidextrousness 694 *skill*; right, offside, starboard; right-hand page, recto; right wing, right-winger; dextral, ambidexter.

Adj. *dextral*, dexter, dextro-; right-hand, starboard, offside; right-handed, dextrous, ambidextral, ambidextrous 694 *skilful*; dextrorse, dextrorsal; dextrorotatory; right-wing.

Adv. *dextrally*, on the right; right-handedly, ambidextrously; dextrorsely; to the right, astarboard.

See: 694.

242 Sinistrality

N. *sinistrality*, left hand, left-handedness; left, near side, on s.; larboard, port; verso; left wing, left-winger; sinistral, southpaw.

Adj. *sinistral*, sinister, sinistrous, left, left-handed; onside, nearside, sinistrorse, sinistrorsal; laevorotatory.

Adv. *sinistrally*, on the left, aport, offside; leftwards; sinisterwise.

Section three: Form

243 Form

N. *form*, substantial f., Platonic f., idea; Gestalt 52 *whole*; essence 3 *substance*; significant form, inner f., inscape 5 *character*; art form 551 *art*, 593 *verse form*; word form 557 *linguistics*; shape, turn, lines, architecture; formation, conformation, configuration, fashion, style, design 331 *structure*; contour, silhouette, relief, profile, frame, outline; figure, cut, set, trim, build, cut of one's jib, lineament 445 *feature*; physiognomy 237 *face*; look, expression, appearance 445 *mien*; posture, attitude, stance; get-up, turnout, rig; type, kind, pattern, stamp, cast, mould, blank 23 *prototype*; format, typeface, typography 587 *print*; morphology, isomorphism.

formation, forming, shaping, creation 164 *production*; expression, formulation 62 *arrangement*; designing, patterning 844 *ornamental art*; weaving, knitting 222 *network*; tailoring 844 *needlework*; throwing 381 *pottery*; moulding 554 *sculpture*; turning, joinery 694 *skill*; etymology, word-formation 557 *linguistics*.

Adj. *formed*, created etc. vb.; receiving form, plastic, fictile; sculptured, carved, moulded, thrown, turned, rounded, squared; shaped, fashioned, fully f., styled, stylized; ready-made, off the peg; matured, ready 669 *prepared*; solid, concrete 324 *dense*; dimensional, two-d., three-d.; isomorphous.

formative, giving form, formal; plastic, glyptic, architectural 331 *structural*.

Vb. *form*, create, make 164 *produce*; formalize, shape, fashion, figure, pattern; throw (pots), blow (glass); turn, round, square; cut, tailor; cut out, silhouette 233 *outline*; sketch, draw 551 *represent*; model, carve, whittle, chisel 554 *sculpt*; hew, rough-h. 46 *cut*; mould, cast; stamp, coin, mint; hammer out, block o., knock o., punch o.; carpenter, mason; forge, smith; knead, work, work up into; construct, build, frame 310 *elevate*; express, formulate, put into shape, pull into s., lick into s., knock into s.

See: 3, 5, 23, 46, 52, 62, **164**, 222, 233, 237, 310, 324, **331**, 381, **445**, 551, 554, 557, 587, 593, 669, 694, 844.

244 Amorphism: absence of form

N. *amorphism*, absence of form; prime matter; confusion, chaos 61 *disorder*; amorphousness, lack of shape, shapelessness; lack of definition, vagueness, fuzziness; rawness, uncouthness 670 *undevelopment*; raw material 631 *materials*; rough diamond; disfigurement, defacement, mutilation, deformation, deformity 246 *distortion*.

Adj. *amorphous*, formless, unformed, inchoate; liquid 335 *fluid*; shapeless, featureless, characterless; messy, chaotic 61 *orderless*; undefined, ill-defined, lacking definition, indistinct, nebulous, vague, fuzzy, blurred 419 *shadowy*; unfashioned, unshapen, unformed, unmade; embryonic 68 *beginning*; raw, unlicked 670 *immature*; unhewn, in the rough 55 *incomplete*; rude, uncouth, barbaric 699 *artless*; rugged 259 *rough*; unshapely 842 *unsightly*; malformed, misshapen, gnarled 246 *deformed*.

Vb. *deform*, deprive of form, unmake, unshape 165 *destroy*; dissolve, melt 337 *liquefy*; knock out of shape, batter 46 *break*; grind, pulp 332 *pulverize*; warp, twist 246 *distort*; deface, disfigure 842 *make ugly*; mutilate, truncate 655 *impair*; jumble, disorder 63 *derange*.

See: 46, 55, 61, 63, 68, 165, 246, 259, 332, 335, 337, 419, 631, 655, 670, 699, 842.

245 Symmetry: regularity of form

N. *symmetry*, bilateral s., radial s., correspondence, proportion 12 *correlation*; balance 28 *equilibrium*; regularity, evenness 16 *uniformity*; arborescence, branching, ramification 219 *parallelism*; shapeliness, regular features, classic f. 841 *beauty*; harmony, congruity, eurhythmy 24 *agreement*; rhythm 141 *periodicity*; finish 646 *perfection*.

Adj. *symmetrical*, balanced 28 *equal*; proportioned, well-p. 12 *correlative*; rhythmical, eurhythmic, harmonious, congruous 24 *agreeing*; congruent, coextensive; corresponding 219 *parallel*; analogous 18 *similar*; smooth, even 16 *uniform*; squared, rounded, round, evensided, isosceles, equilateral 81 *regular*; crystalline; arborescent, dendriform, branching, ramose; formal, classic, comely 841 *shapely*; undeformed, undistorted, unwarped, well set-up 249 *straight*; finished, complete in all its parts 54 *complete*.

See: 12, **16**, 18, **24**, **28**, 54, 81, 141, 219, 249, 646, 841.

246 Distortion: irregularity of form

N. *distortion*, asymmetry, disproportion, disproportionateness, misproportion, want of symmetry 10 *unrelatedness*; imbalance, disequilibrium 29 *inequality*; lop-sidedness, crookedness, skewness 220 *obliquity*; anamorphosis, projection, Mercator's p. 551 *map*; contortion, twisting; thrust, stress, strain, shear; bias, warp; buckle, bend, screw, twist 251 *convolution*; facial distortion, grimace, moue, snarl, rictus 547 *gesture*.

deformity, malformation, monstrosity, abortion 84 *abnormality*; curvature of the spine 248 *curvature*; teratogeny; clubfoot, rickets, valgus 845 *blemish*; ugliness 842 *eyesore*; teratology.

Adj. *distorted*, contorted etc. vb.; irregular, asymmetric, scalene, unsymmetrical, disproportionate 17 *nonuniform*; weighted, biased; not true, not straight; anamorphous, grotesque; out of shape, warped 244 *amorphous*; buckled, twisted, gnarled 251 *convoluted*; wry, awry, askew, crazy, crooked, cock-eyed, on one side 220 *oblique*; slouched, slumped; grimacing, scowling, snarling.

deformed, ugly 842 *unsightly*; misproportioned, ill-proportioned; defective 647 *imperfect*; ill-made, misshapen; hunchbacked, humpbacked, crook-backed, crooked as a ram's horn; bandy, bandy-legged, bow-legged, knock-kneed; pigeon-toed, splay-footed, club-footed, web-footed; round-shouldered, pigeon-chested; snub-nosed, hare-lipped 845 *blemished*; stunted, stumpy 204 *short*; haggard, gaunt 206 *lean*; bloated 195 *fleshy*.

Vb. *distort*, disproportion, weight, bias; contort, screw, twist, knot 251 *twine*; bend, warp 251 *crinkle*; spring, buckle, crumple; strain, sprain, skew, wrest, torture, rack 63 *derange*; misshape, botch 244 *deform*; mangle, batter, knock out of shape 655 *impair*; pervert 552 *misrepresent*; misconstrue 521 *misinterpret*; writhe 251 *wriggle*; wince, grimace, make faces, mop and mow 547 *gesticulate*; snarl, scowl, frown 893 *be sullen*.

See: 10, 17, 29, 63, **84**, 195, 204, 206, **220**, **244**, 248, 251, 521, 547, 551, 552, 647, 655, 842, **845**, 893.

247 Angularity

N. *angularity*, angulation, aduncity, hookedness, crotchet, bracket, crook, hook; bend, scythe, sickle, scimitar 248 *curvature*; chevron, zigzag 220 *obliquity*; V-shape, elbow, knee, knee-joint; shoulder blade, withers 253 *camber*; knuckle, ankle, groin 45 *joint*; crutch, crotch, fluke 222 *cross*; fork, bifurcation, crossways, branching 222 *crossing*; quoin, corner, nook, niche, recess, oriel 194 *compartment*; nose, Roman n., hook n. 254 *protuberance*; wedge, arrowhead 256 *sharp point*; broad arrow, cusp; flexure 261 *fold*; indentation 260 *notch*.

angle, right a., acute a., obtuse a., salient a., reentrant a., spherical a., solid a., dihedral a.

angular measure, goniometry, trigonometry, altimetry; angular elevation, angular distance, angular velocity; zenith distance; second, degree, minute; radian; goniometer, altimeter; clinometer, level, theodolite; transit circle; sextant, quadrant; protractor, set square.

angular figure, triangle, isosceles t., equilateral t., scalene t., spherical t., trigon; parallelogram, rectangle, square, quadrangle, quadrature; quadrilateral, lozenge, diamond; rhomb, rhombus, rhomboid; trapezium, trapezoid; tetragon, polygon, pentagon, hexagon, heptagon, octagon, decagon, dodecahedron, icosahedron; cube, pyramid, wedge; prism, parallelepiped; Platonic bodies.

Adj. *angular*, hooked, uncinate, hook-nosed, aquiline, rostrate; unciform, falciform, falcate 248 *curved*; angled, sharp-a., cornered; staggered, crooked, zigzag 220 *oblique*; jagged, serrated, crinkled 260 *notched*; jointed, geniculate, elbowed; akimbo; knock-kneed; crotched, forked, bifurcate, furcate, furcular, V-shaped.

angulated, triangular, trigonal, trilateral; wedge-shaped, cuneate, cuneiform, fusiform; rectangular, right-angled, orthogonal; square, square-shaped, foursquare, quadrangular, quadrilateral, four-sided, squared; diamond-shaped, lozenge-s.; trapezoidal; multilateral, polygonal, decahedral, polyhedral; cubical, rhomboidal, pyramidal.

Vb. *make angular*, angle, make corners, corner; hook, crook, bend 248 *make curved*; wrinkle, fold 251 *crinkle*; zigzag 220 *be oblique*; fork, bifurcate, divaricate, branch, ramify 294 *diverge*; go off at a tangent 282 *deviate*.

See: 45, 194, **220**, 222, **248**, 251, 253, 254, 256, 260, 261, 282, 294.

248 Curvature

N. *curvature*, curvation; incurvature, incurvation, inward curve 255 *concavity*; outward curve 253 *convexity*; flexure, flexion, inflection, bending 261 *fold*; arcuation, sweep; bowing, stooping 311 *obeisance*; bending down, deflection; turning away, swerve, detour 282 *deviation*; downward bend 309 *descent*; recurvature, retroflexion 221 *inversion*; curling, curliness, sinuosity 251 *convolution*; aduncity 247 *angularity*; curvature of the spine 246 *deformity*.

curve, slight c. 253 *camber*; elbow 247 *angularity*; turn, bend, sharp b., hairpin b., U-turn; horseshoe, oxbow; bay, bight 345 *gulf*; figure of eight 250 *loop*; ogee, S-shape; tracery, curl 251 *convolution*; festoon, swag 844 *pattern*; bow, Cupid's b., rainbow 250 *arc*; arch, ogee a., spring of an a., arcade, vault 253 *dome*; sickle, scimitar, crescent, lunula, half-moon, meniscus, lens; trajectory, catenary, parabola, hyperbola, conic section; caustic, cardioid, conchoid; arch (of the foot), instep; swan neck.

Adj. *curved*, cambered etc. vb.; flexed, bent 220 *oblique*; bowed, stooping 311 *lowered*; curviform, bowlike, curvilineal, curvilinear; rounded, curvaceous, curvy, bosomy, wavy, billowy 251 *undulatory*; aquiline, hook-nosed, parrot-beaked 247 *angular*; rostrate, beaked, beaklike, bill-shaped; bent back, recurved, recurvate, retroflex; retroussé, turned-up, tip-tilted 221 *inverted*; circumflex; ogival, vaulted 253 *arched*; bow-legged 246 *deformed*; down-curving 309 *descending*; hooked, adunc, falciform, falcate; semicircular 250 *round*; crescent, lunular, lunate, lunar, semilunar, horned; meniscal, lenticular; reniform; cordiform, cordate, heart-shaped, bell-s., pear-s.

Vb. *be curved*, - bent etc. adj.; curve, swerve, bend, loop, camber, arch, sweep, sag, swag, give, give in the middle 217 *hang*; reenter, recurve; intort 251 *twine*; curvet 312 *leap*.

make curved, bend, crook 247 *make angular*; turn, round 250 *make round*; bend in, incurvate, inflect; bend back, recurve, retroflect 221 *invert*; bend over, bend down, bow, incline 311 *stoop*; turn over 261 *fold*; turn away 282 *deflect*; arcuate, arch, arch over; coil 251 *twine*; loop, curl, wave 251 *crinkle*; loop the loop, make figures of eight.

See: 217, 220, 221, 246, 247, **250**, **251**, **253**, **255**, 261, 282, 309, 311, 312, 345, 844.

249 Straightness

N. *straightness*, directness, rectilinearity; perpendicularity 215 *verticality*; inflexibility, rigidity 326 *hardness*; chord, radius 203 *line*; straight line, right l., direct l., beeline; Roman road; straight stretch, straight, reach; short cut 200 *short distance*.

Adj. *straight*, direct, even, right, true; in a line, linear; straight-lined, rectilinear, rectilineal; perpendicular 215 *vertical*; unbent, unwarped, undistorted; stiff, inflexible 326 *rigid*; uncurled, straightened, unfrizzed, dekinked; dead straight, undeviating, unswerving, undeflected, on the beam, straight as an arrow.

Vb. *be straight*, - direct etc. adj.; steer straight, follow the great circle; go straight, have no turning, not incline, not bend, not turn, not deviate, not deviate to either side, turn neither right nor left, make a beeline for.

straighten, make straight, align; iron out 216 *flatten*; unbend (a bow); uncross (legs); dekink, uncurl 258 *smooth*; stretch tight; unwrap 62 *unravel*; uncoil, unroll, unfurl, unfold 316 *evolve*.

Adv. *straight on*, directly, as the crow flies 281 *towards*; straight, plumb.

See: 62, 200, 203, **215**, **216**, 258, 281, 316, 326.

250 Circularity: simple circularity

N. *circularity*, orbicularity, roundness, rondure 252 *rotundity*; annularity.

circle, full c., circumference 233 *outline*; great circle, equator; orb, annulus; roundel, roundlet; areola; plate, saucer; round, disc, disk, discus; coin, button, sequin; washer, hoop, ring, quoit; eye, iris; eyelet, loophole, keyhole 263 *orifice*; circular course, circuit, circus, roundabout; zodiac; fairy ring; smoke ring.

loop, figure of eight 251 *convolution*; bow, knot; ringlet, curl 259 *hair*; circlet, bracelet, armlet, torque 844 *finery*; crown, coronet 743 *regalia*; corona, aureole, halo; wreath, garland 228 *headgear*; collar, neckband, necklace 228 *neckwear*; band, cordon, sash, girdle 228 *belt*; baldric, bandolier 47 *girdle*; lasso, lariat 47 *halter*.

wheel, pulley, castor 315 *rotator*; hub, felloe, tyre; rubber tyre, tubeless t., inner tube, outer t.; roller 252 *rotundity*.

arc, semicircle, half-circle, hemicycle, lunette; half-moon, crescent, rainbow 248 *curve*; sector, quadrant, sextant; ellipse, oval, ovule; ellipsoid, cycloid, epicycloid.

orbit, cycle, epicycle, circuit, ecliptic; circulation 314 *circuition*.

Adj. *round*, rounded, circular, cyclic, discoid; orbicular, ringlike, ringed, annular, annulate, annulose, semicircular, hemicyclic; oval, ovate, elliptic, ovoid, egg-shaped, crescent-s., pear-s. 248 *curved*; cycloidal, spherical 252 *rotund*.

Vb. *make round*, - oval etc. adj.; round, turn.

go round, girdle, encircle 230 *surround*; describe a circle 233 *outline*; move round, circulate, orbit, go into o. 314 *circle*.

See: 47, 228, 230, **233**, **248**, **251**, **252**, 259, 263, 314, 315, 743, 844.

251 Convolution: complex circularity

N. *convolution*, involution, circumvolution; intricacy; flexuosity, anfractuosity, sinuosity, sinuousness; tortuosity, tortuousness, torsion, intorsion; reticulation 222 *network*; twine, twist 208 *fibre*; ripple 350 *wave*; wrinkle, corrugation 261 *fold*; indentation, ragged edge 260 *notch*; waviness, undulation, ogee 248 *curve*.

coil, roll, twist; turban, puggaree 228 *headgear*; Turk's head 47 *ligature*; spiral, helix; screw, screw-thread, worm, corkscrew; spring, wound s., coiled s.; whorl, snail-shell, ammonite; whirlpool 350 *eddy*, 315 *vortex*; verticil, tendril 366 *plant*; scollop, scallop, scalloped edge 234 *edging*; kink, curl; ringlet, lovelock 259 *hair*; scroll, volute, fiddlehead, flourish, twirl, curlicue, squiggle 844 *ornamentation*.

meandering, meander, winding course, crankiness; winding, windings and turnings, twists and turns, circumbendibus 282 *deviation*; labyrinth, maze 61 *complexity*; switchback, zigzag 220 *obliquity*.

serpent, snake, eel, worm 365 *reptile*; wriggler, looper, sidewinder.

Adj. *convoluted*, twisted, contorted, intorted 246 *distorted*; tortile, cranky, ambagious; winding, looping, twining, anfractuous, sinuous, tortuous, flexuous; indented, ragged 260 *notched*; crumpled, buckled 261 *folded*.

labyrinthine, mazy, Daedalian, meandering, serpentine; twisting, turning 314 *circuitous*.

snaky, serpentine, serpentiform, anguine, eel-like, anguilliform, wormlike, vermiform, vermicular; squiggly, squirming, wriggling, peristaltic; S-shaped, sigmoid.

undulatory, undulating, rolling, heaving; up-and-down, switchback; crinkle-crankle (wall), wavy, curly, frizzy, kinky, crinkly; crimped, curled, permed; scolloped, wrinkled, corrugated, indented, ragged 260 *notched*; Flamboyant, Decorated.

coiled, spiral, helical, cochlear; convolute, involute, turbinate, whorled, scroll-like, verticillate; wound, wound up; coiling, spiralling.

intricate, involved, complicated, knotted 61 *complex*.

Vb. *twine*, twist, twirl, roll, coil, corkscrew, convolute, spiral 315 *rotate*; wreathe, entwine 222 *enlace*; be convuluted, twisted etc. adj.; turn and twist, bend 248 *be curved*.

crinkle, crimp, frizz, crisp, curl; wave, undulate, ripple, popple; wrinkle, corrugate 261 *fold*; indent, scallop, scollop 260 *notch*; crumple 246 *distort*.

meander, loop, snake, crankle, twist and turn, zigzag, corkscrew. **See** *twine*.

wriggle, writhe, squirm, shimmy, shake; move sinuously, worm.

Adv. *in and out*, round about.

See: 47, 61, 208, 220, **222**, 228, 234, 246, **248**, 259, 260, 261, 282, 314, **315**, 350, 365, 366, 844.

252 Rotundity

N. *rotundity*, rondure, roundness, orbicularity 250 *circularity*; sphericity, sphericality, spheroidicity; globularity, globosity, cylindricity, cylindricality, gibbosity, gibbousness 253 *convexity*.

sphere, globe, spheroid, prolate s., oblate s., ellipsoid, globoid, geoid; hollow sphere, bladder; balloon 276 *airship*; soap bubble 355 *bubble*; ball, football, pelota, wood (bowls), billiard ball, marble, ally, taw; cannonball, bullet, shot, pellet; bead, pill, pea, boll, oakapple, puffball, spherule, globule; drop, droplet, dewdrop, inkdrop, blot; vesicle, bulb, onion, knob, pommel 253 *swelling*; boulder, rolling stone; hemisphere, hump, mushroom 253 *dome*; round head, bullet h., turnip h.

cylinder, roll, rolypoly; roller, rolling pin; round, rung, rundle; round tower, column; bole, trunk, stalk; pipe, drainpipe 263 *tube*; funnel, chimneypot; round box, hat b., pillbox; drum, barrel.

cone, conoid; shadow cone, penumbra; sugarloaf 253 *dome*; cornet, horn 194 *cup*; top, spinning t., peg t.; pear shape, bell s., egg s.

Adj. *rotund*, orbicular 250 *round*; spherical, sphery, spherular; globular, global, globose, globoid; round-headed, bullet-headed, brachycephalic; beady, beadlike, moniliform; hemispherical; spheroidal, ovoid, oviform, egg-shaped; cylindrical, columnar, tubular; cigar-shaped 256 *tapering*; conic, conical; conoid, conoidal; bell-shaped, campanulate, napiform, turnip-shaped; pyriform, pear-shaped, heart-shaped; humped, gibbous; bulbous 253 *convex*; pot-bellied 195 *fleshy*; sphered, balled, rolled up.

Vb. *round*, make spherical; form into a

sphere, form into a globe etc.n.; sphere, globe, ball, bead; balloon 253 *be convex*; coil up, roll, roll up 315 *rotate*.

See: 194, 195, **250**, **253**, 256, 263, 276, 315, 355.

253 Convexity

N. *convexity*, convexness; arcuation, arching 248 *curvature*; sphericity 252 *rotundity*; gibbosity, bulginess, humpiness, bulge, bump; projection, protrusion, protuberance 254 *prominence*; excrescency, tumescence, tumidity, swelling 197 *dilation*; paunchiness 195 *bulk*; pimpliness, wartiness; double convexity, lenticular form; lens 442 *optical device*.

swelling, bump, lump, bulge, growth, excrescence, gall, knot, nodosity, node, nodule; exostosis, apophysis, condyle, knuckle; oedema, emphysema; sarcoma, tumour; bubo, goitre; Adam's apple; bunion, corn, blain, wart, wen, verruca; boil, carbuncle, furuncle, sty, pimple, papula, blister, vesicle; polyp, adenoids, haemorrhoids, piles; proud flesh, weal, welt; cauliflower ear; drop 252 *sphere*; air bubble, soap b. 355 *bubble*; boss, torus, knob, nub, nubble; bulb, button, bud; belly, potbelly, corporation, paunch 195 *bulk*; billow, swell 350 *wave*.

bosom, bust, breast, breasts; boobs, bristols, knockers, tits; mamma, mamilla, papilla, nipple, pap, dug, teat, udder; thorax, chest; cuirass, breastplate.

dome, cupola, vault 226 *roof*; beehive, skep; brow, forehead 237 *face*; skull, cranium, bald head 213 *head*; hemisphere, arch of heaven; anticline, hog's back, mound; hummock, hillock, mamelon, sugarloaf 209 *small hill*; molehill, mushroom, umbrella.

earthwork, tumulus; tell 548 *monument*; barrow, round b., long b.; hill fort, circumvallation 713 *defences*; cursus, embankment, levee.

camber, gentle curve 248 *curve*; arch, bow, rainbow; hump, humpback, hunchback 246 *deformity*; shoulders, calf, elbow 247 *angularity*.

Adj. *convex*, protruding 254 *projecting*; hemispherical, domelike 252 *rotund*; lentiform, lenticular; biconvex, gibbous, humpy, lumpy; curvaceous, bosomy, billowy 248 *curved*; billowing, bulging, bellying, ballooning, bouffant; swelling, swollen 197 *expanded*; bloated, potbellied, barrel-chested 195 *fleshy*; turgid, tumid, tumescent, tumorous, tuberous; nubbly 259 *rough*; verrucose, warty, papulose, pimply; blistery, vesicular.

arched, arcuate, cambered, bowed 248 *curved*; rounded; hillocky, hummocky, anticlinal; mammiform.

Vb. *be convex*, camber, arch, bow; swell, belly, bulge, bag, balloon; make convex, emboss, chase, beat out 254 *jut*.

See: **195**, **197**, 209, 213, 226, 237, 246, 247, **248**, **252**, **254**, 259, 350, 355, 442, 548, 713.

254 Prominence

N. *prominence*, eminence 209 *high land*; conspicuousness 443 *visibility*; solar prominence, solar flare, tongue, tongue of flame.

projection, salient, salient angle 247 *angle*; outstretched arm, forefinger, index f.; bowsprit, cathead, outrigger; tongue of land, spit, point, mull, promontory, foreland, headland, naze, ness 344 *land*; peninsula 349 *island*; spur, foothill; jetty, mole, breakwater, groyne, pier 662 *shelter*; outwork 713 *fortification*; pilaster, buttress 218 *prop*; shelf, sill, ledge, soffit, balcony; eaves 226 *roof*; overhang, rake 220 *obliquity*; flange, lip 234 *edge*; nozzle, spout; tang, tongue; tenon 45 *joint*; snag, stump, outcrop; landmark 209 *high structure*.

protuberance, bump 253 *swelling*; prominent feature; nose, snout, schnozzle, conk; bill, beak, rostrum; muzzle, proboscis, trunk; antenna 378 *feeler*; chin, mentum, jaw, brow, beetle brow 237 *face*; figurehead 237 *prow*; horn, antler 256 *sharp point*.

relievo, relief, basso relievo, alto r., mezzo r., low relief, bas r., high r.; embossment 844 *ornamental art*; cameo 554 *sculpture*.

Adj. *projecting*, jutting, prominent, salient, bold; protuberant, protruding, bulging, popping etc. vb.; bug-eyed, goggle-e., pop-e.; toothy; beetle-browed, overhung; underhung, undershot; repoussé, raised, embossed, in relief, in high r., in low r.; ridged, nobbly 259 *rough*.

Vb. *jut*, project, protrude, pout, pop, pop out, start o.; stand out, stick o., poke o., hang o. 443 *be visible*; bristle up, prick up, cock up 259 *roughen*; shoot up, swell up 197 *expand*; overhang, hang over, beetle

over, impend 217 *hang*.
See: 45, 197, 209, **217**, 218, 220, 226, 234, 237, 247, **253**, 256, **259**, 344, 349, 378, 443, 554, 662, 713, 844.

255 Concavity

N. *concavity*, concaveness, incurvation, incurvity 248 *curvature*; hollowness 190 *emptiness*; depression, dint, dent, fossa; impression, stamp, imprint, footprint 548 *trace*; intaglio 555 *engraving*; ploughing, furrowing 262 *furrow*; indentation 260 *notch*; gap, lacuna 201 *interval*.
cavity, hollow, niche, nook, cranny, recess, corner 194 *compartment*; hole, den, burrow, warren; chasm, abyss 211 *depth*; cave, cavern, antre; grot, grotto, alcove 194 *arbour*; bowl, cup, saucer, basin, trough 194 *vessel*; sump 649 *sink*; cell, follicle, alveolus, pore 263 *orifice*; dimple, pockmark; saltcellar, armpit; honeycomb, sponge 263 *porosity*; funnel, tunnel 263 *tube*; groove, mortise, socket, pocket 262 *furrow*; antrum, sinus; bay, bight, cove, creek, inlet 345 *gulf*; channel, riverbed, wadi, ditch, moat, canal 351 *conduit*; hole in the ground, dip, depression, pothole, swallowhole, punchbowl, crater, pit.
valley, vale, dale, dell, dingle, combe, cwm, corrie, cirque, U-shaped valley, river valley, strath; glen, dip, depression, slade; ravine, chine, gill, clough, gorge, canyon, gully 201 *gap*.
excavation, dugout, grave, gravepit 364 *tomb*; opencast mining; vertical excavation, shaft, borehole, well, mine, coal m., pit, coal p., colliery, quarry 632 *store*; gallery, working g., adit, sap, trench, burrow, warren; underground railway, tube 263 *tunnel*; archaeological excavation, dig; cutting, cut.
excavator, miner, coal-m., quarrier; archaeologist, digger; dredger, drag-line; sapper, burrower, tunneller; ditcher, gravedigger.
Adj. *concave*, hollow, cavernous; vaulted, arched 248 *curved*; hollowed out, scooped o., dug o.; caved in, stove in; depressed, sunk, sunken; biconcave; spoonlike, saucer-shaped, cupped; capsular, funnel-shaped, infundibular; bell-shaped, campanulate; cellular, socketed, alveolate, dented, dimpled, pockmarked; full of holes, honeycombed; spongy, porous 263 *perforated*.
Vb. *be concave*, retreat, retire, cave in; cup, incurve.
make concave, depress, press in, punch in, stamp, impress; buckle, dent, dint, stave in; crush, push in, beat in; excavate, hollow, dig, spade, delve, scrape, scratch, scrabble, trench, canalize 262 *groove*; mine, sap, undermine, burrow, tunnel, bore; honeycomb, perforate 263 *pierce*; scoop out, hollow o., dig o., gouge o., scratch o. 300 *eject*; hole, pit, pockmark; indent 260 *notch*; sink a shaft, make a hole; cut and cover.
See: 190, 194, 201, 211, **248**, 260, **262**, **263**, 300, 345, 351, 364, 548, 555, 632, 649.

256 Sharpness

N. *sharpness*, acuity, acuteness, acumination, pointedness, sting; serration, saw-edge 260 *notch*; spinosity, thorniness, prickliness; acridity 388 *pungency*.
sharp point, sting, prick, point, cusp 213 *vertex*; nail, tack, staple 47 *fastening*; nib, tag, pin, needle, stylus, bodkin, skewer, spit, broach, brochette; lancet, fleam, awl, gimlet, drill, borer, auger 263 *perforator*; arrow, shaft, bolt, quarrel, arrowhead; barb, fluke, swordpoint, rapier, lance, pike 723 *spear*; fishing spear, gaff, harpoon; dagger, dirk, stiletto 723 *side arms*; spike, caltrop, chevaux-de-frise, barbed wire 713 *defences*; spur, rowel; goad, ankus 612 *incentive*; fork, prong, tine, pick, horn, antler; claw, talon, nails 778 *nippers*; spire, flèche, steeple; peak, crag, arête 213 *summit*.
prickle, thorn, brier, bramble, thistle, nettle, cactus; bristle 259 *hair*; beard, awn, spica, spicule; porcupine, hedgehog; spine, needle, quill.
tooth, tusk, tush, fang; first teeth, milk tooth; canine tooth, eyetooth, incisor, grinder, molar, premolar teeth, wisdom t.; pearls, ivories; dentition, front teeth, back t., cheek t.; set of teeth, denture, false teeth, gold t., plate, bridge; comb, saw; cog, ratchet, sprocket, denticle, denticulation 260 *notch*.
sharp edge, cutting e., edge tool; jagged edge, broken glass; cutlery, steel, razor; blade, razor blade; share, ploughshare, coulter 370 *farm tool*; spade, mattock, trowel, shovel; scythe, sickle, hook, reaping h., billhook; cutter, grass c., lawn mower; scissors, barber's s., pinking s.; shears, clippers, secateurs, surgical knife, scalpel, bistoury; chisel, plane, spoke-

shave, scraper, draw-knife 258 *smoother*; knife, bread-k., carver, carving knife, fish k., slicer, skiver; penknife, sheath k., clasp k., jack k., bowie k.; machete, kris, parang, panga; chopper, cleaver, wedge; hatchet, axe, adze; battleaxe 723 *axe*; sword, broadsword, cutlass, scimitar 723 *side arms*.

sharpener, knife s., pencil s., oilstone, whetstone, grindstone; hone, steel, carborundum, file, strop; emery, emery paper, sandpaper.

Adj. *sharp*, stinging, keen, acute; edged, cutting; swordlike, ensiform; pointed, unblunted; sharp-pointed, cusped, cuspidate, mucronate; barbed, spurred; sagittal, arrowy; spiked, spiky, spiny, spinose, spinous, thorny, brambly, briery, thistly; needlelike, acicular, aciculate; prickly, bristly, bristling, awned, bearded 259 *hairy*; hastate, spear-like; studded, muricated, snaggy, craggy, jagged 259 *rough*; comblike, pectinate 260 *notched*; sharp-edged, knife-e., razor-e.; sharp as a razor, keen as a r., sharp as a needle; sharpened, whetted etc. vb.; sharp-set, razor-sharp.

toothed, odontoid; toothy, brick-toothed; tusky, fanged, dental, denticulate, dentiform; cogged, serrated, saw-edged, emarginate 260 *notched*.

tapering, acuminate, fastigiate, conical, pyramidal 293 *convergent*; spired, spiry; horned, cornuted, corniculate; star-shaped, stellate, stellular; spindle-shaped, fusiform, lance-shaped, lanceolate.

Vb. *be sharp*, - stinging etc. adj.; have a point, prick, sting; bristle with; have an edge, bite 46 *cut*; taper, come to a point, end in a point 293 *converge*.

sharpen, edge, put an edge on, whet, hone, oilstone, grind, file, strop; barb, spur, point, acuminate, spiculate; stud.

See: 46, 47, **213**, 258, **259**, **260**, 263, 293, 370, 388, 612, 713, **723**, 778.

257 Bluntness

N. *bluntness*, flatness, bluffness; curves 258 *smoothness*; rustiness, dullness; toothlessness, lack of bite; blunt instrument, foil; blunt edge, blade, flat.

Adj. *unsharpened*, unwhetted; blunt, blunted, unpointed, obtuse; rusty, dull, dull-edged; edgeless, pointless; lacking bite, toothless, edentate; blunt-nosed, stubby, snub, square; round, rounded, curving 248 *curved*; flat, flattened, bluff.

Vb. *blunt*, make blunt, turn, turn the edge; take off the point, bate (a foil); obtund, dull, rust; draw the teeth 161 *disable*; be blunt, not cut, pull, scrape, tear.

See: 161, 248, 258.

258 Smoothness

N. *smoothness*, evenness etc. adj.; smooth texture, silkiness; silk, satin, velvet, velour; fleeciness, down, swansdown 327 *softness*; smooth hair, sleekness; smooth surface, mahogany, marble, glass, ice; dance floor, ice rink; flatness, levelness, lawn, plumb wicket, bowling green, billiard table 216 *horizontality*; tarmac, asphalt, flags 226 *paving*; levigation, polish, varnish, gloss, glaze, shine, finish; slipperiness, slipway, slide; lubricity, oiliness, greasiness 334 *lubrication*; smooth water, dead w., calm, dead c. 266 *quiescence*.

smoother, roller, garden r., road r., steamroller; bulldozer; rolling pin 216 *flattener*; iron, smoothing-i., flatiron, tailor's goose; mangle, wringer; press, hot p., trouser p.; plane, spokeshave, draw knife 256 *sharp edge*; rake, harrow; comb, brush, hairbrush; sandpaper, emery board; file, nail f.; burnisher, turpentine and beeswax; polish, French p., varnish, enamel 226 *facing*; lubricator, grease, oil, grease gun, oilcan 334 *lubricant*.

Adj. *smooth*, nonfrictional, frictionless, nonadhesive, streamlined; without lumps 16 *uniform*; slithery, slippery, skiddy; lubricious, oily, greasy, buttery, soapy; greased, oiled 334 *lubricated*; polished, shiny, varnished, waxed, enamelled, lacquered, glazed; soft, suave, bland, soothing 177 *lenitive*; smooth-textured, silky, silken, satiny, velvety; downy, woolly 259 *fleecy*; marble, glassy; bald, glabrous, clean-shaven 229 *hairless*; sleek, slick, well-brushed, unruffled; combed, carded, raked, harrowed; unwrinkled, uncrumpled; plane, rolled, even, unbroken, level, flush 216 *flat*; glassy, quiet, calm, c. as a millpond 266 *still*; rounded, waterworn 248 *curved*; edgeless, blunt 257 *unsharpened*; smooth-skinned; smooth-haired; smooth as marble, smooth as glass, smooth as ice, smooth as a baby's bottom, smooth as velvet, satin-smooth; slippery as an eel.

Vb. *smooth*, remove friction, streamline; oil, grease, butter 334 *lubricate*; smoothen, plane, planish, even, level; rake, comb; file, rub down 333 *rub*; roll, calender, press, hot-p., uncrease, iron 216 *flatten*; mow, shave, cut 204 *shorten*; smooth over, smooth down, smarm d., slick d., plaster d.; iron out 62 *unravel*; starch, launder 648 *clean*; shine, burnish 417 *make bright*; levigate, buff, polish, glaze, wax, varnish 226 *coat*; pave, tarmac 226 *overlay*.

go smoothly, glide, float, roll, bowl along, run on rails; slip, slide, skid 265 *be in motion*; skate, ski; feel no friction, coast, freewheel.

See: 16, 62, 177, 204, **216**, 226, 229, 248, 256, 257, 259, 265, 266, 327, 333, **334**, 417, 648.

259 Roughness

N. *roughness*, asperity, harshness; salebrosity, broken ground; rough water, choppiness 350 *wave*; rough air, turbulence 352 *wind*; shattered surface, brokenness, jaggedness, broken glass 256 *sharp edge*; serration, saw edge, deckle e. 260 *notch*; ruggedness, cragginess; sierra 209 *high land*; rough going, dirt road; unevenness, joltiness, bumpiness 17 *nonuniformity*; corrugation, rugosity, ripple, ripple mark, corrugated iron 261 *fold*; rut 262 *furrow*; coarseness, coarse grain, knobbliness, nodosity 253 *convexity*; rough surface, washboard, grater, file, sandpaper, emery paper; rough texture, sackcloth, tweed, homespun 222 *textile*; creeping flesh, gooseflesh, horripilation; rough skin, chap, crack; hispidity, scabrousness, bristliness, shagginess; hairiness, villosity; undergrowth, overgrowth 366 *wood*; stubble, burr, bristle, scrubbing brush, awn 256 *prickle*.

hair 208 *filament*; head of h., shock of h., matted h., thatch, fuzz, wool; crop, mop, mane, fleece, shag; bristle, stubble, five o'clock shadow; locks, flowing l.; tresses, curls, ringlet, tight curl; kiss curl; strand, plait, braid; pigtail, ponytail, rat's tails; topknot, forelock, elflock, lovelock, scalplock, dreadlocks; fringe, cowlick, quiff, widow's peak; roll, French pleat, bun, chignon 843 *hairdressing*; false hair, hairpiece, switch, wig, toupee 228 *headgear*; thin hair, wisp; beard, beaver, goatee, imperial, Van Dyke; whiskers, face fungus, sideboards, sideburns, muttonchops, dundrearies; moustache, moustachio, toothbrush, handlebars; eyebrows, eyelashes, cilia; woolliness, fleeciness, downiness, fluffiness, flocculence; down, pubescence, pappus, wool, fur 226 *skin*; tuft, flock, floccule; mohair, cashmere, Angora 208 *fibre*; pile, nap; velvet, velour, plush 327 *softness*; floss, fluff, fuzz, thistledown 323 *lightness*; horsehair 227 *lining*.

plumage, pinion 271 *wing*; plumosity, feathering; quill, rachis, barb, web; feathers, coverts, wing c.; neck feathers, hackle f., hackle; ruff, frill, plume, panache, crest; peacock's feathers, ostrich f., osprey f. 844 *finery*.

Adj. *rough*, unsmooth, uneven, broken; rippling, choppy, storm-tossed; rutty, rutted, pitted, potholed, trampled, poached; bumpy, jolting, bone-breaking; chunky, crisp, roughcast; lumpy, stony, nodular, knobbly, studded, roughened, frosted; muricate, nubbly, slubbed, bouclé; crinkled 251 *undulatory*; knotted, gnarled, knurled, cross-grained, coarse-g., coarse; cracked, chapped 845 *blemished*; lined, wrinkled, corrugated, ridged 262 *furrowed*; rough-edged, deckle-e. 260 *notched*; craggy, cragged, jagged; horripilant, creeping; scabrous, scabby, scaly, blistered, blebby; ruffled, unkempt, unpolished; unbolted, unsifted.

hairy, pilose, villous, crinite; napped, brushed; woolly, fleecy, furry; hirsute, shaggy, shagged, tufty, matted, shockheaded; hispid, bristly, bristling 256 *sharp*; setose, setaceous; wispy, filamentous, plumate, fimbriated, ciliated, fringed, befringed; bewhiskered, bearded, moustached; unshaven, unshorn; unplucked; curly, frizzy, fuzzy, tight-curled, woolly.

downy, pubescent, tomentose, pappose; peachy, velvety, mossy 258 *smooth*; fluffy, feathery, plumose, feathered, fledged.

fleecy, woolly, fluffy, flocculent; lanate, lanuginose.

Vb. *be rough*, - hairy etc. adj.; bristle, bristle up 254 *jut*; creep (of flesh), horripilate; scratch, catch; jolt, bump, jerk 278 *move slowly*.

roughen, roughcast, rough-hew; mill, crenate, serrate, indent, engrail 260 *notch*; stud, boss; crisp, corrugate, wrinkle, ripple, popple 251 *crinkle*; disorder, ruffle, tousle 63 *derange*; rumple, crumple 261 *fold*; rub up the wrong way, set on edge.

Adv. *on edge*, against the grain; in the rough.

See: 17, 63, **208**, 209, 222, 226, 227, 228, 251, 253, 254, **256**, 258, **260**, **261**, **262**, 271, 278, 323, 327, 350, 352, 366, **843**, 844, 845.

260 Notch

N. *notch*, serration, serrulation, saw edge, ragged e. 256 *sharpness*; indentation, deckle edge; machicolation, crenellation 713 *fortification*; nick, snip, cut, gash, kerf; crenation, crenulation; crenature 201 *gap*; indent, dent, dimple 255 *concavity*; picot edge, Vandyke e., scollop, scallop, dogtooth 844 *pattern*; sprocket, cog, ratchet, cogwheel, ratchet w.; saw, hacksaw, circular saw 256 *tooth*; battlement, embrasure, crenel.

Adj. *notched*, indented, jagged, jaggy 256 *sharp*; crenate, crenulate, crenellated; toothed, saw-t., dentate, denticulated; serrated, palmate, emarginate; finely serrated, serrulate; serratodentate.

Vb. *notch*, serrate, tooth, cog; nick, blaze, score, scratch, scotch, scarify, bite, slice 46 *cut*; crenellate, machicolate; indent, scallop, Vandyke; jag, pink, slash; dent, mill, knurl 259 *roughen*; pinch, snip, crimp 261 *fold*.

See: **46**, 201, 255, **256**, 259, 261, 713, 844.

261 Fold

N. *fold*, plication, flexure, flexion, doubling; facing, revers, hem; lapel, cuff, turnup, dog-ear; plait, ply, pleat, box p., accordion p., knife-edge p.; tuck, gather, pucker, ruche, ruffle; flounce, frill; crumple, rumple, crease; wrinkle, ruck; frown, lines, wrinkles, crow's feet 131 *age*; crinkle, crankle; joint, elbow 247 *angularity*; syncline, anticline.

Adj. *folded*, doubled; gathered etc. vb.; plicate, pleated; creasy, wrinkly, puckery; dog-eared; creased, crumpled, crushed 63 *disarranged*; turn-down, turn-over.

Vb. *fold*, double, turn over, bend over, roll; crease, pleat; corrugate, furrow, wrinkle 262 *groove*; rumple, crumple 63 *derange*; curl, frizzle, frizz 251 *crinkle*; pucker, purse; ruffle, cockle up, gather, frill, ruck, shirr, smock; tuck, tuck up, kilt; hem, cuff; turn up, turn down, turn under, double down; enfold, enwrap, wrap, swathe 235 *enclose*; fold up, roll up, furl, reef.

See: 63, 131, 235, 247, 251, **262**.

262 Furrow

N. *furrow*, groove, sulcus, chase, slot, slit, rabbet, mortise; crack, chink, cranny 201 *gap*; trough, hollow 255 *cavity*; glyph, triglyph; flute, fluting, goffering, rifling; chamfer, bezel, incision, gash, slash, scratch, score 46 *scission*; streak, striation 437 *stripe*; wake, wheelmark, rut 548 *trace*; gutter, runnel, ditch, dike, trench, dugout, moat, fosse, channel 351 *conduit*; ravine 255 *valley*; furrowed surface, sulcation, corrugation; corduroy, corrugated iron, washboard, ploughed field; ripple, catspaw 350 *wave*.

Adj. *furrowed*, ploughed etc. vb.; fluted, rifled, goffered; striated, sulcate, bisulcate; canalled, canaliculated; gullied, channelled, rutty; wrinkled, lined 261 *folded*; rippling, wavy 350 *flowing*.

Vb. *groove*, slot, flute, chamfer, rifle; chase; gash, scratch, score, incise 46 *cut*; claw, tear 655 *wound*; striate, streak 437 *variegate*; grave, carve, enchase, bite in, etch, cross-hatch 555 *engrave*; furrow, plough, channel, rut, wrinkle, line; corrugate, goffer 261 *fold*.

See: **46**, 201, 255, **261**, 350, 351, 437, 548, 555, 655.

263 Opening

N. *opening*, throwing open, flinging wide; unstopping, uncorking 229 *uncovering*; pandiculation, stretching oneself 197 *expansion*; yawn, yawning, oscitation; dehiscence, bursting open, splitting; hiation, gaping; hiatus, lacuna, space, interval, ghat 201 *gap*; aperture, split, crack, leak 46 *disunion*; hole, potato; hollow 255 *cavity*; placket 194 *pocket*.

perforation, piercing, tattooing etc. vb.; impalement, puncture, acupuncture, venipuncture; trepanation, trephining; boring, borehole, bore, calibre; pinhole, eyelet.

porosity, porousness, sponge; sieve, sifter, riddle, screen 62 *sorting*; strainer, tea s., colander; grater; holeyness, honeycomb.

orifice, blind o., aperture, slot; oral cavity, mouth, gob, trap, jaws, muzzle; throat, gullet 194 *maw*; sucker; mouthpiece, flue pipe 353 *air pipe*; nozzle, spout, vent, vent-hole, vomitory 298 *outlet*; blower, blowhole, air-hole, spiracle; nasal cavity, nostril, nosehole; inlet, outlet; river-mouth, embouchure; small orifice, ostiole; foramen, pore; breathing pores, stomata; hole, crater, pothole 255 *cavity*; manhole, armhole, keyhole, buttonhole, punch hole, pin h.; pigeonhole 194 *compartment*; eye, eye of a needle, eyelet; deadeye; grummet, ring 250 *loop*.

window, fenestration; shop window, plate-glass w., glass front; embrasure, loophole 713 *fortification*; lattice, grille; fenestella, oeil de boeuf; casement window, leaded w., sash w., bay w., oriel w., dormer w., French w., picture w.; rose window, lancet w. 990 *church interior*; light, lightwell, fanlight, skylight, sunshine roof; companion, cabin window, port, porthole; peephole, keyhole; hagioscope, squint; car window, windscreen, windshield; window frame, casement, sash, mullion, transom; window pane 422 *transparency*.

doorway, archway; doorstep, threshold 68 *entrance*; approach, drive, drive-in, entry 297 *way in*; exit, way out; passage, corridor, gangway, drawbridge 624 *access*; gate, city gates; portal, porch, propylaeum; door, front d., Dutch d.; swing doors, revolving d., double d.; church d., lychgate; back door, postern 238 *rear*; small door, wicket; cat-flap; scuttle, hatch, hatchway; trapdoor, companionway; stairwell; door jamb, gatepost, lintel; concierge 264 *doorkeeper*.

open space 183 *space*; yard, court 185 *place*; opening, clearing, glade; panorama, vista 438 *view*; rolling downs, landscape, open country 348 *plain*; alley, aisle, gangway, thoroughfare 305 *passage*; estuary 345 *gulf*.

tunnel, boring; subway, underpass, underground railway, tube; Channel Tunnel, Chunnel; mine, shaft, pit, gallery, adit 255 *excavation*; cave 255 *cavity*; bolthole, rabbit hole, fox h., mouse h. 192 *dwelling*; funnel 252 *cone*; sewer 351 *drain*.

tube, pipe, duct 351 *conduit*; efflux tube, adjutage; tubule, pipette, cannula; tubing, piping, pipeline, hose; artery, vein, capillary; colon, gut 224 *insides*; funnel, fistula.

chimney, factory c., chimneypot, chimney stack, smokestack, funnel; smokeduct, flue; volcano, fumarole, smokehole 383 *furnace*.

opener, key, master k., skeleton k., passepartout; doorknob, handle; corkscrew, tin opener, can o., bottle o.; aperient, purgative; password, open sesame; passport, safe conduct; pass, ticket 756 *permit*.

perforator, piercer, borer, corer; gimlet, wimble, corkscrew; auger, drill, pneumatic d., road d., dentist's d.; burr, bit, spike b., brace and b.; reamer; trepan, trephine; probe, lancet, stylet, trocar; bodkin, needle, hypodermic n.; awl, bradawl 256 *sharp point*; pin, nail 47 *fastening*; skewer, spit, broach, stiletto 723 *weapon*; punch, card p., puncheon, stapler; dibble; digging stick; pickaxe, pick, ice p.

Adj. *open*, patent, exposed to view 522 *manifest*; unclosed, unstopped, unshut, ajar; unbolted, unbarred, unobstructed, admitting 289 *accessible*; wide-open, agape, gaping; dehiscent; yawning, oscitant; open-mouthed, slack-jawed; opening, aperient; blooming, out.

perforated, pierced etc. vb.; perforate, drilled, bored; honeycombed, riddled; peppered, shot through; cribriform, foraminous; holey, full of holes; windowed, fenestrated, fenestrate.

porous, permeable, pervious, spongy, percolating, leachy, leaky, leaking.

tubular, tubulous, tubulated, cannular, piped; cylindrical 252 *rotund*; funnel-shaped, infundibular; fistulous; vascular, capillary.

Vb. *open*, unclose, unfold, unwrap, unpack, undo, ope; unlock, unlatch, unbolt, open the door, fling wide the gates 299 *admit*; pull out (a drawer); uncover, bare 229 *doff*; unplug, unstop, uncork; unrip, unseam 46 *disunite*; lay open, throw o. 522 *show*; force open, steam o. 176 *force*; cut open, rip o., tear o., crack o.; enlarge a hole, ream; dehisce, fly open, split, gape, yawn; burst, explode; crack at the seams, start, leak; space out 201 *space*; open out, fan o., deploy 75 *be dispersed*; separate, part, hold apart; unclench, open one's hand; bloom, be out.

pierce, transpierce, transfix, impale; gore, run through, stick, pink, lance, bayonet, spear 655 *wound*; spike, skewer, spit; prick, puncture, tattoo; probe, stab, poke; inject; perforate, hole, riddle, pepper, honeycomb; nail, drive, hammer in 279 *strike*; knock holes in, punch, punch full of holes; hull (a ship), scuttle, stave in; tap, drain 304 *extract*; bore, drill, wimble; trephine, trepan; burrow, tunnel, mine 255 *make concave*; cut through, penetrate

297 *enter.*

Adv. *openly,* patently, frankly, unguardedly; on the rooftops; out, out in the open.

See: 46, 47, 62, 68, 75, 176, 183, 185, 192, 194, 197, **201**, 224, 229, 238, 250, 252, **255**, 256, 264, 279, 289, 297, 298, 299, 304, 305, 345, 348, 351, 353, 383, 422, 438, 522, 624, 655, 713, 723, 756, 990.

264 Closure

N. *closure,* closing, shutting etc. vb.; door in one's face; occlusion, stoppage; contraction, strangulation 198 *compression*; sealing off, blockade 232 *circumscription*; encirclement 235 *enclosure*; embolism, obstruction, obturation; infarction, constipation, obstipation, strangury; dead end, cul-de-sac, impasse, blank wall, road block 702 *obstacle*; blind gut, caecum; imperforation, imperviousness, impermeability.

stopper, stopple, cork, plug, bung, peg, spill, spigot; ramrod, rammer, piston; valve, slide v.; wedge, wad, dossil, pledget, tampon; wadding, padding, stuffing, stopping 227 *lining*; dummy, gag, muzzle 748 *fetter*; shutter 421 *screen*; tight bandage, tourniquet 198 *compressor*; damper, choke, cut-out; ventpeg, tap, faucet, stopcock, bibcock; top, lid, cap, cover, seal 226 *covering*; lock, key, bolt, bar 47 *fastening*; door, gate 263 *doorway*; cordon 235 *fence.*

doorkeeper, doorman, gatekeeper, porter, janitor, ostiary; commissionaire, concierge; sentry, sentinel, night watchman 660 *protector*; warden, guard 749 *keeper*; jailer, turnkey, Cerberus, Argus 749 *gaoler.*

Adj. *closed,* unopened, unopenable; shut etc. vb.; shuttered, bolted, barred; stoppered, obturated; unpierced, imperforate, unholed; nonporous, impervious, impermeable 324 *dense*; impenetrable, impassable, unpassable 470 *impracticable*; pathless, untrodden 883 *secluded*; dead-end, blank; clogged up, stuffed up, bunged up; strangulated 198 *contracted*; drawn tight, drawn together 45 *joined.*

sealed off, sealed, hermetically s.; cloistered, claustral; close, unventilated, stuffy, muggy, fuggy, fusty 653 *insalubrious*; staunch, tight, airtight, watertight, proof, waterproof, gasproof, airproof, mouseproof 660 *invulnerable.*

Vb. *close,* shut, occlude, seal; clinch, fix, bind, make tight 45 *tighten*; put the lid on 226 *cover*; batten down the hatches, make all tight; clap to, slam, bang (a door); lock, fasten, snap, snap to; plug, caulk, bung up, cork, stopper, obturate; button, zip up, do up 45 *join*; knit, draw the ends together; clench (fist); block, dam, staunch, choke, throttle, strangle, smother, asphyxiate 702 *obstruct*; blockade 712 *besiege*; enclose, surround, shut in, seal off 232 *circumscribe*; trap, bolt, bar, lock in 747 *imprison*; shut down, clamp d., batten d., ram d., tamp d., cram d.; draw the curtains, put up the shutters.

See: 45, 47, 198, **226**, 227, 232, **235**, 263, 324, 421, 470, 653, 660, 702, 712, 747, 748, 749, 883.

Section four: Motion

265 Motion: successive change of place

N. *motion,* change of position 143 *change*; movement, going, move, march; speed rate, speed, air s., ground s.; pace, tempo; locomotion, motility, mobility, movableness; kinetic energy, motive power, motivity; forward motion, advance, progress, headway 285 *progression*; backward motion 286 *regression,* 290 *recession*; motion towards 289 *approach,* 293 *convergence*; motion away, shift 294 *divergence,* 282 *deviation*; motion into 297 *ingress*; motion out of 298 *egress*; upward motion, rising 308 *ascent*; downward motion, sinking 309 *descent,* 313 *plunge*; motion round, circumnavigation 314 *circuition*; axial motion 315 *rotation,* 316 *evolution*; to and fro movement, fluctuation 317 *oscillation*; irregular motion 318 *agitation*; stir, bustle, unrest, restlessness 678 *activity*; rapid motion 277 *velocity*; slow motion 278 *slowness*; regular motion 16 *uniformity,* 71 *continuity*; recurring movement, rhythm 141 *periodicity*; motion in front 283 *preceding*; motion after 284 *following,* 619 *pursuit*; conduction, conductivity 272 *transference*; current, flow, flux, drift 350 *stream*; course, career, run; traffic, traffic movement, flow of traffic 305 *passing along*; transit 305 *passage*; transportation 272 *transport*; running, walking, foot-slogging 267 *pedestrianism*; riding

267 *equitation*; travel 267 *land travel*, 269 *water travel*, 271 *air travel*; dancing, gliding, sliding, skating, rolling; manoeuvre, manoeuvring, footwork; bodily movement, exercise 162 *athletics*; gesticulation 547 *gesture*; cinematography, motion picture 445 *cinema*; laws of motion, kinematics, kinetics, dynamics; kinesiatrics 658 *therapy*.

gait, rolling g.; walk, port, carriage 688 *conduct*; tread, tramp, footfall, stamp; pace, step, stride; run, lope, jog; jog trot, dog t.; dance step, hop, skip, jump 312 *leap*; skid, slide; waddle, shuffle; swagger, proud step, stalk, strut, goosestep 875 *formality*; march, slow m., quick m., double; trot, piaffer, amble, canter, gallop, hand-g. 267 *equitation*.

Adj. *moving*, rolling etc. vb.; in motion, under way; motive, motory, motor; motile, movable, mobile; progressive, regressive; locomotive, automotive; transitional, shifting 305 *passing*; mercurial 152 *changeful*; unquiet, restless 678 *active*; nomadic 267 *travelling*; drifting, erratic, runaway 282 *deviating*; kinematic, kinematical; kinetic; cinematographic.

Vb. *be in motion*, move, go, hie, gang, wend, trail; gather way 269 *navigate*; budge, stir; stir in the wind, flutter, wave, flap 217 *hang*; march, tramp 267 *walk*; place one's feet, tread; trip, dance 312 *leap*; shuffle, waddle 278 *move slowly*; toddle, patter; run 277 *move fast*; run on wheels, roll, taxi; stream, roll on, drift 350 *flow*; paddle 269 *row*; skitter, slide, slither, skate, ski, toboggan, glide 258 *go smoothly*; fly, volitate, frisk, flit, flitter, dart, hover; climb 308 *ascend*; sink, plunge 309 *descend*; cruise, steam, chug, keep going, proceed 146 *go on*; make one's way, pick one's w., fight one's w., elbow one's w., shoulder one's w. 285 *progress*; pass through, wade t., pass by 305 *pass*; make a move, shift, dodge, duck, shift about, jink, tack, manoeuvre 282 *deviate*; twist 251 *wriggle*; creep, crawl, worm one's way, go on all fours; hover about, hang a. 136 *wait*; move house, change one's address, shift one's quarters; change places 151 *interchange*; move over, make room 190 *go away*; travel, stray 267 *wander*.

move, impart motion, put in m.; render movable, set going, power; put on wheels, put skates under; actuate, switch on 173 *operate*; stir, stir up, jerk, pluck, twitch 318 *agitate*; budge, shift, manhandle, trundle, roll, wheel 188 *displace*; push, shove 279 *impel*; move on, drive, hustle 680 *hasten*; tug, pull 288 *draw*; fling, throw 287 *propel*; convey, transport 272 *transfer*; dispatch 272 *send*; mobilize 74 *bring together*; scatter 75 *disperse*; raise, uplift 310 *elevate*; throw down, drop 311 *let fall*; motion, gesture 547 *gesticulate*; transpose 151 *interchange*.

Adv. *on the move*, under way, on one's w., on the go, on the hop, on the run; in transit; on the march, on the tramp, on the wing.

See: 16, 71, 74, 75, 136, 141, 143, 146, 151, 152, 162, 173, 188, 190, 217, 251, 258, **267**, 269, 271, **272**, 277, 278, 279, 282, 283, 284, 285, 286, 287, 288, 289, **290**, 293, 294, 297, 298, 305, 308, 309, 310, 311, 312, 313, 314, 315, 316, 317, 318, 350, 445, 547, 619, 658, 678, 680, 688, 875.

266 Quiescence

N. *quiescence*, motionlessness; dying down, running down, subsidence 145 *cessation*; rest, stillness; deathliness, deadness; stagnation, stagnancy 679 *inactivity*; pause, truce, standstill 145 *lull*; stand, stoppage, halt; fix, deadlock, lock; full stop, dead s. 145 *stop*; embargo, freeze 757 *prohibition*; immobility, fixity, rigidity, stiffness 326 *hardness*; steadiness, equilibrium 153 *stability*; numbness, trance, faint 375 *insensibility*.

quietude, quiet, quietness, stillness, hush 399 *silence*; tranquillity, peacefulness, no disturbance 717 *peace*; rest 683 *repose*; eternal rest 361 *death*; sleepiness, slumber 679 *sleep*; calm, dead c., flat c. 258 *smoothness*; windlessness, not a breath of air; dead quiet, not a mouse stirring; armchair travel, staying at home; placidity, composure 823 *inexcitability*; passivity, quietism; quietist 717 *pacifist*; tranquillizer 177 *moderator*.

resting place, bivouac 192 *quarters*; roof 192 *home, inn*; shelter, haven 662 *refuge*; place of rest, pillow 218 *bed*; journey's end 295 *goal*; last rest, grave 364 *tomb*.

Adj. *quiescent*, quiet, still; asleep 679 *sleepy*; resting, at rest, becalmed; at anchor, anchored, moored, docked; at a stand, at a standstill, stopped, idle 679 *inactive*; unemployed, out of commission 674 *unused*; dormant, unaroused, dying 361 *dead*; standing, stagnant, vegetating, unprogressive, static, stationary 175 *inert*; sitting, sedentary, chair-borne; on one's back 216 *supine*; disabled, housebound 747 *restrained*; settled, stay-at-home, home-loving, domesticated 828 *content*; untravelled, unadventurous 858 *cautious*; unmoved 860 *indifferent*.

tranquil, undisturbed, sequestered 883 *secluded*; peaceful, restful; unhurried, easy-going 681 *leisurely*; uneventful, without incident 16 *uniform*; calm, windless, airless; unbroken, glassy 258 *smooth*; sunny, halcyon 730 *palmy*; at ease, easeful, comfortable, relaxed 683 *reposeful*; tranquillized,sedated, under sedation; unruffled, unwrinkled, unworried, serene 823 *inexcitable*.

still, unmoving, unstirring, unbudging; not fizzy, flat 387 *tasteless*; immobile, motionless, gestureless; expressionless, deadpan, poker-faced 820 *impassive*; steady, unwinking, unblinking 153 *unchangeable*; standing still, rooted, rooted to the ground 153 *fixed*; transfixed, spellbound; immovable, unable to move, stuck; stiff, frozen 326 *rigid*; benumbed, numb, petrified, paralysed 375 *insensible*; quiet, hushed, soundless 399 *silent*; stock-still, stone-still, still as a statue, still as a post, still as death; quiet as a mouse.

Vb. *be quiescent*, - still etc.adj.; subside, die down 37 *decrease*; pipe down 399 *be silent*; stand still, lie s., keep quiet; stagnate, vegetate 175 *be inert*; stand, mark time 136 *wait*; stay put, sit tight, stand pat, remain in situ, not stir, not budge, remain, abide 144 *stay*; stand to, lie to, ride at anchor; tarry 145 *pause*; rest, sit down, take breath, rest on one's laurels, rest on one's oars, rest and be thankful 683 *repose*; retire, go to bed, doss down 679 *sleep*; settle, settle down 187 *place oneself*; stay at home, not go out 883 *be unsociable*; ground, stick fast; catch, jam, lodge; stand fast, stand firm; not move a muscle, not stir a step, not stir an inch; be at a standstill 145 *cease*.

come to rest, stop, hold, stop short, stop in one's tracks, stop dead in one's tracks, freeze 145 *halt*; pull up, draw up; slow down 278 *decelerate*; anchor, cast a., alight 295 *land*; relax, calm down, rest, pause 683 *repose*.

bring to rest, quiet, make q., quieten, quell, hush 399 *silence*; lull, soothe, calm down 177 *assuage*; lull to sleep, cradle, rock; let alone, let well alone, let sleeping dogs lie 620 *avoid*; bring to a standstill, bring to, lay to, heave to; brake, put the brake on 278 *retard*; stay, immobilize 679 *make inactive*.

Adv. *at a stand*, at a halt; in repose, far from the madding crowd.

Int. stop! stay! halt! whoa! hold! hold hard! hold on! hold it! don't move!

See: 16, 37, 136, 144, **145**, 153, **175**, 177, 187, 192, 216, 218, 258, 278, 295, 326, 361, 364, 375, 387, 399, 620, 662, 674, 679, 681, 683, 717, 730, 747, 757, 820, 823, 828, 858, 860, 883.

267 Land travel

N. *land travel*, travel, travelling, wayfaring; seeing the world, globe-trotting, tourism; walking, riding, driving, motoring, cycling, biking; journey, voyage, peregrination, odyssey; course, passage, sweep; pilgrimage, hajj; quest, expedition, safari, trek, field trip; reconnaissance, exploration, orienteering, youth hostelling; visit, trip, business t., pleasure t., tour, grand t., coach t.; circuit, turn, round, patrol, commuting; round trip, day t. 314 *circuition*; jaunt, hop, spin; ride, bike r., joy r., drive, lift, free l.; excursion, outing, airing; ramble, constitutional, promenade. **See** *pedestrianism*.

wandering, wanderlust, nomadism; vagrancy, vagabondage, vagabondism; no fixed address; roving, rambling, walkabout, waltzing Matilda; tramping, traipsing, flitting, gadding, gallivanting; itchy feet; migration, völkerwanderung, emigration 298 *egress*; immigration 297 *ingress*; transmigration 305 *passage*.

pedestrianism, walking, going on foot, footing it, Shanks's pony; foot-slogging, stumping, tramping, marching, backpacking; ambulation, perambulation; circumambulation, walkabout 314 *circuition*; walk, promenade, constitutional; stroll, saunter, amble, ramble; hike, tramp, march, walking tour; run, cross-country run, jog, trot, jog t., lope 265 *gait*; paddle, paddling, wading; foot race, heel-and-toe walking, marathon 716 *racing*; stalking, stalk 619 *chase*; prowling, loitering; sleepwalking, noctambulation, noctambulism, somnambulism.

marching, campaigning, campaign; manoeuvres, marching and countermarching, advance, retreat; march, forced m., route m., quick march, slow m.; march past, parade, cavalcade, procession 875 *formality*; column, file, cortege, train, caravan.

equitation, equestrianism, horsemanship, manège, dressage 694 *skill*; show jumping, steeplechasing, point-to-point racing 716 *contest*; horse racing; riding, bareback r. 162 *athletics*; haute école, caracole, piaffer, curvet 265 *gait*.

conveyance, lift, escalator 274 *conveyor*; feet, own two f. 214 *foot*; legs, Shanks's pony; horseback, mount 273 *horse*; bicycle, car, bus, train, coach, taxi, ambulance 274 *vehicle*; traffic, wheeled t., motor t., road t. 305 *passing along*.

leg, limb, foreleg, hindleg; shank, shin, calf; thigh, ham, hamstrings; knee, kneecap 247 *angularity*; legs, pegs, pins 218 *prop*; stumps, stilts; stump, wooden leg, artificial l. 150 *substitute*; bow legs, bandy l. 845 *blemish*; thick legs, piano l.; long legs, spindle shanks.

itinerary, route 624 *way*; march, course 281 *direction*; route map, road m., plan, chart 551 *map*; guide, Baedeker, timetable, Bradshaw 524 *guidebook*; milestone, fingerpost 547 *signpost*; halt, stop, stopover, terminus 145 *stopping place*.

Adj. *travelling*, journeying, itinerant, vagrant, wayfaring, on the road; travel-stained, dusty 649 *dirty*; travelled, much-t.; touring, globe-trotting, rubbernecking; migratory, passing through, stopping over, visiting 305 *passing*; nomadic, nomad, floating, unsettled, restless; of no fixed address, homeless, rootless, déraciné(e) 59 *extraneous*; footloose, errant, roving, roaming, rambling, hiking, wandering 282 *deviating*; ambulant, strolling, peripatetic; tramping, vagabond; walking, pedestrian, ambulatory, perambulatory; marching, foot-slogging; gadding, flitting, traipsing, gallivanting; automotive, locomotive, self-moving, self-driven 265 *moving*; noctivagant, somnambulant, sleep-walking.

legged, bow-l., bandy-l. 845 *blemished*; thighed, strong-t.; well-calved, well-hocked; long-legged, leggy 209 *tall*; spindly, spindle-shanked 206 *lean*; piano-legged, thick-ankled 205 *thick*.

Vb. *travel*, fare, journey, peregrinate; tour, see the world, visit, explore 484 *discover*; get around, knock about, go places, sightsee, rubberneck; pilgrimage, go on a pilgrimage; make a journey, go on a j.; go on safari, trek, hump bluey; hike, backpack; be always on the move, live out of a suitcase; set out, fare forth, take wing 296 *depart*; migrate, emigrate, immigrate, settle 187 *place oneself*; shuttle, commute; take oneself off, swan off, slope o.; go to, hie to, repair to, resort to, betake oneself to 295 *arrive*, 882 *visit*; go 265 *be in motion*; wend, wend one's way, stir one's stumps, bend one's steps, shape one's course, tread a path, follow the road; make one's way, pick one's way, thread one's w., force a w., plough through; jog on, trudge on, shuffle on, pad on, plod on, tramp on, march on, chug on 146 *sustain*; course, race, post 277 *move fast*; proceed, advance 285 *progress*; coast, free-wheel, glide, slide, skate, ski, skim, roll along, bowl a., fly a. 258 *go smoothly*.

traverse, cross, range, pass through, range t. 305 *pass*; go round, beat the bounds 314 *circle*; go the rounds, make one's rounds, patrol; scout, reconnoitre 438 *scan*; scour, sweep, sweep through 297 *burst in*.

wander, nomadize, migrate; rove, roam, bum around; ramble, amble, stroll, saunter, mosey along, potter, dawdle, walk about, trail around; gad, traipse, gallivant, gad about, hover, flit about, dart a. 265 *be in motion*; prowl, skulk 523 *lurk*; straggle, trail 75 *be dispersed*; lose the way, wander away 282 *stray*.

walk, step, tread, pace, stride; stride out 277 *move fast*; strut, stalk, prance, mince 871 *be proud*; tread lightly, tiptoe, trip, skip, dance, curvet 312 *leap*; tread heavily, lumber, clump, stamp, tramp, goosestep; toddle, patter, pad; totter, stagger, lurch, reel, stumble 317 *oscillate*; limp, hobble, waddle, shuffle, shamble, dawdle 278 *move slowly*; paddle, wade; go on foot, go by Shanks's pony, foot it, hoof it, hike, footslog, wear out shoe leather; plod, stump, trudge, jog; go, go for a walk, ambulate, perambulate, circumambulate, pace up and down; go for a run *or* a jog, take the air, take one's constitutional; march, quick march, slow march, troop; file, file past, defile, march in procession 65 *come after*; walk behind 284 *follow*; walk in front 283 *precede*.

ride, mount, take horse, hack; trot, amble, tittup, canter, gallop; prance, caper, curvet, piaffe, caracole, passage; cycle, bicycle, bike, motorcycle; freewheel; drive, motor; go by bike, go by car, go by bus, go by coach, go by taxi; go by road, go by tube, go by train; go by air 271 *fly*; take a lift, cadge a l., thumb a l., hitch-hike.

Adv. *on foot*, on the beat; on hoof, on horseback, on Shanks's pony *or* mare; en route 272 *in transit*; by road, by rail, awheel.

Int. come along! move along there! get along! get going! get out! git! go away! be off! buzz off! hop it! skedaddle! scram!

See: 59, 65, 75, 145, 146, 150, 162, 187, 205, 206, 209, 214, 218, 247, 258, **265**, 271, 272, **273**, **274**, 277, 278, 281, 282, 283, 284, 285, 295, 296, 297, 298, 305, 312, 314, 317, 438, 484, 523, 524, 547, 551, 619, 624, 649, 694, 716, 845, 871, 875, 882.

268 Traveller

N. *traveller*, itinerant, wayfarer, viator, peregrinator; explorer, adventurer, voyager 270 *mariner*; air traveller, spaceman *or* -woman 271 *aeronaut*; pioneer, pathfinder, explorer 66 *precursor*; alpinist, mountaineer, cragsman 308 *climber*; pilgrim, palmer, hajji; walker, hiker, rambler, trekker; backpacker, camper, caravanner, youth hosteller; globe-trotter, tourist, rubberneck, sightseer 441 *spectator*; tripper, excursionist; sunseeker, holidaymaker, visitor; roundsman, hawker 794 *pedlar*; travelling salesman, commercial traveller 793 *seller*; messenger, errandboy 529 *courier*; daily traveller, commuter, straphanger; Odysseus, Ulysses, Gulliver, Marco Polo.

wanderer, migrant, bird of passage, visitant 365 *bird*; floating population, nomad, bedouin; gipsy, didicoi, Romany, Bohemian, zigane; rover, ranger, rambler, promenader, stroller; strolling player, wandering minstrel, touring company 594 *entertainer*; rolling stone, drifter, vagrant, vagabond, tramp, knight of the road; swagman, sundowner, hobo, bum, bummer; loafer, beachcomber 679 *idler*; emigrant, émigré, refugee, deportee, exile 59 *foreigner*; runaway, fugitive, escapee 620 *avoider*; déraciné(e), homeless wanderer 883 *solitary*; waif, stray, destitute, street beggar 801 *poor person*; Wandering Jew, Flying Dutchman.

pedestrian, foot passenger, walker, tramper; jogger, sprinter, runner 716 *contender*; toddler; wader, paddler; skater, skier; skateboarder, roller-skater; hiker, hitch-h., foot-slogger; marcher 722 *infantry*; somnambulist, sleepwalker; prowler, loiterer; footpad 789 *robber*.

rider, horse-rider, camel-r., cameleer; elephant-rider, mahout; horseman, horsewoman, equestrian, equestrienne; postilion, postboy 529 *courier*; mounted police, Mounties; cavalier, knight, knight errant 722 *cavalry*; hunt, huntsman 619 *hunter*; jockey, steeplechaser, show jumper 716 *contender*; trainer, breaker 369 *breeder*; roughrider, bareback r., broncobuster, cowboy, cowgirl, cowpuncher, gaucho; cyclist, bicyclist, pedal-pusher, rough-stuffer; circus rider, trick rider 162 *athlete*; motorcyclist, moped rider, scooterist; back-seat driver, passenger, pillion p.

driver, drover, teamster, muleteer; charioteer, coachman, whip, Jehu; carter, waggoner, drayman; car driver, chauffeur, motorist, roadhog 277 *speeder*; joy rider; L-driver 538 *beginner*; taxi driver, cab d., cabby; bus driver, coach d.; lorry d., truck d., van d., trucker, routier, teamster; tractor d.; motorman, train driver, engine d.; stoker, footplateman, fireman; guard, conductor, ticket collector; pilot 271 *aeronaut*.

See: 59, 66, 162, **270**, **271**, 277, 308, 365, 369, 441, 529, 538, 594, 619, 620, 679, 716, 722, 789, 793, 794, 801, 883.

269 Water travel

N. *water travel*, ocean t., sea t., river t., canal t., inland navigation; seafaring, nautical life, life on the ocean wave; navigation, voyaging, sailing, cruising; coasting, longshore sailing; boating, yachting, rowing (**see** *aquatics*); voyage, navigation, cruise, sail; course, run, passage, crossing, ferry c.; circumnavigation 314 *circuition*; marine exploration, submarine e. 484 *discovery*; sea adventures, naval exploits; sea trip, river t., breath of sea air 685 *refreshment*; way, headway, steerage way, sternway, seaway 265 *motion*; leeway, driftway 282 *deviation*; wake, track, wash, backwash 350 *eddy*; sea-path, ocean lane, steamer route, sea lane, approaches 624 *route*; boat, sailing ship 275 *ship*; sailor 270 *mariner*.

navigation, piloting, steering, pilotage 689 *directorship*; astronavigation, celestial navigation; plane sailing, plain s., spherical s., great-circle s., parallel s.; compass reading, dead reckoning 465 *measurement*; pilotship, helmsmanship, seamanship 694 *skill*; nautical experience, weather eye, sea legs; naval exercises, naval manoeuvres, fleet operations, naval tactics 688 *tactics*.

aquatics, boating, sailing, yachting, cruising; rowing, sculling, canoeing; yacht racing, speedboat r., ocean r. 716 *racing*; water skiing, surf riding, surfing, wind s., watersports 837 *sport*; natation, swimming, floating; stroke, breast s., side s., back s., crawl, trudgen, butterfly, dog paddle; diving, plunging 313 *plunge*; wading, paddling; swimsuit 228 *beachwear*.

sailing aid, navigational instrument, sextant, quadrant 247 *angular measure*; chronometer, ship's c. 117 *timekeeper*; log, line; lead, plummet 211 *depth*; anchor 662 *safeguard*; compass, astrocompass, magnetic c., ship's c.; needle, magnetic n.; card, compass c. *or* rose; binnacle; gyrocompass 689 *directorship*; radar 484 *detector*; helm, wheel, tiller, rudder, steering oar; sea mark, buoy, lighthouse, pharos, lightship 547 *signpost*; chart, Admiralty c., portolano 551 *map*; nautical almanac, ephemeris 524 *guidebook*.

propeller, screw, twin screw, blade, rotor 287 *propellant*; paddle wheel, stern w., floatboard; oar, sweep, paddle, scull; pole, punt p., barge p.; fin, flipper, fish's tail 53 *limb*; sails, canvas 275 *sail*.

Adj. *seafaring*, sea, salty, deep-sea, longshore; sailorlike, sailorly 270 *seamanlike*; nautical, naval 275 *marine*; navigational, navigating, sailing, steaming, plying, coasting, ferrying; sea-going, ocean-g.; at sea, on the high seas, afloat, waterborne, seaborne, on board; pitching, tossing, rolling, wallowing, yawing; seasick, green; seaworthy, tight, snug; navigable, deep.

swimming, natatory, floating, sailing; launched, afloat, buoyant; natatorial, aquatic, like a fish; amphibian.

Vb. *go to sea*, follow the s., join the navy; become a sailor, get one's sea legs; be in sail, sail before the mast; live on board, live afloat; go sailing, boat, yacht; launch, launch a ship, christen a s. 68 *auspicate*.

voyage, sail, go by sea, go by ship, take the sea route; take ship, book one's berth, book a passage, work one's p.; embark, go on board, put to sea, set sail,up anchor 296 *start out*; cross the ocean, cross the Channel 267 *traverse*; disembark, land 295 *arrive*; cruise, visit ports; navigate, steam, ply, run, tramp, ferry; coast, hug the shore; roll, pitch, toss, buffet the waves, tumble, wallow 317 *oscillate*.

navigate, man a ship, work a s., crew; put to sea, set sail; launch, push off, boom off; unmoor, cast off, weigh anchor; raise steam, get up s.; hoist sail, spread canvas; get under way, gather w., make w., carry sail 265 *be in motion*; drop the pilot; set a course, make for, head for 281 *steer for*; read the chart, go by the card 281 *orientate*; pilot, steer, hold the helm, captain 689 *direct*; stroke, cox, coxswain; trim the sails, square, square away; change course, veer, gybe, yaw 282 *deviate*; put about, wear ship 282 *turn round*; run before the wind, scud 277 *move fast*; put the helm up, fall to leeward, pay off; put the helm down, luff, bring into the wind; beat to windward, tack, weather; back and fill; round, double a point, circumnavigate 314 *circle*; be caught amidships 700 *be in difficulty*; careen, list, heel over 220 *be oblique*; turn turtle, capsize, overturn 221 *invert*; ride out the storm, weather the s., keep afloat 667 *escape*; run for port 662 *seek refuge*; lie to, lay to, heave to 266 *bring to rest*; take soundings, heave the lead 465 *measure*; tide over 507 *await*; tow, haul, warp, kedge, clubhaul 288 *draw*; ground, run aground, wreck, be cast away 165 *destroy*; sight land, make a landfall, take on a pilot 289 *approach*; make port; cast anchor, drop a.; moor, tie up, dock, disembark 295 *land*; cross one's bows, take the wind out of one's sails, outmanoeuvre, gain the weather gauge 702 *obstruct*; foul 279 *collide*; back, go astern 286 *regress*; surface, break water 298 *emerge*; flood the tanks, dive 313 *plunge*; shoot, shoot a bridge, shoot the rapids 305 *pass*.

row, ply the oar, get the sweeps out; pull, stroke, scull; feather; catch a crab; ship oars; punt; paddle, canoe; boat; shoot the rapids.

swim, float, sail, ride, ride on an even keel; scud, skim, skitter; surf-ride, surf, water-ski, aquaplane; strike out, breast the current, stem the stream; tread water; dive 313 *plunge*; bathe, dip, duck; wade, paddle, splash about, get wet 341 *be wet.*

Adv. *under way*, under sail, under canvas, under steam; before the mast; on deck, on the bridge, on the quarterdeck; at the helm, at the wheel.

Int. ship ahoy! avast! belay there! all aboard! man overboard! yo-heave-ho! hard aport! hard astarboard! steady as she goes! land ahoy!

See: 53, 68, 117, 165, 211, 220, 221, 228, 247, **265**, 266, 267, **270**, **275**, 277, 279, 281, 282, 286, 287, 288, 289, 295, 296, 298, 305, 313, 314, 317, 341, 350, 465, 484, 507, 524, 547, 551, 624, 662, 667, 685, 688, 689, 694, 700, 702, 716, 837.

270 Mariner

N. *mariner*, sailor, sailorman, seaman, seafarer, seafaring man; salt, old s., seadog, shellback; tar, Jack Tar, limey, matelot; no sailor, bad s., fairweather s., landlubber 697 *bungler*; skipper, master mariner, master, ship m.; mate, boatswain, bosun; coxswain; able seaman, A.B. 696 *expert*; deckhand, swabbie; ship's steward, cabin boy 742 *servant*; shipmates, hearties; crew, complement, ship's c., men, watch 686 *personnel*; trawler, whaler, deep-sea fisherman; sea rover, privateer, buccaneer, sea king, Viking, pirate 789 *robber*; sea scout, sea cadet; argonaut, Jason; Ancient Mariner, Flying Dutchman, Captain Ahab, Sinbad the Sailor; Neptune, Poseidon 343 *sea god*.

navigator, pilot, sailing master, helmsman, steersman, wheelman, man at the wheel, quartermaster; coxswain, cox 690 *leader*; leadsman, lookout man; foretopman, reefer; boatswain, bosun's mate; circumnavigator 314 *circler*; compass, binnacle, gyrocompass 269 *sailing aid*.

nautical personnel, marine, submariner, naval cadet, bluejacket, rating 722 *naval man*; petty officer, midshipman, middy, lieutenant, sub-l., commander, captain, commodore, admiral 741 *naval officer*; Admiralty, Sea Lord; Trinity House, lighthouse keeper, coastguard 660 *protector*; lifeboatman 703 *aider*; river police, naval patrol, harbour p., harbourmaster.

boatman, waterman, rowing man, wet bob; gigsman; galley slave; oar, oarsman, sculler, rower, punter; paddler, canoeist; yachtsman *or* -woman; gondolier, ferryman, Charon; wherryman, bargeman, bargee, lighterman; stevedore, docker, longshoreman; lock keeper.

Adj. *seamanlike*, sailorly, like a sailor 694 *expert*; nautical, naval 275 *marine*.

See: **269**, **275**, 314, 343, 660, 686, 690, 694, 696, 697, 703, **722**, 741, 742, 789.

271 Aeronautics

N. *aeronautics*, aeromechanics, aerodynamics, aerostatics, aerodonetics; aerostation, ballooning; aerospace, astronautics; aeroballistics, rocketry 276 *rocket*; volitation, flight, vertical f., horizontal f.; subsonic f., supersonic f. 277 *velocity*; stratospheric flight, hypersonic f., space f.; aviation, flying, night f., blind f., instrument f.; shoran, teleran; gliding, hang-g.; parachuting, skydiving, free fall; flypast, formation flying, stunt f., aerobatics 875 *ostentation*; skywriting, vapour trail; planing, volplaning, looping the loop; spin, roll, side-slip; volplane, nose dive, pull-out; crash dive, crash, prang 309 *descent*; pancake, landing, belly l., crash l., forced l.; talkdown, touchdown 295 *arrival*; take-off, vertical t. 296 *departure*.

air travel, air transport, airlift 272 *transport*; air service, airline; scheduled flight, charter f.; airlane, airway, air route 624 *route*; flight path, glide p., line of flight 281 *direction*; air space 184 *territory*; takeoff, touchdown, landing, three-point l.; landing field, flying f., airbase; airstrip, runway, tarmac, airfield, aerodrome, airport, heliport, helipad; terminal, air t. 295 *goal*; hangar 192 *stable*; fear of flying, aerophobia; jetlag.

space travel, space flight, manned s.f. 276 *spaceship*; lift-off, blast-off; orbit, flyby; docking, space walk; reentry, splashdown, soft landing; cosmodrome, spaceport; launching pad.

aeronaut, aerostat, balloonist; glider, hang g., sky diver, parachutist; paratrooper 722 *soldier*; aviator, aviatrix, airwoman, airman, birdman; astronaut, cosmonaut, spaceman, spacewoman, space traveller; air traveller, air passenger, jet set 268 *traveller*; air hostess 742 *servant*; flier, pilot, test p., jet p., copilot; automatic pilot, autopilot; navigator, air crew; pilot officer, flying o. 741 *air officer*; aircraftman 722 *air force*; air personnel, ground crew 686 *personnel*; Icarus, Daedalus, Mercury; Pegasus.

wing, pinion, feathers, flight f., wing feather, wing spread 259 *plumage*; swept-back wing, delta w., swing-w., variable w.; aerofoil, aileron, flaps.

Adj. *flying*, on the wing; volitant, volant; fluttering, flitting, hovering 265 *moving*; winged, alar, pinnate, feathered; aerial 340 *airy*; airworthy, airborne; air-to-air; soaring, climbing 308 *ascending*; in-flight; airsick; losing height 309 *descending*; grounded 311 *lowered*; aeronautical, aerospace 276 *aviational*; aerodynamic, aerostatic; aerobatic.

Vb. *fly*, wing, take the w., be on the w.; wing one's way, take one's flight, be wafted, cross the sky, overfly; soar, rise 308 *ascend*; hover, hang over 217 *hang*; flutter, flit 265 *be in motion*; taxi, take off, clear, leave the ground, climb, circle 296 *depart*; be airborne, have lift-off; aviate, glide, plane 258 *go smoothly*; float, drift, drift like thistledown 323 *be light*; stunt, spin, roll, side-slip, loop the loop, volplane; hedgehop, skim the rooftops, buzz 200 *be near*; stall, dive, power-dive, nose-d., spiral 313 *plunge*; crash, prang, force-land, crash-land, pancake, ditch 309 *tumble*; pull out, flatten o.; touch down 295 *land*; bale out, jump, parachute, eject; blast off, lift o., take o.; orbit, go into o. 314 *circle*.

Adv. *in flight*, on the wing, on the beam, in orbit.

See: 184, 192, 200, 217, 258, 259, 265, 268, 272, **276**, 277, 281, 295, 296, 308, 309, 311, 313, 314, 323, 340, 624, 686, **722**, 741, 742, 875.

272 Transference

N. *transference*, change of place, translocation, transplantation, transhipment, transfer, bussing; shifting, shift, drift, longshore d., continental d. 282 *deviation*; posting 751 *mandate*; transposition, metathesis 151 *interchange*; removal, removal, relegation, deportation, expulsion 300 *ejection*; unpacking, unloading, airdrop 188 *displacement*; exportation, export 791 *trade*; mutual transfer 791 *barter*; importation, import 299 *reception*; distribution, logistics 633 *provision*; transmittal, forwarding, sending, remittance, dispatch; recalling, recall, extradition 304 *extraction*; recovery, retrieval 771 *acquisition*; handing over, delivery; takeover 792 *purchase*; conveyance, transfer of property, donation 780 *transfer*; committal, trust 751 *commission*; gaol delivery, habeas corpus, release 746 *liberation*; transition, metastasis; passing over, ferry, ferriage 305 *passage*; transmigration 143 *transformation*; transmission, throughput; conduction, convection; transfusion; decantation; diffusion, dispersal 75 *dispersion*; communication, contact 378 *touch*; contagion, infection, contamination 178 *influence*; transcription, transumption, copying, transliteration 520 *translation*.

transport, transportation; conveyance, carriage, shipping, shipment; carrying, humping, portage, porterage, haulage, draught 288 *traction*; carting, cartage, waggonage, drayage, freightage, air freight, airlift; means of transport, rail, road 274 *vehicle*; sea, canal 275 *ship*; pipeline, conveyor belt 274 *conveyor*.

thing transferred, flotsam, jetsam, driftwood, drift, sea-d.; alluvium, detritus, scree, moraine, sediment, deposit; pledge, hostage, trust 767 *security*; legacy, bequest 781 *gift*; lease 777 *property*; cargo, load, payload, freight; black ivory 742 *slave*; consignment, shipment 193 *contents*; goods, mails; luggage, baggage, impedimenta; container, lorryload, trainload, coachload, busload; person transferred, passenger, rider, commuter 268 *traveller*.

transferrer, testator, conveyancer 781 *giver*; sender, remitter, dispatcher, dispatch clerk, consignor, addresser; shipper, shipping agent, transporter; exporter, importer 794 *merchant*; haulier, removal man, conveyor, ferryman 273 *carrier*; post office, post 531 *postal communications*; communicator, transmitter, diffuser; vector, carrier (of a disease) 651 *sick person*.

Adj. *transferable*, negotiable; transportable, movable, portable; roadworthy, airworthy, seaworthy; portative, transmissive, conductive; transmissible, communicable; contagious 653 *infectious*.

Vb. *transfer*, hand over, deliver 780 *assign*; devise, leave 780 *bequeath*; commit, entrust 751 *commission*; transmit, hand down, hand on, pass on; make over, turn over, hand to, pass to; pass the buck; export, transport, convey, ship, airlift, fly, ferry 273 *carry*; infect, contaminate 178 *influence*; conduct, convect; carry over 38 *add*; transfer itself to, come off on, adhere, stick 48 *cohere*.

transpose, shift, move, tranship 188 *dis-*

place; transfer, switch, shunt, shuffle, castle (chess) 151 *interchange*; detach, detail, draft; relegate, deport, expel 300 *eject*; drag, pull 288 *draw*; push, shove 279 *impel*; containerize 193 *load*; funnel, pour in *or* out, transfuse, decant, strain off, siphon off 300 *empty*; unload, remove 188 *displace*; shovel, ladle, spoon out, bail out, excavate 255 *make concave*; transliterate 520 *translate.*

send, have conveyed, remit, transmit, dispatch; direct, consign, address; post, mail; redirect, readdress, post on, forward; send by hand, send by post; send for, order 627 *require*; send away, detach, detail; send flying 287 *propel.*

Adv. *in transit*, en route, on the way; in the post; in the pipeline; by hand; from hand to hand, from pillar to post.

See: 38, 48, 75, 143, 151, 178, **188**, **193**, 255, 268, **273**, 274, 275, 279, 282, 287, 288, 299, 300, 304, 305, 378, 520, 531, 627, 633, 651, 653, 742, 746, 751, 767, 771, 777, 780, 781, 791, 792, 794.

273 Carrier

N. *carrier*, common c., haulier, carter, waggoner, tranter; shipper, transporter, exporter, importer 272 *transferrer*; ferryman 270 *boatman*; lorry driver, bus d. 268 *driver*; delivery van, lorry, truck, cart, goods train 274 *vehicle*; barge, cargo vessel, freighter, tramp 275 *ship*; chassis, undercarriage 218 *prop*; pallet, container; carrier bag 194 *bag*; conveyor belt, escalator 274 *conveyor.*

bearer, litter b., stretcher b.; caddie, golf c.; shieldbearer, cupbearer 742 *retainer*; porter, coolie, bummaree, stevedore; letter carrier, carrier pigeon, postman *or* -woman, special messenger, King's *or* Queen's m. 529 *courier.*

beast of burden, packhorse, pack-mule, pack train, sumpter-horse, sumpter-mule; ass, she-a., donkey, moke, Neddy, cuddy, burro; ox, oxen, bullock, draught animals 365 *cattle*; sledge dog, husky; llama, camel, dromedary, ship of the desert; elephant 365 *mammal.*

horse, equine species, quadruped, horseflesh; dobbin, gee-gee; nag, Rosinante; mount, steed; stallion, gelding, mare, colt, filly, foal; stud horse, brood mare, stud, stable; circus horse, liberty h.; roan, strawberry r., grey, dapple g., bay, chestnut, sorrel, black, piebald, skewbald, pinto, dun, palomino; winged horse, Pegasus; legendary horse, Al Borak, Bayard, Black Bess; Houyhnhnm.

thoroughbred, purebred, blood-horse, bloodstock; Arab, Barbary horse, Barb; pacer, stepper, high-s., trotter; courser, racehorse, racer, goer, stayer; sprinter 277 *speeder*; steeplechaser, hurdler, fencer, jumper, hunter, foxhunter; Morgan, Tennessee walker, Hanoverian, Lipizzaner.

draught horse, cart-h., dray h.; shaft-horse, trace-h.; carriage-horse, coach-h., post-h.; plough-h., shire h., Clydesdale, punch, Suffolk P., Percheron, pit pony.

warhorse, cavalry h., remount; charger, destrier, courser, steed 722 *cavalry*; Bucephalus, Copenhagen, Marengo.

saddle horse, riding h., cow pony; cow-cutting horse, stock h.; mount, hack, roadster; jade, screw, nag; pad, pad-nag, ambler; mustang, bronco; palfrey, jennet.

pony, cob, galloway, garron, sheltie; Shetland pony, fell p., Welsh p., Dartmoor p., Exmoor p., New Forest p.

Adj. *bearing*, carrier, shouldering, burdened, freighted, loaded, overloaded; pick-a-back.

equine, horsy, horse-faced; roan, grey etc. n.; asinine; mulish.

Vb. *carry*, bear 218 *support*; hump, heave, tote; caddie; stoop one's back to, shoulder, bear on one's back, carry on one's shoulders; fetch, bring, reach; fetch and carry; transport, cart, truck, rail, railroad; ship, waft, raft; lift, fly 272 *transfer*; carry through, carry over, pass o., carry across, traject, ferry; convey, conduct, convoy, escort 89 *accompany*; have a rider, be ridden, be mounted; be saddled with, be burdened w.; be loaded with, be fraught 54 *be complete.*

See: 54, 89, 194, 218, 268, 270, **272**, **274**, **275**, 277, 365, 529, 722, 742.

274 Vehicle

N. *vehicle*, conveyance, public c.; public service vehicle, transport, public t.; vehicular traffic, motorised t., road t., wheeled t.; pedal power, horse p.; sedan chair, palanquin; litter, horse l.; brancard, stretcher, hurdle, crate; ambulance, fire engine; Black Maria, paddy wagon; tumbril, hearse; snowplough, snowmobile, weasel; tractor, caterpillar t., tracked vehicle, bulldozer; amphibian, moon buggy; rollercoaster, switchback, dodgem car; time machine.

sledge, sled, sleigh, dogsleigh, horse s., deer s., kibitzka, carriole; bobsleigh, bobsled, toboggan, luge, coaster, ice yacht; sand y., surfboard; skate, ice s., roller s., skateboard; snowshoes, skis, runner, skids, skibob.

bicycle, cycle, pedal c., bike, push b.; wheel, gridiron, crate; velocipede, hobbyhorse, boneshaker, penny-farthing, Ordinary, Safety, sit-up-and-beg; sports model, racer, tourist, roadster; five-speed, ten-s.; small-wheeler; tandem, randem; monocycle, unicycle, tricycle, trike, quadricycle; motorized bicycle, moped; scooter, motor s., motorcycle, motorbike, trail bike, scrambler; motorcycle combination, sidecar; invalid carriage; cycle-rickshaw, trishaw.

pushcart, perambulator, pram, baby buggy, pushchair; bath chair, wheelchair, invalid c.; rickshaw; barrow, wheelbarrow, hand b., coster b.; handcart, go cart; trolley, truck, float.

cart, ox-c., bullock-c., horse-and-cart; dray, milk float; farm cart, haywain, hay waggon; wain, waggon, covered w., prairie schooner; caravan, trailer, horse-box, loose-b.; dustcart, watercart. **See** *lorry*.

carriage, horse-drawn c., equipage, turnout, rig; chariot, coach, state c., coach and four; barouche, landau, landaulet, berlin, victoria, brougham, phaeton, clarence; surrey, buckboard, buggy, waggonette; travelling carriage, chaise, shay, calèche, calash, britzka, droshky, troika; racing chariot, quadriga; four-in-hand, drag, brake, charabanc; two-wheeler, cabriolet, curricle, tilbury, whisky, jaunting car; trap, gig, ponycart, dogcart, governess cart; carriole, sulky; shandrydan, rattletrap.

war chariot, scythed c.; gun carriage, caisson, limber, ammunition waggon; tank, armoured car 722 *cavalry*; jeep, staff car.

stagecoach, stage, mail coach; diligence, post chaise, omnibus. **See** *bus*.

cab, hackney carriage, horsecab, four-wheeler, growler, hansom, fly; fiacre, droshky; gharry, tonga; taxicab, taxi, minicab; rickshaw, jinrickisha, pedicab, cycle-rickshaw.

bus, horsebus, motorbus; omnibus, double-decker, single-d.; articulated bus, bendibus; autobus, trolleybus, motor coach, coach, postbus, minibus.

tram, horse t., tramcar, trolley, streetcar, cablecar.

automobile, horseless carriage, car, motor car; motor, auto; limousine, gas guzzler; saloon, two-door s., four-d. s.; tourer, roadster, runabout, buggy; hard-top, soft-t., convertible; coupé, sports car; racing car, stock c., dragster, hot-rod; hatchback, estate car, station wagon, shooting brake; Land Rover (tdmk), jeep; police car, patrol c.; veteran car, vintage car, model T; tin Lizzie, banger, bus, jalopy, old crock, rattletrap; beetle, bubble car, minicar; invalid car, three-wheeler; minibus, camper.

lorry, truck, pickup t., dump t.; refuse lorry, dustcart; container lorry, articulated l., roadliner, juggernaut; tanker, bowser; car transporter, low-loader; van, delivery v., removal v., pantechnicon; electric van, float.

train, railway t., passenger t., special t., excursion t., boat t., motorail; express train, through t., intercity t., high speed t., HST, advanced passenger t., APT; slow train, stopping t.; goods train, freight t., freightliner; milk train, mail t., night mail; rolling stock, multiple unit; coach, carriage, compartment, first-class c., second-class c., smoker, nonsmoker; Pullman, wagon-lit, sleeping car, sleeper; restaurant car, dining c., buffet c., observation c.; guard's van, luggage v., brake v., caboose; truck, waggon, tank w., hopper w., trolley; bogie; steam train, diesel t., electric t., tube t., model t.; live rail, third r., overhead wires, pantograph; cable railway, electric r., underground r. 624 *railway*; Flying Scotsman, Golden Arrow, Orient Express.

locomotive, iron horse; diesel engine, diesel, steam engine, pony e., tank e., shunter, cab, tender; choo-choo, puff-puff, puffer, chuffer, Puffing Billy, Rocket; traction engine, steam roller.

conveyor; conveyor belt, escalator, moving staircase, moving pavement; shovel, hod 194 *ladle*; fork, trowel 370 *farm tool*; crane 310 *lifter*.

Adj. *vehicular*, wheeled, on wheels; on rails, on runners, on sleds, on skates; horse-drawn, pedal-driven, motorized, electrified; automobile, automotive, locomotive;

non-stop, high-speed, express, through; stopping, local.
See: 194, 310, 370, **624**, 722.

275 Ship

N. *ship*, vessel, boat, craft, watercraft; bark, barque; great ship, tall s.; little ship, cockleshell; bottom, keel, sail; hooker, tub, hull; hulk, prisonship; Argo, Golden Hind, Noah's Ark; steamer, screw s., steamship, steamboat, motor vessel; paddle steamer, paddleboat, sternwheeler, riverboat, showboat; passenger ship, liner, ocean greyhound, floating palace; channel steamer, ferry; hovercraft, hydrofoil; rotor ship; mail-boat, packet, steam p.; dredger, hopper, icebreaker; transport, hospital ship; storeship, tender, escort vessel; pilot vessel; tug, launch; lightship, weather ship; underwater craft, submarine, U-boat 722 *warship*.
galley, war g., galleass, galliot; pirate ship, privateer, corsair; Viking ship, longship; bireme, trireme, quadrireme, quinquereme.
merchant ship, merchantman, trader; cog, galleon, argosy, dromond, carrack, polacre; caravel, galliot, Indiaman; banana boat, tea clipper; slave ship, slaver; cargo boat, freighter, tramp; coaster, chasse-marée; fly-boat, bilander, lugger, hoy; collier, tanker, oil t., supertanker; container ship.
fishing boat, inshore f. boat.; fishing smack, dogger, hooker, buss, coble; drifter, trawler, purse-seiner; factory ship; whaler, whale-catcher.
sailing ship, sailing boat, sailer; windjammer, clipper, tall ship; square-rigged ship (**see** *rig*); four-masted ship, three-masted s., threemaster; barque, barquentine; two-masted ship, brig, hermaphrodite b., brigantine, schooner, pinnace; frigate, corvette 722 *warship*; cutter, sloop, ketch, yawl; wherry; yacht, racing y.; sailing dinghy, smack; xebec, felucca, caïque, dhow, junk, sampan.
rig, square rig, fore-and-aft rig, lateen r., schooner r., sloop r., cutter r., Bermuda r., gaff r.
sail, sailcloth, canvas; square sail, lugsail, lug, lateen sail, fore-and-aft s., leg-of-mutton s., spanker; course, mainsail, foresail, topsail, topgallant sail, royal, skysail; jib, staysail, spinnaker, balloon sail, studding s.; rigging 47 *tackling*; mast, foremast, mainmast, mizzenmast 218 *prop*.
boat, skiff, foldboat, cockboat; lifeboat; ship's boat, tender, dinghy, pram; longboat, jolly boat; whaleboat, dory; pinnace, cutter, gig; bumboat, surf boat; barge, lighter, pontoon; ferry, ferryboat, canalboat, narrowboat; houseboat; towboat, tugboat, tug; powerboat, motorboat, motor launch; pleasure-boat, cabin cruiser; speedboat.
rowing boat, galley; eight, racing e.; sculler, shell, randan; skiff, dinghy, rubber dinghy; coracle, currach; punt, gondola; canoe, outrigger, dugout; pirogue, proa, kayak, umiak.
raft, liferaft, balsa, catamaran, trimaran; float, pontoon.
shipping, craft, forest of masts; argosy, fleet, flotilla, squadron 722 *navy*; marine, mercantile marine, merchant navy, shipping line; flag of convenience 547 *flag*.
Adj. *marine*, maritime, naval, nautical, seagoing, ocean-g. 269 *seafaring*; sea-worthy, water-w., weatherly; snug, tight, shipshape; rigged, square-r. (**see** *rig*); clinker-built, carvel-b.; flush-decked.
Adv. *afloat*, aboard, on board ship, on shipboard; under sail, under steam, under canvas.
See: 47, 218, **269**, 547, **722**.

276 Aircraft

N. *aircraft* 271 *aeronautics*; aerodyne, flying machine; aeroplane, airplane, crate; plane, monoplane, biplane, triplane; amphibian; hydroplane, seaplane, flying boat; airliner, airbus, transport, freighter; warplane, fighter, bomber 722 *air force*; stratocruiser, jet plane, jet, jumbo j., jump j., supersonic j., turbojet, turboprop; VTOL; helicopter, autogyro, whirlybird, chopper, copter; ornithopter; hovercraft 275 *ship*; glider, sailplane; flying instruments, controls, joystick, rudder; aerofoil, fin, tail; flaps, aileron 271 *wing*; prop 269 *propeller*; cockpit, flight deck; undercarriage, landing gear; parachute, ejector seat 300 *ejector*; test bed, wind tunnel; flight simulator; aerodrome 271 *air travel*.
airship, aerostat, balloon, Montgolfier b., hot-air b.; captive balloon, barrage b., observation b., weather b., blimp; dirigible, Zeppelin; kite, box-k.; parachute, chute; hang glider; magic carpet; balloon-basket, nacelle, car, gondola.
rocket, rocketry; step rocket, multistage r.;

booster; nose cone, warhead; guided missile, intercontinental ballistic m. 723 *missile weapon*; doodlebug, V1, V2.

spaceship, spacecraft, space probe, space capsule, space shuttle; lunar module; space station, sputnik 321 *satellite*; flying saucer, UFO, unidentified flying object.

Adj. *aviational*, aeronautical, aerospace; aerodynamic, aerostatic; astronautical, space-travelling; airworthy 271 *flying*; heavier-than-air, lighter-than-air; supersonic; vertical take-off.

See: 1, 2, 269, **271**, 275, 300, 321, **722**, **723**.

277 Velocity

N. *velocity*, celerity, rapidity, speed, swiftness, fleetness, quickness, liveliness, alacrity, agility; instantaneousness, speed of thought 116 *instantaneity*; no loss of time, promptness, expedition, dispatch; speed, tempo, rate, pace, bat 265 *motion*; speed-rate, miles per hour, knots; Mach number; speed of light, speed of sound, supersonic speed; great speed, lightning s.; maximum speed, express s., full s., full steam; utmost speed, press of sail, full s.; precipitation, hurry, flurry 680 *haste*; reckless speed, breakneck s. 857 *rashness*; streak, blue s., streak of lightning, flash, lightning f.; flight, jet f., supersonic f.; gale, hurricane, tempest, torrent; electricity, telegraph, lightning, greased l.; speed measurement, tachometer, speedometer 465 *gauge*; wind gauge 340 *pneumatics*; log, logline; speed trap 542 *trap*.

spurt, acceleration, speed-up, overtaking; burst, burst of speed, burst of energy; thrust, drive, impetus 279 *impulse*; jump, spring, bound, pounce 312 *leap*; whiz, swoop, swoosh, zip, uprush, zoom; down rush, dive, power d.; flying start, rush, dash, scamper, run, sprint, gallop, tantivy.

speeding, driving, hard d., scorching, racing, burn-up; bowling along, rattling a., batting a.; course, race, career, full c.; full speed, full lick; pace, smart p., rattling p., spanking rate, fair clip; quick march, double, forced march 680 *haste*; clean pair of heels, quick retreat 667 *escape*; race course, speed track 716 *racing*.

speeder, hustler, speed merchant, speed maniac, scorcher, racing driver 268 *driver*; runner, harrier; racer, sprinter; galloper; courser, racehorse 273 *thoroughbred*; greyhound, cheetah, hare, deer, doe, gazelle, antelope; ostrich, eagle, swallow; arrow, arrow from the bow, bullet, cannonball 287 *missile*; jet, rocket; speedboat, clipper 275 *ship*; express, express train; express messenger, Ariel, Mercury 529 *courier*; magic carpet, seven-league boots.

Adj. *speedy*, swift, fast, quick, rapid, nimble, volant; darting, dashing, lively, brisk, smart, snappy, nifty, zippy 174 *vigorous*; wasting no time, expeditious, hustling 680 *hasty*; double-quick, rapid-fire; prompt 135 *early*; immediate 116 *instantaneous*; high-geared, high-speed, adapted for speed, streamlined, souped-up; speeding, racing, ton-up; running, charging, runaway; flying, whizzing, hurtling, pelting; whirling, tempestuous; breakneck, headlong, precipitate 857 *rash*; fleet, fleet of foot, wing-footed, light-f., nimble-f., quick-f.; darting, starting, flashing; swift-moving, agile, nimble, slippery, evasive; mercurial, like quicksilver 152 *changeful*; winged, eagle-w., like a bird; arrowy, like an arrow; like a flash, like greased lightning, like the wind, quick as lightning, quick as thought, quick as the wind, like a bat out of hell; meteoric, electric, telegraphic, transonic, supersonic, hypersonic, jet-propelled.

Vb. *move fast*, move, shift, travel, speed; drive, pelt, streak, flash, shoot; scorch, burn up the miles, scour the plain, tear up the road; scud, careen; skim, nip, cut; bowl along 258 *go smoothly*; sweep along, tear a., rattle a., thunder a., storm a.; tear, rip, zip, rush, dash; fly, wing, whiz, skirr; hurtle, zoom, dive; dash off, tear o., dart o., dash on, dash forward; plunge, lunge, swoop; run, trot, double, lope, spank, gallop; bolt, cut and run, hotfoot it, leg it, scoot, skedaddle, scamper, scurry, skelter, scuttle; show a clean pair of heels 620 *run away*; hare, run like a h., run like the wind, run like mad, run like the clappers; start, dart, dartle, flit; frisk, whisk; spring, bound, leap, jump, pounce; ride hard, put one's best foot forward, stir one's stumps, get cracking, get a move on; hie, hurry, post, haste 680 *hasten*; chase, charge, stampede, career, go full tilt, go full pelt, go full lick, go full bat, go full steam, go all out; break the speed limit, break the sound barrier.

accelerate, speed up, raise the tempo; gather

momentum, impart m., spurt, sprint, put on speed, pick up s., whip up s., step on it, step on the gas, put one's foot down, open the throttle, open up, let it rip; crowd on sail; quicken one's speed, mend one's pace, get a move on; set off at a run, get off to a flying start; make up time, make forced marches; quicken, step up, give one his *or* her head, drive, spur, urge forward, urge on; clap spurs to, lend wings to, put dynamite under, expedite 680 *hasten*.

outstrip, overtake, overhaul, catch up, catch up with; lap, outpace, outrun, outmarch, outsail, outwalk, outdrive 306 *outdo*; gain on, distance, outdistance, leave behind, leave standing; lose, shake off; make the running, have the legs of, romp home, win the race 34 *be superior*.

Adv. *swiftly*, rapidly etc. adj.; trippingly, apace; posthaste, with speed, at express s., at full s., at full tilt; in full career, in full gallop, with whip and spur, all out, flat out, ventre à terre; helter-skelter, headlong, lickety-split, hell for leather; presto, pronto, smartish, p.d.q.; like a shot, like the clappers, in a flash, before you could say Jack Robinson 116 *instantaneously*; in full sail, under press of sail *or* canvas, under full steam, full speed ahead; on eagle's wings, with giant strides; nineteen to the dozen, hand over fist; at a rate of knots, at the double, in double-quick time, as fast as one's legs would carry one; in high gear, at the top of one's speed, for all one is worth; by leaps and bounds, in geometrical progression, like wildfire.

See: 34, **116**, 135, 152, 174, 258, 265, 268, 273, 275, 279, 287, 306, 312, 340, 465, 529, 542, 620, 667, **680**, 716, 857.

278 Slowness

N. *slowness*, slackness, languor 679 *sluggishness*; inertia 175 *inertness*; refusal to be hurried, festina lente, deliberation 823 *inexcitability*; tentativeness, gradualism, Fabianism; hesitation 858 *caution*; reluctance 598 *unwillingness*; go-slow, working to rule 145 *strike*; slowing down, slowdown, deceleration, retardation 113 *protraction*; drag 333 *friction*; brake, curb 747 *restraint*; leisureliness, no hurry, time to spare, leisurely progress, easy stages 681 *leisure*; slow motion, low gear; slow march, dead m.; slow time, andante; slow pace, foot p., snail's p., crawl, creep, dawdle; mincing steps, walk, piaffer, amble, jog trot, dog t. 265 *gait*; limping, hobbling; standing start, slow s.; lagging, lag, time lag 136 *delay*.

slowcoach, snail, slug, tortoise, tardigrade; stopping train, slow t.; funeral procession, cortege; dawdler, loiterer, lingerer; slow starter, late developer; laggard, sluggard, lie-abed, sleepyhead, Weary Willie; sloucher 598 *slacker*; drone 679 *idler*.

Adj. *slow*, painfully s.; slow-paced, low-geared, slow-motion, time-lapse; oozy, trickling, dripping; snail-like, tortoise-l., creeping, crawling, dragging; tardigrade, slow-moving 695 *clumsy*; limping, halting; taking one's time, tardy, dilatory, lagging 136 *late*; long about it, unhurried 681 *leisurely*; sedate 875 *formal*; deliberate 823 *patient*; painstaking 457 *careful*; Fabian, cunctative 858 *cautious*; groping, tentative 461 *experimental*; languid, slack, sluggish 679 *lazy*; apathetic, phlegmatic 375 *insensible*; gradual, stealthy, imperceptible, unnoticeable, invisible.

Vb. *move slowly*, go slow, amble, crawl, creep, inch, inch along, ease a., glide a.; ooze, drip, trickle, dribble 350 *flow*; drift 282 *deviate*; hang over, hover; shamble, slouch, mooch, shuffle, scuff; toddle, waddle, take short steps, mince; plod, trudge, tramp, lumber, stump, stump along; wobble, totter, stagger, lurch; struggle, toil, labour, chug, jolt, bump, creak; limp, hobble, go lame; drag one's steps, flag, falter 684 *be fatigued*; trail, lag, fall behind 284 *follow*; not get started, not start, hang fire, drag one's feet, drag oneself 598 *be unwilling*; tarry, be long about it, not be hurried, take one's time 136 *be late*; laze, maunder, idle 679 *be inactive*; take it easy, linger, stroll, saunter, dawdle 267 *walk*; march in slow time, barely move, hardly beat, tick over; grope, feel one's way 461 *be tentative*; soft-pedal, hesitate 858 *be cautious*; speak slowly, drawl 580 *stammer*.

decelerate, slow down, slow up, ease up, let up, lose momentum; reduce speed, slacken s., slacken one's pace; smell the ground (of ships); relax, slacken, ease off 145 *pause*; lose ground, flag, falter 684 *be fatigued*.

retard, check, curb, rein in, throttle down 177 *moderate*; reef, shorten sail, take in s., strike s 269 *navigate*; brake, put on the b., put on the drag 747 *restrain*; backpedal, backwater, backpaddle, put the engines astern, reverse 286 *regress*; handicap, clip the wings 702 *hinder*.

Adv. *slowly*, deliberately etc. adj.; leisurely, lazily, sluggishly; creepingly, creakily, joltily; at half speed, at low s., in low gear, in bottom g.; with mincing steps, at a foot's pace, at a snail's p., at a funeral p.; with leaden step; on crutches; gingerly; in one's own good time; in slow time, adagio, largo, larghetto, lente andante.

gradatim, gradually etc. adj.; by degrees, by slow d., by inches, little by little, bit by bit, inch by inch, step by step, one at a time, by easy stages.

See: 113, 136, 145, 175, 177, 265, 267, 269, 282, 284, 286, 333, 350, 375, 457, 461, 580, 598, **679**, 681, 684, 695, 702, 747, 823, 858, 875.

279 Impulse

N. *impulse*, impulsion, pressure; impetus, momentum; boost, stir-up 174 *stimulant*; encouragement 612 *incentive*; thrust, push, shove, heave; batting, stroke; throw, fling 287 *propulsion*; lunge, kick 712 *attack*; percussion, beating, tapping, drumming; beat, drumbeat 403 *roll*; recoilless beat, dead b., thud; ramming, bulldozing, hammering; butting, butt (**see** *collision*); concussion, shaking, rattling; shock, impact; slam, bang; flick, clip, tap 378 *touch*; shake, rattle, jolt, jerk, wrench 318 *agitation*; pulsation, pulse 318 *spasm*; science of forces, mechanics, dynamics.

knock, dint, dent 255 *concavity*; rap, tap, clap; dab, pat, fillip, flip, flick; nudge, dig 547 *gesture*; smack, slap; cuff, clout, clump, buffet, box on the ears; blow, fourpenny one; lash, stroke, hit, crack; cut, drive (cricket); thwack, thump, biff, bang; punch, rabbit p., left, right, straight left, uppercut, jab, hook; body blow, wild b., haymaker, swipe; knock-out blow, shrewd b.; stamp, kick; whop, swat; spanking, trouncing, dusting, pasting, licking, leathering, whipping, flogging, thrashing, beating, hammering, pummelling, rain of blows; hiding 963 *corporal punishment*; assault, assault and battery 712 *attack*; exchange of blows, fisticuffs, cut and thrust, hammer and tongs 61 *turmoil*.

collision, encounter, meeting; head-on collision, frontal c.; bird strike; graze, scrape 333 *friction*; clash 14 *contrariety*; cannon, carom; impact, bump, shock, crash, smash, smashup, accident; brunt, charge, force 712 *attack*; collision course 293 *convergence*; multiple collision, pileup 74 *accumulation*.

hammer, sledge h., steam h., trip h.; hammerhead, peen; punch, puncher; beetle, maul, mallet; flail; racket, bat, hockey stick, golf club; tapper, knocker, door k.; cosh, blackjack, knuckle-duster, cudgel, club, mace, bicycle chain, sandbag 723 *weapon*; boxing glove; pestle, anvil; hammerer, cudgeller, pummeller, beater, carpet-b.

ram, battering r., bulldozer; pile driver, monkey; ramrod; rammer, tamper; cue, billiard c., pusher 287 *propellant*.

Adj. *impelling*, pushing etc. vb.; impellent; dynamic, dynamical, thrusting; impelled etc. vb.

Vb. *impel*, fling, heave, throw 287 *propel*; give an impetus, impart momentum; slam, bang 264 *close*; press, press in, press up, press down; push, thrust, shove; ram down, tamp; shove off, push off, pole, punt; hustle, prod, urge, spur 277 *accelerate*; fillip, flip, flick; jerk, shake, rattle, shock, jog, jolt, jostle 318 *agitate*; shoulder, elbow, push out of the way, push around 282 *deflect*; throw out, run out, expel 300 *eject*; frogmarch; drive forward, flog on, whip on; goad 612 *incite*; drive, start, run, set going, set moving 173 *operate*; raise 310 *elevate*; plunge, dip, douse 311 *lower*.

collide, make impact 378 *touch*; impinge 306 *encroach*; come into collision 293 *converge*; meet, encounter, clash; cross swords, fence 712 *strike at*; ram, butt, bunt, batter, dint, dent; batter at, bulldoze 165 *demolish*; cannon into, bump into, bump against; graze, graze against 333 *rub*; butt against, collide a.; drive into, crash i., smash i., run i., run down, run over; clash with, collide w., foul, fall foul of; run one's head against, run into a brick wall, run against, dash a. 712 *charge*; clash against, grate a., bark one's shins, stub one's toe; trip, trip over 309 *tumble*; knock together, knock heads t., clash the cymbals, clap one's hands.

strike, smite, hit, land a blow, plant a b., fetch one a b.; aim a blow, hit out at; lunge, lunge at, poke at, strike at; lash out at, let fly; hit wildly, swing, flail, beat the air; strike hard, slam, bang, knock; knock for six, knock into the middle of next week, send flying; knock down, floor 311 *fell*; pat, patter; flip, fillip, tickle; tap, rap, clap; slap, smack; clump, clout, clobber, box the ears of; box, spar 716 *fight;* buffet, punch, thump, thwack, whack, wham, rain blows, pummel, trounce, belabour, beat up, sock it to, let one have it; give one a black eye *or* a bloody nose, make one see stars; pound, batter, bludgeon 332 *pulverize*; biff, bash, dash, slosh, sock, slog, slug, cosh, cudgel, club, mug, spifflicate; blackjack, sandbag, hit over the head, crown; concuss, stun, knock out, leave senseless; spank, wallop, thrash, lash, lam, lambast, beat, whip, cane 963 *flog*; leather, strap, belt, tan one's hide, give a hiding 963 *punish*; thresh, scutch, swingle, flail; hammer, drum; flap, squash, swat 216 *flatten*; paw, stroke 889 *caress*; scratch, maul 655 *wound*; run through, bayonet, pink 263 *pierce*; tear 46 *cut*; throw stones at, stone, pelt, snowball 712 *lapidate*; head (a football); bat, strike a ball, swipe, drive, turn, glance, cut, crack, lift, lob, smash, volley 287 *propel*.

kick, spurn, boot, knee, put the boot in; trample, tread on, stamp on, kneel on; ride over, ride roughshod; spur, dig in one's heels; heel, dribble, shoot (a football).

See: 14, 46, 61, 74, 165, 173, 174, 216, 255, 263, 264, 277, 282, **287**, 293, 300, 306, 309, 310, 311, 318, 332, 333, 378, 403, 547, 612, 655, 712, 716, 723, 889, 963.

280 Recoil

N. *recoil*, revulsion, reaction, retroaction, reflux 148 *reversion*; repercussion, reverberation, echo 404 *resonance*; reflex 417 *reflection*; kick, kickback, backlash; ricochet, cannon, carom; rebound, bounce, spring, springboard, trampoline 328 *elasticity*; ducks and drakes; swing-back, swing of the pendulum 317 *oscillation*; volley, return (at tennis), boomerang; rebuff, repulse 292 *repulsion*; riposte, return fire.

Adj. *recoiling*, rebounding etc. vb.; reactive, repercussive, refluent; retroactive 148 *reverted*.

Vb. *recoil*, react 182 *counteract*; shrink, wince, flinch, jib, shy 620 *avoid*; kick back, hit b.; ricochet, cannon, cannon off; uncoil, spring back, fly b., bound b., rebound; return, swing back 148 *revert*; have repercussions; reverberate, echo 404 *resound*; be reflected, reflect 417 *shine*; return on one's head, boomerang 714 *retaliate*.

See: **148**, 182, 292, 317, 328, 404, 417, 620, 714.

281 Direction

N. *direction*, bearing, compass reading 186 *bearings*; lie of the land 186 *situation*; orientation, collimation, alignment; set, drift 350 *current*; tenor, trend, bending 179 *tendency*; course, beam; beeline, straight shot, line of sight, optical axis 249 *straightness*; course, tack; line, line of march, track, way, path, road 624 *route*; steering, steerage; aim, target 295 *goal*; compass, pelorus 269 *sailing aid*; collimator, sights 442 *optical device*; fingerpost 547 *signpost*; direction finder, range f. 465 *gauge*; orienteering, cross-country race, point-to-point.

compass point, cardinal points, half points, quarter points; quarter, north, east, south, west; magnetic north; rhumb, azimuth.

Adj. *directed*, orientated, directed towards, pointing t., signposted; aimed, well-a., well-directed, well-placed 187 *located*; bound for 617 *intending*; aligned with 219 *parallel*; axial, diagonal 220 *oblique*; sideways 239 *lateral*; facing 240 *opposite*; direct, undeviating, unswerving, straightforward, one-way 249 *straight*; northbound, southbound; northern, northerly, southerly, meridional; western, occidental; eastern, oriental; directive, guiding; showing the way.

Vb. *orientate*, orientate oneself, box the compass, take one's bearings, shoot the sun, check one's course, plot one's c. 269 *navigate*; find which way the wind blows, see how the land lies; take a direction, have a d., bear; direct oneself, ask the way; signpost, direct, show the way, put on the right track 547 *indicate*; pinpoint, locate 187 *place*; keep on the beam 249 *be straight*; face, front 240 *be opposite*.

steer for, steer, shape a course for, set the helm f., be bound f., head f., run f., stand f., make f., aim f.; make towards, bend one's steps to, go to, go towards, go straight for, make a beeline for, march on, align one's march; go straight to the point, hold the line, keep on the beam, keep the nose down 249 *be straight*.

point to, point out, point, point towards, signpost 547 *indicate*; trend, trend towards, incline t., verge, dip, bend 179 *tend*.

aim, level, point; take aim, aim at; train one's sights, draw a bead on, level at; cover, have one covered; collimate, set one's sights; aim well, hit the mark, land, plant 187 *place*.

Adv. *towards*, versus, facing; on the way, on the road to, through, via, by way of; straight, direct, straight forwards; point blank, straight as an arrow; in a direct line, in a straight line, in a line with, in a line for; directly, full tilt at, as the crow flies; upstream, downstream; upwind, downwind; before the wind, close to the w., near the w.; against the w., in the wind's eye, close-hauled; seaward, landward, homeward; downtown; cross-country; in all directions 183 *widely*; from *or* to the four winds; hither, thither; clockwise, anticlockwise, counterclockwise, widdershins; whither, which way?

See: 179, 183, **186**, **187**, 219, 220, 239, 240, 249, 269, 295, 350, 442, 465, 547, 617, 624.

282 Deviation

N. *deviation*, disorientation, misdirection, wrong course, wrong turning; aberration, aberrancy, deflection, refraction; diversion, digression; shift, veer, slew, swing; departure, declension 220 *obliquity*; flexion, swerve, bend 248 *curvature*; branching off, divarication 294 *divergence*; deviousness, detour, bypath, circumbendibus, ambages, long way round 626 *circuit*; vagrancy 267 *wandering*; fall, lapse 495 *error*; wandering mind 456 *abstractedness*; drift, leeway; oblique motion, passaging, crab-walk, sidestep, sideslip; break, leg b., off b., googly (cricket); knight's move (chess); yaw, tack; zigzag, slalom course.

Adj. *deviating*, aberrant, nonconformist, abnormal, deviant 84 *unconformable*; eccentric, off-centre; out of orbit; errant, wandering, rambling, roving, vagrant, loose, footloose 267 *travelling*; undirected, unguided, random, erratic 495 *inexact*; desultory 72 *discontinuous*; abstracted 456 *inattentive*; excursive, digressing; discursive, off the subject 10 *irrelevant*; disorientated, off-course, off-beam, lost, stray, astray; misdirected, misaimed, ill-aimed, off-target, off the mark, wide of the m., wide; off the fairway, in the rough (golf); devious, winding, roundabout 314 *circuitous*; indirect, crooked, zigzag, zigzagging 220 *oblique*; branching, divaricating 294 *divergent*.

Vb. *deviate*, leave the straight, digress, make a detour; branch out, divaricate 294 *diverge*; turn, filter, turn a corner, turn aside, swerve, slew; go out of one's way, depart from one's course; step aside, make way for; alter course, change direction, yaw, tack; veer, back (wind); trend, bend, curve 248 *be curved*; zigzag, twine, twist 251 *meander*; swing, wobble 317 *oscillate*; steer clear of, sheer off; sidle, passage; slide, skid, sideslip; break (cricket); glance, fly off at a tangent 220 *be oblique*; shy, jib, sidestep 620 *avoid*.

turn round, turn about, about turn, wheel, wheel about, face a., face the other way; reverse, reverse direction, return 148 *revert*; go back 286 *turn back*.

stray, err, ramble, rove, drift, divagate, straggle 267 *wander*; go astray, go adrift, miss one's way, lose the w., get lost; lose one's bearings, lose one's sense of direction, take the wrong turning 495 *blunder*; lose track of, lose the thread 456 *be inattentive*.

deflect, bend, crook 220 *make oblique*; warp, skew; put off the scent, misdirect, misaddress 495 *mislead*; avert 713 *parry*; divert, change the course of; sidetrack, draw aside, push a., pull a.; elbow a., edge off; bias, slice, pull, hook, glance, bowl a break, bowl wide (cricket); shuffle, shift, switch, shunt 151 *interchange*; wear ship 269 *navigate*.

Adv. *astray*, adrift; out; wide of the mark, off the mark; right about; round about; erratically, all manner of ways; indirectly, at a tangent, sideways, diagonally 220 *obliquely*; sidling, crabwise.

See: 10, 72, 84, 148, 151, **220**, 248, 251, 267, 269, 286, **294**, 314, 317, 456, 495, 620, 626, 713.

283 Preceding: going before

N. *preceding* 119 *priority*, 64 *precedence*; going before, leading, heading, flying start; preemption, queue-jumping; pride of place, head of the table, head of the river (bumping races); lead, leading role 34 *superiority*; pioneer 66 *precursor*; van, vanguard, avant-garde 237 *front*.

Adj. *foremost*, first; leading etc. vb.
Vb. *precede*, antecede, go before, forerun, herald; usher in, introduce; head, spearhead, lead, be in the van, head the queue; go in front, go in advance, clear the way, light the w., lead the w.; open the ball, lead the dance, guide, conduct 689 *direct*; take the lead, get the lead, have the start on, have a head start; steal a march on, preempt; get in front, jump the queue; get ahead of, lap 277 *outstrip*; be beforehand 135 *be early*; take precedence over, have right of way 64 *come before*.
Adv. *ahead*, before, in advance, in the van, in front, foremost, headmost; primarily, first of all; elders first, women and children first; age before beauty.
See: 34, **64**, **66**, **119**, 135, **237**, 277, 689.

284 Following: going after
N. *following* 65 *sequence*; run, suit 71 *series*; subsequence 120 *posteriority*; pursuit, pursuance 619 *chase*; succession, reversion 780 *transfer*; last place 238 *rear*.
follower, attendant, hanger-on, camp follower, groupie 742 *dependant*; train, tail, wake, cortege, suite, followers 67 *retinue*; following, party, adherent, supporter 703 *aider*; satellite, moon, artificial satellite, space station 276 *spaceship*; trailer, caravan 274 *cart*; tender 275 *ship*.
Adj. *following*, subsequent 65 *sequential*.
Vb. *follow*, come behind, succeed, follow on, follow after, follow close upon, sit on one's tail, follow in the wake of, tread on the heels of, tread in the steps of, follow the footprints of, come to heel 65 *come after*; stick like a shadow, tag after, hang on the skirts of, beset; attend, wait on, dance attendance on 742 *serve*; tag along 89 *accompany*; dog, shadow, trail, tail, track 619 *pursue*; drop behind, fall b., lag, trail, dawdle 278 *move slowly*; bring up the rear 238 *be behind*.
Adv. *behind*, in the rear 238 *rearward*; on the heels of; in the train of, in the wake of, in tow 65 *after*; one after another; later 120 *subsequently*.
See: **65**, **67**, 71, 89, **120**, **238**, 274, 275, 276, 278, 619, 703, 742, 780.

285 Progression: motion forwards
N. *progression*, going forward; procession, march, way, course, career; march of time 111 *course of time*; progress, steady p., forward march 265 *motion*; sudden progress, stride, leap, jump, leaps and bounds 277 *spurt*; irreversibility, irresistible progress, majestic p., flood, tide 350 *current*; gain, ground gained, advance, headway 654 *improvement*; getting ahead, overtaking 283 *preceding*; encroachment 306 *overstepping*; next step, development, evolution 308 *ascent*, 71 *continuity*; mystic progress, purgation, illumination 979 *piety*, 981 *worship*; furtherance, promotion, advancement, preferment; rise, raise, lift, leg-up 310 *elevation*; progressiveness 654 *reformism*; enterprise, go-getting 672 *undertaking*; achievement 727 *success*; economic progress 730 *prosperity*; progressive, improver 654 *reformer*; go-getter, coming man *or* woman, upstart 730 *prosperous person*.
Adj. *progressive*, progressing, enterprising, go-getting, forward-looking, reformist; advancing etc. vb.; profluent, flowing on 265 *moving*; unbroken, irreversible; advanced, up-to-date, abreast of the times 126 *modern*.
Vb. *progress*, proceed 265 *be in motion*; advance, go forward, take a step forward, come on, develop 316 *evolve*; show promise 654 *get better*; get on, do well 730 *prosper*; march on, run on, flow on, pass on, jog on, wag on, rub on, hold on, keep on, slog on 146 *go on*; move with the times 126 *modernize*; maintain progress, never look back, hold one's lead; press on, push on, drive on, push forward, press f., press onwards 680 *hasten*; make a good start, make initial progress, make good p., break the back of; gain, gain ground, make headway, make strides, make rapid s., cover the ground 277 *move fast*; get a move on, get ahead, shoot a., forge a., advance by leaps and bounds; gain on, distance, outdistance, leave behind 277 *outstrip*; gain height, rise, rise higher 308 *climb*; reach towards, reach out to, raise one's sights; make up leeway, recover lost ground 31 *recoup*; gain time, make up t.
promote, further, contribute to, advance 703 *aid*; prefer, upgrade, move up, raise, lift 310 *elevate*; bring forward, push, force, develop 174 *invigorate*; step up, speed up 277 *accelerate*; put ahead, put forward 64 *put in front*; favour, make for, bring on, conduce 156 *cause*.
Adv. *forward*, forwards, onward, forth, on, ahead, forrard; progressively, by leaps and bounds; on the way, on one's way,

under w., en route for, on the road to 272 *in transit*; in progress, in mid p., in sight of.

Int. Forward! Forrard! En avant! Excelsior!

See: 31, 64, 71, 111, 126, 146, 156, 174, **265**, 272, 277, 283, 306, 308, 310, 316, 350, 654, 672, 680, 703, 727, 730, 979, 981.

286 Regression: motion backwards

N. *regression*, regress; reverse direction, retroflexion, retrocession, retrogression, retrogradation, retroaction, backward step 148 *reversion*; motion from, retreat, withdrawal, retirement, disengagement 290 *recession*; regurgitation 300 *voidance*; sternway, reversing, backing, reining back; falling away, decline, drop, fall, slump 655 *deterioration*.

return, remigration, homeward journey; homecoming 295 *arrival*; reentrance, reentry 297 *ingress*; going back, turn of the tide, reflux, refluence, ebb, regurgitation 350 *current*; veering, backing; relapse, backsliding, recidivation 603 *tergiversation*; U-turn, volte-face, about-turn 148 *reversion*; countermarch, countermovement, countermotion 182 *counteraction*; turn, turning point 137 *crisis*; resilience 328 *elasticity*; reflex 280 *recoil*.

Adj. *regressive*, receding, declining, ebbing; refluent, reflex; retrogressive, retrograde, backward; backward-looking, reactionary 125 *retrospective*; retroactive 280 *recoiling*; backing, anticlockwise, counterclockwise; reverse, reversible 148 *reverted*; resilient 328 *elastic*; remigrating, returning, homing, homeward bound.

Vb. *regress*, recede, retrogress, retrograde, retrocede; retreat, sound a r., beat a r.; retire, withdraw, fall back, draw b.; turn away, turn tail 620 *run away*; disengage, back out, back down 753 *resign*; backtrack, backpedal; give way, give ground, lose g.; recede into the distance 446 *disappear*; fall behind, fall astern, drop a. 278 *move slowly*; reverse, back, back water, go backwards; run back, flow back, regurgitate; not hold, slip back; ebb, slump, fall, drop, decline 309 *descend*; bounce back 280 *recoil*.

turn back, put b., retrace one's steps; remigrate, go back, go home, return 148 *revert*; look back, look over one's shoulder, hark back 505 *retrospect*; turn one's back, turn on one's heel; veer round, wheel r., about-face, execute a volte-face 603 *tergiversate*; double, double back, countermarch; start back, jib, shrink 620 *avoid*; come back, come back again, come home; come back to where one started.

Adv. *backwards*, back, astern, in reverse; to the right about.

Int. back! hard astern! hands off!

See: 125, 137, **148**, 182, 278, **280**, **290**, 295, 297, 300, 309, 328, 350, 446, 505, 603, 620, 655, 753.

287 Propulsion

N. *propulsion*, jet p., drive; impulsion, push 279 *impulse*; projection, throwing, tossing, hurling, pelting, slinging, stone-throwing; precipitation; cast, throw, chuck, toss, fling, sling, shy, cock-shy; pot shot, pot, shot, long s.; shooting, firing, discharge, volley 712 *bombardment*; bowling, pitching, throw-in, full toss, yorker, lob (cricket); kick, punt, dribble (football); stroke, drive, swipe 279 *knock*; pull, slice (golf); rally, volley, smash (tennis); ballistics, gunnery, musketry, sniping, pea-shooting; archery, toxophily; marksmanship 694 *skill*; gunshot, bowshot, stone's throw 199 *distance*.

missile, projectile, shell, rocket, cannonball, grapeshot, ball, bullet, shot, small s.; pellet, brickbat, stone, snowball; arrow, dart 723 *missile weapon*; ball, tennis b., golf b., cricket b., hockey b.; football, rugby ball; bowl, boule, wood, jack, puck, curling stone; quoit, discus; javelin; hammer, caber.

propellant, thrust, driving force, jet, steam 160 *energy*; spray, aerosol; thruster, pusher, shover 279 *ram*; tail wind, following w. 352 *wind*; lever, treadle, pedal, bicycle p.; oar, sweep, paddle; screw, blade, paddlewheel 269 *propeller*; coal, petrol, diesel oil 385 *fuel*; gunpowder, dynamite 723 *explosive*; shotgun, rifle 723 *firearm*; revolver 723 *pistol*; airgun, pop gun, water pistol; blowpipe, pea-shooter; catapult, sling, bow 723 *missile weapon*.

shooter, gunman, rifleman, musketeer, pistoleer; gunner, artilleryman 722 *soldiery*; archer, bowman, toxophilite; marksman, markswoman, sharpshooter, sniper, shot, crack s. 696 *proficient person*.

thrower, hurler, caster, pelter, stoner, snowballer; knife-thrower, javelin-t., discus-t., stone-t., slinger; bowler, pitcher, curler.

Adj. *propulsive*, propellant, propelling etc.

vb.; expulsive, explosive, propelled etc. vb.; projectile, missile; ballistic.

Vb. *propel,* launch, project; flight, throw, cast, deliver, heave, pitch, toss, cant, chuck, shy, bung; bowl, lob, york; hurl, fling, sling, catapult; dart, flick; pelt, stone, shower, snowball 712 *lapidate*; precipitate, send flying, send headlong; expel, pitchfork 300 *eject*; blow away, puff a.; blow up, explode, put dynamite under; serve, return, volley, smash, kill (tennis); bat, slam, slog, wham; sky, loft; drive, cut, pull, hook, glance (cricket); slice 279 *strike*; kick, dribble, punt (football); putt, push, shove, shoulder, ease along 279 *impel*; wheel, pedal, roll, bowl, trundle 315 *rotate*; move on, drive, hustle 265 *move*; sweep, sweep up, sweep before one, drive like leaves; put to flight 727 *defeat.*

shoot, fire, open fire, fire off; volley, fire a v.; discharge, explode, let off, set off; let fly, shower with arrows, volley and thunder; draw a bead on, pull the trigger; cannonade, bombard 712 *fire at*; snipe, pot, pot at, loose off at; pepper 263 *pierce.*

See: 160, 199, 263, 265, 269, **279**, 300, 315, 352, 385, 694, 696, **712**, 722, **723**, 727.

288 Traction

N. *traction,* drawing etc. vb.; pulling back, retraction; retractility, retractability; magnetism 291 *attraction*; towage, haulage; draught, pull, haul; tug, tow; towline, towrope; rake, harrow, draw-hoe; trawl, dragnet; drawer, puller, tugger, tower, hauler, haulier; retractor; lugsail, square sail 275 *sail*; windlass 310 *lifter*; tug, tugboat 275 *ship*; tractor, traction engine 274 *locomotive*; lodestone 291 *magnet*; rowing; strain, tug of war 716 *contest*; thing drawn, trailer 274 *cart.*

Adj. *drawing,* pulling etc. vb., tractional, tractive; pulling back, retractive, retractile, retractable; attractive, magnetic 291 *attracting*; tractile, ductile; drawn, horse-d.

Vb. *draw,* pull, haul, hale; trice, warp, kedge 269 *navigate*; tug, tow, take in tow; lug, drag, draggle, trail, trawl; rake, harrow; winch, reel in, wind in, wind up, lift, heave 310 *elevate*; drag down 311 *lower*; suck in 299 *absorb*; pluck, pull out 304 *extract*; wrench 246 *distort*; yank, jerk, twitch, tweak, pluck at, snatch at 318 *agitate*; pull towards 291 *attract*; pull back, draw b., pull in, draw in, retract, sheathe (claws).

Int. yo-heave-ho!

See: 246, 269, 274, 275, **291**, 299, 304, 310, 311, 318, 716.

289 Approach: motion towards

N. *approach,* coming towards, advance 285 *progression*; near approach, approximation 200 *nearness*; flowing towards, afflux 350 *stream*; meeting, confluence 293 *convergence*; access, accession, advent, coming 295 *arrival,* 189 *presence*; approach from behind, overtaking, overlapping 619 *pursuit*; onset 712 *attack*; advances, overture 759 *offer*; means of approach, accessibility, approaches 624 *access.*

Adj. *approaching,* nearing, getting warm etc. vb.; close, approximative 200 *near*; meeting 293 *convergent*; confluent, affluent, tributary; overhanging, hovering, closing in, imminent 155 *impending*; advancing, coming, oncoming, on the way 295 *arriving.*

accessible, approachable, get-at-able; within reach, attainable 469 *possible*; available, obtainable 189 *on the spot*; wayside, roadside, nearby 200 *near*; welcoming, inviting 291 *attracting,* 882 *sociable*; well-paved, made-up, metalled 624 *communicating.*

Vb. *approach,* draw near 200 *be near*; approximate 200 *bring near*; come within range 295 *arrive*; come into view 443 *be visible*; feel the attraction of, be drawn; come to close quarters, come closer, meet 293 *converge*; run down 279 *collide*; near, draw n., get n., go n., come n.; move near, run up to, step up to, sidle up to; roll up 74 *congregate*; come in 297 *enter*; accede, adhere, join 38 *accrue*; waylay, buttonhole; accost 884 *greet*; make up to, make overtures, make passes 889 *court*; nestle, snuggle up to 889 *caress*; lean towards, incline, trend 179 *tend*; move towards, walk t., make t., drift t. 265 *be in motion*; advance 285 *progress*; advance upon, bear down on 712 *attack*; close, close in, close in on 232 *circumscribe*; hover 155 *impend*; gain upon, catch up with, overtake 277 *outstrip*; follow hard, narrow the gap, breathe down one's neck, tread on one's heels, run one close; be in sight of, make the land, make a landfall 295 *land*; hug the coast, hug the shore 269 *navigate.*

Int. this way! come closer! roll up! land ahoy!

See: 38, 74, 155, 179, 189, **200**, 232, 265, 269, 277, 279, 285, 291, **293**, **295**, 297, 350, 443, 469, 619, 624, 712, 759, 882, 884, 889.

290 Recession: motion from

N. *recession*, retirement, withdrawal, retreat, retrocession 286 *regression*; leak 298 *outflow*; emigration, evacuation 296 *departure*; resignation 621 *relinquishment*; flight 667 *escape*; shrinking, flinching 620 *avoidance*; revulsion 280 *recoil*.

Adj. *receding*, ebbing etc. vb.; retreating 286 *regressive*.

Vb. *recede*, retire, withdraw, fall back, draw b., retreat 286 *regress*; ebb, subside, shrink, decline 37 *decrease*; fade from view 446 *disappear*; go, go away, leave, evacuate, emigrate 296 *depart*; go outside, go out, pour out 298 *emerge*; leak, leak out 298 *flow out*; move from, move away, move off, move further, stand off, put space between, widen the gap 199 *be distant*; stand aside, make way, veer away, sheer off 282 *deviate*; drift away 282 *stray*; back away, shrink a., flinch 620 *avoid*; flee 620 *run away*; get away 667 *escape*; go back 286 *turn back*; jump back 280 *recoil*; come off, come away, come unstuck 46 *separate*.

See: 37, 46, 199, 280, 282, **286**, **296**, 298, 446, 620, 621, 667.

291 Attraction

N. *attraction*, pull, drag, draw, tug; drawing to, pulling towards; magnetization, magnetism, magnetic field; gravity, force of g.; itch, itch for 859 *desire*; affinity, sympathy; attractiveness, seductiveness, allure, appeal, sex a.; allurement, seduction, temptation, lure, bait, decoy, charm, siren song 612 *inducement*; charmer, temptress, siren, Circe 612 *motivator*; centre of attraction, cynosure 890 *favourite*.

magnet, bar m., horseshoe m.; coil magnet, solenoid; magnetite, magnetized iron, lodestone; lodestar 520 *guide*; magnetizer.

Adj. *attracting*, drawing etc. vb.; adductive, associative, attractive; magnetic, magnetized; siren, seductive, charming 612 *inducing*; centripetal.

Vb. *attract*, magnetize, pull, drag, tug 288 *draw*; adduct, exercise a pull, draw towards, pull t., drag t., tug t.; appeal, charm, move, pluck at one's heartstrings 821 *impress*; lure, allure, bait 612 *tempt*; decoy 542 *ensnare*.

See: **288**, 520, 542, **612**, 821, 859, 890.

292 Repulsion

N. *repulsion*, repellence; repulsive force, centrifugal f.; repellent quality, repulsiveness 842 *ugliness*; reflection 280 *recoil*; driving off, beating o. 713 *defence*; repulse, rebuff, snub, refusal 607 *rejection*; brush off, dismissal 300 *ejection*.

Adj. *repellent*, repelling etc. vb.; repulsive, off-putting, antipathetic 861 *disliked*; abducent, abductive; centrifugal.

Vb. *repel*, put off, excite nausea 861 *cause dislike*; put away; push away, butt a., butt, head 279 *impel*; drive away, chase a., repulse, beat off, fend off, block, stonewall 713 *parry*; dispel 75 *disperse*; head off, turn away, reflect 282 *deflect*; be deaf to 760 *refuse*; rebuff, snub, brush off, reject one's advances 607 *reject*; give one the bird, cold-shoulder, keep at arm's length, make one keep his *or* her distance 883 *make unwelcome*; show the door to, shut the door in one's face, send one off with a flea in his *or* her ear, send packing, send one about his *or* her business, give one his *or* her marching orders; boot out, sack 300 *dismiss*.

Int. be off! away with you! scram! hop it! get lost!

See: 75, 279, 280, 282, **300**, 607, 713, 760, 842, 861, 883.

293 Convergence

N. *convergence*, mutual approach 289 *approach*; narrowing gap; collision course 279 *collision*; concourse, confluence, conflux, meeting 45 *union*; congress, concurrence, concentration, resort, assembly 74 *assemblage*; closing in, pincer movement 232 *circumscription*; centring, focalization 76 *focus*; narrowing, coming to a point, tapering, taper 206 *narrowness*; converging line, asymptote, tangent; convergent view, perspective, vanishing point 438 *view*.

Adj. *convergent*, converging etc. vb.; focusing, focused; centripetal, centring; confluent, concurrent 45 *conjunctive*; tangential; pointed, conical, pyramidal 256 *tapering*; knock-kneed.

Vb. *converge*, come closer, draw in, close in; narrow the gap; fall in with, come together 295 *meet*; unite, gather together, get t. 74 *congregate*; roll in, pour in, enter in 297 *enter*; close with, intercept, head off, close in upon 232 *circumscribe*; pinch, nip 198 *make smaller*; concentrate, focus, bring into f.; align convergently, toe in; centre, centre on, centre in 225 *centralize*; taper, come to a point, narrow down 206 *be narrow*.

See: 45, 74, 76, 198, 206, 225, 232, 256, 279, **289**, 295, 297, 438.

294 Divergence

N. *divergence* 15 *difference*; complete divergence, contradiction 14 *contrariety*; going apart, divarication; moving apart, parting 46 *separation*; aberration, declination 282 *deviation*; spread, fanning out, deployment 75 *dispersion*; parting of the ways, fork, bifurcation, crossroads, points 222 *crossing*; radiation, ramification, branching out; Y-shape 247 *angularity*; star, rays, spokes.

Adj. *divergent*, diverging etc. vb.; divaricate, separated; radiating, radial, palmate, stellate; centrifugal, centrifuge; aberrant 282 *deviating*.

Vb. *diverge* 15 *differ*; radiate; divaricate, ramify, branch off, branch out; split off, fork, bifurcate; part, part ways, part company 46 *separate*; file off, go one's own way; change direction, switch; glance off, fly off, fly off at a tangent 282 *deviate*; deploy, fan out, spread, scatter 75 *be dispersed*; straddle, spread-eagle; splay, splay apart.

See: 14, 15, **46**, 75, 222, 247, **282**.

295 Arrival

N. *arrival*, advent, accession, appearance, entrance 289 *approach*, 189 *presence*; onset 68 *beginning*; coming, reaching, making; landfall, landing, touchdown, docking, mooring 266 *quiescence*; debarkation, disembarkation 298 *egress*; rejoining, meeting, encounter 154 *event*; greeting, handshake 884 *courteous act*; homecoming 286 *return*; prodigal's return, reception, welcome 876 *celebration*; guest, visitor, visitant, new arrival, recent a., homing pigeon 297 *incomer*; arrival at the winning post, finish, close f., photo f. 716 *contest*; last lap, home stretch.

goal 617 *objective*; terra firma, native land 192 *home*; journey's end, final point, terminus 69 *extremity*; stop, stopover, stage, halt 145 *stopping place*; billet, resting place, landing p., landing stage, pier; port, harbour, haven, anchorage, roadstead 662 *shelter*; dock, dry d., berth 192 *stable*; aerodrome, airport, heliport, terminal, air t. 271 *air travel*; terminus, railway t., railway station, bus s., depot, rendezvous 192 *meeting place*.

Adj. *arriving*, landing etc. vb.; homing, homeward-bound; terminal; nearing 289 *approaching*, 155 *impending*.

Vb. *arrive*, come, reach, fetch up at, get there 189 *be present*; reach one's destination, make land, sight, raise; make a landfall, make port; dock, berth, tie up, moor, drop anchor 266 *come to rest* (**see** *land*); unharness, unhitch, outspan; draw up, pull up, park; home, come h., get h., return h. 286 *regress*; hit, make, win to, gain, attain; finish the race, breast the tape; reach one's goal 725 *carry through*; stand at the door, be on the doorstep, look for a welcome 297 *enter*; make an entrance 297 *burst in*; appear, show up, pop up, turn up, roll up, drop in, blow in 882 *visit*; put in, pull in, stop at, stop over, stop off, break one's journey, stop 145 *pause*; clock in, time one's arrival 135 *be early*; arrive at, find 484 *discover*; arrive at the top 727 *be successful*, 730 *prosper*; be brought, be delivered, come to hand.

land, unload, discharge 188 *displace*; beach, ground, run aground, touch down, make a landing; step ashore, go a., disembark, pour out 298 *emerge*; detrain, debus; get off, get out, get down, alight, light on, perch 309 *descend*; dismount, quit the saddle, set foot to ground.

meet, join, rejoin, see again; receive, greet, welcome, shake hands 882 *be sociable*; go to meet, come to m., meet the train, be at the station; keep a date, rendezvous; come upon, encounter, come in contact, run into, meet by chance; hit, bump into, butt i., knock i., collide with 279 *collide*; burst upon, light u., pitch u; gather, assemble 74 *congregate*.

Int. welcome! welcome home! greetings! hullo! hi! pleased to meet you! aloha! shalom! salaam!

See: 68, **69**, 74, 135, 145, 154, 155, 188, **189**, 192, 266, 271, 279, 286, **289**, **297**, 298, 309, 484, 617, 662, 716, 725, 727, 730, 876, 882, 884.

296 Departure

N. *departure*, leaving, parting, removal, going away; walk-out, exit 298 *egress*; pulling out, emigration 290 *recession*; remigration, going back 286 *return*; migration, exodus, Hegira; hop, flight, flit, moonlight f., decampment, elopement, getaway 667 *escape*; embarkation, going on board 297 *ingress*; mounting, saddling 267 *equitation*; setting out, starting out, outset 68 *start*; takeoff, blast-off 308 *ascent*; zero hour, time of departure, moment of leave-taking; point of departure, port of embarkation; starting point, starting post, stake-boat.

valediction, valedictory, funeral oration, epitaph, obituary 364 *obsequies*; leave-taking, congé, dismissal; goodbyes, goodnights, farewells, adieus; last handshake, waving goodbye 884 *courteous act*; send-off, farewell address; last post, last words, parting shot, Parthian s.; stirrup cup, doch-an-dorris, one for the road, nightcap.

Adj. *departing*, going etc. vb.; valedictory, farewell; parting, leaving, taking leave; outward bound; emigratory.

Vb. *depart*, quit, leave, abandon 621 *relinquish*; retire, withdraw 286 *turn back*; remove, move house, leave the neighbourhood, leave the country, leave home, emigrate, expatriate oneself, absent o. 190 *go away*; leave the nest, take wing; take one's leave, take one's departure, be going, be getting along; bid farewell, say goodbye, say good night, make one's adieus, tear oneself away, part, part company; receive one's congé, get one's marching orders; leave work, cease w. 145 *cease*; clock out, go home 298 *emerge*; quit the scene, leave the stage, bow out, exit, make one's e. 753 *resign*; depart this life 361 *die*.

decamp, up sticks, strike tents, break camp, break up; march out, pack up, clear off; clear out, pull out, evacuate; make tracks, walk one's chalks; be off, beetle o., buzz o., slink o., slope o., swan o., push o., shove o., make oneself scarce; take wing 271 *fly*; vamoose, skedaddle, beat it, hop it, scram, bolt, scuttle, skip, slip away, cut and run 277 *move fast*; flee, take flight, make a break for it 620 *run away*; flit, make a moonlight f., make one's getaway 446 *disappear*; elope, abscond, give one the slip 667 *escape*.

start out, be off, get going, set out 68 *begin*; set forth, sally f., issue f., strike out, light out, march out 298 *emerge*; gird oneself, be ready to start, warm up 669 *make ready*; take ship, embark, go on board 297 *enter*; hoist the Blue Peter, unmoor, cast off, weigh anchor, push off, get under way, set sail, drop the pilot, put out to sea, leave the land behind 269 *navigate*; mount, set foot in the stirrup, bit, bridle, harness, saddle 267 *ride*; hitch up, inspan, pile in, hop on; emplane, entrain; catch a train, catch a plane, catch a bus; pull out, drive off, take off, be on one's way, be in flight, be on the first lap; see off, wish Godspeed, wave goodbye, speed the parting guest.

Int. goodbye! farewell! adieu! au revoir! auf Wiedersehen! a rivederci! be seeing you! cheerio! ciao! bye-bye! ta-ta! so long! pleasant journey! bon voyage! God be with you!

See: 68, 145, **190**, **267**, 269, 271, 277, 286, 290, 297, **298**, 308, 361, 364, 446, 620, 621, 667, 669, 753, 884.

297 Ingress: motion into

N. *ingress*, incoming, entry, entrance; reentry 286 *return*; inflow, influx, flood 350 *stream*; inpouring, inrush; intrusion, trespass 306 *overstepping*; invasion, forced entry, inroad, raid, irruption, incursion 712 *attack*; immersion, diffusion, osmosis; penetration, interpenetration, infiltration, insinuation 231 *interjacency*, 303 *insertion*; immigration, expansionism; indraught, intake 299 *reception*; import, importation 272 *transference*; right of entry, nonrestriction, admission, admittance, access, entrée 756 *permission*; free trade, free market, open-door policy 791 *trade*, 744 *scope*; ticket, pass 756 *permit*; foot in the door 263 *opener*.

way in, way, path 624 *access*; entrance, entry, door 263 *doorway*; mouth, opening 263 *orifice*; intake, inlet 345 *gulf*; channel 351 *conduit*; open door, free port 796 *market*.

incomer, newcomer, Johnny-come-lately; new arrival, new member, new face; new boy 538 *beginner*; visitant, visitor, caller 882 *sociable person*; immigrant, migrant, colonist, settler 59 *foreigner*; stowaway, unwelcome guest 59 *intruder*; invader, raider 712 *attacker*; house-breaker 789 *thief*; entrant, competitor 716 *contender*; person admitted, ticket holder, card h.;

audience, house, gate 441 *onlookers.*

Adj. *incoming*, ingressive, ingoing, inward, inward bound, homing; intrusive, trespassing; irruptive, invasive 712 *attacking*; penetrating, flooding; allowed in, imported.

Vb. *enter*, turn into, go in, come in, move in, drive in, run in, breeze in, venture in, sidle in, step in, walk in, file in; follow in 65 *come after*; set foot in, cross the threshold, darken the doors; let oneself in; unlock the door, turn the key 263 *open*; gain admittance, have entrée to, be invited; look in, drop in, pop in, blow in, call 882 *visit*; board, get aboard; get in, hop in, jump in, pile in; squeeze into, wedge oneself i., pack oneself i., jam oneself i.; creep in, slip in, edge in, slink in, sneak in, steal in; work one's way into, buy one's way into, insinuate oneself; worm into, bore i. 263 *pierce*; bite into, eat i., cut i. 260 *notch*; put one's foot in, tread in, fall into, drop i. 309 *tumble*; sink into, plunge i., dive i. 313 *plunge*; join, enlist in, enrol oneself 58 *be one of*; immigrate, settle in 187 *place oneself*; let in 299 *admit*; put in 303 *insert*; enter oneself, enter for 716 *contend.*

infiltrate, percolate, seep, soak through, go t., soak into, leak i., drip i.; sink in, penetrate, permeate, mix in, interpenetrate, interfuse 43 *mix*; taint, infect 655 *impair*; filter in, wriggle into, worm one's way i., find one's way in.

burst in, irrupt, rush in, charge in, crash in, smash in, break in, storm in 176 *force*; flood, overflow, flow in, pour in, flood in 350 *flow*; crowd in, throng in, roll in, swarm in, press in 74 *congregate*; invade, raid, break through, board, storm, escalade 712 *attack.*

intrude, trespass, gatecrash, outstay one's welcome; horn in, barge in, push in, muscle in, break in upon, burst in u., interrupt 63 *derange*; pick the lock, break in, burgle 788 *steal.*

See: 43, 58, 59, 63, 65, 74, 176, 187, 231, 260, 263, 272, 286, **299**, **303**, 306, 309, 313, 345, 350, 351, 441, 538, 624, 655, 712, 716, 744, 756, 788, 789, 791, 796, 882.

298 Egress: motion out of

N. *egress*, egression, going out; exit, walk-off; walkout, exodus, evacuation 296 *departure*; emigration, expatriation, exile 883 *seclusion*; emergence, emerging, debouchment; emersion, surfacing; emanation, efflux, issue; evaporation, exhalation, effluvium 338 *vaporization*; eruption, outburst 176 *outbreak*; sortie, breakout 667 *escape*; export, exportation 272 *transference*; migrant, emigrant, émigré 59 *foreigner*; expatriate, colonist 191 *settler*; expellee, exile, remittance man.

outflow, effluence, efflux, effluxion, effusion; emission 300 *ejection*; issue, outpouring, gushing, streaming; exudation, oozing, dribbling, weeping; extravasation, bleeding 302 *haemorrhage*; transudation, perspiration, sweating, sweat; percolation, filtration; leak, escape, leakage, seepage 634 *waste*; drain, running sore 772 *loss*; defluxion, outfall, discharge, effluent, drainage, draining 300 *voidance*; overflow, spill, flood 350 *waterfall*; jet, fountain, spring 156 *source*; gush, squirt 350 *stream*; gusher, geyser 300 *ejector*; streaming eyes, runny nose.

outlet, vent, chute; spout, nozzle, tap; pore, blowhole, spiracle 263 *orifice*, 352 *respiration*; sluice, floodgate 351 *conduit*; exhaust, exhaust pipe, adjutage; spout, drainpipe, gargoyle; exit, way out, path 624 *access*; sallyport 263 *doorway*; escape, loophole 667 *means of escape.*

Adj. *outgoing*, outward bound; emergent, issuing, emanating; oozy, runny, leaky; running, leaking, bleeding; effused, extravasated; erupting, eruptive, explosive, volcanic 300 *expulsive*; spent 806 *expended.*

Vb. *emerge*, pop out, project 254 *jut*; pop one's head out, peep out, peer out 443 *be visible*; surface, break water 308 *ascend*; emanate, transpire 526 *be disclosed*; egress, issue, debouch, sally, make a sortie; issue forth, sally f., come f., go f.; issue out of, go out, come o., creep o., sneak o., march o, flounce o., fling o. 267 *walk*; jump out, bale o. 312 *leap*; clear out, evacuate 296 *decamp*; emigrate 267 *travel*; exit, walk off 296 *depart*; erupt, break out, break through, burst the bonds 667 *escape*; get the boot, get the bird, get the push.

flow out, flood o., pour o., stream o. 350 *flow*; gush, spirt, spout, jet 300 *emit*; drain out, run, drip, dribble, trickle, ooze; rise, surge, well out, well up, well over, boil o.; overflow, spill, spill over, slop o.; run off, escape, leak, vent itself, discharge i., disembogue, debouch; bleed, weep, effuse, extravasate; flood, inundate 341 *drench*.

exude, transude, perspire, sweat, steam 379 *be hot*; ooze, seep, seep through, run t., leak t.; percolate, strain, strain out, filter, filtrate, distil; run, dribble, drip, drop, drivel, drool, slaver, slobber, salivate, water at the mouth 341 *be wet*; transpire, exhale 352 *breathe*.

See: 59, 156, 176, 191, 254, 263, 267, 272, **296**, **300**, 302, 308, 312, 338, 341, 350, 351, 352, 379, 443, 526, 624, 634, 667, 772, 806, 883.

299 Reception

N. *reception*, admission, admittance, entrée, access 297 *ingress*; invitation 759 *offer*; receptivity, acceptance; open arms, welcome, effusive w. 876 *celebration*; enlistment, enrolment, naturalization 78 *inclusion*; initiation, baptism 68 *debut*; asylum, sanctuary, shelter 660 *protection*; introduction; importation, import 272 *transference*; radio receiver 531 *telecommunication*; indraught; inbreathing, inhalation 352 *respiration*; sucking, suction; assimilation, digestion, absorption, resorption; engulfing, engulfment, swallowing, ingurgitation; ingestion (of food) 301 *eating*; imbibition, fluid intake 301 *drinking*; intake, consumption 634 *waste*; infusion 303 *insertion*; interjection 231 *interjacency*; admissibility.

Adj. *admitting*, receptive; freely admitting, inviting, welcoming 289 *accessible*; receivable, admissible, acceptable; absorptive, absorbent, hygroscopic; ingestive; digestive, assimilative; introductory, initiatory, baptismal.

Vb. *admit*, readmit; receive, accept, take in; naturalize; grant asylum, afford sanctuary, shelter 660 *safeguard*; welcome, fling wide the gates; invite, call in 759 *offer*; enlist, enrol, take on 622 *employ*; give entrance *or* admittance to, pass in, allow in, allow access, give a ticket to; throw open, open the door 263 *open*; bring in, import, land 272 *transfer*; let in, show in, usher in, introduce 64 *come before*; send in 272 *send*; initiate, baptize 534 *teach*; infiltrate 303 *insert*; take, be given, get 782 *receive*.

absorb, incorporate, engross, assimilate, digest; suck, suck in; soak up, sponge, mop up, blot 342 *dry*; resorb, reabsorb; internalize, take in, ingest, ingurgitate, imbibe; lap up, swallow, swallow up, engulf, engorge, gulp, gobble, devour 301 *eat, drink*; breathe in, inhale 352 *breathe*; sniff, snuff, snuff up, sniff up 394 *smell*; get the taste of 386 *taste*.

See: 64, 68, 78, 231, 263, 272, 289, 297, 301, **303**, 342, 352, 386, 394, 531, 534, 622, 634, 660, 759, 782, 876.

300 Ejection

N. *ejection*, ejaculation, extrusion, expulsion; precipitation 287 *propulsion*; disbarment, striking off, disqualification, excommunication 57 *exclusion*; throwing out, chucking o., bum's rush; drumming out, marching orders; dismissal, discharge, sack, boot, push 607 *rejection*; repatriation, resettlement; deportation, extradition; relegation, exile, banishment 883 *seclusion*; eviction, dislodgment 188 *displacement*; dispossession, deprivation 786 *expropriation*; jettison, throwing overboard 779 *nonretention*; total ejection, clean sweep, elimination 165 *destruction*; emission, effusion, shedding, spilling 298 *outflow*; libation 981 *oblation*; secretion, salivation 302 *excretion*; emissivity, radioactivity 417 *radiation*; expellee, deportee, refugee 883 *outcast*.

ejector, evicter, dispossessor, bailiff; depriver 786 *taker*; displacer, supplanter, superseder 150 *substitute*; expeller, chucker-out, bouncer; expellant, emetic, aperient 658 *purgative*; propellant 723 *explosive*; volcano 383 *furnace*; emitter, radiator, radio transmitter 531 *telecommunication*; ejector seat 276 *aircraft*.

voidance, clearance, clearage, drainage, curettage, aspiration; eruption, eruptiveness 176 *outbreak*; egestion, regurgitation, disgorgement; vomiting, nausea, vomit, puke; eructation, gas, wind, burp, belch, fart; breaking wind, crepitation, belching; elimination, evacuation 302 *excretion*.

Adj. *expulsive*, expellent, extrusive, explosive, eruptive; radiating, emitting, emissive; secretory, salivary; sialogogue; vomitive, vomitory, sickening, emetic; cathartic 302 *excretory*.

vomiting, sick, sickened, nauseated, green, g. around the gills; belching, seasick, airsick, carsick; sick as a dog.

Vb. *eject*, expel, send down 963 *punish*; strike off, strike off the roll, disbar, excommunicate 57 *exclude*; export, send away 272 *transfer*; deport, expatriate, repatriate, resettle; exile, banish, transport 883 *seclude*; extrude, throw up, cast up, wash up, wash ashore; spit out, spew o.; put out, push o., turf o., throw o., chuck o., fling o., bounce 287 *propel*; kick out, boot o., give the bum's rush, throw out on one's ear, bundle out, hustle o.; drum out; precipitate 287 *propel*; pull out 304 *extract*; unearth, root out, weed o., uproot, eradicate, deracinate 165 *destroy*; rub out, scratch o., eliminate 550 *obliterate*; exorcize, rid, get rid of, rid oneself, get shot of; shake off, brush o.; dispossess, expropriate 786 *deprive*; out, oust, evict, dislodge, unhouse, turn out, turn adrift, turn out of house and home 188 *displace*; hunt out, smoke o. 619 *hunt*; jettison, discard, throw away, throw overboard 779 *not retain*; blackball 607 *reject*; ostracize, cut, cut dead, send to Coventry, give the cold shoulder 883 *make unwelcome*; take the place of, supplant, supersede, replace 150 *substitute*.

dismiss, discharge, lay off, make redundant, drop 674 *stop using*; axe, sack, fire, give the sack, give the boot, give the push 779 *not retain*; turn away, send one about his business, send one away with a flea in his ear, send packing, send to Jericho 292 *repel*; see off, shoo o., shoo away 854 *frighten*; show the door, show out, bow o.; bowl out, run o., catch o., take one's wicket; exorcize, tell to go, order off, order away 757 *prohibit*.

empty, drain, void; evacuate, eliminate 302 *excrete*; vent, disgorge, discharge; pour out, decant 272 *transpose*; drink up, drain to the dregs 301 *drink*; drain off, strain off, ladle out, bail o., pump o., suck o., aspirate; run off, siphon o., open the sluices, open the floodgates, turn on the tap 263 *open*; draw off, tap, broach 263 *pierce*; milk, bleed, let blood 304 *extract*; clear, sweep away, clear a., clean up, make a clean sweep of, clear the decks 648 *clean*; clean out, clear out, curette; unload, unlade, unship, unpack 188 *displace*; disembowel, eviscerate, gut, clean, bone, fillet 229 *uncover*; disinfest 648 *purify*; desolate, depopulate, dispeople, unpeople 105 *render few*.

emit, let out, give vent to; send out 272 *send*; emit rays 417 *radiate*; emit a smell, give off, exhale, breathe out, perfume, scent 394 *smell*; vapour, fume, smoke, steam, puff 338 *vaporize*; spit, spatter, sputter, splutter; pour, spill, shed, sprinkle, spray; spurt, squirt, jet, gush 341 *moisten*; extravasate, bleed 298 *flow out*; drip, drop, ooze; dribble, drool, slobber 298 *exude*; sweat, perspire 379 *be hot*; secrete 632 *store*; egest, pass 302 *excrete*; drop (a foal), lay (an egg) 167 *generate*.

vomit, be sick, bring up, throw up, disgorge, retch, keck, gag, upchuck; spew, puke, cat, honk, chunder, ralph; be seasick, feed the fishes; feel nausea, heave.

eruct, eructate, crepitate, belch, burp, gurk; break wind, blow off, fart; hiccup, cough, hawk, clear the throat, expectorate, spit, gob.

See: 57, 105, 150, 165, 167, 176, 188, 229, 263, 272, 276, 287, 292, **298**, 301, **302**, **304**, 338, 341, 379, 383, 394, 417, 531, 550, 607, 619, 632, 648, 658, 674, 723, 757, 779, 786, 854, 883, 963, 981.

301 Food: eating and drinking

N. *eating*, munching etc. vb.; taking food, ingestion; alimentation, nutrition; feeding, drip-f., force-f.; consumption, devouring; swallowing, downing, getting down; manducation, biting, chewing, mastication; rumination, digestion; chewing the cud; pasturing, cropping; eating meals, table, diet, dining, lunching, breakfasting, supping, having tea; communal feeding, messing; dining out 882 *sociability*; partaking, delicate feeding; tasting, nibbling, pecking, licking, playing with one's food; lack of appetite, anorexia; ingurgitation, guzzling, gobbling; overeating, overindulgence 944 *sensualism*, 947 *gluttony*; obesity 195 *bulk*; appetite, voracity, wolfishness 859 *hunger*; omnivorousness, omophagia 464 *indiscrimination*; eating habits, table manners 610 *practice*; flesh-eating, carnivorousness, creophagy, ichthyophagy; anthropophagy, man-eating, cannibalism; herbivorousness, vegetarianism, veganism; edibility, digestibility; food chain, food web.

feasting, eating and drinking, gormandizing, guzzling, swilling; banqueting, eating out; regalement; orgy, Lucullan banquet, state b., feast; reception, wedding breakfast, annual dinner, do 876 *celebration*; harvest supper, beanfeast, beano, bunfight; Christmas dinner, blowout, spread (**see** *meal*); loaded table, festal cheer, groaning board; fleshpots, milk and honey

635 *plenty*; banqueting hall, dining room, mess r., refectory 192 *cafe*.

dieting, dietetics 658 *therapy*; weight-watching, slimming 206 *thinness*; reducing, losing weight 946 *fasting*; diet, balanced d., crash d., macrobiotic d.; nouvelle cuisine, cuisine minceur; regimen, regime, course, dietary, diet sheet; meagre diet, poor table 636 *insufficiency*; malnutrition 651 *disease*; calories, vitamins (**see** *food content*); vitamin pill; dietician, nutritionist, nutrition expert.

gastronomy, gastronomics, gastrology, palate-tickling, epicureanism, epicurism 944 *sensualism*; gourmandise, gourmandism, good living, high l. 947 *gluttony*; dainty palate, refined p. 463 *discrimination*; epicure, gourmet, Lucullus (**see** *eater*).

cookery, cooking, baking, cuisine, haute c.; food preparation, dressing; domestic science, home economics, catering 633 *provision*; food processing (**see** *provisions*); baker, cook, chef, cuisinier, cordon bleu 633 *caterer*; bakery, rotisserie, restaurant 192 *cafe*; kitchen, cookhouse, galley; oven 383 *furnace*; cooking medium, butter, margarine, ghee 357 *oil*; dripping, lard 357 *fat*; yeast 323 *leaven*; recipe, cookery book, cookbook 589 *textbook*.

eater, feeder, consumer, partaker, taster etc. vb.; nibbler, picker, pecker; boarder, messer, messmate; diner, banqueter, feaster, picnicker; diner-out, dining club 882 *sociability*; dainty feeder, connoisseur, gourmet, epicure; gourmand, trencherman, trencherwoman, bon vivant, Lucullus, belly-worshipper 947 *glutton*; flesh-eater, meat-e., carnivore; man-eater, cannibal, anthropophagite; vegetarian, vegan, herbivore; omnivore, hearty eater, hungry e.; wolf, vulture, hyena, locust; teeth, jaws, mandibles 256 *tooth*; mouth, pecker, gullet, stomach, belly, paunch 194 *maw*.

provisions, stores, commissariat; provender, contents of the larder, foodstuff, groceries; tinned *or* canned food, frozen f., dehydrated f., convenience f., junk f.; provisioning, keep, board, entertainment, sustenance 633 *provision*; home-grown food, self-sufficiency; commons, rations, iron r.; helping 783 *portion*; buttery, pantry, larder, stillroom, cellar 632 *storage*; hay box, meat safe; freezer, fridge 384 *refrigerator*.

provender, animal food, fodder, feed, pasture, pasturage, forage; corn, oats, barley, grain, hay, grass, clover, lucerne, silage; beechmast, acorns; foodstuffs, dry feed, winter f.; chickenfeed, pigswill, cattle cake; saltlick.

food, meat, bread, staff of life; aliment, nutriment, liquid n.; alimentation, nutrition; nurture, sustenance, nourishment, food and drink, pabulum, pap; food for the body, food for the mind, food for the spirit; manna; food for the gods, nectar and ambrosia, amrita; daily bread, staple food, wheat, maize, rice, beans, potatoes; foodstuffs, comestibles, edibles, eatables, eats, victuals, viands, provender; grub, tuck, tucker, nosh, scoff, chow; tack, hard t., biscuit, salt pork, pemmican; heavy food, stodge 391 *unsavouriness*; bad food, carrion, offal; wholefood, health food; cheer, good c., good food, good table, regular meals, fleshpots, fat of the land 730 *prosperity*; creature comforts, cakes and ale; delicatessen, delicacies; dainties, titbits, luxuries 637 *superfluity*; garnish, flavouring, sauce 389 *condiment*.

food content, vitamins; calories, roughage, bulk, fibre; minerals, salts; calcium, iron; protein, amino acid; fat, oil, cholesterol, saturated fats, polyunsaturates; carbohydrates, starch; sugar, glucose, sucrose, lactose, fructose 392 *sweet thing*; additive, preservative, artificial flavouring.

mouthful, bite, nibble, morsel 33 *small quantity*; sop, sip, swallow, bolus; gobbet, slice, titbit, bonne bouche; sandwich, snack, crust; petit four, chocolate, sweet, toffee, chewing gum (**see** *sweetmeat*); popcorn, crisps; cud, quid, something to chew; tablet, pill 658 *drug*.

meal, refreshment, fare; light meal, snack, bite to eat; piece, butty, sandwich, open s., hamburger, hot dog; packed lunch, ploughman's l.; square meal, full m., substantial m., heavy meal; sit-down meal, repast, collation, regalement, refection, spread, feed, blowout, beanfeast, beano (**see** *feasting*); junket 837 *festivity*; picnic, fête champêtre, barbecue; austerity lunch, love-feast; chance meal, potluck; breakfast, elevenses, luncheon, lunch, brunch, tiffin; tea, five o'clock, high tea; dinner, supper, fork s., buffet s.; table d'hôte, à la carte; menu, bill of fare, diet sheet 87 *list*; dietary (**see** *dieting*); cover, table, place; help, helping 783 *portion*; serving, serving up, dishing up; waitress service, self-service.

dish, course; main dish, entrée; salad, entremets; dessert, savoury; speciality, pièce de résistance, plat du jour; meat and two veg (**see** *meat*); casserole, stew, Irish s., hotpot, ragout 43 *a mixture*; goulash, curry; pilau, pilaff, paella, risotto; chop suey, chow mein; pasta, ravioli, lasagne, macaroni, spaghetti, noodles; pancake, pizza, taco; pasty, pie, flan, quiche; fricassee, fritters, croquettes; fry-up, mixed grill, kebabs; fondue, soufflé, omelette; egg dish, cheese d., Welsh rarebit, scrambled eggs, poached e., boiled e.; bread and butter, bread and cheese, b. and dripping; réchauffé, rehash, leftovers.

hors-d'oeuvres, antipasto, smorgasbord; starter, appetizer, canapé; soup, cream s., clear s.; broth, brew, potage, consommé; stock, bouillon, julienne, bisque, chowder, puree; mulligatawny, minestrone, borscht, gazpacho, bouillabaisse; cold meats, cooked m., salami, pâté, terrine, galantine; salad, green s., potato s., Russian s., Waldorf s., coleslaw, macedoine; mayonnaise 389 *sauce*.

fish food, fish 365 *marine life*; fish and chips, fish pie, fish cakes, fish fingers, quenelles, kedgeree; white fish, oily f., fresh f., smoked f.; freshwater fish, trout, salmon, eel; seafish, cod, coley, rock salmon, dogfish, whiting, plaice, sole, skate, hake, halibut, haddock, finnan haddie, turbot, mullet, mackerel, herring, brisling, whitebait, sprats; sardine, pilchard, anchovies, tuna, tunny; kippers, bloaters, Bombay duck; seafood, shellfish, oyster, lobster, crayfish, crab, shrimp, prawn, scampi; scallop, cockle, winkle, mussel, whelk, jellied eel; roe, soft r., hard r., caviar.

meat, flesh; human flesh, long pig; red meat, white m.; beef, mutton, lamb, veal, pork, venison, game; pheasant, chicken 365 *table bird*, *poultry*; meat substitute, textured vegetable protein, TVP 150 *substitute*; roast meat, Sunday roast, S. joint, roast beef and Yorkshire pudding; boiled beef and carrots; haggis, black pudding; shepherd's pie, cottage p.; minced meat, mince; meatballs, rissoles, hamburgers; sausage, banger, chipolata, frankfurter; toad in the hole, Cornish pasty, steak and kidney pudding; cut, joint, leg; baron of beef, sirloin; shoulder, hand of pork, skirt, scrag end, breast, brisket; shin, loin, flank, ribs, topside, silverside; cutlet, chop, loin c., chump c., escalope; steak, fillet s., rump s., porterhouse s.; pork pie, ham, bacon, bacon rasher, streaky b., back b., boiled b., gammon; tongue, knuckle, Bath chap, brawn, oxtail, cowheel, pig's trotters, sweetbreads, tripe, chitterlings, pig's fry; offal, kidney, liver 224 *insides*; suet, dripping, crackling; forcemeat, stuffing.

dessert, pudding, sweet; milk pudding, rice p., semolina, tapioca, bread-and-butter pudding; steamed p., suet p., Christmas p., summer p., rolypoly, spotted dick; jam tart, mince pies (**see** *pastries*); crumble, charlotte; stewed fruit, compote, fool; fresh fruit, fruit salad; icecream, sorbet, mousse, soufflé, sundae, trifle, blancmange, jelly, custard 392 *sweet thing*; cheese board.

sweets, boiled s., confectionery; candy, chocolate, caramel, toffee, Turkish delight, marshmallows, mints, liquorice; acid drops, pear d., barley sugar, humbugs, butterscotch, nougat; gob-stopper, aniseed ball, chewing gum, bubble g.; lolly, lollipop 392 *sweet thing*; sweetmeat, comfit, bonbon; crystallized fruit; toffee apple, candyfloss.

fruit, soft fruit, berry, gooseberry, strawberry, raspberry, loganberry, blackberry, bilberry, mulberry; currant, redcurrant, blackcurrant; stone fruit, apricot, peach, nectarine, plum, greengage, damson, cherry; apple, crab a., pippin, russet, pear; citrus fruit, orange, grapefruit, lemon, citron, lime, tangerine, clementine, mandarin; banana, pineapple, grape; rhubarb; date, fig; dried fruit, currant, raisin, sultana, prune; pomegranate, passion fruit, guava, lychee; mango, avocado; melon, water m., cantaloupe, honeydew; pawpaw, papaya; breadfruit; nut, coconut, Brazil nut, cashew n., pecan, peanut, groundnut, monkey nut; almond, walnut, chestnut, hazel nut, cob n., filbert; bottled fruit, preserves 392 *sweet thing*.

vegetable, greens 366 *plant*; root vegetable, tuber, turnip, swede, parsnip, carrot, Jerusalem artichoke; potato, sweet p., yam; spud, baked potato, roast p., boiled p., mashed p., duchesse p., fried p., French fries, chips; green vegetable, cabbage, Chinese c., red c., savoy, cauliflower, broccoli, calabrese, kale, curly k., seakale; sprouts, Brussel s., spring greens; peas, petits pois, mangetout, beans,

French b., broad b., runner b.; okra, sorrel, spinach, chard, asparagus, globe artichoke; leek, onion, shallots, garlic (see *potherb*); marrow, courgette, pumpkin, squash; aubergine, eggplant, capsicum, pepper, chilli; sweetcorn; salads, lettuce, cos l., chicory, endive; spring onion, radish, celery, beetroot; tomato, love-apple; cucumber, beansprouts, bamboo shoots; cress, watercress, mustard and cress; dried vegetables, pulses, lentils, split peas, chick p.; haricot beans, butter b., kidney b., soya b.; edible fungus, mushroom, boletus, truffle; edible seaweed, laver, laverbread, samphire; pease pudding, baked beans, bubble and squeak, sauerkraut, ratatouille.

potherb, herb, culinary h., sweet h., fines herbes, bouquet garni; marjoram, rosemary, sage, mint, parsley, chervil, chives, thyme, basil, savory, tarragon, bayleaf, dill, fennel; coriander, caraway; caper, gherkins; horseradish 389 *condiment*; borage, hops.

cereals, grains, wheat, buckwheat, oats, rye, maize, mealies, corn; rice, brown r., unpolished r.; millet, sorghum; breakfast cereal, cornflakes, muesli, oatmeal, porridge, gruel, skilly, brose; flour, meal, wholemeal, wheat germ, bran; batter, dough; bread, crust, crumb; white bread, sliced b., soda b., brown b., wholemeal b., malt b., granary b., black b., rye b., pumpernickel, corn b., pitta b.; toast, rusk, croutons; loaf, cottage l., tin, farmhouse, bloomer, baguette, French stick; roll, bridge r., bap, croissant, brioche, bun (see *pastries*); crumpet, muffin, scone, teacake, oatcake, bannock; papadum, chapatti, polenta, tortilla, waffle, wafer, crispbread, cracker, cream c.

pastries, confectionery; patty, pasty, turnover, dumpling; tart, flan, puff, pie, piecrust; pastry, shortcrust p., flaky p., puff p., rough p. p., choux p.; patisserie, gateau, cake, lardy c., fruit c., Dundee c., seed c., sponge c., Madeira c., angel c., battenburg c., layer c., cheesecake; fairy cakes, meringue, éclair, macaroon; bun, currant b., Chelsea b., Bath b., doughnut, flapjack, brandysnap, gingerbread, shortbread, cookies, biscuits, digestive b., garibaldi b., custard creams, gingernuts.

dairy product (see *milk*); cream, clotted c., curds, whey, junket, yoghurt; cheese, goat's c., cream c., cottage c.; Cheddar, Cheshire, Leicestershire, Double Gloucester, Caerphilly, Lancashire, Wensleydale, sage Derby, red Windsor; Emmental, Gruyère, Gouda, Edam; Camembert, Brie; Bel Paese, Parmesan; ripe cheese, blue c., blue vinny, Roquefort, Gorgonzola, Stilton, Danish blue.

drinking, imbibing, imbibition, fluid intake; potation; sipping, tasting, wine-tasting 463 *discrimination*; gulping, swilling, soaking, wine-bibbing; drinking to excess 949 *drunkenness*; giving to drink, watering; libation 981 *oblation*; drinker, bibber, swiller, quaffer; toper 949 *drunkard*.

draught, drink, beverage, dram, bevvy; gulp, sip, sup; bottle, bowl, glass 194 *cup*; cuppa, pinta; glassful, bumper; swig, nip, noggin, jigger, tot, slug; peg, double peg, snorter, snifter, chaser; long drink, thirst-quencher; short drink, short; quick one, snort; sundowner, nightcap; loving cup, stirrup c., doch-an-dorris, one for the road; health, toast; mixed drink, concoction, cocktail 43 *mixture*; potion, decoction, infusion 658 *medicine*; divine drink, nectar.

soft drink, teetotal d., nonalcoholic beverage; water, drinking w., filtered w., eau potable, spring water, fountain; soda water, soda, cream s., soda fountain, siphon; table water, mineral w., tonic w., barley w., squash; iced drink, frappé; milk, milk shake; ginger beer, ginger ale, Coca Cola *or* Coke (tdmk); fizz, pop, lemonade, orangeade; cordial, fruit juice, tomato j.; coconut milk; tea, char, pekoe, orange p., Indian t., China t., green t., black t., Russian t., maté, herb t., tisane 658 *tonic*; coffee, café au lait, café noir, black coffee, Irish c., Turkish c., espresso, cappuccino; cocoa (see *milk*); sherbet, syrup, julep, hydromel.

alcoholic drink, strong d., booze, bevvy, wallop, tipple, poison; brew, fermented liquor, intoxicating l. (see *wine*); alcohol, wood a.; malt liquor, John Barleycorn, beer, small b., swipes; draught beer, keg b., bottled b.; strong beer, stingo; ale, real ale; barley wine; stout, lager, bitter, porter, mild, home brew; shandy; cider, rough c., scrumpy; perry, mead, Athole brose; wheat wine, palm w., rice beer, toddy, sake, mescal, tequila; distilled liquor, spirituous l., spirits, ardent s., raw s., aqua vitae, firewater, hooch, moonshine, mountain dew, rotgut, hard stuff;

brandy, cognac, eau-de-vie; gin, sloe g., schnapps, blue ruin; whisky, usquebaugh, Scotch whisky, Scotch; rye, bourbon; Irish whiskey, poteen; vodka, aquavit, ouzo, raki, arrack; rum, demon rum, grog, hot g., punch, rum p.; egg flip, egg nog; cordial, spiced wine, mulled w., negus, posset, hippocras; flavoured wine, cup, claret c.; mixed drink, Pimms (tdmk), gin and tonic, pink gin, highball, brandy and soda, whisky and s.; mint julep; cocktail, Manhattan, Bloody Mary; aperitif, Pernod (tdmk), absinth; liqueur, cassis, curaçao, crème de menthe.

wine, the grape, juice of the g., blood of the g.; red wine, white w., vin rosé; vermouth; spumante, sparkling wine, still w., sweet w., dry w., light w., full-bodied w., vintage w.; vin ordinaire, vin du pays; vino, plonk; table wine, dessert w.; fortified w., sack, sherry, port, Madeira, Marsala; champagne, fizz, bubbly; claret, Burgundy, Beaujolais; hock, Sauternes, Moselle, Riesling, Bordeaux; Tokay, retsina, Chianti.

milk, top of the m., cream; cow's milk, beestings; goat's milk, mare's m., koumiss; mother's milk, breast m.; buttermilk, dried m., skimmed m., condensed m., evaporated m., pasteurized m.; plant milk; milk drink, m. shake, malted m., cocoa, chocolate; curdled milk, curds, junket. **See** *dairy product*.

Adj.*feeding*, eating, grazing etc. vb.; flesh-eating, meat-e.; carnivorous, creophagous, cannibalistic; omophagic, omophagous; insectivorous; herbivorous, graminivorous, frugivorous; vegetarian, vegan; omnivorous 464 *indiscriminating*; greedy, wolfish 947 *gluttonous*; water-drinking, teetotal 942 *temperate*; swilling, tippling, drinking 949 *drunken*; well-fed, well-nourished; nursed, breast-fed; full up, crammed 863 *sated*.

edible, eatable; ritually pure, kosher; esculent, comestible; digestible, predigested; potable, drinkable; milky, lactic; worth eating, palatable, succulent, moreish, palate-tickling, dainty, delicious 386 *tasty*, 390 *savoury*; cereal, wheaten; fermented, distilled, spirituous, alcoholic, hard 949 *intoxicating*; nonalcoholic, soft.

nourishing, feeding, sustaining, nutritious, nutritive, nutritional; alimental, alimentary; dietary, dietetic; fattening, rich, calorific, high in calories; protein-rich, body-building; wholesome 652 *salubrious*.

culinary, dressed, oven-ready, made-up, ready-to-serve; cooked, done to a turn, well-done; al dente; underdone, red, rare, raw; over-cooked, burnt, b. to a cinder; roasted etc. vb. (**see** *cook*); à la meunière, au gratin, au naturel, mornay; gastronomic, epicurean; mensal, prandial, post-p., after-dinner; meal-time.

Vb.*eat*, feed, fare, board, mess; partake 386 *taste*; take a meal, have a feed, break one's fast, break bread; breakfast, lunch, have tea, dine, sup; dine out, regale, feast, banquet, carouse 837 *revel*; eat well, have a good appetite, do justice to, be a good trencherman *or* -woman, ask for more; water at the mouth, drool, raven 859 *be hungry*; fall to, set to, tuck in, lay into; fork in, spoon in, shovel in; stuff oneself, fill one's stomach 863 *sate*; guzzle, gormandize 947 *gluttonize*; put on weight 197 *expand*; work one's way through a meal, take every course, eat up, leave a clean plate; lick the platter clean 165 *consume*; swallow, gulp down, snap up, devour, dispatch, bolt, wolf, make short work of; feed on, live on, fatten on, batten on, prey on; nibble, peck, lick, play with one's food, have a poor appetite; nibble at, peck at, sniff at; ingest, digest 299 *absorb*.

chew, masticate, manducate, champ, chomp, munch, crunch, scrunch; mumble, mouth, worry, gnaw, grind 332 *pulverize*; bite, tear, rend, chew up 46 *cut*.

graze, browse, pasture, crop, feed; ruminate, chew the cud.

drink, imbibe, suck 299 *absorb*; quaff, drink up, drink one's fill, drink like a fish, slake one's thirst, lap, sip; wet one's lips, wet one's whistle; draw the cork, crack a bottle; lap up, soak up, wash down; booze, swill, swig, tipple, tope 949 *get drunk*; toss off one's glass, drain one's g., knock it back; raise one's glass, pledge 876 *toast*; have another, take one for the road; refill one's glass 633 *replenish*; give to drink, wine, water; prepare a drink **or** medicine **or** posset; lay in drink, lay down a cellar 633 *provide*.

feed, nourish, vitaminize; nurture, sustain, board; give to eat, victual, cater, purvey 633 *provide*; nurse, breast-feed, give suck; pasture, graze, put out to grass; fatten, fatten up 197 *enlarge*; dine, wine and dine, feast, banquet, have to dinner, regale with

882 *be hospitable.*

cook, prepare a meal; pressure-cook; put in the oven, bake, brown; roast, spit-roast, pot-r., braise; broil, grill, barbecue, spatchcock, griddle, devil, curry; sauté, fry, deep-f.; fry sunny side up, double-fry (eggs); scramble, poach; boil, parboil; coddle, seethe, simmer, steam; casserole, stew; baste, lard, bard; whip, whisk, beat, blend, liquidize, stir; draw, gut, bone, fillet; stuff, dress, garnish; dice, shred, mince, grate; sauce, flavour, spice 388 *season.*

Int.bon appétit! here's health! here's mud in your eye! bottoms up! down the hatch! slà inte! prosit! skol! cheers!

See:33, 43, 46, 87, 150, 165, 192, 194, 195, 197, 206, 224, 256, 299, 323, 332, 357, 365, 366, 383, 384, **386**, 388, **389**, **390**, 391, **392**, 463, **464**, 589, 610, 632, **633**, 635, 636, 637, 651, 652, 658, 730, 783, 837, 859, 863, 876, 882, 942, 944, 946, **947**, **949**, 981.

302 Excretion

N.*excretion*, discharge, secretion 300 *ejection*; effusion, extravasation; emanation 298 *egress*; exhalation, breathing out 352 *respiration*; exudation, perspiration, sweating, diaphoresis 298 *outflow*; suppuration 651 *infection*; cold, catarrh, hay fever; salivation, expectoration, spitting; coughing, cough; urination, micturition; waterworks; enuresis, incontinence.

haemorrhage, bleeding, extravasation, haemophilia 335 *blood*; menses, catamenia, period, the curse; dysmenorrhoea; leucorrhoea.

defecation, evacuation, elimination, clearance 300 *voidance*; bowel movement, motion; one's natural functions; diarrhoea, the runs 651 *digestive disorders*; constipation.

excrement, waste matter; faeces, stool, excreta, ordure, night soil; coprolite; dung, cowpat, manure, muck; droppings, guano; pee, piss, urine, water; sweat, beads of s., lather; spittle, spit, sputum; saliva, slaver, slobber, froth, foam; rheum, phlegm; catarrh, mucus, snot; matter, pus; afterbirth, lochia; slough, cast, exuviae, pellet; feculence 649 *dirt*.

Adj.*excretory*, secretory; purgative, laxative, aperient; excretive, diuretic; menstrual; diaphoretic, sudorific; perspiratory; faecal, feculent; anal, urinary; rheumy, watery; mucous, phlegmy; cast-off, exuvial.

Vb.*excrete*, secrete; pass, move; move one's bowels, defecate; be taken short, have the runs; relieve oneself, ease o., answer the call of nature, go to the lavatory; urinate, micturate, piddle, pee, piss; have a pee, take a leak; make water, spend a penny; wet oneself; sweat, perspire, steam, glow 379 *be hot*; salivate, slobber, snivel; cough, spit 300 *eruct*; weep 298 *exude*; water at the mouth 859 *be hungry*; foam at the mouth 891 *be angry*; cast, slough, shed one's skin 229 *doff*.

See:229, **298**, **300**, 335, 352, 379, **649**, 651, 859, 891.

303 Insertion: forcible ingress

N.*insertion*, intercalation, interpolation, parenthesis 231 *interjection*; adding 38 *addition*; introduction, insinuation 297 *ingress*; infixation, impaction; planting, transplantation 370 *agriculture*; inoculation, injection, shot 263 *perforation*; infusion, enema; thing inserted, insert, inset; stuffing 227 *lining*.

immersion, submersion, submergence 311 *lowering*; dip, bath 313 *plunge*; baptism 988 *Christian rite*; burial, burial at sea 364 *interment*.

Adj.*inserted*, introduced etc. vb.; added 38 *additional*; intermediate 231 *interjacent*; coffined 364 *buried*.

Vb.*insert*, introduce; weave into 222 *enlace*; put into, thrust i., intrude; poke into, stick i.; transfix, run through 263 *pierce*; ram into, jam i., stuff i., pack i., push i., shove i., tuck i., press i., pop i. 193 *load*; pocket 187 *stow*; ease into place, slide in, fit in; knock into, hammer i., drive i. 279 *impel*; put in, inlay, inset 227 *line*; mount, frame 232 *circumscribe*; subjoin 38 *add*; interpose 231 *put between*; drop in, put in the slot 311 *let fall*; putt, hole out; pot, hole; put in the ground, bury 364 *inter*; sheathe, encapsulate, encase 226 *cover*.

infuse, drop in, instil, pour in 43 *mix*; imbue, imbrue, impregnate 297 *infiltrate*; transfuse, decant 272 *transpose*; squirt in, inject 263 *pierce*.

implant, plant, transplant, plant out; graft, engraft, bud; inoculate, vaccinate; embed, bury; infix, wedge in, impact, dovetail 45 *join*.

immerse, bathe, steep, souse, marinate, soak 341 *drench*; baptize, duck, dip 311 *lower*; submerge, flood; immerse oneself 313 *plunge*.

See: 38, 43, 45, 187, 193, 222, 226, 227, **231**, 232, 263, 272, 279, **297**, 311, 313, 341, 364, 370, 988.

304 Extraction: forcible egress

N. *extraction*, withdrawal, removal 188 *displacement*; elimination, eradication 300 *ejection*; abortion 172 *unproductiveness*; extermination, extirpation 165 *destruction*; extrication, unravelment, disengagement, liberation 668 *deliverance*; evulsion, avulsion, tearing out, ripping o.; cutting out, exsection, excision; Caesarian birth, forceps delivery; expression, squeezing out; suction, sucking out, aspiration; vacuuming, pumping; drawing out, pull, tug, wrench 288 *traction*; digging out 255 *excavation*; mining, quarrying; fishery; distillation 338 *vaporization*; drawing off, tapping, milking; thing extracted, essence, extract.

extractor, gouger; miner, quarrier; wrench, forceps, pincers, pliers, tweezers 778 *nippers*; mangle, squeezer 342 *dryer*; corkscrew, screwdriver 263 *opener*; lever 218 *pivot*; scoop, spoon, shovel; pick, pickaxe; rake; toothpick 648 *cleaning utensil*; vacuum cleaner; excavator, dredge, dredger, dragline; syringe, siphon; aspirator, suction pump; Archimedes' screw, shadoof 341 *irrigator*.

Adj. *extracted*, removed etc. vb.; extractive.

Vb. *extract*, remove, pull 288 *draw*; draw out, elicit, educe; unfold 316 *evolve*; pull out, take o., get o., pluck; withdraw, excise, cut out, rip o., tear o., whip o.; excavate, mine, quarry, dig out, unearth; dredge, dredge up; expel, lever out, winkle o., smoke o. 300 *eject*; extort, wring from; express, press out, squeeze o., gouge o.; force out, wring o., wrench o., drag o.; draw off, milk, tap; syphon off, aspirate, suck, void, pump; wring from, squeeze f., drag f.; pull up, dig up, grub up, rake up; eliminate, weed out, root up, uproot, pluck up by the roots, eradicate, deracinate, extirpate 165 *destroy*; prune, thin out 105 *render few*; distil 338 *vaporize*; extricate, unravel, free 746 *liberate*; unpack, unload 188 *displace*; eviscerate, gut 300 *empty*; unwrap 229 *uncover*; pick out 605 *select*.

See: 105, 165, 172, 188, 218, 229, 255, 263, 288, **300**, 316, 338, 341, 342, 605, 648, 668, 746, 778.

305 Passage: motion through

N. *passage*, transmission 272 *transference*; transportation 272 *transport*; passing, passing through, traversing; transilience 147 *transition*; trespass 306 *overstepping*; transit, traverse, crossing, journey, patrol 267 *land travel*; passage into, penetration, interpenetration, permeation, infiltration; transudation, osmosis, endosmosis 297 *ingress*; exosmosis 298 *egress*; intervention 231 *interjacency*; right of way 624 *access*; stepping-stone, flyover, underpass 624 *bridge*; track, route, orbit 624 *path*; intersection, interchange, junction 222 *crossing*; waterway, channel 351 *conduit*.

passing along, passage, thoroughfare; traffic, pedestrian t., wheeled t., vehicular t.; road traffic, ocean t., air t.; traffic movement, flow of traffic, circulation; walking, crossing, cycling, driving, pulling, pushing, pram-p.; loading, unloading; waiting, parking, kerb-side p., off-street p.; traffic load, traffic density; traffic jam, procession, queue; road user 268 *pedestrian, driver*; passerby.

traffic control, traffic engineering; traffic rules, highway code, Green Cross C. 693 *precept*; traffic lane, bus l., cycle l., one-way street, dual carriageway, clearway 624 *road*; diversion, alternative route 282 *deviation*; white lines, yellow l., cat's-eyes, sleeping policeman; street furniture, traffic lights, lampposts, roundabout; pedestrian crossing, zebra c., pelican c.; Belisha beacon, bollard, refuge, island; car park, parking place, parking zone; parking meter, lay-by; point duty, road patrol, speed trap; traffic police, traffic cop; traffic engineer; traffic warden, meter maid; lollipop man *or* lady.

Adj. *passing*, crossing etc. vb.; transitional, transilient; osmotic.

Vb. *pass*, pass by, leave on one side, skirt, coast 200 *be near*; flash by 277 *move fast*, 114 *be transient*; go past, not stop 146 *go on*, 265 *be in motion*; pass along, join the traffic, circulate, weave; pass through, transit, traverse; shoot through, shoot a bridge, shoot the rapids 269 *navigate*; pass out, come out the other side 298 *emerge*; go through, soak t., percolate, permeate 189 *pervade*; pass and repass, patrol, work over, beat, scour, go over the ground; pass into, penetrate, infiltrate 297 *enter*; bore, perforate 263 *pierce*; thread, thread through, string 45 *connect*; enfilade, rake; open a way, force a passage 297 *burst in*; worm one's way, squeeze through, elbow t., clear the way 285 *progress*; cross, go across, cross over, make a crossing, reach the other side 295 *arrive*; wade across, ford; get through, get past, negotiate; pass beyond 306 *overstep*; repass 286 *turn back*; pass in front, cut across, cross one's bows 702 *obstruct*; step over, straddle, bestride 226 *overlie*; bridge, bridge over 226 *cover*; carry over, carry across, transmit 272 *send*; pass to, hand, reach, pass from hand to hand, hand over 272 *transfer*.

Adv. *en passant*, by the way; on the way, in transit.

See: 45, 114, 146, 147, 189, 200, 222, 226, 231, 263, 265, **267**, 268, 269, **272**, 277, 282, 285, 286, 295, 297, 298, 306, 351, **624**, 693, 702.

306 Overstepping: motion beyond

N. *overstepping*, going beyond 305 *passage*; transcendence 34 *superiority*; excursion, digression 282 *deviation*; violation, transgression, trespass 936 *guilty act*; usurpation, encroachment 916 *arrogation*; infringement, infraction, intrusion 916 *undueness*; expansionism, greediness 859 *desire*; overextension, ribbon development 197 *expansion*; overfulfilment; excessiveness 637 *redundance*; overrating 482 *overestimation*; overdoing it 546 *exaggeration*; overindulgence 943 *intemperance*.

Adj. *surpassing*, transcending etc. vb.; one up on 34 *superior*; overextended, overlong, overhigh; too strong, overpowered; excessive 32 *exorbitant*; out of bounds, out of reach.

Vb. *overstep*, overpass; pass, leave behind; go beyond, go too far, throw out the baby with the bathwater; exceed, exceed the limit; overrun, override, overshoot, overshoot the mark, aim too high; overlap 226 *overlie*; surmount, jump over, leap o., skip o., leap-frog 312 *leap*; step over, cross 305 *pass*; cross the Rubicon, pass the point of no return; overfill, brim over, slop o., spill o. 54 *fill*; overgrow, overspread 637 *superabound*; overdo 546 *exaggerate*; strain, stretch, stretch a point; overbid, overcall one's hand, have one's bluff called, overestimate 482 *overrate*; overindulge 943 *be intemperate*; overstay, oversleep 136 *be late*.

encroach, invade, make inroads on 712 *attack*; infringe, transgress, trespass 954 *be illegal*; poach 788 *steal*; squat, usurp 786 *appropriate*; barge in, horn in 297 *intrude*; overlap, impinge, trench on; entrench upon; eat away, erode 655 *impair*; infest, overrun 297 *burst in*; overflow, flood 341 *drench*.

outdo, exceed, surpass, outclass; transcend, rise above, mount a., soar a., outsoar, outrange, outrival 34 *be superior*; go one better, overcall, overbid, outbid; outwit, overreach 542 *deceive*; outmanoeuvre, outflank, steal a march on; make the running 277 *move fast*; outgo, outpace, outwalk, outmarch, outrun, outride, outjump, outsail, outdistance, distance; overhaul, gain upon, overtake, come in front, shoot ahead; lap, leave standing 277 *outstrip*; leave behind, race, beat, beat hollow 727 *defeat*.

See: 32, **34**, 54, 136, 197, 226, 277, 282, 297, **305**, 312, 341, 482, 542, 546, **637**, 655, 712, 727, 786, 788, 859, 916, 936, 943, 954.

307 Shortfall

N. *shortfall*, falling short etc. vb.; inadequacy 636 *insufficiency*; a minus, deficit, short measure, shortage, loss 42 *decrement*; leeway, drift 282 *deviation*; unfinished state 55 *incompleteness*; nonfulfilment, default, defalcation 726 *noncompletion*; half measures 641 *lost labour*; no go 728 *failure*; fault, defect, shortcoming 647 *imperfection*, 845 *blemish*; something missing, want, lack, need 627 *requirement*.

Adj. *deficient*, short, short of, minus, wanting, lacking, missing; catalectic; underpowered, substandard; undermanned, understaffed, below establishment; half-done, perfunctory 55 *incomplete*; out of one's depth, not up to scratch, inadequate 636 *insufficient*; failing, running short 636 *scarce*; below par 647 *imperfect*; unattained, unreached, tantalizing.

Vb. *fall short*, come s., run s. 636 *not suffice*; not stretch, not reach to; lack, want, be without 627 *require*; underachieve, not make the grade, not come up to scratch; miss, miss the mark; lag 136 *be late*; stop short, fall by the way, not stay the course; break down, get bogged down; fall behind, lose ground, slip back; slump, collapse

286 *regress*; fall through, fall to the ground, come to nothing, end in smoke, fizzle out, fail 728 *miscarry*; labour in vain 641 *waste effort*; tantalize, not come up to expectations 509 *disappoint*.

Adv. *behindhand*, in arrears; not enough; below the mark, far from it; to no purpose, in vain.

See: **42**, 55, 136, 282, 286, 509, 627, **636**, 641, 647, 726, 728, 845.

308 Ascent: motion upwards

N. *ascent*, ascension, lift, upward motion, gaining height; defiance of gravity, levitation; taking off, leaving the ground, takeoff, lift-off, blast-off 296 *departure*; flying up, soaring, spiralling, spiral; zooming, zoom 271 *aeronautics*; culmination 213 *summit*; floating up, surfacing, breaking surface; going up, rising, uprising; rise, upgrowth, upturn; uprush, upsurge, crescendo 36 *increase*; updraught, rising air, rising current, thermal; sunrise, sun-up, dawn 128 *morning*; moonrise, star-rise; mounting, climbing; hill-climbing, mountaineering, alpinism; ladder-scaling, escalade 712 *attack*; jump, vault, pole v., pole jump 312 *leap*; bounce 280 *recoil*; rising ground, hill 209 *high land*; gradient, slope, ramp 220 *incline*; rising pitch 410 *musical note*; means of ascent, stairs, steps, stile, flight of stairs, staircase, spiral s., stairway, landing; ladder, step-l., accommodation l., Jacob's l., companionway; rope ladder, ratlines; stair, step, tread, rung; lift, ski l., escalator 310 *lifter*; fire escape 667 *means of escape*.

climber, mountaineer, alpinist, cragsman *or* -woman, fell walker; steeplejack; rocket, sky r.; soarer, lark, skylark, laverock; gusher, geyser, fountain 350 *stream*.

Adj. *ascending*, rising etc. vb., climbing, scansorial; rearing, rampant; buoyant, floating 323 *light*; supernatant; airborne, gaining height; anabatic, in the ascendant; uphill, steep 215 *vertical*; ladderlike, scalariform; scalable, climbable.

Vb. *ascend*, rise, rise up, go up, leave the ground; defy gravity, levitate; take off, become airborne, fly up 271 *fly*; gain height, mount, soar, spiral, zoom, climb; reach the top, reach the zenith, culminate; float up, bob up, surface, break water; jump up, spring, vault 312 *leap*; bounce 280 *recoil*; push up, grow up, shoot up 36 *grow*; curl upwards; tower, aspire, spire 209 *be high*; gush, spurt, spout, jet, play 298 *flow out*; get up, start up, stand up, rear, rear up, ramp 215 *be vertical*; rise to one's feet, get up 310 *lift oneself*; trend upwards, wind u., slope u., steepen 220 *be oblique*.

climb, walk up, struggle up; mount, make one's way up, work one's way up; go climbing, mountaineer; clamber, scramble, swarm up, shin up, climb like a monkey, go up hand over fist; surmount, top, breast, conquer, scale, scale the heights 209 *be high*; go over the top, escalade 712 *attack*; go upstairs, climb a ladder; mount (a horse), climb into the saddle.

Adv. *up*, uphill, upstairs; upwards 209 *aloft*; excelsior, ever higher; per ardua ad astra.

See: 36, 128, **209**, 213, 215, 220, **271**, 280, 296, 298, **310**, 312, 323, 350, 410, 667, 712.

309 Descent

N. *descent*, declension, declination 282 *deviation*; falling, dropping; cadence; landing; downward trend, spiral, decline, drop, slump 37 *decrease*; sunset, moonset; comedown, demotion 286 *regression*; downfall, débâcle, collapse 165 *ruin*; trip, stumble; titubation, lurch, capsize 221 *overturning*; tumble, crash, spill, fall; cropper, purler; downrush, swoop, stoop, pounce; dive, header, bellyflop 313 *plunge*; nosedive, power-dive 271 *aeronautics*; landing, splashdown 295 *arrival*; sliding down, glissade; subsidence, landslide, avalanche; downdraught 352 *wind*; downpour, shower 350 *rain*; cascade 350 *waterfall*; downthrow (geology); declivity, slope, tilt, dip 220 *incline*; chute, slide, helter-skelter; precipice, sheer drop 215 *verticality*; submergence, sinkage, slippage 311 *lowering*; boring, tunnelling, burrowing, mining, sapping, undermining 255 *excavation*; speleology, pot-holing, caving; descender, faller, tumbler; plunger 313 *diver*; burrower, miner, sapper 255 *excavator*; parachutist 271 *aeronaut*; paratrooper 722 *soldier*; speleologist, pot-holer, caver.

Adj. *descending*, dropping etc. vb.; descendent, declining, declivitous 220 *sloping*; swooping, stooping; tumbledown, falling, tottering; tilting, sinking, foundering; burrowing, sapping; drooping 311 *lowered*; submersible, sinkable.

Vb. *descend*, come down, go d., dip d.; decline, abate, ebb 37 *decrease*; reach a lower level, slump, fall, drop, sink; sink like a lead balloon 322 *weigh*; soak in, seep down 297 *infiltrate*; get lower and lower, reach the depths, touch bottom 210 *be low*; reach one's nadir 35 *be inferior*; sink to the bottom, gravitate, precipitate, settle, set; fall down, fall in, cave in, fall to the ground, collapse; sink in, subside, slip, give way; hang down, prolapse, droop, sag, swag 217 *hang*; go under water, draw, have draught; submerge, fill the tanks, dive 313 *plunge*; drown 313 *founder*; go underground, sink into the earth; dig down, burrow, bore, tunnel, mine, sap, undermine 255 *make concave*; drop from the sky, parachute; swoop, stoop, pounce; fly down, flutter d., float d.; lose height, drop down, swing low; touch down, alight, light, perch 295 *land*; lower oneself, abseil; get down, climb d., step d., get off, fall o., dismount; coast down, slide down, glissade, toboggan; fall like rain, shower, cascade, drip 350 *rain*; take a lower place, come down a peg 286 *regress*; bow down, dip, duck 311 *stoop*; flop, plop, splash down.

tumble, fall; tumble down, fall d.; topple, topple over, heel o., keel o., overbalance, capsize 221 *be inverted*; miss one's footing, slip, slip up, trip, stumble; lose one's balance, titubate, stagger, totter, lurch, tilt, droop 220 *be oblique*; rise and fall, pitch, toss, roll; take a header, dive 313 *plunge*; take a running jump, precipitate oneself 312 *leap*; fall off, take a fall, be thrown, come a cropper, fall heavily, crash to the ground, fall flat on one's face, fall prostrate, bite the dust, measure one's length; plop, plump, plump down 311 *sit down*; slump, sprawl; fall through the air, spiral, spiral down, nosedive, crash, prang.

Adv. *down*, downwards; downhill, downstairs, downstream.

See: 35, 37, 165, **210**, 215, 217, **220**, 221, **255**, 271, 282, 286, 295, 297, **311**, 312, **313**, 322, 350, 352, 722.

310 Elevation

N. *elevation*, raising etc. vb.; erection, uplift, upheaval; picking up, lift; hoist, boost; leg-up 703 *aid*; levitation; exaltation, Assumption; uprising, uptrend, upswing 308 *ascent*; an elevation, eminence 209 *high land*, 254 *prominence*; height above sea level 209 *height*.

lifter, erector, builder, spiderman; raiser, raising agent, yeast 323 *leaven*; lever, jack 218 *pivot*; dredger 304 *extractor*; crane, derrick, hoist, windlass; winch, capstan; rope and pulley, block and tackle, parbuckle, jeers; forklift, elevator, dumb waiter, escalator, lift, ski l., cable railway 274 *conveyor*; hot air, gas, hydrogen, helium; spring, springboard, trampoline; stilts; scaffolding, platform 218 *stand*.

Adj. *elevated*, raised etc. vb.; exalted, uplifted; erectile, erective; erected, set up; upright, erect, upstanding, rampant 215 *vertical*; mounted, on high; towering over, head and shoulders above; lofty, sublime 209 *high*.

Vb. *elevate*, heighten 209 *make higher*; puff up, blow up, swell, leaven 197 *enlarge*; raise, erect, set up, put up, run up, rear up, build up, build; lift, lift up, raise up, heave up; uplift, upraise; jack up, prop 218 *support*; stand on end 215 *make vertical*; prevent from falling, hold up, bear up; prevent from sinking, buoy up; raise aloft, hold a., hold up, wave; hoist, haul up, brail, trice; raise from the ground, pick up, take up; pull up, wind up; weigh, trip (anchor); fish up, drag up, dredge up, pump up 304 *extract*; chair, shoulder, carry shoulder-high; exalt, put on a pedestal 866 *honour*; put on top, mount 213 *crown*; jump up, bounce up 285 *promote*; give a lift, give a leg-up 703 *aid*; throw in the air, throw up, cast up, toss up; sky, loft; send up, shoot up, lob 287 *propel*; perk up (one's head), prick up (one's ears); bristle, bristle up 215 *be vertical*.

lift oneself, arise, rise 308 *ascend*; stand up, get up, pick oneself up, jump up, leap up, spring up, spring to one's feet; pull oneself up; hold oneself up, hold one's head up, draw oneself up to one's full height, stand on tiptoe 215 *be vertical*.

Adv. *on*, on stilts, on tiptoe; on one's legs, on one's hind legs; on the shoulders of, on the back of.

Int. upsy-daisy!

See: 197, **209**, 213, **215**, 218, 254, 274, 285, 287, 304, **308**, 323, 703, 866.

311 Lowering

N. *lowering*, depression, hauling down etc. vb.; pushing down, detrusion 279 *impulse*;

ducking, sousing 313 *plunge*; debasement, demotion, reduction 872 *humiliation*; subversion 149 *revolution*; overthrow, prostration; overturn, upset 221 *overturning*; precipitation, defenestration 287 *propulsion*; keeping under, suppression; a depression, dent, dip, hollow 255 *cavity*; low pressure 340 *weather*.

obeisance, reverence, bow, salaam, kowtow 884 *courtesy*; curtsy, bob, duck, nod 884 *courteous act*; kneeling, genuflexion 920 *respect*.

Adj. *lowered*, depressed etc. vb.; at a low ebb 210 *low*; prostrate 216 *supine*; sedentary, sitting, sit-down; depressive, depressing; submersible.

Vb. *lower*, depress, detrude, push down, thrust d. 279 *impel*; shut down (a lid) 264 *close*; hold down, keep d., hold under 165 *suppress*; lower, let down, take d.; lower a flag, dip, half-mast, haul down, strike; deflate, puncture, flatten, squash, crush 198 *make smaller*; let drop (**see** *let fall*); sink, scuttle, send to the bottom, drown 309 *descend*; duck, souse, douse, dip 313 *plunge*; weigh on, press on 322 *weigh*; capsize, roll over, tip, tilt 221 *invert*; crush, stave in, bash in, dent, hollow 255 *make concave*.

let fall, drop, shed; let go 779 *not retain*; let slip *or* slide through one's fingers; pour, pour out, decant 300 *empty*; spill, slop 341 *moisten*; sprinkle, shower, scatter, dust, dredge; sow, broadcast 75 *disperse*; lay down, put d., set d., throw down, fling d. (**see** *fell*); pitch *or* chuck overboard, drop over the side; precipitate, send headlong 287 *propel*.

fell, trip, topple, tumble, overthrow; prostrate, spread-eagle, lay low, lay one on his back 216 *flatten*; knock down, bowl over, skittle, floor, drop, down 279 *impel*; throw down, cast d., fling d. (**see** *let fall*); pull down, tear d., dash d., raze, level, raze to the ground, pull about one's ears, trample in the dust 165 *demolish*; hew down, cut d., axe 46 *cut*; blow down 352 *blow*; bring down, undermine; shoot down, wing 287 *shoot*.

abase, debase, lower the standard; lower one's sights; demote, reduce to the ranks, cashier 752 *depose*; humble, deflate, puncture, debunk, take down a peg, cut down to size, take the wind out of one's sails 872 *humiliate*; crush, squash 165 *suppress*.

sit down, sit, be seated, sit on the ground, squat, squat on one's hunkers; subside, sink, lower oneself; kneel, recline, stretch oneself out 216 *be horizontal*; roost, nest 683 *repose*; take a seat, seat oneself, park oneself; perch, alight 309 *descend*.

stoop, bend, bend down, get d.; bend over, bend forward, bend backwards; lean forward, lean over backwards; cringe, crouch, cower 721 *knuckle under*; slouch, hunch one's back 248 *make curved*; bow, scrape, duck, bob, curtsy, bob a c. 884 *pay one's respects*; nod, incline one's head, bow down, make obeisance, kiss hands, salaam, prostrate oneself, kowtow 920 *show respect*; kneel, kneel to, genuflect.

See: 46, 75, 149, 165, 198, 210, 216, 221, 248, 255, 264, 279, 287, 300, **309**, **313**, 322, 340, 341, 352, 683, 721, 752, 779, 872, 884, 920.

312 Leap

N. *leap*, saltation, skipping, capering, leapfrogging; jump, hop, skip; spring, bound, vault; high jump, long j., running j.; triple j., hop, skip and a jump; caper, gambol, frolic; kick, high k.; jeté, entrechat; prance, curvet, caracole, capriole, gambade; springy step, light tread 265 *gait*; dance step; dance, reel, jig, Highland fling 837 *dancing*.

jumper, high-j., pole-vaulter, hurdler, steeplechaser; skipper, hopper, leapfrogger; caperer, prancer; dancer, jiver; twister, rock 'n' roller 837 *dance*; tap dancer, clog d., morris d.; ballet d.; dancing girl 594 *entertainer*; kangaroo, goat, chamois, springbok; jerboa, frog, grasshopper, froghopper, flea; bucking horse, bucking bronco; jumping bean; jumping jack, Jack-in-the-box 837 *plaything*.

Adj. *leaping*, jumping etc. vb.; saltatory, saltatorial; skittish, frisky, fresh 819 *lively*; skipping, hopping; dancing, jiving; bobbing, bucking, bouncing; tossing 318 *agitated*.

Vb. *leap*, jump, take a running j.; spring, bound, vault, pole-v., hurdle, jump over the sticks, steeplechase, take one's fences; skip, hop, leapfrog, bob, bounce, rebound, buck, bob up and down 317 *oscillate*; trip, foot it, tread a measure, stamp 837 *dance*; caper, cut capers, gambol, frisk, romp; prance, paw the ground, ramp, rear, plunge; cavort, curvet, caracole; start, give a jump; jump on, pounce; jump up, leap up, spring up 308 *ascend*; jump over, clear; flounce, flounder, jerk 318 *be agitated*; writhe 251 *wriggle*.

Adv. *by leaps and bounds*, on the light fantastic toe, trippingly; at a single bound.

See: 251, 265, **308**, 317, 318, 594, 819, **837**.

313 Plunge

N. *plunge*, swoop, pounce, stoop 309 *descent*; nosedive, power dive 271 *aeronautics*; dive, header, bellyflop; swallow dive, duck d.; dip, ducking; immersion, submergence; crash dive; drowning, sinking.

diver, skin d., scuba d., deepsea d., frogman; underwater swimmer, aquanaut; diving bird, dipper 365 *bird*; submariner; submarine, bathysphere, diving-bell; plunger, sinker, lead, plummet; fathometer 465 *meter*.

Vb. *plunge*, dip, duck, bathe 341 *be wet*; walk the plank, fall in, jump in, plump, plop; dive, make a plunge, take a header, go headfirst; welter, wallow, pitch and toss; souse, douse, immerse, submerse, drown; submerge, flood the tanks, crash-dive 309 *descend*; sink, scuttle, send to the bottom, send to Davy Jones's locker 311 *lower*; sound, fathom, plumb the depths, heave the lead 465 *measure*.

founder, go down 309 *descend*; get out of one's depth; drown, settle down, go to the bottom, go down like a stone 211 *be deep*; plummet, sink, sink like lead, sink like a sack of potatoes 322 *weigh*.

See: 211, 271, 309, 311, 322, 341, 365, 465.

314 Circuition: curvilinear motion

N. *circuition*, circulation, circumambulation, circumnavigation, circling, wheeling, gyre, spiral 315 *rotation*; turning, cornering, turn, U-turn 286 *return*; orbit; lap; circuit, tour, round trip, full circle; figure of eight 250 *loop*; helix 251 *coil*; unwinding 316 *evolution*; circuitousness, roundabout way 626 *circuit*.

circler, circumambulator; circumnavigator 270 *mariner*; roundsman 794 *tradespeople*; patrol, patrolman *or* -woman; moon, satellite 321 *planet*.

Adj. *circuitous*, turning etc. vb.; orbital, ecliptic; geostationary; circumforaneous, peripatetic 267 *travelling*; circumfluent, circumflex 248 *curved*; circumnavigable; devious 626 *roundabout*, 282 *deviating*.

Vb. *circle*, circulate, go the rounds, make the round of; compass, circuit, make a c., lap; tour, do the round trip; go round, skirt; circumambulate, circumnavigate, circumaviate; go round the world, put a girdle round the earth; turn, round, double a point, weather a p.; round a corner, corner, turn a c.; revolve, orbit; wheel, spiral, come full circle, chase one's tail 315 *rotate*; turn round, bend r.; put about, wheel a., face a., turn on one's heel 286 *turn back*; draw a circle, describe a circle 232 *circumscribe*; curve, wind, twist, wind one's way 251 *meander*; make a detour 626 *circuit*.

See: 232, 248, **250**, **251**, 267, 270, 282, 286, **315**, 316, 321, 626, 794.

315 Rotation: motion in a continued circle

N. *rotation*, orbital motion, revolving, orbiting; revolution, full circle; gyration, circling, spiralling; circulation, circumfluence; spinning motion, spin, circumrotation, circumvolution; rolling, volution 285 *progression*; spiral, roll, spin, flat s.; turn, twirl, pirouette, waltz 837 *dance*; whirlabout, whirl, whirr; dizzy round, rat race 678 *overactivity*; dizziness, vertigo; gyrostatics.

vortex, whirl; whirlwind, tornado, cyclone 352 *gale*; waterspout, whirlpool, swirl 350 *eddy*; maelstrom, Charybdis; smoke ring 250 *loop*.

rotator, rotor, spinner; whirligig, teetotum, top, peg t., spinning t., humming t.; roundabout, merry-go-round; churn, whisk; potter's wheel, lathe, circular saw; spinning wheel, spinning jenny; girandole, catherine wheel; flywheel, prayer w., roulette w., wheel of Fortune 250 *wheel*; gyroscope, turntable; gramophone record, disc; wind pump, windmill, fan, sail; propeller, prop, screw; turbine; winder, capstan 310 *lifter*; swivel, hinge; spit, jack; spindle, axle, axis, shaft 218 *pivot*; spool, reel, roller 252 *cylinder*; rolling stone, planet, satellite 268 *wanderer*; whirling dervish; dancer, figure skater; Ixion.

Adj. *rotary*, rotating, spinning etc. vb.; rotatory, circumrotatory; gyratory, gyroscopic, gyrostatic; geostationary; circling, cyclic; vortical, vorticose; cyclonic; vertiginous, dizzy.

Vb. *rotate*, revolve, orbit, go into orbit 314

circle; turn right round, chase one's own tail; spin, spin like a top, twirl, pirouette; corkscrew 251 *twine*; gyre, gyrate, waltz, wheel; whirl, whirr, hum 404 *resound*; mill around, swirl, eddy 350 *flow*; bowl, trundle; set rolling, roll, roll along; spin with one's fingers, twirl, twiddle; churn, whisk 43 *mix*; turn, crank, wind, reel, spool, spin; slew, slew round, swing round, swivel r.; roll up, furl 261 *fold*; roll itself up, curl up, scroll.

Adv. *round and round*, in a circle, in circles, clockwise, anticlockwise, counterclockwise, sunwise, widdershins; head over heels.

See: 43, 218, **250**, **251**, 252, 261, 268, 285, 310, **314**, 350, 352, 404, 678, 837.

316 Evolution: motion in a reverse circle

N. *evolution*, unrolling, unfolding, unfurling; eversion 221 *inversion*; development 157 *growth*; evolutionism 358 *biology*.

Adj. *evolving*, unwinding etc. vb.; evolved etc. vb.; evolutional 358 *biological*.

Vb. *evolve*, unfold, unfurl, unroll, unwind, uncoil, uncurl, untwist, untwine, explicate, disentangle 62 *unravel*; evolute, develop, grow into 147 *be turned to*, 1 *become*; roll back 263 *open*.

See: 1, 62, 147, 157, 221, **263**, 358.

317 Oscillation: reciprocating motion

N. *oscillation*, libration, nutation; harmonic motion, pendular m., swing of the pendulum; vibration, tremor; vibrancy, resonance 141 *periodicity*; pulsation, rhythm; throbbing, drumming, pulse, beat, throb; pitter-patter, flutter, palpitation 318 *agitation*; breathing 352 *respiration*; undulation, wave motion, frequency, frequency band, wavelength 417 *radiation*; sound wave, radio w.; tidal w. 350 *wave*; seismic disturbance, earthquake, tremor 176 *violence*; seismology, seismograph; oscillator, vibrator; pendulum, bob, yoyo 217 *hanging object*. **See** *fluctuation*.

fluctuation, wave motion (**see** *oscillation*); alternation, reciprocation 12 *correlation*; to and fro movement, coming and going, shuttle service; ups and downs, boom and bust, ebb and flow, flux and reflux, systole and diastole; night and day 14 *contrariety*; reeling, lurching, rolling, pitching; roll, pitch, lurch, stagger, reel; shake, nod, wag, dance; springboard 328 *elasticity*; swing, seesaw; rocker, rocking chair, rocking horse; shuttlecock, shuttle; mental fluctuation, wavering, vacillation 601 *irresolution*.

Adj. *oscillating*, undulating etc. vb.; oscillatory, undulatory; swaying, libratory; pulsatory, palpitating; vibrant, vibratory, vibratile; earth-shaking, seismic; pendulous, dangling; reeling, staggery, groggy; rhythmic, rhythmical 141 *periodical*.

Vb. *oscillate*, librate, nutate; emit waves 417 *radiate*; wave, undulate; vibrate, pulsate, pulse, beat, drum; tick, throb, palpitate; respire, pant, heave 352 *breathe*; play, sway, nod; swing, dangle 217 *hang*; seesaw, rock; hunt (trains), lurch, reel, stagger, totter, teeter, waddle, wobble, wamble, wiggle, waggle, wag; bob, bounce, bob up and down, dance 312 *leap*; toss, roll, pitch, tumble, wallow; rattle, chatter, shake; flutter, quiver, shiver 318 *be agitated*; flicker 417 *shine*; echo 404 *resound*. **See** *fluctuate*.

fluctuate, alternate, reciprocate 12 *correlate*; ebb and flow, come and go, pass and repass, shuttle; slosh about, slop a.

brandish, wave, wag, waggle, shake, flourish; wave to and fro, shake up and down, pump; flutter 318 *agitate*.

Adv. *to and fro*, backwards and forwards, back and forth; in and out, up and down, side to side, left to right and right to left; zigzag, seesaw, wibble-wabble; like a yoyo; shuttlewise.

See: 12, 14, **141**, 176, 217, 312, **318**, 328, 350, 352, 404, 417, 601.

318 Agitation: irregular motion

N. *agitation*, irregular motion, jerkiness, fits and starts, unsteadiness 152 *changeableness*; joltiness, bumpiness, broken water, choppiness, pitching, rolling 259 *roughness*; unsteady beam, flicker, twinkle 417 *flash*; sudden motion, start, jump 508 *lack of expectation*; hop 312 *leap*; shake, jig, jiggle; toss 287 *propulsion*; shock, jar, jolt, jerk, judder, jounce, bounce, bump 279 *impulse*; nudge, dig, jog 547 *gesture*; vibration, thrill, throb, pulse, pit-a-pat, palpitation, flutter 317 *oscillation*; shuddering, shudder, shiver, frisson; quiver, quaver, tremor; tremulousness, trembling (**see** *spasm*); restlessness, feverishness, fever; tossing, turning, jactitation; jiving, rock 'n' roll 678 *activity*, 837 *dancing*; itchiness, itch 378 *formication*; twitchiness, twitch, grimacing, grimace; mental agitation, perturbation, disquiet 825 *worry*; trepidation, jumpiness, twitter, flap, butterflies 854 *nervousness*; the shakes, shivers, jumps, jitters, fidgets; aspen, aspen leaf.

spasm, ague, shivering, chattering; twitch, tic, nervous t.; chorea, St Vitus's dance, tarantism; lockjaw, tetanus; cramp, the cramps; throe 377 *pang*; convulsion, paroxysm, access, orgasm 503 *frenzy*; fit, epilepsy, falling sickness 651 *nervous disorders*; pulse, throb 317 *oscillation*; attack, seizure, stroke.

commotion, turbulence, tumult 61 *turmoil*; hurly-burly, hubbub, brouhaha; fever, flurry, rush, bustle 680 *haste*; furore 503 *frenzy*; fuss, bother, kerfuffle 678 *restlessness*; racket, din 400 *loudness*; stir, ferment 821 *excitation*; boiling, fermentation, ebullition, effervescence 355 *bubble*; ground swell, heavy sea 350 *wave*; squall, tempest, thunderstorm, magnetic storm 176 *storm*; whirlpool 315 *vortex*; whirlwind 352 *gale*; disturbance, atmospherics.

Adj. *agitated*, shaken, fluttering, waving, brandished; shaking etc. vb.; troubled, unquiet 678 *active*; feverish, fevered, restless; scratchy, jittery, jumpy, twitchy, flustered, all of a twitter, in a flap, in a flutter 854 *nervous*; hopping, leaping, like a cat on hot bricks; breathless, panting; twitching, itchy; convulsive, spasmodic, spastic; saltatory; skittish 819 *lively*; flighty 456 *light-minded*; doddering, shaky, wavery, tremulous, atremble; thrilling, vibrating 317 *oscillating*.

Vb. *be agitated*, ripple, popple, boil 355 *bubble*; stir, move, dash; shake, tremble, quiver, quaver, shiver; have a fever, throw a fit; writhe, squirm, twitch 251 *wriggle*; toss, turn, toss about, thresh a.; kick, plunge, rear 176 *be violent*; flounder, flop, wallow, roll, reel, pitch 317 *fluctuate*; sway 220 *be oblique*; pulse, beat, thrill, vibrate, judder, shudder; wag, waggle, wobble, stagger, lurch, dodder, totter, teeter, dither 317 *oscillate*; whirr, whirl 315 *rotate*; jig around, jig up and down, jump about, hop, bob, bounce, dance 312 *leap*; flicker, twinkle, gutter, sputter 417 *shine*; flap, flutter, twitter, start, jump; throb, pant, palpitate, miss a beat, go pit-a-pat 821 *be excited*; bustle, rush, mill around 61 *rampage*; ramp, roar 891 *be angry*.

agitate, disturb, rumple, ruffle, untidy 63 *derange*; discompose, perturb, worry 827 *trouble*; ripple, puddle, muddy; stir, stir up 43 *mix*; whisk, whip, beat, churn 315 *rotate*; shake up, shake; wag, waggle, wave, flourish 317 *brandish*; flutter, fly (a flag); jog, joggle, jiggle, jolt, jounce, nudge, dig; jerk, pluck, twitch.

effervesce, froth, spume, foam, foam at the mouth, bubble up 355 *bubble*; boil, boil over, seethe, simmer, sizzle, spit 379 *be hot*; ferment, work.

Adv. *jerkily*, pit-a-pat; convulsively etc. adj.; by fits and starts, with a hop, skip and a jump; spasmodically, in fits, in spasms.

See: 43, 61, 63, 152, 176, 220, 251, 259, 279, 287, 312, **315**, **317**, 350, 352, **355**, 377, 378, 379, 400, 417, 456, 503, 508, 547, 651, 678, 680, 819, 821, 825, 827, 837, 854, 891.

Class three

Matter

Section one: Matter in general

319 Materiality

N. *materiality,* materialness, empirical world, world of experience; corporeity, corporeality, corporality, bodiliness; material existence, world of nature 3 *substantiality*; physical being, physical condition 1 *existence*; plenum 321 *world*; concreteness, tangibility, palpability, solidity 324 *density*; weight 322 *gravity*; personality, individuality 80 *speciality*; embodiment, incarnation, reincarnation, metempsychosis; realization, materialization; positivism, materialism, dialectical m.; unspirituality, worldliness, sensuality 944 *sensualism*; materialist, realist, positivist.

matter, brute m., stuff; plenum; hyle, prime matter; mass, material, fabric, body, frame 331 *structure*; substance, solid s., corpus; organic matter, flesh, flesh and blood, plasma, protoplasm 358 *organism*; real world, world of nature, Nature.

object, tangible o., bird in the hand; inanimate object, still life; physical presence, body, flesh and blood, real person 371 *person*; thing, gadget, something, commodity, article, item; stocks and stones 359 *mineral*; raw material 631 *materials.*

element, elementary unit, sense datum; principle, first p. 68 *origin*; the four elements, earth, air, fire, water; unit of being, monad; factor, ingredient 58 *component*; chemical element, basic substance; isotope; physical element, atom, molecule; elementary particle, electron, neutron, meson, proton, quark 196 *minuteness*; nucleus, nucleon; photon; quantum; ion.

physics, physical science, natural s., science of matter; natural history 358 *biology*; chemistry, organic c., inorganic c., physical c.; mechanics, Newtonian m., quantum m., theory of relativity; thermodynamics; electromagnetism; atomic physics, nuclear physics 160 *nucleonics*; applied physics, technology 694 *skill*; natural philosophy, experimental p. 490 *science*; chemist, physicist, scientist.

Adj. *material,* hylic; real, natural; massy, solid, concrete, palpable, tangible, ponderable, sensible, weighty; physical, spatiotemporal; objective, impersonal, neuter; hypostatic 3 *substantial*; incarnate, embodied; corporal, somatic, corporeal, bodily, fleshly, of flesh and blood, carnal; reincarnated, realized, materialized; materialistic, worldly, unspiritual 944 *sensual.*

Vb. *materialize,* substantialize, substantiate, hypostatize, corporealize, reify; objectify 223 *externalize*; realize, make real, body forth; embody, incarnate, personify.

See: 1, 3, 58, 68, 80, 160, 196, 223, **321,** 322, 324, 331, **358, 359,** 371, 490, 631, 694, 944.

320 Immateriality

N. *immateriality,* unreality 4 *insubstantiality*; incorporeity, incorporeality, dematerialization, disembodiment, imponderability, intangibility, ghostliness, shadowiness; immaterialism, idealism, Platonism; spirituality, otherworldliness; animism; spiritualism 984 *occultism*; other world, world of spirits, eternity 115 *perpetuity*; animist, spiritualist 984 *occultist*; idealist 449 *philosopher*; astral body 970 *ghost.*

subjectivity, personality, selfhood, myself, me, yours truly 80 *self*; ego, id, superego; Conscious, Unconscious; psyche, higher self, spiritual s. 447 *spirit.*

Adj. *immaterial,* without mass; incorporeal, incorporate; abstract 447 *mental*; airy, aery, ghostly, shadowy 4 *insubstantial*; imponderable, intangible; bodiless, unembodied, discarnate, disembodied; supernal, extramundane, unearthly, transcendent; supersensory, psychic, spiritistic, astral 984 *psychical*; spiritual, otherworldly 973 *religious*; personal, subjective; illusory 513 *imaginary*.

Vb. *disembody*, spiritualize, dematerialize, disincarnate.

See: 4, 80, 115, **447**, 449, 513, 970, 973, **984**.

321 Universe

N. *universe*, omneity 52 *whole*; world, creation, all c.; sum of things, plenum, matter and antimatter 319 *matter*; cosmos, macrocosm, microcosm; space-time continuum; expanding universe, metagalaxy; outer space, deep s., intergalactic s.; void; cosmogony, nebular hypothesis, planetesimal h.; big bang theory, steady state t. 68 *start*.

world, wide w., four corners of the earth; home of man, sublunary sphere; earth, mother e., Gaea; middle earth, planet e., spaceship e.; globe, sphere, terrestrial s., terraqueous globe, geoid; geosphere, biosphere; terrestrial surface, crust; subcrust, moho; plate tectonics, continental drift 344 *land*; waters of the earth 343 *ocean*; atlas, world-map 551 *map*; Old World, New World 184 *region*; earthshine; geocentric system, Ptolemaic s.; personal world 8 *circumstance*.

heavens, sky, welkin, empyrean, ether, ethereal sphere, celestial s., hemisphere; firmament, vault of heaven; primum mobile, music of the spheres; night sky, starlit s., aurora borealis, merry dancers, northern lights, aurora australis; zodiacal light, gegenschein 417 *glow*.

star, fixed s., heavenly body, celestial b. 420 *luminary*; sidereal sphere, starry host, host of heaven; asterism, constellation, Great Bear, Little B., Plough, Big Dipper, Charles' Wain, Cassiopeia's Chair, Pleiades, Orion, Orion's belt, Southern Cross; starlight, starshine; main sequence, spectral type; blue star, white s., yellow s., red s; double star, binary, spectroscopic b., eclipsing b., eclipsing variable; multiple star; variable star, cepheid; giant, supergiant, red giant; subgiant, dwarf, red d., white d.; X-ray star, radio s. 417 *radiation*; quasi-stellar object, quasar, pulsar, neutron star, black hole; nova, supernova; Pole Star, North Star, Polaris; Pointers; Dog star, Sirius; Star of David, Star of Bethlehem; Milky Way, Galaxy; star cluster, globular c., galaxy, radio g.; island universe; stellar motion, proper m., radial velocity.

nebula, galactic n., planetary n., protogalaxy, protostar; cosmic dust, interstellar matter; Magellanic cloud, nebula, spiral n.

zodiac, signs of the z., Aries (the Ram), Taurus (the Bull), Gemini (the Twins), Cancer (the Crab), Leo (the Lion), Virgo (the Virgin), Libra (the Balance), Scorpio (the Scorpion), Sagittarius (the Archer), Capricorn (the Goat), Aquarius (the Watercarrier), Pisces (the Fishes); ecliptic; house, mansion, lunar m.

planet, major p., minor p., inferior p., superior p.; asteroid, planetoid; Mercury; Venus, morning star, evening s., Lucifer, Vesper, Hesperus; Mars, red planet; Earth, Jupiter, Saturn, Uranus, Neptune, Pluto; comet, wandering star, Halley's comet; planetary orbit, cometary o., parabolic o., hyperbolic o. 315 *rotation*.

meteor, falling star, shooting s., fireball, bolide; meteorite, aerolite, siderite, chondrite; chondrule; meteoroid; micrometeorite; meteor shower; radiant point.

sun, day-star, orb of day, eye of heaven; midnight sun; parhelion, mock sun; sunlight, photosphere, chromosphere; facula, flocculus, granule, sun spot, prominence, solar flare, corona; solar wind; Sol, Helios, Phoebus, Apollo; solar system, heliocentric s., Copernican s.

moon, satellite; new moon, waxing moon, waning m., half-m., crescent m., horned m., gibbous m., full m., harvest m., hunter's m.; paraselene, mock moon; moonscape, crater, mare, rill; Queen of the night, Selene, Luna, Diana, Phoebe, Cynthia, Hecate, Astarte; man in the moon; parish lantern; moonlight, moonshine.

satellite, moon; earth satellite, artificial s., orbiter, sputnik, moonlet, biosatellite, weather satellite, communications s., comsat; space station, skylab; space shuttle 276 *spaceship*, astronaut 271 *aeronaut*.

astronomy, star lore, stargazing, star watching; satellite tracking· radioastronomy;

astrophysics; exobiology; astrophotography; selenography, selenology; uranography; astrology, horoscope 511 *divination*; observatory, planetarium; tracking station; telescope, refracting t., reflecting t., Newtonian t., Cassegrainian t., Gregorian t. 442 *telescope*; astronomical telescope, altazimuth, equatorial; transit instrument; radio telescope, parabolic reflector, dish; spectroscope, spectrohelioscope, spectroheliograph 551 *photography*; orrery, celestial globe, astrolabe; planisphere; astronomer, radio a., astrophysicist; stargazer, star-watcher; astrologer.

uranometry, uranography; right ascension, declination, hour; hour circle, great c., ecliptic; celestial pole, galactic p., celestial equator, galactic e.; equinoctial line, equinoctial point; equinoctial colure, solstitial c.; equinox, vernal e., first point of Aries, autumnal equinox; solstice, summer s., winter s.; geocentric latitude *or* longtitude, heliocentric latitude *or* longitude, galactic latitude *or* longitude; node, ascending n., descending n.; libration, nutation; precession, precession of the equinoxes.

cosmography, cosmology, cosmogony, cosmogonist, cosmographer.

earth sciences, geography, orography, oceanography, physiography, geomorphology; geology, geodesy, geodetics; geographer, geodesist, geologist; hydrology, hydrography.

Adj. *cosmic*, universal, cosmical, cosmological, cosmogonic, cosmographical; interstellar, interplanetary, intermundane; galactic, intragalactic; extragalactic, ultramundane 59 *extraneous*; metagalactic.

celestial, heavenly, ethereal, empyreal; starry, star-spangled; sidereal, astral, stellar; solar, heliacal, zodiacal; lunar, lunate; lunisolar; nebular, nebulous; heliocentric, geocentric; cometary, meteoric; meteoritic; equinoctial, solstitial.

planetary, planetoidal, asteroidal, satellitic; Mercurian, Venusian, Martian, Jovian, Saturnian, Neptunian, Plutonian.

telluric, tellurian, terrestrial, terrene, terraqueous; sublunary, subastral; Old-World, New-World; polar, circumpolar, equatorial; worldwide, world, global, international, universal 183 *spacious*; worldly, earthly.

astronomic, astronomical, astrophysical, stargazing, star-watching; astrological, telescopic, spectroscopic.

geographic, geographical, oceanographic, orographical; geological, geomorphic; geodesic, geodetic, physiographic; hydrographic, hydrological.

Adv. *under the sun*, on the face of the globe, here below, on earth.

See: 8, 52, 59, 68, 183, 184, 271, 276, 315, 319, 343, 344, **417**, 420, **442**, 511, 551.

322 Gravity

N. *gravity*, gravitation, force of gravity, gravitational pull; gravity feed; weight, weightiness, heaviness, ponderousness, ponderosity 195 *bulk*; specific gravity; pressure, displacement, sinkage, draught; encumbrance, load, lading, freight; burden, burthen; ballast, makeweight, counterpoise 31 *offset*; mass, lump 324 *solid body*; lump of, weight of, mass of; plummet 313 *diver*; weight, bob, sinker, lead, stone, millstone; statics.

weighing, ponderation; balancing, equipoise 28 *equalization*; weights, avoirdupois weight, troy w., apothecaries' w.; grain, carat, scruple, pennyweight, drachm; ounce, pound, stone, quarter, quintal, hundredweight, ton; gram, kilogram, kilo; megaton, kiloton; axle load, laden weight.

scales, weighing machine; steelyard, weighbeam; balance, spring b.; pan, scale, weight; platform scale, weighbridge.

Adj. *weighty*, heavy, ponderous; leaden, heavy as lead; weighing etc. vb.; cumbersome, cumbrous 195 *unwieldy*; lumpish, massive 324 *dense*; pressing, incumbent, superincumbent, oppressive; ponderable, having weight, weighing, with a weight of; weighted, loaded, laden, charged, burdened; overweighted, overburdened, overloaded, top-heavy 29 *unequal*; gravitational, gravitative.

Vb. *weigh*, have weight, exert w.; weigh the same, balance 28 *be equal*; counterpoise, counterweigh 31 *compensate*; outweigh, overweigh, overbalance 34 *predominate*; tip the scales, turn the s., depress the s.; wallow, sink, gravitate, settle 313 *founder*, 309 *descend*; weigh heavy, be h., lie h.; press, weigh on, weigh one down, hang like a millstone 311 *lower*; load, cumber 702 *hinder*; try the weight of, take the w. of, find the w. of, put on the scales, lay in the scale 465 *measure*; weigh oneself, stand on the scales.

make heavy, weight, hang weights on; charge, burden, overweight, overburden, overload 193 *load*; gain weight, put on w. 195 *be large*.

Adv. *weightily*, heavily, leadenly; like a ton of bricks, like a lead balloon.

See: 28, 29, **31**, 34, 193, **195**, 309, 311, 313, **324**, 465, 702.

323 Lightness

N. *lightness*,portability; thinness, air, ether 325 *rarity*; buoyancy; volatility 338 *vaporization*; weightlessness, imponderability, imponderableness; defiance of gravity, levitation 308 *ascent*; feather, thistledown, cobweb, gossamer; fluff, dust, straw 4 *insubstantial thing*; cork, buoy, lifebelt; balloon, bubble; hot air, helium 310 *lifter*.

leaven, raising agent; ferment, enzyme, barm, yeast, baking powder, self-raising flour.

Adj. *light*, underweight 307 *deficient*; lightweight, featherweight; portable, handy 196 *little*; lightsome, light-footed; light on one's feet; light-handed, having a light touch; weightless, without weight, lighter than air; imponderable, unweighable; sublime, ethereal, airy, gaseous, volatile 325 *rare*; uncompressed, doughy, barmy, yeasty, fermenting, zymotic, enzymic; aerated, frothy, foamy, whipped; floating, buoyed up, buoyant, unsinkable; feathery, gossamery, fluffy; light as air, light as a feather, light as a fairy; lightening, unloading; raising, self-raising, leavening.

Vb. *be light*, buoyant, etc. adj.; defy gravity, levitate, surface, float to the surface, float, swim; drift, waft, glide, be airborne 271 *fly*; soar, hover 308 *ascend*.

lighten, make light, make lighter, reduce weight, lose w.; ease 701 *disencumber*; lighten ship, throw overboard, jettison 300 *empty*; volatilize, gasify, vaporize 340 *aerate*; leaven, work; raise, levitate 310 *elevate*.

See: 4, 196, 271, 300, 307, 308, **310**, **325**, 338, **340**, 701.

Section two: Inorganic matter

324 Density

N. *density*, solidity, consistency; compactness, solidness, concreteness, thickness, concentration; incompressibility 326 *hardness*; impenetrability, impermeability; indissolubility, indiscerptibility, indivisibility; coalescence, cohesion, inseparability 48 *coherence*; relative density, specific gravity; densimeter, hydrometer, aerometer.

condensation, consolidation, concentration; constipation; thickening etc. vb.; concretion, nucleation; solidification, consolidation; coagulation, thrombosis; congealment, gelatinization; glaciation; ossification, petrifaction, fossilization 326 *hardening*; crystallization; sedimentation, precipitation; condenser, compressor, thickener, gelatine, rennet, pepsin 354 *thickening*.

solid body, solid; block, mass 319 *matter*; knot, nugget, lump, burl; condensation, nucleus, hard core; aggregate, conglomerate, concretion; concrete, cement; stone, crystal, hardpan 344 *rock*; precipitate, deposit, sediment, silt, clay, cake, clod, clump; bone, ossicle; gristle, cartilage 329 *toughness*; coagulum, curd, clot, blood-c.; solid mass, phalanx, serried ranks; forest, thicket; wall, blank w. 702 *obstacle*.

Adj. *dense*, thick, crass; close, heavy, stuffy (air); foggy, murky, to be cut with a knife; lumpy, ropy, grumous, clotted, curdled; caked, matted, knotted, tangled 48 *cohesive*; consistent, monolithic; firm, close-textured, knotty, gnarled; substantial, massy, massive 322 *weighty*; concrete, solid, frozen, solidified etc. vb.; crystalline, crystallized; condensed, nucleated; costive, constipated; compact, close-packed, firm-p. 54 *full*; thickset, thick-growing, thick, bushy, luxuriant 635 *plenteous*; serried, massed, densely arrayed 74 *assembled*; incompressible, inelastic 326 *rigid*; impenetrable, impermeable, impervious, without holes; indivisible, indiscerptible, infrangible, unbreakable 162 *strong*.

indissoluble, insoluble, infusible; undissolved, unliquefied, unmelted, unthawed, deep-frozen; precipitated, sedimentary.

solidifying, binding, constipating; freezing, congealing; styptic, astringent, haemostatic.

Vb. *be dense*, - solid etc. adj.; become solid, solidify, consolidate; conglomerate, cement 48 *cohere*; condense, nucleate, form a core *or* kernel; densify, thicken, inspissate; precipitate, deposit; freeze, glaciate 380 *be cold*; set, gelatinize, jellify, jell; congeal, coagulate, clot, curdle; cake, crust; crystallize; fossilize, petrify, ossify 326 *harden*; compact, compress, firm down, contract, squeeze 198 *make smaller*; pack, squeeze in, cram, ram down 193 *load*; mass, crowd 74 *bring together*; bind, constipate; precipitate, deposit.

See: 48, 54, 74, 162, 193, 198, 319, 322, **326**, 329, 344, 354, 380, 635, 702.

325 Rarity

N. *rarity*, low pressure, vacuum, near v. 190 *emptiness*; compressibility, sponginess 327 *softness*; tenuity, subtility, fineness 206 *thinness*; lack of substance 4 *insubstantiality*, 323 lightness; incorporeality, ethereality 320 *immateriality*; airiness, windiness, ether, gas 336 *gaseousness*, 340 *air*; rarefaction, expansion, pressure reduction, attenuation; subtilization, etherealization.

Adj. *rare*, tenuous, thin, fine, subtile, subtle; flimsy, slight 4 *insubstantial*; low-pressure, uncompressed; compressible, spongy 328 *elastic*; rarefied, aerated 336 *gaseous*; void, hollow 190 *empty*; ethereal, aery 323 *light*; airy, incorporeal 320 *immaterial*; wispy, straggly 75 *unassembled*.

Vb. *rarefy*, reduce the pressure, expand; make a vacuum, pump out, exhaust 300 *empty*; subtilize, attenuate, refine, thin; dilute, adulterate 163 *weaken*; gasify, volatilize 338 *vaporize*.

See: 4, 75, 163, 190, 206, 300, 320, 323, 327, 328, 336, 338, 340.

326 Hardness

N. *hardness*, unyielding quality, intractability, renitency, resistance 329 *toughness*; starchiness, stiffness, rigour, rigidity, inflexibility; inextensibility, inelasticity; firmness, temper; callosity, callousness; grittiness, stoniness, rockiness, cragginess; grit, stone, pebble; flint, silica, quartz, granite, marble, diamond 344 *rock*; adamant, metal, duralumin; steel, hard s., iron, wrought i., cast i.; nails, hardware, stoneware; cement, concrete, reinforced c., ferroconcrete; brick, baked b.; block, board, heartwood, duramen; hardwood, teak, oak, heart of o. 366 *wood*; bone, gristle, cartilage; a callosity, callus, corn; horn, ivory; crust, shell, hard s.; hard core, hard centre, jaw-breaker; brick wall; stiffener, starch, wax; whalebone, corset, splint 218 *prop*.

hardening, induration; toughening, stiffening, backing; starching; steeling, tempering; vulcanization; petrifaction, lapidification, fossilization; crystallization, vitrification, glaciation; ossification; sclerosis, hardening of the arteries.

Adj. *hard*, adamantine; unbreakable, shatterproof 162 *strong*; fortified, armoured, armour-plated; steeled, proof; iron, cast-i.; steel, steely; hard as iron, hard as steel, hard as stone, rock-hard; sun-baked; stony, rocky, flinty; gritty, gravelly, pebbly; lithic, granitic; crystalline, vitreous, glassy; horny, corneous; callous, calloused; bony, osseous, ossific; cartilaginous, gristly 329 *tough*; hardened, indurate, indurated, tempered, case-hardened; vitrified, petrified, fossilized, ossified; icy, frozen, frozen solid, frozen over.

rigid, stubborn, resistant, intractable, unmalleable, unadaptable; firm, inflexible, unbending 162 *unyielding*; incompressible, inelastic, unsprung; starchy, starched; boned, reinforced; muscle-bound 695 *clumsy*; braced, tense, taut, tight, set, solid; crisp 330 *brittle*; stiff, stark, stiff as a poker, stiff as a ramrod, stiff as a board.

Vb. *harden*, render hard etc. adj.; steel 162 *strengthen*; indurate, temper, vulcanize, toughen; crisp, bake 381 *heat*; petrify, fossilize, ossify; calcify, vitrify, crystallize 324 *be dense*; glaciate, freeze 382 *refrigerate*; stiffen, back, bone, starch, wax (a moustache), tauten 45 *tighten*.

See: 45, 162, 218, 324, **329**, 330, 344, 366, 381, 382, 695.

327 Softness

N. *softness*, tenderness; pliableness etc. adj.; compliance 739 *obedience*; pliancy, pliability, flexibility, plasticity, ductility, tractability; malleability, adaptability; suppleness, litheness; springiness, springing, suspension 328 *elasticity*; extendibility, extensibility; impressibility, doughiness 356 *pulpiness*; sponginess, flaccidity, flabbiness, floppiness; laxity, looseness

354 *semiliquidity*; sogginess, squelchiness, marshiness 347 *marsh*; flocculence, downiness; velvetiness; butter, grease, oil, wax, putty, paste, plasticine (tdmk), clay, dough, soap, plastic; padding, wadding, pad 227 *lining*; cushion, pillow, armchair, feather bed 376 *euphoria*; velvet, plush, down, fluff, fleece 259 *hair*; feathers 259 *plumage*; snow, snowflake 323 *lightness*.

Adj. *soft*, not tough, tender 301 *edible*; melting 335 *fluid*; giving, yielding, compressible; springy, sprung 328 *elastic*; pneumatic, cushiony, pillowed, padded, podgy; impressible, as wax, waxy, doughy, argilaceous; spongy, soggy, mushy, squelchy 347 *marshy*; medullary, pithy; squashy, juicy, overripe 356 *pulpy*; fleecy, flocculent 259 *downy*; turfy, mossy, grassy; velvety, silky 258 *smooth*; unstiffened, unstarched, limp; flaccid, flabby, floppy; unstrung, relaxed, slack, loose; soft as butter, soft as wax, soft as soap, soft as down, soft as velvet, soft as silk; tender as a chicken; softening, emollient 177 *lenitive*.

flexible, whippy, bendable; pliant, pliable; ductile, tractile, malleable, tractable, mouldable, plastic, thermoplastic; extensile, stretchable 328 *elastic*; lithe, lithesome, willowy, supple, lissom, limber, loose-limbed, double-jointed; acrobatic 162 *athletic*.

Vb. *soften*, render soft, tenderize; mellow 669 *mature*; oil, grease 334 *lubricate*; knead, massage, mash, pulp, squash 332 *pulverize*; macerate, steep 341 *drench*; melt, thaw 337 *liquefy*; cushion, pillow; relax, unstring 46 *disunite*; yield, give, give way, relax, bend, unbend 328 *be elastic*.

See: 46, 162, 177, 227, 258, 259, 301, 323, **328**, 332, 334, 335, 337, 341, 347, **354**, **356**, 376, 669, 739.

328 Elasticity

N. *elasticity*, give, stretch; spring, springiness; suspension; stretchability, tensibility, extensibility; resilience, bounce 280 *recoil*; buoyancy, rubber, india r., foam r., elastomer; caoutchouc, guttapercha; whalebone, baleen; elastic; rubber band, rubber ball; gum, chewing g., bubble g.

Adj. *elastic*, stretchy, stretchable, tensile, extensile, extensible; rubbery, springy, bouncy, resilient 280 *recoiling*; buoyant; sprung, well-s.; ductile 327 *soft*.

Vb. *be elastic* - tensile etc. adj.; bounce, spring, spring back 280 *recoil*; stretch, give.

See: 280, **327**.

329 Toughness

N. *toughness*, durability, infrangibility 162 *strength*; tenacity, cohesion 48 *coherence*; viscidity 354 *semiliquidity*; leatheriness, inedibility, indigestibility; leather, gristle, cartilage 326 *hardness*.

Adj. *tough*, durable, resisting; close-woven, strong-fibred 162 *strong*; tenacious, retentive, clinging, sticky 48 *cohesive*; viscid 354 *semiliquid*; infrangible, unbreakable, untearable, shockproof, shatter-proof; vulcanized, toughened; tanned, weatherbeaten; hardboiled, overdone; stringy, sinewy, woody, fibrous; gristly, cartilaginous; rubbery, leathery, coriaceous, tough as old boots *or* shoe leather; indigestible, inedible; nonelastic, inelastic, unsprung, unyielding, stubborn 326 *rigid*.

Vb. *be tough*, - durable, etc. adj.; resist fracture, be unbreakable; toughen, tan, case-harden; mercerize, vulcanize, temper, anneal 162 *strengthen*.

See: 48, **162**, 326, 354.

330 Brittleness

N. *brittleness*, crispness etc. adj.; frangibility; friability, friableness, crumbliness 332 *powderiness*; fissility 46 *scission*; laminability, flakiness 207 *lamina*; fragility, frailty, flimsiness 163 *weakness*; bubble, eggshell, pie crust, matchwood, shale, slate; glass, porcelain 381 *pottery*; windowpane, glasshouse, house of cards, sandcastle 163 *weak thing*.

Adj. *brittle*, breakable, frangible; inelastic 326 *rigid*; fragile, brittle as glass; papery, like parchment; shattery, shivery, splintery; friable, crumbly 332 *powdery*; crisp, crispy, short, flaky, laminable; fissile, splitting; scissile, lacerable, tearable 46 *severable*; frail, delicate, flimsy, eggshell 163 *weak*; gimcrack, crazy, jerry-built 4 *insubstantial*; tumbledown 655 *dilapidated*; ready to break, ready to burst, explosive.

Vb. *be brittle*, - fragile etc. adj.; fracture 46 *break*; crack, snap; star, craze; chip, split, shatter, shiver, fragment; splinter, break off, snap off; burst, fly, explode; give way, fall in, crash 309 *tumble*; fall to pieces 655 *deteriorate*; wear thin; crumble 332 *pul-*

verize; live in a glass house.
Int. fragile! with care!
See: 4, **46**, **163**, 207, 309, 326, **332**, 381, 655.

331 Structure. Texture

N. *structure*, organization, pattern, plan; complex, syndrome 52 *whole*; mould, shape, build 243 *form*; constitution, make-up, set-up, content, substance 56 *composition*; construction, make, works, workings; architecture, tectonics, architectonics; fabric, work, brickwork, stonework, woodwork, timberwork, studwork 631 *materials*; substructure, superstructure 164 *edifice*; scaffold, framework, chassis, shell 218 *frame*; nogging, infilling 303 *insertion*; lamination, cleavage 207 *stratification*; body, carcass, person, physique, anatomy 358 *organism*; bony structure, skeleton, bone, horn; science of structure, organology, physiology, histology 358 *biology*.
texture, contexture, network 222 *crossing*; tissue, fabric, stuff 222 *textile*; staple, denier 208 *fibre*; web, weave, warp and woof, warp and weft 222 *weaving*; nap, pile 259 *hair*; granular texture, granulation, grain, grit; fineness of grain 258 *smoothness*; coarseness of grain 259 *roughness*; surface 223 *exteriority*; feel 378 *touch*.
Adj. *structural*, organic; skeletal; anatomical; organismal, organological; organizational, constructional; tectonic, architectural.
textural, textile, woven 222 *crossed*; fine-woven, close-w.; ribbed, twilled; grained, granular; fine-grained, silky, satiny 258 *smooth*; coarse-grained, gritty 259 *rough*; fine, fine-spun, delicate, gossamery, filmy; coarse, homespun, tweedy 259 *hairy*.
See: 52, 56, 164, 207, 208, 218, **222**, 223, **243**, **258**, **259**, 303, 358, 378, 631.

332 Powderiness

N. *powderiness*, friability, crumbliness 330 *brittleness*; dustiness 649 *dirt*; sandiness, grittiness; granulation; friability, crumbliness 330 *brittleness*; pulverization, levigation, trituration; attrition, detrition, attenuation, disintegration, erosion 51 *decomposition*; grinding, milling; abrasion, filing 333 *friction*; fragmentation, comminution 46 *disunion*; dusting, powdering, frosting.
powder, face p., talcum p.; talc, chalk; pollen, spore, microspore, sporule; dust, coaldust, soot, ash 649 *dirt*; flour, farina; grist, meal, bran; sawdust, filings; powdery deposit, efflorescence, flowers; scurf, dandruff; debris, detritus 41 *leavings*; sand, grit, gravel, shingle; grain, seed, crumb 53 *piece*; granule, grain of powder 33 *small thing*; flake, snowflake; smut, smoke, column of s., smoke cloud, dust c.; fog, smog 355 *cloud*; dust storm, dust devil, fen blow 176 *storm*.
pulverizer, miller, grinder; roller, crusher, masher, atomizer; mill, millstone, muller, quern, quernstone; pestle, pestle and mortar; hand mill, coffee m., pepper m.; grater, grindstone, file; abrasive, sandpaper, emery paper; molar 256 *tooth*; chopper 256 *sharp edge*; sledgehammer 279 *hammer*; bulldozer 279 *ram*.
Adj. *powdery*, pulverulent; chalky, dusty, dust-covered, sooty, smoky 649 *dirty*; sandy, sabulous, arenaceous 342 *dry*; farinaceous, branny, floury, mealy; granulated, granular; gritty, gravelly; flaky, furfuraceous, efflorescent; grated, milled, ground, sifted, sieved; crumbling, crumbled; crumbly, friable 330 *brittle*.
Vb. *pulverize*, powder, reduce to p., grind to p.; triturate, levigate, granulate; crush, kibble, mash, smash, comminute, shatter, fragment, disintegrate 46 *break*; grind, mill, mince, beat, bruise, pound, bray; knead; crumble, crumb, rub in (pastry); crunch, scrunch 301 *chew*; chip, flake, grate, scrape, rasp, file, abrade, rub down 333 *rub*; weather, wear down, rust, erode 51 *decompose*.
See: 33, 41, **46**, **51**, 53, 176, 256, 279, 301, **330**, **333**, 342, 355, 649.

333 Friction

N. *friction*, frictional force, drag 278 *slowness*; rubbing etc. vb.; attrition, rubbing against, rubbing together 279 *collision*; rubbing out, erasure 550 *obliteration*; abrasion, scraping; filing 332 *powderiness*; wearing away, erosion 165 *destruction*; scrape, graze, scratch; brushing, rub; polish, levigation, elbow grease; shampoo, massage, facial m., facial 843 *beautification*; pumice stone; eraser, rubber, rosin; whetstone 256 *sharpener*; masseur, masseuse, shampooer 843 *beautician*.
Adj. *rubbing*, frictional, fretting, grating; abrasive; fricative.

Vb. *rub*, rub against, strike (a match); gnash, grind; fret, fray, chafe, gall; graze, scratch, bark, take the skin off 655 *wound*; rub off, abrade; skin, flay; scuff, scrape, scrub, scour, burnish; brush, rub down, towel, curry, currycomb 648 *clean*; polish, buff, levigate 258 *smooth*; rub out, erase 550 *obliterate*; gnaw, erode, wear away 165 *consume*; rasp, file, grind 332 *pulverize*; knead, shampoo, massage; rub in; anoint 334 *lubricate*; wax, rosin, chalk (one's cue); grate, be rusty, catch, stick, snag; rub gently, stroke 889 *caress*; iron 258 *smooth*.

See: 165, 256, 258, 278, 279, **332**, 334, 550, 648, 655, 843, 889.

334 Lubrication

N. *lubrication*, greasing; anointment, unction, oiling etc. vb.; lubricity 357 *unctuousness*; nonfriction 258 *smoothness*.

lubricant, graphite, plumbago, black lead; glycerine, wax, grease, axle g. 357 *oil*; soap, lather 648 *cleanser*; saliva, spit, spittle, synovia; ointment, salve 658 *balm*; emollient, lenitive 357 *unguent*; lubricator, oil-can, grease-gun.

Adj. *lubricated*, greased etc. vb.; nonfrictional, smooth-running, well-oiled, well-greased; not rusty, silent.

Vb. *lubricate*, oil, grease, wax, soap, lather; butter 357 *grease*; anoint, pour balm.

See: 258, 357, 648, 658.

335 Fluidity

N. *fluidity*, fluidness, liquidity, liquidness; wateriness, rheuminess 339 *water*; juiciness, sappiness 356 *pulpiness*; nonviscosity, noncoagulation, haemophilia; solubility, solubleness, liquescence 337 *liquefaction*; gaseous character 336 *gaseousness*; viscosity 354 *semiliquidity*; hydrology, hydrometry, hydrostatics, hydrodynamics; hydraulics, hydrokinetics; fluid mechanics.

fluid, elastic f. 336 *gas*; nonelastic fluid, liquid; water, running w. 339 *water*; drink 301 *draught*; milk, whey; juice, sap, latex; humour, chyle, rheum, mucus, saliva 302 *excrement*; serum, lymph, plasma; ichor, pus, matter, sanies; gore (**see** *blood*); hydrocele, dropsy 651 *disease*.

blood, claret; lifeblood 360 *life*; bloodstream, circulation; red blood 162 *vitality*; blue blood 868 *nobility*; blood of the gods, ichor; gore, cruor, grume; clot, blood c. 324 *solid body*; corpuscle, red c., white c., platelet; lymph, plasma, serum, blood s.; haemoglobin, haematosis, sanguification; blood group, Rhesus factor; blood count; haematics, haematology.

Adj. *fluid*, fluidic, fluidal 244 *amorphous*; liquid, not solid, not gaseous; in suspension; not congealing, uncongealed; unclotted, clear, clarified; soluble, liquescent, melting 337 *liquefied*; viscous 354 *viscid*; fluent, running 350 *flowing*; runny, rheumy, phlegmy 339 *watery*; succulent, juicy, sappy, squashy 354 *semiliquid*; serous, sanious, ichorous; pussy, mattery, suppurating 653 *toxic*.

sanguineous, haematic, haemic, haemal; serous, lymphatic, plasmatic; bloody, sanguinary 431 *bloodstained*; gory, bleeding; haemophilic, haemolytic.

See: 162, 244, 301, 302, 324, 336, 337, 339, 350, 354, 356, 360, 431, 651, 653, 868.

336 Gaseousness

N. *gaseousness*, vaporousness etc adj.; windiness, flatulence 352 *wind*; aeration, gasification; volatility 338 *vaporization*; aerostatics, aerodynamics 340 *pneumatics*.

gas, vapour, elastic fluid; ether 340 *air*; effluvium, exhalation, miasma 298 *egress*; flatus 352 *wind*; fumes, reek, smoke; steam, water vapour 355 *cloud*; laughing gas, coal g., natural g., methane 385 *fuel*; marsh gas, poison g. 659 *poison*; damp, after-d., black d., choke d., fire d.; gasbag 194 *bladder*; balloon 276 *airship*; gasworks, gas plant, gasification p. 687 *workshop*; gasholder, gasometer 632 *storage*; gaslight, neon light 420 *lamp*; gas stove 383 *furnace*; gas meter 465 *meter*.

Adj. *gaseous*, gasiform; vaporous, steamy, volatile, evaporable 338 *vaporific*; aerial, aeriform, ethereal 340 *airy*; carbonated, effervescent 355 *bubbly*; gassy, windy, flatulent; effluvial, miasmic 659 *baneful*; pneumatic, aerostatic, aerodynamic.

Vb. *gasify*, vapour, steam, emit vapour 338 *vaporize*; let off steam, blow off s. 300 *emit*; turn on the gas; oxygenate 340 *aerate*; carbonate; hydrogenate, hydrogenize.

See: 194, 276, 298, 300, **338**, 340, **352**, 355, 383, 385, 420, 465, 632, 659, 687.

337 Liquefaction

N. *liquefaction*, liquidization; fluidization; solubility, deliquescence 335 *fluidity*; fusion 43 *mixture*; lixiviation, dissolution; thaw, melting, unfreezing 381 *heating*; solvent, dissolvent, flux, diluent, menstruum, alkahest; liquefier, liquefacient; liquidizer; anticoagulant 658 *antidote*.

solution, decoction, infusion; aqua; suspension; flux, lixivium, lye.

Adj. *liquefied*, molten; runny, liquescent, uncongealed, deliquescent; liquefacient, solvent; soluble, dissoluble, liquefiable, fusible 335 *fluid*; in suspension.

Vb. *liquefy*, liquidize, render liquid, unclot, clarify 350 *make flow*; liquate, dissolve, deliquesce, run 350 *flow*; unfreeze, thaw, melt, smelt 381 *heat*; melt down, fuse, render, clarify; leach, lixiviate; hold in solution, fluidize; cast, found.

See: 43, **335**, **350**, 381, 658.

338 Vaporization

N. *vaporization*, gasification; exhalation 355 *cloud*; evaporation, volatilization, distillation, sublimation; steaming, fumigation, vapourability, volatility; atomization.

vaporizer, evaporater; atomizer, spray, aerosol; retort, still, distillery, vaporimeter.

Adj. *vaporific*, volatilized etc. vb.; reeking; vapouring, steaming etc. vb.; vaporous, vapoury, vapourish; steamy, gassy, smoky; evaporable, vaporable, vaporizable, volatile.

Vb. *vaporize*, evaporate; render vaporous, render gaseous; aerify 336 *gasify*; volatilize, distil, sublime, sublimate, exhale, transpire, emit vapour, blow off steam 300 *emit*; smoke, fume, reek, steam; fumigate, spray; make a spray, atomize.

See: 300, 336, 355.

339 Water

N. *water*, H_2O; heavy water D_2O; hard water, soft w.; drinking water, tap w., Adam's ale; mineral w., soda w. 301 *soft drink*; water vapour, steam 355 *cloud*; rain water 350 *rain*; spring water, running w., fresh w. 350 *stream*; holy water 988 *ritual object*; weeping, tears 836 *lamentation*; sweat, saliva 335 *fluid*; high water, high tide, spring t., neap t., low water 350 *wave*; standing water, still w. 346 *lake*; sea water, salt w., brine, briny 343 *ocean*; water cure, taking the waters 658 *therapy*; bath water, bath, shower, douche, splash 648 *ablutions*; lotion, lavender water 843 *cosmetic*; diluent, adulteration, dilution 655 *impairment*; wateriness, damp, wet; watering, spargefaction 341 *moistening*; jug, ewer 194 *vessel*; tap, standpipe, hydrant 351 *conduit*; waterer, hose 341 *irrigator*; water supply, waterworks; well, aquafer w., artesian w., borehole 632 *store*; hydrometry 341 *hygrometry*.

Adj. *watery*, aqueous, aquatic, lymphatic 335 *fluid*; hydro-, hydrated, hydrous; hydrological, hydrographic 321 *geographic*; adulterated, diluted 163 *weak*; still, noneffervescent; fizzy, effervescent; wet, moist, drenching 341 *humid*; balneary 648 *cleansing*; hydrotherapeutic; sudorific 658 *medical*.

Vb. *add water*, water, water down, adulterate, dilute 163 *weaken*; steep, soak, liquor; irrigate, drench 341 *moisten*; combine with water, hydrate; slake 51 *decompose*.

See: 51, 163, 194, 301, 321, 335, **341**, 343, 346, **350**, 351, 355, 632, 648, 655, 658, 836, 843, 988.

340 Air

N. *air* 336 *gas*; thin air, ether 325 *rarity*; cushion of air, air pocket 190 *emptiness*; blast 352 *wind*; common air, oxygen, nitrogen, argon; welkin, blue, blue sky 355 *cloud*; open air, open, out of doors, exposure 183 *space*; sea air, ozone; fresh air, country a., smokeless zone 648 *cleanness*; airing 342 *desiccation*; aeration 338 *vaporization*; fanning 352 *ventilation*; air-conditioning, air-cooling 382 *refrigeration*; ventilator, blower, fan, air-conditioner 384 *refrigerator*; air-filter 648 *cleanser*; humidifier 341 *moisture*.

atmosphere, troposphere, tropopause, stratosphere, ionosphere; mesosphere, exosphere; aerosphere; Heaviside layer, Kennelly-Heaviside l, Appleton l.; ozone l., isothermal l.; radiation layer, Van Allen belt; aeronomy, aerospace; greenhouse effect 381 *heating*.

weather, the elements; fair weather, fine w., halcyon days; dry spell, heat wave 379 *heat*; windless weather, doldrums; atmospheric pressure, anticyclone, high pressure; cyclone, depression, low pressure; rough weather 176 *storm*, 352 *gale*; bad weather, foul w., wet w. 350 *rain*; cold weather 380 *wintriness*; changeable weather, rise and fall of the barometer; meteorology, micrometeorology; weather forecast 511 *prediction*; isobar, millibar; glass, mercury, barometer; vane, weathervane, weathercock; hygrometer 341 *hygrometry*; weather ship, weather station, rain gauge, Stevenson's screen; weather-prophet, weatherman *or* -woman, meteorologist; clime, climate, microclimate; climatology, climatography; climatologist.

pneumatics, aerodynamics, aerography, aerology, barometry 352 *anemometry*; aerometer, barometer, aneroid b., barograph, barogram.

Adj. *airy*, ethereal 4 *insubstantial*; skyey, aerial, aeriform; pneumatic, containing air, aerated, oxygenated; inflated, blown up 197 *expanded*; flatulent 336 *gaseous*; breezy 352 *windy*; well-ventilated, fresh, air-conditioned 382 *cooled*; meteorological, weather-wise; atmospheric, barometric; cyclonic, anticyclonic; high-pressure 324 *dense*; low-pressure 325 *rare*; climatic, climatological.

Vb. *aerate*, oxygenate; air, expose 342 *dry*; ventilate, freshen 648 *clean*; fan, winnow, make a draught 352 *blow*; take the air 352 *breathe*.

Adv. *alfresco*, out of doors, in the open air, in the open, under the open sky, à la belle étoile.

See: 4, 176, 183, 190, 197, 324, 325, 336, 338, 341, 342, 350, **352**, 355, 379, 380, 381, 382, 384, 511, 648.

341 Moisture

N. *moisture*, humidity, sap, juice 335 *fluid*; dampness, wetness, moistness, dewiness; dew point; dankness, condensation, rising damp; sogginess, swampiness, marshiness; saturation, saturation point 54 *plenitude*; leakiness 298 *outflow*; raininess, showeriness; rainfall, high r., wet weather 350 *rain*; damp, wet; spray, spindrift, froth, foam 355 *bubble*; mist, fog, fog bank 355 *cloud*; Scotch mist, drizzle, drip, dew, night d., morning d.; drop, raindrop, dewdrop, teardrop; wet eyes, tears 836 *lamentation*; saliva, salivation, slabber, slobber, spit, spittle 302 *excrement*; ooze, slime, mud, squelch, fen 347 *marsh*; soaked object, sop.

moistening, humidification, bedewing, damping, wetting, drenching, soaking, saturation, deluge 350 *rain*; spargefaction, sprinkling, sprinkle, aspersion, ducking, submersion 303 *immersion*; overflow, flood, inundation 350 *waterfall*; wash, bath 648 *ablutions*; baptism 988 *Christian rite*; infiltration, percolation, leaching; irrigation, watering, spraying, hosing.

irrigator, sprinkler, waterer, water-cart; watering can; spray, rose; hose, garden h., syringe, squirt; pump, fire engine; shadoof, noria, Archimedes' screw, swipe; water butt, dam, reservoir 632 *store*; sluice, water pipe 351 *conduit*.

hygrometry, hydrography, hydrology; hygrometer, udometer, rain gauge, pluviometer, Nilometer 465 *gauge*; hygroscope, weatherhouse.

Adj. *humid*, moistened, wet 339 *watery*; pluvious, pluvial; drizzling, drizzly 350 *rainy*; undried, damp, moist, dripping; dank, muggy, foggy, misty 355 *cloudy*; steaming, reeking; undrained, oozy, muddy, slimy, sloppy, slushy, squashy, squelchy, splashy, plashy, fenny 347 *marshy*; dewy, fresh, bedewed; juicy, sappy 335 *fluid*; dribbling, drip-dropping, seeping, percolating; wetted, steeped, sprinkled; dabbled; gory, bloody 335 *sanguineous*.

drenched, saturated; watered, irrigated; soaking, sopping, streaming, soggy, sodden, soaked, deluged; wet through, wet to the skin, wringing wet, dripping w., sopping wet; wallowing, waterlogged, awash, swamped, drowned.

Vb. *be wet*, - moist etc. adj.; be soggy, squelch, suck; slobber, salivate, sweat, perspire 298 *exude*; steam, reek 300 *emit*; percolate, seep 297 *infiltrate*; weep, bleed, stream; ooze, drip, leak 298 *flow out*; trickle, drizzle, rain, pour, rain cats and dogs 350 *rain*; get wet, - drenched etc. adj.; not have a dry stitch; dip, duck, dive 313 *plunge*; bathe, wash; wallow; paddle, wade, ford.

moisten, humidify, wet, dampen; dilute, hydrate 339 *add water*; lick, lap, wash; plash, splosh, splash, splatter; spill, slop; flood, spray, shower, spatter, bespatter, sprinkle, besprinkle, sparge, syringe; bedew, bedabble, dabble; baste 303 *infuse*.

drench, saturate, imbrue, imbue; soak, deluge, wet through, make run with; leach, lixiviate; wash, lave, bathe; hose down, sluice, slosh, rinse 648 *clean*; baptize 988 *perform ritual*; plunge, dip, duck, submerge, drown 303 *immerse*; swamp, flood, inundate, flood out, waterlog; dunk, douse, souse, steep; macerate, marinate; pickle, brine 666 *preserve*.

irrigate, water, supply w., hose, pump; inundate, flood, overflow, submerge; percolate 297 *infiltrate*; squirt, inject.

See: 54, 297, 298, 300, 302, 303, 313, 335, **339**, 347, **350**, 351, 355, 465, 632, 648, 666, 836, 988.

342 Dryness

N. *dryness*, aridity; need for water, thirst 859 *hunger*; drought, drouth, low rainfall, rainlessness, desert conditions; sandiness, sands 172 *desert*; dry climate, dry season; sun, sunniness 379 *heat*.

desiccation, exsiccation, drying, drying up; airing, evaporation 338 *vaporization*; draining, drainage; dehydration, insolation, sunning 381 *heating*; bleaching, fading, withering, searing 426 *achromatism*; blotting, mopping 648 *cleansing*.

dryer, dehydrator, desiccator, evaporator; dehydrant, siccative, silica gel, sand, blotting paper, blotter, blotting; absorbent, absorbent material; mop, swab, sponge, towel, towelling; hair dryer, spin d., tumble d.; wringer, mangle; airer 217 *hanger*; airing cupboard.

Adj. *dry*, needing water, thirsty 859 *hungry*; unirrigated, irrigable; arid, rainless, waterless, riverless; sandy, dusty 332 *powdery*; bare, brown, grassless; desert, Saharan; anhydrous, dehydrated, desiccated; shrivelled, withered, sere, faded 426 *colourless*; dried up, sapless, juiceless, mummified, parchment-like; sunned, insolated; aired; sun-dried, wind-d., bleached; burnt, scorched, baked, parched 379 *hot*; free from rain, sunny, fine, cloudless, fair; dried out, drained, evaporated; squeezed dry, wrung out, mangled; protected from wet, waterproofed, waterproof, rainproof, showerproof, dampproof; watertight, tight, snug, proof; greaseproof; unwetted, unmoistened, dry-footed, dry-shod; out of water, high and dry; dry as a bone, dry as a biscuit; adapted to drought, xerophilous; nongreasy, nonskid, skidproof.

Vb. *be dry*, - thirsty etc. adj.; keep dry, wear waterproof clothing; hold off the wet, keep watertight; dry up, evaporate 338 *vaporize*; become dry, dry off, dry out.

dry, dehumidify, desiccate, exsiccate, freeze-dry; dehydrate; ditch, drain, pump out, suck dry 300 *empty*; wring out, mangle; spin-dry, tumble-d., drip-d.; hang out, peg o., air, evaporate 338 *vaporize*; sun, expose to sunlight, insolate, sun-dry; smoke, kipper, cure; parch, scorch, bake, burn 381 *heat*; sere, shrivel, bleach; mummify 666 *preserve*; dry up, stop the flow 350 *staunch*; blot, blot up, mop, mop up, soak up, sponge 299 *absorb*; swab, wipe, wipe up, wipe dry.

See: **172**, 217, 299, 300, 332, 338, 350, 379, 381, 426, 648, 666, 859.

343 Ocean

N. *ocean*, sea, blue, salt water, brine, briny; waters, billows, waves, tide 350 *wave*; Davy Jones's locker; main, deep, deep sea; high seas, great waters; trackless deep, watery waste; herring pond, drink; sea lane, shipping lane; ocean floor, sea bed, sea bottom, ooze, benthos; the seven seas; Atlantic Ocean, Pacific O., Arctic O., Antarctic Ocean, Red Sea, Mediterranean, Baltic, North Sea, Irish S.; Tethys.

sea god, Oceanus, Neptune, Poseidon, Triton; Nereus, merman 970 *mythical being*.

sea nymph, Oceanid, Nereid, siren; Amphitrite, Thetis; Calypso, Undine; mermaid; bathing beauty; water sprite 970 *fairy*.

oceanography, hydrography, bathymetry; sea survey, Admiralty chart; bathysphere, bathyscaphe; oceanographer, hydrographer.

Adj. *oceanic*, thalassic, pelagic, pelagian; sea, marine, maritime; ocean-going, sea-g., seaworthy 269 *seafaring*; submarine, subaqueous, subaquatic, subaqua, undersea, underwater; benthic; abyssal 211 *deep*; hydrographic, bathymetric.

Adv. *at sea*, on the sea, on the high seas; afloat.

See: 211, **269**, **350**, 970.

344 Land

N. *land*, dry l., terra firma; earth, ground, crust, earth's c. 321 *world*; continent, mainland; heartland, hinterland; midland, inland, interior 224 *interiority*; peninsula, delta, promontory, tongue of land 254 *projection*; isthmus, neck of land, landbridge; terrain, heights, highlands 209 *high land*; lowlands 210 *lowness*; reclaimed land, polder; steppe, fields 348 *plain*; wilderness 172 *desert*; oasis, Fertile

Crescent; isle 349 *island*; zone, clime; country, district, tract 184 *region*; territory, possessions, acres, estate, real e. 777 *lands*; physical features, landscape, scenery; topography, geography, stratigraphy, geology 321 *earth sciences*; landsman, landlubber, continental, mainlander, islander 191 *dweller*.

shore, coastline 233 *outline*; coast, rocky c., ironbound c. 234 *edge*; strand, beach, sands, shingle; seaboard, seashore, seaside; sea cliff, sea wall; plage, lido, riviera; bank, river bank, riverside, lea, water meadow, washlands; submerged coast, continental shelf.

soil, glebe, farmland, arable land 370 *farm*; pasture 348 *grassland*; deposit, glacial d., aeolian d., moraine, loess, geest, silt, alluvium, alluvion; topsoil, sand, dust, subsoil; mould, leaf m., humus; loam, clay, bole, marl; fuller's earth; argil, potter's clay, china clay, kaolin 381 *pottery*; flinty soil, gravel; stone, pebble, flint; turf, sod, clod 53 *piece*.

rock, cliff, scar, crag; stone, boulder; submerged rock, reef; stack, skerry; dyke, sill, batholith; igneous rock, plutonic r., granite, basalt, hypabyssal rock; volcanic r.; volcanic glass, obsidian; magma, lava, lapilli, tuff; sedimentary rock, sandstone, shale, limestone, chalk, conglomerate; metamorphic rock, schist, marble; massive rock, bedded r.; metal-bearing rock, ore 359 *mineralogy*; precious stone, semi-p. s. 844 *gem*.

Adj. *territorial*, terrestrial, farming, agricultural 370 *agrarian*; terrigenous, terrene 321 *telluric*; earthy, alluvial, silty, sandy, loamy; clayey, marly; chalky; flinty, pebbly, gravelly, stony, rocky; granitic, marble; slaty, shaly; Pre-Cambrian 141 *seasonal*; geological, morphological, orographical, topographical.

coastal, littoral, riparian, riverine, riverside, seaside; shore, onshore.

inland, continental, midland, mainland, interior, central.

Adv. *on land*, on dry l., by l., overland, ashore, on shore, longshore; between the tides.

See: 53, 141, 172, **184**, 191, **209**, 210, 224, 233, **234**, 254, **321**, 348, 349, **359**, 370, 381, 777, 844.

345 Gulf: inlet

N. *gulf*, bay, bight, cove, creek, reach, lagoon; natural harbour, road, roadstead; inlet, outlet, fleet, bayou; arm of the sea, fjord, sea loch; drowned valley, ria; mouth, estuary; firth, frith, kyle; sound, strait, belt, gut, channel.

346 Lake.

N. *lake*, lagoon, land-locked water; loch, lough, llyn; fresh-water lake, salt l.; inland sea, Dead Sea; oxbow lake, mortlake; broad, broads; sheet of water, standing w., stagnant w., backwater; mud flat, wash 347 *marsh*; pool, tarn, mere, pond, dewpond; fishpond, stew; swimming pool, swimming bath; millpond, millpool; artificial lake, dam, reservoir 632 *storage*; well 339 *water*; basin, tank, cistern, sump 649 *sink*; ditch, irrigation d., dike 351 *drain*; waterhole, puddle, splash, wallow.

Adj. *lacustrine*, lake-dwelling, landlocked.

See: 339, 347, **351**, 632, 649.

347 Marsh

N. *marsh*, morass; marshland, slobland, wetlands; washlands, flats, mud f., salt f., salt marsh; fen, carr, moor; moss, bog, peat b., quaking b., quag, quagmire, quicksand; playa, salina, saltpan; mudhole, wallow, slough, mire, mud, ooze; swamp, everglade, swamp-forest, mangrove swamp; sudd; Slough of Despond.

Adj. *marshy*, paludal; moorish, moory; swampy, boggy, fenny; oozy, quaggy, poached, trampled; squashy, squelchy, spongy 327 *soft*; slushy 354 *semiliquid*; muddy, miry 649 *dirty*; undrained, waterlogged 341 *drenched*.

See: 327, 341, **354**, 649.

348 Plain

N. *plain*, peneplain; dene, dale, flood plain, levels 216 *horizontality*; river basin, lowlands 255 *valley*; flats 347 *marsh*; delta, alluvial plain; sands, desert s., waste 172 *desert*; tundra; ice plain, ice field, ice floe 380 *ice*; grasslands, steppe, prairie, pampas, savanna, llanos, campos; heath, common, wold, downland, downs, moor, moorland, fell; upland, plateau, tableland, mesa 209 *high land*; bush, veld, range, open country, rolling c. 183 *space*; champaign, campagna; fields, green belt, park-

land, national park 263 *open space*; lowlands, low countries 210 *lowness*.
grassland, pasture, pasturage, grazing 369 *animal husbandry*; sheeprun, sheepwalk; field, meadow, water m., mead, lea; chase, park, grounds; green, greensward, sward, lawn, turf.
Adj. *campestral*, rural; flat, open, steppe-like, rolling.
See: 172, 183, 209, 210, **216**, 255, 263, 347, 369, 380.

349 Island
N. *island*, isle, islet, skerry; river island, eyot, ait, holm; lagoon island, atoll, reef, coral r.; cay, key; sandbank, bar; floating island, iceberg; 'all-but island', peninsula; island continent; island universe, galaxy 321 *star*; archipelago; insularity 883 *seclusion*; islander, islesman 191 *dweller*.
Adj. *insular*, sea-girt; islanded, isolated, marooned; isleted, archipelagic.
See: 191, 321, 883.

350 Stream: water in motion
N. *stream*, running water, watercourse, river, subterranean r.; navigable river, waterway; tributary, branch, feeder, distributary; streamlet, rivulet, brook, brooklet, bourne, burn, rill, beck, gill, runnel, runlet; freshet, torrent, mountain t., force; arroyo, wadi; spring, fountain, fountainhead, headwaters 156 *source*; jet, spout, gush; geyser, hot spring, well 632 *store*.
current, flow, set, flux 285 *progression*; effluence 298 *egress*; confluence 293 *convergence*; inflow 297 *ingress*; outflow, reflux 286 *regression*; undercurrent, undertow, crosscurrent, rip tide 182 *counteraction*; tide, spring t., neap t.; tidal flow, tidal current, ebb and flow, tidal rise and fall 317 *fluctuation*; tideway, bore, eagre; race, tidal r., millrace, millstream; tap, standpipe, hydrant 351 *conduit*; bloodstream, circulation 314 *circuition*.
eddy, whirlpool, swirl, maelstrom 315 *vortex*; surge, reflux 290 *recession*; wash, backwash, wake 67 *sequel*.
waterfall, falls, cataract, Niagara; cascade, force, rapids, shoot, weir; water power 160 *sources of energy*; flush, chute, spillway, sluice; overflow, spill; fresh, freshet; flood, flash f., spate, inundation, deluge, cataclysm 341 *moistening*, 298 *outflow*.
wave, bow w.; wash, swash, backwash; ripple, cat's-paw 262 *furrow*; swell, ground s.; billow, roller, comber, beach c.; breaker, surf, spume, white horses, white-cap; tidal wave, tsunami; bore, eagre; rip, overfall; broken water, choppiness 259 *roughness*; sea, choppy s., long s., short s., heavy s., angry s; waviness, undulation.
rain, rainfall 341 *moisture*; precipitation; drizzle, mizzle, Scotch mist; sleet, hail 380 *wintriness*; shower, downpour, deluge, drencher, soaker, cloudburst, thunderstorm 176 *storm*; flurry 352 *gale*; pouring rain, teeming r., drenching r., driving r., torrential r.; raininess, wet spell, foul weather; rainy season, the rains, monsoon; lovely weather for ducks; plash, patter; dropping, dripping etc. vb.; rain-making, cloud-seeding; hyetograph; rain gauge 341 *hygrometry*.
Adj. *flowing*, falling etc. vb.; runny 335 *fluid*; fluent, profluent, affluent; riverine, fluvial, fluviatile, tidal; making, running, coursing, racing; streaming; in flood, in spate; flooding, inundatory, cataclysmic; surging, rolling, rippling, purling, eddying; popply, choppy 259 *rough*; winding, meandering 251 *labyrinthine*; oozy, sluggish 278 *slow*; pouring, sheeting, lashing, driving, dripping, dropping; gushing, spirting, spouting 298 *outgoing*; inflowing 297 *incoming*.
rainy, showery, drizzly, spitting, spotting; wet 341 *humid*.
Vb. *flow*, run, course, pour; ebb, regurgitate 286 *regress*; swirl, eddy 315 *rotate*; surge, break, dash, ripple, popple, wrinkle; roll, swell; buck, bounce 312 *leap*; gush, rush, spurt, spout, spew, jet, play, squirt, splutter; well, well up, bubble up, issue 298 *emerge*; pour, stream; trickle, dribble 298 *exude*; drip, drop 309 *descend*; plash, lap, wash, swash, slosh, splash 341 *moisten*; flow softly, purl, trill, murmur, babble, bubble, burble, gurgle, guggle; glide, slide; flow over, overflow, cascade, flood, inundate, deluge 341 *drench*; flow into, fall i., drain i., empty i., spill i., leak i., distil i. 297 *enter*; run off, discharge itself 298 *flow out*; flow through, leak, ooze, percolate 305 *pass*; ooze, wind 251 *meander*.
rain, shower, stream, pour, pelt; snow, sleet, hail; fall, come down, bucket down, rain hard, pour with rain, rain in torrents, rain cats and dogs; sheet, come down in sheets; patter, drizzle, mizzle, drip, drop, spit, sprinkle; be wet, rain and rain, set

in.

make flow, cause to f., send out a stream 300 *emit*; make *or* pass water 302 *excrete*; broach, tap, turn on the t., open the cocks, open the sluice gates 263 *open*; pour, pour out, spill 311 *let fall*; transfuse, decant 272 *transpose*; pump out, drain out 300 *empty*; water 341 *irrigate*; unclot, clear, clarify, melt 337 *liquefy*.

staunch, stop the flow, stem the course 342 *dry*; apply a tourniquet; stop a leak, plug 264 *close*; obstruct the flow, stem, dam, dam up 702 *obstruct*.

See: 67, 156, 160, 176, 182, 251, 259, 262, 263, 264, 272, 278, 285, 286, 290, 293, 297, **298**, **300**, 302, 305, 309, 311, 312, 314, 315, 317, 335, 337, **341**, 342, **351**, 352, 380, 632, 702.

351 Conduit

N. *conduit*, water channel, tideway, riverbed; arroyo, wadi; trough, basin, river b., drainage b.; canyon, ravine, gorge, gully 255 *valley*; inland waterways, canal system; canal, channel, watercourse; ditch, dike; trench, moat, runnel; Irish bridge; gutter, leat, mill race; duct, aqueduct; plumbing, water pipe, main, water m.; pipe, hosepipe, hose; standpipe, hydrant, siphon, tap, spout, funnel 263 *tube*; valve, penstock, flume, sluice, weir, lock, floodgate, watergate, spillway; chute 350 *waterfall*; oilpipe, pipeline 272 *transferrer*; gullet, throat; neck (of a bottle); blood vessel, vein, artery, aorta, carotid, jugular vein; veinlet, capillary.

drain, gully, gutter, gargoyle, waterspout; scupper, overflow, wastepipe, drainpipe 298 *outlet*; covered drain, culvert; open drain, ditch, sewer 649 *sink*; intestine, colon, alimentary canal; catheter 300 *voidance*.

See: 255, **263**, **272**, 298, 300, 350, **649**.

352 Wind: air in motion

N. *wind* 340 *air*; draught, downdraught, updraught, thermal; windiness etc. adj.; blowiness, gustiness, breeziness, squalliness, storminess, weather; blast, blow (**see** *breeze*, *gale*); air stream, jet s.; current, air c., crosswind, headwind 182 *counteraction*; tailwind, following wind 287 *propellant*; air flow, slip stream; air pocket; windlessness, calm air 266 *quietude*; cold draught, cold wind, raw w., icy blast; hot wind, sirocco, leveche, khamsin, harmattan; seasonal wind, monsoon, Etesian winds; regular wind, prevailing w., trade w., antitrades, Brave West Winds, Roaring Forties; north wind, Boreas, bise, mistral, tramontano; south wind, föhn, chinook; east wind, Eurus, levanter; west wind, westerly, Zephyr, Favonius; wind god, Aeolus, cave of Aeolus.

anemometry, aerodynamics 340 *pneumatics*; wind rose; Beaufort scale; anemometer, wind gauge, weathercock, weathervane, windsock, windcone.

breeze, zephyr; breath, breath of air, waft, whiff, puff, gust, capful of wind; light breeze, gentle b., fresh b., stiff b., spanking b.; sea breeze, cooling b.

gale, half g., fresh g., strong wind, high w., howling w.; blow, hard b., blast, gust, flurry, flaw; squall, black s., white s.; storm-wind, nor'wester, sou'wester, hurricane, whirlwind, cyclone, tornado, twister, typhoon, simoom 315 *vortex*; thunderstorm, dust storm, dust devil, blizzard 176 *storm*; weather, dirty w., ugly w., stormy w., windy w., gale force.

blowing, insufflation, inflation 197 *dilation*; blowing up, pumping, pumping up; pumping out 300 *voidance*; pump, air p., stirrup p., bicycle p.; bellows, windbag, bagpipe; woodwind, brass 414 *musical instrument*; blowpipe; exhaust pipe, exhaust 298 *outlet*.

ventilation, airing 340 *air*; crossventilation, draught; fanning, cooling; ventilator 353 *air pipe*; blower, fan, electric f., punkah, air-conditioner 384 *refrigerator*.

respiration, breathing, breathing in and out, inhalation, exhalation, expiration, inspiration; stomach wind, flatus, windiness, flatulence, eructation, belch; gills, lungs, bellows; respirator, iron lung, oxygen tent; windpipe 353 *air pipe*; sneezing, coughing, cough, whooping c., croup 651 *respiratory disease*; sigh, sob, gulp, hiccup, catching of the breath, yawn; hard breathing, panting; wheeze, rattle, death r.

Adj. *windy*, airy, exposed, draughty, breezy, blowy; ventilated, fresh; blowing, gusty, squally; blusterous, blustery, dirty, foul, stormy, tempestuous, boisterous 176 *violent*; windswept, windblown; stormtossed, storm-bound; flatulent; fizzy, gassy 336 *gaseous*; aeolian, favonian, boreal, zephyrous; cyclonic; gale-force, hurricane-f.

puffing, huffing; snorting, wheezing;

wheezy, asthmatic, stertorous, panting, heaving; breathless 318 *agitated*; sniffling, snuffly, sneezy; pulmonary, pulmonic, pulmonate; coughing, chesty.

Vb. *blow*, puff, blast; freshen, blow up, get up, blow hard, blow great guns, blow a hurricane, rage, storm 176 *be violent*; wail, howl, roar 409 *ululate*; screech, scream, whistle, pipe, sing in the shrouds 407 *shrill*; hum, moan, mutter, sough, sigh 401 *sound faint*; stream in the air, wave, flap, shake, flutter 318 *agitate*; draw, make a draught, ventilate, fan 382 *refrigerate*; blow along, waft 287 *propel*; veer, back 282 *deviate*; die down, drop, abate.

breathe, respire, breathe in, inhale; draw a deep breath, fill one's lungs; breathe out, exhale; aspirate, puff, huff, whiff, whiffle; sniff, sniffle, snuffle, snort; breathe hard, breathe heavily, gasp, pant, heave; wheeze, sneeze, cough 407 *rasp*; sigh, sob, gulp, suck one's breath, catch the b., hiccup, yawn; belch, burp 300 *eruct*.

blow up, pump up, inflate 197 *enlarge*; pump out, exhaust 300 *empty*.

See: 176, 182, 197, 266, 282, 287, 298, 300, 315, 318, 336, **340**, **353**, 382, 384, 401, 407, 409, 414, 651.

353 Air pipe

N. *air pipe*, airway, air-passage, windway, air shaft, air well; wind tunnel, smoke tunnel; blowpipe, peashooter 287 *propellant*; windpipe, trachea, larynx; bronchia, bronchus; throat, gullet; nose, nostril, spiracle, blowhole, nozzle, vent, mouthpiece 263 *orifice*; flue pipe, mouth organ 414 *organ*; gas main, gas pipe; tobacco pipe, pipe, briar, hookah 388 *tobacco*; funnel, flue, exhaust pipe 263 *chimney*; airbrick, air duct, ventilator, grating, louvre, air hole 263 *window*.

See: 263, 287, 388, 414.

354 Semiliquidity

N. *semiliquidity*, mucosity, viscidity; clamminess, ropiness; thickness, stodginess; semiliquid, colloid, emulsion, grume, gore, albumen, mucus, mucilage, phlegm, clot 324 *solid body*; pus, matter; juice, sap 335 *fluidity*; soup, slop, gruel, cream, curds 356 *pulpiness*; molten lava; oil slick; mud, slush, sludge, thaw, ooze, slime; sullage, silt 347 *marsh*.

thickening, inspissation, coagulation, curdling, clotting 324 *condensation*; gelation, gelatinization; emulsification; thickener, starch, flour; gelatine, isinglass, pectin.

viscidity, viscosity, glutinousness, glueyness, gumminess, stickiness, treacliness, adhesiveness 48 *coherence*; glue, gluten, gum 47 *adhesive*; emulsion, colloid; glair, size, paste, glaze, slip; gel, jelly; treacle, jam, syrup, honey, goo; wax, mastic 357 *resin*.

Adj. *semiliquid*, semifluid; stodgy, starchy, thick, soupy, curdy, lumpy, ropy 324 *dense*; unclarified, curdled, clotted, coagulated, jellied, gelatinous, pulpy, juicy, sappy, milky, creamy, lactescent, lacteal; emulsive; colloidal; thawing, half-frozen, half-melted, mushy, slushy, sloppy, waterlogged, muddy, squashy, squishy, squidgy, squelchy 347 *marshy*.

viscid, viscous, glutinous, gummy, gooey 48 *cohesive*; slimy, clammy, sticky, tacky; jammy, treacly, syrupy, gluey; glairy, glaireous; mucilaginous, mucous.

Vb. *thicken*, inspissate, congeal 324 *be dense*; coagulate 48 *cohere*; emulsify; gelatinize, gel, jelly, jell; starch 326 *harden*; curdle, clot; churn, whip up, beat up, mash, pulp 332 *pulverize*; muddy, puddle 649 *make unclean*.

See: 47, **48**, **324**, 326, 332, 335, 347, 356, 357, 649.

355 Bubble. Cloud: air and water mixed

N. *bubble*, bubbles, suds, soapsuds, lather, foam, froth; head, top; sea foam, spume, surf, spray, spindrift 341 *moisture*; mousse, soufflé, meringue, candyfloss; yeast, barm 323 *leaven*; scum 649 *dirt*; bubbling, boiling, ebullition, effervescence; fermentation, yeastiness, fizziness, fizz.

cloud, cloudlet, scud, rack; cloudbank, cloudscape; rain cloud, storm c.; woolpack, cumulus, altocumulus, cirrus, cirrocumulus, stratus, cirrostratus, nimbus, nimbostratus; mackerel sky, mare's tail; vapour, steam 338 *vaporization*; brume, haze, mist, fog, smog, pea-souper; cloudiness, film 419 *dimness*; nebulosity 321 *nebula*; nephology, nephoscope.

Adj. *bubbly*, bubbling etc. vb.; effervescent, fizzy, sparkling 336 *gaseous*; mousseux, foaming, foamy; spumy, spumous; with a head on, frothy, soapy, lathery; yeasty, aerated 323 *light*; scummy 649 *dirty*.

cloudy, clouded, overcast, overclouded;

nubilous, nebulous; cirrose, thick, foggy, hazy, misty, brumous 419 *dim*; vaporous, steamy, steaming 338 *vaporific*.
Vb. *bubble*, spume, foam, froth, cream, form a head; mantle, scum; boil, simmer, fizzle, gurgle 318 *effervesce*; work, ferment, fizz, sparkle; aerate, carbonate; steam 338 *vaporize*.
cloud, cloud over, overcast, overcloud; be cloudy, - misty etc. adj.; becloud, befog, fog over, mist up 419 *be dim*.
See: 318, 321, 323, 336, 338, 341, 419, 649.

356 Pulpiness
N. *pulpiness*, doughiness, sponginess; fleshiness, juiciness, sappiness 327 *softness*; poultice, pulp, pith, paste, putty, porridge, pap, puree; mush, mash, squash; dough, batter, sponge; soft fruit, stewed f.; jam 354 *viscidity*; mousse 355 *bubble*; ooze, slush 354 *semiliquidity*; papier mâché, wood pulp; pulping, mastication; steeping, maceration.
Adj. *pulpy*, pulpous, pulped, mashed, crushed, pureed 354 *semiliquid*; mushy, pappy 327 *soft*; succulent, juicy, sappy, squashy, ripe, overripe 669 *matured*; flabby, dimply 195 *fleshy*; doughy, pasty; macerated, steeped 341 *drenched*; soggy, spongy 347 *marshy*.
See: 195, **327**, 341, **347**, **354**, 355, 669.

357 Unctuousness
N. *unctuousness*, unctuosity, oiliness, greasiness, lubricity, soapiness 334 *lubrication*; fattiness, pinguidity; saponification; anointment, unction.
oil, volatile o., essential o.; animal oil, whale o., sperm o., train o., cod-liver o.; vegetable oil, olive o., coconut o., linseed o., cotton-seed o., castor o., rape o., groundnut o., palm o.; mineral oil, shale o., rock o., crude o., petroleum; refined oil, coal o.; fuel oil, paraffin, kerosene, petrol, gasoline, gas 385 *fuel*; lubricating oil 334 *lubricant*.
fat, animal f., grease, adipocere; blubber, tallow, spermaceti; sebum, wax, beeswax, ceresin; suet, lard, dripping, bacon fat 301 *cookery*; glycerine, stearin, olein; butyrin; margarine, butter, clarified b., ghee; milk fats, cream, Devonshire c., Cornish c.; top of the milk; buttermilk; soap, carbolic s., soft s., liquid s., soap flakes 648 *cleanser*.
unguent, salve, unction, ointment, cerate; liniment, embrocation, lanolin; spikenard, nard; pomade, brilliantine; cream, cold cream 843 *cosmetic*.
resin, resinoid, rosin, colophony, gum, gum arabic, tragacanth, myrrh, frankincense, camphor, labdanum; lac, amber, ambergris; pitch, tar, bitumen, asphalt; varnish, copal, mastic, megilp, shellac, lacquer, japan; synthetic resin, epoxy r., polyurethane, plastics.
Adj. *fatty*, pinguid, fat, adipose, blubbery 195 *fleshy*; sebaceous, cereous, waxy, waxen; lardaceous, lardy; saponaceous, soapy; butyraceous, buttery, creamy, milky, rich 390 *savoury*.
unctuous, unguentary, unguineous, greasy, oily, oleaginous; anointed, dripping with oil, basted; slippery, greased, oiled 334 *lubricated*.
resinous, resiny, resinoid, resiniferous; bituminous, pitchy, tarry, asphaltic 354 *viscid*; myrrhic, gummous, gummy; varnished, japanned.
Vb. *grease*, oil, anoint 334 *lubricate*; baste; butter, butter up; saponify; resinify, resin, rosin.
See: 195, 301, **334**, **354**, 385, 390, 648, 843.

Section three: Organic matter

358 Organisms: living matter
N. *organism*, organic matter, animate m.; organized world, organized nature, organic n., living n., living beings; animal and vegetable kingdom, flora and fauna, biota; ecosystem; biotype 77 *breed*; living matter 360 *life*; microscopic life 196 *microorganism*; cell, protoplasm, cytoplasm, nucleoplasm; nucleus, nucleolus; nucleic acid, RNA, DNA; germ plasm; chromatin, chromosome, chromatid, gene 5 *heredity*; albumen, protein; enzyme, globulin; organic remains 125 *fossil*.
biology, microbiology; biotechnology; natural history, nature study; biochemistry, biophysics, developmental biology, molecular b., cell b., cytology, cytogenetics; histology; morphology, embryology; anatomy, physiology 331 *structure*; zoography 367 *zoology*; phytography 368 *botany*; ecology, bionomics; ethology, biogeography; marine biology; genetics,

biogenetics, eugenics, genetic engineering; sociobiology; ontogeny, phylogeny; evolution, natural selection, survival of the fittest; Darwinism, Lamarckism, neo-Darwinism; biogenesis; vitalism; mechanism; naturalist, biologist, zoologist, ecologist; evolutionist, Darwinist.

Adj. *organic*, organized; biogenic; cellular, unicellular, multicellular; plasmic, protoplasmic, cytoplasmic.

biological, physiological, zoological, palaeontological; biogenetic; vitalistic; evolutionistic, evolutionary, Darwinian.

See: 5, 77, 125, 196, 331, **360**, 367, 368.

359 Mineral: inorganic matter

N. *mineral*, mineral world, mineral kingdom; inorganic matter, unorganized m., inanimate m., brute m.; earth's crust 344 *rock*; ore, metal, noble m., precious m., base m.; alloy 43 *a mixture*; mineralogical deposit, coal measures 632 *store*.

mineralogy, geology, lithology, petrography, petrology; metallurgy, metallography; speleology, glaciology 321 *earth sciences*.

Adj. *inorganic*, unorganized; inanimate, azoic; mineral, nonanimal, nonvegetable; mineralogical, petrological; metallurgical, metallic.

See: 43, 321, **344**, 632.

360 Life

N. *life*, living, being alive, animate existence, being 1 *existence*; the living, living and breathing world; living being, being, soul, spirit; plant life 366 *vegetable life*; animal life 365 *animality*; human life 371 *humankind*; gift of life, birth, nativity 68 *origin*; new birth, revivification 656 *revival*; life to come 124 *future state*; immortal life 971 *heaven*; imparting life, vivification, vitalization, animation; vitality, vital force, vital principle, élan vital, life force; soul 447 *spirit*; beating heart, strong pulse; hold on life, survival, cat's nine lives, longevity 113 *long duration*; animal spirits, liveliness, animation 819 *moral sensibility*; wind, breath, breathing 352 *respiration*; vital air, breath of life, breath of one's nostrils; lifeblood, heart's blood 5 *essential part*; vital spark, vital flame; seat of life, heart, artery; vital necessity, nourishment, staff of life 301 *food*; biological function, parenthood, motherhood, fatherhood 167 *propagation*; sex, sexual activity 45 *coition*; living matter, protoplasm, bioplasm, tissue, living t.; macromolecule, bioplast; cell, unicellular organism 358 *organism*; cooperative living, symbiosis 706 *association*; life-support system; lifetime, one's born days; life expectancy, life span, life cycle; capacity for life, viability, viableness 469 *possibility*.

Adj. *alive*, living, quick, live; breathing, alive and kicking; animated 819 *lively*; in life, incarnate, in the flesh; not dead, surviving, in the land of the living, above ground, on this side of the grave; long-lived, tenacious of life 113 *lasting*; capable of life, viable; vital, vivifying, Promethean; vivified, enlivened 656 *restored*; biotic, symbiotic, biological; protoplasmatic, protoplasmic, protoplastic, bioplasmic.

born, born alive; begotten, fathered, sired; mothered, dammed; foaled, dropped; out of, by 11 *akin*; spawned, littered; laid, new-l., hatched 164 *produced*.

Vb. *live*, be alive, have life; respire, draw breath 352 *breathe*; exist, subsist 1 *be*; live one's life, walk the earth; come to life, come to, liven, liven up, quicken, revive 656 *be restored*; not die, be spared, survive 41 *be left*; cheat death, have nine lives; live in 192 *dwell*.

be born, come into the world, first see the light 68 *begin*; have one's nativity, be incarnated; fetch breath, draw b.; be begotten, be conceived.

vitalize, give birth to, beget, conceive, support life 167 *generate*; vivify, liven, enliven, breathe life into, bring to life 174 *invigorate*; revitalize, put new life into, reanimate 656 *revive*; support life, provide a living; provide for, keep alive, keep body and soul together, keep the wolf from the door 301 *feed*.

See: 1, 5, 11, 41, 45, 68, 113, 124, 164, **167**, 174, 192, 301, 352, **358**, **365**, **366**, **371**, 447, 469, 656, 706, 819, 971.

361 Death

N. *death*, no life 2 *extinction*; process of death, dying (**see** *decease*); Dance of Death, mortality, perishability, ephemerality 114 *transience*; sentence of death, doom, crack of d., knell, death k.; execution, martyrdom; deathblow, quietus 362 *killing*; mortification, autolysis 51 *decay*; the beyond, the great divide, the great adventure, crossing the bar; deathliness, rest, eternal r., long sleep, big s. 266 *quietude*; Abraham's bosom 971 *heaven*; the grave 364 *tomb*; hand of death, jaws of d., shadow of d., shades of d.; nether regions, Stygian darkness, Hades 972 *hell*; Death, the Grim Reaper, the Great Leveller; Angel of Death, Azrael; Lord of the Underworld, Pluto; post mortem, autopsy 364 *inquest*; mortuary, charnel house, morgue 364 *cemetery*.

decease, clinical death, brain d.; end of life, extinction, exit, demise, curtains 69 *end*; departure, passing, passing away, passing over; natural death, easy d., quiet end, euthanasia 376 *euphoria*; release, happy r., welcome end; loss of life, fatality, fatal casualty; sudden death, violent d., untimely end; death by drowning, watery grave; death on the roads; fatal disease, mortal illness 651 *disease*; dying day, last hour; valley of the shadow of death; deathbed, deathwatch, death scene; last agony, last gasp, last breath, dying b.; swan song, death rattle, rigor mortis 69 *finality*; extreme unction; passing bell 364 *obsequies*.

the dead, forefathers 66 *precursor*; loved ones, dear departed, saints, souls 968 *saint*; the shades, the spirits, ghosts, phantoms 970 *ghost*; dead body 363 *corpse*; next world 124 *future state*; world of spirits, underworld, netherworld, halls of death, Sheol; Jordan, Styx; Hades, Stygian shore 972 *mythic hell*; Elysian fields, meads of asphodel, happy hunting grounds 971 *mythic heaven*.

death roll, mortality, fatality, death toll, death rate; bill of mortality, casualty list; necrology, death register 87 *list*; death certificate 548 *record*; martyrology; obituary, deaths column, death notice; the dead, the fallen, the lost; casualties, the dead and dying.

Adj. *dying*, expiring etc. vb.; mortal, ephemeral, perishable 114 *transient*; moribund, half-dead, with one foot in the grave, deathlike, deathly; deathly pale; given over, given up, despaired of, all over with, not long for this world; done for, had it; slipping, going, slipping away, sinking; sick unto death 651 *sick*; on one's death bed, at death's door; in extremis; one's hour having come, one's number being up, sands of life running out, death knocking at the door, life hanging by a thread; at the last gasp, struggling for breath; on one's last legs, at the point of death; sentenced to death, under sentence of death, fated to die, fey, doomed.

dead, deceased, demised, no more; passed over, passed away, released, departed, gone, gone before; long gone, dead and gone, dead and buried, in the grave, six feet under 364 *buried*; born dead, stillborn; lifeless, breathless, still; extinct, inanimate, exanimate, bereft of life; stone dead, cold, stiff; dead as mutton, dead as a doornail; kaput, done for, under hatches, gone for a burton; off the hook, out of one's misery; departed this life, out of this world, called to one's eternal rest, gathered to one's fathers, in Abraham's bosom, asleep in Jesus, numbered with the dead; launched into eternity, behind the veil, on the other side, beyond the grave, beyond mortal ken; gone to Elysium, gone to the happy hunting-grounds; defunct, late, lamented, late-lamented, regretted, sainted, of sainted memory; martyred, slaughtered, massacred, killed.

Vb. *die* (**see** *perish*); be dead, lie in the grave, be gone, be no more, cease to be, cease to live 2 *pass away*; die young, not make old bones; die a natural death, die in bed; end one's life, decease, predecease; succumb, expire, stop breathing, give up the ghost, breathe one's last; close one's eyes, fall asleep, sleep one's last sleep; pass, pass over, be taken; depart this life 296 *depart*; ring down the curtain, end one's earthly career, shuffle off this mortal coil, pay the debt of nature, go the way of all flesh, go to one's reward, go to one's last home, go to one's long account; cross the bar *or* the Styx *or* the River Jordan; enter the Celestial City; join the majority, join the choir invisible, join the angels, meet one's Maker, go to glory, reach a better world, awake to life immortal; croak, peg out, snuff it; cop it, have bought it, have had one's chips; conk out, pop off, go west, go for a burton, pop one's clogs, hop the twig, kick the bucket, bite the dust, turn up one's toes, push up the daisies.

perish, die out, become extinct 2 *pass away*; go to the wall 165 *be destroyed*; wilt, wither, come to dust, turn to d. 51 *decompose*; meet one's death, meet one's end, meet one's fate; die in harness, die with one's boots on; die hard, die fighting; get killed, be killed, fall, fall in action, lose one's life, be lost; relinquish one's life, lay down one's l., surrender one's l.; become a martyr, give one's life for another, make the supreme sacrifice; catch one's death, die untimely, snuff out like a candle, drop down dead; meet a sticky end, die a violent death, break one's neck; bleed to death; drown, go to Davy Jones's locker 313 *founder*; be put to death, suffer execution, die the death, walk the plank, receive one's death warrant; commit suicide 362 *kill oneself.*

Adv. *post-obit*, post mortem; in the event of death; posthumously.

See: 2, 51, 66, 69, 87, 114, 124, 165, 266, 296, 313, **362, 363, 364**, 376, 548, 651, 968, 970, 971, 972.

362 Killing: destruction of life

N. *killing*, slaying 165 *destruction*; destruction of life; taking life, dealing death; blood sports, hunting, shooting 619 *chase*; blood-shedding, blood-letting; vivisection; selective killing, cull; mercy killing, euthanasia; murder, assassination, bumping off (**see** *homicide*); poisoning, drowning, suffocation, strangulation, hanging; ritual killing, immolation, sacrifice; martyrization, martyrdom; crucifixion, execution 963 *capital punishment*; judicial murder, auto da fé, burning alive, the stake; dispatch, deathblow, coup de grace, final stroke, quietus; violent death, fatal accident, fatal casualty, death on the roads, car crash, train c., plane crash.

homicide, manslaughter; murder, capital m.; assassination; thuggery; crime passionel 911 *jealousy*; regicide, tyrannicide, parricide, patricide, matricide, uxoricide, fratricide; infanticide, exposure of infants; genocide (**see** *slaughter*).

suicide, self-slaughter, self-destruction, felo de se; self-immolation, suttee, hara-kiri; mass suicide, Gadarene swine, lemmings.

slaughter, bloodshed, high casualties, butchery, carnage; wholesale murder, bloodbath, massacre, noyade, fusillade, battue, holocaust; pogrom, purge, liquidation, decimation, extermination, annihilation 165 *destruction*; genocide, Final Solution; war, battle 718 *warfare*; Roman holiday, gladiatorial combat 716 *duel*; Massacre of the Innocents, Sicilian Vespers, Night of the Long Knives.

slaughterhouse, abattoir, knacker's yard, shambles; bullring 724 *arena*; field of battle; battlefield 724 *battleground*; field of blood, Aceldama; gas chamber, Auschwitz, Belsen.

killer, slayer, man of blood; mercy killer 905 *pity*; soldier, guerrilla 722 *combatant*; slaughterer, butcher, knacker; huntsman 619 *hunter*; trapper, rat catcher, rodent officer, pest exterminator; toreador, picador, matador 162 *athlete*; executioner, hangman 963 *punisher*; homicide (**see** *murderer*); lynch mob; homicidal maniac, pathological killer, psychopath; headhunter, cannibal; beast of prey, maneater; block, gibbet, axe, guillotine, scaffold 964 *means of execution*; insecticide, fungicide, pesticide, poison 659 *bane*.

murderer, homicide, killer, Cain; assassin, terrorist; poisoner, strangler, garrotter, thug; hatchet man, gangster, gunman; bravo, desperado, cutthroat 904 *ruffian*; parricide, regicide, tyrannicide; suicide, kamikaze.

Adj. *deadly*, killing, lethal; fell, mortal, fatal, deathly; involving life, capital; death-bringing, malignant, poisonous 653 *toxic*; asphyxiant, suffocating, stifling; unhealthy, miasmic 653 *insalubrious*; inoperable, incurable.

murderous, slaughterous, homicidal, genocidal; suicidal, self-destructive; internecine, death-dealing, trigger-happy; sanguinary, ensanguined, bloody, gory, bloodstained, red-handed; bloodthirsty, thirsting for blood 898 *cruel*; headhunting, man-eating, cannibalistic.

Vb. *kill*, slay, take life, end l., deprive of l.; do in, do for 165 *destroy*; cut off, nip in the bud, shorten one's life; put down, put to sleep; hasten one's end, bring down to the grave; drive to one's death, work to d., put to d., send to the scaffold, hang, behead, guillotine, electrocute 963 *execute*; stone, stone to death 712 *lapidate*; string up, lynch; make away with, do away w., dispatch, send out of the world, get rid of, send one to his *or* her account, launch into eternity; deal a deathblow, give the coup de grace, put one out of his *or* her misery, give one his *or* her quietus; shed blood, knife, sabre, spear, put to the sword, lance, bayonet, stab, run through 263 *pierce*; shoot down, pick off, pistol, blow the brains out 287 *shoot*; strangle, wring the neck of, garrotte, choke, suffocate, smother, stifle, drown; wall up, bury alive;

smite, brain, spill the brains of, poleaxe, sandbag 279 *strike*; send to the stake, burn alive, roast a. 381 *burn*; immolate, sacrifice, offer up; martyr, martyrize; condemn to death, sign the death warrant, ring the knell 961 *condemn*.

slaughter, butcher, poleaxe, cut the throat of, drain the lifeblood of; massacre, slay en masse, smite hip and thigh, put to the sword; decimate, scupper, wipe out; cut to pieces, cut to ribbons, cut down, shoot d., mow d.; steep one's hands in blood, wade in b., give no quarter, spare none 906 *be pitiless*; annihilate, exterminate, liquidate, purge, send to the gas chamber, commit genocide 165 *destroy*.

murder, commit m., assassinate, finish off, do in, do for, fix, settle, bump off, rub out; make to walk the plank; smother, suffocate, strangle, poison, gas.

kill oneself, do oneself in, do away with oneself, commit suicide, suicide, put an end to one's life; commit hara-kiri, commit suttee; hang oneself, shoot o., blow out one's brains, cut one's throat, slash one's wrists; fall on one's sword, die Roman fashion; put one's head in the oven, gas oneself; take poison, take an overdose; jump overboard, drown oneself; get oneself killed, have a fatal accident 361 *perish*.

Adv. *in at the death*, in at the kill.

Int. no quarter! cry havoc!

See: 162, **165**, 263, 279, 287, **361**, 381, 619, 653, 659, 712, 716, 718, 722, 724, 898, 904, 905, 906, 911, 961, **963**, **964**.

363 Corpse

N. *corpse*, corse, dead body, body; dead man *or* woman, victim; defunct, goner, stiff; cadaver, carcass, skeleton, bones, dry b.; death's-head, skull, memento mori; embalmed corpse, mummy; reliquiae, mortal remains, relics, ashes; clay, dust, earth; tenement of clay; carrion, food for worms, food for fishes; long pig 301 *meat*; organic remains 125 *fossil*; shade, manes, zombie 970 *ghost*.

Adj. *cadaverous*, corpselike; deathlike, deathly; stiff, carrion.

See: 125, 301, 970.

364 Interment

N. *interment*, burial, sepulture, entombment; urn burial; disposal of the dead, burial customs, inhumation, cremation, incineration, embalming, mummification; embalmment, myrrh, spices, natron; coffin, cist, shell, casket, Canopic jar, urn, cinerary u., funeral u.; sarcophagus, mummy-case; pyre, funeral pile, burning-ghat, crematorium; mortuary, morgue, charnel house; bone-urn, ossuary; funeral parlour; sexton, gravedigger; undertaker, funeral director; mortician; embalmer.

obsequies, exequies; mourning, weeping and wailing, wake 836 *lamentation*; lying-in-state; last rites, burial service; funeral rites, funeral solemnity, funeral procession, cortege; knell, passing bell; dead march, muffled drum, last post, taps; memorial service, requiem, funeral hymn, Dies irae, funeral oration; elegy, dirge 836 *lament*; inscription, epitaph, obituary, lapidary phrases; sepulchral monument, tombstone, gravestone, headstone, ledger; brass; hatchment; cross, war memorial; cenotaph 548 *monument*; necrologist, obituary-writer; monumental mason.

funeral, hearse, bier, pall, catafalque, coffin; mourner, weeper, keener; mute, pall-bearer; lychgate (**see** *obsequies*).

grave clothes, cerements, cerecloth, shroud, winding sheet, mummy wrapping.

cemetery, burial place, boneyard, golgotha; churchyard, graveyard, God's Acre; catacombs, columbarium, cinerarium; tower of silence; necropolis, city of the dead; garden of remembrance.

tomb, vault, crypt; burial chamber, mummy c.; pyramid, mastaba; mausoleum, sepulchre; pantheon; grave, narrow house, long home; common grave, mass grave, plague pit; grave pit, cist, beehive tomb, shaft t.; barrow 253 *earthwork*; cromlech, dolmen, menhir 548 *monument*; shrine, memorial, cenotaph.

inquest 459 *enquiry*; necropsy, autopsy, post-mortem; exhumation, disinterment, disentombment.

Adj. *buried*, interred, coffined, urned etc. vb.; laid to rest, in the grave, below ground, under g., six feet under, pushing up the daisies 361 *dead*.

funereal, funerary, funebrial; sombre, sad 428 *black*; mourning; elegiac, mortuary, cinerary, crematory, sepulchral; obsequial, obituary; lapidary, epitaphic; necrological, dirgelike 836 *lamenting*.

Vb. *inter*, inhume, bury; lay out, prepare for burial, close the eyes; embalm, mummify; coffin, encoffin; urn, entomb, ensepulchre; lay in the grave, consign to earth, lay to rest, put to bed with a shovel; burn on the pyre, cremate, incinerate 381 *burn*; pay one's last respects, go to a funeral, toll the knell, sound the last post; mourn, keen, hold a wake 836 *lament*.

exhume, disinter, unbury; disentomb; unearth, dig up.

Adv. *in memoriam*, post-obitum, post-mortem, beneath the sod; hic jacet, RIP.

See: 253, **361**, 381, 428, 459, 548, **836**.

365 Animality. Animal

N. *animality*, animal life, wild life; animal kingdom, fauna, brute creation; physique, flesh, flesh and blood; animalization, zoomorphism, Pan; animalism 944 *sensualism*.

animal, created being, living thing; birds, beasts and fishes; creature, brute, beast, dumb animal, creeping thing; protozoan, metazoan; zoophyte 196 *microorganism*; mammal, amphibian, fish, bird, reptile; worm, mollusc, arthropod; crustacean, insect, arachnid; invertebrate, vertebrate; biped, quadruped; carnivore, herbivore, insectivore, omnivore, ruminant, man-eater; wild animal, game, big game; prey, beast of prey; pack, flock, herd 74 *group*; stock, livestock 369 *stock farm*; tame animal, domestic a.; pet a., household pet, goldfish, cagebird, hamster, guinea pig, tortoise; young animal 132 *young creature*; draught animal 273 *horse, beast of burden*; endangered species, blue whale, oryx; extinct animal, dodo, auk, aurochs; prehistoric animal, pterodactyl, ichthyosaur, plesiosaur, dinosaur, brontosaurus, tyrannosaurus rex, megathere, mammoth, mastodon; fabulous beast, heraldic b., unicorn, griffin 84 *rara avis*.

mammal, viviparous animal; man 371 *humankind*; primate, ape, anthropoid ape, gorilla, orang-outang, chimpanzee, gibbon, baboon, mandrill, monkey; marmoset, lemur; marsupial, kangaroo, wallaby, wombat, koala bear, opossum; rodent, rat, mouse, field m., dormouse, shrew, vole, porcupine, mongoose, chipmunk, skunk, polecat, squirrel; insectivorous mammal, aardvark, ant-eater, mole; nocturnal mammal, bat, bush baby, raccoon, badger, hedgehog; carnivorous mammal, stoat, weasel, ferret; fox, dog f., vixen, Reynard; jackal, hyena, lion (**see** *cat*); herbivorous mammal (**see** *sheep* etc.); hare, rabbit, bunny; aquatic mammal, otter, beaver, water rat, water vole; marine mammal, walrus, seal, sea lion; cetacean, dolphin, porpoise, whale, sperm w., right w.; pachyderm, elephant, tusker, rhinoceros, hippopotamus; bear, polar b., brown b., grizzly b., bruin; giant panda; ungulate, giraffe, zebra (**see** *cattle*); deer, stag, hart, buck, doe, fawn, pricket; red deer, fallow d., roe d., muntjac; reindeer, caribou; elk, moose; gazelle, antelope, chamois, springbok, eland, hartebeest, wildebeest, gnu; horse, donkey, camel 273 *beast of burden*.

bird, winged thing, fowl, fowls of the air; fledgling, squab 132 *young creature*; avifauna, birdlife; cagebird, canary, budgerigar; talking bird, parrot, polly, macaw, mynah bird; songbird, songster, warbler, nightingale, philomel, bulbul, lark, thrush, throstle, mavis, blackbird, linnet; curlew, plover, lapwing, peewit; dove, turtle d., ring d., pigeon, wood p.; woodpecker, yaffle, jay, magpie, pie; jackdaw, rook, raven, crow; finch, goldfinch, greenfinch, chaffinch; tit, blue t., great t., wren, robin, sparrow, hedge s., house s.; yellowhammer, wagtail, pied w.; exotic bird, humming b., sunbird, weaver b., b. of paradise, lyrebird; hoopoe, golden oriole; bird of passage, summer visitor, migrant, cuckoo, swallow, swift, martin; winter visitor, redwing, fieldfare, snow bunting; flightless bird, emu, ostrich, rhea, cassowary, kiwi, penguin; nightbird, owl, barn o., screech o., nightjar; scavenging bird, vulture, marabou, carrion crow; bird of prey, raptor, eagle, golden e., bird of Jove, King of birds; kite, kestrel, harrier, osprey, buzzard, hawk, sparrow-hawk, falcon, peregrine f., hobby, merlin, shrike; fishing bird, pelican, kingfisher, gannet, cormorant, shag, skua, Arctic s.; gull, herring g., kittiwake, tern, oyster-catcher, puffin, guillemot; ocean bird, albatross, shearwater, petrel, stormy p., Mother Carey's chickens; marsh bird, wader, stork, crane, demoiselle c., avocet, heron, bittern; spoonbill, ibis, flamingo; water bird, waterfowl, swan, cob, pen, cygnet; duck, drake, duckling; goose, gander, gosling; merganser, pintail, pochard, teal, mallard, widgeon; moorhen, coot, lily-trotter, diver, dipper, grebe, dab-chick.

table bird, game b., woodcock, wood pigeon, squab; peafowl, peacock, peahen; grouse, ptarmigan, capercaillie, pheasant, partridge, quail; goose, duck, snipe; turkey, gobbler; guinea fowl.

poultry, fowl, hen, biddy; cock, cockerel, rooster, Chanticleer; chicken, pullet; spring chicken, boiler, broiler, roaster, capon; Rhode Island Red, Leghorn, bantam.

cattle, kine, livestock 369 *stock farm*; bull, cow, calf, heifer, fatling, yearling; bullock, steer; beef cattle, Highland c., Aberdeen Angus, Hereford, Charolais; dairy cattle, milch cow, Guernsey, Jersey, Friesian; dual-purpose cattle, Redpoll, shorthorn; zebu, brahmin; ox, oxen; buffalo, bison; yak, musk ox; goat, billy g., nanny g., mountain g., ibex.

sheep, ram, tup, wether, bell w., ewe, lamb, baa-l., lambkin; teg; Southdown, Lincoln, Cheviot, merino; mountain sheep, mouflon.

pig, swine, boar, tusker, warthog; hog, sow, piglet, pigling, sucking pig, shoat, porker; Large White, Wessex Saddleback, Berkshire, Tamworth.

dog, canine, bow-wow, man's best friend; bitch, whelp, pup, puppy; cur, hound, tyke, pooch, mutt; mongrel, pariah dog, pye-d.; guide dog, house d., watch d., bandog, police d., bloodhound, mastiff; sheepdog, Old English S., collie; Dobermann pinscher, bull terrier; bulldog, boxer; wolfhound, borzoi, Afghan hound, Alsatian, Dalmatian; Great Dane; St Bernard; greyhound, courser, whippet; foxhound, staghound, beagle; basset, dachshund; gun dog, retriever, golden r., Labrador r., pointer, setter, Irish s.; terrier, smooth-haired t., wire-h. t., fox t., Sealyham, Scottish t., Scottie; spaniel, cocker s., springer s., King Charles s.; show dog, fancy d., toy d., chihuahua, Pomeranian, chow; lap dog, pekinese, peke, pug; Welsh corgi; poodle, French p., miniature p., toy p.; husky, sledge dog; wild dog, dingo; wolf, coyote.

cat, feline; grimalkin, moggie, puss, pussy, kitten, kit, kitty-cat, pussycat; tom, tom cat, queen c., tabby; mouser; Cheshire Cat; Persian c., Siamese c., Manx c., calico c., tortoiseshell c., marmalade c., tabby c.; big cat, lion, lioness, King of Beasts; tiger, leopard, cheetah, panther, puma, jaguar, cougar, ocelot; wildcat, bobcat, lynx.

amphibian, frog, bullfrog, tree frog; frogspawn, tadpole; paddock, toad, natterjack; newt, eft; salamander, axolotl.

reptile, ophidian, serpent, sea s.; snake, water s., harmless s., grass s., smooth s.; venomous s., viper, adder, asp; cobra, king c., hamadryad; puff adder, mamba, horned viper, rattlesnake; anaconda, boa constrictor, python; crocodile, alligator, cayman; lizard, legless l., slowworm, blindworm; chameleon, iguana, monitor, gecko; turtle, tortoise, terrapin.

marine life, denizens of the deep; marine organisms, nekton, benthos; cetacean (see *mammal*); sea urchin, sea horse, sea anemone, coral, coral reef, jellyfish, Portuguese man of war, starfish, brittle-star; shellfish, mollusc, bivalve, clam, oyster, mussel, cockle; whelk, winkle, limpet; cephalopod, cuttlefish, squid, octopus; crustacean, crab, lobster, crayfish, shrimp; barnacle.

fish, flying f., swordfish, angelfish, dogfish, moray eel, shark; piranha, barracuda; stingray, electric ray; marlin, tunny fish, turbot, bass, conger eel 301 *fish food*; coelacanth; pipefish, blenny, goby, wrasse; pike, roach, perch, dace, bream, carp; trout, grayling; salmon, grilse; eel, elver, lamprey; minnow, gudgeon, stickleback.

insect, larva, pupa, imago; winged insect, fly, house f., horse f., gadfly, bluebottle; mayfly, caddis fly; gnat, midge, tsetse fly, mosquito; greenfly, blackfly, aphid; ladybird, lacewing, hoverfly; firefly, glowworm; dragonfly, crane fly, daddy longlegs; butterfly, moth, hawk m., clothes m.; bee, bumble bee, humble b., honey b., queen b., worker b., drone; wasp, hornet; beetle, stag b., dung b., cockroach; insect pests, vermin, parasites, bug, bed bug, flea, louse, nit, mite, tick, jigger; woodworm, weevil, borer, cockchafer, deathwatch beetle 659 *blight*; pismire, emmet, ant, soldier a., worker a., white a., termite; stick insect, praying mantis; locust, grasshopper, cicada, cricket.

creepy-crawly, grub, maggot, caterpillar, looper, inchworm; worm, earthworm, lugworm, wireworm, roundworm, flatworm, tapeworm, fluke; myriapod, centipede, millipede; slug, snail; earwig, woodlouse; spider, money s.; black widow s., tarantula; scorpion 904 *noxious animal*.

Adj. *animal*, animalcular; brutish, beastly, bestial; feral, domestic; human, manly, subhuman; therianthropic, theriomorphic, zoomorphic; zoological; vertebrate, invertebrate; mammalian, warm-blooded; primatial, anthropoid, simian; equine, asinine, mulish; deerlike, cervine; bovine, taurine, ruminant; ovine, sheepish; goatlike, goatish; porcine, piggy; bearish, ursine; elephantine; canine, doggy; lupine, wolfish; feline, catlike, cattish, tigerish, leonine; vulpine, foxy; avian, birdlike; aquiline, vulturine; passerine; owlish; dovelike; gallinaceous, anserine; cold-blooded, fishy, piscine, molluscan, molluscoid; amphibian, amphibious, salientian; reptilian, saurian, ophidian, snaky, serpentine, viperish; vermicular, wormy, weevilly; verminous; lepidopterous, entomological.

See: 74, 84, **132**, **196**, **273**, **301**, 369, 371, 659, 904, 944.

366 Vegetable life

N. *vegetable life*, vegetable kingdom; flora, vegetation; biomass; flowering, blooming, florescence; lushness, rankness, luxuriance 635 *plenty*, 171 *abundance*; Flora, Pan; faun, dryad, hamadryad, wood nymph 967 *nymph*.

wood, timber, lumber, softwood, hardwood, heartwood, sapwood; forest, virgin f., primeval f.; rain f., jungle; coniferous forest, taiga; bush, heath, scrub, maquis, chapparal; greenwood, woodland, bocage, copse, coppice, spinney; thicket, brake, covert; park, chase, game preserve; hurst, holt; plantation, arboretum, pinetum, pinery; orchard, orangery 370 *garden*; grove, clump; clearing, glade; brushwood, underwood, undergrowth; bushiness, bushes, shrubbery, windbreak, hedge, hedgerow.

forestry, dendrology, silviculture, tree-planting, afforestation, conservation; woodman, forester, verderer; woodcutter, lumberman, lumberjack; dendrologist 370 *gardener*.

tree, shrub, bush, sapling, scion, stock; pollard; bonsai; shoot, sucker, trunk, bole; limb, branch, bough, twig; conifer, coniferous tree, greenwood t., evergreen t., deciduous t., softwood t., hardwood t., ironwood t.; fruit tree, nut t., timber t.; mahogany, ebony, teak, walnut, oak, elm, ash, beech, sycamore, maple, plane, lime, linden; horse chestnut, copper beech; cedar of Lebanon, redwood, larch, fir, Douglas fir, spruce, pine, Scots p.; poplar, Lombardy p., aspen, alder, sallow, willow, weeping w., pussy w.; birch, silver b., rowan, mountain ash; crab apple, sweet chestnut; hazel, elder, spindle, hawthorn, may, blackthorn, sloe; privet, yew, holly, ivy, box, bay, laurel; rhododendron, camellia, azalea; magnolia, laburnum, lilac; wisteria, Virginia creeper; acacia, jacaranda; palm, date p., coconut p., oil p.; baobab, banyan, mangrove; gum tree, eucalyptus, rubber tree 370 *agriculture*.

foliage, foliation, frondescence; greenery, verdure; leafiness, leafage; herbage; umbrage; limb, branch, bough, twig, shoot; spray, sprig; treetop; leaf, simple l., compound l.; frond, flag, blade; leaflet, foliole; pine needle; seed-leaf, cotyledon; leaf-stalk, petiole, stipule, node, stalk, stem; tendril, prickle, thorn.

plant, growing thing, herb, wort, weed; root, tuber, rhizome, bulb, corm 156 *source*; stolon, rootstock, cutting 132 *young plant*; thallophyte, gametophyte, sporophyte; culinary herb 301 *potherb*; medicinal herb 658 *remedy*; food plant, fodder 301 *vegetable*, *fruit*, *provender*; national plant, rose, leek, daffodil, thistle, shamrock; garden plant, pansy, carnation, lily; lavender, honeysuckle 396 *fragrance*; wild plant, daisy, dandelion, buttercup; water plant, water lily, flag; desert plant, cactus, succulent; prickly plant, bramble, gorse; insectivorous plant, Venus's flytrap, sundew; deadly nightshade 659 *poisonous plant*; trailing plant, creeper, climber, twiner, vine, bine, liana; parasite, mistletoe; nonflowering plant, horsetail, fern, bracken; moss, clubmoss, bog m., sphagnum; liverwort; lichen, fungus, mushroom, toadstool, agaric, puffball; mould, penicillin; seaweed, wrack, bladderwrack, kelp, gulfweed; algae 196 *microorganism*.

flower, floweret, floret, blossom, bloom, bud, burgeon; inflorescence, head, corymb, panicle, cyme, umbel, spike, catkin; petal, sepal; corolla, calyx; ovary, ovule, receptacle; pistil, style, stigma, stamen, anther, pollen; nectary; fruit, berry, nut, drupe; seed vessel, pod, capsule, cone; pip, spore, seed 156 *source*; annual, biennial, perennial; house plant, pot p.; hothouse p., exotic; garden flower, wild flower; flowerbed, seedbed; gardening, horticulture, floriculture 370 *garden*.

grass, mowing g., hay; pasture, pasturage, herbage 348 *grassland*; verdure, turf, sod, lawn; meadow grass, rye g., couch g., bent g., fescue; sedge, rush, bulrush, reed, papyrus; marram grass, esparto g.; Pampas grass, elephant g., bamboo, sugar cane; grain plant, wheat, oats, barley, rye, millet, sorghum, rice 301 *cereals*; grain, husk, chaff, stubble, straw.

Adj. *vegetal*, vegetative, vegetable, botanical; evergreen; deciduous; hardy, half-hardy; horticultural, floricultural; floral, flowery, blooming; rank, lush, overgrown; weedy, weed-ridden; leafy, verdant, verdurous 434 *green*; grassy, mossy; turfy; gramineous, graminiferous, herbaceous, herbal; leguminous, cruciferous, composite, umbelliferous; foliate, trifoliate, pinnate; fungous, fungoid, fungiform; exogenous, endogenous; dicotyledonous, monocotyledonous.

arboreal, arboreous, dendriform, dendritic, arborescent, treelike; forested, timbered; woodland, woody, wooded, sylvan, arboraceous; grovy, bosky; wild, jungly, scrubby; bushy, shrubby; afforested, planted; dendrologous, dendrological.

wooden, wood, woody, ligneous, ligniform; hard-grained, soft-grained.

Vb. *vegetate*, germinate, sprout, shoot 36 *grow*; plant, garden, botanize 370 *cultivate*; forest, afforest, reforest, replant.

See: 36, **132**, 156, 171, 196, **301**, 348, **370**, 396, 434, 635, 658, 659, 967.

367 Zoology: the science of animals

N. *zoology*, zoography, zootomy; zoogeography; animal physiology, comparative p., morphology 331 *structure*; embryology 358 *biology*; anatomy, comparative a.; ethology; anthropography 371 *anthropology*; ornithology, bird lore, bird watching; ichthyology, herpetology, ophiology, mammalogy, malacology, helminthology, entomology, conchology; palaeontology; taxidermy.

zoologist, ornithologist, ichthyologist, entomologist, lepidopterist, anatomist, anthropologist etc. n.

Adj. *zoological*, entomological etc. n.

See: 331, **358**, 371.

368 Botany: the science of plants

N. *botany*, phytography, phytogeography, phytotomy; taxonomy; plant physiology, plant pathology; plant ecology; dendrology 366 *forestry*; agrostology; mycology, fungology, bryology, algology; palaeobotany; botanical garden 370 *garden*; hortus siccus, herbarium, herbal; botanist, herbalist, taxonomist etc. n.

Adj. *botanical*, dendrological etc. n.

Vb. *botanize*, herbalize.

See: 366, 370.

369 Animal husbandry

N. *animal husbandry*, animal management; training, manège; thremmatology, breeding, stock-b., rearing; domestication, taming etc. vb.; veterinary science; horse-breeding, cattle-raising; dairy farming, beef f. 365 *cattle*; sheep farming, pig-keeping, goat-k., bee-k., poultry farming; stirpiculture, pisciculture, aviculture, apiculture, sericulture; veterinary surgeon, vet, horse doctor 658 *doctor*; ostler, groom, stable boy 742 *servant*; farrier, blacksmith; keeper, gamekeeper, gillie; game warden.

stock farm, stud f., stud; dairy farm, cattle f., ranch; fish farm, trout f., hatchery; fish pond, fish tank; duck pond; pig farm, piggery; beehive, hive, apiary; pasture, grazing, sheeprun, sheepwalk 348 *grassland*; poultry farm, chicken run, hen r., free range; broiler house, battery, deep litter; factory farm.

cattle pen, byre 192 *stable*; sheepfold 235 *enclosure*; hutch, coop, hencoop, henhouse; cowshed, pigsty; swannery; bird cage, aviary.

zoo, zoological gardens, menagerie, circus; Noah's Ark; aviary, vivarium, terrarium, aquarium; reptile house, monkey temple; bear pit; wildlife park, safari p.; game park, game reserve.

breeder, stock b., horse b.; trainer, animal t., lion-tamer; cattle farmer, sheep f., pig-keeper, bee-k., apiarist; fancier, bird-f., pigeon-f.

herdsman, cowherd; stockman, cattleman, cowman, rancher; cowboy, cowgirl, cow-puncher; broncobuster, gaucho; shepherd, shepherdess; goatherd; goosegirl; milkmaid, dairymaid; kennel maid.

Adj. *tamed*, broken, broken in; gentle, docile; domestic, domesticated; reared, raised, bred; purebred, thoroughbred, half-bred; stirpicultural.

Vb. *break in*, tame, domesticate, acclimatize 610 *habituate*; train 534 *teach*; back, mount, whip, spur 267 *ride*; yoke, harness, hitch, bridle, saddle; round up, herd, corral, cage 235 *enclose*.

breed stock, breed, rear, raise, grow, hatch, culture, incubate, nurture, fatten; ranch, farm 370 *cultivate*.

groom, currycomb, rub down, stable, bed down; tend, herd, shepherd; shear, fleece; milk; drench, water, fodder 301 *feed*.

See: 192, 235, 267, 301, 348, **365**, **370**, 534, 610, 658, 742.

370 Agriculture

N. *agriculture*, agronomy, agronomics, rural economy; agribusiness 622 *business*; cultivation, ploughing, contour p., sowing, reaping; growth, harvest, produce, crop, vintage 632 *store*; cash crop, catch c., fodder c.; husbandry, farming, mixed f., contract f., factory f., intensive f., subsistence f., dry f., organic f.; monoculture; cattle farming, dairy f. 369 *animal husbandry*; cereal farming, arable f.; hydroponics, tray agriculture, tank farming; irrigation 341 *moistening*; geoponics, tillage, tilth, spadework; green fingers; floriculture, flower-growing; horticulture, gardening, market g.; indoor g., bonsai; vegetable growing, fruit g., mushroom g.; viticulture, viniculture, wine-growing, vine-dressing; arboriculture, silviculture, afforestation 366 *forestry*; landscape gardening, landscape architecture; water, dung, manure 171 *fertilizer*; fodder, winter feed 301 *provender*; silage, ensilage 632 *storage*.

farm, home f., grange; arable farm, dairy f., sheep f., cattle f. 369 *stock farm*; ranch, hacienda; model farm; farmstead, farmhouse; farmyard, barnyard 235 *enclosure*; state farm, collective f., kolkhoz, kibbutz; farmland, arable land, ploughed land, fallow 344 *soil*; rice paddy, paddyfield; herbage, pasturage, pasture, fields, meadows 348 *grassland*; demesne, manor farm, estate, holding, smallholding, croft 777 *lands*; allotment, kitchen garden; market garden, hop g.; nursery, garden centre; vineyard; fruit farm, orchard; tea garden, tea estate, coffee e., sugar plantation, rubber p.

garden, botanical g., flower g., rose g., knot g., Dutch g., herb g., rock g., alpine g., indoor g., winter g.; vegetable garden, cabbage patch, kitchen garden, allotment; fruit garden, orchard; arboretum, pinery 366 *wood*; patch, plot, grass p., grass, greensward, lawn, park 235 *enclosure*; shrubbery, border, herbaceous b., bed, flowerbed, parterre 844 *ornamental art*; seedbed, frame, cold f., propagator 167 *propagation*; cloche, conservatory, hothouse, greenhouse, glasshouse, orangery; jardinière, flowerpot.

farmer, husbandman, farm manager, bailiff; cultivator, planter, tea p.; agronomist, agriculturalist; tiller of the soil, peasant, kulak, moujik, paysan; serf; villein; sharecropper, métayer, tenant farmer; gentleman farmer, yeoman; smallholder, crofter, allotment-holder; fruit grower, fruit farmer, orchardist; wine-grower, vineyardist; farm hand, farm labourer, agricultural worker; land girl; ploughman, tractor driver, sower, reaper, harvester, gleaner; thresher; picker, hop p., fruit p., vintager; agricultural folk, farming community, peasantry; rustic, Giles 869 *country-dweller*.

gardener, horticulturist, flower grower; topiarist, landscape gardener; seedsman, nurseryman *or* -woman; market gardener; hop-grower, fruit-g., vine-grower, vinedresser; arborist, arboriculturalist, silviculturist 366 *forestry*; planter, digger, delver, Adam.

farm tool, plough, ploughshare, coulter; harrow, chain h., spike h.; spade, fork, hoe, draw h., Dutch h., rake, trowel; dibble, digging stick; drill; hayrake, hayfork, pitchfork; scythe, sickle, reaping hook, shears, secateurs 256 *sharp edge*; flail, winnowing fan; winepress, ciderpress; mowing machine, reaper, thresher, binder, baler, combine harvester, pea viner; silage cutter *or* forager; tractor; hay waggon, hay wain, haystack; elevator, barn, hayloft, silo 632 *storage*.

Adj. *agrarian*, peasant, farming; agrestic, georgic, bucolic, pastoral, rural, rustic, agricultural, agronomic, geoponic; predial, manorial, collective; arable, cultivable; ploughed, dug, planted etc. vb.

horticultural, garden, gardening, topiary; silvicultural; herbal; cultured, forced, hothouse, exotic.

Vb. *cultivate*, bring under cultivation 171 *make fruitful*; farm, ranch, garden, grow; till, till the soil, scratch the s.; dig, double-dig, delve, spade, dibble; seed, sow, broadcast, scatter the seed, set, plant, prick out, dibble in, puddle in, transplant, plant out, bed o.; plough, harrow, rake, hoe; weed, prune, top and lop, thin out 204 *shorten*; graft, engraft 303 *implant*; layer, take cuttings; force, fertilize, topdress, mulch, dung, manure 174 *invigorate*; grass over, sod, rotate the crop; leave fallow 674 *not use*; harvest, gather in 632 *store*; glean, reap, mow, cut, scythe, cut a swathe; bind, bale, stook, sheaf; flail, thresh, winnow, sift, bolt 46 *separate*; crop, pluck, pick, gather; tread out the grapes; ensile, ensilage; improve one's land 654 *make better*; fence in 235 *enclose*; ditch, drain, reclaim; water 341 *irrigate*.

See: 46, 167, **171**, 174, 204, 235, 256, 301, 303, 341, 344, 348, **366**, 369, 622, 632, 654, 674, 777, 844, 869.

371 Humankind

N. *humankind*, mankind, womankind; humanity, human nature; flesh, mortality; generations of man, peoples of the earth; the world, everyone, everybody, the living, ourselves; human race, human species, hominid, Homo Sapiens, man; tellurian, earthling; human being, Adam, Eve, Adamite, lords of creation; civilized humanity, political animal, civilized world 654 *civilization*; uncivilized humanity, barbarians, savages; primitive humanity, bushmen, aborigines; early humanity, primeval h., Stone-Age h., Cro-Magnon man, Neanderthal man, cavemen and - women, troglodytes; apemen and - women, Pithecanthropus, Australopithecus, Peking man, Java man; bionic person, cyborg, android; ethnic type 11 *race*.

anthropology, anthropography; anthropometrics, craniometry, craniology; anthropogenesis, somatology; ethnology, ethnography, folklore, mythology; social anthropology, demography; social science, humanitarianism 901 *sociology*; humanism; anthroposophy; anthropomorphism, pathetic fallacy; anthropologist, craniologist, ethnographer, demographer, folklorist, humanist.

person, individual, human being, everyman, everywoman; creature, fellow c., mortal, body, bod; a being, soul, living s.; God's image; one, somebody, someone, so-and-so, such a one; party, customer, character, type, element; chap, fellow 372 *male*; girl, female 373 *woman*; personage, figure, person of note, VIP 638 *bigwig*; celebrity, star 890 *favourite*; dramatis personae, all those concerned 686 *personnel*; unit, head, hand, nose.

social group, society, community 74 *group*; kinship group 11 *family*; primitive society, tribalism; organized society, international s., comity of nations 706 *cooperation*; community at large, people, persons, folk; public, general p., man *or* woman in the street, you and me 79 *generality*; population, populace, citizenry 191 *inhabitants*; the masses 869 *commonalty*; stratified society, social classes 869 *lower classes, middle c.*, 868 *upper class, aristocracy*.

nation, nationality, statehood, nationalism, national consciousness, race c.; Pan-Slavism, Pan-Africanism, Negritude; ultranationalism, chauvinism, jingoism, expansionism, imperialism, colonialism; civil society, body politic, people, demos; state, city s., welfare s., civil s., nation s., multiracial s.; realm, commonwealth 733 *political organization*; democracy, republic 733 *government*.

Adj. *human*, creaturely, mortal, fleshly; earthborn, tellurian; anthropoid, hominoid; subhuman 35 *inferior*; anthropological, ethnographical, racial 11 *ethnic*; humanistic; anthropocentric, anthropomorphic; personal, individual.

national, state, civic, civil, public, general, communal, tribal, social, societal; cosmopolitan, international.

See: **11**, 35, 74, 79, 191, 372, 373, 638, 654, 686, 706, 733, 868, 869, 890, 901.

372 Male

N. *male*, male sex, man, he, him; Adam; manliness, masculinity, manhood; virility, machismo; male chauvinism, male exclusiveness; male-dominated society, patriarchy; mannishness, virilism; gentleman, sir, esquire, master; lord, my l., his lordship; Mr, mister, monsieur, Herr, señor, don, dom, senhor, signor, sahib; tovarich, comrade, citoyen; squire, guvnor, guv; buster, Mac, Jock; mate, buddy, pal 880 *chum*; goodman, wight, swain; gaffer, buffer 133 *old man*; fellow, guy, scout, bloke, chap, chappie, johnny, gent; codger, card, cove, joker; blade, rake, gay dog 952 *libertine*; he-man, caveman, macho; male chauvinist pig, MCP; sissy 163 *weakling*; homosexual 84 *nonconformist*; eunuch, castrato; escort, beau, boy friend; bachelor, widower; bridegroom 894 *bridal party*; married man, husband, house h. 894 *spouse*; family man, paterfamilias, patriarch; father 169 *paternity*; uncle, brother, nephew; lad, boy 132 *youngster*; son 170 *sonship*; spear side; stag party, menfolk.

male animal, jack, cock, cockerel, rooster; drake, gander, cob; buck, stag, hart; horse, stallion, entire horse, stud h., colt; bull, bull-calf, bullock, ox, steer; boar, hog; ram, tup; he-goat, billy g.; dog, dog fox, tom cat; gelding, capon 161 *eunuch*.

Adj. *male*, masculine, manly, gentlemanly, chivalrous; virile, macho; mannish, manlike, butch, unfeminine, unwomanly.

See: 84, **132**, **133**, 161, 163, 169, 170, 880, 894, 952.

373 Female

N. *female*, feminine gender, she, her, -ess; femineity, feminality, muliebrity; femininity, feminineness, the eternal feminine; womanhood 134 *adultness*; womanliness, girlishness; feminism, women's rights, Women's Lib *or* Liberation; matriarchy, gynarchy, gynocracy, regiment of women; womanishness, effeminacy, androgyny 163 *weakness*; gynaecology, gyniatrics; obstetrics 167 *propagation*.

womankind, second sex, female s., fair s., gentle s., weaker s.; the distaff side, womenfolk, women, matronage; hen party; women's quarters, zenana, purdah, seraglio, harem.

woman, Eve, she; girl, little g., young g. 132 *youngster*; virgin, maiden; nun, unmarried woman, old maid 895 *spinster*; bachelor girl, career woman; feminist, sister, women's libber; suffragette; bride, married woman, wife, 'trouble and strife', squaw, widow, matron 894 *spouse*; dowager 133 *old woman*; mother, grandmother 169 *maternity*; unmarried mother, working wife *or* mother, housewife; aunt, niece, sister, daughter; wench, lass, nymph; colleen, damsel; petticoat, skirt, doll, chick, bird; honey, hinny, baby; grisette, midinette; brunette, blonde, platinum b., redhead; girl friend, sweetheart 887 *loved one*; moll, bint, crumpet, bit of fluff; broad, courtesan 952 *loose woman*; lesbian 84 *nonconformist*; minx, hussy, baggage, jade; shrew, virago, Amazon; goddess, Venus, Juno, Diana.

lady, gentlewoman; dame; milady, her ladyship, donna; madam, ma'am, marm, mistress, Mrs, missus, Ms, miss, madame, mademoiselle, Frau, Fraulein; signora, signorina, señora, señorita, memsahib; goody, goodwife.

female animal, hen, pen, bitch; mare, filly; cow, heifer; sow, gilt; ewe, ewelamb; nanny goat; hind, doe; vixen, tigress, lioness.

Adj. *female*, she, feminine, petticoat, girlish, womanly, ladylike, maidenly, matronly; child-bearing 167 *generative*; feminist, feministic; viraginous, amazonian; lesbian; womanish, effeminate, unmanly, pansy; feminized, androgynous.

See: 84, **132**, **133**, 134, 163, 167, 169, 887, 894, 895, 952.

374 Physical sensibility

N. *sensibility*, sensitivity, responsiveness; sensitiveness, soreness, tenderness, delicateness; exposed nerve, unhealed wound; perceptivity, awareness, consciousness 819 *moral sensibility*; physical sensibility *or* susceptivity, susceptibility, passibility; hyperaesthesia, allergy; funny bone; sensuousness, aestheticism, aesthetics; aesthete 846 *people of taste*; touchy person, sensitive plant, thin skin 892 *irascibility*.

sense, sense-perception; sensory apparatus, sense organ, nervous system, sensorium; five senses; touch, hearing, taste, smell, sight; sensation, impression 818 *feeling*; effect, response, reaction, reflex, synaesthesia; autosuggestion, autohypnosis; sixth sense, extrasensory perception, ESP; telepathy, thought-transference 984 *psychics*.

Adj. *sentient*, perceptive, sensitive, sensitized; sensible, susceptible, passible; sensory, perceptual; sensuous, aesthetic 818 *feeling*; percipient, aware, conscious 490 *knowing*; acute, sharp, keen 377 *painful*; ticklish, itchy; tender, raw, sore, exposed; impressionable, alive, alive to, warm, responsive; allergic, oversensitive, hypersensitive 819 *impressible*.

striking, keen, sharp, poignant, acute, vivid, clear, lively; electrifying 821 *exciting*; sudden, sensational 821 *impressive*.

Vb. *have feeling*, sense, become aware;

come to one's senses, awaken, wake up; perceive, realize 490 *know*; be sensible of 818 *feel*; react, tingle 819 *be sensitive*; have all one's senses, hear, see, touch, taste, smell; be alert, have one's wits about one.

cause feeling, stir the senses, stir the blood; stir, disturb 318 *agitate*; arouse, awaken, excite, make *or* produce an impression 821 *impress*; arrest, astonish, cause a sensation 508 *surprise*; sharpen, cultivate 174 *invigorate*; refine, aestheticize; increase sensitivity, sensitize; hurt 377 *give pain*.

Adv. *to the quick*, to the heart, on the raw.

See: 174, 318, 377, 490, 508, **818**, **819**, **821**, 846, 892, 984.

375 Physical insensibility

N. *insensibility*, physical i., impassibility, insensitiveness; mental insensibility, imperceptiveness, obtuseness 499 *unintelligence*; impassivity 820 *moral insensibility*; insentience, anaesthesia; analgesia; narcotization, hypnosis, hypnotism, autohypnosis; suspended animation; apoplexy, paralysis, palsy; numbness; catalepsy, stupor, coma, trance, drugged t., freak-out; faint, swoon, blackout, syncope, unconsciousness, senselessness; narcolepsy, narcotism, sleeping sickness 651 *disease*; narcosis, twilight sleep, drugged s. 679 *sleep*; Sleeping Beauty, Rip van Winkle.

anaesthetic, dope 658 *drug*; local anaesthetic, general a.; ether, chloroform, morphine, cocaine, novocaine, chloral; gas, nitrous oxide, laughing gas; gas and air, epidural, pethidene; narcotic, sleeping tablets, knockout drops, draught 679 *soporific*; opium, laudanum; painkiller, analgesic 177 *moderator*; acupuncture.

Adj. *insensible*, insensitive, insentient, insensate; obtuse, dull, imperceptive 499 *unintelligent*; unaware, oblivious; unhearing 416 *deaf*; unseeing 439 *blind*; senseless, sense-bereft, unconscious; inert 679 *inactive*; inanimate, out cold, dead 266 *quiescent*; numb, benumbed, frozen; paralysed, paralytic, palsied; doped, dopey, drugged; freaked out, spaced o.; stoned 949 *dead drunk*; anaesthetized, hypnotized; punch-drunk, dazed, stupefied; semiconscious, in a trance; cataleptic, comatose; anaesthetic, analgesic; hypnotic, mesmeric 679 *soporific*.

unfeeling, cold, callous, inured, indurated, toughened, hardened, case-h.; pachydermatous, thick-skinned; stony, impassible, proof, shockproof 820 *impassive*.

Vb. *be insensible*, - insentient etc. adj.; not react 679 *be inactive*; have a thick skin 820 *be insensitive*; harden oneself, indurate, cease to feel; become insensible, lose consciousness, pass out, black o., faint, swoon; go into a coma.

render insensible, make insensible; obtund, blunt, deaden; paralyse, benumb; freeze 382 *refrigerate*; put to sleep, send to sleep, hypnotize, mesmerize 679 *make inactive*; anaesthetize, put under, gas, chloroform; narcotize, drug, dope; dull, stupefy; stun, concuss, brain, knock out, render unconscious 279 *strike*; pall, cloy 863 *sate*.

See: 177, 266, 279, 382, 416, 439, 499, 651, 658, **679**, **820**, 863, 949.

376 Physical pleasure

N. *pleasure*, physical p., sensual p., sensuous p.; sexual p., s. satisfaction; thrill 821 *excitation*; enjoyment, gratification, sensuousness, sensuality; self-indulgence, animal gratification, luxuriousness, hedonism 944 *sensualism*; dissipation, round of pleasure 943 *intemperance*; rest 685 *refreshment*; treat, diversion, entertainment, divertissement 837 *amusement*; feast 301 *feasting*; good feeding, relish 386 *taste*; gusto, zest, keen appreciation; mental *or* spiritual pleasure, delight, happiness, ecstasy 824 *joy*.

euphoria, well-being, contentment 828 *content*, 824 *happiness*; physical well-being 650 *health*; easeful living, gracious l.; ease, convenience, comfort, cosiness, snugness, creature comforts; luxury, luxuries 637 *superfluity*; lap of luxury 800 *wealth*; feather bed, bed of down, bed of roses, velvet, cushion, pillow 327 *softness*; peace, quiet, rest 683 *repose*; quiet dreams 679 *sleep*; painlessness, euthanasia.

Adj. *pleasant*, pleasure-giving 826 *pleasurable*; pleasing, tickling, titillating; delightful, delightsome; welcome, grateful, gratifying, satisfying 685 *refreshing*; genial, congenial, cordial, heart-warming; nice, agreeable, enjoyable 837 *amusing*; palatable, delicious 386 *tasty*; sugary 392 *sweet*; perfumed 396 *fragrant*; tuneful 410 *melodious*; lovely 841 *beautiful*.

comfortable, affording comfort, comfy, homely, snug, cosy, warm, comforting, restful 683 *reposeful*; painless, peaceful

266 *tranquil*; convenient, easy, cushy; easeful, downy 327 *soft*; luxurious, de luxe; enjoying comfort, euphoric, in comfort, at one's ease, slippered; pampered, featherbedded; happy, gratified 828 *content*; relieved 685 *refreshed*.

sensuous, of the senses, appealing to the s.; bodily, physical 319 *material*; voluptuous, pleasure-loving, enjoying, epicurean, hedonistic 944 *sensual*.

Vb. *enjoy*, relish, like, quite l.; feel pleasure, experience p., take p. in 824 *be pleased*; thrill to 821 *be excited*; luxuriate in, revel in, riot in, bask in, roll in, wallow in; gloat on, gloat over, get a kick out of; lick one's lips, smack one's l. 386 *taste*; live on the fat of the land, live comfortably, live in comfort 730 *prosper*; give pleasure 826 *please*.

Adv. *in comfort*, at one's ease; in clover, on velvet, on a bed of roses.

See: 266, 301, 319, 327, 386, 392, 396, 410, 637, 650, 679, 683, 685, 730, 800, 821, 824, **826**, 828, 837, 841, 943, **944**.

377 Physical pain

N. *pain*, physical p., bodily p.; discomfort, malaise, inconvenience; distress, thin time, hell 731 *adversity*; exhaustion, weariness, strain 684 *fatigue*; hurt, bruise, sprain; cut, gash 655 *wound*; aching, smarting; heartache, anguish, agony 825 *suffering*; slow death, death by inches, torment, torture; crucifixion, martyrdom, vivisection; rack, wheel, thumbscrew 964 *instrument of torture*; painfulness, soreness, tenderness; painful aftermath, hangover 949 *crapulence*.

pang, thrill, throes; stab, twinge, nip, pinch; pins and needles 378 *formication*; stitch, crick, cramp, convulsion 318 *spasm*; smart, sting, sharp pain, shooting p., darting p., gnawing p.; ache, headache, splitting head, migraine, megrim; toothache, earache; stomachache, bellyache, gripes, colic, collywobbles; neuritis, neuralgia, angina; arthritis, rheumatoid a., rheumatism, fibrositis; sciatica, lumbago, backache 651 *ill health*.

Adj. *painful*, paining, aching, agonizing, excruciating, exquisite; harrowing, racking, tormenting; poignant 827 *distressing*; burning, biting, stabbing, lancinating, shooting, tingling, smarting, throbbing; sore, raw, tender, exposed; bitter, bittersweet 393 *sour*; disagreeable, uncomfortable, inconvenient 827 *unpleasant*.

pained, hurt, tortured, martyred etc. vb.; suffering, aching, flinching, wincing, quivering, writhing.

Vb. *give pain*, ache, hurt, pain, sting; inflict pain, excruciate, put to torture, lacerate, torment, twist the arm of 963 *torture*; flog, crucify, martyr 963 *punish*; vivisect, tear, lacerate 46 *cut*; touch the quick; prick, stab 263 *pierce*; gripe, nip, pinch, tweak, twinge, shoot, throb; devour, bite, gnaw; grind, grate, jar, set on edge; fret, chafe, gall 333 *rub*; irritate 832 *aggravate*; put on the rack, break on the wheel; kill by inches, prolong the agony; grate on the ear 411 *discord*; inconvenience, annoy, distress 827 *trouble*.

feel pain, suffer p., feel the pangs 825 *suffer*; agonize, ache, smart, chafe; twitch, wince, flinch, writhe, squirm, creep, shiver, quiver 318 *be agitated*; tingle, get pins and needles; sit on thorns, have a thin time, be a martyr, go through it 731 *have trouble*; shriek, yell, scream, howl, groan 408 *cry*; weep 836 *lament*; lick one's wounds.

See: 46, 263, 318, 333, 378, 393, 408, 411, 651, 655, 684, 731, **825**, **827**, 832, 836, 949, 963, 964.

378 Touch: sensation of touch

N. *touch*, tactility, palpability; handling, feeling, palpation, manipulation; massage, kneading, squeeze, pressure 333 *friction*; graze, contact 202 *contiguity*; light touch, lambency; stroke, pat, caress; flick, flip, tap 279 *knock*; sense of touch, fine t., precision 494 *accuracy*; delicacy, artistry 694 *skill*.

formication, titillation, tickling sensation; creeps, gooseflesh; tingle, tingling, pins-and-needles; scratchiness, itchiness, itch, urtication; urticaria, nettlerash, hives; rash, dhobi's itch, prickly heat 651 *skin disease*; pediculosis 649 *uncleanness*.

feeler, organ of touch, palp, palpus, antenna, whisker, tentacle; proboscis, tongue; digit, forefinger, thumb (**see** *finger*); green fingers; hand, paw, palm, flipper, mitt.

finger, forefinger, index, middle finger, ring f., little f., pinkie; thumb, pollex; hallux, big toe 214 *foot*; five fingers, bunch of fives, bone sandwich; 'pickers and stealers'; hand, fist 778 *nippers*; fingernail, talon, claw.

Adj. *tactual*, tactile; palpal, tentacular; prehensile 778 *retentive*; touching, licking, grazing etc. vb.; touchable, tangible, palpable 319 *material*; light of touch, light-handed, heavy-h. 695 *clumsy*.

handed, with hands; right-handed 241 *dextral*; left-handed 242 *sinistral*; thumbed, fingered, polydactyl; digitate, digital, manual; five-finger.

Vb. *touch*, make contact, come into c.; graze, scrape, shave, brush, glance; kiss, osculate 202 *be contiguous*; impinge, overlap; hit, meet 279 *collide*; feel, palpate; finger, thumb, take between finger and thumb, pinch, nip, massage 333 *rub*; palm, run the hand over, pass the fingers o.; stroke, pat down 258 *smooth*; wipe, sweep 648 *clean*; touch lightly, tap, pat, dab, flick, flip, tickle, scratch; lip, lap, lick, tongue; nuzzle, rub noses; paw, fondle 889 *caress*; handle, twiddle, fiddle with; manipulate, wield, ply, manhandle 173 *operate*; touch roughly, bruise, crush 377 *give pain*; fumble, grope, grabble, scrabble; put out a feeler 461 *be tentative*.

itch, tickle, tingle, creep, crawl, have gooseflesh, have the creeps; prick, prickle, titillate, urticate, scratch; thrill, excite, irritate, inflame 374 *cause feeling*.

See: 173, **202**, 214, 241, 242, 258, 279, 319, 333, 374, 377, 461, 494, 648, 649, 651, 694, 695, **778**, 889.

379 Heat

N. *heat*, caloric; phlogiston; radiant heat; convected heat; incalescence, recalescence, decalescence; emission of heat, diathermancy; incandescence, flame, glow, flush, blush; warmth, fervour, ardour; tepidity, lukewarmness; specific heat, blood h., body h.; sweat, swelter; fever heat, pyrexia, fever, hectic, inflammation 651 *disease*; high temperature, white heat; ebullition, boiling point, flash p., melting p.; torrid heat, tropical h., sweltering h., summer h., high summer, flaming June; dog days, heat haze 128 *summer*; heat wave, scorcher, roaster, sizzler; hot wind, simoom, sirocco; hot springs, thermal s., thermae, geyser, hot water, steam; tropics, torrid zone; sun, midday s., sunshine, solar heat, insolation 381 *heating*.

fire, devouring element, flames; bonfire, bale fire, watch f., beacon f.; St Elmo's f. 417 *glow*; hellfire; death fire, pyre 364 *obsequies*; coal fire, gas f., electric f. 383 *furnace*; Greek fire, wild f. 723 *bomb*; deflagration, conflagration, holocaust; heath fire, forest f.; fireball, blaze, flame, tongue of f., sheet of f., wall of f.; spark, scintillation, flicker, arc 417 *flash*; flare 420 *torch*; eruption, volcano; pyrotechnics 420 *fireworks*; arson 381 *incendiarism*; fire worship 981 *worship*; salamander, phoenix.

thermometry, heat measurement; degree, kelvin, Kelvin scale; thermometer, differential t., clinical t., Fahrenheit t., centigrade *or* Celsius t., Réaumur t.; thermoscope, thermopile, thermostat, air-conditioner; pyrometer, calorimeter; thermal unit, British Thermal Unit, BTU, therm, calorie; solar constant; thermodynamics; thermography, thermograph.

Adj. *hot*, heated, superheated, overheated; inflamed, fervent, fervid; flaming, glowing, red-hot, white-h.; like an oven, hot as hell; piping hot, smoking h.; hot as pepper 388 *pungent*; incalescent, recalescent; feverish, febrile, fevered; sweltering, sudorific, sweating, perspiring; steaming, smoking; running with sweat, dripping with s.; on the boil, boiling, ebullient, scalding; tropical, torrid, scorching, grilling, broiling, searing, blistering, baking, toasting, roasting etc. vb.; scorched, scalded 381 *heated*; thirsty, burning, parched 342 *dry*; running a temperature, in a fever, in a lather, in a sweat, in a muck s.

fiery, ardent, burning, blazing, flaming, flaring; unquenched, unextinguished; smoking, smouldering; ablaze, afire, on fire, in flames; candescent, incandescent, molten, glowing, aglow 431 *red*; pyrogenic, igneous, pyrogenous; ignited, lit, alight, kindled, enkindled; volcanic, erupting, plutonic.

warm, tepid, lukewarm, unfrozen; temperate, mild, genial, balmy; fair, set f., sunny, sunshiny 417 *undimmed*; summery, aestival; tropical, equatorial; torrid, sultry; stuffy, close, muggy; overheated, uncooled, unventilated; oppressive, suffocating, stifling 653 *insalubrious*; warm as toast; snug 376 *comfortable*; at room temperature, at blood heat; caloric, calorific, calorimetric; thermic, thermal, isothermal.

Vb. *be hot*, be warm, get warm etc. adj.; recalesce, incandesce; burn, kindle, catch fire, take f., draw; blaze, flare, flame, flame up, burst into flame, go up in flames; glow, flush; smoke, smoulder, reek, fume, steam 300 *emit*; boil, seethe 318 *effervesce*; toast, grill, roast, sizzle, crackle, frizzle, fry, bake 381 *burn*; get burnt, scorch, boil dry; bask, sun oneself, sunbathe; get sunburnt, tan; swelter, sweat, perspire, glow; melt, thaw 337 *liquefy*; thirst, parch 342 *be dry*; stifle, pant, gasp for breath, fight for air; be in a fever, be feverish, have a fever, run a temperature; keep warm, wrap up.

See: 128, 300, 318, 337, 342, 364, 376, **381**, 383, 388, **417**, **420**, 431, 651, 653, 723, 981.

380 Cold

N. *coldness*, low temperature, drop in t.; cool, coolness, freshness; cold, freezing c., zero temperature, zero, absolute z.; freezing point; frigidity, gelidity; iciness, frostiness; sensation of cold, chilliness, algidity, rigour, hypothermia, shivering, shivers, chattering of the teeth, gooseflesh, goose pimples, frostbite, chilblains; chill, catching cold; cold climate, high latitudes, Frigid Zone, Siberia, North Pole, South P.; Arctic, Antarctica; snowline, permafrost; glacial epoch, Ice Age; polar bear, Eskimo.

wintriness, winter, depth of w., hard w., severe w.; nip in the air, cold snap; cold weather, cold front; inclemency, wintry weather, arctic conditions, polar temperature, degrees of frost; snowstorm, hailstorm, blizzard; frost, Jack Frost, frostwork, rime, hoarfrost, white frost, sharp f., hard f.; sleet, hail, hailstone, silver thaw, black ice, freeze.

snow, snowfall, snowflake, snow crystal; avalanche, snow slip, snowdrift; snowstorm, flurry of snow, the old woman plucking her geese; snowball, snowman; snowplough, snowshoe; winter sports 837 *sport*.

ice, dry i., ice cube; hailstone, icicle; ice cap, ice field, ice sheet, ice shelf, floe, ice f., iceberg, berg, ice front, glacier, icefall, serac; shelf ice, pack i.; driven snow, frozen s., névé, frozen sea; icebreaker, ice yacht; ice house, icebox 384 *refrigerator*; ice action, glaciation 382 *refrigeration*; glaciology.

Adj. *cold*, without heat, impervious to heat, adiathermanous; cool, temperate; shady, chill, chilly, parky, nippy; unheated, unwarmed, unthawed; fresh, raw, keen, bitter, nipping, biting, piercing; inclement, freezing, gelid, ice-cold, bitterly c., below zero; frigid, brumal 129 *wintry*; winterbound, frosty, frostbound, snowy, snow-covered, mantled in snow, blanketed in s.; slushy, sleety, icy; glacial, ice-capped, glaciered, glaciated; boreal, polar, arctic, Siberian.

chilly, feeling cold, acold; shivering, chattering, shivery, algid, aguish; blue, blue with cold; shrammed, perished, perishing, starved with cold, chilled to the bone, frozen, frostbitten, frost-nipped; like ice, cold as charity, cold as a frog, cold as marble, stone-cold, cold as death.

Vb. *be cold*, - chilly etc. adj.; grow cold, lose heat, drop in temperature; feel cold, chatter, shiver, tremble, shake, quake, quiver, shudder; freeze, starve, perish with cold; catch cold, get a chill; chill 382 *refrigerate*.

Adv. *frostily*, frigidly, bitterly, coldly.

See: 129, **382**, 384, 837.

381 Heating

N. *heating*, superheating, increase of temperature, calefaction, torrefaction; diathermy; diathermancy; transcalency; calorific value, thermal efficiency; warming, keeping warm; space heating, central h., district heating system 383 *heater*; insolation, sunning 342 *desiccation*; melting, thawing 337 *liquefaction*; smelting, scorification, cupellation; boiling, ebullition; baking, cooking 301 *cookery*; decoction, distillation; antifreeze mixture.

burning, combustion; inflammation, kindling, ignition; reheat, afterburning; deflagration, conflagration 379 *fire*; incineration, calcination; roasting; cremation 364 *interment*; suttee, self-burning 362 *suicide*; auto-da-fé, holocaust 981 *oblation*; cauterization, cautery, branding; scorching, singeing, charring, carbonization; inflammability, combustibility; burner 383 *furnace*; cauterizer, caustic, moxa, vitriol; hot iron, branding i., brand; match, touchpaper 385 *lighter*; stoker, fireman; burn mark, burn, brand, singe, scald, sunburn, tan.

incendiarism, arson, fire-raising, pyromania; incendiary, arsonist, fire-raiser, fire-bug; firebrand, revolutionary 738 *agitator*.

warm clothes, furs, woollens, woollies, red flannel, thermal underwear; parka, wrap, muffler, muff; winter coat 228 *overcoat*; blanket 226 *coverlet*; padding, wadding 227 *lining*.

ash, ashes, volcanic ash, lava, tuff; carbon, soot, smut, lamp-black, smoke; product of combustion, clinker, charcoal, ember, cinder, coke, slag, dross, scoria, oxide, bone-ash.

pottery, ceramics; earthenware, stoneware, lustre ware, glazed w.; majolica, faience, chinaware, porcelain; crockery, china, bone c., Wedgwood c., Spode c., Worcester c., Doulton c., Chelsea c., Staffordshire c., Derby c., Sèvres c., Dresden c.; delft, willow pattern, terracotta; tile, encaustic t., brick, sun-dried b., mud b., adobe; pot, urn 194 *vessel*.

Adj. *heated*, superheated 379 *hot*; centrally-heated, winterized; lit, kindled, fired; incinerated, burnt, burnt out, burnt down, gutted; cooked, roasted, toasted, grilled, baked; réchauffé, hotted up, warmed up; melted, fused, molten; overheated; steamy, smoky; scorched, charred, singed, branded; bronzed, tanned, sun-t., sunburnt.

heating, warming etc. vb.; calefactory, calefactive, calorific, caustic, burning; solid-fuel, coal-burning, oil-fired; incendiary, inflammatory; thermoplastic, thermosetting; diathermic, diathermanous; inflammable 385 *combustible*; antifreeze.

Vb. *heat*, raise the temperature, warm; provide heating, winterize; keep the cold out, take the chill off; hot up, warm up, stoke up; rub one's hands, stamp one's feet; thaw, thaw out; inflame, foment, poultice; overheat, stew, stifle, suffocate; insolate, sun, parch, shrivel, sear 342 *dry*; torrefy, toast, bake, grill, fry, roast 301 *cook*; melt, defrost, deice 337 *liquefy*; smelt, cupel, scorify; fuse, weld, vulcanize, cast, found.

kindle, enkindle, ignite, light, strike a l.; apply the match, set fire to, touch off 385 *fire*; rekindle, relume; fuel, stoke, feed the flames, fan the fire, add fuel to the f., poke the f., stir the f., blow the f.; lay the fire, make the f., rub two sticks together.

burn, burn up, burn out, gut; commit to the flames, consign to the f.; make a bonfire of, send to the stake; fire, set fire to, set on fire; cremate, incinerate, burn to ashes; boil dry 342 *dry*; carbonize, calcine, oxidize, corrode; coal, char, singe, scorch, tan; cauterize, brand, burn in; scald.

See: 194, 226, 227, 228, 301, 337, **342**, 362, 364, **379**, **383**, **385**, 738, 981.

382 Refrigeration

N. *refrigeration*, cooling, reduction of temperature; icing etc. vb.; freezing, freezing up, glaciation, gelation, congelation 380 *ice*; solidification 324 *condensation*; exposure; ventilation, air-conditioning; cold storage 384 *refrigerator*; cryonic suspension 364 *interment*.

incombustibility, noninflammability, fire resistance; asbestos, amiantus.

extinguisher, fire e.; foam, water, hose, sprinkler, hydrant, standpipe; fire engine, fire brigade, fire station; fireman, fire-fighter.

Adj. *cooled*, chilled etc. vb.; ventilated, air-conditioned; iced up; frozen, deep-frozen, freeze-dried; ice-capped; glaciated; frosted, iced, glacé, frappé; with ice, on the rocks 380 *cold*; cooling etc. vb.; frigorific, refrigerative, refrigeratory.

incombustible, unburnable; uninflammable, noninflammable; fire-resistant, fireproof, flameproof; asbestive; damped, wetted 341 *drenched*.

Vb. *refrigerate*, cool, air-cool, water-c., fan, air-condition, freshen up 685 *refresh*; ventilate, air 340 *aerate*; reduce the temperature, turn off the heat; keep the heat out, keep the sun off, shade, shadow 421 *screen*; frost, freeze, congeal, glaciate; deep-freeze, freeze-dry, lyophilize; make ice, ice; ice up, ice over; chill, benumb, starve, nip, pinch, bite, pierce, chill to the marrow, make one's teeth chatter; expose to the cold, frost-bite.

extinguish, quench, snuff, put out, blow o., snuff o.; choke, stifle, smother 165 *suppress*; damp, douse, damp down, bank d.; rake out, stamp o., stub o.; stop burning, go out, burn o., die down.

See: 165, 324, 340, 341, 364, **380**, **384**, 421, 685.

383 Furnace

N. *furnace*, fiery f.; the stake 964 *means of execution*; volcano, solfatara, fumarole; touchhole, gun barrel; forge, blast furnace, reverberatory f., kiln, lime k., brick k.; oast, oasthouse; incinerator, destructor; crematory, crematorium; brazier, stove, kitchen s., charcoal s., gas s., electric s., primus s., oil s.; oven, gas o., electric o., microwave o.; range, kitchen r., kitchener; cooker, oil c., gas c., electric c.; gas ring, burner, Bunsen b.; blowlamp, oxyacetylene lamp; fire, open f., coal f., log f. 379 *fire*; brand 385 *lighter*; firebox, fireplace, grate, hearth, ingle; fire-irons, andirons, firedog; poker, tongs, shovel; hob, trivet; fireguard, fender; flue 263 *chimney*.

heater, space h., paraffin h., radiator, solar panel; hot-air duct, hypocaust; hot-water pipe, hot-water heater, immersion h., geyser, boiler, back b., copper, kettle, electric k. 194 *cauldron*; hotplate; warming pan, hot-water bottle; electric blanket, footwarmer; still, retort, alembic, crucible 461 *testing agent*; blowpipe, bellows, tuyère, damper; hot baths, thermae, Turkish bath, sauna 648 *ablutions*; hotbed, hothouse, conservatory 370 *garden*; sun trap, solarium; kitchen, galley, cookhouse, caboose; gridiron, grill, frying pan, saucepan; toaster, electric t.; iron, electric i., soldering i., curling tongs; heating agent, flame, sunlight 381 *heating*; gas, electricity, solar energy 160 *sources of energy*; steam, hot air; wood, coal 385 *fuel*.

See: 160, 194, 263, 370, **379**, **381**, **385**, 461, 648, 964.

384 Refrigerator

N. *refrigerator*, cooler; ventilator, fan, punkah, air-conditioner; cooling-room, frigidarium; refrigerating plant, fridge, chiller, cooler, wine c., ice bucket; coolant, freezing mixture, snow, ice; icehouse, icebox, ice pack, cold p., icebag; ice-cubes, rocks; cold storage, freezer, deep-freeze 382 *refrigeration*.

See: **382**.

385 Fuel

N. *fuel*, inflammable material, combustible, food for the flames; firing, kindling; wood, brushwood, firewood, faggot, log, Yule l.; biomass 366 *vegetable life*; turf, peat; cow dung, camel d.; lignite, brown coal, wood c., charcoal; fossil fuel, coal, natural gas, petroleum 357 *oil*, 336 *gas*; nuclear fuel, uranium, plutonium 160 *nucleonics*; petrol, high octane p., three-star, four-s.; juice, gasoline; diesel oil, derv; paraffin, kerosene; alcohol, spirit, methylated s.; North Sea gas, coal g., acetylene, propane, butane, methane, biogas.

coal, black diamond, sea coal, hard c., anthracite, cannel coal, bituminous c.; briquette; coal dust, culm, slack; coal seam, coal deposit, coal measure, coalfield 632 *store*; cinders, embers 381 *ash*; coke, gas c.; smokeless fuel.

lighter, fire-l., cigarette l., igniter, light, pilot l., illuminant, taper, spill, candle 420 *torch*; coal, ember, brand, firebrand; fire ship, incendiary bomb 723 *bomb*; wick, fuse, touchpaper, match, slow m.; linstock, portfire, percussion cap, detonator; safety match, friction m., lucifer, vesta, fusee; flint, steel, tinder, touchwood, punk, spunk, amadou; tinderbox, matchbox.

fumigator, incense, joss stick, sulphur, brimstone.

Adj. *combustible*, burnable, inflammable, incendiary, explosive; carboniferous, carbonaceous, coal-bearing, coaly.

Vb. *fire*, stoke, feed, fuel, coal, add fuel to the flames; mend the fire; put a match to 381 *kindle*.

See: 160, 336, 357, 366, **381**, 420, 632, 723.

386 Taste

N. *taste*, sapor, sapidity, savour; flavour, flavouring; smack, smatch, tang, twang, aftertaste; relish, gusto, zest, appetite 859 *liking*; tasting, gustation; palate, tongue, tastebuds; tooth, sweet t., stomach.

Adj. *tasty*, sapid, saporous, palatable, full of flavour, flavourful, mouth-watering, tempting, appetizing 390 *savoury*; well-seasoned, salty, peppery, tangy 388 *pungent*; flavoured, spiced, spicy, racy, rich, strong, full-flavoured, full-bodied, fruity, hoppy, generous, well-matured, mellow, vintage; gustatory, gustative.

Vb. *taste*, find palatable, lick one's lips, smack one's lips, roll on the tongue, lick one's fingers 376 *enjoy*; savour, sample, try; sip, lick, sup, nibble 301 *eat*; have a taste, taste of, savour of, smack of 18 *resemble*; taste good, tickle the palate 390 *make appetizing*.

See: 18, **301**, 376, 388, **390**, 859.

387 Insipidity

N. *insipidity*, vapidity, vapidness, jejuneness, flatness, staleness, tastelessness etc. adj.; water, milk and water, pap, slops, catlap.

Adj. *tasteless*, without taste, devoid of taste;

jejune, vapid, insipid, watery, milk-and-water; mild, underproof; with water, diluted, adulterated 163 *weakened*; wishy-washy, sloppy; unappetizing 391 *unsavoury*; flat, stale; savourless, zestless, flavourless, unflavoured, unspiced, unseasoned; unsavoured, untasted.

See: 163, **391**.

388 Pungency

N. *pungency*, piquancy, poignancy, sting, kick, bite, edge; burning taste, causticity; hot taste, spiciness; sharp taste, acridity, sharpness, acerbity, acidity 393 *sourness*; roughness, harshness; strong taste, strength, tang, twang, raciness; bad taste 391 *unsavouriness*; salt, brine, pepper, pickle, spice 389 *condiment*; sal volatile, smelling salts 656 *revival*; cordial, pick-me-up, bracer 174 *stimulant*; dram, nip, tot 301 *draught*; hemp, marijuana 658 *drug*.

tobacco, baccy, snout, nicotine; the weed, fragrant w., Indian w., filthy w.; tobacco leaf, Virginia tobacco, Turkish t., latakia, perique; blend, smoking mixture; snuff, rappee, maccaboy; plug of tobacco, plug, quid, fid, twist; chewing tobacco, pipe t., flake, cavendish, shag; cigar, cigarillo, cheroot, panatella, perfecto, Havana, corona; smoke, cigarette, cig, ciggie, fag, gasper, stinker, coffin-nail; reefer, joint 949 *drug-taking*; filter tip, cork tip, low-tar cigarette, high-tar c., menthol c., roll-up; butt, stub, fag-end, dog-end; tobacco pipe, clay p., dudeen, churchwarden; briar, corncob; meerschaum; hubble-bubble, hookah, narghile; pipe of peace, calumet; bowl, stem; dottle, tobacco juice; smoker's cough; snuff taker, snuffer; tobacco chewer; smoker, pipe s., cigarette s., cigar s., chain s.; tobacconist, cigarette machine; snuff box, cigarette case, cigar c., cigarette box, cigar box; humidor; pipe rack; pipe cleaner, reamer; tobacco pouch, tobacco jar; smokeroom; smoker, smoking compartment.

Adj. *pungent*, penetrating, strong; stinging, mordant, biting 256 *sharp*; caustic, burning, smoky; harsh 259 *rough*; bitter, acrid, tart, astringent 393 *sour*; heady, overproof; full-flavoured, nutty 386 *tasty*; strong-flavoured, high, gamy, off; highly-seasoned, spicy, spiced, curried; hot, gingery, peppery, hot as pepper; zesty, tangy, minty, piquant, aromatic 390 *savoury*.

salty, salt, brackish, briny, saline, pickled; salt as the sea, salt as Lot's wife.

Vb. *be pungent*, sting, bite the tongue, set the teeth on edge, make the eyes water.

season, salt, brine, marinate, souse, pickle; flavour, sauce; spice, pepper, devil, curry; smoke, smoke-dry, kipper 666 *preserve*.

smoke, use tobacco, indulge, smoke a pipe, pull, draw, suck, inhale; take a drag; puff, blow smoke rings; chain-smoke, smoke like a chimney; chew a quid; snuff, take snuff, take a pinch.

See: 174, 256, 259, 301, 386, **389**, 390, **391**, **393**, 656, 658, 666, 949.

389 Condiment

N. *condiment*, seasoning, flavouring, dressing, relish, garnish; chaudfroid, aspic; salt, garlic s., celery s.; mustard, French m.; pepper, cayenne, paprika, chilli, caper; black pepper, peppercorn; curry powder, turmeric; onion, garlic 301 *pot-herb*; spicery, spices, spice, allspice, mace, cinnamon, ginger, nutmeg, clove, caraway seed, vanilla pod.

sauce, roux; gravy, stock; brown sauce, white s., béchamel; parsley sauce, bread s., tartar s., mint s., horseradish s., sauce piquante; apple sauce, cranberry s. 392 *sweet thing*; tomato sauce, ketchup; chilli sauce, tabasco s. (tdmk), soy s., Worcester s.; chutney, sweet c., mango c., pickles, piccalilli, pickled onions; salad dressing, mayonnaise, vinaigrette.

Vb. *spice* 388 *season*.

See: **301**, **388**, 392.

390 Savouriness

N. *savouriness*, right taste, tastiness, palatability; raciness, fine flavour, full f., richness; body, bouquet; savoury, relish, appetizer; delicacy, dainty, titbit, bonne bouche 301 *mouthful*; cocktail snacks, hors d'oeuvre; game, venison, turtle, caviar; ambrosia, nectar; epicure's delight.

Adj. *savoury*, nice, good, good to eat, worth eating; seasoned, flavoured, spicy 386 *tasty*; well-dressed, well-cooked, done to a turn; tempting, appetizing, aromatic, zestful, piquant 388 *pungent*; to one's taste, palatable, toothsome, sweet; dainty, delicate; delectable, delicious, exquisite, choice, epicurean; ambrosial, nectareous, fit for the gods; scrumptious, yummy, moreish; fresh, crisp; ripe, mellow, luscious, juicy, succulent; creamy, rich, velvety; gamy, racy, high; rare-flavoured, full-f., vintage.

Vb. *make appetizing*, spice, ginger, pep up 388 *season*; be savoury, tempt the appetite, tickle the palate, flatter the p.; smell good, taste good, taste sweet 392 *sweeten*; like, relish, savour, lap up, smack the lips, roll on one's tongue, lick one's fingers, water at the mouth 386 *taste*.

Int. yum-yum! mmm!

See: 301, **386**, **388**, **392**.

391 Unsavouriness

N. *unsavouriness*, unpalatability, nasty taste, wrong t.; rankness, rottenness, unwholesomeness 653 *insalubrity*; roughness, coarseness, plain cooking 573 *plainness*; acerbity, acridity 393 *sourness*; austerity, prison fare, bread and water; aloes, rue; bitter pill, gall and wormwood; emetic, sickener 659 *poison*.

Adj. *unsavoury*, flat 387 *tasteless*; unpalatable, unappetizing, uninviting; coarse, raw, undressed 670 *uncooked*; badly cooked, overdone, burnt; uneatable, inedible; stale, hard, leathery 329 *tough*; soggy 327 *soft*; sugarless, unsweetened; rough 388 *pungent*; bitter, acrid, acid 393 *sour*; undrinkable, corked; rank, rancid, putrid, rotten, gone off, high, stinking 397 *fetid*; nasty, repulsive, foul, revolting, disgusting, loathsome 827 *unpleasant*; sickly, cloying, mawkish; sickening, emetic, nauseous, nauseating 861 *disliked*; poisonous 653 *toxic*.

Vb. *be unpalatable*, - unappetizing etc. adj.; taste horrid; disgust, repel, sicken, nauseate, turn the stomach 861 *cause dislike*; poison; lose its savour, pall.

Int. ugh! yuk!

See: 327, 329, 387, 388, 393, 397, 573, 653, 659, 670, 827, 861.

392 Sweetness

N. *sweetness*, sweetening, dulcification; sugariness, saccharinity; sweet tooth; saccharimeter.

sweet thing, sweetening, honey, honeycomb, honeypot, honeydew; honeysuckle 396 *fragrance*; saccharin, sucrose, glucose, dextrose, fructose, lactose, galactose; sugar, cane s., beet s., malt s., milk s., invert s.; granulated s., castor s., demerara; molasses, syrup, maple s., treacle; sweet sauce, custard, condensed milk; sweet drink, julep, nectar, hydromel, mead, metheglin; conserve, preserve; candied peel, glacé cherries; jam, marmalade, jelly; marzipan, icing, sugar coating; fudge, candy, sugar c. 301 *sweets*; jujube, cachou, lozenge, pastille; lollipop, ice cream, candyfloss, rock; confectionery, confection, cake 301 *pastries, dessert*.

Adj. *sweet*, sweet to the taste, sweetened, honeyed, candied, crystallized; iced, glacé; sugared, sugary, saccharine, honey-bearing, melliferous; ambrosial, nectareous, luscious, delicious 376 *pleasant*; sweet as honey, sweet as sugar, sweet as a nut 390 *savoury*.

Vb. *sweeten*, sugar, candy, crystallize, ice; sugar the pill, coat the p.; dulcify, saccharize; sweeten wine, mull.

See: **301**, 376, 390, 396.

393 Sourness

N. *sourness*, acerbity; astringency; tartness, bitterness, vinegariness; sharpness 388 *pungency*; acidity, acidosis; acid, argol, tartar; lemon, vinegar; sloe, crab apple; verjuice, alum, bitter aloes, bitters; gall, wormwood, absinth.

Adj. *sour*, sourish, acid, acidy, acidulous, acidulated, subacid, acescent, acetous, acetic, acid-forming, tartaric; acerbic, crabbed, tart, bitter, bitter as gall; sharp, astringent 388 *pungent*; vinegary, sour as vinegar 391 *unsavoury*; unripe, green, hard, rough 670 *immature*; sugarless, unsugared; unsweetened, dry.

Vb. *be sour*, - acid etc. adj.; sour, turn, turn sour; acetify, acidify, acidulate; ferment; set one's teeth on edge.

See: **388**, 391, 670.

394 Odour

N. *odour*, smell, aroma, bouquet, nose; sweet smell, perfume, essence 396 *fragrance*; bad smell, stink 397 *stench*; exhalation, effluvium, emanation; smoke, fume, reek; breath, whiff, waft; strong smell, odorousness, redolence; tang, scent, trail 548 *trace*; olfaction, sense of smell, act of smelling; olfactories, smeller, nostril, nosehole, nose 254 *protuberance*; good nose, keen-scentedness, flair.

Adj. *odorous*, endowed with scent, odoriferous, smelling; scented, perfumed 396 *fragrant*; graveolent, strong, heady, heavy, full-bodied 388 *pungent*; smelly, redolent, nidorous, reeking; malodorous, whiffy, niffy 397 *fetid*; smelt, reaching one's nostrils; olfactory; keen-scented, sharp-nosed.

Vb. *smell*, have an odour, reach one's nostrils; smell of, breathe of, smell strongly of, reek of, reek; give out a smell, exhale; smell a mile off; smell out, scent, nose, wind, get wind of 484 *detect*; get a whiff of; snuff, snuff up, sniff, breathe in, inhale 352 *breathe*; cause to smell, scent, perfume, incense, fumigate.

See: 254, 352, **388**, **396**, **397**, 484, 548.

395 Indorousness

N. *inodorousness*, odourlessness, scentlessness; absence of smell, want of s.; loss of s.; inability to smell, anosmia; noselessness, lack of flair; deodorant, deodorizer, fumes, incense, pastille; deodorization, fumigation, ventilation, purification 648 *cleansing*.

Adj. *odourless*, inodorous, scentless, without smell, wanting s.; unscented, unperfumed; deodorized; deodorizing; noseless, without sense of smell, without flair.

Vb. *have no smell*, not smell; be inodorous, - scentless etc. adj.; deodorize, take away the smell, defumigate; ventilate, clear the air 648 *purify*; lose the scent 495 *err*; hold one's nose.

See: 495, **648**.

396 Fragrance

N. *fragrance*, sweet smell, sweet savour, balminess; redolence, aroma, bouquet 394 *odour*; violet, rose; bank of violets, bed of roses; flower garden, rose g. 370 *garden*; buttonhole, boutonnière, nosegay; thurification, fumigation; perfumery, perfumer.

scent, perfume, aromatic p., aromatic gum; balm, myrrh, incense, frankincense, spikenard; spicery 389 *condiment*; breath-sweetener, cloves, cachou; musk, civet, ambergris, camphor; sandalwood, patchouli; essential oil, otto, attar; lavender, thyme, spearmint, chypre, vanilla, citronella oil; frangipani, bergamot, orris root, tonka bean; honeysuckle, woodruff, new-mown hay; toilet water, lavender w., rose w., attar of roses, eau-de-cologne; pomade, hair oil; face powder, scented soap 843 *cosmetic*; mothball, lavender bag, sachet; pomander, potpourri, scent bottle, smelling b., vinaigrette; joss stick, censer, thurible.

Adj. *fragrant*, redolent, odorous, odoriferous, aromatic, scented, perfumed 376 *pleasant*; incense-breathing, balmy, ambrosial; sweet-scented, sweetly-perfumed; thuriferous, perfumatory; musky, spicy, fruity; rose-scented, fragrant as a rose; laid up in lavender.

Vb. *be fragrant*, smell sweet, smell like a rose, have a perfume, scent, perfume, fumigate, thurify, cense; embalm, lay up in lavender.

See: 370, 376, 389, **394**, 843.

397 Stench

N. *stench*, fetor, fetidity, fetidness, offensiveness; offence to the nose, bad smell, bad odour, foul o., malodour; body odour, BO, armpits; foul breath, halitosis; stink, pong, reek; noxious stench, mephitis; fumes, miasma 336 *gas*; smell of death, taint, corruption, rancidity, putrefaction 51 *decay*; foulness 649 *dirt*; mustiness, fustiness, staleness, stale air, frowst, fug; fungus, stinkhorn, garlic, asafoetida; hydrogen sulphide, ammonia; skunk, polecat; stinkard, stinker, stinkpot, stink bomb, bad egg; dung 302 *excrement*; latrine, sewer 649 *sink*.

Adj. *fetid*, graveolent, strong-smelling, heavy, strong; reeking, nidorous; ill-smelling, malodorous, not of roses; smelly, whiffy, niffy, pongy, humming; stinking, rank, hircine, foxy; fruity, gamy, high; bad, gone b., tainted, rancid; putrid, suppurating, gangrenous 51 *decomposed*; stale, airless, musty, fusty, frowsty, frowzy, fuggy, smoky, unventilated, stuffy, suffocating; foul, noisome, noxious, sulphurous, ammoniacal, mephitic, miasmic 653 *toxic*; acrid, burning 388 *pungent*; nasty, disagreeable, offensive 827 *unpleasant*.

Vb. *stink*, smell, reek, pong, niff, hum; make a smell, fart, blow off; have a bad smell, smell strong, smell offensive; smell bad 51 *decompose*; stink in the nostrils, stink to high heaven, make one hold one's nose; smell like a bad egg, smell like a drain; stink like a goat, stink like a polecat; overpower with stink, stink out.

See: 51, 302, 336, **388**, 649, 653, **827**.

398 Sound

N. *sound*, auditory effect, distinctness; audibility, reception 415 *hearing*; sounding, sonancy, sound-making; audio, mono, monophonic sound, binaural s., stereophonic s., stereo, quadraphonic sound; sound waves, vibrations 417 *radiation*; electronic sound, sound effect; sound track, voice-over; sonority, sonorousness 404 *resonance*; noise, loud sound 400 *loudness*; low sound, softness 401 *faintness*; quality of sound, tone, pitch, level, cadence; accent, intonation, twang, timbre 577 *voice*; tune, strain 410 *melody*, 412 *music*; types of sound 402 *bang*, 403 *roll*, 404 *resonance*, 405 *nonresonance*, 406 *sibilation*, 407 *stridor*, 408 *cry*, 409 *ululation*, 411 *discord*; transmission of sound, telephone, radio 531 *telecommunication*; recorded sound, high fidelity, hi-fi; record-player 414 *gramophone*; loudspeaker 415 *hearing aid*; unit of sound, decibel, phon, sone; sonic barrier, sound b.

acoustics, phonics; phonology, phonography; phonetics; acoustician, sound engineer; phonetician, phoneticist, phonographer; audiometer, sonometer.

speech sound, simple s., phone, syllable, disyllable, polysyllable; consonant, fricative, affricate, plosive, implosive, spirant, liquid, sibilant; dental, alveolar, labial, bilabial, labiodental, nasal, palatal, guttural, velar, labiovelar; aspiration, inspiration, expiration; rough breathing, smooth b.; stop, glottal s.; click; sonant, sonorant, mute, aspirate, surd; semivowel; glide, glide sound; voiced breath, vowel, front v., middle v., back v.; vocoid, contoid; diphthong, triphthong 577 *voice*; rising diphthong, falling d.; monophthongization, diphthongization; vowel gradation, ablaut; umlaut; assimilation, dissimilation; sandhi; vocable 559 *word*; sound symbol, phonogram, International Phonetic Alphabet, IPA 586 *script*.

Adj. *sounding*, soniferous, sonant; sonic; supersonic; plain, audible, distinct, heard; resounding, sonorous 404 *resonant*; stentorian 400 *loud*; auditory, acoustic; electrophonic, radiophonic; monaural, monophonic, mono; binaural, stereophonic, stereo, high fidelity, hi-fi; audio, audiovisual; phonic, phonetic; voiced 577 *vocal*; monophthongal, diphthongal; consonantal; vocalic, vowelled; surd, unvoiced, voiceless.

Vb. *sound*, produce s., give out s., emit s. 415 *be heard*; make a noise 400 *be loud*, 404 *resound*; phoneticize, phonate, vocalize 577 *voice*.

See: **400**, **401**, **402**, **403**, **404**, **405**, **406**, **407**, **408**, **409**, 410, 411, 412, 414, **415**, 417, 531, 559, **577**, 586.

399 Silence

N. *silence*, soundlessness, inaudibility, not a sound, not a squeak; stillness, hush, lull, rest, peace, quiet 266 *quiescence*; muteness, speechlessness 578 *voicelessness*; solemn silence, awful s., pin-drop s., dead s., perfect s., deathly hush.

Adj. *silent*, still, stilly, hushed; calm, peaceful, quiet 266 *quiescent*; soft, faint 401 *muted*; noiseless, soundless, inaudible; soundproof; aphonic, speechless, tongueless, mute 578 *voiceless*; unsounded, unuttered, unspoken; solemn, awful, deathlike, silent as the grave.

Vb. *be silent*, not open one's mouth, not say a word, hold one's tongue 582 *be taciturn*; not speak 578 *be mute*; be still, make no noise, make not a sound; become silent, relapse into silence, pipe down, be quiet, lose one's voice.

silence, still, lull, hush, quiet, quieten, make silent; play down, soft-pedal; stifle, muffle, gag, stop, stop one's mouth, muzzle, put the lid on, put to silence 578 *make mute*; drown, drown the noise.

Int. hush! sh! silence! quiet! peace! soft! whist! hold your tongue! keep your mouth shut! shut up! keep your trap shut! dry up! cut the cackle! stow it! mum's the word!

See: 266, **401**, **578**, **582**.

400 Loudness

N. *loudness*, distinctness, audibility 398 *sound*; noise, loud n., ear-splitting n.; high volume; broken silence, shattered s., knock, knocking; burst of sound, report, loud r., sonic boom, slam, clap, thunderclap, burst, shell b., explosion 402 *bang*; siren, alarm, honk, toot 665 *danger signal*; prolonged noise, reverberation, plangency, boom, rattle 403 *roll*; thunder, rattling t., war in heaven 176 *storm*; dashing, surging, hissing 406 *sibilation*; fire, gunfire, artillery, blitz 712 *bombardment*; stridency, brassiness, shrillness, blast, blare, bray, fanfare, flourish 407 *stridor*; trumpet blast, clarion call, view halloo 547 *call*; sonority, organ notes, clang, clangour 404 *resonance*; ringing tones; bells, peal, chimes 412 *campanology*; diapason, swell, crescendo, fortissimo, tutti, full blast, full chorus; vociferation, clamour, outcry, roaring, shouting, bawling, yelling, screaming, whoop, shout, howl, shriek, scream, roar 408 *cry*, 409 *ululation*; loud laughter, cachinnation 835 *laughter*; loud breathing, stertorousness 352 *respiration*; noisiness, din, row, deafening r., racket, crash, clash, clatter, hubbub, hullabaloo, ballyhoo, song and dance, slamming, banging, stamping, chanting, hooting, uproar, tumult, bedlam, pandemonium, all hell let loose 61 *turmoil*.

megaphone, amplifier, loud pedal; public address system, loudhailer, loudspeaker, speaker, microphone, mike; ear trumpet 415 *hearing aid*; loud instrument, whistle, siren, hooter, horn, klaxon, gong; rattle, bullroarer; buzzer, bell, alarm, door knocker; trumpet, brass; stentorian voice, lungs, good l., lungs of brass, iron throat; Stentor, town crier.

Adj. *loud*, distinct, audible, heard; turned right up, at full volume; noisy, full of noise, rackety, uproarious, rowdy, rumbustious 61 *disorderly*; multisonous, many-tongued 411 *discordant*; clamorous, clamant, shouting, yelling, whooping, screaming, bellowing 408 *crying*; bigmouthed, loud-m.; sonorous, booming, deep, full, powerful; lusty, full-throated, stentorian, brazen-mouthed, trumpet-tongued; ringing, carrying; deafening, dinning; piercing, ear-splitting, ear-rending; thundering, thunderous, rattling, crashing; pealing, clangorous, plangent; shrill, high-sounding 407 *strident*; blaring, brassy; echoing, resounding 404 *resonant*; swelling, crescendo; fortissimo, enough to waken the dead.

Vb. *be loud*, - noisy etc. adj.; break the silence; speak up, give tongue, raise the voice, strain one's v.; call, catcall, caterwaul; skirl, scream, whistle 407 *shrill*; vociferate, shout 408 *cry*; cachinnate 835 *laugh*; clap, stamp, raise the roof; roar, bellow, howl 409 *ululate*; din, sound, boom, reverberate 404 *resound*; rattle, thunder, fulminate, storm, clash; ring, peal, clang, crash; bray, blare; slam 402 *bang*; burst, explode, detonate, go off; knock, knock hard, hammer, drill; deafen, stun; split the ears, rend the eardrums, ring in the ear; swell, fill the air; rend the skies, make the welkin ring, rattle the windows, awake the echoes, waken the dead; raise Cain, kick up a shindy, make the devil of a row 61 *rampage*.

Adv. *loudly*, distinctly etc. adj.; noisily, dinningly; aloud, at the top of one's voice, lustily; in full cry, full blast, full chorus; fortissimo, crescendo.

See: 61, 176, 352, 398, **402**, **403**, **404**, 406, **407**, **408**, **409**, 411, 412, 415, 547, 665, 712, 835.

401 Faintness

N. *faintness*, softness, indistinctness, inaudibility; less sound, low volume, reduction of sound, s.-proofing, noise abatement; dull sound, thud, thump, bump 405 *nonresonance*; whisper, susurration; breath, bated b., muffled tones 578 *voicelessness*; undertone, undercurrent of sound; murmur, hum, drone 403 *roll*; sigh, sough, moan; scratch, squeak, creak, pop; tick, click; tinkle, clink, chink; buzz, whirr; purr, purl, plash, swish; burble, gurgle; rustle, frou-frou; patter, pitter-p., pit-a-pat; soft footfall, pad; soft voice, quiet tone, conversation level.

silencer, noise queller, mute, damper, muffler, soft pedal 414 *mute*; cork, double-glazing; rubber soles; grease, oil 334 *lubricant*; ear plugs.

Adj. *muted*, distant, faint, inaudible, barely audible, just caught, sotto voce; just heard, half-h.; trembling in the air, dying away; weak, feeble, unemphatic, unstressed, unaccented; soft, low, gentle; purling, rippling; piano, subdued, hushed, stealthy, whispered; dull, dead 405 *nonresonant*; muffled, stifled, bated 407 *hoarse*.

Vb. *sound faint*, drop one's voice, whisper, breathe, murmur, mutter 578 *speak low*; sing low, hum, croon, purr; buzz, drone; purl, babble, ripple, plash, lap, gurgle, guggle 350 *flow*; tinkle, chime; moan, sigh, sough 352 *blow*; rustle, swish; tremble, melt; float on the air, steal on the air, melt on the a., die on the ear, fade away, sink into silence; squeak, creak; plop, pop; tick, click; clink, chink; thud, thump 405 *sound dead*.

mute, soften, dull, deaden, dampen, soft-pedal; turn down the volume; hush, muffle, stifle 399 *silence*.

Adv. *faintly*, in a whisper, with bated breath, under one's breath, between the teeth; sotto voce, aside, in an undertone;

piano, pianissimo; à la sourdine; inaudibly, distantly, out of earshot.
See: 334, 350, 352, 399, 403, **405**, 407, 414, **578**.

402 Bang: sudden and violent noise
N. *bang*, report, explosion, detonation, blast, blowout, backfire, sonic boom; peal, thunderclap, crash 400 *loudness*; crepitation, crackling, crackle; smack, crack, snap; slap, clap, tap, rap, rat-tat; knock, slam; pop, plop, plunk; burst, burst of fire, firing, crackle of musketry; volley, round, salvo; shot, pistol-s.; cracker, banger, squib; bomb, grenade; gun, rifle, shot gun, pop g. 723 *firearm*.
Adj. *rapping*, banging etc. vb.
Vb. *crackle*, crepitate; sizzle, fizzle, spit 318 *effervesce*; crack, split; click, rattle; snap, clap, rap, tap, slap, smack; plop, plonk, plunk.
bang, slam, wham, clash, crash, boom; explode, blast, detonate; pop, go p.; backfire; burst, burst on the ear 400 *be loud*.
See: 318, **400**, 723.

403 Roll: repeated and protracted sounds
N. *roll*, rumbling, grumbling; mutter, murmur, background m., rhubarb rhubarb; din, rattle, racket, clack, clatter, chatter; booming, clang, ping, reverberation 404 *resonance*; chugging; knocking, drumming, tattoo, devil's t., rub-a-dub, rat-a-tat, pit-a-pat; peal, carillon 412 *campanology*; dingdong, tick-tock, cuckoo 106 *repetition*; trill, tremolo, vibrato 410 *musical note*; quaver; hum, whirr, buzz, drone, bombination; humming top, bee in a bottle; ringing, singing; drumfire, barrage, cannonade, machine gun.
Adj. *rolling*, roaring etc. vb.; reverberant 404 *resonant*; dingdong, monotonous 106 *repeated*.
Vb. *roll*, drum, tattoo, beat a t.; tap, thrum; chug, rev up; drum in the ear; boom, roar, din in the ear; grumble, rumble, drone, hum, whirr, bombinate; trill, chime, peal, toll; tick, beat 317 *oscillate*; rattle, chatter, clatter, clack; reverberate, clang, ping, ring, sing, sing in the ear; quaver, shake, tremble, vibrate; patter 401 *sound faint*.
See: 106, 317, 401, **404**, 410, 412.

404 Resonance
N. *resonance*, sonorousness; vibration 317 *oscillation*; reverberation, reflection; lingering note, echo 106 *recurrence*; twang, twanging; ringing, ringing in the ear, singing, tinnitus; bell ringing, tintinnabulation 412 *campanology*; peal, carillon; sonority, boom; clang, clangour, plangency; brass 400 *loudness*; peal, blare, bray, flourish, tucket; sounding brass, tinkling cymbal; tinkle, jingle; chink, clink; ping, ring, chime; low note, deep n., grave n., bass n., pedal n. 410 *musical note*; low voice, basso, basso profondo, bass, baritone, bass b., contralto.
Adj. *resonant*, vibrant, reverberant, reverberative; fruity, carrying 400 *loud*; resounding etc. vb.; booming, echoing, lingering; sonorous, reboant, plangent; ringing, tintinnabulary; basso, deep-toned, deep-sounding, deep-mouthed; booming, hollow, sepulchral.
Vb. *resound*, vibrate, reverberate, echo, reecho 403 *roll*; whirr, buzz; hum, ring in the ear, sing; ping, ring, ding; jingle, jangle, chink, clink, clank, clunk; ting, tinkle; twang, thrum; gong, chime, tintinnabulate; tootle, toot, trumpet, blare, bray 400 *be loud*.
See: 106, 317, **400**, **403**, 410, 412.

405 Nonresonance
N. *nonresonance*, nonvibration, dead sound, dull s.; thud, thump, bump; plump, plop, plonk, plunk; cracked bell 411 *discord*; muffled drums 401 *faintness*; mute, damper, sordino 401 *silencer*.
Adj. *nonresonant*, muffled, damped 401 *muted*; dead, dull, heavy; cracked 407 *hoarse*; soundproof 399 *silent*.
Vb. *sound dead*, be nonresonant, not vibrate, arouse no echoes, fall dead on the ear; tink, click, flap; thump, thud, bump, pound; stop the vibrations, damp the reverberations; soft-pedal, muffle, damp, stop, soften, deaden, stifle, silence 401 *mute*.
See: 399, **401**, 407, 411.

406 Sibilation: hissing sound
N. *sibilation*, sibilance, hissing, hiss; assibilation, sigma, sibilant; sputter, splutter; splash, plash; rustle, frou-frou 407 *stridor*; sucking noise, squelch; swish, swoosh, escape of air; hisser, goose, serpent.
Adj. *sibilant*, sibilatory, hissing etc. vb.; wheezy, asthmatic.
Vb. *hiss*, sibilate, assibilate; snort, wheeze, snuffle, whistle; buzz, fizz, fizzle, sizzle,

sputter, splutter, spit; splash, plash 318 *effervesce*; swish, swoosh, whiz; squelch, suck; rustle 407 *rasp*.

See: 318, 407.

407 Stridor: harsh sound

N. *stridor*, stridency, discordance, cacophony 411 *discord*; roughness, raucousness, hoarseness, huskiness, gruffness; harsh sound, aspirate, guttural; squeakiness, rustiness 333 *friction*; scrape, scratch, creak, squeak; stridulation, screechiness; shriek, screech, squawk, yawp, yelp 409 *ululation*; high pitch, shrillness, piping, whistling, wolf whistle; bleep; piercing note, high n., acute n., sharp n. 410 *musical note*; high voice, soprano, treble, falsetto, tenor, countertenor; nasality, twang, drone; skirl, brassiness, brass, blare, tantara 400 *loudness*; pipe, fife, piccolo, penny whistle 414 *flute*.

Adj. *strident*, stridulous, stridulatory; unoiled, grating, rusty, creaky, creaking, jarring (**see** *hoarse*); harsh, brassy, brazen, metallic; high, high-pitched, high-toned, acute, shrill, piping, bleeping; penetrating, piercing, tinny, ear-splitting 400 *loud*; blaring, braying; dry, reedy, squeaky, squawky, screechy, scratchy; cracked 405 *nonresonant*; sharp, flat, inharmonious, cacophonous 411 *discordant*.

hoarse, husky, throaty, guttural, raucous, rough, gruff; rasping, scraping, creaking; grunting, growling; hollow, deep, sepulchral; snoring, stertorous.

Vb. *rasp*, stridulate, grate, crunch, scrunch, grind, saw, scrape, scratch, squeak; snore, snort; cough, hawk, clear the throat, choke, gasp, sob, catch the breath; bray, croak, caw, screech 409 *ululate*; grunt, speak in the throat, burr, aspirate, gutturalize; crack, break (of the voice); jar, grate on the ear, set the teeth on edge, clash, jangle, twang, clank, clink 411 *discord*.

shrill, stridulate, bleep; play the bagpipes, drone, skirl; trumpet, blare 400 *be loud*; pipe, flute, wind the horn 413 *play music*; whistle, catcall, caterwaul 408 *cry*; scream, squeal, yelp, screech, squawk; buzz, hum, whine 409 *ululate*; split the ears, go right through one, strain, crack one's voice, strain one's vocal chords.

See: 333, **400**, 405, **408**, **409**, 410, **411**, 413, 414.

408 Human cry

N. *cry*, animal cry 409 *ululation*; human cry, exclamation, ejaculation 577 *voice*; utterances 579 *speech*; talk, chat, conversation 584 *interlocution*; raised voice, vociferation, vociferousness, clamorousness, shouting, outcry, clamour, hullabaloo 400 *loudness*; yodel, song, chant, chorus 412 *vocal music*; shout, yell, whoop, bawl; howl, scream, shriek 407 *stridor*, 377 *pain*; halloo, hail 547 *call*; view halloo, tallyho, hue and cry 619 *chase*; cheer, hurrah, huzza 835 *rejoicing*; cachinnation, laugh, giggle 835 *laughter*; hoot, boo 924 *disapprobation*; plaint, complaint 762 *deprecation*; plaintiveness, sob, sigh 836 *lamentation*; caterwaul, squeal, wail, whine, boohoo; grunt, gasp 352 *respiration*; shouter, bawler, yeller; rooter, cheerer; crier, barker; town crier.

Adj. *crying*, bawling, clamant, clamorous; loud, vocal, vociferous; stentorian, full-throated, full-lunged, lusty; rousing, cheering; sobbing, blubbing 836 *lamenting*.

Vb. *cry*, cry out, exclaim, ejaculate, pipe up 579 *speak*; call, call out, hail 884 *greet*; raise a cry, whoop; hoot, boo, whistle 924 *disapprove*; cheer, hurrah (**see** *vociferate*); scream, screech, yowl, howl, groan 377 *feel pain*; cachinnate, snigger, giggle 835 *laugh*; caterwaul, squall, boohoo, whine, whimper, wail, fret, mewl, pule 836 *weep*; yammer, moan, sob, sigh 836 *lament*; mutter, grumble 401 *sound faint*, 829 *be discontented*; gasp, grunt, snort, snore 352 *breathe*; squeak, squawk, yap, bark 409 *ululate*.

vociferate, clamour, start shouting, shout, bawl, yell, holler; chant, chorus 413 *sing*; cheer, give three cheers, hurrah, huzza, exult 835 *rejoice*; cheer for, root for; hiss, hoot, boo, bawl out, shout down 924 *disapprove*; roar, bellow 409 *ululate*; yell, cry out, sing o., thunder o.; raise the voice, give v., strain one's lungs, crack one's throat, make oneself hoarse, shout at the top of one's voice, shout at the top of one's lungs 400 *be loud*.

See: 352, 377, **400**, 401, 407, 409, 412, 413, 547, 577, **579**, 584, 619, 762, 829, 835, 836, 884, 924.

409 Ululation: animal sounds

N. *ululation*, animal noise, howling, belling, wailing; barking, baying; buzzing, humming, bombination, drone; twittering, chirruping; warble, call, cry, note, woodnote, birdsong; squeak, cheep, twitter, tweet-tweet; buzz, hum; croak, caw, coo, hiss, quack, cluck, squawk, screech, yawp; baa, moo, neigh, whinny, hee-haw; cock-a-doodle-doo, cuckoo, tu-whit tu-whoo; miaow, mew, bark, yelp, yap, snap, snarl, growl. **See** *ululate*.

Adj. *ululant*, reboant; deep-mouthed, full-m.; full-throated 400 *loud*; roaring, lowing, cackling etc. vb.

Vb. *ululate*, cry, call, give tongue; squawk, screech, yawp; caterwaul, yowl, howl, wail; roar, bellow, bell; hum, drone, buzz, bombinate, bombilate; spit 406 *hiss*; woof, bark, bay, bay at the moon; yelp, yap; snap, snarl, growl, whine; trumpet, bell, troat; bray, neigh, whinny, whicker; bleat, baa; low, moo; miaow, mew, mewl, purr; quack, cackle, gaggle; gobble, gabble, cluck, clack; grunt, gruntle, snort, squeal; pipe, pule; chatter, sing, chirp, chirrup, cheep, peep, tweet, twitter, chuckle, churr, whirr, coo; caw, croak; hoot, honk, boom; grate, stridulate, squeak 407 *rasp*; sing like a bird, warble, carol, whistle 413 *sing*.

See: 400, 406, 407, 413.

410 Melody: concord

N. *melody*, musicality 412 *music*; musicalness, melodiousness, musical quality, tonality, euphony, euphoniousness; harmoniousness, chime, harmony, concord, concert 24 *agreement*; consonance, assonance, attunement; unison, homophony; resolution (of a discord), cadence, perfect c.; harmonics, harmonization, counterpoint, polyphony; faux-bourdon, faburden, thorough bass, continuo, figured bass, ground b.; part, second, chorus; orchestration, instrumentation; tone, tone colour; phrasing 413 *musical skill*; phrase, passage, theme, leitmotiv, coda; movement 412 *musical piece*.

musical note, note, keys, keyboard, manual, pedal point; black notes, white n., sharp, flat, double f., double sharp, accidental, natural, tone, semitone; keynote, fundamental note; tonic, supertonic, mediant, subdominant, dominant, submediant, subtonic, leading note; interval, second, third, fourth, fifth, sixth, seventh, octave, ninth; diatesseron, diapason; gamut, scale (**see** *key*); chord, common c., triad, tetrachord, arpeggio; grace note, grace, ornament, crush note, appoggiatura, acciaccatura, mordent, turn, shake, trill, tremolo, vibrato, cadenza; tone, tonality, register, pitch, concert p., high p., low p.; high note 407 *stridor*; low note 404 *resonance*; undertone, overtone, harmonic, upper partial; sustained note, monotone, drone; phrase, flourish 412 *tune*; bugle call 547 *call*.

notation, musical n., tonic solfa, solfège, solfeggio, solmization; written music, sheet m., score; signature, time s., key s., clef, treble c., bass c., tenor c., alto c.; bar, stave, staff; line, ledger l., space, brace; rest, pause, interval; breve, semibreve, minim, crotchet, quaver, semiquaver, demisemiquaver, hemidemisemiquaver.

tempo, time, beat; rhythm 593 *prosody*; measure, timing; syncopation; upbeat, downbeat; suspension, long note, short n., suspended n.; prolonged n.; tempo rubato; rallentando, andante, adagio.

key, signature, clef, modulation, transposition, major key, minor k.; scale, gamut, major scale, minor s., diatonic s., chromatic s., harmonic s., melodic s., enharmonic s., twelve-tone s.; series, tone row; mode, Lydian m., Phrygian m., Dorian m., Mixolydian; Indian mode, raga.

Adj. *melodious*, melodic, musical, canorous, lilting, tuneful, singable, catchy; tinkling, low, soft 401 *muted*; sweet, dulcet, velvet, mellifluous, Orphean; high-fidelity, clear, clear as a bell, ringing, chiming; silvery, silver-toned, silver-tongued; fine-toned, full-t. 404 *resonant*; euphonious, euphonic, true, well-pitched.

harmonious, harmonizing, concordant, consonant 24 *agreeing*; in pitch; in chorus; assonant, rhyming, matching 18 *similar*; symphonic, symphonious, polyphonic; unisonous, homophonic, monophonic; monotonous, droning, intoning.

harmonic, enharmonic, diatonic, chromatic; tonal, atonal, polytonal, sharp, flat, twelve-toned, dodecaphonic; keyed, modal, minor, major, Dorian, Lydian.

Vb. *harmonize*, concert, have the right pitch, blend, chime 24 *accord*; chorus 413 *sing*; attune, tune, tune up, pitch, string 24 *adjust*; be in key, be in unison, be on the beat; compose, melodize, put to music, symphonize, orchestrate 413 *compose music*; modulate, transpose; resolve a discord, restore harmony.

See: 18, **24**, 401, 404, 407, **412**, **413**, 547, 593.

411 Discord

N. *discord*, conflict of sounds, discordance, dissonance, disharmony 25 *disagreement*; atonality, twelve-tone scale, tone row; imperfect cadence; preparation (of a discord); harshness, hoarseness, cacophony 407 *stridor*; confused sounds, Babel, cat's concert, caterwauling 400 *loudness*; row, din, noise, pandemonium, bedlam, tumult, racket 61 *turmoil*; atmospherics, wow, flutter.

Adj. *discordant*, dissonant, jangling, discording 25 *disagreeing*; conflicting 14 *contrary*; jarring, grating, scraping, rasping, harsh, raucous, cacophonous 407 *strident*; inharmonious, unharmonized; unmelodious, unmusical, untuneful; untuned, cracked; off pitch, off key, out of tune, sharp, flat; atonal, toneless, tuneless, droning, singsong.

Vb. *discord*, lack harmony 25 *disagree*; jangle, jar, grate, clash, crash; saw, scrape 407 *rasp*; be harsh, be out of tune; play sharp, play flat; thrum, drone, whine; prepare a discord; render discordant.

See: 14, **25**, 61, 400, **407**.

412 Music

N. *music*, harmony; sweet music 410 *melody*; musicianship 413 *musical skill*; minstrelsy, music-making, playing; strumming, thrumming, vamping; improvisation; writing music, composing, composition; instrumental music, pipe m., military m.; counterpoint, contrapuntal music; classical music, chamber m., organ m., choral m., operatic m., ballet m., sacred m., soul m.; light music, popular m., pop; descriptive music, programme m.; electronic m., musique concrète; recorded music, canned m., piped m., musical wallpaper, muzak (tdmk); disco music, dance m., waltztime; hot music, syncopation, jazz, progressive j., modern j., cool j., blue note, blues, mainstream jazz, traditional j., trad, Dixieland, ragtime, swing, bebop, bop, stride piano, boogie-woogie; jive, rock 'n' roll, rock music, hard r., heavy metal, new wave, punk; ska, reggae; rhythm 'n' blues, country and western, blue grass, folk; written music, the music, score, full s.; performance, recital, concert, orchestral c., choral c., promenade c., prom; jam session, gig, one-night stand; singsong; music festival, eisteddfod; school of music, conservatoire; Tin Pan Alley.

campanology, bell ringing, hand r.; ringing, chiming; carillon, chime, peal; full p., muffled p.; touch; method-ringing, change-r., hunting, dodging, making place; hunt, hunt forward, hunt backward, dodge; round; changes; method, Grandsire, Plain Bob, Treble Bob, Stedman; set of bells, doubles, triples, caters, cinques; minor, major, royal; maximus; bell, Great Tom, Great Paul, Tsar Kolokol; treble bell, tenor b. 414 *gong*; church bell 547 *call*; bell ringer, campanologist.

tune, melody, strain; theme song, signature tune; descant; reprise, refrain; melodic line; air, popular a., aria, solo; peal, chime, carillon; flourish, sennet, tucket; phrase, passage, measure; siren strains.

musical piece, piece, composition, opus, work, piece of music; tape, recording 414 *gramophone*; orchestration, instrumentation; arrangement, adaptation, setting, transcription; accompaniment, obbligato; voluntary, prelude, overture, intermezzo, finale; incidental music, background m.; romance, rhapsody, extravaganza, impromptu, fantasia, caprice, capriccio, humoresque, divertissement, divertimento, variations, raga; medley, potpourri; étude, study; suite, fugue, canon, toccata; sonata, sonatina, concerto, symphony, sinfonietta; symphonic poem, tone p.; pastorale, scherzo, rondo, gigue, jig, reel; passacaglia, chaconne, gavotte, minuet, tarantella, mazurka, polonaise, polka, waltz 837 *dance*; march, bridal m., wedding m., dead m., funeral m., dirge, pibroch; nocturne, serenade, berceuse; introductory phrase, anacrusis; statement, exposition, development, recapitulation, variation; theme, motive, leitmotiv; movement; passage, phrase; chord 410 *musical note*; cadenza, coda.

vocal music, singing, vocalism, lyricism; vocalization; scat singing; part, singing p.; opera, operetta, light opera, comic o., opéra bouffe, musical comedy, musical 594 *stage play*; choir-singing, oratorio, cantata, chorale; hymn-singing, psalmody, hymnology; descant, chant, plain c., Gregorian c., Ambrosian c., plainsong; cantus, c. firmus, cantillation, recitative;

bel canto, coloratura, bravura; singing practice, solfège, sol-fa, solmization; introit, anthem, canticle, psalm 981 *hymn*; song, lay, roundelay, carol, lyric, lilt; canzonet, cavatina, lieder, lied, ballad; folk song, popular *or* pop s., top twenty, hit parade; ditty, shanty, calypso; spiritual, blues; part song, glee, madrigal, round, catch, canon; chorus, refrain, burden; choral hymn, antiphony, dithyramb; boat song, barcarole; lullaby, cradle song, berceuse; serenade, aubade; bridal hymn, wedding h., epithalamium, prothalamium; love song, amorous ditty; song, birdsong, bird call, dawn chorus; requiem, dirge, threnody, coronach 836 *lament*; musical declamation, recitative; words to be sung, libretto; songbook, hymnbook, psalter.

duet, duo, trio, quartet, quintet, sextet, septet, octet; concerto, concerto grosso, solo, monody; ensemble, tutti.

Adj. *musical* 410 *melodious*; philharmonic, symphonic; melodic, arioso, cantabile; vocal, singable; operatic, recitative; lyric, melic; choral, dithyrambic; hymnal, psalmodic; harmonized 410 *harmonious*; contrapuntal; orchestrated, scored; set, set to music, arranged; instrumental, orchestral, for strings; blue, cool; hot, jazzy, syncopated, swinging, swung.

Adv. *adagio*, lento, largo, larghetto, andante, andantino, maestoso, moderato; allegro, allegretto; spiritoso, vivace, accelerando, presto, prestissimo; piano, mezzo-p., pianissimo, forte, mezzo-f., fortissimo, sforzando, con brio, capriccioso, scherzando; glissando, legato, sostenuto; staccato; crescendo, diminuendo, rallentando; affettuoso, cantabile, parlante; tremolo, pizzicato, vibrato; rubato; da capo.

See: 410, 413, 414, 547, 594, 836, **837**, 981.

413 Musician

N. *musician*, artiste, virtuoso, soloist; bravura player 696 *proficient person*; player, executant, performer, concert artist; ripieno 40 *extra*; bard, minstrel, jongleur, troubadour, trovatore, minnesinger; street musician, busker; composer, symphonist, contrapuntist; scorer, arranger, harmonist; syncopator, jazzman, swinger, cat; music writer, librettist, song writer, lyrics w., lyricist, liederwriter, hymnwriter, hymnographer, psalmist; music teacher, répétiteur, music master, kapellmeister, master of the music, bandmaster, conductor (**see** *orchestra*); the Muses, Apollo, Pan, Orpheus, Amphion; music lover, music critic, concertgoer, operagoer 504 *enthusiast*.

instrumentalist, player, piano p., pianist, accompanist; keyboard performer, organist, cembalist, harpsichordist, accordionist, concertina player; violinist, fiddler, scraper; violist, cellist; harper, harpist, lyre player, lute p., lutanist, sitarist, guitarist, mandolinist, banjoist; strummer, thrummer; piper, fifer, piccolo player, flautist, flutist, clarinettist, oboist, bassoonist; saxophonist, horn player, trumpeter, bugler; cornetist; bell ringer, carilloneur, campanologist; drummer, drummer boy, drum major; percussionist, timpanist; organ-grinder, hurdy-gurdy man.

orchestra, symphony o., chamber o., sinfonietta, quartet, quintet; ensemble, wind e.; strings, brass, woodwind, percussion, drums; band, string b., jazz b., ragtime b.; brass b., military b., pipe b.; skiffle group, steel band; rock b. *or* group, punk b. *or* g., pop g.; conductor, maestro, bandmaster; bandleader, leader, first violin; orchestral player, bandsman.

vocalist, singer, songster, warbler, caroller, chanter; chantress, chanteuse, songstress; siren, mermaid, Lorelei; melodist, troubadour, madrigal singer, minstrel, wandering m.; ballad singer, folk s., pop s.; serenader, crooner, jazz singer, scat s.; opera singer, prima donna, diva; cantatrice, coloratura; aria singer, lieder s.; castrato, treble, soprano, mezzo-s., contralto, alto, tenor, countertenor, baritone, bass b., bass, basso, basso profondo; songbird, nightingale, philomel, lark, thrush, mavis, blackbird 365 *bird*.

choir, chorus, waits, wassailers, carol singers, glee club, barbershop quartet; choir festival, massed choirs, eisteddfod; chorister, choirboy; precentor, cantor, choirmaster, choirleader.

musical skill, musical ability, musical appreciation; musicianship, bardship, minstrelsy; performance, execution, fingering, touch, phrasing, expression; virtuosity, bravura 694 *skill*.

Adj. *musicianly*, fond of music, knowing music, musical; minstrel, Orphean, bardic; vocal, coloratura, lyric, choral; plainsong, Gregorian, melodic 410 *melodious*; instrumental, orchestral, symphonic, contrapuntal; songful, warbling, carolling etc. vb.; scored, arranged, composed; in music, to m.

Vb. *be musical*, learn music, teach m., like m., read m., sight-read; have a good ear, have perfect pitch.

compose music, compose, write music, put to music, set to m., score, arrange, transpose, orchestrate, arrange in parts, supply the counterpoint, harmonize, melodize, improvise, extemporize.

play music, play, perform, execute, render, interpret; pick out a tune; conduct, wield the baton, beat time, mark the time; syncopate; play the piano, accompany; pedal, vamp, strum; brush the ivories, tickle the i., thump the keyboard; harp, pluck, sweep the strings, strike the lyre, pluck the guitar; thrum, twang; fiddle, bow, scrape, saw; play the concertina, squeeze the box, grind the organ; wind, wind the horn, blow, bugle, blow the b., sound the horn, sound, trumpet, sound the t., toot, tootle; pipe, flute, whistle; clash the cymbals; drum, tattoo, beat, tap, ruffle, beat the drum 403 *roll*; ring, peal the bells, ring a change; toll, knell; tune, string, set to concert pitch; practise, do scales, improvise, extemporize, play a voluntary, prelude; begin playing, strike up; give an encore.

sing, vocalize, chant, hymn; intone, cantillate, descant; warble, carol, lilt, trill, croon, hum, whistle, yodel; sol-fa; harmonize, sing seconds; chorus, choir; sing to, serenade; sing the praises, minstrel; chirp, chirrup, twitter, pipe 409 *ululate*; purr 401 *sound faint*.

See: 40, 365, 401, 403, 409, **410**, 504, 694, 696.

414 Musical instruments

N. *musical instrument*, band, music, concert 413 *orchestra*; strings, brass, wind, woodwind, percussion; sounding board, diaphragm, sound box; synthesizer.

harp, stringed instrument, Aeolian harp; lyre, lute, sitar; theorbo; cithara, cithern, zither, gittern, guitar, electric g., mandolin, ukulele, banjo, balalaika, zither; psaltery, vina; plectrum, fret.

viol, violin, Cremona, Stradivarius, fiddle, kit, crowd, rebec; viola *or* tenor violin, viola d'amore, viola da gamba *or* bass viol, cello *or* violoncello, double bass *or* contrabasso; musical saw; bow, fiddlestick; string, catgut; bridge; resin.

piano, pianoforte, grand piano, concert grand, baby g.; upright piano, cottage p.; virginals, dulcimer, harpsichord, cembalo, spinet, clavichord, celesta; piano-organ, player piano, pianola (tdmk); clavier, keyboard, manual, keys, ivories; loud pedal, soft p., damper.

organ, pipe o., church o., Hammond o., electric *or* electronic o., steam o., calliope; reed organ, harmonium, American organ, melodeon; mouth organ, harmonica; kazoo, comb; accordion, piano a., concertina; barrel organ, hurdy-gurdy; great organ, swell o., choir o.; organ pipe, flue p., organ stop, flue s.; manual, keyboard.

flute, fife, piccolo, flageolet, cornetto, recorder; woodwind, reed instrument, clarinet, bass c., basset horn; saxophone, sax, tenor s.; shawm, hautboy, oboe, tenor o., cor Anglais; bassoon, double b.; ocarina; pipe, oaten p., reed, straw; bagpipes, musette; pan pipes, Pandean p., syrinx; nose flute; whistle, penny w., tin w.; pitch-pipe; mouthpiece, embouchure.

horn, brass; bugle horn, post h., hunting h.; bugle, trumpet, clarion; alpenhorn, French horn, flugelhorn, saxhorn, althorn, helicon horn, bass h., sousaphone; euphonium, ophicleide, serpent, bombardon; cornet, trombone, sackbut, tuba, saxtuba, bass tuba; conch, shell.

gong, bell, tintinnabulum; treble bell, tenor b.; church bell, alarm bell, tocsin 665 *danger signal*; tintinnabulation, peal, carillon, chimes, bells; bones, rattle, clappers, castanets, maracas; cymbals; xylophone, marimba; vibraphone, vibes; musical glasses, harmonica; tubular bell, glockenspiel; triangle; tuning fork; Jew's harp; sounding board; percussion instrument.

drum, big d., bass d., tenor d., side d., snare d., kettle d., timpani; war drum, tomtom; tabor, tambourine; tabla.

gramophone, record player, phonograph, radiogram; tape recorder, cassette r., high-fidelity system, hi-fi, stereo set, music centre; playback; recording, tape r., tape, cassette; talking book; gramophone record, disc, platter, long-playing record,

LP, EP, 33, 45, 78; album, single, track 548 *registration*; musical box, jukebox; head, needle, stylus, pickup, cartridge; deck, turntable; amplifier, speaker, tweeter, woofer.

mute, damper, sordino, pedal, soft p., celeste 401 *silencer*.

See: 33, 45, 78, 401, **413**, 548, 665.

415 Hearing

N. *hearing*, audition 398 *acoustics*; sense of hearing, good h.; good ear, sharp e., acute e., quick e., sensitive e., musical e., ear for music; audibility, reception, good r.; earshot, carrying distance, range, reach; something to hear, earful.

listening, hearkening 455 *attention*; auscultation, aural examination 459 *enquiry*; listening-in, tuning-in; lip-reading 520 *interpretation*; eavesdropping, overhearing, wire-tapping, bugging 523 *latency*; sound recording 548 *record*; audition, voice testing 461 *experiment*; interview, audience, hearing 584 *conference*; legal hearing 959 *legal trial*.

listener, hearer, audience, auditorium; stalls, pit, gallery 441 *spectator*; radio listener, radio ham; hi-fi enthusiast, audiophile; disciple, lecture-goer 538 *learner*; monitor, auditor, examiner 459 *questioner*; eavesdropper, little pitcher 453 *inquisitive person*.

ear, auditory apparatus, auditory nerve, acoustic organ; lug, lobe, auricle, pinna, earhole, lughole; aural cavity, cochlea, eardrum, tympanum; auditory canal, labyrinth; otology; otologist, hearing specialist.

hearing aid, deaf-aid, ear trumpet; hearing instrument, stethoscope, otoscope; loudspeaker, loudhailer, tannoy, public address system 528 *publication*; microphone, mike, amplifier 400 *megaphone*; speaking tube; telephone, phone, blower; receiver, earpiece, headphones, earphones; walkie-talkie 531 *telecommunication*; sound recorder, asdic, sonar, magnetic tape, Dictaphone (tdmk) 549 *recording instrument*; radiogram 414 *gramophone*, 531 *broadcasting*.

Adj. *auditory*, hearing, auricular, aural; audiovisual 398 *sounding*; otological, stethoscopic; auditive, acoustic, audile, keen-eared, sharp-e., open-e.; listening, tuned in; prick-eared, ears flapping, all ears 455 *attentive*; within earshot, audible, heard 398 *sounding*.

Vb. *hear*, catch; list, listen, examine by ear, auscultate, put one's ear to; lip-read 520 *interpret*; listen in, switch on, tune in, adjust the receiver; prepare to hear, lift the receiver; overhear, eavesdrop, listen at keyholes, keep one's ears open; intercept, bug, tap, tap the wires; hearken, give ear, lend an e., incline one's e.; give audience, interview, grant an interview 459 *interrogate*; hear confession 526 *confess*; listen with both ears, be all ears, hang on the lips of, lap up 455 *be attentive*; strain one's ears, prick up one's e.; catch a sound, pick up a message; be told, hear it said, come to one's ears 524 *be informed*.

be heard, become audible, reach the ear, fill the e., sound in the e., fall on the e. 398 *sound*; ring in the e. 400 *be loud*; gain a hearing, have an audience; go out on the air, be broadcast.

Adv. *in earshot*, in one's hearing.

See: **398**, 400, **414**, 441, 453, 455, 459, 461, 520, 523, 524, 526, 528, 531, 538, 548, 549, 584, 959.

416 Deafness

N. *deafness*, defective hearing, imperfect h., hardness of hearing; deaf ears, deaf-mutism; deaf-and-dumb speech, dactylology; deaf-and-dumb person, deaf-mute, the deaf and dumb; inaudibility 399 *silence*.

Adj. *deaf*, earless, dull of ear, hard of hearing, stone-deaf, deaf as a post, deaf as mutton, deaf and dumb, deaf-mute; deafened, stunned, unable to hear; deaf to, unhearing, not listening 456 *inattentive*; deaf to music, tone-deaf, unmusical; hard to hear 401 *muted*; inaudible, out of earshot, out of hearing 399 *silent*.

Vb. *be deaf*, not hear, hear nothing, fail to catch; not listen, refuse to hear, shut one's ears, stop one's e., close one's e., plug one's e. 458 *disregard*; turn a deaf ear to 760 *refuse*; be hard of hearing, use a hearing aid; lip-read, use lip-reading 520 *translate*; talk with one's fingers.

deafen, make deaf, stun, split the eardrum, drown one's voice 400 *be loud*.

See: 399, 400, 401, 456, 458, 520, 760.

417 Light

N. *light*, daylight, light of day, noonday, noontide, noon, broad day 128 *morning*; sunbeam, sunlight, sun 420 *luminary*;

starlight, moonlight, moonshine, earthshine; half-light, twilight 419 *dimness*; artificial light, candlelight, firelight 420 *lighting*; illumination, irradiation, splendour, resplendence, effulgence, refulgence, intensity, brightness, vividness, brilliance; luminousness, luminosity, luminance, candle power, magnitude; incandescence, radiance (**see** *glow*); sheen, shine, gloss, lustre (**see** *reflection*); blaze, blaze of light, sheet of l., flood of l.; glare, dazzle, dazzlement; flare, flame 379 *fire*; halo, nimbus, glory, gloriole, aureole, corona; variegated light, spectrum, visible s., iridescence, rainbow 437 *variegation*; coloration, riot of colour 425 *colour*; white 427 *whiteness*.

flash, fulguration, coruscation; lightning, lightning flash; beam, stream, shaft, bar, ray, pencil; streak, meteor flash; scintillation, sparkle, spark; glint, glitter, play, play of light; blink, twinkle, twinkling, flicker, flickering, glimmer, gleam, shimmer, shimmering; spangle, tinsel; strobe light, searchlight 420 *lamp*; firefly 420 *glow-worm*.

glow, flush, sunset glow, afterglow, alpenglow, dawn, sunset; steady flame, steady beam; lambency, lambent light, soft l.; aurora, aurora borealis, aurora australis; northern lights; zodiacal light 321 *heavens*; radiance, incandescence 379 *heat*; luminescence, fluorescence, phosphorescence, thermoluminescence; ignis fatuus, will-o'-the-wisp, St Elmo's fire 420 *glow-worm*.

radiation, visible r., invisible r.; background r.; actinism, emission, absorption; radioactivity, irradiation 160 *nucleonics*; radioisotope; particle counter, Geiger c.; fallout, mushroom cloud 659 *poison*; radiation belt, Van Allen layer 340 *atmosphere*; radio wave, frequency w. 398 *sound*; sky wave, ground w.; long w., short w., medium w. 317 *oscillation*; wavelength, waveband; high frequency, VHF, UHF; interference, static 160 *electricity*; electromagnetic radiation, microwave; infrared radiation, radiant heat *or* energy; visible light; black l.; ultraviolet radiation; X-ray, gamma r., alpha r., beta r., cosmic radiation, cosmic noise; magnetic storm; photon; photoelectric cell; curie, millicurie, roentgen, rem; half-life.

reflection, refraction, double r.; diffraction, dispersion, scattering, interference, polarization; albedo, polish, gloss, sheen, shine, lustre; glare, dazzle, blink, ice b.; reflecting surface, reflector 442 *mirror*; mirror image, hologram 551 *image*.

light contrast, tonality, chiaroscuro; value, light and shade, black and white, halftone, mezzotint; highlights.

optics, electro-optics, fibre optics; photics, photometry, actinometry; dioptrics, catoptrics, spectroscopy 442 *optical device*; holography 551 *photography*; radioscopy, radiometry, radiology; magnification, magnifying power 197 *expansion*.

Adj. *luminous*, luminiferous, lucid, lucent; light, lit, well-lit, floodlit, flooded with light; bright, gay, shining, fulgent, resplendent, splendent, splendid, brilliant, flamboyant, vivid; colourful 425 *coloured*; radiant, effulgent, refulgent; dazzling, blinding, glaring, lurid, garish; incandescent, flaring, flaming, aflame, aglow, ablaze 379 *fiery*; glowing, blushing, auroral, rutilant 431 *red*; luminescent, fluorescent, phosphorescent, noctilucous; soft, lambent, playing; beaming; glittery, flashing, glinting etc. vb.; scintillant, scintillating, sparkling; lustrous, shiny, sheeny, glossy; reflecting, catoptric; refractive, dioptric; optical, photometric; photosensitive.

undimmed, clear, bright, fair, set f.; cloudless, shadowless, unclouded, unshaded; sunny, sunshiny; moonlit, starlit, starry; light as day, bright as noonday, bright as silver; burnished, polished, glassy, gleaming; lucid, pellucid, diaphanous, translucent 422 *transparent*.

radiating, radiant; cosmic, cosmogenic; radioactive, irradiated, hot; reflective, reflecting.

Vb. *shine*, be bright, burn, blaze, flame, flare 379 *be hot*; glow, incandesce, phosphoresce; shine full, glare, dazzle, bedazzle, blind; play, dance; flash, fulgurate, coruscate; glisten, glister, blink; glimmer, flicker, twinkle; glitter, shimmer, glance; scintillate, sparkle, spark; shine again, reflect; take a shine, come up, gleam, glint.

radiate, beam, shoot, shoot out rays 300 *emit*; reflect, refract; be radioactive, bombard; X-ray.

make bright, lighten, dispel the darkness, dawn, rise, wax (moon); clear, clear up, lift, brighten; light, strike a l., ignite 381 *kindle*; light up, switch on; show a light, hang out a l.; shed lustre, throw light on; shine upon, flood with light, irradiate, illuminate, illume, relume; shine within, shine through 443 *be visible*; transilluminate, pass light through; polish, burnish, rub up 648 *clean*.

See: 128, 160, 197, 300, 317, 321, 340, 379, 381, 398, 419, **420**, 422, 425, 427, 431, 437, **442**, **443**, 551, 648, 659.

418 Darkness

N. *darkness*, dark; black 428 *blackness*; night, dark n., nightfall; dead of night, witching time 129 *midnight*; pitchy darkness, thick d., tangible d., total d.; Cimmerian darkness, Stygian gloom, Erebus; obscurity, murk, gloom, dusk 421 *obfuscation*; shadiness, shadows 419 *dimness*; shade, dense s., shadow, umbra, penumbra; silhouette, skiagraph, negative, radiograph, shadowgraph 551 *photography*; skiagraphy; dark place, darkroom; cavern, mine, dungeon, depths.

obscuration, obfuscation, darkening 419 *dimness*; blackout, dimout, fadeout, fade; occultation, eclipse, total e. 446 *disappearance*; extinction of light, lights out; Tenebrae 988 *ritual act*; sunset, sundown 129 *evening*; blackening, adumbration, shading, hatching, cross-h.; distribution of shade, chiaroscuro; dark lantern; snuffer, dimmer, dip switch, off s.

Adj. *dark*, subfusc, sombre, dark-coloured, swart, swarthy 428 *black*; darksome, obscure, pitch-dark, pitchy, sooty, inky, black as night; cavernous, dark as a tunnel, black as a pit; Cimmerian, Stygian, Tartarean; caliginous, murky; funereal, gloomy, dreary, dismal, sombre; louring, lurid 419 *dim*; tenebrous, shady, umbrageous 419 *shadowy*; all black, silhouetted; shaded, darkened 421 *screened*; darkling, benighted; nocturnal, noctivagant; hidden, veiled, secret 523 *occult*.

unlit, unlighted, unilluminated; not shining, lightless; sunless, moonless, starless; eclipsed, overshadowed, overcast 421 *screened*; misted, befogged, clouded, beclouded, cloudy 423 *opaque*; switched off, extinguished; dipped, dimmed, blacked out; obscured, obfuscated.

Vb. *be dark*, grow d., darkle; lour, gather; fade out 419 *be dim*; lurk in the shadows 523 *lurk*; look black, gloom.

darken, black, brown; black out, dim o.; lower the light, dim the l., turn down the wick; occult, eclipse, mantle 226 *cover*; curtain, shutter, veil 421 *screen*; obscure, obfuscate; befog, dim, tone down 419 *bedim*; overcast, overcloud, overshadow, cast in the shade, spread gloom; spread a shade, cast a shadow; adumbrate, silhouette 551 *represent*; shade, hatch, cross-h., fill in; paint over 440 *blur*; underexpose 428 *blacken*.

snuff out, extinguish, quench, put out the light, pinch out, blow o., switch off, dip, douse.

Adv. *darkling*, in the dark, in the shade, in the shadows; at night, by night.

See: 129, 226, **419**, **421**, 423, **428**, 440, 446, 523, 551, 988.

419 Dimness

N. *dimness*, indistinctness, vagueness, fuzziness, blur, soft focus; loom; faintness, paleness 426 *achromatism*; grey 429 *greyness*; dullness, lacklustre, lack of sparkle; no reflection, matt finish; leaden skies; cloudiness, smokiness, poor visibility, white-out 423 *opacity*; mistiness, fogginess, nebulosity; murk, gloom 418 *darkness*; fog, mist 355 *cloud*; shadowiness, shadow, shade, shadow of a shade; spectre 440 *visual fallacy*.

half-light, semidarkness, bad light; waning light, gloaming 129 *evening*; shades of evening, twilight, dusk, crepuscule; owl-light; daybreak, break of day, demi-jour, grey dawn; penumbra, half-shadow, partial eclipse, annular e.

glimmer, flicker 417 *flash*; 'ineffectual fire', noctiluca, firefly 420 *glow-worm*; side lights, dipped l., dips; candlelight, firelight 417 *light*; ember, hot coal; smoky light, tallow candle, dip; dark lantern 420 *lamp*; moonbeam, moonlight, starlight, earthlight, earthshine.

Adj. *dim*, darkish, darksome; dusky, dusk, twilight, crepuscular; wan, dun, subfusc, grey, pale 426 *colourless*; faint, faded, waning; indistinct, blurred, bleary; glassy, dull, lustreless, lacklustre, leaden; flat, matt; filmy, hazy, foggy, fogbound, misty, obnubilated, nebulous 355 *cloudy*; thick, smoky, sooty, muddy 423 *opaque*; dingy, grimy, rusty, rusted, mildewed, unpolished, unburnished 649 *dirty*.

shadowy, umbrageous, shady, shaded, overspread, overshadowed, overcast, overclouded 226 *covered*; vague, indistinct, undefined, obscure, confused, fuzzy, blurry, looming; deceptive; half-seen, half-glimpsed, withdrawn, half-hidden 444 *invisible*; half-lit, partially eclipsed 418 *unlit*; dreamlike, ghostly 4 *insubstantial*; coming and going 446 *disappearing*.

Vb. *be dim*, - faint etc. adj.; be indistinct, loom; grow grey, fade, wane, fade out, pale, grow p. 426 *lose colour*; lour, gloom, darkle; glimmer, flicker, gutter, sputter; lurk in the shade, be lost in the shadows 523 *lurk*.

bedim, dim, dip; lower *or* turn down the lights, fade out 418 *snuff out*; obscure, blur the outline, blear 440 *blur*; smirch, smear, besmirch, besmear, sully; rust, mildew, begrime, muddy, dirty 649 *make unclean*; smoke, fog, mist, befog, becloud 423 *make opaque*; overshadow, overcast; shade, shadow, veil, veil the brightness 226 *cover*; shade in, hatch 418 *darken*.

Adv. *dimly*, vaguely, indistinctly etc. adj.; in the half-light, in the gloaming.

See: 4, 129, 226, 355, 417, **418**, 420, **423**, 426, 429, **440**, 444, 446, 523, 649.

420 Luminary: source of light

N. *luminary*, illuminant 417 *light*; naked light, flame 379 *fire*; flare, gas f. (**see** *lamp*); source of light, orb of day 321 *sun*; orb of night 321 *moon*; starlight 321 *star*; bright star, first magnitude s., Sirius, Aldebaran, Betelgeuse, Canopus, Alpha Centauri; evening star, Hesperus, Vesper, Venus; morning star, Lucifer; shooting star, fireball 321 *meteor*; galaxy, Milky Way, northern lights 321 *heavens*; lightning, bolt of l., sheet l., forked l., ball l., summer l., lightning flash, levin; scintilla, spark, sparkle 417 *flash*.

glow-worm 417 *glow*; firefly, noctiluca; fata morgana, ignis fatuus, will-o'-the-wisp, friar's lantern, Jack-o'-lantern; fireball, St Elmo's fire, corposant; phosphorescent light, corpse-candle; firedrake, fiery dragon.

torch, brand, coal, ember; torchlight, link, flambeau, cresset, match 385 *lighter*; candle, bougie, tallow candle, wax c.; taper, wax t.; spill, wick, dip, rushlight, nightlight, naked light, flare, gas jet, burner, Bunsen b.; torchbearer, linkboy.

lamp, lamplight; lantern, lanthorn, bull's-eye; safety lamp, Davy l., miner's l., acetylene l.; oil lamp, hurricane l., paraffin l., spirit l.; gas lamp, incandescent l., gas mantle, mantle; electric lamp, flash l., flash gun, torch, flashlight, searchlight, arc light, floodlight; headlamp, headlight, side light; anti-dazzle l., foglamp; stop-light, tail light, reflector; bulb, flashbulb, flashcube, photoflood, electric bulb, light b., filament; strobe light, stroboscope, strobe; vapour light, neon l., strip l.; street l., mercury vapour lamp, sodium l.; Chinese lantern, fairy lights; magic lantern, projector; light fitting, chandelier, gaselier, lustre, electrolier, candelabra, girandole; standard lamp, table l., sun l., sunray l.; lamppost, standard; socket, bracket, pricket; sconce, candle holder, candlestick; linkboy, lamplighter.

lighting, illumination, irradiation 417 *light*; artificial lighting, street l.; indirect lighting; gas lighting, electric l., neon l., daylight l., fluorescent l.; floodlighting, son et lumière, limelight, spotlight, footlights, houselights.

signal light, warning l. 665 *danger signal*; traffic light, red l., green l., amber l., stop-light, trafficator, winker; Very light, Bengal l., rocket, star shell, parachute flare, flare; flare path, beacon, beacon fire, balefire 547 *signal*; lighthouse, lightship.

fireworks, illuminations, firework display, pyrotechnics; sky rocket, Roman candle, Catherine wheel, sparkler; banger 723 *explosive*; Bengal light.

Adj. *luminescent*, luminous, self-l., incandescent, shining; phosphoric, phosphorescent, fluorescent, neon; radiant 417 *radiating*; colourful 425 *coloured*; illuminated, well-lit; bright, gay.

Vb. *illuminate*, light up, light 417 *shine*, *make bright*.

See: **321**, 379, 385, **417**, 425, 547, 665, 723.

421 Screen

N. *screen*, shield 660 *protection*; covert 662 *shelter*; bower 194 *arbour*; shady nook 418 *darkness*; sunshade, parasol; sun hat, sola topee 226 *shade*; awning 226 *canopy*; sunscreen, visor; lampshade; eyeshade, blinkers; eyelid, eyelashes 438 *eye*; dark glasses, tinted g., sun g. 442 *eyeglass*; smoked glass, frosted g., reeded g., opaque g., polarized g. 424 *semitransparency*; stained glass 437 *variegation*; partition, wall, hedge 235 *fence*; filter 57 *exclusion*; mask 527 *disguise*; hood, veil, mantle 228 *cloak*.

curtain 226 *shade*; window curtain, net c., bead c.; shade, blind, sunblind; persiennes, jalousie, venetian blind, roller b.; shutter, deadlight.

obfuscation, smoke screen; fog, mist 341 *moisture*; pall, cloud, dust, film, scale 423 *opacity*.

Adj. *screened*, sheltered; sunproof, cool 380 *cold*; shady, umbrageous, bowery 419 *shadowy*; blindfolded, hooded 439 *blind*; screening, impervious, impermeable.

Vb. *screen*, shield, shelter 660 *safeguard*; protect 713 *defend*; ward off, fend off 713 *parry*; blanket, keep off, keep out, filter out 57 *exclude*; cover up, veil, hood 226 *cover*; mask, hide, shroud 525 *conceal*; intercept 702 *obstruct*; blinker, blindfold 439 *blind*; keep out the light, shade, shadow, darken; curtain, curtain off, canopy, draw the curtains, pull down the blind, spread the awning; put up the shutters, close the s. 264 *close*; cloud, fog, mist 419 *bedim*; smoke, frost, glaze, film 423 *make opaque*.

See: 57, 194, **226**, 228, 235, 264, 341, 380, 418, **419**, **423**, 424, 437, 438, 439, 442, 525, 527, 660, 662, 702, 713.

422 Transparency

N. *transparency*, transmission of light, transillumination; translucence, lucency, diaphaneity, unobstructed vision; thinness, gauziness; lucidity, pellucidity, limpidity; clearness, clarity; glassiness; vitreousness; transparent medium, hyaline, water, ice, crystal, perspex (tdmk), cellophane (tdmk), glass, crown g., flint g., sheet g., plate g., optical g., magnifying g., lens, eyepiece 442 *eyeglass*; pane, window p.; sheer silk, gossamer, gauze, lace, chiffon 4 *insubstantial thing*.

Adj. *transparent*, diaphanous, revealing, sheer, see-through; thin, fine, filmy, gauzy, pellucid, translucid; translucent; lucent 424 *semitransparent*; liquid, limpid; crystal, crystalline, hyaline, vitreous, glassy; clear, serene, lucid; crystal-clear, clear as crystal.

Vb. *be transparent*, - translucent etc. adj.; transmit light, show through; shine through, transilluminate, pass light through 417 *make bright*; render transparent, clarify.

See: 4, **417**, 424, 442.

423 Opacity

N. *opacity*, opaqueness; thickness, solidity 324 *density*; filminess, frost; turbidity, muddiness, dirtiness 649 *dirt*; devitrification; fog, mist, dense fog, smog, peasouper 355 *cloud*; film, scale 421 *screen*; smoke-cloud, smoke screen 421 *obfuscation*.

Adj. *opaque*, nontransparent, thick, impervious to light, blank, windowless; not clear, unclarified, devitrified; cloudy, milky, filmy, turbid, muddy, muddied, puddled; foggy, hazy, misty, murky, smoky, sooty, fuliginous 419 *dim*; unwashed, uncleaned 649 *dirty*; vaporous, fumy; coated, frosted, misted, clouded.

Vb. *make opaque*, devitrify; cloud, cloud over, thicken; frost, film, smoke 419 *bedim*; obfuscate; scumble, overpaint 226 *coat*; be opaque, obstruct the light 421 *screen*.

See: 226, 324, 355, 419, **421**, 649.

424 Semitransparency

N. *semitransparency*, milkiness, lactescence; pearliness, opalescence; smoked glass, ground g., frosted g., tinted spectacles, dark glasses; gauze, muslin, net; pearl, opal 437 *variegation*; horn, mica; tissue, tissue paper.

Adj. *semitransparent*, semipellucid, semiopaque, semidiaphanous, gauzy, filmy; translucent, opalescent, opaline, milky, lactescent, pearly; frosted, matt, misty, smoked 419 *dim*, 355 *cloudy*.

See: 355, 419, 437.

425 Colour

N. *colour*, natural c., pure c., positive c., neutral c., primitive c., primary c.; three primaries, complementary colour, secondary c., tertiary c.; chromatism, chromatic aberration; range of colour, chromatic scale; prism, spectrum, rainbow 437 *variegation*; mixture of colours, harmony, discord; colour scheme, palette; coloration 553 *painting*; colour photography, Technicolor (tdmk); riot of colour, splash 437 *variegation*; heraldic colour, tincture, metal, fur 547 *heraldry*.

chromatics, science of colour, colorimetry, chromatology, spectrum analysis, spectrometer; colorimeter, tintometer; spectroscope, prism.

hue, colour quality, chroma, chromaticity, saturation, tone, value; brilliance, intensity, warmth, loudness; softness, deadness, dullness; coloration, livery; pigmentation, colouring, complexion, natural colour; hue of health, flush, blush, glow; ruddiness 431 *redness*; sickly hue, pallor 426 *achromatism*; faded hue, discoloration; tint, shade, nuance, cast, dye; tinge, patina; half-tone, half-light, mezzotint.

pigment, colouring matter, rouge, warpaint 843 *cosmetic*; dyestuff, dye, fast d.; natural d., vegetable d., madder, cochineal 431 *red pigment*; indigo 436 *purpleness*; woad 435 *blueness*; artificial dye, synthetic d., aniline d.; stain, fixative, mordant; wash, colourwash, whitewash, distemper; paint, oil paints, watercolours 553 *art equipment*.

Adj. *coloured*, in colour, painted, toned, tinct, tinged, dyed, double-d., tinted etc. vb.; colorific, tinctorial; fast, unfading, constant; colourful, chromatic, polychromatic; monochromatic 16 *uniform*; prismatic, spectroscopic; technicoloured, kaleidoscopic, many-coloured, particoloured 437 *variegated*.

florid, colourful, high-coloured, full-c., deep-c., bright-hued; ruddy 431 *red*; intense, deep, strong, emphatic; unfaded, vivid, brilliant 417 *luminous*; warm, glowing, rich, gorgeous; painted, gay, bright; jazzy, gaudy, garish, showy, flashy; glaring, flaring, flaunting, spectacular; harsh, raw, crude; lurid, loud, screaming, shrieking; clashing, discordant 25 *disagreeing*.

soft-hued, soft, quiet, tender, delicate, refined; pearly, creamy 427 *whitish*; light, pale, pastel, muted; dull, flat, matt, dead; simple, sober, sad 573 *plain*; sombre, dark 428 *black*; drab, dingy, faded; patinated, weathered, mellow; matching, toning, harmonious 24 *agreeing*.

Vb. *colour*, lay on the c., colour in, crayon, daub 553 *paint*; rouge 431 *redden*, 843 *primp*; pigment, tattoo; dye, dip, imbue, imbrue; woad 435 *blue*; tint, touch up; shade, shadow 428 *blacken*; tincture, tinge; wash, colourwash, distemper, lacquer 226 *coat*; stain, run, discolour; come off (e.g. on one's fingers); tan, weather, mellow; illuminate, miniate, emblazon; whitewash, silver 427 *whiten*; yellow 433 *gild*; enamel 437 *variegate*.

See: 16, 24, 25, 226, 417, 426, 427, 428, 431, 433, 435, 436, **437**, 547, **553**, 573, 843.

426 Achromatism: absence of colour

N. *achromatism*, achromaticity, colourlessness; decoloration, discoloration, etiolation, fading, bleaching 427 *whiteness*; overexposure 551 *photography*; pallor, pallidity, paleness; lightness, faintness etc. adj.; no colour, anaemia, bloodlessness; pigment deficiency, albinism; neutral tint; monochrome; black and white; albino, blond(e), platinum b., peroxide b.

bleacher, decolorant, peroxide, bleaching powder, bleach, lime.

Adj. *colourless*, hueless, toneless, neutral; uncoloured, achromatic; decoloured, discoloured; bleached, etiolated, overexposed; faint, faded, fading; unpigmented, albino, light-skinned, fair, blond 433 *yellow*, 427 *whitish*; lustreless, glossless, mousy; bloodless, anaemic; without colour, drained of colour, drained of blood; washed out, washy; pale, pallid 427 *white*; ashy, ashen, ashen-hued, livid, tallow-faced, whey-f.; pasty, doughy, mealy, sallow, sickly 651 *unhealthy*; dingy, dull, leaden 429 *grey*; blank, glassy, lacklustre; lurid, ghastly, wan 419 *dim*; deathly, cadaverous, pale as death, pale as ashes 361 *dead*.

Vb. *lose colour* 419 *be dim*; pale, fade, bleach, blanch, turn pale, change countenance 427 *whiten*; run, come out in the wash.

decolorize, achromatize, fade, etiolate; blanch, bleach, peroxide 427 *whiten*; deprive of colour, drain of c., wash out; tone down, deaden, weaken; pale, dim 419 *bedim*; dull, tarnish, discolour 649 *make unclean*.

See: 361, **419**, **427**, 429, 433, 551, 649, 651.

427 Whiteness

N. *whiteness*, albescence, etiolation; lack of pigment, albinism 426 *achromatism*; whitishness, lactescence, creaminess, pearliness; hoariness, canescence; white light 417 *light*; white heat 379 *heat*; white man, white woman, white, paleface; albino.

white thing, alabaster, marble; hoar frost, snow, driven s.; chalk, paper, milk, flour, salt, ivory, lily, swan; albino; silver, white metal, white gold, pewter, platinum; pearl, teeth; white patch, blaze.

whiting, blanco, white lead, pipeclay; whitewash, white paint, Chinese white, Paris w., flake w., zinc w., titanium w.

Adj. *white*, candid, pure, albescent; dazzling, light, bright 417 *luminous*; silvered, silvery, silver, argent, argental, argentine; alabaster, marble; chalky, snowy, snow-capped, snow-covered; hoar, frosty, frosted; foaming, spumy, foam-flecked; soapy, lathery; white hot 379 *hot*; white as marble, white as alabaster, white like ivory, white as a lily, white as milk, white as a sheet; pure white, lily-white, milk-w., snow-w., white-skinned, Caucasian; lacking pigment, albinotic; whitened, white-washed, bleached 648 *clean*.

whitish, pearly, milky, creamy 424 *semi-transparent*; ivory, waxen, sallow, pale 426 *colourless*; off-white, half-w.; oyster-w., mushroom, magnolia; unbleached, ecru 430 *brown*; canescent, hoary, grizzled 429 *grey*; pepper-and-salt 437 *mottled*; blond, fair, Nordic; ash-blond(e), platinum b., fair-haired, flaxen-h., tow-headed; dusty, white with dust.

Vb. *whiten*, white, blanco, pipeclay, white-wash, calcimine, wash 648 *clean*; blanch, bleach; pale, fade 426 *decolorize*; frost, silver, grizzle.

See: 379, **417**, 424, **426**, 429, 430, 437, 648.

428 Blackness

N. *blackness*, nigrescence, nigritude 418 *darkness*; inkiness, lividity, black, sable; melanism, swarthiness, swartness, duskiness, pigmentation, pigment, dark colouring, colour; depth, deep tone; black and white, chiaroscuro 437 *chequer*; blackening, darkening 418 *obscuration*; black man, black woman, black, Negro, Negress, Negrillo, Negrito; coloured man *or* woman, coloured; Ethiopian, blackamoor.

black thing, coal, charcoal, soot, pitch, tar; ebony, jet, ink, smut; bruise, black eye; blackberry, sloe; crow, raven, blackbird; black clothes, crepe, mourning.

black pigment, blacking, lampblack, black-lead; ivory black, blue-b., nigrosine; ink, Indian i., printer's i.; japan, niello; burnt cork; melanin.

Adj. *black*, sable; jetty, ebon; inky, pitchy, black as thunder 418 *dark*; sooty, fuliginous, smoky, smudgy, smutty 649 *dirty*; blackened, singed, charred; black-haired, black-locked, raven-haired; black-eyed, sloe-e.; dark, brunette; black-skinned, Negroid, Ethiopian; pigmented, coloured; melanistic; sombre, gloomy, mourning 364 *funereal*; coal-black, jet-b., sloe-b., pitch-b.; blue-b.; deep, of the deepest dye; black as coal, black as jet, black as pitch, black as my hat, black as the ace of spades, black as a tinker's pot; nocturnal, black as night, black as midnight 129 *vespertine*.

blackish, rather black, nigrescent; swarthy, swart, black-faced, dusky, dark, dark-skinned, tanned, sun-t.; coloured, pigmented; livid, black and blue; low-toned, low in tone 419 *dim*.

Vb. *blacken*, black, japan, ink, ink in; dirty, blot, smudge, smirch 649 *make unclean*; deepen 418 *darken*; singe, char 381 *burn*.

See: 129, 364, 381, **418**, 419, 437, 649.

429 Greyness

N. *greyness*, neutral tint, grisaille; pepper and salt, grey hairs, hoary head; pewter, silver; gunmetal, ashes, slate; grey, Payne's g.; dove g. etc. adj.; oyster, taupe.

Adj. *grey*, neutral, dull, sombre, leaden, livid; cool, quiet; canescent, greying, grizzled, grizzly, hoary, hoar; silvery, silvered, pearly, frosted 427 *whitish*; light-grey, powder-g., ash-g., dove-g., pearl-g.; mouse-coloured, mousy, dun, drab, donkey-grey; steely, steel-grey, iron-g., charcoal-g.; bluish-grey, slate-coloured; greyish, ashen, ashy, smoky, fuliginous, cinereous; dapple-grey.

See: 427.

430 Brownness

N. *brownness*, brown, bronze, copper, amber; tobacco leaf, dead l., autumn colours; cinnamon, coffee, chocolate; butterscotch, caramel, toffee, burnt almond; walnut, mahogany; dark skin *or* complexion, suntan; brunette.

brown pigment, bistre, ochre, sepia, raw sienna, burnt s., raw umber, burnt u., Vandyke brown.

Adj. *brown*, bronze, mahogany etc. n.; browned, toasted; bronzed, tanned, sunburnt; dark, brunette; nut-brown, hazel; light brown, ecru, oatmeal, beige, buff, fawn, biscuit, mushroom, café-au-lait; brownish, greyish-brown, dun, drab, mud-coloured; yellowish-brown, snuff-coloured, feuille morte, khaki; tawny, tan, foxy; reddish-brown, bay, roan, sorrel, chestnut, auburn, copper-coloured; russet, rust-coloured, liver-c., maroon; purple-brown, puce; dark brown, peat-b., mocha, chocolate, coffee-coloured etc. n.; fuscous, sub-fusc; brown as a berry, brown as mahogany.

Vb. *embrown*, brown, bronze, tan, sunburn; singe, char, toast 381 *burn*.

See: 381.

431 Redness

N. *redness*, rubescence, blush, flush, hectic f.; fireglow, sunset, dawn 417 *glow*; rubefaction, reddening, warmth; rosiness, ruddiness, bloom, red cheeks, apple c., cherry lips; high colour, floridness, rubicundity; red colour, crimson, scarlet, red etc. adj.; carnation, rose, geranium, poppy; cherry, tomato; burgundy, port, claret; gore 335 *blood*; ruby, garnet, cornelian; flame 379 *fire*; red ink, rubric; red planet, Mars; redbreast, robin r.; redskin, Red Indian; redhead, gingernob.

red pigment, red dye, murex, cochineal, carmine, kermes; dragon's blood; cinnabar, vermilion; ruddle, madder, rose m.; alizarin, crimson lake, Venetian red, rosaniline, solferino; red ochre, red lead, minium; rouge, lipstick 843 *cosmetic*.

Adj. *red*, reddish; ruddy, rubicund, sanguine, florid, blowzy; warm, hot, fiery, glowing, red-hot 379 *hot*; flushed, fevered; erubescent, rubescent, flushing, blushing; red-cheeked, rosy-c.; bright red, red as a lobster, red as a beetroot; red-haired, ginger-h.; carroty, sandy, auburn, titian-red, flame-coloured; rufous, rufescent; russet, rusty, rust-coloured, ferruginous, rubiginous 430 *brown*; pink, rose-p., roseate, rosy, rose-coloured, peach-c., flesh-c., flesh-pink, shell-p., salmon-p., shocking-p.; coral, carnation, damask, crushed strawberry; crimson, cherry-red, cerise, carmine, cramoisy; Tyrian purple, fuchsine, fuchsia, magenta, maroon 436 *purple*; wine-coloured, wine-dark; oxblood, sang-de-boeuf; sanguine, murrey, gules; scarlet, cardinal-red, vermilion, vermeil, pillarbox red, Turkey r.; dyed red, reddened, rouged, painted.

bloodstained, bloodshot; blood-red; sanguine; sanguinary, ensanguined, incarnadine, bloody, gory.

Vb. *redden*, rubefy, rubricate, miniate; rouge, raddle 843 *primp*; incarnadine, dye red, stain with blood; flush, blush, glow; mantle, colour, colour up, crimson, go red.

See: 335, 379, 417, 430, 436, 843.

432 Orange

N. *orange*, red and yellow, gold, old gold; or, tenné; copper, amber; sunflower, marigold; apricot, tangerine; marmalade; ochre, Mars orange, cadmium o., henna.

Adj. *orange*, apricot etc. n.; ochreous, luteous, cupreous, coppery, ginger, tan; orangeish, orangey, orange-coloured, flame-c., copper-c., brass-c., brassy.

433 Yellowness

N. *yellowness*, yellow, sunshine y. etc. adj.; brass, gold, old gold, topaz, amber, old ivory; sulphur, brimstone; buttercup, daffodil, primrose, dandelion; lemon, honey; saffron, mustard; biliousness, jaundice, yellow fever; sallow skin, fair hair; blonde, ash b., platinum b., strawberry b.

yellow pigment, gamboge, cadmium yellow, chrome y., Indian y., Naples y., lemon y., orpiment; yellow ochre, massicot, weld, luteolin, xanthin.

Adj. *yellow*, gold, amber etc. n.; tawny, fulvous, sandy; fair-haired, golden-h. 427 *whitish*; creamy, cream-coloured, buff-c.; honey-c., straw-c., fallow; pale yellow, acid y., lemon y.; primrose y., jasmine, citrine, chartreuse, champagne; canary yellow, sunshine y., sulphur y., mustard y.; golden, aureate, gilt, gilded; deep yellow, luteous; yellowy, yellowish, flavescent, xanthic; sallow, jaundiced, bilious; yellow as parchment, yellow as butter.

Vb. *gild*, yellow.

See: 427.

434 Greenness

N. *greenness*, green etc. adj.; verdancy, greenery, greenwood; verdure, viridity, viridescence; grass, moss, turf, green leaf 366 *foliage*; lime, greengage; jade, emerald, malachite, beryl, aquamarine, olivine, chrysoprase, verd antique; verdigris, patina; celadon, reseda, mignonette; Lincoln green; loden; vert.

green pigment, terre verte, viridian, verditer, bice, green bice, Paris green; chlorophyll.

Adj. *green*, viridescent, verdant; verdurous,

grassy, leafy; grass-green, leaf-g., moss-g.; emerald, sea-green 435 *blue*; jade green, sap g., bottle g.; sage g., willow g.; pea g., apple g., lime g., chartreuse; eau-de-Nil, avocado, olive, olive-green, olivaceous; glaucous, greenish, virescent; vert.

See: 366, 435.

435 Blueness

N. *blueness*, blue, cyan, azure; blue sky, blue sea; sapphire, aquamarine, turquoise, lapis lazuli; bluebell, cornflower, forget-me-not; gentian blue etc. adj.; bluishness, cyanosis; lividness, lividity.

blue pigment, blue dye, bice, indigo, woad; Prussian blue, French b., ultramarine, cobalt, cobalt blue, zaffre, smalt; blue-bag.

Adj. *blue*, cyanic, azure, azury; cerulean, sky-blue; duck-egg blue, eggshell b., turquoise; light blue, pale blue, ice-b., powder-b., Cambridge-b.; air-force b., Saxe-b., slate-b., steel-b., electric-b.; sapphire, aquamarine, peacock-blue, kingfisher-b., royal-b., ultramarine, deep blue, dark b., Oxford-b., midnight-b., navy-b., navy; indigo, perse; hyacinthine, blue-black, black and blue, livid; cold, steely, bluish, blue with cold.

Vb. *blue*, turn blue; dye blue, woad.

436 Purpleness

N. *purpleness*, purple, blue and red; imperial purple; amethyst; lavender, violet, heliotrope, heather, foxglove; plum, damson, aubergine; Tyrian purple, gentian violet; amaranth, lilac, mauve; purpure.

Adj. *purple*, plum etc. n.; purplish, purpled; violet, violaceous, mauve, lavender, lilac; purple-red, fuchsia, magenta, plum-coloured, puce; hyacinthine, heliotrope; dark purple, mulberry, murrey; livid, purple with rage; black and blue 435 *blue*.

Vb. *empurple*, purple.

See: 435.

437 Variegation

N. *variegation*, variety, diversification, diversity 15 *difference*; dancing light, glancing l. 417 *light*; play of colour, shot colours, iridescence, irisation; tiger's eye, opal, nacre, mother-of-pearl; shot silk, moire, pigeon's neck, gorge-de-pigeon; dichromatism, trichromatism; dichroism, trichroism, tricolour, polychromy 425 *colour*; peacock, peacock's tail, peacock butterfly, tortoiseshell, chameleon; Joseph's coat, motley, harlequin, patchwork; mixture of colour, medley of c., riot of c.; enamelwork, enamelling; stained glass, kaleidoscope; rainbow, rainbow effect, band of colour, spectrum, prism.

chequer, check, hound's tooth, pepper-and-salt; plaid, tartan; chessboard; marquetry, parquetry, inlay, inlaid work 844 *ornamental art*; mosaic, tessellation, tesserae, crazy paving 43 *medley*.

stripe, stria, striation; line, streak, band, bar; agate; zebra, tiger; streakiness, mackerel sky; crack, craze, crackle; reticulation 222 *network*.

maculation, mottle, dappling, stippling, marbling; spottiness, patchiness 17 *nonuniformity*; patch, speck, speckle, macula, spots, pockmarks, freckle, foxing 845 *blemish*; fleck, dot, polka d.; blotch, splotch, splodge, splash; leopard, Dalmatian.

Adj. *variegated*, fretted etc. vb.; diversified, daedal; patterned, embroidered, worked 844 *ornamental*; polychromatic, colourful 425 *florid*; bicolour, tricolour; dichroic, dichromatic, trichromatic, trichroic; many-hued, many-coloured, multi-c., parti-c., motley, patched, random, crazy, of all colours; kaleidoscopic 82 *multiform*; plaid, tartan; rainbow-coloured, rainbow, iridal, iridian; prismatic, spectral; mosaic, tessellated, parquet; paned, panelled.

iridescent, irisated, versicolour, chameleon; nacreous, mother-of-pearl; opalescent, opaline, pearly 424 *semitransparent*; shot, shot through with, gorge-de-pigeon, pavonine, moiré, watered, chatoyant, cymophanous.

pied, parti-coloured, black-and-white, pepper-and-salt, grizzled, piebald, skewbald, roan, pinto, chequered, check, dappled, patchy.

mottled, marbled, jaspered, veined, reticulated; studded, maculose, spotted, spotty, patchy; speckled, speckledy, freckled; streaky, streaked, striated, lined, barred, banded, striped 222 *crossed*; brindled, tabby; pocked, pockmarked 845 *blemished*; cloudy, powdered, dusted, dusty.

Vb. *variegate*, diversify, fret, pattern; punctuate; chequer, check, counterchange; patch 656 *repair*; embroider, work 844 *decorate*; braid, quilt; damascene, inlay, tessellate, tile; stud, pepper, dot with, mottle, speckle, freckle, spangle, spot; sprinkle, powder, dust; tattoo, stipple, dapple; streak, stripe, striate; craze, crack 330 *be brittle*; marble, vein, cloud 423 *make opaque*; stain, blot, discolour 649 *make unclean*; make iridescent, irisate; interchange colour, play.

See: 15, **17**, 43, 82, 222, 330, 417, 423, 424, **425**, 649, 656, 844, 845.

438 Vision

N. *vision*, sight, power of s., light-grasp; eyesight; seeing, visualization, mind's eye 513 *imagination*; perception, recognition; acuity (of vision), good sight, keen s., sharp s., long s., far s., normal s.; defective vision, short sight 440 *dim sight*; second sight 984 *occultism*; type of vision, double vision, stereoscopic v., binocular v.; aided vision, magnification; tired vision, winking, blinking; eye-testing, sight-t.; oculist, optician, ophthalmologist 417 *optics*; dream 440 *visual fallacy*.

eye, visual organ, organ of vision, eyeball, iris, pupil, white, cornea, retina, optic nerve; optics, orbs, sparklers, peepers, weepers; windows of the soul; saucer eyes, goggle e.; eyelashes, eyelid 421 *screen*; lashes, sweeping l.; naked eye, unaided e.; clear eye, sharp e., piercing e., penetrating e., gimlet e., X-ray e.; weak eyes 440 *dim sight*; dull eye, glass e. 439 *blindness*; evil eye 983 *sorcery*; hawk, eagle, cat, lynx; Argus; basilisk, cockatrice, Gorgon.

look, regard, glance, side g., squint; tail *or* corner of the eye; glint, blink, flash; penetrating glance, gaze, steady g.; observation, contemplation, watch; stare, fixed s.; come-hither look, glad eye, sheep's eyes, ogle, leer 889 *wooing*; wink 524 *hint*; grimace, dirty look, scowl, evil eye; peep, peek, glimpse, rapid g., half an eye.

inspection, ocular i., ocular demonstration 443 *visibility*; examination, visual e., autopsy 459 *enquiry*; view, preview 522 *manifestation*; oversight, supervision 689 *management*; survey, overview; sweep, reconnaissance, reconnoitre, recce, tour of inspection; sight-seeing, rubbernecking; look, butcher's, lookaround, look-see, dekko, once-over, coup d'oeil, rapid survey, rapid glance; second glance, double take; review, revision; viewing, home v. 445 *cinema*, 531 *broadcasting*; discernment, catching sight, espial, view, first v., first sight; looking round, observation, prying, spying; espionage; peeping, scopophilia, voyeurism, peeping Tom.

view, full v., eyeful; vista, prospect, outlook, perspective; aspect 445 *appearance*; panorama, bird's-eye view, commanding v., unimpeded v.; horizon, false h.; line of sight, line of vision; range of view, purview, ken; field of view, amphitheatre; scene, setting, stage 594 *theatre*; angle of vision, slant, point of view, viewpoint, standpoint; observation point, vantage p., lookout, crow's nest, watchtower 209 *high structure*; belvedere, gazebo; camera obscura; astrodome, conning tower; observatory, observation balloon; stand, grandstand, stall, ringside seat 441 *onlookers*; loophole, peephole, hagioscope 263 *window*.

Adj. *seeing*, glimpsing etc. vb.; visual, perceptible 443 *visible*; panoramic, perspectival; ocular, ophthalmic; optical; stereoscopic, binocular; orthoptic, perspicacious, clear-sighted, sharp-s., sharp-eyed, keen-e., gimlet-e., eagle-e., hawk-e., lynx-e.; vigilant, all eyes, Argus-eyed; second-sighted, visionary 513 *imaginative*.

Vb. *see*, behold, visualize, use one's eyes; see truly, keep in perspective; perceive, discern, distinguish, make out, pick o., recognize, ken 490 *know*; take in, see at a glance 498 *be wise*; descry, discover 484 *detect*; sight, espy, spy, spot, observe 455 *notice*; lay eyes on, clap eyes on, catch sight of, sight, raise land; catch a glimpse of, glimpse; view, command a view of, hold in view, have in sight; see with one's own eyes, witness, look on, be a spectator 441 *watch*; dream, see visions, see things 513 *imagine*; see in the dark, have second sight 510 *foresee*; become visible 443 *be visible*.

gaze, regard, quiz, gaze at, look, look at; look full in the face, look in the eyes; look intently, eye, stare, peer; stare at, stare hard, goggle, gape, gawk, gawp; focus, rivet one's eyes, fix one's gaze; glare, glower, look daggers, look black 891 *be angry*; glance, glance at; squint, look askance, look down one's nose; wink, blink 524 *hint*; make eyes at, give the glad eye, ogle, leer 889 *court*; feast one's eyes on, gloat over 824 *be pleased*; steal a glance, peep, peek, take a peep; direct one's gaze, cock one's eye, cast one's eyes on, bend one's looks on, turn one's eyes on; notice, take n., look upon 455 *be attentive*; lift up one's eyes, look up; look down, look round, look in front; look ahead 858 *be cautious*; look away, drop one's eyes, avert the e. 439 *be blind*; look at each other, exchange glances, make eye contact.

scan, scrutinize, inspect, examine, take stock of, look one up and down; contemplate, pore, pore over 536 *study*; look over, look through, read t., riffle t., leaf t., skim t.; have *or* take a look at, have a dekko, have a butcher's, take a gander *or* a squint at, run one's eye over; see, go and see, take in, sight-see, rubberneck; make a pilgrimage, go to see 882 *visit*; view, survey, sweep, reconnoitre; scout, spy out the land; peep, peek 453 *be curious*; spy, pry, snoop; observe, keep under observation, watch 457 *invigilate*; hold in view, keep in sight; watch out for, look out f. 507 *await*; keep watch, look out, keep an eye out for, keep a weather eye open for, keep looking, keep one's eyes skinned *or* peeled; strain one's eyes, peer; squint at, squinny; crane, crane one's neck, stand on tiptoe.

Adv. *at sight*, at first sight, at the first blush, prima facie; in view 443 *visibly*; in sight of; with one's eyes open.

Int. look! view halloo! land ahoy!

See: 209, 263, 417, 421, 439, 440, **441**, **443**, **445**, 453, 455, 457, 459, 484, 490, 498, 507, 510, 513, 522, 524, 531, 536, 594, 689, 824, 858, 882, 889, 891, 983, 984.

439 Blindness

N. *blindness*, lack of vision; lack of light 418 *darkness*; unawareness 491 *ignorance*; sightlessness, eyelessness; eye disease, amaurosis, amblyopia, glaucoma, river blindness, cataract; night blindness, snow b., colour b.; dim-sightedness 440 *dim sight*; blind side, blind spot 444 *invisibility*; tunnel vision; blind eye 456 *inattention*; word blindness, dyslexia; glass eye, artificial e.; blind man *or* woman, the blind; sandman 679 *sleep*; aid for the blind, Braille, talking book; white stick, guide dog.

Adj. *blind*, sightless, eyeless, visionless, dark; unseeing, undiscerning, unperceiving, unnoticing, unobserving 456 *inattentive*; blinded, blindfold, blinkered; in the dark, benighted; cataractous, glaucomatous, amaurotic 440 *dim-sighted*; stone-blind, gravel-blind, sand-blind; blind as a mole, blind as a bat, blind as an owl, blind as a beetle.

Vb. *be blind*, not use one's eyes; go blind, lose one's sight, lose one's eyes; not see; lose sight of; grope in the dark, feel one's way 461 *be tentative*; have the eyes bandaged, wear blinkers; be blind to 491 *not know*; ignore, have a blind spot, not see for looking, not see what is under one's nose; not see the wood for the trees; not look, shut the eyes to, avert the eyes, turn away the e., look the other way 458 *disregard*; not bear the light, blink, wink, squint 440 *be dim-sighted*.

blind, render b., deprive of sight; put one's eyes out, gouge one's eyes o.; dazzle, daze; darken, obscure, eclipse 419 *bedim*; screen from sight; blinker, blindfold, bandage 421 *screen*; hoodwink, bluff, throw dust in one's eyes 495 *mislead*.

See: 418, 419, 421, **440**, 444, 456, 458, 461, 491, 495, 679.

440 Dim-sightedness: imperfect vision

N. *dim sight*, weak s., failing s., dim-sightedness, dull-sightedness; near-blindness, purblindness 439 *blindness*; half-vision, partial v., blurred v., imperfect v., defective v.; weak eyes, eyestrain, bleariness; amblyopia, half-sight, short s., near s., near-sightedness, myopia; presbyopia, long sight, far s.; double sight, double vision, confusion of v.; astigmatism, cataract, film; glaucoma, iridization; scotoma, dizziness, swimming; colour-blindness, daltonism, dichromatism; snow-blindness, day-blindness; night-blindness, nyctalopia, moon-blindness; ophthalmia, ophthalmitis; conjunctivitis, pink eye; obliquity of vision, cast; convergent vision, strabismus, squint, cross-eye; wall-eye, cock-e., swivel e.; miosis; wink, blink, nictitation, nystagmus; obstructed vision, eyeshade, blinker, veil, curtain 421 *screen*; blind side, blind spot 444 *invisibility*.

visual fallacy, anamorphosis 246 *distortion*; refraction 417 *reflection*; aberration of light 282 *deviation*; false light 552 *misrepresentation*; illusion, optical i., trick of light, trick of the eyesight, phantasm, phantasmagoria, spectre of the Brocken, fata morgana, mirage 542 *deception*; ignis fatuus, will-o'-the-wisp 420 *glow-worm*; phantom, spectre, wraith, apparition 970 *ghost*; vision, dream 513 *fantasy*; distorting mirror, magic m., magic lantern 442 *optical device*.

Adj. *dim-sighted*, purblind, half-blind, gravel-b., dark; weak-eyed, bespectacled; myopic, short-sighted, near-s.; presbyopic, long-sighted, astigmatic; colour-blind, dichromatic; dim-eyed, one-e., monocular; wall-eyed, squinting; strabismal, strabismic, cross-eyed; boss-eyed, cock-e., swivel-e., goggle-e., bug-e. 845 *blemished*; miotic, nystagmic; bleary-eyed, blinking, dazzled, dazed; blinded, temporarily b. 439 *blind*; swimming, dizzy; amaurotic, cataractous, glaucomatous.

Vb. *be dim-sighted*, - myopic etc. adj.; not see well, need spectacles, change one's glasses; have a mist before the eyes, have a film over the e., get something in one's e.; grope, peer, screw up the eyes, squint; blink, bat the eyelid; wink, nictitate; see double, grow dazzled, dazzle, swim; grow blurred, dim, fail; see through a glass darkly.

blur, render indistinct, confuse; glare, dazzle, bedazzle, daze 417 *shine*; darken, dim, mist, fog, smoke, smudge 419 *bedim*; be indistinct, loom 419 *be dim*.

See: 246, 282, 417, **419**, 420, 421, **439**, 442, 444, 513, 542, 552, 845, 970.

441 Spectator

N. *spectator*, beholder; seer, mystic 513 *visionary*; looker, viewer, observer, watcher; inspector, examiner, scrutator, scrutinizer 690 *manager*; waiter, attendant 742 *servant*; witness, eyewitness; passerby, bystander, onlooker; looker-on, gazer, starer, gaper, goggler; eyer, ogler, voyeur, scopophiliac, peeping Tom; window shopper; sightseer, rubberneck, tourist, globetrotter 268 *traveller*; stargazer, astronomer; bird watcher, train spotter, lookout 484 *detector*; watchman, night-w., watch, sentinel, sentry 664 *warner*; patrolman, patrol 314 *circler*; scout, spy, snoop 459 *detective*; filmgoer, cinemagoer 445 *cinema*; theatregoer 594 *playgoer*; televiewer, viewer, TV addict, square-eyes; captive audience.

onlookers, audience, auditorium, sea of faces; box office, gate; house, gallery, gods, circle, dress c., pit, stalls; grandstand, terraces, the Kop; crowd, supporters, followers, aficionados, fans 707 *patron*, 504 *enthusiast*.

Vb. *watch*, spectate, look on, look at, look in, view 438 *see*; witness 189 *be present*; follow, follow with the eyes, observe, attend 455 *be attentive*; eye, ogle, quiz; gape, gawk, stare; spy, spy out, scout, scout out 438 *scan*.

See: 189, 268, 314, **438**, 445, 455, 459, 484, 504, 513, 594, 664, 690, 707, 742.

442 Optical instrument

N. *optical device*, optical instrument; glass, crystal 422 *transparency*; optic, lens, meniscus, achromatic lens, chromatic l., astigmatic l., anastigmatic l., bifocal l.; telephoto l., zoom l., wide-angle l., fisheye l.; eyepiece, ocular, objective; sunglass, burning glass; optometer, ophthalmoscope, skiascope, retinoscope 417 *optics*; helioscope, coronagraph; prism, spectroscope, spectrometer, diffraction grating, polariscope; kaleidoscope; stroboscope; thaumatrope; stereoscope, stereopticon; photometer, light meter, exposure m., actinometer, radiometer; visual display unit, VDU 86 *data processing*; projector, slide *or* film p., overhead p., epidiascope, episcope, magic lantern 445 *cinema*; microfilm reader, slide viewer 551 *photography*.

eyeglass, spectacles, specs, goggles, giglamps; glasses, reading g., steel-rimmed g., horn-rimmed g., pince-nez, sunglasses, dark glasses, Polaroid (tdmk) g., photochromic g., bifocal g., bifocals; thick glasses, pebble g.; contact lens; lorgnette, monocle; magnifying glass, hand lens, loupe; oculist, optician, ophthalmologist; optometrist, optometry.

telescope, refractor, reflector; terrestrial telescope, achromatic t., inverting t., condé t., astronomical t. 321 *astronomy*; collimator; sight, finder, viewfinder, rangefinder; periscope; spyglass, night glass; binoculars, prism b., field glasses, opera g.

microscope, electron m., photomicroscope, ultramicroscope 196 *microscopy*.

mirror, reflector; metal mirror, distorting m., concave m., speculum; rear-view mirror, wing m.; glass, looking g., pier g., cheval g., full-length mirror, hand m.

camera, camera lucida, camera obscura, spectrograph 321 *astronomy*; pin-hole camera, box c., single-lens reflex c., slr, twin-l.r.c.; hand-held c., cinecamera, television camera, videopack, ENG; electric eye, closed-circuit television 484 *detector*; shutter, aperture, stop; flashgun 420 *lamp*; film 551 *photography*.

See: 86, 196, **321**, 417, 420, 422, **445**, 484, **551**.

443 Visibility

N. *visibility*, perceptibility, observability; visuality, presence to the eyes 445 *appearance*; apparency, sight, exposure; distinctness, clearness, clarity, definition, conspicuity, conspicuousness, prominence; eyewitness, ocular proof, visible evidence, object lesson 522 *manifestation*; visual aid 534 *teaching*; scene, field of view 438 *view*; atmospheric visibility, seeing, high visibility, low v.; limit of visibility, ceiling, horizon, visible distance, eyeshot 183 *range*; landmark, seamark 547 *signpost*.

Adj. *visible*, seeable, viewable; perceptible, perceivable, discernible, observable, detectable; noticeable, remarkable; recognizable, unmistakable, palpable; symptomatic 547 *indicating*; apparent 445 *appearing*; evident, showing 522 *manifest*; exposed, open, naked, outcropping, exposed to view, open to v.; sighted, in view, in full v.; before one's eyes, under one's nose 189 *on the spot*; visible to the naked eye, macroscopic; telescopic, just visible, at the limit of vision; panoramic, stereoscopic, periscopic.

obvious, showing, for all to see 522 *shown*; plain, clear, clear-cut, crystal-clear, as clear as day; definite, well-defined, well-marked; distinct, unblurred, in focus; unclouded, undisguised, uncovered, unhidden; spectacular, conspicuous, pointed, prominent, salient; eye-catching, striking, shining 417 *luminous*; glaring, staring; pronounced, in bold relief, in strong r., in high r., highlighted, spotlit; visualized, vivid, eidetic; under one's nose, staring one in the face, plain to see, plain as plain, plain as a pikestaff, plain as the nose on your face.

Vb. *be visible*, become visible, be seen, -obvious etc. adj.; show, show through, shine t. 422 *be transparent*; speak for itself, attract attention, leap to the eye 455 *attract notice*; meet the eye; hit, strike, catch the eye, stand out, act as a landmark; come to light, dawn upon; loom, heave in sight, come into view, show its face 445 *appear*; pop up, crop up, turn up, show up 295 *arrive*; spring up, start up, arise 68 *begin*; surface, break s. 308 *ascend*; emanate, come out, creep out 298 *emerge*; stick out, project 254 *jut*; show, materialize, develop; manifest itself, expose i., betray i. 522 *be plain*; symptomize 547 *indicate*; come on the stage, make one's entry 297 *enter*; come forward, stand f., advance; fill the eyes, dazzle, glare; shine forth, break through the clouds 417 *shine*; have no secrets, live in the public eye; remain visible, stay in sight, float before one's eyes; make visible, expose 522 *manifest*.

Adv. *visibly*, clearly etc. adj.; in sight of, before one's eyes, within eyeshot; on show, on view.

See: 68, 183, 189, 254, 295, 297, 298, 308, 417, 422, **438**, **445**, 455, **522**, 534, 547.

444 Invisibility

N. *invisibility*, nonappearance 190 *absence*; vanishing 446 *disappearance*; imperceptibility, indistinctness, vagueness, indefiniteness; poor visibility, obscurity 419 *dimness*; remoteness, distance 199 *farness*; littleness, smallness 196 *minuteness*; sequestration, privacy 883 *seclusion*; submergence 523 *latency*; disguisement, hiding 525 *concealment*; mystification, mystery 525 *secrecy*; smoke screen, mist, fog, veil, curtain 421 *obfuscation*; blind spot, blind eye 439 *blindness*; blind corner 663 *pitfall*; hidden menace 661 *danger*; impermeability, blank wall 423 *opacity*; black light 417 *radiation*.

Adj. *invisible*, imperceptible, unapparent, unnoticeable, indiscernible; indistinguishable, unrecognizable; unseen, unsighted; viewless, sightless; unnoticed, unregarded 458 *neglected*; out of sight, out of eyeshot 446 *disappearing*; not in sight, remote 199 *distant*; sequestered 883 *secluded*; hidden, lurking 523 *latent*; disguised, camouflaged 525 *concealed*; shadowy, dark, secret, mysterious 421 *screened*; obscured, eclipsed, darkened, dark 418 *unlit*.

indistinct, partly-seen, half-s.; unclear, ill-defined, ill-marked, undefined, indefinite, indistinct 419 *dim*; faint, inconspicuous, microscopic 196 *minute*; confused, vague, blurred, blurry, out of focus; fuzzy, misty, hazy 424 *semitransparent*.

Vb. *be unseen*, lie out of sight; hide, go to earth, lie in ambush 523 *lurk*; escape notice, blush unseen 872 *be humble*;

become invisible, pale, fade, die 419 *be dim*; move out of sight, be lost to view, vanish 446 *disappear*; make invisible, hide away, submerge 525 *conceal*; veil 421 *screen*; darken, eclipse 419 *bedim*.

Adv. *invisibly*, silently 525 *stealthily*; behind the scenes; in the dark.

See: 190, 196, 199, 417, 418, **419**, 421, 423, 424, 439, **446**, 458, **523**, **525**, 661, 663, 872, 883.

445 Appearance

N. *appearance*, phenomenon; apparency 443 *visibility*; first appearance, rise, arising 68 *beginning*; becoming, realization, materialization, embodiment, presence 1 *existence*; showing, exhibition, display, view, preview, demonstration 522 *manifestation*; shadowing forth 511 *prediction*, 471 *probability*; revelation 484 *discovery*; externals, outside, superficies 223 *exteriority*; appearances, look of things; visual impact, face value, first blush; impression, effect; image, pose, front, public face 541 *duplicity*; veneer, show, seeming, semblance; side, aspect, facet; phase, guise, garb 228 *dressing*; colour, light, outline, shape, dimension 243 *form*; set, hang, look; respect, light, angle, slant, point *or* angle of view 438 *view*; a manifestation, emanation, theophany; vision 513 *fantasy*; false appearance, mirage, hallucination, illusion 440 *visual fallacy*; apparition, phantasm, spectre 970 *ghost*; reflection, image, mirror i. 18 *similarity*; mental image, afterimage; likeness 551 *representation*; visual 551 *image*.

spectacle, impressiveness, effectiveness, impression, effect; speciousness, meretriciousness, decoration 844 *ornamentation*; feast for the eyes, eyeful, vision, sight, scene; scenery, landscape, seascape, cloudscape, townscape; panorama, bird's-eye view 438 *view*; display, lavish d., pageantry, pageant, parade, review 875 *ostentation*; revue, extravaganza, pantomime, floor show 594 *stage show*; television, video 531 *broadcasting*; illuminations, son et lumière; pyrotechnics 420 *fireworks*; presentation, show, exhibition, exposition 522 *exhibit*; art exhibition 553 *picture*; visual entertainment, peep show, slide s., film s., picture s., home movies; phantasmagoria, kaleidoscope 437 *variegation*; panorama, diorama, cyclorama; staging, tableau, transformation scene; set, decor, setting, backcloth, background 594 *stage set*.

cinema, cinematography; screen, big s., silver s., Hollywood, film industry; film studio, film production, film-making, shooting 551 *photography*; direction, continuity, cutting, montage, projection; photoplay, screenplay, scenario, script, shooting s.; credits, titles; special effects, animation; voiceover, sound effects, soundtrack; cinematograph, projector 442 *optical device*; picture house, picture palace, circuit cinema, drive-in c., nickelodeon, bioscope, cinematheque, flea pit 594 *theatre*; film director, film star 594 *actor*; filmgoer, cineast 504 *enthusiast*.

film, films, pictures, motion p., moving p., movies, flicks, celluloid; Technicolor (tdmk), 3-D, Cinerama (tdmk), Cinemascope (tdmk); silent film, sound f., talkie; X certificate, A c., AA c., U c.; big picture, B p., supporting film, short, newsreel, trailer; cartoon, animated c., travelogue, documentary, feature film, cinéma vérité; art film, new wave, nouvelle vague; epic, blockbuster, extravaganza, musical, box-office movie, low-budget m.; weepie, creepie, thriller, spine-chiller, cliffhanger, war film, horror f., Hammer (tdmk) pic.; blue movie, skinflick; biopic; Western, spaghetti w., horse opera, cop o., space o.; oldie, remake; rush, preview; general release.

mien, look, face; play of features, expression; brow, countenance, looks; complexion, colour, cast; air, demeanour, carriage, bearing, deportment, poise, presence; gesture, posture, behaviour 688 *conduct*.

feature, trait, mark, lineament; lines, cut, shape, fashion, figure 243 *form*; outline, contour, relief, elevation, profile, silhouette; visage, physiognomy, cut of one's jib 237 *face*.

Adj. *appearing*, apparent, phenomenal; seeming, specious, ostensible; deceptive 542 *deceiving*; outward, external, superficial 223 *exterior*; salient, outcropping, showing, on view 443 *visible*; visual, video-; open to view, exhibited, hung 522 *shown*; impressive, effective, spectacular 875 *showy*; decorative, meretricious 844 *ornamental*; showing itself, revealed, theophanic 522 *manifest*; visionary, dreamlike 513 *imaginary*.

Vb. *appear*, show, show through 443 *be*

visible; seem, look so 18 *resemble*; have the look of, wear the look of, present the appearance of, exhibit the form of, assume the guise of, take the shape of; figure in, display oneself, cut a figure 875 *be ostentatious*; be on show, be on exhibition; appear on television, star in; exhibit 522 *manifest*; start, rise, arise; dawn, break 68 *begin*; eventuate 154 *happen*; materialize, pop up 295 *arrive*; walk 970 *haunt*.

Adv. *apparently*, manifestly, distinctly 443 *visibly*; ostensibly, seemingly, to all appearances, as it seems, to the eye, at first sight, at first blush; on the face of it; to the view, in the eyes of; on view, on show, on exhibition.

See: 1, 3, 18, 68, 154, 223, 228, 237, 243, 295, 420, 437, **438**, **440**, 442, **443**, 471, 484, 504, 511, 513, **522**, 531, 541, **542**, **551**, 553, 594, 688, 844, 875, 970.

446 Disappearance

N. *disappearance*, loss, vanishing; disappearing trick, vanishing t. 542 *sleight*; flight 667 *escape*; exit 296 *departure*; evanescence, evaporation 338 *vaporization*; dematerialization, dissipation, dissolution 51 *decomposition*; extinction 2 *nonexistence*; occultation, eclipse 418 *obscuration*; dissolving views, fadeout; vanishing point, thin air 444 *invisibility*.

Adj. *disappearing*, vanishing; evanescent 114 *transient*; dissipated, dispersed; missing, vanished 190 *absent*; lost, lost to sight, lost to view 444 *invisible*; gone to earth 525 *concealed*; gone 2 *extinct*.

Vb. *disappear*, vanish, do the vanishing trick; dematerialize, melt into thin air; evanesce, evaporate 338 *vaporize*; dissolve, melt, melt away 337 *liquefy*; wear away, wear off, dwindle, dwindle to vanishing point 37 *decrease*; fade, fade out, pale 426 *lose colour*; fade away 114 *be transient*; be occulted, suffer an eclipse 419 *be dim*; disperse, dissipate, diffuse, scatter 75 *be dispersed*; absent oneself, fail to appear, play truant 190 *be absent*; go, be gone, depart 296 *decamp*; run away, get a. 667 *escape*; hide, lie low, be in hiding 523 *lurk*; cover one's tracks, leave no trace 525 *conceal*; sink from view, be lost to sight 444 *be unseen*; retire from view, seclude oneself 883 *seclude*; become extinct 2 *pass away*; make disappear, erase, dispel 550 *obliterate*.

See: 2, 37, 51, 75, 114, 190, 296, 337, 338, 418, 419, 426, **444**, 523, 525, 542, 550, 667, 883.

Class four

Intellect: *the exercise of the mind*

4.1 Formation of ideas

Section one: General

447 Intellect

N. *intellect*, mind, psyche, mentality; affect 817 *affections*; conation 595 *will*; understanding, intellection, conception; thinking principle, intellectual faculty, cogitative f.; rationality, reasoning power; reason, discursive r., association of ideas 475 *reasoning*; philosophy 449 *thought*; awareness, sense, consciousness, self-c., stream of c. 455 *attention*; cognition, perception, apperception, percipience, insight; extrasensory perception, instinct 476 *intuition*; flair, judgment 463 *discrimination*; intellectualism, intellectuality; mental capacity, brains, wits, senses, sense, grey matter 498 *intelligence*; great intellect, genius; mental evolution, psychogenesis; seat of thought, organ of t., brain, cerebrum, cerebellum, cortex 213 *head*; electroencephalograph; alpha waves; sensorium 818 *feeling*; healthy mind 502 *sanity*; diseased mind 503 *psychopathy*; mind over matter 984 *occultism*.

spirit, soul, geist, mind, inner m., inner sense; heart, heart's core, breast, bosom, inner man 5 *essential part*; double, ka, ba, genius 80 *self*; psyche, pneuma, id, ego, superego, animus, anima, self, subliminal s., the unconscious, the subconscious; personality, dual p., multiple p., split p. 503 *psychopathy*; spiritualism, spiritism, psychomancy, psychical research 984 *occultism*; spiritualist, occultist.

psychology, science of mind, metapsychology; parapsychology 984 *psychics*; abnormal psychology 503 *psychopathy*; Freudian psychology, Jungian p., Adlerian p.; Gestalt psychology, configuration theory; behaviourism; crowd psychology; personality testing, psychometry 459 *enquiry*; psychopathology, psychiatry, antipsychiatry, psychotherapy, psychoanalysis 658 *therapy*; psychosurgery 658 *surgery*; psychophysiology, psychobiology, psychophysics.

psychologist, psychoanalyst, psychiatrist, psychotherapist 658 *doctor*; head shrinker, shrink, trick cyclist.

Adj. *mental*, thinking, endowed with reason, reasoning 475 *rational*; cerebral, intellective, intellectual, conceptive, noological, noetic, conceptual, abstract; theoretical 512 *suppositional*; unconcrete 320 *immaterial*; perceptual, percipient, perceptive; cognitive, cognizant 490 *knowing*; conscious, self-c., subjective.

psychic, psychological; psychogenic, psychosomatic; subconscious, subliminal; spiritualistic, mediumistic, psychomantic 984 *psychical*; spiritual, otherworldly 320 *immaterial*.

Vb. *cognize*, perceive, apperceive 490 *know*; realize, sense, become aware of, become conscious of; objectify 223 *externalize*; note 438 *see*; advert, mark 455 *notice*; ratiocinate 475 *reason*; use one's head, understand 498 *be wise*; conceptualize, intellectualize 449 *think*; conceive, invent 484 *discover*; ideate 513 *imagine*; appreciate 480 *estimate*.

See: 5, 80, 213, 223, 320, 438, **449**, 455, 459, 463, **475**, 476, 480, 484, 490, 498, 502, 503, 512, 513, 595, 658, 817, 818, **984**.

448 Absence of intellect

N. *absence of intellect*, unintelligence; brute creation 365 *animality*; vegetation 366 *vegetable life*; inanimate nature, stocks and stones; instinct, brute i. 476 *intuition*;

unreason, vacuity, brainlessness, mindlessness 450 *absence of thought*; brain damage, disordered intellect, unsound mind 503 *insanity*.

Adj. *mindless*, unintelligent; animal, vegetable; mineral, inanimate 359 *inorganic*; unreasoning 450 *unthinking*; instinctive, brute 476 *intuitive*; unoriginal, uninventive, unidea'd 20 *imitative*; brainless, empty-headed 499 *foolish*; moronic, wanting 503 *insane*.

See: 20, 359, 365, 366, **450**, **476**, 499, 503.

449 Thought

N. *thought*, mental process, thinking; mental act, ideation; intellectual exercise, mental e., mental action, mentation, cogitation 447 *intellect*; cerebration, lucubration, headwork, thinking cap; brainwork, brainfag; hard thinking, hard thought, concentrated t., concentration 455 *attention*; deep thought, profound t., depth of t., profundity 498 *wisdom*; abstract thought, imageless t.; conceptual thinking, thoughts, ideas 451 *idea*; conception, ideation, workings of the mind, inmost thoughts 513 *ideality*; flow of ideas, current of thought, train of t.; association of ideas, reason 475 *reasoning*; brown study, reverie, musing, wandering thoughts 456 *abstractedness*; thinking out, excogitation (**see** *meditation*); invention, inventiveness 513 *imagination*; second thoughts, afterthought, reconsideration 67 *sequel*; retrospection, hindsight 505 *memory*; mature thought 669 *preparation*; forethought, prudence 510 *foresight*; thought transference, telepathy 984 *psychics*.

meditation, thoughtfulness, speculation 459 *enquiry*; lateral thinking; reflection, deep r., brooding, rumination, consideration, pondering; contemplation 438 *inspection*; absorption, pensiveness; introspection, self-communing 5 *intrinsicality*; transcendental meditation, TM; religious contemplation, retreat, mysticism 979 *piety*; deliberation, taking counsel 691 *advice*; excogitation, thinking out 480 *judgment*; examination, close study, concentration, application 536 *study*.

philosophy, ontology, teleology, metaphysics, ethics; speculation, philosophical thought, abstract t., systematic t.; scientific thought, science, natural philosophy; philosophical doctrine, philosophical system, philosophical theory, ideology 512 *supposition*; school of philosophy 485 *opinion*; monism, dualism, pluralism; idealism, subjective i., objective i., conceptualism, transcendentalism; phenomenalism, phenomenology, realism, nominalism, positivism, logical p., analytic philosophy 475 *reasoning*; existentialism, voluntarism; determinism, mechanism; vitalism; holism, organicism, structuralism, functionalism, reductionism, reductivism; rationalism, humanism, hedonism, eudaemonism; utilitarianism, materialism; empiricism, probabilism, pragmatism; relativism, relativity; agnosticism, scepticism, irrationalism 486 *doubt*; eclecticism; atheism 974 *irreligion*; nihilism, fatalism 596 *fate*; Pythagoreanism, Platonism, Aristotelianism; Scepticism, Stoicism, Epicureanism, Cynicism; Neo-Platonism, gnosticism; scholasticism, Thomism; Cartesianism, Kantianism, Hegelianism, Neo-H., dialectical materialism, Marxism; anthroposophy, theosophy; Hinduism, Buddhism, Sufism, Vedanta, Yoga, Zen 973 *religion*.

philosopher, thinker, man *or* woman of thought 492 *intellectual*; metaphysician, existentialist, etc. (**see** *philosophy*); school of philosophers, Eleatics, Peripatetics, Academy, Garden, Porch, Lyceum; Diogenes 945 *ascetic*.

Adj. *thoughtful*, conceptive, speculative (**see** *philosophic*); cogitative, deliberative; full of thought, pensive, meditative, ruminant, ruminative, contemplative, reflective; self-communing, introspective; wrapt in thought, lost in t., deep in t.; absorbed 455 *obsessed*; musing, dreaming, dreamy 456 *abstracted*; concentrating, concentrated 455 *attentive*; studying 536 *studious*; thoughtful for others, considerate 901 *philanthropic*; prudent 510 *foreseeing*.

philosophic, metaphysical, ontological, speculative, abstract, conceptual, ideological, systematic, rational, logical.

Vb. *think*, ween, trow 512 *suppose*; conceive, form ideas, ideate; fancy 513 *imagine*; devote thought to, bestow thought upon, think about, cogitate (**see** *meditate*); employ one's mind, use one's brain, put on one's thinking cap; concentrate, collect one's thoughts, pull one's wits together 455 *be attentive*; bend the mind, apply the m., trouble one's head about, lucubrate, cerebrate, mull, mull over, puzzle over, work over, hammer out 536 *study*; think hard, beat one's brains, cudgel one's b., rack one's b., worry at; think through, reason out 475 *reason*; think out, think up, excogitate, invent 484 *discover*; devise 623 *plan*; take into one's head, entertain a notion, harbour a n., have an idea, toy with an i., kick an i. around; cherish an i. 485 *believe*; become obsessed, get a bee in one's bonnet 481 *be biased*; bear in mind, be mindful, think on 505 *remember*.

meditate, ruminate, chew the cud, chew over, digest; wonder about, debate, enquire into 459 *enquire*; reflect, contemplate, study; speculate, philosophize, theorize; intellectualize 447 *cognize*; think about, consider, take into account, take into consideration; take stock of, ponder, weigh 480 *estimate*; think over, turn o., revolve, run over in the mind 505 *memorize*; bethink oneself, reconsider, review, reexamine, have second thoughts, think better of; take counsel, advise with, consult one's pillow, sleep on it 691 *consult*; commune with oneself, introspect; brood, brood upon, muse, fall into a brown study; go into retreat.

dawn upon, occur to, flash on the mind, cross the m., come to m.; come into one's head, strike one; suggest itself, present itself to the mind.

cause thought, provoke *or* challenge t., make one think, make an impression 821 *impress*; penetrate, sink in, fasten on the mind, become an idée fixe, obsess 481 *bias*.

engross, absorb, preoccupy, monopolize; engross one's thoughts, run in one's head, occupy the mind, fill the m., be uppermost in one's mind, come first in one's thoughts; prey on one's mind, haunt, obsess 481 *bias*; fascinate 983 *bewitch*.

Adv. *in mind*, on one's mind, on the brain; under consideration; taking into consideration, bearing in mind, all things considered; on reflection, on consideration, on second thoughts, after due thought; come to think of it.

See: 5, 67, 438, **447**, 451, **455**, 456, 459, **475**, 480, 481, 484, 485, 486, 492, 498, 505, 510, 512, 513, 536, 596, 623, 669, 691, 821, 901, 945, 973, 974, 979, 983, 984.

450 Absence of thought

N. *absence of thought*, inability to think 448 *absence of intellect*; blank mind, fallow m. 491 *ignorance*; vacancy, abstraction 456 *abstractedness*; inanity, vacuity, blankness, fatuity, empty head 499 *unintelligence*; want of thought, thoughtlessness 456 *inattention*; conditioned reflex, automatism; knee-jerk response, gut reaction; instinctiveness, instinct 476 *intuition*; stocks and stones.

Adj. *unthinking*, unreflecting, unphilosophic, unintellectual 448 *mindless*; incapable of thought, idealess, unidea'd, unimaginative, uninventive 20 *imitative*; automatic, instinctive 476 *intuitive*; blank, vacant, empty-headed 190 *empty*; incogitant, not thinking 456 *inattentive*; unoccupied, relaxed; thoughtless, inconsiderate 932 *selfish*; irrational 477 *illogical*; dull-witted, stolid, stupid, wanting 499 *unintelligent*; inanimate, animal, vegetable, mineral.

unthought, unthought of, inconceivable, incogitable, unconsidered, undreamt, not to be thought of, not to be dreamt of 470 *impossible*.

Vb. *not think*, not reflect; leave the mind fallow *or* unoccupied, leave one's mind uncultivated 491 *not know*; be blank, be vacant; not think of, put out of one's mind, dismiss from one's thoughts, laugh off 458 *disregard*; dream, indulge in reveries 456 *be inattentive*; go by instinct 476 *intuit*; think wrongly 481 *misjudge*.

See: 20, 190, **448**, 456, 458, 470, 476, 477, 481, 491, **499**, 932.

451 Idea

N. *idea*, noumenon, notion, abstraction, a thought; object of thought, abstract idea, concept; mere idea, theory 512 *supposition*; percept, image, mental i.; Platonic idea, archetype 23 *prototype*; conception, perception, apprehension 447 *intellect*; reflection, observation 449 *thought*; impression, conceit, fancy 513 *imagination*; product of imagination, figment, fiction; associated ideas, complex; stream of consciousness, free association of ideas; invention, brain-child; brain wave, happy thought 484 *discovery*; wheeze, wrinkle, device 623 *contrivance*; what one thinks, view, point of v., slant, attitude 485 *opinion*; principle, leading idea, main idea; one idea, idée fixe 481 *prejudgment*.

Adj. *ideational*, conceptual 449 *thoughtful*; theoretical 512 *suppositional*; notional, ideal 513 *imaginary*.

See: 23, 447, 449, 481, 484, 485, **512**, 513, 623.

452 Topic

N. *topic*, subject of thought, food for t., mental pabulum; gossip, rumour 529 *news*; subject matter, subject; contents, chapter, section, head, main h. 53 *subdivision*; what it is about, argument, plot, theme, message; text, commonplace, burden, motif; musical topic, statement, leitmotiv 412 *musical piece*; concern, interest, human i.; matter, affair, situation 8 *circumstance*; shop 622 *business*; topic for discussion, business on hand, agenda, order paper 623 *policy*; item on the agenda, motion 761 *request*; resolution 480 *judgment*; problem, headache 459 *question*; heart of the question, gist, pith; theorem, proposition 512 *supposition*; thesis, case, point 475 *argument*; issue, moot point, debatable p., point at issue; field, field of enquiry, field of study 536 *study*.

Adj. *topical*, thematic; challenging, thought-provoking; mooted, debatable 474 *uncertain*; thought about, uppermost in the mind, fit for consideration.

Adv. *in question*, in the mind, on the brain, in one's thoughts; on foot, on the tapis, on the agenda; before the house, under consideration, under discussion.

See: 8, 53, 412, 459, 474, 475, 480, 512, 529, 536, 622, 623, 761.

Section two: Precursory conditions and operations

453 Curiosity: desire for knowledge

N. *curiosity*, intellectual c., speculativeness, enquiring mind, thirst *or* itch for knowledge 536 *study*; interest, itch, inquisitiveness, curiousness; zeal, meddlesomeness, officiousness, nosiness 678 *overactivity*; wanting to know; asking questions, quizzing 459 *question*; sightseeing, rubbernecking, thirst for travel 267 *land travel*; morbid curiosity, ghoulishness; voyeurism 951 *impurity*.

inquisitive person, examiner, cross-e., inquisitor, interrogator, questioner, enfant terrible 459 *enquirer*; nosy parker, stickybeak; busybody, gossip 678 *meddler*; newshound, gossip columnist 529 *news reporter*; seeker, searcher, explorer, experimentalist 461 *experimenter*; sightseer, globetrotter, rubberneck 441 *spectator*; snoop, snooper, spy 459 *detective*; eavesdropper, interceptor, phone-tapper 415 *listener*; Paul Pry, peeping Tom.

Adj. *inquisitive*, curious, interested; speculating, searching, seeking, avid for knowledge 536 *studious*; morbidly curious, ghoulish, prurient; newsmongering, hungering for news, agog, all ears 455 *attentive*; wanting to know, burning with curiosity, consumed with c., eaten up with c.; itching, hungry for; overcurious, nosy, snoopy, prying, spying, peeping, peeking; questioning, inquisitorial 459 *enquiring*; meddlesome, interfering, officious 678 *meddling*.

Vb. *be curious*, want to know, only want to know; seek, look for 459 *search*; test, research 461 *experiment*; feel a concern, be interested, take an interest; show interest, show curiosity, prick up one's ears 455 *be attentive*; mosey around, dip into; dig up, nose out, pick up news; peep, peek, spy 438 *scan*; snoop, pry, nose into 459 *enquire*; eavesdrop, tap the line, intercept, bug, listen, listen in 415 *hear*; poke *or* stick one's nose in, be nosy, interfere, act the busybody 678 *meddle*; ask questions, quiz, question 459 *interrogate*; look, stare, stand and stare, gape, gawk 438 *gaze*.

Int. well? what news? what's going on? who? what? where? when? how? why? why on earth?

See: 267, 415, 438, 441, **455**, **459**, 461, 529, 536, 678, 951.

454 Incuriosity

N. *incuriosity*, lack of interest, incuriousness, no questions, mental inertia; uninterest, unconcern, no interest, insouciance 860 *indifference*; apathy, phlegmatism 820 *moral insensibility*; adiaphorism, indifferentism; blunted curiosity 863 *satiety*.

Adj. *incurious*, uninquisitive, unreflecting 450 *unthinking*; without interest, uninterested; aloof, distant; blasé, unadmiring 865 *unastonished*; wearied 838 *bored*; unconcerned, uninvolved 860 *indifferent*; listless, inert, apathetic 820 *impassive*.

Vb. *be incurious*, - indifferent etc. adj.; have

no curiosity, not think about, take no interest 456 *be inattentive*; feel no concern, couldn't care less, not trouble oneself, not bother with 860 *be indifferent*; mind one's own business, go one's own way 820 *be insensitive*; see nothing, hear n., look the other way 458 *disregard*.

See: 450, 456, 458, 820, 838, **860**, 863, 865.

455 Attention

N. *attention*, notice, regard 438 *look*; consideration 449 *thought*; heed, alertness, readiness, attentiveness, solicitude, observance 457 *carefulness*; observation, watchfulness, vigilance, eyes on, watch, guard 457 *surveillance*; wariness, circumspection 858 *caution*; contemplation, introspection 449 *meditation*; intentness, earnestness, seriousness 599 *resolution*; undivided attention, whole a.; whole mind, concentration, application, studiousness, close study 536 *study*; examination, scrutiny, checkup, review 438 *inspection*; close attention, minute a., meticulousness, attention to detail, particularity, minuteness, finicalness, pedantry 494 *accuracy*; diligent attention, diligence, pains, trouble 678 *assiduity*; exclusive attention, rapt a.; single-mindedness; absorption, preoccupation, brown study 456 *inattention*; interest, inquisitive attention 453 *curiosity*; one-track mind, fixation, obsession, monomania 503 *mania*.

Adj. *attentive*, intent, diligent, assiduous 678 *industrious*; considerate, thoughtful 884 *courteous*; heedful, mindful, regardful 457 *careful*; alert, ready, on one's toes, on the qui vive, on the ball, with it; open-eyed, waking, wakeful, awake, wide-a.; awake to, alive to, sensing 819 *sensitive*; aware, conscious, thinking 449 *thoughtful*; observant, sharp-eyed, observing, watching, watchful 457 *vigilant*; attending, rapt, paying attention, missing nothing; all eyes 438 *seeing*; all ears, prick-eared; all attention, undistracted, concentrating, deep in; serious, earnest; eager to learn 536 *studious*; close, minute, nice, meticulous, particular, punctilious 494 *accurate*; finical, pedantic 862 *fastidious*; on the watch, on the lookout 507 *expectant*.

obsessed, interested, overinterested, overcurious 453 *inquisitive*; single-minded, possessed, engrossed, preoccupied, wrapped up in, taken up with, into, hooked on; rapt, enthralled, spellbound; haunted by 854 *fearing*; monomaniacal 503 *crazy*.

Vb. *be attentive*, attend, give attention, pay a.; look to, heed, pay h., mind 457 *be careful*; trouble oneself, care, take trouble, take pains, bother 682 *exert oneself*; listen, prick up one's ears, sit up, sit up and take notice; take seriously, fasten on 638 *make important*; devote *or* give one's attention to, give one's mind to, bend the mind to, direct one's thoughts to 449 *think*; think of nothing else, be obsessed with 481 *be biased*; keep one's eye on the ball, concentrate, miss nothing; watch, be all eyes 438 *gaze*; be all ears, drink in, hang on the lips of 415 *hear*; focus one's mind on, rivet one's attention to, concentrate on, fix on; examine, inspect, scrutinize, vet, review, pass under review 438 *scan*; overhaul, revise 654 *make better*; study closely, pore, mull, read, reread, digest 536 *study*; pay some attention, glance at, look into, dip into, flip through, flick over the leaves, turn the pages.

be mindful, keep in mind, bear in m., have in m., be thinking of 505 *remember*; not forget, think of, spare a thought for, regard, look on 438 *see*; lend an ear to 415 *hear*; take care of, see to 457 *look after*; have regard to, have an eye to, keep in sight, keep in view 617 *intend*; not lose sight of, keep track of 619 *pursue*.

notice, note, take n., register; mark, recognize, spot; take cognizance of, take into consideration, review, reconsider 449 *meditate*; take account of, consider, weigh 480 *judge*; comment upon, remark on, talk about 584 *converse*; mention, just m., mention in passing, touch on 524 *hint*; recall, revert to, hark back 106 *repeat*; think worthy of attention, have time for, spare time f., find time f.; deign to notice, acknowledge, salute 884 *greet*.

attract notice, draw the attention, hold the a., engage the a., focus the a., rivet the a., be the cynosure of all eyes, cut a figure 875 *be ostentatious*; stick out like a sore thumb, arouse notice, arrest one's n., strike one's n.; interest 821 *impress*; excite attention, invite a., claim a., demand a., meet with a.; catch the eye, fall under observation 443 *be visible*; make one see, bring to one's notice 522 *show*; bring forward, call attention to, advertise 528 *publish*; lay the finger on, point the finger, point out, point to 547 *indicate*; stress, underline 532 *emphasize*; occupy, keep guessing 612 *tempt*; fascinate, haunt, monopolize, obsess 449 *engross*; alert, warn 665 *raise the alarm*; call to attention 737 *command*.

Int. see! mark! lo! ecce! behold! lo and behold! look! look here! look out! look alive! look to it! hark! oyez! hey! mind out! nota bene, NB, take notice! warning! cave! take care! watch your step!

See: 106, 415, 438, 443, **449**, 453, 456, **457**, 480, 481, 494, 503, 505, 507, 522, 524, 528, 532, 536, 547, 584, 599, 612, 617, 619, 638, 654, 665, 678, 682, 737, 819, 821, 854, 858, 862, 875, 884.

456 Inattention

N. *inattention*, inadvertence, forgetfulness 506 *oblivion*; oversight, aberration; lapse 495 *error*; lack of interest, lack of observation 454 *incuriosity*; aloofness, detachment, unconcern 860 *indifference*; nonobservance, disregard 458 *negligence*; thoughtlessness, heedlessness 857 *rashness*; want of thought, inconsiderateness 481 *misjudgment*, 932 *selfishness*; aimlessness, desultoriness 282 *deviation*; superficiality, flippancy 212 *shallowness*; étourderie, dizziness, giddiness, light-mindedness, levity, volatility 604 *caprice*; deaf ears 416 *deafness*; unseeing eyes, blind spot, blind side 439 *blindness*; diversion, distraction, red herring 612 *inducement*; absent-mindedness, wandering wits 450 *absence of thought*; stargazer, daydreamer, woolgatherer, Johnny-head-in-air, Walter Mitty; jaywalker; scatterbrain, grasshopper mind, butterfly.

abstractedness, abstraction, absent-mindedness, wandering attention, absence of mind; woolgathering, daydreaming, stargazing, doodling; fit of abstraction, deep musing, reverie, brown study; distraction, preoccupation, divided attention.

Adj. *inattentive*, careless 458 *negligent*; off one's guard 508 *inexpectant*; unobservant, unnoticing 454 *incurious*; unseeing 439 *blind*; unhearing 416 *deaf*; undiscerning 464 *indiscriminating*; unmindful, unheeding, inadvertent, not thinking, unreflecting 450 *unthinking*; not concentrating, half asleep, only half awake; uninterested 860 *indifferent*; apathetic, unaware 820 *impassive*; oblivious 506 *forgetful*; inconsiderate, thoughtless, tactless, heedless, without consideration, regardless 857 *rash*; cavalier, offhand, cursory, superficial 212 *shallow*.

abstracted, distrait(e), absent-minded, absent, far away, not there, not with it, miles away; lost, lost in thought, wrapped in t., rapt, absorbed, in the clouds, stargazing; bemused, sunk in a brown study, deep in reverie, pensive, dreamy, dreaming, daydreaming, mooning, woolgathering; nodding, napping, half-awake 679 *sleepy*.

distracted, preoccupied, engrossed; otherwise engaged, with divided attention; diverted 282 *deviating*; dazed, dazzled, disconcerted, put out, put out of one's stride, put off, put off one's stroke; rattled, unnerved 854 *nervous*.

light-minded, unfixed, unconcentrated, wandering, desultory, trifling; frivolous, flippant, insouciant, light-headed; airy, volatile, mercurial, bird-witted, flighty, giddy, dizzy, écervelé(e); scatty, scatterbrained, harebrained, featherbrained; wild, romping, harum-scarum, rantipole; addled, brainsick 503 *crazy*; inconstant, to one thing constant never 604 *capricious*.

Vb. *be inattentive*, not attend, pay no attention, pay no heed, not listen, hear nothing, see n.; close one's eyes 439 *be blind*; stop one's ears 416 *be deaf*; not register, not notice, not use one's eyes; not hear the penny drop, not click, not catch; overlook, commit an oversight 495 *blunder*; be off one's guard, let slip, be caught out, catch oneself o., catch oneself doing; lose track of, lose sight of; not remember 506 *forget*; dream, drowse, nod 679 *sleep*; not concentrate, trifle, play at; be abstracted, moider, moither, wander, let one's thoughts wander, let one's mind w., let one's wits go bird-nesting, go woolgathering, indulge in reverie, build castles in Spain 513 *imagine*; fall into a brown study, muse, be lost in thought, moon, stargaze; idle, doodle 679 *be inactive*; be distracted, digress, lose the thread, fluff one's lines 282 *stray*; be disconcerted, be rattled 854 *be nervous*; be put off one's stroke, be put out of one's stride 702 *hinder* (**see** *distract*); disregard, ignore 458 *neglect*; have no time for, think nothing of, think little of 922 *hold cheap*.

distract, call away, divert, divert one's attention; make forget, put out of one's head, drive out of one's mind; entice, throw a sop to Cerberus 612 *tempt*; confuse, muddle 63 *derange*; disturb, interrupt 72 *discontinue*; disconcert, upset, perplex, discompose, fluster, bother, flurry, rattle 318 *agitate*; put off one's stroke 702 *obstruct*; daze, dazzle 439 *blind*; bewilder, flummox, throw off the scent 474 *puzzle*; fuddle, addle 503 *make mad*.

escape notice, escape attention, blush unseen, be overlooked 523 *lurk*; fall on deaf ears, pass over one's head, meet a blind spot, not click; not hold the attention, go in at one ear and out at the other, slip one's memory 506 *be forgotten*.

Adv. *inadvertently*, per incuriam, by oversight; rashly, giddily, gaily, lightheartedly.

See: 63, 72, 212, 282, 318, 416, 439, 450, 454, **458**, 464, 474, 481, 495, 503, 506, 508, 513, 523, 604, 612, 679, 702, 820, 854, 857, 860, 922, 932.

457 Carefulness

N. *carefulness*, mindfulness, attentiveness, diligence, pains 678 *assiduity*; heed, care, utmost c. 455 *attention*; anxiety, solicitude 825 *worry*; loving care 897 *benevolence*; tidiness, orderliness, neatness 60 *order*; attention to detail, thoroughness, meticulousness, minuteness, circumstantiality, particularity; nicety, exactness, exactitude 494 *accuracy*; overnicety, pedantry, perfectionism 862 *fastidiousness*; conscience, scruples, scrupulosity 929 *probity*; vigilance, wakefulness, watchfulness, alertness, readiness 669 *preparedness*; circumspection, prudence, wariness 858 *caution*; forethought 510 *foresight*.

surveillance, an eye on, eyes on, watching, guarding, watch and ward 660 *protection*; vigilance, invigilation, inspection; babysitting, chaperonage; lookout, weather eye; vigil, watch, deathwatch; doomwatch; guard, sentry-go; eyes of Argus, taskmaster's eye, watchful e., unsleeping e., lidless e. 438 *eye*; chaperon, duenna, sentry, sentinel 660 *protection*, 749 *keeper*.

Adj. *careful*, thoughtful, considerate, considered, mindful, regardful, heedful 455 *attentive*; taking care, painstaking; solicitous, anxious; cautious, afraid to touch; loving, tender; conscientious, scrupulous, honest 929 *honourable*; diligent, assiduous 678 *industrious*; thorough, thoroughgoing; meticulous, minute, particular, circumstantial; nice, exact 494 *accurate*; pedantic, overcareful, perfectionist 862 *fastidious*; tidy, neat, clean 60 *orderly*; minding the pence, thrifty, penurious, miserly 816 *parsimonious*.

vigilant, alert, ready 669 *prepared*; on the alert, on guard, on the qui vive, on one's toes; watching, watchful, wakeful, wide-awake; observant, sharp-eyed; all eyes, open-eyed, Argus-e., eagle-e. 438 *seeing*; prudent, provident, far-sighted 510 *foreseeing*; surefooted, picking one's steps; circumspect, guarded, wary, looking before and after 858 *cautious*.

Vb. *be careful*, reck, mind, heed, beware 455 *be attentive*; take precautions, think twice, check, recheck 858 *be cautious*; have one's eyes open, have one's wits about one, keep a lookout, look before and after, look right then left, mind one's step, watch one's s.; pick one's steps, feel one's way 461 *be tentative*; be on one's guard, mind one's P's and Q's; mind one's business, count one's money, look after the pence 814 *economize*; tidy, keep t. 62 *arrange*; take a pride in, take pains, do with care, be meticulous, dot one's i's and cross one's t's; try, do one's best 682 *exert oneself*.

look after, look to, see to, take care of 689 *manage*; take charge of, accept responsibility for; care for, mind, tend, keep 660 *safeguard*; sit up with, baby-sit; nurse, foster, cherish 889 *pet*; have regard for, treat gently 920 *respect*; keep an eye, keep a sharp eye on, keep tabs on, monitor; escort, chaperon, play gooseberry; serve 703 *minister to*.

invigilate, stay awake, sit up; keep vigil, watch; stand sentinel; keep watch, keep watch and ward; look out, keep a sharp lookout, watch out for; keep one's eyes peeled, keep one's weather-eye open, sleep with one eye o., keep one's ear to the ground; mount guard, set watch, post sentries, stand to 660 *safeguard*.

Adv. *carefully*, attentively, diligently; studiously, thoroughly; lovingly, tenderly; painfully, anxiously; with care, gingerly, with kid gloves.

See: 60, 62, 438, **455**, 461, 494, 510, 660,

669, 678, 682, 689, 703, 749, 814, 816, 825, **858**, 862, 889, 897, 920, 929.

458 Negligence

N. *negligence*, carelessness 456 *inattention*; neglectfulness, forgetfulness 506 *oblivion*; remissness, neglect, oversight, omission; nonobservance, pretermission, default, laches, culpable negligence 918 *undutifulness*; unwatchfulness, unwariness, unguarded hour *or* minute, unpreparedness 670 *nonpreparation*; disregard, noninterference, laissez-faire 620 *avoidance*; unconcern, insouciance, nonchalance, don't-care attitude 860 *indifference*; recklessness, incautiousness 857 *rashness*; procrastination 136 *delay*; supineness, slackness, laziness 679 *inactivity*; slovenliness, sluttishness, untidiness 61 *disorder*; sloppiness, inaccuracy, inexactitude 495 *inexactness*; offhandedness, casualness, laxness 734 *laxity*; perfunctoriness, superficiality 212 *shallowness*; trifling, scamping, skipping, dodging, botching 695 *bungling*; scamped work, skimped w., botched job, loose ends 728 *failure*; trifler, slacker, waster 679 *idler*; procrastinator, shirker; sloven 61 *slut*.

Adj. *negligent*, neglectful, careless, unmindful 456 *inattentive*; remiss 918 *undutiful*; thoughtless 450 *unthinking*; oblivious 506 *forgetful*; uncaring, insouciant 860 *indifferent*; regardless, reckless 857 *rash*; heedless 769 *nonobservant*; casual, offhand, happy-go-lucky 734 *lax*; sloppy, slipshod, slaphappy, slapdash, unthorough, perfunctory, superficial; hit and miss, hurried 680 *hasty*; inaccurate 495 *inexact*; slack, supine 679 *lazy*; procrastinating 136 *late*; sluttish, untidy, slovenly 649 *dirty*; not looking, unwary, unwatchful, unheedful, unguarded, off guard 508 *inexpectant*; improvident 670 *unprepared*; disregarding, ignoring 620 *avoiding*; lapsed 974 *irreligious*.

neglected, uncared for, untended; ill-kept, unkempt 649 *dirty*; unprotected, unguarded, unchaperoned; deserted; unattended, left alone 621 *relinquished*; lost sight of, unthought of, unheeded, unmissed, unregarded 860 *unwanted*; disregarded, ignored, out in the cold; unconsidered, overlooked, omitted; unnoticed, unmarked, unremarked, unperceived, unobserved 444 *invisible*; in limbo; shelved, pigeonholed, put aside 136 *late*; unread, unstudied, unexamined, unsifted, unscanned, unweighed, unexplored; undone, half-done, perfunctory 726 *uncompleted*; buried, hid under a bushel 674 *unused*.

Vb. *neglect*, omit, pretermit; pass over; lose sight of, overlook 456 *be inattentive*; leave undone, not finish, leave half-done, leave loose ends, do by halves 726 *not complete*; botch, bungle 695 *be clumsy*; slur, skimp, scamp 204 *shorten*; skip, skim, skip over, jump, skim through, not mention, skate over, gloss over, slur over 525 *conceal*; not take seriously, dabble in, play with, trifle, fribble 837 *amuse oneself*.

disregard, ignore, pass over, give the go-by, dodge, shirk, blink 620 *avoid*; allow to pass, let pass, wink at, connive at, take no notice 734 *be lax*; refuse to see, turn a blind eye to, pay no regard to, dismiss 439 *be blind*; forbear, forget it, excuse, overlook 909 *forgive*; leave out of one's calculations, discount 483 *underestimate*; pass by, pass by on the other side 282 *deviate*; turn one's back on, slight, cold-shoulder, cut, cut dead 885 *be rude*; turn a deaf ear to 416 *be deaf*; take lightly, not trouble oneself with, not trouble one's head about 860 *be indifferent*; have no time for, laugh off, pooh-pooh, treat as of no account 922 *hold cheap*; leave out in the cold 57 *exclude*; leave to their own devices, leave in the lurch, desert, abandon 621 *relinquish*.

be neglectful, doze, drowse, nod 679 *sleep*; be off one's guard, omit precautions; be caught napping, oversleep; be caught with one's pants down 508 *not expect*; drift, freewheel, laisser faire, procrastinate, let slide, let slip, let the grass grow under one's feet 677 *not act*; not bother, take it easy, let things go 679 *be inactive*; shelve, pigeonhole, lay aside, push aside, put a., lay a. 136 *put off*; make neglectful, lull, throw off one's guard, put off one's guard, catch napping, catch bending 508 *surprise*.

Adv. *negligently*, per incuriam; anyhow; any old how; cursorily, perfunctorily.

See: 57, 61, 136, 204, 212, 282, 416, 439, 444, 450, **456**, 483, 495, 506, 508, 525, 620, 621, 649, 670, 674, 677, 679, 680, 695, 726, 728, 734, 769, 837, 857, 860, 885, 909, 918, 922, 974.

459 Enquiry

N. *enquiry*, asking, questioning (**see** *interrogation*); challenge (**see** *question*); asking after, asking about, directing oneself, taking information, getting i. 524 *information*; close enquiry, searching e., strict e., witch-hunt, McCarthyism, spy mania (**see** *search*); inquisition, examination, investigation, visitation; checkup, medical; inquest, post mortem, autopsy, audit, trial 959 *legal trial*; public enquiry, secret e.; commission of enquiry, work party (**see** *enquirer*); census, canvass, survey, market research; poll, Gallup p. (tdmk), straw p. *or* vote 605 *vote*; probe, test, means t., check, spot c., trial run 461 *experiment*; review, scrutiny 438 *inspection*; introspection, self-examination; personality testing, Rorschach *or* inkblot test; research, fundamental r., applied r. 536 *study*; analysis, dissection; exploration, reconnaissance, recce, reconnoitre, survey 484 *discovery*; discussion, ventilation, airing, soundings, canvassing, consultation 584 *conference*; speculation, philosophical enquiry, metaphysical e., scientific e. 449 *philosophy*; enquiring mind 453 *curiosity*.

interrogation, questioning, interpellation, asking questions, putting q., formulating q.; forensic examination, examination-in-chief; leading question, cross-examination, cross-question; reexamination; quiz, brains trust; interrogatory; catechism; inquisition, third degree, grilling; dialogue, dialectic, question and answer, interlocution; Socratic method, Socratic elenchus; question time.

question, question mark, interrogation m. 547 *punctuation*; query, request for information; questions, questionnaire 87 *list*; question sheet, question paper, examination p.; interrogatory, interpellation, Parliamentary question; challenge, fair question, plain q.; catch, cross-question, loaded q.; indirect question, feeler, leading question; rhetorical q.; moot point, knotty p., debating p.; quodlibet, question propounded, point at issue 452 *topic*; crucial question, burning q., sixty-four-thousand-dollar q.; controversy, field of c., contention, bone of c. 475 *argument*; problem, poser, stumper, headache, unsolved mystery 530 *enigma*.

exam, examination, oral e., viva voce e., viva; interview, audition 415 *hearing*; practical examination, written e.; test, series of tests, battery; intelligence test, IQ test; eleven-plus, entrance examination, common entrance, matriculation; Certificate of Secondary Education, CSE, sixteen-plus, General Certificate of Education, GCE, 'O' level, 'A' level; baccalaureate; prelims, pre-Meds, Responsions; tripos, Moderations, Mods., Greats, finals; doctorate examination, bar e.; degree level, pass l., honours l.; catechumen 460 *respondent*; examinee, entrant, sitter 461 *testee*.

search, probe, investigation, enquiry; quest, hunt, witch-h., treasure h. 619 *pursuit*; house-search, domiciliary visit, house-to-house search; search of one's person, frisking; rummaging, turning over; exploration, excavation, archaeological e., digging, dig; speleology, potholing; search party; searchlight; search warrant.

police enquiry, investigation, criminal i., detection 484 *discovery*; detective work, shadowing, house-watching; grilling, third degree; Criminal Investigation Department, CID, Federal Bureau of Investigation, FBI, Interpol; secret police, Gestapo.

secret service, espionage, counter-e., spying, intelligence, MI5, CIA, KGB; informer, spy, undercover agent, secret a., cloak-and-dagger man; double agent, inside a.; counterspy; spy ring.

detective, investigator, criminologist; plain-clothes man; enquiry agent, private detective, private eye; hotel detective, store d.; amateur detective; Federal agent, G-man, CID man; tec, sleuth, bloodhound, dick, snooper, nose, spy 524 *informer*; graphologist, handwriting expert; Sherlock Holmes.

enquirer, investigator, prober; asker (**see** *questioner*); journalist 529 *news reporter*; student, seeker, thinker, seeker for truth 449 *philosopher*; searcher, looker, rummager, search party; inventor, discoverer; dowser, water diviner 484 *detector*; prospector, gold-digger; talent scout; scout, spy, surveyor, reconnoitrer; inspector, visitor 438 *inspection*; checker, screener, scrutineer, censor, ombudsman 480 *estimator*; examiner, examining board, board of examiners; tester, test pilot, researcher, research worker, analyst, analyser, dissector 461 *experimenter*; sampler, pollster, canvasser; explorer 268 *traveller.*

questioner, cross-q., cross-examiner, catechizer; interrogator, inquisitor, Grand I.; querist, interpellator, interlocutor, interviewer; challenger, heckler; quizzer, enfant terrible 453 *inquisitive person*; question *or* quiz master; riddler, enigmatist; examiner of conscience, confessor 986 *clergy*.

Adj.*enquiring*, curious, prying, nosy 453 *inquisitive*; quizzing, quizzical; interrogatory, interrogative; examining, catechetical, inquisitional, cross-questioning; elenctic, dialectic, maieutic, heuristic, zetetic; probing, poking, digging, investigative; testing, searching, fact-finding, exploratory, empirical, tentative 461 *experimental*; analytic, diagnostic.

moot, in question, questionable, debatable; problematic, doubtful 474 *uncertain*; knotty, puzzling 700 *difficult*; fit for enquiry, proposed, propounded; undetermined, undecided, untried, left open.

Vb.*enquire*, ask, want to know, seek an answer 491 *not know*; demand 761 *request*; canvass, agitate, air, ventilate, discuss, query, bring in question, subject to examination 475 *argue*; ask for, look for, enquire for, seek (**see** *search*); hunt for 619 *pursue*; enquire into, make enquiries, probe, delve into, dig i., dig down i., go deep i., sound, take a look at, look into, investigate, throw open to enquiry, hold *or* conduct an enquiry, appoint a commission of e., call in Scotland Yard; try, hear 959 *try a case*; review, overhaul, audit, scrutinize, monitor, screen; analyse, dissect, parse, sift, winnow, thrash out; research 536 *study*; consider, examine 449 *meditate*; check, check on; feel the pulse, take the temperature, take soundings; follow up an enquiry, pursue an e., get to the bottom of, fathom, see into, X-ray 438 *scan*; peer, peep, peek, snoop, spy, pry, nose around 453 *be curious*; survey, reconnoitre, case, sus out; explore, feel one's way 461 *be tentative*; test, try, sample, taste 461 *experiment*.

interrogate, ask questions, put q.; interpellate, question; cross-question, cross-examine, reexamine; badger, challenge, heckle; interview, hold a viva; examine, subject to questioning, sound out, probe, quiz, catechize, grill, give the third degree; put to the question 963 *torture*; pump, pick one's brains, suck one dry; move the question, put the q., pop the q.; pose, propose a question, propound a q., frame a q., raise a q., moot a q., moot.

search, seek, look for; conduct a search, rummage, ransack, comb; scrabble, forage, fossick, root about; scour, clean out, turn over, rake o., pick o., turn out, turn inside out, rake through, rifle t., go t., search t., look into every nook and corner; look high and low; quarter the ground, explore every inch, go over with a fine-tooth comb; pry into, peer i., peep i., peek i.; overhaul, frisk, go over, search one's pockets, feel in one's p., search for, feel for, grope for, hunt for, drag for, fish, go fishing, fish for, dig for; leave no stone unturned, explore every avenue 682 *exert oneself*; cast about, seek a clue, follow the trail 619 *pursue*; probe, explore, go in quest of 461 *be tentative*; dig, excavate, archaeologize; prospect, dowse, treasure-hunt, embark on a t-h.

be questionable, - debatable etc. adj.; be open to question, arouse suspicion, call for enquiry, challenge an answer, demand *or* require an explanation; be subject to examination, be open to enquiry, be under investigation.

Adv.*on trial*, under investigation, under enquiry, sub judice; up for enquiry.

in search of, on the track of, cui bono!

See:5, 87, 268, 415, 438, 449, 452, **453**, 460, **461**, 474, 475, 480, **484**, 491, 524, 529, 530, 536, 547, 584, 605, 619, 682, 700, 761, 959, 963, 986.

460 Answer

N.*answer*, reply, response; replication, reaction; answer by post, acknowledgment, return 588 *correspondence*; official reply, rescript; returns, results 548 *record*; feedback 524 *information*; echo, antiphon, antiphony, respond 106 *repetition*; password, countersign 547 *identification*; keyword, open sesame; answering back, backchat, repartee; retort, counterblast, riposte 714 *retaliation*; give and take, question and answer, dialogue 584 *interlocution*; last word, final answer; Parthian shot; clue, key, right answer, explanation 520 *interpretation*; solution 658 *remedy*; enigmatic answer, oracle, Delphic Oracle 530 *enigma*.

rejoinder, counterstatement, reply, rebuttal, rebutter, surrejoinder, surrebutter 479 *confutation*; defence, speech for the defence, reply; refutation, contradiction 533 *negation*, 467 *counterevidence*; countercharge, counteraccusation, tu quoque 928 *accusation*.

respondent, defendant; answerer, responder, replier, correspondent; examinee 461 *testee*; candidate, applicant, entrant, sitter 716 *contender*.

Adj. *answering*, replying etc. vb.; respondent, responsive, echo-like 106 *repeated*; counter 182 *counteracting*; corresponding 588 *epistolary*; antiphonic, antiphonal; corresponding to 12 *correlative*; contradicting 533 *negative*; refuting, rebutting; oracular; conclusive, final, Parthian.

Vb. *answer*, give a., return an a.; reply, write back, acknowledge, respond, be responsive, echo, reecho 106 *repeat*; react, answer back, flash back, come back at, retort, riposte 714 *retaliate*; say in reply, rejoin, rebut, counter 479 *confute*; field; parry, refuse to answer 620 *avoid*; contradict 533 *negate*; be respondent, defend, have the right of reply; provide the answer, have the a. 642 *be expedient*; answer the question, solve the riddle 520 *interpret*; settle, decide 480 *judge*; suit the requirements 642 *be expedient*; answer to, correspond to 12 *correlate*.

Adv. *in reply*, by way of rejoinder; antiphonally.

See: 12, 106, 182, 461, 467, 479, 480, 520, 524, 530, 533, 547, 548, 584, 588, 620, 642, 658, 714, 716, 928.

461 Experiment

N. *experiment*, practical e., scientific e., controlled e.; experimentalism, experimentation, experimental method, verification, verification by experiment; exploration, probe; analysis, examination 459 *enquiry*; object lesson, proof 478 *demonstration*; assay 480 *estimate*; testability; check, test, crucial t., acid t., test case; probation; double-blind test; practical test, trial, trials, try-out, trial run, practice r., dry r., test flight 671 *attempt*; audition, voice test; ordeal, ordeal by fire, ordeal by water 959 *legal trial*; pilot scheme, rough sketch, first draft, sketchbook; first steps, teething troubles 68 *debut*.

empiricism, speculation, guesswork 512 *conjecture*; tentativeness, tentative method; experience, practice, rule of thumb, trial, trial and error, hit and miss; random shot, shot in the dark, leap in the d., gamble 618 *gambling*; instinct, light of nature 476 *intuition*; sampling, random sample, straw vote; feeler 459 *question*; straw to show which way the wind is blowing, kite-flying, trial balloon, ballon d'essai.

experimenter, experimentalist, empiricist, researcher, research worker, analyst, analyser, vivisector; assayer, chemist; tester; test driver, test pilot; speculator, prospector, sourdough, forty-niner; prober, explorer, adventurer 459 *enquirer*; dabbler 493 *sciolist*; gamester 618 *gambler*.

testing agent, criterion, touchstone; standard, yardstick 465 *gauge*; breathalyser; control; reagent, litmus paper, cupel, retort, test tube 147 *crucible*; pyx, pyx chest; proving ground, wind tunnel; simulator, flight s., test track; laboratory.

testee, examinee 460 *respondent*; probationer 538 *beginner*; candidate, entrant, sitter 716 *contender*; subject of experiment, subject, patient; laboratory animal, guinea pig, rat, monkey.

Adj. *experimental*, analytic, analytical, verificatory, probative, probationary, probational; provisional, tentative 618 *speculative*; trial, exploratory 459 *enquiring*; empirical, experiential, guided by experience; venturesome 671 *attempting*; testable, verifiable, in the experimental stage 474 *uncertain*.

Vb. *experiment*, experimentalize, make experiments; check, check on, verify; prove, put to the proof; assay, analyse; research; dabble; experiment upon, vivisect, make a guinea pig of, practise upon; test, put to the t., subject to a t., run a t. on 459 *enquire*; try, try a thing once; try out, give a trial to 671 *attempt*; try one's strength, test one's muscles; give one a try; sample 386 *taste*; take a random sample, take a straw vote; put to the vote 605 *vote*; rehearse, practise 534 *train*; be tested, undergo a test, come to the t.

be tentative, be empirical, seek experience, feel one's way, proceed by trial and error, proceed by guess and by God; feel 378 *touch*; probe, grope, fumble; get the feel of 536 *learn*; put out a feeler, dip a toe in, fly a kite, feel the pulse, consult the barometer, see how the land lies, see how the wind blows; fish, fish for, angle for, bob for, cast one's net, trawl, put out a t.; wait and see, see what happens; try it on, see how far one can go; try one's fortune, try one's luck, speculate 618 *gamble*; venture, explore, prospect 672 *undertake*; probe, sound 459 *enquire*.

Adv. *experimentally*, on test, on trial, on approval, on probation; empirically, by rule of thumb, by trial and error, by the light of nature, by guess and by God; on spec.

See: 68, 147, 378, 386, **459**, 460, 465, 474, 476, 478, 480, 493, 512, 534, 536, 538, 605, 618, **671**, 672, 716, 959.

462 Comparison

N. *comparison*, analogical procedure; comparing, likening; confrontation, collation, juxtaposition, setting side by side 202 *contiguity*; check 459 *enquiry*; comparability, points of comparison, analogy, parallel, likeness, similitude 18 *similarity*; identification 13 *identity*; antithesis 14 *contrariety*; contrast 15 *differentiation*; simile, allegory 519 *metaphor*; standard of comparison, criterion, pattern, model, check list, control 23 *prototype*; comparer, collator.

Adj. *compared*, collated etc. vb.; compared with, likened, set against, measured a., contrasted; comparative, comparable, analogical; relative, correlative; allegorical, metaphorical 519 *figurative*.

Vb. *compare*, collate, confront; set side by side, bring together 202 *juxtapose*; draw a comparison 18 *liken*, 13 *identify*; parallel; contrast 15 *differentiate*; compare and contrast 463 *discriminate*; match, pair, balance 28 *equalize*; view together, check with 12 *correlate*; institute a comparison, draw a parallel; compare to, compare with, criticize; compare notes, match ideas, exchange views.

Adv. *comparatively*, analogically; in comparison, as compared; relatively 12 *correlatively*.

See: 12, 13, 14, **15**, **18**, 23, 28, 202, 459, 463, 519.

463 Discrimination

N. *discrimination*, distinction 15 *differentiation*; discernment, discretion, ability to make distinctions, appreciation of differences, discriminating judgment, connoisseurship 480 *judgment*; insight, perception, acumen, flair 498 *intelligence*; appreciation, careful a., critique, critical appraisal 480 *estimate*; sensitivity 494 *accuracy*; sensibility 819 *moral sensibility*; tact, delicacy, refinement 846 *good taste*; timing, sense of t., sense of occasion; nicety, particularity 862 *fastidiousness*; fine palate 386 *taste*; logical nicety, sublety, hair-splitting 475 *reasoning*; sifting, separation, sorting out 62 *sorting*; selection 605 *choice*; nice difference, shade of d., nuance, fine shade 15 *difference*.

Adj. *discriminating*, discriminative, selective, judicious, discerning, discreet; sensitive 494 *accurate*; fine, delicate, nice, particular 862 *fastidious*; thoughtful, tactful 513 *imaginative*; tasting, appraising, critical 480 *judicial*; distinguishing 15 *distinctive*.

Vb. *discriminate*, distinguish, contradistinguish 15 *differentiate*; compare and contrast 462 *compare*; sort, sort out, sieve, sift; severalize, separate, separate the sheep from the goats, sort the wheat from the chaff 46 *set apart*; pick out 605 *select*; exercise discretion, see the difference, make a distinction, make an exception, draw the line 468 *qualify*; refine, refine upon, split hairs 475 *reason*; criticize, appraise, taste 480 *estimate*; weigh, consider, make a judgment 480 *judge*; discern, have insight; have a feel for, have an eye *or* an ear for; know what's what, know one's way about, know one's stuff, know a hawk from a handsaw 490 *know*; take into account, give weight to 638 *make important*; attribute just value to 913 *be just*.

See: **15**, 46, 62, 386, 462, 468, 475, 480, 490, 494, 498, 513, 605, 638, 819, 846, 862, 913.

464 Indiscrimination

N. *indiscrimination*, lack of discrimination, promiscuousness, promiscuity, universality 79 *generality*; lack of judgment, uncriticalness, simplicity; obtuseness 499 *unintelligence*; indiscretion, want of consideration 857 *rashness*; imperceptivity 439 *blindness*; unimaginativeness, tactlessness, insensitiveness, insensibility 820 *moral insensibility*; tastelessness, lack of refinement, coarseness, vulgarity 847 *bad taste*; inaccuracy 495 *inexactness*; vagueness, loose terms.

Adj. *indiscriminate*, unsorted 61 *orderless*; rolled into one, undistinguished, undifferentiated, same for everybody 16 *uniform*; random, unaimed, undirected; confused, undefined, unmeasured 474 *uncertain*; promiscuous, haphazard, wholesale, blanket 79 *general*.

indiscriminating, unselective, undiscerning, uncritical 499 *unintelligent*; imperceptive, obtuse; tactless, insensitive, unimaginative 820 *impassive*; unrefined, coarse 847 *vulgar*; indiscreet, ill-judged 857 *rash*; tone-deaf 416 *deaf*; colour-blind 439 *blind*; inaccurate 495 *inexact*.

Vb. *not discriminate*, be indiscriminate, avoid precision, confound opposites, be unselective 606 *be neutral*; exercise no discretion 499 *be foolish*; make no distinction, see no difference, swallow whole; roll into one, lump everything together, heap t. 74 *bring together*; jumble, muddle, confuse, confound 63 *derange*; ignore distinctions, obliterate d., average, take an a., smooth out 30 *average out*.

See: 16, 30, 61, 63, 74, **79**, 416, 439, 474, 495, 499, 606, 820, 847, 857.

465 Measurement

N. *measurement*, admeasurement, quantification; mensuration, surveying, triangulation, cadastral survey; geodetics, geodesy; metage 322 *weighing*; posology, dose, dosage 26 *finite quantity*; rating, valuation, evaluation; appraisal, appraisement, assessment, appreciation, estimation 480 *estimate*; calculation, computation, reckoning 86 *numeration*; dead reckoning, gauging; checking, check; reading, reading off; metrics, micrometry 203 *long measure*; trigonometry; second, degree, minute, quadrant 247 *angular measure*; quadrature, cubature.

geometry, plane g., planimetry; solid geometry, stereometry; altimetry, hypsometry; Euclidean geometry, non-Euclidean g.; geometer.

metrology, dimensions, length, breadth, height, depth, thickness 195 *size*; weights and measures, metric system, unit of measurement; weights 322 *weighing*; axle load; linear measure 203 *long measure*; measure of capacity, volume, cubature, cubic contents 183 *measure*; liquid measure, gill, pint, imperial p., quart, gallon, imperial g.; barrel, pipe, hogshead 194 *vessel*; litre; apothecaries' fluid measure, minim, dram; dry measure, peck, bushel, quarter, chaldron; unit of energy, ohm, watt 160 *electricity*; horse power 160 *energy*; candlepower 417 *light*; decibel, sone 398 *sound*.

coordinate, ordinate and abscissa, polar coordinates, latitude and longitude, right ascension and declination, altitude and azimuth; grid reference.

gauge, measure, scale, graduated s.; time scale 117 *chronometry*; balance 322 *scales*; nonius, vernier, micrometer; footrule, yardstick, metre bar; yard measure, tape m., metal rule; chain, link, pole, perch, rod; lead, log, log-line; fathometer, echo sounder; ruler, slide rule; straight-edge, T-square, try s., set s.; dividers, callipers, compass, protractor; sextant, quadrant 269 *sailing aid*; Jacob's staff, theodolite, planisphere, alidade; astrolabe 321 *astronomy*; index, Plimsoll line, Plimsoll mark, bench m. 547 *indication*; high-water mark, tidemark, floodmark, water line 236 *limit*; axis, coordinate; standard, criterion 23 *prototype*; milestone 547 *signpost*.

meter, measuring instrument; goniometer, planimeter; altimeter 209 *altimetry*; bathometer 211 *depth*; thermometer 379 *thermometry*; barometer, anemometer 352 *anemometry*; dynamometer; hygrometer, fluviometer 341 *hygrometry*; gas etc. meter; speed gauge, speedometer, tachograph, odometer, milometer 277 *velocity*; cyclometer, pedometer 267 *land travel*; time gauge, metronome, time switch, parking meter 117 *timekeeper*; micrometer; Geiger counter; seismograph; geophone.

surveyor, land s., quantity s.; topographer, cartographer, oceanographer, hydrographer, geodesist.

appraiser, valuer, loss adjuster, assessor, measurer, surveyor 480 *estimator*.

Adj. *metrical*, mensural; imperial, metric; metrological, modular; dimensional, three-d.; cubic, volumetric, linear, micrometric; cadastral, topographical; geodetic.

measured, surveyed, mapped, plotted, taped; graduated, calibrated; mensurable, measurable, meterable, assessable, computable, calculable.

Vb. *measure*, mensurate, survey, triangulate; compute, calculate, count, reckon 86 *number*; quantify, take the dimensions, measure the length and breadth; size up, calculate the s.; estimate the average 30 *average out*; beat the bounds, pace out, count one's steps; tape, span; calliper, use the dividers; probe, sound, fathom, plumb 313 *plunge*; take soundings, heave the lead; pace, check the speed 117 *time*; balance 322 *weigh*.

gauge, meter, take a reading, read, read off; standardize, fix the standard, set a standard 16 *make uniform*; grade, mark off, calibrate 27 *graduate*; reduce to scale, draw to s., map 551 *represent*.

appraise, gauge, value, cost, rate, set a value on, fix the price of 809 *price*; evaluate, estimate, make an e., form an e.; appreciate, assess 480 *estimate*; form an opinion 480 *judge*; tape, have taped, have the measure of, size up.

mete out, mete, measure out, weigh, weigh out, dole o., divide, share, share out 775 *participate*, 783 *apportion*.

See: 16, 23, 26, 27, 30, 86, 117, 160, 183, 194, 195, 203, 209, 211, 236, 247, 267, 269, 277, 313, 321, 322, 341, 352, 379, 398, 417, 480, 547, 551, 775, 783, 809.

Section three: Materials for reasoning

466 Evidence

N. *evidence*, facts, data, case history; grounds 475 *reasons*; premises 475 *premise*; hearsay, hearsay evidence 524 *report*; indirect evidence, collateral e., secondary e.; circumstantial evidence 8 *circumstance*; constructive evidence 512 *supposition*; prima facie evidence; internal e., presumptive e., direct e., demonstrative e., final e., conclusive e., proof 478 *demonstration*; supporting evidence, corroboration; verification, confirmation 473 *certainty*; rebutting evidence 467 *counterevidence*; one-sided evidence, ex parte e.; piece of evidence, fact, relevant f.; document, exhibit, fingerprints 548 *record*; clue 524 *hint*; symptom, sign, sure s. 547 *indication*; reference, quotation, citation, chapter and verse; one's authorities, documentation; line of evidence, chain of authorities; authority, scripturality, canonicity.

testimony, witness; statement, evidence in chief 524 *information*; admission, confession 526 *disclosure*; one's case, plea 614 *pretext*; word, assertion, allegation 532 *affirmation*; Bible evidence, evidence on oath; sworn evidence, legal e., deposition, affidavit, attestation 532 *oath*; State's evidence, Queen's e.; word of mouth, oral evidence, verbal e.; documentary evidence, written e.; evidence to character, compurgation 927 *vindication*; copy of the evidence, case record, dossier 548 *record*; written contract 765 *compact*; deed, testament 767 *security*.

credential, compurgation 927 *vindication*; testimonial, chit, character, recommendation, references; seal, signature, countersignature, endorsement, docket; voucher, warranty, warrant, certificate, diploma 767 *security*; ticket, passport, visa 756 *permit*; authority, scripture.

witness, eye w. 441 *spectator*; ear witness 415 *listener*; indicator, informant, telltale 524 *informer*; deponent, testifier, swearer, attestor 765 *signatory*; witness to character, compurgator, referee; sponsor 707 *patron*.

Adj. *evidential*, evidentiary, offering evidence; prima facie 445 *appearing*; suggesting, suggestive, significant 514 *meaningful*; showing, indicative, symptomatic 547 *indicating*; indirect, secondary, circumstantial; firsthand, direct, seen, heard; deducible, verifiable 471 *probable*; constructive 512 *suppositional*; cumulative, supporting, corroborative, confirmatory; telling, damning 928 *accusing*; presumptive, reliable 473 *certain*; probative, proving, demonstrative, conclusive, decisive, final 478 *demonstrating*; based on, grounded on; founded on fact, factual, documentary, documented, well-documented 473 *positive*; authentic, well-grounded, well-founded 494 *true*; weighty, authoritative 178 *influential*; biblical, scriptural, canonical 976 *orthodox*; testified, attested, witnessed; spoken to, sworn to; in evidence, on the record 548 *recorded*.

Vb. *evidence*, show, evince, furnish evidence; show signs of, have the makings of 852 *give hope*; betoken, bespeak 551 *represent*; breathe of, tell of, declare witness to 522 *manifest*; lend colour to 471 *make likely*; tell its own tale, speak for itself, speak volumes; have weight, carry w. 178 *influence*; suggest 547 *indicate*; argue, involve 523 *imply*.

testify, witness; take one's oath, swear, be sworn, speak on oath 532 *affirm*; bear witness, take the stand, give evidence, witness for *or* against, speak to, depose, swear to, vouch for, give one's word;

authenticate, certify 473 *make certain*; attest, subscribe, countersign, endorse, sign; plead, state one's case 475 *argue*; admit, avow, acknowledge 526 *confess*; give a character reference, testimonialize, compurgate.

corroborate, support, buttress 162 *strengthen*; sustain, uphold in evidence 927 *vindicate*; bear out, circumstantiate, verify; validate, confirm, ratify, establish, make a case for, make out, make good 473 *make certain*; lead evidence, adduce e.; bring one's witnesses, produce one's w., confront w.; put the evidence, produce the e., document; collect evidence, rake up *or* scrape together e.; concoct evidence, fabricate e. 541 *fake*; countervail 467 *tell against*; adduce, cite the evidence, quote the e., quote the leading case, quote one's authorities, give the reference, give chapter and verse.

See: 8, 162, 178, 415, 441, 445, 467, **471**, **473**, 475, 478, 494, 512, 514, 522, 523, **524**, 526, 532, 541, 547, 548, 551, 614, 707, 756, 765, 767, 852, 927, 928, 976.

467 Counterevidence

N. *counterevidence*, contraindication 14 *contrariety*; answering evidence, opposite e., rebutting e.; evidence against, evidence on the other side, defence, rebuttal 460 *answer*; refutation, disproof 479 *confutation*; denial 533 *negation*; justification 927 *vindication*; oath against oath, one word against another; counteroath, counterprotest, tu quoque argument; conflicting evidence, contradictory e., negative e.; mitigating evidence 468 *qualification*; hostile witness, hostile evidence 603 *tergiversation*.

Adj. *countervailing*, rebutting 460 *answering*; cancelling out, counteractive 182 *counteracting*; cutting both ways, ambiguous 518 *equivocal*; converse, opposite, in the opposite scale 14 *contrary*; denying, negatory 533 *negative*; damaging, telling against, contraindicating; qualificatory 468 *qualifying*.

unattested, unsworn; lacking proof, unproven, not proved 474 *uncertain*; unsupported, uncorroborated; disproved 479 *confuted*; trumped-up, fabricated 541 *false*.

Vb. *tell against*, damage the case; weigh against, countervail; contravene, traverse, run counter, contradict, contraindicate; rebut 479 *confute*; oppose, point the other way 14 *be contrary*; cancel out 182 *counteract*; cut both ways 518 *be equivocal*; prove a negative 533 *negate*; lead counterevidence, lead for the other side; fail to confirm, tell another story, alter the case; not improve, weaken, damage, spoil; undermine, subvert 165 *destroy*; demolish the case, turn the tables, turn the scale, convict of perjury; contradict oneself, turn hostile 603 *tergiversate*.

Adv. *conversely*, per contra, on the other hand, on the other side, in rebuttal, in rejoinder.

See: 14, 165, 182, 460, 468, 474, **479**, 518, 533, 541, 603, 927.

468 Qualification

N. *qualification*, specification 80 *speciality*; prerequisite 627 *requirement*; assumption 512 *supposition*; leaven, colouring, tinge; modification 143 *change*; mitigation 177 *moderation*; stipulation, condition 766 *conditions*; limitation 747 *restriction*; proviso, reservation; exception, salvo, saving clause, escape c., escalator c., penalty c.; exemption 919 *nonliability*; demur, objection, but 704 *opposition*; consideration, concession, allowance; extenuating circumstances; redeeming feature 31 *offset*.

Adj. *qualifying*, qualificative, qualificatory; restricting, limiting; modifying, altering the case; mitigatory 177 *lenitive*; extenuating, palliative, excusing, weakening, colouring, leavening; contingent, provisional 766 *conditional*; discounting, allowing for; saving, excepting, exempting; circumstanced, qualified, not absolute; exceptional, exempted, exempt 919 *nonliable*.

Vb. *qualify*, condition, limit, restrict 747 *restrain*; colour, shade; leaven, alter 143 *modify*; temper, season, palliate, mitigate 177 *moderate*; adulterate 163 *weaken*; excuse 927 *extenuate*; grant, concede, make allowance for, take into account; lessen 37 *abate*; make exceptions 919 *exempt*; introduce new conditions, alter the case; insert a qualifying clause; insist on 627 *require*; relax, relax the rigour of 734 *be lax*; take exception, object, demur, raise an objection 762 *deprecate*.

Adv. *provided*, provided always, with the proviso that, according as, subject to, conditionally, with the understanding that, so *or* as long as; granting, admitting, supposing; allowing for; with a pinch of salt; not absolutely, not invariably; if, if not, unless 8 *if*; though, although, even if.

nevertheless, even so, all the same, for all that, after all; despite, in spite of; but, yet, still, at all events; whether, whether or no.

See: 8, 31, 37, 80, 143, 163, 177, 512, 627, 704, 734, 747, 762, **766**, 919, 927.

469 Possibility

N. *possibility*, potentiality; capacity, viability, viableness, workability 160 *ability*; what is possible, all that is p. 635 *sufficiency*; what may be 124 *futurity*; what might be, the might-have-been 125 *past time*; the possible, the feasible; what one can do, best one can do, limit of one's endeavour; contingency, eventuality, a possibility, chance, off-chance 159 *fair chance*; good chance 137 *opportunity*; bare possibility, ghost of a chance; likelihood 471 *probability*; thinkableness, credibility 485 *belief*; practicability, operability 642 *good policy*; practicableness, feasibility, easiness 701 *facility*; superableness, negotiability; availability, accessibility, approachability; compatibility 24 *agreement*; risk of.

Adj. *possible*, potential, hypothetical; able, capable, viable; arguable, reasonable; feasible, practicable, negotiable 701 *easy*; workable, performable, achievable; doable, operable; attainable, approachable, accessible, obtainable, realizable; superable, surmountable; not too difficult, not impossible, within the bounds of possibility; available, still open, not excluded, not too late; conceivable, thinkable, credible, imaginable; practical, compatible with the circumstances 642 *advisable*; allowable, permissible, legal 756 *permitted*; contingent 124 *future*; on the cards 471 *probable*; only possible, not inevitable, evitable, revocable 620 *avoidable*; liable, tending.

Vb. *be possible*, - feasible etc. adj.; may, might, maybe, might be; might have been, could have b., should have b.; admit of, allow 756 *permit*; bear, be open to, offer an opportunity for; be a possibility, depend, be contingent, lie within the bounds of possibility; stand a chance 471 *be likely*.

make possible, enable 160 *empower*; allow 756 *permit*; clear the path, smoothe the way, remove the obstacles, put in the way of 701 *facilitate*.

Adv. *possibly*, potentially; conceivably, hypothetically, in posse; perhaps, perchance, for all one knows; within reach, within one's grasp; peradventure, haply, mayhap; may be, could be; if possible, if so be; wind and weather permitting, God willing, Deo volente, D.V.

See: 24, 124, 125, 137, 159, 160, **471**, 485, 620, 635, 642, 701, 756.

470 Impossibility

N. *impossibility*, inconceivability etc. adj.; unthinkableness, no chance, not a chance of, not a cat's chance, not a hope 853 *hopelessness*; what cannot be, what can never be; irrevocability, what might-have-been; impasse, deadlock 702 *obstacle*; unfeasibility, impracticability 643 *inexpedience*; no permission 757 *prohibition*; unavailability, inaccessibility, unobtainability, the moon; sour grapes; insuperability, impossible task, no go 700 *hard task*.

Adj. *impossible*, not possible; not allowed, ruled out, excluded, against the rules 757 *prohibited*; not to be thought of, out of the question, hopeless; unnatural, against nature; unreasonable, contrary to reason, self-contradictory 477 *illogical*; unscientific; untrue, incompatible with the facts 495 *erroneous*; too improbable, incredible, inconceivable, unthinkable, unimaginable, unheard of 486 *unbelieved*; miraculous 864 *wonderful*; visionary, idealistic, unrealistic 513 *imaginary*; irrevocable, beyond recall 830 *regretted*.

impracticable, unfeasible, not to be done; unworkable, unviable; unachievable, unrealizable, unsolvable, insoluble, inextricable, too hard, too much for, beyond one 700 *difficult*; incurable, inoperable; insuperable, insurmountable, impassable, unbridgeable, unbridged; impenetrable, unnavigable, not motorable, unscalable; unapproachable, inaccessible, unattainable, unobtainable, unavailable, not to be had, out of reach, beyond one's reach, not within one's grasp; elusive 667 *escaped*.

Vb. *be impossible*, - impracticable etc. adj., exceed possibility, defy nature, fly in the face of reason, have no chance whatever.

make impossible, rule out, exclude, disallow 757 *prohibit*; put out of reach, tantalize, set an impossible task; deny the possibility, eat one's hat if 533 *negate*.

attempt the impossible, labour in vain 641 *waste effort*; have nothing to go upon, grasp at shadows; be in two places at once, square the circle, discover the secret of perpetual motion, discover the philosopher's stone, find the elixir of life, find a needle in a haystack; weave a rope of sand, skin a flint, gather grapes from thorns *or* figs from thistles, get blood from a stone, fetch water in a sieve; make bricks without straw, make a silk purse out of a sow's ear, change a leopard's spots; have one's cake and eat it; write on water, set the Thames on fire.

Adv. *impossibly*, nohow.

See: 477, 486, 495, 513, 533, 641, 643, 667, 700, 702, 757, 830, 853, 864.

471 Probability

N. *probability*, likelihood, likeliness 159 *chance*; good chance, favourable c., reasonable c., fair c., sporting c. 469 *possibility*; prospect, excellent p. 511 *prediction*; fair expectation 507 *expectation*; well-grounded hope 852 *hope*; safe bet 473 *certainty*; real risk, real danger 661 *danger*; natural course 179 *tendency*; presumption, natural p.; presumptive evidence, circumstantial e. 466 *evidence*; credibility; likely belief 485 *belief*; plausibility, reasonableness, good reason 475 *reasons*; verisimilitude, colour, show of, semblance 445 *appearance*; theory of probability; probabilism, probabilist.

Adj. *probable*, likely 180 *liable*; on the cards, in a fair way; natural, to be expected, foreseeable, foreseen; presumable, presumptive; reliable, to be acted on 473 *certain*; hopeful, promising 507 *expected*; looming 155 *impending*; in danger of 661 *vulnerable*; highly possible 469 *possible*.

plausible, specious, colourable; apparent, ostensible, to all intents and purposes 445 *appearing*; logical, reasonable 475 *rational*; convincing, persuasive, believable, easy to believe 485 *credible*; well-grounded, well-founded 494 *true*; ben trovato 24 *apt*.

Vb. *be likely*, - probable etc. adj.; have a chance, be on the cards, stand a chance, run a good c. 469 *be possible*; bid fair to, be in danger of 179 *tend*; show signs, have the makings of, promise 852 *give hope*.

make likely, make probable, increase the chances; involve 523 *imply*; entail 156 *conduce*; put in the way of, promote 703 *aid*; lend colour to, point to 466 *evidence*.

assume, presume, take for granted, flatter oneself 485 *believe*; conjecture, guess, dare say 512 *suppose*; think likely, look for 507 *expect*; read the future, see ahead 510 *foresee*; rely, count upon 473 *be certain*; gather, deduce, infer 475 *reason*.

Adv. *probably*, presumably; in all probability, in all likelihood, as is to be expected; very likely, most l., ten to one, by all odds, Lombard Street to a China orange; seemingly, apparently, on the face of it, to all appearances, prima facie; belike, like enough, as likely as not.

See: 24, 155, 156, 159, 179, 180, 445, 466, **469**, 473, 475, 485, 494, 507, 510, 511, 512, 523, 661, 703, 852.

472 Improbability

N. *improbability*, unlikelihood, doubt, real d. 474 *uncertainty*; little chance, chance in a million, off-chance, small c., poor c., slim c., outside c., long shot; scarcely any chance, not the ghost of a c., no c. 470 *impossibility*; long odds, bare possibility; pious hopes, forlorn hope, small h., poor prospect 508 *lack of expectation*; rare occurrence, rarity 140 *infrequency*; implausibility, traveller's tale, fisherman's yarn 541 *falsehood*.

Adj. *improbable*, unlikely, more than doubtful, dubious 474 *uncertain*; contrary to all reasonable expectations, unforeseeable, unforeseen 508 *unexpected*; hard to believe, fishy, unconvincing, implausible 474 *uncertified*; rare 140 *infrequent*; unheard of, unimaginable, inconceivable 470 *impossible*; stretching the imagination, incredible, too good to be true 486 *unbelieved*.

Vb. *be unlikely*, - improbable, look impossible etc. adj.; have a bare chance, show little hope, offer small chance; be implausible, not wash, be hard to believe, lend no colour to, strain one's credulity 486 *cause doubt*; think unlikely, whistle for 508 *not expect*.

Int. not likely! no fear! not on your life! not a hope! some hopes!

See: 140, **470**, **474**, 486, 508, 541.

473 Certainty

N. *certainty*, objective c., certitude, certain knowledge 490 *knowledge*; certainness, assuredness, sureness; certain issue, inevitability, inexorability, irrevocability, necessity 596 *fate*; inerrancy, freedom from error, infallibilism, infallibility; indubitability, reliability, utter r., unimpeachability 494 *truth*; certainty of meaning, unambiguity, univocity; no case to answer, incontrovertibility, irrefutability, indisputability, proof 478 *demonstration*; authentication, ratification, validation; certification, verification, confirmation; attestation 466 *testimony*; making sure, check 459 *enquiry*; ascertainment 484 *discovery*; dead certainty, cert, dead c., sure thing, safe bet, cinch, open and shut case, foregone conclusion; fact, ascertained f., indubitable f., positive f. 3 *substantiality*; matter of fact, accomplished f., fait accompli 154 *event*; res judicata, settled decision 480 *judgment*; gospel, Bible 511 *oracle*; dogma 976 *orthodoxy*; dictum, ipse dixit, ex cathedra utterance, axiom 496 *maxim*; court of final appeal, judgment seat 956 *tribunal*; last word, ultimatum 766 *conditions*.

positiveness, subjective certainty, moral c.; assurance, confidence, conviction, persuasion 485 *belief*; unshakable opinion, doctrinaire o. 485 *opinion*; idée fixe, fixity, obsession 481 *bias*; dogmatism, orthodoxy, bigotry 602 *opinionatedness*; infallibility, air of i., self-confidence; pontification, laying down the law.

doctrinaire, dogmatist, infallibilist; self-opinionated person 602 *obstinate person*; bigot, fanatic, zealot; oracle, Sir Oracle, knowall 500 *wiseacre*.

Adj. *certain*, sure, solid, unshakable, well-founded, well-grounded 3 *substantial*; reliable 929 *trustworthy*; authoritative, official 494 *genuine*; factual, historical 494 *true*; ascertained, certified, attested, guaranteed, warranted; tested, tried, foolproof 660 *safe*; infallible, unerring, inerrant 540 *veracious*; axiomatic, dogmatic, taken for granted 485 *creedal*; self-evident, axiomatic, evident, apparent; unequivocal, unambiguous, univocal; unmistakable, clear, clear as day 443 *obvious*; inevitable, unavoidable, ineluctable, irrevocable, inexorable 596 *fated*; bound, bound to be, in the bag; sure as fate, sure as death and taxes 124 *future*; inviolable, safe as houses 660 *invulnerable*; verifiable, testable, demonstrable 478 *demonstrated*.

positive, confident, assured, self-assured, certain in one's mind, undoubting, convinced, persuaded, certified, sure 485 *believing*; opinionated, self-o.; dogmatizing, pontifical, oracular 532 *assertive*; dogmatic, doctrinaire 976 *orthodox*; obsessed, bigoted, fanatical 481 *biased*; unshaken, set, fixed, fixed in one's opinions 153 *unchangeable*; clean-cut, clear-c., definite, defined, unambiguous, unambivalent, unequivocal, univocal 516 *intelligible*; convincing 485 *credible*; classified, in its place 62 *arranged*; affirmative, categorical, absolute, unqualified, unreserved, final, ultimate, conclusive, settled, without appeal.

undisputed, beyond doubt, without a shadow of doubt, axiomatic, uncontroversial; unquestioned, undoubted, uncontested, unarguable, indubitable, unquestionable, questionless, incontrovertible, incontestable, unchallengeable, unimpeachable, undeniable, irrefutable, irrefragable, indefeasible.

Vb. *be certain*, - sure etc. adj.; leave no doubt, be clear as day, stand to reason, be axiomatic 475 *be reasonable*; be positive, be assured, satisfy oneself, convince o., feel sure, be clear in one's mind, make no doubt, hold for true 485 *believe*; understand, know for certain 490 *know*; hold to one's opinions, have made up one's mind, dismiss all doubt; depend on it, rely on, bank on, trust in, swear by; gamble on, bet on, go nap on, put one's shirt on, lay one's bottom dollar.

dogmatize, pontificate, lay down the law 532 *affirm*; play the oracle, know all the answers.

make certain, certify, authenticate, ratify, seal, sign 488 *endorse*; guarantee, warrant, assure; finalize, settle, decide 480 *judge*; remove doubt, persuade 485 *convince*; classify 62 *arrange*; make sure, ascertain, check, double-check, verify, confirm, clinch 466 *corroborate*; reassure oneself, take a second look, do a double take; insure against 660 *safeguard*; reinsure 858 *be cautious*; ensure, make inevitable 596 *necessitate*.

Adv. *certainly*, definitely, certes, for sure, to be sure, no doubt, doubtless, indubitably, as sure as eggs is eggs, as sure as God made little green apples, as night follows day, of course, as a matter of c., no question; no two ways about it, no ifs or buts; without fail, sink or swim, rain or shine, come hell or high water, come what may.

See: 3, 62, 124, 153, 154, 443, 459, 466, 475, 478, 480, 481, 484, **485**, 488, 490, 494, 496, 500, 511, 516, 532, 540, **596**, 602, 660, 766, 858, 929, 956, 976.

474 Uncertainty

N. *uncertainty*, unverifiability, incertitude, doubtfulness, dubiousness; ambiguity 518 *equivocalness*; vagueness, haziness, obscurity 418 *darkness*; mist, haze, fog 423 *opacity*; yes and no, indeterminacy, indetermination, borderline case; indefiniteness, roving commission; query, question mark 459 *question*; open question, anybody's guess; nothing to go on, guesswork, guestimate 512 *conjecture*; contingency, doubtful c., doubtful event 159 *chance*; gamble, toss-up, wager 618 *gambling*; leap in the dark, bow at a venture, pig in a poke, blind date; something or other, this or that.

dubiety, dubitation 486 *doubt*; state of doubt, open mind, suspended judgment, open verdict; suspense, waiting 507 *expectation*; doubt, indecision, hesitancy, shilly-shallying, vacillation 317 *fluctuation*; seesaw, floating vote 601 *irresolution*; embarrassment, perplexity, bewilderment, bafflement, nonplus, quandary; dilemma, cleft stick, Morton's fork 530 *enigma*.

unreliability, liability to error, fallibility 495 *error*; insecurity, precariousness, touch and go 661 *danger*; untrustworthiness, treacherousness; fluidity, unsteadiness, variability, changeability 152 *changeableness*; unpredictability, unexpectedness 508 *lack of expectation*; fickleness, capriciousness, whimsicality 604 *caprice*; slipperiness, suppleness 930 *improbity*; lack of security, no guarantee, no collateral, bare word, dicer's oath, scrap of paper.

Adj. *uncertain*, unsure, doubtful, dubious, not axiomatic; unverifiable (**see** *uncertified*); insecure, chancy, risky 661 *unsafe*; treacherous (**see** *unreliable*); subject to chance, at the mercy of events; occasional, sporadic 140 *infrequent*; temporary, provisional 114 *transient*; fluid 152 *unstable*; contingent, depending on 766 *conditional*; unpredictable, unforeseeable 508 *unexpected*; aoristic, indeterminate, undefined, undetermined, unclassified; random 61 *orderless*; indecisive, undecided, open, in suspense; in question, under enquiry; open to question, questionable 459 *moot*; arguable, debatable, disputable, controvertible, controversial; suspicious 472 *improbable*; problematical, hypothetical, speculative 512 *suppositional*; undefinable, borderline; ambiguous 518 *equivocal*; paradoxical 477 *illogical*; oracular, enigmatic, cryptic, obscure 517 *puzzling*; vague, hazy, misty, cloudy 419 *shadowy*; mysterious, veiled 523 *occult*; unsolved, unresolved, unexplained 517 *unintelligible*; perplexing, bewildering, embarrassing, confusing 61 *complex*.

unreliable, undependable, untrustworthy; treacherous 930 *dishonest*; unsteady, unstable, variable, changeable 152 *changeful*; unpredictable, unforeseeable; fickle 604 *capricious*; fallible, open to error 495 *erroneous*; precarious, ticklish, touch and go.

doubting, in doubt, doubtful, dubious, full of doubt, riddled with d., plagued by uncertainty; agnostic, sceptical 486 *unbelieving*; sitting on the fence, in two minds; in suspense, open-minded; distrustful, mistrustful 858 *cautious*; uncertain, unassured, unconfident, diffident; hesitant, undecided, wavering, unsure which way to jump 601 *irresolute*; unable to say, afraid to say; moithered, moidered, mazed, dazed, baffled, perplexed, bewildered, distracted, distraught 517 *puzzled*; nonplussed, stumped, brought to a standstill, at one's wits' end, on the horns of a dilemma; lost, disorientated, guessing, in the dark, abroad, all at sea, adrift, drifting, astray, at a loss, at fault, clueless 491 *ignorant*.

uncertified, unverified, unchecked; awaiting confirmation, unconfirmed, uncorroborated, unauthenticated, unratified, unsigned, unsealed, unwitnessed, unattested; unwarranted, unguaranteed; unauthoritative, unofficial, apocryphal, uncanonical, unauthentic; unproved, undemonstrated; unascertained, untold, uncounted; untried, untested, in the experimental stage.

Vb. *be uncertain*, be contingent, lie in the lap of the gods; hinge on, be dependent on 157 *depend*; be touch and go, hang by a thread, tremble in the balance; be open to question, be ambiguous 518 *be equivocal*; have one's doubts 486 *doubt*; wait and see, wait on events 507 *await*; have a suspicion, suspect, wonder, wonder whether; dither, be in two minds, hover, float, sit on the fence, sway, seesaw, waver, teeter, vacillate, shilly-shally, falter, pause, hesitate 601 *be irresolute*; avoid a decision, boggle, stickle, demur; be in a maze, flounder, drift, be at sea; have nothing to go on, grope, fumble, cast about, beat a., experiment 461 *be tentative*; lose the thread, miss one's way, get lost 282 *stray*; lose the scent, come to a standstill; not know which way to turn, be at one's wits' end, be at a loss, not know what to make of, have no answer, be in a dilemma, be in a quandary; wouldn't swear, could be wrong.

puzzle, perplex, confuse, befuddle, maze, daze, bewilder, baffle, nonplus, flummox, stump, floor 727 *defeat*; mystify, keep one guessing; bamboozle 542 *befool*; fog, fox, throw off the scent 495 *mislead*; plunge in doubt, plague with d. 486 *cause doubt*; make one think, ask for thought, demand reflection.

Adv. *in suspense*, in a state of uncertainty, on the horns of a dilemma, in a maze, in a daze.

See: 61, 114, 140, 152, 157, 159, 282, 317, 418, 419, 423, 459, 461, 472, 477, **486**, 491, 495, 507, 508, 512, 517, 518, 523, 530, 542, 601, 604, 618, 661, 727, 766, 858, 930.

Section four: Reasoning processes

475 Reasoning

N. *reasoning*, ratiocination, force of argument; reason, discursive r.; intuitive reason, lateral thinking 476 *intuition*; sweet reason, reasonableness, rationality; dialectics, art of reasoning, logic; logical process, logical sequence, inference, general i., generalization; distinction 463 *discrimination*; apriorism, apriority, a priori reasoning, deductive r., deduction; induction, inductive reasoning, a posteriori r., empirical r.; rationalism, dialectic 449 *philosophy*; Boolean algebra, set theory, Venn diagram; modern maths 86 *mathematics*; plain reason, simple arithmetic.

premise, postulate, basis of reasoning; universals; principle, general p., first p.; lemma, starting point; assumption, stipulation 512 *supposition*; axiom, self-evident truth 496 *maxim*; datum, data; hypothesis, provisional hypothesis, one's position; Occam's razor.

argumentation, critical examination, analysis 459 *enquiry*; dialectic, Socratic elenchus, dialogue, logical disputation; formal logic, symbolic l.; logical scheme, synthesis; syllogization, sorites, syllogism, major premise, minor p.; quodlibet, proposition, statement, thesis, theorem, problem; predication, lemma, predicate; inference, corollary; dilemma, horns of a d. 474 *uncertainty*; conclusion, logical c., QED 478 *demonstration*; reductio ad absurdum; paradoxical conclusion, paradox 497 *absurdity*.

argument, discussion, symposium, dialogue; swapping opinions, give and take, cut and thrust; opposing arguments, disputation, controversy, debate 489 *dissent*; appeal to reason, set *or* formal argument, plea, pleading, special p., thesis, case; reasons, submission; defensive argument, apologetics, defence; aggressive argument, destructive a., polemics, polemic; conciliatory argument 719 *peace offering*; war of words, paper war 709 *quarrel*; propaganda, pamphleteering 534 *teaching*; controversialism, argumentativeness; hair-splitting, logic-chopping; logomachy; contentiousness, wrangling, jangling 709 *dissension*; bad argument, sophism 477 *sophistry*; legal argument, pleadings 959 *litigation*; argumentum ad hominem, play on the feelings; argument by analogy, parity of reasoning; tu quoque argument, same to you.

reasons, basis of argument, grounds; real reasons 156 *cause*; alleged reason 614 *pretext*; arguments, pros and cons; case, good c., case to answer; sound argument, strong a., cogent a., conclusive a., unanswerable a. 478 *demonstration*; point, valid p., point well taken, clincher.

reasoner, theologian 449 *philosopher*; logician, dialectician, syllogizer; methodist, methodologist; rationalist, euhemerist, demythologizer; sophister 477 *sophist*; casuist; polemic, polemist, polemicist, apologist, controversialist, eristic, controverter; arguer, debater, disputant; proponent, mooter, canvasser; pleader 958 *lawyer*; wrangler 709 *quarreller*; argumentative person, sea lawyer, barrack-room l., logomachist, quibbler, pedant; scholastic, schoolman 492 *intellectual*; mathematician, pure m.

Adj. *rational*, clear-headed, reasoning, reasonable; rationalistic, euhemeristic; ratiocinative, logical; cogent, acceptable, admissible, to the point, pointed, well-grounded, well-argued 9 *relevant*; sensible, fair 913 *just*; dianoetic, discursory, analytic, synthetic; consistent, systematic, methodological; dialectic, discursive, syllogistic, deductive, inductive, epagogic, maieutic, inferential, a posteriori, a priori, universal; axiomatic 473 *certain*; tenable 469 *possible*.

arguing, appealing to reason; polemical, irenic, apologetic; controversial, disputatious, eristic, argumentative, logomachic; quibbling 477 *sophistical*; disputable, controvertible, debatable, arguable 474 *uncertain*.

Vb. *be reasonable* 471 *be likely*; stand to reason, follow, hang together, hold water; appeal to reason; listen to reason, be guided by r., bow to r.; accept the argument, yield to a.; admit, concede, grant, allow 488 *assent*; have a case, have logic on one's side.

reason, philosophize 449 *think*; syllogize, ratiocinate; rationalize, explain away; apply reason, bring reason to bear, put two and two together; infer, educe, deduce, induct; work out, figure o.; explain 520 *interpret*.

argue, argufy, bandy arguments, give and take, cut and thrust; hold an argument, hold a symposium; exchange opinions, discuss, canvass 584 *confer*; debate, dispute, controvert; discept; quibble, split hairs, chop logic; indulge in argument, argue the case, argue the point, take a p., stick to one's p.; stress, strain, work an argument to death 532 *emphasize*; put one's case, plead; propagandize, pamphleteer 534 *teach*; take up the case, defend; attack, polemicize; try conclusions with, cross swords, join issue, demur, cavil 489 *dissent*; analyse, pull to pieces; out-argue, overwhelm with argument, bludgeon 479 *confute*; prove one's case 478 *demonstrate*; have words, wrangle 709 *bicker*; answer back, make a rejoinder 460 *answer*; start an argument, open a discussion; propose, bring up, moot; have the last word.

premise, posit, postulate, stipulate, lay down, assume, hypothesize 512 *suppose*; take for granted, regard as axiomatic, refer to first principles.

Adv. *reasonably*, fairly, rationally, logically; polemically; hypothetically; a priori, a posteriori, a fortiori, how much the more, much less; consequently; for reasons given; in argument, in one's submission.

See: 9, 86, 156, **449**, 459, 460, 463, 469, 471, 473, 474, 476, 477, 478, 479, 488, 489, 492, 496, 497, 512, 520, 532, 534, 584, 614, 709, 719, 913, 958, 959.

476 Intuition: absence of reason

N. *intuition*, instinct, association, Pavlovian response, automatic reaction, gut r., knee-jerk r. 450 *absence of thought*; light of nature, sixth sense, psi, psi faculty; telepathy; insight, second sight, clairvoyance 984 *psychics*; id, subconscious 447 *spirit*; intuitiveness, direct apprehension, unmediated perception, a priori knowledge; divination, dowsing; inspiration, presentiment, impulse 818 *feeling*; feminine logic; rule of thumb; hunch, impression, sense, guesswork; value judgment 481 *bias*; self-deception, wishful thinking; irrationality, illogicality, illogic; unreason 503 *insanity*.

Adj. *intuitive*, instinctive, impulsive; non-discursive, devoid of logic 477 *illogical*; impressionistic, subjective; involuntary 609 *spontaneous*; subconscious 447 *psychic*; above reason, beyond r., noumenal, independent of reason, unknown to logic, inspirational, inspired, clairvoyant, direct, unmediated.

Vb. *intuit*, know by instinct, have a sixth sense; sense, feel in one's bones, have a funny feeling, have a hunch; somehow feel, get the impression; react automatically, react instinctively; play it by ear, go by impressions, rely on intuition, dispense with reason, use feminine logic; guess, have a g., use guesswork, work on a hunch.

Adv. *intuitively*, instinctively, by instinct, by guess and by God, by the light of nature.

See: 447, 450, 477, 481, 503, 609, 818, 984.

477 Sophistry: false reasoning

N. *sophistry*, illogicalness, illogic; feminine logic 476 *intuition*; sophistical reasoning, false r., fallacious r., specious r., evasive r.; rationalization; double think, self-deception; mental reservation, arrière pensée 525 *concealment*; equivocation, mystification; word fencing, casuistry; subtlety, oversubtlety; special pleading, hair-splitting, logic-chopping; claptrap, mere words 515 *empty talk*; logomachy, quibbling, quibble; chicanery, chicane, subterfuge, shuffle, dodge; evasion 614 *pretext*.

sophism, a sophistry, specious argument, insincere a.; exploded argument, fallacious a.; illogicality, fallacy, paralogism; bad logic, loose thinking, sloppy t.; solecism, flaw, logical f., flaw in the argument; begging the question, petitio principii; circular reasoning; ignoratio elenchi; unwarranted conclusion, non sequitur, post hoc ergo propter hoc; contradiction in terms, antilogy; ignotum per ignotius; weak case, bad c., false c.

sophist, sophister, sophistical reasoner, casuist, quibbler, equivocator; caviller, devil's advocate.

Adj. *sophistical*, specious, plausible, ad captandum; evasive, insincere; hollow, empty; deceptive, illusive, illusory; over-refined, oversubtle, fine-spun; pettifogging, captious, quibbling; sophisticated, tortuous; casuistical.

illogical, contrary to reason, irrational, unreasonable; unreasoned, arbitrary; paralogistic, fallacious, fallible; contradictory, self-c., inconsistent, incongruous; unwarranted, invalid, untenable, unsound; unfounded, ungrounded, groundless; inconsequent, inconsequential; incorrect, unscientific, false 495 *erroneous*.

poorly reasoned, unrigorous, inconclusive; unproved, unsustained; weak, feeble; frivolous, airy, flimsy; loose, woolly, muddled, confused; woolly-headed, muddle-h.

Vb. *reason badly*, paralogize, argue in a circle, beg the question, not see the wood for the trees, strain at a gnat and swallow a camel; not have a leg to stand on; talk at random, babble, burble 515 *mean nothing*.

sophisticate, mislead 535 *misteach*; mystify, fetishize 542 *befool*; quibble, cavil, split hairs 475 *argue*; equivocate 518 *be equivocal*; dodge, shuffle, fence 713 *parry*; not come to the point, beat about the bush 570 *be diffuse*; evade 667 *elude*; varnish, gloss over, whitewash 541 *cant*; colour 552 *misrepresent*; pervert, misapply 675 *misuse*; pervert reason, twist the argument, torture logic; prove that white is black.

See: 475, 476, 495, 515, 518, 525, 535, 541, 542, 552, 570, 614, 667, 675, 713.

478 Demonstration

N. *demonstration*, logic of facts, documentation 466 *evidence*; proven fact 494 *truth*; proof, rigorous p.; establishment, conclusive proof, final p.; conclusiveness, irrefragability 473 *certainty*; verification, ascertainment 461 *experiment*; deduction, inference, argument, triumph of a. 475 *reasoning*; exposition, clarification 522 *manifestation*; burden of proof, onus.

Adj. *demonstrating*, demonstrative, probative 466 *evidential*; deducible, inferential, consequential, following 9 *relevant*; apodictic 532 *affirmative*; convincing, proving; conclusive, categorical, decisive, crucial; heuristic 534 *educational*.

demonstrated, evident, in evidence 466 *evidential*; taken as proved, established, granted, allowed; unconfuted, unrefuted, unanswered; open and shut, unanswerable, undeniable, irrefutable, irrefragable, irresistible, incontrovertible 473 *certain*; capable of proof, demonstrable, testable, discoverable.

Vb. *demonstrate*, prove; show, evince 522 *manifest*; justify 927 *vindicate*; bear out 466 *corroborate*; produce the evidence, document, substantiate, establish, verify 466 *evidence*; infer, deduce, draw, draw a conclusion 475 *reason*; settle the question, satisfy 473 *make certain*; make out, make out a case, prove one's point, clinch an argument, have the best of an a. 485 *convince*.

be proved, be demonstrated, prove to be true, emerge, follow, follow of course, stand to reason 475 *be reasonable*; stand, hold water, hold good 494 *be true*.

Adv. *of course*, provedly, undeniably; as already proved; QED.

See: 9, 461, **466, 473**, 475, 485, 494, 522, 532, 534, 927.

479 Confutation

N. *confutation*, refutation, disproof, invalidation; successful cross-examination, elenchus, exposure; conviction 961 *condemnation*; rebuttal, rejoinder, crushing *or* effective r., complete answer 460 *answer*; clincher, finisher, knockdown argument, crowning a.; tu quoque argument, retort, repartee 839 *witticism*; reductio ad absurdum 851 *ridicule*; contradiction, denial, denunciation 533 *negation*; exploded argument, proved fallacy 477 *sophism*.

Adj. *confuted*, disproved etc. vb.; silenced, exposed, without a leg to stand on; convicted 961 *condemned*; convicted on one's own showing, condemned out of one's own mouth; disprovable, refutable, confutable; tending to refutation, refutatory, refutative.

Vb. *confute*, refute, disprove, invalidate; rebut, retort, have an answer, explain away; negative, deny, contradict 533 *negate*; give the lie to, force to withdraw; prove the contrary, show the fallacy of; cut the ground from under; confound, silence, reduce to s., stop the mouth, shut up, floor, gravel, nonplus; condemn one out of his own mouth; show up, expose; convict 961 *condemn*; convict one of unreason, defeat one's logic; blow sky-high, shoot full of holes, puncture, riddle, destroy, explode, demolish one's arguments, knock the bottom out of 165 *demolish*; have, have in one's hand, have one on the hip; overthrow, squash, crush, overwhelm 727 *defeat*; riddle the defence, outargue, triumph in argument, have the better of the a., get the better of, score off; parry, avoid the trap; stand, stand up to argument; dismiss, override, sweep aside, brush a.; brook no denial, affirm the contrary 532 *affirm*.

be confuted, - refuted etc. adj.; fall to the ground, have not a leg to stand on; exhaust one's arguments; have nothing left to say, have no answer.

Adv. *in rebuttal*, in disproof; on the other hand, per contra.

See: 165, **460**, 477, 532, 533, 727, 839, 851, 961.

Section five: Results of reasoning

480 Judgment: conclusion

N. *judgment*, judging (**see** *estimate*); good judgment, discretion 463 *discrimination*; bad judgment, lack of discretion 464 *indiscrimination*; power of judgment, discretionary judgment, arbitrament 733 *authority*; arbitration, umpirage; judgment on facts, verdict, finding; penal judgment, sentence 963 *punishment*; spoken judgment, pronouncement; act of judgment, decision, adjudication, award; order, ruling; order of the court 737 *decree*; interlocutory decree, decree nisi; decree absolute; judgment in appeal, appellate judgment; irrevocable decision; settled decision, res judicata; final judgment, conclusion, conclusion of the matter, result, upshot; moral 496 *maxim*; value judgment 476 *intuition*; reasoned judgment, deduction, inference, corollary 475 *reasoning*; wise judgment, j. of Solomon 498 *wisdom*; fair judgment, unclouded eye 913 *justice*; vox populi, voting, referendum, plebiscite, poll 605 *vote*.

estimate, estimation, view 485 *opinion*; axiology 449 *philosophy*; assessment, valuation, evaluation, calculation 465 *measurement*; consideration, ponderation; comparing, contrasting 462 *comparison*; transvaluation 147 *conversion*; appreciation, appraisal, appraisement 520 *interpretation*; criticism, constructive c. 703 *aid*; destructive criticism 702 *hindrance*; critique, crit, review, notice, press n., comment, comments, observations, remarks 591 *article*; summing up, recapitulation; survey 438 *inspection*; inspection report 524 *report*; favourable report 923 *approbation*; unfavourable report, censure 924 *disapprobation*; legal opinion, counsel's o., second o. 691 *advice*.

estimator, judge, adjudicator; arbitrator, umpire, referee; surveyor, valuer, valuator 465 *appraiser*; inspector, inspecting officer, reporter, examiner, ombudsman 459 *enquirer*; counsellor 691 *adviser*; censor, critic, reviewer 591 *dissertator*; commentator, observer 520 *interpreter*; juror, assessor 957 *jury*; voter, elector 605 *electorate*.

Adj. *judicial*, judicious, judgmatic 463 *discriminating*; shrewd 498 *wise*; unbiased, dispassionate 913 *just*; juridical, juristic, arbitral; judicatory, decretal; determinative, conclusive; moralizing, moralistic, sententious; expressive of opinion, censorial; censorious 924 *disapproving*; critical, appreciative; advisory 691 *advising*.

Vb. *judge*, sit in judgment, hold the scales; arbitrate, referee; hear, try, hear the case, try the cause 955 *hold court*; uphold an objection, disallow an o.; rule, pronounce; find, find for, find against; decree, award, adjudge, adjudicate; decide, settle, conclude; confirm, make absolute; pass judgment, deliver j.; sentence, pass s., doom 961 *condemn*; agree on a verdict, return a v., bring in a v.; consider one's vote 605 *vote*; judge well, see straight; deduce, infer 475 *reason*; gather, collect; sum up, recapitulate; moralize 534 *teach*.

estimate, form an e., make an e., measure, calculate, make 465 *gauge*; value, evaluate, appraise; rate, rank; sum up, size up; conjecture, guess 512 *suppose*; take stock 808 *account*; consider, weigh, ponder, weigh the pros and cons 449 *meditate*; examine, investigate, vet 459 *enquire*; express an opinion, pass an o., report on; commentate, comment, criticize, review 591 *dissertate*; survey, pass under review 438 *scan*; censor, censure 924 *disapprove*.

Adv. *sub judice*, under trial, under sentence.

See: 147, 438, 449, 459, 462, **463**, 464, 465, 475, 476, 485, 496, 498, 512, **520**, 524, 534, 591, 605, 691, 702, 703, 733, 737, 808, 913, 923, 924, 955, 957, 961, 963.

481 Misjudgment. Prejudice

N. *misjudgment*, miscalculation, misreckoning, misconception, wrong impression 495 *error*; loose thinking 495 *inexactness*; bad judgment, poor j. 464 *indiscrimination*; fallibility, gullibility 499 *unintelligence*; obliquity of judgment, misconstruction 521 *misinterpretation*; wrong verdict, miscarriage of justice 914 *injustice*; overvaluation 482 *overestimation*; undervaluation 483 *underestimation*; autosuggestion, self-deception, wishful thinking 542 *deception*; fool's paradise 513 *fantasy*; false dawn 509 *disappointment*.

prejudgment, prejudication, foregone conclusion 608 *predetermination*; preconception, prenotion; parti pris, mind made up; something on the brain, preconceived idea; idée fixe, hangup, fixation, monomania 503 *mania*.

prejudice, prepossession, predilection; partiality, favouritism 914 *injustice*; bias, biased judgment, warped j., jaundiced eye; blind spot, blind side, mote in the eye, beam in the e. 439 *blindness*; onesidedness, party spirit 708 *party*; partisanship, clannishness, cliquishness, esprit de corps; sectionalism, parochialism, provincialism, insularity; odium theologicum 978 *sectarianism*; chauvinism, xenophobia, my country right or wrong; snobbishness, class war, class prejudice; ageism; sexism, sex prejudice; race p., racialism, racism; colour prejudice; colour bar, apartheid, segregation, discrimination 57 *exclusion*; intolerance, persecution, anti-Semitism 888 *hatred*.

narrow mind, narrow-mindedness, small-m., narrow views, narrow sympathies; cramped ideas, confined i.; insularity, parochialism, provincialism; closed mind, one-track m.; one-sidedness, overspecialization; legalism, pedantry, donnishness, hypercriticism 735 *severity*; illiberality, intolerance, dogmatism 473 *positiveness*; bigotry, fanaticism 602 *opinionatedness*; legalist, pedant, stickler 862 *perfectionist*; faddist 504 *crank*; zealot, bigot, fanatic 473 *doctrinaire*; racialist, racist, white supremacist, chauvinist.

bias, unbalance, disequilibrium 29 *inequality*; warp, bent, slant, liability 179 *tendency*; angle, point of view, private opinion 485 *opinion*; parti pris, mind made up (**see** *prejudgment*); infatuation, obsession 503 *eccentricity*; crankiness, whimsicality, fad, craze, bee in one's bonnet 604 *whim*.

Adj. *misjudging*, misconceiving, misinterpreting etc. vb.; miscalculating, in error, out 495 *mistaken*; fallible, gullible 499 *foolish*; wrong, wrong-headed; unseeing 439 *blind*; myopic, purblind, short-sighted 440 *dim-sighted*; misguided, superstitious 487 *credulous*; subjective, unrealistic, visionary, impractical; crankish, faddy, faddish, whimsical 503 *crazy*; besotted, infatuated 887 *enamoured*; haunted, obsessed, hung up, eaten up with.

narrow-minded, petty-m., small-m., narrow, confined, cramped, hidebound; parochial, provincial, insular; pedantic, donnish 735 *severe*; legalistic, literal, literal-minded, unimaginative, matter-of-fact; hypercritical, overscrupulous, fussy 862 *fastidious*; stiff, unbending 602 *obstinate*; dictatorial, dogmatic 473 *positive*; opinionated, opinionative; self-opinioned, self-conceited 871 *proud*.

biased, warped, twisted, swayed; jaundiced, embittered; prejudiced, closed; snobbish, clannish, cliquish 708 *sectional*; partisan, one-sided, party-minded 978 *sectarian*; nationalistic, chauvinistic, jingoistic, xenophobic; racist, racialist; sexist; class-prejudiced, colour-p.; predisposed, prepossessed, preconceived; prejudging 608 *predetermined*; unreasoning, unreasonable 477 *illogical*; discriminatory 914 *unjust*; illiberal, intolerant, persecuting 735 *oppressive*; bigoted, fanatic 602 *obstinate*; blinded 439 *blind*.

Vb. *misjudge*, miscalculate, miscount, misestimate 495 *blunder*; not take into account, reckon without; undervalue, minimize 483 *underestimate*; overestimate, overvalue 482 *overrate*; guess wrong, come to the wrong conclusion, misconjecture, misconceive 521 *misinterpret*; overreach oneself, overplay one's hand; get the wrong sow by the ear 695 *act foolishly*; overspecialize, not see the wood for the trees; not see beyond one's nose 499 *be foolish*; fly in the face of facts 477 *reason badly*.

prejudge, forejudge, judge beforehand, prejudicate 608 *predetermine*; prejudice the issue, precondemn; preconceive, presuppose, presume 475 *premise*; rush to conclusions, jump to c., run away with a notion 857 *be rash*.

bias, warp, twist, bend; jaundice, prejudice, fill with p.; prepossess, predispose 178 *influence*; infatuate, haunt, obsess 449 *engross*.

be biased, - prejudiced etc. adj.; be one-sided, see one side only, show favouritism, favour one side 914 *do wrong*; lean, favour, take sides, have a down on, have it in for, hold it against one, be unfair, discriminate against 735 *oppress*; pontificate 473 *dogmatize*; be obsessed with, lose one's sense of proportion; blind oneself to, have a blind side, have a blind spot 439 *be blind*.

See: 29, 57, 178, 179, 439, 440, 449, 464, 473, 475, 477, 482, 483, 485, 487, **495**, 499, 503, 504, 509, 513, 521, 542, **602**, 604, 608, 695, 708, 735, 857, 862, 871, 887, 888, **914**, 978.

482 Overestimation

N. *overestimation*, overestimate, overenthusiasm, overvaluation 481 *misjudgment*; overstatement 546 *exaggeration*; boasting 877 *boast*; ballyhoo, hype, buildup 528 *publicity*; overpraise, panegyric, gush, hot air 515 *empty talk*; storm in a teacup, much ado about nothing; megalomania, vanity 871 *pride*; overconfidence 857 *rashness*; egotism 932 *selfishness*; overoptimism, optimistic forecast, optimism; unnecessary pessimism, defeatism 853 *hopelessness*; optimist 852 *hope*; pessimist, prophet of doom, doom merchant, Jonah, defeatist; exaggerator, puffer, barker, advertiser 528 *publicizer*.

Adj. *optimistic*, upbeat, sanguine, oversanguine, overconfident; high-pitched, overpitched; enthusiastic, overenthusiastic, raving.

overrated, overestimated, overvalued, overpraised; puffed, puffed-up, cracked-up, hyped-up, overdone 546 *exaggerated*.

Vb. *overrate*, overestimate, count all one's geese swans; overvalue, overprice, set too high a value on 811 *overcharge*; rave, idealize, overprize, overpraise, think too much of; make too much of 546 *exaggerate*; strain, overemphasize, overstress, overdo, play up, overpitch, inflate, magnify 197 *enlarge*; boost, cry up, puff, panegyrize 923 *praise*; attach too much importance to, make mountains out of molehills, catch at straws; maximize, make the most of; make the best of, whitewash.

See: 197, 481, 515, 528, **546**, 811, 852, 853, 857, 871, 877, 923, 932.

483 Underestimation

N. *underestimation*, underestimate, undervaluation, minimization; conservative estimate, modest calculation 177 *moderation*; depreciation 926 *detraction*; understatement, litotes, meiosis; euphemism 950 *prudery*; self-depreciation, overmodesty 872 *humility*; false modesty, mock m., irony 850 *affectation*; pessimism 853 *hopelessness*; pessimist, minimizer, cynic 926 *detractor*.

Adj. *depreciating*, depreciative, depreciatory, derogatory, pejorative, slighting, belittling, pooh-poohing 926 *detracting*; underestimating, minimizing, conservative 177 *moderate*; modest 872 *humble*; pessimistic, despairing 853 *hopeless*; mock-modest 850 *affected*; euphemistic 541 *hypocritical*.

undervalued, underrated, underpriced, insufficiently appreciated, underpraised, unprized, unappreciated; slighted, pooh-poohed 458 *neglected*.

Vb. *underestimate*, underrate, undervalue, underprice; mark down, discount 812 *cheapen*; depreciate, underpraise, run down, cry d., disparage 926 *detract*; slight, pooh-pooh 922 *hold cheap*; misprize, not do justice to, do less than justice 481 *misjudge*; understate, spare one's blushes; euphemize; play down, soft-pedal, slur over; shrug off 458 *disregard*; make little of, minimize; deflate, cut down to size, make light of, belittle, make no account of, set no store by, think too little of 922 *despise*; set at naught, scorn 851 *ridicule*.

See: 177, 458, 481, 541, 812, 850, 851, 853, 872, 922, **926**, 950.

484 Discovery

N. *discovery*, finding, rediscovery; invention; exploration, speleology, potholing; excavation 459 *search*; detective instinct, nose, flair 619 *pursuit*; detection, spotting, espial 438 *inspection*; radiolocation 187 *location*; dowsing, water divining, rhabdomancy; ascertainment 473 *certainty*; exposure, revelation 522 *manifestation*; illumination, realization, disenchantment; accidental discovery, serendipity; a discovery, an invention, an inspiration; strike, find, lucky f., trouvaille, trover, treasure trove; eye-opener 508 *lack of expectation*; solution, explanation 520 *interpretation*; key, open sesame 263 *opener*.

detector, probe; space p., spy satellite 276 *spaceship*; asdic, sonar; early warning system, Earlybird; radar, radar trap; finder, telescopic f. 442 *telescope*; lie detector; sensor; Geiger counter 465 *meter*; metal detector; divining rod, dowsing r.; dowser, water diviner; spotter, scout, talent s.; discoverer, inventor; explorer 268 *traveller*; archaeologist, speleologist, potholer 459 *enquirer*; prospector 461 *experimenter*.

Adj. *discovering*, exploratory 461 *experimental*; on the scent, on the track, on the trail, warm, getting w.; near discovery, ripe for detection.

Vb. *discover*, rediscover, invent, explore, find a way 461 *experiment*; find out, hit it, have it; strike, hit, hit upon; come upon, happen on, stumble on; meet, encounter 154 *meet with*; realize, tumble to, awake to, see the truth, see the light, see as it really is, see in its true colours 516 *understand*; find, locate 187 *place*; recognize, identify 490 *know*; verify, ascertain 473 *make certain*; fish up, dig up, unearth, uncover, disinter, bring to light 522 *manifest*; elicit, worm out, ferret o., nose o., smell o. 459 *search*; get wind of 524 *be informed*.

detect, expose, show up 522 *show*; get at the facts, find a clue, be on the track, be near the truth, be getting warm, see daylight; put one's finger on the spot, hit the nail on the head, saddle the right horse; descry, discern, perceive, notice, spot, sight, catch sight of 438 *see*; sense, trace, pick up; see the cloven hoof, smell a rat; nose, scent, wind, scent out; follow, trace, track down 619 *hunt*; set a trap for, trap, catch out 542 *ensnare*.

Int. eureka! got it!

See: 154, 187, 263, 268, 276, 438, 442, **459**, **461**, 465, 473, 490, 508, 516, 520, 522, 524, 542, 619.

485 Belief

N. *belief*, act of believing, suspension of disbelief; credence, credit; state of belief, assurance, conviction, persuasion; strong feeling, firm impression; confidence, reliance, dependence on, trust, faith; religious belief 973 *religious faith*; full belief, full assurance; uncritical belief 487 *credulity*; implicit belief, firm b., fixed b. 473 *certainty*; obsession, blind belief 481 *prejudice*; instinctive belief 476 *intuition*; subjective belief, self-persuasion, self-conviction; hope and belief, expectation, sanguine e. 852 *hope*; traditional belief, folklore; public belief, popular b., common b., public opinion; credibility 471 *probability*; one's credit, one's word of honour 929 *probity*; token of credit, pledge.

creed, formulated belief, credo, what one holds, what one believes; dogma, Ark of the Covenant 976 *orthodoxy*; precepts, principles, tenets, articles; catechism, articles of faith; rubric, canon, rule 496 *maxim*; declaration of faith, professed belief, profession, confession, confession of faith 526 *disclosure*; doctrine, system, ideology, school, ism 449 *philosophy*; study of creeds, symbolics 973 *theology*.

opinion, one's opinions, one's views, one's conviction, one's persuasion; sentiment, mind, view; point of view, viewpoint, stand, position, attitude, angle 438 *view*; impression 818 *feeling*; conception, concept, thought 451 *idea*; thinking, way of thinking, way of thought, body of opinions, outlook on life, Weltanschauung 449 *philosophy*; assumption, presumption, principle 475 *premise*; theory, hypothesis 512 *supposition*; surmise, guess 512 *conjecture*; conclusion 480 *judgment*.

Adj. *believing*, holding, maintaining, declaring etc. vb.; confident, assured, reliant, unshaken, secure 473 *certain*; sure, cocksure 473 *positive*; convinced, persuaded, satisfied, converted, sold on; imbued with, penetrated w., obsessed w., possessed; firm in, wedded to; confiding, trustful, trusting, unhesitating, undoubting, unquestioning, unsuspecting, unsuspicious 487 *credulous*; conforming, loyal, pious 976 *orthodox*; having opinions, opinionated 481 *biased*.

credible, plausible, believable, tenable, reasonable 469 *possible*; likely, to be expected 471 *probable*; reliable, trustworthy, trusty, fiducial; worthy of credence, deserving belief, commanding b., persuasive, convincing, impressive 178 *influential*; trusted, believed; held, maintained; accepted, credited, accredited; supposed, putative, hypothetical 512 *suppositional*.

creedal, taught, doctrinal, dogmatic, confessional; canonical, orthodox, authoritative, accredited, ex cathedra; of faith, accepted on trust; sacrosanct, unquestioned; undeniable, absolute, unshakable 473 *undisputed*.

Vb. *believe*, be a believer 976 *be orthodox*; credit, put faith in, give faith to; hold, hold to be true; maintain, declare 532 *affirm*; believe religiously, perceive as true, take for gospel, believe for certain, firmly believe; profess, confess, recite the creed; receive, accept, admit, agree 488 *assent*; take on trust, take on credit; buy, swallow, swallow whole 487 *be credulous*; take for granted, assume 475 *premise*; have no doubt, make no d., cast doubt away, know for certain, be convinced, be sold on, be obsessed with 473 *be certain*; rest assured, be easy in one's mind about, be secure in the belief, rest in the b.; have confidence in, confide, trust, rely on, depend on, take one at his *or* her word; give one credit for, pin one's faith on, pin one's hopes on; have faith in, believe in, swear by, reckon on, count on, calculate on, bank on, be told, understand, know 524 *be informed*; come to believe, be converted; realize 484 *discover*; take as proven, grant, allow.

opine, think, conceive, fancy, ween, trow; have a hunch, surmise, guess 512 *suppose*; suspect, rather s.; be under the impression, have the i. 818 *feel*; deem, esteem, apprehend, assume, presume, take it, hold; embrace an opinion, adopt an o., imbibe an o., get hold of an idea, get it into one's head; have views, have a point of view, view as, take as, regard as, consider as, look upon as, set down as, hold for, account; hold an opinion, cherish an o., foster an o.; express an opinion, hazard an o. 532 *affirm*; change one's opinion 603 *recant*.

convince, make believe, assure, persuade, satisfy; make realize, bring home to 478 *demonstrate*; make confident, restore one's faith; convert, win over, bring o., bring round, wean from; bring to the faith, evangelize, spread the gospel; propagate a belief, propagandize, indoctrinate, proselytize 534 *teach*; cram down one's throat; sell an idea to, put over, put across; have the ear of, gain one's confidence, sway one's belief 178 *influence*; compel belief, exact b.; obsess, haunt, mesmerize, hypnotize; come round to, convince oneself, be sold on.

be believed, be widely b., be received; go down, go down well, be swallowed; find ready listeners, find willing ears; carry conviction; find credence, pass current, pass for truth, take hold of the mind, possess the m., dominate the m.

Adv. *credibly*, believably, supposedly, to the best of one's knowledge and belief; faithfully, on faith, on trust, on authority; on the strength of, on the evidence of, in the light of.

See: 178, 438, 449, 451, 469, 471, **473**, 475, 476, 478, 480, **481**, 484, 487, 488, 496, 512, 524, 526, 532, 534, 603, 818, 852, 929, **973**, 976.

486 Unbelief. Doubt

N.*unbelief*, nonbelief, disbelief, incredulity, discredit; disagreement 489 *dissent*; inability to believe, agnosticism; denial, denial of assent 533 *negation*; contrary belief, conviction to the contrary 704 *opposition*; blank unbelief, unfaith, want of faith; infidelity, misbelief 977 *heresy*; atheism 974 *irreligion*; derision, scorn, mockery 851 *ridicule*; change of belief, loss of faith, reversal of opinion, retraction 603 *recantation*; incredibility, implausibility 472 *improbability*.

doubt 474 *dubiety*; half-belief, critical attitude, hesitation, wavering, uncertainty; misgiving, distrust, mistrust; suspiciousness, scrupulosity; scepticism, agnosticism, pyrrhonism; reserve, reservation 468 *qualification*; demur, objection 704 *opposition*; scruple, qualm, suspicion 854 *nervousness*; jealousness 911 *jealousy*.

unbeliever, no believer, disbeliever; heathen, infidel 977 *heretic*; atheist 974 *irreligionist*; sceptic, pyrrhonist, agnostic; doubter, doubting Thomas; dissenter 489 *dissentient*; lapsed believer, retractor, recanter 603 *tergiversator*; denier 533 *negation*; absolute disbeliever, dissenter from all creeds, nullifidian; cynic, nobody's fool; scoffer, mocker, scorner 926 *detractor*.

Adj.*unbelieving*, disbelieving, incredulous, sceptical; heathen, infidel; nullifidian, creedless; unfaithful, lapsed 603 *tergiversating*; doubtful, undecided, wavering 474 *doubting*; suspicious, shy, shy of 854 *nervous*; oversuspicious 911 *jealous*; slow to believe, distrustful, mistrustful; inconvincible, impervious, hard to convince; cynical, hard-boiled, not born yesterday, no flies on 498 *intelligent*.

unbelieved, disbelieved, discredited, exploded; distrusted, mistrusted etc. vb.; incredible, unbelievable 470 *impossible*; inconceivable, unimaginable, staggering 864 *wonderful*; hard to believe, hardly credible; untenable, undeserving of belief, unworthy of credit; open to suspicion, open to doubt, unreliable, suspect, suspicious, questionable, disputable, far-fetched 474 *uncertified*; so-called, pretended.

Vb.*disbelieve*, be incredulous, find hard to believe, explain away, discredit, refuse credit, greet with scepticism, withhold assent, disagree 489 *dissent*; not fall for, not buy; mock, scoff at 851 *ridicule*; deny, deny outright 533 *negate*; refuse to admit, ignore; change one's belief, retract, lapse, relapse 603 *recant*.

doubt, half-believe 474 *be uncertain*; demur, object, cavil, question, scruple, boggle, stick at, have reservations 468 *qualify*; pause, stop and consider, hesitate, waver 601 *be irresolute*; treat with reserve, distrust, mistrust, suspect, have fears 854 *be nervous*; be shy of, shy at; be sceptical, doubt the truth of, take leave to doubt; not trust, set no store by; have questions, have one's doubts, harbour d., cherish d., cherish scruples; entertain suspicions, smell a rat, scent a fallacy; hold back, not go all the way with one 598 *be unwilling*.

cause doubt, cast d., raise questions; involve in suspicion, render suspect; call in question, discredit 926 *defame*; shake, shake one's faith, undermine one's belief; stagger, startle 508 *surprise*; pass belief 472 *be unlikely*; argue against, deter, tempt 613 *dissuade*; impugn, attack 479 *confute*; keep one guessing 517 *be unintelligible*.

Adv.*incredibly*, unbelievably; in utter disbelief.

doubtfully, hesitatingly, with a pinch of salt.

See:468, 470, 472, **474**, 479, 489, 498, 508, 517, 533, 598, 601, 603, 613, 704, 851, 854, 864, 911, 926, **974**, 977.

487 Credulity

N.*credulity*, credulousness; simplicity, gullibility; rash belief, uncritical acceptance 485 *belief*; will to believe, blind faith, unquestioning belief 612 *persuadability*; infatuation, dotage; self-delusion, self-deception, wishful thinking 481 *misjudgment*; superstition, superstitiousness; one's blind side 439 *blindness*; bigotry, fanaticism 602 *opinionatedness*; uncritical orthodoxy 83 *conformity*; credulous person, simpleton, sucker, mug 544 *dupe*.

Adj.*credulous*, believing, persuasible, persuadable, amenable; easily taken in, easily deceived 544 *gullible*; uncynical, unworldly; naive, simple, unsophisticated, green; childish, silly, soft, stupid 499 *foolish*; overcredulous, overtrustful, overconfiding; doting, infatuated; obsessed; superstitious 481 *misjudging*; confiding, trustful, unsuspecting.

Vb.*be credulous*, be easily persuaded; kid oneself; suspend one's judgment 477 *reason badly*; follow implicitly, believe every word, fall for, buy it, take on trust, take for granted, take for gospel 485 *believe*; accept 299 *absorb*; take the bait, rise to the b., swallow, swallow anything, swallow whole, swallow hook, line and sinker 544 *be duped*; run away with an idea *or* a notion, rush to a conclusion; be superstitious, touch wood, keep one's fingers crossed; think the moon is made of green cheese, take the shadow for the substance; catch at straws, hope eternally 482 *overrate*; not hear a word against, dote 481 *be biased*.

See: 83, 299, 439, 477, 481, 482, 485, 499, 544, 602, 612.

488 Assent

N. *assent*, yes, yea, amen; hearty assent; welcome; agreement, concurrence 758 *consent*; acceptance, agreement in principle 597 *willingness*; acquiescence 721 *submission*; acknowledgment, recognition, realization; no denial, admission, clean breast, plea of guilty, self-condemnation 939 *penitence*; confession, avowal 526 *disclosure*; declaration of faith, profession 532 *affirmation*; sanction, nod, OK, imprimatur, thumbs up, go-ahead, green light 756 *permission*; approval 923 *approbation*; concurrent testimony, accordance, corroboration 466 *evidence*; confirmation, verification 478 *demonstration*; validation, ratification; authentication, certification, endorsement, seal, signature, mark, cross; visa, pass 756 *permit*; stamp, rubber s. 547 *label*; favour, sympathy 706 *cooperation*; support 703 *aid*; assentation 925 *flattery*.

consensus, consentience, same mind 24 *agreement*; concordance, harmony, unison 710 *concord*; unanimity, solid vote, general consent, common c., universal agreement, universal testimony; consentaneity, popular belief, public opinion, vox populi, general voice; chorus, single voice; likemindedness, thinking alike, same wavelength, mutual sympathy, two minds with but a single thought 18 *similarity*; bipartisanship, interparty agreement; understanding, bargain 765 *compact*.

assenter, follower 83 *conformist*; fellow traveller, cooperator 707 *collaborator*; assentator, yes-man 925 *flatterer*; the ayes, consentient voice, willing voter; cheerer, acclaimer 923 *commender*; upholder, supporter, active s., abettor 703 *aider*; seconder, assentor 707 *patron*; ratifier, authenticator; subscriber, endorser 765 *signatory*; party, consenting p., covenanter; confessor, professor, declarant.

Adj. *assenting*, assentient 758 *consenting*; consentient, concurring, party to 24 *agreeing*; fellow-travelling, aiding and abetting, collaborating 706 *cooperative*; likeminded, sympathetic, welcoming 880 *friendly*; consentaneous 710 *concordant*; unanimous, solid, with one voice, in chorus; acquiescent 597 *willing*; delighted 824 *pleased*; allowing, granting 756 *permitting*; sanctioning, ratificatory; not opposed, conceding.

assented, acquiesced in, voted, carried, carried by acclamation, carried nem. con., agreed on all hands; unopposed, unanimous; uncontradicted, unquestioned, uncontested, unchallenged, uncontroverted 473 *undisputed*; admitted, granted, conceded 756 *permitted*; ratified, confirmed, signed, sealed; uncontroversial, nonparty, bipartisan.

Vb. *assent*, concur, agree with 24 *accord*; welcome, hail, cheer, acclaim 923 *applaud*; agree on all points, accept in toto, go all the way with, have no reservations 473 *be certain*; accept, agree in principle, like the idea, buy it; not deny, concede, admit, own, acknowledge, grant, allow 475 *be reasonable*; admit the charge, plead guilty, avow 526 *confess*; signify assent, nod a., nod, say aye, say yes, agree to, give one's assent, go along with 758 *consent*; sanction 756 *permit*; ratify (**see** *endorse*); coincide in opinion, voice the same o., see eye to eye; chime in with, echo, ditto, say amen, say hear hear; say the same, chorus; defer to 920 *respect*; be a yes-man, rubber-stamp 925 *flatter*; reciprocate, sympathize 880 *be friendly*; accede, adhere, side with 708 *join a party*; collaborate, go along with 706 *cooperate*; tolerate (**see** *acquiesce*); covenant, agree upon, come to an understanding, have a mutual agreement 765 *contract*.

acquiesce, not oppose, accept, abide by 739 *obey*; tolerate, not mind, put up with, suffer, endure, wear it; sign on the dotted line, toe the l. 721 *submit*; yield, defer to, withdraw one's objections; let the ayes have it, allow 756 *permit*; let it happen, look on 441 *watch*; go with the stream, swim with the s., float with the current, join in the chorus, follow the fashion, run with the pack 83 *conform*.

endorse, second, support, vote for, give one's vote to 703 *patronize*; subscribe to, attest 547 *sign*; seal, stamp, rubberstamp, confirm, ratify, sanction, homologate 758 *consent*; authenticate 473 *make certain*; countersign.

Adv. *consentingly*, willingly, with all one's heart; by consent, in full agreement, all the way, on all points.

unanimously, with one accord, with one voice, with one consent, one and all, in chorus, to a man, nem. con.; by show of hands, by acclamation; on the nod.

Int. amen! amen to that! hear, hear! aye, aye! so be it! well said! as you say! you said it! you can say that again! how right you are! I couldn't agree more! yes indeed! yes.

See: 18, **24**, 83, 441, 466, 473, 475, 478, 526, 532, 547, 597, 703, 706, 707, 708, 710, 721, 739, 756, **758**, 765, 824, 880, 920, 923, 925, 939.

489 Dissent

N. *dissent*, amicable dissent, agreement to disagree; dissidence, difference, confirmed opposition 704 *opposition*; dissentience, no brief for; difference of opinion, diversity of o., dissentient voice, contrary vote, disagreement, discordance, controversy 709 *dissension*; party feeling, party spirit, faction 708 *party*; popular clamour 891 *anger*; disaffection 829 *discontent*; dissatisfaction, disapproval 924 *disapprobation*; repudiation 607 *rejection*; protestantism, nonconformism, schism 978 *sectarianism*; counterculture, alternative life style 84 *nonconformity*; withdrawal, secession 621 *relinquishment*; walkout 145 *strike*; reluctance 598 *unwillingness*; recusancy 738 *disobedience*; noncompliance 769 *nonobservance*; denial, lack of consent 760 *refusal*; contradiction 533 *negation*; recantation, retraction 603 *tergiversation*; doubtfulness 486 *doubt*; cavil, demur, objection, demurrer, reservation 468 *qualification*; protest, expostulation, protestation, hostile demonstration 762 *deprecation*; challenge 711 *defiance*; passive resistance, noncooperation 738 *sedition*.

dissentient, objector, caviller, critic 926 *detractor*; interrupter, heckler, obstructor 702 *hinderer*; dissident, dissenter, protester, protestant; sectary 978 *sectarian*; separatist, seceder 978 *schismatic*; rebel 738 *revolter*; dropout 84 *nonconformist*; grouser 829 *malcontent*; odd man out, minority; splinter group, cave, faction 708 *party*; the noes, the opposition 704 *opposition*; noncooperator, conscientious objector, passive resister 705 *opponent*; challenger, agitator, firebrand, revolutionary 149 *revolutionist*; recanter, apostate 603 *tergiversator*.

Adj. *dissenting*, dissentient, differing, dissident 709 *quarrelling*; agnostic, sceptical, unconvinced, unconverted 486 *unbelieving*; separatist, schismatic 978 *sectarian*; nonconformist 84 *unconformable*; malcontent, dissatisfied 829 *discontented*; recanting, apostate 603 *tergiversating*; unassenting, unconsenting, not consenting 760 *refusing*; protesting 762 *deprecatory*; recusant, noncompliant 769 *nonobservant*; disinclined, loath, reluctant 598 *unwilling*; obstructive 702 *hindering*; challenging 711 *defiant*; resistant 704 *opposing*; intolerant, persecuting 735 *oppressive*.

unadmitted, unacknowledged, negatived, denied 533 *negative*; out of the question, disallowed 757 *prohibited*.

Vb. *dissent*, differ, agree to d. 25 *disagree*; beg to differ, make bold to d., combat an opinion, take one up on 479 *confute*; demur, enter a demurrer, object, raise objections, have reservations, cavil, boggle, scruple 468 *qualify*; protest, raise one's voice against, demonstrate a. 762 *deprecate*; resist 704 *oppose*; challenge 711 *defy*; show reluctance 598 *be unwilling*; withhold assent, say no, shake one's head, not wear it 760 *refuse*; shrug one's shoulders 860 *be indifferent*; disallow 757 *prohibit*; negative, contradict 533 *negate*; repudiate, hold no brief for, not defend; have no notion of, never intend to 607 *reject*; look askance at, not hold with, revolt at the idea 924 *disapprove*; go one's own way, secede, withdraw 621 *relinquish*; recant, retract 603 *apostatize*; argue, wrangle, bicker 709 *quarrel*.

Adv. *no*, on the contrary; at issue with, at variance w.; under protest; in the negative 760 *denyingly*.

Int. God forbid! not on your life! not on

your nelly! over my dead body! ask me another! tell that to the marines! never again! not likely!

See: 25, 84, 145, 149, 468, 479, 486, 533, 598, 603, 607, 621, 702, 704, 705, 708, 709, 711, 735, 738, 757, **760**, 762, 769, 829, 860, 891, 924, 926, 978.

490 Knowledge

N. *knowledge*, ken; knowing, cognition, cognizance, recognition, realization; intellection, apprehension, comprehension, perception, understanding, grasp, mastery 447 *intellect*; conscience, consciousness, awareness; consciousness raising; insight 476 *intuition*; precognition 510 *foresight*; illumination 975 *revelation*; lights, enlightenment 498 *wisdom*; acquired knowledge, learning, lore (**see** *erudition*); folk wisdom, folklore; occult lore 983 *sorcery*; education, background; experience, practical e., acquaintance, acquaintanceship, familiarity, intimacy; private knowledge, privity, being in the know, sharing the secret 524 *information*; no secret, un secret de Polichinelle; public knowledge, notoriety, common knowledge, open secret 528 *publicity*; complete knowledge, omniscience; partial knowledge, intimation, sidelight, glimpse, glimmering, inkling, suggestion 524 *hint*; suspicion, scent; sensory knowledge, impression 818 *feeling*; self-knowledge, introspection; detection, clue 484 *discovery*; specialism, expert knowledge, savoir faire, savvy, know-how, expertise 694 *skill*; half-knowledge, semi-ignorance, smattering 491 *sciolism*; knowability, knowableness, recognizability 516 *intelligibility*; science of knowledge, theory of k., epistemology.

erudition, lore, wisdom, scholarship, letters, literature 536 *learning*; acquired knowledge, general k., practical k., empirical k., experimental k.; academic knowledge, professional k., encylopedic k., universal k., polymathy, pansophy; solid learning, deep l., profound learning; small l., superficial l., smattering, dilettantism 491 *sciolism*; reading, wide r., desultory r.; book-learning, bookishness, bibliomania; pedantry, donnishness; information, precise i., varied i., general i.; mine of information, store of knowledge, encyclopedia 589 *library*; department of learning, faculty 539 *academy*; scholar 492 *intellectual*.

culture, letters 557 *literature*; the humanities, the arts; education, instruction 534 *teaching*; literacy, numeracy; liberal education, scientific e.; autodidactism; self-education, self-instruction; civilization, cultivation, cultivation of the mind; sophistication, acquirements, acquisitions, attainments, accomplishments, proficiency, mastery.

science, exact s., natural s., metascience; natural philosophy, experimental p.; scientific knowledge, systematic k., progressive k., accurate k., verified k., body of k., organized k., applied science, technology; tree of knowledge, ologies and isms.

Adj. *knowing*, all-k., encyclopedic, omniscient 498 *wise*; cognizant, cognitive 447 *mental*; conscious, aware, mindful of 455 *attentive*; alive to, sensible of 819 *impressible*; experienced, no stranger to, at home with, acquainted, familiar with 610 *habituated*; intimate, privy to, sharing the secret, wise to, on to, in the know, in on, behind the scenes 524 *informed*; fly, canny, shrewd 498 *intelligent*; conversant, practised, versed in, proficient 694 *expert*.

instructed, briefed, primed, made acquainted, informed of, au courant 524 *informed*; taught, trained, bred to; lettered, literate; numerate; schooled, educated, well-e.; learned, book-l., bookish, literary; erudite, scholarly 536 *studious*; read in, well-read, widely-r., well-informed, knowledgeable; donnish, scholastic, pedantic; highbrow, intellectual, cultured, cultivated, sophisticated, Bloomsbury, blue-stocking; strong in, well-qualified; professional, specialized 694 *expert*.

known, cognized, perceived, seen, heard; ascertained, verified 473 *certain*; realized, understood; discovered, explored; noted, celebrated, famous 866 *renowned*; no secret, public, notorious 528 *well-known*; familiar, intimate, dear; too familiar, hackneyed, stale, trite; proverbial, household, commonplace, corny, clichéd 610 *usual*; current, prevalent 79 *general*; memorized, known by heart, learnt off 505 *remembered*; knowable, cognizable, cognoscible; teachable, discoverable 516 *intelligible*.

Vb. *know*, savvy, ken, wot, wot of, ween;

have knowledge, be acquainted; apprehend, conceive, catch, grasp, twig, click, have, take in, get 516 *understand*; know entirely, possess, comprehend, master; come to know, realize; get to know, acquaint oneself, familiarize o.; know again, recognize; know the value, appreciate; be conscious of, be aware, have cognizance, be cognizant 447 *cognize*; discern 463 *discriminate*; perceive 438 *see*; examine, study 438 *scan*; go over, mull, con 455 *be attentive*; know well, know full w., be thoroughly acquainted with, see through, read one like a book, have one's measure, have one taped, know inside out; know down to the ground, know like the back of one's hand; know for a fact 473 *be certain*; know of, have knowledge of, know something; be in the know, be in the secret, have the lowdown 524 *be informed*; know by heart, know by rote 505 *memorize*; know backwards, have it pat, have at one's finger tips, be master of, know one's stuff 694 *be expert*; have a little knowledge of 491 *not know*; experience, know by e., learn one's lesson 536 *learn*; know all the answers, be omniscient; know what's what, see one's way, know one's way about 498 *be wise*.

be known, become k., come to one's knowledge, be brought to one's notice, come to one's ears; lie within one's cognizance, be knowable; be public knowledge, be no secret 528 *be published*.

Adv. *knowingly*, with knowledge; learnedly, scientifically; as every schoolchild knows.

See: 79, 438, 447, 455, 463, 473, 476, 484, 491, **492**, **498**, 505, 510, 516, **524**, 528, 534, 536, 539, **557**, 589, 610, **694**, 818, 819, 866, 975, 983.

491 Ignorance

N. *ignorance*, unknowing, nescience; lack of news, no word of; unawareness, unconsciousness 375 *insensibility*; incognizance, nonrecognition, nonrealization; incomprehension, incapacity, backwardness 499 *unintelligence*; inappreciation, philistinism 439 *blindness*; ecological ignorance, bioblindness; obstacle to knowledge, obscurantism; false knowledge, superstition 495 *error*; blind ignorance, abysmal i., crass i.; monumental i.; lack of knowledge, no science; lack of education, no schooling; untaught state, blankness, blank mind, tabula rasa; unacquaintance, unfamiliarity, inexperience, lack of experience, greenness, rawness; gaucherie, awkwardness; inexpertness, amateurishness 695 *unskilfulness*; innocence, simplicity, naivety 699 *artlessness*; nothing to go on, lack of information, general ignorance, anybody's guess, bewilderment 474 *uncertainty*; moral ignorance, unwisdom 499 *folly*; darkness, benightedness, unenlightenment; savagery, heathenism, paganism 982 *idolatry*; Age of Ignorance, Dark Ages; imperfect knowledge, semi-ignorance (**see** *sciolism*); ignorant person, illiterate 493 *ignoramus*; layman, autodidact, amateur, no expert 697 *bungler*; obscurantist; philistine.

unknown thing, obstacle to knowledge; unknown quantity, matter of ignorance; prehistory 125 *antiquity*; sealed book, Greek; Dark Continent, terra incognita, unknown country, unexplored ground, virgin soil; frontiers of knowledge; dark horse, enigma, mystery 530 *secret*; unidentified flying object, UFO; unidentified body; unknown person, Mr *or* Miss X., anonymity 562 *no name*.

sciolism, smattering, smatter, a little learning; glimmering, glimpse, half-glimpse 524 *hint*; vagueness, half-knowledge 495 *inexactness*; unreal knowledge 495 *error*; superficiality 212 *shallowness*; dilettantism, dabbling; affectation of knowledge, pedantry, quackery, charlatanism, bluff 850 *affectation*; smatterer 493 *sciolist*.

Adj. *ignorant*, nescient, unknowing, blank; incognizant, unrealizing, uncomprehending; in ignorance, unwitting; unaware, unconscious, oblivious 375 *insensible*; unhearing, unseeing; unfamiliar with, unacquainted, a stranger to, not at home with; in the dark (**see** *uninstructed*); reduced to guessing, mystified 474 *uncertain*; bewildered, confused, at one's wits' end; clueless, without a clue; blinkered, blindfolded 439 *blind*; groping, tentative 461 *experimental*; lay, amateurish, nonprofessional, unqualified, inexpert 695 *unskilful*; unversed, not conversant, inexperienced, uninitiated, green, raw; innocent of, guiltless 935 *innocent*; naive, simple, unworldly 699 *artless*; knowing no better, gauche, awkward; unenlightened, benighted; savage, uncivilized; pagan, heathenish 982 *idolatrous*; backward, dull, dense, dumb 499 *unintelligent*;

empty-headed, foolish 499 *unwise*; obscurantist, unscientific; dark, superstitious, prescientific 481 *misjudging*; old-fashioned, out of touch, behind the times 125 *retrospective*; unretentive, forgetting 506 *forgetful*; regardless 456 *inattentive*; wilfully ignorant, indifferent 454 *incurious*.

uninstructed, unbriefed, uninformed, unapprized, not told, no wiser, kept in the dark; not rightly informed, misinformed, mistaught, misled, hoodwinked; not fully informed, ill-i., vague about 474 *uncertain*; unschooled, untaught, untutored, untrained; unlettered, illiterate, innumerate, uneducated; unlearned, uncultivated, uncultured, lowbrow; unscholarly, unbookish, unread, philistine; simple, dull, dense, dumb (**see** *ignorant*).

unknown, unbeknown, untold, unheard; unspoken, unsaid, unuttered; unseen, never seen 444 *invisible*; hidden, veiled 525 *concealed*; unrecognized 525 *disguised*; unapprehended, unrealized, unperceived; unexplained 517 *unintelligible*; dark, enigmatic, mysterious 523 *occult*; strange, new, unfamiliar, unprecedented; unnamed 562 *anonymous*; unidentified, unclassified, uninvestigated 458 *neglected*; undiscovered, unexplored, uncharted, unplumbed, unfathomed; untried, untested; virgin, novel 126 *new*; unknowable, undiscoverable; unforeseeable, unpredictable 124 *future*; unknown to fame, unheard of, obscure, humble 639 *unimportant*; lost, missing 190 *absent*; out of mind 506 *forgotten*.

dabbling, smattering, sciolistic; unqualified, quack, bluffing 850 *affected*; half-educated, semiliterate, semieducated; half-baked, shallow, superficial, dilettante.

Vb. *not know*, be ignorant, be in the dark, lack information, have nothing to go on; be unacquainted, not know from Adam; be innocent of, be green, know no better; know not, wist not, cannot say; not know the half of, have no conception, have no notion, have no clue, have no idea, have not the remotest i., not have the foggiest, not have an inkling, can only guess, be reduced to guessing 512 *suppose*; know nothing of, wallow in ignorance; not hear 416 *be deaf*; have a film over one's eyes, not see 439 *be blind*; be at a loss, not know what to make of 474 *be uncertain*; not know the first thing about, have everything to learn 695 *be unskilful*; not know chalk from cheese 464 *not discriminate*; misunderstand 517 *not understand*; misconstrue 481 *misjudge*; half know, know a little, dabble in; half glimpse, guess, suspect, wonder 486 *doubt*; unlearn 506 *forget*; lack interest 454 *be incurious*; refuse to know, ignore 458 *disregard*; make ignorant, unteach 535 *misteach*; keep in the dark, mystify 525 *keep secret*; profess ignorance, shrug one's shoulders 860 *be indifferent*; want to know, ask 459 *enquire*; grope, fumble 461 *be tentative*.

Adv. *ignorantly*, in ignorance, unawares; unconsciously; amateurishly, unscientifically; dimly, through a glass darkly; for all one knows.

See: 124, 125, 126, 190, 212, 375, 416, 439, 444, 454, 456, 458, 459, 461, 464, 474, 481, 486, **493**, 495, **499**, 506, 512, 517, 523, 524, 525, 530, 535, 562, 639, **695**, 697, 699, 850, 860, 935, 982.

492 Scholar

N. *scholar*, savant(e), learned person, erudite p., educated p., man *or* woman of learning, man *or* woman of letters, bookman, bookwoman; don, reader, professor, pedagogue 537 *teacher*; doctor, clerk, scribe, pedant, bookworm; classicist, humanist; polymath, polyhistor, pantologist, encyclopedist; prodigy of learning, mine of information, walking encyclopedia, talking dictionary; student, serious student 538 *learner*; degree-holder, graduate, qualified person, professional, specialist 696 *proficient person*; world of learning, academic circles, senior common room, professoriate.

intellectual, academic, scholastic, schoolman 449 *philosopher*; brain worker; mastermind, brain, genius, prodigy 500 *sage*; know-all, brainbox; highbrow, egghead, bluestocking, bas bleu, brahmin, longhair; culture vulture; intelligentsia, literati, illuminati; man *or* woman of science, scientist, technologist; boffin, backroom boy *or* girl; academician, Immortal; patron of learning, Maecenas.

collector, connoisseur, dilettante 846 *people of taste*; bibliophile, book collector, bibliomaniac; librarian, curator 749 *keeper*; antiquary 125 *antiquarian*; numismatist, phillumenist, philatelist, stamp collector 504 *enthusiast*; collector of words, compiler, lexicographer, philologist 557 *linguist*.

See: 125, 449, **500**, 504, 537, 538, 557, 696, 749, 846.

493 Ignoramus

N. *ignoramus*, know-nothing, illiterate, analphabet, no scholar, lowbrow; philistine 847 *vulgarian*; duffer, wooden spoon, thickhead, numskull 501 *dunce*; blockhead, goof, goose 501 *fool*; greenhorn, novice, raw recruit 538 *beginner*; simpleton, babe, innocent 544 *dupe*; bigot 481 *narrow mind*.

sciolist, smatterer, half-scholar, pedant 500 *wiseacre*; dabbler, dilettante; quack, charlatan 545 *impostor*.

See: 481, 500, **501**, 538, 544, 545, 847.

494 Truth

N. *truth*, the very t., verity, sooth, good s.; rightness, intrinsic truth; basic truth, primary premise; truism 496 *axiom*; consistency, self-c., accordance with fact; truth of the matter, honest truth, living t., plain t., simple t.; sober truth, stern t.; light, light of truth, revealed t., gospel t., gospel, Holy Writ, Bible 975 *revelation*; nature 321 *world*; facts of life 1 *existence*; actuality, historicity 1 *reality*; factualness, fact, matter of f. 3 *substantiality*; home truth, candour, frankness 929 *probity*; naked truth, unvarnished t., unqualified t., unalloyed t.; the t., the whole t. and nothing but the t.; truth-speaking, truthfulness 540 *veracity*; appearance of truth, verisimilitude 471 *probability*.

authenticity, validity, realness, genuineness; the real Simon Pure, the real McCoy, the real thing, the very t., the genuine article, it 13 *identity*; no illusion, not a fake 21 *no imitation*.

accuracy, care for truth, attention to fact; verisimilitude, realism, naturalism, local colour, warts and all; fine adjustment, sensitivity, fidelity, high f., exactitude, exactness, preciseness, precision, mathematical p., clockwork p.; micrometry 465 *measurement*; mot juste, aptness 24 *adaptation*; meticulousness 455 *attention*; pedantry, rigidity, rigour, letter of the law 735 *severity*; literality, literalness 514 *meaning*; true report, the very words 540 *veracity*; chapter and verse, facts, statistics 466 *evidence*.

Adj. *true*, veritable; correct, right, so; real, tangible 3 *substantial*; actual, factual, historical; well-grounded, well-founded; well-argued, well-taken 478 *demonstrated*; literal, truthful 540 *veracious*; true to the facts, true to scale, true to the letter (**see** *accurate*); categorically true, substantially t.; likely, very l. 471 *probable*; ascertained 473 *certain*; unquestionable 473 *undisputed*; consistent, self-c., logical, reasonable 475 *rational*; natural, true to life, true to nature, undistorted, faithful; realistic, objective, unbiased; unromantic, unideal, down to earth; candid, honest, unflattering, warts and all 522 *undisguised*.

genuine, no other, as represented; authentic, veritable, bona fide, valid, guaranteed, official, pukka; sound, solid, reliable, honest 929 *trustworthy*; natural, pure, sterling, hallmarked, true as steel; dinkum, fair d., Simon-Pure; true-born, by birth; rightful, legitimate; unadulterated, unsophisticated, unvarnished, uncoloured, undisguised, undistorted, unexaggerated.

accurate, exact, precise, definite, defined; well-adjusted, well-pitched, high-fidelity, dead-on 24 *adjusted*; well-aimed, direct, straight, dead-centre 281 *directed*; unerring, undeviating; constant, regular 16 *uniform*; punctual, right, correct, true, spot on; never wrong, infallible; close, faithful, representative, photographic; fine, nice, delicate, sensitive; mathematical, scientific, electronic, micrometric; mathematically exact, scientifically e., religiously e.; scrupulous, punctilious, meticulous, strict, severe 455 *attentive*; word for word, literal; literal-minded, rigid, pedantic, just so 862 *fastidious*.

Vb. *be true*, be so, be just so, be the case, happen, exist 1 *be*; hold, hold true, hold good, hold water, wash, stand the test, ring true; conform to fact, prove true, hold together, be consistent; have truth, enshrine a t.; speak the truth, omit nothing 540 *be truthful*; look true, seem real, come alive, copy nature 551 *represent*; square, set, trim 24 *adjust*; substantiate 466 *corroborate*; prove 478 *demonstrate*; be right, be correct, have the right answer; get at the truth, hit the nail on the head 484 *detect*.

Adv. *truly*, verily, undeniably, really, veritably, genuinely, indeed; as a matter of fact 1 *actually*; to tell the truth 540 *truthfully*; strictly speaking; sic, literally, to the letter, word for word; exactly, accurately, precisely, plumb, right, to an inch, to a hair, to a nicety, to a turn, to a T, just right; in every detail, in all respects.

See: 1, 3, 13, 16, 21, 24, 281, 321, 455, 465, 466, 471, 473, 475, 478, 484, 496, 514, 522, **540**, 551, 735, 862, 929, 975.

495 Error

N. *error,* erroneousness, wrongness, unsoundness; silliness 497 *absurdity*; untruth, unreality, nonobjectivity; falsity, unfactualness, nonhistoricity 2 *nonexistence*; errancy, straying from the truth 282 *deviation*; logical error, fallacy, self-contradiction 477 *sophism*; credal error, misbelief, unorthodoxy 977 *heterodoxy*; mists of error, wrong ideas, old wives' tales, superstition 491 *ignorance*; liability to error, fallibility 481 *misjudgment*; subjective error, subjectivity, unrealism, wishful thinking, doublethink, self-deceit, self-deception; misunderstanding, misconception, misconstruction, cross-purposes 521 *misinterpretation*; misguidance 535 *misteaching*; bad memory, forgetfulness 506 *oblivion*; falseness, untruthfulness 541 *falsehood*; illusion, hallucination, mirage 440 *visual fallacy*; false light, false dawn 509 *disappointment*; mental error, delusion 503 *insanity*; flattering hope, dream 513 *fantasy*; false impression, wrong idea (**see** *mistake*); warped notion, prejudice 481 *bias*.

inexactness, inexactitude, inaccuracy, imprecision, nonadjustment; faultiness, systematic error, probable e.; unrigorousness, looseness, laxity, broadness, generalization 79 *generality*; loose thinking 477 *sophistry*; sloppiness, carelessness 458 *negligence*; mistiming 118 *anachronism*; misstatement, misreport, misinformation, bad reporting 552 *misrepresentation*; misquotation (**see** *mistake*); misuse of language, malapropism 565 *solecism*.

mistake, bad idea (**see** *error*); inappropriate move, miscalculation 481 *misjudgment*; blunder, botch-up 695 *bungling*; wrong impression, mistaken identity, wrong person, wrong address; glaring error, bloomer, boner, clanger, howler, schoolboy h., gaffe, bull, Irish b. 497 *absurdity*; loose thread, oversight 456 *inattention*; mishit, bosh shot 728 *failure*; bungle, slip-up, boob, goof; fluff, muff; slip, slip of the pen, slip of the tongue, spoonerism 565 *solecism*; clerical error, typist's e.; typographic error, printer's e., misprint, erratum, corrigendum; inadvertency, trip, stumble; bad tactics, wrong step, faux pas; solecism 847 *bad taste*; blot, flaw 845 *blemish*.

Adj. *erroneous,* erring, wrong; solecistic 565 *ungrammatical*; in error (**see** *mistaken*); unfactual, unhistorical, mythical 2 *unreal*; aberrant 282 *deviating*; wide of the truth, devoid of t. 543 *untrue*; unsound, unscientific, unreasoned, ill-reasoned, self-contradictory 477 *illogical*; implausible 472 *improbable*; baseless, unsubstantiated, uncorroborated, unfounded, ungrounded, disproved 479 *confuted*; exploded, discredited 924 *disapproved*; fallacious, misleading 535 *misteaching*; unauthentic, apocryphal, unscriptural, unbiblical; perverted, unorthodox, heretical 977 *heterodox*; untruthful, lying 541 *false*; not genuine, fake 542 *spurious*; hallucinatory, illusive, illusory, delusive, deceptive 542 *deceiving*; subjective, unrealistic, fantastical 513 *imaginary*; wild, crackpot 497 *absurd*; fallible, liable to error, wrong-headed, perverse, prejudiced 481 *biased*; superstitious 491 *ignorant*.

mistaken, wrongly taken, misunderstood, misconceived; misrepresented, perverted; misread, misprinted; miscalculated, misjudged 481 *misjudging*; in error, misled, misguided; misinformed, ill-informed, deluded 491 *uninstructed*; slipping, blundering 695 *clumsy*; straying, wandering 282 *deviating*; wide, misaimed, misdirected, off-target 25 *unapt*; at fault, out, cold, off the scent, off the track, off the beam, on the wrong tack, on the wrong scent, off the rails, at sea 474 *uncertain*.

inexact, inaccurate; not strict, unrigorous, not literal, free; broad, generalized 79 *general*; not factual, incorrect, misstated, misreported, garbled; imprecise, erratic, wild, hit or miss; insensitive, clumsy; out, wildly o., maladjusted, badly adjusted; untuned, out of tune, out of gear; unsynchronized, slow, losing, fast, gaining; uncorrected, unrevised; faulty, full of faults, flawed, botched, mangled 695 *bungled*; misprinted, misread, mistranslated 521 *misinterpreted*.

Vb. *err,* commit an error, fall into e., go wrong, mistake, make a m.; labour under a misapprehension, bark up the wrong tree; be in the wrong, be mistaken; delude oneself, suffer hallucinations 481 *misjudge*; be misled, be misguided; receive a wrong impression, get hold of the wrong end of the stick, be at cross-purposes, misunderstand, misconceive, misapprehend, get it wrong 517 *not understand*; miscount, misreckon 482 *overrate*, 483 *underestimate*; go astray 282 *stray*; gain, be fast 135 *be early*; lose, be slow, stop 136 *be late*.

blunder, trip, stumble, miss, fault 695 *be clumsy*; slip, slip up, drop a brick, drop a clanger, boob, goof; commit a faux pas, put one's foot in it; betray oneself, give oneself away 526 *disclose*; blot one's copybook, blot, flaw; fluff, muff, botch, bungle; blow it 728 *fail*; play into one's hands 695 *act foolishly*; miscount 481 *misjudge*; misread, misquote, misprint, mistake the meaning, misapprehend, mistranslate 521 *misinterpret*.

mislead, misdirect, give the wrong address 282 *deflect*; misinform, lead into error, lead astray, pervert, cause to err, involve in error, steep in e. 535 *misteach*; beguile, befool, lead one a dance, lead one up the garden path 542 *deceive*; give a false impression, create a false i., falsify, garble 541 *dissemble*; gloze over, whitewash, cover up 525 *conceal*.

See: 2, 25, 79, 118, 135, 136, 282, 440, 456, 458, 472, 474, 477, 479, **481**, 482, 483, 491, 497, 503, 506, 509, 513, 517, 521, 525, 526, 535, **541**, **542**, **543**, 552, 565, **695**, 728, 845, 847, 924, 977.

496 Maxim

N. *maxim*, apophthegm, gnome, adage, saw, proverb, byword, aphorism; dictum, tag, saying, pithy s., stock s., common s., received s., true s., truth; epigram, mot 839 *witticism*; wise maxim, sage reflection; truism, cliché, commonplace, platitude, banality, hackneyed saying, trite remark, statement of the obvious, bromide; motto, watchword, slogan, catchword; formula, mantra; text, sutra, rule, golden r. 693 *precept*; gloss, comment, note, remark, observation 520 *commentary*; moral, edifying story, fable, cautionary tale 590 *narrative*; phylactery, formulary; book of proverbs, collection of sayings; folklore.

axiom, self-evident truth, truism, tautology; principle, postulate, theorem, formula; Sod's Law, Murphy's Law.

Adj. *aphoristic*, gnomic, sententious, proverbial, moralizing 498 *wise*; epigrammatic, piquant, pithy 839 *witty*; terse, snappy 569 *concise*; enigmatic, oracular 517 *puzzling*; common, banal, trite, corny, hackneyed, platitudinous, clichéd, commonplace, stock 610 *usual*; axiomatic 693 *preceptive*.

Adv. *proverbially*, as the saying goes, as they say, to coin a phrase; pithily, in a nutshell; aphoristically, epigrammatically, wittily; by way of moral.

See: 498, 517, 520, 569, 590, 610, **693**, 839.

497 Absurdity

N. *absurdity*, height of a., absurdness 849 *ridiculousness*; ineptitude, inconsequence 10 *irrelevance*; false logic 477 *sophistry*; foolishness, silliness, silly season 499 *folly*; senselessness, futility, fatuity 641 *lost labour*; nonsense verse, amphigory; talking rot, talking through one's hat; rot, rubbish, nonsense, stuff and nonsense, gibberish, jargon, twaddle 515 *silly talk*; rhapsody, romance, romancing, fustian, bombast 546 *exaggeration*; Irish bull, Irishism, malapropism, howler 495 *mistake*; paradox 508 *lack of expectation*; spoonerism, joke 839 *witticism*; pun, equivoque, play on words 518 *equivocalness*; riddle, riddle-me-ree 530 *enigma*; quibble, verbal q. 477 *sophism*; anticlimax, bathos, descent from the sublime to the ridiculous; sell, catch 542 *trickery*.

foolery, antics, fooling about, horsing around, silliness, asininity, tomfoolery, skylarking 837 *revel*; vagary, whimsy, whimsicality 604 *whim*; extravagance, extravaganza; escapade, scrape 700 *predicament*; practical joke, monkey tricks, piece of nonsense; drollery, comicality 849 *ridiculousness*; clowning, buffoonery, burlesque, parody, caricature 851 *ridicule*; farce, mummery, pretence 850 *affectation*; showing off 875 *ostentation*.

Adj. *absurd*, inept 25 *unapt*; ludicrous, laughable, comical, grotesque 849 *ridiculous*; rash, silly, asinine, tomfool 499 *foolish*; nonsensical, senseless 515 *meaningless*; preposterous, without rhyme or reason 477 *illogical*; wild, overdone, extravagant 546 *exaggerated*; pretentious 850 *affected*; frantic 503 *frenzied*; mad, crazy, crackpot, harebrained 495 *erroneous*; fanciful, fantastic 513 *imaginative*; futile, fatuous 641 *useless*; paradoxical 508 *unexpected*; inconsistent 10 *irrelevant*; quibbling 477 *sophistical*; punning 518 *equivocal*; macaronic 43 *mixed*.

Vb. *be absurd*, play the fool, act like a fool, behave like an idiot 499 *be foolish*; fool, fool about, lark about, muck a., horse a., monkey around, play practical jokes 837 *amuse oneself*; be a laughingstock 849 *be ridiculous*; clown, burlesque, parody, caricature, mimic, guy 851 *ridicule*; talk like a fool, talk rot, talk through one's hat, talk gibberish 515 *mean nothing*; talk wildly, rant, rave 503 *be insane*; rhapsodize, romance 546 *exaggerate*.

See: 10, 25, 43, 477, 495, 499, 503, 508, 513, **515**, 518, 530, 542, 546, 604, 641, 700, 837, 839, **849**, 850, 851, 875.

498 Intelligence. Wisdom

N. *intelligence*, thinking power, intellectualism 447 *intellect*; brains, good b., brain, grey matter, head, headpiece, loaf, upper storey; nous, wit, mother w., commonsense; lights, understanding, sense, good s., horse s., savvy, gumption, know-how; wits, sharp w., ready w., quick thinking, quickness, readiness, esprit; ability, capacity, mental c., mental grasp; calibre, mental c., intelligence quotient, IQ; high IQ, forwardness, brightness; braininess, cleverness 694 *aptitude*; mental gifts, giftedness, brilliance, talent, genius; ideas, inspiration, sheer i. 476 *intuition*; brainwave, bright idea 451 *idea*.

sagacity, judgment, good j., cool j., discretion, discernment 463 *discrimination*; perception, perspicacity, clear thought, clear thinking; acumen, sharpness, acuteness, acuity, penetration; practicality, practical mind, shrewdness, long-headedness; level-headedness, balance 502 *sanity*; prudence, forethought, long-sightedness, farsightedness 510 *foresight*; subtleness, subtlety, craft, craftiness 698 *cunning*; worldly wisdom, oneupmanship 694 *skill*; vigilance, alertness, awareness 457 *carefulness*; policy, good p., tact, statesmanship 688 *tactics*.

wisdom, ripe w., wise understanding, mature u., sapience; grasp of intellect, profundity of thought 449 *thought*; depth, depth of mind, breadth of m., reach of m., enlargement of m.; experience, lifelong e., digested e., ripe e., fund of e., ripe knowledge 490 *knowledge*; tolerance, broad-mindedness, catholic outlook; right views, soundness; mental poise, mental balance, sobriety, objectivity, enlightenment.

Adj. *intelligent*, endowed with brains, brainy, clever, forward, bright, bright as a button; brilliant, scintillating, talented, of genius 694 *gifted*; capable, able, practical 694 *skilful*; apt, ready, quick, quick on the uptake, receptive; acute, sharp, sharp as a needle, sharp-witted, quick-w., nimble-w.; alive, aware, on one's toes, with it 455 *attentive*; astute, shrewd, fly, smart, canny, not born yesterday, up to snuff, all there, on the ball; knowing, sophisticated, worldly-wise; too clever by half, over-clever, clever clever; sagacious, provident, prudent, watchful 457 *careful*; farseeing, farsighted, clear-sighted 510 *foreseeing*; discerning 463 *discriminating*; penetrating, perspicacious, clear-headed, long-h., hard-h., calculating; subtle, crafty, wily, foxy, artful 698 *cunning*; politic, statesmanlike.

wise, sage, sapient; thinking, reflecting 449 *thoughtful*; reasoning 475 *rational*; knowledgeable 490 *instructed*; highbrow, intellectual, profound, deep, oracular; sound, sensible, reasonable 502 *sane*; staid, sober 834 *serious*; reliable, responsible 929 *trustworthy*; experienced, cool, collected, unflappable; unperplexed, unbaffled; proof against flattery; balanced, level-headed, realistic, objective; judicious, impartial 913 *just*; tolerant, fair-minded, enlightened, unbiased, nonpartisan; unfanatical, unbigoted, unprejudiced; broad, broad-minded, latitudinarian; tactful, politic 698 *cunning*; wise as a serpent, wise as an owl, wise as Solomon; well-advised, well-considered, well-judged, wisely decided 642 *advisable*.

Vb. *be wise*, - intelligent etc. adj.; use one's wits, use one's head, use one's intelligence; accumulate experience, have a fund of wisdom 490 *know*; have brains, sparkle, scintillate, shine 644 *be good*; have a head on one's shoulders, have one's wits about one, know how many beans make five, see with half an eye, see at a glance; have one's head screwed on the right way, know a thing or two, know what's what, know how to live, get around, know the score; be realistic, be one's age; show foresight 510 *foresee*; know which side one's bread is buttered on, be prudent, take care 858 *be cautious*; grasp, fathom, take in 516 *understand*; discern, see through, penetrate 438 *see*; distinguish 463 *discriminate*; have sense, listen to reason 475 *be reasonable*; plan well, be politic 623 *plan*; have tact, be wise in one's generation 698 *be cunning*; learn from one's mistakes, come to one's senses, repent 939 *be penitent*.

See: 438, 447, **449**, 451, 455, 457, 463, 475, 476, **490**, 502, 510, 516, 623, 642, 644, 688, **694**, 698, 834, 858, 913, 929, 939.

499 Unintelligence. Folly

N. *unintelligence*, lack of intelligence, want of intellect 448 *absence of intellect*; poverty of intellect, clouded i. 503 *insanity*; weakness of intellect, lack of brains, feeble-mindedness, low IQ, low mental age, immaturity, infantilism; hydrocephalus, Down's syndrome, mongolism, mental deficiency; mental handicap, arrested development, retardation, backwardness; imbecility, idiocy; stupidity, slowness, dullness, obtuseness, thick-headedness, crassness, denseness; blockishness, sottishness, oafishness, owlishness, stolidity, hebetude 820 *moral insensibility*; one's weak side, poor head, no head for, no brain; incapacity, ineptitude, incompetence 695 *unskilfulness*; naivety, simplicity, fallibility, gullibility 481 *misjudgment*; inanity, vacuity, vacuousness, no depth, superficiality 212 *shallowness*; unreadiness, delayed reaction; impercipience, tactlessness, awkwardness, gaucherie 464 *indiscrimination*.

folly, foolishness, extravagance, eccentricity 849 *ridiculousness*; tomfool idea, act of folly 497 *foolery*; trifling, levity, frivolity, giddiness 456 *inattention*; irrationality, unreason, illogic 477 *sophistry*; unwisdom, imprudence, indiscretion; fatuity, fatuousness, pointlessness; wild-goose chase 641 *lost labour*; silliness, asininity; brainlessness, idiocy, lunacy, sheer l., utter folly; recklessness, wildness, incaution 857 *rashness*; blind side, obsession, infatuation 481 *misjudgment*; puerility, boyishness, girlishness, childishness 130 *nonage*; second childhood, senility, anility, dotage 131 *old age*; drivelling, babbling, maundering; conceit, empty-headedness 873 *vanity*.

Adj. *unintelligent*, unintellectual, lowbrow; ungifted, untalented, no genius; incompetent 695 *clumsy*; not bright, dull; subnormal, ESN, mentally handicapped, mentally deficient; undeveloped, immature; backward, retarded, feeble-minded, moronic, cretinous, imbecile 503 *insane*; deficient, wanting, not all there, vacant, a button short; limited, weak, weak in the upper storey; impercipient, unperceptive, slow, slow on the uptake; stupid, obtuse, dense, thick, crass, gross, heavy, sottish, stolid, bovine, Boeotian, blockish, oafish, doltish, owlish; dumb, dim, dim-witted, dull-w., slow-w., thick-w., half-w.; dead from the neck up, thick as two short planks, thick as a brick; thick-skulled, addle-brained, clod-pated, bone-headed, muddle-h., muddy-h., puzzle-h.; cracked, barmy 503 *crazy*; nonunderstanding, impenetrable, unteachable, impervious; prosaic, literal, matter-of-fact, unimaginative; muddled, addled, wrong-headed, pig-h. 481 *misjudging*.

foolish, silly, idiotic, imbecile, asinine, apish; nonsensical, senseless, insensate, fatuous, futile, inane 497 *absurd*; ludicrous, laughable 849 *ridiculous*; like a fool, fallible 544 *gullible*; simple, naive 699 *artless*; inexperienced 491 *ignorant*; tactless, gauche, awkward; soft, wet, soppy, sappy, sawney, goody-goody 935 *innocent*; gumptionless, gormless; goofy, gawky, dopey; childish, babyish, puerile, infantile 132 *infantine*; gaga, senile, anile 131 *ageing*; besotted, fond, doting; amorous, sentimental, spoony 887 *enamoured*; dazed, fuddled, maudlin 949 *drunk*; vapouring, babbling, burbling, drivelling, maundering; mindless, witless, brainless (**see** *unintelligent*); shallow, shallow-minded, shallow-headed, superficial, frivolous, anserine, bird-witted, feather-brained, crack-b., rattle-b., scatter-b., hare-b. 456 *light-minded*; fooling, playing the fool, acting the f., misbehaving, boyish; eccentric, unstable, extravagant, wild, madcap, rantipole; scatty, nutty, dotty, daft 503 *crazy*.

unwise, unblessed with wisdom, unenlightened; obscurantist, unscientific 491 *ignorant*; unphilosophical, unintellectual; unreasoning, irrational 477 *illogical*; indiscreet 464 *indiscriminating*; injudicious 481 *misjudging*; undiscerning, unseeing, unforeseeing, short-sighted 439 *blind*; unteachable, insensate; thoughtless 450 *unthinking*; uncalculating, impatient 680 *hasty*; incautious, foolhardy, reckless 857 *rash*; prejudiced, intolerant 481 *narrow-minded*; inconsistent, unbalanced, penny-wise, pound-foolish; unreasonable, against reason; inept, incongruous, unseemly, improper 643 *inexpedient*; ill-considered, ill-advised, ill-judged 495 *mistaken*.

Vb. *be foolish*, maunder, dote, drivel, babble, burble, talk through one's hat 515 *mean nothing*; go haywire, lose one's wits, take leave of one's senses, go off one's rocker 503 *be insane*; be unintelligent, have no brains, have no sense; not see farther than one's nose; never learn, stay bottom of the class; invite ridicule, look like a fool, look foolish 849 *be ridiculous*; make a fool of oneself, play the fool, act the f., act the giddy goat 497 *be absurd*; sow one's wild oats, misbehave 837 *amuse oneself*; burn one's fingers 695 *act foolishly*; go on a fool's errand 641 *waste effort*; plunge into error 495 *err*; miscalculate 481 *misjudge*.

See: 130, 131, 132, 212, 439, 448, 450, 456, 464, 477, 481, 491, 495, **497**, **503**, 515, 544, 641, 643, 680, 695, 699, 820, 837, 849, 857, 873, 887, 935, 949.

500 Sage

N. *sage*, nobody's fool; learned person 492 *scholar*; wise man, wise woman, statesman *or* - woman; elder statesman *or* - woman, counsellor, consultant, authority 691 *adviser*; expert 696 *proficient person*; genius, master mind; master, mentor, guide, guru, pundit 537 *teacher*; rishi, Buddha 973 *religious teacher*; seer, prophet 511 *oracle*; yogi, swami, sannyasi 945 *ascetic*; leading light, shining l., luminary; master spirit, great soul, mahatma; doctor, thinker 449 *philosopher*; egghead, boffin, highbrow 492 *intellectual*; wizard, shaman, witch doctor 983 *sorcerer*; magus, magian, Magi, wise men from the East; Solomon, Daniel, second D., Daniel come to judgment, learned judge; Nestor, Solon, Seven Sages; Grand Old Man, GOM.

wiseacre, wise guy, know-all, smarty-pants 873 *vain person*; smart aleck, clever dick; brains trust; witling, wise fool, wise men of Gotham; wisest fool in Christendom.

See: 449, 492, 511, 537, 691, 696, 873, 945, 973, 983.

501 Fool

N. *fool*, silly f., tomfool, Tom o' Bedlam 504 *madman*; buffoon, clown, comic, jester, zany, merry andrew, harlequin 594 *entertainer*; perfect fool, complete idiot, ass, jackass, donkey, goose, cuckoo; mooncalf, zombie, idiot, congenital i., born fool, natural; mongol, cretin, moron, imbecile, mental defective; half-wit, sot, stupid, silly, silly-billy; stooge, butt 851 *laughing-stock*; madcap 857 *desperado*; addle-head, muddle-h., blunderer, incompetent, twit, clot 697 *bungler*; scatterbrain, birdbrain, featherbrain, rattle-head, giddy-h., flibbertigibbet; trifler 493 *sciolist*; witling 500 *wiseacre*; crackpot, eccentric, odd fellow 504 *crank*; gaffer, old fogy; babbler, burbler, driveller; dotard 133 *old man*.

ninny, simpleton, Simple Simon; tom noddy, charlie; noodle, noddy, nincompoop, moonraker, juggins, muggins, booby, sap, saphead, softhead, big stiff, stick, poor s., dizzy, dope, jerk, gowk, galoot, goof; greenhorn 538 *beginner*; wet, weed, drip, milksop, mollycoddle, goody-goody, softy 163 *weakling*; child, babe 935 *innocent*; sucker, mug 544 *dupe*; gaper, gawker.

dunce, dullard; blockhead, woodenhead, numskull, duffer, dummkopf, dolt, dumb cluck 493 *ignoramus*; fathead, thickhead, bonehead, pinhead, blockhead, dunderhead, blunderhead, muttonhead, knucklehead, chucklehead, puddinghead, jobbernowl; nitwit, dimwit; mutt, chump, clot, clod, clodpoll, clodhopper, oaf, lout, booby, loon, bumpkin; block, stock, stone.

See: 133, 163, 493, 500, **504**, 538, 544, 594, 697, 851, 857, 935.

502 Sanity

N. *sanity*, saneness, soundness, soundness of mind; reasonableness; rationality, reason; balance, mental b.; mental equilibrium; sobriety, common sense; coherence 516 *intelligibility*; lucidity, lucid interval, lucid moment; normality, proper mind, senses; sound mind, mens sana; mental hygiene, mental health.

Adj. *sane*, normal, not neurotic; of sound mind, sound-minded, mentally sound, all there; in one's senses, compos mentis, in one's right mind, in possession of one's faculties; rational, reasonable 498 *intelligent*; commonsensical, sober, sober-minded; fully conscious, in one's sober senses; coherent 516 *intelligible*; lucid, not wandering, clear-headed; undisturbed, balanced, well-b.; cool, calculating 480 *judicial*; sane enough, not certifiable.

Vb. *be sane*, have one's wits, keep one's senses, retain one's reason; be of sound mind, become sane, recover one's mind, come to one's senses, cool down, sober down, sober up, see sense.

make sane, restore to sanity, bring to their senses *or* their right mind; sober, bring round.

Adv. *sanely*, soberly, lucidly; reasonably, in a reasonable spirit, like a reasonable human being.

See: 480, 498, 516.

503 Insanity

N. *insanity*, unsoundness of mind, lunacy, madness, certifiability; mental sickness, mental illness; mental instability, intellectual unbalance; psychopathic condition, abnormal psychology; mental derangement, loss of reason, sick mind, unsound m., darkened m., troubled brain, clouded b., disordered reason, deranged intellect, brain damage; mental decay, senile d., dotage, softening of the brain 131 *age*; dementia, d. praecox, senile d., presenile d.; amentia, mental deficiency, idiocy, congenital i., imbecility, cretinism, mongolism, Down's syndrome, feeblemindedness 499 *unintelligence*; autism, derangement, aberration 84 *abnormality*; fanaticism 481 *prejudice*; psychiatry 447 *psychology*; psychotherapy 658 *therapy*; psychoanalyst, psychiatrist 658 *doctor*.

psychopathy, sociopathy, maladjustment, personality disorder; identity crisis, personal anomie; psychopathic condition, emotional disturbance; neurosis, psychoneurosis, anxiety neurosis, nerves, nervous disorder, neurasthenia; hysteria; attack of nerves, shattered n., nervous breakdown, brainstorm; shellshock, combat fatigue; obsession, compulsion, phobia, claustrophobia, agarophobia 854 *phobia*; paranoia, delusions, hallucinations, folie à deux; split personality, dual p., multiple p.; catatonia, schizophrenia; psychosis; confusion, frustration; hypochondria; depression, depressed state; melancholia, blues 834 *melancholy*; manic depression, cyclothymia, elation. **See** *mania*.

mania, megalomania, persecution mania, religious m.; kleptomania; homicidal mania; nymphomania, satyriasis; monomania. **See** *eccentricity*.

frenzy, furore, frenetic condition; ecstasy, delirium, raving, hysteria; distraction, wandering of the mind 456 *abstractedness*; incoherence 517 *unintelligibility*; delirium tremens, DT's, jimjams 949 *alcoholism*; epilepsy, fit, paroxysm 318 *spasm*; brain fever, calenture, heatstroke, sunstroke; vertigo, dizziness, swimming of the head.

eccentricity, craziness, crankiness, faddishness; queerness, oddness, weirdness, strange behaviour; oddity, twist, kink, craze, fad 84 *abnormality*; a screw loose, bats in the belfry; fixation, hangup, inhibition, repression; complex, inferiority c., Oedipus c., Electra c.; obsession, infatuation, monomania, ruling passion, fixed idea 481 *bias*; hobbyhorse, bee in one's bonnet 604 *whim*.

lunatic asylum, mental home, mental hospital, psychiatric h.; madhouse, Bedlam; booby-hatch, loony-bin, nuthouse, funny farm; locked ward, padded cell 658 *hospital*.

Adj. *insane*, mad, lunatic, moon-struck; of unsound mind, not in one's right m., non compos mentis, out of one's mind, deprived of one's wits, deranged, demented; certifiable, mental; abnormal, psychologically a., sick, mentally ill, of diseased *or* disordered *or* distempered mind; unbalanced, maladjusted; psychopathic; psychotic; neurotic, hysterical; paranoiac, paranoid, schizophrenic, schizoid; manic, maniacal; catatonic, depressive, manic-d., elated; hyperactive; hypochondriac 834 *melancholic*; kleptomaniac; claustrophobic, agoraphobic; autistic; brain-damaged, shell-shocked; imbecile, moronic, idiotic, cretinous, defective, subnormal 499 *unintelligent*; raving mad, stark staring m., mad as a hatter, mad as a March hare (**see** *frenzied*); declared insane, certified; locked up, put away.

crazy, bewildered, wandering, bemused, pixilated, mazed, moidered 456 *abstracted*; not all there, not right in the head; off one's head *or* one's nut, round the bend *or* the twist, up the pole; crazed, demented, driven mad, maddened (**see** *frenzied*); unhinged, unbalanced, off one's rocker; bedevilled, bewitched, deluded; infatuated, obsessed, eaten up with, possessed; fond, doting, besotted 887 *enamoured*; drivelling, gaga, in one's second childhood; touched in the head, touched, wanting; idiotic, scatterbrained, shatterbrained, crack-brained 499 *foolish*; crackers, cracked, scatty, screwy, nutty, nutty as a fruit cake, nuts, bananas, batty, bats, cuckoo, barmy, bonkers, loco; daft, daffy, dappy, dippy, loony, loopy, potty, dotty; cranky, wacky, eccentric, erratic, funny, queer, odd, peculiar 84 *abnormal*; crotchety, whimsical 604 *capricious*; dizzy, giddy 456 *light-minded*.

frenzied, rabid, maddened, madding; horn-mad, furious, foaming at the mouth 891 *angry*; haggard, wild, distraught 825 *suffering*; possessed, possessed with a devil, bedevilled, bacchic, corybantic; frantic, frenetic, demented, like one possessed, beside oneself, uncontrollable; berserk, seeing red, running amok, running wild 176 *violent*; epileptic, having fits; hysterical, delirious, hallucinating, seeing things, raving, rambling, wandering, incoherent, fevered, brain-sick 651 *sick*.

Vb. *be insane*, - mad, - crazy etc. adj.; have bats in the belfry, have a screw loose; dote, drivel 499 *be foolish*; ramble, wander; babble, rave; foam at the mouth; be delirious, see things.

go mad, go off one's head, go off one's rocker, go crackers, become a lunatic, have to be certified; lose one's mind *or* reason, lose one's wits, lose one's marbles, go out of one's mind, crack up; go berserk, run amok, see red, foam at the mouth, lose one's head 891 *get angry*.

make mad, drive m., send m., drive insane, madden; craze, derange, dement; send off one's head *or* out of one's mind; send round the bend *or* the twist, drive up the wall; overthrow one's reason, turn one's brain; blow one's mind 821 *excite*; unhinge, unbalance, send off one's rocker; infuriate, make one see red 891 *enrage*; infatuate, possess, obsess; go to one's head, turn one's h. 542 *befool*.

See: 84, 131, 176, 318, 447, 456, 481, **499**, 517, 542, 604, **651**, 658, 821, 825, 834, 854, 887, 891, 949.

504 Madman

N. *madman*, madwoman, lunatic, mental case; bedlamite, Tom o' Bedlam, candidate for Bedlam; screwball, nut, nutcase, loon, loony; abnormal character, psychopath, psycho; psychopathic personality, unstable p., aggressive p., antisocial p., sociopath; hysteric, neurotic, neuropath; psychotic; obsessive, paranoiac; schizoid; manic-depressive; maenad, bacchante, corybant; raving lunatic, maniac; kleptomaniac, pyromaniac, monomaniac, megalomaniac; dipsomaniac 949 *drunkard*; dope addict, dope fiend, junkie; drug addict 949 *drug-taking*; hypochondriac, melancholic 834 *moper*; idiot, congenital i., natural, cretin, moron 501 *fool*.

crank, crackpot, nut, nutter, crackbrain; eccentric, oddity, oddball 851 *laughingstock*; freak, deviationist 84 *nonconformist*; faddist, fanatic, extremist, nympholept, lunatic fringe; seer, dreamer 513 *visionary*; knight errant, Don Quixote.

enthusiast, energumen 678 *busy person*; zealot 602 *obstinate person*; devotee, aficionado, addict, fiend, nut, freak, bug, buff; fan, supporter 707 *patron*; connoisseur, fancier 846 *people of taste*; radio ham, discophile, balletomane, opera buff, film b., cineast; bibliophile 492 *collector*.

See: 84, 492, 501, 513, 602, 678, 707, 834, 846, 851, 949.

Section six: Extension of thought

505 Memory

N. *memory*, good m., retentiveness, retention; tenacious memory, capacious m., trustworthy m., correct m., exact m., photographic m., eidetic m., ready m., prompt m.; collective memory, race m., atavism; Mnemosyne.

remembrance, exercise of memory, recollection, recall, total r.; anamnesis; commemoration, evocation, mind's eye; rehearsal, recapitulation 106 *repetition*; memorization, remembering, learning by heart 536 *learning*; reminiscence, thoughts of the past, reminiscent vein, retrospection, review, retrospect, hindsight; flashback, recurrence, voice from the past; déjà vu 984 *psychics*; afterthought 67 *sequel*; nostalgia, regrets 830 *regret*; memorabilia, memoirs, reminiscences, recollections; history, narration 590 *narrative*; fame, notoriety, place in history 866 *famousness*; memoranda, things to be remembered.

reminder, memorial, testimonial, commemoration 876 *celebration*; token of remembrance, souvenir, keepsake, relic, memento, autograph; trophy, bust, statue 548 *monument*; remembrancer, keeper of one's conscience, prompter; testifier 466 *witness*; memorandum, memo, chit, note, notebook, aide-mémoire, diary, engagement d.; album, autograph a., photograph a., scrapbook, commonplacebook, promptbook; leading question, prompt, prompting, suggestion, cue 524 *hint*; mnemonic, aid to memory.

mnemonics, mnemotechnics, mnemotechny, art of memory, Pelmanism; mnemonic device, memoria technica, artificial memory, electronic brain; data bank 632 *store*; mnemonist.

Adj. *remembered*, recollected etc. vb.; retained, retained in the memory, not forgotten, unforgotten; green, fresh, fresh in one's memory, of recent memory; present to the mind, uppermost in one's thoughts; of lasting remembrance, of blessed memory, missed, regretted; memorable, unforgettable, not to be forgotten; haunting, persistent, undying; deep-rooted, deep-seated, indelible, ineffaceable, inscribed upon the mind, lodged in one's m., stamped on one's memory, impressed on one's recollection; embalmed in the memory, kept alive in one's mind; got by heart, memorized 490 *known*.

remembering, mindful, faithful to the memory, keeping in mind, holding in remembrance; evocative, memorial, commemorative 876 *celebratory*; reminiscent, recollecting, anecdotic, anecdotal; living in the past, nostalgic; unable to forget, haunted, obsessed, plagued; recalling, reminding, mnemonic, prompting, suggesting.

Vb. *remember*, mind, bring to m., call to m.; recognize, know again 490 *know*; recollect, bethink oneself; not forget, bottle up 778 *retain*; hold in mind, retain the memory of; embalm *or* keep alive in one's thoughts, treasure in one's heart, enshrine in one's memory, store in one's mind, cherish the memory; never forget, be unable to f.; recall, call to mind, think of; keep in mind 455 *be mindful*; reminisce, write one's memoirs; remind oneself, make a note of, write it down. **See** *memorize*.

retrospect, recollect, recall, recapture; reflect, review, think back, think back upon, trace b., retrace, hark back, carry one's thoughts back, cast one's mind b.; bring back to memory, summon up, conjure u., rake up the past, dig up the p., dwell on the p., live in the p.; archaize 125 *look back*; reopen old wounds, renew old days, recapture old times; make an effort to remember, rack one's brains, tax one's memory.

remind, jog one's memory, refresh one's m., renew one's m.; put one in mind of, take one back; drop a hint, prompt, suggest 524 *hint*; not allow one to forget, abide in the memory, haunt, obsess; not let sleeping dogs lie, fan the embers 821 *excite*; turn another's mind back, make one think of, evoke the memory o.; commemorate, memorialize, raise a memorial, redeem from oblivion, keep the memory green, toast 876 *celebrate*; relate, recount, recapitulate 106 *repeat*; petition 761 *request*; write history, narrate 590 *describe*.

memorize, commit to memory, get to know, con 490 *know*; get by heart, learn by rote 536 *learn*; repeat one's lesson 106 *repeat*; fix in one's memory, rivet in one's m., impress on one's m., grave on the mind, hammer into one's head, drive into one's h.; burden the memory with, stuff the mind w., cram the mind w., load the mind w.

be remembered, stay in the memory, stick in the mind, make a lasting impression; recur, recur to one's thoughts 106 *reoccur*; flash across one's mind, ring a bell, set one's memory working; haunt, dwell in one's thoughts, abide in one's memory, run in one's thoughts, haunt one's t., not leave one's t., be at the back of one's mind, lurk in one's mind, rise from the subconscious, emerge into consciousness; make history, live in h., leave a name 866 *have a reputation*; live on 115 *be eternal*.

Adv. *in memory*, in memory of, to the memory of, in memoriam, lest we forget; by heart, by rote, from memory.

See: 67, 106, 115, 125, 455, 466, **490**, 524, 536, **548**, 590, 632, 761, 778, 821, 830, 866, 876, 984.

506 Oblivion

N. *oblivion*, blankness, no recollection; obliviousness, forgetfulness, absent-mindedness 456 *abstractedness*; loss of memory, amnesia, blackout, total blank, mental block; hysterical amnesia, fugue state 503 *insanity*; misrecollection, paramnesia; insensibility, insensibility of the past, no sense of history; forgetfulness of favours 908 *ingratitude*; dim memory, hazy recollection; short memory, defective m., failing m., faulty m., treacherous m.; decay of memory, lapse of m., memory like a sieve; effacement 550 *obliteration*; Lethe, waters of L., waters of oblivion; nepenthe; good riddance.

amnesty, letting bygones be bygones, burial of grievances, burial of the hatchet; pardon, free p., absolution 909 *forgiveness*.

Adj. *forgotten*, clean f., beyond recall; well forgotten, not missed; unremembered, left; in limbo 458 *neglected*; disremembered, misremembered etc. vb.; almost remembered, on the tip of one's tongue; gone out of one's head, passed out of recollection; buried, suppressed, repressed; out of mind, over and done with, dead and buried, sunk in oblivion, amnestied 909 *forgiven*.

forgetful, forgetting, oblivious; sunk in oblivion, steeped in Lethe; insensible, unconscious of the past; not historically minded; unable to remember, suffering from amnesia, amnesic; causing loss of memory, amnestic, Lethean; unmindful, heedless, mindless 458 *negligent*; absent-minded, inclined to forget 456 *abstracted*; willing to forget, unresentful 909 *forgiving*; unwilling to remember, conveniently forgetting 918 *undutiful*; unmindful of favours 908 *ungrateful*.

Vb. *forget*, clean f., not remember, disremember, have no recollection of; not give another thought to, think no more of; wean one's thoughts from, eliminate from one's mind, suppress the memory, consign to oblivion, be oblivious; amnesty, let bygones be bygones, bury the hatchet 909 *forgive*; break with the past, unlearn, efface 550 *obliterate*; suffer from amnesia, lose one's memory, remember nothing; remember wrongly, misremember, misrecollect; be forgetful, have a short memory, need reminding; lose sight of, leave behind, overlook; be absent-minded, fluff one's notes 456 *be inattentive*; forget one's lines, dry; have a short memory, have a memory like a sieve, go in one ear and out of the other, forget one's own name; almost remember, have on the tip of one's tongue, not quite recall, not call to mind, draw a blank.

be forgotten, slip one's memory, escape one's m., fade from one's mind; sink into oblivion, fall into o., drop out of the news; be overlooked 456 *escape notice*.

See: 456, 458, 503, **550**, 908, 909, 918.

507 Expectation

N. *expectation*, state of e., expectancy 455 *attention*; contemplation 617 *intention*; confident expectation, reliance, confidence, trust 473 *certainty*; presumption 475 *premise*; foretaste 135 *anticipation*; optimism, cheerful expectation 833 *cheerfulness*; eager expectation, anxious e., sanguine e. 859 *desire*; ardent expectation, breathless e. 852 *hope*; waiting, suspense 474 *uncertainty*; pessimism, dread, apprehension, apprehensiveness 854 *fear*; anxiety 825 *worry*; waiting for the end 853 *hopelessness*; one's expectations, one's prospects 471 *probability*; reckoning, calculation 480 *estimate*; prospect, lookout, outlook, forecast 511 *prediction*; contingency 469 *possibility*; destiny 596 *fate*; defeated expectation, frustrated e., tantalization, torment of Tantalus 509 *disappointment*; what is expected, the usual thing 610 *practice*.

Adj. *expectant*, expecting, in expectation, in hourly e.; in suspense, on the waiting list, on the short l.; sure, confident 473 *certain*; anticipatory, anticipant of, anticipative, anticipating, banking on; presuming, taking for granted; predicting 510 *foreseeing*; unsurprised 865 *unastonished*; forewarned, forearmed, ready 669 *prepared*; waiting, waiting for, awaiting; on the lookout, on the watch for, standing by, on call 457 *vigilant*; tense, keyed up 821 *excited*; tantalized, on tenterhooks, on the rack, in agonies of expectation, agog 859 *desiring*; optimistic, hopeful, sanguine 852 *hoping*; apprehensive, dreading, worried, anxious 854 *nervous*; pessimistic, expecting the worst 853 *hopeless*; wondering, open-eyed, open-mouthed, curious 453 *inquisitive*; expecting a baby, parturient 167 *fertilized*.

expected, long e.; up to expectation, as one expected, not surprising 865 *unastonish-*

ing; anticipated, presumed, predicted, on the cards, foreseen, foreseeable 471 *probable*; prospective, future, on the horizon 155 *impending*; promised, contemplated, intended, in view, in prospect 617 *intending*; hoped for, longed for 859 *desired*; apprehended, dreaded, feared 854 *frightening*.

Vb. *expect*, look for, have in prospect, face the prospect, face; contemplate, have in mind, hold in view, promise oneself 617 *intend*; reckon, calculate 480 *estimate*; predict, forecast 510 *foresee*; see it coming 865 *not wonder*; think likely, presume, dare say 471 *assume*; be confident, rely on, bank on, count upon 473 *be certain*; count one's chickens before they are hatched 509 *be disappointed*; anticipate, forestall 669 *prepare oneself*; look out for, watch out f., be waiting f., be ready f. 457 *be careful*; stand by, be on call; hang around (**see** *await*); apprehend, dread 854 *fear*; look forward to, hope for 852 *hope*, 859 *desire*; hope and believe, flatter oneself 485 *believe*.

await, be on the waiting list; stand waiting, stand and wait, watch and pray 136 *wait*; queue up, mark time, bide one's t.; stand to attention, stand by, be on call; hold one's breath, be in suspense; keep one waiting; have in store for, be in store for, be expected 155 *impend*; tantalize, make one's mouth water, lead one to expect 859 *cause desire*.

Adv. *expectantly*, in suspense, with bated breath, on edge, on the edge of one's chair; on the waiting list.

See: 135, 136, 155, 167, 453, 455, 457, 469, **471**, 473, 474, 475, 480, 485, 509, **510**, **511**, 596, 610, 617, 669, 821, 825, 833, 852, 853, 854, 859, 865.

508 Lack of expectation

N. *lack of expectation*, no expectation 472 *improbability*; false expectation 509 *disappointment*; inexpectancy, resignation, no hope 853 *hopelessness*; lack of interest, apathy 454 *incuriosity*; unpreparedness 670 *nonpreparation*; unexpectedness, unforeseen contingency, unusual occurrence; unexpected result, miscalculation 495 *error*; lack of warning, surprise, surprisal, disconcertment; the unexpected, the unforeseen, surprise packet, Jack-in-the-box, afterclap; windfall, gift from the gods 615 *benefit*; shock, nasty s., start, jolt, turn; blow, sudden b., staggering b.; bolt from the blue, thunderclap, bombshell; revelation, eye-opener; culture shock; paradox, reversal, peripeteia 221 *inversion*; astonishment, amazement 864 *wonder*; anticlimax, descent from the sublime to the ridiculous.

Adj. *unexpected*, unanticipated, unprepared for, unlooked for, unhoped for; unguessed, unpredicted, unforeseen; unforeseeable, unpredictable 472 *improbable*; unheralded, unannounced; without warning, surprising; arresting, astounding, mind-boggling, eye-opening, staggering, amazing 864 *wonderful*; shocking, startling 854 *frightening*; sudden 116 *instantaneous*; like a bombshell, like a bolt from the blue, dropped from the clouds; uncovenanted, unbargained for, uncatered for 670 *unprepared*; contrary to expectation, against e.; paradoxical 518 *equivocal*; out of one's reckoning, out of one's ken, out of one's experience, unprecedented, unexampled 84 *unusual*; freakish 84 *abnormal*; whimsical 604 *capricious*; full of surprises, unaccountable 517 *puzzling*.

inexpectant, unexpecting, unguessing, unsuspecting, off guard, unguarded 456 *inattentive*; unaware, uninformed 491 *ignorant*; unwarned, not forewarned; surprised, disconcerted, taken by surprise, taken aback, caught napping, caught bending, caught on the hop, on the wrong foot 670 *unprepared*; astonished, amazed, thunderstruck, dumbfounded, dazed, stunned 864 *wondering*; startled, jolted, shocked; without expectations, unhopeful 853 *hopeless*; apathetic, incurious 860 *indifferent*.

Vb. *not expect*, not look for, not contemplate, think unlikely, not foresee 472 *be unlikely*; not hope for 853 *despair*; be caught out, walk into the trap, fall into the t.; be taken aback, be taken by surprise, not bargain for 670 *be unprepared*; get a shock, have a jolt, start, jump, jump out of one's skin; have one's eyes opened, receive a revelation; look surprised, goggle, stare.

surprise, take by s., spring something on one, spring a mine under; catch, trap, ambush 542 *ensnare*; catch unawares, catch napping, catch bending, catch off one's guard; startle, jolt, make one jump, give one a turn; take aback, stagger, stun;

take one's breath away, knock one down with a feather, bowl one over, strike one all of a heap; be one in the eye for 509 *disappoint*; give one a surprise, pull out of the hat; astonish, amaze, astound, dumbfound 864 *be wonderful*; shock, electrify 821 *impress*; flutter the dovecotes, set the cat among the pigeons 63 *derange*; come like a thunderclap; drop from the clouds, come out of the blue; fall upon, burst u., bounce u., spring u., pounce on; steal upon, creep up on; come up from behind, take one on his blind side, appear from nowhere.

Adv. *unexpectedly*, suddenly, abruptly 116 *instantaneously*; all of a sudden, without warning, without notice, unawares; like a thief in the night.

See: 63, 84, 116, 221, 454, 456, **472**, 491, 495, 509, 517, 518, 542, 604, 615, 670, 821, 853, 854, 860, **864**.

509 Disappointment

N. *disappointment*, sad d., bitter d., cruel d.; regrets 830 *regret*; continued disappointment, tantalization, frustration, feeling of f., bafflement; frustrated expectations, blighted hopes, unsatisfied h., betrayed h., hopes unrealized 853 *hopelessness*; false expectation, vain e. 482 *overestimation*; bad news 529 *news*; not what one expected, disenchantment, disillusionment 829 *discontent*; miscalculation 481 *misjudgment*; mirage, false dawn, fool's paradise; shock, blow, setback, balk 702 *hitch*; nonfulfilment, partial success, near failure 726 *noncompletion*; bad luck, trick of fortune, slip 'twixt the cup and the lip 731 *misfortune*; anticlimax 508 *lack of expectation*; one in the eye for, comedown, letdown 872 *humiliation*; damp squib 728 *failure*.

Adj. *disappointed*, expecting otherwise 508 *inexpectant*; frustrated, thwarted 702 *hindered*; baffled, foiled 728 *defeated*; disconcerted, crestfallen, chagrined, humiliated 872 *humbled*; disgruntled, soured 829 *discontented*; sick with disappointment 853 *hopeless*; heartbroken 834 *dejected*; badly served, let down, betrayed, jilted; refused, turned away 607 *rejected*.

disappointing, unsatisfying, unsatisfactory 636 *insufficient*; not up to expectation, less than one's hopes 829 *discontenting*; miscarried, abortive 728 *unsuccessful*; cheating, deceptive 542 *deceiving*.

Vb. *be disappointed*, - unsuccessful etc. adj.; try in vain 728 *fail*; have hoped for something better, not realize one's expectations 307 *fall short*; expect otherwise, be let down, have hoped better of; find to one's cost 830 *regret*; listen to a false prophet 544 *be duped*; laugh on the wrong side of one's face, be crestfallen, look blue, look blank 872 *be humbled*; be sick with disappointment, be sick at heart, be without hope 853 *despair*.

disappoint, not come up to expectations 307 *fall short*; belie one's expectation; defeat one's hopes, dash one's h., crush one's h., blight one's h., deceive one's h., betray one's h.; burst the bubble, disillusion; serve badly, fail one, let one down, leave one in the lurch, not come up to scratch; balk, foil, thwart, frustrate 702 *hinder*; amaze, dumbfound 508 *surprise*; disconcert, humble 872 *humiliate*; betray, play one false 930 *be dishonest*; play one a trick, jilt, bilk 542 *befool*; dash the cup from one's lips, tantalize, leave unsatisfied, discontent, spoil one's pleasure, dissatisfy, sour, embitter with disappointment 829 *cause discontent*; refuse, deny, turn away 607 *reject*.

Adv. *disappointingly*, tantalizingly, so near and yet so far.

See: 307, 481, 482, 508, 529, 542, 544, 607, 636, 702, 726, 728, 731, **829**, 830, **834**, 853, 872, 930.

510 Foresight

N. *foresight*, prevision; anticipation, foretaste; precognition, foreknowledge, prescience, second sight, clairvoyance; premonition, presentiment, foreboding, forewarning 511 *omen*; prognosis, prognostication 511 *prediction*; foregone conclusion 473 *certainty*; programme, prospectus 623 *plan*; forethought, vision, longsightedness 498 *sagacity*; premeditation 608 *predetermination*; prudence, providence 858 *caution*; intelligent anticipation, readiness, provision 669 *preparation*.

Adj. *foreseeing*, foresighted, prospective, prognostic, predictive 511 *predicting*; clairvoyant, second-sighted, prophetic; prescient, farsighted, weather-wise, sagacious 498 *wise*; looking ahead, provident, prudent 858 *cautious*; anticipant, anticipatory 507 *expectant*.

Vb. *foresee*, divine, prophesy, forecast 511

predict; forewarn 664 *warn*; foreknow, see *or* peep *or* pry into the future, read the f., have second sight; have prior information, know in advance 524 *be informed*; see ahead, look a., see it coming, scent, scent from afar, feel in one's bones; look for 507 *expect*; be beforehand, anticipate, forestall 135 *be early*; make provision 669 *prepare*; surmise, make a good guess 512 *suppose*; forejudge 608 *predetermine*; show prudence, plan ahead 623 *plan*; look to the future, have an eye to the f., see how the cat jumps, see how the wind blows 124 *look ahead*; have an eye on the main chance 498 *be wise*; feel one's way, keep a sharp lookout 455 *be attentive*; lay up for a rainy day 633 *provide*; take precautions, provide against 858 *be cautious*.

See: 124, 135, 455, 473, **498**, **507**, **511**, 512, 524, 608, 623, 633, 664, 669, 858.

511 Prediction

N. *prediction*, foretelling, forewarning, prophecy; apocalypse 975 *revelation*; forecast, weather f.; prognostication, prognosis; presentiment, foreboding 510 *foresight*; presage, prefiguration, prefigurement, 1984; programme, prospectus 623 *plan*; announcement, notice, advance n. 528 *publication*; warning, preliminary w., warning shot 665 *danger signal*; prospect 507 *expectation*; shape of things to come, horoscope, fortune; type 23 *prototype*.

divination, clairvoyance; augury, taking the auspices; vaticination, soothsaying; astrology, astromancy, horoscopy, casting nativities; fortune-telling, palmistry, chiromancy; crystal gazing; cartomancy; I Ching; cleromancy, sortilege, casting lots; bibliomancy, oneiromancy, geomancy, hydromancy, pyromancy; necromancy 984 *occultism*; dowsing 484 *discovery*.

omen, portent, presage, writing on the wall; prognostic, symptom, sign 547 *indication*; augury, auspice; forewarning, caution 664 *warning*; harbinger, herald 529 *messenger*; prefigurement, foretoken, type; ominousness, portentousness, gathering clouds, signs of the times 661 *danger*; luck-bringer, black cat 983 *talisman*; portent of bad luck, broken mirror, spilt salt, shooting star; bird of ill omen, owl, raven.

oracle, consultant 500 *sage*; meteorologist, weatherman; calamity prophet, doom merchant, Cassandra 664 *warner*; prophet, prophetess, seer, vaticinator; futurologist, prognosticator, forecaster; soothsayer 983 *sorcerer*; clairvoyant, medium 984 *occultist*; Delphic oracle, Pythian o., Pythoness, Pythia; sibyl, Sibylline books; Old Moore, Nostradamus; Witch of Endor; cards, tarot c., dice, lot; tripod, crystal ball, mirror, tea leaves, palm; Bible, sortes Vergilianae.

diviner, water d., dowser; tipster 618 *gambler*; astrologer, caster of nativities; fortune-teller, gipsy, palmist, crystal-gazer, interpreter of dreams; augur, haruspex.

Adj. *predicting*, predictive, foretelling; presentient, clairvoyant 510 *foreseeing*; fortune-telling; weather-wise; prophetic, vatic, vaticinatory, mantic, fatidical, apocalyptic; oracular, sibylline; monitory, premonitory, foreboding 664 *cautionary*; heralding, prefiguring 66 *precursory*.

presageful, significant, ominous, portentous, big with fate, pregnant with doom; augural, auspicial, haruspical; auspicious, promising, fortunate, favourable 730 *prosperous*; inauspicious, sinister 731 *adverse*.

Vb. *predict*, forecast, make a prediction, prognosticate, make a prognosis; foretell, prophesy, vaticinate, forebode, bode, augur, spell; foretoken, presage, portend; foreshow, foreshadow, prefigure, shadow forth, forerun, herald, be harbinger, usher in 64 *come before*; point to, betoken, typify, signify 547 *indicate*; announce, give notice, notify 528 *advertise*; forewarn, give warning 664 *warn*; look black, lour, menace 900 *threaten*; promise, augur well, bid fair to, give hopes of, hold out hopes, raise expectations, excite e. 852 *give hope*.

divine, auspicate, haruspicate; read the entrails, take the auspices, take the omens; soothsay, vaticinate; cast a horoscope, cast a nativity; cast lots 618 *gamble*; tell fortunes; read the future, read the signs, read the stars; read the cards, read one's hand.

See: 4, 23, 64, 66, 198, 484, 500, 507, 510, 528, 529, 547, 618, 623, 661, 664, 665, 730, 731, 852, 900, 975, 983, **984**.

Section seven: Creative thought

512 Supposition

N. *supposition*, supposal, notion, the idea of 451 *idea*; fancy, conceit 513 *ideality*; pretence, pretending 850 *affectation*; presumption, assumption, presupposition, postulation, postulate 475 *premise*; condition, stipulation 766 *conditions*; proposal, proposition 759 *offer*; submission 475 *argument*; hypothesis, working h., theory, model, theorem 452 *topic*; thesis, position, stand, attitude, orientation, standpoint 485 *opinion*; suggestion, casual s.; suggestiveness 524 *hint*; basis of supposition, clue, data, datum 466 *evidence*; suspicion, hunch, inkling (**see** *conjecture*); instinct 476 *intuition*; association of ideas 449 *thought*; supposability, conjecturability 469 *possibility*.

conjecture, unverified supposition, guess, surmise, suspicion; mere notion, bare supposition, vague suspicion, rough guess, crude estimate; shrewd idea 476 *intuition*; construction, reconstruction; guesswork, guessing, speculation; gamble, shot, shot in the dark 618 *gambling*.

theorist, hypothesist, theorizer, theoretician, model builder, research worker; supposer, surmiser, guesser; academic, critic, armchair c., armchair detective; doctrinarian 473 *doctrinaire*; speculator, thinker 449 *philosopher*; boffin 623 *planner*; speculator 618 *gambler*.

Adj. *suppositional*, supposing etc. vb.; suppositive, notional, conjectural, guessing, propositional, hypothetical, theoretical, armchair, speculative, academic, of academic interest; gratuitous, unverified; suggestive, hinting, allusive, stimulating, thought-provoking.

supposed, conjectured etc. vb.; assumed, presumed, premised, taken, postulated; proposed, mooted 452 *topical*; given, granted, granted for the sake of argument 488 *assented*; suppositive, putative, presumptive; pretended, so-called, quasi; not real 2 *unreal*; alleged, supposititious, fabled, fancied 543 *untrue*; supposable, surmisable, imaginable 513 *imaginary*.

Vb. *suppose*, just s., pretend, fancy, dream 513 *imagine*; think, conceive, take into one's head 485 *opine*; divine, have a hunch 476 *intuit*; surmise, conjecture, guess, hazard a g., make a g.; suppose so, dare say; persuade oneself 485 *believe*; presume, assume, presuppose, presurmise 475 *premise*; posit, lay down, assert 532 *affirm*; take for granted, take, take it, postulate 475 *reason*; speculate, have a theory, hypothesize, theorize 449 *meditate*; sketch, draft, outline 623 *plan*; rely on supposition 618 *gamble*.

propound, propose, mean seriously 759 *offer*; put on the agenda, moot, move, propose a motion 761 *request*; put a case, submit, make one's submission 475 *argue*; put forth, make a suggestion, venture to say, put forward a notion, throw out an idea 691 *advise*; suggest, adumbrate, allude 524 *hint*; put an idea into one's head, urge 612 *motivate*.

Adv. *supposedly*, reputedly, seemingly; on the assumption that, ex hypothesi.

See: 2, **449**, **451**, **452**, 466, 469, 473, 475, 476, 485, 488, 513, 524, 532, 543, 612, 618, 623, 691, 759, 761, 766, 850.

513 Imagination

N. *imagination*, power of i., visual i., vivid i., highly-coloured i., fertile i., bold i., wild i.; fervid i., lively i.; imaginativeness, creativeness; inventiveness, creativity 21 *originality*; ingenuity, resourcefulness 694 *skill*; fancifulness, fantasy, fantasticalness, stretch of the imagination (**see** *ideality*); understanding, insight, empathy, sympathy 819 *moral sensibility*; poetic imagination, frenzy, poetic f., ecstasy, inspiration, afflatus, divine a.; fancy, the mind's eye, visualization, objectification, image-building, imagery, word-painting; artistry, creative work.

ideality, conception 449 thought; idealization, ego ideal; mental image, projection 445 *appearance*; concept, image, conceit, fancy, coinage of the brain, brain-creation, notion 451 *idea*; whim, whimsy, whimwham, crinkum-crankum 497 *absurdity*; vagary 604 *caprice*; figment, f. of the imagination, fiction 541 *falsehood*; work of fiction, story 590 *novel*; science fiction, fairy tale; imaginative exercise, flight of fancy, play of f., uncontrolled imagination, romance, fantasy, extravaganza, rhapsody 546 *exaggeration*; poetic licence 593 *poetry*; quixotry, knight-errantry, skiamachy, shadow boxing.

fantasy, wildest dreams; vision, dream, bad d., nightmare; Jabberwocky 84 *rara avis*; bogey, phantom 970 *ghost*; shadow, vapour 419 *dimness*; mirage, fata morgana 440 *visual fallacy*; delusion, hallucination, chimera 495 *error*; reverie, brown study 456 *abstractedness*; trance, somnambulism 375 *insensibility*; sick fancy, delirium 503 *frenzy*; subjectivity, autosuggestion; wishful thinking 477 *sophistry*; window-shopping, make-believe, daydream, golden dream, pipe d. 859 *desire*; romance, stardust; romanticism, escapism, idealism, Utopianism; Utopia, Erewhon; promised land, El Dorado; Happy Valley, Fortunate Isles, Isles of the Blest; land of Cockaigne, Ruritania, Shangri-La, Atlantis, Lyonesse, Middle Earth, Narnia, San Serif; fairyland, wonderland; cloud-cuckoo-land, dream l., dream world, castles in Spain, castles in the air; pie in the sky, good time coming, millennium 124 *future state*; idle fancy, myth 543 *fable*.

visionary, seer 511 *diviner*; dreamer, day-d., somnambulist 456 *inattention*; fantast, fantasist; idealist, Utopian 901 *philanthropist*; escapist, ostrich 620 *avoider*; romantic, romancer, romanticist, rhapsodist, myth-maker; enthusiast, knight-errant, Don Quixote 504 *crank*; creative worker 556 *artist*.

Adj. *imaginative*, creative, lively, original, idea'd, inventive, fertile, ingenious; resourceful 694 *skilful*; fancy-led, romancing, romantic; high-flown, rhapsodical, carried away 546 *exaggerated*; poetic, fictional; Utopian, idealistic; rhapsodic, enthusiastic; dreaming, in a trance; extravagant, grotesque, bizarre, fantastical, whimsical, airy-fairy, preposterous, impractical, Heath Robinson 497 *absurd*; visionary, otherworldly, quixotic, Laputan; imaginal, visualizing, eidetic, eidotropic.

imaginary, unreal, unsubstantial 4 *insubstantial*; subjective, notional, chimerical, illusory 495 *erroneous*; dreamy, visionary, not of this world, ideal; cloudy, vaporous 419 *shadowy*; unhistorical, fictitious, fabulous, fabled, legendary, mythic, mythological 543 *untrue*; fanciful, fancy-bred, fancied, imagined, fabricated, hatched; dreamed-up; hypothetical 512 *suppositional*; pretended, make-believe.

Vb. *imagine*, ideate 449 *think*; fancy, dream; excogitate, think of, think up, dream up; make up, devise, invent, originate, create, have an inspiration 609 *improvise*; coin, hatch, concoct, fabricate 164 *produce*; visualize, envisage, see in the mind's eye 438 *see*; conceive, form an image of; figure to oneself, picture to o., represent to o.; paint, p. in words, conjure up a vision, objectify, realize, capture, recapture 551 *represent*; use one's imagination, give reins to one's i., run riot in imagination 546 *exaggerate*; play with one's thoughts, pretend, make-believe, daydream 456 *be inattentive*; build Utopias, build castles in the air; see visions, dream dreams; fantasize, idealize, romanticize, fictionalize, rhapsodize 546 *exaggerate*; enter into, empathize, sympathize 516 *understand*.

Adv. *imaginatively*, in imagination, in thought; with imagination; in the mind's eye; with one's head in the clouds.

See: 4, 21, 84, 124, 164, 375, 419, 438, 440, 445, 449, **451**, **456**, 477, 495, 497, 503, 504, 511, 512, 516, 541, **543**, 546, 551, 556, **590**, 593, 604, 609, 620, 694, 819, 859, 901, 970.

4.2 Communication of ideas

Section one: Nature of ideas communicated

514 Meaning

N. *meaning*, idea conveyed, substance, essence, spirit, sum, sum and substance, gist, pith; contents, text, matter, subject m. 452 *topic*; semantic content, deep structure, sense, value, drift, tenor, purport, import, implication, colouring; force, effect; relevance, bearing, scope; meaningfulness, semantic flow, context (**see** *connotation*); expression, mode of e., diction 566 *style*; semantics, semiology 557 *linguistics*.

connotation, denotation, signification, significance, reference, application; construction 520 *interpretation*; context; original meaning, derivation 156 *source*; range of meaning, semantic field, comprehension; extended meaning, extension; intention, main meaning, core m., leading sense; specialized meaning, peculiar m., idiom 80 *speciality*; received meaning, usage, acceptance, accepted meaning 610 *practice*; single meaning, univocity, unambiguity 516 *intelligibility*; double meaning, ambiguity 518 *equivocalness*; many meanings, polysemy; same meaning, equivalent meaning, convertible terms; synonym, synonymousness, synonymity, equivalence 13 *identity*; opposite meaning, antonym, antonymy 14 *contrariety*; contradictory meaning, countersense; changed meaning, semantic shift; level of meaning, literal meaning, literality 573 *plainness*; metaphorical meaning 519 *metaphor*; hidden meaning, esoteric sense 523 *latency*; constructive sense, implied s.; no sense 497 *absurdity*.

Adj. *meaningful*, significant, of moment 638 *important*; substantial, pithy, meaty, full of meaning, replete with m., packed with m., pregnant; meaning etc. vb.; importing, purporting, significative, indicative 547 *indicating*; telling 516 *expressive*; pointed, epigrammatic 839 *witty*; suggestive, evocative, allusive, implicit; express, explicit 573 *plain*; declaratory 532 *affirmative*; interpretative 520 *interpretive*.

semantic, semiological, philological, etymological 557 *linguistic*; connotational, connotative; denotational, denotative; literal, verbal 573 *plain*; metaphorical 519 *figurative*; univocal, unambiguous 516 *intelligible*; polysemous, ambiguous 518 *equivocal*; synonymous, homonymous 13 *identical*; tantamount, equivalent 18 *similar*; tautologous 106 *repeated*; antonymous 14 *contrary*; idiomatic 80 *special*; paraphrastic 520 *interpretive*; obscure 568 *unclear*; clear 567 *perspicuous*; implied, constructive 523 *tacit*; nonsensical 497 *absurd*; without meaning 515 *meaningless*.

Vb. *mean*, have a meaning, bear a sense, mean something; convey a meaning, get across 524 *communicate*; typify, symbolize 547 *indicate*; signify, denote, connote, stand for 551 *represent*; import, purport, intend; point to, add up to, boil down to, spell, involve 523 *imply*; convey, express, declare, assert 532 *affirm*; bespeak, tell of, speak of, breathe of, speak volumes 466 *evidence*; mean to say, be trying to s., be getting at, be driving at, really mean, have in mind, allude to, refer to; be synonymous, have the same meaning, co-refer 13 *be identical*; say it in other words, tautologize 106 *repeat*; mean the same thing, agree in meaning, coincide 24 *accord*; conflict in meaning, be opposed in m. 25 *disagree*; draw a meaning, infer, understand by 516 *understand*.

Adv. *significantly*, meaningly, meaningfully, with meaning, to the effect that 520 *in plain words*; in a sense, in some s.; as meant, as intended, as understood; in the sense that *or* of; according to the book, from the context; literally, verbally, word for word; so to speak 519 *metaphorically*.

See: 13, 14, 18, 24, 25, 80, 106, 156, 452, 466, 497, 515, **516**, 518, 519, 520, 523, 524, 532, 547, 551, 557, 566, 567, 568, 573, 610, 638, 839.

515 Lack of meaning

N. *lack of meaning*, meaninglessness, unmeaningness, absence of meaning, no m., no context; no bearing 10 *irrelevance*; nonsignificance 639 *unimportance*; amphigory 497 *absurdity*; inanity, emptiness, triteness; truism, platitude, cliché 496 *maxim*; mere words, verbalism; unreason, illogicality 477 *sophistry*; invalidity, dead letter, nullity 161 *ineffectuality*; illegibility, scribble, scribbling 586 *script*; daub 552 *misrepresentation*; empty sound, meaningless noise, strumming; sounding brass, tinkling cymbal 400 *loudness*; jargon, rigmarole, gobbledygook, galimatias; abracadabra, hocus-pocus, mumbo jumbo; gibberish, gabble, double Dutch, Greek, Babel 517 *unintelligibility*; incoherence, raving, delirium 503 *frenzy*; double-talk, mystification 530 *enigma*; insincerity 925 *flattery*.

silly talk, senseless t., nonsense 497 *absurdity*; stuff, stuff and nonsense, balderdash, rubbish, load of r., rot, tommyrot; drivel, twaddle, fiddle-faddle, bosh, tosh, tripe, piffle, bilge, bull.

empty talk, idle speeches, sweet nothings, wind, gas, hot air, vapouring, verbiage 570 *diffuseness*; rant, bombast, fustian, rodomontade 877 *boasting*; blether, blah-blah, flapdoodle, flimflam; gup, guff, pi-jaw, eyewash, claptrap, poppycock 543 *fable*; humbug 541 *falsehood*; moonshine, malarkey, hokum, bunkum, bunk, boloney, hooey; flannel, flummery, blarney 925 *flattery*; patter, sales p., spiel;

talk, chatter, prattle, prating, babble, gabble, jabber, jabber jabber, yak yak, rhubarb rhubarb 581 *chatter*.

Adj. *meaningless*, unmeaning, without meaning, Pickwickian; amphigoric, nonsense, nonsensical 497 *absurd*; senseless, null; unexpressive, unidiomatic 25 *unapt*; nonsignificant, insignificant, inane, empty, trivial, trite 639 *unimportant*; fatuous, piffling, blithering; trashy, trumpery, rubbishy; twaddling, waffling, windy, ranting 546 *exaggerated*; incoherent, raving, gibbering 503 *frenzied*.

unmeant, unintentional, involuntary, unintended, unimplied, unalluded to; mistranslated 521 *misinterpreted*; insincere 925 *flattering*.

Vb. *mean nothing*, be unmeaning, have no meaning, make no sense; scribble, scratch, daub, strum; talk bunkum, talk like an idiot 497 *be absurd*; talk, babble, prattle, prate, gabble, gibber, jabber 581 *be loquacious*; talk double dutch, talk gibberish, doubletalk 517 *be unintelligible*; rant 546 *exaggerate*; gush, rave, drivel, drool, blether, waffle, twaddle; vapour, talk hot air, gas 499 *be foolish*; not mean what one says, blarney 925 *flatter*; make nonsense of 521 *misinterpret*; have no meaning for, be Greek to, pass over one's head 474 *puzzle*.

Int. Rubbish! what rot! nonsense! fiddlesticks! etc. n.

See: 10, 25, 161, 400, 474, 477, 496, **497**, 499, 503, **517**, 521, 530, 541, 543, 546, 552, 570, **581**, 586, 639, 877, 925.

516 Intelligibility

N. *intelligibility*, knowability, cognizability; explicability, teachability, penetrability; apprehensibility, comprehensibility, adaptation to the understanding; readability, legibility, decipherability; clearness, clarity, coherence, limpidity, lucidity 567 *perspicuity*; precision, unambiguity 473 *certainty*; simplicity, straightforwardness, plain speaking, plain speech, downright utterance; plain words, plain English, mother tongue; simple eloquence, unadorned style 573 *plainness*; paraphrase, simplification 701 *facility*; amplification, popularization, haute vulgarisation 520 *interpretation*.

Adj. *intelligible*, understandable, penetrable, realizable, comprehensible, apprehensible; coherent 502 *sane*; audible, recognizable, distinguishable, unmistakable; discoverable, cognizable, knowable 490 *known*; explicable, teachable; unambiguous, unequivocal 514 *meaningful*; explicit, positive 473 *certain*; unblurred, distinct, clear-cut, precise 80 *definite*; well-spoken, articulate; plain-spoken, unevasive, unadorned, downright, forthright 573 *plain*; uninvolved, straightforward, simple 701 *easy*; obvious, self-explanatory, easy to understand, easy to grasp, made easy, adapted to the understanding, clear to the meanest capacity; explained, predigested, simplified, popularized, popular, for the million 520 *interpreted*; clear, limpid 422 *transparent*; pellucid, lucid 567 *perspicuous*; readable, legible, decipherable, well-written, printed, in print; luminous, clear as daylight, clear as noonday, plain as a pikestaff 443 *visible*.

expressive, telling, striking, vivid, graphic, highly coloured, emphatic, forceful, strong, strongly worded 590 *descriptive*; illustrative, explicatory 520 *interpretive*; amplifying, paraphrasing, popularizing.

Vb. *be intelligible*, - clear, - easy etc. adj.; be realized, come alive, take on depth; be readable, read easily; make sense, add up, speak to the understanding 475 *be reasonable*; tell its own tale, speak for itself 466 *evidence*; have no secrets, be on the surface 443 *be visible*; be understood, come over, get across, sink in, dawn on; make understood, clarify, clear up, open one's eyes, elucidate 520 *interpret*; make easy, simplify, popularize 701 *facilitate*; recapitulate 106 *repeat*; labour the obvious 532 *emphasize*.

understand, comprehend, apprehend 490 *know*; master 536 *learn*; have, hold, retain 505 *remember*; have understanding 498 *be wise*; see through, penetrate, fathom, get to the bottom of 484 *detect*; spot, descry, discern, distinguish, make out, see at a glance, see with half an eye 438 *see*; recognize, make no mistake 473 *be certain*; grasp, get hold of, seize, seize the meaning, be on to it, cotton on to, dig; get the hang of, take in, register; be with one, follow, savvy; collect, get, catch on, twig; catch one's drift, get the idea, get the picture; realize, get wise to, tumble to, rumble; begin to understand, come to u., have one's eyes opened, see it all; be undeceived, be disillusioned 830 *regret*; get to know, be told 524 *be informed.*

Adv. *intelligibly,* expressively, lucidly, plainly, simply, in words of one syllable; in plain terms, in clear terms, in plain English, for the layman.

See: 80, 106, 422, 438, **443**, 466, 473, 475, 484, 490, 498, 502, 505, **514**, 520, 524, 532, 536, 567, 573, 590, 701, 830.

517 Unintelligibility

N. *unintelligibility,* incomprehensibility, inapprehensibility, unaccountability, inconceivability; inexplicability, impenetrability; perplexity, difficulty 474 *uncertainty;* obscurity 568 *imperspicuity;* ambiguity 518 *equivocalness;* mystification 515 *lack of meaning;* incoherence 503 *insanity;* double Dutch, gibberish; jargon, foreign tongue, private language 560 *dialect, slang;* stammering 580 *speech defect;* undecipherability, illegibility, unreadability; scribble, scrawl 586 *lettering;* inaudibility 401 *faintness;* Greek, sealed book 530 *secret;* hard saying, paradox, knotty point, obscure problem, pons asinorum, crux, riddle, oracular pronouncement 530 *enigma;* mysterious behaviour, Sphinx-like attitude, baffling demeanour.

Adj. *unintelligible,* incomprehensible, inapprehensible, inconceivable, not understandable, not to be understood, inexplicable, unaccountable, not to be accounted for; unknowable, unrecognizable, incognizable, undiscoverable, as Greek to one 491 *unknown;* unfathomable, unbridgeable, unsearchable, inscrutable, impenetrable; blank, poker-faced, expressionless 820 *impassive;* inaudible 401 *muted;* unreadable, illegible, undecipherable, crabbed; undiscernible 444 *invisible;* hidden, arcane 523 *occult;* cryptic, obscure, shrouded in mystery; esoteric 80 *private;* Sphinx-like, enigmatic, oracular (**see** *puzzling*).

puzzling, hard to understand, complex 700 *difficult;* hard, beyond one, over one's head, recondite, abstruse, elusive; enigmatic, mysterious 523 *occult;* half-understood, nebulous, misty, hazy, dim, obscure 419 *shadowy;* clear as mud, clear as ditch water 568 *unclear;* ambiguous 518 *equivocal;* of doubtful meaning, oracular; paradoxical 508 *unexpected;* fishy, strange, odd 84 *abnormal;* unexplained, without a solution, insoluble, unsolvable; unsolved, unresolved 474 *uncertain.*

inexpressible, unspeakable, untranslatable; unpronounceable, unutterable, ineffable; incommunicable, indefinable; profound, deep; mystic, mystical, transcendental.

puzzled, mystified, unable to understand, wondering, out of one's depth, flummoxed, stumped, baffled, perplexed, nonplussed 474 *uncertain.*

Vb. *be unintelligible,* - puzzling, - inexpressible etc. adj.; be hard, be difficult, present a puzzle, make one's head ache *or* swim 474 *puzzle;* talk in riddles, speak oracles 518 *be equivocal;* talk double dutch, talk gibberish 515 *mean nothing;* speak badly 580 *stammer;* write badly, scribble, scrawl; keep one guessing 486 *cause doubt;* perplex, complicate, entangle, confuse 63 *bedevil;* require explanation, have no answer, need an interpreter; be too deep, go over one's head, be beyond one's reach; elude one's grasp, escape one; pass comprehension, baffle understanding.

not understand, not penetrate, not get it; find unintelligible, not make out, not know what to make of, make nothing of, make neither head nor tail of, be unable to account for; puzzle over, find too difficult, be floored by, be stumped by, give up; be out of one's depth 491 *not know;* wonder, be at sea 474 *be uncertain;* not know what one is about, have no grasp of 695 *be unskilful;* have a blind spot 439 *be blind;* misunderstand one another, be at cross-purposes 495 *blunder;* get it into one's head, get one wrong 481 *misjudge;* not register 456 *be inattentive.*

See: 63, 80, 84, 401, 419, 439, 444, 456, **474**, 481, 486, 491, 495, 503, 508, 515, 518, 523, 530, 560, **568**, 580, 586, 695, 700, 820.

518 Equivocalness

N. *equivocalness,* two voices 14 *contrariety;* ambiguity, ambivalence 517 *unintelligibility;* indefiniteness, vagueness 474 *uncertainty;* double meaning, amphibology 514 *connotation;* newspeak, doubletalk, weasel word 515 *lack of meaning;* conundrum, riddle, oracle, oracular utterance 530 *enigma;* mental reservation 525 *concealment;* prevarication, balancing act; equivocation, white lie 543 *untruth;* quibble, quibbling 477 *sophistry;* wordplay, play on words, paronomasia 574 *ornament;* pun, calembour, equivoque, double entendre 839 *witticism*; faux ami, confusible; anagram, acrostic; synonymy, homonymy, polysemy; homonym, homophone 18 *analogue*.

Adj. *equivocal*, not univocal, ambiguous, ambivalent, epicene; double, double-tongued, two-edged; left-handed, back-h.; equivocating, prevaricating, facing both ways; vague, evasive, oracular; amphibolous, homonymous; anagrammatic.

Vb. *be equivocal*, cut both ways; play on words, pun; have two meanings, have a second meaning 514 *mean*; speak oracles, speak with two voices 14 *be contrary*; fudge, waffle, stall, not give a straight answer 620 *avoid*; equivocate, prevaricate, weasel 541 *dissemble*.

See: 14, 18, 474, 477, 514, 515, 517, 525, 530, **541**, 543, 574, 620, 839.

519 Metaphor: figure of speech

N. *metaphor*, mixed m.; transference; allusion, application; misapplication, catachresis; extended metaphor, allegorization, allegory; mystical interpretation, anagoge 520 *interpretation*; fable, parable 534 *teaching*; objective correlative, symbol; symbolism, nonliterality, figurativeness, imagery 513 *imagination*; image, simile, likeness 462 *comparison*; personification, prosopopeia.

trope, figure, figure of speech, turn of s., flourish; manner of speaking, façon de parler; irony, sarcasm 851 *satire*; rhetorical figure 574 *ornament*; metonymy, antonomasia, synecdoche, enallage; anaphora; litotes 483 *underestimation*; hyperbole 546 *exaggeration*; stress, emphasis; euphuism, euphemism, dysphemism 850 *affectation*; colloquialism 573 *plainness*; contrast, antithesis 462 *comparison*; metathesis 221 *inversion*; paronomasia, word-play 518 *equivocalness*.

Adj. *figurative*, metaphorical, tropical; catachrestic; allusive, symbolic, allegorical, anagogic; parabolical; comparative 462 *compared*; euphuistic, tortured, euphemistic 850 *affected*; colloquial 573 *plain*; hyperbolic 546 *exaggerated*; satirical, sarcastic, ironical 851 *derisive*; flowery, florid 574 *ornate*; oratorical 574 *rhetorical*.

Vb. *figure*, image, embody, personify; typify, symbolize 551 *represent*; allegorize, parabolize, fable; prefigure, adumbrate; apply, allude; refer, liken, contrast 462 *compare*; employ metaphor, indulge in tropes 574 *ornament*.

Adv. *metaphorically*, not literally, tropically, figuratively, by allusion; in a way, so to speak, in a manner of speaking.

See: 221, 462, 483, 513, 518, 520, 534, 546, 551, 573, **574**, 850, 851.

520 Interpretation

N. *interpretation*, definition, explanation, explication, exposition, exegesis, epexegesis; elucidation, light, clarification, illumination; illustration, exemplification 83 *example*; resolution, solution, key, clue, the secret 460 *answer*; decipherment, decoding, cracking 484 *discovery*; emendation 654 *amendment*; application, particular interpretation, twist, turn; construction, construe, reading, lection 514 *meaning*; subaudition 514 *connotation*; euhemerism, demythologization; allegorization 519 *metaphor*; accepted reading, usual text, vulgate; alternative reading, variant r.; criticism, textual c., form c., the higher c., literary c., practical c., appreciation, deconstruction, structuralism 557 *literature*; critique, review 480 *estimate*; critical power, critic's gift 480 *judgment*; insight, feeling, sympathy 819 *moral sensibility*.

commentary, comment, editorial c., Targum; scholium, gloss, footnote; inscription, caption, legend 563 *phrase*; motto, moral 693 *precept*; annotation, notes, marginalia, adversaria; exposition 591 *dissertation*; apparatus criticus, critical edition; glossary, lexicon 559 *dictionary*.

translation, version, rendering, free translation, loose rendering; faithful translation, literal t., construe; key, crib; rewording, paraphrase, metaphrase; précis, abridgment, epitome 592 *compendium*; adaptation, simplification, amplification 516 *intelligibility*; transliteration, decoding, decipherment; lip-reading.

hermeneutics, exegetics, science of interpretation, translator's art; epigraphy, palaeography 557 *linguistics*; cryptanalysis, cryptology; diagnostics, symptomatology; semiology, semiotics; graphology; phrenology, palmistry; prophecy 511 *divination*.

interpreter, clarifier, explainer, exponent, expounder, expositor, exegete 537 *teacher*, 973 *religious teacher*; rationalist, rationalizer, euhemerist, demythologizer; editor 528 *publicizer*; Masorete, textual critic; emender, emendator; commentator, annotator, note-maker, glossator, scholiast; glossarist, critic, reviewer, Leavisite 480 *estimator*; oneirocritic 511 *diviner*; medium 984 *spiritualism*; polyglot 557 *linguist*; translator, paraphraser, paraphrast; cipher clerk, cryptographer, encoder; solver, code-breaker; decoder; cryptanalyst, cryptologist; lip-reader; epigraphist, palaeographer 125 *antiquarian*; spokesman, mouthpiece, representative 754 *delegate*; public relations officer 524 *informant*; executant, performer 413 *musician*; player 594 *actor*; poet, novelist, painter, sculptor 556 *artist*.

guide, precedent 83 *example*; lamp, light, star, guiding s.; dragoman, courier, cicerone 690 *director*; showman, demonstrator 522 *exhibitor*.

Adj. *interpretive*, interpretative, constructive; explanatory, explicatory, explicative, elucidatory; expositive, expository 557 *literary*; exegetical, hermeneutic; defining, definitive; illuminating, illustrative, exemplary; glossarial, annotative, scholiastic, editorial; lip-reading, translative, paraphrastic, metaphrastic; polyglot; mediumistic; synonymous, equivalent 28 *equal*; literal, strict, word-for-word 494 *accurate*; faithful 551 *representing*; free 495 *inexact*.

interpreted, glossed etc. vb.; explained, defined, expounded, elucidated, clarified; annotated, commented, commentated, edited; translated, rendered, Englished; deciphered, decoded, cracked.

Vb. *interpret*, define, clarify, make clear, disambiguate; explain, unfold, expound, elucidate 516 *be intelligible*; illustrate 83 *exemplify*; demonstrate 522 *show*; act as guide, show round; comment on, edit, write notes for, annotate, compose a commentary, gloss; read, spell, spell out; adopt a reading, accept an interpretation, construe, put a construction on, understand by, give a sense to, make sense of, ascribe a meaning to 516 *understand*; illuminate, throw light on, enlighten 524 *inform*; account for, find the cause, deduce, infer 475 *reason*; act as interpreter, be spokesman 755 *deputize*; typify, symbolize; popularize, simplify 701 *facilitate*.

translate, make a version, make a key, make a crib; render, do into, turn i., English; retranslate, rehash, reword, rephrase, paraphrase; abridge, amplify, adapt; transliterate, transcribe; cipher, encode, put into code; lip-read.

decipher, crack, crack the cipher, decode; find the meaning, read hieroglyphics; read, spell out, puzzle o., make o., work o.; piece together, find the sense of, find the key to; solve, resolve, enucleate, unravel, unriddle, disentangle, read between the lines.

Adv. *in plain words*, plainly, in plain English; by way of explanation; that is, i.e.; in other words, to wit, namely, viz.; to make it plain, to explain.

See: 28, 83, 125, 413, **460**, 475, **480**, 484, 494, 495, 511, 514, **516**, 519, 522, 524, 528, 537, 551, 556, **557**, 559, 563, 591, 592, 594, 654, 690, 693, 701, 754, 755, 819, 973, 984.

521 Misinterpretation

N. *misinterpretation*, misunderstanding, malentendu, misconstruction, misapprehension, wrong end of the stick; cross-purposes, crossed lines 495 *mistake*; wrong explanation 535 *misteaching*; mistranslation, misconstrue, translator's error; wrong interpretation, false construction; twist, turn, misapplication, perversion 246 *distortion*; strained sense; false reading; false colouring, dark glasses, rose-coloured spectacles; garbling, falsification 552 *misrepresentation*; overdoing it 546 *exaggeration*; depreciation 483 *underestimation*; parody, travesty 851 *ridicule*; abuse of language, misapplication 565 *solecism*.

Adj. *misinterpreted*, misconceived etc. vb., misconstrued, mistranslated 495 *mistaken*; misread, misquoted.

Vb. *misinterpret*, misunderstand, misapprehend, misconceive 481 *misjudge*; get wrong, get one wrong, get hold of the wrong end of the stick 495 *blunder*; misread, misspell 495 *err*; set in a false light 535 *misteach*; mistranslate, misconstrue, put a false sense *or* construction on; give a twist *or* turn, pervert, strain the sense, wrest the meaning, do violence to the m., wrench, twist, twist the words 246 *distort*; equivocate, weasel, play on words 518 *be equivocal*; add a meaning, read into, write i. 38 *add*; leave out, suppress 39 *subtract*;

misrepeat, misquote; falsify, garble 552 *misrepresent*; travesty, parody, caricature, guy 851 *ridicule*; overpraise 482 *overrate*; underpraise 483 *underestimate*; inflate 546 *exaggerate*; traduce, misrepresent 926 *defame*.

See: 38, 39, 246, 481, 482, 483, **495**, 518, 535, 546, 552, 565, 851, 926.

Section two: Modes of communication

522 Manifestation

N. *manifestation*, revelation, unfolding, discovery, daylight, exposure 526 *disclosure*; expression, formulation 532 *affirmation*; proof 466 *evidence*; confrontation 462 *comparison*; presentation, production, projection, enactment 551 *representation*; symbolization, typification 547 *indication*; sign, token 547 *signal*; symptom 511 *omen*; prerelease, preview 438 *view*; showing, demonstration, exhibition; display, showing off 875 *ostentation*; proclamation 528 *publication*; openness, flagrancy 528 *publicity*; candour, plain speaking, plain speech, home truth 573 *plainness*; prominence, conspicuousness 443 *visibility*; apparition, vision, materialization 445 *appearance*; séance 984 *occultism*; Shekinah, glory 965 *theophany*; incarnation, avatar.

exhibit, specimen, sample 83 *example*; piece of evidence, quotation, citation 466 *evidence*; model, mock-up 551 *image*; showpiece, collector's p., museum p., antique, curio; display, show, dress s., mannequin parade 445 *spectacle*; scene 438 *view*; showplace, showroom, showcase, placard, hoarding 528 *advertisement*; sign 547 *label*; shop window, museum, gallery 632 *collection*; retrospective, exhibition, exposition; fair 796 *market*.

exhibitor, advertiser, publicist 528 *publicizer*; displayer, demonstrator; showman; impresario 594 *stage manager*; exhibitionist, peacock 873 *vain person*; model, mannequin; wearer, sporter, flaunter.

Adj. *manifest*, apparent, ostensible 445 *appearing*; plain, clear, defined 80 *definite*; explained, plain as a pikestaff, clear as daylight 516 *intelligible*; unconcealed, showing 443 *visible*; conspicuous, noticeable, notable, prominent, pronounced, signal, marked, striking, in relief, in the foreground, in the limelight 443 *obvious*; open, patent, evident; gross, crass, palpable; self-evident, written all over one, for all to see, unmistakable, recognizable, identifiable, incontestable 473 *certain*; public, famous, notorious 528 *well-known*; catching the eye, eye-catching 875 *showy*; arrant, glaring, stark staring, flagrant, loud, on the rooftops.

undisguised, overt, explicit, express, emphatic 532 *affirmative*; in the open, public; exoteric; unreserved, open, candid, heart-to-heart, off the record 540 *veracious*; free, frank, downright, forthright, straightforward, outspoken, blunt, plain-spoken, no-nonsense 573 *plain*; honest to goodness, honest to God; bold, daring 711 *defiant*; brazen, shameless, immodest, barefaced 951 *impure*; bare, naked, naked and unashamed 229 *uncovered*; flaunting, unconcealed, inconcealable (**see** *manifest*).

shown, manifested etc. vb.; declared, divulged 526 *disclosed*; showing, featured, on show, on display, on 443 *visible*; exhibited, shown off; brought forth, produced; mentioned, brought to one's notice; adduced, cited, quoted; confronted, brought face to face; worn, sported; unfurled, flaunted, waved, brandished; advertised, publicized 528 *published*; expressible, producible, showable.

Vb. *manifest*, reveal, divulge 526 *disclose*; evince, betoken, show signs of 466 *evidence*; bring to light, unearth 484 *discover*; explain, make plain, make obvious 520 *interpret*; expose, lay bare, unroll, unfurl, unsheathe 229 *uncover*; open up, throw open, lay o. 263 *open*; elicit, draw forth, drag out 304 *extract*; invent, bring forth 164 *produce*; bring out, shadow forth, body f.; incorporate, incarnate, personify 223 *externalize*; typify, symbolize, exemplify 547 *indicate*; point up, accentuate, enhance, develop 36 *augment*; throw light on 420 *illuminate*; highlight, spotlight, throw into relief 532 *emphasize*; express, formulate 532 *affirm*; bring, bring up, mention, adduce, cite, quote; bring to the fore, place in the foreground 638 *make important*; bring to notice, produce, trot out, come out with, proclaim, publicize 528 *publish*; show for what it is, show up (**see** *show*); solve, elucidate 520 *decipher*.

show, exhibit, display; set out, expose to view, offer to the v., set before one's eyes, dangle; wave, flourish 317 *brandish*; sport 228 *wear*; flaunt, parade 875 *be ostentatious*; make a show of, affect 850 *be affected*; present, feature, enact 551 *represent*; put on, stage, release 594 *dramatize*; put on television, televise, screen; stage an exhibition, put on show *or* display, hang (a picture); show off, set o., model (garments); put one through his *or* her paces; demonstrate 534 *teach*; show round, show over, point out, draw attention to, bring to notice 547 *indicate*; confront, bring face to face; reflect, image, mirror, hold up the mirror to 20 *imitate*; tear off the mask, show up, expose 526 *disclose*.

be plain, - explicit etc. adj.; show one's face, unveil 229 *doff*; show one's true colours, have no secrets, make no mystery, not try to hide, wear one's heart on one's sleeve; have no shame, wash one's dirty linen in public; show one's mind, speak out, tell to one's face, make no secret of, make no bones about 573 *speak plainly*; speak for itself, tell its own story 516 *be intelligible*; be obvious, stand to reason, go without saying 478 *be proved*; be conspicuous, stand out, stand out a mile 443 *be visible*; show the flag, be seen, show up, show up well, hold the stage, be in the limelight, stand in full view 455 *attract notice*; loom large, stare one in the face 200 *be near*; appear on the horizon, rear its head, transpire, emanate, come to light 445 *appear*.

Adv. *manifestly*, plainly, obviously, palpably, grossly, crassly, openly, publicly, for all to see, notoriously, flagrantly, undisguisedly; at first blush, prima facie; externally, on the face of it, superficially; open and above-board, with cards on the table; frankly, honestly; before God, before all, under the eye of heaven; in full view, in broad daylight, in public, on the stage.

See: 20, 36, 80, 83, 164, 200, 223, 228, 229, 263, 304, 317, 420, 438, **443**, **445**, 455, 462, 466, 473, 478, 484, 511, 516, 520, **526**, **528**, 532, 534, 540, **547**, 551, 573, 594, 632, 638, 711, 796, 850, 873, 875, 951, 965, 984.

523 Latency

N. *latency*, no signs of 525 *concealment*; insidiousness, treachery 930 *perfidy*; dormancy, dormant condition, potentiality 469 *possibility*; esotericism, cabbala 984 *occultism*; occultness, mysticism; hidden meaning, occult m., veiled m. 517 *unintelligibility*; ambiguous advice 511 *oracle*; symbolism, allegory, anagoge 519 *metaphor*; implication, adumbration, symbolization; mystery 530 *secret*; inmost recesses 224 *interiority*; dark 418 *darkness*; shadowiness 419 *dimness*; imperceptibility 444 *invisibility*; more than meets the eye; deceptive appearance, hidden fires, hidden depths; iron hand in a velvet glove; slumbering volcano, sleeping giant 661 *danger*; dark horse, mystery man, anonymity 562 *no name*; Red under the bed, nigger in the woodpile, snake in the grass, mole 663 *pitfall*; hidden hand, wire-puller, strings, friends in high places, friend at court, power behind the throne, éminence grise 178 *influence*; old-boy network, Freemasonry; secret influence, undercurrent; unsoundness, something rotten; innuendo, insinuation, suggestion, overtone 524 *hint*; half-spoken word, sealed lips 582 *taciturnity*; undertone, aside 401 *faintness*; clandestineness, secret society, cabal, intrigue 623 *plot*; ambushment 527 *ambush*; code, invisible writing, cryptography.

Adj. *latent*, lurking, skulking, delitescent 525 *concealed*; dormant, sleeping 679 *inactive*; passive 266 *quiescent*; in abeyance 175 *inert*; potential, undeveloped 469 *possible*; unguessed, unsuspected, crypto- 491 *unknown*; submerged, underlying, subterranean, below the surface 211 *deep*; in the background, behind the scenes, backroom, undercover 421 *screened*; unmanifested, unseen, unspied, undetected, unexposed 444 *invisible*; murky, obscure 418 *dark*; arcane, impenetrable, undiscoverable 517 *unintelligible*; tucked away, sequestered 883 *secluded*; awaiting discovery, undiscovered, unexplored, untracked, untraced, uninvented, unexplained, unsolved.

tacit, unsaid, unspoken, half-spoken, unpronounced, unexpressed; unavowed, sneaking; unvoiced, unmentioned, untold of, unsung; undivulged, unproclaimed, unprofessed, undeclared; unwritten, unpublished, unedited; understood, implied, inferred, implicit, between the lines; implicative, suggestive; inferential, allusive.

occult, mysterious, mystic; symbolic, allegorical, anagogical 519 *figurative*; cryptic, esoteric 984 *cabbalistic*; veiled, muffled, covert; indirect, crooked 220 *oblique*; clandestine, secret, kept quiet; insidious, treacherous 930 *perfidious*; underhand 525 *stealthy*; undiscovered, hush-hush, top-secret; not public, off the record 80 *private*; coded, cryptographic 525 *disguised*.

Vb. *lurk*, hide, be latent, be a stowaway; burrow, stay underground; lie hidden, lie in ambush; lie low, lie low and say nothing, lie doggo, make no sign 266 *be quiescent*; avoid notice, escape observation 444 *be unseen*; evade detection, escape recognition; act behind the scenes, laugh in one's sleeve 541 *dissemble*; creep, slink, tiptoe, walk on tiptoe 525 *be stealthy*; pull the strings, stage-manage, underlie, be at the bottom of 156 *cause*; smoke, smoulder 175 *be inert*.

imply, insinuate, whisper, murmur, suggest 524 *hint*; understand, infer, leave an inference, allude, be allusive; symbolize, connote, carry a suggestion, involve, spell 514 *mean*.

See: 80, 156, 175, 178, 211, 220, 224, 266, 401, 418, 419, 421, **444**, 469, 491, 511, 514, 517, 519, 524, **525**, **527**, 530, **541**, 562, 582, 623, 661, 663, 679, 883, 930, 984.

524 Information

N. *information*, communication of knowledge, transmission of k., dissemination, diffusion, informatics; computerised information, data base, viewdata 86 *data processing*; mailing list, distribution l. 588 *correspondence*; chain of authorities, tradition, hearsay; enlightenment, instruction, briefing 534 *teaching*; thought-transference, intercommunication; sharing of information, communication; mass media 528 *the press*, 531 *broadcasting*; telling, narration 590 *narrative*; notification, announcement, annunciation, intimation, warning, advice, notice, mention, tip, tip-off (**see** *hint*); advertisement, circular 528 *publicity*; common knowledge, general information, gen, info; factual information, background, facts, the goods, documentary 494 *truth*; material, literature 589 *reading matter*; inside information, dope, lowdown, private source, confidence 530 *secret*; earliest information, scoop; stock of information, acquaintance, the know 490 *knowledge*; recorded information, file, dossier 548 *record*; piece of information, word, report, intelligence 529 *news*; a communication, wire, telegram, cable, cablegram 529 *message*; flood of information, spate of news, outpouring; communicativeness, talking 581 *loquacity*; unauthorized communication, indiscretion, leak 526 *disclosure*.

report, review, compte rendu; information called for 459 *enquiry*; paper, Green Paper, White P., Black P.; account, true a., eyewitness a. 590 *narrative*; statement, return 86 *statistics*; specification, estimates 480 *estimate*; progress report, confidential r.; information offered, dispatch, bulletin, communiqué, handout, press release 529 *news*; representation, presentation, case; memorial, petition 761 *entreaty*; remonstrance, round robin 762 *deprecation*; letters, dispatches 588 *correspondence*.

hint, gentle h., whisper, aside 401 *faintness*; indirect hint, intimation; broad hint, signal, nod, wink, look, nudge, kick, gesticulation 547 *gesture*; prompt, cue 505 *reminder*; suggestion, lead, leading question 547 *indication*; caution 664 *warning*; something to go on, tip, tip-off (**see** *information*); word, passing w., word in the ear, word to the wise, verb. sap. 691 *advice*; insinuation, innuendo 926 *calumny*; clue, symptom 520 *interpretation*; sidelight, glimpse, inkling, adumbration 419 *glimmer*; suspicion, inference, guess 512 *conjecture*; good tip, wheeze, dodge, wrinkle 623 *contrivance*.

informant, teller 590 *narrator*; spokesperson 579 *speaker*; mouthpiece, representative 754 *delegate*; announcer, radio a. 531 *broadcaster*; notifier, advertiser, annunciator 528 *publicizer*; harbinger, herald 529 *messenger*; testifier 466 *witness*; one in the know, authority, source; quarter, channel, circle, grapevine; go-between, contact 231 *intermediary*; informed circles, information centre; news agency 528 *the press*; communicator, intelligencer, correspondent, special c., reporter, newshound, commentator, columnist, gossip writer 529 *news reporter*; tipper, tipster 691 *adviser*; guide, topographer; bigmouth, blabbermouth; little bird.

informer, delator 928 *accuser*; spy, snoop, sleuth 459 *detective*; inside agent, mole;

stool pigeon, nark, copper's n., snitch, sneak, nose, blabber, squealer, squeaker, grass, supergrass; eavesdropper, telltale, talebearer, tattler, tattletale, gossip 581 *chatterer*.

guidebook, Baedeker; travelogue, topography; handbook, manual, vade mecum, ABC; timetable, Bradshaw; roadbook, itinerary, route map, chart, plan 551 *map*; gazetteer 589 *reference book*; nautical almanac, ephemeris; telephone directory, phone book; catalogue 87 *directory*; courier 520 *guide*.

Adj. *informative*, communicative, newsy, chatty, gossipy; informatory, informational, instructive, instructional, documentary 534 *educational*; expressive 532 *affirmative*; expository 520 *interpretive*; in writing 586 *written*; oral, verbal, spoken, nuncupative 579 *speaking*; annunciatory 528 *publishing*; advisory 691 *advising*; monitory 664 *cautionary*; explicit, clear 80 *definite*; candid, plainspoken 573 *plain*; overcommunicative, talking, indiscreet 581 *loquacious*; hinting, insinuating, suggesting.

informed, well-i., kept i.; posted, primed, briefed, instructed 490 *knowing*; told, au courant, genned-up, clued-up, wised-up; in the know, in on, in the picture; brought up to date.

Vb. *inform*, certify, advise, beg to a.; intimate, impart, convey (**see** *communicate*); apprise, acquaint, have one know, give to understand; give one the facts, brief, instruct 534 *teach*; let one know, put one in the picture, fill one in on; enlighten, open the mind, fill with information 534 *educate*; point out, direct one's attention 547 *indicate*; insinuate (**see** *hint*); entrust with information, confide, get confidential, mention privately; put one wise, put right, correct, disabuse, undeceive, disillusion; be specific, state, name, signify 80 *specify*; mention, refer to, touch on, speak of 579 *speak*; gossip, spread rumours; be indiscreet, open one's mouth, blurt out, talk 581 *be loquacious*; leak information, break the news, reveal 526 *disclose*; tell, blab, split, grass, snitch, peach, squeal, blow the gaff 526 *confess*; rat, turn Queen's evidence, turn State's e., implicate an accomplice 603 *tergiversate*; betray one, blow the whistle on, sell one down the river; tell tales, tell on, report against; inform against, lay an information against, shop, denounce 928 *accuse*.

communicate, transmit, pass on, pass on information; dispatch news 588 *correspond*; report, cover, make a report, submit a r.; report progress, post, keep posted; get through, get across, put it over; contact, get in touch; convey, bring word, send w., leave w., write 588 *correspond*; flash news, flash, beam; send a message, speak, semaphore 547 *signal*; wire, telegraph, telex, radio; telephone, phone, call, dial, ring, ring up, give one a ring *or* a tinkle *or* a buzz; disseminate, broadcast, telecast, televise; announce, annunciate, notify, give notice, serve n. 528 *advertise*; give out, put out, carry a report, publicize 528 *publish*; retail, recount, narrate 590 *describe*; commune 584 *converse*; swap news, exchange information, pool one's knowledge.

hint, drop a h., adumbrate, suggest, throw out a suggestion; put an idea in one's head; prompt, give the cue 505 *remind*; caution 664 *warn*; tip off 691 *advise*; wink, tip the wink; nudge 547 *gesticulate*; insinuate, breathe, whisper, say in one's ear, touch upon, just mention, mention in passing, say by the way, let fall, imply, allude, leave one to gather, intimate.

be informed, be in possession of the facts 490 *know*; be told, receive information, have it from; keep one's ears open, get to hear of, use one's ears, overhear 415 *hear*; get wind of, scent 484 *discover*; gather, infer, realize 516 *understand*; come to know, get a line on, get a report, get the facts 536 *learn*; open one's eyes, awaken to, become alive to 455 *be attentive*; ask for information, call for a report 459 *enquire*; have information, have the dope, have something to tell; claim to know 532 *affirm*.

Adv. *reportedly*, as stated, on information received, by report, straight from the horse's mouth; in the air, according to rumour, from what one can gather, if one can trust one's ears.

See: 80, 86, 87, 231, 401, 415, 419, 455, 459, 466, 480, 484, **490**, 494, 505, 512, 516, 520, **526**, **528**, **529**, 530, 531, 532, 534, 536, **547**, 548, 551, 573, 579, 581, 584, 586, 588, 589, 590, 603, 623, 664, 691, 754, 761, 762, 926, 928.

525 Concealment

N.*concealment*, confinement, purdah 883 *seclusion*; hiding 523 *latency*; covering up, burial 364 *interment*; occultation 446 *disappearance*; cache 527 *hiding-place*; fig leaf 226 *covering*; disguisement, disguise, camouflage 542 *deception*; masquerade, bal masqué; anonymity, incognito 562 *no name*; smoke screen 421 *screen*; reticence, reserve, closeness, discretion, no word of 582 *taciturnity*; secret thought, mental reservation, arrière pensée, ulterior motive; lack of candour, vagueness, evasion, evasiveness 518 *equivocalness*; mystification 421 *obfuscation*; misinformation 535 *misteaching*; white lie 543 *mental dishonesty*; subterfuge 542 *trickery*; suppression, D notice; suppression of the truth, cover-up 543 *untruth*; deceitfulness, dissimulation 541 *duplicity*.

secrecy, close s. 399 *silence*; secretness, mystery 530 *secret*; seal of secrecy, hearing in camera, auricular confession; secret society, Freemasonry; clandestineness, secretiveness, furtiveness, stealthiness, clandestine behaviour; low profile; underhand dealing 930 *improbity*; conspiracy 623 *plot*; cryptography, cryptogram, cipher, code 517 *unintelligibility*; invisible ink, sympathetic i.

Adj.*concealed*, crypto-, hidden; hiding, lost, perdu; ensconced, in ambush, lying in wait 523 *latent*; confined, incommunicado 747 *imprisoned*; mysterious, recondite, arcane 517 *unintelligible*; cryptic 523 *occult*; private 883 *secluded*; privy, confidential, off the record, unattributable; secret, top secret, restricted, hush-hush, inviolable; inviolate, unrevealed, ex-directory; undisclosed, untold; unsigned, unnamed 562 *anonymous*; covert, behind the scenes; covered 364 *buried*; hooded, veiled, eclipsed 421 *screened*; stifled, suppressed, clandestine, undercover, underground, subterranean 211 *deep*.

disguised, camouflaged; incognito 562 *anonymous*; unrecognized, unrecognizable 491 *unknown*; disfigured, deformed 246 *distorted*; masked 421 *screened*; overpainted 226 *covered*; blotted out 550 *obliterated*; coded, codified, cryptographic 517 *unintelligible*.

stealthy, silent, furtive, sneaking, like a thief; treading softly, catlike, on tiptoe; prowling, skulking, loitering, lurking; clandestine, hugger-mugger, conspiratorial, cloak-and-dagger; hole-and-corner, backdoor, underhand, surreptitious 930 *dishonest*.

reticent, reserved, withdrawn; noncommittal, uncommunicative, uninformative, cagey, evasive; vague, studiously v.; not talking, discreet, silent 582 *taciturn*; tight-lipped, poker-faced; close, secretive, buttoned-up, close as an oyster, clamlike; in one's shell 883 *unsociable*.

Vb.*conceal*, hide, hide away, secrete, ensconce, confine, keep in purdah 883 *seclude*; stow away, lock up, seal up, bottle up 632 *store*; hide underground, bury 364 *inter*; put out of sight, sweep under the carpet, cover up, whitewash, paper over the cracks 226 *cover*; varnish, gloss over 226 *overlay*; overpaint, blot out 550 *obliterate*; slur, slur over, not mention 458 *disregard*; smother, stifle 165 *suppress*; veil, muffle, mask, disguise, camouflage; shroud, becurtain, draw the curtain 421 *screen*; shade, obscure, eclipse 418 *darken*; befog, becloud, obfuscate 419 *bedim*; hide one's identity, assume a mask, masquerade 541 *dissemble*; code, encode, use a cipher 517 *be unintelligible*.

keep secret, keep it dark, keep under wraps, keep close, keep under one's hat; look blank, look poker-faced, keep a straight face, keep mum, keep one's mouth shut, hold one's tongue, not breathe a word, not utter a syllable, not talk, keep one's counsel, make no sign 582 *be taciturn*; be discreet, neither confirm nor deny, make no comment; keep back, reserve, withhold, let it go no further; hush up, cover up, suppress; keep a low profile, keep in the background, stay in the shadows; let not one's right hand know what one's left hand does; blindfold, bamboozle, keep in the dark 542 *deceive*.

be stealthy, - furtive, - evasive etc. adj.; hugger-mugger, conspire 623 *plot*; snoop, sneak, slink, creep; glide, steal, steal along, steal by, steal past; tiptoe, go on t., pussyfoot; prowl, skulk, loiter; be anonymous, stay incognito; wear a mask, assume a disguise 541 *dissemble*; lie doggo 523 *lurk*; evade, shun, hide from, dodge 620 *avoid*; play hide-and-seek, play bo-peep, hide in holes and corners; leave no address, cover one's tracks, take cover, go to earth; go underground, hide out, vanish 446 *disappear*; hide from the light, retire from sight, withdraw into seclusion, bury oneself, stay in one's shell 883 *be unsociable*; lay an ambush 527 *ambush*.

Adv.*secretly*, hugger-mugger, conspiratorially; confidentially, sotto voce, with bated breath; entre nous, between ourselves, between you and me and the gatepost; aside, to oneself, in petto; in one's sleeve; sub rosa, without beat of drum; not for publication, privately, in camera, in closed court, à huis clos, behind closed doors, anonymously, incognito, with nobody any the wiser.

stealthily, furtively, by stealth, like a thief in the night; under cloak of darkness 444 *invisibly*; underhand, by the back door, in a hole-and-corner way; on the sly, on the quiet, on the QT, by subterfuge.

See:165, 211, 226, 246, 364, 399, 418, 419, 421, 444, **446**, 458, 491, 517, 518, **523**, **527**, 530, 535, 541, **542**, 543, 550, 562, **582**, 620, 623, 632, 747, 883, 930.

526 Disclosure

N.*disclosure*, revealment, revelation, apocalypse; daylight, cold light of day; discovery, uncovering; unwelcome discovery, disillusionment 509 *disappointment*; denouement, catastrophe, peripeteia 154 *event*; lid off, exposé, divulgement, divulgence 528 *publication*; exposure, showing up 522 *manifestation*; explanations, clearing the air, showdown; communication, leak, indiscretion 524 *hint*; betrayal, giveaway; cloven hoof, tell-tale sign, blush, self-betrayal; State's evidence, Queen's e. 603 *tergiversation*; acknowledgment, admission, avowal, confession; auricular confession, confessional 939 *penitence*; clean breast, whole truth, cards on the table 494 *truth*.

Adj.*disclosed*, exposed, revealed 522 *shown*; showing 443 *visible*; confessed, avowed, acknowledged; with the lid off 263 *open*; laid bare 229 *uncovered*.

disclosing, uncovering, unclosing, opening; revelatory, apocalyptic, manifesting; epiphanic 975 *revelational*; revealing 422 *transparent*; expository, explicatory, explanatory 520 *interpretive*; divulging 528 *publishing*; communicative 524 *informative*; leaky, indiscreet, garrulous 581 *loquacious*; tell-tale, indicative 547 *indicating*; tale-bearing, betraying; confessing, confessional, penitent 939 *repentant*.

Vb.*disclose*, reveal, expose, take the wraps off 522 *manifest*; bare, lay b., strip b., denude 229 *doff*; unfold, unroll, unfurl, unpack, unwrap 229 *uncover*; unscreen, uncurtain, unveil, lift the veil, draw the v., raise the curtain, let in daylight; unseal, break the seal, unclose 263 *open*; lay open, open up 484 *discover*; catch out 484 *detect*; not hide 422 *be transparent*; give away, betray, blow one's cover; uncloak, unmask, tear off the mask; expose oneself, betray o., give oneself away 495 *blunder*; declare oneself, lift the mask, drop the m., throw off the m., throw off all disguise; show for what it is, cut down to life size, debunk; disabuse, correct, set right, undeceive, disillusion, open the eyes 524 *inform*; take the lid off, unkennel, let the cat out of the bag (**see** *divulge*).

divulge, declare, be open about, express, vent, give vent to 579 *speak*; ventilate, air, canvass, publicize 528 *publish*; let on, blurt out, blow the gaff, talk out of turn, spill the beans, let the cat out of the bag, give the show *or* the game away; speak of, talk, must tell; utter, breathe; let out, leak 524 *communicate*; let drop, let fall 524 *hint*; come out with, spit it out 573 *speak plainly*; get it off one's chest, unbosom oneself, unburden o.; confide, let one into the secret, open one's mind *or* heart to, bare one's soul to; declare one's intentions, show one's hand, show one's cards, put one's cards on the table; report, tell, tell tales out of school, tell on, name names 928 *accuse*; betray the secret, split, peach, squeal, blab 524 *inform*; rat 603 *tergiversate*.

confess, admit, avow, acknowledge; concede, grant, allow, own 488 *assent*; own up, cough up; implicate oneself, plead guilty; talk, sing, sing like a canary; come out with, come across with, come clean, tell all, admit everything, speak the truth 540 *be truthful*; make a clean breast of it, unburden one's conscience, go to confession, recount one's sins 939 *be penitent*; turn Queen's evidence 603 *tergiversate*.

be disclosed, come out, blow up, break 445 *appear*; come out in evidence, come to light 478 *be proved*; show the cloven hoof, show its face, show its true colours, stand revealed 522 *be plain*; transpire, become known 490 *be known*; leak out, ooze o., creep o. 298 *emerge*; peep out, show 443 *be visible*; show through 422 *be transpar-*

ent; come as a revelation, break through the clouds, flash on the mind 449 *dawn upon*; give oneself away, there speaks . . .

See: 154, 229, 263, 298, 422, 443, 445, 449, 478, **484**, 488, 490, 494, 495, 509, 520, **522**, **524**, **528**, 540, 547, 573, 579, 581, 603, 928, 939, 975.

527 Hiding. Disguise

N. *hiding-place*, hide, hideout, hideaway, hole, hidey-h., priesthole 662 *refuge*; lair, den 192 *retreat*; cache, secret place, oubliette; crypt, vault 194 *cellar*; closet, secret drawer, hidden panel, safe place, safe, safe deposit 632 *storage*; recess, corner, nook, cranny, niche, holes and corners, secret passage, underground p.; cover, underground 662 *shelter*; backstairs, backroom, inmost recesses 224 *interiority*.

ambush, ambuscade, ambushment 525 *concealment*; lurking place, spider's web 542 *trap*; catch 663 *pitfall*; stalking horse, Trojan h., decoy, stool pigeon 545 *impostor*; agent provocateur 663 *troublemaker*.

disguise, blind, masquerade 542 *deception*; camouflage, protective colouring 20 *mimicry*; dummy 542 *sham*; veneer 226 *covering*; mask, visor, veil, domino 228 *cloak*; fancy dress; cloud, smoke screen, cover 421 *screen*.

hider, lurker, skulker, stowaway; dodger 620 *avoider*; masker, masquerader; wolf in sheep's clothing 545 *impostor*.

Vb. *ambush*, set an a., lie in a., lie in wait 523 *lurk*; set a trap for 542 *ensnare*; assume a disguise, wear a mask; throw out a smoke-screen, obfuscate; waylay.

See: 20, 192, 194, 224, 226, 228, 421, 523, **525**, **542**, 545, 620, 632, 662, 663.

528 Publication

N. *publication*, spreading abroad, dissemination, divulgation 526 *disclosure*; promulgation, proclamation; edict, ukase, ban 737 *decree*; call-up, summons; cry, rallying c., hue and c., bugle call 547 *call*; beat of drum, flourish of trumpets 400 *loudness*; press conference, press release, advance publicity (**see** *advertisement*); notification, public notice, official bulletin; announcement, pronouncement, pronunciamento, manifesto, programme, platform; the media, mass m.; publishing, book trade, book-selling 589 *book*; broadcasting 531 *telecommunication*; broadcast, telecast, newscast 529 *news*; kite-flying 529 *rumour*; circulation, circular, encyclical.

publicity, limelight, spotlight, public eye; publicness, common knowledge 490 *knowledge*; open discussion, ventilation, canvassing, canvass; openness, flagrancy, blatancy 522 *manifestation*; open secret, open scandal; notoriety, fame 866 *famousness*; currency, wide c.; circulation, wide c., country-wide c.; sale, extensive sales; readership, audience; viewing figures, listening f.; public relations, PR, propaganda; display, showmanship, salesmanship, window dressing 875 *ostentation*; sensationalism, ballyhoo 546 *exaggeration*; publicization, advertising, skywriting; medium of publicity, television, radio 531 *broadcasting*; public address system, loudspeaker, loud hailer 415 *hearing aid*; public comment, journalism, reporting, rapportage, coverage, report, write-up (**see** *the press*); investigative journalism 459 *enquiry*; newsreel, newsletter 529 *news*; sounding board, correspondence column, open letter, letters to the editor; editorial 591 *article*; pulpit, platform, hustings, soapbox 539 *rostrum*; printing press 587 *print*; blaze of publicity, letters of fire *or* of gold, letters a foot high.

advertisement, notice, insertion, advert, ad, small a., classified a.; personal column; agony c.; headline, banner h., streamer, screamer, spread; puff, blurb, buildup, hype, ballyhoo; promotional literature, unsolicited mail, handout, handbill; bill, affiche, poster 522 *exhibit*; billboard, hoarding, placard, sandwich board, display b., notice b., bulletin b.; yellow pages; advertising copy, slogan, jingle; plug, trailer, commercial 531 *broadcasting*; hard sell, soft s., subliminal advertising; Madison Avenue.

the press, fourth estate, Fleet Street, newspaper world, news business, the papers; newspaper, newssheet, sheet, paper, rag, tabloid, comic; serious press, underground p., gutter p., yellow p., tabloid p.; organ, journal, daily paper, daily, quality d., broadsheet, heavy; morning paper, evening p., Sunday p., local p., picture p.; issue, edition, late e., stop-press e., sports e., extra; magazine section, feuilleton, supplement, colour s., trade s.; leaflet, handbill, pamphlet, brochure, open letter, newsletter.

journal, review, magazine, glossy m., pulp m.; part-work, periodical, daily, weekly, monthly, quarterly, annual; gazette, trade journal, house magazine, trade publication 589 *reading matter*.

publicizer, notifier, announcer; herald, trumpet 529 *messenger*; proclaimer, crier, town crier; barker, tout; bill sticker, bill poster, sandwichman; promoter, publicist, publicity agent, press a., advertising a.; adman, advertiser, hidden persuader; copywriter, blurb writer, commercial artist, public relations officer, PRO, propagandist, pamphleteer 537 *preacher*; printer, publisher 589 *bookperson*; reporter, journalist, investigative j. 529 *news reporter*.

Adj. *published*, in print 587 *printed*; in circulation, circulating, passing round, current; in the news, public 490 *known*; open, exoteric; distributed, circularized, disseminated, broadcast; ventilated, well-v.; on the air, on television; multimedia, mixed media.

publishing, declaratory, notificatory.

well-known, public, celebrated, famous, notorious, crying, flagrant, blatant, glaring, sensational 522 *manifest*.

Vb. *publish*, make public, carry a report 524 *communicate*; report, cover, write up; write an open letter, drag into the limelight, bring into the open, reveal 526 *divulge*; highlight, spotlight 532 *emphasize*; radio, broadcast, telecast, televise, relay, diffuse 524 *inform*; spread, circulate, distribute, disseminate, circularize; canvass, ventilate, discuss 475 *argue*; pamphleteer, propagate, propagandize 534 *teach*; use the press 587 *print*; syndicate, serialize, edit, subedit, sub; issue, release, get out, put o., give o., send forth, give to the world, lay before the public; bring to public notice, let it be known; spread a rumour, fly a kite; rumour, bruit about, noise abroad, spread a.; talk about, retail, pass round, put about, bandy a., hawk a., buzz a. 581 *be loquacious*; voice, broach, talk of, speak of, utter, emit 579 *speak*.

proclaim, announce, herald, promulgate, notify; ban, denounce, raise a hue and cry 928 *accuse*; pronounce, declare, go on record 532 *affirm*; make a proclamation, issue a pronouncement, publish a manifesto; celebrate, sound, noise, trumpet, blazon, blaze abroad, cry, shout, scream, thunder 400 *be loud*; declaim, shout from the rooftops 415 *be heard*; beat the big drum, announce with a flourish of trumpets.

advertise, publicize; insert a notice, bill, placard, post, stick up a notice, put up a poster; tell the world, put on the map, put in headlines, headline, splash; put in lights, spotlight, build up, promote; make much of, feature; sell, boost, puff, cry up, crack up, hype up, write up, extol 482 *overrate*; din, din into one's ears, plug 106 *repeat*.

be published, become public, come out; acquire notoriety, hit the headlines, make the front page; circulate, pass current, pass from mouth to mouth, pass round, go the rounds, get about, spread abroad, spread like wildfire, fly about, buzz a.; find a publisher, see oneself in print, get printed, get into the papers; have a circulation, sell well, go like a best-seller 793 *be sold*.

Adv. *publicly*, openly, in open court, with open doors; in the limelight, in the public eye.

See: 106, 400, 415, 459, 475, 482, 490, **522**, 524, **526**, **529**, **531**, 532, 534, 537, 539, 546, 547, 579, 581, 587, **589**, 591, 737, 793, 866, 875, 928.

529 News

N. *news*, good n.; bad news 509 *disappointment*; tidings, glad t.; gospel, evangel 973 *religion*; dispatches, diplomatic bag; intelligence, report, dispatch, word, advice; piece of information, something to tell, titbit 524 *information*; bulletin, communiqué, handout; newspaper report, press notice; news item, news flash 531 *broadcast*; fresh news, stirring n., hot n., latest n., stop-press n.; sensation, scoop, exclusive; old news, stale n.; copy, filler; yarn, story, old s., tall s.; newscast, newsreel 528 *publicity*; news value, newsworthiness.

rumour, unverified news, unconfirmed report; flying rumour, fame; on dit, hearsay, gossip, gup, talk, talk of the town, tittle-tattle 584 *chat*; scandal 926 *calumny*; whisper, buzz, noise, bruit; false report, hoax, canard; grapevine, bush telegraph; kite-flying.

message, oral m., word of mouth, word,

advice, tip 524 *information*; communication 547 *signal*; wireless message, radiogram, cablegram, cable, telegram, wire 531 *telecommunication*; postcard, letters, dispatches 588 *correspondence*, 531 *postal communications*; ring, phone call; errand, embassy 751 *commission*.

news reporter, newspaperman *or* -woman, reporter, cub r., journalist, correspondent, legman, stringer 589 *author*; gentleman *or* lady of the press, pressman *or* -woman, press representative 524 *informant*; newsreader 531 *broadcaster*; newsmonger, quidnunc, gossip, talker 584 *interlocutor*; tattler, chatterer; muckraker, scandalmonger 926 *defamer*; retailer of news 528 *publicizer*; newsagent, newsvendor, newspaper boy *or* girl.

messenger, forerunner 66 *precursor*; harbinger 511 *omen*; announcer, town crier 528 *publicizer*; ambassador, minister, nuncio, legate, spokesman *or* -woman 754 *envoy*; apostle, emissary; flag-bearer, herald, trumpet; summoner, process-server 955 *law officer*; go-between, contact, contact man 231 *intermediary*.

courier, runner, Queen's Messenger, express m., express, dispatch-bearer, dispatch rider, mounted courier; postman 531 *postal communications*; telegraph boy, messenger b., errand b., office b.; call-boy, bellhop, page, buttons, commissionaire; carrier pigeon 273 *carrier*; Iris, Hermes, Mercury, Ariel.

Adj. *rumoured*, talked about, in the news, in the papers; reported, currently r., going about, going the rounds, passing around, bandied about; rife, afloat, in circulation, on everyone's lips; full of news, newsy, gossipy, chatty 524 *informative*; newsworthy.

Vb. *rumour*, fly a kite; send *or* dispatch news 588 *correspond*. **See 524** *inform*, 526 *disclose*, 528 *publish*.

See: 66, 231, 273, 509, 511, **524**, 526, **528**, **531**, 547, 584, 588, **589**, 751, 754, 926, 955, 973.

530 Secret

N. *secret*, profound s.; secret lore, esotery, esotericism, arcanum, mystery 984 *occultism*; confidential matter, sealed orders, hush-hush subject, top-secret file, state secret; confidential communication, confidence; sphinx, man *or* woman of mystery, enigmatic personality, Gioconda smile; Mr X 562 *no name*; dark horse, unknown quantity; unmentionable thing, skeleton in the cupboard; sealed book; unknown country, terra incognita 491 *unknown thing*.

enigma, mystery, puzzle, Chinese p., tangram; problem, poser, brain-twister, teaser; hard nut to crack, hard saying, knotty point, vexed question, crux 700 *difficulty*; cipher, code, cryptogram, hieroglyphics 517 *unintelligibility*; word-puzzle, logogriph, anagram, acrostic, crossword; riddle, riddle-me-ree, conundrum, rebus; charade, dumb c.; intricacy, labyrinth, maze 61 *complexity*.

See: 61, 491, **517**, 562, 700, 984.

531 Communications

N. *telecommunication*, long-distance c., telephony, telegraphy, radio *or* wireless t., comsat; signalling, semaphore, morse 547 *signal*; cable, cablegram, telegram, wire 529 *message*; bush telegraph 529 *rumour*; radar 484 *discovery*; loran, Decca (tdmk); telex, teleprinter, tape machine, ticker; intercom, walkie-talkie, bleeper; microphone 400 *megaphone*; headset 415 *hearing aid*; telephone, radio t., videophone; line, land-l., trunk l., party l., hot l.; telephone exchange, switchboard; wireless operator, radio ham, telegrapher, telephonist.

postal communications, postal services, Postal Union, GPO; post, mail, letters 588 *correspondence*; surface mail, sea m., air m.; parcel post, registered p., recorded delivery, express d.; postcode, postage stamp; pillarbox, postbox, letterbox; post office, sorting o., mailbag; postmaster *or* -mistress, postman *or* -woman 529 *messenger*; pigeon post; diplomatic bag, dispatch box.

broadcasting, the media 528 *publicity*; broadcasting authority, BBC, Beeb, Auntie; IBA, ITA; independent radio *or* television; commercial r. or t., local r. *or* t., cable r. *or* t., pirate r., Citizen's Band r.; transmitter, booster, communications satellite; aerial, antenna; radio waves, wave lengths, modulation, AM, FM 417 *radiation*; radio station, television channel, network; wireless, radio, steam r., cat's whisker, crystal set; portable, transistor, tranny; television, telly, TV, the box, gogglebox, small screen; colour television, black-and-white t., monochrome t.; closed-circuit t. 442 *camera*; videorecorder, videotape 549 *recording instrument*; Teleprompter (tdmk), autocue; teletext, Ceefax (tdmk), Oracle (tdmk), Prestel (tdmk) 524 *information*; Open University; radio listener 415 *listener*; viewer 441 *spectator*.

broadcast, outside b., telecast, simulcast, transmission, relay, live r. 528 *publication*; recording, repeat, transcription 548 *record*; programme, request p., phone-in, telethon, quiz, chat show, music 837 *amusement*; news, newsflash, news roundup 529 *news*; time signal, pips; talk, feature, documentary 524 *report*; soap opera, sitcom, docudrama 594 *drama*; cartoon, film 445 *cinema*; commercial 528 *advertisement*.

broadcaster, announcer, commentator, talking head, newsreader, newscaster 524 *informant*; presenter, front man, anchorman, linkman, compere, question master; disc jockey, DJ, deejay; media personality 866 *person of repute*.

See: 400, 415, 417, 441, 442, 445, 484, 524, 528, 529, 547, 548, 549, 588, 594, 837, 866.

532 Affirmation

N. *affirmation*, affirmance; proposition, subject and predicate; saying, dictum 496 *maxim*; predication, statement; submission, thesis 512 *supposition*; expressed opinion, conclusion 480 *judgment*; voice, choice, suffrage, ballot 605 *vote*; expression, formulation; written statement, prepared text; one's position, one's stand; declaration, profession; allegation 928 *accusation*; assertion, unsupported a., ipse dixit, say-so; asseveration, averment; admission, confession, avowal 526 *disclosure*; corroboration, confirmation, assurance, avouchment, one's word, warrant 466 *testimony*; insistence, vehemence, peremptoriness 571 *vigour*; stress, accent, accent on, emphasis, overstatement; reiteration 106 *repetition*; challenge, provocation 711 *defiance*; protest 762 *deprecation*; appeal, representation, adjuration 761 *entreaty*; observation, remark, interjection 579 *speech*; comment, criticism, positive c., constructive c. 480 *estimate*; assertiveness, self-assertion, push, thrust, drive 174 *vigorousness*; pontification, dogmatism 473 *positiveness*.

oath, Bible o., oath-taking, oath-giving, swearing, assertory oath, adjuration, solemn affirmation, statement on oath, deposition, affidavit 466 *testimony*; promissory oath, word of a gentleman, word of honour, pledge, promise, warrant, guarantee 764 *promise*.

Adj. *affirmative*, affirming, professing etc. vb.; not negative 473 *positive*; predicative; declaratory, declarative 526 *disclosing*; pronouncing, enunciative 528 *publishing*; valid, in force, unretracted, unretractable 473 *undisputed*; committed, pledged, guaranteed, promised 764 *promissory*; earnest, meaning 617 *intending*; solemn, sworn, on oath, formal; affirmable, predicable.

assertive, assertory, saying, telling; assured, dogmatic, confident, self-assured 473 *positive*; pushing, thrustful, trenchant, incisive, pointed, decisive, decided 571 *forceful*; distinct 80 *definite*; express, peremptory, categorical, absolute, brooking no denial, emphatic, insistent; vehement, thundering 176 *violent*; making no bones, flat, broad, round, blunt, strong, outspoken, strongly-worded, straight from the shoulder 573 *plain*; pontifical, of faith, unquestionable, ex cathedra 485 *creedal*; challenging, provocative 711 *defiant*.

Vb. *affirm*, state, express, formulate, set down; declare, pronounce, deliver, enunciate 528 *proclaim*, 579 *orate*; give expression to, voice 579 *speak*; remark, comment, observe, say; state with conviction, be bound, dare swear 485 *opine*; mean what one says, vow, protest; make a statement, make an assertion, assert, predicate; maintain, hold, contend 475 *argue*; make one's point 478 *demonstrate*; advance, urge 512 *propound*; represent, put one's case, submit; appeal, adjure, claim 761 *request*; allege, asseverate, avouch, aver; bear witness 466 *testify*; certify, confirm, warrant, guarantee 466 *corroborate*; commit oneself, go as far as; pledge, engage 764 *promise*; hold out 759 *offer*; profess, avow; admit 526 *confess*; abide by, not retreat, not retract 599 *stand firm*; challenge 711 *defy*; repudiate 533 *negate*; speak up, speak out, say outright, assert roundly, put it bluntly, make no bones about 573 *speak plainly*; be assertive, brook no denial, shout, shout down; claim to know, say so, lay down the law, speak ex cathedra, pontificate 473 *dogmatize*; get on one's soapbox, have one's say, have the last word.

swear, be sworn, swear an oath, take one's o., take one's Bible o.; attest, confirm by oath 466 *corroborate*; outswear 533 *negate*; cross one's heart, solemnly affirm, make solemn affirmation 466 *testify*; kiss the book, swear on the Bible, swear by all that is holy.

emphasize, stress, lay stress on, accent, accentuate; underline, put in italics, italicize, dot the i's and cross the t's; raise one's voice, speak up, shout, thunder, fulminate 400 *be loud*; bang one's fist down, thump the table; be urgent, be insistant, be earnest, urge, enforce; insist, positively i. 737 *command*; say with emphasis, drive home, impress on, rub in; plug, dwell on, say again and again, reaffirm, reassert, labour 106 *repeat*; single out, highlight, enhance, point up 638 *make important*.

Adv. *affirmatively*, positively, without fear of contradiction, ex cathedra; seriously, joking apart, in sober earnest; on oath, on the Bible; in all conscience, upon one's word, upon one's honour 540 *truthfully*.

Int. As I stand here! As God is my witness! Cross my heart and hope to die!

See: 80, 106, 174, 176, 400, 466, **473**, 475, 478, 480, 485, 496, 512, 526, 528, 533, 540, 571, 573, 579, 599, 605, 617, 638, 711, 737, 759, 761, 762, 764, 928.

533 Negation

N. *negation*, negative, nay; denial 760 *refusal*; refusal of belief, disbelief 486 *unbelief*; disagreement 489 *dissent*; contrary assertion, rebuttal, appeal, cross-a. 460 *rejoinder*; refutation, disproof 479 *confutation*; emphatic denial, contradiction, flat c., gainsaying; the lie, démenti; challenge 711 *defiance*; demurrer 468 *qualification*; protest 762 *deprecation*; repudiation, disclaimer, disavowal, disownment, dissociation, nonassociation 607 *rejection*; abnegation, renunciation 621 *relinquishment*; retractation, abjuration, swearing off 603 *recantation*; negative attitude, noncorroboration, inability to confirm; refusal of consent 757 *prohibition*; recusancy 769 *nonobservance*; contravention 738 *disobedience*; cancellation, invalidation, revocation, disallowance 752 *abrogation*.

Adj. *negative*, denying, negating, negatory; adversative, contradictory 14 *contrary*; contravening 738 *disobedient*; protesting 762 *deprecatory*; recusant 769 *nonobservant*; abrogative, revocatory; abnegating, renunciatory 753 *resigning*; denied, disowned.

Vb. *negate*, negative; contravene 738 *disobey*; deny, gainsay, give the lie to, belie, contradict, deny flatly, contradict absolutely, issue a démenti; deny the possibility, eat one's hat if 470 *make impossible*; disaffirm, repudiate, disavow, disclaim, disown 607 *reject*; not confirm, refuse to corroborate; not maintain, hold no brief for 860 *be indifferent*; deny in part, demur, object 468 *qualify*; disagree 489 *dissent*; dissociate oneself 704 *oppose*; affirm the contrary, controvert, traverse, impugn, question, call in q., refute, rebut, disprove 479 *confute*; refuse credence 486 *disbelieve*; protest, appeal against 762 *deprecate*; challenge, stand up to 711 *defy*; thwart 702 *obstruct*; say no, shake one's head, disallow 760 *refuse*; not allow 757 *prohibit*; revoke, invalidate 752 *abrogate*; abnegate, renounce 621 *relinquish*; abjure, forswear, swear off 603 *recant*; go back on one's word 603 *tergiversate*.

Adv. *nay* 489 *no*; negatively; not at all 33 *in no way*.

Int. never! a thousand times no! nothing of the kind! quite the contrary! far from it! anything but! no such thing!

See: 14, 33, 460, 468, 470, 479, 486, **489**, 603, 607, 621, 702, 704, 711, 738, 752, 753, 757, 760, 762, 769, 860.

534 Teaching

N. *teaching*, pedagogy, pedagogics, private teaching, tutoring; education, schooling, upbringing; tutelage, leading strings; direction, guidance, instruction, edification; spoon-feeding, dictation; chalk and talk; programmed learning, direct method, induction 475 *reasoning*; tuition, preparation, coaching, cramming; seminar, teach-in, clinic, workshop, tutorial; initiation, introduction; training, discipline, drill 682 *exercise*; inculcation, catechization, indoctrination, preaching, pulpitry, homiletics; proselytism, propagandism; persuasion, conversion, conviction; conditioning, brainwashing; pamphleteering, propaganda, agitprop 528 *publicity*.

education, liberal e. 490 *culture*; classical education, scientific e., technical e.; religious e., denominational e., secular e.; moral education, moral training; technical training, technological training, vocational t.; coeducation, progressive education, Froebel system, Froebelism, kindergarten method, Montessori system; monitorial system; elementary education, grounding; nursery education, primary e., secondary e., further e., higher e., university e., adult e.; day release, block r.; sandwich course, refresher c.; advanced studies, postgraduate s.; compensatory education, special e., remedial e.; physical education, gymnastics, physical jerks, callisthenics, eurhythmics.

curriculum, course of study 536 *learning*; core curriculum, common core; first lessons, propaedeutics, ABC, the three R's 68 *beginning*; foundation course; set books, prescribed text 589 *textbook*; set task, project, exercise, simulation e., homework, prep; liberal arts, liberal studies; trivium, grammar, rhetoric, logic; quadrivium, arithmetic, geometry, astronomy, music; sixth-form studies, general s.; Greats, finals 459 *exam*; correspondence course, course of lectures, university extension l., classes, evening c., night school 539 *school*.

lecture, talk, illustrated t., radio t. 531 *broadcasting*; reading, prelection, discourse, disquisition; sermon, preachment, homily 579 *oration*; lesson, apologue, parable; problem play 594 *stage play*; readership, lectureship, professorship, chair; lecturer 537 *teacher*.

Adj. *educational*, pedagogic, tutorial; scholastic, scholarly, academic; instructional, informational; audiovisual, instructive 524 *informative*; educative, didactic, hortative; doctrinal, normative; edifying, moralizing, homiletic, preachy; primary, secondary etc. n.; single-sex, coeducational, comprehensive, all-ability; set, streamed, creamed, mixed-ability; extramural, intramural; extracurricular; redbrick, Oxbridge, Ivy League; cultural, humane, scientific, technological; practical, utilitarian; multidisciplinary.

Vb. *educate*, edify (**see** *teach*); breed, rear, nurse, nurture, bring up, develop, form, mould, shape, lick into shape; put to school, send to s., have taught; tutor, teach, school; ground, coach, cram, prime 669 *prepare*; guide 689 *direct*; instruct 524 *inform*; enlighten, illumine, enlarge the mind, open the m.; sharpen the wits, open the eyes; fill with new ideas, stuff with knowledge, cram with facts, spoonfeed with f.; impress on the memory, knock into the head, inculcate, indoctrinate, imbue, impregnate, infuse, instil, infix, implant, engraft, sow the seeds of; disabuse, unteach; chasten, sober.

teach, be a teacher, give lessons, take a class, hold classes; lecture, deliver lectures; tutor, impart instruction; dictate, read out; preach, harangue, sermonize; discourse, hold forth; moralize, point a moral; elucidate, expound 520 *interpret*; train the mind, indoctrinate, inoculate; pamphleteer, disseminate propaganda, propagandize, proselytize, condition, brainwash 178 *influence*.

train, coach 669 *prepare*; take on, take in hand, initiate, tame 369 *break in*; nurse, foster, cultivate; inure, put through the mill, keep one's nose to the grindstone; drill, exercise, practise, make second nature, familiarize, accustom, groom one for 610 *habituate*; show one the ropes; make fit, qualify; house-train, teach manners, teach how to behave.

See: 68, 178, 369, 459, 475, 490, 520, 524, 528, 531, **536**, **537**, **539**, 579, 589, 594, 610, 669, 682, 689.

535 Misteaching

N. *misteaching*, misinstruction, misguidance, misleading, misdirection; quackery, a case of the blind leading the blind; false intelligence, misinformation 552 *misrepresentation*; mystification 421 *obfuscation*; false name 525 *concealment*; wrong attribution, wrong emendation, miscorrection 495 *mistake*; obscurantism 491 *ignorance*; false teaching, bad t., propaganda 541 *falsehood*; perversion 246 *distortion*; false logic, illogic 477 *sophistry*.

Adj. *misteaching*, misguiding etc. vb.; unedifying, propagandist; obscurantist 491 *ignorant*; mistaught, misled, misdirected 495 *mistaken*.

Vb. *misteach*, miseducate, bring up badly; misinstruct, misinform, misname, misdirect, misguide 495 *mislead*; not edify, corrupt, abuse the mind 934 *make wicked*; pervert 246 *distort*; misdescribe 552 *misrepresent*; cry wolf, put on a false scent 542 *deceive*; lie 541 *be false*; preach to the converted, teach one's grandmother to suck eggs; leave no wiser, keep in ignorance, take advantage of one's ignorance; suppress knowledge, unteach; propagandize, brainwash; explain away.

See: 246, 421, 477, 491, 495, 525, 541, 542, 552, 934.

536 Learning

N. *learning*, lore, wide reading, scholarship, attainments 490 *erudition*; acquisition of knowledge, acquisition of skills; thirst for knowledge, intellectual curiosity 453 *curiosity*; pupillage, tutelage, apprenticeship, novitiate, initiation 669 *preparation*; first steps, teething troubles 68 *beginning*; docility, teachability 694 *aptitude*; self-instruction, self-education, self-improvement; culture, cultivation, self-c.; late learning, opsimathy; learned person 492 *scholar*.

study, studying; application, studiousness; cramming, grind, mugging up; studies, course of s., lessons, class, classwork, deskwork; homework, prep, preparation; revision, refresher course, further reading, further study; perusal, reading, close r., attentive r. 455 *attention*; research, research work, field w., investigation 459 *enquiry*.

Adj. *studious*, devoted to studies, academic; partial to reading, bookish, well-read, scholarly, erudite, learned, scholastic 490 *knowing*; sedulous, diligent 678 *industrious*; receptive, teachable, docile 597 *willing*; self-taught, self-instructed, autodidactic; immersed in one's books 455 *attentive*.

Vb. *learn*, pursue one's education, get oneself taught, go to school, attend college, read, take lessons, sit at the feet of, hear lectures, take a course; acquire knowledge, gain information, collect i., glean i., assimilate learning, imbibe, drink in, cram oneself with facts, know one's f. 490 *know*; apprentice oneself, learn one's trade, serve an apprenticeship, article oneself 669 *prepare oneself*; train, practise, exercise 610 *be wont*; get the feel of, get the hang of, master; get by heart, learn by rote 505 *memorize*; complete the course, graduate.

study, prosecute one's studies, apply oneself, burn the midnight oil; do, take up; research into 459 *enquire*; study particularly, specialize, major in; swot, cram, grind, mug, get up, bone up on; revise, go over, brush up; read, peruse, pore over, wade through; thumb, browse, skip, turn the leaves, dip into; be studious, always have one's nose in a book; devote oneself to reading, bury oneself in one's books, become a polymath.

Adv. *studiously*, at one's books; under training, in articles.

See: 68, 453, 455, 459, **490**, **492**, 505, 597, 610, 669, 678, 694.

537 Teacher

N. *teacher*, preceptor, mentor 520 *guide*; minister 986 *pastor*; guru 500 *sage*; instructor, educator; tutor, private t., crammer, coach; governor, governess, nursemaid 749 *keeper*; educationist, educationalist, pedagogue; pedant 500 *wiseacre*; dominie, beak, schoolmarm; master *or* mistress, school teacher, supply t., class t., form t., subject t.; year tutor; house master *or* mistress; assistant teacher, deputy head, head teacher, head, headmaster *or* -mistress, principal; pupil teacher, usher, monitor; prefect, proctor; dean, don, fellow; lecturer, demonstrator, expositor, exponent 520 *interpreter*; prelector, reader, professor, Regius p.; catechist, catechizer; initiator, mystagogue; confidant, consultant 691 *adviser*; teaching staff, faculty, professoriate, senior common room.

trainer, instructor, physical education i., swimming i.; coach, athletics c.; choirmaster; dancing-master; disciplinarian, caner; animal trainer, horse-t., breaker-in, lion-tamer 369 *breeder*.

preacher, lay p. 986 *pastor*; pulpiteer, Boanerges, orator 579 *speaker*; hot gospeller, evangelist; apostle, missionary, pioneer 66 *precursor*; seer, prophet, major p., minor p. 511 *oracle*; pamphleteer, propagandist 528 *publicizer*.

Adj. *pedagogic* 534 *educational*.

See: 66, 369, 500, 511, 520, 528, **534**, 579, 691, 749, 986.

538 Learner

N. *learner*, disciple, follower, chela; proselyte, convert, initiate, catechumen; late learner, opsimath; self-taught person, autodidact; do-it-yourself fan; empiricist 461 *experimenter*; swotter, mugger, bookworm 492 *scholar*; pupil, scholar, schoolboy *or* -girl; day pupil, boarder; sixth-former; schoolfellow, schoolmate, classmate, fellow student; gifted child, fast

learner, high flier; slow learner, late developer, underachiever, remedial pupil; school-leaver; old boy, old girl.
beginner, young idea, novice, debutant; abecedarian; new boy *or* girl, tyro, greenhorn, tenderfoot, neophyte; amateur 987 *lay person*; recruit, raw r., rookie; colt, cadet, trainee, apprentice, articled clerk; probationer, L-driver, examinee 461 *testee*.
student, university s., college s., collegian, seminarist; undergraduate, undergrad, freshman, fresher, sophomore; former student, alumnus, alumna; commoner, pensioner, foundationer, exhibitioner; scholarship-holder, Rhodes Scholar; prize boy, prizeman; honours student; graduand, graduate, postgraduate, fellow; mature student, research worker, researcher, specialist.
class, reception c.; form, grade, remove, shell; set, band, stream; age group, tutor g., vertical grouping, house; lower form, upper f., sixth f.; art class, life c.; study group, workshop; colloquium 584 *conference*; seminar, discussion group 534 *teaching*.
Adj. *studentlike*, schoolboyish 130 *young*; undergraduate, collegiate; pupillary, discipular; scholarly 536 *studious*; preschool; rudimentary, abecedarian; probationary; in leading strings, in statu pupillari.
See: 130, 461, 492, **534**, 536, 584, 987.

539 School

N. *academy*, institute, institution, educational i.; college, lycée, gymnasium; conservatoire, school of music, school of dancing, ballet school, art s., academy of dramatic art; charm school, finishing school; correspondence college; university, university college, campus; Open University; redbrick university, Oxbridge, varsity; college of further *or* higher education; polytechnic, poly; school of philosophy, Academy, Lyceum, Stoa; alma mater, groves of academe.
school, nursery s., crèche, playgroup, kindergarten; infant school, dame s.; private school, independent s., public s., aided s., maintained s., state s., free s.; preparatory school, prep s., crammer; primary school, middle s., secondary s., high s., secondary modern s., grammar s., comprehensive s.; sixth form college; boarding school, day s.; night s., evening classes; convent school, denominational s.; Sunday s.; school for the blind, deaf-and-dumb s., special school, school for the educationally subnormal; community home, approved school; reform s., Borstal; remand home, detention centre; catchment area; blackboard jungle.
training school, nursery, training ground 724 *arena*; training ship, training college, agricultural c., technical c., tech; college of commerce, secretarial college; c. of education; theological college, seminary; law school, medical school, medical college, teaching hospital; military college, staff college; Dartmouth, Sandhurst, Cranwell; West Point.
classroom, schoolroom; study; lecture room, lecture hall, auditorium, amphitheatre; resources area, library; workshop, laboratory, lab, language lab; gymnasium, playing fields; campus; desk, school d.; schoolbook, reader, primer, crib 589 *textbook*; slate, copybook, workbook, exercise book 548 *record*; visual aid, blackboard 445 *spectacle*.
rostrum, bema, tribune, dais, forum; platform, stage, podium, estrade; hustings, soapbox; chair 534 *lecture*; pulpit, lectern, ambo; microphone 531 *broadcasting*; leader page, column 528 *publicity*.
Adj. *scholastic* 534 *educational*.
See: 445, 528, 531, **534**, 548, 589, 724.

540 Veracity

N. *veracity*, veraciousness, truthfulness, truth-telling, truth-speaking; nothing but fact, fidelity, fidelity to fact, verisimilitude, realism, exactitude 494 *accuracy*; openness, frankness, candour 522 *manifestation*; bona fides, honour bright, no kidding; love of truth, honesty, sincerity 929 *probity*; simplicity, ingenuousness 699 *artlessness*; downrightness, plain speaking, plain dealing 573 *plainness*; baldness, plain words, home truth, unvarnished tale, undisguised meaning, unambiguity, true statement, honest truth, sober t. 494 *truth*; clean breast, true confession, unqualified admission 526 *disclosure*; circumstantiality, particularity, full details, nothing omitted 570 *diffuseness*; gate of horn; truth-speaker, no liar, true prophet.
Adj. *veracious*, truthful 494 *true*; telling the truth, veridical, not lying; as good as one's word, reliable 929 *trustworthy*; factual,

sticking to fact, ungarbled, undistorted, bald, unembroidered, unvarnished, unexaggerated, scrupulous, exact, just 494 *accurate*; full, particular, circumstantial 570 *diffuse*; simple, ingenuous 699 *artless*; bona fide, meant, intended; unaffected, unpretentious, unfeigned, undissembling, open, above-board 522 *undisguised*; candid, unreserved, forthcoming; blunt, free, downright, forthright, plain-speaking, outspoken, straightforward, straight from the shoulder, honest to goodness, honest to God 573 *plain*; unambiguous 516 *intelligible*; honest, sincere, true-hearted, on the up and up 929 *honourable*; truly spoken, fulfilled, proved, verified 478 *demonstrated*; infallible, prophetic 511 *presageful*.

Vb. *be truthful*, tell the truth, tell the truth and shame the devil, tell no lie, swear true 532 *swear*; stick to the facts 494 *be true*; speak in earnest, mean it, really mean, honestly m.; not joke, weigh one's words 834 *be serious*; speak one's mind, open one's heart, keep nothing back 522 *show*; come clean, make a clean breast of it, confess the truth 526 *confess*; drop the mask, appear in one's true colours 526 *disclose*; be prophetic 511 *predict*; verify one's words, say truly 478 *demonstrate*.

Adv. *truthfully*, really and truly, bona fide, sincerely, from the bottom of one's heart 494 *truly*; to tell the truth, the whole t., and nothing but the t.; frankly, candidly, without fear or favour; factually, exactly, just as it happened.

See: 478, **494**, 511, 516, **522**, 526, 532, 570, 573, 699, 834, 929.

541 Falsehood

N. *falsehood*, falseness, spuriousness, falsity; treachery, bad faith, Punic f. 930 *perfidy*; untruthfulness, unveracity, mendacity, deceitfulness, malingering; lying, habitual l., pathological l., mythomania; oathbreaking, perjury, false swearing 543 *untruth*; invention of lies, fabrication, fiction; faking, forgery, falsification 542 *deception*; imaginativeness, invention 513 *imagination*; disingenuousness, prevarication, equivocation, evasion, double-talk, shuffling, fencing 518 *equivocalness*; economy of truth, suppressio veri, suggestio falsi; whitewashing, cover-up; casuistry 477 *sophistry*; overstatement 546 *exaggeration*; perversion 246 *distortion*; false colouring, misrepresentation, subreption 521 *misinterpretation*; meretriciousness 875 *ostentation*; humbug, bunkum, boloney, hooey, flimflam 515 *empty talk*; cant, eyewash, hogwash (**see** *duplicity*); euphemism, mealy-mouthedness, blarney, soft soap 925 *flattery*; liar 545 *deceiver*.

duplicity, false conduct, double life, double-dealing 930 *improbity*; guile 542 *trickery*; hollowness, front, facade, outside, show, window-dressing 875 *ostentation*; pretence, hollow p., bluff, act, fake, counterfeit, imposture 542 *sham*; hypocrisy, Tartuffery; acting, play-a., simulation, dissimulation, dissembling, insincerity, tongue in cheek, cant; lip service, cupboard love; pharisaism, false piety; crocodile tears, show of sympathy; Judas kiss; fraud, pious f., legal fiction, diplomatic illness; cheat, cheating, sharp practice; collusion, nod and a wink; put-up job, frame-up 930 *foul play*; quackery, charlatanry, charlatanism 850 *pretension*; low cunning, artfulness 698 *cunning*.

Adj. *false*, not true, truthless, without truth; imagined, made-up; untruthful, lying, unveracious, mendacious 543 *untrue*; perfidious, treacherous, forsworn, perjured; sneaky, artful 698 *cunning*; disingenuous, dishonest, uncandid, unfair, ambiguous, evasive, shuffling 518 *equivocal*; falsified, garbled; meretricious, embellished, touched up, varnished, painted; overdone 546 *exaggerated*; ungenuine, imitated, counterfeit, fake, phoney, sham, pseudo, snide, quack, bogus 542 *spurious*; cheating, deceptive, deceitful, fraudulent 542 *deceiving*; covinous, collusive; fiddled, engineered, rigged, packed; trumped up.

hypocritical, hollow, empty, insincere, diplomatic; put on, imitated, pretended, seeming, feigned; make-believe, acting, play a.; double, two-faced, double-tongued, shifty, sly, treacherous, double-dealing, designing, Machiavellian 930 *perfidious*; sanctimonious, Tartuffian, Pecksniffian, pharisaical; casuistical; plausible, smooth, smooth-tongued, smooth-spoken, oily; creepy, goody-goody; mealy-mouthed, euphemistic 850 *affected*; canting, gushing 925 *flattering*.

Vb. *be false*, - perjured, - forsworn etc. adj.; perjure oneself, bear false witness, swear falsely, swear that black is white; palter,

palter *or* trifle with the truth; lie, tell lies, utter a falsehood, lie in one's teeth *or* one's throat; tell the tale, swing the lead; strain, stretch the truth, tell a tall story 546 *exaggerate*; tell a fib, tell a whopper, lie hard; invent, make believe, make up, romance 513 *imagine*; put a false construction on 521 *misinterpret*; garble, doctor, tamper with, falsify 246 *distort*; overstate, understate 552 *misrepresent*; misreport, misquote, miscite, misinform, cry wolf 535 *misteach*; lull, soothe 925 *flatter*; play false, play a double game 930 *be dishonest*; run with the hare and hunt with the hounds; break faith, betray 603 *tergiversate*.

dissemble, dissimulate, disguise 525 *conceal*; simulate, counterfeit 20 *imitate*; put on, assume, affect, dress up, play-act, play a part, go through the motions, make a show of 594 *act*; feign, pass off for, sham, pretend, sail under false colours; malinger, sham Abraham 542 *deceive*; lack candour, be less than honest, say one thing and mean another; hide the truth, say less than the t., keep something back, fail to declare; fudge the issue, not give a straight answer, prevaricate, beat about the bush, shuffle, dodge, trim 518 *be equivocal*.

cant, gloze, euphemize, mince matters 850 *be affected*; colour, varnish, paint, embroider, dress up; gloss over, gloze o. 477 *sophisticate*; play the hypocrite, act a part, put on an act; say the grapes are sour.

fake, fudge, fabricate, coin, forge, plagiarize, counterfeit 20 *imitate*; get up, trump up, frame; manipulate, fiddle, wangle, rig, pack (a jury); spin, weave, cook, cook up, concoct, hatch, invent 623 *plot*.

Adv. *falsely*, slyly, deceitfully, under false pretences; hypocritically, mendaciously.

See: 20, 246, 477, 513, 515, 518, 521, **525**, 535, **542**, **543**, **545**, 546, 552, 594, 603, 623, 698, 850, 875, 925, **930**.

542 Deception

N. *deception*, kidding, tongue in cheek; circumvention, outwitting; self-deception, wishful thinking 487 *credulity*; infatuation 499 *folly*; fallacy 477 *sophistry*; illusion, delusion, hallucination, imagination's artful aid 495 *error*; deceptiveness, speciousness 523 *latency* (**see** *trap*); false appearance, mockery, mirage, will-o'-the-wisp 440 *visual fallacy*; show, outward s., meretriciousness, paint (**see** *sham*); false reputation, feet of clay; hollowness, bubble 4 *insubstantiality*; falseness, deceit, quackery, imposture, lie, pious fraud 541 *falsehood*; deceitfulness, guile, craft, artfulness 698 *cunning*; hypocrisy, insincerity 541 *duplicity*; treachery, betrayal 930 *perfidy*; machination, hanky-panky, jiggery-pokery, collusion 623 *plot*; fraudulence, cozenage, cheating, cheat, diddling; cheat 545 *deceiver*.

trickery, dupery, swindling, skulduggery, shenanigan; sharp practice, chicane, chicanery, legal c., pettifoggery; swindle, ramp, racket, wangle, fiddle, diddle, swizzle, swiz, sell, fraud, cheat; card-sharping 930 *foul play*; trick, dirty t., bag of tricks, tricks of the trade, confidence trick, fast one, wiles, ruse, shift, dodge, artful d., fetch, blind, feint 698 *stratagem*; wrinkle 623 *contrivance*; bait, gimmick, diversion, red herring, tub to a whale; hoax, bluff, spoof, leg-pull; game, sport, joke, practical j., rag 839 *witticism*; April fooling.

sleight, pass, sleight of hand, legerdemain, prestidigitation, conjuring, hocus-pocus, illusion, ventriloquism; juggling, jugglery, juggle, googly; thimblerig, three-card trick; magic 983 *sorcery*.

trap, deathtrap 527 *ambush*; catch 530 *enigma*; plant, frame-up 930 *foul play*; hook, noose, snare, springe, gin, spring gun, man trap; net, meshes, toils, web; diversion, blind, decoy, decoy duck, bait, lure, sprat to catch a mackerel; baited trap, mouse t., flypaper, lime-twig, bird-lime; booby trap, mine, tripwire, deadfall, pit 663 *pitfall*; trapdoor, sliding panel, false bottom 530 *secret*; fatal gift, poisoned apple, Trojan horse.

sham, false front, veneer 541 *duplicity*; lip service, tokenism; make-believe, pretence 850 *affectation*; paint, whitewash, varnish, gloss; whited sepulchre, man of straw, paper tiger; wolf in sheep's clothing 545 *impostor*; dummy, scarecrow; imitation, simulacrum, facsimile 22 *copy*; trompe-l'oeil, film set 4 *insubstantial thing*; mockery, hollow m.; counterfeit, forgery, fake; masquerade, mummery, mask, cloak, disguise, borrowed plumes, false colours 525 *concealment*; shoddy, Brummagem, jerry-building 641 *rubbish*; imitation ware, tinsel, paste; ormolu, mosaic gold; German silver, Britannia metal.

Adj. *deceiving*, deceitful, lying 543 *untrue*; deceptive 523 *latent*; hallucinatory, illusive, delusive, illusory; specious 445 *appearing*; glib, slick, oily, slippery 258 *smooth*; fraudulent, humbugging, cheating; lulling, soothing 925 *flattering*; beguiling, treacherous, insidious 930 *perfidious*; trumped-up, framed, colourable 541 *false*; feigned, pretended 541 *hypocritical*; juggling, conjuring; tricky, crafty, wily, guileful, artful, on the fiddle 698 *cunning*; collusive, plotting; painted, whitewashed, sugared, coated, plated (**see** *spurious*).

spurious, ungenuine, false, faked, fake; sham, counterfeit 541 *false*; make-believe, mock, ersatz, bogus, phoney; pseudo-, so-called; not natural, artificial, plastic, paste, cultured, imitation; shoddy, rubbishy 641 *useless*; tinsel, meretricious, flash, catchpenny, pinchbeck, Brummagem 812 *cheap*; jerry-built, cardboard, pasteboard 330 *brittle*; adulterated, sophisticated 43 *mixed*; underweight 323 *light*.

Vb. *deceive*, delude, dazzle; beguile, sugar the pill, gild the p., give a false impression, belie; let down 509 *disappoint*; pull the wool over one's eyes, blinker, blindfold 439 *blind*; kid, bluff, bamboozle, hoodwink, hoax, humbug, hornswoggle; throw dust in the eyes, lead up the garden path 495 *mislead*; spoof, mystify 535 *misteach*; play false, leave in the lurch, betray, two-time, double-cross 930 *be dishonest*; intrigue against 623 *plot*; circumvent, overreach, outwit, outmanoeuvre 306 *outdo*; forestall, steal a march on 135 *be early*; pull a fast one, take one for a ride, be too smart for, outsmart 698 *be cunning*; trick, dupe (**see** *befool*); cheat, cozen, con, swindle, sell, rook, do, do down; diddle, do out of, bilk, gyp, fleece, pluck, rip off, shortchange, obtain money by false pretences 788 *defraud*; juggle, conjure, force a card, palm off, foist o.; fob, fob off with; live on one's wits, try it on, practise chicanery, pettifog; gerrymander, tinker with, fiddle, wangle; load the dice, mark the cards, pack the c., stack the deck; play the hypocrite, impose upon 541 *dissemble*; brazen out, put a good face upon, whitewash 541 *cant*; counterfeit 541 *fake*.

befool, fool, make a fool of, make an ass of, make one look silly; mock, make fun of 851 *ridicule*; rag, play tricks on, pull one's leg, have one on, make an April fool of, play a joke on 497 *be absurd*; sport with, trifle w., throw over, jilt; take in, have, dupe, victimize, gull, outwit; trick, trap, catch out, take advantage of, manipulate, twist round one's little finger; kid, spoof, bamboozle, string along (**see** *deceive*); cajole, get round, fawn on, lull, soothe 925 *flatter*; let down, let in for, play fast and loose with, leave in the lurch, leave one holding the baby 509 *disappoint*; send on a fool's errand, send on a wild-goose chase 495 *mislead*.

ensnare, snare, trap, entrap, set a trap for, lay a trap for, lime, lime the twig; enmesh, entangle, net; trip, trip up, catch, catch out, hook, sniggle; bait, bait the trap, bait the hook, dangle a bait, lure, decoy, entice, inveigle 612 *tempt*; lie in wait, waylay 527 *ambush*; nab, nick, kidnap, shanghai 788 *steal*.

Adv. *deceptively*, deceitfully; under cover of, in the garb of, disguisedly; tongue in cheek.

See: 4, 22, 43, 135, 258, 306, 323, 330, 439, 440, 445, 477, 487, 495, 497, 499, 509, **523**, 525, **527**, 530, 535, **541**, **543**, **545**, 612, 623, 641, 663, 698, 788, 812, 839, 850, 851, 925, 930, 983.

543 Untruth

N. *untruth*, thing that is not, reverse of the truth 541 *falsehood*; less than the truth, understatement 483 *underestimation*; more than the truth, overstatement 546 *exaggeration*; lie, downright l., shameless l., barefaced l.; taradiddle, fib, whopper; false statement, terminological inexactitude; broken word, dicer's oath, lover's o., breach of promise 930 *perfidy*; perjury, false oath; false evidence, pack of lies, tissue of l., trumped-up story, frame-up 466 *evidence*; concoction, fiction, fabrication, invention 513 *ideality* (**see** *fable*); false excuse, Bunbury; misstatement, misinformation 535 *misteaching*; misrepresentation, perversion 246 *distortion*; gloss, varnish, garbling, falsification 521 *misinterpretation*; lie factory, propaganda machine; gate of ivory.

mental dishonesty, disingenuousness, economy of truth, half-truth, partial t., near t., half-lie, white l., pious fraud, mental reservation 468 *qualification*; suggestio falsi, suppressio veri 525 *concealment*;

show, make-believe; tongue in cheek, pretence, profession, false plea, excuse 614 *pretext*; evasion, subterfuge, shift, shuffle, ambiguity, doublethink 518 *equivocalness*; self-depreciation, irony, backhanded compliment 850 *affectation*; artificiality, unnaturalness; sham, empty words 541 *duplicity*; Judas kiss 930 *perfidy*; mask 527 *disguise*.

fable, invention, fiction, imaginative exercise 513 *ideality*; story, tale 590 *narrative*; tall story, shaggy dog story, fishy s., fisherman's yarn, traveller's tale 546 *exaggeration*; fairy tale, nursery t., romance, tale, yarn, story, cock-and-bull s., all my eye and Betty Martin 497 *absurdity*; claptrap, gossip, gup, guff, canard 529 *rumour*; old wives' tales; myth, mythology; moonshine, farce, mare's nest, sell, swiz, hoax, humbug, flummery 515 *empty talk*.

Adj. *untrue*, lying, mendacious 541 *false*; trumped-up, framed, cooked, hatched, concocted; far from the truth, nothing less true; mythological, fabulous; unfounded, empty; fictitious, imagined, make-believe, well-invented, ben trovato; faked, artificial, synthetic, factitious; phoney, bogus, soi-disant, so-called 542 *spurious*; overstated 546 *exaggerated*; boasting 877 *boastful*; perjured, forsworn 930 *perfidious*; evasive, shuffling, surreptitious 518 *equivocal*; ironical 850 *affected*; satirical, mocking 851 *derisive*.

Vb. *be untrue*, not hold water, be wide of the mark; sound untrue, not ring true 472 *be unlikely*; lie, be a liar 541 *be false*; spin a yarn, draw the long bow 546 *exaggerate*; make-believe, draw on one's imagination 513 *imagine*; be phoney, pretend, sham, counterfeit, forge, falsify 541 *dissemble*.

See: 246, 466, 468, 472, 483, 497, 513, 515, 518, 521, 525, 527, 529, 535, **541**, **542**, **546**, 590, 614, 850, 851, 877, 930.

544 Dupe

N. *dupe*, fool, old f., April f. 851 *laughingstock*; Simple Simon, Joe Soap 501 *ninny*; credulous fool, gobe-mouche, gudgeon; one easily taken in, easy prey, easy target, sitting duck, soft touch, pushover, cinch; fair game, victim, fall guy, patsy, stooge, mug, sucker, gull, pigeon; dude, greenhorn, innocent 538 *beginner*; puppet, cat's-paw, pawn 628 *instrument*; vulnerable public, admass.

Adj. *gullible* 487 *credulous*; duped, deceived, taken in, had, done, diddled, sold a pup 542 *deceiving*; innocent, green, silly 499 *foolish*.

Vb. *be duped*, be had, be done, be taken in; fall for, walk into the trap, rise, nibble, swallow the bait, swallow hook line and sinker; get taken for a ride; carry the can; catch a Tartar 508 *not expect*.

See: **487**, 499, 501, 508, 538, **542**, 628, 851.

545 Deceiver

N. *deceiver*, kidder, ragger, leg-puller; practical joker, Puck, Loki, Till Eulenspiegel 839 *humorist*; dissembler, actor, shammer, hypocrite, canter, whited sepulchre, Pharisee, Pecksniff, Tartuffe, Uriah Heep, Joseph Surface; false friend, fair-weather f., jilt, jilter; shuffler, turncoat, trimmer, rat 603 *tergiversator*; two-timer, double-crosser, double agent; traitor, Judas 938 *knave*; seducer 952 *libertine*; serpent, snake in the grass, snake in one's bosom 663 *troublemaker*; plotter, intrigant, intriguer, conspirator 623 *planner*; counterfeiter, forger, faker, plagiarizer 20 *imitator*.

liar, confirmed l., pathological l., mythomaniac; Ananias; fibster, fibber, storyteller; romancer, fabulist; imaginative person, yarner, yarn-spinner; angler, traveller 546 *exaggeration*; fabricator, equivocator, palterer; oath-breaker, perjurer, false witness 541 *falsehood*.

impostor, shammer, ringer, malingerer, adventurer, carpetbagger; usurper; cuckoo in the nest 59 *intruder*; ass in the lion's skin, wolf in sheep's clothing; boaster, bluffer, four-flusher; pretender, charlatan, quack, quacksalver, mountebank, saltimbanco 850 *affecter*; fake, fraud, humbug; pseud, pseudo, phoney; masquerader, mummer; front man 525 *concealment*.

trickster, hoaxer, spoofer, hoodwinker, bamboozler; cheat, cheater, cozener; sharper, cardsharp, rook, thimblerigger 542 *trickery*; shyster, pettifogger; swindler, bilker, diddler, shark 789 *defrauder*; slicker, spieler, twister, jobber, rogue 938 *knave*; confidence trickster, con man 477 *sophist*; decoy, stool pigeon, decoy-duck, agent provocateur; fiddler, manipulator, rigger, fixer; wily bird, fox 698 *slyboots*.

conjuror, illusionist, prestidigitator, juggler, ventriloquist; quick-change artist; magician, necromancer 983 *sorcerer*.

See: 20, 59, 477, 525, **541**, **542**, **546**, 603, 623, 663, 698, 789, 839, 850, 938, 952, 983.

546 Exaggeration

N. *exaggeration*, overemphasis, inflation, magnification, enlargement 197 *expansion*; optimism 482 *overestimation*; stretch, strain, straining; extravagance, exaggerated lengths, extremes, immoderation, extremism; overkill; excess, excessiveness, violence 943 *intemperance*; inordinacy, exorbitance, overdoing it, piling Ossa upon Pelion; overacting, histrionics 875 *ostentation*; sensationalism, ballyhoo, puffery 528 *publicity*; overstatement, hyperbole 519 *trope*; adulation 925 *flattery*; colouring, high c. 574 *ornament*; embroidery 38 *addition*; disproportion 246 *distortion*; caricature, burlesque 851 *satire*; exacerbation 832 *aggravation*; big talk 877 *boasting*; rant, ranting, tirade, rodomontade, grandiloquence 574 *magniloquence*; overpraise, excessive loyalty, chauvinism 481 *prejudice*; tall story, yarn, traveller's tale 543 *fable*; teratology, miracle-mongering; flight of fancy, stretch of the imagination 513 *imagination*; fuss, pother, excitement, storm in a teacup, much ado about nothing 318 *commotion*; extremist, exaggerator; sensationalist, miracle-monger, teratologist; Baron Munchausen 545 *liar*.

Adj. *exaggerated*, magnified, enlarged 197 *expanded*; blown up, out of all proportion; added to, embroidered; strained, overemphasized, overweighted, overdone, overstated, overcoloured, inflated, hyperbolical 574 *rhetorical*; overacted, histrionic; melodramatic, blood-and-thunder; bombastic, swelling 877 *boastful*; tall, fanciful, high-flown, steep, egregious, preposterous, outrageous, far-fetched 497 *absurd*; vaulting, lofty, extravagant, excessive, outré, extremist; violent, immoderate 32 *exorbitant*; fulsome, inordinate 637 *superfluous*.

Vb. *exaggerate*, maximize, magnify, expand, inflate, blow up 197 *enlarge*; overamplify, overelaborate; add to, pile up, pile it on 38 *add*; touch up, enhance, heighten, add a flourish, embroider 844 *decorate*; lay it on thick *or* with a trowel, depict in glowing terms; overdo, overcolour, overdraw, overcharge, overload; overweight, overstress, overemphasize 638 *make important*; overpraise, puff, hype up, oversell, cry up 482 *overrate*; make much of, make too much of 925 *flatter*; stretch, strain 246 *distort*; caricature 851 *satirize*; go to all lengths, not know when to stop, protest too much, speak in superlatives, hyperbolize; overact, melodramatize, dramatize, out-Herod Herod; rant, talk big 877 *boast*; run riot, go to extremes, pile Pelion on Ossa; draw the long bow, overshoot the mark, go too far 306 *overstep*; spin a yarn, draw on the imagination, deal in the marvellous, tell travellers' tales 541 *be false*; make mountains out of molehills, make a storm in a tea cup; intensify, exacerbate 832 *aggravate*; overcompensate, lean over backwards.

See: 32, 38, 197, 246, 306, 318, 481, 482, 497, 513, 519, 528, 541, 543, 545, 574, 637, 638, 832, 844, 851, **875**, **877**, **925**, 943.

Section three: Means of communicating ideas

547 Indication

N. *indication*, pointing out, drawing attention, showing 522 *manifestation*; signification, meaning 514 *connotation*; notification 524 *information*; symbolization, symbolism 551 *representation*; symbol, conventional s., x 558 *letter*; secret symbol, hieroglyph 530 *enigma*; sacred symbol, cross, crescent, mandala; magic symbol, pentacle 983 *talisman*; natural symbol, image, type, figure; token, emblem, figurehead (**see** *badge*); something to go by, symptom, sign 466 *evidence*; tell-tale sign, blush 526 *disclosure*; nudge, wink 524 *hint* (**see** *gesture*); straw in the wind, sign of the times 511 *omen*; clue, scent, whiff 484 *discovery*; noise, footfall 398 *sound*; interpretation of symptoms, symptomatology, semiology, semiotics 520 *hermeneutics*; pointer, finger, forefinger, index finger (**see** *indicator*); guide, index, thumb i. 87 *directory*; key 520 *interpretation*; contour lines, hachures; marker, mark; blaze; nick, scratch 260 *notch*; stamp, print, impression; stigma, stigmata; prick, tattooing, tattoo mark 263 *perforation*; scar

845 *blemish*; line, score, stroke; note, side n., catchword (**see** *punctuation*); legend, caption 590 *description*; inscription, epitaph; motto, cipher, monogram; love token, favour. **See** *badge*.

identification, naming 561 *nomenclature*, 77 *classification*; means of identification, brand, earmark, trademark, imprint (**see** *label*); name and address; autograph, signature, hand 586 *script*; fingerprint, footprint, spoor, track, trail 548 *trace*; secret sign, password, open sesame, watchword, countersign, shibboleth; diagnostic, markings, stripes, spots, colour, colouring; characteristic, trait, lineament, outline, form, shape 445 *feature*; personal characteristic, trick, trick of speech, idiolect; mole, scar, birthmark, strawberry mark 845 *blemish*; divining rod 484 *detector*; litmus paper 461 *testing agent*; mark, note.

symbology, symbolization; semiotics, semiology; dactylology; cipher, code 525 *secrecy*; picture writing, hieroglyphics 586 *script*; gipsy signs, scout s.

gesture, gesticulation, sign language, dactylology; deaf-and-dumb language; sign 524 *hint*; pantomime, dumb show, charade, mime; by-play, stage business; body language, kinesics; demeanour, look in one's eyes, tone of one's voice 445 *mien*; motion, move; tic, twitch 318 *spasm*; shrug, shrug of the shoulders; wag of the head, nod, beck, wink, flicker of the eyelash, twinkle, glance, ogle, leer, grimace 438 *look*; smile, laugh 835 *laughter*; touch, kick, nudge, jog, dig in the ribs 279 *knock*; hug, clap on the shoulders; hand-pressure, squeeze of the hand, handshake, grip; push, shove 279 *impulse*; pointing, signal, waving, wave, hand-signal, wave of the hand; raising one's hand, wagging one's forefinger; drumming one's fingers, tapping one's foot, stamp of the foot 822 *excitable state*; clenching one's teeth, gritting one's t. 599 *resolution*; gnashing *or* grinding one's teeth, snap, snapping one's jaws 892 *irascibility*; wringing one's hands, tearing one's hair 836 *lamentation*; clenched fist 711 *defiance*; flag-waving, umbrella-w., hat-w. 876 *celebration*; clap, clapping, hand-c., cheer 923 *applause*; hiss, hissing, hooting, boo, booing, catcall, Bronx cheer, raspberry 924 *disapprobation*; stuck-out tongue 878 *sauciness*; frown, scowl 893 *sullenness*; pout, moue, pursing of the lips 829 *discontent*.

signal 529 *message*; sign, symptom 522 *manifestation*; flash, rocket, Very light, maroon; signalling, railway signal, smoke s., heliograph, semaphore, tick-tack; telegraph, morse 531 *telecommunication*; flashlamp, signal lamp 420 *lamp*; warning light, beacon, beacon fire, bale-f., watch-f. 379 *fire*; warning signal, red flag, warning light, red l., Belisha beacon, green light, all clear 420 *signal light*; alarum, alarm, warning signal, distress s., SOS 665 *danger signal*; whistle, police w.; siren, hooter; bleeper; buzzer, knocker, door-knocker 414 *gong*; bell, doorbell, alarm bell, Lutine b.; church bells, angelus, carillon, sacring bell; time signal, pip, minute gun, dinner gong, dinner bell 117 *chronometry*; passing bell, knell, muffled drum 364 *obsequies*.

indicator, index, pointer, arrow, needle, compass n., magnetic n.; arm, finger, index-f.; hand, hour h. 117 *timekeeper*; Plimsoll line 465 *gauge*; traffic indicator, trafficator, winker; direction finder, radar; white line, cat's-eyes 305 *traffic control*; weathercock, wind sock 340 *weather*.

signpost, direction post, fingerpost, guidepost; milestone, milepost, milliary column, waymark; lighthouse, lightship, buoy 662 *safeguard*; compass 269 *sailing aid*; lodestar, cynosure, guiding star, pole s., Southern Cross 321 *star*; landmark, seamark, Pillars of Hercules; cairn 253 *earthwork*; monument, memorial 505 *reminder*; triangulation point, benchmark; tidemark 236 *limit*.

call, proclamation, ban, hue-and-cry 528 *publication*; shout, hail; invitation; call to prayer, church bell, muezzin's cry 981 *worship*; summons, word, word of command 737 *command*; distress call, Mayday; bugle, trumpet, bugle-call, reveille, assemble, charge, advance, rally, retreat; lights out, last post; peal, sennet, flourish; drum, drumbeat, drum-roll, tattoo, taps 403 *roll*; call to arms, fiery cross; battle cry, war c., rallying c., slogan, catchword, watchword, shibboleth; challenge, countersign.

badge, token, emblem, symbol, sign, totem (**see** *indication*); insignia (**see** *heraldry*); markings, military m., roundel; badge of sovereignty, throne, sceptre, orb, crown 743 *regalia*; mark of authority, badge of office, wand of o., Black Rod, mace, keys 743 *badge of rule*; baton, stars, pips, spurs, stripes, epaulette 743 *badge of rank*; medal, gong, cross, Victoria Cross, George C., Iron C.; order, star, garter, sash, ribbon 729 *decoration*; badge of merit, laurels, bays, wreath, fillet, chaplet, garland 729 *trophy*; colours, blue, half-b., cap, oar; badge of loyalty, favour, rosette, love knot; badge of mourning, black, crepe, widow's weeds 228 *clothing*.

livery, dress, national d. 228 *uniform*; tartan, tie, old school t., blazer; regimental badge, brassard, epaulette, aiguillette, chevron, stripes, pips, wings; flash, hackle, cockade, rosette.

heraldry, armory, blazonry; heraldic register, Roll of Arms; armorial bearings, coat of arms, blazon; achievement, funereal a., hatchment; shield, escutcheon; crest, torse, wreath, helmet, crown, coronet, mantling, lambrequin; supporters, motto; field, quarter, dexter, sinister, chief, base; charge, device, bearing; ordinary, fess, bar, label, pale, bend, bend sinister, chevron, pile, saltire, cross; canton; inescutcheon, bordure, lozenge, fusil, gyron, flanches; marshalling, quartering, impaling, dimidiation; differencing; fess point, honour p., nombril p.; animal charge, lion, unicorn, griffin, cockatrice, eagle, falcon, martlet; floral charge, Tudor rose, cinquefoil, trefoil, planta genista; badge, rebus, antelope, bear and ragged staff, portcullis; national emblem, rose, thistle, leek, daffodil, shamrock, lilies, fleur-de-lis; device, national d., lion and unicorn, spread eagle, bear, hammer and sickle, triskelion; swastika, fylfot; skull and crossbones; heraldic tincture, colour, gules, azure, vert, sable, purpure, tenné, murrey; metal, or, argent; fur, ermine, ermines, erminois, pean, vair, potent; heraldic personnel, College of Arms, Earl Marshal, King of Arms, Lord Lyon K. of A.; herald, herald extraordinary, pursuivant, Bluemantle, Rouge Croix, Rouge Dragon, Portcullis.

flag, ensign, white e., blue e.; red ensign, Red Duster; jack, pilot j., merchant j.; flag of convenience; colours, ship's c., regimental c., King's Colour, Queen's C.; guidon, standard, vexillum, labarum, banner, gonfalon; banneret, bannerol, banderole, oriflamme; pennon, streamer, pennant, swallowtail, triple tail; pendant, broad p., burgee; bunting; Blue Peter, yellow flag; white flag 721 *submission*; eagle, Roman e.; tricolour; Union Jack; Stars and Stripes, Old Glory, Star Spangled Banner; Red Flag; black flag, pirate f., Jolly Roger, skull and crossbones; parts of a flag, hoist, fly, canton; flagpole, flagstaff.

label, mark of identification, tattoo, caste mark (**see** *identification*); ticket, bill, docket, chit, counterfoil, stub, duplicate; tally, tessera, counter, chip; tick, letter, number, check, mark, countermark; sticky label, sticker; tie-on label, tab, tag; name tape, nameplate, nameboard, signboard, fascia; sign, bush, barber's pole, three balls 522 *exhibit*; plate, brass p., trade sign, trademark, logotype, logo, hallmark, cachet, rebus; earmark, brand, stigma, broad arrow; dunce's cap; seal, signet, sigil, stamp, impress, impression; masthead, caption, heading, title, superscription, rubric; imprint, colophon, watermark; bookplate, ex libris, name, name and address; card, visiting c.; birth certificate, identification papers, identity card; passport, pass 756 *permit*; endorsement 466 *credential*; witness, signature, hand, sign manual, autograph, cipher, mark, cross, initials, monogram, paraph; fingerprint, thumbprint, footprint 548 *trace*.

punctuation, punctuation mark, point, stop, full s., period; comma, colon, semicolon; inverted commas, quotation marks, apostrophe, quotes; exclamation mark, question mark; parentheses, brackets, square b., crotchet, crook, brace; hyphen, hyphenation; dash, swung d., dot, caret, omission mark, blank; reference mark, asterisk, asterism, star; obelus, dagger, squiggle; hand, index; accent, grave a., acute a., circumflex a.; diaeresis, cedilla, tilde; diacritical mark, vowel point, macron, breve, umlaut; sigla, stroke, mark of abbreviation, paragraph, virgule; plus sign, minus s., multiplication s., division s., equals s., decimal point; underlining, sublineation; italics, bold type, heavy t. 587 *print-type*.

Adj. *indicating*, indicative, indicatory, pointing; significative, connotative, denotative; expressive, implicative, suggestive, suggesting 514 *meaningful*; figuring, typical, representative, token, symbolic, emblematic, totemistic, nominal, diagrammatic 551 *representing*; telltale, revealing, betraying 526 *disclosing*; signalizing, symptomatic 466 *evidential*; semiological, semiotic; diagnostic, symptomatological; characteristic, personal, individual 80 *special*; demonstrative, explanatory, exponential 520 *interpretive*; ominous, prophetic 511 *presageful*; gesticulatory, pantomimic; signalling, signing, thumbing etc. vb.

heraldic, emblematic; crested, armorial, blazoned, emblazoned etc. vb.; paly, barry; dexter, sinister; gules, azure, vert, purpure, sable, tenné, murrey, or, argent, ermine; fleury, semé, pommé; rampant, gardant, regardant, couchant, statant, sejant, passant.

marked, labelled etc. vb.; recognized, characterized, known by; scarred, branded, stigmatized, earmarked; patterned, sigillate; spotted 437 *mottled*; denoted, numbered, lettered; referenced, indexed; denotable; indelible.

Vb. *indicate*, point 281 *point to*; point out, exhibit 522 *show*; describe heraldically, blazon; mark out, blaze, waymark, signpost; register 548 *record*; name, identify, classify 80 *specify*; index, make an i., reference, supply references, refer; point the way, show the w., guide 689 *direct*; signify, denote, connote, suggest, imply, involve, spell, bespeak, argue 514 *mean*; symbolize, typify, betoken, stand for, be the sign of 551 *represent*; declare 532 *affirm*; signalize, highlight 532 *emphasize*; evince, show signs of, bear the marks of, bear the stamp of, give evidence of, attest, testify, witness to 466 *evidence*; intimate, smack of, smell of 524 *hint*; betray, reveal 526 *disclose*; inform against 524 *inform*; prefigure, forebode, presage 511 *predict*.

mark, mark off, mark out, chalk o., flag o., lay o., demarcate, delimit 236 *limit*; label, ticket, docket, tag, tab, keep tabs on; earmark, designate; note, annotate, put a mark on, trace upon, line, score, underline, underscore; number, letter, page; tick, tick off; nick, scribe 260 *notch*; chalk, chalk up; scratch, scribble, cover 586 *write*; blot, stain, blacken 649 *make unclean*; scar, disfigure 842 *make ugly*; punctuate, dot, dash, cross, cross out, obelize, asterisk; put one's mark on, leave fingerprints *or* footprints; blaze, brand, burn in; stigmatize, prick, tattoo 263 *pierce*; stamp, seal, punch, impress, emboss; imprint, overprint 587 *print*; etch 555 *engrave*; mark heraldically, emblazon, blazon; impale, dimidiate, quarter, difference; marshal, charge.

sign, ratify, countersign 488 *endorse*; autograph, write one's signature, write one's name; put one's hand to, subscribe, undersign; initial, paraph; put one's mark, put one's cross.

gesticulate, pantomime, mime, mimic, suit the action to the word 20 *imitate*; wave one's hands, talk with one's h., saw the air; wave, wag, waggle 318 *agitate*; wave to, hold out one's hand 884 *greet*; wave one's hat, stamp 923 *applaud*; wave one's arms, gesture, motion, sign; point, thumb, beckon, raise one's hand 455 *attract notice*; nod, beck, wink, shrug; jog, nudge, poke, prod, dig in the ribs, clap on the back; look, look volumes, glance, leer, ogle 438 *gaze*; twinkle, smile 835 *laugh*; raise one's eyebrows, wag one's finger, shake one's head 924 *disapprove*; wring one's hands, tear one's hair 836 *lament*; grit one's teeth, clench one's t. 599 *be resolute*; gnash one's teeth 891 *be angry*; snap, bite 893 *be sullen*; grimace, pout, scowl, frown 829 *be discontented*; cock a snook, curl one's lip 922 *despise*; shuffle, scrape one's feet, paw the ground; pat, stroke 889 *caress*.

signal, make a s., hang out a s., send a s., exchange signals, speak 524 *communicate*; tap out a message, semaphore, wigwag, heliograph; flag down, thumb; wave on, wave by, wave through; unfurl the flag, break the f., fly the f., strike the f., dip the f., dip, half-mast, salute; alert, sound the alarm, dial 999 665 *raise the alarm*; beat the drum, sound the trumpets; fire a warning shot 664 *warn*.

Adv. *symbolically*, heraldically; by this token, in token of; in dumb show, in sign language, in pantomime.

See: 20, 77, 80, 87, 117, 228, 236, 253, 260, 263, 269, 279, 281, 305, 318, 321, 340, 364, 379, 398, 403, 414, 420, 437, 438, 445, 455, 461, 465, 466, 484, 488, 505, 511, 514, 520, **522**, 524, 525, 526, 528, 529, 530, 531, 532, 548, 551, 555, 558, 561, 586, 587, 590, 599, 649, 662, 664, 665, 689, 711, 721, 729, 737, 743, 756, 822, 829, 835, 836, 842, 845, 876, 878, 884, 889, 891, 892, 893, 922, 923, 924, 981, 983.

548 Record

N. *record*, recording, documentation; historical record, memoir, chronicle, annals, history 590 *narrative*; biographical record, case history, curriculum vitae 590 *biography*; photograph, portrait, sketch 551 *representation*; file, dossier, rogues' gallery; public record, gazette, official journal, Hansard; official publication, blue book, White Paper; recorded material, minutes, transactions, acta; notes, annotations, marginalia, adversaria, jottings, dottings, cuttings, press c.; memorabilia, memorandum 505 *reminder*; reports, returns, statements 524 *report*; tally, scoresheet, scoreboard; evidentiary record, form, document, muniment; voucher, certificate, diploma, charter 466 *credential*; birth certificate, death c., marriage lines 767 *title deed*; copy, spare c., carbon c. 22 *duplicate*; documentation, records, archives, papers, correspondence; record, book, roll, register, registry, cartulary; tablet, table, notebook, minutebook, logbook, log, diary, journal, commonplace book, scrapbook, album; ledger, cashbook, chequebook 808 *account book*; index, waiting list 87 *list*; card, index c., microcard, microfilm 196 *miniature*; tape, computer t. 86 *data processing*; magnetic tape, pressing 414 *gramophone*; inscription, legend, caption, heading 547 *indication*; wall writing, graffiti 586 *script*.

registration, registry, record-keeping; recording, sound r., tape r.; inscribing, engraving, epigraphy; enrolment, enlistment; booking, reservation; entering, entry, double e., book-keeping, accountancy 808 *accounts*; filing, indexing.

monument, memorial 505 *reminder*; mausoleum 364 *tomb*; statue, bust 551 *image*; brass, tablet, slab, stela, inscription 364 *obsequies*; hatchment, funerary achievement 547 *heraldry*; pillar, column, memorial arch, obelisk, monolith; ancient monument, cromlech, dolmen, menhir, megalith 125 *antiquity*; cairn, barrow, tell 253 *earthwork*; testimonial, cup, ribbon, decoration 729 *trophy*.

trace, vestige, relic, remains 41 *leavings*; track, tracks, footstep, footprint, footmark, hoofmark, pug, tread; spoor, slot; scent, smell, piste; wake, wash, trail, vapour t.; furrow, swath, path; scuffmark, skidmark, tyremark, fingermark, thumb impression 547 *indication*; fingerprint, dabs 466 *evidence*; mark, tidemark, stain, scar, cicatrice, scratch, weal, wale, welt 845 *blemish*.

Adj. *recording*, logging etc. vb.; clerical, annalistic, record-making; self-recording; recordable; monumental, epigraphic, inscriptional 505 *remembering*.

recorded, on record, in the file, documented; filmed, taped; canned, in the can, on wax; filed, indexed, entered, booked, registered; down, put d.; in writing 586 *written*; in print, in black and white 587 *printed*; traceable, vestigial, extant 41 *remaining*.

Vb. *record*, tape-record, telerecord, tape, videotape; film 551 *photograph*; paint 551 *represent*; document, put *or* place on record; docket, file, index, catalogue, store in the archives; inscribe, cut, carve, grave, incise 555 *engrave*; take down, note down, set down in black and white, put in a book, commit to writing 586 *write*; capture on film, preserve for posterity; have printed 587 *print*; write down, jot d.; note, mark, make a note of; minute, calendar; chronicle 590 *describe*.

register, mark up, chalk up, tick off, tally, notch up, score; tabulate, table, enrol, enlist 87 *list*; fill in, fill up, enter, post, book 808 *account*; reserve, put on the list, put on the waiting l.; inscribe, blazon; log, diarize, journalize 505 *remember*.

Adv. *on record*, in the file, in the index, on the books.

See: 22, 41, 86, 87, 125, 196, 253, 364, 414, 466, **505**, 524, 547, **551**, 555, 586, 587, 590, 729, 767, 808, 845.

549 Recorder

N. *recorder*, registrar, record-keeper, archivist, remembrancer; Master of the Rolls; protonotary 958 *notary*; amanuensis, stenographer, scribe; secretary, receptionist; writer, penpusher; clerk, babu; record clerk, tally c., filing c., book-keeper 808 *accountant*; engraver 555 *engraving*; draughtsman 556 *artist*; photographer, cameraman 551 *photography*; sound recordist; filing cabinet, record room, muniment r., Record Office; Recording Angel.

chronicler, annalist, diarist, historian, historiographer, biographer, autobiographer 590 *narrator*; archaeologist 125 *antiquarian*; memorialist 763 *petitioner*;

reporter, journalist, columnist, gossip-writer, newsman 529 *news reporter*; press photographer, candid camera.

recording instrument, recorder, tape r., videotape r., VTR; record, disc 414 *gramophone*; Dictaphone (tdmk), telautograph, teleprinter, tape machine 531 *telecommunication*; cash register, till, checkout; turnstile; seismograph, speedometer 465 *gauge*; flight recorder, black box; time-recorder, stopwatch 117 *timekeeper*; hygrometer 341 *hygrometry*; anemometer 340 *pneumatics*; camera, photocopier; pen, pencil 586 *stationery*.

See: 117, 125, 340, 341, 414, 465, 529, 531, 551, 555, 556, 586, 590, 763, 808, 958.

550 Obliteration

N. *obliteration*, wiping out etc. vb.; erasure, effacement; overprinting, defacement; deletion, blue pencil, censorship; crossing out, cancellation, cancel; annulment, cassation 752 *abrogation*; burial, oblivion 506 *amnesty*; blot, stain 649 *dirt*; tabula rasa, clean slate, clean sweep 149 *revolution*; rubber, eraser, duster, sponge; stripper, abrasive 648 *cleaning utensil*.

Adj. *obliterated*, wiped out, effaced; out of print, leaving no trace, printless, unrecorded, unregistered, unwritten; intestate.

Vb. *obliterate*, remove the traces, cover, cover up 525 *conceal*; overpaint, overprint, deface, make illegible; efface, eliminate, erase, scratch out, rub o.; abrade 333 *rub*; expunge, sponge out, wash o., wipe o.; blot, black out, blot o.; rub off, wipe o., wash o.; take out, cancel, delete, dele; strike out, cross out, score through, censor, blue-pencil; raze 165 *demolish*; wipe off the map, bury, cover 364 *inter*; sink in oblivion 506 *forget*; submerge 311 *lower*; drown 399 *silence*; leave no trace 446 *disappear*; be effaced 506 *be forgotten*.

See: 149, 165, 311, 333, 364, 399, 446, **506**, 525, 648, 649, 752.

551 Representation

N. *representation*, personification, incarnation, embodiment; typifying, typification, figuration, symbolization 547 *indication*; conventional representation, diagram, picture-writing, hieroglyphics 586 *writing*; presentment, presentation, realization, evocation 522 *manifestation*; assuming the part of, personation, impersonation; enactment, performance, doing 594 *acting*; role-playing, sociodrama, psychodrama 658 *therapy*; mimesis, mimicry, noises off, charade, dumb show 20 *imitation*; depiction, characterization 590 *description*; delineation, drawing, technical d., mechanical d., freehand d., illustration, book i., artwork, graphics, iconography 553 *painting*; creation, work of art 164 *product*; impression, likeness, identikit 18 *similarity*; exact likeness, double, facsimile 22 *duplicate*; trace, tracing 233 *outline*; reflection (**see** *image*); portraiture, portrayal; pictorial equivalent, true picture, striking likeness, speaking l., photographic l., realism 553 *picture*; bad likeness, indifferent l. 552 *misrepresentation*; reproduction, lithograph, collotype 555 *printing*; etching 555 *engraving*; design, blueprint, draft, rough d., croquis, cartoon, sketch, outline 623 *plan*; projection, axonometric p., isometric p., isometric drawing.

image, very i., exact i. 22 *duplicate*; eidetic image, clear i.; mental image, after-image 451 *idea*; projection, reflected image, hologram, silhouette, ombres chinoises 417 *reflection*; visual, visual aid 445 *spectacle*; idol, graven image 982 *idolatry*; painted image, icon; putto, cherub; statuary, statue, colossus; statuette, bust, torso, head 554 *sculpture*; effigy, figure, stick f., figurine, figurehead; gargoyle; wax figure, waxwork; dummy, tailor's d., lay figure, manikin; maquette, model, working m.; doll, teddy bear; marionette, fantoccini, puppet, finger p.; snowman, gingerbread man; scarecrow, guy, Guy Fawkes; robot, Dalek, automaton; type, symbol, epitome.

art, architecture 243 *formation*; fine arts, beaux arts; graphic arts 553 *painting*; plastic art 554 *sculpture*; classical art, oriental a., Byzantine a., Renaissance a., quattrocento, cinquecento, baroque, rococo; art nouveau, Jugendstil, art deco, modern art, abstract art; classicism, realism; Surrealism, Expressionism 553 *school of painting*; op art, pop a.; kitsch 847 *bad taste*; aestheticism, functionalism, De Stijl, Bauhaus; functional art, commercial a.; decorative a. 844 *ornamental art*; the minor arts, illumination, calligraphy, weaving, tapestry, embroidery, pottery.

photography, radiography, skiagraphy;

time-lapse photography, aerial p., telephotography, microphotography; cinematography 445 *cinema*; telecine 531 *broadcasting*; photograph, photo, picture, snapshot, snap; plate, film, fast f., slow f., panchromatic f.; exposure, negative, print, contact p., enprint, sepia p., colour p., slide, diapositive, transparency; frame, still; reel, spool, cassette; filmstrip, microfilm, movie, home m. 445 *film*; daguerrotype, heliotype; spectrogram, hologram; photogram, shadowgraph; skiagram, radiograph, X-ray 417 *radiation*; photocopy 22 *copy*; photogravure 555 *printing*; shot, take, close-up, mug shot, pan, zoom, cover shot, tracking s., dissolve, fade; lens 442 *camera*; cameraman, cinematographer, photographer, snapshotter; radiographer.

map, chart, plan, outline, cartogram 86 *statistics*; sketch map, relief m., political m., survey m., Ordnance S. m., road m., star m., planisphere; Admiralty chart; ground plan, ichnography; elevation, side-e.; projection, Mercator's p., orthographic p., conic p.; atlas, world a.; globe; orrery 321 *astronomy*; map-making, cartography.

Adj. *representing*, reflecting etc. vb.; representative 590 *descriptive*; iconic, pictorial, graphic, vivid; emblematic, symbolic, totemistic, hieroglyphic 547 *indicating*; figurative, illustrative, diagrammatic; representational, realistic, naturalistic, true-to-life; primitive, naive, impressionistic, surrealistic, surreal; abstract, nonfigurative, nonobjective, conceptual; artistic, painterly 694 *well-made*; Rembrandtesque, Turneresque; paintable, photogenic; photographic.

represented, drawn, delineated etc. vb.; fairly drawn, well represented; reflected, imaged; painted, pictured; being drawn, sitting for.

Vb. *represent*, stand for, denote, symbolize 514 *mean*; type, typify, incarnate, embody, personify,epitomize; act the part of, assume the role of; personate, impersonate, pose as 542 *deceive*; pose, model, sit for 23 *be an example*; present, enact, perform, do 594 *dramatize*; project, shadow forth, adumbrate, suggest; reflect, image, hold the mirror up to nature; mimic, mime, copy 20 *imitate*; depict, characterize 590 *describe*; delineate, limn, draw, picture, portray, figure; illustrate, emblazon 553 *paint*; hit off, catch a likeness, catch, capture, realize, register 548 *record*; make an image, carve, cast 554 *sculpt*; cut 555 *engrave*; mould, shape 243 *form*; take the shape of, follow the s., mould upon, fashion u.; design, blueprint, draft, sketch out, chalk o., block o. 623 *plan*; diagrammatize, diagram, make a d., construct a figure, describe a circle 233 *outline*; sketch, scrawl, doodle, dash off 609 *improvise*; map, chart, survey, plot.

photograph, photo, take a p. *or* a picture; snapshot, snap, take a s.; take, shoot, film; X-ray, radiograph; expose, develop, process, print, enlarge, blow up, reduce.

See: 18, 20, 22, 23, 86, 164, 233, **243**, 321, 417, **442**, **445**, 451, 514, 522, 531, 542, 547, 548, 552, **553**, **554**, **555**, 586, 590, 594, 609, 623, 658, 694, **844**, 847, 982.

552 Misrepresentation

N. *misrepresentation*, not a true picture 19 *dissimilarity*; false light 541 *falsehood*; unfair picture, bad likeness 914 *injustice*; travesty, parody 546 *exaggeration*; caricature, burlesque, guy 851 *ridicule*; flattering portrait 925 *flattery*; nonrealism, nonrepresentational art 551 *art*; bad art, daubing; daub, botch, scrawl; anamorphosis, deformation, distorted image, false i., distorting mirror 246 *distortion*; misinformation 535 *misteaching*; misevaluation 521 *misinterpretation*.

Adj. *misrepresented*, travestied etc. vb; misrepresenting, unrepresentative, flat, cardboard.

Vb. *misrepresent*, misdescribe 535 *misteach*; deform 246 *distort*; give a twist *or* turn, miscolour, tone down 925 *flatter*; overdramatize 546 *exaggerate*; overdraw, caricature, guy, burlesque, parody, travesty; daub, botch, splash; lie 541 *be false*.

See: 19, **246**, 521, 535, 541, 546, 551, 851, 914, 925.

553 Painting

N. *painting*, graphic art, colouring, rubrication, illumination; daubing, finger painting; washing, colourwashing, tinting, touching up; depicting, drawing, sketching 551 *representation*; artistry, composition, rectilinear c., design, technique, draughtsmanship, brushwork; line, perspective, golden section; treatment, tone, values, atmosphere, ambience; highlight,

local colour, shading, contrast; monotone, monochrome, polychrome 425 *colour*; black and white, chiaroscuro, grisaille.
art style, style of painting, grand style, grand manner 243 *form*; intimate style, genre painting (**see** *art subject*); pasticcio, pastiche; trompe l'oeil; iconography, portrait-painting, portraiture; scenography, scene painting, sign p., poster p., miniature p.; oil painting, watercolour, tempera, gouache; fresco painting, mural p., encaustic p., impasto, secco.
school of painting, the Primitives, Byzantine school, Renaissance s., Sienese s., Florentine s., Venetian s., Dutch s., Flemish s., French s., Spanish s.; Mannerism, baroque, rococo, Pre-Raphaelitism, Neo-Classicism, Realism, Romanticism, Impressionism, Post-Impressionism, Neo-I., Pointillism, Symbolism, Fauvism, Dada, Cubism, Expressionism, Die Brücke, Der Blaue Reiter, Vorticism, Futurism, Surrealism, Abstract Expressionism, Tachism, action painting; minimal art, Minimalism, Conceptualism 551 *art*.
art subject, landscape, seascape, skyscape, cloudscape; scene, prospect, diorama, panorama 438 *view*; interior, conversation piece, still life, pastoral, nocturne, nude; crucifixion, pietà, nativity.
picture, pictorial equivalent 551 *representation*; tableau, mosaic, tapestry; collage, montage, photomontage; frottage, brass rubbing; painting, pastiche; icon, triptych, diptych, panel; fresco, mural, wall painting, poster; canvas, daub; drawing, line d.; sketch, outline, cartoon; oil painting, oleograph, gouache, watercolour, aquarelle, pastel, wash drawing, pen-and-ink d., pencil d., charcoal d.; design, pattern, doodle; cartoon, chad, caricature, silhouette; miniature, vignette, thumbnail sketch, illuminated initial; old master, masterpiece; study, portrait, full-length p., half-l. p., kit-cat, head, profile, full-face portrait; studio portrait, snap, pin-up 551 *photography*; rotogravure, photogravure, chromolithograph, reproduction, photographic r., halftone; aquatint, woodcut 555 *engraving*; print, plate; illustration, fashion plate, picture postcard, cigarette card, tea c., stamp, transfer, scrap, sticker; picture book, scrapbook, photograph album, illustrated work 589 *book*.
art equipment, palette, palette knife, spatula, paintbrush, paintbox, paint tube; paints, oils, oil paint, poster p., acrylic p.; watercolours, tempera, distemper, gouache, gesso, varnish 226 *facing*; ink, crayon, pastel, chalk, charcoal, heelball; pen, pencil; sketchbook 631 *paper*; canvas, easel, picture frame, mount; studio, atelier, art museum, picture gallery; model, sitter, poser, subject.

Adj. *painted*, daubed, scumbled, plastered etc. vb.; graphic, pictorial, scenic, picturesque, decorative 844 *ornamental*; pastel, in paint, in oils, in watercolours, in tempera 425 *coloured*; linear, black-and-white, chiaroscuro, shaded, stippled, sfumato; grisaille 429 *grey*; painterly, paintable 551 *representing*.

Vb. *paint*, wash, lay *or* float a w. 425 *colour*; tint, touch up, retouch, daub; scumble, put on, paint on; lay on the colour, lay it on thick 226 *coat*; splash on the colour, slap on paint; paint a picture, do a portrait, portray, draw, sketch, limn, cartoon 551 *represent*; miniate, rubricate, illuminate; do in oils *or* watercolours *or* tempera, do in black-and-white; ink, chalk, crayon, pencil, stencil, shade, stipple; block in, rough in; pinxit, delineavit, fecit.

See: 226, 243, **425**, 429, 438, **551**, 555, 589, 631, 844.

554 Sculpture

N. *sculpture*, plastic arts 551 *representation*; modelling, figuring 243 *formation*; carving, stone cutting, wood carving; moulding, ceroplastics; paper modelling, origami; petroglyph, rock carving, bone c., shell c., scrimshaw; toreutics 844 *ornamental art*; constructivism 553 *school of painting*; construction, stabile, mobile; kinetic art; statuary; group; statue, colossus; statuette, figurine, bust, torso, head; model, maquette, cast, plaster c., death mask, waxwork 551 *image*; objet trouvé; ceramics 381 *pottery*; glyph, anaglyph, medallion, cameo, intaglio; repoussé, relief, bas-relief, mezzo-rilievo 254 *relievo*; stone, marble, Parian m.; bronze, clay, wax, plasticine, papier-mâché; armature; modelling tool, chisel, burin.

Adj. *glyptic*, sculptured, carved; statuary, sculpturesque, statuesque, marmoreal; anaglyptic, in relief 254 *projecting*; plastic, ceroplastic; toreutic, glyphic.

Vb. *sculpt*, sculpture, sculp, block out, rough-hew 243 *form*; cut, carve, whittle, chisel, chip, scrimshaw; chase, engrave, emboss; model, mould, cast; sculpsit.

See: 243, 254, 381, 551, 553, 844.

555 Engraving. Printing

N. *engraving*, etching, line engraving, plate e., steel e., copper e., chalcography; photogravure; zincography, cerography, glyptography, gem cutting, gem engraving; glass engraving; mezzotint, aquatint; wood engraving, xylography, lignography, woodcut; linoprinting, linocut; scraperboard; silverpoint; drypoint; steel plate, copper p.; stone, block, wood-b.; chisel, graver, burin, burr, needle, drypoint, etching-p., style.

printing, type-p. 587 *print*; plate printing, copperplate p., intaglio p.; lithography, photolithography, photogravure, chromolithography, colour printing; fabric printing, batik; silk-screen printing, serigraphy; stereotype, autotype, heliotype, collotype; stamping, impression; die, punch, stamp.

Vb. *engrave*, grave, incise, cut, undercut; etch, stipple, scrape; bite, bite in; sandblast; impress, stamp; lithograph 587 *print*; mezzotint, aquatint; incisit, sculpsit, imprimit.

See: 587.

556 Artist

N. *artist*, craftsman *or* -woman 686 *artisan*; architect 164 *producer*; art-master *or* mistress, designer, draughtsman *or* -woman; fashion artist, dress-designer, couturier; drawer, sketcher, delineator, limner; copyist; caricaturist, cartoonist; illustrator, commercial artist; painter, colourist, luminist; dauber, amateur, Sunday painter; pavement artist, scene-painter, sign-p.; oil-painter, watercolourist, pastellist; illuminator, miniaturist; portrait painter, landscape p., marine p., genre p., still-life p.; Academician, RA, old master, modern m.; naive painter, primitive; Pre-Raphaelite, Impressionist, Fauve, Dadaist, Cubist, Vorticist, Surrealist, action painter, Minimalist 553 *school of painting*; art historian, iconographer; aesthetician.

sculptor, sculptress, carver, statuary, monumental mason, modeller, wax m., moulder, figurist; image-maker, idol-m.; whittler.

engraver, etcher, aquatinter; lapidary, chaser, gem-engraver, enameller, enamellist; typographer, type-cutter 587 *printer*.

See: 164, **553**, 587, **686**.

557 Language

N. *language*, tongue, speech, idiom, parlance, talk; langue, parole; spoken language, living l.; patter, lingo 560 *dialect*; personal language, idiolect; mother tongue, native t.; vernacular, common speech, demotic s., vulgar tongue; colloquial speech, English as she is spoken 579 *speech*; correct speech, idiomatic s., Queen's English; lingua franca, koine, Swahili, creole, pidgin, pidgin English, bèche-de-mer; sign language, semiology 547 *gesture*; diplomatic language, international l., International Scientific Vocabulary, Basic English; pasigraphy; artificial language, Esperanto, Ido, Volapuk; official language, Mandarin, Hindi, Standard English, BBC English; officialese, translatorese 560 *neology*; machine language 86 *data processing*; learned language, dead l., Latin, Greek, Sanskrit; metalanguage; confusion of tongues, polyglot medley, Babel, babble 61 *confusion*.

language type, inflected language, analytic l., agglutinative l., polysynthetic l., monosyllabic l., tonal l.; language group, family of languages, Aryan, Indo-European, Indo-Germanic, Germanic, Celtic, Romance, Balto-Slavic, Indo-Iranian; Turanian, Ural-Altaic, Finno-Ugric; Afro-Asiatic languages, Hamito-Semitic l.; Sino-Tibetan; Dravidian; Bantu; Austronesian.

linguistics, language study, dialectology, philology, comparative p.; comparative grammar, syntax 564 *grammar*; phonetics 577 *pronunciation*; Grimm's law, Verner's l.; lexicology, lexicography 559 *etymology*; morphology; semiology, semantics 514 *meaning*; onomasiology, onomastics 561 *nomenclature*; sociolinguistics; palaeography 125 *palaeology*; linguistic distribution, linguistic geography; isogloss; speech community; genius of a language, feel of a l., sprachgefühl, sense of idiom; polyglottism, bilingualism.

literature, written language, creative writing, belles lettres 589 *reading matter*; letters, polite l., classics, arts, humanities, literae humaniores 654 *civilization*; Muses, literary circles, republic of letters, PEN 589 *author*; literary genre, fiction, nonfiction 590 *narrative, description*; lyricism, poetry 593 *poem*; plays 594 *drama*; criticism 480 *estimate*; literary criticism 520 *interpretation*; literary style, l. convention 519 *metaphor*; literary movement, Classicism, Sturm und Drang, Romanticism, Symbolism, Idealism, Expressionism, Surrealism, Realism, Naturalism; literary history, history of literature; Golden Age, Silver A., Augustan A., Classical A. 110 *era*; compendium of literature 592 *anthology*; digest, chrestomathy, reader 589 *textbook*.

linguist, language student, philologist, etymologist, lexicographer 559 *etymology*; onomasiologist, semanticist; grammarian 564 *grammar*; phonetician 398 *acoustics*; student of literature, man *or* woman of letters, belletrist 492 *scholar*; classical scholar, oriental s.; Hellenist, Latinist, Sanskritist, Sinologist 125 *antiquarian*; polyglot, bilingual.

Adj. *linguistic*, lingual, philological, etymological, grammatical, morphological; diachronic, synchronic; lexicographical, onomasiological, semiological, semantic; analytic; agglutinative; monosyllabic; tonal, inflected; holophrastic; correct, pure; written, literary, standard; spoken, living, idiomatic; vulgar, colloquial, vernacular, slangy 560 *dialectal*; local, enchorial; current, common, demotic; bilingual, diglot; multilingual, polyglot.

literary, written, polished, polite, humanistic, belletristic; classical, romantic, naturalistic, surrealistic, futuristic, decadent; lettered, learned; formal; critical 520 *interpretive*.

See: 61, 86, 110, 125, 398, 480, 492, 514, 519, 520, 547, **559**, **560**, 561, 564, 577, **579**, 589, 590, 592, 593, 594, 654.

558 Letter

N. *letter*, part of the alphabet; sign, symbol, character, written c. 586 *writing*; alphabet, ABC, abecedary, criss-cross row; initial teaching alphabet, i.t.a., International Phonetic Alphabet, IPA; syllabic alphabet, syllabary; phonogram 398 *speech sound*; Chinese character, ideogram, ideograph; pictogram, cuneiform, hieroglyph 586 *lettering*; ogham alphabet, runic a., futhorc; Greek alphabet, Roman a., Cyrillic a., Hebrew a., Arabic a.; Pinyin; Devanagari; runic letter, wen; lettering, black letter, Gothic, italic; ampersand; big letter, capital l., cap, majuscule; small letter, minuscule; block letter, uncial; cursive; printed letter, letterpress, type, bold t. 587 *print-type*.

initials, first letter; monogram, cipher; anagram, acrostic, acronym.

spoken letter, phone, phoneme; consonant, vowel, syllable 577 *voice*; guttural, liquid, spirant, sonant 398 *speech sound*; polyphone; digraph.

spelling, misspelling; orthography, cacography; phonography, lexigraphy; anagrammatism; spelling game, spelling bee; transliteration 520 *translation*.

Adj. *literal*, in letters, lettered; alphabetic, abecedarian; in syllables, syllabic; Cyrillic; runic, oghamic; cuneiform, hieroglyphic 586 *written*; Gothic, italic, roman, uncial; large, majuscule, capital, initial; small, minuscule; lexigraphical, spelt, orthographic; ciphered, monogrammatic; anacrostic, anagrammatic; phonetic, consonantal, vocalic, voiced 577 *vocal*.

Vb. *spell*, spell out, read, syllable, syllabify; alphabetize; transliterate; letter, form letters 586 *write*; initial 547 *sign*; anagrammatize.

Adv. *alphabetically*, by letters; literatim, letter-for-letter; syllabically, in syllables.

See: **398**, 520, 547, **577**, **586**, **587**.

559 Word

N. *word*, Verbum, Logos 965 *the Deity*; expression, locution 563 *phrase*; term, vocable 561 *name*; phoneme, syllable 398 *speech sound*; semanteme 514 *meaning*; synonym, tautonym 13 *identity*; homonym, homograph, homophone, pun, weasel word 518 *equivocalness*; antonym 14 *contrariety*; etymon, root, false r., back-formation; folk etymology; derivation, derivative, paronym, doublet; morphological unit, morpheme, stem, inflection; part of speech 564 *grammar*; diminutive, pejorative, intensive; enclitic, contraction, abbreviation, acronym, portmanteau word 569 *conciseness*; cliché, catchword, vogue word, buzz w., trigger w., nonce w., new w., loan w. 560 *neology*; rhyming word, assonant 18 *similarity*; four-letter word 573 *plainness*; swearword 899 *malediction*; hard word, jawbreaker, mouthful; long word, polysyllable; short

word, monosyllable; many words, verbiage, wordiness, verbosity 570 *pleonasm*.
dictionary, rhyming d., polyglot d.; lexicon, wordbook, wordstock, word list, glossary, vocabulary; gradus, thesaurus, word-hoard 632 *store*; compilation, concordance, index.
etymology, derivation of words, philology 557 *linguistics*; morphology; semasiology 514 *meaning*; phonology, orthoepy 577 *pronunciation*; onomasiology, terminology 561 *nomenclature*; lexicology, lexicography; logophile, philologist, etymologist, lexicologist, lexicographer, compiler.
Adj. *verbal*, literal; titular, nominal; etymological, lexical, vocabular; philological, lexicographical, glossarial; derivative, conjugate, cognate, paronymous; synonymous, autonymous 514 *semantic*; wordy, verbose 570 *pleonastic*.
Adv. *verbally*, lexically; verbatim, word for word.
See: 13, 14, 18, 398, 514, 518, **557**, 560, **561**, 563, 564, 569, 570, 573, 577, 632, 899, 965.

560 Neology

N. *neology*, neologism, neoterism 126 *newness*; coinage, new word, nonce w., vogue w., buzz w., catch phrase, cliché; imported word, borrowing, loan word, loan translation, calque 559 *word*; unfamiliar word, jawbreaker, newfangled expression, slang e.; technical language, jargon, technical term; barbarism, caconym, hybrid, hybrid expression; corruption, monkish Latin, dog L.; novelese, reporterese, journalese, officialese, telegraphese; baby talk; newspeak, doubletalk 518 *equivocalness*; affected language, archaism, Wardour Street English 850 *affectation*; abuse of language, abuse of terms, malapropism 565 *solecism*; wordplay, spoonerism 839 *witticism*; idioglossia, idiolalia 580 *speech defect*.
dialect, idiom, lingo, patois, vernacular 557 *language*; burr, brogue, accent 577 *pronunciation*; cockney, Geordie, Doric, broad Scots, Lallans; broken English, pidgin E., pidgin; lingua franca, hybrid language; Briticism, Strine, franglais; anglicism, Americanism, Hibernicism, Irishism, gallicism, Teutonism; provincialism, localism, vernacularism; iotacism 580 *speech defect*; word-coiner, neologist; dialectology 557 *linguistics*.
slang, vulgarism, colloquialism; jargon, argot, cant, patter; gipsy lingo, Romany; thieves' Latin, pedlar's French, St Giles Greek, rhyming slang, back slang, pig Latin; backchat, Billingsgate 899 *scurrility*; gibberish, gobbledygook 515 *empty talk*.
Adj. *neological*, neoteric, newfangled, newly coined, not in the dictionary; barbaric, barbarous, unidiomatic, hybrid, corrupt, pidgin; loaned, borrowed, imported, foreign, revived, archaic, obsolete; irregular, solecistic 565 *ungrammatical*.
dialectal, vernacular; Doric, cockney, broad; guttural, nasal, burred; provincial, local; homely, colloquial; unliterary, nonstandard, slangy, argotic, canting, cant; jargonistic, journalistic; technical, special.
Vb. *neologize*, coin words, invent vocabulary; talk slang, jargonize, cant; talk cockney, speak with an accent, burr 577 *voice*.
See: 126, 515, 518, **557**, **559**, 565, **577**, 580, 839, 850, 899.

561 Nomenclature

N. *nomenclature*, naming etc. vb.; eponymy; onomastics, onomatology, terminology, orismology; description, designation, appellation, denomination; antonomasia 519 *trope*; addressing, apostrophe, roll-call 583 *allocution*; christening, naming ceremony, baptism 988 *Christian rite*; study of place names, toponymy.
name, nomen, first name, forename, Christian name, praenomen; middle name(s), surname, patronymic, matronymic, cognomen; maiden name, married n.; appellation, moniker; nickname, pet name, diminutive, byname, sobriquet, agnomen; epithet, description; handle, style 870 *title*; heading, caption 547 *indication*; designation, appellative; name and address, signature 547 *label*; term, cant t., special t., technical t., trade name 560 *neology*; name-child, same name, namesake, synonym, eponym, tautonym; pen name, pseudonym 562 *misnomer*; noun, proper n. 564 *part of speech*; list of names; place name, local n.
nomenclator, terminologist; namer, name-giver, eponym, christener, baptizer; roll-

caller, announcer.

Adj. *named*, called etc. vb.; titled, entitled, christened; known as, alias; so-called, soi-disant; hight, yclept; nominal, titular; binominal; named after, eponymous; fitly named, what one may fairly call; namable.

naming, denominative, appellative, terminological, orismological, onomastic.

Vb. *name*, call, give a name, christen, baptize 988 *perform ritual*; give one's name to; give a handle to, call by the name of, surname, nickname, dub, clepe; give one his *or* her title, sir, bemadam; title, entitle, style, term 80 *specify*; distinguish 463 *discriminate*; define, characterize 547 *mark*; call by name, call the roll, call out the names, announce; blacklist 924 *reprobate*.

be named, own *or* bear *or* go by the name of; rejoice in the name of, answer to; sail under the flag of.

Adv. *by name*; namely; terminologically.

See: 80, 463, 519, **547**, 560, 562, 564, 583, 870, 924, 988.

562 Misnomer

N. *misnomer*, misnaming, miscalling; malapropism 565 *solecism*; wrong name, false n., alias, assumed title; nom de guerre, nom de plume, pen name; stage name, pseudonym, allonym; nickname, pet name 561 *name*; pseudonymity.

no name, anonymity; anon, anonym, certain person, so-and-so, what's his name; Richard Roe, Jane Doe, N or M, Sir or Madam; Miss X, Monsieur un Tel, A. N. Other; what d'you call it, thingummy, thingummyjig, thingamabob, whatsit; this or that; and co., etc.; some, any, what-have-you.

Adj. *misnamed*, miscalled, mistitled etc. vb.; self-christened, self-styled, soi-disant, would-be, so-called, quasi, pseudonymous.

anonymous, unknown, faceless, nameless, without a name; incognito, innominate, unnamed, unsigned; a certain, certain, such; some, any, this or that.

Vb. *misname*, mistake the name of, miscall, misterm, mistitle; nickname, dub 561 *name*; misname oneself, assume an alias; conceal one's name, be anonymous; write under an assumed name, usurp the name of, pass oneself off as 541 *dissemble*.

See: 541, 561, 565.

563 Phrase

N. *phrase*, form of words; subject and predicate; clause, sentence, period, paragraph; collocation, frozen c., expression, locution; idiom, mannerism 80 *speciality*; fixed expression, formula, verbalism, façon de parler; set phrase, set terms; euphemism, metaphor 519 *trope*; catch phrase, slogan; hackneyed expression, well-worn phrase, cliché, commonplace 610 *habit*; saying, motto, moral, epigram 496 *maxim*; lapidary phrase, epitaph 364 *obsequies*; inscription, legend, caption 548 *record*; phrases, empty p., words, compliments 515 *empty talk*; terminology 561 *nomenclature*; surface structure, deep s.; phraseology, phrasing, diction, wording, choice of words, choice of expression, turn of e.; well-turned phrase, rounded p. 575 *elegance*; roundabout phrase, periphrasis, circumlocution 570 *diffuseness*; paraphrase 520 *translation*; written phrase, phraseogram 586 *script*; phrasemonger, phrasemaker, epigraphist, epigrammatist, proverbialist 575 *stylist*.

Adj. *phraseological*, sentential, periodic, in phrases, in sentences; idiomatic; well-rounded, well-couched.

Vb. *phrase*, word, articulate, syllable; reword, rephrase 520 *translate*; express, formulate, put in words, clothe in w., find words for, state 532 *affirm*; sloganize, talk in clichés; put words together, turn a sentence, round a period 566 *show style*.

Adv. *in terms*, in good set t., in round t.; in a phrase.

See: 80, 364, 496, 515, 519, 520, 532, 548, 561, 566, 570, 575, 586, 610.

564 Grammar

N. *grammar*, comparative g., philology 557 *linguistics*; grammatical studies, analysis, parsing, construing; paradigm; accidence, inflection, case, declension; conjugation, mood, voice, tense; number, gender, agreement of g.; accentuation, pointing 547 *punctuation*; umlaut, ablaut, attraction, assimilation, dissimilation 559 *etymology*; syntax, word order, parataxis, asyndeton, ellipsis, apposition; bad grammar 565 *solecism*; good grammar, grammaticalness, correct style, Standard English.

part of speech, substantive, noun, common n., proper n., collective n.; pronoun; adjective; verb, reflexive v., transitive v., intransitive v.; adverb, preposition, copula, conjunction, interjection; subject, object; article, particle, affix, suffix, infix, prefix; inflection, case-ending; formative, morpheme, semanteme; diminutive, intensive, augmentative.

Adj. *grammatical*, correct; syntactic, inflectional; heteroclite, irregular, anomalous; masculine, feminine, neuter; singular, dual, plural; substantival, adjectival, attributive, predicative; verbal, adverbial; participial; prepositional; denominative, deverbative; conjunctive, copulative; comparative, superlative.

Vb. *parse*, analyse, inflect, conjugate, decline; punctuate; construe 520 *interpret*.

See: 520, 547, **557**, 559, 565.

565 Solecism

N. *solecism*, bad grammar, incorrectness, misusage; faulty syntax, anacoluthon; antiphrasis 574 *ornament*; catachresis, cacology; irregularity 560 *dialect*; impropriety, barbarism 560 *neology*; malapropism, bull, slip, Freudian s., slip of the pen, lapsus calami, slip of the tongue, lapsus linguae 495 *mistake*; mispronunciation, dropping one's aitches 580 *speech defect*; misspelling, cacography; verbicide.

Adj. *ungrammatical*, solecistic; irregular, abnormal; faulty, improper, incongruous; misapplied, catachrestic.

Vb. *be ungrammatical*, violate grammar, commit a solecism; break Priscian's head, murder the Queen's English; mispronounce 580 *stammer*; drop one's aitches; misspell 495 *blunder*.

See: **495**, 560, 574, 580.

566 Style

N. *style*, fashion, mode, tone, manner, vein, strain, idiom; one's own style, personal s., idiosyncrasy, mannerism 80 *speciality*; mode of expression, diction, parlance, phrasing, phraseology 563 *phrase*; choice of words, vocabulary, choice v.; literary style, command of language *or* idiom, raciness, power 571 *vigour*; feeling for words, sprachgefühl, sense of language; literary charm, grace 575 *elegance*; word magic, word-spinning 579 *oratory*; weak style 572 *feebleness*; severe style, vernacular s. 573 *plainness*; elaborate style 574 *ornament*; clumsy style 576 *inelegance*.

Adj. *stylistic*, mannered, literary; elegant, ornate, rhetorical; expressive, eloquent, fluent; racy, idiomatic; plain, perspicuous, forceful.

Vb. *show style*, care for words, spin w.; style, express, measure one's words 563 *phrase*.

See: 80, **563**, 571, 572, 573, 574, 575, 576, 579.

567 Perspicuity

N. *perspicuity*, perspicuousness, clearness, clarity, lucidity, limpidity 422 *transparency*; limpid style 516 *intelligibility*; directness 573 *plainness*; definition, definiteness, exactness 494 *accuracy*.

Adj. *perspicuous*, lucid, limpid 422 *transparent*; clear, unambiguous 516 *intelligible*; explicit, clear-cut 80 *definite*; exact 494 *accurate*; uninvolved, direct 573 *plain*.

See: 80, 422, 494, **516**, 573.

568 Imperspicuity

N. *imperspicuity*, unclarity, obscurity 517 *unintelligibility*; cloudiness, fogginess 423 *opacity*; abstraction, abstruseness; complexity, involved style 574 *ornament*; hard words, Johnsonese 700 *difficulty*; imprecision, impreciseness, vagueness 474 *uncertainty*; inaccuracy 495 *inexactness*; ambiguity 518 *equivocalness*; mysteriousness, oracular style 530 *enigma*; profundity 211 *depth*; overcompression, ellipsis 569 *conciseness*; cloud of words, verbiage 570 *diffuseness*.

Adj. *unclear*, imperspicuous, not transparent, muddied, cloudy 423 *opaque*; cloudy, obscure 418 *dark*; oracular, mysterious, enigmatic 517 *unintelligible*; abstruse, profound 211 *deep*; allusive, indirect 523 *latent*; vague, imprecise, indefinite 474 *uncertain*; ambiguous 518 *equivocal*; muddled, confused, tortuous, involved 61 *complex*; harsh, crabbed, stiff 576 *inelegant*; hard, full of long words, Johnsonian 700 *difficult*.

See: 61, 211, 418, 423, 474, 495, **517**, 518, 523, 530, 569, 570, 574, 576, 700.

569 Conciseness

N. *conciseness*, concision, succinctness, brevity, soul of wit; pithiness, pithy saying 496 *maxim*; aphorism, epigram, clerihew 839 *witticism*; economy of words, no words wasted, few words, terseness, laconism, laconicism; compression, telegraphese; overconciseness, brachylogy; ellipsis, syncope, abbreviation, contraction 204 *shortening*; compendiousness, epitome, précis, outline, brief sketch 592 *compendium*; monostich, haiku; compactness, portmanteau word; clipped speech, monosyllabism 582 *taciturnity*; nutshell, the long and the short of it 204 *shortness*.

Adj. *concise*, brief, not long in telling, short and sweet 204 *short*; laconic, monosyllabic, sparing of words 582 *taciturn*; irreducible, succinct; crisp, brisk, to the point; trenchant, incisive; terse, curt, brusque 885 *ungracious*; compendious, condensed, tight-knit, compact; pithy, pregnant, sententious, neat, exact, pointed, aphoristic, epigrammatic; Tacitean; elliptic, telegraphic, contracted, compressed; summary, cut short, abbreviated.

Vb. *be concise*, - brief etc. adj.; need few words, not beat about the bush, come straight to the point, cut the cackle, cut a long story short; telescope, compress, condense, contract, abridge, abbreviate 204 *shorten*; outline, sketch; summarize, sum up, resume 592 *abstract*; allow no words, be short with, cut short, cut off; be sparing with words, waste no w., clip one's w. 582 *be taciturn*; express pithily, epigrammatize 839 *be witty*.

Adv. *concisely*, pithily, summarily, briefly; without wasting words, in brief, in short, in fine, in a word, in a nutshell; to cut a long story short; to sum up.

See: 204, 496, 582, **592**, 839, 885.

570 Diffuseness

N. *diffuseness*, verboseness etc. adj.; profuseness, copiousness, amplitude; amplification, dilation 197 *expansion*; expatiation, circumstantiality, minuteness, blow-by-blow account; fertility, output, productivity 171 *productiveness*; inspiration, vein, flow, outpouring; abundance, overflowing words, exuberance, redundancy 637 *redundance*; richness, rich vocabulary, wealth of terms, verbosity, wordiness, verbiage, flatulence; fluency, nonstop talking, verbal diarrhoea 581 *loquacity*; long-windedness, prolixity, epic length; repetitiveness, reiteration 106 *repetition*; twice-told tale 838 *tedium*; gush, rigmarole, waffle 515 *empty talk*; effusion, tirade, harangue, sermon, speeches 579 *oration*; descant, disquisition 591 *dissertation*.

pleonasm, superfluity, redundancy 637 *redundance*; battology, tautology; circumlocution, roundabout phrases, periphrasis; ambages, beating about the bush 518 *equivocalness*; padding, expletive, filler 40 *extra*; episode, excursus, digression 10 *irrelevance*.

Adj. *diffuse*, verbose, nonstop 581 *loquacious*; profuse, copious, ample, rich; fertile, abundant, voluminous 171 *prolific*; inspired, flowing, fluent; exuberant, overflowing 637 *redundant*; expatiating, circumstantial, detailed, minute; gushing, effusive; flatulent, windy, frothy; turgid, bombastic 574 *rhetorical*; polysyllabic, sesquipedalian, magniloquent 574 *ornate*.

prolix, of many words, long-winded, wordy, prosy, prosing; spun out, made to last, long-drawn-out 113 *protracted*; boring 838 *tedious*; lengthy, epic, never-ending 203 *long*; spreading, diffusive, discursive, excursive, digressing, episodic; rambling, maundering 282 *deviating*; loose-knit, incoherent 61 *orderless*; desultory, pointless 10 *irrelevant*; indirect, circumlocutory, periphrastic, ambagious, roundabout.

pleonastic, redundant, excessive 637 *superfluous*; repetitious, repetitional, repetitive 106 *repeated*; tautologous, tautological; padded, padded out.

Vb. *be diffuse*, - prolix etc. adj.; dilate, expatiate, amplify, particularize, detail, expand, enlarge upon; descant, discourse at length; repeat, tautologize 106 *repeat oneself*; pad, pad out, draw o., spin o., protract 203 *lengthen*; gush, pour out 350 *flow*; let oneself go, rant, harangue, perorate 579 *orate*; use long words, have swallowed the dictionary; launch out on, spin a long yarn 838 *be tedious*; blether on, rabbit on 581 *be loquacious*; wander, waffle, digress 282 *deviate*; ramble, maunder, drivel, yarn, never end; beat about the bush, not come to the point 518 *be equivocal*.

Adv. *diffusely*, in extenso, at great length, on and on, ad nauseam.

See: 10, 40, 61, 106, 113, 171, 197, 203, 282, 350, 515, 518, **574**, 579, **581**, 591, 637, 838.

571 Vigour

N. *vigour* 174 *vigorousness*; power, strength, vitality, drive, force, forcefulness, oomph 160 *energy*; incisiveness, trenchancy, decision; vim, punch, pep, guts; sparkle, verve, élan, panache, vivacity, liveliness, vividness, raciness; spirit, fire, ardour, glow, warmth, fervour, vehemence, enthusiasm, passion 818 *feeling*; bite, piquancy, poignancy, sharpness, mordancy 388 *pungency*; strong language, stress, underlining, emphasis 532 *affirmation*; iteration, reiteration 106 *repetition*; seriousness, solemnity, gravity, weight; impressiveness, loftiness, elevation, sublimity, grandeur, grandiloquence, declamation 574 *magniloquence*; rhetoric 579 *eloquence*.

Adj. *forceful*, powerful 162 *strong*; energetic, peppy, punchy 174 *vigorous*; racy, idiomatic; bold, dashing, spirited, sparkling, vivacious 819 *lively*; warm, glowing, fiery, ardent, enthusiastic, impassioned 818 *fervent*; vehement, emphatic, insistent, reiterative, positive 532 *affirmative*; slashing, cutting, incisive, trenchant 256 *sharp*; pointed, pungent, mordant, salty 839 *witty*; grave, sententious, strongly-worded 834 *serious*; heavy, meaty, solid; weighty, forcible, cogent 740 *compelling*; vivid, graphic, effective 551 *representing*; flowing, inspired 579 *eloquent*; high-toned, lofty, grand, sublime 821 *impressive*.

Adv. *forcefully*, vigorously, energetically, vehemently, with conviction; in glowing terms.

See: 106, 160, 162, **174**, 256, 388, 532, 551, 574, 579, 740, 818, 819, 821, 834, 839.

572 Feebleness

N. *feebleness* 163 *weakness*; weak style, enervated s.; prosiness, frigidity, ineffectiveness, flatness, staleness, vapidity 387 *insipidity*; jejuneness, poverty, thinness; enervation, flaccidity, lack of force, lack of sparkle, lack of conviction; lack of style, baldness 573 *plainness*; anticlimax.

Adj. *feeble*, weak, thin, flat, vapid, insipid 387 *tasteless*; wishy-washy, watery; sloppy, sentimental, schmaltzy, novelettish; meagre, jejune, exhausted; wan, colourless, bald 573 *plain*; languid, flaccid, nerveless, emasculated, tame, conventional; undramatic, unspirited, uninspired, unelevated, unimpassioned, unemphatic; ineffective, cold, frigid, prosaic, uninspiring, unexciting; monotonous, prosy, pedestrian, dull, dry, boring 838 *tedious*; cliché-ridden, hackneyed, platitudinous, stale, pretentious, flatulent, overambitious; forced, overemphatic, forcible-feeble; inane, empty; juvenile, childish; careless, slovenly, slipshod, limping; lame, unconvincing 477 *poorly reasoned*; limp, loose, lax, inexact, disconnected, disjointed, rambling, vapouring 570 *prolix*; poor, trashy 847 *vulgar*.

See: **163**, 387, 477, 570, 573, 838, 847.

573 Plainness

N. *plainness*, naturalness, simplicity, unadorned s. 699 *artlessness*; austerity, severity, baldness, spareness, bareness, starkness; matter-of-factness, plain prose 593 *prose*; plain words, plain English 516 *intelligibility*; home truths 540 *veracity*; homespun, household words; rustic flavour, vernacular, kaleyard school; common speech, vulgar parlance; idiom, natural i.; unaffectedness 874 *modesty*; bluntness, frankness, coarseness, four-letter word, Anglo-Saxon monosyllable.

Adj. *plain*, simple 699 *artless*; austere, severe, disciplined; bald, spare, stark, bare, unfussy; neat 648 *clean*; pure, unadulterated 44 *unmixed*; unadorned, uncoloured, unpainted, unvarnished, unembellished 540 *veracious*; unemphatic, undramatic, unsensational, played down; unassuming, unpretentious 874 *modest*; uninflated, chaste, restrained; unaffected, honest, natural, straightforward; homely, homey, homespun, vernacular; prosaic, sober 834 *serious*; dry, stodgy 838 *tedious*; humdrum, workaday, everyday, commonplace 610 *usual*; unimaginative, uninspired, unpoetical 593 *prosaic*.

Vb. *speak plainly*, call a spade a spade, use plain English 516 *be intelligible*; discipline one's style, moderate one's vocabulary; say outright, tell it like it is, spell it out, tell one straight *or* to his *or* her face; not mince one's words, not beat about the bush, come to the point, come down to brass tacks, talk turkey.

Adv. *plainly*, simply 516 *intelligibly*; prosaically, in prose; in the vernacular, in plain words, in common parlance; directly, point-blank; not to put too fine a point upon it, in words of one syllable.

See: 44, **516**, 540, 593, 610, 648, 699, 834,

838, 874.

574 Ornament

N. *ornament*, embellishment, colour, decoration, embroidery, frills 844 *ornamentation*; floridness, floweriness, flowers of speech, arabesques 563 *phrase*; gongorism, euphuism; preciosity, preciousness, euphemism; rhetoric, flourish of r., purple patch *or* passage, dithyramb; figurativeness, figure of speech 519 *trope*; alliteration, assonance; paralipsis, aposiopesis; antiphrasis, catachresis; palillogy, anaphora, epistrophe; anadiplosis; inversion, anastrophe, hyperbaton, chiasmus; zeugma; metaphor, simile, antithesis.

magniloquence, high tone 579 *eloquence*; grandiloquence, declamation, orotundity 571 *vigour*; overstatement, extravagance, hyperbole 546 *exaggeration*; turgidity, turgescence, flatulence, inflation; pretentiousness, affectation, pomposity 875 *ostentation*; talking big 877 *boasting*; highfalutin, high-sounding words, bombast, rant, fustian, rodomontade 515 *empty talk*; Johnsonese, long words, sesquipedalian w. 570 *diffuseness*.

phrasemonger, fine writer, word-spinner, euphuist 575 *stylist*; rhetorician, orator 579 *speaker*.

Adj. *ornate*, aureate, beautified 844 *ornamented*; rich, luxuriant, florid, flowery; precious, euphuistic, euphemistic; pretentious 850 *affected*; meretricious, flashy, flamboyant, frothy 875 *showy*; brassy, sonorous, clanging 400 *loud*; tropical, alliterative 519 *figurative*; overloaded, stiff, stilted; pedantic, long-worded, sesquipedalian, Johnsonian.

rhetorical, declamatory, oratorical 579 *eloquent*; resonant, sonorous 400 *loud*; ranting, mouthy, orotund; high-pitched, high-flown, high-flying, highfalutin; grandiose, stately; bombastic, pompous, fustian, Ossianic; grandiloquent, magniloquent; inflated, tumid, turgid, swollen, dithyrambic; antithetical, alliterative, metaphorical 519 *figurative*.

Vb. *ornament*, beautify, grace, adorn, enrich 844 *decorate*; charge, overlay, overload; elaborate, load with ornament; euphuize, euphemize; smell of the lamp, overelaborate.

See: 400, 515, **519**, 546, 563, 570, 571, 575, 579, **844**, 850, 875, 877.

575 Elegance

N. *elegance*, style, perfect s.; grace, gracefulness 841 *beauty*; refinement, taste 846 *good taste*; propriety, restraint, distinction, dignity; clarity 567 *perspicuity*; purity, simplicity; naturalness 573 *plainness*; classicism, Atticism; harmony, euphony, concinnity, balance, proportion 245 *symmetry*; rhythm, ease, flow, smoothness, fluency, readiness, felicity, the right word in the right place; neatness, polish, finish; well-turned period, rounded p.; elaboration, artificiality 574 *ornament*.

stylist, stylish writer 574 *phrasemonger*; classical author, classic, purist.

Adj. *elegant*, majestic, stately 841 *beautiful*; graced, graceful; stylish, polite, refined 846 *tasteful*; uncommon, distinguished, dignified; chaste 950 *pure*; good, correct, idiomatic; sensitive, expressive, clear 567 *perspicuous*; simple, natural, unaffected 573 *plain*; unlaboured, ready, easy, smooth, flowing, fluent, tripping, rhythmic, mellifluous, euphonious; harmonious, balanced, well-proportioned 245 *symmetrical*; concinnous, neat, felicitous, happy, right, neatly put, well-turned 694 *well-made*; artistic, wrought, elaborate, artificial; polished, finished, soigné, manicured; restrained, controlled; flawless 646 *perfect*; classic, classical, Attic, Ciceronian, Augustan.

Vb. *be elegant*, show taste 846 *have taste*; have a good style, write well, have a light touch; elaborate, polish, refine 646 *perfect*; grace one's style, turn a period, point an antithesis 566 *show style*.

See: 245, 566, 567, 573, 574, 646, 694, 841, 846, 950.

576 Inelegance

N. *inelegance*, inconcinnity; clumsiness, roughness, uncouthness 699 *artlessness*; coarseness, lack of finish, lack of polish 647 *imperfection*; harshness, cacophony 411 *discord*; lack of flow, stiffness, stiltedness 326 *hardness*; unwieldiness, cumbrousness, sesquipedality; impropriety, barbarism; incorrectness, bad grammar 565 *solecism*; mispronunciation 580 *speech defect*; vulgarism, vulgarity 847 *bad taste*; mannerism, unnaturalness, artificiality 850 *affectation*; exhibitionism 875 *ostentation*; meretriciousness 542 *sham*; lack of restraint, excess 637 *superfluity*;

turgidity, pomposity 574 *magniloquence*.

Adj. *inelegant*, ungraceful, graceless 842 *ugly*; faulty, incorrect; crabbed, tortuous 568 *unclear*; long-winded 570 *diffuse*; unfinished, unpolished, unrefined, unclassical 647 *imperfect*; bald 573 *plain*; coarse, crude, rude, doggerel, uncouth, barbarous 699 *artless*; impolite, tasteless 847 *vulgar*; unchaste, impure, meretricious; unrestrained, immoderate, excessive; turgid, pompous 574 *rhetorical*; forced, laboured, artificial, unnatural, mannered 850 *affected*; ludicrous, grotesque, bathetic 849 *ridiculous*; offensive, repulsive, jarring, grating 861 *disliked*; heavy, ponderous, insensitive; rough, harsh, uneasy, abrupt; halting, cramped, unready, unfluent; clumsy, awkward, gauche; wooden, stiff, stilted 875 *formal*.

See: 326, 411, 542, 565, 568, 570, 573, 574, 580, 637, 647, 699, 842, 847, 849, 850, 861, 875.

577 Voice

N. *voice*, vocal sound 398 *sound*; speaking voice 579 *speech*; singing voice, musical v., fine v. 412 *vocal music*; powerful voice, vociferation, lung power 400 *loudness*; tongue, vocal organs, vocal cords; lungs, bellows; larynx, voice box; syrinx; vocalization, phoneme, vowel, broad v., pure v., diphthong, triphthong, open vowel, closed v., semivowel, voiced consonant, syllable 398 *speech sound*; articulation, clear a., distinctness; utterance, enunciation, delivery, attack; articulate sound 408 *cry*; exclamation, ejaculation, gasp; mutter, whisper, stage w. 401 *faintness*; tone of voice, accents, timbre, pitch, tone, intonation, modulation.

pronunciation, articulation, elocution, enunciation, inflection, accentuation, stress, emphasis; ictus, arsis, thesis; accent, tonic a.; pure accent, correct a.; native accent, broad a., foreign a.; burr, brogue, drawl, twang 560 *dialect*; trill; aspiration, rough breathing, glottal stop; nasality 407 *stridor*; lisping, stammer 580 *speech defect*; mispronunciation 565 *solecism*.

Adj. *vocal*, voiced, oral, aloud, out loud; vocalic, vowel-like, sonant 398 *sounding*; phonetic, enunciative; articulate, distinct, clear; well-spoken, well-sung, in good voice 410 *melodious*; pronounced, uttered, spoken, dictated, read out, read aloud; aspirated 407 *hoarse*; accented, tonal, accentual, accentuated; guttural 407 *hoarse*; shrill 407 *strident*; wheezy 406 *sibilant*.

Vb. *voice*, pronounce, syllable, verbalize, put into words 579 *speak*; mouth, give tongue, give voice, express, utter, enunciate, articulate; vocalize; inflect, modulate; breathe, aspirate, sound one's aitches; trill, roll, burr; accent, stress 532 *emphasize*; raise the voice, lower the v., whisper, stage-w.; exclaim, ejaculate, rap out 408 *cry*; drone, intone, chant, warble, carol, hum 413 *sing*; bellow, shout, vociferate, use one's voice 400 *be loud*; mispronounce, lisp, drawl, swallow one's consonants, speak thickly 580 *stammer*.

See: 398, 400, 401, 406, **407**, 408, 410, 412, 413, 532, 560, 565, **579**, 580.

578 Voicelessness

N. *voicelessness*, aphonia, no voice, loss of v.; difficulty in speaking, dysphonia, inarticulation; thick speech, hoarseness, huskiness, raucousness; muteness 399 *silence*; dumbness, mutism, deaf-m.; harsh voice, unmusical v., tuneless v. 407 *stridor*; childish treble, falsetto; changing voice, breaking v., cracked v.; sob, sobbing; undertone, low voice, small v., muffled tones, whisper, bated breath 401 *faintness*; surd, unvoiced consonant; voiceless speech, sign language, deaf and dumb language 547 *gesture*; mute, deaf-mute.

Adj. *voiceless*, aphonic, dysphonic; unvoiced, surd; breathed, whispered, muffled, low-voiced, inaudible 401 *muted*; mute, dumb, deaf and dumb; incapable of utterance, speechless, tongueless, wordless, at a loss for words; inarticulate, unvocal, tongue-tied; silent, not speaking, mum, mumchance 582 *taciturn*; silenced, gagged; dry, hollow, sepulchral, breaking, cracked, croaking, hoarse as a raven 407 *hoarse*; breathless, out of breath.

Vb. *be mute*, keep mum 582 *be taciturn*; be silent, hold one's tongue 525 *keep secret*; bridle one's tongue, check oneself, dry up, shut up, ring off, hang up; lose one's voice, be struck dumb, lose one's tongue, lose the power of speech; talk with one's hands 547 *gesticulate*; have difficulty in speaking 580 *stammer*.

make mute, strike dumb, dumbfound, take one's breath away, rob one of words; stick in one's throat, choke on; muffle, hush, deaden 401 *mute*; shout down, drown one's voice; muzzle, gag, stifle 165 *suppress*; stop one's mouth, cut out one's tongue; shut one up, cut one short, hang up on; still, hush, put to silence, put to sleep 399 *silence*.

speak low, speak softly, whisper, stage-w. 401 *sound faint*; whisper in one's ear 524 *hint*; lower one's voice, drop one's v.

Adv. *voicelessly*, in hushed tones, in a whisper, with bated breath; in an undertone, sotto voce, under one's breath, in an aside.

See: 165, 399, 401, 407, 524, 525, 547, 580, **582**.

579 Speech

N. *speech*, faculty of s., organ of s., tongue, lips 577 *voice*; parlance 557 *language*; oral communication, word of mouth 524 *report*; spoken word, accents, tones 559 *word*; verbal intercourse, discourse, colloquy, conversation, talk, palaver, prattle, chinwag 584 *interlocution*; address, apostrophe 583 *allocution*; ready speech, fluency, talkativeness, volubility 581 *loquacity*; prolixity, effusion 570 *diffuseness*; cultivated speech, elocution, voice production; mode of speech, articulation, utterance, delivery, enunciation 577 *pronunciation*; ventriloquism; speech without words, sign language, eye l. 547 *gesture*; thing said, speech, dictum, utterance, remark, observation, comment, interjection 532 *affirmation*; fine words 515 *empty talk*; spiel, patter 542 *trickery*.

oration, speech, effusion; one's say, one's piece, a word in edgeways; public speech, formal s., prepared s., discourse, disquisition, address, talk; salutatory, welcoming address 876 *celebration*; panegyric, eulogy; valedictory, farewell address, funeral oration 364 *obsequies*; after-dinner speech, toast, vote of thanks; broadcast, commentary 534 *lecture*; recitation, recital, reading; set speech, declamation, display of oratory (**see** *eloquence*); pulpit eloquence, sermon, preachment, homily, exhortation; platform eloquence, harangue, tub-thumping, rodomontade, earful, mouthful; hostile eloquence, tirade, diatribe, philippic, invective; monologue 585 *soliloquy*; written speech, dictation, paper, screed 591 *dissertation*; proem, preamble, prologue, narration, digression, peroration.

oratory, art of speaking, rhetoric, public speaking, stump oratory, tub-thumping; speech-making, speechifying, speechification; declamation, elocution, vapouring, ranting, rant; vituperation, invective; soapbox 539 *rostrum*; Hyde Park Corner.

eloquence, eloquent tongue, gift of the gab, fluency, articulacy; glossolalia 821 *excitation*; command of words, way with w., word-spinning 566 *style*; power of speech, power 571 *vigour*; grandiloquence, orotundity, sublimity 574 *magniloquence*; elocution, good delivery, impressive diction, rolling periods, burst of eloquence, torrent of words, peroration, purple passage.

speaker, sayer, utterer; talker, spieler, prattler, gossiper 581 *chatterer*; conversationalist, deipnosophist 584 *interlocutor*; speechifier, speech-maker, speech-writer, rhetorician, elocutionist; orator, Public O., oratress, oratrix, public speaker, after-dinner s., toastmaster; improviser, ad-libber; declaimer, ranter, soap-box orator, tub-thumper, haranguer, demagogue 738 *agitator*; word-spinner, spellbinder; lecturer, dissertator; pulpiteer, Boanerges 537 *preacher*; presenter, announcer 531 *broadcaster*; prologue, narrator, chorus 594 *actor*; mouthpiece, spokesman *or* -woman, spokesperson 754 *delegate*; advocate, pleader, mediator 231 *intermediary*; patter merchant, salesperson 793 *seller*; Demosthenes, Cicero; monologist, soliloquizer 585 *soliloquist*.

Adj. *speaking*, talking; able to speak, with a tongue in one's head; anglophone, francophone, bilingual, polyglot; articulate, fluent, outspoken, free-speaking, talkative 581 *loquacious*; oral 577 *vocal*; well-spoken, soft-s., loud-s.; audible, spoken, verbal; plummy, fruity 404 *resonant*; elocutionary.

eloquent, spellbinding, silver-tongued, trumpet-t.; smooth-t. 925 *flattering*; elocutionary, oratorical 574 *rhetorical*; grandiloquent, declamatory 571 *forceful*; tub-thumping, fire-and-brimstone, ranting, word-spinning; rousing 821 *exciting*.

Vb. *speak*, mention, say; utter, articulate 577 *voice*; pronounce, declare 532 *affirm*; let out, blurt out, come clean 526 *divulge*; whisper, breathe 524 *hint*; confabulate, talk, put in a word 584 *converse*; emit, give utterance, deliver oneself of; break silence, open one's mouth *or* lips, find one's tongue; pipe up, speak up, raise one's voice; wag one's tongue, give t., rattle on, gossip, prattle, chatter 581 *be loquacious*; patter, jabber, gabble; sound off, speak one's mind, tell a thing or two, have one's say, talk one's fill, expatiate 570 *be diffuse*; trot out, reel off, recite; read, read aloud, read out, dictate; speak a language, speak with tongues; have a tongue in one's head, speak for oneself; talk with one's hands 547 *gesticulate*.

orate, make speeches, speechify; declaim, deliver a speech; hold forth, spout, be on one's legs; take the floor *or* the stand, rise to speak; preach, preachify, sermonize, harangue; lecture, address 534 *teach*; invoke, apostrophize 583 *speak to*; perorate, mouth, rant, rail, sound off, tubthump; speak like an angel, spellbind, be eloquent, have the gift of the gab; talk to oneself, monologize 585 *soliloquize*; speak off the top of one's head, ad-lib 609 *improvise*.

See: 231, 364, 404, 515, 524, 526, 531, **532**, 534, 537, 539, 542, 547, 557, 559, 566, 570, 571, **574**, **577**, **581**, **583**, **584**, 585, 591, 594, 609, 738, 754, 793, 821, 876, 925.

580 Speech defect

N. *speech defect*, aphasia, loss of speech, aphonia 578 *voicelessness*; paraphasia, paralalia; idioglossia, idiolalia; stammering, stammer, stutter, lallation, lisp; sigmatism 406 *sibilation*; dysphonia, speech impediment, hesitation, drawl, slur; indistinctness, inarticulateness, thick speech, cleft palate; burr, brogue 560 *dialect*; accent, twang, nasal t. 577 *pronunciation*; affectation, plum in one's mouth, Oxford accent, haw-haw 246 *distortion*; speech therapy.

Adj. *stammering*, stuttering etc. vb.; nasal, adenoidal; indistinct, thick, inarticulate; tongue-tied, aphasic; breathless 578 *voiceless*.

Vb. *stammer*, stutter, trip over one's tongue; drawl, hesitate, falter, quaver, hem and ha, hum and haw; mumble, mutter; lisp; lallate; snuffle, snort, sputter, splutter, sibilate; nasalize, speak through the nose, drone; clip one's words, swallow one's w., gabble, slur; blubber, sob; mispronounce 565 *be ungrammatical*.

See: 246, 406, 560, 565, 577, **578**.

581 Loquacity

N. *loquacity*, loquaciousness, garrulity, talkativeness, communicativeness; volubility, runaway tongue, flow of words, fluency 570 *diffuseness*; verbosity, wordiness, prolixity; running on, spate of words, logorrhoea, verbal diarrhoea, inexhaustible vocabulary; patter, spiel, gab, gift of the g. 579 *eloquence*; garrulous old age, anecdotage 505 *remembrance*.

chatter, chattering, gossiping, gabble, jabber, palaver, jaw-jaw, talkee-talkee, yakkety-yak; clack, quack, cackle, babble, prattle; small talk, gossip, idle g., tittletattle; waffle, blether, gush, guff, gas, hot air 515 *empty talk*.

chatterer, ı onstop talker, rapid speaker; chinwag, rattle, chatterbox; gossip, blabber, tattler 529 *news reporter*; magpie, parrot, jay; talker, gabber, driveller, haverer, ranter, quacker, bletherskite; preacher, sermonizer; proser, windbag, gas-bag, gasser; conversationalist 584 *interlocutor*.

Adj. *loquacious*, talkative, garrulous, tongue-wagging, gossiping, tattling; communicative, chatty, gossipy, newsy 524 *informative*; gabbing, babbling, gabbling, gabby, gassy, windy, prosing, verbose, long-winded 570 *prolix*; nonstop, voluble, running on, fluent, glib, ready, effusive, gushing; conversational 584 *conversing*.

Vb. *be loquacious*, - talkative etc. adj.; have a long tongue, chatter, rattle, run on, reel off, talk nineteen to the dozen; gossip, tattle 584 *converse*; clack, quack, gabble, jabber 515 *mean nothing*; talk, jaw, yak, gab, prate, prose, gas, waffle, haver, blether, twitter, ramble on, rabbit on; drone, maunder, drivel; launch out, start talking, shoot; be glib, oil one's tongue; have one's say, talk at length; expatiate, effuse, gush, spout 570 *be diffuse*; outtalk, talk down; talk out, filibuster 113 *spin out*; talk oneself hoarse, talk one's head off, talk the hind leg off a donkey; talk shop, bore 838 *be tedious*; engage in conversation, buttonhole; monopolize the conversation, not let one get a word in edgeways, never stop talking.

Adv. *loquaciously*, glibly, fluently etc. adj.

Int. patati patata! rhubarb rhubarb! blah blah! yak yak!

See: 113, 505, **515**, 524, 529, **570**, 579, 584, 838.

582 Taciturnity

N. *taciturnity*, silent habit 399 *silence*; incommunicativeness, reserve, reticence, guarded utterance 525 *secrecy*; few words, shortness, brusqueness, curtness, gruffness 885 *rudeness*; muteness 578 *voicelessness*; economy of words, laconism 569 *conciseness*; no speaker, no orator; no talker, not a gossip, person of few words; clam, oyster, statue; Trappist.

Adj. *taciturn*, mute, mum 399 *silent*; sparing of words, saying little, monosyllabic, short, curt, laconic, brusque, gruff 569 *concise*; not talking, vowed to silence; incommunicative; withdrawn, reserved, guarded, with sealed lips 525 *reticent*; close, close-mouthed, tight-lipped; not to be drawn, discreet 858 *cautious*; inarticulate, tongue-tied 578 *voiceless*; not hearing 416 *deaf*.

Vb. *be taciturn*, - laconic etc. adj.; spare one's words, use few w. 569 *be concise*; not talk, say nothing, have little to say; observe silence, make no answer; not be drawn, refuse comment, neither confirm nor deny; keep one's counsel 525 *keep secret*; hold one's peace, hold one's tongue, put a bridle on one's t., keep one's mouth *or* one's trap shut; fall silent, relapse into s., pipe down, dry up, run out of words 145 *cease*; be speechless, lose one's tongue 578 *be mute*; waste no words on, save one's breath to cool one's porridge; not mention, leave out, pass over, omit 458 *disregard*.

Int. hush! shut up! mum's the word! no comment! verb. sap! a word to the wise!

See: 145, **399**, 416, 458, 525, 569, 578, 858, 885.

583 Allocution

N. *allocution*, apostrophe; address, lecture, talk, speech, pep talk 579 *oration*; greeting, salutation, hail; invocation, appeal, interjection, interpellation; buttonholing, word in the ear, aside; hearers, audience 415 *listener*.

Adj. *vocative*, salutatory, invocatory.

Vb. *speak to*, speak at; address, talk to, lecture to; turn to, direct one's words at, apostrophize; appeal to, pray to, invoke; sir, bemadam; approach, accost; hail, call to, salute, say good morning 884 *greet*; pass the time of day, parley with 584 *converse*; take aside, buttonhole.

See: 415, 579, 584, 884.

584 Interlocution

N. *interlocution*, parley, colloquy, converse, conversation, causerie, talk; dialogue, question and answer; exchange, repartee, banter, badinage; slanging match 709 *quarrel*; confabulation, confab, verbal intercourse, social i. 882 *sociality*; commerce, communion, intercommunion, communication, intercommunication 524 *information*; duologue, tête-à-tête.

chat, causerie, chinwag, natter; chitchat, talk, small t., table t., idle t., prattle, gossip 529 *rumour*; tattle, tittle-tattle, tongue-wagging 581 *chatter*; fireside chat, cosy chat, tête-à-tête, heart-to-heart.

conference, colloquy, conversations, talks, pourparler, parley, pow-wow, indaba, palaver; discussion, debate, forum, symposium, seminar, teach-in; talkfest, gabfest; controversy, polemics, logomachy 475 *argument*; exchange of views, talks across the table, high-level talks, summit meeting, summit; negotiations, bargaining, treaty-making 765 *treaty*; conclave, convention, meeting, gathering 74 *assembly*; working lunch; reception, conversazione, party 882 *social gathering*; audience, interview, audition 415 *listening*; consultation, putting heads together, huddle, council, war c., round-table conference 691 *advice*.

interlocutor, collocutor, colloquist, dialogist, symposiast; examiner, interviewer, cross-examiner, interpellator 459 *enquirer*; answerer 460 *respondent*; partner, confabulator, conversationalist, talker 581 *chatterer*; gossip, tattler, informant 529 *news reporter*.

Adj. *conversing*, interlocutory, confabulatory; dialogistic, dialogic; conversable, conversational; chatty, gossipy 581 *loquacious*; newsy, communicative 524 *informative*; conferring, in conference, conferential; consultatory, consultative, advisory 691 *advising*.

Vb. *converse*, colloquize, parley, talk together (**see** *confer*); confabulate, pass the time of day; lead one on, draw one out; buttonhole, engage in conversation, carry on a c., join in a c., put in a word, bandy words, exchange w., question, answer; cut in 231 *interfere*; shine in conversation 839 *be witty*; chat, have a chat *or* a natter *or* a good talk; have a cosy chat, be drawn out

579 *speak*; buzz, natter, chinwag, chew the fat, gossip, tattle 581 *be loquacious*; commune with, talk privately, get confidential with, be closeted with; whisper together, talk tête-à-tête, go into a huddle.

confer, talk it over, take counsel, sit in council *or* in conclave, hold a council of war, pow-wow, palaver; canvass, discuss, debate 475 *argue*; parley, negotiate, hold talks; consult with 691 *consult*.

See: 74, 231, 415, 459, 460, **475**, 524, 529, 579, **581**, 691, 709, 765, 839, 882.

585 Soliloquy

N. *soliloquy*, monologue, monody; interior monologue, stream of consciousness; apostrophe; aside; one-man *or* one-woman show, onehander.

soliloquist, soliloquizer, monologist, monodist.

Adj. *soliloquizing*, thinking aloud; monological.

Vb. *soliloquize*, talk to oneself, say to oneself, say aside, think aloud; apostrophize, pray aloud; talk to the four walls, address an empty house, have an audience of one.

586 Writing

N. *writing*, creative w., composition, literary c., authorship, journalism, itch to write, cacoethes scribendi 590 *description*; literary output 557 *literature*; script, copy, writings, works, books 589 *reading matter*; ink-slinging, quill-driving, pen-pushing, hackwork, Grub Street; paperwork 548 *record*; copying, transcribing, transcription, rewriting, overwriting; autography, holography; ways of writing, handwriting, chirography, stylography, cerography; micrography; longhand, longhand reporting; shorthand writing, shorthand, stenography, tachygraphy, lexigraphy, speedwriting, phonography, stenotypy; phonogram, phraseogram; logograph, logogram, stereotype; typewriting, typing 587 *print*; braille; secret writing, cipher, code 530 *secret*; picture writing, ideography, hieroglyphics; sign-writing, skywriting 528 *advertisement*; inscribing, carving, cutting, graving, epigraphy 555 *engraving*; boustrophedon; study of handwriting, graphology.

lettering, formation of letters, stroke, stroke of the pen, up-stroke, down-s., pothook; line, dot, point; flourish, curlicue, squiggle, scroll 251 *convolution*; handwriting, hand, fist; calligraphy, penmanship; fair hand, law h.; cursive hand, flowing h., round h.; script, italic, copperplate; printing, block letters; clumsy hand, cacography, illegible writing, scribble, scrawl, hen tracks 517 *unintelligibility*; letters, characters, alphabet 558 *letter*; runes, pictogram, ideogram; hieroglyph; cuneiform, arrowhead; Linear A, Linear B., Rosetta stone; palaeography.

script, written matter, inscribed page, illuminated address; specimen, calligraph; writing, screed, scrawl, scribble; manuscript, palimpsest, codex 589 *book*; original, one's own hand, autograph, holograph; signature, sign-manual 547 *indication*; copy, transcript, transcription, fair copy 22 *duplicate*; typescript, stencil; newsprint; printed matter 587 *letterpress*; letter, epistle, rescript, written reply 588 *correspondence*; inscription, epigraph, graffito 548 *record*; superscription, caption, heading; illuminated letters, letters of gold.

stationery, writing materials, pen and paper, pen and ink; stylus, reed, quill, pen, quill-p., fountain p., cartridge p., felt-tip p., ballpoint p., biro (tdmk); nib, steel n.; stylograph, stylo; pencil, propelling p., lead p.; crayon, chalk; papyrus, parchment, vellum; foolscap 631 *paper*; writing paper, notepaper, wove paper, laid p., scented p., recycled p.; notebook, pad, jotter; slate, blackboard; inkstand, inkwell; pencil sharpener, penknife; blotting paper, blotter; typewriter, ribbon; stencil.

calligrapher, calligraphist, penman *or* -woman; cacographer, scribbler, scrawler; writer, pen-pusher, scrivener, scribe, clerk 549 *recorder*; copyist, transcriber; sign-writer 528 *publicizer*; epigraphist, inscriber; subscriber, signer, initialler, signatory; creative writer, script w. 589 *author*; letter writer 588 *correspondent*; graphologist, handwriting expert 484 *detector*.

stenographer, shorthand writer, typist, shorthand t., stenotypist, audiotypist.

Adj. *written*, inscribed, inscriptional, epigraphic; in black and white 548 *recorded*; in writing, in longhand, in shorthand; logographic, stenographic; handwritten, manuscript, autograph, holograph;

signed, under one's hand; penned, pencilled, scrawled, scribbled etc. vb.; cursive, copybook, copperplate; italic, calligraphic; demotic, hieratic; ideographic, hieroglyphic, cuneiform; lettered, alphabetical; runic, Gothic, uncial, roman, italic 558 *literal*; perpendicular, upright, sloping, bold, spidery.

Vb. *write*, be literate; form characters, trace c., engrave, inscribe; letter, block, print; flourish, scroll; write well, write a clear hand; write badly, scribble, scrawl, blot, erase, interline, overwrite; put in writing, set down, set down in black and white, commit to paper, write down, jot d., note 548 *record*; transcribe, copy, copy out, make a fair copy, write out, engross; take down, take dictation, take down in shorthand, stenotype, typewrite, type, type out; take down longhand, write in full; throw on paper, draft, formulate, redact; compose, concoct, indite; pen, pencil, dash off; write letters 588 *correspond*; write one's name 547 *sign*; take up the pen, put pen to paper, spill ink, cover reams; be an author, write books 590 *describe*, 591 *dissertate*; write poetry 593 *poetize*.

See: 22, 251, 484, 517, 528, 530, 547, **548**, 549, 555, 557, **558**, 587, **588**, **589**, 590, 591, 593, 631.

587 Print

N. *print*, printing, typing, typewriting 586 *writing*; typography, printing from type, block printing, plate p., offset process, web offset; lithography, litho, photolithography, photolitho 555 *printing*; photocopying 551 *photography*; photocomposition, photosetting, cold type; composition, cold c., hot c., typesetting, hand-setting, make-up; monotype, linotype, stereotype, electrotype; plate, shell; makeready, printing off, running off.

letterpress, linage, printed matter, print, impression, presswork; pressrun; printout, run-off; copy, pull, proof, galley p., bromide, page proof, revise; colophon, imprint 589 *edition*; dummy, trial copy, proof c.; offprint.

print-type, type, stereotype, plate; flong, matrix; broken type, pie; upper case, lower c., capitals, small c., caps; fount, face, typeface, boldface, bold, clarendon, lightface, old face, bastard type; roman, italic, Gothic, black letter 558 *letter*; body, bevel, shoulder, shank, beard, ascender, descender, serif, sanserif; lead, rule, en, em; space, hairspace, quad; type bar, slug, logotype.

type size, point s., type measure, type scale; brilliant, diamond, pearl, ruby, nonpareil, minion, brevier, bourgeois, elite, long primer, small pica, pica, great primer.

press, printing p., printing works, printers; typefoundry; composing machine, c. room, press r., machining r.; handpress, flatbed, platen press, rotary press, Linotype (tdmk), Monotype (tdmk), offset press; galley, chase, forme, quoin, composing stick; roller, brayer, web.

printer, book p., jobbing p., typographer, compositor, typesetter; typefounder, printer's devil, pressman, printer's reader, proof r.

Adj. *printed*, in print 528 *published*; coldtype, hot-metal; set, composed, machined etc. vb.; in type, in italic, in bold, in roman; typographic; leaded, spaced, justified; solid, tight, crowded.

Vb. *print*, stamp; typeset, compose, photocompose; align, register, justify; set up in type, make ready, impose, machine, run off, pull off, print off; collate, foliate; lithograph, litho, offset, stereotype; get ready for the press, send to p., put to bed; see through the press, proofread, correct; have printed, bring out 528 *publish*.

See: 528, 551, **555**, 558, 586, **589**.

588 Correspondence

N. *correspondence*, stream of c., exchange of letters; communication 524 *information*; mailing list, distribution l.; letters, mail, post, postbag 531 *postal communications*; letter, epistle, missive, dispatch, bulletin; love letter, billet doux, greetings card, Valentine 889 *endearment*; postcard, picture p., card, letter c., notelet; air letter, air mail, sea mail; business letter, bill, account, enclosure; open letter 528 *publicity*; unsolicited mail, circular, round robin, chain letter; note, line, chit; answer, acknowledgment; envelope, cover, stamp, seal; postcode.

correspondent, letter writer, penfriend, poison pen; recipient, addressee; foreign correspondent, contributor 529 *news reporter*; contact 524 *informant*.

Adj. *epistolary*, postal, by post; under cover of, enclosed.

Vb. *correspond*, correspond with, exchange letters, maintain *or* keep up a correspondence, keep in touch with 524 *communicate*; use the post, write to, send a letter to, drop a line; compose dispatches, report 524 *inform*; deal with one's correspondence, acknowledge, reply, write back, reply by return 460 *answer*; circularize 528 *publish*; write again, bombard with letters; post off, forward, mail, airmail; stamp, seal, frank, address.

Adv. *by letter*, by mail, through the post; in correspondence, in touch, in contact.

See: 460, **524**, 528, 529, **531**, 889.

589 Book

N. *book*, title, volume, tome, roll, scroll, document; codex, manuscript, MS, palimpsest; script, typescript, unpublished work; published work, publication, bestseller, potboiler; unsold book, remainder; work, standard w., classic; major work, monumental w., magnum opus; opuscule, slim volume; chapbook, booklet, bouquin; illustrated work, picture book, coffee-table b. 553 *picture*; magazine, periodical, rag 528 *journal*; brochure, pamphlet 528 *the press*; bound book, cased book, hardback, softback, limpback, paperback (**see** *edition*).

reading matter, printed word, written w. 586 *writing*; forms, papers, bumf 548 *record*; script, copy; text, the words, libretto, lyrics, scenario, screenplay, book of words; proof, revise, pull 587 *letterpress*; writings, prose literature 593 *prose*; poetical literature 593 *poetry*; classical literature, serious l., light l. 557 *literature*; books for children, juveniles; history, biography, travel 590 *description*; work of fiction 590 *novel*; biographical work, memoirs, memorabilia 590 *biography*; addresses, speeches 579 *oration*; essay, tract, treatise 591 *dissertation*; piece, occasional pieces 591 *article*; miscellanea, marginalia, jottings, thoughts, pensées; poetical works 593 *poem*; selections, flowers 592 *anthology*; dedicatory volume, Festschrift; early works, juvenilia; posthumous works, literary remains; complete works, oeuvre, corpus; newspaper, magazine 528 *journal*; issue, number, back n.; fascicle, part, instalment, serial, sequel.

textbook, school book, reader 539 *classroom*; abecedary, hornbook; primer, grammar, gradus; text, annotated t., prescribed t., required reading; selection 592 *anthology*; standard text, handbook, manual, enchiridion; pocket book (**see** *reference book*).

reference book, work of reference, encyclopedia, cyclopedia 490 *erudition*; lexicon 559 *dictionary*; biographical dictionary, dictionary of quotations, gazetteer, yearbook, annual 87 *directory*; calendar 117 *chronology*; guide 524 *guidebook*; notebook, diary, album 548 *record*; bibliography, publisher's catalogue, reading list.

edition, impression, issue, run; series, set, collection, library; bound edition, library e., de luxe e., school e., popular e., standard e., definitive e., omnibus e., complete e., collected e., complete works; incunabula, editio princeps, first edition, new e., revised e.; reissue, reprint; réchauffé, rehash, scissors-and-paste job; illustrated edition, special e., limited e., expurgated e.; critical e., variorum e.; adaptation, abridgment 592 *compendium*; octodecimo, sextodecimo, duodecimo, octavo, quarto, folio; book production, layout, format; house style; front matter, prelims, preface, prefatory note; dedication, invocation, acknowledgments; title, bastard t., half-t.; flyleaf, title page, endpaper, colophon 547 *label*; table of contents, table of illustrations; errata, corrigenda, addenda; appendix, supplement, index, thumb i., bibliography; caption, heading, headline, running h., footnote; guide word, catchword; margin, head m., foot m., gutter; folio, page, leaf, recto, verso; sheet, forme, signature, quire; chapter, division, part, section; paragraph, clause, passage, excerpt, inset; plate, print, illustration, halftone, line drawing 553 *picture*.

bookbinding, binding, spiral b., stitching, casing, rebinding, stripping; case, slip c., cover, jacket, dust j. 226 *wrapping*; boards, paper b., millboard 631 *paper*; cloth, limp c., linen, scrim, buckram, leather, pigskin, calf, morocco, vellum, parchment; spine, headband; tooling, blind t., gold t., gilding, marbling; bindery, bookbinder.

library, book collection; national library, public l., branch l., reference l., mobile l., lending l., circulating l., book club; bookshelf, bookcase, bookrack, bookends; bookstall, bookshop, booksellers.

bookperson, man *or* woman of letters, litterateur, literary person; reader, bookworm 492 *scholar*; bibliophile, book lover, book collector, bibliomaniac; bibliographer; librarianship, librarian, library assistant; bookselling, bibliopole, stationer, bookseller, antiquarian b., book dealer, secondhand d., bouquinist; publisher, printer 528 *publicizer*; editor, redactor; reviewing, book reviewer, reviewer 480 *estimator*.

author, authoress, writer, creative w., word-painter, word-smith; literary person, man *or* woman of letters; fiction-writer, novelist, historian, biographer 590 *narrator*; essayist, editorialist 591 *dissertator*; prose writer; verse writer 593 *poet*; playwright, librettist, script writer 594 *dramatist*; freelance; copywriter 528 *publicizer*; pressman *or* -woman, journalist 529 *news reporter*; editor, subeditor, copy editor, contributor, correspondent, special c., war c., sports c., columnist, paragraphist, gossip writer, diarist; scribbler, penpusher, hack, Grub Street h., penny-a-liner, inkslinger, potboiler; ghost, ghost writer; reviser, translator, adapter.

Adj. *bibliographical*, in book form; bound, half-b., case-b., cloth-b., hardback, paperback, soft-cover; loose-leaf; tooled, marbled, gilt; bibliophilic, book-loving, antiquarian; in print, out of print.

See: 87, 117, 226, 480, 490, 492, 524, **528**, 529, 539, 547, 548, 553, 557, 559, 579, 586, **587**, **590**, **591**, **592**, **593**, **594**, 631.

590 Description

N. *description*, account, full a.; statement, exposé, statement of facts, summary 524 *report*; brief, abstract, inscription, caption, legend 592 *compendium*; narration, relation, rehearsal, recital, version (**see** *narrative*); reportage, nonfiction, documentary account; specification, characterization, details, particulars 87 *list*; portrayal, delineation, depiction; portrait, sketch, character s., profile, prosopography 551 *representation*; psychic profile, case history 548 *record*; faction, documentary drama; evocation, word-painting, local colour; picture, true p., realism, naturalism; descriptive account, travelogue 524 *guidebook*; vignette, cameo, thumbnail sketch; idyll, eclogue 593 *poem*; eulogy 923 *praise*; parody 851 *satire*; obituary, epitaph, lapidary inscription 364 *obsequies*.

narrative, storyline, plot, subplot, scenario 594 *stage play*; episode 154 *event*; complication 61 *complexity*; dénouement 725 *completion*; dramatic irony, comic relief; stream of consciousness; fantasia 513 *fantasy*; imaginary account, fiction, story, tale, conte, fabliau, romance, fairytale, folk tale; tradition, legend, legendry, mythology, myth, saga, epic, epos; ballad 593 *poem*; allegory, parable, apologue, cautionary tale; yarn 543 *fable*; anecdote, reminiscence 505 *remembrance*; annals, chronicle, history, historiography 548 *record*.

biography, real-life story, human interest; life, curriculum vitae, life story *or* history; experiences, adventures, fortunes; hagiology, hagiography, martyrology, Foxe's Book of Martyrs; obituary, necrology; rogue's gallery, Newgate calendar; personal account, autobiography, confessions, memoirs 505 *remembrance*; diary, journals 548 *record*; personal correspondence, letters 588 *correspondence*.

novel, fiction, tale; roman à clef, Bildungsroman, roman fleuve; antinovel; historical novel, fictional biography, novelization; short story, novelette, novella; light reading, bedside r. 589 *reading matter*; romance, love story, fairy s., adventure s., Western, science fiction, sci-fi; Gothic novel, ghost story; novel of low life, picaresque novel; crime story, detective s., whodunit; cliffhanger, thriller, shocker, penny dreadful, horror comic; paperback, pulp literature; potboiler, trash; popular novel, blockbuster, best-seller 589 *book*.

narrator, describer, delineator, descriptive writer; reporter, relater; raconteur, anecdotist; yarn-spinner, teller of tales, storyteller, fabler, fabulist, mythologist, allegorist; fiction writer 589 *author*; romancer, novelist, fictionist; biographer, Boswell, Plutarch; hagiographer, martyrologist, autobiographer, memoir writer, diarist; historian, historiographer, chronicler, annalist 549 *recorder*; Muse of History, Clio.

Adj. *descriptive*, representational; graphic, colourful, vivid; well-drawn, sharp 551 *representing*; true-to-life, naturalistic, realistic, real-life, photographic, convincing; picturesque, striking; impressionistic, suggestive, evocative, emotive; moving, thrilling 821 *exciting*; traditional, legendary, storied, mythological 519 *figurative*;

epic, heroic, romantic, cloak-and-dagger; picaresque, low-life, kitchen-sink; narrative, historical, biographical, autobiographical; full, detailed, circumstantial 570 *diffuse*; factual, documentary, nonfiction 494 *accurate*; fictitious, fictional, imaginative 513 *imaginary*; Dickensian, Jamesian, Lawrentian, Kafkaesque 557 *literary*.

Vb. *describe*, delineate, limn, draw, picture, depict, paint 551 *represent*; evoke, bring to life, tell vividly, make one see; characterize, particularize, detail, enter into, descend to 80 *specify*; sketch, adumbrate 233 *outline*; relate, recount, rehearse, recite, report, give an account 524 *communicate*; write, write about 548 *record*; narrate, tell, tell a story, yarn, spin a y., unfold a tale; construct a plot, make a story out of; put into a novel, fictionalize, novelize; romance, mythicize, mythologize 513 *imagine*; review, recapitulate 106 *repeat*; reminisce, relive the past 505 *retrospect*.

See: 61, 80, 87, 106, 154, 233, 364, 494, 505, 513, 519, 524, 543, 548, 549, **551**, **557**, 570, 588, **589**, 592, 593, 594, 725, 821, 851, 923.

591 Dissertation

N. *dissertation*, treatise, tract, tractate; exposition, summary 592 *compendium*; theme, thesis 475 *argument*; disquisition, essay, examination, survey 459 *enquiry*; discourse, descant, discussion; excursus, memoir, paper, monograph, study, lucubration; introductory study, prolegomena; screed, harangue, homily, sermon 534 *lecture*; commentary, textbook, almagest.

article, signed a., syndicated a., column; leading article, leader, editorial; essay, causerie, belles-lettres; literary composition, set piece, companion p.; comment, review, notice, critique, criticism, write-up 480 *estimate*.

dissertator, essayist, expositor; pamphleteer, publicist 528 *publicizer*; editor, leader writer, editorialist; writer, belletrist, contributor 589 *author*; reviewer, critic, commentator, pundit 520 *interpreter*.

Adj. *discursive*, disquisitional 475 *arguing*; expository, critical 520 *interpretive*.

Vb. *dissertate*, treat, handle, write about, deal with, do justice to; descant, discourse upon 475 *argue*; pursue a theme, develop a thesis; go into, enquire into, survey; set out, discuss, canvass, ventilate, air one's views; notice, criticize, comment upon, write up; write an essay, do a paper; annotate, commentate 520 *interpret*.

See: 459, 475, 480, 520, 528, 534, 589, 592.

592 Compendium

N. *compendium*, epitome, resumé, summary, brief; contents, heads, analysis; abstract, sum and substance, gist; consolidation, digest, pandect; multum in parvo, précis; aperçu, conspectus, synopsis, bird's-eye view, survey; review, recapitulation, recap; rundown, runthrough; draft, minute, note 548 *record*; sketch, thumbnail s., outline, skeleton; blueprint 623 *plan*; syllabus, prospectus 87 *list*; abridgment, abbreviation 204 *shortening*; contraction, compression 569 *conciseness*.

anthology, treasury, garland, florilegium, flowers, beauties, best pieces; selections, extracts, chrestomathy 589 *textbook*; collection, compilation, collectanea, miscellanea, miscellany; mythography; analects, fugitive pieces, ephemera; gleanings, leaves, pages; cuttings, album, scrapbook, notebook, sketchbook, commonplace book; anthologist.

epitomizer, abridger, abbreviator; abstracter, summarizer, précis-writer, shortener, cutter.

Adj. *compendious*, pithy 569 *concise*; analytical, synoptic; abstracted, abridged 204 *short*; potted, compacted, capsular; collected, excerpted etc. vb.

Vb. *abstract*, sum up, resume, summarize, run over; epitomize, reduce, abbreviate, abridge 204 *shorten*; capsulize, encapsulate; docket 548 *record*; condense, pot, give sum and substance 569 *be concise*; consolidate, compile 87 *list*; collect 74 *bring together*; conflate 50 *combine*; excerpt, glean, select, anthologize; diagrammatize, sketch, sketch out 233 *outline*.

Adv. *in sum*, in substance, in brief 569 *concisely*; at a glance.

See: 50, 74, 87, 204, 233, 548, **569**, 589, 623.

593 Poetry. Prose

N. *poetry*, poesy, balladry, minstrelsy, song; versification (**see** *prosody*); poetic art, poetics; verse, rhyme, numbers; poetic licence; poetic fire, poetic vein, poetic inspiration, numen, afflatus, divine a.; Muses, tuneful Nine, Calliope, Apollo, Orpheus; Parnassus, Helicon, Castalian spring, Pierian s., Hippocrene.

poem, poetic composition; versification, lines, verses, stanzas, strains; narrative verse, heroic poem, epic, epos, Edda, chansons de geste; dramatic poem, lyric drama, verse drama, Greek tragedy, Greek comedy, satyric drama, trilogy, tetralogy 594 *drama*; light verse, vers de société, lyric verse, melic v.; ode, epode, choric ode, Pindaric o., Sapphic o., Horatian o.; palinode; dithyramb; monody, dirge, elegiac poem, elegy; idyll, eclogue; georgic, bucolics; occasional poem, prothalamion, epithalamium; song, hymn, shanty, lay, ballad 412 *vocal music*; war-song, marching song; love song, drinking song, anacreontic; collected poems 592 *anthology*; canto, fit; cycle, sequence.

doggerel, lame verse, balladry; jingle, ditty, runes, nursery rhyme; nonsense verse; clerihew, limerick; cento, macaronic verse, macaronics, Leonine verse, Fescennine v., Hudibrastic v.; mock epic, burlesque, satirical verse.

verse form, sonnet, sestet, Petrarchan *or* Italian sonnet, Shakespearean *or* English s.; ballade, rondeau, virelay, triolet, villanelle, bouts rimés; burden, refrain, envoi; couplet, distich, sloka; haiku, tanka; triplet, tercet, terza rima, quatrain, ghazal; sestina, rhyme royal, ottava rima, Spenserian stanza; accentual verse, syllabic v., metrical v., blank v.; concrete poetry; Sapphics, Alcaics; limping iambics, scazon; free v., vers libres; verse, versicle, stanza, stave, laisse, strophe, antistrophe; stichomythia; broken line, half l., hemistich. **See** *prosody*.

prosody, versification, metrics, metre, syllabic m., measure, numbers, scansion; rhyme, masculine r., feminine r., internal r., eye r.; rhyme scheme; assonance, alliteration; cadence, rhythm, sprung r.; metrical unit, foot; iamb, trochee, spondee, pyrrhic; dactyl, anapaest, tribrach, amphibrach, choriamb; dimeter, trimeter, tetrameter, pentameter, hexameter, heptameter, octameter; iambic pentameters, blank verse; alexandrine, heroic couplet, elegiac c.; anacrusis, arsis, thesis, ictus, beat, stress, accent, accentuation; elision; enjambment, caesura, diaeresis.

poet, major p., minor p., poet laureate; Lake poet, Georgian p., Metaphysical p., beat p.; versemonger, poetaster; prosodist, versifier, metrist, hexametrist, vers-librist; rhymer, rhymester, rhymist, jingler; bard, minstrel, balladist, balladeer, skald, troubadour, trouvère, jongleur, minnesinger, Meistersinger; epic poet, lyric p., lyrist, bucolic poet, dramatic p., dithyrambist, elegist, elegiac poet; sonneteer, ballad-monger; songwriter, librettist; improviser, improvisatore, improvisatrice; reciter, rhapsode, rhapsodist.

prose, not verse, prose rhythm; prose poem; prosaicness, prosaism, prosiness, prose-writing, everyday language 573 *plainness*; prosaist, prose writer 589 *author*.

Adj. *poetic*, poetical, bardic; songful, tuneful; Parnassian, Pierian; heroic, Homeric, Dantesque, Miltonic *or* Miltonian; mock-heroic, satiric; elegiac, lyrical, dithyrambic, rhapsodic; lyric, anacreontic, Pindaric, Sapphic, Horatian; bucolic, eclogic, Virgilian; Augustan 557 *literary*; rhyming, jingling, etc. vb.; doggerel, macaronic; prosodic, accentual, metrical, measured, rhythmic, scanning, scanned; octosyllabic, hendecasyllabic, iambic, trochaic, spondaic, dactylic, anapaestic; catalectic; Petrarchan, Byronic, Shakespearean, Spenserian.

prosaic, pedestrian, unpoetical, unversified; in prose, matter-of-fact 573 *plain*.

Vb. *poetize*, sing, tune one's lyre, mount Pegasus; syllabize, scan; rhyme, chime, jingle; versify, put into verse, put into rhyme; make verses, elegize, compose an epic, write a lyric, write a sonnet; celebrate in verse; berhyme; lampoon 851 *satirize*.

write prose, stick to prose, prose, prosify.

See: 412, **557**, 573, 589, 592, 594, 851.

594 Drama. Ballet

N. *drama*, the drama, the theatre, the stage, the play, the boards, the footlights; theatreland, Broadway, West End; silver screen, Hollywood 445 *cinema*; show business, show biz, dramatic entertainment, straight drama, legitimate theatre, live t.; intimate t., total t., alternative t., street t., the Fringe, off-off-Broadway; repertory, rep; theatricals, amateur t.; masque, charade, dumb show, puppetry, tableau, t. vivant 551 *representation*;

tragic mask, comic m., sock, buskin, cothurnus; Tragic Muse, Melpomene; Comic Muse, Thalia; Thespis.

dramaturgy, play construction, dramatic form 590 *narrative*; dramatic unities; dramatization, theatricals, dramatics; melodramatics, histrionics; theatricality, staginess; bardolatry; good theatre, bad t., good cinema; play writing, scenario w., script w., libretto w.; stagecraft, theatrecraft, histrionic art, Thespian a.; action, movement, plot, subplot 590 *narrative*; characterization 551 *representation*; production, revival; auditions, casting; walk-through, rehearsal, dress r.; direction, stage management; showmanship; staging, stage directions; dialogue, soliloquy, stage whisper, aside, cue; gagging, business, byplay; entrance, exit (see *acting*); rising of the curtain, prologue, chorus; act, scene, opening s., scène à faire, coup de théâtre, deus ex machina, alarums and excursions; curtain, drop of the c., blackout; finale, epilogue; curtain call, encore; interval, intermission, break; enactment, performance, command p., first p., première, preview, first night, gala n.; matinée, first house, second h.; one-night stand, road show; successful production, sell-out, hit, smash h., box-office h., long run.

stage play, play, drama, work; piece, show, vehicle; libretto, scenario, script, text, book of words, prompt book; part, lines 579 *speech*; dramatic representation 551 *representation*; five-act play, one-act p., playlet; sketch, skit; double bill; curtain-raiser, entr'acte, intermezzo, divertissement; monologue, dramatic m.; duologue, two-hander; masque, mystery play, miracle play, morality p., passion p., Oberammergau; commedia dell'arte; No, Kabuki; Greek drama, trilogy, tetralogy, cycle; poetic drama, verse d.; melodrama, blood and thunder; tragedy, high t., classical t.; tragicomedy, comédie larmoyante; comedy, high c., low c., light c., comedy of manners, Restoration comedy; well-made play, problem p., slice-of-life drama, kitchen-sink d., theatre of the absurd, t. of cruelty; black comedy, Grand Guignol, farce, knockabout f., slapstick, burlesque, extravaganza 849 *ridiculousness*; pantomime, panto, harlequinade; musical comedy, musical, light opera, comic o., opera bouffe, grand opera 412 *vocal music*; radio drama, drama-documentary, television play 531 *broadcast*; photoplay, screenplay 445 *cinema*; shadow play, puppet show, Punch and Judy show.

stage show 445 *spectacle*; ice show, circus 837 *amusement*; variety, music hall, vaudeville; revue, intimate r.; Follies, leg show, strip s.; floor show, cabaret; song and dance, act, turn; star turn, transformation scene, set piece, tableau.

ballet, dance, ballet dancing 837 *dancing*; choreography; classical ballet, Russian b., romantic b., modern dance; toe dance, tap d., clog d. 837 *dance*; solo, pas seul, pas de deux; chassé, glissade; arabesque; fouetté, plié, pirouette 315 *rotation*; pas de chat, entrechat, jeté 312 *leap*.

stage set, set, setting, décor, mise-en-scène, scenery, scene 445 *spectacle*; drop curtain, drop, backdrop, backcloth, cyclorama; screen, wings, flat; background, foreground, front stage, upstage, downstage, stage, boards; apron, proscenium, proscenium arch, picture-frame stage; gauze, curtain, fire c., safety c.; trap, star t.; prompt box (see *theatre*); properties, props, costume, theatrical c.; make-up, greasepaint.

theatre, amphitheatre, stadium 724 *arena*; circus, hippodrome; fleapit, picture palace 445 *cinema*; Greek theatre, Elizabethan t., t. in the round, arena t., open-air t.; showboat, pier, pavilion; big top; playhouse, opera house, music hall, vaudeville theatre, variety t.; night club, boîte, cabaret; stage, boards, proscenium, wings, coulisses, flies (see *stage set*); dressing room, green r.; footlights, floats, battens, spotlight, spot, limelight, floodlight, flood, houselights; auditorium, orchestra; seating, stalls, orchestra s., fauteuil, front rows; pit, parterre; box, loge, circle, dress c., upper c., mezzanine; gallery, balcony, gods; front of house, foyer, bar, box office, stage door.

acting, impersonation, mimesis 551 *representation*; interpretation, improvisation, impression, pantomime, miming, taking off 20 *mimicry*; histrionics, play-acting, character-a., the Method; ham-acting, hamming, barnstorming; overacting, staginess, theatricality; repertoire; character, personage, role, creating a r.; starring role, leading r.; part, good p., fat p.; vignette, cameo; supporting part, bit p., speaking p.; walk-on p.; stock part, ingenue, soubrette, confidante, heavy father, injured husband, merry widow, stage villain; principal boy *or* girl; Harlequin, Columbine, Pierrot, Pantaloon, Scaramouche; pantomime dame; chief part, name p.; hero, heroine, antihero; stage fever; stage fright.

actor, actress, Thespian, Roscius; mimic, mime, pantomimist 20 *imitator*; mummer, masker, guisard; play-actor, player, strolling p., trouper, cabotin(e); barnstormer, ham; rep player, character actor; actor-manager, star, star actor *or* actress, star of stage and screen, film star, starlet, matinée idol 890 *favourite*; tragedian, tragedienne; comedian, comedienne, comedy actor *or* actress; opera singer, prima donna, diva; ballet dancer, ballerina, prima b., coryphée; danseur, danseuse, figurant(e); protagonist, lead, second l., leading man, leading lady, juvenile lead, jeune premier; understudy, stand-in 150 *substitute*; lookalike 18 *analogue*; supernumerary, super, extra, bit player; chorus, gentlemen *or* ladies of the chorus; corps de ballet, troupe, company, repertory c., stock c.; dramatis personae, characters, cast; presenter, narrator; prologue 579 *speaker*.

entertainer, public e., performer; artiste, artist, quick-change a., drag a., striptease a.; diseur, diseuse, monologist; impressionist, impersonator; troubadour, minstrel; street musician, busker; crooner, pop singer 413 *vocalist*; comic, stand-up c., comedian, comedienne 839 *humorist*; ventriloquist, fire-eater, juggler 545 *conjuror*; ropewalker, acrobat 162 *athlete*; clown, buffoon, cap and bells 501 *fool*; pierrot, pierrette, Punch, Punchinello; hoofer, dancer, show girl, chorus g., cancan dancer, belly d., gogo d.; dancing girl, nautch g., geisha g.

stagehand, scene shifter; property man, stage carpenter, scene painter; electrician, machinist; sound recordist, special effects man, continuity girl; costumier, wardrobe mistress, wigmaker, make-up artist; prompter, call-boy, programme seller, usher, usherette, doorman.

stage manager, producer, director, regisseur; designer; manager, actor m., business m., press agent; impresario, showman; backer, sponsor, angel.

dramatist, dramaturge; tragic poet, comic p. 593 *poet*; playwright, scenario writer, script w., lyric w., librettist; farceur, gagman, joke-writer 839 *humorist*; choreographer.

playgoer, theatregoer, operagoer; film fan, opera buff, balletomane 504 *enthusiast*; first-nighter; stage-door Johnny; audience, house, packed h., full h., sell-out; stalls, boxes, pit, circle, gods, gallery, balcony; groundling, pittite 441 *spectator*; claque, claqueur; dramatic critic, play *or* film reviewer.

Adj. *dramatic*, dramaturgical; scenic, theatrical, stagy 551 *representing*; operatic, balletic, Terpsichorean, choreographic; live, legitimate; Thespian, Roscian; histrionic, mimetic 20 *imitative*; tragic, buskined; Thalian, comic, tragicomic; farcical, burlesque, knockabout, slapstick 849 *funny*; cathartic, melodramatic, sensational, blood and thunder 821 *exciting*; Brechtian, Shavian, Pinteresque, avant-garde; produced, released, showing, running 522 *shown*; dramatized, acted; badly-acted, hammed up, camped up; hammy, barnstorming; on the stage, acting, play-a.; cast, cast as, miscast; featured, starred, billed, top of the bill; well-cast, all-star; stagestruck, film-struck, theatregoing.

Vb. *dramatize*, be a dramatist, write plays, write for the stage; make a play of, put in a play; adapt for the stage *or* for radio; do a play, put on the stage, stage, mount, produce, direct, stage-manage; rehearse, cut; cast, typecast, give a part, assign a role; star, feature, bill; present, put on, release 522 *show*; open, open for a season; raise *or* ring up the curtain.

act, go on the stage, tread the boards; face the cameras; perform, enact, play, playact, do a play 551 *represent*; personify, personate, impersonate; act the role, take the part; mime, pantomime, take off 20 *imitate*; create a role, play a part, play the lead; play opposite, support; star, co-star, steal the show, take the centre of the stage, upstage, take all the limelight; play to the gallery, ham, ham it up, camp it up, send up, barnstorm, overact, overdramatize 546 *exaggerate*; rant, roar, out-Herod Herod; underact, throw away; walk on; understudy, stand in 150 *substitute*; con one's part, rehearse, say one's lines; cue in; fluff, forget one's lines, dry; ad-lib, gag; dramatize oneself 875 *be ostentatious.*

Adv. *on stage*, offstage, upstage, downstage; backstage; behind the footlights, in the limelight; dramatically.

See: 18, 20, 150, 162, 312, 315, 412, 413, 441, **445**, 501, 504, 522, 531, 545, 546, **551**, 579, 590, 593, 724, 821, **837**, 839, 849, 875, 890.

Class five

Volition: *the exercise of the will*

Class: 5.1 Individual volition

Section one. Volition in general

595 Will

N. *will,* willing, volition; nonconative will, velleity; disposition, inclination, mind, preference 597 *willingness*; conative will, conation, act of will, effort of w. 682 *exertion*; strength of will, willpower, determination 599 *resolution*; controlled will, self-control 942 *temperance*; intent, purpose 617 *intention*; decision 608 *predetermination*; one's will and pleasure 737 *command*; appetency 859 *desire*; one's own sweet will 932 *selfishness*; self-will, wilfulness 602 *obstinacy*; whimsicality 604 *caprice*; acte gratuit; free will, self-determination 744 *independence*; free choice, option, discretion 605 *choice*; unprompted will, voluntariness, voluntaryism, spontaneousness, spontaneity 597 *voluntary work*; primacy of will, voluntarism.

Adj. *volitional,* willing, volitive, conative; unprompted, unasked, unbidden, freewill, spontaneous, original 597 *voluntary*; discretional, discretionary, optional 605 *choosing*; minded, so m. 617 *intending*; self-willed, wilful 602 *obstinate*; arbitrary, autocratic, dictatorial 735 *authoritarian*; independent, self-determined 744 *free*; determined 599 *resolute*; decided, prepense, intentional, willed, intended 608 *predetermined.*

Vb. *will,* exercise the will; impose one's will, have one's w., have one's way, have it all one's own w. 737 *command*; do what one chooses, do as one likes 744 *be free*; be so minded, see fit, think best 605 *choose*; purpose, determine 617 *intend*; wish 859 *desire*; have a mind of one's own, have a will of one's own, be independent, go one's own way, be one's own man *or* woman 734 *please oneself*; exercise one's discretion, judge for oneself 480 *judge*; act on one's own authority, take the responsibility, take it upon oneself; be self-willed, take the law into one's own hands, take the bit between one's teeth 602 *be obstinate*; know one's own mind 599 *be resolute*; volunteer, offer, do of one's own accord, do without prompting 597 *be willing*; originate 156 *cause.*

Adv. *at will,* at pleasure, ad libitum, ad lib, as it seems good; voluntarily, of one's own free will, of one's own accord; spontaneously, for the heck of it.

See: 156, 480, **597**, **599**, 602, 604, 605, 608, **617**, 682, 734, 735, 737, 744, 859, 932, 942.

596 Necessity

N. *necessity,* hard n., stern n., compelling n.; no alternative, no escape, no option, Hobson's choice 606 *no choice*; last shift, last resort 700 *predicament*; inevitability, the inevitable, what must be 155 *destiny*; necessitation, dictation, necessitarianism, determinism, fatalism 608 *predetermination*; pressure of events, force of circumstances, c. beyond one's control, act of God, fatality 154 *event*; no freedom 745 *subjection*; physical necessity, law of nature; force, superior f. 740 *compulsion*; logical necessity, logic, necessary conclusion, proof 478 *demonstration*; legal necessity, force of law 953 *law*; moral necessity, obligation, conscience 917 *duty*; necessitude, indispensability, a necessity, a necessary, a must 627 *requirement*; necessitousness, want, lack 801 *poverty*;

involuntariness, reflex action, reflex, conditioned r.; instinct, impulse, blind i. 476 *intuition*.

fate, inexorable f., lot, inescapable l., cup, portion; weird, karma, kismet; doom, foredoom, predestination, preordination, election 155 *destiny*; book of fate, God's will, will of Allah, will of heaven; fortune 159 *chance*; stars, planets, astral influence; the Fates, Parcae, Norns; Fatal Sisters, Weird S., S. Three, Lachesis, Clotho, Atropos.

fatalist, determinist, predestinarian, necessitarian; pawn, tool, automaton, robot, machine.

Adj. *necessary*, indispensable, requisite 627 *required*; logically necessary, logical, dictated by reason, unanswerable; demonstrable 478 *demonstrated*; necessitating, imperative, compulsive 740 *compelling*; overriding, irresistible, resistless 34 *superior*; compulsory, mandatory, binding 917 *obligatory*; with force of law 953 *legal*; necessitated, inevitable, unavoidable, inescapable, inexorable 473 *certain*; leaving no choice, dictated, imposed, necessitarian, deterministic 606 *choiceless*.

involuntary, instinctive 476 *intuitive*; unpremeditated, unwilled, unintended 618 *unintentional*; unconscious, unthinking, unwitting, blind, impulsive 609 *spontaneous*; unassenting 598 *unwilling*; under a spell 983 *bewitched*; conditioned, reflex, controlled, automatic, machinelike, mechanistic, mechanical.

fated, decided by fate, karmic, fatal; appointed, destined, predestined, ordained, preordained 608 *predetermined*; elect 605 *chosen*; doomed, foredoomed, prejudged, precondemned 961 *condemned*; bound, obliged 745 *subject*.

Vb. *be forced*, compelled etc. adj.; incur the necessity, lie under the n.; admit the necessity, submit to the n. 721 *submit*; be fated, bow to fate, dree one's weird; be cornered, be driven into a corner, be pushed to the wall 700 *be in difficulty*; know no alternative, have no choice, have no option, needs must; make a virtue of necessity; be unable to help it, be made that way; be subject to impulse, be guided by instinct 745 *be subject*.

necessitate, dictate, impose, oblige 740 *compel*; bind by fate, destine, doom, foredoom, predestinate 155 *predestine*; insist, brook no denial, not take no for an answer; leave no choice, impose the necessity, drive into a corner; demand 627 *require*.

Adv. *necessarily*, of necessity, of course, perforce; nothing for it, no help for it, no two ways about it; willy-nilly, nolens volens, bon gré mal gré, coûte que coûte.

See: 34, 154, 155, 159, **473**, 476, 478, 598, 605, 606, 608, 609, 618, 627, 700, 721, **740**, 745, 801, 917, 953, 961, 983.

597 Willingness

N. *willingness*, voluntariness, volunteering; spontaneousness 609 *spontaneity*; free choice, option 605 *choice*; disposition, mind, animus; inclination, leaning, bent, bias, penchant, propensity 179 *tendency*; facility 694 *aptitude*; predisposition, readiness, right mood, favourable humour, receptive frame of mind; cordiality, good will 897 *benevolence*; acquiescence 488 *assent*; compliance 758 *consent*; ready acquiescence, cheerful consent, alacrity, promptness, zeal, earnestness, eagerness, zealousness, ardour, enthusiasm; initiative, forwardness; impatience, overeagerness, overzealousness, ardour of the chase 678 *overactivity*; devotion, self-d., dedication, sacrifice 931 *disinterestedness*; helpfulness 706 *cooperation*; loyalty 739 *obedience*; pliancy, docility, tractability 612 *persuadability*; submissiveness 721 *submission*; obsequiousness 879 *servility*.

voluntary work, voluntary service 901 *philanthropy*; honorary employment, unpaid labour, labour of love, self-appointed task; gratuitous effort, supererogation; freewill offering 781 *gift*.

volunteer, unpaid worker, ready w., willing horse; no shirker, no slouch 678 *busy person*; do-gooder 901 *philanthropist*.

Adj. *willing*, ungrudging, acquiescent 488 *assenting*; compliant, agreeable, content, game for 758 *consenting*; in the mood, in the right m., receptive, favourable, favourably minded, inclined, disposed, well-d., predisposed, amenable; gracious, genial, cordial; happy, pleased, glad, charmed, delighted; ready 669 *prepared*; ready and willing, prompt, quick 678 *active*; forward, anticipating; alacritous, zealous, eager, enthusiastic, dedicated, keen as mustard; overeager, impatient, spoiling for, raring to go; dependable, reliable 768 *observant*; earnest, trying, doing one's best 671 *attempting*; helpful

706 *cooperative*; docile, teachable, biddable, easy-going 24 *agreeing*; loyal 739 *obedient*; submissive 721 *submitting*; obsequious 879 *servile*; fain, desirous, dying to 859 *desiring*; would-be 852 *hoping*; meaning, meaning to 617 *intending*.

voluntary, offered, unprompted, unforced, unsought, unasked, unbidden 609 *spontaneous*; unsolicited, uncalled for, self-imposed; supererogatory, beyond the call of duty; nonmandatory, discretionary, open to choice, optional 605 *chosen*; volunteering, on one's own initiative, off one's own bat, of one's own free will 759 *offering*; gratuitous, free, honorary, unpaid 812 *uncharged*.

Vb. *be willing*, - ready etc. adj.; not mind, have half a mind to; feel like, have a good mind to 595 *will*; yearn to 859 *desire*; mean to 617 *intend*; agree, acquiesce 488 *assent*; show willing, find it in one's heart, comply 758 *consent*; hearken, lend a willing ear, be found willing 739 *obey*; try, do one's best 671 *attempt*; show zeal, go out of one's way to, lean over backwards, overcompensate; collaborate 706 *cooperate*; anticipate, meet halfway; swallow, jump at, leap at; can't wait, be thrilled at the idea; stomach, make no bones about, make no scruple, not scruple, not hesitate, not hold back; choose freely 605 *choose*; volunteer, sacrifice oneself 759 *offer oneself*.

Adv. *willingly*, with a will, readily, cordially, heartily; voluntarily, spontaneously, without being asked 595 *at will*; readily, like a shot, at the drop of a hat; with open arms, with all one's heart, heart and soul, con amore, with a good grace, without demur, nothing loath; fain, as lief; gladly, with pleasure.

See: 24, 179, 488, **595**, **605**, 609, 612, 617, 669, 671, 678, 694, 706, 721, 739, 758, 759, 768, 781, 812, 852, 859, 879, 897, 901, 931.

598 Unwillingness

N. *unwillingness*, disinclination, indisposition, reluctance; disagreement 489 *dissent*; demur, objection 468 *qualification*; protest 762 *deprecation*; renitency, recalcitrance 704 *opposition*; rejection 760 *refusal*; unhelpfuless, noncooperation 702 *hindrance*; dissociation, nonassociation, abstention 190 *absence*; unenthusiasm, lifelessness, want of alacrity, lack of zeal 860 *indifference*; backwardness 278 *slowness*; hesitation 858 *caution*; scruple, qualm of conscience 486 *doubt*; repugnance 861 *dislike*; recoil, aversion, averseness, no stomach for, shrinking 620 *avoidance*; bashfulness 874 *modesty*; nonobservance, noncompliance 738 *disobedience*; indocility, refractoriness, fractiousness; sulks, sulkiness 893 *sullenness*; perfunctoriness, grudging service; undependability, unreliability 474 *uncertainty*; shelving, postponement, procrastination 136 *delay*; laziness 679 *sluggishness*; neglect, remissness 458 *negligence*.

slacker, shirker 679 *idler*; forced labour, unwilling servant 278 *slowcoach*.

Adj. *unwilling*, indisposed, loath, reluctant, averse; not prepared, not minded, not so m., not in the mood 760 *refusing*; unconsenting, unreconciled 489 *dissenting*; renitent, adverse, opposed, unalterably o., irreconcilable 704 *opposing*; demurring, protesting 762 *deprecatory*; squeamish, with no stomach for 861 *disliking*; full of regrets, regretful, with regret 830 *regretting*; hesitant 858 *cautious*; shy, bashful 874 *modest*; shrinking, shirking 620 *avoiding*; unzealous, unenthusiastic, half-hearted, lukewarm; backward, dragging 278 *slow*; unhelpful, uncooperative 702 *hindering*; noncooperating, fractious, restive, recalcitrant, kicking 738 *disobedient*; not trying, perfunctory, unthorough, remiss 458 *negligent*; grudging, sulky 893 *sullen*; unspontaneous, forced, begrudged.

Vb. *be unwilling*, - reluctant etc. adj.; not have the heart to, not stomach 861 *dislike*; disagree, stickle, stick, boggle, scruple 489 *dissent*; object, demur, protest 762 *deprecate*; resist 704 *oppose*; reject 760 *refuse*; recoil, turn away, back a., not face, blench, fight shy, duck, jib, shirk 620 *avoid*; skimp, scamp 458 *neglect*; drag one's feet, look over one's shoulder, hold back, hang back, hesitate, hang fire, go slow 278 *move slowly*; slack, not try, not pull one's weight 679 *be inactive*; not play, noncooperate, dissociate oneself, abstain 702 *obstruct*; grudge, begrudge, make faces, grimace 893 *be sullen*; drag oneself, force o., make o.; do with regret, have regrets 830 *regret*; tear oneself away 296 *depart*.

Adv. *unwillingly*, reluctantly, under protest, under pressure, with a bad grace, in spite of oneself, against one's will, against the grain; regretfully, with regret, with a heavy heart; not for the world.

See: 136, 190, **278**, 296, 458, 468, 474, 486, 489, 620, 679, 702, 704, 738, 760, 762, 830, 858, 860, 861, 874, 893.

599 Resolution

N. *resolution*, sticking point, resoluteness, determination, grim d.; zeal, earnestness, seriousness; resolve, fixed r., mind made up, decision 608 *predetermination*; drive, vigour 174 *vigorousness*; energy, frantic e., desperate e., desperation 678 *activity*; thoroughness 725 *completion*; fixity of purpose, concentration, iron will, will-power 595 *will*; strength of character, self-control, self-restraint, self-mastery, self-conquest, self-command, self-possession; tenacity 600 *perseverance*; aplomb, mettle, daring, dash, élan 712 *attack*; guts, pluck, spunk, grit, backbone, spirit; fortitude, stiff upper lip, moral fibre 855 *courage*; single-mindedness, devotedness, devotion, utter d., self-d., dedication; firm principles, reliability, staunchness, steadiness, constancy, firmness 153 *stability*; insistence, pressure 740 *compulsion*; sternness, relentlessness, ruthlessness, inexorability, implacability 906 *pitilessness*; inflexibility, steeliness 326 *hardness*; iron, cast i., steel, rock; clenched teeth, hearts of oak, bulldog breed 600 *stamina*; Mr Standfast.

Adj. *resolute*, resolved, made up, determined 597 *willing*; desperate, stopping at nothing; serious, earnest, concentrated; intent upon, set u., bent u. 617 *intending*; insistent, pressing, urgent, driving, forceful, energetic, heroic 174 *vigorous*; zealous, thorough, whole-hogging 455 *attentive*; steady, firm, staunch, reliable, constant 153 *unchangeable*; iron-willed, strong-w., strong-minded, decisive, decided, unbending, immovable, unyielding, inflexible, uncompromising, intransigent 602 *obstinate*; stern, grim, inexorable, implacable, relentless, ruthless, merciless 906 *pitiless*; iron, cast-i., steely, tough as steel, hard as iron 326 *hard*; stalwart, undaunted, nothing daunted 855 *unfearing*; steadfast, unwavering, unshaken, unshakable, unshrinking, unflinching, game, tenacious 600 *persevering*; indomitable 727 *unbeaten*; steeled, armoured, proof; self-controlled, self-restrained 942 *temperate*; self-possessed, self-reliant, self-confident; purposive, purposeful, single-minded, whole-hearted, devoted, dedicated.

Vb. *be resolute*, - determined etc. adj.; steel oneself, brace o., set one's face, clench one's teeth, grit one's t. (**see** *stand firm*); make up one's mind, take a resolution, will, resolve, determine, purpose 617 *intend*; decide, fix, seal, conclude, finish with 69 *terminate*; take on oneself, accept responsibility 595 *will*; know one's own mind, insist, press, urge, not take no for an answer 532 *emphasize*; cut through, override, put one's foot down, stand no nonsense; mean business, stick at nothing, not stop at trifles, go to all lengths, push to extremes; go the whole hog, see it through 725 *carry through*; face, face the odds 661 *face danger*; outface, dare 711 *defy*; endure, go through fire and water 825 *suffer*; face the issue, bring to a head, take the bull by the horns; take the plunge, cross the Rubicon, burn one's boats, burn one's bridges, throw away the scabbard, nail one's colours to the mast; be single-minded, set one's heart on, take up, go in for, take up in earnest, devote *or* dedicate oneself, commit oneself, give oneself to, give up everything for; set to, buckle to, go to it, put one's shoulder to the wheel, put one's heart into, grapple, strain 682 *exert oneself.*

stand firm, not be moved, dig in, dig one's toes *or* heels in, stand one's ground, stay put; not budge, not yield, not compromise, not give an inch; never despair, stand fast, hold f., stick f., hold out 600 *persevere*; bear the brunt, have what it takes, fight on, soldier on, stick it out, grin and bear it, endure 825 *suffer*; die hard, die game, die fighting, die with one's boots on; go down with colours flying.

Adv. *resolutely*, seriously, earnestly, in good earnest; at any price, at all costs; in spite of everything, quand même; manfully, like a man; come what may, come hell or high water 600 *persistently*; live or die, neck or nothing, once and for all.

Int. Here goes! Alea jacta est!

See: 69, 153, 174, 326, 455, 532, 595, 597, **600**, 602, 608, 617, 661, 678, 682, 711, 712, 725, 727, 740, 825, **855**, 906, 942.

600 Perseverance

N. *perseverance*, persistence, tenacity, pertinacity, pertinaciousness, stubbornness 602 *obstinacy*; staunchness, constancy, steadfastness 599 *resolution*; single-mindedness, singleness of purpose, concentration 455 *attention*; sedulousness, application, tirelessness, indefatigability, assiduousness, industriousness 678 *assiduity*; doggedness, plodding, hard work 682 *exertion*; endurance, patience, fortitude 825 *suffering*; maintenance 146 *continuance*; ceaselessness 144 *permanence*; iteration, repeated efforts, unflagging e. 106 *repetition*.

stamina, staying power, indefatigability 162 *strength*; grit, true g., backbone, gameness, pluck; bulldog courage 855 *courage*; hard core, diehard, last ditcher, old guard 602 *obstinate person*; trier, stayer, willing worker 686 *worker*.

Adj. *persevering*, persistent, tenacious, stubborn 602 *obstinate*; game, plucky; patient, plodding, dogged, trying hard 678 *industrious*; strenuous 682 *laborious*; steady, unfaltering, unwavering, undrooping, enduring, unflagging, unwearied, untiring, indefatigable; unsleeping, sleepless 457 *vigilant*; unfailing, unremitting, unintermittent, constant 146 *unceasing*; renewed, iterated, reiterated 106 *repeated*; indomitable, unconquerable, unconquered 727 *unbeaten*; undaunted, undiscouraged, game to the last, true to the end 599 *resolute*.

Vb. *persevere*, persist, keep at it, not take no for an answer, hold out for; not despair, never d., never say die, hope on 852 *hope*; endure, have what it takes, come up for more 825 *suffer*; try, keep on trying, try and try again 671 *attempt*; maintain, keep up, follow up 146 *sustain*; plod, slog, slog away, peg a., plug a., hammer a. at, work at 682 *work*; continue, go on, keep on, keep the pot boiling, keep the ball rolling, rally, keep going; not let go, cling, hold fast, maintain one's grip, hang on like grim death 778 *retain*; hang on, stick it out, sweat it out, stay the course, stick with it, see it through, stay till the end; be in at the death, see one buried first, survive 41 *be left*; maintain one's ground, not budge, not stir 602 *be obstinate*; stick to one's guns, hold out, hold out to the last, die in the last ditch, die at one's post 599 *stand firm*; work till one drops, die in harness; labour unceasingly, spare no pains, move heaven and earth 682 *exert oneself*; bring to conclusion, see the end of, complete 725 *carry through*.

Adv. *persistently*, perseveringly, never say die; through thick and thin, through fire and water, sink or swim 599 *resolutely*; repeatedly, unendingly, ceaselessly; to the bitter end.

See: 41, 106, 144, 146, 162, 455, 457, **599**, **602**, 671, 678, 682, 686, 725, 727, 778, 825, 852, 855.

601 Irresolution

N. *irresolution*, infirmity of purpose, faint-heartedness, loss of nerve, no grit 856 *cowardice*; nonperseverance, broken resolve, broken promise 603 *tergiversation*; unsettlement, indecision, uncertainty, floating vote 474 *dubiety*; hesitation, overcaution 858 *caution*; inconstancy, fluctuation, vacillation, blowing hot and cold 152 *changeableness*; levity, fickleness, whimsicality, irresponsibility 604 *caprice*; lack of willpower, lack of drive 175 *inertness*; passivity 679 *inactivity*; good nature, easygoingness, compromise 734 *laxity*; lack of thoroughness, half-heartedness, half measures 726 *non-completion*; lukewarmness, listlessness, apathy 860 *indifference*; no will of one's own, weak will 163 *weakness*; impressibility, suggestibility 612 *persuadability*; pliancy, overpliancy 327 *softness*; obsequiousness 879 *servility*; submissiveness, slavishness 721 *submission*.

waverer, wobbler, dodderer, shilly-shallyer; shuttlecock, butterfly, feather 152 *changeable thing*; floating voter; weathercock, chameleon, turncoat 603 *tergiversator*; faintheart, compromiser.

Adj. *irresolute*, undecided, indecisive, of two minds, vacillating; unable to make up one's mind, undetermined, unresolved, uncertain 474 *doubting*; squeamish, boggling, hesitating 598 *unwilling*; gutless, timid, tremulous, faint-hearted, unheroic, faint, nerveless 856 *cowardly*; shaken, rattled 854 *nervous*; half-hearted, lukewarm 860 *indifferent*; wobbling, unstaunch, unsteadfast, infirm, infirm of purpose 474 *unreliable*; characterless, featureless 175 *inert*; compromising, weak-willed, weak-minded, weak-kneed, spineless 163 *weak*; suggestible, flexible, pliant 327 *soft*; easygoing, good-natured 734 *lax*;

inconstant, variable, temperamental 152 *changeful*; whimsical, mercurial, not to be pinned down 604 *capricious*; emotional, restless, unsteady, without ballast 152 *unstable*; uncommitted, irresponsible, giddy, feather-brained, light 456 *light-minded*; fidgety, impatient, unpersevering; unthorough, superficial 456 *inattentive*; unfaithful 603 *tergiversating*.

Vb. *be irresolute*, - undecided etc. adj.; back away, blink, jib, shy, shirk 620 *avoid*; palter, shuffle, shilly-shally 518 *be equivocal*; fluctuate, vacillate, seesaw, wobble, waver, sway, hover, teeter, dither 317 *oscillate*; not know one's own mind, blow hot and cold, back and fill, hum and haw, will and will not, be in two minds, go round in circles, not know what to do, be at one's wits' end 474 *be uncertain*; leave in suspense, keep undecided, delay, put off a decision 136 *put off*; dally, dilly-dally 136 *wait*; debate, balance 475 *argue*; have second thoughts, hesitate 858 *be cautious*; falter, grow weary 684 *be fatigued*; not persevere, give up 621 *relinquish*; make a compromise, take half measures 770 *compromise*; yield, give way 721 *submit*; change sides, go over 603 *apostatize*.

Adv. *irresolutely*, faint-heartedly, hesitantly; from pillar to post; seesaw; between the devil and the deep blue sea.

See: 136, 152, 163, 175, 317, 327, 456, **474**, 475, 518, 598, 603, **604**, 612, 620, 621, 679, 684, 721, 726, 734, 770, 854, **856**, 858, 860, 879.

602 Obstinacy

N. *obstinacy*, mind of one's own; determination, will 599 *resolution*; grimness, doggedness, tenacity, pertinacity 600 *perseverance*; stubbornness, obduracy, obdurateness; self-will, pigheadedness; inelasticity, inflexibility, woodenness, toughness 326 *hardness*; intransigence, hard line, no compromise; constancy, irreversibility, fixity 153 *stability*; stiff neck, contumacy 715 *resistance*; incorrigibility 940 *impenitence*; indocility, intractability, mulishness, dourness, sulkiness 893 *sullenness*; perversity, wrongheadedness, cussedness, bloody-mindedness.

opinionatedness, self-opinion, opiniativeness 473 *positiveness*; dogmatism, bigotry, zealotry; rigorism, intolerance, fanaticism 735 *severity*; ruling passion, obsession, idée fixe 481 *bias*; blind side 439 *blindness*; illiberality, obscurantism 491 *ignorance*; old school, ancien régime.

obstinate person, stubborn fellow, mule; stick-in-the-mud, Blimp; hard-liner, hard core; fanatic, rigorist, stickler, pedant, dogmatist, zealot, bigot, persecutor 481 *narrow mind*; sticker, stayer; last-ditcher, die-hard, bitter-ender 600 *stamina*; old fogy 504 *crank*.

Adj. *obstinate*, stubborn; bull-headed, pigheaded, mulish, stubborn as a mule; pertinacious, unyielding, firm, determined 599 *resolute*; dogged, tenacious 600 *persevering*; stiff, inelastic, wooden 326 *rigid*; adamant, inflexible, unbending; obdurate, hard-nosed, hardened, case-h.; uncompromising, intransigent; unmoved, uninfluenced, immovable 153 *unchangeable*; inexorable, unappeasable, implacable, merciless 906 *pitiless*; set, wedded to, set in one's ways, hidebound, ultraconservative, blimpish 610 *habituated*; unteachable, obscurantist, impervious, blind, deaf; opinionated, dogmatic, pedantic 473 *positive*; obsessed, bigoted, fanatical 481 *biased*; dour, grim 893 *sullen*; indocile, hard-mouthed, stiff-necked, contumacious 940 *impenitent* (**see** *wilful*); perverse, incorrigible, bloody-minded, plain cussed; possessive, dog-in-the-manger; irremovable, irreversible; persistent, incurable, chronic 113 *lasting*.

wilful, self-willed, froward, wayward, arbitrary; entêté, headstrong, perverse; unruly, jibbing, restive, refractory; irrepressible, ungovernable, unmanageable, intractable, uncontrollable 738 *disobedient*; unpersuadable, incorrigible, contumacious; cross-grained, crotchety 892 *irascible*.

Vb. *be obstinate*, - stubborn etc. adj.; persist 600 *persevere*; brazen it out 940 *be impenitent*; stick to one's guns, stand out, not budge, stay put 599 *stand firm*; insist, brook no denial, not take no for an answer; go one's own way, want one's own w., must have one's w. 734 *please oneself*; be wedded to one's own opinions, not change one's mind 473 *dogmatize*; stay in a rut, cling to custom 610 *be wont*; not listen, stop up one's ears, take no advice, take the bit between one's teeth, damn the consequences 857 *be rash*; not yield to treatment, become chronic 113 *last*.

Adv. *obstinately*, pigheadedly, mulishly,

like a mule; over one's dead body.

See: 113, 153, 326, 439, 473, **481**, 491, 504, **599**, **600**, 610, 715, 734, 735, 738, 857, 892, 893, 906, 940.

603 Tergiversation: Change of allegiance

N. *tergiversation*, change of mind, better thoughts; afterthought, second thoughts 67 *sequel*; change of allegiance, conversion; change of purpose, alteration of plan, new resolve; good resolution, break with the past, repentance 939 *penitence*; revulsion 280 *recoil*; backsliding, recidivism 657 *relapse*; change of direction 282 *deviation*; reversal, about-face, about-turn, U-turn, volte-face, looking back 286 *return*; versatility, slipperiness, suppleness, unreliability, untrustworthiness 930 *improbity*; apostasy, recreancy (**see** *recantation*); defection, desertion 918 *undutifulness*; ratting, going over, treachery 930 *perfidy*; secession, withdrawal 978 *schism*; abandonment 621 *relinquishment*; change of mood, temperament; coquetry 604 *caprice*.

recantation, palinode, eating one's words, retractation, retraction, withdrawal, apology; renunciation, abjuration, forswearing, swearing off 532 *oath*; disavowal, disclaimer, denial 533 *negation*; revocation, revoking, recall 752 *abrogation*.

tergiversator, turncoat, rat; weathercock 152 *changeable thing*; opportunist, timeserver, trimmer, Vicar of Bray 518 *equivocalness*; double-dealer, Janus, two-faced person 545 *deceiver*; jilt, flirt, coquette 604 *caprice*; recanter, recreant, apostate, renegade, forswearer; traitor, betrayer 938 *knave*; quisling, fifth columnist, collaborationist 707 *collaborator*; lost leader, deserter, defector, quitter, ratter; tell-tale, squealer 524 *informer*; strike-breaker, blackleg, scab; deviationist, secessionist, seceder 978 *schismatic*; runaway, bolter, flincher 620 *avoider*; recidivist, backslider 904 *offender*; convert, proselyte 147 *changed person*.

Adj. *tergiversating*, trimming etc. vb.; shuffling 518 *equivocal*; slippery, supple, versatile, treacherous 930 *perfidious*; double-dealing 541 *hypocritical*; reactionary, going back 286 *regressive*; fickle 604 *capricious*; timeserving 925 *flattering*; vacillating 601 *irresolute*; apostate, recanting, renegade; recidivist, relapsed; false, unfaithful, disloyal 918 *undutiful*.

Vb. *tergiversate*, change one's mind, think again, think better of it 601 *be irresolute*; change one's tune, shift one's ground 152 *vary*; get cold feet, back out, scratch, withdraw 753 *resign*; back down, crawl 872 *be humbled*; apologize (**see** *recant*); change front, change round, swerve, tack, wheel about 282 *turn round*; turn one's back on 286 *turn back*; turn over a new leaf, make good resolutions, repent 939 *be penitent*; reform, mend one's ways 654 *get better*; fall back, backslide 657 *relapse*; trim, shuffle, face both ways, run with the hare and hunt with the hounds 518 *be equivocal*; ditch, jilt, throw over, desert, walk out on 918 *fail in duty*; forsake, abandon, wash one's hands of 621 *relinquish*; turn against, play false.

apostatize, turn one's coat, change sides, let the side down, change one's allegiance; switch, switch over, join the opposition, cross over, cross the floor; desert, defect, fall away; blackleg, rat; betray, collaborate 930 *be dishonest*; be off with the old love, jump on the band wagon, follow the rising star.

recant, unsay, eat one's words, eat one's hat; eat humble pie, apologize; take back, go back on, backpedal, backtrack, do a U-turn; recall one's words, resile, withdraw 769 *not observe*; retract, disavow, disclaim, repudiate, deny 533 *negate*; renounce, abjure, forswear, swear off; recall, revoke, rescind 752 *abrogate*.

See: 67, 147, 152, 280, 282, 286, 518, 524, 532, 533, 541, 545, **601**, **604**, 620, 621, 654, 657, 707, 752, 753, 769, 872, 904, 918, 925, 930, 938, 939, 978.

604 Caprice

N. *caprice*, capriciousness, arbitrariness, motivelessness, purposelessness; whimsicality, freakishness, crankiness 497 *absurdity*; faddishness, faddism 481 *bias*; inconsistency 25 *disagreement*; fitfulness, changeability, variability, fickleness, unreliability, levity, giddiness, lightmindedness, irresponsibility 152 *changeableness*; inconstancy, coquettishness, flirtatiousness; playfulness; fretfulness, pettishness 892 *irascibility*.

whim, whimsy, caprice, fancy, megrim, fantastic notion, weird idea 513 *ideality*; passing fancy, impulse 609 *spontaneity*; vagary, sweet will, humour, mood, fit, crotchet, bee in the bonnet, maggot, quirk, kink, fad, craze, freak 503 *eccentricity*; escapade, prank, boutade, wild-goose chase 497 *foolery*; coquetry, flirtation.

Adj. *capricious*, motiveless, purposeless; whimsical, fanciful, fantastic; eccentric, humoursome, temperamental, crotchety, maggoty, freakish, fitful; hysterical, mad 503 *crazy*; prankish, mischievous, wanton, wayward, perverse; faddy, faddish, particular 862 *fastidious*; captious, arbitrary, unreasonable; fretful, moody, contrary 892 *irascible*; undisciplined, refractory 602 *wilful*; erratic, uncertain, unpredictable 508 *unexpected*; volatile, mercurial, skittish, giddy, frivolous 456 *light-minded*; inconsistent, inconstant, variable 152 *unstable*; irresponsible, unreliable, fickle, feckless 603 *tergiversating*; flirtatious, coquettish, playful.

Vb. *be capricious*, - whimsical etc. adj.; submit to a whim, take it into one's head; pick and choose 862 *be fastidious*; chop and change, blow hot and cold 152 *vary*; have a bee in one's bonnet 481 *be biased*; be fickle, take up a thing and drop it; vacillate 601 *be irresolute*; play pranks, play tricks 497 *be absurd*; flirt, coquette 837 *amuse oneself*.

Adv. *capriciously*, fitfully, by fits and starts, now this, now that; as the mood takes one, at one's own sweet will; on impulse.

See: 25, **152**, 456, 481, 497, 503, 508, 513, 601, 602, 603, 609, 837, 862, 892.

605 Choice

N. *choice*, act of choosing, election 463 *discrimination*; picking and choosing, eclecticism 862 *fastidiousness*; picking out, selection; co-option, co-optation, adoption; designation, nomination, appointment 751 *commission*; right of choice, option; freedom of choice, discretion, pick; deliberate choice, decision 480 *judgment*; preference, predilection, partiality, inclination, leaning, bias 179 *tendency*; taste 859 *liking*; availability 759 *offer*; range of choice, selection, list, short l.; possible choice, alternative, embarras de choix; difficult choice, dilemma 474 *dubiety*; limited choice, no real alternative; only choice, Hobson's choice, nothing for it but 606 *no choice*; blind choice 464 *indiscrimination*; better choice, preferability, desirability, greater good, lesser evil 642 *good policy*; one's preference, favour, fancy, first choice, top seed; thing chosen, selection, pickings, gleanings, excerpts; literary selection 592 *anthology*; unlucky choice, bad bargain; unfair choice, favouritism 914 *injustice*.

vote, voice 485 *opinion*; representation, proportional r., cumulative vote, transferable v., majority v., first past the post; casting v.; ballot, secret b., open vote, postal v.; card vote; vote of confidence; vote-counting, show of hands, division, poll, plebiscite, referendum; suffrage, universal s., adult s., manhood s.; franchise, right of representation, votes for women, women's suffrage, suffragettism; parliamentary system, electoral s., ballot box, vox populi; polling, countng heads, counting noses; straw vote, Gallup poll (tdmk), opinion p.; election, general e.; by-election; indirect election, primary e., primary; polls, voting, electioneering, canvassing, hustings, candidature; successful election, return; psephology, psephologist; suffragette, suffragist.

electorate, voters, balloter, elector, electoral college; quorum; electoral roll, voting list; constituent, constituency, marginal c.; borough, pocket b., rotten b.; polling booth, ballot box, voting paper; slate, ticket, manifesto.

Adj. *choosing*, optional, discretional 595 *volitional*; exercising choice, choosy 463 *discriminating*; showing preference, preferential, favouring 923 *approving*; selective, eclectic; co-optative, elective, electoral; voting, enfranchised; vote-catching, electioneering, canvassing; psephological.

chosen, well-c.; worth choosing, not to be sniffed at; preferable, better 642 *advisable*; select, choice, recherché, picked, hand-p. 644 *excellent*; sorted, assorted, seeded 62 *arranged*; elect, designate; elected, returned; adopted, selected; on approval; preferred, special, favourite, fancy, pet; God's own; by appointment.

Vb. *choose*, have a voice, have free will 595 *will*; eliminate the alternatives, make one's choice, make one's bed; shop around, be choosy; exercise one's discretion, accept, opt, opt for, take up an option; elect, co-opt, adopt, put on the list 923 *approve*; would like, favour, fancy, like best; incline, lean, have a bias 179 *tend*; prefer, have a preference, like better, would rather; might as well, might do worse; go in for, take up, be into; think fit, think it best to, decide, make up one's mind 480 *judge*; settle on, fix on, come out for, come down f., plump f., come down on one side, commit oneself; take the plunge, cross the Rubicon, burn one's boats 599 *be resolute*; range oneself, take sides, side, back, support, embrace, espouse, cast in one's lot with 703 *patronize*; take for better or worse 894 *wed*.

select, pick, pick out, single o.; pass 923 *approve*; nominate, appoint 751 *commission*; designate, mark out, mark down 547 *mark*; preselect, earmark, reserve 46 *set apart*; recommend, put up, propose, second 703 *patronize*; excerpt, cull, anthologize 592 *abstract*; glean, winnow, sift 463 *discriminate*; draw the line, separate; skim, skim off, cream, pick the best; indulge one's fancy, pick and choose 862 *be fastidious*.

vote, have a v., have a voice; have the vote, be enfranchised, be on the electoral roll; poll, go to the polls; cast a vote, register one's v., raise one's hand, divide; vote for, vote in, elect, return; vote down 607 *reject*; electioneer, canvass; accept a candidature, stand 759 *offer oneself*; put to the vote, present the alternatives, take a poll, hold a referendum; count heads, count noses; hold an election, go to the country, appeal to the electorate.

Adv. *optionally*, at pleasure; by ballot; alternatively, either . . . or; preferably, rather, sooner; by choice, à la carte.

See: 46, 62, 179, **463**, 464, 474, 480, 485, 547, 592, **595**, 599, 606, 607, 642, 644, 703, 751, 759, 859, 862, 894, 914, 923.

606 Absence of Choice

N. *no choice*, Hobson's c., no alternative 596 *necessity*; dictation 740 *compulsion*; any, the first that comes 464 *indiscrimination*; no favouritism, impartiality, first come first served 913 *justice*; no preference, noncommitment, nonalignment, neutrality, apathy 860 *indifference*; moral apathy, amoralism, amorality; no difference, six of one and half a dozen of the other, 'a plague on both your houses' 28 *equality*; indecision, open mind, openmindedness 474 *dubiety*; floating vote 601 *irresolution*; refusal to vote, abstention 598 *unwillingness*; no election, spoilt ballot paper; disfranchisement, disqualification, no vote, no voice.

Adj. *choiceless*, without alternative, necessitated 596 *necessary*; without a preference, unable to choose, happy either way 625 *neutral*; open-minded, open to conviction, unresolved, undecided, undetermined 601 *irresolute*; uninterested, apathetic 860 *indifferent*; morally neutral, amoral; disinterested, motiveless; without favouritism, impartial 913 *just*; not voting, abstaining 598 *unwilling*; nonvoting, without a vote, voteless, unenfranchised, disfranchised, disqualified; nothing to offer, featureless, characterless 860 *unwanted*.

Vb. *be neutral*, take no sides, make no choice, not vote, refuse to v., withhold one's v., abstain; waive, waive one's choice, stand aside 621 *relinquish*; stand between 625 *be halfway*; sit on the fence 601 *be irresolute*; not care 860 *be indifferent*.

have no choice, have no alternative, have Hobson's choice, take it or leave it, make a virtue of necessity 596 *be forced*; have no voice, have no vote.

Adv. *neither*, neither . . . nor.

See: 28, **464**, 474, **596**, 598, 601, 621, 625, 740, 860, 913.

607 Rejection

N. *rejection*, nonacceptance; nonapproval, disapproval 924 *disapprobation*; repudiation, denial 533 *negation*; apostasy 603 *recantation*; rebuff, repulse, frozen mitt, cold shoulder 760 *refusal*; spurn, kick, more kicks than ha'pence; rejection at the polls, electoral defeat, lost election, nonelection, forfeiture of deposit 728 *defeat*; elimination 300 *ejection*; nonconsideration, counting out, exception, exemption 57 *exclusion*; disuse, discarding, disemployment 674 *nonuse*; discard, reject, wallflower; unpopular cause, lost c.

Adj. *rejected*, thrown out etc. vb.; unsuitable, ineligible, unchosen 860 *unwanted*; unaccepted, returned, sent back, tried and found wanting, declined with thanks 924 *disapproved*; kept out, excluded, cast out 57 *excluded*; unfit for consideration, not be thought of, out of the question 643 *inexpedient*; discarded 674 *disused*.

Vb. *reject*, not accept, decline, say no to, draw the line at, rebuff, repulse, spurn, dismiss out of hand 760 *refuse*; not approve, not pass, return, send back, return with thanks 924 *disapprove*; not consider, pass over, ignore 458 *disregard*; vote against, not vote for, not choose, outvote 489 *dissent*; scrap, discard, ditch, junk, throw away, throw aside, lay a., give up 674 *stop using*; disallow, revoke 752 *abrogate*; set aside, supersede 752 *depose*; expel, cast out, throw o., chuck o., sling o., kick o., fling o. 300 *eject*; sort out 44 *eliminate*; except, count out, exempt 57 *exclude*; blackball, cold-shoulder, turn one's back on, give the brush-off 885 *be rude*; not want, not cater for 883 *make unwelcome*; disclaim, disavow, deny 533 *negate*; abnegate, repudiate, apostatize 603 *recant*; scout, scorn, disdain, laugh at, mock, deride 851 *ridicule*; sniff at, look a gift horse in the mouth 922 *hold cheap*.

See: 44, 57, **300**, 458, 489, 533, 603, 643, 674, 728, 752, 760, 851, 860, 883, 885, 922, **924**.

608 Predetermination

N. *predetermination*, predestination 596 *necessity*; foreordination, preordination 155 *destiny*; decree 595 *will*; premeditation, resolve, project 617 *intention*; prearrangement 669 *preparation*; order of the day, order paper, agenda 622 *business*; frame-up, put-up job, packed jury 623 *plot*; parti pris, closed mind 481 *prejudice*; foregone conclusion, agreed result.

Adj. *predetermined*, decreed, premeditated etc. vb.; appointed, predestined, foreordained 596 *fated*; deliberate, willed, aforethought, prepense 617 *intending*; with a motive, designed, studied, calculated, measured; weighed, considered, advised; devised, controlled, contrived 623 *planned*; put-up, framed, stacked, packed, prearranged 669 *prepared*.

Vb. *predetermine*, destine, appoint, foreordain, predestinate 155 *predestine*; premeditate, preconceive, resolve beforehand 617 *intend*; agree beforehand, preconcert; settle, fix; contrive a result 156 *cause*; contrive, arrange, prearrange 623 *plan*; frame, put up, pack a jury, stack the cards 541 *fake*.

See: 155, 156, 481, 541, 595, 596, **617**, 622, **623**, 669.

609 Spontaneity

N. *spontaneity*, unpremeditation; ad hoc measures, improvisation; extemporization, ad-libbing, impromptu 670 *non-preparation*; involuntariness, reflex, automatic r.; impulsiveness, impulse, blind i. 476 *intuition*; inconsideration, spur of the moment; snap decision; spurt, burst of confidence 526 *disclosure*; inspiration, sudden thought, hunch, flash 451 *idea*.

improviser, extemporizer, improvisatore, improvisatrice; creature of impulse.

Adj. *spontaneous*, offhand, ad hoc, improvised, extemporaneous, extemporary, sudden, snap; makeshift, catch-as-catch-can 670 *unprepared*; impromptu, unpremeditated, uncalculated, unmeditated, unrehearsed 618 *unintentional*; unprompted, unmotivated, unprovoked; unforced 597 *voluntary*; unguarded, incautious 857 *rash*; natural, instinctive, involuntary, automatic, knee-jerk 476 *intuitive*; untaught 699 *artless*; impulsive, emotional 818 *feeling*.

Vb. *improvise*, not prepare, extemporize, vamp, ad-lib 670 *be unprepared*; obey an impulse, act on the spur of the moment 604 *be capricious*; blurt, come out with, say whatever comes into one's head, flash out with; rise to the occasion.

Adv. *extempore*, extemporaneously, impromptu, ad hoc, on the spur of the moment, offhand, off the cuff, off the top of one's head.

See: 451, **476**, 526, 597, 604, 618, 670, 699, 818, 857.

610 Habit

N. *habit*, disposition, habit of mind 5 *temperament*; habitude, assuetude, force of habit; familiarity, second nature; study, occupation; addiction, confirmed habit, daily h., constitutional; trait, idiosyncrasy; knack, trick, mannerism; instinct, leaning 179 *tendency*; bad habit, cacoethes; usage, standard u., long habit, consuetude, custom, standing c., old c.; use, wont 146 *continuance*; inveteracy, prescription 113 *long duration*; tradition, law, precedent; way, ways, the old w.; lifestyle, way of life; beaten track, tramlines, groove, rut; fixed ways, round, daily r., daily grind, métro, boulot, dodo 16 *uniformity*; regularity 141 *periodicity*; run, routine, drill, system 60 *order*; red tape, beadledom, conventionalism, traditionalism, conservatism, old school 83 *conformity*.

practice, common p., usual custom, usual policy, matter of course; conformism, conventionalism, conventionality 83 *conformity*; mores, manners and customs, social usage, behaviour patterns; institution, ritual, observance 988 *rite*; religious observance, cultus 981 *cult*; mode, vogue, craze, order of the day 848 *fashion*; convention, protocol, unwritten law, done thing, the usual thing; recognized procedure, drill; form, good f. 848 *etiquette*; manners, table m., eating habits; rules and regulations, standing order, rules of business, routine 688 *conduct*; spit and polish 60 *order*.

habituation, training 534 *teaching*; inurement, seasoning, hardening 669 *maturation*; naturalization, acclimatization; acquired taste; conditioning, association, reflex, conditioned r., fixation, complex; drill, repetitive job 106 *repetition*.

habitué, creature of habit, addict, drug a., dope fiend 949 *drug-taking*; traditionalist, conventionalist 83 *conformist*; customer, regular, client 792 *purchaser*; frequenter, devotee, fan 504 *enthusiast*.

Adj. *habitual*, customary, familiar 490 *known*; routine, stereotyped 81 *regular*; conventional, traditionary, traditional 976 *orthodox*; inveterate, prescriptive, time-honoured, permanent 113 *lasting*; resulting from habit, occupational; haunting, besetting, clinging, obsessive; habit-forming 612 *inducing*; ingrained, dyed-in-the-wool 5 *intrinsic*; rooted, deep-r., deep-seated, implanted 153 *fixed*; imbued, dyed, soaked, permeated. **See** *usual*.

usual, accustomed, wonted, consuetudinary, traditional; in character, natural; household, familiar, well-known 490 *known*; unoriginal, trite, trodden, beaten, well-worn, hackneyed; banal, commonplace, common, ordinary 79 *general*; set, stock 83 *typical*; prevalent, widespread, obtaining, current 79 *universal*; monthly, daily, everyday, of everyday occurrence 139 *frequent*; practised, done; admitted, acknowledged, received, accepted, accredited, recognized, understood; right, settled, established, professional, official, hallowed by custom 923 *approved*; de rigueur 740 *compelling*; invariable 153 *unchangeable*; in the fashion, in vogue 848 *fashionable*.

habituated, in the habit of, accustomed to, known to; given to, addicted to; dedicated, devoted to, wedded to; used to, familiar with, conversant w., at home in 490 *knowing*; inveterate, confirmed; practised, inured, seasoned, hardened 669 *prepared*; broken in, trained, tame 369 *tamed*; naturalized, acclimatized.

Vb. *be wont*, love to, be known to, be used to, use to; have the habit of, be a creature of habit; go daily, haunt, frequent; make a habit of, take up, go in for; never vary, be set in one's ways, observe routine, move in a rut, stick in a groove, tread the beaten track, go on in the same old way, cling to custom; become a habit, catch on, grow on one, take hold of o., stick; settle, take root; be the rule, obtain, hold good 178 *prevail*; come into use, acquire the force of custom.

habituate, accustom oneself, get used to, get into the way of, get the knack of, get the feel of, get the hang of, play oneself in, get into one's stride; take to, acquire the habit, learn a h., cultivate a h.; fall into a habit; get into a habit, catch oneself doing; keep one's hand in, practise 106 *repeat*; accustom, inure, season, harden, case-harden 534 *train*; domesticate, tame 369 *break in*; radicate, naturalize, acclimatize; implant, ingraft, imbue 534 *teach*; condition, brainwash 178 *influence*.

Adv. *habitually*, regularly, with regularity 141 *periodically*; customarily, wontedly, occupationally, in the habit of; of course, as usual, as is one's wont; mechanically, automatically, by force of habit; in one's stride.

See: 5, 16, 60, 79, 81, **83**, 106, 113, 139, 141, 146, 153, 178, **179**, 369, 490, 504, 534, 612, 669, 688, 740, 792, 848, 923, 949, 976, 981, 988.

611 Desuetude

N. *desuetude*, disusage, discontinuance, disuse 674 *nonuse*; rust, decay 655 *deterioration*; lost habit, lost skill, rustiness, lack of practice 695 *unskilfulness*; discarded custom, forgotten c. 506 *oblivion*, 550 *obliteration*; outgrown custom, outgrowing, weaning 134 *adultness*; new custom 21 *originality*; unwontedness, no such custom, nonprevalence; not the form, not the thing, not protocol, not etiquette, unconventionality 84 *nonconformity*; want of habit, inexperience, unfamiliarity 491 *ignorance*.

Adj. *unwonted*, not customary, not current, nonprevalent; unpractised, not observed, not done; unnecessary, not de rigueur;

unfashionable, bad form, non-U 847 *vulgar*; out of fashion, old-fashioned, defunct 125 *past*; outgrown, discarded 674 *disused*; against custom, unconventional 84 *unconformable*; unsanctified by custom, untraditional, unprecedented, unhackneyed 21 *original*.

unhabituated, unaccustomed, not used to, not in the habit of 769 *nonobservant*; untrained, unbroken, not broken in, untamed, undomesticated; unseasoned, unripe 670 *immature*; unfamiliar, inexperienced, new to, new, raw, fresh, green 491 *uninstructed*; disaccustomed, weaned; dried out; out of the habit, rusty 695 *unskilful*.

Vb. *disaccustom*, wean from, cure of 656 *cure*; disaccustom oneself, break a habit, drop a h., lose a h., kick the h.; wean oneself from, outgrow; give up, throw off, slough, slough off, shed.

be unpractised, - unfashionable etc. adj.; not catch on; try a thing once, not do it again; not be done, offend custom, infringe protocol; lapse, fall into disuse, wear off 127 *be old*; rust 655 *deteriorate*.

See: 21, 84, 125, 127, 134, 491, 506, 550, 655, 656, 670, **674**, 695, 769, 847.

612 Motive

N. *motive*, cause of action, what is behind it 156 *cause*; rationale, reasons, grounds 156 *reason why*; motivation, driving force, impetus, spring, mainspring, what makes one tick 156 *causation*; intention 617 *objective*; ideal, principle, guiding p., guiding star, lodestar, direction 689 *directorship*; aspiration 852 *hope*; ambition 859 *desire*; calling, call 622 *vocation*; conscience, dictate of c., honour 917 *duty*; shame 854 *fear*; personal reasons, ulterior motive 932 *selfishness*; impulse, spur of the moment, inspiration 609 *spontaneity*.

inducement, pressure, instancy, urgency, press, insistence; lobbying 178 *influence*; indirect influence, side pressure; provocation, urging, incitement, encouragement, incitation, instigation, prompting, inspiration 821 *excitation*; support, abetment 703 *aid*; solicitation, invitation 761 *request*; temptation, enticement, allurement, seduction, seductiveness, tantalization, witchery, bewitchment, fascination, charm, sex appeal, attractiveness, magnetism 291 *attraction*; cajolery, blandishment 925 *flattery*; coaxing, teasing, wheedling 889 *endearment*; persuasion, persuasiveness, salesmanship, sales talk 579 *eloquence*; pep talk, trumpet call, rallying cry 547 *call*; exhortation 534 *lecture*; pleading, advocacy 691 *advice*; propaganda, agitprop; advertising, soft sell, hard s. 528 *advertisement*; promises, election p.; bribery, b. and corruption, graft, palm-greasing 962 *reward*; castigation, tongue-lashing; honeyed words, siren song, voice of the tempter, winning ways.

persuadability, docility, tractability, teachableness 597 *willingness*; pliancy, pliability 327 *softness*; susceptibility, susceptivity, suggestibility, impressibility, sensitivity, emotionalism 819 *moral sensibility*; credulousness 487 *credulity*.

incentive, inducement; stimulus, fillip, tickle, prod, spur, goad, lash, whip; rod, big stick, crack of the whip 900 *threat*; energizer, tonic, provocative, carrot, sop, sop to Cerberus 174 *stimulant*; charm 983 *spell*; attraction, lodestone 291 *magnet*; will-o'-the-wisp 440 *visual fallacy*; lure, decoy, decoy duck, bait 542 *trap*; come-on, loss leader, special offer; profit 771 *gain*; cash, gold 797 *money*; pay, salary, perks, pay increase, rise, raise, bonus 804 *payment*; donation, handout 781 *gift*; gratuity, tip, bribe, hush money, slush fund 962 *reward*; political favours, pork barrel; golden apple, forbidden fruit; tempting offer, offer one cannot refuse 759 *offer*.

motivator, mover, prime m. 156 *cause*; manipulator, manager, wire-puller 178 *influence*; manoeuvrer, tactician, strategist 623 *planner*; instigator, prompter, suggester, hinter; inspirer, muse, counsellor 691 *adviser*; abettor, aider and abettor 703 *aider*; agent provocateur 545 *deceiver*; tantalizer, tempter, seducer; seductress, temptress, vamp, femme fatale, siren; Circe, Lorelei; hypnotizer, hypnotist; persuader, orator, rhetorician 579 *speaker*; advocate, pleader; coaxer, wheedler 925 *flatterer*; vote-catcher, vote-snatcher; salesman, advertiser, propagandist 528 *publicizer*; ringleader 690 *leader*; firebrand, rabble-rouser 738 *agitator*; lobbyist, lobby, pressure group, ginger g.

Adj. *inducing*, inciting; incentive, provocative, persuasive; hortatory, protreptic, directive; motivating, wire-pulling, lobbying 178 *influential*; energizing, stimulating, tonic, challenging, encouraging, rousing, inflaming 821 *exciting*; prompting, insinuating, hinting; teasing, tantalizing; inviting, tempting, alluring, attractive 291 *attracting*; magnetic, fascinating, bewitching 983 *sorcerous*; irresistible, hypnotic, mesmeric; habit-forming 610 *habitual*.

induced, brought on 157 *caused*; inspired, motivated, goal-oriented; incited, egged on, spurred on 821 *excited*; receptive, tractable, docile 597 *willing*; spellbound 983 *bewitched*; persuasible 487 *credulous*.

Vb. *motivate*, motive, move, actuate, manipulate 173 *operate*; work upon, play u., act u., operate u. 178 *influence*; weigh, count, be a consideration, sway 178 *prevail*; call the tune, override 34 *predominate*; work on the feelings, appeal, challenge, shame into (**see** *incite*); infect, inject with, infuse into 534 *educate*; interest, intrigue 821 *impress*; charm, fascinate, captivate, hypnotize, spellbind 983 *bewitch*; pull 291 *attract*; push 279 *impel*; force, enforce, pressurize 740 *compel*; bend, incline, dispose; predispose, prejudice 481 *bias*; predestine 608 *predetermine*; lead, direct 689 *manage*; lead astray 495 *mislead*; give a lead, set the fashion, set an example, set the pace 283 *precede*.

incite, energize, galvanize, stimulate 174 *invigorate*; sound the trumpet, encourage, cheer on, root for 855 *give courage*; inspirit, inspire, animate, provoke, rouse, rally 821 *excite*; evoke, call forth, challenge; exhort, invite, urge, insist, press, exert pressure, bring pressure to bear on, lobby; nag, needle, goad, prod, jog, jolt; spur, prick, tickle; whip, lash, flog; spur on, set on, egg on; drive, hurry, hurry up 680 *hasten*; instigate, prompt, put up to; abet, aid and a. 703 *aid*; insinuate, suggest 524 *hint*; advocate, recommend, counsel 691 *advise*; start, kindle 68 *initiate*.

induce, instigate, bring about 156 *cause*; persuade, carry with one 485 *convince*; carry one's point, prevail upon, talk into, push i., drive i., nag i., bully i., browbeat (**see** *motivate*); twist one's arm 740 *compel*; wear down, soften up; bring round, talk round 147 *convert*; bring to one's side, bring over, win o., procure, enlist, engage; talk over, sweet-talk into, cajole, blandish 925 *flatter*; conciliate, appease 719 *pacify*; entice, seduce (**see** *tempt*).

tempt, try, lead into temptation; entice, dangle before one's eyes, make one's mouth water; tantalize, tease; allure, lure, inveigle 542 *ensnare*; coax, wheedle, pat on the back 889 *pet*; pander to, make things easy for, gild the pill, sugar the p. 701 *facilitate*.

bribe, offer an inducement, hold out a carrot 759 *offer*; suborn, seduce, corrupt; square, buy off; oil, grease the palm, give a sop to Cerberus; tip 962 *reward*.

be induced, yield, succumb 721 *submit*; fall for 487 *be credulous*; concede 758 *consent*; obey one's conscience, act on principle; come *or* fall under the influence; feel the urge, hear the call; be infected, catch the bug, not be immune.

See: 34, 68, 147, **156**, 157, 173, 174, **178**, 279, 283, 291, 327, 440, 481, 485, 487, 495, 524, 528, 534, 542, 545, 547, 579, 597, 608, 609, 610, 617, 622, 623, 680, 689, 690, 691, 701, 703, 719, 721, 738, 740, 758, 759, 761, 771, 781, 797, 804, 819, **821**, 852, 854, 855, 859, 889, 900, 917, 925, 932, 962, 983.

613 Dissuasion

N. *dissuasion*, contrary advice; caution 664 *warning*; discouragement, setback 702 *hindrance*; deterrence 854 *intimidation*; objection, expostulation, remonstrance, reproof, admonition 762 *deprecation*; rebuff 715 *resistance*; no encouragement, disincentive; deterrent 665 *danger signal*; contraindication, countersymptom 14 *contrariety*; cold water, damper, wet blanket; killjoy, spoilsport 702 *hinderer*.

Adj. *dissuasive*, discouraging, chilling, damping; reluctant 598 *unwilling*; expostulatory 762 *deprecatory*; monitory, warning against 664 *cautionary*.

Vb. *dissuade*, persuade against, advise a., argue a., convince to the contrary, talk out of 479 *confute*; caution 664 *warn*; remonstrate, castigate 924 *reprove*; expostulate, cry out against, protest a. 762 *deprecate*; shake, stagger, give one pause 486 *cause doubt*; intimidate 900 *threaten*; terrorize, deter, frighten away, daunt, cow 854 *frighten*; choke off, head off, steer one away from, turn one aside 282 *deflect*; wean away from 611 *disaccustom*; hold one back, keep back, act as a drag 747 *restrain*; render averse, disenchant, disillusion, disincline, indispose, disaffect;

set against, turn a., put off, repel, disgust, fill with distaste 861 *cause dislike*; dishearten, discourage, dispirit 834 *depress*; crush, squelch, throw cold water on, dampen, quench, cool, chill, damp the ardour; take the edge off 257 *blunt*; calm, quiet 177 *moderate*.

See: 14, 177, 257, 282, 479, 486, 598, 611, 664, 665, 702, 715, **747**, 762, 834, 854, 861, 900, 924.

614 Pretext

N. *pretext*, ostensible motive, alleged m.; statement, allegation, profession, claim 532 *affirmation*; plea, excuse, defence, apology, apologia, justification 927 *vindication*; let-out, loophole, alibi 667 *means of escape*; locus standi, leg to stand on, peg to hang something on 218 *prop*; shallow pretext, thin excuse, lame e., equivocation 518 *equivocalness*; special pleading, quibble 477 *sophism*; salvo, proviso 468 *qualification*; subterfuge 698 *stratagem*; false plea, pretence, Bunbury, previous engagement, diplomatic illness 543 *untruth*; blind, dust thrown in the eyes 421 *obfuscation*; stalking horse, smoke screen, cloak, cover 421 *screen*; apology for, simulacrum, makeshift 150 *substitute*; colour, gloss, guise 445 *appearance*; bluff, sour grapes.

Adj. *ostensible*, alleged, pretended; specious, plausible; seeming.

excusing, self-e., exculpatory, apologetic, vindicatory, justificatory 927 *vindicating*.

Vb. *plead*, allege, claim, profess 532 *affirm*; pretext, make one's pretext, make a plea of 475 *argue*; make excuses, offer an excuse, excuse oneself, defend o. 927 *justify*; gloss over, palliate 927 *extenuate*; shelter under, take shelter u., take hold as a handle for, use as a stalking horse; make capital out of, cash in on 137 *profit by*; find a loophole, wriggle out of 667 *escape*; bluff, say the grapes are sour; varnish, colour; blind, throw dust in the eyes 542 *befool*; pretend, affect 541 *dissemble*.

Adv. *ostensibly*, as an excuse, as alleged, as claimed; on the plea of, on the pretext of.

See: 137, 150, 218, 421, 445, 468, 475, 477, 518, 532, 541, 542, 543, 667, 698, 927.

615 Good

N. *good*, one's g., what is good for one; the best, supreme good, summum bonum; public weal, common weal, common good; balance of interest, greater good, lesser evil, the greatest happiness of the greatest number, utilitarianism 642 *good policy*; weal, well-being, welfare 730 *prosperity*; riches, gravy 800 *wealth*; luck, good l., fortune, good f.; happy days, happy ending 824 *happiness*; blessing, benison, world of good (**see** *benefit*); well-wishing, benediction 897 *benevolence*.

benefit, something to one's advantage, advantage, interest; service, convenience, behoof, behalf 640 *utility*; crop, harvest, return 771 *acquisition*; profit, increment, unearned i. 771 *gain*; edification, betterment 654 *improvement*; boon 781 *gift*; good turn 897 *kind act*; favour, blessing, blessing in disguise; turn-up for the book, godsend, windfall, piece of luck, treasure trove, find, prize; good thing, desirable object, the very thing, just the t. 859 *desired object*.

Adj. *good*, goodly, fine; blessed, beatific 824 *happy*; gainful 640 *profitable*; advantageous, heaven-sent 644 *beneficial*; worthwhile 644 *valuable*; helpful 706 *cooperative*; praiseworthy, commendable, recommended 923 *approved*; edifying, moral 933 *virtuous*; pleasure-giving 826 *pleasurable*.

Vb. *benefit*, favour, bless; do good, help, serve, avail, be of service 640 *be useful*; edify, advantage, profit; pay, repay 771 *be profitable*; do one a power of good 654 *make better*; turn out well, be all for the best, come right in the end.

flourish, thrive, do well, be on top of the world; rise, rise in the world 730 *prosper*; arrive 727 *succeed*; benefit by, gain by, be the better for, improve 654 *get better*; turn to good account, cash in on 137 *profit by*; make a profit 771 *gain*; make money 800 *get rich*.

Adv. *well*, aright, satisfactorily, favourably, profitably, happily, not amiss, all to the good; to one's advantage, to one's benefit, for the best, in one's best interests; in fine style, on the up and up.

See: 137, 640, **642**, **644**, 654, 706, 727, **730**, 771, 781, 800, 824, 826, 859, 897, 923, 933.

616 Evil

N. *evil*, evil conduct, mischievousness, injuriousness, disservice, injury, dirty trick 930 *foul play*; wrong, injury, outrage 914 *injustice*; crying evil, shame, abuse; curse, scourge, poison, pest, plague, sore, running s. 659 *bane*; ill, ills that flesh is heir to, Pandora's box; sad world, vale of tears; bale, trouble, troubles 731 *adversity*; affliction, bread of a., misery, distress 825 *suffering*; grief, woe 825 *sorrow*; unease, malaise, discomfort 825 *worry*; nuisance 827 *annoyance*; hurt, bodily harm, wound, bruise, cut, gash 377 *pain*; blow, mortal b., buffet, stroke 279 *knock*; outrageous fortune, slings and arrows, calamity, bad luck 731 *misfortune*; casualty, accident 154 *event*; fatality 361 *death*; catastrophe 165 *ruin*; tragedy, sad ending 655 *deterioration*; mischief, devilry, harm, damage 772 *loss*; ill effect, bad result; disadvantage 35 *inferiority*; drawback, fly in the ointment 647 *defect*; setback 702 *hitch*; evil plight 700 *predicament*; indigence 801 *poverty*; sense of injury, grievance 829 *discontent*; vindictiveness 910 *revengefulness*; cause of evil 898 *malevolence*.

Adj. *evil*, wicked 934 *vicious*; black, foul, shameful 914 *wrong*; bad, too bad 645 *damnable*; unlucky, inauspicious, sinister 731 *adverse*; insidious, injurious, prejudicial, disadvantageous 645 *harmful*; trouble-making 898 *maleficent*; troublous 827 *distressing*; fatal, fell, mortal, deathly 362 *deadly*; ruinous, disastrous 165 *destructive*; catastrophic, calamitous, tragic 731 *unfortunate*; all wrong, awry, out of joint.

Adv. *amiss*, wrong, all wrong, awry, sour; unfortunately, unhappily, unluckily; to one's cost, for one's sins; worse luck!

See: 35, 154, 165, 279, 361, 362, 377, **645**, 647, 655, 659, 700, 702, **731**, 772, 801, 825, 827, 829, 898, 910, 914, 930, 934.

Section two: Prospective volition

617 Intention

N. *intention*, intent, intendment, meaning; intentionality, deliberateness; calculation, calculated risk 480 *estimate*; purpose, set p., settled p., determination, predetermination, resolve 599 *resolution*; animus, mind 447 *intellect*; mens rea, criminal intent 936 *guilt*; good intentions 897 *benevolence*; view, prospect, purview; future intention, proposal 124 *looking ahead*; constant intention, study, pursuit, occupation 622 *business*; project, design 623 *plan*; enterprise 672 *undertaking*; ambition 859 *desire*; formulated intention, decision 480 *judgment*; final decision, ultimatum 766 *conditions*; bid, bid for 671 *attempt*; engagement 764 *promise*; solemn threat 900 *threat*; final intention, destination 69 *end*; teleology, final cause 156 *causation*; be-all and end-all, raison d'être 156 *reason why*; trend 179 *tendency*; tendentiousness 523 *latency*.

objective, destination, object, end, end in view, aim; axe to grind; mark, butt, target; target area, bull's-eye 225 *centre*; tape, winning post 295 *goal*; place of pilgrimage, Mecca 76 *focus*; quarry, game, prey 619 *chase*; prize, crown, wreath 729 *trophy*; dream, aspiration, vision 513 *ideality*; heart's desire, Promised Land, El Dorado 859 *desired object*.

Adj. *intending*, intent on, hell-bent 599 *resolute*; intentional, deliberate, voluntary 595 *volitional*; out to, out for, all out f.; having in view, purposive, teleological; studying, serious; minded, so m., disposed, inclined 597 *willing*; prospective, would-be, aspiring, ambitious 859 *desiring*.

intended, for a purpose, tendentious; deliberate, intentional, studied, designed, purposed, purposeful, aforethought 608 *predetermined*.

Vb. *intend*, purpose, propose; have in mind, have in view, have an eye to, contemplate; study, meditate; reckon on, calculate, look for 507 *expect*; foresee the necessity of 510 *foresee*; mean to, really mean, have every intention 599 *be resolute*; have a purpose, harbour a design; resolve, determine, premeditate 608 *predetermine*; project, design, plan for 623 *plan*; take on oneself, shoulder 672 *undertake*; engage 764 *promise*; threaten to 900 *threaten*; intend for, destine f. 155 *predestine*; mark down for, earmark 547 *mark*; hold for, keep f., reserve f.; intend for oneself (**see** *aim at*).

aim at, make one's target, go for, go in for, take up; go after, go all out for, drive at, labour for, study f., strive after 619 *pursue*; try for, bid f., make a bid, endeavour

671 *attempt*; be after, have an eye on, have designs on, promise oneself, propose to oneself, nurse an ambition, aspire to, dream of, think of, talk of 859 *desire*; take aim, point at, level at, train one's sights on, raise one's s., aim high 281 *aim*.

Adv. *purposely*, on purpose, seriously, with one's eyes open, in cold blood, deliberately, pointedly, intentionally; designedly, advisedly, knowingly, wittingly, voluntarily; with malice aforethought; for, for a purpose, in order to; with the intention of, with a view to, with an eye to, with the object of, in pursuance of, pursuant to; by design, as planned, according to plan, as arranged.

See: 69, 76, 124, 155, 156, 179, 225, 281, 295, 447, 480, 507, 510, 513, 523, 547, 595, 597, **599**, 608, 619, 622, **623**, 671, 672, 729, 764, 766, **859**, 897, 900, 936.

618 Nondesign. Gamble

N. *nondesign*, indetermination, indeterminacy, unpredictability 159 *chance*; involuntariness, instinct 609 *spontaneity*; coincidence, mere c. 89 *accompaniment*; accident, fluke, luck, mere l. 154 *event*; good luck, windfall; bad luck, hard l. 616 *evil*; lottery, luck of the draw (**see** *gambling*); sortition, drawing lots, casting l. 159 *equal chance*;sortilege, sortes Biblicae 511 *divination*; lot, wheel of Fortune 596 *fate*; mascot, amulet, charm 983 *talisman*.

gambling, taking a chance, risk-taking; plunge, risk, hazard, Russian roulette 661 *danger*; gamble, potluck 159 *chance*; venture, speculation, flutter 461 *experiment*; shot, random s., shot in the dark, leap in the d., pig in a poke, blind bargain 474 *uncertainty*; bid, throw; toss of a coin, turn of a card; wager, bet, stake, ante, psychic bid; last throw, desperate bid 857 *rashness*; dice, die, bones, ivories; element of risk, game of chance; bingo; fruit machine, one-armed bandit; roulette, rouge et noir 837 *gambling game*; betting, turf, horse-racing, dog-r. 716 *racing*; football pool, pools; draw, lottery, raffle, tombola, sweepstake, premium bond, football pool; gambling on the market, futures.

gaming-house, hell, gambling den; betting shop; casino, pool room, bingo hall, amusement arcade; racecourse, turf; totalizator, tote, pari mutuel.

bourse, exchange, stock e., bucket shop.

gambler, gamester, player, dicer; better, layer, backer, punter; turf accountant, bookmaker, bookie, tout, tipster; enterprising person, risk-taker; gentleman of fortune, venturer, merchant v., adventurer, undertaker, entrepreneur 672 *undertaking*; speculator, piker, plunger, manipulator; bear, bull, stag; experimentalist 461 *experimenter*.

Adj. *unintentional*, nonintentional, inadvertent, unintended, unmeant, not meant 596 *involuntary*; unpurposed, undesigned, unpremeditated, unrehearsed 609 *spontaneous*; accidental, fortuitous, coincidental 159 *casual*.

designless, aimless, planless, purposeless; motiveless 159 *causeless*; happy-go-lucky, devil-may-care; unselective 464 *indiscriminate*; undirected, unguided, random, haphazard 282 *deviating*; wandering, footloose 267 *travelling*.

speculative, experimental 474 *uncertain*; hazardous, risky, chancy, dicey, aleatory; risk-taking, venturesome, adventurous, enterprising.

Vb. *gamble*, game, play, do the pools; throw, dice, bet, stake, wager, lay; call one's hand, overcall; play high, play for high stakes, double the s.; take bets, offer odds, make a book; back, punt; cover a bet, cover, hedge 660 *seek safety*; play the market, speculate, have a flutter 461 *experiment*; hazard, risk, run a r., take risks, push one's luck, tempt Providence; buy blind, buy a pig in a poke 857 *be rash*; venture, chance it, chance one's arm, tempt fortune, try one's luck, trust to chance; spin the wheel, raffle, draw, draw lots, cut straws, cut for aces, spin a coin, toss up.

Adv. *at random*, by the way, incidentally, haphazardly; unintentionally, unwittingly; chancily, riskily; at a venture, by guess and by God, on the off-chance, on spec.

See: 89, 154, **159**, 267, 282, 461, 464, 474, 511, 596, 609, 616, 660, 661, 672, 716, 837, 857, 983.

619 Pursuit

N. *pursuit*, pursuing, pursuance, follow-up 65 *sequence*; hunting, seeking, looking for, quest 459 *search*; tracking, trailing, dogging 284 *following*; hounding, persecution, witch-hunt; persistence 600 *perseverance*; prosecution, execution 725 *effectuation*; activities, affairs 622 *business*.

chase, run, run for one's money; steeplechase, paperchase 716 *racing*; hunt, hunting, hounding, hue and cry, tally-ho; beat, drive, battue, beating; shooting, gunning, hunting, shooting and fishing 837 *sport*; blood sport, fox hunt, stag h.; big-game h., lion h., tiger h.; elephant h., boar h.; pigsticking; stalking, deer s.; hawking, fowling, falconry; fishing, angling, fly fishing, coarse f., sea f.; inshore f., deep-sea f., whaling; beagling, coursing, ratting, trapping, ferreting, rabbiting; fishing tackle, rod and line, bait, fly; fowling-piece 723 *firearm*; fishtrap, rat-trap 542 *trap*; manhunt, dragnet; game, quarry, prey, victim 617 *objective*; catch 771 *acquisition*.

hunter, quester, seeker, searcher 459 *enquirer*; search party; pursuer, dogger, tracker, trailer, shadow; huntsman, huntress; whip, whipper-in; beater; Nimrod, Diana; sportsman, sportswoman 837 *player*; gun, shot, good s., marksman *or* -woman 287 *shooter*; headhunter 362 *killer*; big-game hunter, fox h., deer stalker; poacher, trout-tickler; trapper, rat-catcher, rodent officer; bird catcher, fowler, falconer, hawker; fisherman, piscator, angler, compleat a.; shrimper; trawler, trawlerman, whaler; field, pack, hounds, cry of h.; hound, foxhound, otterhound, bloodhound 365 *dog*; hawk 365 *bird*; beast of prey, man-eater 365 *mammal*; mouser 365 *cat*.

Adj. *pursuing*, pursuant, seeking, questing 459 *enquiring*; in quest of, sent after; on one's tail, chasing, in pursuit, in hot p., in full cry, on the scent, on the trail 284 *following*; hunting, shooting; fishing, piscatorial.

Vb. *pursue*, seek, look for, cast about for; be gunning for, hunt for, fish for, dig for 459 *search*; send after, send for, send out a search party; stalk, prowl after, sneak a.; shadow, dog, track, trail, tail, sit on one's t., dog one's footsteps, follow the scent 284 *follow*; scent out 484 *discover*; witch-hunt, harry, chivvy, persecute 735 *oppress*; chase, give c., hunt, whoop, halloo, hark, cry on; raise the hunt, raise the hue and cry; run down, ride d., rush at, tilt at, ride full tilt at, charge at 712 *charge*; leap at, jump at 312 *leap*; snatch at 786 *take*; mark as one's prey, make one's quarry 617 *aim at*; set one's course 281 *steer for*; run after, set one's cap at, woo 889 *court*; mob, swarm over; be after, make it one's business 617 *intend*; pursue one's ends 622 *busy oneself*; follow up, persist 600 *persevere*; press on 680 *hasten*; push one's way, elbow one's w., fight one's w. 285 *progress*.

hunt, go hunting, go shooting, follow the chase, ride to hounds; go fishing, cast one's net, fish, angle, fly-fish; trawl; whale; shrimp; net, catch 542 *ensnare*; mouse, play cat and m.; stalk, deer-s., fowl, hawk; course; start game, flush, beat, start, start up; set snares, poach.

Adv. *pursuant to*, in pursuance of, in quest of, in search of, on the lookout for, after; on the trail, on the track, on the scent; in hot pursuit, hot on the trail, in full cry.

Int. Halloo! View halloo! Yoicks! Tallyho!

See: 65, 281, 284, 285, 287, 312, 362, 365, **459**, 484, 542, 600, 617, 622, 680, 712, 716, 723, 725, 735, 771, 786, 837, 889.

620 Avoidance

N. *avoidance*, prevention 702 *hindrance*; abstinence, abstention 942 *temperance*; forbearance, refraining 177 *moderation*; refusal 607 *rejection*; inaction, cop-out 679 *inactivity*; passivity 266 *quiescence*; nonintervention, noninvolvement, neutrality 860 *indifference*; evasiveness 518 *equivocalness*; evasive action, dodge, duck, sidestep; delaying action, noncooperation 769 *nonobservance*; centrifugal force; retreat, withdrawal 286 *regression*; evasion, flight 667 *escape*; shy, jibbing, shrinking 854 *fear*; shunning, wide berth, safe distance 199 *distance*; shyness 598 *unwillingness*; shirking 458 *negligence*; skulking 523 *latency*; revulsion 280 *recoil*; defence mechanism, defensive reaction 713 *defence*; repression, suppression 757 *prohibition*; nonattendance 190 *absence*; escapism.

avoider, nondrinker 942 *abstainer*; dodger, sidestepper, evader, tax e., bilker, welsher 545 *trickster*; shrinker, quitter 856 *coward*; shirker, skiver, slacker, sloucher, scrimshanker 679 *idler*; skulker 527 *hider*; draft-dodger, truant, deserter 918 *undutifulness*; apostate, renegade 603 *tergiversator*; runaway, fugitive, refugee, displaced person, escapee 667 *escaper*; escapist 513 *visionary*; head in the sand, ostrich.

Adj. *avoiding*, shunning; evasive, elusive,

slippery, hard to catch; untamed, wild; shy 874 *modest*; blinking, blenching, shrinking, cowering 854 *nervous*; backward, reluctant, noncooperative 598 *unwilling*; noncommittal, unforthcoming 582 *taciturn*; passive, inert 679 *inactive*; not involved, noncommitted, uncommitted 625 *neutral*; centrifugal; fugitive, hunted, runaway, fly-by-night 667 *escaped*; hiding, skulking 523 *latent*; repressive, suppressive; on the defensive.

avoidable, avertable, escapable, preventable; unsought, unattempted.

Vb. *avoid*, not go near, keep off, keep away; bypass, circumvent 282 *deviate*; turn aside, look the other way, cold-shoulder 883 *make unwelcome*; hold aloof, stand apart, have no hand in, not soil one's fingers, keep one's hands clean, wash one's hands of, shun, eschew, leave, let alone, have nothing to do with, not touch with a bargepole; give a miss, give the go-by; fight shy, back away, draw back 290 *recede*; hold off, stand aloof, keep one's distance, keep a respectful d., give a wide berth, sup with a long spoon 199 *be distant*; keep out of the way, keep clear, stand c., get out of the way, make way for; forbear, spare; refrain, abstain, forswear, deny oneself, do without, not touch 942 *be temperate*; pull one's punches 177 *moderate*; hold back, hang b., not try, not attempt, balk at 598 *be unwilling*; shelve, postpone 136 *put off*; pass the buck, get out of; cop out, funk, shirk 458 *neglect*; shrink, flinch, start aside, jib, refuse, shy, blink, blench 854 *be nervous*; take evasive action, lead one a dance, throw one off the scent, play hide-and-seek; sidestep, dodge, duck; deflect, ward off 713 *parry*; duck the issue, avoid the i., fudge the i., get round, obviate, skirt round, fence, hedge, pussyfoot 518 *be equivocal*; evade, escape, give one the slip 667 *elude*; skulk, cower, hide 523 *lurk*; bury one's head in the sand; disown, deny 533 *negate*; repress, suppress 757 *prohibit*; make excuses 614 *plead*; prevent, foil 702 *hinder*.

run away, desert, play truant, jump bail, take French leave 918 *fail in duty*; abscond, welsh, flit, elope 667 *escape*; absent oneself 190 *be absent*; withdraw, retire, retreat, beat a r., turn tail, turn one's back 282 *turn round*; flee, flit, fly, take to flight, run for one's life; be off, make o., slope o., scamper o., bolt, run, cut and run, show a clean pair of heels, take to one's h., beat it, make oneself scarce, scoot, scram, skedaddle 277 *move fast*; slip the cable, part company, break away 296 *decamp*; steal away, sneak off, slink o., shuffle o., creep o.; scuttle, do a bunk.

Int. *hands off!* keep off! beware! forebear!

See: 136, 177, 190, 199, 266, 277, 280, 282, 286, 290, **296**, 458, 513, 518, 523, 527, 533, 545, 582, 598, 603, 607, 614, 625, **667**, 679, 702, 713, 757, 769, 854, 856, 860, 874, 883, 918, 942.

621 Relinquishment

N. *relinquishment*, abandonment; going, leaving, evacuation 296 *departure*; dereliction, desertion, truancy, defection 918 *undutifulness*; withdrawal, secession 978 *schism*; walk-out 145 *strike*; cop-out 620 *avoidance*; yielding, giving up, handing over, cession 780 *transfer*; forgoing, waiver, renunciation 779 *nonretention*; retirement 753 *resignation*; disuse 674 *nonuse*; discontinuance 611 *desuetude*; cancellation, annulment 752 *abrogation*; world well lost 883 *seclusion*.

Adj. *relinquished*, forsaken, cast-off, castaway, marooned, abandoned etc. vb.; waived, forgone 779 *not retained*.

Vb. *relinquish*, drop, let go, leave hold of, unclench, quit one's hold, loosen one's grip 779 *not retain*; surrender, resign, give up, yield; waive, forgo; lower one's sights 872 *be humble*; cede, hand over, transfer 780 *assign*; forfeit 772 *lose*; renounce, swear off, abnegate, recant, change one's mind 603 *tergiversate*; not proceed with, drop the idea, give up the idea, forget it 506 *forget*; wean oneself 611 *disaccustom*; forswear, deny oneself, abstain 620 *avoid*; shed, slough, cast off, divest 229 *doff*; drop, discard, write off 674 *stop using*; lose interest, have other fish to fry 860 *be indifferent*; abdicate, back down, scratch, stand down, withdraw, retire, drop out 753 *resign*; give in, throw in the sponge *or* the towel, throw up the game, throw in one's hand 721 *submit*; leave, quit, move out, vacate, evacuate 296 *depart*; forsake, abandon, run out on, leave stranded, quit one's post, desert 918 *fail in duty*; play truant 190 *be absent*; down tools, strike, come out 145 *cease*; walk out, secede 978 *schismatize*; go over, rat, sell out 603 *apostatize*; throw over, ditch, jilt, break it off, go back on one's word 542 *deceive*; abandon discussion, waste no more time, pass on to the next, shelve, postpone 136 *put off*; annul, cancel 752 *abrogate*.

See: 136, 145, 190, 229, 296, 506, 542, **603**, 611, 620, 674, 721, 752, 753, 772, **779**, 780, 860, 872, 883, 918, 978.

622 Business

N. *business*, affairs, business a., interests, irons in the fire; main business, occupation, concern, care; aim, ambition 617 *intention*; business on hand, case, agenda 154 *affairs*; enterprise, venture, undertaking, pursuit 678 *activity*; routine, business r., office r., round, daily r. 610 *practice*; business life, daily work; business circles, business world, City; economics, the economy; art, technology, industry, commerce, big business; business company 708 *corporation*; agriculture, agribusiness; cottage industry, home-based i.; industrialism, industrialization, industrial arts, manufacture 164 *production*; trade, craft, handicraft, art and mystery 694 *skill*; guild, union, business association 706 *association*; employment, work, avocation (**see** *vocation*); sideline, hobby, pastime 837 *amusement*.

vocation, calling, life work, mission, apostolate 751 *commission*; life, walk of life, career, chosen career, labour of love, self-imposed task 597 *voluntary work*; living, livelihood, daily bread, one's bread and butter; profession, métier, craft, trade; line, line of country (**see** *function*); exacting profession, high calling; religious profession, ministry; cloth, veil, habit 985 *the church*; military profession, arms 718 *war*; naval profession, sea; legal profession 953 *law*; teaching profession, education 534 *teaching*; medical profession, medicine, practice; business profession, industry, commerce 791 *trade*; government service, civil service, administration 689 *management*; public service, public life; social service 901 *sociology*.

job, ploys, activities 678 *activity*; chores, odd jobs, work, task, set task, exercise 682 *labour*; duty, charge, commission, mission, errand, quest 751 *mandate*; employ, service, employment, full e.; hours of work, working day, workday, manhour; occupation, situation, position, berth, incumbency, appointment, post, office; regular employment, full-time job, permanency; temporary job, part-time j.; situation wanted; opening, vacancy; labour exchange, employment agency, Job Centre, Department of Employment.

function, what one has to do; capacity, office, duty; area, realm, province, domain, orbit, sphere; scope, field, terms of reference 183 *range*; beat, round; department, line, line of country; role, part; business, job; responsibility, concern, care, look-out, baby, pigeon.

Adj. *businesslike*, efficient 694 *skilful*; industrious, busy 678 *active*; vocational, professional, career; industrial, technological, commercial, financial, mercantile; labour-intensive, capital-i.; occupational, functional; official, governmental; routine, systematic 60 *orderly*; workaday 610 *habitual*; earning, in employment, employed, self-e., freelance; in hand, on h., on foot 669 *preparatory*.

Vb. *employ*, busy, occupy, take up one's time, fill one's t., keep one engaged; give employment, engage, recruit, hire, enlist, appoint, post 751 *commission*; take on the payroll 804 *pay*; give a situation to, offer a job to, fill a vacancy, staff with, staff; industrialize.

busy oneself, work, work for 742 *serve*; have a profession, be employed, do a job, hold down a j., earn, earn one's living; earn an honest crust, turn an honest penny 771 *acquire*; take on a job, apply for a j., take a situation; be doing, be up and d., bustle 678 *be busy*; concern oneself with, make it one's business, take a hand in 678 *meddle*; work at, ply; engage in, turn to, turn one's hand to, take up, engage in, go in for; have to do, have on one's hands, have one's hands full, take on oneself, bear the burden, bear the brunt, take on one's shoulders 917 *incur a duty*; work with one's hands, work with one's brains; pursue one's hobby 837 *amuse oneself*.

function, work, go 173 *operate*; fill a role, play one's part, carry on; officiate, act, do the offices, discharge the functions, exercise the f., serve as, do duty for, perform the duties, do the work of; substitute, stand in for 755 *deputize*; hold office, hold a portfolio, hold a place, hold down a job, have a job, serve (**see** *busy oneself*).

do business, transact, negotiate 766 *make terms*; ply a trade, ply a craft, exercise a profession, follow a calling, work at a job;

have a business, engage in, carry on, drive a trade, carry on a t., keep shop; do business with, deal w., enter into trade relations 791 *trade*; transact business, attend to one's b., go about one's b.; pursue one's vocation, earn one's living (**see** *busy oneself*); be an employer, be an industrialist; set up in business, open a shop, put up one's sign.

Adv. *professionally*, in businesslike fashion; in the course of, all in the day's work; business as usual.

See: 60, 154, 164, 173, 183, 534, 597, 610, 617, 669, **678**, **682**, 689, 694, 706, 708, 718, 742, 751, 755, 766, 771, 791, 804, 837, 901, 917, 953, 985.

623 Plan

N. *plan*, scheme, design; planning, contrivance; organization, systematization, rationalization, centralization 60 *order*; programme, project, proposal 617 *intention*; proposition, suggestion, motion, resolution (**see** *policy*); master plan, five-year p., detailed p., ground p., floor p., scale drawing, blueprint 551 *map*; diagram, flow chart 86 *statistics*; sketch, outline, draft, first d., memorandum; skeleton, roughcast; model, pattern, pilot scheme 23 *prototype*; proof, revise, proof copy 22 *copy*; drawing board, planning office, back room, operations r., headquarters, base.

policy, forethought 510 *foresight*; statesmanship 498 *wisdom*; course of action, plan of attack, procedure, strategy 688 *tactics*; operational research 459 *enquiry*; address, approach, attack 624 *way*; steps, measures 676 *action*; stroke of policy, coup, coup d'état 676 *deed*; proposed action, scenario, forecast 511 *prediction*; programme, prospectus, platform, plank, ticket, slate; line, party l.; formula 81 *rule*; schedule, agenda, order of the day 622 *business*.

contrivance, expedient, resource, recourse, resort, card, trump c., card up one's sleeve 629 *means*; recipe, nostrum 658 *remedy*; loophole, way out, alternative, answer 667 *means of escape*; artifice, device, gimmick, dodge, ploy, shift, flag of convenience 698 *stratagem*; wangle, fiddle 930 *foul play*; knack, trick 694 *skill*; stunt, wheeze; inspiration, happy thought, bright idea, right i. 451 *idea*; notion, invention; tool, weapon, contraption, gadget 628 *instrument*; ad hoc measure, improvisation 609 *spontaneity*; makeshift, pis aller 150 *substitute*; feat, tour de force; bold move, stroke, masterstroke 676 *deed*.

plot, deep-laid p., intrigue; web, web of intrigue; cabal, conspiracy, inside job; scheme, racket, game 698 *stratagem*; frame-up, machination; manipulation, wire-pulling 612 *motive*; secret influence 523 *latency*; counterplot, countermine 713 *defence*.

planner, contriver, framer, inventor, originator, hatcher; proposer, promoter, projector; founder, author, architect, designer; backroom boy, boffin 696 *expert*; brains, mastermind; organizer, systematizer, systems analyst; strategist, tactician, manoeuvrer; statesman *or* -woman, politician, Machiavellian; wheeler-dealer, schemer, axe-grinder; careerist, go-getter 678 *busy person*; plotter, intriguer, intrigant, spinner, spider; cabal; conspirator 545 *deceiver*.

Adj. *planned*, blueprinted, schematic, worked out, matured 669 *prepared*; organized, systematized 60 *orderly*; under consideration, in draft, in proof; strategic, tactical; framed, plotted, engineered.

planning, contriving, resourceful, ingenious 698 *cunning*; purposeful, scheming, up to something; involved, deep in; intriguing, plotting, conspiratorial; Machiavellian.

Vb. *plan*, form a p., resolve 617 *intend*; approach, approach a problem, attack a p.; make a plan, draw up, design, draft, blueprint; frame, shape 243 *form*; revise, recast 654 *rectify*; project, plan out, work o., sketch o., chalk o., map o., lay o.; programme, draw up a p., lay the foundation; shape a course, mark out a c.; organize, systematize, rationalize, schematize, methodize 60 *order*; schedule, phase, adjust; invent, think up, hit on, fall on 484 *discover*; conceive a plan 513 *imagine*; find a way, make shift to; contrive, devise, engineer; hatch, concoct, mature 669 *prepare*; arrange, prearrange 608 *predetermine*; calculate, think ahead, look a. 498 *be wise*; have a policy, follow a plan, work to a schedule; do everything with a purpose, have an axe to grind, grind one's axe.

plot, scheme, have designs, be up to something, wheel and deal; manipulate, pull strings 178 *influence*; cabal, conspire, intrigue, machinate; concoct, cook up, brew; hatch a plot 698 *be cunning*; dig a pit for, undermine, countermine 542 *ensnare*; work against, manoeuvre a.; frame 541 *fake*.

See: 22, 23, 60, 81, 86, 150, 178, 243, 451, 459, 484, 498, 510, 511, 513, 523, 541, 542, 545, 551, 608, 609, 612, 617, 622, 624, 628, 629, 654, 658, 667, 669, 676, 678, **688**, 694, 696, **698**, 713, 930.

624 Way

N. *way*, route 267 *itinerary*; manner, wise, guise; fashion, style 243 *form*; method, mode, line, approach, address, attack; procedure, process, way of, way of doing things, modus operandi 688 *tactics*; operation, treatment; modus vivendi, working arrangement 770 *compromise*; usual way, routine 610 *practice*; technique, know-how 694 *skill*; going, gait 265 *motion*; way forward, progress 285 *progression*; royal road, primrose path; way of life, lifestyle, behaviour 688 *conduct*. **See** *route*.

access, means of a., right of way, communications; way to, direct approach 289 *approach*; entrance, door 263 *doorway*; side-entrance, back-e., tradesman's e.; adit, drive, gangway; porch, hall, hallway, corridor, vestibule 194 *lobby*; way through, pass, defile 305 *passage*; intersection, junction, crossing; zebra crossing, pedestrian c. 305 *traffic control*; strait, sound 345 *gulf*; channel, fairway, canal 351 *conduit*; lock, stile, turnstile, tollgate; way up, stairs, flight of s., stairway, ladder 308 *ascent*.

bridge, brig, way over; footbridge, flyover, aqueduct; suspension bridge, swing b., bascule b., Bailey b., humpback b., pack-horse b.; viaduct, span; railway bridge; pontoon bridge, floating b., transporter b.; drawbridge; causeway, stepping-stone, gangway, gangplank, catwalk, duck-boards; ford, ferry 305 *passage*; way under, underpass 263 *tunnel*; isthmus, neck.

route, direction, way to *or* from, way through *or* by, way up *or* over, way in *or* out; line, course, march, tack, track, beaten t., beat; trajectory, orbit; lane, traffic l., bus l. 305 *traffic control*; air lane, sea-l., seaway, fairway, waterway, inland w. 351 *conduit*; trade route; short cut, bypass; detour, circumbendibus, roundabout way 626 *circuit*; line of communication, line of retreat, line of advance.

path, pathway, footway, footpath, pavement, sidewalk; towpath, bridlepath, bridleway, ride; byway, lane, green l., track, sheep t., rabbit run, trail, mountain t.; right of way, public footpath; glade, walk, promenade, esplanade, parade, front, sea f., avenue, drive, boulevard, mall; pedestrian precinct, arcade, colonnade, aisle, cloister, ambulatory; race-track, running track, speed t. 724 *arena*; fairway, runway.

road, high r., highway, Queen's h., highways and byways; main road, A road, minor r., B r., dirt r., cinder track; side road, access r., service r., private r.; corniche, switchback; toll road, turnpike, route nationale; thoroughfare, through road, trunk r., arterial r., artery, bypass, ring road; motorway, M-way, autoroute, autobahn, autostrada; expressway, throughway, clearway; slip road, acceleration lane; crossroads, junction, T-junction, turn-off; intersection, roundabout, cloverleaf; crossing, pedestrian c., zebra c. 305 *traffic control*; roadway, carriageway, dual c.; central reservation, crash barrier; cycle track, cycleway; street, high s., one-way s., side s., back s.; alleyway, wynd, alley, blind a., cul de sac; close, avenue 192 *housing*; pavement, kerb, kerbstone; paving, cobbles, setts, paving stone, flagstones; hard shoulder, verge; macadam, tarmac, asphalt, road metal, laterite; surface, road s., skidproof s.; road building, traffic engineering.

railway, railroad, line; permanent way, track, lines, railway l., electrified l., third rail; main line, branch l., loop l.; tramlines, tramway; monorail, cog railway, rack and pinion, funicular, cableway, ropeway, telpher line; overhead railway, elevated r., underground r., electric r., subway, tube, metro 274 *train*; light railway, narrow gauge, standard g.; junction, crossover, level crossing, tunnel, cutting, embankment; siding, marshalling yard, goods y., shunting y., turntable; station, halt, stop, whistle s., platform 145 *stopping place*; signal, gantry, signal box, cabin; rails, points, sleepers, frog, fishplate, ballast.

Adj. *communicating*, granting access 289 *accessible*; through, main, arterial, trunk; bridged, crossed; paved, metalled, cobbled, tarmac; well-paved, well-laid, skid-proof; signposted, waymarked, lit, well-lit; well-used, busy; trodden, beaten.

Adv. *via*, by way of, in transit; on the way, chemin faisant.

how, in what manner? by what means? on what lines?

See: 145, **192**, 194, 243, 263, 265, **267**, 274, 285, 289, **305**, 308, 345, **351**, 610, 626, 688, 694, 724, 770.

625 Middle way

N. *middle way*, middle course, middle of the road, via media; balance, golden mean, happy medium 30 *average*; moderateness, intermediate technology; central position, halfway, halfway house, midstream 30 *middle point*; slack water, half tide; direct course, nondeviation, straight line, short cut, beeline; short circuit 249 *straightness*; noncommittal, neutrality 177 *moderation*; lukewarmness, half measures 601 *irresolution*; mutual concession 770 *compromise*.

moderate, nonextremist, Minimalist, Menshevik; middle-of-the-roader, half-and-halfer; neutral, uncommitted person, uncommitted nation; Laodicean.

Adj. *neutral*, impartial 913 *just*; noncommittal, uncommitted, unattached, free-floating; detached 860 *indifferent*; moderate, nonextreme, unextreme, middle-of-the-road 225 *central*; sitting on the fence, lukewarm, half-and-half 601 *irresolute*; neither one thing nor the other, grey.

undeviating, unswerving, keeping to the middle 225 *central*; looking neither to right nor left, direct 249 *straight*; in between, halfway, midway, intermediate 231 *interjacent*.

Vb. *be midstream*, keep to the middle, steer a middle course, go straight, hold straight on, not deviate, not swerve, look neither to right nor to left.

be halfway, go halfway, meet h., go so far and no further 770 *compromise*; be in between, occupy the centre, hold the scales, balance 28 *equalize*; sit on the fence 474 *be uncertain*.

See: 28, **30**, **177**, 225, 231, 249, 474, 601, 770, 860, 913.

626 Circuit

N. *circuit*, roundabout way, longest w., circuitous route, bypass, detour, loop, loop line, divagation, digression 282 *deviation*; ambages 251 *convolution*; circulation, circumambulation, orbit, round, lap 314 *circuition*; circumference 250 *circle*; full circle, looping the loop.

Adj. *roundabout*, circuitous, indirect, out of the way 251 *convoluted*; circumlocutory 570 *diffuse*; circulatory, circumambulating; rounding, skirting; encompassing, surrounding 230 *circumjacent*.

Vb. *circuit*, round, lap, beat the bounds, go round, make a circuit, loop the loop 314 *circle*; make a detour, go out of one's way 282 *deviate*; turn, bypass, short-circuit 620 *avoid*; lead one a dance, beat about the bush; encircle, embrace, encompass 230 *surround*; keep to the circumference, skirt, edge round.

Adv. *round about*, round the world, in a roundabout way, circuitously, indirectly, from pillar to post.

See: 230, 250, 251, **282**, **314**, 570, 620.

627 Requirement

N. *requirement*, essential, sine qua non, a necessary, a must 596 *necessity*; needs, necessities, necessaries; indent, order, requisition, shopping list; stipulation, prerequisite, prior conditions 766 *conditions*; desideratum, want, lack, need 636 *insufficiency*; gap 190 *absence*; demand, consumer d., call for, run on, seller's market 792 *purchase*; consumption, input, intake; shortage 307 *shortfall*; balance due, what is owing 803 *debt*; claim 761 *request*; ultimatum, injunction 737 *command*.

needfulness, case of need, occasion; necessity for, essentiality, indispensability, desirability; necessitousness, want, pinch 801 *poverty*; exigency, urgency, emergency 137 *crisis*; vitalness, matter of life and death 638 *important matter*; obligation 917 *duty*; bare minimum, the least one can do; face-saving measures.

Adj. *required*, requisite, prerequisite, needful, needed; necessary, essential, vital, indispensable, not to be spared; called for, in request, in demand 859 *desired*; reserved, earmarked, booked; wanted, lacking, missing 190 *absent*.

necessitous, in want, in need, pinched, feeling the pinch; lacking, deprived of; needing badly, craving; destitute 801 *poor*; starving 636 *underfed*.

demanding, crying, crying out for, calling for, imperative, urgent, instant, exigent, pressing, pinching; compulsory 740 *compelling*.

Vb. *require*, need, want, lack 636 *be unsatisfied*; not have, be without, stand in need of, feel the need for, have occasion for; miss, desiderate; need badly, crave 859 *desire*; call for, cry out f., clamour f.; claim, put in a claim for, apply for 761 *request*; find necessary, find indispensable, be unable to do without, must have; consume, take 634 *waste*, 673 *use*; create a need, render necessary, necessitate, oblige 740 *compel*; make demands 737 *demand*; stipulate 766 *give terms*; order, send an order for, indent, requisition; reserve, book, earmark.

Adv. *in need*, in want; necessarily, sine qua non; of necessity, at a pinch.

See: 137, 190, 307, **596**, 634, **636**, 638, 673, 737, 740, 761, 766, 792, 801, 803, 859, 917.

628 Instrumentality

N. *instrumentality*, operation 173 *agency*; occasion 156 *cause*; result 157 *effect*; pressure 178 *influence*; efficacy 160 *power*; occult power, magic 983 *sorcery*; services, help, assistance, midwifery 703 *aid*; support 706 *cooperation*; intervention, intermediacy, interference 678 *activity*; subservience 739 *obedience*; medium 629 *means*; use, employment, application, serviceability, handiness 640 *utility*; use of machinery, instrumentation, mechanization, automation 630 *machine*.

instrument, hand, organ, sense o.; amanuensis, handmaid, lackey, slave, slave of the lamp 742 *servant*; agent, midwife, medium, help, assistant 703 *aider*; go-between 720 *mediator*; catalyst; vehicle; pawn, piece on the board; robot 630 *machine*; cat's paw, stooge, puppet, creature 707 *auxiliary*; weapon, implement, appliance, lever 630 *tool*; magic ring, Aladdin's lamp 983 *spell*; key, skeleton key, master k., passkey 263 *opener*; open sesame, watchword, password, passport, safeconduct, warrant 756 *permit*; stepping-stone 624 *bridge*; channel, high road, highway 624 *road*; push button, switch, controls; device, expedient, makeshift, gadget 623 *contrivance*; card, trump.

Adj. *instrumental*, working 173 *operative*; hand-operated, manual; automatic, push-button 630 *mechanical*; effective, efficient, efficacious, effectual 160 *powerful*; telling, weighty 178 *influential*; magic 983 *magical*; conducive 156 *causal*; practical, applied; serviceable, general-purpose, employable, handy 640 *useful*; ready, available 597 *willing*; forwarding, promoting, assisting, helpful 703 *aiding*; Socratic, maieutic; functional, agential, subservient, ministering; mediational, intermediate, intervening; mediated by.

Vb. *be instrumental*, work, act 173 *operate*; perform 676 *do*; serve, subserve, work for, lend oneself *or* itself to, pander to 703 *minister to*; help, assist 703 *aid*; advance, promote 703 *patronize*; have a hand in 775 *participate*; be to blame for 156 *cause*; be the instrument, be a cat's paw, pull another's chestnuts out of the fire 640 *be useful*; intermediate, interpose, intervene 720 *mediate*; use one's influence, pull strings 178 *influence*; effect 156 *cause*; tend 156 *conduce*; achieve 725 *carry through*.

Adv. *through*, per, by the hand of, by means of, with the help of, thanks to.

See: **156**, 157, 160, 173, 178, 263, 597, 623, 624, 629, **630**, 640, 676, 678, **703**, 706, 707, 720, 725, 739, **742**, 756, 775, 983.

629 Means

N. *means*, ways and m., wherewithal; power, capacity 160 *ability*; strong hand, trumps, aces; conveniences, facilities; appliances, tools, tools of the trade, bag of tricks 630 *tool*; technology 490 *knowledge*; technique, know-how 694 *skill*; wherewithal, matériel, equipment, supplies, stock, munitions, ammunition 633 *provision*; resources, economic r., natural r., raw material 631 *materials*; nuts and bolts 630 *machine*; labour resources, pool of labour, manpower 686 *personnel*; financial resources 800 *wealth*; liquidity 797 *money*; capital, working c. 628 *instrument*; assets, stock-in-trade 777 *property*; stocks and shares, investments, investment portfolio; revenue, income, receipts, credits 807 *receipt*; borrowing capacity, line of credit 802 *credit*; reserves, standby, shot in one's locker, card up one's sleeve, two strings to one's bow 662 *safeguard*; freedom of choice, alternative 605 *choice*; method, measures, steps 624 *way*; cure, specific 658 *remedy*; expedient, device, resort, recourse 623 *contrivance*; makeshift, ad hoc measure 150 *substitute*; let-out 667 *means of escape*; desperate remedy, last resort, last hope, last throw

618 *gambling*.

Vb. *find means*, provide the wherewithal, supply, find, furnish 633 *provide*; equip, fit out 669 *make ready*; finance, raise the money, promote, float; have the means, be in a position to 160 *be able*; contrive, be resourceful, not be at a loss, find a way 623 *plan*; beg, borrow or steal, get by hook or by crook 771 *acquire*.

Adv. *by means of*, with, wherewith; by, using, through; with the aid of; by dint of; by fair means or foul.

See: 150, 160, 490, 605, 618, 623, 624, 628, **630**, **631**, **633**, 658, 662, 667, 669, 686, 694, 771, 777, 797, 800, 802, 807.

630 Tool

N. *tool*, precision t., machine t., implement 628 *instrument*; apparatus, appliance, utensil; weapon, arm 723 *arms*; device, mechanical d., contraption, gadget 623 *contrivance*; doodah, thingummy, whatsit; screw, screwdriver, drill, electric d. 263 *perforator*; wrench, spanner; pliers, tweezers 778 *nippers*; chisel, wedge, edged tool 256 *sharp edge*; rope 47 *cable*; peg, nail 217 *hanger*, 218 *support*; leverage, lever, jemmy, crowbar, handspike, jack 218 *pivot*; grip, lug, helve, haft, shaft, tiller, helm, rudder 218 *handle*; pulley, sheave 250 *wheel*; switch, stopcock; gunlock, trigger; pedal, pole, punt-p. 287 *propulsion*; ram 279 *hammer*; prehistoric tool, flint; tools of the trade, tool-kit, do-it-yourself k., bag of tricks.

machine, mechanical device; machinery, mechanism, works; clockwork, wheelwork, wheels within wheels; nuts and bolts 58 *component*; spring, mainspring, hairspring; gears, gearing, spur gears, bevel g., synchromesh, automatic gear change; motor, engine, internal combustion e., Wankel e., diesel e., steam e.; turbine, dynamo 160 *sources of energy*; servomechanism, servomotor; robot, automaton; computer 86 *data processing*.

mechanics, engineering; electrical e. 160 *electronics*; cybernetics; automatic control, automation, robotics; mechanical power, mechanical advantage; technics, technology, advanced t., high t.

equipment, furniture, appointments; gear, tackle, harness; fittings, fixture 40 *adjunct*; outfit, kit; upholstery, furnishing; trappings, accoutrements 228 *dress*; utensils, impedimenta, paraphernalia, chattels 777 *property*; wares, stock-in-trade 795 *merchandise*; plant 687 *workshop*.

machinist, operator, operative; driver, minder, machine-m. 686 *agent*; engineer, technician, mechanician, mechanic, fitter; tool-user, craftsman 686 *artisan*.

Adj. *mechanical*, mechanized, motorized, powered, power-driven; labour-saving, automatic 628 *instrumental*; robot-like, automated; machine-minded, tool-using.

See: 40, 47, 58, 86, **160**, 217, 218, 228, 250, 256, 263, 279, 287, 623, **628**, 686, 687, 723, 777, 778, 795.

631 Materials

N. *materials*, resources, building blocks 629 *means*; material, stuff, staple, stock 3 *substance*; raw material, grist; meat, fodder 301 *food*; oil, yellowcake 385 *fuel*; chemical feedstock; ore, mineral, metal, pig iron, ingot; clay, adobe, china clay, potter's c., gypsum 344 *soil*; glass 422 *transparency*; plastic, polythene, polystyrene, latex, celluloid (tdmk), fibreglass; rope, yarn, wool 208 *fibre*; leather, hide 226 *skin*; timber, log, faggot, stick 366 *wood*; rafter, board 218 *beam*; plank, planking, plywood, lath, stave 207 *lamina*; stuffing 227 *lining*; cloth, fabric 222 *textile*.

building material, building block, breeze b., brick 381 *pottery*; bricks and mortar, lath and plaster, wattle and daub, cob; studwork 331 *structure*; thatch, slate, tile, shingle 226 *roof*; stone, marble, flint, ashlar, masonry; rendering 226 *facing*; compo, composition, cement, concrete, reinforced c., ferroconcrete; paving material, flag, cobble 226 *paving*; hard core, gravel, tarmac, asphalt 624 *road*.

paper, rag p., pulp, wood p., newsprint; card, Bristol board, calendered paper, art p., cartridge p., carbon p., tissue p., crepe p., sugar p., tracing p., cellophane; papier mâché, cardboard, pasteboard, millboard, strawboard, fibreboard, chipboard, hardboard, plasterboard; sheet, foolscap, quire, ream; notepaper 586 *stationery*.

See: 3, 207, 208, **218**, 222, **226**, 227, 301, **331**, 344, 366, 381, 385, 422, **586**, 624, 629.

632 Store

N. *store*, mass, heap, load, stack, stockpile, buildup 74 *accumulation*; packet, bundle, bagful 26 *quantity*; harvest, crop, vintage, mow 771 *acquisition*; haystack, haycock, hayrick; stock, stock-in-trade 795 *merchandise*; assets, capital, holding, investment 777 *property*; fund, reserve f., reserves, something in hand, backlog; unexpended balance, savings, savings account, nest egg; deposit, hoard, treasure; buried treasure, cache 527 *hiding-place*; bottom drawer, hope chest, trousseau 633 *provision*; pool, kitty; common fund, community chest 775 *joint possession*; quarry, mine, gold-m.; natural resources, natural deposit, mineral d., coal d.; coalfield, coalbed, gasfield, oilfield; coal mine, colliery, working, shaft; coalface, seam, stringer, lode; pipe, pipe vein; vein, rich v.; bonanza, strike 484 *discovery*; well, oil w., gusher; fountain, fount 156 *source*; supply, constant s., stream; tap, pipeline, artesian well 341 *irrigator*; milch cow, treacle well, cornucopia, abundance 635 *plenty*; repertoire, range (**see** *collection*).

storage, stowage, gathering, garnering 74 *accumulation*; conservation, ensilage, bottling 666 *preservation*; safe deposit 660 *protection*; stabling, warehousing; storage, storage space, shelf-room, space, accommodation 183 *room*; boxroom, loft; hold, bunker 194 *cellar*; storeship, supply base, storehouse, storeroom, stockroom; warehouse, goods shed, godown; depository, depot, entrepôt; dock, wharf, garage 192 *stable*; magazine, arsenal, armoury, gunroom; treasure house 799 *treasury*; exchequer, strongroom, vault, coffer, moneybox, moneybag, till, safe, night s., bank; blood b., sperm b.; data bank 86 *data processing*; store of memories 505 *memory*; hive, honeycomb; granary, garner, barn, silo; water tower, reservoir, cistern, tank, gasholder, gasometer; battery, storage b., dry b., wet b.; garage, petrol station, filling s., petrol pump; dump, sump, drain, cesspool, sewage farm 649 *sink*; pantry, larder, buttery, stillroom 194 *chamber*; cupboard, shelf 194 *cabinet*; refrigerator, fridge, deep freeze; portmanteau, holdall, packing case 194 *box*; container, holder, quiver 194 *receptacle*.

collection, set, complete s.; archives, file 548 *record*; folder, bundle, portfolio 74 *accumulation*; museum 125 *antiquity*; gallery, art g.; bookcollection, library, thesaurus 559 *dictionary*; menagerie, aquarium 369 *zoo*; waxworks, exhibition 522 *exhibit*; repertory, repertoire, bag of tricks.

Adj. *stored*, hoarded etc. vb.; in store, in deposit; in hand, held; in reserve, unexpended; banked, funded, invested; available, in stock; spare, supernumerary.

Vb. *store*, stow, pack, bundle 193 *load*; roll up, fold up; lay up, stow away, put a., put in mothballs; dump, garage, stable, warehouse; garner, barn; gather, harvest, reap, mow, pick, glean 370 *cultivate*; stack, heap, pile, amass, accumulate 74 *bring together*; stock up, lay in, bulk-buy, panic buy, stockpile, pile up, build up, build up one's stocks 36 *augment*; take on, take in, fuel, coal, bunker 633 *provide*; fill, fill up, top up, refill, refuel 633 *replenish*; put by, save, keep, hold, file, hang on to, keep by one 778 *retain*; bottle, pickle, conserve 666 *preserve*; leave, set aside, put a., lay by, keep back, keep in hand, reserve; fund, bank, deposit, invest; hoard, treasure, hive; bury, cache, squirrel away, stash a. 525 *conceal*; husband, save up, salt away, make a nest egg, prepare for a rainy day 814 *economize*; equip oneself, put in the bottom drawer 669 *prepare oneself*; pool, put in the kitty 775 *communalize*.

See: 26, 36, **74**, 86, 125, 156, 183, 192, 193, 194, 341, 369, 370, 484, 505, 522, 525, 527, 548, 559, **633**, **635**, 649, 660, **666**, 669, 771, 775, 777, 778, 795, 799, 814.

633 Provision

N. *provision*, providing, furnishing, logistics, equipment 669 *fitting out*; purveyance, catering; service, delivery; self-service; procuring, pandering; feeding, entertainment, bed and breakfast, board and lodging, maintenance; assistance, lending 703 *subvention*; supply, food s., water s., constant s., feed; pipeline 272 *transference*; commissariat, provisioning, supplies, stores, rations, iron r., emergency r., reserves 632 *store*; reinforcement, replenishment, refill, filling-up 54 *plenitude*; food, provender 301 *provisions*; helping, portion 301 *meal*; grist to the mill, fuel to the flame; produce 164 *product*; increase, return 771 *gain*; conservation, resource management 814 *economy*; budgeting, budget 808 *accounts*; possible need 669 *preparation*.

provider, donor 781 *giver*; creditor, moneylender 784 *lender*; wet nurse, feeder;

purser 798 *treasurer*; steward, butler; commissary, quartermaster, storekeeper; supplier, victualler, sutler; provision merchant, ship's chandler, drysalter, grocer, greengrocer, baker, poulterer, fishmonger, butcher, vintner, wine merchant; retailer, middleman, shopkeeper 794 *tradespeople*; procurer, pander, pimp 952 *bawd*.

caterer, purveyor, hotelier, hotelkeeper, restaurateur; innkeeper, alewife, landlord, landlady, mine host, publican; housekeeper, housewife; cook, chef; pastrycook, confectioner.

Adj. *provisioning*, commissarial; self-service; sufficing, all-s. 635 *sufficient*; supplied, provided, all found; well-appointed, three star; available, on tap, on the menu.

Vb. *provide*, afford, offer, lend 781 *give*; provision, find; equip, furnish, arm, man, fit out, kit o. 669 *make ready*; supply, maintain supply, keep supplied; yield 164 *produce*; bring in a supply, pump in; cater, purvey; procure, pander, pimp; service, service an order, meet an o. 793 *sell*; deliver, make deliveries, deliver the goods; hand out, hand round, serve, serve up, dish up; victual, feed, cook for, board, put up, maintain, keep, clothe; stock, keep a s.; budget, make provision, make due p.; provide for oneself, provision o., take on supplies, stock up, lay in a stock 632 *store*; fuel, coal, bunker; gather food, forage, water, take on w.; tap, draw, draw on, milk 304 *extract*; export, import 791 *trade*.

replenish, reinforce, make good, make up; fill up, top up, refill 54 *fill*; revictual, restock, refuel, reload.

See: 54, 164, 272, **301**, 304, **632**, 635, 669, 703, 771, 781, 784, 791, 793, 794, 798, 808, 814, 952.

634 Waste

N. *waste*, wastage 42 *decrement*; leakage, ebb 298 *outflow*; inroads, consumption; intake 627 *requirement*; spending, outlay, expense 806 *expenditure*; using up, depletion, exhaustion, drainage 300 *voidance*; dissipation 75 *dispersion*; evaporation 338 *vaporization*; melting 337 *liquefaction*; damage 772 *loss*; wear and tear, built-in obsolescence 655 *deterioration*; wastefulness, improvidence, lack of economy, lavishness, extravagance, overspending, unnecessary expenditure 815 *prodigality*; overproduction 637 *superfluity*; misapplication, useless expenditure, frittering away 675 *misuse*; vandalism, wilful destruction, destructiveness, sabotage 165 *destruction*; waste product, refuse 641 *rubbish*.

Adj. *wasteful*, extravagant, unnecessary, uneconomic 815 *prodigal*; throwaway 637 *superfluous*; labour-consuming, time-c., energy-c.; damaging 165 *destructive*.

wasted, exhausted, depleted, consumed; gone to waste, gone down the drain; fruitless, bootless 641 *profitless*; ill-spent, misapplied; of no avail, futile, in vain.

Vb. *waste*, consume, make a dent in, make inroads on, wade into; swallow, devour, gobble up 301 *eat*; spend, lay out 806 *expend*; take, use up, exhaust, deplete, drain, suck dry 300 *empty*; dissipate, scatter, throw to the four winds 75 *disperse*; abuse, overwork, overcrop, overfish, overgraze, impoverish, milk dry 675 *misuse*; wear out, erode, damage 655 *impair*; put to the wrong use, misapply, fritter away, cast pearls before swine; make no use of 674 *not use*; labour in vain 641 *waste effort*; be extravagant, overspend, squander, run through, throw away, pour down the drain, burn the candle at both ends 815 *be prodigal*; be careless, slop, spill; be destructive, ruin, destroy, sabotage, vandalize 165 *lay waste*; be wasted, suffer loss, decay 37 *decrease*; leak, ebb away, run low, dry up 298 *flow out*; melt, melt away 337 *liquefy*; evaporate 338 *vaporize*; run out, give o. 636 *not suffice*; burn out, burn away, gutter 381 *burn*; run to seed 655 *deteriorate*; run to waste, go down the drain.

See: 37, 42, 75, 165, 298, 300, 301, 337, 338, 381, 627, 636, 637, **641**, 655, **674**, 675, 772, 806, **815**.

635 Sufficiency

N. *sufficiency*, right amount; right qualities, qualification; right number, quorum; adequacy, enough, pass marks; assets, adequate income, competence, living wage; subsistence farming; self-sufficiency, autarky; exact requirement, no surplus; minimum, no less, bare minimum, least one can do; acceptability, the possible, all that is p. 469 *possibility*; full measure, satisfaction, ample s., contentment, all that could be desired 828 *con-*

tent; fulfilment 725 *completion*; repletion, one's fill, bellyful 863 *satiety*.

plenty, God's p., horn of p., cornucopia 171 *abundance*; outpouring, showers of, flood, spate, streams 350 *stream*; lots, lashings, galore 32 *great quantity*; fullness, copiousness, amplitude 54 *plenitude*; affluence, riches 800 *wealth*; fat of the land, luxury, loaded table, feast, banquet 301 *feasting*; orgy, riot, profusion 815 *prodigality*; richness, fat; fertility, productivity, luxuriance, lushness 171 *productiveness*; foison, harvest, rich h., bumper crop; rich vein, bonanza, ample store, endless supply, more where it came from 632 *store*; more than enough, too much, superabundance 637 *redundance*.

Adj. *sufficient*, sufficing, all-s. 633 *provisioning*; self-sufficient 54 *complete*; enough, adequate, competent; enough to go round; equal to, a match for 28 *equal*; satisfactory, satisfying 828 *contenting*; measured, commensurate, up to the mark; just right, not too much, not too little; barely sufficient, only just enough; makeshift, provisional 150 *substituted*.

plenteous, plentiful, ample, enough and to spare, more than enough 637 *superfluous*; openhanded, generous, lavish 813 *liberal*; extravagant 815 *prodigal*; wholesale, without stint, unsparing, unmeasured, exhaustless, inexhaustible 32 *great*; luxuriant, luxuriating, riotous, rampant, lush, rank, fertile, fat 171 *prolific*; profuse, abundant, copious, overflowing 637 *redundant*; rich, opulent, affluent 800 *moneyed*.

filled, well-f., flush 54 *full*; chock-full, replete, satiated, ready to burst 863 *sated*; satisfied, contented 828 *content*; well-provided, well-stocked, well-furnished 633 *provisioning*; rich in, teeming, crawling with 104 *multitudinous*.

Vb. *suffice*, be enough, do, answer 642 *be expedient*; just do, work, serve, serve as a makeshift; qualify, reach, make the grade 727 *be successful*; pass, pass muster, wash; measure up to, meet requirements, fill the bill; do all that is possible, rise to the occasion; stand, stand up to, take the strain 218 *support*; do what is required 725 *carry out*; fill up, top up, saturate 54 *fill*; refill 633 *replenish*; prove acceptable, satisfy 828 *content*; more than satisfy, satiate, give one his *or* her bellyful 863 *sate*; provide for, make adequate provision 633 *provide*.

abound, be plentiful, proliferate, teem, swarm, bristle with, crawl w. 104 *be many*; riot, luxuriate 171 *be fruitful*; flow, shower, snow, pour, stream, sheet 350 *rain*; brim, overflow, flow with milk and honey 637 *superabound*; roll in, wallow in, swim in 800 *be rich*.

have enough, be satisfied 828 *be content*; eat one's fill 301 *eat*; drink one's fill 301 *drink*; be sated, have had enough, have had one's bellyful, be fed up 829 *be discontented*; have the means 800 *afford*.

Adv. *enough*, sufficiently, tolerably, amply, to the full, to one's heart's content; ad libitum, ad lib, on tap, on demand; abundantly, inexhaustibly, interminably.

See: 28, **32**, **54**, 104, 150, 171, 218, 301, 350, 469, **632**, 633, **637**, 642, 725, 727, 800, 813, 815, **828**, 829, 863.

636 Insufficiency

N. *insufficiency*, not enough, drop in the bucket; nonsatisfaction 829 *discontent*; inadequacy, incompetence; minginess, little enough, nothing to spare, less than somewhat 33 *small quantity*; too few, no quorum 105 *fewness*; deficiency, imperfection 647 *defect*; deficit 55 *incompleteness*; nonfulfilment 726 *noncompletion*; half measures, tinkering, failure, weakness 307 *shortfall*; bankruptcy 805 *insolvency*; bare subsistence, subsistence level, pittance, dole, mite; stinginess, meanness 816 *parsimony*; short allowance, short commons, iron rations, half r.; austerity, Lenten fare, Spartan f., starvation diet, bread and water 945 *asceticism*; fast day 946 *fasting*; malnutrition, vitamin deficiency 651 *disease*.

scarcity, scarceness, paucity 105 *fewness*; dearth, leanness, seven lean years; drought, famine, starvation; infertility 172 *unproductiveness*; shortage 307 *shortfall*; power cut 37 *decrease*; none to spare, short supply, seller's market; scantiness, meagreness; deprivation 801 *poverty*; lack, want, need 627 *needfulness*; ebb, low water 212 *shallowness*.

Adj. *insufficient*, not satisfying, unsatisfactory, disappointing 829 *discontenting*; inadequate, not enough, too little; scant, scanty, skimpy, slender; too small, cramping 33 *small*; deficient, light on, lacking 55 *incomplete*; wanting, found w., poor 35 *inferior*; incompetent, unequal to, not up to it 695 *unskilful*; weak, thin, watery, jejune, unnourishing 4 *insubstantial*; niggardly, miserly; stingy 816 *parsimonious*.

unprovided, unsupplied, unfurnished, ill-furnished, ill-supplied, vacant, bare, unreplenished 190 *empty*; empty-handed 728 *unsuccessful*; unsatisfied, unfilled, unsated 829 *discontented*; unprovided for, unaccommodated; insatiable 859 *greedy*; deficient in, starved of; cramped 702 *hindered*; hard up 801 *poor*; undercapitalized, underfinanced, understaffed, undermanned, shorthanded, under establishment, under strength; stinted, rationed, skimped; not provided, unavailable, off the menu, off 190 *absent*.

underfed, undernourished; half-fed, half-starved, on short commons; unfed, famished, starved, famine-stricken, starving 946 *fasting*; starveling, spare, scurvy, thin, skinny, skin and bone, macerated, stunted 206 *lean*.

scarce, rare 140 *infrequent*; sparse 105 *few*; short, in short supply, at a premium, hard to get, hard to come by, not to be had for love or money, not to be had at any price, unavailable, unprocurable, unobtainable, out of season, out of stock.

Vb. *not suffice*, be insufficient, - inadequate etc. adj.; not meet requirements 647 *be imperfect*; cramp one's style 747 *restrain*; want, lack, need, require, leave a gap 627 *require*; fail 509 *disappoint*; fall below 35 *be inferior*; come short, default 307 *fall short*; run out, dry up; take half measures, tinker, paper over the cracks 726 *not complete*.

be unsatisfied, ask for more, beg for m., come again, take a second helping, still feel hungry 859 *be hungry*; feel dissatisfied, increase one's demands 829 *be discontented*; spurn an offer, reject with contempt 607 *reject*; desiderate, miss, want, feel the lack, stand in need of, feel something is missing 627 *require*; be a glutton for, be unable to have enough of 947 *gluttonize*.

make insufficient, ask too much, expect too much; overwork, overcrop, impoverish, damage 655 *impair*; exhaust, deplete, run down, squander 634 *waste*; grudge, hold back, stint, skimp, ration, put on half rations, put on short commons 816 *be parsimonious*; disinherit, cut off with a shilling 786 *deprive*.

Adv. *insufficiently*, not enough; in default, failing, for want of; at a low ebb.

See: 4, **33**, 35, 37, 55, **105**, 140, 172, 190, 206, 212, 307, 509, 607, 627, 634, 647, 651, 655, 695, 702, 726, 728, 747, 786, **801**, 805, 816, **829**, 859, 945, 946, 947.

637 Redundance

N. *redundance*, redundancy, overspill, overflow, inundation, flood 298 *outflow*; abundance, superabundance, exuberance, luxuriance, riot, profusion 635 *plenty*; richness, bonanza 632 *store*; upsurge, uprush 36 *increase*; avalanche, spate 32 *great quantity*; too many, mob 74 *crowd*; saturation, saturation point 54 *plenitude*; excess 634 *waste*; excessiveness, nimiety, exorbitance, extremes, too much 546 *exaggeration*; overdoing it, overextension, overexpansion, too many irons in the fire 678 *overactivity*; overpoliteness, officiousness; overpraise, overoptimism 482 *overestimation*; overmeasure, overpayment, overweight; burden, load, overload, last straw 322 *gravity*; more than is fair, lion's share 32 *main part*; overindulgence 943 *intemperance*; overfeeding 947 *gluttony*; overdrinking 949 *drunkenness*; engorgement, plethora, congestion 863 *satiety*; more than enough, bellyful 635 *sufficiency*; glut (**see** *superfluity*); fat, fattiness; obesity 651 *disease*.

superfluity, more than is needed, luxury, luxuriousness; gilt on the gingerbread, frills, luxuries, nonessentials, luxury article; overfulfilment, overkill, duplication, supererogation; something over, bonus, cash crop, spare cash, money to burn 40 *extra*; margin, overlap, excess, overplus, surplusage, surplus, balance 41 *remainder*; superfluousness, excrescence, accessory, fifth wheel, parasite 641 *inutility*; padding, expletive, verse-filler 570 *pleonasm*; tautology 570 *diffuseness*; redundancy, underemployment, unemployment 679 *inactivity*; overemployment, overmanning 678 *activity*; too much of a good thing, embarras de richesses, glut, drug on the market; inflation; surfeit, sickener, overdose 863 *satiety*.

Adj. *redundant*, too many, one too m. 104 *many*; overmuch, excessive, immoderate 32 *exorbitant*; overdone 546 *exaggerated*; overflowing, overfull, slopping, running over, brimming over, filled to overflowing 54 *full*; flooding, streaming 350 *flowing*;

snowed under, saturated, supersaturated 341 *drenched*; cloying, satiating 838 *tedious*; cloyed, satiated 863 *sated*; replete, gorged, crammed, stuffed, overfed, bursting; overcharged, overloaded; congested, plethoric; bloated 197 *expanded*.

superfluous, supererogatory; supernumerary; adscititious, excrescent; needless, unnecessary, unrequired, uncalled for 641 *useless*; excessive, more than one asked for 634 *wasteful*; luxury, luxurious, with all the trimmings; surplus, extra, over and above 41 *remaining*; above one's needs, spare, to spare 38 *additional*; de trop, on one's hands, going begging 860 *unwanted*; dispensable, expendable, replaceable.

Vb. *superabound*, riot, luxuriate 635 *abound*; run riot, overproduce, overpopulate 171 *be fruitful*; bristle with, burst w., meet one at every turn, outnumber 104 *be many*; overflow, brim over, well o., ooze at every pore, burst at the seams 54 *be complete*; stream, flood, inundate, burst its banks, deluge, overwhelm 350 *flow*; engulf 299 *absorb*; know no bounds, spread far and wide 306 *overstep*; overlap 183 *extend*; soak, saturate 341 *drench*; stuff, gorge, cram 54 *fill*; congest, choke, suffocate; overdose, oversatisfy, glut, cloy, satiate, sicken 863 *sate*; overfeed, pamper oneself, overeat, overdrink 943 *be intemperate*; overfulfil, oversubscribe, do more than enough; oversell, flood the market; overstock, pile up; overdo, go over the top, overegg the pudding, pile it on, lay it on thick, lay it on with a trowel 546 *exaggerate*; overload, overburden; overcharge, surcharge; lavish, lavish upon 813 *be liberal*; be lavish, make a splash 815 *be prodigal*; roll in, crawl with, stink of 800 *be rich*.

be superfluous, - redundant etc. adj.; go begging, remain on one's hands 41 *be left*; have time on one's hands 679 *be inactive*; do twice over, duplicate; carry coals to Newcastle, gild the lily, teach one's grandmother to suck eggs; labour the obvious, take a sledgehammer to crack a nut, break a butterfly on a wheel, hold a candle to the sun 641 *waste effort*; exceed requirements, have no use 641 *be useless*; go in for luxuries.

Adv. *redundantly*, over and above, too much, overly, excessively, unnecessarily, beyond measure; enough and to spare; in excess of requirements.

See: 32, 36, 38, 40, 41, **54**, 74, 104, 171, 183, 197, 298, 299, 306, 322, 341, 350, 482, 546, 570, 632, 634, **635**, 641, 651, 678, 679, 800, 813, 815, 838, 860, **863**, 943, 947, 949.

638 Importance

N. *importance*, first i., primacy, priority, urgency 64 *precedence*; paramountcy, supremacy 34 *superiority*; essentiality, irreplaceability; import, consequence, significance, weight, weightiness, gravity, seriousness, solemnity; materiality, materialness, substance, pith, moment 3 *substantiality*; interest, consideration, concern 622 *business*; notability, memorability, mark, prominence, distinction, eminence 866 *repute*; influence 866 *prestige*; size, magnitude 32 *greatness*; rank, high standing 27 *degree*; value, excellence, merit 644 *goodness*; use, usefulness 640 *utility*; stress, emphasis, insistence 532 *affirmation*.

important matter, vital concern; turning point 137 *crisis*; breath of life, be-all and end-all; grave affair, not peanuts, no joke, no laughing matter, matter of life and death; notable point, memorandum 505 *reminder*; big news, great n. 529 *news*; great doings, exploit 676 *deed*; landmark, milestone; red-letter day, great d. 876 *special day*.

chief thing, what matters, the thing, great t., main t.; issue, supreme i., crux 452 *topic*; fundamentals, bedrock, fact 1 *reality*; essential, sine qua non 627 *requirement*; priority, first choice 605 *choice*; gist 514 *meaning*; substance 5 *essential part*; highlight, main feature; best part, cream, salt, pick 644 *elite*; keynote, cornerstone, mainstay, linchpin, kingpin; head, spearhead; sum and substance, heart of the matter, heart, core, kernel, nucleus, nub 225 *centre*; hub 218 *pivot*; cardinal point, main p., half the battle 32 *main part*; chief hope, trump card, main chance.

bigwig, personage, notable, notability, personality, heavyweight, somebody 866 *person of repute*; local worthy, pillar of the community; great man *or* woman, VIP, brass hat; his *or* her nibs, big gun, big shot, big noise, big bug, big wheel, big chief, big Daddy, Mr Big; high muck-a-muck, great panjandrum; leading light, master spirit 500 *sage*; kingpin, key person 696 *expert*; first fiddle, prima donna, star, lion, catch, great c. 890 *favourite*; uncrowned king *or* queen, head, chief 34 *superior*; superior person, lords of creation; the greatest 644 *exceller*; grandee 868 *aristocrat*; magnate, mogul, mandarin; baron, tycoon 741 *autocrat*; captains of industry, big battalions, top brass, top people, establishment 733 *authority*; superpower 178 *influence*.

Adj. *important*, weighty, grave, solemn, serious; pregnant, big; of consequence, of consideration, of importance, of concern; considerable, worth considering; world-shattering, earth-shaking, momentous, critical, fateful 137 *timely*; chief, capital, cardinal, staple, major, main, paramount 34 *supreme*; crucial, essential, material, to the point 9 *relevant*; pivotal 225 *central*; basic, fundamental, bedrock, radical, going to the root; primary, prime, foremost, leading; overriding, overruling, uppermost 34 *superior*; worthwhile, not to be despised, not to be overlooked, not to be sneezed at 644 *valuable*; necessary, vital, indispensable, irreplaceable, key 627 *required*; helpful 640 *useful*; significant, telling, trenchant 514 *meaningful*; imperative, urgent, high-priority; overdue 136 *late*; high-level, top-l., summit 213 *topmost*; top-secret 523 *latent*; high, grand, noble 32 *great*.

notable, of mark 32 *remarkable*; memorable, signal, unforgettable 505 *remembered*; first-rate, outstanding, excelling 34 *superior*; ranking, top-rank, top-flight 644 *excellent*; conspicuous, prominent, eminent, distinguished, exalted, august 866 *noteworthy*; dignified, imposing, commanding 821 *impressive*; formidable, powerful 178 *influential*; newsworthy, front-page; eventful, stirring, breathtaking, shattering, earth-shaking, seismic, epoch-making.

Vb. *be important*, matter, be a consideration, bulk large 612 *motivate*; weigh, carry, tell, count, cast a long shadow 178 *influence*; import, signify 514 *mean*; concern, interest, affect 9 *be related*; have priority, come first 34 *predominate*; take the lead 64 *come before*; be something, be somebody 920 *command respect*; take the limelight, deserve notice, make a stir, create a sensation, cut a figure, cut a dash 455 *attract notice*.

make important, give weight to, attach *or* ascribe importance to; seize on, fasten on; bring to the fore, place in the foreground; enhance, highlight; rub in, stress, underline, labour, make a point of 532 *emphasize*; put in capital letters, headline, splash 528 *advertise*; bring to notice, put on the map 528 *proclaim*; write in letters of gold 876 *celebrate*; magnify 197 *enlarge*; make much of 546 *exaggerate*; lionize, honour, glorify, exalt 920 *show respect*; take seriously, make a fuss about, make a stir, make much ado; value, esteem, make much of, set store by, think everything of 920 *respect*; overestimate 482 *overrate*.

Adv. *importantly*, primarily, significantly; materially, largely, in the main, above all, to crown all; par excellence.

See: 1, 3, 5, 9, 27, **32**, **34**, 64, 136, 137, 178, 197, 213, 218, 225, 452, 455, 482, 500, 505, 514, 523, 528, 529, 532, 546, 605, 612, 622, 627, 640, 644, 676, 696, 733, 741, 821, **866**, 868, 876, 890, 920.

639 Unimportance

N. *unimportance*, inconsequence, insignificance, secondariness 35 *inferiority*; immateriality, inessentiality, lack of substance 4 *insubstantiality*; nothingness, nullity 190 *emptiness*; pettiness 33 *smallness*; paltriness, meanness 922 *contemptibility*; triviality, superficiality 212 *shallowness*; flippancy, snap of the fingers, frivolity, floccinaucinihilipilification; worthlessness 812 *cheapness*; uselessness 641 *inutility*; irrelevance, red herring 10 *unrelatedness*.

trifle, inessential, triviality, technicality; nothing, mere n., no matter, no great m., parish pump; accessory, secondary matter, sideshow; nothing in particular, matter of indifference, not the end of the world; no great shakes, nothing to speak of, nothing to boast of, nothing to worry about, storm in a teacup 482 *overestimation*; tithe, fraction 53 *part*; bagatelle, floccinaucity, tinker's cuss, fig, damn, straw, chaff, pin, button, feather, dust; cobweb, gossamer 330 *brittleness*; small item, tuppence, small change, small beer, small potatoes; paltry sum, peanuts, chickenfeed, fleabite; pinprick, scratch; nothing to it, child's play 701 *easy thing*; jest, joke, practical j., farce 837 *amusement*; peccadillo, venial sin; trifles, trivia, minutiae, detail, petty d. 80 *particulars*; whit, jot, tittle, the least bit, trickle, drop in the ocean 33 *small quantity*; cent, brass farthing 33 *small coin*; nonsense, fiddle-faddle 497 *absurdity*; piffle, drivel 515 *empty talk*.

bauble, toy, rattle 837 *plaything*; gewgaw, kickshaw, knick-knack, bric-a-brac; novelty, trinket, bibelot; tinsel, trumpery, frippery, trash, gimcrack; froth, foam 355 *bubble*.

nonentity, nobody, obscurity; man of straw 4 *insubstantial thing*; figurehead, cipher, sleeping partner; fribble, trifler, smatterer, jack of all trades and master of none 697 *bungler*; mediocrity, lightweight, small beer; small fry, small game; banana republic; other ranks, lower orders 869 *commonalty*; second fiddle 35 *inferior*; underling, understrapper 742 *servant*; pawn, pawn in the game, piece on the board, stooge, puppet 628 *instrument*; Cinderella, poor relation 801 *poor person*; pipsqueak, whippersnapper, squirt, squit, trash 867 *object of scorn*.

Adj. *unimportant*, immaterial 4 *insubstantial*; ineffectual, uninfluential, inconsequential, of no consequence, of no great weight; insignificant 515 *meaningless*; off the point 10 *irrelevant*; inessential, nonessential, not vital, fringe; unnecessary, dispensable, expendable; small, petty, trifling, nugatory, flimsy, paltry 33 *inconsiderable*; negligible, inappreciable, not worth considering, out of the running; weak, puny, powerless 161 *impotent*; wretched, measly, miserable, pitiful, pitiable, pathetic; mean, sorry, shabby 801 *poor*; obscure, disregarded, overlooked 458 *neglected*; overrated, beneath notice, beneath contempt 922 *contemptible*; jumped-up, no-account, tinpot, potty; low-level, of second rank, secondary, minor, by-, subsidiary, peripheral 35 *inferior*.

trivial, trifling, piffling, piddling, fiddling, niggling; pettifogging, pinpricking, nitpicking, technical; footling, frivolous, puerile, childish 499 *foolish*; windy, airy, frothy 4 *insubstantial*; superficial 212 *shallow*; slight 33 *small*; lightweight 323 *light*; not serious, forgivable, venial; parish-pump, small-time; twopenny-halfpenny, one-horse, second-rate, third-r.; potty, grotty, rubbishy, trumpery, trashy, tawdry, catchpenny, pinchbeck, pot-boiling, shoddy, gimcrack 645 *bad*; two-a-penny 812 *cheap*; worthless, valueless 641 *useless*; not worthwhile, not worth a thought 922 *contemptible*; toy, token, nominal, symbolic 547 *indicating*; mediocre, nondescript, forgettable, eminently f.; commonplace, ordinary, uneventful 610 *usual*.

Vb. *be unimportant*, - valueless etc. adj.; not matter, weigh light upon, carry no weight, not weigh, not count, count for nothing, cut no ice, signify little; think unimportant, attach no importance to, not overrate, shrug off 458 *disregard*; snap one's fingers at 922 *hold cheap*; reduce one's importance, cut down to size 872 *humiliate*.

Int. no matter! never mind! so what! too bad!

See: 4, 10, **33**, **35**, 53, 80, 161, 190, 212, 323, 330, 355, 458, 482, 497, 499, 515, 547, 610, 628, 641, 645, 697, 701, 742, 801, 812, 837, 867, 869, 872, 922.

640 Utility

N. *utility*, use, usefulness; employability, serviceability, handiness 628 *instrumentality*; efficacy, efficiency 160 *ability*; adequacy 635 *sufficiency*; adaptability, applicability, suitability 642 *good policy*; readiness, availability 189 *presence*; service, avail, help, great h., good stead 703 *aid*; value, worth, merit 644 *goodness*; virtue, function, capacity, potency 160 *power*; advantage, commodity; profitability, earning capacity, productivity 171 *productiveness*; profit, mileage 771 *gain*; convenience, benefit, general b., public utility, common weal, public good 615 *good*; utilitarianism, functionalism; employment, utilization 673 *use*.

Adj. *useful*, utile, of use, helpful, of service 703 *aiding*; sensible, practical, applied, functional; versatile, multipurpose, all-purpose, of all work; practicable, commodious, convenient, expedient 642 *advisable*; handy, ready, rough and r.; at hand, available, on tap; serviceable, fit for, good for, disposable, adaptable, applicable; fit for use, ready for u., usable, reusable, employable; good, valid, current; subsidiary, subservient 628 *instrumental*; able, competent, efficacious, effective, effectual, efficient 160 *powerful*; conducive 179 *tending*; adequate 635 *sufficient*; pragmatic, utilitarian.

profitable, economic, paying, remunerative 771 *gainful*; prolific, fertile 164 *productive*; beneficial, advantageous, to one's advantage, edifying, worthwhile 615 *good*; worth one's salt, worth one's keep, invaluable, priceless 644 *valuable*.

Vb. *be useful*, - of use etc. adj.; avail, prove helpful, be of value, bestead, stand one in good stead; come in handy, have some use, perform a function; function, work 173 *operate*; perform 676 *do*; serve, subserve, serve one's turn, answer 635 *suffice*; suit one's purpose 642 *be expedient*; further one's purpose, help, advance, promote 703 *aid*; do service, do yeoman s. 742 *serve*; conduce 179 *tend*; benefit, profit, advantage 644 *do good*; bear fruit 171 *be fruitful*; pay, pay off, make a profit, be worth one's while 771 *be profitable*.

find useful, have a use for, employ, make use of, utilize 673 *use*; turn to good account, improve on, make capital out of 137 *profit by*; reap the benefit of 771 *gain*; be the better for 654 *get better*.

Adv. *usefully*, serviceably; advantageously; pro bono publico; cui bono? to whose advantage?

See: 137, 160, 164, 171, 173, 179, 189, **615**, 628, 635, **642**, 644, 654, **673**, 676, 703, 742, 771.

641 Inutility

N. *inutility*, uselessness; no function, no purpose, superfluousness 637 *superfluity*; futility, inanity, vanity, vanity of vanities 497 *absurdity*; worthlessness, unemployability; inadequacy 636 *insufficiency*; inefficacy, ineffectualness, inability 161 *impotence*; inefficiency, incompetence, ineptitude 695 *unskilfulness*; unserviceableness, inconvenience, unsuitability, unfitness 643 *inexpedience*; inapplicability, unadaptability; unprofitability, no benefit 172 *unproductiveness*; disservice, mischief, damage, detriment 772 *loss*; unhelpfulness, recalcitrance 598 *unwillingness*.

lost labour, wasted l. 728 *failure*; game not worth the candle; waste of breath, waste of time, dead loss; lost trouble, labour in vain, wild-goose chase, fool's errand; blind alley 702 *obstacle*; labour of Sisyphus, Penelope's web; half measures, tinkering; futilitarian.

rubbish, good riddance, trash, stuff; waste, refuse, lumber, junk, scrap, litter; spoilage, wastage, waste products, waste paper, mullock; scourings, off-s., sweepings, shavings 41 *leavings*; chaff, husks, bran; scraps, bits; crumbs; offal, carrion; dust, muck, debris, slag, clinker, dross, scum 649 *dirt*; peel, orange p.; dead wood, stubble, weeds, tares; odds and ends, bits and pieces, rags and bones, old clothes, cast-offs; reject, throw-out; midden, rubbish heap, scrap h., dustheap, slag heap, dump.

Adj. *useless*, inutile, functionless, purposeless, pointless, Sisyphean; futile 497 *absurd*; unpractical, impracticable, unworkable, effort-wasting, no go; nonfunctional 844 *ornamental*; redundant, nonreturnable 637 *superfluous*; expendable, dispensable, unnecessary, unneeded 860 *unwanted*; unfit, unapt, inapplicable 643 *inexpedient*; fit for nothing, unusable, unemployable, unadaptable; unqualified, inefficient, incompetent 695 *unskilful*; unable, ineffective, feckless, ineffectual 161 *impotent*; nonfunctioning, inoperative, dud, kaput; uncurrent, invalid 752 *abrogated*; unserviceable, out of order, not working 61 *orderless*; broken down, effete, worn out, past work, hors de combat, obsolete, outmoded 127 *antiquated*; hopeless, vain, idle (**see** *profitless*).

profitless, bootless, unavailing; loss-making, unprofitable, not worthwhile, wasteful, not paying, ill-spent 772 *losing*; vain, in vain, abortive 728 *unsuccessful*; nothing to show for 634 *wasted*; unrewarding, unrewarded, thankless; fruitless, barren, sterile 172 *unproductive*; idle 679 *lazy*; worthless, good for nothing, valueless, no earthly use; rubbishy, trashy, no good, not worth powder and shot, not worth the paper it is written on 645 *bad*; unsalable, dear at any price 811 *dear*.

Vb. *be useless*, have no use, waste one's time, be on a hiding to nothing; achieve no purpose, end in futility; not help 702 *hinder*; not work, not function 728 *fail*; refuse to work 677 *not act*; fall by the wayside 172 *be unproductive*; go begging 637 *be superfluous*.

make useless, disqualify, unfit, disarm, take the sting out of 161 *disable*; castrate, emasculate 161 *unman*; cripple, lame, clip the wings 655 *impair*; dismantle, unmount, dismast, unrig, put out of commission, lay up 679 *make inactive*; sabotage, throw a spanner in the works, put a spoke in one's wheel 702 *obstruct*; disassemble, undo, take to pieces, break up 46 *disunite*; deface, withdraw from currency

752 *abrogate*; devalue 812 *cheapen*; pollute, contaminate, lay waste 172 *make sterile*.
waste effort, labour the obvious; waste one's breath, talk to a brick wall; preach to the converted 637 *be superfluous*; lose one's labour, labour in vain, sweat for nothing, flog a dead horse, beat the air, tilt at windmills; cry for the moon 470 *attempt the impossible*; tinker, paper over the cracks, spoil the ship for a ha'porth of tar 726 *not complete*; rearrange the deckchairs on the Titanic 497 *be absurd*.
Adv. *uselessly*, to no purpose; helplessly, ineffectually, to no avail, until one is blue in the face.
See: 41, 46, 61, 127, 161, **172**, 470, 497, 598, 634, 636, **637**, 643, 645, 649, 655, 677, 679, 695, 702, 726, 728, 752, 772, 811, 812, 844, 860.

642 Good policy
N. *good policy*, expediency; answer, right a., advisability, desirability, worthwhileness, suitability 640 *utility*; fitness, propriety 915 *dueness*; high time, due t., right t., proper t., opportunity 137 *occasion*; rule of expediency, convenience, pragmatism, utilitarianism, opportunism, timeserving; profit, advantage 615 *benefit*; facilities, conveniences 629 *means*; an expedient, pis aller 623 *contrivance*.
Adj. *advisable*, commendable; better to, desirable, worthwhile 644 *beneficial*; acceptable 923 *approved*; up one's street, suitable 24 *fit*; fitting, befitting, seemly, proper 913 *right*; owing 915 *due*; in loco, well-timed, auspicious, opportune 137 *timely*; prudent, politic, judicious 498 *wise*; expedient, expediential; advantageous, profitable 640 *useful*; convenient, workable, practical, pragmatic, practicable, negotiable; qualified, cut out for; to the purpose, adapted to, applicable; handy, effective, effectual.
Vb. *be expedient*, not come amiss, serve the time, suit the occasion, befit; be to the purpose, expedite one's end, help 703 *aid*; forward, advance, promote 640 *be useful*; answer, have the desired effect, produce results 156 *conduce*; wash, work, do, serve, be better than nothing, deliver the goods, fill *or* fit the bill 635 *suffice*; achieve one's aim 727 *succeed*; qualify for, fit, be just the thing 24 *accord*; profit, advantage, benefit 644 *do good*.
Adv. *expediently*, conveniently, fittingly, opportunely 615 *well*; in the right place at the right time.
See: 24, 137, 156, 498, **615**, 623, 629, 635, **640**, **644**, 703, 727, 913, 915, 923.

643 Inexpedience
N. *inexpedience*, inexpediency; no answer, not the a., bad policy, counsel of despair 495 *error*; inadvisability, undesirability; unsuitability, unfitness 25 *inaptitude*; impropriety, unfittingness, unseemliness 916 *undueness*; wrongness 914 *wrong*; inopportuneness 138 *untimeliness*; disqualification, disability, handicap 702 *obstacle*; incommodity, inconvenience, disadvantage, detriment; doubtful advantage, mixed blessing, pis aller; last resort 596 *necessity*.
Adj. *inexpedient*, better not, inadvisable, undesirable, uncommendable, not recommended 924 *disapproved*; ill-advised, impolitic, imprudent, injudicious 499 *unwise*; inappropriate, unfitting, malapropos, out of place, unseemly 916 *undue*; not right, improper, objectionable 914 *wrong*; beneath one's dignity, infra dig; unfit, ineligible, inadmissible, unsuitable, unhappy, infelicitous, inept 25 *unapt*; unseasonable, inopportune, untimely, wrongly timed 138 *ill-timed*; unsatisfactory 636 *insufficient*; discommodious, incommodious, inconvenient; detrimental, disadvantageous, hurtful 645 *harmful*; unhealthy, unwholesome 653 *insalubrious*; unprofitable 641 *useless*; unhelpful 702 *hindering*; untoward 731 *adverse*; ill-contrived, awkward 695 *clumsy*; incommodious, cumbersome, lumbering, hulking 195 *unwieldy*.
Vb. *be inexpedient*, - inadvisable etc. adj.; not fit, come amiss, won't do, won't wash, not answer; not help 641 *be useless*; bother, discommode, incommode, put to inconvenience 827 *trouble*; disadvantage, penalize, hurt 645 *harm*; work against 702 *obstruct*; embarrass 700 *be difficult*.
See: 25, 138, 195, 495, 499, 596, 636, 641, 645, 653, 695, 700, 702, 731, 827, 914, 916, 924.

644 Goodness
N. *goodness*, soundness 650 *health*; virtuosity 694 *skill*; quality, good q., classic q., vintage; long suit, good points, redeeming feature; merit, desert, title to

fame; excellence, eminence, supereminence 34 *superiority*; virtue, worth, value 809 *price*; pricelessness, superexcellence 32 *greatness*; flawlessness 646 *perfection*; distilled essence, quintessence 1 *essence*; beneficence 897 *benevolence*; virtuous character 933 *virtue*.

elite, chosen few, chosen people, the saints; pick, prime, flower; cream, crème de la crème, salt of the earth, pick of the bunch, meritocracy; crack troops, corps d'élite; top people 638 *bigwig*; charmed circle, top drawer, upper crust, aristocracy 868 *upper class*; choice bit, titbit, prime cut, pièce de résistance; plum, prize 729 *trophy*.

exceller, nonpareil, nonesuch; prodigy, genius; superman, wonderwoman, wonder, wonder of the world 864 *prodigy*; Admirable Crichton 646 *paragon*; grand fellow, one of the best 937 *good person*; one in a thousand, treasure, perfect t. 890 *favourite*; jewel, pearl, ruby, diamond 844 *gem*; gem of the first water, pearl of price, gold, pure g., refined g.; chef-d'oeuvre, pièce de résistance, collector's piece, museum p. 694 *masterpiece*; record-breaker, best-seller, best ever, absolute end, last word in, best thing since sliced bread; bee's knees, cat's whiskers, cat's pyjamas; the goods, winner, corker, scorcher, humdinger, wow, knockout, hit, smash h.; smasher, charmer 841 *a beauty*; star, idol 890 *favourite*; best of its kind, the tops, the greatest, top of the pops; top-notcher, top seed, first-rater; cock of the walk, toast of the town, Queen of the May, pride of the north; champion, title-holder, world-beater, prizewinner 727 *victor*.

Adj. *excellent*, fine, braw; exemplary, worth imitating; good, good as gold 933 *virtuous*; above par, preferable, better 34 *superior*; very good, first-rate, superexcellent, alpha plus; prime, quality, good q., fine, superfine, most desirable; God's own, superlative, in a class by itself; all-star, of the first water, rare, vintage, classic 646 *perfect*; choice, select, picked, handpicked, tested, exquisite, recherché 605 *chosen*; exclusive, pure 44 *unmixed*; worthy, meritorious 915 *deserving*; admired, admirable, estimable, praiseworthy, creditable 923 *approvable*; famous, great; couleur de rose, lovely 841 *beautiful*; glorious, dazzling, splendid, splendiferous, magnificent, marvellous, wonderful, terrific, sensational, superb.

super, superduper, fantastic, way-out, fabulous, fab, groovy; spot-on, bang-on; top-notch, top-flight (**see** *best*); lovely, glorious, gorgeous, heavenly, out of this world 32 *prodigious*; smashing, stunning, ripping, topping, swell, great, grand, famous, capital, dandy, hunky-dory; scrumptious, delicious, juicy, plummy, jammy 826 *pleasurable*.

best, very b., optimum, A1, champion, tip-top, top-notch, nothing like it; first, first-rate, crack; a cut above, second to none 34 *supreme*; unequalled, unparalleled, unmatched, peerless, matchless, unbeatable, unsurpassable 646 *perfect*; best-ever, record, record-breaking, best-selling 34 *crowning*; capital, cardinal 638 *important*.

valuable, of value, invaluable, inestimable, priceless, above price, costly, rich 811 *of price*; irreplaceable, unique, rare, precious, golden, worth its weight in gold, worth a king's ransom; sterling, gilt-edged, blue-chip, sound, solid.

beneficial, wholesome, healthy, salutary, sound 652 *salubrious*; refreshing, edifying, worthwhile, advantageous, profitable 640 *useful*; favourable, kind, propitious 730 *prosperous*; harmless, hurtless, inoffensive, innocuous 935 *innocent*.

not bad, tolerable, passable, respectable, standard, up to the mark, in good condition, in fair c., fair, satisfactory 635 *sufficient*; nice, decent, pretty good, all right, okay, OK; sound, fresh, unspoiled; unexceptionable, unobjectionable; indifferent, middling, mediocre, ordinary, fifty-fifty, average 30 *median*.

Vb. *be good*, - sound etc. adj.; have quality; have merit, deserve well 915 *deserve*; qualify, stand the test, pass, pass muster 635 *suffice*; challenge comparison, vie, rival, equal the best 28 *be equal*; excel, transcend, overtop, take the prize 34 *be superior*.

do good, have a good effect, edify; do a world of good 652 *be salubrious*; be the making of, make a man of 654 *make better*; help 615 *benefit*; favour, smile on 730 *prosper*; do a favour, do a good turn, confer an obligation, put in one's debt 897 *be benevolent*; not hurt, do no harm, break no bones.

Adv. *aright*, well, rightly, properly, admirably, excellently, famously.

See: 1, 28, 30, 32, **34**, 44, 605, 615, 635, 638, 640, **646**, 650, 652, 654, 694, 727, 729, 730, 809, 811, 826, 841, 844, 864, 868, 890, 897, 915, 923, 933, 935, 937.

645 Badness

N. *badness*, bad qualities, obnoxiousness, nastiness, beastliness, foulness, grossness, rottenness; demerit, unworthiness, worthlessness; low quality, low standard 35 *inferiority*; faultiness, flaw 647 *imperfection*; poor make, shoddiness 641 *inutility*; clumsiness 695 *unskilfulness*; rankness, unsoundness, taint, decay, corruption 655 *deterioration*; disruption, confusion 61 *disorder*; peccancy, morbidity 651 *disease*; harmfulness, hurtfulness, balefulness, ill, hurt, harm, injury, detriment, damage, mischief 616 *evil*; noxiousness, poisonousness, deadliness, virulence 653 *insalubrity*; poison, blight, cancer 659 *bane*; pestilence, sickness 651 *plague*; contamination, centre of infection, plague spot, hotbed 651 *infection*; affair, scandal 867 *slur*; abomination, filth 649 *uncleanness*; sewer 649 *sink*; bitterness, gall, wormwood 393 *sourness*; painfulness, sting, ache, pang, thorn in the flesh 377 *pain*; molestation 827 *annoyance*; anguish 825 *suffering*; harshness, tyranny, maltreatment, oppression, persecution, intolerance 735 *severity*; unkindness, cruelty, malignancy, malignity, spitefulness, spite 898 *malevolence*; depravity, vice 934 *wickedness*; sin 936 *guilt*; bad influence, evil genius; evil spirit 970 *demon*; ill wind, evil star 731 *misfortune*; black magic, evil eye, hoodoo, jinx 983 *sorcery*; curse 899 *malediction*; snake in the grass 663 *troublemaker*; bad character 904 *evildoer*.

Adj. *bad*, arrant, vile, base, evil, ill-conditioned; gross, black; utterly bad, irredeemable, as bad as bad can be; bad of its kind, poor, mean, wretched, grotty, measly, low-grade, not good enough, execrable, awful 35 *inferior*; no good, worthless, cheap-jack, shoddy, tacky, crummy, ropy, punk, pathetic 641 *useless*; unsatisfactory, faulty, flawed 647 *imperfect*; bad at, incompetent, inefficient, unskilled 695 *clumsy*; badly done, mangled, spoiled 695 *bungled*; scruffy, filthy 649 *dirty*; foul, noisome 397 *fetid* (**see** *not nice*); gone bad, rank, not fresh, unsound, affected, tainted 655 *deteriorated*; corrupt, decaying, decayed, rotten to the core 51 *decomposed*; peccant, disordered, infected, envenomed, poisoned, septic 651 *diseased*; irremediable, incurable; depraved, vicious, villainous, accursed 934 *wicked*; heinous, sinful 936 *guilty*; mean, shabby 930 *dishonest*; wrongful, unjust 914 *wrong*; sinister 616 *evil* (**see** *harmful*); undeserving, unworthy, contemptible; shameful, scandalous, disgraceful 867 *discreditable*; sad, melancholy, lamentable, deplorable, pitiable, pitiful, woeful, grievous, sore 827 *distressing*; unendurable 827 *intolerable*; heavy, onerous, burdensome 684 *fatiguing*; too bad 827 *annoying*.

harmful, hurtful, injurious, damaging, detrimental, prejudicial, disadvantageous 643 *inexpedient*; deleterious, corrosive, wasting, consuming 165 *destructive*; pernicious, fatal 362 *deadly*; costly 811 *dear*; disastrous, ruinous, calamitous 731 *adverse*; degenerative, noxious, malign, malignant, unhealthy, unwholesome, noisome, miasmal, infectious 653 *insalubrious*; polluting, poisonous, radioactive 653 *toxic*; unsafe, risky 661 *dangerous*; sinister, ominous, dire, dreadful, baleful, baneful, accursed 616 *evil*; malefic, mischievous, spiteful, malicious, malevolent, ill-disposed; mischief-making, puckish, impish 898 *unkind*; bloody, bloodthirsty, inhuman 898 *cruel*; outrageous, rough, furious 176 *violent*; harsh, intolerant, persecuting 735 *oppressive*; monstrous 32 *exorbitant*.

not nice, unlikable, obnoxious, nasty, beastly, horrid, horrible, terrible, gruesome, grim, ghastly, awful, dreadful, perfectly d.; scruffy 867 *disreputable*; foul, rotten, lousy, putrid, stinking, stinky, sickening, revolting, nauseous, nauseating 861 *disliked*; loathsome, detestable, abominable 888 *hateful*; vulgar, sordid, low, indecent, improper, gross, filthy, obscene 951 *impure*; shocking, disgusting, reprehensible, monstrous, horrendous 924 *disapproved*; plaguy, wretched, miserable 827 *annoying*.

damnable, damned, darned, blasted, confounded, blinking, dratted, bothersome, blankety-blank; execrable, accursed, cursed, hellish, infernal, devilish, diabolic, diabolical.

Vb. *harm*, do h., do one a hurt, do one a mischief, scathe 827 *hurt*; cost one dear

811 *be dear*; disagree with, make one ill; injure, damage, pollute 655 *impair*; corrupt 655 *pervert*; play havoc with 63 *derange*; do no good 641 *be useless*; worsen, make things worse; do evil, work e. 914 *do wrong*; molest, pain 827 *torment*; plague, vex 827 *trouble*; land one in trouble, queer one's pitch, do for; spite, be unkind 898 *be malevolent*.

ill-treat, maltreat, mishandle, abuse 675 *misuse*; ill-use, burden, overburden, put upon, tyrannize, bear hard on, tread on, trample on, victimize, prey upon; persecute 735 *oppress*; wrong, aggrieve 914 *do wrong*; distress 827 *torment*; outrage, violate, force 176 *be violent*; savage, maul, bite, scratch, tear 655 *wound*; stab 263 *pierce*; batter, bruise, buffet 279 *strike*; agonize, rack, crucify 963 *torture*; spite, use despitefully, wreak one's malice on 898 *be malevolent*; crush 165 *destroy*.

Adv. *badly*, amiss, wrong, ill; to one's cost; cruelly 32 *painfully*.

See: 32, **35**, 51, 61, 63, 165, 176, 263, 279, 362, 377, 393, 397, **616**, 641, 643, **647**, 649, 651, 653, **655**, 659, 661, 663, 675, 684, 695, 731, 735, 811, 825, **827**, 861, 867, 888, 898, 899, 904, 914, 924, 930, 934, 936, 951, 963, 970, 983.

646 Perfection

N. *perfection*, sheer p.; finish, classic quality; perfectness, the ideal; nothing wrong with, immaculacy, immaculateness, faultlessness, flawlessness, mint condition; correctness, correctitude, irreproachability; impeccancy, impeccability, infallibility, indefectibility; transcendence 34 *superiority*; quintessence, essence; peak, pinnacle 213 *summit*; height *or* pitch of perfection, acme of p., pink of p., ne plus ultra, extreme, last word; chef d'oeuvre, flawless performance 694 *masterpiece*.

paragon, nonesuch, nonpareil, flower, a beauty, prince of 644 *exceller*; ideal, beau idéal, knight in shining armour, saint, plaster s.; classic, pattern, pattern of perfection, standard, norm, model, mirror, shining example 23 *prototype*; phoenix, rarity 84 *rara avis*; superman, wonderwoman, demigod 864 *prodigy*.

Adj. *perfect*, perfected, finished, brought to perfection, ripened; ripe, fully r. 669 *matured*; just right, ideal, flawless, faultless, impeccable, infallible, indefectible; correct, irreproachable; immaculate, unblemished, unflawed, unstained; spotless, unspotted, without blemish, without a stain; uncontaminated, pure 44 *unmixed*; guiltless 935 *innocent*; sound, uncracked, sound as a bell, right as rain, right as a trivet, in perfect condition; tight, watertight, seaworthy; whole, entire, one hundred per cent; complete 52 *intact*; dazzling, beyond praise 644 *excellent*; consummate, unsurpassable 34 *supreme*; brilliant, masterly 694 *skilful*; pattern, standard, model, classic, classical, Augustan.

undamaged, safe and sound, with a whole skin, unhurt, unscathed, scatheless, no harm done; unscarred, unscratched, unmarked; unmarred, untainted, unspoilt; unreduced, undiminished, without loss, whole, entire 52 *intact*; in the pink 650 *healthy*.

Vb. *perfect*, consummate, bring to perfection; ripen 669 *mature*; correct 654 *rectify*; put the finishing touch 213 *crown*; complete, leave nothing to be desired 725 *carry through*.

Adv. *perfectly*, flawlessly, impeccably, irreproachably, to perfection, to a turn, just as one would wish.

See: 23, 34, 44, 52, 84, **213**, **644**, 650, 654, 669, 694, 725, 864, 935.

647 Imperfection

N. *imperfection*, imperfectness, not one hundred per cent; room for improvement, not one's best; possibility of perfection, perfectibility 654 *improvement*; faultiness, erroneousness, defectibility, fallibility 495 *error*; patchiness, unevenness, curate's egg 17 *nonuniformity*; immaturity, unripeness, underdevelopment, underachievement 670 *undevelopment*; defectiveness, bit missing 55 *incompleteness*; lack, want 627 *requirement*; deficiency, inadequacy 636 *insufficiency*; unsoundness 661 *vulnerability*; failure, failing, weakness 307 *shortfall*; low standard, pass degree; inferior version, poor relation 35 *inferiority*; second best, pis aller, consolation prize, makeshift 150 *substitute*; mediocrity, averageness 30 *average*; loss of fitness, staleness 684 *fatigue*; adulteration 43 *mixture*.

defect, fault 495 *error*; flaw, rift, leak, loophole, crack 201 *gap*; deficiency, limitation 307 *shortfall*; kink, foible, screw loose 503 *eccentricity*; weak point, soft spot, vulnerable point, tragic flaw, chink in one's armour, Achilles' heel 661 *vulnerability*; feet of clay, weak link in the chain 163 *weakness*; scratch, taint, stain, spot, smudge 845 *blemish*; drawback, catch, snag, fly in the ointment 702 *obstacle*.

Adj. *imperfect*, not quite right, not ideal, less than perfect, not classic; fallible, peccable; uneven, patchy, good in parts, like the curate's egg 17 *nonuniform*; faulty, botched 695 *bungled*; flawed, cracked; leaky, not waterproof; wobbly, rickety 163 *flimsy*; unsound 661 *vulnerable*; soiled, shop-s., tainted, stained, marked, scratched 845 *blemished*; overripe, underripe; past its best 655 *deteriorated*; below par, off form; unfit, stale 684 *fatigued*; off-colour, not in the pink 651 *unhealthy*; not good enough, inadequate, deficient, wanting, lacking 636 *insufficient*; defective, not entire 55 *incomplete*; partial, broken 53 *fragmentary*; legless, armless 163 *crippled*; unfilled, half-filled, undermanned, short-handed, below strength 670 *unequipped*; half-finished 55 *unfinished*; unthorough, perfunctory 456 *inattentive*; overwrought, overelaborated, overdone 546 *exaggerated*; warped, twisted, distorted 246 *deformed*; mutilated, maimed, lame 163 *weakened*; undeveloped, raw, crude, untrained, scratch 670 *immature*; makeshift, make-do, rough and ready, provisional 150 *substituted*; secondary 639 *unimportant*; second-best, second-rate 35 *inferior*; poor, unimpressive, negative 645 *bad*; ordinary, much of a muchness, so-so, middling, average 30 *median*; moderate, unheroic; no great shakes, nothing to boast of; only passable, tolerable, bearable, better than nothing 923 *approvable*.

Vb. *be imperfect*, fall short of perfection, have a fault; be defective 307 *fall short*; lie open to criticism, not bear inspection, not pass muster, fail the test, dissatisfy 636 *not suffice*; barely pass, scrape through; fail to gain approval, not impress, not make the grade 924 *incur blame*; have feet of clay 163 *be weak*.

Adv. *imperfectly*, to a limited extent, barely, almost, not quite, all but; with all its faults.

See: 17, 30, 35, 43, 53, 55, 150, 163, 201, 246, 307, 456, 495, 503, 546, 627, **636**, 639, **645**, 651, 654, 655, 661, 670, 684, 695, 702, **845**, 923, 924.

648 Cleanness

N. *cleanness*, freedom from dirt, absence of dust, immaculateness 950 *purity*; freshness, dewiness, whiteness; shine, polish, spit and polish; cleanliness, kid gloves, daintiness 862 *fastidiousness*.

cleansing, clean, spring-cleaning, dry-c.; washing, cleaning up, mopping up, washing up, wiping up; refining, clarification, purification; sprinkling, asperges, lustration, purgation; washing out, flushing, dialysis; purging, defecation 302 *excretion*; airing, ventilation, fumigation 338 *vaporization*; deodorization 395 *inodorousness*; antisepsis, sterilization, disinfection, decontamination, disinfestation, delousing; sanitation, waterborne s., drainage, sewerage, plumbing 652 *hygiene*; water closet, flush 649 *latrine*.

ablutions, washing; hygiene, oral h.; lavage, lavation, douche, flush; wash, catlick, lick and a promise; soaking, bathing, dipping; soaping, lathering, scrubbing, sponging, rinsing, shampoo; dip 313 *plunge*; bath, tub; bathtub, hipbath, bidet; washbasin, washstand, basin and ewer; hot bath, cold b., steam b., vapour b., blanket b., Turkish b., sauna; shower, cold s.; bathroom, washroom, public baths, thermae; hammam, sudatorium; plunge bath, swimming bath, swimming pool; wash, laundry; washtub, washboard, dolly; copper, boiler, washing machine, launderette.

cleanser, purifier; disinfectant, carbolic, deodorant; soda, washing s., detergent, soap, scented s., soap flakes; water, hot w., soap and w., shampoo; mouth wash, gargle; lotion, hand l.; cleansing cream, cold c.; dentifrice, toothpaste; pumice stone, hearthstone, holystone; polish, furniture p., boot p., blacking; wax, varnish; whitewash, paint 427 *whiting*; blacklead 428 *black pigment*; aperient 658 *purgative*; sewer, drainpipe, wastepipe 351 *drain*; waterworks.

cleaning utensil, broom, besom, mop, sponge, swab, scourer; strigil; loofah; duster, feather d., whisk; brush, scrubbing b., nailbrush, toothbrush, toothpick, dental floss; comb, hair brush, clothes b.; dustpan and brush, waste bin, dustbin; carpet sweeper, vacuum cleaner; doormat, foot-scraper; squeegee; pipe cleaner, pullthrough, reamer; windscreen wiper; screen, sieve, riddle, strainer 263 *porosity*; filter, air-f., oil-f.; blotter, eraser 550 *oblit-*

eration; rake, hoe; sprinkler 341 *irrigator*; dishwasher.

cleaning cloth, duster; dishcloth, tea towel; leather, wash-l.; chamois, shammy; flannel, face f., facecloth, towel, bath t.; handkerchief, paper h., tissue; bib, apron, napkin, serviette, place mat, tablemat, doyley, tablecloth; mat 226 *floor-cover*; cover, chair-c., dustsheet 226 *coverlet*.

cleaner, refiner, distiller; dry cleaner, launderer, laundryman, laundress, washerwoman, dhobi; fuller; scrubber, swabber; washer-up, dishwasher, scullion; charwoman, charlady, cleaner, help, home help; scavenger, sweeper, dustman, refuse collector; lavatory attendant, sanitary engineer; chimneysweep, window cleaner; shoeblack, bootblack; barber, hairdresser 843 *beautician*; gleaner, picker; scavenger bird, crow, vulture.

Adj. *clean*, dirt-free; snowy 427 *white*; polished, clean, bright, shining 417 *undimmed*; cleanly, dainty, nice 862 *fastidious*; dewy, fresh; bright as a new pin, fresh as a daisy; cleaned, scrubbed, polished etc. vb.; shaven, shorn, barbered, trimmed; cleaned up, laundered, starched; spruce, natty, spick and span, neat, tidy, well-groomed 60 *orderly*; deodorized, disinfected, aseptic, antiseptic, hygienic, sterilized, sterile 652 *salubrious*; pure, purified, refined, immaculate, spotless, speckless, stainless, unsoiled, unmuddied, untarnished, unsullied, clean as a whistle 646 *perfect*; untouched, blank; ritually clean, kosher 301 *edible*.

cleansing, lustral, purificatory; disinfectant; hygienic, sanitary; purgative, purgatory; detergent, abstersive; ablutionary, balneary.

Vb. *clean*, spring-clean, clean up; remove the dirt, lay the dust; groom, valet, spruce, neaten, trim 62 *arrange*; wash, wipe, wash clean, wipe c., wash up, wipe up *or* down, dry, wring, wring out; sponge, mop, mop up, swab, wash down; scrub, scour; flush, flush out; sandblast, holystone, scrape 333 *rub*; do the washing, launder, starch, iron; bleach, dry-clean; soap, lather, shampoo; bathe, dip, dunk, rinse, swill down, sluice, douche, shower 341 *drench*; dust, whisk, sweep, sweep up, beat, vacuum; brush, brush up; comb, rake; buff, polish; shine, black, blacklead 417 *make bright*; whitewash 427 *whiten*; erase 550 *obliterate*; strip, pick, pick clean, clean out, clear, clear out, rake o., make a clean sweep 300 *eject*.

purify, purge, clean up; bowdlerize, expurgate; sublimate, elevate 654 *make better*; cleanse, lave, lustrate, asperge; purify oneself, wash one's hands of; freshen, ventilate, fan, deodorize, fumigate; edulcorate, desalt, desalinate; decontaminate, disinfect, sterilize, antisepticize, chlorinate, pasteurize 652 *sanitate*; free from impurities, depurate, refine, distil, clarify, rack, skim, scum, despumate; decarbonize; elutriate, strain, filter, percolate, lixiviate, leach; sift, sieve 44 *eliminate*; sort out, weed o.; flush, clean out, wash o., drain 350 *make flow*.

See: 44, 60, 62, 226, 263, 300, 301, 302, 313, 333, 338, 341, 350, 351, 395, 417, 427, 428, 550, 646, 649, **652**, **654**, 658, 843, 862, 950.

649 Uncleanness

N. *uncleanness*, uncleanliness, dirty habits, wallowing, beastliness; soiling, dirtiness (**see** *dirt*); muckiness, miriness 347 *marsh*; scruffiness, grottiness, filthiness; lousiness, pediculosis, phthiriasis; squalidity, squalidness, squalor, slumminess 801 *poverty*; untidiness, sluttishness, slovenliness 61 *disorder*; stink 397 *stench*; pollution, defilement; corruption, taint, putrescence, putrefaction 51 *decomposition*; contamination 651 *infection*; abomination, scatology, obscenity 945 *badness*; unwashed body, dirty linen.

dirt, filth, stain, patch, blot; crud, yuk, muck, mud, sludge, slime; quagmire, bog 347 *marsh*; night soil, dung, droppings, ordure, faeces 302 *excrement*; snot, mucus; dust, mote 332 *powder*; cobweb, grime, smut, smudge, soot, smoke; grounds, grouts, dregs, lees, draff; sweepings, scourings, off-scourings 41 *leavings*; sediment, sedimentation, deposit, precipitate, residuum, fur; scum, dross, froth; scoriae, ashes, cinders, clinker, slag 381 *ash*; drainage, sewerage, effluent; cast-offs, cast skin, exuviae, slough; scurf, dandruff; tartar, plaque; pus, matter, feculence; refuse, garbage, litter 641 *rubbish*; rot, dry r., wet r., rust, mildew, mould, fungus 51 *decay*; carrion, offal; vermin, flea, nit 365 *insect*.

swill, pig-s., hogwash; bilge, bilge-water; ditch-w., dish-w., slops; sewage, drainage; wallow, hog-w., slough.

latrine, privy, heads, jakes, bog, john, loo; closet, earth c., long drop, water closet, WC; cloakroom, powder room, rest r., washroom, lavatory, toilet; urinal, public convenience, comfort station, Ladies, Gents; close-stool, commode, thunder-box, bedpan, chamber pot, potty, jerry 302 *defecation*.

sink, sink of corruption; kitchen sink, draining board; cesspit, cesspool, sump, septic tank, soakaway; gutter, sewer, main, cloaca 351 *drain*; laystall, dunghill, midden, rubbish heap, dust-h., compost h.; dustbin, trashcan 194 *vessel*; coalhole 194 *cellar*; Augean stables, pigsty, pigpen, den; slum, tenement 192 *housing*; shambles 362 *slaughterhouse*; plague-spot 651 *infection*; spittoon, cuspidor.

dirty person, sloven, slattern, slammerkin, drab, draggletail, traipse 61 *slut*; litterbug, litter lout; mudlark, street arab; scavenger 648 *cleaner*; beast, pig, wallower; ratbag, fleabag.

Adj. *unclean*, unhallowed, unholy 980 *profane*; smutty, scatological, obscene, corrupt 951 *impure*; coarse, unrefined, unpurified; septic, festering, poisonous 653 *toxic*; unsterilized, nonsterile 653 *infectious*; sordid, squalid, slummy, insanitary, unhygienic 653 *insalubrious*; foul, offensive, nasty, grotty, yukky; abominable, disgusting, repulsive 645 *not nice*; noisome, nauseous, nauseating, stinking, malodorous 397 *fetid*; uncleanly, unfastidious, beastly, hoggish; grubby, scruffy, scurfy; leprous, scabby; flea-ridden, lousy, pediculous, crawling; faecal, dungy, stercoraceous, excrementitious 302 *excretory*; carious, rotting, rotted, tainted, high; flyblown, maggoty, carrion 51 *decomposed*.

dirty, filthy; dusty, grimy, sooty, smoky; befouled, polluted, littered, rubbish-strewn; thick with dust, unswept; untidy, unkempt, slatternly, sleazy, slovenly, sluttish, bedraggled, frowzy 61 *orderless*; unsoaped, unwashed, unscoured, unrinsed, unwiped; black, dingy, uncleaned, unpolished, unburnished; tarnished, stained, soiled; greasy, oily; clotted, caked, matted, muddied, begrimed, dirt-encrusted; messy, mucky, muddy, slimy 347 *marshy*; thick, turbid; furred up, scummy; musty, fusty, cobwebby; mouldy, rotten 655 *dilapidated*.

Vb. *be unclean*, - dirty etc. adj.; get dirty, collect dust, foul up, clog; rust, mildew, moulder, fester, rot, go bad, addle 51 *decompose*; grow rank, smell 397 *stink*; wallow, roll in the mud.

make unclean, foul, befoul; dirty, soil; grime, begrime, cover with dust; stain, blot, sully, tarnish; muck up, make a mess, untidy 61 *be disordered*; daub, smirch, besmirch, smut, smudge, blur, smoke 419 *bedim*; spot, patch, maculate 437 *variegate*; streak, smear, besmear, grease; cake, clog, bemire, beslime, muddy, roil, rile; draggle, drabble; spatter, bespatter, splash, slobber, slaver 341 *moisten*; poison, taint, infect, corrupt, pollute, contaminate 655 *impair*; defile, profane, desecrate, unhallow 980 *be impious*.

See: 41, 51, 61, 192, 194, 302, 332, 341, 347, 351, 362, 365, 381, 397, 419, 437, 641, 645, 648, **651**, **653**, **655**, 801, 945, 951, 980.

650 Health

N. *health*, rude h., robust h., glowing h., good h.; healthiness, good constitution, health and strength 162 *vitality*; fitness, condition, good c., pink of condition; bloom, rosiness, rosy cheeks, apple c., ruddy complexion; well-being, physical w.; eupepsia 376 *euphoria*; mens sana in corpore sano; whole skin, soundness; incorruptibility 644 *goodness*; long life, longevity, ripe old age 131 *age*; hygiene, healthy state, clean bill of health; goddess of health, Hygeia.

Adj. *healthy*, healthful, wholesome, hygienic, sanitary 652 *salubrious*; in health, in good h., bursting with h., eupeptic, euphoric; fresh, blooming, ruddy, rosy, rosy-cheeked, florid; lusty, bouncing, strapping, hale, hearty, hale and hearty, sound, fit, well, fine, bonny, full of beans 174 *vigorous*; of good constitution, never ill, robust, hardy, strong, vigorous 162 *stalwart*; fighting fit, in condition, in good condition, in the pink, in good nick, in good shape, in good heart, in fine fettle, in fine trim, in fine feather; feeling fine, feeling great; sound in wind and limb, sound as a bell, fit as a fiddle, A1; fresh as a daisy, fresh as April; a picture of health, feeling good; getting well, convalescent, on the mend, on the up-grade, on the up and up, up and about, on one's legs 656 *restored*; pretty well, no worse, as well as can be expected; safe and sound, unharmed 646 *undamaged*.

Vb. *be healthy*, - well etc. adj.; mind one's health, look after oneself; feel fine, bloom, thrive, flourish, enjoy good health; be in the pink, have never felt better; wear well, look young; keep one's health, keep fit, keep well, keep body and soul together, keep on one's legs; have a clean bill of health.

get healthy, - fit etc. adj.; recuperate, be well again, return to health, recover one's health, put on weight, get the colour back in one's cheeks; mend, convalesce, become convalescent, take a fresh lease of life, become a new man *or* woman 656 *revive*.

See: 1, 131, 162, 174, 376, 644, **646**, **652**, **656**.

651 Ill health. Disease

N. *ill health*, bad h., poor h., delicate h., failing h.; delicacy, weak constitution, diathesis; unhealthiness, weakliness, infirmity, debility 163 *weakness*; seediness, loss of condition, manginess; morbidity, indisposition, cachexia; chronic complaint, allergy, hay fever, catarrh; chronic ill health, invalidism, valetudinarianism, hypochondria; nerves 503 *psychopathy*.

illness, loss of health 655 *deterioration*; affliction, disability, handicap, infirmity 163 *weakness*; sickness, indisposition, ailment, complaint, complication; symptoms, syndrome; condition, history of; bout of sickness, visitation, attack, acute a.; spasm, stroke, seizure, apoplexy, fit; shock; poisoning, metal p., food p.; radiation sickness; nausea, waves of n., queasiness, heaving stomach, vomiting; dizziness, vertigo; headache, migraine 377 *pain*; sign of illness, symptom 547 *indication*; temperature, feverishness, fever, ague, shivers, shakes 318 *spasm*; hypothermia, hyperthermia; pyrexia, calenture; delirium 503 *frenzy*; breakdown, collapse; fainting 375 *insensibility*; prostration, coma; terminal disease, fatal illness 361 *decease*; sickbed, deathbed.

disease, malady, distemper, disorder; epidemic disease, endemic d.; infectious disease, communicable d., notifiable d.; debilitating d., killer d.; congenital d.; occupational d., industrial d.; alcoholism, drug addiction; obesity; deficiency disease, malnutrition, avitaminosis, kwashiorkor, beri-beri, pellagra, rickets, scurvy; degenerative disease, wasting d., marasmus, atrophy; traumatic disease, trauma; organic disease, functional d., circulatory d., neurological d., nervous d., epilepsy, falling sickness; musculo-skeletal disease; cardio-vascular d.; heart d.; endocrine disease, diabetes; urogenital disease; venereal d.; dermatological d.; cancer; respiratory disease; gastro-intestinal d.; synergistic triad; virus disease, bacterial d., water-borne d.; febrile disease, sweating sickness; hydrocele, dropsy; fibrosis; brain disease 503 *insanity*.

plague, pest, scourge 659 *bane*; pestilence, infection, contagion; epidemic, pandemic; pneumonic plague, bubonic p., Black Death.

infection, contagion, bug; miasma, pollution, taint; infectiousness, contagiousness 653 *insalubrity*; suppuration, festering, purulence, gangrene; toxicity, sepsis, poisoning 659 *poison*; plague spot, hotbed; vector, carrier, germ-c., host; parasite, worm, toxocara canis 659 *bane*; virus, bacillus, bacteria, germ, pathogen; blood-poisoning, toxaemia, septicaemia, pyaemia; food-poisoning, botulism; gastroenteritis, cholera (**see** *digestive disorders*); parasitical disease, toxocariasis, toxoplasmosis, bilharzia (**see** *tropical disease*); infectious disease, cold, common c., influenza, flu; diphtheria, pneumonia, viral p.; infective hepatitis; tuberculosis; measles, German measles, rubella; whooping-cough, mumps; chickenpox, smallpox, variola; scarlet fever, scarlatina; fever, malarial f., malaria (**see** *tropical disease*); typhus, jail fever; trench f.; typhoid, paratyphoid; glandular fever; poliomyelitis, polio; encephalitis, meningitis; encephalitis lethargica, sleepy sickness; tetanus, lockjaw; rabies, hydrophobia.

tropical disease, fever, malarial fever, malaria, ague; cholera, Asiatic c.; yellow fever, blackwater f., breakbone f., Lassar f., dengue; kala-azar, dumdum fever, leishmaniasis; trypanosomiasis, sleeping sickness; schistosomiasis, bilharzia; ascariasis, hookworm; trachoma, glaucoma, river blindness 439 *blindness*; yaws; leprosy; beri-beri, kwashiorkor.

digestive disorders, indigestion, dyspepsia, liverishness; biliousness, nausea, vomiting, retching; colic, gripes; stomach ache, tummy a., belly a., guts ache; stomach upset, collywobbles, gippy tummy, diarrhoea, traveller's d., gutrot, lurgy, Montezuma's revenge; the runs, the trots, galloping trots 302 *defecation*; diarrhoea and vomiting, D and V, gastroenteritis; dysentery, cholera, typhoid; food poisoning, botulism, Legionnaire's disease; flatulence, wind, belching 300 *voidance*; acidosis, heartburn; hiatus hernia; ulcer, peptic u., gastric u., duodenal u.; gastritis, duodenitis, enteritis, colitis, peritonitis, appendicitis, perforated appendix; jaundice, hepatitis, cirrhosis, cystitis, nephritis, kidney failure; gallstones, haemorrhoids, piles; constipation; cancer of the bowel.

respiratory disease, cough, cold, sore throat, catarrh, coryza; rhinitis, sinusitis, adenoids, tonsillitis, pharyngitis; laryngitis, tracheitis, croup, bronchitis; emphysema, asthma; pleurisy, pneumonia, bronchopneumonia; pneumoconiosis, silicosis, asbestosis, farmer's lung; diphtheria; whooping cough; lung cancer; smoker's cough, graveyard c.; cystic fibrosis; pulmonary tuberculosis, phthisis, consumption.

cardiovascular disease, cardiac d.; carditis, endocarditis, myocarditis, pericarditis, angina pectoris; breast-pang, chest-spasm; bradycardia, tachycardia; gallop rhythm, palpitation, dyspnoea; murmur, heart m.; valve disease, valvular lesion, mitral stenosis; cardiac hypertrophy, enlarged heart, athlete's heart; fatty degeneration of the heart; heart condition, bad heart, weak h., heart trouble; congenital heart disease, hole in the heart; rheumatic heart disease, coronary h. d.; heart failure; heart attack, coronary thrombosis, coronary; cerebral thrombosis, brain haemorrhage, stroke; blood pressure, high b. p., hypertension; hypotension, low blood pressure; vascular disease, atheroma, aneurysm; hardened arteries, arteriosclerosis; arteritis, phlebitis, varicose veins; thrombosis, clot, blood c., embolism, pulmonary e., infarction.

blood disease, anaemia, aplastic a., haemolytic a., haemorrhagic a., pernicious a., sickle-cell a.; leukaemia, Hodgkin's disease, lymphoma; haemophilia; bleeding, internal b., haemorrhage.

cancer, neoplasm, growth; tumour, benign t.; malignant t., cancerous growth; carcinoma, epithelioma, sarcoma, melanoma; rodent ulcer.

skin disease, cutaneous d., skin lesion; mange; lupus; yaws; leprosy; erythema, miliaria, prickly heat; erysipelas, St Anthony's fire; impetigo, tetters, herpes, herpes zoster, shingles; dermatitis, eczema; serpigo, ringworm; prurigo, pruritus, itch, dhobi's i. 378 *formication*; hives, urticaria, nettlerash; thrush; athlete's foot; rash, eruption, breaking out, acne, spots, blackheads; pustule, papula, pimple; goitre, cyst, blister, wart, verruca 253 *swelling*; macula, mole, freckle, birthmark, pockmark 845 *blemish*.

venereal disease, VD, pox; syphilis, gonorrhoea, the clap; venereal ulcer, chancre, syphilitic sore.

ulcer, ulceration, gathering, festering, purulence; inflammation, lesion 655 *wound*; scald, burn, first-degree b.; sore, boil, abscess, fistula; cyst; blain, chilblain, kibe; corn 253 *swelling*; gangrene, rot 51 *decay*; discharge, pus, matter.

rheumatism, rheumatics; rheumatic fever; muscular rheumatism, myalgia; fibrositis; frozen shoulder, tennis elbow, housemaid's knee, pulled muscle; arthritis, rheumatoid a.; gout 377 *pang*; osteoarthritis; lumbago, sciatica; slipped disc.

nervous disorders, nervous breakdown 503 *psychopathy*; brain tumour; brain haemorrhage, cerebral h., stroke, seizure; hemiplegia, diplegia, paraplegia; general paralysis, atrophy 375 *insensibility*; partial paralysis, paresis; palsy, cerebral p., spasticity; involuntary movements, tremor, tic 318 *spasm*; petit mal, grand mal, epilepsy, falling sickness; infantile paralysis, poliomyelitis, polio; spina bifida; Parkinson's disease; Huntington's chorea, St Vitus's dance; multiple sclerosis; muscular dystrophy; myasthenia gravis; motor neurone disease.

animal disease, veterinary d.; distemper, foot-and-mouth disease, swine fever; myxomatosis; rinderpest, murrain; anthrax, sheeprot, bloat; liver fluke, worms; megrims, staggers; glanders, farcy, sweeny, spavin, thrush; Newcastle disease, fowl pest; psittacosis; hard pad; mange; rabies.

sick person, sufferer; patient, in-p., out-p.; case, stretcher c., hospital c.; mental case 504 *madman*; invalid, chronic i.; valetudinarian, hypochondriac, martyr to ill health; consumptive, asthmatic, bronchitic, dyspeptic, diabetic; haemophiliac, bleeder; insomniac; neuropath, addict, alcoholic; spastic, arthritic, paralytic; paraplegic, disabled person; crock, old c., cripple 163 *weakling*; sick list.

pathology, forensic p.; diagnosis, prognosis; aetiology, nosology, epidemiology, bacteriology, parasitology 658 *therapy*.

Adj. *unhealthy*, unsound, sickly; infirm, decrepit, weakly 163 *weak*; delicate, of weak constitution, liable to illness, always ill; in bad health, in poor h.; in poor condition, mangy; undernourished, malnourished 636 *underfed*; peaked, emaciated; sallow, pale, anaemic 426 *colourless*; bilious 434 *green*; jaundiced 433 *yellow*; invalid, valetudinarian; pill-popping, hypochondriac.

sick, ill, unwell, not well, indisposed, out of sorts, under the weather, off-colour, below par; queasy, nauseated, green around the gills; in poor shape, in bad nick; in a bad way, poorly, seedy, squeamish, groggy, grotty, queer, ailing; sickening for, showing symptoms of; feverish, headachy, off one's food, off one's oats; confined, laid up, bedridden, on one's back, in bed, in hospital, on the sick list, invalided, hospitalized; run down, exhausted 684 *fatigued*; seized, taken ill, taken bad; prostrate, collapsed; in a coma 375 *insensible*; on the danger list, not allowed visitors; critical, serious, comfortable; chronic, incurable, inoperable; mortally ill, moribund 361 *dying*; peaky, drooping, flagging, pining, languishing, wasting away, in a decline.

diseased, pathological, disordered, distempered; affected, infected, plague-stricken; contaminated, tainted, vitiated, rotten, rotting, gangrenous 51 *decomposed*; peccant, morbid, morbific, pathogenic; iatrogenic; psychosomatic 447 *mental*; infectious, contagious; poisonous, festering, purulent 653 *toxic*; degenerative, consumptive, phthistic, phthisical, tuberculous, tubercular; diabetic, dropsical, hydrocephalic; anaemic; bloodless, leukaemic, haemophilic; arthritic, rheumatic, rheumatoid, rheumaticky, creaking; rickety, palsied, paralysed, paralytic, spastic, epileptic; leprous; carcinomatous, cancerous, cankered; syphilitic, venereal; swollen, oedematous; gouty; bronchial, throaty, bronchitic, croupy, sniffly, full of cold, bunged up; asthmatic; allergic; pyretic, febrile, fevered, shivering, aguish, feverish, delirious; sore, tender; ulcerous, ulcerated, inflamed; spotty, pimply, erythematous, erysipelatous; spavined, broken-winded; mangy.

Vb. *be ill*, - sick etc. adj.; enjoy poor health; ail, suffer, labour under, undergo treatment; have a complaint *or* an affliction, be a chronic invalid; not feel well, complain of; feel queer etc. adj.; feel sick 300 *vomit*; lose one's health, sicken, fall sick, fall ill; catch, catch an infection, catch a bug, contract a disease; break out with, go down with; be seized, be stricken, be taken, be taken bad, not feel so good; have a stroke, collapse; be laid up, take to one's bed; be invalided out; languish, pine, peak, droop, waste away, go into a decline, fall into a consumption; fail, flag, lose strength, get worse, sink, fade away 655 *deteriorate*; grow weak 163 *be weak*.

Adv. *morbidly*, unhealthily 653 *unwholesomely*; in sickness; in hospital, in the doctor's hands, under treatment.

See: 51, 163, 253, 300, 302, 318, 361, 375, **377**, 378, 426, 433, 434, 439, 447, 503, 504, 547, 636, 653, **655**, 658, 659, 684, 845.

652 Salubrity

N. *salubrity*, healthiness, state of health; well-being 650 *health*; salubriousness, healthfulness, wholesomeness; whole food, health food; smokeless zone, ventilation, fresh air, open a., sea a., ozone 340 *air*; sunshine, outdoors, out of doors; benign climate, genial c.; health resort.

hygiene, sanitation, cleanliness 648 *cleanness*; preventive medicine, prophylaxis 658 *prophylactic*; quarantine, cordon sanitaire 660 *protection*; immunity, immunization, inoculation, vaccination, pasteurization; antisepsis, sterilization, disinfection, chlorination; sanatorium, spa 658 *hospital*; hot springs, thermae 658 *therapy*; keeping fit, jogging, cycling, constitutional 682 *exercise*; hygienics.

sanitarian, hygienist, sanitationist, sanitary inspector, public health inspector; sanitary engineer; medical officer; fresh-air fiend, sun-worshipper, naturist, nudist.

Adj. *salubrious*, healthful, healthy, wholesome; pure, fresh 648 *clean*; ventilated, well-v., air-conditioned; tonic, bracing, invigorating, refreshing 656 *restorative*; hygienic, sanitary, disinfected, chlorinated, pasteurized, sterilized, sterile, aseptic, antiseptic; sanative, sanatory; prophylactic, immunizing, protective 658 *remedial*; good for, salutary, what the doctor ordered 644 *beneficial*; nutritious, nourishing, body-building, health-giving; noninjurious, harmless, benign, nonmalignant; uninfectious, noninfectious, innoxious, innocuous; immune, immunized, vaccinated, inoculated, protected 660 *invulnerable*.

Vb. *be salubrious*, - bracing etc. adj.; be good for one's health, agree with one; have a good climate; prevent disease; keep fit 650 *be healthy*.

sanitate, disinfect, boil, sterilize, antisepticize, chlorinate, pasteurize; immunize, inoculate, vaccinate; quarantine, put in q., isolate 883 *seclude*; ventilate 340 *aerate*; freshen 648 *purify*; cleanse 648 *clean*; drain 342 *dry*; conserve 666 *preserve*.

Adv. *healthily*, wholesomely, salubriously, hygienically.

See: 340, 342, **644**, **648**, **650**, 656, 658, 660, 666, 682, 883.

653 Insalubrity

N. *insalubrity*, unhealthiness, unwholesomeness; uncleanliness, lack of hygiene, lack of sanitation; dirty habits, verminousness 649 *uncleanness*; unhealthy conditions, unwholesome surroundings; condemned housing, slum; mephitis, bad air, bad climate; smoke haze, smog; infectiousness, contagiousness; bad drains, sewer 649 *sink*; infectious person, carrier, germ-c., vector; germ, microbe 196 *microorganism*; miasma, contagion 651 *infection*; pollution, radioactivity, fallout; deadliness, poisonousness 659 *bane*.

Adj. *insalubrious*, unwholesome, unhealthy; bad for one's health, insanitary, unhygienic 649 *unclean*; bad, nasty, noxious, miasmal, injurious 645 *harmful*; radioactive, carcinogenic; verminous, flea-ridden, rat-infested; undrained 347 *marshy*; stagnant, foul, polluted, undrinkable, inedible; indigestible, unnutritious; unsound, not fresh, stale, gone bad 655 *deteriorated*; unventilated, windowless, airless 264 *sealed off*; smoke-filled, stuffy; overheated, underheated.

infectious, morbific, pathogenic; infective, germ-carrying; contagious, catching, taking, communicable; pestiferous, pestilent, plague-stricken; malarious, malarial, aguish; epidemic, pandemic, endemic; epizootic, enzootic, sporadic; unsterilized, nonsterile, infected 649 *dirty*.

toxic, poisonous, mephitic, pestilential, germ-laden; venomous, envenomed, poisoned, steeped in poison; gathering, festering, septic, pussy, purulent, suppurating; lethal 362 *deadly*.

Adv. *unwholesomely*, insalubriously, poisonously; unhealthily, unhygienically; morbidly.

See: 196, 264, 347, 362, **645**, **649**, **651**, 655, 659.

654 Improvement

N. *improvement*, betterment, amelioration, melioration; uplift, regeneration; good influence, the making of 178 *influence*; change for the better, transfiguration 143 *transformation*; conversion, new leaf 939 *penitence*; revival, recovery 656 *restoration*; evolution, development, perfectibility; elaboration, enrichment; decoration 844 *ornamentation*; advance, onward march, march of time, progress 285 *progression*; furtherance, advancement, preferment, promotion, kick upstairs, rise, raise, lift, jump 308 *ascent*; upturn, upswing 310 *elevation*; revaluation, enhancement 36 *increase*.

amendment, mending etc. vb.; renovation 656 *repair*; reorganization 62 *arrangement*; reformation, reform, radical r. (**see** *reformism*); Borstal 539 *school*; purification, sublimation 648 *cleansing*; refining, rectification; castigation, correction, redaction, revision, red ink, blue pencil; emendation, recension, revised edition, new e., improved version 589 *edition*; revise, proof, corrected copy; second thoughts, better t., review, reconsideration, reexamination; further reflections 67 *sequel*; polish, finishing touch 725 *completion*; perfectionism 862 *fastidiousness*.

civilization, culture, kultur; Western civilization, Eastern c., ancient c., modern c.; black culture, Negritude; civility, refinement 846 *good taste*; training, proper upbringing 534 *education*; cultivation, polish, improvement of the mind 490 *culture*; eurhythmics, callisthenics 682 *exercise*; telesis, euthenics.

reformism, meliorism, perfectionism, idealism; Moral Re-Armament; liberalism, socialism, radicalism; extremism, revolution 738 *sedition*; feminism, progressivism; gradualism, Fabianism; social engineering 901 *sociology*.

reformer, improver, repairer, restorer 656 *mender*; emender, corrector, editor, reviser; progressive, progressist, progressionist; gradualist, Fabian 625 *moderate*; liberal, radical, feminist; extremist, revolutionary 738 *agitator*; socialist, communist, Marxist, Red; reformist, New Dealer; idealist, Utopian 513 *visionary*; sociologist, social worker 901 *philanthropist*.

Adj. *improved*, bettered, enhanced; touched up 843 *beautified*; reformed, revised 34 *superior*; better, better off, all the better for; looking up, on the mend; better advised, wiser 498 *wise*; improvable, corrigible, curable, reformable, perfectible.

improving, reformative, reformatory, remedial 656 *restorative*; reforming, reformist, progressive, radical; civilizing, cultural; idealistic, perfectionist, Utopian, millenarian, chiliastic; perfectionist 862 *fastidious*.

Vb. *get better*, grow b., improve, mend, take a turn for the better, turn the corner; pick up, rally, revive, recover 656 *be restored*; make progress, make headway, advance, develop, evolve 285 *progress*; mellow, ripen 669 *mature*; bear fruit 171 *be fruitful*; rise 308 *ascend*; graduate 727 *succeed*; rise in the world, better oneself, make one's way 730 *prosper*; mend one's ways, reform, turn over a new leaf, go straight 939 *be penitent*; improve oneself, learn by experience 536 *learn*; take advantage of, make capital out of, cash in on 137 *profit by*.

make better, better, improve, ameliorate, meliorate, reform; make improvements, improve upon, refine u.; polish, elaborate, enrich, enhance; do one a power of good 644 *do good*; improve out of all recognition, transfigure 147 *transform*; make, be the making of, have a good influence, leaven 178 *influence*; uplift, regenerate; refine, elevate, sublimate 648 *purify*; civilize, socialize, teach manners; mend 656 *repair*; restore 656 *cure*; recruit, revive, infuse fresh blood into 685 *refresh*; soften, lenify, mitigate, palliate 177 *moderate*; forward, advance, upgrade 285 *promote*; foster, encourage, bring to fruition 669 *mature*; make the most of, get the best out of 673 *use*; develop, open up, reclaim; till, weed, dress, water 370 *cultivate*; tidy, tidy up, neaten 62 *arrange*; spruce up, freshen up 648 *clean*; do up, vamp up, tone up; renovate, refurbish, renew, give a face lift; bring up to date 126 *modernize*; touch up 841 *beautify*; improve on nature, make up, titivate 843 *primp*; embellish, adorn, ornament 844 *decorate*.

rectify, put right, set right, straighten, straighten out 24 *adjust*; mend, patch 656 *repair*; correct, debug, make corrections, blue-pencil, proof-read, remove errors; revise, redact, edit, amend, emend; rewrite, redraft, retell, recast, remould, refashion, remodel, recreate, reform; reorganize 62 *regularize*; make improvements, streamline; review, reexamine, reconsider; correct one's mistakes, stop in time, think again, think better of, have second thoughts.

See: 24, 34, 36, 62, 67, 126, 137, 143, 147, 171, 177, 178, **285**, 308, 310, 370, 490, 498, 513, 534, 536, 539, 589, 625, 644, 648, **656**, 669, 673, 682, 685, 725, 727, 730, 738, 841, 843, 844, 846, 862, 901, 939.

655 Deterioration

N. *deterioration*, debasement, coarsening; cheapening, devaluation; retrogradation, retrogression, slipping back, losing ground 286 *regression*; reversion to type, throwback 5 *heredity*; decline, ebb 37 *decrease*; twilight, fading 419 *dimness*; falling off, downtrend, downturn, slump, depression, recession; impoverishment 801 *poverty*; law of diminishing returns; Gresham's law; Malthusianism; exhaustion 634 *waste*; vitiation, corruption, perversion, prostitution, depravation, degeneration, loss of morale, degeneracy, degenerateness, decadence, depravity 934 *wickedness*; downward course, primrose path 309 *descent*; recidivism 603 *tergiversation*; setback 657 *relapse*; bad ending, tragedy 731 *misfortune*.

dilapidation, collapse, ruination 165 *destruction*; planning blight; lack of maintenance, disrepair, neglect 458 *negligence*; slum, back street 801 *poverty*; ravages of time, wear and tear, erosion, corrosion, oxidization, rustiness, rust, moth and rust, rot, canker, corruption, putrefaction, rottenness 51 *decay*; mouldiness, mildew 659 *blight*; decrepitude, senility

131 *old age*; atrophy 651 *disease*; ruin, wreck, mere w., perfect w., physical w., shadow of one's former self.

impairment, spoiling 675 *misuse*; detriment, damage, spoilage, waste 772 *loss*; discoloration, weathering, patina; pollution, contamination, defilement 649 *uncleanness*; ulceration, poisoning, autointoxication, contamination 651 *infection*; adulteration, sophistication, watering down 43 *mixture*; assault, insult, outrage 712 *attack*; ruination, demolition 165 *destruction*; injuriousness, injury, mischief, harm 165 *havoc*; disablement, crippling, laming, hobbling, nobbling, disabling, mutilation, weakening 163 *weakness*; sprain, strain, pulled muscle, dislocation; disorganization, bedevilment, sabotage, demoralization 63 *derangement*; exacerbation 832 *aggravation*.

wound, injury, trauma; open wound, fresh w., bloody nose; sore, running s. 651 *ulcer*; laceration, lesion; cut, gash, incision, abrasion, nick, snick, scratch 46 *scission*; stab, prick, jab, puncture 263 *perforation*; contusion, bruise, bump, discoloration, black eye, shiner, thick ear 253 *swelling*; burn, scald; rupture, hernia; broken head, broken bones, fracture; scar, mark, cicatrice 845 *blemish*.

Adj. *deteriorated*, not improved, the worse for; exacerbated 832 *aggravated*; spoilt, impaired, damaged, hurt, ruined etc. vb.; worn out, effete, exhausted, worthless 641 *useless*; stale, gone bad, rotten 645 *bad*; corked, flat 387 *tasteless*; undermined, sapped, shaken 163 *weakened*; tired, overtired, done in, washed up 684 *fatigued*; no better, deteriorating, worse, getting w., worse and worse, in a bad way, far gone, on one's last legs; failing, past one's best, declining, in decline, on the d.; senile, senescent 131 *ageing*; on the way out, on the downgrade, on the downward path; falling, slipping, nodding, tottering 309 *descending*; faded, withered, sere, decaying 51 *decomposed*; wasting away, ebbing, at low ebb; slumping, falling off 37 *decreasing*; degenerative, retrogressive, retrograde, unprogressive, unimproved, backward 286 *regressive*; lapsed, recidivist 603 *tergiversating*; degenerate, depraved, corrupt 934 *vicious*; come down in the world, impoverished 801 *poor*.

dilapidated, the worse for wear, falling to pieces, in disrepair, in shreds, in ruins; broken, cracked, leaking; battered, weather-beaten, storm-tossed; decrepit, ruinous, ramshackle, tottery, shaky, rickety, tumbledown, run-down, on its last legs 163 *weakened*; slummy, condemned; worn, well-w., frayed, shabby, tatty, dingy, holey, in holes, in tatters, in rags, out-at-elbows; worn out, worn to a frazzle, worn to a shadow, reduced to a skeleton, done for 641 *useless*; seedy, down at heel, down and out 801 *poor*; rusty, rotten, mildewed, mouldering, moss-grown, moth-eaten, worm-e., dog-eared 51 *decomposed*.

Vb. *deteriorate*, not improve, get no better; worsen, get worse, go from bad to worse, take a turn for the worse; slip, slide, go downhill; have seen better days; not maintain improvement 657 *relapse*; fall off, slump, decline, wane, ebb, sink, fail 37 *decrease*; slip back, retrograde, revert 286 *regress*; lapse 603 *tergiversate*; degenerate, let oneself go, ruin oneself, go to pieces, run to seed, hit the skids 165 *be destroyed*; tread the primrose path, go to the bad 934 *be wicked*; disintegrate, fall apart, collapse, break down, fall, totter, droop, stoop 309 *tumble*; contract, shrink 198 *become small*; wear out, age 131 *grow old*; fade, wither, wilt, shrivel, perish, crumble, moulder, mildew, grow moss; go to rack and ruin; weather, rust, rot, decay 51 *decompose*; spoil, stale, lose its taste, lose its flavour, go flat, go off, go sour, turn 391 *be unpalatable*; go bad, smell 397 *stink*; corrupt, putrefy, rankle, fester, suppurate, gangrene 51 *decompose*; sicken 651 *be ill*; do worse, make things worse, jump from the frying pan into the fire, go farther and fare worse 832 *aggravate*.

pervert, deform, warp, twist 246 *distort*; abuse, prostitute 675 *misuse*; deprave 951 *debauch*; vitiate, corrupt 934 *make wicked*; lower, degrade, debase 311 *abase*; brutalize, dehumanize, barbarize; denature, denaturalize 147 *transform*; denationalize, detribalize; propagandize, brainwash 535 *misteach*.

impair, damage, damnify, hurt, injure, scathe 645 *harm*; mess up, muck up, untidy 63 *jumble*; play havoc with 63 *derange*; disorganize, dismantle, dismast; spoil, maul, mar, botch 695 *be clumsy*; touch, tinker, tamper, meddle with, fool w., monkey w. 678 *meddle*; not improve, worsen, deteriorate, exacerbate, embitter

832 *aggravate*; do no good, kill with kindness 499 *be foolish*; degrade, lower, coarsen 847 *vulgarize*; devalue, debase 812 *cheapen*; blacken, blot, spot, stain, uglify 842 *make ugly*; scar, mark, wrinkle 845 *blemish*; deface, disfigure, deform, warp 246 *distort*; corrupt, vitiate (**see** *pervert*); mutilate, maim, lame, cripple 161 *disable*; scotch, pinion, clip the wings, cramp, hamper 702 *hinder*; castrate 161 *unman*; expurgate, eviscerate, bowdlerize; curtail, dock 204 *shorten*; cream off, skim, take the heart out of; adulterate, sophisticate, alloy 43 *mix*; denature, deactivate 679 *make inactive*; subvert, shake, sap, mine, undermine, demoralize 163 *weaken*; honeycomb, bore, gnaw, gnaw at the roots, eat away, fret, erode, corrode, rust, rot, mildew 51 *decompose*; blight, blast, wither; ravage, waste, scorch, overrun 165 *lay waste*; vandalize, wreck, ruin 165 *destroy*; crumble 332 *pulverize*; dilapidate, fray, wear out, reduce to rags; exhaust, consume, use up 634 *waste*; infect, contaminate, poison, envenom, ulcerate; taint, canker, foul, pollute 649 *make unclean*; defile, desecrate, profane 980 *be impious*.

wound, scotch, draw blood, let b.; tear, rend, lacerate, mangle, rip 46 *disunite*; maul, savage 176 *be violent*; black one's eye, bloody one's nose; bite, scratch, claw; gash, hack, incise 46 *cut*; scarify, score 262 *groove*; nick 260 *notch*; sting, prick, pink, stab, gore, run through 263 *pierce*; bruise, contuse, buffet 279 *strike*; crush, grind 332 *pulverize*; chafe 333 *rub*; smash 46 *break*; graze, pepper, wing.

See:5, 37, 43, 46, **51**, 63, 131, 147, 161, 163, **165**, 176, 198, 204, 246, 253, 260, 262, 263, 279, 286, 309, 311, 332, 333, 387, 391, 397, 419, 458, 499, 535, 603, 634, 641, 645, 649, 651, 657, 659, 675, 678, 679, 684, 695, 702, 712, 731, 772, 801, 812, 832, 842, 845, 847, 934, 951, 980.

656 Restoration

N. *restoration*,returning, giving back, retrocession 787 *restitution*; redress, amends, reparation, reparations 941 *atonement*; finding again, getting back, retrieval, recovery 786 *taking*; reestablishment, reinstallation, reinvestment, recall, replacement, reinstatement, reinstalment; rehabilitation; replanting, reafforestation, reclamation, recycling; rescue, salvage, redemption, ransom, salvation 668 *deliverance*; reconstitution, reerection, rebuilding, reformation, reconstruction, reorganization; readjustment; remodelling 654 *amendment*; reconversion; reaction, counter-reformation 182 *counteraction*; resumption, return to normal, derestriction; recruitment, reinforcement 162 *strengthening*; replenishment 633 *provision*.

repair, reparation, repairs, running r., renovation, renewal, reconditioning, redintegration, reassembling; rectification, emendation; restoration, making like new; mending, invisible m., darning, patching, patching up; cobbling, soling, heeling, tinkering etc. vb.; clout, patch, darn, insertion, reinforcement; new look, facelift 843 *beautification*.

revival, recruitment, recovery 685 *refreshment*; renewal, reawakening, revivescence, resurgence, recovery, rally, comeback; fresh spurt, new energy; economic recovery, economic miracle, boom 730 *prosperity*; reactivation, revivification, reanimation, resuscitation, artificial respiration, kiss of life; rejuvenation, rejuvenescence, second youth, Indian summer; face-lift, new look; rebirth, renaissance, new birth, second b.; palingenesis, regeneration, regeneracy; new life, resurrection, awaking from the dead, recall from the grave; resurrection day 124 *future state*.

recuperation, recovery, pulling through, cure; healing, mending; cicatrization, closing, scabbing over, healing o.; convalescence, restoration to health 658 *remedy*; moderation, easing 831 *relief*; psychological cure, catharsis, abreaction; curability.

mender, repairer, renovator, painter, decorator, interior d.; emendator, rectifier; rebuilder, restorer, refurbisher; patcher, darner, cobbler, shoe-repairer; knife grinder, tinker, plumber, fixer, handyman; salvor, salvager; curer, healer, bonesetter 658 *doctor*; faith healer; psychiatrist; reformist 654 *reformer*.

Adj. *restored*, revived, refreshed etc. vb.; remade, reconditioned, reproofed; redone, rectified 654 *improved*; like new, renewed; saved, born again 979 *sanctified*; reborn, redivivus, renascent, resurgent, like a phoenix from the ashes; alive and kicking 650 *healthy*; cured, none the worse, better, convalescent, on the mend, pulling through; in one's right mind, back to normal, oneself again; retrievable, restorable, recoverable; mendable, amendable; medicable, curable, sanable, operable; found, recovered, salvaged, reclaimed.

restorative, reparative, analeptic, recuperative, curative, sanative, healing, medicated, medicinal 658 *remedial*.

Vb. *be restored*, recover, come round, come to, revive, pick up, rally 685 *be refreshed*; pull through, get over, get up, get well, convalesce, recuperate; turn the corner 654 *get better*; weather the storm, survive, live through; reawake, live again, resurrect, come to life again, arise from the dead, return from the grave; reappear, make a comeback, take on a new lease of life; sleep off, be oneself again, bounce back, snap out of it, come up smiling; pick oneself up, find one's feet again; return to normal, get back to n., go on as before; resume, start again 68 *begin*; look like new, undergo repairs.

restore, give back, hand b., retrocede, yield up 787 *restitute*; make amends 941 *atone*; put back, bring b., replace; recall, reappoint, reinstall, reestablish, rehabilitate; reconstitute, reconstruct, reform, reorganize 654 *make better*; valet 648 *clean*; renovate, renew, rebuild, reerect, remake, redo; overhaul, service, refit, refurbish, make like new 126 *modernize*; make whole, redintegrate; reforest, reafforest, replant, reclaim; recycle, reprocess; revalidate, reinforce, build up one's strength 162 *strengthen*; fill up 633 *replenish*; rally, reassemble 74 *bring together*; redeem, ransom, rescue, salvage 668 *deliver*; release, derestrict 746 *liberate*.

revive, revivify, revitalize, resuscitate, regenerate, recall to life, resurrect, reanimate, rekindle; breathe fresh life into, rejuvenate; freshen, recruit 685 *refresh*.

cure, heal, make well, cure of, break of; nurse, physic, medicate 658 *doctor*; bandage, bind up one's wounds; nurse through, work a cure, snatch from the grave, restore to health, set up, set on one's feet again; set (a bone); cicatrize, heal over, skin o., scab o., close, knit together; right itself, put itself right, work its own cure.

repair, do repairs; amend, emend, right, set to rights, put right, remedy 654 *rectify*; overhaul, mend, fix; cobble, resole, heel; reface, retread, recover, resurface, thatch 226 *cover*; reline 227 *line*; darn, patch, patch up; stop, fill (teeth); make over, do up, touch up, freshen up, retouch, revamp, plaster up, fill in the cracks, paper over; seal, stop a gap, plug a hole 350 *staunch*; caulk 264 *close*; splice, bind 45 *tie*; pick up the pieces, piece together, refit, reassemble, cannibalize 45 *join*; give a face-lift, refurbish, recondition, renovate, renew, remodel, reform.

retrieve, get back, recover, regain, retake, recapture; find again, reclaim, claim back, compensate oneself 31 *recoup*; make up for, make up time, make up leeway.

See: 31, 45, 68, 74, 124, 126, 162, 182, 226, 227, 264, 350, 633, 648, 650, **654**, **658**, 668, **685**, 730, 746, 786, 787, 831, 843, 941, 979.

657 Relapse

N. *relapse*, lapse, falling back; throwback, return 148 *reversion*; retrogression, retrogradation 286 *regression*; sinking, falling off, fall 655 *deterioration*; backsliding, recidivism, apostasy 603 *tergiversation*; recrudescence, reinfection, recurrence, fresh outbreak.

Vb. *relapse*, slip back, slide b., sink b., fall b.; throw back, return, retrogress 286 *regress*; degenerate 655 *deteriorate*; backslide, recidivate, lapse, fall from grace 603 *apostatize*; fall off again, revert to 148 *revert*; have a relapse, suffer a recurrence, not maintain an improvement.

See: **148**, 286, 603, **655**.

658 Remedy

N. *remedy*, succour, help 703 *aid*; oil on troubled waters 177 *moderator*; remedial measure, corrective, correction 654 *amendment*; redress, amends 787 *restitution*; expiation 941 *atonement*; cure, certain c. 656 *recuperation*; medicinal value, healing gift, healing quality *or* property; sovereign remedy, specific r., specific, answer, right a., solution; prescribed remedy, prescription, recipe, formula, nostrum; quack remedy, patent medicine; sovereign remedy, panacea, heal-all, cure-all, catholicon; elixir, elixir vitae, philosopher's stone.

medicine, materia medica, pharmacopoeia; vegetable remedy, herbal r., galenical, herb, medicinal h., simple; balm, balsam;

medication, medicament, patent medicine, proprietary drug, ethical d. (**see** *drug*); placebo; pill, bolus, tablet, tabloid, capsule, lozenge; physic, draught, potion, elixir; decoction, infusion; dose, booster d.; drench; drops, drip; injection, jab, shot; preparation, mixture, powder, electuary, linctus; plaster (**see** *surgical dressing*); spray, inhaler; medicine chest, medicine bottle.

prophylactic, preventive; sanitation, sanitary precaution, cordon sanitaire, quarantine 652 *hygiene*; prophylaxis, immunization, inoculation, vaccination; vaccine, triple v., BCG, TAB; antimalarial pill, quinine; antisepsis, disinfection, sterilization; antiseptic, disinfectant, iodine, carbolic, boric acid, boracic a.; bactericide, germicide, insecticide 659 *poison*; fumigant, fumigator; dentifrice, toothpaste, tooth powder 648 *cleanser*; mouthwash, gargle; fluoridation, fluoride.

antidote, counterirritant, antihistamine; counterpoison, antiserum, antitoxin, mithridate, theriac; antiemetic; antipyretic, febrifuge, quinine; vermifuge, anthelmintic; antigen, antibody, interferon; antibiosis, antibiotic; immunosuppressant; antispasmodic, anticonvulsant; sedative, muscle relaxant; anticoagulant; antacid, analgesic, painkiller. **See** *drug*.

purgative, purge, cathartic, laxative, aperient; castor oil, Epsom salts, health s., senna pods; cascara, milk of magnesia; diuretic; expectorant, emetic, nauseant, ipecacuanha; carminative, digestive, liquorice, dill water; douche, enema.

tonic, restorative; cordial, tonic water, tonic wine; reviver, refresher, pick-me-up 174 *stimulant*; caffeine, nicotine, alcohol; spirits, smelling salts, sal volatile, hartshorn; infusion, tisane, herb tea; coca, betel nut, ginseng; vitamin tablet, iron pill.

drug, synthetic drug, wonder d., miracle d.; antibiotic, sulpha drug, sulphonomide; penicillin; aureomycin, streptomycin, insulin, cortisone; hormone, steroid; progesterone, oestrogen; contraceptive pill 172 *contraception*; analgesic, aspirin, codeine 375 *anaesthetic*; tranquillizer, antidepressant, sedative; barbiturate, sleeping pill 679 *soporific*; narcotic, dope, morphia, morphine, opium, cocaine; intoxicant, stimulant 949 *drug-taking*; lotus, nepenthe, kef.

balm, balsam, oil, soothing syrup, emollient 177 *moderator*; salve, ointment; cream, face c. 843 *cosmetic*; lanolin, liniment, embrocation; lotion, wash; eyewash, collyrium; placebo.

surgical dressing, dressing, lint, gauze; swab; bandage, roller, sling, splint, cast, plaster of Paris; tourniquet; fingerstall; patch; application, external a., plaster, sticking p., corn p., court p., mustard p.; cataplasm, fomentation, poultice, compress; tampon, tent, roll, pledget; pessary, suppository; traumatic.

medical art, leechcraft; therapeutics, art of healing, healing touch 656 *recuperation*; medical advice, practice, medical p.; allopathy, homoeopathy, naturopathy, nature cure; medicine, clinical m., preventive m., fringe m., folk m.; acupuncture; radiography, tomography; diagnosis, prognosis 651 *pathology*; healing, gift of h., laying on of hands, faith healing, Christian Science; sexology, gynaecology, midwifery 167 *obstetrics*; gerontology, geriatrics, paediatrics; orthopaedics, ophthalmology, neurology, dermatology, ear, nose and throat, ENT, cardiology, oncology; radiotherapy; psychodiagnostics, psychopathology, bacteriology, microbiology, virology, immunology; pharmaceutics, pharmacology, posology; veterinary medicine.

surgery, general surgery, brain s., heart s., open-heart s.; plastic surgery, cosmetic s., rhinoplasty, prosthesis, prosthetics; manipulative surgery, chiropractic; operation, surgical o., op.; phlebotomy, venesection; bleeding, blood-letting, cupping, transfusion, perfusion; dialysis; D and C, dilatation and curettage; transplant; cauterization; amputation, trephination, trepanning, lobotomy, tonsillectomy, appendicectomy, appendectomy, colostomy, laparotomy; mastectomy, vasectomy; dentistry, bridging, drawing, extracting, stopping, filling, crowning; massage, chiropody, pedicure, manicure; electrolysis.

therapy, therapeutics, medical care; treatment, medical t., clinical t.; nursing, bedside manner; first aid, aftercare; course, cure, faith c., nature c., cold-water c., hydrotherapy; regimen, diet, dietary; bone-setting, orthopaedics, osteopathy, osteotherapy; hypnotherapy; hormone therapy; immunotherapy; chemotherapy; physiotherapy, occupational therapy; radiotherapy, phototherapy; heat treatment; electrotherapy, shock treatment, ECT, EST; mental treatment, clinical psychology; child psychology; psychotherapy, psychiatry, psychoanalysis 447 *psychology*; group therapy, behaviour t., aversion t., Gestalt t., primal t.; acupuncture; catheterization; intravenous injection, dripfeed; fomentation, poulticing.

hospital, infirmary, general hospital, maternity h., children's h.; mental hospital 503 *lunatic asylum*; dispensary, clinic, antenatal c.; nursing home, convalescent h., rest h.; home for the dying, hospice; lazaret, lazaretto, lazar-house, leper asylum, leper colony; hospital ship, hospital train; stretcher, ambulance; ward, hospital w., casualty w., isolation w., sick bay, sickroom, sickbed; hospital bed, ripple b.; tent, oxygen t., iron lung; respirator, life-support system, heart-lung machine, kidney m.; incubator, intensive care unit; x-ray machine, scanner; dressing station, first-aid s., casualty s.; operating room, operating theatre, operating table; consulting room, surgery, clinic, community health centre; sanatorium, spa, hydro, watering place; pump room, baths, hot springs, thermae; solarium, sun lamp.

doctor, physician; leech, quack, charlatan; veterinary surgeon, vet, horse-doctor; herbalist, herb doctor; faith healer, layer-on of hands, Christian Scientist; allopath, homoeopath, naturopath; acupuncturist; hakim, barefoot doctor, flying d.; witch-doctor, medicine man 983 *sorcerer*; medic, medical student; houseman, intern, registrar; medical practitioner, general p., GP; locum tenens, locum; clinician, therapeutist, healer; surgeon, plastic s., neurosurgeon; sawbones; medical officer, health o., sanitary inspector; medical adviser, consultant, specialist; diagnostician, pathologist, forensic p.; alienist, psychiatrist, psychoanalyst, neurologist; paramedic, anaesthetist, radiographer; physiotherapist, occupational therapist, speech t.; paediatrician, geriatrician; obstetrician, midwife; gynaecologist; sexologist; dermatologist, haematologist; biochemist, microbiologist; radiotherapist; orthopaedist, osteopath, bonesetter, chiropractor, masseur, masseuse; pedicurist, chiropodist, manicurist; ophthalmologist, optician, ophthalmic optician, oculist; aurist; dentist, dental surgeon, orthodontist; nutritionist, dietician; medical profession, Harley Street, National Health Service; Red Cross, St John's Ambulance; Aesculapius, Hippocrates, Galen.

druggist, apothecary, chemist, pharmaceutical c., pharmacist; dispenser, posologist, pharmacologist; chemist's, pharmacy.

nurse, male n., probationer n., student n., staff n.; charge n., sister, night s., ward s., theatre s.; matron; State Enrolled Nurse, SEN; State Registered Nurse, SRN; registered sick children's nurse, RSCN; special nurse, day n., night n.; district nurse, home n.; health visitor; nursing auxiliary, ward orderly, dresser, medical attendant, stretcher-bearer, ambulanceman; almoner, hospital social worker 901 *sociology*; Florence Nightingale, lady with a lamp.

Adj. *remedial*, corrective, analeptic, curative, first-aid 656 *restorative*; helpful 644 *beneficial*; therapeutic, medicinal, healing, curing, hygienic, salutiferous 652 *salubrious*; specific, sovereign; panacean, all-healing; soothing, paregoric, balsamic, demulcent, emollient, palliative 177 *lenitive*; anodyne, analgesic, narcotic, hypnotic, anaesthetic 375 *insensible*; peptic, digestive; purging 648 *cleansing*; cathartic, emetic, vomitory, laxative; antidotal 182 *counteracting*; theriacal; prophylactic, disinfectant, antiseptic; antipyretic, febrifugal; tonic, stimulative; dietetic, alimentary, nutritive, nutritional.

medical, pathological, physicianly, Aesculapian, Hippocratic, Galenic; allopathic, homoeopathic, herbal; surgical, anaplastic, rhinoplastic, orthopaedic; vulnerary, traumatic; obstetric, obstetrical; clinical; medicable, operable, curable.

Vb. *remedy*, fix, put right, correct 656 *restore*; succour, help 703 *aid*; apply a remedy, treat, heal, work a cure 656 *cure*; palliate, soothe, neutralize 831 *relieve*.

doctor, be a d., practise, have a practice; treat, prescribe, advise; attend 703 *minister to*; tend, nurse; give first aid, give the kiss of life 656 *revive*; hospitalize, put on the sick list, put to bed; physic, medicate, drench, dose, purge; inject, give a jab; dress, bind, swathe, bandage; stop the bleeding, apply a tourniquet 350 *staunch*; poultice, plaster, foment; set, put in splints; drug, dope, anaesthetize; operate, use the knife, cut open, amputate; trepan, trephine; curette; cauterize; bleed, phlebotomize; transfuse, perfuse; massage, rub, manipulate; draw, extract, pull, stop, fill, crown; pedicure, manicure; immunize, vaccinate, inoculate; sterilize, pasteurize, antisepticize, disinfect 652 *sanitate*.

See: 167, 172, 174, 177, 182, 350, 375, 447, 503, 644, 648, **651**, 652, 654, **656**, 659, 679, 703, 787, 831, 843, 901, 941, **949**, 983.

659 Bane

N. *bane,* cause of injury, malevolent influence; curse, plague, infestation, pest, scourge, ruin 616 *evil*; malady 651 *disease*; weakness, bad habit, besetting sin 934 *vice*; hell, cup, visitation, affliction 731 *adversity*; woe, funeral 825 *sorrow*; cross, trial; bore 838 *tedium*; bugbear, bête noire 827 *annoyance*; burden, imposition, white elephant; thorn in the flesh, stone round one's neck; stress, strain, perpetual worry, constant anxiety, torment, nagging pain 825 *worry*; running sore 651 *ulcer*; bitterness, acid, gall, wormwood 393 *sourness*; sickener, emetic 391 *unsavouriness*; bite, sting, poison dart, serpent's tooth, fang, briar, nettle 256 *sharp point*; source of trouble, hornet's nest 663 *pitfall*; viper, adder, serpent 365 *reptile*; snake, snake in the grass 663 *troublemaker*; parasite, leech, threadworm, tapeworm 365 *insect, creepy-crawly*; mosquito, wasp 904 *noxious animal*; locust 168 *destroyer*; oppressor, holy terror 735 *tyrant*.

blight, rot, dry r., wet r.; mildew, mould, rust, fungus; moth, woodworm, cankerworm, canker, cancer 51 *decay*; visitation 651 *plague*; frost, nip, cold 380 *coldness*; drought 342 *desiccation*.

poison, poisonousness, virulence, venomousness, toxicity; bad food, bad water, pollution; bacteria, salmonella, bacillus, germ, virus 651 *infection*; teratogen, carcinogen; chemical weapon, biological w.; venom, toxicant, toxin; deadly poison, snake p., rat p., ratsbane, germicide, insecticide, pesticide; fungicide, herbicide, weed-killer, defoliant, dioxin, paraquat, derris, DDT; acid, corrosive; hemlock, atropine, arsenic, strychnine, cyanide, prussic acid, vitriol; nicotine 388 *tobacco*; asphyxiant, poison gas, nerve g., lewisite, mustard gas, tear g., CS gas; carbon monoxide, carbon dioxide, choke damp; foul air, mephitis, miasma, effluvium, sewer gas 653 *insalubrity*; atmospheric pollution, smog; lead pollution; uranium, plutonium; radioactivity, radioactive cloud, mushroom, fallout, strontium 90 417 *radiation*; dope, opium, heroin 658 *drug*, 949 *drug-taking*; intoxicant, depressant 949 *alcoholism*; lethal dose, overdose; toxicology.

poisonous plant, hemlock, deadly nightshade, belladonna, datura, henbane, monkshood, aconite, hellebore; nux vomica, upas tree.

poisoning, venenation 362 *homicide*; blood poisoning, toxaemia 651 *infection*; food poisoning, botulism; chemical poisoning; germ warfare 718 *warfare*; poisoner 362 *murderer*.

Adj. *baneful,* pestilent, noisome 645 *harmful*; blighting, withering, virulent, poisonous, venomous 653 *toxic*; cursed, accursed 616 *evil*.

See: 51, 90, 168, 256, 342, 362, 365, 380, 388, 391, 393, 417, **616**, 645, **651**, 653, 658, 663, 718, 731, 735, 825, **827**, 838, 904, 934, 949.

660 Safety

N. *safety,* safeness, security; invulnerability, impregnability, immunity, charmed life; safety in numbers 104 *multitude*; secure position, permanent post, safe job; social security, welfare state 901 *sociology*; safe distance, wide berth 620 *avoidance*; all clear, coast c., danger past, storm blown over; guarantee, warrant 473 *certainty*; sense of security, assurance, confidence 855 *courage*; safety valve 667 *means of escape*; close shave, narrow escape 667 *escape*; rescue 668 *deliverance*.

protection, conservation 666 *preservation*; insurance, surety 858 *caution*; patronage, auspices, aegis, fatherly eye 703 *aid*; protectorate, guardianship, wardenship, wardship, tutelage, custody, protective c. 747 *restraint*; custodianship, safekeeping, keeping, charge, safe hands, grasp, grip, embrace 778 *retention*; ward, watch and w. 457 *surveillance*; safeguard, precaution, preventive measure 713 *defence*; sanitary precaution, immunization, prophylaxis, quarantine, cordon sanitaire 652 *hygiene*; segregation 883 *seclusion*; cushion, buffer; screen, cover; umbrella 662 *shelter*; means of protection, deterrent 723 *weapon*; safe-conduct, passport, pass 756 *permit*; escort, convoy, guard 722 *armed force*; defence, sure d., bastion, bulwark, tower of strength 713 *defences*; haven, sanctuary, asylum 662 *refuge*; anchor, sheet a. 662 *safeguard*; moat, ditch, palisade, stockade 235 *fence*; shield, breastplate, panoply, armour plate 713 *armour*.

protector, protectress, guardian, tutor; guardian angel, patron saint, tutelary god, liege lord, feudal l., patroness, fairy godmother 707 *patron*; defender, preserver, shepherd; bodyguard, lifeguard, strong-arm man, bouncer; vigilante 713 *defender*; conservator, custodian, curator, warden; warder, guard, security g., coastguard; chaperon, duenna, governess, nursemaid, nanny, baby-sitter 749 *keeper*; watcher, lookout, watch, watchman, night w. 664 *warner*; firewatcher, fire fighter, fireman; policeman *or* -woman, police constable, police sergeant, sheriff; copper, cop 955 *police*; private eye 459 *detective*; sentry, sentinel, garrison, security forces 722 *soldiery*; watchdog, guard dog, police d. 365 *dog*; Cerberus, Argus 457 *surveillance*.

Adj. *safe*, without risk, unhazardous; assured, secure, sure, snug; safe and sound, spared 666 *preserved*; with a whole skin, intact, unharmed 646 *undamaged*; garrisoned, well-defended; insured, covered; immunized, vaccinated, inoculated; disinfected, hygienic 652 *salubrious*; in safety, in security, on the safe side, on sure ground, on terra firma; in harbour, in port, at anchor; above water, high and dry; out of the wood, out of danger, out of harm's way; clear, in the clear, unaccused, unthreatened, unmolested; unexposed, unhazarded; under shelter, sheltered, shielded, screened, protected etc. vb.; patronized, under the wing of; in safe hands, held, in custody, behind bars, under lock and key 747 *imprisoned*; reliable, guaranteed, warranted 929 *trustworthy*; benign, harmless, unthreatening 615 *good*.

invulnerable, immune, impregnable, sacrosanct; inexpugnable, unassailable, unattackable, unbreakable, unchallengeable; founded on a rock, defensible, tenable 162 *strong*; proof, foolproof; weatherproof, waterproof, leakproof, gasproof, fireproof, bulletproof, bombproof, shatterproof; snug, tight, seaworthy, airworthy; armoured, steel-clad, panoplied.

tutelary, custodial, guardian, protective, shepherdlike; ready to die for 931 *disinterested*; watchful 457 *vigilant*; fail-safe; doubly sure, belt and braces; keeping, protecting 666 *preserving*; antiseptic, disinfectant 652 *salubrious*.

Vb. *be safe*, - invulnerable etc. adj.; find safety, reach s., come through, save one's bacon 667 *escape*; land on one's feet, keep one's head above water, weather the storm, ride it out; keep a whole skin, bear a charmed life, have nine lives; be snug, nestle, stay at home, be under shelter, have a roof over one's head; be under cover 523 *lurk*; keep a safe distance, give a wide berth 620 *avoid*.

safeguard, keep safe, guard, protect; spare 905 *show mercy*; stand up for, go bail for 713 *defend*; cover up for, shield; champion 703 *patronize*; grant asylum, afford sanctuary; keep, conserve 666 *preserve*; treasure, hoard 632 *store*; keep in custody 747 *imprison*; ward, watch over, care for, mother, take under one's wing; nurse, foster, cherish; have charge of, take charge of, keep an eye on, chaperon 457 *look after*; hide, put in a safe place 525 *conceal*; cushion, cocoon 218 *support*; insulate, earth; cover, shroud, cloak, shade 421 *screen*; keep under cover, garage, lock up; take in, house, shelter; ensconce, enfold, embrace 235 *enclose*; make safe, secure, fortify 162 *strengthen*; entrench, fence in, fence round 232 *circumscribe*; arm, armour, armour-plate; shepherd, convoy, escort; flank, support; garrison, mount guard; immunize, inoculate, vaccinate; pasteurize, chlorinate, disinfect 652 *sanitate*; give assurances, warrant, guarantee 473 *make certain*; keep order, police, patrol.

seek safety, demand assurances, take precautions, play safe, take no chances, be on the safe side 858 *be cautious*; dig in, lie low 523 *lurk*; run away 667 *escape*; cut and run 277 *move fast*; live to fight another day, think better of it; shorten sail, run for port, take refuge 662 *seek refuge*.

Adv. *under shelter*, under cover, in the lee of; under the aegis of; out of harm's way, safely, with impunity.

See: 104, 162, 218, 232, 235, 277, 365, 421, 457, 459, 473, 523, 525, 615, 620, 632, 646, 652, **662**, 664, **666**, 667, 668, **703**, 707, 713, 722, 723, 747, 749, 756, 778, 855, 858, 883, 901, 905, 929, 931, 955.

661 Danger

N. *danger,* peril; dangerousness, perilousness, shadow of death, jaws of d., lion's mouth, dragon's lair; Scylla and Charybdis; dangerous situation, unhealthy s., desperate s., parlous state, forlorn hope 700 *predicament*; emergency 137 *crisis*; insecurity, jeopardy, risk, hazard, ticklishness, precariousness, slipperiness, ticklish business, razor's edge 474 *uncertainty*; black spot, snag 663 *pitfall*; trap, death t. 527 *ambush*; endangerment, imperilment, hazarding, dangerous course; venturesomeness, daring, overdaring 857 *rashness*; venture, risky v. 672 *undertaking*; leap in the dark 618 *gambling*; slippery slope, road to ruin 655 *deterioration*; sword of Damocles, menace 900 *threat*; sense of danger, apprehension, fears 854 *nervousness*; cause for alarm, rocks ahead, breakers a., storm brewing, gathering clouds, cloud on the horizon 665 *danger signal*; narrow escape, hairbreadth e., close shave, near thing 667 *escape.*

vulnerability, nonimmunity, susceptibility, danger of 180 *liability*; security risk; exposure, nakedness, defencelessness 161 *helplessness*; instability, insecurity 152 *changeableness*; easy target, sitting duck; exposed part, vulnerable point, chink in the armour, Achilles' heel 163 *weakness*; tender spot, soft s., soft underbelly 327 *softness*; unsoundness, feet of clay, human error 647 *imperfection*; weaker brethren.

Adj. *dangerous,* perilous, fraught with danger, treacherous, beset with perils; unlit, unfrequented 854 *frightening*; risky, snaggy, hazardous, venturous, venturesome, dicey, dodgy, chancy 618 *speculative*; serious, ugly, nasty, critical, at flashpoint; at stake, in question; menacing, ominous, foreboding, alarming 900 *threatening*; toxic, poisonous 645 *harmful*; unhealthy, infectious 653 *insalubrious*; inflammable, explosive, radioactive.

unsafe, not safe, slippery, treacherous, untrustworthy 474 *unreliable*; insecure, unsecure, unsound, precarious, dicky; top-heavy, unsteady 152 *unstable*; shaky, tottering, crumbling, ramshackle, rickety, frail 655 *dilapidated*; jerry-built, gimcrack, crazy 163 *weak*; built on sand, on shaky foundations; leaky, waterlogged; critical, ticklish, touch and go, hanging by a thread, trembling in the balance, on the edge, on the brink, on the verge.

vulnerable, expugnable, in danger of, not immune 180 *liable*; open to, wide open, exposed, naked, bare 229 *uncovered*; unarmoured, unfortified, undefended, unprotected, at the mercy of 161 *defenceless*; unshielded, shelterless, helpless, guideless; unguarded, unescorted, unshepherded, unsupported, unflanked, isolated, out on a limb; unwarned, off one's guard 508 *inexpectant.*

endangered, in danger, in peril etc. n.; facing death, in a bad way; slipping, drifting; on the rocks, in shoal water; on slippery ground, on thin ice; in a tight corner, surrounded, trapped, under fire; in the lion's den, on the razor's edge; between two fires, between the devil and the deep blue sea, between Scylla and Charybdis; on the run, not out of the wood; at bay, with one's back to the wall, at the last stand, reduced to the last extremity; under sentence, with a noose round one's neck, awaiting execution 961 *condemned.*

Vb. *be in danger,* run the risk of 180 *be liable*; run into danger, enter the lion's den, walk into a trap; tread on dangerous ground, skate on thin ice, get out of one's depth, sail too near the wind, ride the tiger, play with fire, sit on a powder barrel, sleep on a volcano; lean on a broken reed, feel the ground give way, have to run for it; hang by a thread, tremble in the balance, hover on the brink 474 *be uncertain*; totter, slip, slide 309 *tumble*; get lost 282 *stray.*

face danger, face death, dice with death; take one's life in one's hands 855 *be courageous*; expose oneself, lay oneself open to; stand in the breach 711 *defy*; look danger in the face, look down a gun barrel; face heavy odds, have the odds against one; engage in a forlorn hope, challenge fate, tempt providence, court disaster; take a tiger by the tail, put one's head in the lion's mouth 857 *be rash*; run the gauntlet, come under fire; venture, dare, risk it, take a chance, stick one's neck out 618 *gamble.*

endanger, be dangerous, spell danger, expose to d., put in jeopardy, face with, confront w.; imperil, hazard, jeopardize, compromise; risk, stake, venture 618 *gamble*; drive headlong, run on the rocks, drive dangerously, drive without due care and attention, put one in fear of his *or* her life; be dangerous, threaten danger, loom, forebode, bode ill, menace 900 *threaten*; warm up, hot up; run one hard, overtake 306 *outdo*.

See:137, 152, 161, 163, 180, 229, 282, 306, 309, 327, 474, 508, 527, 618, 645, 647, 653, 655, **663**, **665**, 667, 672, **700**, 711, 854, 855, 857, 900, 961.

662 Refuge. Safeguard

N. *refuge,*sanctuary, asylum, retreat, safe place; traffic island, zebra crossing; last resort, funkhole, bolthole, foxhole, burrow; trench, dugout, airraid shelter, fallout s.; earth, hole, den, lair, covert, nest, lap, hearth 192 *home*; defensible space, privacy; sanctum 194 *chamber*; cloister, cell, hermitage, ivory tower 192 *retreat*; sanctum sanctorum, temple, ark, acropolis, citadel; wall, rampart, bulwark, bastion; stronghold, fastness 713 *fort*; keep, ward; secret place 527 *hiding-place*; dungeon 748 *prison*; rock, Rock of Ages, pillar, tower, tower of strength, mainstay 218 *prop*.

shelter, cover, roof, roof over one's head; covert, earth, hole; fold, sheepfold, pinfold; lee; lee wall, windbreak, hedge 235 *fence*; camp, stockade 235 *enclosure*; shield, wing; fireguard, fender, bumper, mudguard, windscreen 421 *screen*; umbrella, oilskins; sun helmet, sunglasses, goggles, ear muffs, ear plugs; shinguard, pads; protective clothing, overalls; haven, harbour, port; harbourage, anchorage, quay, jetty, ghat, marina, dock 192 *stable*; padded cell 503 *lunatic asylum*; halfway house, sheltered housing; almshouse, old people's home, children's home, dog's h., charitable institution, hospice, home for the dying; Welfare State.

safeguard, means of safety, protection 660 *safety*; precautions 702 *hindrance*; crush barrier, guardrail, railing; mail 713 *armour*; arms, deterrent 723 *weapon*; respirator, gas mask; safety device, dead man's handle, safety catch, safety valve, lightning conductor, fuse, earth; crash helmet; ejector-seat, parachute; safety net; lifeboat, rubber dinghy, life raft 275 *raft*; life belt, life jacket, buoyancy j., Mae West, lifeline, breeches buoy; rope, plank 667 *means of escape*; anchor, kedge, grapnel, grappling iron, killick, drogue; lead, reins, brake 748 *fetter*; bolt, bar, lock, key 264 *stopper*; ballast 31 *offset*; mole, breakwater, groyne, sea wall, embankment; lighthouse, lightship 269 *sailing aid*; jury mast, spare parts 40 *extra*.

Vb. *seek refuge,* take refuge 660 *seek safety*; take to the woods, take to the hills; turn to, throw oneself in the arms of, shelter under the wing of, put up one's umbrella; claim sanctuary, seek political asylum; clasp the knees of, nestle under one's wing, hide behind the skirts of; make port, reach safety, reach home, find shelter; lock oneself in, bolt the door, bar the entrance, let down the portcullis, raise the drawbridge.

See:31, 40, 192, 194, 218, 235, 264, 269, 275, 421, 503, 527, **660**, **667**, 702, 713, 723, 748.

663 Pitfall: source of danger

N. *pitfall*, pit, trap for the unwary, catch; snag, pons asinorum 702 *obstacle*; booby trap, death t., firetrap, minefield 542 *trap*; surprise 508 *lack of expectation*; lying in wait 527 *ambush*; sleeping dog; thin ice; quagmire 347 *marsh*; quicksands, sandbar; shoal, shoal water, breakers, shallows 212 *shallowness*; reef, sunken r., coral r., rock; ironbound coast, lee shore; steep, chasm, abyss, crevasse, precipice 209 *high land*; rapids, crosscurrent, undertow 350 *current*; vortex, maelstrom, whirlpool 350 *eddy*; tidal wave, flash flood 350 *wave*; storm, squall, hurricane 352 *gale*; volcano 383 *furnace*; dynamite, time bomb, powder keg 723 *explosive*; trouble-spot 661 *danger*; plague-spot, hotbed 651 *infection*; source of trouble, hornet's nest, hazard 659 *bane*.

troublemaker, mischiefmaker, stirrer, wrecker; ill-wisher 881 *enemy*; firebrand 738 *agitator*; dangerous person, ugly customer, undesirable, delinquent 904 *ruffian*; nigger in the woodpile, snake in the grass, viper in the bosom; hidden hand 178 *influence*; yellow peril, red p.; Nemesis 910 *avenger*.

See:178, 209, 212, 347, 350, 352, 383, 508, 527, **542**, 651, 659, **661**, **702**, 723, 738, 881, 904, 910.

664 Warning

N. *warning,*caution, caveat; example, warning e., lesson, object l.; notice, advance n. 524 *information*; word, word in the ear, word to the wise, tip, tip-off, wink, nudge

524 *hint*; whistle-blowing 528 *publication*; final warning, final notice, ultimatum 737 *demand*; monition, admonition, admonishment 924 *reprimand*; deterrent 613 *dissuasion*; protest, expostulation 762 *deprecation*; warning shot, s. across the bows; foreboding, premonition 511 *prediction*; voice, voice of conscience, warning voice 917 *conscience*; alarm, siren, foghorn, fog signal, storm s., alert, red alert 665 *danger signal*; Mother Carey's chickens, stormy petrel, bird of ill omen 511 *omen*; gathering cloud, cloud on the horizon, war cloud 661 *danger*; signs of the times, writing on the wall, symptom, sign 547 *indication*; knell, death k. 364 *obsequies*; beacon, light 547 *signal, indicator*; menace 900 *threat*.

warner, admonisher 691 *adviser*; prophet, Cassandra 511 *diviner*; flagman, signaller; lighthouse-keeper; watchman, lookout, watch 457 *surveillance*; scout, spy; picket, sentinel, sentry 660 *protector*; advance guard, rearguard; watchdog.

Adj. *cautionary*, hinting, warning, monitory, admonitory; protesting 762 *deprecatory*; exemplary, instructive 524 *informative*; symptomatic, prognostic 547 *indicating*; premonitory, boding, ill-omened, ominous 511 *presageful*; menacing, minatory 900 *threatening*; deterrent 854 *frightening*.

warned, cautioned etc. vb.; once bitten 858 *cautious*; forewarned 507 *expectant*; forearmed 669 *prepared*.

Vb. *warn*, caution; give fair warning, give notice, notify 524 *inform*; drop a hint, tip off, blow the whistle on 524 *hint*; counsel 691 *advise*; put one in mind of 505 *remind*; admonish 924 *reprove*; spell danger, forewarn 511 *predict*; forearm, put one on his *or* her guard, alert 669 *prepare*; lour, menace 900 *threaten*; issue a caveat, advise against 613 *dissuade*; remonstrate, protest 762 *deprecate*; sound the alarm 665 *raise the alarm*.

be warned, receive notice; beware, take heed, watch one's step 457 *be careful*; be taught a lesson, learn one's l., profit by the example.

Int. look out! watch out! cave! mind your step! look where you are going!

See: 364, 457, 505, 507, 511, **524**, 528, 547, 613, **660**, 661, **665**, 669, 691, 737, 762, 854, 858, 900, 917, 924.

665 Danger signal

N. *danger signal*, note of warning 664 *warning*; murmur, muttering 829 *discontent*; writing on the wall, black cap, evil omen 511 *omen*; storm cone, gale warning; warning sound, alarum, alarm clock, alarm bell, burglar alarm, fire alarm, fire bell, foghorn, fog signal, bell buoy, motor horn, klaxon, bicycle bell, police whistle; blast, honk, toot 400 *loudness*; alarm, church bell, curfew, tocsin, siren, alert, red a.; tattoo, beat of drum, trumpet-call 547 *call*; war cry, battle c., rallying cry; fiery cross; warning light, red l., Very l., beacon; red flag, yellow f.; distress signal, SOS 547 *signal*; sign of alarm, start, tremor, sweat, hair on end 854 *fear*.

false alarm, cry of 'wolf', scare, hoax; bugbear, bugaboo, bogey, nightmare, bad dream 854 *intimidation*; blank cartridge, flash in the pan 4 *insubstantiality*; canard 543 *untruth*; scaremonger 854 *alarmist*.

Vb. *raise the alarm*, sound the a., give the a., dial 999, alert, arouse, scare, startle 854 *frighten*; sound one's horn, honk, toot; turn out the guard, raise a hue and cry, cry blue murder 528 *proclaim*; give a false alarm, cry 'wolf', cry too soon; sound a warning, toll, knell.

See: 4, 400, 511, 528, 543, **547**, 664, 829, 854.

666 Preservation

N. *preservation*, safekeeping, keeping alive; safe conduct 660 *protection*; saving, salvation 668 *deliverance*; conservation, conservancy; perpetuation, prolongation 144 *permanence*; upkeep, maintenance, support 633 *provision*; service, servicing, valeting 648 *cleansing*; insulation, heat retention; saving up 632 *storage*; reservation 814 *economy*; self-preservation 932 *selfishness*; game reserve, nature r., bird sanctuary, conservation area, listed building; protected species; taxidermy, mummification, embalmment, embalming 364 *interment*; cold storage, freezing, deep-freezing 382 *refrigeration*; boiling, drying, sun-d., dehydration 342 *desiccation*; canning, tinning, packing; sterilization 652 *hygiene*; preventive medicine, quarantine, cordon sanitaire.

preserver, life-saver, saviour, rescuer, deliverer 668 *deliverance*; amulet, charm, mascot 983 *talisman*; preservation order; preservative, ice, amber, formaldehyde;

camphor, mothball, lavender; spice, pickle, brine, aspic 389 *condiment*; freezer 384 *refrigerator*; thermos flask (tdmk); silo; cannery, canning factory, bottling plant; safety device, seat belt, gas mask 662 *safeguard*; incubator, respirator, iron lung, life support system; embalmer, mummifier; canner, bottler; conservationist, environmentalist 660 *protector*.

Adj. *preserving*, conserving etc. vb.; energy-saving; preservative, conservative; prophylactic, protective, preventive, hygienic 652 *salubrious*.

preserved, well-p., kept, well-k., fresh, undecayed, intact, whole 646 *perfect*; frozen, on ice, in the fridge; pickled, salted, corned, tinned, canned, potted, bottled; mummified, embalmed; laid up in lavender, treasured 632 *stored*; conserved, protected 660 *safe*.

Vb. *preserve*, conserve, keep alive, keep fresh, freeze, keep on ice 382 *refrigerate*; embalm, mummify, stuff; pickle, salt 388 *season*; souse, marinate; cure, smoke, kipper, dehydrate, sun-dry 342 *dry*; pot, bottle, tin, can; protect, paint, varnish, whitewash, creosote, waterproof; maintain, keep up, keep in good repair, service 656 *repair*; prop up, shore up 218 *support*; keep alive, feed, sustain, provision, supply 633 *provide*; keep safe, keep under cover, garage 660 *safeguard*; save up, bottle up 632 *store*; reserve, save 814 *economize*; nurse, tend 658 *doctor*; cherish, treasure 457 *look after*; not let go, hug, hold 778 *retain*; keep going, prolong; save, save alive, rescue 668 *deliver*.

See: 144, 218, 342, 364, 382, 384, 388, 389, 457, **632**, 633, 646, 648, 652, 656, 658, **660**, **662**, 668, 778, 814, 932, 983.

667 Escape

N. *escape*, leak, leakage, loss 298 *egress*; extrication, delivery, rescue 668 *deliverance*; riddance, good r. 831 *relief*; getaway, breakout; decampment, flight, flit, moonlight f., French leave 296 *departure*; withdrawal, retreat, hasty r. 286 *regression*; disappearing trick 446 *disappearance*; elopement, runaway match; evasion, truancy, tax-dodging 620 *avoidance*; narrow escape, hairbreadth e., close shave, close call, narrow squeak, near thing 661 *danger*; let-off, discharge, reprieve 960 *acquittal*; setting free 746 *liberation*; immunity, impunity, exemption 919 *nonliability*; escapology, escapism.

means of escape, exit, emergency e., way out, back door, secret passage 298 *egress*; ladder, fire escape, escape hatch; drawbridge 624 *bridge*; vent, safety valve 662 *safeguard*; dodge, device, trick 623 *contrivance*; loophole, escape clause, let-out, get-out 468 *qualification*.

escaper, escapee, runaway; truant, escaped prisoner, prison-breaker; fugitive, refugee; survivor; escapist; escapologist, Houdini.

Adj. *escaped*, fled, flown, stolen away; eloping, truant; fugitive, runaway; slippery, elusive 620 *avoiding*; free, at large, scot free, acquitted; relieved, rid of, well out of, well rid of; exempt 919 *nonliable*.

Vb. *escape*, find *or* win freedom 746 *achieve liberty*; effect one's escape, make good one's e., make a getaway, break gaol, break out of prison; abscond, jump bail, flit, elope, skip, take French leave, go AWOL 620 *run away*; steal away, sneak off, duck and run, make oneself scarce, beat a hasty retreat 296 *decamp*; slip through, break t., break out, break loose, break away, get free, break one's chains, slip one's lead; get out, bluff one's way o., sneak o. 298 *emerge*; get away, slip through one's fingers; get off, get off lightly, secure an acquittal, go scot-free, go unpunished; scrape through, save one's bacon, weather the storm, survive; get away with it, secure exemption, wriggle out of 919 *be exempt*; rid oneself, be well rid of, find relief 831 *be relieved*; leak, leak away 298 *flow out*.

elude, evade, welsh, abscond, dodge 620 *avoid*; lie low 523 *lurk*; give one the slip, shake off, throw off the scent, give one a run for one's money; escape notice, be found to be missing 190 *be absent*.

See: 190, 286, **296**, 298, 446, 468, 523, **620**, 623, 624, 661, 662, 668, 746, 831, 919, 960.

668 Deliverance

N. *deliverance*, delivery, extrication 304 *extraction*; disencumberment, riddance 831 *relief*; emancipation 746 *liberation*; rescue, life-saving; salvage, retrieval 656 *restoration*; salvation, redemption 965 *divine function*; ransom, buying off 792 *purchase*; release, let-off, amnesty; discharge, reprieve, reprieval 960 *acquittal*; day of grace, respite 136 *delay*; truce, standstill 145 *cessation*; way out, let-out 667 *escape*; dispensation, exemption 919 *nonliability*.

Adj. *extricable*, rescuable, deliverable, redeemable, fit for release.

Vb. *deliver*, save, rescue, come to the r., snatch from the jaws of death, throw a lifeline; get one out of 304 *extract*; extricate 62 *unravel*; unloose, untie, unbind 46 *disunite*; disburden 701 *disencumber*; rid, save from 831 *relieve*; release, unlock, unbar; emancipate, free, set free, set at large 746 *liberate*; let one off, get one off 960 *acquit*; deliver oneself 667 *escape*; save oneself, rid oneself, get rid of, be rid of; snatch a brand from the burning, be the salvation of; redeem, ransom, buy off 792 *purchase*; salvage, retrieve, recover, bring back 656 *restore*; spare, excuse, dispense from 919 *exempt*.

Int. to the rescue! all hands to the pump! help!

See: 46, 62, 136, 145, 304, 656, **667**, 701, 746, 792, 831, 919, 960, 965.

669 Preparation

N. *preparation*, preparing, making ready; clearance, clearing the decks; preliminaries, preliminary step, tuning, priming, loading; mobilization 718 *war measures*; preliminary course, trial run, trial, trials 461 *experiment*; practice, rehearsal, dress r.; brief, briefing; training, inurement 534 *teaching*; novitiate 68 *beginning*; study, prep, homework 536 *learning*; spadework 682 *labour*; groundwork, foundation 218 *basis*; scaffold, scaffolding 218 *frame*; planning, rough sketch, first draft, outline, blueprint, scheme, pilot s. 623 *plan*; shadow cabinet, shadow factory; arrangement, prearrangement, premeditation 608 *predetermination*; consultation, preconsultation 691 *advice*; forethought, anticipation, precautions 510 *foresight*; bottom drawer, nest egg 632 *store*.

fitting out, provisioning, furnishing, logistics 633 *provision*; appointment, commission, equipment, marshalling, array, armament; promotion, company-promoting; inauguration, flotation, launching 68 *debut*.

maturation, ripening, bringing to a head; seasoning, hardening, acclimatization; brewing, hatching, gestation, incubation, sitting 167 *propagation*; nursing, nurture; cultivation, tillage, sowing, planting 370 *agriculture*; bloom, florescence, efflorescence; fructification, fruition 725 *completion*.

preparedness, readiness, ripeness, mellowness, maturity; puberty, nubility 134 *adultness*; fitness, shipshape condition, height of training, pitch of perfection 646 *perfection*.

preparer, coach 537 *trainer*; torch-bearer, trail-blazer, pioneer, bridge-builder 66 *precursor*; sappers and miners 722 *soldiery*; paver, paviour; loader, packer, stevedore; fitter, equipper, provisioner 633 *provider*; cultivator, agriculturalist, ploughman, sower, planter 370 *farmer*; brewer, cook 301 *cookery*.

Adj. *preparatory*, preparative; preparing etc. adj.; precautionary, preliminary 64 *preceding*; provisional, stopgap 150 *substituted*; brewing, cooking, stewing; brooding, hatching, incubating, maturing; in embryo; in preparation, on foot, on the stocks, on the anvil; in store, in the offing, forthcoming 155 *impending*; under consideration, agitated for, mooted 623 *planned*; under training, learning 536 *studious*.

prepared, ready, alert 457 *vigilant*; made ready, readied, in readiness, at the ready; mobilized, standing by, on call; all set, ready to go, raring to go; teed up, keyed up, psyched up, spoiling for; trained, fully t., qualified, well-prepared, practised, in practice, at concert pitch, word-perfect; primed, briefed, instructed 524 *informed*; forewarned, forearmed 664 *warned*; saddled, in the saddle; tight, snug, battened down; groomed, fully dressed, in one's best bib and tucker, in full feather, dressed to kill, got up to k., in full warpaint 228 *dressed*; accoutred, armed, in armour, in harness, fully armed, armed to the teeth, armed at all points; rigged, rigged out, equipped, furnished, fully f., well-appointed, provided 633 *provisioning*; in store, in hand 632 *stored*; in reserve, ready to hand, ready for use; fit for use, in working order, operational.

matured, ripened, cooked, digested, hatched etc. vb.; ripe, mellow, mature, seasoned, weathered, hardened; tried, experienced, veteran 694 *expert*; adult, grown, full-g., fledged, full-f. 134 *grown-up*; out, in flower, florescent, flowering, fruiting; overripe, overmature; well-cooked, well-done; elaborated, wrought, highly w., worked up, laboured, smelling of the lamp; deep-laid; perfected 725 *completed*.

ready-made, ready-mixed, cut and dried, ready to use, ready-to-wear, off the peg; ready-formed, ready-furnished; prefabricated; processed, oven-ready; predigested, precooked, instant.

Vb. *prepare*, take steps, take measures; make preparations, make ready, pave the way, show the w., bridge, build a b., lead up to, pioneer 64 *come before*; choose one's ground, lay the foundations, do the groundwork, provide the basis; predispose, incline, soften up; prepare the ground, sow the seed 370 *cultivate*; set to work, address oneself to 68 *begin*; rough-hew, cut out, block o.; sketch, outline, blueprint 623 *plan*; plot, concert, prearrange 608 *predetermine*; prepare for, forearm, guard against, insure, take precautions, prepare for a rainy day 660 *seek safety*; anticipate 507 *expect*.

make ready, ready, have r., finish one's preparations; set in order, put in readiness; stow, stow away, pack 632 *store*; batten down the hatches; commission, put in c.; put one's house in order, put in working order, bring up to scratch, wind up, screw up, tune, tune up, adjust 62 *arrange*; settle preliminaries, clear the decks, close the ranks; array, mobilize 74 *bring together*; whet the knife, shuffle the cards, tee up; set, cock, prime, load; raise steam, warm up, crank, crank up, rev up, get into gear; equip, crew, man; fit, fit out, furnish, kit out, rig out, dress; arm, provide with arms, provide with teeth 633 *provide*; improvise, rustle up; rehearse, drill, groom, exercise, lick into shape 534 *train*; inure, acclimatize 610 *habituate*; coach, brief, bring one up to date 524 *inform*.

mature, mellow, ripen, bring to fruition 646 *perfect*; force, bring on 174 *invigorate*; bring to a head 725 *climax*; stew, brew 301 *cook*; gestate, hatch, incubate, breed 369 *breed stock*; grow, farm 370 *cultivate*; fledge, nurse, nurture; elaborate, work out 725 *carry through*; season, weather, smoke, dry, cure; temper, season 326 *harden*.

prepare oneself, brace o., compose o.; qualify oneself, serve an apprenticeship; study, brief oneself, do one's homework; train, exercise, rehearse, practise 536 *learn*; gird up one's loins, roll up one's sleeves; limber up, warm up, flex one's muscles; buckle on one's armour, take sword in hand, shoulder arms; be prepared, stand ready, stand by, hold oneself in readiness, keep one's powder dry.

Adv. *in preparation*, in anticipation, in readiness, just in case; in hand, in train, under way, under construction.

See: 62, 64, **66**, 68, 74, 134, 150, 155, 167, 174, 218, 228, 301, 326, 369, 370, 457, 461, 507, **510**, 524, 534, 536, 537, 608, 610, **623**, 632, 633, 646, 660, 664, 682, 691, 694, 718, 722, **725**.

670 Nonpreparation

N. *nonpreparation*, lack of preparation; potluck; unpreparedness, unreadiness; lack of training, want of practice; disqualification, unfitness; rawness, immaturity, crudity, greenness, unripeness 126 *newness*; belatedness 136 *lateness*; improvidence, nonprovision, neglect 458 *negligence*; no deliberation 857 *rashness*; hastiness, precipitance, rush 680 *haste*; improvisation, impromptu, snap answer 609 *spontaneity*; surprise 508 *lack of expectation*; forwardness, precocity 135 *earliness*; imperfection 55 *incompleteness*.

undevelopment, delayed maturity, slow ripening; state of nature, native state, virgin soil; untilled ground 458 *negligence*; raw material, unlicked cub, rough diamond; late developer; rough copy, unfinished attempt; embryo, abortion.

Adj. *unprepared*, unready, not ready, backward, behindhand 136 *late*; unorganized, unarranged, makeshift; without preparation, ad hoc, ad lib, extemporized, improvised, impromptu, snap, catch-as-catch-can, off the top of one's head 609 *spontaneous*; unstudied 699 *artless*; rash, careless 458 *negligent*; rush, precipitant, overhasty 680 *hasty*; unguarded, exposed, with one's trousers down 661 *vulnerable*; unwarned, caught unawares, taken off guard, caught napping, on the wrong foot, unexpecting 508 *inexpectant*; at sixes and sevens 61 *orderless*; shiftless, improvident, unthrifty, thoughtless, happy-go-lucky 456 *light-minded*; scratch, untrained, untaught, untutored 491 *uninstructed*; undrilled, unpractised, unexercised, unrehearsed 611 *unhabituated*; in a state of nature, uncultivated, unworked, untilled,

fallow, virgin 674 *unused*.
immature, ungrown, half-grown, unripe, green, underripe, half-ripe, unripened, unmellowed, unseasoned; unblown, half-blown; unfledged, unlicked, callow, wet behind the ears; nonadult, adolescent, juvenile, boyish, girlish 130 *young*; undeveloped, half-developed, half-baked, raw 647 *imperfect*; underdeveloped, backward 136 *late*; unhatched, unborn, embryonic, rudimentary 68 *beginning*; half-formed, unformed, unfashioned, unhewn, unwrought, unworked, roughhewn, uncut, unpolished, half-finished, unfinished; undigested, ill-digested; before time, premature, abortive, at half-cock 728 *unsuccessful*; untrained, apprentice, undergraduate 695 *unskilled*; crude, coarse, rude, savage, uncivilized 699 *artless*; early matured, forced, precocious.
uncooked, raw, red, rare, underdone; half-baked, cold, unwarmed; unprepared, undressed, ungarnished; indigestible, inedible 329 *tough*.
unequipped, untrimmed, unrigged, dismasted, dismantled, undressed 229 *uncovered*; unfurnished, half-furnished, ill-provided 307 *deficient*; unfitted, unqualified, disqualified.
Vb. *be unprepared*, - unready etc. adj.; lack preparation 55 *be incomplete*; lie fallow, rust 655 *deteriorate*; want practice, need training; not plan, make no preparations, offer potluck, extemporize 609 *improvise*; live from day to day, let tomorrow take care of itself; be premature, go off at half-cock 135 *be early*; take no precautions, drop one's guard 456 *be inattentive*; catch unawares 508 *surprise*.
Adv. *unreadily*, extempore, off the cuff, ad hoc, off-hand.
See: 55, 61, 68, 126, 130, 135, 136, 229, 307, 329, 456, **458**, 491, **508**, **609**, 611, 647, 655, 661, 674, 680, 695, 699, 728, 857.

671 Attempt

N. *attempt*, essay, bid; step, move, gambit 676 *deed*; endeavour, struggle, strain, effort 682 *exertion*; tackle, try, some attempt; good try, stout t., brave t., valiant effort; best effort, one's level best, best one can do; random effort, catch-as-catch-can; determined effort, set, dead s. 712 *attack*; trial, probation 461 *experiment*; go at, shot at, stab at, jab at, crack at, whack at, bash at; first attempt, first go, first shot, first offence 68 *debut*; final attempt, last bid, last throw; venture, adventure, quest, speculation, operation, exercise 672 *undertaking*; aim, goal 617 *objective*; straining after, high endeavour, perfectionism 862 *fastidiousness*.
trier, bidder, tackler, essayer 852 *hoper*; tester 461 *experimenter*; searcher, quester 459 *enquirer*; struggler, striver, fighter 716 *contender*; idealist 862 *perfectionist*; lobbyist, activist 654 *reformer*; undertaker, contractor, entrepreneur, jobber.
Adj. *attempting*, tackling, trying, striving, doing one's best 597 *willing*; game, nothing daunted 599 *resolute*; questing, searching 459 *enquiring*; tentative, catch-as-catch-can; testing, probationary, on approval 461 *experimental*; ambitious, venturesome, daring 672 *enterprising*.
Vb. *attempt*, essay, try; seek to, aim, make it one's a. 617 *intend*; angle for, fish for, seek 459 *search*; offer, bid, make a b.; make an attempt, make shift to, make the effort, do something about, not just stand there; endeavour, struggle, strive, try hard, try and try again 599 *be resolute*; do one's best, do one's damnedest, go all out, redouble one's efforts 682 *exert oneself*; pull hard, push h., strain, sweat 682 *work*; tackle, take on, try one's hand at, have a go, give it a try, give it a whirl, have a shot at, have a crack at, have a stab at 672 *undertake*; get down to, get to grips with, take the bull by the horns, make a go of; take a chance, chance one's arm, try one's luck, tempt providence, venture, speculate 618 *gamble*; test, make trial of 461 *experiment*; put out a feeler, dip in a toe, fly a kite 461 *be tentative*; be ambitious, attempt too much, bite off more than one can chew, die in the attempt 728 *fail*.
Int. Here goes! nothing venture, nothing gain *or* nothing win!
See: 68, 459, **461**, 597, 599, 617, 618, 654, **672**, 676, **682**, 712, 716, 728, 852, 862.

672 Undertaking

N. *undertaking*, job, task, assignment; self-imposed task, labour of love, pilgrimage 597 *voluntary work*; contract, engagement, obligation 764 *promise*; operation, exercise; programme, project, design 623 *plan*; tall order, big undertaking 700 *hard task*; enterprise, emprise; quest, search, adventure 459 *enquiry*; venture, speculation 618 *gambling*; occupation, matter in hand 622 *business*; struggle, effort, campaign 671 *attempt*.

Adj. *enterprising*, pioneering, adventurous, venturesome, daring; go-ahead, progressive; opportunist, alive to opportunity; ambitious 859 *desiring*; overambitious 857 *rash*; responsible, shouldering responsibility.

Vb. *undertake*, engage in, apply oneself to, address o. to, take up, go in for, devote oneself to; venture on, take on, tackle 671 *attempt*; go about, take in hand, turn *or* put *or* set one's hand to; set forward, set going 68 *initiate*; proceed to, embark on, launch into, plunge into, fall to, set to, buckle to, put one's best foot forward, set one's shoulder to the wheel, set one's hand to the plough 68 *begin*; grasp the nettle 855 *be courageous*; assume responsibility, take charge of 689 *manage*; execute 725 *carry out*; set up shop, have irons in the fire 622 *busy oneself*; take on one's shoulders, take upon oneself, assume an obligation 917 *incur a duty*; engage to, commit oneself 764 *promise*; get involved, let oneself in for, volunteer 597 *be willing*; take on too much, bite off more than one can chew, have too many irons in the fire 678 *be busy*; show enterprise, pioneer; venture, dare 661 *face danger*; apprentice oneself 669 *prepare oneself*.

See: 68, 459, 597, 618, 622, 623, 661, 669, **671**, 678, 689, 700, 725, 764, 855, 857, 859, 917.

673 Use

N. *use*, usufruct, enjoyment, disposal 773 *possession*; conversion to use, conversion, utilization, exploitation; employment, application, appliance; exercise 610 *practice*; resort, recourse; mode of use, treatment, good usage, proper treatment 457 *carefulness*; ill-treatment, hard usage, wrong use 675 *misuse*; effect of use, wear, wear and tear 655 *dilapidation*; exhaustion, consumption 634 *waste*; reuse, palimpsest; usefulness, benefit, service 642 *good policy*; serviceability, practicality, convertibility, applicability 640 *utility*; office, purpose, point 622 *function*; long use, wont 610 *habit*.

Adj. *used*, applied, employed etc. vb.; in service, in use, in constant u., in practice; used up, consumed, worn, threadbare, second-hand, well-used, well-thumbed, dog-eared, well-worn 655 *dilapidated*; beaten, well-trodden 490 *known*; hackneyed, stale; pragmatical, practical, utilitarian 642 *advisable*; makeshift, provisional 150 *substituted*; subservient, like wax *or* putty in one's hands 628 *instrumental*; available, usable, employable, utilizable, convertible 640 *useful*; at one's service, consumable, disposable.

Vb. *use*, employ, exercise, practise, put into practice; apply, exert, bring to bear, administer; spend on, give to, devote to, consecrate to, dedicate to; assign to, allot (**see** *dispose of*); utilize, make use of, harness, convert, convert to use 640 *find useful*; reuse, recycle, exploit, get mileage out of, use to the full, get the best out of, make the most of, exhaust the possibilities; milk, drain 304 *extract*; put to good use, turn to account, capitalize on, make capital out of, use to advantage, make hay with 137 *profit by*; make play with, play on, trade on, cash in on; play off, play off against; make a tool *or* handle of; make a pawn *or* cat's-paw of, take advantage of 542 *befool*; put to use, wear, wear out, use up, consume 634 *waste*; handle, thumb 378 *touch*; tread, follow, beat (a path); work, drive, manipulate 173 *operate*; wield, ply, brandish; overwork, tax, task 684 *fatigue*; prepare for use, work on, work up, mould 243 *form*.

avail oneself of, take up, adopt, try; resort to, run to, have recourse to, fall back on, draw on; impose on, presume on; press into service, enlist in one's s.; make do with, make shift w., do what one can w., make the best of.

dispose of, command; have at one's disposal, control, have at one's command, do what one likes with; allot, assign 783 *apportion*; spare, have to s.; requisition, call in; call into play, set in motion, set in action, set going, deploy 612 *motivate*; enjoy, have the usufruct 773 *possess*; consume, expend, absorb, use up 634 *waste*.

See: 137, 150, 173, 243, 304, 378, 457, 490, 542, 610, 612, 622, 628, **634**, **640**, **642**, 655, 675, 684, 773, 783.

674 Nonuse

N. *nonuse*, abeyance, suspension 677 *inaction*; nonavailability 190 *absence*; stagnation, unemployment 679 *inactivity*; forbearance, abstinence 620 *avoidance*; savings 632 *store*; disuse, obsolescence, superannuation 611 *desuetude*; dismissal

300 *ejection*; waiver, giving up, surrender 621 *relinquishment*; withdrawal, cancellation 752 *abrogation*; unsuitability 643 *inexpedience*; uselessness, write-off 641 *inutility*.

Adj. *unused*, not used; not available 190 *absent*; out of order, not in service, unusable, unemployable 641 *useless*; unpracticable 643 *inexpedient*; unutilized, unapplied, unconverted; nonconvertible, nonreturnable; undisposed of, in hand, reserved, saved 632 *stored*; on the spike, pigeonholed; spare, extra; unspent, unconsumed 666 *preserved*; untilled, unexploited, untapped, lying idle *or* fallow; unessayed, untried; unexercised, in abeyance, suspended; untrodden, unbeaten; untouched, unhandled, unopened 126 *new*; ungathered, unplucked, left to rot 634 *wasted*; unnecessary, not wanted, not required, redundant 860 *unwanted*; unrequired, free, vacant; dispensed with, waived; underused, not made use of, resting, unemployed, idle 679 *inactive*; jobless, out of work.

disused, derelict, discarded, cast-off, jettisoned, scrapped, written off; sacked, discharged, laid off etc. vb.; laid up, mothballed, in mothballs, out of commission, rusting, on the scrap heap; in limbo 458 *neglected*; done with, used up, run down, worn out; on the shelf, retired; out of use, superseded, superannuated, obsolete, discredited 127 *antiquated*.

Vb. *not use*, not utilize, hold in abeyance; not touch, have no use for; abstain, forbear, hold off, do without 620 *avoid*; dispense with, waive, not proceed with 621 *relinquish*; overlook, disregard 458 *neglect*; underuse, underutilize; spare, save, reserve, keep in hand 632 *store*; not accept, decline 607 *reject*.

stop using, disuse, leave off 145 *cease*; outgrow 611 *disaccustom*; leave to rust, lay up, put in mothballs, put out of commission, dismantle 641 *make useless*; have done with, lay aside, put on the shelf, hang up; pension off, put out to grass; discard, dump, ditch, scrap, write off; jettison, throw away, throw overboard 300 *eject*; slough, cast off 229 *doff*; give up, relinquish, resign 779 *not retain*; suspend, withdraw, cancel 752 *abrogate*; discharge, lay off, pay off, make redundant 300 *dismiss*; drop, supersede, replace 150 *substitute*; be unused, rust 655 *deteriorate*.

See: 126, 127, 145, 150, 190, 229, 300, 458, 607, **611**, 620, 621, 632, 634, **641**, 643, 655, 666, 677, 679, 752, 779, 860.

675 Misuse

N. *misuse*, abuse, wrong use; misemployment, misapplication; misdirection, mismanagement, maladministration 695 *bungling*; misappropriation, malpractice 788 *peculation*; perversion 246 *distortion*; prostitution, violation; profanation, desecration 980 *impiety*; pollution 649 *uncleanness*; overuse, overgrazing, overcropping, overfishing; extravagance 634 *waste*; misusage, mishandling, mistreatment, maltreatment, ill-treatment, force 176 *violence*; outrage, injury 616 *evil*.

Vb. *misuse*, abuse; use wrongly, misemploy, put to bad use, misdirect; divert, manipulate, misappropriate 788 *defraud*; violate, desecrate, take in vain 980 *be impious*; prostitute 655 *pervert*; pollute 649 *make unclean*; do violence to 176 *force*; strain 246 *distort*; take advantage of, exploit 673 *use*; manhandle, knock about 645 *ill-treat*; maltreat 735 *oppress*; misgovern, misrule, mishandle, mismanage 695 *be unskilful*; overwork, overtask, overtax 684 *fatigue*; work hard, wear out 655 *impair*; squander, fritter away 634 *waste*; misapply, use a sledgehammer to crack a nut 641 *waste effort*.

See: 176, 246, 616, **634**, 641, 645, 649, 655, 673, 684, 695, 735, 788, 980.

Section three: Voluntary action

676 Action

N. *action*, doing, performance; steps, measures, move 623 *policy*; transaction, enactment, commission, perpetration; dispatch, execution, effectuation, accomplishment 725 *completion*; procedure, routine, praxis 610 *practice*; behaviour 688 *conduct*; movement, play, swing 265 *motion*; operation, working, interaction, evolution 173 *agency*; force, pressure 178 *influence*; work, labour 682 *exertion*; militancy, activism, activeness, drama 678 *activity*; occupation 622 *business*; manufacture 164 *production*; employment 673 *use*; effort, endeavour, campaign, crusade, war on 671 *attempt*; implementation, administration, handling 689 *management*.

deed, act, overt a.; action, exploit, beau geste, feat, achievement 855 *prowess*; bad deed, crime 930 *foul play*; stunt, tour de force 875 *ostentation*; gesture, measure, step, move 623 *policy*; manoeuvre, evolution 688 *tactics*; stroke, blow, coup, coup de main, coup d'état 623 *contrivance*; job, task, operation, exercise 672 *undertaking*; proceeding, transaction, deal, doings, dealings 154 *affairs*; work, handiwork, workmanship, craftsmanship 694 *skill*; pièce de résistance, chef d'oeuvre 694 *masterpiece*; drama, scene; acts 590 *narrative*.

doer, man *or* woman of action, activist 678 *busy person*; practical person, realist; achiever, finisher; hero, heroine 855 *brave person*; practitioner 696 *expert*; stunt man *or* woman, player 594 *actor*; executant, performer; perpetrator, committer; offender, criminal 904 *evildoer*; mover, controller, manipulator 612 *motivator*; operator 686 *agent*; contractor, undertaker, entrepreneur; action group, campaigner, canvasser; executor, executive, administrator, manager 690 *director*; hand, workman, operative 686 *worker*; craftsman, craftswoman 686 *artisan*; creative worker 556 *artist*.

Adj. *doing*, acting, operating, performing, committing etc. vb.; in the act, red-handed; working, at work, in action, in operation, in harness 173 *operative*; up and doing, industrious, busy 678 *active*; occupational 610 *habitual*.

Vb. *do*, act, perform; be in action, come into operation 173 *operate*; militate, act upon 178 *influence*; manipulate 612 *motivate*; use tactics, twist, turn, manoeuvre 698 *be cunning*; do something, lift a finger; proceed, proceed with, get on with, get going, move, take action, take steps; try 671 *attempt*; tackle, take on 672 *undertake*; adopt a measure, enact, legislate 953 *make legal*; do the deed, perpetrate, commit, achieve, accomplish, complete 725 *carry through*; do the needful, take care of, dispatch, execute, implement, fulfil, put into practice 725 *carry out*; solemnize, observe; do great deeds, make history, win renown 866 *have a reputation*; practise, exercise, carry on, discharge, prosecute, pursue, wage, ply, ply one's trade, employ oneself 622 *busy oneself*; officiate, do one's stuff 622 *function*; transact, proceed 622 *do business*; administer, administrate, manage, control 689 *direct*; have to do with 688 *deal with*; sweat, labour, campaign, canvass 682 *work*; exploit, make the most of 673 *use*; intervene, strike a blow for 703 *aid*; have a hand in, be active in, play a part in 775 *participate*; deal in, have a finger in, get mixed up in 678 *meddle*; conduct oneself, indulge in 688 *behave*; play about, lark around, fool a. 497 *be absurd*; stunt, show off 875 *be ostentatious*.

Adv. *in the act*, in flagrante delicto, red-handed; in the midst of, in the thick of; while one's hand is in, while one is about it.

See: 154, 164, **173**, 178, 265, 497, 556, 590, 594, 610, 612, 622, 623, 671, **672**, 673, **678**, 682, 686, **688**, 689, 690, 694, 696, 698, 703, 725, 775, 855, 866, 875, 904, 930, 953.

677 Inaction

N. *inaction*, nonaction, nothing doing, inertia 175 *inertness*; inability to act 161 *impotence*; failure to act, neglect 458 *negligence*; abstinence from action, abstention, refraining 620 *avoidance*; passive resistance 711 *defiance*; suspension, abeyance, dormancy 674 *nonuse*; deadlock, stalemate 145 *stop*; immobility, paralysis, impassivity 375 *insensibility*; passivity, stagnation, vegetation, doldrums, stillness, quiet, calm 266 *quiescence*; time on one's hands, idle hours, dolce far niente 681 *leisure*; rest 683 *repose*; nonemployment, underemployment, unemployment; no work, sinecure; loafing, idleness, indolence 679 *inactivity*; Fabian policy, do-nothingism 136 *delay*; lack of progress 655 *deterioration*; noninterference, nonintervention 860 *indifference*; head in the sand, defeatism 856 *cowardice*.

Adj. *nonactive*, inoperative, idle, suspended, in abeyance 679 *inactive*; passive, dull, sluggish 175 *inert*; unoccupied, leisured 681 *leisurely*; do-nothing, unprogressive, ostrich-like; Fabian, cunctative, delaying, procrastinating; defeatist 853 *hopeless*; stationary, motionless, immobile 266 *quiescent*; cold, extinct; not stirring, without a sign of life, dead-and-alive 361 *dead*; laid off, unemployed, jobless, out of work, on the dole, without employment 674 *unused*; incapable of action 161 *impo-*

tent; benumbed, paralysed 375 *insensible*; apathetic, phlegmatic 820 *impassive*; neutral 860 *indifferent*; unhearing 416 *deaf*.

Vb. *not act*, fail to a., refuse to a., hang fire 598 *be unwilling*; refrain, abstain, pass the buck 620 *avoid*; look on, stand by 441 *watch*; watch and wait, wait and see, bide one's time 136 *wait*; procrastinate 136 *put off*; live and let live, let it rip, let things take their course, laisser aller, laisser faire, let sleeping dogs lie, let well alone; hold no brief for, stay neutral, sit on the fence 860 *be indifferent*; do nothing, tolerate, turn a blind eye 458 *disregard*; sit tight, not move, not budge, not stir, show no sign, not lift a finger, not even attempt 175 *be inert*; rest on one's oars, rest on one's laurels, relax one's efforts; drift, slide, coast, free-wheel; have no hope 853 *despair*; let pass, let go by, leave alone, let a., give it a miss 458 *neglect*; stay still, keep quiet 266 *be quiescent*; sit back, relax 683 *repose*; have no function 641 *be useless*; have nothing to do, kick one's heels 681 *have leisure*; pause, desist 145 *cease*; rust, lie idle, stay on the shelf, lie fallow 674 *not use*; have no life, lie dead 361 *die*.

Adv. *without action*, without movement; nothing doing, hands in one's pockets, with folded arms; with the job half done.

See: 136, 145, 161, **175**, 266, 361, 375, 416, 441, 458, 598, 620, 641, 655, **674**, **679**, **681**, **683**, 711, 820, 853, 856, 860.

678 Activity

N. *activity*, activeness, activism, militancy 676 *action*; interest, active i. 775 *participation*; social activity, group a. 882 *sociability*; activation 612 *motive*; excitation 174 *stimulation*; agitation, movement, mass m. 738 *sedition*; life, stir 265 *motion*; nimbleness, briskness, smartness, alacrity, promptitude 597 *willingness*; readiness 135 *punctuality*; quickness, dispatch, expedition 277 *velocity*; spurt, burst, fit 318 *spasm*; hurry, flurry, hurry-scurry, hustle, bustle, overhaste, frantic haste 680 *haste*; fuss, bother, botheration, ado, to-do, racketing, tumult, frenzy 61 *turmoil*; whirl, scramble, mad s., rat race, maelstrom 315 *vortex*; drama, great doings, much ado, thick of things, thick of the action, the fray; plenty to do, irons in the fire 622 *business*; call on one's time, press of business; pressure of work, no sinecure; high street, marketplace, heavy traffic; press, madding crowd, seething mob; hum, hive, hive of industry 687 *workshop*.

restlessness, pottering, fiddling, aimless activity, desultoriness, no concentration 456 *inattention*; unquiet, fidgets, fidgetiness 318 *agitation*; jumpiness 822 *excitability*; fever, fret 503 *frenzy*; eagerness, enthusiasm, ardour, fervour, abandon, vehemence 818 *warm feeling*; vigour, energy, ceaseless e., dynamic e., dynamism, aggressiveness, militancy, enterprise, initiative, push, drive, go, get-up-and-go, pep 174 *vigorousness*; vivacity, spirit, animation, liveliness, vitality 360 *life*; watchfulness, wakefulness, vigilance 457 *carefulness*; sleeplessness, insomnia.

assiduity, application, concentration, intentness 455 *attention*; sedulity, industriousness, industry, laboriousness, legwork, drudgery 682 *labour*; determination, earnestness, empressement 599 *resolution*; tirelessness, indefatigability 600 *perseverance*; studiousness, painstaking, diligence; whole-heartedness, devotedness.

overactivity, overextension, overexpansion, excess 637 *redundance*; Parkinson's law; displacement activity, futile a., chasing one's own tail 641 *lost labour*; song and dance 318 *commotion*; hyperthyroidism, overexertion; officiousness, beadledom, meddlesomeness, interference, intrusiveness, interruption, meddling, interfering, finger in every pie; tampering, intrigue 623 *plot*.

busy person, new broom, enthusiast, bustler, hustler, someone in a hurry; zealot, fanatic 602 *obstinate person*; slogger, no slouch, hard worker, tireless w., high-pressure w., Stakhanovite, demon for work, glutton for w., workaholic 686 *worker*; factotum, maid-of-all-work, housewife, drudge, dogsbody, fag, slave, galley s., Trojan; horse, beaver, ant, bee; eager beaver, busy bee, workhorse; person of active habits, man *or* woman of action, activist, militant 676 *doer*; participator; sharp fellow, live wire, dynamo, powerhouse, whiz kid, go-getter, pusher, thruster; careerist.

meddler, dabbler, stirrer, interferer, intermeddler, officious person, spoilsport, nosy parker, ultracrepidarian, busybody

453 *inquisitive person*; tamperer, intriguer 623 *planner*; kibitzer, back-seat driver 691 *adviser*; fusspot, nuisance.

Adj. *active*, stirring 265 *moving*; going, working, incessant 146 *unceasing*; expeditious 622 *businesslike*; able, able-bodied 162 *strong*; quick, brisk, nippy, spry, smart, gleg 277 *speedy*; nimble, light-footed, lightsome, tripping; energetic, forceful, thrustful 174 *vigorous*; pushing, go-getting, up-and-coming 672 *enterprising*; frisky, coltish, dashing, sprightly, spirited, mettlesome, live, alive and kicking, full of beans, animated, vivacious 819 *lively*; eager, ardent, perfervid 818 *fervent*; fierce, desperate 599 *resolute*; enthusiastic, zealous, prompt, instant, ready, on one's toes 597 *willing*; awake, alert, watchful, wakeful, on the qui vive 457 *vigilant*; sleepless, restless, feverish, fretful, tossing, dancing, fidgety, jumpy, fussy, nervy, like a cat on hot bricks 318 *agitated*; frantic, demonic 503 *frenzied*; hyperactive, overactive 822 *excitable*; involved, engagé; aggressive, militant, up in arms 718 *warlike*.

busy, bustling, hustling, humming, lively, eventful; coming and going, rushing to and fro, as though one's life depended on it; pottering, doing chores; up and doing, stirring, astir, afoot, on the move, on the go, on the trot, in full swing; slogging, hard at work, hard at it, up to one's eyes, fully engaged; in harness, at work, at one's desk; occupied, fully o., employed, over-e.; fussing like a hen with one chicken, busy as a bee.

industrious, studious, sedulous, assiduous 600 *persevering*; labouring, hardworking, plodding, slogging 682 *laborious*; unflagging, unwearied, unsleeping, tireless, indefatigable, keeping long hours, never-tiring, never-resting, never-sleeping; efficient, workmanlike 622 *businesslike*.

meddling, overbusy, officious, pushy, interfering, meddlesome, intrusive, intriguing; dabbling; participating, in the business.

Vb. *be active*, show interest, interest oneself in, trouble oneself, join in 775 *participate*; be stirring, stir, come and go, rush to and fro 265 *move*; run riot, have one's fling 61 *rampage*; not sleep, wake up, rouse oneself, bestir o., stir one's stumps, be up and doing; hum, thrive 730 *prosper*; make progress 285 *progress*; keep moving, keep on the go, keep the pot boiling 146 *go on*; push, shove, thrust, drive 279 *impel*; elbow one's way 174 *be vigorous*; rush, surge 350 *flow*; roar, rage, bluster 352 *blow*; explode, burst 176 *be violent*; dash, fly, run 277 *move fast*; make the effort, do one's best 671 *attempt*; take pains 455 *be attentive*; buckle to, put one's shoulder to the wheel 682 *exert oneself*; persist, beaver away 600 *persevere*; polish off, dispatch, make short work of, not let the grass grow under one's feet; rise to the occasion, work wonders 727 *be successful*; jump to it, show zeal, make the sparks fly, make things hum 676 *do*; burn with zeal, be on fire 597 *be willing*; be on one's toes, anticipate, wake, watch 457 *be careful*; seize the opportunity, take one's chance 137 *profit by*; assert oneself, not take it lying down, be up in arms, react, react sharply, show fight 711 *defy*; protest, agitate, demonstrate, kick up a shindy, raise the dust 762 *deprecate*.

be busy, keep b., have irons in the fire 622 *busy oneself*; bustle, hurry, scurry 680 *hasten*; live in a whirl, join the rat race, go all ways at once, run round in circles; chase one's own tail 641 *waste effort*; not know which way to turn 700 *be in difficulty*; have one's hands full, be rushed off one's feet, have not a moment to spare *or* to call one's own, have no time to lose, rise early, go to bed late, burn the midnight oil; fuss, fret, fume, stamp with impatience 822 *be excitable*; have other things to do, have other fish to fry 138 *be engaged*; slave, slog 682 *work*; overwork, overdo it, make work, make heavy weather of, never stop, improve the shining hour; affect zeal 850 *be affected*.

meddle, intermeddle, interpose, intervene, interfere, be officious, not mind one's own business, have a finger in every pie; poke one's nose in, shove one's oar in, butt in 297 *intrude*; pester, bother, dun, annoy 827 *trouble*; be bossy, boss, boss one around, tyrannize 735 *oppress*; tinker, tamper, touch 655 *impair*.

Adv. *actively*, on the go, on one's toes; full tilt, whole hog; with might and main, for all one is worth, for dear life.

Int. wakey wakey! rise and shine! shake a leg! get going!

See: 61, 135, 137, 138, 146, 162, **174**, 176, 265, 277, 279, 285, 297, 315, 318, 350, 352, 360, 453, 455, 456, 457, 503, 597, 599, 600, 602, 612, 622, 623, 637, 641,

655, 671, 672, **676**, 680, **682**, 686, 687, 691, 700, 711, 718, 727, 730, 735, 738, 762, 775, 818, 819, 822, 827, 850, 882.

679 Inactivity

N.*inactivity*, inactiveness 677 *inaction*; inertia, heaviness, torpor 175 *inertness*; lull, suspension, suspended animation 145 *cessation*; immobility, stillness, slack period, doldrums, grave, morgue 266 *quiescence*; no progress, stagnation 655 *deterioration*; rust, rustiness 674 *nonuse*; slump, recession 37 *decrease*; unemployment, shutdown; absenteeism 598 *unwillingness*; procrastination, mañana 136 *delay*; idleness, indolence, loafing; idle hours 681 *leisure*.

sluggishness, lethargy, laziness, indolence, sloth; remissness 458 *negligence*; dawdling, slow progress 278 *slowness*; stiffness, debility 163 *weakness*; inanimation, lifelessness; languor, lentor, dullness, listlessness 820 *moral insensibility*; stupor, torpor, torpidity, numbness 375 *insensibility*; apathy 860 *indifference*; phlegm, impassivity 823 *inexcitability*; supineness, no resistance, line of least r. 721 *submission*.

sleepiness, tiredness, weariness, lassitude 684 *fatigue*; somnolence, doziness, drowsiness, heaviness, nodding; oscitation, oscitancy, yawning; tired eyes, heavy lids, sand in the eyes; dreaminess 513 *fantasy*.

sleep, slumber, kip, bye-byes; deep sleep, sound s., heavy s., beauty s.; untroubled sleep, sleep of the just; half-sleep, drowse; light sleep, nap, catnap, forty winks, shuteye, snooze, doze, siesta 683 *repose*; winter sleep, summer s., hibernation, aestivation; unconsciousness, coma, trance, catalepsy, hypnosis 375 *insensibility*; sleepwalking, somnambulism; sleepy sickness 651 *disease*; dreams, gate of ivory, g. of horn; Morpheus, sandman; dreamland, Land of Nod; cot, cradle, pillow, bed.

soporific, somnifacient, sleeping draught, nightcap; sleeping pill, sedative, barbiturate; opiate, poppy, opium, morphine 375 *anaesthetic*; lullaby, berceuse, cradlesong.

idler, drone, lazybones, lie-abed, loafer, lounger, flâneur, sloucher, sluggard; slacker, skiver, clock-watcher; Weary Willie, moper, sleepyhead; dawdler 278 *slowcoach*; hobo, bum, tramp 268 *wanderer*; mendicant 763 *beggar*; spiv, parasite, cadger, sponger, scrounger, freeloader; layabout, good-for-nothing, ne'er-do-well, wastrel, slubberdegullion; floater, drifter, free-wheeler; opium-eater, lotus-e., waiter on Providence 596 *fatalist*; nonworker, sinecurist, rentier; fainéant, dummy, passenger, sleeping partner, absentee landlord; idle rich, leisured classes; dreamer, sleeper, slumberer, dozer, drowser; hibernator, dormouse, hedgehog; Seven Sleepers, Rip van Winkle, Sleeping Beauty.

Adj.*inactive*, motionless, stationary, at a standstill, still, hushed, extinct 266 *quiescent*; suspended, discontinued, taken off, not working, not operating, not in use, laid up, out of commission 674 *disused*; inanimate, lifeless, exanimate 175 *inert*; torpid, benumbed, unconscious, dopey, drugged 375 *insensible*; sluggish, stiff, rusty 677 *nonactive*; lymphatic, listless, lackadaisical 834 *dejected*; tired, faint, languid, languorous 684 *fatigued*; dull, heavy, leaden, lumpish, stolid 820 *impassive*; unresisting, supine, submissive 721 *submitting*; uninterested 454 *incurious*; apathetic 860 *indifferent*; lethargic, unaroused, unawakened 823 *inexcitable*; nonparticipating, sleeping 190 *absent*; leisured, idle, empty, unoccupied, disengaged 681 *leisurely*; on strike, out, locked o.

lazy, bone-l., do-nothing, fainéant; slothful, sluggish, work-shy, indolent, idle, bone-idle, spivvish, parasitical; idling, lolling, loafing 681 *leisurely*; dawdling 278 *slow*; tardy, laggard, dilatory, procrastinating 136 *late*; slack, remiss, careless 458 *negligent*.

sleepy, ready for bed, tired 684 *fatigued*; half-awake, half-asleep; slumberous, somnolent, heavy-eyed, stupid with sleep; drowsy, dozy, dopey, groggy, nodding, yawning; napping, dozing; asleep, dreaming, snoring, fast asleep, sound a., dead to the world; unconscious, out; dormant, hibernating, comatose; in dreamland, in the land of Nod, in the arms of Morpheus, in bed.

soporific, somnific, somniferous, sleep-inducing, sedative, hypnotic.

Vb.*be inactive*, do nothing, rust, stagnate, vegetate, smoulder, hang fire 677 *not act*; let the grass grow under one's feet, delay 136 *put off*; not bother, take it easy, let things go, laisser faire 458 *be neglectful*; hang about, kick one's heels 136 *wait*; slouch, lag, loiter, dawdle 278 *move slowly*; dally, drag one's feet 136 *be late*; stand, sit, lie, lollop, loll, lounge, laze, rest, take it easy 683 *repose*; lie down on the job, slack, skive, shirk 620 *avoid*; not work, fold one's arms, sit around; have nothing to do, loaf, idle, mooch about, moon a., while away the time, kill t., twiddle one's thumbs; waste time, drone away, consume the golden hours, trifle, dabble, fribble, fiddle-faddle, fritter away the time, piddle, potter, putter 641 *waste effort*; slow down, come to a standstill 278 *decelerate*; dilly-dally, hesitate 474 *be uncertain*; droop, faint, fail, languish, slacken 266 *come to rest*; slump 37 *decrease*; be still, be hushed 266 *be quiescent*; discontinue, stop, come to an end 145 *cease*; strike, come out.

sleep, slumber, snooze, nap, catnap; aestivate, hibernate; sleep soundly, sleep well, sleep like a log, sleep like a top, sleep like a little child; dream; snore, drive pigs to market; go to sleep, nod off, drop off, fall asleep, take a nap, have a kip, have forty winks; close one's eyes, feel sleepy, yawn, nod, doze, drowse; go to bed, turn in, doss down, kip d., shake d., hit the hay; settle down, bed d., roost, perch.

make inactive, put to sleep, put to bed, seal up the eyelids; send to sleep, lull, rock, cradle; soothe 177 *assuage*; deaden, paralyse, benumb, dope, drug, narcotize, put out 375 *render insensible*; stiffen, cramp, immobilize 747 *fetter*; lay up, put out of commission 674 *stop using*; dismantle 641 *make useless*; pay off, stand o., lay o. 300 *dismiss*.

See: 37, 136, 145, 163, **175**, 177, 190, 266, 268, 278, 300, **375**, 454, 458, 474, 513, 596, 598, 620, 641, 651, 655, 674, **677**, **681**, **683**, 684, 721, 747, 763, 820, 823, 834, 860.

680 Haste

N. *haste*, hurry, scurry, hurry-scurry, hustle, bustle, flurry, whirl, scramble 678 *activity*; flap, flutter, fidget, fuss 318 *agitation*; rush, rush job 670 *nonpreparation*; feverish haste, tearing hurry, race against time, no time to lose 136 *lateness*; immediacy, urgency 638 *importance*; push, drive, expedition, dispatch 277 *velocity*; hastening, acceleration, forced march, dash 277 *spurt*; overhaste, precipitance, precipitateness, impetuosity 857 *rashness*; inability to wait, hastiness, impatience 822 *excitability*.

Adj. *hasty*, overhasty, impetuous, impulsive, hot-headed, precipitant 857 *rash*; feverish, impatient, all impatience, ardent 818 *fervent*; pushing, shoving; uncontrolled, boisterous, furious 176 *violent*; precipitate, headlong, breathless, breakneck 277 *speedy*; expeditious, prompt, without delay; hasting, hastening, making speed; in haste, in all h., hotfoot, running, racing; in a hurry, unable to wait, pressed for time, hard-pressed, driven; done in haste, hurried, scamped, slapdash, cursory 458 *negligent*; rough and ready, forced, rushed, rush, last-minute 670 *unprepared*; rushed into, railroaded; allowing no time, brooking no delay, urgent, immediate 638 *important*.

Vb. *hasten*, expedite, dispatch; urge, drive, spur, goad, whip, lash, flog 612 *incite*; bundle off, hustle away; rush, allow no time, brook no delay; be hasty, be precipitate, rush headlong 857 *be rash*; haste, make haste; post, race, run, dash off, tear off 277 *move fast*; catch up, make up for lost time, overtake 277 *outstrip*; spurt, dash, make a forced march 277 *accelerate*; hurry, scurry, hustle, bustle, fret, fume, fidget, rush to and fro, dart to and fro 678 *be active*; be in a hurry, have no time to spare, have no time to lose, act without ceremony, cut short the preliminaries, brush aside; cut corners, rush one's fences; rush through, dash through, make short work of; be pressed for time, work against time *or* to a deadline, work under pressure, think on one's feet; do at the last moment 136 *be late*; lose no time, lose not a moment, make every minute count; hasten away, cut and run, make oneself scarce, not be seen for dust 296 *decamp*.

Adv. *hastily*, hurriedly, precipitately, helter-skelter, pell-mell, feverishly, post-haste, hotfoot, apace 277 *swiftly*; with all haste, at short notice, on the spur of the moment; immediately, urgently, with urgency, under pressure, by forced marches, with not a moment to lose.

Int. hurry up! be quick! buck up! look lively! look sharp! get a move on! get a wiggle on! step on it! quick march! at the double!

See: 136, 176, **277**, 296, 318, 458, 612, 638,

670, 678, 818, 822, 857.

681 Leisure

N. *leisure*, spare time, free t., convenience; spare hours, vacant moments, odd m.; time on one's hands, time to kill; not enough work, sinecure; no work, idleness, dolce far niente; off duty, time off, day off, holiday, half-h., break, vacation, leave, furlough 679 *inactivity*; time to spare, no hurry, ample time, all the time in the world; rest, ease, relaxation 683 *repose*; no more work, retirement 753 *resignation*.

Adj. *leisurely*, deliberate, unhurried 278 *slow*; at one's convenience, in one's own time, at any odd moment; leisured, at leisure, disengaged, unoccupied 683 *reposeful*; at a loose end, at ease; off duty, on holiday, on vacation, on leave, on furlough; retired, in retirement; affording leisure, labour-saving.

Vb. *have leisure*, have time enough, have plenty of time, have all the time in the world, have time to spare; be master of one's time, take one's ease, spend, pass, while away; see no cause for haste, be in no hurry, take one's time 278 *move slowly*; want something to do, find time hang heavy on one's hands 679 *be inactive*; take a holiday 683 *repose*; give up work, go into retirement, retire 753 *resign*; find time for, save labour.

See: 278, **679**, **683**, 753.

682 Exertion

N. *exertion*, effort, struggle 671 *attempt*; straining, strain, stress, might and main; tug, pull, stretch, heave, lift, throw; drive, force, pressure, full p., maximum p., applied energy 160 *energy*; ergonomics; ado, trouble, toil and t., mighty efforts, the hard way; muscle, elbow grease, sweat of one's brow; pains, taking pains, operoseness 678 *assiduity*; elaboration, artificiality; overwork, overexertion 678 *overactivity*; extra work, overtime, busman's holiday; battle, campaign, fray.

exercise, practice, regular p., drill, training, work-out, the barre (ballet) 669 *preparation*; physical education, PE, keeping fit, jogging, cycling, constitutional; gymnastics 162 *athletics*; yoga, isometrics, eurhythmics, callisthenics; games, sports, races 837 *sport*.

labour, industry, work, hard w., heavy w., uphill w., warm w., punishing w., long haul; spadework, donkeywork; legwork; manual labour, sweat of one's brow; housework, chores, daily grind, toil, travail, swink, drudgery, slavery, sweat, fag, grind, strain, treadmill, grindstone; hack work; bull; penal work, hard labour, picking oakum, breaking stones 963 *penalty*; forced labour, corvée 740 *compulsion*; fatigue, fatigue duty, spell of d. 917 *duty*; piecework, taskwork, homework, outwork; journeywork; task, chore, job, operation, exercise 676 *deed*; shift, trick, stint, stretch, bout, spell of work 110 *period*; job of work, stroke of w., hand's turn; working life, working day, manhours, womanhours.

Adj. *labouring*, born to toil, horny-handed; working, drudging, sweating, grinding, etc. vb.; on the go, hard at it 678 *busy*; hardworking, laborious 678 *industrious*; slogging, plodding 600 *persevering*; strenuous, energetic 678 *active*; painstaking, thorough 455 *attentive*; exercising, taking exercise, practising; gymnastic, athletic.

laborious, full of labour, involving effort; crushing, killing, backbreaking; gruelling, punishing, exhausting; toilsome, troublesome, weary, wearisome, painful, burdensome; heroic, Herculean; arduous, hard, warm, heavy, uphill 700 *difficult*; hard-fought, hard-won; thorough, painstaking, laboured; elaborate, artificial; detailed, fiddling; effort-wasting 641 *useless*.

Vb. *exert oneself*, apply oneself, put one's best foot forward, make an effort, try 671 *attempt*; struggle, strain, strive, sweat blood; trouble oneself, bestir oneself, put oneself out, bend over backwards; spare no effort, turn every stone, do one's utmost, try one's best, use one's best endeavours, do all one can, go to any lengths, move heaven and earth; go all out, pull out all the stops, put one's heart and soul into it, put out one's whole strength, put one's back into it, strain every nerve, use every muscle 678 *be active*; love one's job, have one's heart in one's work 597 *be willing*; force one's way, drive through, wade t.; hammer at, slog at 600 *persevere*; battle, campaign, take action 676 *do*.

work, labour, toil, moil, drudge, fag, grind, slog, sweat, work up a lather; sweat blood; pull, haul, tug, shove, hump, heave, ply the oar; dig, spade, lumber; do the work, soil one's hands; spit on one's palms, get down to it, set about, set to, take one's coat off 68 *begin*; keep at it, plod 600 *persevere*; work hard, work overtime, moonlight, work double shift, work double tides, work all hours, work night and day, burn the midnight oil 678 *be busy*; slave, slave away, work one's fingers to the bone, work like a galley slave, work like a horse, work like a Trojan; work oneself to death; overdo it, make work; work for, serve 703 *minister to*; put to work, overwork, task, tax 684 *fatigue*.

Adv. *laboriously*, the hard way; manually, by hand; by the sweat of one's brow; arduously, strenuously, energetically; lustily, heartily, heart and soul, with might and main, with all one's might, tooth and nail, hammer and tongs, for all one is worth.

See: 68, 110, 160, 162, 455, 597, 600, 641, 669, **671**, **676**, **678**, 684, 700, 703, 740, 837, 917, 963.

683 Repose

N. *repose*, rest, rest from one's labours 679 *inactivity*; restfulness, ease, comfort 376 *euphoria*; peace and quiet, tranquillity 266 *quiescence*; sweet sleep, happy dreams 679 *sleep*; relaxation, breathing space, breather 685 *refreshment*; pause, respite, let-up, recess, break 145 *lull*; interval 108 *interim*; holiday, vacation, leave, furlough, day off, sabbatical year 681 *leisure*; day of rest, Sabbath, Lord's day.

Adj. *reposeful*, restful, easeful, relaxing; slippered, unbuttoned, in one's shirt-sleeves, carefree, casual, relaxed, laid-back, at ease 828 *content*; cushioned, pillowed, snug 376 *comfortable*; peaceful, quiet 266 *tranquil*; leisured, sabbatical, vacational, holiday 681 *leisurely*; post-prandial, after-dinner.

Vb. *repose*, rest, take a rest, take it easy, take one's ease, sit back, put one's feet up; recline, lie down, loll, lounge, laze, sprawl 216 *be horizontal*; perch, roost 311 *sit down*; couch, go to bed, kip down, go to sleep 679 *sleep*; relax, wind down, unwind, unbend, forget work, put on one's slippers, rest and be thankful; breathe, take a breather 685 *be refreshed*; slack off, let up, slow down; rest on one's oars 266 *come to rest*; take time off *or* out, take a holiday, go on leave 681 *have leisure*.

Adv. *at rest*, reposefully, restfully, peacefully, on holiday, on vacation.

See: 108, 145, 216, 266, 311, 376, **679**, **681**, **685**, 828.

684 Fatigue

N. *fatigue*, tiredness, weariness, lassitude, languor, lethargy; physical fatigue, aching muscles; mental fatigue, brain-fag, staleness; jadedness, distress; limit of endurance, exhaustion, collapse, prostration; strain, overtiredness, overexertion 682 *exertion*; shortness of breath, hard breathing, laboured b., panting, palpitations 352 *respiration*; languishment, faintness, fainting, faint, swoon, blackout 375 *insensibility*.

Adj. *fatigued*, tired, ready for bed 679 *sleepy*; asleep on one's feet, tired out, exhausted, spent; done, done up, done in, pooped, fagged, fagged out, knocked up, washed up, washed out, clapped o., tuckered o., worn to a frazzle; stupid with fatigue, dull, stale; strained, overworked, overtired, overfatigued, overstrained; dog-tired, dog-weary, bone-weary, tired to death, dropping, ready to drop, on one's last legs, all in, dead beat, beat, whacked, knackered, flaked out, flat o.; more dead than alive, swooning, fainting, prostrate; stiff, aching, sore, toilworn; way-worn, footsore, footweary, walked off one's feet; tired-eyed, heavy-e., hollow-e.; tired-looking, haggard, worn; faint, drooping, flagging, languid, languorous; still tired, unrefreshed; tired of, bored with 838 *bored*; jaded, satiated 863 *sated*.

panting, out of breath, short of b.; blown, breathless, gasping, puffing and blowing, snorting, winded, broken-w. 352 *puffing*.

fatiguing, gruelling, punishing 682 *laborious*; tiresome, wearisome; wearing, exacting, demanding; irksome, trying 838 *tedious*.

Vb. *be fatigued*, - fagged etc. adj.; tire oneself out, overdo it, overtax one's strength; get weary, ache in every muscle *or* limb, gasp, pant, puff, blow, grunt 352 *breathe*; languish, droop, drop, sink, flag, fail 163 *be weak*; stagger, faint, swoon, feel giddy; yawn, nod, drowse 679 *sleep*; succumb, drop, collapse, flake out, crack up, crock up, pack up; cry out for rest, have no strength left, be at the end of one's strength; can go no further, can do no more, must have a rest, must sit down; overwork, get stale, need a rest, need a break, need a change, need a holiday.

fatigue, tire, tire out, wear, wear out, exhaust, do up, fag, whack, knock up, crock up, prostrate; double up, wind; demand too much, task, tax, strain, work, drive, overdrive, flog, overwork, overtax, overtask, overburden, overstrain; enervate, drain, take it out of, distress, harass, irk, jade 827 *trouble*; tire to death, weary, bore, send to sleep 838 *be tedious*; keep from sleep, deprive of s., allow no rest.

See: 163, 352, 375, **679**, **682**, 827, 838, 863.

685 Refreshment

N. *refreshment*, breather, breath of air 683 *repose*; break, recess 145 *lull*; renewal, recreation, recruitment, recuperation 656 *restoration*; reanimation 656 *revival*; easing 831 *relief*; stimulation, refresher, reviver, nineteenth hole 174 *stimulant*; refreshments, refection 301 *food*; wash, wash and brush up 648 *cleansing*.

Adj. *refreshing*, thirst-quenching; cooling, cool 380 *cold*; comforting 831 *relieving*; bracing, reviving, recreative, recreational, recruiting 656 *restorative*; easy on, labour-saving 683 *reposeful*.

refreshed, freshened up, breathed, recovered, revived, enlivened 656 *restored*; like a giant refreshed, twice the man *or* woman one was; perked up, ready for more.

Vb. *refresh*, freshen, freshen up 648 *clean*; air, fan, ventilate 340 *aerate*; shade, cool, cool off, cool one down 382 *refrigerate*; brace, stimulate 174 *invigorate*; recruit, recreate, revive, reanimate, reinvigorate, recuperate 656 *restore*; ease 831 *relieve*; allow rest, give a breather; offer food 301 *feed*.

be refreshed, breathe, draw breath, get one's breath back, regain *or* recover one's breath, take a deep b., fill one's lungs; respire, clear one's head; come to, perk up, get one's second wind, feel like a giant refreshed; revive 656 *be restored*; mop one's brow, stretch one's legs, renew oneself, refresh o., take a breather, sleep it off; have a change, have a rest 683 *repose*.

See: 145, 174, 301, 340, 380, 382, 648, **656**, **683**, 831.

686 Agent

N. *agent*, operator, actor, performer, player, executant, practitioner; perpetrator 676 *doer*; minister, tool 628 *instrument*; functionary 741 *officer*; representative 754 *delegate*; deputizer, spokesman 755 *deputy*; proxy 150 *substitute*; executor, executrix, executive, administrator, dealer; middleman 794 *merchant*; employer, manufacturer, industrialist 164 *producer*.

worker, voluntary w. 597 *volunteer*; social worker 901 *philanthropist*; independent worker, freelance, self-employed person; organization man 83 *conformist*; trade unionist 775 *participator*; toiler, moiler, drudge, dogsbody, fag, erk, hack; menial, factotum, wallah, maid-of-all-work, domestic servant 742 *servant*; hewer of wood and drawer of water, beast of burden 742 *slave*; ant, beaver, Stakhanovite 678 *busy person*; professional person, business man, business woman, career w., breadwinner, earner, salary e., wage e., wage slave, employee; brain worker, boffin; clerical worker, desk w., white-collar w., black-coat w.; office w., girl Friday, man Friday; shop assistant 793 *seller*; charwoman, dustman 648 *cleaner*; labourer, casual l., day l., agricultural l., farm worker 370 *farmer*; piece-worker, manual w., blue-collar w.; working man *or* woman, working girl, workman, hand, operative, factory worker, factory hand; navvy, roadman; ganger, plate-layer; docker, stevedore, packer; porter, coolie.

artisan, artificer, tradesman, technician; skilled worker, semi-skilled w., master 696 *proficient person*; journeyman, apprentice 538 *learner*; craftsman *or* -woman, potter, turner, joiner, cabinet-maker, carpenter, chippie, carver, woodworker, sawyer, cooper; wright, wheelwright, wainwright, coach-builder; shipwright, boat-builder; builder, architect, master mason, mason, housebuilder, bricklayer, plasterer, tiler, thatcher, painter, decorator; forger, metalworker, smith, blacksmith, tinsmith, goldsmith, silversmith, gunsmith, locksmith; tinker, knife-grinder; collier, miner, face-worker, steelworker, foundryman; mechanic, machinist, fitter; engineer, civil e., mining e.; powerworker, waterworker; plumber, welder, electrician, gas-fitter; weaver, spinner, tailor, cutter, needlewoman 228 *clothier*; watchmaker, clockmaker; jeweller; glass-blower.

personnel, staff, force, company, gang, squad, crew, complement, cadre 74 *band*; dramatis personae 594 *actor*; co-worker, fellow w., mate, colleague, associate, partner 707 *colleague*; workpeople, hands, men, payroll; labour, casual l.; labour pool, labour force, manpower, working classes, proletariat.

See: 74, 83, 150, **164**, 228, 370, 538, 594, 597, 628, 648, **676**, **678**, **696**, 707, 741, 742, 754, 755, 775, 793, 794, 901.

687 Workshop

N. *workshop*, studio, atelier; workroom, study, library; laboratory, research l.; plant, installation; works, factory, manufactory; workshop, yard; sweatshop; mill, cotton m., loom; sawmill, paper mill; foundry, metalworks; steelyard, steelworks, smelter; blast furnace, forge, smithy, stithy 383 *furnace*; powerhouse, power station, gasworks 160 *energy*; quarry, mine 632 *store*; colliery, coalmine, pit, coalface; tin mine, stannary; mint; arsenal, armoury; dockyard, shipyard, slips; wharf, dock 192 *stable*; construction site, building s.; refinery, distillery, brewery, maltings; shop, shopfloor, bench, production line; nursery 370 *farm*; dairy, creamery 369 *stock farm*; kitchen, laundry; office, bureau, business house, firm, company; offices, secretariat, Whitehall; manufacturing town, hive of industry 678 *activity*.

See: 160, 192, 369, 370, 383, 632, 678.

688 Conduct

N. *conduct*, behaviour, deportment; bearing, personal b., comportment, carriage, port; demeanour, attitude, posture 445 *mien*; aspect, look, look in one's eyes 445 *appearance*; tone, tone of voice, delivery 577 *voice*; motion, action, gesticulation 547 *gesture*; mode of behaviour, fashion, style; manner, guise, air; poise, dignity, presence; graciousness, good manners 884 *courtesy*; ungraciousness, boorishness, rudeness, bad manners 885 *discourtesy*; pose, role-playing 850 *affectation*; mental attitude, outlook 485 *opinion*; mood 818 *feeling*; good behaviour 933 *virtue*; misbehaviour, misconduct 934 *wickedness*; democratic behaviour, common touch; past behaviour, record, track r., history; reward of conduct, deserts 915 *dueness*; way of life, ethos, morals, principles, ideals, customs, manners, lifestyle 610 *habit*; proposed conduct, line of action 623 *policy*; career, course, race, walk, walk of life 622 *vocation*; observance, routine, rules of business 610 *practice*; procedure, process, method, modus operandi 624 *way*; treatment, handling, manipulation, direction 689 *management*; gentle handling, kid gloves, velvet glove 736 *leniency*; rough handling, jackboot, iron hand 735 *severity*; dealings, transactions 154 *affairs*; deeds 676 *deed*; behaviourism.

tactics, strategy, campaign, plan of c., programme 623 *plan*; line, party l. 623 *policy*; political science, art of the possible, politics, realpolitik, statesmanship 733 *governance*; lifemanship, gamesmanship, one-upmanship 698 *cunning*; brinkmanship, generalship, seamanship 694 *skill*; manoeuvres, manoeuvring, marching and countermarching, jockeying, jockeying for position; tactical advantage, vantage ground 34 *advantage*; playing for time 136 *delay*; manoeuvre, shift 623 *contrivance*; move, gambit 676 *deed*; game, little g. 698 *stratagem*.

Adj. *behaving*, behavioural, behaviouristic; psychological; tactical, strategical; political, statesmanlike 622 *businesslike*.

Vb. *behave*, act 676 *do*; behave well, mind one's p's and q's, play the game 933 *be virtuous*; behave badly, break all the rules, misbehave, try it on, carry on 934 *be wicked*; deserve well of, deserve ill of; keep out of mischief, be on one's best behaviour; gesture 547 *gesticulate*; posture, pose, affect 850 *be affected*; conduct oneself, behave o., carry o., bear o., deport o., acquit o., comport o., demean o.; set an example, lead a good life, lead a bad l.; indulge in 678 *be active*; play one's part 775 *participate*; pursue, follow one's career, conduct one's affairs 622 *busy oneself*; follow a course, shape a c., steer a c. 281 *steer for*; paddle one's own canoe, shift for oneself 744 *be free*; employ tactics, manoeuvre, jockey, twist, turn; behave towards, treat.

deal with, have on one's plate, have to do with 676 *do*; handle, manipulate 173 *operate*; conduct, carry on, run 689 *manage*; see to, cope with, do the needful; transact, enact, execute, dispatch, carry through, put into practice 725 *carry out*; work out

623 *plan*; work at, work through, wade t. 682 *work*; go through, read 536 *study*.

See: 34, 136, 154, 173, 281, 445, 485, 536, 547, 577, **610**, 622, 623, 624, **676**, 678, 682, 689, 694, 698, 725, 733, 735, 736, 744, 775, 818, 850, 884, 885, 915, 933, 934.

689 Management

N. *management*, conduct, conduct of affairs, manipulation, running, handling; managership, stewardship, proctorship, agency 751 *commission*; care, charge, control 733 *authority*; superintendence, oversight 457 *surveillance*; patronage 660 *protection*; art of management, tact, way with 694 *skill*; business management, work study, time and motion s., operational research, cost-benefit analysis; organization, decision-making 623 *policy*; housekeeping, housewifery, husbandry, economics, political economy; statecraft, statesmanship; government 733 *governance*; ménage, regimen, regime, dispensation; regulation, law-making 953 *legislation*; reins, reins of government, ministry, cabinet, inner c.; staff work, administration; bureaucracy, civil service; secretariat, government office 687 *workshop*.

directorship, direction, responsibility, control, supreme c. 737 *command*; dictatorship, leadership, premiership, chairmanship, captaincy 34 *superiority*; guidance, steering, steerage, pilotage, steersmanship; pole star, lodestar 520 *guide*; controls, helm, rudder, wheel, tiller, joystick; needle, magnetic n., compass, binnacle; gyrocompass, gyropilot, autopilot 269 *sailing aid*; direction-finding, beam, radar 281 *direction*; remote control.

Adj. *directing*, directorial, leading, hegemonic; directional, guiding, steering, at the helm; governing, controlling, gubernatorial, holding the reins, in the chair 733 *authoritative*; dictatorial 735 *authoritarian*; supervisory, managing, managerial; executive, administrative; legislative, nomothetic; high-level, top-l. 638 *important*; economic, political; official, bureaucratic 733 *governmental*.

Vb. *manage*, manipulate, manoeuvre, pull the strings 178 *influence*; have taped, have the measure of 490 *know*; handle, conduct, run, carry on; minister, administer, prescribe; supervise, superintend, oversee, caretake 457 *invigilate*; nurse 457 *look after*; have charge of, have in one's charge, hold the portfolio, hold the purse strings, hold the reins 612 *motivate* (**see** *direct*); keep order, police, regulate; legislate, pass laws 953 *make legal*; control, govern, sway 733 *rule*; know how to manage, have a way with.

direct, lead, pioneer, precede 64 *come before*; boss, dictate 737 *command*; be in charge, wear the trousers; hold office, hold a responsible position, have responsibility; mastermind, have overall responsibility; assume r. 917 *incur a duty*; preside, take the chair, be in the chair; head, captain, skipper, stroke; pilot, cox, steer, take the helm, hold the tiller 269 *navigate*; point 281 *point to*; show the way 547 *indicate*; shepherd, guide, conduct, lead on; introduce, compere; escort 89 *accompany*; channel, canalize, funnel; route, train, lead, lead over, lead through 281 *steer for*.

Adv. *in control*, in charge, at the helm, at the wheel, on the bridge, in the driving seat, in the saddle, in the chair, at the head; ex officio.

See: 34, 64, 89, 178, 269, **281**, 457, 490, 520, 547, 612, 623, 638, 660, 687, 694, **733**, 735, 737, 751, 917, 953.

690 Director

N. *director*, governing body 741 *governor*; steering committee; cabinet, inner c. 692 *council*; board of directors, board, chair; staff, brass, top b., management; manager, controller; legislator, law-giver, lawmaker; employer, capitalist, boss 741 *master*; headman, chief, head of the household, head of state 34 *superior*; principal, head, headmaster *or* -mistress, rector, moderator, dean, vice-chancellor, chancellor; president, vice-p.; chairperson, chairman, chairwoman, speaker; premier, prime minister; captain, skipper; stroke, cox, master 270 *mariner*; steersman, helmsman 270 *navigator*; pilot 520 *guide*; forerunner 66 *precursor*; drill sergeant 537 *trainer*; director of studies 537 *teacher*; backseat driver 691 *adviser*; kingmaker, wire-puller, animator 612 *motivator*; hidden hand 178 *influence*.

leader, charismatic l., judge (Old Testament) 741 *governor*; messiah, mahdi; leader of the House, leader of the opposition; spearhead, centre forward; shepherd, teamster, drover 369 *herdsman*; bell-wether; fugleman, file-leader; pace-maker; symposiarch, toastmaster, master of ceremonies, MC; high priest, mystagogue; coryphaeus, chorus-leader, choragus, conductor, leader of the orchestra, first violin; precentor; drum major; Führer, Duce 741 *autocrat*; ringleader, demagogue, tribune; rabble-rouser 738 *agitator*; captain, condottiere.

manager, person in responsibility, responsible person; man *or* woman in charge, key person, kingpin 638 *bigwig*; procurator, administrator, executive, executor 676 *doer*; statesman *or* -woman, politician; economist, political e.; housekeeper, chatelaine, housewife; steward, bailiff, farm manager, reeve, greeve; agent, factor 754 *consignee*; superintendent, supervisor, inspector, overseer, foreman *or* -woman, ganger, gaffer; warden, house master *or* mistress, matron, nurse, tutor 660 *protector*; proctor, disciplinarian; party manager, whip; custodian, caretaker, curator, librarian 749 *keeper*; master of hounds, whipper-in, huntsman; circus manager, ringmaster; compere.

official, office-holder, office-bearer, Jack-in-office, tin god; marshal, steward; shop steward; government servant, public s., civil s., apparatchik 742 *servant*; officer of state, high official, vizier, grand v., minister, cabinet m., secretary of state, secretary-general, secretary, under-s.; permanent s., bureaucrat, Eurocrat, mandarin 741 *officer*; judicial officer, district o., magistrate 733 *position of authority*; commissioner, prefect, intendant; consul, proconsul, praetor, quaestor, aedile, tribune; first secretary, counsellor 754 *envoy*; alderman, mayor 692 *councillor*; functionary, party official, petty o., clerk; school prefect, monitor.

See: 34, 66, 178, 270, 369, 520, 537, 612, **638**, 660, 676, 691, 692, **733**, 738, **741**, 742, 749, 754.

691 Advice

N. *advice*, word of a., piece of a., counsel; words of wisdom, rede 498 *wisdom*; counselling 658 *therapy*; criticism, constructive c. 480 *estimate*; didacticism, moralizing, moral injunction, prescription 693 *precept*; caution 664 *warning*; recommendation, proposition, proposal, motion 512 *supposition*; suggestion, submonition, submission; tip, word to the wise 524 *hint*; guidance, briefing, instruction 524 *information*; charge, charge to the jury 959 *legal trial*; taking counsel, deliberation, consultation, mutual c., huddle, heads together, powwow, parley 584 *conference*; seeking advice, reference, referment 692 *council*; advice against 762 *deprecation*.

adviser, counsellor, consultant, trouble-shooter; professional consultant 696 *expert*; referee, arbiter 480 *estimator*; prescriber, commender, advocate, recommender, mover, prompter 612 *motivator*; medical adviser, therapist 658 *doctor*; legal adviser, counsel 958 *lawyer*; guide, philosopher and friend, mentor, confidant 537 *teacher*; monitor, admonisher, remembrancer 505 *reminder*; Nestor, Egeria, Dutch uncle; oracle, wise man 500 *sage*; backseat driver, busybody 678 *meddler*; committee of enquiry, consultative body 692 *council*.

Adj. *advising*, advisory, consultative, deliberative; hortative, recommendatory 612 *inducing*; advising against 613 *dissuasive*; admonitory, warning 664 *cautionary*; didactic; moral, moralizing.

Vb. *advise*, give advice, counsel, offer c.; think best, recommend, prescribe, advocate, commend; propose, move, put to, submit, suggest 512 *propound*; prompt 524 *hint*; press, urge, exhort 612 *incite*; advise against 613 *dissuade*; admonish 664 *warn*; enjoin, charge, dictate 737 *command*; advise aptly 642 *be expedient*.

consult, seek advice, refer; call in, call on; refer to arbitration, hold a public enquiry; confide in, be closeted with, have at one's elbow; take advice, listen to, be advised; accept advice, take one's cue from, submit one's judgment to another's, follow advice; sit in council, sit in conclave, put heads together, advise with, hold a consultation, hold a council of war, deliberate, parley, sit round a table, compare notes 584 *confer*.

See: 480, 498, 500, 505, 512, 524, 537, 584, 612, 613, 642, 658, 664, 678, **692**, **693**, 696, 737, 762, 958, 959.

692 Council

N. *council*, council board, round table; council chamber, board room; Star Chamber, court 956 *tribunal*; Privy Council, presidium; ecclesiastical council, Curia, consistory, Bench of Bishops; vestry; cabinet, kitchen c.; panel, quango, think tank, board, advisory b., consultative body, Royal Commission; conventicle, congregation 74 *assembly*; conclave, convocation 985 *synod*; convention, congress, meeting, top-level m., summit; durbar, diet; folkmoot, moot, comitia, ecclesia; federal council, League of Nations, United Nations, UN, UNO, Security Council; municipal council, county c., district c., town c., parish c.; zemstvo, soviet; council of elders, genro, Sanhedrin; sitting, session, séance, audience, hearing 584 *conference*.

parliament, European P., Mother of Parliaments, Westminster, Upper House, House of Lords, House of Peers, 'another place'; Lower House, House of Commons; senate, senatus; legislature, legislative assembly, deliberative a., consultative a., witenagemot; Duma, Reichsrat, Reichstag; States-General, National Assembly, Chambre des Députés, Bundesrat, Bundestag; Rigsdag, Storting, Folketing, Cortes, Dail, Seanad, Knesset, Majlis; Supreme Soviet; Congress, Senate; House of Representatives; quorum, division.

councillor, privy councillor; senator, conscript fathers, Areopagite, Sanhedrist; peer, life peer; Lords Spiritual, L. Temporal; representative, deputy, congressman *or* -woman, Member of Parliament, MP 754 *delegate*; backbencher, lobby fodder; parliamentarian, legislator; municipal councillor, mayor, alderman 690 *official*.

Adj. *parliamentary*, senatorial, congressional; unicameral, bicameral; curule, conciliar; convocational, synodal.

See: 74, 584, 690, 754, 956, 985.

693 Precept

N. *precept*, firm advice 691 *advice*; direction, instruction, general i.; injunction, charge 737 *command*; commission 751 *mandate*; order, written o., writ 737 *warrant*; rescript, decretal 480 *judgment*; prescript, prescription, ordinance, regulation 737 *decree*; canon, form, norm, formula, formulary, rubric; guidelines 81 *rule*; principle, rule, golden r., moral 496 *maxim*; recipe, receipt 658 *remedy*; commandment, statute, enactment, act, code, penal c., corpus juris 953 *legislation*; tenet, article, set of rules, constitution; ticket, party line; Ten Commandments, Twelve Tables, laws of the Medes and the Persians; canon law, common l., unwritten l. 953 *law*; rule of custom, convention 610 *practice*; technicality, nice point 530 *enigma*; precedent, leading case, text 83 *example*.

Adj. *preceptive*, prescriptive, decretal, mandatory, binding; canonical, rubrical, statutory 953 *legal*; moralizing 496 *aphoristic*; customary, conventional 610 *usual*.

See: 81, 83, 480, **496**, 530, 610, 658, 691, **737**, 751, 953.

694 Skill

N. *skill*, skilfulness, dexterity, dexterousness, handiness, ambidexterity; grace, style 575 *elegance*; neatness, deftness, adroitness, address; ease 701 *facility*; proficiency, competence, efficiency; faculty, capability, capacity 160 *ability*; many-sidedness, all-round capacity, versatility, ambidextrousness, amphibiousness; adaptability, flexibility, suppleness; touch, grip, control; mastery, mastership, wizardry, virtuosity, excellence, prowess 644 *goodness*; strong point, métier, forte, strong suit; acquirement, attainment, accomplishment, skills; seamanship, airmanship, horsemanship, marksmanship; experience, expertise, professionalism; specialism; technology, science, know-how, technique, technical knowledge, practical k. 490 *knowledge*; practical ability, clever hands, deft fingers; craftsmanship, art, artistry, delicacy, fine workmanship, art that conceals art; finish, execution 646 *perfection*; ingenuity, resourcefulness, craft, craftiness 698 *cunning*; cleverness, sharpness, nous, worldly wisdom, sophistication, lifemanship 498 *sagacity*; savoir faire, finesse, tact, discretion 463 *discrimination*; feat of skill, trick, gimmick, dodge 623 *contrivance*; sleight of hand, conjuring 542 *sleight*; funambulism, rope-dancing, tightrope walking; brinkmanship 688 *tactics*; skilful use, exploitation 673 *use*.

aptitude, inborn a., innate ability, good head for; bent, natural b. 179 *tendency*; faculty, endowment, gift, flair; turn, knack, green fingers; talent, genius, genius for; aptness, fitness, qualification.

masterpiece, chef-d'oeuvre, a beauty; pièce de résistance, masterwork, magnum opus; workmanlike job, craftsman's j.; stroke of genius, masterstroke, coup-de-maître, feat, exploit, hat trick 676 *deed*; tour de force, bravura, fireworks; ace, trump, clincher 644 *exceller*; work of art, objet d'art, curio, collector's piece *or* item.

Adj. *skilful*, good, good at, top-flight, first-rate 644 *excellent*; skilled, crack; apt, handy, dexterous, ambidextrous, deft, slick, adroit, agile, nimble, neat; nimble-fingered, green-f.; surefooted; cunning, clever, quick, shrewd, smart, ingenious 498 *intelligent*; politic, diplomatic, statesmanlike 498 *wise*; adaptable, flexible, resourceful, ready; many-sided, versatile; ready for anything, panurgic; sound, able, competent, efficient, competitive; wizard, masterful, masterly, like a master, magisterial, accomplished, finished 646 *perfect*.

gifted, naturally g.; of many parts, talented, endowed, well-e., born for, cut out for.

expert, experienced, veteran, seasoned, tried, versed in, up in, well up in, au fait 490 *instructed*; skilled, trained, practised, well-p. 669 *prepared*; finished, passed, specialized 669 *matured*; proficient, qualified, competent, up to the mark; efficient, professional 622 *businesslike*.

well-made, well-crafted; craftily contrived, deep-laid; finished, felicitous, happy; artistic, artificial, sophisticated, stylish 575 *elegant*; daedal, cunning; shipshape, workmanlike.

Vb. *be skilful*, - deft etc. adj.; be good at, do well 644 *be good*; shine, excel 34 *be superior*; have a turn for, have a gift for, be born for, show aptitude, show a talent for; have the knack, have the trick of, have the right touch; be in practice, be on form, be in good f., have one's eye in, have one's hand in; play one's cards well, not put a foot wrong, know just when to stop; use skilfully, exploit, squeeze the last ounce out of 673 *use*; take advantage of, make hay while the sun shines 137 *profit by*; live by one's wits, get around, know all the answers, know what's what, have one's wits about one 498 *be wise*; exercise discretion 463 *discriminate*.

be expert, turn professional; be master of one's profession, be good at one's job, know one's stuff *or* one's onions, have the know-how; acquire the technique, qualify oneself 536 *learn*; have experience, be an old hand, know the ropes, know all the ins and outs, know backwards, be up to every trick, take in one's stride 490 *know*; display one's skill, play with, demonstrate, stunt 875 *be ostentatious*.

Adv. *skilfully*, craftily, artfully etc. adj.; well, with skill, like a master; handily, neatly, featly; stylishly, artistically; knowledgeably, expertly, scientifically; faultlessly, like a machine; naturally, as to the manner born, in one's stride.

See: 34, 137, 160, 179, 463, **490**, **498**, 536, 542, 575, 622, 623, **644**, 646, 669, 673, 676, 688, 698, 701, 875.

695 Unskilfulness

N. *unskilfulness*, want of skill, no gift for; lack of practice, rustiness 674 *nonuse*; rawness, unripeness, immaturity 670 *undevelopment*; inexperience, inexpertness 491 *ignorance*; incapacity, inability, incompetence, inefficiency 161 *ineffectuality*; Peter principle; disqualification, lack of proficiency; quackery, charlatanism 850 *pretension*; clumsiness, unhandiness, lubberliness, left-handedness, awkwardness, gaucherie (**see** *bungling*); backwardness, slowness 499 *unintelligence*; booby prize, wooden spoon.

bungling, botching, tinkering, half-measures, pale imitation, travesty 726 *noncompletion*; bungle, botch, dog's breakfast, pig's ear, cock-up, shambles; off day, poor performance, poor show, bad job, unsatisfactory work, flop 728 *failure*; missed chance 138 *untimeliness*; hamhandedness, dropped catch, fumble, foozle, muff, fluff, miss, mishit, slice, bosh shot, overthrow, misthrow, misfire, own goal 495 *mistake*; thoughtlessness 456 *inattention*; tactlessness, heavy-handedness; infelicity, indiscretion 464 *indiscrimination*; mishandling, misapplication 675 *misuse*; too many cooks; mismanagement, misrule, misgovernment, maladministration 481 *misjudgment*; misconduct, antics; much ado about nothing, wild-goose chase 641 *lost labour*.

Adj. *unskilful*, ungifted, untalented, unendowed, unaccomplished; stick-in-the-mud, unversatile 679 *inactive*; disqualified, unadapted, unadaptable, unfit, inept 25 *unapt*; unable, incapable 161 *impotent*; incompetent, inefficient, ineffectual; unpractical, unbusinesslike, unstatesmanlike, undiplomatic; impolitic, ill-considered, stupid, foolish 499 *unwise*;

thoughtless 456 *inattentive*; wild, giddy, happy-go-lucky 456 *light-minded*; feckless, futile; not up to scratch, failed 728 *unsuccessful*; inadequate 636 *insufficient*.

unskilled, raw, green, unripe, undeveloped 670 *immature*; uninitiated, under training, untrained, half-skilled, semi-s. 670 *unprepared*; unqualified, inexpert, scratch, inexperienced, ignorant, unversed, unconversant, untaught 491 *uninstructed*; nonprofessional, ham, lay, amateurish, amateur; unscientific, unsound, charlatan, quack, quackish; specious, pretentious 850 *affected*.

clumsy, awkward, gauche, gawkish, boorish, uncouth 885 *discourteous*; stuttering 580 *stammering*; tactless 464 *indiscriminating*; bumbling, bungling; lubberly, unhandy, maladroit, all thumbs, butter-fingered; left-handed, cack-h., one-h., heavy-h., ham-h., heavy-footed; ungainly, lumbering, hulking, gangling, stumbling, shambling; stiff, rusty 674 *unused*; unaccustomed, unpractised, out of practice, out of training, off form 611 *unhabituated*; losing one's touch, slipping; slovenly, slatternly, slapdash 458 *negligent*; fumbling, groping, tentative 461 *experimental*; ungraceful, graceless, clownish 576 *inelegant*; top-heavy, lopsided 29 *unequal*; cumbersome, ponderous, clumsily built, ungainly, unmanageable, unsteerable 195 *unwieldy*; unadjusted 495 *inexact*.

bungled, badly done, botched, foozled, messed up, mismanaged, mishandled etc. vb.; faulty 647 *imperfect*; misguided, ill-advised, ill-considered, ill-judged; ill-prepared, unplanned 670 *unprepared*; ill-contrived, ill-devised, cobbled together; unhappy, infelicitous; crude, rough and ready, inartistic, amateurish, home-made, do-it-yourself 699 *artless*; slapdash, superficial, perfunctory 458 *neglected*; half-baked 726 *uncompleted*.

Vb. *be unskilful*, - inept, - unqualified etc. adj.; not know how 491 *not know*; show one's ignorance, go the wrong way about it, start at the wrong end; do things by halves, tinker, paper over the cracks 726 *not complete*; burn one's fingers, catch a Tartar, reckon without one's host 508 *not expect*; maladminister, mishandle, mismanage, misconduct, misrule, misgovern; misapply 675 *misuse*; misdirect 495 *blunder*; forget one's words, miss one's cue 506 *forget*; ham, overact, underact; lose one's cunning, lose one's skill, go rusty, get out of practice 611 *disaccustom*; come a cropper, come unstuck 728 *fail*; lose one's nerve, lose one's head 854 *be nervous*.

act foolishly, not know what one is about, act in one's own worst interests, stand in one's own light, cut one's own throat, cut off one's nose to spite one's face, throw out the baby with the bath water, make a fool of oneself 497 *be absurd*; become an object lesson, quarrel with one's bread and butter, bite the hand that feeds one, kill the goose that lays the golden eggs, spoil the ship for a ha'porth of tar, bring one's house about one's ears, knock one's head against a brick wall, put the cart before the horse, have too many eggs in one basket; bite off more than one can chew, have too many irons in the fire; spoil one's chances 138 *lose a chance*; put a square peg in a round hole, put new wine into old bottles 495 *blunder*; labour in vain 470 *attempt the impossible*; go on a fool's errand 641 *waste effort*; strain at a gnat and swallow a camel.

be clumsy, lumber, bumble, galumph, hulk, get in the way, stand in the light; trip, trip over, stumble, blunder; not look where one is going 456 *be inattentive*; stutter 580 *stammer*; fumble, grope, flounder 461 *be tentative*; take two bites at a cherry, muff, fluff, foozle; pull, slice, mishit, misthrow; overthrow, overshoot 306 *overstep*; play into the hands of, give a catch, give a chance; spill, slop, drop, drop a catch, drop a sitter 311 *let fall*; catch a crab; bungle, drop a brick, put one's foot in it, make a faux pas, get egg on one's face 495 *blunder*; botch, spoil, mar, blot 655 *impair*; fool with 678 *meddle*; make a mess of it, make a hash of it 728 *miscarry*; do a bad job, make a poor fist at 728 *fail*.

See: 25, 29, 138, 161, 195, 306, 311, 456, 458, 461, 464, 470, 481, **491**, **495**, **497**, 499, 506, 508, 576, 580, 611, 636, **641**, 647, 655, 670, 674, 675, 678, 679, 699, 726, **728**, 850, 854, 885.

696 Proficient person

N. *proficient person*, sound player, expert, adept, dab hand, dabster; do-it-yourself type, all-rounder, Jack of all trades, handyman, Admirable Crichton 646 *paragon*; Renaissance man, person of many parts; maître, master, past m., graduate, cordon bleu; intellectual, mastermind 500 *sage*; genius, wizard 864 *prodigy*; magician 545 *conjuror*; maestro, virtuoso; bravura player 413 *musician*; prima donna, first fiddle, top sawyer, prize-winner, gold-medallist, champion, title-holder, cup-h., dan, black belt, ace 644 *exceller*; picked man, seeded player, white hope; crack shot, dead s. 287 *shooter*; acrobat, gymnast 162 *athlete*.

expert, no novice, practitioner; professional, pro, specialist, authority, doyen, professor 537 *teacher*; pundit, savant, polymath, walking encyclopaedia 492 *scholar*; veteran, old hand, old stager, old soldier, warhorse, sea dog, shellback; practised hand, practised eye; sophisticate, knowing person, smart customer, cunning fellow 698 *slyboots*; sharp, sharper 545 *trickster*; cosmopolitan, citizen of the world, man *or* woman about town, man *or* woman of the world, businessman *or* -woman, career woman, careerist; tactician, strategist, politician; diplomat, diplomatist; artist, craftsman *or* -woman; technician, skilled worker 686 *artisan*; experienced hand, right person for the job, key man *or* woman; consultant 691 *adviser*; boffin, backroom boy 623 *planner*; cognoscente, connoisseur, fancier.

See: 162, 287, 413, 492, 500, 537, 545, 623, **644**, 646, 686, 691, 698, 864.

697 Bungler

N. *bungler*, failure 728 *loser*; bad learner, one's despair; incompetent, botcher, tinkerer; bumbler, blunderer, blunderhead, marplot, bungling idiot; mismanager, fumbler, muffer, muff, butterfingers; lump, lout, clumsy l., clumsy clot, hulk, lubber, looby, swab, bull in a china shop; duffer, stooge, clown, buffoon, booby, galoot, clot, clod, stick, hick, oaf, ass 501 *fool*; slob, sloven, slattern 61 *slut*; scribbler, dauber, bad hand, poor h., rabbit; bad shot, poor s., no marksman; amateur, dabbler; jack of all trades and master of none; novice, greenhorn, colt, raw recruit, sorcerer's apprentice 538 *beginner*; quack 545 *impostor*; landlubber, fair-weather sailor, freshwater s., horse marine; ass in a lion's skin, jackdaw in peacock's feathers; fish out of water, square peg in a round hole 25 *misfit*.

See: 25, 61, 501, 538, 545, 728.

698 Cunning

N. *cunning*, craft 694 *skill*; lore 490 *knowledge*; resourcefulness, inventiveness, ingenuity 513 *imagination*; guile, gamesmanship, cunningness, craftiness, artfulness, subtlety, wiliness, slyness, foxiness; stealthiness, stealth 523 *latency*; cageyness 525 *secrecy*; suppleness, slipperiness, shiftiness; knavery, chicanery, chicane 930 *foul play*; finesse, jugglery 542 *sleight*; cheating, circumvention 542 *deception*; double-dealing, imposture 541 *duplicity*; smoothness 925 *flattery*; disguise 525 *concealment*; wheeling and dealing, manoeuvring, temporizing 688 *tactics*; policy, diplomacy, Machiavellianism, realpolitik; jobbery, gerrymandering 930 *improbity*; underhand dealing, sharp practice; backdoor influence 178 *influence*; intrigue 623 *plot*.

stratagem, ruse, wiles, art, artifice, resource, resort, device, wrinkle, ploy, shift, dodge 623 *contrivance*; machination, game, little g. 623 *plot*; subterfuge, evasion; excuse 614 *pretext*; white lie 543 *mental dishonesty*; cheat 542 *deception*; trick, old t., box of tricks, tricks of the trade, rules of the game 542 *trickery*; feint, catch, net, web, ambush, Trojan horse, stalking h. 542 *trap*; ditch, pit 663 *pitfall*; Parthian shot; web of cunning, web of deceit; blind, dust thrown in the eyes, flag of convenience 542 *sham*; thin end of the wedge, manoeuvre, move 688 *tactics*.

slyboots, crafty fellow, artful dodger, wily person, serpent, snake, fox, Reynard; lurker 527 *hider*; snake in the grass 663 *troublemaker*; fraud, shammer, dissembler, hypocrite, double-crosser 545 *deceiver*; cheat, sharper 545 *trickster*; juggler 545 *conjuror*; smoothie, glib tongue 925 *flatterer*; diplomatist, Machiavelli, intriguer, plotter, schemer 623 *planner*; strategist, tactician, manoeuvrer, wheeler-dealer; wire-puller 612 *motivator*.

Adj. *cunning*, learned, knowledgeable 498 *wise*; crafty, artful, sly, wily, subtle, serpentine, foxy, vulpine, feline; full of ruses, tricky, tricksy; secret 525 *stealthy*; scheming, contriving, practising, plotting, intriguing, Machiavellian 623 *planning*; knowing, fly, slick, smart, sophisticated, urbane; canny, pawky, sharp, astute, shrewd, acute; too clever for, too clever by half, up to everything, not to be caught napping, no flies on, not born yesterday 498 *intelligent*; not to be drawn, cagey 525 *reticent*; experienced 694 *skilful*; resourceful, ingenious; tactical, strategical, deep-laid, well-planned; full of snares, insidious 930 *perfidious*; shifty, slippery, timeserving, temporizing 518 *equivocal*; deceitful, flattering 542 *deceiving*; knavish 930 *rascally*; crooked, devious 930 *dishonest*.

Vb. *be cunning*, - sly etc. adj.; play the fox, try a ruse, finesse, shift, dodge, juggle, manoeuvre, jockey, double-cross, twist, turn 251 *wriggle*; lie low 523 *lurk*; intrigue, scheme, play a deep game, spin a web, weave a plot, have an axe to grind, have an eye to the main chance 623 *plot*; contrive, wangle, devise 623 *plan*; monkey about with, play tricks w., tinker, gerrymander; circumvent, overreach, pull a fast one, steal a march on, trick, cheat 542 *deceive*; sweet-talk, blarney 925 *flatter*; temporize, play for time; be too clever for, be one up on, outsmart, outwit, go one better, know a trick worth two of that 306 *outdo*; be too quick for, snatch from under one's nose, pip at the post; waylay, dig a pit for, undermine, bait the trap 527 *ambush*; introduce the thin end of the wedge, get one's foot in the door; match in cunning, see the catch, avoid the trap; have a card up one's sleeve, have a shot in one's locker; know all the answers, live by one's wits.

Adv. *cunningly*, artfully, slily, on the sly.

See: 178, 251, 306, **490**, **498**, 513, 518, 523, 525, 527, 541, **542**, 543, 545, 612, 614, 623, 663, 688, 694, 925, 930.

699 Artlessness

N. *artlessness*, simplicity, simple-mindedness; naivety, ingenuousness, guilelessness 935 *innocence*; inexperience, unworldliness; unaffectedness, unsophistication, naturalness, freedom from artifice 573 *plainness*; sincerity, candour, frankness; bluntness, matter-of-factness, outspokenness 540 *veracity*; truth, honesty 929 *probity*; uncivilized state, primitiveness, savagery; darkness, barbarism, no science, no art 491 *ignorance*; indifference to art, philistinism; no artistry 647 *imperfection*; uncouthness, vulgarity, crudity 847 *bad taste*.

ingenue, ingenuous person, unsophisticated p., Candide; child of nature, savage, noble s.; enfant terrible; lamb, babe in arms 935 *innocent*; simpleton 501 *ninny*; greenhorn, novice 538 *beginner*; rough diamond, plain man, philistine; simple soul, pure heart; provincial, yokel, rustic, country cousin 869 *country-dweller*.

Adj. *artless*, without art, without artifice, without tricks; unstudied, unprepared; uncomplicated, uncontrived 44 *simple*; unadorned, unvarnished 573 *plain*; native, natural, unartificial, homespun, home-made; do-it-yourself 695 *unskilled*; in a state of nature, uncivilized, wild, savage, primitive, unguided, untutored, unlearned, unscientific, backward 491 *ignorant*; Arcadian, unsophisticated, ingenuous, naive, childlike 935 *innocent*; born yesterday, unworldly, simple-minded, callow, wet behind the ears; guileless, free from guile, unsuspicious, confiding; unaffected, unconstrained, unreserved, uninhibited 609 *spontaneous*; candid, frank, open, undissembling, straightforward 540 *veracious*; undesigning, single, single-hearted, true, honest, sincere 929 *honourable*; above-board, on the level; blunt, outspoken, free-spoken; transparent 522 *undisguised*; unpoetical, prosaic, no-nonsense, matter-of-fact, literal, literal-minded 494 *accurate*; shy, inarticulate, unassuming, unpretentious, unpretending 874 *modest*; inartistic, philistine; unmusical, tone-deaf 416 *deaf*; unrefined, unpolished, uncultured, uncouth 847 *vulgar*; hoydenish 847 *ill-bred*.

Vb. *be artless*, - natural etc. adj.; live in a state of nature, know no better; have no guile, have no tricks 935 *be innocent*; have no affectations, eschew artifice; confide, wear one's heart upon one's sleeve; look one in the face, look one straight in the eyes, call a spade a spade, say what is in one's mind 573 *speak plainly*; not mince one's words 540 *be truthful*.

Adv. *artlessly*, without art, without pretensions, without affectation; frankly, sincerely, openly, with an open heart.

See: 44, 416, 491, 494, 501, 522, 538, **540**, **573**, 609, 647, 695, 847, 869, 874, 929, 935.

Section four: Antagonism

700 Difficulty

N. *difficulty*, hardness, arduousness, laboriousness, the hard way 682 *exertion*; impracticability, no go, nonstarter 470 *impossibility*; intricacy, perplexity, inextricability, involvement 61 *complexity*; complication 832 *aggravation*; obscurity, impenetrability 517 *unintelligibility*; inconvenience, awkwardness, embarrassment 643 *inexpedience*; drag 333 *friction*; rough ground, hard going, bad patch 259 *roughness*; quagmire, slough 347 *marsh*; knot, Gordian k. 251 *coil*; problem, thorny p., crux, hard nut to crack, poser, teaser, puzzle, headache 530 *enigma*; impediment, handicap, obstacle, snag, rub, where the shoe pinches 702 *hindrance*; teething troubles 702 *hitch*; maze, crooked path 251 *convolution*; cul-de-sac, dead end, impasse, blank wall 264 *closure*; deadlock, standstill, stoppage 145 *stop*; stress, brunt, burden 684 *fatigue*; trial, ordeal, temptation, tribulation, vexation 825 *suffering*; trouble, sea of troubles 731 *adversity*; difficult person, handful, one's despair, kittle cattle; hot potato.

hard task, test, real t., trial of strength; labours of Hercules, Herculean task, superhuman t., thankless t., never-ending t., Sisyphean labour; task, job, work cut out, hard row to hoe, no picnic; handful, tall order, tough assignment, stiff job, hard work, uphill struggle 682 *labour*.

predicament, embarrassment, false position, delicate situation; nonplus, quandary, dilemma, cleft stick; borderline case 474 *dubiety*; catch-22 situation; fix, jam, hole, scrape, hot water, trouble, fine kettle of fish, pickle, stew, imbroglio, mess, muddle; pinch, strait, straits, pass, pretty p.; slippery slope, sticky wicket, tight corner, ticklish situation, hot seat 661 *danger*; critical situation, exigency, emergency 137 *crisis*.

Adj. *difficult*, hard, tough, formidable; steep, arduous, uphill; inconvenient, onerous, burdensome, irksome, toilsome, bothersome, plaguy 682 *laborious*; exacting, demanding 684 *fatiguing*; big, of Herculean *or* Sisyphean proportions, insuperable, impracticable 470 *impossible*; offering a problem, problematic, more easily said than done; delicate, ticklish, tricky; embarrassing, awkward, unwieldy, unmanageable, hard to cope with, not easily tackled; out of hand, intractable, refractory 738 *disobedient*; stubborn, unyielding, perverse 602 *obstinate*; ill-behaved, naughty 934 *wicked*; perplexing, clueless, obscure 517 *unintelligible*; knotty, complex, complicated, inextricable, labyrinthine 251 *intricate*; impenetrable, impassable, trackless, pathless, unnavigable; thorny, rugged, craggy 259 *rough*; sticky, critical 661 *dangerous*.

in difficulties, hampered 702 *hindered*; labouring, labouring under difficulties; in a quandary, in a dilemma, in a cleft stick, between two stools, between Scylla and Charybdis, between the devil and the deep blue sea 474 *doubting*; baffled, clueless, nonplussed 517 *puzzled*; in a jam, in a fix, on the hook, up a gum tree, in a spot, in a hole, in a scrape, in hot water, in the soup, in a pickle; in deep water, out of one's depth, under fire, not out of the wood, in danger, in the hot seat 661 *endangered*; worried, beset with difficulties, harassed with problems, tormented with anxiety 825 *suffering*; under pressure, up against it, hard pressed, sore p., hard put to it, driven to extremities; in dire straits, in distressed circumstances; left holding the baby, left in the lurch; at one's wits end, at the end of one's tether, cornered, at bay, with one's back against the wall; stuck, stuck fast, aground 728 *grounded*.

Vb. *be difficult*, - hard etc. adj.; make things difficult, make difficulties for; complicate, complicate matters 63 *bedevil*; put one on the spot, inconvenience, put to i., bother, irk, plague, try one's patience, lead one a merry dance, be a thorn in one's flesh, go against the grain 827 *trouble*; present difficulties, set one a problem, pose, perplex, baffle, nonplus, stump 474 *puzzle*; encumber, clog, hamper, obstruct 702 *hinder*; make things worse 832 *aggravate*; lead to an impasse, create deadlock 470 *make impossible*; go hard with, run one hard, drive to the wall 661 *endanger*.

be in difficulty, have a problem; tread carefully, walk among eggs, pick one's way 461 *be tentative*; have one's hands full, have more than one can cope with 678 *be busy*; not know which way to turn, be at a loss 474 *be uncertain*; have difficulties, have one's work cut out, be put to it, be put to trouble, have trouble with; run into trouble, fall into difficulties, strike a bad patch; be asking for trouble, fish in troubled waters; let oneself in for, cop it, catch a packet, catch a Tartar, have a wolf by the ears, have a tiger by the tail, stir up a hornet's nest; have a hard time of it 731 *have trouble*; bear the brunt, feel the pinch 825 *suffer*; have more than enough, sink under the burden 684 *be fatigued*; invite difficulty, make it hard for oneself, bring it on oneself, make a problem of, make heavy weather of, flounder; stick, come unstuck 728 *miscarry*; do it the hard way, swim upstream, breast the current, struggle, fight 716 *contend*; have to face it, live dangerously 661 *face danger*; labour under difficulties, labour under a disadvantage, have one hand tied behind one's back, be handicapped by.

Adv. *with difficulty*, with much ado, hardly; the hard way, uphill, against the stream, against the wind, against the grain; despite, in spite of, in the teeth of; at a pinch; in difficulty.

See: 22, 61, 63, 137, 145, 251, 259, 264, 333, 347, 461, 470, **474**, 517, 530, 602, 643, **661**, 678, 682, 684, **702**, 716, 728, 731, 738, 825, 827, 832, 934.

701 Facility

N. *facility*, easiness, ease, convenience, comfort; flexibility, pliancy 327 *softness*; capability, capacity, feasibility 469 *possibility*; comprehensibility 516 *intelligibility*; facilitation, easing, making easy, simplification, smoothing, disencumbrance, disentanglement, disengagement, removal of difficulties 746 *liberation*; free hand, full play, full scope, clean slate 744 *scope*; facilities, provision for 703 *aid*; leave 756 *permission*; simplicity, no complication 44 *simpleness*; straightforwardness, no difficulty, no competition; an open-and-shut case; no friction, easy going, calm seas 258 *smoothness*; fair wind, clear coast, clear road 137 *opportunity*; straight road, royal r., highway, primrose path 624 *road*; downhill 309 *descent*.

easy thing, no trouble, a pleasure, child's play, kid's stuff; soft option, short work, light work, cushy number, sinecure 679 *inactivity*; picnic, doddle 837 *amusement*; chickenfeed, piece of cake, money for jam *or* old rope; easy money, fast buck; smooth sailing, plain s., easy ride; nothing to it, sitter, easy target, sitting duck; easy meat, soft touch; pushover, walkover 727 *victory*; cinch, sure thing, dead cert 473 *certainty*.

Adj. *easy*, facile, undemanding, cushy; effortless, painless; light, short; frictionless 258 *smooth*; uncomplicated 44 *simple*; not hard, not difficult, foolproof; easy as pie, easily done, easily managed, no sooner said than done; as easy as falling off a log, as simple as ABC; feasible 469 *possible*; easing, facilitating, helpful 703 *aiding*; downhill, downstream, with the current, with the tide; convenient 376 *comfortable*; approachable, within reach 289 *accessible*; open to all 263 *open*; comprehensible, for the million 516 *intelligible*.

tractable, manageable, easy-going 597 *willing*; submissive 721 *submitting*; yielding, malleable, ductile, pliant 327 *flexible*; smooth-running, well-oiled, frictionless; handy, manoeuvrable, labour-saving.

facilitated, simplified, made easy; disembarrassed, disencumbered, disburdened, untrammelled, unloaded, light; disengaged, unimpeded, unobstructed, untrammelled, unfettered, unrestrained 744 *unconfined*; aided, given a chance, given a leg up, helped on one's way; in one's element, at home, quite at home, at ease 376 *comfortable*.

Vb. *be easy*, - simple etc. adj.; require no effort, present no difficulties, give no trouble, make no demands; be open to all, be had for the asking; come out easily, be easily solved, have a simple answer 516 *be intelligible*; run well, go w., work w., go like clockwork 258 *go smoothly*.

do easily, have no trouble, see one's way to; make nothing of, make light of, make no bones about, make short work of, do it standing on one's head, do it with one hand tied behind one's back; have it all one's own way, carry all before one, have it in the bag, hold all the trumps, win hands down, win at a canter, have a walkover 727 *win*; sail home, coast h., free-wheel; be at ease, be at home, be in one's element, take in one's stride, take to like a duck to water; take it easy 685 *be refreshed*; not strain oneself, drift with the tide, swim with the stream 721 *submit*; spare effort, save oneself trouble, take the easy way out, take the line of least resistance, look for a short cut.

facilitate, ease, make easy; iron out 258

smooth; grease, oil 334 *lubricate*; explain, simplify, vulgarize, popularize 520 *interpret*; provide the means, enable 160 *empower*; make way for, not stand in the way, leave it open, allow 756 *permit*; give a chance to, put one in the way of 469 *make possible*; help, help on, speed, expedite 703 *aid*; pioneer, open up, clear the way, blaze a trail, make a path for 64 *come before*; pave the way, bridge the gap; give full play to, make an opening for, leave open, leave a loophole 744 *give scope*.

disencumber, free, liberate, unshackle, unfetter 668 *deliver*; clear, clear the ground, weed, clear away, unclog 648 *clean*; derestrict, deobstruct; cut through red tape; disengage, disentangle, extricate 62 *unravel*; unknot, untie 46 *disunite*; cut the knot, cut the Gordian k. 46 *cut*; ease, lighten, take off one's shoulders, unload, unburden, disburden, ease the burden, alleviate, obviate 831 *relieve*.

Adv. *easily*, readily, smoothly, like clockwork; on wheels, swimmingly; effortlessly, with no effort, by the flick of a switch; without difficulty, just like that; without a hitch, without let or hindrance, freely, without obstruction, on the nod; on easy terms.

See: 44, 46, 62, 64, 137, 160, 258, 263, 289, 309, 327, 334, 376, 469, 473, 516, 520, 597, 624, 648, 668, 679, 685, **703**, 721, 727, 744, 746, 756, 831, 837.

702 Hindrance

N. *hindrance*, let or h., impediment, rub; inhibition, fixation, hangup, block; stalling, thwarting, obstruction, frustration; hampering, shackling, clogging etc. vb.; stopping up, blockage, blocking, shutting 264 *closure*; blockade, siege 712 *attack*; limitation, restriction, control, squeeze 747 *restraint*; arrest 747 *detention*; check, retardation, retardment, deceleration 278 *slowness*; drag 333 *friction*; interference, meddling 678 *overactivity*; interruption, interception, interposition, intervention 231 *interjacency*; obtrusion 303 *insertion*; objection 762 *deprecation*; obstructiveness, picketing, sabotage 704 *opposition*; countermeasure, strikebreaking, lockout 182 *counteraction*; defence 715 *resistance*; discouragement, active d., disincentive 613 *dissuasion*; hostility 924 *disapprobation*; blacking, boycott 620 *avoidance*; forestalling, prevention; prophylaxis, sanitation 652 *hygiene*; sterilization, birth control 172 *contraception*; ban, embargo 757 *prohibition*; capacity for hindrance, nuisance value.

obstacle, impediment, hindrance, nuisance, drawback, inconvenience, handicap 700 *difficulty*; bunker, hazard; bottleneck, blockage, road block, traffic jam, logjam; a hindrance, tie, tether 47 *bond*; previous engagement 138 *untimeliness*; red tape, regulations; snag, block, stop, stymie; stumbling block, tripwire, hurdle, hedge, ditch, moat; jump, water-j.; something in the way, lion in the path (**see** *hinderer*); barrier, bulkhead, wall, brick w., sea w., groyne, boom, dam, weir, dike, embankment 662 *safeguard*; bulwark, breastplate, buffer, parapet, portcullis, barbed wire 713 *defences*; fence, blockade 235 *enclosure*; curtain, Iron Curtain 231 *partition*; stile, gate, turnstile, tollgate; crosswind, headwind, crosscurrent; impasse, deadlock, stalemate, vicious circle, catch-22; cul-de-sac, blind alley, dead end.

hitch, unexpected obstacle, snag, catch, lightning strike 145 *strike*; repulse, rebuff 760 *refusal*; contretemps, spot of trouble; teething troubles; technical hitch, breakdown, failure, engine f., engine trouble; puncture, flat; leak, burst pipe; fuse, short circuit; stoppage, holdup, setback 145 *stop*; something wrong, screw loose, spanner in the works, fly in the ointment.

encumbrance, handicap, liability; drag, clog, shackle, chain 748 *fetter*; trammels, meshes, toils; impedimenta, baggage, lumber; cross, millstone, albatross round one's neck, weight on one's shoulders, dead weight 322 *gravity*; pack, fardel, burden, load, overload, last straw; onus, incubus, Old Man of the Sea; family commitments, dependants; mortgage, debts 803 *debt*.

hinderer, hindrance; red herring 10 *irrelevance*; wet blanket, damper, spoilsport, killjoy; marplot 697 *bungler*; dog in the manger, thwarter, frustrator; interceptor, fielder; obstructor, staller; obstructionist, filibuster, saboteur; botherer, heckler, interrupter, interjector, barracker; intervener, interferer 678 *meddler*; interloper, intruder, gatecrasher, uninvited guest 59 *intruder*; mischiefmaker, spoiler, poltergeist, gremlin 663 *troublemaker*; challenger 705 *opponent*; rival, competitor 716 contender.

Adj. *hindering*, impeding, obstructive, stalling, delaying, dragging; frustrating, thwarting etc. vb.; cross, contrary, unfavourable 731 *adverse*; restrictive, cramping, clogging 747 *restraining*; prohibitive, preventive 757 *prohibiting*; prophylactic, counteractive 182 *counteracting*; upsetting, disconcerting, offputting; intrusive, obtrusive, not wanted 59 *extraneous*; interloping, intercepting, interfering 678 *meddling*; blocking, in the way, in the light; inconvenient 643 *inexpedient*; hard, rough, snaggy 700 *difficult*; onerous, crushing, burdensome, cumbrous 322 *weighty*; tripping, entangling; choking, strangling, stifling; disincentive, discouraging; disheartening, damping 613 *dissuasive*; unhelpful, uncooperative, unaccommodating 598 *unwilling*; defensive, oppositional 704 *opposing*.

hindered, clogged, waterlogged, cramped, overgrown; handicapped, encumbered, burdened with, lumbered w., saddled w., stuck w.; frustrated, thwarted, stymied etc. vb.; up against a brick wall; held up, delayed, held back, stuck, becalmed, wind-bound, fog-b. 747 *restrained*; stopped, prevented 757 *prohibited*; in check, hard-pressed, cornered, treed 700 *in difficulties*; heavy-laden, overburdened 684 *fatigued*; left in the lurch, unaided, single-handed; marooned, stranded, left high and dry.

Vb. *hinder*, hamper, obstruct, impede; bother, annoy, inconvenience 827 *trouble*; embarrass, disconcert, upset, disorder 63 *derange*; trip, trip up, get under one's feet; tangle, entangle, enmesh 542 *ensnare*; get in the way, stand in one's light, cross one's path; come between, intervene, interpose 678 *meddle*; intercept, cut off, head off, undermine, cut the ground from under one's feet, pull the rug from under one's f.; nip, nip in the bud, stifle, choke; gag, muzzle 578 *make mute*; suffocate, repress 165 *suppress*; quell, shoot down, kill stone dead 362 *kill*; hamper, burden, cumber, encumber; press, press down, hang like a millstone round one's neck 322 *weigh*; load with, saddle w. 193 *load*; cramp, handicap; shackle, trammel, tie one's hands, tie hand and foot 747 *fetter*; put under house arrest; restrict, circumscribe *limit*; check, brake, be a drag on, hold 747 *restrain*; hold up, slow down, set one back 278 *retard*; lame, cripple, hobble, hamstring, paralyse 161 *disable*; scotch, wing 655 *wound*; clip the wings, cramp the style of, take the wind out of one's sails; discountenance, put out of countenance 867 *shame*; intimidate, deter 854 *frighten*; discourage, dishearten 613 *dissuade*; be the spectre at the feast, mar, spoil 655 *impair*; damp, damp down, throw cold water on; snub, rebuff 760 *refuse*.

obstruct, intervene, interpose, interfere 678 *meddle*; obtrude, interlope 297 *intrude*; stymie, snooker, stand in the way 231 *lie between*; buzz, jostle, crowd, squeeze; sit on one's tail 284 *follow*; stop, intercept, occlude, stop up, block, block up, wall up 264 *close*; jam, jam tight, foul up, cause a stoppage, bring to a standstill; bandage, bind 350 *staunch*; dam, dam up, earth up, embank; divert, draw off 495 *mislead*; fend off, stave off, stall off 713 *parry*; barricade 235 *enclose*; fence, hedge in, blockade 232 *circumscribe*; deny access, keep out 57 *exclude*; prevent, not allow, inhibit, ban, bar, debar 757 *prohibit*.

be obstructive, make it hard for, give trouble, play up 700 *be difficult*; put off, stall, stonewall; not play ball, noncooperate 598 *be unwilling*; baffle, foil, stymie, balk, be a dog in the manger; counter 182 *counteract*; check, countercheck, thwart, frustrate; object, raise objections 704 *oppose*; interrupt, interject, heckle, barrack; refuse a hearing, shout down 400 *be loud*; take evasive action 620 *avoid*; talk out, filibuster 581 *be loquacious*; play for time, protract, drag out 113 *spin out*; strike 145 *halt*; picket, molest; sabotage, throw a spanner in the works, gum up the works, spike the guns, put a spoke in one's wheel; cross one's bows, take the wind out of one's sails.

See: 10, 22, 47, 57, 59, 63, 113, 138, 145, 161, 165, 172, 182, 193, 231, 232, 235, 236, 264, 278, 284, 297, 303, 322, 333, 350, 362, 400, 495, 542, 578, 581, 598, 613, 620, 643, 652, 655, 662, 663, 678, 684, 697, **700**, **704**, 705, 712, 713, 715, 716, 731, **747**, 748, 757, 760, 762, 803, 827, 854, 867, 924.

703 Aid

N. *aid*, assistance, help, helping hand, leg-up, lift, boost; succour, rescue 668 *deliverance*; comfort, support, moral s., backing, seconding, abetment, encouragement; reinforcement 162 *strengthening*; helpfulness, willing help, cordial assistance 706 *cooperation*; service, ministry, ministration, subministration 897 *kind act*; interest, friendly i., kindly i., good offices; custom 792 *purchase*; patronage, auspices, sponsorship, countenance, suffrage, favour 660 *protection*, 178 *influence*; good will, charity, sympathy, tea and s. 897 *benevolence*; intercession 981 *prayers*; advocacy, championship; good advice, constructive criticism 691 *advice*; promotion, furtherance, advancement 654 *improvement*; nursing, spoonfeeding; first aid, medical assistance 658 *medical art*; relief, easing 685 *refreshment*; preferential treatment, most favoured nation t.; favourable conditions, favourable circumstances 730 *prosperity*; fair wind, following w., tail w. 287 *propulsion*; facilitation, facilities, magic carpet, magic wand, Aladdin's lamp 701 *facility*; self-help, do-it-yourself 744 *independence*.

subvention, economic aid, monetary help, pecuniary assistance; donation 781 *gift*; charity 901 *philanthropy*; social security, benefit, unemployment b., sick b., supplementary b.; loan, temporary accommodation 802 *credit*; subsidy, hand-out, bounty, grant, allowance, expense account; stipend, bursary, scholarship 962 *reward*; supplies, maintenance, support, keep, upkeep, free board and lodging 633 *provision*; manna, manna in the wilderness 301 *food*; soup kitchen.

aider, help, helper, assister, assistant, lieutenant, henchman, aide, right-hand man, man Friday, girl F.; stand-by, support, prop, mainstay; tower of strength, rock 660 *protector*; hand-holder, ministering angel; district nurse, social worker, counsellor 691 *adviser*; good neighbour, good Samaritan, friend in need; ally, brother-in-arms 707 *collaborator*; relieving force, reinforcements, recruits 707 *auxiliary*; deus ex machina, genie of the lamp, fairy godmother 903 *benefactor*; promoter, sponsor 707 *patron*; booster, friendly critic 923 *commender*; abettor, instigator 612 *motivator*; factor, useful ingredient 58 *component*; springboard, jumping-off ground 628 *instrument*.

Adj. *aiding*, helpful, obliging 706 *cooperative*; kind, well-disposed, well-intentioned 897 *benevolent*; neighbourly 880 *friendly*; favourable, propitious; supporting, seconding, abetting; supportive, encouraging 612 *inducing*; of service, of help, of great assistance 640 *useful*; constructive, well-meant; morale-boosting; assistant, auxiliary, subsidiary, ancillary, accessory; in aid of, contributory, promoting; at one's beck and call, subservient 742 *serving*; assisting 628 *instrumental*.

Vb. *aid*, help, assist, lend a hand, bear a h., give a helping hand 706 *cooperate*; lend one's aid, render assistance; hold out a hand to, take by the hand, take under one's wing, take in tow, give a lift to; hold one's hand, spoonfeed; be kind to, do one a good turn, give a leg up, help a lame dog over a stile 897 *be benevolent*; help one out, tide one over, see one through; oblige, accommodate, lend money to 784 *lend*; put up the money, subsidize; facilitate, speed, lend wings to, further, advance, boost 285 *promote*; abet, instigate, foment, nourish, feed the flame, fan the f. 612 *induce*; make for, contribute to, be accessory to, be a factor in 156 *conduce*; lend support to, boost one's morale, back up, stand by, bolster, prop up 218 *support*; comfort, sustain, hearten, give heart to, encourage, rally, embolden 855 *give courage*; succour, come to the help of, send help to, bail out, help o., relieve 668 *deliver*; step into the breach, reinforce, fortify 162 *strengthen*; ease 685 *refresh*; set one on his *or* her feet 656 *restore*.

patronize, favour, smile on, shine on 730 *be auspicious*; sponsor, back, guarantee, go bail for; recommend, put up for; propose, second; countenance, give countenance to, connive at, protect 660 *safeguard*; join, enlist under 78 *be included*; contribute to, subscribe to, lend one's name 488 *endorse*; take an interest in 880 *befriend*; espouse the cause of, take one's part, side with, champion, take up the cudgels for, stick up for, stand up f., stand by 713 *defend*; canvass for, root f., vote f. 605 *vote*; give moral support to, pray for, intercede; pay for, pay the piper 804 *defray*; entertain, keep, cherish, foster, nurse, wet-nurse, mother 889 *pet*; bestow one's custom, buy from 792 *purchase*.

minister to, wait on, do for, help, oblige 742 *serve*; give first aid to, nurse 658 *doctor*; squire, valet, mother; subserve, be of service to, make oneself useful to 640 *be useful*; anticipate the wishes of 597 *be willing*; pander to, toady, humour, suck up to 925 *flatter*; slave, do all one can for, do everything for 682 *work*; be assistant to, make oneself the tool of 628 *be instrumental.*

Adv. *in aid of*, in the cause of, for the sake of, on behalf of; under the aegis *or* auspices of, by the aid of, thanks to; in the service of, in the name of.

See: 58, 78, 156, 162, 178, 218, 285, 287, 301, 488, 597, 605, 612, 628, 633, 640, 654, 656, 658, 660, 668, 682, 685, 691, 701, **706**, **707**, 713, 730, 742, 744, 781, 784, 792, 802, 804, 855, 880, 889, 897, 901, 903, 923, 925, 962, 981.

704 Opposition

N. *opposition*, antagonism, hostility 881 *enmity*; clashing, conflict, friction, lack of harmony 709 *dissension*; dissociation, nonassociation, noncooperation, unhelpful attitude 598 *unwillingness*; repugnance 861 *dislike*; contrariness, cussedness, recalcitrance 602 *obstinacy*; impugnation, counterargument 479 *confutation*; contradiction, denial 533 *negation*; challenge 711 *defiance*; oppugnation, firm opposition, stout o., stand 715 *resistance*; contravention, infringement 738 *revolt*; going against, siding a., voting a. 924 *disapprobation*; withdrawal, walkout 489 *dissent*; physical opposition, headwind, crosscurrent 702 *obstacle*; mutual opposition, cross purposes, tug of war, battle of wills; faction, rivalry, emulation, competition 716 *contention*; political opposition, the Opposition, Her Majesty's O., the other side, wrong s.; underground, alternative society 84 *nonconformity*.

opposites, contraries, extremes, opposite poles 14 *contrariety*; rivals, duellists, competitors 716 *contender*; opposite parties, factions, cat and dog 709 *quarreller*; town and gown, the right and the left, management and workers, Labour and Conservative, Democrat and Republican.

Adj. *opposing*, oppositional, opposed; in opposition, on the other side, on the wrong s.; anti, against, agin; antagonistic, hostile, unfriendly, antipathetic, unsympathetic 881 *inimical*; unfavourable, unpropitious 731 *adverse*; cross, thwarting 702 *hindering*; contradictory 14 *contrary*; cussed, bloody-minded, bolshie 602 *obstinate*; refractory, recalcitrant 738 *disobedient*; resistant 182 *counteracting*; clashing, conflicting, at variance, at odds with 709 *quarrelling*; militant, up in arms, at daggers drawn 716 *contending*; fronting, facing, face to face, eyeball to eyeball 237 *frontal*; polarized, at opposite extremes 240 *opposite*; mutually opposed, rival, competitive 911 *jealous*.

Vb. *oppose*, go against, militate a. 14 *be contrary*; side against, stand a., hold out a., fight a., dig one's heels in 715 *resist*; set one's face against, make a dead set a. 607 *reject*; object, kick, protest, protest against 762 *deprecate*; run one's head against, beat a. 279 *collide*; vote against, vote down 924 *disapprove*; not support, dissociate oneself; contradict, belie 533 *negate*; counter 479 *confute*; work against 182 *counteract*; countermine, thwart, baffle, foil 702 *be obstructive*; be at cross purposes, play at c. p.; stand up to, challenge, dare 711 *defy*; set at naught 922 *hold cheap*; flout, fly in the face of 738 *disobey*; rebuff, spurn, give one a slap in the face, slam the door in one's f. 760 *refuse*; emulate, rival, match oneself with, compete with, bid against 716 *contend*; set against, pit a., match a.

withstand, confront, face, look in the f., stand up to 661 *face danger*; rise against 738 *revolt*; take on, meet, encounter, cross swords with 716 *fight*; struggle against, breast, stem, breast the tide, stem the t., swim against the stream; cope with, grapple w., wrestle w. 678 *be active*; not be beaten 599 *stand firm*; hold one's own, bear the brunt 715 *resist*.

Adv. *in opposition*, against, versus, agin; in conflict with, against the tide, against the stream, against the wind, with the wind in one's teeth, against the grain, in the teeth of, in the face of, in defiance of, in spite of, despite.

See: 14, 84, 182, 237, 240, 279, 479, 489, 533, 598, 599, 602, 607, 661, 678, **702**, **709**, 711, **715**, 716, 731, 738, 760, 762, 861, 881, 911, 922, 924.

705 Opponent

N. *opponent*, opposer, lion in the path; adversary, antagonist, foe, foeman 881 *enemy*; assailant 712 *attacker*; opposing party, opposition p., the opposition, opposite camp; factionist, partisan; obstructionist, filibusterer 702 *hinderer*; independent party, cross benches; die-hard, bitter-ender, last-ditcher, irreconcilable; reactionary, counter-revolutionary, obscurantist; objector, conscientious o. 489 *dissentient*; resister, passive r.; dissident, noncooperator 829 *malcontent*; agitator, terrorist, extremist 738 *revolter*; challenger, rival, emulator, corrival, competitor, runner-up; fighter, contestant, duellist; entrant, the field, all comers 716 *contender*; brawler, wrangler 709 *quarreller*; common enemy, public e., universal foe, outlaw 904 *offender*.

See: **489**, 702, 709, 712, **716**, 738, 829, 881, 904.

706 Cooperation

N. *cooperation*, helpfulness 597 *willingness*; contribution, coagency, synergy, symbiosis; duet, double harness, tandem; collaboration, joint effort, combined operation; team work, working together, concerted effort; relay, relay race, team r.; team spirit, esprit de corps; lack of friction, unanimity, agreement, concurrence, bipartisanship 710 *concord*; clanship, clannishness, party spirit, cliquishness, partisanship, old school tie; connivance, collusion, abetment 612 *inducement*; conspiracy, complot 623 *plot*; complicity, participation, worker p.; sympathy 880 *friendliness*; fraternity, solidarity, fellowship, freemasonry, fellow feeling, comradeship, fellow-travelling; common cause, mutual assistance, helping one another, networking, back-scratching, log-rolling; reciprocity, give and take, mutual concession 770 *compromise*; mutual advice, consultation 584 *conference*.

association, coming together; colleagueship, copartnership, partnership 775 *participation*; nationalization, internationalization 775 *joint possession*; pooling, pool, kitty; membership, affiliation 78 *inclusion*; connection, hookup, tie-up 9 *relation*; consociation, ecosystem; combination, consolidation, centralization 45 *union*; integration, solidarity 52 *whole*; unification 88 *unity*; amalgamation, fusion, merger; voluntary association, coalition, alliance, league, federation, confederation, confederacy, umbrella organization; axis, united front, common f., popular f. 708 *political party*; an association, fellowship, college, club, sodality, fraternity 708 *community*; set, clique, cell 708 *party*; workers' association, trade union, chapel; business association, company, joint-stock c., syndicate, combine, consortium, trust, cartel, ring 708 *corporation*; housing association, economic community, cooperative, workers' c., commune 708 *community*.

Adj. *cooperative*, helpful 703 *aiding*; en rapport 710 *concordant*; symbiotic, synergic; collaborating, in double harness, in tandem; married, associating, associated, leagued, in league, hand in glove with; bipartisan; federal 708 *corporate*.

Vb. *cooperate*, collaborate, work together, pull t., work in t., work as a team; hunt in pairs, run in double harness; team up, join forces, go into partnership 775 *participate*; show willing, play ball, reciprocate, respond; lend oneself to, espouse 703 *patronize*; join in, take part, enter into, take a hand in, pitch in; rally round 703 *aid*; hang together, hold t., sail *or* row in the same boat, stand shoulder to shoulder, stand by each other, sink or swim together; be in league with, make common cause with, take in each other's washing; network, band together, gang up, associate, league, confederate, federate, ally; coalesce, merge, unite 43 *be mixed*; combine, make common cause, club together; understand one another, think alike; conspire 623 *plot*; lay heads together, get into a huddle 691 *consult*; collude, connive, play another's game; work for an understanding, treat with, negotiate 766 *make terms*.

Adv. *cooperatively*, hand in hand, jointly, unanimously, as one man, as one.

Int. All together now! Harambee!

See: 9, 43, **45**, 52, 78, 88, 584, 597, 612, 623, 691, **703**, **708**, 710, 766, 770, 775, 880.

707 Auxiliary

N. *auxiliary*, relay, recruit, fresh troops, reinforcement; second line, paramilitary formation 722 *soldiery*; ally, brother-in-arms, confederate (**see** *colleague*); coadjutor, adjuvant, assistant, helper, helpmate, helping hand 703 *aider*; right-hand man, second, tower of strength; adjutant, lieutenant, aide-de-camp; amanuensis, secretary, clerk; midwife, handmaid; dogsbody 742 *servant*; acolyte, server; best man, bridesmaid; friend in need 880 *friend*; hanger-on, satellite, henchman, sidekick, follower 742 *dependant*; disciple, adherent, votary 978 *sectarian*;

loyalist, legitimist; stooge, cat's-paw, puppet 628 *instrument*; shadow, familiar 89 *concomitant*; jackal, running dog, creature, âme damnée.

collaborator, cooperator, co-worker, fellow w.; team-mate, yoke-fellow; sympathizer, fellow traveller, fifth column, fifth columnist.

colleague, associate, confrère, fellow, brother, sister; co-director, partner, sharer 775 *participator*; comrade, companion, boon c., playmate; confidant(e), alter ego, second self, faithful companion, fidus Achates; mate, chum, pal, buddy, crony 880 *friend*; helpmate, better half 894 *spouse*; standby, stalwart; ally, confederate; accomplice, accessory, abettor, aider and abettor, fellow conspirator, partner in crime; co-religionist; one's fellows, one's own side.

patron, defender, guardian angel 660 *protector*; well-wisher, sympathizer; champion, advocate, friend at court; supporter, sponsor, backer, guarantor; proposer, seconder, voter; partisan, votary, aficionado, fan 887 *lover*; good friend, Jack at a pinch, friend in need, deus ex machina; fairy godmother, rich uncle, sugar daddy 903 *benefactor*; promoter, founder; patron of art, Maecenas 492 *collector*; customer, client 792 *purchaser*.

See: 89, 492, 628, 660, **703**, 722, 742, 775, 792, 880, 887, 894, 903, 978.

708 Party

N. *party*, movement; group, class 77 *classification*; subsect, confession, communion, denomination, church 978 *sect*; faction, cabal, cave, splinter group 489 *dissentient*; circle, inner c., charmed c., kitchen cabinet; set, clique, in-crowd, coterie, galère; caucus, junta, camarilla, politburo, committee, club, cell, cadre; ring, closed shop; team, eight, eleven, fifteen; crew, complement 686 *personnel*; troupe, company 594 *actor*; gang, knot, bunch, outfit 74 *band*; horde 74 *crowd*; side, camp.

political party, right, left, centre; Conservative, Tories, Unionists, National Front; Liberals, Radicals, Whigs; Socialists, Labour, Liblab, Social Democrats; Democrats, Republicans; Nationalists; Ecologists, Greens; New Left, Workers' ...olutionary Party, International ...ists, Trotskyists, Marxists, Commu... Bolsheviks, Mensheviks; Fascists, Nazis, Falangists; Blackshirts, Brownshirts; Jacobins, Girondists; coalition, popular front, bloc; citoyen, comrade, tovarich, Red, commie, Trot; socialist, labourite, Fabian, syndicalist; anarchist 738 *revolter*; rightwinger, rightist, true blue; left-winger, leftist, leftie, pinko; populist, democrat; moderate, centrist; party worker, party member, politician, politico; militant, activist 676 *doer*.

society, partnership, coalition, combination, combine 706 *association*; league, alliance, axis; federation, confederation, confederacy; economic association, cooperative, Bund, union, Benelux, EEC, Common Market, free trade area; private society, club 76 *focus*; secret society, Ku Klux Klan, Freemasonry, lodge, cell; friendly society, trade union; chapel; group, division, branch, local b.; youth movement, Boy Scouts, Cubs, Rovers, Rangers, Girl Guides, Brownies; Pioneers, Komsomol; Women's Institute, Townswomen's Guild, Mother's Union; Daughters of the American Revolution, DAR; fellow, honorary f., associate, member; party member, paid-up m., card-carrying m.; comrade, trade unionist; corresponding member, branch m., affiliate 58 *component*.

community, fellowship, brotherhood, body, congregation, band of brothers, fraternity, confraternity, sorority, sisterhood; guild, sodality; race, tribe, clan, sect 11 *family*; order 77 *classification*; social class 371 *social group*; state, nation s., multiracial s. 371 *nation*.

corporation, body; incorporated society, body corporate, mayor and corporation 692 *council*; company, livery c., joint-stock c., limited liability c., holding c.; multinational c.; firm, concern, joint c., partnership; house, business h.; establishment, organization, institute; trust, combine, monopoly, cartel, syndicate, conglomerate 706 *association*; trade association, chamber of commerce, guild, cooperative society; consumers' association.

Adj. *corporate*, incorporate, corporative, joint-stock; joint, partnered, bonded, banded, leagued, federal, federative; allied, federate, confederate; social, clubbable 882 *sociable*; fraternal, comradely 880 *friendly*; cooperative, syndicalist; communal 775 *sharing*.

sectional, factional, denominational, Masonic 978 *sectarian*; partisan, clannish, cliquish, cliquey, exclusive; class-conscious; nationalistic 481 *biased*; rightist, right-wing, true-blue; right of centre, left of c.; leftist, left-wing, pink, red; Whiggish, Tory; radical, conservative.

Vb. *join a party*, put one's name down, subscribe; join, swell the ranks, become a member, take out membership; sign on, enlist, enrol oneself, get elected; sneak in, creep in 297 *enter*; belong to, fit in, make one of 78 *be included*; align oneself, side with, take sides, range oneself with, team up w. 706 *cooperate*; club together, associate, ally, league, federate; cement a union, merge; found a party, lead a p.

Adv. *in league*, in partnership, in the same boat, in cahoots with, hand in glove w.; hand in hand, side by side, shoulder to shoulder, back to back; all together, en masse, jointly, collectively; unitedly, as one; with all the rest, in the swim.

See: 11, 58, **74**, 76, 77, 78, 297, 371, 481, 489, 594, 676, 686, 692, **706**, 738, 775, 880, 882, 978.

709 Dissension

N. *dissension*, disagreement 489 *dissent*; noncooperation 704 *opposition*; disharmony, dissonance, disaccord, jar, jangle, jarring note, discordant n. 411 *discord*; recrimination 714 *retaliation*; bickering, sniping, cat-and-dog life; differences, odds, variance, friction, tension, unpleasantness; soreness 891 *resentment*; no love lost, hostility, mutual h. 888 *hatred*; disunity, disunion, internal dissension, infighting, muttering in the ranks, house divided against itself 25 *disagreement*; rift, cleavage, cleavage of opinion, parting of the ways, separation 294 *divergence*; split, faction 978 *schism*; misunderstanding, cross purposes 481 *misjudgment*; breach, rupture, open r., severance of relations, recall of ambassadors; challenge 711 *defiance*; ultimatum, declaration of war 718 *war*.

quarrelsomeness, factiousness, litigiousness; aggressiveness, combativeness, pugnacity, warlike behaviour 718 *bellicosity*; provocativeness, trailing one's coat 711 *defiance*; cantankerousness, awkwardness, prickliness, fieriness 892 *irascibility*; shrewishness, sharp tongue 899 *scurrility*; contentiousness 716 *contention*; rivalry 911 *jealousy*; thirst for revenge 910 *revengefulness*; mischievousness, mischief, spite 898 *malevolence*; apple of discord, spirit of mischief; Ate, Mars.

quarrel, open q.; feud, blood f., vendetta 910 *revenge*; war 718 *warfare*; strife 716 *contention*; conflict, clash 279 *collision*; legal battle 959 *litigation*; controversy, dispute, wrangle, argy-bargy; polemic, battle of arguments, paper war 475 *argument*; wordy warfare, words, war of w., high w., raised voices, stormy exchange, altercation, set-to, abuse, slanging match 899 *scurrility*; jar, spat, tiff, squabble, jangle, wrangle, barney, hassle, squall, storm in a teacup; rumpus, hubbub, racket, row, shindy, commotion, scrimmage, fracas, brawl, fisticuffs, breach of the peace 61 *turmoil*; gang warfare, street fighting, riot 716 *fight*.

casus belli, root of the trouble; flashpoint, breaking point; tender spot, sore point; apple of discord, bone of contention, bone to pick; disputed point, point at issue, area of disagreement, battleground.

quarreller, disputer, wrangler; controversialist 475 *reasoner*; duellist, rival, emulator 716 *contender*; strange bedfellows, Kilkenny cats, Montagues and Capulets; quarrelmonger, mischief-maker 663 *troublemaker*; scold, bitter tongue 892 *shrew*; aggressor 712 *attacker*.

Adj. *quarrelling*, discordant, discrepant, clashing, conflicting 14 *contrary*; on bad terms, feuding, at odds, at sixes and sevens, at loggerheads, at variance, at daggers drawn, up in arms 881 *inimical*; divided, factious, schismatic 489 *dissenting*; mutinous, rebellious 738 *disobedient*; uncooperative, noncooperating 704 *opposing*; sore 891 *resentful*; awkward, cantankerous 892 *irascible*; sulky 893 *sullen*; implacable 910 *revengeful*; litigant, litigious 959 *litigating*; quarrelsome, nonpacific, bellicose 718 *warlike*; pugnacious, combative, spoiling for a fight, trailing one's coat, belligerent, aggressive, militant 712 *attacking*; abusive, shrewish, scolding, scurrilous 899 *cursing*; argumentative, contentious, disputatious, wrangling, polemical, controversial 475 *arguing*.

Vb. *quarrel*, disagree 489 *dissent*; clash, conflict 279 *collide*; cross swords with, be at one another's throats; misunderstand, be at cross purposes, pull different ways, be at variance, have differences, have a bone to pick 15 *differ*; recriminate 714 *retaliate*; fall out, go one's separate ways, part company, split, break with; break away 978 *schismatize*; break off relations, declare war 718 *go to war*; go to law, take it to court 959 *litigate*; dispute, try conclusions with 479 *confute*; have a feud with, carry on a vendetta 910 *be revengeful*; turn sulky, sulk 893 *be sullen*; noncooperate 704 *oppose*.

make quarrels, pick q., start something, pick a fight, start it; look for trouble, be spoiling for a fight, make something of it, trail one's coat, challenge 711 *defy*; irritate, rub up the wrong way, tread on one's toes, provoke 891 *enrage*; have a bone to pick, have a crow to pluck; cherish a feud, enjoy a quarrel 881 *make enemies*; embroil, entangle, estrange, set at odds, set at variance, set by the ears 888 *excite hate*; create discord, sound a discordant note 411 *discord*; sow dissension, stir up strife, be a quarrelmonger, make mischief, make trouble, put the cat among the pigeons; divide, draw apart, disunite, come between, drive a wedge b. 46 *sunder*; widen the breach, fan the flame 832 *aggravate*; set against, pit a., match with; egg on, incite 612 *motivate*.

bicker, spat, tiff, squabble; nag, henpeck, jar, spar, spar with, live a cat-and-dog life; jangle, wrangle, dispute with, go at it hammer and tongs 475 *argue*; scold 899 *cuss*; have words with, altercate, pick a bone w., pluck a crow w., row, row with; brawl, kick up a shindy, disturb the peace, make the fur fly, raise the dust 61 *rampage*.

See: 14, 15, 25, 46, 61, 279, 294, 411, 475, 479, 481, **489**, 612, 663, 704, 711, 712, 714, **716**, 718, 738, 832, 881, 888, 891, 892, 893, 898, 899, 910, 911, 959, 978.

710 Concord

N. *concord*, harmony 410 *melody*; unison, unity, duet 24 *agreement*; unanimity, bipartisanship 488 *consensus*; lack of friction, understanding, good u., mutual u., rapport; solidarity, team spirit 706 *cooperation*; reciprocity 12 *correlation*; sympathy, fellow feeling 887 *love*; compatibility, coexistence, amity 880 *friendship*; rap-chement, détente, reunion, reconcili- conciliation, peacemaking 719 *ation*; good offices, arbitration 720 *mediation*; entente cordiale, happy family, the best of friends, sweetness and light, love and peace 717 *peace*; goodwill, goodwill amongst men, honeymoon period.

Adj. *concordant*, blended 410 *harmonious*; en rapport, eye to eye, unanimous, of one mind, bipartisan 24 *agreeing*; coexistent, compatible, united, cemented, bonded, allied, leagued; fraternal, loving, amicable, on good terms 880 *friendly*; frictionless, happy, peaceable, pacific, at peace 717 *peaceful*; conciliatory 719 *pacificatory*.

Vb. *concord* 410 *harmonize*; bring into concord 719 *pacify*; agree 24 *accord*; hit it off, see eye to eye, play a duet, chime in with, pull together 706 *cooperate*; reciprocate, respond, run parallel 181 *concur*; fraternize 880 *be friendly*; keep the peace, remain at peace 717 *be at peace*.

See: 12, 24, 181, 410, 488, **706**, **717**, **719**, 720, 880, 887.

711 Defiance

N. *defiance*, dare, daring, challenge, gage, gauntlet, hat in the ring; bold front, brave face 855 *courage*; war dance, war cry, war whoop, war song, battle cry 900 *threat*; brazenness 878 *insolence*; demonstration, display, bravura 875 *ostentation*.

Adj. *defiant*, defying, challenging, provocative, bellicose, militant 718 *warlike*; saucy, insulting 878 *insolent*; mutinous, rebellious 738 *disobedient*; greatly daring 855 *courageous*; stiff-necked 871 *proud*; reckless, trigger-happy 857 *rash*.

Vb. *defy*, challenge, take one up on 489 *dissent*; stand up to 704 *oppose*; caution 664 *warn*; throw in one's teeth, throw down the gauntlet, throw one's hat in the ring; demand satisfaction, call out, send one's seconds; dare, outdare, beard; brave, run the gauntlet 661 *face danger*; laugh to scorn, laugh in one's face, laugh in one's beard, set at naught, snap one's fingers at 922 *hold cheap*; bid defiance to, set at d., hurl d.; call one's bluff, double the bid; show fight, bare one's teeth, show one's fangs, double one's fist, clench one's f., shake one's f. 900 *threaten*; refuse to bow down to 871 *be proud*; look big, throw out one's chest, beat one's c., show a bold front; wave a banner 317 *brandish*; march, demonstrate, hold a demonstration, stage a sit-in, not be moved; cock a snook 878 *be insolent*; ask for trouble 709 *make* *quarrels*; crow over, shout 727 *triumph*; crow, bluster, brag 877 *boast*.

Adv. *defiantly*, challengingly, in defiance of, in one's teeth, to one's face, under the very nose of; in open rebellion.

Int. do your worst! come on if you dare!

See: 317, 489, 661, 664, **704**, 709, 718, 727, 738, 855, 857, 871, 875, 877, 878, 900, 922.

712 Attack

N. *attack*, hostile a., best method of defence; pugnacity, combativeness, aggressiveness 718 *bellicosity*; aggression, unprovoked a. 914 *injustice*; stab in the back 930 *foul play*; mugging, assault, assault and battery, grievous bodily harm 176 *violence*; armed attack, offensive, drive, push, thrust, pincer movement 688 *tactics*; run at, dead set at; onslaught, onset, rush, shock, charge; sally, sortie, breakout, breakthrough; counterattack 714 *retaliation*; shock tactics, blitzkrieg, coup de main, surprise; encroachment, infringement 306 *overstepping*; invasion, incursion, irruption, overrunning 297 *ingress*; raid, foray 788 *brigandage*; blitz, air raid, air attack, sea a., land a.; night attack, camisado; storm, taking by s., escalade; boarding; investment, siege, blockade 230 *surroundings*; challenge, tilt.

terror tactics, war of nerves 854 *intimidation*; war to the knife 735 *severity*; whiff of grapeshot, shot across the bows; dragonnade, noyade, bloodbath 362 *slaughter*; devastation, laying waste 165 *havoc*.

bombardment, cannonade, barrage, strafe, blitz; broadside, volley, salvo; bomb-dropping, bombing, strategic b., tactical b., saturation b.; firing, shooting, fire, gunfire, machine-gun f., rifle f., fusillade, burst of fire, rapid f., cross-f., plunging f.; raking f., enfilade; antiaircraft fire, flak; sharpshooting, sniping; gunnery, musketry.

lunge, thrust, home-t., foin, pass, passado, quarte and tierce; cut, cut and thrust, stoccado, stab, jab; bayonet, cold steel; punch, swipe, kick 279 *knock*.

attacker, assailant, aggressor; hawk, militant; spearhead, storm troops, shock t., strike force; fighter pilot, air ace, bomber 722 *armed force*; sharpshooter, sniper; terrorist, guerrilla; invader, raider; besieger, blockader, stormer, escalader.

Adj. *attacking*, assailing, assaulting etc. vb.; pugnacious, combative, aggressive, on the offensive 718 *warlike*; hawkish, militant, spoiling for a fight, hostile 881 *inimical*; up in arms, on the warpath 718 *warring*; storming, charging, boarding, going over the top.

Vb. *attack*, be spoiling for a fight; start a fight, declare war 718 *go to war*; strike the first blow, fire the first shot; assault, assail, make a dead set at, go for, set on, pounce upon, fall u., pitch into, sail i., have at; attack tooth and nail, savage, maul, draw blood 655 *wound*; launch out at, let fly at, let one have it, round on; surprise, take by s., blitz, overwhelm; move in, invade 306 *encroach*; raid, foray, overrun, infest 297 *burst in*; show fight, take the offensive, assume the o., go over to the o., go over to the attack; counterattack 714 *retaliate*; thrust, push 279 *impel*; erupt, sally, make a sortie, break out, break through 298 *emerge*; board, lay aboard, grapple; escalade, storm, take by storm, carry, capture 727 *overmaster*; ravage, make havoc, scorch, burn 165 *lay waste*; harry, drive, beat, corner, bring to bay 619 *hunt*; challenge, enter the lists 711 *defy*; take on 704 *oppose*; take up the cudgels, draw the sword, couch one's lance, break a lance 716 *fight*.

besiege, lay siege to, beleaguer, invest, surround, beset, blockade 235 *enclose*; sap, mine, undermine, spring a mine.

strike at, raise one's hand against; lay about one, swipe, flail, hammer 279 *strike, kick*; go berserk, run amok 176 *be violent*; have at, have a fling at, fetch a blow, have a cut at, lash out at; beat up, mug; clash, ram 279 *collide*; make a pass at, lunge; close with, grapple w., come to close quarters, fight hand to hand, cut and thrust; push, butt, thrust, poke at, thrust at; stab, spear, lance, bayonet, run through, cut down 263 *pierce*; strike home, lay low, bring down 311 *abase*; stab in the back 930 *be dishonest*.

charge, sound the c., advance against, march a., ride a., drive a., sail a., fly a.; go over the top; bear down on, come upon; rush, mob 61 *rampage*; make a rush, rush at, run at, dash at, tilt at, ride full tilt at; ride down, run down, ram, shock 279 *collide*.

fire at, shoot at, fire upon; fire a shot at, take a potshot, pop at, snipe, pick off 287 *shoot*; shoot down, bring d.; torpedo, sink; soften up, strafe, bombard, blitz, cannonade, shell, fusillade, pepper; bomb, throw bombs, drop b., lay eggs, plaster, prang; open fire, let fly, volley; volley and thunder, rattle, blast, pour a broadside into, rake, straddle, enfilade; take aim, level, draw a bead on 281 *aim*.

lapidate, stone, throw a stone, heave a brick; shy, sling, pelt; hurl at 287 *propel*.

Adv. *aggressively*, offensively, on the offensive, on the attack, on the warpath.

See: 61, 165, **176**, 230, 235, 263, 279, 281, 287, 297, 298, 306, 311, 362, 619, 655, 688, 704, 711, 714, **716**, **718**, 722, 727, 735, 788, 854, 881, 914, 930.

713 Defence

N. *defence*, the defensive, self-defence 715 *resistance*; art of self-defence, boxing 716 *pugilism*; judo, jujitsu 716 *wrestling*; counter, counterstroke, parry, warding off 182 *counteraction*; defensiveness 854 *nervousness*; posture of defence, guard; defensive alliance, balance of power; safekeeping 666 *preservation*; self-protection 660 *protection*; a defence, rampart, bulwark, screen, buffer, fender, bumper 662 *safeguard*; deterrent 723 *weapon*; munitions 723 *ammunition*.

defences, lines, entrenchment, fieldwork, redoubt, redan, lunette; breastwork, parados, contravallation; outwork, circumvallation; earthwork, embankment, mound; sandbags; mole, boom; wall, barricade, fence 235 *barrier*; abatis, palisade, paling, stockade; moat, ditch, dike, fosse; trench, dugout; tripwire, booby trap 542 *trap*; barbed wire, barbed wire entanglements; spike, caltrop, chevaux de frise; antitank obstacles, dragon's teeth; Maginot Line, Siegfried L., Hadrian's Wall, Great Wall of China; airraid shelter, fallout s., bunker 662 *shelter*; barrage, antiaircraft fire, flak; barrage balloon; wooden walls; minefield, mine, countermine; smokescreen 421 *screen*.

fortification (**see** *fort*); circumvallation, bulwark, rampart, wall; parapet, battlements, machicolation, embrasure, casemate, merlon, loophole; banquette, barbette, emplacement, gun e.; vallum, scarp, escarp, counterscarp, glacis; curtain, bastion; ravelin, demilune, outwork, demibastion; buttress, abutment; gabion, gabionade.

fort, fortress, fortalice, stronghold, fastness; citadel, capitol, acropolis 662 *refuge*; castle, keep, ward, barbican, tower, turret, bartizan, donjon; portcullis, drawbridge; gate, postern, sally port; peel, Martello tower, pillbox; blockhouse, strong point; laager, zareba, encampment 235 *enclosure*; Roman camp, castrum; British camp 253 *earthwork*.

armour, harness; full armour, panoply; mail, chain m.; scale armour, splint a., armour plate; breastplate, backplate; cuirass, lorica, plastron; hauberk, habergeon, brigandine, coat of mail, corslet; helmet, helm, casque, basinet, sallet, morion; visor, beaver; siege cap, steel helmet, tin hat; shako, bearskin, busby 228 *headgear*; greaves, gauntlet, vambrace; shield, buckler, scutum, target; pavis, mantelet, testudo; protective clothing, riot shield, gas mask 662 *safeguard*.

defender, champion 927 *vindicator*; patron 703 *aider*; knight-errant, paladin; loyalist, legitimist, patriot; bodyguard, lifeguard, Praetorian Guard 722 *soldier*; watch, sentry, sentinel; patrol, patrolman; garrison, picket, guard, escort, rearguard; Home Guard, Territorials, militia, thin red line 722 *soldiery*; fireman, firefighter, firewatcher; civil defence corps; guardian, warden 660 *protector*; warder, custodian 749 *keeper*; deliverer, rescuer 668 *deliverance*; title-defender, titleholder.

Adj. *defending*, challenged, on the defensive 715 *resisting*; defensive, protective, antitank, antiaircraft 660 *tutelary*; exculpatory, self-excusing 927 *vindicating*.

defended, armoured, armour-plated; heavy-armed, mailed, mail-clad, armour-c., iron-c.; panoplied, accoutred, harnessed, armed to the teeth, armed at all points *or* cap-a-pie 669 *prepared*; moated, palisaded, barricaded, walled, fortified, machicolated, castellated, battlemented, loopholed; entrenched, dug in; defensible, proof, bombproof, bulletproof 660 *invulnerable*.

Vb. *defend*, guard, protect, keep, watch, ward 660 *safeguard*; fence, hedge, moat 232 *circumscribe*; palisade, barricade 235 *enclose*; block 702 *obstruct*; cushion, pad, shield, curtain, cover 421 *screen*; cloak 525 *conceal*; provide with arms, munition, arm, accoutre 669 *make ready*; harness, armour, clothe in a., armour-plate;

reinforce, fortify, crenellate, machicolate 162 *strengthen*; entrench, dig in 599 *stand firm*; stand in front, stand by; garrison, man, man the defences, man the breach, stop the gap; champion 927 *vindicate*; fight for, take up arms for, break a lance for, take up the cudgels for, cover up f. 703 *patronize*; rescue, come to the r. 668 *deliver*.

parry, counter, riposte, fence, fend, fend off, ward o., hold o., keep o., fight o., stave o., hold *or* keep at bay, keep at arm's length 620 *avoid*; turn, avert 282 *deflect*; play, play with, keep in play; stall, stonewall, block 702 *obstruct*; act on the defensive, fight a defensive battle, play for a draw, stalemate; fight back, show fight, give a warm reception to 715 *resist*; butt away, repulse 292 *repel*; bear the brunt, hold one's own 704 *withstand*; fall back on 673 *avail oneself of*; beat a strategic retreat 286 *turn back*; survive, scrape through, live to fight another day 667 *escape*.

Adv. *defensively*, on the defensive, at bay; in defence, pro patria, in self-defence.

See: 162, 182, 228, 232, 235, 253, 282, 286, 292, 421, 525, 542, 599, 620, **660**, **662**, 666, 667, 668, 669, 673, 702, 703, 704, 715, 716, **722**, **723**, 749, 854, 927.

714 Retaliation

N. *retaliation*, reprisal, lex talionis 910 *revenge*; requital, recompense, quittance, comeuppance 962 *reward*; desert, deserts 915 *dueness*; punitive action, poetic justice, retribution, Nemesis 963 *punishment*; reaction, boomerang, backlash 280 *recoil*; counter, counterstroke, counterblast, counterplot, countermine 182 *counteraction*; counterattack, sally, sortie 712 *attack*; recrimination, answering back, riposte, retort 460 *rejoinder*; returning good for evil, heaping coals of fire; reciprocation, like for like, tit for tat, quid pro quo, measure for measure, blow for blow, an eye for an eye and a tooth for a tooth, a Roland for an Oliver, biter bit, a game at which two can play; potential retaliation, deterrent 854 *intimidation*.

Adj. *retaliatory*, in retaliation, in reprisal, in self-defence; retaliative, retributive, punitive, recriminatory; like for like, reciprocal; rightly served.

Vb. *retaliate*, exact compensation 31 *recoup*; take reprisals 963 *punish*; counter, riposte 713 *parry*; make a requital, pay one out, pay off old scores, wipe out a score, square the account, be quits, get even with, get upsides with, get one's own back, sort one out 910 *avenge*; requite, reward; serve rightly, teach one a lesson; do unto others as you would be done by, return good for evil; reciprocate, give and take, return like for like; return the compliment, give as good as one gets, pay one in his own coin, give a quid pro quo; return, retort, cap, answer back 460 *answer*; recriminate 928 *accuse*; react, boomerang 280 *recoil*; round on, kick back, hit b., not take it lying down 715 *resist*; turn the tables on, hoist one with his own petard, make one laugh on the other side of his face, have the last laugh.

be rightly served, serve one right, have had one's lesson; have to pay compensation 787 *restitute*; find one's match, catch a tiger by the tail; get one's deserts, get what was coming to one, get a dose of one's own medicine 963 *be punished*.

Adv. *en revanche*, by way of return, in requital.

Int. it serves you right! take that! put that in your pipe and smoke it! the laugh's on you! now who's laughing!

See: 31, 182, 280, 460, **712**, 713, 715, 787, 854, **910**, 915, 928, 962, 963.

715 Resistance

N. *resistance*, stand, firm s., brave front 704 *opposition*; intractability 602 *obstinacy*; reluctance, renitency 598 *unwillingness*; repugnance 861 *dislike*; objection, demur 468 *qualification*; recalcitrance, kicking, protest 762 *deprecation*; noncooperation, passive resistance, civil disobedience; rising, insurrection, resistance movement, backlash 738 *revolt*; self-defence 713 *defence*; repulsion, repulse, rebuff, bloody nose 760 *refusal*; refusal to work 145 *strike*.

Adj. *resisting*, standing firm against 704 *opposing*; protesting, unconsenting, reluctant 598 *unwilling*; recalcitrant, renitent, unsubmissive, mutinous 738 *disobedient*; stubborn 602 *obstinate*; holding out, unyielding, unconquerable, indomitable, unsubdued, undefeated 727 *unbeaten*; resistant, tough, proof, proofed, bulletproof, waterproof; repugnant, repelling 292 *repellent*.

Vb. *resist*, offer resistance, give a warm

reception, stand against 704 *withstand*; obstruct 702 *hinder*; challenge, stand out against 711 *defy*; confront, outface 661 *face danger*; struggle against, contend with, stem the tide 704 *oppose*; recalcitrate, kick, kick against the pricks, protest 762 *deprecate*; demur, object 468 *qualify*; down tools, come out 145 *cease*; engineer a strike, call out 145 *halt*; mutiny, rise, not take it lying down 738 *revolt*; make a stand, fight off, keep at arm's length, keep at bay, hold off 713 *parry*; make a fight of it 716 *contend*; hold out, not submit, stand one's ground, not give way 599 *stand firm*; bear up, bear the brunt, endure 825 *suffer*; be proof against, not admit, repel, rebuff 760 *refuse*; resist temptation, not be tempted; last 113 *outlast*.

Int. No surrender!

See: 113, 145, 292, 468, 598, 599, **602**, 661, 702, **704**, 711, 713, 716, 727, 738, 760, 762, 825, 861.

716 Contention

N. *contention*, strife, tussle, conflict, clash, running battle 709 *dissension*; combat, fighting, war 718 *warfare*; debate, dispute, controversy, polemics, paper warfare, ink-slinging 475 *argument*; altercation, words, war of w. 709 *quarrel*; stakes, bone of contention 709 *casus belli*; competition, rivalry, emulation 911 *jealousy*; competitiveness, gamesmanship, survival of the fittest, rat race; cut-throat competition, war to the knife, no holds barred; sports, athletics 837 *sport*.

contest, trial, trial of strength, test of endurance, marathon, pentathlon, decathlon, tug-of-war 682 *exertion*; tussle, struggle 671 *attempt*; bitter struggle, needle match; equal contest, dingdong fight; close finish, photo f. 200 *short distance*; competition, open c., free-for-all; knockout competition, tournament; tourney, joust, tilt; prize competition, stakes, Ashes; match, test m.; concours, rally; event, handicap, run-off; heat, final, semifinal, quarterfinal, Cup tie; set, game, rubber; sporting event, wager, bet 837 *sport*; field day 837 *amusement*; Derby Day (**see** *racing*); athletics, gymnastics; gymkhana, horseshow, rodeo; games, Highland Games, Olympic G., Olympics; Wimbledon, Wembley, Lords 724 *arena*.

racing, speed contest 277 *speeding*; races, race, foot r., flat r., sprint, dash; road race, marathon; long-distance race, cross-country r.; slalom, obstacle race; sack r., egg and spoon r.; relay race, team r.; the Turf, horse racing, sport of kings; point-to-point, steeplechase, hurdles, sticks 312 *leap*; motor race, motor rally, dirt-track racing, stockcar r., speedway, motocross; cycle race, Tour de France; dog racing; boat race, yacht r., America's Cup competition; regatta, eights, Henley; Epsom, Ascot, racecourse, track, stadium 724 *arena*.

pugilism, noble art of self-defence, boxing, shadow b., sparring, milling, fisticuffs; prize fighting, boxing match, prizefight; mill, spar, clinch, in-fighting; round, bout; the ring, the fancy 837 *sport*.

wrestling, jujitsu, judo, karate, kung fu; all-in wrestling, catch-as-catch-can, no holds barred; catch, hold; wrestle, grapple, wrestling match.

duel, triangular d.; affair of honour, pistols for two and coffee for one; single combat, gladiatorial c.; jousting, tilting, tourney, tournament; fencing, swordplay, singlestick, quarterstaff, kendo; hand-to-hand fighting, close grips; bullfight, tauromachy; cockfight; bullring, cockpit, lists 724 *arena*.

fight, hostilities, appeal to arms 718 *warfare*; battle royal, free fight, free-for-all, rough and tumble, roughhouse, horseplay, shindy, scuffle, scrum, scrimmage, scramble, dogfight, mêlée, fracas, uproar, rumpus, ructions 61 *turmoil*; gang warfare, street fight, riot, rumble; brawl, broil 709 *quarrel*; punch-up, fisticuffs, blows, hard knocks; give and take, cut and thrust; affray, set-to, tussle; running fight, dingdong f., close fighting, hand-to-hand f.; close grips, close quarters; combat, fray, clash, conflict 279 *collision*; encounter, dustup, scrap, brush; skirmish, skirmishing; engagement, action, pitched battle, stand-up fight, shoot-out 718 *battle*; deed of arms, feat of a., passage of a. 676 *deed*; campaign, struggle; death struggle, death grapple, war to the knife, fight to the death; Armageddon, theomachy, gigantomachy; field of battle, battlefield 724 *battleground*.

contender, struggler, striver; tussler, fighter, battler, gamecock; gladiator, bullfighter 722 *combatant*; prizefighter 722 *pugilist*; duellist 709 *quarreller*; fencer, swordsman; candidate, entrant, examinee; competitor, rival, corrival, emulator; challenger, runner-up, finalist; front runner, favourite, top seed; starter, also-ran, the field, all comers; contestant, pothunter; racer, runner 162 *athlete*; sprinter 277 *speeder*.

Adj. *contending*, struggling, grappling etc. vb.; rival, rivalling, racing, outdoing 306 *surpassing*; competing, in the same business; agonistic, sporting; starting, running, in the running; athletic, palaestric, pugilistic, gladiatorial; contentious, quarrelsome 709 *quarrelling*; irritable 892 *irascible*; aggressive, combative, fight-hungry, spoiling for a fight, pugnacious, bellicose, warmongering 718 *warlike*; at loggerheads, at odds, at war, belligerent 718 *warring*; competitive, keen, cutthroat; hand-to-hand, close, at close quarters; keenly contested, dingdong; close-run; well-fought, fought to the finish.

Vb. *contend*, combat, strive, struggle, battle, fight, tussle, wrestle, grapple 671 *attempt*; oppose, put up a fight 715 *resist*; argue for, stick out for, make a point of, insist 532 *emphasize*; contest, compete, challenge, stake, wager, bet; play, play against, match oneself, vie with, race, run a race; emulate, rival 911 *be jealous*; outrival 306 *outdo*; enter, enter for, take on, enter the lists, descend into the arena, take up the challenge, pick up the gauntlet; couch one's lance, tilt with, joust w., break a lance w.; take on, try a fall, try conclusions with, close w., grapple w., engage w., lock horns w. 712 *strike at*; have a hard fight, fight to a finish.

fight, break the peace, have a fight, scuffle, row, scrimmage, scrap, set to 176 *be violent*; pitch into, sail i. 712 *attack*; lay about one 712 *strike at*; mix it, join in the mêlée; square up to, come to blows, exchange b., give hard knocks, give and take; box, spar, pummel, jostle, hit, kick, scratch, bite 279 *strike*; fall foul of, join issue with 709 *quarrel*; duel, call out, give satisfaction; encounter, have a brush with, scrap w., exchange shots, skirmish; take on, engage, fight a pitched battle 718 *give battle*; come to grips, come to close quarters, close with, grapple, lock horns; fence, cross swords, measure s.; fight hand to hand, use cold steel; appeal to arms 718 *go to war*; combat, campaign, fight the good fight 718 *wage war*; fight hard, fight like fiends, fight it out, fight to the last man 599 *be resolute*.

See: 61, 162, 176, 200, 277, 279, 306, 312, 475, 532, 599, 671, 676, 682, **709**, 712, 715, 718, 722, 724, 837, 892, 911.

717 Peace

N. *peace*, state of p., peacefulness, peace and quiet, a quiet life 266 *quiescence*; harmony 710 *concord*; piping times of peace 730 *palmy days*; peacetime, Civvy Street; universal peace, Pax Romana; law and order 60 *order*; end of hostilities, demobilization 145 *cessation*; truce, uneasy t., armistice 145 *lull*; freedom from war, cold w., coexistence, armed neutrality; neutrality, nonalignment; noninvolvement 860 *indifference*; nonintervention 620 *avoidance*; peaceableness, nonaggression 177 *moderation*; cordial relations 880 *friendship*; pacifism, peace at any price, nonviolence, ahimsa; disarmament, peacemaking, irenics 719 *pacification*; pipe of peace, calumet; league of peace, peace treaty, nonaggression pact 765 *treaty*; burial of the hatchet 506 *amnesty*.

pacifist, man *or* woman of peace, peacelover, peacemonger, dove; peace party 177 *moderator*; neutral, civilian, noncombatant, nonbelligerent; passive resister, conscientious objector, conchie; peacemaker 720 *mediator*.

Adj. *peaceful*, quiet, halcyon 266 *tranquil*; piping 730 *palmy*; without war, without bloodshed, bloodless; harmless, dovelike 935 *innocent*; mild-mannered, easy-going 884 *amiable*; uncompetitive, uncontentious; peaceable, law-abiding, peaceloving, pacific, unmilitary, unwarlike, unmilitant, unaggressive, war-weary; pacifist, nonviolent; unarmed, noncombatant, civilian; unresisting, passive, submissive 721 *submitting*; peacemaking, conciliatory, irenic 720 *mediatory*; without enemies, at peace; not at war, neutral; postwar, prewar, interwar; peacetime.

Vb. *be at peace*, enjoy p., stay at p., observe neutrality, keep out of war, keep out of trouble; mean no harm, be pacific 935 *be innocent*; keep the peace, avoid bloodshed; work for peace, make p. 720 *mediate*; beat swords into ploughshares, make the lion lie down with the lamb, smoke the pipe of peace.

Adv. *peacefully*, peaceably, pacifically; without violence, bloodlessly; quietly,

tranquilly, in peace, at p.
See: 60, 145, 177, 266, 506, 620, 710, **719**, **720**, 721, 730, 765, 860, 880, 884, 935.

718 War

N. *war*, arms, the sword; grim-visaged war, horrida bella, ultima ratio regum; appeal to arms, arbitrament of war, fortune of w.; undeclared war, cold w., armed neutrality; paper war, polemic 709 *quarrel*; war of nerves, sabre-rattling, gunboat diplomacy 854 *intimidation*; half-war, doubtful w., phoney w.; disguised war, intervention, armed i., police action; real war, hot w.; internecine war, civil w., war of revolution, war of independence; wars of religion, holy war, crusade, jihad; aggressive war, war of expansion; limited war, localized w.; triphibious war, w. on all fronts; major war, general w., world w., global w.; total war, blitzkrieg, atomic war, nuclear w., push-button war; war of attrition, truceless war, war to the knife, war to the death, no holds barred; war to end all wars, Armageddon; pomp and circumstance of war, chivalry, shining armour, rows of scarlet, nodding plumes; martial music, drums, bugle, trumpet; call to arms, bugle call 547 *call*; battle cry, war whoop, war song 711 *defiance*; god of war, Ares, Mars, Bellona. **See** *warfare*.

belligerency, state of war, state of siege; resort to arms, declaration of war, outbreak of w., militancy, hostilities; wartime, wartime conditions, time of war.

bellicosity, war fever; love of war, warlike habits, military spirit, pugnacity, combativeness, aggressiveness, hawkishness, militancy 709 *quarrelsomeness*; militarism, expansionism; jingoism, chauvinism 481 *prejudice*.

art of war, warcraft, siegecraft, strategy, grand s. 688 *tactics*; castrametation 713 *fortification*; generalship, soldiership, seamanship, airmanship 694 *skill*; ballistics, gunnery, musketry practice; drill, training 534 *teaching*; staffwork, logistics, planning 623 *plan*; military evolutions, manoeuvres; military experience 490 *knowledge*.

war measures, war footing, war preparations, arming 669 *preparation*; call to arms, clarion call, fiery cross 547 *call*; war effort, war work, call-up, mobilization, recruitment, conscription, national service, military duty; volunteering, joining up; rationing; blackout; censorship; internment.

warfare, war, warpath, making war, waging w.; deeds of blood, bloodshed, battles, sieges 176 *violence*; fighting, campaigning, soldiering, active service; military service, naval s., air s.; bombing, saturation b. 712 *bombardment*; raiding, sea r.; besieging, blockading, investment 235 *enclosure*; aerial warfare, naval w., submarine w., undersea w., chemical w., gas w., germ w., bacteriological w., atomic w., nuclear w., theatre nuclear w., tactical n. w.; economic warfare, blockade, attrition, scorched earth policy; psychological warfare, propaganda; offensive warfare 712 *attack*; defensive warfare 713 *defence*; mobile warfare, static w., trench w., desert w., jungle w.; bush-fighting, guerrilla warfare; campaign, expedition; operations, land o., sea o., naval o., air o., combined o., joint o., amphibious o.; incursion, invasion, raid; order, word of command, orders 737 *command*; password, watchword; battle cry, slogan 547 *call*; plan of campaign, battle orders 623 *plan*.

battle, pitched b., battle royal 716 *fight*; line of battle, order of b., array; line, firing l., first l., front l., front, battle f., battle station; armed conflict, action, scrap, skirmish, brush, collision, clash; offensive, blitz 712 *attack*; defensive battle, stand 713 *defence*; engagement, naval e., sea fight, air f., dogfight; arena, battlefield, field of battle, theatre of war, area of hostilities 724 *battleground*.

Adj. *warring*, on the warpath; campaigning, battling etc. vb.; at war, in a state of w.; belligerent, militant, engaged in war, mobilized, uniformed, under arms, in the army, at the front, on active service; militant, up in arms; armed, sword in hand 669 *prepared*; arrayed, embattled; engaged, at grips, at loggerheads 709 *quarrelling*; on the offensive 712 *attacking*.

warlike, militaristic, bellicose, hawkish, unpacific; militant, aggressive, pugnacious, combative; war-loving, fierce, untamed 898 *cruel*; bloodthirsty, battle-hungry, war-fevered; military, paramilitary, martial, exercised in arms, bearing a.; veteran, battle-scarred; knightly, chivalrous; soldierly, soldierlike; military, naval; operational, strategical, tactical.

Vb. *go to war,* resort to arms; declare war, open hostilities, let slip the dogs of war; appeal to arms, unsheathe the sword, throw away the scabbard, whet the sword, take up the cudgels 716 *fight*; take to arms, fly to a., rise, rebel 738 *revolt*; raise one's banner, set up one's standard, call to arms, send round the fiery cross; arm, militarize, mobilize, put on a war footing; call up, call to the colours, recruit, conscript; join the army, join up, enlist, enrol, put on uniform, take a commission.

wage war, make w., go on the warpath, march to war, engage in hostilities, war, war against, war upon; campaign, open a c., take the field; go on active service, shoulder a musket, smell powder, flesh one's sword; soldier, be at the front; take the offensive, invade 712 *attack*; keep the field, hold one's ground 599 *stand firm*; act on the defensive 713 *defend*; manoeuvre, march, countermarch; blockade, beleaguer, besiege, invest 230 *surround*; shed blood, put to the sword 362 *slaughter*; ravage, burn, scorch 165 *lay waste*; press the button 165 *demolish, be destroyed.*

give battle, battle, offer b., accept b.; join battle, meet on the battlefield; engage, provoke an engagement; combat, fight it out 716 *fight*; take a position, choose one's ground, dig in; rally, close the ranks, stand, make a s. 715 *resist*; sound the charge, go over the top 712 *charge*; open fire 712 *fire at*; skirmish, brush with 716 *contend.*

Adv. *at war,* at the sword's point, at the point of the bayonet, in the thick of the fray, at the cannon's mouth.

See: 165, 176, 230, 235, 362, 481, 490, 534, 547, 599, 623, 669, 688, 694, 709, 711, **712, 713,** 715, **716,** 724, 737, 738, 854, 898.

719 Pacification

N. *pacification,* pacifying, peacemaking; conciliation, appeasement, mollification 177 *moderation*; reconciliation, reconcilement, détente, improved relations, rapprochement; accommodation, adjustment 24 *agreement*; composition of differences 770 *compromise*; good offices 720 *mediation*; convention, entente, understanding, peace treaty, nonaggression pact, SALT 765 *treaty*; suspension of hostilities, truce, armistice, cease-fire 145 *lull*; disarmament, demobilization, disbanding; nonproliferation; nuclear disarmament, nuclear-free zone; imposed peace, forced reconciliation 740 *compulsion.*

peace offering, eirenicon, irenics 177 *moderator*; propitiation, appeasement 736 *leniency*; olive branch, overture, peaceful approach, hand of friendship, outstretched hand 880 *friendliness*; flag of truce, white flag, pipe of peace, calumet 717 *peace*; wergild, blood money, compensation 787 *restitution*; fair offer, easy terms 177 *moderation*; plea for peace 506 *amnesty*; mercy 909 *forgiveness.*

Adj. *pacificatory,* conciliatory, placatory, propitiatory; irenic 880 *friendly*; disarming, soothing 177 *lenitive*; peacemaking, mediatory; pacified, happy 828 *content.*

Vb. *pacify,* make peace, impose p., give peace to; allay, tranquillize, mollify, soothe 177 *assuage*; smooth one's ruffled feathers, pour balm into one's wounds, heal 656 *cure*; hold out the olive branch, hold out one's hand, return a soft answer, coo like a dove 880 *be friendly*; conciliate, propitiate, disarm, reconcile, placate, appease, satisfy 828 *content*; pour oil on troubled waters 266 *bring to rest*; restore harmony 410 *harmonize*; win over, bring to terms, meet halfway 770 *compromise*; compose differences, settle d., accommodate 24 *adjust*; bridge over, bring together 720 *mediate*; show mercy 736 *be lenient*; grant a truce, grant an armistice, grant peace 766 *give terms*; keep the peace 717 *be at peace.*

make peace, stop fighting, cry quits, break it up 145 *cease*; bury the hatchet, let bygones be bygones, forgive and forget 506 *forget*; shake hands, make it up, make friends, patch up a quarrel, come to an understanding, agree to differ; lay down one's arms, sheathe the sword, beat swords into ploughshares; make a truce, suspend hostilities, demilitarize, disarm, demobilize; close the gates of Janus, smoke the pipe of peace.

See: 24, 145, 177, 266, 410, 506, 656, 717, 720, 736, 740, 765, 766, 770, 787, 828, 880, 909.

720 Mediation

N. *mediation,* good offices, mediatorship, intercession; umpirage, arbitration; intervention, interposition 231 *interjacency*; intermeddling 678 *overactivity*; statesmanship, diplomacy; parley, negotiation 584 *conference*.

mediator, common friend, middleman, matchmaker, go-between, negotiator 231 *intermediary*; arbitrator, umpire, referee 480 *estimator*; diplomat, diplomatist, representative, attorney, agent, press a., spokesperson 754 *delegate*; intercessor, pleader, propitiator; moderating influence, peace party 177 *moderator*; pacifier, pacificator, troubleshooter, ombudsman; marriage guidance counsellor 691 *adviser*; peacemaker, dove.

Adj. *mediatory*, mediatorial, intercessory, intercessorial, propitiatory 719 *pacificatory*.

Vb. *mediate*, intervene, intermeddle 678 *meddle*; step in, put oneself between, interpose 231 *put between*; proffer one's good offices, offer one's intercession, intercede for, beg off, propitiate; run messages for, be a go-between; bring together, negotiate, act as agent; arbitrate, umpire 480 *judge*; compose differences 719 *pacify*.

See: 177, **231**, 480, 584, 678, 691, **719**, 754.

721 Submission

N. *submission*, submissiveness 739 *obedience*; subservience, slavishness 745 *servitude*; acquiescence, compliance, consent 488 *assent*; supineness, peace at any price, line of least resistance, nonresistance, passiveness, resignation, fatalism 679 *inactivity*; yielding, giving way, white flag, capitulation, surrender, unconditional s., cession, abandonment 621 *relinquishment*; deference, humble submission 872 *humility*; act of submission, homage 739 *loyalty*; kneeling, genuflexion, kowtow, prostration 311 *obeisance*; defeatist, quitter; mouse, doormat 856 *coward*.

Adj. *submitting*, surrendering etc. vb.; quiet, meek, unresisting, nonresisting, law-abiding 717 *peaceful*; submissive 739 *obedient*; fatalistic, resigned, acquiescent 488 *assenting*; pliant, malleable 327 *soft*; weak-kneed, bending; crouching, crawling, lying down, supine, prostrate; kneeling, on bended knees 872 *humble*.

Vb. *submit*, yield, give in; not resist, not insist, defer to; bow to, make a virtue of necessity, yield with a good grace, admit defeat, yield the palm 728 *be defeated*; resign oneself, be resigned 488 *acquiesce*; accept 488 *assent*; shrug one's shoulders 860 *be indifferent*; withdraw, make way for, draw in one's horns 286 *turn back*; not contest, let judgment go by default 679 *be inactive*; cease resistance, stop fighting, have no fight left, give up, cry quits, have had enough, throw up the sponge, throw in the towel, surrender, hold up one's hands, show the white flag, ask for terms; surrender on terms, capitulate; throw oneself on another's mercy; give oneself up, yield oneself, throw down one's arms, hand over one's sword, give one's parole; haul down the flag, strike one's colours; renounce authority, deliver the keys.

knuckle under, succumb, be out for the count, cave in, collapse; sag, wilt, faint, drop 684 *be fatigued*; show no fight, take the line of least resistance, bow before the storm; be submissive, learn obedience, bow one's neck to the yoke, do homage 745 *be subject*; take one's medicine, swallow the pill 963 *be punished*; apologize, eat humble pie, eat dirt 872 *be humble*; take it, take it from one, take it lying down, pocket the insult, grin and bear it, suffer in patience, digest, stomach, put up with 825 *suffer*; bend, bow, kneel, kowtow, crouch, cringe, crawl 311 *stoop*; grovel, lick the dust, lick the boots of, kiss the rod; fall on one's knees, throw oneself at the feet of, beg for mercy, cry *or* howl for m. 905 *ask mercy*.

See: 286, 311, 327, 488, 621, 679, 684, 717, 728, **739**, 745, 825, 856, 860, **872**, 905, 963.

722 Combatant. Army. Navy. Air Force

N. *combatant*, fighter, struggler 716 *contender*; aggressor, assailant, assaulter 712 *attacker*; besieger, stormer, escalader; stormtroops, shock troops; belligerent, fighting man, warrior, brave; bodyguard 713 *defender*; gunman, strongarm man 362 *killer*; bully, bravo, rough, rowdy 904 *ruffian*; fire-eater, swashbuckler, swaggerer, miles gloriosus 877 *boaster*; duellist 709 *quarreller*; swordsman, sabreur, foilsman, fencer, sword, good s.; gladiator, retiarius 162 *athlete*; fighting cock, gamecock; bullfighter, toreador, matador, picador; grappler, wrestler, jujitsuist, judoist 716 *wrestling*; competitor 716 *contender*; champion, champ 644 *exceller*; jouster, tilter; knight, knight-errant, paladin 707 *patron*; wrangler, disputer, controversialist 475 *reasoner*; barrister, advocate 959 *litigant*.

pugilist, pug, boxer, bruiser, sparring partner; flyweight, bantamweight, featherweight, welterweight, middleweight, cruiserweight, heavyweight; slogger 716 *pugilism*.

militarist, jingoist, chauvinist, expansionist, militant, warmonger, hawk; crusader, Ghazi; Kshatriya, Samurai, Mameluke; professional soldier, freelance, mercenary (**see** *soldier*); soldier of fortune, adventurer, condottiere; freebooter, marauder, pirate, privateer, buccaneer 789 *robber*.

soldier, army man, pongo; military man, long-term soldier, regular; soldiery, troops (**see** *armed force*); campaigner, old c., conquistador; old soldier, veteran, Chelsea pensioner; fighting man, warrior, brave, myrmidon; man-at-arms, redcoat, legionary, legionnaire, centurion; vexillary, standard-bearer, colour escort, colour sergeant, ensign, cornet; heavy-armed soldier, hoplite; light-armed soldier, peltast; velites, skirmishers; sharpshooter, sniper, franc-tireur 287 *shooter*; auxiliary, Territorial, Home Guard, militiaman, fencible; yeomanry, yeoman; irregular, irregular troops, moss-trooper, cateran, kern, gallowglass, rapparee, bashi-bazouk; raider, tip-and-run r.; guerrilla, partisan, freedom fighter, fedayeen; underground fighter, Maquis; picked troops 644 *elite*; guards, housecarls 660 *protector* (**see** *armed force*); effective, enlisted man; reservist; volunteer; pressed man; conscript, recruit, rookie; serviceman, Tommy, Tommy Atkins, GI, doughboy, Aussie, Anzac, poilu, sepoy, Gurkha, askari; woman soldier, female warrior, Amazon; battlemaid, Valkyrie; Wren, WRAF, WRAC.

soldiery, cannon fodder, food for powder; gallant company, merry men, heroes; the ranks, other r.; private, private soldier, common s., man-at-arms; slinger, archer, bowman, crossbowman, arbalester; spearman, pikeman, halberdier, lancer; arquebusier, matchlockman, musketeer, fusilier, rifleman, pistoleer, carabineer, bazookaman, grenadier, bombardier, gunner, machine gunner, artilleryman; pioneer, sapper, miner, engineer; signalman; corporal, sergeant, lieutenant 741 *army officer*.

army, host, camp; phalanx, legion; cohorts, big battalions; horde, mass 104 *multitude*; warlike people, martial race; nation in arms, general levy, arrière-ban; National Guard, Home G.; militia, yeomanry; regular army, standing a., professional a., mercenary a., volunteer a., Territorial A., conscript a., draft; the services, armed forces, air arm, fleet air arm, fleet.

armed force, forces, troops, contingents, effectives, men, personnel; armament, armada; corps d'élite, ceremonial troops, guards, household troops; Household Cavalry, Royal Horse Guards, The Blues and Royals, Life Guards, Foot Guards; Swiss G., Praetorian G., Varangian G., Immortals, janissaries; picked troops, crack t., shock t., storm t.; spearhead, expeditionary force, striking f., flying column; parachute troops, paratroops, commando, Commandos, task force, raiding party, guerrilla force; combat troops, field army, line, thin red l., front l., front-line troops, first echelon; wing, van, vanguard, rear, rearguard, centre, main body; second echelon, base troops, reserves, recruits, reinforcements, draft, levy 707 *auxiliary*; base, staff; detachment, picket, party, detail; patrol, night patrol, night watch, sentry, sentinel, vedette 660 *protector*; garrison, occupying force, occupation troops, army of occupation.

formation, array, line; square, phalanx; legion, cohort, century, decury, maniple; column, file, rank; unit, group, detachment, corps, army c., division, armoured d., panzer d.; brigade, rifle b., light b., heavy b.; artillery brigade, battery; regiment, cavalry r., squadron, troop; battalion, company, platoon, section, squad, detail, party 74 *band*.

infantry, line i., bayonets, foot regiment, infantryman, foot soldier, foot, peon; footslogger, PBI; mountain infantry, light i.; chasseur, jaeger, Zouave.

cavalry, yeomanry; heavy cavalry, light c., sabres, horse, light h., cavalry regiment; horseman, cameleer, rider; mounted troops, mounted rifles, mounted police, mounted infantry, horse artillery; horse soldier, cavalryman, yeoman; trooper, sowar; chivalry, knight; man-at-arms, lancer, uhlan, hussar, cuirassier, dragoon, light d., heavy d.; Ironsides, Cossack, spahi; rough-rider; armour, armoured car, armoured personnel carrier; tank,

Panzer; charger, destrier 273 *warhorse*.

navy, sea power, Admiralty; sail, wooden walls; fleet arm, naval armament, armada; fleet, flotilla, squadron.

naval man, naval service, navy, senior service; admiral, Sea Lord 741 *naval officer*; sailor 270 *mariner*; bluejacket, man-o'-war man, able seaman, rating, pressed man; foretopman; powder monkey; cabin boy; gobby, gob, swab, swabbie; marine, jolly, leatherneck, limey; submariner, naval airman 270 *nautical personnel*; Royal Navy, RN, WRNS; Royal Marines; Royal Naval Reserve RNR, RNVR, Wavy Navy.

warship, war vessel, war galley, bireme, trireme, quinquereme, galleon, galleass 275 *ship*; raider, privateer, pirate ship; man-o'-war, ship of the line, armoured vessel, capital ship, battleship, dreadnought; monitor, ironclad; cruiser, light c., armoured c., battle c.; frigate, corvette; mosquito boat, fast patrol b., PT b.; gunboat, motor torpedo boat, E-boat; destroyer; fire ship, blockship; minelayer, minesweeper; submarine, nuclear s., U-boat; Q-ship, mystery s.; aircraft carrier, fleet c.; landing craft, duck, amphibian; transport, troopship; tender, store ship, depot s., parent s., guard s., hospital s.; flagship, flotilla leader.

air force, RAF, WRAF, USAF; Royal Air Force Volunteer Reserve; air arm, flying corps, air service, fleet air arm; squadron, flight, group, wing; warplane 276 *aircraft*; battle plane, bomber, fighter b., heavy b., light b., fighter, night f., interceptor, ground-attack aircraft, interdictor; flying boat, patrol plane, scout; transport plane, troop-carrier; Zeppelin, captive balloon, barrage b. 276 *airship*; air troops, airborne division; parachute troops, paratroopers; aircraftman, ground staff; fighter pilot, bomber p., navigator, observer, air crew.

See:74, 104, 162, **270**, 273, 275, **276**, 287, 362, 475, 644, 660, 707, 709, 712, 713, **716**, **741**, 789, 877, 904, 959.

723 Arms

N. *arms* (**see** *weapon*); arming, armament, munitioning, munitions; armaments, arms race; nuclear deterrent 713 *defence*; arms traffic, gun-running; ballistics, rocketry, gunnery, musketry, archery, bowmanship.

arsenal, armoury, gun room, gun rack, ammunition chest; arms depot 632 *storage*; magazine, powder m., powder barrel, powder keg, powder flask, powder horn; caisson, ammunition box; bullet-pouch, cartridge belt, bandolier; arrow-case, quiver; scabbard, sheath; holster 194 *receptacle*.

weapon, arm, deterrent; deadly weapon, defensive w.; armour, plate, mail 713 *defence*; offensive weapon 712 *attack*; conventional weapon, nuclear w., theatre n. w., tactical n. w. 718 *warfare*; secret weapon, death ray, laser; germ warfare, chemical w.; gas, war g., poison g., mustard g., nerve g. 659 *poison*; natural weapon, teeth, claws, nails 256 *sharp point*.

missile weapon, javelin, harpoon, dart; bolas, lasso; boomerang, woomera, throwstick; arrow, barbed a., shaft, bolt, quarrel; arrowhead, barb; stone, brick, brickbat; slingstone, shot, ball, bullet, pellet, fléchette, shell, star s., gas s., shrapnel, whizzbang, rocket, MIRV (**see** *ammunition*); bow, longbow, crossbow, arbalest, ballista, catapult, mangonel, sling; blowpipe; bazooka, rocket-thrower (**see** *gun*); cruise missile, guided m., ballistic m., ICBM, intercontinental ballistic missile, surface-to-air m. 287 *missile*; antimissile missile, ABM.

club, mace, knobkerrie, knobstick, warhammer 279 *hammer*; battering ram 279 *ram*; bat, staff, stave, stick, switch, lathi, quarterstaff; life-preserver, bludgeon, truncheon, cudgel, shillelagh, blackjack, sandbag, knuckle-duster, brass knuckles, cosh, bicycle chain.

spear, harpoon, gaff; lance, javelin, jerid, pike, assegai; partisan, bill, halberd 256 *sharp point*.

axe, battleaxe, tomahawk, hatchet, halberd, bill, gisarme; poleaxe, chopper 256 *sharp edge*.

sidearms, sword; steel, cold steel, naked s.; broadsword, glaive, claymore, two-edged sword, two-handed s.; cutlass, hanger, short sword, swordstick; sabre, scimitar, yataghan, falchion, snickersnee; blade, fine b., trusty b., bilbo, Toledo; rapier, tuck; fencing sword, épée, foil; dagger, bayonet, dirk, skean, poniard, dudgeon, misericord, stylet, stiletto 256 *sharp point*; machete, kukri, kris, parang, panga; knife, bowie k., flick k., switchblade 256 *sharp edge.*

firearm, small arms, hand gun, arquebus, hackbut; matchlock, wheel-lock, flintlock, fusil, musket, Brown Bess; blunderbuss, muzzleloader, smoothbore, carbine; breechloader, chassepot, needlegun; rifle, magazine r., repeating r., Winchester; fowling piece, sporting gun, shotgun, sawn-off s., single-barrelled gun, double-barrelled g., elephant g.; Enfield rifle, Lee-Enfield, Lee-Metford, Martini-Henry, Mauser, Snider; bore, calibre; muzzle; trigger, lock; magazine; breech, butt, gunstock; sight, backsight; ramrod.

pistol, duelling p., horse p.; petronel, pistolet; six-shooter, Colt (tdmk), revolver, repeater, zipgun, rod, gat, shooting iron, automatic.

gun, guns, ordnance, cannonry, artillery, light a., heavy a., mountain a.; horse artillery, galloping guns; battery, broadside; artillery park, gun p.; cannon, brass c., bombard, falconet, swivel, jingal, basilisk, petard, carronade, culverin; mortar; piece, field piece, field gun, siege g.; great gun, heavy g., cannon royal, seventy-four, heavy metal, Big Bertha; howitzer, trench-mortar, minethrower, minenwerfer, Minnie, trench gun; antiaircraft gun, antitank g., ack-ack, Bofors gun, bazooka; assault gun, quick-firing g., Gatling g., mitrailleuse, pom-pom, Maxim, Lewis gun, machine g., M 60 machine g., light machine g., Bren g., Sten g., submachine g., Thompson submachine g., tommy g.; flamethrower; guncarriage, limber, caisson; gun emplacement, rocket site, launching pad, silo.

ammunition, live a., live shot; round of ammunition, round; powder and shot; shot, round s., case s., grape s., chain s., small s., mitraille, buckshot; ball, cannonball, bullet, expanding b., soft-nosed b., dumdum b.; projectile 287 *missile*; slug, stone, pellet; shell, shrapnel; flak, ack-ack; wad, cartouche, cartridge, live c.; spent cartridge, dud; cartridge belt, cartridge clip; cartridge case.

explosive, propellant; powder, gunpowder; saltpetre, high explosive, lyddite, melinite, cordite, gun cotton, dynamite, gelignite, TNT, nitroglycerine; cap, detonator, fuse; priming, charge, warhead, atomic w.; fissionable material.

bomb, explosive device; shell, bombshell; grenade, hand g., pineapple, Molotov cocktail; megaton bomb, atom b., A-bomb, nuclear b., hydrogen b., H-bomb; neutron b., enhanced radiation b.; mushroom cloud, fallout; blockbuster; cluster bomb, fragmentation b.; firebomb, incendiary bomb, napalm b.; carcass, Greek fire; mine, landmine, magnetic mine, acoustic m., limpet; booby trap 542 *trap*; depth charge, torpedo, tin fish; flying bomb, V-1, doodlebug, V-2; rocket bomb; time bomb, infernal machine.

See: 1, 2, 60, 194, 256, 279, 287, 542, 632, 659, 712, 713, 718.

724 Arena

N. *arena*, field, field of action; ground, terrain; centre, scene, stage, theatre; hustings, platform, floor; amphitheatre, coliseum, stadium, stand, grandstand; campus, Campus Martius, Champs de Mars, parade ground, training g.; forum, marketplace 76 *focus*; hippodrome, circus, course, racecourse, turf; track, running t., cinder t., dog t.; ring, bullring, boxing r., ropes; rink, skating r., ice r.; palaestra, gymnasium, gym; range, shooting r., rifle r., butts; playground, beach, lido, pier, fairground 837 *pleasure ground*; recreation ground, playing field, football f., pitch, cricket p.; court, tennis c., badminton c., squash c.; putting green, bowling g., bowling alley, skittle a.; lists, tiltyard; cockpit, beargarden; chessboard, checkerboard; bridge table; auction room; examination hall; courtroom 956 *lawcourt*.

battleground, battlefield, field of battle; field of blood, Aceldama; theatre of war, combat zone, no-go area; front, front line, firing l., trenches, no-man's-land; sector, salient, bulge, pocket; beachhead, bridgehead; encampment, tented field; disputed territory 718 *battle*.

See: 76, 718, 837, 956.

Section five: Results of action

725 Completion

N. *completion*, finish, termination, conclusion, end of the matter 69 *end*; terminus 295 *goal*; issue, upshot 154 *event*; result, end r., final r., end product 157 *effect*; fullness 54 *completeness*; fulfilment 635 *sufficiency*; maturity, fruition, readiness, perfect r. 669 *preparedness*; consummation, culmination, ne plus ultra 646 *perfection*; exhaustiveness, thoroughness 455 *attention*; elaboration, rounding off, finishing off, mopping up, winding up; roofing, topping out; top, crown, superstructure 213 *summit*; missing link 627 *requirement*; last touch, last stroke, crowning s., final s., finishing s., coup de grace, clincher; achievement, fait accompli, work done, finished product (**see** *effectuation*); boiling point, danger p., breaking p., last straw 236 *limit*; climax, payoff; resolution, solution, dénouement, catastrophe, last act, final curtain 69 *finality*.

effectuation, carrying through *or* out; execution, discharge, implementation; dispatch, performance 676 *action*; accomplishment, achievement, realization 727 *success*; elaboration, working out.

Adj. *completive*, completing, perfective; crowning, culminating 213 *topmost*; finishing, conclusive, final, last 69 *ending*; unanswerable, crushing; thorough, thoroughgoing, wholehogging 599 *resolute*.

completed, full, full-blown 54 *complete*; done, well d., achieved, accomplished etc. vb.; wrought out, highly wrought, elaborate 646 *perfect*; sewn up, buttoned up, in the can, under one's belt, secured 727 *successful*.

Vb. *carry through*, follow t., follow up; drive home, clinch, seal, set the seal on, seal up; clear up, mop up, wipe up, finish off, polish off; dispose of, dispatch, give the coup de grace; complete, consummate, put the finishing touch, top out 54 *make complete*; elaborate, hammer out, work o. 646 *perfect*; ripen, bring to a head, bring to the boil 669 *mature*; sit out, see out, see it through (**see** *carry out*); get through, get shot of, dispose of, wrap up, bring to its close 69 *terminate*; set at rest 266 *bring to rest*.

carry out, see through, effect, enact 676 *do*; dispatch, execute, discharge, implement, effectuate, realize, compass, bring about, accomplish, fulfil, consummate, achieve 727 *succeed*; make short work of, make no bones of; do thoroughly, leave no loose ends, not do by halves, go the whole hog, be in at the death; deliver the goods, bring home the bacon, be as good as one's word, fill the bill.

climax, cap, crown all 213 *crown*; culminate, reach its peak; scale the heights, conquer Everest; reach boiling point, come to a crisis; reach the limit, touch bottom; put the lid on, add the last straw; come to its end, attain one's e., come to fruition, touch the goal 295 *arrive*; have enough of, be through with 635 *have enough*.

See: 54, 69, 154, 157, 213, 236, 266, 295, 455, 599, 627, 635, 646, 669, 676, **727**.

726 Noncompletion

N. *noncompletion*, no success 728 *failure*; nonperformance, nonexecution, neglect 458 *negligence*; nonfulfilment 636 *insufficiency*; deficiency, deficit 307 *shortfall*; lack 55 *incompleteness*; unripeness, immaturity 670 *undevelopment*; never-ending task, painting the Forth Bridge, Penelope's web, Sisyphean labour, argument in a circle, recurring decimal 71 *continuity*; perfunctoriness, superficiality, a lick and a promise 456 *inattention*; tinkering, work undone, job half-done, loose ends; no decision, lack of finality, no result, drawn game; stalemate, deadlock; semicompletion, launching stage.

Adj. *uncompleted*, partial, fragmentary 55 *incomplete*; not finalized 55 *unfinished*; undone, unperformed, unexecuted, unachieved, unaccomplished; unrealized, half-done, half-finished, half-begun, hardly b. 458 *neglected*; half-baked, underdone, unripe 670 *immature*; unthorough, perfunctory, superficial; not cleared up, left hanging, left in the air; lacking finish, unelaborated, not worked out, inchoate, sketchy, in outline 647 *imperfect*; unbleached, unprocessed, semiprocessed; never-ending 71 *continuous*.

Vb. *not complete*, hardly begin, leave undone, leave in the air, leave hanging 458 *neglect*; skip, scamp, do by halves, tinker, paper over the cracks 636 *not suffice*; scotch the snake not kill it 655 *wound*; give up, not follow up, not follow through; fall out, drop o., not stay the course; fall short of one's goal, fall down on 728 *fail*; defer, postpone, put off till tomorrow 136 *put off*.

Adv. *on the stocks*, under construction, on the anvil, in preparation, in process of.

See: 55, 71, 136, 307, 456, 458, 636, 647, 655, 670, **728**.

727 Success

N. *success*, sweet smell of s., glory 866 *famousness*; success all round, happy outcome, happy ending, favourable issue; success story, progress, steady advance, Godspeed, time well spent 285 *progression*; fresh advance, breakthrough; one's day, continued success, run of luck, good fortune 730 *prosperity*; lead, temporary l., first blood 34 *advantage*; momentary success, flash in the pan; exploit, feat, achievement 676 *deed*; accomplishment, goal 725 *completion*; a success, feather in one's cap, triumph, hit, smash h., triumphant success, howling s., succès fou; good hit, winning h., good shot 694 *skill*; beginner's luck, lucky stroke, fluke 618 *nondesign*; hat trick, stroke of genius, masterstroke 694 *masterpiece*; trump, trump card, winning c., card up one's sleeve 623 *contrivance*; success in examination, pass, qualification; match-winning 34 *superiority*.

victory, infliction of defeat, beating, whipping, licking, trouncing 728 *defeat*; conquest, subdual 745 *subjection*; successful attack, taking by storm, escalade 712 *attack*; honours of battle, the best of it; win, game and match; outright win, complete victory, checkmate; narrow win, Pyrrhic victory, well-fought field; easy win, runaway victory, love game, walk-over, pushover, picnic 701 *easy thing*; crushing victory, quelling v., slam, grand s.; kill, knockout, KO; mastery, ascendancy, upper hand, whip h., edge, winning position, certain victory 34 *advantage*; no defeat, stalemate 28 *draw*; celebration of victory, triumph, ovation, epinician ode 876 *celebration*.

victor, winner, champion, top dog, world-beater, medallist, prizewinner, first, double f. 644 *exceller*; winning side, the winners; triumpher, conquering hero, Alexander, Tamburlaine; conqueror, conquistador; defeater, beater, vanquisher, overcomer, subjugator, subduer, queller; master, mistress, master *or* mistress of the field, master *or* mistress of the situation; a success, successful rival, successful person, self-made man *or* woman, man *or* woman to watch, rising star 730 *prosperous person*.

Adj. *successful*, effective, efficacious; crushing, quelling; efficient; sovereign 658 *remedial*; well-spent, fruitful 640 *profitable*; happy, lucky; felicitous, masterly 694 *skilful*; ever-victorious, unbeatable (**see** *unbeaten*); never-failing, surefire, foolproof; unerring, infallible, surefooted 473 *certain*; home and dry 725 *completed*; prizewinning, victorious, world-beating 644 *excellent*; winning, leading, up, one up 34 *superior*; on top, in the ascendant, rising, on the up and up, going places, sitting pretty 730 *prosperous*; triumphant, crowning; triumphal, epinician, victorious; crowned with success, flushed with victory; glorious 866 *renowned*.

unbeaten, undefeated, unbowed, unsubdued, unquelled, unvanquished 599 *resolute*; unbeatable, unconquerable, ever-victorious, invincible.

Vb. *succeed*, succeed in, effect, accomplish, achieve, compass 725 *carry through*; be successful, make out, win one's spurs; make a success of, make a go of, make short work of, rise to the occasion; make good, rise, do well, get promotion, work one's way up the ladder, come to the top 730 *prosper*; pass, make the grade, qualify, graduate, come off well, give a good account of oneself, come well out of it, come off with flying colours, come out on top, have the best of it 34 *be superior*; advance, break through, make a breakthrough 285 *progress*; strive to some purpose, gain one's end, reach one's goal, secure one's object, obtain one's objective, attain one's purpose; pull it off, bring it off, be as good as one's word, bring home the bacon; have a success, score a s., make the big time, make a hit, make a killing, go over big; hit the jackpot, break the bank; score a point, win a p., carry a p.; arrive, be a success, get around, make one's mark, click.

be successful, be efficacious, be effective, come off, come right in the end; answer, answer the purpose, do the trick, ring the bell, show results, turn out well; turn up trumps, rise to the occasion, do oneself proud; do the job, do wonders, do marvels; compass, manage 676 *do*; work, act, work like magic, act like a charm 173 *operate*; take effect, tell, pull its weight 178 *influence*; pay off, pay dividends, bear fruit 171 *be fruitful*; get it, hit it, hit the nail on the head; play one's hand well, not put a foot wrong, never go w.; be surefooted, keep on the right side of; have the ball at one's feet, hold all the trumps; be irresistible, not know the meaning of failure, brush obstacles aside 701 *do easily*; not know when one is beaten, come up smiling 599 *be resolute*; avoid defeat, hold one's own, maintain one's position 599 *stand firm*.

triumph, have one's day, be crowned with success, wear the laurels of victory 876 *celebrate*; crow, crow over 877 *boast*; score, score off, be one up on; triumph over difficulties, contrive a success, manage, make it, win through; surmount, overcome obstacles, get over a snag, sweep difficulties out of the way; find a loophole, find a way out 667 *escape*; make headway against, stem the tide, weather the storm 715 *resist*; reap the fruits, reap the harvest 771 *gain*.

overmaster, be too much for, be more than a match for 34 *be superior*; master, overcome, overpower, overmatch, overthrow, overturn, override, overtrump 306 *outdo*; have the advantage, take the a., seize the a., hold the a., keep the a., prevail 34 *predominate*; have one on the hip, have one by the short hairs; checkmate, trump, ruff; conquer, vanquish, quell, subdue, subject, suppress, put down, crush 745 *subjugate*; capture, carry, take, storm, take by s., escalade 712 *attack*.

defeat (**see** *overmaster*); discomfit, dash, put another's nose out of joint, cook one's goose; repulse, rebuff 292 *repel*; confound, dismay 854 *frighten*; best, be too good for, get the better of, get the upper hand, get the whip h. 34 *be superior*; worst, outplay, outpoint, outflank, outmanoeuvre, outclass, outshine 306 *outdo*; disconcert, cut the ground from under one's feet, trip, lay by the heels 702 *obstruct*; baffle, gravel, nonplus 474 *puzzle*; defeat easily, knock spots off, wipe the floor with; beat, lick, thrash, whip, trounce, swamp, overwhelm, crush, drub, give a drubbing, roll in the dust, trample underfoot, trample upon; beat hollow, rout, put to flight, scatter 75 *disperse*; silence, put the lid on, put hors de combat, put out of court 165 *suppress*; down one's opponent, flatten, crush, put out for the count, knock out; knock for six, hit for s.; bowl out, skittle o.; run hard, corner, drive to the wall, check, put in check 661 *endanger*; put an end to, wipe out, do for, settle, fix, dish 165 *destroy*; sink, send to the bottom 313 *plunge*; break, bankrupt 801 *impoverish*.

win, win the battle, carry the day, achieve victory, defeat the enemy, down one's opponent (**see** *defeat*); be victorious, remain in possession of the field, claim the victory; come off best, come off with flying colours; win hands down, carry *or* sweep all before one, have it all one's own way, romp home, have a walkover, walk off with, waltz away with 701 *do easily*; win on points, scrape home, survive; win the last battle, win the last round; win the match, take the prize, take the cup, gain the palm, wear the crown, wear the laurel wreath; become champion, beat all comers, rule OK 34 *be superior*.

Adv. *successfully*, swimmingly, marvellously well; to some purpose, to good p., with good result, with good effect, with magical e.; to one's heart's content, beyond one's fondest dreams, beyond all expectation; with flying colours, in triumph.

See: 28, **34**, 75, 165, 171, 173, 178, 285, 292, 306, 313, 473, 474, 599, 618, 623, 640, **644**, 658, 661, 667, 676, 694, 701, 702, 712, 715, 725, 728, **730**, 745, 771, 801, 854, 866, 876, 877.

728 Failure

N. *failure*, nonsuccess, lack of success, negative result; no luck, off day 731 *misfortune*; nonfulfilment 726 *noncompletion*; frustration 702 *hindrance*; inefficacy, ineffectiveness 161 *ineffectuality*; vain attempt, abortive a., wild-goose chase, futile effort, no result 641 *lost labour*; mess, muddle, bungle 695 *bungling*; abortion, miscarriage 172 *unproductiveness*; hopeless failure, sad f., damp squib, washout, fiasco, flop, non-event; no ball, bosh shot, misfire, slip, omission, faux pas 495 *mistake*; no go, dead stop, halt 145 *stop*; engine failure, electrical fault, seizing up, breakdown 702 *hitch*; collapse, fall, stumble, trip 309 *descent*; incapacity 163 *weakness*; anticlimax 509 *disappointment*; losses 772 *loss*; bankruptcy 805 *insolvency*.

defeat, bafflement, bewilderment, puzzlement 474 *uncertainty*; nonplus, deadlock, stalemate 145 *stop*; lost battle, repulse, rebuff, bloody nose, check, reverse; no move left, checkmate, mate, fool's m.; the worst of it, discomfiture, beating, drubbing, hiding, licking, thrashing, trouncing; retreat; flight 290 *recession*; dispersal

75 *dispersion*; stampede, panic 854 *fear*; rout, landslide; fall, downfall, collapse, débâcle; wreck, perdition, graveyard 165 *ruin*; lost cause, losing game, losing battle; deathblow, quietus; utter defeat, total d., final d., Waterloo; conquest, subjugation 745 *subjection*.

loser, unsuccessful competitor, baffled enemy, defeated rival; also-ran, non-starter; has-been, extinct volcano; defeatist, pessimist, misery 834 *moper*; fumbler 697 *bungler*; dud, failure, flop, lemon; sacrifice, victim, prey 544 *dupe*; born loser 731 *unlucky person*; underdog 35 *inferior*; underachiever, early leaver; dropout 25 *misfit*; bankrupt, insolvent 805 *nonpayer*; the losers, losing side, the defeated, the conquered, the vanquished, the fallen.

Adj. *unsuccessful*, ineffective, pale; inglorious, obscure, unrewarded, empty-handed; unlucky 731 *unfortunate*; vain, bootless, negative, fruitless, profitless; dud, misfired, hanging fire; miscarried, stillborn, aborted, abortive, premature; jilted, ditched; manqué, failed, ploughed, flunked; unplaced, losing, failing; vincible; stumbling, tripping, groping, wandering, out of one's depth 474 *uncertain*.

defeated, beaten, bested, worsted, pipped, dished, done for; baffled, thwarted, foiled 702 *hindered*; disconcerted, dashed, discomfited, hoist with one's own petard; outmanoeuvred, outmatched, outplayed, outvoted; outclassed, outshone 35 *inferior*; thrashed, licked, whacked; on the losing side, among the also-rans, unplaced, out of the running; in retreat, in flight 290 *receding*; routed, scattered, put to flight; swamped, overwhelmed, sunk; overborne, overthrown, struck down, knocked out, kaput, brought low, fallen; captured, made a prey, victimized, sacrificed.

grounded, stranded, wrecked, washed up, left high and dry; on the rocks, on one's beam-ends 165 *destroyed*; unhorsed, dismounted, thrown, brought low; ruined, bankrupt 700 *in difficulties*.

Vb. *fail*, not succeed, have no success, get no results; be unsuccessful, - beaten etc. adj.; fall down on, foozle, muddle, botch, bungle 495 *blunder*; flunk, not make the grade, be found wanting 636 *not suffice*; fail one, let one down 509 *disappoint*; miss the boat 138 *lose a chance*; misdirect, miss one's aim, go wide, miss, hit the wrong target, fall between two stools 282 *deviate*; get nothing out of it, get no change out of it, draw a blank, back the wrong horse, return empty-handed, lose one's pains, labour in vain, have shot one's bolt 641 *waste effort*; kiss goodbye to 772 *lose*; overreach oneself, come a cropper, fall, collapse, slide 309 *tumble*; break down, malfunction, come to pieces, come unstuck; falter, stall, seize, seize up, crock up, pack up, conk out; stop, come to a dead stop, come up against a blank wall, come to a dead end; stick, stick in the mud, get bogged down 145 *cease*; come to a sticky end, come to a bad e. 655 *deteriorate*; go on the rocks, run aground, ground, sink 313 *founder*; make a loss, crash, bust, break, go bankrupt 805 *not pay*.

miscarry, be stillborn, abort; misfire, hang fire, flash in the pan, fizzle out; fall, fall to the ground, crash 309 *tumble*; not come off, come to naught, come to nothing, go by the board, end in futility 641 *be useless*; fail to succeed, fall flat, come to grief; burst, bust, explode, blow up, go up in smoke; flop, prove a fiasco; not go well, go wrong, go amiss, go awry, gang agley, take a turn for the worse, take an ugly turn; do no good, make things worse 832 *aggravate*; dash one's hopes, frustrate one's expectations 509 *disappoint*.

be defeated, lose, lose out, suffer defeat, take a beating, lose the day, lose the battle, lose the match; lose the election, lose one's seat, lose the vote, be outvoted; just lose, just miss, get pipped at the post; get the worst of it, come off second best, go off with one's tail between one's legs, lick one's wounds; lose hands down, come in last, not win a point; take the count, bite the dust; fall, succumb 745 *be subject*; be captured, fall a prey to, be victimized; retreat, lose ground 290 *recede*; take to flight 620 *run away*; admit defeat, had enough, cry quits 721 *submit*; have not a leg to stand on, have the ground cut from under one's feet; go downhill 655 *deteriorate*; go to the wall, go to the dogs 165 *be destroyed*.

Adv. *unsuccessfully*, to no purpose, to little or no p., in vain.

See: 25, 35, 75, 138, 145, 161, 163, 165, 172, 282, 290, 309, 313, 474, 495, 509, 544, 620, 636, **641**, 655, 695, 697, 700, 702,

721, 726, **731**, 745, 772, 805, 832, 834, 854.

729 Trophy

N. *trophy*, sign of success; war trophy, spoils, spolia opima, capture, captives 790 *booty*; scalp, head; scars, wounds 655 *wound*; memorial, war m., memento 505 *reminder*; triumphal arch 548 *monument*; triumph, ovation 876 *celebration*; plum, glittering prizes; benefit, benefit match; prize, first p., consolation p., booby p., wooden spoon 962 *reward*; sports trophy, Ashes, cup, pot, plate, shield; award, Oscar a., Tony a., Emmy a., Golden Rose; bays, laurels, the laurel and the rose, crown, laurel c., bay c., coronal, chaplet, garland, wreath, palm, palm of victory; epinician ode, pat on the back; favour, feather in one's cap, love token 547 *badge*; flying colours 875 *ostentation*; glory 866 *repute*.

decoration, honour 870 *title*; blushing honours, battle h., spurs 866 *honours*; citation, mention in dispatches; rosette, ribbon, sash, cordon bleu; athletic honour, blue, oar; medal, gong, star, cross, garter, order; service stripe, long-service medal, war m., campaign m.; Victoria Cross, VC, Military C., Croix de Guerre, Iron Cross; Distinguished Service Cross, Congressional Medal, Medal of Honour; George Cross, Medal for Merit, Legion of Honour, civic crown.

See:505, **547**, 548, 655, 790, **866**, 870, 875, 876, 962.

730 Prosperity

N. *prosperity*, thriving, health and wealth, having it good 727 *success*; well-being, welfare, weal 824 *happiness*; economic prosperity, booming economy, boom; roaring trade, seller's market, favourable trade balance, no unemployment; luxury, affluence, Easy Street 800 *wealth*; golden touch, Midas t.; fleshpots, fat of the land, milk and honey, chicken in every pot 635 *plenty*; auspiciousness, favour, smiles of fortune, good f., blessings, godsend, crowning mercy, goodness and mercy 615 *good*; bonanza, winning streak, luck, run of l., good l., break, lucky b., luck of the draw 159 *chance*; glory, honour and g., renown 866 *prestige*.

palmy days, heyday, prime, floruit; halcyon days, bright d., summer, sunshine, fair weather, Indian summer, Edwardian s.; piping times 717 *peace*; easy times, life of Riley, place in the sun, clover, velvet, bed of roses 376 *euphoria*; golden times, Golden Age, Saturnia Regna 824 *happiness*; expansive times, Periclean Age, Augustan A., Pax Romana, Elizabethan Age.

prosperous person, man *or* woman of substance, man *or* woman of property 800 *rich person*; successful person, made man, rising man *or* woman; favourite of the gods, child of fortune, lucky fellow, lucky dog; arriviste, upstart, parvenu, nouveau riche, profiteer; celebrity, hero 866 *person of repute*; lion 890 *favourite*.

Adj. *prosperous*, thriving, flourishing, booming 727 *successful*; rising, doing well, up and coming, on the up and up; on the make, profiteering; well set-up, established, well-to-do, well-off, affluent, comfortable, comfortably off 800 *moneyed*; riding high on the hog's back, riding on the crest of a wave, buoyant; fortunate, lucky, born with a silver spoon in one's mouth, born under a lucky star; in clover, on velvet; at ease, in bliss 824 *happy*; fat, sleek, euphoric.

palmy, balmy, halcyon, golden, couleur de rose, rosy; piping, blissful, blessed; providential, favourable, promising, auspicious, propitious, cloudless, clear, fine, fair, set f.; glorious, expansive; euphoric, agreeable, cosy 376 *comfortable*.

Vb. *prosper*, thrive, flourish, have one's day; do well, fare w., have a good time of it 376 *enjoy*; bask in sunshine, make hay, live in clover, lie on velvet, have it easy, have it made, live on milk and honey, live on the fat of the land, 'never have had it so good'; batten on, grow fat, feed well 301 *eat*; blossom, bloom, flower 171 *be fruitful*; win glory 866 *have a reputation*; boom, drive a roaring trade, enjoy a seller's market; profiteer 771 *gain*; get on, go far, rise in the world, work one's way up, make it, arrive 727 *succeed*; make money, make a fortune, strike it rich, make one's pile, feather one's nest 800 *get rich*; run smoothly, run on oiled wheels 258 *go smoothly*; go on swimmingly, swim with the tide, sail before the wind; keep afloat, keep one's head above water, not do badly.

have luck, have all the l., have a stroke of l., have a lucky break, have a run of luck;

strike lucky, strike oil, strike a rich vein, be on to a good thing, get on the gravy train; fall on one's feet, enjoy the smiles of fortune, bear a charmed life, be born under a lucky star, be born with a silver spoon in one's mouth, have the ball at one's feet.

be auspicious, - propitious etc. adj.; promise, promise well, augur well, set fair; favour, prosper, profit 615 *benefit*; look kindly on, smile on, shine on, bless, shed blessings on; water, fertilize, make blossom like the rose; turn out well, take a good turn, take a favourable t., turn up trumps 644 *do good*; glorify 866 *honour*.

Adv. *prosperously*, swimmingly 727 *successfully*; beyond one's wildest dreams, in the swim, in clover, on velvet; in luck's way.

Int. Good luck! all the best! best of British!

See: 159, 171, 258, 301, 376, **615**, 635, 644, 717, **727**, 771, 800, **824**, 866, 890.

731 Adversity

N. *adversity*, adverse circumstances, misfortune, frowns of fortune, mixed blessing (**see** *misfortune*); continual struggle, weary way 700 *difficulty*; hardship, hard life, tough time, no bed of roses 825 *suffering*; groaning, travail 377 *pain*; bad times, hard t., iron age, ice a., dark a., hell upon earth, vale of sorrows 616 *evil*; burden, load, pressure, pressure of the times; ups and downs of life, vicissitude 154 *event*; troubles, sea of t., peck of t., trials, cares, worries 825 *worry*; wretchedness, misery, despondency, Slough of Despond 834 *dejection*; bitter cup, bitter pill 872 *humiliation*; cross, cup of sorrows 825 *sorrow*; curse, blight, blast, plague, scourge, infliction, visitation 659 *bane*; bleakness, cold wind, draught, chill, cold, winter 380 *coldness*; gloom 418 *darkness*; ill wind, cross w.; blow, hard b., blow between the eyes 704 *opposition*; setback, check, rebuff, reverse 728 *defeat*; rub, pinch, plight, funeral 700 *predicament*; poor lookout, trouble ahead; trough, bad patch, rainy day 655 *deterioration*; slump, recession, depression 679 *inactivity*; dark clouds, gathering c. 900 *threat*; decline, fall, downfall 165 *ruin*; broken fortune, want, need, distress, extremity 801 *poverty*.

misfortune, bad fortune, ill f.; bad luck, hard luck; no luck, no luck this time, no success 728 *failure*; evil dispensation, evil star, malign influence 645 *badness*; hard case, raw deal, rotten hand, chicane, yarborough; hard lot, hard fate, hard lines; ill hap, mishap, mischance, misadventure, contretemps, accident, casualty 159 *chance*; disaster, calamity, catastrophe, the worst.

unlucky person, poor unfortunate, constant loser, poor risk; star-crossed lover, sport of fortune, plaything of fate, Jonah; down-and-out 728 *loser*; underdog 35 *inferior*; new poor 801 *poor person*; lame dog, lame duck 163 *weakling*; scapegoat, victim, wretch, poor w. 825 *sufferer*; prey 544 *dupe*.

Adj. *adverse*, hostile, frowning, ominous, sinister, inauspicious, unfavourable; bleak, cold, hard; opposed, cross, thwart, contrary, untoward 704 *opposing*; malign 645 *harmful*; dire, dreadful, ruinous 165 *destructive*; disastrous, calamitous, catastrophic; too bad 645 *bad*.

unprosperous, unblest, inglorious 728 *unsuccessful*; unwell, in poor shape; not doing well, in low water, badly off, not well off 801 *poor*; in trouble, up against it, in adverse circumstances, clouded, under a cloud 700 *in difficulties*; declining, on the wane, on the down grade, on the road to ruin 655 *deteriorated*; in the wars, in a bad way, in an evil plight, in dire straits, in extremities.

unfortunate, ill-fated, unlucky, ill-starred, star-crossed, blasted; fraught, futureless; unblest, luckless, hapless, poor, wretched, forlorn, miserable, undone, unhappy; stricken, doomed, accursed; not lucky, out of luck, down on one's luck; out of favour, under a cloud 924 *disapproved*; born under an evil star; accident-prone.

Vb. *have trouble*, be in t., be born to t., be one's own worst enemy; stew in one's own juice; be fortune's sport, be the victim of fate, have no luck, get more kicks than ha'pence; be in for it, go through it, be hard pressed, be up against it, fall foul of 700 *be in difficulty*; strike a bad patch 825 *suffer*; suffer humiliation 872 *be humbled*; come to grief 728 *miscarry*; feel the pinch, feel the draught, fall on evil days, have seen better d. 801 *be poor*; go downhill, go down in the world, fall from grace, decline 655 *deteriorate*; sink 313 *founder*; come to a bad end 728 *fail*; go to rack and ruin, go to the dogs 165 *be destroyed*; go hard with, be difficult for 700 *be difficult*.

Adv. *in adversity*, from bad to worse, out of the frying pan into the fire; unfortunately, unhappily; as ill luck would have it, by mischance, by misadventure.

See: 35, 154, 159, 163, 165, 313, 377, 380, 418, 544, **616**, 645, 655, 659, 679, 700, 704, **728**, 801, **825**, 834, 872, 900, 924.

732 Averageness

N. *averageness*, mediocrity 30 *average*; golden mean, neither too much nor too little; common lot, ups and downs, mixed blessing; average circumstances, moderate c., a modest competence, enough to get by; modesty, plain living, no excess 177 *moderation*; respectability, middle class, bourgeoisie 869 *middle classes*; Main Street, suburbia, subtopia, villadom; common man, everyman, man in the street 869 *commoner*.

Adj. *middling*, average, mediocre; neither good nor bad, betwixt and between, middlebrow; ordinary, commonplace 30 *median*; common, representative 83 *typical*; nonextreme 177 *moderate*; decent, quiet 874 *modest*; not striking, undistinguished, inglorious, nothing to boast of; minor, second-rate, second best 35 *inferior*; fair, fair to middling; so-so, all right, OK, adequate; unobjectionable, tolerable, passable, fifty-fifty, much of a muchness; medium, middle, colourless, grey 625 *neutral*.

Vb. *be middling*, - mediocre etc. adj.; follow the mean 30 *average out*; pass muster 635 *suffice*; jog on, manage well enough, go on quietly, avoid excess, keep to the middle 625 *be halfway*; never set the Thames on fire; leave something to be desired 647 *be imperfect*.

See: **30**, 35, 83, 177, 625, 635, 647, 869, 874.

5.2 Social volition

Section one: General social volition

733 Authority

N. *authority*, power; powers that be, 'they', the Establishment, ruling classes 741 *master*; the Government, the Administration, Whitehall 690 *director*; right, divine r., prerogative, royal p.; dynasticism, legitimacy; law, rightful power, legal p., lawful authority 953 *legality*; legislative assembly 692 *parliament*; delegated authority, regency, committee 751 *commission*; office of authority, office, place (**see** *position of authority*); portfolio 955 *jurisdiction*; vicarious authority, power behind the throne 178 *influence*; indirect authority, patronage, prestige, credit; leadership, hegemony 689 *directorship*; ascendancy, preponderance, predominance, supremacy 34 *superiority*; pride of place, seniority, priority 64 *precedence*; majesty, royalty, kingliness, crown, kingly c. 868 *nobility*; lordliness, authoritativeness, dignity; purse strings, financial control; sea power, Admiralty, trident, Britannia; acquisition of power, succession, legitimate s., accession; seizure of power, usurpation.

governance, rule, sway, iron s., reins of government, direction, command 689 *directorship*; control, supreme c.; hold, grip, clutches 778 *retention*; domination, mastery, whip hand, effective control, reach, long arm; dominion, joint d., condominium, sovereignty, suzerainty, raj, overlordship, supremacy 34 *superiority*; reign, regnancy, regency, dynasty; foreign rule, heteronomy, empery, empire, rod of e. 745 *subjection*; imperialism, colonialism, neocolonialism; white supremacy, black power; regime, regiment, regimen; state control, statism, dirigisme, paternalism; bureaucracy, apparat, civil service, officialism, beadledom, bumbledom, red tape; Parkinson's law 197 *expansion*.

despotism, benevolent d., paternalism; one-man rule, monocracy, tyranny; dictatorship, Caesarism, tsarism, Stalinism; absolutism, autocracy, autarchy, absolute monarchy; statism, omnicompetent state, state socialism, state capitalism; dictatorship of the proletariat; totalitarianism;

police state, rule of terror 735 *brute force.*

government, direction 689 *management;* form of government, state system, polity; politics, politicking; constitutional government, constitutionalism, rule of law 953 *legality;* misgovernment 734 *anarchy;* theocracy, thearchy, priestly government, hierocracy, clericalism 985 *ecclesiasticism;* monarchy, constitutional m., monarchical government, kingship; republicanism, federalism; tribal system, tribalism; patriarchy, matriarchate; feudalism, feudality; benevolent despotism, paternalism; squirearchy, aristocracy, meritocracy, oligarchy, minority rule, elitism; gynarchy, gynocracy 373 *womankind;* gerontocracy, senatorial government; duumvirate, triumvirate; rule of wealth, plutocracy; representative government, parliamentary g., government by the ballot box, party system 708 *political party,* 605 *vote;* democracy, egalitarianism, people's rule, government of the people, by the people, for the people; democracy unlimited, demagogy, demagoguery, popular will, vox populi; majority rule, one man one vote; isocracy, pantisocracy, pluralism, collectivism, proletarianism, dictatorship of the proletariat; communism, Leninism, Marxism-L., Castroism, Maoism, Titoism; party rule, Bolshevism, Fascism, Nazism, National Socialism; committee rule, sovietism; imperium in imperio, stratocracy, army rule, military government, martial law; ochlocracy, mobocracy, mob rule, mob law; syndicalism, socialism, guild s., Fabianism, statism; bureaucracy, technocracy; self-government, autonomy, home rule 744 *independence;* puppet government 628 *instrument;* caretaker government, regency, interregnum; sphere of influence, mandate, mandated territory.

position of authority, post, place, office, high o., office of power, office of dignity; kingship, kinghood, tsardom, royalty, regality; regency, regentship, protectorship; rulership, chieftainship, sheikhdom, emirate, principate, lordship, seigniory; rajahship, sultanate, caliphate, governorship, viceroyalty; satrapy, ethnarchy; consulate, consulship, proconsulate, prefecture, tribunate, aedileship; magistrature, magistracy; mayoralty, aldermanship; headship, presidentship, presidency, premiership, chairmanship 689 *directorship;* overlordship, superintendency, inspectorship; masterdom, mastership; government post, Cabinet seat; seat of government, capital, metropolis, palace, White House, Kremlin, Number Ten, Whitehall; secretariat 687 *workshop.*

political organization, body politic; state, nation s., commonwealth; country, realm, kingdom, republic, city state, city, free c., polis; temple state; federation, confederation; principality, duchy, archduchy, dukedom, palatinate; empire, dominion, colony, dependency, protectorate, mandate, mandated territory 184 *territory;* free world, Communist bloc, Third World 184 *region;* superpower 34 *superiority;* banana republic 35 *inferiority;* buffer state 231 *interjacency;* province, county 184 *district;* body politic, corporative state, social s., welfare s.; laws, constitution.

Adj. *authoritative,* empowered, competent; in office, in authority, clothed with a., magisterial, official, ex officio; mandatory, binding, compulsory 740 *compelling;* magistral, masterful, domineering; commanding, lordly, dignified, majestic; overruling, imperious, bossy; peremptory, arbitrary, absolute, autocratic, tyrannical, dictatorial, totalitarian 735 *authoritarian;* powerful, puissant 162 *strong;* hegemonic, leading 178 *influential;* preeminent, preponderant, predominant, prepollent, dominant, paramount 34 *supreme.*

ruling, reigning, regnant, regnal; sovereign, holding the sceptre, on the throne; royal, regal, majestic, kinglike, kingly, queenly, princely, lordly; dynastic; imperial; magisterial; governing, controlling, dictating etc. vb.

governmental, gubernatorial, political, constitutional; administrative, ministerial, official, bureaucratic, centralized; technocratic; matriarchal, patriarchal; monarchical, feudal, aristocratic, oligarchic, plutocratic, democratic, popular, classless, republican; self-governing, autonomous, autarchic 744 *independent.*

Vb. *rule,* hold sway, reign, reign supreme, sit on the throne, wear the crown, wield the sceptre; govern, control 737 *command;* manage, hold the reins, hold office 689 *direct;* have a place, occupy a post, fill a p.; be in power, have authority, wield a., exercise a., exert a., use one's a.; rule absolutely, tyrannize 735 *oppress;* dictate, lay down the law; plan, give laws to, legislate for; divide and rule, Balkanize; keep order, police.

take authority, mount the throne, ascend the t., accede to the t., succeed to the t., take office, take command, assume c., take over; assume authority, form a government; gain power, get a hold on, get the whip hand, take control; seize power, get the power into one's hands, usurp, usurp the throne.

dominate, have the power, have the prestige; preponderate, turn the scale, hold all the aces 34 *predominate*; lord it over, boss, rule the roost, wear the trousers 737 *command*; have the mastery, have the upper hand, have the whip h., call the tune 727 *overmaster*; have in one's power, have over a barrel; lead by the nose, twist round one's little finger, have under one's thumb, hold in the palm of one's hand 178 *influence*; regiment, discipline, drill, drive 735 *be severe*; dictate, coerce 740 *compel*; subject to one's influence, hold down, hold under 745 *subjugate*; override, overrule, overawe; have it all one's own way, do as one wishes 744 *be free.*

be governed, have laws, have a constitution; be ruled, be swayed by, be dictated to; be under authority, owe obedience, owe fealty, owe loyalty 745 *be subject.*

Adv.*by authority,* in the name of, de par le Roi; by warrant of, in virtue of one's authority.

See:34, 35, 64, 162, 178, 184, 197, 231, 373, 605, 628, 687, 689, 690, 692, 708, 727, 734, 735, **737**, 740, **741**, 744, 745, 751, 778, 868, 953, 955, 985.

734 Laxity: absence of authority

N.*laxity,* slackness, remissness, indifference 458 *negligence*; laissez-faire 744 *scope*; informality, lack of ceremony 769 *nonobservance*; looseness, loosening, relaxation, derestriction 746 *liberation*; loose organization, unbinding, decentralization 46 *disunion*; connivance 756 *permission*; indulgence, toleration, licence, overindulgence, permissiveness 736 *leniency*; line of least resistance 721 *submission*; weak will, feeble grasp, weak administration, crumbling power 163 *weakness*; no grip, no drive, no push, inertia 175 *inertness*; no control, no restrictions, noninterference, abdication of authority, surrender of control 753 *resignation*; renunciation 621 *relinquishment*; concession 770 *compromise*; King Log.

anarchy, breakdown of law and order, no authority, writ not running; free-for-all, every man for himself; disorder, disorganization, chaos 61 *turmoil*; licence, insubordination, indiscipline 738 *disobedience*; anarchism, nihilism, antinomianism 769 *nonobservance*; interregnum, power vacuum, powerlessness 161 *impotence*; misrule, misgovernment; mob law, lynch l., reign of terror 954 *lawlessness*; defiance of authority, unauthorized power, usurpation 916 *arrogation*; dethronement, deposition, uncrowning 752 *deposal.*

Adj.*lax,* loose, slack; devolved, decentralized; disorganized, unorganized 61 *orderless*; feeble, soft 163 *weak*; crippled 163 *weakened*; slipshod, remiss 458 *negligent*; uncaring 860 *indifferent*; relaxed, unstrict, informal, not standing on ceremony; free-and-easy, happy-go-lucky 744 *unconfined*; permissive, tolerant, undemanding, easy, gentle, indulgent, overindulgent 736 *lenient*; weak-willed, weak-kneed 601 *irresolute*; unassertive, unmasterful, lacking authority, uninfluential.

anarchic, anarchical; ungoverned, uncontrolled, unbridled, unsubmissive; insubordinate 878 *insolent*; rebellious 738 *disobedient*; disorderly, unruly 738 *riotous*; unauthorized 954 *illegal*; lawless, nihilistic, anarchistic, antinomian 769 *nonobservant.*

Vb.*be lax,* not enforce; hold a loose rein, give one their head, give rope enough 744 *give scope*; waive the rules, stretch a point, connive at; tolerate, put up with, suffer; laisser faire, laisser aller 756 *permit,* let it rip 677 *notact*; let one get away with, not say boo to a goose; spoonfeed, indulge, spoil 736 *be lenient*; make concessions 770 *compromise*; relax, unbind 46 *disunite*; lose control 161 *be impotent*; renounce authority 621 *relinquish*; stand down, abdicate 753 *resign*; misrule, misgovern, mismanage, reduce to chaos 63 *derange.*

please oneself, let oneself go, indulge oneself 943 *be intemperate*; be a law unto oneself, stand in no awe of, defy authority, resist control 738 *disobey*; take on oneself, act without authority, act without instructions, act on one's own responsibility; arrogate, usurp authority 916 *be undue.*

unthrone, dethrone, uncrown, unseat, overthrow, force to resign 752 *depose*; usurp, snatch the sceptre, seize the crown.

See: 46, 61, 63, 161, 163, 175, 458, 601, 621, 677, 721, **736**, **738**, **744**, 746, 752, 753, 756, 769, 770, 860, 878, 916, 943, 954.

735 Severity

N. *severity*, no weakness, rigorousness, strictness, stringency; formalism, pedantry; high standards 862 *fastidiousness*; rigidity, inflexibility 326 *hardness*; discipline, firm control, strong hand, tight h., tight grasp 733 *authority*; rod of iron, heavy hand, Draconian laws; harshness, rigour, extremity, extremes; no concession, no compromise, letter of the law, pound of flesh; intolerance, rigorism, fanaticism, bigotry 602 *opinionatedness*; press laws, censorship, suppression 747 *restraint*; blue laws, puritanism 950 *prudery*; infliction, visitation, inquisition, persecution, exploitation, harassment, oppression, Rachmanism; spite, victimization 910 *revenge*; callousness, lack of mercy, inclemency, inexorability, no appeal 906 *pitilessness*; harsh treatment, the hard way, tender mercies, cruelty 898 *inhumanity*; self-mortification, self-denial, austerity 945 *asceticism*.

brute force, naked f.; rule of might, big battalions, gunboat diplomacy 160 *power*; coercion, bludgeoning 740 *compulsion*; bloodiness 176 *violence*; subjugation 745 *subjection*; arbitrary power, absolutism, autocracy, dictatorship 733 *despotism*; tyranny, liberticide; Fascism, Nazism, Hitlerism, Stalinism, totalitarianism; Prussianism, militarism; martial law, iron rule, iron hand, mailed fist, jackboot, bludgeon.

tyrant, rigorist, pedant, precisian, formalist, stickler, red-tapist; petty tyrant, Jack-in-office; disciplinarian, martinet, sergeant major; militarist, jackboot; hanging judge; heavy father, Dutch uncle; Big Brother, authoritarian, despot, dictator 741 *autocrat*; boss, commissar, gauleiter; inquisitor, persecutor; oppressor, bully, hard master, taskmaster, slave-driver; extortioner, bloodsucker, tax-gatherer, publican, predator, harpy; vulture, octopus; Moloch, ogre, brute 938 *monster*; hard-liner; King Stork.

Adj. *severe*, austere, Spartan 945 *ascetic*; strict, rigorous, extreme; strait-laced, puritanical, prudish; donnish, pedagogic, formalistic, pedantic; bigoted, fanatical; hypercritical 862 *fastidious*; intolerant, censorious 924 *disapproving*; unbending, rigid 326 *hard*; hard as nails, hard-headed, hard-boiled, flinty, dour; inflexible, obdurate, uncompromising 602 *obstinate*; inexorable, relentless, merciless, unsparing, implacable, unforgiving 906 *pitiless*; heavy, stern, stiff; punitive; stringent, Draconian, drastic, savage.

authoritarian, masterful, domineering, lordly, arrogant, haughty 878 *insolent*; despotic, absolute, unfettered, arbitrary; totalitarian, Fascist; dictatorial, autocratic; antidemocratic, undemocratic; coercive, imperative, compulsive 740 *compelling*; fussy, bossy, governessy.

oppressive, hard on 914 *unjust*; tyrannical, despotic; tyrannous, harsh, overharsh; grinding, withering, exigent, exacting, grasping, griping, extortionate, exploitive, predatory; persecuting, inquisitorial, searching, unsparing; high-handed, overbearing, domineering; heavy-handed, ungentle, rough, bloody 176 *violent*; brutal, ogreish 898 *cruel*.

Vb. *be severe*, - harsh, - strict etc. adj.; stand no nonsense, be cruel to be kind; exert authority, put one's foot down, discipline; bear hard on, deal hardly with, lay a heavy hand on; permit no liberties, keep a tight rein on 747 *restrain*; be down on, have a down on (**see** *oppress*); come down on, come down like a ton of bricks, crack down on, stamp on, put a stop to, clamp down on 165 *suppress*; not tolerate, persecute, hunt down 619 *pursue*; ill-treat, mishandle, abuse 675 *misuse*; treat rough, get tough with, pull no punches; inflict, visit on, visit with, chastise 963 *punish*; mete out stern punishment, wreak vengeance 910 *avenge*; exact reprisals 714 *retaliate*; strain one's authority 954 *be illegal*; be extreme, have one's pound of flesh; harden one's heart, show no mercy 906 *be pitiless*; give no quarter, put to the sword 362 *slaughter*.

oppress, tyrannize, play the tyrant, be despotic, take liberties, abuse one's authority 734 *please oneself*; assume, arrogate 916 *be undue*; domineer, lord it; overawe, intimidate, terrorize 854 *frighten*; bludgeon 740 *compel*; shove around, boss a., put upon; bully, bait, harass, plague, annoy 827 *torment*; persecute, spite, victimize 898 *be malevolent*; break, break the spirit, tame 369 *break in*; task, tax, drive 684 *fatigue*; overtax, exploit, extort, squeeze, grind, grind the faces of the poor; trample, tread down, tread underfoot, stamp on, hold down 165 *suppress*; enslave 745 *subjugate*; ride roughshod, injure, inflict injustice 914 *do wrong*; misgovern, misrule; rule with a rod of iron; whip, scourge, rack, put the screws on 963 *torture*; shed blood, dye with b. 362 *murder*; be heavy, weigh on, burden, crush 322 *weigh*.

Adv. *severely*, sternly, strictly etc. adj.; tyrannically, despotically, arbitrarily; high-handedly, heavy-handedly; cruelly, mercilessly.

See: 160, 165, 176, 322, 326, 362, 369, 602, 619, 675, 684, 714, 733, 734, **740**, **741**, 745, 747, 827, 854, 862, 878, 898, **906**, 910, 914, 916, 924, 938, 945, 950, 954, 963.

736 Leniency

N. *leniency*, softness 734 *laxity*; mildness, gentleness, tenderness; forbearance, soft answer 823 *patience*; pardon 909 *forgiveness*; quarter, mercy, lenity, clemency, mercifulness, compassion 905 *pity*; humanity, kindness 897 *benevolence*; favour, sop, concession; indulgence, toleration; sufferance, allowance, leave 756 *permission*; connivance, complaisance; justice with mercy 177 *moderation*; light rein, light hand, velvet glove, kid gloves; wet, liberal, soggy l.

Adj. *lenient*, soft, gentle, mild, mild as milk; indulgent, tolerant; conniving, complaisant; easy, easy-going, low-pressure, undemanding 734 *lax*; forbearing, longsuffering 823 *patient*; clement, merciful 909 *forgiving*; tender 905 *pitying*; too soft, overmerciful.

Vb. *be lenient*, show consideration, make no demands, make few d.; deal gently, handle tenderly, go easy, pull one's punches, temper the wind to the shorn lamb 177 *moderate*; featherbed, spoonfeed, spoil, indulge, humour 889 *pet*; gratify, favour 925 *flatter*; tolerate, allow, connive 756 *permit*; stretch a point 734 *be lax*; concede 758 *consent*; not press, refrain, forbear 823 *be patient*; pity, spare, give quarter 905 *show mercy*; pardon 909 *forgive*; amnesty 506 *forget*; relax, humanize 897 *be benevolent*.

See: 177, 506, **734**, 756, 758, 823, 889, 897, **905**, 909, 925.

737 Command

N. *command*, royal c., invitation, summons; commandment, ordinance; injunction, imposition; dictation, bidding, behest, hest, will and pleasure; dictum, say-so 532 *affirmation*; charge, commission, appointment 751 *mandate*; instructions, rules, regulations; brief 524 *information*; directive, order, order of the day, marching orders; word of command, word; beck, nod, sign 547 *gesture*; signal, bugle call, trumpet c. 547 *call*; whip, three-line w.; categorical imperative, dictate 740 *compulsion*; negative command, taboo, ban, embargo, proscription 757 *prohibition*; countermand, counterorder 752 *abrogation*.

decree, edict, fiat, ukase, firman, ipse dixit; law, canon, rescript, prescript 693 *precept*; bull, papal decree, decretal; circular, encyclical; ordinance, order in council; decree nisi, decree absolute; decision, placet, senatus consultum 480 *judgment*; enactment, act 953 *legislation*; plebiscite, electoral mandate 605 *vote*; dictate, diktat, dictation.

demand, demand as of right, claim, revendication 915 dueness; requisition 761 *request*; notice, warning n., final n., final demand, ultimatum; blackmail 900 *threat*; imposition, exaction, levy, tax demand 809 *tax*.

warrant, search w., commission, brevet, authorization, written authority, letters patent, passport 756 *permit*; writ, summons, subpoena, citation, mandamus, habeas corpus 959 *legal process*.

Adj. *commanding*, imperative, imperatival, categorical, dictatorial; jussive, mandatory, obligatory, peremptory, compulsive 740 *compelling*; decretory, decretal; exacting obedience 733 *authoritative*; decisive, conclusive, final; demanding, insistent, clamant, vocal.

Vb. *command*, bid, invite; order, tell, issue a command, give an order, send an o.; signal, call, nod, beck, motion, sign, make a s. 547 *gesticulate*; wink, tip the wink 524 *hint*; direct, give a directive, instruct, brief, circularize, send round instructions; rule, lay down, enjoin; give a mandate, charge, call upon 751 *commission*; impose, lay upon, set a task, make obligatory 917 *impose a duty*; detail, tell off; call together, convene 74 *bring together*; send for, summon; cite, subpoena, issue a writ 959 *litigate*; send back, remand; dictate, enforce obedience, put one's foot down 740 *compel*; countermand 752 *abrogate*; lay an embargo, ban, taboo, proscribe 757 *prohibit*.

decree, pass a d., sign a d., pass an order in council, issue a ukase; promulgate 528 *proclaim*; declare, say, say so, lay down the law 532 *affirm*; signify one's will and pleasure, prescribe, ordain, appoint 608 *predetermine*; enact, make law, pass a l., legislate 953 *make legal*; pass judgment, give j., rule, give a ruling 480 *judge*.

demand, require, requisition 627 *require*; order, order up, indent 761 *request*; make demands on, send a final demand, give final notice, present an ultimatum, demand with threats, blackmail 900 *threaten*; present one's claim, make claims upon, revendicate, reclaim 915 *claim*; demand payment, dun, bill, invoice; charge 809 *price*; exact, levy 809 *tax*.

Adv. *commandingly*, imperatively, categorically, authoritatively; at the word of command.

See: 74, 480, 524, 528, 532, 547, 605, 608, 627, 693, **733**, 740, 751, 752, 756, 757, **761**, 809, 900, 915, 917, 953, 959.

738 Disobedience

N. *disobedience*, indiscipline, unbiddableness, refractoriness 598 *unwillingness*; naughtiness, misbehaviour, mischief-making, monkey tricks; delinquency 934 *wickedness*; insubordination, mutinousness, mutineering; refusal to obey orders, defiance of o. 711 *defiance*; disregard of orders, noncompliance 769 *nonobservance*; disloyalty, defection, desertion 918 *undutifulness*; violation of orders, violation of the law, infraction, infringement, criminality, crime, sin 936 *guilty act*; noncooperation, civil disobedience, passive resistance 715 *resistance*; conscientious objection 704 *opposition*; obstructionism 702 *hindrance*; murmuring, restlessness 829 *discontent*; seditiousness, sansculottism (**see** *sedition*); wildness 954 *lawlessness*; banditry, mafia 788 *brigandage*.

revolt, mutiny; direct action 145 *strike*; faction 709 *dissension*; breakaway, secession 978 *schism*; defection 603 *tergiversation*; explosive situation, restlessness, restiveness 318 *agitation*; sabotage, wrecking activities 165 *destruction*; breach of the peace, disturbance, disorder, riot, street r., rioting, gang warfare, streetfighting, émeute, tumult, barricades 61 *turmoil*; rebellion, insurrection, rising, uprising 176 *outbreak*; putsch, coup d'état; resistance movement, insurgency 715 *resistance*; subversion 149 *revolution*; terrorism 954 *lawlessness*; civil war 718 *war*; regicide, tyrannicide 362 *homicide*.

sedition, seditiousness; agitation, cabal, intrigue 623 *plot*; agitprop, subversion, infiltration, fifth-columnism; underground activities 523 *latency*; terrorism, anarchism, nihilism; treasonable activities, disloyalty, treason, high t., lese-majesty 930 *perfidy*.

revolter, awkward person, difficult character, handful 700 *difficulty*; naughty child, scamp, scapegrace, little monkey 938 *bad person*; mutineer, rebel, frondeur; demonstrator, striker 705 *opponent*; secessionist, seceder, splinter group 978 *schismatic*; Titoist, deviationist, dissident 829 *malcontent*; blackleg, scab, nonstriker 84 *nonconformist*; independent, maverick, lone wolf; seditionary, seditionist; traitor, quisling, fifth columnist 603 *tergiversator*; tyrannicide, regicide; insurrectionist, insurgent; guerrilla, partisan; resistance, underground, Maquis; Black Panther, Black Muslim, Rastafarian, Rasta; Provisional, Provo; extremist, Jacobin,sansculotte, carbonaro, Bolshevist, Trotskyist, Red, red republican 149 *revolutionist*; counter-revolutionary, reactionary, monarchist, White Russian, chouan; terrorist, anarchist, nihilist; mafia, bandit 789 *robber*; rebel against all laws, antinomian.

agitator, disruptive influence, agent provocateur; protester, demonstrator, counterdemonstrator, marcher; tub-thumper, ranter, rabble-rouser, demagogue; firebrand, mischief-maker 663 *troublemaker*; seditionist, sedition-monger; Red, communist, commie, bolshie; suffragette, women's libber; Digger, Leveller; ringleader, Spartacus, Wat Tyler, Jack Cade, John Brown, Young Turk.

rioter, street r., brawler, rowdy 904 *ruffian*; saboteur, wrecker, Luddite; secret society, Ku Klux Klan.

Adj. *disobedient*, undisciplined, badly disciplined; disobeying, naughty, mischievous, misbehaving; unfilial, undaughterly; unbiddable, awkward, difficult, self-willed, wayward, restive, impatient of control, vicious, unruly, unmanageable 176 *violent*; intractable, ungovernable 598 *unwilling*; insubordinate, mutinous, rebellious, bolshie, bloody-minded; contrary 704 *opposing*; nonconformist 84 *unconformable*; unsubmissive, recusant, uncomplying, uncompliant 769 *nonobservant*; recalcitrant 715 *resisting*; challenging 711 *defiant*; refractory, perverse, froward 602 *obstinate*; subversive, revolutionary, reactionary; seditious, troublemaking; traitorous, disloyal 918 *undutiful*; antinomian 734 *anarchic*; gate-crashing, intrusive, uninvited, unbidden; wild, untamed, feral, savage.

riotous, rioting, out of control; anarchic, tumultuary, rumbustious, rowdy, unruly, wild, rackety 61 *disorderly*; law-breaking 954 *lawless*; mutinous, insurrectionary, rebellious, in rebellion, up in arms 715 *resisting*.

Vb. *disobey*, not obey, not listen; be disobedient, misbehave, get into mischief; flout authority, not comply with 769 *not observe*; not do as one is told, disobey orders, show insubordination 711 *defy*; defy the whip, cross-vote; snap one's fingers, fly in the face of 704 *oppose*; set the law at defiance, break the law, commit a crime 954 *be illegal*; violate, infringe, transgress, trespass 306 *encroach*; turn restive, kick, chafe, fret, champ at the bit, play up; kick over the traces, take the bit between one's teeth, bolt, take French leave, take the law into one's own hands, be a law unto oneself 734 *please oneself*.

revolt, rebel, mutiny; down tools, strike, come out 145 *cease*; sabotage 702 *obstruct*; undermine, work underground; secede, break away 978 *schismatize*; betray 603 *tergiversate*; agitate, demonstrate, protest 762 *deprecate*; kick up a stink, raise Cain, start a riot, stage a revolt, lead a rebellion 715 *resist*; rise, rise up, rise in arms, throw off the yoke, renounce allegiance, fight for independence 746 *achieve liberty*; overthrow, upset 149 *revolutionize*.

See: 61, 84, 145, 149, 165, 176, 306, 318, 362, 523, **598**, 602, 603, 623, 663, 700, 702, **704**, 705, 709, 711, **715**, 718, 734, 746, 762, 769, 788, 789, 829, 904, 918, 930, 934, 936, 938, 954, 978.

739 Obedience

N. *obedience*, compliance 768 *observance*; goodness, meekness, biddability, tractability, pliancy, malleability 327 *softness*; readiness 597 *willingness*; nonresistance, submissiveness, acquiescence 721 *submission*; passiveness, passivity 679 *inactivity*; dutifulness, morale, discipline 917 *duty*; deference, obsequiousness, slavishness 879 *servility*; tameness, docility; dumb driven cattle 742 *slave*.

loyalty, constancy, devotion, fidelity, faithfulness, good faith 929 *probity*; allegiance, fealty, homage, service, deference, submission; vote of confidence.

Adj. *obedient*, complying, compliant, cooperating, conforming 768 *observant*; loyal, leal, faithful, true-blue, steadfast, constant; devoted, dedicated, sworn; offering homage, submissive 721 *submitting*; law-abiding 717 *peaceful*; complaisant, amenable, docile; good, well-behaved; filial, daughterly; ready 597 *willing*; acquiescent, resigned, unresisting, nonresisting, passive 679 *inactive*; meek, biddable, dutiful, under discipline; at one's beck and call, at one's orders, on a string, on a lead, under control; disciplined, regimented 917 *obliged*; trained, manageable, tame; respectful, deferential, subservient, obsequious, slavish 879 *servile*.

Vb. *obey*, comply, do to order, act upon 768 *observe*; sign on the dotted line, toe the l., come to heel 83 *conform*; assent 758 *consent*; listen, hearken, heed, mind, obey orders, attend to instructions, do as one is told; observe discipline, wait for the word of command; hold oneself ready, put oneself at one's service 597 *be willing*; answer the helm, obey the rein; obey the whip, vote to order, follow the party line; do one's bidding, come at one's call, wait upon, follow, follow to the world's end 742 *serve*; be loyal, owe loyalty, bear allegiance, pay homage, offer h. 768 *keep faith*; be under, pay tribute 745 *be subject*; know one's duty 917 *do one's duty*; make oneself useful, do Trojan service 703 *minister to*; yield, defer to, bow, bend, stoop, be submissive 721 *submit*; grovel, cringe 879 *be servile*; play second fiddle 35 *be inferior*.

Adv. *obediently*, submissively etc. adj.; under orders, to order, as ordered, in obedience to; yours to command, at your service.

See: 35, 83, 327, 597, 679, 703, 717, **721**, **742**, 745, 758, **768**, 879, 917, 929.

740 Compulsion

N. *compulsion*, spur of necessity 596 *necessity*; law of nature 953 *law*; act of God, force majeure; moral compulsion 917 *conscience*; Hobson's choice 606 *no choice*; dictation, coercion, regimentation; arm-twisting, blackmail 900 *threat*; negative compulsion 747 *restraint*; sanction, sanctions 963 *penalty*; enforcement, constraint, duress, force, main force, physical f.; right of the stronger, mailed fist, big stick, bludgeon, strong arm, strongarm tactics 735 *brute force*; force-feeding; impressment, pressgang, conscription, call-up, draft 718 *war measures*; exaction, extortion 786 *taking*; slavery, corvée, forced labour, labour camp 745 *servitude*; command performance 737 *command*.

Adj. *compelling*, compulsive, involuntary, of necessity, unavoidable, inevitable 596 *necessary*; imperative, dictatorial, peremptory 737 *commanding*; compulsory, mandatory, binding 917 *obligatory*; urgent, pressing; overriding, constraining, coercive; omnipotent, irresistible, not to be trifled with 160 *powerful*; forcible, forceful, cogent; high-pressure, sledgehammer, strongarm, bludgeoning 735 *oppressive*.

Vb. *compel*, constrain, coerce 176 *force*; enforce, put into force; dictate, necessitate, oblige, bind; order 737 *command*; impose 917 *impose a duty*; make one, leave no option; leave no escape, pin down, tie d.; impress, draft, conscript; drive, dragoon, regiment, discipline; force one's hand, bulldoze, steamroller, railroad, pressgang, bully into; bludgeon 735 *oppress*; take by force, requisition, commandeer, extort, exact, wring from, drag f. 786 *take*; apply pressure, lean on, squeeze, turn the heat on, put the screws on, twist one's arm 963 *torture*; blackmail, hijack, hold to ransom 900 *threaten*; be peremptory, insist, make a point of, press, urge 532 *emphasize*; brook no denial, not take no for an answer 532 *affirm*; compel to accept, force upon, ram down one's throat, inflict, foist, fob off on; force-feed; hold back 747 *restrain*.

Adv. *by force*, perforce, compulsorily, of necessity, on compulsion, under pressure, under protest, under duress, nolens volens; forcibly, by force majeure, by main force; vi et armis; at the sword's point, at gunpoint.

See: 160, 176, 532, **596**, 606, 718, **735**, **737**, 745, 747, 786, 900, 917, 953, 963.

741 Master

N. *master*, mistress; master *or* mistress of, captor, possessor 776 *owner*; sire, lord, lady, dame; liege, lord, lord paramount, overlord, lord's lord, suzerain; protector 707 *patron*; seigneur, lord of the manor, squire, laird 868 *aristocrat*; lord and master, man of the house 372 *male*; lady of the house, landlady 373 *lady*; senator, oligarch, plutocrat; sir, madam 870 *title*; goodman, goodwife; patriarch, matriarch 169 *parentage*; senior, head, principal, provost 34 *superior*; schoolmaster *or* -mistress 537 *teacher*; president, chairperson, speaker 690 *director*; employer, captain of industry, capitalist, boss, governor, guvnor, guv 690 *manager*; leader, caudillo, duce, führer (**see** *autocrat*); cock of the walk, lords of creation 638 *bigwig*; ruling class, ruling party, dominant interest, vested i., the Establishment; the authorities, principalities and powers, the powers that be, 'them', Westminster, the Government, Whitehall, Pentagon 733 *government*; staff, High Command 689 *directorship*.

autocrat, absolute ruler, absolute monarch; despot, tyrant, dictator, duce, führer, Big Brother; tycoon, boss, shogun, Great Cham 638 *bigwig*; petty tyrant, satrap, gauleiter, commissar, Jack-in-office, tin god, little Hitler 690 *official*.

sovereign, suzerain, crowned head, anointed king *or* queen; Majesty, Highness, Royal H., Excellency; dynasty, house, royal h., royal line, royal blood; royalty, monarch, king, queen, Rex, Regina; divine king, Pharaoh, Inca; imperator, emperor, empress; Caesar, Kaiser, Kaiserin, Tsar *or* Czar, Tsarina *or* Czarina, Tsarevitch *or* Czarevich; prince, princess, Infante, Infanta, Dauphin, Prince of Wales, Crown Prince *or* Princess, Great King, King of Kings, Padishah, Shah, Sophy; khan, Great Khan; Celestial Emperor; Mikado; Mogul, Sultan, Sultana; Negus, Prester John; pope, pontiff, Dalai Lama, Aga Khan; caliph, Commander of the Faithful.

potentate, dynast, ruler; chief, chieftain, headman, induna, cacique, sachem, sagamore, sheikh; prince, pendragon, princeling, rajah, rani, maharajah, maharani; emir, sirdar, sherif; nawab, begum; archduke, duke, duchess, burgrave, margrave, margravine, Palatine, Elector, Electress; regent, Prince Regent.

governor, military g., lieutenant-g., High Commissioner, Governor-General, Crown Representative, viceroy, vicereine, khedive; proconsul, satrap, hetman, stadholder, ethnarch, tetrarch; grand vizier, bey, pasha, bashaw; ecclesiastical governor, Prince Bishop; exarch, eparch, patriarch, metropolitan, archbishop, cardinal 986 *ecclesiarch*; imam, ayatollah 690 *leader*.

officer, person in office, p. in authority; functionary, mandarin, nabob, bureaucrat, apparatchik 690 *official*; civil servant, public s. 742 *servant*; gauleiter, commissar; chief officer, prime minister, grand vizier, vizier, wazir, dewan, chancellor, vice-c., Pooh-Bah; constable, marshal, seneschal, warden; burgomaster, mayor, Lord M., Lady M., mayoress, alderman, provost, bailie, city father, councillor; dignitary, local worthy 866 *person of repute*; sheriff, bailiff; justice, justice of the peace, alcalde, hakim 957 *judge*; magistrate, chief m., archon, podestà; president, doge; consul, proconsul, praetor, quaestor, aedile; prefect, intendant, district officer; commissioner, deputy c.; revenue officer, collector, headman; lictor, mace-bearer, beadle, bedel; process-server, pursuivant, tipstaff 955 *law officer*; sexton, verger 986 *church officer*; courier 529 *messenger*; party official, whip.

naval officer, Sea Lord; admiral of the fleet, admiral, vice-a., rear-a., commodore, captain, commander, lieutenant-c., lieutenant, flag-l., sub-l., petty officer, leading seaman 270 *nautical personnel*; trierarch, navarch.

army officer, staff, High Command, staff officer, brass hat; commissioned officer, brevet o.; marshal, field m., commander-in-chief, seraskier, generalissimo, general, lieutenant-g., major-g.; brigadier, colonel, lieutenant-c., major, captain, lieutenant, second l., subaltern; ensign, cornet; warrant officer, noncommissioned o., NCO, sergeant major, company s. m., staff s., colour s., sergeant, corporal, lance corporal; adjutant, aide-de-camp, quartermaster, orderly officer; imperator, military tribune, legate, centurion, decurion, vexillary; chiliarch, hipparch; subahdar 722 *soldiery*; war minister, warlord, commanding officer, commander, commandant; military rank 27 *degree*.

air officer, marshal of the air force, air marshal, air commodore, group captain, wing commander, squadron leader, flight lieutenant, flying officer, pilot o., warrant o., flight sergeant 722 *air force*.

See: 27, 34, 169, 270, 372, 373, 529, 537, **638**, 689, **690**, 707, 722, **733**, 742, 776, 866, 868, 870, 955, 957, 986.

742 Servant

N. *servant*, public s., civil s. 690 *official*; unpaid servant, fag, slave; general servant, factotum, chief cook and bottle washer 678 *busy person*; humble servant, menial; orderly, attendant; verger 986 *church officer*; subordinate, underling, understrapper 35 *inferior*; subaltern, helper, assistant, secretary, right-hand man 703 *aider*; paid servant, mercenary, hireling, employee, hand, hired man; odd-job man, handyman, labourer, peon 686 *worker*; hewer of wood and drawer of water, hack, drudge, dogsbody, erk; farmhand 370 *farmer*; shepherd, cowherd, milkmaid 369 *herdsman*; shop assistant 793 *seller*; steward, stewardess, cabin boy; waiter, waitress, head waiter, wine w.; bartender, barman, barmaid, pot boy, tapster 192 *tavern*; stableman, ostler, groom, stable boy *or* lad, postilion; errand boy, messenger, runner 529 *courier*; doorman, commissionaire, janitor, concierge 264 *doorkeeper*; porter, night p.; caddie 273 *bearer*; callboy, page boy, bellboy, bellhop, buttons; boots, sweeper 648 *cleaner*; caretaker, housekeeper (**see** *domestic*); occasional servant, help, daily, char, charwoman, cleaning lady; universal aunt; baby-sitter; nurse, nursemaid 749 *keeper*; companion, confidante.

domestic, staff; servant's hall 686 *personnel*; servitor, domestic servant, general s., manservant, man, serving m.; footman, flunkey, lackey; servant girl, abigail, maid, maidservant, handmaid, parlour maid, housemaid, chambermaid, femme de chambre; domestic drudge, maid of all work, tweeny, skivvy, slavey; kitchen maid, scullery m., dairy m., laundry m.; kitchen boy, turnspit, scullion, washer-up, housekeeper, butler, cook; steward, chaplain, governess, tutor, nurse, nanny; personal servant, body s., page, squire, valet, gentleman's gentleman, batman; lady's maid, waiting woman; nursemaid, ayah, amah, bonne, au pair; gyp, scout, bed-maker; outdoor staff, gardener, under-g., groom; coachman, chauffeur 268 *driver*.

retainer, follower, following, suite, train, cortege 67 *retinue*; court, courtier; attendant, usher, gillie; bodyguard, housecarl, henchman, squire, page, page of honour, donzel, armour-bearer, shield-b., train-b.; household staff, majordomo, chamberlain, equerry, steward, bailiff, castellan, chatelain, seneschal; chatelaine, housekeeper; cellarer, butler, cup-bearer; chaplain, beadsman; lady-in-waiting, companion, confidante; governess, nurse, nanny 749 *keeper*.

dependant, clientèle, client; hanger-on, parasite, satellite, camp follower, creature, jackal, âme damnée 284 *follower*; stooge, puppet 628 *instrument*; subordinate 35 *inferior*; minion, myrmidon, lackey, flunkey (**see** *domestic*); man, henchman, liegeman, vassal; pensioner, beadsman; apprentice, protégé(e), ward, charge, nursling, foster child.

subject, state s., national, citizen 191 *native*; liege, vassal; people, citizenry 869 *commonalty*; subject population, dependency, colony, satellite.

slave, thrall, bondman, bondwoman, bondmaid, slave girl; helot, helotry, hewer of wood and drawer of water; serf, ascriptus glebae, villein; galley slave, wage s., sweated labour 686 *worker*; hierodule, temple prostitute; odalisque, eunuch; chattel, puppet, pawn; machine, robot 628 *instrument*; captive, chaingang 750 *prisoner*.

Adj. *serving*, ministering, fagging 703 *aiding*; in service, in domestic s., menial; working, in employment, on the payroll; on the staff, in the train of; at one's beck and call 739 *obedient*; unfree, unfranchised, unprivileged; in servitude, in slavery, in captivity, in bonds 745 *subject*.

Vb. *serve*, be in service, wait upon, wait on hand and foot 703 *minister to*; live in, be on hand 89 *accompany*; attend upon, follow 739 *obey*; tend, squire, valet, dress; char, do chores, do for, oblige; fag for, dogsbody for, do service, make oneself useful 640 *be useful*; work for 622 *function*.

See: 35, 67, 89, 191, 192, 264, 268, 273, 284, 369, 370, 529, 622, 628, 640, **648**, 678, **686**, **690**, 703, 739, **745**, 749, 750, 793, 869, 986.

743 Badge of rule

N. *regalia*, royal trappings, emblem of royalty, insignia of r.; crown, kingly c., orb, sceptre; coronet, tiara, diadem; rod of empire, sword of state 733 *authority*; robe of state, coronation robes, royal robe; ermine, royal purple; throne, peacock t., royal seat, seat of kings; ensign 547 *flag*; royal standard, royal arms 547 *heraldry*; lion, eagle, fleur-de-lis; Prince of Wales's feathers; uraeus.

badge of rule, emblem of authority, staff, wand, wand of office, verge, rod, Black Rod, baton, truncheon, gavel; herald's wand, caduceus; signet, seal, privy s., keys, ring; sword of state, sword of justice, mace, fasces, axes; pastoral staff, crosier; ankh, ansate cross; woolsack, chair, bench; sartorial insignia, triple crown, mitre, bishop's hat, cardinal's hat., shovel h., biretta; bishop's apron, gaiters 989 *canonicals*; judge's cap, black c. 961 *condemnation*; peer's cap, cap of maintenance, cap of dignity; robe, mantle, toga.

badge of rank, sword, belt, sash, spurs, cocked hat, epaulette, tab 547 *badge*; uniform 547 *livery*; brass, star, pips, crown, crossed batons; gold braid, scrambled egg; chevron, stripe, anchor, curl, brassard, armlet; garter, order 729 *decoration*.

See: **547**, 729, 733, 961, 989.

744 Freedom

N. *freedom*, liberty, being at large; freedom of action, initiative; free will 595 *will*; free thought, free speech, freedom of the press, academic f., the four freedoms; rights, civil rights, equal r. 915 *dueness*; privilege, prerogative, exemption, immunity, diplomatic i. 919 *nonliability*; liberalism, libertarianism, latitudinarianism; licence, artistic l.; excess of freedom, indiscipline 738 *disobedience*; free love 951 *illicit love*; laisser faire, noninterference, nonintervention; noninvolvement, neutralism 860 *indifference*; nonalignment, cross benches; isolationism, isolation, splendid i. 883 *seclusion*; emancipation, setting free 746 *liberation*; women's liberation, women's lib; gay l.; enfranchisement, naturalization, citizenship; franchise, secret ballot 605 *vote*.

independence, freedom of action, unilaterality; freedom of choice 605 *choice*; no allegiance, floating vote; freedom of thought, emancipation, bohemianism 84 *nonconformity*; unmarried state, bachelorhood 895 *celibacy*; individualism, self-expression, individuality 80 *speciality*; self-determination, statehood, nationhood, national status 371 *nation*; autonomy, autarchy, self-government, self-rule, home r.; autarky, self-sufficiency 635 *sufficiency*; freehold 777 *property*; independent means, competence 800 *wealth*.

scope, free s., full s., play, free p., full p. 183 *range*; swing, rope, long r.; manoeuvrability, leverage; field, room, living r., lebensraum, living space, elbowroom, searoom, wide berth, leeway, margin, clearance 183 *room*; latitude, liberty, Liberty Hall; permissive society; informality, unconstraint; fling, licence, excess 734 *laxity*; one's head, one's own way, one's own devices; ball at one's feet 137 *opportunity*; facilities, the run of, free hand, blank cheque, carte blanche; free-for-all, free field, free enterprise, free trade, free port, free market, open m., free-trade area; open country, high seas.

free person, freeman, burgess, burgher, citizen, free c., voter; no slave, ex-slave, freedman, freedwoman; ex-convict, released prisoner; escapee 667 *escaper*; free agent, freelance; independent, crossbencher; isolationist, neutral 625 *moderate*; free-trader; freethinker, latitudinarian, liberal; libertarian, Bohemian, individualist 84 *nonconformist*; lone wolf 883 *solitary*.

Adj. *free*, freeborn, enfranchised; heart-whole, fancy-free; scot-free 960 *acquitted*; on the loose, at large 667 *escaped*; released, freed 746 *liberated*; free as air, free as the wind, free as a bird; footloose, go-as-you-please, ranging 267 *travelling*; ranging freely, having full play (**see** *unconfined*); licensed, chartered, privileged 756 *permitted*; exempt, immune 919 *nonliable*; free-speaking, plain-spoken 573 *plain*; free-thinking, emancipated, broad, broadminded, latitudinarian (**see** *independent*); unbiased, unprejudiced, independent, uninfluenced 913 *just*; free and easy, all things to all men 882 *sociable*; loose, licentious, unbridled, incontinent, wanton 951 *impure*; at leisure, out of harness, retired; relaxed, unbuttoned, at home, at ease 681 *leisurely*; free of cost, gratis, unpaid for 812 *uncharged*; unclaimed, going begging 860 *unwanted*; free for all, unreserved 289 *accessible*.

unconfined, uncribbed, uncabined, untrammelled, unshackled, unfettered, unbridled, uncurbed, unchained, unbound, unmuzzled; unchecked, unrestrained, unregulated, ungoverned; unprevented, unhindered, unimpeded, unobstructed; uninhibited, informal, dégagé(e), casual, freewheeling; free-range, wandering, random; left to one's own devices.

independent, unnecessitated, uncontrolled; uninduced, unilateral 609 *spontaneous*; unforced, uncompelled, uninfluenced; unattached, detached 860 *indifferent*; free to choose, uncommitted, uninvolved; nonpartisan, unaffiliated 625 *neutral*; isolationist 883 *unsociable*; unvanquished, unconquered, unconquerable, irrepressible 727 *unbeaten*; enjoying liberty, unsubjected, unenslaved, not discriminated against; autonomous, autarchic, self-governing, self-ruling; autarkic, self-sufficient, self-supporting, self-contained, self-motivated, inner-directed; self-reliant, one's own master; ungoverned, masterless, owning no master, ungovernable 734 *anarchic*; self-employed, one's own boss, free-lance; unofficial, cowboy, wildcat; free-minded, free-spirited, free-souled; single, bachelor 895 *unwedded*; individualistic, unconventional 84 *unconformable*; breakaway 489 *dissenting*.

unconditional, unconditioned, without strings, no strings attached; catch-as-catch-can, free-for-all, no holds barred; unrestricted, unlimited, absolute; open, wide open; discretionary, arbitrary; freehold, allodial.

Vb. *be free*, enjoy liberty; go free, get f., save oneself 667 *escape*; take French leave 738 *disobey*; have the run of, be free of, have the freedom of, range, have scope, have play, have a free hand, have elbowroom; have plenty of rope, have one's head; feel at home, make oneself at home; feel free, be oneself, let oneself go, let it all hang out, let one's hair down 683 *repose*; have one's fling, have one's way, have it one's own w., cut loose, drop out, do as one likes *or* chooses 734 *please oneself*; follow one's bent, do one's own thing; go as you please, drift, wander, roam 282 *stray*; go one's own way, go it alone, shift for oneself, fend for oneself, paddle one's own canoe, stand alone; have a will of one's own 595 *will*; have a free mind, be independent, call no man master, be one's own man; stand up for one's rights, defy the whip, cross-vote 711 *defy*; stand on one's own feet, be self-sufficient, ask no favours 635 *suffice*; take liberties, make free with, presume, presume on 878 *be insolent*; dare, venture, make bold to, permit oneself.

give scope, allow initiative, give one his *or* her head, allow full play, give free rein to, allow enough rope 734 *be lax*; give a free hand, give the run of 701 *facilitate*; release, set free, enfranchise 746 *liberate*; let, license, charter 756 *permit*; let alone, not interfere, live and let live, laisser aller, laisser faire; leave one to his *or* her own devices; leave it open, leave to one's own choice; keep the door open.

Adv. *freely*, liberally, ad libitum, at will.

See: 80, 84, 137, 183, 267, 282, 289, 371, 489, 573, 595, 605, 609, 625, 635, 667, 681, 683, 701, 711, 727, **734**, 738, **746**, 756, 777, 800, 812, 860, 878, 882, 883, 895, 913, 915, 919, 951, 960.

745 Subjection

N. *subjection*, subordination; subordinate position, inferior rank, cadetship, juniority, inferior status, satellite s. 35 *inferiority*; creaturehood; dependence, tutelage, guardianship, wardship, apron strings, leading s.; apprenticeship 536 *learning*; mutual dependence, symbiosis 12 *correlation*; subjecthood, allegiance, nationality, citizenship; subjugation, conquest, colonialism; loss of freedom, disfranchisement, enslavement 721 *submission*; constraint, discipline 747 *restraint*; oppression 735 *severity*; yoke 748 *fetter*; slavishness 879 *servility*.

service, domestic s., government s., employ, employment; servitorship, flunkeydom, flunkeyism 739 *obedience*; tribute, suit and service; vassalage, feudality, feudalism 739 *loyalty*; compulsory service, corvée, forced labour 740 *compulsion*; conscription 718 *war measures*.

servitude, involuntary s., slavery, abject s.; enslavement, captivity, thraldom, bondage, yoke; helotry, helotism, serfdom, villeinage, peonage.

Adj. *subjected*, dominated etc. vb.; subjugated, overborne, overwhelmed 728 *defeated*; subdued, pacified; taken prisoner, deprived of freedom, in chains 747 *restrained*; discriminated against, underprivileged, disfranchised; colonized, enslaved, reduced to slavery, sold into s.; in harness 742 *serving*; under the yoke, under the heel; oppressed, downtrodden, underfoot; treated like dirt, henpecked, browbeaten; the sport of, the plaything of, kicked around like a football; regimented, planned; brought to heel, quelled, domesticated 369 *tamed*; eating out of one's hand, submissive 721 *submitting*; subservient, slavish 879 *servile*.

subject, unfree, not independent, unfranchised, unprivileged; satellite, satellitic; bond, bound, tributary, colonial; owing service, owing fealty, liege, vassal, feudal, feudatory 739 *obedient*; under, subordinate, of lower rank, junior, cadet 35 *inferior*; dependent, in chancery, in statu pupillari; tied to one's apron strings; subject to, liable to, exposed to 180 *liable*; a slave to 610 *habituated*; in the hands of, in the clutches of, under the control of, in the power of, at the mercy of, under the sway of, under one's thumb; not able to call one's soul one's own; having no say in, voiceless; parasitical, hanging on 879 *servile*; paid, in the pay of; encumbranced, mortgaged 917 *obliged*.

Vb. *be subject*, live under, own the sway of, pay tribute, be under 739 *obey*; obey the whip, vote to order; depend on, lean on, hang on 35 *be inferior*; be a doormat, let oneself be trampled on, let oneself be kicked around; serve, live in subjection, be a slave; lose one's independence 721 *submit*; pawn, mortgage 780 *assign*; sacrifice one's freedom, have no will of one's own, be a tool 628 *be instrumental*; cringe, fawn 879 *be servile*.

subjugate, subdue, reduce, subject 727 *overmaster*; colonize, annex, mediatize; take captive, lead in triumph, drag at one's chariot wheels 727 *triumph*; take, capture, lead captive, lay one's yoke upon, reduce to servitude, enslave, sell into slavery; fetter, bind, hold in bondage 747 *imprison*;

rob of freedom, disfranchise; trample on, tread on, treat like dirt 735 *oppress*; keep under, keep down, hold d., repress, sit on, stamp out 165 *suppress*; enthral, captivate 821 *impress*; enchant 983 *bewitch*; dominate, lead by the nose 178 *influence*; discipline, regiment; tame, quell 369 *break in*; have eating out of one's hand, bring to heel, have at one's beck and call; make one's plaything, do what one likes with 673 *dispose of*.

See: 12, **35**, 165, 178, 180, 369, 536, 610, 628, 673, 718, 721, 727, 728, **735**, 739, 740, **742**, **747**, **748**, 780, 821, 879, 917, 983.

746 Liberation

N. *liberation*, setting free, unshackling, unbinding, release, discharge 960 *acquittal*; free expression, abreaction, catharsis 818 *feeling*; unravelling, extrication, disinvolvement 46 *separation*; riddance, good r. 831 *relief*; rescue, redemption, salvation, moksha 668 *deliverance*; manumission, emancipation, enfranchisement; parole, bail; liberalization, relaxation (of control) 734 *laxity*; decontrol, derationing 752 *abrogation*; demobilization, disbandment 75 *dispersion*; forgiveness of sins, absolution 909 *forgiveness*; acquittance, deed of release, quittance, quitclaim.

Adj. *liberated*, rescued, delivered, saved 668 *extricable*; rid of, relieved; paroled, set free, freed, manumitted, unbound 744 *unconfined*; released, enlarged, discharged, acquitted; emancipated, enfranchised etc. vb.

Vb. *liberate*, rescue, save 668 *deliver*; dispense 919 *exempt*; pardon 909 *forgive*; discharge, absolve, let off the hook 960 *acquit*; make free, emancipate, manumit; enfranchise, give the vote; grant equal rights, end discrimination; release, free, set free, set at liberty, let out; release conditionally, parole 766 *give terms*; strike off the fetters, unfetter, unshackle, unchain; unbar, unbolt, unlock 263 *open*; loosen, unloose, loose, unbind, untie, disentangle, extricate, disengage, clear 62 *unravel*; unstop, uncork, ungag, unmuzzle; uncoop, uncage, unkennel; unleash, let off the lead; let loose, leave to wander, turn adrift; license, charter; give play to 744 *give scope*; let out, vent, give vent to 300 *empty*; leave hold, unhand, let go 779 *not retain*; relax, liberalize 734 *be lax*; lift, lift off 831 *relieve*; lift controls, decontrol, deration 752 *abrogate*; demobilize, disband, send home 75 *disperse*; unyoke, unharness, unload 701 *disencumber*; disentail, pay off the mortgage, clear the debt.

achieve liberty, gain one's freedom, breathe freely; get the bit between one's teeth, assert oneself, claim freedom of action; fight for independence 738 *revolt*; free oneself, shake oneself free; break loose, burst one's bonds, throw off the yoke, cast off one's shackles, slip the collar, kick over the traces, get away 667 *escape*.

See: 46, 62, 75, 263, 300, 667, 668, 701, 734, 738, **744**, 752, 766, 779, 818, 831, 909, 919, 960.

747 Restraint

N. *restraint*, self-r., self-control 942 *temperance*; reserve, inhibitions; suppression, repression, coercion, constraint 740 *compulsion*; cramp, check 702 *hindrance*; curb, drag, brake, snaffle, bridle 748 *fetter*; arrest, retardation, deceleration 278 *slowness*; prevention, veto, ban, bar, embargo 757 *prohibition*; legal restraint, Official Secrets Act, D-notice 953 *law*; control, strict c., discipline 733 *authority*; censorship 550 *obliteration*; press laws 735 *severity*; binding over 963 *penalty*.

restriction, limitation, limiting factor 236 *limit*; localization, keeping within limits 232 *circumscription*; speed limit, restricted area; restriction on movement, no-go area, curfew; constriction, squeeze 198 *compression*; duress, pressure 740 *compulsion*; control, food c., rationing; restrictive practice, restraint of trade, exclusive rights, exclusivity 57 *exclusion*; monopoly, price ring, cartel, closed shop; ring, circle, charmed c.; protection, protectionism, mercantilism, mercantile system, protective s., tariff, tariff wall; retrenchment, cuts 814 *economy*; economic pressure, freeze, price control, credit squeeze; blockade, starving out; monopolist, protectionist, restrictionist, mercantilist, monetarist.

detention, preventive d., custody, protective c. 660 *protection*; arrest, house a., restriction on movement; custodianship, keeping, guarding, keep, care, charge, ward; quarantine, internment; remand, refusal of bail; lettre de cachet; captivity, duress, durance, durance vile; bondage, slavery

745 *servitude*; entombment, burial 364 *interment*; herding, impoundment, immurement, confinement, solitary c., incarceration, imprisonment; sentence, time, a stretch, porridge; penology, penologist.

Adj. *restraining*, checking etc. vb.; restrictive, conditional, with strings; limiting, limitary; custodial, keeping; cramping, hidebound; straitlaced, unbending, unyielding, strict 735 *severe*; stiff 326 *rigid*; tight 206 *narrow*; straitening, confining, close 198 *compressive*; confined, poky; coercive, coactive 740 *compelling*; repressive, inhibiting 757 *prohibiting*; monopolistic, protectionist, protective, mercantilist.

restrained, self-r., self-controlled 942 *temperate*; pent up, bottled up; reserved, shy; disciplined, controlled, under control 739 *obedient*; on a lead, kept on a leash, kept under restraint 232 *circumscribed*; pinned, pinned down, kept under 745 *subjected*; on parole 917 *obliged*; protected, rationed; limited, restricted, scant, tight; cramped, hampered, trammelled, shackled 702 *hindered*; tied, bound, gagged; held up, weatherbound, fogbound, snowbound.

imprisoned, confined, detained, kept in; landlocked 232 *circumscribed*; entombed, confined 364 *buried*; quarantined, in quarantine; interned, in internment; under detention, under house arrest, kept close, incommunicado; under arrest, laid by the heels, in custody; refused bail, on remand; behind bars, incarcerated, locked up 750 *captive*; inside, in jug, in clink, in quod, in a cell; gated, confined to barracks; herded, corralled, penned up, impounded; in irons, fettered, shackled; pilloried, in the stocks; serving a sentence, doing time, doing porridge; caged, in captivity, trapped.

Vb. *restrain*, hold back, pull b.; arrest, check, curb, rein in, brake, put a brake on, put a drag on, act as a brake 278 *retard*; cramp, clog, hamper 702 *hinder*; swathe, bind, tie hand and foot 45 *tie*; call a halt, stop, put a stop to 145 *halt*; inhibit, veto, ban, bar 757 *prohibit*; bridle, discipline, control 735 *be severe*; subdue 745 *subjugate*; restrain oneself,control o., bite back, keep one's cool, keep one's hair *or* shirt on 823 *keep calm*; grip, hold, pin, keep a tight hold *or* rein on, hold in leash, hold in check 778 *retain*; hold in, keep in, fight down, fight back, bottle up; restrict, tighten, hem in, limit, keep within bounds, stop from spreading, localize, cordon off, draw the line 232 *circumscribe*; damp down, pour cold water on, assuage 177 *moderate*; hold down, slap d., clamp down on, crack down on, keep under, sit on, jump on, repress 165 *suppress*; muzzle, gag, silence 578 *make mute*; censor, black out 550 *obliterate*; restrict access, debar from, rope off, keep out 57 *exclude*; restrict imports, put on a tariff; restrict supplies, withhold, keep back, stint; restrict consumption, ration, dole out, be sparing, retrench 814 *economize*; try to stop, resist 704 *oppose*; police, patrol, keep order.

arrest, make an a., apprehend, lay by the heels, catch, cop, nab, collar, pinch, nick, pick up; haul in, run in; handcuff, put the handcuffs on, snap the bracelets on (**see** *fetter*); take, make a prisoner, take prisoner, capture, lead captive; kidnap, seize, take hostage; put under arrest, take into custody, take charge of, clap in jail, hold.

fetter, manacle, bind, pinion, tie up, handcuff, put in irons; pillory, put in the stocks, tether, picket 45 *tie*; shackle, trammel, hobble; enchain, chain, load with chains; make conditions, attach strings.

imprison, confine, immure, quarantine, intern; hold, detain, keep in, gate; keep in detention, keep under arrest, keep close, hold incommunicado; cloister 883 *seclude*; entomb, bury 364 *inter*; wall up, seal up; coop up, cage, kennel, impound, corral, herd, pen, cabin, box up, shut up, shut in, trap 235 *enclose*; put in a straitjacket; incarcerate, throw into prison, send to p., commit to p., remand, give in charge; jug, lock up; turn the key on, keep under lock and key, put in a cell, keep behind bars, clap in irons; keep prisoner, keep in captivity, keep in custody, refuse bail.

See: 45, 57, 145, 165, 177, 198, 206, 232, 235, 236, 278, 326, 364, 550, 578, 660, **702**, 704, 733, 735, 739, 740, 745, 748, **750**, 757, 778, 814, 823, 883, 917, 942, 953, 963.

748 Prison

N. *prison*, prison-house, house of correction; panopticon; open prison, prison without bars, halfway house; penitentiary, reformatory, Borstal; approved school, remand home, community h.; assessment centre, detention c.; sin bin; prison ship, hulks; dungeon, oubliette, black hole, limbo; Bastille, Tower; debtor's prison, Marshalsea, Fleet; Newgate, Wormwood Scrubs, Holloway; Sing Sing, Alcatraz; criminal lunatic asylum, Broadmoor.

gaol, jail, quod, clink, jug, can, stir, big house; glasshouse, brig.

lockup, choky, calaboose, nick, police station; guardroom, guardhouse, roundhouse; cooler, cell, prison c., condemned c., Death Row; dungeon cell, dungeon, oubliette, torture chamber; prison van, Black Maria, saladière; dock, bar; pound, pen, cage, coop, kennel 235 *enclosure*; ghetto, reserve; stocks, pillory; lock, padlock, bolt, bar, barred window.

prison camp, detention c., internment c., prisoner of war c., Stalag; concentration camp, Belsen, Auschwitz, Buchenwald; labour camp, Gulag, re-education camp; penal settlement *or* colony, Botany Bay, Devil's Island.

fetter, shackle, trammels, bond, chain, ball and c., ring-bolt, irons, gyves, bilboes, hobble; manacle, pinion, handcuff, bracelet, darbies; straitjacket, corset; muzzle, gag, bit, bridle, snaffle, headstall, halter; rein, bearing r., martingale; reins, ribbons, traces; yoke, collar, harness; curb, brake, skid, clog, drag 702 *hindrance*; lead, tether, rope, leading string, apron strings 47 *halter*.

See: 47, 235, **702**.

749 Keeper

N. *keeper*, custodian, curator; archivist, record keeper 549 *recorder*; charge officer, officer in charge; caretaker, concierge, housekeeper; castellan, seneschal, chatelaine, warden; ranger, gamekeeper; guard, escort, convoy; garrison 713 *defender*; watchdog, sentry, sentinel, lookout, watchman, night w., watch, coastguard, lighthouse keeper 660 *protector*; invigilator, tutor, chaperon, duenna, governess, nurse, foster n., wet n., nanny, nursemaid, baby-sitter 742 *domestic*; foster parent, adoptive p.; guardian, legal g.; probation officer 901 *philanthropist*.

gaoler, jailer, turnkey, warder, wardress, prison guard, prison officer, screw; prison governor; Argus.

See: 549, **660**, 713, 742, 901.

750 Prisoner

N. *prisoner*, captive, capture, prisoner of war, POW; parolee, ticket-of-leave man; close prisoner, person under arrest; political prisoner, prisoner of conscience; detainee, prisoner of state; prisoner at the bar, defendant, accused 928 *accused person*; first offender, Borstal boy; persistent offender, old lag, jailbird 904 *offender*; gaol inmate, prisoner behind bars, guest of Her Majesty; condemned prisoner, convict; lifer; trusty; chain gang, galley slave 742 *slave*; hostage, kidnap victim 767 *security*.

Adj. *captive*, imprisoned, chained, fettered, shackled, in chains, in irons, behind bars, under lock and key, cooling one's heels; jailed, in prison, in Dartmoor, in Borstal, inside 747 *imprisoned*; in the pillory, in the stocks, in the galleys; in custody, under arrest, without bail, remanded; detained, under detention, detained at Her Majesty's pleasure.

See: 742, **747**, 767, **904**, 928.

751 Commission: vicarious authority

N. *commission*, vicarious authority; committal, delegation; devolution, decentralization; deputation, legation, mission, embassy 754 *envoy*; regency, vice-r., regentship, vice-royalty 733 *authority*; representation, procuratory, proxy; card vote; agency, factorage, trusteeship, executorship 689 *management*; clerkship, public service, civil s., bureaucracy 733 *government*.

mandate, trust, charge 737 *command*; commission, assignment, appointment, office, task, errand, mission; enterprise 672 *undertaking*; nomination, return, election 605 *vote*; posting, translation, transfer 272 *transference*; investment, investiture, installation, induction, inauguration, ordination, enthronement, coronation; power of attorney, written authority, charter, writ 737 *warrant*; brevet, diploma 756 *permit*; terms of reference 766 *conditions*; responsibility, care, cure (of souls); ward, charge.

Adj. *commissioned*, empowered, entrusted etc. vb.; deputed, delegated, accredited; vicarious, representational, agential.

Vb. *commission*, put in c.; empower, authorize, charge, sanction, charter, license 756 *permit*; post, accredit, appoint, collate, assign, name, nominate; engage, hire, staff 622 *employ*; invest, induct, install, ordain; raise to the throne, enthrone, crown, anoint; commit, put in one's hands, turn over to, leave it to; consign, entrust, trust with, grant powers of attorney; delegate, depute, send on a mission, send on an errand, send out, return, elect, give a mandate 605 *vote*.

Adv. *by proxy*, per procurationem, p.p., by delegated authority.

See: 272, 605, 622, 672, 689, **733**, **737**, **754**, 756, 766.

752 Abrogation

N. *abrogation*, annulment, invalidation; voidance, nullification, disallowance, vacation, defeasance; cancelling, cancellation, cassation, suppression; recall, repeal, revocation, revoking, rescission; abolition, abolishment, dissolution; neonomianism 126 *newness*; repudiation 533 *negation*; retractation 603 *recantation*; suspension, discontinuance, disuse, dead letter 674 *nonuse*; reversal, undoing 148 *reversion*; counterorder, countermand, nolle prosequi; reprieve.

deposal, deposition, dethronement; demotion, degradation; disestablishment, disendowment; deconsecration, secularization; discharge, congé, dismissal, sack, removal 300 *ejection*; unfrocking 963 *punishment*; ousting, deprivation, divestment 786 *expropriation*; replacement, supersession 150 *substitution*; recall, transfer, relief 272 *transference*.

Adj. *abrogated*, voided, vacated, set aside, quashed, cancelled etc. vb.; void, null and void; functus officio, dead; dormant, sleeping 674 *unused*; recalled, revoked.

Vb. *abrogate*, annul, disannul, cancel; scrub, scrub out, rub o., wipe o. 550 *obliterate*; invalidate, abolish, dissolve, nullify, void, vacate, render null and void; quash, set aside, reverse, overrule; repeal, revoke, recall; rescind, tear up; unmake, undo 148 *revert*; countermand, counterorder; disclaim, disown, deny 533 *negate*; repudiate, retract 603 *recant*; ignore 458 *disregard*; call off, call a halt 747 *restrain*; suspend, discontinue, write off, make a dead letter of 674 *stop using*; unwish, unwill, wish undone 830 *regret*; not proceed with 621 *relinquish*.

depose, discrown, uncrown, dethrone; unseat; divest 786 *deprive*; unfrock; disbench, disbar, strike off the roll 57 *exclude*; disaffiliate, disestablish, disendow; deconsecrate, secularize; suspend, cashier 300 *dismiss*; ease out, edge o., oust 300 *eject*; demote, degrade, reduce to the ranks; recall, relieve, supersede, replace, remove 272 *transfer*.

See: 57, 126, 148, 150, 272, 300, 458, 533, 550, 603, 621, 674, 747, 786, 830, 963.

753 Resignation

N. *resignation*, demission; retirement, retiral; leaving, withdrawal 296 *departure*; pension, compensation, golden handshake 962 *reward*; waiver, surrender, abandonment, abdication, renunciation 621 *relinquishment*; abjuration, disclaimer 533 *negation*; state of retirement 681 *leisure*; feeling of resignation, acquiescence 721 *submission*; abdicator, resigner, quitter; person in retirement, pensioner.

Adj. *resigning*, abdicating, renunciatory; outgoing, former, retired, quondam, onetime, ci-devant; emeritus.

Vb. *resign*, tender one's resignation, send in one's papers, demit, lay down one's office, break one's staff; be relieved, hand over, vacate, vacate office; vacate one's seat, apply for the Chiltern Hundreds; stand down, stand aside, make way for, leave it to; sign off, declare (cricket); scratch, withdraw, back out, retire from the contest, throw in one's hand, surrender, give up 721 *submit*; quit, throw up, chuck it; ask for one's cards; sign away, give a. 780 *assign*; abdicate, abandon, renounce 621 *relinquish*; retire, go into retirement; be pensioned off; finish one's term, conclude one's term of office; decline to stand again, not renew the fight, refuse battle; waive, disclaim, abjure 533 *negate*; retract 603 *recant*.

See: 296, 533, 603, **621**, 681, **721**, 780, 962.

754 Consignee

N. *consignee*, committee, steering c., panel, quango 692 *council*; counsellor, wise man, team of experts, working party 691 *adviser*; bailee, stakeholder; nominee, appointee, licensee; trustee, executor 686 *agent*; factor, one's man of business, bailiff, steward 690 *manager*; caretaker, curator 749 *keeper*; representative (**see** *del-*

egate); legal representative, attorney, counsel, advocate 958 *law agent*; proxy 755 *deputy*; negotiator, middleman, broker, stockbroker 231 *intermediary*; underwriter, insurer; purser, bursar 798 *treasurer*; rent collector, tax c., revenue c., income-tax officer; office-bearer, secretary of state 741 *officer*; functionary 690 *official*.

delegate, walking d., shop steward; nominee, representative, elected r., member; official representative, commissary, commissioner; man *or* woman on the spot, correspondent, war c., one's own c., special c. 588 *correspondent*; emissary, special messenger 529 *messenger*; plenipotentiary (**see** *envoy*); delegation, trade d., mission.

envoy, emissary, legate, ablegate, nuncio, papal n., internuncio, permanent representative, resident, ambassador, ambassadress, High Commissioner, chargé d'affaires; ambassador at large; corps diplomatique, diplomatic corps; minister, diplomat; consul, vice-c.; first secretary, attaché; embassy, legation, mission, consulate, High Commission; diplomatist, negotiator, plenipotentiary.

See: 231, 529, 588, **686**, **690**, 691, 692, **741**, 749, 755, 798, 958.

755 Deputy

N. *deputy*, surrogate, alternate, proxy; scapegoat, substitute, locum tenens, understudy, stand-in 150 *substitution*; pro-, vice-, vice-gerent, vice-regent, viceroy, vice-president, vice-chairman, vice-chancellor, vice-admiral, vice-captain, vice-consul; proconsul, propraetor; vicar, vicar-general; second-in-command, deputy prime minister 741 *officer*; right-hand man, lieutenant, secretary 703 *aider*; alter ego, power behind the throne 612 *motivator*; caretaker government; heir, heir apparent, successor designate 776 *beneficiary*; spokesperson, mouthpiece, herald 529 *messenger*; second, advocate, champion 707 *patron*; agent, factor, attorney 754 *consignee*.

Adj. *deputizing*, representing, acting for, agential; vice-, pro-; diplomatic, ambassadorial, plenipotentiary; standing-in for 150 *substituted*; negotiatory, intermediary 231 *interjacent*.

Vb. *deputize*, act for 622 *function*; act on behalf of, represent, hold a mandate for, hold a proxy f., appear f., sit f., speak f., answer f., hold a brief f., state the case f.; hold in trust, manage the business of, be executor 689 *manage*; negotiate, be broker for, replace, stand for, stand in the stead of, do duty for, stand in another's shoes 150 *substitute*; be the whipping boy, act as scapegoat.

Adv. *on behalf*, for, pro; by proxy.

See: **150**, 231, 529, 612, 622, 689, 703, 707, 741, **754**, 776.

Section two: Special social volition

756 Permission

N. *permission*, general p., liberty 744 *freedom*; leave, sanction, clearance; vouchsafement, accordance, grant; licence, authorization, warrant; allowance, sufferance, tolerance, toleration, indulgence 736 *leniency*; acquiescence, passive consent, implied c. 758 *consent*; connivance 703 *aid*; blessing, approval 923 *approbation*; grace, grace and favour 897 *benevolence*; concession, dispensation, exemption 919 *nonliability*; release 746 *liberation*.

permit, express permission, written p.; authority, law 737 *warrant*; commission 751 *mandate*; brevet, grant, charter, patent, letters p.; pass, password; passport, passbook, visa, safe-conduct; ticket, chit; licence, driving l.; free hand, carte blanche, blank cheque 744 *scope*; leave, compassionate l., leave of absence, furlough, holiday; parole, ticket of leave; clearance, all clear, green light, go-ahead; nihil obstat, imprimatur.

Adj. *permitting*, permissive, indulgent, complaisant, tolerant 736 *lenient*; conniving 703 *aiding*.

permitted, allowed etc. vb.; licit, legalized 953 *legal*; licensed, chartered, patent; unforbidden, unprohibited, open, optional, discretional, without strings 744 *unconditional*; permissible, allowable; printable, sayable; passed.

Vb. *permit*, let 469 *make possible*; give permission, grant leave, grant, accord, vouchsafe 781 *give*; nod, say yes 758 *consent*; bless, give one's blessing; go out of one's way to 759 *offer*; sanction, pass 923 *approve*; entitle, authorize, warrant, charter, patent, license, enable 160 *empower*; ratify, legalize 953 *make legal*; restore permission, decontrol; lift, lift a ban, dispense, release 919 *exempt*; clear, give clearance 746 *liberate*; give the go-ahead, give the all clear, give the green light, tip the wink; recognize, concede, allow 488 *assent*; give one a chance, let one try; make it easy for, favour, privilege, indulge 701 *facilitate*; leave the way open, open the door to, open the floodgates 263 *open*; foster, encourage 156 *conduce*; humour 823 *be patient*; suffer, tolerate, put up with, brook 736 *be lenient*; connive, shut one's eyes to, wink at 734 *be lax*; laisser faire, laisser aller, allow a free hand, give carte blanche, issue a blank cheque 744 *give scope*; permit oneself, allow o., take the liberty 734 *please oneself*.

ask leave, beg l., beg permission, ask if one may, ask one's blessing; apply for leave; seek a favour, petition 761 *request*; get leave, have permission; receive a charter, take out a patent.

Adv. *by leave*, with permission, by favour of, under licence; permissibly, allowably, legally, legitimately, licitly.

See: 156, 160, 263, 469, 488, 701, 703, **734**, **736**, 737, **744**, 746, 751, 758, 759, 761, 781, 823, 897, 919, 923, 953.

757 Prohibition

N. *prohibition*, inhibition, interdiction, disallowance, injunction; countermand, counterorder; intervention, interference; interdict, veto, ban, embargo, outlawry; restriction, curfew 747 *restraint*; proscription, taboo, Index; rejection, thumbs down 760 *refusal*; nonrecognition, intolerance 924 *disapprobation*; prohibition of drink, licensing laws 942 *temperance*; sumptuary law 814 *economy*; repressive legislation, censorship, press laws, repression, suppression 735 *severity*; abolition, cancellation, suspension 752 *abrogation*; blackout, news b. 550 *obliteration*; forbidden fruit, contraband article 859 *desired object*.

Adj. *prohibiting*, prohibitory, forbidding, prohibitive, excessive 470 *impossible*; repressive 747 *restraining*; penal 963 *punitive*; hostile 881 *inimical*; exclusive 57 *excluding*.

prohibited, forbidden, verboten, not allowed; barred, banned, under ban; censored, blue-pencilled, blacked-out; contraband, illicit, unlawful, outlawed, against the law 954 *illegal*; verboten, taboo, untouchable, blacked; frowned on, not to be thought of, not done; not to be spoken, unmentionable, unsayable, unprintable; out of bounds 57 *excluded*.

Vb. *prohibit*, forbid; disallow, veto, refuse permission, withhold p., refuse leave, forbid the banns 760 *refuse*; withdraw permission, cancel leave; countermand, counterorder, revoke, suspend 752 *abrogate*; inhibit, prevent 702 *hinder*; restrict, stop 747 *restrain*; ban, interdict, taboo, proscribe, outlaw; black, declare b.; impose a ban, place out of bounds; bar, debar, warn off, shut the door on 57 *exclude*; excommunicate 300 *eject*; repress, stifle, kill 165 *suppress*; censor, blue-pencil, black out 550 *obliterate*; not tolerate, put one's foot down 735 *be severe*; frown on, not countenance, not brook 924 *disapprove*; discourage 613 *dissuade*; clip, narrow, pinch, cramp 232 *circumscribe*; draw the line, block; intervene, interpose, interfere, dash the cup from one's lips.

See: 57, 165, 232, 300, 470, 550, 613, 702, 735, **747**, 752, **760**, 814, 859, 881, 924, 942, 954, 963.

758 Consent

N. *consent*, free c., full c., willing c. 597 *willingness*; implied consent, implicit c.; agreement 488 *assent*; compliance 768 *observance*; concession, grant, accord; acquiescence, acceptance, entertainment, allowance 756 *permission*; sanction, endorsement, ratification, confirmation; partial consent 770 *compromise*.

Adj. *consenting*, agreeable, compliant, ready, ready enough 597 *willing*; winking at, conniving 703 *aiding*; yielding 721 *submitting*.

Vb. *consent*, say yes, nod; give consent, ratify, confirm 488 *endorse*; sanction, pass 756 *permit*; give one's approval 923 *approve*; tolerate, recognize, allow, connive 736 *be lenient*; agree, fall in with, accede 488 *assent*; not say no, entertain the idea; have no objection 488 *acquiesce*; be persuaded, come over, come round 612 *be induced*; consent unwillingly, force oneself; yield, give way 721 *submit*; comply, grant a request, do as asked; grant, accord, concede, vouchsafe 781 *give*; deign, condescend 884 *be courteous*; listen, hearken 415 *hear*; turn a willing ear, go halfway to meet 597 *be willing*; meet one's wishes, do all one is asked 828 *content*; accept, take one at one's word, take up an offer, jump at; clinch a deal, close with, settle 766 *make terms*.

See: 415, **488**, 597, 612, 703, 721, 736, **756**, 766, 768, 770, 781, 828, 884, 923.

759 Offer

N. *offer*, fair o., proffer; improper offer, bribery, bribe 612 *inducement*; tender, bid, takeover b.; declaration, motion, proposition, proposal; approach, overture, advance, invitation; tentative approach, feeler; present, presentation, offering, gratuity, sacrifice 781 *gift*; dedication, consecration; candidature, application, solicitation 761 *request*.

Adj. *offering*, inviting; offered, advertised 522 *shown*; open, available; on offer, on the market, up for grabs; on hire, to let, for sale; open to bid, up for auction.

Vb. *offer*, proffer, hold out, make an offer, bid, tender; present, lay at one's feet, place in one's hands 781 *give*; dedicate, consecrate; sacrifice to; introduce, broach, move, propose, make a proposition, put forward, suggest 512 *propound*; not wait to be asked, approach, approach with, make overtures, make advances, hold out one's hand; keep the door ajar, keep one's offer open; induce 612 *bribe*; invite, send an invitation, ask one in 882 *be hospitable*; hawk, hawk about, invite tenders, offer for sale 793 *sell*; auction, declare the bidding open; cater, cater for 633 *provide*; make available, place at one's disposal, make a present of 469 *make possible*; pose, confront with.

offer oneself, sacrifice o.; stand, be a candidate, compete, run for, enter 716 *contend*; volunteer, come forward 597 *be willing*; apply, put in for 761 *request*; be on offer, look for takers, go begging.

See: 469, 512, 522, 597, **612**, 633, 716, 761, **781**, 793, 882.

760 Refusal

N. *refusal*, nonacceptance, declining, turning down, thumbs down 607 *rejection*; denial, negative answer, no, nay 533 *negation*; uncompromising answer, flat refusal, point-blank r., peremptory r. 711 *defiance*; repulse, rebuff, slap in the face 292 *repulsion*; no facilities, denial policy 715 *resistance*; withholding 778 *retention*; recalcitrance 738 *disobedience*; noncompliance 769 *nonobservance*; recusancy 598 *unwillingness*; objection, protest 762 *deprecation*; self-denial 945 *asceticism*; restraint 942 *temperance*; renunciation, abnegation 621 *relinquishment*.

Adj. *refusing*, denying, withholding, rejecting etc. vb.; recusant, noncompliant, uncompliant 769 *nonobservant*; jibbing, objecting, demurring 762 *deprecatory*; deaf to, unhearing 598 *unwilling*.

refused, not granted, turned down, disallowed, ungratified, rebuffed etc. vb.; inadmissible, not permitted 757 *prohibited*; out of the question 470 *impossible*; unoffered, withheld 778 *retained*.

Vb. *refuse*, say no, shake one's head; excuse oneself, send one's apologies; disagree 489 *dissent*; deny, negative, repudiate, disclaim 533 *negate*; decline, turn down, spurn 607 *reject*; deny firmly, repulse, rebuff, tell one where to get off 292 *repel*; turn away 300 *dismiss*; resist persuasion, be unmoved, harden one's heart 602 *be obstinate*; not hear, not listen, turn a deaf ear 416 *be deaf*; not give, close one's hand, close one's purse; turn one's back on; hang fire, hang back 598 *be unwilling*; beg off, back down; turn from, have nothing to do with, shy at, jib at 620 *avoid*; debar, keep out, shut the door 57 *exclude*; not want, not cater for; look askance at, frown on, dislike, disfavour, discountenance, not hear of 924 *disapprove*; refuse permission, not allow 757 *prohibit*; not consent, set one's face against 715 *resist*; oppose 704 *withstand*; kick, protest 762 *deprecate*; not comply 769 *not observe*; grudge, begrudge, withhold, keep from 778 *retain*; deny oneself, waive, renounce, give up 621 *relinquish*; deprive oneself, go without, do w. 945 *be ascetic*.

Adv. *denyingly*, with a refusal, without acceptance; no, never, on no account, nothing doing, not likely, not on one's life, over one's dead body, not for all the tea in China.

See: 57, 292, 300, 416, 470, **489**, 533, 598, 602, 607, 620, 621, 704, 711, 715, 738, **757**, 762, 769, 778, 924, 942, 945.

761 Request

N. *request*, simple r., modest r., humble petition; negative request 762 *deprecation*; asking, first time of a.; canvass, canvassing, hawking 793 *sale*; strong request, forcible demand, requisition; last demand, final d., last time of asking, ultimatum 737 *demand*; demand with threats, blackmail 900 *threat*; assertion of one's rights, claim, counterclaim 915 *dueness*; consumer demand, steady d., seller's market 627 *requirement*; postulate 475 *premise*; proposition, proposal, motion, prompting, suggestion; overture, approach 759 *offer*; bid, application, suit; petition, memorial, round robin; prayer, appeal, plea (**see** *entreaty*); pressure, instance, insistence, urgency 740 *compulsion*; clamour, cry, cri de coeur; dunning, importunity; soliciting, accosting, solicitation, invitation, temptation; mendicancy, begging, street-b., panhandling; appeal for funds, begging letter, flag day, bazaar, charity performance; advertising 528 *advertisement*; small ad, 'wanted' column; wish, want 859 *desire*.

entreaty, imploring, beseeching; submission, humble s., clasped hands, bended knees; supplication, prayer 981 *prayers*; appeal, invocation, apostrophe 583 *allocution*; solemn entreaty, adjuration, conjuration, obsecration; incantation, imprecation.

Adj. *requesting*, asking, inviting, begging etc. vb.; mendicant, alms-seeking; invitatory 759 *offering*; claiming 627 *demanding*; insisting, insistent; clamorous, importunate, pressing, urgent, instant.

supplicatory, entreating, suppliant, praying, prayerful; on bended knees, with folded hands, cap in hand; precatory, precative; imploratory, beseeching, with tears in one's eyes; adjuratory, invocatory, imprecatory.

Vb. *request*, ask, invite, solicit; make overtures, approach, accost 759 *offer*; sue for, woo, pop the question 889 *court*; seek, look for 459 *search*; fish for, angle for; need, call for, clamour f. 627 *require*; crave, make a request, prefer an appeal, beg a favour, ask a boon, have a request to make, make bold to ask, trouble one for 859 *desire*; apply, make application, put in for, bid, bid for, make a bid f.; apply to, call on, appeal to, run to, address oneself to, go cap in hand to; tout, hawk, canvass, solicit orders 793 *sell*; petition, memorialize; press a claim, expect 915 *claim*; make demands 737 *demand*; blackmail 900 *threaten*; be instant, insist 532 *emphasize*; urge, persuade 612 *induce*; coax, wheedle, cajole; importune, ply, press, dun, besiege, beset; knock at the door, demand entrance; touch, touch for 785 *borrow*; requisition 786 *take*; raise money, tax 786 *levy*; formulate one's demands, state one's terms, send an ultimatum 766 *give terms*.

beg, cadge, crave, sponge, play the parasite; bum, scrounge, sorn; thumb a lift, hitch-hike; panhandle, hold out one's hand, beg one's bread, go from door to door, knock at doors; appeal for funds, pass the hat, make a collection, raise subscriptions 786 *levy*; beg in vain, whistle for 627 *require*.

entreat, make entreaty, beg hard; supplicate, be a suppliant; pray, implore, beseech, appeal, conjure, adjure, obtest, obsecrate; invoke, imprecate; apostrophize, appeal to, call on 583 *speak to*; address one's prayers to, pray to 981 *offer worship*; kneel to, go down on one's knees, fall at one's feet; gain by entreaty, impetrate 771 *acquire*.

See: 459, 475, 528, 532, 583, 612, 627, **737**, 740, 759, 762, 766, 771, 785, 786, 793, 859, 889, 900, 915, **981**.

762 Deprecation: negative request

N. *deprecation*, negative request, contrary advice 613 *dissuasion*; begging off, plea for mercy, crossed fingers; intercession, mediation 981 *prayers*; counterpetition, counterclaim 761 *request*; murmur, cheep, squeal, complaint 829 *discontent*; exception, demur, expostulation, remonstrance, protest 704 *opposition*; reaction, backlash 182 *counteraction*; gesture of protest, tut-tut, raised eyebrows, groans, jeers 924 *disapprobation*; open letter, round robin; demonstration, indignation meeting, march, hunger m.; noncompliance 760 *refusal*.

Adj. *deprecatory* 613 *dissuasive*; protesting, protestant, expostulatory; clamant, vocal; intercessory, mediatorial; averting, apotropaic.

Vb. *deprecate*, ask one not to, advise against, have a better idea, make a counterproposal 613 *dissuade*; avert the omen, touch wood, knock on w., cross one's fingers, keep one's fingers crossed 983 *practise sorcery*; beg off, plead for, intercede 720 *mediate*; pray, appeal 761 *entreat*; cry for mercy 905 *ask mercy*; show embarrassment, tut-tut, shake one's head, raise one's eyebrows 924 *disapprove*;

remonstrate, expostulate 924 *reprove*; jeer, groan, stamp 926 *detract*; murmur, beef, complain 829 *be discontented*; object, take exception to; demur, jib, kick, squeal, protest against, appeal a., petition a., lobby a., campaign a., raise one's voice a., cry out a., cry blue murder 704 *oppose*; demonstrate, hold an indignation meeting; strike, come out, walk o. 145 *cease*.

See: 145, 182, **613**, 704, 720, 760, 761, 829, 905, 924, 926, 981, 983.

763 Petitioner

N. *petitioner*, humble p., suppliant, supplicant; appealer, appellant; claimant, pretender; postulant, aspirant, expectant; solicitor, asker, seeker, enquirer, advertiser; customer, bidder, tenderer; suitor, courter, wooer; canvasser, hawker, touter, tout, barker, spieler; dun, dunner; pressure group, lobby, lobbyist; applicant, candidate, entrant; competitor, runner 716 *contender*; complainer, grouser 829 *malcontent*.

beggar, street b., professional b., schnorrer, panhandler; mendicant, mendicant friar, fakir, sannyasi; tramp, bum 268 *wanderer*; cadger, borrower, scrounger, sorner, hitch-hiker; sponger, parasite 879 *toady*.

See: 268, 716, **829**, 879.

Section three: Conditional social volition

764 Promise

N. *promise*, promise-making, pollicitation 759 *offer*; undertaking, preengagement, commitment; affiance, betrothal, engagement 894 *marriage*; troth, plight, plighted word, word, one's solemn w., parole, word of honour, sacred pledge, vow, marriage v. 532 *oath*; declaration, solemn d. 532 *affirmation*; declared intention 617 *intention*; profession, professions, fair words; assurance, pledge, credit, honour, warrant, warranty, guarantee, insurance 767 *security*; voluntary commitment, gentlemen's agreement, mutual a. 765 *compact*; covenant, bond, promise to pay 803 *debt*; obligation, debt of honour 917 *duty*; firm date, delivery d. 672 *undertaking*; promiser, promise-maker, votary; engager, party 765 *signatory*.

Adj. *promissory*, promising, votive; on oath, under o., under hand and seal; on credit, on parole.

promised, covenanted, guaranteed, secured 767 *pledged*; engaged, bespoke, reserved; betrothed, affianced; committed, in for it; bound, obligated 917 *obliged*.

Vb. *promise*, say one will 532 *affirm*; hold out, proffer 759 *offer*; make a promise, give one's word, pledge one's w.; vow, vow and protest, take one's oath on it 532 *swear*; vouch for, go bail for, warrant, guarantee, assure, confirm, secure, insure, underwrite 767 *give security*; pledge, stake; pledge one's honour, stake one's credit; engage, enter into an engagement, give a firm date 672 *undertake*; make a gentleman's agreement, commit oneself, bind oneself, be bound, covenant 765 *contract*; accept an obligation, take on oneself, answer for, accept responsibility 917 *incur a duty*; accept a liability, promise to pay, incur a debt of honour 785 *borrow*; bespeak, preengage, reserve 617 *intend*; plight one's troth, exchange vows 894 *wed*.

take a pledge, demand security 473 *make certain*; put on oath, administer an o., adjure, swear, make one s. 466 *testify*; make one promise, exact a p.; take on credit, take one's word, accept one's parole, parole 485 *believe*; rely on, expect 473 *be certain*.

Adv. *as promised*, according to contract, duly; professedly, truly 540 *truthfully*; upon one's word, upon one's honour, cross one's heart 532 *affirmatively*.

See: 466, 473, 485, **532**, 540, 617, 672, 759, **765**, **767**, 785, 803, 894, 917.

765 Compact

N. *compact*, contract, bargain, agreement, mutual a., mutual undertaking 672 *undertaking*; gentleman's agreement, debt of honour 764 *promise*; mutual pledge, exchange of vows; engagement, betrothal 894 *marriage*; covenant, bond 767 *security*; league, alliance, cartel 706 *cooperation*; pact, convention, understanding 24 *agreement*; private understanding, something between them; secret pact, conspiracy 623 *plot*; negotiation 766 *conditions*; deal, give and take 770 *compromise*; adjustment, composition, arrangement, settlement; completion, ratification, confirmation 488 *assent*; seal, sigil, signet, signature, countersignature;

deed of agreement, indenture 767 *title deed.*
treaty, international agreement; Treaty of Rome, Warsaw Pact; peace treaty, nonaggression pact 719 *pacification;* convention, concordat, protocol; Geneva Convention.
signatory, signer, countersigner, subscriber, the undersigned; swearer, attestor, attestant 466 *witness;* endorser, ratifier; adherent, party, consenting p. 488 *assenter;* covenanter, contractor, contracting party; treaty-maker, negotiator 720 *mediator.*
Adj. *contractual,* conventional, consensual 488 *assenting;* bilateral, multilateral; agreed to, negotiated, signed, countersigned, sworn, ratified; covenanted, signed, sealed and delivered; under one's hand and seal.
Vb. *contract,* enter into a contract, engage 672 *undertake;* precontract 764 *promise;* covenant, make a compact, strike a bargain, sign a pact, shake hands on, do a deal, clinch a d.; join in a compact, adhere; league, ally 706 *cooperate;* treat, negotiate 791 *bargain;* give and take 770 *compromise;* stipulate 766 *give terms;* agree, come to an agreement, arrive at a formula, come to terms 766 *make terms;* conclude, close, settle; indent, execute, sign, subscribe, ratify, attest, confirm 488 *endorse;* insure, underwrite 767 *give security.*
See: 24, 466, **488**, 623, 672, 706, 719, 720, **764**, **766**, **767**, 770, 791, 894.

766 Conditions

N. *conditions,* making terms, treaty-making, diplomacy, negotiation, bargaining, collective b.; hard bargaining, horse-trading 791 *barter;* formula, terms, set t., written t., stated t., terms for agreement; final terms, ultimatum, time limit 900 *threat;* dictated terms 740 *compulsion;* part of the bargain, condition, set of terms, frame of reference; articles, articles of agreement; provision, clause, entrenched c., escape c., saving c., proviso, limitation, strings, reservation, exception, small print 468 *qualification;* stipulation, sine qua non, essential clause 627 *requirement;* rule 693 *precept;* contractual terms, embodied t. 765 *treaty;* terms of reference 751 *mandate.*
Adj. *conditional,* with strings attached, stipulatory, qualificatory, provisory 468 *qualifying;* limiting, subject to terms, conditioned, contingent, provisional; guarded, safeguarded, entrenched; binding 917 *obligatory.*
Vb. *give terms,* propose conditions; condition, bind, tie down, attach strings; hold out for, insist on, make demands 737 *demand;* stipulate, make it a sine qua non 627 *require;* allow no exception 735 *be severe;* insert a proviso, leave a loophole 468 *qualify;* fix the terms, impose the conditions, write the articles, draft the clauses; add a clause, write in.
make terms, negotiate, treat, be in treaty, parley, hold conversations 584 *confer;* deal with, treat w., negotiate w.; make overtures, throw out a feeler 461 *be tentative;* haggle, higgle 791 *bargain;* proffer, make proposals, make a counterproposal 759 *offer;* give and take, yield a point, stretch a p. 770 *compromise;* negotiate a treaty, hammer out a formula, do a deal 765 *contract.*
Adv. *on terms,* on one's own t.; conditionally, provisionally, subject to, with a reservation; strictly, to the letter.
See: 461, **468**, 584, 627, 693, 735, 737, 740, 751, 759, **765**, 770, 791, 900, 917.

767 Security

N. *security,* precaution 858 *caution;* guarantee, warranty, authorization, writ 737 *warrant;* word of honour 764 *promise;* sponsorship, sponsion, patronage 660 *protection;* suretyship, surety, bail, caution, replevin, recognizance, personal r., parole; gage, pledge, pawn, hostage; stake, stake money, deposit, earnest, handsel, token, instalment; colour of one's money, earnest m., caution m.; token payment, down p. 804 *payment;* indemnity, insurance, underwriting 660 *safety;* transfer of security, hypothecation, mortgage, bottomry 780 *transfer;* collateral, collateral security, real s., bailor, sponsor, underwriter 707 *patron.*
title deed, deed, instrument; unilateral deed, deed poll; bilateral deed, indenture; charter, covenant, bond 765 *compact;* receipt, IOU, voucher, acquittance, quittance; certificate, authentication, marriage lines; verification, seal, stamp, signature, endorsement, acceptance 466 *credential;* valuable security, banknote, treasury note, promissory n., note of hand, bill, treasury bill, bill of exchange;

blue chip, gilt-edged security; portfolio, scrip, share, debenture; mortgage deed, policy, insurance p.; will, testament, codicil, certificate of probate; muniments, archives 548 *record*.

Adj. *pledged*, pawned, popped, deposited; up the spout, in hock, in pawn, on deposit; on lease, on mortgage; on bail, on recognizance.

secured, covered, hedged, insured, mortgaged; gilt-edged, copper-bottomed; guaranteed, covenanted 764 *promised*.

Vb. *give bail*, go b., bail one out, go surety, give s.; take bail, take recognizance, release on bail; hold in pledge, keep in pawn 764 *take a pledge*.

give security, offer collateral, hypothecate, mortgage; pledge, pawn, pop, hock 785 *borrow*; guarantee, warrant 473 *make certain*; authenticate, verify 466 *corroborate*; execute, endorse, seal, stamp, sign, countersign, subscribe, give one's signature 488 *endorse*; accept, grant a receipt, write an IOU 782 *receive*; vouch for 764 *promise*; secure, indemnify, insure, assure, underwrite 660 *safeguard*.

See: 466, 473, 488, 548, 660, 707, 737, **764**, 765, 780, 782, 785, 804, 858.

768 Observance

N. *observance*, close o. 610 *practice*; full observance, fulfilment, satisfaction 635 *sufficiency*; diligence, conscientiousness; adherence to, attention to; paying respect to, acknowledgment; performance, discharge, acquittal 676 *action*; compliance 739 *obedience*; conformance 83 *conformity*; attachment, fidelity, faith, good f. 739 *loyalty*; sense of responsibility, dependability, reliability 929 *probity*.

Adj. *observant*, practising 676 *doing*; heedful, watchful, careful of, attentive to 455 *attentive*; conscientious, diligent, earnest, religious, punctilious; overconscientious, perfectionist 862 *fastidious*; literal, pedantic, exact 494 *accurate*; responsible, reliable, dependable 929 *trustworthy*; loyal, true, compliant 739 *obedient*; adherent to, adhering to 83 *conformable*; faithful 929 *honourable*.

Vb. *observe*, heed, respect, regard, have regard to, pay respect to, acknowledge, pay attention to, attend to 455 *be attentive*; keep, practise, adhere to, cling to, follow, hold by, abide by, be loyal to 83 *conform*; comply 739 *obey*; fulfil, discharge, perform, execute, carry out, carry out to the letter 676 *do*; satisfy 635 *suffice*.

keep faith, be faithful to, have loyalty; discharge one's functions 917 *do one's duty*; honour one's obligations, meet one's o., be as good as one's word, make good one's promise, keep one's p., fulfil one's engagement, be true to the spirit of, stand by 929 *be honourable*; come up to scratch, redeem one's pledge, pay one's debt, pay up 804 *pay*; give one his *or* her due 915 *grant claims*.

Adv. *with observance*, faithfully, religiously, loyally; literally, meticulously, according to the spirit of, to the full.

See: 83, 455, 494, 610, 635, 676, **739**, 804, 862, 915, **917**, **929**.

769 Nonobservance

N. *nonobservance*, inobservance; informality, indifference 734 *laxity*; inattention, omission, laches 458 *negligence*; nonadherence 84 *nonconformity*; abhorrence 607 *rejection*; anarchism 734 *anarchy*; nonperformance, nonfeasance 679 *inactivity*; nonfulfilment, shortcoming 726 *noncompletion*; infringement, violation, transgression 306 *overstepping*; noncompliance, disloyalty 738 *disobedience*; protest 762 *deprecation*; disregard, discourtesy 921 *disrespect*; bad faith, breach of f., breach of promise 930 *perfidy*; retractation 603 *tergiversation*; repudiation, denial 533 *negation*; failure, bankruptcy 805 *insolvency*; forfeiture 963 *penalty*.

Adj. *nonobservant*, nonpractising, lapsed; nonconforming, standing out, blacklegging, nonadhering, nonconformist 84 *unconformable*; inattentive to, disregarding, neglectful 458 *negligent*; unprofessional, uncanonical; maverick, cowboy; indifferent, informal 734 *lax*; noncompliant 738 *disobedient*; transgressive, infringing, unlawful 954 *lawbreaking*; disloyal 918 *undutiful*; unfaithful 930 *perfidious*; anarchical 734 *anarchic*.

Vb. *not observe*, not practise, abhor 607 *reject*; not conform, not adhere, not follow, stand out 84 *be unconformable*; discard 674 *stop using*; set aside 752 *abrogate*; omit, ignore, skip 458 *neglect*; disregard, slight, show no respect for, snap one's fingers at 921 *not respect*; stretch a point 734 *be lax*; violate, do violence to, drive a coach and horses through, trample underfoot 176 *force*; transgress 306 *overstep*; not comply with 738 *disobey*; desert 918 *fail in duty*; fail, not come up to scratch 636 *not suffice*; perform less than one promised 726 *not complete*; break faith, break one's promise, break one's word, neglect one's vow, repudiate one's obligations, dishonour 533 *negate*; not fulfil one's engagement, renege on, go back on, back out, cancel 603 *tergiversate*; prove unreliable 930 *be dishonest*; give the go-by, cut, shirk, dodge, evade, elude 620 *avoid*; shuffle, palter, quibble, fob off, equivocate 518 *be equivocal*; forfeit, incur a penalty 963 *be punished*.

See: 84, 176, 306, 458, 518, 533, 603, 607, 620, 636, 674, 679, 726, 734, **738**, 752, 762, 805, **918**, 921, **930**, 954, 963.

770 Compromise

N. *compromise*, noninsistence, concession; mutual concession, give and take, adjustment, formula 765 *compact*; composition, commutation; second best, pis aller, half a loaf 35 *inferiority*; modus vivendi, working arrangement 624 *way*; splitting the difference 30 *average*; halfway 625 *middle way*; balancing act.

Vb. *compromise*, make a c., find a formula, find a basis; make mutual concessions, give and take, meet one halfway 625 *be halfway*; live and let live, not insist, stretch a point 734 *be lax*; strike an average, take the mean, go half and half, go Dutch, split the difference 30 *average out*; compound, commute 150 *substitute*; compose differences, adjust d., arbitrate, go to arbitration; patch up, bridge over 719 *pacify*; take the good with the bad, take what is offered, make a virtue of necessity, take the will for the deed; make the best of a bad job.

See: 30, 35, 150, 624, **625**, 719, 734, 765.

Section four: Possessive relations

771 Acquisition

N. *acquisition*, getting, winning; breadwinning, earning; acquirement, obtainment, procurement; collection 74 *assemblage*; realization, profit-taking 793 *sale*; conversion, encashment 780 *transfer*; fund-raising; milking, exploitation, profiteering; money-grubbing 816 *avarice*; heap, stack, pile, pool, scoop, jackpot 74 *accumulation*; trover, finding, picking up, totting 484 *discovery*; finding again, recovery, retrieval, revendication, recoupment 656 *restoration*; redemption 792 *purchase*; appropriation 786 *taking*; subreption, theft 788 *stealing*; inheritance, heirship, patrimony; thing acquired, acquest, find, trouvaille, windfall, treasure, treasure trove; something for nothing, free gift 781 *gift*; legacy, bequest; gratuity, baksheesh 962 *reward*; benefit match, prize, plum 729 *trophy*; gravy 615 *benefit*; easy money 701 *facility*; pelf, lucre 797 *money*; plunder 790 *booty*.

earnings, income, earned i., wage, salary, screw, pay packet, productivity bonus 804 *pay*; rate for the job, pay scale, differential; pension, superannuation, compensation, 'golden handshake'; remuneration, emolument 962 *reward*; allowance, expense account; pickings, perquisite, perks, fringe benefits; salvage, totting; commission, rake-off 810 *discount*; return, net r., gross r., receipts, proceeds, turnover, takings, revenue, taxes 807 *receipt*; reaping, harvest, vintage, crop, cash c., catch c., second c., aftermath, gleanings; output, produce 164 *product*.

gain, thrift, savings 814 *economy*; no loss, credit side, profit, net p., paper p., capital gain, winnings; dividend, share-out 775 *participation*; usury, interest, high i., compound i., simple i. 36 *increment*; paying transaction, profitable t., lucrative deal, successful speculation; pay increase, rise, raise 36 *increase*; advantage, benefit; selfish advantage, personal benefit, main chance 932 *selfishness*.

Adj. *acquiring*, acquisitive, accumulative; on the make, getting, winning 730 *prosperous*; hoarding, saving; greedy 816 *avaricious*.

gainful, paying, money-making, money-spinning, lucrative, remunerative 962 *rewarding*; advantageous 640 *profitable*; fruitful, fertile 164 *productive*; stipendiary, paid, remunerated, breadwinning.

acquired, had, got; ill-gotten; inherited, patrimonial; on the credit side.

Vb. *acquire*, get, come by; get by effort, earn, gain, obtain, procure, get at; find, strike, come across, come by, pick up, pitch upon, light u. 484 *discover*; get hold of, get possession of, lay one's hands on, make one's own, annex 786 *appropriate*; win, capture, catch, land, net, bag 786 *take*; pick, glean, fill one's pockets; gather, reap, crop, harvest; derive, draw, tap, milk, mine 304 *extract*; collect, accumulate, heap, pile up 74 *bring together*; scrape together, rake t.; collect funds, raise, levy, raise the wind; save, save up, hoard 632 *store*; get by purchase, buy, preempt 792 *purchase*; get in advance, reserve, book, engage 135 *be early*; get somehow, beg, borrow or steal; get a living, earn a l., win one's bread, turn an honest penny, keep the wolf from the door 622 *busy oneself*; get money, draw a salary, draw a pension, receive one's wages; have an income, be in receipt of, have a turnover, gross, take 782 *receive*; turn into money, convert, cash, encash, realize, clear, make; get back, come by one's own, recover, salvage, recycle, regain, redeem, recapture, reconquer 656 *retrieve*; take back, resume, reassume, reclaim; compensate oneself, recover one's losses 31 *recoup*; recover one's costs, break even, balance accounts 28 *equalize*; attain, reach; come in for, catch, incur.

inherit, come into, be left, receive a legacy; succeed, succeed to, step into the shoes of, be the heir of.

gain, profit, make a p., reap a p., earn a dividend; make, win; make money, coin m., line one's pockets 730 *prosper*; make a fortune, make a killing, make one's pile, rake in the shekels, turn a pretty penny 800 *get rich*; scoop, make a s., win, win the jackpot, break the bank; see one's advantage, sell at a profit; draw one's interest, collect one's profit, credit to one's account.

be profitable, profit, repay, be worthwhile 640 *be useful*; pay, pay well; bring in, gross, yield 164 *produce*; bring in a return, pay a dividend, show a profit 730 *prosper*; accrue, roll in, bring grist to the mill, stick to one's fingers.

See: 28, 31, **36**, 74, 135, 164, 304, 484, 615, 622, 632, 640, 656, 701, 729, 730, 775, 780, 781, 782, **786**, 788, 790, **792**, 793, 797, 800, 804, 807, 810, 814, 816, 932, 962.

772 Loss

N. *loss*, deprivation, privation, bereavement; dispossession, eviction 786 *expropriation*; sacrifice, forfeiture, forfeit, lapse 963 *penalty*; hopeless loss, dead l., total l., utter l., irretrievable l., irreparable l., perdition 165 *ruin*; depreciation 655 *deterioration*; diminishing returns 42 *decrement*; setback, check, reverse; loss of profit, lack of p.; overdraft, failure, bankruptcy 805 *insolvency*; consumption 806 *expenditure*; nonrecovery, spilt milk, wastage, leakage 634 *waste*; dissipation, evaporation, drain 37 *decrease*; riddance, good r. 746 *liberation*; losing battle 728 *defeat*.

Adj. *losing*, unprofitable 641 *profitless*; squandering 815 *prodigal*; the worse for wear 655 *deteriorated*; forfeiting, sacrificing, sacrificial; deprived, dispossessed, robbed; denuded, stripped of, shorn of, bereft, bereaved; minus, without, lacking; rid of, quit of; set back, out of pocket, down, in the red, overdrawn, broke, bankrupt, insolvent 805 *nonpaying*; nonprofitmaking 931 *disinterested*.

lost, long l., gone, gone for ever; gone by the board 458 *neglected*; vanished, flown out of the window 446 *disappearing*; missing, mislaid 188 *misplaced*; untraced, untraceable, lost, stolen or strayed 190 *absent*; rid, off one's hands; wanting, lacking, short 307 *deficient*; irrecoverable, irreclaimable, irretrievable, irredeemable, unsalvageable, nonrecyclable 634 *wasted*; spent, gone down the drain, squandered 806 *expended*; forfeit, forfeited, sacrificed.

Vb. *lose*, not find, be unable to f., look in vain for; mislay 188 *misplace*; miss, let slip, let slip through one's fingers, kiss *or* say good-bye to 138 *lose a chance*; have nothing to show for, squander, throw away 634 *waste*; deserve to lose, forfeit, sacrifice; spill, allow to leak, pour down the drain; throw good money after bad, sink 806 *expend*; not improve matters, be the worse for 832 *aggravate*; be a loser, burn one's fingers 731 *have trouble*; lose one's stake, lose one's bet, pay out; make no profit, be down, be out of pocket; be set back, incur losses, meet with l., sell at a loss; be unable to pay, break, go broke, go bankrupt 805 *not pay*; overdraw, be overdrawn, be in the red, be minus.

be lost, be missing, be declared m. 190 *be absent*; lapse, go down the drain, go down the spout, go to pot 165 *be destroyed*; melt away 446 *disappear*; be a good riddance 831 *relieve*.

See: **37**, 42, 138, 165, 188, 190, 307, 446,

458, **634**, 641, 655, 728, 731, 746, 786, 805, 806, 815, 831, 832, 931, 963.

773 Possession

N. *possession*, right of p., de jure p., ownership, proprietorship, rightful possession, lawful p., enjoyment, usufruct, uti possidetis; seisin, occupancy, nine points of the law, bird in the hand; mastery, hold, grasp, grip, de facto possession 778 *retention*; haves and have-nots 776 *possessor*; a possession 777 *property*; tenancy, holding 777 *estate*; tenure, fee, fief, feud, feudality, seigniory, socage, villeinage; long possession, prescription 610 *habit*; exclusive possession, sole p., monopoly, corner, ring; preoccupancy, preemption, squatting; future possession, expectations, heirship, heirdom, inheritance, heritage, patrimony, reversion, remaindership; taking possession, impropriation, appropriation, making one's own, claiming, hoisting one's flag over 786 *taking*.

Adj. *possessing*, seized of, having, holding, owning, enjoying etc. vb.; proprietorial, having possessions, propertied, landed; possessed of, in possession, occupying, squatting; endowed with, blest w., fraught w., instinct w.; exclusive, monopolistic, possessive.

possessed, enjoyed, had, held etc. vb.; in the possession of, in the ownership of, in one's hand, in one's grasp; in the bank, in one's account, to one's name, to one's credit; at one's disposal, on hand, in store; proper, personal 80 *special*; belonging, one's own, one's very o., unshared, private; monopolized by, engrossed by, devoured by; booked, reserved, engaged, occupied; included in, inherent, appertaining, attaching; unsold, undisposed of, on one's hands.

Vb. *possess*, be possessed of, own, have; die possessed of 780 *bequeath*; hold, have and hold, have a firm grip on, hold in one's grasp, grip 778 *retain*; have at one's command, have absolute disposal of, command 673 *dispose of*; call one's own, boast of 915 *claim*; contain, include 78 *comprise*; fill, occupy; squat, sit in, sit on, settle upon, inhabit; enjoy, have for one's own 673 *use*; have all to oneself, be a dog in the manger, monopolize, hog, corner, corner the market; get, take possession, make one's own, impropriate 786 *take*; recover, reoccupy, re-enter 656 *retrieve*; preoccupy, preempt, reserve, book, engage 135 *be early*; come into, come in for, succeed 771 *inherit*.

belong, be vested, be v. in, belong to; go with, be included in, inhere 78 *be included*; be subject to, owe service to 745 *be subject*.

Adv. *possessively*, monopolistically; in one's own right, by right of possession.

See: 78, 80, 135, 610, 656, 673, 745, 771, 776, 777, **778**, 780, **786**, 915.

774 Nonownership

N. *nonownership*, nonpossession, nonoccupancy, vacancy; tenancy, temporary lease; dependence 745 *subjection*; pauperism 801 *poverty*; loss of possession 786 *expropriation*; deprivation, disentitlement 772 *loss*; no-man's-land, debatable territory, Tom Tiddler's ground 190 *emptiness*.

Adj. *not owning*, not possessing, dependent 745 *subject*; dispossessed, disentitled; owning nothing, destitute, penniless, propertyless 801 *poor*; unblest with; lacking, minus, without 627 *required*.

unpossessed, unattached, not belonging; masterless, ownerless, nobody's, no man's; international, common; not owned, unowned, unappropriated; unclaimed, disowned; up for grabs, anybody's; unheld, unoccupied, untenanted, unleased; vacant 190 *empty*; derelict, abandoned 779 *not retained*; unobtained, unacquired, untaken, going begging 860 *unwanted*.

See: 190, 627, 745, 772, 779, 786, 801, 860.

775 Joint Possession

N. *joint possession*, possession in common; joint tenancy, tenancy in common; gavelkind; joint ownership, common o.; common land, common, global commons; public property, public domain 777 *property*; joint government, condominium 733 *political organization*; joint stock, common stock, pool, kitty 632 *store*; cooperative system, mutualism 706 *cooperation*; nationalization, public ownership, state o., socialism, communism, collectivism; community of possessions, community of women; collective farm, collective, commune, kolkhoz, kibbutz 370 *farm*; sharecropping, métayage.

participation, membership, affiliation 78 *inclusion*; sharing, co-sharing, partnership, co-p., profit-sharing 706 *association*; Dutch treat, bottle party, dividend, share-out; share, fair s., lot, whack 783 *portion*; complicity, involvement, sympathy; fellow feeling, sympathetic strike, joint action.

participator, member, partner, co-p., sharer, partaker 707 *colleague*; parcener, coheir, joint h.; shareholder, stockholder 776 *possessor*; co-tenant, joint t., flat-mate, room-m., tenants in common, housing association; sharecropper, métayer 370 *farmer*; cooperator, mutualist; trade unionist; collectivist, socialist, communist; commune-dweller, kibbutznik; sympathizer, contributor 707 *patron*.

Adj. *sharing*, joint, profit-sharing, cooperative; common, communal, international, global; collective, socialistic, communistic; partaking, participating, participatory, in on, involved, in the same boat 708 *corporate*; in the swim, in the thick of things; sympathetic, condoling.

Vb. *participate*, have a hand in, join in, sit in, be in on 706 *cooperate*; partake of, share in, take a share, come in for a s.; share, go shares, go halves, go fifty-fifty, share and share alike 783 *apportion*; share expenses, go Dutch 804 *defray*.

communalize, socialize, mutualize, nationalize, internationalize, communize; put in the kitty, pool, hold in common, have all in c.

Adv. *in common*, by shares, share and share alike; jointly, collectively, unitedly, communally.

See: 78, 370, 632, **706**, 707, 708, 733, 776, 777, **783**, 804.

776 Possessor

N. *possessor*, holder, person in possession; taker, captor, conqueror; trespasser, squatter; monopolizer, dog in the manger; occupant, lodger, occupier, incumbent; mortgagee, bailee, trustee; renter, hirer, lessee, leaseholder, copyholder, rent-payer; tenantry, tenant, protected t., council t.; house-owner, householder, freeholder, franklin, yeoman; feudatory, feoffee, tenant in fee, vassal 742 *dependant*; peasant, serf, villein, kulak, moujik 370 *farmer*; subtenant, undertenant.

owner, monarch, monarch of all one surveys; master, mistress, proprietor, proprietress; purchaser, buyer 792 *purchaser*; lord, lord paramount, lord of the manor, mesne lord, feoffer; landed gentry, landed interest; squire, laird 868 *aristocracy*; man *or* woman of property, property-owner, property-holder, shareholder, stockholder, landholder, zamindar, landowner, landlord, landlady; mortgagor; testator, testatrix, bequeather, devisor 781 *giver*.

beneficiary, feoffee, releasee, grantee; impropriator, lay i. 782 *recipient*; incumbent 986 *cleric*; devisee, legatee; inheritor, heritor, expectant, successor, successor apparent, tanist; next of kin 11 *kinsman*; heir *or* heiress, expectant h., heir of the body, heir-at-law, heir in tail, heir apparent, heir presumptive; crown prince 741 *sovereign*; reversioner, remainderman; coheir, joint heir 775 *participator*.

See: 11, 370, 741, 742, 775, 781, **782**, **792**, 868, 986.

777 Property

N. *property*, meum et tuum, suum cuique; possession, possessions, one's all; stake, venture; personalty, personal property, public p., common p.; church property, temporalities; chose in possession, chattel, real property, immovables (**see** *lands*); movables, personal estate, goods and chattels, appurtenances, belongings, paraphernalia, effects, personal e., impedimenta, baggage, bag and baggage, things, what one stands up in; cargo, lading 193 *contents*; goods, wares, stock, stock-in-trade 795 *merchandise*; plant, fixtures, furniture.

estate, estate and effects, assets, frozen a., liquid a., assets and liabilities; circumstances, what one is worth, what one will cut up for; resources 629 *means*; substance, capital, one's money, one's fortune 800 *wealth*; revenue, income, rent-roll 807 *receipt*; valuables, securities, stocks and shares, portfolio; stake, holding, investment; copyright, patent; chose in action, claim, demand, debts; right, title, interest; living 985 *benefice*; lease, tenure, freehold, copyhold, fee, fee simple, fee tail; tenement, hereditament.

lands, land, acres, broad a., acreage, grounds; estate, landed e., property, landed p.; real estate, real property, realty; hereditament, tenement, holding, tenure, allodium, freehold, copyhold, fief, feud, manor, honour, seigniory, lordship, domain, demesne; messuage, toft, plot 184 *territory*; farm, home f., ranch, hacienda;

crown lands, common land, common 775 *joint possession*; dependency, dominion 733 *political organization*.

dower, dowry, dot, portion, marriage p., jointure, marriage settlement; allotment, allowance, pin money; alimony, patrimony, birthright 915 *dueness*; appanage, heritage; inheritance, legacy, bequest; heirloom; expectations, remainder, reversion; limitation, entail; mortmain.

Adj. *proprietary*, branded, patented; movable, immovable, real, personal; propertied, landed, predial, manorial, seigniorial, feudal, allodial, freehold, leasehold, copyhold; patrimonial, hereditary, heritable, testamentary; entailed, limited; dowered, endowed, established.

Vb. *dower*, endow, possess with, bless w. 781 *give*; devise 780 *bequeath*; grant, allot 780 *assign*; possess, put in possession, install 751 *commission*; establish, found.

See: 184, 193, 629, 733, 751, 775, 780, 781, 795, **800**, 807, 915, 985.

778 Retention

N. *retention*, prehensility, tenacity; stickiness 354 *viscidity*; tenaciousness, retentiveness, holding on, hanging on, clinging to, prehension; handhold, foothold, toehold 218 *support*; bridgehead, beachhead 34 *advantage*; clutches, grip, iron g., vicelike g., gripe, grasp, hold, firm h., stranglehold, half-nelson; squeeze 198 *compression*; clinch, lock; hug, bear h., embrace, clasp, cuddle 889 *endearment*; keep, ward, keeping in 747 *detention*; finders keepers 760 *refusal*; containment, holding action, pincer movement 235 *enclosure*; plug, stop 264 *stopper*; ligament 47 *bond*.

nippers, pincers, tweezers, pliers, wrench, tongs, forceps, vice, clamp 47 *fastening*; talon, claw, nails 256 *sharp point*; tentacle, hook, tendril 378 *feeler*; teeth, fangs 256 *tooth*; paw, hand, fingers 378 *finger*; fist, clenched f.

Adj. *retentive*, tenacious, prehensile; vicelike, retaining 747 *restraining*; clinging, adhesive, sticky, gummy, gooey 48 *cohesive*; firm, indissoluble, unshakable 45 *tied*; tight, strangling, throttling; tightfisted 816 *parsimonious*; shut fast 264 *closed*.

retained, in the grip of, gripped, pinioned, pinned, clutched, strangled; fast, stuck f., bound, held; kept in, detained 747 *imprisoned*; penned, held in, contained 232 *circumscribed*; saved, kept 666 *preserved*; booked, reserved, engaged; not for sale; unforfeited, kept back, withheld 760 *refused*; uncommunicated, esoteric, incommunicable 523 *occult*; nontransferable, inalienable; entailed, in mortmain.

Vb. *retain*, hold; grab, buttonhole, hold back 702 *obstruct*; hold up, catch, steady 218 *support*; hold on, hold fast, hold tight, keep a firm hold of, maintain one's hold, not let go; cling to, hang on to, freeze on to, stick to, adhere 48 *agglutinate*; fasten on, grip, gripe, grasp, grapple, clench, clinch, lock; hug, clasp, clutch, embrace; pin, pin down, hold d.; have by the throat, throttle, strangle, keep a stranglehold on, get a half-nelson on, tighten one's grip 747 *restrain*; fix one's teeth in, dig one's nails in, dig one's toes in, hang on like a bulldog, hang on for dear life; keep in, detain 747 *imprison*; contain, keep within limits, draw the line 235 *enclose*; keep to oneself, keep in one's own hands, keep back, withhold 525 *keep secret*; keep in hand, have in hand, not dispose of 632 *store*; save, keep 666 *preserve*; not part with, keep back, withhold 760 *refuse*.

See: 34, 45, **47**, 48, 198, 218, 232, 235, 256, 264, 354, 378, 523, 525, 632, 666, 702, **747**, 760, 816, 889.

779 Nonretention

N. *nonretention*, parting with, disposal, alienation 780 *transfer*; selling off 793 *sale*; letting go, leaving hold of, release 746 *liberation*; unfreezing, decontrol; dispensation, exemption 919 *nonliability*; dissolution (of a marriage) 896 *divorce*; cession, abandonment, renunciation 621 *relinquishment*; cancellation 752 *abrogation*; disuse 611 *desuetude*; availability, salability, disposability; unsoundness, leaking, leak 298 *outflow*.

derelict, deserted village, abandoned position; jetsam, flotsam 641 *rubbish*; castoff, slough; waif, stray, foundling, orphan, maroon, outcast, pariah.

Adj. *not retained*, not kept, under notice to quit; alienated, disposed of, sold off; left behind 41 *remaining*; dispensed with, abandoned 621 *relinquished*; released 746 *liberated*; fired, made redundant, given the sack *or* the chop; derelict, unclaimed, unappropriated; unowned 774 *unpossessed*; disowned, divorced, disinherited;

heritable, inheritable, transferable; available, for sale 793 *salable*; givable, bestowable.

Vb. *not retain*, part with, alienate, transfer 780 *assign*; sell off, dispose of 793 *sell*; be open-handed 815 *be prodigal*; free, let go, let slip, unhand, leave hold of, relax one's grip, release one's hold; unlock, unclinch, unclench 263 *open*; unbind, untie, disentangle 46 *disunite*; forgo, dispense with, do without, spare, give up, waive, abandon, cede, yield 621 *relinquish*; renounce, abjure 603 *recant*; cancel, revoke 752 *abrogate*; lift, lift restrictions, derestrict, decontrol, deration 746 *liberate*; supersede, replace 150 *substitute*; wash one's hands of, disown, disclaim 533 *negate*; dissolve (a marriage) 896 *divorce*; disinherit, cut off with a shilling 801 *impoverish*; marry off 894 *marry*; get rid of, cast off, ditch, jettison, throw overboard 300 *eject*; cast away, abandon, maroon; pension off, invalid out, retire; discharge, give notice to quit, ease out, kick o. 300 *dismiss*; lay off, stand o.; drop, discard 674 *stop using*; withdraw, abandon one's position 753 *resign*; lose friends, estrange 881 *make enemies*; sit loose to 860 *be indifferent*; let out, leak 300 *emit*.

See: 41, **46**, 150, 263, 298, 300, 533, 603, 611, **621**, 641, 674, 746, 752, 753, 774, **780**, 793, 801, 815, 860, 881, 894, 896, 919.

780 Transfer (of property)

N. *transfer*, transmission, consignment, delivery, handover 272 *transference*; enfeoffment, feoffment, impropriation; settlement, limitation; conveyancing, conveyance; bequeathal; assignment; alienation 779 *nonretention*; demise, devise, bequest 781 *gift*; lease, let, rental, hire; buying, bargain and sale 793 *sale*; trade 791 *barter*; conversion, exchange 151 *interchange*; nationalization, privatization; change of hands, changeover 150 *substitution*; devolution, delegation 751 *commission*; heritability, succession, reversion, inheritance; pledge, pawn, hostage.

Adj. *transferred*, made over; borrowed, lent, pawned, leased, rented, hired; transferable, conveyable, alienable, exchangeable, negotiable; heritable, reversional, reversionary; givable, bestowable.

Vb. *assign*, convey, transfer by deed; transfer by will (see *bequeath*); grant, sign away, give a. 781 *give*; let, rent, hire 784 *lease*; alienate 793 *sell*; negotiate, barter 791 *trade*; change over 150 *substitute*; exchange, convert 151 *interchange*; confer, confer ownership, put in possession, impropriate, invest with, enfeoff; commit, devolve, delegate, entrust 751 *commission*; give away, marry off 894 *marry*; deliver, give delivery, transmit, hand over, make o., unload on, pass to, pass the buck 272 *transfer*; pledge, pawn 784 *lend*; transfer ownership, withdraw a gift, give to another; disinherit, cut off 801 *impoverish*; dispossess, expropriate, relieve of 786 *deprive*; transfer to the state, nationalize, municipalize 775 *communalize*.

bequeath, will, will and bequeath, devise, demise; grant, assign; leave, leave by will, make a bequest, leave a legacy; make a will, make one's last will and testament, put in one's will, add a codicil; leave a fortune, cut up well 800 *be rich*; have something to leave.

change hands, pass to another, come into the hands of; change places, be transferred, pass, shift; revert to, devolve upon; pass from one to another, pass from hand to hand, circulate, go the rounds 314 *circle*; succeed, inherit 771 *acquire*.

See: 150, 151, 272, 314, 751, 771, 775, 779, **781**, 784, 786, 791, 793, 800, 801, 894.

781 Giving

N. *giving*, bestowal, donation; alms-giving, charity 901 *philanthropy*; generosity, generous giving 813 *liberality*; contribution, subscription to 703 *subvention*; prize-giving, presentation, award 962 *reward*; delivery, commitment, consignment, conveyance 780 *transfer*; endowment, settlement 777 *dower*; grant, accordance, presentment, conferment; investment, investiture, enfeoffment, infeudation; bequeathal, leaving, will-making.

gift, fairing, keepsake, token; present, birthday p., Christmas p.; good-luck present, handsel; Christmas box, whip-round, tip, fee, honorarium, baksheesh, gratuity, pourboire, trinkgeld, drink money 962 *reward*; token, consideration; bribe, sweetener, douceur 612 *inducement*; prize, award, presentation 729 *trophy*; benefit, benefit match, benefit performance; alms, Maundy money, dole, benefaction, charity 901 *philanthropy*; food parcel, free meal; bounty, manna; largesse, donation, donative, hand-out; bonus, bonanza; something extra, extras; perks, perquisites, expense account; grant, allowance, subsidy, aid 703 *subvention*; boon, grace, favour, service, labour of love 597 *voluntary work*; free gift, outright g., ex gratia payment; piece of luck, windfall 771 *acquisition*; repayment, unsolicited r., conscience money 804 *payment*; forced loan, benevolence, tribute 809 *tax*; bequest, legacy 780 *transfer*.

offering, dedication, consecration; votive offering 979 *piety*; peace offering, thank o., offertory, collection, sacrifice, self-s. 981 *oblation*; Easter offering, Peter's pence; widow's mite; contribution, subscription, flag day; ante, stake.

giver, donor, bestower; rewarder, tipper, briber; grantor, feoffer; presenter, awarder, prize-giver; settlor, testator, legator, devisor, bequeather; subscriber, contributor; sacrificer 981 *worshipper*; tributary, tribute-payer 742 *subject*; almoner, almsgiver, blood donor 903 *benefactor*; generous giver, distributor of largesse, Lady Bountiful, rich uncle, Santa Claus, Father Christmas 813 *good giver*.

Adj. *giving*, granting etc. vb.; tributary 745 *subject*; subscribing, contributory 703 *aiding*; alms-giving, charitable, eleemosynary, compassionate 897 *benevolent*; sacrificial, votive, sacrificing, oblatory 981 *worshipping*; generous, bountiful 813 *liberal*.

given, bestowed, gifted; given away, gratuitous, gratis, for nothing, free 812 *uncharged*; givable, bestowable, allowed, allowable, concessional 756 *permitted*.

Vb. *give*, bestow, lend, render; afford, provide; vouchsafe, favour with, honour w., indulge w., show favour, grant a boon 736 *be lenient*; grant, accord 756 *permit*; gift, donate, make a present of; give by will, leave 780 *bequeath*; dower, endow, enrich; give a prize, present, award 962 *reward*; confer, bestow upon, vest, invest with; dedicate, consecrate, vow to 759 *offer*; devote, offer up, immolate, sacrifice 981 *offer worship*; spare for, have time for; give a present, gratify, tip, consider, remember, cross one's palm with silver; grease the palm 612 *bribe*; bestow alms, give to charity 897 *philanthropize*; give freely, open one's purse, put one's hand in one's pocket, lavish, pour out, shower upon 813 *be liberal*; spare, give free, give away, not charge; stand, treat, entertain 882 *be hospitable*; give out, dispense, dole out, mete o., share o., allot, deal out 783 *apportion*; contribute, subscribe, pay towards, subsidize, help, help with money 703 *aid*; have a whip-round, pass round the hat; pay one's share *or* whack, chip in 775 *participate*; part with, fork out, shell o. 804 *pay*; share, share with, impart 524 *communicate*; render one's due, furnish one's quota 917 *do one's duty*; give one his *or* her due 915 *grant claims*; pay tribute; give up, cede, yield 621 *relinquish*; hand over, give o., make o., deliver 780 *assign*; commit, consign, entrust 751 *commission*; dispatch 272 *send*.

See: 272, 524, 597, 612, 621, 703, 729, 736, 742, 745, 751, 756, 759, 771, 775, 777, **780**, **783**, 804, 809, 812, **813**, 882, **897**, 901, 903, 915, 917, 962, 979, 981.

782 Receiving

N. *receiving*, admittance 299 *reception*; getting 771 *acquisition*; acceptance, recipience, assumption; inheritance, succession, heirship; collection, collectorship, receivership, receipt of custom; a receipt, windfall 781 *gift*; toll, tribute, dues, receipts, proceeds, winnings, takings 771 *earnings*; receiving end.

recipient, acceptor, receiver, taker, biter; trustee 754 *consignee*; addressee 588 *correspondent*; buyer 792 *purchaser*; donee, grantee, assignee, allottee, licensee, patentee, concessionnaire, lessee, releasee; devisee, legatee, inheritor, heir, successor 776 *beneficiary*; payee, earner, stipendiary, wage-earner; pensioner, old-age p., pensionary, annuitant; remittance man 742 *dependant*; winner, prize-w., scholar, exhibitioner; object of charity 763 *beggar*; one at the receiving end 825 *sufferer*.

receiver, official r., liquidator 798 *treasurer*; payee, collector, bill-c., debt-c., rent-c., tax-c., tax-farmer, publican; income-tax officer, excise o., excisemen, customs officer, douanier; booking clerk; shareholder, bond-holder, rentier.

Adj. *receiving*, recipient; receptive, welcoming; impressionable 819 *sensitive*; paid, stipendiary, wage-earning; pensionary, pensioned; awarded, given, favoured.

Vb. *receive*, be given, have from; get 771 *acquire*; collect, take up, levy, toll 786 *take*; gross, net, pocket, pouch; be in receipt of, have received; get one's share; accept, take in 299 *admit*; accept from, take f., draw, encash, be paid; have an income, draw a pension; inherit, succeed to, come into, come in for; receipt, give a r., acknowledge.

be received, be drawn, be receipted; be credited, be added unto 38 *accrue*; come to hand, come in, roll in; pass into one's hands, stick to one's fingers, fall to one's share, fall to one's lot.

See: 38, 299, 588, 742, 754, 763, **771**, 776, 781, 786, 792, 798, 819, 825.

783 Apportionment

N. *apportionment*, appointment, assignment, allotment, allocation, appropriation; division, partition, repartition, sharing out; shares, fair s., distribution, deal, new d.; dispensing, dispensation, administration; demarcation, delimitation 236 *limit*; place, assigned p., allotted sphere, seat, station 27 *degree*; public sector, private s.

portion, share, share-out, cut, split; dividend, interim d., final d.; allocation, allotment; lot, contingent; proportion, ratio; quantum, quota; halves, bigger half, moiety 53 *part*; deal, hand (at cards); dole, mess, modicum, pittance, allowance; ration, iron rations, ration book, coupon; dose, dosage, measure, dollop, whack, helping, slice, slice of the cake 53 *piece*; rake-off, commission 810 *discount*; stake, ante; allotted task, taskwork, task, stint 682 *labour*.

Vb. *apportion*, allot, allocate, appropriate; appoint, assign; assign a part, cast, cast for a role; assign a place, detail, billet; partition, zone; demarcate, delimit 236 *limit*; divide, carve up, split, cut; halve 92 *bisect*; go shares 775 *participate*; share, share out, divvy up, distribute, spread around; dispense, administer, serve, deal, deal out, portion out, dole out, parcel out, dish out 781 *give*; mete out, measure, admeasure, ration, dose; divide proportionately, prorate; get a share, take one's whack.

Adv. *pro rata*, to each according to his share; proportionately, respectively, each to each, per head, per capita.

See: 27, **53**, 92, 236, 682, 775, **781**, 810.

784 Lending

N. *lending*, hiring, leasing, farming out; letting, subletting, subinfeudation; lending at interest, usury, giving credit 802 *credit*; investment; mortgage, bridging loan; advance, imprest, loan, accommodation, temporary a.; lending on security, pawnbroking; lease, long l.; let, sublet.

pawnshop, pawnbroker's, mont-de-piété, pop-shop, hock s.; bank, credit company, finance c., building society, International Monetary Fund, World Bank.

lender, creditor; harsh creditor, extortioner; investor, financier, banker; moneylender, usurer, loan shark, Shylock; pawnbroker, uncle; mortgagee, lessor, hirer, renter; backer, angel; seller on credit, tallyman; hire-purchase dealer.

Adj. *lending*, investing, laying out; usurious, extortionate; lent, loaned, on credit.

Vb. *lend*, loan, put out at interest; advance, accommodate, allow credit, give one a loan 802 *credit*; lend on security; put up the money, back, finance; invest, sink; risk one's money 791 *speculate*.

lease, let, demise, let out, hire out, let out on hire, farm out; sublet, subinfeudate.

Adv. *on loan*, on credit, on advance; on security.

See: 791, 802.

785 Borrowing

N. *borrowing*, touching; request for credit, loan application; loan transaction, mortgage 803 *debt*; credit account, credit card; hire purchase, HP, instalment plan, the never-never; pledging, pawning; temporary misappropriation, joyride 788 *stealing*; something borrowed, loan, repayable amount 784 *lending*; forced loan, benevolence 809 *tax*; unauthorized borrowing, infringement, plagiarism, copying 20 *imitation*; borrowed plumes 542 *deception*.

Vb. *borrow*, borrow from, touch, touch for 761 *request*; hypothecate, mortgage, pawn, pledge, pop, hock 767 *give security*; take a loan, exact a benevolence; use a credit card, get credit, get accommodation, take on loan, take on credit, take on tick; buy in instalments, buy on hire purchase *or* the never-never 792 *purchase*; incur liabilities, run into debt 803 *be in debt*; promise to pay, ask for credit, apply for a loan, raise a loan, raise the wind, float a loan; invite investment, issue debentures, accept deposits; beg, borrow, or steal 771 *acquire*; cheat, crib, plagiarize, infringe 20 *copy*.

hire, rent, farm, lease, take on lease, charter.

See: 20, 542, 761, 767, 771, 784, 788, 792, **803**, 809.

786 Taking

N. *taking*, snatching; seizure, capture, rape; taking hold, grasp, prehension, apprehension 778 *retention*; taking possession, assuming ownership, appropriation, assumption 916 *arrogation*; requisition, commandeering, compulsory purchase 771 *acquisition*; compulsory saving, postwar credit 785 *borrowing*; exaction, taxation, raising taxes, impost, levy, capital l. 809 *tax*; taking back, recovery, retrieval, recoupment; taking away, removal 188 *displacement*; furtive removal 788 *stealing*; cadging, scrounging, totting; bodily removal, abduction, press gang, kidnapping, slave-raiding, piracy; raid 788 *spoliation*; thing taken, take, haul, catch, capture, prize, plum 790 *booty*; receipts, takings, winnings, pickings, gleanings 771 *earnings*.

expropriation, dispossession, angary; forcible seizure, attachment, distraint, distress, foreclosure; eviction, expulsion 300 *ejection*; takeover, deprivation, divestment 752 *abrogation*; hiving off, asset-stripping; disinheritance 780 *transfer*; taking without compensation, confiscation, capital levy; exaction, extortion; swindle, rip-off; impounding, sequestration.

rapacity, rapaciousness, thirst for loot; avidity, thirst 859 *hunger*; greed, insatiable g., insatiability 816 *avarice*; vampirism, blood-sucking; extortion, blackmail.

taker, appropriator, remover; seizer, snatcher, grabber; spoiler, raider, pillager, marauder, ransacker, sacker, looter, despoiler 789 *robber*; kidnapper, abductor, press gang; slave-raider, slaver; captor, capturer 741 *master*; usurper, arrogator; extortioner, blackmailer; locust, devourer 168 *destroyer*; bloodsucker, leech, parasite, vampire, harpy, vulture, wolf, shark; beast of prey, predator; confiscator, sequestrator 782 *receiver*; expropriator, disseisor; asset-stripper.

Adj. *taking*, abstractive, deductive; grasping, extortionate, rapacious, wolfish, vulturine; devouring, all-d., all-engulfing, voracious, ravening, ravenous 859 *hungry*; raptorial, predatory 788 *thieving*; privative, expropriatory, confiscatory; commandeering, requisitory; acquisitive, possessive 771 *acquiring*.

Vb. *take*, accept, be given 782 *receive*; take over, take back (**see** *appropriate*); take in, let in 299 *admit*; take up, snatch up; take in advance, anticipate 135 *be early*; take hold, fasten on, clutch, grip, cling 778 *retain*; lay hands upon, seize, snatch, grab, pounce, pounce on, spring; snatch at, reach, reach out for, make a long arm; grasp at, clutch at, grab at, make a grab, scramble for, rush f.; capture, rape, storm, take by s. 727 *overmaster*; conquer, captive, lead c. 745 *subjugate*; catch, overtake, intercept 277 *outstrip*; apprehend, take into custody, make an arrest, nab, nobble, collar, lay by the heels 747 *arrest*; make sure of, fasten, pinion 747 *fetter*; hook, trap, snare, lime 542 *ensnare*; net, land, bag, pocket, pouch; gross, have a turnover 771 *acquire*; gather, accumulate, collect 74 *bring together*; cull, pick, pluck; reap, crop, harvest, glean 370 *cultivate*; scrounge, tot, ransack 459 *search*; pick up, snap up, snaffle; knock off, help oneself 788 *steal*; pick clean, strip 229 *uncover*; remove, withdraw (**see** *take away*); deduct 39 *subtract*; take out, unload, unlade 188 *displace*; draw, draw out, draw off, milk, tap, mine 304 *extract*; take the lot, sweep the board, scoop the pool.

appropriate, take to *or* for oneself, make one's own, annex; pirate, plagiarize 20 *copy*; take possession, stake one's claim; take over, assume, assume ownership, impropriate 773 *possess*; enter into, come i., succeed 771 *inherit*; install oneself, seat o. 187 *place oneself*; overrun, swarm over, people, populate, occupy, settle, colonize; win, conquer; take back, get back one's own, recover, resume, repossess, recapture, reconquer 656 *retrieve*; reclaim 915 *claim*; commandeer, requisition 737 *demand*; nationalize, secularize 775 *communalize*; denationalize, privatize; usurp, arrogate, trespass, squat 916 *be undue*; dispossess (**see** *deprive*); treat as one's own, make free with; monopolize, hog, be a dog in the manger; sweep everything into one's net, engulf, suck in, suck up, swallow 299 *absorb*; devour, eat up. **See** *fleece.*

levy, raise, extort, exact, wrest from, wring f., force f. 304 *extract*; compel to lend 785 *borrow*; exact tribute, make pay, collect a toll; raise taxes 809 *tax*; overtax, rack-rent, suck dry (**see** *fleece*); draw off, exhaust, drain 300 *empty*; wring, squeeze, squeeze to the last drop, squeeze till the pips squeak 735 *oppress*; divert resources, sequestrate.

take away, remove, shift, unload 188 *displace*; send away 272 *send*; lighten 701 *disencumber*; hive off, abstract, relieve of 788 *steal*; remove bodily, escort 89 *accompany*; kidnap, crimp, shanghai, press, impress, abduct, ravish, carry off, bear off, bear away; hurry off with, run away w., run off w., elope w., clear off w. 296 *decamp*; raid, loot, plunder 788 *rob*.

deprive, bereave, orphan, widow; divest, denude, strip 229 *uncover*; unfrock, unthrone 752 *depose*; dispossess, usurp 916 *disentitle*; oust, evict, expel 300 *eject*; expropriate, confiscate, sequester, sequestrate, distrain, foreclose; disinherit, cut out of one's will, cut off, cut off with a shilling.

fleece, pluck, skin, shear, gut; strip, strip bare 229 *uncover*; take to the cleaners, rip off; swindle, cheat 542 *deceive*; blackmail, bleed, bleed white, sponge, suck, suck like a leech, suck dry; soak, sting; mulct 788 *defraud*; devour, eat up, eat out of house and home 301 *eat*; take one's all, bankrupt, leave one without a penny *or* cent 801 *impoverish*.

See: 20, 39, 74, 89, 135, 168, 187, 188, 229, 272, 277, 296, 299, 300, 301, 304, 370, 459, 542, 656, 701, 727, 735, 737, 741, 745, 747, 752, **771**, **773**, 775, 778, 780, 782, 785, 788, 789, 790, 801, 809, 816, 859, 915, 916.

787 Restitution

N. *restitution*, giving back, return, reversion; bringing back, repatriation; reinstatement, reenthronement, reinvestment; rehabilitation 656 *restoration*; redemption, ransom, rescue 668 *deliverance*; recuperation, replevin, recovery; compensation, indemnification; repayment, recoupment; refund, reimbursement; indemnity, damages 963 *penalty*; amends, reparation 941 *atonement*.

Adj. *restoring*, restitutory, refunding; indemnificatory, compensatory 941 *atoning*.

Vb. *restitute*, make restitution 656 *restore*; return, render, give back 779 *not retain*; pay up, cough up 804 *pay*; refund, repay, recoup, reimburse; indemnify, pay an indemnity, pay damages, compensate, make it up to; pay compensation, make reparation, make amends 941 *atone*; bring back, repatriate; ransom, redeem 668 *deliver*; reinstate, reinvest, rehabilitate, set up again, raise one to his feet, restore one to favour; recover 656 *retrieve*.

See: **656**, 668, 779, 804, 941, 963.

788 Stealing

N. *stealing*, thieving, lifting, robbing etc. vb.; theft, larceny, petty l., grand l., compound l.; pilfering, filching, robbing the till, pickpocketing, shoplifting; burglary, house-breaking, breaking and entering; safe-blowing, s.-breaking, s.-cracking; robbery, highway r., gang r., dacoity, thuggee; robbery with violence, stickup, holdup, bag-snatching, mugging, smash and grab raid; cattle-raiding, c.-rustling; rape, abduction, kidnapping, hijack; slave-raiding; body-snatching; abstraction, removal 786 *taking*; literary theft, cribbing, plagiarism, pirating, copyright infringement 20 *imitation*; temporary misappropriation, joyride 785 *borrowing*; thievery, act of theft; job, fiddle.

brigandage, banditry, outlawry, piracy, buccaneering, filibustering; privateering, letters of marque 718 *warfare*; raiding, raid, razzia, foray 712 *attack*.

spoliation, plundering, looting, pillage; cattle-rustling (**see** *brigandage*); sack, sacking; depredations, rapine, ravaging 165 *havoc*.

peculation, embezzlement, misappropriation, malversation, breach of trust, fraudulent conversion; blackmail, extortion, protection racket; daylight robbery, rip-off; moonlighting, tax evasion, fraud, fiddle, swindle, cheating; confidence trick, skin game 542 *deception*.

thievishness, thievery, light-fingeredness, light fingers, kleptomania; predacity 786 *rapacity*; dishonesty, crookedness, unreliability 930 *improbity*; burglarious intent, intention to steal; den of thieves, thieves' kitchen.

Adj. *thieving*, in the act of theft; with intent to steal; thievish, light-fingered; kleptomaniac; furacious, larcenous, burglarious; predatory, predacious, raptorial; piratical, buccaneering, filibustering, privateering, raiding, marauding; scrounging, foraging; fraudulent, on the fiddle 930 *dishonest.*

Vb. *steal,* lift, thieve, pilfer, shoplift, help oneself; be light-fingered, pick pockets, have a finger in the till; pick locks, blow a safe; burgle, burglarize, house-break; rob, relieve of; rifle, sack, clean out; swipe, nobble, nick, pinch, half-inch, pocket, bone, prig, snaffle, snitch, knock off 786 *take*; forage, scrounge; lift cattle, rustle, drive off, make off with; abduct, kidnap, shanghai; abstract, purloin, filch; sneak off with, walk off w., make away w., spirit away; crib, copy, plagiarize, infringe copyright, pirate 20 *copy*; smuggle, run, bootleg, poach, hijack, skyjack.

defraud, embezzle, peculate, misappropriate, purloin, let stick to one's fingers; fiddle, cook the books, commit breach of trust, obtain money on false pretences; con, swindle, cheat, diddle, chisel, do out of, bilk 542 *deceive*; rook, pigeon, gull, dupe; pluck, skin, rip off 786 *fleece.*

rob, rob with violence, mug; commit highway robbery, hold up, stick up; pirate, sail under the skull and crossbones, buccaneer, filibuster, maraud, reave, raid; foray, forage, scrounge; strip, gut, ransack, rifle; plunder, pillage, loot, sack, put to the s., despoil, ravage, spoil 165 *lay waste*; make a prey of, victimize, blackmail, demand money with menaces; extort, screw, squeeze 735 *oppress.*

See: 20, 165, 542, 712, 718, 735, 785, **786**, **930**.

789 Thief

N. *thief,* thieving fraternity, swell mob, light-fingered gentry, den of thieves; crook, Artful Dodger; pickers and stealers, light fingers; kleptomaniac, stealer, lifter, filcher, purloiner, pilferer, petty thief, larcenist; sneaker, sneak thief, shoplifter; pickpocket, dip, cutpurse, bag-snatcher; cattle thief, rustler; burglar, cat b., house-breaker, safe-b., safe-blower, cracksman, picklock, yegg, yeggman; poacher, bootlegger, smuggler, runner, night r., gun r.; abductor, kidnapper 786 *taker*; slaver, slave-raider; body-snatcher, resurrectionist; fence, receiver of stolen property; plagiarist, infringer, pirate.

robber, robber band, forty thieves; brigand, bandit, outlaw, Robin Hood; footpad, highwayman, knight of the road, Dick Turpin, Jonathan Wild; mugger, thug, dacoit, gang-robber 904 *ruffian*; gangster, racketeer; gunman, hijacker; sea rover, pirate, buccaneer, picaroon, corsair, filibuster, privateer; Captain Kidd, Long John Silver; reaver, marauder, raider, freebooter, moss-trooper, cateran, rapparee; plunderer, pillager, sacker, ravager, spoiler, despoiler, depredator; wrecker.

defrauder, embezzler, peculator, fiddler, diddler; defaulter, welsher; swindler, sharper, cheat, shark, con man, chevalier d'industrie 545 *trickster*; forger, counterfeiter, coin-clipper.

See: 545, 786, 904.

790 Booty

N. *booty,* spoil, spoils; spoils of war, spolia opima 729 *trophy*; plunder, loot, pillage; prey, victim, quarry; find, strike, prize, purchase, haul, catch 771 *gain*; pickings, tottings; stolen article, stolen goods, swag; moonshine, hooch, bootleg, contraband; illicit gains, graft, boodle, blackmail; pork barrel 703 *subvention.*

See: 703, 729, 771.

791 Barter

N. *barter,* exchange, fair e., swap 151 *interchange*; exchange of goods, payment in kind, truck, truck system; traffic, trading, dealing, buying and selling; factorage, factorship, brokerage, agiotage, arbitrage, jobbing, stock-jobbing, share-pushing; negotiation, bargaining, hard b., higgling, haggling, horse-trading.

trade, commercial intercourse; trading, exporting 272 *transference*; visible trade, invisible t.; foreign trade, home *or* domestic t.; protection, trade restrictions 747 *restriction*; free trade, open market 796 *market*; traffic, drug t., white slave t., slave trade; smuggling, black market; retail trade 793 *sale*; capitalism, free enterprise, laisser faire 744 *scope*; free market economy, boom and bust 317 *fluctuation*; profit-making, mutual profit; tied aid, dollar diplomacy 612 *inducement*; commerce, business affairs 622 *business*; private enterprise, state e.; private sector, public s.; venture, business v. 672 *undertaking*; speculation 618 *gambling*; transaction, commercial t., deal, business d., bargain, negotiation 765 *compact*; clientele, custom 792 *purchase*.

Adj. *trading*, trafficking, exchanging; swapping, au pair; commercial, commercialistic, mercantile; wholesale, retail; exchangeable, marketable, merchantable 793 *salable*; for profit 618 *speculative*.

Vb. *trade*, exchange 151 *interchange*; barter, truck, swap, do a s.; traffic in, merchandise in; buy and sell, buy cheap and sell dear, export and import; open a trade, drive a t., merchant 622 *do business*; trade in, deal in, handle; deal in stolen property, fence; turn over, turn over one's stock 793 *sell*; commercialize, put on a business footing; trade with, do business w., deal w., have dealings w., open an account w.; finance, back, promote; look to one's profit, have an eye to business, go out for trade; be a thorough businessman *or* -woman, know the price of everything and the value of nothing.

speculate, venture, risk 618 *gamble*; invest, sink one's capital in, put one's money to work; rig the market, racketeer, profiteer; deal in the black market, sell under the counter; deal in futures, dabble in shares, play the market, go bust; go on the Stock Exchange, operate, bull, bear, stag.

bargain, negotiate, chaffer; push up, beat down; huckster, haggle, higgle, dicker, argy-bargy 766 *make terms*; bid for, make a bid, make a takeover bid, preempt; raise the bid, outbid 759 *offer*; overbid 482 *overrate*; underbid 483 *underestimate*; stickle, stick out for, hold out for, state one's terms, ask for, charge 766 *give terms*; settle for, take; drive a bargain, do a deal, shake hands on 765 *contract*.

Adv. *in trade*, in commerce, in business, in the marketplace, on Change; across the counter, under the counter.

See: 151, 272, 317, 482, 483, 612, 618, **622**, 672, 744, 747, 759, 765, 766, 792, 793, 796.

792 Purchase

N. *purchase*, buying; buying up, takeover, cornering, forestalling, preemption; redemption, ransom 668 *deliverance*; purchase on account, purchase on credit, hire purchase, the never-never 785 *borrowing*; shopping, window s., spending, shopping spree 806 *expenditure*; shopping by post, mail order; regular buying, custom, patronage, consumer demand 627 *requirement*; buying over, bribery 612 *inducement*; bid, take-over b. 759 *offer*; first refusal, right of purchase; a purchase, buy, good b., bargain, real b., one's money's worth; purchases, shopping list, requirements.

purchaser, buyer, emptor, preemptor; vendee, transferee, consignee; buyer of labour, employer; shopper, window-s.; customer, patron, client, clientele, consumer; offerer, bidder, highest b.; taker, acceptor; bargainer, haggler; ransomer, redeemer; share-buyer, bull, stag.

Adj. *bought*, paid for, ransomed, redeemed; purchased, bribed; purchasable, bribable; worth buying 644 *valuable*.

buying, redemptive, purchasing, shopping, marketing; cash and carry, cash on delivery, C.O.D., preemptive, bidding, bargaining, haggling; in the market for; bullish.

Vb. *purchase*, make a p., complete a p.; buy, acquire by purchase 771 *acquire*; shop, window-s., market, go shopping; have a shopping list 627 *require*; make a good buy, get one's money's worth; buy outright, buy over the counter, pay cash for; buy on credit, buy on hire purchase; buy on account, buy on tick 785 *borrow*; pay by cheque *or* by Giro, buy in 632 *store*; buy up, preempt, corner, make a corner in; buy out, make a take-over bid; buy over, square, suborn 612 *bribe*; buy back, redeem, repurchase, ransom 668 *deliver*; pay for, bear the cost of 804 *defray*; buy oneself in, invest in, sink one's money in 791 *speculate*; buy service, rent 785 *hire*; bid, bid for, bid up 759 *offer*; buy shares, bull, stag.

See: 612, 627, 632, 644, 668, 759, 771, **785**, **791**, 804, **806**.

793 Sale

N. *sale*, selling, vendition; putting on sale, marketing; disposal 779 *nonretention*; clearance, sell-out; clearance sale, stocktaking s., white s., jumble s., sale of work, bazaar; sale of office, simony 930 *improbity*; exclusive sale, monopoly, oligopoly 747 *restraint*; public sale, auctioneering, auction, sale by a., roup, Dutch auction, vendue; good market, market for; sales, good s., boom 730 *prosperity*; bad sales 731 *adversity*; salesmanship, service, sales talk, pitch, sales patter, spiel; hard sell, soft s. 528 *advertisement*;

market research 459 *enquiry*; salability, vendibility, marketability; vendible, thing sold, seller, best-s., selling line 795 *merchandise*.

seller, vendor, consignor, transferor; share-seller, bear; auctioneer; market trader, barrow boy, costermonger, hawker 794 *pedlar*; shopkeeper, dealer 633 *caterer*; wholesaler, marketer, retailer 794 *tradespeople*; sales representative, rep, door-to-door salesman; traveller, commercial t., travelling salesman *or* -woman, knight of the road; agent, canvasser, tout; shop walker, shop assistant, shop girl, salesman, saleswoman; clerk, booking c., ticket agent; roundsman, milkman.

Adj. *salable*, vendible, marketable, on sale; sold, sold out; in demand, sought after, called for; available, on the market, up for sale; bearish; on auction, under the hammer.

Vb. *sell*, make a sale; flog, dispose of; market, put on sale, offer for s., have for s., vend; bring to market, unload on the market, dump; hawk, peddle, push; canvass, tout; cater for the market 633 *provide*; put up for sale, auction, auction off, sell by a., bring under the hammer, sell to the highest bidder, knock down to; wholesale; retail, sell over the counter; turn over one's stock 791 *trade*; realize one's capital, encash; sell at a profit 771 *gain*; sell at a loss 772 *lose*; undercut 812 *cheapen*; sell off, remainder; sell up, sell out, wind up 145 *cease*; clear stock, hold a sale; sell again, re-sell; sell forward.

be sold, be on sale, come under the hammer 780 *change hands*; sell, have a sale, have a market, meet a demand, be in d., sell well, sell like hot cakes, sell out, boom; be a selling line, be a best-seller; sell badly, stay on the shelf.

See: 145, 459, 528, 633, 730, 731, 747, 771, 772, 779, 780, **791**, **794**, **795**, 812, 930.

794 Merchant

N. *merchant*, merchant prince, merchant venturer; liveryman, livery company, guild, chamber of commerce, concern, firm 708 *corporation*; business person, man *or* woman of business; entrepreneur, speculator, operator 618 *gambler*; trafficker, fence; slaver, slave trader; importer, exporter; wholesale merchant, wholesaler; merchandiser, dealer, chandler; middleman, broker, stockbroker; stock-jobber, share-pusher; estate agent, house a.; financier, company promoter; banker 784 *lender*; money-changer, cambist.

tradespeople, tradesfolk; tradesman, retailer, middleman, regrater, tallyman; shopkeeper, storekeeper 793 *seller*; monger, ironmonger, mercer, haberdasher, grocer, provision merchant 633 *caterer*.

pedlar, peddler 793 *seller*; rag-and-bone man; itinerant tradesman, street seller, hawker, huckster, colporteur, bagman, chapman, cheapjack; coster, costermonger, barrow boy; market trader, stallkeeper; sutler, vivandière 633 *caterer*.

See: 618, 633, 708, 784, **793**.

795 Merchandise

N. *merchandise*, article of commerce, line, staple; article, commodity, salable c., vendible, stock, stock-in-trade, range, repertoire 632 *store*; freight, cargo 193 *contents*; stuff, things for sale, supplies, wares, goods, capital g., durables; shop goods, consumer g., consumer durables; perishable goods, canned g., dry g., white g., sundries.

See: 193, 632.

796 Market

N. *market*, daily m., weekly m., mart; open market, free trade area, Common Market, Comecon; free market, open-door policy 791 *trade*; black market, underground economy, black e.; seller's market, buyer's m.; marketplace, market cross, forum, agora 76 *focus*; street market, flea m., Petticoat Lane; auction room, Christie's, Sotheby's; fair, world f., international f., trade f., industries f., horse f., goose f., motor show; exhibition, exposition, shop window 522 *exhibit*; corn market, wheat pit, corn exchange; exchange, Stock E., Change, bourse, kerb market, bucket shop; Wall Street, Rialto; toll booth, custom house.

emporium, free port, entrepôt, depot, warehouse 632 *storage*; wharf, quay; trading centre, trading post; general market, bazaar, arcade, covered market, pedestrian precinct, shopping centre.

shop, retailer's; store, multiple s., department s., chain s.; emporium, bazaar, boutique, bargain basement, supermarket, hypermarket, superstore, cash and carry;

concern, firm, establishment, house, trading h.; corner shop, stall, booth, stand, newstand, kiosk, barrow, vending machine, slot m.; counter, shop window, window display; premises, place of business 687 *workshop*.

See: 76, 522, 632, 687, **791**.

797 Money

N. *money*, Lsd, pounds, shillings and pence; pelf, Mammon 800 *wealth*; lucre, filthy l., root of all evil; medium of exchange, circulating medium, cash nexus; currency, decimal c., managed c., fluctuating c., hard c., soft c.; sound currency, honest money, legal tender; money of account, sterling, pound s.; precious metal, gold, ringing g., clinking g.; silver, siller (**see** *bullion*); ready money, the ready, the best, cash, spot c., hard c., petty c.; change, small c., coppers 33 *small coin*; pocket money, pin m.; spending m.; paltry sum, chickenfeed, peanuts.

shekels, dibs, shiners, spondulicks, brass, tin, rhino, dough, lolly, sugar, bread; boodle, swag, loot, gravy; soap, palm oil 612 *incentive*.

funds, temporary f., hot money; liquidity, account, bank a., current a., deposit a., money in the bank, bank annuities; liquid assets; wherewithal, the needful 629 *means*; sinews of war, ready money, the ready, finances, exchequer, financial provision, cash flow, cash supplies, monies, treasure 633 *provision*; remittance 804 *payment*; funds for investment, capital; funds in hand, reserves, balances, sterling b.; sum of money, amount, figure, sum, round s., lump s.; quid, smacker, oncer; fiver, tenner, pony, monkey, grand; mint of money, wads, scads, pile, packet, stacks, millions, billions, crores, lakhs 32 *great quantity*; moneybags, purse, bottomless p. 632 *store*.

finance, high f., world of finance; financial control, money power, purse strings, power of the purse, almighty dollar; money dealings, cash transaction; money market, Eurodollar m., exchange 796 *market*; exchange rate, valuta, parity, par 28 *equality*; snake; floating pound; devaluation, depreciation, falling exchange rate 655 *deterioration*; rising exchange rate, strong pound 654 *improvement*; bimetallism; gold standard; green pound; managed currency, equalization fund, sinking f., revolving f.; deficit finance, inflation, inflationary spiral; disinflation, deflation; stagflation; reflation.

coinage, minting, issue; metallic currency, stamped coinage, gold c., silver c., electrum c., copper c., nickel c., billon c., bronze c.; specie, minted coinage, coin, piece, coin of the realm; monetary unit, monetary denomination; guinea, sovereign, half s.; pound, quid; crown, half c., florin, shilling, bob, sixpence, tanner, threepenny bit, penny, bun p., copper, halfpenny, ship h.; farthing; decimal coinage, fifty p, ten p, five p, two p, one p, half p; dollar, buck, simoleon; half dollar, quarter, dime, nickel, cent; ten-dollar piece, eagle; napoleon, louis d'or; franc, new f.; mark, Deutschmark, Ostmark; guilder, krona, krone, lira, drachma, peseta, escudo, peso, dinar, rupee, rand, yuan, yen, zloty, rouble; obol, talent, shekel, solidus, bezant, ducat, angel, noble, real, pistole, piece of eight; change, small c., centime, pfennig, piastre, kopek, cash 33 *small coin*; shell money, cowrie, wampum; numismatics, numismatology, chrysology.

paper money, fiat m., fiduciary currency, assignat; bankroll, wad; note, banknote, treasury note, pound n., five-p. n., ten-p. n., bill, dollar b., greenback, buck, ten-dollar bill, sawbuck; bill of exchange, negotiable instrument; draft, order, money o., postal o., check, cheque, certified c., giro c., traveller's c., letter of credit; promissory note, note of hand, IOU; coupon, warrant, scrip, certificate, bond, premium b. 767 *security*.

false money, bad m., counterfeit m., base coin, snide; forged note, flash n., forgery; dud cheque 805 *nonpayment*; clipped coinage, depreciated currency, devalued c.; demonetized coinage, withdrawn c., obsolete c.

bullion, bar, gold b., ingot, nugget; solid gold, solid silver; precious metal, yellow m., platinum, gold, white g., electrum, silver, billon.

minter, moneyer, mint master; coiner, forger; money-dealer, money-changer, cambist 794 *merchant*; cashier 798 *treasurer*; financier, capitalist; moneyed man, moneybags 800 *rich person*.

Adj. *monetary*, numismatic, chrysological; pecuniary, financial, fiscal, budgetary, sumptuary; coined, stamped, minted, issued; nummary, fiduciary; gold-based, sterling, sound, solvent 800 *rich*; inflationary, deflationary; clipped, devalued, depreciated; withdrawn, demonetized.

Vb. *mint*, coin, stamp; monetize, issue, circulate; pass, utter; forge, counterfeit.

demonetize, withdraw, withdraw from circulation, call in an issue; clip, debase the coinage; devalue, depreciate, inflate 812 *cheapen*.

draw money, cash, encash, realize, turn into cash, draw upon, cash a cheque, endorse a c., write a c. 804 *pay*.

See: 28, 32, 33, 612, 629, 632, 633, 654, 655, 767, 794, 796, **798**, **800**, 804, 805, 812.

798 Treasurer

N. *treasurer*, honorary t.; bursar, purser, quaestor; cashier, teller, croupier; depositary, stakeholder, trustee, steward 754 *consignee*; liquidator 782 *receiver*; bookkeeper 808 *accountant*; banker, financier; keeper of the purse, paymaster, almoner, controller, Chancellor of the Exchequer, Secretary of the Treasury, Governor of the Bank of England; mint master 797 *minter*; giro, bank 799 *treasury*.

See: 754, 782, 797, 799, 808.

799 Treasury

N. *treasury*, treasure house, thesaurus; exchequer, fisc, public purse; reserves, fund 632 *store*; counting house, custom house; bursary, almonry; bank, Bank of England, Old Lady of Threadneedle Street; savings bank, Post Office savings b., penny b., building society; coffer, chest 194 *box*; treasure chest, depository 632 *storage*; strongroom, strongbox, safe, safe deposit, cash box, moneybox, piggybank, stocking, mattress; till, cash register, cash desk, slot machine; receipt of custom, box office, gate, turnstile; moneybag, purse, purse strings 194 *pocket*; wallet, billfold, wad, rouleau 194 *case*.

See: 194, **632**.

800 Wealth

N. *wealth*, Mammon, lucre, pelf, brass, moneybags 797 *money*; moneymaking, golden touch, Midas t., philosopher's stone; riches, fleshpots, fat of the land 635 *plenty*; luxury 637 *superfluity*; opulence, affluence 730 *prosperity*; ease, comfort, easy circumstances, comfortable c. 376 *euphoria*; solvency, soundness, creditworthiness 802 *credit*; solidity, substance 3 *substantiality*; independence, competence, self-sufficiency 635 *sufficiency*; high income, surtax bracket 782 *receiving*; gains 771 *gain*; resources, substantial r., well-lined purse, capital 629 *means*; liquid assets, bank account; limitless resources, bottomless purse, purse of Fortunatus, goose that lays golden eggs; nest egg 632 *store*; tidy sum, power of money, mint of m., pots of m., pile, scads, wads, packet, cool million 32 *great quantity*; fortune, handsome f., large inheritance, ample endowment; broad acres, estates, possessions 777 *property*; bonanza, mine, gold m.; El Dorado, Golconda, riches of Solomon, king's ransom; plutocracy, capitalism.

rich person, wealthy p., well-to-do p., man *or* woman of means; baron, tycoon, oil magnate, nabob, moneybags, millionaire, multi-m., millionairess; Croesus, Midas, Dives, Plutus; moneymaker, moneyspinner, fat cat, capitalist, plutocrat, bloated p.; heir to riches, heiress, poor little rich girl 776 *beneficiary*; the haves, moneyed class, propertied c., leisured c., jeunesse dorée, jet set 848 *beau monde*; new rich, nouveau riche, parvenu, self-made man 730 *prosperous person*; plutocracy, timocracy.

Adj. *rich*, richly endowed, lush, fertile 171 *prolific*; abundant 635 *plenteous*; richly furnished, luxurious, upholstered, plush, plushy, ritzy, slap-up; diamond-studded, glittering 875 *ostentatious*; wealthy, blest with this world's goods, well-endowed, well-provided for, born in the purple, born with a silver spoon in one's mouth; opulent, affluent 730 *prosperous*; well-off, well-to-do, well-situated, in easy circumstances, comfortably off, well-housed, well-paid, overpaid 376 *comfortable*.

moneyed, propertied, worth a lot, worth a packet, worth millions; made of money, lousy with m., rolling in m., rolling, dripping, loaded; stinking rich, filthy r., disgustingly r.; rich as Croesus, rich as Solomon; in funds, in cash, in credit, in the black; well-heeled, flush, in the money, in the dough, quids in, doing nicely thankyou; credit-worthy, solvent, sound, able to pay; out of debt, all straight 804 *paying*.

Vb. *be rich*, be full to overflowing, turn all to gold 637 *superabound*; have money, have a power of m., have means, draw a large income; be rolling in money, stink of m., wallow in riches; be born in the purple, be born with a silver spoon in one's mouth; be sitting on a goldmine, be raking it in; be flush, be in funds etc. adj.; have credit, command capital, have money to burn; die rich 780 *bequeath*.

afford, have the means, have the wherewithal, be able to pay, be solvent, make both ends meet, keep one's head above water, keep the wolf from the door, keep up with the Joneses 635 *have enough*.

get rich, come into money 771 *inherit*; do all right for oneself 730 *prosper*; enrich oneself, make money, mint m., coin m., spin m., rake in the shekels, laugh all the way to the bank; make a packet, make a pile, make a bomb, make a fortune, feather one's nest, line one's pocket, strike it rich, hit the jackpot, win the pools, have one's ship come home 771 *gain*; seek riches, worship the golden calf, pay tribute to Mammon.

make rich, enrich, make one's fortune, put money in one's pocket, line one's p.; leave one a fortune 780 *bequeath*; enhance 36 *augment*; improve 654 *make better*.

See: 3, 32, 36, 171, 376, 629, 632, **635**, **637**, 654, **730**, 771, 776, 777, 780, 782, **797**, 802, 804, 848, 875.

801 Poverty

N. *poverty*, Lady Poverty 945 *asceticism*; renunciation of wealth, voluntary poverty 931 *disinterestedness*; impecuniosity, financial embarrassment, difficulties, Queer Street 805 *insolvency*; impoverishment, loss of fortune, beggary, mendicancy; utter poverty, penury, pennilessness, pauperism, destitution; privation, indigence, neediness, necessitousness, necessity, dire n., need, want, pinch 627 *requirement*; bare cupboard, empty larder 636 *scarcity*; wolf at the door, famine 946 *fasting*; light pocket, empty purse, insufficient income, slender means, meagre resources, reduced circumstances, straitened c., low water 636 *insufficiency*; straits, distress, belt-tightening 825 *suffering*; grinding poverty, subsistence level, hand-to-mouth existence, mere e., bare e.; poorness, meanness, meagreness, shabbiness, seediness, beggarliness, raggedness, shreds and tatters; general poverty, recession, slump, depression 655 *deterioration*; squalor, public s., slum, substandard housing 655 *dilapidation*; workhouse, poorhouse.

poor person, broken man *or* woman, bankrupt, insolvent 805 *nonpayer*; hermit, sannyasi 945 *ascetic*; pauper, indigent, poor beggar, rag-picker, starveling, vagrant, tramp, down-and-out 763 *beggar*; slum-dweller, underdog; the poor, new poor, the have-nots, the underprivileged 869 *lower classes*; Cinderella 867 *object of scorn*; poor white, white trash; poor relation 35 *inferior*; Job, Lazarus.

Adj. *poor*, not well-off, badly o., poorly o., hard up, not blest with this world's goods; lowpaid, underpaid, underprivileged; hard up, impecunious, short, short of funds, short of cash, out of pocket, in the red; skint, cleaned out, bust, broke, flat b., stony b., bankrupt, insolvent 805 *nonpaying*; reduced to poverty *or* beggary, on the breadline, in the dole queue; impoverished, pauperized, broken, beggared; dispossessed, deprived, stripped, fleeced, robbed; penurious, poverty-stricken; needy, indigent, in want, in need 627 *necessitous*; homeless, shelterless; hungry 636 *underfed*; in distress, straitened, pinched, hard put to it, put to one's shifts, on one's uppers, on one's beam ends, not knowing which way to turn 700 *in difficulties*; unable to make both ends meet, unable to pay one's way, unable to keep the wolf from the door; unprovided for, dowerless, portionless; penniless, moneyless, destitute; down to one's last penny, without a bean, without a cent, without a sou, without prospects, with nothing to hope for.

beggarly, starveling, shabby, seedy, down at heel, out at elbows, down and out, in rags, tattered, patched, barefoot, threadbare, tatty 655 *dilapidated*; scruffy, squalid, mean, slummy, back-street 649 *dirty*; poverty-stricken, pinched with poverty, poor as a church mouse, poor as Job.

Vb. *be poor*, earn little or nothing, live on a pittance, eke out a livelihood, scratch a living, scrape an existence, live from hand to mouth; feel the pinch, fall on hard times, be in dire straits, have to watch the pennies, be unable to afford; beg for one's bread, sing for one's supper; starve 859 *be hungry*; want, lack 627 *require*; not have a penny, not have two halfpennies to rub together; have no prospects, have no more shots in one's locker; become poor, go broke 805 *not pay*; decline in fortune, lose one's money, come down in the world 655 *deteriorate*; go on the parish, go on relief, go to the workhouse; go on the dole, claim supplementary benefit.

impoverish, reduce to poverty, leave destitute, beggar, pauperize; ruin 165 *destroy*; rob, strip 786 *fleece*; dispossess, disinherit, cut off with a shilling 786 *deprive*.

See: 35, 165, 627, **636**, 649, 655, 700, 763, 786, 805, 825, 859, 867, 869, 931, 945, 946.

802 Credit

N. *credit*, repute, reputation 866 *prestige*; creditworthiness, sound proposition; trust, confidence, reliability 929 *probity*; borrowing capacity, limit of credit; line of credit, tick; banker's credit, letter of c., credit card, credit note, sum to one's account, credit a., the black; credits, balances, credit balance 807 *receipt*; postponed payment, unpaid bill, account, score, tally, bill 808 *accounts*; national credit, floating debt 803 *debt*; loan, mortgage 784 *lending*; sum entrusted, sum voted, vote.

creditor, importunate c., dun; mortgagee, pledgee 784 *lender*; depositor, investor.

Vb. *credit*, give *or* furnish c., extend c., forgo repayment, grant a loan 784 *lend*; place to one's credit, credit one's account; grant, vote; await payment, charge to one's account, sell on credit; take credit, open an account, keep an account with, run up an account, run up a bill 785 *borrow*.

See: **784**, 785, 803, 807, 808, 866, 929.

803 Debt

N. *debt*, indebtedness, state of i. 785 *borrowing*; liability, obligation, commitment; encumbrance, mortgage 767 *security*; something owing, debit, charge; what one owes, debts, bills, hire-purchase debt; national debt, floating d., funded d.; promise to pay, debt of honour, unsecured debt 764 *promise*; bad debt, write-off 772 *loss*; good debt 771 *gain*; tally, account, account owing; deficit, overdraft, balance to pay 307 *shortfall*; inability to pay 805 *insolvency*; payment refused, frozen balance, blocked account, frozen assets 805 *nonpayment*; deferred payment 802 *credit*; overdue payment, arrears, accumulated a., back pay, back rent; no more credit, foreclosure.

interest, simple i., compound i., high i., excessive i., usury, pound of flesh 784 *lending*; premium, rate of interest, bank rate.

debtor, loanee, borrower, loan applicant; obligor, drawee; mortgagor, pledgor; bad debtor, defaulter, insolvent 805 *nonpayer*.

Adj. *indebted*, in debt, in hock, borrowing, indebted; pledged, liable, committed, responsible, answerable, bound 917 *obliged*; owing, overdrawn, in the red; encumbered, mortgaged; deep in debt, plunged in d., burdened with d., over head and ears in d., in Queer Street 700 *in difficulties*; defaulting, unable to pay, insolvent 805 *nonpaying*; at the mercy of one's creditors, in the hands of the receiver.

owed, unpaid, still u.; owing, due, overdue, in arrears; outstanding, unbalanced; on the debit side, chargeable, payable, debited, on credit, on deposit, repayable, returnable, bearing, payable on delivery, C.O.D.

Vb. *be in debt*, owe, have to repay; owe money, pay interest; accept a charge, be debited with, be liable; get credit, overdraw (one's account); get on tick, buy on hire purchase *or* the never-never 785 *borrow*; live on credit, buy on c., use a credit card, keep an account with, have charged to one's a.; run up an account, run into debt; be in the red, be overdrawn; leave one's bills unpaid, cheat one's creditors, bilk, welsh, do a moonlight flit 805 *not pay*; back another's credit, make oneself responsible, stand surety for 917 *incur a duty*.

See: 307, 700, 764, 767, 771, 772, 784, **785**, 802, 805, 917.

804 Payment

N. *payment*, paying for, bearing the cost, defrayment; paying off, discharge, quittance, acquittance, release, satisfaction, full s., liquidation, clearance, settlement, settlement on account; receipted payment, receipt in full 807 *receipt*; cash payment, down p., ready money 797 *money*; first payment, earnest, earnest money, handsel, deposit; instalment, standing order; deferred payment, hire purchase 785 *borrowing*; due payment, subscription, tribute 809 *tax*; voluntary payment, contribution, collection 781 *offering*; payment in lieu, composition 150 *substitution*; repayment, compensation, indemnity 787 *restitution*; disbursement, remittance 806 *expenditure*.

pay, payout, payoff, pay packet, pay day, wages bill, wages, salary 771 *earnings*; grant, grant-in-aid, subsidy 703 *subvention*; salary, pension, annuity, remuneration, emolument, fee, garnish, bribe 962 *reward*; cut, commission 810 *discount*; something paid, contribution, subscription, collection, tribute 809 *tax*; damages, indemnity 963 *penalty*; compensation, redundancy pay, golden handshake; payer, paymaster, purser, cashier 798 *treasurer*.

Adj. *paying*, disbursing 806 *expending*; paying in full, paying cash, unindebted; out of debt, owing nothing.

Vb. *pay*, disburse 806 *expend*; contribute 781 *give*; pay in kind, barter 791 *trade*; make payment, pay out, shell o., fork o., stump up, cough up; come across, do the needful, unloose the purse strings, open one's purse; pay a high price, pay through the nose; pay back, repay, reimburse, compensate 787 *restitute*; tickle the palm, grease the palm 612 *bribe*; pay wages, remunerate, tip 962 *reward*; pay in advance, ante up, pay on sight, pay on call, pay on demand; pay by cheque *or* by giro; pay on the nail, pay on the dot, pay cash, pay cash down, put d.; honour (a bill), pay up, pay in full, meet, satisfy, redeem, discharge, get a receipt; clear, liquidate, settle, settle an account, clear accounts with, balance accounts w., square accounts w. 808 *account*; settle accounts with, settle a score; pay off old scores, pay one out 714 *retaliate*.

defray, pay for, defray the cost, bear the c., stand the c., put up funds; pay one's way, pay one's shot; foot the bill, meet the b., pick up the b., pay the piper; buy a round, stand treat, treat 781 *give*; share expenses, go Dutch 775 *participate*.

Adv. *cash down*, money d.; cash on delivery, C.O.D.; with ready money, on the nail, on the dot, on demand; to the tune of.

See: 150, 612, 703, 714, 771, 775, 781, 785, 787, 791, 797, 798, **806**, 807, 808, 809, 810, 962, 963.

805 Nonpayment

N. *nonpayment*, default; defalcation 930 *improbity*; reduced payment, stoppage, deduction 963 *penalty*; moratorium, embargo, freeze; dishonouring, refusal to pay, protest, repudiation 760 *refusal*; tax avoidance, tax evasion 620 *avoidance*; deferred payment, hire purchase 785 *borrowing*; cancellation of debts 752 *abrogation*; waste-paper bonds, protested bill, dishonoured cheque, bogus c., dud c., bouncing c.; depreciation, devaluation, devalued currency 797 *false money*.

insolvency, inability to pay, failure to meet one's obligations; crash, failure; failure of credit, run upon a bank; bankruptcy, bankruptcy court, bankruptcy proceedings; nothing to pay with, nothing in the kitty, overdrawn account, overdraft 636 *insufficiency*; unpayable debt 803 *debt*.

nonpayer, defaulter, defalcator, embezzler, tax dodger 789 *defrauder*; bilker, welsher, absconder; failure, lame duck; bankrupt, discharged b., undischarged b., insolvent debtor.

Adj. *nonpaying*, defaulting, behindhand, in arrears; unable to pay, insolvent, bankrupt; hopelessly in debt, always owing 803 *indebted*; beggared, ruined 801 *poor*.

Vb. *not pay*, default, embezzle, swindle 788 *defraud*; fall into arrears, get behindhand; stop payment, withhold p., freeze, block; refuse payment, protest a bill; disallow payment; fiddle one's income tax, practise tax evasion 930 *be dishonest*; divert, sequester 786 *deprive*; bounce one's cheque, dishonour, repudiate; become insolvent, go bankrupt, go through the bankruptcy court, get whitewashed; sink, fail, break, go bust, crash, wind up, go into liquidation; evade one's creditors, welsh, bilk 542 *deceive*; abscond 296 *decamp*; be unable to pay 801 *be poor*; go off the gold standard, devalue *or* depreciate the currency 797 *demonetize*; keep one's purse shut 816 *be parsimonious*; cancel a debt, wipe the slate clean, discharge a bankrupt 752 *abrogate*.

See: 296, 542, 620, 636, 752, 760, 785, 786, 788, 789, 797, 801, 803, 816, 930, 963.

806 Expenditure

N. *expenditure*, spending, disbursement 804 *payment*; cost of living; outgoings, overheads, costs, cost incurred, expenses, out-of-pocket e., expense account; expense, outlay, investment; dissaving, disinvestment, run on savings; fee, tax 804 *pay*; extravagance, spending spree 815 *prodigality*.

Adj. *expending*, spending, sumptuary; generous 813 *liberal*; extravagant, splashing out, throwing one's money around 815 *prodigal*; out of pocket, lighter in one's purse.

expended, spent, disbursed, paid, paid out; laid out, invested; costing, at one's expense.

Vb. *expend*, spend; buy 792 *purchase*; lay out, invest, sink money; be out of pocket, incur costs, incur expenses; afford, stand, bear the cost, meet charges, disburse, pay out 804 *pay*; run down one's account, draw on one's savings, dissave, disinvest; untie the purse-strings, open one's purse, empty one's pocket; give money, donate 781 *give*; spare no expense, do it proud, be lavish 813 *be liberal*; fling money around, splash out, blow, blow one's cash 815 *be prodigal*; use up, spend up, consume, run through, get t. 634 *waste*.

See: 634, 781, 792, **804**, 813, 815.

807 Receipt

N. *receipt*, voucher, acknowledgment of payment; money received, credits, revenue, royalty, rents, rent-roll, dues; customs, taxes 809 *tax*; money coming in, turnover, takings, proceeds, returns, receipts, gross r., net r., box-office r., gate money, gate; income, national i., private i., privy purse; emolument, regular income, pay, half p., salary, wages 771 *earnings*; remuneration 962 *reward*; pension, annuity, tontine; allowance, personal a.; pocket money, spending m.; inadequate allowance, pittance; alimony, maintenance; scholarship 771 *acquisition*; interest, return, rake-off; winnings, profits, gross p., net p., capital gain 771 *gain*; bonus, premium 40 *extra*; prize 729 *trophy*; draw, lucky d.; legacy, inheritance 777 *dower*.

Adj. *received*, paid, receipted, acknowledged, acknowledged with thanks.

Vb. see 771 *acquire*, 782 *receive, be received*, 786 *take*.

See: 40, 729, 771, 777, **782**, 786, 809, 962.

808 Accounts

N. *accounts*, accountancy, accounting, commercial arithmetic; book-keeping, entry, double e., single e.; audit, inspection of accounts; account, profit and loss a., balance sheet, debit and credit, receipts and expenditures; budgeting, budget, budget estimates 633 *provision*; running account, current a., cash a., suspense a., expense a.; statement of account, account rendered, compte rendu, statement, bill, waybill, invoice, manifest 87 *list*; account paid, account settled 804 *payment*; reckoning, computation, score, tally, facts and figures 86 *numeration*.

account book, pass b., cheque b.; cash b., day b., journal, ledger, register, books 548 *record*.

accountant, chartered a., certified public a.; cost accountant, bookkeeper, storekeeper; cashier 798 *treasurer*; inspector of accounts, examiner of a., auditor; actuary, statistician.

Adj. *accounting*, bookkeeping, in charge of accounts; actuarial, reckoning, computing, inventorial, budgetary; accountable.

Vb. *account*, keep the books, keep accounts; make up an account, cast an a.; budget, prepare a b.; cost, value, write up, write down 480 *estimate*; book, enter, journalize, post, carry over, debit, credit 548 *register*; prepare a balance sheet, balance accounts; settle accounts, square a., finalize a., wind up a.; prepare a statement, present an account, charge, bill, invoice; overcharge, surcharge, undercharge 809 *price*; cook the accounts *or* the books, falsify the a., fiddle, garble, doctor 788 *defraud*; audit, inspect accounts, examine the a., go through the books; take stock, check s., inventory, catalogue 87 *list*.

See: 86, 87, 480, **548**, 633, 788, 798, 804, 809.

809 Price

N. *price*, selling p., world p., market p., standard p., list p.; rate, going r., rate for the job; piece rate, flat r.; high rate, ceiling 811 *dearness*; low rate, floor 812 *cheapness*; price control, fixed price, prix fixe 747 *restraint*; value, face v., par v., fair v., worth, money's w., what it will fetch; scarcity value, famine price; price list, tariff; quoted price, quotation, price charged; amount, figure, sum asked for; ransom, fine 963 *penalty*; demand, dues, charge; surcharge, supplement 40 *extra*; overcharge, excessive charge, extortion, ransom; fare, flat f., hire, rental, rent, ground r., house r., quit r.; fee, entrance *or* admission fee; refresher, commission, rake-off; charges, freight c., freightage, wharfage, lighterage; salvage; postage; cover charge, corkage; bill, invoice, reckoning, shot.

cost, buying price, purchase p.; damage, costs, expenses 806 *expenditure*; business costs, running c., overheads; wages, wage bill; legal costs, damages 963 *penalty*; cost of living, cost of living index.

tax, taxes, dues; taxation, tax demand 737 *demand*; rating, assessment, appraisement, valorization 480 *estimate*; cess, rate, general r., water r.; levy, toll, duty; imposition, impost; charge, scot, scot and lot (**see** *price*); exaction, forced loan, aid, benevolence 740 *compulsion*; forced savings 785 *borrowing*; punitive tax 963 *penalty*; tribute, danegeld, blackmail, ransom 804 *payment*; ecclesiastical tax, Peter's pence, tithe, tenths; National Insurance; poll tax, capitation t.; estate duty, death duty; direct taxation, income tax, PAYE, surtax, supertax, company tax, corporation t., excess profits t.; capital levy, capital gains tax 786 *expropriation*; indirect taxation, excise, customs, tariff, tonnage and poundage; local tax, octroi; purchase tax, sales t., value-added tax, VAT; salt tax, gabelle; feudal tax, scutage.

Adj. *priced*, charged, fixed; chargeable, leviable, taxable, assessable, ratable, customable, dutiable, excisable; ad valorem; to the tune of, for the price of; taxed, rated, assessed; paid, stipendiary.

Vb. *price*, cost, assess, value, rate 480 *estimate*; put a price on, set a price on; place a value on, fix a price for; raise a price, lower a p.; control the p., fix the p.; ask a price, charge, require 737 *demand*; bill, invoice.

cost, be worth, fetch, bring in; amount to, come to, mount up to; be priced at, be valued at; bear a price, have a p., have its p.; sell for, go f., be going f., change hands for, realize.

tax, lay a tax on, impose a tax; fix a tariff, levy a rate, assess for tax, value, valorize; toll, excise, subject to duty, make dutiable; raise taxes, collect t., take a toll 786 *levy*; take a collection, pass round the hat 761 *beg*; fine, punish by f., mulct 963 *punish*.

See: 40, 480, 737, 740, 747, 761, 785, **786**, 804, 806, **811**, 812, 963.

810 Discount

N. *discount*, something off, reduction, rebate, cut 42 *decrement*; stoppage, deduction; concession, allowance, margin, special price; tare, tare and tret; drawback, backwardation, contango; cut price, cut rate, special offer, loss leader 612 *incentive*; bargain price, bargain sale 812 *cheapness*; poundage, percentage; agio, brokerage; one's cut, commission, rake-off.

Vb. *discount*, deduct 39 *subtract*; allow a margin, tare; reduce, depreciate, abate, rebate 37 *abate*; offer a discount, allow a d.; mark down, take off, cut, slash 812 *cheapen*; let stick to one's fingers, rake off, take a discount, take one's percentage.

Adv. *at a discount*, below par, less than the market rate.

See: 37, 39, 42, 612, 812.

811 Dearness

N. *dearness*, costliness, expensiveness; value, high v., high worth, pricelessness; famine price, scarcity value, rarity, dearth 636 *scarcity*; exorbitance, extortion, rack rents, rip-off; overcharge, excessive charge, unfair price, bad value, poor v.; bad bargain, high price, fancy p., luxury p.; cost, high c., heavy c., pretty penny; tax on one's pocket, ruinous charge; rising costs, rising prices, sellers' market, bull m., climbing prices, soaring p.; cheap money, inflation, inflationary pressure, bullish tendency.

Adj. *dear*, high-priced, pricy, expensive, ritzy, upmarket; costly, multimillion; extravagant, dearly-bought; dear at the price, overrated, overcharged, overpriced, overpaid; exorbitant, excessive, extortionate, preposterous; steep, stiff, sky-high; beyond one's means, prohibitive, more than one can afford, more than one's pocket can stand; dear at any price 641 *useless*; rising in price, hardening, rising, soaring, climbing, mounting, inflationary; bullish.

of price, of value, of worth 644 *valuable*; priceless, beyond price, above p.; unpayable; invaluable 640 *useful*; inestimable, worth a king's ransom, worth its weight in gold, worth a fortune; precious, rare, scarce, like gold dust 140 *infrequent*; at a premium, not to be had for love or money.

Vb. *be dear,* cost a lot, cost a packet, cost a pretty penny, be high-priced, hurt one's pocket, make a hole in one's p.; gain in value, rise in price, harden; go up, appreciate, escalate, soar, mount, climb; get too dear, price itself out of the market; prove expensive, cost one dear, cost a fortune, cost the earth.

overcharge, overprice, sell dear, oversell, ask too much; profiteer, soak, sting, bleed, skin, extort, charge rack rents, rip off, short-change, hold to ransom 786 *fleece*; put up prices, mark up; bull, raise the price, raise the bid, bid up, auction 793 *sell.*

pay too much, pay through the nose, pay the devil, be stung, be ripped off, be had, be done; pay high, pay dear, buy a white elephant; achieve a Pyrrhic victory; pay beyond one's means, ruin oneself.

Adv. *dearly,* dear, at a price, at great cost, at heavy c., at huge expense; exorbitantly, extravagantly.

See: 140, 636, 640, 641, **644**, **786**, 793.

812 Cheapness

N. *cheapness,* inexpensiveness, affordability; good value, value for money, money's worth, snip, bargain, good b., bon marché; sale goods, seconds, rejects; low price, reasonable charge, reasonableness; cheap rate, off-peak r., off-season r., concessional r., excursion fare, railcard 810 *discount*; nominal price, reduced p., knock-down p., cut p., bargain p., budget p., popular p., competitive p., sale p., sacrificial p., giveaway p., rockbottom p.; peppercorn rent, easy terms; buyers' market, sluggish m.; Dutch auction; falling prices. declining p., bearishness; depreciation, fall, slump; deflation; glut, drug on the market 635 *plenty*; superfluity 637 *redundance.*

no charge, absence of c., nominal c. 781 *gift*; gratuitousness, labour of love 597 *voluntary work*; free trade, free port; free entry, free admission, free seats, free pass, free ticket; free quarters, grace and favour; free board, free service, free delivery; everything for nothing.

Adj. *cheap,* inexpensive, uncostly, moderate, reasonable, fair; affordable, within one's means, easy on the pocket; cheap to make, low-budget; substandard, shop-soiled; economical, economy, economy size; not dear, worth its price, worth the money; low, low-priced, cheap-p., cheap at the price, cheap at half the p.; dirt-cheap, going cheap, going for a song, for peanuts; bargain-rate, bargain-basement, downmarket, cut-price, concessional, sale-price, reduced, r. to clear; marked down, half-price; tourist-class, off-season; easy to buy, two-a-penny; worth nothing, cheap and nasty, cheapjack, catchpenny, Brummagem 641 *useless*; cheapening, bearish, falling, declining, slumping; unsalable, unmarketable; unchargeable, valueless 860 *unwanted*; underpaid, underpriced.

uncharged, not charged for, gratuitous, complimentary; gratis, for nothing, for love, for kicks, for nix, for the asking; costing nothing, free, scot-f., free of charge, for free; zero-rated, untaxed, tax-free, rent-f., post-f., post-paid, carriage-p., f.o.b.; including extras; unpaid, unsalaried, honorary 597 *voluntary*; given away, unbought, as a gift 781 *given*; costless, free, gratis and for nothing.

Vb. *be cheap,* - inexpensive etc. adj.; cost little, be economical, be easily afforded, be easy on the pocket; be worth the money, be cheap at the price; be bought for a song, be picked up for nothing, go dirt-cheap; cost nothing, be without charge, be free, be had for the asking; cheapen, get cheaper, fall in price, depreciate, come down, decline, sag, fall, drift, slump, plunge, plummet.

cheapen, lower, lower the price, reduce the p.; put a low price on, keep cheap, lower one's charges, trim one's prices, mark down, cut, slash; undercharge, underrate, let go for a song, sacrifice, give away, make a present of 781 *give*; beat down, undercut, undersell, engage in cut-throat competition; dump, unload; flood the market, glut 637 *superabound*; depress the market, bear.

Adv. *cheaply,* on the cheap; at cost price, at prime cost, at wholesale prices, at a discount, for a song, for nothing, on the house.

See: 597, 635, 637, 641, **781**, 810, 860.

813 Liberality

N. *liberality,* liberalness, bounteousness, bountifulness, munificence, generosity

931 *disinterestedness*; open-handedness, open heart, open hand, open purse, hospitality, open house 882 *sociability*; free hand, blank cheque, carte blanche 744 *scope*; cornucopia 635 *plenty*; lavishness 815 *prodigality*; bounty, largesse 781 *gift*; handsome offer, sporting o. 759 *offer*; benefaction, charity 897 *kind act*.

good giver, free g., princely g., generous g., cheerful g., liberal donor, unselfish d., blood d., kidney d.; good spender, good tipper; Lady Bountiful, Father Christmas, Santa Claus, rich uncle 903 *benefactor*.

Adj. *liberal*, free, free-spending, free-handed, open-h., lavish 815 *prodigal*; large-hearted, free-h. 931 *disinterested*; bountiful, charitable 897 *benevolent*; hospitable 882 *sociable*; handsome, generous, munificent, splendid, slap-up; lordly, princely, royal, right royal; ungrudging, unstinting, unsparing, unfailing; in liberal quantities, abundant, ample, bounteous, profuse, full, pressed down and running over 635 *plenteous*; overflowing 637 *redundant*.

Vb. *be liberal*, - generous etc. adj.; lavish, shower largesse, shower upon 781 *give*; unbelt, open the purse strings; give generously, give with both hands, give the shirt off one's back; give till it hurts 897 *philanthropize*; give more than asked, overpay, pay well, tip w.; keep open house 882 *be hospitable*; do one proud, not count the cost, spare no expense; give carte blanche, give a blank cheque 744 *give scope*; spend freely, not ask for the change, throw one's money around 815 *be prodigal*.

Adv. *liberally*, ungrudgingly, with open hand, with both hands.

See: 635, 637, 744, 759, 781, **815**, 882, **897**, 903, 931.

814 Economy

N. *economy*, thrift, thriftiness, frugality; prudence, care, carefulness; husbandry, good h., good housekeeping, good housewifery; sound stewardship, good management, careful m.; watchful eye on expense, avoidance of waste, sumptuary law, credit squeeze 747 *restriction*; economy drive, economy measures; time-saving, labour-s., time and motion study; husbanding of resources, economizing, saving, sparing, pinching, paring, cheese-p.; retrenchment, economies, cuts; savings, hoarded s. 632 *store*; conservation, energy-saving; economizer 816 *niggard*; economist, monetarist; conservationist 666 *preserver*; good housewife, careful steward.

Adj. *economical*, time-saving, labour-s., energy-s., money-s., cost-reducing, cost-cutting; money-conscious, chary of expense, counting every penny 816 *parsimonious*; thrifty, careful, prudent, canny, frugal, saving, sparing, spare; unlavish, meagre, Spartan, sparse; marginal, with nothing to spare.

Vb. *economize*, be economical, - sparing etc. adj.; husband one's resources, avoid extravagance, keep costs down, waste nothing, find a use for everything, recycle, reuse; keep within one's budget, keep within compass, cut one's coat according to one's cloth, make both ends meet; watch expenses, pare e., cut costs, cut down expenditure, trim e., cut back, make economies, retrench, tighten one's belt; pinch, scrape, look after the pennies 816 *be parsimonious*; save, spare, hoard 632 *store*; plough back, reinvest, get interest on one's money, not leave money idle, make every penny work 800 *get rich*.

Adv. *sparingly*, economically, frugally, nothing in excess.

See: **632**, 666, 747, 800, **816**.

815 Prodigality

N. *prodigality*, lavishness, profusion, profuseness 637 *redundance*; idle display, idle expenditure, conspicuous consumption 875 *ostentation*; extravagance, wasteful expenditure, spendthrift e., reckless e.; wastefulness, profligacy, dissipation, squandering, squandermania, orgy of spending, spending spree, splurge 634 *waste*; unthriftiness, improvidence, indifference to economy, no attempt at economy, uncontrolled expenditure, unregulated e., deficit finance; misapplication, misuse of funds 675 *misuse*; money burning a hole in one's pocket.

prodigal, prodigal son, spender, big s., free s., reckless s., waster, wastrel, profligate, spend-all, spendthrift, scattergood, squanderer.

Adj. *prodigal*, lavish 813 *liberal*; profuse, overlavish, overliberal; extravagant, regardless of cost, wasteful, squandering, profligate; uneconomic, uneconomical, unthrifty, thriftless, spendthrift, improvident, dissipative, reckless, dissipated;

penny wise and pound foolish.

Vb. *be prodigal*, prodigalize, go the pace, blow one's money, blue one's m.; overspend, pour out money, splash money around, throw one's money around, flash pound notes; splurge, spend money like water, pour one's money through a sieve; burn one's money, run through one's savings, exhaust one's resources, spend to the last farthing, spend up to the hilt, splurge out, blow everything, waste one's inheritance, consume one's substance, squander 634 *waste*; play ducks and drakes, burn the candle at both ends, fritter away, throw a., fling a., gamble a., dissipate, scatter to the winds, pour down the drain; not count the cost, keep no check on expenditure; have no money sense, think money grows on trees; misspend, fool one's money away, throw good money after bad, throw the helve after the hatchet; have no thought for the morrow, spend more than one has, overdraw; eat up one's capital, kill the goose that lays the golden eggs; save nothing, put nothing by, keep nothing for a rainy day.

Adv. *prodigally*, profusely, recklessly; like a prodigal, like a spendthrift.

Int. hang the expense! a short life and a merry one! easy come, easy go!

See: 634, 637, 675, **813**, 875.

816 Parsimony

N. *parsimony*, parsimoniousness; credit squeeze 814 *economy*; false economy, misplaced e., policy of penny wise and pound foolish; cheese-paring, scrimping, pinching, scraping, penny-pinching; tightfistedness, niggardliness, meanness, minginess, stinginess, miserliness; illiberality, ungenerosity, uncharitableness, grudging hand, closed purse 932 *selfishness*.

avarice, cupidity, acquisitiveness, possessiveness; money-grubbing, itching palm; rapacity, avidity, greed 859 *desire*; mercenariness, venality.

niggard, skinflint, screw, scrimp, scraper, pinchfist, penny pincher, pinchpenny, tightwad, meanie; grudging giver, no tipper; miser, money-grubber, lickpenny, muckworm; cadger; saver, hoarder, squirrel, magpie; hunks, churl, codger, curmudgeon; usurer 784 *lender*; Harpagon, Scrooge.

Adj. *parsimonious*, careful 814 *economical*; too careful, overeconomical, overfrugal, frugal to excess; money-conscious, penny-wise, miserly, mean, mingy, stingy, near, close, tight; tight-fisted, close-f., hard-f. 778 *retentive*; grudging, curmudgeonly, churlish, illiberal, ungenerous, uncharitable, empty-handed, giftless; penurious, chary, sparing, pinching, scraping, scrimping, shabby, small-minded.

avaricious, grasping, griping, monopolistic 932 *selfish*; possessive, acquisitive 771 *acquiring*; hoarding, saving; pinching; miserly; cadging; money-grubbing, money-conscious, money-mad, covetous 859 *greedy*; usurious, rapacious, extortionate; mercenary, venal, sordid.

Vb. *be parsimonious*, - niggardly etc. adj.; keep one's purse shut 778 *retain*; grudge, begrudge, withhold, keep back 760 *refuse*; dole out, stint, skimp, starve, spare 636 *make insufficient*; scrape, scrimp, pinch 814 *economize*; screw, rack-rent, skin a flint 786 *fleece*; be penny-wise, spoil the ship for a ha'porth of tar; starve oneself, live like a pauper; hoard wealth, never spend a penny; grudge every farthing, beat down, haggle 791 *bargain*; cadge, beg, borrow; hoard, sit on, keep for oneself 932 *be selfish*.

Adv. *parsimoniously*, niggardly, sparingly, on a shoestring.

See: 636, 760, 771, 778, 784, 786, 791, **814**, 859, **932**.

Class six

Emotion, religion and morality

Section one: General

817 Affections

N. *affections,* qualities, instincts; passions, feelings, emotions, emotional life; nature, disposition 5 *character;* spirit, temper, tone, grain, mettle 5 *temperament;* cast of mind, habit of m., trait 7 *state;* personality, psychology, mentality, outlook, mental and spiritual make-up, inherited characteristics 5 *heredity;* being, innermost b., breast, bosom, heart, soul, core, inmost soul, inner man, cockles of the heart, heart of hearts 5 *essential part,* 447 *spirit;* animus, attitude, frame of mind, state of m., vein, strain, humour, mood; predilection, predisposition, inclinations, turn, bent, bias 179 *tendency;* passion, ruling p., master p. 481 *prejudice;* heartstrings 818 *feeling;* fullness of heart; heyday of the blood; force of character; anthropomorphism, pathetic fallacy.

Adj. *with affections,* affected, characterized, formed, moulded, cast, tempered, framed; instinct with, imbued w., penetrated w., eaten up w., possessed w., obsessed w., devoured w.; inborn, inbred, congenital 5 *genetic;* deep-rooted, ineffaceable 5 *intrinsic;* emotional, demonstrative 818 *feeling.*

See: **5**, 7, 179, 447, 481, **818**.

818 Feeling

N. *feeling,* experience, emotional life, affect; sentience, sensation, sense of 374 *sense;* emotion, crystallized e., sentiment; true feeling, sincerity 540 *veracity;* impulse 609 *spontaneity;* intuition, instinct; responsiveness, response, reaction, fellow feeling, sympathy, involvement, personal i. 880 *friendliness;* vibrations, vibes; empathy, appreciation, realization, understanding 490 *knowledge;* impression, deep feeling, deep sense of 819 *moral sensibility;* religious feeling, unction 979 *piety;* finer feelings 897 *benevolence;* tender feelings 887 *love;* hard feelings 891 *resentment;* stirred feeling, thrill, kick 318 *spasm;* shock, turn 508 *lack of expectation;* pathos 825 *suffering;* release of feeling, catharthis, abreaction; actuating feeling, animus, emotionality, emotionalism, affectivity 822 *excitability;* sentimentality, romanticism; manifestation of feeling, demonstration, demonstrativeness; expression, facial e., play of features 547 *gesture;* blush, flush, hectic f., suffusion; tingling, gooseflesh, tremor, trembling, quiver, flutter, flurry, palpitation, pulsation, heaving, panting, throbbing 318 *agitation;* stew, ferment 318 *commotion;* swelling heart, lump in one's throat, tears in one's eyes; control of feeling, stoicism, endurance, stiff upper lip 823 *patience.*

warm feeling, glow; cordiality, empressement, effusiveness, heartiness, full heart, overflowing h.; hot head, impatience; unction, earnestness 834 *seriousness;* eagerness, keenness, fervour, ardour, vehemence, enthusiasm, dash, fire 174 *vigorousness;* vigour, zeal 678 *activity;* fanaticism, mania 481 *prejudice;* emotion, passion, ecstasy, inspiration, elevation, transports 822 *excitable state.*

Adj. *feeling,* affective, sensible, sensorial, sensory 374 *sentient;* spirited, vivacious, lively 819 *sensitive;* sensuous 944 *sensual;* experiencing, living; enduring, bearing 825 *suffering;* intuitive, sensitive, vibrant, responsive, reacting; involved, sympathetic, condoling 775 *sharing;* tenderhearted 819 *impressible;* emotional, passionate, full of feeling; unctuous, soulful; intense, tense 821 *excited;* cordial, hearty; gushing, effusive; sentimental, romantic; mawkish, maudlin, schmaltzy, treacly, soppy, sloppy, slushy; thrilling, tingling, throbbing; blushing, flushing.

impressed, affected, influenced; stirred, aroused, moved, touched 821 *excited*; struck, awed, awestruck, overwhelmed, struck all of a heap; penetrated, imbued with, aflame w., consumed w., devoured by, inspired by; rapt, enraptured, enthralled, ecstatic; lyrical, raving 822 *excitable*.

fervent, fervid, perfervid, passionate, ardent, tense, intense; eager, breathless, panting, throbbing; impassioned, vehement, earnest, zealous; enthusiastic, exuberant, bubbling; hot-headed, warm-blooded, impetuous, impatient 822 *excitable*; warm, fiery, glowing, burning, red-hot, flaming, boiling 379 *hot*; hysterical, delirious, overwrought, worked up, feverish, hectic 503 *frenzied*; strong, uncontrollable, furious 176 *violent*.

felt, experienced, lived; heartfelt, cordial, hearty, warm, sincerely felt, sincere 540 *veracious*; deeply-felt, deep-seated, visceral, profound 211 *deep*; stirring, soul-s., heart-warming, heart-swelling; emotive, strong, overwhelming, traumatic 821 *impressive*; smart, acute, keen, poignant, piercing, trenchant 256 *sharp*; caustic, burning, smarting 388 *pungent*; penetrating, absorbing; thrilling, tingling, rapturous, ecstatic 826 *pleasurable*; pathetic, affecting 827 *distressing*.

Vb. *feel*, sense, receive an impression; entertain, entertain feelings, have f., cherish f., harbour f., feel deeply, take to heart 819 *be sensitive*; know the feeling, experience, live, live through, go t., pass t., taste; bear, endure, undergo, smart, smart under 825 *suffer*; suffer with, feel w., sympathize, condole, share 775 *participate*; respond, react, tingle, warm to, fire, kindle, catch, catch the infection, be inspired 821 *be excited*; cause feeling 821 *impress*.

show feeling, exhibit f., show signs of emotion; demonstrate, not hide one's feelings 522 *manifest*; enthuse, go into ecstasies 824 *be pleased*; fly into a passion 891 *get angry*; turn colour, change c., look blue, look black; go livid, go black in the face, go purple 428 *blacken*; look pale, blench, turn pale, go white 427 *whiten*; colour, blush, flush, glow, mantle, turn red, turn crimson, go red in the face 431 *redden*; quiver, tremble, wince; flutter, shake, quake 318 *be agitated*; tingle, thrill, vibrate, throb, beat faster 317 *oscillate*; palpitate, pant, heave, draw a deep breath 352 *breathe*; reel, lurch, stagger; stutter 580 *stammer*.

Adv. *feelingly*, unctuously, earnestly, con amore, heart and soul; with a full heart, with a swelling h., with a bursting h., with a melting h., sympathetically; cordially, heartily, devoutly, sincerely, from the bottom of one's heart.

See: 174, 176, 211, 256, 317, 318, 352, 374, 379, 388, 427, 428, 431, 481, 490, 503, 508, 522, 540, 547, 580, 609, 678, 775, **819**, **821**, **822**, 823, 824, 825, 826, 827, 834, 880, 887, 891, 897, 944, 979.

819 Sensibility

N. *moral sensibility*, sensitivity, sensitiveness, soul; touchiness, prickliness, irritability 892 *irascibility*; raw feelings, tender f., thin skin, soft spot, tender spot, Achilles' heel; sore point, where the shoe pinches 891 *resentment*; impressibility, affectibility, susceptibility; plasticity, malleability 327 *softness*; finer feelings, sentiments; sentimentality, sentimentalism; tenderness, affection 887 *love*; spirit, spiritedness, vivacity, vivaciousness, liveliness, verve 571 *vigour*; emotionalism, ebullience, effervescence 822 *excitability*; fastidiousness, finickiness, aestheticism 463 *discrimination*; temperament, mobility, changeability 152 *changeableness*; physical sensitivity 374 *sensibility*; touchy person, moody p., sensitive plant, bundle of nerves.

Adj. *impressible*, malleable, plastic 327 *soft*; sensible, aware, conscious of, awake to, alive to, responsive 374 *sentient*; impressed with, touched, moved, touched to the quick 818 *impressed*; persuasible 612 *induced*; impressionable 822 *excitable*; susceptible, susceptive; romantic, sentimental; soppy, wet, sentimentalizing, gushing; emotional, warm-hearted; soft, tender, tender-hearted, soft-h., compassionate 905 *pitying*.

sensitive, sensitized; tingling, sore, raw, tender 374 *sentient*; aesthetic, fastidious, particular 463 *discriminating*; oversensitive, hypersensitive, all feeling 822 *excitable*; touchy, irritable, impatient, thin-skinned, easily stung, easily aroused 892 *irascible*.

lively, alive, tremblingly a.; vital, vivacious, animated; gamesome, skittish 833 *merry*;

irrepressible, ebullient, effervescent; mettlesome, spirited, high-s., lively-minded, spirituel(le); alert, aware, on one's toes 455 *attentive*; overquick, impatient; nervous, highly-strung, overstrung, temperamental; mobile, changeable; enthusiastic, impassioned 818 *fervent*; overenthusiastic, overzealous, fanatic; lively in style, expressive, racy 571 *forceful.*

Vb. *be sensitive*, - sentimental etc. adj.; have a soft heart, take it to heart, soften one's heart, let one's heart be touched, weep for 905 *pity*; tingle 318 *be agitated.*

Adv. *on the raw*, to the quick, to the heart, where the shoe pinches, where it hurts most.

See: 152, 318, 327, 374, 455, 463, 571, 612, **818**, **822**, 833, 887, 891, 892, 905.

820 Insensibility

N. *moral insensibility*, lack of sensitivity, insensitiveness; insentience, lack of sensation, numbness, stupor 375 *insensibility*; inertia 175 *inertness*; lethargy 679 *inactivity*; quietism, stagnation, vegetation 266 *quiescence*; woodenness, blockishness, obtuseness, stupidity, dullness, no imagination 499 *unintelligence*; slowness, delayed reaction 456 *inattention*; uninterest 454 *incuriosity*; nonchalance, insouciance, unconcern, detachment, apathy 860 *indifference*; no nerves, imperturbation, phlegm, stolidness, calmness, steadiness, coolness, sangfroid 823 *inexcitability*; no feelings, aloofness, impassibility, impassivity, impassiveness; repression, repression of feeling, stoicism 823 *patience*; inscrutability, poker face, deadpan expression 834 *seriousness*; insensitivity, coarseness, philistinism 699 *artlessness*; imperception, thick skin, rhinoceros hide; no pride, no honour; cold heart, frigidity; unsusceptibility, unimpressibility, dourness; unsentimentality, cynicism; callousness 326 *hardness*; lack of feeling, dry eyes, no heart, heart of stone, heart of marble, brutishness, brutality, brutalization 898 *inhumanity*; no joy, no humour, no life, not a spark, no animation 838 *tedium*; no admiration for 865 *lack of wonder.*

unfeeling person, iceberg, icicle, cold fish, cold heart, cold-blooded animal; stoic, ascetic; stock, stone, block, marble.

Adj. *impassive*, unconscious 375 *insensible*; unsusceptible, insensitive, unimaginative; unresponsive, unimpressionable, unimpressible 823 *inexcitable*; phlegmatic, stolid; wooden, blockish; bovine; dull, slow 499 *unintelligent*; unemotional, passionless, impassible; proof, proof against, steeled a.; stoical, ascetic, controlled, undemonstrative; unconcerned, aloof, distant, detached 860 *indifferent*; unaffected, calm 266 *tranquil*; steady, unruffled, unshaken, unshocked, unshockable; imperturbable, without nerves, cool; inscrutable, blank, expressionless, deadpan, poker-faced; unseeing 439 *blind*; unhearing 416 *deaf*; unsentimental, cynical; impersonal, dispassionate, without warmth, reserved, unforthcoming, stony, frigid, frozen, icy, cold, cold-blooded, cold-hearted, cold as charity; unfeeling, heartless, soulless, inhuman; unsmitten, heart-free, fancy-f., heart-whole; unloving, unaffectionate, undemonstrative.

apathetic, unenthusiastic, unambitious; unimpassioned, uninspired, unexcited, unwarmed, unmoved, unstirred, untouched, unsmitten, unstruck, unaroused, unstung; half-hearted, lukewarm, Laodicean 860 *indifferent*; uninterested 454 *incurious*; nonchalant, insouciant, pococurante, careless, regardless, neglectful 458 *negligent*; unspirited, spiritless, lackadaisical; lotus-eating, vegetative, stagnant 266 *quiescent*; sluggish, supine 679 *inactive*; passive 175 *inert*; blunted 257 *unsharpened*; cloyed 863 *sated*; torpid, numb, benumbed, paralysed, comatose 375 *insensible.*

thick-skinned, pachydermatous; impenetrable, impervious; blind to, deaf to, dead to, closed to; obtuse, unimaginative, insensitive; callous, insensate, tough, toughened, hardened, case-h. 326 *hard*; hard-bitten, hard-boiled, inured 669 *matured*; shameless, unblushing, unmoral, amoral.

Vb. *be insensitive*, - impassive etc. adj.; have no sensation, have no feelings 375 *be insensible*; not see, miss the point of, be blind to 439 *be blind*; lack animation, lack spirit, lack verve; harden oneself, steel o., harden one's heart against, own no pity 906 *be pitiless*; feel indifference 860 *be indifferent*; feel no emotion, despise e., have no finer feelings, be a philistine, nil admirari 865 *not wonder*; show no regard for 922 *despise*; take no interest 454 *be incurious*; ignore 458 *disregard*; control one's feelings, quell one's desires 942 *be temperate*; stagnate, vegetate 679 *be inactive*; not stir, not turn a hair, not bat an eyelid 599 *be resolute*.

make insensitive, benumb 375 *render insensible*; render callous, steel, toughen 326 *harden*; sear, dry up 342 *dry*; deafen, stop the ears 399 *silence*; shut the eyes of 439 *blind*; brutalize 655 *pervert*; stale, coarsen 847 *vulgarize*; satiate, cloy 863 *sate*; deaden, obtund, take the edge off 257 *blunt*.

Adv. *in cold blood*, with dry eyes, without emotion, with steady pulse; without enthusiasm.

See: 175, 257, 266, 326, 342, **375**, 399, 416, 439, 454, 456, 458, 499, 599, 655, 669, 679, 699, **823**, 834, 838, 847, 860, 863, 865, 898, 906, 922, 942.

821 Excitation

N. *excitation*, rousing, arousal, stirring up, working up, whipping up; galvanization, electrification 174 *stimulation*; possession, inspiration, afflatus, exhilaration, intoxication, headiness; evocation, calling forth; encouragement, animation, incitement, invitation, appeal 612 *inducement*; provocation, irritation, casus belli; impression, image, impact 178 *influence*; fascination, bewitchment, enchantment 983 *sorcery*; rapture, ravishment 824 *joy*; emotional appeal, human interest, sentiment, sentimentalism, sob-stuff, pathos; sensationalism, thrill-seeking, melodrama; scandal-mongering, muck-raking 926 *detraction*; excitement, high pressure, tension 160 *energy*; state of excitement, perturbation, effervescence, ebullience 318 *agitation*; shock, thrill, kicks 318 *spasm*; stew, ferment, tizzy, flurry, furore 318 *commotion*; pitch of excitement, fever pitch, orgasm 503 *frenzy*; climax 137 *crisis*; excited feeling, passion, emotion, enthusiasm, lyricism 818 *feeling*; fuss, drama 822 *excitable state*; temper, fury, rage 891 *anger*; interest 453 *curiosity*; amazement 864 *wonder*; awe 854 *fear*.

excitant, stimulator, agent provocateur, rabble-rouser, tub-thumper 738 *agitator*; sensationalist, sob sister, scandalmonger; headline, banner h. 528 *publicity*; fillip, ginger, tonic, pick-me-up 174 *stimulant*; upper, pep pill 949 *drug-taking*; sting, prick, goad, spur, whip, lash 612 *incentive*; fan; irritant, gadfly.

Adj. *excited*, activated, stimulated, stung etc. vb.; busy, astir, bustling, rushing 678 *active*; ebullient, effervescent, boiling, seething 355 *bubbly*; tense, wrought up, strung up, keyed up, wound up; overheated, feverish, hectic; delirious, frantic 503 *frenzied*; glowing 818 *fervent*; heated, flushed 379 *hot*; red-hot with excitement, violent 176 *furious*; hot under the collar, hot and bothered; seeing red, wild, mad, livid, foaming at the mouth, frothing, ramping, stamping, roaring, raging 891 *angry*; avid, eager, itching, agog, thrill-seeking, watering at the mouth 859 *desiring*; tingling, atremble, aquiver 818 *feeling*; flurried, atwitter, all of a flutter 318 *agitated*; restless, restive, overexcited, overwrought, distraught, distracted, distrait(e); freaked out, on a high, on a trip; beside oneself, hysterical, out of control, uncontrollable, running amok, carried away, a prey to passion; turned on, hyped up; crazy about 887 *enamoured*; inspired, possessed, impassioned, enthusiastic, lyrical, raving 822 *excitable*.

exciting, stimulating, sparkling, intoxicating, heady, exhilarating; provocative, piquant, tantalizing; salty, spicy, appetizing; alluring 887 *lovable*; evocative, emotive, suggestive; suspenseful, cliff-hanging, hair-raising, spine-chilling; thrilling, agitating; moving, affecting, inspiring, possessing; heating, kindling, rousing, stirring, soul-s., heart-swelling, heart-thrilling; cheering, rousing, rabble-r.; sensational, dramatic, melodramatic, stunning, mind-boggling, mind-blowing; interesting, gripping, absorbing, enthralling.

impressive, imposing, grand, stately; dignified, majestic, regal, royal, kingly, queenly 868 *noble*; awe-inspiring, sublime, humbling; overwhelming, overpowering; picturesque, scenic; striking, arresting, dramatic; telling, forceful 178 *influential*.

Vb. *excite*, affect, infect 178 *influence*; warm the heart 833 *cheer*; touch, move, draw tears 834 *sadden*; impassion, touch the heartstrings, strike a chord, arouse the emotions, stir the feelings, play on one's f.; quicken the pulse, startle, electrify, galvanize; warm the blood, raise the temperature, raise to fever pitch, bring to the boil, make one's blood boil 381 *heat*;

inflame, enkindle, kindle, draw a spark, set on fire 381 *burn*; sting, pique, irritate 891 *enrage*; tantalize, tease 827 *torment*; touch on the raw, cut to the quick; rip up, open the wound 827 *hurt*; work on, work up, whip up 612 *incite*; breathe into, enthuse, inspire, possess; stir, rouse, arouse, wake, awaken, turn on (**see** *animate*); evoke, summon up, call forth; thrill, exhilarate, intoxicate; transport, send, send into ecstasies 826 *delight*.

animate, vivify, enliven, quicken 360 *vitalize*; revive, rekindle, resuscitate, breathe fresh life into, bring in new blood 656 *restore*; inspire, inspirit, put one on his mettle; infuse courage into, encourage, hearten 855 *give courage*; give an edge, put teeth into, whet 256 *sharpen*; urge, nag, spur, goad, lash 277 *accelerate*; jolt, jog, shake up; fillip, give a fillip to, stimulate, ginger 174 *invigorate*; cherish, foster, foment 162 *strengthen*; fuel, intensify, fan, fan the flame, blow on the coals, stir the embers.

impress, sink in, leave an impression; project *or* present an image; interest, hold, grip, absorb; intrigue, rouse curiosity, make one sit up; strike, claim attention, rivet the a. 455 *attract notice*; affect 178 *influence*; let sink in, bring home to, drive home 532 *emphasize*; come home to, make one realize, penetrate, pierce 516 *be intelligible*; arrest, shake, smite, stun, amaze, astound, stagger 508 *surprise*; stupefy, gorgonize, petrify 864 *be wonderful*; dazzle, fill with admiration; inspire with awe, humble; take one's breath away, overwhelm; oppress, perturb, disquiet, upset, unsettle, distress, worry 827 *trouble*.

be excited, lose one's cool; flare, flare up, flame, burn 379 *be hot*; sizzle, seethe, boil, explode 318 *effervesce*; catch the infection, thrill to 818 *feel*; tingle, tremble 822 *be excitable*; quiver, flutter, palpitate 318 *be agitated*; mantle, flush 818 *show feeling*; squirm, writhe 251 *wriggle*; dance, stamp, ramp; jump 312 *leap*; toss and turn, be unable to sleep.

Adv. *excitedly*, uncontrollably, frenziedly; all agog, with one's heart in one's mouth, with beating heart, with hair on end; aquiver, atremble.

See: 137, 160, 162, **174**, 176, 178, 251, 256, 277, 312, **318**, 355, 360, 379, 381, 453, 455, 503, 508, 516, 528, 532, 612, 656, 678, 738, **818**, **822**, 824, 826, 827, 833, 834, 854, 855, 859, 864, 868, 887, 891, 926, 949, 983.

822 Excitability

N. *excitability*, excitableness, explosiveness, inflammability; instability, temperament, emotionalism; hot blood, hot temper, irritability, scratchiness, touchiness 892 *irascibility*; impatience, nonendurance; incontinence; intolerance, fanaticism 481 *bias*; passionateness, vehemence, impetuosity, recklessness, headstrong behaviour 857 *rashness*; hastiness 680 *haste*; effervescence, ebullition; turbulence, boisterousness; restlessness, fidgetiness, fidgets, nerves, flap 318 *agitation*.

excitable state, exhilaration, elevation, elation, intoxication, abandon, abandonment; thrill, transport, trip, high, ecstasy, inspiration, lyricism 818 *feeling*; fever, fever of excitement, fret, fume, perturbation, trepidation, bother, fuss, flurry, whirl 318 *agitation*; warmth 379 *heat*; ferment, pother, stew; gust, storm, tempest 352 *gale*; effervescence, ebullition, outburst, outbreak, explosion, scene, song and dance 318 *commotion*; brainstorm, hysterics, delirium, fit, agony 503 *frenzy*; distraction, madness 503 *insanity*; mania, passion, master p., ruling p.; rage, towering r., fury 176 *violence*; temper, tantrums, rampage 891 *anger*.

Adj. *excitable*, sensitized, oversensitive, raw 819 *sensitive*; passionate, emotional; susceptible, romantic; out for thrills, thrill-loving, thrill-seeking, looking for kicks; suggestible, inflammable, like tinder; unstable, easily exhilarated, easily depressed; easily impressed, impressionable, impressible; variable, temperamental, mercurial, volatile 152 *changeful*; fitful 604 *capricious*; restless, unquiet, nervy, fidgety, edgy, on edge, ruffled 318 *agitated*; highly-strung, nervous, skittish, mettlesome 819 *lively*; easily provoked, irritable, fiery, hot-tempered, hot-headed 892 *irascible*; impatient, trigger-happy 680 *hasty*; impetuous, impulsive, madcap 857 *rash*; savage, fierce; vehement, boisterous, rumbustious, tempestuous, turbulent, stormy, uproarious, clamorous 176 *violent*; restive, uncontrollable 738 *riotous*; effervescent, simmering, seething, boiling; volcanic, explosive, ready to burst; fanatical, unbalanced, intolerant;

rabid 176 *furious*; feverish, febrile, frantic, hysterical, delirious 503 *frenzied*; dancing, stamping; like a cat on hot bricks, like a cat on a hot tin roof; tense, electric; elated, inspired, raving, lyrical 821 *excited*.

Vb. *be excitable*, - impatient etc. adj.; show impatience, fret, fume, stamp; shuffle, chafe, fidget, champ at the bit; show excitement, show temperament 818 *show feeling*; tingle with, be itching to; be on edge, have nerves, be in a stew, be in a fuss, flap 318 *be agitated*; start, jump 854 *be nervous*; be under strain, break down, be on the verge of a breakdown; have a temper 892 *be irascible*; foam, froth, throw fits, have hysterics 503 *go mad*; abandon oneself, let oneself go, go wild, run riot, run amok, get out of control, see red; storm, rush about 61 *rampage*; ramp, rage, roar 176 *be violent*; fly into a temper, fly off the handle, burst out, break o., explode, create 891 *get angry*; kindle, burn, smoulder, catch fire, flare up 821 *be excited*.

See: 61, 152, 176, 318, 352, 379, 481, 503, 604, 680, 738, **818**, **819**, **821**, 854, 857, 891, 892.

823 Inexcitability

N. *inexcitability*, imperturbability, good temper; calmness, steadiness, composure; coolness, cool, sangfroid, nonchalance; frigidity, coldness, impassibility 820 *moral insensibility*; unruffled state, tranquillity 266 *quietude*; serenity, placidity, peace of mind, calm of m. 828 *content*; equanimity, balance, poise, even temper, level t., philosophic t., philosophy, balanced mind 28 *equilibrium*; self-possession, self-command, self-control, self-restraint 942 *temperance*; repression, self-r., stoicism 945 *asceticism*; detachment, nonattachment, dispassion, dispassionateness 860 *indifference*; gravity, staidness, demureness, sobriety 834 *seriousness*; quietism, Quakerism; sweetness, gentleness 884 *courtesy*; tameness, meekness, lack of spirit, lack of mettle 734 *laxity*; tranquillization, soothing 177 *moderation*.

patience, patience of Job; forbearance, endurance, longsuffering, longanimity; tolerance, toleration, refusal to be provoked; stoicism; resignation, acquiescence 721 *submission*.

Adj. *inexcitable*, impassible, dispassionate, cold, frigid, heavy, dull 820 *impassive*; stable 153 *unchangeable*; not given to worry, unworrying, unworried, cool, cool as a cucumber, imperturbable, unflappable; cool-headed, level-h.; steady, composed, controlled; self-controlled, moderate 942 *temperate*; inscrutable, deadpan; deliberate, unhurried, unhasty 278 *slow*; even, level, equable 16 *uniform*; not irritable, good-tempered, even-t., easy-going, sunny; staid, sedate, sober, sober-minded, demure, reserved, grave 834 *serious*; quiet, unemphatic 266 *quiescent*; placid, unruffled, calm, serene 266 *tranquil*; sweet, gentle, mild, lamblike, meek 935 *innocent*; mild as milk 177 *moderate*; unwarlike 717 *peaceful*; easy, easygoing, undemanding 736 *lenient*; comfortable, gemütlich 828 *content*; philosophic, unambitious 860 *indifferent*; acquiescent, resigned, submissive 739 *obedient*; spiritless, lackadaisical, torpid, passive 175 *inert*; calmed down, in a reasonable frame of mind, tame 369 *tamed*; unenthusiastic, unsentimental, unromantic, unpoetic, earthbound 593 *prosaic*.

patient, meek, like patience on a monument, armed with patience; tolerant, long-suffering, longanimous, forbearing, enduring; stoic, stoical, philosophic, philosophical, uncomplaining.

Vb. *keep calm*, be composed, be collected; compose oneself, collect o., keep cool, keep a cool head; master one's feelings, swallow one's resentment, control one's temper, keep one's cool, keep one's hair *or* shirt on; not turn a hair, not bat an eyelid 820 *be insensitive*; relax, not excite oneself, not worry, stop worrying, take things easy, take things as they come 683 *repose*; resign oneself, take in good part, take philosophically, have patience, be resigned 721 *submit*.

be patient, show patience, show restraint, forbear; put up with, stand, stand for, tolerate, bear, endure, support, sustain, suffer, abide; resign oneself, grin and bear it, put a brave face on it; brook, take, take it from, swallow, digest, stomach, pocket 721 *knuckle under*; turn the other cheek 909 *forgive*; be tolerant, live and let live, condone 736 *be lenient*; turn a blind eye, overlook 734 *be lax*; allow 756 *permit*; ignore provocation, keep the peace 717 *be at peace*; find a modus vivendi, coexist 770 *compromise.*

tranquillize, steady, moderate, moderate one's transports, sober down 177 *assuage*; calm, rock, lull 266 *bring to rest*; cool down, compose 719 *pacify*; make one's mind easy, set one's mind at rest 831 *relieve*; control, repress 747 *restrain*.

See: 16, 28, 153, 175, **177**, **266**, 278, 369, 593, 683, 717, 719, 721, 734, 736, 739, 747, 756, 770, **820**, 828, 831, 834, 860, 884, 909, 935, 942, 945.

Section two: Personal emotion

824 Joy

N. *joy* 376 *pleasure*; great pleasure, keen p.; sensation of pleasure, enjoyment, thrill, kick, piquancy 826 *pleasurableness*; joyfulness, joyousness 835 *rejoicing*; delight, gladness, rapture, exaltation, exhilaration, transports of delight; abandonment, ecstasy, enchantment, bewitchment, ravishment; unholy joy, gloating, schadenfreude, malice 898 *malevolence*; life of pleasure, joys of life, rose-strewn path; halcyon days, holidays, honeymoon 730 *palmy days*.

happiness, felicity, good fortune, wellbeing, snugness, comfort, ease 376 *euphoria*; unalloyed delight, rose without a thorn; flourishing time, Saturnia Regna, golden age, age of Aquarius 730 *prosperity*; blessedness, bliss, beatitude, summum bonum; seventh heaven, cloud nine, nirvana, Paradise, Elysium, Garden of Eden, Fortunate Isles, Isles of the Blessed, Hesperides, Arcadia, Cockaigne 513 *fantasy*; happy valley, bower of bliss, home sweet home.

enjoyment, gratification, satisfaction, fulfilment 828 *content*; delectation, relish, zest, gusto; indulgence, luxuriation, wallowing 943 *intemperance*; full life, eudaemonism, hedonism, Epicureanism 944 *sensualism*; glee, merry-making, lark, frolic, gambol 833 *merriment*; fun, treat, excursion, outing 837 *amusement*; refreshment, good cheer, cakes and ale, beer and skittles, panem et circenses 301 *eating*.

Adj. *pleased*, well-p., glad, not sorry; welcoming, receiving with open arms; satisfied, happy 828 *content*; gratified, flattered, chuffed, pleased as Punch; over the moon, on top of the world; enjoying, loving it, tickled, tickled to death, tickled pink 837 *amused*; exhilarated 833 *merry*; euphoric, walking on air; exalted, elated, overjoyed 833 *jubilant*; cheering, shouting 835 *rejoicing*; delighted, transported, enraptured, ravished, rapturous, ecstatic, raving 923 *approving*; in raptures, in ecstasies, in transports, in the seventh heaven, on cloud nine; captivated, charmed, enchanted, fascinated 818 *impressed*; maliciously pleased, gloating.

happy, happy as a king, happy as a sandboy, happy as a lark, happy as the day is long; blithe, joyful, joyous, gladsome 833 *merry*; beaming, smiling 835 *laughing*; radiant, radiating joy, sparkling, starry-eyed; felicitous, lucky, fortunate, to be congratulated 730 *prosperous*; blissful, blest, blessed, beatified; in felicity, in bliss, in paradise; at ease, made comfortable 376 *comfortable*.

Vb. *be pleased*, - glad etc. adj.; have the pleasure; feel *or* experience pleasure, hug oneself, congratulate o., purr, purr with pleasure, dance with p., jump for joy 833 *be cheerful*; laugh, smile 835 *rejoice*; get pleasure from, get a kick out of, take pleasure in, delight in, rejoice in; go into ecstasies, rave, rave about 818 *show feeling*; indulge in, have time for, luxuriate in, solace oneself with, refresh oneself w., bask in, wallow, spoil oneself 376 *enjoy*; have fun 837 *amuse oneself*; gloat, gloat over; savour, appreciate, relish, smack one's lips 386 *taste*; take a fancy to, like 887 *love*; think well of 923 *approve*; take in good part, take no offence.

See: 301, 376, 386, 513, **730**, 818, 826, **828**, **833**, **835**, 837, 887, 898, 923, 943, 944.

825 Suffering

N. *suffering*, heartache, Weltschmerz, lacrimae rerum 834 *melancholy*; longing, homesickness, nostalgia 859 *desire*; unsatisfied desire 829 *discontent*; weariness 684 *fatigue*; weight on the spirit, nightmare, incubus; affliction, distress, dolour, anguish, angst, agony, torture, torment, mental t. 377 *pain*; twinge, stab, smart, sting, thorn 377 *pang*; bitter cup 827 *painfulness*; Passion, Crucifixion, Calvary, martyrdom; rack, the stake 963 *punishment*; purgatory, hell, pains of h., damnation, eternal d. 961 *condemnation*; bed of nails, bed of thorns, no bed of roses 700 *difficulty*; unpleasantness, mauvais quart d'heure; inconvenience, disagreeableness, discomfort, malaise; the hard way, trial, ordeal; shock, blow, infliction, visitation, tribulation 659 *bane*; extremity, death's door 651 *illness*; living death, death in life, fate worse than death 616 *evil*; dystopia; evil days, unhappy times, iron age 731 *adversity*.

sorrow, grief, sadness, mournfulness, gloom 834 *dejection*; dole, dolour, woe, wretchedness, misery, depths of m.; prostration, despair, desolation 853 *hopelessness*; unhappiness, infelicity, tale of woe 731 *adversity*; weariness of spirit, heavy heart, aching h., bleeding h., broken h.; displeasure, dissatisfaction 829 *discontent*; vexation, bitterness, mortification, chagrin, heart-burning, fretting, repining, remorse 830 *regret*.

worry, worrying, worriedness, unease, uneasiness, discomfort, disquiet, unquiet, inquietude, fret, fretting 318 *agitation*; discomposure, dismay, distress 63 *derangement*; phobia, hangup; something on one's mind, weight on one's m., anxiety, concern, solicitude, thought, care; responsibility, weight of r., load, burden; strain, tension, premenstrual t., PMT; a worry, worries, cares, cares of the world; trouble, troubles 616 *evil*; bother, botheration, annoyance, irritation, pest, thorn in the flesh, death of 659 *bane*; bothersome task 838 *bore*; something to worry about, lookout, funeral; headache, teaser, puzzle, problem 530 *enigma*.

sufferer, victim, scapegoat, sacrifice; prey, shorn lamb 544 *dupe*; willing sacrifice, martyr; object of compassion, wretch, poor w., misery 731 *unlucky person*; patient 651 *sick person*.

Adj. *suffering*, ill 651 *sick*; agonizing, writhing, aching, griped, in pain, on a bed of p., ravaged with p., bleeding, harrowed, on the rack, in torment, in hell 377 *pained*; inconvenienced, uncomfortable, ill at ease; anguished, distressed, upset; worked up 818 *fervent*; anxious, unhappy about, worried, troubled, disquieted, apprehensive, dismayed 854 *nervous*; sick with worry, cut up about, in a state 316 *agitated*; discomposed, disconcerted 63 *disarranged*; ill-used, maltreated, severely handled, on the receiving end; longsuffering, downtrodden 745 *subjected*; victimized, made a prey, sacrificed; stricken, wounded; heavy-laden, crushed 684 *fatigued*; careworn, sad-looking, worried-l., harassed-l.; woeful, woebegone, haggard, wild-eyed.

unhappy, infelicitous, unlucky, accursed 731 *unfortunate*; despairing 853 *hopeless*; doomed 961 *condemned*; to be pitied, pitiable, poor, wretched, miserable; sad, melancholy, despondent, disconsolate; cut up, heart-broken, broken-hearted, heavy-h., sick at heart; sorrowful, sorrowing, grieved, grieving, grief-stricken, woebegone 834 *dejected*; plunged in grief, weeping, weepy, wet-eyed, tearful, in tears 836 *lamenting*; nostalgic, longing 859 *desiring*; displeased, dissatisfied, disappointed 829 *discontented*; offended, vexed, annoyed, pained 924 *disapproving*; piqued, chagrined, mortified, humiliated 891 *resentful*; sickened, disgusted, nauseated 861 *disliking*; sorry, remorseful, compunctious, regretful 830 *regretting*.

Vb. *suffer*, undergo, endure, go through, experience 818 *feel*; bear, endure, put up with; bear pain, suffer p., suffer torments, bleed; hurt oneself, be hurt, smart, chafe, ache 377 *feel pain*; wince, flinch, agonize, writhe, squirm 251 *wriggle*; take up one's cross, become a martyr, sacrifice oneself; take one's punishment, take it on the chin 599 *stand firm*; have a thin time, have a bad t., go through it, have trouble enough 731 *have trouble*; trouble oneself, distress o., fuss, worry, worry to death, fret, agonize, be on pins and needles 318 *be agitated*; mind, let weigh upon one, take it badly, take it to heart; sorrow, passion, grieve, weep, sigh, take on 836 *lament*; pity oneself, be despondent 834 *be dejected*; have regrets, kick oneself 830 *regret*.

See: 63, 251, 316, 318, **377**, 530, 544, 599, 616, 651, 659, 684, 700, 731, 745, 818, 827, **829**, 830, **834**, **836**, 838, 853, 854, 859, 861, 891, 924, 961, 963.

826 Pleasurableness

N. *pleasurableness*, pleasures of, pleasantness, niceness, delectableness, delectability, delightfulness, amenity, sunny side, bright s.; invitingness, attractiveness, appeal, sex a., come-hither look 291 *attraction*; winning ways 925 *flattery*; amiability, winsomeness, charm, fascination, enchantment, witchery, loveliness, sight for sore eyes 841 *beauty*; joyfulness, honeymoon 824 *joy*; something nice, a little of what one fancies, a delight, a treat, a joy; novelty, pastime, fun 837 *amusement*; interest, human i.; melody, harmony 412 *music*; tastiness, deliciousness 390 *savouriness*; spice, zest, relish; dainty, titbit, sweet 392 *sweetness*; manna in the wilderness, balm 685 *refreshment*; land flowing with milk and honey 635 *plenty*; peace, perfect p., peace and quiet, tranquillity 266 *quietude*, 681 *leisure*; pipedream 513 *fantasy*.

Adj. *pleasurable*, pleasant, nice, good; pleasure-giving 837 *amusing*; pleasing, agreeable, grateful, gratifying, flattering; acceptable, welcome, welcome as the flowers in May; well-liked, to one's taste, to one's liking, just what the doctor ordered; wonderful, marvellous, splendid 644 *excellent*; frictionless, painless 376 *comfortable*; easeful, refreshing 683 *reposeful*; peaceful, quiet 266 *tranquil*; bowery, luxurious, voluptuous 376 *sensuous*; genial, warm, sunny 833 *cheering*; delightful, delectable, delicious, exquisite, choice; luscious, juicy 356 *pulpy*; delicate, tasty 390 *savoury*; sugary 392 *sweet*; dulcet, musical, harmonious 410 *melodious*; picturesque, scenic, lovely 841 *beautiful*; amiable, dear, winning, endearing 887 *lovable*; attractive, fetching, appealing, interesting 291 *attracting*; seductive, enticing, inviting, captivating; charming, enchanting, bewitching, ravishing, siren, Circean; haunting, thrilling, heart-melting, heart-warming 821 *exciting*; homely, cosy; pastoral, idyllic; Elysian, paradisal, heavenly, out of this world; beatific, blessed, blissful 824 *happy*.

Vb. *please*, give pleasure, afford p., yield p., agree with; make things pleasant 925 *flatter*; lull, soothe 177 *assuage*; comfort 833 *cheer*; put at ease, make comfortable 831 *relieve*; sugar, gild the pill 392 *sweeten*; stroke, pat, pet, baby, coddle, nurse 889 *caress*; indulge, pander to 734 *be lax*; charm, interest 837 *amuse*; rejoice, gladden, make happy; gratify, satisfy, crown one's wishes, leave nothing more to be desired 828 *content*; bless, crown one's bliss, raise to the seventh heaven, beatify.

delight, surprise with joy; rejoice, exhilarate, elate, elevate, uplift; rejoice one's heart, warm the cockles of one's h., do one's heart good; thrill, intoxicate, ravish; transport, turn on, send, send one into raptures *or* ecstasies 821 *excite*; make music in one's ears 925 *flatter*; take one's fancy, tickle one's f. 887 *excite love*; tickle one's palate 390 *make appetizing*; regale, refresh; tickle, tickle one to death, titillate, tease, tantalize; entrance, enrapture; enchant, charm, becharm 983 *bewitch*; take one's breath away 821 *impress*; allure, seduce 291 *attract*.

See: 177, 266, 291, 356, **376**, 390, 392, 410, 412, 513, 635, 644, 681, 683, 685, 734, 821, **824**, **828**, 831, **833**, 837, 841, 887, 889, 925, 983.

827 Painfulness

N. *painfulness*, painful treatment, harshness, roughness, harassment, persecution 735 *severity*; hurtfulness, harmfulness 645 *badness*; disagreeableness, unpleasantness; loathsomeness, hatefulness, beastliness 616 *evil*; grimness 842 *ugliness*; hideosity 842 *eyesore*; friction, chafing, irritation, ulceration, inflammation, exacerbation 832 *aggravation*; soreness, tenderness 377 *pain*; irritability, inflammability 822 *excitability*; sore subject, sore point, rub, soft spot, tender s. 819 *moral sensibility*; sore, running s., ulcer, thorn in the flesh, pinprick, where the shoe pinches 659 *bane*; shock 508 *lack of expectation*; unpalatability, disgust, nausea, sickener 391 *unsavouriness*; sharpness, bitterness, bitter cup, bitter draught, bitter pill, gall and wormwood, vinegar 393 *sourness*; bread of affliction 731 *adversity*; tribulation, ordeal, cross 825 *suffering*; trouble, care 825 *worry*; dreariness, cheerlessness; pitifulness, pathos; sorry sight, pathetic s., painful s., sad spectacle, object of pity 731 *unlucky person*; heavy news 825 *sorrow*; disenchantment, disillusionment 509 *disappointment*; hornet's nest, hot water 700 *predicament*.

annoyance, vexation, death of, pest, curse, plague, pain in the neck 659 *bane*; botheration, embarrassment 825 *worry*; cause for annoyance, interference, nuisance, pinprick; burden, drag 702 *encumbrance*; grievance, complaint; hardship, troubles 616 *evil*; last straw, limit; offence, affront, insult, provocation 921 *indignity*; molestation, infestation, persecution, malignity 898 *malevolence*; feeling of annoyance, displeasure, mortification 891 *resentment*; menace, enfant terrible.

Adj. *paining*, hurting, aching, sore, tender; dolorous, agonizing, racking, purgatorial

377 *painful*; scathing, searing, scalding, burning, sharp, shooting, biting, nipping, gnawing, throbbing; caustic, corrosive, vitriolic; harsh, hard, rough, cruel 735 *severe*; grinding, gruelling, punishing, searching, exquisite, excruciating, extreme; hurtful, harmful, poisonous 659 *baneful*.

unpleasant, unpleasing, disagreeable; uncomfortable, comfortless, joyless, dreary, dismal, depressing 834 *cheerless*; unattractive, uninviting, unappealing; hideous 842 *ugly*; unwelcome, undesired, unacceptable 860 *unwanted*; thankless, unpopular, displeasing 924 *disapproved*; disappointing, unsatisfactory 829 *discontenting*; distasteful, unpalatable, off 391 *unsavoury*; foul, nasty, beastly, horrible 645 *not nice*; malodorous, stinking 397 *fetid*; bitter, sharp 393 *sour*; invidious, obnoxious, offensive, objectionable, undesirable, odious, hateful, loathsome, nauseous, slimy, disgusting, revolting, repellent 861 *disliked*; execrable, accursed 645 *damnable*.

annoying, too bad; troublesome, embarrassing, worrying; bothersome, bothering, wearisome, irksome, tiresome, boring 838 *tedious*; burdensome, onerous, oppressive 322 *weighty*; disappointing, unlucky, unfortunate, untoward 731 *adverse*; awkward, unaccommodating, impossible, pesky, plaguy, harassing 702 *hindering*; importunate, pestering; teasing, trying, irritating, vexatious, aggravating, provoking, maddening, infuriating; galling, stinging, biting, mortifying.

distressing, afflicting, crushing, grievous; moving, affecting, touching, grieving; shocking, traumatic; harrowing, heartbreaking, heart-rending, tear-jerking; pathetic, tragic, tragical, sad, woeful, rueful, mournful, pitiful, lamentable, deplorable 905 *pitiable*; ghastly, grim, dreadful, appalling, horrifying, horrific, nerve-racking 854 *frightening*.

intolerable, insufferable, impossible, insupportable, unendurable, unbearable 32 *exorbitant*; past bearing, past enduring, not to be borne, not to be endured, not to be put up with; extreme, beyond the limits of tolerance, more than flesh and blood can stand, enough to make one mad, enough to make a parson swear, enough to try the patience of Job, enough to provoke a saint.

Vb. *hurt*, injure 645 *harm*; pain, cause p. 377 *give pain*; bite, cut, tear, rend 655 *wound*; wound the feelings, hurt the f., gall, pique, nettle, mortify 891 *huff*; rub up the wrong way, tread on one's corns; touch a soft spot, cut to the quick, pierce the heart, rend the heartstrings, draw tears, grieve, afflict, distress 834 *sadden*; plunge into sorrow, bring grief to one's heart, plant an arrow in one's breast, plant a thorn in one's side; corrode, embitter, exacerbate, rub salt in the wound, gnaw, chafe, rankle, fester 832 *aggravate*; offend, aggrieve (**see** *displease*); insult, affront 921 *not respect*.

torment, martyr; harrow, rack, put to the r., break on the wheel 963 *torture*; give the third degree, give one the works; put through the hoop, give one a bad time, maltreat, bait, bully, rag, bullyrag, persecute, assail 735 *oppress*; be offensive, snap at, bark at 885 *be rude*; importune, dun, beset, besiege 737 *demand*; haunt, obsess; annoy, do it to a.; tease, pester, plague, nag, henpeck, badger, worry, try, chivvy, harass, harry, heckle; molest, bother, vex, provoke, peeve, ruffle, irritate, needle, sting, chafe, fret, bug, gall, irk, roil, rile 891 *enrage*.

trouble, discomfort, disquiet, disturb, agitate, discompose, disconcert, throw one out, upset, incommode 63 *derange*; worry, embarrass, perplex 474 *puzzle*; exercise, tire 684 *fatigue*; weary, bore 838 *be tedious*; obsess, haunt, bedevil; weigh upon one, prey on the mind, weigh on the spirits, deject 834 *depress*; infest, get in one's hair, dog one's footsteps, get under one's feet, get in one's way, thwart 702 *obstruct*.

displease, not please, not appeal, find no favour 924 *incur blame*; grate, jar, disagree with, grate on, jar on, get on one's nerves, set one's teeth on edge, go against the grain, give one the pip, give one a pain, get one's goat, get under one's skin; disenchant, disillusion, undeceive 509 *disappoint*; dissatisfy, give cause for complaint, aggrieve 829 *cause discontent*; offend, shock, horrify, scandalize, disgust, revolt, repel, put one off, sicken, nauseate, fill one with loathing, stink in the nostrils, stick in the throat, stick in the gizzard, make one's gorge rise, turn one's stomach, make one sick, make one vomit, make one throw up 861 *cause dislike*; make one's flesh creep, make one's blood run cold, curdle the blood, appal 854 *frighten*.

See: 32, 63, 322, **377**, 391, 393, 397, 474, 508, 509, 616, 645, 655, 659, 684, 700, 702, 731, 735, 737, 819, 822, **825**, **829**, 832, 834, 838, 842, 854, 860, 861, 885, 891, 898, 905, 921, 924, 963.

828 Content

N. *content*, contentment, contentedness, satisfaction, entire s., complacency; self-complacency, self-satisfaction, smugness 873 *vanity*; measure of content, half-smile, ray of comfort; serenity, quietism, tranquillity, resignation 266 *quietude*; ease of mind, trouble-free m., easy m., peace of m., heart's ease, nothing left to worry about 376 *euphoria*; conciliation, reconciliation 719 *pacification*; snugness, cosiness, comfort, sitting pretty; wish-fulfilment, desires fulfilled, ambition achieved, port after stormy seas 730 *prosperity*; acquiescence 758 *consent*; resignation 721 *submission*.

Adj. *content*, contented, satisfied, well-s. 824 *happy*; appeased, pacified 717 *peaceful*; cosy, snug 376 *comfortable*; at ease 683 *reposeful*; easy in mind, smiling 833 *cheerful*; flattered 824 *pleased*; with nothing left to wish for, with no desire unfulfilled, having nothing to grumble at 863 *sated*; unrepining, uncomplaining, with no regrets, without complaints; unenvious, unjealous 931 *disinterested*; philosophic, without desire, without passion 823 *inexcitable*; resigned, acquiescent 721 *submitting*; fairly content, better satisfied; easily pleased, easygoing 736 *lenient*; secure 660 *safe*; unmolested, untroubled, unworried, unafflicted, unvexed, unplagued; blessed with contentment, thankful, gratified 907 *grateful*.

contenting, satisfying, satisfactory 635 *sufficient*; lulling, pacifying, appeasing 719 *pacificatory*; tolerable, bearable, endurable, livable; unobjectionable, passable, acceptable 923 *approvable*; desirable, wished for, all that is wished for 859 *desired*.

Vb. *be content*, - satisfied etc. adj.; purr, purr with content 824 *be pleased*; rest and be thankful, rest satisfied, take the good that the gods provide, count one's blessings; be thankful, have much to be thankful for 907 *be grateful*; have all one could ask for, have one's wish, attain one's desire, fulfil one's ambition 730 *prosper*; congratulate oneself, hug o. 835 *rejoice*; be at ease, be at home, sit pat, sit pretty 376 *enjoy*; be reconciled 719 *make peace*; get over it, take comfort 831 *be relieved*; rest content, take in good part; take things as they come, make the best of, complain of nothing, have no complaints, have nothing to grouse about, have no regrets, not repine; put up with, acquiesce 721 *submit*.

content, make contented, satisfy, gratify, make one's day 826 *please*; meet with approval, go down well 923 *be praised*; make happy, bless with contentment; grant a boon 781 *give*; crown one's wishes, leave no desire unfulfilled, quench one's thirst 863 *sate*; comfort 833 *cheer*; bring comfort to, speak peace to 831 *relieve*; be kind to 897 *philanthropize*; lull, set at ease, set at rest; propitiate, disarm, reconcile, conciliate, appease 719 *pacify*.

Adv. *contentedly*, complacently, with satisfaction, to one's heart's content, as one would wish.

See: 266, **376**, 635, 660, 683, 717, 719, 721, 730, 736, 758, 781, 823, **824**, 826, 831, 833, 835, 859, 863, 873, 897, 907, 923, 931.

829 Discontent

N. *discontent*, discontentment, disgruntlement; displeasure, pain, dissatisfaction, acute d. 924 *disapprobation*; cold comfort, not what one expected 509 *disappointment*; soreness, irritation, chagrin, pique, mortification, heart-burning, bitterness, bile, spleen 891 *resentment*; uneasiness, disquiet 825 *worry*; grief, vexation of spirit 825 *sorrow*; maladjustment, strain, tension; restlessness, unrest, state of u., restiveness 738 *disobedience*; agitation 318 *commotion*; finickiness, faddiness, hypercriticism, perfectionism, nit-picking 862 *fastidiousness*; querulousness 709 *quarrelsomeness*; ill will 912 *envy*; competition 911 *jealousy*; chip on one's shoulder, grievance, grudge, gripe, complaint 709 *quarrel*; weariness, world-w., melancholy, ennui 834 *dejection*; sulkiness, sulks, dirty look, grimace, scowl, frown 893 *sullenness*; groan, curse 899 *malediction*; cheep, squeak, murmur, murmuring, whispering campaign 762 *deprecation*.

malcontent, grumbler, grouch, grouser,

mutterer, croaker, complainer, whiner, bleater, bellyacher, Jonah 834 *moper*; plaintiff 763 *petitioner*; faultfinder, nit-picker, critic, censurer, envier 709 *quarreller*; person with a grievance, someone with a chip on their shoulder, angry young man; laudator temporis acti; dissident, dropout 738 *revolter*; murmurer, seditionist 738 *agitator*; indignation meeting, protest m.; the Opposition, Her Majesty's O., Government in Exile; irreconcilable, bitter-ender, last-ditcher, diehard 705 *opponent*; hard taskmaster 735 *tyrant*.

Adj. *discontented*, displeased, not best pleased; dissatisfied 924 *disapproving*; unsatisfied, ungratified, frustrated 509 *disappointed*; defeated 728 *unsuccessful*; malcontent, dissident 489 *dissenting*; non-cooperative, obstructive 702 *hindering*; restless, restive 738 *disobedient*; disgruntled, ill-content, weary, browned off, cheesed o., fed up to the back teeth 838 *bored*, 825 *unhappy*; repining 830 *regretting*; sad, uncomforted, unconsoled, unrelieved, disconsolate 834 *dejected*; ill-disposed, grudging, jealous, envious; bileful, spleenful, bitter, embittered, soured 393 *sour*; peevish, testy, cross, sulky, sulking, pouting 893 *sullen*; grouchy, grumbling, grousing, whining, murmuring, swearing 899 *cursing*; protesting 762 *deprecatory*; unflattered, smarting, sore, mortified, insulted, affronted, piqued, vexed, put out, annoyed 891 *resentful*; fretful, querulous, petulant, complaining; hard to please, hard to satisfy, never satisfied, exigent, exacting 862 *fastidious*; fault-finding, critical, hypercritical, censorious 926 *detracting*; irreconcilable, hostile 881 *inimical*; resisting 704 *opposing*.

discontenting, unsatisfactory, unsatisfying 636 *insufficient*; sickening, nauseating 861 *disliked*; boring 838 *tedious*; displeasing, upsetting, mortifying 827 *annoying*; frustrating 509 *disappointing*; baffling, obstructive 702 *hindering*; discouraging, disheartening 613 *dissuasive*.

Vb. *be discontented*, - dissatisfied etc. adj.; be critical, crab, carp, criticize, find fault 862 *be fastidious*; lack, miss, feel something is missing 627 *require*; sneer, groan, jeer 924 *disapprove*; mind, take offence, take in bad part, take amiss, take ill, take to heart, take on, be offended, smart under 891 *resent*; get out of bed the wrong side, get the hump, sulk 893 *be sullen*; look blue, look glum, make a wry face, pull a long f. 834 *be dejected*; moan, mutter, murmur, whine, whinge, bleat, beef, protest, complain, object, cry blue murder 762 *deprecate*; bellyache, grumble, grouse, croak, snap; wail 836 *lament*; be aggrieved, have a grievance, cherish a g., have a chip on one's shoulder; join the opposition 704 *oppose*; rise up, be up in arms about 738 *revolt*; grudge 912 *envy*; quarrel with one's bread and butter 709 *quarrel*; not know when one is well off, look a gift horse in the mouth; make a meal of it 598 *be unwilling*; refuse to be satisfied, ask for one's money back, return 607 *reject*; repine 830 *regret*.

cause discontent, dissatisfy 636 *not suffice*; leave dissatisfied, leave room for complaint 509 *disappoint*; spoil for one, spoil one's pleasure, get one down 834 *depress*; dishearten, discourage 613 *dissuade*; sour, embitter, disgruntle; upset, chafe, fret, niggle, bite, put on edge, put out of humour, irritate 891 *huff*; put out of countenance, mortify 872 *humiliate*; offend, cause resentment 827 *displease*; shock, scandalize 924 *incur blame*; nauseate, sicken, disgust 861 *cause dislike*; arouse discontent, sow the seeds of d., sow dragon's teeth, sow the wind, make trouble, stir up t., agitate 738 *revolt*.

See: 318, 393, 489, 509, 598, 607, 613, 627, 636, 702, 704, 705, 709, 728, 735, 738, 762, 763, 825, **827**, 830, **834**, 836, 838, 861, 862, 872, 881, **891**, **893**, 899, 911, 912, 924, 926.

830 Regret

N. *regret*, regretfulness, regretting, repining; mortification, heart-burning 891 *resentment*; futile regret, vain r., crying over spilt milk; soul-searching, self-reproach, remorse, contrition, repentance, compunction, qualms, pangs of conscience, regrets, apologies 939 *penitence*; disillusion, second thoughts, better t. 67 *sequel*; longing, desiderium, homesickness, maladie du pays, nostalgia, nostalgie de la boue 859 *desire*; sense of loss 737 *demand*; matter of regret, pity of it.

Adj. *regretting*, missing, homesick, nostalgic, wistful; harking back, looking over one's shoulder 125 *retrospective*; mortified, repining, bitter 891 *resentful*; irreconcilable, inconsolable 836 *lament-*

ing; compunctious, regretful, remorseful, rueful, conscience-stricken, sorry, full of regrets, apologetic, soul-searching, penitent 939 *repentant*; undeceived, disillusioned, sadder and wiser.

regretted, much r., sadly missed, badly wanted; regrettable, deplorable, much to be deplored, too bad, a shame, a crying s.

Vb. *regret*, rue, deplore, rue the day; curse one's folly, never forgive oneself, blame o., accuse o., reproach o., kick o., bite one's tongue; unwish, wish undone, repine, wring one's hands, cry over spilt milk, spend time in vain regrets 836 *lament*; want one's time over again, sigh for the good old days, fight one's battles over again, reopen old wounds, hark back, evoke the past 505 *retrospect*; look back, look over one's shoulder; miss, sadly m., miss badly, regret the loss, want back; long for, pine for, hanker after, be homesick 859 *desire*; express regrets, apologize, feel compunction, feel remorse, be sorry 939 *be penitent*; ask for another chance 905 *ask mercy*; deplore, deprecate, lament 924 *disapprove*; feel mortified, gnash one's teeth 891 *resent*; have cause for regret, have had one's lesson 963 *be punished*.

See: 67, 125, 505, 737, **836**, 859, 891, 905, 924, **939**, 963.

831 Relief

N. *relief*, rest 685 *refreshment*; easing, alleviation, mitigation, palliation, abatement 177 *moderation*; good riddance; exemption 668 *deliverance*; solace, consolation, comfort, ray of c., crumb of c.; silver lining, break in the clouds 852 *hope*; feeling better, load off one's mind, sigh of relief 656 *revival*; lulling, lullaby, cradle song, berceuse; soothing, salve 658 *balm*; painkiller, analgesic 375 *anaesthetic*; sedative, sleeping pill 679 *soporific*; pillow 218 *cushion*; comforter, consoler, ray of sunshine.

Adj. *relieving*, soothing, smoothing, balsamic 685 *refreshing*; lulling, assuaging, pain-killing, analgesic, anodyne 177 *lenitive*; curative, restorative 658 *remedial*; consoling, consolatory, comforting.

Vb. *relieve*, ease, soften, cushion; relax, lessen the strain; temper 177 *moderate*; lift, raise, take off, lighten, unburden, disburden, take a load off one's mind 701 *disencumber*; spare, exempt from 919 *exempt*; save 668 *deliver*; console, dry the eyes, wipe the e., wipe away the tears, solace, comfort, bring c., offer a crumb of c., give hope; cheer up, buck up, encourage, hearten, pat on the back 833 *cheer*; shade, cool, fan, ventilate 685 *refresh*; restore, repair 656 *cure*; bandage, bind up, poultice 658 *doctor*; calm, soothe, nurse, pour balm, pour oil, palliate, mitigate, moderate, alleviate 177 *assuage*; smooth the brow, take out the wrinkles 258 *smooth*; stroke, pat 889 *caress*; cradle, lull, put to sleep 679 *sleep*; anaesthetize, kill the pain 375 *render insensible*; take pity on, put out of one's misery, give the coup de grace 905 *pity*.

be relieved, relieve oneself, ease o., obtain relief; feel relief, heave a sigh of r., draw a long breath, breathe again; console oneself, solace o.; take comfort, feel better, dry one's eyes, smile again 833 *be cheerful*; recover from the blow, get over it, come to, be oneself again, pull oneself together, snap out of it, buck up, perk up, sleep off 656 *be restored*; rest content 828 *be content*.

See: **177**, 218, 258, 375, **656**, 658, 668, 679, 685, 701, 828, 833, 852, 889, 905, 919.

832 Aggravation

N. *aggravation*, exacerbation, exasperation, irritation, embittering, embitterment; enhancement, augmentation 36 *increase*; intensification 162 *strengthening*; heightening, deepening, adding to 482 *overestimation*; making worse 655 *deterioration*; complication 700 *difficulty*; irritant 821 *excitant*.

Adj. *aggravated*, intensified; exacerbated, complicated; unrelieved, unmitigated, made worse, not improved 655 *deteriorated*; aggravable.

Vb. *aggravate*, intensify 162 *strengthen*; enhance, heighten, deepen; increase 36 *augment*; worsen, make worse, render w., make things w., not improve matters 655 *deteriorate*; add insult to injury, rub salt in the wound, rub it in; exacerbate, embitter, further embitter, sour, envenom, inflame 821 *excite*; exasperate, irritate 891 *enrage*; add fuel to the flames, fan the embers; complicate, make bad worse, go from bad to worse, jump from the frying pan into the fire.

Adv. *aggravatedly*, worse and worse, from bad to worse, out of the frying pan into

the fire.
Int. so much the worse! tant pis!
See: 36, 162, 482, 655, 700, 821, 891.

833 Cheerfulness

N. *cheerfulness*, alacrity 597 *willingness*; optimism, hopefulness 852 *hope*; cheeriness, happiness, blitheness 824 *joy*; geniality, sunniness, breeziness, smiles, good humour, bon naturel; vitality, spirits, animal s., high s., joie de vivre 360 *life*; light-heartedness, sunshine in the soul, light heart, optimistic outlook, carefree mind 828 *content*; liveliness, sparkle, vivacity, animation, exhilaration, elevation 822 *excitable state*; life and soul of the party, party spirit, conviviality 882 *sociability*; optimist, perennial o., Pollyanna, Mr Micawber.

merriment, laughter and joy; cheer, good c.; exhilaration, high spirits, abandon; jollity, joviality, jocularity, gaiety, glee, mirth, hilarity 835 *laughter*; levity, frivolity 499 *folly*; merry-making, fun, fun and games, sport, good s. 837 *amusement*; jubilation, jubilee 876 *celebration*.

Adj. *cheerful*, cheery, blithe, blithesome 824 *happy*; hearty, genial, convivial 882 *sociable*; sanguine, optimistic, rose-coloured; smiling, sunny, bright, beaming, radiant 835 *laughing*; breezy, of good cheer, in high spirits, in good s., in a good humour; in good heart, unrepining, optimistic, upbeat, hopeful, buoyant, resilient, irrepressible; carefree, light-hearted, happy-go-lucky; debonair, bonny, buxom, bouncing; pert, jaunty, perky, chirpy, chipper, spry, spirited, sprightly, vivacious, animated, vital, sparkling, full of beans, full of pep, bright-eyed and bushy-tailed, on the top of one's form 819 *lively*; alacritous 597 *willing*.

merry, joyous, joyful, merry as a cricket, happy as a sandboy, happy as a king, gay as a lark, happy as the day is long; ebullient, effervescent, sparkling, mirth-loving, laughter-l., waggish, jocular 839 *witty*; gay, light, frivolous 456 *light-minded*; playful, sportive, frisky, gamesome, frolicsome, kittenish 837 *amusing*; roguish, arch, sly, tricksy, full of tricks; merry-making, mirthful, jocund, jovial, jolly, joking, dancing, laughing, singing, drinking, anacreontic; wild, rackety, shouting, roaring with laughter, hilarious, uproarious, rip-roaring, rollicking, rattling, splitting one's sides, tickled pink 837 *amused*.

jubilant, jubilating, overjoyed, gleeful, gleesome, delighted 824 *pleased*; chuffed, elated, flushed, exulting, exultant, triumphant, cock-a-hoop 727 *successful*; triumphing, celebrating, riotous, rioting 876 *celebratory*.

cheering, exhilarating, enlivening, encouraging etc. vb.; warming, heart-w., raising the spirits, exhilarating, animating, intoxicating 821 *exciting*; optimistic, tonic, comforting, like a ray of sunshine, just what the doctor ordered; balmy, palmy, bracing, invigorating 652 *salubrious*.

Vb. *be cheerful*, be in good spirits, be in good humour, be in good heart; keep cheerful, look on the bright side, keep one's spirits up 852 *hope*; keep one's pecker up, grin and bear it, make the best of it, put a good face upon it 599 *be resolute*; take heart, snap out of it, cheer up, perk up, buck up 831 *be relieved*; brighten, liven up, grow animated, let oneself go, abandon oneself, drive dull care away; radiate good humour, smile, beam, sparkle; dance, sing, carol, lilt, chirrup, chirp, whistle, laugh 835 *rejoice*; whoop, cheer 876 *celebrate*; have fun, frisk, frolic, rollick, romp, gambol, sport, disport oneself, enjoy o., have a good time 837 *amuse oneself*; throw a party, make whoopee 882 *be sociable*.

cheer, gladden, warm, warm the heart 828 *content*; comfort, console 831 *relieve*; rejoice the heart, put in a good humour 826 *please*; inspire, enliven 821 *animate*; exhilarate, elate 826 *delight*; encourage, inspirit, hearten, raise the spirits, buck up, jolly along, bolster, bolster up 855 *give courage*; act like a tonic, energize 174 *invigorate*.

Adv. *cheerfully*, willingly, joyfully, gladly, gaily, joyously, light-heartedly, optimistically, without a care in the world; airily, breezily; allegro, con brio.

See: 174, 360, 456, 499, 597, 599, 652, 727, 819, 821, 822, **824**, **826**, **828**, 831, **835**, 837, 839, 852, 855, 876, 882.

834 Dejection. Seriousness

N. *dejection*, joylessness, unhappiness, cheerlessness, dreariness, dejectedness, low spirits, dumps, doldrums; droopiness, spiritlessness, dispiritedness, sinking heart; disillusion 509 *disappointment*; defeatism, pessimism, cynicism, despair, death wish, suicidal tendency 853 *hopelessness*; weariness, oppression, enervation, exhaustion 684 *fatigue*; oppression of spirit, heartache, heaviness, sadness, misery, wretchedness, disconsolateness, dolefulness 825 *sorrow*; despondency, prostration, languishment; Slough of Despond, grey dawn; gloominess, gloom, settled g.; glumness, dejected look, long face, face as long as a fiddle; haggardness, funereal aspect, downcast countenance, lacklustre eye; cause of dejection, sorry sight, memento mori, depressant 838 *bore*; gloom and doom, care, thought, trouble 825 *worry*.

melancholy, melancholia, hypochondria; neurosis, neurasthenia; depression, cafard, black mood, blue devils, blues, horrors, mopes, moping, mopishness, sighing, sigh; dismals, vapours, megrims, spleen, bile 829 *discontent*; disgust of life, world-weariness, taedium vitae, Weltschmerz, angst, mal du siècle, nostalgia, homesickness 825 *suffering*.

seriousness, earnestness; gravity, solemnity, sobriety, demureness, staidness, grimness 893 *sullenness*; primness, humourlessness, heaviness, dullness; straight face, poker f., dead pan; sternness, heavy stuff; earnest, dead e.; no laughing matter, chastening thought.

moper, croaker, complainer, Jonah 829 *malcontent*; sourpuss, crosspatch, bear with a sore head; pessimist, damper, wet blanket, killjoy, spoilsport; Job's comforter, misery, sobersides; death's-head, skeleton at the feast, gloom and doom merchant; hypochondriac, malade imaginaire, seek-sorrow, self-tormentor.

Adj. *dejected*, joyless, dreary, cheerless, unhappy, sad (**see** *melancholic*); gloomy, despondent, desponding, downbeat, unhopeful, pessimistic, defeatist, despairing 853 *hopeless*; beaten, overcome 728 *defeated*; discouraged, disheartened, dismayed; dispirited, unnerved, unmanned 854 *nervous*; troubled, worried 825 *suffering*; downcast, downhearted, droopy, low, down, down in the mouth, low-spirited, depressed; out of sorts, not oneself, out of spirits; sluggish, listless, spiritless, lackadaisical 679 *inactive*; lacklustre 419 *dim*; out of countenance, discountenanced, humbled, crushed, chap-fallen, chop-f., crestfallen, ready to cry 509 *disappointed*; browned off, cheesed off, pissed off, sick as a parrot 829 *discontented*; in the doldrums, in low water, out of luck 731 *unprosperous*; chastened, sobered, sadder and wiser 830 *regretting*; vexed, chagrined, mortified, cut up; subdued, piano; cynical, disillusioned 509 *disappointed*.

melancholic, atrabilious, vapourish, hypochondriacal; blue, feeling blue, down in the dumps; jaundiced, sour, hipped, hippish; thoughtful, pensive, penseroso, full of thought; melancholy, sad, triste; saddened, cut up, heavy, heavy-hearted, full of heaviness, sick at heart, heart-sick, soul-s. 825 *unhappy*; sorry, rueful 830 *regretting*; mournful, doleful, woeful, tearful, lachrymose 836 *lamenting*; uncheerful, cheerless, joyless, dreary, comfortless; forlorn, miserable, wretched, unrelieved, refusing comfort, disconsolate; sorry for oneself, self-pitying, wallowing in self-pity; moody, sulky, sulking 893 *sullen*; mopish, dull, dismal, gloomy, morose, glum, sunk in gloom; long-faced, long in the face, woebegone; wan, haggard, careworn.

serious, sober, sober as a judge, sobersided, solemn, sedate, stolid, staid, demure, muted, grave, stern, Puritanical 735 *severe*; sour, dour, Puritan, grim, grim-visaged, dark, frowning, scowling, forbidding, saturnine 893 *sullen*; unlaughing, unsmiling; inscrutable, straight-faced, po-f., poker-f., deadpan; prim, unlively, humourless; unfunny, unwitty, without a laugh in it, heavy, dull, solid 838 *tedious*; chastening, sobering.

cheerless, comfortless, uncomforting, unconsoling; uncongenial, uninviting; depressing, unrelieved, dreary, dull, flat 838 *tedious*; dismal, lugubrious, funereal, gloomy, dark, forbidding; drab, grey, sombre, sombrous, overcast, clouded, murky, louring; ungenial, cold.

Vb. *be dejected*, despond, lose heart, admit defeat 853 *despair*; succumb, lie down 728 *be defeated*; languish, sink, droop, sag, wilt, flag, give up 684 *be fatigued*; look downcast, look blue, hang the head, pull a long face, laugh on the wrong side of one's mouth; mope, brood 449 *think*; lay to heart, take to h., sulk 893 *be sullen*; eat one's heart out, yearn, long 859 *desire*; sigh, grieve 829 *be discontented*; groan

825 *suffer*; weep 836 *lament*; repine 830 *regret*.

be serious, not smile, repress a s.; not laugh, keep a straight face, keep one's countenance, maintain one's gravity, recover one's g., sober up; look grave, look glum; lack sparkle, lack humour, not see the joke, take oneself seriously, be a bore 838 *be tedious*; sober, chasten.

sadden, grieve, grieve to the heart, bring grief, bring sorrow; turn one's hair grey, break one's heart, pluck at one's heartstrings, make one's heart bleed; draw tears, touch the heart, melt the h., leave not a dry eye 821 *impress*; annoy, pain, spoil one's pleasure 829 *cause discontent*; deny comfort, render disconsolate, drive to despair 853 *leave no hope*; crush, overcome, overwhelm, prostrate; orphan, bereave 786 *deprive*.

depress, deject, get one down; cause alarm and despondency, dismay, dishearten, discourage, dispirit, take the heart out of, unman, unnerve 854 *frighten*; spoil the fun, take the joy out of, cast a shadow, cast a gloom over 418 *darken*; damp, dampen, damp the spirits, put a damper on, be a wet blanket, throw cold water, frown upon 613 *dissuade*; dash one's hopes 509 *disappoint*; dull the spirits, prey on the mind, weigh heavy on one's heart, oppress the breast; make the heart sick, disgust 827 *displease*; strain, weary 684 *fatigue*; bore 838 *be tedious*; chasten, sober 534 *teach*.

See:418, 419, 449, 509, 534, 613, 679, 684, 728, 731, 735, 786, 821, **825**, **827**, **829**, 830, **836**, 838, 853, 854, 859, 893.

835 Rejoicing

N. *rejoicing*, manifestation of joy 837 *festivity*; jubilation, jubilee, triumph, exultation 876 *celebration*; congratulations, felicitation, self-congratulation, mutual c. 886 *congratulation*; plaudits, clapping, shout, yell 923 *applause*; cheers, rousing c., three c., huzza, hurrah, hosanna, halleluja 923 *praise*; thanksgiving 907 *thanks*; paean, psalm, Te Deum 981 *hymn*; raptures, elation 824 *joy*; revelling, revels 837 *revel*; merrymaking, abandon, abandonment 833 *merriment*.

laughter, faculty of l., risibility; loud laughter, hearty l., rollicking l., Homeric l.; roar of laughter, shout of l., burst of l., peal of l., shrieks of l., gales of l., immoderate l., cachinnation; mocking laughter, derision 851 *ridicule*; laugh, belly l., horse l., guffaw, fou rire; chuckle, throaty c., chortle, gurgle, cackle, crow, coo; giggle, snigger, snicker, titter, tee-hee; fit of laughing, the giggles; smile, sweet s., simper, smirk, grin, broad g., sardonic g.; inclination to laughter, twinkle, half-smile; humour, sense of h. 839 *wit*; laughableness, laughing matter, comedy, farce 497 *absurdity*.

laugher, chuckler, grinner, smirker etc. vb.; Cheshire cat; mocker, derider 926 *detractor*; rejoicer, rollicker 837 *reveller*; god of ridicule, Momus; comic muse, Thalia.

Adj. *rejoicing*, revelling, rollicking, cheering, shouting, yelling etc. vb.; exultant, flushed, elated 833 *jubilant*; lyrical, ecstatic 923 *approving*.

laughing, guffawing etc. vb.; splitting one's sides, creased, doubled up, convulsed with laughter, dying with l., rolling in the aisles; humorous; mocking 851 *derisive*; laughable, risible, derisory 849 *ridiculous*; comic, comical, funny, farcical 497 *absurd*.

Vb. *rejoice*, be joyful, sing for joy, shout for j., leap for j., dance for j., dance, skip 312 *leap*; clap, clap one's hands, throw one's cap in the air, whoop, cheer, huzza, hurrah 923 *applaud*; shout, yell oneself hoarse 408 *vociferate*; carol 413 *sing*; sing paeans, shout hosannahs, sound the trumpet 923 *praise*; exult, crow, jubilate 876 *celebrate*; felicitate 886 *congratulate*; bless, give thanks, thank one's lucky stars 907 *thank*; abandon oneself, let oneself go, let one's hair down, paint the town red, riot, go mad for joy , dance in the streets, maffick 61 *rampage*; make merry 833 *be cheerful*; have a good time, frolic, frisk, rollick 837 *revel*; have a party, celebrate 882 *be sociable*; feel pleased, congratulate oneself, hug o., rub one's hands, smack one's lips, gloat 824 *be pleased*; purr, coo, gurgle; sigh for pleasure, cry for joy.

laugh, laugh outright, start laughing, burst out l., get the giggles, bubble with laughter; hoot, chuckle, chortle, crow, cackle; giggle, snigger, snicker, titter, tee-hee; make merry over, laugh at, laugh in one's sleeve *or* one's beard, mock, deride 851 *ridicule*; laugh loudly, cachinnate; shake, fall about, roll around, hold one's sides, split one's s., be in stitches, burst with laughter, split with l., rock with l., roll with l., shriek with l., hoot with l., roar with l., choke with l., die with l., kill oneself laughing, laugh fit to burst.

smile, break into a s., grin, show one's teeth; grimace, curl one's lip, grin like a Cheshire cat; smirk, simper; twinkle, beam, flash a smile.

Int. cheers! three c.! huzza! hurrah! hooray! hosannah! hallelujah! glory be! hail the conquering hero!

See: 61, 312, 408, 413, 497, **824**, **833**, 837, 839, 849, 851, **876**, 882, 886, 907, 923, 926, 981.

836 Lamentation

N. *lamentation*, lamenting, ululation, wail, wail of woe, groaning, weeping, wailing; plangency, weeping and wailing, weeping and gnashing of teeth, beating the breast, tearing one's hair; mourning, deep m. 364 *obsequies*; rending one's garments, sackcloth and ashes; widow's weeds, weepers, crepe, black; cypress, willow; Wailing Wall; crying, sobbing, sighing, blubbering, whimpering, whining, greeting, grizzling, snivelling etc. vb.; tears, tearfulness, dolefulness 834 *dejection*; tenderness, melting mood, starting tears, tears of pity 905 *pity*; wet eyes, red e., swollen e.; eyes swimming *or* brimming with tears; falling tears, fit of t., flood of t., burst of t.; breakdown, hysterics; cry, good c.; tear, teardrop; heaving breast, sob, sigh, groan, moan, whimper, whine, grizzle, bawl, boo-hoo.

lament, plaint, complaint, jeremiad, dirge, knell, requiem, threnody, elegy, epicedium, death song, swansong, funeral oration 364 *obsequies*; keen, coronach, wake 905 *condolence*; howl, shriek, scream, outcry 409 *ululation*; tears of grief, tears of rage; sobstuff, sob-story, hard-luck s., tale of woe; de profundis, cri de coeur; show of grief, crocodile tears 542 *sham*.

weeper, wailer, keener, lamenter, threnodist, elegist; mourner, professional m., mute 364 *funeral*; sobber, sigher, grizzler, sniveller, whimperer, whiner, blubberer, crybaby; complainer, grouser 829 *malcontent*; Jeremiah, Niobe; dying duck, dying swan.

Adj. *lamenting*, crying etc. vb.; lachrymatory, tear-shedding, tear-dropping; in tears, bathed in t., dissolved in t.; tearful, lachrymose; wet-eyed, red-e., with moist eyes; close to tears, on the verge of t., ready to cry; mourning, mournful, doleful, lugubrious 825 *unhappy*; woeful, woebegone, haggard, wild-eyed, wringing one's hands 834 *dejected*; complaining, plangent, plaintive, singing the blues; elegiac, epicedial, threnodic, threnodial, dirgelike 364 *funereal*; condoling, in mourning, in black, in funeral garments, in sackcloth and ashes; half-masted, at half-mast; whining, fretful, querulous, with a hard-luck story, with a tale of woe; pathetic, pitiful, lamentable, fit for tears, tear-jerking 905 *pitiable*; lamented, deplorable 830 *regretted*.

Vb. *lament*, grieve, sorrow, sigh, heave a s. 825 *suffer*; deplore 830 *regret*; condole, commiserate 905 *pity*; grieve for, sigh for, weep over, cry o., bewail, bemoan, elegize, threnodize; bury with lamentation, sing the dirge, sing a requiem, toll the knell 364 *inter*; mourn, wail, keen; express grief, put on black, go into mourning, wear m., wear the willow, put on sackcloth and ashes, wring one's hands, beat the breast, tear one's hair, roll in the dust; take on, carry on, take it badly; complain, beef, bellyache, grouse, tell one's tale of woe 829 *be discontented*.

weep, wail, greet, pipe one's eye; shed tears, drop t., burst into t., melt in t., dissolve in t.; hold back one's tears, be ready to cry; give way to tears, break down, cry, cry like a child, cry like a baby, boo-hoo, bawl, cry one's eyes out; howl, cry out, squall, yell, yammer, clamour, scream, shriek 409 *ululate*; sob, sigh, moan, groan 825 *suffer*; snivel, grizzle, blubber, pule, whine, whinge, whimper; get ready to cry, weep without cause, cry for nothing, cry out before one is hurt.

Adv. *tearfully*, painfully, de profundis.

See: 364, 409, 542, **825**, 829, 830, 834, 905.

837 Amusement

N. *amusement*, pleasure, interest, delight 826 *pleasurableness*; diversion, divertissement, entertainment, light e., popular e.; dramatic entertainment, happening 594 *drama*; radio, television 531 *broadcasting*; pastime, hobby, labour of love 597 *voluntary work*; solace, recreation 685 *refreshment*; relaxation 683 *repose*; holiday, Bank h. 681 *leisure*; April Fool's Day, gala day, red-letter d. 876 *special day*; play, sport, fun, good clean f., good cheer, jollity, joviality, jocundity 833 *merriment*; occasion, do, show, junket, Gaudy night 876 *celebration*; outing, excursion, jaunt, day out, pleasure trip; treat, Sunday school t., wayzgoose, fête champêtre, picnic (**see** *festivity*); conversazione, garden party, bunfight, fête, flower show, gymkhana, jamboree 74 *assembly*; game, game of chance, game of skill; whist drive, bridge party (**see** *card game*); round games, party g. (**see** *indoor game*).

festivity, playtime, holiday-making, holidaying; visiting 882 *social round*; fun 835 *laughter*; beer and skittles 824 *enjoyment*; social whirl, round of pleasure, round of gaiety; seeing life, high life, night l.; good time; living it up, burning the candle at both ends, a short life and a merry one 943 *intemperance*; festival, high f., fair, funfair, fun of the fair, kermess, carnival, fiesta, Jahrmarkt, mi-carême, gala; masque, mummery; festivities, fun and games, merrymaking, revels, Saturnalia, Mardi Gras 833 *merriment*; high day, feast d., May D., Derby D. 876 *special day*; carousal, wassail, wake 301 *feasting*; conviviality, house-warming, party, Dutch p., bottle p. 882 *social gathering*; drinking party, drinking bout, bender 301 *drinking*; orgy, carouse 949 *drunkenness*; bust, binge, beano, blowout; barbecue, ox-roasting, clambake, bump supper, harvest s., beanfeast, dinner, annual d., banquet 301 *meal*.

revel, rout, rave-up, knees-up, jollification, whoopee, fun, great f., high old time; fun fast and furious, high jinks, spree, junket, junketing, horseplay; night out, night on the tiles; bonfire, pyrotechnics, Fifth of November 420 *fireworks*; play, game, romp, rollick, frolic, lark, skylarking, escapade, antic, prank, rag, trick, monkey tricks 497 *foolery*.

pleasure ground, park, deer p., national p., chase, grouse moor; green, village g., common; arbour, gardens, pleasure g., winter g. 192 *pleasance*; seaside, Riviera, lido, bathing beach, holiday camp; playground, recreation ground, playing field, links, golf course; rink, skating r., ice r.; tennis court, bowling green, croquet lawn 724 *arena*; circus, fair, swing, swingboats, roundabout, merry-go-round, carousel, scenic railway, switchback, big wheel, big dipper, tunnel of love, ghost train; dodgems; seesaw, slide, helter-skelter.

place of amusement, fairground, funfair, shooting gallery, amusement arcade; skittle alley, bowling a., covered court, billiard room, pool r., assembly r., pump r.; concert hall, music h., vaudeville, hippodrome; picture palace 445 *cinema*; playhouse 594 *theatre*; ballroom, dance floor; dance hall, palais de danse, discotheque, disco; cabaret, night club, clip joint; bingo hall, casino, kursaal 618 *gaming-house*.

sport, outdoor life; sportsmanship, gamesmanship 694 *skill*; sports, field s., track events; games, gymnastics 162 *athletics*, 312 *leap*, 716 *contest*, *racing*, *pugilism*, *wrestling*; outdoor sports, cycling, hiking, rambling, orienteering, camping, picnicking; running, jogging; riding, pony-trekking; archery, shooting, clay-pigeon s.; hunting, shooting and fishing 619 *chase*; water sports, swimming, bathing, surf-riding, wind surfing; skin diving, subaqua, water skiing, aquaplaning, boating, rowing, yachting, sailing 269 *aquatics*; rock-climbing, mountaineering, Alpinism 308 *ascent*; exploring, caving, speleology 309 *descent*; winter sports, skiing, Langlauf, ski-jumping, bobsleighing, tobogganning, luging, skating, ice s., ice hockey; curling; flying, gliding, hang g. 271 *aeronautics*; tourism, touring, travelling, exploration 267 *land travel*.

ball game, pat-ball, bat and ball game; King Willow, cricket, French c.; baseball, softball, rounders; tennis, lawn t., real t., table t., pingpong; badminton, battledore and shuttlecock; squash, rackets; handball, volleyball; fives, pelota; netball, basketball; football, Association f., soccer; Rugby football, R. Union, R. League, rugger; lacrosse, hockey, ice h.; polo, water polo; croquet, putting, golf, clock g., crazy g.; skittles, ninepins, bowls, curling; marbles, dibs; quoits, deck q., hoop-la; billiards, snooker, pool; bagatelle, pinball, bar billiards, shove ha'penny, shovelboard.

indoor game, nursery g., parlour g., panel g., round g., party g.; musical bumps, musical chairs, hunt the thimble, hunt the slipper, postman's knock, kiss in the ring, oranges and lemons, nuts in May; sardines, rabbits, murders; forfeits, guessing game; quiz, twenty questions; charades, dumb c., crambo, dumb c., parson's cat, I-spy; word game, spelling bee, Scrabble (tdmk); riddles, crosswords, acrostics; paper game, consequences, noughts and crosses, battleships, boxes; darts, dominoes, mah-jong, tiddly-winks, jigsaw puzzle.

board game, chess, three-dimensional c.; draughts, checkers, Chinese c., halma, fox and hounds; backgammon; ludo, snakes and ladders, crown and anchor, Monopoly (tdmk), go.

children's games, skipping, swinging, jumping, ring-a-ring-o'-roses; leapfrog, hopscotch 312 *leap*; touch, tag, he, chain he, hide-and-seek, follow-my-leader, Simon says, blind man's buff, hares and hounds, cowboys and Indians, cops and robbers, prisoner's base, Tom Tiddler's ground.

card game, cards, game of cards, rubber of whist, rubber of bridge; boston, whist, solo w., auction w., auction bridge, contract b.; nap, napoleon; skat; euchre, écarté, loo, picquet, cribbage, quadrille, bezique, pinocle; rummy, gin r., canasta, hearts, black Maria, casino, Newmarket, speculation, spite and malice, chase the ace, cheat; solo, solitaire, patience; snap, beggar-my-neighbour, draw-the-well-dry, old maid, racing demon, slapjack, Happy Families, pelmanism; lotto, housey-housey, bingo; vingt-et-un, pontoon, black jack; brag, poker, strip p., stud p., seven-card stud p.; banker, baccarat, faro, fantan, chemin de fer, chemmy; monte, three-card m. See *gambling game*.

gambling game, dice g., craps, dice, dicing; roulette, rouge et noir; coin-spinning, heads and tails, raffle, tombola, sweepstake, football pool 618 *gambling*.

dancing, dance, ball, nautch; bal masqué, masquerade; bal costumé, fancy dress dance; thé dansant, tea dance, ceilidh, square dance, hoe-down; hop, jam session, disco; ballet dancing, classical d. 594 *ballet*; folk dancing, country d., Scottish c. d., old-time d., sequence d., ballroom dancing; choreography; eurhythmics; muse of dancing, Terpsichore.

dance, war dance, sword d., corroboree; shuffle, soft-shoe s., cakewalk; solo dance, pas seul; clog dance, step d., tap d., toe d.; fan dance, dance of the seven veils, hula-hula; high kicks, cancan; belly dance, danse du ventre; gipsy dance, flamenco; country dance, morris d., barn d., square d., contredanse, hay; sailor's dance, hornpipe, keel row; folk dance, Russian d., Cossack d., polonaise, mazurka, czardas; jig, Irish j., Walls of Limerick, Waves of Torres; fling, Highland f.; reel, Virginia r., Scotch r., eightsome, foursome, Strathspey, Gay Gordons, Petronella, Duke of Perth, strip the willow, Dashing White Sergeant, Sir Roger de Coverley; rigadoon, tarantella, bolero, fandango, farandole, galliard, écossaise, gavotte, quadrille, cotillion, minuet, pavane, saraband, allemande, galop, schottische, polka; valse, waltz, last w., Viennese w., hesitation w., St Bernard; valeta, lancers; foxtrot, turkey trot, quickstep; Charleston, black bottom, blues, one-step, two-s., Boston t-s., paso-doble, tango, rumba, samba, mambo, bossa nova, habanera, beguine, conga, conga line, cha-cha; Boomps-a-Daisy, hokey-cokey, Lambeth Walk, Palais Glide; stomp, bop, bebop, shimmy, jive, rock 'n' roll, twist; excuse-me dance, Paul Jones, snowball; dancer, tap d., clog d., ballet d., ballerina, corps de ballet 594 *actor*; high-kicker, cancan dancer, gogo d. 594 *entertainer*; waltzer, foxtrotter, shuffler, hoofer, jiver, jitterbug, bebopper, disco dancer 312 *jumper*.

plaything, bauble, knick-knack, souvenir, trinket, toy 639 *bauble*; children's toy, rattle, bricks, building b., meccano (tdmk); Jack-in-the-box, teddy bear, doll, china d., rag d., doll's house, doll's pram; top, whipping t., teetotum, yo-yo, diabolo; jacks, fivestones, marbles; ball, balloon 252 *sphere*; hoop, skipping rope, stilts, pogo stick, rocking horse, hobby h., tricycle; roller skates, skateboard, surfboard; popgun, airgun, water pistol; toy soldier, tin s., lead s.; model, model yacht, model aeroplane, clockwork train, model railway; magic lantern, peep show, toy theatre 522 *exhibit*; puppet show, marionettes, Punch and Judy 551 *image*; pintable, billiard table; card, cards, pack, stack, deck; domino, tile; draught, counter, chip; tiddly-wink; chess piece, pawn, knight, bishop, castle *or* rook, queen, king.

player, sportsman *or* -woman, sporting man *or* woman; competitor, pot-hunter 716 *contender*; games-player, all-rounder; ball-player, footballer, forward, striker, defence, goalkeeper; cricketer, batsman, fielder, wicket-keeper, bowler; hockey-player, tennis-p.; marksman, archer 287 *shooter*; shot-putter 287 *thrower*; dicer, gamester 618 *gambler*; card-player, chess-p., chess tiger, chess rabbit; fellow sportsman *or* -woman, playmate 707 *colleague*.

reveller, merry-maker, rioter, roisterer, gamboller, rollicker, frolicker; skylarker, ragger; drinker, drunk 949 *drunkard*; feaster, diner-out 301 *eater*; party-goer 882 *sociable person*; pleasure-seeker, thrill-s.; playboy, good-time girl; debauchee 952 *libertine*; holidaymaker, excursionist, day-tripper, tourist 268 *traveller*; Lord of Misrule, master of the revels, master of ceremonies, MC, toastmaster; symposiarch, arbiter elegantiarum.

Adj. *amusing*, entertaining, diverting etc. vb.; fun-making, sportive, full of fun 833 *merry*; setting out to please, pleasant 826 *pleasurable*; laughable, ridiculous, clownish 849 *funny*; recreative, recreational 685 *refreshing*; festal, festive, holiday.

amused, entertained, tickled 824 *pleased*; having fun, festive, sportive, rompish, rollicking, roisterous, prankish, playful, kittenish, roguish, waggish, jolly, jovial; out to enjoy oneself, in festal mood, in holiday spirit 835 *rejoicing*; horsy, sporty, sporting, gamesome, games-playing 162 *athletic*; disporting, playing, at play; working for pleasure, following one's hobby; entertainable, easy to please, ready to be amused.

Vb. *amuse*, interest, entertain, beguile, divert, tickle, make one laugh, take one out of oneself; tickle the fancy, titillate, please 826 *delight*; recreate 685 *refresh*; solace, enliven 833 *cheer*; treat, regale, take out, take for an outing; raise a smile, wake laughter, stir l., convulse with l., set the table in a roar, have them rolling in the aisles, wow, slay, be the death of 849 *be ridiculous*; humour, keep amused, put in a good humour; give a party, play the host *or* hostess 882 *be hospitable*; be a sport, be a good s., be great fun.

amuse oneself, kill time, while away the t., pass the t. 681 *have leisure*; pursue one's hobby, dabble in; play, play at, have fun, enjoy oneself, drown care 833 *be cheerful*; make holiday, take a h., go a-Maying, have an outing, have a field day, have a ball; sport, disport oneself; take one's pleasure, dally, toy, wanton; frisk, frolic, rollick, romp, gambol, caper; cut capers, play tricks, play pranks, lark around, skylark, fool about, play the fool 497 *be absurd*; jest, jape 839 *be witty*; play cards, take a hand; game, dice 618 *gamble*; play games, be devoted to sport; live the outdoor life, camp, picnic; sail, yacht, fly; hunt, shoot, fish; play golf; ride, trek, hike, ramble; run, race, jump; bathe, swim, dive; skate, ski, toboggan.

dance, join the dance, go dancing; tap-dance, waltz, foxtrot, Charleston, tango, rumba, jive, jitterbug, stomp, bop, twist, rock 'n' roll; whirl 315 *rotate*; cavort, caper, jig about, bob up and down; shuffle, hoof, trip, tread a measure, trip the light fantastic toe 312 *leap*.

revel, make merry, make whoopee, celebrate 835 *rejoice*; drive dull care away, make it a party, have a good time; let oneself go, let one's hair down, let off steam; go on the razzle, go on a bender, have a night out, have a night on the tiles, live it up, paint the town red; junket, roister, drown care; feast, banquet, quaff, carouse, wassail, make the rafters ring; go on a binge, go pub-crawling 301 *drink*; drown one's sorrows 949 *get drunk*; sow one's wild oats, burn the candle at both ends; stay up till all hours, never go home till morning.

Int. carpe diem! eat, drink and be merry! on with the dance! vogue la galère! gaudeamus igitur!

See: 74, 162, 192, 252, 267, 268, 269, 271, 287, 301, 308, 309, 312, 315, 420, 445, 497, 522, 531, 551, 594, 597, 618, 619, 639, **681**, 683, 685, 694, 707, 716, 724, **824**, **826**, **833**, 835, **839**, 849, 876, 882, 943, 949, 952.

838 Tedium

N. *tedium*, ennui, taedium vitae, world-weariness, Weltschmerz 834 *melancholy*; lack of interest, uninterest 860 *indifference*; weariness, languor 684 *fatigue*; wearisomeness, tediousness, irksomeness; dryness, stodginess, heaviness; too much of a good thing 863 *satiety*; disgust, loathing, nausea 861 *dislike*; flatness, staleness 387 *insipidity*; stuffiness 840 *dullness*; longueurs, prolixity 570 *diffuseness*; sameness 16 *uniformity*; monotony, dull m. 106 *repetition*; leaden hours, time to kill 679 *inactivity*; thumb-twiddling, devil's tattoo.

bore, utter b., no fun; boring thing, twice-told tale, déjà vu; irk, drag, bind, chore; dull work, boring w.; beaten track, daily round 610 *habit*; grindstone, treadmill 682 *labour*; boring person, bromide, pain in the neck, dryasdust, proser, buttonholer, pub bore; drip, wet blanket, killjoy, misery 834 *moper*; frump, Mrs Grundy; too much of a good thing.

Adj. *tedious*, uninteresting, devoid of interest, strictly for the birds; unenjoyable, unexciting, uneventful, unentertaining, unamusing, unfunny; slow, dragging, leaden, heavy; dry, dryasdust, arid; flat, stale, insipid 387 *tasteless*; bald 573 *plain*; humdrum, soulless, mundane, suburban, depressing, dreary, stuffy, bourgeois 840 *dull*; stodgy, prosaic, uninspired, unreadable, unread; prosy, long, overlong, long-winded, drawn out 570 *prolix*; drowsy, somnific 679 *soporific*; boring, binding, wearisome, tiresome, irksome; wearing, chronic, mortal 684 *fatiguing*; repetitive, repetitious 106 *repeated*; same, unvarying, invariable, monotonous 16 *uniform*; too much, cloying, satiating; disgusting, nauseating, nauseous.

bored, unentertained, unamused, unexcited; afflicted with boredom, twiddling one's thumbs 679 *inactive*; fed up to the back teeth, browned off, cheesed off, had it up to here 829 *discontented*; stale, weary, jaded 684 *fatigued*; blue, world-weary, weary of life 834 *melancholic*; blasé, uninterested 860 *indifferent*; satiated, cloyed 863 *sated*; nauseated, sick of, sick and tired, fed up, loathing 861 *disliking*.

Vb. *be tedious*, pall, lose its novelty, cloy, glut, jade, satiate 863 *sate*; nauseate, sicken, disgust 861 *cause dislike*; bore, irk, try, weary 684 *fatigue*; bore to death, bore to tears, bore the pants off, bore stiff; weary to distraction, tire out, wear o.; get one down, try one's patience, outstay one's welcome, stay too long; fail to interest, make one yawn, send one to sleep; drag 278 *move slowly*; go on and on, never end; harp on, prove monotonous 106 *repeat oneself*; buttonhole, be prolix 570 *be diffuse*.

Adv. *boringly*, ad nauseam, to death.

See: 16, 106, 278, 387, 570, 573, 610, 679, 682, **684**, 829, **834**, **840**, 860, 861, 863.

839 Wit

N. *wit*, wittiness, pointedness, point, smartness, epigrammatism; esprit, ready wit, verbal readiness; esprit de l'escalier 67 *sequel*; saltiness, salt, Attic s. 575 *elegance*; sparkle, scintillation, brightness 498 *intelligence*; humour, sense of h., pleasant h.; wry humour, pawkiness, dryness, slyness; drollery, pleasantry, waggishness, waggery, facetiousness; jocularity, jocosity, jocoseness 833 *merriment*; comicalness, absurdity 849 *ridiculousness*; lack of seriousness, trifling, flippancy 456 *inattention*; fun, joking, practical j., jesting, tomfoolery, buffoonery, clowning, funny business 497 *foolery*; comic turn, laugh a minute; broad humour, low h., vulgarity 847 *bad taste*; farce, broad f., knockabout comedy, slapstick, custard-pie humour, ham, high camp 594 *dramaturgy*; whimsicality, fancy 604 *whim*; cartoon, comic strip, caricature; biting wit, cruel humour, satire, sarcasm 851 *ridicule*; irony 850 *affectation*; black comedy, gallows humour; word-fencing 477 *sophistry*; wordplay, play on words, punning, equivocation 518 *equivocalness*.

witticism, witty remark, piece of humour, stroke of wit, jeu d'esprit, sally, mot, bon mot, aperçu; spoonerism; epigram, conceit; pun, play on words, equivoque, calembour 518 *equivocalness*; point of the joke, cream of the jest; feed line, punch l., throwaway l.; banter, chaff, badinage, persiflage; retort, repartee, quid pro quo, backchat, backtalk 460 *answer*; sarcasm 851 *satire*; joke, standing j., private j., family j., in-joke; jest, dry j., good one, rib-tickler, side-splitter; quip, jape, quirk, crank, quips and cranks, gag, crack, wisecrack, one-liner; old joke, corny j., stale jest, chestnut, Joe Miller, bromide; practical joke, hoax, legpull; broad jest, dirty joke, blue j., sick j.; story, funny s., shaggy-dog s.; limerick, clerihew.

humorist, wit, bel esprit, epigrammatist, reparteeist; conversationalist; card, character, life and soul of the party, wag, wisecracker, japer, joker, Joe Miller, Sam Weller; jokesmith, funny man, gagman, gagster, punster; banterer, persifleur, leg-puller, ragger, teaser; practical joker 545 *deceiver*; ironist 850 *affecter*; mocker, scoffer, satirist, lampooner 926 *detractor*; comedian, comedienne, comic, standup c., knockabout c. 594 *entertainer*; comic writer, cartoonist, caricaturist; burlesquer, parodist 20 *imitator*; raconteur, raconteuse; jester, court j., wearer of the cap and bells, motley fool, clown, farceur, buffoon, stooge 501 *fool.*

Adj. *witty,* spirituel(le), nimble-witted, quick; Attic 575 *elegant*; pointed, ben trovato, epigrammatic; brilliant, sparkling, smart, clever, too clever by half 498 *intelligent*; salty, racy, piquant; fruity, risqué; snappy, biting, pungent, keen, sharp, sarcastic; ironic, dry, sly, pawky; unserious, facetious, flippant 456 *light-minded*; jocular, jocose, joking, joshing, jokey, waggish, roguish; lively, pleasant, gay, merry and wise 833 *merry*; comic, funny ha-ha, rib-tickling 849 *funny*; comical, humorous, droll; whimsical 604 *capricious*; playful, sportive, fooling 497 *absurd.*

Vb. *be witty,* scintillate, sparkle, flash; jest, joke, crack a j., quip, gag, wisecrack; tell a good story, raise a laugh, set the table in a roar 837 *amuse*; pun, make a p., play on words, equivocate 518 *be equivocal*; fool, jape 497 *be absurd*; play with, tease, chaff, rag, banter, twit, pull one's leg, have one on, make merry with, make fun of, poke fun at, exercise one's wit upon 851 *ridicule*; ham up, camp up; mock, caricature, burlesque 851 *satirize*; retort, flash back, come back at 460 *answer*; have a sense of humour, enjoy a joke, see the point.

Adv. *in jest,* in joke, in fun, in sport, in play; with tongue in cheek.

See: 20, 67, 456, 460, 477, 497, 498, 501, 518, 545, 575, 594, 604, **833**, 837, 847, **849**, 850, **851**, 926.

840 Dullness

N. *dullness,* heaviness 834 *dejection*; stuffiness, dreariness, deadliness; monotony, boringness 838 *tedium*; colourlessness, drabness; lack of sparkle, lack of inspiration, want of originality; stodginess, unreadability, prosiness; staleness, flatness 387 *insipidity*; banality, triteness, superficiality; lack of humour, no sense of h., inability to see a joke, primness, impenetrable gravity, grimness 834 *seriousness*; prosaicness, prose, matter of fact 573 *plainness.*

Adj. *dull,* unamusing, uninteresting, unentertaining, unstimulating, uninspiring; unfunny, uncomical, straight; uncharming, uncaptivating; deadly dull, dull as ditchwater; stuffy, dreary, deadly; pointless, meaningless 838 *tedious*; unvivid, unlively, colourless, drab; flat, bland, vapid, insipid 387 *tasteless*; unimaginative, uninventive, unoriginal, derivative, superficial; stupid 499 *unintelligent*; without laughter, humourless, grave, prim, po-faced, frumpish 834 *serious*; unwitty, unsparkling, unscintillating; graceless, lacking wit 576 *inelegant*; heavy, heavy-footed, clod-hopping, ponderous, sluggish 278 *slow*; stodgy, prosaic, matter-of-fact, pedestrian, unreadable; stale, banal, commonplace, trite, platitudinous 610 *usual.*

Vb. *be dull,* drone on, bore 838 *be tedious*; platitudinize, prose; have no sense of humour, never see a joke, not see the point, miss the cream of the jest.

See: 278, 387, 499, 573, 576, 610, 834, **838**.

841 Beauty

N. *beauty,* pulchritude, the beautiful; ripe perfection, highest p. 646 *perfection*; the sublime, sublimity, grandeur, magnificence, nobility; splendour, gorgeousness, brilliance, brightness, radiance 417 *light*; transfiguration 843 *beautification*; polish, gloss, ornament 844 *ornamentation*; scenic beauty, scenery, view, landscape, seascape, snowscape, cloudscape 445 *spectacle*; form, fair proportions, regular features, classic f. 245 *symmetry*; physical beauty, loveliness, comeliness, fairness, handsomeness, bonniness, prettiness; attraction, attractiveness, agreeableness, charm 826 *pleasurableness*; appeal, glamour, sex appeal, cuteness, kissability; attractions, charms, graces, perfections; good looks, handsome features, pretty face, beaux yeux; eyes of blue, cherry lips, ruby l., pearly teeth, schoolgirl complexion, peaches and cream c.; shapeliness, trim figure, curves, curvaceousness, vital statistics; gracefulness, grace 575 *elegance*; chic, style, dress sense 848 *fashion*; delicacy, refinement 846 *good taste*; appreciation of beauty, aesthetics, aestheticism.

a beauty, thing of beauty, work of art; garden, beauty spot; masterpiece 644 *exceller*; bijou, jewel, pearl, treasure 646 *paragon*; peacock, swan, flower, rosebud, rose, lily; fair one, lady bright; belle, raving beauty, reigning b., toast, idol 890 *favourite*; beau idéal, dream girl; beauty queen, Miss World, bathing belle, pin-up girl, cover girl; pin-up, beefcake, cheesecake; hunk, muscleman, Mr Universe;

fine figure of a man *or* woman; blond(e), brunette, redhead; English rose; dream, vision, poem, picture, perfect p., sight for sore eyes; angel, charmer, dazzler; stunner, knockout, eyeful, good-looker; doll, dolly bird, cookie; glamour puss, glamour girl *or* boy; heartthrob, dreamboat; enchantress, femme fatale, vamp, seductress, siren, witch 983 *sorceress*; smasher, scorcher, lovely, cutie, honey, beaut, peach, dish; sylph, fairy, peri, houri; Grace, the Graces, Venus, Aphrodite, Helen of Troy; Apollo, Hyperion, Endymion, Adonis, Narcissus.

Adj. *beautiful*, pulchritudinous, beauteous, of beauty; lovely, fair, bright, radiant; comely, goodly, bonny, pretty; sweet, sweetly pretty, picture-postcard, pretty-pretty, nice, good enough to eat; pretty as a picture, photogenic; handsome, good-looking, well-favoured; well-built, well-set-up, husky, manly; tall, dark and handsome; gracious, stately, majestic, statuesque, Junoesque; adorable, godlike, goddess-like, divine, 'divinely tall and most divinely fair'; pleasing to the eye, lovely to behold; picturesque, scenic, ornamental; landscaped, well laid-out; artistic, harmonious, well-grouped, well-composed, cunning, curious, quaint 694 *well-made*; aesthetic 846 *tasteful*; exquisite, choice 605 *chosen*; unspotted, unblemished 646 *perfect*.

splendid, sublime, heavenly, superb, fine 644 *excellent*; grand 868 *noble*; glorious, ravishing, rich, gorgeous, highly-coloured 425 *florid*; bright, resplendent, dazzling, beaming, radiant, sparkling, glowing 417 *radiating*; glossy, magnificent, specious 875 *showy*; ornate 844 *ornamented*.

shapely, well-proportioned, regular, classic 245 *symmetrical*; formed, well-f., well-turned; rounded, well-r., well-stacked, buxom, bosomy, curvaceous 248 *curved*; slinky, callipygous; clean-limbed, straight-l., straight, slender, slim, lissom, svelte, willowy 206 *lean*; lightsome, graceful, elegant, chic; petite, dainty, delicate; undeformed, undefaced, unwarped, untwisted 646 *perfect*.

personable, prepossessing, agreeable; comfortable, buxom, sonsy; attractive, dishy, taking, fetching, appealing 826 *pleasurable*; sexy, cute, kissable; charming, entrancing, enchanting, glamorous; lovesome, winsome 887 *lovable*; fresh-faced, clean-cut, wholesome, lusty, blooming, in bloom, ruddy 431 *red*; rosy, rosy-cheeked, apple-c., cherry-lipped, fresh-complexioned, bright-eyed; sightly, becoming, fit to be seen, easy on the eye, passable, not amiss; presentable, proper, decent, neat, natty, tidy, trim; spruce, snappy, dapper, glossy, sleek; well-dressed, well turned out, smart, stylish, classy, soigné(e) 848 *fashionable*; elegant, dainty, delicate, refined 846 *tasteful*.

Vb. *be beautiful*, - splendid etc. adj.; be entrancing 983 *bewitch*; take one's breath away, beggar all description; be photogenic, photograph well; have good looks, have bright eyes; bloom, glow, dazzle 417 *shine*; be dressed to kill; do one credit, win a beauty contest.

beautify, trim, neaten, improve; brighten 417 *make bright*; prettify, bejewel, tattoo 844 *decorate*; set (a jewel); set off, grace, suit, fit, become, go well, show one off, flatter; bring out the highlights, enhance one's looks, glamorize, transfigure; give a face-lift, smarten up; prink, prank, titivate, powder, rouge 843 *primp*.

See: 206, 245, 248, 417, 425, 431, 445, 575, 605, **644**, **646**, 694, 826, 843, **844**, 846, 848, 868, 875, 887, 890, 983.

842 Ugliness

N. *ugliness*, unsightliness, hideousness, repulsiveness; lack of beauty, gracelessness, lumpishness, clumsiness 576 *inelegance*; want of symmetry, asymmetry 246 *distortion*; unshapeliness, lack of form 246 *deformity*; mutilation, disfigurement 845 *blemish*; uglification, disfiguration, defacement; squalor, filth, grottiness 649 *uncleanness*; homeliness, plainness, plain features, ugly face; not much to look at, no beauty, no oil painting, a face to stop a clock; wry face, snarl, forbidding countenance, vinegarish expression, grim look, sour l. 893 *sullenness*; haggardness, haggard look; fading beauty, dim eyes, wrinkles, crowsfeet, hand of time 131 *age*.

eyesore, hideosity, blot, botch, patch 845 *blemish*; aesthetic crime, offence to the eyes; blot on the landscape, architectural monstrosity, satanic mills; ugly person, fright, sight, frump, not one's type; scarecrow, horror, death's-head, gargoyle, grotesque; monster, abortion; harridan, witch; toad, gorilla, baboon, crow; plain

Jane, ugly duckling; satyr, Caliban; gorgon, Medusa; Beast.

Adj. *ugly*, lacking beauty, unbeautiful, unlovely, uncomely, unhandsome; coarse-looking, blowzy, frowzy; ugly as sin, hideous, foul 649 *unclean*; frightful, shocking, monstrous; repulsive, repellent, odious, loathsome 861 *disliked*; beastly, nasty 645 *not nice*; not much to look at, unprepossessing, unpretty, homely, plain, plain-featured, with no looks, without any looks; mousy, frumpish, frumpy; forbidding, ill-favoured, hard-featured, villainous, grim-visaged, grim, saturnine 893 *sullen*.

unsightly, faded, withered, worn, ravaged, wrinkled 131 *ageing*; not worth looking at, not fit to be seen, unseemly; imperfect, marred 845 *blemished*; unshapely, shapeless, formless, irregular, asymmetrical 244 *amorphous*; grotesque, twisted, deformed, disfigured 246 *distorted*; defaced, vandalized, litter-strewn; badly made, ill-proportioned, disproportionate, misshapen; dumpy, squat 196 *dwarfish*; bloated 195 *fleshy*; stained, discoloured, washed out 426 *colourless*; ghastly, wan, grisly, gruesome; tousled, in disarray 61 *orderless*.

graceless, ungraced, ungraceful 576 *inelegant*; inartistic, unaesthetic; unflattering, unbecoming, unattractive; squalid, dingy, poky, dreary, drab; lank, dull, mousy; dowdy, badly dressed, lacking clothes-sense; garish, gaudy, gross, indelicate, coarse 847 *vulgar*; rude, crude, rough, rugged, uncouth 699 *artless*; clumsy, awkward, ungainly, cumbersome, hulky, hulking, slouching, clod-hopping 195 *unwieldy*.

Vb. *be ugly*, lack beauty, have no looks, lose one's l.; fade, wither, age, show one's a. 131 *grow old*; look ill, look a wreck, look a mess, look a fright.

make ugly, uglify; fade, discolour 426 *decolorize*; wither 655 *deteriorate*; soil, sully 649 *make unclean*; spoil, deface, disfigure, mar, blemish, blot; misshape 244 *deform*; pull a face, grimace 893 *be sullen*; torture, twist 246 *distort*; mutilate, vandalize 655 *impair*.

See: 61, 131, 195, 196, 244, 246, 426, 576, **645**, 649, 655, 699, **845**, 847, 861, 893.

843 Beautification

N. *beautification*, beautifying 844 *ornamentation*; transfiguration 143 *transformation*; scenic improvement, landscape gardening 844 *ornamental art*; plastic surgery, cosmetic s., nose-straightening, nose job, skin-grafting, face-lift 658 *surgery*; beauty treatment, skin t., face-lifting, mole-removing, eyebrow-plucking, eyebrow-pencilling; face mask, face pack, mud p., oatmeal p., facial; massage, face m., skin m.; manicure, nail-polishing, buffing; pedicure, chiropody; tattooing 844 *ornamental art*; ear-piercing, nose-p.; sun-tanning, browning; sun lamp, ultraviolet rays; toilet, grooming, make-up, art of m., cosmetology; creaming, rouging, painting, dyeing, powdering, patching; scenting, soaping, shampooing; wash and brush up 648 *ablutions*.

hairdressing, trichology, hair-treatment, scalp massage; barbering, shaving, clipping, trimming, thinning, singeing; depilation, plucking; cutting, haircut, bobbing, shingling; shave, hair cut, wet c., razor c., clip, trim, singe, short back and sides; hair style, coiffure, crop, Eton c., bob, shingle, pageboy, crewcut, cut en brosse, urchin cut, baby doll c., bouffant c.; styling, hair-s., curling, frizzing, waving, setting, hair-straightening, defrizzing; hairdo, restyle, shampoo and set, set, wave, blow w., marcel w., cold w.; permanent w., perm; curl 251 *coil*; bang, fringe, ponytail, chignon, bun; pompadour, beehive, Afro 259 *hair*; false hair, hairpiece, toupee, switch 228 *wig*; curling iron, tongs, curl papers, curlers, rollers; bandeau, Alice band; comb, hairpin, hairgrip, slide; hairnet, snood 228 *headgear*.

hairwash, shampoo, rinse, tinting, colour tone, highlights, lightening, bleach, dye, henna, peroxide; hair spray, lacquer, hair-cream, grease, brilliantine; hair-restorer.

cosmetic, beautifier, glamourizer, aid to beauty, patch, beauty spot; make-up, liquid m., stick m.; paint, greasepaint, warpaint, rouge, pomade, cream, face c., cold c., cleansing c., vanishing c., foundation c., night c., hormone c., lanolin 357 *unguent*; lipstick, lip gloss; nail polish, nail varnish, powder, face p., talcum p.; kohl, mascara, eye shadow, eyeliner; hand lotion, astringent l., aftershave l., suntan l.; scented soap, bath salts, bath oil, bath essence, bubble bath, foam b. 648 *cleanser*; antiperspirant, deodorant; scent, perfume, essence, cologne, eau de c., lavender water, toilet w., cologne stick; eyebrow pencil, false eyelashes; powder puff, compact; vanity case, manicure set, nail file, nail scissors, clippers; shaver, razor, depilatory; toiletry, toiletries.

beauty parlour, beauty salon, parfumerie; boudoir, dressing room, powder r.; health farm.

beautician, beauty specialist; face-lifter, plastic surgeon; make-up artist, tattooer; cosmetician; barber, hairdresser, hair stylist, coiffeur, coiffeuse; trichologist; manicurist, pedicurist, chiropodist.

Adj. *beautified*, transfigured, transformed; prettified, glamorized, bedizened; made-up, rouged, farded, raddled, painted, powdered, scented; curled, bouffant; primped, dressed up, dolled up, tarted up, done up like a dog's dinner, done up to the nines 841 *beautiful*.

Vb. *primp*, prettify, doll up, dress up, bedizen, bejewel; ornament 844 *decorate*; prink, prank, trick out; preen; titivate, make up, put on make-up, apply cosmetics, rouge, paint, shadow, highlight; powder; wear scent; shave, pluck one's eyebrows, varnish one's nails, dye one's hair; curl, wave; have a hairdo, have a facial, have a manicure 841 *beautify*.

See: 143, 228, 251, **259**, 357, 648, 658, **841**, **844**.

844 Ornamentation

N. *ornamentation*, decoration, adornment, garnish; ornate style, ornateness 574 *ornament*; art deco, art nouveau, baroque, rococo; chinoiserie; richness, gilt, gaudiness 875 *ostentation*; enhancement, enrichment, embellishment; setting, background; table decoration, centrepiece, epergne, silver, china, glass; floral decoration, flower arrangement, wreath, garland, bouquet, nosegay, posy, buttonhole; objet d'art, bric-a-brac, curio, bibelot.

ornamental art, gardening, landscape g., topiarism; architecture, landscape a., building; interior decoration, furnishing, draping, painting, decorating; statuary 554 *sculpture*; frieze, dado, cartouche, metope, triglyph; capital, acanthus; pilaster, caryatid, figurehead; boss, cornice, corbel, gargoyle; astragal, moulding, beading, fluting, reeding, chamfering, strapwork, linenfold; fretting, tracery; varnishing 226 *facing*; pargeting, veneering, panelling, graining; ormolu, gilding, gilt, gold leaf; lettering, illumination, illustration, illustrating 551 *art*; stained glass; tie-dyeing, batik; heraldic art 547 *heraldry*; tattooing; etching 555 *engraving*; work, handiwork, handicraft, fancywork, woodwork, fretwork, frostwork; pokerwork, pyrography; open-work, filigree; whittling, carving, scrimshaw; embossing, chasing, intaglio 254 *relievo*; inlay, inset, enamelling, cloisonné,champlevé, mosaic, marquetry 437 *variegation*; metalwork, toreutics; gem-cutting, setting; cut glass, engraved g.; wrought iron.

pattern, motif, print, design, composition 331 *structure*; detail, elaborate d.; geometrical style, Decorated s., rose window, spandrel, cyma, ogee, fleuron, cusp, trefoil, fleur-de-lis; crocket, finial, tracery, scrollwork, fiddlehead, poppyhead, arabesque, flourish, curlicue 251 *coil*; swag, festoon; weave, diaper 331 *texture*; argyle, Arran, paisley 222 *textile*; chevron, key pattern; check 437 *chequer*; pin-stripe 437 *stripe*; spot, dot, polka d. 437 *maculation*; herringbone, zigzag, dogtooth, hound's tooth 220 *obliquity*; watermark 547 *identification*.

needlework, stitchery, tapestry, arras; cross-stitch, sampler; patchwork, appliqué; open work, drawn-thread w.; embroidery, smocking; crochet, lace, broderie anglaise; tatting, knitting 222 *network*; stitch, purl, plain, stocking stitch, garter s., moss s.; gros point, petit p., needle p.; chain stitch, cable s., hem s., stem s., blanket s., feather s., back s., satin s., herringbone s., French knot, lazy-daisy.

trimming, passementerie, piping, valance, border, fringe, frieze, frill, flounce, galloon, gimp 234 *edging*; binding 589 *bookbinding*; trappings; braid, frog, lapel, epaulette, star, rosette, cockade 547 *badge*; bow 47 *fastening*; bobble, pompom; tassel, dangler, bead, bugle; ermine, fur 259 *hair*; feather, ostrich f., osprey, aigrette, plume, panache 259 *plumage*; streamer, ribbon.

finery, togs, glad rags, Sunday best 228 *clothing*; fal-de-lal, frippery, frills and furbelows, ribbons, chiffon, froufrou; gaudery, gaud, trinket, knick-knack, gewgaw, fandangle; tinsel, spangle, sequin, clinquant, diamante, costume jewellery, glass, paste, marcasite, rhinestone 639 *bauble*.

jewellery, bijouterie; crown jewels, diadem, tiara 743 *regalia*; drop, pendant, locket 217 *hanging object*; crucifix; amulet, charm 983 *talisman*; rope, string, necklet, necklace, choker, chain, watch c., albert 250 *loop*; torque, armlet, anklet, bracelet, wristlet, bangle; ring, earring, signet ring, wedding r., eternity r., engagement r., mourning r., dress r. 250 *circle*; cameo, brooch, clasp, fibula, badge, crest; stud, pin, gold p., tie p., collar stud, cufflinks 47 *fastening*; medal, medallion.

gem, jewel, bijou; stone, precious s., semiprecious s.; uncut gem, cut g., cabochon; brilliant, sparkler, diamond, rock, ice; solitaire; carbuncle, ruby, pearl, cultured p., seed p., pink p.; opal, black o., fire o., girasol; sapphire, turquoise, emerald, beryl, aquamarine, chrysoberyl, chrysoprase, alexandrite; garnet, amethyst, topaz, chalcedony, cornelian, sard, jasper, tiger's-eye, agate, onyx, sardonyx; heliotrope, bloodstone, moonstone, cat's-eye, zircon, jacinth, hyacinth, tourmaline, apatite, chrysolite, olivine, peridot; coral, ivory, mother of pearl, jet, amber, jade, lapis lazuli.

Adj. *ornamental*, decorative, nonfunctional, fancy, arty-crafty; intricate, elaborate, quaint, daedal; picturesque, pretty-pretty; scenic, landscape, topiary; geometric; Doric, Ionic, Corinthian, Moresque, Romanesque, Decorated; baroque, rococo.

ornamented, richly o., luxuriant; adorned, decorated, embellished, polished 574 *ornate*; picked out 437 *variegated*; patterned, inwrought, mosaic, inlaid, enamelled, chryselephantine; worked, embroidered, trimmed; wreathed, festooned, garlanded, crowned; overdone, overdecorated, overloaded 847 *vulgar*; overcoloured 425 *florid*; luscious, plush, gilt, begilt, gilded 800 *rich*; gorgeous, garish, glittering, flashy, gaudy, meretricious 875 *showy*.

bedecked, groomed, got up, togged up, wearing, sporting; decked, decked out, bedizened; looking one's best, in one's Sunday best, in full fig, en grande toilette 228 *dressed*; tricked out, dolled up, tarted up, dressed to kill 843 *beautified*; bejewelled, beribboned, festooned, studded, bemedalled.

Vb. *decorate*, adorn, embellish, enhance, enrich; grace, set, set off 574 *ornament*; paint, bejewel; tart up, glamorize, prettify 841 *beautify*; garnish, trim, shape; array, deck, bedeck 228 *dress*; deck out, trick o., prank, preen, titivate 843 *primp*; freshen, smarten, spruce up, furbish, burnish 648 *clean*; bemedal, beribbon, garland, crown 866 *honour*; stud, spangle, bespangle 437 *variegate*; colourwash, whitewash, varnish, grain, japan, lacquer 226 *coat*; enamel, gild, silver; blazon, emblazon, illuminate, illustrate 553 *paint*, 425 *colour*; border, trim 234 *hem*; work, pick out, broider, embroider, tapestry; pattern, inlay, engrave; enchase, encrust, emboss, bead, mould; fret, carve, foliate 262 *groove*, 260 *notch*; enlace, wreathe, festoon, trace, scroll 251 *twine*.

See: 47, 217, 220, 222, 226, 228, 234, 250, 251, 254, 259, 260, 262, 331, 425, 437, 547, 551, 553, 554, 555, **574**, 589, 639, 648, 743, 800, **841**, 843, 847, 866, 875, 983.

845 Blemish

N. *blemish*, no ornament; scar, cicatrice, weal, welt, mark, pockmark; injury, flaw, crack, defect 647 *imperfection*; disfigurement, deformity 246 *distortion*; stigma, blot, blot on the landscape 842 *eyesore*; scribbling, graffiti; blur, blotch, splotch, smudge 550 *obliteration*; smut, patch, smear, stain, tarnish, rust, patina 649 *dirt*; spot, speck, speckle, macula, spottiness 437 *maculation*; freckle, mole, birthmark, strawberry mark; excrescence, pimpliness, pimple, blackhead, carbuncle, wen, wart 253 *swelling*; blotchiness, acne, eczema 651 *skin disease*; harelip, cleft palate; cast, squint; cut, scratch, scald, bruise, black eye, shiner, cauliflower ear, broken nose 655 *wound*.

Adj. *blemished*, defective, flawed, cracked, damaged 647 *imperfect*; tarnished, stained, soiled, flyblown, fleabitten 649 *dirty*; shop-soiled, spoilt 655 *deteriorated*; marked, scarred, marred; foxed, spotted, pitted, pockmarked, maculate; spotty, freckled; squinting, bug-eyed 440 *dim-sighted*; club-footed, pigeon-toed, hammer-t.; knock-kneed, bandy, bandy-legged; hunch-backed, crooked 246 *deformed*.

Vb. *blemish*, flaw, crack, injure, damage

655 *impair*; blot, smudge, stain, smear, sully, soil 649 *make unclean*; stigmatize, brand 547 *mark*; scar, pit, pockmark; mar, spoil, spoil the look of 842 *make ugly*; deface, disfigure, scribble on 244 *deform*.

See: 244, **246**, 253, 437, 440, 547, 550, **647**, 649, 651, **655**, 842.

846 Good Taste

N. *good taste*, tastefulness, taste, refined t., cultivated t.; restraint, simplicity 573 *plainness*; best of taste, choiceness, excellence 644 *goodness*; refinement, delicacy, euphemism 950 *purity*; fine feeling, nice appreciation, discernment, palate 463 *discrimination*; daintiness, finickiness, kid gloves 862 *fastidiousness*; decency, seemliness 848 *etiquette*; tact, consideration, natural courtesy, dignity, manners, polished m., breeding, civility, urbanity, social graces 884 *courtesy*; correctness, propriety, decorum; grace, polish, finish, sophistication, gracious living 575 *elegance*; cultivation, culture, virtu, connoisseurship, amateurship, dilettantism; epicureanism, epicurism; aestheticism, aesthetics, criticism, art c. 480 *judgment*; artistry, virtuosity, flair 694 *skill*.

people of taste, bon ton 848 *beau monde*; sophisticate, connoisseur, cognoscente, amateur, dilettante; epicurean, epicure, gourmet, aesthete, critic, art c. 480 *estimator*; arbiter of taste, arbiter elegantiarum, Beau Nash 848 *fop*; purist, precisian 602 *obstinate person*; euphemist 950 *prude*.

Adj. *tasteful*, gracious, dignified; in good taste, in the best of t.; choice, exquisite 644 *excellent*; simple, unmeretricious 573 *plain*; graceful, Attic, classical 575 *elegant*; chaste, refined, delicate, euphemistic 950 *pure*; aesthetic, artistic 819 *sensitive*; discerning, epicurean 463 *discriminating*; nice, dainty, choosy, finicky 862 *fastidious*; critical, appreciative 480 *judicial*; decent, seemly, becoming 24 *apt*; proper, correct, comme il faut 848 *fashionable*; mannerly 848 *well-bred*.

Vb. *have taste*, show good t., reveal fine feelings 463 *discriminate*; appreciate, value, criticize 480 *judge*; go in for the best, take only the best 862 *be fastidious*.

Adv. *tastefully*, elegantly, in good taste, in the best t.; becomingly, fittingly, properly, agreeably 24 *pertinently*.

See: 24, **463**, 480, 573, 575, 602, **644**, 694, 819, **848**, 862, 884, 950.

847 Bad Taste

N. *bad taste*, tastelessness, poor taste, excruciating t. 645 *badness*; no taste, lack of t.; bad art, kitsch; international airport plastic; commercialism, commercialization, prostitution of talent; yellow press, gutter p.; unrefinement, coarseness, barbarism, vulgarism, vandalism, philistinism, Babbittry 699 *artlessness*; vulgarity, gaudiness, garishness, loudness, blatancy, flagrancy; tawdriness, shoddiness; shoddy, frippery, tinsel, glitter, paste, ersatz, imitation 639 *bauble*; lack of feeling, insensitivity, crassness, grossness; tactlessness, indelicacy, impropriety, unseemliness; bad joke, untimely jest, misplaced wit; nastiness, obscenity 951 *impurity*; unfashionableness, dowdiness, frumpishness; frump, dowdy, square.

ill-breeding, vulgarity, commonness; loudness, heartiness; rusticity, provinciality, inurbanity, incivility, unfashionableness; bad form, incorrectness; bad manners, no manners, gaucherie, boorishness, rudeness, impoliteness 885 *discourtesy*; ungentlemanliness, caddishness; brutishness, savagery; misbehaviour, indecorum, ribaldry; rough behaviour, rowdyism, ruffianism 61 *disorder*.

vulgarian, snob, social climber, cad, bounder; rough diamond, unlicked cub; arriviste, parvenu, nouveau riche; proletarian, prole 869 *commoner*; Goth, Vandal, Philistine, Babbitt; barbarian, savage; yob, punk.

Adj. *vulgar*, undignified; unrefined, unpolished 576 *inelegant*; tasteless, in bad taste, in the worst possible t.; gross, crass, coarse, coarse-grained; unfastidious, not particular; knowing no better, philistine, barbarian 699 *artless*; commercial, commercialized; tawdry, cheap, cheap and nasty, catchpenny, gingerbread, kitschy, ersatz; flashy, meretricious, bedizened 875 *showy*; obtrusive, blatant, loud, screaming, gaudy, garish, raffish; flaunting, shameless, tarted up; fulsome, excessive; schmaltzy, novelettish; overdressed, underdressed; shabby genteel 850 *affected*; not respectable, ungenteel; common, common as muck, low, gutter, sordid 867 *disreputable*; improper, indelicate, indecorous; going too far, beyond the pale, scandalous, indecent, low-minded, ribald, obscene, risqué 951 *impure*.

ill-bred, underbred, badly brought up; unpresentable, not to be taken anywhere; ungentlemanly, unladylike; unfeminine, hoydenish; ungenteel, non-U 869 *plebeian*; loud, hearty; tactless, insensitive, blunt; uncourtly, uncivil, impolite, mannerless, unmannerly, ill-mannered 885 *discourteous*; unfashionable, unsmart, frumpish, dowdy, rustic, provincial, countrified, gone native; crude, rude, boorish, churlish, yobbish, loutish, clodhopping, uncouth, uncultured, uncultivated, unpolished, unrefined 491 *ignorant*; unsophisticated, knowing no better 699 *artless*; unlettered, uncivilized, barbaric; awkward, gauche, lubberly 695 *clumsy*; misbehaving, rowdy, ruffianly, riotous 61 *disorderly*; snobbish, uppity, superior 850 *affected*.

Vb. *vulgarize*, cheapen, coarsen, debase, lower, lower the tone; commercialize, popularize; show bad taste, know no better 491 *not know*; be unfashionable, be out of date.

See: 61, 491, 576, 639, **645**, 695, 699, 850, 867, 869, 875, 885, 951.

848 Fashion. Etiquette

N. *fashion*, style, mode, cut 243 *form*; method 624 *way*; vogue, cult 610 *habit*; prevailing taste, current fashion 126 *modernism*; rage, fad, craze, cry, furore; new look, the latest, latest fashion, what's new 126 *newness*; dernier cri, last word, ne plus ultra; extreme of fashion, height of f., pink of f.; dash 875 *ostentation*; fashionableness, ton, bon t.; stylishness, flair, chic; dress sense, fashion s.; fashion show, mannequin parade 522 *exhibit*; haute couture, elegance, foppishness, dressiness; foppery 850 *affectation*; world of fashion, Vanity Fair, passing show, way of the world.

etiquette, point of e., punctilio 875 *formality*; protocol, convention, custom, conventionality 610 *practice*; snobbery, conventions of society, sanctions of s., done thing, good form; convenances, proprieties, appearances, Mrs Grundy; bienséance, decency, decorum, propriety, right note, correctness 846 *good taste*; civilized behaviour 884 *courtesy*; breeding, good b., polish; gentility, gentlemanliness, ladylike behaviour; manners, good m., refined m., polished m., drawing-room m., court m., best behaviour; grand air, poise, dignity, savoir faire, savvy 688 *conduct*.

beau monde, society, good s., high s., civilized s., civilization; town, best end of town, Mayfair; St James's, court, drawing room, salon; high circles, top drawer, right people, best p., smart set, county s., upper ten 868 *nobility*; cream, upper crust, cream of society 644 *elite*; café society, jeunesse dorée, gilded youth, beautiful people, jet set; hipster, swinger; fashionable person, glass of fashion; man *or* woman about town, man *or* woman of fashion, high stepper, classy dame; slave to fashion, leader of f., Beau Nash; man *or* woman of the world, mondaine, socialite, playboy, clubman, clubwoman, cosmopolitan 882 *sociable person*.

fop, fine gentleman, macaroni, buck, pearly king; fine lady, belle, pearly queen; debutante, deb; dandy, exquisite, beau, Beau Brummel; popinjay, peacock, clothes-horse, fashion plate; coxcomb, puppy, dandiprat, jackanapes; swell, toff, dude, nob, His Nibs, Lady Muck; Ted, mod; spark, blood, blade, buckeen, lad, gay dog; lounge lizard, carpet knight, gallant; ladykiller, squire of dames.

Adj. *fashionable*, modish, stylish, voguish, bon ton; correct, comme il faut; in, in vogue, in fashion, in the latest f., à la mode, chichi; recherché, exquisite, chic, elegant, well-dressed, well-groomed 846 *tasteful*; clothes-conscious, foppish, dressy; high-stepping, dashing, rakish, snazzy, flashy 875 *showy*; dandy, smart, classy, ritzy, swanky, swell, swish, posh; up-to-the-minute, ultrafashionable, newfangled, all the rage 126 *modern*; hip, hep, groovy, trendy, swinging, with it; groomed, dandified, dressed up to the nines, in full dress, en grande tenue 228 *dressed*; in society, in the best s., in the right set, moving in the best circles, knowing the right people, belonging to the best clubs; in the swim 83 *conformable*; snobbish 850 *affected*; conventional, done 610 *usual*.

well-bred, thoroughbred, blue-blooded 868 *noble*; cosmopolitan, sophisticated, civilized, citified, urbane; polished, polite, well brought up, house-trained; U, gentlemanly, ladylike 868 *genteel*; civil, well-mannered, easy-m., good-m., well-spoken 884 *courteous*; courtly, stately, distingué(e), dignified 875 *formal*; poised, dégagé(e), easy, unembarrassed, smooth; correct, decorous, proper, convenable, decent; tactful, diplomatic; considerate 884 *amiable*; punctilious 929 *honourable*.

Vb. *be in fashion*, be done, catch on 610 *be wont*; be all the rage, be the latest 126 *modernize*; get with it, follow the fashion, jump on the band wagon, change with the times 83 *conform*; have the entrée, move in the best circles, be seen in the right places; savoir faire, savoir vivre 882 *be sociable*; entertain 882 *be hospitable*; keep up with the Joneses, keep up appearances; observe decorum, do the right thing; cut a dash, cut a figure, lead the fashion, set the f., set the tone, give a lead; look right, pass; have an air, have style; show flair, dress well, wear the right clothes, dandify 843 *primp*.

Adv. *fashionably*, in style, à la mode; for appearances, for fashion's sake.

See: 83, **126**, 228, 243, 522, 610, 624, 644, 688, 843, **846**, 850, 868, 875, 882, 884, 929.

849 Ridiculousness

N. *ridiculousness*, ludicrousness, risibility, laughability, height of absurdity 497 *absurdity*; funniness, pricelessness, comicality, drollery, waggishness 839 *wit*; quaintness, oddness, queerness, eccentricity 84 *nonconformity*; bathos, anticlimax 509 *disappointment*; boasting 877 *boast*; extravagance, bombast 546 *exaggeration*; comic interlude, light relief; light verse, comic v., doggerel, limerick 839 *witticism*; spoonerism, malapropism, bull; comic turn, comedy, farce, burlesque, slapstick, knockabout, clowning, buffoonery 594 *stage play*; paradox, paradoxicality, Gilbertian situation 508 *lack of expectation*.

Adj. *ridiculous*, ludicrous, preposterous, monstrous, grotesque, fantastic, cockeyed, inappropriate 497 *absurd*; awkward, clownish 695 *clumsy*; silly 499 *foolish*; derisory, contemptible 639 *unimportant*; laughable, risible; bizarre, rum, quaint, odd, queer 84 *unusual*; strange, outlandish 59 *extraneous*; mannered, stilted 850 *affected*; inflated, bombastic, extravagant, outré 546 *exaggerated*; crazy, crackpot, fanciful 513 *imaginary*; whimsical 604 *capricious*; paradoxical.

funny, funny-peculiar 84 *abnormal*; funny-ha-ha, laughter-inducing, good for a laugh 837 *amusing*; comical, droll, drollish, humorous, waggish 839 *witty*; rich, priceless, side-splitting, hilarious, a real hoot, too funny for words; light, comic, seriocomic, tragicomic; mocking, ironical, satirical 851 *derisive*; burlesque, mock-heroic; doggerel; farcical, slapstick, clownish, knockabout; Chaplinesque, Pickwickian, Malvolian, Shavian, Gilbertian.

Vb. *be ridiculous*, make one laugh, excite laughter, raise a laugh; tickle, shake *or* disturb one's gravity, give one the giggles; entertain 837 *amuse*; look silly, be a figure of fun, cut a ridiculous figure, be a laughingstock, fool, play the fool 497 *be absurd*; come down with a bump, descend to bathos, pass from the sublime to the ridiculous; make an exhibition of oneself, put oneself out of court 695 *act foolishly*; poke fun at, make one a laughingstock 851 *ridicule*.

See: 59, 84, 497, 499, 508, 509, 513, 546, 594, 604, 639, 695, **837**, 839, 850, **851**, 877.

850 Affectation

N. *affectation*, cult, fad 848 *fashion*; affectedness, pretentiousness 875 *ostentation*; assumption of airs, grand a. 873 *airs*; posing, posturing, attitudinizing, striking attitudes, high moral tone; pose, public image; artificiality, mannerism, trick, literary affectation, esoteric vocabulary, grandiloquence 574 *magniloquence*; preciosity, euphuism 574 *ornament*; pout, moue, grimace 547 *gesture*; coquetry, minauderie 604 *caprice*; conceit, conceitedness, foppery, foppishness, dandyism, coxcombry 873 *vanity*; euphemism, mock modesty, false shame, mauvaise honte 874 *modesty*; irony, Socratic i., backhanded compliment 851 *ridicule*; insincerity, play-acting, tongue in cheek 541 *duplicity*; staginess, theatricality, histrionics.

pretension, pretensions, false p.; artifice, sham, humbug, quackery, charlatanism, charlatanry 542 *deception*; superficiality, shallowness, shallow profundity 4 *insubstantiality*; stiffness, starchiness, buckram 875 *formality*; pedantry, purism, precisianism 735 *severity*; demureness, prunes and prisms 950 *prudery*; sanctimony, sanctimoniousness 979 *pietism*.

affecter, humbug, quack, charlatan 545 *impostor*; play-actor 594 *actor*; hypocrite, flatterer 545 *deceiver*; bluffer 877 *boaster*; coquette, flirt; mass of affectation, attitudinizer, poser, poseur, poseuse 873 *vain person*; ironist 839 *humorist*; coxcomb, dandy 848 *fop*; grimacer, simperer; formalist, precisian, purist, pedant; know-all 500 *wise guy*; prig, puritan, pietist, goody-goody 950 *prude*; mannerist, euphuist, bluestocking.

Adj. *affected*, full of affectation, self-conscious; studied, mannered, euphuistic, precious, chichi 574 *ornate*; artificial, unnatural, stilted, stiff, starchy 875 *formal*; prim, priggish, prudish, mealy-mouthed, euphemistic, sanctimonious, self-righteous, holier than thou, smug, demure 979 *pietistic*; arch, sly, nudging, winking 833 *merry*; coquettish, coy, cute, twee, too-too, mock-modest, niminy-piminy, mincing, simpering, grimacing, languishing; humbugging, canting, hypocritical, tongue-in-cheek, ironical 542 *deceiving*; bluffing 877 *boastful*; shallow, hollow, specious, pretentious, big-sounding, high-s.; big-mouthed, gushing, fulsome, stagy, theatrical, overdramatized 875 *ostentatious*; dandified, foppish, poncy, camp; conceited, la-di-da, giving oneself airs, showing off, swanking, posturing, posing, striking poses, striking an attitude, attitudinizing 873 *vain*; stuck-up 871 *prideful*; snobbish, social-climbing, keeping up appearances 847 *ill-bred*; bogus 541 *false*; for effect, assumed, put on, insincere, phoney; overdone 546 *exaggerated*.

Vb. *be affected*, affect, put on, wear, assume; pretend, feign, go through the motions, make a show of, bluff 541 *dissemble*; make as if 20 *imitate*; affect zeal 678 *be busy*; perform, act a part, play-act 594 *act*; overact, ham, barnstorm 546 *exaggerate*; try for effect, seek an e., camp it up, play to the gallery; dramatize oneself, attitudinize, strike attitudes, posture, pose, strike a p., prance, mince, ponce about 875 *be ostentatious*; have pretensions, put on airs, give oneself a., put on side, swank, show off 873 *be vain*; air one's knowledge 490 *know*; euphuize 575 *be elegant*; brag, vaunt, talk big 877 *boast*; pout, moue, simper, smirk 835 *smile*; coquette, flirt, languish 887 *excite love*; play the hypocrite 541 *cant*; save appearances, euphemize.

See: 4, 20, 490, 500, 541, 542, 545, 546, 547, 574, 575, 594, 604, 678, 735, 833, 835, 839, 847, 848, 851, 871, **873**, 874, **875**, 877, 887, 950, 979.

851 Ridicule

N. *ridicule*, derision, derisiveness, poking fun; mockery, scoffing, flippancy 921 *disrespect*; sniggering, grinning 835 *laughter*; raillery, teasing, ribbing, banter, persiflage, badinage, leg-pulling, chaff, leg-pull; buffoonery, horseplay, clowning, practical joke 497 *foolery*; grin, snigger, laugh, scoff, mock, fleer 926 *detraction*; irony, tongue in cheek, sarcasm, barbed shaft, backhanded compliment; catcall, hoot, hiss 924 *censure*; personalities, personal remarks, insult 921 *indignity*; ribaldry 839 *witticism*.

satire, denunciation 928 *accusation*; parody, burlesque, travesty, caricature, cartoon 552 *misrepresentation*; skit, spoof, send-up, take-off 20 *mimicry*; squib, lampoon, pasquinade 926 *detraction*.

laughingstock, object of ridicule, figure of fun, butt, universal b., common jest, by-word; sport, game, fair g.; cock-shy, Aunt Sally; April fool, silly f., buffoon, clown, zany 501 *fool*; stooge, butt, foil, feed, straight man; guy, caricature, travesty, mockery of, apology for; eccentric 504 *crank*; original, card, caution, queer fish, odd f.; fogy, old f., geezer, museum piece, mossback, back number, square; fall guy, victim 728 *loser*.

Adj. *derisive*, ridiculing, mocking, chaffing, joshing etc. vb.; flippant 456 *light-minded*; sardonic, sarcastic; disparaging 926 *detracting*; ironical, quizzical; satirical, Hudibrastic 839 *witty*; ribald 847 *vulgar*; burlesque, mock-heroic.

Vb. *ridicule*, deride, pour scorn on, laugh at, grin at, smile at, smirk at; snigger, laugh in one's sleeve; banter, chaff, rally, twit, josh, rib, tease, roast, rag, pull one's leg, poke fun, make merry with, play w., exercise one's wit on, make fun of, make sport of, make a monkey of, take the mickey out of, have one on, kid, fool, make a fool of, make an April fool of, fool to the top of one's bent 542 *befool*; mock, scoff, fleer, jeer 926 *detract*; turn to a jest, make a joke of, turn to ridicule 922 *hold cheap*; take down, deflate, debunk, make one look silly, make one laugh on the other side of his *or* her face 872 *humiliate*.

satirize, lampoon 921 *not respect*; mock, fleer, gibe; mimic, send up, take off 20 *imitate*; parody, travesty, spoof, burlesque, caricature, guy 552 *misrepresent*; expose, show up, denounce, pillory 928 *accuse*.

See: 20, 456, 497, 501, 504, 542, 552, 728, 835, **839**, 847, 872, 921, 922, 924, **926**, 928.

852 Hope

N. *hope*, hopes, expectations, assumption, presumption 507 *expectation*; good hopes, certain h., high h., sanguine expectation, hope and belief, conviction 485 *belief*; reliance, trust, confidence, faith, assurance 473 *certainty*; eager hope 471 *probability*; hope recovered, reassurance 831 *relief*; safe hope, security, anchor, sheet a., mainstay, staff 218 *support*; final hope, last h., last throw 618 *gambling*; ray of hope, beam of h., gleam of h., glimmer of h. 469 *possibility*; good omen, happy o., favourable auspices, promise, fair prospect, bright p. 511 *omen*; blue sky, silver lining; hopefulness, no cause for despair; buoyancy, airiness, breeziness, optimism, enthusiasm 833 *cheerfulness*; wishful thinking, self-deception; rose-coloured spectacles, rosy picture.

aspiration, ambition, purpose 617 *intention*; pious hope, fervent h., fond h., airy h.; vision, pipe dream, golden d., heart's desire, utopianism, chiliasm, millenarianism, Messianism; castles in Spain, El Dorado, fool's paradise 513 *fantasy*; promised land, land of promise, utopia, millennium, the day, Der Tag 617 *objective*.

hoper, aspirant, candidate, waiting list; hopeful, young h.; expectant, heir apparent 776 *beneficiary*; optimist, prisoner of hope; utopian, millenarian, chiliast 513 *visionary*; waiter on Providence, Micawber.

Adj. *hoping*, aspiring, soaring, starry-eyed; ambitious, would-be 617 *intending*; dreaming, dreaming of 513 *imaginative*; hopeful, in hopes 507 *expectant*; happy in the hope, next in succession, in sight of, on the verge of; in high hopes, sanguine, confident 473 *certain*; buoyant, optimistic, airy, uncritical; elated, enthusiastic, flushed 833 *jubilant*; hoping for the best, ever-hoping, undespairing, undiscouraged 855 *unfearing*; Micawberish; not unhopeful, reasonably confident.

promising, full of promise, favourable, auspicious, propitious 730 *prosperous*; bright, fair, golden, roseate, rosy, rose-coloured, couleur de rose; affording hope, hopeful, encouraging, inspiriting; plausible, likely 471 *probable*; utopian, millennial, chiliastic; wishful, self-deluding 477 *illogical*; visionary 513 *imaginary*.

Vb. *hope*, trust, confide, have faith; rest assured, feel confident, hope in, put one's trust in, rely, lean on, bank on, count on, pin one's hopes on, hope and believe 485 *believe*; presume 471 *assume*; speculate, look forward 507 *expect*; hope for, dream of, aspire, promise oneself, soar, aim high 617 *intend*; have a hope, be in hopes, have hopes, have expectations, live in hopes, keep one's fingers crossed; feel hope, cherish h., nourish h., nurse h.; buck up, take heart, take hope, pluck up h., recover h., renew h., see light at the end of the tunnel 831 *be relieved*; remain hopeful, not despair, see no cause for d., not despond 599 *stand firm*; hope on, hope against hope, cling to h., keep hope alive, never say die; catch at a straw, keep one's spirits up, look on the bright side, hope for the best 833 *be cheerful*; keep smiling 600 *persevere*; be hopeful, see life through rose-coloured spectacles; flatter oneself, delude o. 477 *reason badly*; anticipate, count one's chickens before they are hatched 135 *be early*; indulge in wishful thinking, dream 513 *imagine*.

give hope, afford h., foster h., inspire h., raise h., inspirit, encourage, comfort 833 *cheer*; show signs of, have the makings of, promise, show p., promise well, shape up w., augur w., bid fair 471 *be likely*; raise expectations, paint a rosy picture 511 *predict*.

Adv. *hopefully*, expectantly, in all hopefulness, in all confidence; without discouragement, without despair; optimistically, airily, lightly, gaily, uncritically.

Int. nil desperandum! never say die! while there's life, there's hope!

See: 135, 218, 469, 471, 473, 477, 485, 507, 511, 513, 599, 600, 617, 618, 730, 776, 831, 833, 855.

853 Hopelessness

N. *hopelessness*, no hope, loss of hope, discouragement, defeatism, despondency, dismay 834 *dejection*; pessimism, cynicism, despair, desperation, no way out, last hope gone; hopes overthrown, dashed hopes, hope deferred, hope extinguished, cheated hope, frustrated h., deluded h. 509 *disappointment*; resignation 508 *lack of expectation*; not a hope 470 *impossibility*; chimera, vain hope, forlorn h., futile h., impossible h. 513 *fantasy*; message of despair, wan smile; poor lookout, no prospects; hopeless case, dead duck; hopeless situation, bad job, bad business 700 *predicament*; counsel of despair, Job's comforter, misery, pessimist, defeatist 834 *moper*.

Adj. *hopeless*, bereft of hope, without hope, desponding, despairing, in despair, desperate, suicidal; unhopeful, pessimistic, cynical, looking on the black side; defeatist, expecting the worst, fearing the w., resigned to the w.; sunk in despair, inconsolable, disconsolate, comfortless 834 *dejected*; wringing one's hands 836 *lamenting*; cheated of one's last hope 509 *disappointed*; desolate, forlorn; ruined, undone, without resource 731 *unfortunate*.

unpromising, holding out no hope, offering no h., hopeless, comfortless, without comfort 834 *cheerless*; desperate 661 *dangerous*; unpropitious, inauspicious 731 *adverse*; ill-omened, boding ill, threatening, ominous 511 *presageful*; inassuageable, immitigable, irremediable, remediless, incurable, cureless, immedicable, inoperable; past cure, beyond hope, past recall, despaired of; incorrigible, irreparable, irrecoverable, irrevocable, irredeemable, irreclaimable; irreversible, inevitable; impracticable, out of the question 470 *impossible*.

Vb. *despair*, lose heart, lose hope, have no h., hope no more; despond, give way to despair, wring one's hands 834 *be dejected*; have shot one's last bolt, give up hope, reject h., abandon h., relinquish h.; hope for nothing more from, write off 674 *stop using*; give up, turn one's face to the wall 721 *submit*.

leave no hope, offer no h., deny h.; drive to despair, bring to d.; shatter one's last hope 509 *disappoint*; be incurable, - inoperable etc. adj.

See: 470, 508, **509**, 511, 513, 661, 674, 700, 721, 731, **834**, 836.

854 Fear

N. *fear*, healthy f., dread, awe 920 *respect*; abject fear 856 *cowardice*; fright, stage f.; wind up, funk, blue funk; terror, mortal t., panic t.; state of terror, intimidation, trepidation, alarm, false a.; shock, flutter, flap, flat spin 318 *agitation*; fit, fit of terror, scare, stampede, panic 318 *spasm*; flight, sauve qui peut; horror, horripilation, hair on end, cold sweat, blood turning to water; consternation, dismay 853 *hopelessness*; defence mechanism, repression, escapism 620 *avoidance*.

nervousness, want of courage, lack of confidence, cowardliness 856 *cowardice*; self-distrust, diffidence, shyness 874 *modesty*; defensiveness, blustering, bluster 877 *boasting*; timidity, timorousness, fearfulness, hesitation, fighting shy, backing out 620 *avoidance*; loss of nerve, cold feet, fears, suspicions, misgivings, qualms, mistrust, apprehension, apprehensiveness, uneasiness, disquiet, disquietude, solicitude, anxiety, care 825 *worry*; depression, despondency 834 *dejection*; defeatism, pessimism 853 *hopelessness*; perturbation, trepidation, fear and trembling, flutter, tremor, palpitation, blushing, trembling, quaking, shaking, shuddering, shivering, stuttering; nerves, willies, butterflies, collywobbles, creeps, shivers, jumps, jitters, heebie-jeebies 318 *agitation*; gooseflesh, hair on end, knees knocking.

phobia, claustrophobia, agoraphobia, aerophobia, acrophobia, pyrophobia, frigophobia, pogonophobia, autophobia, phobophobia; fear of death; antisemitism, racial prejudice, Gallophobia, xenophobia 888 *hatred*; McCarthyism, spy mania, witch-hunting.

intimidation, deterrence, war of nerves, war cry, sabre-rattling, arms buildup, fee, faw, fum; threatening 900 *threat*; caution 664 *warning*; terror, terrorization, terrorism, reign of terror 735 *severity*; alarmism, scaremongering; sword of Damocles, suspended sentence 963 *punishment*; deterrent, weapon of retaliation 723 *weapon*; object of terror, goblin, hobgoblin 970 *demon*; spook, spectre 970 *ghost*; Gorgon, Medusa, scarecrow, nightmare; bugbear, bugaboo, ogre 938 *monster*; death's head, skull and crossbones.

alarmist, scaremonger, doom merchant, spreader of alarm and despondency, Calamity Jane; defeatist, pessimist; terrorist, terrorizer, intimidator, horrifier, frightener, nerve-shaker, sabre-rattler.

Adj. *fearing*, afeard, afraid, frightened, funky, panicky; overawed 920 *respectful*; intimidated, terrorized, demoralized; in fear, in trepidation, in a fright, in a cold sweat, in a flap, in a flat spin, in a panic; terror-crazed, panic-stricken, panic-struck; stampeding, scared, alarmed, startled; hysterical, having fits, in hysterics; dismayed, in consternation, consternated, flabbergasted; frozen, petrified, stunned; appalled, shocked, horrified, aghast, horror-struck, awestruck, unmanned, scared out of one's wits, numbed with fear, paralysed by f., frightened to death, fainting with fright, white as a sheet, pale as death, pale as a ghost, ashen-faced; more frightened than hurt, suffering from shock.

nervous, defensive, on the d., tense, uptight; waiting for the bomb to drop; defeatist, pessimistic, despairing 853 *hopeless*; timid, timorous, shy, diffident, self-conscious, self-distrustful 874 *modest*; coy, wary, hesitating, shrinking, treading warily 858 *cautious*; doubtful, distrustful, misdoubting, suspicious 474 *doubting*; windy, faint-hearted 601 *irresolute*; disturbed, disquieted, dismayed; apprehensive, uneasy, fearful, dreading, anxious, worried 825 *unhappy*; haunted, haunted by fears, a prey to f., terror-ridden, highly-strung, starting at a sound, afraid of one's own shadow, jittery, jumpy, nervy; tremulous, shaky, shaking, trembling, quaking, cowering, cringing 856 *cowardly*; with one's heart in one's mouth, shaking like a leaf *or* a jelly; on pins and needles, palpitating, breathless 318 *agitated*.

frightening, shocking, startling, alarming etc. vb.; formidable, redoubtable; hazardous, hairy 661 *dangerous*; tremendous, dreadful, fear-inspiring, awe-i., numinous, fearsome, awesome 821 *impressive*; grim, grisly, hideous, ghastly, lurid, frightful, revolting, horrifying, horrific, horrible, terrible, awful, appalling, mind-boggling, mind-blowing; horripilant, hair-raising, blood-curdling; weird, eerie, creepy, scary, ghoulish, nightmarish, gruesome, macabre, sinister; portentous, ominous, direful 511 *presageful*; intimidating, terroristic, sabre-rattling, bullying, hectoring 735 *oppressive*; minatory, menacing 900 *threatening*; bellowing, roaring 400 *loud*; nerve-racking 827 *distressing*.

Vb. *fear*, funk, be afraid, - frightened etc. adj.; stand in fear *or* awe, dread 920 *respect*; flap, be in a f., have the wind up, have the willies; get the wind up, take fright, take alarm; flap, panic, fall into p., stampede, take to flight, fly 620 *run away*; start, jump, flutter 318 *be agitated*; faint, collapse, break down.

quake, shake, tremble, quiver, shiver, shudder, stutter, quaver; quake in one's shoes, shake like a jelly, fear for one's life, be frightened to death, be scared out of one's wits, faint for fear; change colour, blench, pale, go white as a sheet; wince, flinch, shrink, shy, jib 620 *avoid*; quail, cower, crouch, skulk, come to heel 721 *knuckle under*; stand aghast, be horrified, be chilled with fear, freeze, freeze with horror, feel one's blood run cold, feel one's blood turn to water, feel one's hair stand on end.

be nervous, - apprehensive etc. adj.; feel shy 874 *be modest*; have misgivings, suspect, distrust, mistrust 486 *doubt*; shrink, shy, quail, funk it, not face it, put off the evil day; be anxious, dread, consult one's fears, have f., have qualms; hesitate, get cold feet, think twice, have second thoughts, think better of it, not dare 858 *be cautious*; get the wind up, start at one's own shadow, be on edge, sit on thorns 318 *be agitated*.

frighten, fright, affright, play the bogyman, make faces, grimace; scare, panic, stampede; intimidate, put in fear, menace 900 *threaten*; stand over, hang o. 155 *impend*; alarm, cause a., raise the a., cry wolf; scare the living daylights out of, scare stiff, scare half to death; make one jump, give one a fright, give one a turn, startle, flutter, flurry 318 *agitate*; start, flush 619 *hunt*; disquiet, disturb, perturb, prey on the mind, haunt, obsess, beset 827 *trouble*; raise apprehensions, put the wind up, make nervous, rattle, shake, unnerve; play on one's nerves, wring one's n., unstring one's n.; unman, make a coward of, cowardize, demoralize; strike with fear, put the fear of God into, awe, overawe 821 *impress*; quell, subdue, cow 727 *overmaster*; amaze, shock, stagger, flabbergast, stun 508 *surprise*; dismay, confound, abash, disconcert 63 *derange*; frighten off, daunt, deter, discourage 613 *dissuade*; terrorize, institute a reign of terror 735 *oppress*; browbeat, bully 827 *torment*; terrify, horrify, harrow, make aghast; chill, freeze, benumb, paralyse, petrify, rivet, turn to stone, Gorgonize, mesmerize 375 *render insensible*; appal, chill the spine, freeze the blood, make one's blood run cold, turn one's blood to water; make one's hair stand on end *or* curl, make one's flesh creep, make one's knees knock, make one's teeth chatter, frighten out of one's wits.

See:63, 155, **318**, 375, 400, 474, 486, 508, 511, 601, 613, 619, 620, 661, 664, 721, 723, 727, 735, 821, **825**, 827, 834, 853, **856**, 858, 874, 877, 888, 900, 920, 938, 963, 970.

855 Courage

N. *courage,* bravery, valiance, valour, derring-do; moral courage, courage of one's convictions 929 *probity*; VC courage, heroism, gallantry, chivalry; self-confidence, self-reliance, fearlessness, ignorance of fear, intrepidity, daring, nerve; defiance of danger, boldness, hardihood, audacity 857 *rashness*; spirit, mettle, dash, go, élan, panache 174 *vigorousness*; enterprise 672 *undertaking*; tenacity, bulldog courage 600 *perseverance*; undauntedness, high morale, stoutness of heart, firmness, fortitude, determination, resoluteness 599 *resolution*; gameness, pluck, spunk, cojones, guts, heart, great h., stout h., heart of oak, backbone, grit 600 *stamina*; sham courage, Dutch c., pot valour; desperate courage, courage of despair; brave face, bold front 711 *defiance*; fresh courage, encouragement, animation 612 *inducement.*

manliness, manhood 929 *probity*; virtue, chivalry; manly spirit, martial s., heroic qualities, soldierly q., morale, devotion to duty; militancy, aggressiveness, fierceness 718 *bellicosity*; endurance, stiff upper lip 599 *resolution.*

prowess, derring-do, deeds of d., chivalry, knightliness, knighthood, heroism, heroic achievement, knightly deed, gallant act, act of courage, soldierly conduct; feat, feat of arms, emprise, exploit, stroke, bold s. 676 *deed*; desperate venture 857 *rashness*; heroics.

brave person, hero, heroine, VC, GC; knight, paladin; good soldier, stout s., stout fellow, beau sabreur, brave, warrior 722 *soldier*; man, true m., man *or* woman of mettle, man *or* woman of spirit, plucky fellow, game dog, bulldog; daredevil, risk-taker; fire-eater, bully, bravo 857 *desperado*; Galahad, Greatheart, Lionheart; Joan of Arc, Boadicea, Amazon; Don Quixote, Bayard, knight-errant, k. of the Round Table; gallant knight, preux chevalier; the brave, the bravest of the brave; band of heroes, gallant company; forlorn hope, picked troops 644 *elite*; lion, tiger, game-cock, fighting c., bulldog.

Adj. *courageous,* brave, valorous, valiant, gallant, heroic; chivalrous, knightly, knight-like; yeomanly, soldierly, soldier-like, martial, Amazonian 718 *warlike*; stout, doughty, tall, bonny, manful, manly, tough, macho, red-blooded; militant, bellicose, aggressive, fire-eating; fierce, bloody, savage 898 *cruel*; bold 711 *defiant*; dashing, hardy, audacious, daring, venturesome, bold as brass 857 *rash*; adventurous 672 *enterprising*; mettlesome, spirited, high-s., high-hearted, stout-h., lion-hearted, bold as a lion; firm-minded, strong-m., full of courage, full of fight, full of spirit, full of spunk, spunky; full of Dutch courage, pot-valiant; unbowed, unswayed, firm, steady, dogged, indomitable, never say die 600 *persevering*; desperate, determined 599 *resolute*; of high morale, game, plucky, sporting; ready for danger, ready for the fray, ready for anything, unflinching, unshrinking, leading the charge 597 *willing.*

unfearing, unafraid, intrepid, nerveless, with nerves of steel *or* of iron; despising danger, danger-loving; sure of oneself, confident, self-c., self-reliant; fearless, dauntless, dreadless, aweless; unshrinking, untrembling, unblenching; undismayed, undaunted, undashed, unabashed, unawed, unalarmed, unconcerned, unapprehensive, unappalled, unshaken, unshakable.

Vb. *be courageous,*- bold etc. adj.; have what it takes, come up to scratch, show spirit; fight with the best 716 *fight*; venture, adventure, bell the cat, take the plunge, take the bull by the horns 672 *undertake*; dare 661 *face danger*; show fight, brave, face, outface, outdare, beard, affront, snap one's fingers at 711 *defy*; confront, look in the face, look in the eyes; speak out, speak up, stand up and be counted 532 *affirm*; face the music, brave it out, show a bold front, stick to one's guns 599 *stand firm*; go over the top 712 *charge*; laugh at danger, mock at d. 857 *be rash*; show prowess, show valour, win one's spurs; keep one's head 823 *keep calm*; bear up, endure, grin and bear it 825 *suffer*.

take courage, pluck up c., muster c., take heart of grace, nerve oneself, take one's courage in both hands; put a brave face on it, show fight, cast away fear, screw up one's courage 599 *be resolute*; rally, stand 599 *stand firm*.

give courage, infuse c.; animate, put heart into, hearten, nerve, make a man of; embolden, encourage, inspirit, inspire 612 *incite*; buck up, rally 833 *cheer*; pat on the back, keep in countenance, keep in spirits, preserve morale, raise m., keep one's blood up; bolster up, reassure, take away fear, give confidence.

Adv. *bravely*, courageously, stoutly, doughtily, manfully; with one's blood up; with one's head held high.

See: 174, 532, 597, **599**, 600, 612, 644, 661, 672, 676, 711, 712, 716, 718, 722, 823, 825, 833, **857**, 898, 929.

856 Cowardice

N. *cowardice*, abject fear, funk, sheer f. 854 *fear*; cowardliness, craven spirit, no grit, no guts 601 *irresolution*; pusillanimity, timidity, want of courage, lack of daring; absence of morale, faint-heartedness, chicken-heartedness; unmanliness, poltroonery, dastardy, dastardliness; defeatism 853 *hopelessness*; desertion, quitting, shirking 918 *undutifulness*; white feather, yellow streak, low morale, faint heart, chicken liver; pot valiance, Dutch courage, braggadocio 877 *boasting*; cowering, skulking, leading from behind; discretion, better part of valour; safety first, overcaution 858 *caution*; moral cowardice, recantation 603 *tergiversation*.

coward, utter c., faintheart, no hero; funk, poltroon, craven, dastard, yellow-belly, lily-liver, chickenheart, wheyface; scaredycat, fraidycat, cowardy custard; sneak, rat, tell-tale 524 *informer*; runaway 603 *tergiversator*; coward at heart, bully, braggart 877 *boaster*; sissy, milksop, baby, big b., cry-b. 163 *weakling*; skulker, quitter, shirker, flincher, deserter, scuttler; cur, chicken, rabbit, mouse, jellyfish, invertebrate, doormat; scaremonger, defeatist 854 *alarmist*.

Adj. *cowardly*, coward, craven, poltroonish; not so brave, pusillanimous, timid, timorous, fearful, niddering, afraid of one's own shadow, unable to say boo to a goose 854 *nervous*; soft, womanish, babyish, unmanly, sissy 163 *weak*; spiritless, spunkless, without grit, without guts, poor-spirited, weak-minded, faint-hearted, chicken-h., chicken-livered, white-l., yellow-l., milk-l., lily-l., yellow-bellied, chicken; sneaking, skulking, cowering, quailing; dastardly, yellow, abject, base, vile, mean-spirited, currish, recreant, caitiff; unsoldierly, unmilitary, unmartial, unwarlike, unaggressive; cowed, lacking morale, with no fight left 721 *submitting*; defeatist 853 *hopeless*; unheroic, unvaliant, uncourageous, prudent, discreet 858 *cautious*; bashful, shy, coy 874 *modest*; easily frightened, funky, shakable, unstable, unsteady, infirm of purpose 601 *irresolute*.

Vb. *be cowardly*, lack courage, have no fight, have no pluck, have no grit, have no guts, have no heart *or* stomach for, not dare 601 *be irresolute*; lose one's nerve, have cold feet 854 *be nervous*; shrink, funk, shy from, back out, chicken o. 620 *avoid*; hide, slink, skulk, sneak; quail, cower, cringe 721 *knuckle under*; show a yellow streak, show the white feather, show fear, turn tail, cut and run, run for cover, panic, stampede, scuttle, show one's back, desert 620 *run away*; show discretion, live to fight another day, lead from behind, keep well to the rear 858 *be cautious*.

See: 163, 524, **601**, 603, 620, 721, 853, **854**, 858, 874, **877**, 918.

857 Rashness

N. *rashness*, lack of caution, lack of circumspection, incaution, incautiousness, unwariness, heedlessness 456 *inattention*; carelessness, neglect 458 *negligence*; imprudence, improvidence, indiscretion 499 *folly*; lack of consideration, inconsideration, irresponsibility, frivolity, flippancy, levity, light-mindedness; wildness, indiscipline, haughtiness 738 *disobedience*; scorn of the consequences, recklessness, foolhardiness, temerity, audacity, presumption, overconfidence, overdaring; hotheadedness, fieriness, impatience 822 *excitability*; rushing into things, impetuosity, precipitance, hastiness, overhaste 680 *haste*; overenthusiasm, quixotry, quixotism, knight-errantry; dangerous game, playing with fire, brinkmanship, game of chicken; desperation, courage of despair 855 *courage*; needless risk, leap in the dark 661 *danger*; too many eggs in one basket, underinsurance 661 *vulnerability*; reckless gamble, last throw 618 *gambling*; reckless expenditure 815 *prodigality*.

desperado, daredevil, tearaway, madcap, hothead, Hotspur, fire-eater; adventurer, plunger, inveterate gambler 618 *gambler*; harum-scarum, scapegrace, ne'er-do-well; one who sticks at nothing, gunman, terrorist; bully, bravo 904 *ruffian*.

Adj. *rash*, ill-considered, ill-advised, harebrained, foolhardy, wildcat, injudicious, indiscreet, imprudent 499 *unwise*; careless, hit-and-miss, slapdash, free-and-easy, accident-prone 458 *negligent*; unforeseeing, not looking, uncircumspect, incautious, unwary, heedless, thoughtless, inconsiderate, uncalculating 456 *inattentive*; light, frivolous, airy, breezy, flippant, giddy, devil-may-care, harum-scarum, slaphappy, trigger-happy 456 *light-minded*; irresponsible, reckless, regardless, couldn't-care-less, don't-care, damning the consquences, foolhardy, lunatic, wanton, wild, cavalier; bold, daring, temerarious, audacious; overdaring, overbold, madcap, daredevil, do-or-die, neck or nothing, breakneck, suicidal; overambitious, oversanguine, oversure, overconfident 852 *hoping*; overweening, presumptuous, arrogant 878 *insolent*; precipitate, Gadarene, headlong, hell-bent, desperate 680 *hasty*; unchecked, headstrong 602 *wilful*; untaught by experience 491 *ignorant*; impulsive, impatient, hot-blooded, hot-headed, fire-eating, furious 822 *excitable*; danger-loving 855 *unfearing*; venturesome 618 *speculative*; adventurous, risk-taking 672 *enterprising*; improvident, thriftless 815 *prodigal*.

Vb. *be rash*, - reckless etc. adj.; lack caution, want judgment, lean on a broken reed; expose oneself, drop one's guard, stick one's neck out, take unnecessary risks, ride the tiger; not look round, go bull-headed at, charge at, rush at, rush into 680 *hasten*; take a leap in the dark, buy a pig in a poke; ignore the consequences, damn the c.; plunge 618 *gamble*; put all one's eggs into one basket, not be insured, underinsure; not care 456 *be inattentive*; play fast and loose 634 *waste*; spend to the hilt 815 *be prodigal*; play the fool, play with edged tools, play with fire, burn one's fingers; venture to the brink, stand on the edge of a volcano, go out on a limb, risk one's neck, dice with death 661 *face danger*; play a desperate game, court disaster, ask for trouble, tempt providence, push one's luck, rush in where angels fear to tread; anticipate, reckon without one's host, count one's chickens before they are hatched, aim too high 695 *act foolishly*.

Adv. *rashly*, inconsiderately, carelessly, incautiously, lightly, gaily; headlong, recklessly, like Gadarene swine.

See: 456, 458, 491, 499, 602, 618, 634, **661**, 672, **680**, 695, 738, 815, 822, 852, 855, 878, 904.

858 Caution

N. *caution*, cautiousness, wariness, heedfulness, care, heed 457 *carefulness*; hesitation, doubt, second thoughts 854 *nervousness*; instinct of self-preservation 932 *selfishness*; looking before one leaps, looking twice, looking round, circumspection; guardedness, secretiveness, reticence 525 *secrecy*; calculation, careful reckoning, counting the risk, safety first; nothing left to chance 669 *preparation*; deliberation, mature consideration 480 *judgment*; sobriety, balance, level-headedness 834 *seriousness*; prudence, discretion, worldly wisdom 498 *wisdom*; insurance, precaution 662 *safeguard*; forethought 510 *foresight*; Fabianism, Fabian policy 823 *patience*; going slow, watching one's step, one step at a time, festina lente 278 *slowness*; wait-and-see policy, waiting game 136 *delay*.

Adj. *cautious*, chary, wary, watchful 455 *attentive*; heedful 457 *careful*; hesitating, doubtful, suspicious 854 *nervous*; taking no risks, insured, hedging; guarded, secret, secretive, incommunicative, cagey 525 *reticent*; experienced, taught by experience, once bitten, twice shy 669 *prepared*; on one's guard, circumspect, looking round, looking all ways, gingerly, stealthy, feeling one's way, watching one's step, tentative 461 *experimental*; conservative 660 *safe*; responsible 929 *trustworthy*; prudent, prudential, discreet 498 *wise*; noncommittal 625 *neutral*; frugal, counting the cost 814 *economical*; canny, counting the risk; timid, overcautious, unenterprising, unadventurous, overinsured; slow, unhasty, deliberate, Fabian 823 *patient*; sober, cool-headed, level-h., cool; cold-blooded, calm, self-possessed 823 *inexcitable*.

Vb. *be cautious*, beware, take good care 457 *be careful*; take no risks, go by the book, play safe, play for safety, play for a draw; play a waiting game 498 *be wise*; ca' canny, go slow 278 *move slowly*; cover up, cover one's tracks 525 *conceal*; not talk 525 *keep secret*; keep under cover, keep on the safe side, keep in the rear, keep in the background, hide 523 *lurk*; look, look out, see how the land lies 438 *scan*; see how the wind blows, feel one's way, play it by ear 461 *be tentative*; be on one's guard, tread warily, watch one's step, pussyfoot 525 *be stealthy*; look twice, think t. 455 *be mindful*; calculate, reckon 480 *judge*; count the cost, cut one's coat according to one's cloth 814 *economize*; know when to stop, take one's time, reculer pour mieux sauter; let well alone, let sleeping dogs lie, keep aloof, keep well out of 620 *avoid*; consider the consequences 511 *predict*; take precautions 124 *look ahead*; look a gift horse in the mouth 480 *estimate*; assure oneself, make sure 473 *make certain*; cover oneself, insure, take out a policy, reinsure, hedge, overinsure 660 *seek safety*; leave nothing to chance 669 *prepare*.

Adv. *cautiously*, with caution, gingerly, conservatively; softly softly.

See: 124, 136, 278, 438, **455**, 457, 461, 473, 480, 498, 510, 511, 523, 525, 620, 625, **660**, 662, 669, 814, 823, 834, **854**, 929, 932.

859 Desire

N. *desire*, wish, will and pleasure 595 *will*; summons, call, cry 737 *command*; dun 737 *demand*; desideration, wanting, want, need, exigency 627 *requirement*; claim 915 *dueness*; desiderium, nostalgia, homesickness 830 *regret*; wistfulness, longing, hankering, yearning, sheep's eyes; wishing, thinking, daydreaming, daydream 513 *fantasy*; ambition, aspiration 852 *hope*; appetency, yen, urge 279 *impulse*; cacoethes, itch; curiousness, thirst for knowledge, intellectual curiosity 453 *curiosity*; avidity, eagerness, zeal 597 *willingness*; passion, ardour, warmth, impetuosity, impatience 822 *excitability*; rage, fury 503 *frenzy*; monomania 503 *mania*; craving, lust for, appetite, hunger, thirst, hungry look (**see** *hunger*); land-hunger, expansionism; covetousness, cupidity, itching palm 816 *avarice*; graspingness, greediness, greed 786 *rapacity*; voracity, wolfishness, insatiability 947 *gluttony*; concupiscence, lust (**see** *libido*); inordinate desire, incontinence 943 *intemperance*.

hunger, famine, famished condition, empty stomach 946 *fasting*; appetite, good a., sharp a., keen a., voracious a., edge of a.; thirst, thirstiness 342 *dryness*; burning thirst, unquenchable t.; dipsomania 949 *alcoholism*.

liking, fancy, fondness, infatuation 887 *love*; stomach, appetite, zest; relish, tooth, sweet t. 386 *taste*; leaning, penchant, propensity, trend 179 *tendency*; weakness, partiality; affinity, mutual a.; sympathy, involvement 775 *participation*; inclination, mind 617 *intention*; predilection, favour 605 *choice*; whim, whimsy 604 *caprice*; hobby, craze, fad, mania 481 *bias*; fascination, allurement, attraction, temptation, titillation, seduction 612 *inducement*.

libido, Eros, life instinct, sexual urge; erotism, eroticism; concupiscence, sexual desire, carnal d., passion, rut, heat, oestrus; mating season; libidinousness, lickerishness, prurience, lust 951 *unchastity*; nymphomania, priapism, satyriasis 84 *abnormality*.

desired object, one's desire, wish, desire, desirable thing, desideratum 627 *requirement*; catch, prize, plum 729 *trophy*; lion, idol, cynosure 890 *favourite*; forbidden fruit, torment of Tantalus; envy, temptation; magnet, lure, draw 291 *attraction*; princesse lointaine 887 *loved one*; aim, goal, star, ambition, aspiration, dream 617 *objective*; ideal 646 *perfection*; height of one's ambition.

desirer, coveter, envier; wooer, suer, courter 887 *lover*; glutton, sucker for; fancier, amateur, dilettante 492 *collector*; devotee, votary, idolater 981 *worshipper*; well-wisher, favourer, sympathizer 707 *patron*; wisher, aspirant 852 *hoper*; claimant, pretender; candidate, parasite 763 *petitioner*; ambitious person, careerist; seducer 952 *libertine*.

Adj. *desiring*, appetent, desirous, wishing, wishful, tempted, unable to resist; oversexed, lustful, libidinous, concupiscent, rutting, on heat, ruttish, must, oestrous 951 *lecherous*; covetous (**see** *greedy*); craving, needing, wanting 627 *demanding*; missing, nostalgic 830 *regretting*; fain, inclined, minded, set upon, bent upon 617 *intending*; ambitious 852 *hoping*; aspiring, would-be, wistful, longing, yearning, hankering, hungry for; unsatisfied, demanding more; curious, solicitous, sedulous, anxious; eager, keen, mad k., burning, ardent, agog, breathless, impatient, dying for; itching, spoiling for; clamant, vocal; avid, overeager, overinclined, mad for; liking, fond, partial to, with a weakness for.

greedy, acquisitive, possessive 932 *selfish*; ambitious, status-seeking; voracious, omnivorous, open-mouthed 947 *gluttonous*; unsated, unsatisfied, unslaked, quenchless, unquenchable, inappeasable, insatiable, insatiate; rapacious, grasping, retentive 816 *avaricious*; exacting, extortionate 735 *oppressive*.

hungry, hungering; unfilled, empty, foodless, supperless, dinnerless 946 *fasting*; half-starved, starving, famished 636 *underfed*; peckish, ready for, ravenous, hungry as a hunter, pinched with hunger; thirsty, thirsting, athirst, dry, drouthy, parched, parched with thirst.

desired, wanted, liked; likable, desirable, worth having, enviable, in demand; acceptable, welcome; appetizing 826 *pleasurable*; fetching, catchy, attractive, appealing 291 *attracting*; wished, self-sought, invited 597 *voluntary*.

Vb. *desire*, want, desiderate, miss, feel the lack of 627 *require*; ask for, cry out f., clamour f. 737 *demand*; desire the presence of, call, summon, ring for 737 *command*; invite 882 *be hospitable*; wish, make a w., pray; wish otherwise, unwish 830 *regret*; wish for oneself, covet 912 *envy*; promise oneself, have a mind to, set one's heart on, set one's mind on, have designs on, aim at, have at heart 617 *intend*; plan for, angle f., fish f. 623 *plan*; aspire, raise one's eyes to, dream of, dream, daydream 852 *hope*; want a lot, aim high; look for, expect, think one deserves 915 *claim*; wish in vain, whistle for, cry for the moon 695 *act foolishly*; wish for another, pray for, intercede, invoke, wish on, call down on; wish ill 899 *curse*; wish one well 897 *be benevolent*; welcome, be glad of, jump at, catch at, grasp at, clutch at 786 *take*; lean towards 179 *tend*; favour, prefer, select 605 *choose*; crave, itch for, hanker after, long for; long, yearn, pine, languish; pant for, gasp f., burn f., die f., be dying f. 636 *be unsatisfied*; thirst for, hunger f., raven f. (**see** *be hungry*); can't wait, must have; like, have a liking, affect, have a taste for, care for 887 *love*; take to, warm to, fall in love with, dote, dote on, moon after, sigh a., burn 887 *be in love*; ogle, make eyes at, make passes, solicit, woo 889 *court*; set one's cap at, make a dead set at, run after, chase 619 *pursue*; lust, lust for, lust after 951 *be impure*; rut, be on heat.

be hungry, hunger, famish, starve, have an empty stomach, be ready to eat a horse 636 *be unsatisfied*; have a good appetite, open one's mouth for, water at the mouth 301 *eat*; thirst, be athirst, be dry, be dying for a drink.

cause desire, incline 612 *motivate*; arouse desire, provoke d., fill with longing 887 *excite love*; stimulate 821 *excite*; smell good, whet the appetite, make the mouth water 390 *make appetizing*; parch, raise a thirst; dangle, tease, titillate, tantalize 612 *tempt*; allure, seduce, draw 291 *attract*; hold out hope 852 *give hope*.

Adv. *desirously*, wishfully, wistfully, eagerly, with appetite, hungrily, thirstily, greedily; by request, as desired.

See: 84, 179, 279, 291, 301, 342, 386, 390, 453, 481, 492, 503, 513, 595, 597, 604, 605, 612, **617**, 619, 623, **627**, 636, 646, 695, 707, 729, 735, 737, 763, 775, 786, 816, 821, 822, 826, 830, **852**, 882, 887, 889, 890, 897, 899, 912, 915, 932, 943, 946, 947, 949, 951, 952, 981.

860 Indifference

N. *indifference*, unconcern, uninterestedness 454 *incuriosity*; lack of interest, half-heartedness, want of zeal, lukewarmness 598 *unwillingness*; coolness, coldness, faint praise, two cheers 823 *inexcitability*; unsurprise 865 *lack of wonder*; lovelessness, mutual indifference, nothing between them; anorexia, no appetite, loss of a.; inappetence, no desire for; inertia, apathy 679 *inactivity*; nonchalance, insouciance 458 *negligence*; perfunctoriness, carelessness 456 *inattention*; don't-care attitude 734 *laxity*; recklessness, heedlessness 857 *rashness*; promiscuousness 464 *indiscrimination*; amorality, indifferentism; open mind, impartiality, equity 913 *justice*; neutrality 625 *middle way*; nil admirari; six of one and half a dozen of the other; indifferentist, neutralist, neutral 625 *moderate*; Laodicean 598 *slacker*; object of indifference, wallflower.

Adj. *indifferent*, uncaring, unconcerned, insolicitous; uninterested 454 *incurious*; lukewarm, Laodicean, half-hearted 598 *unwilling*; impersonal, passionless, phlegmatic 820 *impassive*; unimpressed, unwondering, unsurprised, blasé 865 *unastonished*; calm, cool, cold 823 *inexcitable*; nonchalant, insouciant, careless, pococurante, perfunctory 458 *negligent*; supine, lackadaisical, listless 679 *inactive*; undesirous, unambitious, unaspiring; don't-care, easy-going 734 *lax*; unresponsive, unmoved, unallured, unattracted, untempted, insensible to 625 *undeviating*; loveless, heart-whole, fancy-free, uninvolved; disenchanted, disillusioned, out of love, cooling off; impartial, inflexible 913 *just*; noncommittal, moderate 625 *neutral*; promiscuous 464 *indiscriminating*; amoral, cynical.

unwanted, unwelcome, de trop; undesired, unwished for, unasked, uninvited, unbidden, unprovoked; loveless, unvalued, uncared for, unmissed 458 *neglected*; unchosen, on the shelf; all one to 606 *choiceless*; insipid, tasteless 391 *unsavoury*; unattractive, unalluring, untempting, undesirable 861 *disliked*.

Vb. *be indifferent*, - unconcerned etc. adj.; see nothing wonderful 865 *not wonder*; not have one's heart in it, take no interest 456 *be inattentive*; not mind, care little for, damn with faint praise; care nothing for, not give a fig *or* a thankyou for, not care a straw about, have no taste for, have no relish f. 861 *dislike*; couldn't care less, take it or leave it; not think twice about, not care, not give a hoot, shrug, shrug off, dismiss, let go, make light of 922 *hold cheap*; not defend, hold no brief for, take neither side 606 *be neutral*; grow indifferent, fall out of love, cool off; not repine, have no regrets; fail to move, leave one cold 820 *make insensitive*.

Int. Never mind! what does it matter! who cares! so what!

See: 391, 454, 456, 458, 464, 598, 606, 625, 679, 734, **820**, 823, 857, 861, 865, 913, 922.

861 Dislike

N. *dislike*, disinclination, no fancy for, no stomach for; reluctance, backwardness 598 *unwillingness*; displeasure 891 *resentment*; dissatisfaction 829 *discontent*; disagreement 489 *dissent*; shyness, aversion 620 *avoidance*; instinctive dislike, sudden *or* instant d., antipathy, allergy; rooted dislike, distaste, disrelish; repugnance, repulsion, disgust, abomination, abhorrence, detestation, loathing; shuddering, horror, mortal h. 854 *fear*; xenophobia 854 *phobia*; prejudice, sectarian p., odium theologicum 481 *bias*; animosity, bad blood, ill feeling, mutual hatred, common h. 888 *hatred*; nausea, queasiness, turn, heaving stomach, vomit 300 *voidance*; sickener, one's fill 863 *satiety*; gall and wormwood, bitterness 393 *sourness*; object of dislike, not one's type, bête noire, pet aversion, Dr Fell.

Adj. *disliking*, not liking, displeased 829 *discontented*; undesirous, disinclined, loath 598 *unwilling*; squeamish, qualmish, queasy; allergic, antipathetic; disagreeing 489 *dissenting*; averse, hostile 881 *inimical*; shy 620 *avoiding*; repelled, abhorring, loathing 888 *hating*; unfriendly, unloverlike, loveless; unsympathetic, out of sympathy; disenchanted, disillusioned, out of love 860 *indifferent*; sick of 863 *sated*; nauseated 300 *vomiting*.

disliked, unwished, undesired, undesirable 860 *unwanted*; unchosen 607 *rejected*; unpopular, out of favour, avoided; disagreeing, not to one's taste, grating, jarring, unrelished, bitter, uncomforting, unconsoling; repugnant, antipathetic, rebarbative, repulsive 292 *repellent*; revolting, abhorrent, loathsome 888 *hateful*; abominable, disgusting 924 *disapproved*; nauseous, nauseating, sickening, fulsome, foul, stinking 391 *unsavoury*; disagreeable, insufferable 827 *intolerable*; loveless, unlovable, unsympathetic; unlovely 842 *ugly*.

Vb. *dislike*, mislike, disrelish, find not to

one's taste; not care for, have no liking f.; have no stomach for, have no heart for 598 *be unwilling*; not choose, prefer not to 607 *reject*; object 762 *deprecate*; mind 891 *resent*; take a dislike to, feel an aversion for, have a down on 481 *be biased*; react against 280 *recoil*; feel sick at, want to heave 300 *vomit*; shun, turn away, shrink from, have no time for 620 *avoid*; look askance at 924 *disapprove*; turn up the nose at, sniff at, sneer at 922 *despise*; make a face, grimace 893 *be sullen*; be unable to abide, not endure, can't stand, detest, loathe, abominate, abhor 888 *hate*; not like the look of, shudder at 854 *fear*; unwish, wish undone 830 *regret*.

cause dislike, disincline, deter 854 *frighten*; go against the grain, rub up the wrong way, antagonize, put one's back up 891 *enrage*; set against, set at odds, make bad blood 888 *excite hate*; satiate, pall, pall on, jade 863 *sate*; disagree with, upset 25 *disagree*; put off, revolt 292 *repel*; offend, grate, jar 827 *displease*; get one's goat, get up one's nose 827 *torment*; disgust, stick in one's throat, nauseate, sicken, make one's gorge rise, turn one's stomach, make one sick; shock, scandalize, make a scandal 924 *incur blame*.

Adv. *ad nauseam*, disgustingly.

Int. ugh! horrible! yuk! revolting!

See: 25, 280, 292, 300, 391, 393, 481, 489, **598**, 607, 620, 762, 827, 829, 830, 842, 854, 860, 863, 881, 888, 891, 893, 922, 924.

862 Fastidiousness

N. *fastidiousness*, niceness, nicety, daintiness, finicalness, finicality, delicacy; discernment, perspicacity, sublety 463 *discrimination*; refinement 846 *good taste*; connoisseurship, epicurism; meticulousness, preciseness, particularity 457 *carefulness*; idealism, casuistry, artistic conscience, overdeveloped c. 917 *conscience*; perfectionism, fussiness, nit-picking, overnicety, over-refinement, hypercriticalness, donnishness, pedantry, hairsplitting; rigorism 735 *severity*; primness, prudishness, Puritanism 950 *prudery*.

perfectionist, idealist, purist, precisian, rigorist, fusspot, fussbudget, pedant, stickler, hard taskmaster; picker and chooser, gourmet, epicure.

Adj. *fastidious*, concerned with quality, quality-minded; nice, mincing, dainty, delicate, epicurean; perspicacious, discerning 463 *discriminating*; particular, demanding, choosy, finicky, finical; overnice, overparticular, scrupulous, meticulous, squeamish, qualmish 455 *attentive*; punctilious, painstaking, conscientious, overconscientious, critical, hypercritical, overcritical, fussy, pernickety, hard to please, fault-finding, censorious 924 *disapproving*; pedantic, donnish, precise, rigorous, exacting, difficult 735 *severe*; prim, puritanical 950 *prudish*.

Vb. *be fastidious*, - choosy etc. adj.; have only the best; pick and choose 605 *choose*; refine, over-refine, split hairs, mince matters 475 *argue*; draw distinctions 463 *discriminate*; find fault 924 *dispraise*; fuss, turn up one's nose, wrinkle one's n., say ugh!; look a gift horse in the mouth, feel superior, disdain 922 *despise*; keep oneself to oneself 883 *be unsociable*.

See: 455, 457, 463, 475, 605, 735, 846, 883, 917, 922, 924, 950.

863 Satiety

N. *satiety*, jadedness, fullness, repletion 54 *plenitude*; overfulness, plethora, stuffing, engorgement, saturation, saturation point 637 *redundance*; glut, surfeit, too much of a good thing 838 *tedium*; overdose, excess 637 *superfluity*; spoiled child, enfant gâté(e).

Adj. *sated*, satiated, satisfied, replete, saturated, brimming 635 *filled*; overfull, surfeited, gorged, glutted, cloyed, sick of; jaded, blasé 838 *bored*.

Vb. *sate*, satiate; satisfy, quench, slake 635 *suffice*; fill up, overfill, saturate 54 *fill*; soak 341 *drench*; stuff, gorge, glut, surfeit, cloy, jade, pall; overdose, overfeed; sicken 861 *cause dislike*; spoil, kill with kindness; bore, weary 838 *be tedious*.

See: 54, 341, 635, 637, 838, 861.

864 Wonder

N. *wonder*, state of wonder, wonderment, raptness; admiration, hero worship 887 *love*; awe, fascination; cry of wonder, gasp of admiration, whistle, wolf w., exclamation, exclamation mark; shocked silence 399 *silence*; open mouth, popping eyes; shock, surprise, surprisal 508 *lack of expectation*; astonishment, astoundment, amazement; stupor, stupefaction; bewilderment, bafflement 474 *uncertainty*; consternation 854 *fear*.

thaumaturgy, wonder-working, miracle-w., spellbinding, magic 983 *sorcery*; wonderful works, thaumatology, teratology; stroke of genius, feat, exploit 676 *deed*; transformation scene, coup de théâtre 594 *dramaturgy*.

prodigy, portent, sign, eye-opener 511 *omen*; something incredible, quite something, phenomenon, miracle, marvel, wonder; drama, sensation, cause célèbre, nine-days' wonder, annus mirabilis; object of wonder *or* admiration, wonderland, fairyland 513 *fantasy*; seven wonders of the world; sight 445 *spectacle*; infant prodigy, genius, man *or* woman of genius 696 *proficient person*; miracle-worker, thaumaturge, wizard 983 *sorcerer*; hero, heroine, wonder boy, dream girl, superwoman, bionic man, whiz kid, Admirable Crichton 646 *paragon*; freak, sport, curiosity, oddity, monster, monstrosity 84 *rara avis*; puzzle 530 *enigma*.

Adj. *wondering*, marvelling, admiring etc. vb.; awed, awestruck, fascinated, spellbound 818 *impressed*; surprised 508 *inexpectant*; astonished, amazed, astounded; in wonderment, rapt, lost in wonder, lost in amazement, unable to believe one's eyes *or* senses; wide-eyed, round-e., pop-e., with one's eyes starting out of one's head; open-mouthed, agape, gaping; dazzled, blinded; dumbfounded, dumb, struck d., inarticulate, speechless, breathless, wordless, left without words, silenced 399 *silent*; bowled over, struck all of a heap, thunderstruck; transfixed, rooted to the spot; dazed, stupefied, bewildered 517 *puzzled*; aghast, flabbergasted; shocked, scandalized 924 *disapproving*.

wonderful, to wonder at, wondrous, marvellous, miraculous, monstrous, prodigious, phenomenal; stupendous, fearful 854 *frightening*; admirable, exquisite 644 *excellent*; record-breaking 644 *best*; striking, overwhelming, awesome, awe-inspiring, breathtaking 821 *impressive*; dramatic, sensational; shocking, scandalizing; rare, exceptional, extraordinary, unprecedented 84 *unusual*; remarkable, noteworthy; strange, passing s., odd, very odd, outré, weird, weird and wonderful, unaccountable, mysterious, enigmatic 517 *puzzling*; exotic, outlandish, unheard of 59 *extraneous*; fantastic 513 *imaginary*; impossible, hardly possible, too good *or* bad to be true 472 *improbable*; unbelievable, incredible, inconceivable, unimaginable, indescribable; unutterable, unspeakable, ineffable 517 *inexpressible*; surprising 508 *unexpected*; mind-boggling, mind-blowing, astounding, amazing, shattering, bewildering etc. vb.; wonder-working, thaumaturgic; magic, like m. 983 *magical*.

Vb. *wonder*, marvel, admire, whistle; hold one's breath, gasp, gasp with admiration; hero-worship 887 *love*; stare, gaze and gaze, goggle at, gawk, open one's eyes wide, rub one's e., not believe one's e.; gape, open one's mouth, stand in amazement, look aghast 508 *not expect*; be awe-struck, be overwhelmed 854 *fear*; have no words to express, not know what to say 399 *be silent*.

be wonderful, - marvellous etc. adj.; do wonders, work miracles, achieve marvels; surpass belief, stagger b. 486 *cause doubt*; beggar all description, baffle d., beat everything; spellbind, enchant 983 *bewitch*; dazzle, strike with admiration, turn one's head 887 *excite love*; strike dumb, awe, electrify 821 *impress*; make one's eyes open, take one's breath away; bowl over, stagger; stun, daze, stupefy, petrify, dumbfound, confound, astound, astonish, amaze, flabbergast 508 *surprise*; baffle, bewilder 474 *puzzle*; startle 854 *frighten*; shock, scandalize 924 *incur blame*.

Adv. *wonderfully*, marvellously, remarkably, splendidly, fearfully; wondrous strange, strange to say, wonderful to relate, mirabile dictu, to the wonder of all.

Int. Amazing! incredible! I don't believe it! well I never! blow me down! did you ever! gosh! wow! how about that! bless my soul! 'pon my word! goodness gracious! whatever next!

See: 59, 84, 399, 445, 472, 474, 486, 508, 511, 513, 517, 530, 594, **644**, **646**, 676, 696, 818, 821, 854, 887, 924, 983.

865 Lack of wonder

N. *lack of wonder*, lack of astonishment, unastonishment, unamazement, unsurprise; awelessness, irreverence, refusal to be impressed, nil admirari; blankness, stony indifference 860 *indifference*; quietism, composure, calmness, serenity, tranquillity 266 *quietude*; imperturbability, equability, impassiveness, cold blood 820 *moral insensibility*; taking for granted 610 *habituation*; lack of imagination, unimaginativeness; disbelief 486 *unbelief*; matter of course, just what one thought, nothing to wonder at, nothing in it.

Adj. *unastonished*, unamazed, unsurprised; unawed 855 *unfearing*; accustomed 610 *habituated*; calm, collected, composed; unimpressionable, phlegmatic, impassive 820 *apathetic*; blasé, undazzled, undazed, unimpressed, unadmiring, unmoved, unstirred, unaroused 860 *indifferent*; cold-blooded, unimaginative; blind to 439 *blind*; disbelieving 486 *unbelieving*; taking for granted, expecting 507 *expectant*.

unastonishing, unsurprising, foreseen 507 *expected*; customary, common, ordinary, unimpressive, all in the day's work, nothing wonderful 610 *usual*.

Vb. *not wonder*, see nothing remarkable 820 *be insensitive*; be blind and deaf to; not believe 486 *disbelieve*; see through 516 *understand*; treat as a matter of course, take for granted, take as one's due; see it coming 507 *expect*; keep one's head 823 *keep calm*.

Int. no wonder! nothing to it! of course! why not! as expected! quite so, naturally.

See: 266, 439, 486, 507, 516, 610, **820**, 823, 855, **860**.

866 Repute

N. *repute*, good r., high r.; reputation, good r., special r.; report, good r.; title to fame, name, honoured n., great n., good n., fair n., character, known c., good c., high c., reputability, respectability 802 *credit*; regard, esteem 920 *respect*; opinion, good o., good odour, favour, high f., popular f.; popularity, vogue 848 *fashion*; acclaim, applause, approval, stamp of a., cachet 923 *approbation*.

prestige, aura, mystique, magic; glamour, dazzle, éclat, lustre, splendour; brilliance, prowess; illustriousness, glory, honour, honour and glory, kudos, succès d'estime (**see** *famousness*); esteem, estimation, account, high a., worship 638 *importance*; face, izzat, caste; degree, rank, ranking, standing, footing, status, honorary s., brevet rank 73 *serial place*; condition, position, position in society; top of the ladder *or* the tree, precedence 34 *superiority*; conspicuousness, prominence, eminence, supereminence 443 *visibility*; distinction, greatness, high rank, exaltedness, majesty 868 *nobility*; impressiveness, dignity, stateliness, solemnity, grandeur, sublimity, awesomeness; name to conjure with 178 *influence*; paramountcy, ascendancy, hegemony, primacy 733 *authority*; leadership, acknowledged l. 689 *directorship*; prestigiousness, snob value.

famousness, title to fame, celebrity, notability, remarkability; illustriousness, renown, stardom, fame, name, note; household name, synonym for; glory 727 *success*; notoriety 867 *disrepute*; talk of the town 528 *publicity*; place in history, posthumous fame 505 *memory*; undying name, immortal n., immortality, deathlessness; remembrance, commemoration, niche in the hall of fame.

honours, honour, blaze of glory, cloud of g., crown of g.; crown, martyr's c.; halo, aureole, nimbus, glory; blushing honours, battle h.; laurels, bays, wreath, garland, favour; feather, feather in one's cap 729 *trophy*; order, star, garter, ribbon, medal 729 *decoration*; spurs, sword, shield, arms 547 *heraldry*; an honour, signal h., distinction, accolade, award 962 *reward*; compliment, flattery, incense, laud, eulogy 923 *praise*; memorial, statue, bust, picture, portrait, niche, plaque, temple, monument 505 *reminder*; title of honour, dignity, handle 870 *title*; patent of nobility, knighthood, baronetcy, peerage 868 *nobility*; academic honour, baccalaureate, doctorate, degree, academic d., honours d., pass d., aegrotat d., honorary d., diploma, certificate 870 *academic title*; source of honour, fount of h., College of Arms; honours list, birthday honours, roll of honour 87 *list*.

dignification, glorification, lionization; honouring, complimenting; crowning, commemoration, coronation 876 *celebration*; sanctification, dedication, consecration, canonization, beatification; deification, apotheosis; enshrinement, enthronement; promotion, advancement, enhancement, aggrandizement 285 *progression*; exaltation 310 *elevation*; ennoblement, knighting; rehabilitation 656 *restoration*.

person of repute, honoured sir, gentle reader; worthy, sound person, good citizen, loyal subject, pillar, pillar of society, pillar of the church, pillar of the state; man *or* woman of honour 929 *honourable* person; knight, dame, peer 868 *person of rank*; somebody, great man, great woman, big shot, big noise, big name, big wheel, VIP 638 *bigwig*; someone of mark, notable, celebrity, notability, figure, public f.; champion 644 *exceller*; lion, star, rising star, luminary; man *or* woman of the hour, heroine of the hour, hero of the day, popular hero; pop singer, idol 890 *favourite*; cynosure, model, mirror 646 *paragon*; cream, cream of society 644 *elite*; choice spirit, master s., leading light 690 *leader*; grand old man, GOM 500 *sage*; noble army, great company, bevy, galaxy, constellation 74 *band*.

Adj. *reputable*, reputed, of repute, of good *or* sound reputation, of credit; creditworthy 929 *trustworthy*; gentlemanly 929 *honourable*; worthy, creditable, meritorious, prestigious 644 *excellent*; esteemed, respectable, regarded, well-r., well thought of 920 *respected*; edifying, moral 933 *virtuous*; in good odour, in favour, in high f. 923 *approved*; popular, modish 848 *fashionable*; sanctioned, allowed, admitted 756 *permitted*.

worshipful, reverend, honourable; admirable 864 *wonderful*; heroic 855 *courageous*; imposing, dignified, august, stately, grand, sublime 821 *impressive*; lofty, high 310 *elevated*; high and mighty, mighty 32 *great*; lordly, princely, kingly, queenly, majestic, royal, regal 868 *noble*; aristocratic, well-born, high-caste, heaven-born; glorious, in glory, full of g., full of honours, honoured, titled, ennobled; time-honoured, ancient, age-old 127 *immemorial*; sacrosanct, sacred, holy 979 *sanctified*; honorific, dignifying.

noteworthy, notable, remarkable, extraordinary 84 *unusual*; fabulous 864 *wonderful*; of mark, of distinction, distinguished, distingué(e) 638 *important*; conspicuous, prominent, public, in the public eye, in the limelight 443 *obvious*; eminent, preeminent, supereminent; peerless, foremost, in the forefront 34 *superior*; ranking, starring, leading, commanding; brilliant, bright, lustrous 417 *luminous*; illustrious, splendid, glorious 875 *ostentatious*.

renowned, celebrated, acclaimed, sung; of renown, of glorious name, of fame; famous, fabled, legendary, famed, far-f.; historic, illustrious, great, noble, glorious 644 *excellent*; notorious 867 *disreputable*; known as, well-known, on the map 490 *known*; of note, noted (see *noteworthy*); talked of, resounding, on all lips, on every tongue, in the news 528 *published*; unfading, never-f., evergreen, imperishable, deathless, immortal, eternal 115 *perpetual*.

Vb. *have a reputation*, enjoy a r., wear a halo; have a good name, have a name to lose; rank, stand high, have status *or* standing, have a position, enjoy consideration, be looked up to, have a name for, be praised f. 920 *command respect*; stand well with, earn golden opinions, do oneself credit, win honour, win renown, gain prestige, gain recognition, build a reputation, earn a name, acquire a character, improve one's credit 923 *be praised*; be somebody, make one's mark 730 *prosper*; win one's spurs, gain one's laurels, take one's degree, graduate 727 *succeed*; cut a figure, cut a dash, cover oneself with glory 875 *be ostentatious*; rise to fame, flash to stardom; shine, excel 644 *be good*; outshine, eclipse, steal the show, throw into the shade, overshadow 34 *be superior*; have precedence, play first fiddle, take the lead, play the l., star 64 *come before*; bask in glory, have fame, have a great name, hand down one's name to posterity; make history, live in h., be sure of immortality 505 *be remembered*.

seek repute, thirst for honour, strive for glory, nurse one's ambition; be conscious of one's reputation, consider one's position, be mindful of one's prestige 871 *be proud*; wear one's honours, show off, flaunt 871 *feel pride*; lord it, queen it, prance, strut 875 *be ostentatious*; brag 877 *boast*.

honour, revere, regard, look up to, hold in respect, hold in honour 920 *respect*; stand in awe of 854 *fear*; bow down to 981 *worship*; know how to value, appreciate, prize, value, tender, treasure 887 *love*; show honour, pay respect, pay due regard, pay one's respects to 920 *show respect*; be polite to 884 *be courteous*; compliment 925 *flatter*; grace with, honour w., dedicate to, inscribe to; praise, sing the praises, laud, glorify, acclaim 923 *applaud*; grant the palm, deck with laurels, make much of, lionize, chair, ask for one's autograph; credit, give c., honour for 907 *thank*; glorify, immortalize, eternize, commemorate, memorialize 505 *remember*; celebrate, renown, blazon 528 *proclaim*; reflect honour, redound to one's honour *or* one's credit, lend distinction *or* lustre to, do credit to, be a credit to.

dignify, glorify, exalt; canonize, beatify, deify, consecrate, dedicate 979 *sanctify*; install, enthrone, crown 751 *commission*; signalize, mark out, distinguish 547 *indicate*; aggrandize, advance, upgrade 285 *promote*; honour, delight to h., confer an h.; bemedal, beribbon 844 *decorate*; bestow a title, create, elevate, raise to the peerage, ennoble; dub, knight, give the accolade; give one his *or* her title, sir, bemadam 561 *name*; take a title, take a handle to one's name, accept a knighthood.

See:32, 34, 64, 73, 74, 84, 87, 115, 127, 178, 285, 310, 417, 443, 490, 500, 505, **528**, 547, 561, 638, 644, 646, 656, 689, 690, **727**, **729**, 730, 733, 751, 756, 802, 821, 844, 848, 854, 855, 864, 867, 868, 870, 871, 875, 876, 877, 884, 887, 890, 907, **920**, **923**, 925, 929, 933, 962, 979, 981.

867 Disrepute

N. *disrepute*, disreputableness, bad reputation, bad name, bad character, shady reputation, past; disesteem 921 *disrespect*; notoriety, infamy, ill repute, ill fame, succès de scandale; no reputation, no standing, ingloriousness, obscurity; bad odour, ill favour, disfavour, discredit, black books, bad light 888 *odium*; derogation, dishonour, disgrace, shame (**see** *slur*), smear campaign 926 *detraction*; ignominy, loss of honour, loss of reputation, faded r., withered laurels, tarnished honour, Watergate; departed glory, Ichabod; loss of face, loss of rank, demotion, degradation, reduction to the ranks, dishonourable discharge; debasement, abasement, comedown 872 *humiliation*; abjectness, baseness, vileness, turpitude 934 *wickedness*.

slur, reproach 924 *censure*; imputation, aspersion, reflection, slander, obloquy, opprobrium, abuse 926 *calumny*; slight, insult 921 *indignity*; scandal, shocking s., disgrace, shame, burning s., crying s.; defilement, pollution 649 *uncleanness*; stain, smear, smudge 649 *dirt*; stigma, brand, mark, black m., spot, blot, tarnish, taint 845 *blemish*; dirty linen; bar sinister, blot on one's scutcheon, badge of infamy, scarlet letter, mark of Cain.

object of scorn, scandalous person, reproach, byword, contempt, discredit 938 *bad person*; reject, the dregs 645 *badness*; Cinderella, poor relation 639 *nonentity*; failure 728 *loser*.

Adj. *disreputable*, not respectable, disrespectable, louche, shifty, shady 930 *rascally*; notorious, infamous, of ill fame, nefarious; arrant 645 *bad*; doubtful, dubious, questionable, objectionable 645 *not nice*; risqué, ribald, improper, indecent, obscene 951 *impure*; not thought much of, held in contempt, despised 922 *contemptible*; characterless, without references, of no repute *or* reputation; petty, pitiful 639 *unimportant*; outcast 607 *rejected*; degraded, base, abject, despicable, odious 888 *hateful*; mean, cheap, low 847 *vulgar*; shabby, squalid, dirty, scruffy 649 *unclean*; poor, down at heel, out at elbows 655 *dilapidated*; in a bad light, under a cloud, in one's bad *or* black books, in the doghouse, unable to show one's face; discredited, disgraced, in disgrace (**see** *inglorious*); reproached 924 *disapproved*; unpopular 861 *disliked*.

discreditable, no credit to, bringing discredit, reflecting upon one, damaging, compromising; ignoble, unworthy; improper, unbecoming 643 *inexpedient*; dishonourable 930 *dishonest*; despicable 922 *contemptible*; censurable 924 *blameworthy*; shameful, shame-making, disgraceful, infamous, unedifying, scandalous, shocking, outrageous, unmentionable, disgusting; too bad 645 *not nice*.

degrading, lowering, demeaning, ignominious, opprobrious, humiliating; derogatory, wounding one's honour; beneath one, beneath one's dignity, infra dig.

inglorious, without repute, without prestige, without note; without a name, nameless 562 *anonymous*; grovelling, unheroic 879 *servile*; unaspiring, unambitious 874 *modest*; unnoted, unremarked, unnoticed, unmentioned 458 *neglected*; renownless, unrenowned, unknown to fame, unheard of, obscure 491 *unknown*; unseen, unheard 444 *invisible*; unhymned, unsung, unglorified, unhonoured, undecorated; titleless 869 *plebeian*; deflated, cut down to size, debunked, humiliated 872 *humbled*; sunk low, shorn of glory, faded, withered, tarnished; stripped of reputation, discredited, creditless, disgraced, dishonoured, out of favour, in eclipse; degraded, demoted, reduced to the ranks.

Vb. *have no repute*, have no reputation, have no character, have no name to lose, have a past; have no credit, rank low, stand low in estimation, have no standing, cut no ice 639 *be unimportant*; be out of favour, be in bad odour, be unpopular, be discredited, be in disgrace, stink in the nostrils; play second fiddle, take a back seat, stay in the background 35 *be inferior*; blush unseen 444 *be unseen*.

lose repute, fall *or* go out of fashion, pass from the public eye; come down in the world, fall, sink 309 *descend*; fade, wither; fall into disrepute, incur discredit, incur dishonour, incur disgrace, achieve notoriety, get a bad name for oneself 924 *incur blame*; spoil one's record, blot one's copybook, disgrace oneself, compromise one's name, risk one's reputation, lose one's r., outlive one's r.; tarnish one's glory, forfeit one's honour, lose one's halo, lose one's good name, earn no credit, earn no honour, win no glory 728 *fail*; come down in the eyes of, forfeit one's good opinion, sink in estimation, suffer in reputation, lose prestige, lose face; admit defeat, slink away, crawl, crouch 721 *knuckle under*; look silly, look foolish, cut a sorry figure, blush for shame, laugh on the wrong side of one's mouth 497 *be absurd*; be exposed, be brought to book 963 *be punished*.

demean oneself, lower o., degrade o.; derogate, condescend, stoop, marry beneath one; compromise one's dignity, make oneself cheap, cheapen oneself, disgrace o., behave unworthily, have no sense of one's position; sacrifice one's pride, forfeit self-respect; have no pride, feel no shame, think no s.

shame, put to s., hold up to s.; pillory, expose, show up, post; scorn, mock 851 *ridicule*; snub, take down a peg or two 872 *humiliate*; discompose, disconcert, put out of countenance, put one's nose out of joint, deflate, cut down to size, debunk; strip of one's honours, deplume, degrade, downgrade, demote, disrate, reduce to the ranks, cashier, disbar, defrock, deprive, strip 963 *punish*; blackball 57 *exclude*; vilify, malign, disparage 926 *defame*; destroy one's reputation, take away one's good name, ruin one's credit; put in a bad light, reflect upon, taint; sully, mar, blacken, tarnish, stain, blot, besmear, smear, bespatter 649 *make unclean*; debase, defile, desecrate, profane 980 *be impious*; stigmatize, brand, cast a slur upon, tar 547 *mark*; dishonour, disgrace, discredit, give a bad name, bring into disrepute, bring shame upon, scandalize, be a public scandal 924 *incur blame*; heap shame upon, heap dirt u., drag through the mire; trample, tread underfoot, outrage 735 *oppress*; contemn, disdain 922 *despise*; make one blush, outrage one's modesty 951 *debauch*; not spare one's blushes, overpraise.

See: 35, 57, 309, 444, 458, 491, 497, 547, 562, 607, 639, 643, 645, 649, 655, 721, 728, 735, 845, 847, 851, 861, 869, **872**, 874, 879, 888, 921, 922, **924**, **926**, 930, 934, 938, 951, 963, 980.

868 Nobility

N. *nobility*, nobleness, distinction, rank, high r., titled r., station, order 27 *degree*; royalty, kingliness, queenliness, princeliness, majesty, prerogative 733 *authority*; birth, high b., gentle b., gentility, noblesse; descent, high d., noble d., ancestry, long a., line, unbroken l., lineage, pedigree, ancient p. 169 *genealogy*; noble family, noble house, ancient h., royal h., dynasty, royal d. 11 *family*; blood, blue b., best b.; bloodstock, caste, high c.; badge of rank, patent of nobility, coat of arms, crest 547 *heraldry*.

aristocracy, patriciate, patrician order; nobility, hereditary n., lesser n., noblesse, ancien régime; lordship, lords, peerage, House of Lords, lords spiritual and temporal; dukedom, earldom, viscountcy, baronetcy; baronage, knightage; landed interest, squirearchy, squiredom; county family, county set, gentry, landed g., gentlefolk; the great, great folk, the high and the mighty, notables; life peerage.

upper class, upper classes, upper ten, upper crust, top layer, top drawer; first families, the quality, best people, better sort, chosen few 644 *elite*; high society, social register, high life, fashionable world 848 *beau monde*; ruling class, the twice-born, the Establishment 733 *authority*; high-ups, Olympians; the haves 800 *rich person*; salaried class, salariat.

aristocrat, patrician, Olympian; person of high caste, Brahman, Rajput; descendant of the Prophet, sayyid; bloodstock, thoroughbred; senator, magnifico, magnate, dignitary; don, grandee, caballero, hidalgo; gentleman, gentlewoman, armiger; squire, squireen, buckeen, laird; boyar, Junker; emperor, king, queen, prince 741 *sovereign*; nob, swell, gent, toff 848 *fop*; panjandrum, superior person 638 *bigwig*.

person of rank, titled person, noble, nobleman *or* -woman, noble lord *or* lady, atheling, seigneur; princeling, lordling, aristo; lordship, milord; peer, hereditary p., life p.; peer of the realm, peeress; Prince of Wales, princess royal, duke, grand d., archduke, duchess; marquis, marquess, marquise, marchioness, margrave, margravine, count, countess, contessa; earl, belted e.; viscount, viscountess, baron, baroness, thane, baronet, knight, banneret, knight-bachelor, knight-banneret; rajah, bey, nawab, begum, emir, khan, sheikh 741 *potentate, governor*.

Adj. *noble*, chivalrous, knightly; gentlemanly, gentlemanlike, ladylike (**see** *genteel*); majestic, royal, regal, every inch a king *or* queen; kingly, queenly, princely, lordly; ducal, baronial, seigneurial; of royal blood, of high birth, of gentle b., of good family, pedigreed, well-born, high-b., born in the purple, born with a silver spoon in one's mouth; thoroughbred, pur sang, blue-blooded; of rank, ennobled, titled, in Debrett, in Burke's Peerage, in the Almanach de Gotha; haughty, high, exalted, high-up, grand 32 *great*.

genteel, patrician, senatorial; aristocratic, Olympian; superior, top-drawer, high-class, upper-c., cabin-c., classy, posh, U, highly respectable, comme il faut; of good breeding 848 *well-bred*.

See: 11, 27, 32, 169, 547, 638, 644, 733, **741**, 800, **848**.

869 Commonalty

N. *commonalty*, commons, third estate, bourgeoisie, middle classes, lower c.; plebs, plebeians; citizenry, demos, democracy; townsfolk, countryfolk; silent majority, grass roots; general public; people at large, populace, the people, the common p., plain p.; vulgar herd, great unwashed; the many, the many-headed, the multitude, the million, hoi polloi; the masses, mass of society, mass of the people, admass, lumpenproletariat, proletariat; the general, rank and file, ragtag and bobtail, Tom, Dick and Harry 79 *everyman*.

rabble, rabblement, mob, horde 74 *crowd*; clamjamphrie, rout, rabble r., rascal multitude, varletry; riffraff, scum, offscourings, dregs of society, canaille, cattle, vermin.

lower classes, lower orders, one's inferiors 35 *inferior*; common sort, small fry, humble folk; working class, servant c.; steerage, steerage class, lower deck; second-class citizens, the have-nots, the under-privileged; proletariat, proles;sansculottes, submerged tenth, slum population; down-and-outs, depressed class, outcasts, outcasts of society, poor whites, white trash; demi-monde, underworld, low company, low life.

middle classes, bourgeoisie 732 *averageness*; professional classes, salaried c., white-collar workers; Brown, Jones and Robinson.

commoner, bourgeois(e), plebeian, pleb; untitled person, plain Mr *or* Mrs; citizen, mere citizen, John Citizen, Joe Bloggs; one of the people, man *or* woman of the p., democrat, republican; proletarian, prole; working man *or* woman 686 *worker*; town-dweller, country-d. 191 *native*; little man, man *or* woman in the street, everyman, everywoman, common type, average t. 30 *common man*; common person, groundling, pittite, galleryite 35 *inferior*; backbencher, private; underling 742 *servant*; ranker, upstart, parvenu, social climber, arriviste, nouveau riche, philistine 847 *vulgarian*; a nobody, nobody one knows, nobody knows who 639 *nonentity*; low-caste person, Sudra, outcaste; untouchable, harijan; villein, serf 742 *slave*.

country-dweller, countryman *or* -woman, yeoman, rustic, Hodge, swain, gaffer, peasant, son *or* daughter of the soil, tiller of the soil, cultivator, ploughman 370 *farmer*; boor, churl, bog-trotter; yokel, hind, chawbacon, clod, clodhopper, rube, hayseed, hick, backwoodsman; bumpkin, country b., Tony Lumpkin, country cousin, provincial, hillbilly; village idiot 501 *ninny*.

low fellow, fellow, varlet 938 *cad*; slum-dweller 801 *poor person*; guttersnipe, mudlark, street arab, gamin, ragamuffin, tatterdemalion, sansculotte; down-and-out, tramp, bum, vagabond 268 *wanderer*;

gaberlunzie, panhandler 763 *beggar*; low type, rough t., bully, ugly customer, plug ugly, ruffian, rowdy, rough, roughneck 904 *ruffian*; rascal 938 *knave*; gangster, hood; criminal, delinquent, juvenile d. 904 *offender*; barbarian, savage, Goth, Vandal, Yahoo.

Adj. *plebeian*, common, simple, untitled, unennobled, without rank, titleless; ignoble, below the salt; below-stairs, servant-class; lower-deck, rank and file 732 *middling*; mean, low, low-down, street-corner 867 *disreputable*; lowly, base-born, low-born, low-caste, of low origin, of mean parentage, of mean extraction; slave-born, servile; humble, of low estate, of humble condition 35 *inferior*; unaristocratic, middle-class, lower m.-c., working-c., cloth-cap, non-U, proletarian; homely, homespun 573 *plain*; obscure 867 *inglorious*; coarse, brutish, uncouth, unpolished 847 *ill-bred*; unfashionable, cockney, bourgeois, Main Street, suburban, provincial, rustic; parvenu, risen from the ranks 847 *vulgar*; boorish, churlish, loutish 885 *ungracious*.

barbaric, barbarous, barbarian, wild, savage, brutish, yobbish; uncivilized, uncultured, without arts, primitive, neolithic 699 *artless*.

See: 30, 35, 74, 79, 191, 268, 370, 501, 573, 639, 686, 699, **732**, **742**, 763, 801, **847**, 867, 885, 904, 938.

870 Title

N. *title*, title to fame, entitlement, claim 915 *dueness*; title of honour, courtesy title, honorific, handle, handle to one's name; honour, distinction, order, knighthood 866 *honours*; dignified style, royal we, editorial we 875 *formality*; mode of address, Royal Highness, Serene H., Excellency, Grace, Lordship, Ladyship, noble, most n., my liege, my lord, my lady, dame; the Honourable, Right Honourable; Reverend, Very R., Right R., Most R., Monsignor, His Holiness; dom, padre; your reverence, your honour, your worship; sire, esquire, sir, dear s., madam, ma'am, master, mister, mistress, miss, Ms; monsieur, madame, mademoiselle; don, señor, señora, señorita; signore, signora, signorina; Herr, mynheer, Frau, Fraulein; babu, sahib, memsahib; bwana, effendi, mirza; citoyen, comrade, tovarich.

academic title, doctor, doctor honoris causa; doctor of philosophy, D Phil, PhD; doctor of literature, D Litt.; doctor of divinity, DD; doctor of laws, LLD; doctor of medicine, MD; doctor of music, Mus D; bachelor of arts, BA; bachelor of literature, B Litt; bachelor of science, BSc; bachelor of education B Ed; bachelor of law, BL; bachelor of music, Mus B; master of arts, MA; master of science, MSc; M Ed; M Litt, M Phil; Professor, Professor Emeritus; reader, lecturer; doctorate, baccalaureate.

See: 866, 875, 915.

871 Pride

N. *pride*, proud heart; proper pride, just p., modest p., natural p., innocent p.; self-esteem, amour propre; self-respect, self-confidence; self-admiration, conceit, self-c., swelled *or* swollen head, swank, side, puffed-out chest 873 *vanity*; snobbery, inverted s. 850 *affectation*; false pride, touchiness, prickliness 819 *moral sensibility*; dignity, reputation 866 *prestige*; stateliness, loftiness; condescension, hauteur, haughtiness, unapproachability, disdain 922 *contempt*; overweening pride, arrogance, hubris 878 *insolence*; swelling pride, pomp, pomposity, grandiosity, show, display 875 *ostentation*; self-praise, vainglory 877 *boasting*; class-consciousness, race-prejudice 481 *prejudice*; object of pride, source of p., boast, joy, pride and j. 890 *favourite*; cynosure, pick, flower 646 *paragon*.

proud person, vain p., snob, parvenu; mass of pride, pride incarnate; swelled head, swank, swankpot; prima donna, high muckamuck 638 *bigwig*; fine gentleman, grande dame 848 *fop*; turkey cock, cock of the walk, swaggerer, bragger 877 *boaster*; purse-proud plutocrat 800 *rich person*; class-conscious person 868 *aristocrat*.

Adj. *proud*, elevated, haughty, lofty, sublime 209 *high*; plumed, crested 875 *showy*; fine, grand 848 *fashionable*; grandiose, dignified, stately, statuesque 821 *impressive*; majestic, royal, kingly, queenly, lordly, aristocratic 868 *noble*; self-respecting, self-confident, proud-hearted, high-souled 855 *courageous*; high-stepping, high-spirited, high-mettled 819 *lively*; stiff-necked 602 *obstinate*; mighty, overmighty 32 *great*; imperious, commanding 733 *authoritative*; high-handed

735 *oppressive*; overweening, overbearing, hubristic, arrogant 878 *insolent*; brazen, unblushing, unabashed, flaunting, hardened 522 *undisguised*.

prideful, full of pride, blown-up with pride, flushed with p., puffed-up, inflated, swelling, swollen; overproud, high and mighty, stuck-up, toffee-nosed, snobbish, nose-in-the-air; upstage, uppish, uppity; on one's dignity, on one's high horse, on stilts; haughty, disdainful, superior, holier than thou, supercilious, hoity-toity, high-hat, patronizing, condescending 922 *despising*; standoffish, aloof, distant, unapproachable, stiff, starchy, unbending, undemocratic 885 *ungracious*; taking pride in, purse-proud, house-p; feeling pride, proud of, bursting with pride, inches taller; strutting, swaggering, vainglorious 877 *boastful*; pleased with oneself, pleased as Punch, like the cat that got the cream; cocky, bumptious, conceited 873 *vain*; pretentious 850 *affected*; swanky, swanking, pompous 875 *showy*; proud as Lucifer, proud as a peacock.

Vb. *be proud*, have one's pride, have one's self-respect, be jealous of one's honour, guard one's reputation, hold one's head high, stand erect, refuse to stoop, bow to no one, stand on one's dignity, mount one's high horse; give oneself airs, toss one's head, hold one's nose in the air, think it beneath one, be too proud to, be too grand to; be stuck-up, swank, show off, swagger, strut 875 *be ostentatious*; condescend, patronize; look down on, disdain 922 *despise*; display hauteur 878 *be insolent*; lord it, queen it, come it over, throw one's weight about, overween 735 *oppress*.

feel pride, swell with p., take pride in, glory in, boast of, not blush for 877 *boast*; hug oneself, congratulate o., pat o. on the back 824 *be pleased*; be flattered, flatter oneself, pride o., pique o., plume o., preen o., think a lot of oneself, think too much of o. 873 *be vain*.

See: 32, 209, 481, 522, 602, 638, 646, 733, 735, 800, 819, 821, 824, 848, 850, 855, 866, 868, **873**, **875**, 877, **878**, 885, 890, 922.

872 Humility. Humiliation

N. *humility*, humbleness, humble spirit 874 *modesty*; abasement, lowness, lowliness; unpretentiousness, quietness; harmlessness, inoffensiveness 935 *innocence*; meekness, resignation, submissiveness 721 *submission*; self-knowledge, self-depreciation, self-abnegation, self-effacement, self-abasement, kenosis 931 *disinterestedness*; condescension, stooping 884 *courtesy*; humble person, no boaster, mouse, violet.

humiliation, abasement, humbling, let-down, setdown, climbdown, comedown, slap in the face 921 *indignity*; crushing retort; rebuke 924 *reprimand*; shame, disgrace 867 *disrepute*; sense of shame, sense of disgrace, blush, suffusion, confusion; shamefaced look, hangdog expression; chastening thought, mortification, hurt pride, injured p., offended dignity 891 *resentment*.

Adj. *humble*, not proud, humble-minded, self-deprecating, poor in spirit, lowly; meek, submissive, resigned, unprotesting 721 *submitting*; self-effacing, self-abnegating 931 *disinterested*; self-abasing, stooping, condescending 884 *courteous*; mouselike, harmless, inoffensive, unoffending 935 *innocent*; unassuming, unpretentious, without airs, without side 874 *modest*; mean, low 639 *unimportant*; of lowly birth 869 *plebeian*.

humbled, broken-spirited, bowed down; chastened, crushed, dashed, abashed, crestfallen, chapfallen, sheepish, disconcerted, out of countenance 834 *dejected*; humiliated, let down, set d., taken d., cut down to size, squashed, deflated, debunked; not proud of, ashamed 939 *repentant*; mortified, shamed, blushing 867 *inglorious*; scorned, rebuked 924 *disapproved*; brought low, discomfited 728 *defeated*.

Vb. *be humble*, - lowly etc. adj.; have no sense of pride, humble oneself 867 *demean oneself*; play second fiddle 874 *be modest*; put others first 931 *be disinterested*; condescend, unbend 884 *be courteous*; stoop, bow down, crawl, sing small, eat humble pie 721 *knuckle under*; put up with insolence, turn the other cheek, stomach, pocket 909 *forgive*.

be humbled, - humiliated etc. adj.; receive a snub, be taken down a peg; be ashamed, be ashamed of oneself, feel shame; blush, colour up 431 *redden*; feel small, hide one's face, hang one's head, avert one's eyes, have nothing to say for oneself, wish to sink through the floor, wish the earth would swallow one up; stop swanking, come off it.

humiliate, humble, chasten, abash, disconcert, put to the blush; lower, take down a peg, debunk, deflate; make one feel small, make one sing small, teach one his *or* her place, make one crawl, rub one's nose in the dirt; snub, cut, crush, squash, sit on, send away with a flea in their ear 885 *be rude*; slight 921 *not respect*; mortify, hurt one's pride, offend one's dignity, lower in all men's eyes, put to shame 867 *shame*; score off, put one's nose out of joint, make a fool of, make one look silly 542 *befool*; put in the shade 306 *outdo*; outstare, outfrown, frown down, wither, daunt 854 *frighten*; get the better of, triumph over, crow o. 727 *overmaster*.

See: 306, 431, 542, 639, 721, 727, 728, 834, 854, **867**, 869, **874**, 884, 885, 891, 909, 921, 924, 931, 935, 939.

873 Vanity

N. *vanity*, emptiness 4 *insubstantiality*; vain pride, empty p., idle p. 871 *pride*; immodesty, conceit, conceitedness, self-importance, megalomania; swank, side, puffed-up chest, swollen head; cockiness, bumptiousness, assurance, self-a.; good opinion of oneself, self-conceit, self-esteem, amour propre; self-satisfaction, smugness; self-love, self-admiration, narcissism; self-complacency, self-approbation, self-praise, self-applause, self-flattery, self-congratulation, self-glorification, vainglory 877 *boasting*; self-sufficiency, self-centredness, egotism 932 *selfishness*; exhibitionism, showing off, self-display 875 *ostentation*; Vanity Fair 848 *beau monde*.

airs, fine a., airs and graces, mannerisms, pretensions, absurd p. 850 *affectation*; swank, pompousness 875 *ostentation*; coxcombry, priggishness, foppery.

vain person, self-admirer, Narcissus; self-centred person, egotist, coxcomb 848 *fop*; exhibitionist, peacock, show-off; know-all, bighead, God's gift to women; smarty-pants, smart aleck, cleverstick, Mr Clever, Miss Clever 500 *wiseacre*; stuffed shirt, pompous twit 4 *insubstantial thing*.

Adj. *vain*, conceited, overweening, stuck-up, proud 871 *prideful*; egotistic, egocentric, self-centred, self-satisfied, self-complacent, full of oneself, self-important 932 *selfish*; smug, complacent, pleased with oneself; self-admiring, self-loving, narcissistic, stuck on oneself; wise in one's own conceit, dogmatic, opinionated, oversubtle, overclever, clever clever, too clever by half 498 *intelligent*; swollen-headed, puffed-up, too big for one's boots, bigheaded, bumptious, cocky, perky, smart-alecky, smart-ass 878 *insolent*; immodest, blatant; showing off, swaggering, vainglorious, self-glorious 877 *boastful*; pompous 875 *ostentatious*; pretentious, soi-disant, so-called; coxcombical, fantastical, putting on airs 850 *affected*.

Vb. *be vain*, - conceited etc. adj.; have a swelled head, have one's head turned; have a high opinion of oneself, set a high value on o., think a lot of o., think too much of o., think oneself the cat's pyjamas, think o. God Almighty; exaggerate one's own merits, blow one's own trumpet 877 *boast*; admire oneself, hug o., flatter o.; plume oneself, preen o., pride o. 871 *feel pride*; swank, strut, show off, put on airs, show one's paces, display one's talents, talk for effect, talk big, not hide one's light under a bushel, push oneself forward 875 *be ostentatious*; lap up flattery, fish for compliments; get above oneself, have pretensions, give oneself airs 850 *be affected*; play the fop, be overconcerned with one's appearance, dress up, dandify 843 *primp*.

make conceited, fill with conceit, puff up, inflate, give a swelled head to, go to one's head, turn one's h. 925 *flatter*; take one at his *or* her own valuation.

Adv. *conceitedly*, vainly, vaingloriously, swankily.

See: 4, 498, 500, 843, 848, **850**, **871**, **875**, 877, 878, 925, 932.

874 Modesty

N. *modesty*, lack of ostentation, unboastfulness, shyness, retiring disposition; diffidence, constraint, self-distrust, timidness, timidity 854 *nervousness*; mauvaise honte, overmodesty, prudishness 950 *prudery*; bashfulness, blushing, blush; pudency, shamefacedness, shockability; chastity 950 *purity*; deprecation, self-depreciation, self-effacement 872 *humility*; unobtrusiveness, unpretentiousness, unassuming nature; demureness, reserve; hidden merit; modest person, shy thing, shrinking violet, mouse.

Adj. *modest*, without vanity, free from

pride; self-effacing, unobtrusive, unseen, unheard 872 *humble*; self-deprecating, unboastful; unassertive, unpushing, unthrustful, unambitious; quiet, unassuming, unpretentious, unpretending; unimposing, unimpressive, moderate, mediocre 639 *unimportant*; shy, retiring, shrinking, timid, diffident, unselfconfident, unsure of oneself 854 *nervous*; overshy, awkward, constrained, embarrassed, inarticulate; deprecating, demurring; bashful, blushful, blushing, rosy; shamefaced, sheepish; reserved, demure, coy; shockable, overmodest, prudish 850 *affected*; chaste 950 *pure*.

Vb. *be modest*, show moderation, ration oneself 942 *be temperate*; not blow one's trumpet, have no ambition, shrink from notoriety; efface oneself, yield precedence 872 *be humble*; play second fiddle, keep in the background, take a back seat, know one's place; blush unseen, shun the limelight, hide one's light under a bushel 456 *escape notice*; not look for praise, do good by stealth and blush to find it fame; retire, creep into one's shell, shrink, hang back, be coy 620 *avoid*; show bashfulness, feel shame, stand blushing, blush, colour, crimson, mantle 431 *redden*; preserve one's modesty 933 *be virtuous*.

Adv. *modestly*, quietly, soberly, demurely; unpretentiously, sans façon, without fuss, without ceremony, privately, without beat of drum.

See: 431, 456, 620, 639, 850, 854, 872, 933, 942, 950.

875 Ostentation. Formality

N. *ostentation*, demonstration, display, parade, show 522 *manifestation*; unconcealment, blatancy, flagrancy, shamelessness, brazenness, exhibitionism 528 *publicity*; ostentatiousness, showiness, magnificence, ideas of m., delusions of grandeur, grandiosity; splendour, brilliance; self-consequence, self-importance 873 *vanity*; pomposity, fuss, swagger, showing off, pretension, pretensions, airs and graces 873 *airs*; swank, side, thrown-out chest, strut; machismo, bravado, heroics 877 *boast*; theatricality, histrionics, dramatization, dramatics, sensationalism 546 *exaggeration*; demonstrativeness, back-slapping, bonhomie 882 *sociability*; showmanship, effect, window-dressing; solemnity (**see** *formality*); grandeur, dignity, stateliness, impressiveness; declamation, rhetoric 574 *magniloquence*; flourish, flourish of trumpets, fanfaronade, big drum 528 *publication*; pageantry, pomp, circumstance, pomp and c., bravery, pride, panache, waving plumes, fine feathers, flying colours, dash, splash, splurge 844 *finery*; frippery, gaudiness, glitter, tinsel 844 *ornamentation*; idle pomp, idle show, false glitter, unsubstantial pageant, mummery, mockery, idle m., hollow m., solemn m. 4 *insubstantiality*; tomfoolery 497 *foolery*; travesty 20 *mimicry*; exterior, gloss, veneer, polish, varnish 223 *exteriority*; pretence, profession 614 *pretext*; insincerity, lip service 542 *deception*.

formality, state, stateliness, dignity; ceremoniousness, stiffness, starchiness; royal we, editorial we 870 *title*; ceremony, ceremonial 988 *ritual*; drill, smartness, spit and polish; correctness, correctitude, protocol, form, good f., right f. 848 *etiquette*; punctilio, punctiliousness, preciseness 455 *attention*; routine, fixed r. 610 *practice*; solemnity, formal occasion, ceremonial o., state o., function, grand f., official f., red carpet 876 *celebration*; full dress, court d., robes, regalia, finery 228 *formal dress*; correct dress 228 *uniform*.

pageant, show 522 *exhibit*; fete, gala, gala performance, tournament, tattoo; field day, great doings 876 *celebration*; son et lumière 445 *spectacle*; set piece, tableau, scene, transformation s., stage effect 594 *stage set*; display, bravura, stunt; pyrotechnics 420 *fireworks*; carnival, Lord Mayor's Show 837 *festivity, revel*; procession, promenade, march-past, flypast; changing the guard, trooping the colour; turnout, review, grand r., parade, array 74 *assembly*.

Adj. *ostentatious*, showy, pompous; aiming at effect, striving for e., done for e.; window-dressing, for show; prestige, for p., for the look of the thing; specious, seeming, hollow 542 *spurious*; consequential, self-important; pretentious, would-be 850 *affected*; showing off, swanking, swanky 873 *vain*; inflated, turgid, orotund, windy, magniloquent, declamatory, high-sounding, high-flown 574 *rhetorical*; grand, highfalutin, splendiferous, splendid, brilliant, magnificent, grandiose, posh; superb, royal 813 *liberal*; sumptuous, diamond-studded, luxurious, de luxe, plushy, ritzy, costly, expensive, expense-account 811 *dear*; painted, glorified, tarted up.

showy, flashy, dressy, dressed to kill, foppish 848 *fashionable*; colourful, lurid, gaudy, gorgeous 425 *florid*; tinsel, glittering, garish 847 *vulgar*; flaming, flaring, flaunting, flagrant, blatant, public; brave, dashing, gallant, gay, jaunty, rakish, sporty; spectacular, scenic, dramatic, histrionic, theatrical, stagy; sensational, daring; exhibitionist, stunting.

formal, dignified, solemn, stately, majestic, grand, fine; ceremonious, standing on ceremony, punctilious, stickling, correct, precise, stiff, starchy; black-tie, white-tie, full-dress; of state, public, official; ceremonial, ritual 988 *ritualistic*; for a special occasion 876 *celebratory*.

Vb. *be ostentatious*, - showy etc. adj.; observe the formalities, stand on ceremony; splurge, cut a dash, make a splash, make a figure; glitter, dazzle 417 *shine*; flaunt, sport 228 *wear*; dress up 843 *primp*; wave, flourish 317 *brandish*; blazon, trumpet, beat the big drum 528 *proclaim*; stage a demonstration, wave banners 711 *defy*; demonstrate, exhibit 522 *show*; act the showman, make a display, put on a show; make the most of, put on a front, window-dress, stage-manage; see to the outside, paper the cracks, polish, veneer 226 *coat*; intend for effect, strive for e., sensationalize; talk for effect, shoot a line 877 *boast*; take the centre of the stage, grab the limelight 455 *attract notice*; put oneself forward, advertise oneself, dramatize o.; play to the gallery, fish for compliments 850 *be affected*; show off, show one's paces, prance, promenade, swan around; parade, march, march past, fly past; peacock, strut, swank, put on side 873 *be vain*; make an exhibition of oneself, make people stare.

See: 4, 20, 74, 223, 226, 228, 317, 417, 420, 425, 445, 455, 497, 522, 528, 542, 546, 574, 594, 610, 614, 711, 811, 813, 837, 843, 844, 847, 848, **850**, 870, **873**, 876, **877**, 882, 988.

876 Celebration

N. *celebration*, performance, solemnization 676 *action*; commemoration 505 *remembrance*; observance, solemn o. 988 *ritual*; ceremony, function, occasion, do; formal occasion, coronation, enthronement, inauguration, installation, presentation 751 *commission*; debut, coming out 68 *beginning*; reception, welcome, hero's w., tickertape w., red-carpet treatment 875 *formality*; official reception 923 *applause*; festive occasion, fete, jubilee, diamond j. 837 *festivity*; jubilation, cheering, ovation, triumph, salute, salvo, tattoo, roll, roll of drums, fanfare, fanfaronade, flourish of trumpets, flying colours, flag waving, mafficking 835 *rejoicing*; flags, streamers, decorations, Chinese lanterns, illuminations; firework display 420 *fireworks*; bonfire 379 *fire*; triumphal arch 729 *trophy*; harvest home, thanksgiving, Te Deum 907 *thanks*; paean, hosanna, halleluja 886 *congratulation*; health, toast.

special day, day to remember, great day, red-letter d., gala d., flag d., field d.; saint's day, feast d., fast d. 988 *holy day*; Armistice Day, D-Day, Remembrance Sunday; Fourth of July, Independence Day, Republic D.; birthday, name day; wedding anniversary, silver wedding, golden w., diamond w., ruby w.; centenary, bicentenary, sesquicentenary 141 *anniversary*.

Adj. *celebratory*, celebrating, signalizing, observing, commemorative 505 *remembering*; occasional, anniversary, centennial, bicentennial, millennial 141 *seasonal*; festive, jubilant 835 *rejoicing*; triumphant, triumphal; welcoming, honorific 886 *congratulatory*.

Vb. *celebrate*, solemnize, perform 676 *do*; hallow, keep holy, keep sacred 979 *sanctify*; commemorate 505 *remember*; honour, observe, keep, keep up, maintain; signalize, make it an occasion, mark the o.; make much of, welcome, kill the fatted calf, do one proud 882 *be hospitable*; do honour to, fete; chair, carry shoulder-high 310 *elevate*; mob, rush 61 *rampage*; garland, wreathe, crown 962 *reward*; lionize, give a hero's welcome, fling wide the gates, roll out the red carpet, hang out the flags, beat a tattoo, blow the trumpets, clash the cymbals, fire a salute, fire a salvo, fire a feu de joie 884 *pay one's respects*; cheer, jubilate, triumph, maffick 835 *rejoice*; make holiday 837 *revel*; instate, present, inaugurate, launch, install, induct 751 *commission;* make one's debut, come out 68 *begin*.

toast, pledge, clink glasses; drink to, raise one's glass to, fill one's glass to, drain a bumper, drink a health 301 *drink*.

Adv. *in honour of*, in memory of, in celebration of, on the occasion of; to mark the o.

See: 61, 68, 141, 301, 310, 379, 420, 505, 676, 729, 751, **835**, 837, 875, 882, 884, **886**, 907, 923, 962, 979, 988.

877 Boasting

N. *boasting*, bragging, boastfulness, vainglory, braggadocio, braggartism; jactation 875 *ostentation*; self-glorification, self-advertisement, swagger, swank, bounce 873 *vanity*; advertisement 528 *publicity*; puffery 482 *overestimation*; grandiloquence, rodomontade, vapouring, gassing, fine talk 515 *empty talk*; swaggering, swashbuckling, heroics, bravado; flag-wagging *or* -waving, chauvinism, jingoism, spread-eagleism 481 *bias*; defensiveness, blustering, bluster 854 *nervousness*; sabre-rattling, intimidation 900 *threat*.

boast, brag, vaunt; puff, hype 528 *advertisement*; gasconade, flourish, fanfaronade, bravado, bombast, rant, rodomontade, fustian, tall talk 546 *exaggeration*; hot air, gas, bunkum 515 *empty talk*; bluff, bounce 542 *deception*; presumptuous challenge 711 *defiance*; big talk, big drum, bluster, hectoring, idle threat 900 *threat*.

boaster, vaunter, swaggerer, braggart, braggadocio, macho; brag, big-mouth, loudmouth, shouter, prater, gasbag; blagueur, blusterer, charlatan, pretender 545 *impostor*; bouncer, bluffer 545 *liar*; swank, show-off 873 *vain person*; swashbuckler, gasconader, Gascon, Thraso, Matamore, Bobadil, Scaramouch, Pistol, miles gloriosus; advertiser, puffer 528 *publicizer*; flourisher, fanfaron, trumpeter; ranter, hot air merchant; jingoist, chauvinist; sabre-rattler, intimidator.

Adj. *boastful*, boasting, bragging, vaunting, big-mouthed; braggart, swaggering 875 *ostentatious*; vainglorious, self-glorifying 873 *vain*; bellicose, sabre-rattling, jingoistic, chauvinistic 718 *warlike*; bluffing, hollow, pretentious, empty 542 *spurious*; bombastic, magniloquent, grandiloquent 546 *exaggerated*; flushed, exultant, triumphant, cock-a-hoop 727 *successful*.

Vb. *boast*, brag, vaunt, gab, gasconade, talk big, shoot a line, bluff, huff and puff, bluster, hector, shout; bid defiance 711 *defy*; vapour, prate, rant, gas 515 *mean nothing*; enlarge, magnify 546 *exaggerate*; trumpet, parade, flaunt, show off 528 *publish*; puff, crack up, cry one's wares 528 *advertise*; sell oneself, advertise o., blow one's own trumpet, bang the big drum 875 *be ostentatious*; flourish, wave 317 *brandish*; play the jingo, rattle the sabre 900 *threaten*; show off, strut, swagger, prance, swank, throw out one's chest 873 *be vain*; gloat, pat oneself on the back, hug oneself 824 *be pleased*; boast of, plume oneself on 871 *be proud*; glory in, crow over 727 *triumph*; jubilate, exult 835 *rejoice*.

See: 317, 481, 482, **515**, 528, 542, 545, **546**, 711, 718, 727, 824, 835, 854, 871, **873**, **875**, 900.

878 Insolence

N. *insolence*, hubris, arrogance, haughtiness, loftiness 871 *pride*; domineering, tyranny 735 *severity*; bravado 711 *defiance*; bluster 900 *threat*; disdain 922 *contempt*; sneer, sneering 926 *detraction*; contumely, contumelious behaviour 899 *scurrility*; assurance, self-a., self-assertion, bumptiousness, cockiness, brashness; presumption 916 *arrogation*; audacity, hardihood, boldness, effrontery, chutzpah, shamelessness, brazenness, blatancy, flagrancy; face, front, hardened f., brazen face.

sauciness, disrespect, impertinence, impudence, pertness; flippancy, nerve, gall, brass, cheek, cool c., neck; lip, mouth, sauce, snook, V-sign 547 *gesture*; taunt, personality, insult, affront 921 *indignity*; rudeness, incivility, throwaway manner 885 *discourtesy*; petulance, defiance, answer, provocation, answering back, backtalk, backchat 460 *rejoinder*; raillery, banter 851 *ridicule*.

insolent person, saucebox, impertinent, jackanapes, cheeky devil; minx, hussy, baggage, madam; whippersnapper, pup, puppy; upstart, beggar on horseback, Jack-in-office, tin god 639 *nonentity*; blusterer, swaggerer, braggart 877 *boaster*; bantam-cock, cockalorum 871 *proud person*; bully, hoodlum, roisterer, swashbuckler, fire-eater, desperado 904 *ruffian*.

Adj. *insolent*, bellicose 718 *warlike*; rebellious 711 *defiant*; sneering 926 *detracting*; insulting, calumnious 921 *disrespectful*; injurious, scurrilous 899 *cursing*; lofty, supercilious, disdainful, contemptuous 922 *despising*; undemocratic, snobbish, haughty, snooty, up-stage, high-hat, high and mighty 871 *proud*; hubristic, arrogant, presumptuous, assuming; brash, bumptious, bouncing 873 *vain*; flagrant, blatant; shameless, lost to shame, unblushing, unabashed, brazen, brazen-faced, bold as brass; bold, hardy, audacious 857 *rash*; overweening, overbearing, domineering, imperious, magisterial, lordly, dictatorial, arbitrary, high-handed, harsh, tyrannical 735 *oppressive*; blustering, bullying, fire-eating, ruffianly 877 *boastful*.

impertinent, pert, malapert, forward, fresh; impudent, saucy, cheeky, brassy, cool, jaunty, perky, cocky, cocksure, flippant, flip; cavalier, offhand, familiar, overfamiliar, free-and-easy, devil-may-care, breezy, airy 921 *disrespectful*; impolite, rude, uncivil, ill-mannered 885 *discourteous*; defiant, answering back, provocative, deliberately p., offensive; personal, ridiculing 851 *derisive*.

Vb. *be insolent*, - arrogant etc. adj.; forget one's manners, get personal 885 *be rude*; have a nerve, cheek, sauce, give lip, taunt, provoke 891 *enrage*; have the audacity to, have the cheek to; retort, answer back 460 *answer*; shout down 479 *confute*; get above oneself, get above one's station, teach one's grandmother to suck eggs; not know one's place, presume, arrogate, assume, take on oneself, make bold to, make free with, get fresh; put on airs, hold one's nose in the air, look one up and down 871 *be proud*; look down on, sneer at 922 *despise*; banter, rally 851 *ridicule*; express contempt, sniff, snort; not give a fig 860 *be indifferent*; cock a snook, put one's tongue out, give the V-sign, send to blazes 711 *defy*; outstare, outlook, outface, brazen it out; take a high tone, lord it, queen it, lord it over; lay down the law, throw one's weight around; hector, bully, browbeat, trample on, ride roughshod over, treat with a high hand 735 *oppress*; swank, swagger, swell, look big 873 *be vain*; brag, talk big 877 *boast*; brook no restraint, own no law, be a law unto oneself 738 *disobey*; defy nemesis, provoke the gods, tempt providence.

Adv. *insolently*, impertinently, pertly; arrogantly, hubristically, outrageously.

See: 460, 479, 547, 639, 711, 718, 735, 738, 851, 857, 860, **871**, 873, **877**, 885, 891, 899, 900, 904, 916, 921, 922, 926.

879 Servility

N. *servility*, slavishness, abject spirit, no pride, lack of self-respect 856 *cowardice*; subservience 721 *submission*; submissiveness, obsequiousness, compliance, pliancy 739 *obedience*; time-serving 603 *tergiversation*; abasement 872 *humility*; prostration, genuflexion, stooping, bent back, bow, scrape, duck, bob 311 *obeisance*; truckling, cringing, crawling, fawning, bootlicking, bumsucking, toadyism, sycophancy, ingratiation 925 *flattery*; flunkeyism 745 *service*; servile condition, slavery 745 *servitude*.

toady, toad-eater; time-server, collaborator, Uncle Tom; yes-man, rubber stamp 488 *assenter*; lickspittle, bootlicker, back-scratcher, bumsucker, groveller, truckler, crawler, creep; hypocrite, creeping Jesus, Uriah Heep 850 *affecter*; spaniel, fawner, courtier, fortune-hunter, tuft-h., lion-h. 925 *flatterer*; sycophant, parasite, leech, sponger, freeloader; jackal, hanger-on, gigolo 742 *dependant*; flunkey, lackey 742 *retainer*; born slave, slave; lapdog, poodle; tool, creature, cat's-paw 628 *instrument*.

Adj. *servile*, not free, dependent 745 *subject*; slavish 856 *cowardly*; mean-spirited, mean, abject, base, tame 745 *subjected*; subservient, submissive, deferential 721 *submitting*; pliant, compliant, supple 739 *obedient*; time-serving 603 *tergiversating*; bowed, stooping, prostrate, grovelling, truckling, bowing, scraping, cringing, cowering, crawling, sneaking, fawning; begging, whining; toadying, toadyish, sycophantic, parasitical; creepy, obsequious, unctuous, soapy, oily, slimy, overcivil, overattentive, ingratiating 925 *flattering*.

Vb. *be servile*, forfeit one's self-respect, stoop to anything 867 *demean oneself*; squirm, roll, sneak, cringe, crouch, creep, crawl, grovel, truckle, kiss the hands of, kiss the hem of one's garment, lick the boots of 721 *knuckle under*; bow, scrape, bend, bob, duck, kowtow, make obeisance, kneel 311 *stoop*; swallow insults 872 *be humble*; make up to, toady to, suck up to, spaniel, fawn, ingratiate oneself, pay court to, curry favour, worm oneself into f. 925 *flatter*; squire, attend, dance attendance on, fetch and carry for 742 *serve*; comply 739 *obey*; be the tool of, do one's dirty work, pander to, stooge for 628 *be instrumental*; whine, wheedle, beg for favours, beg for crumbs 761 *beg*; play the parasite, batten on, sponge, sponge on; jump on the band wagon, run with the hare and hunt with the hounds 83 *conform*; serve the times 603 *tergiversate*.

Adv. *servilely*, slavishly, with servility, with a bow and a scrape, cap in hand, touching one's forelock.

See: 83, 311, 488, 603, 628, 721, 739, **742**, 745, 761, 850, 856, 867, 872, **925**.

Section three: Interpersonal emotion

880 Friendship

N. *friendship*, bonds of f., amity 710 *concord*; compatibility, mateyness, chumminess; friendly relations, relations of friendship, friendly intercourse, social i., hobnobbing 882 *sociality*; companionship, belonging, togetherness; alignment, fellowship, comradeship, sodality, freemasonry, brotherhood, sisterhood 706 *association*; solidarity, support, mutual s. 706 *cooperation*; acquaintanceship, acquaintance, mutual a., familiarity, intimacy 490 *knowledge*; fast friendship, close f., warm f., cordial f., passionate f. 887 *love*; making friends, getting acquainted, introduction, recommendation, commendation; overtures, rapprochement 289 *approach*; renewal of friendship, reconciliation 719 *pacification*.

friendliness, amicability, kindliness, kindness, neighbourliness 884 *courtesy*; heartiness, cordiality, warmth 897 *benevolence*; fraternization, camaraderie, mateyness; hospitality 882 *sociability*; greeting, welcome, open arms, handclasp, handshake, hug, rubbing noses 884 *courteous act*; regard, mutual r. 920 *respect*; goodwill, mutual g.; fellow feeling, sympathy, response 775 *participation*; understanding, friendly u., good u., same wavelength, entente, entente cordiale, honeymoon 710 *concord*; partiality 481 *prejudice*; favouritism, partisanship 914 *injustice*; support, loyal s. 703 *aid*.

friend, girlfriend, boyfriend 887 *loved one*; one's friends and acquaintances, acquaintance, intimate a.; friend of the family, lifelong friend, mutual f., friend's f.; crony, old c. (**see** *chum*); neighbour, good n., fellow townsman *or* -woman, fellow countryman *or* -woman; cousin, clansman 11 *kinsman*; well-wisher, favourer, partisan, backer 707 *patron*; second 660 *protector*; fellow, sister, brother, soul brother *or* sister; confrère, partner, associate 707 *colleague*; ally, brother-in-arms 707 *auxiliary*; collaborator, helper, friend in need 703 *aider*; invitee, guest, welcome g., frequent visitor, persona grata; young friend, protégé(e); host, kind h. 882 *sociable person*; former friend, fairweather f. 603 *tergiversator*.

close friend, best f.; soul mate, kindred spirit; best man, bridesmaid 894 *bridal party*; dear friend, good f., close f., fast f., firm f., loyal f., f. in need; intimate, bosom friend, bosom pal, confidant(e), fidus Achates; alter ego, other self, shadow; comrade, companion, boon c., drinking c.; good friends all, happy family; mutual friends, inseparables, band of brothers *or* sisters, Three Musketeers, David and Jonathan, Ruth and Naomi, Castor and Pollux; two minds with but a single thought, Arcades ambo, birds of a feather.

chum, crony; pal, mate, amigo, cobber, copain, buddy, butty, sidekick; fellow, comrade, shipmate, messmate, roommate, stable companion 707 *colleague*; playmate, classmate, schoolmate, schoolfellow; pen friend, pen pal; hearties, my h.

xenophile, Anglophile, Francophile, Russophile, Sinophile, friend of all the world 901 *philanthropist*.

Adj. *friendly*, nonhostile, amicable, well-affected, devoted 887 *loving*; loyal, faithful, staunch, fast, firm, tested, tried 929 *trustworthy*; fraternal, brotherly, sisterly, cousinly; natural, unstrained, easy, harmonious 710 *concordant*; compatible, congenial, sympathetic, understanding; well-wishing, well-meaning, well-intentioned, philanthropic 897 *benevolent*; hearty, cordial, warm, welcoming, hospitable 882 *sociable*; effusive, demonstrative, back-slapping, hail-fellow-well-met; comradely, chummy, pally, matey; friendly with, good friends w., at home w.; acquainted 490 *knowing*; free and easy, on familiar terms, on visiting t., on intimate t., on the best of t., well in with, intimate, inseparable, thick, thick as thieves, hand in glove.

Vb. *be friendly,* be friends with, get on well w., be on friendly terms w.; have neighbourly relations, have dealings w., rub along w.; fraternize, hobnob, keep company with, keep up w., keep in w., go about together, be inseparable 882 *be sociable*; have friends, make f., win f., have a wide circle of friends, have many friendships, have a large acquaintance; shake hands, clasp h., embrace 884 *greet*; welcome, entertain 882 *be hospitable*; sympathize 516 *understand*; like, warm to, become fond of 887 *love*; mean well, have the best intentions, have the friendliest feelings 897 *be benevolent*.

befriend, acknowledge, know, accept one's friendship; take up, favour, protect 703 *patronize*; overcome hostility, gain one's friendship; extend the right hand of fellowship, make welcome; strike up an acquaintance, scrape an a., knit friendship; break the ice, make overtures 289 *approach*; seek one's friendship, cultivate one's f., pay one's addresses to 889 *court*; take to, warm to, click with, hit it off; fraternize with, frat, hobnob, get pally with, get chummy w., chum up w., make friends w.; make acquainted, make known to each other, introduce, present, commend; renew friendship, become reconciled, shake hands 719 *make peace*.

Adv. *amicably,* in a friendly spirit; as friends, arm in arm; heartily, cordially.

See: 11, 289, 481, 490, 516, 603, 660, 703, 706, 707, 710, 719, 775, **882**, 884, **887**, 889, 894, 897, 901, 914, 920, 929.

881 Enmity

N. *enmity,* inimicality, hostility, antagonism 704 *opposition*; no love lost, unfriendliness, incompatibility, antipathy 861 *dislike*; loathing 888 *hatred*; animosity, animus, spite, grudge, ill feeling, ill will, bad blood, intolerance, persecution 898 *malevolence*; jealousy 912 *envy*; coolness, coldness 380 *ice*; estrangement, alienation, strain, tension, no honeymoon 709 *dissension*; bitterness, bitter feelings, hard f., rancour, soreness 891 *resentment*; unfaithfulness, disloyalty 930 *perfidy*; breach, open b., breach of friendship 709 *quarrel*; hostile act 709 *casus belli*; conflict, hostilities, state of war 718 *belligerency*; vendetta, feud.

enemy, no friend, bad f., unfriend; ex-friend 603 *tergiversator*; traitor, viper in one's bosom 663 *troublemaker*; bad neighbour, ill-wisher; antagonist, opposite side, other s. 705 *opponent*; competitor, rival 716 *contender*; open enemy, foe, foeman, hostile force 722 *combatant*; aggressor 712 *attacker*; enemy within the gates, fifth column, Trojan Horse; public enemy, outlaw, pirate 789 *robber*; personal enemy, declared e., sworn e., bitter e., confirmed e., irreconcilable e., arch enemy; misanthropist, misogynist 902 *misanthrope*; xenophobe, Anglophobe, Francophobe, negrophobe, racialist, anti-Semite 481 *narrow mind*; persona non grata, pet aversion, bête noire 888 *hateful object*.

Adj. *inimical,* unfriendly, not well-inclined, ill-disposed, disaffected; disloyal, unfaithful 930 *perfidious*; aloof, distant, unwelcoming 883 *unsociable*; cool, chilly, frigid, icy 380 *cold*; antipathetic, incompatible, unsympathetic 861 *disliking*; loathing 888 *hating*; hostile, warring, conflicting, actively opposed 704 *opposing*; antagonized, estranged, alienated, unreconciled, irreconcilable; bitter, embittered, rancorous 891 *resentful*; jealous, grudging 912 *envious*; spiteful 898 *malevolent*; bad friends with, on bad terms, not on speaking t.; at feud, at enmity, at variance, at loggerheads, at daggers drawn 709 *quarrelling*; aggressive, militant, belligerent, at war with 718 *warring*; intolerant, persecuting 735 *oppressive*; dangerous, venomous, deadly, fell 659 *baneful*.

Vb. *be inimical,* - unfriendly etc. adj.; show hostility 883 *make unwelcome*; harden one's heart, bear ill will, bear malice 898 *be malevolent*; grudge 912 *envy*; hound, persecute 735 *oppress*; chase, hunt down 619 *hunt*; battle 716 *fight*; make war 718 *wage war*; take offence, take umbrage 891 *resent*; fall out, come to blows 709 *quarrel*; be incompatible, conflict, collide, clash 14 *be contrary*; withstand 704 *oppose*.

make enemies, be unpopular, have no friends 883 *be unsociable*; get across, cause offence, antagonize, irritate 891 *enrage*; estrange, alienate, make bad blood, set by the ears, set at odds 709 *make quarrels*.

See: 14, 380, 481, 603, 619, 659, 663, 704, 705, **709**, 712, 716, 718, 722, 735, 789, 861, 883, **888**, 891, **898**, 902, 912, 930.

882 Sociality

N. *sociality*, relations, community r., race r.; membership, membership of society, intercommunity, consociation 706 *association*; making one of, being one of, belonging; team spirit, esprit de corps; fellowship, comradeship, companionship, society; camaraderie, fraternization, fratting, hobnobbing; social intercourse, familiarity, intimacy, togetherness 880 *friendship*; social circle, home c., family c., one's friends and acquaintances 880 *friend*; social ambition, social climbing; society, claims of society, social demands, the world.

sociability, social activity, group a.; social adjustment, compatibility 83 *conformity*; sociableness, gregariousness, sociable disposition, fondness for company 880 *friendliness*; social success, popularity; social tact, common touch; social graces, savoir vivre, good manners, easy m. 884 *courtesy*; urbanity 846 *good taste*; ability to mix, clubbability; affability, readiness to chat 584 *interlocution*; acceptability, welcome, kind w., hearty w., warm w., smiling reception; greeting, glad hand, handshake, handclasp, embrace 884 *courteous act*; hospitality, entertaining, home from home, open house, Liberty Hall, pot luck 813 *liberality*; good company, good fellowship, geniality, cordiality, heartiness, back-slapping, bonhomie; conviviality, joviality, jollity, merrymaking 824 *enjoyment*; gaiety 837 *revel*; cheer, good c. 301 *food*; eating and drinking, social board, festive b., loving cup 301 *feasting*.

social gathering, forgathering, meeting 74 *assembly*; reunion, get-together, conversazione, social; reception, at home, soirée, levee; entertainment 837 *amusement*; singsong, camp fire; party, hen p., stag p., partie carrée, tête-à-tête; housewarming, house party, weekend p., birthday p., coming-out p.; social meal, feast, banquet 301 *feasting*; communion, love feast, agape 988 *ritual act*; coffee morning, tea party, bun fight, drinks, cocktail party, dinner p., supper p., garden p., picnic, barbecue, bottle party 837 *festivity*; dance, ball, hop, disco 837 *dancing*.

social round, social activities, social whirl, season, social s., social entertainment; social calls, round of visits; seeing one's friends, visiting, calling, dropping in; weekending, stay, visit, formal v., call, courtesy c.; visiting terms, frequentation, haunting 880 *friendship*; social demands, engagement; dating, trysting; rendezvous, assignation, date, blind d.; meeting place, club, pub, local 76 *focus*.

sociable person, active member, keen m.; caller, visitor, dropper-in, frequenter, habitué; convivial person, bon vivant, good fellow, charming companion; good mixer, good company, life and soul of the party; social success, catch, lion 890 *favourite*; jolly person, boon companion, hobnobber, clubman, club woman; active member of the community, good neighbour 880 *friend*; hostess, host, mine h.; guest, welcome g., one of the family; diner-out, parasite, freeloader, gatecrasher; gadabout, social butterfly; socialite, ornament of society, social climber 848 *beau monde*.

Adj. *sociable*, gregarious, social, sociably disposed, extrovert, outgoing, fond of company, party-minded; companionable, fraternizing, affable, conversable, chatty, gossipy, fond of talk, always ready for a chat; clubbable, clubby; cosy, folksy; neighbourly, matey, pally 880 *friendly*; hospitable, welcoming, smiling, cordial, warm, hearty, back-slapping, hail-fellow-well-met; convivial, festive, Christmassy, jolly, jovial 833 *merry*; lively, witty 837 *amusing*; urbane 884 *courteous*; easy, free-and-easy, easy-mannered; unbuttoned, post-prandial, after-dinner 683 *reposeful*.

welcomed, feted, entertained; welcome, ever-w., quite one of the family; popular, liked, sought-after, socially successful, invited, getting around, first on the invitation list.

Vb. *be sociable*, - gregarious etc. adj.; enjoy society, like company, love a party; have friends, make friends easily, hobnob, fraternize, socialize, mix with 880 *be friendly*; mix well, be a good mixer, get around, know how to live, mix in society, go out, dine o., go to parties, accept invitations, cadge i., gate-crash; have fun, live it up 837 *amuse oneself*; join in, get together, make it a party, club together, go Dutch, share, go shares 775 *participate*; take pot luck, eat off the same platter 301 *eat*; join in a bottle, crack a b. 301 *drink*; pledge 876 *toast*; carouse 837 *revel*; make oneself welcome, make oneself at home, become one of the family; relax, unbend 683 *repose*; chat to 584 *converse*; make engagements, date, make a date; make friends, make friendly overtures 880 *befriend*; introduce oneself, exchange names; extend one's friendships, enlarge one's circle of acquaintances; keep up with, keep in w., write to 588 *correspond*.

visit, see people, go visiting, go for a visit, pay a v., be one's guest, sojourn, stay, weekend; keep up with, keep in w., keep in touch, see one's friends; go and see, look one up, call, call in, look in, drop in; wait on, leave a card; exchange visits, be on visiting terms.

be hospitable, keep open house 813 *be liberal*; invite, have round, ask in, be at home to, receive, open one's home to; welcome, make w., bid one w., welcome with open arms, hug, embrace 884 *greet*; act the host, do the honours, preside; do proud, kill the fatted calf 876 *celebrate*; send invitations, have company, entertain, regale 301 *feed*; give a party, throw a p. 837 *revel*; accept, take in, cater for, provide entertainment 633 *provide*.

Adv. *sociably*, hospitably, in friendly fashion, like friends, en famille; arm in arm, hand in hand.

See: 74, 76, 83, 301, 584, 588, 633, 683, **706**, 775, 813, 824, 833, 837, 846, 848, 876, **880**, 884, 890, 988.

883 Unsociability. Seclusion

N. *unsociability*, unsociableness, unsocial habits, shyness 620 *avoidance*; introversion, autism; refusal to mix, keeping one's own company, keeping oneself to oneself; staying at home, home life, domesticity; singleness 895 *celibacy*; inhospitality 816 *parsimony*; standoffishness, unapproachability, distance, aloofness, lonely pride 871 *pride*; unfriendliness, coolness, coldness, moroseness, savageness 893 *sullenness*; cut, cut direct 885 *discourtesy*; silence, lack of conversation 582 *taciturnity*; ostracism, boycott 57 *exclusion*; blacklist 607 *rejection*.

seclusion, privacy, private world, world of one's own; island universe 321 *star*; peace and quiet 266 *quietude*; home life, domesticity; loneliness, solitariness, solitude; retreat, retirement, withdrawal; hiddenness 523 *latency*; confinement, purdah 525 *concealment*; isolation, splendid i. 744 *independence*; division, estrangement 46 *separation*; renunciation 621 *relinquishment*; renunciation of the world, coenobitism 985 *monasticism*; self-exile, expatriation; sequestration, segregation, rustication, excommunication, quarantine, deportation, banishment, exile 57 *exclusion*; reserve, reservation, ghetto, native quarter, harem; gaol 748 *prison*; sequestered nook, godforsaken hole, back of beyond; island, desert, wilderness; hide-out, hideaway 527 *hiding-place*; den, study, sanctum, cloister, cell, hermitage 192 *retreat*; ivory tower, private quarters, shell; backwater, rus in urbe.

solitary, unsocial person, iceberg; lonely person, lonely heart; loner, lone wolf, rogue elephant; isolationist, island; introvert; stay-at-home, home-body; ruralist, troglodyte, cave-dweller; recluse, coenobite, anchorite, anchoress, hermit, eremite, marabout; stylite, pillar monk, Diogenes and his tub; maroon, castaway 779 *derelict*; Robinson Crusoe, Alexander Selkirk.

outcast, pariah, leper, outsider; outcaste, untouchable, harijan; expatriate, alien 59 *foreigner*; exile, expellee, deportee, evacuee, refugee, displaced person, homeless p., stateless p.; proscribed person, outlaw, bandit; Ishmael, vagabond 268 *wanderer*; waif, stray 779 *derelict*; reject, flotsam and jetsam 641 *rubbish*.

Adj. *unsociable*, unsocial, antisocial, introverted, morose, not fit to live with; unassimilated, foreign 59 *extraneous*; unclubbable, stay-at-home, home-keeping, quiet, domestic; inhospitable, unwelcoming, forbidding, hostile, unneighbourly, unfriendly, misanthropic; distant, aloof, unbending, stiff; stand-offish, offish, haughty 871 *prideful*; unwelcoming, frosty, icy, cold 893 *sullen*; unforthcoming, in one's shell; unconversational, uncommunicative, close, silent 582 *taciturn*; cool, impersonal 860 *indifferent*; solitary, lonely, lone 88 *alone*; shy, retiring, withdrawn, afraid of company, avoiding society 620 *avoiding*; wild, feral; celibate, unmarried 895 *unwedded*; anchoretic, eremetic, the world forgetting, by the world forgot.

friendless, unfriended, lorn, forlorn, desolate, forsaken; lonely, lonesome, solitary; on one's own, without company 88 *alone*; cold-shouldered, uninvited, without introductions; unpopular, avoided 860 *unwanted*; blacklisted, blackballed, ostracized, boycotted, sent to Coventry 57 *excluded*; expelled, disbarred, deported, exiled; under embargo, banned 757 *prohibited*.

secluded, private, sequestered, cloistered, hidden, buried, tucked away 523 *latent*; veiled, behind the veil, in purdah 421 *screened*; quiet, lonely, isolated, enisled; remote, out of the way; godforsaken, unvisited, unfrequented, unexplored, unseen, unfamiliar, off the beaten track 491 *unknown*; uninhabited, deserted, desert, desolate 190 *empty*.

Vb. *be unsociable*, keep one's own company, keep oneself to oneself, shun company, see no one, talk to nobody; go it alone, play a lone hand; keep out, stay o., stew in one's own juice; stay in one's shell, shut oneself up, immure oneself, remain private, maintain one's privacy, stand aloof 620 *avoid*; stay at home, cultivate one's garden, bury oneself, vegetate 266 *be quiescent*; retire, go into retirement, give up one's friends, leave the world, make a retreat, take the veil; live in seclusion, live in purdah.

make unwelcome, frown on 924 *disapprove*; repel, keep at arm's length, make one keep his distance, treat coolly; not acknowledge, ignore, cut, cut dead 885 *be rude*; cold-shoulder, turn one's back on, shut the door on; rebuff, give one the brush-off; turn out, turf o., cast o., expel 300 *eject*; ostracize, boycott, send to Coventry, blacklist, blackball 57 *exclude*; have no time for, refuse to meet, refuse to mix with, refuse to associate w., have nothing to do with, treat as a leper, treat as an outsider 620 *avoid*; excommunicate, banish, exile, outlaw, ban 963 *punish*.

seclude, sequester, island, isolate, quarantine, segregate; keep in private, keep in purdah; confine, shut up 747 *imprison*.

See: 46, 57, 59, 88, 190, 192, 266, 268, 300, 321, 421, 491, 523, 525, 527, 582, 607, 620, 621, 641, 744, 747, 748, 757, 779, 816, 860, 871, 885, 893, 895, 924, 963, 985.

884 Courtesy

N. *courtesy*, chivalry, knightliness, gallantry; deference 920 *respect*; consideration, condescension 872 *humility*; graciousness, politeness, civility, urbanity, mannerliness, manners, good m., noble m., good behaviour, best b.; good breeding, gentlemanliness, ladylikeness, gentility 846 *good taste*; tactfulness, diplomacy; courtliness, correctness, correctitude 875 *formality*; comity, amenity, amiability, sweetness, niceness, obligingness, kindness, kindliness 897 *benevolence*; gentleness, mildness 736 *leniency*; easy temper, good humour, complaisance 734 *laxity*; agreeableness, affability, suavity, blandness, common touch, social tact 882 *sociability*; smooth tongue 925 *flattery*.

courteous act, act of courtesy, polite act, graceful gesture, courtesy, civility, favour, charity, kindness 897 *kind act*; soft answer 736 *leniency*; compliment 886 *congratulation*; kind words, fair w., sweet w. 889 *endearment*; introduction, presentation 880 *friendliness*; welcome, polite w., reception, invitation; acknowledgment, recognition, mark of r., nod, salutation, salute, greeting, affectionate g., welcoming gesture, smile, kiss, hug, squeeze, handclasp, handshake 920 *respects*; salaam, kowtow, bow, curtsy 311 *obeisance*; terms of courtesy, respects, regards, kind r., best r., duty, remembrances, love, best wishes; love and kisses, farewell 296 *valediction*.

Adj. *courteous*, chivalrous, knightly, generous 868 *noble*; courtly, gallant, old-world, correct 875 *formal*; polite, civil, urbane, gentle, gentlemanly, ladylike, dignified, well-mannered, fine-m. 848 *well-bred*; gracious, condescending 872 *humble*; deferential, mannerly 920 *respectful*; on one's best behaviour, anxious to please 455 *attentive*; obliging, complaisant, kind 897 *benevolent*; conciliatory, sweet 719 *pacificatory*; agreeable, suave, bland, smooth, ingratiating, well-spoken, fair-s., honey-tongued 925 *flattering*; obsequious 879 *servile*.

amiable, nice, sweet, winning 887 *lovable*; affable, friendly 882 *sociable*; considerate, kind 897 *benevolent*; inoffensive, harmless 935 *innocent*; gentle, easy, mild, soft-spoken 736 *lenient*; good-tempered, sweet-t., unruffled 823 *inexcitable*; well-behaved, good 739 *obedient*; pacific, peaceable 717 *peaceful*.

Vb. *be courteous*, be on one's best behaviour, mind one's P's and Q's; mind one's manners, display good m.; show courtesy, treat with politeness, treat with deference 920 *respect*; give one his *or* her title, call sir, call madam; oblige, put oneself out 703 *aid*; condescend 872 *be humble*; notice, have time for 455 *be attentive*; conciliate, speak fair 719 *pacify*; not forget one's manners, keep a civil tongue in one's head, make oneself agreeable, be all things to all men; take no offence, take in good part, return a soft answer 823 *be patient*; become courteous, mend one's manners, express regrets 941 *atone*.

pay one's respects, give one's regards, send one's r., offer one's duty; send one's compliments, do one the honour; pay compliments 925 *flatter*; drink to, pledge 876 *toast*; homage, pay h., show one's respect, kneel, kiss hands 920 *show respect*; honour, crown, wreathe, garland, chair, give a hero's welcome 876 *celebrate*.

greet, send greetings (**see** *pay one's respects*); flag 547 *signal*; accost, sidle up 289 *approach*; acknowledge, recognize, hold out one's hand 455 *notice*; shout one's greeting, hail 408 *vociferate*; nod, wave, smile, kiss one's fingers, blow a kiss; say hallo, bid good morning 583 *speak to*; salute, make salutation, raise one's hat, uncap, uncover; touch one's cap, tug one's forelock; bend, bow, bob, duck, curtsy, salaam, make obeisance, kiss hands, prostrate oneself, kowtow 311 *stoop*; shake hands, clasp h., shake the hand, press *or* squeeze *or* wring *or* pump the hand, press the flesh; advance to meet 920 *show respect*; escort 89 *accompany*; make a salute, fire a s., present arms, parade, turn out 876 *celebrate*; receive, do the honours; welcome, welcome in, welcome home 882 *be sociable*; welcome with open arms 824 *be pleased*; open one's arms, embrace, hug, kiss 889 *caress*; usher, usher in, present, introduce 299 *admit*.

Adv. *courteously*, politely, with respect, with all due deference; condescendingly, graciously.

See: 89, 289, 296, 299, 311, 408, 455, 547, 583, 703, 717, 719, 734, 736, 739, 823, 824, 846, **848**, 868, 872, 875, 876, 879, **880**, **882**, 886, 887, 889, 897, 920, 925, 935, 941.

885 Discourtesy

N. *discourtesy*, impoliteness, bad manners, deplorable m., sheer bad m., shocking bad m.; no manners, mannerlessness, failure of courtesy, want of chivalry, lack of politeness, lack of manners, scant courtesy, incivility, inurbanity; churlishness, uncouthness, boorishness 847 *ill-breeding*; unpleasantness, nastiness, beastliness; misbehaviour, misconduct, unbecoming conduct; tactlessness, inconsiderateness, want of consideration.

rudeness, ungraciousness, gruffness, bluntness; sharpness, tartness, acerbity, acrimony, asperity; ungentleness, roughness, harshness 735 *severity*; offhandedness 456 *inattention*; brusquerie, shortness, short answer, plain a. 569 *conciseness*; sarcasm 851 *ridicule*; excessive frankness, unparliamentary language, bad l., rude words, virulence 899 *scurrility*; rebuff, insult 921 *indignity*; personalities, impertinence, pertness, sauce, lip, cheek, truculence 878 *insolence*; impatience, interruption, shouting 822 *excitability*; black look, sour l., scowl, frown 893 *sullenness*; a discourtesy, act of d., piece of bad manners.

rude person, no true knight, no gentleman, no lady; savage, barbarian, brute, lout, boor, loudmouth, mannerless brat, unlicked cub 878 *insolent person*; curmudgeon, crab, bear; sourpuss, crosspatch, groucher, grouser, sulker 829 *malcontent*.

Adj. *discourteous*, unknightly, ungallant, unchivalrous, unhandsome; uncourtly, unceremonious, ungentlemanly, unladylike; inurbane, impolite, uncivil, rude; mannerless, unmannerly, ill-mannered, bad-m., boorish, loutish, uncouth, brutish, beastly, savage, barbarian 847 *ill-bred*; insolent, impudent; cheeky, saucy, pert, forward 878 *impertinent*; unpleasant, disagreeable; cool, not anxious to please, unaccommodating, uncomplaisant 860 *indifferent*; offhanded, cavalier, airy, breezy, tactless, inconsiderate 456 *inattentive*.

ungracious, unsmiling, grim 834 *serious*; gruff, grunting, growling, bearish 893 *sullen*; peevish, testy 892 *irascible*; difficult, surly, churlish, unfriendly, unneighbourly 883 *unsociable*; grousing, grumbling, swearing 829 *discontented*; ungentle, rough, rugged, harsh, brutal 735 *severe*; bluff, free, frank, overfrank, blunt, overblunt; brusque, short 569 *concise*; tart, sharp, biting, acrimonious 388 *pungent*; sarcastic, uncomplimentary, unflattering 926 *detracting*; foul-mouthed, foul-spoken, abusive, vituperative 899 *cursing*;

contumelious, offensive, injurious, insulting, truculent 921 *disrespectful*.

Vb. *be rude*, - mannerless etc. adj.; want manners, have no m., flout etiquette; know no better 699 *be artless*; forget one's manners, display bad manners, show discourtesy 878 *be insolent*; show no thought for others, show no regard for one's feelings 921 *not respect*; have no time for 456 *be inattentive*; treat rudely, be beastly to, snub, turn one's back on, cold-shoulder, cut, ignore, look right through, cut dead 883 *make unwelcome*; show one the door, send away with a flea in one's ear 300 *eject*; cause offence, ruffle one's feelings 891 *huff*; insult, abuse; take liberties, make free with, make bold; stare, ogle 438 *gaze*; make one blush 867 *shame*; lose one's temper, shout, interrupt 891 *get angry*; curse, swear, damn 899 *cuss*; snarl, growl, frown, scowl, lour, pout, sulk 893 *be sullen*.

Adv. *impolitely*, discourteously, like a boor, like an ill-mannered fellow.

See: 300, 388, 438, 456, 569, 699, 735, 822, 829, 834, **847**, 851, 860, 867, **878**, 883, 891, 892, 893, 899, **921**, 926.

886 Congratulation

N. *congratulation*, felicitation, gratulation, congratulations, felicitations, compliments, best c., compliments of the season; good wishes, best w., happy returns; salute, toast; welcome, hero's w., official reception 876 *celebration*; thanks 907 *gratitude*.

Adj. *congratulatory*, gratulatory, complimentary; honorific, triumphal, welcoming 876 *celebratory*.

Vb. *congratulate*, felicitate, compliment; offer one's congratulations, wish one joy, give one joy, wish many happy returns, wish a merry Christmas and a happy New Year, offer the season's greetings; send one's congratulations, send one's compliments 884 *pay one's respects*; sanction a triumph, accord an ovation, give one a hero's welcome, give three cheers, clap 923 *applaud*; fete, mob, rush, lionize 876 *celebrate*; congratulate oneself, hug o., thank one's lucky stars 824 *be pleased*; thank Heaven 907 *be grateful*.

See: 824, 876, 884, 907, 923.

887 Love

N. *love*, affection, friendship, charity, Eros; agape, brotherly love, sisterly l., Christian l.; true love, real thing; natural affection, parental a., maternal a., mother-love, protective l., protectiveness 931 *disinterestedness*; possessive love, possessiveness 911 *jealousy*; conjugal love, uxoriousness; closeness, intimacy; sentiment 818 *feeling*; kindness, tenderness 897 *benevolence*; Platonic love 880 *friendship*; two hearts that beat as one, mutual love, mutual affection, mutual attraction, compatibility, sympathy, fellow feeling, understanding; fondness, liking, predilection, inclination 179 *tendency*; preference 605 *choice*; fancy 604 *caprice*; attachment, sentimental a., firm a.; devotion, loyal d., patriotism 739 *loyalty*; courtly love, gallantry; sentimentality, susceptibility, amorousness 819 *moral sensibility*; power of love, fascination, enchantment, bewitchment 983 *sorcery*; lovesickness, Cupid's sting, yearning, longing 859 *desire*; amativeness, amorism, eroticism, lust 859 *libido*; regard 920 *respect*; admiration, hero-worship 864 *wonder*; dawn of love, first l., calf l., puppy l., young l.; crush, pash, infatuation; madness 503 *insanity*; worship 982 *idolatry*; romantic love, l. at first sight, passion, tender p., fire of love, flames of l., enthusiasm, rapture, ecstasy, transport, transports of love 822 *excitable state*; erotomania, abnormal affection 84 *abnormality*; love psychology, narcissism, Oedipus complex, Electra c.; love-hate, odi et amo.

lovableness, amiability, attractiveness, popularity, gift of pleasing; winsomeness, charm, fascination, appeal, sex a., attractions, charms, beauties; winning ways, pleasing qualities, endearing q.; coquetry, flirtatiousness; sentimental value.

love affair, romantic a., affair of the heart, affaire de coeur; romance, love and the world well lost; flirtation, amour, amourette, entanglement; loves, amours; free love; liaison, intrigue, seduction, adultery 951 *illicit love*; falling in love, something between them; course of love, the old old story; betrothal, engagement, wedding bells 894 *marriage*; broken engagement, broken romance, broken heart.

love-making, flirting, coquetting, spooning, canoodling, billing and cooing 889 *endearment*; courtship, courting, walking out, sighing, suing, pressing one's suit, laying siege 889 *wooing*; pursuit of love, hoping for conquests, flirting, coquetry, philandering; gallantry, dalliance, dallying, toying, chambering and wantonness, libertinage 951 *unchastity*; bestowal of love, favours.

love-nest, abode of love, bower, Bower of Bliss; honeymoon cottage, bridal suite, nuptial chamber, bridal bed; harem, seraglio.

lover, love, true l., sweetheart; young man, boyfriend, Romeo; swain, beau, gallant, spark, cavalier, squire, escort, date; steady, fiancé; wooer, courter, suitor, follower, captive, admirer, hero-worshipper, adorer, votary worshipper; aficionado, fan, devoted following, fan club; sugar daddy, dotard; cicisbeo, gigolo, squire of dames, ladies' man, lady-killer, seducer, Lothario, Don Juan, Casanova; paramour, amorist 952 *libertine*; flirt, coquette, philanderer; gold-digger, vamp.

loved one, beloved, love, true love, soul mate, heart's desire, light of one's life, one's own 890 *darling*; intimate 880 *close friend*; favoured suitor, lucky man, intended, betrothed, affianced, fiancé(e), bride-to-be 894 *spouse*; conquest, inamorata, lady-love, girlfriend, girl, bird, honey, baby, sweetie; angel, princess, goddess; sweetheart, valentine, flame, old f.; idol, hero; heartthrob, maiden's prayer, dream man, dream girl, princesse lointaine 859 *desired object*; Phyllis, Dulcinea, Amaryllis; favourite, mistress, leman, concubine 952 *kept woman*; dangerous woman, femme fatale.

lovers, pair of lovers, loving couple, engaged c., turtledoves, lovebirds; Daphnis and Chloe, Aucassin and Nicolette, Harlequin and Columbine; star-crossed lovers, tragic l., Pyramus and Thisbe, Romeo and Juliet, Hero and Leander, Tristan and Isolde, Lancelot and Guinevere, Troilus and Cressida; historic lovers, Héloïse and Abélard, Dante and Beatrice, Petrarch and Laura, Antony and Cleopatra.

love god, goddess of love, Venus, Aphrodite, Astarte, Freya; Amor, Eros, Kama, Cupid, blind boy; cupidon, amoretto.

love emblem, myrtle, turtledove; Cupid's bow, Cupid's arrows, Cupid's dart, Cupid's torch; golden arrow, leaden a.; pierced heart, bleeding h., broken h. 889 *love token*.

Adj. *loving*, brotherly, sisterly; loyal, patriotic 931 *disinterested*; wooing, courting, cuddling, making love 889 *caressing*; affectionate, cuddlesome, demonstrative; tender, motherly, wifely, conjugal; loverlike, loverly, gallant, romantic, sentimental, lovesick; mooning, moping, lovelorn, languishing 834 *dejected*; attached to, fond of, fond, uxorious, doting; possessive 911 *jealous*; admiring, adoring, devoted, enslaved (**see** *enamoured*); flirtatious, coquettish 604 *capricious*; amatory, amorous, amative, ardent, passionate 818 *fervent*; yearning 859 *desiring*; lustful, concupiscent, libidinous 951 *lecherous*.

enamoured, in love, fallen in l., falling in l., inclined to, sweet on, soft on, keen on, set on, stuck on, gone on, sold on; struck with, taken w., smitten, bitten, caught, hooked; charmed, enchanted, fascinated 983 *bewitched*; mad on, infatuated, besotted, crazy about, wild a., head over heels in love 503 *crazy*; happily in love, blissfully in l. 824 *happy*; rapturous, ecstatic 821 *excited*.

lovable, likable, congenial, sympathetic, to one's liking, to one's taste, to one's fancy, after one's own heart 859 *desired*; lovesome, winsome, loveworthy 884 *amiable*; sweet, angelic, divine, adorable; lovely, graceful, good-looking 841 *beautiful*; interesting, intriguing, attractive, seductive, alluring 291 *attracting*; prepossessing, appealing, engaging, winning, endearing, captivating, irresistible; cuddly, desirable, kissable; charming, enchanting, bewitching 983 *sorcerous*; liked, beloved, endeared to, dear, darling, pet, fancy, favourite.

erotic, aphrodisiac, erotogenic, erogenous; sexy, pornographic 951 *impure*; amatory 821 *excited*.

Vb. *love*, like, care, rather care for, quite like, take pleasure in, be partial to, take an interest in; sympathize with, feel w., be fond of, have a soft spot for; be susceptible, have a heart, have a warm h.; bear love towards, hold in affection, hold dear, care for, cherish, cling to, embrace; appreciate, value, prize, treasure, think the world of, regard, admire, revere 920 *respect*; adore, worship, idolize, only have eyes for 982 *idolatrize*; live for, live only f.; burn with love, be on fire with passion (**see** *be in love*); make love, bestow one's favours 45 *unite with*; make much of, spoil, pet, fondle, drool over, slobber o. 889 *caress.*

be in love, burn, sweat, faint, die of *or* for love 361 *die*; burn with love, glow with ardour, flame with passion, love to distraction, dote 503 *be insane*; take a fancy to, take a shine to, cotton on to, take to, warm to, be taken with, be sweet on, dig; carry a torch for, look with passion on 859 *desire*; form an attachment, fall for, fall in love, get infatuated, get hooked on, have it bad; go crazy over, be nuts on 503 *go mad*; set one's heart on, lose one's heart, bestow one's affections; declare one's love, offer one's heart to, woo, sue, sigh, press one's suit, make one's addresses 889 *court*; set one's cap at, chase 619 *pursue*; enjoy one's favours; honeymoon 894 *wed.*

excite love, arouse desire 859 *cause desire*; warm, inflame 381 *heat*; rouse, stir, flutter, enrapture, enthral 821 *excite*; dazzle, bedazzle, charm, enchant, fascinate 983 *bewitch*; allure, draw 291 *attract*; make oneself attractive 843 *primp*; lure, bait, tantalize, seduce 612 *tempt*; lead on, flirt, coquette, philander, break hearts; toy, vamp 889 *caress*; smile, leer, make eyes at, ogle, wink 889 *court*; catch one's eye 455 *attract notice*; enamour, take one's fancy, steal one's heart, gain one's affections, engage the a.; make a hit, bowl over, sweep off one's feet, turn one's head, infatuate 503 *make mad*; make a conquest, captivate 745 *subjugate*; catch, lead to the altar 894 *wed*; endear, endear oneself, ingratiate o., insinuate o., wind oneself into the affections; be loved, be amiable, be lovable, make oneself a favourite, become a f., be the rage; steal every heart, set all hearts on fire, have a place in every heart; curry favour 925 *flatter.*

Adv.*affectionately*, kindly, lovingly, tenderly 457 *carefully*; fondly, dotingly, madly.

See:45, 84, 179, 291, 361, 381, 455, 457, 503, 604, 605, 612, 619, 739, 745, 818, 819, 821, 822, 824, 834, 841, 843, 859, 864, 880, 884, **889**, **890**, 894, 897, 911, 920, 925, 931, 951, 952, 982, 983.

888 Hatred

N.*hatred*, hate, no love lost; love-hate, odi et amo; revulsion of feeling, disillusion; aversion, antipathy, allergy, nausea 861 *dislike*; intense dislike, repugnance, detestation, loathing, abhorrence, abomination; disfavour, displeasure (**see** *odium*); disaffection, estrangement, alienation 709 *dissension*; hostility, antagonism 881 *enmity*; animosity, ill feeling, bad blood, bitterness, acrimony, rancour 891 *resentment*; malice, ill will, evil eye, spite, grudge, ancient g. 898 *malevolence*; jealousy 912 *envy*; wrath 891 *anger*; execration, hymn of hate 899 *malediction*; scowl, snap, snarl, baring one's fangs 893 *sullenness*; phobia, xenophobia, Anglophobia, anti-Semitism, racialism, racism, colour prejudice 481 *prejudice*; misogyny 902 *misanthropy.*

odium, disfavour, unpopularity 924 *disapprobation*; discredit, bad odour, black books 867 *disrepute*; odiousness, hatefulness, loathsomeness, beastliness, obnoxiousness; despicability, despisedness 922 *contemptibility.*

hateful object, anathema; unwelcome necessity, bitter pill; abomination, filth; object of one's hate 881 *enemy*; not one's type, one's aversion, pet a., bête noire, bugbear, Dr Fell, nobody's darling; pest, menace, good riddance 659 *bane*; rotter 938 *cad*; heretic, blackleg, scab 603 *tergiversator.*

Adj.*hating*, loathing, envying etc. vb.; loveless; antipathetic, revolted, disgusted 861 *disliking*; set against 704 *opposing*; averse, abhorrent, antagonistic, hostile, antagonized, snarling 881 *inimical*; envious, spiteful, spleenful, malicious, full of malice, malignant 898 *malevolent*; bitter, rancorous 891 *resentful*; full of hate, implacable; vindictive 910 *revengeful*; virulent, execrative 899 *cursing*; out of love, disillusioned 509 *disappointed.*

hateful, odious, unlovable, unloved; invidious, antagonizing, obnoxious, pestilential 659 *baneful*; beastly, nasty, horrid 645 *not nice*; abhorrent, loathsome, abominable; accursed, execrable, execrated 899 *cursed*; offensive, repulsive, repellent, nauseous, nauseating, revolting, disgusting 861 *disliked*; bitter, sharp 393 *sour*; unwelcome 860 *unwanted.*

hated, loathed etc. vb.; uncared for 458 *neglected*; out of favour, unpopular 861 *disliked*; in one's bad books, discredited 924 *disapproved*; loveless, unloved; unvalued, unmissed, unregretted, unlamented, unmourned, unwept; unchosen, refused, spurned, condemned, jilted, lovelorn, crossed in love 607 *rejected*.

Vb. *hate*, bear hatred, have no love for; hate one's guts; loathe, abominate, detest, abhor, hold in horror; turn away from, shrink f. 620 *avoid*; revolt from, recoil at 280 *recoil*; can't bear, can't stand 861 *dislike*; find loathsome, find obnoxious; not choose, refuse 607 *reject*; spurn, contemn 922 *despise*; execrate, hold accursed, denounce 899 *curse*; bear malice, have a down on 898 *be malevolent*; feel envy 912 *envy*; bear a grudge, have it in for 910 *be revengeful*, 891 *resent*; scowl, growl, snap, snarl, bare one's fangs 893 *be sullen*; insult 878 *be insolent*; conceive a hatred for, fall out of love, turn to hate.

excite hate, grate, jar 292 *repel*; cause loathing, disgust, nauseate, stink in the nostrils 861 *cause dislike*; shock, horrify 924 *incur blame*; antagonize, destroy goodwill, estrange, alienate, sow dissension, set by the ears, set at each others' throats, create bad blood, end friendship, turn all to hate 881 *make enemies*; poison, envenom, embitter, exacerbate 832 *aggravate*; exasperate, incense 891 *enrage*.

See: 280, 292, 393, 458, 481, 509, 603, 607, 620, 645, 659, 704, 709, 832, 860, **861**, 867, 878, **881**, **891**, 893, 898, 899, 902, 910, 912, 922, 924, 938.

889 Endearment

N. *endearment*, blandishments, compliments 925 *flattery*; loving words, affectionate speeches, pretty s., pretty names, pet name; soft nothings, sweet n., lovers' vows; affectionate behaviour, dalliance, billing and cooing, holding hands, slap and tickle, footsie; fondling, cuddling, canoodling, petting, necking, smooching, snogging, kissing, osculation; caress, embracement, embrace, clasp, hug, bear h., cuddle, squeeze, pressure, fond p.; salute, buss, kiss, butterfly k., French k., smacker; nibble, bite; stroke, tickle, slap, pat, pinch, nip 378 *touch*; familiarity, overfamiliarity, advances, pass.

wooing, courting, spooning, flirting; play, love-p., lovemaking; wink, side-glance, glad eye, come hither look, ogle, oeillade, amorous glance, sheep's eyes, fond look, languishing l., sigh; flirtation, philandering, coquetry, gallantry, amorous intentions, honourable i.; courtship, suit, love s., addresses, advances 887 *love-making*; serenade, aubade, love song, love lyric, amorous ditty, caterwauling; love letter, billet-doux; love poem, sonnet; proposal, engagement, betrothal 894 *marriage*.

love token, true lover's knot, favour, ribbon, glove; ring, engagement r., wedding r., eternity r.; valentine, love letter, billet-doux; language of flowers, posy, red roses; arrow, heart 887 *love emblem*; tattoo.

Adj. *caressing*, clinging, toying, fondling etc. vb.; demonstrative, affectionate 887 *loving*; soppy, spoony, lovey-dovey; cuddlesome, flirtatious, coquettish; wooing, sighing, suing.

Vb. *pet*, pamper, spoil, spoonfeed, mother, smother, kill with kindness; cosset, cocker, coddle; make much of, be all over one; treasure 887 *love*; cherish, foster 660 *safeguard*; nurse, lap, rock, cradle, baby; coo, sing to, croon over; coax, wheedle 925 *flatter*.

caress, love, fondle, dandle, take in one's lap; play with, stroke, smooth, pat, paw, pinch one's cheek, pat one on the head, chuck under the chin; osculate, kiss, buss, brush one's cheek; embrace, enlace, enfold, lap, fold in one's arms, press to one's bosom, hang on one's neck, fly into the arms of; open one's arms, clasp, hug, hold one tight, cling, not let go 778 *retain*; squeeze, press, cuddle; snuggle, nestle, nuzzle, nibble; play, romp, wanton, toy, trifle, dally, spark; make dalliance, make love, carry on, canoodle, spoon, bill and coo, hold hands, slap and tickle, pet, neck, snog, smooch, play footsie; vamp 887 *excite love*; (of animals) lick, fawn, rub oneself against; (of a crowd) mob, rush, snatch at, be all over, swarm over.

court, make advances, give the glad eye; make eyes at, make sheep's e., ogle, leer, eye 438 *gaze*; get off with, try to get off with, become familiar, get fresh, make a pass at, make passes; gallivant, philander, flirt, coquette 887 *excite love*; be sweet on 887 *be in love*; set one's cap at, run after, chase 619 *pursue*; squire, escort 89 *accompany*; hang round, wait on 284 *follow*; date, make a date, take out; walk out with, go steady; sue, woo, go a-wooing, go courting, pay court to, pay one's addresses to, pay attentions to, pay suit to, press one's suit; lay siege to one's affections, whisper sweet nothings, speak fondly to; serenade, caterwaul; sigh, sigh at the feet of, pine, languish 887 *love*; offer one's heart, offer one's hand, offer one's fortune; ask for the hand of, propose, propose marriage, pop the question, plight one's troth, become engaged, announce one's engagement, publish the banns, make a match 894 *wed*.

See: 89, 284, 378, 438, 619, 660, 778, **887**, 894, 925.

890 Darling. Favourite

N. *darling*, dear, my dear; dear friend; dearest, dear one, only one; one's own, one's all; truelove, love, beloved 887 *loved one*; heart, dear h.; sweetheart, fancy, valentine; sweeting, sweetling, sweetie, sugar, honey, honeybaby, honeybunch; precious, jewel, treasure; chéri(e), chou, mavourneen; angel, angel child, cherub; pippin, poppet, popsy, moppet, mopsy; pet, petkins, lamb, precious l., chick, chicken, duck, ducks, ducky, dearie, lovey.

favourite, darling, mignon; spoiled darling, spoiled child, enfant gâté, fondling, cosset, mother's darling, teacher's pet; jewel, heart's-blood, apple of one's eye, blue-eyed boy; persona grata, someone after one's own heart, one of the best, good man, good chap, fine fellow, marvellous woman, Mr *or* Miss Right; the tops, salt of the earth; brick, sport, good s., real s.; first choice, front runner, top seed, only possible choice 644 *exceller*; someone to be proud of, boast, pride, p. and joy; national figure, favourite son, grand old man, man *or* woman of the hour 866 *person of repute*; idol, hero, heroine, golden girl *or* boy; screen goddess, media personality, star, film s.; general favourite, universal f., cynosure, toast of the town; world's sweetheart, Queen of Hearts, pinup girl 841 *a beauty*; centre of attraction, cynosure, honeypot 291 *attraction*; catch, lion 859 *desired object*.

See: 291, 644, 841, 859, 866, **887**.

891 Resentment. Anger

N. *resentment*, displeasure, dissatisfaction 829 *discontent*; huffiness, ill humour, sulks 893 *sullenness*; sternness 735 *severity*; heart-burning, heart-swelling, rankling, rancour, soreness, painful feelings; slow burn, growing impatience; indignation (**see** *anger*); umbrage, offence, taking o., huff, tiff, pique; bile, spleen, gall; acerbity, acrimony, bitterness, bitter resentment, hard feelings; virulence, hate 888 *hatred*; animosity, grudge, ancient g., bone to pick, crow to pluck 881 *enmity*; vindictiveness, revengefulness, spite 910 *revenge*; malice 898 *malevolence*; impatience, fierceness, hot blood 892 *irascibility*; cause of offence, red rag to a bull, sore point, dangerous subject; pinprick, irritation 827 *annoyance*; provocation, aggravation, insult, affront, last straw 921 *indignity*; wrong, injury 914 *injustice*.

anger, wrathfulness, irritation, exasperation, vexation, indignation; dudgeon, high d., wrath, ire, choler; rage, tearing r., fury, raging f., passion, towering p. 822 *excitable state*; crossness, temper, tantrum, tizzy, paddy, paddywhack, fume, fret, pet, fit of temper, burst of anger, outburst, explosion, storm, stew, ferment, taking, paroxysm, tears of rage 318 *agitation*; rampage, fire and fury, gnashing the teeth, stamping the foot; shout, roar 400 *loudness*; fierceness, angry look, glare, frown, scowl; growl, snarl, bark, bite, snap, snappishness, asperity 892 *irascibility*; warmth, heat, high words, angry w. 709 *quarrel*; box on the ear, rap on the knuckles, slap in the face 921 *indignity*; blows, fisticuffs 716 *fight*.

Fury, Erinys, Alecto, Megaera, Tisiphone, Furies, Eumenides 910 *avenger*.

Adj. *resentful*, piqued, stung, galled, huffed, miffed; stung, hurt, sore, smarting 829 *discontented*; surprised, pained, hurt, offended; warm, indignant; unresigned, reproachful 924 *disapproving*; bitter, embittered, acrimonious, full of hate, rancorous, virulent 888 *hating*; full of spleen, spleenful, splenetic, spiteful 898 *malevolent*; full of revenge, vindictive 910 *revengeful*; jealous, green with envy 912 *envious*; grudging 598 *unwilling*.

angry, displeased, not amused, stern, frowning 834 *serious*; impatient, cross, waxy, ratty, wild, mad, livid; wroth, wrathy, wrathful, ireful, irate; peeved, nettled, rattled, annoyed, irritated, vexed, provoked, stung; worked up, wrought up, het up, hot, hot under the collar; angry with, mad at; indignant, angered, incensed, infuriated, beside oneself with rage; shirty, in a temper, in a paddy, in a wax, in a huff, in a rage, in a boiling r., in a fury, in a taking, in a passion; warm, fuming, boiling, burning; speechless, stuttering, gnashing, spitting with fury, crying with rage; raging, foaming, savage, violent 176 *furious*; apoplectic, rabid, foaming at the mouth, mad as a hornet, hopping m., dancing, rampaging, rampageous 503 *frenzied*; seeing red, berserk; roaring, ramping, rearing; snarling, snapping, glaring, glowering 893 *sullen*; red with anger, flushed with rage, red-eyed, bloodshot 431 *red*; blue in the face; pale with anger; dangerous, fierce 892 *irascible*.

Vb. *resent*, be piqued, - offended etc. adj.; find intolerable, not bear, be unable to stomach 825 *suffer*; feel, mind, have a chip on one's shoulder, feel resentment, smart under 829 *be discontented*; take amiss, take ill, take the wrong way, not see the joke; feel insulted, take offence, take umbrage, take exception to 709 *quarrel*; jib, take in ill part, take in bad p., get sore, cut up rough; burn, smoulder, sizzle, simmer, boil with indignation; express resentment, vent one's spleen, indulge one's spite 898 *be malevolent*; take to heart, let it rankle, remember an injury, cherish a grudge, bear malice 910 *be revengeful*; go green with envy 912 *envy*.

get angry, get cross, get wild, get mad; get peeved, get sore, get in a pet, go spare; kindle, grow warm, grow heated, colour, redden, flush with anger; take fire, flare up, start up, rear up, ramp; bridle, bristle, raise one's hackles, arch one's back; lose patience, lose one's temper, lose control of one's t., forget oneself; throw a tantrum, stamp, shout; get one's dander up, get one's monkey up, fall into a passion, fly into a temper, fly off the handle; let fly, burst out, let off steam, boil over, blow up, flip one's lid, blow one's top, explode; see red, go berserk, go mad, foam at the mouth 822 *be excitable*.

be angry, - impatient etc. adj.; show impatience, interrupt, chafe, fret, fume, fuss, flounce, dance, ramp, stamp, champ, champ at the bit, paw the ground; carry on, create, perform, make a scene, make a row, go on the warpath 61 *rampage*; turn nasty, cut up rough, raise Cain; rage, rant, roar, bellow, bluster, storm, thunder, fulminate 400 *be loud*; look like thunder, look black, look daggers, glare, glower, frown, scowl, growl, snarl 893 *be sullen*; spit, snap, lash out; gnash one's teeth, grind one's t., weep with rage, boil with r., quiver with r., shake with passion, swell with fury, burst with indignation, stamp with rage, dance with fury, lash one's tail 821 *be excited*; breathe fire and fury, out-Lear Lear; let fly, express one's feelings, vent one's spleen 176 *be violent*.

huff, miff, pique, sting, nettle, rankle, smart; ruffle the dignity, wound, wound the feelings 827 *hurt*; antagonize, put one's back up, rub up the wrong way, get across, give umbrage, offend, cause offence, cause lasting o., embitter 888 *excite hate*; stick in the throat, raise one's gorge 861 *cause dislike*; affront, insult, outrage 921 *not respect*.

enrage, upset, discompose, ruffle, disturb one's equanimity, ruffle one's temper, irritate, rile, peeve; annoy, vex, pester, bug, bother 827 *trouble*; get on one's nerves, get under one's skin, get one's goat, give one the pip; do it to annoy, tease, bait, pinprick, needle 827 *torment*; bite, fret, nag, gnaw; put out of patience, put in an ill humour, try one's patience, exasperate; push too far, make one lose one's temper, put into a temper, work into a passion; anger, incense, infuriate, madden, drive mad; goad, sting, taunt, trail one's coat, invite a quarrel; drive into a fury, lash into f., whip up one's anger, rouse one's ire, rouse one's choler, kindle one's wrath, excite indignation, stir the blood, stir one's bile, make one's gorge rise, raise one's hackles, get one's dander up; make one's blood boil, make one see red; cause resentment, embitter, envenom, poison; exasperate, add fuel to the flames 832 *aggravate*; embroil, set at loggerheads, set by the ears 709 *make quarrels*.

Adv. *angrily*, resentfully, bitterly; warmly, heatedly; with one's hackles up; in anger, in fury, in the heat of the moment, in the height of passion, with one's monkey up, with one's dander up.

See: 61, 176, 318, 400, 431, 503, 598, 709, 716, 735, 821, 822, 825, 827, **829**, 832, 834, 861, 881, 888, **892**, **893**, 898, 910, 912, 914, 921, 924.

892 Irascibility

N. *irascibility*, choler, quick passions, irritability, impatience 822 *excitability*; grumpiness, gruffness 883 *unsociability*; sharpness, tartness, asperity, gall, bile, vinegar 393 *sourness*; sensitivity 819 *moral sensibility*; huffiness, touchiness, prickliness, readiness to take offence, pugnacity, bellicosity 709 *quarrelsomeness*; temperament, testiness, pepperiness, peevishness, petulance; captiousness, uncertain temper, doubtful t., sharp t., short t.; hot temper, fierce t., fiery t.; limited patience, snappishness, a word and a blow; fierceness, dangerousness, hot blood, fieriness, inflammable nature; bad temper, dangerous t., foul t., nasty t., evil t.

shrew, scold, fishwife; spitfire, termagant, virago, vixen, battleaxe, harridan, fury, Xanthippe; Tartar, hornet; bear 902 *misanthrope*; crosspatch, mad dog; fiery person, redhead.

Adj. *irascible*, impatient, choleric, irritable, peppery, testy, crusty, peevish, crotchety, cranky, cross-grained; short-tempered, hot-t., sharp-t., uncertain-t.; prickly, touchy, tetchy, huffy, umbrageous, thin-skinned 819 *sensitive*; inflammable, like tinder; hot-blooded, fierce, fiery, passionate 822 *excitable*; quick, warm, hasty, overhasty, trigger-happy 857 *rash*; quick-tempered, easily roused 709 *quarrelling*; scolding, shrewish, vixenish; sharp-tongued 899 *cursing*; petulant, cantankerous, snarling, querulous; captious, bitter, vinegary 393 *sour*; splenetic, spleenful, bilious, liverish, gouty; scratchy, snuffy, snappy, snappish, waspish; tart, sharp, short; uptight, edgy; fractious, fretful, moody, temperamental, changeable; gruff, grumpy, pettish, ratty, like a bear with a sore head 829 *discontented*; ill-humoured, cross, stroppy 893 *sullen*.

Vb. *be irascible*, have a temper, have an uncontrollable t.; have a devil in one; snort, bark, snap, bite 893 *be sullen*; snap one's head off, bite one's head off, jump down one's throat 891 *get angry*.

See: 393, 709, 819, **822**, 829, 857, 883, 891, **893**, 899, 902.

893 Sullenness

N. *sullenness*, sternness, grimness 834 *seriousness*; sulkiness, ill humour, pettishness; morosity, surliness, churlishness, crabbedness, crustiness, unsociableness 883 *unsociability*; vinegar 393 *sourness*; grumpiness, grouchiness, pout, grimace 829 *discontent*; gruffness 885 *discourtesy*; crossness, peevishness, ill temper, bad t., savage t., shocking t. 892 *irascibility*; spleen, bile, liver; sulks, fit of the s., the pouts, mulligrubs, dumps, grouch, bouderie, moodiness, temperament; cafard, the blues, blue devils 834 *melancholy*; black look, hangdog l.; glare, glower, lour, frown, scowl; snort, growl, snarl, snap, bite; 'curses not loud but deep'.

Adj. *sullen*, forbidding, ugly; gloomy, saturnine, overcast, cloudy, sunless 418 *dark*; glowering, scowling; stern, frowning, unsmiling, grim 834 *serious*; sulky, sulking, cross, cross as two sticks, out of temper, out of humour, out of sorts, misanthropic 883 *unsociable*; surly, morose, dyspeptic, crabbed, crusty, cross-grained, difficult; snarling, snapping, snappish, shrewish, vixenish, cantankerous, quarrelsome, stroppy 709 *quarrelling*; refractory, jibbing 738 *disobedient*; grouchy, grumbling, grumpy 829 *discontented*; acid, tart, vinegary 393 *sour*; gruff, rough, abrupt, brusque 885 *discourteous*; temperamental, moody, humoursome, up and down 152 *changeful*; bilious, jaundiced, dyspeptic; blue, down, down in the dumps, depressed, melancholy 834 *melancholic*; petulant, pettish, peevish, shirty, ill-tempered, bad-t. 892 *irascible*; smouldering, sultry.

Vb. *be sullen*, gloom, glower, glare, lour; look black, scowl, frown, knit one's brows; bare one's teeth, show one's fangs, spit; snap, snarl, growl, snort; make a face, grimace, pout, sulk 883 *be unsociable*; mope, have the blues 834 *be dejected*; get out of bed on the wrong side; grouch, grouse, carp, crab, complain, grumble, mutter, smoulder 829 *be discontented*.

Adv. *sullenly*, sulkily, gloomily, ill-humouredly, with a bad grace 598 *unwillingly*.

See: 152, 393, 418, 598, 709, 738, **829**, **834**, 883, 885, 892.

894 Marriage

N. *marriage*, matrimony, holy m., sacrament of m., one flesh; wedlock, wedded state, married s., state of matrimony, wedded bliss; match, union, alliance, partnership; conjugality, conjugal knot, nuptial bond, marriage tie, marriage bed, bed and board, cohabitation, living as man and wife, life together; husbandhood, husbandship; wifehood, wifeship; coverture, matronage, matronhood; banns, marriage certificate, marriage lines; marriage god, Hymen, Hera, Juno.

type of marriage, matrimonial arrangement, monogamy, monandry, bigamy, polygamy, Mormonism, polygyny, polyandry; digamy, deuterogamy, second marriage, remarriage, levirate; endogamy, exogamy; arranged match, marriage of convenience; love-match; mixed marriage, intermarriage, miscegenation 43 *mixture*; mismarriage, mésalliance, misalliance, morganatic marriage, left-handed m.; companionate marriage, temporary m., trial m., open m., common-law m.; free union, free love, concubinage; ménage à trois; compulsory marriage, forcible wedlock, shotgun wedding; abduction, Sabine rape.

wedding, getting married, match, matchmaking, betrothal, engagement; nuptial vows, marriage v., ring, wedding r.; bridal, nuptials, spousals, hymenal rites; leading to the altar, tying the knot, getting spliced; marriage rites, marriage ceremony; wedding service, nuptial mass, nuptial benediction 988 *Christian rite*; church wedding, white w., civil marriage, registry-office m.; Gretna Green marriage, run-away match, elopement; solemn wedding, quiet w.; torch of Hymen, nuptial song, hymeneal, prothalamium, epithalamium; wedding day, wedding bells; marriage feast, wedding breakfast, reception; honeymoon; silver wedding, golden w., wedding anniversary 876 *special day*.

bridal party, groomsman, best man, paranymph, maid *or* matron of honour, bridesmaid, page, train-bearer; attendant, usher.

spouse, espouser, espoused; one's promised, one's betrothed 887 *loved one*; marriage partner, man, wife; spouses, man and wife, Mr and Mrs, Darby and Joan, Philemon and Baucis; married couple, young marrieds, bridal pair, newlyweds, honeymooners; bride, blushing b., young matron; bridegroom, benedick; consort, partner, mate, yoke-mate, helpmate, helpmeet, better half, soul-mate, affinity; married man, husband, goodman, hubbie, man, old man, lord and master; much-married man, henpecked husband; injured husband 952 *cuckold*; married woman, wedded wife, lawful w., lady, matron, feme covert, partner of one's bed and board; wife of one's bosom, woman, old w., missus, wifey, old dutch, rib, grey mare, trouble and strife, Duchess of Fife, joy of my life; squaw, broadwife; faithful spouse, monogamist; digamist, second husband, second wife, bigamous w.; common-law husband *or* wife, wife *or* husband in all but name.

polygamist, polygynist, much-married man, owner of a harem, Turk, Mormon, Solomon; Bluebeard; bigamist.

matchmaker, matrimonial agent, marriage-broker, go-between; marriage bureau, lonely hearts club, personal column; marriage guidance counsellor 720 *mediator*.

nubility, marriageable age, fitness for marriage, marriageability; eligibility, suitability, good match, proper m., suitable m.; suitable party, eligible p., welcome suitor 887 *lover*.

Adj. *married*, partnered, paired, mated, matched; tied, spliced, hitched, in double harness; espoused, wedded, united, made man and wife, made one, joined in holy matrimony, bone of one's bone and flesh of one's flesh; monogamous; polygynous, polygamous, polyandrous; much-married, polygamistic; remarried, digamous, bigamous; just married, newly m., newly-wed, honeymooning; mismarried, ill-matched.

marriageable, nubile, fit for marriage, ripe for m., of age, of marriageable a.; eligible, suitable; handfast, betrothed, promised, engaged, affianced, plighted, bespoke.

matrimonial, marital, connubial, concubinary; premarital, postmarital, extramarital; nuptial, bridal, spousal, hymeneal, epithalamic, epithalamial; conjugal, wifely, matronly, husbandly; digamous, bigamous; polygamous, polygynous, polyandrous; endogamous, exogamous; morganatic.

Vb. *marry*, marry off, find a husband *or* wife for, match, mate; matchmake, make a match, arrange a m.; betroth, affiance, espouse, publish the banns, announce the engagement; bestow in marriage, give in marriage, give away; join in marriage, make fast in wedlock, declare man and wife; join, couple, splice, hitch, tie the knot.

wed, marry, espouse; take *or* find a wife *or* a husband; ask for the hand of 889 *court*; quit the single state, take the plunge, get married, get hitched, get spliced, mate with, marry oneself to, unite oneself with, give oneself in marriage, bestow one's hand, accept a proposal, plight one's troth, become engaged, put up the banns;

lead to the altar, walk down the aisle, say 'I do', take for better or worse, be made one 45 *unite with*; pair off, mate, couple; honeymoon, cohabit, set up house together, share bed and board, live as man and wife, live together, live in sin; marry well, make a good match; mismarry, make a bad match, repent at leisure; make a love match 887 *be in love*; marry in haste, run away, elope; contract marriage, make an honest woman of, go through a form of marriage; marry again, remarry; commit bigamy; intermarry, miscegenate.

Adv. *matrimonially*, in the way of marriage; bigamously, polygamously, morganatically.

See: 43, 45, 720, 876, **887**, 889, 952, 988.

895 Celibacy

N. *celibacy*, singleness, single state, single blessedness 744 *independence*; bachelorhood, bachelorship, bachelordom; misogamy, misogyny 883 *unsociability*; spinsterhood, spinsterdom; monkhood, the veil 985 *monasticism*; maidenhood, virginity 950 *purity*.

celibate, unmarried man, single m., bachelor, Benedick; confirmed bachelor, born b., old b., gay b., not the marrying kind; enemy of marriage, misogamist, misogynist 902 *misanthrope*; Encratite, monastic 986 *monk*; hermit 883 *solitary*; monastic order, celibate o. 985 *holy orders*.

spinster, unmarried woman, feme sole, bachelor girl; maid unwed, debutante; maid, maiden, virgo intacta; maiden aunt, old maid; vestal, vestal virgin 986 *nun*; Amazon, Diana, Artemis.

Adj. *unwedded*, unwed, unmarried; unpartnered, single, mateless, unmated; spouseless, wifeless, husbandless; unwooed, unasked, on the shelf; free, uncaught, heart-whole, fancy-free 744 *independent*; maidenly, virgin, virginal, vestal 950 *pure*; spinster, spinsterlike, spinsterish, old-maidish; bachelor, bachelor-like; celibate, monkish, nunnish 986 *monastic*.

Vb. *live single*, stay unmarried, live in single blessedness; refuse marriage, keep heart-whole 744 *be free*; have no offers, receive no proposals; live like a hermit 883 *be unsociable*; take the veil 986 *take orders*.

See: 744, 883, 902, 950, 985, 986.

896 Divorce. Widowhood

N. *divorce*, dissolution of marriage, divorcement, putting away, repudiation; bill of divorcement, divorce decree, decree nisi, decree absolute; separation, legal s., judicial s.; annulment, decree of nullity; no marriage, nonconsummation; nullity, impediment, diriment i., prohibited degree, consanguinity, affinity; desertion, living apart, separate maintenance, alimony; marriage on the rocks, broken marriage, broken engagement, forbidding the banns; divorce court, divorce case; divorced person, divorcee, divorcé(e), nor wife nor maid; corespondent; single parent.

widowhood, widowerhood, viduity, dowagerhood; grass widowhood; widows' weeds 228 *formal dress*; widower, widow, widow woman, relict; dowager, dowager duchess; war widow, grass w., grass widower, Merry Widow.

Adj. *divorced*, deserted, separated, living apart; dissolved.

widowed, husbandless, wifeless; vidual.

Vb. *divorce*, separate, split up, go one's separate ways, live separately, live apart, desert 621 *relinquish*; unmarry, untie the knot 46 *disunite*; put away, sue for divorce, file a divorce suit; wear the horns, be cuckolded; get a divorce, revert to bachelorhood, regain one's freedom; put asunder, dissolve marriage, annul a m., grant a decree of nullity, grant a divorce, pronounce a decree absolute.

be widowed, outlive one's spouse, lose one's wife, mourn one's husband, put on widow's weeds.

widow, bereave, make a widow *or* widower, leave one's wife a widow.

See: 46, 228, 621.

897 Benevolence

N. *benevolence*, good will, helpfulness 880 *friendliness*; ahimsa, harmlessness 935 *innocence*; benignity, kindly disposition, heart of gold; amiability, bonhomie 882 *sociability*; milk of human kindness, goodness of nature, warmth of heart, warm-heartedness, kind-heartedness, kindliness, kindness, loving-k., goodness and mercy, charity, Christian c. 887 *love*; godly love, brotherly l., brotherliness, fraternal feeling 880 *friendship*; tenderness, consideration 736 *leniency*; understanding, responsiveness, caring, concern, fellow feeling, empathy, sympathy, overflowing s. 818 *feeling*; condolence 905 *pity*; decent feeling, humanity, humaneness, humanitarianism 901 *philanthropy*; utilitarianism 901 *sociology*; charitableness, hospitality, beneficence, unselfishness, generosity, magnanimity 813 *liberality*; gentleness, softness, mildness, tolerance, toleration 734 *laxity*; placability, mercy 909 *forgiveness*; God's love, grace of God; blessing, benediction.

kind act, kindness, favour, service; good deed, charitable d.; charity, deed of c., relief, alms, almsgiving 781 *giving*; prayers, good offices, kind o., good turn, helpful act 703 *aid*; labour of love 597 *voluntary work*.

kind person, bon enfant, Christian; good sort, good neighbour, good Samaritan, well-wisher 880 *friend*; sympathizer 707 *patron*; altruist, idealist, do-gooder 901 *philanthropist*.

Adj. *benevolent*, well meant, well-intentioned, with the best intentions, for the best 880 *friendly*; out of kindness, to oblige; out of charity, eleemosynary; good of one, so good of; sympathetic, wishing well, well-wishing, favouring, praying for; kindly disposed, benign, benignant, kindly, kind-hearted, overflowing with kindness, full of the milk of human k., warm-hearted, large-h., golden-h.; kind, good, human, decent, Christian; affectionate 887 *loving*; fatherly, paternal; motherly, maternal; brotherly, fraternal; sisterly, cousinly; good-humoured, good-natured, easy, sweet, gentle 884 *amiable*; placable, merciful 909 *forgiving*; tolerant, indulgent 734 *lax*; humane, considerate 736 *lenient*; soft-hearted, tender; pitiful, sympathizing, condolent 905 *pitying*; genial, hospitable 882 *sociable*; bounteous, bountiful 813 *liberal*; generous, magnanimous, unselfish, unenvious, unjealous, altruistic 931 *disinterested*; beneficent, charitable, humanitarian, doing good 901 *philanthropic*; obliging, accommodating, helpful 703 *aiding*; tactful, complaisant, gracious, gallant, chivalrous, chivalric 884 *courteous*.

Vb. *be benevolent*, - kind etc. adj.; feel the springs of charity, have one's heart in the right place; show concern, care for, feel for; sympathize, understand, feel as for oneself, enter into another's feelings, put oneself in another's place, do as one would be done by, practise the golden rule; return good for evil, love one's enemy 909 *forgive*; wish well, pray for, bless, give one's blessing, bestow a benediction; bear good will, wish the best for, have the right intentions, have the best i., mean well; look with a favourable eye, favour 703 *patronize*; benefit 644 *do good*; be a good Samaritan, do a good turn, render a service, oblige, put one under an obligation 703 *aid*; humanize, reform 654 *make better*.

philanthropize, do good, go about doing good, do good works, have a social conscience, serve the community, show public spirit, care; get involved 678 *be active*; reform, improve; relieve the poor, go slumming; visit, nurse 703 *minister to*; mother 889 *pet*.

Adv. *benevolently*, kindly, tenderly, lovingly, charitably, generously; in kindness, in charity, in love and peace, out of kindness, to oblige; mercifully, by the grace of God.

See: 597, **644**, 654, 678, 703, 707, 734, 736, 781, 813, 818, **880**, 882, 884, 887, 889, **901**, **905**, 909, **931**, 935.

898 Malevolence

N. *malevolence*, ill will 881 *enmity*; truculence, cussedness, bitchiness, beastliness, evil intent, bad intention, worst intentions, cloven hoof; spite, gall, spitefulness, viciousness, despite, malignity, malignancy, malice, deliberate m., malice prepense, malice aforethought; bad blood, hate 888 *hatred*; venom, virulence, deadliness, balefulness 659 *bane*; bitterness, acrimony, acerbity 393 *sourness*; mordacity 388 *pungency*; rancour, spleen 891 *resentment*; gloating, Schadenfreude, unholy joy 912 *envy*; evil eye 983 *spell*.

inhumanity, misanthropy, lack of humanity, inconsiderateness, lack of concern; lack of charity, uncharitableness; intolerance, persecution 735 *severity*; harshness, mercilessness, implacability, hardness of heart, obduracy, heart of marble, heart of stone 906 *pitilessness*; cold feelings, unkindness; callousness 326 *hardness*; cruelty, barbarity, bloodthirstiness, bloodiness, bloodlust; barbarism, savagery, ferocity, barbarousness, savageness, ferociousness; atrociousness, outrageousness; sadism, fiendishness, devilishness 934 *wickedness*; truculence, brutality, ruffianism; destructiveness, vandalism 165 *destruction*.

cruel act, cruel conduct, brutality; ill-treatment, bad t., ill usage 675 *misuse*; unkindness, disservice, ill turn; victimization, bullying, 'tender mercies' 735 *severity*; foul play, bloodshed 176 *violence*; excess, extremes; act of inhumanity, inhuman deed, atrocity, outrage, devilry; cruelty, cruelties, torture, tortures, barbarity, barbarities; cannibalism, murder 362 *homicide*; mass murder, genocide 362 *slaughter*.

Adj. *malevolent*, ill-wishing, ill-willed, evil-intentioned, ill-disposed, meaning harm 661 *dangerous*; ill-natured, churlish 893 *sullen*; nasty, bloody-minded, bitchy, cussed 602 *wilful*; malicious, catty, spiteful 926 *detracting*; mischievous, mischief-making (**see** *maleficent*); baleful, squint-eyed, malign, malignant 645 *harmful*; vicious, viperous, venomous 362 *deadly*; black-hearted, full of spite 888 *hating*; jealous 912 *envious*; disloyal, treacherous 930 *perfidious*; bitter, rancorous 891 *resentful*; implacable, unforgiving, merciless 906 *pitiless*; vindictive, gloating 910 *revengeful*; hostile, fell 881 *inimical*; intolerant, persecuting 735 *oppressive*.

maleficent, malefic, hurtful, damaging 645 *harmful*; poisonous, venomous, virulent, caustic, mordacious 659 *baneful*; working evil, spreading evil, mischief-making, spreading mischief 645 *bad*.

unkind, unamiable, ill-natured 893 *sullen*; unkindly, unbenevolent, unloving, unaffectionate, untender, stepmotherly, unmaternal, unbrotherly, unfraternal, undaughterly, unfilial, unchristian; cold, unfriendly, hostile, misanthropic 881 *inimical*; unforthcoming, uncordial, inhospitable 883 *unsociable*; uncooperative, unhelpful, disobliging; ungenerous, uncharitable, unforgiving; mean, nasty; rude, harsh, gruff, beastly 885 *ungracious*; unsympathetic, unresponsive, uncaring, unfeeling, insensible, unmoved 820 *impassive*; stern 735 *severe*; unsqueamish, tough, hardboiled, hardbitten 326 *hard*; inhuman, unnatural.

cruel, grim, fell; steely, grim-faced, cold-eyed, steely-e., hard-hearted, flint-h., stony-h.; callous, cold-blooded; heartless, ruthless, merciless 906 *pitiless*; tyrannical 735 *oppressive*; gloating, sadistic; bloodthirsty, cannibalistic 362 *murderous*; bloody 176 *violent*; excessive, extreme; atrocious, outrageous; feral, tigerish, wolfish; unnatural, subhuman, dehumanized, brutalized, brutish; brutal, rough, truculent, fierce, ferocious; savage, barbarous, wild, untamed, untamable, tameless; inhuman, ghoulish, fiendish, devilish, diabolical, demoniacal, satanic, hellish, infernal.

Vb. *be malevolent*, bear malice, cherish a grudge, have it in for 888 *hate*; show ill will, betray the cloven hoof; show envy 912 *envy*; disoblige, spite, do one a bad turn; go to extremes, do one's worst, wreak one's spite, break a butterfly on a wheel, have no mercy 906 *be pitiless*; take one's revenge, take it out of, victimize, gloat 910 *be revengeful*; take it out on, bully, maltreat 645 *ill-treat*; molest, hurt, injure, annoy 645 *harm*; malign, run down, throw stones at 926 *detract*; tease, harry, hound, persecute, tyrannize, torture 735 *oppress*; raven, thirst for blood 362 *slaughter*; rankle, fester, poison, be a thorn in the flesh; create havoc, blight, blast 165 *lay waste*; cast the evil eye 983 *bewitch*.

Adv. *malevolently*, with evil intent, with the worst intentions; unkindly, spitefully, out of spite.

See: 165, 176, 326, 362, 388, 393, 602, **645**, 659, 661, 675, 735, 820, **881**, 883, 885, 888, 891, 893, **906**, 910, 912, 926, 930, 934, 983.

899 Malediction

N. *malediction*, malison, curse, imprecation, anathema; evil eye 983 *spell*; no blessing, ill wishes, bad wishes, 'curses not loud but deep' 898 *malevolence*; execration, denunciation, commination 900 *threat*; onslaught 712 *attack*; fulmination, thunder, thunders of the Vatican; ban, proscription, excommunication; exorcism, bell, book and candle.

scurrility, ribaldry, vulgarity; profanity, swearing, profane s., cursing and swearing, blasting, effing and blinding; bad language, foul l., filthy l., blue l., shocking l., strong l., unparliamentary l., Limehouse, Billingsgate; naughty word, expletive, swearword, oath, swear, damn, curse, cuss, tinker's c.; invective, vituperation, abuse, volley of a.; mutual abuse, slanging match, stormy exchange; vain abuse, empty curse, more bark than bite 900 *threat*; no compliment, aspersion, reflection, vilification, slander 926 *calumny*; cheek, sauce 878 *sauciness*; personal remarks, epithet, insult 921 *indignity*; contumely, scorn 922 *contempt*; scolding, rough edge of one's tongue, lambasting, tongue-lashing 924 *reproach*.

Adj. *maledictory*, cursing, maledictive, imprecatory, anathematizing, comminatory, fulminatory, denunciatory, damnatory.

cursing, evil-speaking, swearing, damning, blasting; profane, foul-mouthed, foul-tongued, foul-spoken, unparliamentary, scurrilous, scurrile, ribald 847 *vulgar*; sulphurous, blue; viperish, vituperative, abusive, vitriolic, injurious, vilipendious, reproachful 924 *disapproving*; contumelious, scornful 922 *despising*.

cursed, wished, wished on one; accursed, unblest, execrable; anathematized, under a ban, excommunicated, damned 961 *condemned*; under a spell 983 *bewitched*.

Vb. *curse*, cast the evil eye 983 *bewitch*; accurse, wish ill 898 *be malevolent*; wish on, call down on; wish one joy of; curse with bell, book and candle, curse up hill and down dale; anathematize, imprecate, invoke curses on, execrate, hold up to execration; fulminate, thunder against, inveigh 924 *reprove*; denounce 928 *accuse*; excommunicate, damn 961 *condemn*; round upon, confound, send to the devil, send to blazes; abuse, vituperate, revile, rail, chide, heap abuse, pour vitriol 924 *reprobate*; bespatter, throw mud 926 *detract*.

cuss, curse, swear, damn, blast; blaspheme 980 *be impious*; swear like a trooper, use expletives, use Billingsgate, curse and swear, eff and blind, turn the air blue; slang, slangwhang, abuse, blackguard 924 *reprobate*; rail at, scold, give the rough edge of one's tongue.

Int. curse! a curse on! a plague on! woe to! woe betide! ill betide! confusion seize! confound it! devil take it! blast! damn! dang! darn! drat! hang! the deuce! the dickens!

See: 712, 847, 878, **898**, 900, 921, 922, 924, 926, 928, 961, 980, 983.

900 Threat

N. *threat*, menace; commination, fulmination 899 *malediction*; minacity, threatfulness, ominousness; challenge, dare 711 *defiance*; blackmail 737 *demand*; battle cry, war whoop, sabre-rattling, war of nerves 854 *intimidation*; deterrent, big stick 723 *weapon*; black cloud, gathering clouds 511 *omen*; hidden fires, secret weapon 663 *pitfall*; impending danger, sword of Damocles 661 *danger*; danger signal, fair warning, writing on the wall 664 *warning*; bluster, idle threat, hollow t. 877 *boast*; bark, growl, snarl 893 *sullenness*.

Adj. *threatening*, menacing, minatory, minatorial, minacious; sabre-rattling 711 *defiant*; blustering, bullying, hectoring 877 *boastful*; muttering, grumbling 893 *sullen*; bodeful, portentous, ominous, foreboding 511 *presageful*; hovering, louring, hanging over 155 *impending*; ready to spring, growling, snarling 891 *angry*; abusive 899 *cursing*; comminatory 899 *maledictory*; deterrent 854 *frightening*; nasty, unpleasant 661 *dangerous*.

Vb. *threaten*, menace, use threats, hold out t., utter t.; demand with menaces, blackmail 737 *demand*; hijack, hold to ransom; frighten, deter, intimidate, bully, wave the big stick 854 *frighten*; roar, bellow 408 *vociferate*; fulminate, thunder 899 *curse*; bark, talk big, bluster, hector 877 *boast*; shake, wave, flaunt 317 *brandish*; rattle the sabre, clench the fist, draw one's sword, make a pass 711 *defy*; bare the fangs, snarl, growl, mutter 893 *be sullen*; bristle, spit, look daggers, grow nasty 891 *get angry*; pull a gun on, hold at gunpoint; draw a bead on, cover, have one covered, keep one c. 281 *aim*; gather, mass, lour, hang over, hover 155 *impend*; bode ill, presage, disaster, mean no good, promise trouble, spell danger 511 *predict*; serve notice, caution, forewarn 664 *warn*; breathe revenge, promise r., threaten reprisals 910 *be revengeful*.

Adv. *threateningly*, menacingly, on pain of death.

See: 155, 281, 317, 408, 511, **661**, 663, 664, 711, 723, 737, **854**, 877, 891, 893, 899, 910.

901 Philanthropy

N. *philanthropy*, humanitarianism, humanity, humaneness, the golden rule 897 *benevolence*; humanism, cosmopolitanism, internationalism; altruism 931 *disinterestedness*; idealism, ideals 933 *virtue*; universal benevolence, the greatest happiness of the greatest number, utilitarianism, Benthamism; common good, socialism, communism; passion for improvement, urge to set the world to rights 654 *reformism*; chivalry, knight-errantry; dedication, crusading spirit, missionary s., nonconformist conscience, social c.; good works, mission, civilizing m., 'white man's burden'; Holy War, jihad, crusade, campaign, cause, good c.; voluntary agency, charitable foundation, charity 703 *aid*.

sociology, social science, social engineering, social planning; poor relief, benefit, dole; social services, Welfare State; community service, social service, social work, slumming, good works.

patriotism, civic ideals, good citizenship, public spirit, concern for the community, love of one's country; local patriotism, parochialism; nationalism, chauvinism, my country right or wrong; irredentism, Zionism.

philanthropist, friend of the human race 903 *benefactor*; humanitarian, do-gooder, social worker, slummer 897 *kind person*; community service worker, VSO, Peace Corps 597 *volunteer*; paladin, champion, crusader, knight, knight errant; Messiah 690 *leader*; missionary, person with a mission, dedicated soul, bodhisattva; ideologist, idealist, altruist, flower people 513 *visionary*; reformist 654 *reformer*; utilitarian, Benthamite; Utopian, millenarian, chiliast; populist, humanist, cosmopolite, cosmopolitan, citizen of the world, internationalist.

patriot, lover of one's country, fighter for one's c.; father *or* mother of the people; nationalist, chauvinist, irredentist, Zionist.

Adj. *philanthropic*, humanitarian, humane, human 897 *benevolent*; charitable, aid-giving 703 *aiding*; enlightened, humanistic, liberal; cosmopolitan, international, internationally minded; idealistic, altruistic 931 *disinterested*; visionary, dedicated; sociological, socialistic, communistic; utilitarian.

patriotic, civically minded, public-spirited, community-minded; irredentist, nationalistic, chauvinistic; loyal, true, true-blue.

Vb. *be charitable* 897 *philanthropize*.

Adv. *pro bono publico*.

See: 513, 597, 654, 690, 703, **897**, **903**, 931, 933.

902 Misanthropy

N. *misanthropy*, hatred of mankind, distrust of one's fellows, disillusionment with society, cynicism 883 *unsociability*; misandry, misogyny; moroseness 893 *sullenness*; inhumanity, incivism; egotism.

misanthrope, misanthropist, hater of the human race, man-hater, woman-h., misogynist; cynic, Diogenes, Alceste; egotist; no patriot, defeatist; world-hater, unsocial animal 883 *solitary*; bear, crosspatch, sulker 829 *malcontent*.

Adj. *misanthropic*, inhuman, antisocial 883 *unsociable*; cynical; uncivic, unpatriotic, defeatist.

Vb. *misanthropize*, become a misanthrope, lose faith in humankind.

Adv. *misanthropically*, cynically.

See: 829, 883, 893.

903 Benefactor

N. *benefactor*, benefactress 901 *philanthropist*; Lady Bountiful, Father Christmas, Santa Claus 781 *giver*; fairy godmother, guardian angel, tutelary saint, good genius 660 *protector*; founder, foundress, supporter 707 *patron*; tyrannicide, pater patriae, protector of the people 901 *patriot*; saviour, ransomer, redeemer, deliverer, rescuer 668 *deliverance*; champion 713 *defender*; Lady Godiva, Good Samaritan 897 *kind person*; good neighbour 880 *friend*; helper, present help in time of trouble 703 *aider*; salt of the earth, saint 937 *good person*.

See: 660, 668, 703, 707, 713, 781, 880, 897, 901, 937.

904 Evildoer

N. *evildoer*, malefactor, wrongdoer, sinner 934 *wickedness*; villain, blackguard, bad lot, baddy; one up to no good, mischief-maker 663 *troublemaker*; scamp, monkey, imp of mischief, little devil, holy terror; gossip, slanderer, calumniator 926 *detractor*; snake in the grass, viper in the bosom, traitor 545 *deceiver*; obstructionist, saboteur 702 *hinderer*; spoiler, despoiler, wrecker, defacer, vandal, Hun, iconoclast 168 *destroyer*; terrorist, nihilist, anarchist 738 *revolter*; incendiary, arsonist 381 *incendiarism*; disturber of the peace 738 *rioter*.

ruffian, blackguard, rogue, scoundrel 938 *knave*; lout, hooligan, hoodlum, larrikin 869 *low fellow*; Hell's Angel, yob, yobbo, punk; bully, terror, terror of the neighbourhood; rough, tough, rowdy, ugly customer, plug-ugly, bruiser, thug, apache; bravo, desperado, assassin, hired a.; cutthroat, hatchet man, gunman, killer, butcher 362 *murderer*; genocide, mass murderer; plague, scourge, scourge of the human race, Attila 659 *bane*; petty tyrant, gauleiter 735 *tyrant*; brute, savage b., beast, savage, barbarian, ape-man, caveman; cannibal, head-hunter; homicidal maniac 504 *madman*.

offender, sinner, black sheep 938 *bad person*; suspect; culprit, guilty person, lawbreaker; criminal, villain, crook, malefactor, malfeasant, wrongdoer, misdemeanant, felon; delinquent, juvenile d., first offender; recidivist, backslider, old offender, hardened o., lag, old l., convict, ex-c., jailbird; lifer, gallowsbird, 'quare fellow'; parolee, probationer, ticket-of-leave man; mafioso, mobster, gangster, racketeer; housebreaker 789 *thief, robber*; forger 789 *defrauder*; blackmailer, bloodsucker; poisoner 362 *murderer*; outlaw, public enemy 881 *enemy*; intruder, trespasser; criminal world, underworld, Mafia 934 *wickedness*.

hellhag, hellhound, fiend, devil incarnate; hellcat, bitch, virago 892 *shrew*; she-devil, fury, harpy, siren; ogre, ogress, witch, vampire, werewolf 938 *monster*.

noxious animal, brute, beast, wild b.; beast of prey, predator; tiger, man-eater, wolf, hyena, jackal, fox; kite, vulture 365 *bird*; snake, serpent, viper 365 *reptile*; cockatrice, basilisk, salamander 84 *rara avis*; scorpion, wasp, hornet; pest, locust, Colorado beetle, deathwatch b. 365 *insect*; rat 659 *bane*; wild cat, mad dog, rogue elephant.

See: 84, 168, 362, 365, 381, 504, 545, 659, 663, 702, 735, 738, **789**, 869, 881, 892, 926, 934, **938**.

905 Pity

N. *pity*, springs of p., ruth; remorse, compunction 830 *regret*; charity, compassion, bowels of c., compassionateness, humanity 897 *benevolence*; soft heart, tender h., bleeding h.; gentleness, softness 736 *leniency*; commiseration, touched feelings, melting mood, tears of sympathy 825 *sorrow*; Weltschmerz, lacrimae rerum 834 *dejection*; sympathy, empathy, understanding, deep u., fellow feeling (**see** *condolence*); self-pity, self-compassion, self-commiseration, tears for oneself.

condolence, commiseration, sympathetic grief, sympathy, fellow feeling, fellowship in sorrow 775 *participation*; consolation, comfort 831 *relief*; professional condolence, keen, coronach, wake 836 *lament*.

mercy, tender mercies, quarter, grace; second chance; mercifulness, clemency, lenity, placability, forbearance, longsuffering 909 *forgiveness*; light sentence 963 *penalty*; let-off 960 *acquittal*.

Adj. *pitying*, compassionate, sympathetic, understanding, condolent, commiserating; sorry for, feeling for; merciful, clement, full of mercy 736 *lenient*; melting, tender, tender-hearted, soft, soft-hearted 819 *impressible*; weak 734 *lax*; unhardened, easily touched, easily moved; placable, disposed to mercy 909 *forgiving*; remorseful, compunctious; humane, charitable 897 *benevolent*; forbearing 823 *patient*.

pitiable, pitiful, piteous, pathetic, heartrending; deserving pity, demanding p., claiming p., challenging sympathy; arousing compassion.

Vb. *pity*, feel p., weep for p.; show compassion, show pity, take pity on; sympathize, sympathize with, enter into one's feelings, feel for, feel with, share the grief of 775 *participate*; sorrow, grieve, bleed for, feel sorry for, weep f., lament f., commiserate, condole, condole with, express one's condolences, send one's c.; yearn over 836 *lament*; console, comfort, offer consolation, afford c., wipe away one's tears 833 *cheer*; have pity, have compassion, melt, thaw, relent 909 *forgive*.

show mercy, have m., offer m., spare, spare the life of, give quarter; commute (a sentence), pardon, amnesty; forget one's anger 909 *forgive*; be slow to anger, forbear; give one a break, give one a second chance 736 *be lenient*; relent, unbend, not proceed to extremes, relax one's rigour, show consideration, not be too hard upon, go easy on, let one down gently; put out of one's misery, give the coup de grace, be cruel to be kind.

ask mercy, plead for m., appeal for m., pray for m., beg for m., throw oneself upon another's mercy, fall at one's feet, cry mercy, ask for quarter, plead for one's life; excite pity, move to compassion, propitiate, disarm, melt, thaw, soften 719 *pacify*.

Int. alas! poor thing! for pity's sake! for mercy's s.! for the love of God! have mercy! have a heart!

See: 719, 734, 736, 775, 819, 823, 825, 830, 831, 833, 834, 836, **897**, **909**, 960, 963.

906 Pitilessness

N. *pitilessness*, lack of pity, heartlessness, ruthlessness, mercilessness, unmercifulness; inclemency, intolerance, rigour 735 *severity*; callousness, hardness of heart 898 *inhumanity*; inflexibility 326 *hardness*; inexorability, relentlessness, remorselessness, unforgivingness 910 *revengefulness*; letter of the law, pound of flesh; no pity, no heart, short shrift, no quarter.

Adj. *pitiless*, unpitying, uncompassionate, uncondoling, uncomforting, unconsoling, unfeeling, unresponsive 820 *impassive*; unsympathising, unsympathetic; unmelting, unmoved, tearless, dry-eyed; hardhearted, stony-h.; unsqueamish, callous, tough, hardened 326 *hard*; harsh, rigorous, intolerant, persecuting 735 *severe*; brutal, sadistic 898 *cruel*; merciless, ruthless, heartless; indisposed to mercy, inclement, unmerciful, unrelenting, relentless, remorseless, inflexible, inexorable, implacable; unforgiving, unpardoning, vindictive 910 *revengeful*.

Vb. *be pitiless*, - ruthless etc. adj.; have no heart, have no compassion, have no pity, know no p.; not be moved, turn a deaf ear; show no pity, show no mercy, give no quarter, spare none; harden one's heart, be deaf to appeal, admit no excuse; not tolerate, persecute 735 *be severe*; stand on the letter of the law, insist on one's pound of flesh 735 *be severe*; take one's revenge 910 *avenge*.

See: 326, 735, 820, **898**, 910.

907 Gratitude

N. *gratitude*, gratefulness, thankfulness, grateful heart, feeling of obligation, sense of o.; grateful acceptance, appreciativeness, appreciation, lively sense of favours received.

thanks, hearty t.; giving thanks, vote of t., thankyou; thanksgiving, benediction, blessing; praises, Te Deum 876 *celebration*; grace, bismillah, grace before meals; thankyou letter, bread-and-butter l., Collins; credit, credit title, acknowledgment, grateful a., recognition, grateful r., ungrudging r., full praise; tribute 923 *praise*; thank-offering, parting present, recognition of one's services, token of one's gratitude, tip 962 *reward*; requital, return, favour returned 714 *retaliation*.

Adj. *grateful*, thankful, appreciative; showing appreciation, thanking, blessing, praising; acknowledging favours, crediting, giving credit; obliged, much o., under obligation, beholden, indebted.

Vb. *be grateful*, have a grateful heart, overflow with gratitude; thank one's lucky stars, praise Heaven; feel an obligation, cherish a favour, never forget; accept gratefully, pocket thankfully, receive with open arms, not look a gift horse in the mouth; be privileged, have the honour to.

thank, give thanks, render t., return t., express t., pour out one's t., praise, bless; acknowledge, express acknowledgments, credit, give c., give full c. 158 *attribute*; appreciate, show appreciation, tip 962 *reward*; return a favour, requite, repay, repay with interest; return with thanks 787 *restitute*.

Adv. *gratefully*, thankfully, with gratitude, with thanks, with interest.

Int. thanks! many t.! much obliged! thank you! thank goodness! thank Heaven! Heaven be praised!

See: 158, 714, 787, 876, 923, 962.

908 Ingratitude

N. *ingratitude*, lack of gratitude, lack of appreciation, ungratefulness, unthankfulness, thanklessness; grudging thanks, cold t., more kicks than ha'pence; no sense of obligation, indifference to favours, 'benefits forgot' 506 *oblivion*; no reward, unrewardingness, thankless task, thankless office; thankless person, ingrate, ungrateful wretch.

Adj. *ungrateful*, unthankful 885 *discourteous*; unobliged, not obliged, unbeholden; unmindful 506 *forgetful*; unmindful of favours, insensible of benefits, incapable of gratitude 820 *apathetic*.

unthanked, unappreciated, thankless, without credit, unacknowledged, forgotten; rewardless, bootless, unrewarding, unrewarded, unrequited, ill-requited, untipped.

Vb. *be ungrateful*, show ingratitude, admit no obligation, acknowledge no favour;

take for granted, take as one's due; not thank, omit to t., forget to t.; see no reason to thank, grudge thanks, not give a thank-you for, look a gift horse in the mouth; forget a kindness, return evil for good.

Int. thank you for nothing! no thanks to.

See: 506, 820, 885.

909 Forgiveness

N. *forgiveness*, pardon, free p., full p., reprieve 506 *amnesty*; indemnity, grace, indulgence, plenary i. 905 *mercy*; cancellation, remission, absolution 960 *acquittal*; condonation; justification, exculpation, exoneration, excuse 927 *vindication*; mutual forgiveness, reconciliation 719 *pacification*; forgiving nature, mercifulness, placability, lenity 905 *pity*; longsuffering, forbearance 823 *patience*; forgiver, pardoner.

Adj. *forgiving*, merciful, placable, condoning, admitting excuses, conciliatory; willing to forgive 736 *lenient*; magnanimous 897 *benevolent*; unreproachful, unresentful, forbearing, longsuffering 823 *patient*; reluctant to punish, more in sorrow than in anger.

forgiven, pardoned, forgiven and forgotten, amnestied, reprieved; remitted, cancelled, blotted out; condoned, excused, exonerated, let off 960 *acquitted*; absolved, shriven; unresented, unavenged, unrevenged, unpunished, unchastened; pardonable, forgivable, venial, excusable.

Vb. *forgive*, pardon, reprieve, amnesty, forgive and forget, think no more of, not give another thought 506 *forget*; remit, absolve, assoil, shrive; cancel, blot out, wipe the slate clean 550 *obliterate*; relent, unbend, accept an apology 736 *be lenient*; be merciful, not be too hard upon, let one down gently, let one off the hook 905 *show mercy*; bear with, put up w., forbear, tolerate, make allowances 823 *be patient*; take no offence, bear no malice, take in good part, pocket, stomach, not hold it against one; forget an injury, ignore a wrong, overlook, pass over, not punish, leave unavenged, turn the other cheek; return good for evil 897 *be benevolent*; connive, wink at, condone, not make an issue of 458 *disregard*; excuse, find excuses for 927 *justify*; recommend for pardon, intercede 720 *mediate*; exculpate, exonerate 960 *acquit*; be ready to forgive, make the first move, bury the hatchet, let bygones be bygones, make it up, shake hands, kiss and be friends, be reconciled 880 *be friendly*; restore to favour, kill the fatted calf 876 *celebrate*.

beg pardon, plead for forgiveness, offer apologies, ask for absolution 905 *ask mercy*; propitiate, placate 941 *atone*.

Adv. *forgivingly*, without resentment, more in sorrow than in anger.

See: 458, 506, 550, 719, 720, 736, 823, 876, 880, **897**, **905**, 927, 941, 960.

910 Revenge

N. *revengefulness*, thirst for revenge; vindictiveness, spitefulness, spite 898 *malevolence*; ruthlessness 906 *pitilessness*; remorselessness, relentlessness, implacability, irreconcilability, unappeasability; unappeasable resentment, deadly rancour 891 *resentment*.

revenge, sweet r.; crime passionel 911 *jealousy*; vengeance, avengement, day of reckoning 963 *punishment*; victimization, reprisal, reprisals, punitive expedition 714 *retaliation*; lex talionis, eye for an eye, tooth for a tooth; vendetta, feud, blood f. 881 *enmity*.

avenger, vindicator, punisher, revanchist; Nemesis, Eumenides, avenging furies.

Adj. *revengeful*, vengeful, breathing vengeance, thirsting for revenge; avenging, taking vengeance, retaliative 714 *retaliatory*; at feud 881 *inimical*; unforgiving, unforgetting, implacable, unappeasable, unrelenting, relentless, remorseless 906 *pitiless*; vindictive, spiteful 898 *malevolent*; rancorous 891 *resentful*; enjoying revenge, gloating.

Vb. *avenge*, avenge oneself, revenge o., take one's revenge, exact r., take vengeance, wreak v., take the law into one's own hands; exact retribution, get one's own back, repay, pay out, pay off *or* settle old scores, square an account, give someone what was coming to them; get back at, give tit for tat 714 *retaliate*; sate one's vengeance, have one's fill of revenge, enjoy one's r., gloat.

be revengeful, - vindictive etc. adj.; get one's knife into 898 *be malevolent*; bear malice, cry out for revenge, breathe r., promise vengeance 888 *hate*; nurse one's revenge, harbour a grudge, carry on a feud, have a rod in pickle, have a crow to pluck, have a score *or* accounts to settle 881 *be inimi-*

cal; let it rankle, remember an injury, brood on one's wrongs, refuse to forget 891 *resent*.

See: **714**, 881, 888, 891, **898**, 906, 911, 963.

911 Jealousy

N. *jealousy*, pangs of j., jealousness; jaundiced eye, green-eyed monster; distrust, mistrust 486 *doubt*; heart-burning 891 *resentment*; enviousness 912 *envy*; hate 888 *hatred*; inferiority complex, emulation, competitiveness, competition, rivalry, jealous r. 716 *contention*; possessiveness 887 *love*; sexual jealousy, eternal triangle, crime passionel 910 *revenge*; object of jealousy, competitor, rival, hated r., the other man, the other woman; Othello.

Adj. *jealous*, green-eyed, yellow-e., jaundiced, envying 912 *envious*; devoured with jealousy, eaten up with j.; possessive 887 *loving*; suspicious, mistrusting, distrustful 474 *doubting*; emulative, competitive, rival, competing.

Vb. *be jealous*, scent a rival, suspect, mistrust, distrust 486 *doubt*; view with jealousy, view with a jaundiced eye 912 *envy*; resent another's superiority, nurse an inferiority complex; brook no rival, resent competition; strive to keep for oneself, not allow out of one's sight.

See: 474, 486, 716, 887, 888, 891, 910, 912.

912 Envy

N. *envy*, envious eye, enviousness, covetousness 859 *desire*; rivalry 716 *contention*; envious rivalry 911 *jealousy*; ill will, spite, spleen, bile 898 *malevolence*; mortification, unwilling admiration, grudging praise.

Adj. *envious*, envying, envious-eyed, green with envy 911 *jealous*; greedy, unsated, unsatisfied 829 *discontented*; covetous, longing 859 *desiring*; grudging; mortified 891 *resentful*.

Vb. *envy*, view with e., cast envious looks, turn green with e., resent; covet, crave, lust after, must have for oneself, long to change places with 859 *desire*.

See: 716, 829, 859, 891, 898, 911.

Section four: Morality

913 Right

N. *right*, rightfulness, rightness, fitness, what ought to be, what should be; obligation 917 *duty*; fittingness, seemliness, propriety, decency 848 *etiquette*; normality 83 *conformity*; rules, rules and regulations 693 *precept*; ethicalness, morality, good morals 917 *morals*; righteousness 933 *virtue*; rectitude, uprightness, honour 929 *probity*; one's right, one's due, deserts, merits, claim 915 *dueness*.

justice, freedom from wrong, justifiability; righting wrong, redress; reform 654 *reformism*; tardy justice, overdue reform; even-handed justice, impartial j.; scales of justice, justice under the law, process of l. 953 *legality*; retribution, retributive justice, poetic j. 962 *reward*; give and take, lex talionis 714 *retaliation*; fair-mindedness, objectivity, disinterestedness, detachment, impartiality, equalness 28 *equality*; equity, equitableness, reasonableness, fairness; fair deal, square d., fair treatment, fair play; no discrimination, equal opportunity; good law, Queensberry rules; Astraea, Themis, Nemesis.

Adj. *right*, rightful, proper, right and p., meet and right; fitting, suitable 24 *fit*; good 917 *ethical*; put right, redressed, reformed 654 *improved*; normal, standard, classical 83 *conformable*.

just, upright, righteous, right-minded, on the side of the angels 933 *virtuous*; fair-minded, disinterested, unprejudiced, unbiased, unswerving, undeflected 625 *neutral*; detached, impersonal, dispassionate, objective, open-minded; equal, egalitarian, impartial, even-handed; fair, square, fair and s., equitable, reasonable, fair enough; in the right, justifiable, justified, unchallengeable, unchallenged, unimpeachable; legitimate, according to law 953 *legal*; sporting, sportsmanlike 929 *honourable*; deserved, well-d., earned, merited, well-m. 915 *due*; overdue, demanded, claimed, rightly c., claimable 627 *required*.

Vb. *be right*, behove 915 *be due*; have justice, have good cause, be in the right, have right on one's side.

be just, - impartial etc. adj.; play the game 929 *be honourable*; do justice, give the devil his due, give full marks to, hand it to 915 *grant claims*; see justice done, see fair play, hold the scales even, hear both sides, go by merit, consider on its merits 480 *judge*; temper justice with mercy 905 *show mercy*; see one righted, right a wrong, redress, remedy, mend, reform, put right 654 *rectify*; serve one right 714 *retaliate*; try to be fair, lean over backwards, overcompensate; hide nothing, declare one's interest.

Adv. *rightly*, justly, justifiably, with justice; in the right, within one's rights; like a judge, impartially, indifferently, equally, without distinction, without respect of persons, without fear or favour, fairly, without favouritism; on its merits.

See: 24, 28, 83, 480, 625, 627, 654, 693, 714, 848, 905, **915**, **917**, **929**, 933, 953, 962.

914 Wrong

N. *wrong*, wrongness, something wrong, oddness, queerness 84 *abnormality*; something rotten, curse, bane, scandal 645 *badness*; disgrace, shame, crying s., dishonour 867 *slur*; impropriety, indecorum 847 *bad taste*; wrongheadedness, unreasonableness 481 *misjudgment*; unjustifiability, what ought not to be, what must not be 916 *undueness*; inexcusability, culpability, guiltiness 936 *guilt*; immorality, vice, sin 934 *wickedness*; dishonesty, unrighteousness 930 *improbity*; irregularity, illegitimacy, criminality, crime, lawlessness 954 *illegality*; wrongfulness, misdoing, misfeasance, transgression, trespass, encroachment; delict, misdeed, offence 936 *guilty act*; a wrong, injustice, tort, mischief, outrage, foul 930 *foul play*; sense of wrong, complaint, charge 928 *accusation*; grievance, just g. 891 *resentment*; wrong-doer, immoralist, unjust judge 938 *bad person*.

injustice, no justice; miscarriage of justice, wrong verdict 481 *misjudgment*; corrupt justice, uneven scales, warped judgment, packed jury 481 *bias*; one-sidedness, inequity, unfairness; discrimination, race d., sex d.; partiality, leaning, favouritism, favour, nepotism; preferential treatment, positive discrimination; partisanship, party spirit, old school tie 481 *prejudice*; unlawfulness, no law 954 *illegality*; justice denied, right withheld, privilege curtailed 916 *undueness*; unfair advantage, 'heads I win, tails you lose'; no equality, wolf and the lamb 29 *inequality*; not cricket 930 *foul play*; imposition, robbing Peter to pay Paul.

Adj. *wrong*, not right 645 *bad*; odd, queer, suspect 84 *abnormal*; unfitting, unseemly, improper 847 *vulgar*; wrongheaded, unreasonable 481 *misjudging*; wrong from the start, out of court, inadmissible; irregular, against the rules, foul, unauthorized, unwarranted 757 *prohibited*; wrongful, illegitimate, illicit, tortious, felonious, criminal 954 *illegal*; condemnable, culpable, in the wrong, offside 936 *guilty*; unwarrantable, inexcusable, unpardonable, unforgivable, unjustifiable (**see** *unjust*); open to objection, objectionable, reprehensible, scandalous 861 *disliked*; injurious, mischievous 645 *harmful*; unrighteous 930 *dishonest*; iniquitous, sinful, vicious, immoral 934 *wicked*.

unjust, unjustifiable; uneven, weighted 29 *unequal*; inequitable, iniquitous, unfair; hard, hard on 735 *severe*; foul, not playing the game, below the belt, unsportsmanlike; discriminatory, favouring, one-sided, leaning to one side, partial, partisan, prejudiced 481 *biased*; selling justice 930 *venal*; wresting the law 954 *illegal*.

Vb. *be wrong*, - unjust etc. adj.; be in the wrong, go wrong, err 655 *deteriorate*.

do wrong, wrong, hurt, injure, do an injury 645 *harm*; be hard on, have a down on 735 *be severe*; not play the game, not play cricket, hit below the belt; break the rules, commit a foul; commit a tort, commit a crime, break the law, wrest the l., pervert the l. 954 *be illegal*; transgress, infringe, trespass 306 *encroach*; wink at, connive at; leave unrighted, leave unremedied; do less than justice, withhold justice, deny j., deny one's rights; weight, load the scales, pack the jury, rig the jury; lean, lean to one side, discriminate against, show partiality, show favouritism, discriminate 481 *be biased*; favour 703 *patronize*; go too far, overcompensate, lean over backwards; commit, perpetrate.

Adv. *wrongly*, unrightfully, unjustly, wrongfully, illegally; criminally, with criminal intent.

See: 29, 84, 306, **481**, 645, 655, 703, 735, 757, 847, 861, 867, 891, **916**, 928, **930**, 934, 936, 938, 954.

915 Dueness

N. *dueness*, what is due, what is owing; accountability, responsibility, obligation 917 *duty*; from each according to his ability and to each according to his need; the least one can do, bare minimum; what one looks for, expectations; payability, dues 804 *payment*; something owed, indebtedness 803 *debt*; tribute, credit 158 *attribution*; recognition, acknowledgment 907 *thanks*; something to be said for, case for; qualification, merits, deserts, just d. 913 *right*; justification 927 *vindication*; entitlement, claim, title 913 *right*; birthright, patriality, patrimony 777 *dower*; interest, vested i., vested right, prescriptive r., absolute r., indefeasible r., inalienable r.; legal right, easement, prescription, ancient lights; human rights, women's r. 744 *freedom*; constitutional right, civil rights, bill of r., Magna Carta; privilege, exemption, immunity 919 *nonliability*; prerogative, privilege; charter, warrant, licence 756 *permit*; liberty, franchise; bond, security 767 *title deed*; patent, copyright; recovery of rights, restoration, revendication, compensation 787 *restitution*; owner, title-holder 776 *possessor*; heir 776 *beneficiary*; claimant, plaintiff, appellant; person with a grievance 763 *petitioner*.

Adj. *due*, owing, payable 803 *owed*; ascribable, attributable, assignable; merited, well-m., deserved, well-d., richly-d., condign, earned, well-e., coming to one; admitted, allowed, sanctioned, warranted, licit, lawful 756 *permitted*; constitutional, entrenched, untouchable, uninfringeable, unchallengeable, unimpeachable, inviolable; privileged, sacrosanct; confirmed, vested, prescriptive, inalienable, imprescriptible; secured by law, legalized, legitimate, rightful, of right, de jure 953 *legal*; claimable, heritable, inheritable, earmarked, reserved; expected, fit, fitting, befitting 913 *right*; proper, en règle 642 *advisable*.

deserving, meriting, worthy of, worthy, meritorious, emeritus, honoris causa; grant-worthy, credit-w.; justifiable, justified; entitled, having the right, having the title, claiming the right, asserting one's privilege, standing up for one's rights.

Vb. *be due*, - owing etc. adj.; ought, ought to be, should be, should have been; be one's due, be due to, have it coming; be the least one can offer, be the least one can do, be the bare minimum; behove, befit, beseem 917 *be one's duty*.

claim, claim as a right, lay claim to, stake a c., take possession 786 *appropriate*; claim unduly, arrogate; demand one's rights, assert one's r., stand up for one's r., vindicate one's r., insist on one's r., stand on one's r.; draw on, come down on for, take one's toll 786 *levy*; call in (debts), reclaim 656 *retrieve*; publish one's claims, declare one's right; sue, demand redress 761 *request*; enforce a claim, exercise a right; establish a right, patent, copyright.

have a right, expect, have a right to e., claim; be entitled, be privileged, have the right to, have a claim to, make out a case for 478 *demonstrate*; justify, substantiate 927 *vindicate*; have the law on one's side, have the court in one's favour, get a favourable verdict.

deserve, merit, be worthy, be found w., have a claim on; earn, receive one's due, meet with one's deserts, get one's d.; have it coming to one, have only oneself to thank; sow the wind and reap the whirlwind.

grant claims, give every man his due 913 *be just*; ascribe, assign, credit 158 *attribute*; hand it to, acknowledge, recognize 907 *thank*; allow a claim, sanction a c., warrant, authorize 756 *permit*; admit a right, acknowledge a claim, satisfy a c., pay one's dues, honour, meet an obligation, honour a bill 804 *pay*; privilege, give a right, confer a r., give one a title; allot, prescribe 783 *apportion*; legalize, legitimize 953 *make legal*; confirm, validate 488 *endorse*.

Adv. *duly*, by right, in one's own right, by law, de jure, ex officio, by divine right; as expected of one, as required of one.

See: 158, 478, 488, 642, 656, 744, 756, 761, 763, 767, 776, 777, 783, 786, 787, 803, 804, 907, **913**, **917**, 919, 927, 953.

916 Undueness

N. *undueness*, not what one expects *or* would expect 508 *lack of expectation*; not the thing, impropriety, unseemliness, indecorum 847 *bad taste*; unfittingness 643 *inexpedience*; unworthiness, demerit 934 *vice*; illicitness, illegitimacy, bastardy 954 *illegality*; no thanks to 908 *ingratitude*; absence of right, want of title, failure of t., nonentitlement; no claim, no right, no title, false t., weak t., empty t., courtesy t.; gratuitousness, gratuity, bonus, grace marks, unearned increment; inordinacy, excessiveness, too much, overpayment

637 *redundance*; imposition, exaction 735 *severity*; unfair share, lion's s. 32 *main part*; violation, breach, infraction, infringement, encroachment 306 *overstepping*; profanation, desecration 980 *impiety*.

arrogation, assumption, unjustified a., presumption, unwarranted p., swollen claims; pretendership, usurpation, tyranny; misappropriation 786 *expropriation*; encroachment, inroad, trespass 306 *overstepping*.

loss of right, disentitlement, disfranchisement, disqualification; denaturalization, detribalization 147 *conversion*; forfeiture 772 *loss*; dismissal, deprivation, dethronement 752 *deposal*; ouster, dispossession 786 *expropriation*; seizure, forcible s., robbery 788 *stealing*; cancellation 752 *abrogation*; waiver, abdication 621 *relinquishment*.

usurper, arrogator 735 *tyrant*; pretender 545 *impostor*; desecrator; violator, infringer, encroacher, trespasser, squatter, cuckoo in the nest.

Adj. *undue*, not owing, unattributable; unowed, gratuitous, by favour; not expected, unlooked for, uncalled for 508 *unexpected*; inappropriate, improper, unseemly, unfitting, unbefitting 643 *inexpedient*; preposterous, not to be thought of, out of the question 497 *absurd*.

unwarranted, unwarrantable; unauthorized, unsanctioned, unlicensed, unchartered, unconstitutional; unrightful, unlegalized, illicit, illegitimate, ultra vires 954 *illegal*; arrogated, usurped, stolen, borrowed; excessive, presumptuous, assuming 878 *insolent*; unjustified, unjustifiable 914 *wrong*; undeserved, unmerited, unearned; overpaid, underpaid; invalid, weak; forfeited, forfeit; false, bastard 542 *spurious*; fictitious, would-be 850 *affected*.

unentitled, without title, uncrowned; unqualified, without qualifications, unempowered, incompetent; unworthy, undeserving, meritless, unmeritorious; underprivileged, unprivileged, without rights, unchartered, unfranchised, voteless; disentitled, discrowned; dethroned, deposed; disqualified, invalidated, disfranchised, defrocked; deprived, bereft, dispossessed.

Vb. *be undue*, - undeserved etc. adj.; not be due, be unclaimed, be unclaimable; show bad taste, misbecome, ill beseem 847 *vulgarize*; presume, arrogate 878 *be insolent*; usurp, borrow 788 *steal*; be given an inch and take an ell; trespass, squat 306 *encroach*; infringe, break, violate 954 *be illegal*; desecrate, profane 980 *be impious*.

disentitle, uncrown, dethrone 752 *depose*; disqualify, unfrock, disfranchise, alienize, denaturalize, detribalize, denationalize; invalidate 752 *abrogate*; disallow 757 *prohibit*; dispossess, expropriate 786 *deprive*; forfeit, declare f.; defeat a claim, mock the claims of; make illegitimate, illegalize 954 *make illegal*; bastardize, debase 655 *impair*.

Adv. *unduly*, improperly; undeservedly, without desert, no thanks to.

See: 32, 147, 306, 497, 508, 542, 545, 621, 637, 643, 655, 735, **752**, 757, 772, 786, 788, 847, 850, 878, 908, 914, 934, **954**, 980.

917 Duty

N. *duty*, what ought to be done, what is up to one, the right thing, the proper t., the decent t.; one's duty, bounden d., imperative d., inescapable d.; obligation, liability, onus, responsibility, accountability 915 *dueness*; fealty, allegiance, loyalty 739 *obedience*; sense of duty, dutifulness, duteousness 597 *willingness*; discharge of duty, performance, acquittal, discharge 768 *observance*; call of duty, claims of conscience, case of c.; bond, tie, engagement, commitment, word, pledge 764 *promise*; task, office, charge 751 *commission*; walk of life, station, profession 622 *vocation*.

conscience, professional c., tender c., nonconformist c., exacting c., peremptory c.; categorical imperative, inner voice, 'still, small voice', 'stern daughter of the voice of God'.

code of duty, code of honour, unwritten code, professional c., bushido; Decalogue, Ten Commandments, Hippocratic oath 693 *precept*.

morals, morality 933 *virtue*; honour 929 *probity*; moral principles, ideals, high i., standards, high s., professional s.; ethics, religious e., humanist e., professional e.; ethology, deontology, casuistry, ethical philosophy, moral p., moral science, idealism, humanism, utilitarianism, behaviourism 449 *philosophy*.

Adj. *obliged,* duty-bound, on duty, bound by duty, called by d.; under duty, in duty bound, in the line of duty; obligated, beholden, under obligation; tied, bound, sworn, pledged, committed, engaged; unexempted, liable, chargeable, answerable, responsible, accountable; in honour bound, bound in conscience, answerable to God; plagued by conscience, conscience-stricken 939 *repentant*; conscientious 768 *observant*; duteous, dutiful 739 *obedient*; vowed, under a vow.

obligatory, incumbent, imposed, behoving, up to one; binding, de rigueur, compulsory, mandatory, peremptory, operative 740 *compelling*; inescapable, unavoidable; strict, unconditional, categorical.

ethical, moral 933 *virtuous*; honest, decent 929 *honourable*; moralistic, ethological, casuistical; moralizing; humanistic, idealistic; utilitarian.

Vb. *be one's duty,* be incumbent, behove, become, befit 915 *be due*; devolve on, belong to, be up to, pertain to, fall to, arise from one's functions, be part of the job; lie at one's door, rest with, rest on one's shoulders.

incur a duty, make it one's d., take on oneself, accept responsibility, shoulder one's r.; make oneself liable, commit oneself, pledge o., engage for 764 *promise*; assume one's functions, enter upon one's office, receive a posting; have the office, have the function, have the charge, have the duty; owe it to oneself, feel it up to one; feel duty's call, accept the c., answer the c., submit to one's vocation.

do one's duty, fulfil one's d. 739 *obey*; discharge, acquit, perform, do the needful 676 *do*; do one's bit, play one's part; perform one's office, discharge one's functions 768 *observe*; be on duty, stay at one's post, go down with one's ship; come up to what is expected of one, not be found wanting; keep faith with one's conscience, meet one's obligations, discharge an obligation, make good one's promise, redeem a pledge, be as good as one's word; honour, meet, pay up 804 *pay*.

impose a duty, require, oblige, look to, call upon; devolve, call to office, swear one in, offer a post, post 751 *commission*; assign a duty, saddle with, detail, order, enjoin, decree 737 *command*; tax, task, overtask 684 *fatigue*; exact 735 *be severe*; demand obedience, expect it of one 507 *expect*; bind, condition 766 *give terms*; bind over, take security 764 *take a pledge*.

Adv. *on duty,* at one's post; under an obligation; in the line of duty, as in duty bound; with a clear conscience; for conscience' sake.

See: 449, 507, 597, 622, 676, 684, 693, 735, 737, **739**, 740, 751, 764, 766, 768, 804, **915**, **929**, 933, 939.

918 Undutifulness

N. *undutifulness,* default, want of duty, dereliction of d.; neglect, laches, culpable negligence 458 *negligence*; undutifulness, unduteousness 921 *disrespect*; malingering, evasion of duty, cop-out 620 *avoidance*; nonpractice, nonperformance 769 *nonobservance*; idleness, laziness 679 *sluggishness*; forgetfulness 506 *oblivion*; noncooperation, want of alacrity 598 *unwillingness*; truancy, absenteeism 190 *absence*; absconding 667 *escape*; infraction, violation, breach of orders, indiscipline, mutiny, rebellion 738 *disobedience*; incompetence, mismanagement 695 *bungling*; obstruction, sabotage 702 *hindrance*; desertion, defection 603 *tergiversation*; disloyalty, treachery 930 *perfidy*; secession, breakaway 978 *schism*; irresponsibility, escapism; truant, absentee, malingerer, defaulter 620 *avoider*; slacker 679 *idler*; deserter, absconder 667 *escaper*; betrayer, traitor 603 *tergiversator*; saboteur 702 *hinderer*; mutineer, rebel 738 *revolter*; seceder 978 *schismatic*.

Adj. *undutiful,* wanting in duty, uncooperative 598 *unwilling*; unduteous, unfilial, undaughterly 921 *disrespectful*; mutinous, rebellious 738 *disobedient*; disloyal, treacherous 930 *perfidious*; irresponsible, unreliable; truant, absentee 190 *absent*; absconding 667 *escaped*.

Vb. *fail in duty,* neglect one's d. 458 *neglect*; ignore one's obligations 458 *disregard*; oversleep 679 *sleep*; default, let one down, leave one in the lurch 509 *disappoint*; mismanage, bungle 495 *blunder*; not remember 506 *forget*; shirk, evade, wriggle out of, malinger, dodge the column 620 *avoid*; wash one's hands of, pass the buck 919 *be exempt*; play truant, overstay leave 190 *be absent*; abscond 667 *escape*; quit, scuttle, scarper 296 *decamp*; abandon, abandon one's post, desert, desert the colours 621 *relinquish*; break orders, disobey o., violate o., exceed one's instructions 738 *disobey*; mutiny, rebel 738 *revolt*; be disloyal, prove treacherous, betray 603 *tergiversate*; sabotage 702 *obstruct*; noncooperate, withdraw, walk out, break away, secede 978 *schismatize*.

See: 190, 296, 458, 495, 506, 509, 598, 603, **620**, 621, 667, 679, 695, 702, **738**, 769, 919, 921, **930**, 978.

919 Nonliability

N. *nonliability*, nonresponsibility, exemption, dispensation; conscience clause, escape c., force majeure 468 *qualification*; immunity, impunity, privilege, special treatment, benefit of clergy; extraterritoriality, diplomatic immunity; franchise, charter 915 *dueness*; independence, liberty, the four freedoms 744 *freedom*; licence, leave 756 *permission*; aegrotat, certificate of exemption 756 *permit*; excuse, exoneration, exculpation 960 *acquittal*; absolution, pardon, amnesty 909 *forgiveness*; discharge, release 746 *liberation*; renunciation 621 *relinquishment*; evasion of responsibility, escapism, self-exemption, washing one's hands, passing the buck 753 *resignation*.

Adj. *nonliable*, not responsible, not answerable, unaccountable, unpunishable; excused, exonerated, scot-free 960 *acquitted*; dispensed, exempted, privileged, prerogatived; shielded, protected; untouched, exempt, immune; unaffected, well out of; independent, free-born 744 *free*; tax-free, post-f., duty-f. 812 *uncharged*.

Vb. *exempt*, set apart, set aside; eliminate, count out, rule o. 57 *exclude*; excuse, exonerate, exculpate 960 *acquit*; grant absolution, absolve, pardon 909 *forgive*; spare 905 *show mercy*; grant immunity, privilege, charter 756 *permit*; license, dispense, give dispensation, grant impunity; amnesty 506 *forget*; enfranchise, manumit, set at liberty, release 746 *liberate*; pass over, stretch a point 736 *be lenient*.

be exempt, - exempted etc. adj.; owe no responsibility, have no liability, not come within the scope of; enjoy immunity, enjoy impunity, enjoy a privileged position, enjoy independence 744 *be free*; spare oneself the necessity, exempt oneself, excuse oneself, absent oneself, take leave, go on leave 190 *go away*; transfer the responsibility, pass the buck, shift the blame 272 *transfer*; evade *or* escape liability, get away with 667 *escape*; own *or* admit no responsibility, wash one's hands of 918 *fail in duty*.

See: 57, 190, 272, 468, 506, 621, 667, 736, **744**, 746, 753, 756, 812, 905, 909, 915, 918, 960.

920 Respect

N. *respect*, regard, consideration, esteem 923 *approbation*; high standing, honour, favour 866 *repute*; polite regard, attention, attentions, flattering a. 884 *courtesy*; due respect, respectfulness, deference, humbleness 872 *humility*; obsequiousness 879 *servility*; humble service, devotion 739 *loyalty*; admiration, awe 864 *wonder*; terror 854 *fear*; reverence, veneration, adoration 981 *worship*.

respects, regards, duty, kind regards, greetings 884 *courteous act*; red carpet, guard of honour, address of welcome, illuminated address, salutation, salaam; nod, bob, duck, bow, scrape, curtsy, genuflexion, prostration, kowtow 311 *obeisance*; reverence, homage; salute, presenting arms; honours of war, flags flying.

Adj. *respectful*, deferential, knowing one's place 872 *humble*; obsequious, bootlicking 879 *servile*; submissive 721 *submitting*; reverent, reverential 981 *worshipping*; admiring, awestruck 864 *wondering*; polite 884 *courteous*; ceremonious, at the salute, cap in hand, bare-headed; kneeling, on one's knees, prostrate; bobbing, bowing, scraping, bending; obeisant, showing respect, rising, standing, on one's feet, all standing.

respected, admired, honoured, esteemed, revered 866 *reputable*; respectable, reverend, venerable; time-honoured 866 *worshipful*; imposing 821 *impressive*.

Vb. *respect*, entertain r. for, hold in r., hold in honour, think well of, rank high, place h., look up to, esteem, regard, value; admire 864 *wonder*; reverence, venerate, exalt, magnify 866 *honour*; adore 981 *worship*; idolize 982 *idolatrize*; revere, stand in awe of, have a wholesome respect for 854 *fear*; know one's place, defer to 721 *submit*; pay tribute to, take one's hat off to 923 *praise*; do homage to, make much of, lionize, carry shoulder-high 876 *celebrate*.

show respect, render honour, pay homage,

do the honours 884 *pay one's respects*; make way for, leave room for, keep one's distance, know one's place; welcome, hail, salute, present arms, turn out the guard, roll out the red carpet 884 *greet*; cheer, drink to 876 *toast*; bob, duck, bow, bow and scrape, curtsy, kneel, kowtow, prostrate oneself 311 *stoop*; observe decorum, stand on ceremony, stand, rise, rise to one's feet, rise from one's seat, uncover, stand bareheaded; humble oneself, condescend 872 *be humble*.

command respect, inspire r., awe, strike with a., overawe, impose 821 *impress*; enjoy a reputation, rank high, stand h., stand well in the eyes of all 866 *have a reputation*; compel respect, demand r., command admiration 864 *be wonderful*; dazzle, bedazzle 875 *be ostentatious*; receive respect, gain honour, gain a reputation 923 *be praised*.

Adv. *respectfully*, humbly, with all respect, with due r.; obsequiously, deferentially, reverentially, reverently; saving your grace, saving your presence.

See: 311, 721, 739, 821, 854, 864, **866**, 872, 875, 876, 879, **884**, 923, 981, 982.

921 Disrespect

N. *disrespect*, want of respect, scant r., disrespectfulness, irreverence, impoliteness, incivility, discourtesy 885 *rudeness*; dishonour, disfavour 924 *disapprobation*; neglect, undervaluation 483 *underestimation*; low esteem 867 *disrepute*; depreciation, disparagement 926 *detraction*; contumely 899 *scurrility*; scorn 922 *contempt*; mockery 851 *ridicule*; desecration 980 *impiety*.

indignity, humiliation, affront, insult, slight, snub, slap in the face, outrage 878 *insolence*; snook, V-sign 878 *sauciness*; gibe, taunt, jeer 922 *contempt*; quip, sarcasm, mock, flout 851 *ridicule*; hiss, hoot, boo, catcall, brickbat, rotten eggs 924 *disapprobation*.

Adj. *disrespectful*, wanting in respect, slighting, neglectful 458 *negligent*; insubordinate 738 *disobedient*; irreverent, irreverential, aweless 865 *unastonished*; sacrilegious 980 *profane*; outspoken, overcandid 573 *plain*; rude, impolite 885 *discourteous*; airy, breezy, offhand, offhanded, cavalier, familiar, cheeky, saucy 878 *impertinent*; insulting, outrageous 878 *insolent*; flouting, jeering, gibing, scoffing, mocking, satirical, cynical, sarcastic 851 *derisive*; injurious, contumelious, scurrilous 899 *cursing*; denigratory, depreciative, pejorative 483 *depreciating*; snobbish, supercilious, disdainful, scornful 922 *despising*; unflattering, uncomplimentary 924 *disapproving*.

unrespected, disrespected, held in low esteem, of no account 867 *disreputable*; ignored, disregarded, disobeyed, unregarded, unsaluted, ungreeted 458 *neglected*; unenvied, unadmired, unflattered, unreverenced, unrevered, unworshipped; underrated, denigrated, disparaged 483 *undervalued*; looked down on, spat on 922 *contemptible*.

Vb. *not respect*, deny r., be disrespectful; be unable to respect, have no respect for, have no regard f., have no use f. 924 *disapprove*; misprize, undervalue, underrate 483 *underestimate*; look down on, have a low opinion of, disdain, scorn 922 *despise*; run down, denigrate, disparage 926 *defame*; spit on, toss aside 607 *reject*; show disrespect, show no respect, lack courtesy, remain seated, remain covered, keep one's hat on, push aside, shove a., crowd, jostle 885 *be rude*; ignore, turn one's back 458 *disregard*; snub, slight, insult, affront, outrage 872 *humiliate*; dishonour, disgrace, put to shame, drag in the mud 867 *shame*; trifle with, treat lightly 922 *hold cheap*; cheapen, lower, degrade 847 *vulgarize*; have no awe, not reverence, desecrate, profane 980 *be impious*; call names, abuse 899 *curse*; taunt, twit, cock a snook 878 *be insolent*; laugh at, guy, scoff, mock, flout, deride 851 *ridicule*; make mouths at, jeer, hiss, hoot, heckle, boo, point at, spit at 924 *reprobate*; mob, hound, chase 619 *pursue*; pelt, stone, heave a brick 712 *lapidate*.

Adv. *disrespectfully*, irreverently, profanely, sacrilegiously; mockingly, derisively.

See: 458, 483, 573, 607, 619, 712, 738, 847, 851, 865, 867, 872, **878**, **885**, 899, 922, 924, 926, 980.

922 Contempt

N. *contempt*, sovereign c., supreme c., utter c., unutterable c.; scorn, disdain, disdainfulness, superiority, loftiness 871 *pride*; contemptuousness, sniffiness; snootiness, superciliousness, snobbishness 850 *affectation*; superior airs, scornful eye, smile of contempt, curl of the lip, snort, sniff; slight, humiliation 921 *indignity*; sneer, dig at 926 *detraction*; derision, scoffing 851 *ridicule*; snub, rebuff 885 *discourtesy*.

contemptibility, unworthiness, despisedness, insignificance, puerility, pitiability, futility 639 *unimportance*; pettiness, meanness, littleness, paltriness 33 *smallness*; cause for shame, byword of reproach 867 *object of scorn*.

Adj. *despising*, full of contempt, contemptuous, disdainful, holier than thou, snooty, snuffy, sniffy, snobbish; haughty, lofty, airy, supercilious 871 *proud*; scornful, withering, jeering, sneering, booing 924 *disapproving*; disrespectful, impertinent 878 *insolent*; slighting, pooh-poohing 483 *depreciating*.

contemptible, despicable, beneath contempt; abject, worthless, misbegotten 645 *bad*; petty, paltry, little, mean 33 *small*; spurned, spat on 607 *rejected*; scorned, despised, contemned, low in one's estimation 921 *unrespected*; trifling, pitiable, futile, of no account 639 *unimportant*.

Vb. *despise*, contemn, hold in contempt, feel utter contempt for, have no use for 921 *not respect*; look down on, consider beneath one, be too good for, be too grand for 871 *be proud*; disdain, spurn, sniff at, snort at 607 *reject*; come it over, turn up one's nose, wrinkle the n., curl one's lip, toss one's head, snort; snub, turn one's back on 885 *be rude*; scorn, whistle, hiss, boo, point at, point the finger of scorn 924 *reprobate*; laugh at, have a dig at, laugh to scorn, scoff, scout, flout, gibe, jeer, mock, deride 851 *ridicule*; push around, trample on, ride roughshod over 735 *oppress*; disgrace, roll in the mire 867 *shame*.

hold cheap, misprize, have a low opinion of 921 *not respect*; ignore, dismiss, discount, take no account of 458 *disregard*; belittle, disparage, fail to appreciate, underrate, undervalue 483 *underestimate*; decry 926 *detract*; set no value on, set no store by, think nothing of, think small beer of, not care a rap for, not care a straw, not give a hoot *or* a damn, laugh at, treat as a laughing matter, snap one's fingers at, shrug away, pooh-pooh; slight, trifle with, treat lightly, treat like dirt, lower, degrade 872 *humiliate*.

Adv. *contemptuously*, disdainfully, scornfully, with contempt, with disdain.

contemptibly, pitiably, miserably; to one's utter contempt.

See: 33, 458, 483, 607, 639, 645, 735, 850, 851, 867, 871, 872, 878, 885, **921**, 924, 926.

923 Approbation

N. *approbation*, approval, sober a., modified rapture; satisfaction 828 *content*; appreciation, recognition 907 *gratitude*; good opinion, golden opinions, kudos, credit 866 *prestige*; regard, admiration, esteem 920 *respect*; good books, good graces, grace, favour, popularity, affection 887 *love*; adoption, acceptance, welcome, favourable reception 299 *reception*; sanction 756 *permission*; nod of approval, seal of a., blessing; nod, wink, thumbs up, consent 488 *assent*; countenance, patronage, championship, advocacy 703 *aid*; friendly notice, favourable review 480 *estimate*; good word, kind w., testimonial, reference, commendation, recommendation 466 *credential*.

praise, loud p., lyrical p., praise and glory, laud, laudation, benediction, blessing; compliment, high c., encomium, eulogy, panegyric, glorification, adulation, idolatry 925 *flattery*; hero worship 864 *wonder*; overpraise 482 *overestimation*; faint praise, two cheers; shout of praise, hosanna, alleluia; praises, song of praise, hymn of p., paean of p., dithyramb, doxology, Gloria, Te Deum; tribute, credit, due credit 907 *thanks*; complimentary reference, bouquet, accolade, citation, honourable mention, commendation, glowing terms; official biography, hagiography; self-praise, self-glorification 877 *boasting*; name in lights, letters of gold; puff, blurb 528 *advertisement*.

applause, clamorous a., acclaim, universal a.; enthusiasm, excitement 821 *excitation*; warm reception, hero's welcome 876 *celebration*; acclamation, plaudits, clapping, stamping, whistling, cheering; clap, three cheers, paean, hosanna; thunderous applause, peal of a., shout of a., chorus of a., round of a., salvo of a., storm of a., ovation, standing o.; encore, curtain call; bouquet, pat on the back.

commender, praiser, laudator, encomiast, eulogist, panegyrist; clapper, shouter, claqueur, claque; approver, friendly critic, admirer, devoted a., hero-worshipper, fan club; advocate, recommender, supporter, speaker for the motion 707 *patron*; inscriber, dedicator; advertiser, blurb-writer, puffer, booster; agent, tout, touter, barker 528 *publicizer*; canvasser, electioneer, election agent.

Adj. *approving*, uncensorious, uncomplaining, satisfied 828 *content*; favouring, supporting, advocating 703 *aiding*; appreciative 907 *grateful*; approbatory, favourable, friendly, well-inclined; complimentary, commendatory, laudatory, eulogistic, encomiastic, panegyrical, lyrical; admiring, hero-worshipping, idolatrous; lavish, generous; fulsome, overpraising, uncritical, undiscriminating; acclamatory, clapping, thunderous 400 *loud*; dithyrambic, ecstatic, in raptures 821 *excited*.

approvable, admissible, permissible, acceptable; worthwhile 640 *useful*; deserving, meritorious, commendable, laudable, estimable, worthy, praiseworthy, creditable, admirable, uncensurable, unimpeachable, beyond all praise 646 *perfect*; enviable, desirable 859 *desired*.

approved, passed, tested, tried; uncensured, free from blame, stamped with approval, blessed; popular, in favour, in high f., in the good graces of, in good odour, in high esteem, thought well of 866 *reputable*; praised etc. vb.; commended, highly c.; favoured, backed, odds on 605 *chosen*.

Vb. *approve*, see nothing wrong with, sound pleased, have no fault to find, have nothing but praise for, think highly of 920 *respect*; like well 887 *love*; think well of, admire, esteem, value, prize, treasure, cherish, set store by 866 *honour*; appreciate, give credit, salute, take one's hat off to, hand it to, give full marks; think no worse of, think the better of; count it to one's credit, see the good points, see the good in one, think good, think perfect; think desirable 912 *envy*; think the best, award the palm; see to be good, find g., pronounce g., mark with approbation, give the seal *or* stamp of approval; accept, pass, tick, give marks for; nod, wink, nod one's approval, give one's assent 488 *assent*; sanction, bless, give one's blessing 756 *permit*; ratify 488 *endorse*; commend, recommend, advocate, support, back, favour, countenance, stand up for, speak up f., put in a good word for, give one a reference *or* a testimonial 703 *patronize*.

praise, compliment, pay compliments 925 *flatter*; speak well of, speak highly of, swear by; bless 907 *thank*; salute, pay tribute to, hand it to, take one's hat off to; commend, give praise, laud, eulogize, panegyrize, praise to the skies, sound the praises, sing the p., hymn the p., swell the p., doxologize, exalt, extol, glorify, magnify; wax lyrical, get carried away; not spare one's blushes 546 *exaggerate*; puff, inflate, overpraise, overestimate 482 *overrate*; lionize, hero-worship, idolize 982 *idolatrize*; trumpet, write up, cry up, hype up, crack up, boost 528 *advertise*; praise oneself, glorify o. 877 *boast*.

applaud, receive with applause, welcome, hail, hail with satisfaction; acclaim, receive with acclamation, clap, clap one's hands, give a big hand, stamp, whistle, bring the house down, raise the roof; cheer, raise a c., give three cheers, give three times three; cheer to the echo, shout for, root for; clap on the back, pat on the back; welcome, congratulate, garland, chair 876 *celebrate*; drink to 876 *toast*.

be praised, - praiseworthy etc. adj.; get a citation, be mentioned in dispatches; recommend oneself 866 *seek repute*; find favour, win praise, gain credit, earn golden opinions 866 *have a reputation*; get a compliment, receive a tribute, get a hand, get a clap, get a cheer; receive an ovation, take the house by storm 727 *triumph*; deserve praise, be to one's credit, redound to the honour; pass, do, pass muster, pass the test.

Adv. *approvingly*, admiringly, with admiration, with praises, with compliments; ungrudgingly, without demur; enviously.

commendably, admirably, wonderfully, unimpeachably; acceptably, satisfactorily, to satisfaction, to approval.

Int. bravo! well done! hear hear! encore! bis! three cheers! hurrah! hosanna!

See: 299, 400, 466, 480, 482, 488, 528, 546, 605, 640, 646, 703, 707, 727, 756, 821, 828, 859, 864, **866**, 876, 877, 887, 907, 912, **920**, 925, 982.

924 Disapprobation

N. *disapprobation*, disapproval, dissatisfaction 829 *discontent*; nonapproval, return 607 *rejection*; no permission 760 *refusal*; disfavour, displeasure, unpopularity 861 *dislike*; low opinion 921 *disrespect*; bad books 867 *disrepute*; disparagement, decrial, crabbing, carping, niggling 926 *detraction*; censoriousness, fault-finding 862 *fastidiousness*; hostility 881 *enmity*; objection, exception, cavil 468 *qualification*; complaint, clamour, outcry, protest, tut-tut 762 *deprecation*; indignation 891 *anger*; sibilation, hissing, hiss, boo, slow handclap, whistle, catcall 851 *ridicule*; ostracism, boycott, bar, colour b., ban, nonadmission 57 *exclusion*; blackball, blacklist, Index.

censure, dispraise, discommendation, blame, reprehension, impeachment, inculpation 928 *accusation*; home truth, no compliment, left-handed c., back-handed c.; criticism, hostile c., stricture; hypercriticism, fault-finding; hostile attack, slashing a., onslaught 712 *attack*; bad press, critical review, hostile r., slashing r., slating; open letter, tirade, jeremiad, philippic, diatribe 704 *opposition*; conviction 961 *condemnation*; false accusation 928 *false charge*; slur, slander, insinuation, innuendo 926 *calumny*; brand, stigma.

reproach, reproaches; recriminations 709 *quarrel*; home truths, invective, vituperation, calling names, bawling out, shouting down 899 *scurrility*; execration 899 *malediction*; personal remarks, aspersion, reflection 921 *indignity*; taunt, sneer 878 *insolence*; sarcasm, irony, satire, biting wit, biting tongue, dig, cut, hit, brickbat 851 *ridicule*; rough side of one's tongue, tongue-lashing, hard words, cutting w., bitter w. (see *reprimand*); silent reproach, disapproving look, dirty l., black l. 893 *sullenness*.

reprimand, remonstrance 762 *deprecation*; stricture, animadversion, reprehension, reprobation; censure, rebuke, reproof, snub; rocket, raspberry; piece of one's mind, expression of displeasure, mark of d., black mark; castigation, correction, rap over the knuckles, box on the ears 963 *punishment*; inculpation, admonition, admonishment, objurgation, tongue-lashing, chiding, upbraiding, scolding, rating, slating, strafing, trouncing, lambasting, dressing down, blowing up, roasting, wigging, carpeting, mauvais quart d'heure; talking to, lecture, curtain l., jobation.

disapprover, no friend, no admirer; nonsupporter, nonvoter; damper, wet blanket, spoilsport, misery 834 *moper*; pussyfoot, puritan, rigorist 950 *prude*; attacker, opposer 705 *opponent*; critic, hostile c., captious c., knocker, fault-finder; reprover, castigator, censurer, censor; satirist, lampooner, mocker 926 *detractor*; brander, stigmatizer; misogynist 902 *misanthrope*; grouser, groucher 829 *malcontent*.

Adj. *disapproving*, unapproving, unable to approve, not amused, unamused; shocked, scandalized; unadmiring, unimpressed; disillusioned 509 *disappointed*; sparing of praise, grudging; silent 582 *taciturn*; disapprobatory, unfavourable, hostile 881 *inimical*; objecting, protesting, clamorous 762 *deprecatory*; reproachful, chiding, scolding, upbraiding, vituperative 899 *maledictory*; critical, unflattering, uncomplimentary; withering, hard-hitting, strongly worded; overcritical, hypercritical, captious, fault-finding, niggling, carping; disparaging, defamatory, damaging 926 *detracting*; caustic, sharp, bitter, venomous, trenchant, mordant; sarcastic, sardonic, cynical 851 *derisive*; censorious, holier than thou; blaming, faulting, censuring, reprimanding, recriminative, denunciatory, accusatory, condemning, damning, damnatory 928 *accusing*.

disapproved, unapproved, blacklisted, blackballed 607 *rejected*; unsatisfactory, found wanting 636 *insufficient*; ploughed, failed 728 *unsuccessful*; cancelled 752 *abrogated*; deleted, censored 550 *obliterated*; fallen foul of, out of favour, under a cloud; unpraised, dispraised, criticized, decried, run down, slandered, calumniated; lectured, henpecked, nagged, reprimanded, scolded, chidden; on the mat, on the carpet; unregretted, unlamented, unbewailed, unpitied 861 *disliked*; hooted, hissed, hissed off the stage; discredited, disowned, out; in bad odour, in one's bad books 867 *disreputable*.

blameworthy, not good enough, too bad; blamable, exceptionable, open to criticism, censurable, condemnable 645 *bad*; reprehensible, dishonourable, unjustifiable 867 *discreditable*; unpraiseworthy, uncommendable, not to be recommended, not to be thought of; reprobate, culpable, to blame 928 *accusable*.

Vb. *disapprove*, not admire, hold no brief for, fail to appreciate, have no praise for, not think much of, think little of, take a dim view of; think the worse of, think ill of 922 *despise*; not pass, fail, plough; return 607 *reject*; disallow 757 *prohibit*; cancel 752 *abrogate*; censor 550 *obliterate*; withhold approval, look grave, shake one's head, not hold with 489 *dissent*; disfavour, reprehend, lament, deplore 830 *regret*; abhor, reprobate 861 *dislike*; wash one's hands of, disown, look askance, avoid, ignore; keep at a distance, draw the line, ostracize, ban, bar, blacklist 57 *exclude*; protest, tut-tut, remonstrate, object, take exception to, demur 762 *deprecate*; discountenance, show disapproval, exclaim, shout down, bawl d., hoot, boo, bay, heckle, hiss, whistle, give the bird, drive off the stage; throw mud, throw rotten eggs, throw bricks *or* stones 712 *lapidate*; hound, chase, mob, lynch; make a face, make a moue, make mouths at, spit; look black 893 *be sullen*; look daggers 891 *be angry*.

dispraise, discommend, not recommend, give no marks to, damn with faint praise, damn 961 *condemn*; criticize, fault, find f., pick holes, niggle, crab, cavil, depreciate, run down, belittle, pan 926 *detract*; oppose, tilt at, shoot at, throw the book at 712 *attack*; weigh in, pitch into, hit out at, let fly, lay into, lam into, savage, maul, slash, slate, scourge, flay, put the boot in; inveigh, thunder, fulminate, storm against, rage a. 61 *rampage*; shout down, cry shame, slang, call names; gird, rail, revile, abuse, heap a., pour vitriol, objurgate, anathematize, execrate 899 *curse*; vilify, blacken 926 *defame*; stigmatize, brand, pillory; expose, denounce, recriminate 928 *accuse*; sneer, twit, taunt 921 *not respect*.

reprove, reprehend, reproach, rebuke, administer a r., snub; call to order, caution, wag one's finger, read the Riot Act 664 *warn*; book, give one a black mark; censure, reprimand, take to task, rap over the knuckles, box the ears; tick off, tell off, have one's head for, carpet, have on the carpet, haul over the coals; remonstrate, expostulate, admonish, castigate, chide, correct; lecture, read one a lecture, give one a talking to, give one a wigging, give one a dressing-down, lambast, trounce, roast, browbeat, blow up, tear a strip off, come down hard on, come down on like a ton of bricks, chastise 963 *punish*.

blame, find fault, carp, pick holes in; get at, henpeck 709 *bicker*; reprehend, hold to blame, pick on, put the blame on, hold responsible; throw the first stone, inculpate, incriminate, complain against, impute, impeach, charge, criminate 928 *accuse*; round on, return the charge, recriminate 714 *retaliate*; think the worst of 961 *condemn*.

reprobate, reproach, heap reproaches on; upbraid, slate, rate, berate, rail, strafe, shend, revile, abuse, blackguard 899 *curse*; go for, inveigh against, bawl out, scold, tongue-lash, lash, excoriate, give the rough edge of one's tongue, rail in good set terms against, give one a piece of one's mind, give one what for, give it to one straight from the shoulder, not pull one's punches.

incur blame, take the blame, take the rap, carry the can, catch it; be held responsible, have to answer for; be open to criticism, blot one's copy book, get a bad name 867 *lose repute*; be up on a charge, stand accused; stand corrected; be an example, be a scandal, scandalize, shock, revolt 861 *cause dislike*.

Adv. *disapprovingly*, reluctantly, against one's better judgment, under protest; reproachfully, complainingly.

See: 57, 61, 468, 489, 509, 550, 582, 607, 636, 645, 664, 704, 705, 709, 712, 714, 728, 752, 757, 760, 762, 829, 830, 834, 851, 861, 862, 867, 878, 881, 891, 893, 899, 902, 921, **922**, **926**, 928, 950, 961, **963**.

925 Flattery

N. *flattery*, cajolery, wheedling, taffy, blarney, blandiloquence, blandishments, sweet talk; flannel, soft soap, soft sawder, salve, lip-salve, rosewater, incense, adulation; voice of the charmer, honeyed words, sweet nothings 889 *endearment*; compliment, pretty speeches; coquetry, winning ways; fawning, backscratching; assentation, obsequiousness, flunkeyism, sycophancy, toadying 879 *servility*; unctuousness, smarminess, euphemism, insincerity, hypocrisy, tongue in cheek, lip-homage 542 *sham*.

flatterer, adulator, cajoler, wheedler; coquette, charmer; tout, puffer, booster, claqueur, claque 923 *commender*; courtier, yes-man 488 *assenter*; creep, fawner, sycophant, parasite, minion, hanger-on 879 *toady*; fair-weather friend, hypocrite 545 *deceiver*.

Adj. *flattering*, overpraising, overdone 546 *exaggerated*; boosting, puffing; complimentary, overcomplimentary, full of compliments; fulsome, adulatory; sugary, saccharine; cajoling, wheedling, coaxing, blarneying, blandiloquent; mealy-mouthed, glozing, canting; smooth-tongued, honey-t., bland; smooth, oily, unctuous, soapy, slimy, smarmy; obsequious, all over one, courtly, fawning, crawling, back-scratching, sycophantic 879 *servile*; specious, plausible, beguiling, ingratiating, insinuating; lulling, soothing; vote-catching, vote-snatching; false, insincere, tongue-in-cheek, unreliable 541 *hypocritical*.

Vb. *flatter*, deal in flattery, have kissed the Blarney Stone; compliment 923 *praise*; overpraise, overdo it, lay it on thick, lay it on with a trowel, not spare one's blushes; puff, boost, cry up 482 *overrate*; adulate, burn incense to, assail with flattery, turn one's head 873 *make conceited*; butter up, sawder, soft-soap; blarney, flannel; sweet-talk, sugar; wheedle, coax, cajole, coo; lull, soothe, beguile 542 *deceive*; humour, jolly along, pander to; gild the pill, make things pleasant, tell people what they want to hear; blandish, smooth, smarm; press the flesh, make much of, be all over one 889 *caress*; fawn, fawn on, cultivate, court, pay court to, play the courtier, massage one's ego; smirk 835 *smile*; scratch one's back, curry favour, make up to, suck up to; truckle to, toady to, pander to 879 *be servile*; insinuate oneself, get on the right side of, creep into one's good graces; flatter oneself, have a swelled head 873 *be vain*.

Adv. *flatteringly*, speciously; ad captandum.

See: 482, 488, 541, **542**, 545, 546, 835, 873, **879**, 889, 923.

926 Detraction

N. *detraction*, faint praise, two cheers, understatement 483 *underestimation*; criticism, hostile c., destructive c., bad review, bad press 924 *disapprobation*; onslaught 712 *attack*; vivisection, hatchet job; impeachment 928 *accusation*; exposure, bad light 867 *disrepute*; decrial, disparagement, depreciation, running down; lowering, derogation; slighting language, scorn 922 *contempt*; envenomed tongue 899 *malediction*; contumely, obloquy, vilification, abuse, invective 899 *scurrility*; calumniation, defamation, traducement 543 *untruth*; backbiting, cattiness, spite 898 *malevolence*; aspersion, reflection, snide remark (**see** *calumny*); whisper, innuendo, insinuation, imputation, whispering campaign; smear campaign, mud-slinging, smirching, denigration, character assassination; brand, stigma; muck-raking, scandal-mongering; nil admirari, disillusionment, cynicism 865 *lack of wonder*.

calumny, slander, libel, false report, roorback 543 *untruth*; a defamation, defamatory remark, damaging report; smear, smear-word, dirty word 867 *slur*; offensive remark, personal r., personality, insult, taunt, dig at, brickbat 921 *indignity*; scoff, sarcasm 851 *ridicule*; sneer, sniff; caricature 552 *misrepresentation*; skit, lampoon, pasquinade, squib 851 *satire*; scandal, scandalous talk, malicious gossip, bad mouth.

detractor, decrier, disparager, depreciator, slighter, despiser; nonadmirer, debunker, deflater, cynic; mocker, scoffer, satirizer, satirist, lampooner; castigator, denouncer, reprover, censurer, censor 924 *disapprover*; no respecter of persons, no flatterer, candid friend, candid critic; critic, hostile c., destructive c., attacker; arch-critic, chief accuser, impeacher 928 *accuser*; captious critic, knocker, Zoilus; fault-finder, carper, caviller, niggler, nit-picker, hair-splitter; heckler, barracker 702 *hinderer*; philistine 847 *vulgarian*.

defamer, calumniator, traducer, destroyer of reputations, hatchet man; smircher, smearer, slanderer, libeller; backbiter, gossiper, scandal-monger, muck-raker; gossip columnist, gutter press; denigrator, mud-slinger; brander, stigmatizer; vituperator, reviler; scold, Thersites 892 *shrew*; poison pen.

Adj. *detracting*, derogatory, pejorative; disparaging, depreciatory, decrying, crying down, slighting, contemptuous 922 *despising*; whispering, insinuating, blackening, denigratory, mud-slinging, smearing; compromising, damaging; scandalous, calumnious, calumniatory, defamatory, slanderous, libellous; insulting 921 *disrespectful*; contumelious, injurious, abusive, scurrilous 899 *cursing*; shrewish, scolding, caustic, bitter, venomous, denunciatory, castigatory, accusatory, blaming 924 *dis-*

approving; sarcastic, mocking, **scoffing,** sneering, cynical, snide 851 *derisive*; **catty,** spiteful 898 *malevolent*; **unflattering, can-**did 573 *plain*.

Vb. *detract*, derogate, depreciate, **disparage,** run down, sell short; **debunk, deflate,** puncture, cut down to size 921 *not respect*; minimize 483 *underestimate*; **belittle,** slight 922 *hold cheap*; sneer at, sniff at 922 *despise*; decry, cry down, damn with faint praise, fail to appreciate 924 *disapprove*; find nothing to praise, criticize, knock, slam, fault, find f., pick holes in, slash, slate, pull to pieces, tear to ribbons 924 *dispraise*; caricature, guy 552 *misrepresent*; lampoon, dip one's pen in gall 851 *satirize*; scoff, mock 851 *ridicule*; make catty remarks, get in a dig at; whisper, insinuate, cast aspersions.

defame, dishonour, damage, compromise, scandalize, degrade, lower, put to shame 867 *shame*; give a dog a bad name, lower *or* lessen one's reputation, destroy one's good name; denounce, expose, pillory, stigmatize, brand 928 *accuse*; calumniate, libel, slander, traduce, malign; vilify, denigrate, blacken, tarnish, sully; reflect upon, put in a bad light; speak ill of, speak evil, gossip, badmouth, make scandal, talk about, backbite, talk behind one's back; discredit 486 *cause doubt*; smear, besmear, smirch, besmirch, spatter, bespatter, throw mud, fling dirt, drag in the gutter 649 *make unclean*; hound, witch-hunt 619 *hunt*; look for scandal, smell evil, muckrake, rake about in the gutter 619 *pursue*.

See: 483, 486, 543, 552, 573, 619, 649, 702, 712, 847, 851, 865, **867**, 892, 898, 899, 921, 922, **924**, **928**.

927 Vindication

N. *vindication*, restoration, rehabilitation 787 *restitution*; triumph of justice, right triumphant, wrong righted, right asserted, truth established; exoneration, exculpation, clearance 960 *acquittal*; justification, good grounds, just cause, every excuse; compurgation, apologetics, self-defence, apologia, defence, legal d., good d., successful d.; alibi, plea, excuse, whitewash, gloss 614 *pretext*; fair excuse, good e., just e. 494 *truth*; partial excuse, extenuation, palliation, mitigation, mitigating circumstance, extenuating c., palliative 468 *qualification*; counterargument 479 *confutation*; reply, reply for the defence, rebuttal 460 *rejoinder*; recrimination, **tu quoque, countercharge,** charge retorted; **justifiable charge,** true bill 928 *accusation*; **bringing to book,** poetic justice, just punishment 963 *punishment*.

vindicator, punisher 910 *avenger*; apologist, advocate, defender, champion; justifier, excuser, whitewasher; compurgator, oath-helper, character witness 466 *witness*; self-defender, defendant 928 *accused person*.

Adj. *vindicating*, vindicatory, vindicative, avenging; apologetic, exculpatory, justifying, defending; extenuatory, mitigating, palliative.

vindicable, justifiable, maintainable, defensible, arguable; specious, plausible; allowable, warrantable, unobjectionable 756 *permitted*; excusable, having some excuse, pardonable, forgivable, venial, expiable; vindicated, justified, within one's rights, not guilty 935 *innocent*; justified by the event 494 *true*.

Vb. *vindicate*, revenge 910 *avenge*; do justice to, give the devil his due 915 *grant claims*; set right, restore, rehabilitate 787 *restitute*; maintain, speak up for, argue f., contend f., advocate 475 *argue*; undertake to prove, bear out, confirm, make good, prove the truth of, prove 478 *demonstrate*; champion, stand up for, stick up for 713 *defend*; support, offer moral support 703 *patronize*.

justify, warrant, justify by the event, give grounds for, provide justification, furnish an excuse, give a handle, give one cause; put one in the right, put one in the clear, clear, exonerate, exculpate 960 *acquit*; give colour to, colour, whitewash, varnish, gloss; salve one's conscience, justify oneself, defend o. 614 *plead*; plead one's own cause, say in defence, rebut the charge, plead ignorance.

extenuate, excuse, make excuses for, make allowances; palliate, mitigate, soften, mince one's words, soft-pedal, slur, slur over, gloss, gloss over, varnish, whitewash; take the will for the deed 736 *be lenient*.

See: 460, 466, 468, 475, 478, 479, 494, 614, 703, 713, 736, 756, **787**, 910, 915, 928, 935, **960**, 963.

928 Accusation

N. *accusation*, complaint, charge, home truth; censure, blame, stricture 924 *reproach*; challenge 711 *defiance*; inculpation, crimination; countercharge, recrimination, tu quoque argument 460 *rejoinder*; twit, taunt 921 *indignity*; imputation, allegation, information, delation, denunciation; plaint, suit, action 959 *litigation*; prosecution, impeachment, arraignment, indictment, citation, summons; bill of indictment, true bill; gravamen, substance of a charge, main c.; case, case to answer, case for the prosecution 475 *reasons*; items in the indictment, particular charge, count 466 *evidence*.

false charge, faked c., cooked-up c., trumped-up c., put-up job, frame-up; false information, perjured testimony, hostile evidence, suspect e., false e.; counterfeit evidence, plant; illegal prosecution, vexatious p.; lie, libel, slander, scandal, stigma 926 *calumny*.

accuser, complainant, plaintiff, petitioner, appellant, libellant, litigant; challenger, denouncer, charger; grass, nark, copper's n. 524 *informer*; common informer, delator, relator; impeacher, indicter, prosecutor, public p., procurator fiscal; libeller, slanderer, calumniator, stigmatizer 926 *defamer*; hostile witness 881 *enemy*; the finger of suspicion.

accused person, the accused, prisoner, prisoner at the bar; defendant, respondent, corespondent; culprit; suspect, victim of suspicion, marked man; slandered person, libellee, victim.

Adj. *accusing*, alleging, accusatory, denunciatory, criminatory, recriminatory; incriminating, pointing to; imputative, stigmatizing, damnatory, condemnatory; tale-bearing, sycophantic, calumnious, defamatory 926 *detracting*; suspicious 924 *disapproving*.

accused, informed against, reported a., complained a., suspect; under suspicion, under a cloud; denounced, impeached etc. vb.; charged, up on a charge, prosecuted, hauled up, booked, summoned; awaiting trial, on bail, remanded; slandered, libelled, calumniated 924 *disapproved*.

accusable, imputable; actionable, suable, chargeable, justiciable, liable to prosecution; inexcusable, unpardonable, unforgivable, indefensible, unjustifiable 924 *blameworthy*; without excuse, without defence, condemnable 934 *heinous*; undefended 661 *vulnerable*.

Vb. *accuse*, challenge 711 *defy*; taunt, twit 878 *be insolent*; point, point a finger at, cast the first stone, throw in one's teeth, reproach 924 *reprove*; stigmatize, brand, pillory, gibbet, cast a slur on, calumniate 926 *defame*; impute, charge with, saddle w., tax w., hold against, lay to one's charge, lay at one's door, hold responsible, make r.; pick on, fix on, hold to blame, put the blame on, pin on, bring home to 924 *blame*; point at, expose, show up, name, name names 526 *divulge*; denounce, inform against, tell, tell on, peach on, blab, split on, turn Queen's evidence 524 *inform*; involve, implicate, inculpate, incriminate; recriminate, countercharge, rebut the charge, retort the c., turn the tables upon 479 *confute*; make one a scapegoat, shift the blame; accuse oneself, admit the charge, plead guilty 526 *confess*; involve oneself, implicate o., lay oneself open, put oneself out of court.

indict, impeach, arraign, inform against, complain a., lodge a complaint, lay an information against; complain, charge, bring a charge, swear an indictment 959 *litigate*; book, cite, summon, prosecute, sue; bring an action, bring a suit, bring a case; haul up, put on trial, put in the dock; throw the book at 712 *attack*; charge falsely, lie against 541 *be false*; frame, trump up a charge, cook the evidence, use false e., fake the e., plant the e. 541 *fake*.

Adv. *accusingly*, censoriously.

See: 460, 466, 475, 479, 524, 526, 541, 661, 711, 712, 878, 881, 921, **924**, **926**, 934, 959.

929 Probity

N. *probity*, rectitude, uprightness, goodness, sanctity 933 *virtue*; stainlessness 950 *purity*; good character, moral fibre, honesty, soundness, incorruptibility, integrity; high character, nobleness, nobility; honourableness, decent feelings, tender conscience; honour, personal h., sense of h., principles; conscientiousness 768 *observance*; scrupulousness, scrupulosity, punctiliousness, meticulousness 457 *carefulness*; ingenuousness, single-heartedness; trustworthiness, reliability, sense of responsibility; truthfulness 540 *veracity*; candour, plain-speaking 573 *plainness*; sincerity, good faith, bona fides 494 *truth*; fidelity, faith, troth, faithfulness, trustiness, constancy 739 *loyalty*; clean hands 935 *innocence*; impartiality, fairness, sportsmanship 913 *justice*; respectability 866 *repute*; gentlemanliness, chivalry; principle, point of honour, punctilio, code, code of honour, bushido 913 *right*; court of justice, court of honour, field of h.

honourable person, honest p., man of honour, woman of her word, sound character, trusty soul 937 *good person*; true lady, perfect gentleman, true knight, preux chevalier, galant homme; Galahad, Parsifal; fair fighter, clean f., fair player, good loser, sportsman, sportswoman, sport, good sport, trump, brick, good sort, true Brit.

Adj. *honourable*, upright, erect, of integrity, of honour 933 *virtuous*; correct, strict; law-abiding, honest, strictly h., on the level; principled, high-p., on the up-and-up; scrupulous, conscientious, soul-searching; incorruptible, unbribable, not to be bought off; incorrupt, immaculate 935 *innocent*; stainless, unstained, untarnished, unsullied 648 *clean*; noble, high-minded, pure-m. 950 *pure*; ingenuous, unsuspicious, guileless, unworldly 699 *artless*; good, straight, straight as a die, square, on the square, one hundred per cent; fair, fair-dealing, equitable, impartial 913 *just*; sporting, sportsmanlike, playing the game; gentlemanly, chivalrous, knightly, sans peur et sans reproche; jealous of one's honour, careful of one's reputation, respectable 866 *reputable*; saintly 979 *pious*.

trustworthy, creditworthy, reliable, dependable, tried, tested, proven; trusty, true-hearted, true-blue, true to the core, sure, staunch, single-hearted, constant, unchanging, faithful, loyal 739 *obedient*; responsible, duteous, dutiful 768 *observant*; conscientious, religious, scrupulous, meticulous, punctilious 457 *careful*; candid, frank, open, open and above-board, open-hearted, transparent, ingenuous, without guile 494 *true*; straightforward, truthful, truth-speaking, as good as one's word 540 *veracious*; unperjured, unperfidious, untreacherous.

Vb. *be honourable*, - chivalrous etc. adj.; behave well, behave like a gentleman 933 *be virtuous*; deal honourably, play fair, play the game 913 *be just*; be a sport, be a brick, turn up trumps; preserve one's honour, fear God 979 *be pious*; keep faith, keep one's promise, be as good as one's word; hate a lie, stick to the truth, speak the truth and shame the devil 540 *be truthful*; go straight, reform, turn over a new leaf 654 *get better*.

See: 457, 494, **540**, 573, 648, 654, 699, 739, 768, 866, 913, **933**, 935, 937, 950, 979.

930 Improbity

N. *improbity*, dishonesty; lack of probity, lack of conscience, lack of principle; suppleness, flexibility, laxity; unconscientiousness 456 *inattention*; unscrupulousness, opportunism; insincerity, disingenuousness, unstraightforwardness, untrustworthiness, unreliability, undependability, untruthfulness 541 *falsehood*; unfairness, partiality 914 *injustice*; shuffling, slipperiness, snakiness, artfulness; fishiness, suspiciousness, shadiness, obliquity, twistiness, deviousness, crookedness, crooked paths; corruption, corruptibility, venality, bribability, graft, jobbery, nepotism, simony, barratry; Tammanyism; baseness, shabbiness, abjectness, abjection, debasement, shamefulness, disgrace, dishonour, shame 867 *disrepute*; worthlessness, good-for-nothingness, villainousness, villainy, knavery, roguery, rascality, spivvery, skulduggery, racketeering; criminality, crime, complicity 954 *lawbreaking*; turpitude, moral t. 934 *wickedness*.

perfidy, perfidiousness, faithlessness, unfaithfulness, infidelity, unfaith 543 *untruth*; bad faith, Punic f., questionable f.; divided allegiance, wavering loyalty, disloyalty 738 *disobedience*; double-dealing, double-crossing, Judas kiss 541 *duplicity*; volte-face 603 *tergiversation*; defection, desertion 918 *undutifulness*; betrayal, treachery, stab in the back, sell-out; treason, high t. 738 *sedition*; fifth column, Trojan horse; breach of faith, broken word, broken faith, broken promise, breach of p., oath forsworn, scrap of paper; cry of treason, Perfide Albion!

foul play, dirty trick, stab in the back; not playing the game, foul 914 *wrong*; professional foul 623 *contrivance*; trick, shuffle, chicane, chicanery 542 *trickery*; practice, sharp p., heads I win tails you lose; fishy transaction, dirty work, job, deal, ramp, racket; fiddle, wangle, manipulation, gerrymandering, hanky-panky, monkey business; tax evasion 620 *avoidance*; malversation 788 *peculation*; crime, felony 954 *lawbreaking*.

Adj. *dishonest*, not on the level 914 *wrong*; not particular, unfastidious, unsqueamish; unprincipled, unscrupulous, conscienceless; shameless, dead to honour, lost to shame; unethical, immoral 934 *wicked*; shaky, untrustworthy, unreliable, undependable, not to be trusted; supple, flexible 603 *tergiversating*; disingenuous, unstraightforward, untruthful, uncandid 543 *untrue*; two-faced, insincere 541 *hypocritical*; creeping, crawling; tricky, artful, dodging, opportunist, slippery, snaky, foxy 698 *cunning*; shifty, shuffling, prevaricating 518 *equivocal*; designing, scheming; sneaking, underhand 523 *latent*; up to something, on the fiddle; not straight, unstraight, indirect, bent, crooked, devious, oblique, tortuous, winding 251 *labyrinthine*; insidious, dark, sinister; shady, fishy, suspicious, doubtful, questionable; fraudulent 542 *spurious*; illicit 954 *illegal*; foul 645 *bad*; unclean 649 *dirty*; mean, shabby, dishonourable, infamous 867 *disreputable*; derogatory, unworthy, undignified; inglorious, ignominious 867 *degrading*; ignoble, unchivalrous, ungentlemanly; unsporting, unsportsmanlike, unfair.

rascally, criminal, felonious 954 *lawless*; knavish, picaresque, spivvish; infamous, blackguard, villainous; scurvy, scabby, arrant, low, low-down, base, vile, currish; mean, shabby, paltry, pettifogging, abject, wretched, contemptible 639 *unimportant*; time-serving, crawling 925 *flattering*.

venal, corruptible, purchasable, bribable, hireling, mercenary 792 *bought*; corrupt, jobbing, grafting, simoniacal, nepotistic; barratrous, selling justice.

perfidious, treacherous, unfaithful, inconstant, faithless 541 *false*; double-dealing, double-crossing, time-serving 541 *hypocritical*; disloyal 603 *tergiversating*; false-hearted, guileful, traitorous, treasonous, treasonable, disloyal, untrue 738 *disobedient*; plotting, scheming, intriguing 623 *planning*; insidious, dark, Machiavellian; cheating 542 *deceiving*; fraudulent 542 *spurious*.

Vb. *be dishonest*, - dishonourable etc. adj.; have no morals, forget one's principles, yield to temptation, be lost to shame; lack honesty, live dishonestly, live by one's wits, lead a life of crime 954 *be illegal*; fiddle, finagle, wangle, gerrymander, start a racket, racketeer; defalcate, peculate 788 *defraud*; cheat, swindle 542 *deceive*; betray, play false, do the dirty on, stab in the back; play double, double-cross 541 *dissemble*; fawn 925 *flatter*; break faith, break one's word, go back on one's promises, tell lies 541 *be false*; shuffle, dodge, prevaricate 518 *be equivocal*; sell out, sell down the river 603 *apostatize*; sink into crime, sell one's honour, stoop to 867 *lose repute*; smack of dishonesty, smell fishy.

Adv. *dishonestly*; shamelessly, by fair means or foul; treacherously, mala fide; knavishly, villainously, without regard for honesty.

See: 251, 456, 518, 523, **541**, 542, 543, 603, 620, 623, 639, 645, 649, 698, 738, 788, 792, 867, 914, 918, 925, **934**, 954.

931 Disinterestedness

N. *disinterestedness*, impartiality 913 *justice*; unselfishness, unpossessiveness, selflessness, no thought for self, self-effacement 872 *humility*; self-control, self-abnegation, self-denial, self-surrender, self-sacrifice, self-immolation, self-devotion, martyrdom; rising above oneself, heroism, stoicism 855 *courage*; loftiness of purpose, elevation of soul, idealism, ideals, high i.; sublimity, elevation, loftiness, nobility, magnanimity; knightliness, chivalry, knight-errantry, quixotry; generosity, liberality, liberalism 897 *benevolence*; purity of motive, dedication, consecration, labour of love; loyalty, faith, faithfulness 929 *probity*; patriotism 901 *philanthropy*; altruism, thought for others, consideration, considerateness, kindness 884 *courtesy*; compassion 905 *pity*; charity 887 *love*.

Adj. *disinterested*, impartial, without self-interest 913 *just*; self-controlled, stoical 942 *temperate*; incorruptible, uncorrupted, unbought, unbribed, honest 929 *honourable*; self-effacing, modest 872 *humble*; unjealous, unpossessive, unenvious, ungrudging; unselfish, selfless, self-forgetful; self-denying, self-sacrificing, ready to die for, martyr-like; devoted, dedicated, consecrated; loyal, faithful; heroic 855 *courageous*; thoughtful, considerate, kind 884 *courteous*; altruistic, philanthropic, patriotic 897 *benevolent*; pure, unmixed; undesigning; sacrificial, unmercenary, for love, non-profitmaking; idealistic, quixotic, high-minded, lofty, elevated, sublime, noble, great-hearted, magnanimous, chivalrous, knightly; generous, liberal, unsparing 781 *giving*.

Vb. *be disinterested*, - unselfish etc. adj.; sacrifice, make a s., sacrifice oneself, devote o., live for, die f.; do as one would be done by, think of others, put oneself last, take a back seat 872 *be humble*; rise above petty considerations, rise above oneself, surrender personal considerations; have no axe to grind, have nothing to gain, do for its own sake.

See: 781, 855, 872, 884, 887, 897, 901, 905, 913, 929, 942.

932 Selfishness

N. *selfishness*, self-consideration, self-love, self-admiration, narcissism, self-worship, self-approbation, self-praise 873 *vanity*; self-pity, self-indulgence, ego trip 943 *intemperance*; self-absorption, egocentricity; egoism, egotism, individualism, particularism; self-preservation, everyone for themselves; axe to grind, personal considerations, personal motives, private ends, personal advantage, selfish benefit; self-seeking, self-serving, self-aggrandizement, self-interest, concern for number one; no thought for others, 'I'm all right, Jack'; charity that begins at home, cupboard love; illiberality, no magnanimity, mean-mindedness, pettiness, paltriness; meanness, miserliness, niggardliness 816 *parsimony*; greed, acquisitiveness 816 *avarice*; possessiveness 911 *jealousy*; worldliness, worldly wisdom; 'heads I win tails you lose' 914 *injustice*; careerism, selfish ambition, naked a., ruthless a.; power politics.

egotist, egoist, self-centred person, narcissist 873 *vain person*; particularist, individualist, mass of selfishness; self-seeker; careerist, arriviste, go-getter, adventurer, gold-digger, fortune-hunter; money-grubber, miser 816 *niggard*; monopolist, dog in the manger, hog, road h.; opportunist, time-server, worldling.

Adj. *selfish*, egocentric, self-centred, self-absorbed, wrapped up in oneself; egoistic, egotistic, egotistical; personal, individualistic, concerned with number one; self-interested, self-regarding, self-considering, self-seeking; self-indulgent 943 *intemperate*; self-loving, self-admiring, narcissistic 873 *vain*; not altruistic, with an interest; unphilanthropic, unneighbourly; unpatriotic; uncharitable, unsympathetic, cold-hearted 898 *unkind*; unhandsome, mean, mean-minded, petty, paltry; illiberal, ungenerous, niggardly 816 *parsimonious*; acquisitive, money-grubbing, mercenary 816 *avaricious*; venal 930 *dishonest*; covetous 912 *envious*; hoggish, hogging, monopolistic 859 *greedy*; possessive, dog-in-the-manger; competitive 911 *jealous*; self-serving, designing, axe-grinding; go-getting, on the make, gold-digging, opportunist, time-serving, careerist; unidealistic, materialistic, mundane, worldly, earthly, worldly-minded, worldly-wise.

Vb. *be selfish*, - egoistic etc. adj.; put oneself first, think only of oneself, take care of number one; love oneself, indulge o., look after o., coddle o., cosset o., have only oneself to please; feather one's nest, look out for oneself, have an eye to the main chance, know on which side one's bread is buttered; keep for oneself, hang on to, hog, monopolize, be a dog in the manger 778 *retain*; have personal motives, have private ends, have an axe to grind, have one's own game to play; pursue one's interests, advance one's own i., sacrifice the interests of others.

Adv. *selfishly*, self-regardingly, only for oneself; on the make, for profit; ungenerously, illiberally; for one's own sake, from personal motives, for private ends; jealously, possessively.

See: 778, 816, 859, 873, 898, 911, 912, 914, 930, 943.

933 Virtue

N. *virtue*, virtuousness, moral strength, moral tone; goodness, sheer g.; saintliness, holiness, spirituality, odour of sanctity 979 *sanctity*; righteousness 913 *justice*; uprightness, rectitude, moral r., character, integrity, honour, personal h. 929 *probity*; perfect honour, stainlessness, irreproachability; avoidance of guilt, guiltlessness 935 *innocence*; morality, ethics 917 *morals*; sexual morality, temperance, chastity 950 *purity*; straight and narrow, virtuous conduct, Christian c., good behaviour, well-spent life, duty done; good conscience, conscious rectitude; self-improvement, moral rearmament.

virtues, cardinal v., moral v., moral laws; theological virtues, faith, hope, charity; natural virtues, prudence, justice, temperance, fortitude; qualities, fine q., saving quality, saving grace; a virtue, good fault, fault on the right side; worth, merit, desert; excellence, perfections 646 *perfection*; nobleness, magnanimity, altruism, unselfishness 931 *disinterestedness*; idealism, ideals; self-control 942 *temperance*.

Adj. *virtuous*, moral 917 *ethical*; good, good as gold 644 *excellent*; stainless, without a spot on one's character 950 *pure*; guiltless 935 *innocent*; irreproachable, impeccable, above temptation 646 *perfect*; saint-like, seraphic, angelic, saintly, holy 979 *sanctified*; principled, well-p., right-minded, on the side of the angels 913 *right*; righteous 913 *just*; upright, sterling, honest 929 *honourable*; duteous, dutiful 739 *obedient*; unselfish 931 *disinterested*; generous, magnanimous, idealistic, well-intentioned, philanthropic 897 *benevolent*; sober 942 *temperate*; chaste, virginal; proper, edifying, improving, exemplary; elevated, sublimated; meritorious, worthy, praiseworthy, commendable 923 *approved*.

Vb. *be virtuous*, - good etc. adj.; have all the virtues, be a shining light, qualify for sainthood 644 *be good*; behave, be on one's good *or* best behaviour; practise virtue, resist temptation, command one's passions 942 *be temperate*; rise superior to, have a soul above; keep to the straight and narrow path, follow one's conscience, walk humbly with one's God, fight the good fight; discharge one's obligations 917 *do one's duty*; go straight, keep s. 929 *be honourable*; love good, hate wrong 913 *be just*; hear no evil, see no evil, speak no evil; edify, set a good example, shame the devil 644 *do good*.

Adv. *virtuously*, well, with merit; righteously, purely, innocently; holily.

See: 644, 646, 739, 897, **913**, 917, 923, **929**, 931, 935, 942, 950, 979.

934 Wickedness

N. *wickedness*, principle of evil 645 *badness*; Devil, cloven hoof 969 *Satan*; fallen nature, Old Adam; unrighteousness, iniquity, sinfulness, sin 914 *wrong*; peccability, loss of innocence 936 *guilt*; ungodliness 980 *impiety*; ignorance of good, no morals; amorality, amoralism 860 *indifference*; hardness of heart 898 *malevolence*; wilfulness, stubbornness 602 *obstinacy*; waywardness, naughtiness, bad behaviour 738 *disobedience*; immorality, turpitude, moral t.; loose morals, carnality, profligacy 951 *impurity*; demoralization, degeneration, degeneracy, vitiation, degradation 655 *deterioration*; recidivism, backsliding 603 *tergiversation*; vice, corruption, depravity 645 *badness*; flagitiousness, heinousness, shamelessness, flagrancy; bad character, viciousness, unworthiness, baseness, vileness; villainy, knavery, roguery 930 *foul play*; laxity, want of principle, dishonesty 930 *improbity*; crime, criminality 954 *lawbreaking*; devilry, hellishness 898 *inhumanity*; devil worship, diabolism 982 *idolatry*; shame, scandal, abomination, enormity, infamy 867 *disrepute*; infamous conduct, misbehaviour, delinquency, wrongdoing, evil-doing, transgression, evil courses, wicked ways, career of crime; primrose path, slippery slope; low life, criminal world, underworld, demimonde; den of vice, sink of iniquity 649 *sink*.

vice, fault, demerit, unworthiness; human weakness, moral w., infirmity, frailty, foible 163 *weakness*; imperfection, shortcoming, defect, deficiency, failing, flaw, weak point, weak side, weakness of the flesh; trespass, injury, outrage, enormity 914 *wrong*; sin, besetting s., capital s., deadly s.; seven deadly sins, pride, covetousness, lust, anger, gluttony, envy, sloth; venial sin, small fault, slight transgression, peccadillo, scrape; impropriety, indecorum 847 *bad taste*; offence 936 *guilty act*; crime, felony, deadly crime, capital c. 954 *illegality*.

Adj. *wicked*, virtueless, unvirtuous, immoral; amoral, amoralistic 860 *indifferent*; lax, unprincipled, unscrupulous, conscienceless 930 *dishonest*; unblushing, hardened, callous, shameless, brazen, flaunting; ungodly, irreligious, profane 980 *impious*; iniquitous, unrighteous 914 *unjust*; evil 645 *bad*; evil-minded, bad-hearted, black-hearted 898 *malevolent*; evil-doing 898 *maleficent*; misbehaving, bad, naughty 738 *disobedient*; weak (**see** *frail*); peccant, erring, sinning, transgressing; sinful, full of sin 936 *guilty*; unworthy, undeserving, unmeritorious;

graceless, not in a state of grace, reprobate; hopeless, incorrigible, irreclaimable, unredeemed, irredeemable; accursed, godforsaken; hellish, infernal, devilish, fiendish, Mephistophelean, satanic 969 *diabolic*.

vicious, steeped in vice, sunk in iniquity; good-for-nothing, ne'er-do-well; hopeless, past praying for; punk, worthless, unworthy, meritless, graceless 924 *disapproved*; villainous, knavish, miscreant, double-dyed 930 *rascally*; improper, unseemly, indecent, unedifying 847 *vulgar*; without morals, immoral; unvirtuous, intemperate 951 *unchaste*; profligate, abandoned, characterless, lost to virtue, lost to shame 867 *disreputable*; vitiated, corrupt, degraded, demoralized, debauched, ruined, depraved, perverted, degenerate, sick, rotten, rotten to the core 655 *deteriorated*; brutalized, brutal 898 *cruel*.

frail, infirm, feeble 163 *weak*; having a weaker side, having one's foibles, human, only h., too h. 734 *lax*; suggestible, easily tempted 661 *vulnerable*; not above temptation, not impeccable, not perfect, fallen 647 *imperfect*; slipping, sliding, recidivous 603 *tergiversating*.

heinous, heavy, grave, serious, deadly; black, scarlet, of deepest dye; abysmal, hellish, infernal; sinful, immoral 914 *wrong*; demoralizing, unedifying, contra bonos mores; criminal, nefarious, felonious 954 *lawbreaking*; flagitious, monstrous, flagrant, scandalous, scandalizing, infamous, shameful, disgraceful, shocking, outrageous, obscene; gross, foul, rank; base, vile, abominable, accursed; mean, shabby, despicable 645 *bad*; blameworthy, culpable 928 *accusable*; reprehensible, indefensible, unjustifiable 916 *unwarranted*; atrocious, brutal 898 *cruel*; unforgivable, unpardonable, inexcusable, irremissible, inexpiable, unatonable.

Vb. *be wicked*, - vicious, - sinful etc. adj.; not be in a state of grace, scoff at virtue; fall from grace, spoil one's record, blot one's copybook, lapse, relapse, backslide 603 *tergiversate*; fall into evil ways, go to the bad *or* to the dogs 655 *deteriorate*; do wrong, transgress, misbehave, misdemean oneself, carry on, be naughty, sow one's wild oats; trespass, offend, sin, commit s.; leave the straight and narrow, deviate from the paths of virtue, err, stray, slip, trip, stumble, fall; have one's foibles, have one's weak side 163 *be weak*.

make wicked, render evil, corrupt, demoralize, deform one's character, brutalize 655 *pervert*; mislead, lead astray, seduce 612 *tempt*; set a bad example, teach wickedness, dehumanize, brutalize, diabolize.

Adv. *wickedly*, wrongly, sinfully; viciously, vilely, devilishly; unforgivably, unpardonably, irredeemably, inexpiably; to one's discredit.

See: 163, 602, 603, 612, 645, 647, 649, 655, 661, 734, 738, 847, 860, 867, 898, **914**, 916, 924, 928, **930**, **936**, 951, 954, 969, 980, 982.

935 Innocence

N. *innocence*, blessed i., freedom from guilt, guiltlessness, clean hands; conscious innocence, clear conscience, irreproachability; nothing to declare, nothing to confess; inculpability, blamelessness, freedom from blame, every excuse; declared innocence 960 *acquittal*; ignorance of evil 491 *ignorance*; inexperience, unworldliness 699 *artlessness*; playfulness, harmlessness, inoffensiveness, innocent intentions, pure motives; freedom from sin, unfallen state, purity of heart, state of grace 933 *virtue*; undefilement, stainlessness 950 *purity*; incorruption, incorruptibility 929 *probity*; impeccability 646 *perfection*; days of innocence, golden age 824 *happiness*.

innocent, Holy Innocents, babe, newborn babe, babe unborn, babes and sucklings; child, ingenue; lamb, dove; angel, pure soul; milksop, goody-goody; one in the right, innocent party, injured p., not the culprit.

Adj. *innocent*, pure, unspotted, stainless, unblemished, spotless, immaculate 648 *clean*; incorrupt, uncorrupted, undefiled; unfallen, sinless, free from sin, unerring, impeccable 646 *perfect*; green, inexperienced, naive, knowing no better, unhardened, unversed in crime 491 *ignorant*; unworldly, guileless 699 *artless*; well-meaning, well-intentioned 897 *benevolent*; innocuous, harmless, inoffensive, playful, gentle, lamb-like, dove-like, child-like, angelic; wide-eyed, looking as if butter would not melt in one's mouth; innocent as a lamb *or* a dove, innocent as a babe unborn, innocent as a child; shockable, goody-goody; Arcadian.

guiltless, free from guilt, not responsible, not guilty 960 *acquitted*; more sinned against than sinning; falsely accused, misunderstood; clean-handed, bloodless; blameless, faultless, unblameworthy, not culpable; irreproachable, above suspicion; unobjectionable, unexceptionable, unimpeachable, entirely defensible, with every excuse 923 *approvable*; pardonable, forgivable, excusable, venial, exculpable, expiable.

Vb. *be innocent*, know no wrong, wrong no one, have no guile 929 *be honourable*; live in a state of grace, not fall from g. 933 *be virtuous*; have every excuse, have no need to blush, have clean hands, have a clear conscience, have nothing to be ashamed of, have nothing to confess *or* declare; have the best intentions, mean no harm; know no better 699 *be artless*; stand free of blame, stand above suspicion; acquit oneself, salve one's conscience.

Adv. *innocently*, blamelessly, harmlessly; with the best intentions; with clean hands, with a clear conscience, with an easy c.

See: 491, 646, 648, 699, 824, 897, 923, 929, **933**, 950, 960.

936 Guilt

N. *guilt*, guiltiness, blood g., red-handedness; culpability; criminality, delinquency 954 *illegality*; sinfulness, original sin 934 *wickedness*; involvement, complicity; liability, one's fault; burden of guilt 702 *encumbrance*; blame, censure 924 *reproach*; guilt complex 503 *eccentricity*; guilty feelings, conscious guilt, guilty conscience, bad c.; guilty behaviour, suspicious conduct, blush, stammer, embarrassment; admitted guilt, confessed g., confession 526 *disclosure*; twinge of conscience, remorse, shame 939 *penitence*.

guilty act, sin, deadly s., venial s. 934 *vice*; misdeed, wicked deed, misdoing, sinning, transgression, trespass, offence, crime, corpus delicti 954 *illegality*; misdemeanour, felony; misconduct, misbehaviour, malpractice, malversation; infamous conduct, unprofessional c.; indiscretion, impropriety, peccadillo; naughtiness, scrape; lapse, slip, faux pas, blunder 495 *mistake*; omission, sin of o. 458 *negligence*; culpable omission, laches; fault, failure, dereliction of duty 918 *undutifulness*; injustice, delict, tort, injury 914 *wrong*; enormity, atrocity, outrage 898 *cruel act*.

Adj. *guilty*, found g., convicted 961 *condemned*; thought guilty, suspected, blamed, censured, made responsible 924 *disapproved*; responsible 180 *liable*; in the wrong, at fault, to blame, culpable, chargeable 928 *accusable*; blameful, shameful, reprehensible, censurable 924 *blameworthy*; unjustifiable, without excuse, inexcusable, unpardonable, unforgivable; inexpiable, mortal, deadly 934 *heinous*; trespassing, transgressing, peccant, sinful 934 *wicked*; criminal 954 *illegal*; blood-guilty 362 *murderous*; red-handed, caught in the act, surprised in the attempt; caught with one's hand in the till; hangdog, sheepish, shamefaced, blushing, ashamed.

Vb. *be guilty*, be at fault, bear the blame; have sins upon one's conscience, have crimes to answer for, have blood on one's hands; be caught in the act, be caught red-handed; acknowledge one's guilt, have nothing to say for oneself, plead guilty 526 *confess*; have no excuse, stand condemned; trespass, transgress, sin 934 *be wicked*.

Adv. *guiltily*, criminally; inexcusably, without excuse; red-handed, in the very act, flagrante delicto.

See: 180, 362, 458, 495, 503, 526, 702, 898, 914, 918, 924, 928, 934, 939, 954, 961.

937 Good Person

N. *good person*, fine human being, sterling character, exemplary c. 929 *honourable person*; pillar of society, model of virtue, salt of the earth, shining light, perfection 646 *paragon*; Christian, true C.; saint 979 *pietist*; mahatma, maharishi, great saint; seraph, angel 935 *innocent*; heart of gold 897 *kind person*; good neighbour, Good Samaritan 903 *benefactor*; idealist 901 *philanthropist*; the best, one of the b., one in a million, the tops 890 *favourite*; hero, heroine 855 *brave person*; goody, good guy, good sort, stout fellow, brick, trump, sport; rough diamond, ugly duckling.

See: **646**, 855, 890, 897, 901, 903, 929, 935, **979**.

938 Bad Person

N. *bad person*, evil p., no saint, sinner, hardened s., limb of Satan, Antichrist 904 *evildoer*; fallen angel, backslider, recidivist, lost sheep, lost soul, âme damnée, one without morals, immoralist; reprobate, slubberdegullion, scapegrace, good-for-nothing, ne'er-do-well, black sheep, the despair of; scallywag, scamp; rake, roué, profligate 952 *libertine*; wanton, hussy 952 *loose woman*; wastrel, waster, prodigal son 815 *prodigal*; scandalous person, reproach, outcast, dregs, riffraff, trash, scum 867 *object of scorn*; nasty type, ugly customer, undesirable, bad 'un, wrong 'un, badmash, thug, bully, roughneck 904 *ruffian*; bad lot, bad egg, bad hat, bad character, bad guy, baddy, villain; bad influence, bad example; bad child, naughty c., terror, holy t., enfant terrible, whelp, monkey, little m., little devil 663 *troublemaker*.

knave, scurvy k., varlet, vagabond, varmint, caitiff, wretch, rascal, rapscallion 869 *low fellow*; rogue, prince of rogues; criminal 904 *offender*; thief, pirate, freebooter 789 *robber*; villain, blackguard, scoundrel, miscreant; cheat, liar, crook; impostor, twister, con-man 545 *trickster*; sneak, grass, squealer, rat 524 *informer*; renegade, recreant 603 *tergiversator*; betrayer, traitor, archtraitor, quisling, Judas; animal, dog, hound, swine, snake, serpent, viper, reptile, vermin 904 *noxious animal*.

cad, nasty bit of work, scoundrel, blackguard; rotter, blighter, bastard, dastard, bounder, heel, slob, scab, son of a bitch; stinker, skunk, dirty dog, filthy beast; pimp, pander, pervert, degenerate; cur, hound, swine, rat, worm; louse, insect, vermin; pig, beast, horrid b., cat, bitch; the end, absolute e.

monster, shocker, horror, unspeakable villain; monster of cruelty, brute, savage, sadist; ogre 735 *tyrant*; Juggernaut, Moloch; public enemy number one; monster of wickedness, monster of iniquity *or* depravity, fiend, demon, ghoul 969 *devil*; hellhound, fury 904 *hellhag*; devil in human shape, devil incarnate, fiend i., ape-man, gorilla, King Kong, Frankenstein's monster, bogey, terror, nightmare.

See: 524, 545, 603, 663, 735, 789, 815, 867, 869, **904**, 952, 969.

939 Penitence

N. *penitence*, repentance, contrition, attrition, compunction, remorse, self-reproach 830 *regret*; self-accusation, self-condemnation, humble confession 526 *disclosure*; confession 988 *Christian rite*; self-humiliation 872 *humility*; guilt-feeling, weight on one's mind, voice of conscience, uneasy c., unquiet c., bad c., twinge of c., qualms of c., pangs of c., stings of c., pricks of c. 936 *guilt*; awakened conscience 603 *recantation*; last-minute repentance, deathbed r.; sackcloth and ashes, white sheet, stool of repentance 941 *penance*; apology 941 *atonement*; half-repentance, grudging apology.

penitent, confessor; flagellant 945 *ascetic*; magdalen, prodigal son, returned prodigal, a sadder and a wiser man; reformed character, brand plucked from the burning.

Adj. *repentant*, contrite, remorseful, regretful, sorry, apologetic, full of regrets 830 *regretting*; ashamed 872 *humbled*; unhardened, softened, melted, weeping 836 *lamenting*; compunctious, relenting, conscience-stricken, conscience-smitten, pricked by conscience, plagued by c.; self-reproachful, self-accusing, self-convicted, self-condemned; confessing, in the confessional; penitent, penitential, penitentiary, doing penance 941 *atoning*; chastened, sobered, awakened; reclaimed, reformed, converted, regenerate, born again.

Vb. *be penitent*, repent, show compunction, feel shame, blush for s., feel sorry, say one is s., express regrets, apologize; reproach oneself, blame o., reprove o., accuse o., convict o., condemn o.; go to confession, acknowledge one's faults 526 *confess*; do penance, wear a white sheet, repent in sackcloth and ashes 941 *atone*; bewail one's sins, sing Miserere, sing De Profundis 836 *lament*; beat one's breast, scourge oneself; eat humble pie 721 *knuckle under*; rue, have regrets, wish undone 830 *regret*; think again, think better of, stop in time; learn one's lesson, learn from experience 536 *learn*; reform, be reformed, be reclaimed, turn over a new leaf 654 *get better*; see the light, be converted, put on the new man, turn from sin 147 *be turned to*; recant one's error 603 *recant*.

Adv. *penitently*, like a penitent, on the stool of repentance, in sackcloth and ashes; repentantly, regretfully.

Int. sorry! mea culpa! repent! for pity!

See: 147, 526, 536, 603, 654, 721, 830, 836,

872, 936, **941**, 945, 988.

940 Impenitence

N. *impenitence*, lack of contrition; contumacy, recusance, refusal to recant, obduracy, stubbornness 602 *obstinacy*; hardness of heart, induration 326 *hardness*; no apologies, no regrets, no compunction 906 *pitilessness*; incorrigibility, seared conscience, unawakened c., sleeping c.; hardened sinner, despair of 938 *bad person*.

Adj. *impenitent*, unregretting, unapologizing, unrecanting, recusant; contumacious, obdurate, inveterate, stubborn 602 *obstinate*; unconfessing, unrepentant, uncontrite; unregretful, without regrets; unrelenting, relentless 600 *persevering*; without compunction, without a pang, heartless 898 *cruel*; unsoftened, unmoved; hard, hardened, case-h.; conscienceless, unashamed, unblushing, brazen; incorrigible, irreclaimable, irredeemable, hopeless, despaired of, lost 934 *wicked*; unconfessed, unshriven; unchastened, unreformed, unregenerate, unreconciled; unreclaimed, unconverted.

unrepented, unregretted, unapologized for, unatoned.

Vb. *be impenitent*, make no excuses, offer no apologies, have no regrets, would do it again; not see the light, refuse to recant 602 *be obstinate*; make no confession, die and make no sign, die in one's sins, die in contumacy; stay unreconciled, want no forgiveness; feel no compunction, harden one's heart, steel one's h. 906 *be pitiless*.

Adv. *impenitently*, unashamedly, unblushingly; without compunction, with no regrets.

See: 326, 600, **602**, 898, 906, 934, 938.

941 Atonement

N. *atonement*, making amends, amends, amende honorable, apology, full a., satisfaction; reparation, compensation, indemnity, indemnification, blood money, wergild, conscience money 787 *restitution*; repayment, quittance, quits; composition 770 *compromise*.

propitiation, expiation, satisfaction, reconciliation, conciliation 719 *pacification*; reclamation, redemption 965 *divine function*; sacrifice, offering, burnt o., peace o., sin o. 981 *oblation*; sin-eater, scapegoat, whipping boy, chopping block 150 *substitute*.

penance, shrift, confession, acknowledgment 939 *penitence*; sacrament of penance, penitential exercise, austerities, fasting, flagellation 945 *asceticism*; lustration, purgation 648 *cleansing*; purgatorial torments, purgatory; penitent form, anxious seat, stool of repentance, cutty stool, corner 964 *pillory*; white sheet, sanbenito; sackcloth and ashes 836 *lamentation*.

Adj. *atoning*, making amends 939 *repentant*; reparatory, compensatory, indemnificatory 787 *restoring*; conciliatory, apologetic; propitiatory, expiatory, piacular, purgatorial, lustral 648 *cleansing*; sacrificial 759 *offering*; penitential, penitentiary, doing penance, undergoing p. 963 *punitive*.

Vb. *atone*, salve one's conscience, make amends, make reparation, offer r., indemnify, compensate, pay compensation, make it up to; apologize, make apologies, offer one's a. 909 *beg pardon*; propitiate, conciliate 719 *pacify*; give satisfaction, offer s. 787 *restitute*; redeem one's error, repair one's fault, make up for, make matters right, be restored to favour; sacrifice to, offer sacrifice; expiate, pay the penalty, pay the forfeit, pay the cost, smart for it 963 *be punished*; become the whipping boy, make oneself the scapegoat 931 *be disinterested*; reclaim, redeem.

do penance, undergo p., perform penitential exercises; pray, fast, flagellate oneself, scourge o.; purge one's contempt *or* one's offences, suffer purgatory; put on sackcloth and ashes, stand in the corner, sit on the stool of repentance; take one's punishment, swallow one's medicine 963 *be punished*; salve one's conscience, go to confession 526 *confess*.

See: 150, 526, 648, 719, 759, 770, 787, 836, 909, 931, **939**, 945, 963, 964, 965, 981.

942 Temperance

N. *temperance*, temperateness, nothing in excess 177 *moderation*; self-denial 931 *disinterestedness*; self-restraint, self-control, self-discipline, stoicism 747 *restraint*; continence, chastity 950 *purity*; soberness 948 *sobriety*; forbearance 620 *avoidance*; renunciation 621 *relinquishment*; abstemiousness, abstinence, abstention, total abstinence, teetotalism; enforced abstention, prohibition, prohibitionism 747 *restriction*; vegetarianism, veganism;

dieting 946 *fasting*; frugality 814 *economy*; plain living, simple life; frugal diet 945 *asceticism*.

abstainer, total a., teetotaller 948 *sober person*; prohibitionist, pussyfoot; nonsmoker; vegetarian, fruitarian, vegan; dropout, advocate of the simple life; dieter, faster; enemy of excess, Spartan 945 *ascetic*.

Adj. *temperate*, not excessive, within bounds, within reasonable limits; measured, tempered 177 *moderate*; plain, Spartan, sparing 814 *economical*; frugal 816 *parsimonious*; forbearing, abstemious, abstinent 620 *avoiding*; dry, teetotal 948 *sober*; vegan, vegetarian, ungreedy, self-controlled, self-disciplined, continent 747 *restrained*; chaste 950 *pure*; self-denying 945 *ascetic*.

Vb. *be temperate*, - moderate etc. adj.; moderate, temper, keep within bounds, observe a limit, avoid excess, know when one has had enough, know when to stop 177 *be moderate*; keep sober 948 *be sober*; forbear, refrain, abstain 620 *avoid*; control oneself, contain o. 747 *restrain*; deny oneself 945 *be ascetic*; go dry, take the pledge, sign the p.; give up, swear off; ration oneself, tighten one's belt 946 *starve*; diet, go on a d. 206 *make thin*.

See: 177, 206, 620, 621, 747, 814, 816, 931, **945**, 946, **948**, 950.

943 Intemperance

N. *intemperance*, want of moderation, immoderation, unrestraint, abandon; excess, excessiveness, luxury 637 *redundance*; too much 637 *superfluity*; wastefulness, extravagance, waste, consumer society 815 *prodigality*; want of self-control, indiscipline, incontinence 734 *laxity*; indulgence, self-i., overindulgence; addiction, bad habit 610 *habit*; drug habit 949 *drug-taking*; high living, dissipation, licentiousness, debauchery 944 *sensualism*; overeating 947 *gluttony*; intoxication, hangover 949 *drunkenness*.

Adj. *intemperate*, immoderate, exceeding, excessive 637 *redundant*; untempered, unmeasured, unlimited 635 *plenteous*; unfrugal, wasteful, extravagant, profligate, spendthrift 815 *prodigal*; luxurious 637 *superfluous*; unascetic, unspartan, indulgent, self-i., overindulgent, denying oneself nothing; unrestrained, uncontrolled, lacking self-control, undisciplined 738 *riotous*; incontinent 951 *unchaste*; unsober, nonteetotal 949 *drunk*; animal 944 *sensual*.

Vb. *be intemperate*, - immoderate etc. adj.; roll in, luxuriate, plunge, wallow; lack self-control, want discipline, lose control 734 *be lax*; deny oneself nothing, indulge oneself, give oneself up to 734 *please oneself*; have one's fling, sow one's wild oats 815 *be prodigal*; run to excess, run riot, exceed 306 *overstep*; observe no limits, go to any lengths, stick at nothing, not know when to stop, overindulge, burn the candle at both ends 634 *waste*; live it up, go on a binge 837 *revel*; overdrink, drink like a fish, drink to excess 949 *get drunk*; eat to excess, gorge, overeat, pig it, make oneself sick 947 *gluttonize*; be incontinent, grow dissipated 951 *be impure*; addict oneself, become a slave to habit 610 *be wont*.

Adv. *intemperately*, immoderately, excessively, with abandon; without moderation, without control; incontinently, licentiously; not wisely but too well.

See: 306, 610, 634, 635, 637, 734, 738, 815, 837, **944**, **947**, **949**, 951.

944 Sensualism

N. *sensualism*, life of the senses, unspirituality, earthiness, materialism 319 *materiality*; cultivation of the senses, sensuality, carnality, sexuality, the flesh; grossness, beastliness, bestiality, animalism, hoggishness, wallowing; craze for excitement 822 *excitability*; love of pleasure, search for p., hedonism, epicurism, epicureanism, eudaemonism 376 *pleasure*; sybaritism, voluptuousness, voluptuosity, softness, luxuriousness, dolce vita; luxury, lap of l. 637 *superfluity*; full life, wine of l., life of pleasure, high living, fast l., wine, women and song 824 *enjoyment*; dissipation, abandon 943 *intemperance*; licentiousness, dissoluteness, debauchery 951 *impurity*; indulgence, self-i., overindulgence, greediness, gourmandise 947 *gluttony*; eating and drinking, Lucullan banquet 301 *feasting*; orgy, debauch, saturnalia, Bacchanalia 837 *revel*.

sensualist, animal, pig, swine, hog, wallower; no ascetic, hedonist, playboy, pleasure-lover, thrill-seeker; luxury-lover, sybarite, voluptuary; eudaemonist, epicurean, free-liver, bon viveur; epicure, gourmet, gourmand 947 *glutton*; hard drinker 949 *drunkard*; loose liver, profligate, rake 952 *libertine*; drug addict 949 *drug-taking*; degenerate, decadent; sadist, masochist.

Adj. *sensual*, earthy, gross, unspiritual 319 *material*; fleshly, carnal, bodily; sexual, venereal 887 *erotic*; animal, bestial, beastly, brutish, swinish, hoggish, wallowing; Circean, pleasure-giving 826 *pleasurable*; sybaritic, voluptuous, pleasure-loving, thrill-seeking, living for kicks; hedonistic, eudaemonistic, epicurean, Lucullan, luxury-loving, luxurious; pampered, indulged, self-i., overindulged; overfed 947 *gluttonous*; high-living, fast-l., incontinent 943 *intemperate*; licentious, dissipated, debauched 951 *impure*; riotous, orgiastic, Bacchanalian 949 *drunken*.

Vb. *be sensual*, - voluptuous etc. adj.; cultivate one's senses, be the slave of one's desires, live for pleasure, wallow in luxury, live well, live off the fat of the land 730 *prosper*; indulge oneself, pamper o., do oneself proud; run riot, go the pace, burn the candle at both ends 943 *be intemperate*.

Adv. *sensually*, voluptuously, bestially, hoggishly, swinishly.

See: 301, 319, **376**, 637, 730, 822, 824, 826, 837, 887, **943**, 947, 949, 951, 952.

945 Asceticism

N. *asceticism*, austerity, mortification, self-m., self-chastisement, self-torture, self-mutilation; maceration, flagellation 941 *penance*; ascetic practice, Encratism, yoga; anchoritism, eremitism 883 *seclusion*; Cynicism, Diogenes and his tub 883 *unsociability*; holy poverty 801 *poverty*; plain living, simple fare, dinner of herbs, Spartan fare, Lenten f. 946 *fasting*; fast day 946 *fast*; self-denial 942 *temperance*; frugality 814 *economy*; Puritanism, Sabbatarianism; sackcloth, hair shirt, cilice.

ascetic, spiritual athlete, gymnosophist, yogi, sannyasi, fakir, dervish, fire-walker; hermit, eremite, anchoret, anchorite, anchoress, recluse 883 *solitary*; Cynic, Diogenes; flagellant 939 *penitent*; water-drinker 948 *sober person*; faster, Encratite 942 *abstainer*; Puritan, Plymouth Brethren, Sabbatarian; spoilsport, killjoy, pussyfoot 702 *hinderer*.

Adj. *ascetic*, yogic, self-mortifying, fasting, flagellating; hermit-like, eremitical, anchoretic; puritanical; Sabbatarian; austere, rigorous 735 *severe*; Spartan, unpampered 942 *temperate*; water-drinking 948 *sober*; plain, wholesome 652 *salubrious*.

Vb. *be ascetic*, live like a Spartan; fast, live on air 946 *starve*; live like a hermit, wear a hair shirt, put on sackcloth; control one's senses, lie on nails, walk through fire.

Adv. *ascetically*, austerely, abstinently, simply, plainly, frugally, painfully.

See: 652, 702, 735, 801, 814, 883, 939, 941, **942**, **946**, 948.

946 Fasting

N. *fasting*, abstinence from food; no appetite, anorexia, a. nervosa 651 *ill health*; cutting down 301 *dieting*; keeping fast, strict fast, xerophagy; Lenten fare, bread and water, spare diet, meagre d., starvation d., soupe maigre 945 *asceticism*; iron rations, short commons 636 *scarcity*; no food, starvation, utter s., famishment, inanition 859 *hunger*.

fast, fast day, Friday, Good Friday, Lent, Ramadan; day of abstinence, meatless day, fish d., jour maigre 945 *asceticism*; hunger strike 145 *strike*.

Adj. *fasting*, not eating, off one's food; abstinent 942 *temperate*; keeping fast, keeping Lent; without food, unfed, empty, dinnerless, supperless; poorly fed, half-starved 636 *underfed*; starved, starving, clemmed, famished, famishing, dying for food, wasting away 206 *lean*; wanting food 859 *hungry*; sparing, frugal 814 *economical*; scanty 636 *scarce*; meagre, thin, poor, Spartan; Lenten.

Vb. *starve*, famish, clem 859 *be hungry*; macerate, waste with hunger, show one's bones; have no food, have nothing to eat, live on water, live on air, dine with Duke Humphrey 801 *be poor*; fast, go without food, abstain from f., eat no meat; keep Lent, keep Ramadan; lay off food, give up eating, eat nothing, refuse one's food, go on hunger strike; eat less, diet, go on a d., reduce, take off weight 37 *abate*; tighten one's belt, go on short commons, live on iron rations; eat sparingly, make a little go a long way, control one's appetite 942 *be temperate*; keep a poor table 816 *be parsimonious*.

See: 37, 145, 206, 301, 636, 651, 801, 814, 816, 859, 942, **945**.

947 Gluttony

N. *gluttony*, greediness, greed, rapacity, insatiability, gulosity, voracity, voraciousness, wolfishness, hoggishness, piggishness; edacity, polyphagia, insatiable appetite 859 *hunger*; good living, high l., indulgence, overeating, overfeeding 943 *intemperance*; guzzling, gorging, gormandizing, gluttonizing, pampered appetite, belly worship, gourmandise, epicureanism, epicurism, pleasures of the table 301 *gastronomy*; bust, blowout, masses of food 301 *feasting*.

glutton, glutton for food, guzzler, gormandizer, bolter, gorger, crammer, stuffer; locust, wolf, vulture, cormorant, pig, hog; vampire, blood-sucker; trencherman *or* -woman, good eater, hearty e. 301 *eater*; coarse feeder, greedy-guts, greedy pig; gourmand, gastronome, gourmet, epicure, bon vivant, Lucullus.

Adj. *gluttonous*, rapacious, ventripotent 859 *greedy*; devouring, voracious, edacious, wolfish; omnivorous, all-swallowing, all-engulfing 464 *indiscriminating*; starving, insatiable, never full 859 *hungry*; pampered, full-fed, overfed, eating one's fill 301 *feeding*; guzzling, gormandizing, gorging, stuffing, cramming, belly-worshipping, licking one's lips, licking one's chops, watering at the mouth; gastronomic, epicurean.

Vb. *gluttonize*, gormandize; guzzle, bolt, wolf, scoff, gobble, gobble up, devour, gulp down; fill oneself, gorge, cram, stuff; glut oneself, overeat 301 *eat*; have the run of one's teeth, eat one's head off, eat out of house and home; have a good appetite, ply a good knife and fork; eat like a trooper, eat like a horse, eat like a pig, have two feet in the trough, make a beast of oneself, have eyes bigger than one's stomach; make oneself sick; indulge one's appetite, pamper one's a., tickle one's palate; savour one's food, lick one's lips, lick one's chops, water at the mouth; keep a good table, have the best cook; like one's food, worship one's belly, live only for eating.

Adv. *gluttonously*, ravenously, wolfishly, hungrily; at a gulp, with one bite; gastronomically.

See: 301, 464, 859, **943**.

948 Sobriety

N. *sobriety*, soberness 942 *temperance*; water-drinking, tea-d., teetotalism, pussyfootism; state of sobriety, unintoxicated state, clear head, unfuddled brain, no hangover; dry area.

sober person, moderate drinker, no toper; nonaddict, nonalcoholic; water-drinker, tea-d., teetotaller, total abstainer 942 *abstainer*; Rechabite, Band of Hope, temperance society, Alcoholics Anonymous; prohibitionist, pussyfoot.

Adj. *sober*, abstinent, abstemious 620 *avoiding*; water-drinking, tea-d. 942 *temperate*; not drinking, off drink, drying out, on the water-waggon; teetotal, pussyfoot, prohibitionist, dry; unintoxicated, unfuddled, clear-headed, with a clear head, sober as a judge, stone-cold sober; sobered, come to one's senses, sobered up, without a hangover; dried out, off the bottle; unfermented, nonalcoholic, soft.

Vb. *be sober*, - abstemious, etc. adj.; drink water, prefer soft drinks; not drink, not imbibe, keep off liquor, never touch drink, drink moderately 942 *be temperate*; dry out, come off (drugs); go on the water-waggon, give up alcohol, become teetotal, sign the pledge, join the Band of Hope; go dry, turn prohibitionist; carry one's liquor, hold one's l., keep a clear head, be sober as a judge; sober up, clear one's head, get the fumes out of one's brain, get rid of a hangover, sleep it off.

Adv. *soberly*, with sobriety, abstemiously.

See: 620, **942**.

949 Drunkenness. Drug-taking

N. *drunkenness*, excessive drinking 943 *intemperance*; ebriosity, insobriety, inebriety, temulency; bibulousness, winebibbing, weakness for liquor, fondness for the bottle; sottishness, beeriness, vinousness; influence of liquor, inspiration, exhilaration 821 *excitation*; Dutch courage 855 *courage*; intoxication, inebriation, befuddlement, fuddledness, blackout; hiccoughing, hiccup, thick speech 580 *speech defect*; tipsiness, wooziness, staggering, titubancy 317 *oscillation*; getting drunk, one over the eight, drop too much, hard drinking, swilling, soaking 301 *drinking*; compotation, potation, deep potations, libations, libation to Bacchus; hair of the dog that bit one; flowing bowl, booze, liquor, John Barleycorn 301 *alcoholic* *drink*, *wine*; drinking bout, jag, lush, blind, binge, spree, bender, pub-crawl, orgy of drinking, Bacchanalia 837 *revel*; Bacchus, Dionysus.

crapulence, crapulousness; morning after the night before, hangover, thick head, sick headache.

alcoholism, alcoholic addiction, dipsomania 503 *mania*; delirium tremens, dt's, the horrors, heebiejeebies, jimjams, pink elephants; grog-blossom, red nose.

drug-taking, smoking, snorting, sniffing, glue-s., hitting up, shooting up, injecting, mainlining; pill-popping; hard drug, soft d.; joint, reefer, roach; shot, fix; narcotic, dope; nicotine 388 *tobacco*; cannabis, marijuana, ganja, hemp, hashish, hash, bhang, kef, pot, grass; cocaine, coke, snow; heroin, horse, smack; methadone; downers, barbiturates, barbs, morphia, morphine, opium 658 *drug*; stimulant, pep pill, amphetamine, speed, purple hearts, dexies, uppers 821 *excitant*; intoxicant, hallucinogen, LSD, acid, mescalin, peyote; drug addiction, drug abuse, drug dependence, habit 943 *intemperance*; drying out, withdrawal symptoms, cold turkey; drug addict, dope fiend, freak; head, acidhead, junkie, mainliner; pusher.

drunkard, habitual d., inebriate, drunk, sot, lush; slave to drink, wino, alcoholic, dipsomaniac, pathological drunk; drinker, social d., hard d., secret d.; bibber, wine-b., tippler, toper, boozer, swiller, soaker, old soak, souse, sponge, wineskin; love-pot, tosspot, barfly, frothblower, thirsty soul; devotee of Bacchus, Bacchanal, Bacchant(e), maenad, Silenus; carouser, pub-crawler 837 *reveller*.

Adj. *drunk*, inebriated, intoxicated, under the influence, having had a drop too much; in one's cups, in liquor, the worse for l.; half-seas over, three sheets in the wind, one over the eight; boozed up, ginned up, liquored up, lit up, flushed, merry, happy, high, elevated, exhilarated 821 *excited*; comfortably drunk, feeling no pain, mellow, full, fou, primed, well-p., tanked up, bevvied up; gloriously drunk, roaring d., fighting d., pot-valiant, drunk and disorderly 61 *disorderly*.

tipsy, tiddly, squiffy, tight, half-cut, pissed, Brahms and Liszt; well-oiled, pickled, canned, bottled, stewed, fried, well-lubricated; smashed, sloshed, sozzled, soaked, soused, plastered; pixilated, fuddled, muddled, flustered; maudlin, tearful, tired and emotional; drunken, boozy, muzzy, woozy; glazed, glassy-eyed, pie-e., seeing double; dizzy, giddy, reeling, staggering 317 *oscillating*; hiccupping 580 *stammering*.

dead drunk, stinking d., stinko, stoned; blind drunk, blind, blotto; legless, paralytic; gone, shot, stiff, out, in a drunken stupor; under the table, dead to the world; drunk as a lord, drunk as a fiddler's bitch; drunk as an owl, drunk as David's sow; pissed as a newt, fou as a coot.

crapulous, crapulent, with a hangover, with a thick head; dizzy, giddy, sick.

drugged, doped, high, zonked, spaced out, freaked o., in a trance; stoned, incapacitated 375 *insensible*; turned on, hooked on drugs, addicted.

drunken, inebriate 943 *intemperate*; habitually drunk, always tight, never sober; sottish, sodden, gin-s., boozy, beery, vinous, smelling of drink, stinking of liquor; thirsty, bibulous, fond of a drink; tippling, boozing, toping, swilling, swigging, hard-drinking; pub-crawling, carousing, wassailing; red-nosed, bloodshot, gouty, liverish; given to drink, a slave to d., addicted to d., on the bottle, alcoholic, dipsomaniac.

intoxicating, poisonous, inebriating, inebriative, temulent; exhilarating, going to the head, heady, winy, like wine 821 *exciting*; stimulant, intoxicant; opiate, narcotic; hallucinatory, psychedelic, psychotropic, mind-bending, mind-blowing; addictive, habit-forming; alcoholic, spirituous, vinous, beery; not soft, hard, potent, double-strength, overproof 162 *strong*; neat 44 *unmixed*.

Vb. *be drunk*, - tipsy etc. adj.; be under the influence of liquor, have had too much; have a weak head, not hold one's liquor, succumb, be overcome, pass out; hiccup, stutter 580 *stammer*; see double, not walk straight, lurch, stagger, reel 317 *oscillate*.

get drunk, have too much, drink deep, drink hard, drink like a fish, drink to get tight; liquor up, tank up, crack a bottle, knock back a few, bend one's elbow, lush, bib, tipple, fuddle, booze, tope, guzzle, swig, swill, soak, souse, hit the bottle 301 *drink*; go on the spree, go on a blind *or* a bender, go on the fuddle, go pub-crawling, pub-crawl; drown one's sorrows, commune with the spirits; quaff, carouse, wassail, sacrifice to Bacchus 837 *revel*.

drug oneself, smoke, sniff, snort, inject oneself, shoot, mainline; turn on, trip out, take a trip; freak out.

inebriate, be intoxicating, - heady etc. adj.; exhilarate, elevate 821 *excite*; go to one's head, make one's head swim, fuddle, befuddle, stupefy; make drunk, tipsify; drink one under the table.

See:44, 61, 162, **301**, 317, 375, 388, 503, 580, 658, 821, **837**, 855, **943**.

950 Purity

N.*purity*, faultlessness 646 *perfection*; sinlessness, immaculacy 935 *innocence*; moral purity, morals, good m., morality 933 *virtue*; decency, propriety, delicacy 846 *good taste*; pudency, shame, bashfulness 874 *modesty*; chastity, continence, Encratism 942 *temperance*; coldness, frigidity 820 *moral insensibility*; honour, one's h.; virginity, maidenhood, maidenhead 895 *celibacy*.

prudery, prudishness, squeamishness, shockability; overmodesty, false modesty, false shame, mauvaise honte 874 *modesty*; demureness, gravity 834 *seriousness*; priggishness, primness, coyness 850 *affectation*; sanctimony, sanctimoniousness 979 *pietism*; Puritanism, blue laws 735 *severity*; euphemism, Grundyism, genteelism, mealy-mouthedness; censorship, expurgation, bowdlerization 550 *obliteration*.

virgin, maiden, vestal, vestal virgin, virgo intacta, maid, old maid, spinster 895 *celibate*; Encratite, religious celibate 986 *monk, nun*; Joseph, Galahad; virtuous woman, Procne, Lucretia; Diana, Artemis.

prude, prig, Victorian, euphemist 850 *affecter*; Puritan, wowser; guardian of morality, censor, Watch Committee, Mrs Grundy.

Adj.*pure*, faultless 646 *perfect*; undefiled, unfallen, sinless 935 *innocent*; maidenly, virgin, virginal, vestal, untouched 895 *unwedded*; blushful, blushing, rosy 874 *modest*; coy, shy 620 *avoiding*; chaste, continent 942 *temperate*; unmovable, unassailable, impregnable, incorruptible 929 *honourable*; unfeeling 820 *impassive*; frigid 380 *cold*; immaculate, spotless, snowy 427 *white*; good, moral 933 *virtuous*; Platonic, sublimated, elevated, purified; decent, decorous, delicate, refined 846 *tasteful*; edifying, printable, quotable, repeatable, mentionable, virginibus puerisque 648 *clean*; censored, bowdlerized, expurgated, edited.

prudish, squeamish, shockable, Victorian; prim 850 *affected*; overdelicate, overmodest; old-maidish, straitlaced, narrow-minded, puritan, priggish; holy, sanctimonious 979 *pietistic*.

See:380, 427, 550, 620, 646, 648, 735, 820, 834, 846, 850, 874, 895, 929, **933**, 935, 942, 979, 986.

951 Impurity

N.*impurity*, impure thoughts, filthiness, defilement 649 *uncleanness*; indelicacy 847 *bad taste*; indecency, immodesty, impudicity, shamelessness, exhibitionism; coarseness, grossness, nastiness; ribaldry, bawdry, bawdiness, salaciousness; loose talk, filthy t., blue story, smoking-room s., double entendre, equivoque; smut, dirt, filth, obscenity, obscene literature, adult l., curious l., erotic l., erotica; pornography, hard-core p., soft porn, girlie magazine; banned book; blue film, skin flick; prurience, voyeurism, scopophilia.

unchastity, lightness, promiscuity, wantonness; incontinence, easy virtue, no morals, amorality; permissive society 734 *laxity*; vice, immorality, sexual delinquency; sex consciousness, roving eye; lickerishness, prurience, concupiscence, lust 859 *libido*; carnality, sexuality, eroticism, erotism, fleshliness, the flesh 944 *sensualism*; sex-indulgence, sexiness, lasciviousness, lewdness, salacity, lubricity; dissoluteness, dissipation, debauchery, licentiousness, licence, libertinism, libertinage, gallantry; seduction, defloration; venery, lechery, priapism, fornication, wenching, womanizing, whoring; harlotry, whorishness.

illicit love, guilty l., unlawful desires, forbidden fruit; extramarital relations, criminal conversation, unlawful carnal knowledge; incestuous affection, incest; homosexuality, Lesbianism 84 *abnormality*; perversion, pederasty, buggery, sodomy, bestiality; satyriasis, priapism, nymphomania; adultery, unfaithfulness, infidelity, marital i., cuckolding, cuckoldry; wife-swapping; eternal triangle, liaison, intrigue, amour, amourette, seduction 887 *love affair*; free love, unwedded cohabitation, irregular union, concubinage, companionate marriage 894 *type of mar-*

riage.

rape, ravishment, violation, indecent assault, grope; gang bang; sex crime, sex murder.

social evil, harlot's trade, harlotry, whoredom; oldest profession, Mrs Warren's p.; streetwalking, prostitution, open p.; public indecency, indecent exposure, flashing; pimping, pandering, brothel-keeping, living on immoral earnings, white slave traffic; vice squad.

brothel, bordello, bagnio, stews; whorehouse, bawdy-house, disorderly h., house of ill fame, house of ill repute; knocking-shop; red-light district.

Adj. *impure*, defiling, defiled, unclean, nasty 649 *dirty*; unwholesome 653 *insalubrious*; indelicate, not for the squeamish; vulgar, coarse, gross; ribald, broad, free, loose; strong, racy, bawdy, Fescennine, Rabelaisian; uncensored, unexpurgated, unbowdlerized; suggestive, provocative, piquant, titillating, near the knuckle; spicy, juicy, fruity; immoral, risqué, equivocal, nudge-nudge wink-wink; naughty, wicked, blue; unmentionable, unquotable, unprintable; smutty, filthy, scrofulous, scabrous, scatological, stinking, rank, offensive; indecent, obscene, lewd, salacious, lubricious; licentious, pornographic; prurient, erotic, phallic, ithyphallic, priapic; sexual, sexy, hot.

unchaste, unvirtuous 934 *vicious*; susceptible, not impregnable 934 *frail*; fallen, seduced, prostituted, taken advantage of; of easy virtue, of loose morals, amoral, immoral; incontinent, light, wanton, loose, fast, naughty; wild, rackety; immodest, daring, revealing; unblushing, shameless, flaunting, scarlet, meretricious, whorish, tarty; promiscuous, sleeping around; streetwalking, on the game; Paphian, Aphrodisian.

lecherous, carnal, fleshly, carnal-minded, voluptuous 944 *sensual*; libidinous, lascivious, lustful, lickerish, goatish; prurient, concupiscent 859 *desiring*; rampant, on heat, rutting, ruttish; hot, sexed-up, randy; sex-conscious, man-c., woman-c.; oversexed, sex-mad, sex-crazy, priapic, nymphomaniac; perverted, bestial; lewd, licentious, libertine, free, loose, rakish; depraved, debauched, dissolute, dissipated, profligate 934 *vicious*; whoremongering, brothel-haunting.

extramarital, irregular, concubinary; unlawful, incestuous; homosexual, Lesbian 84 *abnormal*; adulterous, unfaithful; committing adultery, anticipating marriage; bed-hopping, promiscuous.

Vb. *be impure*, - unchaste etc. adj.; be immoral, have no morals; be unfaithful, deceive one's spouse, break the marriage vow, commit adultery, cuckold; be dissipated 943 *be intemperate*; fornicate, womanize, whore, wench, haunt brothels; keep a mistress, have a lover; lech, lust, rut, be on heat, be hot 859 *desire*; be promiscuous, sleep around; become a prostitute, street-walk, be on the streets; pimp, pander, procure, keep a brothel.

debauch, defile, smirch 649 *make unclean*; proposition, seduce, lead astray; take advantage of, have one's way with, take one's pleasure with; dishonour, deflower, wreck, ruin, disgrace 867 *shame*; prostitute, make a whore of; lay, knock off, bed, lie with, sleep w. 45 *unite with*; rape, commit r., ravish, violate, molest, abuse, outrage, interfere with, assault, indecently a.

Adv. *impurely*, immodestly, shamelessly; loosely, bawdily, sexily, erotically; lewdly, salaciously, suggestively; carnally, sexually 944 *sensually*; lustfully, pruriently, concupiscently.

See: 45, 84, 649, 653, 734, 847, 859, 867, 887, 894, **934**, 943, **944**.

952 Libertine

N. *libertine*, no Joseph; gay bachelor, not the marrying kind; philanderer, flirt; free-lover, loose fellow, fast man, gay dog, rip, rake, rakehell, roué, debauchee, profligate 944 *sensualist*; lady-killer, gallant, squire of dames; fancy man, gigolo, sugar daddy; seducer, deceiver, gay d., false lover, Lothario 887 *lover*; corespondent, adulterer, cuckolder, bed-hopper, wife-swapper; immoralist, amorist, Don Juan, Casanova; wolf, woman-hunter, woman-chaser, skirt-c., kerb-crawler; womanizer, fornicator, stud; whoremonger, whore-master; voyeur, lecher, flasher, satyr, goat, dirty old man; sex maniac, raper, rapist, ravisher; catamite, male prostitute; pederast, sodomite, pervert 84 *nonconformist*.

cuckold, deceived husband, injured h., complaisant h.; wearer of horns.

loose woman, light w., light o' love, wanton, easy lay; fast woman, sexpot, hot stuff;

woman of easy virtue, w. of doubtful reputation, demi-rep, one no better than she should be; flirt, piece, bit, bint, wench, floozy, jade, hussy; nymphet, sex kitten, Lolita, groupie; baggage, trash, trollop, trull, drab, slut; tart, chippy, scrubber, pick-up; vamp, adventuress, temptress, seductress, femme fatale, scarlet woman, painted w., Jezebel, Delilah; adultress, other woman; nymphomaniac, Messalina.

kept woman, fancy w., mistress, paramour, leman, hetaera, concubine, unofficial wife 887 *loved one*; bit of fluff, floozie, doxy, moll.

prostitute, common p., pro; white slave, fallen woman, erring sister; frail sisterhood, demi-monde; harlot, trollop, whore, strumpet; streetwalker, woman of the streets, broad, hustler, hooker, scrubber; pick-up, casual conquest, call girl; fille de joie, f. de nuit, poule, cocotte, courtesan; demi-mondaine, demi-rep; Aspasia, Thais; Cyprian, Paphian; odalisque, temple prostitute 742 *slave*.

bawd, go-between, pimp, ponce, pander, procurer, procuress, mack, brothel-keeper, madam; white slaver.

See: 84, 742, 887, **944**.

953 Legality

N. *legality*, formality, form, formula, rite, due process 959 *litigation*; form of law, letter of the l., four corners of the l. (**see** *law*); respect for law, constitutionality, constitutionalism; good law, judgment according to the l. 480 *judgment*; justice under the law 913 *justice*; keeping within the law, lawfulness, legitimateness, legitimacy, validity.

legislation, legislature, legislatorship, law-giving, law-making, constitution-m.; codification; legalization, legitimization, validation, ratification, confirmation 532 *affirmation*; passing into law, enacting, enactment, regulation, regulation by law, regulation by statute; plebiscite 605 *vote*; plebiscitum, psephism, popular decree; law, statute, ordinance, order, standing o., bylaw 737 *decree*; canon, rule, edict, rescript 693 *precept*; legislator, lawgiver, lawmaker.

law, law and equity, the law; body of law, corpus juris, constitution, written c., unwritten c.; charter, institution; codification, codified law, statute book, legal code, pandect, Twelve Tables, Ten Commandments, Pentateuch; penal code, civil c., Napoleonic c.; written law, statute l., common l., unwritten l., natural l.; personal law, private l., canon l., ecclesiastical l.; international law, jus gentium, law of nations, law of the sea, law of the air; law of commerce, commercial law, lex mercatoria, law of contract, law of crime, criminal law, civil l., constitutional l., law of the land; arm of the law, legal process 955 *jurisdiction*; writ, summons, lawsuit 959 *legal trial*.

jurisprudence, nomology, science of law, knowledge of l., legal learning; law consultancy, legal advice.

Adj. *legal*, lawful 913 *just*; law-abiding 739 *obedient*; legitimate, competent; licit, licensed, permissible, allowable 756 *permitted*; within the law, sanctioned by law, according to l., de jure, legally sound, good in law; statutable, statutory, constitutional; nomothetic, law-giving, legislatorial, legislational, legislative, decretal; legislated, enacted, passed, voted, made law, ordained, decreed, ordered, by order; legalized, legitimized, brought within the law; liable *or* amenable to law, actionable, justiciable, triable, cognizable 928 *accusable*; fit for legislation, suitable for enactment; pertaining to law, jurisprudential, nomological, learned in the law.

Vb. *be legal*, - legitimate etc. adj.; stand up in law; come within the law, respect the l., abide by the l., keep within the l., stay the right side of the l.

make legal, legalize, legitimize, validate, confirm, ratify, formalize 488 *endorse*; vest, establish 153 *stabilize*; legislate, make laws, give l.; pass, enact, ordain, enforce 737 *decree*.

Adv. *legally*, by law, by order; legitimately, de jure, in the eye of the law.

See: 153, 480, 488, 532, 605, 693, **737**, 739, 756, 913, 928, **955**, **959**.

954 Illegality

N. *illegality*, bad law, legal flaw, loophole, irregularity, error of law, mistake of l.; wrong verdict, bad judgment 481 *misjudgment*; contradictory law, antinomy; miscarriage of justice 914 *injustice*; wrong side of the law, unlawfulness; unauthorization, incompetence, illicitness, illegitimacy, impermissibility 757 *prohibition*.

lawbreaking, breach of law, violation of l.,

transgression, contravention, infringement, encroachment 306 *overstepping*; trespass, offence, offence against the law, tort, civil wrong; champerty, malpractice 930 *foul play*; shadiness, dishonesty 930 *improbity*; criminality 936 *guilt*; criminal activity, criminal offence, indictable o., crime, capital c., misdemeanour, felony; misprision, misfeasance, malfeasance, wrongdoing 914 *wrong*; criminology, criminal statistics; criminal 904 *offender*.

lawlessness, antinomianism; outlawry, disfranchisement; no law, absence of l., paralysis of authority, breakdown of law and order, crime wave 734 *anarchy*; summary justice, vigilantism; kangaroo court, gang rule, mob law, lynch l.; riot, race r., rioting, hooliganism, ruffianism, rebellion 738 *revolt*; coup d'état, usurpation 916 *arrogation*; arbitrary rule, arbitrariness, negation of law, abolition of l.; martial law; mailed fist, jackboot 735 *brute force*.

bastardy, bar *or* bend *or* baton sinister; bastardization, illegitimacy; bastard, illegitimate child, natural c., love c., by-blow, spurious offspring, offspring of adultery, fruit of a.

Adj. *illegal*, illegitimate, illicit; contraband, black-market, hot; impermissible, verboten 757 *prohibited*; unauthorized, incompetent, without authority, unwarrantable, informal, unofficial; unlawful, wrongous, wrongful 914 *wrong*; unlegislated, not covered by law, exceeding the l., bad in law; unchartered, unconstitutional, unstatutory; no longer law, superseded, suspended, null and void, annulled 752 *abrogated*; irregular, contrary to law, not according to l., unknown to l.; injudicial, extrajudicial; on the wrong side of the law, against the l.; outside the law, outlawed, out of bounds; tortious, actionable, cognizable, justiciable, triable, punishable 928 *accusable*.

lawbreaking, trespassing, transgressing, infringing, encroaching; sinning 934 *wicked*; offending 936 *guilty*; criminal, felonious; fraudulent, shady 930 *dishonest*.

lawless, antinomian, without law, chaotic 734 *anarchic*; ungovernable, licentious 738 *riotous*; violent, summary; arbitrary, irresponsible, unanswerable, unaccountable; unofficial, cowboy; above the law, overmighty; despotic, tyrannical 735 *oppressive*.

bastard, illegitimate, spurious; misbegotten, adulterine, baseborn; born out of wedlock, born on the wrong side of the blanket; without a father, without a name, without benefit of clergy; bastardized.

Vb. *be illegal*, be bad in law, break the law, violate the l., offend against the l., circumvent the l., disregard the statute; wrest the law, twist *or* strain the l., torture the l.; be lawless, defy the law, drive a coach and horses through the l. 914 *do wrong*; take the law into one's own hands, exceed one's authority, encroach 734 *please oneself*; have no law, know no l., stand above the law; stand outside the law, suffer outlawry.

make illegal, - unlawful etc. adj.; put outside the law, outlaw; illegalize 757 *prohibit*; forbid by law, penalize 963 *punish*; bastardize, illegitimize; suspend, annul, cancel, make the law a dead letter 752 *abrogate*.

Adv. *illegally*, illicitly, illegitimately, unlawfully, criminally; on the black market, under the counter.

See: 306, 481, 734, 735, 738, 752, **757**, 904, **914**, 916, 928, **930**, 934, 936, 963.

955 Jurisdiction

N. *jurisdiction*, portfolio 622 *function*; judicature, magistracy, commission of the peace; mayoralty, shrievalty, bumbledom; competence, legal c., legal authority, arm of the law 733 *authority*; administration of justice, legal administration, Home Office; local jurisdiction, local authority, corporation, municipality, county council, district c., parish c., bailiwick 692 *council*; vigilance committee, watch c. 956 *tribunal*; office, bureau, secretariat 687 *workshop*; legal authority, competence, cognizance 751 *mandate*.

law officer, legal administrator, Lord Chancellor, Attorney General, Lord Advocate, Solicitor General, Queen's Proctor; Crown Counsel, public prosecutor; judge advocate, procurator fiscal, district attorney 957 *judge*; mayor, Lord M., sheriff 733 *position of authority*; court officer, clerk of the court, tipstaff, bailiff; summoner, process-server, catchpoll, Bow-street runner; apparitor, beadle, macebearer 690 *official*.

police, forces of law and order, long arm of

the law; police force, the force, the fuzz; Scotland Yard; constabulary, gendarmerie, military police, transport p.; police officer, limb of the law, policeman *or* -woman, constable, special c., copper, cop, traffic c., patrolman *or* -woman; bobby, flatfoot, rozzer, dick, flic; police sergeant, police inspector, police superintendent, commissioner of police, chief constable, provost marshal; watch, posse comitatus; Special Patrol Group, SPG; plain-clothes man 459 *detective*.

Adj. *jurisdictional*, jurisdictive, competent; executive, administrative, administrational, directive 689 *directing*; justiciary, judiciary, juridical; justiciable, subject to jurisdiction, liable to the law.

Vb. *hold court*, administer justice, sit on the bench, sit in judgment 480 *judge*; hear complaints, hear causes 959 *try a case*; be seized of, take cognizance, take judicial notice.

See: 459, 480, 622, 687, 689, 690, 692, **733**, 751, **956**, **957**, **959**.

956 Tribunal

N. *tribunal*, seat of justice, woolsack, throne; judgment seat, bar, bar of justice; court of conscience, tribunal of penance, confessional, Judgment Day; forum, ecclesia, wardmote 692 *council*; public opinion, vox populi, electorate; judicatory, bench, board, bench of judges, panel of j., judge and jury; judicial assembly, Areopagus; commission of the peace; Justices of the Peace.

lawcourt, court, open c.; court of law, court of justice, criminal court, civil c.; Federal Court, High Court, Court of Justiciary; District Court, County Court; Supreme Court, appellate court, Court of Appeal; C. of Cassation; Court of Exchequer, Star Chamber; House of Lords 692 *parliament*; High Court of Justice, Queen's Bench, Queen's Bench Division, Court of Criminal Appeal; Admiralty Division; Probate Court, Divorce C.; Court of Chancery, court of equity, c. of arbitration; Court of Common Pleas; Eyre of Justice, court of oyer and terminer, circuit court; assizes; Court of Session, sessions, quarter s., petty s.; Central Criminal Court, Old Bailey; magistrate's court, juvenile c., police c.; coroner's court; court of piepowder *or* pie poudre; court of record, feudal c., manorial c., Stannary C., court baron, court leet; guild court, hustings; court-martial, drumhead court, summary c.

ecclesiastical court, C. of Arches, Papal C., Curia; Inquisition, Holy Office.

courtroom, courthouse, lawcourts, bench, woolsack, jury box; judgment seat, mercy s.; dock, bar; witness box.

Adj. *judicatory*, judicial, justiciary, curial, inquisitional, Rhadamanthine; original, appellate 955 *jurisdictional*.

See: 692, 955.

957 Judge

N. *judge*, justice, justiceship, your Lordship, my lud, m'lud; justiciary, podestà; verderer; Lord Chancellor, Lord Chief Justice, Master of the Rolls, Lords of Appeal; military judge, Judge Advocate General; chief justice, puisné judge, county court j., recorder, Common Serjeant; sessions judge, assize j., circuit j.; district judge, subordinate j.; magistrate, district m., city m., police m., stipiendary m.; coroner; honorary magistrate, justice of the peace, JP; bench, judiciary; hanging judge, Judge Jeffreys.

magistracy, the beak, his *or* her Worship, his *or* her Honour, his nibs, her nibs; arbiter, umpire, referee, assessor, arbitrator, ombudsman 480 *estimator*; Recording Angel 549 *recorder*; Solomon, Rhadamanthus, Daniel come to judgment.

jury, twelve good men and true, twelve just men, twelve men in a box; grand jury, special j., common j., petty j., trial j., coroner's j.; vetted j., rigged j.; juror's panel, jury list; juror, juryman *or* -woman, jurat; foreman *or* forewoman of the jury.

See: **480**, 549.

958 Lawyer

N. *lawyer*, practising l., legal practitioner, member of the legal profession, man *or* woman of law; common lawyer, canon l., civil l., criminal l.; one called to the bar, barrister, barrister-at-law, advocate, counsel, learned c.; junior barrister, stuff gown, junior counsel; senior barrister, bencher, bencher of the Inns of Court; silk gown, silk, leading counsel, King's C., K.C., Queen's C., Q.C.; serjeant, serjeant-at-law; circuit barrister, circuiteer; Philadelphia lawyer 696 *expert*; shyster, pettifogger, crooked lawyer.

law agent, attorney, public a., attorney at law, proctor, procurator; Writer to the Signet, solicitor before the Supreme Court; solicitor, legal adviser; legal representative, legal agent, pleader, advocate; equity draftsman; conveyancer.

notary, notary public, commissioner for oaths; scrivener, petition-writer; clerk of the court 955 *law officer*; solicitor's clerk, barrister's c., barrister's devil.

jurist, jurisconsult, legal adviser, legal expert, legal light, master of jurisprudence, pundit, legist, legalist, canonist; student of law, law student.

bar, civil b., criminal b., English bar, Scottish b., junior b., senior b.; Inns of Chancery, Inns of Court, Gray's Inn, Lincoln's I., Inner Temple, Middle T.; profession of law, legal profession, the Robe; barristership, advocacy, pleading; solicitorship, attorneyship; legal consultancy.

Adj. *jurisprudential*, learned in the law, called to the bar, at the b., practising at the b., barristerial, forensic; notarial.

Vb. *do law*, study l., go in for l., take up l.; eat one's dinners, be called to the bar; take silk, be called within the bar; practise at the bar, accept a brief, take a case, advocate, plead; practice law.

See: 696, **955**.

959 Litigation

N. *litigation*, going to law, litigiousness 709 *quarrelsomeness*; legal dispute 709 *quarrel*; issue, legal i., matter for judgment, case for decision; lawsuit, suit at law, suit, case, cause, action; prosecution, arraignment, impeachment, charge 928 *accusation*; test case 461 *experiment*; claim, counter c. 915 *dueness*; plea, petition 761 *request*; affidavit, written statement, averment, pleading, demurrer 532 *affirmation*.

legal process, proceedings, legal procedure, course of law, arm of the l. 955 *jurisdiction*; citation, subpoena, summons, search warrant 737 *warrant*; arrest, apprehension, detention, committal 747 *restraint*; habeas corpus, bail, surety, security, recognizance, personal r.; injunction, stay order; writ, certiorari, nisi prius.

legal trial, trial, fair t., justice seen to be done; trial by law, trial by jury, trial at the bar, trial in court, assize, sessions 956 *lawcourt*; inquest, inquisition, examination 459 *enquiry*; hearing, prosecution, defence; hearing of evidence, taking of e., recording of e. 466 *evidence*; examination, cross-e., re-e., objection sustained, objection overruled 466 *testimony*; pleadings, arguments 475 *reasoning*; counterargument, rebutter, rebuttal 460 *rejoinder*; proof 478 *demonstration*; disproof 479 *confutation*; summing up, charge to the jury; ruling, finding, decision, verdict 480 *judgment*; majority verdict, hung jury; favourable verdict 960 *acquittal*; unfavourable verdict 961 *condemnation*; execution of judgment 963 *punishment*; appeal, motion of a.; successful appeal, reversal of judgment, retrial; precedent, case law; law reports; cause list; case record, dossier 548 *record*.

litigant, litigator, libellant, party, party to a suit, suitor 763 *petitioner*; claimant, plaintiff, defendant, appellant, respondent, objector, intervener; accused, prisoner at the bar 928 *accused person*; litigious person, common informer 524 *informer*; prosecutor 928 *accuser*.

Adj. *litigating*, at law with, litigant, suing 928 *accusing*; going to law, appearing in court; contesting, objecting, disputing 475 *arguing*; litigious 709 *quarrelling*.

litigated, on trial, coram judice; argued, disputed, contested; up for trial, brought before the court, submitted for judgment, offered for arbitration; sub judice, on the cause list, down for hearing, ready for h.; litigable, disputable, arguable, suable, actionable, justiciable 928 *accusable*.

Vb. *litigate*, go to law, appeal to l., set the law in motion, institute legal proceedings, start an action, bring a suit, file a s., petition 761 *request*; prepare a case, prepare a brief, brief counsel; file a claim, contest at law 915 *claim*; have the law on one, take one to court, haul before the c., make one a party, sue, implead, arraign, impeach, accuse, charge, prefer charges, press c. 928 *indict*; cite, summon, serve notice on; prosecute, put on trial, bring to justice, bring to trial, bring to the bar; argue one's case, advocate, plead, call evidence 475 *argue*.

try a case, take cognizance, put down for hearing, empanel a jury, hear a cause; call witnesses, examine, cross-examine, take statements; sit in judgment, rule, find, decide, adjudicate 480 *judge*; close the pleadings, sum up, charge the jury; bring in a verdict, pronounce sentence; commit

for trial.
stand trial, come before, come up for trial, be put on t., stand in the dock; plead guilty, plead not guilty; plead to the charge, ask to be tried, submit to judgment, hear sentence; defend an action, put in one's defence, make one's d.

Adv. *in litigation*, at law, in court, before the judge; sub judice, pendente lite; litigiously.

See: 459, 460, 461, 466, 475, 478, 479, 480, 524, 532, 548, 709, 737, 747, 761, 763, **915**, **928**, **955**, 956, 960, 961, 963.

960 Acquittal

N. *acquittal*, favourable verdict, verdict of not guilty, verdict of not proven, benefit of the doubt; clearance, exculpation, exoneration 935 *innocence*; absolution, discharge; let-off, thumbs up 746 *liberation*; whitewashing, justification, compurgation 927 *vindication*; successful defence, defeat of the prosecution; nonsuit, case dismissed; no case, withdrawal of the charge, quashing, quietus; reprieve, pardon 909 *forgiveness*; nonprosecution, exemption, impunity 919 *nonliability*.

Adj. *acquitted*, not guilty 935 *guiltless*; clear, cleared, in the clear, exonerated, exculpated, vindicated; uncondemned, unpunished, unchastised, immune, exempted, exempt 919 *nonliable*; let off, let off the hook, discharged, without a stain on one's character 746 *liberated*; reprieved 909 *forgiven*; recommended for mercy.

Vb. *acquit*, find *or* pronounce not guilty, prove innocent, justify, whitewash, get one off 927 *vindicate*; clear, absolve, exonerate, exculpate; find there is no case to answer, not press charges, not prosecute 919 *exempt*; discharge, let go, let off 746 *liberate*; reprieve, respite, pardon, remit the penalty 909 *forgive*; quash, quash the conviction, set aside the sentence, allow an appeal 752 *abrogate*.

See: 746, 752, 909, 919, 927, 935.

961 Condemnation

N. *condemnation*, unfavourable verdict, hostile v.; finding of guilty, conviction; successful prosecution, unsuccessful defence; final condemnation, damnation, perdition; blacklist, Index 924 *disapprobation*; excommunication 899 *malediction*; doom, judgment, sentence 963 *punishment*; writing on the wall 511 *omen*; outlawry, price on one's head, proscription, attainder; death warrant, condemned cell, execution chamber, Death Row; black cap, thumbs down.

Adj. *condemned*, found guilty, made liable; convicted, sentenced; proscribed, outlawed, with a price on one's head; self-convicted, confessing; without a case, having no case, without a leg to stand on; nonsuited 924 *disapproved*; lost, damned, in hell, burning, frying.

Vb. *condemn*, prove guilty, bring home the charge; find liable, find against, nonsuit; find guilty, pronounce g., convict, sentence; sentence to death, put on the black cap, sign one's death warrant; reject one's defence, reject one's appeal 607 *reject*; proscribe, attaint, outlaw, bar, put a price on one's head 954 *make illegal*; blacklist 924 *disapprove*; damn, excommunicate 899 *curse*; convict oneself, stand condemned out of one's own mouth 936 *be guilty*; plead guilty 526 *confess*.

See: 511, 526, 607, 899, **924**, 936, 954, 963.

962 Reward

N. *reward*, guerdon, remuneration, recompense; meed, deserts, just d. 913 *justice*; recognition, acknowledgment, thanks 907 *gratitude*; tribute, deserved t., proof of regard 923 *praise*; prize-giving, award, presentation, prize, Nobel P.; crown, cup, pot, shield, certificate, medal 729 *trophy*; consolation prize, booby p.; honour 729 *decoration*; birthday honours 866 *honours*; letters after one's name, peerdom 870 *title*; prize money, cash p., jackpot; prize fellowship, scholarship, bursary, stipend, exhibition 703 *subvention*; reward for service, fee, retainer, refresher, honorarium, payment, remuneration, emolument, pension, salary, wage, wages, increment 804 *pay*; productivity bonus, overtime pay 612 *incentive*; perquisite, perks, expense account, fringe benefits; income, turnover 771 *earnings*; return, profitable r., profit, margin of p. 771 *gain*; compensation, indemnification, satisfaction; consideration, quid pro quo 31 *offset*; comeuppance 714 *retaliation*; reparation 787 *restitution*; bounty, gratuity, golden handshake; commission, dastur, rake-off, kickback; tip, solatium, douceur, pourboire, trinkgeld, baksheesh 781 *gift*;

tempting offer 759 *offer*; bait, lure, bribe 612 *incentive*; hush money, smart m., protection m., blackmail.

Adj. *rewarding*, prize-giving; generous, open-handed 813 *liberal*; paying, profitable, remunerative 771 *gainful*; promising 759 *offering*; compensatory, indemnificatory, reparatory 787 *restoring*; retributive 714 *retaliatory*.

Vb. *reward*, recompense; award, present, give a prize, offer a reward; bestow a medal, honour with a title 866 *honour*; recognize, acknowledge, pay tribute, thank, show one's gratitude 907 *be grateful*; remunerate 804 *pay*; satisfy, tip 781 *give*; tip well 813 *be liberal*; repay, requite 714 *retaliate*; compensate, indemnify, make reparation 787 *restitute*; offer a bribe, win over 612 *bribe*.

be rewarded, gain a reward, win a prize, get a medal, receive a title; get paid, draw a salary, earn an income, have a gainful occupation 771 *acquire*; accept payment, accept a gratification 782 *receive*; take a bribe, have one's palm greased; have one's reward, get one's deserts, receive one's due 915 *deserve*; get one's comeuppance 714 *be rightly served*; reap, reap a profit 771 *gain*; reap the fruits, reap the whirlwind.

Adv. *rewardingly*, profitably; for a consideration, as a reward, in compensation, for one's pains.

See: 31, **612**, 703, 714, **729**, 759, 771, **781**, 782, 787, 804, 813, 866, 870, 907, 913, 915, 923.

963 Punishment

N. *punishment*, sentence 961 *condemnation*; execution of sentence, exaction of penalty, penalization, victimization; chastisement, heads rolling; chastening, castigation, carpeting 924 *reprimand*; disciplinary action, discipline; dose, pill, bitter p., hard lines, infliction, trial, visitation, punishing experience 731 *adversity*; just deserts, meet reward, comeuppance 915 *dueness*; doom, judgment, day of j., day of reckoning, divine justice 913 *justice*; poetic justice, retributive j., retribution, Nemesis; reckoning, repayment 787 *restitution*; requital, reprisal 714 *retaliation*; avengement 910 *revenge*; penance, self-punishment 941 *atonement*; self-mortification, self-discipline 945 *asceticism*; hara-kiri 362 *suicide*; penology, penologist.

corporal punishment, bodily chastisement, smacking, slapping, trouncing, hiding, dusting, beating, thrashing, t. of a lifetime; caning, whipping, flogging, birching; scourging, flagellation, running the gauntlet; ducking, keel-hauling; slap, smack, rap, rap over the knuckles, box on the ear; drubbing, blow, buffet, cuff, clout, stroke, stripe 279 *knock*; third degree, torture, peine forte et dure, racking, strappado, breaking on the wheel, death by a thousand cuts 377 *pain*.

capital punishment, extreme penalty 361 *death*; death sentence, death warrant; execution 362 *killing*; decapitation, beheading, guillotining, decollation; traitor's death, hanging, drawing and quartering; strangulation, garrotte, bowstringing; hanging, long drop; electrocution; stoning, lapidation; crucifixion, impalement, flaying alive; burning, burning at the stake, auto da fé; drowning, noyade; massacre, mass murder, mass execution, purge, genocide 362 *slaughter*; martyrdom, martyrization, persecution to the death; illegal execution, lynching, lynch law; judicial murder.

penalty, injury, damage 772 *loss*; infliction, imposition, task, lines; prescribed punishment, sentence, penalization, pains and penalties, penal code, penology; devil to pay, liability, legal l. 915 *dueness*; damages, costs, compensation, restoration 787 *restitution*; amercement, fining, mulct, fine, deodand, compulsory payment 804 *payment*; ransom 809 *price*; forfeit, forfeiture, sequestration, escheat, confiscation, deprivation 786 *expropriation*; keeping in, gating, imprisonment 747 *detention*; suspension, rustication; binding over 747 *restraint*; penal servitude, hard labour, galley service, galleys; transportation; expulsion, deportation 300 *ejection*; ostracism, banishment, exile, proscription, ban, outlawing 57 *exclusion*; reprisal 714 *retaliation*.

punisher, vindicator, retaliator 910 *avenger*; inflicter, chastiser, castigator, corrector, chastener, discipliner; persecutor 735 *tyrant*; sentencer, justiciary, magistrate, court, law 957 *judge*; whipper, caner, flogger, flagellator; torturer, inquisitor; executioner, headsman, hangman, Jack Ketch; garrotter, bow-stringer; firing squad; lyncher 362 *murderer*.

Adj. *punitive*, penological, penal, punitory; castigatory, disciplinary, corrective; vindictive, retributive 910 *revengeful*; in reprisal 714 *retaliatory*; penalizing, fining; confiscatory, expropriatory 786 *taking*; scourging, flagellatory, torturing 377 *painful*.

punishable, liable, amerceable, mulctable; indictable 928 *accusable*; deserving punishment, asking for it.

Vb. *punish*, visit, afflict 827 *hurt*; persecute, victimize, make an example of 735 *be severe*; inflict, impose, inflict punishment, administer correction, take disciplinary action; give one a lesson, chasten, discipline, correct, chastise, castigate; reprimand, strafe, rebuke, rap across the knuckles, have one's head for 924 *reprove*; throw the book at, come down hard on, come down on like a ton of bricks, give one what for; penalize, impose a penalty, sentence 961 *condemn*; execute justice, execute judgment, execute a sentence, carry out a s.; exact a penalty, exact retribution, settle with, get even w., pay one out 714 *retaliate*; settle, fix, bring to book, give one what was coming to him, revenge oneself 910 *avenge*; amerce, mulct, fine, forfeit, deprive, sequestrate, confiscate 786 *take away*; unfrock, demote, degrade, downgrade, reduce to the ranks, suspend 867 *shame*; stand in a corner, send out of the room; tar and feather, toss in a blanket; pillory, set in the stocks; masthead; duck, keelhaul; picket, spread-eagle; lock up 747 *imprison*; transport; condemn to the galleys.

spank, paddle, slap, smack, slipper, paddle; cuff, clout, box on the ears, rap over the knuckles; drub, trounce, beat, belt, strap, leather, lather, larrup, wallop, welt, tan, cane, birch, switch, whack, dust, tan one's hide, beat black and blue 279 *strike*.

flog, whip, horsewhip, thrash, hide, belabour, cudgel, fustigate 279 *strike*; scourge, give stripes, give strokes, give one the cat; lash, lay on the l., flay, flay one's back, lay one's back open; flail, flagellate, bastinado.

torture, give the third degree; give one the works 377 *give pain*; put to the torture, thumbscrew, rack, put on the r., break on the wheel, mutilate, kneecap; persecute, martyrize 827 *torment*.

execute, punish with death, put to death 362 *kill*; lynch 362 *murder*; dismember, tear limb from limb; decimate; crucify, impale; flay, flay alive; stone, stone to death 712 *lapidate*; shoot, fusillade, stand against a wall; burn, burn alive, burn at the stake, send to the s.; bow-string, garrotte, strangle; gibbet, hang, hang by the neck, string up, bring to the gallows; hang, draw and quarter; send to the scaffold, bring to the block, strike off one's head, behead, decapitate, decollate, guillotine; electrocute, send to the chair; gas, put in the gas chamber; commit genocide, hold mass executions, purge, massacre 362 *slaughter*.

be punished, suffer punishment, take the consequences, be for the high jump, have it coming to one, catch it, catch it in the neck; take the rap, stand the racket, face the music; take one's medicine, take one's gruel, hold one's hand out; get what one was asking for, get one's deserts; regret it, smart for it; come to execution, lay one's head on the block; come to the gallows, take a ride to Tyburn, dance upon nothing, swing; pay for it with one's head, die the death.

Int. off with his head! à la lanterne!

See: 57, 279, 300, 361, **362**, 377, 712, 714, 731, 735, 747, 772, 786, 787, 804, 809, **827**, 867, 910, 913, 915, **924**, 928, 941, 945, 957, 961.

964 Means of Punishment

N. *scourge*, birch, birch-rod, cat, cat-o'-nine-tails, rope's end, knout, cowhide, sjambok, chabouk, kourbash; whip, horsewhip, switch, quirt; lash, strap, tawse, thong, belt; cane, rattan; stick, big s., rod, ferule, cudgel, ruler 723 *club*; rubber hose, bicycle chain, sandbag.

pillory, stocks, whipping post, ducking stool, cucking stool; corner, dunce's cap; stool of repentance, cutty stool; chain, irons, bilboes 748 *fetter*; prison house, prison 748 *gaol*.

instrument of torture, rack, thumbscrew, iron boot, pilliwinks; Iron Maiden, triangle, wheel, treadmill; torture chamber.

means of execution, scaffold, block, gallows, gibbet, Tyburn tree; cross; stake; Tarpeian rock; hemlock 659 *poison*; bullet, wall; axe, headsman's a., guillotine, maiden, widow-maker; hempen collar, halter, rope, noose, drop; garrotte, bowstring; electric chair, hot seat; death chamber, lethal c., gas c.; condemned cell, Death Row 961 *condemnation*.

See: 659, 723, 748, 961.

Section five: Religion

965 Divineness

N. *divineness*, divinity, deity; godhood, godhead, godship; divine principle, Brahma; numen, numinousness, mana; being of God, divine essence, perfection, the Good the True and the Beautiful; love, Fatherhood; Brahmahood, nirvana; impersonal God, Atman, Paramatman, oversoul, world soul; Ens Entium, First Cause, primum mobile 156 *source*; divine nature, God's ways, Providence.

divine attribute, being 1 *existence*; perfect being 646 *perfection*; oneness 88 *unity*; infinitude 107 *infinity*; immanence, omnipresence 189 *presence*; omniscience, wisdom 490 *knowledge*; omnipotence, almightiness 160 *power*; timelessness, eternity 115 *perpetuity*; immutability, changelessness 153 *stability*; truth, sanctity, holiness, goodness, justice, mercy; transcendence, sublimity, supremacy, sovereignty, majesty, glory, light; glory of the Lord, Shekinah.

the Deity, God, personal god, Supreme Being, Divine B., Alpha and Omega; the Infinite, the Eternal, the All-wise, the Almighty, the Most High; the All-holy, the All-merciful; Ruler of Heaven and Earth, Judge of all men, Maker of all things, Creator, Preserver; Allah; Elohim, Yahweh, Jehovah, Adonai, ineffable name, I AM; name of God, Tetragrammaton; God of Abraham, God of Moses, Lord of Hosts, God of our fathers; our Father; Demiurge; All-Father, Great Spirit, manitou; Ahura Mazda, Ormuzd; Krishna.

Trinity, triad, Hindu Triad, Brahma, Siva, Vishnu; Holy Trinity, Hypostatic Union; Triune God, Three Persons in one God, Three in One and One in Three; God the Father, God the Son, God the Holy Ghost.

Holy Ghost, third person of the Trinity; the Spirit, Holy Spirit, Spirit of Truth; Paraclete, Comforter, Consoler; Dove.

God the Son, second person of the Trinity, Word, Logos, Son of God, the Only Begotten, Word made flesh, Incarnate Son; Messiah, Son of David, rod of Jesse, the Lord's Anointed, Christ; Immanuel; Lamb of God, Son of Man, Man of Sorrows; Son of Mary, Jesus, Jesu, Jesus Christ; Holy Infant, Christ Child, Child of Bethlehem; Jesus of Nazareth, the Nazarene, the Galilean; the Good Shepherd, Saviour, Redeemer, Friend; Lord, Master; Rock of Ages, Bread of Life, True Vine; the Way the Truth and the Life; Light of the World, Sun of Righteousness; King of Kings, King of Heaven, King of Glory, Prince of Peace.

divine function, creation, preservation, judgment; mercy, compassion, forgiveness; inspiration, unction, regeneration, comfort, strengthening, consolation, grace, prevenient g.; propitiation, atonement, redemption, justification, salvation, mediation, intercession.

theophany, divine manifestation, divine emanation, descent, descent to earth, divine intervention, incarnation; transfiguration; Shekinah, Glory of the Lord; avatar, avatar of Vishnu, Krishna.

theocracy, divine government, divine dispensation, God's law, Kingdom of God; God's ways, God's dealings, providence, special p., deus ex machina.

Adj. *divine*, holy, hallowed, sanctified, sacred, sacrosanct, heavenly, celestial; transcendental, sublime, ineffable; numinous, mystical, religious, spiritual, superhuman, supernatural, transcendent; unearthly, supramundane, extramundane, not of this world; providential; theophanic; theocratic.

godlike, divine, superhuman; transcendent, immanent; omnipresent 189 *ubiquitous*; immeasurable 107 *infinite*; absolute, undefined, self-existent, living 1 *existing*; timeless, eternal, everlasting, immortal 115 *perpetual*; immutable, unchanging, changeless 144 *permanent*; almighty, all-powerful, omnipotent 160 *powerful*; creative 160 *dynamic*; prescient, providential 510 *foreseeing*; all-wise, all-seeing, all-knowing, omniscient 490 *knowing*; oracular 511 *predicting*; all-merciful, merciful 909 *forgiving*; compassionate 905 *pitying*; parent-like 887 *loving*; holy, all-h., worshipped 979 *sanctified*; sovereign 34 *supreme*; majestic 733 *authoritative*; transfigured, glorious, all-g. 866 *worshipful*; theomorphic, incarnate, in the image of

God, deified; messianic, anointed; Christly, Christlike.
deistic, theistic, Yahwistic, Elohistic.
redemptive, intercessional, mediatory, propitiatory; incarnational; soteriological, messianic.
Adv. *divinely*, as God; under God, by God's will, Deo volente, D.V.; by divine right, jure divino; redemptively, as a saviour.
See: 1, 34, 88, 107, 115, 144, 153, 156, 160, 189, 490, 510, 511, 646, 733, 866, 887, 905, 909, 979.

966 Deities in general

N. *deity*, god, goddess, deva, devi; the gods, the immortals; Olympian 967 *Olympian deity*; the unknown god, pagan g., false g., idol; godling, petty god, inferior g., subordinate g. 967 *lesser deity*; demigod, half-god, divine hero, deified person, divine king; object of worship, fetish, totem 982 *idol*; mumbo jumbo; theogony; pantheon.
mythic deity, nature god *or* goddess, Pan, Flora; earth goddess, Gaia; mother earth, mother goddess, earth mother, Great Mother, Magna Mater, Cybele, Ishtar, Astarte, Isis; fertility god, Adonis, Tammuz, Marduk, Atys; god of the underworld, Pluto, Dis 967 *Chthonian deity*; sky god, Zeus, Jupiter; storm god, Indra, wind god, Aeolus; sun god, Apollo, Hyperion, Helios, Ra, Mithras; river god, sea g., Poseidon, Neptune, Varuna; war god *or* goddess, Mars, Bellona; god *or* goddess of love, Cupid, Eros, Venus, Aphrodite; household gods, Teraphim, Lares, Penates; the Fates, the Norns 596 *fate*.
Adj. *mythological*, mythical; theogonic; deiform, theomorphic, deific, deified.
See: 596, 967, 982.

967 Pantheon: classical and nonclassical deities

N. *classical deities*, gods and goddesses of Greece and Rome, Graeco-Roman pantheon; Homeric deities, Hesiodic theogony; primeval deities, Erebus, Nox; Ge, Gaia, Tellus, Uranus, Cronus, Saturn, Rhea, Ops; Pontus, Oceanus, Tethys; Helios, Sol, Hyperion, Phaëthon; Titan, Atlas, Prometheus; Giant, Enceladus; the Fates, Parcae, Clotho, Lachesis, Atropos.
Olympian deity, Olympian, Zeus, Jupiter, Jove, president of the immortals; Pluto, Hades; Poseidon, Neptune; Apollo, Phoebus; Hermes, Mercury; Ares, Mars; Hephaestus, Vulcan; Dionysus, Bacchus; Hera, Juno; Demeter, Ceres; Persephone, Proserpina; Athena, Minerva; Aphrodite, Venus; Artemis, Diana; Eros, Cupid; Iris; Hebe.
Chthonian deity, Ge, Gaia, Dis Pater, Orcus, Hades, Pluto, Persephone; Erectheus, Trophonius, Pytho; Eumenides, Erinys, Furies.
lesser deity, Pan, Silvanus, Flora, Faunus, Silenus; Aurora, Eos; Luna, Selene; Aeolus, Boreas 352 *wind*; Triton, Nereus, Proteus, Glaucus; Ate, Eris, Bellona, Nike; Astraea; Muses, tuneful Nine, Erato, Euterpe, Terpsichore, Polyhymnia, Clio, Calliope, Melpomene, Thalia, Urania; Asclepius, Aesculapius; Hypnos, Somnus, Morpheus; Hymen; Hestia, Vesta; Lares, Penates; local god, genius loci.
nymph, wood n., tree n., dryad, hamadryad; mountain nymph, oread; water nymph, naiad; sea nymph, nereid, Oceanid; Thetis, Calypso, Callisto; Pleiades, Maia; Latona, Leto; siren 970 *mythical being*.
demigod, divine offspring, divine hero; Heracles, Hercules; Dioscuri, Castor and Pollux, Castor and Polydeuces; Perseus, Achilles, Aeneas, Memnon.
Hindu deities, Brahmanic d., Vedic d.; Dyaus Pitar, Prithivi; Varuna (sky), Mitra (light), Indra (thunder), Agni (fire), Surya (sun); Trimurti, Brahma, Siva, Vishnu; Sakti, Uma *or* Parvat, Kali *or* Durga; Ganesha (luck-bringer), Karttikeya (fertility), Sarasvati (learning), Hanuman (monkey-god), Sitala (smallpox), Manasa (snakes), Lakshmi (wealth and fortune).
Egyptian deities, Nun, Atum; Shu (air), Tefnut (moisture), Nut (sky), Geb (earth), Osiris, Isis, Set, Nephthys; Ra *or* Re, Amon- *or* Amun-Ra, Atum-Ra, Aton; Horus, elder Horus, Ra-Harakhte, Khepera; Amon, Min (all-father), Hathor (all-mother), Neith, Anata; Ptah (creator), Ma'at (truth), Imhotep (peace), Bes (dancing), Serapis (underworld); theriomorphic deity, theriocephalous d.; Apis (sacred bull), Thoth (ibis), Anubis (jackal), Sekhmet (lioness), Sebek (crocodile), Bast (cat), Setekh (hound), Uadjit (cobra), Taurt (hippopotamus).

Semitic deities, Nammu, Anu, Enlil, Enki *or* Ea; Shamash, Sin, Adad; Bel, Marduk; El, Baal, Aleyan-Baal; Moloch, Rimmon, Asshur; great mother, Ishtar, Ashtoreth, Astarte, Asherah, Inanna, Anat; fertility god, Tammuz, Atys; Mot, Allatu.

Nordic deities, Aesir, Vanir; Odin *or* Wotan, Frigg his wife; Thor (thunder god), his wife Sif, his son Ull; Tiu *or* Tyr (war), Heimdall, Balder the beautiful, Vidar the silent, Hoder the blind, Bragi (god of poetry), Hermoder (messenger), Vali (youngest son of Odin); Frey *or* Freyr (peace, fertility), Freya *or* Freyja (goddess of love), Njord *or* Nerthus (wealth and ships), Hoenir, Odmir; Skadi; Loki (evil and strife), Hel (goddess of the dead); Aegir (ocean), his wife Ran, Mimir (guardian of the spring of wisdom), Ymir (father of the Giants).

Celtic deities, Dagda, Math, Magog, Oengus *or* Dwyn; Ogma, Belinus, Esos, Teutates, Taranis; Mabon, Borvo *or* Bormo; Epona; Bilé *or* Beli, Govannon or Goibniu (smith), Diancecht (medecine), Lludd *or* Nudd *or* Nuada (sun); Gwydion, Amaethon; Lleu *or* Lug (light), Dylan (darkness); sea gods, Ler *or* Llyr, Bran *or* Branwen, Manannan *or* Manawydan; Dana *or* Don, Morrigan (war), Brigit, Blathnat, Arianrod, Blodeuwedd, Creirwy (love), Keridwen (poetry), Rhiannon (underworld).

Aztec deities, Nahuan d.; Cipactli (earth dragon); Coatlicue (ancient earth goddess); Red Tezcatlipoca, Black T., White T., Blue T., Xipe Topec (spring), Quetzalcoatl (culture), Huitzilopochtli(warrior); god and goddess of creation, Tonacatecuhtli, Tonacacihuatl; deities of fertility, Cihuacoatl, Chicomecoatl, Centeotl, Tlazolteotl, Xochipilli; Tlaloc (rain), Chalchiuhtlicue (water); Xiuhtecuhtli (fire), Tonatiuh (sun), Tecciztecatl, Metztli (moon), Mixcoatl (sky), Mictlantecuhtli (death).

See: 352, **970**.

968 Angel. Saint. Madonna.

N. *angel*, archangel, heavenly host, angelic h., choir invisible; heavenly hierarchy, thrones, principalities and powers; seraph, seraphim, cherub, cherubim; ministering spirit, Michael, Gabriel, Raphael, Uriel, Zadkiel; Israfel, Azrael, angel of death; guardian angel, tutelary spirit; angelhood, archangelship; angelophany; angelolatry; angelology.

saint, patron s., s. and martyr, the blessed ...; glorified soul, soul in bliss, Church triumphant.

Madonna, Our Lady, Blessed Virgin Mary, Mother of God, Mater Dolorosa; Queen of Heaven, Queen of Angels, Stella Maris; Mariolatry.

Adj. *angelic*, angelical, archangelic, seraphic, cherubic; saintly, glorified, celestial.

Vb. *angelize*, angelify; beatify 979 *sanctify*.

See: 979.

969 Devil

N. *Satan*, Lucifer, fallen angel, rebel a.; Archfiend, Prince of Darkness, Prince of this world; serpent, Old S., Tempter, Adversary, Antichrist, Common Enemy, Enemy of mankind; Diabolus, Father of Lies; evil genie, Shaitan, Eblis; King of Hell, angel of the bottomless pit, Apollyon, Abaddon; the foul fiend, the Devil, the Evil One, Wicked O.; spirit of evil, principle of e., Ahriman, Angra Mainyu.

Mephisto, Mephistopheles, His Satanic Majesty, the old one, the Old Gentleman, Old Nick, Old Harry, Old Scratch, Auld Hornie, Clootie.

devil, fiend; devilkin, deviling, devilet, familiar, imp, imp of Satan, devil's spawn 938 *bad person*; Tutivillus, Asmodeus, Azazel 970 *demon*; malevolent spirit, unclean s., dybbuk; powers of darkness, diabolic hierarchy; damned spirit, fallen angel, lost soul, sinner, dweller in Pandemonium, denizen of Hell; Mammon, Belial, Beelzebub, Lord of the Flies; devildom, devilship, devilhood, demonship; horns, cloven hoof.

diabolism, devilry, demonry, diablerie 898 *inhumanity*; Satanism, devilism; devil worship, demonism, polydaemonism, demonolatry; demonomania, demoniac possession; witchcraft, black magic, Black Mass 983 *sorcery*; Satanology, demonology; demonization.

diabolist, Satanist, devil-worshipper, demonolater, demonist; demonologist, demonologer.

Adj. *diabolic*, diabolical, devil-like, satanic, Mephistophelean, fiendish, demonic, demoniacal, devilish 898 *malevolent*;

infernal, hellish, hell-born; devil-worshipping, demonolatrous; demoniac, possessed; demonological.

Vb. *diabolize*, demonize; possess, bedevil 983 *bewitch*.

See: 898, 938, **970**, 983.

970 Fairy

N. *fairy*, fairy world, magic w., elfland, fairyland, faerie; fairy folk, good f., little people; fairy being, fay, peri; good fairy, fairy godmother 903 *benefactor*; bad fairy, witch 983 *sorceress*; fairy queen, Mab, Queen M., Titania; fairy king, Oberon, Erl King; Puck, Robin Goodfellow; spirit of air, Ariel; elemental spirit, sylph, sylphid; genius; fairy ring, pixie r.; fairyism, fairy lore, fairy tales, folklore.

elf, elves, elfin folk, alfar, hidden folk, pixie, piskie, brownie, kobold; gnome, dwarf, Nibelung; troll, trow; orc, goblin, flibbertigibbet; imp, sprite, hobgoblin; changeling; leprechaun, cluricaune; pigwidgin; poltergeist, gremlin, dybbuk; Puck, Hob, Robin Goodfellow; elvishness, goblinry.

ghost, spirit, departed s.; shades, souls of the dead, Manes, lemures; revived corpse, zombie; visitant, revenant, haunter, walker, poltergeist, duppy; spook, spectre, apparition, phantom, phantasm, shape, shade, wraith, presence, doppelganger, fetch 440 *visual fallacy*; control 984 *spiritualism*; White Lady, Herne the Hunter, Black Shuck.

demon, cacodemon, flibbertigibbet, Friar Rush; imp, familiar, familiar spirit 969 *devil*; afreet, rakshasa; daeva, asura; she-demon, lamia, banshee; kelpie, troll, troll woman; ogre, ogress, giant, giantess, Baba Yaga; bugbear, bugaboo, bogle, bogey, bogey man, bunyip 938 *monster*; ghoul, vampire, lycanthrope, loup garou, werewolf, werefolk; incubus, succubus, succuba, nightmare; fury, harpy; Gorgon; ogreishness, ghoulishness.

mythical being 968 *angel*, 969 *devil*; demon, genie, jinn; houri; Valkyrie, battlemaid; centaur, satyr, faun; sea nymph, river n., water n., Oceanid, Naiad, water elf, kelpie, nix, nixie; merfolk, merman, mermaid; Lorelei, siren; water spirit, Undine 967 *nymph*; Lady of the Lake, Old Man of the Sea; Merlin 983 *sorcerer*; Wayland Smith, Green Man, Wodwose; yeti, Abominable Snowman, Leviathan, phoenix 84 *rara avis*.

Adj. *fairylike*, fairy, nymphean; sylph-like 206 *lean*; dwarf-like 196 *dwarfish*; gigantic 195 *huge*; monstrous, ogreish, devilish, demonic 969 *diabolic*; vampirish, lycanthropic; gorgonian; elf-like, elfin, elvish, impish, Puckish 898 *maleficent*; magic 983 *magical*; mythical, mythic, folklorish 513 *imaginary*.

spooky, spookish, ghostly, ghoulish; haunted, hagridden; nightmarish, macabre 854 *frightening*; weird, uncanny, unearthly, eldritch 84 *abnormal*; eerie, numinous, supernatural, supernormal; spectral, apparitional, wraith-like; disembodied, discarnate 320 *immaterial*; ectoplasmic, astral, spiritualistic, mediumistic 984 *psychical*.

Vb. *haunt*, visit, walk; ghost, gibber, mop and mow.

Adv. *spookishly*, spectrally, uncannily, nightmarishly; elfishly, puckishly; with its head tucked underneath its arm.

See: 84, 195, 196, 206, 320, 440, 513, 854, 898, 903, 938, **967**, 968, **969**, 983, 984.

971 Heaven

N. *heaven*, presence of God, abode of G., throne of G., kingdom of G., kingdom of heaven, heavenly kingdom, kingdom come; Paradise, abode of the blest, abode of the saints, land of the leal; Abraham's bosom, eternal home, happy h.; eternal rest, celestial bliss, blessed state; nirvana, seventh heaven; the Millennium, earthly paradise, Zion, Land of Beulah, New Jerusalem, Holy City, Celestial C.; afterlife, eternal life, eternity 124 *future state*; resurrection; assumption, translation, glorification; deification, apotheosis.

mythic heaven, Olympus; Valhalla, Asgard; Elysium, Elysian fields, happy hunting grounds; Earthly Paradise, Eden, Garden of E., garden of the Hesperides, Islands of the Blest, Isle of Avalon 513 *fantasy*.

Adj. *paradisiac*, paradisiacal, paradisal; heavenly, celestial, supernal, eternal; beatific, blessed, blissful 824 *happy*; resurrectional, glorified; Elysian, Olympian; millennial.

See: 124, **513**, 824.

972 Hell

N. *hell*, place of the dead, lower world, nether w., nether regions, infernal r., underworld; grave, limbo, Sheol, Hades; purgatory; perdition, place of the damned, inferno, Satan's palace, Pandemonium; abyss, bottomless pit, Abaddon; place of torment, Tophet, Gehenna, lake of fire and brimstone; hellfire, everlasting fire, unquenchable f.

mythic hell, Hel, Niflheim; realm of Pluto, Hades, Tartarus, Avernus, Erebus; river of hell, Acheron, Styx, Cocytus, Phlegethon, Lethe; Stygian ferryman, Charon; infernal watchdog, Cerberus; infernal judge, Minos, Rhadamanthus; nether gods, Chthonians, Pluto, Osiris 967 *Chthonian deity*.

Adj. *infernal*, bottomless 211 *deep*; Chthonian, subterranean 210 *low*; hellish, Plutonian, Avernal, Tartarean; Acherontic, Stygian, Lethean; Cerberian; Rhadamanthine; damned, devilish 969 *diabolic*.

See: 210, 211, 967, 969.

973 Religion

N. *religion*, religious instinct 872 *humility*; religious feeling 979 *piety*; Messianism 507 *expectation*; search for truth, religious quest; natural religion, deism; primitive religion, early faith; paganism 982 *idolatry*; nature religion, orgiastic r., mystery r., mysteries, Eleusinian m., Orphism; dharma, revealed religion, historical r., incarnational r., sacramental r.; mysticism, Sufism; yoga, hathayoga, dharmayoga, jnanayoga, karmayoga, bhaktiyoga; Eightfold Path; theosophy 449 *philosophy*; theolatry 981 *worship*; religious cult, state religion, official r. 981 *cult*; untheological religion, creedless r., personal r.; no religion, atheism 974 *irreligion*.

deism, belief in a god, theism; animism, pantheism, polytheism, henotheism, monotheism, dualism; gnosticism.

religious faith, faith 485 *belief*; Christianity, the Cross; Judaism; Islam, Muhammedanism, the Crescent; Baha'ism, Zoroastrianism, Mazdaism; Vedic religion, Dharma; Hinduism, Brahmanism, Vedantism, Tantrism; Vaishnavism 978 *sectarianism*; Sikhism; Jainism; Buddhism, Theravada, Hinayana, Mahayana, Zen; Shintoism; Taoism, Confucianism; Theosophy; Scientology.

theology, study of religion; natural theology, revealed f.; religious knowledge, religious learning, divinity; scholastic theology, scholasticism, Thomism; Rabbinism; isagogics, theological exegesis; typology; demythologization; Christology; soteriology, theodicy; eschatology; hagiology, hagiography, iconology; dogmatics, dogmatic theology; symbolics, creedal theology; tradition, deposit of faith; teaching, doctrine, religious d., received d., defined d.; definition, canon; doxy, dogma, tenet; articles of faith, credo 485 *creed*; confession, Thirty-nine Articles; fundamentalism 976 *orthodoxism*; Bibliology, higher criticism; comparative religion.

theologian, theologue; divinity student, divine; doctor, doctor of the Church; doctor of the Law, rabbi, scribe, mufti, mullah; schoolman, scholastic, scholastic theologian, Thomist, Talmudist, canonist; theogonist, hagiologist, hagiographer, iconologist; psalmist, hymnographer, hymnwriter; textualist, Masorete; Bible critic, higher c.; scripturalist, fundamentalist, rabbinist.

religious teacher, prophet, rishi, inspired writer; guru, maharishi 500 *sage*; evangelist, apostle, missionary; reformer, religious r.; expected leader, Messiah, Mahdi, Invisible Imam, twelfth avatar of Vishnu; founder of Christianity, Christ, Jesus Christ; Prophet of God, Muhammad, Mohammed *or* Mahomet; Zoroaster *or* Zarathustra; Ramakrishna, Baha'ullah; Buddha, Gautama; Confucius, Lao-tzu; Joseph Smith, Mary Baker Eddy, Madame Blavatsky; expounder, hierophant, gospeller, catechist 520 *interpreter*.

religionist, deist, theist; monotheist, henotheist, polytheist, pantheist; animist, fetishist 982 *idolater*; pagan, gentile 974 *heathen*; people of the book; adherent, believer, true b., orthodoxist 976 *the orthodox*; militant 979 *zealot*; Christian, Nazarene; Jew; Muslim, Moslem, Islamite, Mussulman, Muhammadan; Sunnite, Shi'ite 978 *non-Christian sect*; Sufi, dervish; Baha'i; Parsee, Zoroastrian; Hindu, gymnosophist, Brahmanist; Sikh; Jain; Buddhist, Zen B.; Tantrist; Taoist; Confucianist; Shintoist; Theosophist; Mormon 978 *sect*; Rosicrucian 984 *occultist*; gnostic 977 *heretic*.

Adj. *religious*, divine, holy, sacred, spiritual, sacramental; deistic, theistic, animistic, pantheistic, henotheistic, monotheistic, dualistic; Christian, Islamic, Moslem, Jewish, Judaistic, Mosaic; Baha'i, Zoroastrian, Avestan; Confucian, Taoistic; Buddhistic, Hinduistic, Vedic, Brahmanic, Upanishadic, Vedantic; yogic, mystic, Sufic; devotional, devout, practising 981 *worshipping*.

theological, theosophical, scholastic, rabbinical; doctrinal, dogmatic, creedal, canonical; Christological, soteriological; doxological 988 *ritualistic*; hagiological, iconological.

See: 449, 485, 500, 507, 520, 872, 974, 976, 977, **978**, 979, 981, 982, 984, 988.

974 Irreligion

N. *irreligion*, unreligiousness, unspirituality; nothing sacred, profaneness, ungodliness, godlessness 980 *impiety*; false religion, heathenism 982 *idolatry*; no religion, atheism, nullifidianism, dissent from all creeds, disbelief 486 *unbelief*; agnosticism, scepticism, Pyrrhonism 486 *doubt*; probabilism, euhemerism 449 *philosophy*; lack of faith, want of f., infidelity; lapse, lapse from faith, recidivism, backsliding 603 *tergiversation*; paganization, dechristianization, post-Christian state; amoralism, apathy, indifferentism 860 *indifference*.

antichristianity, antichristianism 704 *opposition*; paganism, heathenism, heathendom; Satanism 969 *diabolism*; free thinking, free thought, rationalism, positivism, nihilism 449 *philosophy*; hylotheism, materialism; secularism, worldliness, fleshliness 944 *sensualism*; Mammonism 816 *avarice*.

irreligionist, Antichrist; nullifidian, dissenter, dissenter from all creeds, no believer, atheist 486 *unbeliever*; rationalist, euhemerist, freethinker; agnostic, sceptic, Pyrrhonist; nihilist, materialist, positivist; secularist, Mammonist, Mammonite, worldling, amoralist, indifferentist.

heathen, non-Christian, pagan, paynim; misbeliever, infidel, giaour; gentile, the uncircumcised, the unbaptized, the unconverted; apostate, backslider, lapsed Christian 603 *tergiversator*.

Adj. *irreligious*, having no religion, without r., without a god, godless, altarless, profane 980 *impious*; nihilistic, atheistic, atheistical; creedless, nullifidian, agnostic, doubting, sceptical, Pyrrhonian, Pyrrhonic 486 *unbelieving*; free-thinking, rationalizing, rationalistic, euhemeristic; nonreligious, nonworshipping, nonpractising, nontheological, noncreedal 769 *nonobservant*; undevout, unreligious, unspiritual, ungodly 934 *wicked*; amoral, morally neutral 860 *indifferent*; secular, mundane, of this world, worldly, materialistic, Main Street 932 *selfish*; Mammonistic 944 *sensual*; lacking faith, faithless, backsliding, recidivous, lapsed, paganized, post-Christian 603 *tergiversating*; unchristian, non-Christian; antireligious, anti-Christian, anti-Church, anticlerical.

heathenish, unholy, unhallowed, unsanctified, unblest, unconsecrated 980 *profane*; unchristian, unbaptized, unconfirmed; gentile, uncircumcised; heathen, pagan, infidel; pre-Christian, unconverted, in darkness 491 *uninstructed*.

Vb. *be irreligious*, - atheistic etc. adj.; have no religion, lack faith; remain unconverted 486 *disbelieve*; shut one's eyes to the light, love darkness, serve Mammon; lose one's faith, give up the Church 603 *apostatize*; have no use for religion, scoff at r.; euhemerize, demythologize, rationalize; persecute the faith, deny God, blaspheme 980 *be impious*.

paganize, heathenize, dechristianize; desanctify, deconsecrate, undedicate, secularize.

See: 449, 486, 491, 603, 704, 769, 816, 860, 932, 934, **944**, 969, **980**, **982**.

975 Revelation

N. *revelation*, divine r., apocalypse 526 *disclosure*; illumination 417 *light*; afflatus, divine a., inspiration, divine i.; prophecy, prophetic inspiration; intuition, mystical i., mysticism; direct communication, the Law, Mosaic L., Ten Commandments; divine message, God's word, gospel, gospel message; God revealed, theophany, burning bush, epiphany, incarnation, Word made flesh; avatar, emanation, divine e.

scripture, Word of God, inspired text, sacred t., sacred writings; Holy Scripture, Holy Writ, Bible, Holy B., the Book, the Good Book, the Word; Wyclif's Bible, Geneva *or* Breeches B., King James's Bible, Authorized Version, Revised V., Jerusalem Bible, New English B., Good News B.; Vulgate, Douai Version, Greek version, Septuagint; canonical writings, canonical books, canon; Old Testament,

Pentateuch, Hexateuch, Octateuch, Major Prophets, Minor P.; Torah, the Law and the Prophets, Hagiographa; New Testament, Gospels, Synoptic G., Epistles, Pastoral E., Pauline E., Johannine E., Petrine E.; Acts of the Apostles, Revelation, Apocalypse; noncanonical writings, Apocrypha, agrapha, logia, sayings, noncanonical gospel; patristic writings; psalter, psalmbook, breviary, missal; prayer book, Book of Common Prayer 981 *prayers*; hymn book, hymnal 981 *hymn*; post-Biblical writings (Hebrew), Targum, Talmud, Mishnah, Gemara; textual commentary, Masorah, Higher Criticism; fundamentalism, scripturalism.

non-Biblical scripture, Koran, the Glorious Koran, Qur'an; Hadith, Sunna; Hindu scripture, Veda, the Four Vedas, Rigveda, Yajurveda, Samaveda, Atharvaveda; Brahmana, Upanishad, Purana; Bhagavad Gita; sruti, smriti, shastra, sutra, tantra; Granth; Buddhist scripture, Pitaka, Tripitaka, Nikaya, Dhammapada; Iranian and Zoroastrian scripture, Avesta, Zend-Avesta; Book of the Dead (Egyptian); Book of Mormon.

Adj. *revelational*, inspirational, mystic; inspired, prophetic, revealed, epiphanous; visional; apocalyptic; prophetic, evangelical; mystagogic.

scriptural, sacred, holy; hierographic, hieratic; revealed, inspired, prophetic; canonical 733 *authoritative*; biblical, Mosaic, pre-exilic, exilic, postexilic; gospel, evangelistic, apostolic; subapostolic, patristic, homiletic; Talmudic, Mishnaic; Koranic, uncreated; Vedic, Upanishadic, Puranic; textuary, textual, Masoretic.

See: 417, 526, 733, 981.

976 Orthodoxy

N. *orthodoxy*, orthodoxness, correct opinion, right belief; sound theology, Trinitarianism; religious truth, gospel t., pure Gospel 494 *truth*; scripturality, canonicity; the Faith, the true faith, the whole f., deposit of f., 'the faith once delivered unto the saints'; primitive faith, early Church, Apostolic age; ecumenicalism, catholicity, Catholicism; formulated faith, credo 485 *creed*; Apostles' Creed, Nicene C., Athanasian C.; Thirty-nine Articles, Tridentine decrees; textuary, catechism, Church Catechism.

orthodoxism, strictness, strict interpretation; scripturalism, textualism, fundamentalism, literalism, precisianism; Karaism (Jewish); traditionalism, institutionalism, ecclesiasticism, churchianity 985 *the church*; sound churchmanship 83 *conformity*; Christian practice 768 *observance*; intolerance, heresy-hunting, persecution; suppression of heresy, extermination of error, Counter-Reformation; religious censorship, Holy Office 956 *tribunal*; Inquisition 459 *interrogation*; Index, Index Expurgatorius, Index Librorum Prohibitorum 924 *disapprobation*; guaranteed orthodoxy, imprimatur 923 *approbation*.

Christendom, Christian world, the Church; undivided Church; Christian fellowship, communion of saints; Holy Church, Mother C.; Bride of Christ; Body of Christ, universal Church; Church militant, Church on earth, visible Church; invisible Church, Church triumphant; established Church, recognized C., denominational C.; Orthodox C., Eastern Orthodox C., Armenian C., Coptic C.; Church of Rome, Roman Catholic and Apostolic C.; Church of England, Episcopalian C.; Church of Scotland; Church of South India; Reformed Church, Protestant C., Lutheran C., Calvinist C.; Ecumenical Council, World Council of Churches.

Catholicism, Orthodoxy, Eastern O.; Roman Catholicism, Romanism, popery, papistry, ultramontanism, Scarlet Woman; Counter-Reformation; Old Catholicism; Anglicanism, Episcopalianism, prelacy; Anglo-Catholicism, High Church; Tractarianism, Oxford Movement.

Protestantism, the Reformation, Anglicanism, Lutheranism, Zwinglianism, Calvinism; Presbyterianism, Congregationalism, United Reformed Church, Baptists; Quakerism, Society of Friends; Wesleyanism, Methodism, Primitive M. 978 *sect*.

Catholic, Orthodox, Eastern O.; Greek O., Russian O., Coptic; Roman Catholic, Romanist, papist, ultramontanist; Old Catholic, Anglo-C., Anglican, Episcopalian, High-Churchman, Tractarian.

Protestant, reformer, Anglican, Lutheran, Zwinglian, Calvinist, Huguenot, Anabaptist; Presbyterian, Congregationalist, Baptist, Wesleyan, Methodist, Wesleyan M., Primitive M.; Quaker, Friend; Plymouth

Brother.

church member, churchman *or* -woman, church-goer, pillar of the church; Christian, disciple of Christ, follower of C.; the baptized, the confirmed; practising Christian, communicant 981 *worshipper*; the saints, the faithful, the body of the f., church people, chapel p.; congregation, coreligionist, fellow-worshipper.

the orthodox, the believing, the faithful, the converted; born-again Christian, evangelical; believer, true b.; pillar of orthodoxy, conformer 83 *conformist*; traditionalist, scripturalist, textualist, literalist, fundamentalist 973 *theologian*.

Adj. *orthodox*, holding the faith, reciting the creed 485 *believing*; right-minded, sound, balanced 480 *judicial*; nonheretical, unschismatical 488 *assenting*; undivided 52 *whole*; unswerving, undeviating, loyal, devout 739 *obedient*; practising, conforming, conventional 83 *conformable*; churchy 979 *pietistic*; precise, strict, pedantic; hyperorthodox, overreligious, holier than thou; intolerant, witch-hunting, heresy-h., inquisitional 459 *enquiring*; correct 494 *accurate*; of faith, to be believed, doctrinal 485 *creedal*; authoritative, defined, canonical, biblical, scriptural, evangelical, gospel 494 *genuine*; textual, literal, fundamentalist, fundamentalistic; Trinitarian; Athanasian; catholic, ecumenical, universal; accepted, held, widely h., believed, generally b. 485 *credible*; traditional, customary 610 *usual*.

Roman Catholic, Catholic, Roman, Romish, Romanist, Romanizing, ultramontanist; popish, papistic.

Anglican, episcopalian; Tractarian, Anglo-Catholic, High-Church, high, spiky; Low-Church; Broad-C., Latitudinarian.

Protestant, reformed; denominational 978 *sectarian*; Lutheran, Zwinglian, Calvinist, Calvinistic; Presbyterian, Congregational, United Reformed, Baptist, Methodist, Wesleyan, Quaker; bishopless, nonepiscopal.

Vb. *be orthodox*, - catholic etc. adj.; hold the faith, recite the creeds 485 *believe*; support the church, go to c. 83 *conform*; catholicize, Romanize; Protestantize; Anglicanize; Lutheranize; Calvinize; Presbyterianize.

Adv. *orthodoxly*, catholicly, ecumenically.

See: 52, **83**, 459, 480, **485**, 488, 494, 610, 739, 768, 923, 924, 956, 973, **978**, 979, 981, 985.

977 Heterodoxy

N. *heterodoxy*, other men's doxy; unorthodoxy, unauthorized belief, unauthorized doubts, personal judgment; erroneous opinion, wrong belief, misbelief, false creed, superstition 495 *error*; strange doctrine, new teaching, bad t.; perversion of the truth 535 *misteaching*; doubtful orthodoxy, heretical tendency, latitudinarianism, modernism, Higher Criticism; unscripturality, noncatholicity, partial truth; heresy, rank h.

heresy, heathen theology, Gnosticism; Monarchianism, Arianism; Socinianism; Unitarianism; Apollinarianism, Nestorianism; Monophysitism, Monothelitism; Pelagianism; Montanism, Donatism, Manichaeism, Albigensianism, Antinomianism; Lollardy; Erastianism, antipapalism.

heretic, arch-h., heresiarch; Gnostic, Manichee; Monarchian, Unitarian; Arius, Arian; Socinus, Socinian; Nestorius, Nestorian; Eutyches, Apollinaris, Apollinarian; Monophysite, Monothelite; Pelagius; Montanus, millenarian; Donatist; Manichaean, Cathar, Paulician, Albigensian; Antinomian; Wycliffite, Lollard, Hussite; Waldenses.

Adj. *heterodox*, differing, unconventional 15 *different*; dissentient 489 *dissenting*; nondoctrinaire, nonconformist 84 *unconformable*; uncatholic, antipapal; less than orthodox, erroneous 495 *mistaken*; unorthodox, unbiblical, unscriptural, unauthorized, unsanctioned, proscribed 757 *prohibited*; heretical, anathematized, damnable 961 *condemned*.

heretical, heretic; heathen, Gnostic, Manichean, Monarchian, Unitarian, Socinian; Arian, Eutychian, Apollinarian, Nestorian, Monophysitic, Monothelite; Pelagian; Montanist; Manichaean, Albigensian; Antinomian, Waldensian, Wycliffite, Lollard, Hussite.

Vb. *declare heretical*, anathematize 961 *condemn*.

be heretical, - unorthodox etc. adj.

Adv. *heretically*, unorthodoxly.

See: 15, **84**, 489, 495, 535, 757, 961.

978 Sectarianism

N. *sectarianism*, particularism, exclusiveness, clannishness, sectionalism 481 *prejudice*; bigotry 481 *bias*; party-mindedness, party spirit, factiousness 709 *quarrelsomeness*; independence, separatism, schismaticalness, schismatical tendency 738 *disobedience*; denominationalism, nonconformism, nonconformity 489 *dissent*; Lutheranism, Calvinism, Anabaptism, Pietism, Moravianism, Puritanism 976 *Protestantism*; Puseyism, Tractarianism 976 *Catholicism*.

schism, division, divisions, differences 709 *quarrel*; dissociation, breakaway, secession, withdrawal 46 *separation*; nonrecognition, mutual excommunication 883 *seclusion*; recusancy 769 *nonobservance*; religious schism, Great Schism.

church party, Judaizers, Ebionites; Homoousians, Homoiousians; ultramontanists, papalists; Gallicans; Erastians; High-Church party, Episcopalians, Puseyites, Tractarians 976 *Catholic*; Low-Church party, Evangelicals, Puritans 976 *Protestant*; Broad Church party, Latitudinarians, Modernists; Universalists.

sect, division, off-shoot, branch, group, faction 708 *party*; order, religious o., brotherhood, sisterhood 708 *community*; nonconformist sect, chapel, conventicle 976 *Protestantism*; Society of Friends, Friends, Quakers; Unitarians; Moravians; Plymouth Brethren; Churches of Christ; Sabbatarians, Seventh-day Adventists; Church of Christ Scientist; Church of Jesus Christ of the Latter-Day Saints, Mormons; Jehovah's Witnesses; Salvation Army, Salvationists; Oxford Group, Moral Re-Armament.

non-Christian sect, Jewish s.; Orthodox Jews, Reform J.; Pharisees, Sadducees; Hasidim, Rabbinists; Karaites; Nazarites, Essenes; pagano-Christian sect, Gnostics, Mandaeans, Euchites; Islamic sect, Sunnis, Shi'ites, Sufis, Wahhabis; Black Muslims; Rastafarians, Rastas; Hindu sect, Vedantists, Vaishnavas, Saivas, Shaktas; Brahmo, Hare Krishna sect; Tantrists, Pure Land sect, Jodo s. 973 *religious faith*.

sectarian, particularist; follower, adherent, devotee; Sectary, Dissenter, Nonconformist, Independent; Puritan, Shaker; Quaker, Friend; Pentecostalist; Presbyterian, Covenanter 976 *Protestant*; Salvationist; Christian Scientist; Jehovah's Witness; Unitarian; Seventh-day Adventist, Mennonite; Mormon; Moonie; Christadelphian, Scientologist, Gnostic 977 *heretic*.

schismatic, separated brother; schismatics, separated brethren; separatist, separationist; seceder, secessionist; factionary, factionist 709 *quarreller*; rebel, mutineer 738 *revolter*; recusant, nonjuror; dissident, dissenter, nonconformist 489 *dissentient*; wrong believer 977 *heretic*; apostate 603 *tergiversator*.

Adj. *sectarian*, particularist; party-minded, partisan 481 *biased*; clannish, exclusive 708 *sectional*; Judaizer, Ebionite; Gallican; Erastian; High-Church, Episcopalian 976 *Anglican*; Low-Church, Evangelical 976 *Protestant*; Puritan, Independent, Presbyterian, Covenanting; revivalist, Pentecostalist; Vaishnavite, Saiva, Shakta, Tantrist; Ramakrishna; Rastafarian; Sunni, Shi'ite, Sufic; Essene, Pharisaic, Sadducean, Hasidic; Gnostic.

schismatical, schismatic, secessionist, seceding, breakaway; divided, separated 46 *separate*; excommunicated, excommunicable 977 *heretical*; dissentient, nonconformist 489 *dissenting*; recusant 769 *nonobservant*; rebellious, rebel, contumacious 738 *disobedient*; apostate 603 *tergiversating*.

Vb. *sectarianize*, follow a sect 708 *join a party*.

schismatize, commit schism, separate, divide, withdraw, secede, break away, hive off 603 *apostatize*; be in a state of schism, be contumacious 738 *disobey*.

See: 46, 481, **489**, 603, 708, 709, 738, 769, 883, 973, **976**, **977**.

979 Piety

N. *piety*, piousness, goodness 933 *virtue*; reverence, veneration, honour, decent respect 920 *respect*; affection, kind feeling, friendly f. 897 *benevolence*; dutifulness, loyalty, conformity, attendance at worship 768 *observance*; churchmanship, sound c. 976 *orthodoxy*; religiousness, religion, theism 973 *deism*; religious feeling, pious sentiment, theopathy; fear of God, godly fear 854 *fear*; submissiveness, humbleness 872 *humility*; pious belief, faith, trust, trust in God 485 *belief*; devotion, dedication, self-surrender 931 *disinterestedness*; devoutness, sincerity, earnestness, unction; enthusiasm, fervour, zeal, muscular Christianity; inspiration, exaltation, speaking in tongues, glossolalia 821 *excitation*; adoration, prostration 981 *worship*; prayerfulness, meditation, retreat; contemplation, mysticism, communion with God, mystic communion 973 *religion*; faith healing 656 *restoration*; act of piety, pious duty, charity 901 *philanthropy*; pious fiction, edifying reading, tract, sermon; Christian behaviour, Christian life; pilgrimage, hajj.

sanctity, holiness, hallowedness, sacredness, sacrosanctity; goodness, cardinal virtues, theological v. 933 *virtue*; cooperation with grace, synergism; state of grace, odour of sanctity 950 *purity*; godliness, saintliness, holy character; spirituality, unworldliness, otherworldliness; spiritual life, life in God; sainthood, blessedness, blessed state; enlightenment, Buddhahood; conversion, regeneration, rebirth, new birth 656 *revival*; sanctification, justification, adoption 965 *divine function*; canonization, beatification, consecration, dedication 866 *dignification*.

pietism, show of piety, sanctimony; sanctimoniousness, unction, cant 542 *sham*; religionism, religiosity, religious mania; overpiety, overorthodoxy 976 *orthodoxism*; scrupulosity, tender conscience; austerity 945 *asceticism*; formalism, precisianism, Puritanism 481 *narrow mind*; literalness, fundamentalism, Bible-worship, bibliolatry 494 *accuracy*; sabbatarianism 978 *sectarianism*; churchianity, churchiness, sacerdotalism, ritualism 985 *ecclesiasticism*; preachiness, unctuousness; odium theologicum 888 *hatred*; bigotry, fanaticism 481 *prejudice*; persecution, witch-hunting, heresy-h. 735 *severity*; crusading spirit, missionary s., salvationism 901 *philanthropy*.

pietist, pious person, real saint 937 *good person*; children of God, c. of light; the good, the righteous, the just; conformist 488 *assenter*; professing Christian, practising C., communicant 981 *worshipper*; confessor, martyr; beatified person, saint, bodhisattva, marabout; man *or* woman of prayer, contemplative, mystic, Sufi; holy man, sadhu, sannyasi, bhikshu, fakir, dervish 945 *ascetic*; hermit, anchorite 883 *solitary*; monk, nun, religious 986 *clergy*; devotee, dedicated soul; convert, neophyte, catechumen, ordinand 538 *learner*; believer, true b., the faithful 976 *church member*; the chosen people, the elect, children of delight; pilgrim, palmer, hajji; votary.

zealot, religionist, enthusiast, wowser, fanatic, bigot, image-breaker, iconoclast; formalist, precisian, Puritan; Pharisee, scribe, scribes and Pharisees; the unco guid; fundamentalist, Bible-worshipper, bibliolater, Sabbatarian 978 *sectarian*; bible-puncher, sermonizer, pulpiteer 537 *preacher*; evangelical, salvationist, hot-gospeller; missionary 901 *philanthropist*; revivalist, speaker in tongues, faith healer; champion of the faith, crusader, militant Christian; militant Islamite, Ghazi; persecutor 735 *tyrant*.

Adj. *pious*, good, kind 897 *benevolent*, 933 *virtuous*; decent, reverent 920 *respectful*; faithful, true, loyal, devoted 739 *obedient*; conforming, traditional 768 *observant*; believing, holding the faith 976 *orthodox*; sincere, practising, professing, confessing 540 *veracious*; pure, pure in heart, holy-minded, heavenly-m.; unworldly, otherworldly, spiritual; godly, God-fearing, religious, devout; praying, prayerful, psalm-singing 981 *worshipping*; in retreat, meditative, contemplative, mystic; holy, saintly, saintlike, sainted; Christian, Christ-like, full of grace.

pietistic, ardent, fervent, seraphic; enthusiastic, inspired; austere 945 *ascetic*; hermit-like, anchoretic 883 *unsociable*; earnest, pi, religiose, overreligious, overpious, overdevout, overrighteous, self-righteous, holier than thou; overstrict, precise, Puritan 678 *meddling*; formalistic, Pharisaic, ritualistic 978 *sectarian*; priest-ridden, churchy; psalm-singing, hymn-s.; preachy, sanctimonious, canting 850 *affected*; goody-goody, too good to be true 933 *virtuous*; crusading, evangelical, missionary-minded.

sanctified, made holy, consecrated, dedicated, enshrined; reverend, holy, sacred, solemn, sacrosanct 866 *worshipful*; haloed, sainted, canonized, beatified; adopted, justified; chosen; saved, redeemed, ransomed 746 *liberated*; regenerate, renewed, reborn, born again 656 *restored*.

Vb. *be pious*, - religious etc. adj.; be holy, wear a halo; mind heavenly things, think of God; fear God 854 *fear*; have faith 485 *believe*; keep the faith, fight the good fight

162 *be strong*; walk humbly with one's God, humble oneself 872 *be humble*; go to church, attend divine worship; pray, say one's prayers 981 *worship*; kneel, genuflect, bow 311 *stoop*; cross oneself, make the sign of the cross; make offering, sacrifice, devote 759 *offer*; give alms and oblations, lend to God 781 *give*; give to the poor 897 *be benevolent*; glorify God 923 *praise*; give God the glory 907 *thank*; revere, show reverence 920 *show respect*; hearken, listen 739 *obey*; sermonize, preachify, preach at 534 *teach*; let one's light shine, set a good example.

become pious, be converted, experience religion, get religion; change one's religion, go over 603 *tergiversate*; see the light, see the error of one's ways 603 *recant*; mend one's ways, reform, repent, receive Christ 939 *be penitent*; enter the church, become ordained, take holy orders, take vows, take the veil 986 *take orders*; be a pilgrim, go on a pilgrimage, perform the hajj.

make pious, bring religion to, bring to God, proselytize, convert 485 *convince*; Christianize, win for Christ, baptize, receive into the church 299 *admit*; Islamize, Judaize; depaganize, spiritualize 648 *purify*; edify, confirm, strengthen one's faith, confirm in the f. 162 *strengthen*; inspire, fill with grace, uplift 654 *make better*; redeem, regenerate 656 *restore*.

sanctify, hallow, make holy, keep h. 866 *honour*; spiritualize, consecrate, dedicate, enshrine 866 *dignify*; make a saint of, saint, canonize, beatify, invest with a halo; bless, pronounce a blessing, make the sign of the cross.

See: 162, 299, 311, 481, 485, 488, 494, 534, 537, 538, 540, 542, 603, 648, 654, 656, 678, 735, 739, 746, 759, 768, 781, 821, 850, 854, 866, 872, 883, 888, 897, 901, 907, 920, 923, 931, **933**, 937, 939, 945, 950, 965, 973, 976, 978, **981**, 985, 986.

980 Impiety

N. *impiety*, impiousness; irreverence, disregard 921 *disrespect*; nonworship, lack of piety, lack of reverence; godlessness 974 *irreligion*; scoffing, mockery, derision 851 *ridicule*; scorn, pride 922 *contempt*; sacrilegiousness, profanity; blasphemy, cursing, swearing 899 *malediction*; sacrilege, desecration, violation, profanation, perversion, abuse 675 *misuse*; unrighteousness, consciencelessness, immorality, sin, pervertedness 934 *wickedness*; hardening, stubbornness 940 *impenitence*; regression 655 *deterioration*; backsliding, apostasy 603 *tergiversation*; profaneness, unholiness, worldliness, materialism 319 *materiality*; amoralism, indifferentism 464 *indiscrimination*; misdirected devotion 982 *idolatry*; paganism, heathenism; rejection, reprobation 924 *disapprobation*.

false piety, sham p. 541 *falsehood*; solemn mockery, mummery 542 *sham*; sanctimony, sanctimoniousness, Pharisaism 979 *pietism*; hypocrisy, religious h., lip service 541 *duplicity*; cant 850 *affectation*.

impious person, blasphemer, curser, swearer 899 *malediction*; mocker, scorner, contemner, defamer, calumniator 926 *detractor*; sacrilegious person, desecrator, violator, profaner 904 *offender*; profane person, nonworshipper, gentile, pagan, infidel, unbeliever 974 *heathen*; misbeliever 982 *idolater*; disbeliever, atheist, sceptic 974 *irreligionist*; indifferentist, amoralist; worldling, materialist, immoralist 944 *sensualist*; sinner, reprobate, the wicked, the unrighteous, sons of Belial, children of darkness 938 *bad person*; recidivist, backslider, apostate, adulterous generation 603 *tergiversator*; fallen angel, Tempter, Wicked One 969 *Satan*; hypocrite, religious h., Tartuffe 545 *deceiver*; canter, lip-worshipper 850 *affecter*.

Adj. *impious*, ungodly, antireligious, anti-Christian, antichurch, anticlerical 704 *opposing*; recusant, dissenting 977 *heretical*; unbelieving, nonbelieving, atheistical, godless 974 *irreligious*; nonworshipping, undevout, nonpractising 769 *nonobservant*; misbelieving 982 *idolatrous*; scoffing, mocking, deriding 851 *derisive*; blaspheming, blasphemous, swearing 899 *cursing*; irreligious, irreverent, without reverence 921 *disrespectful*; sacrilegious, profaning, desecrating, violating, iconoclastic 954 *lawless*; unawed, brazen, bold 855 *unfearing*; hard, unmoved, unfeeling 898 *cruel*; sinning, sinful, impure, hardened, perverted, reprobate, unregenerate 934 *wicked*; backsliding, apostate 603 *tergiversating*; canting, sanctimonious 850 *affected*; pharisaical 541 *hypocritical*.

profane, unholy, unhallowed, unsanctified, unblest; forsaken by God, accursed;

undedicated, unconsecrated, deconsecrated, secularized; infidel, pagan, gentile; paganized, dechristianized 974 *heathenish.*

Vb. *be impious,* - sacrilegious etc. adj.; rebel against God 871 *be proud;* sin 934 *be wicked;* swear, blaspheme, take the name of the Lord in vain 899 *curse;* have no reverence, show no respect 921 *not respect;* profane, desecrate, violate 675 *misuse;* commit sacrilege, lay profane hands on, defile, sully 649 *make unclean;* misbelieve, worship false gods; cant, beat one's breast 850 *be affected;* play the hypocrite, play false 541 *dissemble;* backslide 603 *apostatize;* sin against the light, grow hardened, harden one's heart 655 *deteriorate.*

See: 319, 464, 541, 542, 545, 603, 649, 655, 675, 704, 769, 850, 851, 855, 871, 898, 899, 904, 921, 922, 924, 926, **934**, 938, 940, 944, 954, 969, **974**, 977, 979, 982.

981 Worship

N. *worship,* honour, reverence, homage 920 *respect;* holy fear, awe 854 *fear;* veneration, adoration, prostration of the soul; humbling oneself, humbleness 872 *humility;* devotion, devotedness, bhakti 979 *piety;* prayer, one's devotions, one's prayers; retreat, quiet time, meditation, contemplation, communion.

cult, mystique; type of worship, service 917 *duty;* service of God, supreme worship, latria; inferior worship, dulia, hyperdulia; Christolatry, Mariolatry; iconolatry, image-worship; false worship 982 *idolatry.*

act of worship, rites, mysteries 988 *rite;* laud, laudation, praises, doxology 923 *praise;* glorification, giving glory, extolment 866 *dignification;* hymning, hymn-singing, psalm-s., psalmody, plainsong, chanting 412 *vocal music;* thanksgiving, blessing, benediction 907 *thanks;* offering, oblation, almsgiving, sacrifice, making s., sacrificing, offering (**see** *oblation*); praying, saying one's prayers, reciting the rosary; self-examination 939 *penitence;* self-denial, self-discipline 945 *asceticism;* keeping fast 946 *fasting;* hajj, pilgrimage 267 *wandering.*

prayers, orisons, devotions; private devotion, retreat, contemplation 449 *meditation;* prayer, bidding prayer; impetration, petition, petitionary prayer 761 *request;* invocation, invocatory prayer 583 *allocution;* intercession, intercessory prayer, arrow p. 762 *deprecation;* suffrage, prayers for the dead, vigils; special prayer, intention; rogation, supplication, solemn s., litany, solemn l.; comminatory prayer, commination, denunciation 900 *threat;* imprecation, imprecatory prayer 899 *malediction;* excommunication, ban 883 *seclusion;* exorcism 300 *ejection;* benediction, benedicite, benison, grace 907 *thanks;* prayer for the day, collect; liturgical prayer, the Lord's Prayer, Paternoster, Our Father; Ave, Ave Maria, Hail Mary; Kyrie Eleison, Sursum Corda, Sanctus; Nunc Dimittis; dismissal, blessing; rosary, beads, beadroll; prayer-wheel; prayer book, missal, breviary, book of hours; call to prayer, muezzin's cry 547 *call.*

hymn, song, psalm, metrical p.; religious song, spiritual; processional hymn, recessional; introit; plainsong, Gregorian chant, Ambrosian c., descant 412 *vocal music;* anthem, cantata, motet; antiphon, response; canticle, Te Deum, Benedicite; song of praise, paean, Magnificat; doxology, Gloria; greater doxology, Gloria in Excelsis; lesser doxology, Gloria Patri; paean, halleluja, hosanna; Homeric hymn; Vedic hymn; hymn-singing, hymnody; psalm-singing, psalmody; hymnbook, hymnal, psalter; Vedic hymns, Rigveda, Samaveda; hymnology, hymnography.

oblation, offertory, collection, alms and oblations 781 *offering;* pew rent, pewage; libation, incense, censing 988 *rite;* dedication, consecration 866 *dignification;* votive offering, de voto o.; thank-offering 907 *gratitude;* sin-offering, victim, scapegoat 150 *substitute;* burnt offering, holocaust; sacrifice, devotion; immolation, hecatomb 362 *slaughter;* human sacrifice 362 *homicide;* self-sacrifice, self-devotion 931 *disinterestedness;* self-immolation, suttee 362 *suicide;* expiation, propitiation 941 *atonement;* a humble and a contrite heart 939 *penitence.*

public worship, common prayer, intercommunion; agape, love-feast; service, divine service, divine office, mass, matins, evensong, benediction 988 *church service;* psalm-singing, psalmody, hymn-singing 412 *vocal music;* church, church-going, chapel-g. 979 *piety;* meeting for prayer, gathering for worship 74 *assembly*; prayer meeting, revival m.; open-air service, mission s., street evangelism, revivalism; temple worship, state religion 973 *religion*.

worshipper, fellow w., coreligionist 976 *church member*; adorer, venerator; votary, devotee, oblate 979 *pietist*; glorifier, hymner, praiser, idolizer, admirer, ardent a., humble a. 923 *commender*; follower, server 742 *servant*; image-worshipper, iconolater 982 *idolater*; sacrificer, offerer 781 *giver*; invocator, invoker, caller 583 *allocution*; supplicator, supplicant, suppliant 763 *petitioner*; man *or* woman of prayer, beadsman, intercessor; contemplative, mystic, Sufi, visionary; dervish, marabout, enthusiast, revivalist, prophet 973 *religious teacher*; celebrant, officiant 986 *clergy*; communicant, churchgoer, chapelgoer, temple worshipper; congregation, the faithful 976 *church member*; psalm-singer, hymn-s., psalmodist, chanter, cantor; psalmist, hymn-writer, hymnologist 988 *ritualist*; pilgrim, palmer, hajji 268 *traveller*.

Adj. *worshipping*, - adoring etc. vb.; worshipping falsely 982 *idolatrous*; devout, devoted 979 *pious*; reverent, reverential 920 *respectful*; prayerful, fervent 761 *supplicatory*; meditating, praying, interceding; in the act of worship, communicating; kneeling, on one's knees; at one's prayers, at one's devotions, in retreat; regular in worship, church-going, chapel-g., communicant 976 *orthodox*; participating in worship, hymn-singing, psalm-s.; celebrating, officiating, ministering 988 *ritualistic*; mystic, mystical.

devotional, appertaining to worship 988 *ritualistic*; worshipful, solemn, sacred, holy 979 *sanctified*; revered, worshipped 920 *respected*; sacramental, mystic, mystical; invocatory; precatory, intercessory, petitionary 761 *supplicatory*; imprecatory 899 *maledictory*; sacrificial; oblationary, votive, ex voto 759 *offering*; doxological, giving glory, praising 923 *approving*.

Vb. *worship*, honour, revere, venerate, adore 920 *respect*; honour and obey 854 *fear*; do worship to, pay homage to, acknowledge 917 *do one's duty*; pay divine honours to, make a god of one, deify, apotheosize 982 *idolatrize*; bow down before, kneel to, genuflect, humble oneself, prostrate o. 872 *be humbled*; lift up one's heart, bless, give thanks 907 *thank*; extol, laud, magnify, glorify, give glory to, doxologize 923 *praise*; hymn, anthem, celebrate 413 *sing*; light candles to, burn incense before; call on, invoke, address 583 *speak to*; petition, beseech, supplicate, intercede, make intercession, pray over 761 *entreat*; pray, say a prayer, say one's prayers, recite the rosary, tell one's beads; meditate, contemplate, commune with God 979 *be pious*.

offer worship, celebrate, officiate, minister, administer the sacraments 988 *perform ritual*; lead the congregation, lead in prayer; sacrifice, make s., offer up 781 *give*; sacrifice to, propitiate, appease 719 *pacify*; vow, make vows 764 *promise*; praise not only with one's lips, live a life of praise; dedicate, consecrate 979 *sanctify*; take vows, enter holy orders 986 *take orders*; go on a pilgrimage 267 *travel*; go to church, go to chapel, go to meeting, meet for prayer 979 *be pious*; go to service, hear Mass, take the sacraments, receive the Eucharist, communicate, take Holy Communion, share in the Lord's Supper; fast, observe Lent 946 *starve*; deny oneself, practise asceticism 945 *be ascetic*; go into retreat 449 *meditate*; chant psalms, sing hymns, sing praises, carol 413 *sing*; shout halleluja, doxologize 923 *praise*.

Int. Alleluia! Halleluja! Hosanna! Glory be to God! Holy, Holy, Holy! Lift up your hearts, Sursum Corda! Lord, have mercy, Kyrie Eleison! Our Father; Lord, bless us! God save!

See: 74, 150, 267, 268, 300, 362, 412, 413, 449, 547, 583, 719, 742, 759, 761, 762, 763, 764, 781, 854, 866, 872, 883, 899, 900, 907, 917, 920, **923**, 931, 939, 941, 945, 946, 973, 976, 979, 982, 986, **988**.

982 Idolatry

N. *idolatry*, idolatrousness, false worship, superstition 981 *worship*; heathenism, paganism 973 *religion*; fetishism, anthropomorphism, zoomorphism; iconolatry, image worship; idolism, idol worship, idolomania; idolomancy, mumbo jumbo, hocus-pocus 983 *sorcery*; cult, cargo c.; sacrifice, human s. 981 *oblation*; heliolatry, sun worship; star worship, Sabaism; pyrolatry, fire worship; zoolatry, animal worship; ophiolatry, snake worship; necrolatry, demonolatry, devil worship 969 *diabolism*; Mammonism, worship of wealth; bibliolatry, ecclesiolatry.

deification, god-making, apotheosis; idolization, hero worship 920 *respect*; king worship, emperor w. 981 *worship*.

idol, statue 554 *sculpture*; image, graven i., molten i.; cult image, fetish, totem pole; linga, yoni; golden calf 966 *deity*; godling, joss; teraphim, lares et penates, totem; Mumbo-Jumbo; Juggernaut, Baal, Moloch.

idolater, idolatress; idol-worshipper, idolatrizer; anthropomorphite; fetishist, totemist; iconolater, image-worshipper 981 *worshipper*; heliolater, sun-worshipper; pyrolater, fire-worshipper; bibliolater, ecclesiolater 979 *pietist*; Mammonist, Mammon-worshipper; demonolater, demonist, devil-worshipper 969 *diabolist*; pagan, heathendom 974 *heathen*; idolizer, deifier 923 *commender*; idol-maker, image-m., maker of graven images.

Adj. *idolatrous*, pagan, heathen 974 *heathenish*; fetishistic; anthropomorphic, theriomorphic; fire-worshipping, sun-w., star-w.; devil-worshipping 969 *diabolic*.

Vb. *idolatrize*, worship idols, worship the golden calf, bow down to a graven image; anthropomorphize, make God in one's own image; deify, apotheosize 979 *sanctify*; idealize, idolize, put on a pedestal 923 *praise*; heathenize 974 *paganize*.

Adv. *idolatrously*, heathenishly.

See: 554, 920, 923, 966, 969, 973, 974, 979, **981**, **983**.

983 Sorcery

N. *sorcery*, spellbinding, witchery, magic arts, enchantments; witchcraft, sortilege; Magianism, gramarye, magic lore 490 *knowledge*; wizardry, magic skill 694 *skill*; wonder-working, miracle-mongering 864 *thaumaturgy*; magic, jugglery, illusionism 542 *sleight*; sympathetic magic, influence 612 *inducement*; white magic, theurgy; black magic, black art, necromancy, diablerie 969 *diabolism*; priestcraft, superstition, witch-doctoring, shamanism; obeah, obi, voodooism, voodoo, hoodoo; psychomancy, spirit-raising 511 *divination*, 984 *occultism*; spirit-laying, ghost-l., exorcism 988 *rite*; magic rite, conjuration, invocation, incantation; ghost dance; coven, witches' sabbath, witches' coven; Walpurgisnacht, Hallowe'en; witching hour.

spell, charm, enchantment, cantrip, hoodoo, curse; evil eye, jinx, hex, influence; bewitchment, fascination 291 *attraction*; obsession, possession, demoniacal p., bedevilment, nympholepsy; Dionysiac frenzy 503 *frenzy*; incantation, rune; magic sign, pass; magic word, magic formula, abraxas, open sesame, abracadabra; hocus pocus, mumbo jumbo, fee faw fum 515 *lack of meaning*; philtre, love potion (**see** *magic instrument*).

talisman, charm, countercharm; cross, phylactery; St Christopher medal 662 *safeguard*; juju, obeah, fetish 982 *idol*; periapt, amulet, mascot, lucky charm; luck-bringer, hare's foot, four-leaf clover, horseshoe, black cat; pentacle, pentagram 547 *indication*; swastika, fylfot, gammadion; scarab; birthstone; emblem, flag, national f.; relic, holy r.; palladium 662 *refuge*.

magic instrument, bell, book and candle, wizard's cap, witches' broomstick; magic recipe, witches' brew, hell-broth, witches' cauldron; philtre, potion, moly; wand, fairy w.; magic ring, wishing cap; Aladdin's lamp, purse of Fortunatus, peau de chagrin; magic mirror, magic sword, flying carpet; seven-league boots; Excalibur; cap of darkness, cloak of invisibility; wish-fulfiller, wishing well, wishbone, merrythought; divining rod 484 *detector*.

sorcerer, wise man, seer, soothsayer, Chaldean, sortileger 511 *diviner*; astrologer, alchemist 984 *occultist*; Druid, Druidess; magus, mage, Magian, the Magi; thaumaturgist, wonder-worker, miracle-w. 864 *thaumaturgy*; shaman, witchdoctor, medicine man, fetishist 982 *idolater*; obeah man, voodooist, hoodooist, spirit-raiser 984 *occultist*; conjuror, exorcist; charmer, snake-c.; juggler, illusionist 545 *conjuror*; spellbinder, enchanter, wizard, warlock; magician, theurgist; necromancer 969 *diabolist*; familiar, imp, evil spirit 969 *devil*; sorcerer's apprentice; Merlin, Prospero, Gandalf; Faust, Pied Piper.

sorceress, wise woman, sibyl 511 *diviner*; enchantress, witch, weird sister; hag, hell-cat; succubus, succuba; lamia; fairy godmother, wicked fairy, Morgan le Fay 970 *fairy*; Witch of Endor, Hecate, Circe, Medea.

Adj. *sorcerous*, sortilegious; wizardly, witch-like; Circean; magician, Chaldean;

thaumaturgic 864 *wonderful*; theurgical; necromantic 969 *diabolic*; shamanistic, voodooistic; spell-like, incantatory, runic; conjuring, spirit-raising; witching, spellbinding, enchanting, fascinating 291 *attracting*; malignant, blighting, blasting, withering, casting the evil eye, overlooking 898 *maleficent*; occult, esoteric 984 *cabbalistic*.

magical, witching; otherworldly, supernatural, uncanny, eldritch, weird 970 *fairylike*; talismanic, phylacteric 660 *tutelary*; having magic power, magic, charmed, enchanted 178 *influential*.

bewitched, witched, ensorcelled, tranced, enchanted, charmed, becharmed, fey; hypnotized, fascinated, spellbound, under a spell, under a charm; overlooked, under the evil eye; under a curse, cursed; blighted, blasted, withered; hag-ridden, haunted, beghosted.

Vb. *practise sorcery*, - witchcraft etc. n.; cast horoscopes, cast a nativity 511 *divine*; do magic, weave spells; make wax effigies; speak mystically, recite a spell, recite an incantation, say the magic word, make passes; conjure, invoke, call up; raise spirits, command s.; exorcize, lay ghosts; wave a wand, rub the magic ring; put on seven-league boots; ride a broomstick.

bewitch, witch, charm, becharm, enchant, fascinate 291 *attract*; hypnotize; magic, magic away; spellbind, cast a spell on, lay under a spell; hoodoo, voodoo; overlook, cast the evil eye, blight, blast 898 *be malevolent*; put a curse on, lay under a curse 899 *curse*; lay under a ban, taboo, make t. 757 *prohibit*; hag-ride, walk, ghost 970 *haunt*.

Adv. *sorcerously*, by means of enchantment; as under a spell.

See: 178, 291, 484, 490, 503, **511**, 515, 542, 545, 547, 612, 660, 662, 694, 757, 864, 898, 899, 969, 970, 982, **984**, 988.

984 Occultism

N. *occultism*, esotericism, hermeticism, mysticism, transcendentalism 973 *religion*; mystical interpretation, cabbalism, cabbala, gematria; theosophy, reincarnationism; yogism; sciosophy, hyperphysics, metapsychics; supernaturalism, psychicism, pseudopsychology; secret art, esoteric science, occult lore, alchemy, astrology, psychomancy, spiritualism, magic 983 *sorcery*; sortilege 511 *divination*; fortune-telling, crystal-gazing, palmistry, chiromancy 511 *prediction*; clairvoyance, second sight 438 *vision*; sixth sense 476 *intuition*; animal magnetism, mesmerism, hypnotism; hypnosis, hypnotic trance 375 *insensibility*.

psychics, parapsychology, psychism 447 *psychology*; psychic science, psychical research; paranormal perception, extrasensory p., ESP; telaesthesia, clairaudience, clairvoyance, second sight 476 *intuition*; psychokinesis, fork-bending; telepathy, telergy; thought-reading, mind-r., thought transference; precognition, psi faculty; déjà vu.

spiritualism, spiritism; spirit communication, psychomancy 983 *sorcery*; sciomancy 511 *divination*; mediumism, mediumship; séance, sitting; astral body, spirit b., ethereal b. 320 *immateriality*; spirit manifestation, materialization, ectoplasm 319 *materiality*; apport, telekinesis; poltergeists; spirit-rapping, table-tapping, table-turning; automatism, automatic writing, spirit w., psychography 586 *writing*; spirit message, psychogram; spiritualistic apparatus, psychograph, planchette, ouija board; control 970 *ghost*; ghost-hunting; psychical research.

occultist, mystic, transcendentalist, supernaturalist; esoteric, cabbalist; reincarnationist; theosophist, yogi; spiritualist, believer in spiritualism; Rosicrucian; alchemist 983 *sorcerer*; astrologer, fortune-teller, crystal-gazer, palmist 511 *diviner*; Cagliostro, Dr Dee, Friar Bungay, Mesmer.

psychic, clairvoyant, clairaudient; telepath, telepathist; mind reader, thought r.; mesmerist, hypnotist; medium, spirit-rapper, automatist, psychographer, spirit-writer; seer, prophet 511 *oracle*; dowser, water diviner 484 *detector*.

psychist, parapsychologist, metapsychologist, psychophysicist, psychical researcher.

Adj. *cabbalistic*, esoteric, hermetic, cryptic, hidden 523 *occult*; dark, mysterious 491 *unknown*; mystic, transcendental, supernatural 973 *religious*; theosophical, reincarnational; Rosicrucian; astrological, alchemic, necromantic 983 *sorcerous*; ghosty, poltergeistish 970 *spooky*.

psychical, psychic, fey, second-sighted; prophetic 511 *predicting*; telepathic, clairvoyant, clairaudient; thought-reading, mind-r.; spiritualistic, mediumistic; ectoplasmic, telekinetic, spirit-rapping; mesmeric, hypnotic.

paranormal, parapsychological, metapsychological, supernatural, preternatural, hyperphysical, supranormal, supranatural.

Vb. *practise occultism*, mysticize, theosophize; cabbalize; alchemize 147 *transform*; astrologize 511 *divine*; hypnotize, mesmerize; practise spiritualism, dabble in s.; hold a séance; practise mediumship, have a control, go into a trance, rap tables, write spirit messages; materialize, dematerialize; study spiritualism, engage in psychical research.

See: 147, 319, 320, 375, 438, 447, 476, 484, 491, **511**, 523, 586, **970**, 973, **983**.

985 The Church

N. *the church*, churchdom, pale of the church 976 *Christendom*; priestly government, hierocracy, theocracy 733 *authority*; the elect, priestly nation, kingdom of priests; church government, Canterbury, Vatican 733 *government*; ecclesiastical order, hierarchy 60 *order*; papalism, papacy, popedom; popishness, ultramontanism; prelatism, prelacy; archiepiscopacy, episcopacy, episcopalianism; presbytery, presbyterianism, congregationalism, independence 978 *sectarianism*; ecclesiology, ecclesiologist.

ecclesiasticism, clericalism, sacerdotalism; priestliness, priesthood, brahmanhood; priestdom, priestcraft; Brahmanism; ecclesiastical privilege, benefit of clergy 919 *nonliability*; ecclesiastical censorship, Holy Office, Index Expurgatorius 757 *prohibition*.

monasticism, monastic life, monachism 895 *celibacy*; cenobitism 883 *seclusion*; monkhood, monkishness 945 *asceticism*.

church ministry, ecclesiastical vocation, call, call to the ministry 622 *vocation*; apostleship, apostolate, mission, overseas m., inner-city m. 147 *conversion*; working priesthood, industrial p. 775 *participation*; pastorate, pastorship, cure, cure of souls; spiritual comfort, spiritual leadership 901 *philanthropy*; spiritual guidance, confession, absolution 988 *ministration*; preaching, homiletics 534 *teaching*.

holy orders, orders, minor o. 986 *cleric*; apostolic succession, ordination, consecration; induction, reading in; installation, enthronement; nomination, presentation, appointment 751 *commission*; preferment, translation, elevation 285 *progression*.

church office 689 *management*; ecclesiastical rank; priesthood; apostolate, apostleship; pontificate, papacy, Holy See, Vatican; cardinalate, cardinalship; patriarchate, exarchate, metropolitanate; primacy, primateship; archiepiscopate, archbishopric; see, bishopric, episcopate, episcopacy, prelacy, prelature; abbotship, abbacy, abbotric; priorate, priorship; archdeaconry, archdeaconate, archdeaconship; deanery, deanship; canonry, canonicate; prebendaryship; deaconate, deaconship; diaconate, subdiaconate; presbyterate, presbytership, eldership, moderatorship, ministership, pastorship, pastorate; rectorship, vicarship, vicariate; curacy, cure of souls; chaplainship, chaplaincy, chaplainry; incumbency, tenure, benefice 773 *possession*.

parish, deanery; presbytery; diocese, bishopric, see, archbishopric; metropolitanate, patriarchate, province 184 *district*.

benefice, incumbency, tenure; living, rectorship, parsonage; glebe, tithe; prebend, prebendal stall, canonry; temporalities, church lands, church endowments 777 *property*; patronage, advowson, right of presentation.

synod, provincial s., convocation, general council, ecumenical c. 692 *council*; college of cardinals, consistory, conclave; bench of bishops, episcopal bench; chapter, vestry; kirk session, presbytery, synod, Sanhedrin 956 *tribunal*; consistorial court, Court of Arches 956 *ecclesiastical court*.

Adj. *ecclesiastical*, ecclestiastic, churchly, ecclesiological, theocratic; infallible 733 *authoritative*; hierocratic, priest-ridden, ultramontane 976 *orthodox*; apostolic; hierarchical, pontifical, papal 976 *Roman Catholic*; patriarchal, metropolitan; archiepiscopal, episcopal, prelatic, prelatical 986 *clerical*; episcopalian, presbyterian 978 *sectarian*; prioral, abbatial; conciliar, synodic, presbyteral, capitular; Sanhedral, consistorial; provincial, diocesan, parochial.

priestly, sacerdotal, hieratic, Aaronic, Levitical; Brahmanic; sacramental, spiritual; ministering, apostolic, pastoral.

Vb. *be ecclesiastical*, be churchly, - priestly

etc. adj.; episcopize, prelatize; frock, ordain, order, consecrate, enthrone; cowl, tonsure, make a monk of; call, confer, nominate, present; benefice, prefer, bestow a living 781 *give*; translate 272 *transfer*; elevate 285 *promote*; beatify, canonize, saint 979 *sanctify*; enter the church 986 *take orders*.

Adv. *ecclesiastically*, church-wise.

See: 60, 147, 184, 272, 285, 534, 622, 689, 692, 733, 751, 757, 773, 775, 777, 781, 883, 895, 901, 919, 945, 956, 976, 978, 979, **986**, 988.

986 Clergy

N. *clergy*, hierarchy; clerical order, parsondom, the cloth, the pulpit, the ministry; sacerdotal order, priesthood, secular clergy, regular clergy, religious.

cleric, clerical; clerk in holy orders, priest, deacon, subdeacon, acolyte, exorcist, lector, ostiary; churchman *or* -woman, ecclesiastic, divine; Doctor of Divinity; clergyman, man *or* woman of the cloth, minister of the Gospel, servant of God; reverend, father, father in God; padre, sky pilot, Holy Joe; beneficed clergyman, beneficiary, pluralist, parson, rector, incumbent, residentiary 776 *possessor*; hedge-priest, priestling 639 *nonentity*; ordinand, seminarist 538 *learner*.

pastor, shepherd, father in God, minister, woman m., parish priest, curé, rector, vicar, perpetual curate, curate, abbé; chaplain; confessor, father c., penitentiary; spiritual director, spiritual adviser; pardoner; friar; preaching order, predicant; pulpiteer, lay preacher 537 *preacher*; field preacher, missioner, missionary 901 *philanthropist*; evangelist, revivalist, salvationist, hot-gospeller.

ecclesiarch, ecclesiastical potentate, hierarch, dignitary 741 *governor*; pope, Supreme Pontiff, Holy Father, Vicar of Christ, Bishop of Rome; cardinal, prince of the church; patriarch, exarch, metropolitan, primate, archbishop; prelate, diocesan, bishop; suffragan, assistant bishop, 'episcopal curate'; bench of bishops, episcopate, Lords Spiritual; archpriest, archpresbyter; archdeacon, deacon, subdeacon; dean, subdean, rural dean; canon, canon regular, canon secular, residentiary; prebendary, capitular; archimandrite; Superior, Mother S.; abbot, abbess; prior, prioress, Grand Prior; elder, presbyter, moderator.

monk, monastic 895 *celibate*; hermit, cenobite, Desert Father 883 *solitary*; Orthodox monk, caloyer; Islamic monk, santon, marabout; Sufi 979 *pietist*; dervish, fakir 945 *ascetic*; Buddhist monk, pongye, bonze; brother, regular, conventual; superior, archimandrite, abbot, prior; novice, lay brother; friar, begging f., mendicant f., discalced f., barefoot f.; monks, religious; fraternity, brotherhood, lay b., friary; order, religious o. 708 *community*; Black Monk, Benedictine, Cistercian, Bernardine, Trappist; Carthusian; Cluniac; Gilbertine; Premonstratensian, Mathurin, Trinitarian; Dominicans, Friars Majors, Black Friars; Franciscans, Poverelli, Grey Friars, Friars Minors, Capuchins; Augustines, Austin Friars; Carmelites, White Friars; Crutched Friars; Beghards; teaching order, missionary o., Society of Jesus, Jesuits; crusading order, Templars, Knights Templars; Hospitallers, Knights Hospitallers, Knights of the Hospital of St John of Jerusalem, Knights of Malta.

nun, clergywoman; anchoress, recluse; religious, bride of Christ; sister, mother; novice, postulant; lay sister; Superioress, Mother Superior, abbess, prioress, canoness, deaconess; sisterhood, lay s., beguinage, Beguine; Carmelites, Ursulines, Poor Clares, Little Sisters of the Poor, Sisters of Mercy.

church officer, elder, presbyter, deacon 741 *officer*; priest, chantry p., chaplain; curate in charge, minister; lay preacher, lay reader; acolyte, server, altar boy; crucifer, thurifer 988 *ritualist*; chorister, choirboy, precentor, succentor, cantor 413 *choir*; sidesman *or* -woman; churchwarden; clerk, vestry c., parish c.; beadle, verger, pew-opener; sacristan, sexton; grave digger, bellringer.

priest, chief p., high p., archpriest, hierophant; priestess, vestal, Pythia, Pythoness, prophetess, prophet 511 *oracle*; Levite; rabbi; imam, mufti; Brahman; bonze, lama, Dalai L., Panchen L.; pontifex, pontiff, flamen, archflamen; Druid, Druidess; shaman, witch doctor.

church title, Holy Father; Eminence; Monsignor, Monseigneur; Lordship, Lord Spiritual; Most Reverend, Right R., Very R.; the Reverend; parson, rector, vicar; father, brother, Dom; mother, sister.

monastery, monkery, bonzery, lamasery; friary; priory, abbey; cloister, convent, nunnery, beguinage; ashram, hermitage 192 *retreat*; community house 192 *abode*; theological college, seminary 539 *training school*; cell 194 *chamber*.

parsonage, presbytery, rectory, vicarage; manse; deanery, archdeaconry 192 *abode*; palace, bishop's p., patriarchate; Lambeth, Vatican; close, cathedral c., precincts 235 *enclosure*.

Adj. *clerical*, in orders, in holy o.; regular; secular; ordained, consecrated; gaitered, aproned, mitred 989 *vestured*; prebendal, beneficed, pluralistic; unbeneficed, glebeless, lay; parsonical, rectorial, vicarial; pastoral, ministerial, presbyteral, sacerdotal 985 *priestly*; diaconal, subdiaconal, archidiaconal, prelatical, episcopal 985 *ecclesiastical*.

monastic, monasterial, cloistral, cloisterly; cloistered, conventual, enclosed 232 *circumscribed*; monkish, monachic, celibate 895 *unwedded*; contemplative, in retreat; cowled, veiled 989 *vestured*; tonsured, shaven and shorn.

Vb. *take orders*, be ordained, enter the church, enter the ministry, wear the cloth; take vows, take the tonsure, take the cowl; take the veil, become a nun; enter a monastery *or* a nunnery, renounce the world.

Adv. *clerically*, parsonically.

See: 192, 194, 232, 235, 413, 511, 537, 538, 539, 639, 708, 741, 776, 883, 895, 901, 945, 979, **985**, 988, 989.

987 Laity

N. *laity*, temporalty, lay people, people, civilians 869 *commonalty*; cure, charge, parish; flock, sheep, fold; diocesans, parishioners; brethren, congregation, society 976 *church member*; lay brethren, lay sisterhood, lay community 708 *community*; the profane, the worldly.

secularity, laicity; laicization, secularization, deconsecration.

lay person, laic; lay rector, lay deacon; lay brother, lay sister; catechumen, ordinand, seminarist, novice, postulant 538 *learner*; lay preacher, lay reader; elder, deacon, deaconess 986 *church officer*; parishioner, diocesan, member of the flock 976 *church member*; laicizer, secularizer.

Adj. *laical*, congregational, parochial; laic, lay, nonclerical, nonpriestly, unordained, not in orders; nonecclesiastical, unclerical, unpriestly, secular; temporal, in the world, of the w., nonreligious 974 *irreligious*; profane, unholy, unconsecrated; laicized, secularized, deconsecrated.

Vb. *laicize*, secularize, undedicate, deconsecrate.

See: 538, 708, 869, 974, **976**, 986.

988 Ritual

N. *ritual*, procedure, way of doing things, method 624 *way*; prescribed procedure, due order 60 *order*; form, order, liturgy 610 *practice*; symbolization, symbolism 519 *metaphor*; ceremonial, ceremony 875 *formality*.

ritualism, ceremonialism, ceremony, formalism; liturgics.

rite, mode of worship 981 *cult*; institution, observance, ritual practice 610 *practice*; form, order, ordinance, rubric, formula, formulary 693 *precept*; ceremony, solemnity, sacrament, mystery 876 *celebration*; rites, mysteries 551 *representation*; initiatory rite, rite of passage, circumcision, initiation, baptism 299 *reception*; christening (**see** *Christian rite*); non-Christian rites, salat, puja.

ministration, functioning, officiation, performance 676 *action*; administration, celebration, solemnization; the pulpit, sermon, address, preaching 534 *teaching*; homily 534 *lecture*; sacred rhetoric, homiletics 579 *oratory*; pastorship, pastoral care, cure of souls; pastoral epistle, pastoral letter; confession, auricular c.; shrift, absolution, penance.

Christian rite, rites of the Church; sacrament, the seven sacraments; baptism, infant b., christening 299 *reception*; immersion, total i. 303 *immersion*; affusion 341 *moistening*; laying on of hands, confirmation, First Communion; Holy Communion, Eucharist, reservation of the sacraments; penitential rites 941 *penance*; absolution 960 *acquittal*; Holy Matrimony 894 *marriage*; Holy Orders 985 *the church*; Holy Unction, chrism; visitation of the sick, extreme unction, last rites, viaticum; burial of the dead; requiem mass; liturgy, order of service, order of baptism, marriage service, solemnization of matrimony, nuptial mass; churching of women; ordination, ordering of deacons, ordering of priests; consecration, consecration of bishops; exorcism

300 *ejection*; excommunication, ban, bell, book and candle; canonization, beatification 866 *dignification*; dedication, undedication.

Holy Communion, Eucharist, Blessed E.; mass, high m., missa solemnis; sung m., missa cantata; low mass; public mass, private m.; communion, the Lord's Supper; preparation, confession, asperges; service of the book, introit, the Kyries, the Gloria, the Lesson, the Gradual, the Collects, the Gospel, the creed; service of the Altar, the offertory, offertory sentence, offertory prayers, the biddings; the blessing, the thanksgiving, Sursum Corda, Preface, Sanctus, Great Amen; the breaking of the bread, the commixture; the Pax; consecration; elevation of the Host; Agnus Dei; the Communion; kiss of peace; prayers of thanksgiving, the dismissal; the blessing.

the sacrament, the Holy Sacrament, the Blessed Eucharist; Corpus Christi, body and blood of Christ; real presence, transubstantiation, consubstantiation, impanation; the elements, bread and wine, altar bread; consecrated bread, host; reserved sacrament; viaticum.

church service, office, duty, service 981 *act of worship*; liturgy, celebration, concelebration; canonical hours, matins, lauds, prime, terce, sext, none, vespers, compline; the little hours; morning prayer, matins; evening prayer, evensong, benediction; Tenebrae; vigil, midnight mass, watchnight service; devotional service, three-hour s.; novena.

ritual act, symbolic act, sacramental, symbolism 551 *representation*; lustration, purification 648 *cleansing*; thurification, incense-burning 338 *vaporization*; sprinkling, aspersion, asperges 341 *moistening*; circumambulation 314 *circuition*; procession 285 *progression*; stations of the Cross 981 *act of worship*; obeisance, bowing, kneeling, genuflexion, prostration, homage 920 *respects*; crossing oneself, signation, sign of the cross 547 *gesture*; Eucharistic rite, breaking the bread; intinction; elevating of the Host; kiss of peace.

ritual object, cross, rood, Holy Rood, crucifix; altar, Lord's table, communion t.; altar furniture, altar cloth, candle, candlestick; communion wine, communion bread; cup, chalice, Grail, Holy Grail, Sangrail; cruet; paten, ciborium, pyx, pyx chest, tabernacle; monstrance, chrism, chrismatory; collection plate, salver; incense, incensory, censer, thurible; holy water; aspergillum; aspersorium; piscina; sacring bell, Sanctus bell; font, baptismal f., baptistery; baptismal garment, chrisom, christening gown; wedding garment, bridal veil, wedding ring; devotional object, relics, sacred relics; reliquary, shrine, casket 194 *box*; icon, Pietà, Holy Sepulchre, stations of the Cross 551 *image*; osculatory, pax; Agnus Dei, rosary, beads, beadroll 981 *prayers*; votive candle; non-Christian objects, Ark of the Covenant, Mercy-seat; seven-branched candlestick; shewbread; laver; hyssop; sackcloth and ashes; libation dish, patina; joss stick; prayer wheel; altar of incense; urim, thummim; temple veil.

ritualist, ceremonialist, sabbatarian, formalist; liturgist, litanist; sacramentarian, sacramentalist; celebrant, minister 986 *priest*; server, acolyte; thurifer; crucifer, processionist.

office-book, service-b., ordinal, lectionary; liturgy, litany; formulary, rubric, canon 693 *precept*; book of hours, breviary; missal, mass-book; prayer book, Book of Common Prayer, Alternative Service Book 981 *prayers*; beads, rosary.

hymnal, hymn book, choir b.; psalter, psalm-book, book of psalms 981 *hymn*.

holy day, feast, feast day, festival 837 *festivity*; fast day, meatless d. 946 *fast*; high day, day of observance, day of obligation 876 *celebration*; Sabbath, Sabbath-day, day of rest 681 *leisure*; Lord's Day, Sunday; saint's day 141 *anniversary*; All Hallows, All Saints, All Souls, Lady Day, Feast of the Annunciation; Candlemas, Feast of the Purification; Feast of the Assumption; Lammas, Martinmas, Michaelmas; Advent; Christmas, Christmastide, Yuletide, Noel, Nativity, Epiphany, Twelfth Night; Lent, Shrove Tuesday, Ash Wednesday, Maundy Thursday, Good Friday; Holy Week, Passion Week; Easter, Eastertide, Easter Sunday; Ascension Day; Whitsuntide, Whitsun, Pentecost; Corpus Christi; Trinity Sunday; Passover; Feast of Weeks, Pentecost; Feast of Tabernacles, Feast of Ingathering; Feast of the Dedication, Hanukkah; Day of Atonement, Yom Kippur; Ramadan, Bairam; Muharram.

Adj.*ritual*, procedural; formal, solemn, ceremonial, liturgical; processional, recessional; symbolic, representational 551 *representing*; sacramental, Eucharistic; chrismal; baptismal; sacrificial, paschal; festal, pentecostal; fasting, Lenten; prescribed, ordained; unleavened; kosher; consecrated, blessed.

ritualistic, ceremonious, ceremonial, formulistic; sabbatarian; observant of ritual, addicted to r.

Vb.*perform ritual*, perform the rites, say office, celebrate, concelebrate, officiate; take the service, lead worship 981 *offer worship*; baptize, christen, confirm, ordain, lay on hands; minister, administer the sacraments, give communion; sacrifice, offer s., make s.; offer prayers, bless, give benediction; anathematize, ban, ban with bell, book and candle; excommunicate, unchurch, unfrock; dedicate, consecrate, deconsecrate; purify, lustrate, asperge; cense, burn incense; anoint, give extreme unction; confess, absolve, pronounce absolution, shrive; take communion, receive the sacraments; bow, kneel, genuflect, prostrate oneself; sign oneself, cross o., make the sign of the cross; take holy water; tell one's beads, say one's rosary; make one's stations; process, go in procession; circumambulate; fast, flagellate oneself, do penance.

ritualize, ceremonialize, institute a rite, organize a cult; sabbatize, sacramentalize, observe, keep, keep holy.

Adv.*ritually*, ceremonially; symbolically, sacramentally; liturgically.

See:60, 141, 194, 285, 299, 300, 303, 314, 338, 341, 519, 534, 547, 551, 579, 610, 624, 648, 676, 681, 693, 837, 866, **875**, **876**, 894, 920, 941, 946, 960, **981**, 985, 986.

989 Canonicals

N.*canonicals*, clericals, clerical dress, cloth, clerical black 228 *dress*; frock, soutane, cassock, scapular; cloak, gown, Geneva g. 228 *cloak*; robe, cowl, hood, capuche; lappet, bands, Geneva b.; clerical collar, dog c.; chimere, lawn sleeves; apron, gaiters, shovel hat; cardinal's hat; priests' cap, biretta, black b., purple b., red b.; skullcap, calotte, zucchetto; Salvation Army bonnet 228 *headgear*; tonsure, shaven crown 229 *bareness*; prayer-cap; tallith.

vestments, ephod, priestly vesture, canonical robes; pontificalia, pontificals; cassock, surplice, rochet; cope, tunicle, dalmatic, alb 228 *robe*; amice, chasuble; stole, deacon's s.; scarf, tippet, pallium; cingulum 47 *girdle*; maniple, fanon; mitre, tiara, triple crown 743 *regalia*; papal vestment, orale; crosier, crook, staff, pastoral s. 743 *badge of rank*; pectoral 222 *cross*; episcopal ring; orphrey *or* orfray, ecclesiastical embroidery 844 *ornamentation*.

Adj.*vestmental*, vestmentary, vestiary; canonical, pontifical.

vestured, robed 228 *dressed*; surpliced, stoled etc. n.; cowled, hooded, veiled 986 *monastic*; gaitered, aproned 986 *clerical*; mitred, crosiered; wearing the triple crown, tiara'd.

See:47, 222, **228**, 229, 743, 844, 986.

990 Temple

N.*temple*, fane, pantheon; shrine, sacellum; joss house, teocalli 982 *idolatry*; house of God, tabernacle, the Temple, House of the Lord; place of worship 981 *worship*; masjid, mosque; house of prayer, oratory; sacred edifice, pagoda, stupa, tope, dagoba, ziggurat 164 *edifice*; torii, toran, gopuram 263 *doorway*.

holy place, holy ground, sacred precinct, temenos; sacrarium, sanctuary, adytum, cella, naos; Ark of the Covenant, Mercy-seat, Sanctum, Holy of Holies, oracle; martyry, sacred tomb, marabout, sepulchre, Holy Sepulchre; graveyard, God's Acre 364 *cemetery*; place of pilgrimage; Holy City, Zion, Jerusalem; Mecca, Benares.

church, house of God; parish church, daughter c., chapel of ease; cathedral, minster, procathedral; basilica; abbey; kirk, chapel, tabernacle, temple, bethel, ebenezer; conventicle, meeting house, prayer h.; house of prayer, oratory, chantry, chantry chapel; synagogue, mosque.

altar, high a., sacrarium, sanctuary; altar stone, altar slab; altar table, Lord's t., communion t.; altar bread 988 *the sacrament*; altar pyx; prothesis, credence, credence table 988 *ritual object*; canopy, baldachin, altarpiece, diptych, triptych, altar screen, reredos; altar cloth, altar frontal, antependium; predella, altar rails.

church utensil, font, baptistry; ambry, stoup, piscina; chalice, paten 988 *ritual object*; pulpit, lectern; Bible, chained B., hymnal, prayer book 981 *prayers*; hassock, kneeler; salver, collection plate, offertory bag; organ, harmonium; bell, church b., carillon 412 *campanology*.

church interior, nave, aisle, apse, ambulatory, transept; chancel, choir, sanctuary; hagioscope, squint; chancel screen, rood screen, jube, rood loft, gallery, organ loft; stall, choir s., sedile, sedilia, misericord; pew, box pew; pulpit, ambo; lectern; chapel, side c., Lady c.; confessional; clerestory, triforium; spandrel; stained glass, stained-glass window, rose w., Jesse w.; calvary, stations of the Cross, Easter sepulchre; baptistry, font; sacristy, vestry; undercroft, crypt, vault; rood, cross, crucifix.

church exterior, porch, narthex, galilee; tympanum 263 *doorway*; tower, steeple, spire 209 *high structure*; bell tower, bell-cote, belfry, campanile; buttress, flying b. 218 *prop*; cloister, ambulatory; chapter house, presbytery 692 *council*; churchyard, kirkyard, lychgate; close 235 *enclosure*.

Adj. *churchlike*, basilican, cathedral-like, cathedralesque; cruciform 222 *crossed*; apsidal 248 *curved*; Romanesque, Norman, Gothic, Early English, Decorated, Perpendicular, baroque, Puginesque, Gothic revival.

See: 164, 209, 218, 222, 235, 248, 263, 364, 412, 692, **981**, 982, 988.

A

a
one 88 adj.
A1
supreme 34 adj.
best 644 adj.
healthy 650 adj.
aback
rearward 238 adv.
abacus
counting instrument 86 n.
abaft
rearward 238 adv.
abandon
exclude 57 vb.
depart 296 vb.
disregard 458 vb.
tergiversate 603 vb.
relinquish 621 vb.
resign 753 vb.
not retain 779 vb.
excitable state 822 n.
merriment 833 n.
rejoicing 835 n.
intemperance 943 n.
sensualism 944 n.
— hope
despair 853 vb.
— one's post
fail in duty 918 vb.
abandoned
remaining 41 adj.
separate 46 adj.
unpossessed 774 adj.
not retained 779 adj.
vicious 934 adj.
abandonment
tergiversation 603 n.
relinquishment 621 n.
submission 721 n.
resignation 753 n.
nonretention 779 n.
excitable state 822 n.
joy 824 n.
rejoicing 835 n.
abase
abase 311 vb.
pervert 655 vb.
abasement
disrepute 867 n.
humiliation 872 n.
humility 872 n.
servility 879 n.
abash
frighten 854 vb.
humiliate 872 vb.
abate
abate 37 vb.
decrease 37 vb.
weaken 163 vb.
moderate 177 vb.
blow 352 vb.
qualify 468 vb.
discount 810 vb.
abatement
diminution 37 n.
contraction 198 n.
relief 831 n.
abattoir
slaughterhouse 362 n.
abbess
ecclesiarch 986 n.
nun 986 n.
abbey
house 192 n.
monastery 986 n.
church 990 n.
abbot
ecclesiarch 986 n.
monk 986 n.
abbotship
church office 985 n.
abbreviate
subtract 39 vb.
shorten 204 vb.
be concise 569 vb.
abstract 592 vb.
abbreviation
smallness 33 n.
diminution 37 n.
contraction 198 n.
word 559 n.
compendium 592 n.
ABC
beginning 68 n.
directory 87 n.
guidebook 524 n.
curriculum 534 n.
letter 558 n.
abdicate
relinquish 621 vb.
be lax 734 vb.
resign 753 vb.
abdication
resignation 753 n.
loss of right 916 n.
abdomen
maw 194 n.
insides 224 n.
abduct
take away 786 vb.
steal 788 vb.
abduction
type of marriage 894 n.
abductor
taker 786 n.
thief 789 n.
abeam
sideways 239 adv.
abed
supine 216 adj.
aberrant
nonuniform 17 adj.
unconformable 84 adj.
erroneous 495 adj.
aberration
abnormality 84 n.
displacement 188 n.
deviation 282 n.
divergence 294 n.
inattention 456 n.
insanity 503 n.
abet
conduce 156 vb.
concur 181 vb.
incite 612 vb.
aid 703 vb.
abetment
inducement 612 n.
cooperation 706 n.
abettor
cause 156 n.
assenter 488 n.
motivator 612 n.
aider 703 n.
colleague 707 n.
abeyance
extinction 2 n.
lull 145 n.
nonuse 674 n.
inaction 677 n.
abhor
not observe 769 vb.
dislike 861 vb.
hate 888 vb.
disapprove 924 vb.
abide
be 1 vb.
continue 108 vb.
last 113 vb.
stay 144 vb.
go on 146 vb.
dwell 192 vb.
be quiescent 266 vb.
be patient 823 vb.
— by
acquiesce 488 vb.
affirm 532 vb.
observe 768 vb.
ability
intrinsicality 5 n.
ability 160 n.
influence 178 n.
possibility 469 n.
intelligence 498 n.
means 629 n.
utility 640 n.
skill 694 n.
ab initio
initially 68 adv.
abject
cowardly 856 adj.
disreputable 867 adj.
servile 879 adj.
contemptible 922 adj.
rascally 930 adj.
abjure
negate 533 vb.
recant 603 vb.
resign 753 vb.
not retain 779 vb.
ablaze
fiery 379 adj.
luminous 417 adj.
able
powerful 160 adj.
possible 469 adj.
intelligent 498 adj.
useful 640 adj.
active 678 adj.
skilful 694 adj.
(See **ability** *)*
able-bodied
stalwart 162 adj.
active 678 adj.
ablegate
envoy 754 n.
able seaman
mariner 270 n.
naval man 722 n.
ablutions
ablutions 648 n.
abnegate
negate 533 vb.
reject 607 vb.
relinquish 621 vb.
abnormal
nonuniform 17 adj.
abnormal 84 adj.
misplaced 188 adj.
deviating 282 adj.
crazy 503 adj.
insane 503 adj.
unexpected 508 adj.
puzzling 517 adj.
funny 849 adj.
wrong 914 adj.
spooky 970 adj.
abnormality
misfit 25 n.
abnormality 84 n.
deformity 246 n.
eccentricity 503 n.
illicit love 951 n.
abnormal psychology
psychology 447 n.
insanity 503 n.
aboard
here 189 adv.
afloat 275 adv.
abode
district 184 n.
station 187 n.
abode 192 n.
abolish
nullify 2 vb.
destroy 165 vb.
abrogate 752 vb.
abolition
revolution 149 n.
destruction 165 n.
abrogation 752 n.
prohibition 757 n.
abolitionist
revolutionist 149 n.
abominable
not nice 645 adj.
unclean 649 adj.
disliked 861 adj.
hateful 888 adj.
heinous 934 adj.
Abominable Snowman
mythical being 970 n.

abominably
extremely 32 adv.
abomination
badness 645 n.
uncleanness 649 n.
dislike 861 n.
hateful object 888 n.
hatred 888 n.
wickedness 934 n.
aboriginal
beginning 68 adj.
primal 127 adj.
native 191 n., adj.
aborigine
earliness 135 n.
humankind 371 n.
abort
suppress 165 vb.
be unproductive 172 vb.
miscarry 728 vb.
abortion
abnormality 84 n.
deformity 246 n.
undevelopment 670 n.
failure 728 n.
eyesore 842 n.
abortive
unproductive 172 adj.
disappointing 509 adj.
profitless 641 adj.
unsuccessful 728 adj.
abound
abound 635 vb.
superabound 637 vb.
(See **abundance** *)*
about
concerning 9 adv.
about 33 adv.
nearly 200 adv.
around 230 adv.
about, be
be near 200 vb.
about to
prospectively 124 adv.
tending 179 adj.
about to be
impending 155 adj.
about-turn
reversion 148 n.
turn round 282 vb.
return 286 n.
tergiversation 603 n.
above
before 64 adv.
aloft 209 adv.
above all
eminently 34 adv.
importantly 638 adv.
above average
superior 34 adj.
above-board
veracious 540 adj.
artless 699 adj.
above-mentioned
preceding 64 adj.
repeated 106 adj.
prior 119 adj.
above par
beyond 34 adv.
excellent 644 adj.
above price
valuable 644 adj.
of price 811 adj.
above suspicion
guiltless 935 adj.
above temptation
virtuous 933 adj.
above the law
lawless 954 adj.
ab ovo
initially 68 adv.
abracadabra
lack of meaning 515 n.
spell 983 n.
abrade
abate 37 vb.
subtract 39 vb.
uncover 229 vb.
pulverize 332 vb.
rub 333 vb.
obliterate 550 vb.
abrasion
wound 655 n.
abrasive
pulverizer 332 n.
rubbing 333 adj.
obliteration 550 n.
abreaction
recuperation 656 n.
liberation 746 n.
feeling 818 n.
abreast
equal 28 adj.
in parallel 219 adv.
sideways 239 adv.
abreast of the times
progressive 285 adj.
abridge
abate 37 vb.
subtract 39 vb.
make smaller 198 vb.
shorten 204 vb.
translate 520 vb.
be concise 569 vb.
abstract 592 vb.
abridgment
edition 589 n.
compendium 592 n.
abroad
abroad 59 adv.
afar 199 adv.
abrogate
nullify 2 vb.
disable 161 vb.
suppress 165 vb.
negate 533 vb.
recant 603 vb.
reject 607 vb.
relinquish 621 vb.
make useless 641 vb.
stop using 674 vb.
liberate 746 vb.
abrogate 752 vb.
prohibit 757 vb.
not observe 769 vb.
not retain 779 vb.
disentitle 916 vb.
make illegal 954 vb.
abrogation
revolution 149 n.
obliteration 550 n.
abrogation 752 n.
abrupt
instantaneous 116 adj.
violent 176 adj.
vertical 215 adj.
sloping 220 adj.
inelegant 576 adj.
sullen 893 adj.
abruptly
unexpectedly 508 adv.
abscess
ulcer 651 n.
abscission
subtraction 39 n.
scission 46 n.
abscond
decamp 296 vb.
run away 620 vb.
escape 667 vb.
not pay 805 vb.
fail in duty 918 vb.
abseil
descend 309 vb.
absence
nonexistence 2 n.
absence 190 n.
farness 199 n.
invisibility 444 n.
avoidance 620 n.
requirement 627 n.
undutifulness 918 n.
absence of mind
abstractedness 456 n.
absent
nonexistent 2 adj.
incomplete 55 adj.
misplaced 188 adj.
absent 190 adj.
disappearing 446 adj.
abstracted 456 adj.
required 627 adj.
unprovided 636 adj.
unused 674 adj.
inactive 679 adj.
lost 772 adj.
undutiful 918 adj.
absenteeism
absence 190 n.
inactivity 679 n.
undutifulness 918 n.
absent-minded
abstracted 456 adj.
forgetful 506 adj.
absent oneself
be absent 190 vb.
depart 296 vb.
disappear 446 vb.
run away 620 vb.
be exempt 919 vb.
absinth, absinthe
alcoholic drink 301 n.
sourness 393 n.
absolute
existing 1 adj.
unrelated 10 adj.
absolute 32 adj.
complete 54 adj.
one 88 adj.
positive 473 adj.
creedal 485 adj.
assertive 532 adj.
authoritative 733 adj.
authoritarian 735 adj.
unconditional 744 adj.
godlike 965 adj.
absolute end
exceller 644 n.
cad 938 n.
absolutely
positively 32 adv.
absolutely it
identity 13 n.
no imitation 21 n.
absolute monarch
autocrat 741 n.
absoluteness
unrelatedness 10 n.
simpleness 44 n.
unity 88 n.
absolute zero
coldness 380 n.
absolution
amnesty 506 n.
liberation 746 n.
forgiveness 909 n.
nonliability 919 n.
acquittal 960 n.
church ministry 985 n.
Christian rite 988 n.
absolutism
despotism 733 n.
brute force 735 n.
absolve
liberate 746 vb.
forgive 909 vb.
exempt 919 vb.
acquit 960 vb.
perform ritual 988 vb.
absorb
add 38 vb.
combine 50 vb.
contain 56 vb.
consume 165 vb.
hold within 224 vb.
absorb 299 vb.
drink 301 vb.

eat 301 vb.
dry 342 vb.
engross 449 vb.
dispose of 673 vb.
appropriate 786 vb.
impress 821 vb.
absorbed
conformable 83 adj.
thoughtful 449 adj.
abstracted 456 adj.
absorbent
admitting 299 adj.
dryer 342 n.
absorbing
felt 818 adj.
exciting 821 adj.
absorption
identity 13 n.
combination 50 n.
reception 299 n.
radiation 417 n.
meditation 449 n.
attention 455 n.
abstain
be unwilling 598 vb.
be neutral 606 vb.
avoid 620 vb.
relinquish 621 vb.
not use 674 vb.
not act 677 vb.
be temperate 942 vb.
abstainer
avoider 620 n.
abstainer 942 n.
ascetic 945 n.
sober person 948 n.
abstemious
temperate 942 adj.
sober 948 adj.
abstention
unwillingness 598 n.
no choice 606 n.
avoidance 620 n.
inaction 677 n.
temperance 942 n.
abstinence
avoidance 620 n.
nonuse 674 n.
temperance 942 n.
abstinent
temperate 942 adj.
fasting 946 adj.
sober 948 adj.
abstract
insubstantial 4 adj.
subtract 39 vb.
shorten 204 vb.
immaterial 320 adj.
mental 447 adj.
philosophic 449 adj.
be concise 569 vb.
description 590 n.
compendium 592 n.
abstract 592 vb.
select 605 vb.
take away 786 vb.
steal 788 vb.
abstract art
art 551 n.
abstracted
thoughtful 449 adj.
abstracted 456 adj.
crazy 503 adj.
forgetful 506 adj.
compendious 592 adj.
abstractedness
thought 449 n.
absence of thought 450 n.
abstractedness 456 n.
frenzy 503 n.
fantasy 513 n.
abstraction
insubstantiality 4 n.
insubstantial thing 4 n.
subtraction 39 n.
disunion 46 n.
separation 46 n.
absence of thought 450 n.
idea 451 n.
abstractedness 456 n.
imperspicuity 568 n.
stealing 788 n.
abstractive
taking 786 adj.
abstruse
puzzling 517 adj.
unclear 568 adj.
absurd
disagreeing 25 adj.
erroneous 495 adj.
absurd 497 adj.
foolish 499 adj.
imaginative 513 adj.
meaningless 515 adj.
exaggerated 546 adj.
useless 641 adj.
laughing 835 adj.
witty 839 adj.
ridiculous 849 adj.
absurdity
insubstantiality 4 n.
ineffectuality 161 n.
argumentation 475 n.
error 495 n.
absurdity 497 n.
ideality 513 n.
lack of meaning 515 n.
fable 543 n.
caprice 604 n.
trifle 639 n.
inutility 641 n.
laughter 835 n.
wit 839 n.
ridiculousness 849 n.
abundance
greatness 32 n.
great quantity 32 n.
abundance 171 n.
store 632 n.
plenty 635 n.
redundance 637 n.
abundant
many 104 adj.
rich 800 adj.
liberal 813 adj.
abuse
force 176 vb.
evil 616 n.
waste 634 vb.
ill-treat 645 vb.
pervert 655 vb.
misuse 675 n.vb.
quarrel 709 n.
be severe 735 vb.
slur 867 n.
be rude 885 vb.
scurrility 899 n.
curse 899 vb.
not respect 921 vb.
dispraise 924 vb.
reprobate 924 vb.
detraction 926 n.
debauch 951 vb.
impiety 980 n.
— one's authority
oppress 735 vb.
abuse of language
misinterpretation 521 n.
neology 560 n.
abusive
quarrelling 709 adj.
ungracious 885 adj.
cursing 899 adj.
threatening 900 adj.
detracting 926 adj.
abut
be near 200 vb.
be contiguous 202 vb.
abutment
contiguity 202 n.
prop 218 n.
abysmal
deep 211 adj.
heinous 934 adj.
abyss
space 183 n.
gap 201 n.
depth 211 n.
cavity 255 n.
pitfall 663 n.
hell 972 n.
academic
irrelevant 10 adj.
intellectual 492 n.
scholar 492 n.
theorist 512 n.
suppositional 512 adj.
educational 534 adj.
studious 536 adj.
academic dress
formal dress 228 n.
academic freedom
freedom 744 n.
academic knowledge
erudition 490 n.
academic title
honours 866 n.
academic title 870 n.
Academy
philosopher 449 n.
academy 539 n.
acanthus
ornamental art 844 n.
accede
approach 289 vb.
assent 488 vb.
consent 758 vb.
— to the throne
take authority 733 vb.
accelerando
adagio 412 adv.
accelerate
augment 36 vb.
be early 135 vb.
be vigorous 174 vb.
accelerate 277 vb.
impel 279 vb.
promote 285 vb.
hasten 680 vb.
animate 821 vb.
accent
sound 398 n.
affirmation 532 n.
emphasize 532 vb.
punctuation 547 n.
dialect 560 n.
pronunciation 577 n.
speech defect 580 n.
prosody 593 n.
accents
voice 577 n.
speech 579 n.
accentuate
manifest 522 vb.
emphasize 532 vb.
accentuation
grammar 564 n.
pronunciation 577 n.
prosody 593 n.
accept
admit 299 vb.
believe 485 vb.
be credulous 487 vb.
acquiesce 488 vb.
assent 488 vb.
choose 605 vb.
submit 721 vb.
consent 758 vb.
give security 767 vb.
receive 782 vb.
take 786 vb.
be hospitable 882 vb.
approve 923 vb.
— an apology
forgive 909 vb.
— a proposal
wed 894 vb.
— responsibility (for)
look after 457 vb.
promise 764 vb.
incur a duty 917 vb.

acceptability
sufficiency 635 n.
sociability 882 n.
acceptable
admitting 299 adj.
rational 475 adj.
advisable 642 adj.
pleasurable 826 adj.
contenting 828 adj.
desired 859 adj.
approvable 923 adj.
acceptance
reception 299 n.
assent 488 n.
connotation 514 n.
consent 758 n.
title deed 767 n.
receiving 782 n.
approbation 923 n.
accepted
credible 485 adj.
usual 610 adj.
orthodox 976 adj.
accepted meaning
connotation 514 n.
accepted reading
interpretation 520 n.
access
bond 47 n.
entrance 68 n.
doorway 263 n.
approach 289 n.
ingress 297 n.
way in 297 n.
outlet 298 n.
reception 299 n.
passage 305 n.
spasm 318 n.
access 624 n.
accessible
near 200 adj.
open 263 adj.
accessible 289 adj.
admitting 299 adj.
possible 469 adj.
communicating 624 adj.
easy 701 adj.
free 744 adj.
accession
increment 36 n.
addition 38 n.
approach 289 n.
arrival 295 n.
authority 733 n.
accessories
dressing 228 n.
accessory
extrinsicality 6 n.
extrinsic 6 adj.
adjunct 40 n.
concomitant 89 n.
accompanying 89 adj.
superfluity 637 n.
trifle 639 n.
aiding 703 adj.
colleague 707 n.
accident
event 154 n.
chance 159 n.
collision 279 n.
evil 616 n.
nondesign 618 n.
misfortune 731 n.
accidental
extrinsic 6 adj.
casual 159 adj.
musical note 410 n.
unintentional 618 adj.
accident-prone
unfortunate 731 adj.
rash 857 adj.
accidie
inertness 175 n.
acclaim
assent 488 vb.
repute 866 n.
honour 866 vb.
applause 923 n.
applaud 923 vb.
acclimatize, acclimatise
make conform 83 vb.
break in 369 vb.
habituate 610 vb.
make ready 669 vb.
acclivity
incline 220 n.
accolade
honours 866 n.
praise 923 n.
accommodate
adjust 24 vb.
equalize 28 vb.
comprise 78 vb.
make conform 83 vb.
place 187 vb.
aid 703 vb.
pacify 719 vb.
lend 784 vb.
— oneself
conform 83 vb.
accommodating
benevolent 897 adj.
accommodation
room 183 n.
quarters 192 n.
storage 632 n.
accompaniment
addition 38 n.
accompaniment 89 n.
concomitant 89 n.
contiguity 202 n.
musical piece 412 n.
accompanist
instrumentalist 413 n.
accompany
accompany 89 vb.
synchronize 123 vb.
concur 181 vb.
follow 284 vb.
play music 413 vb.
serve 742 vb.
court 889 vb.
accomplice
concomitant 89 n.
colleague 707 n.
accomplish
produce 164 vb.
do 676 vb.
carry out 725 vb.
succeed 727 vb.
accomplished
skilful 694 adj.
accomplished fact
certainty 473 n.
accomplishments
culture 490 n.
accord
be related 9 vb.
be identical 13 vb.
be uniform 16 vb.
resemble 18 vb.
agreement 24 n.
accord 24 vb.
be equal 28 vb.
be in order 60 vb.
conform 83 vb.
concur 181 vb.
harmonize 410 vb.
assent 488 vb.
be expedient 642 vb.
concord 710 vb.
permit 756 vb.
consent 758 n.
give 781 vb.
according as
accordingly 8 adv.
provided 468 adv.
according to
agreeing 24 adj.
conformably 83 adv.
according to plan
conformably 83 adv.
purposely 617 adv.
according to rule
orderly 60 adj.
regular 81 adj.
regulated 83 adj.
accordion
organ 414 n.
accost
approach 289 vb.
speak to 583 vb.
request 761 vb.
greet 884 vb.
accouchement
obstetrics 167 n.
account
statistics 86 n.
number 86 vb.
list 87 n.
estimate 480 vb.
opine 485 vb.
report 524 n.
register 548 vb.
correspondence 588 n.
description 590 n.
funds 797 n.
credit 802 n.
debt 803 n.
pay 804 vb.
accounts 808 n.
account 808 vb.
prestige 866 n.
— for
cause 156 vb.
account for 158 vb.
interpret 520 vb.
accountability
liability 180 n.
dueness 915 n.
duty 917 n.
accountancy
numeration 86 n.
registration 548 n.
accounts 808 n.
accountant
enumerator 86 n.
recorder 549 n.
treasurer 798 n.
accountant 808 n.
account book
account book 808 n.
accounts
numeration 86 n.
registration 548 n.
provision 633 n.
credit 802 n.
accounts 808 n.
accoutred
prepared 669 adj.
defended 713 adj.
accoutrements
dressing 228 n.
equipment 630 n.
accredited
credible 485 adj.
creedal 485 adj.
usual 610 adj.
commissioned 751 adj.
accretion
increment 36 n.
addition 38 n.
adjunct 40 n.
extraneousness 59 n.
expansion 197 n.
accrue
be extrinsic 6 vb.
augment 36 vb.
accrue 38 vb.
result 157 vb.
approach 289 vb.
be profitable 771 vb.
be received 782 vb.
accumulate
grow 36 vb.
join 45 vb.
bring together 74 vb.
store 632 vb.
acquire 771 vb.
take 786 vb.
accumulation
great quantity 32 n.
increase 36 n.

medley 43 n.
accumulation 74 n.
collection 632 n.
storage 632 n.
acquisition 771 n.
accuracy
similarity 18 n.
mimicry 20 n.
attention 455 n.
carefulness 457 n.
discrimination 463 n.
accuracy 494 n.
veracity 540 n.
accurate
adjusted 24 adj.
attentive 455 adj.
careful 457 adj.
discriminating 463 adj.
accurate 494 adj.
veracious 540 adj.
descriptive 590 adj.
accursed
bad 645 adj.
damnable 645 adj.
harmful 645 adj.
baneful 659 adj.
unfortunate 731 adj.
unhappy 825 adj.
unpleasant 827 adj.
hateful 888 adj.
cursed 899 adj.
heinous 934 adj.
wicked 934 adj.
profane 980 adj.
accusable
blameworthy 924 adj.
accusable 928 adj.
heinous 934 adj.
guilty 936 adj.
illegal 954 adj.
punishable 963 adj.
accusation
affirmation 532 n.
wrong 914 n.
detraction 926 n.
accusation 928 n.
litigation 959 n.
accuse
attribute 158 vb.
inform 524 vb.
blame 924 vb.
defame 926 vb.
accuse 928 vb.
litigate 959 vb.
— oneself
regret 830 vb.
be penitent 939 vb.
accused, the
prisoner 750 n.
accused person 928 n.
litigant 959 n.
accuser
informer 524 n.
detractor 926 n.
accuser 928 n.
litigant 959 n.
accustom
train 534 vb.
habituate 610 vb.
accustomed
usual 610 adj.
unastonished 865 adj.
ace
unit 88 n.
masterpiece 694 n.
proficient person 696 n.
ace in the hole
advantage 34 n.
acerbity
pungency 388 n.
unsavouriness 391 n.
sourness 393 n.
rudeness 885 n.
resentment 891 n.
malevolence 898 n.
acetous
sour 393 adj.
acetylene
fuel 385 n.
ace up one's sleeve
advantage 34 n.
ache
pang 377 n.
feel pain 377 vb.
give pain 377 vb.
badness 645 n.
suffer 825 vb.
Acheron
mythic hell 972 n.
achievable
possible 469 adj.
achieve
terminate 69 vb.
produce 164 vb.
be instrumental 628 vb.
do 676 vb.
carry out 725 vb.
succeed 727 vb.
— no purpose
be useless 641 vb.
achievement
production 164 n.
progression 285 n.
heraldry 547 n.
deed 676 n.
completion 725 n.
effectuation 725 n.
success 727 n.
Achilles' heel
weakness 163 n.
defect 647 n.
vulnerability 661 n.
moral sensibility 819 n.
aching
pain 377 n.
pained 377 adj.
painful 377 adj.
fatigued 684 adj.
suffering 825 adj.
paining 827 adj.
aching heart
sorrow 825 n.
achromatism
achromatism 426 n.
whiteness 427 n.
acid
destroyer 168 n.
keen 174 adj.
unsavoury 391 adj.
sourness 393 n.
sour 393 adj.
bane 659 n.
poison 659 n.
sullen 893 adj.
drug-taking 949 n.
acidity
pungency 388 n.
sourness 393 n.
acid test
experiment 461 n.
acidulous
sour 393 adj.
ack-ack
ammunition 723 n.
gun 723 n.
acknowledge
attribute 158 vb.
notice 455 vb.
answer 460 vb.
testify 466 vb.
assent 488 vb.
confess 526 vb.
correspond 588 vb.
observe 768 vb.
receive 782 vb.
befriend 880 vb.
greet 884 vb.
thank 907 vb.
grant claims 915 vb.
reward 962 vb.
worship 981 vb.
acknowledged
usual 610 adj.
received 807 adj.
acknowledgment
attribution 158 n.
answer 460 n.
assent 488 n.
disclosure 526 n.
correspondence 588 n.
observance 768 n.
courteous act 884 n.
thanks 907 n.
dueness 915 n.
reward 962 n.
acme
summit 213 n.
acme of perfection
perfection 646 n.
acne
skin disease 651 n.
blemish 845 n.
acolyte
auxiliary 707 n.
church officer 986 n.
cleric 986 n.
ritualist 988 n.
acoustics
acoustics 398 n.
hearing 415 n.
linguist 557 n.
acquaint
inform 524 vb.
acquaintance
knowledge 490 n.
information 524 n.
friend 880 n.
friendship 880 n.
acquainted
knowing 490 adj.
friendly 880 adj.
acquest
acquisition 771 n.
acquiesce
acquiesce 488 vb.
acquiescence
conformity 83 n.
concurrence 181 n.
assent 488 n.
willingness 597 n.
submission 721 n.
obedience 739 n.
resignation 753 n.
permission 756 n.
consent 758 n.
patience 823 n.
content 828 n.
acquiescent
agreeing 24 adj.
inexcitable 823 adj.
acquire
bring together 74 vb.
find means 629 vb.
acquire 771 vb.
receive 782 vb.
borrow 785 vb.
take 786 vb.
purchase 792 vb.
be rewarded 962 vb.
— the habit
habituate 610 vb.
acquired
extrinsic 6 adj.
acquired characteristic
extrinsicality 6 n.
acquired taste
habituation 610 n.
acquirements
culture 490 n.
skill 694 n.
acquisition
assemblage 74 n.
transference 272 n.
benefit 615 n.
acquisition 771 n.
gift 781 n.
receiving 782 n.
taking 786 n.
acquisitive
acquiring 771 adj.
taking 786 adj.
avaricious 816 adj.
greedy 859 adj.
selfish 932 adj.

acquit
deliver 668 vb.
liberate 746 vb.
forgive 909 vb.
do one's duty 917 vb.
exempt 919 vb.
acquit 960 vb.
— oneself
behave 688 vb.
acquittal
escape 667 n.
liberation 746 n.
observance 768 n.
mercy 905 n.
forgiveness 909 n.
duty 917 n.
nonliability 919 n.
vindication 927 n.
innocence 935 n.
legal trial 959 n.
acquittal 960 n.
acquittance
title deed 767 n.
payment 804 n.
acreage
measure 183 n.
acres
land 344 n.
lands 777 n.
acrid
keen 174 adj.
pungent 388 adj.
unsavoury 391 adj.
fetid 397 adj.
acrimonious
ungracious 885 adj.
resentful 891 adj.
acrimony
keenness 174 n.
hatred 888 n.
malevolence 898 n.
acrobat
equilibrium 28 n.
athlete 162 n.
entertainer 594 n.
proficient person 696 n.
acrobatic
athletic 162 adj.
flexible 327 adj.
acrobatics
athletics 162 n.
acronym
initials 558 n.
word 559 n.
across
obliquely 220 adv.
across 222 adv.
across-the-board
general 79 adj.
acrostic
equivocalness 518 n.
enigma 530 n.
initials 558 n.
acrylic fibre
fibre 208 n.
act
imitate 20 vb.
operate 173 vb.
duplicity 541 n.
dissemble 541 vb.
dramaturgy 594 n.
stage show 594 n.
act 594 vb.
function 622 vb.
be instrumental 628 vb.
deed 676 n.
do 676 vb.
behave 688 vb.
precept 693 n.
be successful 727 vb.
decree 737 n.
be affected 850 vb.
— a part
cant 541 vb.
be affected 850 vb.
— for
substitute 150 vb.
deputize 755 vb.
— in one's own worst interests
act foolishly 695 vb.
— the fool
be foolish 499 vb.
— the part of
substitute 150 vb.
represent 551 vb.
— upon
operate 173 vb.
motivate 612 vb.
do 676 vb.
obey 739 vb.
— without authority
please oneself 734 vb.
acted upon
operative 173 adj.
acte gratuit
will 595 n.
acting
ephemeral 114 adj.
substituted 150 adj.
operative 173 adj.
hypocritical 541 adj.
representation 551 n.
acting 594 n.
dramatic 594 adj.
actinism
radiation 417 n.
actinometer
optical device 442 n.
action
event 154 n.
production 164 n.
agency 173 n.
dramaturgy 594 n.
policy 623 n.
action 676 n.
deed 676 n.
activity 678 n.
conduct 688 n.
fight 716 n.
battle 718 n.
effectuation 725 n.
observance 768 n.
accusation 928 n.
litigation 959 n.
actionable
accusable 928 adj.
legal 953 adj.
illegal 954 adj.
activation
stimulation 174 n.
activity 678 n.
activator
alterer 143 n.
stimulant 174 n.
active
eventful 154 adj.
stalwart 162 adj.
operative 173 adj.
vigorous 174 adj.
influential 178 adj.
moving 265 adj.
agitated 318 adj.
willing 597 adj.
businesslike 622 adj.
doing 676 adj.
active 678 adj.
labouring 682 adj.
excited 821 adj.
active member of the community
sociable person 882 n.
active service
warfare 718 n.
activism
action 676 n.
activity 678 n.
activist
trier 671 n.
doer 676 n.
busy person 678 n.
political party 708 n.
activities
pursuit 619 n.
job 622 n.
activity
vigorousness 174 n.
motion 265 n.
agitation 318 n.
business 622 n.
job 622 n.
instrumentality 628 n.
action 676 n.
activity 678 n.
haste 680 n.
workshop 687 n.
act of God
ruin 165 n.
necessity 596 n.
compulsion 740 n.
act of will
will 595 n.
act of worship
act of worship 981 n.
ritual act 988 n.
actor
imitator 20 n.
cinema 445 n.
deceiver 545 n.
actor 594 n.
doer 676 n.
agent 686 n.
dance 837 n.
affecter 850 n.
actor manager
stage manager 594 n.
actress
actor 594 n.
acts
deed 676 n.
Acts of the Apostles
scripture 975 n.
actual
real 1 adj.
present 121 adj.
true 494 adj.
actual fact
event 154 n.
actuality
reality 1 n.
truth 494 n.
actuary
enumerator 86 n.
accountant 808 n.
actuate
operate 173 vb.
influence 178 vb.
move 265 vb.
motivate 612 vb.
acuity
sharpness 256 n.
vision 438 n.
sagacity 498 n.
acumen
discrimination 463 n.
sagacity 498 n.
acupuncture
perforation 263 n.
anaesthetic 375 n.
therapy 658 n.
acute
keen 174 adj.
violent 176 adj.
sharp 256 adj.
sentient 374 adj.
striking 374 adj.
strident 407 adj.
intelligent 498 adj.
cunning 698 adj.
felt 818 adj.
acute accent
punctuation 547 n.
acute angle
angle 247 n.
acute ear
hearing 415 n.
acuteness
sharpness 256 n.
sagacity 498 n.
AD
anno domini 108 adv.
adage
maxim 496 n.
adagio
slowly 278 adv.
tempo 410 n.
adagio 412 adv.

Adam
gardener 370 n.
humankind 371 n.
male 372 n.
Adam and Eve
precursor 66 n.
parentage 169 n.
adamant
obstinate 602 adj.
adamantine
strong 162 adj.
hard 326 adj.
Adam's apple
swelling 253 n.
adapt
adjust 24 vb.
modify 143 vb.
translate 520 vb.
— for radio/the stage
dramatize 594 vb.
— oneself
conform 83 vb.
adaptability
softness 327 n.
adaptable
fit 24 adj.
conformable 83 adj.
useful 640 adj.
skilful 694 adj.
adaptation
adaptation 24 n.
conformity 83 n.
transformation 143 n.
musical piece 412 n.
translation 520 n.
edition 589 n.
adapted to
advisable 642 adj.
adapter
alterer 143 n.
author 589 n.
ad captandum
sophistical 477 adj.
flatteringly 925 adv.
add
augment 36 vb.
add 38 vb.
affix 45 vb.
join 45 vb.
agglutinate 48 vb.
combine 50 vb.
fill 54 vb.
put in front 64 vb.
place after 65 vb.
do sums 86 vb.
modify 143 vb.
enlarge 197 vb.
insert 303 vb.
misinterpret 521 vb.
exaggerate 546 vb.
— fuel to the fire/ flames
make violent 176 vb.
kindle 381 vb.
aggravate 832 vb.
enrage 891 vb.
— insult to injury
aggravate 832 vb.
— up
add 38 vb.
be intelligible 516 vb.
— up to
number 86 vb.
mean 514 vb.
addendum
addition 38 n.
adjunct 40 n.
extra 40 n.
edition 589 n.
adder
reptile 365 n.
bane 659 n.
addict
enthusiast 504 n.
habitué 610 n.
sick person 651 n.
drug-taking 949 n.
addiction
habit 610 n.
intemperance 943 n.
addictive
intoxicating 949 adj.
addition
increase 36 n.
increment 36 n.
addition 38 n.
adjunct 40 n.
mixture 43 n.
joining together 45 n.
whole 52 n.
sequence 65 n.
numerical result 85 n.
numerical operation 86 n.
protraction 113 n.
expansion 197 n.
insertion 303 n.
exaggeration 546 n.
additional
extrinsic 6 adj.
additional 38 adj.
included 78 adj.
superfluous 637 adj.
additive
additional 38 adj.
extra 40 n.
component 58 n.
food content 301 n.
addle
make sterile 172 vb.
distract 456 vb.
be unclean 649 vb.
addled
unproductive 172 adj.
light-minded 456 adj.
unintelligent 499 adj.
addle-head
fool 501 n.
address
place 185 n.
situation 186 n.
locality 187 n.
abode 192 n.
send 272 vb.
oration 579 n.
speech 579 n.
orate 579 vb.
allocution 583 n.
speak to 583 vb.
correspond 588 vb.
way 624 n.
skill 694 n.
— oneself to
begin 60 vb.
prepare 669 vb.
undertake 672 vb.
request 761 vb.
addressee
resident 191 n.
correspondent 588 n.
recipient 782 n.
addresses
reading matter 589 n.
wooing 889 n.
address of welcome
respects 920 n.
adduce
corroborate 466 vb.
manifest 522 vb.
adductive
attracting 291 adj.
adenoids
swelling 253 n.
respiratory disease 651 n.
adept
proficient person 696 n.
adequate
powerful 160 adj.
sufficient 635 adj.
useful 640 adj.
middling 732 adj.
à deux
dual 90 adj.
adhere
accrue 38 vb.
unite with 45 vb.
cohere 48 vb.
be contiguous 202 vb.
transfer 272 vb.
approach 289 vb.
assent 488 vb.
contract 765 vb.
retain 778 vb.
— to
observe 768 vb.
adherent
follower 284 n.
auxiliary 707 n.
signatory 765 n.
religionist 973 n.
sectarian 978 n.
adhesion
coherence 48 n.
contiguity 202 n.
adhesive
conjunctive 45 adj.
joined 45 adj.
adhesive 47 n.
coherence 48 n.
cohesive 48 adj.
viscidity 354 n.
retentive 778 adj.
ad hoc
specially 80 adv.
spontaneous 609 adj.
extempore 609 adv.
unprepared 670 adj.
unreadily 670 adv.
ad hoc measure
contrivance 623 n.
means 629 n.
ad hominem
specially 80 adv.
adieus
valediction 296 n.
ad infinitum
infinitely 107 adv.
adipose
fatty 357 adj.
adit
excavation 255 n.
tunnel 263 n.
access 624 n.
adjacent
near 200 adj.
contiguous 202 adj.
adjective
adjunct 40 n.
part of speech 564 n.
adjoin
be near 200 vb.
be contiguous 202 vb.
adjourn
put off 136 vb.
pause 145 vb.
adjournment
interim 108 n.
delay 136 n.
adjudge
judge 480 vb.
adjudicate
judge 480 vb.
try a case 959 vb.
adjudicator
estimator 480 n.
adjunct
extrinsicality 6 n.
addition 38 n.
adjunct 40 n.
part 53 n.
component 58 n.
concomitant 89 n.
adjuration
oath 532 n.
entreaty 761 n.
adjure
affirm 532 vb.
entreat 761 vb.

take a pledge 764 vb.
adjust
adjust 24 vb.
equalize 28 vb.
order 60 vb.
regularize 62 vb.
make conform 83 vb.
time 117 vb.
synchronize 123 vb.
modify 143 vb.
moderate 177 vb.
harmonize 410 vb.
plan 623 vb.
rectify 654 vb.
make ready 669 vb.
pacify 719 vb.
— oneself
conform 83 vb.
adjusted
adjusted 24 adj.
conformable 83 adj.
tailored 228 adj.
accurate 494 adj.
adjustment
adaptation 24 n.
equalization 28 n.
conformity 83 n.
change 143 n.
moderation 177 n.
pacification 719 n.
compact 765 n.
compromise 770 n.
adjutant
auxiliary 707 n.
army officer 741 n.
Adlerian psychology
psychology 447 n.
ad-lib
orate 579 vb.
act 594 vb.
improvise 609 vb.
unprepared 670 adj.
ad lib, ad libitum
often 139 adv.
at will 595 adv.
enough 635 adv.
freely 744 adv.
adman
publicizer 528 n.
admass
dupe 544 n.
commonalty 869 n.
administer
use 673 vb.
do 676 vb.
manage 689 vb.
apportion 783 vb.
— an oath
take a pledge 764 vb.
— justice
hold court 955 vb.
— the sacraments
perform ritual 988 vb.
administration
arrangement 62 n.
vocation 622 n.
action 676 n.
management 689 n.
apportionment 783 n.
ministration 988 n.
Administration, the
authority 733 n.
administrative
directing 689 adj.
governmental 733 adj.
jurisdictional 955 adj.
administrator
doer 676 n.
agent 686 n.
manager 690 n.
admirable
excellent 644 adj.
wonderful 864 adj.
worshipful 866 adj.
approvable 923 adj.
Admirable Crichton
exceller 644 n.
proficient person 696 n.
prodigy 864 n.
admiral
nautical personnel 270 n.
naval man 722 n.
naval officer 741 n.
Admiralty
nautical personnel 270 n.
navy 722 n.
authority 733 n.
admiration
wonder 864 n.
love 887 n.
respect 920 n.
approbation 923 n.
admired
excellent 644 adj.
respected 920 adj.
admire oneself
be vain 873 vb.
admirer
lover 887 n.
commender 923 n.
worshipper 981 n.
admissible
apt 24 adj.
included 78 adj.
numerable 86 adj.
admitting 299 adj.
rational 475 adj.
approvable 923 adj.
admission
inclusion 78 n.
ingress 297 n.
reception 299 n.
testimony 466 n.
assent 488 n.
disclosure 526 n.
affirmation 532 n.
admit
add 38 vb.
admit 299 vb.
testify 466 vb.
be reasonable 475 vb.
believe 485 vb.
assent 488 vb.
confess 526 vb.
affirm 532 vb.
receive 782 vb.
— defeat
submit 721 vb.
be defeated 728 vb.
be dejected 834 vb.
— of
be possible 469 vb.
— the necessity
be forced 596 vb.
admittance
ingress 297 n.
reception 299 n.
receiving 782 n.
admitted
included 78 adj.
assented 488 adj.
usual 610 adj.
reputable 866 adj.
due 915 adj.
admitting
open 263 adj.
admitting 299 adj.
provided 468 adv.
admixture
mixture 43 n.
tincture 43 n.
admonish
warn 664 vb.
advise 691 vb.
reprove 924 vb.
admonition
dissuasion 613 n.
warning 664 n.
reprimand 924 n.
ad nauseam
repeatedly 106 adv.
diffusely 570 adv.
boringly 838 adv.
ad nauseam 861 adv.
ado
activity 678 n.
exertion 682 n.
adobe
pottery 381 n.
materials 631 n.
adolescence
youth 130 n.
adolescent
young 130 adj.
youngster 132 n.
immature 670 adj.
Adonis
a beauty 841 n.
mythic deity 966 n.
adopt
be akin 11 vb.
choose 605 vb.
avail oneself of 673 vb.
adoption
parentage 169 n.
choice 605 n.
approbation 923 n.
adorable
beautiful 841 adj.
lovable 887 adj.
adoration
respect 920 n.
piety 979 n.
worship 981 n.
adore
love 887 vb.
respect 920 vb.
worship 981 vb.
adorn
ornament 574 vb.
make better 654 vb.
decorate 844 vb.
adrift
irrelevant 10 adj.
unrelated 10 adj.
separate 46 adj.
apart 46 adv.
unassembled 75 adj.
astray 282 adv.
doubting 474 adj.
adroit
skilful 694 adj.
adscititious
extrinsic 6 adj.
additional 38 adj.
superfluous 637 adj.
adulation
exaggeration 546 n.
praise 923 n.
flattery 925 n.
adult
adult 134 n.
grown-up 134 adj.
matured 669 adj.
adulterate
mix 43 vb.
modify 143 vb.
weaken 163 vb.
rarefy 325 vb.
add water 339 vb.
qualify 468 vb.
impair 655 vb.
adulterated
spurious 542 adj.
adulterer
libertine 952 n.
adulterous
extramarital 951 adj.
adultery
love affair 887 n.
illicit love 951 n.
adultness
middle age 131 n.
adultness 134 n.
female 373 n.
desuetude 611 n.
preparedness 669 n.
adultress
loose woman 952 n.
adumbrate
predestine 155 vb.

darken 418 vb.
propound 512 vb.
figure 519 vb.
hint 524 vb.
represent 551 vb.
describe 590 vb.
adumbration
similarity 18 n.
copy 22 n.
latency 523 n.
advance
increase 36 n.
grow 36 vb.
part 53 n.
put in front 64 vb.
elapse 111 vb.
early 135 adj.
go on 146 vb.
conduce 156 vb.
motion 265 n.
marching 267 n.
travel 267 vb.
progression 285 n.
progress 285 vb.
promote 285 vb.
approach 289 n.vb.
be visible 443 vb.
affirm 532 vb.
call 547 n.
be instrumental 628 vb.
be useful 640 vb.
be expedient 642 vb.
improvement 654 n.
get better 654 vb.
make better 654 vb.
aid 703 vb.
succeed 727 vb.
offer 759 n.
lending 784 n.
lend 784 vb.
dignify 866 vb.
— against
charge 712 vb.
advanced
modern 126 adj.
early 135 adj.
progressive 285 adj.
advanced in years
ageing 131 adj.
advance guard
front 237 n.
warner 664 n.
advancement
increase 36 n.
progression 285 n.
improvement 654 n.
aid 703 n.
dignification 866 n.
advance notice
prediction 511 n.
warning 664 n.
advances
approach 289 n.
endearment 889 n.
wooing 889 n.
advantage
advantage 34 n.
fair chance 159 n.
power 160 n.
benefit 615 n.vb.
utility 640 n.
be useful 640 vb.
good policy 642 n.
be expedient 642 vb.
tactics 688 n.
success 727 n.
victory 727 n.
gain 771 n.
retention 778 n.
advent
futurity 124 n.
event 154 n.
approach 289 n.
arrival 295 n.
Advent
holy day 988 n.
adventitious
extrinsic 6 adj.
circumstantial 8 adj.
additional 38 adj.
casual 159 adj.
adventure
event 154 n.
attempt 671 n.
undertaking 672 n.
be courageous 855 vb.
adventurer
traveller 268 n.
experimenter 461 n.
impostor 545 n.
gambler 618 n.
militarist 722 n.
desperado 857 n.
egotist 932 n.
adventures
biography 590 n.
adventuress
loose woman 952 n.
adventure story
novel 590 n.
adventurous
speculative 618 adj.
enterprising 672 adj.
courageous 855 adj.
rash 857 adj.
adverb
adjunct 40 n.
part of speech 564 n.
adversary
opponent 705 n.
adverse
contrary 14 adj.
inopportune 138 adj.
presageful 511 adj.
unwilling 598 adj.
evil 616 adj.
inexpedient 643 adj.
harmful 645 adj.
hindering 702 adj.
opposing 704 adj.
adverse 731 adj.
annoying 827 adj.
unpromising 853 adj.
adversity
ruin 165 n.
pain 377 n.
evil 616 n.
bane 659 n.
difficulty 700 n.
adversity 731 n.
sorrow 825 n.
suffering 825 n.
painfulness 827 n.
punishment 963 n.
advertise
attract notice 455 vb.
predict 511 vb.
communicate 524 vb.
advertise 528 vb.
make important 638 vb.
boast 877 vb.
praise 923 vb.
— oneself
be ostentatious 875 vb.
boast 877 vb.
advertisement
exhibit 522 n.
information 524 n.
advertisement 528 n.
writing 586 n.
inducement 612 n.
request 761 n.
sale 793 n.
boast 877 n.
boasting 877 n.
praise 923 n.
advertising
publicity 528 n.
advice
estimate 480 n.
hint 524 n.
information 524 n.
message 529 n.
news 529 n.
conference 584 n.
inducement 612 n.
preparation 669 n.
advice 691 n.
precept 693 n.
aid 703 n.
advisable
fit 24 adj.
opportune 137 adj.
operative 173 adj.
possible 469 adj.
wise 498 adj.
chosen 605 adj.
useful 640 adj.
advisable 642 adj.
due 915 adj.
advise
propound 512 vb.
hint 524 vb.
inform 524 vb.
incite 612 vb.
doctor 658 vb.
warn 664 vb.
advise 691 vb.
— against
dissuade 613 vb.
warn 664 vb.
advise 691 vb.
deprecate 762 vb.
advisedly
purposely 617 adv.
adviser
estimator 480 n.
sage 500 n.
informant 524 n.
teacher 537 n.
motivator 612 n.
warner 664 n.
meddler 678 n.
director 690 n.
adviser 691 n.
expert 696 n.
aider 703 n.
mediator 720 n.
consignee 754 n.
advisory board
council 692 n.
advocate
intermediary 231 n.
speaker 579 n.
motivator 612 n.
incite 612 vb.
adviser 691 n.
advise 691 vb.
patron 707 n.
combatant 722 n.
consignee 754 n.
deputy 755 n.
commender 923 n.
approve 923 vb.
vindicator 927 n.
vindicate 927 vb.
lawyer 958 n.
litigate 959 vb.
adytum
chamber 194 n.
holy place 990 n.
adze
sharp edge 256 n.
aedile
official 690 n.
officer 741 n.
aegis
protection 660 n.
aegrotat
nonliability 919 n.
aeolian
windy 352 adj.
aeon
era 110 n.
aeonian
perpetual 115 adj.
aerate
lighten 323 vb.
gasify 336 vb.
aerate 340 vb.
sanitate 652 vb.
refresh 685 vb.
aerated
rare 325 adj.
airy 340 adj.
bubbly 355 adj.
aerial
high 209 adj.
flying 271 adj.

gaseous 336 adj.
airy 340 adj.
broadcasting 531 n.
aerie, aery
(See **eyrie** *)*
aeroballistics
aeronautics 271 n.
aerobatics
aeronautics 271 n.
aerodrome
air travel 271 n.
aircraft 276 n.
aerodynamic
flying 271 adj.
aviational 276 adj.
aerodynamics
aeronautics 271 n.
pneumatics 340 n.
anemometry 352 n.
aerodyne
aircraft 276 n.
aerofoil
wing 271 n.
aircraft 276 n.
aeronaut
traveller 268 n.
aeronaut 271 n.
aeronautics
aeronautics 271 n.
aircraft 276 n.
ascent 308 n.
descent 309 n.
plunge 313 n.
sport 837 n.
aeroplane
aircraft 276 n.
aerosol
propellant 287 n.
vaporizer 338 n.
aerospace
aeronautics 271 n.
flying 271 adj.
aviational 276 adj.
atmosphere 340 n.
aerostat
airship 276 n.
Aesir
Nordic deities 967 n.
aesthete
sensibility 374 n.
people of taste 846 n.
aesthetic
sentient 374 adj.
sensitive 819 adj.
beautiful 841 adj.
tasteful 846 adj.
aestheticism
sensibility 374 n.
art 551 n.
moral sensibility 819 n.
beauty 841 n.
good taste 846 n.
aesthetics
sensibility 374 n.
beauty 841 n.
good taste 846 n.
aetiology
causation 156 n.
attribution 158 n.
pathology 651 n.
afar
afar 199 adv.
affability
sociability 882 n.
courtesy 884 n.
affair
topic 452 n.
badness 645 n.
affair of honour
duel 716 n.
affair of the heart
love affair 887 n.
affairs
affairs 154 n.
event 154 n.
pursuit 619 n.
business 622 n.
deed 676 n.
conduct 688 n.
affect
be related 9 vb.
modify 143 vb.
influence 178 vb.
tend 179 vb.
intellect 447 n.
show 522 vb.
dissemble 541 vb.
plead 614 vb.
be important 638 vb.
behave 688 vb.
feeling 818 n.
excite 821 vb.
impress 821 vb.
be affected 850 vb.
desire 859 vb.
affectation
imitation 20 n.
mimicry 20 n.
conformity 83 n.
underestimation 483 n.
foolery 497 n.
trope 519 n.
sham 542 n.
neology 560 n.
magniloquence 574 n.
speech defect 580 n.
conduct 688 n.
fashion 848 n.
affectation 850 n.
pride 871 n.
airs 873 n.
prudery 950 n.
false piety 980 n.
affectation of knowledge
sciolism 491 n.
affected
absurd 497 adj.
untrue 543 adj.
inelegant 576 adj.
diseased 651 adj.
impressed 818 adj.
ridiculous 849 adj.
affected 850 adj.
vain 873 adj.
ostentatious 875 adj.
(See **affect, affectation** *)*
affecting
felt 818 adj.
exciting 821 adj.
distressing 827 adj.
affection
moral sensibility 819 n.
love 887 n.
affectionate
loving 887 adj.
caressing 889 adj.
benevolent 897 adj.
affections
temperament 5 n.
state 7 n.
influence 178 n.
intellect 447 n.
affections 817 n.
affidavit
testimony 466 n.
oath 532 n.
litigation 959 n.
affiliation
relation 9 n.
consanguinity 11 n.
attribution 158 n.
association 706 n.
participation 775 n.
affinity
relation 9 n.
consanguinity 11 n.
similarity 18 n.
tendency 179 n.
attraction 291 n.
liking 859 n.
spouse 894 n.
affirm
testify 466 vb.
dogmatize 473 vb.
confute 479 vb.
believe 485 vb.
opine 485 vb.
suppose 512 vb.
mean 514 vb.
proclaim 528 vb.
affirm 532 vb.
indicate 547 vb.
speak 579 vb.
plead 614 vb.
decree 737 vb.
promise 764 vb.
affirmation
testimony 466 n.
assent 488 n.
affirmation 532 n.
promise 764 n.
affirmative
positive 473 adj.
demonstrating 478 adj.
affirmative 532 adj.
forceful 571 adj.
affix
add 38 vb.
adjunct 40 n.
affix 45 vb.
agglutinate 48 vb.
sequel 67 n.
part of speech 564 n.
afflatus
imagination 513 n.
poetry 593 n.
excitation 821 n.
revelation 975 n.
afflict
hurt 827 vb.
punish 963 vb.
affliction
evil 616 n.
illness 651 n.
bane 659 n.
suffering 825 n.
affluence
plenty 635 n.
prosperity 730 n.
wealth 800 n.
afford
provide 633 vb.
have enough 635 vb.
give 781 vb.
afford 800 vb.
expend 806 vb.
affordable
cheap 812 adj.
afforestation
forestry 366 n.
agriculture 370 n.
affray
turmoil 61 n.
fight 716 n.
affront
annoyance 827 n.
hurt 827 vb.
be courageous 855 vb.
sauciness 878 n.
resentment 891 n.
huff 891 vb.
indignity 921 n.
not respect 921 vb.
affronted
discontented 829 adj.
aficionado
enthusiast 504 n.
patron 707 n.
lover 887 n.
afield
afar 199 adv.
afire
fiery 379 adj.
aflame
luminous 417 adj.
aflame with
impressed 818 adj.
afloat
existing 1 adj.
happening 154 adj.
seafaring 269 adj.
swimming 269 adj.
afloat 275 adv.
at sea 343 adv.
rumoured 529 adj.

afoot
existing 1 adj.
busy 678 adj.
aforesaid
preceding 64 adj.
repeated 106 adj.
prior 119 adj.
aforethought
predetermined 608 adj.
intended 617 adj.
aforetime
before 119 adv.
formerly 125 adv.
a fortiori
eminently 34 adv.
reasonably 475 adv.
afraid
fearing 854 adj.
afraid of one's own shadow
nervous 854 adj.
cowardly 856 adj.
afraid to touch
careful 457 adj.
afresh
again 106 adv.
newly 126 adv.
Africanize
transform 147 vb.
aft
rearward 238 adv.
after
after 65 adv.
subsequent 120 adj.
subsequently 120 adv.
back 238 adj.
rearward 238 adv.
behind 284 adv.
pursuant to 619 adv.
after a fashion
partially 33 adv.
after all
in return 31 adv.
nevertheless 468 adv.
after, be
aim at 617 vb.
pursue 619 vb.
afterbirth
obstetrics 167 n.
aftercare
therapy 658 n.
afterclap
sequel 67 n.
lack of expectation 508 n.
after-dinner
subsequent 120 adj.
culinary 301 adj.
reposeful 683 adj.
sociable 882 adj.
after due thought
in mind 449 adv.
aftereffect
sequel 67 n.
afterglow
remainder 41 n.
sequel 67 n.
glow 417 n.
afterimage
appearance 445 n.
image 551 n.
afterlife
sequel 67 n.
future state 124 n.
heaven 971 n.
aftermath
sequel 67 n.
posteriority 120 n.
effect 157 n.
afternoon
evening 129 n.
vespertine 129 adj.
after one's own heart
lovable 887 adj.
afterpart
sequel 67 n.
poop 238 n.
rear 238 n.
afters
sequel 67 n.
aftertaste
sequel 67 n.
taste 386 n.
after the fashion of
similar 18 adj.
afterthought
sequel 67 n.
lateness 136 n.
thought 449 n.
remembrance 505 n.
tergiversation 603 n.
after time
late 136 adj.adv.
afterwards
after 65 adv.
subsequently 120 adv.
afterworld
sequel 67 n.
destiny 155 n.
again
twice 91 adv.adv.
again 106 adv.
again and again
repeatedly 106 adv.
often 139 adv.
against
although 182 adv.
against 240 adv.
opposing 704 adj.
in opposition 704 adv.
against nature
impossible 470 adj.
against one's better judgment
disapprovingly 924 adv.
against one's will
unwillingly 598 adv.
against the grain
on edge 259 adv.
unwillingly 598 adv.
with difficulty 700 adv.
in opposition 704 adv.
against the law
prohibited 757 adj.
illegal 954 adj.
against the rules
unconformable 84 adj.
impossible 470 adj.
wrong 914 adj.
against the stream
with difficulty 700 adv.
in opposition 704 adv.
agape
open 263 adj.
wondering 864 adj.
social gathering 882 n.
love 887 n.
public worship 981 n.
agate
stripe 437 n.
gem 844 n.
age
date 108 n.
pass time 108 vb.
era 110 n.
chronology 117 n.
oldness 127 n.
be old 127 vb.
age 131 n.
grow old 131 vb.
helplessness 161 n.
deteriorate 655 vb.
age, an
long duration 113 n.
aged
ageing 131 adj.
age group
group 74 n.
classification 77 n.
contemporary 123 n.
class 538 n.
ageing
antiquated 127 adj.
ageing 131 adj.
weak 163 adj.
deteriorated 655 adj.
ageism
prejudice 481 n.
ageless
perpetual 115 adj.
young 130 adj.
agelong
lasting 113 adj.
perpetual 115 adj.
agency
agency 173 n.
instrumentality 628 n.
action 676 n.
management 689 n.
commission 751 n.
agenda
affairs 154 n.
topic 452 n.
predetermination 608 n.
business 622 n.
policy 623 n.
agent
inferior 35 n.
substitute 150 n.
cause 156 n.
producer 164 n.
intermediary 231 n.
instrument 628 n.
machinist 630 n.
doer 676 n.
agent 686 n.
manager 690 n.
mediator 720 n.
consignee 754 n.
deputy 755 n.
seller 793 n.
commender 923 n.
agent provocateur
ambush 527 n.
trickster 545 n.
motivator 612 n.
agitator 738 n.
excitant 821 n.
Age of Enlightenment
era 110 n.
age-old
immemorial 127 adj.
worshipful 866 adj.
agglomeration
coherence 48 n.
accumulation 74 n.
agglutinate
add 38 vb.
affix 45 vb.
join 45 vb.
agglutinate 48 vb.
retain 778 vb.
aggrandizement, aggrandisement
greatness 32 n.
increase 36 n.
expansion 197 n.
dignification 866 n.
aggravate
augment 36 vb.
make violent 176 vb.
give pain 377 vb.
exaggerate 546 vb.
deteriorate 655 vb.
impair 655 vb.
be difficult 700 vb.
make quarrels 709 vb.
miscarry 728 vb.
hurt 827 vb.
aggravate 832 vb.
excite hate 888 vb.
enrage 891 vb.
aggravating
annoying 827 adj.
aggregate
all 52 n.
bring together 74 vb.
numerical result 85 n.

solid body 324 n.
aggregation
combination 50 n.
accumulation 74 n.
aggression
attack 712 n.
aggressive
vigorous 174 adj.
violent 176 adj.
active 678 adj.
quarrelling 709 adj.
attacking 712 adj.
contending 716 adj.
warlike 718 adj.
courageous 855 adj.
inimical 881 adj.
aggressiveness
vitality 162 n.
vigorousness 174 n.
restlessness 678 n.
quarrelsomeness 709 n.
attack 712 n.
bellicosity 718 n.
aggressor
quarreller 709 n.
attacker 712 n.
combatant 722 n.
enemy 881 n.
aggrieve
ill-treat 645 vb.
displease 827 vb.
hurt 827 vb.
aggrieved, be
be discontented 829 vb.
aghast
fearing 854 adj.
wondering 864 adj.
agile
speedy 277 adj.
skilful 694 adj.
agitate
derange 63 vb.
jumble 63 vb.
move 265 vb.
impel 279 vb.
brandish 317 vb.
agitate 318 vb.
cause feeling 374 vb.
distract 456 vb.
enquire 459 vb.
gesticulate 547 vb.
be active 678 vb.
revolt 738 vb.
trouble 827 vb.
cause discontent 829 vb.
— against
counteract 182 vb.
agitated
disorderly 61 adj.
fitful 142 adj.
violent 176 adj.
agitated 318 adj.
puffing 352 adj.
excited 821 adj.
suffering 825 adj.
nervous 854 adj.
agitation
derangement 63 n.
changeableness 152 n.
stimulation 174 n.
outbreak 176 n.
motion 265 n.
oscillation 317 n.
agitation 318 n.
restlessness 678 n.
haste 680 n.
revolt 738 n.
sedition 738 n.
feeling 818 n.
excitation 821 n.
excitable state 822 n.
worry 825 n.
discontent 829 n.
fear 854 n.
anger 891 n.
agitator
revolutionist 149 n.
violent creature 176 n.
dissentient 489 n.
speaker 579 n.
motivator 612 n.
reformer 654 n.
troublemaker 663 n.
leader 690 n.
opponent 705 n.
agitator 738 n.
excitant 821 n.
malcontent 829 n.
agitprop
teaching 534 n.
inducement 612 n.
sedition 738 n.
aglow
fiery 379 adj.
luminous 417 adj.
agnostic
doubting 474 adj.
unbeliever 486 n.
dissenting 489 adj.
irreligionist 974 n.
irreligious 974 adj.
agnosticism
philosophy 449 n.
doubt 486 n.
unbelief 486 n.
irreligion 974 n.
ago
not now 122 adv.
formerly 125 adv.
agog
inquisitive 453 adj.
expectant 507 adj.
excited 821 adj.
desiring 859 adj.
agonize, agonise
feel pain 377 vb.
ill-treat 645 vb.
suffer 825 vb.
agony
pain 377 n.
excitable state 822 n.
suffering 825 n.
agony column
advertisement 528 n.
agoraphobia
psychopathy 503 n.
phobia 854 n.
agrarian
territorial 344 adj.
agrarian 370 adj.
agree
accord 24 vb.
concur 181 vb.
believe 485 vb.
be willing 597 vb.
concord 710 vb.
consent 758 vb.
contract 765 vb.
— to differ
dissent 489 vb.
make peace 719 vb.
— with one
be salubrious 652 vb.
agreeable
agreeing 24 adj.
conformable 83 adj.
pleasant 376 adj.
willing 597 adj.
palmy 730 adj.
consenting 758 adj.
pleasurable 826 adj.
personable 841 adj.
courteous 884 adj.
agreeably
tastefully 846 adv.
agreement
identity 13 n.
uniformity 16 n.
similarity 18 n.
agreement 24 n.
equality 28 n.
conformity 83 n.
concurrence 181 n.
symmetry 245 n.
melody 410 n.
assent 488 n.
consensus 488 n.
cooperation 706 n.
concord 710 n.
pacification 719 n.
consent 758 n.
compact 765 n.
agribusiness
agriculture 370 n.
business 622 n.
agricultural
territorial 344 adj.
agrarian 370 adj.
agriculturalist, agriculturist
producer 164 n.
farmer 370 n.
preparer 669 n.
agricultural worker
farmer 370 n.
agriculture
production 164 n.
agriculture 370 n.
maturation 669 n.
agronomics
agriculture 370 n.
agronomist
farmer 370 n.
aground
in difficulties 700 adj.
ague
spasm 318 n.
illness 651 n.
tropical disease 651 n.
ahead
superior 34 adj.
before 64 adv.
future 124 adj.
beyond 199 adv.
in front 237 adv.
ahead 283 adv.
forward 285 adv.
ahead of its time
early 135 adj.
ahimsa
peace 717 n.
benevolence 897 n.
Ahriman
Satan 969 n.
Ahura Mazda
the Deity 965 n.
aid
strengthening 162 n.
support 218 n.vb.
incite 612 vb.
instrumentality 628 n.
utility 640 n.
be expedient 642 vb.
remedy 658 n.
facility 701 n.
facilitate 701 vb.
aid 703 n.vb.
cooperate 706 vb.
gift 781 n.
kind act 897 n.
philanthropy 901 n.
— and abet
incite 612 vb.
aide-de-camp
auxiliary 707 n.
army officer 741 n.
aide-mémoire
reminder 505 n.
aider
cause 156 n.
motivator 612 n.
instrument 628 n.
aider 703 n.
auxiliary 707 n.
defender 713 n.
servant 742 n.
friend 880 n.
benefactor 903 n.
aid-giving
philanthropic 901 adj.
aiguillette
livery 547 n.
aileron
equilibrium 28 n.

wing 271 n.
aircraft 276 n.
ailing
sick 651 adj.
ailment
illness 651 n.
aim
place 187 vb.
direction 281 n.
aim 281 vb.
objective 617 n.
attempt 671 n.vb.
fire at 712 vb.
desired object 859 n.
— at
aim 281 vb.
aim at 617 vb.
pursue 619 vb.
desire 859 vb.
— high
hope 852 vb.
— too high
overstep 306 vb.
be rash 857 vb.
aimless
orderless 61 adj.
designless 618 adj.
aimless activity
restlessness 678 n.
aimlessness
inattention 456 n.
air
insubstantial thing 4 n.
initiate 68 vb.
element 319 n.
lightness 323 n.
rarity 325 n.
gas 336 n.
air 340 n.
aerate 340 vb.
dry 342 vb.
ventilation 352 n.
wind 352 n.
tune 412 n.
mien 445 n.
enquire 459 vb.
divulge 526 vb.
salubrity 652 n.
refresh 685 vb.
conduct 688 n.
— one's knowledge
be affected 850 vb.
— one's views
dissertate 591 vb.
air base
station 187 n.
air travel 271 n.
airbed
bed 218 n.
airborne
high 209 adj.
flying 271 adj.
ascending 308 adj.
airbus
aircraft 276 n.
air commodore
air officer 741 n.
air-conditioned
airy 340 adj.
cooled 382 adj.
salubrious 652 adj.
air-conditioner
ventilation 352 n.
aircraft
aircraft 276 n.
air force 722 n.
aircraft carrier
warship 722 n.
air crew
aeronaut 271 n.
air force 722 n.
air current
wind 352 n.
airdrop
transference 272 n.
airer
hanger 217 n.
dryer 342 n.
airfield
air travel 271 n.
air force
aeronaut 271 n.
aircraft 276 n.
air force 722 n.
air officer 741 n.
air freight
transport 272 n.
airgun
propellant 287 n.
plaything 837 n.
air-hole
orifice 263 n.
air pipe 353 n.
air hostess
aeronaut 271 n.
airily
cheerfully 833 adv.
hopefully 852 adv.
airiness
rarity 325 n.
hope 852 n.
airing
enquiry 459 n.
airlane
air travel 271 n.
route 624 n.
airless
tranquil 266 adj.
fetid 397 adj.
insalubrious 653 adj.
air letter
correspondence 588 n.
airlift
air travel 271 n.
transport 272 n.
transfer 272 vb.
airline
air travel 271 n.
airliner
aircraft 276 n.
air lock
intermediary 231 n.
air mail
postal communications 531 n.
correspondence 588 n.
correspond 588 vb.
airman, airwoman
aeronaut 271 n.
air marshal
air officer 741 n.
air pipe
orifice 263 n.
respiration 352 n.
ventilation 352 n.
air pipe 353 n.
airplane
aircraft 276 n.
air pocket
emptiness 190 n.
air 340 n.
wind 352 n.
airport
air travel 271 n.
goal 295 n.
airproof
sealed off 264 adj.
air raid
attack 712 n.
airraid shelter
refuge 662 n.
defences 713 n.
air route
air travel 271 n.
airs
affectation 850 n.
airs 873 n.
ostentation 875 n.
air shaft
air pipe 353 n.
airship
sphere 252 n.
airship 276 n.
gas 336 n.
air force 722 n.
airsick
flying 271 adj.
vomiting 300 adj.
airspace
territory 184 n.
air travel 271 n.
air stream
wind 352 n.
airstrip
air travel 271 n.
airtight
sealed off 264 adj.
airtight container
small box 194 n.
air-to-air
flying 271 adj.
air travel
motion 265 n.
air travel 271 n.
aircraft 276 n.
airway
air travel 271 n.
air pipe 353 n.
airworthy
flying 271 adj.
transferable 272 adj.
aviational 276 adj.
invulnerable 660 adj.
airy
insubstantial 4 adj.
flying 271 adj.
light 323 adj.
gaseous 336 adj.
airy 340 adj.
windy 352 adj.
light-minded 456 adj.
trivial 639 adj.
hoping 852 adj.
rash 857 adj.
impertinent 878 adj.
discourteous 885 adj.
disrespectful 921 adj.
despising 922 adj.
airy-fairy
imaginative 513 adj.
aisle
open space 263 n.
path 624 n.
church interior 990 n.
ait
island 349 n.
ajar
open 263 adj.
akimbo
angular 247 adj.
akin
relative 9 adj.
akin 11 adj.
similar 18 adj.
included 78 adj.
near 200 adj.
born 360 adj.
à la
similar 18 adj.
alabaster
white thing 427 n.
à la carte
meal 301 n.
optionally 605 adv.
alacritous
vigorous 174 adj.
willing 597 adj.
cheerful 833 adj.
alacrity
velocity 277 n.
willingness 597 n.
activity 678 n.
cheerfulness 833 n.
Aladdin's lamp
instrument 628 n.
aid 703 n.
magic instrument 983 n.
à la mode
modern 126 adj.
fashionable 848 adj.
fashionably 848 adv.
alarm
loudness 400 n.
megaphone 400 n.

signal 547 n.
warning 664 n.
danger signal 665 n.
fear 854 n.
frighten 854 vb.
alarming
dangerous 661 adj.
frightening 854 adj.
alarmist
false alarm 665 n.
alarmist 854 n.
alarums and excursions
dramaturgy 594 n.
alb
vestments 989 n.
albatross
bird 365 n.
encumbrance 702 n.
albedo
reflection 417 n.
albescence
whiteness 427 n.
Albigensian
heretic 977 n.
albino
colourless 426 adj.
whiteness 427 n.
white thing 427 n.
album
gramophone 414 n.
reminder 505 n.
record 548 n.
reference book 589 n.
anthology 592 n.
albumen
semiliquidity 354 n.
organism 358 n.
alchemist
alterer 143 n.
sorcerer 983 n.
occultist 984 n.
alchemy
conversion 147 n.
occultism 984 n.
alcohol
stimulant 174 n.
alcoholic drink 301 n.
fuel 385 n.
tonic 658 n.
alcoholic
strong 162 adj.
edible 301 adj.
sick person 651 n.
drunkard 949 n.
drunken 949 adj.
intoxicating 949 adj.
Alcoholics Anonymous
sober person 948 n.
alcoholism
disease 651 n.
alcoholism 949 n.
alcove
arbour 194 n.
cavity 255 n.
al dente
culinary 301 adj.
alderman
official 690 n.
councillor 692 n.
officer 741 n.
ale
alcoholic drink 301 n.
aleatory
casual 159 adj.
speculative 618 adj.
alehouse
tavern 192 n.
alembic
crucible 147 n.
heater 383 n.
alert
attentive 455 adj.
attract notice 455 vb.
vigilant 457 adj.
signal 547 vb.
warning 664 n.
warn 664 vb.
danger signal 665 n.
raise the alarm 665 vb.
prepared 669 adj.
active 678 adj.
lively 819 adj.
alertness
attention 455 n.
carefulness 457 n.
sagacity 498 n.
A level
exam 459 n.
alexandrine
prosody 593 n.
al fresco
externally 223 adv.
alfresco 340 adv.
algae
microorganism 196 n.
plant 366 n.
algebra
mathematics 86 n.
algidity
coldness 380 n.
Algol
data processing 86 n.
algorithm
mathematics 86 n.
numeration 86 n.
alias
named 561 adj.
misnomer 562 n.
alibi
absence 190 n.
pretext 614 n.
vindication 927 n.
alidade
gauge 465 n.
alien
extrinsic 6 adj.
unrelated 10 adj.
separate 46 adj.
foreigner 59 n.
extraneous 59 adj.
unconformable 84 adj.
outcast 883 n.
alienate
set apart 46 vb.
not retain 779 vb.
assign 780 vb.
make enemies 881 vb.
excite hate 888 vb.
alienation
nonretention 779 n.
transfer 780 n.
enmity 881 n.
hatred 888 n.
alien element
unrelatedness 10 n.
dissimilarity 19 n.
extraneousness 59 n.
alight
place oneself 187 vb.
come to rest 266 vb.
land 295 vb.
descend 309 vb.
sit down 311 vb.
fiery 379 adj.
align
make uniform 16 vb.
adjust 24 vb.
arrange 62 vb.
flatten 216 vb.
straighten 249 vb.
print 587 vb.
— oneself
join a party 708 vb.
alignment
direction 281 n.
friendship 880 n.
alike
similar 18 adj.
aliment
food 301 n.
alimentary
nourishing 301 adj.
remedial 658 adj.
alimony
dower 777 n.
receipt 807 n.
divorce 896 n.
A-line
tailored 228 adj.
aliquant, aliquot
part 53 n.
numerical element 85 n.
alive
existing 1 adj.
alive 360 adj.
sentient 374 adj.
intelligent 498 adj.
lively 819 adj.
alive and kicking
alive 360 adj.
restored 656 adj.
active 678 adj.
alive to
sentient 374 adj.
attentive 455 adj.
knowing 490 adj.
impressible 819 adj.
alive with
multitudinous 104 adj.
alkahest
liquefaction 337 n.
all
great quantity 32 n.
all 52 n.
completeness 54 n.
everyman 79 n.
universal 79 adj.
all-ability
educational 534 adj.
Allah
the Deity 965 n.
all along
while 108 adv.
all along 113 adv.
until now 121 adv.
all and sundry
everyman 79 n.
all anyhow
nonuniformly 17 adv.
orderless 61 adj.
confusedly 61 adv.
all at once
instantaneously 116 adv.
all at sea
doubting 474 adj.
allay
abate 37 vb.
assuage 177 vb.
pacify 719 vb.
all but
almost 33 adv.
on the whole 52 adv.
nearly 200 adv.
imperfectly 647 adv.
all change
interchange 151 n.
all clear
signal 547 n.
safety 660 n.
permit 756 n.
all comers
opponent 705 n.
contender 716 n.
all correct
in order 60 adv.
all day
all along 113 adv.
all ears
auditory 415 adj.
inquisitive 453 adj.
attentive 455 adj.
allegation
testimony 466 n.
affirmation 532 n.
pretext 614 n.
accusation 928 n.
alleged
supposed 512 adj.
ostensible 614 adj.

allegiance
loyalty 739 n.
subjection 745 n.
duty 917 n.
allegorical
compared 462 adj.
figurative 519 adj.
occult 523 adj.
allegory
assimilation 18 n.
comparison 462 n.
metaphor 519 n.
latency 523 n.
narrative 590 n.
allegretto
adagio 412 adv.
allegro
adagio 412 adv.
cheerfully 833 adv.
allelomorph
heredity 5 n.
alleluia
praise 923 n.
Alleluia!
981 int.
all-embracing
extensive 32 adj.
comprehensive 52 adj.
inclusive 78 adj.
general 79 adj.
allergy
sensibility 374 n.
ill health 651 n.
dislike 861 n.
hatred 888 n.
alleviate
abate 37 vb.
assuage 177 vb.
disencumber 701 vb.
relieve 831 vb.
alley
open space 263 n.
road 624 n.
all eyes
seeing 438 adj.
attentive 455 adj.
vigilant 457 adj.
All-Father
the Deity 965 n.
all for the best, be
benefit 615 vb.
all found
provisioning 633 adj.
all hands
everyman 79 n.
all hell let loose
turmoil 61 n.
loudness 400 n.
alliance
relation 9 n.
consanguinity 11 n.
union 45 n.
combination 50 n.
concurrence 181 n.
association 706 n.
society 708 n.
compact 765 n.
marriage 894 n.
alligator
skin 226 n.
reptile 365 n.
all-in
inclusive 78 adj.
all in
fatigued 684 adj.
all in all
on an average 30 adv.
on the whole 52 adv.
all in good time
opportunely 137 adv.
in the future 155 adv.
all in the day's work
professionally 622 adv.
unastonishing 865 adj.
alliteration
assimilation 18 n.
recurrence 106 n.
ornament 574 n.
prosody 593 n.
all-knowing
knowing 490 adj.
godlike 965 adj.
all manner of
different 15 adj.
multiform 82 adj.
all-merciful
godlike 965 adj.
all my eye and Betty Martin
fable 543 n.
all my own work
originality 21 n.
allocation
arrangement 62 n.
apportionment 783 n.
portion 783 n.
allocution
nomenclature 561 n.
speech 579 n.
allocution 583 n.
entreaty 761 n.
prayers 981 n.
allodial
unconditional 744 adj.
proprietary 777 adj.
all of a piece
uniform 16 adj.
simple 44 adj.
one 88 adj.
all of a sudden
instantaneously 116 adv.
unexpectedly 508 adv.
all off
ending 69 adj.
all one
equivalent 28 adj.
all one's life
for a long time 113 adv.
all one to
unwanted 860 adj.
allopathy
medical art 658 n.
allot
quantify 26 vb.
arrange 62 vb.
disperse 75 vb.
dispose of 673 vb.
use 673 vb.
dower 777 vb.
give 781 vb.
apportion 783 vb.
grant claims 915 vb.
allotment
piece 53 n.
farm 370 n.
garden 370 n.
portion 783 n.
all out
completely 54 adv.
swiftly 277 adv.
all over, be
be complete 54 vb.
end 69 vb.
all over one, be
pet 889 vb.
flatter 925 vb.
all over the place
nonuniformly 17 adv.
confusedly 61 adv.
here 189 adv.
all over with
dying 361 adj.
allow
subtract 39 vb.
attribute 158 vb.
be possible 469 vb.
make possible 469 vb.
be reasonable 475 vb.
believe 485 vb.
acquiesce 488 vb.
assent 488 vb.
confess 526 vb.
facilitate 701 vb.
be lenient 736 vb.
permit 756 vb.
consent 758 vb.
be patient 823 vb.
— a claim
grant claims 915 vb.
— an appeal
acquit 960 vb.
— for
set off 31 vb.
— full play
give scope 744 vb.
— in
admit 299 vb.
— no rest
fatigue 684 vb.
— oneself
permit 756 vb.
— to lapse
lose a chance 138 vb.
— to pass
disregard 458 vb.
allowable
possible 469 adj.
permitted 756 adj.
given 781 adj.
vindicable 927 adj.
legal 953 adj.
allowance
offset 31 n.
extra 40 n.
decrement 42 n.
qualification 468 n.
subvention 703 n.
leniency 736 n.
permission 756 n.
consent 758 n.
earnings 771 n.
dower 777 n.
gift 781 n.
portion 783 n.
receipt 807 n.
discount 810 n.
alloy
a mixture 43 n.
mix 43 vb.
compound 50 n.
mineral 359 n.
impair 655 vb.
all-powerful
strong 162 adj.
godlike 965 adj.
all-purpose
useful 640 adj.
all right
not bad 644 adj.
middling 732 adj.
all round
throughout 54 adv.
all-rounder
multiformity 82 n.
athlete 162 n.
proficient person 696 n.
player 837 n.
All Saints
holy day 988 n.
all set
prepared 669 adj.
all shapes and sizes
nonuniformity 17 n.
all sorts
medley 43 n.
everyman 79 n.
All Souls
holy day 988 n.
allspice
condiment 389 n.
all-star
dramatic 594 adj.
excellent 644 adj.
all talk
insubstantial thing 4 n.
all that could be desired
sufficiency 635 n.
all the better for
superior 34 adj.

improved 654 adj.
all the more
eminently 34 adv.
crescendo 36 adv.
all the rage
fashionable 848 adj.
all there
intelligent 498 adj.
sane 502 adj.
all the same
nevertheless 468 adv.
all the time
while 108 adv.
all the time in the world
leisure 681 n.
all the way
throughout 54 adv.
consentingly 488 adv.
all the year round
all along 113 adv.
all things considered
on the whole 52 adv.
in mind 449 adv.
all thumbs
clumsy 695 adj.
all together
conjointly 45 adv.
collectively 52 adv.
together 74 adv.
with 89 adv.
in league 708 adv.
all told
completely 54 adv.
all to the good
well 615 adv.
allude
relate 9 vb.
propound 512 vb.
mean 514 vb.
figure 519 vb.
imply 523 vb.
hint 524 vb.
all up with, be
be destroyed 165 vb.
allure
influence 178 vb.
attraction 291 n.
attract 291 vb.
tempt 612 vb.
delight 826 vb.
cause desire 859 vb.
excite love 887 vb.
allusion
referral 9 n.
metaphor 519 n.
allusive
relevant 9 adj.
suppositional 512 adj.
meaningful 514 adj.
figurative 519 adj.
tacit 523 adj.
unclear 568 adj.
alluvial
territorial 344 adj.
alluvium
leavings 41 n.
thing transferred 272 n.
soil 344 n.
all-wise
godlike 965 adj.
ally
join 45 vb.
combine 50 vb.
aider 703 n.
cooperate 706 vb.
auxiliary 707 n.
colleague 707 n.
join a party 708 vb.
contract 765 vb.
friend 880 n.
almagest
dissertation 591 n.
alma mater
academy 539 n.
almanac
directory 87 n.
chronology 117 n.
almighty
powerful 160 adj.
godlike 965 adj.
Almighty, the
the Deity 965 n.
almond
fruit 301 n.
almoner
nurse 658 n.
giver 781 n.
treasurer 798 n.
almost
almost 33 adv.
on the whole 52 adv.
nearly 200 adv.
imperfectly 647 adv.
almost all
main part 32 n.
chief part 52 n.
alms
gift 781 n.
kind act 897 n.
alms-giving
giving 781 n.
kind act 897 n.
act of worship 981 n.
almshouse
retreat 192 n.
shelter 662 n.
aloes
unsavouriness 391 n.
aloft
overhanging 209 adj.
aloft 209 adv.
up 308 adv.
alone
unrelated 10 adj.
separate 46 adj.
alone 88 adj.
singly 88 adv.
friendless 883 adj.
unsociable 883 adj.
along
longwise 203 adv.
alongside
near 200 adv.
in parallel 219 adv.
sideways 239 adv.
along with
in addition 38 adv.
with 89 adv.
synchronously 123 adv.
aloof
distant 199 adj.
incurious 454 adj.
impassive 820 adj.
prideful 871 adj.
inimical 881 adj.
unsociable 883 adj.
aloofness
noncoherence 49 n.
inattention 456 n.
unsociability 883 n.
aloud
loudly 400 adv.
vocal 577 adj.
alpaca
fibre 208 n.
textile 222 n.
alpenglow
glow 417 n.
alpha
beginning 68 n.
Alpha and Omega
all 52 n.
the Deity 965 n.
alphabet
beginning 68 n.
list 87 n.
letter 558 n.
lettering 586 n.
alphabetical order
order 60 n.
alphanumeric
computerized 86 adj.
alpha plus
excellent 644 adj.
alpha ray
radiation 417 n.
alpha waves
intellect 447 n.
alpine
alpine 209 adj.
alpinism
ascent 308 n.
Alps
high land 209 n.
already
before 119 adv.
at present 121 adv.
retrospectively 125 adv.
also
in addition 38 adv.
also-ran
inferior 35 n.
contender 716 n.
loser 728 n.
altar
ritual object 988 n.
altar 990 n.
altar bread
the sacrament 988 n.
altazimuth
astronomy 321 n.
alter
change 143 vb.
modify 143 vb.
qualify 468 vb.
— course
deviate 282 vb.
— the case
tell against 467 vb.
qualify 468 vb.
alterable
changeful 152 adj.
unstable 152 adj.
alteration
difference 15 n.
change 143 n.
transition 147 n.
alteration of plan
tergiversation 603 n.
altercation
quarrel 709 n.
contention 716 n.
alter ego
identity 13 n.
analogue 18 n.
colleague 707 n.
deputy 755 n.
close friend 880 n.
alternate
correlative 12 adj.
correlate 12 vb.
sequential 65 adj.
come after 65 vb.
discontinuous 72 adj.
be discontinuous 72 vb.
periodical 141 adj.
be periodic 141 vb.
substitute 150 n.
vary 152 vb.
fluctuate 317 vb.
deputy 755 n.
alternating current
electricity 160 n.
alternative
changeable 143 adj.
substitute 150 n.
choice 605 n.
contrivance 623 n.
means 629 n.
alternative life style
dissent 489 n.
alternatively
instead 150 adv.
optionally 605 adv.
alternative reading
interpretation 520 n.
alternator
electronics 160 n.
although
in return 31 adv.
although 182 adv.
provided 468 adv.
altimetry
altimetry 209 n.
angular measure 247 n.
geometry 465 n.

meter 465 n.
altitude
degree 27 n.
superiority 34 n.
height 209 n.
alto
vocalist 413 n.
altogether
on the whole 52 adv.
completely 54 adv.
altruism
philanthropy 901 n.
disinterestedness 931 n.
virtues 933 n.
altruist
kind person 897 n.
philanthropist 901 n.
altruistic
benevolent 897 adj.
philanthropic 901 adj.
disinterested 931 adj.
alum
sourness 393 n.
alumnus, alumna
student 538 n.
alveolus
cavity 255 n.
always
generally 79 adv.
while 108 adv.
a.m.
o'clock 117 adv.
morning 128 n.
at sunrise 128 adv.
amalgam
a mixture 43 n.
compound 50 n.
amalgamate
mix 43 vb.
combine 50 vb.
amalgamation
association 706 n.
amanuensis
recorder 549 n.
instrument 628 n.
auxiliary 707 n.
amaranthine
perpetual 115 adj.
amass
join 45 vb.
bring together 74 vb.
store 632 vb.
amateur
ignorance 491 n.
beginner 538 n.
artist 556 n.
unskilled 695 adj.
bungler 697 n.
people of taste 846 n.
desirer 859 n.
amateurish
ignorant 491 adj.
bungled 695 adj.
unskilled 695 adj.
amateurship
good taste 846 n.
amateur theatricals
drama 594 n.
amative
loving 887 adj.
amatory
erotic 887 adj.
loving 887 adj.
amaurotic
blind 439 adj.
dim-sighted 440 adj.
amaze
surprise 508 vb.
disappoint 509 vb.
impress 821 vb.
frighten 854 vb.
be wonderful 864 vb.
amazement
lack of expectation 508 n.
excitation 821 n.
wonder 864 n.
amazing
prodigious 32 adj.
Amazon
athlete 162 n.
woman 373 n.
soldier 722 n.
brave person 855 n.
amazonian
manly 162 adj.
ambages
deviation 282 n.
pleonasm 570 n.
circuit 626 n.
ambassador, ambassadress
messenger 529 n.
envoy 754 n.
amber
resin 357 n.
brownness 430 n.
yellow 433 adj.
preserver 666 n.
gem 844 n.
ambergris
resin 357 n.
scent 396 n.
ambidextrous
dual 90 adj.
double 91 adj.
dextral 241 adj.
skilful 694 adj.
ambience
surroundings 230 n.
ambiguity
disagreement 25 n.
equivocalness 518 n.
mental dishonesty 543 n.
ambiguous
unconformable 84 adj.
countervailing 467 adj.
uncertain 474 adj.
semantic 514 adj.
puzzling 517 adj.
equivocal 518 adj.
false 541 adj.
unclear 568 adj.
ambition
motive 612 n.
intention 617 n.
business 622 n.
aspiration 852 n.
desire 859 n.
desired object 859 n.
ambitious
attempting 671 adj.
enterprising 672 adj.
hoping 852 adj.
ambivalence
contrariety 14 n.
disagreement 25 n.
equivocalness 518 n.
amble
gait 265 n.
pedestrianism 267 n.
ride 267 vb.
wander 267 vb.
slowness 278 n.
move slowly 278 vb.
amblyopia
blindness 439 n.
dim sight 440 n.
ambrosia
savouriness 390 n.
ambrosial
savoury 390 adj.
sweet 392 adj.
fragrant 396 adj.
Ambrosian chant
vocal music 412 n.
hymn 981 n.
ambulance
conveyance 267 n.
vehicle 274 n.
hospital 658 n.
ambulate
walk 267 vb.
ambulatory
travelling 267 adj.
path 624 n.
church exterior 990 n.
church interior 990 n.
ambuscade
ambush 527 n.
ambush
surprise 508 vb.
latency 523 n.
be stealthy 525 vb.
ambush 527 n.vb.
trap 542 n.
ensnare 542 vb.
danger 661 n.
pitfall 663 n.
stratagem 698 n.
be cunning 698 vb.
âme damnée
auxiliary 707 n.
dependant 742 n.
bad person 938 n.
ameliorate
make better 654 vb.
amen
assent 488 n., int.
amenable
liable 180 adj.
credulous 487 adj.
willing 597 adj.
obedient 739 adj.
amend
rectify 654 vb.
repair 656 vb.
amende honorable
atonement 941 n.
amendment
compensation 31 n.
interpretation 520 n.
amendment 654 n.
restoration 656 n.
remedy 658 n.
amends
compensation 31 n.
offset 31 n.
restoration 656 n.
remedy 658 n.
restitution 787 n.
atonement 941 n.
amenity
pleasurableness 826 n.
courtesy 884 n.
amentia
insanity 503 n.
amercement
penalty 963 n.
Americanism
dialect 560 n.
Americanize, Americanise
transform 147 vb.
amethyst
purpleness 436 n.
gem 844 n.
amiability
courtesy 884 n.
amiable
peaceful 717 adj.
pleasurable 826 adj.
well-bred 848 adj.
amiable 884 adj.
lovable 887 adj.
benevolent 897 adj.
amicable
concordant 710 adj.
friendly 880 adj.
amid, amidst
among 43 adv.
between 231 adv.
amino acid
food content 301 n.
amiss
inopportunely 138 adv.
amiss 616 adv.
badly 645 adv.
amity
concord 710 n.
friendship 880 n.
ammonite
fossil 125 n.
coil 251 n.

ammunition
means 629 n.
defence 713 n.
ammunition 723 n.
ammunition box
arsenal 723 n.
amnesia
oblivion 506 n.
amnesty
amnesty 506 n.
forget 506 vb.
obliteration 550 n.
deliverance 668 n.
peace 717 n.
peace offering 719 n.
be lenient 736 vb.
show mercy 905 vb.
forgiveness 909 n.
forgive 909 vb.
nonliability 919 n.
exempt 919 vb.
amoeba
small animal 33 n.
microorganism 196 n.
among, amongst
among 43 adv.
centrally 225 adv.
between 231 adv.
amoral
thick-skinned 820 adj.
indifferent 860 adj.
wicked 934 adj.
unchaste 951 adj.
irreligious 974 adj.
amoralist
irreligionist 974 n.
impious person 980 n.
amorality
no choice 606 n.
indifference 860 n.
wickedness 934 n.
unchastity 951 n.
amorist
lover 887 n.
libertine 952 n.
amorous
foolish 499 adj.
loving 887 adj.
amorphism
nonuniformity 17 n.
amorphism 244 n.
amorphous
incomplete 55 adj.
orderless 61 adj.
amorphous 244 adj.
distorted 246 adj.
fluid 335 adj.
unsightly 842 adj.
amount
quantity 26 n.
funds 797 n.
price 809 n.
amount to
number 86 vb.
cost 809 vb.
amour
love affair 887 n.
illicit love 951 n.
amour propre
pride 871 n.
vanity 873 n.
amp, ampere
electronics 160 n.
ampersand
letter 558 n.
amphetamine
drug-taking 949 n.
amphibian
swimming 269 adj.
vehicle 274 n.
amphibian 365 n.
animal 365 n.adj.
amphibious
unconformable 84 adj.
dual 90 adj.
double 91 adj.
amphibiousness
skill 694 n.
amphibology
equivocalness 518 n.
amphigory, amphigouri
absurdity 497 n.
lack of meaning 515 n.
amphitheatre
theatre 594 n.
arena 724 n.
amphora
vessel 194 n.
ample
great 32 adj.
many 104 adj.
spacious 183 adj.
fleshy 195 adj.
large 195 adj.
broad 205 adj.
diffuse 570 adj.
plenteous 635 adj.
liberal 813 adj.
amplification
increase 36 n.
expansion 197 n.
intelligibility 516 n.
translation 520 n.
diffuseness 570 n.
amplifier
megaphone 400 n.
gramophone 414 n.
hearing aid 415 n.
amplitude
quantity 26 n.
degree 27 n.
greatness 32 n.
plenitude 54 n.
range 183 n.
size 195 n.
breadth 205 n.
diffuseness 570 n.
plenty 635 n.
ampoule
receptacle 194 n.
amputate
subtract 39 vb.
sunder 46 vb.
doctor 658 vb.
amulet
preserver 666 n.
jewellery 844 n.
talisman 983 n.
amuse
please 826 vb.
amuse 837 vb.
be witty 839 vb.
be ridiculous 849 vb.
amusement
pleasure 376 n.
trifle 639 n.
easy thing 701 n.
enjoyment 824 n.
pleasurableness 826 n.
merriment 833 n.
amusement 837 n.
social gathering 882 n.
amusement arcade
gaming-house 618 n.
place of amusement 837 n.
amusing
pleasant 376 adj.
pleasurable 826 adj.
merry 833 adj.
amusing 837 adj.
funny 849 adj.
sociable 882 adj.
an
one 88 adj.
Anabaptist
Protestant 976 n.
anabatic
ascending 308 adj.
anachronism
anachronism 118 n.
different time 122 n.
untimeliness 138 n.
inexactness 495 n.
anachronistic
anachronistic 118 adj.
not contemporary 122 adj.
antiquated 127 adj.
ill-timed 138 adj.
anacoluthon
discontinuity 72 n.
solecism 565 n.
anaconda
reptile 365 n.
anacreontic
poem 593 n.
poetic 593 adj.
merry 833 adj.
anacrusis
musical piece 412 n.
prosody 593 n.
anaemia
weakness 163 n.
achromatism 426 n.
blood disease 651 n.
anaemic
unhealthy 651 adj.
anaesthesia
insensibility 375 n.
anaesthetic
moderator 177 n.
anaesthetic 375 n.
insensible 375 adj.
drug 658 n.
remedial 658 adj.
soporific 679 n.
relief 831 n.
anaesthetist
doctor 658 n.
anaesthetize, anaesthetise
render insensible 375 vb.
doctor 658 vb.
relieve 831 vb.
anagoge
metaphor 519 n.
latency 523 n.
anagram
interchange 151 n.
equivocalness 518 n.
enigma 530 n.
initials 558 n.
anal
back 238 adj.
excretory 302 adj.
analeptic
restorative 656 adj.
remedial 658 adj.
analgesia
insensibility 375 n.
analgesic
anaesthetic 375 n.
insensible 375 adj.
antidote 658 n.
drug 658 n.
remedial 658 adj.
relief 831 n.
relieving 831 adj.
analogical
similar 18 adj.
compared 462 adj.
analogous
relative 9 adj.
correlative 12 adj.
similar 18 adj.
symmetrical 245 adj.
analogue
identity 13 n.
analogue 18 n.
copy 22 n.
computerized 86 adj.
analogy
relativeness 9 n.
similarity 18 n.
comparison 462 n.
analphabet
ignoramus 493 n.
analyse
sunder 46 vb.
decompose 51 vb.
class 62 vb.
enquire 459 vb.
experiment 461 vb.

argue 475 vb.
parse 564 vb.
analysis
separation 46 n.
decomposition 51 n.
arrangement 62 n.
numerical operation 86 n.
enquiry 459 n.
experiment 461 n.
argumentation 475 n.
grammar 564 n.
analyst
enquirer 459 n.
experimenter 461 n.
analytic, – al
enquiring 459 adj.
experimental 461 adj.
rational 475 adj.
linguistic 557 adj.
anamnesis
remembrance 505 n.
anamorphosis
distortion 246 n.
visual fallacy 440 n.
misrepresentation 552 n.
anapaest
prosody 593 n.
anaphora
repetition 106 n.
trope 519 n.
ornament 574 n.
anaphrodisiac
moderator 177 n.
anarchic, anarchical
disorderly 61 adj.
anarchic 734 adj.
disobedient 738 adj.
riotous 738 adj.
independent 744 adj.
nonobservant 769 adj.
lawless 954 adj.
anarchism
sedition 738 n.
anarchist
anarchist 61 n.
revolutionist 149 n.
destroyer 168 n.
violent creature 176 n.
political party 708 n.
revolter 738 n.
evildoer 904 n.
anarchy
disorder 61 n.
anarchy 734 n.
nonobservance 769 n.
lawlessness 954 n.
anastrophe
inversion 221 n.
ornament 574 n.
anathema
hateful object 888 n.
malediction 899 n.
anathematize, anathematise
curse 899 vb.
dispraise 924 vb.
declare heretical 977 vb.
perform ritual 988 vb.
anatomical
structural 331 adj.
anatomist
zoologist 367 n.
anatomization
decomposition 51 n.
anatomize, anatomise
sunder 46 vb.
class 62 vb.
anatomy
structure 331 n.
biology 358 n.
zoology 367 n.
ancestor
precursor 66 n.
source 156 n.
paternity 169 n.
ancestral
former 125 adj.
immemorial 127 adj.
parental 169 adj.
ancestress
maternity 169 n.
ancestry
heredity 5 n.
consanguinity 11 n.
origin 68 n.
source 156 n.
genealogy 169 n.
nobility 868 n.
anchor
affix 45 vb.
coupling 47 n.
place 187 vb.
place oneself 187 vb.
dwell 192 vb.
come to rest 266 vb.
sailing aid 269 n.
protection 660 n.
safeguard 662 n.
badge of rank 743 n.
hope 852 n.
anchorage
station 187 n.
goal 295 n.
shelter 662 n.
anchored
fixed 153 adj.
quiescent 266 adj.
anchoress
solitary 883 n.
ascetic 945 n.
nun 986 n.
anchorite
solitary 883 n.
ascetic 945 n.
pietist 979 n.
ancien régime
past time 125 n.
archaism 127 n.
aristocracy 868 n.
ancient
great 32 adj.
former 125 adj.
past 125 adj.
olden 127 adj.
worshipful 866 adj.
ancient lights
dueness 915 n.
ancient monument
antiquity 125 n.
monument 548 n.
ancient pedigree
nobility 868 n.
ancients, the
precursor 66 n.
antiquity 125 n.
ancillary
inferior 35 adj.
aiding 703 adj.
ancon
shelf 218 n.
and
in addition 38 adv.
andante
slowness 278 n.
tempo 410 n.
adagio 412 adv.
andirons
furnace 383 n.
androgyne
nonconformist 84 n.
and so
accordingly 8 adv.
consequently 157 adv.
and so forth, and so on
in addition 38 adv.
anecdotage
old age 131 n.
loquacity 581 n.
anecdotal
unrelated 10 adj.
remembering 505 adj.
anecdote
narrative 590 n.
anemometer
recording instrument 549 n.
anemometry
pneumatics 340 n.
anemometry 352 n.
meter 465 n.
aneurysm
cardiovascular disease 651 n.
anew
again 106 adv.
newly 126 adv.
anfractuosity
convolution 251 n.
angary
expropriation 786 n.
angel
stage manager 594 n.
lender 784 n.
coinage 797 n.
a beauty 841 n.
loved one 887 n.
darling 890 n.
innocent 935 n.
good person 937 n.
angel 968 n.
mythical being 970 n.
angelic, angelical
lovable 887 adj.
virtuous 933 adj.
innocent 935 adj.
angelic 968 adj.
angel of death
destroyer 168 n.
angel 968 n.
angelus
signal 547 n.
anger
excitation 821 n.
excitable state 822 n.
hatred 888 n.
anger 891 n.
enrage 891 vb.
disapprobation 924 n.
vice 934 n.
angina
pang 377 n.
angle
angle 247 n.
make angular 247 vb.
projection 254 n.
appearance 445 n.
bias 481 n.
opinion 485 n.
hunt 619 vb.
— for
be tentative 461 vb.
attempt 671 vb.
request 761 vb.
desire 859 vb.
angle of vision
view 438 n.
Anglican
Protestant 976 n.
Anglican 976 adj.
sectarian 978 adj.
anglicism
dialect 560 n.
Anglo-Catholic
Catholic 976 n.
Anglican 976 adj.
Anglophile
xenophile 880 n.
Anglophobe
enemy 881 n.
anglophone
speaking 579 adj.
Anglo-Saxon monosyllable
plainness 573 n.
Angora
fibre 208 n.
textile 222 n.
hair 259 n.

angry
furious 176 adj.
frenzied 503 adj.
excited 821 adj.
angry 891 adj.
threatening 900 adj.
angry young man
nonconformist 84 n.
malcontent 829 n.
angst
suffering 825 n.
melancholy 834 n.
anguine
snaky 251 adj.
anguish
pain 377 n.
badness 645 n.
suffering 825 n.
angular
oblique 220 adj.
crossed 222 adj.
angular 247 adj.
curved 248 adj.
angularity
joint 45 n.
nonconformity 84 n.
obliquity 220 n.
angularity 247 n.
curvature 248 n.
camber 253 n.
leg 267 n.
divergence 294 n.
anhydrous
dry 342 adj.
aniline dye
pigment 425 n.
anility
old age 131 n.
folly 499 n.
anima
spirit 447 n.
animadversion
reprimand 924 n.
animal
young creature 132 n.
animal 365 n.adj.
mindless 448 adj.
unthinking 450 adj.
knave 938 n.
intemperate 943 adj.
sensualist 944 n.
sensual 944 adj.
animal and vegetable kingdom
organism 358 n.
animal cry
cry 408 n.
animalcule
microorganism 196 n.
animal disease
animal disease 651 n.
animal food
provender 301 n.
animal husbandry
production 164 n.
propagation 167 n.
animal husbandry 369 n.
agriculture 370 n.
animalism
animality 365 n.
sensualism 944 n.
animality
life 360 n.
animality 365 n.
absence of intellect 448 n.
animal life
life 360 n.
animality 365 n.
animal management
animal husbandry 369 n.
animal spirits
vitality 162 n.
life 360 n.
cheerfulness 833 n.
animal trainer
breeder 369 n.
trainer 537 n.
animal worship
idolatry 982 n.
animate
strengthen 162 vb.
invigorate 174 vb.
incite 612 vb.
animate 821 vb.
cheer 833 vb.
give courage 855 vb.
animated
alive 360 adj.
active 678 adj.
lively 819 adj.
cheerful 833 adj.
animated cartoon
film 445 n.
animate existence
life 360 n.
animate matter
organism 358 n.
animation
life 360 n.
cinema 445 n.
restlessness 678 n.
excitation 821 n.
cheerfulness 833 n.
courage 855 n.
animator
director 690 n.
animism
immateriality 320 n.
deism 973 n.
animosity
dislike 861 n.
enmity 881 n.
hatred 888 n.
resentment 891 n.
animus
spirit 447 n.
willingness 597 n.
intention 617 n.
affections 817 n.
feeling 818 n.
enmity 881 n.
ankh
cross 222 n.
badge of rule 743 n.
ankle
joint 45 n.
foot 214 n.
angularity 247 n.
ankle-deep
deep 211 adj.
shallow 212 adj.
ankle-length
long 203 adj.
anklet
jewellery 844 n.
ankus
sharp point 256 n.
annalist
chronologist 117 n.
chronicler 549 n.
narrator 590 n.
annals
chronology 117 n.
record 548 n.
narrative 590 n.
anneal
be tough 329 vb.
annex
add 38 vb.
connect 45 vb.
subjugate 745 vb.
acquire 771 vb.
appropriate 786 vb.
annexation
addition 38 n.
joining together 45 n.
annexe
adjunct 40 n.
annihilate
nullify 2 vb.
abate 37 vb.
destroy 165 vb.
slaughter 362 vb.
anniversary
date 108 n.
period 110 n.
anniversary 141 n.
seasonal 141 adj.
special day 876 n.
celebratory 876 adj.
holy day 988 n.
anno domini
anno domini 108 adv.
old age 131 n.
annotate
interpret 520 vb.
mark 547 vb.
dissertate 591 vb.
annotated text
textbook 589 n.
annotation
commentary 520 n.
record 548 n.
announce
predict 511 vb.
communicate 524 vb.
proclaim 528 vb.
name 561 vb.
— itself
happen 154 vb.
announcement
prediction 511 n.
information 524 n.
publication 528 n.
announcer
precursor 66 n.
informant 524 n.
publicizer 528 n.
messenger 529 n.
broadcaster 531 n.
nomenclator 561 n.
speaker 579 n.
annoy
give pain 377 vb.
meddle 678 vb.
hinder 702 vb.
oppress 735 vb.
torment 827 vb.
sadden 834 vb.
enrage 891 vb.
be malevolent 898 vb.
annoyance
evil 616 n.
badness 645 n.
bane 659 n.
worry 825 n.
annoyance 827 n.
resentment 891 n.
annoyed
unhappy 825 adj.
discontented 829 adj.
angry 891 adj.
annoying
bad 645 adj.
not nice 645 adj.
annoying 827 adj.
discontenting 829 adj.
annual
periodic 110 adj.
ephemeral 114 adj.
seasonal 141 adj.
flower 366 n.
journal 528 n.
reference book 589 n.
annuitant
recipient 782 n.
annuity
pay 804 n.
receipt 807 n.
annul
destroy 165 vb.
relinquish 621 vb.
abrogate 752 vb.
divorce 896 vb.
make illegal 954 vb.
annular
round 250 adj.
annulled
illegal 954 adj.
annulment
obliteration 550 n.
relinquishment 621 n.

abrogation 752 n.
divorce 896 n.
annunciate
communicate 524 vb.
annus mirabilis
period 110 n.
prodigy 864 n.
anode
electricity 160 n.
anodyne
moderator 177 n.
lenitive 177 adj.
remedial 658 adj.
relieving 831 adj.
anoint
overlay 226 vb.
rub 333 vb.
lubricate 334 vb.
grease 357 vb.
commission 751 vb.
perform ritual 988 vb.
anointed
godlike 965 adj.
anointed king/queen
sovereign 741 n.
anointment
lubrication 334 n.
unctuousness 357 n.
anomalous
orderless 61 adj.
abnormal 84 adj.
grammatical 564 adj.
anomaly
disorder 61 n.
nonconformity 84 n.
anon
betimes 135 adv.
anonymity
unknown thing 491 n.
latency 523 n.
concealment 525 n.
no name 562 n.
anonymous
disguised 525 adj.
anonymous 562 adj.
inglorious 867 adj.
anorak
jacket 228 n.
anorexia
indifference 860 n.
fasting 946 n.
anosmia
inodorousness 395 n.
another
different 15 adj.
additional 38 adj.
sequential 65 adj.
another story
variant 15 n.
another time
different time 122 n.
ansate cross
cross 222 n.
badge of rule 743 n.
anserine
animal 365 adj.
foolish 499 adj.
answer
accord 24 vb.
numerical result 85 n.
reason why 156 n.
answer 460 n.vb.
counterevidence 467 n.
argue 475 vb.
confutation 479 n.
converse 584 vb.
correspondence 588 n.
correspond 588 vb.
contrivance 623 n.
suffice 635 vb.
be useful 640 vb.
good policy 642 n.
be expedient 642 vb.
remedy 658 n.
retaliate 714 vb.
be successful 727 vb.
be witty 839 vb.
— back
interchange 151 vb.
answer 460 vb.
argue 475 vb.
retaliate 714 vb.
be insolent 878 vb.
— for
be liable 180 vb.
deputize 755 vb.
promise 764 vb.
— the purpose
be successful 727 vb.
— to
be related 9 vb.
correlate 12 vb.
resemble 18 vb.
answer 460 vb.
be named 561 vb.
answerable
causal 156 adj.
liable 180 adj.
indebted 803 adj.
obliged 917 adj.
answerer
respondent 460 n.
interlocutor 584 n.
ant
small animal 33 n.
insect 365 n.
busy person 678 n.
worker 686 n.
antacid
antidote 658 n.
antagonism
contrariety 14 n.
counteraction 182 n.
opposition 704 n.
enmity 881 n.
hatred 888 n.
antagonist
opponent 705 n.
enemy 881 n.
antagonize, antagonise
counteract 182 vb.
cause dislike 861 vb.
make enemies 881 vb.
excite hate 888 vb.
huff 891 vb.
Antarctica
coldness 380 n.
ante
before 64 adv.
gambling 618 n.
offering 781 n.
portion 783 n.
antecede
be before 119 vb.
precede 283 vb.
antecedence
precedence 64 n.
priority 119 n.
antecedent
precursor 66 n.
antedate
come before 64 vb.
misdate 118 vb.
antediluvian
prior 119 adj.
antiquated 127 adj.
primal 127 adj.
antelope
speeder 277 n.
mammal 365 n.
antenatal
prior 119 adj.
fertilized 167 adj.
antenna
filament 208 n.
protuberance 254 n.
feeler 378 n.
broadcasting 531 n.
antependium
altar 990 n.
antepenultimate
ending 69 adj.
anteposition
precedence 64 n.
anterior
preceding 64 adj.
prior 119 adj.
frontal 237 adj.
anteroom
lobby 194 n.
ante up
pay 804 vb.
anthem
vocal music 412 n.
hymn 981 n.
worship 981 vb.
anther
flower 366 n.
anthill
nest 192 n.
small hill 209 n.
anthology
composition 56 n.
assemblage 74 n.
literature 557 n.
textbook 589 n.
anthology 592 n.
poem 593 n.
choice 605 n.
anthracite
coal 385 n.
anthrax
animal disease 651 n.
anthropocentric
human 371 adj.
anthropoid
animal 365 adj.
human 371 adj.
anthropoid ape
mammal 365 n.
anthropological
human 371 adj.
anthropologist
anthropology 371 n.
zoologist 367 n.
anthropology
zoology 367 n.
anthropology 371 n.
anthropomorphic
human 371 adj.
idolatrous 982 adj.
anti-
contrary 14 adj.
opposing 704 adj.
antiaircraft
defending 713 adj.
antiaircraft gun
gun 723 n.
antibiotic
antidote 658 n.
drug 658 n.
antibody
antidote 658 n.
Antichrist
bad person 938 n.
Satan 969 n.
irreligionist 974 n.
anti-Christian
irreligious 974 adj.
impious 980 adj.
antichristianism
antichristianity 974 n.
anticipate
misdate 118 vb.
do before 119 vb.
look ahead 124 vb.
be early 135 vb.
expect 507 vb.
foresee 510 vb.
be willing 597 vb.
prepare 669 vb.
be active 678 vb.
take 786 vb.
hope 852 vb.
be rash 857 vb.
anticipation
precursor 66 n.
anticipation 135 n.
expectation 507 n.
foresight 510 n.
preparation 669 n.
anticipatory
expectant 507 adj.

foreseeing 510 adj.
anticlerical
irreligious 974 adj.
impious 980 adj.
anticlimax
decrease 37 n.
absurdity 497 n.
lack of expectation 508 n.
disappointment 509 n.
feebleness 572 n.
failure 728 n.
ridiculousness 849 n.
anticlinal
sloping 220 adj.
arched 253 adj.
anticline
dome 253 n.
fold 261 n.
anticlockwise
towards 281 adv.
regressive 286 adj.
round and round 315 adv.
anticoagulant
liquefaction 337 n.
antidote 658 n.
anticonvulsant
antidote 658 n.
antics
foolery 497 n.
bungling 695 n.
revel 837 n.
anticyclone
weather 340 n.
antidepressant
drug 658 n.
antidote
contrariety 14 n.
moderator 177 n.
counteraction 182 n.
liquefaction 337 n.
antidote 658 n.
antifreeze
heating 381 adj.
antigen
antidote 658 n.
antihero
acting 594 n.
antihistamine
antidote 658 n.
antilogarithm
numerical element 85 n.
antilogy
contrariety 14 n.
sophism 477 n.
antimalarial pill
prophylactic 658 n.
antimissile missile
missile weapon 723 n.
antinomian
anarchic 734 adj.
revolter 738 n.
disobedient 738 adj.
lawless 954 adj.
heretic 977 n.
antinomy
contrariety 14 n.
illegality 954 n.
antinovel
novel 590 n.
antipasto
hors-d'oeuvres 301 n.
antipathetic
contrary 14 adj.
disagreeing 25 adj.
unconformable 84 adj.
counteracting 182 adj.
repellent 292 adj.
opposing 704 adj.
disliked 861 adj.
disliking 861 adj.
inimical 881 adj.
hating 888 adj.
antipathy
contrariety 14 n.
difference 15 n.
counteraction 182 n.
dislike 861 n.
enmity 881 n.
hatred 888 n.
antiperspirant
cosmetic 843 n.
antiphon
answer 460 n.
hymn 981 n.
antipodal, antipodean
contrary 14 adj.
distant 199 adj.
inverted 221 adj.
opposite 240 adj.
antipodes
extremity 69 n.
farness 199 n.
contraposition 240 n.
antipyretic
antidote 658 n.
remedial 658 adj.
antiquarian
antiquarian 125 n.
olden 127 adj.
collector 492 n.
chronicler 549 n.
bibliographical 589 adj.
antiquary
antiquarian 125 n.
collector 492 n.
antiquated
anachronistic 118 adj.
not contemporary 122 adj.
past 125 adj.
antiquated 127 adj.
ageing 131 adj.
useless 641 adj.
disused 674 adj.
antique
archaism 127 n.
olden 127 adj.
antiquity
time 108 n.
era 110 n.
long duration 113 n.
antiquity 125 n.
past time 125 n.
oldness 127 n.
monument 548 n.
collection 632 n.
antireligious
irreligious 974 adj.
impious 980 adj.
anti-Semite
enemy 881 n.
anti-Semitism
prejudice 481 n.
phobia 854 n.
hatred 888 n.
antiseptic
clean 648 adj.
salubrious 652 adj.
prophylactic 658 n.
remedial 658 adj.
tutelary 660 adj.
antisepticize, antisepticise
purify 648 vb.
sanitate 652 vb.
doctor 658 vb.
antisocial
unsociable 883 adj.
misanthropic 902 adj.
antispasmodic
antidote 658 n.
antithesis
contrariety 14 n.
difference 15 n.
contraposition 240 n.
comparison 462 n.
trope 519 n.
ornament 574 n.
antithetic, antithetical
contrary 14 adj.
rhetorical 574 adj.
antitoxin
antidote 658 n.
antitype
prototype 23 n.
antler
protuberance 254 n.
sharp point 256 n.
antonomasia
trope 519 n.
nomenclature 561 n.
antonym
contrariety 14 n.
connotation 514 n.
word 559 n.
antrum
cavity 255 n.
anus
buttocks 238 n.
anvil
stand 218 n.
hammer 279 n.
anxiety
carefulness 457 n.
expectation 507 n.
worry 825 n.
nervousness 854 n.
anxiety neurosis
psychopathy 503 n.
anxious
careful 457 adj.
expectant 507 adj.
suffering 825 adj.
nervous 854 adj.
desiring 859 adj.
anxious to please
courteous 884 adj.
any
quantitative 26 adj.
universal 79 adj.
no name 562 n.
anonymous 562 adj.
no choice 606 n.
anybody's
unpossessed 774 adj.
anybody's guess
uncertainty 474 n.
ignorance 491 n.
anyhow
confusedly 61 adv.
negligently 458 adv.
any old how
negligently 458 adv.
anyone
everyman 79 n.
anything
everyman 79 n.
anything but
contrary 14 adj.
different 15 adj.
any time
not now 122 adv.
any time but this
different time 122 n.
aorist
time 108 n.
apace
swiftly 277 adv.
hastily 680 adv.
apart
separate 46 adj.
apart 46 adv.
afar 199 adv.
apart from
exclusive of 57 adv.
apartheid
separation 46 n.
exclusion 57 n.
prejudice 481 n.
apartment
flat 192 n.
chamber 194 n.
apathetic
inert 175 adj.
slow 278 adj.
incurious 454 adj.
inattentive 456 adj.
inexpectant 508 adj.
choiceless 606 adj.
nonactive 677 adj.
inactive 679 adj.
apathetic 820 adj.
apathy
indifference 860 n.

ape
imitator 20 n.
imitate 20 vb.
mammal 365 n.
ape-man
humankind 371 n.
ruffian 904 n.
monster 938 n.
aperçu
compendium 592 n.
witticism 839 n.
aperient
opener 263 n.
excretory 302 adj.
cleanser 648 n.
purgative 658 n.
aperitif
prelude 66 n.
stimulant 174 n.
alcoholic drink 301 n.
aperture
opening 263 n.
orifice 263 n.
camera 442 n.
apex
summit 213 n.
vertex 213 n.
aphasia
speech defect 580 n.
aphelion
distance 199 n.
aphid
insect 365 n.
aphonia, aphony
voicelessness 578 n.
speech defect 580 n.
aphonic
silent 399 adj.
voiceless 578 adj.
aphorism
maxim 496 n.
conciseness 569 n.
aphoristic
aphoristic 496 adj.
concise 569 adj.
preceptive 693 adj.
aphrodisiac
stimulant 174 n.
erotic 887 adj.
Aphrodite
a beauty 841 n.
love god 887 n.
Olympian deity 967 n.
apiary
nest 192 n.
stock farm 369 n.
apiculture
animal husbandry 369 n.
apiece
severally 80 adv.
apishness
mimicry 20 n.
aplomb
stability 153 n.
resolution 599 n.
apocalypse
ruin 165 n.
prediction 511 n.
disclosure 526 n.
revelation 975 n.
scripture 975 n.
apocope
shortening 204 n.
Apocrypha
scripture 975 n.
apocryphal
uncertified 474 adj.
erroneous 495 adj.
apodictic
demonstrating 478 adj.
apogee
distance 199 n.
summit 213 n.
Apollo
sun 321 n.
musician 413 n.
poetry 593 n.
a beauty 841 n.
Olympian deity 967 n.
Apollyon
Satan 969 n.
apologetic
excusing 614 adj.
regretting 830 adj.
repentant 939 adj.
atoning 941 adj.
apologetics, apologia
argument 475 n.
pretext 614 n.
vindication 927 n.
apologies
regret 830 n.
apologist
reasoner 475 n.
vindicator 927 n.
apologize, apologise
recant 603 vb.
tergiversate 603 vb.
knuckle under 721 vb.
regret 830 vb.
be penitent 939 vb.
atone 941 vb.
apologue
narrative 590 n.
apology
recantation 603 n.
pretext 614 n.
penitence 939 n.
atonement 941 n.
apology for
copy 22 n.
pretext 614 n.
laughingstock 851 n.
apophthegm
maxim 496 n.
apoplectic
angry 891 adj.
apoplexy
helplessness 161 n.
insensibility 375 n.
illness 651 n.
aport
sinistrally 242 adv.
apostasy
tergiversation 603 n.
rejection 607 n.
relapse 657 n.
impiety 980 n.
apostate
changed person 147 n.
dissentient 489 n.
tergiversator 603 n.
heathen 974 n.
schismatic 978 n.
impious person 980 n.
impious 980 adj.
apostatize, apostatise
apostatize 603 vb.
reject 607 vb.
relinquish 621 vb.
relapse 657 vb.
be irreligious 974 vb.
a posteriori
rational 475 adj.
apostle
messenger 529 n.
preacher 537 n.
religious teacher 973 n.
Apostles' Creed
orthodoxy 976 n.
apostolate
vocation 622 n.
church ministry 985 n.
church office 985 n.
apostolic
scriptural 975 adj.
ecclesiastical 985 adj.
priestly 985 adj.
apostolic succession
holy orders 985 n.
apostrophe
punctuation 547 n.
nomenclature 561 n.
speech 579 n.
allocution 583 n.
soliloquy 585 n.
entreaty 761 n.
apothecary
druggist 658 n.
apotheosis
dignification 866 n.
heaven 971 n.
deification 982 n.
apotheosize, apotheosise
worship 981 vb.
idolatrize 982 vb.
appal
displease 827 vb.
frighten 854 vb.
appanage
adjunct 40 n.
dower 777 n.
apparat
governance 733 n.
apparatchik
official 690 n.
officer 741 n.
apparatus
tool 630 n.
apparatus criticus
commentary 520 n.
apparel
clothing 228 n.
dress 228 vb.
apparent
visible 443 adj.
appearing 445 adj.
plausible 471 adj.
certain 473 adj.
manifest 522 adj.
apparition
visual fallacy 440 n.
appearance 445 n.
manifestation 522 n.
ghost 970 n.
apparitor
law officer 955 n.
appeal
influence 178 vb.
attraction 291 n.
attract 291 vb.
affirmation 532 n.
affirm 532 vb.
negation 533 n.
allocution 583 n.
motivate 612 vb.
entreaty 761 n.
request 761 n.
entreat 761 vb.
deprecate 762 vb.
excitation 821 n.
pleasurableness 826 n.
beauty 841 n.
lovableness 887 n.
legal trial 959 n.
— against
negate 533 vb.
deprecate 762 vb.
— for mercy
ask mercy 905 vb.
— to
speak to 583 vb.
entreat 761 vb.
request 761 vb.
— to arms
fight 716 vb.
go to war 718 vb.
— to reason
be reasonable 475 vb.
appealer
petitioner 763 n.
appear
begin 68 vb.
arrive 295 vb.
be visible 443 vb.
appear 445 vb.
be plain 522 vb.
be disclosed 526 vb.
— for
deputize 755 vb.

— from nowhere
surprise 508 vb.
appearance
modality 7 n.
circumstance 8 n.
similarity 18 n.
beginning 68 n.
exteriority 223 n.
form 243 n.
arrival 295 n.
view 438 n.
visibility 443 n.
appearance 445 n.
probability 471 n.
ideality 513 n.
manifestation 522 n.
pretext 614 n.
conduct 688 n.
appearances
etiquette 848 n.
appearing
evidential 466 adj.
plausible 471 adj.
deceiving 542 adj.
appease
assuage 177 vb.
induce 612 vb.
pacify 719 vb.
content 828 vb.
offer worship 981 vb.
appeasement
peace offering 719 n.
appellant
petitioner 763 n.
dueness 915 n.
accuser 928 n.
litigant 959 n.
appellate
judicatory 956 adj.
appellation
name 561 n.
nomenclature 561 n.
append
add 38 vb.
place after 65 vb.
hang 217 vb.
appendage
adjunct 40 n.
limb 53 n.
sequel 67 n.
concomitant 89 n.
appendicitis
digestive disorders 651 n.
appendix
addition 38 n.
adjunct 40 n.
sequel 67 n.
extremity 69 n.
hanging object 217 n.
edition 589 n.
apperceive
cognize 447 vb.
appertaining
relative 9 adj.
possessed 773 adj.
appertain to
be one of 58 vb.
be included 78 vb.
appetency, appetence
relation 9 n.
will 595 n.
desire 859 n.
appetite
eating 301 n.
taste 386 n.
desire 859 n.
hunger 859 n.
liking 859 n.
appetizer, appetiser
prelude 66 n.
stimulant 174 n.
hors d'oeuvres 301 n.
savouriness 390 n.
appetizing, appetising
tasty 386 adj.
savoury 390 adj.
exciting 821 adj.
desired 859 adj.
applaud
assent 488 vb.
gesticulate 547 vb.
rejoice 835 vb.
honour 866 vb.
congratulate 886 vb.
applaud 923 vb.
apple
fruit 301 n.
apple of discord
casus belli 709 n.
quarrelsomeness 709 n.
apple of one's eye
favourite 890 n.
appliance
causal means 156 n.
instrument 628 n.
means 629 n.
tool 630 n.
use 673 n.
applicable
relevant 9 adj.
apt 24 adj.
operative 173 adj.
useful 640 adj.
advisable 642 adj.
applicant
respondent 460 n.
petitioner 763 n.
application
referral 9 n.
relevance 9 n.
meditation 449 n.
attention 455 n.
connotation 514 n.
metaphor 519 n.
interpretation 520 n.
study 536 n.
perseverance 600 n.
instrumentality 628 n.
surgical dressing 658 n.
use 673 n.
assiduity 678 n.
offer 759 n.
request 761 n.
applied
instrumental 628 adj.
useful 640 adj.
used 673 adj.
applied technology
smallness 33 n.
appliqué
needlework 844 n.
apply
relate 9 vb.
figure 519 vb.
use 673 vb.
offer oneself 759 vb.
request 761 vb.
— for
require 627 vb.
— oneself
study 536 vb.
undertake 672 vb.
exert oneself 682 vb.
— the mind
think 449 vb.
appoggiatura
musical note 410 n.
appoint
select 605 vb.
predetermine 608 vb.
employ 622 vb.
decree 737 vb.
commission 751 vb.
apportion 783 vb.
appointed
fated 596 adj.
predetermined 608 adj.
appointee
consignee 754 n.
appointment
choice 605 n.
job 622 n.
fitting out 669 n.
command 737 n.
mandate 751 n.
apportionment 783 n.
holy orders 985 n.
apportion
quantify 26 vb.
sunder 46 vb.
decompose 51 vb.
part 53 vb.
arrange 62 vb.
disperse 75 vb.
bisect 92 vb.
mete out 465 vb.
dispose of 673 vb.
participate 775 vb.
give 781 vb.
apportion 783 vb.
grant claims 915 vb.
appositeness
relevance 9 n.
fitness 24 n.
apposition
contiguity 202 n.
grammar 564 n.
appraise
discriminate 463 vb.
appraise 465 vb.
estimate 480 vb.
appreciate
grow 36 vb.
cognize 447 vb.
appraise 465 vb.
know 490 vb.
be dear 811 vb.
be pleased 824 vb.
have taste 846 vb.
honour 866 vb.
love 887 vb.
thank 907 vb.
approve 923 vb.
appreciation
increase 36 n.
discrimination 463 n.
measurement 465 n.
estimate 480 n.
interpretation 520 n.
feeling 818 n.
gratitude 907 n.
approbation 923 n.
appreciative
judicial 480 adj.
tasteful 846 adj.
grateful 907 adj.
approving 923 adj.
apprehend
opine 485 vb.
know 490 vb.
expect 507 vb.
understand 516 vb.
arrest 747 vb.
take 786 vb.
apprehensible
intelligible 516 adj.
apprehension
idea 451 n.
knowledge 490 n.
expectation 507 n.
danger 661 n.
taking 786 n.
nervousness 854 n.
legal process 959 n.
apprehensive
expectant 507 adj.
suffering 825 adj.
nervous 854 adj.
apprentice
beginner 538 n.
immature 670 adj.
artisan 686 n.
dependant 742 n.
apprentice oneself
learn 536 vb.
undertake 672 vb.
apprise
inform 524 vb.
approach
relativeness 9 n.
resemble 18 vb.
beginning 68 n.
entrance 68 n.
futurity 124 n.
be to come 124 vb.

event 154 n.
destiny 155 n.
impend 155 vb.
tend 179 vb.
nearness 200 n.
doorway 263 n.
motion 265 n.
navigate 269 vb.
approach 289 n.vb.
convergence 293 n.
arrival 295 n.
speak to 583 vb.
policy 623 n.
plan 623 vb.
access 624 n.
offer 759 n.vb.
request 761 n.vb.
befriend 880 vb.
greet 884 vb.

approachable
accessible 289 adj.
possible 469 adj.
easy 701 adj.

approbation
estimate 480 n.
assent 488 n.
permission 756 n.
repute 866 n.
respect 920 n.
approbation 923 n.
orthodoxism 976 n.

appropriate
circumstantial 8 adj.
relevant 9 adj.
apt 24 adj.
special 80 adj.
acquire 771 vb.
apportion 783 vb.
appropriate 786 vb.
claim 915 vb.

approvable
excellent 644 adj.
contenting 828 adj.
approvable 923 adj.

approval
assent 488 n.
permission 756 n.
repute 866 n.
approbation 923 n.

approve
choose 605 vb.
select 605 vb.
permit 756 vb.
consent 758 vb.
be pleased 824 vb.
approve 923 vb.

approved
usual 610 adj.

approved school
school 539 n.
prison 748 n.

approximate
similar 18 adj.
liken 18 vb.
near 200 adj.
be near 200 vb.
bring near 200 vb.
approach 289 vb.

approximately
almost 33 adv.
nearly 200 adv.

approximation
relativeness 9 n.
similarity 18 n.
numerical operation 86 n.
nearness 200 n.
approach 289 n.

appurtenance(s)
addition 38 n.
adjunct 40 n.
component 58 n.
concomitant 89 n.
property 777 n.

appurtenant
relative 9 adj.

apricot
fruit 301 n.
orange 432 n.

April fool
dupe 544 n.
laughingstock 851 n.

April shower
brief span 114 n.
changable thing 152 n.

a priori
intrinsic 5 adj.
rational 475 n.

apron
apron 228 n.
stage set 594 n.
cleaning cloth 648 n.
canonicals 989 n.

apron strings
subjection 745 n.
fetter 748 n.

apropos
concerning 9 adv.
apt 24 adj.
incidentally 137 adv.

apse
church interior 990 n.

apt
relevant 9 adj.
apt 24 adj.
special 80 adj.
opportune 137 adj.
plausible 471 adj.
intelligent 498 adj.
skilful 694 adj.
tasteful 846 adj.

aptitude
fitness 24 n.
ability 160 n.
tendency 179 n.
intelligence 498 n.
learning 536 n.
willingness 597 n.
aptitude 694 n.

apt to
tending 179 adj.
liable 180 adj.

aquamarine
greenness 434 n.
blueness 435 n.
gem 844 n.

aquanaut
diver 313 n.

aquaplane
swim 269 vb.

aquarelle
picture 553 n.

aquarium
zoo 369 n.
collection 632 n.

Aquarius
zodiac 321 n.

aquatic
swimming 269 adj.
watery 339 adj.

aquatics
aquatics 269 n.
sport 837 n.

aquatint
picture 553 n.
engraving 555 n.
engrave 555 vb.

aqua vitae
alcoholic drink 301 n.

aqueduct
conduit 351 n.
bridge 624 n.

aqueous
watery 339 adj.

aquiline
angular 247 adj.
curved 248 adj.
animal 365 adj.

arabesque
crossing 222 n.
ornament 574 n.
ballet 594 n.
pattern 844 n.

Arabic alphabet
letter 558 n.

Arabic numerals
number 85 n.

arable
agrarian 370 adj.

arable land
soil 344 n.
farm 370 n.

arachnid
animal 365 n.

arbiter
adviser 691 n.
magistracy 957 n.

arbiter elegantiarum
reveller 837 n.
people of taste 846 n.

arbitrage
barter 791 n.

arbitral
judicial 480 adj.

arbitrament
judgment 480 n.

arbitrarily
severely 735 adv.

arbitrary
unrelated 10 adj.
unconformable 84 adj.
illogical 477 adj.
volitional 595 adj.
wilful 602 adj.
capricious 604 adj.
authoritative 733 adj.
authoritarian 735 adj.
unconditional 744 adj.
insolent 878 adj.
lawless 954 adj.

arbitrary power
brute force 735 n.

arbitrate
judge 480 vb.
mediate 720 vb.
compromise 770 vb.

arbitrator
estimator 480 n.
mediator 720 n.
magistracy 957 n.

arboreal
arboreal 366 adj.

arborescence
symmetry 245 n.

arboretum
wood 366 n.
garden 370 n.

arbour
pavilion 192 n.
arbour 194 n.
screen 421 n.
pleasure ground 837 n.

arc
part 53 n.
curve 248 n.
arc 250 n.
fire 379 n.

arcade
pavilion 192 n.
curve 248 n.
path 624 n.
emporium 796 n.

Arcadia
happiness 824 n.

Arcadian
artless 699 adj.
innocent 935 adj.

arcane
unintelligible 517 adj.
latent 523 adj.
concealed 525 adj.

arch
consummate 32 adj.
supreme 34 adj.
bond 47 n.
foot 214 n.
prop 218 n.
curve 248 n.
be curved 248 vb.
make curved 248 vb.
camber 253 n.
be convex 253 vb.
merry 833 adj.
affected 850 adj.

archaeological excavation
search 459 n.
archaeologist
antiquarian 125 n.
excavator 255 n.
detector 484 n.
chronicler 549 n.
archaeology
palaeology 125 n.
archaic
antiquated 127 adj.
olden 127 adj.
archaism
antiquity 125 n.
archaism 127 n.
reversion 148 n.
neology 560 n.
archangel
angel 968 n.
archbishop
governor 741 n.
ecclesiarch 986 n.
archbishopric
district 184 n.
church office 985 n.
parish 985 n.
archdeacon
ecclesiarch 986 n.
archduchy
political organization 733 n.
archduke
potentate 741 n.
person of rank 868 n.
arched
curved 248 adj.
arched 253 adj.
concave 255 adj.
arch enemy
enemy 881 n.
archer
shooter 287 n.
soldiery 722 n.
player 837 n.
archery
sport 837 n.
archetypal
original 21 adj.
archetype
prototype 23 n.
idea 451 n.
archimandrite
ecclesiarch 986 n.
monk 986 n.
Archimedes' screw
extractor 304 n.
irrigator 341 n.
archipelago
island 349 n.
architect
producer 164 n.
artist 556 n.
planner 623 n.
artisan 686 n.
architect-designed
produced 164 adj.
architectural 192 adj.
architectonics
structure 331 n.
architectural
architectural 192 adj.
formative 243 adj.
structural 331 adj.
architectural monstrosity
eyesore 842 n.
architecture
composition 56 n.
arrangement 62 n.
production 164 n.
form 243 n.
structure 331 n.
art 551 n.
ornamental art 844 n.
architrave
summit 213 n.
beam 218 n.
archives
record 548 n.
collection 632 n.
title deed 767 n.
archivist
recorder 549 n.
keeper 749 n.
archpriest
ecclesiarch 986 n.
priest 986 n.
archway
doorway 263 n.
arc light
lamp 420 n.
arctic
opposite 240 adj.
cold 380 adj.
Arctic
coldness 380 n.
arcuate
make curved 248 vb.
arched 253 adj.
ardent
fiery 379 adj.
forceful 571 adj.
active 678 adj.
hasty 680 adj.
fervent 818 adj.
desiring 859 adj.
loving 887 adj.
pietistic 979 adj.
ardent admirer
worshipper 981 n.
ardour
heat 379 n.
vigour 571 n.
willingness 597 n.
restlessness 678 n.
warm feeling 818 n.
desire 859 n.
arduous
laborious 682 adj.
difficult 700 adj.
area
quantity 26 n.
greatness 32 n.
measure 183 n.
space 183 n.
region 184 n.
place 185 n.
size 195 n.
function 622 n.
arena
athletics 162 n.
range 183 n.
region 184 n.
contest 716 n.
battle 718 n.
arena 724 n.
pleasure ground 837 n.
arenaceous
powdery 332 adj.
areola
circle 250 n.
Ares
war 718 n.
Olympian deity 967 n.
arête
sharp point 256 n.
argent
white 427 adj.
heraldry 547 n.
heraldic 547 adj.
argil
soil 344 n.
argilaceous
soft 327 adj.
argon
air 340 n.
argosy
merchant ship 275 n.
shipping 275 n.
argot
slang 560 n.
arguable
possible 469 adj.
uncertain 474 adj.
argue
disagree 25 vb.
testify 466 vb.
argue 475 vb.
sophisticate 477 vb.
dissent 489 vb.
propound 512 vb.
publish 528 vb.
affirm 532 vb.
indicate 547 vb.
confer 584 vb.
dissertate 591 vb.
plead 614 vb.
bicker 709 vb.
vindicate 927 vb.
litigate 959 vb.
— against
cause doubt 486 vb.
dissuade 613 vb.
— for
contend 716 vb.
— in a circle
reason badly 477 vb.
argufy
argue 475 vb.
argument
disagreement 25 n.
topic 452 n.
question 459 n.
argument 475 n.
demonstration 478 n.
supposition 512 n.
conference 584 n.
dissertation 591 n.
quarrel 709 n.
contention 716 n.
argumentation
argumentation 475 n.
argumentative
arguing 475 adj.
quarrelling 709 adj.
Argus
doorkeeper 264 n.
eye 438 n.
protector 660 n.
gaoler 749 n.
Argus-eyed
seeing 438 adj.
vigilant 457 adj.
argy-bargy
quarrel 709 n.
bargain 791 vb.
aria
tune 412 n.
Arian
heretic 977 n.
heretical 977 adj.
arid
unproductive 172 adj.
dry 342 adj.
tedious 838 adj.
aridity
desert 172 n.
dryness 342 n.
Ariel
speeder 277 n.
courier 529 n.
fairy 970 n.
Aries
zodiac 321 n.
aright
well 615 adv.
aright 644 adv.
arioso
musical 412 adj.
arise
become 1 vb.
begin 68 vb.
happen 154 vb.
lift oneself 310 vb.
be visible 443 vb.
appear 445 vb.
— from
result 157 vb.
— from the dead
be restored 656 vb.
aristocracy
superior 34 n.
superiority 34 n.

social group 371 n.
elite 644 n.
government 733 n.
owner 776 n.
aristocracy 868 n.
aristocrat
bigwig 638 n.
master 741 n.
aristocrat 868 n.
proud person 871 n.
Aristotelianism
philosophy 449 n.
arithmetic
mathematics 86 n.
curriculum 534 n.
arithmetical
numerical 85 adj.
statistical 86 adj.
arithmetical progression
series 71 n.
ratio 85 n.
arithmetician
enumerator 86 n.
ark
retreat 192 n.
box 194 n.
refuge 662 n.
Ark of the Covenant
creed 485 n.
ritual object 988 n.
holy place 990 n.
arm
adjunct 40 n.
limb 53 n.
extremity 69 n.
empower 160 vb.
prop 218 n.
sleeve 228 n.
indicator 547 n.
tool 630 n.
provide 633 vb.
safeguard 660 vb.
make ready 669 vb.
defend 713 vb.
go to war 718 vb.
weapon 723 n.
armada
armed force 722 n.
navy 722 n.
Armageddon
fight 716 n.
war 718 n.
armament
fitting out 669 n.
armed force 722 n.
arms 723 n.
armature
sculpture 554 n.
armband
belt 228 n.
armchair
seat 218 n.
softness 327 n.
suppositional 512 adj.
armchair critic
theorist 512 n.
armchair travel
quietude 266 n.
armed
strong 162 adj.
prepared 669 adj.
warring 718 adj.
armed conflict
battle 718 n.
armed force(s)
band 74 n.
protection 660 n.
attacker 712 n.
armed force 722 n.
army 722 n.
armed intervention
war 718 n.
Armenian Church
Christendom 976 n.
armhole
sleeve 228 n.
orifice 263 n.
armiger
aristocrat 868 n.
arm in arm
joined 45 adj.
with 89 adv.
near 200 adv.
contiguously 202 adv.
across 222 adv.
amicably 880 adv.
sociably 882 adv.
armistice
lull 145 n.
peace 717 n.
pacification 719 n.
Armistice Day
special day 876 n.
armless
fragmentary 53 adj.
incomplete 55 adj.
crippled 163 adj.
imperfect 647 adj.
armlet
belt 228 n.
loop 250 n.
badge of rank 743 n.
jewellery 844 n.
arm of the law
law 953 n.
jurisdiction 955 n.
legal process 959 n.
arm of the sea
gulf 345 n.
armorial
heraldic 547 adj.
armour
covering 226 n.
headgear 228 n.
legwear 228 n.
protection 660 n.
safeguard 660 vb.
safeguard 662 n.
armour 713 n.
defend 713 vb.
cavalry 722 n.
weapon 723 n.
armour-bearer
retainer 742 n.
armoured
hard 326 adj.
resolute 599 adj.
invulnerable 660 adj.
defended 713 adj.
armoured car
war chariot 274 n.
cavalry 722 n.
armoured cruiser
warship 722 n.
armoured division
formation 722 n.
armour plate
covering 226 n.
protection 660 n.
safeguard 660 vb.
armour 713 n.
defend 713 vb.
armoury
accumulation 74 n.
storage 632 n.
workshop 687 n.
arsenal 723 n.
armpit
cavity 255 n.
arms
garment 228 n.
vocation 622 n.
tool 630 n.
safeguard 662 n.
war 718 n.
arms 723 n.
honours 866 n.
arms buildup
intimidation 854 n.
arms depot
arsenal 723 n.
arm's length
long measure 203 n.
arm-twisting
compulsion 740 n.
army
multitude 104 n.
army 722 n.
Army List
directory 87 n.
list 87 n.
army officer
soldiery 722 n.
army officer 741 n.
army of occupation
armed force 722 n.
army rule
government 733 n.
aroma
odour 394 n.
fragrance 396 n.
aromatic
pungent 388 adj.
savoury 390 adj.
fragrant 396 adj.
aromatic perfume
scent 396 n.
around
nearly 200 adv.
around 230 adv.
around the clock
continuously 71 adv.
arouse
cause 156 vb.
cause feeling 374 vb.
raise the alarm 665 vb.
excite 821 vb.
— desire
cause desire 859 vb.
excite love 887 vb.
— suspicion
be questionable 459 vb.
aroused
impressed 818 adj.
arpeggio
musical note 410 n.
arquebus
firearm 723 n.
arraign
indict 928 vb.
litigate 959 vb.
Arran
pattern 844 n.
arrange
adjust 24 vb.
compose 56 vb.
order 60 vb.
arrange 62 vb.
modify 143 vb.
produce 164 vb.
place 187 vb.
compose music 413 vb.
be careful 457 vb.
make certain 473 vb.
predetermine 608 vb.
plan 623 vb.
clean 648 vb.
make better 654 vb.
make ready 669 vb.
arranged match
type of marriage 894 n.
arrangement
adaptation 24 n.
composition 56 n.
order 60 n.
arrangement 62 n.
series 71 n.
assemblage 74 n.
classification 77 n.
regularity 81 n.
formation 243 n.
musical piece 412 n.
amendment 654 n.
preparation 669 n.
compact 765 n.
arrant
consummate 32 adj.
manifest 522 adj.
bad 645 adj.
disreputable 867 adj.
rascally 930 adj.
array
order 60 n.

arrangement 62 n.
arrange 62 vb.
series 71 n.
multitude 104 n.
place 187 vb.
dressing 228 n.
dress 228 vb.
fitting out 669 n.
make ready 669 vb.
battle 718 n.
formation 722 n.
decorate 844 vb.
pageant 875 n.
arrears
debt 803 n.
arrest
cessation 145 n.
halt 145 vb.
cause feeling 374 vb.
hindrance 702 n.
detention 747 n.
restraint 747 n.
arrest 747 vb.
restrain 747 vb.
take 786 vb.
impress 821 vb.
legal process 959 n.
— one's notice
attract notice 455 vb.
arrested development
unintelligence 499 n.
arresting
unexpected 508 adj.
impressive 821 adj.
arrière pensée
sophistry 477 n.
concealment 525 n.
arrival
union 45 n.
intruder 59 n.
beginning 68 n.
approach 289 n.
arrival 295 n.
arrive
happen 154 vb.
be present 189 vb.
travel 267 vb.
voyage 269 vb.
approach 289 vb.
arrive 295 vb.
appear 445 vb.
flourish 615 vb.
climax 725 vb.
succeed 727 vb.
prosper 730 vb.
arriviste
prosperous person 730 n.
vulgarian 847 n.
commoner 869 n.
egotist 932 n.
arrogance
pride 871 n.
insolence 878 n.
arrogant
authoritarian 735 adj.
rash 857 adj.
proud 871 adj.
insolent 878 adj.
arrogate
please oneself 734 vb.
oppress 735 vb.
appropriate 786 vb.
be insolent 878 vb.
claim 915 vb.
be undue 916 vb.
arrogation
overstepping 306 n.
taking 786 n.
insolence 878 n.
arrogation 916 n.
lawlessness 954 n.
arrow
sharp point 256 n.
speeder 277 n.
missile 287 n.
indicator 547 n.
missile weapon 723 n.
love token 889 n.
arrowhead
angularity 247 n.
sharp point 256 n.
lettering 586 n.
missile weapon 723 n.
arrowshot
short distance 200 n.
arroyo
stream 350 n.
conduit 351 n.
arse
buttocks 238 n.
arsenal
accumulation 74 n.
storage 632 n.
workshop 687 n.
arsenal 723 n.
arsenic
poison 659 n.
arsis
pronunciation 577 n.
prosody 593 n.
arson
destruction 165 n.
fire 379 n.
incendiarism 381 n.
arsy-versy
inversely 221 adv.
art
composition 56 n.
production 164 n.
form 243 n.
art 551 n.
misrepresentation 552 n.
school of painting 553 n.
business 622 n.
skill 694 n.
stratagem 698 n.
ornamental art 844 n.
art critic
people of taste 846 n.
Artemis
spinster 895 n.
virgin 950 n.
Olympian deity 967 n.
art equipment
pigment 425 n.
art equipment 553 n.
arterial
communicating 624 adj.
arterial road
road 624 n.
arteriosclerosis
cardiovascular disease 651 n.
artery
essential part 5 n.
tube 263 n.
conduit 351 n.
life 360 n.
road 624 n.
artesian well
water 339 n.
store 632 n.
art exhibition
spectacle 445 n.
art form
form 243 n.
artful
intelligent 498 adj.
false 541 adj.
deceiving 542 adj.
cunning 698 adj.
dishonest 930 adj.
artful dodger
slyboots 698 n.
artfully
skilfully 694 adv.
art gallery
collection 632 n.
arthritic
impotent 161 adj.
crippled 163 adj.
sick person 651 n.
diseased 651 adj.
arthritis
pang 377 n.
rheumatism 651 n.
arthropod
animal 365 n.
article
arrangement 62 n.
product 164 n.
object 319 n.
estimate 480 n.
publicity 528 n.
part of speech 564 n.
reading matter 589 n.
article 591 n.
precept 693 n.
merchandise 795 n.
articled clerk
beginner 538 n.
article of clothing
garment 228 n.
article oneself
learn 536 vb.
articles
conditions 766 n.
articles of faith
creed 485 n.
theology 973 n.
articulate
join 45 vb.
intelligible 516 adj.
phrase 563 vb.
vocal 577 adj.
voice 577 vb.
speaking 579 adj.
speak 579 vb.
articulation
pronunciation 577 n.
artifact, artefact
product 164 n.
artifice
contrivance 623 n.
stratagem 698 n.
pretension 850 n.
artificer
producer 164 n.
artisan 686 n.
artificial
simulating 18 adj.
produced 164 adj.
spurious 542 adj.
untrue 543 adj.
elegant 575 adj.
inelegant 576 adj.
laborious 682 adj.
well-made 694 adj.
affected 850 adj.
artificial fibre
fibre 208 n.
artificial flavouring
food content 301 n.
artificial insemination
propagation 167 n.
artificial limb
substitute 150 n.
artificial respiration
revival 656 n.
artillery
loudness 400 n.
gun 723 n.
artillery brigade
formation 722 n.
artilleryman
shooter 287 n.
soldiery 722 n.
artisan
producer 164 n.
artist 556 n.
machinist 630 n.
doer 676 n.
artisan 686 n.
expert 696 n.
artist
imitator 20 n.
producer 164 n.
visionary 513 n.
interpreter 520 n.

recorder 549 n.
artist 556 n.
entertainer 594 n.
doer 676 n.
expert 696 n.
artiste
musician 413 n.
entertainer 594 n.
artistic
representing 551 adj.
elegant 575 adj.
well-made 694 adj.
beautiful 841 adj.
tasteful 846 adj.
artistry
touch 378 n.
imagination 513 n.
painting 553 n.
skill 694 n.
good taste 846 n.
artist's model
living model 23 n.
artless
simple 44 adj.
amorphous 244 adj.
ignorant 491 adj.
foolish 499 adj.
veracious 540 adj.
plain 573 adj.
inelegant 576 adj.
spontaneous 609 adj.
immature 670 adj.
unprepared 670 adj.
bungled 695 adj.
artless 699 adj.
graceless 842 adj.
ill-bred 847 adj.
vulgar 847 adj.
barbaric 869 adj.
honourable 929 adj.
innocent 935 adj.
art master/mistress
artist 556 n.
art nouveau
art 551 n.
ornamentation 844 n.
art of the possible
tactics 688 n.
arts
culture 490 n.
literature 557 n.
art school
academy 539 n.
art style
art style 553 n.
art subject
art subject 553 n.
art that conceals art
skill 694 n.
artwork
representation 551 n.
arty-crafty
ornamental 844 adj.
Aryan
language type 557 n.
as
similarly 18 adv.
asafoetida
stench 397 n.
as a matter of course
conformably 83 adv.
certainly 473 adv.
as a matter of fact
truly 494 adv.
as a result
consequently 157 adv.
as arranged
purposely 617 adv.
as ... as can be
completely 54 adv.
as a start
initially 68 adv.
as a whole
wholly 52 adv.
as before
as before 144 adv.
asbestos
incombustibility 382 n.
asbestosis
respiratory disease 651 n.
as broad as it is long
equivalent 28 adj.
ascend
be great 32 vb.
grow 36 vb.
be high 209 vb.
fly 271 vb.
emerge 298 vb.
ascend 308 vb.
lift oneself 310 vb.
leap 312 vb.
be light 323 vb.
be visible 443 vb.
— the throne
take authority 733 vb.
ascendancy, ascendance
superiority 34 n.
power 160 n.
influence 178 n.
victory 727 n.
authority 733 n.
prestige 866 n.
ascender
print-type 587 n.
ascending order
increase 36 n.
series 71 n.
expansion 197 n.
Ascension Day
holy day 988 n.
ascent
series 71 n.
vertex 213 n.
incline 220 n.
motion 265 n.
progression 285 n.
ascent 308 n.
elevation 310 n.
access 624 n.
ascertain
make certain 473 vb.
discover 484 vb.
ascertained
certain 473 adj.
known 490 adj.
true 494 adj.
ascetic
philosopher 449 n.
sage 500 n.
severe 735 adj.
impassive 820 adj.
penitent 939 n.
abstainer 942 n.
temperate 942 adj.
ascetic 945 n.adj.
pietist 979 n.
pietistic 979 adj.
monk 986 n.
asceticism
poverty 801 n.
penance 941 n.
asceticism 945 n.
fast 946 n.
monasticism 985 n.
ascribe
attribute 158 vb.
grant claims 915 vb.
asdic
hearing aid 415 n.
detector 484 n.
as directed
in order 60 adv.
aseity
existence 1 n.
aseptic
clean 648 adj.
salubrious 652 adj.
asexual
simple 44 adj.
as far as possible
completely 54 adv.
as far as the eye can see
afar 199 adv.
as follows
after 65 adv.
Asgard
mythic heaven 971 n.
as good as
equivalent 28 adj.
equally 28 adv.
on the whole 52 adv.
completely 54 adv.
nearly 200 adv.
as good as one's word
veracious 540 adj.
trustworthy 929 adj.
as good as one's word, be
carry out 725 vb.
keep faith 768 vb.
as good luck would have it
by chance 159 adv.
ash
powder 332 n.
tree 366 n.
ash 381 n.
coal 385 n.
dirt 649 n.
ashamed
humbled 872 adj.
guilty 936 adj.
repentant 939 adj.
ash-blond(e)
whitish 427 adj.
yellowness 433 n.
ashen
colourless 426 adj.
grey 429 adj.
ashen-faced
fearing 854 adj.
ashes
remainder 41 n.
corpse 363 n.
Ashes
contest 716 n.
trophy 729 n.
ashlar
facing 226 n.
building material 631 n.
ashore
on land 344 adv.
ashram
retreat 192 n.
monastery 986 n.
Ash Wednesday
holy day 988 n.
ashy
colourless 426 adj.
grey 429 adj.
aside
sideways 239 adv.
faintly 401 adv.
latency 523 n.
hint 524 n.
secretly 525 adv.
allocution 583 n.
soliloquy 585 n.
dramaturgy 594 n.
as if
similarly 18 adv.
as ill luck would have it
inopportunely 138 adv.
by chance 159 adv.
in adversity 731 adv.
asinine
equine 273 adj.
animal 365 adj.
absurd 497 adj.
foolish 499 adj.
as it turns out
accordingly 8 adv.
as it were
similarly 18 adv.
ask
enquire 459 vb.
not know 491 vb.
request 761 vb.

— for
enquire 459 vb.
bargain 791 vb.
desire 859 vb.
— for one's cards
resign 753 vb.
— for one's money back
be discontented 829 vb.
— for quarter
ask mercy 905 vb.
— for the hand of
court 889 vb.
wed 894 vb.
— for trouble
defy 711 vb.
be rash 857 vb.
— in
be hospitable 882 vb.
— leave
ask leave 756 vb.
— mercy
knuckle under 721 vb.
regret 830 vb.
ask mercy 905 vb.
beg pardon 909 vb.
— questions
be curious 453 vb.
interrogate 459 vb.
— the way
orientate 281 vb.
— too much
make insufficient 636 vb.
overcharge 811 vb.
askance
obliquely 220 adv.
sideways 239 adv.
askari
soldier 722 n.
askew
unequal 29 adj.
orderless 61 adj.
oblique 220 adj.
obliquely 220 adv.
distorted 246 adj.
asking for it
punishable 963 adj.
aslant
oblique 220 adj.
obliquely 220 adv.
asleep
quiescent 266 adj.
sleepy 679 adj.
as long as
provided 468 adj.
provisionally 112 adv.
as night follows day
certainly 473 adv.
as one
conjointly 45 adv.
together 74 adv.
cooperatively 706 adv.
in league 708 adv.
asparagus
vegetable 301 n.
aspect
modality 7 n.
circumstance 8 n.
situation 186 n.
view 438 n.
appearance 445 n.
conduct 688 n.
aspen
agitation 318 n.
tree 366 n.
asperge
purify 648 vb.
perform ritual 988 vb.
aspergillum
ritual object 988 n.
asperity
roughness 259 n.
rudeness 885 n.
anger 891 n.
irascibility 892 n.
aspersion
moistening 341 n.
slur 867 n.
scurrility 899 n.
reproach 924 n.
detraction 926 n.
ritual act 988 n.
aspersorium
ritual object 988 n.
asphalt
paving 226 n.
smoothness 258 n.
resin 357 n.
road 624 n.
building material 631 n.
asphyxiant
deadly 362 adj.
poison 659 n.
asphyxiate
close 264 vb.
aspic
condiment 389 n.
preserver 666 n.
aspirant
petitioner 763 n.
hoper 852 n.
desirer 859 n.
aspirate
empty 300 vb.
extract 304 vb.
breathe 352 vb.
speech sound 398 n.
stridor 407 n.
rasp 407 vb.
voice 577 vb.
aspiration
motive 612 n.
objective 617 n.
aspiration 852 n.
desire 859 n.
aspire
ascend 308 vb.
hope 852 vb.
desire 859 vb.
— to
aim at 617 vb.
aspirin
drug 658 n.
asquint
obliquely 220 adv.
sideways 239 adv.
as regards
concerning 9 adv.
as required of one
duly 915 adv.
ass
beast of burden 273 n.
fool 501 n.
bungler 697 n.
assail
attack 712 vb.
torment 827 vb.
assailant
opponent 705 n.
attacker 712 n.
combatant 722 n.
assassin
destroyer 168 n.
violent creature 176 n.
murderer 362 n.
ruffian 904 n.
assassination
homicide 362 n.
killing 362 n.
assault
outbreak 176 n.
knock 279 n.
impairment 655 n.
attack 712 n.vb.
debauch 951 vb.
assay
experiment 461 n. vb.
assegai
spear 723 n.
assemblage
combination 50 n.
arrangement 62 n.
assemblage 74 n.
acquisition 771 n.
assemble
join 45 vb.
compose 56 vb.
bring together 74 vb.
congregate 74 vb.
produce 164 vb.
meet 295 vb.
call 547 n.
assembly
union 45 n.
combination 50 n.
assembly 74 n.
production 164 n.
convergence 293 n.
conference 584 n.
council 692 n.
amusement 837 n.
pageant 875 n.
social gathering 882 n.
public worship 981 n.
assembly line
continuity 71 n.
production 164 n.
assembly rooms
meeting place 192 n.
place of amusement 837 n.
assent
agreement 24 n.
concurrence 181 n.
believe 485 vb.
assent 488 n.vb.
willingness 597 n.
submission 721 n.
obey 739 vb.
permit 756 vb.
consent 758 n.vb.
compact 765 n.
approbation 923 n.
assenter
assenter 488 n.
signatory 765 n.
toady 879 n.
flatterer 925 n.
pietist 979 n.
assenting
orthodox 976 adj.
assert
suppose 512 vb.
mean 514 vb.
affirm 532 vb.
— oneself
influence 178 vb.
be active 678 vb.
achieve liberty 746 vb.
— one's rights
claim 915 vb.
assertion
testimony 466 n.
affirmation 532 n.
assertive
strong 162 adj.
positive 473 adj.
assertive 532 adj.
assess
appraise 465 vb.
price 809 vb.
assessment
measurement 465 n.
estimate 480 n.
tax 809 n.
assessment centre
prison 748 n.
assessor
appraiser 465 n.
estimator 480 n.
magistracy 957 n.
assets
means 629 n.
store 632 n.
sufficiency 635 n.
estate 777 n.
asset-stripper
taker 786 n.
asseverate
affirm 532 vb.

assibilate
hiss 406 vb.
assiduity
attention 455 n.
carefulness 457 n.
perseverance 600 n.
assiduity 678 n.
exertion 682 n.
assiduous
frequent 139 adj.
assign
arrange 62 vb.
place 187 vb.
transfer 272 vb.
dispose of 673 vb.
commission 751 vb.
dower 777 vb.
assign 780 vb.
bequeath 780 vb.
give 781 vb.
apportion 783 vb.
grant claims 915 vb.
— a place
apportion 783 vb.
— a role
dramatize 594 vb.
— to
attribute 158 vb.
use 673 vb.
assignat
paper money 797 n.
assignation
social round 882 n.
assignee
recipient 782 n.
assignment
undertaking 672 n.
mandate 751 n.
transfer 780 n.
apportionment 783 n.
assignment of cause
attribution 158 n.
assimilate
identify 13 vb.
make uniform 16 vb.
combine 50 vb.
make conform 83 vb.
transform 147 vb.
absorb 299 vb.
assimilated
conformable 83 adj.
converted 147 adj.
assimilation
uniformity 16 n.
assimilation 18 n.
imitation 20 n.
adaptation 24 n.
simplification 44 n.
combination 50 n.
inclusion 78 n.
conformity 83 n.
conversion 147 n.
reception 299 n.
speech sound 398 n.
grammar 564 n.
ass in a lion's skin
misfit 25 n.
imposter 545 n.
bungler 697 n.
assist
aid 703 vb.
— at
be present 189 vb.
assistance
instrumentality 628 n.
provision 633 n.
aid 703 n.
assistant
inferior 35 n.
instrument 628 n.
aider 703 n.
auxiliary 707 n.
servant 742 n.
assize(s)
lawcourt 956 n.
legal trial 959 n.
assize judge
judge 957 n.
as... so...
correlatively 12 adv.
associate
join 45 vb.
combine 50 vb.
congregate 74 vb.
concomitant 89 n.
personnel 686 n.
cooperate 706 vb.
colleague 707 n.
society 708 n.
join a party 708 vb.
friend 880 n.
— with
accompany 89 vb.
association
relation 9 n.
union 45 n.
combination 50 n.
group 74 n.
unity 88 n.
accompaniment 89 n.
concurrence 181 n.
intuition 476 n.
habituation 610 n.
business 622 n.
association 706 n.
corporation 708 n.
society 708 n.
participation 775 n.
friendship 880 n.
sociality 882 n.
association of ideas
intellect 447 n.
thought 449 n.
supposition 512 n.
assonance
assimilation 18 n.
recurrence 106 n.
melody 410 n.
ornament 574 n.
prosody 593 n.
as soon as
synchronously 123 adv.
assorted
different 15 adj.
uniform 16 adj.
arranged 62 adj.
chosen 605 adj.
assortment
uniformity 16 n.
medley 43 n.
arrangement 62 n.
series 71 n.
accumulation 74 n.
bunch 74 n.
sort 77 n.
assuage
assuage 177 vb.
bring to rest 266 vb.
pacify 719 vb.
restrain 747 vb.
tranquillize 823 vb.
relieve 831 vb.
as such
intrinsically 5 adv.
assuetude
habit 610 n.
assume
account for 158 vb.
wear 228 vb.
assume 471 vb.
premise 475 vb.
believe 485 vb.
opine 485 vb.
expect 507 vb.
suppose 512 vb.
dissemble 541 vb.
appropriate 786 vb.
be affected 850 vb.
hope 852 vb.
be insolent 878 vb.
— a disguise
be stealthy 525 vb.
— command
take authority 733 vb.
— responsibility
undertake 672 vb.
direct 689 vb.
— the role of
represent 551 vb.
assumed
supposed 512 adj.
affected 850 adj.
assumed title
misnomer 562 n.
assuming
if 8 adv.
insolent 878 adj.
unwarranted 916 adj.
assumption
attribution 158 n.
qualification 468 n.
premise 475 n.
opinion 485 n.
supposition 512 n.
receiving 782 n.
taking 786 n.
hope 852 n.
arrogation 916 n.
heaven 971 n.
Assumption
elevation 310 n.
assurance
calculation of chance 159 n.
positiveness 473 n.
belief 485 n.
affirmation 532 n.
safety 660 n.
promise 764 n.
hope 852 n.
vanity 873 n.
insolence 878 n.
assure
make certain 473 vb.
convince 485 vb.
promise 764 vb.
give security 767 vb.
— oneself
be cautious 858 vb.
assured
positive 473 adj.
believing 485 adj.
assertive 532 adj.
safe 660 adj.
Astarte
moon 321 n.
love god 887 n.
mythic deity 966 n.
asterisk
punctuation 547 n.
mark 547 vb.
asterism
star 321 n.
punctuation 547 n.
astern
rearward 238 adv.
backwards 286 adv.
asteroid
planet 321 n.
as the case may be
accordingly 8 adv.
by chance 159 adv.
as the crow flies
straight on 249 adv.
towards 281 adv.
as the mood takes one
capriciously 604 adv.
asthenia
weakness 163 n.
as the saying goes
proverbially 496 adv.
as things are
conditionally 7 adv.
as things go
eventually 154 adv.
asthma
respiratory disease 651 n.
asthmatic
puffing 352 adj.
sibilant 406 adj.
sick person 651 n.
diseased 651 adj.

astigmatic
dim-sighted 440 adj.
astir
busy 678 adj.
excited 821 adj.
as to
concerning 9 adv.
astonish
cause feeling 374 vb.
surprise 508 vb.
be wonderful 864 vb.
astonishing
prodigious 32 adj.
unusual 84 adj.
astonishment
lack of expectation 508 n.
wonder 864 n.
astound
surprise 508 vb.
impress 821 vb.
be wonderful 864 vb.
Astraea
justice 913 n.
lesser deity 967 n.
astragal
ornamental art 844 n.
astrakhan
skin 226 n.
astral
immaterial 320 adj.
celestial 321 adj.
spooky 970 adj.
astral body
immateriality 320 n.
spiritualism 984 n.
astray
unrelated 10 adj.
unassembled 75 adj.
unconformable 84 adj.
deviating 282 adj.
astray 282 adv.
doubting 474 adj.
astriction
joining together 45 n.
compression 198 n.
astride
astride 218 adv.
astringent
conjunctive 45 adj.
compressor 198 n.
compressive 198 adj.
solidifying 324 adj.
pungent 388 adj.
sour 393 adj.
astringent lotion
cosmetic 843 n.
astrocompass
sailing aid 269 n.
astrodome
view 438 n.
astrolabe
astronomy 321 n.
gauge 465 n.
astrologer
astronomy 321 n.
diviner 511 n.
sorcerer 983 n.
occultist 984 n.
astronaut
aeronaut 271 n.
satellite 321 n.
astronavigation
navigation 269 n.
astronomer
astronomy 321 n.
spectator 441 n.
astronomical
exorbitant 32 adj.
astronomic 321 adj.
astronomical almanac
chronology 117 n.
astronomical telescope
astronomy 321 n.
telescope 442 n.
astronomical unit
long measure 203 n.
astronomy
astronomy 321 n.
astrophysics
astronomy 321 n.
astute
intelligent 498 adj.
cunning 698 adj.
asunder
separate 46 adj.
apart 46 adv.
afar 199 adv.
as usual
conformably 83 adv.
habitually 610 adv.
as well as
in addition 38 adv.
asylum
retreat 192 n.
reception 299 n.
protection 660 n.
refuge 662 n.
asymmetrical, asymmetric
unrelated 10 adj.
nonuniform 17 adj.
unequal 29 adj.
abnormal 84 adj.
distorted 246 adj.
unsightly 842 adj.
asymptote
convergence 293 n.
as you were
reversibly 148 adv.
at a glance
in sum 592 adv.
at a guess
about 33 adv.
at a gulp
gluttonously 947 adv.
at a later date
subsequently 120 adv.
at all costs
resolutely 599 adv.
at all events
in return 31 adv.
nevertheless 468 adv.
at all times
perpetually 139 adv.
at a loose end
leisurely 681 adj.
at a loss, be
be uncertain 474 vb.
not know 491 vb.
be in difficulty 700 vb.
at a loss for words
voiceless 578 adj.
at a low ebb
under 210 adv.
lowered 311 adj.
insufficiently 636 adv.
at an angle
obliquely 220 adv.
at anchor
fixed 153 adj.
located 187 adj.
quiescent 266 adj.
safe 660 adj.
at any moment
in the future 155 adv.
at any price
resolutely 599 adv.
at any rate
in return 31 adv.
at a pinch
in need 627 adv.
with difficulty 700 adv.
at a premium
scarce 636 adj.
of price 811 adj.
at a price
dearly 811 adv.
at arm's length
afar 199 adv.
at a standstill
as before 144 adv.
quiescent 266 adj.
inactive 679 adj.
at a stretch
continuously 71 adv.
at a stroke
instantaneously 116 adv.
atavism
heredity 5 n.
consanguinity 11 n.
recurrence 106 n.
reversion 148 n.
reproduction 166 n.
influence 178 n.
memory 505 n.
ataxia
helplessness 161 n.
at bay
endangered 661 adj.
in difficulties 700 adj.
defensively 713 adv.
at close quarters
near 200 adj.adv.
contending 716 adj.
at crack of dawn
at sunrise 128 adv.
at daggers drawn
opposing 704 adj.
quarrelling 709 adj.
inimical 881 adj.
at death's door
dying 361 adj.
Ate
quarrelsomeness 709 n.
lesser deity 967 n.
at ease
tranquil 266 adj.
leisurely 681 adj.
reposeful 683 adj.
facilitated 701 adj.
prosperous 730 adj.
free 744 adj.
happy 824 adj.
content 828 adj.
atelier
chamber 194 n.
art equipment 553 n.
workshop 687 n.
at every turn
widely 183 adv.
at fault
doubting 474 adj.
mistaken 495 adj.
guilty 936 adj.
at first sight
at sight 438 adv.
apparently 445 adv.
at flashpoint
dangerous 661 adj.
at full length
completely 54 adv.
longwise 203 adv.
horizontally 216 adv.
at full speed
swiftly 277 adv.
at full tilt
vigorously 174 adv.
swiftly 277 adv.
at great cost
dearly 811 adv.
at great length
diffusely 570 adv.
at gunpoint
by force 740 adv.
athanasia
perpetuity 115 n.
Athanasian Creed
orthodoxy 976 n.
at hand
early 135 adj.
impending 155 adj.
on the spot 189 adj.
near 200 adj.
useful 640 adj.
atheism
philosophy 449 n.
unbelief 486 n.
irreligion 974 n.

Athena, Athene
Olympian deity 967 n.
athlete
athlete 162 n.
entertainer 594 n.
proficient person 696 n.
contender 716 n.
athlete's foot
skin disease 651 n.
athletics
athletics 162 n.
motion 265 n.
equitation 267 n.
exercise 682 n.
contention 716 n.
contest 716 n.
sport 837 n.
at home
apt 24 adj.
on the spot 189 adj.
residing 192 adj.
social gathering 882 n.
at home in
habituated 610 adj.
at home with
knowing 490 adj.
friendly 880 adj.
athwart
oblique 220 adj.
across 222 adv.
at intervals
discontinuously 72 adv.
periodically 141 adv.
at intervals 201 adv.
Atlantic Ocean
ocean 343 n.
Atlantis
fantasy 513 n.
at large
escaped 667 adj.
free 744 adj.
atlas
arrangement 62 n.
directory 87 n.
world 321 n.
map 551 n.
Atlas
athlete 162 n.
prop 218 n.
classical deities 967 n.
at last
finally 69 adv.
at last 113 adv.
late 136 adv.
at law
in litigation 959 adv.
at least
in return 31 adv.
slightly 33 adv.
at leisure
leisurely 681 adj.
free 744 adj.
at loggerheads
disagreeing 25 adj.
quarrelling 709 adj.
contending 716 adj.
warring 718 adj.
inimical 881 adj.
at low ebb
small 33 adj.
less 35 adv.
diminuendo 37 adv.
deteriorated 655 adj.
atman
self 80 n.
Atman
divineness 965 n.
atmosphere
influence 178 n.
surroundings 230 n.
atmosphere 340 n.
radiation 417 n.
atmospheric
airy 340 adj.
atmospheric pressure
weather 340 n.
atmospherics
commotion 318 n.
discord 411 n.
at night
post meridiem 129 adv.
darkling 418 adv.
at no time
never 109 adv.
at odds
disagreeing 25 adj.
opposing 704 adj.
quarrelling 709 adj.
contending 716 adj.
atoll
island 349 n.
atom
small thing 33 n.
unit 88 n.
minuteness 196 n.
element 319 n.
atom bomb
bomb 723 n.
atomic
dynamic 160 adj.
minute 196 adj.
atomic energy
energy 160 n.
atomic physics
physics 319 n.
atomic pile
nucleonics 160 n.
atomic warhead
explosive 723 n.
atomize, atomise
decompose 51 vb.
demolish 165 vb.
vaporize 338 vb.
atomizer, atomiser
pulverizer 332 n.
vaporizer 338 n.
atom-smasher
nucleonics 160 n.
atonal
harmonic 410 adj.
discordant 411 adj.
at once
instantaneously 116 adv.
at one
agreeing 24 adj.
at one another's throats, be
quarrel 709 vb.
at one fell swoop
instantaneously 116 adv.
violently 176 adv.
atonement
compensation 31 n.
substitution 150 n.
restoration 656 n.
restitution 787 n.
penitence 939 n.
atonement 941 n.
divine function 965 n.
at one's beck and call
aiding 703 adj.
obedient 739 adj.
serving 742 adj.
at one's convenience
leisurely 681 adj.
at one's ease
comfortable 376 adj.
in comfort 376 adv.
at one's elbow/fingertips
near 200 adv.
at one's orders
obedient 739 adj.
at one's own sweet will
capriciously 604 adv.
at one's post
on duty 917 adv.
at one's service
used 673 adj.
possessed 773 adj.
at one's side
near 200 adv.
at one's wits' end
doubting 474 adj.
ignorant 491 adj.
in difficulties 700 adj.
at one with
concurrent 181 adj.
atony
weakness 163 n.
atop
aloft 209 adv.
atop 213 adv.
at peace
concordant 710 adj.
peaceful 717 adj.
peacefully 717 adv.
at play
amused 837 adj.
at pleasure
at will 595 adv.
optionally 605 adv.
at present
at present 121 adv.
atrabilious
melancholic 834 adj.
at random
by chance 159 adv.
at random 618 adv.
at regular intervals
in order 60 adv.
periodically 141 adv.
at rest
fixed 153 adj.
inactively 175 adv.
quiescent 266 adj.
at rest 683 adv.
at right angles
vertically 215 adv.
atrocious
cruel 898 adj.
heinous 934 adj.
atrocity
violence 176 n.
cruel act 898 n.
guilty act 936 n.
at room temperature
warm 379 adj.
atrophy
helplessness 161 n.
contraction 198 n.
disease 651 n.
nervous disorders 651 n.
dilapidation 655 n.
atropine
poison 659 n.
Atropos
fate 596 n.
classical deities 967 n.
at sea
seafaring 269 adj.
at sea 343 adv.
at sea, be
be uncertain 474 vb.
not understand 517 vb.
at short notice
brief 114 adj.
suddenly 135 adv.
hastily 680 adv.
at sight
at sight 438 adv.
at sixes and sevens
confusedly 61 adv.
unprepared 670 adj.
quarrelling 709 adj.
at stake
dangerous 661 adj.
attach
add 38 vb.
affix 45 vb.
connect 45 vb.
attaché
envoy 754 n.
attaché case
box 194 n.
attached to
loving 887 adj.
attachment
adjunct 40 n.

joining together 45 n.
part 53 n.
observance 768 n.
expropriation 786 n.
love 887 n.

attack
begin 68 vb.
be vigorous 174 vb.
outbreak 176 n.
knock 279 n.
approach 289 n.
burst in 297 vb.
encroach 306 vb.
spasm 318 n.
argue 475 vb.
cause doubt 486 vb.
voice 577 n.
resolution 599 n.
policy 623 n.
way 624 n.
illness 651 n.
impairment 655 n.
attempt 671 n.
attack 712 n.vb.
fight 716 vb.
battle 718 n.
wage war 718 vb.
brigandage 788 n.
censure 924 n.
dispraise 924 vb.
detraction 926 n.
indict 928 vb.

attacker
intruder 59 n.
destroyer 168 n.
opponent 705 n.
quarreller 709 n.
attacker 712 n.
combatant 722 n.
enemy 881 n.
detractor 926 n.

attack of nerves
psychopathy 503 n.

attain
arrive 295 vb.
acquire 771 vb.

— one's desire
be content 828 vb.

— one's purpose
succeed 727 vb.

attainable
accessible 289 adj.
possible 469 adj.

attainder
condemnation 961 n.

attainments
culture 490 n.
learning 536 n.
skill 694 n.

attar
scent 396 n.

attempt
experiment 461 vb.
be willing 597 vb.
persevere 600 vb.
intention 617 n.
aim at 617 vb.
attempt 671 n.vb.
undertaking 672 n.
action 676 n.
do 676 vb.
exert oneself 682 vb.

— the impossible
attempt the impossible 470 vb.
waste effort 641 vb.
act foolishly 695 vb.

attend
accompany 89 vb.
be present 189 vb.
follow 284 vb.
watch 441 vb.
be attentive 455 vb.
doctor 658 vb.
be servile 879 vb.

— upon
serve 742 vb.

attendant
concomitant 89 n.
follower 284 n.
retainer 742 n.
bridal party 894 n.

attention
listening 415 n.
attention 455 n.
carefulness 457 n.
accuracy 494 n.
expectation 507 n.
study 536 n.
perseverance 600 n.
assiduity 678 n.
respect 920 n.

attentive, be
hear 415 vb.
gaze 438 vb.
watch 441 vb.
think 449 vb.
be attentive 455 vb.
be careful 457 vb.
be active 678 vb.
observe 768 vb.
be courteous 884 vb.

attenuate
abate 37 vb.
make smaller 198 vb.
narrow 206 adj.
make thin 206 vb.
rarefy 325 vb.

attest
testify 466 vb.
endorse 488 vb.
swear 532 vb.
indicate 547 vb.
contract 765 vb.

attested
evidential 466 adj.
certain 473 adj.

at the beginning
initially 68 adv.

at the bottom of
causal 156 adj.

at the bottom of, be
be inside 224 vb.
lurk 523 vb.

at the breast
infantine 132 adj.

at the double
swiftly 277 adv.

at the drop of a hat
instantaneously 116 adv.
suddenly 135 adv.
willingly 597 adv.

at the eleventh hour
late 136 adv.
timely 137 adj.
opportunely 137 adv.

at the end
after 65 adv.

at the end of one's tether
in difficulties 700 adj.

at the first opportunity
betimes 135 adv.

at the helm
under way 269 adv.
directing 689 adj.
in control 689 adv.

at the last gasp
dying 361 adj.

at the mercy of
liable 180 adj.
vulnerable 661 adj.
subject 745 adj.

at the ready
prepared 669 adj.

at the salute
respectful 920 adj.

at the same time
in return 31 adv.
synchronously 123 adv.

at the top
great 32 adj.
atop 213 adv.

at the top of one's voice
loudly 400 adv.

at the wheel
under way 269 adv.
in control 689 adv.

at this moment
at present 121 adv.

attic
attic 194 n.
vertex 213 n.

Attic
elegant 575 adj.
witty 839 adj.
tasteful 846 adj.

at times
sometimes 139 adv.

attire
dressing 228 n.
dress 228 vb.

attitude
state 7 n.
circumstance 8 n.
situation 186 n.
form 243 n.
idea 451 n.
opinion 485 n.
supposition 512 n.
conduct 688 n.
affections 817 n.

attitudinize, attitudinise
be affected 850 vb.

attorney
mediator 720 n.
consignee 754 n.
deputy 755 n.
law agent 958 n.

attract
bring together 74 vb.
influence 178 vb.
draw 288 vb.
attract 291 vb.
motivate 612 vb.
delight 826 vb.
cause desire 859 vb.
excite love 887 vb.
bewitch 983 vb.

— notice
be visible 443 vb.
attract notice 455 vb.
be plain 522 vb.
gesticulate 547 vb.
impress 821 vb.
be ostentatious 875 vb.

attraction
focus 76 n.
energy 160 n.
influence 178 n.
tendency 179 n.
attraction 291 n.
grammar 564 n.
incentive 612 n.
inducement 612 n.
pleasurableness 826 n.
beauty 841 n.
desired object 859 n.
liking 859 n.
favourite 890 n.
spell 983 n.

attractive
influential 178 adj.
drawing 288 adj.
attracting 291 adj.
inducing 612 adj.
pleasurable 826 adj.
personable 841 adj.
desired 859 adj.
lovable 887 adj.

attractiveness
beauty 841 n.

attribute
essential part 5 n.
speciality 80 n.
concomitant 89 n.
attribution 158 n.
attribute 158 vb.
ability 160 n.
thank 907 vb.
grant claims 915 vb.

attributed to
caused 157 adj.

attributive
grammatical 564 adj.
attrition
decrease 37 n.
powderiness 332 n.
friction 333 n.
warfare 718 n.
penitence 939 n.
attune
adjust 24 vb.
harmonize 410 vb.
at variance
disagreeing 25 adj.
opposing 704 adj.
quarrelling 709 adj.
inimical 881 adj.
at war
contending 716 adj.
at war 718 adv.
inimical 881 adj.
at will
at will 595 adv.
willingly 597 adv.
freely 744 adv.
at work
operative 173 adj.
doing 676 adj.
busy 678 adj.
at your service
obediently 739 adv.
atypical
nonuniform 17 adj.
dissimilar 19 adj.
inimitable 21 adj.
abnormal 84 adj.
aubade
vocal music 412 n.
wooing 889 n.
auberge
inn 192 n.
aubergine
vegetable 301 n.
purpleness 436 n.
auburn
brown 430 adj.
red 431 adj.
au courant
instructed 490 adj.
informed 524 adj.
auction
offer 759 vb.
sale 793 n.
sell 793 vb.
overcharge 811 vb.
auction room
market 796 n.
audacity
courage 855 n.
rashness 857 n.
insolence 878 n.
audible
sounding 398 adj.
loud 400 adj.
auditory 415 adj.
intelligible 516 adj.
speaking 579 adj.
audience
incomer 297 n.
listener 415 n.
listening 415 n.
onlookers 441 n.
allocution 583 n.
conference 584 n.
playgoer 594 n.
council 692 n.
audio
sound 398 n.
sounding 398 adj.
audiotypist
stenographer 586 n.
audiovisual
sounding 398 adj.
auditory 415 adj.
educational 534 adj.
audit
number 86 vb.
enquiry 459 n.
enquire 459 vb.
accounts 808 n.
account 808 vb.
audition
hearing 415 n.
listening 415 n.
exam 459 n.
experiment 461 n.
conference 584 n.
dramaturgy 594 n.
auditor
listener 415 n.
accountant 808 n.
auditorium
listener 415 n.
onlookers 441 n.
classroom 539 n.
theatre 594 n.
auditory
sounding 398 adj.
auditory 415 adj.
au fait
expert 694 adj.
Augean stables
sink 649 n.
auger
sharp point 256 n.
perforator 263 n.
augment
be great 32 vb.
augment 36 vb.
add 38 vb.
be many 104 vb.
strengthen 162 vb.
enlarge 197 vb.
store 632 vb.
aggravate 832 vb.
augmentative
part of speech 564 n.
augur
diviner 511 n.
predict 511 vb.
— well
predict 511 vb.
be auspicious 730 vb.
give hope 852 vb.
august
great 32 adj.
notable 638 adj.
worshipful 866 adj.
Augustan
elegant 575 adj.
poetic 593 adj.
perfect 646 adj.
Augustan Age
literature 557 n.
palmy days 730 n.
auk
animal 365 n.
auld lang syne
past time 125 n.
au naturel
uncovered 229 adj.
culinary 301 adj.
aunt
kinsman 11 n.
woman 373 n.
Aunt Sally
laughingstock 851 n.
au pair
interchanged 151 adj.
in exchange 151 adv.
resident 191 n.
domestic 742 n.
trading 791 adj.
aura
surroundings 230 n.
prestige 866 n.
aural
auditory 415 adj.
aural examination
listening 415 n.
aureate
ornate 574 adj.
aureole
loop 250 n.
light 417 n.
honours 866 n.
auricular
auditory 415 adj.
auricular confession
secrecy 525 n.
disclosure 526 n.
ministration 988 n.
aurora
glow 417 n.
Aurora
morning 128 n.
lesser deity 967 n.
aurora borealis
heavens 321 n.
glow 417 n.
auroral
matinal 128 adj.
lateral 239 adj.
luminous 417 adj.
Auschwitz
slaughterhouse 362 n.
prison camp 748 n.
auscultation
listening 415 n.
auspice
omen 511 n.
auspices
protection 660 n.
aid 703 n.
auspicious
circumstantial 8 adj.
opportune 137 adj.
presageful 511 adj.
advisable 642 adj.
palmy 730 adj.
promising 852 adj.
austere
plain 573 adj.
severe 735 adj.
ascetic 945 adj.
pietistic 979 adj.
austerities
penance 941 n.
austerity
unsavouriness 391 n.
plainness 573 n.
insufficiency 636 n.
severity 735 n.
asceticism 945 n.
pietism 979 n.
austerity lunch
meal 301 n.
Australopithecus
humankind 371 n.
autarchic
governmental 733 adj.
independent 744 adj.
autarchy
despotism 733 n.
independence 744 n.
autarkic
independent 744 adj.
autarky
sufficiency 635 n.
independence 744 n.
authentic
inimitable 21 adj.
evidential 466 adj.
genuine 494 adj.
authenticate
testify 466 vb.
make certain 473 vb.
endorse 488 vb.
give security 767 vb.
authenticity
identity 13 n.
no imitation 21 n.
authenticity 494 n.
author
cause 156 n.
producer 164 n.
news reporter 529 n.
literature 557 n.
author 589 n.
narrator 590 n.
dissertator 591 n.
prose 593 n.
authoress
author 589 n.
authoritarian
volitional 595 adj.
directing 689 adj.
authoritative 733 adj.
tyrant 735 n.

authoritarian 735 adj.
authoritative
powerful 160 adj.
influential 178 adj.
evidential 466 adj.
certain 473 adj.
creedal 485 adj.
directing 689 adj.
authoritative 733 adj.
commanding 737 adj.
scriptural 975 adj.
orthodox 976 adj.
authorities, the
master 741 n.
authority
greatness 32 n.
superiority 34 n.
precedence 64 n.
power 160 n.
influence 178 n.
credential 466 n.
evidence 466 n.
sage 500 n.
informant 524 n.
bigwig 638 n.
management 689 n.
expert 696 n.
authority 733 n.
severity 735 n.
regalia 743 n.
commission 751 n.
permit 756 n.
prestige 866 n.
jurisdiction 955 n.
authorization
warrant 737 n.
authorize, authorise
empower 160 vb.
commission 751 vb.
permit 756 vb.
grant claims 915 vb.
Authorized Version
scripture 975 n.
autism
intrinsicality 5 n.
insanity 503 n.
unsociability 883 n.
autobiographer
chronicler 549 n.
narrator 590 n.
autobiography
biography 590 n.
autochthonous
native 191 adj.
autocracy
despotism 733 n.
brute force 735 n.
autocrat
bigwig 638 n.
leader 690 n.
tyrant 735 n.
autocrat 741 n.
autocratic
volitional 595 adj.
authoritative 733 adj.
authoritarian 735 adj.
autocue
broadcasting 531 n.
auto da fé
killing 362 n.
burning 381 n.
capital punishment 963 n.
autodidact
ignorance 491 n.
learner 538 n.
autodidactic
studious 536 adj.
autogenesis
propagation 167 n.
autograph
no imitation 21 n.
identification 547 n.
label 547 n.
sign 547 vb.
script 586 n.
written 586 adj.
autograph album
reminder 505 n.
autohypnosis
sense 374 n.
insensibility 375 n.
autointoxication
impairment 655 n.
autolysis
death 361 n.
automate
computerize 86 vb.
empower 160 vb.
produce 164 vb.
automated
mechanical 630 adj.
automatic
computerized 86 adj.
unthinking 450 adj.
involuntary 596 adj.
spontaneous 609 adj.
instrumental 628 adj.
mechanical 630 adj.
pistol 723 n.
automatically
habitually 610 adv.
automatic writing
spiritualism 984 n.
automation
electronics 160 n.
production 164 n.
instrumentality 628 n.
mechanics 630 n.
automatism
absence of thought 450 n.
spiritualism 984 n.
automatist
psychic 984 n.
automaton
image 551 n.
fatalist 596 n.
machine 630 n.
automobile
automobile 274 n.
vehicular 274 adj.
automotive
moving 265 adj.
travelling 267 adj.
vehicular 274 adj.
autonomous
governmental 733 adj.
independent 744 adj.
autonymous
verbal 559 adj.
autopilot
aeronaut 271 n.
directorship 689 n.
autopsy
death 361 n.
inquest 364 n.
inspection 438 n.
enquiry 459 n.
autoroute
road 624 n.
autosuggestion
sense 374 n.
misjudgment 481 n.
fantasy 513 n.
autotype
printing 555 n.
autumn
period 110 n.
oldness 127 n.
autumn 129 n.
auxiliary
inferior 35 n.adj.
additional 38 adj.
extra 40 n.
substitute 150 n.
prop 218 n.
instrument 628 n.
aider 703 n.
aiding 703 adj.
auxiliary 707 n.
armed force 722 n.
soldier 722 n.
avail
benefit 615 vb.
utility 640 n.
be useful 640 vb.
— oneself of
avail oneself of 673 vb.
availability
choice 605 n.
available
on the spot 189 adj.
accessible 289 adj.
possible 469 adj.
instrumental 628 adj.
stored 632 adj.
provisioning 633 adj.
useful 640 adj.
used 673 adj.
offering 759 adj.
not retained 779 adj.
salable 793 adj.
avalanche
revolution 149 n.
descent 309 n.
snow 380 n.
redundance 637 n.
avant-garde
preceding 64 adj.
precursor 66 n.
modernist 126 n.
modern 126 adj.
front 237 n.
preceding 283 n.
avant-propos
prelude 66 n.
avarice
acquisition 771 n.
rapacity 786 n.
avarice 816 n.
desire 859 n.
selfishness 932 n.
avatar
transformation 143 n.
manifestation 522 n.
theophany 965 n.
revelation 975 n.
Ave Maria
prayers 981 n.
avenge
retaliate 714 vb.
be pitiless 906 vb.
avenge 910 vb.
vindicate 927 vb.
punish 963 vb.
avenger
Fury 891 n.
avenger 910 n.
avenue
housing 192 n.
pleasance 192 n.
path 624 n.
road 624 n.
aver
affirm 532 vb.
average
average 30 n.
median 30 adj.
average out 30 vb.
inconsiderable 33 adj.
middle 70 n.
generality 79 n.
general 79 adj.
typical 83 adj.
not discriminate 464 vb.
middle way 625 n.
not bad 644 adj.
imperfect 647 adj.
averageness 732 n.
middling 732 adj.
compromise 770 n.
— out
measure 465 vb.
compromise 770 vb.
averages
statistics 86 n.
average specimen
common man 30 n.
aversion
unwillingness 598 n.
dislike 861 n.
hatred 888 n.

aversion therapy
therapy 658 n.
avert
deflect 282 vb.
parry 713 vb.
— one's eyes
gaze 438 vb.
be blind 439 vb.
be humbled 872 vb.
— the omen
deprecate 762 vb.
avertable
avoidable 620 adj.
avian
animal 365 adj.
aviary
nest 192 n.
zoo 369 n.
aviation
aeronautics 271 n.
aviator, aviatrix
aeronaut 271 n.
aviculture
animal husbandry 369 n.
avid
excited 821 adj.
desiring 859 adj.
avid for knowledge
inquisitive 453 adj.
avidity
rapacity 786 n.
avarice 816 n.
desire 859 n.
avifauna
bird 365 n.
avocado
fruit 301 n.
green 434 adj.
avocation
business 622 n.
avoid
exclude 57 vb.
be absent 190 vb.
recoil 280 vb.
deviate 282 vb.
turn back 286 vb.
disregard 458 vb.
be stealthy 525 vb.
be unwilling 598 vb.
avoid 620 vb.
circuit 626 vb.
elude 667 vb.
not use 674 vb.
not act 677 vb.
parry 713 vb.
refuse 760 vb.
not observe 769 vb.
be cautious 858 vb.
dislike 861 vb.
be unsociable 883 vb.
make unwelcome 883 vb.
fail in duty 918 vb.
— bloodshed
be at peace 717 vb.
— defeat
be successful 727 vb.
— notice
lurk 523 vb.
avoidance
avoidance 620 n.
escape 667 n.
nonpayment 805 n.
undutifulness 918 n.
temperance 942 n.
avoided
separate 46 adj.
disliked 861 adj.
friendless 883 adj.
avoirdupois
finite quantity 26 n.
bulk 195 n.
weighing 322 n.
avouch
affirm 532 vb.
avow
testify 466 vb.
assent 488 vb.
confess 526 vb.
affirm 532 vb.
avulsion
scission 46 n.
extraction 304 n.
avuncular
akin 11 adj.
await
look ahead 124 vb.
wait 136 vb.
await 507 vb.
awaiting confirmation
uncertified 474 adj.
awaiting trial
accused 928 adj.
awake
attentive 455 adj.
active 678 adj.
awaken
cause 156 vb.
cause feeling 374 vb.
have feeling 374 vb.
excite 821 vb.
awake to
attentive 455 adj.
discover 484 vb.
impressible 819 adj.
award
judgment 480 n.
judge 480 vb.
trophy 729 n.
gift 781 n.
giving 781 n.
give 781 vb.
honours 866 n.
reward 962 n.vb.
— the palm
approve 923 vb.
aware
sentient 374 adj.
attentive 455 adj.
knowing 490 adj.
intelligent 498 adj.
impressible 819 adj.
lively 819 adj.
awareness
sensibility 374 n.
intellect 447 n.
knowledge 490 n.
sagacity 498 n.
awash
drenched 341 adj.
away
absent 190 adj.
distant 199 adj.
afar 199 adv.
awe
excitation 821 n.
fear 854 n.
frighten 854 vb.
wonder 864 n.
be wonderful 864 vb.
respect 920 n.
command respect 920 vb.
worship 981 n.
awe-inspiring
impressive 821 adj.
frightening 854 adj.
wonderful 864 adj.
aweless
unfearing 855 adj.
disrespectful 921 adj.
awelessness
lack of wonder 865 n.
awesome
frightening 854 adj.
wonderful 864 adj.
awesomeness
prestige 866 n.
awestruck
impressed 818 adj.
fearing 854 adj.
wondering 864 adj.
respectful 920 adj.
awful
silent 399 adj.
bad 645 adj.
not nice 645 adj.
frightening 854 adj.
awfully
extremely 32 adv.
awheel
on foot 267 adv.
awhile
transiently 114 adv.
awkward
unconformable 84 adj.
unwieldy 195 adj.
ignorant 491 adj.
foolish 499 adj.
inelegant 576 adj.
inexpedient 643 adj.
clumsy 695 adj.
difficult 700 adj.
quarrelling 709 adj.
disobedient 738 adj.
annoying 827 adj.
graceless 842 adj.
ill-bred 847 adj.
ridiculous 849 adj.
modest 874 adj.
awkward age
youth 130 n.
awkward situation
circumstance 8 n.
complexity 61 n.
awl
sharp point 256 n.
perforator 263 n.
awn
prickle 256 n.
roughness 259 n.
awning
canopy 226 n.
screen 421 n.
AWOL
absent 190 adj.
awry
unequal 29 adj.
orderless 61 adj.
oblique 220 adj.
distorted 246 adj.
evil 616 adj.
amiss 616 adv.
axe
destroy 165 vb.
shorten 204 vb.
sharp edge 256 n.
dismiss 300 vb.
fell 311 vb.
killer 362 n.
axe 723 n.
means of execution 964 n.
axe-grinder
planner 623 n.
axe to grind
objective 617 n.
selfishness 932 n.
axial
central 225 adj.
directed 281 adj.
axiology
estimate 480 n.
axiom
certainty 473 n.
premise 475 n.
truth 494 n.
axiom 496 n.
axiomatic
certain 473 adj.
aphoristic 496 adj.
axis
pivot 218 n.
centre 225 n.
rotator 315 n.
gauge 465 n.
association 706 n.
society 708 n.
axle
pivot 218 n.
rotator 315 n.
axle grease
lubricant 334 n.
axle load
weighing 322 n.
metrology 465 n.
axonometric projection
representation 551 n.
ayah
domestic 742 n.

ayatollah
governor 741 n.
ayes, the
assenter 488 n.
azimuth
horizontality 216 n.
compass point 281 n.
azimuth circle
verticality 215 n.
azoic
inorganic 359 adj.
Azrael
death 361 n.
angel 968 n.
azure
blueness 435 n.
heraldry 547 n.
azygous
alone 88 adj.

B

ba
identity 13 n.
analogue 18 n.
spirit 447 n.
BA
academic title 870 n.
baa
ululation 409 n.
ululate 409 vb.
Baal
Semitic deities 967 n.
idol 982 n.
Baba Yaga
demon 970 n.
Babbitt
conformist 83 n.
vulgarian 847 n.
babble
flow 350 vb.
sound faint 401 vb.
reason badly 477 vb.
be foolish 499 vb.
be insane 503 vb.
empty talk 515 n.
mean nothing 515 vb.
language 557 n.
chatter 581 n.
babe
child 132 n.
ignoramus 493 n.
ninny 501 n.
innocent 935 n.
babe-in-arms
weakling 163 n.
ingenue 699 n.
Babel
confusion 61 n.
discord 411 n.
lack of meaning 515 n.
language 557 n.
babes and sucklings
innocent 935 n.
baboon
mammal 365 n.
eyesore 842 n.
babu
recorder 549 n.
title 870 n.
baby
child 132 n.
infantine 132 adj.
weakling 163 n.
little 196 adj.
function 622 n.
please 826 vb.
coward 856 n.
loved one 887 n.
pet 889 vb.
baby boom
productiveness 171 n.
baby buggy
pushcart 274 n.
babyhood
beginning 68 n.
youth 130 n.
helplessness 161 n.
babyish
infantine 132 adj.
weak 163 adj.
foolish 499 adj.
cowardly 856 adj.
baby-sit
look after 457 vb.
baby-sitter
protector 660 n.
servant 742 n.
keeper 749 n.
baby talk
neology 560 n.
baccalaureate
exam 459 n.
honours 866 n.
academic title 870 n.
baccarat
card game 837 n.
Bacchanalia
turmoil 61 n.
sensualism 944 n.
drunkenness 949 n.
Bacchant(e)
madman 504 n.
drunkard 949 n.
Bacchic
disorderly 61 adj.
frenzied 503 adj.
Bacchus
drunkenness 949 n.
Olympian deity 967 n.
bachelor
unit 88 n.
male 372 n.
independent 744 adj.
celibate 895 n.
unwedded 895 adj.
bachelor girl
woman 373 n.
spinster 895 n.
bachelor of arts, BA
academic title 870 n.
bacillus
microorganism 196 n.
infection 651 n.
poison 659 n.
back
prop 218 n.
be inverted 221 vb.
line 227 vb.
rear 238 n.
back 238 adj.
be behind 238 vb.
contraposition 240 n.
deviate 282 vb.
regress 286 vb.
backwards 286 adv.
harden 326 vb.
blow 352 vb.
break in 369 vb.
choose 605 vb.
gamble 618 vb.
patronize 703 vb.
lend 784 vb.
trade 791 vb.
approve 923 vb.
— and fill
navigate 269 vb.
be irresolute 601 vb.
— away
recede 290 vb.
be unwilling 598 vb.
be irresolute 601 vb.
avoid 620 vb.
— down
revert 148 vb.
regress 286 vb.
tergiversate 603 vb.
relinquish 621 vb.
refuse 760 vb.
— out
regress 286 vb.
tergiversate 603 vb.
resign 753 vb.
not observe 769 vb.
be cowardly 856 vb.
— the wrong horse
fail 728 vb.
— up
support 218 vb.
be behind 238 vb.
aid 703 vb.
— water
retard 278 vb.
regress 286 vb.
backache
pang 377 n.
back and forth
to and fro 317 adv.
backbencher
inferior 35 n.
councillor 692 n.
commoner 869 n.
backbite
defame 926 vb.
backbone
essential part 5 n.
vitality 162 n.
vigorousness 174 n.
pillar 218 n.
prop 218 n.
centre 225 n.
rear 238 n.
resolution 599 n.
stamina 600 n.
courage 855 n.
backbreaking
laborious 682 adj.
backchat
answer 460 n.
slang 560 n.
witticism 839 n.
sauciness 878 n.
backcloth
spectacle 445 n.
stage set 594 n.
back door
rear 238 n.
doorway 263 n.
stealthy 525 adj.
means of escape 667 n.
backdrop
rear 238 n.
stage set 594 n.
back-end
autumn 129 n.
rear 238 n.
back entrance
rear 238 n.
access 624 n.
backer
stage manager 594 n.
gambler 618 n.
patron 707 n.
lender 784 n.
friend 880 n.
backfire
reversion 148 n.
counteraction 182 n.
bang 402 n.vb.
back formation
word 559 n.
backgammon
board game 837 n.
background
circumstance 8 n.
concomitant 89 n.
accompanying 89 adj.
distance 199 n.
surroundings 230 n.
rear 238 n.
spectacle 445 n.
knowledge 490 n.
information 524 n.
stage set 594 n.
ornamentation 844 n.
backhanded
equivocal 518 adj.

backhanded compliment
mental dishonesty 543 n.
affectation 850 n.
ridicule 851 n.
censure 924 n.
backing
lining 227 n.
aid 703 n.
backlash
reversion 148 n.
effect 157 n.
counteraction 182 n.
recoil 280 n.
retaliation 714 n.
resistance 715 n.
deprecation 762 n.
backlog
store 632 n.
back number
archaism 127 n.
reading matter 589 n.
laughingstock 851 n.
back of
rearward 238 adv.
back of beyond
district 184 n.
farness 199 n.
seclusion 883 n.
backpack
bag 194 n.
travel 267 vb.
back pay
debt 803 n.
backpedal
retard 278 vb.
regress 286 vb.
recant 603 vb.
backrest
prop 218 n.
backroom
latent 523 adj.
hiding-place 527 n.
plan 623 n.
backroom boy/girl
intellectual 492 n.
planner 623 n.
expert 696 n.
backscratcher
toady 879 n.
back-scratching
cooperation 706 n.
flattery 925 n.
back seat
inferiority 35 n.
rear 238 n.
back-seat driver
rider 268 n.
meddler 678 n.
director 690 n.
adviser 691 n.
backside
buttocks 238 n.
rear 238 n.
back slang
slang 560 n.
back-slapping
ostentation 875 n.
friendly 880 adj.
sociability 882 n.
sociable 882 adj.
backslide
revert 148 vb.
tergiversate 603 vb.
relapse 657 vb.
be wicked 934 vb.
be impious 980 vb.
backslider
tergiversator 603 n.
offender 904 n.
heathen 974 n.
impious person 980 n.
backstage
rear 238 n.
on stage 594 adv.
backstairs
hiding-place 527 n.
back stitch
needlework 844 n.
back street
road 624 n.
dilapidation 655 n.
beggarly 801 adj.
back stroke
aquatics 269 n.
backtalk
witticism 839 n.
sauciness 878 n.
back-to-back
small house 192 n.
architectural 192 adj.
rearward 238 adv.
against 240 adv.
in league 708 adv.
back-to-front
inverted 221 adj.
inversely 221 adv.
backtrack
regress 286 vb.
recant 603 vb.
backward
late 136 adj.
rearward 238 adv.
regressive 286 adj.
ignorant 491 adj.
unintelligent 499 adj.
unwilling 598 adj.
avoiding 620 adj.
deteriorated 655 adj.
immature 670 adj.
unprepared 670 adj.
artless 699 adj.
backwardation
discount 810 n.
backward-looking
retrospective 125 adj.
regressive 286 adj.
backwards
backwards 286 adv.
backwards and forwards
in exchange 151 adv.
to and fro 317 adv.
backwash
effect 157 n.
water travel 269 n.
eddy 350 n.
wave 350 n.
backwater
lake 346 n.
seclusion 883 n.
backwoods
district 184 n.
backwoodsman
absence 190 n.
country-dweller 869 n.
backyard
place 185 n.
bacon
meat 301 n.
bacteria
microorganism 196 n.
infection 651 n.
poison 659 n.
bacteriology
pathology 651 n.
medical art 658 n.
bad
inferior 35 adj.
decomposed 51 adj.
fetid 397 adj.
evil 616 adj.
trivial 639 adj.
profitless 641 adj.
bad 645 adj.
imperfect 647 adj.
insalubrious 653 adj.
deteriorated 655 adj.
adverse 731 adj.
disreputable 867 adj.
maleficent 898 adj.
wrong 914 adj.
contemptible 922 adj.
blameworthy 924 adj.
dishonest 930 adj.
heinous 934 adj.
wicked 934 adj.
bad air
insalubrity 653 n.
bad apple
alterer 143 n.
bad art
misrepresentation 552 n.
bad taste 847 n.
bad at
bad 645 adj.
bad bargain
choice 605 n.
dearness 811 n.
bad behaviour
wickedness 934 n.
bad blood
dislike 861 n.
enmity 881 n.
hatred 888 n.
malevolence 898 n.
bad books
disapprobation 924 n.
bad business
hopelessness 853 n.
bad case
sophism 477 n.
bad character
badness 645 n.
disrepute 867 n.
wickedness 934 n.
bad person 938 n.
bad conscience
guilt 936 n.
penitence 939 n.
bad dream
fantasy 513 n.
false alarm 665 n.
baddy
evildoer 904 n.
bad person 938 n.
bad example
irrelevance 10 n.
bad person 938 n.
bad faith
falsehood 541 n.
nonobservance 769 n.
perfidy 930 n.
bad fit
misfit 25 n.
bad form
unwonted 611 adj.
ill-breeding 847 n.
badge
badge 547 n.
heraldry 547 n.
trophy 729 n.
badge of rank 743 n.
jewellery 844 n.
badge of infamy
slur 867 n.
badger
mammal 365 n.
interrogate 459 vb.
torment 827 vb.
bad grammar
grammar 564 n.
solecism 565 n.
inelegance 576 n.
bad habit
habit 610 n.
bane 659 n.
intemperance 943 n.
bad hand
bungler 697 n.
bad health
ill health 651 n.
bad heart
cardiovascular disease 651 n.
bad idea
mistake 495 n.

badinage
interlocution 584 n.
witticism 839 n.
ridicule 851 n.
bad influence
alterer 143 n.
badness 645 n.
bad person 938 n.
bad job
bungling 695 n.
hopelessness 853 n.
bad language
rudeness 885 n.
scurrility 899 n.
bad light
half-light 419 n.
disrepute 867 n.
detraction 926 n.
bad likeness
dissimilarity 19 n.
representation 551 n.
misrepresentation 552 n.
bad logic
sophism 477 n.
bad lot
evildoer 904 n.
bad person 938 n.
bad luck
chance 159 n.
disappointment 509 n.
evil 616 n.
nondesign 618 n.
misfortune 731 n.
badly
painfully 32 adv.
slightly 33 adv.
badly 645 adv.
badly brought up
ill-bred 847 adj.
disobedient 738 adj.
badly off
unprosperous 731 adj.
poor 801 adj.
bad manners
conduct 688 n.
ill-breeding 847 n.
discourtesy 885 n.
bad match
misfit 25 n.
badminton
ball game 837 n.
bad money
false money 797 n.
bad-mouth
calumny 926 n.
defame 926 vb.
bad name
disrepute 867 n.
bad news
disappointment 509 n.
news 529 n.
bad odour
stench 397 n.
disrepute 867 n.
odium 888 n.
bad patch
difficulty 700 n.
adversity 731 n.
bad person
offender 904 n.
bad person 938 n.
devil 969 n.
bad policy
inexpedience 643 n.
bad press
censure 924 n.
detraction 926 n.
bad reputation
disrepute 867 n.
bad smell
odour 394 n.
stench 397 n.
bad tactics
mistake 495 n.
bad taste
pungency 388 n.
indiscrimination 464 n.
mistake 495 n.
art 551 n.
inelegance 576 n.
artlessness 699 n.
wit 839 n.
bad taste 847 n.
impurity 951 n.
bad temper
irascibility 892 n.
sullenness 893 n.
bad times
adversity 731 n.
bad value
dearness 811 n.
bad wishes
malediction 899 n.
Baedeker
itinerary 267 n.
guidebook 524 n.
baffle
puzzle 474 vb.
be difficult 700 vb.
be obstructive 702 vb.
oppose 704 vb.
defeat 727 vb.
be wonderful 864 vb.
— description
be wonderful 864 vb.
— understanding
be unintelligible 517 vb.
baffled
impotent 161 adj.
puzzled 517 adj.
defeated 728 adj.
bag
bunch 74 n.
bag 194 n.
be convex 253 vb.
carrier 273 n.
acquire 771 vb.
take 786 vb.
bag and baggage
property 777 n.
bagatelle
trifle 639 n.
ball game 837 n.
bagful
finite quantity 26 n.
store 632 n.
baggage
box 194 n.
thing transferred 272 n.
encumbrance 702 n.
property 777 n.
insolent person 878 n.
loose woman 952 n.
baggy
nonadhesive 49 adj.
spacious 183 adj.
large 195 adj.
broad 205 adj.
hanging 217 adj.
bagpipes
flute 414 n.
bags
great quantity 32 n.
trousers 228 n.
bag-snatcher
thief 789 n.
Baha'ism
religious faith 973 n.
bail
liberation 746 n.
security 767 n.
legal process 959 n.
bailee
consignee 754 n.
possessor 776 n.
bailey
place 185 n.
bailie
officer 741 n.
bailiff
ejector 300 n.
farmer 370 n.
manager 690 n.
officer 741 n.
retainer 742 n.
consignee 754 n.
law officer 955 n.
bailiwick
district 184 n.
jurisdiction 955 n.
bail out
transpose 272 vb.
empty 300 vb.
aid 703 vb.
give bail 767 vb.
bain-marie
cauldron 194 n.
Bairam
holy day 988 n.
bairn
child 132 n.
bait
attraction 291 n.
attract 291 vb.
trap 542 n.
trickery 542 n.
ensnare 542 vb.
incentive 612 n.
chase 619 n.
oppress 735 vb.
torment 827 vb.
excite love 887 vb.
enrage 891 vb.
reward 962 n.
— the trap
ensnare 542 vb.
be cunning 698 vb.
baize
textile 222 n.
bake
cook 301 vb.
harden 326 vb.
dry 342 vb.
be hot 379 vb.
heat 381 vb.
baker
cookery 301 n.
provider 633 n.
baker's dozen
over five 99 n.
baking powder
leaven 323 n.
baksheesh
acquisition 771 n.
gift 781 n.
reward 962 n.
balalaika
harp 414 n.
balance
relate 9 vb.
correlate 12 vb.
adjust 24 vb.
equilibrium 28 n.
equalize 28 vb.
average 30 n.
set off 31 vb.
remainder 41 n.
part 53 n.
completeness 54 n.
stability 153 n.
stabilize 153 vb.
symmetry 245 n.
scales 322 n.
compare 462 vb.
measure 465 vb.
sagacity 498 n.
sanity 502 n.
elegance 575 n.
be irresolute 601 vb.
middle way 625 n.
superfluity 637 n.
inexcitability 823 n.
caution 858 n.
— accounts with
pay 804 vb.
account 808 vb.
balance due
requirement 627 n.
balance of power
defence 713 n.
balances
funds 797 n.
credit 802 n.

balance sheet
accounts 808 n.
balance to pay
debt 803 n.
balancing act
equivocalness 518 n.
compromise 770 n.
balcony
lobby 194 n.
projection 254 n.
theatre 594 n.
bald
hairless 229 adj.
smooth 258 adj.
veracious 540 adj.
feeble 572 adj.
plain 573 adj.
inelegant 576 adj.
tedious 838 adj.
baldachin
canopy 226 n.
altar 990 n.
balderdash
silly talk 515 n.
baldric
belt 228 n.
loop 250 n.
bale
bunch 74 n.
stow 187 vb.
cultivate 370 vb.
evil 616 n.
— out
fly 271 vb.
emerge 298 vb.
bale fire
fire 379 n.
signal light 420 n.
signal 547 n.
baleful
harmful 645 adj.
malevolent 898 adj.
baler
ladle 194 n.
farm tool 370 n.
balk, baulk
beam 218 n.
partition 231 n.
disappointment 509 n.
disappoint 509 vb.
be obstructive 702 vb.
— at
avoid 620 vb.
Balkanize
rule 733 vb.
ball
sphere 252 n.
round 252 vb.
missile 287 n.
ammunition 723 n.
missile weapon 723 n.
dancing 837 n.
plaything 837 n.
social gathering 882 n.
ballad
vocal music 412 n.
narrative 590 n.
poem 593 n.
balladist
poet 593 n.
balladry
doggerel 593 n.
poetry 593 n.
ballad singer
vocalist 413 n.
ball and chain
fetter 748 n.
ballast
offset 31 n.
compensate 31 vb.
stabilizer 153 n.
gravity 322 n.
railway 624 n.
safeguard 662 n.
ball at one's feet
scope 744 n.
ballerina
actor 594 n.
dance 837 n.
ballet
composition 56 n.
ballet 594 n.
dancing 837 n.
ballet dancer
jumper 312 n.
actor 594 n.
dance 837 n.
balletomane
enthusiast 504 n.
playgoer 594 n.
ballet school
academy 539 n.
ball game
ball game 837 n.
ballistic missile
missile weapon 723 n.
ballistics
propulsion 287 n.
art of war 718 n.
arms 723 n.
ballon d'essai
empiricism 461 n.
balloon
bladder 194 n.
expand 197 vb.
circumscription 232 n.
outline 233 n.
sphere 252 n.
round 252 vb.
be convex 253 vb.
airship 276 n.
lightness 323 n.
gas 336 n.
plaything 837 n.
balloonist
aeronaut 271 n.
ballot
affirmation 532 n.
vote 605 n.
ballot box
electorate 605 n.
ball-player
player 837 n.
ballpoint pen
stationery 586 n.
ballroom
place of amusement 837 n.
ballroom dancing
dancing 837 n.
ballyhoo
loudness 400 n.
overestimation 482 n.
advertisement 528 n.
publicity 528 n.
exaggeration 546 n.
balm
moderator 177 n.
lubricant 334 n.
scent 396 n.
balm 658 n.
medicine 658 n.
pleasurableness 826 n.
relief 831 n.
bal masqué
concealment 525 n.
dancing 837 n.
balmy
warm 379 adj.
fragrant 396 adj.
palmy 730 adj.
cheering 833 adj.
balsa
raft 275 n.
balsam
balm 658 n.
medicine 658 n.
Baltic
ocean 343 n.
baluster
pillar 218 n.
balustrade
handle 218 n.
barrier 235 n.
fence 235 n.
bambino
child 132 n.
bamboo
grass 366 n.
bamboozle
puzzle 474 vb.
keep secret 525 vb.
befool 542 vb.
deceive 542 vb.
bamboozler
trickster 545 n.
ban
exclusion 57 n.
exclude 57 vb.
publication 528 n.
proclaim 528 vb.
call 547 n.
hindrance 702 n.
obstruct 702 vb.
command 737 n.vb.
restraint 747 n.
restrain 747 vb.
prohibition 757 n.
prohibit 757 vb.
make unwelcome 883 vb.
malediction 899 n.
disapprobation 924 n.
disapprove 924 vb.
penalty 963 n.
— with bell, book and candle
perform ritual 988 vb.
banal
aphoristic 496 adj.
usual 610 adj.
dull 840 adj.
banana
fruit 301 n.
banana republic
nonentity 639 n.
political organization 733 n.
bananas
crazy 503 adj.
band
bond 47 n.
girdle 47 n.
ligature 47 n.
band 74 n.
classification 77 n.
compressor 198 n.
strip 208 n.
outline 233 n.
loop 250 n.
orchestra 413 n.
stripe 437 n.
class 538 n.
personnel 686 n.
party 708 n.
formation 722 n.
bandage
tie 45 vb.
ligature 47 n.
compressor 198 n.
strip 208 n.
prop 218 n.
support 218 vb.
wrapping 226 n.
cover 226 vb.
blind 439 vb.
cure 656 vb.
surgical dressing 658 n.
doctor 658 vb.
obstruct 702 vb.
relieve 831 vb.
bandanna
headgear 228 n.
bandeau
girdle 47 n.
hairdressing 843 n.
banded
arranged 62 adj.
assembled 74 adj.
mottled 437 adj.
corporate 708 adj.
bandit
revolter 738 n.
robber 789 n.

outcast 883 n.
bandleader
timekeeper 117 n.
orchestra 413 n.
bandmaster
musician 413 n.
band of brothers
band 74 n.
community 708 n.
close friend 880 n.
Band of Hope
sober person 948 n.
bandolier
belt 228 n.
arsenal 723 n.
bands
canonicals 989 n.
bandsman
orchestra 413 n.
bandstand
pavilion 192 n.
band together
combine 50 vb.
congregate 74 vb.
cooperate 706 vb.
bandy about
publish 528 vb.
— words
interchange 151 vb.
converse 584 vb.
bandy-legged
deformed 246 adj.
legged 267 adj.
blemished 845 adj.
bane
destroyer 168 n.
influence 178 n.
killer 362 n.
evil 616 n.
badness 645 n.
infection 651 n.
plague 651 n.
insalubrity 653 n.
bane 659 n.
pitfall 663 n.
adversity 731 n.
suffering 825 n.
worry 825 n.
annoyance 827 n.
painfulness 827 n.
hateful object 888 n.
malevolence 898 n.
noxious animal 904 n.
ruffian 904 n.
wrong 914 n.
bang
be vigorous 174 vb.
close 264 vb.
impulse 279 n.
knock 279 n.
impel 279 vb.
strike 279 vb.
loudness 400 n.
be loud 400 vb.
bang 402 n.vb.
hairdressing 843 n.
— one's fist down
emphasize 532 vb.
— the big drum
boast 877 vb.
banger
automobile 274 n.
meat 301 n.
bang 402 n.
fireworks 420 n.
bangle
jewellery 844 n.
bang-on
super 644 adj.
banish
exclude 57 vb.
displace 188 vb.
eject 300 vb.
make unwelcome 883 vb.
banishment
penalty 963 n.
banister
pillar 218 n.
banjo
harp 414 n.
bank
high land 209 n.
seat 218 n.
incline 220 n.
be oblique 220 vb.
edge 234 n.
laterality 239 n.
shore 344 n.
storage 632 n.
store 632 vb.
pawnshop 784 n.
treasurer 798 n.
treasury 799 n.
— down
extinguish 382 vb.
— on
be certain 473 vb.
believe 485 vb.
expect 507 vb.
hope 852 vb.
bank account
funds 797 n.
wealth 800 n.
banker
lender 784 n.
merchant 794 n.
treasurer 798 n.
Bank Holiday
amusement 837 n.
banknote
title deed 767 n.
paper money 797 n.
bank rate
interest 803 n.
bankrupt
defeat 727 vb.
loser 728 n.
grounded 728 adj.
fleece 786 vb.
poor person 801 n.
poor 801 adj.
nonpayer 805 n.
nonpaying 805 adj.
bankruptcy
insufficiency 636 n.
failure 728 n.
nonobservance 769 n.
loss 772 n.
insolvency 805 n.
banned book
impurity 951 n.
banner
flag 547 n.
banns
marriage 894 n.
banquet
eat 301 vb.
feed 301 vb.
plenty 635 n.
festivity 837 n.
revel 837 vb.
social gathering 882 n.
banquette
stand 218 n.
fortification 713 n.
banshee
demon 970 n.
bantam
small animal 33 n.
dwarf 196 n.
poultry 365 n.
bantamweight
pugilist 722 n.
banter
interlocution 584 n.
witticism 839 n.
be witty 839 vb.
ridicule 851 n.vb.
sauciness 878 n.
be insolent 878 vb.
baptism
reception 299 n.
immersion 303 n.
moistening 341 n.
nomenclature 561 n.
Christian rite 988 n.
rite 988 n.
baptism of fire
debut 68 n.
Baptist
Protestant 976 n.adj.
baptistry
church interior 990 n.
church utensil 990 n.
baptize, baptise
name 561 vb.
baptized, the
church member 976 n.
bar
degree 27 n.
in deduction 39 adv.
fastening 47 n.
exclusion 57 n.
exclude 57 vb.
exclusive of 57 adv.
tavern 192 n.
chamber 194 n.
line 203 n.
prop 218 n.
barrier 235 n.
stopper 264 n.
close 264 vb.
island 349 n.
notation 410 n.
flash 417 n.
stripe 437 n.
heraldry 547 n.
safeguard 662 n.
obstruct 702 vb.
restraint 747 n.
restrain 747 vb.
lockup 748 n.
prohibit 757 vb.
bullion 797 n.
disapprobation 924 n.
disapprove 924 vb.
courtroom 956 n.
tribunal 956 n.
bar 958 n.
condemn 961 vb.
barb
filament 208 n.
sharp point 256 n.
sharpen 256 vb.
plumage 259 n.
missile weapon 723 n.
barbarian
extraneous 59 adj.
destroyer 168 n.
violent creature 176 n.
vulgarian 847 n.
vulgar 847 adj.
low fellow 869 n.
barbaric 869 adj.
rude person 885 n.
discourteous 885 adj.
ruffian 904 n.
barbaric
amorphous 244 adj.
neological 560 adj.
ill-bred 847 adj.
barbaric 869 adj.
barbarism
neology 560 n.
solecism 565 n.
inelegance 576 n.
artlessness 699 n.
bad taste 847 n.
inhumanity 898 n.
barbarity
violence 176 n.
cruel act 898 n.
inhumanity 898 n.
barbarize, barbarise
pervert 655 vb.
barbarous
violent 176 adj.
neological 560 adj.
inelegant 576 adj.
barbaric 869 adj.
cruel 898 adj.
barbecue
meal 301 n.
cook 301 vb.
festivity 837 n.

social gathering 882 n.
barbed shaft
ridicule 851 n.
barbed wire
fence 235 n.
sharp point 256 n.
obstacle 702 n.
defences 713 n.
barber
cleaner 648 n.
beautician 843 n.
barbering
hairdressing 843 n.
barbican
fort 713 n.
barbiturate(s)
moderator 177 n.
drug 658 n.
soporific 679 n.
drug-taking 949 n.
barcarole
vocal music 412 n.
bard
cook 301 vb.
musician 413 n.
poet 593 n.
bardolatry
dramaturgy 594 n.
bare
inconsiderable 33 adj.
simple 44 adj.
weakened 163 adj.
unproductive 172 adj.
empty 190 adj.
uncovered 229 adj.
uncover 229 vb.
open 263 vb.
dry 342 adj.
undisguised 522 adj.
disclose 526 vb.
plain 573 adj.
unprovided 636 adj.
vulnerable 661 adj.
— one's teeth
defy 711 vb.
be sullen 893 vb.
threaten 900 vb.
bareback riding
equitation 267 n.
barefaced
undisguised 522 adj.
barefaced lie
untruth 543 n.
barefoot
uncovered 229 adj.
beggarly 801 adj.
bareheaded
uncovered 229 adj.
respectful 920 adj.
barely
slightly 33 adv.
imperfectly 647 adv.
bare minimum
needfulness 627 n.
sufficiency 635 n.
dueness 915 n.
bargain
consensus 488 n.
compact 765 n.
contract 765 vb.
make terms 766 vb.
trade 791 n.
bargain 791 vb.
purchase 792 n.
cheapness 812 n.
be parsimonious 816 vb.
bargain basement
shop 796 n.
cheap 812 adj.
barge
carrier 273 n.
boat 275 n.
barge in
intrude 297 vb.
encroach 306 vb.
baritone
resonance 404 n.
vocalist 413 n.
bark
layer 207 n.
skin 226 n.
uncover 229 vb.
ship 275 n.
rub 333 vb.
cry 408 vb.
ululation 409 n.
ululate 409 vb.
anger 891 n.
be irascible 892 vb.
threat 900 n.
threaten 900 vb.
— up the wrong tree
err 495 vb.
barker
overestimation 482 n.
publicizer 528 n.
petitioner 763 n.
commender 923 n.
barley
provender 301 n.
grass 366 n.
barm
leaven 323 n.
bubble 355 n.
barmaid, barman
servant 742 n.
barmy
light 323 adj.
unintelligent 499 adj.
crazy 503 adj.
barn
farm tool 370 n.
storage 632 n.
store 632 vb.
barnacle
coherence 48 n.
marine life 365 n.
barn dance
dance 837 n.
barney
quarrel 709 n.
barnstorm
act 594 vb.
be affected 850 vb.
barnyard
farm 370 n.
barometer
pneumatics 340 n.
weather 340 n.
meter 465 n.
baron
bigwig 638 n.
rich person 800 n.
person of rank 868 n.
baronetcy
honours 866 n.
aristocracy 868 n.
baronial
noble 868 adj.
baroque
art 551 n.
school of painting 553 n.
ornamentation 844 n.
ornamental 844 adj.
churchlike 990 adj.
barouche
carriage 274 n.
barque
sailing ship 275 n.
barrack(s)
quarters 192 n.
be obstructive 702 vb.
barracker
hinderer 702 n.
detractor 926 n.
barrack-room lawyer
reasoner 475 n.
barrage
roll 403 n.
bombardment 712 n.
defences 713 n.
barrage balloon
airship 276 n.
defences 713 n.
air force 722 n.
barratry
improbity 930 n.
barred
excluded 57 adj.
crossed 222 adj.
closed 264 adj.
mottled 437 adj.
prohibited 757 adj.
barrel
vat 194 n.
cylinder 252 n.
metrology 465 n.
barrel organ
organ 414 n.
barren
impotent 161 adj.
unproductive 172 adj.
profitless 641 adj.
barricade
exclusion 57 n.
barrier 235 n.
obstruct 702 vb.
defences 713 n.
defend 713 vb.
barricades
revolt 738 n.
barrier
exclusion 57 n.
outline 233 n.
barrier 235 n.
obstacle 702 n.
defences 713 n.
barrister
lawyer 958 n.
barrow
small hill 209 n.
earthwork 253 n.
pushcart 274 n.
tomb 364 n.
monument 548 n.
shop 796 n.
barrow boy
seller 793 n.
pedlar 794 n.
bar sinister
slur 867 n.
bastardy 954 n.
bartender
servant 742 n.
barter
equivalence 28 n.
interchange 151 n. vb.
transference 272 n.
conditions 766 n.
transfer 780 n.
barter 791 n.
trade 791 vb.
basalt
rock 344 n.
bas bleu
intellectual 492 n.
base
inferiority 35 n.
extremity 69 n.
serial place 73 n.
source 156 n.
situation 186 n.
station 187 n.
place 187 vb.
abode 192 n.
cellar 194 n.
lowness 210 n.
base 214 n.
basis 218 n.
support 218 vb.
limit 236 n.
heraldry 547 n.
plan 623 n.
bad 645 adj.
armed force 722 n.
cowardly 856 adj.
disreputable 867 adj.
servile 879 adj.
rascally 930 adj.
heinous 934 adj.
baseball
ball game 837 n.

base-born
plebeian 869 adj.
bastard 954 adj.
baseless
unreal 2 adj.
erroneous 495 adj.
basement
cellar 194 n.
base 214 n.
base metal
mineral 359 n.
bash
strike 279 vb.
bash at
attempt 671 n.
bashaw
governor 741 n.
bashfulness
unwillingness 598 n.
modesty 874 n.
purity 950 n.
basic
intrinsic 5 adj.
simple 44 adj.
fundamental 156 adj.
undermost 214 adj.
important 638 adj.
BASIC
data processing 86 n.
basics
reality 1 n.
basic substance
element 319 n.
basil
potherb 301 n.
basilica
church 990 n.
basilisk
rara avis 84 n.
eye 438 n.
noxious animal 904 n.
basin
bowl 194 n.
cavity 255 n.
lake 346 n.
conduit 351 n.
basis
reason why 156 n.
base 214 n.
basis 218 n.
bask
be hot 379 vb.
— in
enjoy 376 vb.
be pleased 824 vb.
— in glory
have a reputation 866 vb.
basket
basket 194 n.
basketball
ball game 837 n.
basketwork
basket 194 n.
network 222 n.
basque
edging 234 n.
bas relief
relievo 254 n.
sculpture 554 n.
bass
fish 365 n.
resonance 404 n.
vocalist 413 n.
bassinet
basket 194 n.
bed 218 n.
bassoon
flute 414 n.
bast
ligature 47 n.
fibre 208 n.
bastard
unwarranted 916 adj.
cad 938 n.
bastardy 954 n.
bastard 954 adj.
baste
tie 45 vb.
cook 301 vb.
moisten 341 vb.
grease 357 vb.
bastinado
flog 963 vb.
bastion
protection 660 n.
refuge 662 n.
fortification 713 n.
bat
velocity 277 n.
hammer 279 n.
strike 279 vb.
propel 287 vb.
mammal 365 n.
club 723 n.
batch
finite quantity 26 n.
bunch 74 n.
group 74 n.
bated breath
faintness 401 n.
voicelessness 578 n.
bath
vessel 194 n.
immersion 303 n.
water 339 n.
moistening 341 n.
ablutions 648 n.
bath chair
pushcart 274 n.
bathe
swim 269 vb.
immerse 303 vb.
plunge 313 vb.
be wet 341 vb.
drench 341 vb.
clean 648 vb.
amuse oneself 837 vb.
bathetic
inelegant 576 adj.
bathing suit
beachwear 228 n.
bath oil
cosmetic 843 n.
batholith
rock 344 n.
bathometer
depth 211 n.
meter 465 n.
bathos
absurdity 497 n.
ridiculousness 849 n.
bathrobe
informal dress 228 n.
bathroom
chamber 194 n.
ablutions 648 n.
bathysphere
depth 211 n.
diver 313 n.
oceanography 343 n.
batik
textile 222 n.
printing 555 n.
ornamental art 844 n.
batiste
textile 222 n.
batman
domestic 742 n.
baton
prop 218 n.
badge 547 n.
badge of rule 743 n.
bats in the belfry
eccentricity 503 n.
batsman
player 837 n.
battalion(s)
multitude 104 n.
formation 722 n.
batten
fastening 47 n.
strip 208 n.
— down
close 264 vb.
— on
eat 301 vb.
prosper 730 vb.
be servile 879 vb.
battened down
prepared 669 adj.
batter
demolish 165 vb.
obliquity 220 n.
deform 244 vb.
distort 246 vb.
collide 279 vb.
strike 279 vb.
cereals 301 n.
pulpiness 356 n.
ill-treat 645 vb.
battered
dilapidated 655 adj.
battering ram
ram 279 n.
club 723 n.
battery
accumulation 74 n.
causal means 156 n.
electronics 160 n.
stable 192 n.
stock farm 369 n.
exam 459 n.
storage 632 n.
formation 722 n.
gun 723 n.
battle
slaughter 362 n.
exertion 682 n.
exert oneself 682 vb.
fight 716 n.
contend 716 vb.
battle 718 n.
give battle 718 vb.
battleground 724 n.
be inimical 881 vb.
battleaxe
sharp edge 256 n.
axe 723 n.
shrew 892 n.
battle cruiser
warship 722 n.
battle cry
call 547 n.
danger signal 665 n.
defiance 711 n.
war 718 n.
warfare 718 n.
threat 900 n.
battledress
uniform 228 n.
battlefield
slaughterhouse 362 n.
fight 716 n.
battle 718 n.
battleground 724 n.
battleground
casus belli 709 n.
battleground 724 n.
battle honours
decoration 729 n.
honours 866 n.
battlements
summit 213 n.
notch 260 n.
fortification 713 n.
battle of wills
opposition 704 n.
battle orders
warfare 718 n.
battle-scarred
warlike 718 adj.
battleship
warship 722 n.
battology
pleonasm 570 n.
battue
slaughter 362 n.
chase 619 n.
batty
crazy 503 adj.
bauble
insubstantial thing 4 n.
bauble 639 n.
plaything 837 n.
finery 844 n.
bad taste 847 n.

Bauhaus
art 551 n.
bawd
bawd 952 n.
bawdy
impure 951 adj.
bawdy-house
brothel 951 n.
bawl
cry 408 n.
vociferate 408 vb.
lamentation 836 n.
weep 836 vb.
— down
disapprove 924 vb.
— out
vociferate 408 vb.
reprobate 924 vb.
bay
compartment 194 n.
curve 248 n.
cavity 255 n.
horse 273 n.
gulf 345 n.
tree 366 n.
ululate 409 vb.
brown 430 adj.
disapprove 924 vb.
bayonet
pierce 263 vb.
strike 279 vb.
kill 362 vb.
lunge 712 n.
strike at 712 vb.
sidearms 723 n.
bayou
gulf 345 n.
bays
badge 547 n.
trophy 729 n.
honours 866 n.
bazaar
sale 793 n.
emporium 796 n.
shop 796 n.
bazooka
gun 723 n.
missile weapon 723 n.
BBC
broadcasting 531 n.
BC
anno domini 108 adv.
prior 119 adj.
be
be 1 vb.
be now 121 vb.
be situated 186 vb.
be present 189 vb.
live 360 vb.
be true 494 vb.
beach
edge 234 n.
land 295 vb.
shore 344 n.
arena 724 n.
beachcomber
wanderer 268 n.
wave 350 n.
beachhead
battleground 724 n.
retention 778 n.
beacon
fire 379 n.
signal light 420 n.
signal 547 n.
warning 664 n.
danger signal 665 n.
bead
sphere 252 n.
round 252 vb.
trimming 844 n.
decorate 844 vb.
beadle
officer 741 n.
law officer 955 n.
church officer 986 n.
beadledom
habit 610 n.
overactivity 678 n.
governance 733 n.
beadroll
list 87 n.
prayers 981 n.
beads
prayers 981 n.
ritual object 988 n.
beagle
dog 365 n.
beagling
chase 619 n.
beak
prow 237 n.
protuberance 254 n.
teacher 537 n.
magistracy 957 n.
beaked
curved 248 adj.
beaker
cup 194 n.
'be-all and end-all'
all 52 n.
intention 617 n.
important matter 638 n.
beam
beam 218 n.
roof 226 n.
laterality 239 n.
direction 281 n.
flash 417 n.
radiate 417 vb.
communicate 524 vb.
materials 631 n.
directorship 689 n.
be cheerful 833 vb.
smile 835 vb.
beaming
luminous 417 adj.
happy 824 adj.
cheerful 833 adj.
splendid 841 adj.
beam in the eye
prejudice 481 n.
beamy
broad 205 adj.
bean
small coin 33 n.
head 213 n.
beanfeast
feasting 301 n.
meal 301 n.
festivity 837 n.
beanpole
thinness 206 n.
tall creature 209 n.
beans
food 301 n.
vegetable 301 n.
bear
reproduce itself 167 vb.
be fruitful 171 vb.
support 218 vb.
carry 273 vb.
orientate 281 vb.
mammal 365 n.
be possible 469 vb.
gambler 618 n.
speculate 791 vb.
seller 793 n.
cheapen 812 vb.
feel 818 vb.
be patient 823 vb.
suffer 825 vb.
rude person 885 n.
shrew 892 n.
misanthrope 902 n.
— a charmed life
be safe 660 vb.
have luck 730 vb.
— a grudge
hate 888 vb.
— a hand
aid 703 vb.
— away
take away 786 vb.
— down on
approach 289 vb.
charge 712 vb.
— fruit
reproduce itself 167 vb.
be useful 640 vb.
get better 654 vb.
be successful 727 vb.
— hard on
be violent 176 vb.
ill-treat 645 vb.
be severe 735 vb.
— in mind
think 449 vb.
be mindful 455 vb.
— malice
be inimical 881 vb.
hate 888 vb.
resent 891 vb.
be malevolent 898 vb.
be revengeful 910 vb.
— no malice
forgive 909 vb.
— off
take away 786 vb.
— one company
accompany 89 vb.
— oneself
behave 688 vb.
— out
corroborate 466 vb.
demonstrate 478 vb.
vindicate 927 vb.
— pain
suffer 825 vb.
— the blame
be guilty 936 vb.
— the brunt
stand firm 599 vb.
busy oneself 622 vb.
be in difficulty 700 vb.
withstand 704 vb.
parry 713 vb.
resist 715 vb.
— the cost
defray 804 vb.
expend 806 vb.
— up
support 218 vb.
elevate 310 vb.
resist 715 vb.
be courageous 855 vb.
— upon
be related 9 vb.
operate 173 vb.
influence 178 vb.
— with
forgive 909 vb.
— witness
testify 466 vb.
affirm 532 vb.
— young
produce 164 vb.
bearable
imperfect 647 adj.
contenting 828 adj.
beard
adultness 134 n.
filament 208 n.
prickle 256 n.
hair 259 n.
print-type 587 n.
defy 711 vb.
be courageous 855 vb.
beardless
young 130 adj.
hairless 229 adj.
bearer
bearer 273 n.
servant 742 n.
beargarden
turmoil 61 n.
arena 724 n.
bear hug
retention 778 n.
endearment 889 n.
bearing
relation 9 n.
pivot 218 n.
prop 218 n.
bearing 273 adj.

direction 281 n.
mien 445 n.
meaning 514 n.
heraldry 547 n.
conduct 688 n.
owed 803 adj.
feeling 818 adj.
bearing on
concerning 9 adv.
relative 9 adj.
apt 24 adj.
bearing rein
fetter 748 n.
bearings
bearings 186 n.
direction 281 n.
bearish
animal 365 adj.
salable 793 adj.
cheap 812 adj.
ungracious 885 adj.
bear pit
zoo 369 n.
bearskin
headgear 228 n.
armour 713 n.
bear with a sore head
moper 834 n.
bear with a sore head, like a
irascible 892 adj.
beast
inferior 35 n.
violent creature 176 n.
animal 365 n.
dirty person 649 n.
eyesore 842 n.
noxious animal 904 n.
ruffian 904 n.
cad 938 n.
beastly
extremely 32 adv.
animal 365 adj.
not nice 645 adj.
unclean 649 adj.
unpleasant 827 adj.
ugly 842 adj.
discourteous 885 adj.
hateful 888 adj.
unkind 898 adj.
sensual 944 adj.
beast of burden
beast of burden 273 n.
worker 686 n.
beast of prey
killer 362 n.
animal 365 n.
hunter 619 n.
noxious animal 904 n.
beat
be superior 34 vb.
periodicity 141 n.
be periodic 141 vb.
territory 184 n.
place 185 n.
impulse 279 n.
strike 279 vb.
cook 301 vb.
pass 305 vb.
outdo 306 vb.
oscillation 317 n.
oscillate 317 vb.
agitate 318 vb.
be agitated 318 vb.
pulverize 332 vb.
roll 403 vb.
tempo 410 n.
play music 413 vb.
prosody 593 n.
chase 619 n.
hunt 619 vb.
function 622 n.
route 624 n.
clean 648 vb.
use 673 vb.
fatigued 684 adj.
attack 712 vb.
defeat 727 vb.
spank 963 vb.
— about the bush
sophisticate 477 vb.
dissemble 541 vb.
be diffuse 570 vb.
circuit 626 vb.
— all comers
be superior 34 vb.
win 727 vb.
— a retreat
regress 286 vb.
run away 620 vb.
escape 667 vb.
— a tattoo
roll 403 vb.
celebrate 876 vb.
— down
demolish 165 vb.
bargain 791 vb.
cheapen 812 vb.
be parsimonious 816 vb.
— faster
show feeling 818 vb.
— flat
flatten 216 vb.
— hollow
be superior 34 vb.
outdo 306 vb.
defeat 727 vb.
— in
make concave 255 vb.
— it
decamp 296 vb.
run away 620 vb.
— off
repel 292 vb.
— one's brains
think 449 vb.
— one's breast
be penitent 939 vb.
— swords into ploughshares
be at peace 717 vb.
make peace 719 vb.
— the air
strike 279 vb.
waste effort 641 vb.
— the big drum
proclaim 528 vb.
be ostentatious 875 vb.
— the bounds
limit 236 vb.
traverse 267 vb.
measure 465 vb.
circuit 626 vb.
— the breast
lament 836 vb.
— the drum
play music 413 vb.
signal 547 vb.
— the record
be superior 34 vb.
— time
time 117 vb.
play music 413 vb.
— up
strike 279 vb.
thicken 354 vb.
strike at 712 vb.
beaten track
habit 610 n.
route 624 n.
bore 838 n.
beatific
good 615 adj.
pleasurable 826 adj.
paradisiac 971 adj.
beatify
please 826 vb.
dignify 866 vb.
angelize 968 vb.
sanctify 979 vb.
be ecclesiastical 985 vb.
beating
corporal punishment 963 n.
beatitude
happiness 824 n.
beau
male 372 n.
fop 848 n.
lover 887 n.
Beaufort scale
anemometry 352 n.
beau geste
deed 676 n.
beau idéal
paragon 646 n.
a beauty 841 n.
Beaujolais
wine 301 n.
beau monde
rich person 800 n.
people of taste 846 n.
beau monde 848 n.
upper class 868 n.
beauteous
beautiful 841 adj.
beautiful
pleasant 376 adj.
elegant 575 adj.
excellent 644 adj.
pleasurable 826 adj.
beautiful 841 adj.
beautified 843 adj.
lovable 887 adj.
beautify
ornament 574 vb.
make better 654 vb.
beautify 841 vb.
primp 843 vb.
decorate 844 vb.
beauty
symmetry 245 n.
elegance 575 n.
pleasurableness 826 n.
beauty 841 n.
beauty, a
exceller 644 n.
paragon 646 n.
masterpiece 694 n.
a beauty 841 n.
favourite 890 n.
beauty spot
a beauty 841 n.
cosmetic 843 n.
beaux arts
art 551 n.
beaux yeux
beauty 841 n.
beaver
headgear 228 n.
hair 259 n.
mammal 365 n.
busy person 678 n.
worker 686 n.
armour 713 n.
beaver away
be active 678 vb.
bebop
music 412 n.
dance 837 n.
becalmed
quiescent 266 adj.
hindered 702 adj.
because (of)
causally 156 adv.
consequently 157 adv.
hence 158 adv.
beck
stream 350 n.
gesture 547 n.
gesticulate 547 vb.
command 737 n.vb.
beckon
gesticulate 547 vb.
become
become 1 vb.
be turned to 147 vb.
happen 154 vb.
evolve 316 vb.
becoming
agreeing 24 adj.
personable 841 adj.
tasteful 846 adj.

bed
unite with 45 vb.
place 187 vb.
layer 207 n.
base 214 n.
basis 218 n.
bed 218 n.
resting place 266 n.
garden 370 n.
sleep 679 n.
debauch 951 vb.
— down
place 187 vb.
groom 369 vb.
sleep 679 vb.
— out
cultivate 370 vb.
bed and breakfast
inn 192 n.
provision 633 n.
bedaub
coat 226 vb.
bedazzle
shine 417 vb.
blur 440 vb.
excite love 887 vb.
command respect 920 vb.
bed bug
insect 365 n.
bedclothes
coverlet 226 n.
bedding
stratification 207 n.
bed 218 n.
coverlet 226 n.
bedeck
decorate 844 vb.
bedevil
bedevil 63 vb.
destroy 165 vb.
be difficult 700 vb.
trouble 827 vb.
diabolize 969 vb.
bedevilment
impairment 655 n.
spell 983 n.
bedew
moisten 341 vb.
bedim
darken 418 vb.
bedim 419 vb.
blur 440 vb.
conceal 525 vb.
make unclean 649 vb.
bedizen
dress 228 vb.
primp 843 vb.
bedlam
confusion 61 n.
turmoil 61 n.
loudness 400 n.
discord 411 n.
lunatic asylum 503 n.
bed of nails
suffering 825 n.
bed of Procrustes
equalization 28 n.
bed of roses
euphoria 376 n.
fragrance 396 n.
palmy days 730 n.
bedouin
dweller 191 n.
wanderer 268 n.
bedpan
vessel 194 n.
latrine 649 n.
bedraggled
orderless 61 adj.
dirty 649 adj.
bedridden
sick 651 adj.
bedrock
reality 1 n.
simpleness 44 n.
permanence 144 n.
fixture 153 n.
source 156 n.
base 214 n.
basis 218 n.
chief thing 638 n.
important 638 adj.
bedroom
chamber 194 n.
bedside manner
therapy 658 n.
bedside reading
novel 590 n.
bed-sitter
flat 192 n.
bedtime
clock time 117 n.
evening 129 n.
vespertine 129 adj.
bee
insect 365 n.
busy person 678 n.
beech
tree 366 n.
beef
meat 301 n.
deprecate 762 vb.
be discontented 829 vb.
lament 836 vb.
— up
strengthen 162 vb.
beefcake
a beauty 841 n.
beefy
stalwart 162 adj.
fleshy 195 adj.
beehive
nest 192 n.
stock farm 369 n.
bee in one's bonnet
bias 481 n.
eccentricity 503 n.
whim 604 n.
bee-keeping
animal husbandry 369 n.
beeline
short distance 200 n.
straightness 249 n.
direction 281 n.
middle way 625 n.
Beelzebub
devil 969 n.
beer
alcoholic drink 301 n.
beer and skittles
enjoyment 824 n.
festivity 837 n.
beer cellar
tavern 192 n.
beery
drunken 949 adj.
intoxicating 949 adj.
bee's knees
exceller 644 n.
beestings
milk 301 n.
beeswax
fat 357 n.
beetle
be high 209 vb.
hammer 279 n.
insect 365 n.
— off
decamp 296 vb.
beetle-browed
projecting 254 adj.
beetle-crusher
foot 214 n.
beetling
overhanging 209 adj.
hanging 217 adj.
beetroot
vegetable 301 n.
befall
happen 154 vb.
befitting
fit 24 adj.
advisable 642 adj.
due 915 adj.
befog
cloud 355 vb.
darken 418 vb.
bedim 419 vb.
conceal 525 vb.
befool
puzzle 474 vb.
sophisticate 477 vb.
mislead 495 vb.
befool 542 vb.
ridicule 851 vb.
humiliate 872 vb.
before
before 64 adv.
before(in time) 119 adv.
here 189 adv.
in front 237 adv.
ahead 283 adv.
before Christ
anno domini 108 adv.
before God
manifestly 522 adv.
beforehand
before 119 adv.
beforehand 135 adv.
before-mentioned
preceding 64 adj.
before one's eyes
on the spot 189 adj.
in front 237 adv.
visible 443 adj.
visibly 443 adv.
before one's time
beforehand 135 adv.
before the Flood
anciently 127 adv.
before the mast
under way 269 adv.
before time
anachronistic 118 adj.
immature 670 adj.
before you could say knife
instantaneously 116 adv.
swiftly 277 adv.
befoul
make unclean 649 vb.
befriend
patronize 703 vb.
befriend 880 vb.
befuddle
puzzle 474 n.
inebriate 949 vb.
befuddlement
drunkenness 949 n.
beg
borrow 785 vb.
beg 761 vb.
— a favour
request 761 vb.
—, borrow or steal
find means 629 vb.
acquire 771 vb.
— for favours
be servile 879 vb.
— for mercy
knuckle under 721 vb.
ask mercy 905 vb.
— for one's bread
be poor 801 vb.
— leave
ask leave 756 vb.
— off
mediate 720 vb.
refuse 760 vb.
deprecate 762 vb.
— pardon
beg pardon 909 vb.
atone 941 vb.
— permission
ask leave 756 vb.
— the question
reason badly 477 vb.
— to advise
inform 524 vb.
— to differ
dissent 489 vb.
beget
cause 156 vb.

generate 167 vb.
vitalize 360 vb.
begetter
paternity 169 n.
beggar
beggar 763 n.
poor person 801 n.
impoverish 801 vb.
low fellow 869 n.
beggarliness
inferiority 35 n.
poverty 801 n.
beggar on horseback
insolent person 878 n.
begin
become 1 vb.
come before 64 vb.
begin 68 vb.
revert 148 vb.
cause 156 vb.
start out 296 vb.
be born 360 vb.
appear 445 vb.
prepare 669 vb.
undertake 672 vb.
— again
begin 68 vb.
repeat 106 vb.
beginner
ignoramus 493 n.
beginner 538 n.
bungler 697 n.
ingenue 699 n.
beginner's luck
success 727 n.
beginning
prelude 66 n.
beginning 68 n.adj.
new 126 adj.
primal 127 adj.
youth 130 n.
earliness 135 n.
source 156 n.
begotten
produced 164 adj.
born 360 adj.
begrime
bedim 419 vb.
make unclean 649 vb.
begrudge
be unwilling 598 vb.
refuse 760 vb.
be parsimonious 816 vb.
beguile
mislead 495 vb.
deceive 542 vb.
amuse 837 vb.
flatter 925 vb.
begum
potentate 741 n.
person of rank 868 n.
behalf
benefit 615 n.
behave
do 676 vb.
behave 688 vb.
be virtuous 933 vb.
— badly
behave 688 vb.
— like a gentleman
be honourable 929 vb.
— like an idiot
be absurd 497 vb.
— naturally
accord 24 vb.
— unworthily
demean oneself 867 vb.
behaviour
mien 445 n.
way 624 n.
action 676 n.
conduct 688 n.
behaviourism
psychology 447 n.
behaviour therapy
therapy 658 n.
behead
subtract 39 vb.
sunder 46 vb.
shorten 204 vb.
kill 362 vb.
execute 963 vb.
beheading
capital punishment 963 n.
behemoth
giant 195 n.
behest
command 737 n.
behind
buttocks 238 n.
rear 238 n.
rearward 238 adv.
behind 284 adv.
behind bars
safe 660 adj.
imprisoned 747 adj.
captive 750 adj.
behind closed doors
secretly 525 adv.
behindhand
late 136 adj.
behindhand 307 adv.
unprepared 670 adj.
nonpaying 805 adj.
behind one
past 125 adj.
behind one's back
not here 190 adv.
behind the scenes
causally 156 adv.
rearward 238 adv.
invisibly 444 adv.
knowing 490 adj.
latent 523 adj.
concealed 525 adj.
behind the times
anachronistic 118 adj.
not contemporary 122 adj.
antiquated 127 adj.
ignorant 491 adj.
behold
see 438 vb.
beholden
grateful 907 adj.
obliged 917 adj.
beholder
spectator 441 n.
behove
be right 913 vb.
be due 915 vb.
be one's duty 917 vb.
beige
brown 430 adj.
being
existence 1 n.
existing 1 adj.
self 80 n.
life 360 n.
affections 817 n.
being, a
person 371 n.
bejewel
beautify 841 vb.
primp 843 vb.
decorate 844 vb.
belabour
strike 279 vb.
flog 963 vb.
belated
late 136 adj.
belatedness
nonpreparation 670 n.
belay
tie 45 vb.
bel canto
vocal music 412 n.
belch
voidance 300 n.
eruct 300 vb.
respiration 352 n.
breathe 352 vb.
beleaguer
circumscribe 232 vb.
besiege 712 vb.
wage war 718 vb.
bel esprit
humorist 839 n.
belfry
high structure 209 n.
head 213 n.
church exterior 990 n.
Belial
devil 969 n.
belie
disappoint 509 vb.
negate 533 vb.
deceive 542 vb.
oppose 704 vb.
belief
positiveness 473 n.
belief 485 n.
credulity 487 n.
hope 852 n.
religious faith 973 n.
belief in a god
deism 973 n.
believable
plausible 471 adj.
credible 485 adj.
believe
think 449 vb.
assume 471 vb.
be certain 473 vb.
believe 485 vb.
be credulous 487 vb.
expect 507 vb.
suppose 512 vb.
hope 852 vb.
be orthodox 976 vb.
be pious 979 vb.
— every word
be credulous 487 vb.
believer
religionist 973 n.
the orthodox 976 n.
pietist 979 n.
belittle
abate 37 vb.
underestimate 483 vb.
hold cheap 922 vb.
dispraise 924 vb.
detract 926 vb.
bell
timekeeper 117 n.
ululate 409 vb.
campanology 412 n.
gong 414 n.
signal 547 n.
church utensil 990 n.
— the cat
be courageous 855 vb.
belladonna
poisonous plant 659 n.
bell, book and candle
malediction 899 n.
bell-bottomed
broad 205 adj.
bellboy, bellhop
courier 529 n.
servant 742 n.
bell buoy
danger signal 665 n.
belle
a beauty 841 n.
fop 848 n.
belle époque
era 110 n.
belles lettres
literature 557 n.
article 591 n.
bellicose
violent 176 adj.
quarrelling 709 adj.
defiant 711 adj.
contending 716 adj.
warlike 718 adj.
courageous 855 adj.
boastful 877 adj.
insolent 878 adj.

bellicosity
irascibility 892 n.
belligerent
quarrelling 709 adj.
contending 716 adj.
warring 718 adj.
combatant 722 n.
inimical 881 adj.
bellow
be loud 400 vb.
vociferate 408 vb.
ululate 409 vb.
voice 577 vb.
be angry 891 vb.
threaten 900 vb.
bellows
blowing 352 n.
respiration 352 n.
heater 383 n.
voice 577 n.
bell ringing
campanology 412 n.
bell-shaped
curved 248 adj.
rotund 252 adj.
concave 255 adj.
bell tower
church exterior 990 n.
bell wether
sheep 365 n.
leader 690 n.
belly
maw 194 n.
expand 197 vb.
insides 224 n.
swelling 253 n.
be convex 253 vb.
eater 301 n.
bellyache
pang 377 n.
digestive disorders 651 n.
be discontented 829 vb.
lament 836 vb.
bellyacher
malcontent 829 n.
bellyband
girdle 47 n.
bellyflop
descent 309 n.
plunge 313 n.
bellyful
plenitude 54 n.
sufficiency 635 n.
redundance 637 n.
belly laugh
laughter 835 n.
belly worship
gluttony 947 n.
belong (to)
be intrinsic 5 vb.
be related 9 vb.
accord 24 vb.
be one of 58 vb.
be included 78 vb.
accompany 89 vb.
join a party 708 vb.
belong 773 vb.
belonging
friendship 880 n.
sociality 882 n.
belongings
property 777 n.
beloved
loved one 887 n.
lovable 887 adj.
darling 890 n.
below
after 65 adv.
under 210 adv.
below ground
buried 364 adj.
below par
unequal 29 adj.
less 35 adv.
under 210 adv.
deficient 307 adj.
imperfect 647 adj.
sick 651 adj.
at a discount 810 adv.
below stairs
under 210 adv.
plebeian 869 adj.
below the belt
unjust 914 adj.
below the salt
plebeian 869 adj.
below the surface
low 210 adj.
latent 523 adj.
below zero
cold 380 adj.
belt
girdle 47 n.
region 184 n.
compressor 198 n.
belt 228 n.
loop 250 n.
strike 279 vb.
gulf 345 n.
badge of rank 743 n.
spank 963 vb.
scourge 964 n.
belt and braces
tutelary 660 adj.
belted earl
person of rank 868 n.
belt-tightening
poverty 801 n.
belvedere
view 438 n.
bemadam
name 561 vb.
speak to 583 vb.
dignify 866 vb.
bemedal
decorate 844 vb.
dignify 866 vb.
bemoan
lament 836 vb.
bemused
abstracted 456 adj.
crazy 503 adj.
bench
seat 218 n.
stand 218 n.
workshop 687 n.
badge of rule 743 n.
courtroom 956 n.
tribunal 956 n.
judge 957 n.
bench mark
gauge 465 n.
signpost 547 n.
bench of bishops
council 629 n.
synod 985 n.
ecclesiarch 986 n.
bend
break 46 vb.
ligature 47 n.
derange 63 vb.
conform 83 vb.
make conform 83 vb.
modify 143 vb.
obliquity 220 n.
be oblique 220 vb.
make oblique 220 vb.
distortion 246 n.
distort 246 vb.
angularity 247 n.
make angular 247 vb.
curve 248 n.
be curved 248 vb.
make curved 248 vb.
twine 251 vb.
point to 281 vb.
deviation 282 n.
deflect 282 vb.
deviate 282 vb.
stoop 311 vb.
soften 327 vb.
bias 481 vb.
heraldry 547 n.
motivate 612 vb.
knuckle under 721 vb.
obey 739 vb.
be servile 879 vb.
greet 884 vb.
— backwards
be behind 238 vb.
— down
make curved 248 vb.
stoop 311 vb.
— one's steps
travel 267 vb.
steer for 281 vb.
— over
be oblique 220 vb.
make curved 248 vb.
fold 261 vb.
stoop 311 vb.
— over backwards
exert oneself 682 vb.
— round
circle 314 vb.
— the mind
think 449 vb.
bendable
flexible 327 adj.
bended knees
entreaty 761 n.
bender
festivity 837 n.
drunkenness 949 n.
beneath
less 35 adv.
under 210 adv.
beneath contempt
unimportant 639 adj.
contemptible 922 adj.
beneath one's dignity
inexpedient 643 adj.
degrading 867 adj.
benedicite
prayers 981 n.
Benedictine
monk 986 n.
benediction
good 615 n.
benevolence 897 n.
thanks 907 n.
praise 923 n.
act of worship 981 n.
prayers 981 n.
benefaction
gift 781 n.
liberality 813 n.
benefactor, benefactress
aider 703 n.
patron 707 n.
giver 781 n.
good giver 813 n.
philanthropist 901 n.
benefactor 903 n.
good person 937 n.
benefice
estate 777 n.
benefice 985 n.
beneficence
goodness 644 n.
benevolence 897 n.
beneficial
good 615 adj.
profitable 640 adj.
advisable 642 adj.
beneficial 644 adj.
salubrious 652 adj.
remedial 658 adj.
beneficiary
beneficiary 776 n.
recipient 782 n.
benefit
advantage 34 n.
benefit 615 n.vb.
utility 640 n.
be useful 640 vb.
be expedient 642 vb.
do good 644 vb.
use 673 n.
subvention 703 n.
acquisition 771 n.
gain 771 n.
gift 781 n.

be benevolent 897 vb.
sociology 901 n.
benefit of the doubt
acquittal 960 n.
benefit performance
gift 781 n.
benevolent
aiding 703 adj.
giving 781 adj.
liberal 813 adj.
friendly 880 adj.
amiable 884 adj.
courteous 884 adj.
benevolent 897 adj.
philanthropic 901 adj.
pitying 905 adj.
forgiving 909 adj.
disinterested 931 adj.
virtuous 933 adj.
innocent 935 adj.
pious 979 adj.
benighted
vespertine 129 adj.
late 136 adj.
dark 418 adj.
blind 439 adj.
ignorant 491 adj.
benign
salubrious 652 adj.
safe 660 adj.
benevolent 897 adj.
benison
prayers 981 n.
bent
abnormal 84 adj.
tendency 179 n.
oblique 220 adj.
curved 248 adj.
bias 481 n.
willingness 597 n.
aptitude 694 n.
affections 817 n.
dishonest 930 adj.
Benthamism
philanthropy 901 n.
benthos
ocean 343 n.
marine life 365 n.
ben trovato
plausible 471 adj.
untrue 543 adj.
witty 839 adj.
bent upon
resolute 599 adj.
desiring 859 adj.
benumb
make inactive 679 vb.
benumbed
still 266 adj.
insensible 375 adj.
nonactive 677 adj.
inactive 679 adj.
apathetic 820 adj.
bequeath
transfer 272 vb.
dower 777 vb.
bequeath 780 vb.
give 781 vb.
make rich 800 vb.
bequest
thing transferred 272 n.
acquisition 771 n.
dower 777 n.
transfer 780 n.
gift 781 n.
berate
reprobate 924 vb.
berceuse
musical piece 412 n.
soporific 679 n.
relief 831 n.
bereave
deprive 786 vb.
sadden 834 vb.
widow 896 vb.
bereavement
loss 772 n.
bereft
defenceless 161 adj.
losing 772 adj.
unentitled 916 adj.
bereft of hope
hopeless 853 adj.
beret
headgear 228 n.
beribbon
decorate 844 vb.
dignify 866 vb.
beri-beri
tropical disease 651 n.
berlin
carriage 274 n.
Berlin Wall
partition 231 n.
berry
product 164 n.
fruit 301 n.
flower 366 n.
berserk
furious 176 adj.
frenzied 503 adj.
angry 891 adj.
berth
place 187 vb.
quarters 192 n.
stable 192 n.
dwell 192 vb.
goal 295 n.
arrive 295 vb.
job 622 n.
beryl
greenness 434 n.
gem 844 n.
beseech
entreat 761 vb.
worship 981 vb.
beset
surround 230 vb.
circumscribe 232 vb.
follow 284 vb.
besiege 712 vb.
request 761 vb.
torment 827 vb.
frighten 854 vb.
besetting
universal 79 adj.
habitual 610 adj.
besetting sin
bane 659 n.
vice 934 n.
beside
near 200 adv.
sideways 239 adv.
beside oneself
frenzied 503 adj.
excited 821 adj.
angry 891 adj.
besides
in addition 38 adv.
beside the point
irrelevant 10 adj.
besiege
surround 230 vb.
circumscribe 232 vb.
besiege 712 vb.
wage war 718 vb.
request 761 vb.
torment 827 vb.
besilver
coat 226 vb.
beslime
make unclean 649 vb.
besmear, besmirch
overlay 226 vb.
bedim 419 vb.
make unclean 649 vb.
shame 867 vb.
defame 926 vb.
besotted
misjudging 481 adj.
foolish 499 adj.
crazy 503 adj.
enamoured 887 adj.
bespangle
decorate 844 vb.
bespatter
disperse 75 vb.
moisten 341 vb.
make unclean 649 vb.
shame 867 vb.
curse 899 vb.
defame 926 vb.
bespeak
evidence 466 vb.
mean 514 vb.
indicate 547 vb.
promise 764 vb.
bespectacled
dim-sighted 440 adj.
bespoke
tailored 228 adj.
besprinkle
mix 43 vb.
disperse 75 vb.
moisten 341 vb.
best
great 32 adj.
crowning 34 adj.
supreme 34 adj.
be superior 34 vb.
topmost 213 adj.
best 644 adj.
defeat 727 vb.
best, the
good 615 n.
money 797 n.
good person 937 n.
best behaviour
etiquette 848 n.
courtesy 884 n.
best bib and tucker
clothing 228 n.
bested
defeated 728 adj.
bestial
animal 365 adj.
sensual 944 adj.
lecherous 951 adj.
bestir oneself
be active 678 vb.
exert oneself 682 vb.
best man
auxiliary 707 n.
close friend 880 n.
bridal party 894 n.
best of its kind
exceller 644 n.
best of it, the
victory 727 n.
best one can do
possibility 469 n.
attempt 671 n.
bestow
place 187 vb.
give 781 vb.
best part
main part 32 n.
chief part 52 n.
chief thing 638 n.
best people
superior 34 n.
beau monde 848 n.
upper class 868 n.
bestraddle
be high 209 vb.
overlie 226 vb.
bestrew
disperse 75 vb.
bestride
connect 45 vb.
influence 178 vb.
extend 183 vb.
be broad 205 vb.
be high 209 vb.
overlie 226 vb.
pass 305 vb.
best-seller
book 589 n.
novel 590 n.
exceller 644 n.
sale 793 n.
best wishes
courteous act 884 n.
congratulation 886 n.
bet
gambling 618 n.
gamble 618 vb.

contest 716 n.
contend 716 vb.
— on
be certain 473 vb.
betake oneself to
travel 267 vb.
beta ray
radiation 417 n.
bête noire
bane 659 n.
dislike 861 n.
enemy 881 n.
hateful object 888 n.
bethink oneself
meditate 449 vb.
remember 505 vb.
betide
happen 154 vb.
betimes, be
be early 135 vb.
betoken
evidence 466 vb.
predict 511 vb.
manifest 522 vb.
indicate 547 vb.
betray
disappoint 509 vb.
disclose 526 vb.
be false 541 vb.
deceive 542 vb.
indicate 547 vb.
apostatize 603 vb.
revolt 738 vb.
fail in duty 918 vb.
be dishonest 930 vb.
betrothal
promise 764 n.
compact 765 n.
love affair 887 n.
wooing 889 n.
wedding 894 n.
betrothed
joined 45 adj.
promised 764 adj.
loved one 887 n.
marriageable 894 adj.
better
superior 34 adj.
be superior 34 vb.
chosen 605 adj.
gambler 618 n.
excellent 644 adj.
improved 654 adj.
make better 654 vb.
restored 656 adj.
better half
colleague 707 n.
spouse 894 n.
betterment
benefit 615 n.
improvement 654 n.
better not
inexpedient 643 adj.
better off
improved 654 adj.
better than nothing
imperfect 647 adj.
better thoughts
sequel 67 n.
tergiversation 603 n.
amendment 654 n.
regret 830 n.
better to
advisable 642 adj.
betting
gambling 618 n.
between
correlatively 12 adv.
between 231 adv.
between ourselves
secretly 525 adv.
between the devil and the deep blue sea
irresolutely 601 adv.
endangered 661 adj.
in difficulties 700 adj.
between the lines
tacit 523 adj.
between two stools
in difficulties 700 adj.
between whiles
while 108 adv.
betwixt
between 231 adv.
betwixt and between
middle 70 adj.
between 231 adv.
middling 732 adj.
bevel
cut 46 vb.
obliquity 220 n.
oblique 220 adj.
make oblique 220 vb.
print-type 587 n.
beverage
draught 301 n.
bevy
group 74 n.
certain quantity 104 n.
bewail
lament 836 vb.
beware
be careful 457 vb.
be warned 664 vb.
be cautious 858 vb.
bewhiskered
hairy 259 adj.
bewilder
distract 456 vb.
puzzle 474 vb.
be wonderful 864 vb.
bewildered
doubting 474 adj.
ignorant 491 adj
crazy 503 adj.
wondering 864 adj.
bewitch
engross 449 vb.
motivate 612 vb.
subjugate 745 vb.
delight 826 vb.
be beautiful 841 vb.
excite love 887 vb.
be malevolent 898 vb.
curse 899 vb.
diabolize 969 vb.
bewitch 983 vb.
bewitched
converted 147 adj.
crazy 503 adj.
involuntary 596 adj.
induced 612 adj.
enamoured 887 adj.
cursed 899 adj.
bewitched 983 adj.
bewitchment
spell 983 n.
bey
governor 741 n.
person of rank 868 n.
beyond
beyond 34 adv.
removed 199 adj.
beyond 199 adv.
beyond, the
death 361 n.
beyond all expectation
successfully 727 adv.
beyond compare
extremely 32 adv.
supreme 34 adj.
beyond doubt
undisputed 473 adj.
beyond one
impracticable 470 adj.
puzzling 517 adj.
beyond one's means
dear 811 adj.
beyond one's wildest dreams
prosperously 730 adv.
beyond praise
perfect 646 adj.
beyond the call of duty
voluntary 597 adj.
beyond the grave
dead 361 adj.
beyond the pale
excluded 57 adj.
vulgar 847 adj.
bezel
obliquity 220 n.
furrow 262 n.
bhakti
worship 981 n.
bhang
drug-taking 949 n.
bi-
dual 90 adj.
bias
inequality 29 n.
influence 178 vb.
tendency 179 n.
tend 179 vb.
obliquity 220 n.
make oblique 220 vb.
distortion 246 n.
distort 246 vb.
deflect 282 vb.
bias 481 n.
prejudice 481 n.
bias 481 vb.
error 495 n.
eccentricity 503 n.
opinionatedness 602 n.
caprice 604 n.
choice 605 n.
motivate 612 vb.
affections 817 n.
liking 859 n.
dislike 861 n.
injustice 914 n.
biased
biased 481 adj.
unjust 914 adj.
biased judgment
prejudice 481 n.
bib
apron 228 n.
garment 228 n.
cleaning cloth 648 n.
Bible
certainty 473 n.
truth 494 n.
oracle 511 n.
scripture 975 n.
Bible oath
oath 532 n.
bible-puncher
zealot 979 n.
Bible-worship
pietism 979 n.
biblical
evidential 466 adj.
scriptural 975 adj.
orthodox 976 adj.
bibliographer
bookperson 589 n.
bibliography
list 87 n.
edition 589 n.
reference book 589 n.
bibliolatry
pietism 979 n.
idolatry 982 n.
bibliophile
collector 492 n.
enthusiast 504 n.
bookperson 589 n.
bibulous
drunken 949 adj.
bicameral
dual 90 adj.
parliamentary 692 adj.
bicentenary
fifth and over 99 adj.
anniversary 141 n.
special day 876 n.

biceps
vitality 162 n.
bicker
disagree 25 vb.
argue 475 vb.
dissent 489 vb.
bicker 709 vb.
bicolour
variegated 437 adj.
bicycle
conveyance 267 n.
ride 267 vb.
bicycle 274 n.
bicycle chain
club 723 n.
scourge 964 n.
bicyclist
rider 268 n.
bid
intention 617 n.
gambling 618 n.
attempt 671 n.vb.
command 737 vb.
offer 759 n.vb.
request 761 n.vb.
purchase 792 n.vb.
— against
oppose 704 vb.
— defiance to
defy 711 vb.
— fair to
tend 179 vb.
be likely 471 vb.
predict 511 vb.
give hope 852 vb.
— farewell
depart 296 vb.
— for
bargain 791 vb.
biddable
willing 597 adj.
obedient 739 adj.
bidding
command 737 n.
bide one's time
wait 136 vb.
await 507 vb.
not act 677 vb.
bidet
ablutions 648 n.
biennial
periodic 110 adj.
seasonal 141 adj.
flower 366 n.
bienséance
etiquette 848 n.
bier
bed 218 n.
funeral 364 n.
biff
knock 279 n.
strike 279 vb.
bifid
bisected 92 adj.
bifocal
dual 90 adj.
bifocals
eyeglass 442 n.
biform
dual 90 adj.
double 91 adj.
bifurcate
bisected 92 adj.
bifurcate 92 vb.
cross 222 vb.
angular 247 adj.
make angular 247 vb.
diverge 294 vb.
big
great 32 adj.
large 195 adj.
important 638 adj.
difficult 700 adj.
bigamist
polygamist 894 n.
big battalions
bigwig 638 n.
army 722 n.
brute force 735 n.
Big Brother
tyrant 735 n.
autocrat 741 n.
big business
business 622 n.
big Daddy
bigwig 638 n.
big drum
drum 414 n.
ostentation 875 n.
boast 877 n.
big game
animal 365 n.
big-game hunter
hunter 619 n.
bigger
expanded 197 adj.
biggest slice of the cake
chief part 52 n.
bighead
vain person 873 n.
bight
curve 248 n.
cavity 255 n.
gulf 345 n.
bigmouth
informant 524 n.
boaster 877 n.
big name
person of repute 866 n.
big noise
influence 178 n.
bigwig 638 n.
person of repute 866 n.
bigot
doctrinaire 473 n.
narrow mind 481 n.
ignoramus 493 n.
obstinate person 602 n.
zealot 979 n.
bigotry
narrow mind 481 n.
credulity 487 n.
opinionatedness 602 n.
severity 735 n.
sectarianism 978 n.
pietism 979 n.
big shot
influence 178 n.
bigwig 638 n.
person of repute 866 n.
big spender
prodigal 815 n.
big stick
incentive 612 n.
compulsion 740 n.
threat 900 n.
scourge 964 n.
big talk
exaggeration 546 n.
boast 877 n.
big top
canopy 226 n.
theatre 594 n.
bigwig
superior 34 n.
bigwig 638 n.
elite 644 n.
manager 690 n.
master 741 n.
person of repute 866 n.
aristocrat 868 n.
proud person 871 n.
big with fate
presageful 511 adj.
bijou
little 196 adj.
a beauty 841 n.
gem 844 n.
bijouterie
jewellery 844 n.
bike
ride 267 vb.
bicycle 274 n.
bikini
beachwear 228 n.
bilabial
speech sound 398 n.
bilateral
correlative 12 adj.
dual 90 adj.
lateral 239 adj.
contractual 765 adj.
bilboes
fetter 748 n.
pillory 964 n.
Bildungsroman
novel 590 n.
bile
discontent 829 n.
melancholy 834 n.
resentment 891 n.
irascibility 892 n.
sullenness 893 n.
envy 912 n.
bilge
leavings 41 n.
base 214 n.
silly talk 515 n.
swill 649 n.
bilharzia
infection 651 n.
tropical disease 651 n.
bilingual
linguist 557 n.
linguistic 557 adj.
speaking 579 adj.
bilious
yellow 433 adj.
unhealthy 651 adj.
irascible 892 adj.
sullen 893 adj.
bilk
disappoint 509 vb.
deceive 542 vb.
defraud 788 vb.
be in debt 803 vb.
not pay 805 vb.
bilker
trickster 545 n.
avoider 620 n.
nonpayer 805 n.
bill
numerical result 85 n.
list 87 n.
protuberance 254 n.
advertisement 528 n.
advertise 528 vb.
label 547 n.
correspondence 588 n.
dramatize 594 vb.
axe 723 n.
spear 723 n.
demand 737 vb.
title deed 767 n.
paper money 797 n.
credit 802 n.
accounts 808 n.
account 808 vb.
price 809 n.
price 809 vb.
bill and coo
caress 889 vb.
billboard
advertisement 528 n.
bill-collector
receiver 782 n.
billet
stopping place 145 n.
place 185 n.
quarters 192 n.
goal 295 n.
apportion 783 vb.
billiards
ball game 837 n.
Billingsgate
slang 560 n.
scurrility 899 n.

billion
over one hundred 99 n.
billions
funds 797 n.
bill of exchange
title deed 767 n.
paper money 797 n.
bill of fare
list 87 n.
meal 301 n.
bill of indictment
accusation 928 n.
bill of lading
list 87 n.
bill of mortality
death roll 361 n.
bill of rights
dueness 915 n.
billon
a mixture 43 n.
bullion 797 n.
billow
high water 209 n.
swelling 253 n.
wave 350 n.
billows
ocean 343 n.
billowy
curved 248 adj.
convex 253 adj.
bills
debt 803 n.
billycan
cauldron 194 n.
billy goat
cattle 365 n.
male animal 372 n.
bimetallism
finance 797 n.
bin
vessel 194 n.
binary
computerized 86 adj.
dual 90 adj.
star 321 n.
binaural
sounding 398 adj.
bind
tie 45 vb.
combine 50 vb.
bring together 74 vb.
stabilize 153 vb.
make smaller 198 vb.
cover 226 vb.
close 264 vb.
be dense 324 vb.
cultivate 370 vb.
repair 656 vb.
doctor 658 vb.
obstruct 702 vb.
compel 740 vb.
subjugate 745 vb.
fetter 747 vb.
restrain 747 vb.
give terms 766 vb.
bore 838 n.
impose a duty 917 vb.
— oneself
promise 764 vb.
binding
joining together 45 n.
ligature 47 n.
compressive 198 adj.
wrapping 226 n.
edging 234 n.
solidifying 324 adj.
bookbinding 589 n.
necessary 596 adj.
preceptive 693 adj.
authoritative 733 adj.
compelling 740 adj.
conditional 766 adj.
tedious 838 adj.
trimming 844 n.
obligatory 917 adj.
binding over
restraint 747 n.
penalty 963 n.
binge
festivity 837 n.
drunkenness 949 n.
bingo
gambling 618 n.
card game 837 n.
bingo hall
gaming-house 618 n.
place of amusement 837 n.
binnacle
sailing aid 269 n.
binocular
seeing 438 adj.
binoculars
telescope 442 n.
binomial
dual 90 adj.
binominal
named 561 adj.
bioblindness
ignorance 491 n.
biochemist
doctor 658 n.
biochemistry
biology 358 n.
biodegradable
severable 46 adj.
decomposable 51 adj.
ephemeral 114 adj.
biogas
fuel 385 n.
biogenesis
propagation 167 n.
biology 358 n.
biogenic
organic 358 adj.
biogeography
biology 358 n.
biographer
chronicler 549 n.
author 589 n.
narrator 590 n.
biographical
descriptive 590 adj.
biography
record 548 n.
reading matter 589 n.
biography 590 n.
biological
biological 358 adj.
alive 360 adj.
biological weapon
poison 659 n.
biology
heredity 5 n.
propagation 167 n.
evolution 316 n.
physics 319 n.
structure 331 n.
biology 358 n.
zoology 367 n.
biomass
vegetable life 366 n.
fuel 385 n.
bionic man
prodigy 864 n.
bionomics
biology 358 n.
biophysics
biology 358 n.
bioplast
life 360 n.
biorhythm
regular return 141 n.
biosphere
world 321 n.
biota
organism 358 n.
biotechnology
biology 358 n.
biotic
alive 360 adj.
biotype
prototype 23 n.
situation 186 n.
organism 358 n.
bipartisan
agreeing 24 adj.
dual 90 adj.
assented 488 adj.
cooperative 706 adj.
concordant 710 adj.
bipartite
disunited 46 adj.
bisected 92 adj.
biped
duality 90 n.
animal 365 n.
biplane
aircraft 276 n.
birch
tree 366 n.
spank 963 vb.
scourge 964 n.
bird
young creature 132 n.
wanderer 268 n.
diver 313 n.
animal 365 n.
bird 365 n.
woman 373 n.
vocalist 413 n.
hunter 619 n.
loved one 887 n.
noxious animal 904 n.
bird cage
cattle pen 369 n.
bird call
vocal music 412 n.
bird catcher
hunter 619 n.
bird-fancier
breeder 369 n.
bird in the hand
presence 189 n.
object 319 n.
possession 773 n.
birdlime
adhesive 47 n.
trap 542 n.
bird lore
zoology 367 n.
birdman
aeronaut 271 n.
bird of ill omen
omen 511 n.
warning 664 n.
bird of passage
brief span 114 n.
wanderer 268 n.
bird 365 n.
bird of prey
bird 365 n.
bird sanctuary
preservation 666 n.
birds and the bees
propagation 167 n.
bird's-eye view
whole 52 n.
generality 79 n.
view 438 n.
spectacle 445 n.
compendium 592 n.
birds of a feather
analogue 18 n.
close friend 880 n.
birdsong
ululation 409 n.
vocal music 412 n.
bird strike
collision 279 n.
bird watcher
spectator 441 n.
bird-witted
light-minded 456 adj.
foolish 499 adj.
bireme
galley 275 n.
warship 722 n.
biretta
headgear 228 n.
badge of rule 743 n.
canonicals 989 n.
biro
stationery 586 n.

birth
beginning 68 n.
origin 68 n.
obstetrics 167 n.
propagation 167 n.
genealogy 169 n.
life 360 n.
nobility 868 n.
birth certificate
label 547 n.
record 548 n.
birth control
contraception 172 n.
hindrance 702 n.
birthday
date 108 n.
anniversary 141 n.
special day 876 n.
birthday suit
bareness 229 n.
birthmark
identification 547 n.
skin disease 651 n.
blemish 845 n.
birthplace
source 156 n.
place 185 n.
home 192 n.
birth rate
statistics 86 n.
propagation 167 n.
birthright
priority 119 n.
dower 777 n.
dueness 915 n.
birthstone
talisman 983 n.
bis
again 106 adv.
biscuit
food 301 n.
pastries 301 n.
brown 430 adj.
bisect
sunder 46 vb.
bisect 92 vb.
apportion 783 vb.
bisection
equalization 28 n.
bisection 92 n.
bisexual
abnormal 84 adj.
double 91 adj.
generative 167 adj.
bisexuality
abnormality 84 n.
bishop
ecclesiarch 986 n.
bishopric
district 184 n.
church office 985 n.
parish 985 n.
bison
cattle 365 n.
bissextile
seasonal 141 adj.
bistre
brown pigment 430 n.
bistro
café 192 n.
bit
finite quantity 26 n.
small quantity 33 n.
piece 53 n.
component 58 n.
data processing 86 n.
perforator 263 n.
fetter 748 n.
bit, a
partially 33 adv.
bit by bit
by degrees 27 adv.
separately 46 adv.
piecemeal 53 adv.
severally 80 adv.
gradatim 278 adv.
bitch
dog 365 n.
female animal 373 n.
hellhag 904 n.
cad 938 n.
bitchiness
malevolence 898 n.
bite
small quantity 33 n.
cut 46 vb.
piece 53 n.
vigorousness 174 n.
be violent 176 vb.
be sharp 256 vb.
notch 260 vb.
meal 301 n.
mouthful 301 n.
chew 301 vb.
give pain 377 vb.
refrigerate 382 vb.
pungency 388 n.
gesticulate 547 vb.
engrave 555 vb.
vigour 571 n.
ill-treat 645 vb.
wound 655 vb.
bane 659 n.
fight 716 vb.
hurt 827 vb.
cause discontent 829 vb.
endearment 889 n.
anger 891 n.
enrage 891 vb.
be irascible 892 vb.
sullenness 893 n.
— back
restrain 747 vb.
— off more than one can chew
attempt 671 vb.
undertake 672 vb.
act foolishly 695 vb.
— one's head off
be irascible 892 vb.
— one's tongue
regret 830 vb.
— the dust
be destroyed 165 vb.
tumble 309 vb.
die 361 vb.
be defeated 728 vb.
— the hand that feeds one
act foolishly 695 vb.
biter bit
retaliation 714 n.
biting
keen 174 adj.
painful 377 adj.
cold 380 adj.
pungent 388 adj.
witty 839 adj.
ungracious 885 adj.
bit missing
imperfection 647 n.
bit of fluff
woman 373 n.
kept woman 952 n.
bit part
acting 594 n.
bits and pieces
medley 43 n.
piece 53 n.
rubbish 641 n.
bitten
enamoured 887 adj.
bitter
alcoholic drink 301 n.
painful 377 adj.
cold 380 adj.
pungent 388 adj.
unsavoury 391 adj.
sour 393 adj.
unpleasant 827 adj.
discontented 829 adj.
regretting 830 adj.
disliked 861 adj.
inimical 881 adj.
hateful 888 adj.
hating 888 adj.
resentful 891 adj.
irascible 892 adj.
malevolent 898 adj.
disapproving 924 adj.
detracting 926 adj.
bitter cup
adversity 731 n.
suffering 825 n.
painfulness 827 n.
bitter end
finality 69 n.
bitterly
extremely 32 adv.
greatly 32 adv.
painfully 32 adv.
frostily 380 adv.
angrily 891 adv.
bitter pill
unsavouriness 391 n.
adversity 731 n.
painfulness 827 n.
hateful object 888 n.
punishment 963 n.
bittersweet
contrary 14 adj.
painful 377 adj.
bitter words
reproach 924 n.
bitty
fragmentary 53 adj.
incomplete 55 adj.
discontinuous 72 adj.
exiguous 196 adj.
bitumen
resin 357 n.
bivalve
marine life 365 n.
bivouac
station 187 n.
place oneself 187 vb.
abode 192 n.
dwell 192 vb.
resting place 266 n.
bizarre
unusual 84 adj.
imaginative 513 adj.
ridiculous 849 adj.
blab
inform 524 vb.
divulge 526 vb.
accuse 928 vb.
blabber
informer 524 n.
chatterer 581 n.
black
set apart 46 vb.
exclude 57 vb.
formal dress 228 n.
funereal 364 adj.
darkness 418 n.
dark 418 adj.
darken 418 vb.
blackness 428 n.
black 428 adj.
blacken 428 vb.
evil 616 adj.
bad 645 adj.
clean 648 vb.
dirty 649 adj.
prohibit 757 vb.
lamentation 836 n.
heinous 934 adj.
— out
be insensible 375 vb.
darken 418 vb.
obliterate 550 vb.
restrain 747 vb.
prohibit 757 vb.
black, the
credit 802 n.
black and blue
blackish 428 adj.
blue 435 adj.
purple 436 adj.
black and white
polarity 14 n.
light contrast 417 n.
achromatism 426 n.
blackness 428 n.
pied 437 adj.
black art
sorcery 983 n.
blackball
exclusion 57 n.
exclude 57 vb.

eject 300 vb.
reject 607 vb.
shame 867 vb.
make unwelcome 883 vb.
disapprobation 924 n.
black belt
proficient person 696 n.
blackberry
fruit 301 n.
blackbird
bird 365 n.
vocalist 413 n.
blackboard
classroom 539 n.
stationery 586 n.
black books
disrepute 867 n.
odium 888 n.
black box
recording instrument 549 n.
black cap
danger signal 665 n.
badge of rule 743 n.
condemnation 961 n.
black cat
omen 511 n.
talisman 983 n.
black cloud
threat 900 n.
black comedy
stage play 594 n.
wit 839 n.
black culture
civilization 654 n.
blackcurrant
fruit 301 n.
black damp
gas 336 n.
Black Death
plague 651 n.
black diamond
coal 385 n.
black economy
market 796 n.
blacked
prohibited 757 adj.
blacken
darken 418 vb.
blacken 428 vb.
mark 547 vb.
impair 655 vb.
show feeling 818 vb.
shame 867 vb.
dispraise 924 vb.
defame 926 vb.
black eye
wound 655 n.
blemish 845 n.
blackguard
cuss 899 vb.
evildoer 904 n.
ruffian 904 n.
reprobate 924 vb.
rascally 930 adj.
cad 938 n.
knave 938 n.
blackhead
blemish 845 n.
black-hearted
malevolent 898 adj.
wicked 934 adj.
black hole
star 321 n.
prison 748 n.
black ice
wintriness 380 n.
blacking
black pigment 428 n.
cleanser 648 n.
black ivory
thing transferred 272 n.
blackjack
vessel 194 n.
hammer 279 n.
strike 279 vb.
club 723 n.
card game 837 n.
black lead
lubricant 334 n.
black pigment 428 n.
cleanser 648 n.
blackleg
nonconformist 84 n.
tergiversator 603 n.
apostatize 603 vb.
revolter 738 n.
hateful object 888 n.
blacklegging
nonobservant 769 adj.
black letter
letter 558 n.
print-type 587 n.
black light
radiation 417 n.
invisibility 444 n.
blacklist
set apart 46 vb.
list 87 n.
name 561 vb.
unsociability 883 n.
make unwelcome 883 vb.
disapprobation 924 n.
disapprove 924 vb.
condemnation 961 n.
condemn 961 vb.
blacklisted
friendless 883 adj.
disapproved 924 adj.
black look
rudeness 885 n.
sullenness 893 n.
reproach 924 n.
black magic
badness 645 n.
diabolism 969 n.
sorcery 983 n.
blackmail
demand 737 n.vb.
compulsion 740 n.
compel 740 vb.
request 761 n.vb.
rapacity 786 n.
fleece 786 vb.
peculation 788 n.
rob 788 vb.
booty 790 n.
tax 809 n.
threat 900 n.
threaten 900 vb.
reward 962 n.
blackmailer
taker 786 n.
offender 904 n.
black man/woman
blackness 428 n.
Black Maria
vehicle 274 n.
lockup 748 n.
black mark
slur 867 n.
reprimand 924 n.
black market
trade 791 n.
market 796 n.
illegal 954 adj.
Black Mass
diabolism 969 n.
black mood
melancholy 834 n.
Black Muslim
revolter 738 n.
non-Christian sect 978 n.
blackness
darkness 418 n.
blackness 428 n.
blackout
insensibility 375 n.
obscuration 418 n.
oblivion 506 n.
dramaturgy 594 n.
fatigue 684 n.
war measures 718 n.
prohibition 757 n.
drunkenness 949 n.
Black Panther
revolter 738 n.
Black Paper
report 524 n.
black power
governance 733 n.
black pudding
meat 301 n.
Black Rod
badge 547 n.
badge of rule 743 n.
black sheep
offender 904 n.
bad person 938 n.
Blackshirts
political party 708 n.
black-skinned
black 428 adj.
blacksmith
animal husbandry 369 n.
artisan 686 n.
black spot
danger 661 n.
black-tie
formal 875 adj.
bladder
bladder 194 n.
sphere 252 n.
bladder-like
expanded 197 adj.
blade
sharp edge 256 n.
propeller 269 n.
propellant 287 n.
foliage 366 n.
male 372 n.
sidearms 723 n.
fop 848 n.
blagueur
boaster 877 n.
blah-blah
empty talk 515 n.
blamable
blameworthy 924 adj.
blame
censure 924 n.
blame 924 vb.
accusation 928 n.
accuse 928 vb.
guilt 936 n.
— for
attribute 158 vb.
— oneself
regret 830 vb.
be penitent 939 vb.
blameless
guiltless 935 adj.
blameworthy
discreditable 867 adj.
blameworthy 924 adj.
accusable 928 adj.
heinous 934 adj.
guilty 936 adj.
blanch
decolorize 426 vb.
lose colour 426 vb.
whiten 427 vb.
blancmange
dessert 301 n.
bland
lenitive 177 adj.
smooth 258 adj.
dull 840 adj.
courteous 884 adj.
flattering 925 adj.
blandiloquence
flattery 925 n.
blandish
induce 612 vb.
flatter 925 vb.
blandishments
inducement 612 n.
endearment 889 n.
flattery 925 n.
blank
nonexistence 2 n.
insubstantial 4 adj.

uniform 16 adj.
zero 103 n.
emptiness 190 n.
empty 190 adj.
form 243 n.
closed 264 adj.
opaque 423 adj.
colourless 426 adj.
unthinking 450 adj.
ignorant 491 adj.
unintelligible 517 adj.
punctuation 547 n.
clean 648 adj.
impassive 820 adj.
blank cartridge
emptiness 190 n.
false alarm 665 n.
blank cheque
scope 744 n.
permit 756 n.
liberality 813 n.
blanket
inclusive 78 adj.
general 79 adj.
suppress 165 vb.
moderate 177 vb.
coverlet 226 n.
cover 226 vb.
warm clothes 381 n.
screen 421 vb.
indiscriminate 464 adj.
blankety-blank
damnable 645 adj.
blankness
absence of thought 450 n.
ignorance 491 n.
oblivion 506 n.
lack of wonder 865 n.
blank verse
prosody 593 n.
verse form 593 n.
blank wall
closure 264 n.
solid body 324 n.
invisibility 444 n.
difficulty 700 n.
blare
loudness 400 n.
be loud 400 vb.
resonance 404 n.
resound 404 vb.
stridor 407 n.
shrill 407 vb.
blarney
empty talk 515 n.
mean nothing 515 vb.
falsehood 541 n.
be cunning 698 vb.
flattery 925 n.
flatter 925 vb.
blasé
incurious 454 adj.
bored 838 adj.
indifferent 860 adj.
sated 863 adj.
unastonished 865 adj.
blaspheme
cuss 899 vb.
be irreligious 974 vb.
be impious 980 vb.
blast
outbreak 176 n.
air 340 n.
gale 352 n.
wind 352 n.
blow 352 vb.
loudness 400 n.
bang 402 n.vb.
impair 655 vb.
danger signal 665 n.
fire at 712 vb.
adversity 731 n.
be malevolent 898 vb.
cuss 899 vb.
bewitch 983 vb.
— off
fly 271 vb.
blasted
unproductive 172 adj.
damnable 645 adj.
unfortunate 731 adj.
bewitched 983 adj.
blast furnace
furnace 383 n.
workshop 687 n.
blast-off
space travel 271 n.
departure 296 n.
ascent 308 n.
blatant
flagrant 32 adj.
well-known 528 adj.
vulgar 847 adj.
vain 873 adj.
showy 875 adj.
insolent 878 adj.
blaze
notch 260 vb.
fire 379 n.
be hot 379 vb.
light 417 n.
shine 417 vb.
white thing 427 n.
indication 547 n.
indicate 547 vb.
mark 547 vb.
— abroad
proclaim 528 vb.
— a trail
come before 64 vb.
facilitate 701 vb.
blaze of glory
honours 866 n.
blazer
jacket 228 n.
livery 547 n.
blazon
heraldry 547 n.
indicate 547 vb.
register 548 vb.
decorate 844 vb.
honour 866 vb.
be ostentatious 875 vb.
blazoned
heraldic 547 adj.
blazonry
heraldry 547 n.
bleach
dry 342 vb.
bleacher 426 n.
decolorize 426 vb.
lose colour 426 vb.
whiten 427 vb.
clean 648 vb.
hairwash 843 n.
bleached
colourless 426 adj.
white 427 adj.
bleak
wintry 129 adj.
unproductive 172 adj.
empty 190 adj.
adverse 731 adj.
bleariness
dim sight 440 n.
bleary
dim 419 adj.
bleat
ululate 409 vb.
be discontented 829 vb.
bleater
malcontent 829 n.
bleed
flow out 298 vb.
emit 300 vb.
empty 300 vb.
be wet 341 vb.
doctor 658 vb.
fleece 786 vb.
overcharge 811 vb.
suffer 825 vb.
— for
pity 905 vb.
bleeding
outflow 298 n.
haemorrhage 302 n.
sanguineous 335 adj.
bleeding heart
sorrow 825 n.
love emblem 887 n.
pity 905 n.
bleep
stridor 407 n.
shrill 407 vb.
bleeper
telecommunication 531 n.
signal 547 n.
blemish
inferiority 35 n.
tincture 43 n.
weakness 163 n.
deformity 246 n.
shortfall 307 n.
maculation 437 n.
mistake 495 n.
identification 547 n.
trace 548 n.
defect 647 n.
skin disease 651 n.
wound 655 n.
impair 655 vb.
eyesore 842 n.
ugliness 842 n.
make ugly 842 vb.
blemish 845 n.vb.
slur 867 n.
blench
be unwilling 598 vb.
avoid 620 vb.
show feeling 818 vb.
quake 854 vb.
blend
a mixture 43 n.
mix 43 vb.
compound 50 n.
combine 50 vb.
produce 164 vb.
cook 301 vb.
tobacco 388 n.
harmonize 410 vb.
bless
benefit 615 vb.
be auspicious 730 vb.
permit 756 vb.
please 826 vb.
rejoice 835 vb.
be benevolent 897 vb.
thank 907 vb.
approve 923 vb.
praise 923 vb.
sanctify 979 vb.
worship 981 vb.
perform ritual 988 vb.
blessed
good 615 adj.
palmy 730 adj.
happy 824 adj.
pleasurable 826 adj.
approved 923 adj.
paradisiac 971 adj.
ritual 988 adj.
blessed..., the
saint 968 n.
Blessed Eucharist
Holy Communion 988 n.
blessedness
happiness 824 n.
sanctity 979 n.
Blessed Virgin Mary
Madonna 968 n.
blessing
benefit 615 n.
(See **bless** *)*
blest
happy 824 adj.
blest with
possessing 773 adj.
blether, blather
empty talk 515 n.

mean nothing 515 vb.
be diffuse 570 vb.
chatter 581 n.
be loquacious 581 vb.
blight
decay 51 n.
destroyer 168 n.
insect 365 n.
badness 645 n.
dilapidation 655 n.
impair 655 vb.
blight 659 n.
adversity 731 n.
be malevolent 898 vb.
bewitch 983 vb.
blighted hopes
disappointment 509 n.
blighter
cad 938 n.
blimp
airship 276 n.
obstinate person 602 n.
blind
shade 226 n.
insensible 375 adj.
shine 417 vb.
curtain 421 n.
screen 421 vb.
blind 439 adj.vb.
dim-sighted 440 adj.
inattentive 456 adj.
distract 456 vb.
indiscriminating 464 adj.
biased 481 adj.
misjudging 481 adj.
ignorant 491 adj.
unwise 499 adj.
disguise 527 n.
trap 542 n.
trickery 542 n.
deceive 542 vb.
involuntary 596 adj.
obstinate 602 adj.
pretext 614 n.
stratagem 698 n.
impassive 820 adj.
make insensitive 820 vb.
unastonished 865 adj.
drunkenness 949 n.
dead drunk 949 adj.
blind alley
road 624 n.
lost labour 641 n.
obstacle 702 n.
blind bargain
gambling 618 n.
blind corner
invisibility 444 n.
blind date
uncertainty 474 n.
social round 882 n.
blindfold
screen 421 vb.
blind 439 adj.vb.
keep secret 525 vb.
deceive 542 vb.
blind leading the blind
misteaching 535 n.
blind side
blindness 439 n.
dim sight 440 n.
prejudice 481 n.
folly 499 n.
opinionatedness 602 n.
blind spot
blindness 439 n.
invisibility 444 n.
inattention 456 n.
prejudice 481 n.
blind to
thick-skinned 820 adj.
unastonished 865 adj.
blink
flash 417 n.
shine 417 vb.
look 438 n.
gaze 438 vb.
be blind 439 vb.
be dim-sighted 440 vb.
disregard 458 vb.
be irresolute 601 vb.
avoid 620 vb.
blinker
screen 421 vb.
blind 439 vb.
dim sight 440 n.
deceive 542 vb.
blinkered
ignorant 491 adj.
bliss
happiness 824 n.
blissful
palmy 730 adj.
happy 824 adj.
pleasurable 826 adj.
paradisiac 971 adj.
blister
bladder 194 n.
swelling 253 n.
skin disease 651 n.
blistered
rough 259 adj.
blistering
hot 379 adj.
blithe
happy 824 adj.
cheerful 833 adj.
blithering
meaningless 515 adj.
blitz
havoc 165 n.
demolish 165 vb.
loudness 400 n.
attack 712 n., vb.
bombardment 712 n.
fire at 712 vb.
blitzkrieg
attack 712 n.
war 718 n.
blizzard
storm 176 n.
gale 352 n.
wintriness 380 n.
bloated
increasing 36 adj.
fleshy 195 adj.
expanded 197 adj.
deformed 246 adj.
convex 253 adj.
redundant 637 adj.
unsightly 842 adj.
bloaters
fish food 301 n.
bloc
political party 708 n.
block
housing 192 n.
bulk 195 n.
head 213 n.
stand 218 n.
close 264 vb.
repel 292 vb.
solid body 324 n.
hardness 326 n.
dunce 501 n.
engraving 555 n.
write 586 vb.
hindrance 702 n.
obstacle 702 n.
obstruct 702 vb.
defend 713 vb.
parry 713 vb.
prohibit 757 vb.
not pay 805 vb.
unfeeling person 820 n.
means of execution 964 n.
— in
paint 553 vb.
— out
outline 233 vb.
form 243 vb.
represent 551 vb.
sculpt 554 vb.
prepare 669 vb.
— up
obstruct 702 vb.
blockade
surround 230 vb.
circumscription 232 n.
circumscribe 232 vb.
closure 264 n.
close 264 vb.
hindrance 702 n.
obstacle 702 n.
obstruct 702 vb.
attack 712 n.
besiege 712 vb.
warfare 718 n.
wage war 718 vb.
restriction 747 n.
blockage
stop 145 n.
hindrance 702 n.
obstacle 702 n.
block and tackle
lifter 310 n.
blockbuster
destroyer 168 n.
film 445 n.
novel 590 n.
bomb 723 n.
blockhead
ignoramus 493 n.
dunce 501 n.
blockhouse
fort 713 n.
blockishness
unintelligence 499 n.
moral insensibility 820 n.
block letter
letter 558 n.
block of flats
flat 192 n.
block release
education 534 n.
bloke
male 372 n.
blond(e)
achromatism 426 n.
colourless 426 adj.
whitish 427 adj.
yellowness 433 n.
a beauty 841 n.
blood
consanguinity 11 n.
auspicate 68 vb.
breed 77 n.
genealogy 169 n.
vigorousness 174 n.
haemorrhage 302 n.
blood 335 n.
redness 431 n.
fop 848 n.
nobility 868 n.
blood-and-thunder
exaggerated 546 adj.
stage play 594 n.
dramatic 594 adj.
bloodbath
slaughter 362 n.
terror tactics 712 n.
blood-curdling
frightening 854 adj.
blood disease
blood disease 651 n.
blood donor
giver 781 n.
good giver 813 n.
blood feud
quarrel 709 n.
revenge 910 n.
blood group
classification 77 n.
blood 335 n.
blood heat
heat 379 n.
bloodhound
dog 365 n.

detective 459 n.
hunter 619 n.
bloodiness
brute force 735 n.
inhumanity 898 n.
bloodless
insubstantial 4 adj.
weak 163 adj.
colourless 426 adj.
diseased 651 adj.
peaceful 717 adj.
guiltless 935 adj.
blood-letting
killing 362 n.
surgery 658 n.
blood lust
violence 176 n.
inhumanity 898 n.
blood money
peace offering 719 n.
atonement 941 n.
blood on one's hands
be guilty 936 vb.
blood-poisoning
infection 651 n.
poisoning 659 n.
blood pressure
cardiovascular disease 651 n.
blood-red
bloodstained 431 adj.
blood relation
kinsman 11 n.
bloodshed
slaughter 362 n.
warfare 718 n.
cruel act 898 n.
bloodshot
bloodstained 431 adj.
angry 891 adj.
drunken 949 adj.
blood sports
killing 362 n.
chase 619 n.
bloodstained
sanguineous 335 adj.
murderous 362 adj.
bloodstained 431 adj.
bloodstock
thoroughbred 273 n.
aristocrat 868 n.
nobility 868 n.
bloodstone
gem 844 n.
bloodsucker
tyrant 735 n.
taker 786 n.
offender 904 n.
glutton 947 n.
bloodthirsty
furious 176 adj.
murderous 362 adj.
harmful 645 adj.
warlike 718 adj.
cruel 898 adj.
bloody
violent 176 adj.
sanguineous 335 adj.
humid 341 adj.
murderous 362 adj.
bloodstained 431 adj.
harmful 645 adj.
oppressive 735 adj.
courageous 855 adj.
cruel 898 adj.
bloody-minded
obstinate 602 adj.
opposing 704 adj.
disobedient 738 adj.
malevolent 898 adj.
bloody nose
wound 655 n.
resistance 715 n.
defeat 728 n.
bloom
salad days 130 n.
adultness 134 n.
reproduce itself 167 vb.
be fruitful 171 vb.
expand 197 vb.
layer 207 n.
open 263 vb.
flower 366 n.
redness 431 n.
health 650 n.
be healthy 650 vb.
maturation 669 n.
prosper 730 vb.
be beautiful 841 vb.
bloomer
mistake 495 n.
bloomers
trousers 228 n.
underwear 228 n.
blooming
young 130 adj.
grown-up 134 adj.
vigorous 174 adj.
open 263 adj.
vegetable life 366 n.
vegetal 366 adj.
healthy 650 adj.
personable 841 adj.
blossom
grow 36 vb.
growth 157 n.
product 164 n.
be fruitful 171 vb.
expand 197 vb.
flower 366 n.
prosper 730 vb.
blossom-time
spring 128 n.
blot
tincture 43 n.
sphere 252 n.
absorb 299 vb.
dry 342 vb.
blacken 428 vb.
variegate 437 vb.
mistake 495 n.
blunder 495 vb.
mark 547 vb.
obliteration 550 n.
obliterate 550 vb.
write 586 vb.
dirt 649 n.
make unclean 649 vb.
impair 655 vb.
be clumsy 695 vb.
eyesore 842 n.
make ugly 842 vb.
blemish 845 n.vb.
slur 867 n.
shame 867 vb.
— one's copybook
blunder 495 vb.
lose repute 867 vb.
incur blame 924 vb.
be wicked 934 vb.
— out
destroy 165 vb.
conceal 525 vb.
obliterate 550 vb.
forgive 909 vb.
blotch
maculation 437 n.
blemish 845 n.
blot on the landscape
eyesore 842 n.
blotter
dryer 342 n.
stationery 586 n.
cleaning utensil 648 n.
blotto
dead drunk 949 adj.
blouse
shirt 228 n.
blouson
jacket 228 n.
blow
be violent 176 vb.
expand 197 vb.
form 243 vb.
knock 279 n.
aerate 340 vb.
gale 352 n.
wind 352 n.
blow 352 vb.
play music 413 vb.
lack of expectation 508 n.
disappointment 509 n.
evil 616 n.
deed 676 n.
be fatigued 684 vb.
adversity 731 n.
expend 806 vb.
suffering 825 n.
corporal punishment 963 n.
— down
demolish 165 vb.
fell 311 vb.
— hot and cold
change 143 vb.
vary 152 vb.
be irresolute 601 vb.
be capricious 604 vb.
— in
arrive 295 vb.
enter 297 vb.
— it
blunder 495 vb.
— off
eruct 300 vb.
stink 397 vb.
— one's cover
disclose 526 vb.
— one's mind
make mad 503 vb.
— one's money
be prodigal 815 vb.
— one's own trumpet
be vain 873 vb.
boast 877 vb.
— one's top
get angry 891 vb.
— open
force 176 vb.
— out
nullify 2 vb.
suppress 165 vb.
extinguish 382 vb.
snuff out 418 vb.
— over
be past 125 vb.
cease 145 vb.
— sky-high
demolish 165 vb.
confute 479 vb.
— the whistle on
inform 524 vb.
warn 664 vb.
— up
augment 36 vb.
break 46 vb.
rend 46 vb.
be dispersed 75 vb.
demolish 165 vb.
be violent 176 vb.
force 176 vb.
enlarge 197 vb.
propel 287 vb.
elevate 310 vb.
blow up 352 vb.
be disclosed 526 vb.
exaggerate 546 vb.
photograph 551 vb.
miscarry 728 vb.
get angry 891 vb.
reprove 924 vb.
blow-by-blow account
diffuseness 570 n.
blower
orifice 263 n.
air 340 n.
ventilation 352 n.
hearing aid 415 n.
blowhole
orifice 263 n.
outlet 298 n.
air pipe 353 n.
blowing hot and cold
irresolution 601 n.
blowlamp
furnace 383 n.

blown
panting 684 adj.
blowout
feasting 301 n.
bang 402 n.
festivity 837 n.
gluttony 947 n.
blowpipe
propellant 287 n.
blowing 352 n.
air pipe 353 n.
heater 383 n.
missile weapon 723 n.
blows
fight 716 n.
anger 891 n.
blow wave
hairdressing 843 n.
blowy
windy 352 adj.
blowzy
red 431 adj.
ugly 842 adj.
blubber
fat 357 n.
stammer 580 vb.
weep 836 vb.
bludgeon
strike 279 vb.
argue 475 vb.
club 723 n.
brute force 735 n.
oppress 735 vb.
compulsion 740 n.
compel 740 vb.
blue
air 340 n.
ocean 343 n.
chilly 380 adj.
musical 412 adj.
blueness 435 n.
blue 435 adj.vb.
badge 547 n.
decoration 729 n.
melancholic 834 adj.
bored 838 adj.
sullen 893 adj.
cursing 899 adj.
impure 951 adj.
— one's money
be prodigal 815 vb.
Blue
athlete 162 n.
blue-black
black 428 adj.
blue 435 adj.
blue blood
genealogy 169 n.
nobility 868 n.
blue book
record 548 n.
bluebottle
insect 365 n.
blue-chip
valuable 644 adj.
title deed 767 n.
blue-collar worker
worker 686 n.
blue-eyed boy
favourite 890 n.
blue film
impurity 951 n.
bluejacket
nautical personnel 270 n.
naval man 722 n.
blue joke
witticism 839 n.
blue language
scurrility 899 n.
blue laws
severity 735 n.
prudery 950 n.
blue moon
neverness 109 n.
blue-pencil
subtract 39 vb.
moderate 177 vb.
obliteration 550 n.
obliterate 550 vb.
amendment 654 n.
rectify 654 vb.
prohibit 757 vb.
Blue Peter
flag 547 n.
blueprint
prototype 23 n.
representation 551 n.
represent 551 vb.
compendium 592 n.
plan 623 n.vb.
preparation 669 n.
prepare 669 vb.
blues
music 412 n.
vocal music 412 n.
psychopathy 503 n.
melancholy 834 n.
sullenness 893 n.
blue-stocking
instructed 490 adj.
intellectual 492 n.
affecter 850 n.
blue streak
velocity 277 n.
bluff
violent 176 adj.
high land 209 n.
verticality 215 n.
blind 439 vb.
sciolism 491 n.
duplicity 541 n.
trickery 542 n.
deceive 542 vb.
pretext 614 n.
plead 614 vb.
be affected 850 vb.
boast 877 n.vb.
ungracious 885 adj.
— one's way out
escape 667 vb.
bluish
blue 435 adj.
blunder
stray 282 vb.
misjudge 481 vb.
mistake 495 n.
blunder 495 vb.
misinterpret 521 vb.
disclose 526 vb.
be ungrammatical 565 vb.
act foolishly 695 vb.
be clumsy 695 vb.
be unskilful 695 vb.
fail 728 vb.
— upon
chance 159 vb.
blunderbuss
firearm 723 n.
blunderer
fool 501 n.
bungler 697 n.
blunt
weaken 163 vb.
moderate 177 vb.
short 204 adj.
low 210 adj.
unsharpened 257 adj.
blunt 257 vb.
smooth 258 adj.
render insensible 375 vb.
undisguised 522 adj.
assertive 532 adj.
veracious 540 adj.
artless 699 adj.
make insensitive 820 vb.
ill-bred 847 adj.
ungracious 885 adj.
blunted
unsharpened 257 adj.
apathetic 820 adj.
bluntness
bluntness 257 n.
plainness 573 n.
artlessness 699 n.
rudeness 885 n.
blur
dimness 419 n.
bedim 419 vb.
blur 440 vb.
make unclean 649 vb.
blemish 845 n.
blurb
advertisement 528 n.
praise 923 n.
blurred
amorphous 244 adj.
dim 419 adj.
indistinct 444 adj.
blurt out
inform 524 vb.
divulge 526 vb.
speak 579 vb.
blush
heat 379 n.
hue 425 n.
redness 431 n.
redden 431 vb.
disclosure 526 n.
indication 547 n.
feeling 818 n.
show feeling 818 vb.
humiliation 872 n.
be humbled 872 vb.
modesty 874 n.
be modest 874 vb.
guilt 936 n.
— for shame
lose repute 867 vb.
be penitent 939 vb.
— unseen
be unseen 444 vb.
escape notice 456 vb.
have no repute 867 vb.
be modest 874 vb.
blushful
modest 874 adj.
pure 950 adj.
bluster
ineffectuality 161 n.
violence 176 n.
be violent 176 vb.
be active 678 vb.
defy 711 vb.
nervousness 854 n.
boast 877 n., vb.
boasting 877 n.
insolence 878 n.
be angry 891 vb.
threat 900 n.
threaten 900 vb.
blustery
violent 176 adj.
windy 352 adj.
boa constrictor
compressor 198 n.
reptile 365 n.
Boanerges
preacher 537 n.
speaker 579 n.
boar
pig 365 n.
male animal 372 n.
board
lamina 207 n.
shelf 218 n.
stand 218 n.
burst in 297 vb.
enter 297 vb.
provisions 301 n.
eat 301 vb.
feed 301 vb.
hardness 326 n.
materials 631 n.
provide 633 vb.
director 690 n.
council 692 n.
attack 712 vb.
tribunal 956 n.
— out
dwell 192 vb.
board and lodging
provision 633 n.
boarder
resident 191 n.
eater 301 n.
learner 538 n.

board game
board game 837 n.
boarding house
quarters 192 n.
boarding school
quarters 192 n.
school 539 n.
board meeting
assembly 74 n.
board of directors
director 690 n.
board room
council 692 n.
boards
wrapping 226 n.
bookbinding 589 n.
stage set 594 n.
theatre 594 n.
boast
comprise 78 vb.
overestimation 482 n.
exaggerate 546 vb.
defy 711 vb.
triumph 727 vb.
ridiculousness 849 n.
be affected 850 vb.
seek repute 866 vb.
pride 871 n.
feel pride 871 vb.
be vain 873 vb.
ostentation 875 n.
be ostentatious 875 vb.
boast 877 n.vb.
be insolent 878 vb.
favourite 890 n.
threat 900 n.
— of
possess 773 vb.
boaster
impostor 545 n.
boaster 877 n.
boasting
overestimation 482 n.
empty talk 515 n.
untrue 543 adj.
exaggeration 546 n.
magniloquence 574 n.
ridiculousness 849 n.
pride 871 n.
vanity 873 n.
boasting 877 n.
boastful 877 adj.
boat
water travel 269 n.
go to sea 269 vb.
boat 275 n.
ship 275 n.
boater
headgear 228 n.
boathouse
stable 192 n.
boating
aquatics 269 n.
water travel 269 n.
sport 837 n.
boatman
boatman 270 n.
carrier 273 n.
boatswain
mariner 270 n.
navigator 270 n.
bob
timekeeper 117 n.
shortness 204 n.
shorten 204 vb.
hang 217 vb.
obeisance 311 n.
stoop 311 vb.
leap 312 vb.
oscillation 317 n.
oscillate 317 vb.
be agitated 318 vb.
gravity 322 n.
coinage 797 n.
hairdressing 843 n.
servility 879 n.
be servile 879 vb.
greet 884 vb.
respects 920 n.
show respect 920 vb.
— up
ascend 308 vb.
— up and down
leap 312 vb.
oscillate 317 vb.
dance 837 vb.
bobble
hanging object 217 n.
trimming 844 n.
bobby
police 955 n.
bobsleigh
sledge 274 n.
bod
person 371 n.
bode
predict 511 vb.
— ill
endanger 661 vb.
threaten 900 vb.
bodhisattva
philanthropist 901 n.
pietist 979 n.
bodice
garment 228 n.
bodiless
insubstantial 4 adj.
immaterial 320 adj.
bodily
substantially 3 adv.
collectively 52 adv.
violently 176 adv.
material 319 adj.
sensuous 376 adj.
sensual 944 adj.
body
substance 3 n.
quantity 26 n.
main part 32 n.
chief part 52 n.
middle 70 n.
band 74 n.
frame 218 n.
matter 319 n.
object 319 n.
structure 331 n.
corpse 363 n.
person 371 n.
savouriness 390 n.
print-type 587 n.
community 708 n.
corporation 708 n.
— forth
make extrinsic 6 vb.
externalize 223 vb.
materialize 319 vb.
manifest 522 vb.
body and soul
wholly 52 adv.
body-building
nourishing 301 adj.
salubrious 652 adj.
bodyguard
concomitant 89 n.
protector 660 n.
defender 713 n.
combatant 722 n.
retainer 742 n.
body language
gesture 547 n.
body politic
nation 371 n.
political organization 733 n.
boffin
intellectual 492 n.
sage 500 n.
theorist 512 n.
planner 623 n.
worker 686 n.
expert 696 n.
bog
marsh 347 n.
dirt 649 n.
latrine 649 n.
bogey, bogy, bogie
fantasy 513 n.
false alarm 665 n.
monster 938 n.
demon 970 n.
bogged down
late 136 adj.
boggle
be uncertain 474 vb.
doubt 486 vb.
dissent 489 vb.
be unwilling 598 vb.
boggling
irresolute 601 adj.
boggy
marshy 347 adj.
bogus
false 541 adj.
spurious 542 adj.
untrue 543 adj.
affected 850 adj.
Bohemian
nonconformist 84 n.
unconformable 84 adj.
wanderer 268 n.
free person 744 n.
boil
swelling 253 n.
cook 301 vb.
be agitated 318 vb.
effervesce 318 vb.
bubble 355 vb.
be hot 379 vb.
ulcer 651 n.
sanitate 652 vb.
be excited 821 vb.
— down
abate 37 vb.
make smaller 198 vb.
shorten 204 vb.
— down to
be intrinsic 5 vb.
mean 514 vb.
— over
be violent 176 vb.
flow out 298 vb.
effervesce 318 vb.
get angry 891 vb.
boiler
cauldron 194 n.
poultry 365 n.
heater 383 n.
ablutions 648 n.
boiler suit
suit 228 n.
boiling
furious 176 adj.
hot 379 adj.
heating 381 n.
preservation 666 n.
fervent 818 adj.
excited 821 adj.
angry 891 adj.
boiling point
heat 379 n.
completion 725 n.
boisterous
disorderly 61 adj.
violent 176 adj.
windy 352 adj.
hasty 680 adj.
excitable 822 adj.
bold
projecting 254 adj.
undisguised 522 adj.
forceful 571 adj.
written 586 adj.
print-type 587 n.
courageous 855 adj.
rash 857 adj.
insolent 878 adj.
impious 980 adj.
boldface
print-type 587 n.
bold front
defiance 711 n.
courage 855 n.
bole
chief part 52 n.
cylinder 252 n.
soil 344 n.
tree 366 n.
bolero
jacket 228 n.

dance 837 n.
bolide
meteor 321 n.
boll
receptacle 194 n.
sphere 252 n.
bollard
fastening 47 n.
traffic control 305 n.
boloney
empty talk 515 n.
falsehood 541 n.
Bolsheviks
political party 708 n.
Bolshevism
government 733 n.
Bolshevist
revolter 738 n.
bolshie
opposing 704 adj.
agitator 738 n.
disobedient 738 adj.
bolster (up)
cushion 218 n.
support 218 vb.
aid 703 vb.
cheer 833 vb.
give courage 855 vb.
bolt
affix 45 vb.
fastening 47 n.
bunch 74 n.
textile 222 n.
barrier 235 n.
sharp point 256 n.
stopper 264 n.
close 264 vb.
move fast 277 vb.
decamp 296 vb.
eat 301 vb.
cultivate 370 vb.
run away 620 vb.
safeguard 662 n.
missile weapon 723 n.
disobey 738 vb.
lockup 748 n.
gluttonize 947 vb.
bolted
closed 264 adj.
bolt from the blue
lack of expectation 508 n.
bolthole
tunnel 263 n.
refuge 662 n.
bolt of lightning
luminary 420 n.
bolus
mouthful 301 n.
medicine 658 n.
bomb
nucleonics 160 n.
demolish 165 vb.
destroyer 168 n.
bang 402 n.
fire at 712 vb.
bomb 723 n.
bombard
demolish 165 vb.
shoot 287 vb.
radiate 417 vb.
fire at 712 vb.
bombardier
soldiery 722 n.
bombardment
havoc 165 n.
loudness 400 n.
bombardment 712 n.
warfare 718 n.
bombast
empty talk 515 n.
magniloquence 574 n.
boast 877 n.
bombastic
exaggerated 546 adj.
diffuse 570 adj.
rhetorical 574 adj.
ridiculous 849 adj.
boastful 877 adj.
bomber
aircraft 276 n.
attacker 712 n.
air force 722 n.
bombinate, bombilate
roll 403 vb.
ululate 409 vb.
bombproof
unyielding 162 adj.
invulnerable 660 adj.
defended 713 adj.
bombshell
lack of expectation 508 n.
bomb 723 n.
bona fide
genuine 494 adj.
veracious 540 adj.
truthfully 540 adv.
bona fides
probity 929 n.
bonanza
store 632 n.
plenty 635 n.
redundance 637 n.
prosperity 730 n.
gift 781 n.
wealth 800 n.
bonbon
sweets 301 n.
bonce
head 213 n.
bond
relation 9 n.
union 45 n.
bond 47 n.
intermediary 231 n.
obstacle 702 n.
subject 745 adj.
fetter 748 n.
promise 764 n.
compact 765 n.
title deed 767 n.
retention 778 n.
paper money 797 n.
dueness 915 n.
duty 917 n.
bondage
servitude 745 n.
detention 747 n.
bonds of friendship
friendship 880 n.
bone
empty 300 vb.
cook 301 vb.
solid body 324 n.
hardness 326 n.
structure 331 n.
steal 788 vb.
— up on
study 536 vb.
boned
rigid 326 adj.
bonehead
dunce 501 n.
boneless
impotent 161 adj.
bonemeal
fertilizer 171 n.
bone of contention
question 459 n.
casus belli 709 n.
contention 716 n.
boner
mistake 495 n.
bones
remainder 41 n.
corpse 363 n.
gong 414 n.
gambling 618 n.
bone-setter
mender 656 n.
doctor 658 n.
boneshaker
bicycle 274 n.
bone to pick
casus belli 709 n.
resentment 891 n.
bonfire
fire 379 n.
revel 837 n.
celebration 876 n.
bon gré mal gré
necessarily 596 adv.
bonhomie
ostentation 875 n.
sociability 882 n.
benevolence 897 n.
bonkers
crazy 503 adj.
bon marché
cheapness 812 n.
bon mot
witticism 839 n.
bonne bouche
mouthful 301 n.
savouriness 390 n.
bonnet
covering 226 n.
headgear 228 n.
bonny
healthy 650 adj.
cheerful 833 adj.
beautiful 841 adj.
courageous 855 adj.
bonsai
tree 366 n.
agriculture 370 n.
bon ton
people of taste 846 n.
fashion 848 n.
fashionable 848 adj.
bonus
inequality 29 n.
extra 40 n.
incentive 612 n.
superfluity 637 n.
gift 781 n.
receipt 807 n.
undueness 916 n.
bon vivant
eater 301 n.
sociable person 882 n.
glutton 947 n.
bon viveur
sensualist 944 n.
bon voyage!
296 int.
bony
lean 206 adj.
hard 326 adj.
bonze
monk 986 n.
priest 986 n.
boo
cry 408 n.vb.
vociferate 408 vb.
gesture 547 n.
indignity 921 n.
not respect 921 vb.
despise 922 vb.
disapprobation 924 n.
disapprove 924 vb.
boob
mistake 495 n.
blunder 495 vb.
booby
dunce 501 n.
ninny 501 n.
bungler 697 n.
booby prize
unskilfulness 695 n.
trophy 729 n.
reward 962 n.
booby trap
trap 542 n.
pitfall 663 n.
defences 713 n.
bomb 723 n.
boodle
booty 790 n.
shekels 797 n.
boogie-woogie
music 412 n.
boohoo
cry 408 n.vb.
lamentation 836 n.
weep 836 vb.
book
list 87 vb.
be early 135 vb.

publication 528 n.
record 548 n.
register 548 vb.
script 586 n.
book 589 n.
novel 590 n.
require 627 vb.
acquire 771 vb.
account 808 vb.
reprove 924 vb.
indict 928 vb.
Book, the
scripture 975 n.
bookbinder
bookbinding 589 n.
bookcase
cabinet 194 n.
library 589 n.
book collection
library 589 n.
collection 632 n.
book-collector
collector 492 n.
bookperson 589 n.
bookie
gambler 618 n.
booking
registration 548 n.
booking clerk
receiver 782 n.
seller 793 n.
bookish
instructed 490 adj.
studious 536 adj.
bookkeeper
enumerator 86 n.
recorder 549 n.
treasurer 798 n.
accountant 808 n.
booklet
book 589 n.
book lover
bookperson 589 n.
bookmaker
gambler 618 n.
bookmaking
calculation of chance 159 n.
Book of Common Prayer
scripture 975 n.
office-book 988 n.
bookplate
label 547 n.
bookseller
bookperson 589 n.
bookshelf
library 589 n.
bookshop
library 589 n.
book trade
publication 528 n.
bookworm
scholar 492 n.
learner 538 n.
bookperson 589 n.
Boolean algebra
reasoning 475 n.
boom
grow 36 vb.
productiveness 171 n.
prop 218 n.
loudness 400 n.
be loud 400 vb.
bang 402 vb.
roll 403 vb.
resonance 404 n.
ululate 409 vb.
revival 656 n.
obstacle 702 n.
defences 713 n.
prosperity 730 n.
prosper 730 vb.
sale 793 n.
be sold 793 vb.
boom and bust
fluctuation 317 n.
trade 791 n.
boomerang
recoil 280 n.vb.
retaliation 714 n.
retaliate 714 vb.
missile weapon 723 n.
boon
benefit 615 n.
gift 781 n.
boon companion
concomitant 89 n.
colleague 707 n.
close friend 880 n.
sociable person 882 n.
boorish
clumsy 695 adj.
ill-bred 847 adj.
plebeian 869 adj.
discourteous 885 adj.
boost
increase 36 n.
augment 36 vb.
stimulation 174 n.
invigorate 174 vb.
impulse 279 n.
elevation 310 n.
overrate 482 vb.
advertise 528 vb.
aid 703 n.vb.
praise 923 vb.
flatter 925 vb.
booster
rocket 276 n.
boot
box 194 n.
kick 279 vb.
ejection 300 n.
— out
repel 292 vb.
eject 300 vb.
booth
small house 192 n.
compartment 194 n.
shop 796 n.
bootleg
steal 788 vb.
booty 790 n.
bootless
wasted 634 adj.
profitless 641 adj.
unsuccessful 728 adj.
unthanked 908 adj.
bootlicker
toady 879 n.
boot polish
cleanser 648 n.
boots
footwear 228 n.
servant 742 n.
booty
trophy 729 n.
acquisition 771 n.
booty 790 n.
booze
alcoholic drink 301 n.
drink 301 vb.
drunkenness 949 n.
get drunk 949 vb.
boozer
tavern 192 n.
drunkard 949 n.
boozy
drunken 949 adj.
tipsy 949 adj.
bop
music 412 n.
dance 837 n.vb.
bordello
brothel 951 n.
border
entrance 68 n.
be near 200 vb.
contiguity 202 n.
surroundings 230 n.
circumscribe 232 vb.
edge 234 n.
edging 234 n.
marginal 234 adj.
hem 234 vb.
limit 236 n.
limited 236 adj.
flank 239 vb.
garden 370 n.
trimming 844 n.
decorate 844 vb.
borderer
dweller 191 n.
borderland
contiguity 202 n.
borderline
limited 236 adj.
uncertain 474 adj.
Borders
district 184 n.
bore
enlarge 197 vb.
breadth 205 n.
make concave 255 vb.
perforation 263 n.
pierce 263 vb.
pass 305 vb.
descend 309 vb.
current 350 n.
wave 350 n.
be loquacious 581 vb.
impair 655 vb.
bane 659 n.
fatigue 684 vb.
firearm 723 n.
trouble 827 vb.
depress 834 vb.
bore 838 n.
be tedious 838 vb.
be dull 840 vb.
sate 863 vb.
borehole
excavation 255 n.
perforation 263 n.
water 339 n.
borer
sharp point 256 n.
perforator 263 n.
insect 365 n.
boring
feeble 572 adj.
boring person
bore 838 n.
born
produced 164 adj.
born 360 adj.
born, be
become 1 vb.
begin 68 vb.
happen 154 vb.
reproduce itself 167 vb.
be born 360 vb.
born again
restored 656 adj.
repentant 939 adj.
sanctified 979 adj.
born-again Christian
the orthodox 976 n.
born for
gifted 694 adj.
born in the purple
rich 800 adj.
noble 868 adj.
born like it, be
be intrinsic 5 vb.
born of
caused 157 adj.
born with a silver spoon in one's mouth
prosperous 730 adj.
rich 800 adj.
noble 868 adj.
born yesterday
artless 699 adj.
borough
district 184 n.
electorate 605 n.
borrow
copy 20 vb.
borrow 785 vb.
be in debt 803 vb.
be parsimonious 816 vb.
borrowed
neological 560 adj.
transferred 780 adj.

unwarranted 916 adj.
borrowed plumes
sham 542 n.
borrowed time
opportunity 137 n.
Borstal
school 539 n.
amendment 654 n.
prison 748 n.
bosh
silly talk 515 n.
bosom
interiority 224 n.
garment 228 n.
bosom 253 n.
spirit 447 n.
affections 817 n.
bosom friend
close friend 880 n.
bosomy
fleshy 195 adj.
curved 248 adj.
convex 253 adj.
shapely 841 adj.
boss
superior 34 n.
swelling 253 n.
roughen 259 vb.
direct 689 vb.
director 690 n.
dominate 733 vb.
tyrant 735 n.
autocrat 741 n.
master 741 n.
ornamental art 844 n.
— around
oppress 735 vb.
bossy
authoritative 733 adj.
authoritarian 735 adj.
bosun
mariner 270 n.
Boswell
narrator 590 n.
botanical
vegetal 366 adj.
botanical 368 adj.
botany
biology 358 n.
botany 368 n.
botch, bodge
distort 246 vb.
neglect 458 vb.
blunder 495 vb.
misrepresentation 552 n.
misrepresent 552 vb.
impair 655 vb.
bungling 695 n.
be clumsy 695 vb.
fail 728 vb.
eyesore 842 n.
botch-up
mistake 495 n.
both
dual 90 adj.
bother
commotion 318 n.
be attentive 455 vb.
distract 456 vb.
be inexpedient 643 vb.
activity 678 n.
meddle 678 vb.
be difficult 700 vb.
hinder 702 vb.
excitable state 822 n.
worry 825 n.
torment 827 vb.
enrage 891 vb.
bothersome
annoying 827 adj.
bothy
small house 192 n.
bottle
vessel 194 n.
draught 301 n.
store 632 vb.
preserve 666 vb.
— up
remember 505 vb.
conceal 525 vb.
preserve 666 vb.
restrain 747 vb.
bottleneck
contraction 198 n.
narrowness 206 n.
obstacle 702 n.
bottle party
participation 775 n.
festivity 837 n.
social gathering 882 n.
bottom
extremity 69 n.
lowness 210 n.
depth 211 n.
base 214 n.
undermost 214 adj.
support 218 vb.
buttocks 238 n.
ship 275 n.
bottom drawer
store 632 n.
preparation 669 n.
bottomless
deep 211 adj.
infernal 972 adj.
bottomless purse
funds 797 n.
wealth 800 n.
bottom rung
serial place 73 n.
bottom up
inverted 221 adj.
botulism
digestive disorders 651 n.
infection 651 n.
poisoning 659 n.
boudoir
chamber 194 n.
beauty parlour 843 n.
bouffant
tailored 228 adj.
convex 253 adj.
beautified 843 adj.
bough
branch 53 n.
foliage 366 n.
tree 366 n.
bouillon
hors-d'oeuvres 301 n.
boulder
bulk 195 n.
sphere 252 n.
rock 344 n.
boulevard
pleasance 192 n.
path 624 n.
bounce
recoil 280 n.
eject 300 vb.
ascent 308 n.
ascend 308 vb.
leap 312 vb.
oscillate 317 vb.
agitation 318 n.
be agitated 318 vb.
elasticity 328 n.
be elastic 328 vb.
boasting 877 n.
— back
be restored 656 vb.
bouncer
ejector 300 n.
protector 660 n.
bouncing
vigorous 174 adj.
leaping 312 adj.
healthy 650 adj.
cheerful 833 adj.
insolent 878 adj.
bouncing cheque
nonpayment 805 n.
bound
tied 45 adj.
hem 234 vb.
limit 236 vb.
spurt 277 n.
move fast 277 vb.
leap 312 n.vb.
certain 473 adj.
bibliographical 589 adj.
fated 596 adj.
subject 745 adj.
restrained 747 adj.
promised 764 adj.
retained 778 adj.
indebted 803 adj.
obliged 917 adj.
— back
recoil 280 vb.
bound, be
affirm 532 vb.
promise 764 vb.
boundary
separation 46 n.
extremity 69 n.
edge 234 n.
limit 236 n.
limited 236 adj.
boundary wall
fence 235 n.
bounden duty
duty 917 n.
bounder
vulgarian 847 n.
cad 938 n.
bound for
directed 281 adj.
boundless
infinite 107 adj.
spacious 183 adj.
bounds
region 184 n.
place 185 n.
outline 233 n.
edge 234 n.
bound to be
certain 473 adj.
bounteous
liberal 813 adj.
benevolent 897 adj.
bountiful
giving 781 adj.
liberal 813 adj.
benevolent 897 adj.
bounty
subvention 703 n.
gift 781 n.
liberality 813 n.
reward 962 n.
bouquet
bunch 74 n.
savouriness 390 n.
odour 394 n.
fragrance 396 n.
ornamentation 844 n.
applause 923 n.
praise 923 n.
bouquet garni
potherb 301 n.
bourbon
alcoholic drink 301 n.
bourgeois
commoner 869 n.
plebeian 869 adj.
bourgeois ethic
conformity 83 n.
bourgeoisie
averageness 732 n.
commonalty 869 n.
middle classes 869 n.
bourn, bourne
limit 236 n.
stream 350 n.
bourse
bourse 618 n.
market 796 n.
bout
period 110 n.
labour 682 n.
pugilism 716 n.

boutade
whim 604 n.
boutique
clothier 228 n.
shop 796 n.
bovine
animal 365 adj.
unintelligent 499 adj.
impassive 820 adj.
bow
prow 237 n.
curve 248 n.
make curved 248 vb.
loop 250 n.
camber 253 n.
be convex 253 vb.
propellant 287 n.
obeisance 311 n.
stoop 311 vb.
play music 413 vb.
viol 414 n.
knuckle under 721 vb.
missile weapon 723 n.
obey 739 vb.
trimming 844 n.
servility 879 n.
be servile 879 vb.
courteous act 884 n.
greet 884 vb.
respects 920 n.
show respect 920 vb.
be pious 979 vb.
perform ritual 988 vb.
— down (to)
descend 309 vb.
stoop 311 vb.
honour 866 vb.
be humble 872 vb.
worship 981 vb.
— out
depart 296 vb.
dismiss 300 vb.
— to
be inferior 35 vb.
submit 721 vb.
— to fate
be forced 596 vb.
— to no one
be proud 871 vb.
— to reason
be reasonable 475 vb.
bow at a venture
uncertainty 474 n.
bowdlerize, bowdlerise
subtract 39 vb.
purify 648 vb.
impair 655 vb.
bowdlerizer
alterer 143 n.
bowel movement
defecation 302 n.
bowels
insides 224 n.
bower
pavilion 192 n.
arbour 194 n.
screen 421 n.
love-nest 887 n.
bowl
bowl 194 n.
cavity 255 n.
propel 287 vb.
draught 301 n.
rotate 315 vb.
— along
go smoothly 258 vb.
travel 267 vb.
move fast 277 vb.
— out
dismiss 300 vb.
defeat 727 vb.
— over
disable 161 vb.
fell 311 vb.
surprise 508 vb.
be wonderful 864 vb.
excite love 887 vb.
bow-legged
deformed 246 adj.
curved 248 adj.
legged 267 adj.
bowler
headgear 228 n.
thrower 287 n.
player 837 n.
bowline
tackling 47 n.
bowling alley
arena 724 n.
place of amusement 837 n.
bowling green
horizontality 216 n.
smoothness 258 n.
arena 724 n.
pleasure ground 837 n.
bowls
ball game 837 n.
bowman
shooter 287 n.
soldiery 722 n.
bowshot
short distance 200 n.
propulsion 287 n.
bowsprit
prow 237 n.
projection 254 n.
bow-string
execute 963 vb.
means of execution 964 n.
bow tie
neckwear 228 n.
box
box 194 n.
compartment 194 n.
cover 226 vb.
circumscribe 232 vb.
enclosure 235 n.
enclose 235 vb.
strike 279 vb.
tree 366 n.
theatre 594 n.
storage 632 n.
fight 716 vb.
— on the ears
spank 963 vb.
— the compass
orientate 281 vb.
box, the
broadcasting 531 n.
boxer
dog 365 n.
pugilist 722 n.
boxing
defence 713 n.
pugilism 716 n.
box office
onlookers 441 n.
theatre 594 n.
treasury 799 n.
box on the ears
knock 279 n.
reprimand 924 n.
box room
chamber 194 n.
storage 632 n.
boy
youngster 132 n.
male 372 n.
boycott
separation 46 n.
set apart 46 vb.
exclusion 57 n.
exclude 57 vb.
hindrance 702 n.
unsociability 883 n.
make unwelcome 883 vb.
disapprobation 924 n.
boy friend
male 372 n.
friend 880 n.
lover 887 n.
boyhood
youth 130 n.
boyish
young 130 adj.
infantine 132 adj.
foolish 499 adj.
immature 670 adj.
bra
underwear 228 n.
brace
tighten 45 vb.
fastening 47 n.
group 74 n.
duality 90 n.
strengthen 162 vb.
prop 218 n.
support 218 vb.
notation 410 n.
punctuation 547 n.
refresh 685 vb.
— oneself
be resolute 599 vb.
prepare oneself 669 vb.
brace and bit
perforator 263 n.
braced
rigid 326 adj.
bracelet
loop 250 n.
fetter 748 n.
jewellery 844 n.
bracer
stimulant 174 n.
pungency 388 n.
braces
fastening 47 n.
hanger 217 n.
underwear 228 n.
bracing
vigorous 174 adj.
salubrious 652 adj.
refreshing 685 adj.
cheering 833 adj.
bracken
plant 366 n.
bracket
equalize 28 vb.
join 45 vb.
bond 47 n.
classification 77 n.
pair 90 vb.
prop 218 n.
shelf 218 n.
put between 231 vb.
angularity 247 n.
lamp 420 n.
— with
liken 18 vb.
brackets
punctuation 547 n.
brackish
salty 388 adj.
bradawl
perforator 263 n.
Bradshaw
directory 87 n.
itinerary 267 n.
guidebook 524 n.
brae
high land 209 n.
brag
defy 711 vb.
card game 837 n.
be affected 850 vb.
seek repute 866 vb.
boast 877 n., vb.
boaster 877 n.
be insolent 878 vb.
braggart
coward 856 n.
boaster 877 n.
boastful 877 adj.
insolent person 878 n.
Brahma
divineness 965 n.
Trinity 965 n.
Hindu deities 967 n.
Brahman, Brahmin
cattle 365 n.
aristocrat 868 n.
priest 986 n.

Brahmanism
religious faith 973 n.
Brahmin
intellectual 492 n.
Brahmo
non-Christian sect 978 n.
braid
tie 45 vb.
ligature 47 n.
strip 208 n.
crossing 222 n.
weave 222 vb.
hair 259 n.
variegate 437 vb.
trimming 844 n.
brail
tighten 45 vb.
elevate 310 vb.
braille
writing 586 n.
brain
head 213 n.
kill 362 vb.
render insensible 375 vb.
intellect 447 n.
intellectual 492 n.
intelligence 498 n.
brainchild
product 164 n.
idea 451 n.
brain damage
absence of intellect 448 n.
insanity 503 n.
brainfag
thought 449 n.
fatigue 684 n.
brainless
mindless 448 adj.
foolish 499 adj.
brains
intellect 447 n.
intelligence 498 n.
planner 623 n.
brainstorm
psychopathy 503 n.
excitable state 822 n.
brains trust
interrogation 459 n.
wiseacre 500 n.
brain-twister
enigma 530 n.
brainwash
convert 147 vb.
influence 178 vb.
teach 534 vb.
misteach 535 vb.
habituate 610 vb.
pervert 655 vb.
brain wave
idea 451 n.
intelligence 498 n.
brainwork
thought 449 n.
brainy
intelligent 498 adj.
braise
cook 301 vb.
brake
halt 145 vb.
moderator 177 n.
bring to rest 266 vb.
carriage 274 n.
slowness 278 n.
retard 278 vb.
wood 366 n.
safeguard 662 n.
hinder 702 vb.
restraint 747 n.
restrain 747 vb.
fetter 748 n.
bramble
prickle 256 n.
plant 366 n.
bran
leavings 41 n.
cereals 301 n.
powder 332 n.
branch
adjunct 40 n.
branch 53 n.
be dispersed 75 vb.
classification 77 n.
descendant 170 n.
extend 183 vb.
filament 208 n.
make angular 247 vb.
stream 350 n.
foliage 366 n.
tree 366 n.
society 708 n.
sect 978 n.
— off
bifurcate 92 vb.
diverge 294 vb.
— out
be dispersed 75 vb.
deviate 282 vb.
diverge 294 vb.
branched
brachial 53 adj.
branching
symmetry 245 n.
branch line
railway 624 n.
brand
sort 77 n.
burning 381 n.
burn 381 vb.
furnace 383 n.
lighter 385 n.
torch 420 n.
identification 547 n.
label 547 n.
mark 547 vb.
blemish 845 vb.
slur 867 n.
shame 867 vb.
censure 924 n.
dispraise 924 vb.
detraction 926 n.
defame 926 vb.
accuse 928 vb.
branded
marked 547 adj.
proprietary 777 adj.
brandish
brandish 317 vb.
agitate 318 vb.
show 522 vb.
use 673 vb.
defy 711 vb.
be ostentatious 875 vb.
boast 877 vb.
threaten 900 vb.
brand-new
new 126 adj.
brandy
alcoholic drink 301 n.
brashness
insolence 878 n.
brashy
fragmentary 53 adj.
brass
a mixture 43 n.
blowing 352 n.
resonance 404 n.
stridor 407 n.
orchestra 413 n.
horn 414 n.
yellowness 433 n.
monument 548 n.
director 690 n.
badge of rank 743 n.
shekels 797 n.
wealth 800 n.
sauciness 878 n.
brassard
livery 547 n.
badge of rank 743 n.
brass farthing
trifle 639 n.
brass hat
bigwig 638 n.
army officer 741 n.
brassiere
underwear 228 n.
brass knuckles
club 723 n.
brass plate
label 547 n.
brass rubbing
picture 553 n.
brass tacks
reality 1 n.
brassy
loud 400 adj.
strident 407 adj.
orange 432 adj.
ornate 574 adj.
impertinent 878 adj.
brat
child 132 n.
brattice
lining 227 n.
partition 231 n.
bravado
ostentation 875 n.
boast 877 n.
boasting 877 n.
insolence 878 n.
brave
be in front 237 vb.
defy 711 vb.
combatant 722 n.
brave person 855 n.
courageous 855 adj.
showy 875 adj.
— it out
be courageous 855 vb.
bravo
violent creature 176 n.
murderer 362 n.
combatant 722 n.
brave person 855 n.
desperado 857 n.
ruffian 904 n.
923 int.
bravura
musical skill 413 n.
masterpiece 694 n.
defiance 711 n.
bravura player
proficient person 696 n.
braw
excellent 644 adj.
brawl
turmoil 61 n.
quarrel 709 n.
bicker 709 vb.
fight 716 n.
brawler
rioter 738 n.
brawn
vitality 162 n.
meat 301 n.
brawny
stalwart 162 adj.
fleshy 195 adj.
bray
pulverize 332 vb.
be loud 400 vb.
resound 404 vb.
rasp 407 vb.
ululate 409 vb.
braze
join 45 vb.
agglutinate 48 vb.
brazen
strident 407 adj.
undisguised 522 adj.
proud 871 adj.
insolent 878 adj.
wicked 934 adj.
impenitent 940 adj.
impious 980 adj.
— it out
be obstinate 602 vb.
be insolent 878 vb.
brazier
furnace 383 n.
breach
disagreement 25 n.
disunion 46 n.

gap 201 n.
dissension 709 n.
enmity 881 n.
undueness 916 n.
breach of promise
untruth 543 n.
nonobservance 769 n.
perfidy 930 n.
breach of the peace
turmoil 61 n.
quarrel 709 n.
revolt 738 n.
bread
cereals 301 n.
food 301 n.
shekels 797 n.
bread-and-butter, one's
vocation 622 n.
bread and water
unsavouriness 391 n.
insufficiency 636 n.
fasting 946 n.
bread and wine
the sacrament 988 n.
breadth
greatness 32 n.
measure 183 n.
size 195 n.
breadth 205 n.
metrology 465 n.
breadth of mind
wisdom 498 n.
breadwinner
worker 686 n.
breadwinning
gainful 771 adj.
break
disunion 46 n.
break 46 vb.
separate 46 vb.
incompleteness 55 n.
series 71 n.
discontinuity 72 n.
discontinue 72 vb.
interim 108 n.
opportunity 137 n.
change 143 n.
lull 145 n.
continuance 146 n.
demolish 165 vb.
force 176 vb.
gap 201 n.
interval 201 n.
deviate 282 vb.
be brittle 330 vb.
pulverize 332 vb.
flow 350 vb.
rasp 407 vb.
be disclosed 526 vb.
wound 655 vb.
leisure 681 n.
repose 683 n.
refreshment 685 n.
defeat 727 vb.
fail 728 vb.
prosperity 730 n.
oppress 735 vb.
lose 772 vb.
be undue 916 vb.
— a habit
be unconformable 84 vb.
disaccustom 611 vb.
— away
separate 46 vb.
be dispersed 75 vb.
run away 620 vb.
escape 667 vb.
quarrel 709 vb.
revolt 738 vb.
fail in duty 918 vb.
schismatize 978 vb.
— down
simplify 44 vb.
disunite 46 vb.
decompose 51 vb.
demolish 165 vb.
fall short 307 vb.
deteriorate 655 vb.
fail 728 vb.
be excitable 822 vb.
weep 836 vb.
fear 854 vb.
— even
be equal 28 vb.
acquire 771 vb.
— faith
be false 541 vb.
not observe 769 vb.
be dishonest 930 vb.
— in
burst in 297 vb.
intrude 297 vb.
break in 369 vb.
train 534 vb.
habituate 610 vb.
oppress 735 vb.
subjugate 745 vb.
— in on
derange 63 vb.
mistime 138 vb.
intrude 297 vb.
— loose
escape 667 vb.
achieve liberty 746 vb.
— new ground
initiate 68 vb.
— of
cure 656 vb.
— off
be incomplete 55 vb.
discontinue 72 vb.
cease 145 vb.
be brittle 330 vb.
relinquish 621 vb.
— off relations
quarrel 709 vb.
— one's back
load 193 vb.
— one's heart
sadden 834 vb.
— one's neck
perish 361 vb.
— one's word
not observe 769 vb.
be dishonest 930 vb.
— on the wheel
give pain 377 vb.
torment 827 vb.
torture 963 vb.
— orders
fail in duty 918 vb.
— out
begin 68 vb.
be violent 176 vb.
emerge 298 vb.
escape 667 vb.
attack 712 vb.
be excitable 822 vb.
— ranks
be dispersed 75 vb.
— the back of
progress 285 vb.
— the bank
succeed 727 vb.
gain 771 vb.
— the ice
initiate 68 vb.
befriend 880 vb.
— the law
disobey 738 vb.
do wrong 914 vb.
be illegal 954 vb.
— the news
inform 524 vb.
— the peace
be violent 176 vb.
fight 716 vb.
— the rules
do wrong 914 vb.
— through
emerge 298 vb.
be visible 443 vb.
be disclosed 526 vb.
escape 667 vb.
attack 712 vb.
succeed 727 vb.
— through the clouds
be disclosed 526 vb.
— up
break 46 vb.
disunite 46 vb.
separate 46 vb.
sunder 46 vb.
decompose 51 vb.
be disordered 61 vb.
be dispersed 75 vb.
disperse 75 vb.
be destroyed 165 vb.
demolish 165 vb.
decamp 296 vb.
make useless 641 vb.
— wind
eruct 300 vb.
— with
quarrel 709 vb.
— with custom
be unconformable 84 vb.
— with the past
change 143 n.
revolutionize 149 vb.
forget 506 vb.
tergiversation 603 n.
breakable
brittle 330 adj.
breakaway
independent 744 adj.
schismatical 978 adj.
breakdown
stop 145 n.
helplessness 161 n.
ruin 165 n.
illness 651 n.
hitch 702 n.
failure 728 n.
breakdown of law and order
anarchy 734 n.
lawlessness 954 n.
breaker
vat 194 n.
wave 350 n.
breaker-in
trainer 537 n.
breakfast
meal 301 n.
eat 301 vb.
breaking point
casus belli 709 n.
completion 725 n.
break in the clouds
relief 831 n.
breakneck
sloping 220 adj.
speedy 277 adj.
hasty 680 adj.
rash 857 adj.
break of day
morning 128 n.
half-light 419 n.
breakout
egress 298 n.
escape 667 n.
breakthrough
success 727 n.
breakup
finality 69 n.
ruin 165 n.
breakwater
projection 254 n.
safeguard 662 n.
breast
interiority 224 n.
be in front 237 vb.
bosom 253 n.
climb 308 vb.
spirit 447 n.
withstand 704 vb.
affections 817 n.
breast-feed
feed 301 vb.
breastplate
protection 660 n.
armour 713 n.
breastwork
defences 713 n.
breath
insubstantial thing 4 n.
small quantity 33 n.

instant 116 n.
breeze 352 n.
life 360 n.
odour 394 n.
faintness 401 n.
breathalyser
testing agent 461 n.
breathe
be 1 vb.
breathe 352 vb.
live 360 vb.
smell 394 vb.
sound faint 401 vb.
cry 408 vb.
hint 524 vb.
divulge 526 vb.
voice 577 vb.
speak 579 vb.
repose 683 vb.
be refreshed 685 vb.
show feeling 818 vb.
— again
be relieved 831 vb.
— down one's neck
impend 155 vb.
approach 289 vb.
— fresh life into
vitalize 360 vb.
revive 656 vb.
animate 821 vb.
— in
absorb 299 vb.
breathe 352 vb.
smell 394 vb.
— of
evidence 466 vb.
mean 514 vb.
— one's last
die 361 vb.
— out
emit 300 vb.
breathe 352 vb.
breather
lull 145 n.
repose 683 n.
refreshment 685 n.
breathing
oscillation 317 n.
respiration 352 n.
life 360 n.
alive 360 adj.
breathing space
lull 145 n.
repose 683 n.
breathless
agitated 318 adj.
puffing 352 adj.
dead 361 adj.
voiceless 578 adj.
stammering 580 adj.
hasty 680 adj.
panting 684 adj.
fervent 818 adj.
nervous 854 adj.
desiring 859 adj.
wondering 864 adj.
breath of air
breeze 352 n.
refreshment 685 n.
breath of life
life 360 n.
important matter 638 n.
breathtaking
prodigious 32 adj.
notable 638 adj.
wonderful 864 adj.
bred
produced 164 adj.
tamed 369 adj.
bred in the bone
genetic 5 adj.
bred to
instructed 490 adj.
breech
firearm 723 n.
breeches
trousers 228 n.
breed
character 5 n.
race 11 n.
augment 36 vb.
grow 36 vb.
group 74 n.
breed 77 n.
produce 164 vb.
reproduce 166 vb.
generate 167 vb.
reproduce itself 167 vb.
posterity 170 n.
organism 358 n.
breed stock 369 vb.
educate 534 vb.
mature 669 vb.
— with
unite with 45 vb.
breeder
producer 164 n.
breeder 369 n.
trainer 537 n.
breeding
good taste 846 n.
etiquette 848 n.
breeding-ground
seedbed 156 n.
breeze
breeze 352 n.
breezy
airy 340 adj.
windy 352 adj.
cheerful 833 adj.
rash 857 adj.
discourteous 885 adj.
disrespectful 921 adj.
bressummer
beam 218 n.
brethren
laity 987 n.
breve
notation 410 n.
punctuation 547 n.
brevet
warrant 737 n.
mandate 751 n.
permit 756 n.
breviary
scripture 975 n.
prayers 981 n.
office-book 988 n.
brevity
smallness 33 n.
brief span 114 n.
shortness 204 n.
conciseness 569 n.
brew
a mixture 43 n.
mix 43 vb.
alcoholic drink 301 n.
plot 623 vb.
mature 669 vb.
brewery
workshop 687 n.
brewing
impending 155 adj.
briar
(See **brier** *)*
bribable
venal 930 adj.
bribe
offset 31 n.
compensate 31 vb.
incentive 612 n.
bribe 612 vb.
offer 759 n.vb.
gift 781 n.
give 781 vb.
purchase 792 vb.
pay 804 n.vb.
reward 962 n.vb.
bribery
inducement 612 n.
offer 759 n.
purchase 792 n.
bric-a-brac
bauble 639 n.
ornamentation 844 n.
brick
architectural 192 adj.
hardness 326 n.
pottery 381 n.
building material 631 n.
missile weapon 723 n.
favourite 890 n.
honourable person 929 n.
good person 937 n.
brickbat
missile 287 n.
indignity 921 n.
reproach 924 n.
calumny 926 n.
bricklayer
artisan 686 n.
bricks
plaything 837 n.
bricks and mortar
edifice 164 n.
housing 192 n.
building material 631 n.
brick wall
barrier 235 n.
obstacle 702 n.
brickwork
edifice 164 n.
structure 331 n.
bridal
wedding 894 n.
matrimonial 894 adj.
bride
woman 373 n.
spouse 894 n.
bridegroom
male 372 n.
spouse 894 n.
bridesmaid
auxiliary 707 n.
close friend 880 n.
bridal party 894 n.
bridge
connect 45 vb.
bond 47 n.
vertex 213 n.
tooth 256 n.
passage 305 n.
pass 305 vb.
bridge 624 n.
card game 837 n.
— over
pass 305 vb.
compromise 770 vb.
— the gap
facilitate 701 vb.
bridge-builder
preparer 669 n.
bridgehead
front 237 n.
battleground 724 n.
retention 778 n.
bridle
affix 45 vb.
start out 296 vb.
break in 369 vb.
restraint 747 n.
restrain 747 vb.
fetter 748 n.
get angry 891 vb.
bridlepath
path 624 n.
brief
small 33 adj.
brief 114 adj.
short 204 adj.
inform 524 vb.
concise 569 adj.
description 590 n.
compendium 592 n.
preparation 669 n.
make ready 669 vb.
command 737 n.vb.
— counsel
litigate 959 vb.
briefcase
case 194 n.
briefed
instructed 490 adj.
informed 524 adj.
prepared 669 adj.

briefing
information 524 n.
preparation 669 n.
advice 691 n.
briefs
underwear 228 n.
brier, briar
prickle 256 n.
tobacco 388 n.
bane 659 n.
brig
sailing ship 275 n.
bridge 624 n.
gaol 748 n.
brigade
group 74 n.
formation 722 n.
brigadier
army officer 741 n.
brigand
robber 789 n.
brigandage
attack 712 n.
brigandage 788 n.
bright
luminous 417 adj.
undimmed 417 adj.
luminescent 420 adj.
florid 425 adj.
white 427 adj.
intelligent 498 adj.
clean 648 adj.
cheerful 833 adj.
beautiful 841 adj.
splendid 841 adj.
promising 852 adj.
noteworthy 866 adj.
brighten
make bright 417 vb.
be cheerful 833 vb.
beautify 841 vb.
bright-eyed
personable 841 adj.
cheerful 833 adj.
bright idea
intelligence 498 n.
contrivance 623 n.
brightness
light 417 n.
intelligence 498 n.
wit 839 n.
beauty 841 n.
bright side
pleasurableness 826 n.
bright young thing
modernist 126 n.
brilliance
light 417 n.
hue 425 n.
intelligence 498 n.
beauty 841 n.
prestige 866 n.
ostentation 875 n.
brilliant
luminous 417 adj.
florid 425 adj.
intelligent 498 adj.
perfect 646 adj.
witty 839 adj.
gem 844 n.
noteworthy 866 adj.
ostentatious 875 adj.
brilliantine
adhesive 47 n.
unguent 357 n.
hairwash 843 n.
brim
be complete 54 vb.
fill 54 vb.
edge 234 n.
abound 635 vb.
— over
superabound 637 vb.
brimful, brimfull
full 54 adj.
brimstone
fumigator 385 n.
yellowness 433 n.
brindled
mottled 437 adj.
brine
water 339 n.
drench 341 vb.
ocean 343 n.
pungency 388 n.
season 388 vb.
preserver 666 n.
bring
carry 273 vb.
manifest 522 vb.
— about
happen 154 vb.
cause 156 vb.
produce 164 vb.
induce 612 vb.
carry out 725 vb.
— back
replace 187 vb.
restore 656 vb.
deliver 668 vb.
restitute 787 vb.
— down
fell 311 vb.
fire at 712 vb.
strike at 712 vb.
— forth
reproduce itself 167 vb.
manifest 522 vb.
— forward
promote 285 vb.
attract notice 455 vb.
— home the bacon
carry out 725 vb.
succeed 727 vb.
— home to
attribute 158 vb.
convince 485 vb.
impress 821 vb.
accuse 928 vb.
— in
admit 299 vb.
be profitable 771 vb.
cost 809 vb.
— into being
generate 167 vb.
— into disrepute
shame 867 vb.
— into play
operate 173 vb.
— into the world
generate 167 vb.
— it off
succeed 727 vb.
— it on oneself
be in difficulty 700 vb.
— on
cause 156 vb.
promote 285 vb.
mature 669 vb.
— out
cause 156 vb.
manifest 522 vb.
print 587 vb.
— round
convince 485 vb.
make sane 502 vb.
induce 612 vb.
— the house down
applaud 923 vb.
— to
augment 36 vb.
add 38 vb.
bring to rest 266 vb.
— to a head
augment 36 vb.
mature 669 vb.
carry through 725 vb.
— to an end
terminate 69 vb.
— to a point
focus 76 vb.
— to a standstill
halt 145 vb.
bring to rest 266 vb.
obstruct 702 vb.
— to bear
use 673 vb.
— to book
punish 963 vb.
— to fruition
make better 654 vb.
mature 669 vb.
— together
join 45 vb.
combine 50 vb.
compose 56 vb.
arrange 62 vb.
bring together 74 vb.
compare 462 vb.
pacify 719 vb.
mediate 720 vb.
acquire 771 vb.
— to life
vitalize 360 vb.
describe 590 vb.
— to light
discover 484 vb.
manifest 522 vb.
— to mind
remember 505 vb.
— to notice
attract notice 455 vb.
manifest 522 vb.
make important 638 vb.
— to pass
cause 156 vb.
— to rest
bring to rest 266 vb.
tranquillize 823 vb.
— up
produce 164 vb.
vomit 300 vb.
argue 475 vb.
manifest 522 vb.
educate 534 vb.
— up badly
misteach 535 vb.
brink
extremity 69 n.
nearness 200 n.
edge 234 n.
brinkmanship
tactics 688 n.
skill 694 n.
rashness 857 n.
briny
water 339 n.
ocean 343 n.
salty 388 adj.
brisk
brief 114 adj.
vigorous 174 adj.
speedy 277 adj.
concise 569 adj.
active 678 adj.
bristle
be vertical 215 vb.
prickle 256 n.
hair 259 n.
roughness 259 n.
be rough 259 vb.
elevate 310 vb.
get angry 891 vb.
threaten 900 vb.
— with
be many 104 vb.
be sharp 256 vb.
abound 635 vb.
superabound 637 vb.
Bristol fashion
orderly 60 adj.
Briticism
dialect 560 n.
Britisher
native 191 n.
Briton
native 191 n.
brittle
ephemeral 114 adj.
flimsy 163 adj.
rigid 326 adj.
brittle 330 adj.
brittleness
transience 114 n.
weakness 163 n.
weak thing 163 n.
brittleness 330 n.

broach
initiate 68 vb.
cause 156 vb.
sharp point 256 n.
perforator 263 n.
empty 300 vb.
make flow 350 vb.
publish 528 vb.
offer 759 vb.
broad
great 32 adj.
general 79 adj.
spacious 183 adj.
large 195 adj.
broad 205 adj.
lake 346 n.
inexact 495 adj.
wise 498 adj.
assertive 532 adj.
dialectal 560 adj.
free 744 adj.
impure 951 adj.
prostitute 952 n.
broad arrow
angularity 247 n.
label 547 n.
broad-based
inclusive 78 adj.
general 79 adj.
broadcast
disperse 75 vb.
generalize 79 vb.
let fall 311 vb.
cultivate 370 vb.
communicate 524 vb.
publication 528 n.
published 528 adj.
publish 528 vb.
news 529 n.
broadcast 531 n.
broadcast, be
be heard 415 vb.
broadcasting
broadcasting 531 n.
Broad-Church
Anglican 976 adj.
broadcloth
textile 222 n.
broaden
augment 36 vb.
generalize 79 vb.
enlarge 197 vb.
expand 197 vb.
be broad 205 vb.
broad-minded
wise 498 adj.
free 744 adj.
Broadmoor
prison 748 n.
broads
lake 346 n.
broadsheet
the press 528 n.
broadside
laterality 239 n.
bombardment 712 n.
gun 723 n.
broadside on
sideways 239 adv.
broadsword
sharp edge 256 n.
sidearms 723 n.
Broadway
drama 594 n.
broadways
broadways 205 adv.
Brobdingnagian
giant 195 n.
huge 195 adj.
brocade
textile 222 n.
broccoli
vegetable 301 n.
brochette
fastening 47 n.
sharp point 256 n.
brochure
the press 528 n.
book 589 n.
broderie anglaise
needlework 844 n.
brogue
speciality 80 n.
dialect 560 n.
pronunciation 577 n.
speech defect 580 n.
brogues
footwear 228 n.
broil
cook 301 vb.
fight 716 n.
broiler
poultry 365 n.
broke
losing 772 adj.
poor 801 adj.
broken
disunited 46 adj.
fragmentary 53 adj.
discontinuous 72 adj.
weakened 163 adj.
rough 259 adj.
tamed 369 adj.
imperfect 647 adj.
dilapidated 655 adj.
poor 801 adj.
broken bones
wound 655 n.
broken down
useless 641 adj.
broken heart
sorrow 825 n.
love affair 887 n.
broken in
tamed 369 adj.
habituated 610 adj.
broken marriage
divorce 896 n.
broken reed
ineffectuality 161 n.
weak thing 163 n.
broken thread
discontinuity 72 n.
broken-winded
diseased 651 adj.
panting 684 adj.
broken word
untruth 543 n.
perfidy 930 n.
broker
intermediary 231 n.
consignee 754 n.
merchant 794 n.
brokerage
barter 791 n.
discount 810 n.
broker for, be
deputize 755 vb.
brolly
shade 226 n.
bromide
moderator 177 n.
maxim 496 n.
bore 838 n.
witticism 839 n.
bronchitis
respiratory disease 651 n.
bronco
saddle horse 273 n.
brontosaurus
animal 365 n.
Bronx cheer
gesture 547 n.
bronze
a mixture 43 n.
brownness 430 n.
brown 430 adj.
embrown 430 vb.
sculpture 554 n.
brooch
fastening 47 n.
jewellery 844 n.
brood
group 74 n.
certain quantity 104 n.
young creature 132 n.
posterity 170 n.
meditate 449 vb.
be dejected 834 vb.
— upon
meditate 449 vb.
be revengeful 910 vb.
broody
fertilized 167 adj.
brook
stream 350 n.
permit 756 vb.
be patient 823 vb.
— no delay
hasten 680 vb.
— no denial
confute 479 vb.
affirm 532 vb.
necessitate 596 vb.
be obstinate 602 vb.
compel 740 vb.
broom
cleaning utensil 648 n.
broomstick
thinness 206 n.
broth
hors-d'oeuvres 301 n.
brothel
brothel 951 n.
brothel-keeper
bawd 952 n.
brother
kinsman 11 n.
be akin 11 vb.
analogue 18 n.
compeer 28 n.
male 372 n.
colleague 707 n.
friend 880 n.
church title 986 n.
monk 986 n.
brotherhood
family 11 n.
group 74 n.
community 708 n.
friendship 880 n.
sect 978 n.
monk 986 n.
brotherly
akin 11 adj.
friendly 880 adj.
loving 887 adj.
benevolent 897 adj.
brouhaha
commotion 318 n.
brow
head 213 n.
vertex 213 n.
face 237 n.
dome 253 n.
protuberance 254 n.
mien 445 n.
browbeat
induce 612 vb.
frighten 854 vb.
be insolent 878 vb.
reprove 924 vb.
browbeaten
subjected 745 adj.
brown
cook 301 vb.
dry 342 adj.
darken 418 vb.
brownness 430 n.
brown 430 adj.
embrown 430 vb.
browned off
discontented 829 adj.
dejected 834 adj.
bored 838 adj.
brownie
elf 970 n.
Brownshirts
political party 708 n.
brown study
thought 449 n.
attention 455 n.
abstractedness 456 n.
fantasy 513 n.
browse
graze 301 vb.
study 536 vb.

bruise
force 176 vb.
pulverize 332 vb.
pain 377 n.
touch 378 vb.
ill-treat 645 vb.
wound 655 n.vb.
blemish 845 n.
bruiser
athlete 162 n.
pugilist 722 n.
ruffian 904 n.
bruit about
publish 528 vb.
brumal
wintry 129 adj.
cold 380 adj.
Brummagem
sham 542 n.
spurious 542 adj.
cheap 812 adj.
brunch
meal 301 n.
brunette
woman 373 n.
black 428 adj.
brown 430 adj.
a beauty 841 n.
brunt
difficulty 700 n.
brush
district 184 n.
be near 200 vb.
be contiguous 202 vb.
rear 238 n.
smoother 258 n.
rub 333 vb.
touch 378 vb.
cleaning utensil 648 n.
clean 648 vb.
fight 716 n.
battle 718 n.
— aside
confute 479 vb.
hasten 680 vb.
— up
study 536 vb.
clean 648 vb.
brush-off
repulsion 292 n.
brushwood
wood 366 n.
fuel 385 n.
brushwork
painting 553 n.
brusque
violent 176 adj.
concise 569 adj.
taciturn 582 adj.
ungracious 885 adj.
sullen 893 adj.
brutal
violent 176 adj.
oppressive 735 adj.
ungracious 885 adj.
cruel 898 adj.
pitiless 906 adj.
heinous 934 adj.
vicious 934 adj.
brutality
violence 176 n.
moral insensibility 820 n.
cruel act 898 n.
inhumanity 898 n.
brutalize, brutalise
pervert 655 vb.
make insensitive 820 vb.
make wicked 934 vb.
brutalized
cruel 898 adj.
vicious 934 adj.
brute
violent creature 176 n.
animal 365 n.
mindless 448 adj.
tyrant 735 n.
rude person 885 n.
noxious animal 904 n.
ruffian 904 n.
monster 938 n.
brute creation
animality 365 n.
absence of intellect 448 n.
brute force
strength 162 n.
violence 176 n.
despotism 733 n.
brute force 735 n.
compulsion 740 n.
lawlessness 954 n.
brutish
animal 365 adj.
barbaric 869 adj.
plebeian 869 adj.
discourteous 885 adj.
cruel 898 adj.
sensual 944 adj.
brutishness
moral insensibility 820 n.
ill-breeding 847 n.
BSc
academic title 870 n.
BTU
thermometry 379 n.
bubble
insubstantial thing 4 n.
brief span 114 n.
bladder 194 n.
sphere 252 n.
effervesce 318 vb.
lightness 323 n.
brittleness 330 n.
flow 350 vb.
bubble 355 n.vb.
deception 542 n.
bauble 639 n.
bubbly
wine 301 n.
gaseous 336 adj.
bubbly 355 adj.
excited 821 adj.
buccaneer
mariner 270 n.
militarist 722 n.
rob 788 vb.
robber 789 n.
buck
leap 312 vb.
mammal 365 n.
male animal 372 n.
coinage 797 n.
paper money 797 n.
fop 848 n.
— up
be relieved 831 vb.
relieve 831 vb.
be cheerful 833 vb.
cheer 833 vb.
hope 852 vb.
give courage 855 vb.
bucket
vessel 194 n.
bucket down
rain 350 vb.
bucket shop
bourse 618 n.
market 796 n.
buckle
join 45 vb.
fastening 47 n.
distortion 246 n.
distort 246 vb.
make concave 255 vb.
— to
be resolute 599 vb.
undertake 672 vb.
be active 678 vb.
buckler
armour 713 n.
buckram
bookbinding 589 n.
pretension 850 n.
buckshot
ammunition 723 n.
buckskin
skin 226 n.
bucolic
agrarian 370 adj.
poetic 593 adj.
bud
grow 36 vb.
origin 68 n.
source 156 n.
growth 157 n.
result 157 vb.
generate 167 vb.
expand 197 vb.
swelling 253 n.
implant 303 vb.
flower 366 n.
Buddha
sage 500 n.
religious teacher 973 n.
Buddhahood
sanctity 979 n.
Buddhism
philosophy 449 n.
religious faith 973 n.
Buddhist
religionist 973 n.
budding
beginning 68 adj.
new 126 adj.
young 130 adj.
expanded 197 adj.
buddy
male 372 n.
colleague 707 n.
chum 880 n.
budge
be in motion 265 vb.
move 265 vb.
budgerigar
bird 365 n.
budget
provision 633 n.
provide 633 vb.
accounts 808 n.
account 808 vb.
budget price
cheapness 812 n.
buff
skin 226 n.
smooth 258 vb.
rub 333 vb.
brown 430 adj.
yellow 433 adj.
enthusiast 504 n.
clean 648 vb.
buffalo
cattle 365 n.
buffer
intermediary 231 n.
male 372 n.
protection 660 n.
obstacle 702 n.
defence 713 n.
buffer state
contiguity 202 n.
intermediary 231 n.
political organization 733 n.
buffet
café 192 n.
cabinet 194 n.
knock 279 n.
strike 279 vb.
evil 616 n.
ill-treat 645 vb.
wound 655 vb.
corporal punishment 963 n.
buffoon
fool 501 n.
entertainer 594 n.
bungler 697 n.
humorist 839 n.
laughingstock 851 n.
buffoonery
foolery 497 n.
wit 839 n.
ridiculousness 849 n.

bug
microorganism 196 n.
insect 365 n.
hear 415 vb.
be curious 453 vb.
enthusiast 504 n.
infection 651 n.
torment 827 vb.
enrage 891 vb.
bugbear
bane 659 n.
false alarm 665 n.
intimidation 854 n.
hateful object 888 n.
demon 970 n.
buggery
illicit love 951 n.
bugging
listening 415 n.
Buggins's turn
sequence 65 n.
buggy
automobile 274 n.
carriage 274 n.
bugle
play music 413 vb.
horn 414 n.
call 547 n.
war 718 n.
build
composition 56 n.
compose 56 vb.
produce 164 vb.
form 243 n.vb.
elevate 310 vb.
structure 331 n.
— up
augment 36 vb.
make complete 54 vb.
bring together 74 vb.
strengthen 162 vb.
urbanize 192 vb.
enlarge 197 vb.
make higher 209 vb.
elevate 310 vb.
advertise 528 vb.
store 632 vb.
builder
producer 164 n.
lifter 310 n.
artisan 686 n.
building
edifice 164 n.
production 164 n.
house 192 n.
housing 192 n.
ornamental art 844 n.
building block
building material 631 n.
materials 631 n.
building society
pawnshop 784 n.
treasury 799 n.
buildup
increase 36 n.
composition 56 n.
overestimation 482 n.
advertisement 528 n.
store 632 n.
built-in
intrinsic 5 adj.
component 58 adj.
accompanying 89 adj.
interior 224 adj.
built-in obsolescence
waste 634 n.
built on a rock
fixed 153 adj.
built on sand
unstable 152 adj.
unsafe 661 adj.
built over
covered 226 adj.
built-up
urban 192 adj.
built-up area
district 184 n.
housing 192 n.
bulb
source 156 n.
sphere 252 n.
swelling 253 n.
plant 366 n.
lamp 420 n.
bulbous
expanded 197 adj.
rotund 252 adj.
bulge
increment 36 n.
grow 36 vb.
convexity 253 n.
swelling 253 n.
be convex 253 vb.
battleground 724 n.
bulging
full 54 adj.
convex 253 adj.
projecting 254 adj.
bulk
quantity 26 n.
main part 32 n.
be great 32 vb.
chief part 52 n.
greater number 104 n.
bulk 195 n.
thickness 205 n.
convexity 253 n.
food content 301 n.
— large
be great 32 vb.
be important 638 vb.
bulkhead
partition 231 n.
obstacle 702 n.
bulky
substantial 3 adj.
great 32 adj.
large 195 adj.
bull
cattle 365 n.
male animal 372 n.
mistake 495 n.
silly talk 515 n.
solecism 565 n.
labour 682 n.
decree 737 n.
speculate 791 vb.
purchaser 792 n.
overcharge 811 vb.
ridiculousness 849 n.
bulldog
dog 365 n.
brave person 855 n.
bulldoze
demolish 165 vb.
compel 740 vb.
bulldozer
destroyer 168 n.
flattener 216 n.
smoother 258 n.
vehicle 274 n.
ram 279 n.
pulverizer 332 n.
bullet
sphere 252 n.
speeder 277 n.
missile 287 n.
ammunition 723 n.
missile weapon 723 n.
means of execution 964 n.
bulletin
report 524 n.
news 529 n.
correspondence 588 n.
bulletproof
invulnerable 660 adj.
defended 713 adj.
bullfight
duel 716 n.
bullfighter
contender 716 n.
combatant 722 n.
bull-headed
obstinate 602 adj.
bull in a china shop
turmoil 61 n.
bungler 697 n.
bullion
bullion 797 n.
bullish
buying 792 adj.
dear 811 adj.
bullock
eunuch 161 n.
beast of burden 273 n.
cattle 365 n.
male animal 372 n.
bullring
arena 724 n.
bull's-eye
centre 225 n.
lamp 420 n.
objective 617 n.
bully
violent creature 176 n.
combatant 722 n.
tyrant 735 n.
oppress 735 vb.
torment 827 vb.
frighten 854 vb.
coward 856 n.
desperado 857 n.
low fellow 869 n.
insolent person 878 n.
be insolent 878 vb.
be malevolent 898 vb.
threaten 900 vb.
ruffian 904 n.
bad person 938 n.
— into
induce 612 vb.
compel 740 vb.
bulrush
grass 366 n.
bulwark
prop 218 n.
protection 660 n.
refuge 662 n.
obstacle 702 n.
defence 713 n.
fortification 713 n.
bum
wanderer 268 n.
idler 679 n.
beggar 763 n.
low fellow 869 n.
bum around
wander 267 vb.
bumble
be clumsy 695 vb.
bumble bee
insect 365 n.
bumbledom
governance 733 n.
jurisdiction 955 n.
bumbler
bungler 697 n.
bumf
reading matter 589 n.
bump
convexity 253 n.
swelling 253 n.
protuberance 254 n.
be rough 259 vb.
move slowly 278 vb.
collision 279 n.
agitation 318 n.
nonresonance 405 n.
wound 655 n.
— into
collide 279 vb.
meet 295 vb.
— off
murder 362 vb.
— up
augment 36 vb.
invigorate 174 vb.
bumper
plenitude 54 n.
intermediary 231 n.
draught 301 n.

shelter 662 n.
defence 713 n.
bumper crop
plenty 635 n.
bumper-to-bumper
contiguous 202 adj.
bumpkin
dunce 501 n.
country-dweller 869 n.
bumptious
prideful 871 adj.
vain 873 adj.
insolent 878 adj.
bumpy
nonuniform 17 adj.
discontinuous 72 adj.
rough 259 adj.
bum's rush
ejection 300 n.
bumsucker
toady 879 n.
bun
hair 259 n.
cereals 301 n.
pastries 301 n.
hairdressing 843 n.
Bunbury
untruth 543 n.
pretext 614 n.
bunch
cohere 48 vb.
band 74 n.
bunch 74 n.
crowd 74 n.
bring together 74 vb.
congregate 74 vb.
party 708 n.
bundle
bunch 74 n.
bring together 74 vb.
bag 194 n.
collection 632 n.
store 632 n.vb.
— off
hasten 680 vb.
eject 300 vb.
bundle of nerves
moral sensibility 819 n.
bunfight
feasting 301 n.
amusement 837 n.
social gathering 882 n.
bung
covering 226 n.
stopper 264 n.
propel 287 vb.
bungalow
house 192 n.
bunged up
closed 264 adj.
diseased 651 adj.
bungle
lose a chance 138 vb.
neglect 458 vb.
mistake 495 n.
blunder 495 vb.
bungling 695 n.
be clumsy 695 vb.
failure 728 n.
fail 728 vb.
bungler
fool 501 n.
bungler 697 n.
hinderer 702 n.
bunion
swelling 253 n.
bunk
bed 218 n.
empty talk 515 n.
bunker
cellar 194 n.
storage 632 n.
obstacle 702 n.
defences 713 n.
bunk-house
inn 192 n.
bunkum
empty talk 515 n.
falsehood 541 n.
boast 877 n.
Bunsen burner
furnace 383 n.
bunt
collide 279 vb.
bunting
flag 547 n.
buoy
sailing aid 269 n.
signpost 547 n.
buoyancy
energy 160 n.
lightness 323 n.
elasticity 328 n.
hope 852 n.
buoyant
swimming 269 adj.
cheerful 833 adj.
hoping 852 adj.
buoy up
support 218 vb.
elevate 310 vb.
bur
coherence 48 n.
burble
flow 350 vb.
faintness 401 n.
reason badly 477 vb.
be foolish 499 vb.
burden
load 193 vb.
gravity 322 n.
make heavy 322 vb.
vocal music 412 n.
topic 452 n.
verse form 593 n.
redundance 637 n.
ill-treat 645 vb.
bane 659 n.
difficulty 700 n.
encumbrance 702 n.
hinder 702 vb.
adversity 731 n.
oppress 735 vb.
worry 825 n.
annoyance 827 n.
burdened
bearing 273 adj.
burden of proof
demonstration 478 n.
burdensome
bad 645 adj.
laborious 682 adj.
difficult 700 adj.
hindering 702 adj.
annoying 827 adj.
bureau
cabinet 194 n.
workshop 687 n.
jurisdiction 955 n.
bureaucracy
management 689 n.
governance 733 n.
government 733 n.
bureaucrat
official 690 n.
officer 741 n.
burgee
flag 547 n.
burgeon
grow 36 vb.
reproduce itself 167 vb.
be fruitful 171 vb.
expand 197 vb.
flower 366 n.
burgeoning
young 130 adj.
burgh
housing 192 n.
burgher
native 191 n.
free person 744 n.
burglar
thief 789 n.
burglary
stealing 788 n.
burgle
intrude 297 vb.
steal 788 vb.
burgomaster
officer 741 n.
burgundy
wine 301 n.
redness 431 n.
burial
immersion 303 n.
interment 364 n.
concealment 525 n.
obliteration 550 n.
detention 747 n.
burial chamber
tomb 364 n.
burial of the dead
Christian rite 988 n.
burial of the hatchet
amnesty 506 n.
peace 717 n.
burial place
cemetery 364 n.
burial service
obsequies 364 n.
buried
deep 211 adj.
inserted 303 adj.
dead 361 adj.
buried 364 adj.
neglected 458 adj.
forgotten 506 adj.
concealed 525 adj.
imprisoned 747 adj.
secluded 883 adj.
burin
engraving 555 n.
burka
robe 228 n.
Burke's Peerage
directory 87 n.
burl
solid body 324 n.
burlesque
imitate 20 vb.
foolery 497 n.
exaggeration 546 n.
misrepresentation 552 n.
doggerel 593 n.
stage play 594 n.
be witty 839 vb.
funny 849 adj.
satire 851 n.
satirize 851 vb.
burly
stalwart 162 adj.
fleshy 195 adj.
burn
destroy 165 vb.
lay waste 165 vb.
dry 342 vb.
stream 350 n.
inter 364 vb.
be hot 379 vb.
burning 381 n.
burn 381 vb.
shine 417 vb.
blacken 428 vb.
embrown 430 vb.
waste 634 vb.
wound 655 n.
attack 712 vb.
be excited 821 vb.
desire 859 vb.
be in love 887 vb.
resent 891 vb.
— alive
kill 362 vb.
execute 963 vb.
— in
mark 547 vb.
— incense
worship 981 vb.
perform ritual 988 vb.
— one's boats/ bridges
initiate 68 vb.
be resolute 599 vb.
choose 605 vb.
— one's fingers
be foolish 499 vb.
be unskilful 695 vb.

lose 772 vb.
be rash 857 vb.
— out
burn 381 vb.
extinguish 382 vb.
waste 634 vb.
— the candle at both ends
waste 634 vb.
be prodigal 815 vb.
revel 837 vb.
be intemperate 943 vb.
— the midnight oil
be late 136 vb.
study 536 vb.
be busy 678 vb.
work 682 vb.
— up
destroy 165 vb.
burn 381 vb.
burnable
combustible 385 adj.
burner
burning 381 n.
furnace 383 n.
torch 420 n.
burning
painful 377 adj.
fiery 379 adj.
burning 381 n.
pungent 388 adj.
fervent 818 adj.
burnish
smooth 258 vb.
rub 333 vb.
make bright 417 vb.
decorate 844 vb.
burnous
cloak 228 n.
burnt
culinary 301 adj.
dry 342 adj.
heated 381 adj.
unsavoury 391 adj.
burnt offering
propitiation 941 n.
oblation 981 n.
burnt out
weakened 163 adj.
burn-up
speeding 277 n.
burp
eruct 300 vb.
breathe 352 vb.
burr
roughness 259 n.
perforator 263 n.
rasp 407 vb.
engraving 555 n.
dialect 560 n.
neologize 560 vb.
pronunciation 577 n.
voice 577 vb.
speech defect 580 n.
burro
beast of burden 273 n.
burrow
place oneself 187 vb.
dwelling 192 n.
dwell 192 vb.
cavity 255 n.
excavation 255 n.
make concave 255 vb.
pierce 263 vb.
descend 309 vb.
lurk 523 vb.
refuge 662 n.
bursar
consignee 754 n.
treasurer 798 n.
bursary
subvention 703 n.
reward 962 n.
burst
break 46 vb.
rend 46 vb.
be dispersed 75 vb.
instant 116 n.
outbreak 176 n.
be violent 176 vb.
open 263 vb.
spurt 277 n.
be brittle 330 vb.
be loud 400 vb.
bang 402 vb.
activity 678 n.
miscarry 728 vb.
— forth
begin 68 vb.
expand 197 vb.
— in
burst in 297 vb.
— into flame
be hot 379 vb.
— into tears
weep 836 vb.
— in upon
intrude 297 vb.
— out
be violent 176 vb.
be excitable 822 vb.
get angry 891 vb.
— upon
meet 295 vb.
surprise 508 vb.
— with
superabound 637 vb.
bursting at the seams
full 54 adj.
redundant 637 adj.
bury
implant 303 vb.
insert 303 vb.
inter 364 vb.
conceal 525 vb.
obliterate 550 vb.
store 632 vb.
imprison 747 vb.
— one's head in the sand
avoid 620 vb.
— the hatchet
forget 506 vb.
make peace 719 vb.
forgive 909 vb.
bus
conveyance 267 n.
automobile 274 n.
bus 274 n.
busby
headgear 228 n.
armour 713 n.
bus driver
driver 268 n.
carrier 273 n.
bush
desert 172 n.
district 184 n.
lining 227 n.
plain 348 n.
tree 366 n.
wood 366 n.
bushel
great quantity 32 n.
certain quantity 104 n.
metrology 465 n.
bush-fighting
warfare 718 n.
bush hat
headgear 228 n.
bushido
code of duty 917 n.
probity 929 n.
bushmen
humankind 371 n.
bush telegraph
rumour 529 n.
telecommunication 531 n.
bushy
dense 324 adj.
arboreal 366 adj.
business
affairs 154 n.
production 164 n.
topic 452 n.
dramaturgy 594 n.
intention 617 n.
pursuit 619 n.
business 622 n.
function 622 n.
policy 623 n.
importance 638 n.
undertaking 672 n.
action 676 n.
activity 678 n.
trade 791 n.
business association
business 622 n.
association 706 n.
business deal
trade 791 n.
business house
workshop 687 n.
corporation 708 n.
businesslike
orderly 60 adj.
businesslike 622 adj.
industrious 678 adj.
busker
musician 413 n.
entertainer 594 n.
buskin
footwear 228 n.
drama 594 n.
busman's holiday
exertion 682 n.
buss
fishing boat 275 n.
endearment 889 n.
caress 889 vb.
bussing
transference 272 n.
bus stop
stopping place 145 n.
bust
break 46 vb.
bosom 253 n.
monument 548 n.
image 551 n.
sculpture 554 n.
fail 728 vb.
miscarry 728 vb.
poor 801 adj.
festivity 837 n.
honours 866 n.
gluttony 947 n.
bustee
housing 192 n.
buster
male 372 n.
bustle
garment 228 n.
motion 265 n.
commotion 318 n.
be agitated 318 vb.
busy oneself 622 vb.
activity 678 n.
be busy 678 vb.
haste 680 n.
hasten 680 vb.
bustling
eventful 154 adj.
busy 678 adj.
excited 821 adj.
busy
eventful 154 adj.
influential 178 adj.
businesslike 622 adj.
employ 622 vb.
doing 676 adj.
busy 678 adj.
labouring 682 adj.
excited 821 adj.
— oneself
pursue 619 vb.
busy oneself 622 vb.
undertake 672 vb.
do 676 vb.
be busy 678 vb.
busybody
inquisitive person 453 n.
meddler 678 n.
adviser 691 n.
busy person
enthusiast 504 n.
volunteer 597 n.
busy person 678 n.
but
in return 31 adv.

unconformably 84 adv.
qualification 468 n.
nevertheless 468 adv.
butane
fuel 385 n.
butch
male 372 adj.
butcher
violent creature 176 n.
killer 362 n.
slaughter 362 vb.
provider 633 n.
ruffian 904 n.
butler
provider 633 n.
retainer 742 n.
butt
vat 194 n.
impulse 279 n.
collide 279 vb.
tobacco 388 n.
fool 501 n.
objective 617 n.
strike at 712 vb.
firearm 723 n.
laughingstock 851 n.
— away
repel 292 vb.
parry 713 vb.
— in
interfere 231 vb.
meddle 678 vb.
butte
small hill 209 n.
butt end
remainder 41 n.
extremity 69 n.
butter
overlay 226 vb.
smooth 258 vb.
cookery 301 n.
softness 327 n.
lubricate 334 vb.
fat 357 n.
grease 357 vb.
— up
flatter 925 vb.
buttercup
plant 366 n.
yellowness 433 n.
butterfingers
bungler 697 n.
butterflies
agitation 318 n.
nervousness 854 n.
butterfly
insect 365 n.
inattention 456 n.
waverer 601 n.
buttermilk
milk 301 n.
fat 357 n.
butterscotch
sweets 301 n.
brownness 430 n.
buttocks
buttocks 238 n.
button
fastening 47 n.
swelling 253 n.
close 264 vb.
trifle 639 n.
— up
join 45 vb.
wear 228 vb.
buttoned-up
reticent 525 adj.
completed 725 adj.
buttonhole
fastening 47 n.
orifice 263 n.
approach 289 vb.
fragrance 396 n.
be loquacious 581 vb.
speak to 583 vb.
converse 584 vb.
retain 778 vb.
be tedious 838 vb.
ornamentation 844 n.
button-through
tailored 228 adj.
buttress
stabilizer 153 n.
strengthen 162 vb.
prop 218 n.
support 218 vb.
projection 254 n.
corroborate 466 vb.
fortification 713 n.
church exterior 990 n.
butts
arena 724 n.
butty
meal 301 n.
chum 880 n.
buxom
fleshy 195 adj.
cheerful 833 adj.
personable 841 adj.
shapely 841 adj.
buy
believe 485 vb.
acquire 771 vb.
purchase 792 n.vb.
expend 806 vb.
— and sell
trade 791 vb.
— a pig in a poke
gamble 618 vb.
be rash 857 vb.
— off
bribe 612 vb.
deliver 668 vb.
buyer
owner 776 n.
recipient 782 n.
purchaser 792 n.
buyer's market
market 796 n.
cheapness 812 n.
buzz
be near 200 vb.
fly 271 vb.
faintness 401 n.
sound faint 401 vb.
roll 403 n.
resound 404 vb.
hiss 406 vb.
ululate 409 vb.
rumour 529 n.
converse 584 vb.
obstruct 702 vb.
— off
decamp 296 vb.
buzzard
bird 365 n.
buzzer
megaphone 400 n.
signal 547 n.
buzz word
word 559 n.
neology 560 n.
by
akin 11 adj.
before 119 adv.
caused 157 adj.
by means of 629 adv.
by accident
by chance 159 adv.
by a head
at intervals 201 adv.
by and by
prospectively 124 adv.
by and large
on the whole 52 adv.
generally 79 adv.
by appointment
chosen 605 adj.
by-blow
bastardy 954 n.
by chance
by chance 159 adv.
by degrees
by degrees 27 adv.
piecemeal 53 adv.
gradatim 278 adv.
by design
purposely 617 adv.
by dint of
powerfully 160 adv.
by means of 629 adv.
by-election
substitution 150 n.
vote 605 n.
by fair means or foul
by means of 629 adv.
dishonestly 930 adv.
by far
eminently 34 adv.
by fits and starts
confusedly 61 adv.
fitfully 142 adv.
jerkily 318 adv.
capriciously 604 adv.
by force
violently 176 adv.
by force 740 adv.
bygone
past 125 adj.
archaism 127 n.
by guess and by God
experimentally 461 adv.
intuitively 476 adv.
at random 618 adv.
by halves
incompletely 55 adv.
by hand
in transit 272 adv.
laboriously 682 adv.
by heart
in memory 505 adv.
by inches
by degrees 27 adv.
piecemeal 53 adv.
gradatim 278 adv.
by instalments
piecemeal 53 adv.
by instinct
intuitively 476 adv.
bylaw, byelaw
rule 81 n.
legislation 953 n.
legally 953 adv.
by law
duly 915 adv.
by leaps and bounds
swiftly 277 adv.
forward 285 adv.
by leaps and bounds 312 adv.
by means of
through 628 adv.
by means of 629 adv.
byname
name 561 n.
by no means
in no way 33 adv.
by oneself
alone 88 adj.
singly 88 adv.
by order
legally 953 adv.
bypass
avoid 620 vb.
road 624 n.
circuit 626 vb.
byplay
gesture 547 n.
dramaturgy 594 n.
by-product
extra 40 n.
sequel 67 n.
concomitant 89 n.
effect 157 n.
product 164 n.
by proxy
instead 150 adv.
by proxy 751 adv.
on behalf 755 adv.
byre
stable 192 n.
cattle pen 369 n.
by request
desirously 859 adv.

by right
duly 915 adv.
bystander
presence 189 n.
spectator 441 n.
by storm
violently 176 adv.
byte
data processing 86 n.
by the back door
stealthily 525 adv.
by the book
in order 60 adv.
to rule 81 adv.
conformably 83 adv.
by the clock
to rule 81 adv.
by the light of nature
experimentally 461 adv.
intuitively 476 adv.
by the skin of one's teeth
slightly 33 adv.
by the way
concerning 9 adv.
unrelatedly 10 adv.
incidentally 137 adv.
en passant 305 adv.
at random 618 adv.
by trial and error
experimentally 461 adv.
byway
path 624 n.
by way of
towards 281 adv.
via 624 adv.
by way of explanation
in plain words 520 adv.
byword
maxim 496 n.
laughingstock 851 n.
object of scorn 867 n.
Byzantine
olden 127 adj.
Byzantine art
art 551 n.

C

cab
cab 274 n.
locomotive 274 n.
cabal
planner 623 n.
plot 623 n.
party 708 n.
cabaret
stage show 594 n.
theatre 594 n.
place of amusement 837 n.
cabbage
inertness 175 n.
vegetable 301 n.
cabbala
latency 523 n.
occultism 984 n.
cabby
driver 268 n.
caber
missile 287 n.
cabin
small house 192 n.
chamber 194 n.
cabin boy
mariner 270 n.
naval man 722 n.
servant 742 n.
cabin cruiser
boat 275 n.
cabinet
cabinet 194 n.
chamber 194 n.
stand 218 n.
storage 632 n.
management 689 n.
director 690 n.
council 692 n.
cabinet-maker
artisan 686 n.
Cabinet seat
position of authority 733 n.
cable
cable 47 n.
electronics 160 n.
fibre 208 n.
information 524 n.
message 529 n.
telecommunication 531 n.
cablecar
tram 274 n.
cable railway
train 274 n.
lifter 310 n.
cableway
railway 624 n.
cabochon
gem 844 n.
caboose
train 274 n.
heater 383 n.
cabriolet
carriage 274 n.
cache
concealment 525 n.
hiding-place 527 n.
store 632 n.
cachet
label 547 n.
repute 866 n.
cachexia
weakness 163 n.
ill health 651 n.
cachinnation
loudness 400 n.
cry 408 n.
laughter 835 n.
cachou
sweet thing 392 n.
scent 396 n.
cack-handed
clumsy 695 adj.
cackle
ululate 409 vb.
chatter 581 n.
laughter 835 n.
laugh 835 vb.
cacography
spelling 558 n.
lettering 586 n.
cacology
solecism 565 n.
cacophony
stridor 407 n.
discord 411 n.
inelegance 576 n.
cactus
prickle 256 n.
plant 366 n.
cad
vulgarian 847 n.
low fellow 869 n.
hateful object 888 n.
cad 938 n.
cadastral
listed 87 adj.
metrical 465 adj.
cadaver
corpse 363 n.
cadaverous
lean 206 adj.
cadaverous 363 adj.
colourless 426 adj.
caddie, caddy
bearer 273 n.
carry 273 vb.
servant 742 n.
cadence
descent 309 n.
sound 398 n.
melody 410 n.
prosody 593 n.
cadenza
musical note 410 n.
musical piece 412 n.
cadet
posteriority 120 n.
young 130 adj.
beginner 538 n.
cadge
beg 761 vb.
be parsimonious 816 vb.
cadger
idler 679 n.
beggar 763 n.
niggard 816 n.
cadre
band 74 n.
personnel 686 n.
party 708 n.
caduceus
badge of rule 743 n.
caducity
transience 114 n.
old age 131 n.
weakness 163 n.
Caesar
sovereign 741 n.
Caesarian section
obstetrics 167 n.
caesura
separation 46 n.
discontinuity 72 n.
prosody 593 n.
cafard
melancholy 834 n.
sullenness 893 n.
café, cafeteria
café 192 n.
cookery 301 n.
café au lait
soft drink 310 n.
brown 430 adj.
caffeine
tonic 658 n.
caftan, kaftan
robe 228 n.
shirt 228 n.
cage
stable 192 n.
compartment 194 n.
receptacle 194 n.
circumscribe 232 vb.
enclosure 235 n.
enclose 235 vb.
break in 369 vb.
imprison 747 vb.
lockup 748 n.
cagebird
bird 365 n.
cagey
reticent 525 adj.
cunning 698 adj.
cautious 858 adj.
Cain
murderer 362 n.
Cainozoic
secular 110 adj.
cairn
small hill 209 n.
signpost 547 n.
monument 548 n.
caisson
box 194 n.
arsenal 723 n.
cajole
befool 542 vb.
induce 612 vb.
request 761 vb.
flatter 925 vb.
cajolery
inducement 612 n.
flattery 925 n.
cake
cohere 48 vb.
pastries 301 n.
solid body 324 n.
be dense 324 vb.
sweet thing 392 n.
make unclean 649 vb.
caked
dense 324 adj.
dirty 649 adj.

cakes and ale
food 301 n.
enjoyment 824 n.
cakewalk
dance 837 n.
calabash
vessel 194 n.
calaboose
lockup 748 n.
calamitous
evil 616 adj.
harmful 645 adj.
adverse 731 adj.
calamity
evil 616 n.
misfortune 731 n.
calcify
harden 326 vb.
calcination
burning 381 n.
calcium
food content 301 n.
calculate
do sums 86 vb.
measure 465 vb.
estimate 480 vb.
expect 507 vb.
intend 617 vb.
plan 623 vb.
be cautious 858 vb.
— on
belive 485 vb.
calculated (to)
tending 179 adj.
predetermined 608 adj.
calculating
intelligent 498 adj.
calculation
numeration 86 n.
measurement 465 n.
estimate 480 n.
expectation 507 n.
intention 617 n.
caution 858 n.
calculator
counting instrument 86 n.
enumerator 86 n.
calculus
mathematics 86 n.
calefaction
heating 381 n.
calendar
directory 87 n.
list 87 n.
fix the time 108 vb.
chronology 117 n.
record 548 vb.
reference book 589 n.
calendar month
period 110 n.
calendrical
chronological 117 adj.
calends, kalends
date 108 n.
calf
young creature 132 n.
skin 226 n.
leg 267 n.
cattle 365 n.
bookbinding 589 n.
calf love
love 887 n.
calibrate
graduate 27 vb.
gauge 465 vb.
calibre
sort 77 n.
size 195 n.
breadth 205 n.
intelligence 498 n.
firearm 723 n.
calico
textile 222 n.
caliph
sovereign 741 n.
caliphate
position of authority 733 n.
call
enter 297 vb.
loudness 400 n.
be loud 400 vb.
cry 408 n.vb.
ululation 409 n.
ululate 409 vb.
musical note 410 n.
communicate 524 vb.
publication 528 n.
call 547 n.
name 561 vb.
motive 612 n.
command 737 n.vb.
desire 859 n.vb.
social round 882 n.
visit 882 vb.
prayers 981 n.
church ministry 985 n.
— a halt
halt 145 vb.
restrain 747 vb.
abrogate 752 vb.
— a spade a spade
speak plainly 573 vb.
be artless 699 vb.
— attention to
attract notice 455 vb.
— away
distract 456 vb.
— down on
desire 859 vb.
curse 899 vb.
— for
require 627 vb.
request 761 vb.
— forth
incite 612 vb.
excite 821 vb.
— in
bring together 74 vb.
admit 299 vb.
consult 691 vb.
visit 882 vb.
claim 915 vb.
— in question
cause doubt 486 vb.
negate 533 vb.
— into being
initiate 68 vb.
generate 167 vb.
— into play
dispose of 673 vb.
— it a day
terminate 69 vb.
cease 145 vb.
— names
not respect 921 vb.
dispraise 924 vb.
— off
halt 145 vb.
abrogate 752 vb.
— on
consult 691 vb.
entreat 761 vb.
request 761 vb.
worship 981 vb.
— one's bluff
defy 711 vb.
— one's own
possess 773 vb.
— out
halt 145 vb.
cry 408 vb.
resist 715 vb.
fight 716 vb.
— over
number 86 vb.
— sir/madam
be courteous 884 vb.
— the roll
number 86 vb.
name 561 vb.
— the tune
motivate 612 vb.
dominate 733 vb.
— to
speak to 583 vb.
— to mind
remember 505 vb.
— to order
order 60 vb.
reprove 924 vb.
— upon
command 737 vb.
impose a duty 917 vb.
callboy
stagehand 594 n.
servant 742 n.
called
named 561 adj.
called for
required 627 adj.
salable 793 adj.
called-up
assembled 74 adj.
caller
incomer 297 n.
sociable person 882 n.
call girl
prostitute 952 n.
calligraphy
art 551 n.
lettering 586 n.
calling
vocation 622 n.
social round 882 n.
callipers
gauge 465 n.
callisthenics
athletics 162 n.
exercise 682 n.
call of duty
duty 917 n.
callous
hard 326 adj.
unfeeling 375 adj.
thick-skinned 820 adj.
cruel 898 adj.
pitiless 906 adj.
wicked 934 adj.
calloused
hard 326 adj.
callousness
moral insensibility 820 n.
inhumanity 898 n.
callow
young 130 adj.
immature 670 adj.
artless 699 adj.
call to arms
call 547 n.
war measures 718 n.
call to prayer
call 547 n.
prayers 981 n.
call-up
assemblage 74 n.
war measures 718 n.
calm
moderation 177 n.
moderate 177 adj.
assuage 177 vb.
flat 216 adj.
smoothness 258 n.
smooth 258 adj.
quietude 266 n.
tranquil 266 adj.
silent 399 adj.
dissuade 613 vb.
inaction 677 n.
impassive 820 adj.
inexcitable 823 adj.
tranquillize 823 vb.
relieve 831 vb.
indifferent 860 adj.
unastonished 865 adj.
calmative
moderator 177 n.

calm before the storm
reversion 148 n.
caloric
heat 379 n.
warm 379 adj.
calorie(s)
energy 160 n.
food content 301 n.
dieting 301 n.
thermometry 379 n.
calorific
heating 381 adj.
calumniate
defame 926 vb.
accuse 928 vb.
calumny
rumour 529 n.
slur 867 n.
scurrility 899 n.
censure 924 n.
calumny 926 n.
false charge 928 n.
calvary
suffering 825 n.
church interior 990 n.
calve
reproduce itself 167 vb.
Calvinism
Protestantism 976 n.
sectarianism 978 n.
calypso
vocal music 412 n.
calyx
receptacle 194 n.
flower 366 n.
camaraderie
friendliness 880 n.
sociality 882 n.
camber
obliquity 220 n.
make oblique 220 vb.
curve 248 n.
camber 253 n.
be convex 253 vb.
cambric
textile 222 n.
camel
beast of burden 273 n.
mammal 365 n.
cameleer
rider 268 n.
cavalry 722 n.
camellia
tree 366 n.
cameo
relievo 254 n.
sculpture 554 n.
description 590 n.
acting 594 n.
jewellery 844 n.
camera
camera 442 n.
broadcasting 531 n.
recording instrument 549 n.
photography 551 n.
cameraman
recorder 549 n.
photography 551 n.
camouflage
assimilation 18 n.
mimicry 20 n.
transform 147 vb.
conceal 525 vb.
disguise 527 n.
camouflaged
invisible 444 adj.
disguised 525 adj.
camp
station 187 n.
place oneself 187 vb.
abode 192 n.
dwell 192 vb.
shelter 662 n.
party 708 n.
army 722 n.
amuse oneself 837 vb.
affected 850 adj.
— it up
act 594 vb.
be witty 839 vb.
be affected 850 vb.
campaign
marching 267 n.
undertaking 672 n.
action 676 n.
do 676 vb.
exertion 682 n.
exert oneself 682 vb.
tactics 688 n.
fight 716 n.vb.
warfare 718 n.
wage war 718 vb.
— against
deprecate 762 vb.
campaigner
doer 676 n.
soldier 722 n.
campanile
high structure 209 n.
church exterior 990 n.
campanologist
campanology 412 n.
instrumentalist 413 n.
campanulate
concave 255 adj.
camper
traveller 268 n.
automobile 274 n.
campfire
focus 76 n.
social gathering 882 n.
camp follower
follower 284 n.
dependant 742 n.
camphor
resin 357 n.
scent 396 n.
preserver 666 n.
campus
focus 76 n.
meeting place 192 n.
academy 539 n.
can
be able 160 vb.
cup 194 n.
small box 194 n.
vessel 194 n.
preserve 666 vb.
gaol 748 n.
canal
cavity 255 n.
transport 272 n.
conduit 351 n.
access 624 n.
canalize, canalise
make concave 255 vb.
direct 689 vb.
canapé
hors-d'oeuvres 301 n.
canard
rumour 529 n.
fable 543 n.
false alarm 665 n.
canary
bird 365 n.
canasta
card game 837 n.
cancan
dance 837 n.
cancan dancer
entertainer 594 n.
cancel
nullify 2 vb.
set off 31 vb.
destroy 165 vb.
counteract 182 vb.
obliterate 550 vb.
relinquish 621 vb.
stop using 674 vb.
abrogate 752 vb.
not observe 769 vb.
not retain 779 vb.
forgive 909 vb.
— out
be contrary 14 vb.
counteract 182 vb.
tell against 467 vb.
cancellation
negation 533 n.
cancer
badness 645 n.
cancer 651 n.
blight 659 n.
Cancer
zodiac 321 n.
candelabra
lamp 420 n.
candid
true 494 adj.
undisguised 522 adj.
informative 524 adj.
veracious 540 adj.
artless 699 adj.
detracting 926 adj.
trustworthy 929 adj.
candidate
respondent 460 n.
testee 461 n.
contender 716 n.
petitioner 763 n.
hoper 852 n.
desirer 859 n.
candidate, be a
offer oneself 759 vb.
candidature
vote 605 n.
offer 759 n.
Candide
ingenue 699 n.
candle
lighter 385 n.
torch 420 n.
ritual object 988 n.
candlelight
evening 129 n.
light 417 n.
glimmer 419 n.
Candlemas
holy day 988 n.
candle power
light 417 n.
metrology 465 n.
candlestick
lamp 420 n.
ritual object 988 n.
candlewick
textile 222 n.
candour
truth 494 n.
manifestation 522 n.
veracity 540 n.
artlessness 699 n.
probity 929 n.
candy
sweets 301 n.
sweet thing 392 n.
sweeten 392 vb.
cane
prop 218 n.
strike 279 vb.
spank 963 vb.
scourge 964 n.
canescent
grey 429 adj.
canine
dog 365 n.
animal 365 adj.
caning
corporal punishment 963 n.
canister
box 194 n.
small box 194 n.
canker
dilapidation 655 n.
blight 659 n.
cankered
diseased 651 adj.
cannabis
drug-taking 949 n.
canned
recorded 548 adj.
preserved 666 adj.
tipsy 949 adj.

canned goods
merchandise 795 n.
canned music
music 412 n.
cannibal
eater 301 n.
killer 362 n.
ruffian 904 n.
cannibalism
eating 301 n.
cannibalize, cannibalise
sunder 46 vb.
repair 656 vb.
cannon
gun 723 n.
cannonade
shoot 287 vb.
roll 403 n.
bombardment 712 n.
fire at 712 vb.
cannonball
sphere 252 n.
speeder 277 n.
missile 287 n.
ammunition 723 n.
cannon fodder
soldiery 722 n.
cannon into
collide 279 vb.
— off
recoil 280 vb.
cannot
be impotent 161 vb.
canny
knowing 490 adj.
intelligent 498 adj.
cunning 698 adj.
economical 814 adj.
cautious 858 adj.
canoe
row 269 vb.
rowing boat 275 n.
canoeing
aquatics 269 n.
canon
rule 81 n.
musical piece 412 n.
creed 485 n.
precept 693 n.
decree 737 n.
legislation 953 n.
theology 973 n.
scripture 975 n.
ecclesiarch 986 n.
office-book 988 n.
canoness
nun 986 n.
canonical
regulated 83 adj.
orthodox 976 adj.
canonical books
scripture 975 n.
canonical hours
church service 988 n.
canonical robes
vestments 989 n.
canonize, canonise
dignify 866 vb.
sanctify 979 vb.
canon law
precept 693 n.
law 953 n.
canopy
pavilion 192 n.
canopy 226 n.
screen 421 n., vb.
altar 990 n.
cant
obliquity 220 n.
be oblique 220 vb.
make oblique 220 vb.
propel 287 vb.
duplicity 541 n.
falsehood 541 n.
cant 541 vb.
slang 560 n.
dialectal 560 adj.
neologize 560 vb.
be affected 850 vb.
pietism 979 n.
false piety 980 n.
be impious 980 vb.
cantabile
musical 412 adj.
adagio 412 adv.
cantankerous
quarrelling 709 adj.
irascible 892 adj.
sullen 893 adj.
cantata
vocal music 412 n.
hymn 981 n.
canteen
café 192 n.
box 194 n.
canter
gait 265 n.
ride 267 vb.
canticle
vocal music 412 n.
hymn 981 n.
cantilever
prop 218 n.
canting
affected 850 adj.
canto
subdivision 53 n.
poem 593 n.
canton
district 184 n.
flag 547 n.
heraldry 547 n.
cantonment
station 187 n.
abode 192 n.
cantor
choir 413 n.
worshipper 981 n.
church officer 986 n.
can't stand
dislike 861 vb.
hate 888 vb.
canvas
textile 222 n.
canopy 226 n.
sail 275 n.
art equipment 553 n.
picture 553 n.
canvass
enquiry 459 n.
enquire 459 vb.
argue 475 vb.
publicity 528 n.
publish 528 vb.
confer 584 vb.
dissertate 591 vb.
vote 605 vb.
do 676 vb.
request 761 n.vb.
sell 793 vb.
canvasser
seller 793 n.
commender 923 n.
canyon
gap 201 n.
high land 209 n.
valley 255 n.
cap
be superior 34 vb.
culminate 34 vb.
vertex 213 n.
crown 213 vb.
covering 226 n.
cover 226 vb.
headgear 228 n.
stopper 264 n.
badge 547 n.
retaliate 714 vb.
explosive 723 n.
climax 725 vb.
capability
fitness 24 n.
ability 160 n.
influence 178 n.
skill 694 n.
facility 701 n.
capable
intrinsic 5 adj.
fit 24 adj.
powerful 160 adj.
possible 469 adj.
intelligent 498 adj.
capacious
great 32 adj.
spacious 183 adj.
recipient 194 adj.
large 195 adj.
capacity
essential part 5 n.
greatness 32 n.
plenitude 54 n.
inclusion 78 n.
ability 160 n.
room 183 n.
size 195 n.
limit 236 n.
possibility 469 n.
intelligence 498 n.
function 622 n.
means 629 n.
utility 640 n.
skill 694 n.
facility 701 n.
cap and bells
entertainer 594 n.
cap and gown
formal dress 228 n.
caparison
coverlet 226 n.
dressing 228 n.
dress 228 vb.
cape
cloak 228 n.
caper
ride 267 vb.
leap 312 n.vb.
condiment 389 n.
amuse oneself 837 vb.
dance 837 vb.
capillary
filament 208 n.
tube 263 n.
conduit 351 n.
cap in hand
supplicatory 761 adj.
servilely 879 adv.
respectful 920 adj.
capital
supreme 34 adj.
summit 213 n.
deadly 362 adj.
literal 558 adj.
means 629 n.
store 632 n.
important 638 adj.
best 644 adj.
super 644 adj.
position of authority 733 n.
estate 777 n.
funds 797 n.
wealth 800 n.
ornamental art 844 n.
capital city
city 184 n.
capital crime
vice 934 n.
lawbreaking 954 n.
capital-intensive
businesslike 622 adj.
capitalism
trade 791 n.
wealth 800 n.
capitalist
director 690 n.
master 741 n.
minter 797 n.
rich person 800 n.
capitalize, capitalise
profit by 137 vb.
use 673 vb.
capital letter
letter 558 n.
capital levy
taking 786 n.
tax 809 n.
capital punishment
capital punishment 963 n.

capitals
print-type 587 n.
capitation
numeration 86 n.
statistics 86 n.
capitulation
submission 721 n.
cap of maintenance
badge of rule 743 n.
capon
eunuch 161 n.
poultry 365 n.
male animal 372 n.
caponize, caponise
unman 161 vb.
caprice
musical piece 412 n.
ideality 513 n.
caprice 604 n.
whim 604 n.
affectation 850 n.
liking 859 n.
capricious
multiform 82 adj.
unconformable 84 adj.
transient 114 adj.
fitful 142 adj.
changeful 152 adj.
light-minded 456 adj.
unreliable 474 adj.
unexpected 508 adj.
tergiversating 603 adj.
capricious 604 adj.
capriciousness
fitfulness 142 n.
Capricorn
zodiac 321 n.
capsize
be unequal 29 vb.
derange 63 vb.
be inverted 221 vb.
invert 221 vb.
lower 311 vb.
capstan
lifter 310 n.
rotator 315 n.
capstone
summit 213 n.
capsule
receptacle 194 n.
covering 226 n.
flower 366 n.
medicine 658 n.
capsulize, capsulise
abstract 592 vb.
captain
come first 34 vb.
navigate 269 vb.
nautical personnel 270 n.
direct 689 vb.
director 690 n.
leader 690 n.
army officer 741 n.
naval officer 741 n.
captaincy
precedence 64 n.
directorship 689 n.
captain of industry
bigwig 638 n.
master 741 n.
caption
commentary 520 n.
indication 547 n.
label 547 n.
name 561 n.
phrase 563 n.
script 586 n.
edition 589 n.
captious
sophistical 477 adj.
capricious 604 adj.
irascible 892 adj.
disapproving 924 adj.
captivate
motivate 612 vb.
excite love 887 vb.
captivating
pleasurable 826 adj.
lovable 887 adj.
captive
slave 742 n.
imprisoned 747 adj.
prisoner 750 n.
captive 750 adj.
captivity
servitude 745 n.
detention 747 n.
captor
master 741 n.
possessor 776 n.
taker 786 n.
capture
imagine 513 vb.
represent 551 vb.
overmaster 727 vb.
trophy 729 n.
subjugate 745 vb.
arrest 747 vb.
acquire 771 vb.
taking 786 n.
take 786 vb.
— on film
record 548 vb.
car
automobile 274 n.
caracole
equitation 267 n.
leap 312 n.vb.
carafe
vessel 194 n.
caramel
sweets 301 n.
brownness 430 n.
carapace
covering 226 n.
carat
weighing 322 n.
caravan
procession 71 n.
small house 192 n.
marching 267 n.
cart 274 n.
follower 284 n.
caravanner
traveller 268 n.
caraway
potherb 301 n.
condiment 389 n.
carbine
firearm 723 n.
carbohydrates
food content 301 n.
carbolic
cleanser 648 n.
prophylactic 658 n.
carbon
duplicate 22 n.
ash 381 n.
carbonate
gasify 336 vb.
bubble 355 vb.
carbon copy
duplicate 22 n.
record 548 n.
carbon dioxide
poison 659 n.
carbonize, carbonise
burn 381 vb.
carbon monoxide
poison 659 n.
carbon paper
paper 631 n.
carboy
vessel 194 n.
carbuncle
swelling 253 n.
gem 844 n.
blemish 845 n.
carcass
structure 331 n.
corpse 363 n.
carcinogen
poison 659 n.
carcinogenic
insalubrious 653 adj.
card
unravel 62 vb.
nonconformist 84 n.
lamina 207 n.
sailing aid 269 n.
male 372 n.
label 547 n.
record 548 n.
correspondence 588 n.
contrivance 623 n.
instrument 628 n.
paper 631 n.
plaything 837 n.
humorist 839 n.
laughingstock 851 n.
cardboard
lamina 207 n.
spurious 542 adj.
misrepresented 552 adj.
paper 631 n.
card game
card game 837 n.
cardiac disease
cardiovascular disease 651 n.
cardigan
jersey 228 n.
cardinal
intrinsic 5 adj.
supreme 34 adj.
numerical 85 adj.
important 638 adj.
best 644 adj.
governor 741 n.
ecclesiarch 986 n.
cardinal points
compass point 281 n.
cardinal virtues
virtues 933 n.
sanctity 979 n.
card index
sorting 62 n.
list 87 n.
cardiology
medical art 658 n.
cardiovascular disease
cardiovascular disease 651 n.
card-player
player 837 n.
card punch
data processing 86 n.
perforator 263 n.
cards
oracle 511 n.
card game 837 n.
plaything 837 n.
cardsharp
trickster 545 n.
cards on the table
disclosure 526 n.
card up one's sleeve
contrivance 623 n.
means 629 n.
success 727 n.
card vote
vote 605 n.
commission 751 n.
care
be attentive 455 vb.
carefulness 457 n.
business 622 n.
function 622 n.
management 689 n.
detention 747 n.
mandate 751 n.
economy 814 n.
worry 825 n.
painfulness 827 n.
dejection 834 n.
nervousness 854 n.
caution 858 n.
love 887 vb.
philanthropize 897 vb.
— for
look after 457 vb.
safeguard 660 vb.
desire 859 vb.
love 887 vb.

be benevolent 897 vb.
careen
be oblique 220 vb.
move fast 277 vb.
career
continuity 71 n.
motion 265 n.
speeding 277 n.
move fast 277 vb.
progression 285 n.
vocation 622 n.
businesslike 622 adj.
conduct 688 n.
careerist
planner 623 n.
busy person 678 n.
expert 696 n.
desirer 859 n.
egotist 932 n.
selfish 932 adj.
career woman
woman 373 n.
worker 686 n.
expert 696 n.
carefree
reposeful 683 adj.
cheerful 833 adj.
careful
slow 278 adj.
attentive 455 adj.
careful 457 adj.
economical 814 adj.
parsimonious 816 adj.
cautious 858 adj.
carefulness
carefulness 457 n.
careful of
observant 768 adj.
careless
orderless 61 adj.
inattentive 456 adj.
negligent 458 adj.
unprepared 670 adj.
lazy 679 adj.
apathetic 820 adj.
rash 857 adj.
indifferent 860 adj.
careless, be
waste 634 vb.
carelessness
negligence 458 n.
inexactness 495 n.
rashness 857 n.
indifference 860 n.
cares
adversity 731 n.
worry 825 n.
caress
touch 378 n.vb.
please 826 vb.
love 887 vb.
endearment 889 n.
caress 889 vb.
caret
punctuation 547 n.
caretaker
manager 690 n.
servant 742 n.
keeper 749 n.
consignee 754 n.
caretaker government
government 733 n.
deputy 755 n.
careworn
suffering 825 adj.
melancholic 834 adj.
cargo
contents 193 n.
thing transferred 272 n.
merchandise 795 n.
cargo boat
carrier 273 n.
merchant ship 275 n.
cargo cult
idolatry 982 n.
caricature
dissimilarity 19 n.
imitate 20 vb.
misinterpret 521 vb.
exaggerate 546 vb.
misrepresentation 552 n.
misrepresent 552 vb.
picture 553 n.
be witty 839 vb.
laughingstock 851 n.
satire 851 n.
satirize 851 vb.
calumny 926 n.
detract 926 vb.
caricaturist
imitator 20 n.
artist 556 n.
humorist 839 n.
caries
decay 51 n.
carillon
campanology 412 n.
tune 412 n.
Carmelites
monk 986 n.
nun 986 n.
carminative
purgative 658 n.
carmine
red pigment 431 n.
red 431 adj.
carnage
havoc 165 n.
slaughter 362 n.
carnal
material 319 adj.
sensual 944 adj.
lecherous 951 adj.
carnal desire
libido 859 n.
carnal knowledge
coition 45 n.
carnation
plant 366 n.
redness 431 n.
carnelian
(See **cornelian** *)*
carnival
festivity 837 n.
pageant 875 n.
carnivore
eater 301 n.
animal 365 n.
carnivorous
feeding 301 adj.
carol
ululate 409 vb.
vocal music 412 n.
sing 413 vb.
voice 577 vb.
be cheerful 833 vb.
rejoice 835 vb.
offer worship 981 vb.
caroller
vocalist 413 n.
carotid
conduit 351 n.
carousal
festivity 837 n.
carouse
eat 301 vb.
revel 837 vb.
be sociable 882 vb.
get drunk 949 vb.
carouser
drunkard 949 n.
carp
fish 365 n.
be discontented 829 vb.
be sullen 893 vb.
blame 924 vb.
car park
enclosure 235 n.
traffic control 305 n.
carpenter
form 243 vb.
artisan 686 n.
carpet
base 214 n.
floor-cover 226 n.
reprove 924 vb.
carpetbagger
impostor 545 n.
carport
stable 192 n.
carrel
compartment 194 n.
carriage
prop 218 n.
gait 265 n.
transport 272 n.
carriage 274 n.
train 274 n.
mien 445 n.
conduct 688 n.
carriage-paid
uncharged 812 adj.
carriageway
road 624 n.
carried
assented 488 adj.
carried away
imaginative 513 adj.
excited 821 adj.
carried over
remaining 41 adj.
carrier
prop 218 n.
transferrer 272 n.
carrier 273 n.
courier 529 n.
infection 651 n.
insalubrity 653 n.
carrier pigeon
bearer 273 n.
courier 529 n.
carriole
carriage 274 n.
sledge 274 n.
carrion
decay 51 n.
food 301 n.
corpse 363 n.
rubbish 641 n.
dirt 649 n.
unclean 649 adj.
carrot
vegetable 301 n.
incentive 612 n.
carroty
red 431 adj.
carry
reproduce itself 167 vb.
tend 179 vb.
range 183 n.
be distant 199 vb.
support 218 vb.
wear 228 vb.
carry 273 vb.
be important 638 vb.
attack 712 vb.
overmaster 727 vb.
— across
carry 273 vb.
pass 305 vb.
— all before one
do easily 701 vb.
win 727 vb.
— coals to Newcastle
be superfluous 637 vb.
— conviction
be believed 485 vb.
— no weight
be unimportant 639 vb.
— off
take away 786 vb.
— on
go on 146 vb.
do business 622 vb.
function 622 vb.
do 676 vb.
behave 688 vb.
manage 689 vb.
lament 836 vb.
caress 889 vb.
be angry 891 vb.
be wicked 934 vb.
— one's bat
go on 146 vb.

— out
make complete 54 vb.
undertake 672 vb.
do 676 vb.
carry out 725 vb.
observe 768 vb.
— over
add 38 vb.
do sums 86 vb.
transfer 272 vb.
carry 273 vb.
pass 305 vb.
account 808 vb.
— shoulder-high
elevate 310 vb.
celebrate 876 vb.
respect 920 vb.
— the can
be duped 544 vb.
incur blame 924 vb.
— the day
win 727 vb.
— through
make complete 54 vb.
terminate 69 vb.
go on 146 vb.
persevere 600 vb.
be instrumental 628 vb.
perfect 646 vb.
mature 669 vb.
do 676 vb.
deal with 688 vb.
carry through 725 vb.
succeed 727 vb.
— weight
influence 178 vb.
evidence 466 vb.
— with one
influence 178 vb.
induce 612 vb.
carrying
loud 400 adj.
resonant 404 adj.
carsick
vomiting 300 adj.
cart
carry 273 vb.
cart 274 n.
— away
displace 188 vb.
carte blanche
scope 744 n.
permit 756 n.
liberality 813 n.
cartel
association 706 n.
corporation 708 n.
restriction 747 n.
compact 765 n.
carter
driver 268 n.
carrier 273 n.
Cartesianism
philosophy 449 n.
carthorse
draught horse 273 n.
cartilage
hardness 326 n.
toughness 329 n.
cartogram
statistics 86 n.
map 551 n.
cartographer
surveyor 465 n.
carton
small box 194 n.
cartoon
copy 22 n.
film 445 n.
representation 551 n.
picture 553 n.
wit 839 n.
satire 851 n.
cartoonist
artist 556 n.
humorist 839 n.
car transporter
lorry 274 n.
cartridge
gramophone 414 n.
ammunition 723 n.
cartridge belt
arsenal 723 n.
cartwheel
overturning 221 n.
carve
cut 46 vb.
sunder 46 vb.
produce 164 vb.
form 243 vb.
groove 262 vb.
record 548 vb.
represent 551 vb.
sculpt 554 vb.
decorate 844 vb.
— up
apportion 783 vb.
carving knife
sharp edge 256 n.
caryatid
pillar 218 n.
ornamental art 844 n.
Casanova
lover 887 n.
libertine 952 n.
cascade
descent 309 n.
descend 309 vb.
waterfall 350 n.
flow 350 vb.
case
state 7 n.
example 83 n.
event 154 n.
box 194 n.
case 194 n.
cover 226 vb.
enclosure 235 n.
topic 452 n.
enquire 459 vb.
argument 475 n.
reasons 475 n.
report 524 n.
grammar 564 n.
bookbinding 589 n.
business 622 n.
sick person 651 n.
treasury 799 n.
accusation 928 n.
litigation 959 n.
case, be the
be 1 vb.
be true 494 vb.
cased book
book 589 n.
case dismissed
acquittal 960 n.
case for
dueness 915 n.
case-hardened
strong 162 adj.
hard 326 adj.
unfeeling 375 adj.
obstinate 602 adj.
thick-skinned 820 adj.
impenitent 940 adj.
case history
evidence 466 n.
record 548 n.
description 590 n.
case in point
relevance 9 n.
fitness 24 n.
example 83 n.
casement
window 263 n.
cash
incentive 612 n.
coinage 797 n.
money 797 n.
draw money 797 vb.
— in on
profit by 137 vb.
plead 614 vb.
flourish 615 vb.
get better 654 vb.
use 673 vb.
cash and carry
buying 792 adj.
shop 796 n.
cashbook
record 548 n.
account book 808 n.
cash box
treasury 799 n.
cash crop
agriculture 370 n.
superfluity 637 n.
earnings 771 n.
cash desk
treasury 799 n.
cash down
cash down 804 adv.
cash flow
funds 797 n.
cashier
abase 311 vb.
depose 752 vb.
minter 797 n.
treasurer 798 n.
pay 804 n.
accountant 808 n.
shame 867 vb.
cashmere
fibre 208 n.
textile 222 n.
hair 259 n.
cash nexus
money 797 n.
cash payment
payment 804 n.
cash register
counting instrument 86 n.
recording instrument 549 n.
treasury 799 n.
casino
gaming-house 618 n.
place of amusement 837 n.
cask
vat 194 n.
casket
small box 194 n.
interment 364 n.
ritual object 988 n.
casque
armour 713 n.
Cassandra
oracle 511 n.
warner 664 n.
cassation
obliteration 550 n.
abrogation 752 n.
casserole
cauldron 194 n.
dish 301 n.
cook 301 vb.
cassette
gramophone 414 n.
photography 551 n.
cassock
robe 228 n.
canonicals 989 n.
vestments 989 n.
cast
character 5 n.
copy 22 n.
band 74 n.
number 86 vb.
tendency 179 n.
doff 229 vb.
form 243 n.vb.
propel 287 vb.
excrement 302 n.
hue 425 n.
dim sight 440 n.
mien 445 n.
represent 551 vb.
sculpture 554 n.
sculpt 554 vb.
actor 594 n.
dramatize 594 vb.
surgical dressing 658 n.
blemish 845 n.
— about(for)
search 459 vb.

be uncertain 474 vb.
pursue 619 vb.
— a long shadow
be important 638 vb.
— a nativity
divine 511 vb.
practise sorcery 983 vb.
— anchor
place oneself 187 vb.
come to rest 266 vb.
navigate 269 vb.
— a shadow
darken 418 vb.
depress 834 vb.
— a spell on
bewitch 983 vb.
— aspersions
detract 926 vb.
— a vote
vote 605 vb.
— away
not retain 779 vb.
— horoscopes
practise sorcery 983 vb.
— in one's lot with
choose 605 vb.
— its skin
doff 229 vb.
— off
navigate 269 vb.
start out 296 vb.
not retain 779 vb.
— one's net
be tentative 461 vb.
hunt 619 vb.
— out
reject 607 vb.
make unwelcome 883 vb.
— pearls before swine
waste 634 vb.
— the evil eye
be malevolent 898 vb.
curse 899 vb.
bewitch 983 vb.
castanets
gong 414 n.
castaway
solitary 883 n.
caste
breed 77 n.
classification 77 n.
particularism 80 n.
prestige 866 n.
nobility 868 n.
castellated
defended 713 adj.
caste mark
label 547 n.
caste system
exclusion 57 n.
castigate
dissuade 613 vb.
reprove 924 vb.
punish 963 vb.
casting lots
divination 511 n.
nondesign 618 n.
casting vote
inequality 29 n.
influence 178 n.
vote 605 n.
cast in the same mould
similar 18 adj.
cast iron
hardness 326 n.
resolution 599 n.
castle
house 192 n.
transpose 272 vb.
fort 713 n.
castles in Spain/in the air
fantasy 513 n.
aspiration 852 n.
cast-off
remaining 41 adj.
separate 46 adj.
relinquished 621 adj.
disused 674 adj.
derelict 779 n.
cast-offs
clothing 228 n.
rubbish 641 n.
cast of mind
affections 817 n.
castor, caster
small box 194 n.
wheel 250 n.
castor oil
oil 357 n.
purgative 658 n.
castrate
unman 161 vb.
make sterile 172 vb.
impair 655 vb.
castrated
impotent 161 adj.
castrato
eunuch 161 n.
male 372 n.
vocalist 413 n.
Castroism
government 733 n.
castrum
fort 713 n.
casual
orderless 61 adj.
casual 159 adj.
negligent 458 adj.
unintentional 618 adj.
reposeful 683 adj.
unconfined 744 adj.
casual labour
personnel 686 n.
casuals
informal dress 228 n.
footwear 228 n.
casualty
event 154 n.
chance 159 n.
misfortune 731 n.
casualty list
death roll 361 n.
casualty ward
hospital 658 n.
casuist
reasoner 475 n.
sophist 477 n.
casuistry
sophistry 477 n.
falsehood 541 n.
fastidiousness 862 n.
morals 917 n.
cat
vomit 300 vb.
cat 365 n.
musician 413 n.
eye 438 n.
cad 938 n.
scourge 964 n.
catachrestic
figurative 519 adj.
ungrammatical 565 adj.
cataclysm
revolution 149 n.
havoc 165 n.
outbreak 176 n.
waterfall 350 n.
catacombs
cemetery 364 n.
catafalque
funeral 364 n.
catalepsy
insensibility 375 n.
sleep 679 n.
catalogue
arrangement 62 n.
class 62 vb.
list 87 n.vb.
guidebook 524 n.
record 548 vb.
account 808 vb.
catalysis
decomposition 51 n.
change 143 n.
catalyst
alterer 143 n.
stimulant 174 n.
instrument 628 n.
catamaran
raft 275 n.
catamite
libertine 952 n.
cat and dog
opposites 704 n.
cat-and-dog life
dissension 709 n.
catapult
propellant 287 n.
propel 287 vb.
missile weapon 723 n.
cataract
high water 209 n.
waterfall 350 n.
blindness 439 n.
dim sight 440 n.
catarrh
excretion 302 n.
respiratory disease 651 n.
catastrophe
end 69 n.
revolution 149 n.
event 154 n.
ruin 165 n.
evil 616 n.
completion 725 n.
misfortune 731 n.
catatonia
psychopathy 503 n.
catcall
gesture 547 n.
ridicule 851 n.
indignity 921 n.
disapprobation 924 n.
catch
fastening 47 n.
bring together 74 vb.
halt 145 vb.
be rough 259 vb.
rub 333 vb.
vocal music 412 n.
hear 415 vb.
question 459 n.
know 490 vb.
surprise 508 vb.
trap 542 n.
ensnare 542 vb.
represent 551 vb.
hunt 619 vb.
defect 647 n.
be ill 651 vb.
pitfall 663 n.
stratagem 698 n.
predicament 700 n.
hitch 702 n.
wrestling 716 n.
arrest 747 vb.
acquire 771 vb.
take 786 vb.
booty 790 n.
feel 818 vb.
desired object 859 n.
sociable person 882 n.
excite love 887 vb.
favourite 890 n.
— a crab
row 269 vb.
be clumsy 695 vb.
— a glimpse of
see 438 vb.
— a likeness
represent 551 vb.
— an infection
be ill 651 vb.
— a sound
hear 415 vb.
— at a straw
hope 852 vb.
— a train
start out 296 vb.
— bending
surprise 508 vb.

— fire
be hot 379 vb.
be excitable 822 vb.
— it
incur blame 924 vb.
be punished 963 vb.
— on
prevail 178 vb.
understand 516 vb.
be wont 610 vb.
be in fashion 848 vb.
— one's eye
be visible 443 vb.
attract notice 455 vb.
excite love 887 vb.
— out
dismiss 300 vb.
detect 484 vb.
befool 542 vb.
— sight of
see 438 vb.
detect 484 vb.
— the breath
breathe 352 vb.
rasp 407 vb.
— unawares
surprise 508 vb.
be unprepared 670 vb.
— up with
outstrip 277 vb.
approach 289 vb.
catch-22 (situation)
predicament 700 n.
catch-all
receptacle 194 n.
catch-as-catch-can
attempting 671 adj.
wrestling 716 n.
unconditional 744 adj.
catch crop
agriculture 370 n.
earnings 771 n.
catching
influential 178 adj.
infectious 653 adj.
catchment area
territory 184 n.
school 539 n.
catchpenny
spurious 542 adj.
catchphrase
neology 560 n.
phrase 563 n.
catchword
maxim 496 n.
call 547 n.
word 559 n.
edition 589 n.
catchy
melodious 410 adj.
desired 859 adj.
catechism
interrogation 459 n.
creed 485 n.
orthodoxy 976 n.
catechist
teacher 537 n.
religious teacher 973 n.
catechumen
learner 538 n.
categorical
positive 473 adj.
demonstrating 478 adj.
assertive 532 adj.
commanding 737 adj.
obligatory 917 adj.
categorical imperative
command 737 n.
conscience 917 n.
categorization, categorisation
arrangement 62 n.
category
state 7 n.
classification 77 n.
catenary
continuous 71 adj.
curve 248 n.
cater
feed 301 vb.
provide 633 vb.
offer 759 vb.
catering
cookery 301 n.
provision 633 n.
caterpillar
young creature 132 n.
creepy-crawly 365 n.
caterwaul
be loud 400 vb.
ululate 409 vb.
caterwauling
discord 411 n.
Cathar
heretic 977 n.
catharsis
recuperation 656 n.
liberation 746 n.
feeling 818 n.
cathartic
dramatic 594 adj.
purgative 658 n.
remedial 658 adj.
cathedral
church 990 n.
cathedral close
parsonage 986 n.
Catherine wheel
rotator 315 n.
fireworks 420 n.
catheter
drain 351 n.
catheterization
therapy 658 n.
cathode
electricity 160 n.
catholic
universal 79 adj.
Catholic
Catholic 976 n.
Roman Catholic 976 adj.
church party 978 n.
Catholicism
Catholicism 976 n.
orthodoxy 976 n.
sectarianism 978 n.
catkin
flower 366 n.
catlap
insipidity 387 n.
catlick
ablutions 648 n.
catlike
animal 365 adj.
stealthy 525 adj.
catnap
sleep 679 n.vb.
cat on hot bricks, like a
agitated 318 adj.
active 678 n.
excitable 822 adj.
cat-o'-nine-tails
scourge 964 n.
cat's concert
discord 411 n.
cat's cradle
crossing 222 n.
cat's eye
traffic control 305 n.
gem 844 n.
cat's paw
wave 350 n.
dupe 544 n.
instrument 628 n.
auxiliary 707 n.
toady 879 n.
catsuit
suit 228 n.
cat's whiskers/ pyjamas
exceller 644 n.
cattle
beast of burden 273 n.
cattle 365 n.
animal husbandry 369 n.
rabble 869 n.
cattle cake
provender 301 n.
cattle farm
stock farm 369 n.
farm 370 n.
cattle farming
agriculture 370 n.
cattleman
herdsman 369 n.
cattle pen
enclosure 235 n.
cattle pen 369 n.
cattle-rustling
spoliation 788 n.
cattle thief
thief 789 n.
catty
malevolent 898 adj.
detracting 926 adj.
catwalk
bridge 624 n.
Caucasian
ethnic 11 adj.
white 427 adj.
caucus
assemblage 74 n.
party 708 n.
caudal
ending 69 adj.
back 238 adj.
caudillo
master 741 n.
caught in the act
guilty 936 adj.
caught napping
inexpectant 508 adj.
unprepared 670 adj.
caul
obstetrics 167 n.
cauldron
crucible 147 n.
cauldron 194 n.
heater 383 n.
cauliflower
vegetable 301 n.
cauliflower ear
swelling 253 n.
blemish 845 n.
caulk
close 264 vb.
repair 656 vb.
causal
causal 156 adj.
influential 178 adj.
instrumental 628 adj.
causation
causation 156 n.
agency 173 n.
motive 612 n.
intention 617 n.
causative
causal 156 adj.
cause
cause 156 n.
reason why 156 n.
cause 156 vb.
produce 164 vb.
influence 178 n.
promote 285 vb.
reasons 475 n.
predetermine 608 vb.
motivator 612 n.
motive 612 n.
induce 612 vb.
instrumentality 628 n.
be instrumental 628 vb.
philanthropy 901 n.
litigation 959 n.
— offence
make enemies 881 vb.

be rude 885 vb.
huff 891 vb.
— pain
hurt 827 vb.
— resentment
cause discontent 829 vb.
— thought
cause thought 449 vb.
cause and effect
relativeness 9 n.
causation 156 n.
cause célèbre
prodigy 864 n.
cause for alarm
danger 661 n.
causeless
causeless 159 adj.
designless 618 adj.
causerie
chat 584 n.
interlocution 584 n.
article 591 n.
causeway
bond 47 n.
bridge 624 n.
caustic
keen 174 adj.
curve 248 n.
burning 381 n.
pungent 388 adj.
felt 818 adj.
paining 827 adj.
maleficent 898 adj.
disapproving 924 adj.
detracting 926 adj.
cauterize, cauterise
burn 381 vb.
doctor 658 vb.
caution
attention 455 n.
carefulness 457 n.
foresight 510 n.
omen 511 n.
hint 524 n.
dissuade 613 vb.
warning 664 n.
warn 664 vb.
advice 691 n.
laughingstock 851 n.
intimidation 854 n.
caution 858 n.
reprove 924 vb.
cautionary
advising 691 adj.
cautionary tale
maxim 496 n.
narrative 590 n.
caution money
security 767 n.
cautious
slow 278 adj.
careful 457 adj.
doubting 474 adj.
foreseeing 510 adj.
taciturn 582 adj.
unwilling 598 adj.
warned 664 adj.
nervous 854 adj.
cowardly 856 adj.
cautious 858 adj.
cavalcade
procession 71 n.
marching 267 n.
cavalier
rider 268 n.
inattentive 456 adj.
rash 857 adj.
impertinent 878 adj.
discourteous 885 adj.
lover 887 n.
disrespectful 921 adj.
cavalry
rider 268 n.
warhorse 273 n.
cavalry 722 n.
cave
dwelling 192 n.
receptacle 194 n.
depth 211 n.
interiority 224 n.
cavity 255 n.
tunnel 263 n.
dissentient 489 n.
party 708 n.
caveat
warning 664 n.
cave-dweller
dweller 191 n.
cave in
break 46 vb.
be concave 255 vb.
descend 309 vb.
knuckle under 721 vb.
caveman
violent creature 176 n.
male 372 n.
ruffian 904 n.
cavemen and -women
dweller 191 n.
humankind 371 n.
cavern
cavity 255 n.
darkness 418 n.
cavernous
spacious 183 adj.
deep 211 adj.
caviar
fish food 301 n.
savouriness 390 n.
cavil
argue 475 vb.
sophisticate 477 vb.
doubt 486 vb.
dissent 489 n.vb.
disapprobation 924 n.
dispraise 924 vb.
caviller
sophist 477 n.
dissentient 489 n.
detractor 926 n.
caving
descent 309 n.
sport 837 n.
cavity
receptacle 194 n.
gap 201 n.
depth 211 n.
cavity 255 n.
opening 263 n.
orifice 263 n.
cavity wall
barrier 235 n.
cavort
leap 312 vb.
dance 837 vb.
caw
rasp 407 vb.
ululation 409 n.
cease
end 69 vb.
cease 145 vb.
be quiescent 266 vb.
relinquish 621 vb.
stop using 674 vb.
be inactive 679 vb.
make peace 719 vb.
fail 728 vb.
cease-fire
lull 145 n.
pacification 719 n.
ceaseless
continuous 71 adj.
perpetual 115 adj.
ceaselessly
persistently 600 adv.
cedar
tree 366 n.
cede
relinquish 621 vb.
not retain 779 vb.
give 781 vb.
cedilla
punctuation 547 n.
Ceefax
broadcasting 531 n.
ceilidh
dancing 837 n.
ceiling
finite quantity 26 n.
height 209 n.
vertex 213 n.
roof 226 n.
limit 236 n.
visibility 443 n.
price 809 n.
celebrant
worshipper 981 n.
ritualist 988 n.
celebrate
remind 505 vb.
proclaim 528 vb.
rejoice 835 vb.
revel 837 vb.
honour 866 vb.
celebrate 876 vb.
be hospitable 882 vb.
congratulate 886 vb.
respect 920 vb.
applaud 923 vb.
worship 981 vb.
perform ritual 988 vb.
celebrated
known 490 adj.
well-known 528 adj.
renowned 866 adj.
celebration
feasting 301 n.
victory 727 n.
trophy 729 n.
merriment 833 n.
rejoicing 835 n.
pageant 875 n.
celebration 876 n.
congratulation 886 n.
church service 988 n.
holy day 988 n.
(See **celebrate** *)*
celebratory
celebratory 876 adj.
celebrity
person of repute 866 n.
celery
vegetable 301 n.
celesta
piano 414 n.
celeste
mute 414 n.
celestial
celestial 321 adj.
divine 965 adj.
angelic 968 adj.
paradisiac 971 adj.
Celestial City
heaven 971 n.
celibacy
celibacy 895 n.
celibate
alone 88 adj.
unproductive 172 adj.
unsociable 883 adj.
celibate 895 n.
unwedded 895 adj.
virgin 950 n.
monk 986 n.
cell
electronics 160 n.
retreat 192 n.
compartment 194 n.
minuteness 196 n.
enclosure 235 n.
cavity 255 n.
organism 358 n.
life 360 n.
refuge 662 n.
association 706 n.
party 708 n.
society 708 n.
lockup 748 n.
seclusion 883 n.
monastery 986 n.
cellar
cellar 194 n.
lowness 210 n.
depth 211 n.

base 214 n.
provisions 301 n.
storage 632 n.
cellarer
retainer 742 n.
cellist
instrumentalist 413 n.
cello
viol 414 n.
cellophane
wrapping 226 n.
transparency 422 n.
paper 631 n.
cellular
cellular 194 adj.
concave 255 adj.
organic 358 adj.
celluloid
film 445 n.
materials 631 n.
Celt
native 191 n.
Celtic deities
Celtic deities 967 n.
Celtic fringe
foreigner 59 n.
cement
join 45 vb.
adhesive 47 n.
bond 47 n.
agglutinate 48 vb.
overlay 226 vb.
solid body 324 n.
hardness 326 n.
building material 631 n.
cemetery
death 361 n.
cemetery 364 n.
holy place 990 n.
cenobite
monk 986 n.
cenotaph
obsequies 364 n.
tomb 364 n.
censer
scent 396 n.
ritual object 988 n.
censor
exclude 57 vb.
alterer 143 n.
enquirer 459 n.
estimator 480 n.
obliterate 550 vb.
restrain 747 vb.
prohibit 757 vb.
disapprover 924 n.
disapprove 924 vb.
detractor 926 n.
prude 950 n.
censored
prohibited 757 adj.
disapproved 924 adj.
pure 950 adj.
censorious
judicial 480 adj.
severe 735 adj.
discontented 829 adj.
fastidious 862 adj.
disapproving 924 adj.
censorship
obliteration 550 n.
severity 735 n.
censurable
discreditable 867 adj.
blameworthy 924 adj.
guilty 936 adj.
censure
estimate 480 n.vb.
slur 867 n.
censure 924 n.
reprimand 924 n.
reprove 924 vb.
accusation 928 n.
guilt 936 n.
census
numeration 86 n.
statistics 86 n.
list 87 n.
enquiry 459 n.
census-taker
enumerator 86 n.
cent
small coin 33 n.
trifle 639 n.
coinage 797 n.
centaur
rara avis 84 n.
mythical being 970 n.
centenarian
hundred 99 n.
old person 133 n.
centenary
hundred 99 n.
anniversary 141 n.
special day 876 n.
centennial
fifth and over 99 adj.
periodic 110 adj.
seasonal 141 adj.
celebratory 876 adj.
centime
small coin 33 n.
coinage 797 n.
centimetre
long measure 203 n.
shortness 204 n.
centipede
creepy-crawly 365 n.
cento
a mixture 43 n.
doggerel 593 n.
central
intrinsic 5 adj.
middle 70 adj.
fundamental 156 adj.
interior 224 adj.
central 225 adj.
inland 344 adj.
neutral 625 adj.
undeviating 625 adj.
important 638 adj.
central heating
heating 381 n.
centralization, centralisation
uniformity 16 n.
combination 50 n.
arrangement 62 n.
accumulation 74 n.
centrality 225 n.
plan 623 n.
association 706 n.
centralized
governmental 733 adj.
centre
essence 1 n.
essential part 5 n.
middle point 30 n.
middle 70 n.
bring together 74 vb.
focus 76 n.
interiority 224 n.
centre 225 n.
centralize 225 vb.
converge 293 vb.
political party 708 n.
armed force 722 n.
arena 724 n.
— on
focus 76 vb.
converge 293 vb.
centreboard
stabilizer 153 n.
pivot 218 n.
centre forward
front 237 n.
leader 690 n.
centre of attraction
focus 76 n.
attraction 291 n.
favourite 890 n.
centrepiece
ornamentation 844 n.
centrifugal
unassembled 75 adj.
exterior 223 adj.
repellent 292 adj.
divergent 294 adj.
avoiding 620 adj.
centripetal
central 225 adj.
attracting 291 adj.
convergent 293 adj.
centrist
political party 708 n.
centurion
hundred 99 n.
army officer 741 n.
century
hundred 99 n.
period 110 n.
cephalic
topmost 213 adj.
cepheid
star 321 n.
ceramics
pottery 381 n.
sculpture 554 n.
Cerberus
three 93 n.
doorkeeper 264 n.
protector 660 n.
mythic hell 972 n.
cereal farming
agriculture 370 n.
cereals
cereals 301 n.
grass 366 n.
cerebral
mental 447 adj.
cerebral haemorrhage
nervous disorders 651 n.
cerebral thrombosis
cardiovascular disease 651 n.
cerebrate
think 449 vb.
cerecloth
grave clothes 364 n.
ceremonial
formality 875 n.
formal 875 adj.
ritual 988 n.adj.
ritualistic 988 adj.
ceremonial occasion
formality 875 n.
ceremonious
formal 875 adj.
respectful 920 adj.
ritualistic 988 adj.
ceremony
formality 875 n.
celebration 876 n.
rite 988 n.
Ceres
fertilizer 171 n.
Olympian deity 967 n.
cerise
red 431 adj.
cerography
engraving 555 n.
writing 586 n.
ceroplastic
glyptic 554 adj.
cert
certainty 473 n.
certain
quantitative 26 adj.
definite 80 adj.
unchangeable 153 adj.
impending 155 adj.
certain 473 adj.
demonstrated 478 adj.
known 490 adj.
true 494 adj.
expectant 507 adj.
manifest 522 adj.
necessary 596 adj.
hoping 852 adj.
certain, a
one 88 adj.
anonymous 562 adj.

certain, be
assume 471 vb.
be certain 473 vb.
believe 485 vb.
know 490 vb.
expect 507 vb.
certainty
safety 660 n.
easy thing 701 n.
(See **certain** *)*
certifiable
insane 503 adj.
certificate
credential 466 n.
record 548 n.
title deed 767 n.
paper money 797 n.
honours 866 n.
reward 962 n.
certified
certain 473 adj.
positive 473 adj.
insane 503 adj.
certify
testify 466 vb.
make certain 473 vb.
inform 524 vb.
affirm 532 vb.
certitude
certainty 473 n.
cervix
pillar 218 n.
cessation
finality 69 n.
discontinuity 72 n.
cessation 145 n.
quiescence 266 n.
inactivity 679 n.
cession
relinquishment 621 n.
nonretention 779 n.
cesspit, cesspool
receptacle 194 n.
sink 649 n.
cetacean
mammal 365 n.
marine life 365 n.
ceteris paribus
equally 28 adv.
cha-cha
dance 837 n.
chaconne
musical piece 412 n.
chafe
rub 333 vb.
feel pain 377 vb.
give pain 377 vb.
wound 655 vb.
be excitable 822 vb.
suffer 825 vb.
hurt 827 vb.
torment 827 vb.
cause discontent 829 vb.
be angry 891 vb.
chaff
leavings 41 n.
grass 366 n.
trifle 639 n.
rubbish 641 n.
witticism 839 n.
be witty 839 vb.
ridicule 851 n.vb.
chaffinch
bird 365 n.
chagrin
sorrow 825 n.
discontent 829 n.
chagrined
disappointed 509 adj.
unhappy 825 adj.
dejected 834 adj.
chain
bond 47 n.
cable 47 n.
coherence 48 n.
continuity 71 n.
series 71 n.
long measure 203 n.
high land 209 n.
gauge 465 n.
encumbrance 702 n.
fetter 747 vb.
fetter 748 n.
jewellery 844 n.
— together
connect 45 vb.
chained
captive 750 adj.
chaingang
slave 742 n.
prisoner 750 n.
chain letter
correspondence 588 n.
chain mail
armour 713 n.
chain of reasoning
relevance 9 n.
chain reaction
continuity 71 n.
chain-smoke
smoke 388 vb.
chain store
shop 796 n.
chair
seat 218 n.
lecture 534 n.
rostrum 539 n.
director 690 n.
badge of rule 743 n.
honour 866 vb.
celebrate 876 vb.
pay one's respects 884 vb.
applaud 923 vb.
chairborne
quiescent 266 adj.
chairman, chairwoman
director 690 n.
chairmanship
directorship 689 n.
position of authority 733 n.
chaise
carriage 274 n.
chaise longue
seat 218 n.
chalcedony
gem 844 n.
Chaldean
sorcerer 983 n.
chalet
house 192 n.
small house 192 n.
chalice
cup 194 n.
ritual object 988 n.
chalk
powder 332 n.
rock 344 n.
white thing 427 n.
mark 547 vb.
art equipment 553 n.
paint 553 vb.
stationery 586 n.
— out
limit 236 vb.
mark 547 vb.
represent 551 vb.
plan 623 vb.
— up
mark 547 vb.
register 548 vb.
challenge
question 459 n.
interrogate 459 vb.
dissent 489 n.vb.
affirmation 532 n.
negation 533 n.
call 547 n.
motivate 612 vb.
opposition 704 n.
oppose 704 vb.
dissension 709 n.
make quarrels 709 vb.
defiance 711 n.
defy 711 vb.
attack 712 vb.
resist 715 vb.
contend 716 vb.
threat 900 n.
accusation 928 n.
challenging
topical 452 adj.
chamber
flat 192 n.
chamber 194 n.
chamberlain
retainer 742 n.
chambermaid
domestic 742 n.
chamber music
music 412 n.
chamber of commerce
corporation 708 n.
merchant 794 n.
chamber pot
vessel 194 n.
latrine 649 n.
chambers
quarters 192 n.
chameleon
changeable thing 152 n.
reptile 365 n.
variegation 437 n.
iridescent 437 adj.
chamfer
make oblique 220 vb.
furrow 262 n.
groove 262 vb.
chamfering
ornamental art 844 n.
chamois
skin 226 n.
jumper 312 n.
mammal 365 n.
cleaning cloth 648 n.
champ
chew 301 vb.
combatant 722 n.
— at the bit
disobey 738 vb.
be excitable 822 vb.
be angry 891 vb.
champagne
wine 301 n.
champaign
plain 348 n.
champion
superior 34 n.
supreme 34 adj.
athlete 162 n.
exceller 644 n.
best 644 adj.
safeguard 660 vb.
proficient person 696 n.
patronize 703 vb.
patron 707 n.
defender 713 n.
defend 713 vb.
combatant 722 n.
victor 727 n.
deputy 755 n.
person of repute 866 n.
philanthropist 901 n.
benefactor 903 n.
vindicator 927 n.
vindicate 927 vb.
champion of the faith
zealot 979 n.
championship
superiority 34 n.
chance
extrinsicality 6 n.
opportunity 137 n.
event 154 n.
happen 154 vb.
chance 159 n., vb.
casual 159 adj.
possibility 469 n.
probability 471 n.
uncertainty 474 n.
fate 596 n.

gambling 618 n.
nondesign 618 n.
— it
gamble 618 vb.
chance in a million
chance 159 n.
improbability 472 n.
chancel
church interior 990 n.
chancellor
director 690 n.
officer 741 n.
Chancellor of the Exchequer
treasurer 798 n.
chancy
casual 159 adj.
uncertain 474 adj.
speculative 618 adj.
dangerous 661 adj.
chandelier
hanging object 217 n.
lamp 420 n.
chandler
merchant 794 n.
change
differ 15 vb.
make unlike 19 vb.
fitfulness 142 n.
change 143 n.vb.
be turned to 147 vb.
quid pro quo 150 n.
changeableness 152 n.
vary 152 vb.
influence 178 vb.
wear 228 vb.
doff 229 vb.
coinage 797 n.
money 797 n.
— a leopard's spots
attempt the impossible 470 vb.
— colour
lose colour 426 vb.
show feeling 818 vb.
quake 854 vb.
— direction
deviate 282 vb.
diverge 294 vb.
— for
substitute 150 vb.
— gradually
shade off 27 vb.
— hands
change hands 780 vb.
be sold 793 vb.
— into
become 1 vb.
— one's mind
vary 152 vb.
tergiversate 603 vb.
relinquish 621 vb.
— one's tune
differ 15 vb.
change 143 vb.
tergiversate 603 vb.
— places
be in motion 265 vb.
change hands 780 vb.
— round
modify 143 vb.
displace 188 vb.
— sides
be irresolute 601 vb.
apostatize 603 vb.
— the face of
transform 147 vb.
revolutionize 149 vb.
— with the times
be in fashion 848 vb.
Change
market 796 n.
changeable
nonuniform 17 adj.
multiform 82 adj.
transient 114 adj.
changeable 143 adj.
converted 147 adj.
changeful 152 adj.
unreliable 474 adj.
lively 819 adj.
irascible 892 adj.
changeableness
changeableness 152 n.
irresolution 601 n.
caprice 604 n.
changeable thing
changeable thing 152 n.
waverer 601 n.
tergiversator 603 n.
change for the better
change 143 n.
improvement 654 n.
changeful
nonuniform 17 adj.
multiform 82 adj.
transient 114 adj.
fitful 142 adj.
changeful 152 adj.
unreliable 474 adj.
irresolute 601 adj.
excitable 822 adj.
sullen 893 adj.
changeless
unchangeable 153 adj.
godlike 965 adj.
changeling
child 132 n.
substitute 150 n.
elf 970 n.
change of life
middle age 131 n.
changeover
transfer 780 n.
change ringing
campanology 412 n.
channel
cavity 255 n.
furrow 262 n.
passage 305 n.
gulf 345 n.
conduit 351 n.
informant 524 n.
access 624 n.
instrument 628 n.
direct 689 vb.
chant
repeat oneself 106 vb.
cry 408 n.
vociferate 408 vb.
vocal music 412 n.
sing 413 vb.
voice 577 vb.
— psalms
offer worship 981 vb.
chantry chapel
church 990 n.
chaos
noncoherence 49 n.
decomposition 51 n.
confusion 61 n.
disorder 61 n.
havoc 165 n.
amorphism 244 n.
anarchy 734 n.
chaotic
orderless 61 adj.
lawless 954 adj.
chap
roughness 259 n.
person 371 n.
male 372 n.
chapatti
cereals 301 n.
chapel
association 706 n.
society 708 n.
sect 978 n.
church 990 n.
church interior 990 n.
chapelgoer
church member 976 n.
worshipper 981 n.
chaperon
accompany 89 vb.
surveillance 457 n.
look after 457 vb.
protector 660 n.
safeguard 660 vb.
keeper 749 n.
chapfallen, chopfallen
dejected 834 adj.
humbled 872 adj.
chaplain
retainer 742 n.
church officer 986 n.
pastor 986 n.
chaplaincy
church office 985 n.
chaplet
trophy 729 n.
chappals
footwear 228 n.
chapped
rough 259 adj.
chappie
male 372 n.
chaps, chops
threshold 234 n.
laterality 239 n.
chapter
subdivision 53 n.
topic 452 n.
edition 589 n.
synod 985 n.
chapter and verse
evidence 466 n.
accuracy 494 n.
chapter house
church exterior 990 n.
chapter of accidents
affairs 154 n.
chance 159 n.
char
burn 381 vb.
blacken 428 vb.
servant 742 n.
serve 742 vb.
charabanc
carriage 274 n.
character
character 5 n.
modality 7 n.
sort 77 n.
speciality 80 n.
nonconformist 84 n.
number 85 n.
form 243 n.
person 371 n.
credential 466 n.
letter 558 n.
acting 594 n.
affections 817 n.
humorist 839 n.
repute 866 n.
virtue 933 n.
character assassination
detraction 926 n.
characteristic
characteristic 5 adj.
intrinsic 5 adj.
distinctive 15 adj.
speciality 80 n.
special 80 adj.
tendency 179 n.
identification 547 n.
indicating 547 adj.
characterization, characterisation
representation 551 n.
description 590 n.
dramaturgy 594 n.
characterized
marked 547 adj.
with affections 817 adj.
characterless
insubstantial 4 adj.
uniform 16 adj.
irresolute 601 adj.
character sketch
description 590 n.

character witness
vindicator 927 n.
charade(s)
sham 542 n.
representation 551 n.
indoor game 837 n.
charcoal
ash 381 n.
fuel 385 n.
black thing 428 n.
art equipment 553 n.
charge
fill 54 vb.
empower 160 vb.
be violent 176 vb.
load 193 vb.
move fast 277 vb.
collide 279 vb.
make heavy 322 vb.
call 547 n.
heraldry 547 n.
mark 547 vb.
job 622 n.
protection 660 n.
management 689 n.
advise 691 vb.
precept 693 n.
attack 712 n.
charge 712 vb.
give battle 718 vb.
explosive 723 n.
command 737 n.vb.
demand 737 vb.
dependant 742 n.
detention 747 n.
mandate 751 n.
commission 751 vb.
account 808 vb.
price 809 n.vb.
duty 917 n.
blame 924 vb.
accusation 928 n.
litigate 959 vb.
— at
pursue 619 vb.
be rash 857 vb.
— in
burst in 297 vb.
— to one's account
credit 802 vb.
— with
attribute 158 vb.
accuse 928 vb.
chargé d'affaires
envoy 754 n.
charge nurse
nurse 658 n.
charger
plate 194 n.
warhorse 273 n.
cavalry 722 n.
accuser 928 n.
chariot
carriage 274 n.
charioteer
driver 268 n.
charisma
power 160 n.
influence 178 n.
charismatic
influential 178 adj.
charismatic leader
leader 690 n.
charitable
giving 781 adj.
liberal 813 adj.
benevolent 897 adj.
philanthropic 901 adj.
pitying 905 adj.
charity
aid 703 n.
subvention 703 n.
gift 781 n.
giving 781 n.
liberality 813 n.
courteous act 884 n.
love 887 n.
benevolence 897 n.
kind act 897 n.
philanthropy 901 n.
pity 905 n.
disinterestedness 931 n.
virtues 933 n.
piety 979 n.
charity that begins at home
selfishness 932 n.
charlady
cleaner 648 n.
charlatan
sciolist 493 n.
impostor 545 n.
doctor 658 n.
unskilled 695 adj.
affecter 850 n.
boaster 877 n.
Charleston
dance 837 n.
charlie
ninny 501 n.
charlotte
dessert 301 n.
charm
attraction 291 n.
attract 291 vb.
inducement 612 n.
motivate 612 vb.
preserver 666 n.
delight 826 vb.
please 826 vb.
beauty 841 n.
jewellery 844 n.
lovableness 887 n.
excite love 887 vb.
spell 983 n.
talisman 983 n.
bewitch 983 vb.
charmed circle
elite 644 n.
party 708 n.
charmed life
safety 660 n.
charmer
a beauty 841 n.
flatterer 925 n.
sorcerer 983 n.
charming
attracting 291 adj.
pleasurable 826 adj.
personable 841 adj.
lovable 887 adj.
charms
beauty 841 n.
lovableness 887 n.
charnel house
death 361 n.
interment 364 n.
Charon
boatman 270 n.
mythic hell 972 n.
chart
list 87 n.
sailing aid 269 n.
guidebook 524 n.
map 551 n.
represent 551 vb.
charter
record 548 n.
give scope 744 vb.
liberate 746 vb.
mandate 751 n.
commission 751 vb.
permit 756 n.vb.
title deed 767 n.
hire 785 vb.
dueness 915 n.
nonliability 919 n.
law 953 n.
chartered accountant
accountant 808 n.
charter flight
air travel 271 n.
chartreuse
yellow 433 adj.
green 434 adj.
charwoman
cleaner 648 n.
chary
parsimonious 816 adj.
cautious 858 adj.
chase
groove 262 vb.
move fast 277 vb.
killing 362 n.
cry 408 n.
sculpt 554 vb.
press 587 n.
chase 619 n.
pursue 619 vb.
pleasure ground 837 n.
sport 837 n.
desire 859 vb.
court 889 vb.
— away
repel 292 vb.
— one's own tail
rotate 315 vb.
be busy 678 vb.
chaser
draught 301 n.
chasm
disunion 46 n.
gap 201 n.
depth 211 n.
cavity 255 n.
pitfall 663 n.
chassis
base 214 n.
frame 218 n.
prop 218 n.
structure 331 n.
chaste
plain 573 adj.
elegant 575 adj.
tasteful 846 adj.
modest 874 adj.
virtuous 933 adj.
temperate 942 adj.
pure 950 adj.
chasten
moderate 177 vb.
educate 534 vb.
be serious 834 vb.
depress 834 vb.
humiliate 872 vb.
punish 963 vb.
chastened
repentant 939 adj.
chastise
be severe 735 vb.
reprove 924 vb.
punish 963 vb.
chastisement
punishment 963 n.
chastity
contraception 172 n.
modesty 874 n.
virtue 933 n.
temperance 942 n.
purity 950 n.
chasuble
vestments 989 n.
chat
rumour 529 n.
chat 584 n.
converse 584 vb.
château
house 192 n.
chatelaine
keeper 749 n.
chatoyant
iridescent 437 adj.
chat show
broadcast 531 n.
chattel
slave 742 n.
property 777 n.
chatter
be cold 380 vb.
roll 403 n.
ululate 409 vb.
empty talk 515 n.
speak 579 vb.
chatter 581 n.
be loquacious 581 vb.
chat 584 n.
chatterbox
chatterer 581 n.
chattering
spasm 318 n.
chilly 380 adj.

chatty
informative 524 adj.
loquacious 581 adj.
conversing 584 adj.
sociable 882 adj.
chauffeur
driver 268 n.
domestic 742 n.
chauvinism
nation 371 n.
prejudice 481 n.
bellicosity 718 n.
boasting 877 n.
patriotism 901 n.
chauvinist
narrow mind 481 n.
militarist 722 n.
patriot 901 n.
cheap
inferior 35 adj.
spurious 542 adj.
cheap 812 adj.
vulgar 847 adj.
disreputable 867 adj.
cheapen
underestimate 483 vb.
impair 655 vb.
demonetize 797 vb.
discount 810 vb.
cheapen 812 vb.
vulgarize 847 vb.
not respect 921 vb.
— oneself
demean oneself 867 vb.
cheap-jack
bad 645 adj.
cheap 812 adj.
cheapness
inferiority 35 n.
cheapness 812 n.
cheat
duplicity 541 n.
deception 542 n.
trickery 542 n.
deceive 542 vb.
trickster 545 n.
slyboots 698 n.
stratagem 698 n.
be cunning 698 vb.
fleece 786 vb.
defraud 788 vb.
defrauder 789 n.
be dishonest 930 vb.
knave 938 n.
check
number 86 vb.
delay 136 n.
stop 145 n.
halt 145 vb.
moderation 177 n.
moderate 177 vb.
counteraction 182 n.
retard 278 vb.
chequer 437 n.
pied 437 adj.
variegate 437 vb.
be careful 457 vb.
enquiry 459 n.
enquire 459 vb.
experiment 461 N. vb.
comparison 462 n.
measurement 465 n.
make certain 473 vb.
label 547 n.
hindrance 702 n.
be obstructive 702 vb.
hinder 702 vb.
defeat 727 vb.
defeat 728 n.
adversity 731 n.
restraint 747 n.
restrain 747 vb.
paper money 797 n.
pattern 844 n.
— on
enquire 459 vb.
experiment 461 vb.
— oneself
be mute 578 vb.
checklist
list 87 n.
comparison 462 n.
checkmate
halt 145 vb.
overmaster 727 vb.
defeat 728 n.
checkout
recording instrument 549 n.
checkup
attention 455 n.
enquiry 459 n.
Cheddar
dairy product 301 n.
cheek
laterality 239 n.
sauciness 878 n.
be insolent 878 vb.
rudeness 885 n.
scurrility 899 n.
cheek by jowl
with 89 adv.
near 200 adv.
contiguously 202 adv.
sideways 239 adv.
cheeky
impertinent 878 adj.
discourteous 885 adj.
disrespectful 921 adj.
cheep
ululation 409 n.
ululate 409 vb.
cheer
invigorate 174 vb.
food 301 n.
cry 408 n.vb.
vociferate 408 vb.
gesture 547 n.
please 826 vb.
relieve 831 vb.
merriment 833 n.
be cheerful 833 vb.
cheer 833 vb.
rejoice 835 vb.
give hope 852 vb.
give courage 855 vb.
celebrate 876 vb.
sociability 882 n.
show respect 920 vb.
applaud 923 vb.
— on
incite 612 vb.
— up
relieve 831 vb.
be cheerful 833 vb.
cheerful
content 828 adj.
cheerful 833 adj.
cheerfulness
vitality 162 n.
expectation 507 n.
cheerfulness 833 n.
hope 852 n.
cheerio!
296 int.
cheerless
unpleasant 827 adj.
cheerless 834 adj.
dejected 834 adj.
melancholic 834 adj.
unpromising 853 adj.
cheers!
301 int.
835 int.
cheery
cheerful 833 adj.
cheese
dairy product 301 n.
cheese board
dessert 301 n.
cheesecake
pastries 301 n.
a beauty 841 n.
cheesecloth
textile 222 n.
cheesed off
discontented 829 adj.
dejected 834 adj.
bored 838 adj.
cheese-paring
economy 814 n.
parsimony 816 n.
cheetah
speeder 277 n.
cat 365 n.
chef
cookery 301 n.
caterer 633 n.
chef d'oeuvre
product 164 n.
exceller 644 n.
perfection 646 n.
deed 676 n.
masterpiece 694 n.
chemical warfare
poisoning 659 n.
warfare 718 n.
weapon 723 n.
chemise
dress 228 n.
underwear 228 n.
chemist
alterer 143 n.
physics 319 n.
experimenter 461 n.
druggist 658 n.
chemistry
physics 319 n.
chemotherapy
therapy 658 n.
chenille
textile 222 n.
cheque
paper money 797 n.
chequebook
record 548 n.
account book 808 n.
chequer
chequer 437 n.
variegate 437 vb.
pattern 844 n.
chequered
changeable 143 adj.
pied 437 adj.
cherish
look after 457 vb.
safeguard 660 vb.
preserve 666 vb.
patronize 703 vb.
love 887 vb.
pet 889 vb.
approve 923 vb.
— the memory
remember 505 vb.
cheroot
tobacco 388 n.
cherry
fruit 301 n.
redness 431 n.
cherub
child 132 n.
image 551 n.
darling 890 n.
angel 968 n.
cherubic
angelic 968 adj.
cherubim
angel 968 n.
chervil
potherb 301 n.
Cheshire Cat
cat 365 n.
laugher 835 n.
chess
board game 837 n.
chessboard
chequer 437 n.
arena 724 n.
chess piece
plaything 837 n.
chess-player
player 837 n.
chest
box 194 n.
insides 224 n.
bosom 253 n.
treasury 799 n.
chesterfield
seat 218 n.

chestnut
repetition 106 n.
horse 273 n.
fruit 301 n.
brown 430 adj.
witticism 839 n.
chest of drawers
cabinet 194 n.
chesty
puffing 352 adj.
cheval glass
mirror 442 n.
chevalier d'industrie
defrauder 789 n.
chevaux-de-frise
sharp point 256 n.
defences 713 n.
chevron
obliquity 220 n.
angularity 247 n.
heraldry 547 n.
livery 547 n.
badge of rank 743 n.
pattern 844 n.
chew
rend 46 vb.
chew 301 vb.
pulverize 332 vb.
— a quid
smoke 388 vb.
— over
meditate 449 vb.
— the fat
converse 584 vb.
chewing gum
sweets 301 n.
elasticity 328 n.
Chianti
wine 301 n.
chiaroscuro
light contrast 417 n.
painting 553 n.
chiasmus
inversion 221 n.
ornament 574 n.
chic
beauty 841 n.
shapely 841 adj.
fashion 848 n.
fashionable 848 adj.
chicanery
sophistry 477 n.
trickery 542 n.
cunning 698 n.
foul play 930 n.
chichi
fashionable 848 adj.
affected 850 adj.
chick
young creature 132 n.
youngster 132 n.
woman 373 n.
darling 890 n.
chicken
young creature 132 n.
meat 301 n.
poultry 365 n.
coward 856 n.
cowardly 856 adj.
chickenfeed
provender 301 n.
trifle 639 n.
easy thing 701 n.
money 797 n.
chicken out
be cowardly 856 vb.
chickenpox
infection 651 n.
chicken run
stock farm 369 n.
chicken wire
network 222 n.
chick peas
vegetable 301 n.
chicory
vegetable 301 n.
chide
curse 899 vb.
reprove 924 vb.
chief
superior 34 n.
supreme 34 adj.
first 68 adj.
central 225 adj.
heraldry 547 n.
bigwig 638 n.
important 638 adj.
director 690 n.
potentate 741 n.
chieftain
potentate 741 n.
chieftainship
position of authority 733 n.
chiffon
textile 222 n.
transparency 422 n.
finery 844 n.
chiffonier
cabinet 194 n.
chignon
hair 259 n.
hairdressing 843 n.
chilblain(s)
coldness 380 n.
ulcer 651 n.
child
child 132 n.
descendant 170 n.
posterity 170 n.
dwarf 196 n.
ninny 501 n.
innocent 935 n.
childbirth
obstetrics 167 n.
childhood
youth 130 n.
childish
young 130 adj.
infantine 132 adj.
foolish 499 adj.
feeble 572 adj.
trivial 639 adj.
childless
unproductive 172 adj.
childlike
infantine 132 adj.
artless 699 adj.
innocent 935 adj.
child of fortune
prosperous person 730 n.
child of nature
ingenue 699 n.
children's home
shelter 662 n.
child's play
trifle 639 n.
easy thing 701 n.
chiliad
over one hundred 99 n.
chiliasm
aspiration 852 n.
chill
moderate 177 vb.
coldness 380 n.
cold 380 adj.
be cold 380 vb.
refrigerate 382 vb.
dissuade 613 vb.
adversity 731 n.
frighten 854 vb.
chiller
refrigerator 384 n.
chilli
vegetable 301 n.
condiment 389 n.
chilly
chilly 380 adj.
cold 380 adj.
inimical 881 adj.
chime
sound faint 401 vb.
resound 404 vb.
melody 410 n.
harmonize 410 vb.
campanology 412 n.
tune 412 n.
— in
accord 24 vb.
concord 710 vb.
chimera
insubstantial thing 4 n.
rara avis 84 n.
fantasy 513 n.
hopelessness 853 n.
chimerical
insubstantial 4 adj.
imaginary 513 adj.
chimney
gap 201 n.
chimney 263 n.
air pipe 353 n.
furnace 383 n.
chimney corner
home 192 n.
chimneysweep
cleaner 648 n.
chimpanzee
mammal 365 n.
chin
face 237 n.
protuberance 254 n.
china
weak thing 163 n.
pottery 381 n.
ornamentation 844 n.
china clay
soil 344 n.
materials 631 n.
chinaware
receptacle 194 n.
pottery 381 n.
chinchilla
skin 226 n.
chine
centre 225 n.
rear 238 n.
valley 255 n.
Chinese boxes
stratification 207 n.
Chinese lantern
lamp 420 n.
celebration 876 n.
Chinese puzzle
enigma 530 n.
chink
gap 201 n.
narrowness 206 n.
furrow 262 n.
faintness 401 n.
sound faint 401 vb.
resonance 404 n.
resound 404 vb.
chink in one's armour
defect 647 n.
vulnerability 661 n.
chinoiserie
ornamentation 844 n.
chinook
wind 352 n.
chintz
textile 222 n.
chinwag
speech 579 n.
chatterer 581 n.
chat 584 n.
converse 584 vb.
chip
small thing 33 n.
break 46 vb.
cut 46 vb.
piece 53 n.
microelectronics 196 n.
be brittle 330 vb.
pulverize 332 vb.
label 547 n.
sculpt 554 vb.
plaything 837 n.
— away
make smaller 198 vb.

— in
discontinue 72 vb.
interfere 231 vb.
give 781 vb.
chipboard
paper 631 n.
chipmunk
mammal 365 n.
chip off the old block
analogue 18 n.
descendant 170 n.
chipolata
meat 301 n.
chip on one's shoulder
discontent 829 n.
chipper
cheerful 833 adj.
chippings
paving 226 n.
chippy
café 192 n.
loose woman 952 n.
chips
vegetable 301 n.
chirography
writing 586 n.
chiromancy
divination 511 n.
occultism 984 n.
chiropodist
doctor 658 n.
beautician 843 n.
chiropractic
surgery 658 n.
chiropractor
doctor 658 n.
chirp, chirrup
ululate 409 vb.
sing 413 vb.
be cheerful 833 vb.
chirpy
cheerful 833 adj.
chisel
cut 46 vb.
produce 164 vb.
form 243 vb.
sharp edge 256 n.
sculpture 554 n.
sculpt 554 vb.
engraving 555 n.
tool 630 n.
defraud 788 vb.
chit
youngster 132 n.
dwarf 196 n.
credential 466 n.
label 547 n.
correspondence 588 n.
chitchat
chat 584 n.
chiton
robe 228 n.
chitterlings
meat 301 n.
chivalric
benevolent 897 adj.
chivalrous
male 372 adj.
courageous 855 adj.
noble 868 adj.
courteous 884 adj.
benevolent 897 adj.
honourable 929 adj.
disinterested 931 adj.
chivalry
cavalry 722 n.
prowess 855 n.
philanthropy 901 n.
chives
potherb 301 n.
chivvy
pursue 619 vb.
torment 827 vb.
chloral
anaesthetic 375 n.
chlorinate
purify 648 vb.
sanitate 652 vb.
safeguard 660 vb.
chloroform
anaesthetic 375 n.
render insensible 375 vb.
chlorophyll
green pigment 434 n.
chock
prop 218 n.
chock-a-block
full 54 adj.
filled 635 adj.
chocolate
milk 301 n.
mouthful 301 n.
sweets 301 n.
brown 430 adj.
choice
unusual 84 adj.
opportunity 137 n.
savoury 390 adj.
discrimination 463 n.
will 595 n.
willingness 597 n.
choice 605 n.
chosen 605 adj.
excellent 644 adj.
beautiful 841 adj.
tasteful 846 adj.
liking 859 n.
love 887 n.
choiceless
necessary 596 adj.
choiceless 606 adj.
choice of words
phrase 563 n.
style 566 n.
choir
choir 413 n.
sing 413 vb.
church officer 986 n.
church interior 990 n.
choke
stopper 264 n.
close 264 vb.
kill 362 vb.
extinguish 382 vb.
rasp 407 vb.
superabound 637 vb.
hinder 702 vb.
— off
dissuade 613 vb.
choke damp
gas 336 n.
poison 659 n.
choker
jewellery 844 n.
choky
lockup 748 n.
choler
anger 891 n.
irascibility 892 n.
cholera
digestive disorders 651 n.
infection 651 n.
tropical disease 651 n.
choleric
irascible 892 adj.
cholesterol
food content 301 n.
choli
shirt 228 n.
choose
will 595 vb.
be willing 597 vb.
choose 605 vb.
desire 859 vb.
choosy
choosing 605 adj.
tasteful 846 adj.
fastidious 862 adj.
chop
cut 46 vb.
piece 53 n.
meat 301 n.
— and change
change 143 vb.
vary 152 vb.
be capricious 604 vb.
— logic
argue 475 vb.
— up
cut 46 vb.
shorten 204 vb.
chopper
sharp edge 256 n.
aircraft 276 n.
pulverizer 332 n.
axe 723 n.
choppiness
roughness 259 n.
agitation 318 n.
wave 350 n.
choppy
nonuniform 17 adj.
rough 259 adj.
flowing 350 adj.
chop suey
dish 301 n.
choral
musical 412 adj.
musicianly 413 adj.
choral music
music 412 n.
chord
combination 50 n.
straightness 249 n.
musical note 410 n.
musical piece 412 n.
chore
labour 682 n.
bore 838 n.
choreographer
dramatist 594 n.
choreography
composition 56 n.
arrangement 62 n.
ballet 594 n.
dancing 837 n.
choric ode
poem 593 n.
chorister
choir 413 n.
church officer 986 n.
chortle
laughter 835 n.
laugh 835 vb.
chorus
do likewise 20 vb.
agreement 24 n.
accord 24 vb.
combination 50 n.
repetition 106 n.
repeat oneself 106 vb.
synchronize 123 vb.
periodicity 141 n.
cry 408 n.
vociferate 408 vb.
melody 410 n.
harmonize 410 vb.
vocal music 412 n.
choir 413 n.
sing 413 vb.
consensus 488 n.
speaker 579 n.
actor 594 n.
dramaturgy 594 n.
chorus girl
entertainer 594 n.
chosen
superior 34 adj.
separate 46 adj.
fated 596 adj.
voluntary 597 adj.
chosen 605 adj.
excellent 644 adj.
approved 923 adj.
sanctified 979 adj.
chosen career
vocation 622 n.
chosen few
particularism 80 n.
elite 644 n.
upper class 868 n.
chosen people
elite 644 n.
pietist 979 n.
chow
food 301 n.

dog 365 n.
chow mein
dish 301 n.
chrestomathy
literature 557 n.
anthology 592 n.
Christ
God the Son 965 n.
religious teacher 973 n.
Christadelphian
sectarian 978 n.
christen
auspicate 68 vb.
name 561 vb.
perform ritual 988 vb.
Christendom
Christendom 976 n.
the church 985 n.
christening
nomenclature 561 n.
Christian rite 988 n.
Christian
religionist 973 n.
religious 973 adj.
church member 976 n.
pious 979 adj.
Christian behaviour
virtue 933 n.
piety 979 n.
Christian charity
benevolence 897 n.
Christian fellowship
Christendom 976 n.
Christianity
religious faith 973 n.
Christian practice
orthodoxism 976 n.
Christian rite
Christian rite 988 n.
Christian Science
medical art 658 n.
Christian Scientist
doctor 658 n.
sectarian 978 n.
Christlike
godlike 965 adj.
pious 979 adj.
Christmas
winter 129 n.
holy day 988 n.
Christmas box
gift 781 n.
Christmas dinner
feasting 301 n.
Christmas present
gift 781 n.
Christmassy
sociable 882 adj.
Christology
theology 973 n.
chroma
hue 425 n.
chromatic
harmonic 410 adj.
coloured 425 adj.
chromatic scale
key 410 n.
chromatin
organism 358 n.
chromatism
colour 425 n.
chrome yellow
yellow pigment 433 n.
chromolithography
printing 555 n.
chromosome
heredity 5 n.
organism 358 n.
chronic
lasting 113 adj.
obstinate 602 adj.
sick 651 adj.
tedious 838 adj.
chronic invalid
sick person 651 n.
chronicle
chronology 117 n.
time 117 vb.
record 548 n.vb.
narrative 590 n.
chronicler
antiquarian 125 n.
chronicler 549 n.
narrator 590 n.
chronograph
timekeeper 117 n.
chronological
chronological 117 adj.
chronological error
anachronism 118 n.
chronology
directory 87 n.
date 108 n.
chronology 117 n.
reference book 589 n.
chronometer
timekeeper 117 n.
sailing aid 269 n.
chronometry
chronometry 117 n.
chrysalis
young creature 132 n.
source 156 n.
chryselephantine
ornamented 844 adj.
chrysoberyl
gem 844 n.
chrysoprase
greenness 434 n.
gem 844 n.
Chthonian
infernal 972 adj.
chubby
fleshy 195 adj.
chuck
propulsion 287 n.
propel 287 vb.
— it
resign 753 vb.
— out
eject 300 vb.
reject 607 vb.
— under the chin
caress 889 vb.
chucker-out
athlete 162 n.
ejector 300 n.
chuckle
ululate 409 vb.
laughter 835 n.
laugh 835 vb.
chuffed
pleased 824 adj.
jubilant 833 adj.
chug
be in motion 265 vb.
move slowly 278 vb.
roll 403 vb.
chum
male 372 n.
colleague 707 n.
chum 880 n.
chummy
friendly 880 adj.
chump
head 213 n.
dunce 501 n.
chunk
piece 53 n.
bulk 195 n.
chunky
fleshy 195 adj.
rough 259 adj.
church
public worship 981 n.
church 990 n.
Church, the
Christendom 976 n.
orthodoxism 976 n.
the church 985 n.
church bell(s)
campanology 412 n.
signal 547 n.
call 547 n.
church utensil 990 n.
Churches of Christ
sect 978 n.
church exterior
church exterior 990 n.
church-goer
church member 976 n.
worshipper 981 n.
churching of women
Christian rite 988 n.
church interior
church interior 990 n.
church lands
benefice 985 n.
churchman, churchwoman
church member 976 n.
cleric 986 n.
church member
church member 976 n.
worshipper 981 n.
laity 987 n.
Church militant
Christendom 976 n.
Church of Christ Scientist
sect 978 n.
Church of England
Christendom 976 n.
church office
degree 27 n.
church office 985 n.
church officer
church officer 986 n.
lay person 987 n.
Church of Rome
Christendom 976 n.
Church of Scotland
Christendom 976 n.
church service
public worship 981 n.
church service 988 n.
Church triumphant
saint 968 n.
Christendom 976 n.
church utensil
church utensil 990 n.
churchwarden
tobacco 388 n.
church officer 986 n.
churchy
orthodox 976 adj.
pietistic 979 adj.
churchyard
cemetery 364 n.
church exterior 990 n.
churl
niggard 816 n.
country-dweller 869 n.
churlish
parsimonious 816 adj.
ill-bred 847 adj.
plebeian 869 adj.
ungracious 885 adj.
malevolent 898 adj.
churn
vessel 194 n.
agitate 318 vb.
— out
produce 164 vb.
churr
ululate 409 vb.
chute
obliquity 220 n.
outlet 298 n.
descent 309 n.
waterfall 350 n.
chutney
sauce 389 n.

chutzpah
insolence 878 n.
CIA
secret service 459 n.
cicada
insect 365 n.
cicatrice, cicatrix
trace 548 n.
wound 655 n.
blemish 845 n.
cicerone
guide 520 n.
Ciceronian
elegant 575 adj.
CID
police enquiry 459 n.
cider
alcoholic drink 301 n.
ci-devant
prior 119 adj.
resigning 753 adj.
CID man
detective 459 n.
cigar, cigarette
tobacco 388 n.
cigarette card
picture 553 n.
cigar-shaped
rotund 252 adj.
cilium
filament 208 n.
hair 259 n.
Cimmerian
dark 418 adj.
cinch
girdle 47 n.
certainty 473 n.
easy thing 701 n.
Cinderella
nonentity 639 n.
object of scorn 867 n.
cinders
ash 381 n.
coal 385 n.
dirt 649 n.
cinder track
road 624 n.
arena 724 n.
cineast
cinema 445 n.
enthusiast 504 n.
cinecamera
camera 442 n.
cinema
cinema 445 n.
place of amusement 837 n.
cinemagoer
spectator 441 n.
cinematography
motion 265 n.
cinema 445 n.
photography 551 n.
cinerary
funereal 364 adj.
cinnamon
condiment 389 n.
brownness 430 n.
cinquecento
art 551 n.
cipher, cypher
nonexistence 2 n.
insubstantial thing 4 n.
number 85 n.
zero 103 n.
translate 520 vb.
secrecy 525 n.
enigma 530 n.
indication 547 n.
label 547 n.
symbology 547 n.
initials 558 n.
writing 586 n.
nonentity 639 n.
circa
nearly 200 adv.
Circean
pleasurable 826 adj.
sensual 944 adj.
sorcerous 983 adj.
circle
continuity 71 n.
group 74 n.
be periodic 141 vb.
surround 230 vb.
circumscription 232 n.
outline 233 n.
circle 250 n.
go round 250 vb.
traverse 267 vb.
navigate 269 vb.
fly 271 vb.
circle 314 vb.
theatre 594 n.
circuit 626 n.vb.
party 708 n.
restriction 747 n.
circlet
outline 233 n.
loop 250 n.
circuit
whole 52 n.
continuity 71 n.
regular return 141 n.
revolution 149 n.
electricity 160 n.
region 184 n.
surroundings 230 n.
outline 233 n.
circle 250 n.
orbit 250 n.
land travel 267 n.
circuition 314 n.
circle 314 vb.
route 624 n.
circuit 626 n.vb.
circuition
circuit 626 n.
circuitous
labyrinthine 251 adj.
deviating 282 adj.
circuitous 314 adj.
roundabout 626 adj.
circular
continuous 71 adj.
round 250 adj.
information 524 n.
publication 528 n.
correspondence 588 n.
decree 737 n.
circularity
circularity 250 n.
circularize, circularise
publish 528 vb.
correspond 588 vb.
command 737 vb.
circular reasoning
sophism 477 n.
circulate
disperse 75 vb.
go round 250 vb.
pass 305 vb.
circle 314 vb.
be published 528 vb.
publish 528 vb.
change hands 780 vb.
mint 797 vb.
circulation
blood 335 n.
circuit 626 n.
circumambulate
walk 267 vb.
circle 314 vb.
perform ritual 988 vb.
circumbendibus
meandering 251 n.
deviation 282 n.
circumcision
scission 46 n.
rite 988 n.
circumference
region 184 n.
size 195 n.
distance 199 n.
exteriority 223 n.
surroundings 230 n.
outline 233 n.
limit 236 n.
circle 250 n.
circuit 626 n.
circumflex
curved 248 adj.
punctuation 547 n.
circumjacent
circumjacent 230 adj.
circumlocution
phrase 563 n.
pleonasm 570 n.
circumnavigation
motion 265 n.
water travel 269 n.
circuition 314 n.
circumscribe
surround 230 vb.
circumscribe 232 vb.
outline 233 vb.
enclose 235 vb.
limit 236 vb.
hinder 702 vb.
obstruct 702 vb.
restrain 747 vb.
circumscribed
circumscribed 232 adj.
circumspect
vigilant 457 adj.
cautious 858 adj.
circumspection
attention 455 n.
carefulness 457 n.
caution 858 n.
circumstance
state 7 n.
circumstance 8 n.
relation 9 n.
degree 27 n.
concomitant 89 n.
affairs 154 n.
event 154 n.
influence 178 n.
ostentation 875 n.
circumstances
circumstance 8 n.
particulars 80 n.
estate 777 n.
circumstantial
circumstantial 8 adj.
complete 54 adj.
definite 80 adj.
careful 457 adj.
evidential 466 adj.
veracious 540 adj.
diffuse 570 adj.
descriptive 590 adj.
circumstantial evidence
evidence 466 n.
probability 471 n.
circumvent
deceive 542 vb.
avoid 620 vb.
be cunning 698 vb.
circus
housing 192 n.
circle 250 n.
zoo 369 n.
stage show 594 n.
arena 724 n.
pleasure ground 837 n.
cirque
valley 255 n.
cirrhosis
digestive disorders 651 n.
cirrus
cloud 355 n.
cissy
(See **sissy** *)*
Cistercian
monk 986 n.
cistern
vat 194 n.
lake 346 n.
storage 632 n.

citadel
refuge 662 n.
fort 713 n.
citation
referral 9 n.
evidence 466 n.
decoration 729 n.
warrant 737 n.
praise 923 n.
cite
specify 80 vb.
exemplify 83 vb.
repeat 106 vb.
citified
urban 192 adj.
well-bred 848 adj.
citizen
native 191 n.
subject 742 n.
free person 744 n.
commoner 869 n.
citizenry
inhabitants 191 n.
social group 371 n.
commonalty 869 n.
citizenship
freedom 744 n.
citrus fruit
fruit 301 n.
city
city 184 n.
abode 192 n.
housing 192 n.
City
city 184 n.
business 622 n.
city-dweller
dweller 191 n.
city father
officer 741 n.
city state
nation 371 n.
political organization 733 n.
civet
scent 396 n.
civic
national 371 adj.
civic centre
focus 76 n.
civic ideals
patriotism 901 n.
civil
national 371 adj.
well-bred 848 adj.
courteous 884 adj.
civil code
law 953 n.
civil defence
defender 713 n.
civil disobedience
resistance 715 n.
disobedience 738 n.
civil engineering
production 164 n.
civilian
pacifist 717 n.
peaceful 717 adj.
civility
civilization 654 n.
good taste 846 n.
courteous act 884 n.
courtesy 884 n.
civilization, civilisation
humankind 371 n.
culture 490 n.
literature 557 n.
civilization 654 n.
beau monde 848 n.
civilize, civilise
make better 654 vb.
civilized
well-bred 848 adj.
civilized behaviour
etiquette 848 n.
civil law
law 953 n.
civil rights
freedom 744 n.
dueness 915 n.
civil servant
official 690 n.
officer 741 n.
servant 742 n.
civil service
vocation 622 n.
management 689 n.
governance 733 n.
commission 751 n.
civil war
war 718 n.
revolt 738 n.
civvies
informal dress 228 n.
Civvy Street
peace 717 n.
clack
roll 403 n.vb.
ululate 409 vb.
chatter 581 n.
be loquacious 581 vb.
clad
dressed 228 adj.
cladding
facing 226 n.
claim
territory 184 n.
enclosure 235 n.
affirm 532 vb.
pretext 614 n.
plead 614 vb.
requirement 627 n.
require 627 vb.
demand 737 n.vb.
request 761 n.vb.
estate 777 n.
appropriate 786 vb.
desire 859 n.vb.
title 870 n.
dueness 915 n.
claim 915 vb.
have a right 915 vb.
litigate 959 vb.
— attention
attract notice 455 vb.
impress 821 vb.
— back
retrieve 656 vb.
claimant
petitioner 763 n.
desirer 859 n.
dueness 915 n.
litigant 959 n.
clairvoyance
intuition 476 n.
occultism 984 n.
psychics 984 n.
clairvoyant
psychic 984 n.
psychical 984 adj.
clam
marine life 365 n.
taciturnity 582 n.
clamant
loud 400 adj.
desiring 859 adj.
clamber
climb 308 vb.
clamlike
reticent 525 adj.
clammy
viscid 354 adj.
clamour
loudness 400 n.
cry 408 n.
vociferate 408 vb.
request 761 n.
weep 836 vb.
disapprobation 924 n.
— for
require 627 vb.
request 761 vb.
desire 859 vb.
clamp
affix 45 vb.
fastening 47 n.
close 264 vb.
nippers 778 n.
— down on
be severe 735 vb.
restrain 747 vb.
clan
race 11 n.
group 74 n.
breed 77 n.
genealogy 169 n.
community 708 n.
clandestine
occult 523 adj.
concealed 525 adj.
stealthy 525 adj.
clang
loudness 400 n.
be loud 400 vb.
roll 403 n.vb.
resonance 404 n.
clanger
mistake 495 n.
clangour
loudness 400 n.
resonance 404 n.
clank
resound 404 vb.
rasp 407 vb.
clannish
ethnic 11 adj.
biased 481 adj.
sectional 708 adj.
sectarian 978 adj.
clansman
kinsman 11 n.
friend 880 n.
clap
knock 279 n.
strike 279 vb.
loudness 400 n.
be loud 400 vb.
bang 402 n.
crackle 402 vb.
gesture 547 n.
rejoice 835 vb.
congratulate 886 vb.
applause 923 n.
applaud 923 vb.
— eyes on
see 438 vb.
— on the back
gesticulate 547 vb.
applaud 923 vb.
clap, the
venereal disease 651 n.
clapped out
impotent 161 adj.
fatigued 684 adj.
claptrap
sophistry 477 n.
empty talk 515 n.
fable 543 n.
claque
playgoer 594 n.
commender 923 n.
flatterer 925 n.
claret
wine 301 n.
blood 335 n.
redness 431 n.
clarification
demonstration 478 n.
interpretation 520 n.
clarify
eliminate 44 vb.
liquefy 337 vb.
make flow 350 vb.
be transparent 422 vb.
be intelligible 516 vb.
interpret 520 vb.
purify 648 vb.
clarinet
flute 414 n.
clarinettist
instrumentalist 413 n.
clarion call
loudness 400 n.
war measures 718 n.

clarity
transparency 422 n.
visibility 443 n.
intelligibility 516 n.
perspicuity 567 n.
elegance 575 n.
clash
contrariety 14 n.
be contrary 14 vb.
disagreement 25 n.
disagree 25 vb.
violence 176 n.
collision 279 n.
collide 279 vb.
loudness 400 n.
be loud 400 vb.
bang 402 vb.
rasp 407 vb.
discord 411 vb.
quarrel 709 n.vb.
strike at 712 vb.
contention 716 n.
battle 718 n.
be inimical 881 vb.
clashing
disagreeing 25 adj.
florid 425 adj.
clasp
fastening 47 n.
cohere 48 vb.
circumscribe 232 vb.
retention 778 n.
retain 778 vb.
jewellery 844 n.
endearment 889 n.
caress 889 vb.
— hands
be friendly 880 vb.
greet 884 vb.
clasp knife
sharp edge 256 n.
class
degree 27 n.
graduate 27 vb.
arrangement 62 n.
class 62 vb.
group 74 n.
breed 77 n.
classification 77 n.
number with 78 vb.
contemporary 123 n.
study 536 n.
class 538 n.
party 708 n.
class-conscious
sectional 708 adj.
class consciousness
particularism 80 n.
pride 871 n.
classes
curriculum 534 n.
classic
prototypal 23 adj.
supreme 34 adj.
olden 127 adj.
tailored 228 adj.
symmetrical 245 adj.
stylist 575 n.
elegant 575 adj.
book 589 n.
excellent 644 adj.
paragon 646 n.
perfect 646 adj.
shapely 841 adj.
classical
architectural 192 adj.
literary 557 adj.
tasteful 846 adj.
right 913 adj.
Classical Age
antiquity 125 n.
literature 557 n.
classicism
art 551 n.
literature 557 n.
elegance 575 n.
classicist
antiquarian 125 n.
scholar 492 n.
classification
relation 9 n.
subdivision 53 n.
arrangement 62 n.
series 71 n.
classification 77 n.
identification 547 n.
classified
orderly 60 adj.
arranged 62 adj.
positive 473 adj.
classified ad
advertisement 528 n.
classified with
included 78 adj.
classify
class 62 vb.
classmate
learner 538 n.
chum 880 n.
class prejudice
prejudice 481 n.
classroom
classroom 539 n.
classy
personable 841 adj.
fashionable 848 adj.
genteel 868 adj.
clatter
loudness 400 n.
roll 403 n.vb.
clause
subdivision 53 n.
phrase 563 n.
conditions 766 n.
claustral
sealed off 264 adj.
claustrophobia
psychopathy 503 n.
phobia 854 n.
claustrophobic
circumjacent 230 adj.
insane 503 adj.
claw
rend 46 vb.
coupling 47 n.
foot 214 n.
sharp point 256 n.
finger 378 n.
wound 655 vb.
weapon 723 n.
nippers 778 n.
clay
adhesive 47 n.
changeable thing 152 n.
solid body 324 n.
softness 327 n.
soil 344 n.
corpse 363 n.
sculpture 554 n.
materials 631 n.
claymore
sidearms 723 n.
clay-pigeon shooting
sport 837 n.
clay pipe
tobacco 388 n.
clean
unmixed 44 adj.
completely 54 adv.
new 126 adj.
empty 190 adj.
empty 300 vb.
make bright 417 vb.
whiten 427 vb.
careful 457 adj.
plain 573 adj.
cleansing 648 n.
clean 648 adj.vb.
salubrious 652 adj.
sanitate 652 vb.
make better 654 vb.
honourable 929 adj.
pure 950 adj.
— out
empty 300 vb.
search 459 vb.
clean 648 vb.
purify 648 vb.
steal 788 vb.
— up
unravel 62 vb.
empty 300 vb.
clean 648 vb.
purify 648 vb.
clean breast
assent 488 n.
disclosure 526 n.
veracity 540 n.
clean-cut
definite 80 adj.
positive 473 adj.
cleaned
clean 648 adj.
cleaner
cleaner 648 n.
clean hands
probity 929 n.
innocence 935 n.
clean-limbed
shapely 841 adj.
cleanliness
cleanness 648 n.
hygiene 652 n.
clean pair of heels
speeding 277 n.
cleanse
eliminate 44 vb.
purify 648 vb.
sanitate 652 vb.
cleanser
cleanser 648 n.
clean-shaven
hairless 229 adj.
smooth 258 adj.
cleansing
ritual act 988 n.
cleansing cream
cleanser 648 n.
cosmetic 843 n.
clean slate
obliteration 550 n.
facility 701 n.
clean sweep
revolution 149 n.
ejection 300 n.
clear
unmixed 44 adj.
eliminate 44 vb.
orderly 60 adj.
space 201 vb.
be high 209 vb.
fly 271 vb.
empty 300 vb.
leap 312 vb.
fluid 335 adj.
make flow 350 vb.
striking 374 adj.
melodious 410 adj.
undimmed 417 adj.
make bright 417 vb.
transparent 422 adj.
obvious 443 adj.
certain 473 adj.
semantic 514 adj.
intelligible 516 adj.
manifest 522 adj.
perspicuous 567 adj.
elegant 575 adj.
vocal 577 adj.
clean 648 vb.
safe 660 adj.
disencumber 701 vb.
liberate 746 vb.
permit 756 vb.
acquire 771 vb.
pay 804 vb.
justify 927 vb.
acquitted 960 adj.
acquit 960 vb.
— away
displace 188 vb.
empty 300 vb.
disencumber 701 vb.
— off (with)
decamp 296 vb.
take away 786 vb.
— out
decamp 296 vb.
emerge 298 vb.
empty 300 vb.
clean 648 vb.

— stock
sell 793 vb.
— the decks
make ready 669 vb.
disencumber 701 vb.
— the throat
eruct 300 vb.
rasp 407 vb.
— the way/path
come before 64 vb.
precede 283 vb.
make possible 469 vb.
facilitate 701 vb.
— up
cease 145 vb.
make bright 417 vb.
be intelligible 516 vb.
carry through 725 vb.
clearance
elimination 44 n.
room 183 n.
interval 201 n.
voidance 300 n.
preparation 669 n.
scope 744 n.
permission 756 n.
permit 756 n.
sale 793 n.
clear as ditch water
puzzling 517 adj.
clear coast
facility 701 n.
clear conscience
innocence 935 n.
clear-cut
definite 80 adj.
obvious 443 adj.
positive 473 adj.
intelligible 516 adj.
perspicuous 567 adj.
clear field
opportunity 137 n.
clear-headed
rational 475 adj.
intelligent 498 adj.
sane 502 adj.
sober 948 adj.
clearing
open space 263 n.
wood 366 n.
clearness
transparency 422 n.
visibility 443 n.
intelligibility 516 n.
perspicuity 567 n.
clear of
beyond 199 adv.
clear-sighted
seeing 438 adj.
intelligent 498 adj.
clear thinking
sagacity 498 n.
clearway
traffic control 305 n.
road 624 n.
cleat
fastening 47 n.
cleavage
disunion 46 n.
scission 46 n.
structure 331 n.
dissension 709 n.
cleave
sunder 46 vb.
bisect 92 vb.
— to
cohere 48 vb.
cleaver
sharp edge 256 n.
clef
key 410 n.
notation 410 n.
cleft
disunion 46 n.
disunited 46 adj.
bisected 92 adj.
gap 201 n.
cleft palate
speech defect 580 n.
blemish 845 n.
cleft stick
dubiety 474 n.
predicament 700 n.
clemency
leniency 736 n.
mercy 905 n.
clementine
fruit 301 n.
clench
make smaller 198 vb.
close 264 vb.
retain 778 vb.
— one's fist
defy 711 vb.
threaten 900 vb.
— one's teeth
gesticulate 547 vb.
be resolute 599 vb.
clenched fist
gesture 547 n.
nippers 778 n.
clerestory
church interior 990 n.
clergy
clergy 986 n.
clergyman
cleric 986 n.
clerical
recording 548 adj.
ecclesiastical 985 adj.
clerical 986 adj.
clerical collar
canonicals 989 n.
clericalism
government 733 n.
ecclesiasticism 985 n.
clerical worker
worker 686 n.
clerihew
doggerel 593 n.
witticism 839 n.
clerk
scholar 492 n.
recorder 549 n.
calligrapher 586 n.
official 690 n.
auxiliary 707 n.
seller 793 n.
church officer 986 n.
cleric 986 n.
clever
intelligent 498 adj.
skilful 694 adj.
witty 839 adj.
clever clever
vain 873 adj.
clever dick
wiseacre 500 n.
cleverness
intelligence 498 n.
skill 694 n.
cliché
repetition 106 n.
maxim 496 n.
lack of meaning 515 n.
neology 560 n.
phrase 563 n.
cliché-ridden
feeble 572 adj.
click
fastening 47 n.
speech sound 398 n.
sound faint 401 vb.
crackle 402 vb.
sound dead 405 vb.
know 490 vb.
succeed 727 vb.
— with
befriend 880 vb.
client
habitué 610 n.
patron 707 n.
dependant 742 n.
purchaser 792 n.
clientele
trade 791 n.
cliff
high land 209 n.
verticality 215 n.
incline 220 n.
rock 344 n.
cliff-hanging
exciting 821 adj.
climacteric
serial place 73 n.
middle age 131 n.
climactic
crowning 34 adj.
climate
influence 178 n.
tendency 179 n.
region 184 n.
weather 340 n.
climatic
airy 340 adj.
climatology
weather 340 n.
climax
superiority 34 n.
culminate 34 vb.
be complete 54 vb.
serial place 73 n.
summit 213 n.
crown 213 vb.
mature 669 vb.
completion 725 n.
climax 725 vb.
excitation 821 n.
climb
grow 36 vb.
high land 209 n.
be oblique 220 vb.
be in motion 265 vb.
fly 271 vb.
progress 285 vb.
ascend 308 vb.
climb 308 vb.
— down
descend 309 vb.
climbdown
humiliation 872 n.
climber
traveller 268 n.
climber 308 n.
plant 366 n.
clime
region 184 n.
weather 340 n.
land 344 n.
clinch
affix 45 vb.
unite with 45 vb.
ligature 47 n.
cohere 48 vb.
close 264 vb.
make certain 473 vb.
pugilism 716 n.
carry through 725 vb.
retention 778 n.
retain 778 vb.
— a deal
consent 758 vb.
contract 765 vb.
clincher
end 69 n.
reasons 475 n.
confutation 479 n.
masterpiece 694 n.
completion 725 n.
cling
cohere 48 vb.
persevere 600 vb.
caress 889 vb.
— to
be near 200 vb.
observe 768 vb.
retain 778 vb.
love 887 vb.
— to custom
be obstinate 602 vb.
be wont 610 vb.
clinging
cohesive 48 adj.
habitual 610 adj.

caressing 889 adj.
retentive 778 adj.
clinic
teaching 534 n.
hospital 658 n.
clinical
medical 658 adj.
clinical medicine
medical art 658 n.
clinical psychology
therapy 658 n.
clink
faintness 401 n.
sound faint 401 vb.
resonance 404 n.
resound 404 vb.
gaol 748 n.
— glasses
toast 876 vb.
clinker
ash 381 n.
rubbish 641 n.
dirt 649 n.
clinker-built
layered 207 adj.
marine 275 adj.
clinometer
angular measure 247 n.
clip
abate 37 vb.
subtract 39 vb.
connect 45 vb.
cut 46 vb.
fastening 47 n.
make smaller 198 vb.
shorten 204 vb.
impulse 279 n.
hairdressing 843 n.
— one's words
be concise 569 vb.
stammer 580 vb.
— the wings
disable 161 vb.
retard 278 vb.
make useless 641 vb.
impair 655 vb.
hinder 702 vb.
clip joint
place of amusement 837 n.
clipped coinage
false money 797 n.
clipper
sailing ship 275 n.
speeder 277 n.
clippers
sharp edge 256 n.
clipping(s)
small thing 33 n.
piece 53 n.
clique
band 74 n.
association 706 n.
party 708 n.
cliquish, cliquey
excluding 57 adj.
biased 481 adj.
sectional 708 adj.
clitoris
genitalia 167 n.
cloaca
sink 649 n.
cloak
wrapping 226 n.
cloak 228 n.
screen 421 n.
disguise 527 n.
sham 542 n.
pretext 614 n.
safeguard 660 vb.
canonicals 989 n.
cloak-and-dagger
stealthy 525 adj.
descriptive 590 adj.
cloak-and-dagger man
secret service 459 n.
cloakroom
chamber 194 n.
latrine 649 n.
clobber
clothing 228 n.
strike 279 vb.
cloche
headgear 228 n.
garden 370 n.
clock
timekeeper 117 n.
clock in
begin 68 vb.
time 117 vb.
arrive 295 vb.
— out
end 69 vb.
time 117 vb.
depart 296 vb.
clockmaker
timekeeper 117 n.
clock-watcher
idler 679 n.
clockwise
towards 281 adv.
round and round 315 adv.
clockwork
complexity 61 n.
machine 630 n.
plaything 837 n.
clockwork, like
uniformly 16 adv.
periodical 141 adj.
easily 701 adv.
clod
piece 53 n.n.
bulk 195 n.
solid body 324 n.
soil 344 n.
dunce 501 n.
bungler 697 n.
country-dweller 869 n.
clod-hopping
dull 840 adj.
graceless 842 adj.
ill-bred 847 adj.
clog
footwear 228 n.
be unclean 649 vb.
make unclean 649 vb.
be difficult 700 vb.
restrain 747 vb.
clogged up
closed 264 adj.
clogging
hindering 702 adj.
cloister
retreat 192 n.
enclosure 235 n.
enclose 235 vb.
refuge 662 n.
imprison 747 vb.
seclusion 883 n.
monastery 986 n.
church exterior 990 n.
cloistered
circumscribed 232 adj.
sealed off 264 adj.
secluded 883 adj.
clone
analogue 18 n.
copy 22 n.
reproduce 166 vb.
close
similar 18 adj.
firm 45 adj.
join 45 vb.
end 69 n.vb.
terminate 69 vb.
cease 145 vb.
impending 155 adj.
housing 192 n.
near 200 adj.
contiguous 202 adj.
narrow 206 adj.
enclosure 235 n.
close 264 vb.
approaching 289 adj.
approach 289 vb.
dense 324 adj.
warm 379 adj.
accurate 494 adj.
reticent 525 adj.
taciturn 582 adj.
road 624 n.
cure 656 vb.
obstruct 702 vb.
contract 765 vb.
parsimonious 816 adj.
unsociable 883 adj.
parsonage 986 n.
church exterior 990 n.
— a gap
join 45 vb.
— down
terminate 69 vb.
— in
circumscribe 232 vb.
approach 289 vb.
converge 293 vb.
— one's ears
be deaf 416 vb.
— one's eyes
die 361 vb.
be inattentive 456 vb.
sleep 679 vb.
— one's hand
refuse 760 vb.
— the ranks
cohere 48 vb.
be near 200 vb.
make ready 669 vb.
give battle 718 vb.
— up
become small 198 vb.
be near 200 vb.
— with
cohere 48 vb.
converge 293 vb.
strike at 712 vb.
fight 716 vb.
consent 758 vb.
close at hand
future 124 adj.
near 200 adv.
close attention
attention 455 n.
close behind
near 200 adv.
rearward 238 adv.
close call
escape 667 n.
(See **close shave** *)*
close contact
contiguity 202 n.
closed circuit
electricity 160 n.
closed-circuit television
camera 442 n.
broadcasting 531 n.
closed door
exclusion 57 n.
closed mind
narrow mind 481 n.
predetermination 608 n.
closed shop
uniformity 16 n.
exclusion 57 n.
party 708 n.
restriction 747 n.
close finish
short distance 200 n.
contest 716 n.
close-fisted
parsimonious 816 adj.
close-fitting
adjusted 24 adj.
cohesive 48 adj.
close friend
close friend 880 n.
loved one 887 n.
close grips
short distance 200 n.
duel 716 n.
close-hauled
towards 281 adv.

closeness
union 45 n.
nearness 200 n.
narrowness 206 n.
love 887 n.
close of day
evening 129 n.
close-packed
dense 324 adj.
close quarters
short distance 200 n.
close-run
near 200 adj.
contending 716 adj.
close season
interim 108 n.
period 110 n.
lull 145 n.
close-set
firm 45 adj.
close shave
safety 660 n.
danger 661 n.
escape 667 n.
closet
cabinet 194 n.
chamber 194 n.
hiding-place 527 n.
latrine 649 n.
closeted with, be
converse 584 vb.
consult 691 vb.
close-textured
dense 324 adj.
close-up
photography 551 n.
close-woven
tough 329 adj.
textural 331 adj.
closure
end 69 n.
stop 145 n.
closure 264 n.
hindrance 702 n.
clot
solid body 324 n.
be dense 324 vb.
blood 335 n.
semiliquidity 354 n.
thicken 354 vb.
dunce 501 n.
fool 501 n.
bungler 697 n.
cloth
product 164 n.
textile 222 n.
bookbinding 589 n.
vocation 622 n.
materials 631 n.
canonicals 989 n.
cloth, the
clergy 986 n.
cloth-cap
plebeian 869 adj.
clothe
dress 228 vb.
provide 633 vb.
clothed
dressed 228 adj.
clothes
clothing 228 n.
clothes-conscious
fashionable 848 adj.
clotheshorse
hanger 217 n.
frame 218 n.
fop 848 n.
clothier
clothier 228 n.
artisan 686 n.
clothing
clothing 228 n.
dressing 228 n.
badge 547 n.
finery 844 n.
clotted
dense 324 adj.
semiliquid 354 adj.
cloud
certain quantity 104 n.
vaporization 338 n.
air 340 n.
moisture 341 n.
cloud 355 n., vb.
dimness 419 n.
obfuscation 421 n.
screen 421 vb.
make opaque 423 vb.
disguise 527 n.
— the issue
be unrelated 10 vb.
cloudburst
storm 176 n.
rain 350 n.
cloud-capp'd
high 209 adj.
cloud-cuckoo-land
fantasy 513 n.
clouded
cloudy 355 adj.
unlit 418 adj.
opaque 423 adj.
unprosperous 731 adj.
cheerless 834 adj.
clouded brain
unintelligence 499 n.
insanity 503 n.
cloudiness
imperspicuity 568 n.
cloudless
dry 342 adj.
undimmed 417 adj.
palmy 730 adj.
cloud nine
happiness 824 n.
cloud on the horizon
danger 661 n.
warning 664 n.
cloudscape
cloud 355 n.
spectacle 445 n.
art subject 553 n.
beauty 841 n.
cloudy
humid 341 adj.
cloudy 355 adj.
dim 419 adj.
opaque 423 adj.
mottled 437 adj.
uncertain 474 adj.
imaginary 513 adj.
unclear 568 adj.
sullen 893 adj.
clout
influence 178 n.
knock 279 n.
strike 279 vb.
repair 656 n.
corporal punishment 963 n.
spank 963 vb.
clove(s)
condiment 389 n.
scent 396 n.
clove hitch
ligature 47 n.
cloven
disunited 46 adj.
bisected 92 adj.
spaced 201 adj.
cloven hoof
foot 214 n.
disclosure 526 n.
malevolence 898 n.
wickedness 934 n.
devil 969 n.
clover
provender 301 n.
palmy days 730 n.
clown
be absurd 497 vb.
fool 501 n.
entertainer 594 n.
bungler 697 n.
humorist 839 n.
laughingstock 851 n.
clowning
foolery 497 n.
ridiculousness 849 n.
clownish
clumsy 695 adj.
amusing 837 adj.
funny 849 adj.
ridiculous 849 adj.
cloy
render insensible 375 vb.
superabound 637 vb.
make insensitive 820 vb.
be tedious 838 vb.
sate 863 vb.
cloying
unsavoury 391 adj.
club
group 74 n.
focus 76 n.
meeting place 192 n.
hammer 279 n.
strike 279 vb.
association 706 n.
party 708 n.
society 708 n.
club 723 n.
social round 882 n.
scourge 964 n.
— together
cooperate 706 vb.
join a party 708 vb.
be sociable 882 vb.
clubbability
sociability 882 n.
clubfoot
deformity 246 n.
clubhouse
meeting place 192 n.
clubman, clubwoman
beau monde 848 n.
sociable person 882 n.
cluck
ululation 409 n.
ululate 409 vb.
clue
answer 460 n.
evidence 466 n.
knowledge 490 n.
supposition 512 n.
interpretation 520 n.
hint 524 n.
indication 547 n.
clued-up
informed 524 adj.
clueless
doubting 474 adj.
ignorant 491 adj.
difficult 700 adj.
in difficulties 700 adj.
clump
bunch 74 n.
walk 267 vb.
knock 279 n.
strike 279 vb.
solid body 324 n.
wood 366 n.
clumsiness
unskilfulness 695 n.
clumsy
unapt 25 adj.
unequal 29 adj.
unwieldy 195 adj.
slow 278 adj.
inexact 495 adj.
mistaken 495 adj.
inelegant 576 adj.
inexpedient 643 adj.
bad 645 adj.
clumsy 695 adj.
graceless 842 adj.
ridiculous 849 adj.
clunk
resound 404 vb.
cluster
crowd 74 n.
group 74 n.
congregate 74 vb.
clutch
group 74 n.
certain quantity 104 n.

young creature 132 n.
retain 778 vb.
take 786 vb.
— at
take 786 vb.
desire 859 vb.
clutches
governance 733 n.
retention 778 n.
clutter
confusion 61 n.
jumble 63 vb.
be many 104 vb.
coach
conveyance 267 n.
bus 274 n.
carriage 274 n.
train 274 n.
educate 534 vb.
train 534 vb.
teacher 537 n.
trainer 537 n.
preparer 669 n.
make ready 669 vb.
coachbuilder
artisan 686 n.
coachhouse
stable 192 n.
coachload
certain quantity 104 n.
thing transferred 272 n.
coachman
driver 268 n.
domestic 742 n.
coadjutor
auxiliary 707 n.
coagulate
cohere 48 vb.
be dense 324 vb.
thicken 354 vb.
coagulation
union 45 n.
coal
sources of energy 160 n.
heater 383 n.
coal 385 n.
fuel 385 n.
fire 385 vb.
torch 420 n.
black thing 428 n.
coalesce
be identical 13 vb.
combine 50 vb.
cooperate 706 vb.
coalfield
coal 385 n.
store 632 n.
coal fire
fire 379 n.
furnace 383 n.
coal gas
gas 336 n.
fuel 385 n.
coalhole
cellar 194 n.
coalition
union 45 n.
association 706 n.
political party 708 n.
society 708 n.
coal measures
mineral 359 n.
coal 385 n.
coal mine
excavation 255 n.
store 632 n.
workshop 687 n.
coaming
edge 234 n.
coarse
rough 259 adj.
textural 331 adj.
unsavoury 391 adj.
indiscriminating 464 adj.
inelegant 576 adj.
unclean 649 adj.
immature 670 adj.
graceless 842 adj.
vulgar 847 adj.
plebeian 869 adj.
impure 951 adj.
coarse fishing
chase 619 n.
coarse-looking
ugly 842 adj.
coarsen
impair 655 vb.
make insensitive 820 vb.
vulgarize 847 vb.
coarseness
roughness 259 n.
unsavouriness 391 n.
indiscrimination 464 n.
plainness 573 n.
inelegance 576 n.
moral insensibility 820 n.
bad taste 847 n.
impurity 951 n.
coarsening
deterioration 655 n.
coast
edge 234 n.
laterality 239 n.
flank 239 vb.
go smoothly 258 vb.
travel 267 vb.
voyage 269 vb.
pass 305 vb.
shore 344 n.
not act 677 vb.
do easily 701 vb.
— down
descend 309 vb.
coastal
marginal 234 adj.
coastal 344 adj.
coast clear
safety 660 n.
coaster
stand 218 n.
sledge 274 n.
merchant ship 275 n.
coastguard
nautical personnel 270 n.
protector 660 n.
keeper 749 n.
coastline
outline 233 n.
edge 234 n.
shore 344 n.
coat
layer 207 n.
laminate 207 vb.
skin 226 n.
wrapping 226 n.
coat 226 vb.
line 227 vb.
jacket 228 n.
overcoat 228 n.
colour 425 vb.
paint 553 vb.
decorate 844 vb.
— the pill
sweeten 392 vb.
coating
layer 207 n.
covering 226 n.
facing 226 n.
lining 227 n.
coat of arms
heraldry 547 n.
nobility 868 n.
coat of mail
armour 713 n.
coat of paint
facing 226 n.
coat tails
hanging object 217 n.
garment 228 n.
coax
tempt 612 vb.
request 761 vb.
pet 889 vb.
flatter 925 vb.
cob
architectural 192 adj.
pony 273 n.
fruit 301 n.
bird 365 n.
building material 631 n.
cobalt
blue pigment 435 n.
cobber
chum 880 n.
cobble(s)
paving 226 n.
road 624 n.
building material 631 n.
repair 656 vb.
cobbled together
produced 164 adj.
bungled 695 adj.
cobbler
clothier 228 n.
mender 656 n.
coble
fishing boat 275 n.
Cobol
data processing 86 n.
cobra
reptile 365 n.
cobweb
weak thing 163 n.
filament 208 n.
network 222 n.
lightness 323 n.
trifle 639 n.
dirt 649 n.
cobwebs of antiquity
oldness 127 n.
cocaine
anaesthetic 375 n.
drug 658 n.
drug-taking 949 n.
coccyx
buttocks 238 n.
cochineal
red pigment 431 n.
cochlea
ear 415 n.
cock
poultry 365 n.
male animal 372 n.
make ready 669 vb.
— a snook
gesticulate 547 vb.
defy 711 vb.
be insolent 878 vb.
not respect 921 vb.
— up
make vertical 215 vb.
jut 254 vb.
cockade
livery 547 n.
trimming 844 n.
cock-a-hoop
jubilant 833 adj.
boastful 877 adj.
Cockaigne
city 184 n.
happiness 824 n.
cock and bull story
insubstantial thing 4 n.
fable 543 n.
cockatrice
rara avis 84 n.
eye 438 n.
heraldry 547 n.
noxious animal 904 n.
cockcrow
morning 128 n.
cocked hat
headgear 228 n.
badge of rank 743 n.
cock-eyed
oblique 220 adj.
distorted 246 adj.

dim-sighted 440 adj.
ridiculous 849 adj.
cockiness
vanity 873 n.
insolence 878 n.
cockle
fish food 301 n.
marine life 365 n.
cockleshell
ship 275 n.
cockles of the heart
affections 817 n.
cockney
native 191 n.
dialect 560 n.
plebeian 869 adj.
cock of the walk
exceller 644 n.
master 741 n.
proud person 871 n.
cockpit
chamber 194 n.
aircraft 276 n.
arena 724 n.
cockroach
insect 365 n.
cockshut
evening 129 n.
cock-shy
propulsion 287 n.
laughingstock 851 n.
cocksure
believing 485 adj.
impertinent 878 adj.
cocktail
a mixture 43 n.
alcoholic drink 301 n.
draught 301 n.
cocktail party
social gathering 882 n.
cocky
prideful 871 adj.
vain 873 adj.
impertinent 878 adj.
cocoa
milk 301 n.
soft drink 301 n.
coconut
fruit 301 n.
coconut matting
floor-cover 226 n.
cocoon
young creature 132 n.
source 156 n.
receptacle 194 n.
wrapping 226 n.
safeguard 660 vb.
cod
fish food 301 n.
C.O.D.
buying 792 adj.
owed 803 adj.
cash down 804 adv.
coda
adjunct 40 n.
sequel 67 n.
end 69 n.
rear 238 n.
melody 410 n.
musical piece 412 n.
coddle
cook 301 vb.
please 826 vb.
pet 889 vb.
code
arrangement 62 n.
rule 81 n.
latency 523 n.
secrecy 525 n.
conceal 525 vb.
enigma 530 n.
symbology 547 n.
writing 586 n.
precept 693 n.
probity 929 n.
code-breaker
interpreter 520 n.
codeine
drug 658 n.
code of honour
code of duty 917 n.
probity 929 n.
codex
script 586 n.
book 589 n.
codicil
adjunct 40 n.
sequel 67 n.
title deed 767 n.
codification
law 953 n.
legislation 953 n.
codify
class 62 vb.
coeducation
education 534 n.
coefficient
numerical element 85 n.
coequal
compeer 28 n.
equal 28 adj.
coerce
dominate 733 vb.
compel 740 vb.
coercion
brute force 735 n.
compulsion 740 n.
restraint 747 n.
coeval
contemporary 123 n.
synchronous 123 adj.
coexistence
accompaniment 89 n.
synchronism 123 n.
contiguity 202 n.
concord 710 n.
peace 717 n.
coffee
soft drink 301 n.
brownness 430 n.
coffee bar
café 192 n.
coffee-coloured
brown 430 adj.
coffee estate
farm 370 n.
coffee mill
pulverizer 332 n.
coffee morning
social gathering 882 n.
coffeepot
cauldron 194 n.
coffer
box 194 n.
storage 632 n.
treasury 799 n.
coffin
box 194 n.
funeral 364 n.
interment 364 n.
cog
tooth 256 n.
notch 260 n.vb.
cogent
powerful 160 adj.
rational 475 adj.
forceful 571 adj.
compelling 740 adj.
cogged
toothed 256 adj.
cogitate
think 449 vb.
cognac
alcoholic drink 301 n.
cognate
akin 11 adj.
cognition
intellect 447 n.
knowledge 490 n.
cognitive
mental 447 adj.
cognizable, cognisable
known 490 adj.
intelligible 516 adj.
legal 953 adj.
cognizance
knowledge 490 n.
jurisdiction 955 n.
cognoscente
expert 696 n.
people of taste 846 n.
cogwheel
notch 260 n.
cohabit
unite with 45 vb.
wed 894 vb.
cohere
unite with 45 vb.
cohere 48 vb.
thicken 354 vb.
coherence
coherence 48 n.
coherent
sane 502 adj.
intelligible 516 adj.
cohesion
union 45 n.
coherence 48 n.
density 324 n.
toughness 329 n.
cohesive
conjunctive 45 adj.
cohesive 48 adj.
viscid 354 adj.
retentive 778 adj.
cohort(s)
formation 722 n.
army 722 n.
coif
headgear 228 n.
coiffeur, coiffeuse
beautician 843 n.
coiffure
wig 228 n.
hairdressing 843 n.
coil
complexity 61 n.
contraception 172 n.
make curved 248 vb.
coil 251 n.
twine 251 vb.
hairdressing 843 n.
pattern 844 n.
— up
round 252 vb.
coin
imagine 513 vb.
fake 541 vb.
coinage 797 n.
mint 797 vb.
— money
gain 771 vb.
get rich 800 vb.
— words
neologize 560 vb.
coinage
small coin 33 n.
neology 560 n.
coinage 797 n.
coincide
be identical 13 vb.
accord 24 vb.
accompany 89 vb.
synchronize 123 vb.
coincidence
concomitant 89 n.
synchronism 123 n.
event 154 n.
chance 159 n.
nondesign 618 n.
coincidental
casual 159 adj.
unintentional 618 adj.
coincidentally
unrelatedly 10 adv.
coiner
minter 797 n.
coitus
coition 45 n.
propagation 167 n.
coke
ash 381 n.
coal 385 n.
drug-taking 949 n.

col
narrowness 206 n.
high land 209 n.
cold
wintry 129 adj.
dead 361 adj.
unfeeling 375 adj.
coldness 380 n.
cold 380 adj.
cooled 382 adj.
blue 435 adj.
mistaken 495 adj.
infection 651 n.
respiratory disease 651 n.
uncooked 670 adj.
refreshing 685 adj.
adversity 731 n.
impassive 820 adj.
inexcitable 823 adj.
cheerless 834 adj.
indifferent 860 adj.
inimical 881 adj.
unsociable 883 adj.
unkind 898 adj.
pure 950 adj.
cold-blooded
animal 365 adj.
impassive 820 adj.
cautious 858 adj.
unastonished 865 adj.
cruel 898 adj.
cold comfort
discontent 829 n.
cold cream
cleanser 648 n.
cosmetic 843 n.
cold-eyed
cruel 898 adj.
cold feet
nervousness 854 n.
cold fish
unfeeling person 820 n.
cold frame
garden 370 n.
cold front
wintriness 380 n.
cold-hearted
impassive 820 adj.
selfish 932 adj.
cold light of day
disclosure 526 n.
coldness
coldness 380 n.
(See **cold** *)*
cold-shoulder
exclude 57 vb.
repel 292 vb.
disregard 458 vb.
rejection 607 n.
reject 607 vb.
avoid 620 vb.
make unwelcome 883 vb.
be rude 885 vb.
cold-shouldered
friendless 883 adj.
cold shower
moderator 177 n.
ablutions 648 n.
cold steel
lunge 712 n.
sidearms 723 n.
cold storage
delay 136 n.
refrigeration 382 n.
refrigerator 384 n.
preservation 666 n.
cold sweat
fear 854 n.
cold turkey
drug-taking 949 n.
cold war
peace 717 n.
war 718 n.
cold water
moderator 177 n.
dissuasion 613 n.
cold wind
wind 352 n.
adversity 731 n.
coleslaw
hors-d'oeuvres 301 n.
colic
pang 377 n.
digestive disorders 651 n.
colitis
digestive disorders 651 n.
collaborate
assent 488 vb.
be willing 597 vb.
apostatize 603 vb.
cooperate 706 vb.
collaboration
cooperation 706 n.
collaborator
tergiversator 603 n.
aider 703 n.
collaborator 707 n.
toady 879 n.
friend 880 n.
collage
combination 50 n.
picture 553 n.
collapse
decomposition 51 n.
cease 145 vb.
helplessness 161 n.
be impotent 161 vb.
weakness 163 n.
ruin 165 n.
descent 309 n.
descend 309 vb.
illness 651 n.
be ill 651 vb.
dilapidation 655 n.
deteriorate 655 vb.
fatigue 684 n.
be fatigued 684 vb.
knuckle under 721 vb.
defeat 728 n.
failure 728 n.
fail 728 vb.
collar
halter 47 n.
garment 228 n.
neckwear 228 n.
arrest 747 vb.
fetter 748 n.
take 786 vb.
collar stud
jewellery 844 n.
collate
compare 462 vb.
print 587 vb.
collateral
kinsman 11 n.
akin 11 adj.
accompanying 89 adj.
parallel 219 adj.
security 767 n.
collation
meal 301 n.
comparison 462 n.
colleague
personnel 686 n.
colleague 707 n.
friend 880 n.
collect
bring together 74 vb.
congregate 74 vb.
acquire 771 vb.
receive 782 vb.
take 786 vb.
prayers 981 n.
— oneself
keep calm 823 vb.
— one's thoughts
think 449 vb.
collected
wise 498 adj.
unastonished 865 adj.
collection
arrangement 62 n.
accumulation 74 n.
assemblage 74 n.
exhibit 522 n.
edition 589 n.
anthology 592 n.
collection 632 n.
acquisition 771 n.
receiving 782 n.
oblation 981 n.
collective
general 79 adj.
joint possession 775 n.
sharing 775 adj.
collective bargaining
conditions 766 n.
collective farm
farm 370 n.
joint possession 775 n.
collectively
collectively 52 adv.
together 74 adv.
with 89 adv.
in league 708 adv.
in common 775 adv.
collective noun
assemblage 74 n.
part of speech 564 n.
collectivism
government 733 n.
joint possession 775 n.
collector
accumulator 74 n.
collector 492 n.
enthusiast 504 n.
desirer 859 n.
collector's piece
exhibit 522 n.
exceller 644 n.
masterpiece 694 n.
colleen
youngster 132 n.
woman 373 n.
college
academy 539 n.
association 706 n.
College of Arms
heraldry 547 n.
honours 866 n.
college of cardinals
synod 985 n.
college of commerce
training school 539 n.
college student
student 538 n.
collide
disagree 25 vb.
collide 279 vb.
meet 295 vb.
touch 378 vb.
oppose 704 vb.
quarrel 709 vb.
strike at 712 vb.
be inimical 881 vb.
colliery
excavation 255 n.
store 632 n.
workshop 687 n.
collimate
be parallel 219 vb.
aim 281 vb.
collision
disagreement 25 n.
violence 176 n.
counteraction 182 n.
collision 279 n.
convergence 293 n.
friction 333 n.
quarrel 709 n.
battle 718 n.
collision course
convergence 293 n.
collocation
arrangement 62 n.
assemblage 74 n.
location 187 n.
phrase 563 n.
colloquial
figurative 519 adj.
linguistic 557 adj.
dialectal 560 adj.

colloquialism
trope 519 n.
slang 560 n.
colloquy
speech 579 n.
conference 584 n.
interlocution 584 n.
collotype
copy 22 n.
representation 551 n.
printing 555 n.
collude
concur 181 vb.
cooperate 706 vb.
collusion
concurrence 181 n.
duplicity 541 n.
deception 542 n.
cooperation 706 n.
collywobbles
pang 377 n.
digestive disorders 651 n.
nervousness 854 n.
cologne
cosmetic 843 n.
colon
insides 224 n.
tube 263 n.
drain 351 n.
punctuation 547 n.
colonel
army officer 741 n.
colonial
foreigner 59 n.
settler 191 n.
subject 745 adj.
colonialism
nation 371 n.
governance 733 n.
subjection 745 n.
colonist
settler 191 n.
incomer 297 n.
egress 298 n.
colonize, colonise
place oneself 187 vb.
dwell 192 vb.
subjugate 745 vb.
appropriate 786 vb.
colonnade
series 71 n.
pavilion 192 n.
path 624 n.
colony
crowd 74 n.
certain quantity 104 n.
descendant 170 n.
territory 184 n.
station 187 n.
inhabitants 191 n.
political organization 733 n.
subject 742 n.
colophon
label 547 n.
letterpress 587 n.
edition 589 n.
coloration
light 417 n.
colour 425 n.
hue 425 n.
coloratura
vocal music 412 n.
vocalist 413 n.
musicianly 413 adj.
colossal
enormous 32 adj.
huge 195 adj.
tall 209 adj.
colossus
giant 195 n.
high structure 209 n.
tall creature 209 n.
sculpture 554 n.
colostomy
surgery 658 n.
colour
character 5 n.
tincture 43 n.
be mixed 43 vb.
mix 43 vb.
sort 77 n.
modify 143 vb.
influence 178 vb.
prevail 178 vb.
light 417 n.
colour 425 n.vb.
redden 431 vb.
variegation 437 n.
appearance 445 n.
mien 445 n.
qualify 468 vb.
probability 471 n.
sophisticate 477 vb.
cant 541 vb.
heraldry 547 n.
identification 547 n.
paint 553 vb.
ornament 574 n.
pretext 614 n.
show feeling 818 vb.
decorate 844 vb.
be modest 874 vb.
get angry 891 vb.
justify 927 vb.
— in
colour 425 vb.
— up
redden 431 vb.
be humbled 872 vb.
colourable
plausible 471 adj.
deceiving 542 adj.
colour bar
exclusion 57 n.
prejudice 481 n.
colour-blind
dim-sighted 440 adj.
indiscriminating 464 adj.
coloured
coloured 425 adj.
painted 553 adj.
coloured man/woman
blackness 428 n.
colour escort
soldier 722 n.
colourful
luminous 417 adj.
luminescent 420 adj.
coloured 425 adj.
florid 425 adj.
variegated 437 adj.
descriptive 590 adj.
showy 875 adj.
colouring
hue 425 n.
qualification 468 n.
meaning 514 n.
exaggeration 546 n.
identification 547 n.
painting 553 n.
colouring matter
pigment 425 n.
colourist
artist 556 n.
colourless
insubstantial 4 adj.
weak 163 adj.
weakly 163 adj.
dim 419 adj.
colourless 426 adj.
whitish 427 adj.
feeble 572 adj.
unhealthy 651 adj.
middling 732 adj.
dull 840 adj.
colour prejudice
prejudice 481 n.
hatred 888 n.
colours
clothing 228 n.
badge 547 n.
flag 547 n.
colour sergeant
soldier 722 n.
army officer 741 n.
colour supplement
the press 528 n.
colourwash
coat 226 vb.
pigment 425 n.
colour 425 vb.
decorate 844 vb.
colporteur
pedlar 794 n.
colt
young creature 132 n.
horse 273 n.
male animal 372 n.
beginner 538 n.
bungler 697 n.
pistol 723 n.
coltish
infantine 132 adj.
active 678 adj.
column
high structure 209 n.
pillar 218 n.
cylinder 252 n.
marching 267 n.
rostrum 539 n.
monument 548 n.
article 591 n.
formation 722 n.
columnist
informant 524 n.
chronicler 549 n.
author 589 n.
coma
helplessness 161 n.
insensibility 375 n.
illness 651 n.
sleep 679 n.
comatose
impotent 161 adj.
insensible 375 adj.
sleepy 679 adj.
apathetic 820 adj.
comb
tooth 256 n.
smoother 258 n.
smooth 258 vb.
organ 414 n.
search 459 vb.
cleaning utensil 648 n.
clean 648 vb.
hairdressing 843 n.
— out
unravel 62 vb.
combat
contention 716 n.
fight 716 n., vb.
give battle 718 vb.
— an opinion
dissent 489 vb.
combatant
combatant 722 n.
enemy 881 n.
combat fatigue
psychopathy 503 n.
combative
quarrelling 709 adj.
attacking 712 adj.
contending 716 adj.
warlike 718 adj.
combat troops
armed force 722 n.
combat zone
battleground 724 n.
combe
valley 255 n.
comber
wave 350 n.
combination
a mixture 43 n.
mixture 43 n.
joining together 45 n.
union 45 n.
combination 50 n.
composition 56 n.
assemblage 74 n.
numerical operation 86 n.
unity 88 n.
association 706 n.
society 708 n.
combination lock
fastening 47 n.

combine
combine 50 vb.
cooperate 706 vb.
(See **combination** *)*
combined
mixed 43 adj.
joined 45 adj.
combined 50 adj.
concurrent 181 adj.
combined operation(s)
cooperation 706 n.
warfare 718 n.
combine harvester
farm tool 370 n.
combustible
fuel 385 n.
combustible 385 adj.
combustion
burning 381 n.
come
arrive 295 vb.
— about
be 1 vb.
happen 154 vb.
— a cropper
tumble 309 vb.
be unskilful 695 vb.
fail 728 vb.
— across
acquire 771 vb.
pay 804 vb.
— after
come after 65 vb.
run on 71 vb.
ensue 120 vb.
be behind 238 vb.
follow 284 vb.
— and go
fluctuate 317 vb.
be active 678 vb.
— apart
separate 46 vb.
— away
recede 290 vb.
— back
turn back 286 vb.
— back at
answer 460 vb.
be witty 839 vb.
— before
come before 64 vb.
be before 119 vb.
be early 135 vb.
stand trial 959 vb.
— behind
follow 284 vb.
— between
interfere 231 vb.
lie between 231 vb.
hinder 702 vb.
make quarrels 709 vb.
— by
acquire 771 vb.
— clean
confess 526 vb.
be truthful 540 vb.
speak 579 vb.
— closer
approach 289 vb.
converge 293 vb.
— down
descend 309 vb.
rain 350 vb.
be cheap 812 vb.
— down in the world
be poor 801 vb.
lose repute 867 vb.
— down on
be severe 735 vb.
reprove 924 vb.
punish 963 vb.
— down on for
claim 915 vb.
— down on one side
choose 605 vb.
— down with a bump
be ridiculous 849 vb.
— first
come first 34 vb.
be important 638 vb.
— first in one's thoughts
engross 449 vb.
— forth
emerge 298 vb.
— forward
be visible 443 vb.
offer oneself 759 vb.
— from
result 157 vb.
— home
turn back 286 vb.
arrive 295 vb.
— home to
impress 821 vb.
— in
be included 78 vb.
enter 297 vb.
be received 782 vb.
— in for
acquire 771 vb.
— in handy
be useful 640 vb.
— into
inherit 771 vb.
possess 773 vb.
receive 782 vb.
get rich 800 vb.
— into existence
become 1 vb.
happen 154 vb.
— into one's head
dawn upon 449 vb.
— into operation
do 676 vb.
— into the hands of
change hands 780 vb.
— into the world
begin 68 vb.
be born 360 vb.
— into use
be wont 610 vb.
— into view
approach 289 vb.
be visible 443 vb.
— it over
be proud 871 vb.
despise 922 vb.
— naturally to
accord 24 vb.
— near
approach 289 vb.
— next
come after 65 vb.
— of
result 157 vb.
— of age
come of age 134 vb.
— off
cease 145 vb.
happen 154 vb.
recede 290 vb.
be successful 727 vb.
be sober 948 vb.
— off it
be humbled 872 vb.
— off on
cohere 48 vb.
transfer 272 vb.
colour 425 vb.
— on
impend 155 vb.
progress 285 vb.
— out
begin 68 vb.
cease 145 vb.
emerge 298 vb.
be visible 443 vb.
be disclosed 526 vb.
be published 528 vb.
resist 715 vb.
revolt 738 vb.
— out for
choose 605 vb.
— out on top
succeed 727 vb.
— out with
confess 526 vb.
divulge 526 vb.
improvise 609 vb.
— over
be intelligible 516 vb.
consent 758 vb.
— round (again)
be periodic 141 vb.
be restored 656 vb.
— round to
convince 485 vb.
consent 758 vb.
— short
be inferior 35 vb.
fall short 307 vb.
not suffice 636 vb.
— through
be safe 660 vb.
— to
number 86 vb.
be turned to 147 vb.
be restored 656 vb.
cost 809 vb.
— to a head
culminate 34 vb.
be complete 54 vb.
— to an end
end 69 vb.
cease 145 vb.
— to bits
separate 46 vb.
— to blows
fight 716 vb.
be inimical 881 vb.
— together
congregate 74 vb.
converge 293 vb.
— to grief
miscarry 728 vb.
have trouble 731 vb.
— to hand
arrive 295 vb.
be received 782 vb.
— to heel
accompany 89 vb.
obey 739 vb.
— to life (again)
live 360 vb.
be restored 656 vb.
— to light
be visible 443 vb.
be plain 522 vb.
be disclosed 526 vb.
— to mind
dawn upon 449 vb.
— to nothing
be unproductive 172 vb.
miscarry 728 vb.
— to one's ears
hear 415 vb.
be known 490 vb.
— to one's senses
have feeling 374 vb.
be wise 498 vb.
be sane 502 vb.
sober 948 adj.
— to pass
happen 154 vb.
— to rest
come to rest 266 vb.
repose 683 vb.
— to the fore
be in front 237 vb.
— to the point
specify 80 vb.
speak plainly 573 vb.
— under
be included 78 vb.
— under the hammer
be sold 793 vb.
— unstuck
separate 46 vb.
be in difficulty 700 vb.
fail 728 vb.
— upon
meet 295 vb.
discover 484 vb.
comeback
revival 656 n.
Comecon
market 796 n.

comedian, comedienne
actor 594 n.
entertainer 594 n.
humorist 839 n.
comedown
disappointment 509 n.
humiliation 872 n.
comedy
stage play 594 n.
laughter 835 n.
ridiculousness 849 n.
come hell or high water
certainly 473 adv.
resolutely 599 adv.
come-hither look
look 438 n.
pleasurableness 826 n.
wooing 889 n.
comely
symmetrical 245 adj.
beautiful 841 adj.
come-on
incentive 612 n.
comestibles
food 301 n.
comet
planet 321 n.
comeuppance
punishment 963 n.
come what may
certainly 473 adv.
resolutely 599 adv.
comfit
sweets 301 n.
comfort
assuage 177 vb.
euphoria 376 n.
repose 683 n.
aid 703 n.vb.
wealth 800 n.
happiness 824 n.
content 828 n.vb.
relief 831 n.
relieve 831 vb.
cheer 833 vb.
give hope 852 vb.
condolence 905 n.
pity 905 vb.
comfortable
adjusted 24 adj.
tranquil 266 adj.
comfortable 376 adj.
reposeful 683 adj.
easy 701 adj.
palmy 730 adj.
prosperous 730 adj.
rich 800 adj.
happy 824 adj.
pleasurable 826 adj.
content 828 adj.
comforter
wrapping 226 n.
neckwear 228 n.
relief 831 n.
Comforter, the
Holy Ghost 965 n.
comforting
lenitive 177 adj.
comfortable 376 adj.
refreshing 685 adj.
relieving 831 adj.
cheering 833 adj.
comfortless
unpleasant 827 adj.
cheerless 834 adj.
melancholic 834 adj.
hopeless 853 adj.
unpromising 853 adj.
comic
fool 501 n.
the press 528 n.
entertainer 594 n.
dramatic 594 adj.
laughing 835 adj.
humorist 839 n.
witty 839 adj.
funny 849 adj.
comical
absurd 497 adj.
witty 839 adj.
funny 849 adj.
coming
future 124 adj.
(See **come** *)*
coming out
debut 68 n.
coming to one
due 915 adj.
comity
courtesy 884 n.
comity of nations
social group 371 n.
comma
punctuation 547 n.
command
advantage 34 n.
be superior 34 vb.
be high 209 vb.
will 595 n.vb.
dispose of 673 vb.
directorship 689 n.
direct 689 vb.
warfare 718 n.
governance 733 n.
dominate 733 vb.
rule 733 vb.
command 737 n.vb.
mandate 751 n.
possess 773 vb.
desire 859 vb.
impose a duty 917 vb.
— one's passions
be virtuous 933 vb.
— respect
be important 638 vb.
have a reputation 866 vb.
command respect 920 vb.
commandant
army officer 741 n.
commandeer
compel 740 vb.
appropriate 786 vb.
commander
superior 34 n.
army officer 741 n.
naval officer 741 n.
commanding
superior 34 adj.
influential 178 adj.
notable 638 adj.
authoritative 733 adj.
commanding 737 adj.
noteworthy 866 adj.
proud 871 adj.
commandment
precept 693 n.
command 737 n.
commando
armed force 722 n.
command of language
style 566 n.
eloquence 579 n.
command performance
dramaturgy 594 n.
commedia dell'arte
stage play 594 n.
comme il faut
tasteful 846 adj.
fashionable 848 adj.
genteel 868 adj.
commemorate
remind 505 vb.
honour 866 vb.
celebrate 876 vb.
commemoration
remembrance 505 n.
commemorative
remembering 505 adj.
celebratory 876 adj.
commence
begin 68 vb.
commencement
beginning 68 n.
commend
advise 691 vb.
befriend 880 vb.
approve 923 vb.
praise 923 vb.
commendable
good 615 adj.
advisable 642 adj.
approvable 923 adj.
virtuous 933 adj.
commendation
friendship 880 n.
approbation 923 n.
praise 923 n.
commensurable
numerical 85 adj.
numerable 86 adj.
commensurate
relative 9 adj.
agreeing 24 adj.
numerable 86 adj.
sufficient 635 adj.
comment
estimate 480 n.vb.
commentary 520 n.
affirmation 532 n.
affirm 532 vb.
speech 579 n.
article 591 n.
— on
interpret 520 vb.
commentary
commentary 520 n.
oration 579 n.
commentator
estimator 480 n.
interpreter 520 n.
informant 524 n.
broadcaster 531 n.
dissertator 591 n.
commerce
business 622 n.
vocation 622 n.
trade 791 n.
commercial
advertisement 528 n.
broadcast 531 n.
businesslike 622 adj.
trading 791 adj.
vulgar 847 adj.
commercialism
bad taste 847 n.
commercialize, commercialise
trade 791 vb.
vulgarize 847 vb.
commercial traveller
traveller 268 n.
seller 793 n.
commination
malediction 899 n.
threat 900 n.
prayers 981 n.
comminute
break 46 vb.
pulverize 332 vb.
commiserate
lament 836 vb.
pity 905 vb.
commissar
tyrant 735 n.
autocrat 741 n.
officer 741 n.
commissariat
provision 633 n.
commissary
provider 633 n.
delegate 754 n.
commission
auspicate 68 vb.
band 74 n.
message 529 n.
select 605 vb.
job 622 n.
employ 622 vb.
fitting out 669 n.
make ready 669 vb.
action 676 n.
authority 733 n.

command 737 n., vb.
warrant 737 n.
commission 751 n., vb.
mandate 751 n.
permit 756 n.
earnings 771 n.
transfer 780 n.
assign 780 vb.
pay 804 n.
dignify 866 vb.
duty 917 n.
impose a duty 917 vb.
commissionaire
doorkeeper 264 n.
courier 529 n.
commissioned officer
army officer 741 n.
commissioner
official 690 n.
officer 741 n.
delegate 754 n.
commissioner for oaths
notary 958 n.
commission of enquiry
enquiry 459 n.
commit
transfer 272 vb.
do 676 vb.
commission 751 vb.
assign 780 vb.
give 781 vb.
do wrong 914 vb.
— for trial
try a case 959 vb.
— oneself
affirm 532 vb.
be resolute 599 vb.
choose 605 vb.
undertake 672 vb.
promise 764 vb.
incur a duty 917 vb.
— to memory
memorize 505 vb.
— to writing
record 548 vb.
write 586 vb.
commitment
promise 764 n.
giving 781 n.
debt 803 n.
duty 917 n.
committal
transference 272 n.
commission 751 n.
legal process 959 n.
committed
promised 764 adj.
indebted 803 adj.
obliged 917 adj.
committee
band 74 n.
party 708 n.
authority 733 n.
consignee 754 n.
commode
cabinet 194 n.
latrine 649 n.
commodious
spacious 183 adj.
useful 640 adj.
commodity
object 319 n.
utility 640 n.
merchandise 795 n.
commodore
nautical personnel 270 n.
naval officer 741 n.
common
inferior 35 adj.
general 79 adj.
typical 83 adj.
frequent 139 adj.
plain 348 n.
usual 610 adj.
middling 732 adj.
unpossessed 774 adj.
sharing 775 adj.
lands 777 n.
pleasure ground 837 n.
vulgar 847 adj.
unastonishing 865 adj.
plebeian 869 adj.
commonalty
everyman 79 n.
social group 371 n.
commonalty 869 n.
common cause
cooperation 706 n.
common core
curriculum 534 n.
common denominator
relation 9 n.
numerical element 85 n.
commoner
common man 30 n.
student 538 n.
commoner 869 n.
common good
good 615 n.
philanthropy 901 n.
common knowledge
knowledge 490 n.
information 524 n.
publicity 528 n.
common land
joint possession 775 n.
lands 777 n.
common law
tradition 127 n.
precept 693 n.
law 953 n.
common-law husband/wife
spouse 894 n.
commonly
often 139 adv.
common man
common man 30 n.
everyman 79 n.
averageness 732 n.
commoner 869 n.
Common Market
society 708 n.
market 796 n.
commonness
inferiority 35 n.
generality 79 n.
ill-breeding 847 n.
common noun
part of speech 564 n.
common or garden
typical 83 adj.
common ownership
joint possession 775 n.
commonplace
median 30 adj.
general 79 adj.
typical 83 adj.
topic 452 n.
known 490 adj.
maxim 496 n.
aphoristic 496 adj.
phrase 563 n.
plain 573 adj.
usual 610 adj.
trivial 639 adj.
middling 732 adj.
dull 840 adj.
Common Prayer
public worship 981 n.
commons
provisions 301 n.
commonalty 869 n.
commonsense
intelligence 498 n.
sanity 502 n.
common touch
conduct 688 n.
sociability 882 n.
courtesy 884 n.
commonwealth
territory 184 n.
nation 371 n.
political organization 733 n.
commotion
turmoil 61 n.
violence 176 n.
commotion 318 n.
overactivity 678 n.
excitable state 822 n.
discontent 829 n.
communal
national 371 adj.
corporate 708 adj.
sharing 775 adj.
communalize, communalise
communalize 775 vb.
communally
in common 775 adv.
commune
district 184 n.
inhabitants 191 n.
association 706 n.
joint possession 775 n.
commune with
converse 584 vb.
communicate 524 vb.
communicable
transferable 272 adj.
infectious 653 adj.
communicant
church member 976 n.
pietist 979 n.
worshipper 981 n.
communicate
connect 45 vb.
communicate 524 vb.
divulge 526 vb.
publish 528 vb.
signal 547 vb.
correspond 588 vb.
describe 590 vb.
offer worship 981 vb.
communicating
accessible 289 adj.
communicating 624 adj.
communication
message 529 n.
interlocution 584 n.
communications
access 624 n.
communications satellite
satellite 321 n.
broadcasting 531 n.
communicative
informative 524 adj.
disclosing 526 adj.
loquacious 581 adj.
conversing 584 adj.
communion
interlocution 584 n.
party 708 n.
Holy Communion 988 n.
communion of saints
Christendom 976 n.
communiqué
report 524 n.
news 529 n.
communism
government 733 n.
joint possession 775 n.
communist
reformer 654 n.
agitator 738 n.
participator 775 n.
Communist bloc
political organization 733 n.
communistic
sharing 775 adj.
philanthropic 901 adj.

Communists
political party 708 n.
community
inhabitants 191 n.
social group 371 n.
association 706 n.
community 708 n.
sect 978 n.
monk 986 n.
community centre
focus 76 n.
meeting place 192 n.
community chest
store 632 n.
community home
school 539 n.
prison 748 n.
community of possessions
joint possession 775 n.
community relations
sociality 882 n.
community service
sociology 901 n.
commutation
compensation 31 n.
substitution 150 n.
interchange 151 n.
commute
substitute 150 vb.
interchange 151 vb.
travel 267 vb.
compromise 770 vb.
show mercy 905 vb.
commuter
dweller 191 n.
traveller 268 n.
compact
small 33 adj.
little 196 adj.
make smaller 198 vb.
short 204 adj.
dense 324 adj.
be dense 324 vb.
consensus 488 n.
concise 569 adj.
promise 764 n.
compact 765 n.
cosmetic 843 n.
compaction
coherence 48 n.
compression 198 n.
companion
analogue 18 n.
union 45 n.
concomitant 89 n.
colleague 707 n.
retainer 742 n.
close friend 880 n.
companionable
sociable 882 adj.
companionship
accompaniment 89 n.
friendship 880 n.
sociality 882 n.
companionway
doorway 263 n.
ascent 308 n.
company
assembly 74 n.
band 74 n.
accompaniment 89 n.
actor 594 n.
personnel 686 n.
workshop 687 n.
association 706 n.
corporation 708 n.
party 708 n.
formation 722 n.
comparable
equivalent 28 adj.
comparative
relative 9 adj.
distinctive 15 adj.
comparative 27 adj.
superior 34 adj.
compared 462 adj.
figurative 519 adj.
grammatical 564 adj.
comparatively
slightly 33 adv.
comparatively 462 adv.
compare
relate 9 vb.
liken 18 vb.
graduate 27 vb.
compare 462 vb.
discriminate 463 vb.
figure 519 vb.
— notes
consult 691 vb.
comparison
relativeness 9 n.
assimilation 18 n.
joining together 45 n.
comparison 462 n.
estimate 480 n.
metaphor 519 n.
trope 519 n.
compartment
subdivision 53 n.
classification 77 n.
compartment 194 n.
train 274 n.
compartmentalize, compartmentalise
set apart 46 vb.
part 53 vb.
compartmentalized
fragmentary 53 adj.
cellular 194 adj.
compass
ability 160 n.
be able 160 vb.
range 183 n.
distance 199 n.
surroundings 230 n.
surround 230 vb.
outline 233 n.
sailing aid 269 n.
navigator 270 n.
direction 281 n.
gauge 465 n.
directorship 689 n.
succeed 727 vb.
compass direction
bearings 186 n.
compassion
leniency 736 n.
pity 905 n.
compassionate
impressible 819 adj.
pitying 905 adj.
compassionate leave
permit 756 n.
compass needle
indicator 547 n.
compass point
laterality 239 n.
compass point 281 n.
compatible
agreeing 24 adj.
possible 469 adj.
concordant 710 adj.
friendly 880 adj.
compatriot
kinsman 11 n.
compeer
compeer 28 n.
contemporary 123 n.
compel
be able 160 vb.
necessitate 596 vb.
induce 612 vb.
motivate 612 vb.
command 737 vb.
compel 740 vb.
compelling
causal 156 adj.
powerful 160 adj.
strong 162 adj.
influential 178 adj.
forceful 571 adj.
necessary 596 adj.
demanding 627 adj.
authoritative 733 adj.
authoritarian 735 adj.
commanding 737 adj.
compelling 740 adj.
obligatory 917 adj.
compendious
small 33 adj.
short 204 adj.
concise 569 adj.
compendious 592 adj.
compendium
combination 50 n.
conciseness 569 n.
compendium 592 n.
compensate
adjust 24 vb.
equalize 28 vb.
compensate 31 vb.
restitute 787 vb.
pay 804 vb.
atone 941 vb.
reward 962 vb.
compensation
compensation 31 n.
offset 31 n.
substitution 150 n.
restitution 787 n.
payment 804 n.
compensatory
compensatory 31 adj.
counteracting 182 adj.
rewarding 962 adj.
compere
broadcaster 531 n.
direct 689 vb.
compete
contend 716 vb.
offer oneself 759 vb.
competence
ability 160 n.
sufficiency 635 n.
skill 694 n.
independence 744 n.
wealth 800 n.
jurisdiction 955 n.
competent
powerful 160 adj.
sufficient 635 adj.
useful 640 adj.
expert 694 adj.
skilful 694 adj.
authoritative 733 adj.
legal 953 adj.
jurisdictional 955 adj.
competition
opposition 704 n.
contention 716 n.
contest 716 n.
jealousy 911 n.
competitive
equal 28 adj.
contending 716 adj.
competitiveness
contention 716 n.
jealousy 911 n.
competitor
compeer 28 n.
incomer 297 n.
opponent 705 n.
contender 716 n.
combatant 722 n.
player 837 n.
compilation
anthology 592 n.
compile
compose 56 vb.
bring together 74 vb.
abstract 592 vb.
compiler
collector 492 n.
etymology 559 n.
complacency
content 828 n.
complacent
vain 873 adj.

complain
deprecate 762 vb.
be discontented 829 vb.
lament 836 vb.
be sullen 893 vb.
indict 928 vb.
complainant
accuser 928 n.
complainer
petitioner 763 n.
malcontent 829 n.
moper 834 n.
weeper 836 n.
complaint
cry 408 n.
illness 651 n.
deprecation 762 n.
annoyance 827 n.
discontent 829 n.
lament 836 n.
wrong 914 n.
disapprobation 924 n.
accusation 928 n.
complaisant
conformable 83 adj.
lenient 736 adj.
obedient 739 adj.
permitting 756 adj.
courteous 884 adj.
benevolent 897 adj.
complaisant husband
cuckold 952 n.
complement
analogue 18 n.
plenitude 54 n.
make complete 54 vb.
component 58 n.
band 74 n.
inclusion 78 n.
numerical element 85 n.
concomitant 89 n.
personnel 686 n.
complementary
correlative 12 adj.
complete 54 adj.
complete
consummate 32 adj.
whole 52 adj.
complete 54 adj.
make complete 54 vb.
persevere 600 vb.
sufficient 635 adj.
perfect 646 adj. vb.
do 676 vb.
completed 725 adj.
carry through 725 vb.
completeness
whole 52 n.
completeness 54 n.
completion 725 n.
complete set
all 52 n.
inclusion 78 n.
collection 632 n.
complete works
edition 589 n.
completion
completeness 54 n.
plenitude 54 n.
maturation 669 n.
completion 725 n.
(See **complete** *)*
completive
crowning 34 adj.
complete 54 adj.
ending 69 adj.
completive 725 adj.
complex
mixed 43 adj.
whole 52 n.
complex 61 adj.
crossed 222 adj.
intricate 251 adj.
structure 331 n.
idea 451 n.
eccentricity 503 n.
puzzling 517 adj.
unclear 568 adj.
habituation 610 n.
difficult 700 adj.
complexion
modality 7 n.
state 7 n.
hue 425 n.
mien 445 n.
complexity
complexity 61 n.
enigma 530 n.
imperspicuity 568 n.
compliance
concurrence 181 n.
softness 327 n.
willingness 597 n.
submission 721 n.
obedience 739 n.
consent 758 n.
observance 768 n.
servility 879 n.
compliant
willing 597 adj.
servile 879 adj.
complicate
bedevil 63 vb.
aggravate 832 vb.
complicated
complex 61 adj.
intricate 251 adj.
difficult 700 adj.
complication
complexity 61 n.
narrative 590 n.
illness 651 n.
difficulty 700 n.
aggravation 832 n.
complicity
cooperation 706 n.
participation 775 n.
improbity 930 n.
guilt 936 n.
compliment
honours 866 n.
honour 866 vb.
congratulate 886 vb.
praise 923 n.vb.
flattery 925 n.
flatter 925 vb.
complimentary
uncharged 812 adj.
congratulatory 886 adj.
approving 923 adj.
flattering 925 adj.
compline
church service 988 n.
comply
obey 739 vb.
(See **compliance** *)*
— with
conform 83 vb.
compo
facing 226 n.
building material 631 n.
component
component 58 n.adj.
included 78 adj.
accompanying 89 adj.
contents 193 n.
element 319 n.
machine 630 n.
comportment
conduct 688 n.
comport oneself
behave 688 vb.
— with
accord 24 vb.
compose
combine 50 vb.
compose 56 vb.
constitute 56 vb.
arrange 62 vb.
be included 78 vb.
produce 164 vb.
compose music 413 vb.
write 586 vb.
print 587 vb.
— oneself
prepare oneself 669 vb.
keep calm 823 vb.
composed
inexcitable 823 adj.
unastonished 865 adj.
composer
producer 164 n.
musician 413 n.
composite
mixed 43 adj.
joined 45 adj.
compound 50 n.
plural 101 adj.
vegetal 366 adj.
composition
a mixture 43 n.
combination 50 n.
compound 50 n.
composition 56 n.
arrangement 62 n.
assemblage 74 n.
inclusion 78 n.
production 164 n.
structure 331 n.
musical piece 412 n.
painting 553 n.
writing 586 n.
print 587 n.
building material 631 n.
compact 765 n.
compromise 770 n.
payment 804 n.
pattern 844 n.
compositor
printer 587 n.
compos mentis
sane 502 adj.
compost
fertilizer 171 n.
make fruitful 171 vb.
compostable
decomposable 51 adj.
composure
quietude 266 n.
inexcitability 823 n.
lack of wonder 865 n.
compound
a mixture 43 n.
mix 43 vb.
compound 50 n.
combine 50 vb.
composition 56 n.
product 164 n.
enclosure 235 n.
compromise 770 vb.
compound interest
gain 771 n.
interest 803 n.
comprehend
contain 56 vb.
comprise 78 vb.
know 490 vb.
understand 516 vb.
comprehensible
intelligible 516 adj.
easy 701 adj.
comprehension
inclusion 78 n.
knowledge 490 n.
connotation 514 n.
comprehensive
extensive 32 adj.
comprehensive 52 adj.
complete 54 adj.
inclusive 78 adj.
general 79 adj.
school 539 n.
compress
tighten 45 vb.
make smaller 198 vb.
shorten 204 vb.
make thin 206 vb.

be dense 324 vb.
be concise 569 vb.
surgical dressing 658 n.
compressible
rare 325 adj.
soft 327 adj.
compression
smallness 33 n.
diminution 37 n.
energy 160 n.
compression 198 n.
narrowing 206 n.
compendium 592 n.
restriction 747 n.
compressor
ligature 47 n.
compressor 198 n.
comprise
contain 56 vb.
comprise 78 vb.
compromise
adaptation 24 n.
middle point 30 n.
average out 30 vb.
set off 31 vb.
substitute 150 n.
moderation 177 n.
be irresolute 601 vb.
middle way 625 n.
be halfway 625 vb.
endanger 661 vb.
laxity 734 n.
be lax 734 vb.
consent 758 n.
compact 765 n.
make terms 766 vb.
compromise 770 n. vb.
defame 926 vb.
compromising
discreditable 867 adj.
compte rendu
report 524 n.
accounts 808 n.
compulsion
psychopathy 503 n.
necessity 596 n.
no choice 606 n.
brute force 735 n.
command 737 n.
compulsion 740 n.
restraint 747 n.
compulsive
powerful 160 adj.
strong 162 adj.
necessary 596 adj.
authoritarian 735 adj.
commanding 737 adj.
compelling 740 adj.
compulsory
authoritative 733 adj.
obligatory 917 adj.
compunction
regret 830 n.
pity 905 n.
penitence 939 n.
compunctious
unhappy 825 adj.
compurgate
testify 466 vb.
compurgator
witness 466 n.
vindicator 927 n.
computation
data processing 86 n.
numeration 86 n.
accounts 808 n.
compute
computerize 86 vb.
do sums 86 vb.
measure 465 vb.
computer
counting instrument 86 n.
enumerator 86 n.
computer electronics
electronics 160 n.
computerize
computerize 86 vb.
computer program
data processing 86 n.
computer programmer
enumerator 86 n.
computing
data processing 86 n.
accounting 808 adj.
comrade
male 372 n.
colleague 707 n.
political party 708 n.
society 708 n.
title 870 n.
chum 880 n.
comradeship
cooperation 706 n.
friendship 880 n.
sociality 882 n.
comsat
satellite 321 n.
telecommunication 531 n.
con
know 490 vb.
memorize 505 vb.
deceive 542 vb.
defraud 788 vb.
con amore
willingly 597 adv.
feelingly 818 adv.
conation
intellect 447 n.
will 595 n.
con brio
vigorously 174 adv.
adagio 412 adv.
cheerfully 833 adv.
concatenation
joining together 45 n.
continuity 71 n.
concave
concave 255 adj.
concavity
curvature 248 n.
concavity 255 n.
conceal
contain 56 vb.
suppress 165 vb.
cover 226 vb.
screen 421 vb.
be unseen 444 vb.
conceal 525 vb.
dissemble 541 vb.
obliterate 550 vb.
safeguard 660 vb.
concealment
dissimilarity 19 n.
invisibility 444 n.
sophistry 477 n.
equivocalness 518 n.
latency 523 n.
concealment 525 n.
ambush 527 n.
misteaching 535 n.
sham 542 n.
mental dishonesty 543 n.
cunning 698 n.n.
seclusion 883 n.
concede
set off 31 vb.
qualify 468 vb.
be reasonable 475 vb.
assent 488 vb.
confess 526 vb.
be induced 612 vb.
be lenient 736 vb.
permit 756 vb.
consent 758 vb.
conceit
idea 451 n.
folly 499 n.
supposition 512 n.
ideality 513 n.
witticism 839 n.
affectation 850 n.
pride 871 n.
vanity 873 n.
conceited
affected 850 adj.
prideful 871 adj.
vain 873 adj.
conceivable
possible 469 adj.
conceive
produce 164 vb.
reproduce itself 167 vb.
be fruitful 171 vb.
vitalize 360 vb.
cognize 447 vb.
think 449 vb.
opine 485 vb.
know 490 vb.
suppose 512 vb.
imagine 513 vb.
conceived, be
be born 360 vb.
concentrate
augment 36 vb.
bring together 74 vb.
congregate 74 vb.
focus 76 vb.
centralize 225 vb.
converge 293 vb.
think 449 vb.
be attentive 455 vb.
concentration
density 324 n.
thought 449 n.
perseverance 600 n.
assiduity 678 n.
(See **concentrate***)*
concentration camp
prison camp 748 n.
concentric
parallel 219 adj.
central 225 adj.
concept
idea 451 n.
opinion 485 n.
ideality 513 n.
conception
origin 68 n.
product 164 n.
propagation 167 n.
intellect 447 n.
thought 449 n.
idea 451 n.
opinion 485 n.
ideality 513 n.
conceptual
mental 447 adj.
philosophic 449 adj.
ideational 451 adj.
representing 551 adj.
conceptualize, conceptualise
cognize 447 vb.
concern
be related 9 vb.
affairs 154 n.
topic 452 n.
business 622 n.
function 622 n.
importance 638 n.
be important 638 vb.
corporation 708 n.
merchant 794 n.
shop 796 n.
worry 825 n.
benevolence 897 n.
— oneself with
busy oneself 622 vb.
concerning
relative 9 adj.
concerning 9 adv.
concert
agreement 24 n.
concurrence 181 n.
harmonize 410 vb.
music 412 n.
prepare 669 vb.
concert artist
musician 413 n.
concerted effort
cooperation 706 n.
concert hall
meeting place 192 n.

place of amusement 837 n.
concertina
organ 414 n.
concerto
musical piece 412 n.
concert pitch
musical note 410 n.
concert pitch, at
prepared 669 adj.
concession
offset 31 n.
qualification 468 n.
laxity 734 n.
leniency 736 n.
permission 756 n.
consent 758 n.
compromise 770 n.
discount 810 n.
concessional
cheap 812 adj.
concessionnaire
recipient 782 n.
conch
horn 414 n.
conchie
pacifist 717 n.
conchology
zoology 367 n.
concierge
doorkeeper 264 n.
keeper 749 n.
conciliate
induce 612 vb.
pacify 719 vb.
content 828 vb.
be courteous 884 vb.
atone 941 vb.
conciliatory
concordant 710 adj.
pacificatory 719 adj.
forgiving 909 adj.
concinnity
elegance 575 n.
concise
brief 114 adj.
short 204 adj.
aphoristic 496 adj.
concise 569 adj.
compendious 592 adj.
conciseness
conciseness 569 n.
concision
shortness 204 n.
conciseness 569 n.
conclave
assembly 74 n.
conference 584 n.
council 692 n.
synod 985 n.
conclude
end 69 vb.
terminate 69 vb.
judge 480 vb.
be resolute 599 vb.
contract 765 vb.
conclusion
sequel 67 n.
end 69 n.
finality 69 n.
argumentation 475 n.
judgment 480 n.
opinion 485 n.
completion 725 n.
conclusive
ending 69 adj.
answering 460 adj.
evidential 466 adj.
positive 473 adj.
demonstrating 478 adj.
judicial 480 adj.
completive 725 adj.
commanding 737 adj.
concoct
imagine 513 vb.
fake 541 vb.
write 586 vb.
plan 623 vb.
plot 623 vb.
concoction
a mixture 43 n.
production 164 n.
draught 301 n.
untruth 543 n.
concomitant
concomitant 89 n.
accompanying 89 adj.
synchronous 123 adj.
concord
agreement 24 n.
concurrence 181 n.
melody 410 n.
consensus 488 n.
cooperation 706 n.
concord 710 n.
peace 717 n.
friendliness 880 n.
concordance
agreement 24 n.
dictionary 559 n.
concordat
agreement 24 n.
treaty 765 n.
concourse
assembly 74 n.
convergence 293 n.
concrete
real 1 adj.
substantial 3 adj.
coherence 48 n.
definite 80 adj.
architectural 192 adj.
formed 243 adj.
material 319 adj.
solid body 324 n.
dense 324 adj.
hardness 326 n.
building material 631 n.
concrete jungle
housing 192 n.
concreteness
substantiality 3 n.
materiality 319 n.
density 324 n.
concretion
substance 3 n.
union 45 n.
condensation 324 n.
solid body 324 n.
concubinage
type of marriage 894 n.
illicit love 951 n.
concubine
loved one 887 n.
kept woman 952 n.
concupiscence
libido 859 n.
unchastity 951 n.
concur
accord 24 vb.
accompany 89 vb.
synchronize 123 vb.
concur 181 vb.
assent 488 vb.
concord 710 vb.
concurrence
agreement 24 n.
event 154 n.
concurrence 181 n.
assent 488 n.
concurrent
concurrent 181 adj.
parallel 219 adj.
convergent 293 adj.
concurrently
synchronously 123 adv.
concurrently 181 adv.
concuss
strike 279 vb.
render insensible 375 vb.
condemn
judge 480 vb.
blame 924 vb.
condemn 961 vb.
punish 963 vb.
declare heretical 977 vb.
condemnable
wrong 914 adj.
blameworthy 924 adj.
accusable 928 adj.
condemnation
ruin 165 n.
censure 924 n.
condemnation 961 n.
condemned
fated 596 adj.
dilapidated 655 adj.
hated 888 adj.
cursed 899 adj.
guilty 936 adj.
condemned 961 adj.
condemned cell
lockup 748 n.
condemned out of one's own mouth
confuted 479 adj.
condensation
contraction 198 n.
condensation 324 n.
moisture 341 n.
thickening 354 n.
condense
make smaller 198 vb.
be dense 324 vb.
be concise 569 vb.
abstract 592 vb.
condescend
consent 758 vb.
demean oneself 867 vb.
be humble 872 vb.
show respect 920 vb.
condescension
pride 871 n.
humility 872 n.
courtesy 884 n.
condign
due 915 adj.
condiment
pungency 388 n.
condiment 389 n.
condition
state 7 n.
qualification 468 n.
qualify 468 vb.
supposition 512 n.
teach 534 vb.
habituate 610 vb.
health 650 n.
illness 651 n.
conditions 766 n.
prestige 866 n.
conditional
qualifying 468 adj.
uncertain 474 adj.
restraining 747 adj.
conditional 766 adj.
conditionally
conditionally 7 adv.
if 8 adv.
relatively 9 adv.
provided 468 adv.
conditioned reflex
absence of thought 450 n.
necessity 596 n.
habituation 610 n.
conditions
circumstance 8 n.
requirement 627 n.
conditions 766 n.
condole
feel 818 vb.
lament 836 vb.
pity 905 vb.
condolence
condolence 905 n.
condom
contraception 172 n.
condominium
governance 733 n.

joint possession 775 n.
condone
be patient 823 vb.
forgive 909 vb.
conduce
conduce 156 vb.
tend 179 vb.
be liable 180 vb.
promote 285 vb.
make likely 471 vb.
be instrumental 628 vb.
be expedient 642 vb.
aid 703 vb.
conducive
tending 179 adj.
conduct
accompany 89 vb.
transfer 272 vb.
precede 283 vb.
play music 413 vb.
mien 445 n.
practice 610 n.
action 676 n.
conduct 688 n.
deal with 688 vb.
management 689 n.
direct 689 vb.
manage 689 vb.
— oneself
do 676 vb.
behave 688 vb.
conduction
electricity 160 n.
motion 265 n.
transference 272 n.
conductor
timekeeper 117 n.
electricity 160 n.
driver 268 n.
musician 413 n.
leader 690 n.
conduit
tube 263 n.
irrigator 341 n.
conduit 351 n.
cone
cone 252 n.
flower 366 n.
confabulate
speak 579 vb.
converse 584 vb.
confabulation
interlocution 584 n.
confection
a mixture 43 n.
product 164 n.
sweet thing 392 n.
confectioner
caterer 633 n.
confectionery
pastries 301 n.
sweets 301 n.
confederacy
association 706 n.
society 708 n.
confederate
auxiliary 707 n.
colleague 707 n.
confederation
combination 50 n.
association 706 n.
society 708 n.
political organization 733 n.
confer
confer 584 vb.
consult 691 vb.
assign 780 vb.
give 781 vb.
— an honour
dignify 866 vb.
conference
assembly 74 n.
listening 415 n.
enquiry 459 n.
conference 584 n.
council 692 n.
confess
believe 485 vb.
confess 526 vb.
affirm 532 vb.
be truthful 540 vb.
be guilty 936 vb.
be penitent 939 vb.
perform ritual 988 vb.
confession
testimony 466 n.
creed 485 n.
assent 488 n.
disclosure 526 n.
party 708 n.
guilt 936 n.
penitence 939 n.
penance 941 n.
theology 973 n.
ministration 988 n.
confessional
tribunal 956 n.
church interior 990 n.
confessions
biography 590 n.
confessor
questioner 459 n.
pietist 979 n.
pastor 986 n.
confetti
small thing 33 n.
confidant(e)
adviser 691 n.
retainer 742 n.
close friend 880 n.
confide
believe 485 vb.
divulge 526 vb.
be artless 699 vb.
hope 852 vb.
— in
consult 691 vb.
confidence
positiveness 473 n.
belief 485 n.
expectation 507 n.
information 524 n.
secret 530 n.
safety 660 n.
credit 802 n.
hope 852 n.
confidence trick
trickery 542 n.
peculation 788 n.
confident
unfearing 855 adj.
(See **confidence***)*
confidential
concealed 525 adj.
configuration
form 243 n.
configuration theory
psychology 447 n.
confine
limit 236 vb.
imprison 747 vb.
seclude 883 vb.
confined
circumscribed 232 adj.
sick 651 adj.
imprisoned 747 adj.
confined ideas
narrow mind 481 n.
confinement
obstetrics 167 n.
confines
region 184 n.
near place 200 n.
edge 234 n.
confirm
stabilize 153 vb.
strengthen 162 vb.
corroborate 466 vb.
make certain 473 vb.
endorse 488 vb.
affirm 532 vb.
consent 758 vb.
promise 764 vb.
contract 765 vb.
grant claims 915 vb.
vindicate 927 vb.
make legal 953 vb.
make pious 979 vb.
confirmation
evidence 466 n.
Christian rite 988 n.
confirmed
established 153 adj.
habituated 610 adj.
confiscate
deprive 786 vb.
punish 963 vb.
confiscation
expropriation 786 n.
penalty 963 n.
conflagration
fire 379 n.
burning 381 n.
conflation
combination 50 n.
conflict
contrariety 14 n.
differ 15 vb.
disagreement 25 n.
disagree 25 vb.
counteraction 182 n.
opposition 704 n.
quarrel 709 n.vb.
contention 716 n.
fight 716 n.
enmity 881 n.
be inimical 881 vb.
confluence
union 45 n.
convergence 293 n.
current 350 n.
conform
be uniform 16 vb.
do likewise 20 vb.
adjust 24 vb.
conform 83 vb.
make conform 83 vb.
modify 143 vb.
acquiesce 488 vb.
obey 739 vb.
observe 768 vb.
be in fashion 848 vb.
be servile 879 vb.
be orthodox 976 vb.
conformable
agreeimg 24 adj.
conformable 83 adj.
observant 768 adj.
conformance
conformance 24 n.
conformity 83 n.
conformation
adaptation 24 n.
composition 56 n.
conformity 83 n.
production 164 n.
form 243 n.
conformist
conformist 83 n.
assenter 488 n.
habitué 610 n.
the orthodox 976 n.
pietist 979 n.
conformity
uniformity 16 n.
conformance 24 n.
regularity 81 n.
conformity 83 n.
habit 610 n.
practice 610 n.
observance 768 n.
orthodoxism 976 n.
confound
bedevil 63 vb.
derange 63 vb.
not discriminate 464 vb.
confute 479 vb.
defeat 727 vb.
frighten 854 vb.
curse 899 vb.
confounded
damnable 645 adj.
confoundedly
extremely 32 adv.
confraternity
community 708 n.

confrère
colleague 707 n.
friend 880 n.
confront
be present 189 vb.
be opposite 240 vb.
compare 462 vb.
show 522 vb.
withstand 704 vb.
resist 715 vb.
be courageous 855 vb.
— with
endanger 661 vb.
offer 759 vb.
confrontation
manifestation 522 n.
Confucianism
religious faith 973 n.
Confucius
religious teacher 973 n.
confusable
identical 13 adj.
confuse
bedevil 63 vb.
derange 63 vb.
blur 440 vb.
distract 456 vb.
not discriminate 464 vb.
puzzle 474 vb.
be unintelligible 517 vb.
confused
mixed 43 adj.
orderless 61 adj.
indistinct 444 adj.
indiscriminate 464 adj.
poorly reasoned 477 adj.
ignorant 491 adj.
unclear 568 adj.
confusible
equivocalness 518 n.
confusion
medley 43 n.
confusion 61 n.
havoc 165 n.
amorphism 244 n.
psychopathy 503 n.
humiliation 872 n.
confutation
vindication 927 n.
confute
answer 460 vb.
tell against 467 vb.
argue 475 vb.
confute 479 vb.
cause doubt 486 vb.
dissent 489 vb.
negate 533 vb.
dissuade 613 vb.
oppose 704 vb.
quarrel 709 vb.
accuse 928 vb.
confuted
erroneous 495 adj.
conga
dance 837 n.
congé
valediction 296 n.
deposal 752 n.
congeal
be dense 324 vb.
thicken 354 vb.
refrigerate 382 vb.
congealment
coherence 48 n.
condensation 324 n.
congeneric, congenerous
akin 11 adj.
similar 18 adj.
congenial
agreeing 24 adj.
pleasant 376 adj.
friendly 880 adj.
lovable 887 adj.
congenital
genetic 5 adj.
congenital disease
disease 651 n.
congenital idiocy
insanity 503 n.
congestion
crowd 74 n.
redundance 637 n.
conglomerate
cohere 48 vb.
bring together 74 vb.
congregate 74 vb.
solid body 324 n.
rock 344 n.
corporation 708 n.
conglomeration
medley 43 n.
coherence 48 n.
accumulation 74 n.
congratulate
rejoice 835 vb.
congratulate 886 vb.
applaud 923 vb.
— oneself
be pleased 824 vb.
be content 828 vb.
rejoice 835 vb.
feel pride 871 vb.
congratulation
rejoicing 835 n.
celebration 876 n.
courteous act 884 n.
congratulation 886 n
congratulatory
celebratory 876 adj.
congratulatory 886 adj.
congregate
congregate 74 vb.
be many 104 vb.
meet 295 vb.
congregation
assembly 74 n.
council 692 n.
community 708 n.
church member 976 n.
worshipper 981 n.
laity 987 n.
congregational
laical 987 adj.
Congregationalism
Protestantism 976 n.
congress
union 45 n.
convergence 293 n.
council 692 n.
Congress
parliament 692 n.
congressman, congresswoman
councillor 692 n.
congruent
identical 13 adj.
agreeing 24 adj.
equal 28 adj.
symmetrical 245 adj.
congruity
similarity 18 n.
conformance 24 n.
symmetry 245 n.
congruous
agreeing 24 adj.
symmetrical 245 adj.
conic
rotund 252 adj.
conical
rotund 252 adj.
tapering 256 adj.
convergent 293 adj.
conic section
curve 248 n.
conifer
tree 366 n.
conjectural
suppositional 512 adj.
conjecture
attribution 158 n.
empiricism 461 n.
assume 471 vb.
uncertainty 474 n.
estimate 480 vb.
opinion 485 n.
conjecture 512 n.
suppose 512 vb.
conjoin
add 38 vb.
join 45 vb.
conjoint
joined 45 adj.
combined 50 adj.
conjugal
loving 887 adj.
matrimonial 894 adj.
conjugate
combined 50 adj.
dual 90 adj.
verbal 559 adj.
parse 564 vb.
conjugation
differentiation 15 n.
arrangement 62 n.
grammar 564 n.
conjunct
joined 45 adj.
conjunction
union 45 n.
concurrence 181 n.
contiguity 202 n.
part of speech 564 n.
conjunctive
additional 38 adj.
conjunctive 45 adj.
convergent 293 adj.
grammatical 564 adj.
conjunctivitis
dim sight 440 n.
conjuncture
juncture 8 n.
occasion 137 n.
conjure
modify 143 vb.
deceive 542 vb.
entreat 761 vb.
practise sorcery 983 vb.
— up
imagine 513 vb.
conjuring
sleight 542 n.
deceiving 542 adj.
skill 694 n.
conjuror
conjuror 545 n.
entertainer 594 n.
proficient person 696 n.
sorcerer 983 n.
conk
head 213 n.
face 237 n.
protuberance 254 n.
conk out
die 361 vb.
fail 728 vb.
con man
trickster 545 n.
defrauder 789 n.
knave 938 n.
connatural
genetic 5 adj.
connect
relate 9 vb.
connect 45 vb.
continue 71 vb.
be contiguous 202 vb.
pass 305 vb.
— with
relate 9 vb.
attribute 158 vb.
connection
relation 9 n.
consanguinity 11 n.
union 45 n.
bond 47 n.
coherence 48 n.
association 706 n.
conning tower
view 438 n.

connivance
cooperation 706 n.
laxity 734 n.
leniency 736 n.
permission 756 n.
connive at
disregard 458 vb.
patronize 703 vb.
be lax 734 vb.
consent 758 vb.
do wrong 914 vb.
connoisseur
collector 492 n.
enthusiast 504 n.
expert 696 n.
people of taste 846 n.
connoisseurship
discrimination 463 n.
good taste 846 n.
fastidiousness 862 n.
connotation
connotation 514 n.
equivocalness 518 n.
interpretation 520 n.
indication 547 n.
connote
mean 514 vb.
imply 523 vb.
indicate 547 vb.
connubial
matrimonial 894 adj.
conquer
climb 308 vb.
overmaster 727 vb.
appropriate 786 vb.
take 786 vb.
conqueror
victor 727 n.
possessor 776 n.
conquest
victory 727 n.
defeat 728 n.
subjection 745 n.
loved one 887 n.
conquistador
soldier 722 n.
victor 727 n.
consanguineous
akin 11 adj.
conscience
knowledge 490 n.
motive 612 n.
warning 664 n.
conscience 917 n.
conscience clause
nonliability 919 n.
conscienceless
dishonest 930 adj.
wicked 934 adj.
impenitent 940 adj.
conscience money
gift 781 n.
atonement 941 n.
conscience-stricken, conscience-smitten
regretting 830 adj.
obliged 917 adj.
repentant 939 adj.
conscientious
careful 457 adj.
observant 768 adj.
fastidious 862 adj.
obliged 917 adj.
honourable 929 adj.
trustworthy 929 adj.
conscientious objection
disobedience 738 n.
conscientious objector
dissentient 489 n.
opponent 705 n.
pacifist 717 n.
conscious (of)
sentient 374 adj.
mental 447 adj.
attentive 455 adj.
knowing 490 adj.
impressible 819 adj.
Conscious, the
subjectivity 320 n.
consciousness
sensibility 374 n.
intellect 447 n.
knowledge 490 n.
conscript
go to war 718 vb.
soldier 722 n.
compel 740 vb.
conscription
war measures 718 n.
compulsion 740 n.
service 745 n.
consecrate
offer 759 vb.
give 781 vb.
dignify 866 vb.
sanctify 979 vb.
offer worship 981 vb.
be ecclesiastical 985 vb.
perform ritual 988 vb.
— to
use 673 vb.
consecrated bread
the sacrament 988 n.
consecration
disinterestedness 931 n.
(See **consecrate** *)*
consecutive
relative 9 adj.
sequential 65 adj.
continuous 71 adj.
consensual
agreeing 24 adj.
contractual 765 adj.
consensus
agreement 24 n.
concurrence 181 n.
consensus 488 n.
concord 710 n.
consent
agreement 24 n.
accord 24 vb.
assent 488 n.vb.
willingness 597 n.
be willing 597 vb.
be induced 612 vb.
submission 721 n.
be lenient 736 vb.
obey 739 vb.
permission 756 n.
permit 756 vb.
consent 758 n.vb.
approbation 923 n.
consequence
sequence 65 n.
sequel 67 n.
event 154 n.
effect 157 n.
importance 638 n.
consequences
indoor game 837 n.
consequential
eventual 154 adj.
caused 157 adj.
demonstrating 478 adj.
ostentatious 875 adj.
consequently
after 65 adv.
consequently 157 adv.
reasonably 475 adv.
conservancy
preservation 666 n.
conservation
permanence 144 n.
storage 632 n.
provision 633 n.
protection 660 n.
preservation 666 n.
economy 814 n.
conservationist
preserver 666 n.
conservatism
permanence 144 n.
habit 610 n.
conservative
antiquated 127 adj.
permanent 144 adj.
depreciating 483 adj.
preserving 666 adj.
sectional 708 adj.
cautious 858 adj.
Conservative
political party 708 n.
conservatoire
music 412 n.
academy 539 n.
conservator
protector 660 n.
preserver 666 n.
conservatory
seedbed 156 n.
arbour 194 n.
garden 370 n.
heater 383 n.
conserve
set apart 46 vb.
sweet thing 392 n.
store 632 vb.
sanitate 652 vb.
safeguard 660 vb.
preserve 666 vb.
consider
meditate 449 vb.
notice 455 vb.
enquire 459 vb.
discriminate 463 vb.
estimate 480 vb.
considerable
substantial 3 adj.
great 32 adj.
many 104 adj.
large 195 adj.
important 638 adj.
considerate
thoughtful 449 adj.
attentive 455 adj.
careful 457 adj.
well-bred 848 adj.
amiable 884 adj.
benevolent 897 adj.
disinterested 931 adj.
consideration
quid pro quo 150 n.
meditation 449 n.
attention 455 n.
qualification 468 n.
estimate 480 n.
gift 781 n.
courtesy 884 n.
benevolence 897 n.
respect 920 n.
disinterestedness 931 n.
reward 962 n.
consideration, be a
motivate 612 vb.
be important 638 vb.
considered
careful 457 adj.
predetermined 608 adj.
consign
send 272 vb.
commission 751 vb.
give 781 vb.
consignee
consignee 754 n.
recipient 782 n.
consignment
thing transferred 272 n.
transfer 780 n.
giving 781 n.
consignor
transferrer 272 n.
seller 793 n.
consistency
uniformity 16 n.
conformance 24 n.
regularity 81 n.
density 324 n.
truth 494 n.
consistent
rational 475 adj.

consistent with
agreeing 24 adj.
conformable 83 adj.
consist in
be 1 vb.
consist of
contain 56 vb.
comprise 78 vb.
consistorial
ecclesiastical 985 adj.
consistory
council 692 n.
synod 985 n.
consolation
relief 831 n.
condolence 905 n.
consolation prize
imperfection 647 n.
trophy 729 n.
reward 962 n.
console
cabinet 194 n.
shelf 218 n.
relieve 831 vb.
cheer 833 vb.
pity 905 vb.
— oneself
be relieved 831 vb.
consolidate
join 45 vb.
cohere 48 vb.
bring together 74 vb.
centralize 225 vb.
be dense 324 vb.
abstract 592 vb.
consolidation
contraction 198 n.
association 706 n.
consommé
hors-d'oeuvres 301 n.
consonance
agreement 24 n.
melody 410 n.
consonant
agreeing 24 adj.
speech sound 398 n.
harmonious 410 adj.
spoken letter 558 n.
consort
concomitant 89 n.
spouse 894 n.
consortium
agreement 24 n.
association 706 n.
consort with
accompany 89 vb.
conspectus
combination 50 n.
whole 52 n.
generality 79 n.
compendium 592 n.
conspicuous
obvious 443 adj.
manifest 522 adj.
notable 638 adj.
noteworthy 866 adj.
conspicuous by one's absence, be
be absent 190 vb.
conspicuous consumption
prodigality 815 n.
conspicuously
remarkably 32 adv.
conspicuousness
prominence 254 n.
visibility 443 n.
manifestation 522 n.
prestige 866 n.
conspiracy
assemblage 74 n.
concurrence 181 n.
secrecy 525 n.
plot 623 n.
cooperation 706 n.
compact 765 n.
conspirator
deceiver 545 n.
planner 623 n.
conspiratorial
stealthy 525 adj.
planning 623 adj.
conspire
plot 623 vb.
(See **conspiracy** *)*
constable
officer 741 n.
police 955 n.
constabulary
police 955 n.
constancy
uniformity 16 n.
regularity 81 n.
stability 153 n.
resolution 599 n.
perseverance 600 n.
obstinacy 602 n.
loyalty 739 n.
probity 929 n.
constant
characteristic 5 adj.
identity 13 n.
identical 13 adj.
uniform 16 adj.
continuous 71 adj.
regular 81 adj.
number 85 n.
lasting 113 adj.
perpetual 115 adj.
frequent 139 adj.
periodical 141 adj.
fixture 153 n.
unchangeable 153 adj.
accurate 494 adj.
resolute 599 adj.
persevering 600 adj.
obedient 739 adj.
trustworthy 929 adj.
constantly
for ever 115 adv.
perpetually 139 adv.
constellation
group 74 n.
star 321 n.
person of repute 866 n.
consternation
fear 854 n.
wonder 864 n.
constipating
compressive 198 adj.
solidifying 324 adj.
constipation
closure 264 n.
defecation 302 n.
condensation 324 n.
digestive disorders 651 n.
constituency
district 184 n.
electorate 605 n.
constituent(s)
part 53 n.
component 58 n.adj.
included 78 adj.
contents 193 n.
electorate 605 n.
constitute
constitute 56 vb.
be one of 58 vb.
be included 78 vb.
produce 164 vb.
constitution
character 5 n.
composition 56 n.
beginning 68 n.
inclusion 78 n.
structure 331 n.
precept 693 n.
political organization 733 n.
law 953 n.
constitutional
intrinsic 5 adj.
habit 610 n.
hygiene 652 n.
exercise 682 n.
governmental 733 adj.
due 915 adj.
legal 953 adj.
constitutionalism
government 733 n.
legality 953 n.
constitutive principle
essence 1 n.
constraint
compulsion 740 n.
subjection 745 n.
restraint 747 n.
modesty 874 n.
constrict
tighten 45 vb.
make smaller 198 vb.
constriction
compression 198 n.
narrowing 206 n.
restriction 747 n.
constrictor
compressor 198 n.
construct
compose 56 vb.
produce 164 vb.
form 243 vb.
— a figure
outline 233 vb.
represent 551 vb.
construction
composition 56 n.n.
arrangement 62 n.
production 164 n.
structure 331 n.
conjecture 512 n.
connotation 514 n.
interpretation 520 n.
sculpture 554 n.
constructional
structural 331 adj.
constructive
productive 164 adj.
semantic 514 adj.
interpretive 520 adj.
aiding 703 adj.
constructive criticism
estimate 480 n.
advice 691 n.
constructivism
sculpture 554 n.
constructor
producer 164 n.
construe
interpretation 520 n.
translation 520 n.
interpret 520 vb.
parse 564 vb.
consubstantiality
identity 13 n.
unity 88 n.
consubstantiation
the sacrament 988 n.
consuetude
habit 610 n.
consul
official 690 n.
officer 741 n.
envoy 754 n.
consulate
position of authority 733 n.
envoy 754 n.
consult
confer 584 vb.
consult 691 vb.
— one's pillow
wait 136 vb.
meditate 449 vb.
consultant
sage 500 n.
oracle 511 n.
teacher 537 n.
doctor 658 n.
adviser 691 n.
expert 696 n.
consultation
enquiry 459 n.
conference 584 n.
advice 691 n.
cooperation 706 n.
consultative body
council 692 n.

consulting room
hospital 658 n.
consume
abate 37 vb.
decompose 51 vb.
consume 165 vb.
destroy 165 vb.
eat 301 vb.
require 627 vb.
waste 634 vb.
impair 655 vb.
dispose of 673 vb.
use 673 vb.
expend 806 vb.
consumed with
impressed 818 adj.
consumer
eater 301 n.
purchaser 792 n.
consumer demand
requirement 627 n.
request 761 n.
purchase 792 n.
consumer durables
merchandise 795 n.
consumers' association
corporation 708 n.
consumer society
intemperance 943 n.
consummate
consummate 32 adj.
complete 54 adj.
terminate 69 vb.
crown 213 vb.
perfect 646 adj. vb.
carry through 725 vb.
consummation
coition 45 n.
completion 725 n.
consumption
decrease 37 n.
thinness 206 n.
reception 299 n.
eating 301 n.
requirement 627 n.
waste 634 n.
respiratory disease 651 n.
use 673 n.
loss 772 n.
consumptive
sick person 651 n.
diseased 651 adj.
contact
union 45 n.
connect 45 vb.
contiguity 202 n.
be contiguous 202 vb.
transference 272 n.
touch 378 n.
informant 524 n.
communicate 524 vb.
messenger 529 n.
correspondent 588 n.
contact lens
eyeglass 442 n.
contact print
copy 22 n.
photography 551 n.
contagion
infection 651 n.
plague 651 n.
contagious
influential 178 adj.
transferable 272 adj.
diseased 651 adj.
infectious 653 adj.
contain
contain 56 vb.
comprise 78 vb.
surround 230 vb.
possess 773 vb.
retain 778 vb.
— oneself
be temperate 942 vb.
container
receptacle 194 n.
thing transferred 272 n.
carrier 273 n.
storage 632 n.
containerize, containerise
load 193 vb.
transpose 272 vb.
containment
surroundings 230 n.
circumscription 232 n.
retention 778 n.
contaminate
be mixed 43 vb.
influence 178 vb.
transfer 272 vb.
make useless 641 vb.
make unclean 649 vb.
impair 655 vb.
contaminated
diseased 651 adj.
contamination
badness 645 n.
impairment 655 n.
(See **contaminate** *)*
contemplate
scan 438 vb.
meditate 449 vb.
expect 507 vb.
intend 617 vb.
worship 981 vb.
contemplation
look 438 n.
meditation 449 n.
attention 455 n.
expectation 507 n.
piety 979 n.
prayers 981 n.
worship 981 n.
contemplative
thoughtful 449 adj.
pious 979 adj.
monastic 986 adj.
contemporaneous
accompanying 89 adj.
present 121 adj.
synchronous 123 adj.
contemporary
accompanying 89 adj.
present time 121 n.
present 121 adj.
contemporary 123 n.
synchronous 123 adj.
modern 126 adj.
contempt
object of scorn 867 n.
pride 871 n.
insolence 878 n.
scurrility 899 n.
disrespect 921 n.
indignity 921 n.
contempt 922 n.
detraction 926 n.
impiety 980 n.
contemptible
inferior 35 adj.
trivial 639 adj.
unimportant 639 adj.
bad 645 adj.
ridiculous 849 adj.
discreditable 867 adj.
disreputable 867 adj.
unrespected 921 adj.
contemptible 922 adj.
rascally 930 adj.
contemptuous
insolent 878 adj.
despising 922 adj.
detracting 926 adj.
contend
do likewise 20 vb.
affirm 532 vb.
oppose 704 vb.
resist 715 vb.
contend 716 vb.
give battle 718 vb.
offer oneself 759 vb.
contender
athlete 162 n.
contender 716 n.
player 837 n.
content
structure 331 n.
euphoria 376 n.
comfortable 376 adj.
willing 597 adj.
sufficiency 635 n.
filled 635 adj.
suffice 635 vb.
reposeful 683 adj.
pacify 719 vb.
inexcitability 823 n.
inexcitable 823 adj.
enjoyment 824 n.
pleased 824 adj.
please 826 vb.
content 828 n. adj.
content 828 vb.
cheerfulness 833 n.
cheer 833 vb.
approving 923 adj.
contention
question 459 n.
argument 475 n.
opposition 704 n.
quarrel 709 n.
quarrelsomeness 709 n.
contention 716 n.
jealousy 911 n.
contentious
quarrelling 709 adj.
contending 716 adj.
contentment
euphoria 376 n.
sufficiency 635 n.
content 828 n.
contents
finite quantity 26 n.
component 58 n.
bunch 74 n.
contents 193 n.
topic 452 n.
meaning 514 n.
compendium 592 n.
conterminous
ending 69 adj.
synchronous 123 adj.
contiguous 202 adj.
limited 236 adj.
contessa
person of rank 868 n.
contest
athletics 162 n.
contest 716 n.
contend 716 vb.
sport 837 n.
— at law
litigate 959 vb.
contestant
opponent 705 n.
contender 716 n.
context
circumstance 8 n.
relation 9 n.
concomitant 89 n.
connotation 514 n.
meaning 514 n.
contiguity
nearness 200 n.
contiguity 202 n.
touch 378 n.
contiguous
near 200 adj.
contiguous 202 adj.
continence
temperance 942 n.
purity 950 n.
continent
region 184 n.
land 344 n.
temperate 942 adj.
pure 950 adj.

continental
foreigner 59 n.
extraneous 59 adj.
regional 184 adj.
dweller 191 n.
land 344 n.
inland 344 adj.
continental drift
transference 272 n.
world 321 n.
continental shelf
territory 184 n.
shore 344 n.
contingency
juncture 8 n.
event 154 n.
chance 159 n.
contingent
extrinsic 6 adj.
circumstantial 8 adj.
part 53 n.
eventual 154 adj.
caused 157 adj.
casual 159 adj.
liable 180 adj.
qualifying 468 adj.
possible 469 adj.
uncertain 474 adj.
conditional 766 adj.
contingents
armed force 722 n.
continual
continuous 71 adj.
perpetual 115 adj.
frequent 139 adj.
unceasing 146 adj.
continuance
uniformity 16 n.
sequence 65 n.
continuity 71 n.
course of time 111 n.
durability 113 n.
perpetuity 115 n.
present time 121 n.
permanence 144 n.
continuance 146 n.
perseverance 600 n.
habit 610 n.
continuation
adjunct 40 n.
sequel 67 n.
continuity 71 n.
continuance 146 n.
continue
be 1 vb.
continue 71 vb.
run on 71 vb.
lengthen 203 vb.
(See **continuance, continuity** *)*
continuity
uniformity 16 n.
order 60 n.
sequence 65 n.
continuity 71 n.
recurrence 106 n.
perpetuity 115 n.
frequency 139 n.
periodicity 141 n.
continuance 146 n.
contiguity 202 n.
motion 265 n.
progression 285 n.
cinema 445 n.
continuity girl
stagehand 594 n.
continuo
melody 410 n.
continuous
continuous 71 adj.
(See **continuity** *)*
continuum
continuity 71 n.
space 183 n.
contort
distort 246 vb.
contorted
convoluted 251 adj.
contortionist
athlete 162 n.
contour
outline 233 n.
form 243 n.
feature 445 n.
contour lines
indication 547 n.
contour ploughing
agriculture 370 n.
contra-
contrary 14 adj.
contraband
prohibited 757 adj.
booty 790 n.
illegal 954 adj.
contraception
impotence 161 n.
contraception 172 n.
drug 658 n.
hindrance 702 n.
contraceptive
contraception 172 n.
contract
abate 37 vb.
decrease 37 vb.
be little 196 vb.
become small 198 vb.
make smaller 198 vb.
shorten 204 vb.
make thin 206 vb.
be dense 324 vb.
be concise 569 vb.
undertaking 672 n.
promise 764 vb.
compact 765 n.
contract 765 vb.
make terms 766 vb.
bargain 791 vb.
— a disease
be ill 651 vb.
— marriage
wed 894 vb.
contract bridge
card game 837 n.
contractibility
compression 198 n.
contractility
compression 198 n.
contraction
joining together 45 n.
contraction 198 n.
closure 264 n.
word 559 n.
conciseness 569 n.
compendium 592 n.
(See **contract** *)*
contractions
obstetrics 167 n.
contractor
trier 671 n.
doer 676 n.
signatory 765 n.
contractual
agreeing 24 adj.
contractual 765 adj.
contradict
be contrary 14 vb.
disagree 25 vb.
answer 460 vb.
tell against 467 vb.
confute 479 vb.
dissent 489 vb.
negate 533 vb.
oppose 704 vb.
— oneself
tell against 467 vb.
contradiction
contrariety 14 n.
disagreement 25 n.
divergence 294 n.
rejoinder 460 n.
confutation 479 n.
dissent 489 n.
negation 533 n.
opposition 704 n.
contradiction in terms
sophism 477 n.
contradictory
illogical 477 adj.
(See **contradiction** *)*
contradistinction
contrariety 14 n.
differentiation 15 n.
contradistinguish
discriminate 463 vb.
contraindicate
be contrary 14 vb.
tell against 467 vb.
contralto
resonance 404 n.
vocalist 413 n.
contraposition
contraposition 240 n.
contraption
contrivance 623 n.
tool 630 n.
contrapuntal
musical 412 adj.
contraries
polarity 14 n.
opposites 704 n.
contrariety
word 559 n.
(See **contrary** *)*
contrariwise
correlatively 12 adv.
contrarily 14 adv.
inversely 221 adv.
against 240 adv.
contrary
contrary 14 adj.
different 15 adj.
nonuniform 17 adj.
disagreeing 25 adj.
unconformable 84 adj.
counteracting 182 adj.
inverted 221 adj.
opposite 240 adj.adj.
discordant 411 adj.
countervailing 467 adj.
semantic 514 adj.
negative 533 adj.
capricious 604 adj.
hindering 702 adj.
opposing 704 adj.
adverse 731 adj.
disobedient 738 adj.
contrary to
although 182 adv.
contrast
contrariety 14 n.
be contrary 14 vb.
difference 15 n.
differ 15 vb.
dissimilarity 19 n.
nonconformity 84 n.
comparison 462 n.
compare 462 vb.
trope 519 n.
figure 519 vb.
painting 553 n.
contravene
be contrary 14 vb.
tell against 467 vb.
negate 533 vb.
contravention
lawbreaking 954 n.
contretemps
untimeliness 138 n.
hitch 702 n.
misfortune 731 n.
contribute
give 781 vb.
pay 804 vb.
— to
augment 36 vb.
conduce 156 vb.
tend 179 vb.
promote 285 vb.
aid 703 vb.
patronize 703 vb.
contributing
influential 178 adj.
concurrent 181 adj.
contribution
addition 38 n.
cooperation 706 n.
giving 781 n.
offering 781 n.

pay 804 n.
payment 804 n.
contributor
cause 156 n.
correspondent 588 n.
author 589 n.
participator 775 n.
giver 781 n.
contrition
regret 830 n.
penitence 939 n.
contrivance
arrangement 62 n.
idea 451 n.
trickery 542 n.
contrivance 623 n.
plan 623 n.
instrument 628 n.
means 629 n.
tool 630 n.
good policy 642 n.
tactics 688 n.
skill 694 n.
stratagem 698 n.
contrive
cause 156 vb.
produce 164 vb.
predetermine 608 vb.
plan 623 vb.
find means 629 vb.
be cunning 698 vb.
contrived
predetermined 608 adj.
control
order 60 vb.
power 160 n.
be able 160 vb.
moderation 177 n.
moderate 177 vb.
influence 178 n.
prevail 178 vb.
testing agent 461 n.
dispose of 673 vb.
do 676 vb.
management 689 n.
manage 689 vb.
skill 694 n.
hindrance 702 n.
governance 733 n.
rule 733 vb.
restraint 747 n.
restrain 747 vb.
tranquillize 823 vb.
ghost 970 n.
spiritualism 984 n.
— oneself
restrain 747 vb.
be temperate 942 vb.
controlled
elegant 575 adj.
involuntary 596 adj.
predetermined 608 adj.
restrained 747 adj.
impassive 820 adj.
inexcitable 823 adj.
controller
moderator 177 n.
doer 676 n.
director 690 n.
treasurer 798 n.
controls
aircraft 276 n.
instrument 628 n.
directorship 689 n.
controversial
uncertain 474 adj.
arguing 475 adj.
quarrelling 709 adj.
controversy
disagreement 25 n.
question 459 n.
argument 475 n.
dissent 489 n.
quarrel 709 n.
contention 716 n.
controvert
argue 475 vb.
negate 533 vb.
contumacious
obstinate 602 adj.
wilful 602 adj.
impenitent 940 adj.
schismatical 978 adj.
contumelious
ungracious 885 adj.
cursing 899 adj.
disrespectful 921 adj.
detracting 926 adj.
contumely
insolence 878 n.
scurrility 899 n.
disrespect 921 n.
detraction 926 n.
contusion
wound 655 n.
conundrum
equivocalness 518 n.
enigma 530 n.
conurbation
city 184 n.
housing 192 n.
convalesce
get healthy 650 vb.
be restored 656 vb.
convalescence
recuperation 656 n.
convalescent home
hospital 658 n.
convection
transference 272 n.
convenances
etiquette 848 n.
convene
bring together 74 vb.
command 737 vb.
convener
accumulator 74 n.
convenience
opportunity 137 n.
euphoria 376 n.
benefit 615 n.
utility 640 n.
good policy 642 n.
leisure 681 n.
facility 701 n.
convenient
advisable 642 adj.
convent
quarters 192 n.
monastery 986 n.
conventicle
assembly 74 n.
sect 978 n.
convention
agreement 24 n.
assembly 74 n.
conformity 83 n.
conference 584 n.
practice 610 n.
council 692 n.
precept 693 n.
compact 765 n.
etiquette 848 n.
conventional
imitative 20 adj.
regular 81 adj.
conformable 83 adj.
typical 83 adj.
feeble 572 adj.
habitual 610 adj.
preceptive 693 adj.
contractual 765 adj.
fashionable 848 adj.
orthodox 976 adj.
conventionalist
conformist 83 n.
habitué 610 n.
conventionality
conformity 83 n.
(See **convention** *)*
conventionalize, conventionalise
make uniform 16 vb.
make conform 83 vb.
conventual
monk 986 n.
monastic 986 adj.
converge
focus 76 vb.
converge 293 vb.
convergence
union 45 n.
assembly 74 n.
focus 76 n.
nearness 200 n.
contiguity 202 n.
narrowing 206 n.
collision 279 n.
approach 289 n.
convergence 293 n.
conversant (with)
knowing 490 adj.
habituated 610 adj.
conversation
speech 579 n.
interlocution 584 n.
conversational
loquacious 581 adj.
conversing 584 adj.
conversationalist
speaker 579 n.
chatterer 581 n.
interlocutor 584 n.
humorist 839 n.
conversazione
conference 584 n.
amusement 837 n.
social gathering 882 n.
converse
contrariety 14 n.
contrary 14 adj.
countervailing 467 adj.
speak 579 vb.
be loquacious 581 vb.
speak to 583 vb.
converse 584 vb.
be sociable 882 vb.
conversely
contrarily 14 adv.
in exchange 151 adv.
conversely 467 adv.
conversion
transformation 143 n.
conversion 147 n.
teaching 534 n.
tergiversation 603 n.
improvement 654 n.
use 673 n.
transfer 780 n.
sanctity 979 n.
convert
make unlike 19 vb.
modify 143 vb.
changed person 147 n.
convert 147 vb.
interchange 151 vb.
convince 485 vb.
learner 538 n.
tergiversator 603 n.
induce 612 vb.
use 673 vb.
acquire 771 vb.
assign 780 vb.
pietist 979 n.
make pious 979 vb.
converted
believing 485 adj.
repentant 939 adj.
converter
alterer 143 n.
convertible
equivalent 28 adj.
interchanged 151 adj.
automobile 274 n.
convex
convex 253 adj.
convexity
curvature 248 n.
rotundity 252 n.
convexity 253 n.
roughness 259 n.
convey
move 265 vb.

transfer 272 vb.
carry 273 vb.
mean 514 vb.
communicate 524 vb.
inform 524 vb.
assign 780 vb.

conveyance
conveyance 267 n.
transference 272 n.
transport 272 n.
vehicle 274 n.
transfer 780 n.
giving 781 n.

conveyancer
transferrer 272 n.
law agent 958 n.

conveyor
conveyance 267 n.
transferrer 272 n.
transport 272 n.
carrier 273 n.
conveyor 274 n.
lifter 310 n.

conveyor belt
continuity 71 n.
conveyor 274 n.

convict
confute 479 vb.
prisoner 750 n.
offender 904 n.
condemn 961 vb.

convicted
guilty 936 adj.

conviction
positiveness 473 n.
confutation 479 n.
belief 485 n.
teaching 534 n.
hope 852 n.
condemnation 961 n.

convince
convert 147 vb.
influence 178 vb.
make certain 473 vb.
demonstrate 478 vb.
convince 485 vb.
induce 612 vb.

— to the contrary
dissuade 613 vb.

convinced
positive 473 adj.
believing 485 adj.

convincing
plausible 471 adj.
positive 473 adj.
demonstrating 478 adj.
credible 485 adj.
descriptive 590 adj.

convivial
cheerful 833 adj.
sociable 882 adj.

conviviality
cheerfulness 833 n.
festivity 837 n.
sociability 882 n.

convocation
assembly 74 n.
council 692 n.
synod 985 n.

convoke
bring together 74 vb.

convoluted
distorted 246 adj.
convoluted 251 adj.
roundabout 626 adj.

convolution
complexity 61 n.
crossing 222 n.
curve 248 n.
loop 250 n.
convolution 251 n.

convoy
accompany 89 vb.
carry 273 vb.
protection 660 n.
safeguard 660 vb.
keeper 749 n.

convulse
derange 63 vb.

— with laughter
amuse 837 vb.

convulsion
disorder 61 n.
turmoil 61 n.
derangement 63 n.
revolution 149 n.
outbreak 176 n.
spasm 318 n.
pang 377 n.

cony
skin 226 n.

coo
ululation 409 n.
ululate 409 vb.
rejoice 835 vb.
pet 889 vb.
flatter 925 vb.

cook
cookery 301 n.
cook 301 vb.
heat 381 vb.
fake 541 vb.
caterer 633 n.
preparer 669 n.
mature 669 vb.
domestic 742 n.

— for
provide 633 vb.

— one's goose
destroy 165 vb.
defeat 727 vb.

— the books
defraud 788 vb.
account 808 vb.

— the evidence
indict 928 vb.

— up
fake 541 vb.
plot 623 vb.

cooker
furnace 383 n.

cookery
cookery 301 n.

cookery book
cookery 301 n.

cookhouse
chamber 194 n.
cookery 301 n.
heater 383 n.

cookie, cooky
pastries 301 n.
a beauty 841 n.

cooking
impending 155 adj.
cookery 301 n.
preparatory 669 adj.

cool
moderate 177 Adj. vb.
coldness 380 n.
cold 380 adj.
refrigerate 382 vb.
musical 412 adj.
screened 421 adj.
wise 498 adj.
sane 502 adj.
dissuade 613 vb.
refreshing 685 adj.
refresh 685 vb.
impassive 820 adj.
inexcitability 823 n.
inexcitable 823 adj.
relieve 831 vb.
cautious 858 adj.
indifferent 860 adj.
impertinent 878 adj.
inimical 881 adj.
unsociable 883 adj.
discourteous 885 adj.

— down
be sane 502 vb.
tranquillize 823 vb.

— off
refresh 685 vb.
be indifferent 860 vb.

— one's heels
wait 136 vb.

coolant
nucleonics 160 n.
refrigerator 384 n.

cooler
moderator 177 n.
refrigerator 384 n.
lockup 748 n.

coolie
bearer 273 n.
worker 686 n.

cooling
ventilation 352 n.
refrigeration 382 n.

cooling-off period
delay 136 n.
lull 145 n.

coop
stable 192 n.
cattle pen 369 n.
lockup 748 n.

cooper
artisan 686 n.

cooperate
cooperate 706 vb.

cooperation
combination 50 n.
causation 156 n.
production 164 n.
agency 173 n.
concurrence 181 n.
assent 488 n.
willingness 597 n.
instrumentality 628 n.
aid 703 n.
cooperation 706 n.
concord 710 n.
joint possession 775 n.
friendship 880 n.

cooperative
willing 597 adj.
aiding 703 adj.
association 706 n.
cooperative 706 adj.
society 708 n.
corporate 708 adj.
sharing 775 adj.

cooperator
assenter 488 n.
collaborator 707 n.
participator 775 n.

co-opt
choose 605 vb.

coop up
imprison 747 vb.

coordinate
equal 28 adj.
regularize 62 vb.
coordinate 465 n.
gauge 465 n.

coordinates
suit 228 n.

coot
bird 365 n.

cop
protector 660 n.
arrest 747 vb.
police 955 n.

— it
die 361 vb.
be in difficulty 700 vb.

— out
avoid 620 vb.

copartnership
association 706 n.
participation 775 n.

cope
vestments 989 n.

cope (with)
be equal 28 vb.
deal with 688 vb.
withstand 704 vb.

Copernican system
centrality 225 n.
sun 321 n.

coping
summit 213 n.

copious
prolific 171 adj.
diffuse 570 adj.
plenteous 635 adj.

cop-out
avoidance 620 n.
undutifulness 918 n.
copper
cauldron 194 n.
heater 383 n.
brownness 430 n.
orange 432 n.
protector 660 n.
coinage 797 n.
police 955 n.
copper-bottomed
secured 767 adj.
copper-coloured
brown 430 adj.
orange 432 adj.
copperplate
engraving 555 n.
lettering 586 n.
written 586 adj.
coppice
wood 366 n.
coprolite
excrement 302 n.
copse
wood 366 n.
Coptic Church
Christendom 976 n.
copula
bond 47 n.
part of speech 564 n.
copulation
coition 45 n.
propagation 167 n.
copulative
conjunctive 45 adj.
grammatical 564 adj.
copy
identity 13 n.
analogue 18 n.
imitation 20 n.
copy 20 vb.
copy 22 n.
prototype 23 n.
conform 83 vb.
duplication 91 n.
double 91 vb.
repeat 106 vb.
reproduction 166 n.
reproduce 166 vb.
news 529 n.
sham 542 n.
record 548 n.
photography 551 n.
represent 551 vb.
script 586 n.
writing 586 n.
write 586 vb.
letterpress 587 n.
reading matter 589 n.
borrow 785 vb.
steal 788 vb.
copybook
prototypal 23 adj.
regulated 83 adj.
copycat
imitator 20 n.
conformist 83 n.
copy editor
author 589 n.
copyhold
estate 777 n.
lands 777 n.
proprietary 777 adj.
copyholder
possessor 776 n.
copyist
imitator 20 n.
artist 556 n.
calligrapher 586 n.
copyright
dueness 915 n.
claim 915 vb.
copywriter
publicizer 528 n.
coquetry
affectation 850 n.
love-making 887 n.
wooing 889 n.
flattery 925 n.
coquette
tergiversator 603 n.
be capricious 604 vb.
affecter 850 n.
be affected 850 vb.
lover 887 n.
excite love 887 vb.
court 889 vb.
flatterer 925 n.
coracle
rowing boat 275 n.
coral
fossil 125 n.
marine life 365 n.
red 431 adj.
gem 844 n.
coral reef
island 349 n.
corbel
shelf 218 n.
ornamental art 844 n.
cord
cable 47 n.
ligature 47 n.
fibre 208 n.
cordage
tackling 47 n.
cordial
soft drink 301 n.
pleasant 376 adj.
willing 597 adj.
tonic 658 n.
feeling 818 adj.
felt 818 adj.
friendly 880 adj.
sociable 882 adj.
cordiality
warm feeling 818 n.
cordite
explosive 723 n.
cordon
barrier 235 n.
enclose 235 vb.
— off
circumscribe 232 vb.
restrain 747 vb.
cordon bleu
cookery 301 n.
proficient person 696 n.
cordon sanitaire
prophylactic 658 n.
protection 660 n.
corduroy
textile 222 n.
furrow 262 n.
core
essence 1 n.
substance 3 n.
essential part 5 n.
focus 76 n.
centre 225 n.
chief thing 638 n.
affections 817 n.
core curriculum
curriculum 534 n.
corespondent
divorce 896 n.
accused person 928 n.
coriaceous
tough 329 adj.
coriander
potherb 301 n.
Corinthian
ornamental 844 adj.
cork
covering 226 n.
stopper 264 n.
close 264 vb.
lightness 323 n.
silencer 401 n.
corkage
price 809 n.
corked
unsavoury 391 adj.
deteriorated 655 adj.
corker
exceller 644 n.
corkscrew
coil 251 n.
twine 251 vb.
opener 263 n.
perforator 263 n.
extractor 304 n.
rotate 315 vb.
corm
plant 366 n.
cormorant
bird 365 n.
glutton 947 n.
corn
swelling 253 n.
cereals 301 n.
provender 301 n.
hardness 326 n.
ulcer 651 n.
cornea
eye 438 n.
cornelian, carnelian
redness 431 n.
gem 844 n.
corner
circumstance 8 n.
place 185 n.
angularity 247 n.
make angular 247 vb.
cavity 255 n.
circle 314 vb.
hiding-place 527 n.
attack 712 vb.
defeat 727 vb.
possession 773 n.
possess 773 vb.
purchase 792 vb.
penance 941 n.
pillory 964 n.
— the market
be early 135 vb.
cornered
in difficulties 700 adj.
hindered 702 adj.
cornerstone
prop 218 n.
chief thing 638 n.
cornerwise
obliquely 220 adv.
cornet
cone 252 n.
horn 414 n.
army officer 741 n.
corn exchange
market 796 n.
cornflakes
cereals 301 n.
cornice
summit 213 n.
edge 234 n.
ornamental art 844 n.
corniche
road 624 n.
cornucopia
abundance 171 n.
store 632 n.
plenty 635 n.
liberality 813 n.
corny
known 490 adj.
aphoristic 496 adj.
corolla
flower 366 n.
corollary
adjunct 40 n.
concomitant 89 n.
effect 157 n.
argumentation 475 n.
judgment 480 n.
corona
loop 250 n.
sun 321 n.
light 417 n.
coronach
vocal music 412 n.
lament 836 n.
condolence 905 n.
coronary
cardiovascular disease 651 n.

coronation
dignification 866 n.
celebration 876 n.
coronation robes
regalia 743 n.
coroner
judge 957 n.
coroner's court
lawcourt 956 n.
coronet
headgear 228 n.
loop 250 n.
heraldry 547 n.
regalia 743 n.
corporal
material 319 adj.
soldiery 722 n.
army officer 741 n.
corporal punishment
corporal punishment 963 n.
corporate
joined 45 adj.
corporate 708 adj.
corporation
maw 194 n.
bulk 195 n.
business 622 n.
association 706 n.
corporation 708 n.
corporeal
substantial 3 adj.
material 319 adj.
corps
band 74 n.
formation 722 n.
corps de ballet
actor 594 n.
dance 837 n.
corps d'élite
elite 644 n.
corps diplomatique
envoy 754 n.
corpse
remainder 41 n.
decay 51 n.
the dead 361 n.
corpse 363 n.
corpulence
bulk 195 n.
thickness 205 n.
corpus
great quantity 32 n.
whole 52 n.
assemblage 74 n.
matter 319 n.
reading matter 589 n.
Corpus Christi
holy day 988 n.
corpuscle
minuteness 196 n.
blood 335 n.
corral
bring together 74 vb.
circumscribe 232 vb.
enclosure 235 n.
break in 369 vb.
imprison 747 vb.
correct
orderly 60 adj.
regulated 83 adj.
modify 143 vb.
moderate 177 vb.
accurate 494 adj.
true 494 adj.
inform 524 vb.
disclose 526 vb.
linguistic 557 adj.
grammatical 564 adj.
elegant 575 adj.
print 587 vb.
perfect 646 adj. vb.
rectify 654 vb.
remedy 658 vb.
tasteful 846 adj.
fashionable 848 adj.
well-bred 848 adj.
formal 875 adj.
courteous 884 adj.
reprove 924 vb.
honourable 929 adj.
punish 963 vb.
orthodox 976 adj.
correction
amendment 654 n.
correctitude
formality 875 n.
corrective
counteracting 182 adj.
remedy 658 n.
remedial 658 adj.
punitive 963 adj.
correlate
correlate 12 vb.
analogue 18 n.
adjust 24 vb.
depend 157 vb.
compare 462 vb.
correlation
relativeness 9 n.
correlation 12 n.
similarity 18 n.
equalization 28 n.
statistics 86 n.
interchange 151 n.
symmetry 245 n.
correlative
correlative 12 adj.
agreeing 24 adj.
answering 460 adj.
correspond
be related 9 vb.
correlate 12 vb.
accord 24 vb.
conform 83 vb.
be parallel 219 vb.
communicate 524 vb.
write 586 vb.
correspond 588 vb.
— to
resemble 18 vb.
answer 460 vb.
correspondence
similarity 18 n.
symmetry 245 n.
report 524 n.
message 529 n.
postal communications 531 n.
correspondence 588 n.
correspondence column
publicity 528 n.
correspondence course
curriculum 534 n.
correspondent
informant 524 n.
news reporter 529 n.
correspondent 588 n.
delegate 754 n.
corresponding
agreeing 24 adj.
equivalent 28 adj.
corridor
entrance 68 n.
region 184 n.
lobby 194 n.
access 624 n.
corrie
valley 255 n.
corrigendum
mistake 495 n.
corroborate
corroborate 466 vb.
make certain 473 vb.
demonstrate 478 vb.
affirm 532 vb.
corroboration
evidence 466 n.
assent 488 n.
affirmation 532 n.
corroboree
dance 837 n.
corrode
burn 381 vb.
impair 655 vb.
hurt 827 vb.
corrosion
dilapidation 655 n.
corrosive
destroyer 168 n.
keen 174 adj.
harmful 645 adj.
poison 659 n.
paining 827 adj.
corrugate
crinkle 251 vb.
roughen 259 vb.
fold 261 vb.
groove 262 vb.
corrugated
undulatory 251 adj.
corrugated iron
roof 226 n.
corrupt
decompose 51 vb.
misteach 535 vb.
bribe 612 vb.
bad 645 adj.
harm 645 vb.
unclean 649 adj.
make unclean 649 vb.
deteriorated 655 adj.
impair 655 vb.
pervert 655 vb.
venal 930 adj.
vicious 934 adj.
make wicked 934 vb.
corruptible
venal 930 adj.
corruption
decay 51 n.
stench 397 n.
neology 560 n.
badness 645 n.
uncleanness 649 n.
deterioration 655 n.
dilapidation 655 n.
improbity 930 n.
wickedness 934 n.
corsage
garment 228 n.
corsair
galley 275 n.
robber 789 n.
corset
compressor 198 n.
prop 218 n.
underwear 228 n.
corslet
armour 713 n.
cortège
retinue 67 n.
procession 71 n.
obsequies 364 n.
cortex
exteriority 223 n.
skin 226 n.
intellect 447 n.
cortisone
drug 658 n.
coruscation
flash 417 n.
corvée
labour 682 n.
compulsion 740 n.
service 745 n.
corvette
sailing ship 275 n.
warship 722 n.
corybantic
frenzied 503 adj.
corymb
flower 366 n.
cosecant
ratio 85 n.
cosh
hammer 279 n.
strike 279 vb.
club 723 n.
cosine
ratio 85 n.
cosiness
euphoria 376 n.
content 828 n.

cosmetic
scent 396 n.
balm 658 n.
cosmetic 843 n.
cosmetician
beautician 843 n.
cosmetic surgery
surgery 658 n.
beautification 843 n.
cosmic
extensive 32 adj.
comprehensive 52 adj.
cosmic 321 adj.
radiating 417 adj.
cosmic dust
nebula 321 n.
cosmic radiation
radiation 417 n.
cosmogony
cosmography 321 n.
universe 321 n.
cosmography
situation 186 n.
cosmography 321 n.
cosmological
cosmic 321 adj.
cosmonaut
aeronaut 271 n.
cosmopolitan
universal 79 adj.
urban 192 adj.
national 371 adj.
expert 696 n.
beau monde 848 n.
well-bred 848 adj.
philanthropist 901 n.
philanthropic 901 adj.
cosmos
whole 52 n.
arrangement 62 n.
universe 321 n.
Cossack
cavalry 722 n.
cosset
pet 889 vb.
cost
appraise 465 vb.
account 808 vb.
cost 809 n.vb.
price 809 vb.
dearness 811 n.
— nothing
be cheap 812 vb.
co-star
act 594 vb.
cost-benefit analysis
management 689 n.
cost-cutting
economical 814 adj.
costermonger
seller 793 n.
pedlar 794 n.
costly
destructive 165 adj.
valuable 644 adj.
harmful 645 adj.
dear 811 adj.
ostentatious 875 adj.
cost of living
statistics 86 n.
expenditure 806 n.
cost 809 n.
costs
offset 31 n.
expenditure 806 n.
cost 809 n.
penalty 963 n.
costume
suit 228 n.
stage set 594 n.
costume jewellery
finery 844 n.
costumier
clothier 228 n.
stagehand 594 n.
cosy
comfortable 376 adj.
palmy 730 adj.
pleasurable 826 adj.
content 828 adj.
sociable 882 adj.
cot
small house 192 n.
bed 218 n.
sleep 679 n.
cotangent
ratio 85 n.
coterie
band 74 n.
group 74 n.
classification 77 n.
party 708 n.
cothurnus
drama 594 n.
cotillion
dance 837 n.
cottage
small house 192 n.
cottage industry
business 622 n.
cottage pie
meat 301 n.
cottager
resident 191 n.
cotton
fibre 208 n.
textile 222 n.
cotton mill
workshop 687 n.
cotton on to
understand 516 vb.
be in love 887 vb.
cotton wool
fibre 208 n.
cotyledon
foliage 366 n.
couch
be horizontal 216 vb.
bed 218 n.
seat 218 n.
repose 683 vb.
couchant
heraldic 547 adj.
cougar
cat 365 n.
cough
eruct 300 vb.
excretion 302 n.
excrete 302 vb.
respiration 352 n.
breathe 352 vb.
rasp 407 vb.
respiratory disease 651 n.
— up
confess 526 vb.
restitute 787 vb.
pay 804 vb.
could be
possible 469 adv.
couldn't care less
be incurious 454 vb.
rash 857 adj.
be indifferent 860 vb.
couleur de rose
excellent 644 adj.
palmy 730 adj.
promising 852 adj.
coulisses
theatre 594 n.
couloir
gap 201 n.
coulter
sharp edge 256 n.
farm tool 370 n.
council
assembly 74 n.
conference 584 n.
director 690 n.
adviser 691 n.
council 692 n.
corporation 708 n.
tribunal 956 n.
synod 985 n.
councillor
official 690 n.
councillor 692 n.
officer 741 n.
counsel
incite 612 vb.
warn 664 vb.
advice 691 n.
adviser 691 n.
advise 691 vb.
consignee 754 n.
lawyer 958 n.
counsellor
sage 500 n.
motivator 612 n.
adviser 691 n.
aider 703 n.
count
comprise 78 vb.
numeration 86 n.
number 86 vb.
measure 465 vb.
motivate 612 vb.
be important 638 vb.
person of rank 868 n.
accusation 928 n.
— as
substitute 150 vb.
— for nothing
be unimportant 639 vb.
— heads
number 86 vb.
vote 605 vb.
— it to one's credit
approve 923 vb.
— on
believe 485 vb.
hope 852 vb.
— one's blessings
be content 828 vb.
— one's chickens before they are hatched
expect 507 vb.
hope 852 vb.
be rash 857 vb.
— out
exclude 57 vb.
reject 607 vb.
exempt 919 vb.
— the cost
be cautious 858 vb.
— upon
assume 471 vb.
expect 507 vb.
— with
number with 78 vb.
countdown
start 68 n.
number 86 vb.
countenance
face 237 n.
mien 445 n.
patronize 703 vb.
approbation 923 n.
approve 923 vb.
counter
contrary 14 adj.
enumerator 86 n.
counteract 182 vb.
shelf 218 n.
stand 218 n.
answering 460 adj.
answer 460 vb.
be obstructive 702 vb.
oppose 704 vb.
parry 713 vb.
retaliate 714 vb.
shop 796 n.
plaything 837 n.
counteract
set off 31 vb.
weaken 163 vb.
influence 178 vb.
counteract 182 vb.
tell against 467 vb.
oppose 704 vb.
counteracting
remedial 658 adj.
counteraction
reversion 148 n.
counteraction 182 n.
(See **counteract** *)*
counterargument
vindication 927 n.

counterattack
attack 712 vb.
retaliation 714 n.
counterattraction
offset 31 n.
influence 178 n.
counterbalance
offset 31 n.
counteract 182 vb.
counterblast
answer 460 n.
retaliation 714 n.
counterchange
interchange 151 vb.
variegate 437 vb.
countercharge
rejoinder 460 n.
accusation 928 n.
countercheck
be obstructive 702 vb.
counterclaim
deprecation 762 n.
litigation 959 n.
counterclockwise
towards 281 adv.
regressive 286 adj.
round and round 315 adv.
counterculture
dissent 489 n.
counterespionage
secret service 459 n.
counterevidence
counterevidence 467 n.
counterfeit
imitation 20 n.
imitative 20 adj.
copy 20 vb.
copy 22 n.
false 541 adj.
dissemble 541 vb.
fake 541 vb.
sham 542 n.
spurious 542 adj.
deceive 542 vb.
be untrue 543 vb.
counterfeiter
deceiver 545 n.
defrauder 789 n.
counterfoil
label 547 n.
counterirritant
antidote 658 n.
countermand
command 737 vb.
abrogate 752 vb.
prohibit 757 vb.
countermarch
turn back 286 vb.
countermeasure
hindrance 702 n.
countermine
plot 623 n.vb.
oppose 704 vb.
defences 713 n.
retaliation 714 n.
countermove
counteraction 182 n.
counterorder
abrogation 752 n.
counterpane
coverlet 226 n.
counterpart
identity 13 n.
analogue 18 n.
copy 22 n.
counterplot
plot 623 n.
retaliation 714 n.
counterpoint
combination 50 n.
melody 410 n.
music 412 n.
counterpoise
equalization 28 n.
equalize 28 vb.
offset 31 n.
counteract 182 vb.
gravity 322 n.
counterpoison
antidote 658 n.
Counter-Reformation
Catholicism 976 n.
orthodoxism 976 n.
counter-revolution
reversion 148 n.
revolution 149 n.
counter-revolutionary
opponent 705 n.
revolter 738 n.
countersign
endorse 488 vb.
call 547 n.
identification 547 n.
sign 547 vb.
countersignature
credential 466 n.
countersigner
signatory 765 n.
counterspy
secret service 459 n.
counterstroke
defence 713 n.
retaliation 714 n.
countertenor
vocalist 413 n.
countervail
be equal 28 vb.
set off 31 vb.
counteract 182 vb.
tell against 467 vb.
counterweight
offset 31 n.
stabilizer 153 n.
countess
person of rank 868 n.
counting house
treasury 799 n.
countless
multitudinous 104 adj.
infinite 107 adj.
countrified
provincial 192 adj.
ill-bred 847 adj.
country
region 184 n.
regional 184 adj.
land 344 n.
political organization 733 n.
country and western
music 412 n.
country cousin
ingenue 699 n.
country-dweller 869 n.
country dancing
dancing 837 n.
country-dweller
dweller 191 n.
native 191 n.
farmer 370 n.
country-dweller 869 n.
countryman, countrywoman
country-dweller 869 n.
country seat
abode 192 n.
countryside
district 184 n.
county
district 184 n.
political organization 733 n.
county council
council 692 n.
jurisdiction 955 n.
county set
beau monde 848 n.
aristocracy 868 n.
coup
policy 623 n.
deed 676 n.
coup de grace
end 69 n.
ruin 165 n.
killing 362 n.
completion 725 n.
coup de main
violence 176 n.
attack 712 n.
coup d'état
revolution 149 n.
deed 676 n.
revolt 738 n.
lawlessness 954 n.
coup de théâtre
dramaturgy 594 n.
thaumaturgy 864 n.
coup d'oeil
inspection 438 n.
coupé
automobile 274 n.
couple
analogue 18 n.
join 45 vb.
unite with 45 vb.
combine 50 vb.
duality 90 n.
marry 894 vb.
couplet
verse form 593 n.
coupling
coition 45 n.
joining together 45 n.
coupling 47 n.
coupon
portion 783 n.
paper money 797 n.
courage
resolution 599 n.
courage 855 n.
courageous
manly 162 adj.
courageous 855 adj.
courageous, be
face danger 661 vb.
courgette
vegetable 301 n.
courier
bearer 273 n.
speeder 277 n.
guide 520 n.
courier 529 n.
course
order 60 n.
continuity 71 n.
time 108 n.
tendency 179 n.
layer 207 n.
motion 265 n.
itinerary 267 n.
water travel 269 n.
sail 275 n.
speeding 277 n.
direction 281 n.
progression 285 n.
dieting 301 n.
dish 301 n.
flow 350 vb.
hunt 619 vb.
route 624 n.
therapy 658 n.
conduct 688 n.
arena 724 n.
course of action
policy 623 n.
course of events
affairs 154 n.
course of law
legal process 959 n.
course of studies
curriculum 534 n.
study 536 n.
course of time
course of time 111 n.
courser
thoroughbred 273 n.
speeder 277 n.
court
place 185 n.
housing 192 n.
open space 263 n.
council 692 n.
arena 724 n.
retainer 742 n.
beau monde 848 n.

be in love 887 vb.
court 889 vb.
flatter 925 vb.
lawcourt 956 n.
— disaster
face danger 661 vb.
be rash 857 vb.
court dress
formal dress 228 n.
formality 875 n.
courteous
attentive 455 adj.
well-bred 848 adj.
sociable 882 adj.
courteous 884 adj.
benevolent 897 adj.
respectful 920 adj.
courtesan
prostitute 952 n.
courtesy
etiquette 848 n.
courtesy 884 n.
(See **courteous** *)*
courtesy title
title 870 n.
undueness 916 n.
courthouse
courtroom 956 n.
courtier
retainer 742 n.
toady 879 n.
flatterer 925 n.
courting
love-making 887 n.
wooing 889 n.
courtly
well-bred 848 adj.
courteous 884 adj.
flattering 925 adj.
court-martial
lawcourt 956 n.
court officer
law officer 955 n.
court of law
lawcourt 956 n.
courtroom
arena 724 n.
courtroom 956 n.
courtship
love-making 887 n.
wooing 889 n.
courtyard
place 185 n.
enclosure 235 n.
cousin
kinsman 11 n.
friend 880 n.
couturier, couturière
clothier 228 n.
artist 556 n.
cove
cavity 255 n.
gulf 345 n.
coven
assembly 74 n.
sorcery 983 n.
covenant
promise 764 n.vb.
compact 765 n.
contract 765 vb.
title deed 767 n.
covenanter
assenter 488 n.
signatory 765 n.
sectarian 978 n.
cover
offset 31 n.
unite with 45 vb.
fill 54 vb.
comprise 78 vb.
suppress 165 vb.
extend 183 vb.
load 193 vb.
receptacle 194 n.
be high 209 vb.
hang 217 vb.
covering 226 n.
cover 226 vb.
line 227 vb.
dress 228 vb.
stopper 264 n.
close 264 vb.
aim 281 vb.
meal 301 n.
pass 305 vb.
darken 418 vb.
screen 421 vb.
communicate 524 vb.
conceal 525 vb.
disguise 527 n.
hiding-place 527 n.
publish 528 vb.
mark 547 vb.
obliterate 550 vb.
correspondence 588 n.
bookbinding 589 n.
pretext 614 n.
cleaning cloth 648 n.
protection 660 n.
safeguard 660 vb.
shelter 662 n.
defend 713 vb.
threaten 900 vb.
— oneself
be cautious 858 vb.
— one's tracks
disappear 446 vb.
be stealthy 525 vb.
be cautious 858 vb.
— the ground
progress 285 vb.
— up
mislead 495 vb.
conceal 525 vb.
obliterate 550 vb.
coverage
inclusion 78 n.
range 183 n.
publicity 528 n.
cover charge
price 809 n.
cover girl
a beauty 841 n.
coverlet
coverlet 226 n.
covert
plumage 259 n.
wood 366 n.
occult 523 adj.
concealed 525 adj.
shelter 662 n.
cover-up
concealment 525 n.
falsehood 541 n.
covet
desire 859 vb.
envy 912 vb.
covetous
avaricious 816 adj.
desiring 859 adj.
envious 912 adj.
selfish 932 adj.
covey
group 74 n.
certain quantity 104 n.
cow
cattle 365 n.
female animal 373 n.
dissuade 613 vb.
frighten 854 vb.
coward
weakling 163 n.
avoider 620 n.
coward 856 n.
cowardice
irresolution 601 n.
nervousness 854 n.
cowardice 856 n.
cowboy
rider 268 n.
herdsman 369 n.
independent 744 adj.
nonobservant 769 adj.
lawless 954 adj.
cower
stoop 311 vb.
avoid 620 vb.
quake 854 vb.
be cowardly 856 vb.
cowgirl
rider 268 n.
herdsman 369 n.
cowherd
herdsman 369 n.
cowhide
scourge 964 n.
cowl
covering 226 n.
headgear 228 n.
canonicals 989 n.
cowled
monastic 986 adj.
cowlick
hair 259 n.
co-worker
concomitant 89 n.
personnel 686 n.
collaborator 707 n.
cowpat
excrement 302 n.
cowpuncher
rider 268 n.
herdsman 369 n.
cowshed
stable 192 n.
cattle pen 369 n.
cox, coxswain
navigator 270 n.
direct 689 vb.
coxcomb
fop 848 n.
affecter 850 n.
vain person 873 n.
coy
affected 850 adj.
modest 874 adj.
coyness
prudery 950 n.
cozen
deceive 542 vb.
crab
fish food 301 n.
marine life 365 n.
be discontented 829 vb.
rude person 885 n.
be sullen 893 vb.
dispraise 924 vb.
crabbed
sour 393 adj.
unintelligible 517 adj.
unclear 568 adj.
inelegant 576 adj.
sullen 893 adj.
crabwise
obliquely 220 adv.
sideways 239 adv.
astray 282 adv.
crack
disunion 46 n.
break 46 vb.
discontinuity 72 n.
instant 116 n.
weakness 163 n.
gap 201 n.
space 201 vb.
narrowness 206 n.
roughness 259 n.
furrow 262 n.
opening 263 n.
knock 279 n.
strike 279 vb.
be brittle 330 vb.
bang 402 n.
crackle 402 vb.
rasp 407 vb.
stripe 437 n.
decipher 520 vb.
best 644 adj.
defect 647 n.
skilful 694 adj.
witticism 839 n.
blemish 845 n.vb.
— a bottle
drink 301 vb.
be sociable 882 vb.
— a joke
be witty 839 vb.

— down on
be severe 735 vb.
restrain 747 vb.
— up
go mad 503 vb.
advertise 528 vb.
boast 877 vb.
praise 923 vb.
crack at
attempt 671 n.
crack-brained
foolish 499 adj.
crazy 503 adj.
cracked
nonresonant 405 adj.
strident 407 adj.
discordant 411 adj.
crazy 503 adj.
voiceless 578 adj.
imperfect 647 adj.
blemished 845 adj.
(See **crack** *)*
cracked-up
overrated 482 adj.
cracker
cereals 301 n.
bang 402 n.
crackers
crazy 503 adj.
crackle
be hot 379 vb.
bang 402 n.
crackle 402 vb.
stripe 437 n.
crack of doom
finality 69 n.
future state 124 n.
ruin 165 n.
crack of the whip
stimulant 174 n.
incentive 612 n.
crackpot
erroneous 495 adj.
absurd 497 adj.
fool 501 n.
crank 504 n.
ridiculous 849 adj.
crack shot
shooter 287 n.
proficient person 696 n.
cracksman
thief 789 n.
crack troops
elite 644 n.
armed force 722 n.
cradle
origin 68 n.
nonage 130 n.
seedbed 156 n.
assuage 177 vb.
place 187 vb.
home 192 n.
basket 194 n.
bed 218 n.
support 218 vb.
bring to rest 266 vb.
sleep 679 n.
relieve 831 vb.
pet 889 vb.
cradle song
vocal music 412 n.
soporific 679 n.
craft
ship 275 n.
sagacity 498 n.
deception 542 n.
business 622 n.
vocation 622 n.
skill 694 n.
cunning 698 n.
craftsman, craftswoman
producer 164 n.
artist 556 n.
doer 676 n.
artisan 686 n.
expert 696 n.
craftsmanship
skill 694 n.
crafty
intelligent 498 adj.
deceiving 542 adj.
cunning 698 adj.
crafty fellow
slyboots 698 n.
crag
high land 209 n.
sharp point 256 n.
rock 344 n.
craggy
sharp 256 adj.
rough 259 adj.
difficult 700 adj.
cram
fill 54 vb.
bring together 74 vb.
load 193 vb.
make smaller 198 vb.
be dense 324 vb.
educate 534 vb.
study 536 vb.
superabound 637 vb.
gluttonize 947 vb.
crammer
teacher 537 n.
school 539 n.
glutton 947 n.
cramp
fastening 47 n.
weaken 163 vb.
make smaller 198 vb.
spasm 318 n.
pang 377 n.
impair 655 vb.
make inactive 679 vb.
hinder 702 vb.
restrain 747 vb.
prohibit 757 vb.
— one's style
disable 161 vb.
not suffice 636 vb.
hinder 702 vb.
cramped
little 196 adj.
narrow-minded 481 adj.
inelegant 576 adj.
crane
conveyor 274 n.
lifter 310 n.
bird 365 n.
crane one's neck
scan 438 vb.
craniology
head 213 n.
anthropology 371 n.
cranium
head 213 n.
dome 253 n.
crank
nonconformist 84 n.
handle 218 n.
rotate 315 vb.
narrow mind 481 n.
fool 501 n.
crank 504 n.
visionary 513 n.
witticism 839 n.
laughingstock 851 n.
— up
make ready 669 vb.
crankiness
caprice 604 n.
cranky
crazy 503 adj.
irascible 892 adj.
crannog
dwelling 192 n.
cranny
compartment 194 n.
cavity 255 n.
furrow 262 n.
hiding-place 527 n.
craps
gambling game 837 n.
crapulence
sequel 67 n.
crapulence 949 n.
craquelure
network 222 n.
crash
revolution 149 n.
ruin 165 n.
textile 222 n.
fly 271 vb.
collision 279 n.
descent 309 n.
tumble 309 vb.
be brittle 330 vb.
loudness 400 n.
bang 402 n.
discord 411 vb.
fail 728 vb.
miscarry 728 vb.
insolvency 805 n.
crash barrier
road 624 n.
crash dive
aeronautics 271 n.
plunge 313 n.
crash helmet
headgear 228 n.
safeguard 662 n.
crash landing
aeronautics 271 n.
crass
consummate 32 adj.
unintelligent 499 adj.
vulgar 847 adj.
crate
basket 194 n.
vehicle 274 n.
aircraft 276 n.
crater
cavity 255 n.
orifice 263 n.
moon 321 n.
cravat
neckwear 228 n.
crave
require 627 vb.
beg 761 vb.
request 761 vb.
desire 859 vb.
envy 912 vb.
craven
cowardly 856 adj.
craw
maw 194 n.
crawl
be low 210 vb.
be in motion 265 vb.
aquatics 269 n.
slowness 278 n.
move slowly 278 vb.
itch 378 vb.
knuckle under 721 vb.
lose repute 867 vb.
be humble 872 vb.
be servile 879 vb.
— with
be many 104 vb.
abound 635 vb.
superabound 637 vb.
crawler
toady 879 n.
crawling
multitudinous 104 adj.
unclean 649 adj.
(See **crawl** *)*
crayfish
fish food 301 n.
marine life 365 n.
crayon
colour 425 vb.
art equipment 553 n.
paint 553 vb.
stationery 586 n.
craze
be brittle 330 vb.
variegate 437 vb.
bias 481 n.
eccentricity 503 n.
make mad 503 vb.
whim 604 n.
practice 610 n.

fashion 848 n.
liking 859 n.
crazy
flimsy 163 adj.
distorted 246 adj.
brittle 330 adj.
variegated 437 adj.
obsessed 455 adj.
misjudging 481 adj.
absurd 497 adj.
foolish 499 adj.
unintelligent 499 adj.
crazy 503 adj.
capricious 604 adj.
unsafe 661 adj.
ridiculous 849 adj.
enamoured 887 adj.
crazy about
excited 821 adj.
enamoured 887 adj.
crazy paving
nonuniformity 17 n.
paving 226 n.
chequer 437 n.
creak
move slowly 278 vb.
sound faint 401 vb.
stridor 407 n.
cream
dairy product 301 n.
milk 301 n.
semiliquidity 354 n.
fat 357 n.
unguent 357 n.
select 605 vb.
chief thing 638 n.
elite 644 n.
balm 658 n.
cosmetic 843 n.
beau monde 848 n.
person of repute 866 n.
— off
impair 655 vb.
cream-coloured
yellow 433 adj.
cream soda
soft drink 301 n.
creamy
semiliquid 354 adj.
fatty 357 adj.
savoury 390 adj.
soft-hued 425 adj.
whitish 427 adj.
yellow 433 adj.
crease
joint 45 n.
jumble 63 vb.
place 185 n.
fold 261 n.vb.
creased
folded 261 adj.
laughing 835 adj.
create
cause 156 vb.
produce 164 vb.
form 243 vb.
imagine 513 vb.
be excitable 822 vb.
dignify 866 vb.
be angry 891 vb.
— a role
act 594 vb.
creation
existence 1 n.
originality 21 n.
beginning 68 n.
antiquity 125 n.
causation 156 n.
product 164 n.
production 164 n.
dress 228 n.
formation 243 n.
universe 321 n.
representation 551 n.
creative
original 21 adj.
productive 164 adj.
imaginative 513 adj.
godlike 965 adj.
creative worker
producer 164 n.
visionary 513 n.
doer 676 n.
creative writing
literature 557 n.
writing 586 n.
creator
cause 156 n.
producer 164 n.
Creator
the Deity 965 n.
creature
substance 3 n.
product 164 n.
animal 365 n.
person 371 n.
instrument 628 n.
auxiliary 707 n.
dependant 742 n.
toady 879 n.
creature comforts
food 301 n.
euphoria 376 n.
creaturehood
subjection 745 n.
creature of habit
repetition 106 n.
habitué 610 n.
crèche
school 539 n.
credence
belief 485 n.
altar 990 n.
credential
credential 466 n.
title deed 767 n.
approbation 923 n.
credibility gap
disagreement 25 n.
credible
possible 469 adj.
plausible 471 adj.
credible 485 adj.
credit
attribute 158 vb.
influence 178 n.
belief 485 n.
believe 485 vb.
means 629 n.
subvention 703 n.
authority 733 n.
promise 764 n.
lending 784 n.
lend 784 vb.
wealth 800 n.
credit 802 n.vb.
debt 803 n.
account 808 vb.
repute 866 n.
honour 866 vb.
thanks 907 n.
thank 907 vb.
dueness 915 n.
approbation 923 n.
praise 923 n.
— with
attribute 158 vb.
creditable
excellent 644 adj.
reputable 866 adj.
approvable 923 adj.
credit account
borrowing 785 n.
credit 802 n.
credit card
borrowing 785 n.
credit 802 n.
creditless
inglorious 867 adj.
credit note
credit 802 n.
creditor
provider 633 n.
lender 784 n.
creditor 802 n.
credit side
gain 771 n.
credit squeeze
restriction 747 n.
economy 814 n.
parsimony 816 n.
credit title
attribution 158 n.
thanks 907 n.
credit to, be a
honour 866 vb.
credit-worthy
moneyed 800 adj.
reputable 866 adj.
deserving 915 adj.
trustworthy 929 adj.
credo
creed 485 n.
theology 973 n.
orthodoxy 976 n.
credulity
belief 485 n.
credulity 487 n.
deception 542 n.
persuadability 612 n.
credulous
misjudging 481 adj.
credulous 487 adj.
gullible 544 adj.
induced 612 adj.
creed
creed 485 n.
theology 973 n.
orthodoxy 976 n.
creedless
unbelieving 486 adj.
irreligious 974 adj.
creek
gap 201 n.
cavity 255 n.
gulf 345 n.
creel
basket 194 n.
creep
drag on 113 vb.
be rough 259 vb.
be in motion 265 vb.
slowness 278 n.
move slowly 278 vb.
feel pain 377 vb.
itch 378 vb.
lurk 523 vb.
be stealthy 525 vb.
toady 879 n.
be servile 879 vb.
flatterer 925 n.
— in
enter 297 vb.
— off
run away 620 vb.
— out
emerge 298 vb.
be visible 443 vb.
— up on
surprise 508 vb.
creeper
plant 366 n.
creepie
film 445 n.
creeping Jesus
toady 879 n.
creeps
formication 378 n.
nervousness 854 n.
creepy
hypocritical 541 adj.
frightening 854 adj.
servile 879 adj.
creepy-crawly
creepy-crawly 365 n.
bane 659 n.
cremation
interment 364 n.
burning 381 n.
crematorium
interment 364 n.
furnace 383 n.
crème de la crème
elite 644 n.
crenation
edging 234 n.
notch 260 n.
crenellate
notch 260 vb.
defend 713 vb.
creole
language 557 n.
Creole
hybrid 43 n.

settler 191 n.
creosote
coat 226 vb.
preserve 666 vb.
crepe, crèpe
black thing 428 n.
lamentation 836 n.
crepitate
eruct 300 vb.
crackle 402 vb.
crepuscular
vespertine 129 adj.
dim 419 adj.
crescendo
increase 36 n.
crescendo 36 adv.
expansion 197 n.
ascent 308 n.
loudness 400 n.
loudly 400 adv.
crescent
housing 192 n.
curve 248 n.
arc 250 n.
moon 321 n.
Crescent, the
religious faith 973 n.
crescent-shaped
round 250 adj.
cress
vegetable 301 n.
cresset
torch 420 n.
crest
superiority 34 n.
high land 209 n.
summit 213 n.
crown 213 vb.
plumage 259 n.
heraldry 547 n.
jewellery 844 n.
nobility 868 n.
crestfallen
disappointed 509 adj.
dejected 834 adj.
humbled 872 adj.
cretin
fool 501 n.
cretinous
unintelligent 499 adj.
cretonne
textile 222 n.
crevasse
gap 201 n.
pitfall 663 n.
crevice
gap 201 n.
crew
component 58 n.
band 74 n.
operate 173 vb.
navigate 269 vb.
mariner 270 n.
make ready 669 vb.
personnel 686 n.
party 708 n.
crew cut
shortness 204 n.
hairdressing 843 n.
crib
copy 20 vb.
copy 22 n.
basket 194 n.
bed 218 n.
translation 520 n.
classroom 539 n.
borrow 785 vb.
steal 788 vb.
cribbage
card game 837 n.
crick
pang 377 n.
cricket
insect 365 n.
ball game 837 n.
cricketer
player 837 n.
cricket pitch
arena 724 n.
cri de coeur
request 761 n.
lament 836 n.
crier
cry 408 n.
publicizer 528 n.
crime
deed 676 n.
disobedience 738 n.
wrong 914 n.
foul play 930 n.
improbity 930 n.
vice 934 n.
wickedness 934 n.
guilty act 936 n.
lawbreaking 954 n.
crime passionel
homicide 362 n.
revenge 910 n.
jealousy 911 n.
crime story
novel 590 n.
crime wave
lawlessness 954 n.
criminal
nonconformist 84 n.
low fellow 869 n.
offender 904 n.
wrong 914 adj.
rascally 930 adj.
heinous 934 adj.
guilty 936 adj.
knave 938 n.
lawbreaking 954 n. adj.
criminal court
lawcourt 956 n.
criminal investigation
police enquiry 459 n.
criminal offence
lawbreaking 954 n.
criminal world
offender 904 n.
wickedness 934 n.
criminologist
detective 459 n.
crimp
crinkle 251 vb.
notch 260 vb.
crimson
red 431 adj.
redden 431 vb.
be modest 874 vb.
cringe
stoop 311 vb.
knuckle under 721 vb.
be subject 745 vb.
be cowardly 856 vb.
be servile 879 vb.
crinkle
distort 246 vb.
crinkle 251 vb.
roughen 259 vb.
fold 261 n.
crinkle-crankle
undulatory 251 adj.
crinoline
skirt 228 n.
cripple
disable 161 vb.
weaken 163 vb.
make useless 641 vb.
sick person 651 n.
impair 655 vb.
hinder 702 vb.
crippled
crippled 163 adj.
imperfect 647 adj.
crisis
juncture 8 n.
degree 27 n.
present time 121 n.
crisis 137 n.
event 154 n.
summit 213 n.
important matter 638 n.
danger 661 n.
predicament 700 n.
excitation 821 n.
crisp
crinkle 251 vb.
roughen 259 vb.
rigid 326 adj.
harden 326 vb.
brittle 330 adj.
savoury 390 adj.
concise 569 adj.
crisps
mouthful 301 n.
crisscross
crossing 222 n.
crossed 222 adj.
criterion
prototype 23 n.
testing agent 461 n.
comparison 462 n.
gauge 465 n.
critic
estimator 480 n.
dissentient 489 n.
theorist 512 n.
interpreter 520 n.
dissertator 591 n.
malcontent 829 n.
people of taste 846 n.
disapprover 924 n.
detractor 926 n.
critical
circumstantial 8 adj.
crucial 137 adj.
eventful 154 adj.
discriminating 463 adj.
judicial 480 adj.
literary 557 adj.
discursive 591 adj.
important 638 adj.
sick 651 adj.
dangerous 661 adj.
difficult 700 adj.
discontented 829 adj.
tasteful 846 adj.
fastidious 862 adj.
disapproving 924 adj.
critical moment
juncture 8 n.
critical path analysis
mathematics 86 n.
criticism
estimate 480 n.
interpretation 520 n.
affirmation 532 n.
literature 557 n.
article 591 n.
advice 691 n.
good taste 846 n.
censure 924 n.
detraction 926 n.
criticize, criticise
compare 462 vb.
discriminate 463 vb.
be discontented 829 vb.
critique
estimate 480 n.
(See **criticism** *)*
croak
die 361 vb.
rasp 407 vb.
ululation 409 n.
ululate 409 vb.
be discontented 829 vb.
croaker
malcontent 829 n.
moper 834 n.
croaking
voiceless 578 adj.
crochet
tie 45 vb.
network 222 n.
weave 222 vb.
needlework 844 n.
crock
vessel 194 n.
sick person 651 n.
crockery
receptacle 194 n.
pottery 381 n.

crocket
pattern 844 n.
Crockford
directory 87 n.
crock up
be fatigued 684 vb.
fatigue 684 vb.
fail 728 vb.
crocodile
procession 71 n.
line 203 n.
skin 226 n.
reptile 365 n.
crocodile tears
duplicity 541 n.
lament 836 n.
Croesus
rich person 800 n.
croft
house 192 n.
enclosure 235 n.
farm 370 n.
crofter
resident 191 n.
farmer 370 n.
croissant
cereals 301 n.
Croix de Guerre
decoration 729 n.
Cro-Magnon man
humankind 371 n.
cromlech
tomb 364 n.
monument 548 n.
crone
old woman 133 n.
crony
colleague 707 n.
chum 880 n.
friend 880 n.
crook
prop 218 n.
make oblique 220 vb.
angularity 247 n.
make angular 247 vb.
make curved 248 vb.
thief 789 n.
offender 904 n.
knave 938 n.
vestments 989 n.
crook-backed
deformed 246 adj.
crooked
oblique 220 adj.
distorted 246 adj.
angular 247 adj.
deviating 282 adj.
cunning 698 adj.
blemished 845 adj.
dishonest 930 adj.
croon
sound faint 401 vb.
sing 413 vb.
crooner
vocalist 413 n.
entertainer 594 n.
crop
great quantity 32 n.
growth 157 n.
product 164 n.
maw 194 n.
shorten 204 vb.
graze 301 vb.
agriculture 370 n.
cultivate 370 vb.
benefit 615 n.
store 632 n.
earnings 771 n.
acquire 771 vb.
take 786 vb.
hairdressing 843 n.
— up
begin 68 vb.
happen 154 vb.
chance 159 vb.
be visible 443 vb.
crop-full
full 54 adj.
cropper
descent 309 n.
croquet
ball game 837 n.
croquettes
dish 301 n.
crore
over one hundred 99 n.
crosier
badge of rule 743 n.
vestments 989 n.
cross
hybrid 43 n.
mix 43 vb.
counteract 182 vb.
be oblique 220 vb.
cross 222 n.vb.
angularity 247 n.
traverse 267 vb.
pass 305 vb.
overstep 306 vb.
assent 488 n.
badge 547 n.
label 547 n.
mark 547 vb.
bane 659 n.
encumbrance 702 n.
hindering 702 adj.
opposing 704 adj.
decoration 729 n.
adversity 731 n.
adverse 731 adj.
painfulness 827 n.
discontented 829 adj.
angry 891 adj.
irascible 892 adj.
sullen 893 adj.
means of execution 964 n.
talisman 983 n.
ritual object 988 n.
vestments 989 n.
church interior 990 n.
— oneself
be pious 979 vb.
perform ritual 988 vb.
— one's fingers
deprecate 762 vb.
— one's heart
swear 532 vb.
as promised 764 adv.
— one's path
hinder 702 vb.
— out
subtract 39 vb.
mark 547 vb.
obliterate 550 vb.
— over
cross 222 vb.
pass 305 vb.
apostatize 603 vb.
— swords (with)
argue 475 vb.
quarrel 709 vb.
fight 716 vb.
— the bar
die 361 vb.
— the floor
apostatize 603 vb.
— the mind
dawn upon 449 vb.
— the ocean
voyage 269 vb.
— the Rubicon
initiate 68 vb.
overstep 306 vb.
be resolute 599 vb.
choose 605 vb.
— the threshold
enter 297 vb.
Cross, the
religious faith 973 n.
crossbar
beam 218 n.
cross 222 n.
cross-bencher
opponent 705 n.
free person 744 n.
crossbones
cross 222 n.
crossbow
missile weapon 723 n.
cross-bred
mixed 43 adj.
cross-connection
union 45 n.
cross-country
towards 281 adv.
cross-country race
pedestrianism 267 n.
racing 716 n.
crosscurrent
counteraction 182 n.
contraposition 240 n.
current 350 n.
pitfall 663 n.
obstacle 702 n.
opposition 704 n.
crossed
textural 331 adj.
mottled 437 adj.
communicating 624 adj.
(See **cross***)*
crossed in love
hated 888 adj.
crossed lines
misinterpretation 521 n.
cross-examine
interrogate 459 vb.
try a case 959 vb.
cross-examiner
inquisitive person 453 n.
questioner 459 n.
interlocutor 584 n.
cross-eyed
dim-sighted 440 adj.
cross-fertilize
mix 43 vb.
cross-fire
bombardment 712 n.
cross-grained
rough 259 adj.
wilful 602 adj.
irascible 892 adj.
sullen 893 adj.
cross-hatch
groove 262 vb.
darken 418 vb.
crossing
joint 45 n.
crossing 222 n.
water travel 269 n.
passage 305 n.
access 624 n.
road 624 n.
cross-legged
crossed 222 adj.
crosspatch
moper 834 n.
rude person 885 n.
shrew 892 n.
misanthrope 902 n.
cross-purposes
error 495 n.
misinterpretation 521 n.
opposition 704 n.
dissension 709 n.
cross-question
question 459 n.
interrogate 459 vb.
cross-reference
referral 9 n.
class 62 vb.
crossroads
juncture 8 n.
joint 45 n.
focus 76 n.
crossing 222 n.
divergence 294 n.
road 624 n.
cross-section
example 83 n.
cross-stitch
needlework 844 n.
crosstree
prop 218 n.

cross-vote
disobey 738 vb.
be free 744 vb.
crosswind
wind 352 n.
obstacle 702 n.
adversity 731 n.
crosswise
obliquely 220 adv.
across 222 adv.
crossword
enigma 530 n.
indoor game 837 n.
crotch
angularity 247 n.
crotchet
angularity 247 n.
notation 410 n.
whim 604 n.
crotchety
unconformable 84 adj.
crazy 503 adj.
wilful 602 adj.
capricious 604 adj.
irascible 892 adj.
crouch
be low 210 vb.
stoop 311 vb.
knuckle under 721 vb.
quake 854 vb.
be servile 879 vb.
croup
buttocks 238 n.
respiratory disease 651 n.
croupier
treasurer 798 n.
crow
bird 365 n.
black thing 428 n.
cleaner 648 n.
triumph 727 vb.
laughter 835 n.
rejoice 835 vb.
boast 877 vb.
crowbar
tool 630 n.
crowd
medley 43 n.
confusion 61 n.
crowd 74 n.
multitude 104 n.
be many 104 vb.
be near 200 vb.
be contiguous 202 vb.
be dense 324 vb.
onlookers 441 n.
obstruct 702 vb.
party 708 n.
rabble 869 n.
crowded
firm 45 adj.
multitudinous 104 adj.
crown
completeness 54 n.
head 213 n.
summit 213 n.
vertex 213 n.
crown 213 vb.
limit 236 vb.
loop 250 n.
strike 279 vb.
badge 547 n.
heraldry 547 n.
objective 617 n.
perfect 646 vb.
doctor 658 vb.
completion 725 n.
climax 725 vb.
trophy 729 n.
authority 733 n.
badge of rank 743 n.
regalia 743 n.
commission 751 vb.
coinage 797 n.
decorate 844 vb.
honours 866 n.
dignify 866 vb.
pay one's respects 884 vb.
reward 962 n.
— all
culminate 34 vb.
climax 725 vb.
crowned head
sovereign 741 n.
crown of glory
honours 866 n.
Crown Prince/ Princess
sovereign 741 n.
crow's feet
fold 261 n.
ugliness 842 n.
crow's nest
high structure 209 n.
vertex 213 n.
view 438 n.
crow to pluck
resentment 891 n.
crucial
circumstantial 8 adj.
crucial 137 adj.
fundamental 156 adj.
demonstrating 478 adj.
important 638 adj.
crucial moment
juncture 8 n.
crisis 137 n.
crucible
crucible 147 n.
heater 383 n.
testing agent 461 n.
crucifix
cross 222 n.
jewellery 844 n.
ritual object 988 n.
church interior 990 n.
crucifixion
killing 362 n.
pain 377 n.
art subject 553 n.
suffering 825 n.
capital punishment 963 n.
cruciform
crossed 222 adj.
churchlike 990 adj.
crucify
give pain 377 vb.
ill-treat 645 vb.
execute 963 vb.
crud
dirt 649 n.
crude
incomplete 55 adj.
beginning 68 adj.
florid 425 adj.
inelegant 576 adj.
imperfect 647 adj.
immature 670 adj.
bungled 695 adj.
graceless 842 adj.
ill-bred 847 adj.
crude oil
oil 357 n.
cruel
violent 176 adj.
murderous 362 adj.
harmful 645 adj.
warlike 718 adj.
oppressive 735 adj.
paining 827 adj.
cruel 898 adj.
pitiless 906 adj.
heinous 934 adj.
vicious 934 adj.
cruelly
painfully 32 adv.
badly 645 adv.
severely 735 adv.
cruel to be kind, be
be severe 735 vb.
show mercy 905 vb.
cruelty
badness 645 n.
severity 735 n.
cruel act 898 n.
inhumanity 898 n.
cruise
be in motion 265 vb.
water travel 269 n.
voyage 269 vb.
cruise missile
missile weapon 723 n.
cruiser
warship 722 n.
cruiserweight
pugilist 722 n.
crumb(s)
small thing 33 n.
leavings 41 n.
piece 53 n.
powder 332 n.
crumble
break 46 vb.
decompose 51 vb.
be weak 163 vb.
be destroyed 165 vb.
dessert 301 n.
be brittle 330 vb.
pulverize 332 vb.
deteriorate 655 vb.
impair 655 vb.
crumbling
antiquated 127 adj.
weakened 163 adj.
destroyed 165 adj.
powdery 332 adj.
unsafe 661 adj.
crumbly
fragmentary 53 adj.
brittle 330 adj.
powdery 332 adj.
crumb of comfort
relief 831 n.
crummy
inferior 35 adj.
bad 645 adj.
crumpet
head 213 n.
cereals 301 n.
woman 373 n.
crumple
jumble 63 vb.
make smaller 198 vb.
distort 246 vb.
crinkle 251 vb.
roughen 259 vb.
fold 261 n.vb.
— up
be destroyed 165 vb.
crunch
rend 46 vb.
chew 301 vb.
pulverize 332 vb.
rasp 407 vb.
crupper
buttocks 238 n.
crusade
action 676 n.
war 718 n.
philanthropy 901 n.
crusader
militarist 722 n.
philanthropist 901 n.
zealot 979 n.
cruse
vessel 194 n.
crush
jumble 63 vb.
crowd 74 n.
demolish 165 vb.
force 176 vb.
make smaller 198 vb.
make concave 255 vb.
lower 311 vb.
pulverize 332 vb.
touch 378 vb.
confute 479 vb.
dissuade 613 vb.
ill-treat 645 vb.
wound 655 vb.
defeat 727 vb.

overmaster 727 vb.
oppress 735 vb.
sadden 834 vb.
humiliate 872 vb.
love 887 n.
crush barrier
safeguard 662 n.
crushed
destroyed 165 adj.
folded 261 adj.
pulpy 356 adj.
suffering 825 adj.
dejected 834 adj.
humbled 872 adj.
crusher
pulverizer 332 n.
crushing
destructive 165 adj.
laborious 682 adj.
hindering 702 adj.
completive 725 adj.
successful 727 adj.
distressing 827 adj.
crushing blow
ruin 165 n.
crust
piece 53 n.
exteriority 223 n.
covering 226 n.
skin 226 n.
cereals 301 n.
mouthful 301 n.
hardness 326 n.
land 344 n.
crustacean
animal 365 n.
marine life 365 n.
crusty
irascible 892 adj.
sullen 893 adj.
crutch
prop 218 n.
garment 228 n.
angularity 247 n.
crux
cross 222 n.
unintelligibility 517 n.
enigma 530 n.
chief thing 638 n.
difficulty 700 n.
cry
feel pain 377 vb.
loudness 400 n.
be loud 400 vb.
shrill 407 vb.
cry 408 n.vb.
ululation 409 n.
proclaim 528 vb.
voice 577 n.vb.
request 761 n.
lamentation 836 n.
weep 836 vb.
desire 859 n.
— blue murder
raise the alarm 665 vb.
deprecate 762 vb.
be discontented 829 vb.
— down
underestimate 483 vb.
detract 926 vb.
— for joy
rejoice 835 vb.
— for mercy
knuckle under 721 vb.
deprecate 762 vb.
ask mercy 905 vb.
— for the moon
waste effort 641 vb.
desire 859 vb.
— one's wares
boast 877 vb.
— out
cry 408 vb.
vociferate 408 vb.
weep 836 vb.
— out against
dissuade 613 vb.
deprecate 762 vb.
— out for
require 627 vb.
desire 859 vb.
— over spilt milk
regret 830 vb.
— quits
make peace 719 vb.
submit 721 vb.
— up
overrate 482 vb.
advertise 528 vb.
exaggerate 546 vb.
praise 923 vb.
flatter 925 vb.
— wolf
misteach 535 vb.
be false 541 vb.
raise the alarm 665 vb.
frighten 854 vb.
crybaby
weakling 163 n.
weeper 836 n.
coward 856 n.
crying shame
slur 867 n.
wrong 914 n.
cryonic suspension
refrigeration 382 n.
crypt
cellar 194 n.
depth 211 n.
tomb 364 n.
church interior 990 n.
cryptanalysis
hermeneutics 520 n.
cryptic
uncertain 474 adj.
unintelligible 517 adj.
occult 523 adj.
concealed 525 adj.
cabbalistic 984 adj.
crypto-
latent 523 adj.
concealed 525 adj.
cryptogram
secrecy 525 n.
enigma 530 n.
cryptographer
interpreter 520 n.
crystal
minuteness 196 n.
solid body 324 n.
transparency 422 n.
transparent 422 adj.
optical device 442 n.
crystal ball
oracle 511 n.
crystal-clear
transparent 422 adj.
obvious 443 adj.
crystal-gazer
diviner 511 n.
occultist 984 n.
crystalline
symmetrical 245 adj.
dense 324 adj.
hard 326 adj.
transparent 422 adj.
crystallization
conversion 147 n.
condensation 324 n.
hardening 326 n.
crystallize, crystallise
harden 326 vb.
sweeten 392 vb.
crystal set
broadcasting 531 n.
CSE
exam 459 n.
CS gas
poison 659 n.
cub
young creature 132 n.
youngster 132 n.
reproduce itself 167 vb.
cubbyhole
retreat 192 n.
compartment 194 n.
cube
do sums 86 vb.
treble 94 vb.
angular figure 247 n.
cube root
numerical element 85 n.
cubic
spatial 183 adj.
metrical 465 adj.
cubicle
chamber 194 n.
compartment 194 n.
Cubism
school of painting 553 n.
cub reporter
news reporter 529 n.
cucking stool
pillory 964 n.
cuckold
be impure 951 vb.
cuckold 952 n.
cuckoo
repetition 106 n.
resident 191 n.
bird 365 n.
ululation 409 n.
fool 501 n.
crazy 503 adj.
cuckoo in the nest
intruder 59 n.
impostor 545 n.
usurper 916 n.
cucumber
vegetable 301 n.
cud
mouthful 301 n.
cuddle
be near 200 vb.
retention 778 n.
endearment 889 n.
caress 889 vb.
cuddly
lovable 887 adj.
cudgel
hammer 279 n.
strike 279 vb.
club 723 n.
flog 963 vb.
scourge 964 n.
cudgel one's brains
think 449 vb.
cue
ram 279 n.
reminder 505 n.
hint 524 n.
dramaturgy 594 n.
cuff
garment 228 n.
sleeve 228 n.
fold 261 n.
knock 279 n.
corporal punishment 963 n.
spank 963 vb.
cufflink
fastening 47 n.
jewellery 844 n.
cui bono
in search of 459 adv.
usefully 640 adv.
cuirass
armour 713 n.
cuirassier
cavalry 722 n.
Cuisenaire rods
counting instrument 86 n.
cuisine
cookery 301 n.
cuisine minceur
dieting 301 n.
cul-de-sac
closure 264 n.
road 624 n.

obstacle 702 n.
culinary
culinary 301 adj.
culinary herb
potherb 301 n.
plant 366 n.
cull
killing 362 n.
select 605 vb.
take 786 vb.
culm
coal 385 n.
culminate
culminate 34 vb.
be complete 54 vb.
be high 209 vb.
crown 213 vb.
ascend 308 vb.
climax 725 vb.
culottes
skirt 228 n.
culpable
wrong 914 adj.
blameworthy 924 adj.
heinous 934 adj.
guilty 936 adj.
culpable negligence
negligence 458 n.
undutifulness 918 n.
culprit
offender 904 n.
accused person 928 n.
cult
fashion 848 n.
affectation 850 n.
religion 973 n.
cult 981 n.
idolatry 982 n.
cult image
idol 982 n.
cultivate
produce 164 vb.
make fruitful 171 vb.
cultivate 370 vb.
cause feeling 374 vb.
train 534 vb.
make better 654 vb.
mature 669 vb.
prepare 669 vb.
flatter 925 vb.
cultivated
instructed 490 adj.
cultivation
agriculture 370 n.
culture 490 n.
learning 536 n.
civilization 654 n.
maturation 669 n.
good taste 846 n.
cultivator
farmer 370 n.
country-dweller 869 n.
cultural
educational 534 adj.
improving 654 adj.
culture
culture 490 n.
education 534 n.
learning 536 n.
civilization 654 n.
good taste 846 n.
cultured
horticultural 370 adj.
instructed 490 adj.
spurious 542 adj.
cultured pearl
gem 844 n.
culture shock
lack of expectation 508 n.
culvert
drain 351 n.
cumber
weigh 322 vb.
hinder 702 vb.
cumbersome
unwieldy 195 adj.
weighty 322 adj.
clumsy 695 adj.
graceless 842 adj.
cummerbund
belt 228 n.
cumulative
increasing 36 adj.
evidential 466 adj.
cumulativeness
increase 36 n.
continuity 71 n.
cumulative vote
vote 605 n.
cumulus
cloud 355 n.
cunctation
delay 136 n.
cuneiform
angulated 247 adj.
letter 558 n.
lettering 586 n.
cunning
sagacity 498 n.
wise 498 adj.
duplicity 541 n.
deceiving 542 adj.
tactics 688 n.
skill 694 n.
skilful 694 adj.
well-made 694 adj.
cunning 698 n.adj.
dishonest 930 adj.
cup
cup 194 n.
support 218 vb.
cavity 255 n.
be concave 255 vb.
alcoholic drink 301 n.
monument 548 n.
fate 596 n.
bane 659 n.
trophy 729 n.
reward 962 n.
ritual object 988 n.
cupbearer
bearer 273 n.
retainer 742 n.
cupboard
cabinet 194 n.
storage 632 n.
cupboard love
duplicity 541 n.
selfishness 932 n.
cupel
testing agent 461 n.
cupful
small quantity 33 n.
contents 193 n.
Cupid
love god 887 n.
mythic deity 966 n.
cupidity
avarice 816 n.
desire 859 n.
Cupid's sting
love 887 n.
cup of sorrows
adversity 731 n.
cupola
high structure 209 n.
roof 226 n.
dome 253 n.
cuppa
draught 301 n.
cupping
surgery 658 n.
cup tie
contest 716 n.
cur
dog 365 n.
coward 856 n.
cad 938 n.
curable
improved 654 adj.
restored 656 adj.
medical 658 adj.
curate
pastor 986 n.
curate's egg
imperfection 647 n.
curative
restorative 656 adj.
remedial 658 adj.
relieving 831 adj.
curator
protector 660 n.
manager 690 n.
keeper 749 n.
consignee 754 n.
curb
moderate 177 vb.
retard 278 vb.
restrain 747 vb.
fetter 748 n.
curdle
be dense 324 vb.
thicken 354 vb.
curds
dairy product 301 n.
semiliquidity 354 n.
cure
counteract 182 vb.
means 629 n.
make better 654 vb.
recuperation 656 n.
cure 656 vb.
remedy 658 n., vb.
therapy 658 n.
preserve 666 vb.
mature 669 vb.
relieve 831 vb.
— of
disaccustom 611 vb.
cure 656 vb.
curé
pastor 986 n.
cure-all
remedy 658 n.
cureless
unpromising 853 adj.
cure of souls
church ministry 985 n.
curettage
voidance 300 n.
curfew
evening 129 n.
danger signal 665 n.
restriction 747 n.
prohibition 757 n.
Curia
council 692 n.
ecclesiastical court 956 n.
curie
radiation 417 n.
curio
exhibit 522 n.
masterpiece 694 n.
ornamentation 844 n.
curiosity
nonconformist 84 n.
curiosity 453 n.
enquiry 459 n.
learning 536 n.
excitation 821 n.
desire 859 n.
prodigy 864 n.
curious
beautiful 841 adj.
desiring 859 adj.
curl
filament 208 n.
curve 248 n.
loop 250 n.
coil 251 n.
crinkle 251 vb.
fold 261 vb.
hairdressing 843 n.
primp 843 vb.
— one's lip
gesticulate 547 vb.
smile 835 vb.
despise 922 vb.
— up
rotate 315 vb.
curlers
fastening 47 n.
hairdressing 843 n.

curlicue
coil 251 n.
lettering 586 n.
pattern 844 n.
curls
hair 259 n.
curly
undulatory 251 adj.
hairy 259 adj.
curmudgeon
niggard 816 n.
rude person 885 n.
currant
fruit 301 n.
currency
generality 79 n.
publicity 528 n.
money 797 n.
current
general 79 adj.
present 121 adj.
happening 154 adj.
motion 265 n.
direction 281 n.
progression 285 n.
current 350 n.
wind 352 n.
known 490 adj.
published 528 adj.
usual 610 adj.
useful 640 adj.
current account
funds 797 n.
current affairs
affairs 154 n.
curricle
carriage 274 n.
curriculum
curriculum 534 n.
curriculum vitae
record 548 n.
biography 590 n.
curry
dish 301 n.
season 388 vb.
— favour
be servile 879 vb.
flatter 925 vb.
currycomb
rub 333 vb.
groom 369 vb.
curry powder
condiment 389 n.
curse
influence 178 n.
haemorrhage 302 n.
evil 616 n.
badness 645 n.
bane 659 n.
adversity 731 n.
annoyance 827 n.
discontent 829 n.
hate 888 vb.
malediction 899 n.
scurrility 899 n.
curse 899 vb.
cuss 899 vb.
threaten 900 vb.
reprobate 924 vb.
condemn 961 vb.
be impious 980 vb.
spell 983 n.
bewitch 983 vb.
curse with bell, book and candle
curse 899 vb.
perform ritual 988 vb.
cursed
damnable 645 adj.
cursed 899 adj.
bewitched 983 adj.
cursing and swearing
scurrility 899 n.
cursive
letter 558 n.
written 586 adj.
cursory
inconsiderable 33 adj.
transient 114 adj.
inattentive 456 adj.
hasty 680 adj.
curt
concise 569 adj.
taciturn 582 adj.
curtail
subtract 39 vb.
cut 46 vb.
sunder 46 vb.
shorten 204 vb.
impair 655 vb.
curtain
separation 46 n.
exclusion 57 n.
end 69 n.
hang 217 vb.
shade 226 n.
partition 231 n.
darken 418 vb.
curtain 421 n.
screen 421 vb.
invisibility 444 n.
dramaturgy 594 n.
stage set 594 n.
fortification 713 n.
curtain call
recurrence 106 n.
dramaturgy 594 n.
applause 923 n.
curtain lecture
reprimand 924 n.
curtain-raiser
beginning 68 n.
stage play 594 n.
curtains
finality 69 n.
decease 361 n.
curtsy, curtsey
obeisance 311 n.
stoop 311 vb.
courteous act 884 n.
respects 920 n.
show respect 920 vb.
curvaceous
curved 248 adj.
convex 253 adj.
shapely 841 adj.
curvature
obliquity 220 n.
deformity 246 n.
curvature 248 n.
curve
make oblique 220 vb.
curve 248 n.
be curved 248 vb.
arc 250 n.
camber 253 n.
deviate 282 vb.
curves
bluntness 257 n.
beauty 841 n.
curvet
equitation 267 n.
leap 312 n.vb.
cushion
moderator 177 n.
moderate 177 vb.
cushion 218 n.
support 218 vb.
intermediary 231 n.
put between 231 vb.
softness 327 n.
soften 327 vb.
euphoria 376 n.
protection 660 n.
defend 713 vb.
relieve 831 vb.
cushy
comfortable 376 adj.
easy 701 adj.
cusp
extremity 69 n.
sharp point 256 n.
pattern 844 n.
cuss
cuss 899 vb.
cussedness
obstinacy 602 n.
opposition 704 n.
malevolence 898 n.
custard
dessert 301 n.
sweet thing 392 n.
custodial
tutelary 660 adj.
restraining 747 adj.
custodian
protector 660 n.
manager 690 n.
defender 713 n.
keeper 749 n.
custody
protection 660 n.
detention 747 n.
custom
order 60 n.
continuity 71 n.
generality 79 n.
regularity 81 n.
tradition 127 n.
permanence 144 n.
habit 610 n.
aid 703 n.
trade 791 n.
purchase 792 n.
etiquette 848 n.
customary
general 79 adj.
regular 81 adj.
habitual 610 adj.
preceptive 693 adj.
unastonishing 865 adj.
orthodox 976 adj.
customer
person 371 n.
habitué 610 n.
patron 707 n.
purchaser 792 n.
customs
conduct 688 n.
receipt 807 n.
tax 809 n.
customs barrier
exclusion 57 n.
customs house
market 796 n.
treasury 799 n.
customs officer
receiver 782 n.
cut
adjust 24 vb.
diminution 37 n.
subtract 39 vb.
decrement 42 n.
cut 46 vb.
piece 53 n.
discontinuity 72 n.
be absent 190 vb.
make smaller 198 vb.
shorten 204 vb.
form 243 n.vb.
form 243 vb.
excavation 255 n.
be sharp 256 vb.
notch 260 vb.
move fast 277 vb.
strike 279 vb.
propel 287 vb.
meat 301 n.
fell 311 vb.
cultivate 370 vb.
pain 377 n.
give pain 377 vb.
disregard 458 vb.
sculpt 554 vb.
engrave 555 vb.
wound 655 n.vb.
lunge 712 n.
not observe 769 vb.
portion 783 n.
pay 804 n.
discount 810 n.
cheapen 812 vb.
hurt 827 vb.
blemish 845 n.
fashion 848 n.
humiliate 872 vb.
make unwelcome 883 vb.
be rude 885 vb.
— across
be oblique 220 vb.

pass 305 vb.
— a dash
be important 638 vb.
have a reputation 866 vb.
be ostentatious 875 vb.
— adrift
separate 46 vb.
— a figure
appear 445 vb.
attract notice 455 vb.
be in fashion 848 vb.
— and run
move fast 277 vb.
decamp 296 vb.
run away 620 vb.
— back
abate 37 vb.
subtract 39 vb.
shorten 204 vb.
economize 814 vb.
— both ways
tell against 467 vb.
be equivocal 518 vb.
— corners
hasten 680 vb.
— costs
economize 814 vb.
— dead
make unwelcome 883 vb.
be rude 885 vb.
— down
demolish 165 vb.
fell 311 vb.
slaughter 362 vb.
— down to size
make conform 83 vb.
be unimportant 639 vb.
humbled 872 adj.
detract 926 vb.
— ice
influence 178 vb.
— in
converse 584 vb.
— it out!
145 int.
— loose
separate 46 vb.
be free 744 vb.
— no ice
be impotent 161 vb.
be unimportant 639 vb.
have no repute 867 vb.
— off
cut 46 vb.
set apart 46 vb.
suppress 165 vb.
circumscribe 232 vb.
kill 362 vb.
hinder 702 vb.
deprive 786 vb.
impoverish 801 vb.
— off one's nose to spite one's face
act foolishly 695 vb.
— one's coat according to one's cloth
economize 814 vb.
be cautious 858 vb.
— open
cut 46 vb.
open 263 vb.
doctor 658 vb.
— out
form 243 vb.
extract 304 vb.
prepare 669 vb.
— short
halt 145 vb.
suppress 165 vb.
shorten 204 vb.
be concise 569 vb.
make mute 578 vb.
— the Gordian knot
disunite 46 vb.
disencumber 701 vb.
— the ground from under
confute 479 vb.
defeat 727 vb.
— through
pierce 263 vb.
— to the quick
excite 821 vb.
hurt 827 vb.
— up rough
be angry 891 vb.
resent 891 vb.
— up well
bequeath 780 vb.
cut above, a
superior 34 adj.
best 644 adj.
cut and dried
arranged 62 adj.
definite 80 adj.
ready-made 669 adj.
cut and thrust
argument 475 n.
fight 716 n.
cutaneous
dermal 226 adj.
cute
personable 841 adj.
affected 850 adj.
cut glass
ornamental art 844 n.
cuticle
skin 226 n.
cutlass
sharp edge 256 n.
sidearms 723 n.
cutlery
sharp edge 256 n.
cutlet
meat 301 n.
cut of one's jib
form 243 n.
feature 445 n.
cut out for
fit 24 adj.
advisable 642 adj.
gifted 694 adj.
cut price
discount 810 n.
cheapness 812 n.
cuts
restriction 747 n.
economy 814 n.
cutter
shortener 204 n.
sharp edge 256 n.
boat 275 n.
artisan 686 n.
cutthroat
destructive 165 adj.
murderer 362 n.
contending 716 adj.
ruffian 904 n.
cutting
scission 46 n.
excavation 255 n.
sharp 256 adj.
plant 366 n.
cinema 445 n.
forceful 571 adj.
writing 586 n.
railway 624 n.
hairdressing 843 n.
cuttings
record 548 n.
anthology 592 n.
cuttlefish
marine life 365 n.
cut up
unhappy 825 adj.
dejected 834 adj.
melancholic 834 adj.
cwm
valley 255 n.
cyan
blueness 435 n.
cyanide
poison 659 n.
cybernetics
data processing 86 n.
mechanics 630 n.
cycle
recurrence 106 n.
era 110 n.
regular return 141 n.
orbit 250 n.
ride 267 vb.
bicycle 274 n.
poem 593 n.
cycle track
road 624 n.
cyclic
periodical 141 adj.
cycling
land travel 267 n.
exercise 682 n.
sport 837 n.
cyclist
rider 268 n.
cyclone
storm 176 n.
vortex 315 n.
weather 340 n.
gale 352 n.
Cyclops
giant 195 n.
cyclostyle
copy 20 vb.
cyclotron
nucleonics 160 n.
cygnet
young creature 132 n.
bird 365 n.
cylinder
cylinder 252 n.
cylindrical
rotund 252 adj.
tubular 263 adj.
cymbals
gong 414 n.
cyme
flower 366 n.
cynic
underestimation 483 n.
unbeliever 486 n.
misanthrope 902 n.
detractor 926 n.
Cynic
ascetic 945 n.
cynical
unbelieving 486 adj.
misanthropic 902 adj.
detracting 926 adj.
cynicism
moral insensibility 820 n.
dejection 834 n.
hopelessness 853 n.
misanthropy 902 n.
detraction 926 n.
cynosure
prototype 23 n.
focus 76 n.
attraction 291 n.
desired object 859 n.
person of repute 866 n.
favourite 890 n.n.
cypress
lamentation 836 n.
Cyrillic alphabet
letter 558 n.
cyst
bladder 194 n.
ulcer 651 n.
cystic fibrosis
respiratory disease 651 n.
cystitis
digestive disorders 651 n.
cytology
biology 358 n.
cytoplasm
organism 358 n.

czar
(See **tsar** *)*
czardas
dance 837 n.

D

dab
small thing 33 n.
knock 279 n.
touch 378 vb.
dabble
moisten 341 vb.
experiment 461 vb.
be inactive 679 vb.
— in
not know 491 vb.
amuse oneself 837 vb.
dabbler
experimenter 461 n.
sciolist 493 n.
meddler 678 n.
bungler 697 n.
dab hand, dabster
proficient person 696 n.
dabs
trace 548 n.
da capo
again 106 adv.
dachshund
dog 365 n.
dacoit
robber 789 n.
dactyl
prosody 593 n.
dactylology
deafness 416 n.
gesture 547 n.
symbology 547 n.
dad, daddy
paternity 169 n.
Dada
school of painting 553 n.
daddy longlegs
insect 365 n.
dado
base 214 n.
ornamental art 844 n.
daedal
variegated 437 adj.
well-made 694 adj.
ornamental 844 adj.
Daedalian
labyrinthine 251 adj.
daffodil
plant 366 n.
yellowness 433 n.
heraldry 547 n.
daft
foolish 499 adj.
crazy 503 adj.
dagger
sharp point 256 n.
punctuation 547 n.
sidearms 723 n.
daguerrotype
photography 551 n.
Dail
parliament 692 n.
daily
often 139 adv.
seasonal 141 adj.
periodically 141 adv.
journal 528 n.
the press 528 n.
usual 610 adj.
servant 742 n.
daily bread
food 301 n.
vocation 622 n.
daily round
uniformity 16 n.
continuity 71 n.
regular return 141 n.
habit 610 n.
business 622 n.
dainties
food 301 n.
daintiness
cleanness 648 n.
good taste 846 n.
fastidiousness 862 n.
dainty
small 33 adj.
flimsy 163 adj.
little 196 adj.
edible 301 adj.
savoury 390 adj.
clean 648 adj.
pleasurableness 826 n.
personable 841 adj.
shapely 841 adj.
tasteful 846 adj.
fastidious 862 adj.
dairy
chamber 194 n.
workshop 687 n.
dairy farming
animal husbandry 369 n.
agriculture 370 n.
dairymaid
herdsman 369 n.
domestic 742 n.
dairy product
dairy product 301 n.
dais
stand 218 n.
rostrum 539 n.
daisy
plant 366 n.
daisy-cutter
lowness 210 n.
dak bungalow
inn 192 n.
Dalai Lama
sovereign 741 n.
dale
valley 255 n.
Dalek
image 551 n.
dalesman, daleswoman
dweller 191 n.
dalliance
love-making 887 n.
endearment 889 n.
dally
be late 136 vb.
be irresolute 601 vb.
be inactive 679 vb.
amuse oneself 837 vb.
caress 889 vb.
Dalmatian
dog 365 n.
maculation 437 n.
dalmatic
vestments 989 n.
daltonism
dim sight 440 n.
dam
exclusion 57 n.
maternity 169 n.
irrigator 341 n.
lake 346 n.
dam (up)
close 264 vb.
staunch 350 vb.
obstruct 702 vb.
damage
break 46 vb.
derange 63 vb.
weaken 163 vb.
lay waste 165 vb.
tell against 467 vb.
evil 616 n.
waste 634 n.vb.
inutility 641 n.
badness 645 n.
harm 645 vb.
impairment 655 n.
impair 655 vb.
cost 809 n.
blemish 845 vb.
defame 926 vb.
damages
restitution 787 n.
cost 809 n.
penalty 963 n.
damaging
harmful 645 adj.
discreditable 867 adj.
maleficent 898 adj.
damascene
variegate 437 vb.
damask
textile 222 n.
red 431 adj.
dame
lady 373 n.
master 741 n.
person of repute 866 n.
title 870 n.
damn
trifle 639 n.
scurrility 899 n.
curse 899 vb.
cuss 899 vb.
dispraise 924 vb.
condemn 961 vb.
— the consequences
be obstinate 602 vb.
be rash 857 vb.
— with faint praise
be indifferent 860 vb.
dispraise 924 vb.
detract 926 vb.
damnable
evil 616 adj.
damnable 645 adj.
unpleasant 827 adj.
damnably
extremely 32 adv.
damnation
future state 124 n.
suffering 825 n.
condemnation 961 n.
damnatory
maledictory 899 adj.
disapproving 924 adj.
accusing 928 adj.
damned
damnable 645 adj.
cursed 899 adj.
condemned 961 adj.
infernal 972 adj.
damning
evidential 466 adj.
damp
gas 336 n.
water 339 n.
moisture 341 n.
humid 341 adj.
extinguish 382 vb.
sound dead 405 vb.
(See **dampen** *)*
— down
abate 37 vb.
hinder 702 vb.
restrain 747 vb.
damp course
base 214 n.
dampen
moderate 177 vb.
moisten 341 vb.
mute 401 vb.
dissuade 613 vb.
depress 834 vb.
damper
moderator 177 n.
stopper 264 n.
heater 383 n.
silencer 401 n.
nonresonance 405 n.
mute 414 n.
moper 834 n.
disapprover 924 n.
dampness
moisture 341 n.

damp-proof
unyielding 162 adj.
dry 342 adj.
damp squib
disappointment 509 n.
failure 728 n.
damsel
youngster 132 n.
woman 373 n.
damson
fruit 301 n.
purpleness 436 n.
dance
composition 56 n.
be in motion 265 vb.
leap 312 vb.
rotation 315 n.
oscillate 317 vb.
be agitated 318 vb.
musical piece 412 n.
shine 417 vb.
ballet 594 n.
be excited 821 vb.
be cheerful 833 vb.
dance 837 n., vb.
dancing 837 n.
social gathering 882 n.
— attendance on
accompany 89 vb.
follow 284 vb.
be servile 879 vb.
— for joy
rejoice 835 vb.
— upon nothing
be punished 963 vb.
— with fury
be angry 891 vb.
dance floor
smoothness 258 n.
place of amusement 837 n.
dancer
jumper 312 n.
entertainer 594 n.
dance 837 n.
dance step
gait 265 n.
leap 312 n.
dancing
ballet 594 n.
dancing 837 n.
(See **dance** *)*
dancing girl
jumper 312 n.
entertainer 594 n.
dandelion
plant 366 n.
dandified
fashionable 848 adj.
affected 850 adj.
dandle
caress 889 vb.
dandruff
powder 332 n.
dirt 649 n.
dandy
super 644 adj.
fop 848 n.
fashionable 848 adj.
affecter 850 n.
danger
probability 471 n.
unreliability 474 n.
omen 511 n.
latency 523 n.
danger 661 n.
pitfall 663 n.
predicament 700 n.
threat 900 n.
danger-loving
unfearing 855 adj.
rash 857 adj.
dangerous
harmful 645 adj.
dangerous 661 adj.
difficult 700 adj.
frightening 854 adj.
inimical 881 adj.
angry 891 adj.
malevolent 898 adj.
threatening 900 adj.
danger signal
prediction 511 n.
signal 547 n.
warning 664 n.
danger signal 665 n.
threat 900 n.
dangle
come unstuck 49 vb.
hang 217 vb.
oscillate 317 vb.
show 522 vb.
tempt 612 vb.
cause desire 859 vb.
Daniel
sage 500 n.
dank
humid 341 adj.
danseur, danseuse
actor 594 n.
dapper
orderly 60 adj.
personable 841 adj.
dapple
variegate 437 vb.
dappled
mixed 43 adj.
pied 437 adj.
Darby and Joan
duality 90 n.
old couple 133 n.
spouse 894 n.
dare
be resolute 599 vb.
face danger 661 vb.
undertake 672 vb.
defiance 711 n.
defy 711 vb.
be free 744 vb.
be courageous 855 vb.
threat 900 n.
— say
assume 471 vb.
expect 507 vb.
suppose 512 vb.
— swear
affirm 532 vb.
daredevil
brave person 855 n.
desperado 857 n.
rash 857 adj.
daring
undisguised 522 adj.
rash 857 adj.
showy 875 adj.
unchaste 951 adj.
(See **dare** *)*
dark
evening 129 n.
darkness 418 n.
dark 418 adj.
soft-hued 425 adj.
black 428 adj.adj.
brown 430 adj.
blind 439 adj.
dim-sighted 440 adj.
invisible 444 adj.adj.
ignorant 491 adj.
unknown 491 adj.
latent 523 adj.
unclear 568 adj.
cheerless 834 adj.
serious 834 adj.
sullen 893 adj.
dishonest 930 adj.
cabbalistic 984 adj.
Dark Ages
era 110 n.
antiquity 125 n.
ignorance 491 n.
dark clouds
adversity 731 n.
Dark Continent
unknown thing 491 n.
darken
darken 418 vb.
bedim 419 vb.
screen 421 vb.
blacken 428 vb.
blind 439 vb.
blur 440 vb.
be unseen 444 vb.
conceal 525 vb.
depress 834 vb.
dark glasses
shade 226 n.
screen 421 n.
semitransparency 424 n.
eyeglass 442 n.
dark horse
unknown thing 491 n.
latency 523 n.
secret 530 n.
darkness
darkness 418 n.
uncertainty 474 n.
ignorance 491 n.
(See **dark** *)*
dark-skinned
blackish 428 adj.
darling
loved one 887 n.
lovable 887 adj.
darling 890 n.
favourite 890 n.
darn
repair 656 n.
darned
damnable 645 adj.
dart
vary 152 vb.
be in motion 265 vb.
move fast 277 vb.
missile 287 n.
propel 287 vb.
missile weapon 723 n.
— about
wander 267 vb.
darts
indoor game 837 n.
Darwinism
biology 358 n.
dash
small quantity 33 n.
tincture 43 n.
vigorousness 174 n.
be violent 176 vb.
spurt 277 n.
move fast 277 vb.
strike 279 vb.
be agitated 318 vb.
flow 350 vb.
punctuation 547 n.
mark 547 vb.
resolution 599 n.
be active 678 vb.
haste 680 n.
hasten 680 vb.
racing 716 n.
defeat 727 vb.
warm feeling 818 n.
fashion 848 n.
courage 855 n.
ostentation 875 n.
— against
collide 279 vb.
— at
charge 712 vb.
— down
fell 311 vb.
— off
move fast 277 vb.
represent 551 vb.
write 586 vb.
hasten 680 vb.
— one's hopes
disappoint 509 vb.
miscarry 728 vb.
depress 834 vb.
dashed
defeated 728 adj.
humbled 872 adj.
dashed hopes
hopelessness 853 n.
dashiki
shirt 228 n.
dashing
forceful 571 adj.

courageous 855 adj.
(See **dash** *)*
dastard
coward 856 n.
cad 938 n.
dastardly
cowardly 856 adj.
data
data processing 86 n.
evidence 466 n.
premise 475 n.
supposition 512 n.
data bank
data processing 86 n.
mnemonics 505 n.
storage 632 n.
data base
information 524 n.
data processing
data processing 86 n.
electronics 160 n.
microelectronics 196 n.
optical device 442 n.
information 524 n.
record 548 n.
language 557 n.
date
date 108 n.
fix the time 108 vb.
chronology 117 n.
fruit 301 n.
social round 882 n.
be sociable 882 vb.
lover 887 n.
dated
dated 108 adj.
antiquated 127 adj.
dateless
perpetual 115 adj.
date line
dividing line 92 n.
clock time 117 n.
datum
premise 475 n.
(See **data** *)*
daub
coat 226 vb.
colour 425 vb.
lack of meaning 515 n.
misrepresentation 552 n.
picture 553 n.
paint 553 vb.
make unclean 649 vb.
dauber
artist 556 n.
bungler 697 n.
daughter
descendant 170 n.
woman 373 n.
daughterly
filial 170 adj.
obedient 739 adj.
daunt
dissuade 613 vb.
frighten 854 vb.
humiliate 872 vb.
dauntless
unfearing 855 adj.
Dauphin
sovereign 741 n.
davit
hanger 217 n.
Davy Jones's locker
ocean 343 n.
Davy lamp
lamp 420 n.
dawdle
drag on 113 vb.
be late 136 vb.
walk 267 vb.
wander 267 vb.
slowness 278 n.
move slowly 278 vb.
be inactive 679 vb.
dawdler
slowcoach 278 n.
idler 679 n.
dawn
precursor 66 n.
beginning 68 n.
begin 68 vb.
primal 127 adj.
morning 128 n.
glow 417 n.
make bright 417 vb.
redness 431 n.
appear 445 vb.
— on/upon
be visible 443 vb.
down upon 449 vb.
be intelligible 516 vb.
dawn chorus
morning 128 n.
vocal music 412 n.
day
date 108 n.
period 110 n.
day after day
repeatedly 106 adv.
perpetually 139 adv.
day and night
polarity 14 n.
perpetually 139 adv.
day book
account book 808 n.
daybreak
morning 128 n.
half-light 419 n.
day by day
repeatedly 106 adv.
while 108 adv.
all along 113 adv.
day centre
meeting place 192 n.
daydream
fantasy 513 n.
imagine 513 vb.
desire 859 n.vb.
daydreaming
abstractedness 456 n.
desire 859 n.
day in day out
all along 113 adv.
daylight
morning 128 n.
interval 201 n.
light 417 n.
manifestation 522 n.
disclosure 526 n.
daylight saving
clock time 117 n.
day of abstinence
fast 946 n.
day off
lull 145 n.
leisure 681 n.
repose 683 n.
Day of Judgment
finality 69 n.
punishment 963 n.
day of obligation
holy day 988 n.
day of reckoning
revenge 910 n.
punishment 963 n.
day of rest
repose 683 n.
holy day 988 n.
day of the week
date 108 n.
regular return 141 n.
day out
amusement 837 n.
day pupil
learner 538 n.
day release
education 534 n.
days
time 108 n.
era 110 n.
days of grace
delay 136 n.
daystar
morning 128 n.
sun 321 n.
daytime
morning 128 n.
matinal 128 adj.
day to remember
special day 876 n.
day trip
land travel 267 n.
day-tripper
reveller 837 n.
daze
blur 440 vb.
distract 456 vb.
puzzle 474 vb.
dazed
insensible 375 adj.
dim-sighted 440 adj.
distracted 456 adj.
doubting 474 adj.
foolish 499 adj.
inexpectant 508 adj.
wondering 864 adj.
dazzle
light 417 n.
reflection 417 n.
shine 417 vb.
blind 439 vb.
blur 440 vb.
distract 456 vb.
deceive 542 vb.
impress 821 vb.
be beautiful 841 vb.
be wonderful 864 vb.
prestige 866 n.
be ostentatious 875 vb.
excite love 887 vb.
command respect 920 vb.
dazzler
a beauty 841 n.
dazzling
excellent 644 adj.
splendid 841 adj.
D-day
start 68 n.
date 108 n.
special day 876 n.
DDT
poison 659 n.
deacon, deaconess
church officer 986 n.
lay person 987 n.
deaconship
church office 985 n.
deactivate
weaken 163 vb.
assuage 177 vb.
counteract 182 vb.
impair 655 vb.
deactivated
inert 175 adj.
dead
extinct 2 adj.
past 125 adj.
inert 175 adj.
quiescent 266 adj.
dead 361 adj.
buried 364 adj.
insensible 375 adj.
muted 401 adj.
nonresonant 405 adj.
soft-hued 425 adj.
colourless 426 adj.
nonactive 677 adj.
abrogated 752 adj.
dead, the
death roll 361 n.
dead and buried
past 125 adj.
forgotten 506 adj.
dead as the dodo
extinct 2 adj.
past 125 adj.
dead beat
fatigued 684 adj.
dead body
corpse 363 n.
dead centre
centre 225 n.
accurate 494 adj.
dead cert
certainty 473 n.

easy thing 701 n.
dead drunk
insensible 375 adj.
dead drunk 949 adj.
dead duck
hopelessness 853 n.
dead earnest
seriousness 834 n.
deaden
assuage 177 vb.
render insensible 375 vb.
mute 401 vb.
sound dead 405 vb.
decolorize 426 vb.
make mute 578 vb.
make inactive 679 vb.
make insensitive 820 vb.
dead end
stopping place 145 n.
closure 264 n.
obstacle 702 n.
deadfall
trap 542 n.
dead from the neck up
unintelligent 499 adj.
dead heat
draw 28 n.
synchronism 123 n.
dead letter
ineffectuality 161 n.
lack of meaning 515 n.
abrogation 752 n.
deadlight
curtain 421 n.
deadline
finality 69 n.
limit 236 n.
deadlock
draw 28 n.
stop 145 n.
impossibility 470 n.
inaction 677 n.
difficulty 700 n.
noncompletion 726 n.
defeat 728 n.
dead loss
lost labour 641 n.
loss 772 n.
deadly
destructive 165 adj.
deadly 362 adj.
evil 616 adj.
harmful 645 adj.
toxic 653 adj.
dull 840 adj.
inimical 881 adj.
malevolent 898 adj.
heinous 934 adj.
deadly poison
poison 659 n.
deadly sin
vice 934 n.
guilty act 936 n.
dead man/woman
corpse 363 n.
dead man's handle
safeguard 662 n.
dead march
slowness 278 n.
obsequies 364 n.
musical piece 412 n.
dead of night
midnight 129 n.
darkness 418 n.
dead-on
accurate 494 adj.
deadpan
impassive 820 adj.
inexcitable 823 adj.
serious 834 adj.
dead reckoning
numeration 86 n.
navigation 269 n.
measurement 465 n.
dead set
attempt 671 n.
dead shot
proficient person 696 n.
dead spit of
analogue 18 n.
dead stop
stop 145 n.
quiescence 266 n.
failure 728 n.
dead to
thick-skinned 820 adj.
dead to the world
sleepy 679 adj.
dead drunk 949 adj.
dead water
smoothness 258 n.
dead weight
encumbrance 702 n.
dead wood
rubbish 641 n.
deaf
insensible 375 adj.
deaf 416 adj.
inattentive 456 adj.
indiscriminating 464 adj.
obstinate 602 adj.
nonactive 677 adj.
impassive 820 adj.
deaf-aid
hearing aid 415 n.
deaf and dumb
deaf 416 adj.
voiceless 578 adj.
deaf-and-dumb language
gesture 547 n.
deafen
be loud 400 vb.
deafen 416 vb.
make insensitive 820 vb.
deaf-mute
deafness 416 n.
voicelessness 578 n.
deafness
deafness 416 n.
deaf to
deaf 416 adj.
refusing 760 adj.
thick-skinned 820 adj.
deaf to, be
repel 292 vb.
be pitiless 906 vb.
deal
great quantity 32 n.
arrange 62 vb.
deed 676 n.
compact 765 n.
apportionment 783 n.
trade 791 n.
— in
do 676 vb.
trade 791 vb.
— out
disperse 75 vb.
give 781 vb.
apportion 783 vb.
— with
be related 9 vb.
dissertate 591 vb.
do business 622 vb.
deal with 688 vb.
make terms 766 vb.
trade 791 vb.
dealer
agent 686 n.
seller 793 n.
merchant 794 n.
dealings
deed 676 n.
conduct 688 n.
dean
teacher 537 n.
director 690 n.
ecclesiarch 986 n.
deanery
church office 985 n.
parish 985 n.
parsonage 986 n.
dear
known 490 adj.
profitless 641 adj.
harmful 645 adj.
dear 811 adj.
pleasurable 826 adj.
lovable 887 adj.
darling 890 n.
dearest
darling 890 n.
dearly
greatly 32 adv.
dear Sir
title 870 n.
dearth
unproductiveness 172 n.
scarcity 636 n.
dearness 811 n.
death
extinction 2 n.
decay 51 n.
destroyer 168 n.
quietude 266 n.
death 361 n.
capital punishment 963 n.
deathbed
late 136 adj.
decease 361 n.
illness 651 n.
death blow
end 69 n.
death 361 n.
killing 362 n.
defeat 728 n.
death-bringing
deadly 362 adj.
death chamber
means of execution 964 n.
death-dealing
murderous 362 adj.
death duty
tax 809 n.
death in life
suffering 825 n.
death knell
death 361 n.
warning 664 n.
deathless
perpetual 115 adj.
renowned 866 adj.
deathlike
dying 361 adj.
cadaverous 363 adj.
deathliness
quiescence 266 n.
death 361 n.
deathly
dying 361 adj.
deadly 362 adj.
cadaverous 363 adj.
colourless 426 adj.
evil 616 adj.
death mask
copy 22 n.
sculpture 554 n.
death of
worry 825 n.
annoyance 827 n.
death of, be the
amuse 837 vb.
death rate
statistics 86 n.
death roll 361 n.
death rattle
respiration 352 n.
decease 361 n.
death ray
weapon 723 n.
death roll
death roll 361 n.
Death Row
lockup 748 n.
condemnation 961 n.
death sentence
capital punishment 963 n.

death's-head
corpse 363 n.
moper 834 n.
eyesore 842 n.
intimidation 854 n.
death toll
death roll 361 n.
death trap
trap 542 n.
danger 661 n.
pitfall 663 n.
death warrant
condemnation 961 n.
capital punishment 963 n.
deathwatch
decease 361 n.
surveillance 457 n.
deathwatch beetle
noxious animal 904 n.
death wish
dejection 834 n.
debacle
revolution 149 n.
ruin 165 n.
defeat 728 n.
debag
uncover 229 vb.
debar
exclude 57 vb.
obstruct 702 vb.
prohibit 757 vb.
refuse 760 vb.
debase
impair 655 vb.
pervert 655 vb.
vulgarize 847 vb.
shame 867 vb.
disentitle 916 vb.
— the coinage
demonetize 797 vb.
debatable
topical 452 adj.
moot 459 adj.
uncertain 474 adj.
arguing 475 adj.
debatable territory
territory 184 n.
nonownership 774 n.
debate
meditate 449 vb.
argument 475 n.
argue 475 vb.
conference 584 n.
confer 584 vb.
be irresolute 601 vb.
contention 716 n.
debater
reasoner 475 n.
debauch
pervert 655 vb.
shame 867 vb.
sensualism 944 n.
debauch 951 vb.
debauched
vicious 934 adj.
sensual 944 adj.
lecherous 951 adj.
debauchee
reveller 837 n.
libertine 952 n.
debauchery
intemperance 943 n.
sensualism 944 n.
unchastity 951 n.
debenture
title deed 767 n.
debilitate
weaken 163 vb.
debilitating disease
disease 651 n.
debility
weakness 163 n.
ill health 651 n.
debit
debt 803 n.
account 808 vb.
debonair
cheerful 833 adj.
debouch
emerge 298 vb.
flow out 298 vb.
Debrett
directory 87 n.
debris
remainder 41 n.
piece 53 n.
accumulation 74 n.
powder 332 n.
rubbish 641 n.
debt
encumbrance 702 n.
debt 803 n.
dueness 915 n.
debt-collector
receiver 782 n.
debt of honour
promise 764 n.
compact 765 n.
debtor
debtor 803 n.
debug
unravel 62 vb.
computerize 86 vb.
rectify 654 vb.
debunk
disclose 526 vb.
ridicule 851 vb.
shame 867 vb.
humiliate 872 vb.
detract 926 vb.
debus
land 295 vb.
debut
debut 68 n.
reception 299 n.
celebration 876 n.
debutant(e)
beginner 538 n.
fop 848 n.
decade
over five 99 n.
period 110 n.
decadence
deterioration 655 n.
decadent
literary 557 adj.
sensualist 944 n.
decagon
angular figure 247 n.
Decalogue
code of duty 917 n.
decamp
go away 190 vb.
decamp 296 vb.
disappear 446 vb.
run away 620 vb.
hasten 680 vb.
decant
transpose 272 vb.
empty 300 vb.
infuse 303 vb.
make flow 350 vb.
decanter
vessel 194 n.
decapitate
subtract 39 vb.
sunder 46 vb.
execute 963 vb.
decarbonize, decarbonise
purify 648 vb.
decathlon
contest 716 n.
decay
decrease 37 n.vb.
decay 51 n.
decompose 51 vb.
oldness 127 n.
be old 127 vb.
destroyer 168 n.
death 361 n.
desuetude 611 n.
waste 634 vb.
badness 645 n.
dirt 649 n.
dilapidation 655 n.
deteriorate 655 vb.
blight 659 n.
decease
end 69 n.
decease 361 n.
die 361 vb.
deceit
deception 542 n.
deceitful
false 541 adj.
deceiving 542 adj.
cunning 698 adj.
deceive
mislead 495 vb.
keep secret 525 vb.
misteach 535 vb.
dissemble 541 vb.
deceive 542 vb.
be cunning 698 vb.
defraud 788 vb.
flatter 925 vb.
be dishonest 930 vb.
be impure 951 vb.
deceived
gullible 544 adj.
deceived husband
cuckold 952 n.
deceiver
deceiver 545 n.
slyboots 698 n.
affecter 850 n.
flatterer 925 n.
libertine 952 n.
deceiving
simulating 18 adj.
appearing 445 adj.
disappointing 509 adj.
deceleration
delay 136 n.
slowness 278 n.
hindrance 702 n.
restraint 747 n.
decency
good taste 846 n.
etiquette 848 n.
right 913 n.
purity 950 n.
decennium
period 110 n.
decent
not bad 644 adj.
middling 732 adj.
personable 841 adj.
tasteful 846 adj.
well-bred 848 adj.
ethical 917 adj.
pure 950 adj.
decentralization, decentralisation
nonuniformity 17 n.
decomposition 51 n.
arrangement 62 n.
dispersion 75 n.
laxity 734 n.
commission 751 n.
deception
insubstantiality 4 n.
visual fallacy 440 n.
concealment 525 n.
disguise 527 n.
deception 542 n.
deceptive
simulating 18 adj.
shadowy 419 adj.
appearing 445 adj.
sophistical 477 adj.
erroneous 495 adj.
disappointing 509 adj.
false 541 adj.
deceiving 542 adj.
dechristianization, dechristianisation
irreligion 974 n.
decibel
sound 398 n.
metrology 465 n.
decide
terminate 69 vb.
cause 156 vb.
answer 460 vb.
make certain 473 vb.
judge 480 vb.
be resolute 599 vb.

choose 605 vb.
try a case 959 vb.
decided
assertive 532 adj.
volitional 595 adj.
resolute 599 adj.
deciduous
ephemeral 114 adj.
vegetal 366 adj.
decimal
numerical element 85 n.
decimal point
punctuation 547 n.
decimal system
numeration 86 n.
decimate
render few 105 vb.
weaken 163 vb.
destroy 165 vb.
slaughter 362 vb.
execute 963 vb.
decipher
decipher 520 vb.
manifest 522 vb.
decipherable
intelligible 516 adj.
decipherment
interpretation 520 n.
translation 520 n.
decision
judgment 480 n.
vigour 571 n.
will 595 n.
resolution 599 n.
choice 605 n.
intention 617 n.
decree 737 n.
legal trial 959 n.
decision-making
management 689 n.
decisive
crucial 137 adj.
causal 156 adj.
influential 178 adj.
evidential 466 adj.
demonstrating 478 adj.
assertive 532 adj.
resolute 599 adj.
commanding 737 adj.
decisive factor
cause 156 n.
deck
compartment 194 n.
layer 207 n.
basis 218 n.
paving 226 n.
roof 226 n.
overlay 226 vb.
dress 228 vb.
gramophone 414 n.
plaything 837 n.
decorate 844 vb.
— out
decorate 844 vb.
deck chair
seat 218 n.
deckhand
mariner 270 n.
deckle edge
edging 234 n.
roughness 259 n.
notch 260 n.
declaim
proclaim 528 vb.
orate 579 vb.
declaimer
speaker 579 n.
declamation
vigour 571 n.
magniloquence 574 n.
oration 579 n.
oratory 579 n.
ostentation 875 n.
declarant
foreigner 59 n.
assenter 488 n.
declaration
affirmation 532 n.
offer 759 n.
promise 764 n.
declaration of faith
creed 485 n.
declare
believe 485 vb.
mean 514 vb.
divulge 526 vb.
proclaim 528 vb.
affirm 532 vb.
indicate 547 vb.
speak 579 vb.
decree 737 vb.
resign 753 vb.
declare war
go to war 718 vb.
declassify
derange 63 vb.
declension
decrease 37 n.
change 143 n.
grammar 564 n.
declination
bearings 186 n.
divergence 294 n.
descent 309 n.
uranometry 321 n.
decline
inferiority 35 n.
decrease 37 n.vb.
oldness 127 n.
weakness 163 n.
be weak 163 vb.
be oblique 220 vb.
regression 286 n.
recede 290 vb.
descent 309 n.
descend 309 vb.
parse 564 vb.
reject 607 vb.
deterioration 655 n.
deteriorate 655 vb.
not use 674 vb.
adversity 731 n.
refuse 760 vb.
declining years
old age 131 n.
declivity
incline 220 n.
descent 309 n.
decoction
draught 301 n.
solution 337 n.
heating 381 n.
medicine 658 n.
decode
decipher 520 vb.
decoder
interpreter 520 n.
decollate
execute 963 vb.
décolleté
bareness 229 n.
decolorant
bleacher 426 n.
decolorize, decolorise
decolorize 426 vb.
whiten 427 vb.
decomposable
decomposable 51 adj.
ephemeral 114 adj.
decompose
simplify 44 vb.
disunite 46 vb.
decompose 51 vb.
disperse 75 vb.
perish 361 vb.
be unclean 649 vb.
deteriorate 655 Vb. vb.
decomposition
noncoherence 49 n.
deconsecrate
depose 752 vb.
paganize 974 vb.
laicize 987 vb.
deconsecrated
profane 980 adj.
deconstruction
interpretation 520 n.
decontaminate
purify 648 vb.
decontrol
revert 148 vb.
liberate 746 vb.
permit 756 vb.
nonretention 779 n.
decor
spectacle 445 n.
stage set 594 n.
decorate
transform 147 vb.
coat 226 vb.
exaggerate 546 vb.
ornament 574 vb.
make better 654 vb.
beautify 841 vb.
decorate 844 vb.
dignify 866 vb.
Decorated
undulatory 251 adj.
ornamental 844 adj.
churchlike 990 adj.
decoration
decoration 729 n.
badge of rank 743 n.
ornamentation 844 n.
honours 866 n.
reward 962 n.
(See **decorate** *)*
decorative
painted 553 adj.
ornamental 844 adj.
decorator
alterer 143 n.
mender 656 n.
artisan 686 n.
decorous
fit 24 adj.
orderly 60 adj.
well-bred 848 adj.
pure 950 adj.
decorticate
uncover 229 vb.
decorum
good taste 846 n.
etiquette 848 n.
decoy
attraction 291 n.
ambush 527 n.
trap 542 n.
ensnare 542 vb.
trickster 545 n.
incentive 612 n.
decrease
decrease 37 n.vb.
subtract 39 vb.
be weak 163 vb.
unproductiveness 172 n.
become small 198 vb.
waste 634 vb.
scarcity 636 n.
deterioration 655 n.
loss 772 n.
decreasing
lesser 35 adj.
few 105 adj.
decreasingly
diminuendo 37 adv.
decree
judgment 480 n.
publication 528 n.
predetermination 608 n.
precept 693 n.
decree 737 n.vb.
impose a duty 917 vb.
legislation 953 n.
decree absolute
divorce 896 n.
decree nisi
divorce 896 n.
decrement
decrease 37 n.
subtraction 39 n.
decrement 42 n.
deficit 55 n.

contraction 198 n.
shortfall 307 n.
waste 634 n.
loss 772 n.
discount 810 n.
decrepit
ageing 131 adj.
weak 163 adj.
unhealthy 651 adj.
dilapidated 655 adj.
decried
disapproved 924 adj.
decry
hold cheap 922 vb.
detract 926 vb.
decumbent
supine 216 adj.
dedicate
offer 759 vb.
give 781 vb.
dignify 866 vb.
sanctify 979 vb.
offer worship 981 vb.
— to
use 673 vb.
honour 866 vb.
dedicated
willing 597 adj.
resolute 599 adj.
habituated 610 adj.
obedient 739 adj.
philanthropic 901 adj.
disinterested 931 adj.
dedication
edition 589 n.
offering 781 n.
deduce
assume 471 vb.
reason 475 vb.
demonstrate 478 vb.
judge 480 vb.
interpret 520 vb.
deduct
subtract 39 vb.
disunite 46 vb.
take 786 vb.
discount 810 vb.
deduction
diminution 37 n.
subtraction 39 n.
decrement 42 n.
reasoning 475 n.
discount 810 n.
deductive
rational 475 adj.
deed
affairs 154 n.
deed 676 n.
conduct 688 n.
title deed 767 n.
prowess 855 n.
deejay
broadcaster 531 n.
deem
opine 485 vb.
deep
spacious 183 adj.
low 210 adj.
deep 211 adj.
ocean 343 n.
loud 400 adj.
hoarse 407 adj.
wise 498 adj.
inexpressible 517 adj.
latent 523 adj.
unclear 568 adj.
felt 818 adj.
infernal 972 adj.
deep-coloured
florid 425 adj.
deep down
intrinsic 5 adj.
inside 224 adv.
deepen
augment 36 vb.
enlarge 197 vb.
be deep 211 vb.
blacken 428 vb.
aggravate 832 vb.
deep-freeze
refrigerate 382 vb.
refrigerator 384 n.
storage 632 n.
preservation 666 n.
deep-fry
cook 301 vb.
deep in
attentive 455 adj.
planning 623 adj.
deep-laid
matured 669 adj.
well-made 694 adj.
cunning 698 adj.
deep litter
stock farm 369 n.
deep-rooted
intrinsic 5 adj.
lasting 113 adj.
fixed 153 adj.
strong 162 adj.
deep 211 adj.
remembered 505 adj.
habitual 610 adj.
with affections 817 adj.
deep-sea
deep 211 adj.
seafaring 269 adj.
ocean 343 n.
deep-seated
intrinsic 5 adj.
lasting 113 adj.
fixed 153 adj.
deep 211 adj.
interior 224 adj.
remembered 505 adj.
habitual 610 adj.
felt 818 adj.
deep structure
meaning 514 n.
phrase 563 n.
deer
speeder 277 n.
mammal 365 n.
deerstalker
headgear 228 n.
hunter 619 n.
deface
destroy 165 vb.
deform 244 vb.
obliterate 550 vb.
make useless 641 vb.
impair 655 vb.
make ugly 842 vb.
blemish 845 vb.
defalcate
be dishonest 930 vb.
defalcation
deficit 55 n.
shortfall 307 n.
nonpayment 805 n.
defamation
detraction 926 n.
defamatory
disapproving 924 adj.
detracting 926 adj.
accusing 928 adj.
defame
cause doubt 486 vb.
shame 867 vb.
dispraise 924 vb.
defame 926 vb.
accuse 928 vb.
default
deficit 55 n.
shortfall 307 n.
negligence 458 n.
not suffice 636 vb.
nonpayment 805 n.
fail in duty 918 vb.
defeasance
abrogation 752 n.
defeat
ruin 165 n.
outdo 306 vb.
puzzle 474 vb.
confute 479 vb.
defeat 727 vb.
defeat 728 n.
defeated
inferior 35 adj.
defeated 728 adj.
dejected 834 adj.
defeated, the
loser 728 n.
defeatism
overestimation 482 n.
inaction 677 n.
dejection 834 n.
hopelessness 853 n.
nervousness 854 n.
cowardice 856 n.
defeatist
alarmist 854 n.
coward 856 n.
misanthrope 902 n.
defecation
defecation 302 n.
latrine 649 n.
defect
inferiority 35 n.
deficit 55 n.
render few 105 vb.
weakness 163 n.
shortfall 307 n.
apostatize 603 vb.
evil 616 n.
insufficiency 636 n.
defect 647 n.
blemish 845 n.
vice 934 n.
defection
tergiversation 603 n.
relinquishment 621 n.
disobedience 738 n.
revolt 738 n.
undutifulness 918 n.
perfidy 930 n.
defective
incomplete 55 adj.
deformed 246 adj.
insane 503 adj.
imperfect 647 adj.
blemished 845 adj.
defence
counteraction 182 n.
rejoinder 460 n.
counterevidence 467 n.
argument 475 n.
pretext 614 n.
avoidance 620 n.
plot 623 n.
protection 660 n.
hindrance 702 n.
defence 713 n.
warfare 718 n.
arms 723 n.
vindication 927 n.
legal trial 959 n.
defenceless
defenceless 161 adj.
weak 163 adj.
vulnerable 661 adj.
defence mechanism
avoidance 620 n.
fear 854 n.
defences
earthwork 253 n.
protection 660 n.
obstacle 702 n.
defences 713 n.
defend
argue 475 vb.
safeguard 660 vb.
patronize 703 vb.
defend 713 vb.
wage war 718 vb.
defendant
respondent 460 n.
prisoner 750 n.
vindicator 927 n.
accused person 928 n.
litigant 959 n.
defender
protector 660 n.
patron 707 n.
defender 713 n.

keeper 749 n.
vindicator 927 n.
defenestration
lowering 311 n.
defensible
invulnerable 660 adj.
defended 713 adj.
vindicable 927 adj.
defensible space
territory 184 n.
refuge 662 n.
defensive
hindering 702 adj.
defending 713 adj.
nervous 854 adj.
defer
put off 136 vb.
not complete 726 vb.
— to
acquiesce 488 vb.
(See **deference** *)*
deference
submission 721 n.
loyalty 739 n.
obedience 739 n.
courtesy 884 n.
respect 920 n.
deferential
servile 879 adj.
respectful 920 adj.
deferment
delay 136 n.
nonpayment 805 n.
defiance
dissent 489 n.
affirmation 532 n.
negation 533 n.
gesture 547 n.
opposition 704 n.
dissension 709 n.
defiance 711 n.
disobedience 738 n.
refusal 760 n.
courage 855 n.
boast 877 n.
insolence 878 n.
defiant
unconformable 84 adj.
undisguised 522 adj.
deficiency
inferiority 35 n.
incompleteness 55 n.
insufficiency 636 n.
defect 647 n.
imperfection 647 n.
noncompletion 726 n.
vice 934 n.
deficiency disease
disease 651 n.
deficient
small 33 adj.
deficient 307 adj.
unintelligent 499 adj.
(See **deficiency** *)*
deficit
deficit 55 n.
shortfall 307 n.
insufficiency 636 n.
noncompletion 726 n.
debt 803 n.
deficit finance
finance 797 n.
prodigality 815 n.
defile
gap 201 n.
narrowness 206 n.
walk 267 vb.
access 624 n.
make unclean 649 vb.
impair 655 vb.
shame 867 vb.
debauch 951 vb.
be impious 980 vb.
defilement
uncleanness 649 n.
define
arrange 62 vb.
specify 80 vb.
limit 236 vb.
interpret 520 vb.
name 561 vb.
definite
definite 80 adj.
limited 236 adj.
obvious 443 adj.
positive 473 adj.
accurate 494 adj.
intelligible 516 adj.
manifest 522 adj.
informative 524 adj.
assertive 532 adj.
perspicuous 567 adj.
definitely
positively 32 adv.
certainly 473 adv.
definition
limit 236 n.
visibility 443 n.
interpretation 520 n.
perspicuity 567 n.
definitive
ending 69 adj.
definite 80 adj.
interpretive 520 adj.
deflate
abate 37 vb.
disable 161 vb.
make smaller 198 vb.
abase 311 vb.
lower 311 vb.
underestimate 483 vb.
ridicule 851 vb.
shame 867 vb.
humiliate 872 vb.
detract 926 vb.
deflation
decrease 37 n.
contraction 198 n.
finance 797 n.
cheapness 812 n.
deflationary
monetary 797 adj.
deflect
make oblique 220 vb.
make curved 248 vb.
deflect 282 vb.
repel 292 vb.
dissuade 613 vb.
avoid 620 vb.
parry 713 vb.
deflection
curvature 248 n.
deviation 282 n.
deflower
unite with 45 vb.
debauch 951 vb.
defoliant
poison 659 n.
defoliate
lay waste 165 vb.
defoliation
unproductiveness 172 n.
deforest
lay waste 165 vb.
make sterile 172 vb.
deform
force 176 vb.
deform 244 vb.
distort 246 vb.
misrepresent 552 vb.
impair 655 vb.
make ugly 842 vb.
blemish 845 vb.
deformed
abnormal 84 adj.
crippled 163 adj.
imperfect 647 adj.
deformity
amorphism 244 n.
deformity 246 n.
camber 253 n.
(See **deform** *)*
defraud
deceive 542 vb.
misuse 675 vb.
fleece 786 vb.
defraud 788 vb.
be dishonest 930 vb.
defrauder
trickster 545 n.
defrauder 789 n.
defrayment
payment 804 n.
defrock
shame 867 vb.
defrocked
unentitled 916 adj.
defrost
heat 381 vb.
deft
skilful 694 adj.
defumigate
have no smell 395 vb.
defunct
extinct 2 adj.
dead 361 adj.
corpse 363 n.
unwonted 611 adj.
defy
dissent 489 vb.
affirm 532 vb.
negate 533 vb.
be resolute 599 vb.
face danger 661 vb.
oppose 704 vb.
defy 711 vb.
resist 715 vb.
disobey 738 vb.
be free 744 vb.
be courageous 855 vb.
boast 877 vb.
be insolent 878 vb.
— authority
please oneself 734 vb.
— gravity
ascend 308 vb.
be light 323 vb.
— nature
be impossible 470 vb.
dégagé(e)
unconfined 744 adj.
well-bred 848 adj.
degauss
counteract 182 vb.
degeneracy
deterioration 655 n.
wickedness 934 n.
degenerate
decrease 37 vb.
changed person 147 n.
be turned to 147 vb.
deteriorated 655 adj.
deteriorate 655 vb.
relapse 657 vb.
vicious 934 adj.
cad 938 n.
sensualist 944 n.
degenerative
harmful 645 adj.
diseased 651 adj.
degradation
diminution 37 n.
deposal 752 n.
disrepute 867 n.
wickedness 934 n.
degrade
abate 37 vb.
impair 655 vb.
pervert 655 vb.
depose 752 vb.
shame 867 vb.
not respect 921 vb.
hold cheap 922 vb.
defame 926 vb.
punish 963 vb.
degree
relativeness 9 n.
degree 27 n.
series 71 n.
situation 186 n.

angular measure 247 n.
thermometry 379 n.
measurement 465 n.
importance 638 n.
honours 866 n.
prestige 866 n.
nobility 868 n.
degree-holder
scholar 492 n.
degree of latitude
long measure 203 n.
degree of longitude
long measure 203 n.
dehumanize, dehumanise
pervert 655 vb.
make wicked 934 vb.
dehumanized
cruel 898 adj.
dehumidify
dry 342 vb.
dehydrate
make smaller 198 vb.
dry 342 vb.
preserve 666 vb.
deice
heat 381 vb.
deification
dignification 866 n.
heaven 971 n.
deification 982 n.
deified
godlike 965 adj.
mythological 966 adj.
deify
dignify 866 vb.
worship 981 vb.
idolatrize 982 vb.
deign
consent 758 vb.
deism
deism 973 n.
religion 973 n.
deist
religionist 973 n.
deity
divineness 965 n.
deity 966 n.
idol 982 n.
Deity, the
cause 156 n.
the Deity 965 n.
déjà vu
remembrance 505 n.
bore 838 n.
psychics 984 n.
dejected
disappointed 509 adj.
unhappy 825 adj.
discontented 829 adj.
dejected 834 adj.
lamenting 836 adj.
hopeless 853 adj.
dejection
dejection 834 n.
de jure
due 915 adj.
duly 915 adv.
legal 953 adj.
legally 953 adv.
dekko
inspection 438 n.
delay
protraction 113 n.
delay 136 n.
put off 136 vb.
lull 145 n.
slowness 278 n.
unwillingness 598 n.
be irresolute 601 vb.
inaction 677 n.
be inactive 679 vb.
caution 858 n.
delayed
late 136 adj.
hindered 702 adj.
delaying action
avoidance 620 n.
delectable
savoury 390 adj.
pleasurable 826 adj.
delectation
enjoyment 824 n.
delegate
agent 686 n.
councillor 692 n.
mediator 720 n.
commission 751 vb.
delegate 754 n.
assign 780 vb.
delegation
commission 751 n.
delete
subtract 39 vb.
destroy 165 vb.
obliterate 550 vb.
deleterious
harmful 645 adj.
delft
pottery 381 n.
deliberate
slow 278 adj.
predetermined 608 adj.
intended 617 adj.
leisurely 681 adj.
consult 691 vb.
inexcitable 823 adj.
cautious 858 adj.
deliberation
slowness 278 n.
meditation 449 n.
advice 691 n.
caution 858 n.
delicacies
food 301 n.
delicacy
weakness 163 n.
touch 378 n.
savouriness 390 n.
discrimination 463 n.
ill health 651 n.
skill 694 n.
beauty 841 n.
good taste 846 n.
fastidiousness 862 n.
purity 950 n.
delicate
insubstantial 4 adj.
flimsy 163 adj.
brittle 330 adj.
textural 331 adj.
soft-hued 425 adj.
accurate 494 adj.
difficult 700 adj.
pleasurable 826 adj.
delicate situation
predicament 700 n.
delicatessen
food 301 n.
delicious
edible 301 adj.
pleasant 376 adj.
savoury 390 adj.
sweet 392 adj.
super 644 adj.
pleasurable 826 adj.
delight
pleasure 376 n.
excite 821 vb.
joy 824 n.
delight 826 vb.
amusement 837 n.
delighted
assenting 488 adj.
willing 597 adj.
pleased 824 adj.
jubilant 833 adj.
delightful
pleasant 376 adj.
pleasurable 826 adj.
Delilah
loose woman 952 n.
delimit
limit 236 vb.
mark 547 vb.
apportion 783 vb.
delineate
outline 233 vb.
represent 551 vb.
describe 590 vb.
delineator
artist 556 n.
narrator 590 n.
delinquency
disobedience 738 n.
wickedness 934 n.
guilt 936 n.
delinquent
troublemaker 663 n.
low fellow 869 n.
offender 904 n.
deliquesce
liquefy 337 vb.
delirious
frenzied 503 adj.
diseased 651 adj.
fervent 818 adj.
excited 821 adj.
excitable 822 adj.
delirium
frenzy 503 n.
fantasy 513 n.
lack of meaning 515 n.
illness 651 n.
excitable state 822 n.
delirium tremens
alcoholism 949 n.
deliver
transfer 272 vb.
propel 287 vb.
affirm 532 vb.
provide 633 vb.
restore 656 vb.
preserve 666 vb.
deliver 668 vb.
disencumber 701 vb.
aid 703 vb.
liberate 746 vb.
assign 780 vb.
give 781 vb.
restitute 787 vb.
relieve 831 vb.
— the goods
provide 633 vb.
be expedient 642 vb.
carry out 725 vb.
deliverance
extraction 304 n.
safety 660 n.
escape 667 n.
aid 703 n.
(See **deliver** *)*
deliverer
preserver 666 n.
defender 713 n.
benefactor 903 n.
delivery
obstetrics 167 n.
transference 272 n.
voice 577 n.
speech 579 n.
provision 633 n.
deliverance 668 n.
conduct 688 n.
transfer 780 n.
dell
valley 255 n.
delousing
cleansing 648 n.
delta
land 344 n.
plain 348 n.
delude
deceive 542 vb.
— oneself
err 495 vb.
hope 852 vb.
deluge
crowd 74 n.
drench 341 vb.
rain 350 n.
waterfall 350 n.
superabound 637 vb.
delusion
error 495 n.
fantasy 513 n.

deception 542 n.
delusions
psychopathy 503 n.
de luxe
comfortable 376 adj.
ostentatious 875 adj.
delve
make concave 255 vb.
cultivate 370 vb.
— into
enquire 459 vb.
demagnetize
counteract 182 vb.
demagogue
speaker 579 n.
leader 690 n.
agitator 738 n.
demagogy
government 733 n.
demand
enquire 459 vb.
necessitate 596 vb.
requirement 627 n.
require 627 vb.
demand 737 n.vb.
request 761 n.vb.
desire 859 vb.
— one's rights
claim 915 vb.
— with menaces
threaten 900 vb.
demanding
fatiguing 684 adj.
difficult 700 adj.
fastidious 862 adj.
demarcate
limit 236 vb.
mark 547 vb.
apportion 783 vb.
dematerialize, dematerialise
pass away 2 vb.
disembody 320 vb.
disappear 446 vb.
practise occultism 984 vb.
demeaning
degrading 867 adj.
demean oneself
behave 688 vb.
demean oneself 867 vb.
be humble 872 vb.
be servile 879 vb.
demeanour
mien 445 n.
gesture 547 n.
conduct 688 n.
demented
crazy 503 adj.
insane 503 adj.
démenti
negation 533 n.
dementia
insanity 503 n.
demerit
undueness 916 n.
vice 934 n.
demesne
farm 370 n.
lands 777 n.
demi-
bisected 92 adj.
demigod
paragon 646 n.
deity 966 n.
demigod 967 n.
demijohn
vessel 194 n.
demilitarize, demilitarise
make peace 719 vb.
demi-monde
lower classes 869 n.
wickedness 934 n.
prostitute 952 n.
demise
decease 361 n.
transfer 780 n.
bequeath 780 vb.
lease 784 vb.
demission
resignation 753 n.
Demiurge
the Deity 965 n.
demobilization, demobilisation
dispersion 75 n.
peace 717 n.
pacification 719 n.
liberation 746 n.
democracy
nation 371 n.
government 733 n.
commonalty 869 n.
democrat
political party 708 n.
commoner 869 n.
democratic
equal 28 adj.
governmental 733 adj.
démodé
antiquated 127 adj.
demography
statistics 86 n.
anthropology 371 n.
demolish
break 46 vb.
revolutionize 149 vb.
demolish 165 vb.
force 176 vb.
fell 311 vb.
confute 479 vb.
obliterate 550 vb.
demolition
destruction 165 n.
impairment 655 n.
demon
violent creature 176 n.
badness 645 n.
monster 938 n.
devil 969 n.
demon 970 n.
mythical being 970 n.
demonetize, demonetise
demonetize 797 vb.
demonetized
monetary 797 adj.
demoniac, demoniacal
cruel 898 adj.
diabolic 969 adj.
demoniac possession
spell 983 n.
demonic, demonical
diabolic 969 adj.
fairylike 970 adj.
demonolatry
diabolism 969 n.
idolatry 982 n.
demonstrable
certain 473 adj.
demonstrated 478 adj.
necessary 596 adj.
demonstrate
demonstrate 478 vb.
interpret 520 vb.
show 522 vb.
be expert 694 vb.
defy 711 vb.
revolt 738 vb.
deprecate 762 vb.
show feeling 818 vb.
demonstrated
demonstrated 478 adj.
true 494 adj.
demonstration
assemblage 74 n.
evidence 466 n.
reasons 475 n.
(See **demonstrate** *)*
demonstrative
demonstrating 478 adj.
indicating 547 adj.
with affections 817 adj.
caressing 889 adj.
demonstrativeness
feeling 818 n.
ostentation 875 n.
demonstrator
guide 520 n.
exhibitor 522 n.
teacher 537 n.
agitator 738 n.
revolter 738 n.
demoralize, demoralise
impair 655 vb.
frighten 854 vb.
demoralized
impotent 161 adj.
fearing 854 adj.
demos
nation 371 n.
commonalty 869 n.
demote
depose 752 vb.
shame 867 vb.
punish 963 vb.
demotic
linguistic 557 adj.
written 586 adj.
demulcent
moderator 177 n.
lenitive 177 adj.
remedial 658 adj.
demur
qualification 468 n.
argue 475 vb.
doubt 486 vb.
dissent 489 n.vb.
negate 533 vb.
be unwilling 598 vb.
resist 715 vb.
deprecate 762 vb.
disapprove 924 vb.
demure
inexcitable 823 adj.
serious 834 adj.
affected 850 adj.
modest 874 adj.
demurrer
dissent 489 n.
demythologization, demythologisation
interpretation 520 n.
theology 973 n.
den
dwelling 192 n.
retreat 192 n.
chamber 194 n.
hiding-place 527 n.
sink 649 n.
refuge 662 n.
seclusion 883 n.
denationalize, denationalise
derange 63 vb.
pervert 655 vb.
appropriate 786 vb.
disentitle 916 vb.
denaturalize, denaturalise
transform 147 vb.
pervert 655 vb.
disentitle 916 vb.
denature
modify 143 vb.
weaken 163 vb.
impair 655 vb.
pervert 655 vb.
dendrochronology
chronology 117 n.
dendrology
forestry 366 n.
botany 368 n.
dene
plain 348 n.
denial
confutation 479 n.
unbelief 486 n.
dissent 489 n.
negation 533 n.
recantation 603 n.
rejection 607 n.
opposition 704 n.
refusal 760 n.

denier
fibre 208 n.
texture 331 n.
denigrate
not respect 921 vb.
defame 926 vb.
denim
textile 222 n.
denims
trousers 228 n.
denizen
dweller 191 n.
denomination
classification 77 n.
nomenclature 561 n.
party 708 n.
denominational
sectional 708 adj.
Protestant 976 adj.
denominator
numerical element 85 n.
denotation
connotation 514 n.
denote
specify 80 vb.
mean 514 vb.
indicate 547 vb.
represent 551 vb.
denouement
end 69 n.
effect 157 n.
disclosure 526 n.
narrative 590 n.
completion 725 n.
denounce
inform 524 vb.
proclaim 528 vb.
satirize 851 vb.
hate 888 vb.
curse 899 vb.
dispraise 924 vb.
defame 926 vb.
accuse 928 vb.
de novo
initially 68 adv.
again 106 adv.
dense
firm 45 adj.
assembled 74 adj.
multitudinous 104 adj.
unyielding 162 adj.
contracted 198 adj.
thick 205 adj.
closed 264 adj.
dense 324 adj.
ignorant 491 adj.
uninstructed 491 adj.
unintelligent 499 adj.
density
materiality 319 n.
density 324 n.
opacity 423 n.
dent
concavity 255 n.
notch 260 n.vb.
knock 279 n.
lowering 311 n.
dental
toothed 256 adj.
speech sound 398 n.
dentate
notched 260 adj.
dentifrice
cleanser 648 n.
dentist
doctor 658 n.
denude
subtract 39 vb.
disunite 46 vb.
uncover 229 vb.
disclose 526 vb.
deprive 786 vb.
denuded
weakened 163 adj.
losing 772 adj.
denunciation
confutation 479 n.
satire 851 n.
malediction 899 n.
accusation 928 n.
denunciatory
maledictory 899 adj.
disapproving 924 adj.
deny
be contrary 14 vb.
exclude 57 vb.
confute 479 vb.
disbelieve 486 vb.
disappoint 509 vb.
negate 533 vb.
recant 603 vb.
reject 607 vb.
avoid 620 vb.
abrogate 752 vb.
refuse 760 vb.
— oneself
avoid 620 vb.
relinquish 621 vb.
be temperate 942 vb.
— the possibility
negate 533 vb.
deodorant
inodorousness 395 n.
cleanser 648 n.
cosmetic 843 n.
deodorize, deodorise
have no smell 395 vb.
purify 648 vb.
deontology
morals 917 n.
Deo volente
possibly 469 adv.
divinely 965 adv.
depart
go away 190 vb.
travel 267 vb.
recede 290 vb.
depart 296 vb.
die 361 vb.
disappear 446 vb.
— from
differ 15 vb.
department
subdivision 53 n.
classification 77 n.
district 184 n.
function 622 n.
departmentalized, departmentalised
fragmentary 53 adj.
department store
shop 796 n.
departure
start 68 n.
deviation 282 n.
departure 296 n.
egress 298 n.
ascent 308 n.
resignation 753 n.
(See **depart** *)*
depend
depend 157 vb.
be possible 469 vb.
be uncertain 474 vb.
— on
be certain 473 vb.
believe 485 vb.
be subject 745 vb.
dependable
willing 597 adj.
observant 768 adj.
trustworthy 929 adj.
dependant
inferior 35 n.
follower 284 n.
encumbrance 702 n.
auxiliary 707 n.
dependant 742 n.
recipient 782 n.
dependence
subjection 745 n.
nonownership 774 n.
dependency
territory 184 n.
political organization 733 n.
subject 742 n.
lands 777 n.
dependent
inferior 35 adj.
subject 745 adj.
not owning 774 adj.
servile 879 adj.
dependent on
caused 157 adj.
liable 180 adj.
depending on
accordingly 8 adv.
uncertain 474 adj.
depict
represent 551 vb.
describe 590 vb.
depilation
uncovering 229 n.
depilatory
stripper 229 n.
cosmetic 843 n.
deplete
waste 634 vb.
make insufficient 636 vb.
deplorable
bad 645 adj.
distressing 827 adj.
regretted 830 adj.
deplore
regret 830 vb.
lament 836 vb.
disapprove 924 vb.
deploy
place 187 vb.
expand 197 vb.
flank 239 vb.
open 263 vb.
diverge 294 vb.
dispose of 673 vb.
deplume
uncover 229 vb.
shame 867 vb.
deponent
witness 466 n.
depopulate
lay waste 165 vb.
empty 300 vb.
deport
exclude 57 vb.
transpose 272 vb.
eject 300 vb.
deportee
wanderer 268 n.
ejection 300 n.
outcast 883 n.
deportment
mien 445 n.
conduct 688 n.
deposal
deposal 752 n.
depose
testify 466 vb.
unthrone 734 vb.
depose 752 vb.
disentitle 916 vb.
deposed
powerless 161 adj.
unentitled 916 adj.
deposit
leavings 41 n.
part 53 n.
place 187 vb.
thing transferred 272 n.
solid body 324 n.
be dense 324 vb.
soil 344 n.
store 632 n.vb.
dirt 649 n.
security 767 n.
payment 804 n.
deposition
location 187 n.
testimony 466 n.
oath 532 n.
deposal 752 n.
depositor
creditor 802 n.
depository
storage 632 n.
treasury 799 n.
depot
station 187 n.

storage 632 n.
emporium 796 n.
deprave
pervert 655 vb.
depraved
bad 645 adj.
deteriorated 655 adj.
vicious 934 adj.
lecherous 951 adj.
depravity
wickedness 934 n.
deprecate
oppose 704 vb.
resist 715 vb.
deprecate 762 vb.
be discontented 829 vb.
regret 830 vb.
disapprove 924 vb.
deprecation
dissent 489 n.
unwillingness 598 n.
dissuasion 613 n.
warning 664 n.
deprecation 762 n.
modesty 874 n.
deprecatory
deprecatory 762 adj.
depreciate
abate 37 vb.
underestimate 483 vb.
demonetize 797 vb.
discount 810 vb.
be cheap 812 vb.
dispraise 924 vb.
detract 926 vb.
depreciation
decrement 42 n.
misinterpretation 521 n.
loss 772 n.
depredations
havoc 165 n.
spoliation 788 n.
depredator
robber 789 n.
depress
make concave 255 vb.
lower 311 vb.
trouble 827 vb.
cause discontent 829 vb.
depress 834 vb.
depressed state
psychopathy 503 n.
depressing
unpleasant 827 adj.
cheerless 834 adj.
tedious 838 adj.
depression
lowness 210 n.
depth 211 n.
concavity 255 n.
valley 255 n.
lowering 311 n.
weather 340 n.
deterioration 655 n.
adversity 731 n.
poverty 801 n.
melancholy 834 n.
deprivation
separation 46 n.
absence 190 n.
ejection 300 n.
deposal 752 n.
loss 772 n.
nonownership 774 n.
expropriation 786 n.
loss of right 916 n.
deprive
weaken 163 vb.
make insufficient 636 vb.
deprive 786 vb.
impoverish 801 vb.
not pay 805 vb.
disentitle 916 vb.
punish 963 vb.
— oneself
refuse 760 vb.
deprived
necessitous 627 adj.
de profundis
tearfully 836 adv.
depth
greatness 32 n.
measure 183 n.
size 195 n.
depth 211 n.
interiority 224 n.
metrology 465 n.
wisdom 498 n.
imperspicuity 568 n.
depth charge
bomb 723 n.
depths
rear 238 n.
darkness 418 n.
deputation
commission 751 n.
depute
commission 751 vb.
deputize, deputise
substitute 150 vb.
deputize 755 vb.
deputy
inferior 35 n.
substitute 150 n.
agent 686 n.
councillor 692 n.
consignee 754 n.
deputy 755 n.
deracinate
destroy 165 vb.
eject 300 vb.
extract 304 vb.
déraciné(e)
foreigner 59 n.
displaced 188 adj.
wanderer 268 n.
derail
derange 63 vb.
displace 188 vb.
derange
derange 63 vb.
disperse 75 vb.
deform 244 vb.
intrude 297 vb.
agitate 318 vb.
distract 456 vb.
make mad 503 vb.
impair 655 vb.
hinder 702 vb.
trouble 827 vb.
deranged
insane 503 adj.
derangement
disorder 61 n.
(See **derange** *)*
deration
liberate 746 vb.
not retain 779 vb.
derby
headgear 228 n.
Derby day
contest 716 n.
festivity 837 n.
derelict
survivor 41 n.
disused 674 adj.
unpossessed 774 adj.
derelict 779 n.
not retained 779 adj.
outcast 883 n.
dereliction
relinquishment 621 n.
undutifulness 918 n.
guilty act 936 n.
derestrict
revert 148 vb.
restore 656 vb.
not retain 779 vb.
derestriction
laxity 734 n.
deride
reject 607 vb.
laugh 835 vb.
ridicule 851 vb.
not respect 921 vb.
despise 922 vb.
de rigueur
usual 610 adj.
obligatory 917 adj.
derision
unbelief 486 n.
laughter 835 n.
ridicule 851 n.
contempt 922 n.
derisive
laughing 835 adj.
funny 849 adj.
derisive 851 adj.
disrespectful 921 adj.
detracting 926 adj.
derisory
ridiculous 849 adj.
derivation
origin 68 n.
reversion 148 n.
source 156 n.
effect 157 n.
attribution 158 n.
connotation 514 n.
etymology 559 n.
derivative
imitative 20 adj.
numerical element 85 n.
caused 157 adj.
word 559 n.
dull 840 adj.
derive (from)
result 157 vb.
attribute 158 vb.
acquire 771 vb.
dermatitis
skin disease 651 n.
dermatology
medical art 658 n.
dermis
skin 226 n.
dernier cri
modernism 126 n.
fashion 848 n.
derogate
demean oneself 867 vb.
detract 926 vb.
derogatory
depreciating 483 adj.
degrading 867 adj.
detracting 926 adj.
derrick
lifter 310 n.
derrière
buttocks 238 n.
derring-do
courage 855 n.
prowess 855 n.
derris
poison 659 n.
Der Tag
aspiration 852 n.
derv
fuel 385 n.
dervish
ascetic 945 n.
religionist 973 n.
pietist 979 n.
worshipper 981 n.
desalinate
purify 648 vb.
desanctify
paganize 974 vb.
descant
tune 412 n.
sing 413 vb.
be diffuse 570 vb.
dissertate 591 vb.
hymn 981 n.
descend
land 295 vb.
descend 309 vb.
lower 311 vb.
plunge 313 vb.
— from
result 157 vb.
descendant
survivor 41 n.
successor 67 n.
descendant 170 n.
descendants
posteriority 120 n.

futurity 124 n.
descending order
decrease 37 n.
series 71 n.
contraction 198 n.
descent
consanguinity 11 n.
decrease 37 n.
sequence 65 n.
continuity 71 n.
posteriority 120 n.
source 156 n.
genealogy 169 n.
sonship 170 n.
presence 189 n.
depth 211 n.
incline 220 n.
motion 265 n.
descent 309 n.
plunge 313 n.
deterioration 655 n.
nobility 868 n.
theophany 965 n.
describe
communicate 524 vb.
represent 551 vb.
write 586 vb.
describe 590 vb.
— a circle
circle 314 vb.
description
assimilation 18 n.
indication 547 n.
representation 551 n.
literature 557 n.
name 561 n.
writing 586 n.
description 590 n.
descriptive
expressive 516 adj.
representing 551 adj.
descriptive 590 adj.
descry
see 438 vb.
detect 484 vb.
understand 516 vb.
desecrate
make unclean 649 vb.
impair 655 vb.
misuse 675 vb.
shame 867 vb.
be undue 916 vb.
not respect 921 vb.
be impious 980 vb.
desecrator
impious person 980 n.
desert
havoc 165 n.
desert 172 n.
unproductive 172 adj.
emptiness 190 n.
dryness 342 n.
plain 348 n.
tergiversate 603 vb.
run away 620 vb.
relinquish 621 vb.
not observe 769 vb.
be cowardly 856 vb.
seclusion 883 n.
fail in duty 918 vb.
deserted
alone 88 adj.
empty 190 adj.
neglected 458 adj.
secluded 883 adj.
deserter
tergiversator 603 n.
avoider 620 n.
coward 856 n.
undutifulness 918 n.
desertion
disobedience 738 n.
divorce 896 n.
perfidy 930 n.
(See **desert** *)*
deserts
conduct 688 n.
retaliation 714 n.
dueness 915 n.
reward 962 n.
deserve
be good 644 vb.
behave 688 vb.
deserve 915 vb.
be rewarded 962 vb.
deserved
just 913 adj.
due 915 adj.
deserving
excellent 644 adj.
approvable 923 adj.
déshabillé
informal dress 228 n.
uncovering 229 n.
desiccation
desiccation 342 n.
preservation 666 n.
desideratum
requirement 627 n.
desired object 859 n.
design
prototype 23 n.
composition 56 n.
production 164 n.
form 243 n.
representation 551 n.
picture 553 n.
intend 617 vb.
plan 623 n.vb.
undertaking 672 n.
pattern 844 n.
designate
specify 80 vb.
subsequent 120 adj.
future 124 adj.
mark 547 vb.
chosen 605 adj.
select 605 vb.
designation
classification 77 n.
name 561 n.
nomenclature 561 n.
designed
architectural 192 adj.
predetermined 608 adj.
intended 617 adj.
designer
producer 164 n.
artist 556 n.
stage manager 594 n.
planner 623 n.
designing
hypocritical 541 adj.
dishonest 930 adj.
designless
casual 159 adj.
designless 618 adj.
desirability
choice 605 n.
needfulness 627 n.
good policy 642 n.
desirable
advisable 642 adj.
contenting 828 adj.
desired 859 adj.
lovable 887 adj.
approvable 923 adj.
desire
attraction 291 n.
fantasy 513 n.
will 595 n.vb.
motive 612 n.
intention 617 n.
require 627 vb.
request 761 n.vb.
suffering 825 n.
desire 859 n.
desired object 859 n.
desire 859 vb.
love 887 n.
be in love 887 vb.
envy 912 n.vb.
desirous
willing 597 adj.
desiring 859 adj.
desist
discontinue 72 vb.
cease 145 vb.
not act 677 vb.
desk
cabinet 194 n.
stand 218 n.
classroom 539 n.
deskwork
study 536 n.
desolate
lay waste 165 vb.
unproductive 172 adj.
empty 190 adj.
empty 300 vb.
hopeless 853 adj.
friendless 883 adj.
secluded 883 adj.
desolation
havoc 165 n.
desert 172 n.
emptiness 190 n.
sorrow 825 n.
despair
not expect 508 vb.
be disappointed 509 vb.
sorrow 825 n.
be dejected 834 vb.
hopelessness 853 n.
despair 853 vb.
despaired of
dying 361 adj.
unpromising 853 adj.
impenitent 940 adj.
despair of, the
bad person 938 n.
despatch
(See **dispatch** *)*
desperado
violent creature 176 n.
murderer 362 n.
desperado 857 n.
ruffian 904 n.
desperate
consummate 32 adj.
furious 176 adj.
resolute 599 adj.
active 678 adj.
hopeless 853 adj.
unpromising 853 adj.
courageous 855 adj.
rash 857 adj.
desperation
resolution 599 n.
despicability
odium 888 n.
despicable
discreditable 867 adj.
disreputable 867 adj.
contemptible 922 adj.
heinous 934 adj.
despise
underestimate 483 vb.
gesticulate 547 vb.
be fastidious 862 vb.
be proud 871 vb.
be insolent 878 vb.
hate 888 vb.
not respect 921 vb.
despise 922 vb.
disapprove 924 vb.
despite
in defiance of 25 adv.
although 182 adv.
nevertheless 468 adv.
with difficulty 700 adv.
in opposition 704 adv.
despoil
lay waste 165 vb.
rob 788 vb.

despondent
unhappy 825 adj.
dejected 834 adj.
hopeless 853 adj.
despot
tyrant 735 n.
autocrat 741 n.
despotic
authoritarian 735 adj.
oppressive 735 adj.
lawless 954 adj.
despotism
despotism 733 n.
brute force 735 n.
dessert
dessert 301 n.
sweet thing 392 n.
dessertspoon
ladle 194 n.
destination
stopping place 145 n.
intention 617 n.
objective 617 n.
destined
future 124 adj.
impending 155 adj.
fated 596 adj.
destine for
intend 617 vb.
destiny
futurity 124 n.
destiny 155 n.
cause 156 n.
fate 596 n.
necessity 596 n.
predetermination 608 n.
destitute
wanderer 268 n.
necessitous 627 adj.
not owning 774 adj.
poor 801 adj.
destitution
poverty 801 n.
destroy
nullify 2 vb.
disunite 46 vb.
destroy 165 vb.
deform 244 vb.
kill 362 vb.
slaughter 362 vb.
confute 479 vb.
waste 634 vb.
impair 655 vb.
defeat 727 vb.
impoverish 801 vb.
destroyed, be
be defeated 728 vb.
destroyer
revolutionist 149 n.
destroyer 168 n.
violent creature 176 n.
flattener 216 n.
bane 659 n.
warship 722 n.
destroyer of reputations
defamer 926 n.
destruct
destroy 165 vb.
destruction
extinction 2 n.
decomposition 51 n.
disorder 61 n.
finality 69 n.
destruction 165 n.
outbreak 176 n.
slaughter 362 n.
waste 634 n.
destructive
destructive 165 adj.
violent 176 adj.
evil 616 adj.
wasteful 634 adj.
harmful 645 adj.
adverse 731 adj.
destructive criticism
estimate 480 n.
detraction 926 n.
destructor
furnace 383 n.
desuetude
desuetude 611 n.
nonuse 674 n.
desultoriness
inattention 456 n.
restlessness 678 n.
desultory
orderless 61 adj.
discontinuous 72 adj.
fitful 142 adj.
deviating 282 adj.
light-minded 456 adj.
detach
disunite 46 vb.
unstick 49 vb.
disperse 75 vb.
send 272 vb.
transpose 272 vb.
detached
unrelated 10 adj.
nonadhesive 49 adj.
architectural 192 adj.
neutral 625 adj.
independent 744 adj.
impassive 820 adj.
just 913 adj.
detachment
part 53 n.
armed force 722 n.
inexcitability 823 n.
detail
small quantity 33 n.
part 53 n.
specify 80 vb.
send 272 vb.
be diffuse 570 vb.
describe 590 vb.
trifle 639 n.
formation 722 n.
command 737 vb.
apportion 783 vb.
pattern 844 n.
detailed
complete 54 adj.
definite 80 adj.
diffuse 570 adj.
descriptive 590 adj.
laborious 682 adj.
details
particulars 80 n.
description 590 n.
detain
imprison 747 vb.
retain 778 vb.
detained
captive 750 adj.
detainee
prisoner 750 n.
detect
smell 394 vb.
see 438 vb.
detect 484 vb.
understand 516 vb.
disclose 526 vb.
detectable
visible 443 adj.
detection
police enquiry 459 n.
discovery 484 n.
knowledge 490 n.
detective
inquisitive person 453 n.
detective 459 n.
detector
detector 484 n.
détente
moderation 177 n.
concord 710 n.
pacification 719 n.
detention
delay 136 n.
hindrance 702 n.
detention 747 n.
retention 778 n.
penalty 963 n.
detention centre
school 539 n.
prison 748 n.
deter
cause doubt 486 vb.
dissuade 613 vb.
hinder 702 vb.
frighten 854 vb.
cause dislike 861 vb.
threaten 900 vb.
detergent
cleanser 648 n.
deteriorate
decompose 51 vb.
waste 634 vb.
deteriorate 655 vb.
impair 655 vb.
stop using 674 vb.
make ugly 842 vb.
(See **deterioration** *)*
deterioration
inferiority 35 n.
decrease 37 n.
old age 131 n.
change 143 n.
weakness 163 n.
ruin 165 n.
regression 286 n.
desuetude 611 n.
badness 645 n.
illness 651 n.
deterioration 655 n.
relapse 657 n.
inactivity 679 n.
loss 772 n.
aggravation 832 n.
wickedness 934 n.
determinant
cause 156 n.
determinate
definite 80 adj.
determination
will 595 n.
resolution 599 n.
obstinacy 602 n.
intention 617 n.
assiduity 678 n.
courage 855 n.
determine
arrange 62 vb.
terminate 69 vb.
specify 80 vb.
cause 156 vb.
will 595 vb.
be resolute 599 vb.
intend 617 vb.
determined
resolute 599 adj.
obstinate 602 adj.
courageous 855 adj.
determinism
philosophy 449 n.
necessity 596 n.
determinist
fatalist 596 n.
deterrence
dissuasion 613 n.
intimidation 854 n.
deterrent
counteraction 182 n.
dissuasion 613 n.
protection 660 n.
safeguard 662 n.
warning 664 n.
cautionary 664 adj.
defence 713 n.
retaliation 714 n.
weapon 723 n.
intimidation 854 n.
threat 900 n.
detest
dislike 861 vb.
hate 888 vb.
detestable
not nice 645 adj.
dethrone
unthrone 734 vb.
depose 752 vb.
disentitle 916 vb.
detonate
be violent 176 vb.
be loud 400 vb.
bang 402 vb.

detonator
lighter 385 n.
explosive 723 n.
detour
deviation 282 n.
route 624 n.
circuit 626 n.
detract (from)
subtract 39 vb.
underestimate 483 vb.
ridicule 851 vb.
hold cheap 922 vb.
detract 926 vb.
detraction
diminution 37 n.
underestimation 483 n.
detraction 926 n.
detribalize, detribalise
transform 147 vb.
pervert 655 vb.
disentitle 916 vb.
detriment
impairment 655 n.
detrimental
inexpedient 643 adj.
harmful 645 adj.
detritus
leavings 41 n.
accumulation 74 n.
powder 332 n.
de trop
superfluous 637 adj.
unwanted 860 adj.
deuce
draw 28 n.
duality 90 n.
deucedly
extremely 32 adv.
deus ex machina
dramaturgy 594 n.
aider 703 n.
patron 707 n.
theocracy 965 n.
devaluation
deterioration 655 n.
finance 797 n.
nonpayment 805 n.
devalue
make useless 641 vb.
demonetize 797 vb.
devastate
lay waste 165 vb.
devastation
havoc 165 n.
terror tactics 712 n.
develop
become 1 vb.
augment 36 vb.
grow 36 vb.
result 157 vb.
produce 164 vb.
urbanize 192 vb.
enlarge 197 vb.
progress 285 vb.
evolve 316 vb.
manifest 522 vb.
educate 534 vb.
photograph 551 vb.
get better 654 vb.
make better 654 vb.
development
adultness 134 n.
conversion 147 n.
growth 157 n.
production 164 n.
propagation 167 n.
expansion 197 n.
progression 285 n.
musical piece 412 n.
improvement 654 n.
deviant
nonconformist 84 n.
abnormal 84 adj.
deviate
differ 15 vb.
separate 46 vb.
vary 152 vb.
make oblique 220 vb.
deviate 282 vb.
diverge 294 vb.
disregard 458 vb.
be diffuse 570 vb.
avoid 620 vb.
circuit 626 vb.
deviation
irrelevance 10 n.
nonuniformity 17 n.
nonconformity 84 n.
statistics 86 n.
change 143 n.
displacement 188 n.
meandering 251 n.
deviation 282 n.
error 495 n.
tergiversation 603 n.
deviationist
nonconformist 84 n.
crank 504 n.
tergiversator 603 n.
revolter 738 n.
device
idea 451 n.
heraldry 547 n.
contrivance 623 n.
instrument 628 n.
means 629 n.
tool 630 n.
means of escape 667 n.
stratagem 698 n.
devil
violent creature 176 n.
cook 301 vb.
season 388 vb.
monster 938 n.
devil 969 n.
demon 970 n.
mythical being 970 n.
Devil, The
wickedness 934 n.
Satan 969 n.
devilish
damnable 645 adj.
cruel 898 adj.
wicked 934 adj.
diabolic 969 adj.
fairylike 970 adj.
infernal 972 adj.
devilishly
extremely 32 adv.
devil-may-care
designless 618 adj.
rash 857 adj.
impertinent 878 adj.
devilry
evil 616 n.
cruel act 898 n.
wickedness 934 n.
diabolism 969 n.
devil's advocate
sophist 477 n.
Devil's Island
prison camp 748 n.
devil's tattoo
roll 403 n.
tedium 838 n.
devil to pay
turmoil 61 n.
penalty 963 n.
devil worship
wickedness 934 n.
diabolism 969 n.
idolatry 982 n.
devious
deviating 282 adj.
circuitous 314 adj.
cunning 698 adj.
dishonest 930 adj.
devise
think 449 vb.
imagine 513 vb.
plan 623 vb.
be cunning 698 vb.
dower 777 vb.
bequeath 780 vb.
devitalize, devitalise
unman 161 vb.
weaken 163 vb.
devitrify
make opaque 423 vb.
devoid
empty 190 adj.
devolution
decomposition 51 n.
commission 751 n.
transfer 780 n.
devolve
assign 780 vb.
impose a duty 917 vb.
— on
change hands 780 vb.
be one's duty 917 vb.
devote (to)
use 673 vb.
give 781 vb.
be pious 979 vb.
— oneself to
undertake 672 vb.
be disinterested 931 vb.
devoted
resolute 599 adj.
obedient 739 adj.
loving 887 adj.
disinterested 931 adj.
pious 979 adj.
worshipping 981 adj.
devoted to
habituated 610 adj.
devotee
enthusiast 504 n.
habitué 610 n.
desirer 859 n.
sectarian 978 n.
pietist 979 n.
worshipper 981 n.
devotion
resolution 599 n.
loyalty 739 n.
love 887 n.
respect 920 n.
piety 979 n.
worship 981 n.
devotional
religious 973 adj.
devotional 981 adj.
de voto offering
oblation 981 n.
devour
consume 165 vb.
destroy 165 vb.
absorb 299 vb.
eat 301 vb.
give pain 377 vb.
waste 634 vb.
appropriate 786 vb.
fleece 786 vb.
gluttonize 947 vb.
devoured by
possessed 773 adj.
impressed 818 adj.
devout
religious 973 adj.
orthodox 976 adj.
pious 979 adj.
worshipping 981 adj.
devoutly
feelingly 818 adv.
dew
moisture 341 n.
dewfall
evening 129 n.
dewpond
lake 346 n.
dewy
new 126 adj.
matinal 128 adj.
humid 341 adj.
clean 648 adj.
dexter
heraldic 547 adj.
dexterity
skill 694 n.
dexterous, dextrous
dextral 241 adj.

skilful 694 adj.
dextral
dextrality 241 n.
handed 378 adj.
dextrose
sweet thing 392 n.
dharma
religion 973 n.
Dharma
religious faith 973 n.
dhobi
cleaner 648 n.
dhobi's itch
formication 378 n.
skin disease 651 n.
dhoti
loincloth 228 n.
dhow
sailing ship 275 n.
di-
dual 90 adj.
diabetes
disease 651 n.
diabetic
sick person 651 n.
diablerie
diabolism 969 n.
sorcery 983 n.
diabolic
wicked 934 adj.
diabolic 969 adj.
fairylike 970 adj.
infernal 972 adj.
idolatrous 982 adj.
sorcerous 983 adj.
diabolical
damnable 645 adj.
cruel 898 adj.
diabolism
wickedness 934 n.
diabolism 969 n.
antichristianity 974 n.
idolatry 982 n.
sorcery 983 n.
diabolo
plaything 837 n.
diachronic
retrospective 125 adj.
linguistic 557 adj.
diaconate
church office 985 n.
diacritical mark
punctuation 547 n.
diadem
regalia 743 n.
jewellery 844 n.
diaeresis
punctuation 547 n.
prosody 593 n.
diagnosis
character 5 n.
classification 77 n.
pathology 651 n.
medical art 658 n.
diagnostic
characteristic 5 adj.
distinctive 15 adj.
special 80 adj.
identification 547 n.
diagonal
dividing line 92 n.
oblique 220 adj.
directed 281 adj.
diagram
copy 22 n.
outline 233 n.
representation 551 n.
plan 623 n.
diagrammatic
indicating 547 adj.
representing 551 adj.
dial
timekeeper 117 n.
face 237 n.
communicate 524 vb.
signal 547 vb.
dialect
language 557 n.
dialect 560 n.
pronunciation 577 n.
speech defect 580 n.
dialectic(s)
interrogation 459 n.
argumentation 475 n.
reasoning 475 n.
rational 475 adj.
dialectical materialism
materiality 319 n.
philosophy 449 n.
dialectician
reasoner 475 n.
dialogue
interrogation 459 n.
answer 460 n.
argumentation 475 n.
interlocution 584 n.
dramaturgy 594 n.
dialysis
cleansing 648 n.
diamante
finery 844 n.
diameter
dividing line 92 n.
breadth 205 n.
diametrically opposite
contrary 14 adj.
opposite 240 adj.
diamond
angular figure 247 n.
hardness 326 n.
exceller 644 n.
gem 844 n.
diamond jubilee
anniversary 141 n.
celebration 876 n.
diamond-studded
rich 800 adj.
ostentatious 875 adj.
Diana
moon 321 n.
woman 373 n.
hunter 619 n.
spinster 895 n.
virgin 950 n.
Olympian deity 967 n.
diapason
loudness 400 n.
musical note 410 n.
diaper
loincloth 228 n.
pattern 844 n.
diaphanous
transparent 422 adj.
diaphragm
middle 70 n.
contraception 172 n.
partition 231 n.
musical instrument 414 n.
diapositive
photography 551 n.
diarist
chronologist 117 n.
chronicler 549 n.
author 589 n.
narrator 590 n.
diarrhoea
defecation 302 n.
digestive disorders 651 n.
diary
chronology 117 n.
reminder 505 n.
record 548 n.
reference book 589 n.
biography 590 n.
Diaspora
dispersion 75 n.
diastole
dilation 197 n.
diathermic
heating 381 adj.
diathesis
ill health 651 n.
diatonic scale
key 410 n.
diatribe
oration 579 n.
censure 924 n.
dibble
perforator 263 n.
farm tool 370 n.
cultivate 370 vb.
dice
cut 46 vb.
oracle 511 n.
gamble 618 vb.
gambling game 837 n.
— with death
face danger 661 vb.
be rash 857 vb.
dicer
gambler 618 n.
player 837 n.
dicer's oath
unreliability 474 n.
untruth 543 n.
dicey
casual 159 adj.
speculative 618 adj.
dangerous 661 adj.
dichotomy
disunion 46 n.
bisection 92 n.
dichromatic
variegated 437 adj.
dim-sighted 440 adj.
dick
detective 459 n.
dicker
bargain 791 vb.
Dick Turpin
robber 789 n.
dicky, dickey
seat 218 n.
garment 228 n.
unsafe 661 adj.
Dictaphone
hearing aid 415 n.
recording instrument 549 n.
dictate
speak 579 vb.
necessitate 596 vb.
direct 689 vb.
advise 691 vb.
dominate 733 vb.
rule 733 vb.
decree 737 n.
compel 740 vb.
dictation
teaching 534 n.
no choice 606 n.
command 737 n.
dictator
tyrant 735 n.
autocrat 741 n.
dictatorial
narrow-minded 481 adj.
volitional 595 adj.
directing 689 adj.
authoritative 733 adj.
authoritarian 735 adj.
commanding 737 adj.
compelling 740 adj.
insolent 878 adj.
dictatorship
directorship 689 n.
despotism 733 n.
brute force 735 n.
diction
meaning 514 n.
phrase 563 n.
style 566 n.
dictionary
word list 87 n.
dictionary 559 n.
reference book 589 n.
collection 632 n.
dictum
maxim 496 n.

affirmation 532 n.
speech 579 n.
didactic
educational 534 adj.
advising 691 adj.
diddle
deceive 542 vb.
defraud 788 vb.
diddled
gullible 544 adj.
diddler
trickster 545 n.
defrauder 789 n.
didicoi
wanderer 268 n.
die
mould 23 n.
end 69 vb.
die 361 vb.
printing 555 n.
gambling 618 n.
— away
shade off 27 vb.
decrease 37 vb.
cease 145 vb.
sound faint 401 vb.
— down
be quiescent 266 vb.
extinguish 382 vb.
— fighting
perish 361 vb.
stand firm 599 vb.
— for
desire 859 vb.
be in love 887 vb.
be disinterested 931 vb.
— in harness
perish 361 vb.
persevere 600 vb.
— in one's sins
be impenitent 940 vb.
— out
pass away 2 vb.
end 69 vb.
perish 361 vb.
— the death
perish 361 vb.
be punished 963 vb.
died out
extinct 2 adj.
past 125 adj.
diehard
stamina 600 n.
obstinate person 602 n.
malcontent 829 n.
diesel engine
locomotive 274 n.
machine 630 n.
diesel oil
propellant 287 n.
fuel 385 n.
Dies irae
obsequies 364 n.
dies non
neverness 109 n.
diet
make smaller 198 vb.
dieting 301 n.
therapy 658 n.
council 692 n.
be temperate 942 vb.
starve 946 vb.
dieter
abstainer 942 n.
dietician, dietitian
dieting 301 n.
doctor 658 n.
differ
differ 15 vb.
quarrel 709 vb.
difference
unrelatedness 10 n.
contrariety 14 n.
difference 15 n.
dissimilarity 19 n.
disagreement 25 n.
inequality 29 n.
remainder 41 n.
change 143 n.
divergence 294 n.
discrimination 463 n.
dissent 489 n.
dissension 709 n.
schism 978 n.
different
different 15 adj.
nonuniform 17 adj.
superior 34 adj.
extraneous 59 adj.
special 80 adj.
multiform 82 adj.
converted 147 adj.
changeful 152 adj.
differentiae
speciality 80 n.
differential
difference 15 n.
degree 27 n.
numerical element 85 n.
earnings 771 n.
differential calculus
mathematics 86 n.
differentiate
differentiate 15 vb.
set apart 46 vb.
specify 80 vb.
discriminate 463 vb.
difficult
impracticable 470 adj.
puzzling 517 adj.
unclear 568 adj.
laborious 682 adj.
difficult 700 adj.
hindering 702 adj.
disobedient 738 adj.
fastidious 862 adj.
ungracious 885 adj.
sullen 893 adj.
difficulty
complexity 61 n.
unintelligibility 517 n.
enigma 530 n.
imperspicuity 568 n.
difficulty 700 n.
obstacle 702 n.
adversity 731 n.
suffering 825 n.
diffidence
nervousness 854 n.
modesty 874 n.
diffident
doubting 474 adj.
diffraction
dispersion 75 n.
reflection 417 n.
diffuse
disperse 75 vb.
generalize 79 vb.
publish 528 vb.
diffuse 570 adj.
diffuseness
diffuseness 570 n.
loquacity 581 n.
diffusion
dispersion 75 n.
presence 189 n.
transference 272 n.
ingress 297 n.
information 524 n.
diffusive
prolix 570 adj.
dig
antiquity 125 n.
excavation 255 n.
make concave 255 vb.
knock 279 n.
cultivate 370 vb.
search 459 n.vb.
understand 516 vb.
work 682 vb.
reproach 924 n.
— a pit for
plot 623 vb.
be cunning 698 vb.
— for
search 459 vb.
pursue 619 vb.
— in
place oneself 187 vb.
stand firm 599 vb.
seek safety 660 vb.
defend 713 vb.
give battle 718 vb.
— one's nails in
retain 778 vb.
— one's toes/heels in
stay 144 vb.
stand firm 599 vb.
oppose 704 vb.
— out
make concave 255 vb.
extract 304 vb.
— up
extract 304 vb.
exhume 364 vb.
be curious 453 vb.
discover 484 vb.
— up the past
look back 125 vb.
retrospect 505 vb.
dig at
contempt 922 n.
calumny 926 n.
digest
arrangement 62 n.
class 62 vb.
modify 143 vb.
absorb 299 vb.
eat 301 vb.
meditate 449 vb.
be attentive 455 vb.
literature 557 n.
compendium 592 n.
knuckle under 721 vb.
be patient 823 vb.
digestible
edible 301 adj.
digestion
reception 299 n.
eating 301 n.
digestive
remedial 658 adj.
digger
excavator 255 n.
gardener 370 n.
Digger
agitator 738 n.
dig in the ribs
gesture 547 n.
digit
number 85 n.
feeler 378 n.
digital
numerical 85 adj.
computerized 86 adj.
handed 378 adj.
digital computer
counting instrument 86 n.
dignification
dignification 866 n.
dignified
elegant 575 adj.
authoritative 733 adj.
impressive 821 adj.
tasteful 846 adj.
well-bred 848 adj.
worshipful 866 adj.
proud 871 adj.
formal 875 adj.
courteous 884 adj.
dignify
dignify 866 vb.
dignitary
officer 741 n.
aristocrat 868 n.
ecclesiarch 986 n.
dignity
elegance 575 n.
conduct 688 n.
authority 733 n.
good taste 846 n.
etiquette 848 n.

honours 866 n.
prestige 866 n.
pride 871 n.
formality 875 n.
ostentation 875 n.
digraph
spoken letter 558 n.
digress
deviate 282 vb.
be inattentive 456 vb.
be diffuse 570 vb.
digression
deviation 282 n.
pleonasm 570 n.
circuit 626 n.
digressive
unrelated 10 adj.
digs
quarters 192 n.
dike, dyke
gap 201 n.
fence 235 n.
furrow 262 n.
rock 344 n.
lake 346 n.
conduit 351 n.
obstacle 702 n.
defences 713 n.
diktat
decree 737 n.
dilapidated
antiquated 127 adj.
weakened 163 adj.
dirty 649 adj.
unsafe 661 adj.
used 673 adj.
beggarly 801 adj.
dilapidation
decay 51 n.
destruction 165 n.
dilapidation 655 n.
dilatation and curettage
surgery 658 n.
dilate
grow 36 vb.
expand 197 vb.
be diffuse 570 vb.
dilation
increase 36 n.
dilation 197 n.
convexity 253 n.
diffuseness 570 n.
dilatory
late 136 adj.
slow 278 adj.
lazy 679 adj.
dilemma
circumstance 8 n.
dubiety 474 n.
argumentation 475 n.
choice 605 n.
predicament 700 n.
dilettante
dabbling 491 adj.
collector 492 n.
sciolist 493 n.
people of taste 846 n.
desirer 859 n.
diligence
stagecoach 274 n.
attention 455 n.
carefulness 457 n.
assiduity 678 n.
observance 768 n.
diligent
studious 536 adj.
dill
potherb 301 n.
dill water
purgative 658 n.
dilly-dally
be late 136 vb.
be irresolute 601 vb.
be inactive 679 vb.
dilute
weaken 163 vb.
rarefy 325 vb.
add water 339 vb.
moisten 341 vb.
dim
darken 418 vb.
dim 419 adj.
bedim 419 vb.
decolorize 426 vb.
blur 440 vb.
indistinct 444 adj.
unintelligent 499 adj.
puzzling 517 adj.
dime
small coin 33 n.
coinage 797 n.
dimension
quantity 26 n.
measure 183 n.
appearance 445 n.
dimensional
formed 243 adj.
metrical 465 adj.
dimensions
size 195 n.
metrology 465 n.
diminish
abate 37 vb.
render few 105 vb.
moderate 177 vb.
diminishing returns
decrease 37 n.
loss 772 n.
diminuendo
diminuendo 37 adv.
diminution
smallness 33 n.
diminution 37 n.
subtraction 39 n.
decrement 42 n.
contraction 198 n.
diminutive
small 33 adj.
little 196 adj.
word 559 n.
name 561 n.
dimity
textile 222 n.
dimness
darkness 418 n.
dimness 419 n.
invisibility 444 n.
latency 523 n.
dimple
cavity 255 n.
notch 260 n.
dimpled
fleshy 195 adj.
dim sight
dim sight 440 n.
dimwit
dunce 501 n.
dim-witted
unintelligent 499 adj.
din
commotion 318 n.
loudness 400 n.
roll 403 n.
discord 411 n.
dinar
coinage 797 n.
dine
eat 301 vb.
feed 301 vb.
— out
be sociable 882 vb.
diner
café 192 n.
eater 301 n.
diner-out
reveller 837 n.
sociable person 882 n.
dingdong
equal 28 adj.
repeated 106 adj.
roll 403 n.
contending 716 adj.
dinghy
rowing boat 275 n.
dingle
valley 255 n.
dingo
dog 365 n.
dingy
dim 419 adj.
soft-hued 425 adj.
colourless 426 adj.
dirty 649 adj.
dilapidated 655 adj.
graceless 842 adj.
din into one's ears
repeat oneself 106 vb.
advertise 528 vb.
dinkum
genuine 494 adj.
dinky
orderly 60 adj.
little 196 adj.
dinner
meal 301 n.
festivity 837 n.
dinnerless
hungry 859 adj.
fasting 946 adj.
dinner of herbs
asceticism 945 n.
dinner party
social gathering 882 n.
dinosaur
fossil 125 n.
archaism 127 n.
giant 195 n.
animal 365 n.
dint
power 160 n.
be vigorous 174 vb.
concavity 255 n.
make concave 255 vb.
knock 279 n.
collide 279 vb.
diocesan
ecclesiastical 985 adj.
ecclesiarch 986 n.
lay person 987 n.
diocese
district 184 n.
parish 985 n.
Diogenes
philosopher 449 n.
solitary 883 n.
misanthrope 902 n.
ascetic 945 n.
Dionysiac
disorderly 61 adj.
Dionysus
drunkenness 949 n.
Olympian deity 967 n.
diorama
spectacle 445 n.
art subject 553 n.
dioxin
poison 659 n.
dip
incline 220 n.
be oblique 220 vb.
cavity 255 n.
valley 255 n.
swim 269 vb.
impel 279 vb.
point to 281 vb.
immersion 303 n.
immerse 303 vb.
descent 309 n.
descend 309 vb.
lower 311 vb.
plunge 313 n.vb.
drench 341 vb.
snuff out 418 vb.
glimmer 419 n.
bedim 419 vb.
torch 420 n.
colour 425 vb.
signal 547 vb.
ablutions 648 n.
clean 648 vb.
thief 789 n.
— a toe in
be tentative 461 vb.

— into
be curious 453 vb.
be attentive 455 vb.
study 536 vb.
diphtheria
infection 651 n.
respiratory disease 651 n.
diphthong
speech sound 398 n.
voice 577 n.
diploma
credential 466 n.
record 548 n.
mandate 751 n.
honours 866 n.
diplomacy
cunning 698 n.
mediation 720 n.
conditions 766 n.
courtesy 884 n.
diplomat
expert 696 n.
mediator 720 n.
envoy 754 n.
diplomatic
hypocritical 541 adj.
skilful 694 adj.
diplomatic bag
news 529 n.
postal communications 531 n.
diplomatic corps
envoy 754 n.
diplomatic illness
duplicity 541 n.
pretext 614 n.
diplomatic immunity
freedom 744 n.
nonliability 919 n.
diplomatist
expert 696 n.
slyboots 698 n.
mediator 720 n.
envoy 754 n.
dipped lights
glimmer 419 n.
dipper
ladle 194 n.
diver 313 n.
bird 365 n.
dipsomania
hunger 859 n.
alcoholism 949 n.
dipsomaniac
madman 504 n.
drunkard 949 n.
diptych
picture 553 n.
altar 990 n.
dire
harmful 645 adj.
adverse 731 adj.
direct
simple 44 adj.
orderly 60 adj.
continuous 71 adj.
straight 249 adj.
send 272 vb.
directed 281 adj.
orientate 281 vb.
towards 281 adv.
intuitive 476 adj.
accurate 494 adj.
educate 534 vb.
indicate 547 vb.
perspicuous 567 adj.
dramatize 594 vb.
motivate 612 vb.
undeviating 625 adj.
do 676 vb.
direct 689 vb.
rule 733 vb.
command 737 vb.
direct action
revolt 738 n.
direction
tendency 179 n.
bearings 186 n.
itinerary 267 n.
direction 281 n.
cinema 445 n.
teaching 534 n.
dramaturgy 594 n.
motive 612 n.
route 624 n.
directorship 689 n.
precept 693 n.
governance 733 n.
direction finder
direction 281 n.
indicator 547 n.
directive
command 737 n.
direct line
straightness 249 n.
directly
instantaneously 116 adv.
suddenly 135 adv.
straight on 249 adv.
towards 281 adv.
plainly 573 adv.
direct method
teaching 534 n.
directness
continuity 71 n.
straightness 249 n.
perspicuity 567 n.
director
superior 34 n.
guide 520 n.
stage manager 594 n.
director 690 n.
authority 733 n.
master 741 n.
directorship
directorship 689 n.
position of authority 733 n.
directory
directory 87 n.
guidebook 524 n.
reference book 589 n.
direful
frightening 854 adj.
dirge
obsequies 364 n.
musical piece 412 n.
poem 593 n.
lament 836 n.
dirgelike
funereal 364 adj.
lamenting 836 adj.
dirigible
airship 276 n.
dirigisme
governance 733 n.
dirk
sharp point 256 n.
sidearms 723 n.
dirndl
skirt 228 n.
dirt
leavings 41 n.
excrement 302 n.
rubbish 641 n.
dirt 649 n.
blemish 845 n.
slur 867 n.
impurity 951 n.
dirt road
roughness 259 n.
road 624 n.
dirty
orderless 61 adj.
opaque 423 adj.
blacken 428 vb.
neglected 458 adj.
bad 645 adj.
dirty 649 adj.
make unclean 649 vb.
blemished 845 adj.
disreputable 867 adj.
dishonest 930 adj.
impure 951 adj.
dirty habits
uncleanness 649 n.
insalubrity 653 n.
dirty joke
witticism 839 n.
dirty look
look 438 n.
discontent 829 n.
reproach 924 n.
dirty person
slut 61 n.
dirty person 649 n.
dirty trick
trickery 542 n.
evil 616 n.
foul play 930 n.
dirty weather
storm 176 n.
gale 352 n.
dirty word
calumny 926 n.
dirty work
foul play 930 n.
disability
inexpedience 643 n.
illness 651 n.
disable
disable 161 vb.
weaken 163 vb.
make useless 641 vb.
impair 655 vb.
hinder 702 vb.
disablement
impairment 655 n.
disabuse
inform 524 vb.
disclose 526 vb.
educate 534 vb.
disaccustom
disaccustom 611 vb.
stop using 674 vb.
disadvantage
inferiority 35 n.
evil 616 n.
inexpedience 643 n.
disadvantageous
harmful 645 adj.
disaffect
dissuade 613 vb.
disaffected
inimical 881 adj.
disaffection
dissent 489 n.
disaffiliate
depose 752 vb.
disaffirm
negate 533 vb.
disagree
be contrary 14 vb.
differ 15 vb.
disagree 25 vb.
disbelieve 486 vb.
dissent 489 vb.
negate 533 vb.
be unwilling 598 vb.
quarrel 709 vb.
refuse 760 vb.
cause dislike 861 vb.
— with
harm 645 vb.
displease 827 vb.
cause dislike 861 vb.
disagreeable
painful 377 adj.
fetid 397 adj.
unpleasant 827 adj.
disliked 861 adj.
discourteous 885 adj.
disagreement
dissimilarity 19 n.
disagreement 25 n.
nonconformity 84 n.
discord 411 n.
dissension 709 n.
(See **disagree** *)*
disallow
exclude 57 vb.
make impossible 470 vb.
dissent 489 vb.
negate 533 vb.
reject 607 vb.
prohibit 757 vb.
disentitle 916 vb.
disapprove 924 vb.

disallowed
refused 760 adj.
disappear
be transient 114 vb.
cease 145 vb.
go away 190 vb.
recede 290 vb.
disappear 446 vb.
obliterate 550 vb.
be lost 772 vb.
disappearance
absence 190 n.
obscuration 418 n.
invisibility 444 n.
disappearance 446 n.
concealment 525 n.
escape 667 n.
disappoint
fall short 307 vb.
disappoint 509 vb.
deceive 542 vb.
not suffice 636 vb.
miscarry 728 vb.
displease 827 vb.
cause discontent 829 vb.
depress 834 vb.
leave no hope 853 vb.
fail in duty 918 vb.
disappointment
disappointment 509 n.
disapprobation
disapprobation 924 n.
disapproval
dissent 489 n.
rejection 607 n.
disapprobation 924 n.
disapprove
oppose 704 vb.
deprecate 762 vb.
be discontented 829 vb.
dislike 861 vb.
make unwelcome 883 vb.
not respect 921 vb.
disapprove 924 vb.
detract 926 vb.
condemn 961 vb.
disapproved
unconformable 84 adj.
not nice 645 adj.
disliked 861 adj.
disreputable 867 adj.
disarm
disable 161 vb.
weaken 163 vb.
assuage 177 vb.
be moderate 177 vb.
make useless 641 vb.
make peace 719 vb.
disarmament
peace 717 n.
disarmed
defenceless 161 adj.
weakened 163 adj.
disarming
lenitive 177 adj.
pacificatory 719 adj.
disarrange
derange 63 vb.
disarranged
orderless 61 adj.
disarranged 63 adj.
disarray
disorder 61 n.
disaster
ruin 165 n.
misfortune 731 n.
disaster area
havoc 165 n.
disastrous
evil 616 adj.
harmful 645 adj.
adverse 731 adj.
disavow
negate 533 vb.
recant 603 vb.
reject 607 vb.
disband
disunite 46 vb.
decompose 51 vb.
disperse 75 vb.
liberate 746 vb.
disbar
exclude 57 vb.
eject 300 vb.
depose 752 vb.
shame 867 vb.
disbelief
unbelief 486 n.
negation 533 n.
lack of wonder 865 n.
irreligion 974 n.
disbeliever
unbeliever 486 n.
impious person 980 n.
disburden
deliver 668 vb.
disencumber 701 vb.
relieve 831 vb.
disburse
pay 804 vb.
expend 806 vb.
disc, disk
lamina 207 n.
circle 250 n.
gramophone 414 n.
discard
leave over 41 vb.
eject 300 vb.
rejection 607 n.
reject 607 vb.
relinquish 621 vb.
stop using 674 vb.
not observe 769 vb.
not retain 779 vb.
discarnate
immaterial 320 adj.
spooky 970 adj.
discern
see 438 vb.
discriminate 463 vb.
detect 484 vb.
know 490 vb.
be wise 498 vb.
understand 516 vb.
discernible
visible 443 adj.
discerning
discriminating 463 adj.
intelligent 498 adj.
tasteful 846 adj.
fastidious 862 adj.
discernment
discrimination 463 n.
good taste 846 n.
discharge
propulsion 287 n.
shoot 287 vb.
land 295 vb.
outflow 298 n.
ejection 300 n.
dismiss 300 vb.
empty 300 vb.
excretion 302 n.
escape 667 n.
deliverance 668 n.
stop using 674 vb.
do 676 vb.
effectuation 725 n.
carry out 725 vb.
liberation 746 n.
deposal 752 n.
observance 768 n.
not retain 779 vb.
payment 804 n.
do one's duty 917 vb.
nonliability 919 n.
acquittal 960 n.
disciple
listener 415 n.
learner 538 n.
auxiliary 707 n.
church member 976 n.
disciplinarian
trainer 537 n.
manager 690 n.
tyrant 735 n.
disciplinary
punitive 963 adj.
discipline
order 60 n.
teaching 534 n.
dominate 733 vb.
severity 735 n.
obedience 739 n.
compel 740 vb.
subjugate 745 vb.
restraint 747 n.
punish 963 vb.
disciplined
orderly 60 adj.
plain 573 adj.
obedient 739 adj.
disc jockey
broadcaster 531 n.
disclaim
negate 533 vb.
recant 603 vb.
reject 607 vb.
abrogate 752 vb.
resign 753 vb.
refuse 760 vb.
not retain 779 vb.
disclose
uncover 229 vb.
manifest 522 vb.
inform 524 vb.
disclose 526 vb.
indicate 547 vb.
disclosure
testimony 466 n.
disclosure 526 n.
publication 528 n.
revelation 975 n.
disco, discotheque
dancing 837 n.
place of amusement 837 n.
social gathering 882 n.
discoloration
hue 425 n.
achromatism 426 n.
impairment 655 n.
discoloured
unsightly 842 adj.
discomfited
humbled 872 adj.
discomfort
pain 377 n.
evil 616 n.
suffering 825 n.
worry 825 n.
trouble 827 vb.
discompose
derange 63 vb.
agitate 318 vb.
distract 456 vb.
trouble 827 vb.
discomposure
disorder 61 n.
worry 825 n.
disconcert
derange 63 vb.
distract 456 vb.
disappoint 509 vb.
hinder 702 vb.
trouble 827 vb.
frighten 854 vb.
shame 867 vb.
humiliate 872 vb.
disconcerted
inexpectant 508 adj.
suffering 825 adj.
disconnect
disunite 46 vb.
discontinue 72 vb.
disconnected
unrelated 10 adj.
disconsolate
unhappy 825 adj.
discontented 829 adj.

melancholic 834 adj.
hopeless 853 adj.
discontent
disapprobation 924 n.
discontented
dissenting 489 adj.
disappointed 509 adj.
unprovided 636 adj.
unhappy 825 adj.
discontented 829 adj.
dejected 834 adj.
bored 838 adj.
disliking 861 adj.
resentful 891 adj.
sullen 893 adj.
envious 912 adj.
discontinuance
cessation 145 n.
stop 145 n.
desuetude 611 n.
relinquishment 621 n.
abrogation 752 n.
discontinue
terminate 69 vb.
cease 145 vb.
discontinuity
unrelatedness 10 n.
disunion 46 n.
discontinuity 72 n.
fitfulness 142 n.
cessation 145 n.
interval 201 n.
discord
disagreement 25 n.
medley 43 n.
disorder 61 n.
stridor 407 n.
discord 411 n.vb.
dissension 709 n.
discordant
unrelated 10 adj.
contrary 14 adj.
disagreeing 25 adj.
strident 407 adj.
discordant 411 adj.
florid 425 adj.
quarrelling 709 adj.
discotheque
(See **disco** *)*
discount
subtract 39 vb.
decrement 42 n.
disregard 458 vb.
underestimate 483 vb.
discount 810 n.vb.
discountenance
disapprove 924 vb.
discourage
dissuade 613 vb.
hinder 702 vb.
prohibit 757 vb.
cause discontent 829 vb.
depress 834 vb.
frighten 854 vb.
discouragement
hopelessness 853 n.
discourse
lecture 534 n.
teach 534 vb.
oration 579 n.
speech 579 n.
dissertation 591 n.
discourteous
impertinent 878 adj.
discourtesy
ill-breeding 847 n.
unsociability 883 n.
discourtesy 885 n.
disrespect 921 n.
discover
come before 64 vb.
initiate 68 vb.
meet with 154 vb.
produce 164 vb.
see 438 vb.
think 449 vb.
discover 484 vb.
manifest 522 vb.
be informed 524 vb.
discovered
known 490 adj.
discoverer
precursor 66 n.
producer 164 n.
enquirer 459 n.
detector 484 n.
discovery
beginning 68 n.
appearance 445 n.
idea 451 n.
enquiry 459 n.
discovery 484 n.
knowledge 490 n.
divination 511 n.
interpretation 520 n.
manifestation 522 n.
disclosure 526 n.
discredit
unbelief 486 n.
cause doubt 486 vb.
disbelieve 486 vb.
disrepute 867 n.
object of scorn 867 n.
shame 867 vb.
odium 888 n.
defame 926 vb.
discreditable
bad 645 adj.
discreditable 867 adj.
blameworthy 924 adj.
discredited
erroneous 495 adj.
disused 674 adj.
disapproved 924 adj.
discreet
discriminating 463 adj.
reticent 525 adj.
taciturn 582 adj.
cautious 858 adj.
discrepancy
difference 15 n.
disagreement 25 n.
discrete
separate 46 adj.
discontinuous 72 adj.
discretion
discrimination 463 n.
judgment 480 n.
sagacity 498 n.
concealment 525 n.
will 595 n.
choice 605 n.
skill 694 n.
caution 858 n.
discretionary
volitional 595 adj.
voluntary 597 adj.
unconditional 744 adj.
discriminate
differentiate 15 vb.
make unlike 19 vb.
set apart 46 vb.
specify 80 vb.
compare 462 vb.
discriminate 463 vb.
be wise 498 vb.
select 605 vb.
be skilful 694 vb.
have taste 846 vb.
be fastidious 862 vb.
— against
be biased 481 vb.
do wrong 914 vb.
discrimination
discrimination 463 n.
judgment 480 n.
prejudice 481 n.
moral sensibility 819 n.
injustice 914 n.
discriminatory
biased 481 adj.
unjust 914 adj.
discursive
deviating 282 adj.
rational 475 adj.
prolix 570 adj.
discursive 591 adj.
discus
circle 250 n.
missile 287 n.
discuss
argue 475 vb.
confer 584 vb.
dissertate 591 vb.
discussion
enquiry 459 n.
argument 475 n.
conference 584 n.
discussion group
assembly 74 n.
class 538 n.
disdain
reject 607 vb.
be fastidious 862 vb.
shame 867 vb.
pride 871 n.
be proud 871 vb.
insolence 878 n.
not respect 921 vb.
contempt 922 n.
despise 922 vb.
disease
disease 651 n.
bane 659 n.
disembark
land 295 vb.
disembarrassed
facilitated 701 adj.
disembodied
immaterial 320 adj.
spooky 970 adj.
disembowel
empty 300 vb.
disembroil
unravel 62 vb.
disenchanted
indifferent 860 adj.
disliking 861 adj.
disenchantment
reversion 148 n.
discovery 484 n.
disappointment 509 n.
painfulness 827 n.
disencumber
lighten 323 vb.
deliver 668 vb.
disencumber 701 vb.
liberate 746 vb.
take away 786 vb.
relieve 831 vb.
disendow
depose 752 vb.
disengage
disunite 46 vb.
regress 286 vb.
disencumber 701 vb.
liberate 746 vb.
disengaged
inactive 679 adj.
leisurely 681 adj.
disentangle
simplify 44 vb.
disunite 46 vb.
unravel 62 vb.
decipher 520 vb.
disencumber 701 vb.
liberate 746 vb.
not retain 779 vb.
disequilibrium
inequality 29 n.
disestablish
depose 752 vb.
diseur, diseuse
entertainer 594 n.
disfavour
disrepute 867 n.
odium 888 n.
disrespect 921 n.
disapprobation 924 n.
disfigure
deform 244 vb.

mark 547 vb.
impair 655 vb.
make ugly 842 vb.
blemish 845 vb.
disfigured
disguised 525 adj.
unsightly 842 adj.
disfranchise
subjugate 745 vb.
disentitle 916 vb.
disfranchisement
no choice 606 n.
disgorge
empty 300 vb.
vomit 300 vb.
disgrace
disrepute 867 n.
shame 867 vb.
humiliation 872 n.
wrong 914 n.
not respect 921 vb.
improbity 930 n.
— oneself
lose repute 867 vb.
disgraceful
bad 645 adj.
discreditable 867 adj.
heinous 934 adj.
disgruntled
disappointed 509 adj.
discontented 829 adj.
disguise
make unlike 19 vb.
mimicry 20 n.
imitate 20 vb.
transform 147 vb.
conceal 525 vb.
disguise 527 n.
sham 542 n.
cunning 698 n.
disguised
invisible 444 adj.
unknown 491 adj.
disgust
be unpalatable 391 vb.
displease 827 vb.
cause discontent 829 vb.
dislike 861 n.
excite hate 888 vb.
disgusting
unsavoury 391 adj.
not nice 645 adj.
unclean 649 adj.
unpleasant 827 adj.
tedious 838 adj.
disliked 861 adj.
discreditable 867 adj.
hateful 888 adj.
disgustingly
ad nauseam 861 adv.
dish
destroy 165 vb.
plate 194 n.
dish 301 n.
defeat 727 vb.
a beauty 841 n.
— out
apportion 783 vb.
— up
provide 633 vb.
dishabille
informal dress 228 n.
uncovering 229 n.
disharmony
disagreement 25 n.
disorder 61 n.
discord 411 n.
dissension 709 n.
dishcloth
cleaning cloth 648 n.
dishearten
dissuade 613 vb.
hinder 702 vb.
cause discontent 829 vb.
depress 834 vb.
disheartened
dejected 834 adj.
dishevel
jumble 63 vb.
enlace 222 vb.
dishevelment
disorder 61 n.
derangement 63 n.
dishonest
false 541 adj.
thieving 788 adj.
discreditable 867 adj.
dishonest 930 adj.
dishonesty
improbity 930 n.
dishonour
not pay 805 vb.
disrepute 867 n.
shame 867 vb.
wrong 914 n.
disrespect 921 n.
not respect 921 vb.
defame 926 vb.
improbity 930 n.
debauch 951 vb.
dishonourable
discreditable 867 adj.
blameworthy 924 adj.
dishonest 930 adj.
dishwasher
cleaner 648 n.
cleaning utensil 648 n.
dishwater
weak thing 163 n.
swill 649 n.
dishy
personable 841 adj.
disillusion
disappoint 509 vb.
disclose 526 vb.
dissuade 613 vb.
displease 827 vb.
dejection 834 n.
hatred 888 n.
disillusioned
regretting 830 adj.
indifferent 860 adj.
disliking 861 adj.
disincentive
dissuasion 613 n.
hindrance 702 n.
disinclination
unwillingness 598 n.
dislike 861 n.
disincline
dissuade 613 vb.
cause dislike 861 vb.
disinfect
make sterile 172 vb.
purify 648 vb.
sanitate 652 vb.
doctor 658 vb.
safeguard 660 vb.
disinfectant
cleanser 648 n.
prophylactic 658 n.
disinfection
hygiene 652 n.
disinfestation
cleansing 648 n.
disinflation
finance 797 n.
disingenuous
false 541 adj.
dishonest 930 adj.
disinherit
not retain 779 vb.
deprive 786 vb.
impoverish 801 vb.
disintegrate
break 46 vb.
disunite 46 vb.
separate 46 vb.
decompose 51 vb.
be dispersed 75 vb.
pulverize 332 vb.
deteriorate 655 vb.
disintegration
decomposition 51 n.
disinter
exhume 364 vb.
discover 484 vb.
disinterested
benevolent 897 adj.
philanthropic 901 adj.
just 913 adj.
disinterested 931 adj.
disinterment
inquest 364 n.
disjecta membra
piece 53 n.
dispersion 75 n.
disjoin
disunite 46 vb.
disjointed
feeble 572 adj.
disjunctive
separate 46 adj.
disk
(See **disc** *)*
dislike
unwillingness 598 n.
be unwilling 598 vb.
resistance 715 n.
refuse 760 vb.
dislike 861 n.vb.
enmity 881 n.
hatred 888 n.
hate 888 vb.
disapprobation 924 n.
disapprove 924 vb.
disliked
disagreeing 25 adj.
repellent 292 adj.
unsavoury 391 adj.
not nice 645 adj.
unpleasant 827 adj.
unwanted 860 adj.
disliked 861 adj.
hated 888 adj.
wrong 914 adj.
disapproved 924 adj.
dislocate
disunite 46 vb.
derange 63 vb.
disable 161 vb.
force 176 vb.
displace 188 vb.
dislocation
impairment 655 n.
dislodge
derange 63 vb.
displace 188 vb.
eject 300 vb.
disloyal
changeful 152 adj.
tergiversating 603 adj.
disobedient 738 adj.
nonobservant 769 adj.
inimical 881 adj.
malevolent 898 adj.
undutiful 918 adj.
perfidious 930 adj.
dismal
dark 418 adj.
unpleasant 827 adj.
cheerless 834 adj.
melancholic 834 adj.
dismantle
break 46 vb.
weaken 163 vb.
demolish 165 vb.
make useless 641 vb.
impair 655 vb.
stop using 674 vb.
make inactive 679 vb.
dismantled
unequipped 670 adj.
dismay
defeat 727 vb.
worry 825 n.
depress 834 vb.
hopelessness 853 n.

fear 854 n.
frighten 854 vb.
dismember
rend 46 vb.
sunder 46 vb.
execute 963 vb.
dismemberment
decomposition 51 n.
dismiss
exclude 57 vb.
disperse 75 vb.
dismiss 300 vb.
disregard 458 vb.
confute 479 vb.
depose 752 vb.
refuse 760 vb.
not retain 779 vb.
be indifferent 860 vb.
hold cheap 922 vb.
— out of hand
reject 607 vb.
dismissal
valediction 296 n.
ejection 300 n.
loss of right 916 n.
dismount
unstick 49 vb.
descend 309 vb.
disobedience
disorder 61 n.
disobedience 738 n.
refusal 760 n.
disobedient
revolutionary 149 adj.
unwilling 598 adj.
wilful 602 adj.
difficult 700 adj.
opposing 704 adj.
defiant 711 adj.
resisting 715 adj.
anarchic 734 adj.
disobedient 738 adj.
nonobservant 769 adj.
sullen 893 adj.
undutiful 918 adj.
disrespectful 921 adj.
disobey
be contrary 14 vb.
please oneself 734 vb.
disobey 738 vb.
be insolent 878 vb.
disoblige
be malevolent 898 vb.
disorder
decompose 51 vb.
disorder 61 n.
derangement 63 n.
derange 63 vb.
discontinuity 72 n.
disperse 75 vb.
amorphism 244 n.
deform 244 vb.
badness 645 n.
uncleanness 649 n.
disease 651 n.
hinder 702 vb.
anarchy 734 n.
revolt 738 n.
disordered reason
insanity 503 n.
disorderly
disorderly 61 adj.
violent 176 adj.
anarchic 734 adj.
riotous 738 adj.
ill-bred 847 adj.
drunk 949 adj.
disorderly house
brothel 951 n.
disorganize, disorganise
derange 63 vb.
impair 655 vb.
disorganized
orderless 61 adj.
lax 734 adj.
disorientate
derange 63 vb.
displace 188 vb.
disorientated
deviating 282 adj.
doubting 474 adj.
disown
negate 533 vb.
avoid 620 vb.
abrogate 752 vb.
not retain 779 vb.
disapprove 924 vb.
disparage
underestimate 483 vb.
shame 867 vb.
not respect 921 vb.
hold cheap 922 vb.
detract 926 vb.
disparaging
derisive 851 adj.
disapproving 924 adj.
detracting 926 adj.
disparity
unrelatedness 10 n.
difference 15 n.
dissimilarity 19 n.
disagreement 25 n.
inequality 29 n.
dispassionate
judicial 480 adj.
impassive 820 adj.
inexcitable 823 adj.
just 913 adj.
dispatch, despatch
punctuality 135 n.
displace 188 vb.
move 265 vb.
transference 272 n.
send 272 vb.
velocity 277 n.
eat 301 vb.
kill 362 vb.
report 524 n.
news 529 n.
correspondence 588 n.
do 676 vb.
activity 678 n.
haste 680 n.
hasten 680 vb.
deal with 688 vb.
effectuation 725 n.
carry out 725 vb.
dispatch box
box 194 n.
postal communications 531 n.
dispatch clerk
transferrer 272 n.
dispatches
report 524 n.
message 529 n.
news 529 n.
dispatch rider
courier 529 n.
dispel
disunite 46 vb.
disperse 75 vb.
destroy 165 vb.
displace 188 vb.
repel 292 vb.
disappear 446 vb.
dispensable
superfluous 637 adj.
unimportant 639 adj.
useless 641 adj.
dispensary
hospital 658 n.
dispensation
deliverance 668 n.
management 689 n.
permission 756 n.
nonretention 779 n.
apportionment 783 n.
nonliability 919 n.
dispense
disperse 75 vb.
liberate 746 vb.
permit 756 vb.
give 781 vb.
apportion 783 vb.
exempt 919 vb.
— with
not use 674 vb.
not retain 779 vb.
dispenser
druggist 658 n.
dispersal
diminution 37 n.
disunion 46 n.
dispersion 75 n.
transference 272 n.
defeat 728 n.
disperse
disunite 46 vb.
separate 46 vb.
be dispersed 75 vb.
disperse 75 vb.
disappear 446 vb.
waste 634 vb.
dispersion
separation 46 n.
noncoherence 49 n.
dispersion 75 n.
divergence 294 n.
reflection 417 n.
dispirit
dissuade 613 vb.
depress 834 vb.
displace
exclude 57 vb.
derange 63 vb.
substitute 150 vb.
displace 188 vb.
move 265 vb.
transpose 272 vb.
eject 300 vb.
extract 304 vb.
take away 786 vb.
displaced person
outcast 883 n.
displacement
displacement 188 n.
depth 211 n.
gravity 322 n.
(See **displace** *)*
displacement activity
overactivity 678 n.
display
accumulation 74 n.
appearance 445 n.
spectacle 445 n.
exhibit 522 n.
manifestation 522 n.
show 522 vb.
publicity 528 n.
pride 871 n.
ostentation 875 n.
pageant 875 n.
displease
displease 827 vb.
cause discontent 829 vb.
depress 834 vb.
cause dislike 861 vb.
displeased
unhappy 825 adj.
discontented 829 adj.
angry 891 adj.
displeasure
sorrow 825 n.
annoyance 827 n.
discontent 829 n.
dislike 861 n.
hatred 888 n.
resentment 891 n.
disapprobation 924 n.
disport oneself
be cheerful 833 vb.
amuse oneself 837 vb.
disposable
decomposable 51 adj.
ephemeral 114 adj.
useful 640 adj.
used 673 adj.

disposal
arrangement 62 n.
use 673 n.
nonretention 779 n.
sale 793 n.
dispose
order 60 vb.
arrange 62 vb.
influence 178 vb.
tend 179 vb.
motivate 612 vb.
— of
dispose of 673 vb.
carry through 725 vb.
possess 773 vb.
not retain 779 vb.
sell 793 vb.
disposed
willing 597 adj.
intending 617 adj.
disposition
temperament 5 n.
state 7 n.
order 60 n.
arrangement 62 n.
location 187 n.
will 595 n.
willingness 597 n.
habit 610 n.
affections 817 n.
dispossess
eject 300 vb.
assign 780 vb.
appropriate 786 vb.
impoverish 801 vb.
disentitle 916 vb.
dispossessed
losing 772 adj.
not owning 774 adj.
poor 801 adj.
unentitled 916 adj.
dispraise
censure 924 n.
dispraise 924 vb.
detract 926 vb.
disproof
counterevidence 467 n.
confutation 479 n.
disproportion
unrelatedness 10 n.
disagreement 25 n.
inequality 29 n.
distortion 246 n.
exaggeration 546 n.
disproportionate
unrelated 10 adj.
disagreeing 25 adj.
unequal 29 adj.
distorted 246 adj.
unsightly 842 adj.
disprove
confute 479 vb.
negate 533 vb.
disputable
uncertain 474 adj.
arguing 475 adj.
unbelieved 486 adj.
litigated 959 adj.
disputant
reasoner 475 n.
disputation
argument 475 n.
disputatious
arguing 475 adj.
quarrelling 709 adj.
dispute
disagree 25 vb.
argue 475 vb.
quarrel 709 n.vb.
contention 716 n.
disputer
quarreller 709 n.
combatant 722 n.
disqualification
impotence 161 n.
ejection 300 n.
inexpedience 643 n.
nonpreparation 670 n.
unskilfulness 695 n.
loss of right 916 n.
disqualify
exclude 57 vb.
disable 161 vb.
make useless 641 vb.
disentitle 916 vb.
disquiet
changeableness 152 n.
agitation 318 n.
impress 821 vb.
worry 825 n.
trouble 827 vb.
discontent 829 n.
nervousness 854 n.
frighten 854 vb.
disquisition
lecture 534 n.
diffuseness 570 n.
oration 579 n.
dissertation 591 n.
disregard
exclude 57 vb.
be deaf 416 vb.
be blind 439 vb.
not think 450 vb.
be incurious 454 vb.
inattention 456 n.
be inattentive 456 vb.
negligence 458 n.
disregard 458 vb.
underestimate 483 vb.
not know 491 vb.
reject 607 vb.
not use 674 vb.
abrogate 752 vb.
not observe 769 vb.
be insensitive 820 vb.
fail in duty 918 vb.
not respect 921 vb.
hold cheap 922 vb.
impiety 980 n.
disregarded
neglected 458 adj.
unimportant 639 adj.
unrespected 921 adj.
disrelish
dislike 861 n.vb.
disremember
forget 506 vb.
disrepair
dilapidation 655 n.
disreputable
not nice 645 adj.
vulgar 847 adj.
disreputable 867 adj.
unrespected 921 adj.
disapproved 924 adj.
dishonest 930 adj.
disrepute
disrepute 867 n.
odium 888 n.
disrespect
ridicule 851 n.
sauciness 878 n.
undutifulness 918 n.
disrespect 921 n.
impiety 980 n.
disrespectful
impertinent 878 adj.
ungracious 885 adj.
undutiful 918 adj.
disrespectful 921 adj.
disrobe
doff 229 vb.
disruption
separation 46 n.
discontinuity 72 n.
destruction 165 n.
disruptive influence
agitator 738 n.
dissatisfaction
incompleteness 55 n.
dissent 489 n.
sorrow 825 n.
discontent 829 n.
dislike 861 n.
resentment 891 n.
disapprobation 924 n.
dissatisfy
disappoint 509 vb.
be imperfect 647 vb.
displease 827 vb.
cause discontent 829 vb.
dissect
sunder 46 vb.
decompose 51 vb.
class 62 vb.
enquire 459 vb.
dissemble
make unlike 19 vb.
mislead 495 vb.
be equivocal 518 vb.
conceal 525 vb.
dissemble 541 vb.
deceive 542 vb.
be affected 850 vb.
be dishonest 930 vb.
dissembler
deceiver 545 n.
slyboots 698 n.
disseminate
disperse 75 vb.
communicate 524 vb.
publish 528 vb.
dissension
disagreement 25 n.
argument 475 n.
dissent 489 n.
dissension 709 n.
contention 716 n.
dissent
nonconformity 84 n.
unbelief 486 n.
dissent 489 n.vb.
negation 533 n.
dissension 709 n.
refuse 760 vb.
disapprove 924 vb.
sectarianism 978 n.
dissenter
misfit 25 n.
nonconformist 84 n.
unbeliever 486 n.
dissentient 489 n.
irreligionist 974 n.
schismatic 978 n.
dissertate
write 586 vb.
dissertate 591 vb.
dissertation
commentary 520 n.
diffuseness 570 n.
dissertation 591 n.
disservice
evil 616 n.
inutility 641 n.
cruel act 898 n.
dissever
disunite 46 vb.
dissident
misfit 25 n.
nonconformist 84 n.
unconformable 84 adj.
dissentient 489 n.
dissenting 489 adj.
opponent 705 n.
revolter 738 n.
malcontent 829 n.
discontented 829 adj.
schismatic 978 n.
dissimilar
different 15 adj.
nonuniform 17 adj.
dissimilar 19 adj.
unequal 29 adj.
dissimilarity
unrelatedness 10 n.
polarity 14 n.
dissimilarity 19 n.
originality 21 n.
misrepresentation 552 n.
dissimulate
dissemble 541 vb.

dissimulation
mimicry 20 n.
concealment 525 n.
duplicity 541 n.
dissipate
disperse 75 vb.
destroy 165 vb.
disappear 446 vb.
waste 634 vb.
be prodigal 815 vb.
dissipated
prodigal 815 adj.
sensual 944 adj.
lecherous 951 adj.
dissipation
pleasure 376 n.
intemperance 943 n.
dissociate oneself
negate 533 vb.
be unwilling 598 vb.
oppose 704 vb.
dissociation
disunion 46 n.
schism 978 n.
dissoluble
liquefied 337 adj.
dissoluteness
sensualism 944 n.
unchastity 951 n.
dissolution
disunion 46 n.
separation 46 n.
decomposition 51 n.
disorder 61 n.
finality 69 n.
destruction 165 n.
disappearance 446 n.
abrogation 752 n.
nonretention 779 n.
dissolution of marriage
divorce 896 n.
dissolve
pass away 2 vb.
shade off 27 vb.
decompose 51 vb.
be dispersed 75 vb.
deform 244 vb.
liquefy 337 vb.
photography 551 n.
— in tears
weep 836 vb.
dissonance
disagreement 25 n.
discord 411 n.
dissension 709 n.
dissuade
cause doubt 486 vb.
dissuade 613 vb.
warn 664 vb.
advise 691 vb.
hinder 702 vb.
deprecate 762 vb.
cause discontent 829 vb.
frighten 854 vb.
dissuasion
dissuasion 613 n.
distaff
weaving 222 n.
distaff side
race 11 n.
womankind 373 n.
distal
distant 199 adj.
distance
range 183 n.
distance 199 n.
length 203 n.
outstrip 277 vb.
outdo 306 vb.
unsociability 883 n.
distance between
interval 201 n.
distance of time
long duration 113 n.
antiquity 125 n.
distant
dissimilar 19 adj.
extraneous 59 adj.
distant 199 adj.
muted 401 adj.
invisible 444 adj.
incurious 454 adj.
impassive 820 adj.
prideful 871 adj.
inimical 881 adj.
unsociable 883 adj.
distant future
futurity 124 n.
distant past
past time 125 n.
distant relation
kinsman 11 n.
distaste
dislike 861 n.
distasteful
unpleasant 827 adj.
distemper
facing 226 n.
colour 425 vb.
animal disease 651 n.
disease 651 n.
distend
augment 36 vb.
enlarge 197 vb.
expand 197 vb.
distich
duality 90 n.
verse form 593 n.
distil
eliminate 44 vb.
exude 298 vb.
extract 304 vb.
vaporize 338 vb.
purify 648 vb.
distillation
essential part 5 n.
heating 381 n.
distilled liquor
alcoholic drink 301 n.
distillery
vaporizer 338 n.
workshop 687 n.
distinct
different 15 adj.
dissimilar 19 adj.
separate 46 adj.
definite 80 adj.
sounding 398 adj.
loud 400 adj.
obvious 443 adj.
intelligible 516 adj.
assertive 532 adj.
vocal 577 adj.
distinction
differentiation 15 n.
speciality 80 n.
discrimination 463 n.
reasoning 475 n.
elegance 575 n.
importance 638 n.
honours 866 n.
prestige 866 n.
nobility 868 n.
title 870 n.
distinctive
distinctive 15 adj.
special 80 adj.
distinctly
loudly 400 adv.
apparently 445 adv.
distingué(e)
well-bred 848 adj.
noteworthy 866 adj.
distinguish
differentiate 15 vb.
make unlike 19 vb.
set apart 46 vb.
see 438 vb.
discriminate 463 vb.
be wise 498 vb.
understand 516 vb.
name 561 vb.
dignify 866 vb.
distinguished
remarkable 32 adj.
superior 34 adj.
elegant 575 adj.
notable 638 adj.
noteworthy 866 adj.
distort
make unlike 19 vb.
transform 147 vb.
force 176 vb.
make oblique 220 vb.
deform 244 vb.
distort 246 vb.
misinterpret 521 vb.
misteach 535 vb.
be false 541 vb.
exaggerate 546 vb.
misrepresent 552 vb.
impair 655 vb.
misuse 675 vb.
make ugly 842 vb.
distorted
abnormal 84 adj.
convoluted 251 adj.
disguised 525 adj.
imperfect 647 adj.
distorting mirror
visual fallacy 440 n.
misrepresentation 552 n.
distortion
unrelatedness 10 n.
disagreement 25 n.
distortion 246 n.
visual fallacy 440 n.
untruth 543 n.
blemish 845 n.
(See **distort** *)*
distract
derange 63 vb.
distract 456 vb.
distracted
distracted 456 adj.
doubting 474 adj.
excited 821 adj.
distraction
abstractedness 456 n.
inattention 456 n.
frenzy 503 n.
excitable state 822 n.
distrain
deprive 786 vb.
distrait(e)
abstracted 456 adj.
excited 821 adj.
distraught
doubting 474 adj.
frenzied 503 adj.
excited 821 adj.
distress
pain 377 n.
give pain 377 vb.
evil 616 n.
ill-treat 645 vb.
fatigue 684 n.
adversity 731 n.
poverty 801 n.
impress 821 vb.
suffering 825 n.
worry 825 n.
hurt 827 vb.
distressing
felt 818 adj.
distressing 827 adj.
frightening 854 adj.
distress signal
signal 547 n.
danger signal 665 n.
distributary
stream 350 n.
distribute
arrange 62 vb.
publish 528 vb.
apportion 783 vb.
distribution
dispersion 75 n.
transference 272 n.
distribution curve
statistics 86 n.
distributor
electronics 160 n.
giver 781 n.

district
district 184 n.
regional 184 adj.
place 185 n.
locality 187 n.
abode 192 n.
housing 192 n.
land 344 n.
political organization 733 n.
parish 985 n.
district attorney
law officer 955 n.
district council
council 692 n.
jurisdiction 955 n.
district heating system
heating 381 n.
district nurse
nurse 658 n.
aider 703 n.
distrust
doubt 486 n.vb.
be nervous 854 vb.
be jealous 911 vb.
distrustful
doubting 474 adj.
disturb
decompose 51 vb.
derange 63 vb.
mistime 138 vb.
displace 188 vb.
agitate 318 vb.
cause feeling 374 vb.
distract 456 vb.
trouble 827 vb.
frighten 854 vb.
disturbance
turmoil 61 n.
commotion 318 n.
revolt 738 n.
disturbed
violent 176 adj.
nervous 854 adj.
disunion, disunity
disagreement 25 n.
disunion 46 n.
disorder 61 n.
dissension 709 n.
disunite
disunite 46 vb.
disunited
disunited 46 adj.
decomposed 51 adj.
fragmentary 53 adj.
orderless 61 adj.
disuse
rejection 607 n.
desuetude 611 n.
relinquishment 621 n.
nonuse 674 n.
stop using 674 vb.
abrogation 752 n.
nonretention 779 n.
disused
antiquated 127 adj.
disused 674 adj.
disyllable
speech sound 398 n.
ditch
partition 231 n.
cavity 255 n.
furrow 262 n.
fly 271 vb.
dry 342 vb.
drain 351 n.
tergiversate 603 vb.
reject 607 vb.
relinquish 621 vb.
stop using 674 vb.
defences 713 n.
not retain 779 vb.
ditchwater
swill 649 n.
dither
be agitated 318 vb.
be uncertain 474 vb.
be irresolute 601 vb.
dithyrambic
rhetorical 574 adj.
poetic 593 adj.
ditto
identity 13 n.
do likewise 20 vb.
repeat 106 vb.
again 106 adv.
assent 488 vb.
ditty
vocal music 412 n.
doggerel 593 n.
ditty bag
bag 194 n.
diuretic
excretory 302 adj.
purgative 658 n.
diurnal
matinal 128 adj.
seasonal 141 adj.
diva
vocalist 413 n.
actor 594 n.
divagate
stray 282 vb.
divan
bed 218 n.
seat 218 n.
divaricate
deviate 282 vb.
diverge 294 vb.
dive
tavern 192 n.
swim 269 vb.
fly 271 vb.
move fast 277 vb.
descent 309 n.
descend 309 vb.
plunge 313 n.vb.
amuse oneself 837 vb.
diver
depth 211 n.
diver 313 n.
bird 365 n.
diverge
disagree 25 vb.
separate 46 vb.
be dispersed 75 vb.
bifurcate 92 vb.
deviate 282 vb.
diverge 294 vb.
divergence, divergency
difference 15 n.
nonuniformity 17 n.
dissimilarity 19 n.
dissension 709 n.
divers
different 15 adj.
multiform 82 adj.
many 104 adj.
diverse
different 15 adj.
nonuniform 17 adj.
dissimilar 19 adj.
multiform 82 adj.
diversify
modify 143 vb.
variegate 437 vb.
diversion
irrelevance 10 n.
deviation 282 n.
traffic control 305 n.
pleasure 376 n.
inattention 456 n.
trap 542 n.
amusement 837 n.
diversity
unrelatedness 10 n.
variegation 437 n.
(See **diverse** *)*
divert
make oblique 220 vb.
deflect 282 vb.
distract 456 vb.
misuse 675 vb.
obstruct 702 vb.
amuse 837 vb.
divertimento
musical piece 412 n.
divertissement
pleasure 376 n.
musical piece 412 n.
stage play 594 n.
amusement 837 n.
Dives
rich person 800 n.
divest
uncover 229 vb.
relinquish 621 vb.
depose 752 vb.
deprive 786 vb.
divide
sunder 46 vb.
part 53 vb.
class 62 vb.
do sums 86 vb.
bisect 92 vb.
summit 213 n.
partition 231 n.
limit 236 n.
mete out 465 vb.
vote 605 vb.
make quarrels 709 vb.
apportion 783 vb.
schismatize 978 vb.
divided
disunited 46 adj.
fragmentary 53 adj.
quarrelling 709 adj.
schismatical 978 adj.
dividend
part 53 n.
numerical element 85 n.
gain 771 n.
participation 775 n.
portion 783 n.
dividers
gauge 465 n.
divination
intuition 476 n.
divination 511 n.
hermeneutics 520 n.
sorcery 983 n.
occultism 984 n.
divine
foresee 510 vb.
divine 511 vb.
suppose 512 vb.
beautiful 841 adj.
lovable 887 adj.
divine 965 adj.
godlike 965 adj.
theologian 973 n.
religious 973 adj.
cleric 986 n.
diviner
diviner 511 n.
visionary 513 n.
interpreter 520 n.
warner 664 n.
sorcerer 983 n.
occultist 984 n.
divine revelation
revelation 975 n.
divine right
authority 733 n.
divine service
public worship 981 n.
divining rod
detector 484 n.
magic instrument 983 n.
divinity
divineness 965 n.
theology 973 n.
divinity student
theologian 973 n.
divisible
severable 46 adj.
numerical 85 adj.
division
scission 46 n.
decomposition 51 n.
subdivision 53 n.
discontinuity 72 n.
classification 77 n.
numerical operation 86 n.
district 184 n.
partition 231 n.

vote 605 n.
parliament 692 n.
society 708 n.
formation 722 n.
apportionment 783 n.
schism 978 n.
divorce
separation 46 n.
disunite 46 vb.
divorce 896 n.vb.
divorcee
divorce 896 n.
divot
piece 53 n.
divulge
manifest 522 vb.
divulge 526 vb.
publish 528 vb.
speak 579 vb.
accuse 928 vb.
divvy up
apportion 783 vb.
dixie
cauldron 194 n.
Dixieland
music 412 n.
dizziness
rotation 315 n.
dim sight 440 n.
frenzy 503 n.
illness 651 n.
dizzy
unequal 29 adj.
high 209 adj.
rotary 315 adj.
light-minded 456 adj.
crazy 503 adj.
tipsy 949 adj.
DJ
broadcaster 531 n.
djinn
(See **jinn** *)*
DNA
heredity 5 n.
organism 358 n.
D-notice
restraint 747 n.
do
be in a state of 7 vb.
accord 24 vb.
cause 156 vb.
be able 160 vb.
produce 164 vb.
operate 173 vb.
study 536 vb.
deceive 542 vb.
represent 551 vb.
be instrumental 628 vb.
suffice 635 vb.
be useful 640 vb.
be expedient 642 vb.
do 676 vb.
be active 678 vb.
deal with 688 vb.
carry out 725 vb.
observe 768 vb.
celebration 876 n.
— again
repeat 106 vb.
— a job
busy oneself 622 vb.
— all one can
exert oneself 682 vb.
minister to 703 vb.
— all right for oneself
get rich 800 vb.
— as one likes
will 595 vb.
dominate 733 vb.
be free 744 vb.
— as one would be done by
be benevolent 897 vb.
be disinterested 931 vb.
— as others do
conform 83 vb.
— away with
destroy 165 vb.
kill 362 vb.
— by halves
neglect 458 vb.
not complete 726 vb.
— down
deceive 542 vb.
— duty for
substitute 150 vb.
function 622 vb.
deputize 755 vb.
— for
destroy 165 vb.
kill 362 vb.
murder 362 vb.
harm 645 vb.
minister to 703 vb.
defeat 727 vb.
serve 742 vb.
— in
destroy 165 vb.
murder 362 vb.
— instead
compensate 31 vb.
— into
translate 520 vb.
— its job
operate 173 vb.
— justice to
eat 301 vb.
vindicate 927 vb.
— one's best
be careful 457 vb.
be willing 597 vb.
attempt 671 vb.
be active 678 vb.
— one's bit
do one's duty 917 vb.
— one's dirty work
be servile 879 vb.
— one's duty
keep faith 768 vb.
do one's duty 917 vb.
— oneself in
kill oneself 362 vb.
— one's own thing
be unconformable 84 vb.
be free 744 vb.
— one's utmost
exert oneself 682 vb.
— out of
deceive 542 vb.
defraud 788 vb.
— proud
be liberal 813 vb.
be hospitable 882 vb.
— the dirty on
be dishonest 930 vb.
— the honours
be hospitable 882 vb.
greet 884 vb.
show respect 920 vb.
— the needful
do 676 vb.
deal with 688 vb.
pay 804 vb.
— the trick
be successful 727 vb.
— up
join 45 vb.
modernize 126 vb.
close 264 vb.
make better 654 vb.
repair 656 vb.
fatigue 684 vb.
— well
progress 285 vb.
flourish 615 vb.
be skilful 694 vb.
succeed 727 vb.
prosper 730 vb.
— without
not use 674 vb.
refuse 760 vb.
not retain 779 vb.
dobbin
horse 273 n.
doch-an-dorris
valediction 296 n.
draught 301 n.
docile
tamed 369 adj.
studious 536 adj.
willing 597 adj.
induced 612 adj.
obedient 739 adj.
docility
persuadability 612 n.
dock
subtract 39 vb.
cut 46 vb.
place 187 vb.
stable 192 n.
shorten 204 vb.
arrive 295 vb.
storage 632 n.
impair 655 vb.
shelter 662 n.
courtroom 956 n.
docker
displacement 188 n.
boatman 270 n.
worker 686 n.
docket
class 62 vb.
list 87 n.vb.
credential 466 n.
label 547 n.
mark 547 vb.
record 548 vb.
abstract 592 vb.
docking
diminution 37 n.
space travel 271 n.
arrival 295 n.
doctor
mix 43 vb.
modify 143 vb.
psychologist 447 n.
scholar 492 n.
be false 541 vb.
mender 656 n.
doctor 658 n.vb.
academic title 870 n.
theologian 973 n.
doctorate
honours 866 n.
academic title 870 n.
doctrinaire
doctrinaire 473 n.
positive 473 adj.
narrow mind 481 n.
theorist 512 n.
doctrinal
creedal 485 adj.
educational 534 adj.
theological 973 adj.
orthodox 976 adj.
doctrine
creed 485 n.
theology 973 n.
document
evidence 466 n.
corroborate 466 vb.
demonstrate 478 vb.
record 548 n.vb.
documentary
film 445 n.
evidential 466 adj.
informative 524 adj.
broadcast 531 n.
descriptive 590 adj.
documentation
evidence 466 n.
demonstration 478 n.
record 548 n.n.
dodderer
waverer 601 n.
doddering
ageing 131 adj.
weak 163 adj.
agitated 318 adj.
doddle
easy thing 701 n.
dodecahedron
over five 99 n.

angular figure 247 n.
dodge
vary 152 vb.
be oblique 220 vb.
campanology 412 n.
disregard 458 vb.
sophistry 477 n.
be stealthy 525 vb.
dissemble 541 vb.
trickery 542 n.
avoid 620 vb.
contrivance 623 n.
elude 667 vb.
stratagem 698 n.
be cunning 698 vb.
not observe 769 vb.
be dishonest 930 vb.
— the column
fail in duty 918 vb.
dodgems
pleasure ground 837 n.
dodger
hider 527 n.
avoider 620 n.
dodgy
dangerous 661 adj.
dodo
archaism 127 n.
animal 365 n.
doe
speeder 277 n.
female animal 373 n.
doer
producer 164 n.
doer 676 n.
busy person 678 n.
doeskin
textile 222 n.
skin 226 n.
doff
doff 229 vb.
dog
accompany 89 vb.
follow 284 vb.
dog 365 n.
male animal 372 n.
pursue 619 vb.
knave 938 n.
dogcart
carriage 274 n.
dog collar
neckwear 228 n.
canonicals 989 n.
dog days
summer 128 n.
heat 379 n.
doge
officer 741 n.
dog-eared
folded 261 adj.
dilapidated 655 adj.
used 673 adj.
dogend
tobacco 388 n.
dogfight
fight 716 n.
battle 718 n.
dogfish
fish food 301 n.
fish 365 n.
dogged
persevering 600 adj.
obstinate 602 adj.
courageous 855 adj.
doggerel
inelegant 576 adj.
doggerel 593 n.
ridiculousness 849 n.
dog in the manger
hinderer 702 n.
possessor 776 n.
egotist 932 n.
selfish 932 adj.
dog-in-the-manger policy
exclusion 57 n.
dogma
certainty 473 n.
creed 485 n.
theology 973 n.
dogmatic
certain 473 adj.
positive 473 adj.
narrow-minded 481 adj.
creedal 485 adj.
assertive 532 adj.
obstinate 602 adj.
theological 973 adj.
dogmatist
doctrinaire 473 n.
obstinate person 602 n.
do-gooder
volunteer 597 n.
kind person 897 n.
philanthropist 901 n.
dogsbody
busy person 678 n.
worker 686 n.
auxiliary 707 n.
servant 742 n.
dog's breakfast
bungling 695 n.
dog-tired
fatigued 684 adj.
dogtooth
notch 260 n.
pattern 844 n.
dog track
meeting place 192 n.
arena 724 n.
dog trot
gait 265 n.
slowness 278 n.
dogwatch
period 110 n.
doing
production 164 n.
agency 173 n.
representation 551 n.
action 676 n.
doing 676 adj.
doings
affairs 154 n.
deed 676 n.
doing time
imprisoned 747 adj.
doing well
prosperous 730 adj.
do-it-yourself
bungled 695 adj.
artless 699 adj.
dolce far niente
inaction 677 n.
leisure 681 n.
dolce vita
sensualism 944 n.
doldrums
weather 340 n.
inaction 677 n.
inactivity 679 n.
dejection 834 n.
dole
small quantity 33 n.
insufficiency 636 n.
gift 781 n.
portion 783 n.
sociology 901 n.
doleful
melancholic 834 adj.
lamenting 836 adj.
dole out
mete out 465 vb.
give 781 vb.
apportion 783 vb.
be parsimonious 816 vb.
doll
dwarf 196 n.
woman 373 n.
image 551 n.
plaything 837 n.
a beauty 841 n.
dollar
coinage 797 n.
dollar bill
paper money 797 n.
dollar diplomacy
trade 791 n.
dolled up
beautified 843 adj.
bedecked 844 adj.
dollop
piece 53 n.
portion 783 n.
doll's house
plaything 837 n.
dolly bird
a beauty 841 n.
dolmen
tomb 364 n.
monument 548 n.
dolorous
paining 827 adj.
dolour
sorrow 825 n.
suffering 825 n.
dolphin
mammal 365 n.
dolt
dunce 501 n.
doltish
unintelligent 499 adj.
Dom
church title 986 n.
domain
classification 77 n.
territory 184 n.
function 622 n.
lands 777 n.
dome
edifice 164 n.
house 192 n.
high structure 209 n.
head 213 n.
roof 226 n.
sphere 252 n.
dome 253 n.
Domesday Book
list 87 n.
domestic
native 191 adj.
provincial 192 adj.
interior 224 adj.
animal 365 adj.
tamed 369 adj.
domestic 742 n.
unsociable 883 adj.
domesticate
break in 369 vb.
habituate 610 vb.
domesticated
located 187 adj.
native 191 adj.
tamed 369 adj.
domesticity
unsociability 883 n.
domestic science
cookery 301 n.
domestic service
service 745 n.
domicile
abode 192 n.
domiciled
residing 192 adj.
domiciliary
native 191 adj.
dominance
influence 178 n.
dominant
supreme 34 adj.
influential 178 adj.
musical note 410 n.
authoritative 733 adj.
dominant characteristic
speciality 80 n.
dominate
be able 160 vb.
influence 178 vb.
prevail 178 vb.
be high 209 vb.
dominate 733 vb.
subjugate 745 vb.
domination
superiority 34 n.
influence 178 n.
governance 733 n.

domineering
authoritarian 735 adj.
oppressive 735 adj.
insolent 878 adj.
Dominican
monk 986 n.
dominie
teacher 537 n.
dominion
territory 184 n.
governance 733 n.
political organization 733 n.
lands 777 n.
domino
cloak 228 n.
disguise 527 n.
dominoes
indoor game 837 n.
domino theory
continuity 71 n.
don
wear 228 vb.
male 372 n.
scholar 492 n.
teacher 537 n.
aristocrat 868 n.
title 870 n.
donate
give 781 vb.
expend 806 vb.
donation
transference 272 n.
subvention 703 n.
gift 781 n.
done
past 125 adj.
usual 610 adj.
completed 725 adj.
fashionable 848 adj.
done, be
pay too much 811 vb.
done for
destroyed 165 adj.
dying 361 adj.
defeated 728 adj.
done in/up
deteriorated 655 adj.
fatigued 684 adj.
done thing
practice 610 n.
etiquette 848 n.
done to a turn
culinary 301 adj.
savoury 390 adj.
done up to the nines
beautified 843 adj.
done with
disused 674 adj.
donjon
fort 713 n.
Don Juan
lover 887 n.
libertine 952 n.
donkey
beast of burden 273 n.
fool 501 n.
donkey's years
long duration 113 n.
donkeywork
labour 682 n.
donna
lady 373 n.
donnish
narrow-minded 481 adj.
instructed 490 adj.
severe 735 adj.
fastidious 862 adj.
Donnybrook
turmoil 61 n.
donor
propagation 167 n.
provider 633 n.
giver 781 n.
do-nothing
nonactive 677 adj.
lazy 679 adj.
Don Quixote
crank 504 n.
visionary 513 n.
brave person 855 n.
don't-care
rash 857 adj.
indifferent 860 adj.
doodah
tool 630 n.
doodle
be inattentive 456 vb.
picture 553 n.
doodlebug
rocket 276 n.
bomb 723 n.
doom
finality 69 n.
predestine 155 vb.
ruin 165 n.
death 361 n.
fate 596 n.
condemnation 961 n.
punishment 963 n.
doomed
ephemeral 114 adj.
destroyed 165 adj.
dying 361 adj.
fated 596 adj.
unfortunate 731 adj.
unhappy 825 adj.
doom merchant
overestimation 482 n.
oracle 511 n.
alarmist 854 n.
doomsday
future state 124 n.
doomwatch
surveillance 457 n.
door
threshold 234 n.
barrier 235 n.
doorway 263 n.
stopper 264 n.
way in 297 n.
access 624 n.
doorbell
signal 547 n.
do-or-die
rash 857 adj.
door in one's face
closure 264 n.
door jamb
pillar 218 n.
doorway 263 n.
doorkeeper
doorkeeper 264 n.
doorknob
opener 263 n.
door knocker
hammer 279 n.
signal 547 n.
doorman
doorkeeper 264 n.
doormat
weakling 163 n.
floor-cover 226 n.
cleaning utensil 648 n.
submission 721 n.
coward 856 n.
doorstep
doorway 263 n.
doorway
entrance 68 n.
doorway 263 n.
way in 297 n.
access 624 n.
dope
anaesthetic 375 n.
render insensible 375 vb.
ninny 501 n.
information 524 n.
drug 658 n.
doctor 658 vb.
poison 659 n.
make inactive 679 vb.
drug-taking 949 n.
doped
insensible 375 adj.
drugged 949 adj.
dope fiend
madman 504 n.
habitué 610 n.
drug-taking 949 n.
dopey, dopy
foolish 499 adj.
inactive 679 adj.
sleepy 679 adj.
doppelgänger
analogue 18 n.
ghost 970 n.
Doppler effect
displacement 188 n.
Doric
dialectal 560 adj.
ornamental 844 adj.
dormancy
inaction 677 n.
dormant
inert 175 adj.
quiescent 266 adj.
latent 523 adj.
abrogated 752 adj.
dormitory
quarters 192 n.
chamber 194 n.
dormitory suburb
district 184 n.
dormouse
mammal 365 n.
idler 679 n.
dorp
housing 192 n.
dorsal
back 238 adj.
dose
finite quantity 26 n.
measurement 465 n.
medicine 658 n.
portion 783 n.
punishment 963 n.
doss down
dwell 192 vb.
sleep 679 vb.
dosshouse
inn 192 n.
dossier
information 524 n.
record 548 n.
dot
small thing 33 n.
place 185 n.
maculation 437 n.
punctuation 547 n.
mark 547 vb.
lettering 586 n.
dower 777 n.
pattern 844 n.
— the i's and cross the t's
be careful 457 vb.
emphasize 532 vb.
dotage
old age 131 n.
folly 499 n.
insanity 503 n.
dotard
old man 133 n.
dote
be credulous 487 vb.
be foolish 499 vb.
be insane 503 vb.
be in love 887 vb.
— on
desire 859 vb.
dottle
leavings 41 n.
tobacco 388 n.
dotty
foolish 499 adj.
crazy 503 adj.
double
identity 13 n.
analogue 18 n.
augment 36 vb.
dual 90 adj.
double 91 vb.
substitute 150 n.
invigorate 174 vb.
enlarge 197 vb.
fold 261 vb.

gait 265 n.
speeding 277 n.
turn back 286 vb.
spirit 447 n.
equivocal 518 adj.
hypocritical 541 adj.
representation 551 n.
— up
disable 161 vb.
fatigue 684 vb.
double agent
secret service 459 n.
deceiver 545 n.
double-barrelled
dual 90 adj.
double bass
viol 414 n.
double-blind test
experiment 461 n.
double-breasted
tailored 228 adj.
double-check
make certain 473 vb.
double chin
bulk 195 n.
double-cross
deceive 542 vb.
be cunning 698 vb.
be dishonest 930 vb.
double-crosser
deceiver 545 n.
slyboots 698 n.
perfidy 930 n.
double-dealing
duplicity 541 n.
hypocritical 541 adj.
tergiversating 603 adj.
cunning 698 n.
perfidy 930 n.
double-decker
stratification 207 n.
bus 274 n.
doubled up
laughing 835 adj.
double Dutch
lack of meaning 515 n.
unintelligibility 517 n.
double-dyed
consummate 32 adj.
coloured 425 adj.
vicious 934 adj.
double entendre
equivocalness 518 n.
impurity 951 n.
double figures
over five 99 n.
double first
victor 727 n.
double-fronted
architectural 192 adj.
double-glazing
lining 227 n.
barrier 235 n.
silencer 401 n.
double harness
duality 90 n.
cooperation 706 n.
double-jointed
flexible 327 adj.
double life
duality 90 n.
duplicity 541 n.
double meaning
connotation 514 n.
equivocalness 518 n.
doublet
jacket 228 n.
word 559 n.
double take
sequel 67 n.
inspection 438 n.
double-talk
lack of meaning 515 n.
equivocalness 518 n.
neology 560 n.
doublethink
sophistry 477 n.
mental dishonesty 543 n.
doubly
greatly 32 adv.
twice 91 adv.
doubt
dubiety 474 n.
be uncertain 474 vb.
doubt 486 n. vb.
not know 491 vb.
doubtful
moot 459 adj.
doubting 474 adj.
uncertain 474 adj.
unbelieving 486 adj.
nervous 854 adj.
cautious 858 adj.
disreputable 867 adj.
dishonest 930 adj.
doubtless
certainly 473 adv.
douceur
gift 781 n.
reward 962 n.
douche
water 339 n.
ablutions 648 n.
therapy 658 n.
dough
cereals 301 n.
softness 327 n.
pulpiness 356 n.
shekels 797 n.
doughnut
pastries 301 n.
doughty
stalwart 162 adj.
courageous 855 adj.
doughy
soft 327 adj.
pulpy 356 adj.
colourless 426 adj.
dour
obstinate 602 adj.
severe 735 adj.
serious 834 adj.
douse, dowse
plunge 313 vb.
drench 341 vb.
extinguish 382 vb.
snuff out 418 vb.
dove
bird 365 n.
pacifist 717 n.
mediator 720 n.
innocent 935 n.
Dove
Holy Ghost 965 n.
dovetail
accord 24 vb.
joint 45 n.
join 45 vb.
introduce 231 vb.
dowager
old woman 133 n.
woman 373 n.
widowhood 896 n.
dowdy
graceless 842 adj.
bad taste 847 n.
ill-bred 847 adj.
dowel
fastening 47 n.
dower
dower 777 n.
give 781 vb.
down
filament 208 n.
under 210 adv.
vertically 215 adv.
smoothness 258 n.
hair 259 n.
down 309 adv.
fell 311 vb.
softness 327 n.
recorded 548 adj.
losing 772 adj.
dejected 834 adj.
sullen 893 adj.
— tools
cease 145 vb.
revolt 738 vb.
down-and-out
unlucky person 731 n.
poor person 801 n.
low fellow 869 n.
down at heel
dilapidated 655 adj.
beggarly 801 adj.
downbeat
tempo 410 n.
dejected 834 adj.
downcast
dejected 834 adj.
downdraught
descent 309 n.
wind 352 n.
downers
drug-taking 949 n.
downfall
ruin 165 n.
descent 309 n.
defeat 728 n.
adversity 731 n.
downgrade
shame 867 vb.
punish 963 vb.
downhearted
dejected 834 adj.
downhill
sloping 220 adj.
down 309 adv.
easy 701 adj.
downmarket
cheap 812 adj.
down on, be
be severe 735 vb.
down on one's luck
unfortunate 731 adj.
down payment
security 767 n.
payment 804 n.
downpour
rain 350 n.
downright
consummate 32 adj.
positively 32 adv.
simple 44 adj.
complete 54 adj.
intelligible 516 adj.
undisguised 522 adj.
veracious 540 adj.
downs
high land 209 n.
plain 348 n.
Down's syndrome
unintelligence 499 n.
downstage
on stage 594 adv.
downstairs
under 210 adv.
down 309 adv.
downstream
towards 281 adv.
down 309 adv.
easy 701 adj.
downthrow
descent 309 n.
down to earth
true 494 adj.
down to the ground
completely 54 adv.
downtown
city 184 n.
downtrodden
subjected 745 adj.
suffering 825 adj.
downturn
deterioration 655 n.
down under
beyond 199 adv.
downwards
under 210 adv.
down 309 adv.
downward trend
decrease 37 n.
descent 309 n.
downwind
towards 281 adv.
downy
fibrous 208 adj.
smooth 258 adj.

downy 259 adj.
soft 327 adj.
comfortable 376 adj.
dowry
dower 777 n.
dowse
search 459 vb.
dowser
enquirer 459 n.
detector 484 n.
diviner 511 n.
doxology
hymn 981 n.
doyen
seniority 131 n.
expert 696 n.
doze
be neglectful 458 vb.
sleep 679 n.vb.
dozen
over five 99 n.
drab
uniform 16 adj.
soft-hued 425 adj.
dirty person 649 n.
cheerless 834 adj.
dull 840 adj.
graceless 842 adj.
loose woman 952 n.
drabble
make unclean 649 vb.
drabness
dullness 840 n.
drachm
weighing 322 n.
drachma
coinage 797 n.
Draconian
severe 735 adj.
draff
dirt 649 n.
draft
copy 22 n.
prototype 23 n.
compose 56 vb.
representation 551 n.
write 586 vb.
compendium 592 n.
plan 623 n.vb.
army 722 n.
compulsion 740 n.
paper money 797 n.
draft-dodger
avoider 620 n.
drag
be pending 136 vb.
counteraction 182 n.
be long 203 vb.
slowness 278 n.
draw 288 vb.
attraction 291 n.
friction 333 n.
difficulty 700 n.
encumbrance 702 n.
restraint 747 n.
fetter 748 n.
annoyance 827 n.
bore 838 n.
be tedious 838 vb.
— for
search 459 vb.
— from
extract 304 vb.
compel 740 vb.
— in by the heels
be unrelated 10 vb.
— on
continue 108 vb.
drag on 113 vb.
be pending 136 vb.
— one's feet
move slowly 278 vb.
be unwilling 598 vb.
be inactive 679 vb.
— out
spin out 113 vb.
extract 304 vb.
manifest 522 vb.
— towards
attract 291 vb.
— up
elevate 310 vb.
drag artist(e)
imitator 20 n.
entertainer 594 n.
draggle
hang 217 vb.
make unclean 649 vb.
draggletail
slut 61 n.
dirty person 649 n.
drag-line
excavator 255 n.
extractor 304 n.
dragnet
generality 79 n.
network 222 n.
chase 619 n.
dragoman
guide 520 n.
dragon
rara avis 84 n.
violent creature 176 n.
dragonfly
insect 365 n.
dragon's teeth
defences 713 n.
dragoon
cavalry 722 n.
compel 740 vb.
dragster
automobile 274 n.
drain
pierce 263 vb.
outflow 298 n.
empty 300 vb.
dry 342 vb.
drain 351 n.
cultivate 370 vb.
waste 634 vb.
cleanser 648 n.
sink 649 n.
sanitate 652 vb.
use 673 vb.
fatigue 684 vb.
loss 772 n.
levy 786 vb.
— away
decrease 37 vb.
— into
flow 350 vb.
— of colour
decolorize 426 vb.
— off
empty 300 vb.
— one's glass
drink 301 vb.
— out
flow out 298 vb.
make flow 350 vb.
drainage
outflow 298 n.
voidance 300 n.
waste 634 n.
cleansing 648 n.
dirt 649 n.
swill 649 n.
drainpipe
cylinder 252 n.
outlet 298 n.
drain 351 n.
cleanser 648 n.
dram
draught 301 n.
metrology 465 n.
drama
broadcast 531 n.
literature 557 n.
drama 594 n.
stage play 594 n.
action 676 n.
activity 678 n.
excitation 821 n.
dramatic
dramatic 594 adj.
exciting 821 adj.
impressive 821 adj.
wonderful 864 adj.
showy 875 adj.
dramatic critic
playgoer 594 n.
dramatic irony
narrative 590 n.
dramatics
dramaturgy 594 n.
ostentation 875 n.
dramatis personae
list 87 n.
person 371 n.
actor 594 n.
personnel 686 n.
dramatist
author 589 n.
dramatist 594 n.
dramatize, dramatise
show 522 vb.
exaggerate 546 vb.
represent 551 vb.
dramatize 594 vb.
— oneself
act 594 vb.
be affected 850 vb.
be ostentatious 875 vb.
dramaturgy
dramaturgy 594 n.
drape
hang 217 vb.
dress 228 vb.
draper
clothier 228 n.
draperies
hanging object 217 n.
robe 228 n.
drastic
vigorous 174 adj.
severe 735 adj.
drastically
extremely 32 adv.
draught
depth 211 n.
transport 272 n.
traction 288 n.
draught 301 n.
gravity 322 n.
wind 352 n.
medicine 658 n.
adversity 731 n.
plaything 837 n.
draught animals
beast of burden 273 n.
draughts
board game 837 n.
draughtsman, draughtswoman
recorder 549 n.
artist 556 n.
draughtsmanship
painting 553 n.
draughty
windy 352 adj.
draw
copy 20 vb.
draw 28 n.
be equal 28 vb.
compose 56 vb.
bring together 74 vb.
displace 188 vb.
make thin 206 vb.
uncover 229 vb.
outline 233 vb.
form 243 vb.
draw 288 vb.
attraction 291 n.
attract 291 vb.
cook 301 vb.
extract 304 vb.
blow 352 vb.
be hot 379 vb.
smoke 388 vb.
represent 551 vb.
paint 553 vb.
describe 590 vb.
gambling 618 n.
provide 633 vb.
acquire 771 vb.
receive 782 vb.
take 786 vb.
receipt 807 n.
desired object 859 n.
excite love 887 vb.

— a bead on
aim 281 vb.
shoot 287 vb.
fire at 712 vb.
threaten 900 vb.
— a blank
forget 506 vb.
fail 728 vb.
— aside
deflect 282 vb.
— attention to
show 522 vb.
— back
regress 286 vb.
recede 290 vb.
avoid 620 vb.
— blood
wound 655 vb.
attack 712 vb.
— breath
be 1 vb.
be born 360 vb.
live 360 vb.
be refreshed 685 vb.
— in
make smaller 198 vb.
— in one's horns
submit 721 vb.
— lots
gamble 618 vb.
— near
be near 200 vb.
approach 289 vb.
— off
empty 300 vb.
extract 304 vb.
obstruct 702 vb.
take 786 vb.
— on
avail oneself of 673 vb.
claim 915 vb.
— one out
converse 584 vb.
— out
spin out 113 vb.
enlarge 197 vb.
lengthen 203 vb.
extract 304 vb.
be diffuse 570 vb.
— stumps
terminate 69 vb.
— the curtains
close 264 vb.
screen 421 vb.
conceal 525 vb.
— the line
exclude 57 vb.
limit 236 vb.
discriminate 463 vb.
reject 607 vb.
restrain 747 vb.
prohibit 757 vb.
disapprove 924 vb.
— the teeth
disable 161 vb.
blunt 257 vb.
— to a close
end 69 vb.
— together
join 45 vb.
bring together 74 vb.
make smaller 198 vb.
close 264 vb.
— towards
attract 291 vb.
— up
compose 56 vb.
be in order 60 vb.
come to rest 266 vb.
plan 623 vb.
drawback
decrement 42 n.
defect 647 n.
obstacle 702 n.
drawbridge
doorway 263 n.
bridge 624 n.
fort 713 n.
drawer
compartment 194 n.
traction 288 n.
artist 556 n.
drawers
underwear 228 n.
draw hoe
traction 288 n.
farm tool 370 n.
drawing
copy 22 n.
representation 551 n.
picture 553 n.
drawing board
plan 623 n.
drawing pin
fastening 47 n.
drawl
pronunciation 577 n.
voice 577 vb.
speech defect 580 n.
drawn
equal 28 adj.
lean 206 adj.
represented 551 adj.
drawn game
draw 28 n.
noncompletion 726 n.
drawn out
protracted 113 adj.
tedious 838 adj.
drawstring
fastening 47 n.
ligature 47 n.
dray
cart 274 n.
drayman
driver 268 n.
dread
expect 507 vb.
fear 854 n.vb.
dreadful
prodigious 32 adj.
harmful 645 adj.
not nice 645 adj.
adverse 731 adj.
distressing 827 adj.
frightening 854 adj.
dreadlocks
hair 259 n.
dream
insubstantial thing 4 n.
vision 438 n.
see 438 vb.
visual fallacy 440 n.
not think 450 vb.
be inattentive 456 vb.
error 495 n.
suppose 512 vb.
fantasy 513 n.
objective 617 n.
sleep 679 vb.
a beauty 841 n.
hope 852 vb.
desired object 859 n.
— of
aim at 617 vb.
hope 852 vb.
desire 859 vb.
— up
imagine 513 vb.
dreamer
crank 504 n.
visionary 513 n.
idler 679 n.
dreamland
fantasy 513 n.
sleep 679 n.
dreamlike
shadowy 419 adj.
appearing 445 adj.
dream world
fantasy 513 n.
dreamy
insubstantial 4 adj.
thoughtful 449 adj.
abstracted 456 adj.
imaginary 513 adj.
dreary
dark 418 adj.
unpleasant 827 adj.
cheerless 834 adj.
dejected 834 adj.
melancholic 834 adj.
tedious 838 adj.
dull 840 adj.
graceless 842 adj.
dredge
extract 304 vb.
dredger
excavator 255 n.
ship 275 n.
extractor 304 n.
lifter 310 n.
dree one's weird
be forced 596 vb.
dregs
inferior 35 n.
leavings 41 n.
extremity 69 n.
dirt 649 n.
rabble 869 n.
object of scorn 867 n.
bad person 938 n.
drench
soften 327 vb.
add water 339 vb.
drench 341 vb.
groom 369 vb.
superabound 637 vb.
clean 648 vb.
medicine 658 n.
sate 863 vb.
drenching rain
rain 350 n.
dress
be uniform 16 vb.
adjust 24 vb.
equalize 28 vb.
cover 226 vb.
dress 228 n.vb.
cook 301 vb.
livery 547 n.
equipment 630 n.
doctor 658 vb.
make ready 669 vb.
decorate 844 vb.
— up
dress 228 vb.
wear 228 vb.
cant 541 vb.
dissemble 541 vb.
primp 843 vb.
be vain 873 vb.
be ostentatious 875 vb.
dressage
equitation 267 n.
dress circle
onlookers 441 n.
theatre 594 n.
dressed
dressed 228 adj.
dressed up
beautified 843 adj.
bedecked 844 adj.
fashionable 848 adj.
dresser
cabinet 194 n.
shelf 218 n.
stand 218 n.
clothier 228 n.
nurse 658 n.
dressing
condiment 389 n.
surgical dressing 658 n.
dressing down
reprimand 924 n.
dressing gown
informal dress 228 n.
dressing station
hospital 658 n.
dressmaker
clothier 228 n.
dress rehearsal
dramaturgy 594 n.
preparation 669 n.

dress sense
beauty 841 n.
fashion 848 n.
dressy
fashionable 848 adj.
showy 875 adj.
drey
nest 192 n.
dribble
small quantity 33 n.
move slowly 278 vb.
kick 279 vb.
propel 287 vb.
exude 298 vb.
flow out 298 vb.
emit 300 vb.
flow 350 vb.
driblet
finite quantity 26 n.
small thing 33 n.
dried out
dry 342 adj.
unhabituated 611 adj.
sober 948 adj.
dried up
unproductive 172 adj.
dry 342 adj.
drift
leavings 41 n.
accumulation 74 n.
vary 152 vb.
tendency 179 n.
distance 199 n.
be in motion 265 vb.
fly 271 vb.
thing transferred 272 n.
move slowly 278 vb.
direction 281 n.
deviation 282 n.
shortfall 307 n.
be light 323 vb.
be neglectful 458 vb.
be uncertain 474 vb.
meaning 514 n.
not act 677 vb.
be free 744 vb.
— away
be dispersed 75 vb.
recede 290 vb.
— with the tide
conform 83 vb.
do easily 701 vb.
drifter
wanderer 268 n.
fishing boat 275 n.
idler 679 n.
driftwood
thing transferred 272 n.
drill
make uniform 16 vb.
regularity 81 n.
make conform 83 vb.
textile 222 n.
sharp point 256 n.
perforator 263 n.
farm tool 370 n.
train 534 vb.
habituation 610 n.
practice 610 n.
tool 630 n.
make ready 669 vb.
exercise 682 n.
art of war 718 n.
dominate 733 vb.
formality 875 n.
drink
absorb 299 vb.
draught 301 n.
drink 301 vb.
fluid 335 n.
ocean 343 n.
revel 837 vb.
get drunk 949 vb.
— a health
toast 876 vb.
— in
be attentive 455 vb.
learn 536 vb.
— one's fill
drink 301 vb.
have enough 635 vb.
— one under the table
inebriate 949 vb.
— to
toast 876 vb.
pay one's respects 884 vb.
applaud 923 vb.
— to excess
be intemperate 943 vb.
get drunk 949 vb.
— up
empty 300 vb.
drinkable
edible 301 adj.
drinker
drinking 301 n.
reveller 837 n.
drunkard 949 n.
drinking bout
festivity 837 n.
drunkenness 949 n.
drinking water
soft drink 301 n.
water 339 n.
drinks
social gathering 882 n.
drip
weakling 163 n.
exude 298 vb.
emit 300 vb.
descend 309 vb.
moisture 341 n.
flow 350 vb.
rain 350 vb.
ninny 501 n.
bore 838 n.
drip-dry
dry 342 vb.
dripfeed
eating 301 n.
therapy 658 n.
dripping
meat 301 n.
fat 357 n.
dripping wet
drenched 341 adj.
dripping with
full 54 adj.
drive
energy 160 n.
empower 160 vb.
operate 173 vb.
vigorousness 174 n.
be vigorous 174 vb.
influence 178 n.
move 265 vb.
land travel 267 n.
ride 267 vb.
move fast 277 vb.
impel 279 vb.
propulsion 287 n.
propel 287 vb.
vigour 571 n.
resolution 599 n.
incite 612 vb.
chase 619 n.
path 624 n.
restlessness 678 n.
haste 680 n.
exertion 682 n.
fatigue 684 vb.
attack 712 n.
oppress 735 vb.
compel 740 vb.
— a coach and horses through
not observe 769 vb.
be illegal 954 vb.
— apart
set apart 46 vb.
make quarrels 709 vb.
— at
aim at 617 vb.
— home
emphasize 532 vb.
carry through 725 vb.
impress 821 vb.
— in
affix 45 vb.
enter 297 vb.
— into
collide 279 vb.
insert 303 vb.
induce 612 vb.
— off
repel 292 vb.
start out 296 vb.
steal 788 vb.
— on
progress 285 vb.
— out of one's mind
distract 456 vb.
— to the wall
be difficult 700 vb.
defeat 727 vb.
— up the wall
make mad 503 vb.
— without due care and attention
endanger 661 vb.
drivel
exude 298 vb.
be foolish 499 vb.
be insane 503 vb.
silly talk 515 n.
be diffuse 570 vb.
be loquacious 581 vb.
driveller
fool 501 n.
chatterer 581 n.
driven
dynamic 160 adj.
hasty 680 adj.
driven into a corner, be
be forced 596 vb.
driver
driver 268 n.
machinist 630 n.
driving force
power 160 n.
propellant 287 n.
motive 612 n.
drizzle
moisture 341 n.
be wet 341 vb.
rain 350 n.vb.
droll
witty 839 adj.
funny 849 adj.
drone
uniformity 16 n.
insect 365 n.
sound faint 401 vb.
roll 403 vb.
shrill 407 vb.
ululation 409 n.
musical note 410 n.
voice 577 vb.
be loquacious 581 vb.
idler 679 n.
— away
be inactive 679 vb.
— on
be dull 840 vb.
drool (over)
exude 298 vb.
mean nothing 515 vb.
love 887 vb.
droop
be weak 163 vb.
hang 217 vb.
descend 309 vb.
be ill 651 vb.
deteriorate 655 vb.
be inactive 679 vb.
be fatigued 684 vb.
be dejected 834 vb.
drop
small thing 33 n.
decrease 37 vb.

terminate 69 vb.
be weak 163 vb.
reproduce itself 167 vb.
minuteness 196 n.
depth 211 n.
hanging object 217 n.
sphere 252 n.
exude 298 vb.
dismiss 300 vb.
emit 300 vb.
descend 309 vb.
let fall 311 vb.
moisture 341 n.
flow 350 vb.
rain 350 vb.
stage set 594 n.
relinquish 621 vb.
stop using 674 vb.
be fatigued 684 vb.
be clumsy 695 vb.
not retain 779 vb.
jewellery 844 n.
means of execution 964 n.
— a brick
blunder 495 vb.
be clumsy 695 vb.
— anchor
place oneself 187 vb.
navigate 269 vb.
arrive 295 vb.
— behind
be behind 238 vb.
follow 284 vb.
— from the clouds
surprise 508 vb.
— in
arrive 295 vb.
enter 297 vb.
infuse 303 vb.
insert 303 vb.
visit 882 vb.
— off
sleep 679 vb.
— one's guard
be unprepared 670 vb.
be rash 857 vb.
— out
relinquish 621 vb.
not complete 726 vb.
be free 744 vb.
— the idea
relinquish 621 vb.
— the mask
disclose 526 vb.
be truthful 540 vb.
drop by drop
by degrees 27 adv.
piecemeal 53 adv.
drop in the bucket
small quantity 33 n.
insufficiency 636 n.
trifle 639 n.
droplet
small thing 33 n.
minuteness 196 n.
sphere 252 n.
drop of the curtain
finality 69 n.
dramaturgy 594 n.
dropout
nonconformist 84 n.
dissentient 489 n.
loser 728 n.
malcontent 829 n.
abstainer 942 n.
droppings
excrement 302 n.
dirt 649 n.
drops
medicine 658 n.
dropsy
dilation 197 n.
disease 651 n.
drop too much
drunkenness 949 n.
droshky
cab 274 n.
carriage 274 n.
dross
leavings 41 n.
layer 207 n.
ash 381 n.
rubbish 641 n.
dirt 649 n.
drought
dryness 342 n.
scarcity 636 n.
blight 659 n.
drove
group 74 n.
certain quantity 104 n.
drover
driver 268 n.
leader 690 n.
drown
fill 54 vb.
suppress 165 vb.
descend 309 vb.
lower 311 vb.
founder 313 vb.
drench 341 vb.
perish 361 vb.
kill 362 vb.
silence 399 vb.
obliterate 550 vb.
— one's sorrows
revel 837 vb.
get drunk 949 vb.
— one's voice
deafen 416 vb.
make mute 578 vb.
drowned
deep 211 adj.
drowse
be inattentive 456 vb.
be neglectful 458 vb.
sleep 679 n.vb.
be fatigued 684 vb.
drubbing
defeat 728 n.
corporal punishment 963 n.
drudge
busy person 678 n.
worker 686 n.
servant 742 n.
drudgery
assiduity 678 n.
labour 682 n.
drug
anaesthetic 375 n.
render insensible 375 vb.
drug 658 n.
doctor 658 vb.
poison 659 n.
drug abuse
drug-taking 949 n.
drug addict
madman 504 n.
habitué 610 n.
drug-taking 949 n.
drug addiction
disease 651 n.
drug-taking 949 n.
drugged
impotent 161 adj.
insensible 375 adj.
inactive 679 adj.
drugged 949 adj.
drugget
floor-cover 226 n.
druggist
druggist 658 n.
drug on the market
superfluity 637 n.
cheapness 812 n.
drug-taking
tobacco 388 n.
excitant 821 n.
intemperance 943 n.
drug-taking 949 n.
Druid, Druidess
sorcerer 983 n.
priest 986 n.
drum
vat 194 n.
cylinder 252 n.
strike 279 vb.
oscillate 317 vb.
roll 403 vb.
play music 413 vb.
drum 414 n.
call 547 n.
— out
eject 300 vb.
drumbeat
periodicity 141 n.
impulse 279 n.
call 547 n.
drum major
instrumentalist 413 n.
leader 690 n.
drunk
drunk 949 adj.
drunkard
reveller 837 n.
sensualist 944 n.
drunkard 949 n.
drunken
disorderly 61 adj.
sensual 944 adj.
drunken 949 adj.
tipsy 949 adj.
drunkenness
festivity 837 n.
intemperance 943 n.
drunkenness 949 n.
dry
nonadhesive 49 adj.
unproductive 172 adj.
absorb 299 vb.
powdery 332 adj.
dry 342 adj.vb.
staunch 350 vb.
hot 379 adj.
heat 381 vb.
sour 393 adj.
strident 407 adj.
plain 573 adj.
act 594 vb.
clean 648 vb.
sanitate 652 vb.
preserve 666 vb.
mature 669 vb.
tedious 838 adj.
witty 839 adj.
hungry 859 adj.
temperate 942 adj.
sober 948 adj.
— one's eyes
be relieved 831 vb.
— out
be dry 342 vb.
be sober 948 vb.
— up
decrease 37 vb.
cease 145 vb.
be dry 342 vb.
be mute 578 vb.
waste 634 vb.
not suffice 636 vb.
make insensitive 820 vb.
dryad
vegetable life 366 n.
nymph 967 n.
dryasdust
bore 838 n.
tedious 838 adj.
dry-clean
clean 648 vb.
dry dock
stable 192 n.
goal 295 n.
dryer, drier
extractor 304 n.
dryer 342 n.
dry-eyed
pitiless 906 adj.
dry eyes
moral insensibility 820 n.
dry goods
textile 222 n.
merchandise 795 n.

drying
desiccation 342 n.
preservation 666 n.
drying out
drug-taking 949 n.
dryness
desert 172 n.
dryness 342 n.
tedium 838 n.
wit 839 n.
hunger 859 n.
dry-point
engraving 555 n.
dry rot
dirt 649 n.
blight 659 n.
dry run
experiment 461 n.
dry spell
weather 340 n.
dt's
frenzy 503 n.
alcoholism 949 n.
dual
dual 90 adj.
double 91 adj.
grammatical 564 adj.
dualism
duality 90 n.
philosophy 449 n.
deism 973 n.
dual personality
psychopathy 503 n.
dual-purpose
double 91 adj.
dub
name 561 vb.
misname 562 vb.
dignify 866 vb.
dubiety
dubiety 474 n.
doubt 486 n.
irresolution 601 n.
choice 605 n.
predicament 700 n.
dubious
improbable 472 adj.
doubting 474 adj.
uncertain 474 adj.
disreputable 867 adj.
ducal
noble 868 adj.
ducat
coinage 797 n.
duchess
potentate 741 n.
person of rank 868 n.
duchy
political organization 733 n.
duck
zero 103 n.
textile 222 n.
swim 269 vb.
immerse 303 vb.
descend 309 vb.
obeisance 311 n.
stoop 311 vb.
plunge 313 vb.
drench 341 vb.
bird 365 n.
table bird 365 n.
be unwilling 598 vb.
avoid 620 vb.
darling 890 n.
show respect 920 vb.
duckboards
paving 226 n.
bridge 624 n.
ducking
corporal punishment 963 n.
ducky, ducks
darling 890 n.
duct
tube 263 n.
conduit 351 n.
ductile
drawing 288 adj.
flexible 327 adj.
elastic 328 adj.
tractable 701 adj.
dud
powerless 161 adj.
useless 641 adj.
loser 728 n.
unsuccessful 728 adj.
dud cheque
false money 797 n.
dude
fop 848 n.
dudgeon
anger 891 n.
duds
clothing 228 n.
due
future 124 adj.
impending 155 adj.
advisable 642 adj.
owed 803 adj.
just 913 adj.
due 915 adj.
duel
duel 716 n.
duellist
opponent 705 n.
quarreller 709 n.
contender 716 n.
combatant 722 n.
dueness
attribution 158 n.
right 913 n.
dueness 915 n.
duty 917 n.
duenna
surveillance 457 n.
protector 660 n.
keeper 749 n.
dues
receipt 807 n.
tax 809 n.
duet
duality 90 n.
duet 412 n.
cooperation 706 n.
concord 710 n.
due to
caused 157 adj.
duffel, duffle
textile 222 n.
duffer
ignoramus 493 n.
dunce 501 n.
bungler 697 n.
dugout
excavation 255 n.
rowing boat 275 n.
refuge 662 n.
defences 713 n.
duke
potentate 741 n.
person of rank 868 n.
dukedom
political organization 733 n.
aristocracy 868 n.
dulcet
melodious 410 adj.
pleasurable 826 adj.
dulcify
assuage 177 vb.
sweeten 392 vb.
dulcimer
piano 414 n.
dulia
cult 981 n.
dull
assuage 177 vb.
blunt 257 vb.
render insensible 375 vb.
muted 401 adj.
nonresonant 405 adj.
dim 419 adj.
soft-hued 425 adj.
colourless 426 adj.
grey 429 adj.
ignorant 491 adj.
unintelligent 499 adj.
feeble 572 adj.
inactive 679 adj.
impassive 820 adj.
inexcitable 823 adj.
cheerless 834 adj.
melancholic 834 adj.
serious 834 adj.
tedious 838 adj.
dull 840 adj.
dullness
inertness 175 n.
duly
as promised 764 adv.
duly 915 adv.
dumb
ignorant 491 adj.
unintelligent 499 adj.
voiceless 578 adj.
wondering 864 adj.
dumbfound
surprise 508 vb.
disappoint 509 vb.
make mute 578 vb.
be wonderful 864 vb.
dumb show
gesture 547 n.
representation 551 n.
drama 594 n.
dumbwaiter
cabinet 194 n.
lifter 310 n.
dummy
copy 22 n.
prototype 23 n.
substituted 150 adj.
ineffectuality 161 n.
stopper 264 n.
sham 542 n.
image 551 n.
dump
accumulation 74 n.
small house 192 n.
storage 632 n.
rubbish 641 n.
stop using 674 vb.
sell 793 vb.
cheapen 812 vb.
dumpling
bulk 195 n.
pastries 301 n.
dumps
dejection 834 n.
sullenness 893 n.
dumpy
fleshy 195 adj.
dwarfish 196 adj.
short 204 adj.
thick 205 adj.
dun
horse 273 n.
dim 419 adj.
grey 429 adj.
brown 430 adj.
demand 737 vb.
petitioner 763 n.
creditor 802 n.
torment 827 vb.
dunce
ignoramus 493 n.
dunce 501 n.
dunderhead
dunce 501 n.
dune
small hill 209 n.
dung
fertilizer 171 n.
excrement 302 n.
agriculture 370 n.
cultivate 370 vb.
stench 397 n.
dirt 649 n.
dungarees
trousers 228 n.
dungeon
cellar 194 n.
depth 211 n.
darkness 418 n.
refuge 662 n.
lockup 748 n.
prison 748 n.

dunghill
sink 649 n.
dunk
drench 341 vb.
duo
duality 90 n.
duet 412 n.
duodecimal
fifth and over 99 adj.
duodecimo
miniature 196 n.
little 196 adj.
edition 589 n.
duologue
interlocution 584 n.
stage play 594 n.
dupe
credulity 487 n.
befool 542 vb.
deceive 542 vb.
dupe 544 n.
loser 728 n.
defraud 788 vb.
duped
gullible 544 adj.
duplex
dual 90 adj.
double 91 adj.
flat 192 n.
duplicate
identity 13 n.
copy 20 vb.
duplicate 22 n.
double 91 adj.vb.
repeat 106 vb.
reproduce 166 vb.
label 547 n.
record 548 n.
representation 551 n.
be superfluous 637 vb.
duplicator
imitator 20 n.
duplicity
concealment 525 n.
duplicity 541 n.
deception 542 n.
sham 542 n.
mental dishonesty 543 n.
cunning 698 n.
affectation 850 n.
perfidy 930 n.
false piety 980 n.
duppy
ghost 970 n.
durable
lasting 113 adj.
perpetual 115 adj.
permanent 144 adj.
unchangeable 153 adj.
tough 329 adj.
durables
merchandise 795 n.
duration
time 108 n.
course of time 111 n.
permanence 144 n.
durbar
council 692 n.
duress
compulsion 740 n.
detention 747 n.
restriction 747 n.
during
while 108 adv.
dusk
evening 129 n.
darkness 418 n.
half-light 419 n.
dim 419 adj.
dusky
vespertine 129 adj.
dim 419 adj.
blackish 428 adj.
dust
minuteness 196 n.
overlay 226 vb.
let fall 311 vb.
lightness 323 n.
powder 332 n.
soil 344 n.
corpse 363 n.
obfuscation 421 n.
variegate 437 vb.
trifle 639 n.
rubbish 641 n.
clean 648 vb.
dirt 649 n.
dustbin
cleaning utensil 648 n.
sink 649 n.
dustbowl
desert 172 n.
dust devil
gale 352 n.
duster
overcoat 228 n.
obliteration 550 n.
cleaning cloth 648 n.
dusting
corporal punishment 963 n.
dust jacket/cover
wrapping 226 n.
bookbinding 589 n.
dustman
cleaner 648 n.
worker 686 n.
dustpan and brush
cleaning utensil 648 n.
dustsheet
cleaning cloth 648 n.
dust thrown in the eyes
pretext 614 n.
stratagem 698 n.
dustup
turmoil 61 n.
fight 716 n.
dusty
travelling 267 adj.
powdery 332 adj.
dry 342 adj.
whitish 427 adj.
mottled 437 adj.
dirty 649 adj.
Dutch auction
sale 793 n.
cheapness 812 n.
Dutch cap
contraception 172 n.
Dutch courage
drunkenness 949 n.
Dutch oven
cauldron 194 n.
Dutch treat
participation 775 n.
Dutch uncle
adviser 691 n.
tyrant 735 n.
dutiable
priced 809 adj.
dutiful
obedient 739 adj.
obliged 917 adj.
trustworthy 929 adj.
virtuous 933 adj.
dutifulness
obedience 739 n.
duty
necessity 596 n.
motive 612 n.
job 622 n.
needfulness 627 n.
labour 682 n.
obedience 739 n.
tax 809 n.
right 913 n.
dueness 915 n.
duty 917 n.
respects 920 n.
duty-bound
obliged 917 adj.
duty-free
nonliable 919 adj.
duvet
coverlet 226 n.
dwarf
abate 37 vb.
dwarf 196 n.
elf 970 n.
dwarfish
small 33 adj.
dwarfish 196 adj.
short 204 adj.
unsightly 842 adj.
fairylike 970 adj.
dwell
stay 144 vb.
be situated 186 vb.
place oneself 187 vb.
dwell 192 vb.
— on
emphasize 532 vb.
— on the past
retrospect 505 vb.
dweller
dweller 191 n.
dwelling
dwelling 192 n.
house 192 n.
dwindle
decrease 37 vb.
be weak 163 vb.
become small 198 vb.
disappear 446 vb.
dybbuk
devil 969 n.
elf 970 n.
dye
tincture 43 n.
modify 143 vb.
pigment 425 n.
colour 425 vb.
hairwash 843 n.
dyed-in-the-wool
consummate 32 adj.
permanent 144 adj.
habitual 610 adj.
dyeing
beautification 843 n.
dying
extinct 2 adj.
ephemeral 114 adj.
dying 361 adj.
(See **die** *)*
dying duck
weeper 836 n.
dying race
unproductiveness 172 n.
dyke
(See **dike** *)*
dynamic
dynamic 160 adj.
operative 173 adj.
vigorous 174 adj.
impelling 279 adj.
dynamics
science of forces 162 n.
motion 265 n.
dynamism
energy 160 n.
vigorousness 174 n.
restlessness 678 n.
dynamite
demolish 165 vb.
vigorousness 174 n.
pitfall 663 n.
explosive 723 n.
dynamo
causal means 156 n.
electronics 160 n.
vigorousness 174 n.
machine 630 n.
busy person 678 n.
dynasty
continuity 71 n.
governance 733 n.
sovereign 741 n.
nobility 868 n.
dysentery
digestive disorders 651 n.
dyslexia
blindness 439 n.

dyspepsia
digestive disorders 631 n.
dyspeptic
sick person 651 n.
sullen 893 adj.
dystopia
suffering 825 n.

E

each
universal 79 adj.
severally 80 adv.
each other
correlation 12 n.
correlatively 12 adv.
eager
willing 597 adj.
active 678 adj.
fervent 818 adj.
excited 821 adj.
desiring 859 adj.
eager to learn
attentive 455 adj.
eagle
speeder 277 n.
bird 365 n.
flag 547 n.
heraldry 547 n.
regalia 743 n.
coinage 797 n.
eagle-eyed
seeing 438 adj.
vigilant 457 adj.
ear
growth 157 n.
handle 218 n.
ear 415 n.
ear for
hearing 415 n.
earl
person of rank 868 n.
earldom
aristocracy 868 n.
earlier
before 64 adv.
prior 119 adj.
before 119 adv.
not now 122 adv.
early
anachronistic 118 adj.
past 125 adj.
primal 127 adj.
matinal 128 adj.
early 135 adj.
betimes 135 adv.
ill-timed 138 adj.
early days
beginning 68 n.
early leaver
loser 728 n.
early man
precursor 66 n.
humankind 371 n.
early warning system
detector 484 n.
earmark
label 547 n.
mark 547 vb.
select 605 vb.
intend 617 vb.
require 627 vb.
earmarked
future 124 adj.
due 915 adj.
earn
busy oneself 622 vb.
acquire 771 vb.
deserve 915 vb.
— interest
grow 36 vb.
— one's living
come of age 134 vb.
busy oneself 622 vb.
do business 622 vb.
earned
just 913 adj.
due 915 adj.
earner
worker 686 n.
earnest
attentive 455 adj.
affirmative 532 adj.
willing 597 adj.
resolute 599 adj.
security 767 n.
observant 768 adj.
payment 804 n.
fervent 818 adj.
seriousness 834 n.
pietistic 979 adj.
earnestness
assiduity 678 n.
earnings
earnings 771 n.
receiving 782 n.
receipt 807 n.
reward 962 n.
earphones
hearing aid 415 n.
ear-piercing
beautification 843 n.
ear plugs
silencer 401 n.
shelter 662 n.
earring
hanging object 217 n.
jewellery 844 n.
earshot
short distance 200 n.
hearing 415 n.
ear-splitting
loud 400 adj.
strident 407 adj.
earth
connect 45 vb.
cable 47 n.
electricity 160 n.
dwelling 192 n.
base 214 n.
element 319 n.
world 321 n.
land 344 n.
corpse 363 n.
safeguard 660 vb.
refuge 662 n.
— up
obstruct 702 vb.
earthborn
human 371 adj.
earthbound
native 191 adj.
inexcitable 823 adj.
earthenware
product 164 n.
pottery 381 n.
earthiness
sensualism 944 n.
earthling
humankind 371 n.
earthly
telluric 321 adj.
Earth Mother
fertilizer 171 n.
mythic deity 966 n.
earthquake
destroyer 168 n.
outbreak 176 n.
oscillation 317 n.
earth sciences
situation 186 n.
earth sciences 321 n.
land 344 n.
mineralogy 359 n.
earth-shaking
influential 178 adj.
oscillating 317 adj.
important 638 adj.
notable 638 adj.
earthshine
glimmer 419 n.
earthwork
antiquity 125 n.
earthwork 253 n.
monument 548 n.
defences 713 n.
earthworm
creepy-crawly 365 n.
earthy
territorial 344 adj.
sensual 944 adj.
ear trumpet
megaphone 400 n.
hearing aid 415 n.
earwig
creepy-crawly 365 n.
ease
abate 37 vb.
assuage 177 vb.
lighten 323 vb.
euphoria 376 n.
elegance 575 n.
leisure 681 n.
repose 683 n.
refresh 685 vb.
skill 694 n.
facility 701 n.
disencumber 701 vb.
facilitate 701 vb.
aid 703 vb.
wealth 800 n.
happiness 824 n.
relieve 831 vb.
— along
move slowly 278 vb.
propel 287 vb.
— into place
insert 303 vb.
— off/up
be moderate 177 vb.
decelerate 278 vb.
— oneself
excrete 302 vb.
be relieved 831 vb.
— out
depose 752 vb.
not retain 779 vb.
easel
frame 218 n.
art equipment 553 n.
ease of mind
content 828 n.
easily aroused
sensitive 819 adj.
easily deceived
credulous 487 adj.
easily depressed
excitable 822 adj.
easily done
easy 701 adj.
easily pleased
content 828 adj.
easily provoked
excitable 822 adj.
irascible 892 adj.
easiness
possibility 469 n.
facility 701 n.
east
laterality 239 n.
compass point 281 n.
east and west
polarity 14 n.
region 184 n.
Easter
holy day 988 n.
easterly
lateral 239 adj.
eastern
lateral 239 adj.
directed 281 adj.
Easterner
foreigner 59 n.
Eastertide
spring 128 n.
holy day 988 n.
eastward
lateral 239 adj.
easy
sloping 220 adj.
comfortable 376 adj.
intelligible 516 adj.
elegant 575 adj.
easy 701 adj.
lax 734 adj.
lenient 736 adj.
inexcitable 823 adj.
well-bred 848 adj.
friendly 880 adj.

sociable 882 adj.
amiable 884 adj.
easy circumstances
wealth 800 n.
easy come, easy go
transiently 114 adv.
815 int.
easy-going
tranquil 266 adj.
willing 597 adj.
irresolute 601 adj.
tractable 701 adj.
lenient 736 adj.
inexcitable 823 adj.
content 828 adj.
indifferent 860 adj.
easy-mannered
well-bred 848 adj.
sociable 882 adj.
easy money
easy thing 701 n.
acquisition 771 n.
easy on the eye
personable 841 adj.
easy on the pocket
cheap 812 adj.
easy prey
dupe 544 n.
easy stages
slowness 278 n.
Easy Street
prosperity 730 n.
easy terms
peace offering 719 n.
cheapness 812 n.
easy virtue
unchastity 951 n.
eat
absorb 299 vb.
eat 301 vb.
taste 386 vb.
waste 634 vb.
gluttonize 947 vb.
— away
abate 37 vb.
encroach 306 vb.
impair 655 vb.
— dirt
knuckle under 721 vb.
— humble pie
recant 603 vb.
knuckle under 721 vb.
be humble 872 vb.
be penitent 939 vb.
— one's fill
be complete 54 vb.
have enough 635 vb.
— one's hat if
make impossible 470 vb.
negate 533 vb.
— one's heart out
be dejected 834 vb.
— one's words
recant 603 vb.
— out of house and home
fleece 786 vb.
gluttonize 947 vb.
— up
consume 165 vb.
eat 301 vb.
appropriate 786 vb.
eatable
edible 301 adj.
eatables
food 301 n.
eaten up with
misjudging 481 adj.
crazy 503 adj.
with affections 817 adj.
eater
eater 301 n.
reveller 837 n.
glutton 947 n.
eating and drinking
feasting 301 n.
sociability 882 n.
sensualism 944 n.
eating-house
café 192 n.
eau de cologne
scent 396 n.
cosmetic 843 n.
eaves
roof 226 n.
edge 234 n.
projection 254 n.
eavesdrop
hear 415 vb.
be curious 453 vb.
eavesdropper
listener 415 n.
inquisitive person 453 n.
informer 524 n.
ebb
decrease 37 n.vb.
revert 148 vb.
regress 286 vb.
recede 290 vb.
flow 350 vb.
scarcity 636 n.
deterioration 655 n.
— away
decrease 37 vb.
waste 634 vb.
ebb and flow
periodicity 141 n.
fluctuation 317 n.
current 350 n.
ebb tide
decrease 37 n.
lowness 210 n.
ebony
tree 366 n.
black thing 428 n.
ebullience
stimulation 174 n.
moral sensibility 819 n.
excitation 821 n.
ebullient
merry 833 adj.
ebullition
outbreak 176 n.
bubble 355 n.
excitable state 822 n.
eccentric
misfit 25 n.
unconformable 84 adj.
fitful 142 adj.
crazy 503 adj.
crank 504 n.
capricious 604 adj.
laughingstock 851 n.
eccentricity
originality 21 n.
speciality 80 n.
nonconformity 84 n.
folly 499 n.
eccentricity 503 n.
ecclesiastic
cleric 986 n.
ecclesiastical, ecclesiastic
ecclesiastical 985 adj.
clerical 986 adj.
ecclesiology
the church 985 n.
echelon
series 71 n.
echo
imitation 20 n.
do likewise 20 vb.
copy 22 n.
accord 24 vb.
conform 83 vb.
double 91 vb.
repetition 106 n.
recoil 280 n.vb.
resound 404 vb.
answer 460 n.vb.
assent 488 vb.
echo sounder
gauge 465 n.
éclair
pastries 301 n.
éclat
vigorousness 174 n.
prestige 866 n.
eclectic
mixed 43 adj.
choosing 605 adj.
eclecticism
philosophy 449 n.
eclipse
be superior 34 vb.
obscuration 418 n.
darken 418 vb.
blind 439 vb.
be unseen 444 vb.
disappearance 446 n.
conceal 525 vb.
ecliptic
orbit 250 n.
uranometry 321 n.
eclogue
poem 593 n.
ecodevelopment
production 164 n.
ecological
relative 9 adj.
ecologist
biology 358 n.
economy 814 n.
Ecologists
political party 708 n.
ecology
relation 9 n.
biology 358 n.
economic
profitable 640 adj.
directing 689 adj.
economic aid
subvention 703 n.
economical
cheap 812 adj.
economical 814 adj.
temperate 942 adj.
economic community
association 706 n.
economic miracle
revival 656 n.
economic resources
means 629 n.
economics
business 622 n.
management 689 n.
economist
manager 690 n.
economy 814 n.
economize, economise
be careful 457 vb.
store 632 vb.
preserve 666 vb.
restrain 747 vb.
economize 814 vb.
be cautious 858 vb.
economy
order 60 n.
provision 633 n.
economy 814 n.
temperance 942 n.
economy, the
business 622 n.
economy size
large 195 adj.
cheap 812 adj.
ecosystem
organism 358 n.
association 706 n.
ecru
whitish 427 adj.
brown 430 adj.
ecstasy
pleasure 376 n.
frenzy 503 n.
imagination 513 n.
warm feeling 818 n.
excitable state 822 n.
joy 824 n.
love 887 n.
ecstatic
rejoicing 835 adj.

ECT
therapy 658 n.
ectomorphic
lean 206 adj.
ectopic
unconformable 84 adj.
misplaced 188 adj.
ectoplasm
spiritualism 984 n.
ecumenical
universal 79 adj.
orthodox 976 adj.
ecumenicalism
generality 79 n.
orthodoxy 976 n.
ecumenicity
generality 79 n.
eczema
skin disease 651 n.
blemish 845 n.
Edda
poem 593 n.
eddy
coil 251 n.
vortex 315 n.
rotate 315 vb.
eddy 350 n.
Eden
mythic heaven 971 n.
edge
advantage 34 n.
extremity 69 n.
keenness 174 n.
nearness 200 n.
contiguity 202 n.
outline 233 n.
edge 234 n.
limit 236 n.vb.
laterality 239 n.
sharpen 256 vb.
shore 344 n.
pungency 388 n.
— in
introduce 231 vb.
enter 297 vb.
— off
deflect 282 vb.
— out
depose 752 vb.
edge tool
sharp edge 256 n.
edgewise
obliquely 220 adv.
edging
adjunct 40 n.
edging 234 n.
trimming 844 n.
edgy
excitable 822 adj.
irascible 892 adj.
edible
edible 301 adj.
edict
publication 528 n.
decree 737 n.
legislation 953 n.
edification
teaching 534 n.
benefit 615 n.
edifice
edifice 164 n.
edify
educate 534 vb.
benefit 615 vb.
do good 644 vb.
be virtuous 933 vb.
make pious 979 vb.
edifying
reputable 866 adj.
pure 950 adj.
edit
modify 143 vb.
interpret 520 vb.
publish 528 vb.
rectify 654 vb.
edited
pure 950 adj.
edition
miniature 196 n.
the press 528 n.
edition 589 n.
editor
interpreter 520 n.
author 589 n.
bookperson 589 n.
dissertator 591 n.
reformer 654 n.
editorial
interpretive 520 adj.
publicity 528 n.
article 591 n.
EDP
data processing 86 n.
educate
inform 524 vb.
educate 534 vb.
motivate 612 vb.
educated
instructed 490 adj.
education
culture 490 n.
knowledge 490 n.
education 534 n.
teaching 534 n.
vocation 622 n.
civilization 654 n.
educational
influential 178 adj.
informative 524 adj.
educational 534 adj.
pedagogic 537 adj.
scholastic 539 adj.
educationist, educationalist
teacher 537 n.
educator
teacher 537 n.
educe
extract 304 vb.
reason 475 vb.
edulcorate
purify 648 vb.
EEC
society 708 n.
eel
serpent 251 n.
fish food 301 n.
eerie
frightening 854 adj.
spooky 970 adj.
efface
destroy 165 vb.
forget 506 vb.
obliterate 550 vb.
— oneself
be modest 874 vb.
effect
sequel 67 n.
end 69 n.
event 154 n.
cause 156 vb.
effect 157 n.
product 164 n.
produce 164 vb.
sense 374 n.
appearance 445 n.
spectacle 445 n.
meaning 514 n.
be instrumental 628 vb.
carry out 725 vb.
succeed 727 vb.
ostentation 875 n.
effective
causal 156 adj.
powerful 160 adj.
influential 178 adj.
forceful 571 adj.
instrumental 628 adj.
useful 640 adj.
advisable 642 adj.
soldier 722 n.
successful 727 adj.
effectiveness
agency 173 n.
effects
property 777 n.
effectual
causal 156 adj.
powerful 160 adj.
operative 173 adj.
instrumental 628 adj.
useful 640 adj.
advisable 642 adj.
effectuality
ability 160 n.
effectually
on the whole 52 adv.
completely 54 adv.
effectuate
cause 156 vb.
carry out 725 vb.
effeminacy
weakness 163 n.
female 373 n.
effeminate
weakling 163 n.
weak 163 adj.
female 373 adj.
effendi
title 870 n.
effervesce
effervesce 318 vb.
bubble 355 vb.
hiss 406 vb.
be excited 821 vb.
effervescence
outbreak 176 n.
commotion 318 n.
bubble 355 n.
moral sensibility 819 n.
excitable state 822 n.
effervescent
gaseous 336 adj.
bubbly 355 adj.
lively 819 adj.
excited 821 adj.
merry 833 adj.
effete
impotent 161 adj.
weakened 163 adj.
useless 641 adj.
deteriorated 655 adj.
efficacious
powerful 160 adj.
operative 173 adj.
instrumental 628 adj.
useful 640 adj.
successful 727 adj.
efficacy
ability 160 n.
instrumentality 628 n.
utility 640 n.
efficiency
ability 160 n.
efficient
operative 173 adj.
businesslike 622 adj.
instrumental 628 adj.
useful 640 adj.
industrious 678 adj.
skilful 694 adj.
successful 727 adj.
effigy
copy 22 n.
image 551 n.
efflorescence
propagation 167 n.
powder 332 n.
maturation 669 n.
effluence
outflow 298 n.
current 350 n.
effluent
outflow 298 n.
dirt 649 n.
effluvium
egress 298 n.
gas 336 n.
odour 394 n.
poison 659 n.
efflux
outflow 298 n.
effort
power 160 n.

production 164 n.
vigorousness 174 n.
attempt 671 n.
undertaking 672 n.
action 676 n.
exertion 682 n.
effortless
easy 701 adj.
effort-wasting
useless 641 adj.
laborious 682 adj.
effrontery
insolence 878 n.
effulgence
light 417 n.
effusion
outflow 298 n.
diffuseness 570 n.
oration 579 n.
effusive
diffuse 570 adj.
loquacious 581 adj.
feeling 818 adj.
e.g.
namely 80 adv.
egalitarian
uniformist 16 n.
just 913 adj.
egg
origin 68 n.
source 156 n.
product 164 n.
genitalia 167 n.
egg flip
alcoholic drink 301 n.
egghead
intellectual 492 n.
sage 500 n.
egg on
incite 612 vb.
make quarrels 709 vb.
egg on one's face, get
be clumsy 695 vb.
egg-shaped
round 250 adj.
rotund 252 adj.
eggshell
weak thing 163 n.
brittleness 330 n.
ego
intrinsicality 5 n.
self 80 n.
subjectivity 320 n.
spirit 447 n.
egocentric
vain 873 adj.
selfish 932 adj.
ego ideal
ideality 513 n.
egoism
particularism 80 n.
interiority 224 n.
selfishness 932 n.
egoist
egotist 932 n.
egotism
overestimation 482 n.
vanity 873 n.
misanthropy 902 n.
selfishness 932 n.
egotist
vain person 873 n.
misanthrope 902 n.
egotist 932 n.
ego trip
selfishness 932 n.
egregious
exaggerated 546 adj.
egress
departure 296 n.
egress 298 n.
passage 305 n.
Egyptian deities
Egyptian deities 967 n.
Egyptologist
antiquarian 125 n.
eiderdown
coverlet 226 n.
eidetic
lifelike 18 adj.
obvious 443 adj.
imaginative 513 adj.
eight
band 74 n.
over five 99 n.
rowing boat 275 n.
party 708 n.
eight bells
noon 128 n.
eightsome
dance 837 n.
eighty
twenty and over 99 n.
eisteddfod
assembly 74 n.
music 412 n.
either ... or
optionally 605 adv.
ejaculation
ejection 300 n.
cry 408 n.
voice 577 n.
eject
displace 188 vb.
fly 271 vb.
impel 279 vb.
propel 287 vb.
eject 300 vb.
reject 607 vb.
depose 752 vb.
not retain 779 vb.
deprive 786 vb.
make unwelcome 883 vb.
ejection
repulsion 292 n.
ejection 300 n.
ejector seat
aircraft 276 n.
ejector 300 n.
safeguard 662 n.
eke out
make complete 54 vb.
elaborate
complex 61 adj.
ornament 574 vb.
elegant 575 adj.
mature 669 vb.
laborious 682 adj.
carry through 725 vb.
ornamental 844 adj.
elaboration
improvement 654 n.
élan
vigorousness 174 n.
vigour 571 n.
resolution 599 n.
courage 855 n.
élan vital
life 360 n.
elapse
end 69 vb.
continue 108 vb.
elapse 111 vb.
elapsed
past 125 adj.
elastic
flexible 327 adj.
elasticity 328 n.
elastic 328 adj.
elasticity
strength 162 n.
expansion 197 n.
recoil 280 n.
return 286 n.
softness 327 n.
elasticity 328 n.
elated
excitable 822 adj.
pleased 824 adj.
jubilant 833 adj.
rejoicing 835 adj.
hoping 852 adj.
elation
psychopathy 503 n.
excitable state 822 n.
elbow
joint 45 n.
limb 53 n.
angularity 247 n.
fold 261 n.
impel 279 vb.
— aside
deflect 282 vb.
— one's way
be in motion 265 vb.
pass 305 vb.
elbow grease
friction 333 n.
exertion 682 n.
elbow room
opportunity 137 n.
room 183 n.
scope 744 n.
elder
superior 34 n.
prior 119 adj.
older 131 adj.
tree 366 n.
church officer 986 n.
elderly
ageing 131 adj.
elderly gentleman
old man 133 n.
elderly lady
old woman 133 n.
elders
seniority 131 n.
elder statesman/ stateswoman
sage 500 n.
eldest
precursor 66 n.
prior 119 adj.
older 131 adj.
El Dorado
fantasy 513 n.
wealth 800 n.
aspiration 852 n.
eldritch
spooky 970 adj.
magical 983 adj.
elect
fated 596 adj.
chosen 605 adj.
vote 605 vb.
commission 751 vb.
elect, the
pietist 979 n.
elected representative
delegate 754 n.
election
vote 605 n.
mandate 751 n.
election promises
inducement 612 n.
elector
estimator 480 n.
electorate 605 n.
electoral
choosing 605 adj.
electoral college
electorate 605 n.
electoral roll
list 87 n.
electorate 605 n.
electoral system
vote 605 n.
electorate
list 87 n.
electorate 605 n.
tribunal 956 n.
Electra complex
eccentricity 503 n.
love 887 n.
electric
dynamic 160 adj.
speedy 277 adj.
excitable 822 adj.
electrical engineering
electronics 160 n.
mechanics 630 n.
electric chair
seat 218 n.
means of execution 964 n.

electric eye
camera 442 n.
electrician
stagehand 594 n.
artisan 686 n.
electricity
electricity 160 n.
heater 383 n.
radiation 417 n.
electrify
empower 160 vb.
invigorate 174 vb.
surprise 508 vb.
excite 821 vb.
be wonderful 864 vb.
electrifying
striking 374 adj.
electrocute
kill 362 vb.
execute 963 vb.
electrode
electricity 160 n.
electrodynamics
electricity 160 n.
science of forces 162 n.
electro-encephalograph
intellect 447 n.
electrolysis
decomposition 51 n.
surgery 658 n.
electromagnetism
electricity 160 n.
physics 319 n.
electron
minuteness 196 n.
element 319 n.
electronics
electronics 160 n.
microelectronics 196 n.
mechanics 630 n.
electroplate
coat 226 vb.
electrostatics
electricity 160 n.
science of forces 162 n.
electrotherapy
therapy 658 n.
electrotype
copy 22 n.
print 587 n.
electrum
a mixture 43 n.
bullion 797 n.
electuary
medicine 658 n.
eleemosynary
giving 781 adj.
benevolent 897 adj.
elegance
elegance 575 n.
elegant
apt 24 adj.
stylistic 566 adj.
elegant 575 adj.
well-made 694 adj.
witty 839 adj.
personable 841 adj.
shapely 841 adj.
tasteful 846 adj.
fashionable 848 adj.
elegiac
funereal 364 adj.
poetic 593 adj.
lamenting 836 adj.
elegy
obsequies 364 n.
poem 593 n.
lament 836 n.
element
part 53 n.
component 58 n.
source 156 n.
filament 208 n.
element 319 n.
person 371 n.
elemental
intrinsic 5 adj.
simple 44 adj.
beginning 68 adj.
fundamental 156 adj.
elementary
simple 44 adj.
beginning 68 adj.
elements, the
weather 340 n.
the sacrament 988 n.
elenchus
confutation 479 n.
elephant
giant 195 n.
beast of burden 273 n.
mammal 365 n.
elephantine
large 195 adj.
unwieldy 195 adj.
elevate
make higher 209 vb.
make vertical 215 vb.
promote 285 vb.
elevate 310 vb.
make better 654 vb.
delight 826 vb.
dignify 866 vb.
(See **elevation** *)*
elevated
elevated 310 adj.
worshipful 866 adj.
disinterested 931 adj.
virtuous 933 adj.
drunk 949 adj.
elevation
height 209 n.
elevation 310 n.
feature 445 n.
map 551 n.
vigour 571 n.
improvement 654 n.
warm feeling 818 n.
excitable state 822 n.
cheerfulness 833 n.
dignification 866 n.
disinterestedness 931 n.
holy orders 985 n.
elevation of the Host
Holy Communion 988 n.
elevator
lifter 310 n.
farm tool 370 n.
eleven
band 74 n.
over five 99 n.
party 708 n.
eleven plus
exam 459 n.
elevenses
meal 301 n.
eleventh hour
lateness 136 n.
crisis 137 n.
elf
dwarf 196 n.
elf 970 n.
elfin
little 196 adj.
fairylike 970 adj.
elfland
fairy 970 n.
elflock
hair 259 n.
elicit
cause 156 vb.
extract 304 vb.
discover 484 vb.
manifest 522 vb.
eligible
included 78 adj.
marriageable 894 adj.
Elijah's mantle
sequence 65 n.
eliminate
eliminate 44 vb.
exclude 57 vb.
class 62 vb.
render few 105 vb.
eject 300 vb.
empty 300 vb.
extract 304 vb.
obliterate 550 vb.
reject 607 vb.
purify 648 vb.
exempt 919 vb.
elimination
elimination 44 n.
destruction 165 n.
elision
contraction 198 n.
prosody 593 n.
elite
superior 34 n.
group 74 n.
type size 587 n.
elite 644 n.
beau monde 848 n.
person of repute 866 n.
upper class 868 n.
elitism
government 733 n.
elixir
medicine 658 n.
remedy 658 n.
Elizabethan Age
past time 125 n.
palmy days 730 n.
elk
mammal 365 n.
ellipse
arc 250 n.
ellipsis
grammar 564 n.
imperspicuity 568 n.
conciseness 569 n.
elliptic, elliptical
short 204 adj.
round 250 adj.
concise 569 adj.
elm
tree 366 n.
elocution
pronunciation 577 n.
eloquence 579 n.
oratory 579 n.
elocutionist
speaker 579 n.
Elohistic
deistic 965 adj.
elongate
lengthen 203 vb.
elongation
distance 199 n.
elope
decamp 296 vb.
run away 620 vb.
escape 667 vb.
wed 894 vb.
— with
take away 786 vb.
eloquence
vigour 571 n.
magniloquence 574 n.
eloquence 579 n.
loquacity 581 n.
inducement 612 n.
eloquent
stylistic 566 adj.
forceful 571 adj.
rhetorical 574 adj.
eloquent 579 adj.
else
in addition 38 adv.
elsewhere
not here 190 adv.
elucidate
be intelligible 516 vb.
interpret 520 vb.
manifest 522 vb.
teach 534 vb.
elude
sophisticate 477 vb.
avoid 620 vb.

elude 667 vb.
not observe 769 vb.
elusive
impracticable 470 adj.
puzzling 517 adj.
avoiding 620 adj.
escaped 667 adj.
elvish
fairylike 970 adj.
Elysian fields
the dead 361 n.
mythic heaven 971 n.
Elysium
happiness 824 n.
em
print-type 587 n.
emaciated
lean 206 adj.
unhealthy 651 adj.
emaciation
contraction 198 n.
emanate
result 157 vb.
emerge 298 vb.
be visible 443 vb.
emancipation
deliverance 668 n.
freedom 744 n.
independence 744 n.
liberation 746 n.
emasculate
abate 37 vb.
subtract 39 vb.
unman 161 vb.
make useless 641 vb.
emasculated
impotent 161 adj.
feeble 572 adj.
embalm
inter 364 vb.
be fragrant 396 vb.
preserve 666 vb.
embankment
prop 218 n.
earthwork 253 n.
safeguard 662 n.
obstacle 702 n.
defences 713 n.
embargo
quiescence 266 n.
hindrance 702 n.
restraint 747 n.
prohibition 757 n.
embarkation
start 68 n.
departure 296 n.
embark on
begin 68 vb.
undertake 672 vb.
embarras de choix
choice 605 n.
embarras de richesses
superfluity 637 n.
embarrass
be inexpedient 643 vb.
hinder 702 vb.
trouble 827 vb.
embarrassed
modest 874 adj.
embarrassing
uncertain 474 adj.
difficult 700 adj.
annoying 827 adj.
embarrassment
predicament 700 n.
embassy
message 529 n.
commission 751 n.
envoy 754 n.
embattled
warring 718 adj.
embed
place 187 vb.
support 218 vb.
hold within 224 vb.
implant 303 vb.
embellish
add 38 vb.
make better 654 vb.
decorate 844 vb.
embellishment
ornament 574 n.
ornamentation 844 n.
ember
ash 381 n.
lighter 385 n.
glimmer 419 n.
torch 420 n.
embezzlement
peculation 788 n.
embezzler
defrauder 789 n.
nonpayer 805 n.
embitter
impair 655 vb.
hurt 827 vb.
cause discontent 829 vb.
aggravate 832 vb.
excite hate 888 vb.
enrage 891 vb.
huff 891 vb.
embittered
biased 481 adj.
discontented 829 adj.
inimical 881 adj.
resentful 891 adj.
emblazon
colour 425 vb.
mark 547 vb.
represent 551 vb.
decorate 844 vb.
emblazoned
heraldic 547 adj.
emblem
insubstantial thing 4 n.
badge 547 n.
indication 547 n.
talisman 983 n.
emblematic
representing 551 adj.
emblem of authority
badge of rule 743 n.
emblem of royalty
regalia 743 n.
embodiment
essential part 5 n.
embody
combine 50 vb.
contain 56 vb.
comprise 78 vb.
materialize 319 vb.
figure 519 vb.
represent 551 vb.
embolden
aid 703 vb.
give courage 855 vb.
embolism
closure 264 n.
cardiovascular disease 651 n.
embonpoint
bulk 195 n.
emboss
be convex 253 vb.
mark 547 vb.
sculpt 554 vb.
decorate 844 vb.
embossed
projecting 254 adj.
embouchure
orifice 263 n.
flute 414 n.
embrace
unite with 45 vb.
contain 56 vb.
comprise 78 vb.
surround 230 vb.
circumscribe 232 vb.
enclose 235 vb.
choose 605 vb.
protection 660 n.
retention 778 n.
sociability 882 n.
greet 884 vb.
love 887 vb.
endearment 889 n.
caress 889 vb.
embrasure
notch 260 n.
window 263 n.
fortification 713 n.
embrocation
unguent 357 n.
balm 658 n.
embroider
variegate 437 vb.
cant 541 vb.
exaggerate 546 vb.
decorate 844 vb.
embroidery
adjunct 40 n.
art 551 n.
ornament 574 n.
needlework 844 n.
embroil
bedevil 63 vb.
make quarrels 709 vb.
embroilment
complexity 61 n.
confusion 61 n.
embryo
young creature 132 n.
source 156 n.
undevelopment 670 n.
embryology
biology 358 n.
zoology 367 n.
embryonic
beginning 68 adj.
causal 156 adj.
amorphous 244 adj.
immature 670 adj.
emendation
interpretation 520 n.
amendment 654 n.
repair 656 n.
emerald
greenness 434 n.
gem 844 n.
emerge
begin 68 vb.
result 157 vb.
start out 296 vb.
emerge 298 vb.
flow 350 vb.
be visible 443 vb.
be proved 478 vb.
be disclosed 526 vb.
emergence
beginning 68 n.
egress 298 n.
emergency
juncture 8 n.
crisis 137 n.
event 154 n.
needfulness 627 n.
danger 661 n.
predicament 700 n.
emergency exit
means of escape 667 n.
emergency rations
provision 633 n.
emeritus
resigning 753 adj.
deserving 915 adj.
emery paper
sharpener 256 n.
smoother 258 n.
pulverizer 332 n.
emetic
ejector 300 n.
expulsive 300 adj.
unsavoury 391 adj.
purgative 658 n.
remedial 658 adj.
bane 659 n.
émeute
revolt 738 n.
emigrant
foreigner 59 n.
wanderer 268 n.
egress 298 n.
emigration
wandering 267 n.
departure 296 n.
egress 298 n.

eminence
greatness 32 n.
superiority 34 n.
height 209 n.
high land 209 n.
prominence 254 n.
elevation 310 n.
importance 638 n.
goodness 644 n.
prestige 866 n.
Eminence
church title 986 n.
éminence grise
latency 523 n.
eminent
remarkable 32 adj.
notable 638 adj.
noteworthy 866 adj.
emir
potentate 741 n.
person of rank 868 n.
emirate
position of authority 733 n.
emissary
messenger 529 n.
delegate 754 n.
envoy 754 n.
emission
outflow 298 n.
ejection 300 n.
radiation 417 n.
emit
flow out 298 vb.
emit 300 vb.
radiate 417 vb.
publish 528 vb.
speak 579 vb.
emmet
foreigner 59 n.
insect 365 n.
Emmy award
trophy 729 n.
emollient
lenitive 177 adj.
soft 327 adj.
lubricant 334 n.
balm 658 n.
remedial 658 adj.
emolument
earnings 771 n.
pay 804 n.
receipt 807 n.
reward 962 n.
emotion
influence 178 n.
feeling 818 n.
warm feeling 818 n.
excitation 821 n.
emotional
irresolute 601 adj.
spontaneous 609 adj.
with affections 817 adj.
feeling 818 adj.
impressible 819 adj.
excitable 822 adj.
emotional disturbance
psychopathy 503 n.
emotionalism
persuadability 612 n.
feeling 818 n.
moral sensibility 819 n.
excitability 822 n.
emotional life
affections 817 n.
feeling 818 n.
emotions
affections 817 n.
emotive
descriptive 590 adj.
felt 818 adj.
exciting 821 adj.
empanel
list 87 vb.
try a case 959 vb.
empathize
imagine 513 vb.
empathy
imagination 513 n.
feeling 818 n.
benevolence 897 n.
emperor
sovereign 741 n.
aristocrat 868 n.
emphasis
strengthening 162 n.
trope 519 n.
affirmation 532 n.
vigour 571 n.
pronunciation 577 n.
emphasize, emphasise
emphasize 532 vb.
indicate 547 vb.
make important 638 vb.
emphatic
strong 162 adj.
florid 425 adj.
expressive 516 adj.
undisguised 522 adj.
assertive 532 adj.
forceful 571 adj.
emphysema
swelling 253 n.
respiratory disease 651 n.
empire
territory 184 n.
governance 733 n.
political organization 733 n.
empirical
enquiring 459 adj.
experimental 461 adj.
empiricism
philosophy 449 n.
empiricism 461 n.
empiricist
experimenter 461 n.
learner 538 n.
emplacement
place 185 n.
situation 186 n.
location 187 n.
stand 218 n.
fortification 713 n.
employ
employ 622 vb.
find useful 640 vb.
use 673 vb.
employed
businesslike 622 adj.
used 673 adj.
busy 678 adj.
employee
worker 686 n.
servant 742 n.
employer
agent 686 n.
director 690 n.
master 741 n.
purchaser 792 n.
employment
business 622 n.
job 622 n.
instrumentality 628 n.
utility 640 n.
use 673 n.
action 676 n.
service 745 n.
employment agency
job 622 n.
emporium
emporium 796 n.
shop 796 n.
empower
empower 160 vb.
make possible 469 vb.
commission 751 vb.
permit 756 vb.
empowered
powerful 160 adj.
authoritative 733 adj.
empowering
ability 160 n.
empress
sovereign 741 n.
empressement
assiduity 678 n.
warm feeling 818 n.
empties
emptiness 190 n.
emptiness
nonexistence 2 n.
insubstantiality 4 n.
emptiness 190 n.
air 340 n.
lack of meaning 515 n.
unimportance 639 n.
nonownership 774 n.
vanity 873 n.
empty
subtract 39 vb.
lay waste 165 vb.
unproductive 172 adj.
empty 190 adj.
be absent 190 vb.
make smaller 198 vb.
transpose 272 vb.
empty 300 vb.
lighten 323 vb.
rare 325 adj.
make flow 350 vb.
unthinking 450 adj.
sophistical 477 adj.
meaningless 515 adj.
hypocritical 541 adj.
untrue 543 adj.
feeble 572 adj.
waste 634 vb.
unprovided 636 adj.
inactive 679 adj.
unpossessed 774 adj.
hungry 859 adj.
boastful 877 adj.
secluded 883 adj.
fasting 946 adj.
— into
flow 350 vb.
empty-handed
unprovided 636 adj.
unsuccessful 728 adj.
parsimonious 816 adj.
empty-headed
mindless 448 adj.
unthinking 450 adj.
ignorant 491 adj.
empty-headedness
folly 499 n.
empty husk
remainder 41 n.
empty larder
poverty 801 n.
empty purse
poverty 801 n.
empty seats
nobody 190 n.
empty stomach
hunger 859 n.
empty talk
insubstantial thing 4 n.
empty talk 515 n.
falsehood 541 n.
fable 543 n.
diffuseness 570 n.
chatter 581 n.
boasting 877 n.
empty threats
ineffectuality 161 n.
empty title
undueness 916 n.
empurple
empurple 436 vb.
empyreal
celestial 321 adj.
empyrean
heavens 321 n.
emu
bird 365 n.
emulate
do likewise 20 vb.
oppose 704 vb.
contend 716 vb.

emulation
jealousy 911 n.
emulator
opponent 705 n.
quarreller 709 n.
contender 716 n.
emulsify
thicken 354 vb.
emulsion
facing 226 n.
coat 226 vb.
semiliquidity 354 n.
viscidity 354 n.
en
print-type 587 n.
enable
empower 160 vb.
make possible 469 vb.
facilitate 701 vb.
permit 756 vb.
enact
show 522 vb.
represent 551 vb.
act 594 vb.
do 676 vb.
deal with 688 vb.
carry out 725 vb.
decree 737 vb.
make legal 953 vb.
enactment
dramaturgy 594 n.
action 676 n.
precept 693 n.
enamel
facing 226 n.
smoother 258 n.
colour 425 vb.
decorate 844 vb.
enamelling
variegation 437 n.
ornamental art 844 n.
enamour
excite love 887 vb.
en bloc
collectively 52 adv.
encamp
place oneself 187 vb.
dwell 192 vb.
encampment
station 187 n.
abode 192 n.
fort 713 n.
battleground 724 n.
encapsulate
comprise 78 vb.
cover 226 vb.
insert 303 vb.
abstract 592 vb.
encase
cover 226 vb.
circumscribe 232 vb.
insert 303 vb.
encash
receive 782 vb.
draw money 797 vb.
encaustic painting
pottery 381 n.
art style 553 n.
enceinte
fertilized 167 adj.
enclosure 235 n.
enchain
fetter 747 vb.
enchant
convert 147 vb.
subjugate 745 vb.
delight 826 vb.
be wonderful 864 vb.
excite love 887 vb.
bewitch 983 vb.
enchanted
pleased 824 adj.
magical 983 adj.
enchanter
sorcerer 983 n.
enchanting
personable 841 adj.
lovable 887 adj.
enchantment
excitation 821 n.
joy 824 n.
pleasurableness 826 n.
spell 983 n.
enchantress
a beauty 841 n.
sorceress 983 n.
enchase
groove 262 vb.
decorate 844 vb.
encircle
surround 230 vb.
circumscribe 232 vb.
circuit 626 vb.
encirclement
circumscription 232 n.
closure 264 n.
enclave
region 184 n.
enclitic
word 559 n.
enclose
contain 56 vb.
hold within 224 vb.
circumscribe 232 vb.
enclose 235 vb.
close 264 vb.
safeguard 660 vb.
imprison 747 vb.
enclosed
monastic 986 adj.
enclosure
place 185 n.
contents 193 n.
circumscription 232 n.
enclosure 235 n.
garden 370 n.
correspondence 588 n.
encode
translate 520 vb.
conceal 525 vb.
encomium
praise 923 n.
encompass
comprise 78 vb.
surround 230 vb.
circumscribe 232 vb.
limit 236 vb.
encore
repetition 106 n.
again 106 adv.
dramaturgy 594 n.
applause 923 n.
encounter
event 154 n.
meet with 154 vb.
collision 279 n.
meet 295 vb.
discover 484 vb.
fight 716 n.
encounter group
assembly 74 n.
encourage
conduce 156 vb.
incite 612 vb.
make better 654 vb.
aid 703 vb.
permit 756 vb.
animate 821 vb.
relieve 831 vb.
cheer 833 vb.
give hope 852 vb.
give courage 855 vb.
encouragement
inducement 612 n.
encouraging
influential 178 adj.
promising 852 adj.
encroach
interfere 231 vb.
encroach 306 vb.
be undue 916 vb.
be illegal 954 vb.
encroacher
usurper 916 n.
encroachment
progression 285 n.
overstepping 306 n.
attack 712 n.
wrong 914 n.
arrogation 916 n.
encrust
coat 226 vb.
line 227 vb.
decorate 844 vb.
encumber
be difficult 700 vb.
hinder 702 vb.
encumbrance
gravity 322 n.
encumbrance 702 n.
debt 803 n.
annoyance 827 n.
encyclical
publication 528 n.
decree 737 n.
encyclopedia
reference book 589 n.
encyclopedic
inclusive 78 adj.
general 79 adj.
knowing 490 adj.
end
completeness 54 n.
sequel 67 n.
end 69 n., vb.
extremity 69 n.
be past 125 vb.
stop 145 n.
cease 145 vb.
event 154 n.
ruin 165 n.
destroy 165 vb.
vertex 213 n.
limit 236 n.
decease 361 n.
intention 617 n.
objective 617 n.
completion 725 n.
endanger
endanger 661 vb.
be difficult 700 vb.
endangered species
animal 365 n.
endearing
pleasurable 826 adj.
lovable 887 adj.
endearment
inducement 612 n.
courteous act 884 n.
love-making 887 n.
endearment 889 n.
endeavour
aim at 617 vb.
attempt 671 n.vb.
action 676 n.
endemic
interior 224 adj.
infectious 653 adj.
endive
vegetable 301 n.
endless
multitudinous 104 adj.
infinite 107 adj.
perpetual 115 adj.
endless band
continuity 71 n.
endo-
interior 224 adj.
endocrine
insides 224 n.
end of hostilities
peace 717 n.
end of life
decease 361 n.
end of one's tether
limit 236 n.
end of the matter
finality 69 n.
completion 725 n.
end of the world
finality 69 n.
endomorphic
thick 205 adj.
endorse
testify 466 vb.

endorse 488 vb.
sign 547 vb.
patronize 703 vb.
consent 758 vb.
give security 767 vb.
approve 923 vb.
— a cheque
draw money 797 vb.
endorsement
assent 488 n.
endorser
assenter 488 n.
signatory 765 n.
endow
empower 160 vb.
dower 777 vb.
give 781 vb.
endowed (with)
gifted 694 adj.
possessing 773 adj.
endowment
heredity 5 n.
ability 160 n.
aptitude 694 n.
giving 781 n.
endpaper
edition 589 n.
end product
product 164 n.
completion 725 n.
ends of the earth
edge 234 n.
limit 236 n.
end to end
contiguously 202 adv.
longwise 203 adv.
endurance
durability 113 n.
perpetuity 115 n.
permanence 144 n.
strength 162 n.
perseverance 600 n.
feeling 818 n.
patience 823 n.
manliness 855 n.
endure
be 1 vb.
continue 108 vb.
last 113 vb.
stay 144 vb.
go on 146 vb.
meet with 154 vb.
support 218 vb.
acquiesce 488 vb.
be resolute 599 vb.
stand firm 599 vb.
persevere 600 vb.
resist 715 vb.
feel 818 vb.
be patient 823 vb.
suffer 825 vb.
be courageous 855 vb.
enduring
permanent 144 adj.
endwise
vertically 215 adv.
enema
insertion 303 n.
purgative 658 n.
enemy
troublemaker 663 n.
opponent 705 n.
enemy 881 n.
hateful object 888 n.
energetic
dynamic 160 adj.
vigorous 174 adj.
forceful 571 adj.
resolute 599 adj.
active 678 adj.
labouring 682 adj.
energize, energise
augment 36 vb.
strengthen 162 vb.
invigorate 174 vb.
incite 612 vb.
cheer 833 vb.
energizer
stimulant 174 n.
incentive 612 n.
energumen
enthusiast 504 n.
energy
causal means 156 n.
energy 160 n.
strength 162 n.
vigorousness 174 n.
vigour 571 n.
resolution 599 n.
restlessness 678 n.
exertion 682 n.
energy-consuming
wasteful 634 adj.
energy-saving
preserving 666 adj.
economical 814 adj.
enervate
unman 161 vb.
weaken 163 vb.
fatigue 684 vb.
enervation
weakness 163 n.
feebleness 572 n.
dejection 834 n.
en famille
inside 224 adv.
sociably 882 adv.
enfant gâté
satiety 863 n.
favourite 890 n.
enfant terrible
inquisitive person 453 n.
questioner 459 n.
ingenue 699 n.
annoyance 827 n.
bad person 938 n.
enfeeble
weaken 163 vb.
enfilade
look along 203 vb.
pass 305 vb.
bombardment 712 n.
enfold
hold within 224 vb.
dress 228 vb.
circumscribe 232 vb.
fold 261 vb.
safeguard 660 vb.
caress 889 vb.
enforce
emphasize 532 vb.
motivate 612 vb.
compel 740 vb.
make legal 953 vb.
enfranchise
give scope 744 vb.
liberate 746 vb.
enfranchised, be
vote 605 vb.
ENG
camera 442 n.
engage
join 45 vb.
induce 612 vb.
employ 622 vb.
give battle 718 vb.
commission 751 vb.
promise 764 vb.
acquire 771 vb.
— in
busy oneself 622 Vb.
do business 622 vb.
undertake 672 vb.
engaged
retained 778 adj.
marriageable 894 adj.
engaged couple
lovers 887 n.
engagement
undertaking 672 n.
battle 718 n.
promise 764 n.
compact 765 n.
social round 882 n.
love affair 887 n.
duty 917 n.
engagement book
list 87 n.
reminder 505 n.
engagement ring
jewellery 844 n.
love token 889 n.
engender
generate 167 vb.
engine
causal means 156 n.
machine 630 n.
engineer
cause 156 vb.
produce 164 vb.
plan 623 vb.
machinist 630 n.
artisan 686 n.
engineering
production 164 n.
mechanics 630 n.
English
translate 520 vb.
language 557 n.
Englishman/ Englishwoman
native 191 n.
engorge
absorb 299 vb.
engorgement
redundance 637 n.
satiety 863 n.
engraft
add 38 vb.
affix 45 vb.
implant 303 vb.
cultivate 370 vb.
educate 534 vb.
engrave
cut 46 vb.
groove 262 vb.
mark 547 vb.
record 548 vb.
represent 551 vb.
engrave 555 vb.
write 586 vb.
decorate 844 vb.
engraver
recorder 549 n.
engraver 556 n.
engraving
copy 22 n.
picture 553 n.
engraving 555 n.
engross
absorb 299 vb.
engross 449 vb.
engrossed
obsessed 455 adj.
distracted 456 adj.
possessed 773 adj.
engulf
consume 165 vb.
destroy 165 vb.
absorb 299 vb.
appropriate 786 vb.
enhance
augment 36 vb.
manifest 522 vb.
emphasize 532 vb.
make important 638 vb.
make better 654 vb.
beautify 841 vb.
enhancement
improvement 654 n.
ornamentation 844 n.
dignification 866 n.
enharmonic
harmonic 410 adj.
enigma
question 459 n.
unknown thing 491 n.
enigma 530 n.
difficulty 700 n.
prodigy 864 n.
enigmatic
uncertain 474 adj.
aphoristic 496 adj.
puzzling 517 adj.

unintelligible 517 adj.
unclear 568 adj.
enjoin
advise 691 vb.
command 737 vb.
impose a duty 917 vb.
enjoy
enjoy 376 vb.
dispose of 673 vb.
prosper 730 vb.
possess 773 vb.
be pleased 824 vb.
be content 828 vb.
— oneself
be cheerful 833 vb.
amuse oneself 837 vb.
enjoyable
pleasant 376 adj.
enjoyment
pleasure 376 n.
enjoyment 824 n.
festivity 837 n.
sociability 882 n.
sensualism 944 n.
enkindle
kindle 381 vb.
excite 821 vb.
enlace
enlace 222 vb.
twine 251 vb.
caress 889 vb.
enlarge
augment 36 vb.
enlarge 197 vb.
blow up 352 vb.
exaggerate 546 vb.
photograph 551 vb.
make important 638 vb.
boast 877 vb.
— the mind
educate 534 vb.
— upon
be diffuse 570 vb.
enlighten
interpret 520 vb.
inform 524 vb.
educate 534 vb.
enlightened
wise 498 adj.
philanthropic 901 adj.
enlightenment
knowledge 490 n.
wisdom 498 n.
information 524 n.
sanctity 979 n.
enlist
be included 78 vb.
list 87 vb.
admit 299 vb.
register 548 vb.
induce 612 vb.
employ 622 vb.
join a party 708 vb.
go to war 718 vb.
— in
enter 297 vb.
enlisted man
soldier 722 n.
enliven
strengthen 162 vb.
invigorate 174 vb.
vitalize 360 vb.
animate 821 vb.
cheer 833 vb.
amuse 837 vb.
enlivened
alive 360 adj.
refreshed 685 adj.
en masse
collectively 52 adv.
together 74 adv.
in league 708 adv.
enmesh
enlace 222 vb.
ensnare 542 vb.
hinder 702 vb.
enmity
opposition 704 n.
enmity 881 n.
hatred 888 n.
malevolence 898 n.
ennoble
dignify 866 vb.
ennobled
worshipful 866 adj.
noble 868 adj.
ennui
discontent 829 n.
tedium 838 n.
enormity
greatness 32 n.
hugeness 195 n.
wickedness 934 n.
guilty act 936 n.
enormous
enormous 32 adj.
huge 195 adj.
enough
sufficiency 635 n.
sufficient 635 adj.
enough 635 adv.
enough and to spare
plenteous 635 adj.
redundantly 637 adv.
enough to get by
averageness 732 n.
en passant
incidentally 137 adv.
en passant 305 adv.
enquire, inquire
be curious 453 vb.
enquire 459 vb.
experiment 461 vb.
not know 491 vb.
study 536 vb.
enquirer, inquirer
inquisitive person 453 n.
enquirer 459 n.
experimenter 461 n.
detector 484 n.
interlocutor 584 n.
petitioner 763 n.
enquiry, inquiry
inquest 364 n.
listening 415 n.
inspection 438 n.
meditation 449 n.
enquiry 459 n.
search 459 n.
report 524 n.
dissertation 591 n.
legal trial 959 n.
enrage
make violent 176 vb.
make mad 503 vb.
excite 821 vb.
torment 827 vb.
aggravate 832 vb.
excite hate 888 vb.
enrage 891 vb.
en rapport
cooperative 706 adj.
concordant 710 adj.
enrapture
delight 826 vb.
excite love 887 vb.
en règle
due 915 adj.
enrich
augment 36 vb.
ornament 574 vb.
make better 654 vb.
give 781 vb.
make rich 800 vb.
decorate 844 vb.
enrobe
dress 228 vb.
enrol, enroll
list 87 vb.
admit 299 vb.
register 548 vb.
— oneself
be included 78 vb.
join a party 708 vb.
en route
on foot 267 adv.
in transit 272 adv.
forward 285 adv.
ensanguined
bloodstained 431 adj.
ensconce
place 187 vb.
conceal 525 vb.
safeguard 660 vb.
ensemble
all 52 n.
whole 52 n.
suit 228 n.
orchestra 413 n.
enshrine
circumscribe 232 vb.
sanctify 979 vb.
ensign
flag 547 n.
soldier 722 n.
army officer 741 n.
ensilage
agriculture 370 n.
storage 632 n.
enslave
oppress 735 vb.
subjugate 745 vb.
ensnare
attract 291 vb.
ambush 527 vb.
ensnare 542 vb.
tempt 612 vb.
hunt 619 vb.
plot 623 vb.
take 786 vb.
ensue
come after 65 vb.
ensue 120 vb.
ensure
make certain 473 vb.
entablature
summit 213 n.
entail
conduce 156 vb.
make likely 471 vb.
dower 777 n.
entangle
bedevil 63 vb.
enlace 222 vb.
be unintelligible 517 vb.
ensnare 542 vb.
hinder 702 vb.
make quarrels 709 vb.
entangled
complex 61 adj.
entanglement
love affair 887 n.
entelechy
reality 1 n.
entente
agreement 24 n.
concord 710 n.
pacification 719 n.
friendliness 880 n.
enter
be included 78 vb.
list 87 vb.
pierce 263 vb.
approach 289 vb.
converge 293 vb.
arrive 295 vb.
enter 297 vb.
be visible 443 vb.
register 548 vb.
join a party 708 vb.
contend 716 vb.
offer oneself 759 vb.
account 808 vb.
— for
contend 716 vb.
— into
constitute 56 vb.
be one of 58 vb.
imagine 513 vb.
describe 590 vb.
cooperate 706 vb.
— into a contract
contract 765 vb.
— the church
take orders 986 vb.

— upon
begin 68 vb.
enteritis
digestive disorders 651 n.
enterprise
vigorousness 174 n.
progression 285 n.
intention 617 n.
business 622 n.
undertaking 672 n.
restlessness 678 n.
mandate 751 n.
courage 855 n.
enterprising
speculative 618 adj.
attempting 671 adj.
enterprising 672 adj.
entertain
patronize 703 vb.
give 781 vb.
feel 818 vb.
amuse 837 vb.
be ridiculous 849 vb.
be friendly 880 vb.
be hospitable 882 vb.
— the idea
consent 758 vb.
entertained
amused 837 adj.
entertainer
fool 501 n.
entertainer 594 n.
humorist 839 n.
entertaining
sociability 882 n.
entertainment
provisions 301 n.
pleasure 376 n.
provision 633 n.
amusement 837 n.
social gathering 882 n.
entêté(e)
wilful 602 adj.
enthral, enthrall
subjugate 745 vb.
excite love 887 vb.
enthralled
obsessed 455 adj.
impressed 818 adj.
enthralling
exciting 821 adj.
enthrone
commission 751 vb.
dignify 866 vb.
be ecclesiastical 985 vb.
enthuse
show feeling 818 vb.
excite 821 vb.
enthusiasm
vigorousness 174 n.
vigour 571 n.
willingness 597 n.
restlessness 678 n.
warm feeling 818 n.
excitation 821 n.
hope 852 n.
love 887 n.
applause 923 n.
piety 979 n.
enthusiast
collector 492 n.
enthusiast 504 n.
visionary 513 n.
habitué 610 n.
busy person 678 n.
zealot 979 n.
enthusiastic
optimistic 482 adj.
fervent 818 adj.
lively 819 adj.
hoping 852 adj.
entice
distract 456 vb.
ensnare 542 vb.
induce 612 vb.
tempt 612 vb.
enticing
pleasurable 826 adj.
entire
consummate 32 adj.
simple 44 adj.
whole 52 adj.
complete 54 adj.
perfect 646 adj.
undamaged 646 adj.
entitle
name 561 vb.
permit 756 vb.
entitlement
title 870 n.
dueness 915 n.
entity
existence 1 n.
substance 3 n.
whole 52 n.
unit 88 n.
entomb
inter 364 vb.
imprison 747 vb.
entomological
animal 365 adj.
zoological 367 adj.
entomologist
zoologist 367 n.
entourage
concomitant 89 n.
surroundings 230 n.
entr'acte
stage play 594 n.
entrails
insides 224 n.
entrance
entrance 68 n.
front 237 n.
doorway 263 n.
arrival 295 n.
way in 297 n.
dramaturgy 594 n.
access 624 n.
delight 826 vb.
entrancing
personable 841 adj.
entrant
incomer 297 n.
respondent 460 n.
testee 461 n.
opponent 705 n.
contender 716 n.
petitioner 763 n.
entrap
ensnare 542 vb.
en travesti
imitatively 20 adv.
entreat
entreat 761 vb.
deprecate 762 vb.
worship 981 vb.
entrechat
leap 312 n.
ballet 594 n.
entrée
ingress 297 n.
reception 299 n.
dish 301 n.
entremets
dish 301 n.
entrench, intrench
safeguard 660 vb.
— oneself
place oneself 187 vb.
— upon
encroach 306 vb.
entrenched
permanent 144 adj.
established 153 adj.
strong 162 adj.
defended 713 adj.
conditional 766 adj.
due 915 adj.
entrepôt
storage 632 n.
emporium 796 n.
entrepreneur
gambler 618 n.
trier 671 n.
doer 676 n.
merchant 794 n.
entresol
layer 207 n.
entropy
decomposition 51 n.
entrust
transfer 272 vb.
commission 751 vb.
assign 780 vb.
give 781 vb.
entry
doorway 263 n.
ingress 297 n.
way in 297 n.
registration 548 n.
accounts 808 n.
entwine
connect 45 vb.
unite with 45 vb.
enlace 222 vb.
twine 251 vb.
enumerate
specify 80 vb.
number 86 vb.
list 87 vb.
enumerator
enumerator 86 n.
enunciate
affirm 532 vb.
voice 577 vb.
enunciation
speech 579 n.
enuresis
excretion 302 n.
envelop
comprise 78 vb.
cover 226 vb.
circumscribe 232 vb.
envelope
receptacle 194 n.
covering 226 n.
enclosure 235 n.
correspondence 588 n.
envenom
impair 655 vb.
aggravate 832 vb.
excite hate 888 vb.
enrage 891 vb.
envenomed
bad 645 adj.
toxic 653 adj.
enviable
desired 859 adj.
approvable 923 adj.
envier
malcontent 829 n.
desirer 859 n.
envious
discontented 829 adj.
inimical 881 adj.
resentful 891 adj.
jealous 911 adj.
envious 912 adj.
environ
surround 230 vb.
environment
circumstance 8 n.
relation 9 n.
locality 187 n.
surroundings 230 n.
environmental
circumstantial 8 adj.
relative 9 adj.
environmentalist
preserver 666 n.
environs
locality 187 n.
near place 200 n.
surroundings 230 n.
envisage
imagine 513 vb.
envoi, envoy
adjunct 40 n.
verse form 593 n.
envoy
messenger 529 n.
official 690 n.
envoy 754 n.
envy
discontent 829 n.
be discontented 829 vb.
desired object 859 n.
desire 859 vb.
hate 888 vb.

resent 891 vb.
be malevolent 898 vb.
jealousy 911 n.
be jealous 911 vb.
envy 912 n.vb.
approve 923 vb.
enwrap
fold 261 vb.
enzyme
alterer 143 n.
leaven 323 n.
organism 358 n.
eo-
primal 127 adj.
eolith
antiquity 125 n.
eparch
governor 741 n.
epaulette
badge 547 n.
livery 547 n.
badge of rank 743 n.
trimming 844 n.
épée
sidearms 723 n.
ephemera
brief span 114 n.
anthology 592 n.
ephemeral
ephemeral 114 adj.
ephemerality
transience 114 n.
death 361 n.
ephemeris
chronology 117 n.
ephod
vestments 989 n.
epic
film 445 n.
prolix 570 adj.
narrative 590 n.
descriptive 590 adj.
poem 593 n.
epicene
multiform 82 adj.
abnormal 84 adj.
equivocal 518 adj.
epicentre
centre 225 n.
epicure
eater 301 n.
gastronomy 301 n.
people of taste 846 n.
perfectionist 862 n.
sensualist 944 n.
glutton 947 n.
epicurean
sensuous 376 adj.
people of taste 846 n.
tasteful 846 adj.
fastidious 862 adj.
sensualist 944 n.
sensual 944 adj.
Epicureanism
philosophy 449 n.
enjoyment 824 n.
epidemic
extensive 32 adj.
comprehensive 52 adj.
universal 79 adj.
plague 651 n.
infectious 653 adj.
epidermis
skin 226 n.
epidiascope
optical device 442 n.
epidural
obstetrics 167 n.
anaesthetic 375 n.
epigram
maxim 496 n.
phrase 563 n.
conciseness 569 n.
witticism 839 n.
epigrammatic
aphoristic 496 adj.
epilepsy
spasm 318 n.
frenzy 503 n.
nervous disorders 651 n.
epilogue
sequel 67 n.
extremity 69 n.
dramaturgy 594 n.
epiphany
revelation 975 n.
Epiphany
holy day 988 n.
epiphenomenon
concomitant 89 n.
episcopacy
church office 985 n.
the church 985 n.
episcopal
ecclesiastical 985 adj.
clerical 986 adj.
episcopalian
Anglican 976 adj.
ecclesiastical 985 adj.
Episcopalian
Catholic 976 n.
sectarian 978 adj.
episcopate
church office 985 n.
ecclesiarch 986 n.
episcope
optical device 442 n.
episode
event 154 n.
interjection 231 n.
pleonasm 570 n.
narrative 590 n.
episodic
unrelated 10 adj.
discontinuous 72 adj.
epistemology
knowledge 490 n.
epistle
script 586 n.
correspondence 588 n.
Epistles
scripture 975 n.
epitaph
valediction 296 n.
obsequies 364 n.
indication 547 n.
epithet
name 561 n.
scurrility 899 n.
epitome
miniature 196 n.
image 551 n.
conciseness 569 n.
compendium 592 n.
epitomize, epitomise
represent 551 vb.
epoch
era 110 n.
chronology 117 n.
epoch-making
notable 638 adj.
eponymous
named 561 adj.
Epsom salts
purgative 658 n.
equable
uniform 16 adj.
equal 28 adj.
inexcitable 823 adj.
equal
compeer 28 n.
equal 28 adj.
be equal 28 vb.
equal contest
contest 716 n.
equalitarian
uniformist 16 n.
equality
identity 13 n.
equality 28 n.
synchronism 123 n.
stability 153 n.
equal chance 159 n.
parallelism 219 n.
no choice 606 n.
justice 913 n.
equalization
equalization 28 n.
compensation 31 n.
weighing 322 n.
equalization fund
finance 797 n.
equalize, equalise
correlate 12 vb.
make uniform 16 vb.
adjust 24 vb.
equalize 28 vb.
average out 30 vb.
flatten 216 vb.
equal opportunity
justice 913 n.
equal rights
freedom 744 n.
equal to
powerful 160 adj.
sufficient 635 adj.
equanimity
inexcitability 823 n.
equate
identify 13 vb.
equalize 28 vb.
equation
equivalence 28 n.
numerical result 85 n.
equator
middle 70 n.
dividing line 92 n.
circle 250 n.
equatorial
middle 70 adj.
telluric 321 adj.
warm 379 adj.
equerry
retainer 742 n.
equestrian, equestrienne
rider 268 n.
equestrianism
equitation 267 n.
equidistant
equal 28 adj.
middle 70 adj.
parallel 219 adj.
equilateral
equal 28 adj.
symmetrical 245 adj.
equilibrant
equilibrium 28 n.
equilibrium
equilibrium 28 n.
quiescence 266 n.
inexcitability 823 n.
equine
equine 273 adj.
animal 365 adj.
equinoctial
vernal 128 adj.
autumnal 129 adj.
celestial 321 adj.
equinox
uranometry 321 n.
equip
dress 228 vb.
find means 629 vb.
provide 633 vb.
make ready 669 vb.
equipage
carriage 274 n.
equipment
adjunct 40 n.
contents 193 n.
means 629 n.
equipment 630 n.
provision 633 n.
fitting out 669 n.
equipoise
equilibrium 28 n.
weighing 322 n.
equitable
equal 28 adj.
just 913 adj.
honourable 929 adj.
equitation
gait 265 n.

equitation 267 n.
equity
indifference 860 n.
justice 913 n.
equivalence
identity 13 n.
equivalence 28 n.
connotation 514 n.
equivalent
analogue 18 n.
compeer 28 n.
equivalent 28 adj.
offset 31 n.
quid pro quo 150 n.
interpretive 520 adj.
equivocal
double 91 adj.
uncertain 474 adj.
puzzling 517 adj.
equivocal 518 adj.
unclear 568 adj.
cunning 698 adj.
dishonest 930 adj.
impure 951 adj.
equivocalness
equivocalness 518 n.
concealment 525 n.
mental dishonesty 543 n.
word 559 n.
imperspicuity 568 n.
equivocation
sophistry 477 n.
equivocalness 518 n.
falsehood 541 n.
pretext 614 n.
wit 839 n.
equivocator
sophist 477 n.
liar 545 n.
equivoque
absurdity 497 n.
equivocalness 518 n.
witticism 839 n.
impurity 951 n.
era
date 108 n.
era 110 n.
chronology 117 n.
past time 125 n.
eradicate
revolutionize 149 vb.
destroy 165 vb.
displace 188 vb.
eject 300 vb.
extract 304 vb.
erase
destroy 165 vb.
rub 333 vb.
disappear 446 vb.
obliterate 550 vb.
clean 648 vb.
Erebus
darkness 418 n.
classical deities 967 n.
mythic hell 972 n.
erect
produce 164 vb.
place 187 vb.
vertical 215 adj.
make vertical 215 vb.
elevated 310 adj.
elevate 310 vb.
honourable 929 adj.
erection
edifice 164 n.
eremite
solitary 883 n.
ascetic 945 n.
erg
energy 160 n.
ergo
hence 158 adv.
ergonomics
exertion 682 n.
Erinys
Fury 891 n.
eristic
reasoner 475 n.
arguing 475 adj.
Erl King
fairy 970 n.
ermine
skin 226 n.
heraldry 547 n.
regalia 743 n.
trimming 844 n.
erode
abate 37 vb.
decompose 51 vb.
encroach 306 vb.
pulverize 332 vb.
rub 333 vb.
waste 634 vb.
impair 655 vb.
eroded
unproductive 172 adj.
erogenous
erotic 887 adj.
Eros
libido 859 n.
love 887 n.
love god 887 n.
erosion
destroyer 168 n.
(See **erode***)*
erotic
erotic 887 adj.
sensual 944 adj.
impure 951 adj.
eroticism
libido 859 n.
love 887 n.
unchastity 951 n.
err
stray 282 vb.
err 495 vb.
be wicked 934 vb.
errand
message 529 n.
job 622 n.
mandate 751 n.
errandboy
traveller 268 n.
courier 529 n.
servant 742 n.
errant
travelling 267 adj.
deviating 282 adj.
errata
edition 589 n.
erratic
nonuniform 17 adj.
fitful 142 adj.
unstable 152 adj.
moving 265 adj.
deviating 282 adj.
inexact 495 adj.
crazy 503 adj.
capricious 604 adj.
erratum
mistake 495 n.
erroneous
unreal 2 adj.
illogical 477 adj.
erroneous 495 adj.
imaginary 513 adj.
heterodox 977 adj.
error
deviation 282 n.
misjudgment 481 n.
ignorance 491 n.
error 495 n.
deception 542 n.
inexpedience 643 n.
defect 647 n.
imperfection 647 n.
ersatz
simulating 18 adj.
imitative 20 adj.
substituted 150 adj.
spurious 542 adj.
vulgar 847 adj.
erstwhile
prior 119 adj.
eructation
voidance 300 n.
respiration 352 n.
erudite
instructed 490 adj.
studious 536 adj.
erudite person
scholar 492 n.
erudition
erudition 490 n.
learning 536 n.
erupt
be violent 176 vb.
emerge 298 vb.
attack 712 vb.
eruption
revolution 149 n.
outbreak 176 n.
egress 298 n.
voidance 300 n.
fire 379 n.
skin disease 651 n.
escalade
ascent 308 n.
attack 712 n.
escalate
grow 36 vb.
be dear 811 vb.
escalator
conveyance 267 n.
carrier 273 n.
conveyor 274 n.
ascent 308 n.
lifter 310 n.
escalator clause
qualification 468 n.
escalope
meat 301 n.
escapade
foolery 497 n.
whim 604 n.
revel 837 n.
escape
departure 296 n.
decamp 296 vb.
outflow 298 n.
outlet 298 n.
flow out 298 vb.
disappear 446 vb.
avoidance 620 n.
run away 620 vb.
be safe 660 vb.
seek safety 660 vb.
escape 667 n.vb.
deliverance 668 n.
achieve liberty 746 vb.
be exempt 919 vb.
— notice
be unseen 444 vb.
escape notice 456 vb.
elude 667 vb.
be modest 874 vb.
— one
be forgotten 506 vb.
be unintelligible 517 vb.
escape clause
qualification 468 n.
conditions 766 n.
escape hatch
means of escape 667 n.
escapism
fantasy 513 n.
avoidance 620 n.
escape 667 n.
escapist
visionary 513 n.
escapology
escape 667 n.
escarpment
high land 209 n.
incline 220 n.
eschatology
finality 69 n.
theology 973 n.
escheat
reversion 148 n.
eschew
avoid 620 vb.
escort
concomitant 89 n.
accompany 89 vb.
male 372 n.
look after 457 vb.
protection 660 n.

direct 689 vb.
defender 713 n.
keeper 749 n.
take away 786 vb.
lover 887 n.
court 889 vb.
escritoire
cabinet 194 n.
escudo
coinage 797 n.
escutcheon
heraldry 547 n.
Eskimo
coldness 380 n.
ESN
unintelligent 499 adj.
esoteric
private 80 adj.
unintelligible 517 adj.
occult 523 adj.
cabbalistic 984 adj.
esotericism
latency 523 n.
secret 530 n.
occultism 984 n.
ESP
sense 374 n.
psychics 984 n.
espalier
frame 218 n.
fence 235 n.
especially
eminently 34 adv.
specially 80 adv.
Esperanto
language 557 n.
espial
inspection 438 n.
discovery 484 n.
espionage
inspection 438 n.
secret service 459 n.
esplanade
horizontality 216 n.
path 624 n.
espouse
choose 605 vb.
patronize 703 vb.
cooperate 706 vb.
marry 894 vb.
wed 894 vb.
espresso
soft drink 301 n.
esprit
intelligence 498 n.
wit 839 n.
esprit de corps
prejudice 481 n.
cooperation 706 n.
sociality 882 n.
esprit de l'escalier
sequel 67 n.
lateness 136 n.
wit 839 n.
espy
see 438 vb.
esquire
male 372 n.
title 870 n.
–ess
female 373 n.
essay
reading matter 589 n.
article 591 n.
attempt 671 n.vb.
essayist
author 589 n.
dissertator 591 n.
essence
essence 1 n.
essential part 5 n.
main part 32 n.
simpleness 44 n.
product 164 n.
form 243 n.
extraction 304 n.
odour 394 n.
meaning 514 n.
goodness 644 n.
perfection 646 n.
cosmetic 843 n.
Essenes
non-Christian sect 978 n.
essential
real 1 adj.
intrinsic 5 adj.
absolute 32 adj.
requirement 627 n.
required 627 adj.
chief thing 638 n.
important 638 adj.
essentiality
substantiality 3 n.
essential oil
scent 396 n.
EST
therapy 658 n.
establish
auspicate 68 vb.
perpetuate 115 vb.
stabilize 153 vb.
produce 164 vb.
place 187 vb.
corroborate 466 vb.
demonstrate 478 vb.
dower 777 vb.
make legal 953 vb.
established
immemorial 127 adj.
permanent 144 adj.
powerful 160 adj.
usual 610 adj.
prosperous 730 adj.
established Church
Christendom 976 n.
established order
regularity 81 n.
establishment
location 187 n.
corporation 708 n.
shop 796 n.
(See **establish** *)*
Establishment, the
influence 178 n.
bigwig 638 n.
authority 733 n.
master 741 n.
upper class 868 n.
estate
state 7 n.
territory 184 n.
land 344 n.
farm 370 n.
possession 773 n.
estate 777 n.
lands 777 n.
estate agent
merchant 794 n.
estate duty
tax 809 n.
estates
wealth 800 n.
esteem
opine 485 vb.
make important 638 vb.
prestige 866 n.
repute 866 n.
respect 920 n.vb.
approbation 923 n.
approve 923 vb.
estimable
excellent 644 adj.
approvable 923 adj.
estimate
do sums 86 vb.
cognize 447 vb.
experiment 461 n.
discriminate 463 vb.
measurement 465 n.
estimate 480 n.vb.
expectation 507 n.
interpretation 520 n.
report 524 n.
price 809 vb.
estimation
measurement 465 n.
estimate 480 n.
prestige 866 n.
estimator
appraiser 465 n.
estimator 480 n.
estrade
rostrum 539 n.
estrange
set apart 46 vb.
make quarrels 709 vb.
not retain 779 vb.
make enemies 881 vb.
excite hate 888 vb.
estrangement
enmity 881 n.
seclusion 883 n.
hatred 888 n.
estuary
open space 263 n.
gulf 345 n.
et cetera, etc.
in addition 38 adv.
including 78 adv.
et cetera 101 adv.
etch
outline 233 vb.
groove 262 vb.
mark 547 vb.
engrave 555 vb.
etching
representation 551 n.
engraving 555 n.
ornamental art 844 n.
eternal
existing 1 adj.
infinite 107 adj.
lasting 113 adj.
perpetual 115 adj.
renowned 866 adj.
godlike 965 adj.
paradisiac 971 adj.
Eternal, the
the Deity 965 n.
eternal, be
be eternal 115 vb.
go on 146 vb.
be remembered 505 vb.
eternal life
heaven 971 n.
eternally
uniformly 16 adv.
(See **eternal** *)*
eternal rest
quietude 266 n.
death 361 n.
heaven 971 n.
eternal triangle
jealousy 911 n.
illicit love 951 n.
eternity
existence 1 n.
infinity 107 n.
time 108 n.
neverness 109 n.
perpetuity 115 n.
immateriality 320 n.
divine attribute 965 n.
heaven 971 n.
Etesian winds
wind 352 n.
ether, aether
heavens 321 n.
lightness 323 n.
rarity 325 n.
gas 336 n.
air 340 n.
anaesthetic 375 n.
ethereal
celestial 321 adj.
ethereal body
spiritualism 984 n.
ethical
right 913 adj.
ethical 917 adj.
virtuous 933 adj.
ethical drug
medicine 658 n.

ethics
philosophy 449 n.
morals 917 n.
virtue 933 n.
ethnarch
governor 741 n.
ethnic
ethnic 11 adj.
native 191 adj.
human 371 adj.
ethnic group
race 11 n.
ethnic type
humankind 371 n.
ethnography
anthropology 371 n.
ethnology
anthropology 371 n.
ethology
biology 358 n.
zoology 367 n.
morals 917 n.
ethos
character 5 n.
conduct 688 n.
etiolate
decolorize 426 vb.
etiolation
achromatism 426 n.
whiteness 427 n.
etiquette
conformity 83 n.
practice 610 n.
etiquette 848 n.
formality 875 n.
étourderie
inattention 456 n.
étude
musical piece 412 n.
etymological
semantic 514 adj.
linguistic 557 adj.
verbal 559 adj.
etymology
source 156 n.
formation 243 n.
linguist 557 n.
linguistics 557 n.
etymology 559 n.
Eucharist
Holy Communion 988 n.
eucharistic
ritual 988 adj.
eudaemonism
philosophy 449 n.
enjoyment 824 n.
sensualism 944 n.
eugenics
propagation 167 n.
biology 358 n.
euhemerism
interpretation 520 n.
irreligion 974 n.
euhemeristic
rational 475 adj.
irreligious 974 adj.
eulogist
commender 923 n.
eulogize, eulogise
praise 923 vb.
eulogy
oration 579 n.
description 590 n.
honours 866 n.
praise 923 n.
Eumenides
Fury 891 n.
avenger 910 n.
Chthonian deity 967 n.
eunuch
eunuch 161 n.
male 372 n.
slave 742 n.
eupepsia
health 650 n.
euphemism
underestimation 483 n.
trope 519 n.
falsehood 541 n.
ornament 574 n.
good taste 846 n.
affectation 850 n.
flattery 925 n.
prudery 950 n.
euphemize, euphemise
moderate 177 vb.
euphonium
horn 414 n.
euphony
melody 410 n.
elegance 575 n.
euphoria
euphoria 376 n.
health 650 n.
repose 683 n.
palmy days 730 n.
happiness 824 n.
content 828 n.
euphoric
comfortable 376 adj.
euphuism
trope 519 n.
ornament 574 n.
affectation 850 n.
euphuist
phrasemonger 574 n.
affecter 850 n.
Eurasian
hybrid 43 n.
eureka!
484 int.
eurhythmic
symmetrical 245 adj.
eurhythmics
education 534 n.
exercise 682 n.
dancing 837 n.
Eurocrat
official 690 n.
Europeanize, Europeanise
transform 147 vb.
euthanasia
decease 361 n.
killing 362 n.
euphoria 376 n.
evacuate
be absent 190 vb.
decamp 296 vb.
emerge 298 vb.
empty 300 vb.
relinquish 621 vb.
evacuation
defecation 302 n.
relinquishment 621 n.
evacuee
outcast 883 n.
evade
sophisticate 477 vb.
be stealthy 525 vb.
avoid 620 vb.
elude 667 vb.
not observe 769 vb.
fail in duty 918 vb.
— one's creditors
not pay 805 vb.
evader
avoider 620 n.
evaginate
invert 221 vb.
evaluate
class 62 vb.
appraise 465 vb.
estimate 480 vb.
evanescent
transient 114 adj.
disappearing 446 adj.
evangelical
revelational 975 adj.
the orthodox 976 n.
orthodox 976 adj.
sectarian 978 adj.
zealot 979 n.
pietistic 979 adj.
evangelist
preacher 537 n.
religious teacher 973 n.
pastor 986 n.
evangelistic
scriptural 975 adj.
evangelize, evangelise
convert 147 vb.
convince 485 vb.
evaporate
pass away 2 vb.
decrease 37 vb.
be dispersed 75 vb.
be transient 114 vb.
destroy 165 vb.
become small 198 vb.
vaporize 338 vb.
dry 342 vb.
disappear 446 vb.
waste 634 vb.
evaporation
egress 298 n.
vaporization 338 n.
loss 772 n.
evasion
sophistry 477 n.
concealment 525 n.
falsehood 541 n.
mental dishonesty 543 n.
avoidance 620 n.
escape 667 n.
stratagem 698 n.
evasion of duty
undutifulness 918 n.
evasion of responsibility
nonliability 919 n.
evasive
sophistical 477 adj.
equivocal 518 adj.
reticent 525 adj.
false 541 adj.
untrue 543 adj.
avoiding 620 adj.
eve
precursor 66 n.
priority 119 n.
evening 129 n.
Eve
humankind 371 n.
woman 373 n.
even
uniform 16 adj.
equal 28 adj.
regular 81 adj.
numerical 85 adj.
evening 129 n.
periodical 141 adj.
flat 216 adj.
flatten 216 vb.
symmetrical 245 adj.
straight 249 adj.
smooth 258 adj. vb.
inexcitable 823 adj.
even chance
equal chance 159 n.
even-handed
just 913 adj.
even if
provided 468 adv.
evening
end 69 n.
period 110 n.
evening 129 n.
vespertine 129 adj.
obscuration 418 n.
half-light 419 n.
evening classes
curriculum 534 n.
school 539 n.
evening dress
formal dress 228 n.
evening star
evening 129 n.
planet 321 n.
luminary 420 n.
even keel
equilibrium 28 n.
evenness
uniformity 16 n.
equality 28 n.
periodicity 141 n.

symmetry 245 n.
smoothness 258 n.
even so
in return 31 adv.
nevertheless 468 adv.
evensong
evening 129 n.
public worship 981 n.
church service 988 n.
event
reality 1 n.
event 154 n.
effect 157 n.
nondesign 618 n.
contest 716 n.
completion 725 n.
even temper
inexcitability 823 n.
even tenor
uniformity 16 n.
order 60 n.
eventful
eventful 154 adj.
notable 638 adj.
busy 678 adj.
eventual
circumstantial 8 adj.
future 124 adj.
eventual 154 adj.
caused 157 adj.
eventuality
juncture 8 n.
event 154 n.
possibility 469 n.
eventually
prospectively 124 adv.
eventually 154 adv.
in the future 155 adv.
eventuate
happen 154 vb.
result 157 vb.
appear 445 vb.
ever and always
for ever 115 adv.
evergreen
lasting 113 adj.
perpetual 115 adj.
new 126 adj.
young 130 adj.
unchangeable 153 adj.
vegetal 366 adj.
renowned 866 adj.
everlasting
perpetual 115 adj.
godlike 965 adj.
evermore
for ever 115 adv.
ever since
all along 113 adv.
eversion
change 143 n.
inversion 221 n.
evolution 316 n.
ever so
greatly 32 adv.
every
universal 79 adj.
everybody
all 52 n.
everyman 79 n.
humankind 371 n.
everyday
typical 83 adj.
plain 573 adj.
usual 610 adj.
every inch
wholly 52 adv.
completely 54 adv.
everyman, everywoman
prototype 23 n.
common man 30 n.
all 52 n.
everyman 79 n.
person 371 n.
averageness 732 n.
commoner 869 n.
every man for himself
anarchy 734 n.
selfishness 932 n.
every minute
often 139 adv.
everyone
all 52 n.
everyman 79 n.
humankind 371 n.
every other
sequential 65 adj.
by turns 141 adv.
every so often
sometimes 139 adv.
periodically 141 adv.
at intervals 201 adv.
everywhere
sporadically 75 adv.
widely 183 adv.
here 189 adv.
evict
displace 188 vb.
eject 300 vb.
deprive 786 vb.
evicter
ejector 300 n.
eviction
exclusion 57 n.
ejection 300 n.
loss 772 n.
expropriation 786 n.
evidence
evidence 466 n.vb.
make likely 471 vb.
demonstration 478 n.
exhibit 522 n.
manifestation 522 n.
manifest 522 vb.
indication 547 n.
indicate 547 vb.
trace 548 n.
accusation 928 n.
legal trial 959 n.
evidence against
counterevidence 467 n.
evident
visible 443 adj.
certain 473 adj.
demonstrated 478 adj.
manifest 522 adj.
evidential
evidential 466 adj.
evil
evil 616 n.adj.
badness 645 n.
harmful 645 adj.
bane 659 n.
misuse 675 n.
adversity 731 n.
suffering 825 n.
wicked 934 adj.
evildoer
evildoer 904 n.
bad person 938 n.
evil-doing
wickedness 934 n.
evil eye
malevolence 898 n.
malediction 899 n.
spell 983 n.
evil hour
untimeliness 138 n.
evil intent
malevolence 898 n.
evil omen
danger signal 665 n.
Evil One, the
Satan 969 n.
evil spirit
sorcerer 983 n.
evil star
misfortune 731 n.
evince
evidence 466 vb.
demonstrate 478 vb.
manifest 522 vb.
indicate 547 vb.
eviscerate
weaken 163 vb.
empty 300 vb.
extract 304 vb.
impair 655 vb.
evocation
causation 156 n.
remembrance 505 n.
representation 551 n.
description 590 n.
evocative
meaningful 514 adj.
descriptive 590 adj.
evoke
incite 612 vb.
excite 821 vb.
evolution
existence 1 n.
numerical operation 86 n.
conversion 147 n.
event 154 n.
motion 265 n.
progression 285 n.
evolution 316 n.
biology 358 n.
improvement 654 n.
action 676 n.
evolve
become 1 vb.
unravel 62 vb.
be turned to 147 vb.
result 157 vb.
produce 164 vb.
generate 167 vb.
extract 304 vb.
evolve 316 vb.
get better 654 vb.
ewe
sheep 365 n.
female animal 373 n.
ewer
vessel 194 n.
water 339 n.
ex-
prior 119 adj.
former 125 adj.
exacerbate
augment 36 vb.
make violent 176 vb.
impair 655 vb.
hurt 827 vb.
aggravate 832 vb.
excite hate 888 vb.
exacerbation
increase 36 n.
exaggeration 546 n.
impairment 655 n.
painfulness 827 n.
exact
lifelike 18 adj.
definite 80 adj.
careful 457 adj.
accurate 494 adj.
veracious 540 adj.
perspicuous 567 adj.
concise 569 adj.
demand 737 vb.
compel 740 vb.
observant 768 adj.
levy 786 vb.
impose a duty 917 vb.
exacting
fatiguing 684 adj.
difficult 700 adj.
oppressive 735 adj.
discontented 829 adj.
greedy 859 adj.
fastidious 862 adj.
exaction
demand 737 n.
compulsion 740 n.
taking 786 n.
tax 809 n.
undueness 916 n.
exactitude
carefulness 457 n.
accuracy 494 n.
veracity 540 n.

exaggerate
augment 36 vb.
enlarge 197 vb.
overstep 306 vb.
overrate 482 vb.
be absurd 497 vb.
imagine 513 vb.
misinterpret 521 vb.
be untrue 543 vb.
exaggerate 546 vb.
misrepresent 552 vb.
make important 638 vb.
be affected 850 vb.
boast 877 vb.
exaggerated
exorbitant 32 adj.
unusual 84 adj.
exaggerated 546 adj.
flattering 925 adj.
exaggeration
trope 519 n.
publicity 528 n.
falsehood 541 n.
liar 545 n.
exaggeration 546 n.
magniloquence 574 n.
redundance 637 n.
ostentation 875 n.
exalt
elevate 310 vb.
make important 638 vb.
dignify 866 vb.
respect 920 vb.
praise 923 vb.
exaltation
joy 824 n.
piety 979 n.
exalted
great 32 adj.
noble 868 adj.
examination, exam
inspection 438 n.
meditation 449 n.
attention 455 n.
enquiry 459 n.
exam 459 n.
experiment 461 n.
dissertation 591 n.
legal trial 959 n.
examination paper
question 459 n.
examine
scan 438 vb.
interrogate 459 vb.
estimate 480 vb.
know 490 vb.
try a case 959 vb.
examinee
respondent 460 n.
testee 461 n.
beginner 538 n.
contender 716 n.
examiner
listener 415 n.
spectator 441 n.
inquisitive person 453 n.
enquirer 459 n.
estimator 480 n.
interlocutor 584 n.
example
relevance 9 n.
analogue 18 n.
originality 21 n.
duplicate 22 n.
prototype 23 n.
precursor 66 n.
rule 81 n.
example 83 n.
exhibit 522 n.
warning 664 n.
precept 693 n.
exasperate
make violent 176 vb.
aggravate 832 vb.
excite hate 888 vb.
enrage 891 vb.
ex cathedra
creedal 485 adj.
assertive 532 adj.
affirmatively 532 adv.
excavation
antiquity 125 n.
excavation 255 n.
tunnel 263 n.
extraction 304 n.
descent 309 n.
search 459 n.
discovery 484 n.
exceed
be great 32 vb.
be superior 34 vb.
grow 36 vb.
outdo 306 vb.
overstep 306 vb.
be intemperate 943 vb.
— requirements
be superfluous 637 vb.
exceedingly
extremely 32 adv.
excel
be superior 34 vb.
be good 644 vb.
be skilful 694 vb.
have a reputation 866 vb.
excellence
superiority 34 n.
(See **excellent** *)*
Excellency
sovereign 741 n.
title 870 n.
excellent
great 32 adj.
supreme 34 adj.
notable 638 adj.
excellent 644 adj.
perfect 646 adj.
skilful 694 adj.
pleasurable 826 adj.
splendid 841 adj.
tasteful 846 adj.
wonderful 864 adj.
renowned 866 adj.
virtuous 933 adj.
exceller
exceller 644 n.
proficient person 696 n.
except
if 8 adv.
in deduction 39 adv.
exclusive of 57 adv.
exception
nonuniformity 17 n.
separation 46 n.
exclusion 57 n.
speciality 80 n.
nonconformity 84 n.
qualification 468 n.
rejection 607 n.
deprecation 762 n.
conditions 766 n.
disapprobation 924 n.
exceptionable
blameworthy 924 adj.
exceptional
remarkable 32 adj.
abnormal 84 adj.
wonderful 864 adj.
excerpt
part 53 n.
edition 589 n.
abstract 592 vb.
select 605 vb.
excess
remainder 41 n.
redundance 637 n.
superfluity 637 n.
overactivity 678 n.
satiety 863 n.
cruel act 898 n.
intemperance 943 n.
excessive
exorbitant 32 adj.
violent 176 adj.
surpassing 306 adj.
exaggerated 546 adj.
pleonastic 570 adj.
inelegant 576 adj.
superfluous 637 adj.
dear 811 adj.
cruel 898 adj.
unwarranted 916 adj.
intemperate 943 adj.
excessive drinking
drunkenness 949 n.
excessive frankness
rudeness 885 n.
excessive size
size 195 n.
excess of freedom
freedom 744 n.
exchange
correlation 12 n.
equivalence 28 n.
focus 76 n.
substitution 150 n.
interchange 151 n. vb.
bourse 618 n.
transfer 780 n.
barter 791 n.
trade 791 vb.
market 796 n.
finance 797 n.
— blows
fight 716 vb.
— glances
gaze 438 vb.
— information
communicate 524 vb.
— letters
correspond 588 vb.
— views
compare 462 vb.
— vows
promise 764 vb.
— words
converse 584 vb.
exchequer
storage 632 n.
funds 797 n.
treasury 799 n.
excisable
priced 809 adj.
excise
subtract 39 vb.
extract 304 vb.
tax 809 n.
excitability
restlessness 678 n.
excitability 822 n.
excitable
fervent 818 adj.
impressed 818 adj.
impressible 819 adj.
excited 821 adj.
excitable 822 adj.
rash 857 adj.
irascible 892 adj.
excitant
stimulant 174 n.
excitant 821 n.
drug-taking 949 n.
excite
cause 156 vb.
strengthen 162 vb.
invigorate 174 vb.
make violent 176 vb.
cause feeling 374 vb.
incite 612 vb.
excite 821 vb.
delight 826 vb.
aggravate 832 vb.
cause desire 859 vb.
excite love 887 vb.
excited
expectant 507 adj.
feeling 818 adj.
excited 821 adj.
excitement
stimulation 174 n.
excitation 821 n.

exciting
striking 374 adj.
eloquent 579 adj.
descriptive 590 adj.
dramatic 594 adj.
intoxicating 949 adj.
exclaim
cry 408 vb.
voice 577 vb.
disapprove 924 vb.
exclamation
cry 408 n.
voice 577 n.
wonder 864 n.
exclamation mark
punctuation 547 n.
exclude
set apart 46 vb.
be incomplete 55 vb.
exclude 57 vb.
disregard 458 vb.
make impossible 470 vb.
obstruct 702 vb.
prohibit 757 vb.
refuse 760 vb.
make unwelcome 883 vb.
exempt 919 vb.
excluded
absent 190 adj.
exclusion
elimination 44 n.
separation 46 n.
exclusion 57 n.
exteriority 223 n.
rejection 607 n.
restriction 747 n.
seclusion 883 n.
exclusive
private 80 adj.
news 529 n.
excellent 644 adj.
sectional 708 adj.
possessing 773 adj.
sectarian 978 adj.
exclusiveness
sectarianism 978 n.
exclusive rights
restriction 747 n.
excogitate
think 449 vb.
imagine 513 vb.
excommunicate
exclude 57 vb.
eject 300 vb.
prohibit 757 vb.
make unwelcome 883 vb.
curse 899 vb.
condemn 961 vb.
perform ritual 988 vb.
excommunicated
cursed 899 adj.
schismatical 978 adj.
excoriate
uncover 229 vb.
reprobate 924 vb.
excrement
excrement 302 n.
dirt 649 n.
excrescence
swelling 253 n.
blemish 845 n.
excrescent
superfluous 637 adj.
excrete
emit 300 vb.
empty 300 vb.
excrete 302 vb.
excruciating
painful 377 adj.
paining 827 adj.
excruciatingly
painfully 32 adv.
exculpate
justify 927 vb.
acquit 960 vb.
excursion
land travel 267 n.
amusement 837 n.
excursionist
traveller 268 n.
reveller 837 n.
excursive
deviating 282 adj.
prolix 570 adj.
excuse
reason why 156 n.
disregard 458 vb.
qualify 468 vb.
mental dishonesty 543 n.
pretext 614 n.
stratagem 698 n.
forgive 909 vb.
exempt 919 vb.
vindication 927 n.
— oneself
plead 614 vb.
refuse 760 vb.
be exempt 919 vb.
excused
forgiven 909 adj.
nonliable 919 adj.
ex-directory
concealed 525 adj.
execrable
damnable 645 adj.
execrate
hate 888 vb.
curse 899 vb.
executant
musician 413 n.
doer 676 n.
execute
produce 164 vb.
operate 173 vb.
kill 362 vb.
play music 413 vb.
do 676 vb.
deal with 688 vb.
carry out 725 vb.
observe 768 vb.
execution
capital punishment 963 n.
executioner
killer 362 n.
punisher 963 n.
executive
doer 676 n.
agent 686 n.
manager 690 n.
executor
consignee 754 n.
exegesis
interpretation 520 n.
exemplar
prototype 23 n.
example 83 n.
exemplary
typical 83 adj.
excellent 644 adj.
cautionary 664 adj.
exemplary character
good person 937 n.
exemplify
exemplify 83 vb.
manifest 522 vb.
exempt
liberate 746 vb.
exempt 919 vb.
exempt from
unmixed 44 adj.
absent 190 adj.
exemption
permission 756 n.
nonliability 919 n.
exercise
train 534 vb.
job 622 n.
prepare oneself 669 vb.
use 673 n.vb.
do 676 vb.
exercise 682 n.
trouble 827 vb.
exert
use 673 vb.
— oneself
be vigorous 174 vb.
be attentive 455 vb.
persevere 600 vb.
attempt 671 vb.
be active 678 vb.
exert oneself 682 vb.
exertion
power 160 n.
vigorousness 174 n.
attempt 671 n.
exertion 682 n.
exfoliate
laminate 207 vb.
doff 229 vb.
exhalation
excretion 302 n.
vaporization 338 n.
respiration 352 n.
odour 394 n.
exhale
exude 298 vb.
emit 300 vb.
exhaust
abate 37 vb.
make smaller 198 vb.
outlet 298 n.
rarefy 325 vb.
blowing 352 n.
waste 634 vb.
make insufficient 636 vb.
impair 655 vb.
fatigue 684 vb.
levy 786 vb.
— one's arguments
be confuted 479 vb.
— one's resources
be prodigal 815 vb.
— the possibilities
comprise 78 vb.
use 673 vb.
exhaustion
helplessness 161 n.
weakness 163 n.
use 673 n.
(See **exhaust** *)*
exhaustive
complete 54 adj.
exhaust pipe
outlet 298 n.
air pipe 353 n.
exhibit
evidence 466 n.
show 522 vb.
indicate 547 vb.
market 796 n.
be ostentatious 875 vb.
exhibition
spectacle 445 n.
exhibit 522 n.
collection 632 n.
reward 962 n.
exhibitioner
student 538 n.
recipient 782 n.
exhibitionism
vanity 873 n.
ostentation 875 n.
impurity 951 n.
exhibitor
guide 520 n.
exhibitor 522 n.
exhilarate
excite 821 vb.
delight 826 vb.
cheer 833 vb.
inebriate 949 vb.
exhilaration
excitable state 822 n.
joy 824 n.
merriment 833 n.
drunkenness 949 n.
exhort
incite 612 vb.
advise 691 vb.
exhortation
oration 579 n.
inducement 612 n.
exhume
look back 125 vb.

exhume 364 vb.
exigency, exigence
juncture 8 n.
needfulness 627 n.
predicament 700 n.
desire 859 n.
exigent
demanding 627 adj.
oppressive 735 adj.
discontented 829 adj.
exiguous
small 33 adj.
exiguous 196 adj.
lean 206 adj.
exile
exclusion 57 n.
foreigner 59 n.
displacement 188 n.
wanderer 268 n.
egress 298 n.
eject 300 vb.
outcast 883 n.
seclusion 883 n.
penalty 963 n.
exist
be 1 vb.
be now 121 vb.
be present 189 vb.
live 360 vb.
be true 494 vb.
existence
existence 1 n.
presence 189 n.
materiality 319 n.
life 360 n.
existentialism
existence 1 n.
philosophy 449 n.
exit
doorway 263 n.
departure 296 n.
depart 296 vb.
egress 298 n.
outlet 298 n.
emerge 298 vb.
decease 361 n.
disappearance 446 n.
dramaturgy 594 n.
means of escape 667 n.
ex libris
label 547 n.
exobiology
astronomy 321 n.
exodus
departure 296 n.
egress 298 n.
ex officio
in control 689 adv.
authoritative 733 adj.
duly 915 adv.
exogamous
matrimonial 894 adj.
exogenous
exterior 223 adj.
vegetal 366 adj.
exonerate
forgive 909 vb.
exempt 919 vb.
justify 927 vb.
acquit 960 vb.
exorbitant
exorbitant 32 adj.
surpassing 306 adj.
exaggerated 546 adj.
dear 811 adj.
intolerable 827 adj.
exorcism
sorcery 983 n.
Christian rite 988 n.
exorcize, exorcise
dismiss 300 vb.
exordium
prelude 66 n.
beginning 68 n.
exosphere
atmosphere 340 n.
exoteric
exterior 223 adj.
undisguised 522 adj.
published 528 adj.
exotic
unrelated 10 adj.
dissimilar 19 adj.
extraneous 59 adj.
unconformable 84 adj.
flower 366 n.
horticultural 370 adj.
wonderful 864 adj.
expand
grow 36 vb.
add 38 vb.
enlarge 197 vb.
expand 197 vb.
lengthen 203 vb.
be broad 205 vb.
rarefy 325 vb.
exaggerate 546 vb.
be diffuse 570 vb.
expanse
greatness 32 n.
great quantity 32 n.
space 183 n.
size 195 n.
breadth 205 n.
expansion
increase 36 n.
expansion 197 n.
overstepping 306 n.
diffuseness 570 n.
(See **expand** *)*
expansionism
ingress 297 n.
overstepping 306 n.
nation 371 n.
bellicosity 718 n.
desire 859 n.
expansionist
militarist 722 n.
expansive
inclusive 78 adj.
spacious 183 adj.
expanded 197 adj.
broad 205 adj.
palmy 730 adj.
expatiate
be diffuse 570 vb.
be loquacious 581 vb.
expatriate
foreigner 59 n.
dweller 191 n.
egress 298 n.
outcast 883 n.
expatriation
exclusion 57 n.
egress 298 n.
seclusion 883 n.
expect
look ahead 124 vb.
assume 471 vb.
expect 507 vb.
foresee 510 vb.
intend 617 vb.
prepare 669 vb.
request 761 vb.
hope 852 vb.
desire 859 vb.
not wonder 865 vb.
have a right 915 vb.
impose a duty 917 vb.
— otherwise
be disappointed 509 vb.
— too much
make insufficient 636 vb.
expectancy, expectance
looking ahead 124 n.
expectation 507 n.
expectant
attentive 455 adj.
expectant 507 adj.
warned 664 adj.
hoping 852 adj.
expectant mother
maternity 169 n.
expectation
looking ahead 124 n.
destiny 155 n.
probability 471 n.
belief 485 n.
expectation 507 n.
hope 852 n.
expectations
dower 777 n.
hope 852 n.
dueness 915 n.
expectorant
purgative 658 n.
expectorate
eruct 300 vb.
expediency, expedience
good policy 642 n.
expedient
contrivance 623 n.
means 629 n.
useful 640 adj.
advisable 642 adj.
expedite
accelerate 277 vb.
hasten 680 vb.
facilitate 701 vb.
expedition
land travel 267 n.
activity 678 n.
haste 680 n.
warfare 718 n.
expeditionary force
armed force 722 n.
expeditious
speedy 277 adj.
active 678 adj.
hasty 680 adj.
expel
eliminate 44 vb.
externalize 223 vb.
impel 279 vb.
propel 287 vb.
eject 300 vb.
extract 304 vb.
reject 607 vb.
make unwelcome 883 vb.
expend
waste 634 vb.
dispose of 673 vb.
expend 806 vb.
expendable
superfluous 637 adj.
unimportant 639 adj.
useless 641 adj.
expenditure
loss 772 n.
purchase 792 n.
expenditure 806 n.
expense
waste 634 n.
expenditure 806 n.
expense account
subvention 703 n.
earnings 771 n.
expenditure 806 n.
ostentatious 875 adj.
expenses
expenditure 806 n.
expensive
dear 811 adj.
ostentatious 875 adj.
experience
meet with 154 vb.
empiricism 461 n.
knowledge 490 n.
know 490 vb.
wisdom 498 n.
skill 694 n.
feeling 818 n.
feel 818 vb.
suffer 825 vb.
experienced
wise 498 adj.
matured 669 adj.
expert 694 adj.
cunning 698 adj.

experiences
biography 590 n.
experiment
be curious 453 vb.
enquiry 459 n.
experiment 461 n. vb.
demonstration 478 n.
preparation 669 n.
attempt 671 n.vb.
experimental
new 126 adj.
experimental 461 adj.
discovering 484 adj.
speculative 618 adj.
attempting 671 adj.
cautious 858 adj.
experimentalist
experimenter 461 n.
experimentation
experiment 461 n.
experimenter
enquirer 459 n.
experimenter 461 n.
learner 538 n.
gambler 618 n.
trier 671 n.
expert
instructed 490 adj.
sage 500 n.
planner 623 n.
bigwig 638 n.
matured 669 adj.
adviser 691 n.
expert 694 adj.
expert 696 n.
proficient person 696 n.
expertise
knowledge 490 n.
skill 694 n.
expiate
atone 941 vb.
expiation
compensation 31 n.
propitiation 941 n.
expiration
end 69 n.
respiration 352 n.
speech sound 398 n.
expire
end 69 vb.
elapse 111 vb.
die 361 vb.
expired
past 125 adj.
explain
specify 80 vb.
account for 158 vb.
interpret 520 vb.
manifest 522 vb.
facilitate 701 vb.
— away
reason 475 vb.
confute 479 vb.
disbelieve 486 vb.
misteach 535 vb.
explained
intelligible 516 adj.
explanation
reason why 156 n.
attribution 158 n.
answer 460 n.
discovery 484 n.
interpretation 520 n.
disclosure 526 n.
expletive
pleonasm 570 n.
scurrility 899 n.
explicable
intelligible 516 adj.
explication
interpretation 520 n.
explicit
definite 80 adj.
meaningful 514 adj.
intelligible 516 adj.
undisguised 522 adj.
informative 524 adj.
perspicuous 567 adj.
explode
break 46 vb.
rend 46 vb.
be dispersed 75 vb.
demolish 165 vb.
be violent 176 vb.
open 263 vb.
shoot 287 vb.
be loud 400 vb.
bang 402 vb.
confute 479 vb.
miscarry 728 vb.
be excitable 822 vb.
get angry 891 vb.
exploded
unbelieved 486 adj.
erroneous 495 adj.
exploit
profit by 137 vb.
produce 164 vb.
use 673 vb.
misuse 675 vb.
deed 676 n.
do 676 vb.
be skilful 694 vb.
oppress 735 vb.
prowess 855 n.
thaumaturgy 864 n.
exploration
land travel 267 n.
enquiry 459 n.
search 459 n.
discovery 484 n.
exploratory
precursory 66 adj.
experimental 461 adj.
explore
travel 267 vb.
(See **exploration** *)*
explored
known 490 adj.
explorer
precursor 66 n.
traveller 268 n.
inquisitive person 453 n.
enquirer 459 n.
experimenter 461 n.
detector 484 n.
explosion
revolution 149 n.
havoc 165 n.
outbreak 176 n.
loudness 400 n.
bang 402 n.
excitable state 822 n.
anger 891 n.
explosive
expulsive 300 adj.
combustible 385 adj.
dangerous 661 adj.
explosive 723 n.
excitable 822 adj.
(See **explode** *)*
explosive device
bomb 723 n.
explosive situation
revolt 738 n.
exponent
numerical element 85 n.
interpreter 520 n.
teacher 537 n.
export
transference 272 n.
egress 298 n.
eject 300 vb.
provide 633 vb.
— and import
trade 791 vb.
exporter
transferrer 272 n.
carrier 273 n.
merchant 794 n.
expose
uncover 229 vb.
aerate 340 vb.
be visible 443 vb.
confute 479 vb.
detect 484 vb.
manifest 522 vb.
show 522 vb.
disclose 526 vb.
photograph 551 vb.
satirize 851 vb.
shame 867 vb.
dispraise 924 vb.
defame 926 vb.
accuse 928 vb.
— oneself
disclose 526 vb.
face danger 661 vb.
be rash 857 vb.
exposé
disclosure 526 n.
description 590 n.
exposed
defenceless 161 adj.
weakened 163 adj.
windy 352 adj.
sentient 374 adj.
painful 377 adj.
visible 443 adj.
vulnerable 661 adj.
unprepared 670 adj.
(See **expose** *)*
exposed nerve
sensibility 374 n.
exposed to
liable 180 adj.
subject 745 adj.
exposed to view
open 263 adj.
visible 443 adj.
exposition
musical piece 412 n.
spectacle 445 n.
demonstration 478 n.
commentary 520 n.
interpretation 520 n.
exhibit 522 n.
dissertation 591 n.
market 796 n.
expositor
interpreter 520 n.
teacher 537 n.
dissertator 591 n.
ex post facto
retrospectively 125 adv.
expostulate
reprove 924 vb.
expostulation
dissent 489 n.
dissuasion 613 n.
warning 664 n.
deprecation 762 n.
exposure
liability 180 n.
uncovering 229 n.
air 340 n.
refrigeration 382 n.
visibility 443 n.
confutation 479 n.
discovery 484 n.
manifestation 522 n.
disclosure 526 n.
photography 551 n.
vulnerability 661 n.
detraction 926 n.
exposure meter
optical device 442 n.
exposure of infants
homicide 362 n.
expound
interpret 520 vb.
teach 534 vb.
expounder
interpreter 520 n.
religious teacher 973 n.
express
definite 80 adj.
vehicular 274 adj.
speeder 277 n.
extract 304 vb.
meaningful 514 adj.
mean 514 vb.
undisguised 522 adj.
manifest 522 vb.

divulge 526 vb.
courier 529 n.
assertive 532 adj.
affirm 532 vb.
phrase 563 vb.
voice 577 vb.
express delivery
postal communications 531 n.
expressed in numbers
statistical 86 adj.
expression
number 85 n.
form 243 n.
musical skill 413 n.
mien 445 n.
meaning 514 n.
manifestation 522 n.
affirmation 532 n.
word 559 n.
phrase 563 n.
feeling 818 n.
Expressionism
art 551 n.
school of painting 553 n.
literature 557 n.
expressionless
still 266 adj.
unintelligible 517 adj.
impassive 820 adj.
expressive
meaningful 514 adj.
expressive 516 adj.
informative 524 adj.
indicating 547 adj.
stylistic 566 adj.
elegant 575 adj.
lively 819 adj.
express train
train 274 n.
speeder 277 n.
expressway
road 624 n.
expropriate
eject 300 vb.
assign 780 vb.
deprive 786 vb.
disentitle 916 vb.
expropriation
expropriation 786 n.
expulsion
elimination 44 n.
separation 46 n.
exclusion 57 n.
displacement 188 n.
ejection 300 n.
expropriation 786 n.
penalty 963 n.
(See **expel** *)*
expulsive
propulsive 287 adj.
expulsive 300 adj.
expunge
destroy 165 vb.
obliterate 550 vb.
expurgate
subtract 39 vb.
exclude 57 vb.
purify 648 vb.
impair 655 vb.
expurgated
pure 950 adj.
exquisite
painful 377 adj.
savoury 390 adj.
excellent 644 adj.
pleasurable 826 adj.
paining 827 adj.
beautiful 841 adj.
tasteful 846 adj.
fop 848 n.
fashionable 848 adj.
wonderful 864 adj.
extant
existing 1 adj.
present 121 adj.
recorded 548 adj.
extemporaneous
spontaneous 609 adj.
extempore
instantaneously 116 adv.
extempore 609 adv.
unreadily 670 adv.
extemporize, extemporise
compose music 413 vb.
improvise 609 vb.
be unprepared 670 vb.
extend
augment 36 vb.
add 38 vb.
continue 108 vb.
extend 183 vb.
enlarge 197 vb.
lengthen 203 vb.
— to
fill 54 vb.
extend 183 vb.
be distant 199 vb.
be contiguous 202 vb.
extended
protracted 113 adj.
extensibility
expansion 197 n.
softness 327 n.
elasticity 328 n.
extension
increase 36 n.
adjunct 40 n.
protraction 113 n.
continuance 146 n.
space 183 n.
lobby 194 n.
expansion 197 n.
lengthening 203 n.
connotation 514 n.
extensive
extensive 32 adj.
comprehensive 52 adj.
inclusive 78 adj.
universal 79 adj.
spacious 183 adj.
extent
quantity 26 n.
degree 27 n.
greatness 32 n.
time 108 n.
space 183 n.
size 195 n.
length 203 n.
extenuate
abate 37 vb.
moderate 177 vb.
qualify 468 vb.
plead 614 vb.
extenuate 927 vb.
extenuating circumstances
qualification 468 n.
vindication 927 n.
exterior
extrinsic 6 adj.
extraneous 59 adj.
exteriority 223 n.
exterior 223 adj.
appearing 445 adj.
ostentation 875 n.
exterminate
destroy 165 vb.
slaughter 362 vb.
extermination
destruction 165 n.
extraction 304 n.
slaughter 362 n.
external
extrinsic 6 adj.
separate 46 adj.
exterior 223 adj., n.
appearing 445 adj.
externalize, externalise
make extrinsic 6 vb.
externalize 223 vb.
materialize 319 vb.
cognize 447 vb.
manifest 522 vb.
extinct
extinct 2 adj.
past 125 adj.
dead 361 adj.
nonactive 677 adj.
inactive 679 adj.
extinction
decease 361 n.
disappearance 446 n.
extinguish
suppress 165 vb.
moderate 177 vb.
extinguish 382 vb.
snuff out 418 vb.
extinguisher
destroyer 168 n.
moderator 177 n.
extinguisher 382 n.
extirpate
destroy 165 vb.
extract 304 vb.
extol
advertise 528 vb.
praise 923 vb.
worship 981 vb.
extort
extract 304 vb.
oppress 735 vb.
compel 740 vb.
levy 786 vb.
rob 788 vb.
overcharge 811 vb.
extortionate
exorbitant 32 adj.
dear 811 adj.
avaricious 816 adj.
greedy 859 adj.
extra
increment 36 n.
additional 38 adj.
extra 40 n.n.
exclusive of 57 adv.
component 58 n.
actor 594 n.
superfluity 637 n.
superfluous 637 adj.
unused 674 adj.
extract
part 53 n.
product 164 n.
uncover 229 vb.
draw 288 vb.
empty 300 vb.
extract 304 vb.
doctor 658 vb.
deliver 668 vb.
levy 786 vb.
take 786 vb.
extraction
genealogy 169 n.
extracts
anthology 592 n.
extracurricular
educational 534 adj.
extradite
exclude 57 vb.
extradition
transference 272 n.
ejection 300 n.
extragalactic
extraneous 59 adj.
cosmic 321 adj.
extramarital
extramarital 951 adj.
extramundane
immaterial 320 adj.
divine 965 adj.
extramural
educational 534 adj.
extraneous
extrinsic 6 adj.
unrelated 10 adj.
disagreeing 25 adj.
additional 38 adj.
separate 46 adj.
extraneous 59 adj.
unconformable 84 adj.
exterior 223 adj.

extraordinary
remarkable 32 adj.
unusual 84 adj.
wonderful 864 adj.
noteworthy 866 adj.
extrapolation
numerical operation 86 n.
extrasensory perception
sense 374 n.
intellect 447 n.
psychics 984 n.
extraterrestrial
extraneous 59 adj.
exterior 223 adj.
extraterritoriality
nonliability 919 n.
extravagance
magniloquence 574 n.
misuse 675 n.
prodigality 815 n.
extravagant
exorbitant 32 adj.
violent 176 adj.
absurd 497 adj.
foolish 499 adj.
imaginative 513 adj.
exaggerated 546 adj.
wasteful 634 adj.
plenteous 635 adj.
expending 806 adj.
dear 811 adj.
prodigal 815 adj.
ridiculous 849 adj.
intemperate 943 adj.
extravaganza
musical piece 412 n.
film 445 n.
spectacle 445 n.
foolery 497 n.
ideality 513 n.
extravasation
outflow 298 n.
haemorrhage 302 n.
extreme
exorbitant 32 adj.
complete 54 adj.
extremity 69 n.
ending 69 adj.
violent 176 adj.
limit 236 n.
severe 735 adj.
intolerable 827 adj.
extremely
extremely 32 adv.
eminently 34 adv.
completely 54 adv.
extreme penalty
capital punishment 963 n.
extremes
exaggeration 546 n.
opposites 704 n.
cruel act 898 n.
extreme unction
decease 361 n.
Christian rite 988 n.
extremism
exaggeration 546 n.
reformism 654 n.
extremist
crank 504 n.
reformer 654 n.
opponent 705 n.
revolter 738 n.
extremity, extremities
adjunct 40 n.
end 69 n.
extremity 69 n.
crisis 137 n.
vertex 213 n.
edge 234 n.
limit 236 n.
rear 238 n.
adversity 731 n.
severity 735 n.
suffering 825 n.
extricate
extract 304 vb.
deliver 668 vb.
disencumber 701 vb.
liberate 746 vb.
extrication
escape 667 n.
extrinsic
extrinsic 6 adj.
unrelated 10 adj.
separate 46 adj.
extrovert, extravert
extrinsicality 6 n.
exteriority 223 n.
sociable 882 adj.
extrude
eject 300 vb.
exuberance
productiveness 171 n.
diffuseness 570 n.
redundance 637 n.
exuberant
fervent 818 adj.
exude
exude 298 vb.
emit 300 vb.
be wet 341 vb.
exult
vociferate 408 vb.
rejoice 835 vb.
boast 877 vb.
exultant
jubilant 833 adj.
ex voto
devotional 981 adj.
eye
centre 225 n.
orifice 263 n.
eye 438 n.
gaze 438 vb.
watch 441 vb.
surveillance 457 n.
court 889 vb.
eyeball
eye 438 n.
eyeball to eyeball
near 200 adv.
opposing 704 adj.
eyebrows
hair 259 n.
eye-catching
obvious 443 adj.
manifest 522 adj.
eye disease
blindness 439 n.
eye for an eye
interchange 151 n.
retaliation 714 n.
revenge 910 n.
eyeful
view 438 n.
spectacle 445 n.
a beauty 841 n.
eyeglass
eyeglass 442 n.
eyelashes
filament 208 n.
hair 259 n.
eyeless
crippled 163 adj.
blind 439 adj.
eyelet
fastening 47 n.
circle 250 n.
orifice 263 n.
eyelid
shade 226 n.
screen 421 n.
eyeliner
cosmetic 843 n.
eye on, an
surveillance 457 n.
eye-opener
discovery 484 n.
lack of expectation 508 n.
prodigy 864 n.
eyepiece
optical device 442 n.
eye shade
shade 226 n.
screen 421 n.
eye shadow
cosmetic 843 n.
eyeshot
visibility 443 n.
eyesight
vision 438 n.
eyes on
attention 455 n.
eyesore
eyesore 842 n.
eyestrain
dim sight 440 n.
eye to eye
concordant 710 adj.
eyewash
empty talk 515 n.
falsehood 541 n.
balm 658 n.
eyewitness
spectator 441 n.
witness 466 n.
eyot
island 349 n.
eyrie, eyry, aerie
nest 192 n.
high structure 209 n.

F

fab
super 644 adj.
Fabian
reformer 654 n.
political party 708 n.
Fabianism
slowness 278 n.
caution 858 n.
Fabian policy
delay 136 n.
inaction 677 n.
fable
maxim 496 n.
fantasy 513 n.
fable 543 n.
narrative 590 n.
fabled
supposed 512 adj.
imaginary 513 adj.
renowned 866 adj.
fabric
modality 7 n.
textile 222 n.
matter 319 n.
structure 331 n.
materials 631 n.
fabricate
compose 56 vb.
produce 164 vb.
imagine 513 vb.
fake 541 vb.
fabricated
unattested 467 adj.
imaginary 513 adj.
fabrication
falsehood 541 n.
untruth 543 n.
fabricator
liar 545 n.
fabulist
liar 545 n.
narrator 590 n.
fabulous
unreal 2 adj.
prodigious 32 adj.
imaginary 513 adj.
untrue 543 adj.
super 644 adj.
noteworthy 866 adj.
facade, façade
exteriority 223 n.
face 237 n.
duplicity 541 n.
face
timekeeper 117 n.
impend 155 vb.
be present 189 vb.
exteriority 223 n.
coat 226 vb.
line 227 vb.

face 237 n.
be in front 237 vb.
be opposite 240 vb.
orientate 281 vb.
feature 445 n.
mien 445 n.
print-type 587 n.
be resolute 599 vb.
withstand 704 vb.
be courageous 855 vb.
prestige 866 n.
insolence 878 n.
— about
revert 148 vb.
turn round 282 vb.
— both ways
tergiversate 603 vb.
— death
face danger 661 vb.
— the cameras
act 594 vb.
— the music
be resolute 599 vb.
be courageous 855 vb.
be punished 963 vb.
— up to
be in front 237 vb.
facecloth
cleaning cloth 648 n.
face down
under 210 adv.
supine 216 adj.
inversely 221 adv.
face flannel
cleaning cloth 648 n.
face fungus
hair 259 n.
faceless
uniform 16 adj.
anonymous 562 adj.
face-lift
revival 656 n.
beautification 843 n.
face powder
powder 332 n.
cosmetic 843 n.
face-saving measures
needfulness 627 n.
facet
exteriority 223 n.
appearance 445 n.
facetious
witty 839 adj.
face to face
near 200 adv.
in front 237 adv.
against 240 adv.
opposing 704 adj.
face value
appearance 445 n.
price 809 n.
facial
exterior 223 adj.
beautification 843 n.
facile
easy 701 adj.
facilitate
make possible 469 vb.
facilitate 701 vb.
aid 703 vb.
give scope 744 vb.
facilities
means 629 n.
good policy 642 n.
facility 701 n.
aid 703 n.
scope 744 n.
facility
skill 694 n.
facing
near 200 adj.
facing 226 n.
lining 227 n.
opposite 240 adj.
towards 281 adv.
façon de parler
trope 519 n.
phrase 563 n.
facsimile
copy 22 n.
sham 542 n.
representation 551 n.
fact
reality 1 n.
event 154 n.
evidence 466 n.
certainty 473 n.
truth 494 n.
chief thing 638 n.
fact-finding
enquiring 459 adj.
faction
dissent 489 n.
dissentient 489 n.
description 590 n.
opposition 704 n.
party 708 n.
dissension 709 n.
revolt 738 n.
sect 978 n.
factional
sectional 708 adj.
factiousness
quarrelsomeness 709 n.
sectarianism 978 n.
factitious
untrue 543 adj.
fact of life
reality 1 n.
factor
circumstance 8 n.
part 53 n.
component 58 n.
numerical element 85 n.
cause 156 n.
influence 178 n.
element 319 n.
manager 690 n.
consignee 754 n.
deputy 755 n.
factor (in), be a
be related 9 vb.
aid 703 vb.
factorize, factorise
simplify 44 vb.
factory
production 164 n.
workshop 687 n.
factory farming
production 164 n.
agriculture 370 n.
factory hand
worker 686 n.
factory ship
fishing boat 275 n.
factotum
busy person 678 n.
worker 686 n.
servant 742 n.
facts
evidence 466 n.
accuracy 494 n.
information 524 n.
facts of life
propagation 167 n.
factual
real 1 adj.
evidential 466 adj.
certain 473 adj.
true 494 adj.
veracious 540 adj.
descriptive 590 adj.
faculty
ability 160 n.
erudition 490 n.
teacher 537 n.
aptitude 694 n.
skill 694 n.
fad
eccentricity 503 n.
whim 604 n.
fashion 848 n.
affectation 850 n.
liking 859 n.
faddist
narrow mind 481 n.
crank 504 n.
fade
shade off 27 vb.
decrease 37 vb.
be transient 114 vb.
be old 127 vb.
be weak 163 vb.
be dim 419 vb.
lose colour 426 vb.
photography 551 n.
deteriorate 655 vb.
be ugly 842 vb.
lose repute 867 vb.
— away
end 69 vb.
cease 145 vb.
sound faint 401 vb.
disappear 446 vb.
be ill 651 vb.
faded
dry 342 adj.
soft-hued 425 adj.
colourless 426 adj.
fadeout
obscuration 418 n.
disappearance 446 n.
faeces
excrement 302 n.
dirt 649 n.
faerie
fairy 970 n.
fag
tobacco 388 n.
busy person 678 n.
labour 682 n.
fatigue 684 vb.
servant 742 n.
fag end
remainder 41 n.
extremity 69 n.
tobacco 388 n.
fagged out
fatigued 684 adj.
faggot
bunch 74 n.
fuel 385 n.
faience
pottery 381 n.
fail
be inferior 35 vb.
decrease 37 vb.
lose a chance 138 vb.
cease 145 vb.
be weak 163 vb.
be unproductive 172 vb.
fall short 307 vb.
blunder 495 vb.
be disappointed 509 vb.
not suffice 636 vb.
be useless 641 vb.
be ill 651 vb.
deteriorate 655 vb.
be fatigued 684 vb.
not complete 726 vb.
fail 728 vb.
not observe 769 vb.
not pay 805 vb.
disapprove 924 vb.
— one
disappoint 509 vb.
failing
deficient 307 adj.
vice 934 n.
fail-safe
tutelary 660 adj.
failure
inferiority 35 n.
stop 145 n.
impotence 161 n.
ruin 165 n.
negligence 458 n.
mistake 495 n.
disappointment 509 n.
insufficiency 636 n.
lost labour 641 n.
imperfection 647 n.
bungling 695 n.
bungler 697 n.
hitch 702 n.

noncompletion 726 n.
failure 728 n.
loser 728 n.
misfortune 731 n.
nonobservance 769 n.
loss 772 n.
insolvency 805 n.
object of scorn 867 n.

fain
willingly 597 adv.
desiring 859 adj.

fainéant
idler 679 n.

faint
small 33 adj.
weak 163 adj.
be weak 163 vb.
insensibility 375 n.
be insensible 375 vb.
muted 401 adj.
dim 419 adj.
colourless 426 adj.
indistinct 444 adj.
irresolute 601 adj.
inactive 679 adj.
fatigued 684 adj.
be fatigued 684 vb.

faintheart
waverer 601 n.
coward 856 n.

faint-hearted
irresolute 601 adj.
nervous 854 adj.
cowardly 856 adj.

faintly
slightly 33 adv.

faintness
weakness 163 n.
nonresonance 405 n.
unintelligibility 517 n.
(See **faint** *)*

faint praise
indifference 860 n.
detraction 926 n.

fair
inconsiderable 33 adj.
dry 342 adj.
warm 379 adj.
undimmed 417 adj.
whitish 427 adj.
rational 475 adj.
exhibit 522 n.
not bad 644 adj.
palmy 730 adj.
middling 732 adj.
market 796 n.
cheap 812 adj.
festivity 837 n.
pleasure ground 837 n.
beautiful 841 adj.
promising 852 adj.
just 913 adj.
honourable 929 adj.

fair chance
opportunity 137 n.
fair chance 159 n.
possibility 469 n.
probability 471 n.

fair copy
copy 22 n.
script 586 n.

fair deal
justice 913 n.

fair exchange
equivalence 28 n.
barter 791 n.

fair fighter
honourable person 929 n.

fair game
dupe 544 n.
laughingstock 851 n.

fairground
place of amusement 837 n.

fair-haired
whitish 427 adj.
yellow 433 adj.

fair hand
lettering 586 n.

fairly
greatly 32 adv.
slightly 33 adv.

fair-minded
wise 498 adj.
just 913 adj.

fair one
a beauty 841 n.

fair play
justice 913 n.

fair sex
womankind 373 n.

fair shares
participation 775 n.
apportionment 783 n.

fair-sized
great 32 adj.
large 195 adj.

fair-spoken
courteous 884 adj.

fair trial
legal trial 959 n.

fair warning
threat 900 n.

fairway
access 624 n.
route 624 n.

fair-weather friend
deceiver 545 n.
friend 880 n.

fair wind
facility 701 n.
aid 703 n.

fair words
promise 764 n.
courteous act 884 n.

fairy
nonconformist 84 n.
fairy 970 n.
sorceress 983 n.

fairy godmother
protector 660 n.
patron 707 n.
benefactor 903 n.

fairyland
fantasy 513 n.
prodigy 864 n.
fairy 970 n.

fairy lights
lamp 420 n.

fairy tale
ideality 513 n.
fable 543 n.
narrative 590 n.

fait accompli
reality 1 n.
certainty 473 n.
completion 725 n.

faith
belief 485 n.
observance 768 n.
hope 852 n.
probity 929 n.
virtues 933 n.
religious faith 973 n.
piety 979 n.

Faith, the
orthodoxy 976 n.

faith cure
therapy 658 n.

faithful
lifelike 18 adj.
accurate 494 adj.
true 494 adj.
interpretive 520 adj.
obedient 739 adj.
observant 768 adj.
friendly 880 adj.
trustworthy 929 adj.
disinterested 931 adj.
pious 979 adj.

faithful, the
church member 976 n.
the orthodox 976 n.
pietist 979 n.
worshipper 981 n.

faithfulness
loyalty 739 n.

faithful to, be
keep faith 768 vb.

faith healer
mender 656 n.
doctor 658 n.

faith healing
medical art 658 n.
piety 979 n.

faithless
perfidious 930 adj.
irreligious 974 adj.

fake
imitation 20 n.
copy 22 n.
false 541 adj.
fake 541 vb.
sham 542 n.
spurious 542 adj.
impostor 545 n.

faker
imitator 20 n.
deceiver 545 n.

fakir
beggar 763 n.
ascetic 945 n.
pietist 979 n.

Falangists
political party 708 n.

falcon
bird 365 n.
heraldry 547 n.

falconer
hunter 619 n.

fall
decrease 37 n.vb.
autumn 129 n.
be weak 163 vb.
be destroyed 165 vb.
depth 211 n.
incline 220 n.
deviation 282 n.
regression 286 n.
descent 309 n.
tumble 309 vb.
rain 350 vb.
perish 361 vb.
deteriorate 655 vb.
relapse 657 n.
defeat 728 n.
fail 728 vb.
miscarry 728 vb.
adversity 731 n.
be cheap 812 vb.
lose repute 867 vb.
be wicked 934 vb.

— about
laugh 835 vb.

— apart
separate 46 vb.
deteriorate 655 vb.

— asleep
die 361 vb.
sleep 679 vb.

— away
apostatize 603 vb.

— back
regress 286 vb.
recede 290 vb.

— back on
avail oneself of 673 vb.

— behind
move slowly 278 vb.
follow 284 vb.
fall short 307 vb.

— below
be inferior 35 vb.
not suffice 636 vb.

— down on
not complete 726 vb.
fail 728 vb.

— flat
miscarry 728 vb.

— for
be credulous 487 vb.
be duped 544 vb.
be induced 612 vb.
be in love 887 vb.

— foul of
collide 279 vb.
fight 716 vb.
have trouble 731 vb.
— from grace
relapse 657 vb.
be wicked 934 vb.
— ill
be ill 651 vb.
— in
be uniform 16 vb.
be in order 60 vb.
— in love (with)
desire 859 vb.
be in love 887 vb.
— into
be turned to 147 vb.
— into line
be in order 60 vb.
conform 83 vb.
— in with
conform 83 vb.
converge 293 vb.
consent 758 vb.
— off
separate 46 vb.
tumble 309 vb.
deteriorate 655 vb.
— on one's feet
have luck 730 vb.
— out
disagree 25 vb.
be dispersed 75 vb.
happen 154 vb.
quarrel 709 vb.
— short
be inferior 35 vb.
be incomplete 55 vb.
fall short 307 vb.
disappoint 509 vb.
not suffice 636 vb.
be imperfect 647 vb.
— to
eat 301 vb.
undertake 672 vb.
be one's duty 917 vb.
— to pieces
be brittle 330 vb.
— under
be included 78 vb.
— upon
surprise 508 vb.
attack 712 vb.
fallacious
illogical 477 adj.
erroneous 495 adj.
fallacy
sophism 477 n.
error 495 n.
deception 542 n.
fallen, the
death roll 361 n.
fallen angel
devil 969 n.
fallen woman
prostitute 952 n.
fall guy
dupe 544 n.
laughingstock 851 n.
fallible
unreliable 474 adj.
illogical 477 adj.
misjudging 481 adj.
erroneous 495 adj.
foolish 499 adj.
imperfect 647 adj.
falling off
decrease 37 n.
deterioration 655 n.
relapse 657 n.
falling sickness
spasm 318 n.
nervous disorders 651 n.
falling star
meteor 321 n.
Fallopian tubes
genitalia 167 n.
fallout
sequel 67 n.
nucleonics 160 n.
radiation 417 n.
poison 659 n.
bomb 723 n.
fallout shelter
refuge 662 n.
fallow
unproductive 172 adj.
inert 175 adj.
farm 370 n.
yellow 433 adj.
falls
waterfall 350 n.
false
unreal 2 adj.
illogical 477 adj.
erroneous 495 adj.
false 541 adj.
spurious 542 adj.
untrue 543 adj.
tergiversating 603 adj.
affected 850 adj.
unwarranted 916 adj.
flattering 925 adj.
perfidious 930 adj.
false alarm
insubstantial thing 4 n.
false alarm 665 n.
false dawn
precursor 66 n.
misjudgment 481 n.
error 495 n.
disappointment 509 n.
false economy
parsimony 816 n.
false evidence
untruth 543 n.
false charge 928 n.
false eyelashes
cosmetic 843 n.
false friend
deceiver 545 n.
false hair
hairdressing 843 n.
false-hearted
perfidious 930 adj.
falsehood
error 495 n.
ideality 513 n.
falsehood 541 n.
untruth 543 n.
misrepresentation 552 n.
improbity 930 n.
false horizon
view 438 n.
false impression
error 495 n.
false light
error 495 n.
misrepresentation 552 n.
false logic
absurdity 497 n.
misteaching 535 n.
false lover
libertine 952 n.
false modesty
underestimation 483 n.
prudery 950 n.
false name
misnomer 562 n.
false note
misfit 25 n.
false position
predicament 700 n.
false pretences
deception 542 n.
false shame
affectation 850 n.
prudery 950 n.
falsetto
stridor 407 n.
voicelessness 578 n.
false witness
liar 545 n.
falsify
mislead 495 vb.
misinterpret 521 vb.
be false 541 vb.
be untrue 543 vb.
falsity
falsehood 541 n.
(See **false** *)*
falter
decelerate 278 vb.
be uncertain 474 vb.
stammer 580 vb.
be irresolute 601 vb.
fail 728 vb.
fame
greatness 32 n.
remembrance 505 n.
publicity 528 n.
rumour 529 n.
famousness 866 n.
familial
akin 11 adj.
familiar
interior 224 adj.
known 490 adj.
habitual 610 adj.
usual 610 adj.
auxiliary 707 n.
impertinent 878 adj.
disrespectful 921 adj.
devil 969 n.
demon 970 n.
sorcerer 983 n.
familiarity
knowledge 490 n.
habit 610 n.
friendship 880 n.
sociality 882 n.
endearment 889 n.
familiarize, familiarise
train 534 vb.
— oneself
know 490 vb.
familiar territory
home 192 n.
family
family 11 n.
akin 11 adj.
all 52 n.
subdivision 53 n.
group 74 n.
breed 77 n.
parental 169 adj.
posterity 170 n.
social group 371 n.
community 708 n.
nobility 868 n.
family circle
family 11 n.
sociality 882 n.
family commitments
encumbrance 702 n.
family connection
consanguinity 11 n.
family likeness
similarity 18 n.
family planning
contraception 172 n.
family tree
series 71 n.
list 87 n.
genealogy 169 n.
famine
unproductiveness 172 n.
scarcity 636 n.
poverty 801 n.
hunger 859 n.
famished
underfed 636 adj.
hungry 859 adj.
fasting 946 adj.
famous
great 32 adj.
known 490 adj.
manifest 522 adj.
well-known 528 adj.
excellent 644 adj.
super 644 adj.
renowned 866 adj.
fan
bunch 74 n.

rotator 315 n.
aerate 340 vb.
ventilation 352 n.
refrigerate 382 vb.
enthusiast 504 n.
habitué 610 n.
refresh 685 vb.
patron 707 n.
animate 821 vb.
lover 887 n.
— out
be dispersed 75 vb.
expand 197 vb.
be broad 205 vb.
open 263 vb.
diverge 294 vb.
— the flame
animate 821 vb.
aggravate 832 vb.
fanatic
nonconformist 84 n.
doctrinaire 473 n.
narrow mind 481 n.
biased 481 adj.
crank 504 n.
obstinate person 602 n.
busy person 678 n.
lively 819 adj.
zealot 979 n.
fanatical
positive 473 adj.
severe 735 adj.
excitable 822 adj.
fancier
breeder 369 n.
enthusiast 504 n.
expert 696 n.
desirer 859 n.
fanciful
absurd 497 adj.
imaginary 513 adj.
exaggerated 546 adj.
capricious 604 adj.
ridiculous 849 adj.
fan club
lover 887 n.
commender 923 n.
fancy
think 449 vb.
idea 451 n.
opine 485 vb.
supposition 512 n.
suppose 512 vb.
ideality 513 n.
imagination 513 n.
imagine 513 vb.
whim 604 n.
choice 605 n.
wit 839 n.
ornamental 844 adj.
liking 859 n.
love 887 n.
darling 890 n.
fancy dress
clothing 228 n.
disguise 527 n.
fancy-free
free 744 adj.
impassive 820 adj.
indifferent 860 adj.
unwedded 895 adj.
fancy-led
imaginative 513 adj.
fancy man
libertine 952 n.
fancy woman
kept woman 952 n.
fancywork
ornamental art 844 n.
fandango
dance 837 n.
fanfare
loudness 400 n.
celebration 876 n.
fanfaronade
ostentation 875 n.
celebration 876 n.
boast 877 n.
fang(s)
tooth 256 n.
bane 659 n.
nippers 778 n.
fanlight
window 263 n.
fanon
vestments 989 n.
fantasia
musical piece 412 n.
narrative 590 n.
fantasist
visionary 513 n.
fantasize, fantasise
imagine 513 vb.
fantastic
prodigious 32 adj.
unusual 84 adj.
absurd 497 adj.
capricious 604 adj.
super 644 adj.
ridiculous 849 adj.
wonderful 864 adj.
fantasy
insubstantiality 4 n.
insubstantial thing 4 n.
visual fallacy 440 n.
appearance 445 n.
error 495 n.
fantasy 513 n.
imagination 513 n.
pleasurableness 826 n.
aspiration 852 n.
desire 859 n.
far
distant 199 adj.
afar 199 adv.
far and away
eminently 34 adv.
far and near
widely 183 adv.
far and wide
widely 183 adv.
afar 199 adv.
far away
afar 199 adv.
abstracted 456 adj.
farce
foolery 497 n.
fable 543 n.
stage play 594 n.
trifle 639 n.
laughter 835 n.
wit 839 n.
ridiculousness 849 n.
farceur
dramatist 594 n.
humorist 839 n.
farcical
funny 849 adj.
far cry from, a
dissimilar 19 adj.
afar 199 adv.
fare
be in a state of 7 vb.
travel 267 vb.
meal 301 n.
eat 301 vb.
price 809 n.
farewell
valediction 296 n.
courteous act 884 n.
far-fetched
irrelevant 10 adj.
unbelieved 486 adj.
exaggerated 546 adj.
far-flung
unassembled 75 adj.
spacious 183 adj.
far gone
consummate 32 adj.
deteriorated 655 adj.
farinaceous
powdery 332 adj.
farm
produce 164 vb.
enclosure 235 n.
breed stock 369 vb.
farm 370 n.
cultivate 370 vb.
mature 669 vb.
workshop 687 n.
lands 777 n.
hire 785 vb.
— out
lease 784 vb.
farmer
producer 164 n.
farmer 370 n.
country-dweller 869 n.
farming
territorial 344 adj.
agriculture 370 n.
farmland
soil 344 n.
farm 370 n.
farness
farness 199 n.
farrago
medley 43 n.
confusion 61 n.
far-reaching
extensive 32 adj.
spacious 183 adj.
farrier
animal husbandry 369 n.
farrow
reproduce itself 167 vb.
far-sighted
vigilant 457 adj.
intelligent 498 adj.
foreseeing 510 adj.
fart
voidance 300 n.
farther
distant 199 adj.
beyond 199 adv.
farthest point
extremity 69 n.
limit 236 n.
farthing
small coin 33 n.
coinage 797 n.
fascia
strip 208 n.
face 237 n.
label 547 n.
fascinate
influence 178 vb.
engross 449 vb.
attract notice 455 vb.
motivate 612 vb.
excite love 887 vb.
bewitch 983 vb.
fascination
excitation 821 n.
pleasurableness 826 n.
liking 859 n.
wonder 864 n.
Fascism
government 733 n.
brute force 735 n.
Fascists
political party 708 n.
fashion
modality 7 n.
similarity 18 n.
generality 79 n.
conformity 83 n.
modernism 126 n.
produce 164 vb.
dressing 228 n.
form 243 n.vb.
feature 445 n.
represent 551 vb.
style 566 n.
practice 610 n.
way 624 n.
conduct 688 n.
fashion 848 n.
affectation 850 n.
fashionable
personable 841 adj.
tasteful 846 adj.
fashionable 848 adj.
fashionable person
beau monde 848 n.
fashion plate
fop 848 n.

fast
firm 45 adj.
tied 45 adj.
inseparably 45 adv.
anachronistic 118 adj.
fixed 153 adj.
speedy 277 adj.
coloured 425 adj.
retained 778 adj.
do penance 941 vb.
asceticism 945 n.
be ascetic 945 vb.
fast 946 n.
starve 946 vb.
unchaste 951 adj.
offer worship 981 vb.
fast breeder reactor
nucleonics 160 n.
fast buck
easy thing 701 n.
fast day
fast 946 n.
holy day 988 n.
fast dye
fixture 153 n.
pigment 425 n.
fasten
affix 45 vb.
tighten 45 vb.
close 264 vb.
— on
be attentive 455 vb.
make important 638 vb.
retain 778 vb.
take 786 vb.
— to
hang 217 vb.
fastener
fastening 47 n.
fastening
joining together 45 n.
fastening 47 n.
fast friend
close friend 880 n.
fastidious
attentive 455 adj.
careful 457 adj.
discriminating 463 adj.
narrow-minded 481 adj.
accurate 494 adj.
capricious 604 adj.
clean 648 adj.
severe 735 adj.
observant 768 adj.
sensitive 819 adj.
discontented 829 adj.
tasteful 846 adj.
fastidious 862 adj.
fast living
sensualism 944 n.
fastness
refuge 662 n.
fort 713 n.
fast one
trickery 542 n.
fat
fleshy 195 adj.
expanded 197 adj.
food content 301 n.
fat 357 n.
plenty 635 n.
redundance 637 n.
prosperous 730 adj.
fatal
deadly 362 adj.
fated 596 adj.
evil 616 adj.
harmful 645 adj.
fatalism
philosophy 449 n.
necessity 596 n.
submission 721 n.
fatalist
fatalist 596 n.
fatality
death roll 361 n.
decease 361 n.
necessity 596 n.
fata morgana
visual fallacy 440 n.
fat cat
rich person 800 n.
fate
finality 69 n.
futurity 124 n.
destiny 155 n.
cause 156 n.
chance 159 n.
influence 178 n.
certainty 473 n.
fate 596 n.
nondesign 618 n.
fated
fated 596 adj.
predetermined 608 adj.
fateful
important 638 adj.
Fates, the
fate 596 n.
classical deities 967 n.
fathead
dunce 501 n.
father
kinsman 11 n.
cause 156 n.
generate 167 vb.
male 372 n.
church title 986 n.
cleric 986 n.
— upon
attribute 158 vb.
Father Christmas
giver 781 n.
good giver 813 n.
benefactor 903 n.
fathered
born 360 adj.
father figure
substitute 150 n.
paternity 169 n.
fatherhood
family 11 n.
parentage 169 n.
paternity 169 n.
fatherland
territory 184 n.
home 192 n.
fatherly
parental 169 adj.
benevolent 897 adj.
fatherly eye
protection 660 n.
fathom
long measure 203 n.
be deep 211 vb.
plunge 313 vb.
enquire 459 vb.
measure 465 vb.
be wise 498 vb.
understand 516 vb.
fathomless
deep 211 adj.
fatigue
weakness 163 n.
misuse 675 vb.
sleepiness 679 n.
work 682 vb.
fatigue 684 n.vb.
oppress 735 vb.
suffering 825 n.
trouble 827 vb.
dejection 834 n.
be tedious 838 vb.
fatigue party
band 74 n.
fatigues
uniform 228 n.
fat in the fire
turmoil 61 n.
fatness
bulk 195 n.
fat of the land
food 301 n.
plenty 635 n.
prosperity 730 n.
wealth 800 n.
fat part
acting 594 n.
fatten
grow 36 vb.
enlarge 197 vb.
be broad 205 vb.
feed 301 vb.
breed stock 369 vb.
fatuity
insubstantiality 4 n.
absence of thought 450 n.
absurdity 497 n.
folly 499 n.
fatuous
meaningless 515 adj.
faucet
stopper 264 n.
fault
discontinuity 72 n.
weakness 163 n.
gap 201 n.
shortfall 307 n.
blunder 495 vb.
defect 647 n.
dispraise 924 vb.
detract 926 vb.
vice 934 n.
guilty act 936 n.
faultfinder
malcontent 829 n.
disapprover 924 n.
detractor 926 n.
faultless
perfect 646 adj.
guiltless 935 adj.
pure 950 adj.
faultlessly
skilfully 694 adv.
faulty
inexact 495 adj.
ungrammatical 565 adj.
inelegant 576 adj.
bad 645 adj.
imperfect 647 adj.
bungled 695 adj.
faun
vegetable life 366 n.
mythical being 970 n.
fauna
animality 365 n.
Faust
sorcerer 983 n.
fauteuil
seat 218 n.
theatre 594 n.
Fauvism
school of painting 553 n.
faux ami
equivocalness 518 n.
faux pas
mistake 495 n.
failure 728 n.
guilty act 936 n.
favour
advantage 34 n.
influence 178 n.
promote 285 vb.
be biased 481 vb.
assent 488 n.
badge 547 n.
choose 605 vb.
benefit 615 n.vb.
do good 644 vb.
patronize 703 vb.
trophy 729 n.
be auspicious 730 vb.
be lenient 736 vb.
permit 756 vb.
gift 781 n.
liking 859 n.
honours 866 n.
repute 866 n.
befriend 880 vb.
courteous act 884 n.
love token 889 n.
kind act 897 n.
injustice 914 n.

approbation 923 n.
favourable
opportune 137 adj.
presageful 511 adj.
willing 597 adj.
beneficial 644 adj.
aiding 703 adj.
palmy 730 adj.
promising 852 adj.
approving 923 adj.
favourable chance
fair chance 159 n.
probability 471 n.
favourite
chosen 605 adj.
bigwig 638 n.
exceller 644 n.
contender 716 n.
desired object 859 n.
person of repute 866 n.
sociable person 882 n.
loved one 887 n.
lovable 887 adj.
favourite 890 n.
favouritism
prejudice 481 n.
choice 605 n.
friendliness 880 n.
injustice 914 n.
favours
love-making 887 n.
fawn
young creature 132 n.
mammal 365 n.
brown 430 adj.
be servile 879 vb.
caress 889 vb.
flatter 925 vb.
FBI
police enquiry 459 n.
fealty
loyalty 739 n.
duty 917 n.
fear
expect 507 vb.
motive 612 n.
avoidance 620 n.
fear 854 n.vb.
cowardice 856 n.
dislike 861 n.vb.
wonder 864 n.vb.
honour 866 vb.
respect 920 n.vb.
piety 979 n.
worship 981 n.vb.
fearful
nervous 854 adj.
cowardly 856 adj.
wonderful 864 adj.
fearfully
extremely 32 adv.
fearing the worst
hopeless 853 adj.
fear-inspiring
frightening 854 adj.
fearless
unfearing 855 adj.
fearlessness
courage 855 n.
fears
danger 661 n.
feasible
possible 469 adj.
easy 701 adj.
feast
feasting 301 n.
feed 301 vb.
pleasure 376 n.
plenty 635 n.
revel 837 vb.
social gathering 882 n.
holy day 988 n.
feast day
festivity 837 n.
special day 876 n.
holy day 988 n.
feast for the eyes
spectacle 445 n.
feasting
feasting 301 n.
festivity 837 n.
social gathering 882 n.
sensualism 944 n.
gluttony 947 n.
feat
contrivance 623 n.
deed 676 n.
masterpiece 694 n.
prowess 855 n.
thaumaturgy 864 n.
feather
sort 77 n.
row 269 vb.
lightness 323 n.
waverer 601 n.
trifle 639 n.
trimming 844 n.
— one's nest
prosper 730 vb.
get rich 800 vb.
be selfish 932 vb.
feather bed
softness 327 n.
euphoria 376 n.
featherbed
be lenient 736 vb.
featherbrain
fool 501 n.
featherbrained
light-minded 456 adj.
foolish 499 adj.
feathered
downy 259 adj.
flying 271 adj.
feather in one's cap
success 727 n.
trophy 729 n.
honours 866 n.
feathers
skin 226 n.
plumage 259 n.
wing 271 n.
softness 327 n.
featherweight
light 323 adj.
pugilist 722 n.
feathery
downy 259 adj.
light 323 adj.
feature(s)
character 5 n.
component 58 n.
speciality 80 n.
outline 233 n.
face 237 n.
form 243 n.
feature 445 n.
show 522 vb.
advertise 528 vb.
broadcast 531 n.
identification 547 n.
dramatize 594 vb.
featureless
insubstantial 4 adj.
uniform 16 adj.
empty 190 adj.
amorphous 244 adj.
irresolute 601 adj.
choiceless 606 adj.
febrifuge
antidote 658 n.
febrile
hot 379 adj.
diseased 651 adj.
excitable 822 adj.
feckless
capricious 604 adj.
useless 641 adj.
unskilful 695 adj.
fecund
generative 167 adj.
prolific 171 adj.
federal
cooperative 706 adj.
corporate 708 adj.
federalism
government 733 n.
federate
combine 50 vb.
cooperate 706 vb.
join a party 708 vb.
federation
combination 50 n.
association 706 n.
society 708 n.
political organization 733 n.
fed up
discontented 829 adj.
bored 838 adj.
fee
possession 773 n.
estate 777 n.
gift 781 n.
pay 804 n.
expenditure 806 n.
price 809 n.
reward 962 n.
feeble
small 33 adj.
inferior 35 adj.
powerless 161 adj.
weak 163 adj.
muted 401 adj.
poorly reasoned 477 adj.
feeble 572 adj.
lax 734 adj.
frail 934 adj.
feeble-minded
unintelligent 499 adj.
feed
enlarge 197 vb.
provender 301 n.
eat 301 vb.
feed 301 vb.
vitalize 360 vb.
fire 385 vb.
provision 633 n.
provide 633 vb.
refresh 685 vb.
laughingstock 851 n.
be hospitable 882 vb.
feedback
data processing 86 n.
reversion 148 n.
answer 460 n.
feel
texture 331 n.
have feeling 374 vb.
touch 378 vb.
be tentative 461 vb.
opine 485 vb.
feel 818 vb.
be excited 821 vb.
suffer 825 vb.
resent 891 vb.
— fine
be healthy 650 vb.
— for
search 459 vb.
be benevolent 897 vb.
pity 905 vb.
— free
be free 744 vb.
— in one's bones
intuit 476 vb.
foresee 510 vb.
— like
be willing 597 vb.
— one's way
move slowly 278 vb.
be blind 439 vb.
be careful 457 vb.
enquire 459 vb.
be tentative 461 vb.
be cautious 858 vb.
— the pinch
be in difficulty 700 vb.
have trouble 731 vb.
be poor 801 vb.
— the pulse
enquire 459 vb.
be tentative 461 vb.
— the urge
be induced 612 vb.

— with
feel 818 vb.
love 887 vb.
pity 905 vb.
feeler
filament 208 n.
feeler 378 n.
question 459 n.
empiricism 461 n.
offer 759 n.
feeling
influence 178 n.
sense 374 n.
sentient 374 adj.
touch 378 n.
intuition 476 n.
opinion 485 n.
interpretation 520 n.
vigour 571 n.
liberation 746 n.
with affections 817 adj.
feeling 818 n.adj.
excited 821 adj.
love 887 n.
benevolence 897 n.
feeling for words
style 566 n.
feeling no pain
drunk 949 adj.
feelings
affections 817 n.
feet
foot 214 n.
conveyance 267 n.
feet of clay
weakness 163 n.
defect 647 n.
vulnerability 661 n.
feign
dissemble 541 vb.
be affected 850 vb.
feint
trickery 542 n.
stratagem 698 n.
felicitate
rejoice 835 vb.
congratulate 886 vb.
felicitous
apt 24 adj.
elegant 575 adj.
well-made 694 adj.
successful 727 adj.
felicity
elegance 575 n.
happiness 824 n.
feline
cat 365 n.
animal 365 adj.
cunning 698 adj.
fell
cut 46 vb.
demolish 165 vb.
high land 209 n.
flatten 216 vb.
skin 226 n.
strike 279 vb.
fell 311 vb.
plain 348 n.
deadly 362 adj.
evil 616 adj.
inimical 881 adj.
cruel 898 adj.
felloe, felly
edge 234 n.
wheel 250 n.
fellow
analogue 18 n.
compeer 28 n.
concomitant 89 n.
male 372 n.
teacher 537 n.
student 538 n.
colleague 707 n.
society 708 n.
low fellow 869 n.
chum 880 n.
fellow citizen
native 191 n.
fellow creature
person 371 n.
fellow feeling
bond 47 n.
cooperation 706 n.
concord 710 n.
participation 775 n.
feeling 818 n.
friendliness 880 n.
love 887 n.
benevolence 897 n.
condolence 905 n.
pity 905 n.
fellowship
group 74 n.
association 706 n.
cooperation 706 n.
community 708 n.
friendship 880 n.
sociality 882 n.
fellow traveller
assenter 488 n.
collaborator 707 n.
fellow worker
personnel 686 n.
collaborator 707 n.
fell walker
climber 308 n.
felon
offender 904 n.
felony
foul play 930 n.
vice 934 n.
guilty act 936 n.
lawbreaking 954 n.
felt
textile 222 n.
weave 222 vb.
felt 818 adj.
felucca
sailing ship 275 n.
female
female 373 n.adj.
feminine
generic 77 adj.
female 373 adj.
grammatical 564 adj.
feminine logic
intuition 476 n.
femininity
female 373 n.
feminism
female 373 n.
reformism 654 n.
feminist
woman 373 n.
reformist 654 n.
femme fatale
motivator 612 n.
a beauty 841 n.
fen
moisture 341 n.
marsh 347 n.
fence
partition 231 n.
fence 235 n.
stopper 264 n.
sophisticate 477 vb.
avoid 620 vb.
protection 660 n.
shelter 662 n.
obstacle 702 n.
defences 713 n.
parry 713 vb.
fight 716 vb.
thief 789 n.
trade 791 vb.
fencing
duel 716 n.
fender
furnace 383 n.
shelter 662 n.
fend for oneself
come of age 134 vb.
be free 744 vb.
— off
repel 292 vb.
parry 713 vb.
fenestration
window 263 n.
fennel
potherb 301 n.
feral
animal 365 adj.
disobedient 738 adj.
unsociable 883 adj.
cruel 898 adj.
ferment
turmoil 61 n.
alterer 143 n.
conversion 147 n.
be turned to 147 vb.
stimulation 174 n.
violence 176 n.
commotion 318 n.
effervesce 318 vb.
leaven 323 n.
bubble 355 vb.
be sour 393 vb.
feeling 818 n.
excitation 821 n.
excitable state 822 n.
anger 891 n.
fermented liquor
alcoholic drink 301 n.
fern
plant 366 n.
ferocious
furious 176 adj.
cruel 898 adj.
ferret
mammal 365 n.
ferreting
chase 619 n.
ferret out
discover 484 vb.
ferroconcrete
hardness 326 n.
building material 631 n.
ferrule
covering 226 n.
ferry
voyage 269 vb.
transfer 272 vb.
carry 273 vb.
boat 275 n.
fertile
imaginative 513 adj.
profitable 640 adj.
gainful 771 adj.
rich 800 adj.
(See **fertility** *)*
fertile soil
seedbed 156 n.
fertility
propagation 167 n.
productiveness 171 n.
plenty 635 n.
fertility drug
propagation 167 n.
fertilizer 171 n.
fertility god
mythic deity 966 n.
fertility symbol
fertilizer 171 n.
fertilize, fertilise
make fruitful 171 vb.
invigorate 174 vb.
cultivate 370 vb.
be auspicious 730 vb.
fertilizer
propagation 167 n.
fertilizer 171 n.
agriculture 370 n.
fervent
hot 379 adj.
forceful 571 adj.
active 678 adj.
hasty 680 adj.
fervent 818 adj.
lively 819 adj.
excited 821 adj.
loving 887 adj.
pietistic 979 adj.
worshipping 981 adj.
fervid
hot 379 adj.

fervent 818 adj.
fervour
vigorousness 174 n.
warm feeling 818 n.
fess, fesse
heraldry 547 n.
fester
be unclean 649 vb.
deteriorate 655 vb.
hurt 827 vb.
be malevolent 898 vb.
festering
diseased 651 adj.
toxic 653 adj.
festina lente
slowness 278 n.
caution 858 n.
festival
assembly 74 n.
festivity 837 n.
holy day 988 n.
festive
amusing 837 adj.
celebratory 876 adj.
sociable 882 adj.
festivity
meal 301 n.
rejoicing 835 n.
festivity 837 n.
celebration 876 n.
social gathering 882 n.
festoon
curve 248 n.
pattern 844 n.
decorate 844 vb.
Festschrift
reading matter 589 n.
fetch
analogue 18 n.
carry 273 vb.
trickery 542 n.
cost 809 vb.
ghost 970 n.
— up at
arrive 295 vb.
fetching
pleasurable 826 adj.
personable 841 adj.
desired 859 adj.
fete
amusement 837 n.
pageant 875 n.
celebration 876 n.
congratulate 886 vb.
feted
welcomed 882 adj.
fetid
unsavoury 391 adj.
fetid 397 adj.
bad 645 adj.
unclean 649 adj.
fetish
idol 982 n.
talisman 983 n.
fetishism
idolatry 982 n.
fetlock
foot 214 n.
fetter
tie 45 vb.
fastening 47 n.
make inactive 679 vb.
hinder 702 vb.
subjugate 745 vb.
fetter 747 vb.
fetter 748 n.
fettered
imprisoned 747 adj.
captive 750 adj.
fettle
state 7 n.
feud
quarrel 709 n.
enmity 881 n.
revenge 910 n.
feudal
olden 127 adj.
governmental 733 adj.
subject 745 adj.
proprietary 777 adj.
feudalism
government 733 n.
service 745 n.
feuilleton
the press 528 n.
fever
agitation 318 n.
heat 379 n.
illness 651 n.
tropical disease 651 n.
restlessness 678 n.
excitable state 822 n.
fevered
frenzied 503 adj.
feverish
sick 651 adj.
hasty 680 adj.
fervent 818 adj.
excited 821 adj.
few
inconsiderable 33 adj.
few 105 adj.
infrequent 140 adj.
scarce 636 adj.
few, a
plurality 101 n.
fewness 105 n.
few and far between
discontinuous 72 adj.
unassembled 75 adj.
few 105 adj.
infrequent 140 adj.
seldom 140 adv.
few words
conciseness 569 n.
taciturnity 582 n.
fey
dying 361 adj.
bewitched 983 adj.
psychical 984 adj.
fez
headgear 228 n.
fiancé(e)
loved one 887 n.
lover 887 n.
fiasco
failure 728 n.
fiat
decree 737 n.
fib
untruth 543 n.
fibber
liar 545 n.
fibre
essential part 5 n.
fibre 208 n.
textile 222 n.
food content 301 n.
texture 331 n.
fibreglass
textile 222 n.
materials 631 n.
fibrositis
pang 377 n.
rheumatism 651 n.
fibrous
tough 329 adj.
(See **fibre** *)*
fichu
neckwear 228 n.
fickle
transient 114 adj.
changeable 143 adj.
changeful 152 adj.
unreliable 474 adj.
tergiversating 603 adj.
capricious 604 adj.
fickleness
irresolution 601 n.
fiction
product 164 n.
idea 451 n.
ideality 513 n.
falsehood 541 n.
untruth 543 n.
literature 557 n.
novel 590 n.
fictional
imaginative 513 adj.
descriptive 590 adj.
fiction-writer
author 589 n.
narrator 590 n.
fictitious
unreal 2 adj.
insubstantial 4 adj.
imaginary 513 adj.
untrue 543 adj.
descriptive 590 adj.
unwarranted 916 adj.
fiddle
play music 413 vb.
viol 414 n.
deceive 542 vb.
contrivance 623 n.
defraud 788 vb.
foul play 930 n.
be dishonest 930 vb.
— one's income tax
not pay 805 vb.
— with
modify 143 vb.
touch 378 vb.
fiddle-faddle
silly talk 515 n.
trifle 639 n.
be inactive 679 vb.
fiddlehead
coil 251 n.
pattern 844 n.
fiddler
instrumentalist 413 n.
trickster 545 n.
defrauder 789 n.
fiddling
trivial 639 adj.
laborious 682 adj.
fidelity
accuracy 494 n.
veracity 540 n.
loyalty 739 n.
observance 768 n.
probity 929 n.
fidget
haste 680 n.
be excitable 822 vb.
fidgets
agitation 318 n.
restlessness 678 n.
excitability 822 n.
fidgety
unstable 152 adj.
irresolute 601 adj.
active 678 adj.
excitable 822 adj.
fief
lands 777 n.
field
opportunity 137 n.
range 183 n.
enclosure 235 n.
grassland 348 n.
topic 452 n.
heraldry 547 n.
hunter 619 n.
function 622 n.
arena 724 n.
scope 744 n.
field, the
opponent 705 n.
contender 716 n.
field day
contest 716 n.
pageant 875 n.
special day 876 n.
fielder
hinderer 702 n.
player 837 n.
field glasses
telescope 442 n.
field marshal
army officer 741 n.
fields
land 344 n.
plain 348 n.

farm 370 n.
field sports
sport 837 n.
field trip
land travel 267 n.
field work
study 536 n.
fiend
enthusiast 504 n.
hellhag 904 n.
monster 938 n.
devil 969 n.
fiendish
cruel 898 adj.
wicked 934 adj.
diabolic 969 adj.
fierce
furious 176 adj.
active 678 adj.
warlike 718 adj.
excitable 822 adj.
courageous 855 adj.
angry 891 adj.
irascible 892 adj.
cruel 898 adj.
fierceness
violence 176 n.
fieriness
quarrelsomeness 709 n.
rashness 857 n.
fiery
violent 176 adj.
fiery 379 adj.
luminous 417 adj.
red 431 adj.
forceful 571 adj.
fervent 818 adj.
excitable 822 adj.
irascible 892 adj.
fiery cross
call 547 n.
danger signal 665 n.
war measures 718 n.
fiesta
festivity 837 n.
fife
stridor 407 n.
flute 414 n.
fifteen
band 74 n.
party 708 n.
fifth
fifth and over 99 adj.
musical note 410 n.
fifth column
collaborator 707 n.
perfidy 930 n.
fifth columnist
tergiversator 603 n.
fifty
twenty and over 99 n.
fifty-fifty
equal 28 adj.
equal chance 159 n.
middling 732 adj.
fig
state 7 n.
fruit 301 n.
trifle 639 n.
fight
turmoil 61 n.
be in difficulty 700 vb.
quarrel 709 n.
fight 716 n., vb.
contend 716 vb.
battle 718 n.
go to war 718 vb.
— against
oppose 704 vb.
— back
parry 713 vb.
— down
restrain 747 vb.
— for
defend 713 vb.
— off
parry 713 vb.
resist 715 vb.
— on
stand firm 599 vb.
— one's way
be in motion 265 vb.
pursue 619 vb.
— shy
be unwilling 598 vb.
avoid 620 vb.
fighter
trier 671 n.
opponent 705 n.
contender 716 n.
air force 722 n.
combatant 722 n.
fighting chance
fair chance 159 n.
fighting cock
combatant 722 n.
brave person 855 n.
fighting fit
athletic 162 adj.
healthy 650 adj.
fighting man
combatant 722 n.
soldier 722 n.
fig leaf
loincloth 228 n.
concealment 525 n.
figment
insubstantial thing 4 n.
ideality 513 n.
figurant(e)
actor 594 n.
figuration
representation 551 n.
figurative
semantic 514 adj.
figurative 519 adj.
occult 523 adj.
representing 551 adj.
ornate 574 adj.
figuratively
metaphorically 519 adv.
figure
number 85 n.
do sums 86 vb.
outline 233 n.
form 243 n.vb.
person 371 n.
feature 445 n.
figure 519 vb.
indication 547 n.
image 551 n.
represent 551 vb.
funds 797 n.
price 809 n.
person of repute 866 n.
— in
appear 445 vb.
— out
reason 475 vb.
— to oneself
imagine 513 vb.
figurehead
insubstantial thing 4 n.
ineffectuality 161 n.
prow 237 n.
image 551 n.
nonentity 639 n.
figure-hugging
cohesive 48 adj.
figure of eight
loop 250 n.
circuition 314 n.
figure of fun
laughingstock 851 n.
figure of speech
trope 519 n.
ornament 574 n.
figures
statistics 86 n.
figure skater
rotator 315 n.
filament
thinness 206 n.
filament 208 n.
lamp 420 n.
filch
steal 788 vb.
file
abate 37 vb.
sorting 62 n.
class 62 vb.
procession 71 n.
run on 71 vb.
list 87 n.vb.
put off 136 vb.
receptacle 194 n.
make smaller 198 vb.
sharpener 256 n.
smoother 258 n.
roughness 259 n.
walk 267 vb.
pulverize 332 vb.
rub 333 vb.
information 524 n.
record 548 n.vb.
collection 632 n.
store 632 vb.
formation 722 n.
— a suit
litigate 959 vb.
filial
filial 170 adj.
obedient 739 adj.
filibuster
spin out 113 vb.
delay 136 n.
hinderer 702 n.
opponent 705 n.
filibustering
brigandage 788 n.
filigree
network 222 n.
ornamental art 844 n.
filing cabinet
recorder 549 n.
filings
leavings 41 n.
powder 332 n.
filing system
sorting 62 n.
fill
grow 36 vb.
fill 54 vb.
be many 104 vb.
pervade 189 vb.
load 193 vb.
enlarge 197 vb.
line 227 vb.
store 632 vb.
replenish 633 vb.
suffice 635 vb.
superabound 637 vb.
repair 656 vb.
doctor 658 vb.
sate 863 vb.
— in
augment 36 vb.
darken 418 vb.
register 548 vb.
— one in on
inform 524 vb.
— oneself
gluttonize 947 vb.
— one's time
employ 622 vb.
— out
grow 36 vb.
expand 197 vb.
— the bill
suffice 635 vb.
be expedient 642 vb.
— up
fill 54 vb.
replenish 633 vb.
suffice 635 vb.
sate 863 vb.
fillet
strip 208 n.
headgear 228 n.
cook 301 vb.
fillet steak
meat 301 n.
filling
contents 193 n.
lining 227 n.

surgery 658 n.
fillip
stimulant 174 n.
knock 279 n.
incentive 612 n.
excitant 821 n.
filly
young creature 132 n.
horse 273 n.
female animal 373 n.
film
layer 207 n.
covering 226 n.
cloud 355 n.
obfuscation 421 n.
opacity 423 n.
dim sight 440 n.
camera 442 n.
film 445 n.
broadcast 531 n.
record 548 vb.
photography 551 N.
photograph 551 vb.
film director
cinema 445 n.
filmgoer
spectator 441 n.
cinema 445 n.
film show
spectacle 445 n.
film star
cinema 445 n.
actor 594 n.
favourite 890 n.
filmstrip
photography 551 n.
filmy
textural 331 adj.
dim 419 adj.
transparent 422 adj.
opaque 423 adj.
filter
deviate 282 vb.
exude 298 vb.
screen 421 n.
cleaning utensil 648 n.
purify 648 vb.
— in
infiltrate 297 vb.
filth
badness 645 n.
dirt 649 n.
ugliness 842 n.
hateful object 888 n.
impurity 951 n.
filthy
not nice 645 adj.
filthy language
scurrility 899 n.
fin
limb 53 n.
stabilizer 153 n.
laterality 239 n.
propeller 269 n.
final
ending 69 adj.
answering 460 adj.
positive 473 adj.
contest 716 n.
completive 725 adj.
final cause
cause 156 n.
intention 617 n.
finale
end 69 n.
musical piece 412 n.
dramaturgy 594 n.
finalist
contender 716 n.
finality
completeness 54 n.
finality 69 n.
completion 725 n.
finalize, finalise
make certain 473 vb.
final notice
warning 664 n.
demand 737 n.
final point
goal 295 n.
final result
effect 157 n.
completion 725 n.
finals
exam 459 n.
final stroke
killing 362 n.
finance
find means 629 vb.
lend 784 vb.
finance 797 n.
finances
funds 797 n.
financial
businesslike 622 adj.
monetary 797 adj.
financier
lender 784 n.
merchant 794 n.
minter 797 n.
treasurer 798 n.
finch
bird 365 n.
find
meet with 154 vb.
arrive 295 vb.
judge 480 vb.
discovery 484 n.
discover 484 vb.
benefit 615 n.
find means 629 vb.
provide 633 vb.
acquisition 771 n.
acquire 771 vb.
booty 790 n.
— again
retrieve 656 vb.
— against
judge 480 vb.
condemn 961 vb.
— a needle in a haystack
attempt the impossible 470 vb.
— a way
discover 484 vb.
plan 623 vb.
find means 629 vb.
triumph 727 vb.
— fault
be discontented 829 vb.
be fastidious 862 vb.
dispraise 924 vb.
detract 926 vb.
— favour
be praised 923 vb.
— it in one's heart
be willing 597 vb.
— means
find means 629 vb.
— one's feet again
be restored 656 vb.
— one's match
be rightly served 714 vb.
— one's tongue
speak 579 vb.
— one's way in
infiltrate 297 vb.
— out
discover 484 vb.
— time for
notice 455 vb.
have leisure 681 vb.
— to one's cost
be disappointed 509 vb.
— words for
phrase 563 vb.
finder
telescope 442 n.
detector 484 n.
finders keepers
retention 778 n.
fin de siècle
era 110 n.
finding
judgment 480 n.
discovery 484 n.
acquisition 771 n.
legal trial 959 n.
fine
small 33 adj.
large 195 adj.
narrow 206 adj.
rare 325 adj.
textural 331 adj.
dry 342 adj.
transparent 422 adj.
discriminating 463 adj.
accurate 494 adj.
good 615 adj.
excellent 644 adj.
healthy 650 adj.
palmy 730 adj.
price 809 n.
tax 809 vb.
splendid 841 adj.
proud 871 adj.
formal 875 adj.
penalty 963 n.
punish 963 vb.
fine airs
airs 873 n.
fine arts
art 551 n.
fine feathers
ostentation 875 n.
fine gentleman/lady
fop 848 n.
proud person 871 n.
fine-grained
textural 331 adj.
fine human being
good person 937 n.
fine kettle of fish
predicament 700 n.
finer feelings
feeling 818 n.
moral sensibility 819 n.
finery
clothing 228 n.
finery 844 n.
ostentation 875 n.
fines herbes
potherb 301 n.
fine-spun
narrow 206 adj.
fibrous 208 adj.
textural 331 adj.
sophistical 477 adj.
finesse
skill 694 n.
cunning 698 n.
fine-tuned
adjusted 24 adj.
finger
small thing 33 n.
piece 53 n.
finger 378 n.
touch 378 vb.
indicator 547 n.
nippers 778 n.
finger in every pie
overactivity 678 n.
fingering
musical skill 413 n.
fingermark
trace 548 n.
fingernail
finger 378 n.
finger of suspicion, the
accuser 928 n.
fingerpost
direction 281 n.
signpost 547 n.
fingerprint(s)
remainder 41 n.
evidence 466 n.
identification 547 n.
label 547 n.
trace 548 n.
finial
vertex 213 n.

pattern 844 n.
finical
attentive 455 adj.
fastidious 862 adj.
finickiness
moral sensibility 819 n.
discontent 829 n.
good taste 846 n.
finicky
fastidious 862 adj.
finish
completeness 54 n.
end 69 n. vb.
terminate 69 vb.
cease 145 vb.
smoothness 258 n.
arrival 295 n.
elegance 575 n.
perfection 646 n.
skill 694 n.
completion 725 n.
good taste 846 n.
— off
murder 362 vb.
finished
extinct 2 adj.
consummate 32 adj.
past 125 adj.
well-made 694 adj.
finished article
product 164 n.
finisher
survivor 41 n.
successor 67 n.
confutation 479 n.
finishing school
academy 539 n.
finishing touch
amendment 654 n.
finite
limited 236 adj.
fir
tree 366 n.
fire
destroyer 168 n.
vigorousness 174 n.
shoot 287 vb.
dismiss 300 vb.
element 319 n.
fire 379 n.
kindle 381 vb.
furnace 383 n.
fire 385 vb.
light 417 n.
luminary 420 n.
signal 547 n.
vigour 571 n.
bombardment 712 n.
warm feeling 818 n.
— a salute
celebrate 876 vb.
greet 884 vb.
— at
shoot 287 vb.
fire at 712 vb.
— away
begin 68 vb.
fire alarm
danger signal 665 n.
firearm
firearm 723 n.
fireball
meteor 321 n.
fire 379 n.
luminary 420 n.
firebox
furnace 383 n.
firebrand
violent creature 176 n.
incendiarism 381 n.
lighter 385 n.
dissentient 489 n.
motivator 612 n.
troublemaker 663 n.
agitator 738 n.
firebreak
gap 201 n.
fire brigade
extinguisher 382 n.
fire-bug
incendiarism 381 n.
fired
not retained 779 adj.
fire damp
gas 336 n.
firedrake
rara avis 84 n.
glow-worm 420 n.
fire-eater
violent creature 176 n.
entertainer 594 n.
combatant 722 n.
desperado 857 n.
insolent person 878 n.
fire engine
irrigator 341 n.
extinguisher 382 n.
fire escape
ascent 308 n.
means of escape 667 n.
firefighter
extinguisher 382 n.
protector 660 n.
defender 713 n.
firefly
insect 365 n.
flash 417 n.
glow-worm 420 n.
fireguard
furnace 383 n.
shelter 662 n.
firelight
light 417 n.
glimmer 419 n.
firelighter
lighter 385 n.
fireman
driver 268 n.
extinguisher 382 n.
fireplace
furnace 383 n.
fireproof
coat 226 vb.
incombustible 382 adj.
invulnerable 660 adj.
fire-raising
destruction 165 n.
incendiarism 381 n.
fireside
focus 76 n.
place 185 n.
home 192 n.
firetrap
pitfall 663 n.
fire-walker
ascetic 945 n.
firewatcher
protector 660 n.
defender 713 n.
firewater
alcoholic drink 301 n.
firewood
fuel 385 n.
fireworks
fire 379 n.
fireworks 420 n.
spectacle 445 n.
masterpiece 694 n.
revel 837 n.
celebration 876 n.
fire worship
idolatry 982 n.
firing
propulsion 287 n.
fuel 385 n.
bang 402 n.
bombardment 712 n.
firing line
front 237 n.
battle 718 n.
battleground 724 n.
firing squad
punisher 963 n.
firkin
vat 194 n.
firm
firm 45 adj.
fixed 153 adj.
strong 162 adj.
dense 324 adj.
rigid 326 adj.
resolute 599 adj.
obstinate 602 adj.
workshop 687 n.
corporation 708 n.
retentive 778 adj.
merchant 794 n.
shop 796 n.
courageous 855 adj.
firmament
heavens 321 n.
firmness
permanence 144 n.
(See **firm** *)*
first
original 21 adj.
supreme 34 adj.
first 68 adj.
initially 68 adv.
prior 119 adj.
fundamental 156 adj.
foremost 283 adj.
best 644 adj.
victor 727 n.
first aid
therapy 658 n.
aid 703 n.
first appearance
debut 68 n.
first arrival
earliness 135 n.
first blood
success 727 n.
first blush
beginning 68 n.
appearance 445 n.
firstborn
superior 34 n.
precursor 66 n.
prior 119 adj.
older 131 adj.
First Cause
cause 156 n.
divineness 965 n.
first choice
superior 34 n.
choice 605 n.
chief thing 638 n.
favourite 890 n.
first-class
supreme 34 adj.
first come first served
no choice 606 n.
first draft
incompleteness 55 n.
experiment 461 n.
plan 623 n.
preparation 669 n.
firsthand
original 21 adj.
new 126 adj.
evidential 466 adj.
first impression
beginning 68 n.
first lady
superior 34 n.
first light, at
at sunrise 128 adv.
first night
debut 68 n.
dramaturgy 594 n.
first occurrence
prototype 23 n.
first of all
initially 68 adv.
ahead 283 adv.
first offence
debut 68 n.
attempt 671 n.
first offender
prisoner 750 n.
offender 904 n.
first principle(s)
beginning 68 n.
premise 475 n.

first-rate
supreme 34 adj.
notable 638 adj.
best 644 adj.
excellent 644 adj.
skilful 694 adj.
first sight
beginning 68 n.
inspection 438 n.
first sight, at
at sight 438 adv.
apparently 445 adv.
first steps
debut 68 n.
experiment 461 n.
learning 536 n.
first thing
betimes 135 adv.
first to arrive, be
come before 64 vb.
first violin
orchestra 413 n.
leader 690 n.
firth
gulf 345 n.
fiscal
monetary 797 adj.
fish
fish food 301 n.
fish 365 n.
hunt 619 vb.
amuse oneself 837 vb.
— for
search 459 vb.
be tentative 461 vb.
pursue 619 vb.
desire 859 vb.
— for compliments
be vain 873 vb.
— in troubled waters
be in difficulty 700 vb.
— up
elevate 310 vb.
discover 484 vb.
fish day
fast 946 n.
fisherman
hunter 619 n.
fisherman's yarn
fable 543 n.
fishery
extraction 304 n.
fishmonger
provider 633 n.
fishnet
network 222 n.
fish out of water
misfit 25 n.
nonconformist 84 n.
displacement 188 n.
bungler 697 n.
fishpond
lake 346 n.
stock farm 369 n.
fishwife
shrew 892 n.
fishy
animal 365 adj.
improbable 472 adj.
puzzling 517 adj.
dishonest 930 adj.
fissile
severable 46 adj.
brittle 330 adj.
fission
separation 46 n.
decomposition 51 n.
nucleonics 160 n.
fissure
disunion 46 n.
gap 201 n.
fist
finger 378 n.
lettering 586 n.
nippers 778 n.
fistful
contents 193 n.
fisticuffs
knock 279 n.
quarrel 709 n.
pugilism 716 n.
fit
fit 24 adj.
adjust 24 vb.
join 45 vb.
cohere 48 vb.
make conform 83 vb.
athletic 162 adj.
violence 176 n.
spasm 318 n.
frenzy 503 n.
poem 593 n.
whim 604 n.
advisable 642 adj.
healthy 650 adj.
illness 651 n.
make ready 669 vb.
activity 678 n.
excitable state 822 n.
right 913 adj.
due 915 adj.
— badly
mismatch 25 vb.
— in
accord 24 vb.
conform 83 vb.
load 193 vb.
insert 303 vb.
join a party 708 vb.
— out
dress 228 vb.
find means 629 vb.
provide 633 vb.
make ready 669 vb.
— together
join 45 vb.
combine 50 vb.
fit for
useful 640 adj.
prepared 669 adj.
fit for nothing
useless 641 adj.
fitful
discontinuous 72 adj.
fitful 142 adj.
capricious 604 adj.
excitable 822 adj.
fitness
relevance 9 n.
fitness 24 n.
occasion 137 n.
ability 160 n.
tendency 179 n.
good policy 642 n.
health 650 n.
preparedness 669 n.
aptitude 694 n.
right 913 n.
fits and starts
fitfulness 142 n.
agitation 318 n.
fitter
machinist 630 n.
preparer 669 n.
artisan 686 n.
fitting
relevant 9 adj.
fit 24 adj.
opportune 137 adj.
advisable 642 adj.
right 913 adj.
due 915 adj.
fittings
equipment 630 n.
fit to be seen
personable 841 adj.
fit to burst
full 54 adj.
five
five 99 n.
fifth and over 99 adj.
fiver
funds 797 n.
fives
ball game 837 n.
five senses
sense 374 n.
fivestones
plaything 837 n.
five-toed
footed 214 adj.
fix
affix 45 vb.
arrange 62 vb.
stabilize 153 vb.
place 187 vb.
close 264 vb.
quiescence 266 n.
murder 362 vb.
be resolute 599 vb.
predetermine 608 vb.
repair 656 vb.
remedy 658 vb.
predicament 700 n.
defeat 727 vb.
drug-taking 949 n.
— on
affix 45 vb.
be attentive 455 vb.
choose 605 vb.
accuse 928 vb.
fixation
attention 455 n.
prejudgment 481 n.
eccentricity 503 n.
habituation 610 n.
fixative
adhesive 47 n.
pigment 425 n.
fixed
firm 45 adj.
immemorial 127 adj.
permanent 144 adj.
fixed 153 adj.
strong 162 adj.
located 187 adj.
still 266 adj.
positive 473 adj.
habitual 610 adj.
fixed idea
eccentricity 503 n.
fixed interval
regular return 141 n.
fixer
trickster 545 n.
mender 656 n.
fixity
resolution 599 n.
obstinacy 602 n.
fixture
adjunct 40 n.
joining together 45 n.
part 53 n.
concomitant 89 n.
permanence 144 n.
fixture 153 n.
equipment 630 n.
fixtures
property 777 n.
fizz
vigorousness 174 n.
soft drink 301 n.
wine 301 n.
bubble 355 n.vb.
hiss 406 vb.
fizzle
bubble 355 vb.
crackle 402 vb.
hiss 406 vb.
— out
fall short 307 vb.
miscarry 728 vb.
fizzy
windy 352 adj.
bubbly 355 adj.
fjord
gulf 345 n.
flabbergasted
fearing 854 adj.
wondering 864 adj.
flabby
weak 163 adj.
soft 327 adj.
pulpy 356 adj.
flaccid
weak 163 adj.

inert 175 adj.
soft 327 adj.
feeble 572 adj.
flag
be weak 163 vb.
lamina 207 n.
paving 226 n.
decelerate 278 vb.
plant 366 n.
flag 547 n.
building material 631 n.
be fatigued 684 vb.
be dejected 834 vb.
greet 884 vb.
talisman 983 n.
— down
signal 547 vb.
— out
mark 547 vb.
flag day
request 761 n.
offering 781 n.
special day 876 n.
flagellant
penitent 939 n.
ascetic 945 n.
flagellation
penance 941 n.
asceticism 945 n.
corporal punishment 963 n.
flag lieutenant
naval officer 741 n.
flag of convenience
shipping 275 n.
contrivance 623 n.
stratagem 698 n.
flag of truce
peace offering 719 n.
flagon
vessel 194 n.
flagrancy
manifestation 522 n.
publicity 528 n.
bad taste 847 n.
ostentation 875 n.
insolence 878 n.
flagrant
flagrant 32 adj.
heinous 934 adj.
flagrante delicto
guiltily 936 adv.
flagship
warship 722 n.
flagstaff
high structure 209 n.
prop 218 n.
flag 547 n.
flag-waving
gesture 547 n.
celebration 876 n.
boasting 877 n.
flail
hammer 279 n.
strike 279 vb.
farm tool 370 n.
strike at 712 vb.
flog 963 vb.
flair
discrimination 463 n.
aptitude 694 n.
good taste 846 n.
fashion 848 n.
flak
bombardment 712 n.
ammunition 723 n.
flake
small thing 33 n.
piece 53 n.
lamina 207 n.
powder 332 n.
tobacco 388 n.
flaked out
fatigued 684 adj.
flaky
layered 207 adj.
brittle 330 adj.
powdery 332 adj.
flambeau
torch 420 n.
flamboyant
luminous 417 adj.
ornate 574 adj.
flame
fire 379 n.
heater 383 n.
light 417 n.
shine 417 vb.
luminary 420 n.
redness 431 n.
be excited 821 vb.
loved one 887 n.
flame-coloured
red 431 adj.
orange 432 adj.
flamen
priest 986 n.
flamenco
dance 837 n.
flameproof
incombustible 382 adj.
flamethrower
gun 723 n.
flaming
violent 176 adj.
fiery 379 adj.
luminous 417 adj.
fervent 818 adj.
showy 875 adj.
flamingo
bird 365 n.
flan
dish 301 n.
pastries 301 n.
flâneur
idler 679 n.
flange
edge 234 n.
projection 254 n.
flank
laterality 239 n.
flank 239 vb.
safeguard 660 vb.
flannel
textile 222 n.
empty talk 515 n.
cleaning cloth 648 n.
flattery 925 n.
flannelette
textile 222 n.
flap
adjunct 40 n.
come unstuck 49 vb.
hanging object 217 n.
hang 217 vb.
covering 226 n.
be in motion 265 vb.
strike 279 vb.
agitation 318 n.
be agitated 318 vb.
sound dead 405 vb.
haste 680 n.
excitability 822 n.
fear 854 n.vb.
flaps
aircraft 276 n.
flare
be violent 176 vb.
expand 197 vb.
be broad 205 vb.
be hot 379 vb.
light 417 n.
shine 417 vb.
torch 420 n.
— up
grow 36 vb.
be excited 821 vb.
get angry 891 vb.
flare path
signal light 420 n.
flaring
fiery 379 adj.
florid 425 adj.
showy 875 adj.
flash
instant 116 n.
vary 152 vb.
be violent 176 vb.
move fast 277 vb.
fire 379 n.
flash 417 n.
shine 417 vb.
look 438 n.
communicate 524 vb.
spurious 542 adj.
livery 547 n.
signal 547 n.
spontaneity 609 n.
be witty 839 vb.
— by
pass 305 vb.
— on the mind
dawn upon 449 vb.
be disclosed 526 vb.
flashback
remembrance 505 n.
flashbulb
lamp 420 n.
flasher
stripper 229 n.
libertine 952 n.
flash flood
waterfall 350 n.
pitfall 663 n.
flashgun
lamp 420 n.
camera 442 n.
flash in the pan
insubstantial thing 4 n.
brief span 114 n.
ineffectuality 161 n.
false alarm 665 n.
success 727 n.
miscarry 728 vb.
flashlight
lamp 420 n.
signal 547 n.
flash note
false money 797 n.
flash point
heat 379 n.
casus belli 709 n.
flashy
florid 425 adj.
ornate 574 adj.
ornamented 844 adj.
vulgar 847 adj.
showy 875 adj.
flask
vessel 194 n.
flat
uniform 16 adj.
flat 192 n.
low 210 adj.
flat 216 adj.
horizontally 216 adv.
unsharpened 257 adj.
smooth 258 adj.
still 266 adj.
campestral 348 adj.
tasteless 387 adj.
unsavoury 391 adj.
strident 407 adj.
musical note 410 n.
discordant 411 adj.
dim 419 adj.
soft-hued 425 adj.
assertive 532 adj.
misrepresented 552 adj.
feeble 572 adj.
stage set 594 n.
deteriorated 655 adj.
hitch 702 n.
cheerless 834 adj.
tedious 838 adj.
dull 840 adj.
flat contradiction
negation 533 n.
flat-footed
footed 214 adj.
flatiron
flattener 216 n.
smoother 258 n.
flat mate
participator 775 n.
flat out
swiftly 277 adv.

fatigued 684 adj.
flat rate
price 809 n.
flats
lowness 210 n.
horizontality 216 n.
marsh 347 n.
plain 348 n.
flat spin
rotation 315 n.
fear 854 n.
flatten
demolish 165 vb.
make smaller 198 vb.
flatten 216 vb.
straighten 249 vb.
smooth 258 vb.
strike 279 vb.
fell 311 vb.
defeat 727 vb.
flatter
imitate 20 vb.
mean nothing 515 vb.
befool 542 vb.
exaggerate 546 vb.
misrepresent 552 vb.
induce 612 vb.
please 826 vb.
beautify 841 vb.
honour 866 vb.
be servile 879 vb.
pet 889 vb.
praise 923 vb.
flatter 925 vb.
be dishonest 930 vb.
— oneself
assume 471 vb.
expect 507 vb.
hope 852 vb.
feel pride 871 vb.
be vain 873 vb.
flatter 925 vb.
flatterer
assenter 488 n.
slyboots 698 n.
affecter 850 n.
toady 879 n.
flatterer 925 n.
flattering portrait
misrepresentation 552 n.
flattery
empty talk 515 n.
falsehood 541 n.
servility 879 n.
endearment 889 n.
flattery 925 n.
flatulence
gaseousness 336 n.
respiration 352 n.
diffuseness 570 n.
magniloquence 574 n.
digestive disorders 651 n.
flaunt
show 522 vb.
seek repute 866 vb.
be ostentatious 875 vb.
boast 877 vb.
threaten 900 vb.
flautist
instrumentalist 413 n.
flavour
tincture 43 n.
cook 301 vb.
taste 386 n.
season 388 vb.
flavoured
tasty 386 adj.
savoury 390 adj.
flavouring
condiment 389 n.
flavourless
tasteless 387 adj.
flaw
discontinuity 72 n.
weakness 163 n.
gap 201 n.
gale 352 n.
sophism 477 n.
mistake 495 n.
blunder 495 vb.
badness 645 n.
defect 647 n.
blemish 845 n.vb.
vice 934 n.
flawed
incomplete 55 adj.
imperfect 647 adj.
flawless
consummate 32 adj.
elegant 575 adj.
perfect 646 adj.
flax
fibre 208 n.
flaxen-haired
whitish 427 adj.
flay
disunite 46 vb.
uncover 229 vb.
dispraise 924 vb.
execute 963 vb.
flog 963 vb.
flea
small animal 33 n.
jumper 312 n.
insect 365 n.
dirt 649 n.
fleabag
dirty person 649 n.
fleabite
trifle 639 n.
fleabitten
blemished 845 adj.
fleam
sharp point 256 n.
flea pit
cinema 445 n.
theatre 594 n.
flea-ridden
unclean 649 adj.
insalubrious 653 adj.
flèche
high structure 209 n.
sharp point 256 n.
fleck
small thing 33 n.
maculation 437 n.
fledged
downy 259 adj.
matured 669 adj.
fledgling
new 126 adj.
young creature 132 n.
bird 365 n.
flee
recede 290 vb.
decamp 296 vb.
run away 620 vb.
fleece
skin 226 n.
hair 259 n.
softness 327 n.
fleece 786 vb.
defraud 788 vb.
fleecy
fibrous 208 adj.
smooth 258 adj.
fleecy 259 adj.
soft 327 adj.
fleer
ridicule 851 n.vb.
satirize 851 vb.
fleet
multitude 104 n.
brief 114 adj.
be transient 114 vb.
shipping 275 n.
speedy 277 adj.
gulf 345 n.
navy 722 n.
fleeting
insubstantial 4 adj.
transient 114 adj.
Fleet Street
the press 528 n.
flesh
auspicate 68 vb.
meat 301 n.
matter 319 n.
animality 365 n.
humankind 371 n.
flesh, the
sensualism 944 n.
unchastity 951 n.
flesh and blood
real 1 adj.
substance 3 n.
bulk 195 n.
matter 319 n.
animality 365 n.
flesh-coloured
red 431 adj.
flesh-eating
eating 301 n.
feeding 301 adj.
fleshings
legwear 228 n.
fleshless
lean 206 adj.
fleshly
material 319 adj.
human 371 adj.
sensual 944 adj.
lecherous 951 adj.
fleshpots
feasting 301 n.
food 301 n.
prosperity 730 n.
wealth 800 n.
fleshy
fleshy 195 adj.
expanded 197 adj.
thick 205 adj.
pulpy 356 adj.
unsightly 842 adj.
fleur-de-lis, fleur-de-lys
heraldry 547 n.
regalia 743 n.
pattern 844 n.
fleuron
pattern 844 n.
flex
electronics 160 n.
flexed
curved 248 adj.
flexible
conformable 83 adj.
flexible 327 adj.
irresolute 601 adj.
skilful 694 adj.
tractable 701 adj.
dishonest 930 adj.
flexion
curvature 248 n.
fold 261 n.
deviation 282 n.
flex one's muscles
prepare oneself 669 vb.
flexure
curvature 248 n.
fold 261 n.
flibbertigibbet
fool 501 n.
flick
knock 279 n.
impel 279 vb.
propel 287 vb.
touch 378 n.vb.
— the switch
operate 173 vb.
flicker
small quantity 33 n.
be transient 114 vb.
vary 152 vb.
oscillate 317 vb.
be agitated 318 vb.
fire 379 n.
flash 417 n.
shine 417 vb.
glimmer 419 n.
be dim 419 vb.
flickering
fitful 142 adj.
flicks
film 445 n.

flier, flyer
aeronaut 271 n.
flies
theatre 594 n.
flight
group 74 n.
aeronautics 271 n.
velocity 277 n.
propel 287 vb.
recession 290 n.
departure 296 n.
disappearance 446 n.
avoidance 620 n.
escape 667 n.
air force 722 n.
defeat 728 n.
fear 854 n.
flight lieutenant
air officer 741 n.
flight of fancy
insubstantial thing 4 n.
ideality 513 n.
exaggeration 546 n.
flight of stairs
ascent 308 n.
access 624 n.
flight path
air travel 271 n.
flight recorder
recording instrument 549 n.
flight sergeant
air officer 741 n.
flighty
changeful 152 adj.
agitated 318 adj.
light-minded 456 adj.
flimflam
empty talk 515 n.
falsehood 541 n.
flimsy
insubstantial 4 adj.
duplicate 22 n.
small 33 adj.
flimsy 163 adj.
brittle 330 adj.
poorly reasoned 477 adj.
unimportant 639 adj.
flinch
recoil 280 vb.
feel pain 377 vb.
avoid 620 vb.
suffer 825 vb.
quake 854 vb.
flincher
tergiversator 603 n.
coward 856 n.
fling
move 265 vb.
impel 279 vb.
propel 287 vb.
scope 744 n.
dance 837 n.
— about
jumble 63 vb.
— away
be prodigal 815 vb.
— down
let fall 311 vb.
— out
emerge 298 vb.
eject 300 vb.
reject 607 vb.
— wide the gates
open 263 vb.
admit 299 vb.
flint
hardness 326 n.
soil 344 n.
lighter 385 n.
tool 630 n.
building material 631 n.
flintlock
firearm 723 n.
flinty
hard 326 adj.
territorial 344 adj.
severe 735 adj.
cruel 898 adj.
flip
knock 279 n.
strike 279 vb.
touch 378 n.vb.
impertinent 878 adj.
— one's lid
get angry 891 vb.
— through
be attentive 455 vb.
flippant
light-minded 456 adj.
witty 839 adj.
derisive 851 adj.
rash 857 adj.
impertinent 878 adj.
flipper
limb 53 n.
propeller 269 n.
feeler 378 n.
flip side
rear 238 n.
flirt
tergiversator 603 n.
be capricious 604 vb.
affecter 850 n.
be affected 850 vb.
excite love 887 vb.
court 889 vb.
libertine 952 n.
loose woman 952 n.
flirtation
whim 604 n.
love affair 887 n.
flit
be transient 114 vb.
vary 152 vb.
be in motion 265 vb.
fly 271 vb.
move fast 277 vb.
decamp 296 vb.
run away 620 vb.
escape 667 n.vb.
flitter
be in motion 265 vb.
float
vary 152 vb.
stabilize 153 vb.
hang 217 vb.
go smoothly 258 vb.
swim 269 vb.
fly 271 vb.
pushcart 274 n.
raft 275 n.
be light 323 vb.
be uncertain 474 vb.
find means 629 vb.
— down
descend 309 vb.
— on the air
sound faint 401 vb.
— up
ascend 308 vb.
floater
idler 679 n.
floating population
wanderer 268 n.
floating pound
finance 797 n.
floating vote
dubiety 474 n.
irresolution 601 n.
no choice 606 n.
independence 744 n.
floating voter
changeable thing 152 n.
waverer 601 n.
floats
theatre 594 n.
floccinaucinihilipilification
unimportance 639 n.
floccinaucity
trifle 639 n.
flocculent
fleecy 259 adj.
soft 327 adj.
flock
group 74 n.
certain quantity 104 n.
filament 208 n.
hair 259 n.
animal 365 n.
laity 987 n.
flock together
congregate 74 vb.
floe
ice 380 n.
flog
strike 279 vb.
incite 612 vb.
hasten 680 vb.
fatigue 684 vb.
sell 793 vb.
flog 963 vb.
— a dead horse
waste effort 641 vb.
flogging
corporal punishment 963 n.
flong
print-type 587 n.
flood
great quantity 32 n.
increase 36 n.
crowd 74 n.
congregate 74 vb.
be dispersed 75 vb.
be many 104 vb.
destroyer 168 n.
outbreak 176 n.
high water 209 n.
overlie 226 vb.
progression 285 n.
burst in 297 vb.
flow out 298 vb.
immerse 303 vb.
encroach 306 vb.
irrigate 341 vb.
waterfall 350 n.
flow 350 vb.
plenty 635 n.
superabound 637 vb.
— the market
superabound 637 vb.
cheapen 812 vb.
— the tanks
navigate 269 vb.
plunge 313 vb.
floodgate
outlet 298 n.
conduit 351 n.
floodlight
lamp 420 n.
theatre 594 n.
floodlighting
lighting 420 n.
floor
compartment 194 n.
layer 207 n.
lowness 210 n.
base 214 n.
flatten 216 vb.
basis 218 n.
paving 226 n.
overlay 226 vb.
strike 279 vb.
fell 311 vb.
puzzle 474 vb.
confute 479 vb.
arena 724 n.
price 809 n.
floorboards
paving 226 n.
floor-cover
floor-cover 226 n.
floored by, be
not understand 517 vb.
floor show
spectacle 445 n.
stage show 594 n.
floozy, floosy
loose woman 952 n.
flop
descend 309 vb.
be agitated 318 vb.
bungling 695 n.
failure 728 n.

loser 728 n.
miscarry 728 vb.
floppy
nonadhesive 49 adj.
weak 163 adj.
soft 327 adj.
floppy disk
data processing 86 n.
flora
vegetable life 366 n.
flora and fauna
organism 358 n.
floral
vegetal 366 adj.
florescence
salad days 130 n.
growth 157 n.
vegetable life 366 n.
maturation 669 n.
floriculture
flower 366 n.
agriculture 370 n.
florid
florid 425 adj.
red 431 adj.
ornate 574 adj.
healthy 650 adj.
ornamented 844 adj.
showy 875 adj.
florin
coinage 797 n.
floss
fibre 208 n.
hair 259 n.
flotation
fitting out 669 n.
flotilla
shipping 275 n.
navy 722 n.
flotsam
thing transferred 272 n.
derelict 779 n.
flotsam and jetsam
dispersion 75 n.
outcast 883 n.
flounce
edging 234 n.
fold 261 n.
leap 312 vb.
trimming 844 n.
be angry 891 vb.
flounder
leap 312 vb.
be agitated 318 vb.
be uncertain 474 vb.
be clumsy 695 vb.
be in difficulty 700 vb.
flour
cereals 301 n.
powder 332 n.
thickening 354 n.
flourish
grow 36 vb.
be fruitful 171 vb.
coil 251 n.
brandish 317 vb.
agitate 318 vb.
loudness 400 n.
resonance 404 n.
musical note 410 n.
tune 412 n.
trope 519 n.
show 522 vb.
call 547 n.
ornament 574 n.
lettering 586 n.
flourish 615 vb.
be healthy 650 vb.
prosper 730 vb.
pattern 844 n.
be ostentatious 875 vb.
boast 877 n.vb.
flourish of trumpets
publication 528 n.
ostentation 875 n.
celebration 876 n.
flout
oppose 704 vb.
disobey 738 vb.
not respect 921 vb.
flow
quantity 26 n.
continuity 71 n.
elapse 111 vb.
continuance 146 n.
hang 217 vb.
motion 265 n.
current 350 n.
flow 350 vb.
diffuseness 570 n.
elegance 575 n.
abound 635 vb.
— from
result 157 vb.
— on
progress 285 vb.
— out
flow out 298 vb.
waste 634 vb.
flow chart
statistics 86 n.
plan 623 n.
flower
essential part 5 n.
grow 36 vb.
product 164 n.
reproduce itself 167 vb.
expand 197 vb.
flower 366 n.
elite 644 n.
paragon 646 n.
prosper 730 vb.
a beauty 841 n.
pride 871 n.
flowerbed
flower 366 n.
garden 370 n.
flower grower
gardener 370 n.
flowering
vernal 128 adj.
young 130 adj.
matured 669 adj.
flower people
philanthropist 901 n.
flowerpot
vessel 194 n.
garden 370 n.
flowers
powder 332 n.
anthology 592 n.
flower show
amusement 837 n.
flowers of speech
ornament 574 n.
flowery
vegetal 366 adj.
figurative 519 adj.
ornate 574 adj.
flowing
perpetual 115 adj.
hanging 217 adj.
fluid 335 adj.
flowing 350 adj.
forceful 571 adj.
elegant 575 adj.
flowing hand
lettering 586 n.
flown
absent 190 adj.
escaped 667 adj.
flown out of the window
lost 772 adj.
flow of words
loquacity 581 n.
flu
infection 651 n.
fluctuate
be periodic 141 vb.
vary 152 vb.
fluctuate 317 vb.
be irresolute 601 vb.
fluctuation
dubiety 474 n.
irresolution 601 n.
flue
chimney 263 n.
furnace 383 n.
fluency
eloquence 579 n.
loquacity 581 n.
fluent
fluid 335 adj.
flowing 350 adj.
stylistic 566 adj.
diffuse 570 adj.
elegant 575 adj.
speaking 579 adj.
loquacious 581 adj.
flue pipe
organ 414 n.
fluff
hair 259 n.
lightness 323 n.
softness 327 n.
mistake 495 n.
act 594 vb.
bungling 695 n.
be clumsy 695 vb.
fluffy
downy 259 adj.
fleecy 259 adj.
light 323 adj.
fluid
unstable 152 adj.
amorphous 244 adj.
soft 327 adj.
fluid 335 n.adj.
liquefied 337 adj.
watery 339 adj.
flowing 350 adj.
uncertain 474 adj.
fluke
chance 159 n.
angularity 247 n.
sharp point 256 n.
creepy-crawly 365 n.
nondesign 618 n.
success 727 n.
fluky
casual 159 adj.
flume
conduit 351 n.
flummery
empty talk 515 n.
fable 543 n.
flummox
distract 456 vb.
puzzle 474 vb.
flunk
fail 728 vb.
flunkey, flunky
domestic 742 n.
toady 879 n.
fluorescent
luminous 417 adj.
luminescent 420 adj.
fluoridation
prophylactic 658 n.
flurried
excited 821 adj.
flurry
derange 63 vb.
commotion 318 n.
rain 350 n.
gale 352 n.
distract 456 vb.
activity 678 n.
haste 680 n.
feeling 818 n.
excitable state 822 n.
frighten 854 vb.
flush
uniform 16 adj.
equal 28 adj.
full 54 adj.
flat 216 adj.
smooth 258 adj.
waterfall 350 n.
be hot 379 vb.
glow 417 n.
hue 425 n.
redness 431 n.
hunt 619 vb.
filled 635 adj.
clean 648 vb.
moneyed 800 adj.
show feeling 818 vb.
be excited 821 vb.

flushed
red 431 adj.
excited 821 adj.
rejoicing 835 adj.
drunk 949 adj.
fluster
derange 63 vb.
distract 456 vb.
flustered
agitated 318 adj.
tipsy 949 adj.
flute
groove 262 vb.
shrill 407 vb.
play music 413 vb.
flute 414 n.
fluting
furrow 262 n.
ornamental art 844 n.
flutist
instrumentalist 413 n.
flutter
vary 152 vb.
be in motion 265 vb.
fly 271 vb.
oscillation 317 n.
brandish 317 vb.
agitation 318 n.
be agitated 318 vb.
blow 352 vb.
gambling 618 n.
haste 680 n.
feeling 818 n.
be excited 821 vb.
nervousness 854 n.
frighten 854 vb.
excite love 887 vb.
— the dovecotes
surprise 508 vb.
fluvial
flowing 350 adj.
flux
conversion 147 n.
motion 265 n.
liquefaction 337 n.
current 350 n.
flux and reflux
fluctuation 317 n.
fluxion
numerical element 85 n.
fly
elapse 111 vb.
be transient 114 vb.
garment 228 n.
edge 234 n.
be in motion 265 vb.
fly 271 vb.
cab 274 n.
move fast 277 vb.
decamp 296 vb.
agitate 318 vb.
be light 323 vb.
be brittle 330 vb.
insect 365 n.
knowing 490 adj.
intelligent 498 adj.
flag 547 n.
run away 620 vb.
be active 678 vb.
cunning 698 adj.
fear 854 vb.
— a kite
be tentative 461 vb.
publish 528 vb.
rumour 529 vb.
attempt 671 vb.
— apart
be dispersed 75 vb.
— back
recoil 280 vb.
— in the face of
be contrary 14 vb.
oppose 704 vb.
disobey 738 vb.
— into a passion
show feeling 818 vb.
— off
diverge 294 vb.
— off the handle
be excitable 822 vb.
get angry 891 vb.
— out
be violent 176 vb.
— the flag
signal 547 vb.
flyblown
unclean 649 adj.
blemished 845 adj.
flyby
space travel 271 n.
fly-by-night
avoiding 620 adj.
fly fishing
chase 619 n.
flying
nonadhesive 49 adj.
aeronautics 271 n.
aviational 276 adj.
speedy 277 adj.
sport 837 n.
flying boat
aircraft 276 n.
flying buttress
church exterior 990 n.
flying carpet
magic instrument 983 n.
flying colours
trophy 729 n.
ostentation 875 n.
celebration 876 n.
flying column
armed force 722 n.
Flying Dutchman
wanderer 268 n.
mariner 270 n.
flying field
air travel 271 n.
flying saucer
spaceship 276 n.
flying start
advantage 34 n.
start 68 n.
priority 119 n.
spurt 277 n.
preceding 283 n.
fly in the ointment
evil 616 n.
defect 647 n.
hitch 702 n.
flyleaf
edition 589 n.
flyover
crossing 222 n.
passage 305 n.
bridge 624 n.
flypaper
adhesive 47 n.
trap 542 n.
flypast
aeronautics 271 n.
pageant 875 n.
fly sheet
canopy 226 n.
flyweight
pugilist 722 n.
flywheel
rotator 315 n.
foal
young creature 132 n.
reproduce itself 167 vb.
horse 273 n.
foam
be violent 176 vb.
effervesce 318 vb.
moisture 341 n.
bubble 355 n.vb.
bauble 639 n.
be excitable 822 vb.
— at the mouth
go mad 503 vb.
get angry 891 vb.
foamy
light 323 adj.
bubbly 355 adj.
white 427 adj.
fob off
not observe 769 vb.
— off on
compel 740 vb.
— off with
substitute 150 vb.
deceive 542 vb.
focal
central 225 adj.
focalization, focalisation
centrality 225 n.
convergence 293 n.
focal point
focus 76 n.
focus
adjust 24 vb.
bring together 74 vb.
focus 76 n.vb.
meeting place 192 n.
centre 225 n.
converge 293 vb.
gaze 438 vb.
objective 617 n.
arena 724 n.
— on
congregate 74 vb.
be attentive 455 vb.
— the attention
attract notice 455 vb.
fodder
provender 301 n.
plant 366 n.
groom 369 vb.
agriculture 370 n.
materials 631 n.
foe
opponent 705 n.
enemy 881 n.
foetus
young creature 132 n.
source 156 n.
fog
moisture 341 n.
cloud 355 n.
dimness 419 n.
obfuscation 421 n.
opacity 423 n.
blur 440 vb.
invisibility 444 n.
uncertainty 474 n.
puzzle 474 vb.
foggy
dense 324 adj.
humid 341 adj.
cloudy 355 adj.
dim 419 adj.
opaque 423 adj.
foghorn
warning 664 n.
danger signal 665 n.
fogy, fogey
laughingstock 851 n.
foible
temperament 5 n.
speciality 80 n.
defect 647 n.
vice 934 n.
foil
lamina 207 n.
bluntness 257 n.
disappoint 509 vb.
avoid 620 vb.
be obstructive 702 vb.
oppose 704 vb.
sidearms 723 n.
laughingstock 851 n.
foiled
disappointed 509 adj.
defeated 728 adj.
foist
compel 740 vb.
— in
introduce 231 vb.
— off
deceive 542 vb.
fold
derangement 63 n.
duplication 91 n.
stable 192 n.

garment 228 n.
enclosure 235 n.
make angular 247 vb.
crinkle 251 vb.
fold 261 n.vb.
rotate 315 vb.
shelter 662 n.
laity 987 n.
— in one's arms
enclose 235 vb.
caress 889 vb.
— one's arms
be inactive 679 vb.
— up
cease 145 vb.
make smaller 198 vb.
enclose 235 vb.
fold 261 vb.
folder
sorting 62 n.
receptacle 194 n.
collection 632 n.
foliage
branch 53 n.
foliage 366 n.
greenness 434 n.
foliate
number 86 vb.
layered 207 adj.
folie à deux
psychopathy 503 n.
folio
part 53 n.
edition 589 n.n.
folk
social group 371 n.
music 412 n.
folklore
tradition 127 n.
anthropology 371 n.
belief 485 n.
knowledge 490 n.
maxim 496 n.
fairy 970 n.
folk medicine
medical art 658 n.
folk singer
vocalist 413 n.
folksy
sociable 882 adj.
follicle
compartment 194 n.
cavity 255 n.
follow
do likewise 20 vb.
come after 65 vb.
accompany 89 vb.
ensue 120 vb.
happen 154 vb.
result 157 vb.
be behind 238 vb.
follow 284 vb.
watch 441 vb.
be reasonable 475 vb.
be proved 478 vb.
detect 484 vb.
understand 516 vb.
pursue 619 vb.
use 673 vb.
obey 739 vb.
serve 742 vb.
observe 768 vb.
— in the steps of
conform 83 vb.
— one's bent
be free 744 vb.
— suit
do likewise 20 vb.
conform 83 vb.
— the party line
obey 739 vb.
— the scent
pursue 619 vb.
— the shape
represent 551 vb.
— the trail
search 459 vb.
— through
sustain 146 vb.
carry through 725 vb.
— up
persevere 600 vb.
pursue 619 vb.
follower
imitator 20 n.
retinue 67 n.
conformist 83 n.
concomitant 89 n.
follower 284 n.
learner 538 n.
auxiliary 707 n.
dependant 742 n.
lover 887 n.
sectarian 978 n.
worshipper 981 n.
following wind
propellant 287 n.
aid 703 n.
follow-up
sequel 67 n.
folly
insubstantial thing 4 n.
pavilion 192 n.
ignorance 491 n.
absurdity 497 n.
folly 499 n.
rashness 857 n.
foment
conduce 156 vb.
make violent 176 vb.
heat 381 vb.
doctor 658 vb.
aid 703 vb.
animate 821 vb.
fond
foolish 499 adj.
crazy 503 adj.
desiring 859 adj.
loving 887 adj.
fond hope
aspiration 852 n.
fondle
touch 378 vb.
love 887 vb.
caress 889 vb.
fondly
affectionately 887 adv.
fondness
liking 859 n.
love 887 n.
fondue
dish 301 n.
font
ritual object 988 n.
church interior 990 n.
fontanelle
head 213 n.
food
food 301 n.
materials 631 n.
provision 633 n.
refreshment 685 n.
food chain
continuity 71 n.
eating 301 n.
food content
food content 301 n.
food for thought
topic 452 n.
food poisoning
digestive disorders 651 n.
infection 651 n.
poisoning 659 n.
food preparation
cookery 301 n.
foodstuffs
food 301 n.
provender 301 n.
provisions 301 n.
food supply
provision 633 n.
fool
dessert 301 n.
ignoramus 493 n.
fool 501 n.
befool 542 vb.
dupe 544 n.
entertainer 594 n.
bungler 697 n.
humorist 839 n.
be ridiculous 849 vb.
laughingstock 851 n.
— about
be absurd 497 vb.
amuse oneself 837 vb.
foolery
foolery 497 n.
folly 499 n.
whim 604 n.
revel 837 n.
ostentation 875 n.
foolhardy
unwise 499 adj.
rash 857 adj.
foolish
ageing 131 adj.
mindless 448 adj.
misjudging 481 adj.
credulous 487 adj.
ignorant 491 adj.
absurd 497 adj.
foolish 499 adj.
crazy 503 adj.
gullible 544 adj.
trivial 639 adj.
ridiculous 849 adj.
foolproof
certain 473 adj.
invulnerable 660 adj.
easy 701 adj.
successful 727 adj.
foolscap
stationery 586 n.
paper 631 n.
fool's errand
lost labour 641 n.
fool's paradise
insubstantial thing 4 n.
misjudgment 481 n.
disappointment 509 n.
aspiration 852 n.
foot
extremity 69 n.
long measure 203 n.
lowness 210 n.
base 214 n.
foot 214 n.
conveyance 267 n.
prosody 593 n.
infantry 722 n.
— it
walk 267 vb.
leap 312 vb.
— the bill
defray 804 vb.
footage
distance 199 n.
length 203 n.
football
bladder 194 n.
ball game 837 n.
footballer
player 837 n.
football pool
gambling 618 n.
foot by foot
piecemeal 53 adv.
footed
footed 214 adj.
footfall
gait 265 n.
indication 547 n.
foothill
high land 209 n.
projection 254 n.
foothold
basis 218 n.
support 218 n.
retention 778 n.
footing
state 7 n.
circumstance 8 n.
degree 27 n.
serial place 73 n.
influence 178 n.

situation 186 n.
base 214 n.
basis 218 n.
support 218 n.
prestige 866 n.
foot in the door
ingress 297 n.
footlights
lighting 420 n.
theatre 594 n.
footling
trivial 639 adj.
footloose
travelling 267 adj.
deviating 282 adj.
designless 618 adj.
free 744 adj.
footman
domestic 742 n.
footmark
trace 548 n.
footnote
commentary 520 n.
edition 589 n.
foot pace
slowness 278 n.
footpad
robber 789 n.
footpath
path 624 n.
footplate
stand 218 n.
footplateman
driver 268 n.
foot-pound
energy 160 n.
footprint
concavity 255 n.
identification 547 n.
trace 548 n.
foot race
pedestrianism 267 n.
racing 716 n.
footrest
prop 218 n.
footrule
gauge 465 n.
foot-scraper
cleaning utensil 648 n.
footsie
endearment 889 n.
footslogger
pedestrian 268 n.
infantry 722 n.
footsore
fatigued 684 adj.
footstep
trace 548 n.
footstool
seat 218 n.
footwear
footwear 228 n.
footwork
motion 265 n.
foozle
be clumsy 695 vb.
fail 728 vb.
fop
fop 848 n.
affecter 850 n.
vain person 873 n.
foppish
fashionable 848 adj.
affected 850 adj.
showy 875 adj.
for
hence 158 adv.
purposely 617 adv.
on behalf 755 adv.
forage
provender 301 n.
search 459 vb.
provide 633 vb.
steal 788 vb.
for all one is worth
swiftly 277 adv.
actively 678 adv.
laboriously 682 adv.
for all one knows
by chance 159 adv.
possibly 469 adv.
ignorantly 491 adv.
for all that
in return 31 adv.
in addition 38 adv.
nevertheless 468 adv.
for a long time
while 108 adv.
for a long time 113 adv.
for a time
while 108 adv.
transiently 114 adv.
foray
attack 712 n.vb.
brigandage 788 n.
forbear
disregard 458 vb.
not use 674 vb.
be lenient 736 vb.
be patient 823 vb.
show mercy 905 vb.
forgive 909 vb.
be temperate 942 vb.
forbearance
avoidance 620 n.
mercy 905 n.
forbid
prohibit 757 vb.
— by law
make illegal 954 vb.
— the banns
prohibit 757 vb.
forbidden fruit
incentive 612 n.
desired object 859 n.
forbidding
cheerless 834 adj.
serious 834 adj.
ugly 842 adj.
unsociable 883 adj.
sullen 893 adj.
force
quantity 26 n.
band 74 n.
make conform 83 vb.
cause 156 n.
energy 160 n.
strength 162 n.
agency 173 n.
vigorousness 174 n.
be vigorous 174 vb.
violence 176 n.
force 176 vb.
influence 178 n.vb.
promote 285 vb.
burst in 297 vb.
waterfall 350 n.
cultivate 370 vb.
meaning 514 n.
vigour 571 n.
necessity 596 n.
motivate 612 vb.
ill-treat 645 vb.
mature 669 vb.
misuse 675 n.vb.
action 676 n.
exertion 682 n.
personnel 686 n.
compulsion 740 n.
compel 740 vb.
not observe 769 vb.
— apart
break 46 vb.
sunder 46 vb.
— in
introduce 231 vb.
— oneself
be unwilling 598 vb.
consent 758 vb.
— one's hand
compel 740 vb.
— one's way
exert oneself 682 vb.
— out
extract 304 vb.
forced
irrelevant 10 adj.
horticultural 370 adj.
feeble 572 adj.
inelegant 576 adj.
unwilling 598 adj.
immature 670 adj.
hasty 680 adj.
forced, be
be forced 596 vb.
have no choice 606 vb.
forced labour
labour 682 n.
compulsion 740 n.
service 745 n.
forced landing
aeronautics 271 n.
forced march
marching 267 n.
haste 680 n.
force-feeding
eating 301 n.
compulsion 740 n.
forceful
strong 162 adj.
vigorous 174 adj.
expressive 516 adj.
assertive 532 adj.
forceful 571 adj.
eloquent 579 adj.
resolute 599 adj.
active 678 adj.
compelling 740 adj.
lively 819 adj.
impressive 821 adj.
force majeure
compulsion 740 n.
nonliability 919 n.
force of circumstances
necessity 596 n.
force of habit
habit 610 n.
forceps
extractor 304 n.
nippers 778 n.
forceps delivery
obstetrics 167 n.
forces
armed force 722 n.
forces of law and order
police 955 n.
forcible
powerful 160 adj.
strong 162 adj.
vigorous 174 adj.
violent 176 adj.
forceful 571 adj.
compelling 740 adj.
ford
shallowness 212 n.
pass 305 vb.
bridge 624 n.
for dear life
actively 678 adv.
fore
prior 119 adj.
front 237 n.
frontal 237 adj.
fore and aft
throughout 54 adv.
longwise 203 adv.
forearm
limb 53 n.
forearmed
expectant 507 adj.
warned 664 adj.
prepared 669 adj.
forebear(s)
precursor 66 n.
paternity 169 n.
forebode
predict 511 vb.
indicate 547 vb.
foreboding
foresight 510 n.
prediction 511 n.
dangerous 661 adj.
warning 664 n.
threatening 900 adj.
forecast
looking ahead 124 n.

impending 155 adj.
expectation 507 n.
foresee 510 vb.
predict 511 vb.
policy 623 n.
forecastle
prow 237 n.
foreclosure
expropriation 786 n.
debt 803 n.
forecourt
front 237 n.
foredoom
predestine 155 vb.
fate 596 n.
forefather(s)
paternity 169 n.
the dead 361 n.
forefinger
finger 378 n.
indication 547 n.
forefront
beginning 68 n.
front 237 n.
foregoing
preceding 64 adj.
prior 119 adj.
foregoing 125 adj.
foregone conclusion
certainty 473 n.
prejudgment 481 n.
foresight 510 n.
predetermination 608 n.
foreground
nearness 200 n.
front 237 n.
stage set 594 n.
forehead
head 213 n.
face 237 n.
dome 253 n.
foreign
extrinsic 6 adj.
unrelated 10 adj.
disagreeing 25 adj.
separate 46 adj.
extraneous 59 adj.
neological 560 adj.
foreign body
misfit 25 n.
extraneousness 59 n.
foreigner
foreigner 59 n.
settler 191 n.
wanderer 268 n.
incomer 297 n.
outcast 883 n.
foreign parts
farness 199 n.
forejudge
prejudge 481 vb.
foreknow
foresee 510 vb.
foreland
projection 254 n.
foreleg
leg 267 n.
forelock
front 237 n.
hair 259 n.
foreman, forewoman
superior 34 n.
manager 690 n.
jury 957 n.
foremast
prow 237 n.
sail 275 n.
foremost
supreme 34 adj.
first 68 adj.
foremost 283 adj.
ahead 283 adv.
important 638 adj.
noteworthy 866 adj.
forensic
jurisprudential 958 adj.
foreordain
predestine 155 vb.
predetermine 608 vb.
forepart
front 237 n.
forerunner
precursor 66 n.
messenger 529 n.
foresail
sail 275 n.
foresee
look ahead 124 vb.
be wise 498 vb.
expect 507 vb.
foresee 510 vb.
intend 617 vb.
foreseeable
future 124 adj.
probable 471 adj.
expected 507 adj.
foreseen
expected 507 adj.
unastonishing 865 adj.
foreshadow
be before 119 vb.
predestine 155 vb.
predict 511 vb.
foreshow
predict 511 vb.
foresight
anticipation 135 n.
carefulness 457 n.
sagacity 498 n.
foresight 510 n.
prediction 511 n.
policy 623 n.
preparation 669 n.
caution 858 n.
forest
multitude 104 n.
solid body 324 n.
wood 366 n.
vegetate 366 vb.
forestall
exclude 57 vb.
do before 119 vb.
look ahead 124 vb.
be early 135 vb.
expect 507 vb.
foresee 510 vb.
deceive 542 vb.
forester
forestry 366 n.
forestry
forestry 366 n.
botany 368 n.
agriculture 370 n.
foretaste
precursor 66 n.
example 83 n.
priority 119 n.
expectation 507 n.
foresight 510 n.
foretell
predict 511 vb.
forethought
thought 449 n.
carefulness 457 n.
sagacity 498 n.
foresight 510 n.
policy 623 n.
preparation 669 n.
caution 858 n.
foretoken
omen 511 n.
predict 511 vb.
for ever
continuously 71 adv.
for ever 115 adv.
for every occasion
general 79 adj.
forewarn
foresee 510 vb.
predict 511 vb.
warn 664 vb.
threaten 900 vb.
forewarned
expectant 507 adj.
prepared 669 adj.
forewarning
precursor 66 n.
omen 511 n.
foreword
prelude 66 n.
for example
conformably 83 adv.
forfeit
decrement 42 n.
relinquish 621 vb.
not observe 769 vb.
lose 772 vb.
disentitle 916 vb.
penalty 963 n.
forgather
congregate 74 vb.
forgathering
union 45 n.
assembly 74 n.
social gathering 882 n.
forge
copy 20 vb.
produce 164 vb.
form 243 vb.
furnace 383 n.
fake 541 vb.
workshop 687 n.
mint 797 vb.
— ahead
be in front 237 vb.
progress 285 vb.
forger
imitator 20 n.
deceiver 545 n.
defrauder 789 n.
minter 797 n.
offender 904 n.
forgery
copy 22 n.
sham 542 n.
false money 797 n.
forget
not know 491 vb.
forget 506 vb.
obliterate 550 vb.
relinquish 621 vb.
forgive 909 vb.
fail in duty 918 vb.
— one's manners
be insolent 878 vb.
be rude 885 vb.
forgetful
inattentive 456 adj.
negligent 458 adj.
ignorant 491 adj.
forgetful 506 adj.
ungrateful 908 adj.
forgettable
trivial 639 adj.
forgivable, forgiveable
trivial 639 adj.
forgiven 909 adj.
vindicable 927 adj.
guiltless 935 adj.
forgive
disregard 458 vb.
forget 506 vb.
be lenient 736 vb.
be patient 823 vb.
be benevolent 897 vb.
show mercy 905 vb.
forgive 909 vb.
exempt 919 vb.
acquit 960 vb.
forgiveness
amnesty 506 n.
peace offering 719 n.
forgiveness 909 n.
forgiveness of sins
liberation 746 n.
divine function 965 n.
forgo
relinquish 621 vb.
not retain 779 vb.
for good
finally 69 adv.
for a long time 113 adv.
forgotten
past 125 adj.
unknown 491 adj.
forgotten 506 adj.

unthanked 908 adj.
forgotten, be
pass away 2 vb.
escape notice 456 vb.
fork
bifurcation 92 n.
angularity 247 n.
sharp point 256 n.
diverge 294 vb.
farm tool 370 n.
— out
give 781 vb.
pay 804 vb.
fork-bending
psychics 984 n.
forklift
lifter 310 n.
fork supper
meal 301 n.
forlorn
unfortunate 731 adj.
melancholic 834 adj.
hopeless 853 adj.
friendless 883 adj.
forlorn hope
improbability 472 n.
danger 661 n.
form
modality 7 n.
similarity 18 n.
mould 23 n.
constitute 56 vb.
arrange 62 vb.
sort 77 n.
rule 81 n.
conformity 83 n.
modify 143 vb.
convert 147 vb.
produce 164 vb.
seat 218 n.
form 243 n.vb.
structure 331 n.
appearance 445 n.
educate 534 vb.
class 538 n.
record 548 n.
represent 551 vb.
sculpt 554 vb.
practice 610 n.
beauty 841 n.
fashion 848 n.
formality 875 n.
legality 953 n.
ritual 988 n.
formal
such 7 adj.
regulated 83 adj.
literary 557 adj.
formal 875 adj.
courteous 884 adj.
formaldehyde
preserver 666 n.
formal dress
formal dress 228 n.
formality 875 n.
formalism
severity 735 n.
pietism 979 n.
ritualism 988 n.
formalist
conformist 83 n.
affecter 850 n.
formality
etiquette 848 n.
title 870 n.
formality 875 n.
courtesy 884 n.
legality 953 n.
ritual 988 n.
formal visit
social round 882 n.
format
form 243 n.
edition 589 n.
formation
composition 56 n.
band 74 n.
production 164 n.
form 243 n.
formation 243 n.
formation 722 n.
formative
such 7 adj.
causal 156 adj.
productive 164 adj.
formative 243 adj.
part of speech 564 n.
forme
press 587 n.
edition 589 n.
former
preceding 64 adj.
prior 119 adj.
former 125 adj.
resigning 753 adj.
formerly
before 119 adv.
formerly 125 adv.
anciently 127 adv.
formica
lamina 207 n.
formication
formication 378 n.
skin disease 651 n.
formidable
notable 638 adj.
difficult 700 adj.
frightening 854 adj.
formless
amorphous 244 adj.
unsightly 842 adj.
form of law
legality 953 n.
form of words
phrase 563 n.
forms
reading matter 589 n.
formula
rule 81 n.
number 85 n.
axiom 496 n.
phrase 563 n.
policy 623 n.
remedy 658 n.
precept 693 n.
conditions 766 n.
compromise 770 n.
legality 953 n.
rite 988 n.
formulary
office-book 988 n.
rite 988 n.
formulate
arrange 62 vb.
form 243 vb.
manifest 522 vb.
affirm 532 vb.
phrase 563 vb.
write 586 vb.
fornication
unchastity 951 n.
fornicator
libertine 952 n.
for nothing
given 781 adj.
uncharged 812 adj.
cheaply 812 adv.
for one's own part
specially 80 adv.
for one's own sake
selfishly 932 adv.
for one's pains
rewardingly 962 adv.
for one's sins
amiss 616 adv.
forsake
tergiversate 603 vb.
relinquish 621 vb.
forsaken
alone 88 adj.
relinquished 621 adj.
friendless 883 adj.
for sale
offering 759 adj.
not retained 779 adj.
for show
ostentatious 875 adj.
for starters
initially 68 adv.
for sure
certainly 473 adv.
forswear
negate 533 vb.
recant 603 vb.
avoid 620 vb.
relinquish 621 vb.
forsworn
false 541 adj.
untrue 543 adj.
fort
refuge 662 n.
fort 713 n.
forte
adagio 412 adv.
skill 694 n.
forth
forward 285 adv.
forthcoming
early 135 adj.
impending 155 adj.
veracious 540 adj.
preparatory 669 adj.
for the best
well 615 adv.
benevolent 897 adj.
for the heck of it
at will 595 adv.
for the million
intelligible 516 adj.
easy 701 adj.
for the moment
transiently 114 adv.
for the occasion
present 121 adj.
opportune 137 adj.
for the present
provisionally 112 adv.
transiently 114 adv.
for the sake of
in aid of 703 adv.
for the time being
while 108 adv.
transiently 114 adv.
at present 121 adv.
forthright
intelligible 516 adj.
undisguised 522 adj.
veracious 540 adj.
forthwith
instantaneously 116 adv.
suddenly 135 adv.
fortification
fortification 713 n.
art of war 718 n.
fortified
strong 162 adj.
hard 326 adj.
defended 713 adj.
fortify
strengthen 162 vb.
safeguard 660 vb.
aid 703 vb.
defend 713 vb.
fortiori, a
eminently 34 adv.
reasonably 475 adv.
fortissimo
loudness 400 n.
adagio 412 adv.
fortitude
resolution 599 n.
perseverance 600 n.
courage 855 n.
virtues 933 n.
fortnight
period 110 n.
fortnightly
seasonal 141 adj.
Fortran
data processing 86 n.
fortress
edifice 164 n.
fort 713 n.
fortuitous
extrinsic 6 adj.
casual 159 adj.
unintentional 618 adj.
fortunate
opportune 137 adj.
presageful 511 adj.
prosperous 730 adj.

happy 824 adj.
fortune
changeable thing 152 n.
event 154 n.
chance 159 n.
prediction 511 n.
fate 596 n.
good 615 n.
wealth 800 n.
fortune-hunter
toady 879 n.
egotist 932 n.
fortune-teller
diviner 511 n.
occultist 984 n.
forty
twenty and over 99 n.
forty winks
sleep 679 n.
forum
rostrum 539 n.
conference 584 n.
arena 724 n.
market 796 n.
tribunal 956 n.
for want of
instead 150 adv.
without 190 adv.
insufficiently 636 adv.
forward
early 135 adj.
send 272 vb.
285 int.
intelligent 498 adj.
correspond 588 vb.
willing 597 adj.
be expedient 642 vb.
make better 654 vb.
player 837 n.
impertinent 878 adj.
discourteous 885 adj.
forward, forwards
frontal 237 adj.
forwarding
instrumental 628 adj.
forward-looking
progressive 285 adj.
for years
for a long time 113 adv.
fosse
fence 235 n.
furrow 262 n.
defences 713 n.
fossick
search 459 vb.
fossil
remainder 41 n.
fossil 125 n.
archaism 127 n.
primal 127 adj.
fossil fuel
fuel 385 n.
fossilization, fossilisation
fossil 125 n.
condensation 324 n.
hardening 326 n.
fossilized
past 125 adj.
antiquated 127 adj.
foster
be akin 11 vb.
conduce 156 vb.
look after 457 vb.
train 534 vb.
make better 654 vb.
safeguard 660 vb.
patronize 703 vb.
permit 756 vb.
animate 821 vb.
foster child
family 11 n.
dependant 742 n.
fostering
parentage 169 n.
foster parent
substitute 150 n.
keeper 749 n.
fouetté
ballet 594 n.
foul
collide 279 vb.
windy 352 adj.
unsavoury 391 adj.
fetid 397 adj.
evil 616 adj.
bad 645 adj.
not nice 645 adj.
unclean 649 adj.
make unclean 649 vb.
insalubrious 653 adj.
impair 655 vb.
unpleasant 827 adj.
ugly 842 adj.
disliked 861 adj.
unjust 914 adj.
foul play 930 n.
heinous 934 adj.
— up
obstruct 702 vb.
foul air
poison 659 n.
foul fiend, the
Satan 969 n.
foul language
scurrility 899 n.
foul-mouthed
ungracious 885 adj.
cursing 899 adj.
foul play
evil 616 n.
injustice 914 n.
foul play 930 n.
lawbreaking 954 n.
foul temper
irascibility 892 n.
foul weather
weather 340 n.
rain 350 n.
found
initiate 68 vb.
stabilize 153 vb.
cause 156 vb.
produce 164 vb.
support 218 vb.
liquefy 337 vb.
heat 381 vb.
restored 656 adj.
dower 777 vb.
found, be
be 1 vb.
be situated 186 vb.
foundation(s)
beginning 68 n.
permanence 144 n.
source 156 n.
base 214 n.
basis 218 n.
preparation 669 n.
foundation course
curriculum 534 n.
foundation cream
cosmetic 843 n.
foundation garment
underwear 228 n.
founded on a rock
invulnerable 660 adj.
founded on fact
evidential 466 adj.
founder, foundress
cause 156 n.
producer 164 n.
planner 623 n.
patron 707 n.
benefactor 903 n.
founder
founder 313 vb.
perish 361 vb.
fail 728 vb.
have trouble 731 vb.
foundered
destroyed 165 adj.
deep 211 adj.
founder member, be a
auspicate 68 vb.
founder of Christianity
religious teacher 973 n.
founder of the family
paternity 169 n.
founding father
producer 164 n.
foundling
derelict 779 n.
foundry
crucible 147 n.
workshop 687 n.
foundryman
artisan 686 n.
fount
origin 68 n.
source 156 n.
store 632 n.
fount, font
print-type 587 n.
fountain
source 156 n.
outflow 298 n.
soft drink 301 n.
climber 308 n.
stream 350 n.
store 632 n.
fountainhead
source 156 n.
stream 350 n.
fountain pen
stationery 586 n.
four
quaternity 96 n.
four 96 adj.
four corners of
whole 52 n.
four-flusher
impostor 545 n.
fourfold
fourfold 97 adj.
four freedoms, the
freedom 744 n.
four-in-hand
group 74 n.
quaternity 96 n.
carriage 274 n.
fou rire
laughter 835 n.
four-leaf clover
talisman 983 n.
four-letter word
word 559 n.
plainness 573 n.
fourpenny one
knock 279 n.
four-poster
bed 218 n.
four-sided
angulated 247 adj.
foursome
quaternity 96 n.
dance 837 n.
foursquare
fixed 153 adj.
fourth
quadrisection 98 n.
musical note 410 n.
fourth dimension
time 108 n.
fourth-dimensional
spatial 183 adj.
fourth estate
the press 528 n.
Fourth of July
anniversary 141 n.
special day 876 n.
four-wheeler
cab 274 n.
fowl
bird 365 n.
poultry 365 n.
hunt 619 vb.
fowler
hunter 619 n.
fowling piece
firearm 723 n.
fowl pest
animal disease 651 n.

fox
mammal 365 n.
puzzle 474 vb.
trickster 545 n.
slyboots 698 n.
noxious animal 904 n.
foxglove
purpleness 436 n.
fox hole
tunnel 263 n.
refuge 662 n.
foxhound
dog 365 n.
hunter 619 n.
foxhunter
thoroughbred 273 n.
hunter 619 n.
foxiness
cunning 698 n.
foxing
maculation 437 n.
foxtrot
dance 837 n.vb.
foxy
animal 365 adj.
fetid 397 adj.
brown 430 adj.
intelligent 498 adj.
cunning 698 adj.
dishonest 930 adj.
foyer
lobby 194 n.
theatre 594 n.
fracas
turmoil 61 n.
quarrel 709 n.
fight 716 n.
fraction
quantity 26 n.n.
small quantity 33 n.
part 53 n.
numerical element 85 n.
fraction 102 n.
trifle 639 n.
fractionalize, fractionalise
sunder 46 vb.
fractious
unwilling 598 adj.
irascible 892 adj.
fracture
separation 46 n.
break 46 vb.
discontinuity 72 n.
gap 201 n.
be brittle 330 vb.
wound 655 n.
fragile
insubstantial 4 adj.
small 33 adj.
flimsy 163 adj.
brittle 330 adj.
fragility
transience 114 n.
fragment
small thing 33 n.
break 46 vb.
sunder 46 vb.
piece 53 n.
fraction 102 n.
be brittle 330 vb.
pulverize 332 vb.
fragmentary
incomplete 55 adj.
uncompleted 726 adj.
fragmentation
separation 46 n.
powderiness 332 n.
fragrance
plant 366 n.
fragrance 396 n.
fragrant
pleasant 376 adj.
odorous 394 adj.
fragrant 396 adj.
frail
small 33 adj.
ephemeral 114 adj.
flimsy 163 adj.
basket 194 n.
brittle 330 adj.
unsafe 661 adj.
frail 934 adj.
frailty
vice 934 n.
frame
modality 7 n.
mould 23 n.
affix 45 vb.
produce 164 vb.
basket 194 n.
receptacle 194 n.
hanger 217 n.
frame 218 n.
weaving 222 n.
be exterior 223 vb.
outline 233 n.vb.
edging 234 n.
enclose 235 vb.
form 243 n.vb.
structure 331 n.
garden 370 n.
fake 541 vb.
photography 551 n.
predetermine 608 vb.
plot 623 vb.
preparation 669 n.
indict 928 vb.
frame of mind
state 7 n.
affections 817 n.
frame of reference
referral 9 n.
prototype 23 n.
conditions 766 n.
frame-up
duplicity 541 n.
trap 542 n.
untruth 543 n.
predetermination 608 n.
plot 623 n.
false charge 928 n.
framework
basket 194 n.
frame 218 n.
outline 233 n.
structure 331 n.
franc
coinage 797 n.
franchise
vote 605 n.
freedom 744 n.
dueness 915 n.
nonliability 919 n.
Franciscans
monk 986 n.
Francophile
xenophile 880 n.
Francophobe
enemy 881 n.
Francophone
speaking 579 adj.
franc-tireur
soldier 722 n.
frangible
flimsy 163 adj.
brittle 330 adj.
franglais
dialect 560 n.
frank
undisguised 522 adj.
correspond 588 vb.
artless 699 adj.
ungracious 885 adj.
trustworthy 929 adj.
frankfurter
meat 301 n.
frankincense
resin 357 n.
scent 396 n.
frankness
truth 494 n.
veracity 540 n.
plainness 573 n.
artlessness 699 n.
frantic
disorderly 61 adj.
furious 176 adj.
absurd 497 adj.
frenzied 503 adj.
active 678 adj.
excited 821 adj.
excitable 822 adj.
frap
tighten 45 vb.
frappé
soft drink 301 n.
cooled 382 adj.
fraternal
akin 11 adj.
corporate 708 adj.
concordant 710 adj.
friendly 880 adj.
benevolent 897 adj.
fraternity
family 11 n.
association 706 n.
community 708 n.
monk 986 n.
fraternize, fraternise
accord 24 vb.
combine 50 vb.
concord 710 vb.
be friendly 880 vb.
be sociable 882 vb.
fratricide
homicide 362 n.
Frau
lady 373 n.
title 870 n.
fraud
duplicity 541 n.
trickery 542 n.
impostor 545 n.
slyboots 698 n.
peculation 788 n.
fraudulent
false 541 adj.
deceiving 542 adj.
thieving 788 adj.
dishonest 930 adj.
perfidious 930 adj.
lawbreaking 954 adj.
fraught
full 54 adj.
unfortunate 731 adj.
fraught with danger
dangerous 661 adj.
Fraulein
lady 373 n.
title 870 n.
fray
rend 46 vb.
rub 333 vb.
activity 678 n.
exertion 682 n.
fight 716 n.
frayed
dilapidated 655 adj.
freak
variant 15 n.
misfit 25 n.
nonconformist 84 n.
crank 504 n.
enthusiast 504 n.
whim 604 n.
prodigy 864 n.
drug-taking 949 n.
freaked out
insensible 375 adj.
excited 821 adj.
drugged 949 adj.
freakish
abnormal 84 adj.
unexpected 508 adj.
capricious 604 adj.
freak out
be unconformable 84 vb.
drug oneself 949 vb.
freckle
maculation 437 n.
variegate 437 vb.
blemish 845 n.
freckled
mottled 437 adj.
blemished 845 adj.
free
disunited 46 adj.
unstick 49 vb.

extract 304 vb.
inexact 495 adj.
interpretive 520 adj.
undisguised 522 adj.
veracious 540 adj.
voluntary 597 adj.
escaped 667 adj.
deliver 668 vb.
unused 674 adj.
disencumber 701 vb.
free 744 adj.
liberate 746 vb.
not retain 779 vb.
given 781 adj.
uncharged 812 adj.
liberal 813 adj.
ungracious 885 adj.
unwedded 895 adj.
nonliable 919 adj.
— oneself
separate 46 vb.
achieve liberty 746 vb.
free agent
free person 744 n.
free-and-easy
lax 734 adj.
free 744 adj.
rash 857 adj.
impertinent 878 adj.
friendly 880 adj.
sociable 882 adj.
freebooter
militarist 722 n.
robber 789 n.
knave 938 n.
freeborn
free 744 adj.
nonliable 919 adj.
free choice
will 595 n.
willingness 597 n.
free city
political organization 733 n.
freedman, freedwoman
free person 744 n.
freedom
opportunity 137 n.
freedom 744 n.
permission 756 n.
dueness 915 n.
nonliability 919 n.
freedom fighter
soldier 722 n.
freedom of action
freedom 744 n.
independence 744 n.
freedom of choice
opportunity 137 n.
choice 605 n.
means 629 n.
independence 744 n.
free enterprise
scope 744 n.
trade 791 n.
free entry
no charge 812 n.
free expression
liberation 746 n.
free fall
aeronautics 271 n.
free field
scope 744 n.
free-floating
neutral 625 adj.
free-for-all
turmoil 61 n.
fight 716 n.
anarchy 734 n.
scope 744 n.
unconditional 744 adj.
free from
unmixed 44 adj.
free gift
extra 40 n.
acquisition 771 n.
gift 781 n.
free hand
facility 701 n.
scope 744 n.
permit 756 n.
liberality 813 n.
freehold
unconditional 744 adj.
lands 777 n.
proprietary 777 adj.
freeholder
possessor 776 n.
free house
tavern 192 n.
freelance
author 589 n.
businesslike 622 adj.
worker 686 n.
free person 744 n.
free-liver
sensualist 944 n.
freeloader
idler 679 n.
toady 879 n.
sociable person 882 n.
free love
love affair 887 n.
type of marriage 894 n.
illicit love 951 n.
freely
easily 701 adv.
freely 744 adv.
freeman
free person 744 n.
free market
scope 744 n.
market 796 n.
free-market economy
trade 791 n.
freemartin
eunuch 161 n.
freemasonry
cooperation 706 n.
friendship 880 n.
Freemasonry
latency 523 n.
secrecy 525 n.
society 708 n.
free of charge
uncharged 812 adj.
free pardon
amnesty 506 n.
forgiveness 909 n.
free play
scope 744 n.
free port
scope 744 n.
emporium 796 n.
free range
stock farm 369 n.
free speech
freedom 744 n.
free spender
prodigal 815 n.
free-spoken
artless 699 adj.
freethinker
free person 744 n.
irreligionist 974 n.
free thought
antichristianity 974 n.
free time
leisure 681 n.
free to choose
independent 744 adj.
free trade
ingress 297 n.
scope 744 n.
trade 791 n.
free trade area
society 708 n.
market 796 n.
freewheel
go smoothly 258 vb.
travel 267 vb.
not act 677 vb.
do easily 701 vb.
freewheeler
idler 679 n.
freewheeling
unconfined 744 adj.
free will
will 595 n.
freedom 744 n.
free world
political organization 733 n.
freeze
cohere 48 vb.
halt 145 vb.
come to rest 266 vb.
harden 326 vb.
render insensible 375 vb.
wintriness 380 n.
be cold 380 vb.
refrigerate 382 vb.
preserve 666 vb.
restriction 747 n.
not pay 805 vb.
frighten 854 vb.
quake 854 vb.
freeze-dry
dry 342 vb.
refrigerate 382 vb.
freezer
refrigerator 384 n.
preserver 666 n.
freight
fill 54 vb.
stow 187 vb.
contents 193 n.
thing transferred 272 n.
gravity 322 n.
merchandise 795 n.
freightage
transport 272 n.
price 809 n.
freighter
carrier 273 n.
merchant ship 275 n.
aircraft 276 n.
freightliner
train 274 n.
French leave
absence 190 n.
escape 667 n.
French letter
contraception 172 n.
French polish
smoother 258 n.
frenetic, phrenetic
frenzied 503 adj.
frenzied
disorderly 61 adj.
frenzied 503 adj.
active 678 adj.
excited 821 adj.
angry 891 adj.
frenzy
turmoil 61 n.
violence 176 n.
commotion 318 n.
spasm 318 n.
frenzy 503 n.
fantasy 513 n.
lack of meaning 515 n.
illness 651 n.
restlessness 678 n.
excitable state 822 n.
desire 859 n.
frequency
degree 27 n.
continuity 71 n.
recurrence 106 n.
frequency 139 n.
periodicity 141 n.
electricity 160 n.
oscillation 317 n.
frequency wave
radiation 417 n.
frequent
many 104 adj.
repeated 106 adj.
frequent 139 adj.
be present 189 vb.
dwell 192 vb.

usual 610 adj.
be wont 610 vb.

frequenter
habitué 610 n.
sociable person 882 n.

fresco
picture 553 n.

fresh
different 15 adj.
original 21 adj.
new 126 adj.
matinal 128 adj.
airy 340 adj.
humid 341 adj.
windy 352 adj.
cold 380 adj.
savoury 390 adj.
remembered 505 adj.
unhabituated 611 adj.
not bad 644 adj.
clean 648 adj.
healthy 650 adj.
salubrious 652 adj.
impertinent 878 adj.

fresh air
air 340 n.
salubrity 652 n.

fresh blood
successor 67 n.

fresh-complexioned
personable 841 adj.

freshen
be strong 162 vb.
invigorate 174 vb.
aerate 340 vb.
blow 352 vb.
purify 648 vb.
sanitate 652 vb.
revive 656 vb.
refresh 685 vb.
decorate 844 vb.

fresher, freshman
student 538 n.

freshet
stream 350 n.
waterfall 350 n.

freshly
newly 126 adv.

freshness
originality 21 n.
newness 126 n.
youth 130 n.
(See **fresh** *)*

fresh outbreak
relapse 657 n.

fresh spurt
revival 656 n.

fresh start
start 68 n.

fresh troops
auxiliary 707 n.

fresh water
water 339 n.

freshwater fish
fish food 301 n.

freshwater sailor
bungler 697 n.

fret
rend 46 vb.
rub 333 vb.
give pain 377 vb.
cry 408 vb.
harp 414 n.
variegate 437 vb.
impair 655 vb.
restlessness 678 n.
disobey 738 vb.
excitable state 822 n.
worry 825 n.
torment 827 vb.
cause discontent 829 vb.
decorate 844 vb.
be angry 891 vb.

fretful
capricious 604 adj.
discontented 829 adj.
lamenting 836 adj.
irascible 892 adj.

fretwork
network 222 n.
ornamental art 844 n.

Freudian psychology
psychology 447 n.

friable
flimsy 163 adj.
brittle 330 adj.
powdery 332 adj.

friar
monk 986 n.
pastor 986 n.

friary
monastery 986 n.

fribble
neglect 458 vb.
nonentity 639 n.
be inactive 679 vb.

fricassee
dish 301 n.

fricative
speech sound 398 n.

friction
energy 160 n.
counteraction 182 n.
collision 279 n.
powderiness 332 n.
friction 333 n.
stridor 407 n.
hindrance 702 n.
opposition 704 n.
dissension 709 n.
painfulness 827 n.

frictionless
smooth 258 adj.
easy 701 adj.
concordant 710 adj.
pleasurable 826 adj.

Friday
fast 946 n.

fridge
provisions 301 n.
refrigerator 384 n.
storage 632 n.

friend
colleague 707 n.
friend 880 n.
sociable person 882 n.
kind person 897 n.
benefactor 903 n.

Friend
Protestant 976 n.
sectarian 978 n.

friend at court
influence 178 n.
latency 523 n.
patron 707 n.

friend in need
aider 703 n.
patron 707 n.
friend 880 n.

friendless
separate 46 adj.
alone 88 adj.
defenceless 161 adj.
friendless 883 adj.

friendliness
cooperation 706 n.
peace offering 719 n.

friendly
aiding 703 adj.
concordant 710 adj.
friendly 880 adj.
sociable 882 adj.
amiable 884 adj.
benevolent 897 adj.
approving 923 adj.

friendly critic
aider 703 n.
commender 923 n.

friend of all the world
xenophile 880 n.
philanthropist 901 n.

friendship
concord 710 n.
friendship 880 n.
sociality 882 n.
love 887 n.n.
benevolence 897 n.

Friesian
cattle 365 n.

frieze
textile 222 n.
trimming 844 n.

frigate
sailing ship 275 n.
warship 722 n.

fright
eyesore 842 n.
fear 854 n.

frighten
unman 161 vb.
dissuade 613 vb.
raise the alarm 665 vb.
hinder 702 vb.
depress 834 vb.
frighten 854 vb.
threaten 900 vb.

frightened
fearing 854 adj.

frightener
alarmist 854 n.

frightening
unexpected 508 adj.
dangerous 661 adj.
cautionary 664 adj.
distressing 827 adj.
frightening 854 adj.
wonderful 864 adj.
spooky 970 adj.

frightful
prodigious 32 adj.
ugly 842 adj.
frightening 854 adj.

frightfully
extremely 32 adv.

frigid
cold 380 adj.
feeble 572 adj.
impassive 820 adj.
inexcitable 823 adj.
inimical 881 adj.
pure 950 adj.

frill
edging 234 n.
plumage 259 n.
fold 261 n.vb.
trimming 844 n.

frills
adjunct 40 n.
ornament 574 n.
superfluity 637 n.
finery 844 n.

fringe
extremity 69 n.
contiguity 202 n.
filament 208 n.
edging 234 n.
hair 259 n.
unimportant 639 adj.
hairdressing 843 n.
trimming 844 n.

fringe benefits
earnings 771 n.
reward 962 n.

fringe medicine
medical art 658 n.

frippery
clothing 228 n.
bauble 639 n.
finery 844 n.
bad taste 847 n.
ostentation 875 n.

frisk
move fast 277 vb.
leap 312 vb.
search 459 vb.
be cheerful 833 vb.
rejoice 835 vb.
amuse oneself 837 vb.

frisky
active 678 adj.

frisson
agitation 318 n.

fritter away
abate 37 vb.
waste 634 vb.
misuse 675 vb.
be prodigal 815 vb.
— away time
pass time 108 vb.
be inactive 679 vb.
fritters
dish 301 n.
frivolity
folly 499 n.
unimportance 639 n.
merriment 833 n.
rashness 857 n.
frivolous
light-minded 456 adj.
capricious 604 adj.
frizz
crinkle 251 vb.
fold 261 vb.
frizzle
be hot 379 vb.
frizzy
undulatory 251 adj.
hairy 259 adj.
frock
dress 228 n.
be ecclesiastical 985 vb.
canonicals 989 n.
Froebel system
education 534 n.
frog
fastening 47 n.
jumper 312 n.
amphibian 365 n.
railway 624 n.
trimming 844 n.
frogman
depth 211 n.
diver 313 n.
frogmarch
impel 279 vb.
frolic
leap 312 n.
enjoyment 824 n.
rejoice 835 vb.
revel 837 n.
frolicker
reveller 837 n.
frolicsome
merry 833 adj.
from A to Z
including 78 adv.
from bad to worse
in adversity 731 adv.
aggravatedly 832 adv.
from beginning to end
throughout 54 adv.
from coast to coast
throughout 54 adv.
widely 183 adv.
from first to last
throughout 54 adv.
from hand to hand
contiguously 202 adv.
in transit 272 adv.
from head to foot
throughout 54 adv.
from now on
henceforth 124 adv.
from one end to the other
throughout 54 adv.
from pillar to post
in transit 272 adv.
irresolutely 601 adv.
round about 626 adv.
from pole to pole
widely 183 adv.
from scratch
initially 68 adv.
from the bottom of one's heart
truthfully 540 adv.
feelingly 818 adv.
from the cradle to the grave
for a long time 113 adv.
from the start
initially 68 adv.
subsequently 120 adv.
until now 121 adv.
from time immemorial
retrospectively 125 adv.
from time to time
sometimes 139 adv.
from top to bottom
throughout 54 adv.
aloft 209 adv.
frond
foliage 366 n.
frondeur
revolter 738 n.
front
precedence 64 n.
prelude 66 n.
beginning 68 n.
exteriority 223 n.
coat 226 vb.
edge 234 n.
front 237 n.
frontal 237 adj.
be in front 237 vb.
orientate 281 vb.
preceding 283 n.
appearance 445 n.
duplicity 541 n.
path 624 n.
battle 718 n.
battleground 724 n.
insolence 878 n.
frontage
situation 186 n.
face 237 n.
contraposition 240 n.
frontal
frontal 237 adj.
opposite 240 adj.
opposing 704 adj.
front elevation
face 237 n.
frontier
entrance 68 n.
extremity 69 n.
farness 199 n.
contiguity 202 n.
edge 234 n.
limit 236 n.
frontiersman, frontierswoman
dweller 191 n.
frontiers of knowledge
unknown thing 491 n.
frontispiece
prelude 66 n.
front 237 n.
front line
front 237 n.
armed force 722 n.
front man
broadcaster 531 n.
impostor 545 n.
front matter
edition 589 n.
front-page
notable 638 adj.
front-rank
supreme 34 adj.
front runner
contender 716 n.
favourite 890 n.
frost
cover 226 vb.
wintriness 380 n.
refrigerate 382 vb.
screen 421 vb.
make opaque 423 vb.
whiten 427 vb.
blight 659 n.
frostbite
coldness 380 n.
frostbound
cold 380 adj.
frosted glass
screen 421 n.
semitransparency 424 n.
frosting
covering 226 n.
powderiness 332 n.
frostwork
wintriness 380 n.
ornamental art 844 n.
frosty
cold 380 adj.
white 427 adj.
unsociable 883 adj.
froth
stimulation 174 n.
excrement 302 n.
effervesce 318 vb.
moisture 341 n.
bubble 355 n.vb.
bauble 639 n.
dirt 649 n.
be excitable 822 vb.
frothblower
drunkard 949 n.
frothy
light 323 adj.
bubbly 355 adj.
diffuse 570 adj.
ornate 574 adj.
trivial 639 adj.
frottage
picture 553 n.
frou-frou
faintness 401 n.
sibilation 406 n.
finery 844 n.
frown
distort 246 vb.
fold 261 n.
gesture 547 n.
gesticulate 547 vb.
discontent 829 n.
rudeness 885 n.
anger 891 n.
be sullen 893 vb.
— on/upon
prohibit 757 vb.
refuse 760 vb.
make unwelcome 883 vb.
frowning
adverse 731 adj.
serious 834 adj.
sullen 893 adj.
frowst
stench 397 n.
frowzy
fetid 397 adj.
dirty 649 adj.
ugly 842 adj.
frozen
cohesive 48 adj.
fixed 153 adj.
still 266 adj.
dense 324 adj.
hard 326 adj.
insensible 375 adj.
chilly 380 adj.
cooled 382 adj.
preserved 666 adj.
impassive 820 adj.
fearing 854 adj.
frozen assets
estate 777 n.
debt 803 n.
frozen food
provisions 301 n.
frozen mitt
rejection 607 n.
fructification
maturation 669 n.
fructify
reproduce itself 167 vb.
be fruitful 171 vb.

fructose
food content 301 n.
sweet thing 392 n.
frugal
economical 814 adj.
cautious 858 adj.
temperate 942 adj.
fasting 946 adj.
frugality
asceticism 945 n.
fruit
growth 157 n.
product 164 n.
reproduce itself 167 vb.
fruit 301 n.
flower 366 n.
fruitarian
abstainer 942 n.
fruitful
increasing 36 adj.
productive 164 adj.
prolific 171 adj.
successful 727 adj.
gainful 771 adj.
fruitful, be
prosper 730 vb.
fruit growing
agriculture 370 n.
fruition
propagation 167 n.
maturation 669 n.
completion 725 n.
fruit juice
soft drink 301 n.
fruitless
unproductive 172 adj.
wasted 634 adj.
profitless 641 adj.
unsuccessful 728 adj.
fruit machine
gambling 618 n.
fruit salad
dessert 301 n.
fruity
tasty 386 adj.
fragrant 396 adj.
fetid 397 adj.
resonant 404 adj.
speaking 579 adj.
witty 839 adj.
impure 951 adj.
frump
bore 838 n.
eyesore 842 n.
bad taste 847 n.
frumpish
dull 840 adj.
frustrate
disappoint 509 vb.
be obstructive 702 vb.
hindrance 702 n.
failure 728 n.
frustrated
discontented 829 adj.
frustration
psychopathy 503 n.
disappointment 509 n.
hindrance 702 n.
failure 728 n.
fry
young creature 132 n.
cook 301 vb.
be hot 379 vb.
heat 381 vb.
frying pan
cauldron 194 n.
heater 383 n.
fry-up
dish 301 n.
fuchsia
red 431 adj.
purple 436 adj.
fuddle
distract 456 vb.
inebriate 949 vb.
fuddled
foolish 499 adj.
tipsy 949 adj.
fuddy-duddy
archaism 127 n.
fudge
sweet thing 392 n.
be equivocal 518 vb.
fake 541 vb.
— the issue
avoid 620 vb.
fuel
sources of energy 160 n.
propellant 287 n.
fuel 385 n.
fire 385 vb.
materials 631 n.
provide 633 vb.
animate 821 vb.
fuel cell
electronics 160 n.
fuel rods
nucleonics 160 n.
fug
stench 397 n.
fugacious
transient 114 adj.
fuggy
sealed off 264 adj.
fetid 397 adj.
fugitive
disunited 46 adj.
transient 114 adj.
wanderer 268 n.
avoider 620 n.
escaper 667 n.
fugleman
living model 23 n.
leader 690 n.
fugue
musical piece 412 n.
fugue state
oblivion 506 n.
führer, fuehrer
leader 690 n.
autocrat 741 n.
master 741 n.
fulcrum
pivot 218 n.
centre 225 n.
fulfil
do 676 vb.
carry out 725 vb.
observe 768 vb.
— expectations
happen 154 vb.
fulfilment
completeness 54 n.
sufficiency 635 n.
completion 725 n.
observance 768 n.
enjoyment 824 n.
fuliginous
opaque 423 adj.
black 428 adj.
grey 429 adj.
full
whole 52 adj.
complete 54 adj.
full 54 adj.
assembled 74 adj.
multitudinous 104 adj.
fleshy 195 adj.
broad 205 adj.
loud 400 adj.
veracious 540 adj.
descriptive 590 adj.
filled 635 adj.
completed 725 adj.
drunk 949 adj.
full age
adultness 134 n.
full blast
loudness 400 n.
full-blooded
vigorous 174 adj.
full-blown
complete 54 adj.
grown-up 134 adj.
expanded 197 adj.
completed 725 adj.
full-bodied
tasty 386 adj.
odorous 394 adj.
full circle
revolution 149 n.
circuition 314 n.
rotation 315 n.
full dress
formal dress 228 n.
formality 875 n.
fuller
cleaner 648 n.
fuller's earth
soil 344 n.
full-face portrait
picture 553 n.
full/fully-fledged
complete 54 adj.
grown-up 134 adj.
matured 669 adj.
full frontal
frontal 237 adj.
full/fully-grown
complete 54 adj.
grown-up 134 adj.
matured 669 adj.
full heart
warm feeling 818 n.
full house
plenitude 54 n.
crowd 74 n.
playgoer 594 n.
full-length
comprehensive 52 adj.
long 203 adj.
full life
enjoyment 824 n.
sensualism 944 n.
full measure
plenitude 54 n.
sufficiency 635 n.
fullness, fulness
greatness 32 n.
whole 52 n.
plenitude 54 n.
breadth 205 n.
plenty 635 n.
completion 725 n.
satiety 863 n.
full of beans
vigorous 174 adj.
healthy 650 adj.
active 678 adj.
cheerful 833 adj.
full of oneself
vain 873 adj.
full play
facility 701 n.
scope 744 n.
full pressure
energy 160 n.
exertion 682 n.
full sail
velocity 277 n.
full satisfaction
payment 804 n.
full-scale
extensive 32 adj.
complete 54 adj.
full-size
great 32 adj.
full speed
speeding 277 n.
velocity 277 n.
full steam ahead
vigorously 174 adv.
full stop
quiescence 266 n.
punctuation 547 n.
full-throated
loud 400 adj.
crying 408 adj.
ululant 409 adj.
full tilt
actively 678 adv.
full-time job
job 622 n.
full toss
propulsion 287 n.
full up
feeding 301 adj.
fully
greatly 32 adv.
wholly 52 adv.

completely 54 adv.
fully-fashioned
tailored 228 adj.
formed 243 adj.
fully furnished
complete 54 adj.
inclusive 78 adj.
prepared 669 adj.
fulminate
be violent 176 vb.
be loud 400 vb.
emphasize 532 vb.
be angry 891 vb.
curse 899 vb.
threaten 900 vb.
dispraise 924 vb.
fulsome
exaggerated 546 adj.
vulgar 847 adj.
affected 850 adj.
disliked 861 adj.
approving 923 adj.
flattering 925 adj.
fulvous
yellow 433 adj.
fumarole
chimney 263 n.
furnace 383 n.
fumble
touch 378 vb.
be tentative 461 vb.
be uncertain 474 vb.
be clumsy 695 vb.
fumbler
bungler 697 n.
loser 728 n.
fume
be violent 176 vb.
emit 300 vb.
vaporize 338 vb.
be hot 379 vb.
odour 394 n.
hasten 680 vb.
be excitable 822 vb.
anger 891 n.
be angry 891 vb.
fumes
gas 336 n.
stench 397 n.
fumigant
prophylactic 658 n.
fumigate
vaporize 338 vb.
smell 394 vb.
be fragrant 396 vb.
purify 648 vb.
fun
enjoyment 824 n.
pleasurableness 826 n.
merriment 833 n.
amusement 837 n.
wit 839 n.
fun and games
festivity 837 n.
function
number 85 n.
agency 173 n.
operate 173 vb.
function 622 n.vb.
utility 640 n.
do 676 vb.
serve 742 vb.
formality 875 n.
celebration 876 n.
functional
correlative 12 adj.
operative 173 adj.
businesslike 622 adj.
instrumental 628 adj.
useful 640 adj.
functional disease
disease 651 n.
functionalism
philosophy 449 n.
art 551 n.
utility 640 n.
functionary
agent 686 n.
official 690 n.
officer 741 n.
consignee 754 n.
fund
store 632 n.vb.
treasury 799 n.
fundamental
intrinsic 5 adj.
simple 44 adj.
beginning 68 adj.
fundamental 156 adj.
undermost 214 adj.
supporting 218 adj.
important 638 adj.
fundamentalism
theology 973 n.
scripture 975 n.
orthodoxism 976 n.
pietism 979 n.
fundamentalist
the orthodox 976 n.
zealot 979 n.
fundamental note
musical note 410 n.
fundamentals
reality 1 n.
chief thing 638 n.
fund-raising
acquisition 771 n.
funds
funds 797 n.
funeral
funeral 364 n.
bane 659 n.
worry 825 n.
funeral oration
valediction 296 n.
obsequies 364 n.
oration 579 n.
lament 836 n.
funerary
funereal 364 adj.
funereal
funereal 364 adj.
dark 418 adj.
black 428 adj.
cheerless 834 adj.
lamenting 836 adj.
funfair
place of amusement 837 n.
fungicide
poison 659 n.
fungoid
vegetal 366 adj.
fungology
botany 368 n.
fungus
plant 366 n.
dirt 649 n.
blight 659 n.
funicular
railway 624 n.
funk
avoid 620 vb.
fear 854 n.vb.
be cowardly 856 vb.
funkhole
refuge 662 n.
funnel
cylinder 252 n.
cavity 255 n.
chimney 263 n.
tube 263 n.
transpose 272 vb.
conduit 351 n.
air pipe 353 n.
direct 689 vb.
funnel-shaped
concave 255 adj.
tubular 263 adj.
funny
unusual 84 adj.
crazy 503 adj.
amusing 837 adj.
witty 839 adj.
funny 849 adj.
funny bone
limb 53 n.
sensibility 374 n.
funny man
humorist 839 n.
funny story
witticism 839 n.
fur
covering 226 n.
skin 226 n.
hair 259 n.
heraldry 547 n.
dirt 649 n.
trimming 844 n.
furbish
decorate 844 vb.
furcate
crossed 222 adj.
angular 247 adj.
furfuraceous
powdery 332 adj.
Furies
Fury 891 n.
Chthonian deity 967 n.
furious
destructive 165 adj.
furious 176 adj.
violent 176 adj.
frenzied 503 adj.
harmful 645 adj.
hasty 680 adj.
fervent 818 adj.
excited 821 adj.
excitable 822 adj.
rash 857 adj.
angry 891 adj.
furiously
extremely 32 adv.
furl
fold 261 vb.
rotate 315 vb.
furlong
long measure 203 n.
furlough
absence 190 n.
leisure 681 n.
repose 683 n.
permit 756 n.
furnace
fire 379 n.
furnace 383 n.
workshop 687 n.
furnish
find means 629 vb.
provide 633 vb.
make ready 669 vb.
furnishing(s)
adjunct 40 n.
contents 193 n.
equipment 630 n.
ornamental art 844 n.
furniture
equipment 630 n.
property 777 n.
furore
violence 176 n.
commotion 318 n.
frenzy 503 n.
excitation 821 n.
fashion 848 n.
furred up
dirty 649 adj.
furrier
stripper 229 n.
forrow
concavity 255 n.
roughness 259 n.
fold 261 vb.
furrow 262 n.
groove 262 vb.
trace 548 n.
furry
hairy 259 adj.
further
additional 38 adj.
beyond 199 adv.
promote 285 vb.
aid 703 vb.
— one's purpose
be useful 640 vb.
furtherance
progression 285 n.
improvement 654 n.
aid 703 n.
further education
education 534 n.

furthermore
in addition 38 adv.
further on
beyond 199 adv.
in front 237 adv.
further reading
study 536 n.
furthest
distant 199 adj.
furthest point
limit 236 n.
furtive
stealthy 525 adj.
fury
violent creature 176 n.
excitation 821 n.
excitable state 822 n.
desire 859 n.
anger 891 n.
shrew 892 n.
hellhag 904 n.
demon 970 n.
Fury
Fury 891 n.
fuscous
brown 430 adj.
fuse
join 45 vb.
combine 50 vb.
heat 381 vb.
lighter 385 n.
safeguard 662 n.
hitch 702 n.
explosive 723 n.
fuselage
frame 218 n.
fusiform
angulated 247 adj.
tapering 256 adj.
fusilier
soldiery 722 n.
fusillade
slaughter 362 n.
bombardment 712 n.
execute 963 vb.
fusion
mixture 43 n.
union 45 n.
combination 50 n.
nucleonics 160 n.
liquefaction 337 n.
association 706 n.
fuss
commotion 318 n.
exaggeration 546 n.
activity 678 n.
be busy 678 vb.
haste 680 n.
excitation 821 n.
excitable state 822 n.
suffer 825 vb.
be fastidious 862 vb.
ostentation 875 n.
be angry 891 vb.
fusspot
meddler 678 n.
perfectionist 862 n.
fussy
narrow-minded 481 adj.
active 678 adj.
authoritarian 735 adj.
fastidious 862 adj.
fustian
textile 222 n.
absurdity 497 n.
empty talk 515 n.
magniloquence 574 n.
fustigate
flog 963 vb.
fustiness
stench 397 n.
fusty
antiquated 127 adj.
sealed off 264 adj.
fetid 397 adj.
dirty 649 adj.
futhorc
letter 558 n.
futile
absurd 497 adj.
foolish 499 adj.
wasted 634 adj.
useless 641 adj.
unskilful 695 adj.
contemptible 922 adj.
futile activity
overactivity 678 n.
futilitarian
lost labour 641 n.
futility
ineffectuality 161 n.
(See **futile** *)*
future
subsequent 120 adj.
futurity 124 n.
future 124 adj.
impending 155 adj.
expected 507 adj.
future generations
successor 67 n.
futurity 124 n.
futureless
unfortunate 731 adj.
futures
gambling 618 n.
future state
future state 124 n.
future tense
futurity 124 n.
Futurism
school of painting 553 n.
futurist
modernist 126 n.
futuristic
modern 126 adj.
literary 557 adj.
futurity
futurity 124 n.
destiny 155 n.
possibility 469 n.
futurologist
oracle 511 n.
fuzz
hair 259 n.
fuzzy
amorphous 244 adj.
hairy 259 adj.
shadowy 419 adj.
indistinct 444 adj.
fylfot
quaternity 96 n.
cross 222 n.
heraldry 547 n.
talisman 983 n.

G

gab
loquacity 581 n.
gabardine
textile 222 n.
overcoat 228 n.
gabber
chatterer 581 n.
gabble
ululate 409 vb.
empty talk 515 n.
speak 579 vb.
stammer 580 vb.
be loquacious 581 vb.
gabfest
conference 584 n.
gabion
fortification 713 n.
gable
extremity 69 n.
vertex 213 n.
laterality 239 n.
Gabriel
angel 968 n.
gad about
wander 267 vb.
gadabout
sociable person 882 n.
Gadarene swine, like
violently 176 adv.
rashly 857 adv.
gadfly
insect 365 n.
excitant 821 n.
gadget
object 319 n.
contrivance 623 n.
instrument 628 n.
tool 630 n.
Gaea
(See **Gaia** *)*
gaff
sharp point 256 n.
spear 723 n.
gaffe
mistake 495 n.
gaffer
old man 133 n.
male 372 n.
manager 690 n.
country-dweller 869 n.
gag
stopper 264 n.
vomit 300 vb.
silence 399 vb.
make mute 578 vb.
act 594 vb.
hinder 702 vb.
restrain 747 vb.
fetter 748 n.
witticism 839 n.
gaga
ageing 131 adj.
foolish 499 adj.
crazy 503 adj.
gage
defiance 711 n.
security 767 n.
gaggle
group 74 n.
ululate 409 vb.
gagster, gagman
dramatist 594 n.
humorist 839 n.
Gaia
world 321 n.
mythic deity 966 n.
gaiety
merriment 833 n.
sociability 882 n.
gaily
inadvertently 456 adv.
cheerfully 833 adv.
hopefully 852 adv.
rashly 857 adv.
gain
increment 36 n.
grow 36 vb.
be early 135 vb.
growth 157 n.
product 164 n.
progression 285 n.
arrive 295 vb.
benefit 615 n.
utility 640 n.
triumph 727 vb.
gain 771 n., vb.
acquire 771 vb.
booty 790 n.
get rich 800 vb.
receipt 807 n.
be rewarded 962 vb.
— a footing
prevail 178 vb.
place oneself 187 vb.
— a hearing
influence 178 vb.
be heard 415 vb.
— ground
grow 36 vb.
progress 285 vb.
— on/upon
outstrip 277 vb.
progress 285 vb.
approach 289 vb.

outdo 306 vb.
— one's affections
excite love 887 vb.
— one's confidence
convince 485 vb.
— one's end
succeed 727 vb.
— power
be able 160 vb.
take authority 733 vb.
— recognition
have a reputation 866 vb.
— the upper hand
prevail 178 vb.
— time
spin out 113 vb.
be early 135 vb.
put off 136 vb.
— weight
make heavy 322 vb.
gainful
good 615 adj.
profitable 640 adj.
gainful 771 adj.
rewarding 962 adj.
gaining
anachronistic 118 adj.
inexact 495 adj.
gains
wealth 800 n.
gainsay
negate 533 vb.
gait
gait 265 n.
equitation 267 n.
way 624 n.
gaitered
clerical 986 adj.
gaiters
legwear 228 n.
badge of rule 743 n.
canonicals 989 n.
gala
festivity 837 n.
pageant 875 n.
galactic
cosmic 321 adj.
Galahad
brave person 855 n.
honourable person 929 n.
virgin 950 n.
gala night
dramaturgy 594 n.
galantine
hors-d'oeuvres 301 n.
galaxy
group 74 n.
certain quantity 104 n.
star 321 n.
island 349 n.
luminary 420 n.
person of repute 866 n.
gale
storm 176 n.
commotion 318 n.
gale 352 n.
excitable state 822 n.
gale force
violent 176 adj.
windy 352 adj.
Galenic
medical 658 adj.
galenical
medicine 658 n.
galère
party 708 n.
galilee
church exterior 990 n.
galimatias
lack of meaning 515 n.
gall
swelling 253 n.
rub 333 vb.
give pain 377 vb.
sourness 393 n.
bane 659 n.
torment 827 vb.
sauciness 878 n.
resentment 891 n.
irascibility 892 n.
malevolence 898 n.
gall and wormwood
unsavouriness 391 n.
painfulness 827 n.
dislike 861 n.
gallant
fop 848 n.
courageous 855 adj.
showy 875 adj.
courteous 884 adj.
lover 887 n.
benevolent 897 adj.
libertine 952 n.
gallantry
courage 855 n.
wooing 889 n.
galleon
merchant ship 275 n.
warship 722 n.
gallery
lobby 194 n.
excavation 255 n.
tunnel 263 n.
listener 415 n.
onlookers 441 n.
exhibit 522 n.
playgoer 594 n.
theatre 594 n.
collection 632 n.
church interior 990 n.
galley
chamber 194 n.
galley 275 n.
cookery 301 n.
press 587 n.
galley proof
letterpress 587 n.
galleys
penalty 963 n.
galley slave
boatman 270 n.
busy person 678 n.
slave 742 n.
prisoner 750 n.
galliard
dance 837 n.
Gallican
sectarian 978 adj.
gallicism
dialect 560 n.
galligaskins
trousers 228 n.
gallimaufry
medley 43 n.
gallinaceous
animal 365 adj.
gallipot
vessel 194 n.
gallivant
wander 267 vb.
court 889 vb.
gallon
metrology 465 n.
gallons
great quantity 32 n.
galloon
trimming 844 n.
gallop
be transient 114 vb.
gait 265 n.
ride 267 vb.
move fast 277 vb.
gallop rhythm
cardiovascular disease 651 n.
gallows
hanger 217 n.
means of execution 964 n.
gallowsbird
offender 904 n.
gallows humour
wit 839 n.
gallstones
digestive disorders 651 n.
Gallup poll
statistics 86 n.
enquiry 459 n.
vote 605 n.
galoot
ninny 501 n.
bungler 697 n.
galop
dance 837 n.
galore
great quantity 32 n.
many 104 adj.
plenty 635 n.
galumph
be clumsy 695 vb.
galvanize, galvanise
invigorate 174 vb.
incite 612 vb.
excite 821 vb.
gambade
leap 312 n.
gambit
debut 68 n.
attempt 671 n.
tactics 688 n.
gamble
chance 159 vb.
be tentative 461 vb.
uncertainty 474 n.
suppose 512 vb.
gamble 618 vb.
face danger 661 vb.
speculate 791 vb.
be rash 857 vb.
— away
be prodigal 815 vb.
— on
be certain 473 vb.
gambler
experimenter 461 n.
diviner 511 n.
gambler 618 n.
player 837 n.
desperado 857 n.
gambling
equal chance 159 n.
gambling 618 n.
gambling game 837 n.
gambling den
gaming-house 618 n.
gamboge
yellow pigment 433 n.
gambol
leap 312 n.vb.
enjoyment 824 n.
be cheerful 833 vb.
amuse oneself 837 vb.
gamboller
reveller 837 n.
game
crippled 163 adj.
meat 301 n.
animal 365 n.
savouriness 390 n.
trickery 542 n.
resolute 599 adj.
persevering 600 adj.
objective 617 n.
gamble 618 vb.
chase 619 n.
plot 623 n.
attempting 671 adj.
tactics 688 n.
stratagem 698 n.
contest 716 n.
amusement 837 n.
laughingstock 851 n.
courageous 855 adj.
game at which two can play, a
retaliation 714 n.
game bird
table bird 365 n.

gamecock
contender 716 n.
combatant 722 n.
brave person 855 n.
game for
willing 597 adj.
gamekeeper
animal husbandry 369 n.
keeper 749 n.
game not worth the candle
lost labour 641 n.
game of cards
card game 837 n.
game of chance
gambling 618 n.
amusement 837 n.
game park
zoo 369 n.
game preserve
wood 366 n.
game reserve
zoo 369 n.
preservation 666 n.
games
exercise 682 n.
contest 716 n.
sport 837 n.
gamesmanship
tactics 688 n.
cunning 698 n.
gamesome
lively 819 adj.
merry 833 adj.
gamester
gambler 618 n.
game warden
animal husbandry 369 n.
gamin
low fellow 869 n.
gaming-house
gaming-house 618 n.
place of amusement 837 n.
gammadion
cross 222 n.
talisman 983 n.
gamma ray
radiation 417 n.
gammon
meat 301 n.
gamp
shade 226 n.
gamut
series 71 n.
musical note 410 n.
gamy
pungent 388 adj.
savoury 390 adj.
fetid 397 adj.
gander
bird 365 n.
male animal 372 n.
gang
band 74 n.
be in motion 265 vb.
party 708 n.
— agley
miscarry 728 vb.
— up
congregate 74 vb.
cooperate 706 vb.
— up with
accompany 89 vb.
ganger
worker 686 n.
manager 690 n.
gangling
unwieldy 195 adj.
narrow 206 adj.
clumsy 695 adj.
ganglion
centre 225 n.
gangplank
bridge 624 n.
gangrene
decay 51 n.
infection 651 n.
deteriorate 655 vb.
gang rule
lawlessness 954 n.
gangster
murderer 362 n.
robber 789 n.
low fellow 869 n.
offender 904 n.
gang warfare
turmoil 61 n.
quarrel 709 n.
fight 716 n.
gangway
doorway 263 n.
open space 263 n.
access 624 n.
bridge 624 n.
ganja
drug-taking 949 n.
gannet
bird 365 n.
gantry
stand 218 n.
railway 624 n.
gaol, jail
gaol 748 n.
seclusion 883 n.
gaoler, jailer
doorkeeper 264 n.
gaoler 749 n.
gap
disunion 46 n.
incompleteness 55 n.
discontinuity 72 n.
gap 201 n.
concavity 255 n.
valley 255 n.
opening 263 n.
requirement 627 n.
defect 647 n.
gape
space 201 vb.
be deep 211 vb.
open 263 vb.
gaze 438 vb.
watch 441 vb.
be curious 453 vb.
wonder 864 vb.
gaping
expanded 197 adj.
garage
stable 192 n.
chamber 194 n.
storage 632 n.
store 632 vb.
safeguard 660 vb.
garb
dressing 228 n.
appearance 445 n.
garbage
dirt 649 n.
garble
mislead 495 vb.
misinterpret 521 vb.
be false 541 vb.
garbled
incomplete 55 adj.
inexact 495 adj.
garden
seedbed 156 n.
arbour 194 n.
enclosure 235 n.
garden 370 n.
cultivate 370 vb.
a beauty 841 n.
Garden
philosopher 449 n.
garden city
district 184 n.
gardener
producer 164 n.
gardener 370 n.
domestic 742 n.
gardening
agriculture 370 n.
ornamental art 844 n.
Garden of Eden
happiness 824 n.
mythic heaven 971 n.
garden of remembrance
cemetery 364 n.
garden party
amusement 837 n.
social gathering 882 n.
gardens
pleasance 192 n.
pleasure ground 837 n.
gargantuan
huge 195 adj.
gargle
cleanser 648 n.
prophylactic 658 n.
gargoyle
outlet 298 n.
drain 351 n.
image 551 n.
eyesore 842 n.
ornamental art 844 n.
garish
luminous 417 adj.
florid 425 adj.
graceless 842 adj.
ornamented 844 adj.
vulgar 847 adj.
showy 875 adj.
garland
loop 250 n.
badge 547 n.
anthology 592 n.
trophy 729 n.
ornamentation 844 n.
honours 866 n.
celebrate 876 vb.
pay one's respects 884 vb.
garlic
vegetable 301 n.
condiment 389 n.
stench 397 n.
garment(s)
garment 228 n.
clothing 228 n.
garner
bring together 74 vb.
store 632 vb.
garnet
redness 431 n.
gem 844 n.
garnish
adjunct 40 n.
food 301 n.
condiment 389 n.
decorate 844 vb.
garniture
dressing 228 n.
garret
attic 194 n.
vertex 213 n.
garrison
resident 191 n.
protector 660 n.
defender 713 n.
defend 713 vb.
armed force 722 n.
keeper 749 n.
garrotte
kill 362 vb.
execute 963 vb.
means of execution 964 n.
garrotter
murderer 362 n.
punisher 963 n.
garrulous
disclosing 526 adj.
loquacious 581 adj.
garter
fastening 47 n.
compressor 198 n.
legwear 228 n.
badge 547 n.
decoration 729 n.
badge of rank 743 n.
honours 866 n.
garter stitch
needlework 844 n.
garth
enclosure 235 n.

gas
sources of energy 160 n.
lifter 310 n.
rarity 325 n.
gas 336 n.
air 340 n.
murder 362 vb.
anaesthetic 375 n.
render insensible 375 vb.
heater 383 n.
fuel 385 n.
stench 397 n.
empty talk 515 n.
chatter 581 n.
weapon 723 n.
boast 877 n.vb.
execute 963 vb.
gasbag
bladder 194 n.
chatterer 581 n.
boaster 877 n.
gas chamber
slaughterhouse 362 n.
means of execution 964 n.
Gascon
boaster 877 n.
gasconade
boast 877 n.
gaseous
insubstantial 4 adj.
gaseous 336 adj.
windy 352 adj.
bubbly 355 adj.
gash
cut 46 vb.
gap 201 n.
notch 260 n.
pain 377 n.
wound 655 n.vb.
gasholder
storage 632 n.
gasification
vaporization 338 n.
gaslight
gas 336 n.
lighting 420 n.
gas main
air pipe 353 n.
gas mantle
lamp 420 n.
gas mask
safeguard 662 n.
preserver 666 n.
armour 713 n.
gasoline
oil 357 n.
fuel 385 n.
gasometer
gas 336 n.
storage 632 n.
gas oven
furnace 383 n.
gasp
breathe 352 vb.
rasp 407 vb.
cry 408 n.vb.
voice 577 n.
be fatigued 684 vb.
wonder 864 vb.
gasproof
sealed off 264 adj.
invulnerable 660 adj.
gasser
chatterer 581 n.
gas shell
missile weapon 723 n.
gassy
gaseous 336 adj.
vaporific 338 adj.
windy 352 adj.
Gastarbeiter
foreigner 59 n.
gastroenteritis
digestive disorders 651 n.
infection 651 n.
gastronomic
culinary 301 adj.
gluttonous 947 adj.
gastronomy
gastronomy 301 n.
gluttony 947 n.
gasworks
gas 336 n.
workshop 687 n.
gat
pistol 723 n.
gate
barrier 235 n.
doorway 263 n.
onlookers 441 n.
obstacle 702 n.
fort 713 n.
imprison 747 vb.
receipt 807 n.
gateau
pastries 301 n.
gatecrash
intrude 297 vb.
be sociable 882 vb.
gatecrasher
intruder 59 n.
gatekeeper
doorkeeper 264 n.
gate money
receipt 807 n.
gate of horn
veracity 540 n.
sleep 679 n.
gate of ivory
untruth 543 n.
sleep 679 n.
gatepost
doorway 263 n.
gateway
entrance 68 n.
gather
join 45 vb.
congregate 74 vb.
expand 197 vb.
fold 261 n.vb.
meet 295 vb.
cultivate 370 vb.
be dark 418 vb.
assume 471 vb.
be informed 524 vb.
store 632 vb.
acquire 771 vb.
take 786 vb.
— grapes from thorns
attempt the impossible 470 vb.
— momentum
accelerate 277 vb.
— round
congregate 74 vb.
— together
converge 293 vb.
— way
be in motion 265 vb.
navigate 269 vb.
gathered
tailored 228 adj.
gathered to one's fathers
dead 361 adj.
gatherer
accumulator 74 n.
gathering
assembly 74 n.
conference 584 n.
ulcer 651 n.
toxic 653 adj.
(See **gather** *)*
gathering clouds
omen 511 n.
warning 664 n.
adversity 731 n.
threat 900 n.
gating
penalty 963 n.
Gatling gun
gun 723 n.
gauche
ignorant 491 adj.
foolish 499 adj.
inelegant 576 adj.
clumsy 695 adj.
ill-bred 847 adj.
gaucherie
unskilfulness 695 n.
gaucho
rider 268 n.
herdsman 369 n.
gaudery
finery 844 n.
gaudy
florid 425 adj.
graceless 842 adj.
ornamented 844 adj.
vulgar 847 adj.
showy 875 adj.
gauge
prototype 23 n.
breadth 205 n.
testing agent 461 n.
gauge 465 n.vb.
estimate 480 vb.
indicator 547 n.
gauleiter
tyrant 735 n.
autocrat 741 n.
gaunt
unproductive 172 adj.
lean 206 adj.
deformed 246 adj.
gauntlet
glove 228 n.
defiance 711 n.
armour 713 n.
gauze
textile 222 n.
transparency 422 n.
semitransparency 424 n.
stage set 594 n.
surgical dressing 658 n.
gauzy
insubstantial 4 adj.
gavel
badge of rule 743 n.
gavotte
dance 837 n.
gawk
gaze 438 vb.
watch 441 vb.
be curious 453 vb.
wonder 864 vb.
gawker
ninny 501 n.
gawkish
clumsy 695 adj.
gawky
foolish 499 adj.
gawp
gaze 438 vb.
gay
nonconformist 84 n.
abnormal 84 adj.
luminescent 420 adj.
florid 425 adj.
merry 833 adj.
witty 839 adj.
showy 875 adj.
gay dog
fop 848 n.
libertine 952 n.
gaze
look 438 n.
gaze 438 vb.
be curious 453 vb.
be attentive 455 vb.
wonder 864 vb.
gazebo
arbour 194 n.
view 438 n.
gazelle
speeder 277 n.
mammal 365 n.
gazer
spectator 441 n.
gazette
journal 528 n.
record 548 n.
gazetteer
directory 87 n.
guidebook 524 n.

reference book 589 n.
GCE
exam 459 n.
gear
clothing 228 n.
equipment 630 n.
gears
machine 630 n.
gear to
relate 9 vb.
join 45 vb.
— with
accord 24 vb.
gecko
reptile 365 n.
geezer
laughingstock 851 n.
Gehenna
hell 972 n.
Geiger counter
radiation 417 n.
meter 465 n.
detector 484 n.
geisha girl
entertainer 594 n.
geist
spirit 447 n.
gel
viscidity 354 n.
gelatine
condensation 324 n.
thickening 354 n.
gelatinize, gelatinise
be dense 324 vb.
thicken 354 vb.
gelatinous
semiliquid 354 adj.
geld
subtract 39 vb.
unman 161 vb.
make sterile 172 vb.
gelding
eunuch 161 n.
horse 273 n.
male animal 372 n.
gelignite
explosive 723 n.
gem
rock 344 n.
exceller 644 n.
gem 844 n.
Gemara
scripture 975 n.
gem cutting
engraving 555 n.
ornamental art 844 n.
geminate
double 91 adj. vb.
Gemini
duality 90 n.
zodiac 321 n.
gen
information 524 n.
gender
classification 77 n.
grammar 564 n.
gene
heredity 5 n.
organism 358 n.
genealogy
heredity 5 n.
series 71 n.
list 87 n.
genealogy 169 n.
general
comprehensive 52 adj.
inclusive 78 adj.
general 79 adj.
typical 83 adj.
national 371 adj.
indiscriminate 464 adj.
usual 610 adj.
army officer 741 n.
General Certificate of Education
exam 459 n.
general consent
consensus 488 n.
general election
vote 605 n.
generalissimo
army officer 741 n.
generality
average 30 n.
completeness 54 n.
generality 79 n.
conformity 83 n.
inexactness 495 n.
(See **general** *)*
generalization, generalisation
reasoning 475 n.
inexactness 495 n.
generalize
generalize 79 vb.
general knowledge
erudition 490 n.
generally
on an average 30 adv.
greatly 32 adv.
generally 79 adv.
often 139 adv.
generally believed
orthodox 976 adj.
general post
interchange 151 n.
general practitioner
doctor 658 n.
general principle
premise 475 n.
general public
social group 371 n.
commonalty 869 n.
generalship
tactics 688 n.
art of war 718 n.
general strike
strike 145 n.
general studies
curriculum 534 n.
general voice
consensus 488 n.
generate
unite with 45 vb.
initiate 68 vb.
cause 156 vb.
generate 167 vb.
make fruitful 171 vb.
emit 300 vb.
vitalize 360 vb.
generation
coition 45 n.
era 110 n.
causation 156 n.
propagation 167 n.
generations
long duration 113 n.
generations of man
humankind 371 n.
generative
productive 164 adj.
generative 167 adj.
prolific 171 adj.
female 373 adj.
generator
causal means 156 n.
electronics 160 n.
sources of energy 160 n.
generic
generic 77 adj.
general 79 adj.
generosity
liberality 813 n.
generous
great 32 adj.
many 104 adj.
plenteous 635 adj.
giving 781 adj.
expending 806 adj.
liberal 813 adj.
courteous 884 adj.
benevolent 897 adj.
approving 923 adj.
disinterested 931 adj.
virtuous 933 adj.
rewarding 962 adj.
genesis
origin 68 n.
source 156 n.
propagation 167 n.
genetic
genetic 5 adj.
inherited 157 adj.
generative 167 adj.
genetic engineering
biology 358 n.
genetics
heredity 5 n.
biology 358 n.
Geneva bands
canonicals 989 n.
Geneva Convention
treaty 765 n.
Geneva gown
canonicals 989 n.
genial
pleasant 376 adj.
warm 379 adj.
willing 597 adj.
pleasurable 826 adj.
cheerful 833 adj.
benevolent 897 adj.
genial climate
salubrity 652 n.
geniality
sociability 882 n.
genie
mythical being 970 n.
genie of the lamp
aider 703 n.
genital
generative 167 adj.
genitals
source 156 n.
genitalia 167 n.
genius
identity 13 n.
analogue 18 n.
intellect 447 n.
spirit 447 n.
intellectual 492 n.
intelligence 498 n.
sage 500 n.
exceller 644 n.
aptitude 694 n.
proficient person 696 n.
prodigy 864 n.
fairy 970 n.
genius loci
locality 187 n.
lesser deity 967 n.
genned-up
informed 524 adj.
genocide
destruction 165 n.
slaughter 362 n.
cruel act 898 n.
genotype
breed 77 n.
genre
sort 77 n.
genre painter
artist 556 n.
genre painting
art style 553 n.
genteel
well-bred 848 adj.
genteel 868 adj.
gentile
religionist 973 n.
heathen 974 n.
profane 980 adj.
gentility
etiquette 848 n.
nobility 868 n.
courtesy 884 n.
gentle
moderate 177 adj.
sloping 220 adj.
tamed 369 adj.
muted 401 adj.
lax 734 adj.
lenient 736 adj.
inexcitable 823 adj.
amiable 884 adj.
courteous 884 adj.

benevolent 897 adj.
innocent 935 adj.
gentle birth
nobility 868 n.
gentlefolk
aristocracy 868 n.
gentleman
male 372 n.
aristocrat 868 n.
gentlemanly
male 372 adj.
well-bred 848 adj.
reputable 866 adj.
noble 868 adj.
courteous 884 adj.
honourable 929 adj.
gentleman's agreement
promise 764 n.
compact 765 n.
gentleman's gentleman
domestic 742 n.
gentleness
pity 905 n.
(See **gentle** *)*
gentle sex
womankind 373 n.
gentlewoman
lady 373 n.
aristocrat 868 n.
gentry
aristocracy 868 n.
Gents
latrine 649 n.
genuflect
be pious 979 vb.
genuflexion, genuflection
obeisance 311 n.
submission 721 n.
respects 920 n.
ritual act 988 n.
genuine
certain 473 adj.
genuine 494 adj.
genuineness
identity 13 n.
no imitation 21 n.
authenticity 494 n.
genus
group 74 n.
breed 77 n.
geocentric
central 225 adj.
celestial 321 adj.
geodesic, geodetic
geographic 321 adj.
metrical 465 adj.
geodesist
enumerator 86 n.
earth sciences 321 n.
surveyor 465 n.
geographer
earth sciences 321 n.
geographical, geographic
situated 186 adj.
geographic 321 adj.
geography
situation 186 n.
earth sciences 321 n.
land 344 n.
geoid
sphere 252 n.
world 321 n.
geological
primal 127 adj.
geological period
era 110 n.
geological times
antiquity 125 n.
geologist
earth sciences 321 n.
geology
earth sciences 321 n.
land 344 n.
mineralogy 359 n.
geometer
enumerator 86 n.
geometry 465 n.
geometric, geometrical
statistical 86 adj.
ornamental 844 adj.
geometrical progression
series 71 n.
ratio 85 n.
geometry
mathematics 86 n.
geometry 465 n.
geomorphology
earth sciences 321 n.
geophone
meter 465 n.
geoponics
agriculture 370 n.
Geordie
native 191 n.
dialect 560 n.
George Cross
badge 547 n.
decoration 729 n.
georgette
textile 222 n.
Georgian
olden 127 adj.
georgic
agrarian 370 adj.
poem 593 n.
geosphere
world 321 n.
geostationary
circuitous 314 adj.
rotary 315 adj.
geothermal power
sources of energy 160 n.
geranium
redness 431 n.
geriatric
ageing 131 adj.
geriatrician
doctor 658 n.
geriatrics
gerontology 131 n.
medical art 658 n.
germ
origin 68 n.
source 156 n.
microorganism 196 n.
infection 651 n.
insalubrity 653 n.
poison 659 n.
german
akin 11 adj.
germane
apt 24 adj.
Germanic
language type 557 n.
germicide
prophylactic 658 n.
poison 659 n.
germinal
beginning 68 adj.
causal 156 adj.
generative 167 adj.
germinate
begin 68 vb.
result 157 vb.
reproduce itself 167 vb.
be fruitful 171 vb.
vegetate 366 vb.
germination
propagation 167 n.
germ-laden
toxic 653 adj.
germ warfare
poisoning 659 n.
warfare 718 n.
weapon 723 n.
gerontocracy
seniority 131 n.
government 733 n.
gerontology
gerontology 131 n.
medical art 658 n.
gerrymander
be cunning 698 vb.
be dishonest 930 vb.
gesso
art equipment 553 n.
Gestalt
form 243 n.
Gestalt psychology
psychology 447 n.
Gestapo
police enquiry 459 n.
gestation
propagation 167 n.
maturation 669 n.
gesticulate
gesticulate 547 vb.
be mute 578 vb.
speak 579 vb.
gesticulation
mimicry 20 n.
gesture 547 n.
gesture
distortion 246 n.
motion 265 n.
agitation 318 n.
mien 445 n.
hint 524 n.
gesture 547 n.
gesticulate 547 vb.
deed 676 n.
conduct 688 n.
command 737 n.
affectation 850 n.
sauciness 878 n.
ritual act 988 n.
get
be turned to 147 vb.
generate 167 vb.
know 490 vb.
understand 516 vb.
acquire 771 vb.
possess 773 vb.
receive 782 vb.
— about
be published 528 vb.
— above oneself
be vain 873 vb.
be insolent 878 vb.
— across
mean 514 vb.
be intelligible 516 vb.
communicate 524 vb.
make enemies 881 vb.
huff 891 vb.
— ahead (of)
come before 64 vb.
precede 283 vb.
progress 285 vb.
— a hold on
take authority 733 vb.
— a kick out of
enjoy 376 vb.
be pleased 824 vb.
— a move on
accelerate 277 vb.
move fast 277 vb.
progress 285 vb.
— around
travel 267 vb.
be wise 498 vb.
be skilful 694 vb.
succeed 727 vb.
be sociable 882 vb.
— a shock
not expect 508 vb.
— at
blame 924 vb.
— away
recede 290 vb.
disappear 446 vb.
escape 667 vb.
achieve liberty 746 vb.
— away with (it)
escape 667 vb.
be exempt 919 vb.
— a whiff of
smell 394 vb.
— a word in
interfere 231 vb.
— back
recoup 31 vb.

retrieve 656 vb.
— back at
avenge 910 vb.
— behindhand
not pay 805 vb.
— better
progress 285 vb.
flourish 615 vb.
get better 654 vb.
be restored 656 vb.
— between
interfere 231 vb.
— blood from a stone
attempt the impossible 470 vb.
— bogged down
fall short 307 vb.
fail 728 vb.
— by heart
memorize 505 vb.
learn 536 vb.
— by hook or by crook
find means 629 vb.
— cold feet
tergiversate 603 vb.
be nervous 854 vb.
— cracking
begin 68 vb.
move fast 277 vb.
— down
land 295 vb.
descend 309 vb.
stoop 311 vb.
— down to (it)
attempt 671 vb.
work 682 vb.
— dressed
wear 228 vb.
— even with
retaliate 714 vb.
punish 963 vb.
— going
start out 296 vb.
do 676 vb.
— hold of
understand 516 vb.
acquire 771 vb.
— hold of an idea
opine 485 vb.
— hold of the wrong end of the stick
err 495 vb.
misinterpret 521 vb.
— in
bring together 74 vb.
enter 297 vb.
— in front
precede 283 vb.
— in the way
be near 200 vb.
be clumsy 695 vb.
hinder 702 vb.
trouble 827 vb.
— into
wear 228 vb.
— into one's stride
habituate 610 vb.
— into proportion
relate 9 vb.
— into the way of
habituate 610 vb.
— in touch
be contiguous 202 vb.
communicate 524 vb.
— involved
undertake 672 vb.
philanthropize 897 vb.
— it into one's head
opine 485 vb.
not understand 517 vb.
— it off one's chest
divulge 526 vb.
— it wrong
err 495 vb.
misinterpret 521 vb.
— lost!
292 int.
— more kicks than ha'pence
have trouble 731 vb.
— nothing out of it
fail 728 vb.
— off
land 295 vb.
descend 309 vb.
— off lightly
escape 667 vb.
— off with
court 889 vb.
— on
progress 285 vb.
prosper 730 vb.
— one down
cause discontent 829 vb.
depress 834 vb.
be tedious 838 vb.
— one off
deliver 668 vb.
acquit 960 vb.
— one's deserts
be rightly served 714 vb.
deserve 915 vb.
be rewarded 962 vb.
be punished 963 vb.
— one's knife into
be revengeful 910 vb.
— one's own back
revert 148 vb.
retaliate 714 vb.
avenge 910 vb.
— one wrong
not understand 517 vb.
misinterpret 521 vb.
— on one's nerves
displease 827 vb.
enrage 891 vb.
— on the gravy train
have luck 730 vb.
— on the right side of
flatter 925 vb.
— on with
accord 24 vb.
do 676 vb.
be friendly 880 vb.
— out
land 295 vb.
extract 304 vb.
publish 528 vb.
escape 667 vb.
— out of
avoid 620 vb.
— out of bed the wrong side
be discontented 829 vb.
be sullen 893 vb.
— out of practice
be unskilful 695 vb.
— out of the way
avoid 620 vb.
— over
be restored 656 vb.
triumph 727 vb.
— over it
be content 828 vb.
be relieved 831 vb.
— religion
become pious 979 vb.
— rich
flourish 615 vb.
prosper 730 vb.
gain 771 vb.
get rich 800 vb.
— rid of
eliminate 44 vb.
destroy 165 vb.
eject 300 vb.
kill 362 vb.
deliver 668 vb.
not retain 779 vb.
— round
be unconformable 84 vb.
befool 542 vb.
avoid 620 vb.
— the best out of
make better 654 vb.
use 673 vb.
— the better of
be superior 34 vb.
confute 479 vb.
defeat 727 vb.
humiliate 872 vb.
— the bit between one's teeth
achieve liberty 746 vb.
— the feel of
be tentative 461 vb.
— the hang of
understand 516 vb.
learn 536 vb.
habituate 610 vb.
— the impression
intuit 476 vb.
— the push
emerge 298 vb.
— the upper hand
defeat 727 vb.
— the wind up
be nervous 854 vb.
fear 854 vb.
— the worst of it
be defeated 728 vb.
— through
terminate 69 vb.
pass 305 vb.
communicate 524 vb.
carry through 725 vb.
expend 806 vb.
— together
congregate 74 vb.
converge 293 vb.
— to grips with
attempt 671 vb.
— to hear of
be informed 524 vb.
— to the bottom of
enquire 459 vb.
understand 516 vb.
— under one's feet
hinder 702 vb.
trouble 827 vb.
— under one's skin
displease 827 vb.
enrage 891 vb.
— under way
initiate 68 vb.
navigate 269 vb.
start out 296 vb.
— up
produce 164 vb.
ascend 308 vb.vb.
lift oneself 310 vb.
blow 352 vb.
study 536 vb.
fake 541 vb.
be restored 656 vb.
— up steam
be vigorous 174 vb.
navigate 269 vb.
— used to
habituate 610 vb.
— what was coming to one
be rightly served 714 vb.
be punished 963 vb.
— wind of
smell 394 vb.
discover 484 vb.
be informed 524 vb.
— wise to
understand 516 vb.
— with it
modernize 126 vb.
be in fashion 848 vb.
— worse
be inferior 35 vb.
be ill 651 vb.
deteriorate 655 vb.

get-at-able
accessible 289 adj.
getting on
ageing 131 adj.
getting warm
near 200 adj.
approaching 289 adj.
discovering 484 adj.
get-together
social gathering 882 n.
getup
form 243 n.
gewgaw
bauble 639 n.
finery 844 n.
geyser
outflow 298 n.
climber 308 n.
stream 350 n.
heater 383 n.
gharry
cab 274 n.
ghastly
colourless 426 adj.
not nice 645 adj.
distressing 827 adj.
unsightly 842 adj.
frightening 854 adj.
ghat
gap 201 n.
opening 263 n.
shelter 662 n.
ghazal
verse form 593 n.
Ghazi
militarist 722 n.
zealot 979 n.
ghee, ghi
cookery 301 n.
fat 357 n.
ghetto
exclusion 57 n.
housing 192 n.
seclusion 883 n.
ghost
insubstantial thing 4 n.
immateriality 320 n.
the dead 361 n.
visual fallacy 440 n.
fantasy 513 n.
ghost 970 n.
ghost-hunting
spiritualism 984 n.
ghostly
insubstantial 4 adj.
immaterial 320 adj.
shadowy 419 adj.
spooky 970 adj.
ghost of a chance
possibility 469 n.
ghost writer
substitute 150 n.
author 589 n.
ghoul
monster 938 n.
demon 970 n.
ghoulish
inquisitive 453 adj.
frightening 854 adj.
cruel 898 adj.
spooky 970 adj.
GI
soldier 722 n.
giant
enormous 32 adj.
giant 195 n.
tall creature 209 n.
demon 970 n.
giaour
heathen 974 n.
gibber
mean nothing 515 vb.
haunt 970 vb.
gibberish
absurdity 497 n.
lack of meaning 515 n.
unintelligibility 517 n.
slang 560 n.
gibbet
hanger 217 n.
killer 362 n.
means of execution 964 n.
gibbous
rotund 252 adj.
convex 253 adj.
gibe, jibe
satirize 851 vb.
indignity 921 n.
despise 922 vb.
giddiness
weakness 163 n.
folly 499 n.
giddy
changeful 152 adj.
light-minded 456 adj.
crazy 503 adj.
irresolute 601 adj.
capricious 604 adj.
unskilful 695 adj.
rash 857 adj.
tipsy 949 adj.
gift
extra 40 n.
ability 160 n.
tendency 179 n.
incentive 612 n.
benefit 615 n.
aptitude 694 n.
subvention 703 n.
offer 759 n.
acquisition 771 n.
gift 781 n.
no charge 812 n.
gifted
intelligent 498 adj.
gifted 694 adj.
gift from the gods
lack of expectation 508 n.
giftless
parsimonious 816 adj.
gift of the gab
eloquence 579 n.
loquacity 581 n.
gig
carriage 274 n.
boat 275 n.
music 412 n.
gigantic
enormous 32 adj.
stalwart 162 adj.
huge 195 adj.
tall 209 adj.
fairylike 970 adj.
giggle
laugh 835 vb.
giggles, the
laughter 835 n.
gigolo
toady 879 n.
lover 887 n.
Gilbertian
funny 849 adj.
gild
coat 226 vb.
gild 433 vb.
decorate 844 vb.
— the lily
be superfluous 637 vb.
— the pill
deceive 542 vb.
tempt 612 vb.
please 826 vb.
flatter 925 vb.
gilded youth
beau monde 848 n.
gilding
bookbinding 589 n.
ornamental art 844 n.
Giles
farmer 370·n.
gilet
jacket 228 n.
gill
valley 255 n.
stream 350 n.
metrology 465 n.
gillie
animal husbandry 369 n.
retainer 742 n.
gills
laterality 239 n.
respiration 352 n.
gilt
female animal 373 n.
yellow 433 adj.
ornamentation 844 n.
ornamented 844 adj.
gilt-edged
valuable 644 adj.
secured 767 adj.
gilt on the gingerbread
superfluity 637 n.
gimcrack
flimsy 163 adj.
brittle 330 adj.
bauble 639 n.
trivial 639 adj.
unsafe 661 adj.
gimlet
sharp point 256 n.
perforator 263 n.
gimlet-eyed
seeing 438 adj.
gimmick
trickery 542 n.
contrivance 623 n.
skill 694 n.
gimp
trimming 844 n.
gin
alcoholic drink 301 n.
trap 542 n.
ginger
vigorousness 174 n.
condiment 389 n.
make appetizing 390 vb.
orange 432 adj.
excitant 821 n.
animate 821 vb.
ginger beer
soft drink 301 n.
gingerbread
pastries 301 n.
vulgar 847 adj.
ginger group
motivator 612 n.
ginger-haired
red 431 adj.
gingerly
moderately 177 adv.
slowly 278 adv.
carefully 457 adv.
cautiously 858 adv.
gingery
pungent 388 adj.
gingham
textile 222 n.
ginseng
tonic 658 n.
gin-sodden
drunken 949 adj.
Gioconda smile
secret 530 n.
gippy tummy
digestive disorders 651 n.
gipsy, gypsy
nonconformist 84 n.
wanderer 268 n.
diviner 511 n.
giraffe
tall creature 209 n.
mammal 365 n.
girandole
rotator 315 n.
lamp 420 n.

gird
tie 45 vb.
dispraise 924 vb.
— oneself
start out 296 vb.
prepare oneself 669 vb.
girder
bond 47 n.
beam 218 n.
girdle
girdle 47 n.
cauldron 194 n.
compressor 198 n.
belt 228 n.
underwear 228 n.
surround 230 vb.
loop 250 n.
go round 250 vb.
girl
youngster 132 n.
person 371 n.
woman 373 n.
girl Friday
worker 686 n.
aider 703 n.
girlfriend
friend 880 n.
loved one 887 n.
Girl Guides
society 708 n.
girlhood
youth 130 n.
girlie magazine
impurity 951 n.
girlish
young 130 adj.
infantine 132 adj.
female 373 adj.
immature 670 adj.
giro
treasurer 798 n.
girth
greatness 32 n.
girdle 47 n.
size 195 n.
gist
substance 3 n.
essential part 5 n.
chief part 52 n.
topic 452 n.
meaning 514 n.
compendium 592 n.
chief thing 638 n.
givable, giveable
not retained 779 adj.
transferred 780 adj.
given 781 adj.
give
be curved 248 vb.
soften 327 vb.
elasticity 328 n.
provide 633 vb.
offer 759 vb.
give 781 vb.
apportion 783 vb.
expend 806 vb.
be liberal 813 vb.
reward 962 vb.
— a big hand
applaud 923 vb.
— a dog a bad name
shame 867 vb.
defame 926 vb.
— a false impression
mislead 495 vb.
deceive 542 vb.
— a free hand
give scope 744 vb.
— a good account of oneself
succeed 727 vb.
— a lead
motivate 612 vb.
be in fashion 848 vb.
— as good as one gets
interchange 151 vb.
retaliate 714 vb.
— away
disclose 526 vb.
assign 780 vb.
cheapen 812 vb.
marry 894 vb.
— a wide berth
be distant 199 vb.
avoid 620 vb.
be safe 660 vb.
— back
revert 148 vb.
restore 656 vb.
restitute 787 vb.
— birth (to)
reproduce itself 167 vb.
be fruitful 171 vb.
vitalize 360 vb.
— every man his due
grant claims 915 vb.
— ground
regress 286 vb.
— grounds for
justify 927 vb.
— in
relinquish 621 vb.
submit 721 vb.
— it a miss
avoid 620 vb.
not act 677 vb.
— it a try
attempt 671 vb.
— notice
predict 511 vb.
communicate 524 vb.
warn 664 vb.
— occasion for
cause 156 vb.
— off
emit 300 vb.
— one a piece of one's mind
reprobate 924 vb.
— one a turn
surprise 508 vb.
frighten 854 vb.
— one cause
justify 927 vb.
— one credit for
believe 485 vb.
— one his/her due
keep faith 768 vb.
give 781 vb.
— one his/her head
accelerate 277 vb.
give scope 744 vb.
— one joy
congratulate 886 vb.
— one pause
dissuade 613 vb.
— one's blessing
permit 756 vb.
be benevolent 897 vb.
approve 923 vb.
— oneself airs
be affected 850 vb.
be proud 871 vb.
be vain 873 vb.
— oneself away
blunder 495 vb.
disclose 526 vb.
— oneself up
submit 721 vb.
— oneself up to
be intemperate 943 vb.
— one's mind to
be attentive 455 vb.
— one's word
testify 466 vb.
promise 764 vb.
— one the brush-off
repel 292 vb.
reject 607 vb.
make unwelcome 883 vb.
— one the facts
inform 524 vb.
— one the giggles
be ridiculous 849 vb.
— one the pip
displease 827 vb.
enrage 891 vb.
— one the slip
decamp 296 vb.
avoid 620 vb.
elude 667 vb.
— one the works
torment 827 vb.
torture 963 vb.
— one what for
reprobate 924 vb.
punish 963 vb.
— out
communicate 524 vb.
publish 528 vb.
— over
cease 145 vb.
— pleasure
enjoy 376 vb.
please 826 vb.
— points to
equalize 28 vb.
— quarter
be lenient 736 vb.
show mercy 905 vb.
— rise to
conduce 156 vb.
— satisfaction
fight 716 vb.
atone 941 vb.
— the devil his due
be just 913 vb.
vindicate 927 vb.
— the glad eye
gaze 438 vb.
court 889 vb.
— the go-ahead
permit 756 vb.
— the go-by
disregard 458 vb.
avoid 620 vb.
not observe 769 vb.
— the lie to
confute 479 vb.
negate 533 vb.
— the game away
divulge 526 vb.
— tongue
be loud 400 vb.
ululate 409 vb.
voice 577 vb.
speak 579 vb.
— to the poor
be pious 979 vb.
— to the world
publish 528 vb.
— to understand
inform 524 vb.
— up
cease 145 vb.
not understand 517 vb.
be irresolute 601 vb.
reject 607 vb.
disaccustom 611 vb.
relinquish 621 vb.
stop using 674 vb.
submit 721 vb.
not complete 726 vb.
resign 753 vb.
not retain 779 vb.
give 781 vb.
be dejected 834 vb.
despair 853 vb.
be temperate 942 vb.
— up the ghost
die 361 vb.
— vent to
emit 300 vb.
divulge 526 vb.
liberate 746 vb.
— way
be weak 163 vb.
regress 286 vb.
descend 309 vb.
be brittle 330 vb.
be irresolute 601 vb.
consent 758 vb.
give-and-take
interchange 151 n.
argument 475 n.

cooperation 706 n.
fight 716 n.
compromise 770 n.
giveaway
disclosure 526 n.
given
existing 1 adj.
circumstantial 8 adj.
prior 119 adj.
supposed 512 adj.
given 781 adj.
uncharged 812 adj.
given away
given 781 adj.
uncharged 812 adj.
given the sack
not retained 779 adj.
given to
habituated 610 adj.
given up
dying 361 adj.
giver
provider 633 n.
giver 781 n.
benefactor 903 n.
giving way
submission 721 n.
gizzard
maw 194 n.
glabrous
smooth 258 adj.
glacé
cooled 382 adj.
sweet 392 adj.
glacial
cold 380 adj.
glaciation
condensation 324 n.
hardening 326 n.
ice 380 n.
refrigeration 382 n.
glacier
ice 380 n.
glacis
incline 220 n.
fortification 713 n.
glad
willing 597 adj.
pleased 824 adj.
gladden
please 826 vb.
cheer 833 vb.
glade
open space 263 n.
wood 366 n.
path 624 n.
glad eye
look 438 n.
wooing 889 n.
glad hand
sociability 882 n.
gladiator
contender 716 n.
combatant 722 n.
gladly
willingly 597 adv.
cheerfully 833 adv.
gladness
joy 824 n.
glad rags
clothing 228 n.
finery 844 n.
Gladstone bag
bag 194 n.
glair
viscidity 354 n.
glamorize, glamorise
beautify 841 vb.
decorate 844 vb.
glamorous, glamourous
personable 841 adj.
glamour
beauty 841 n.
prestige 866 n.
glamour girl/boy
a beauty 841 n.
glance
deviate 282 vb.
propel 287 vb.
touch 378 vb.
shine 417 vb.
look 438 n.
gesture 547 n.
— at
gaze 438 vb.
be attentive 455 vb.
glancing
lateral 239 adj.
gland
insides 224 n.
glandular fever
infection 651 n.
glare
light 417 n.
shine 417 vb.
gaze 438 vb.
blur 440 vb.
be angry 891 vb.
glaring
flagrant 32 adj.
luminous 417 adj.
florid 425 adj.
obvious 443 adj.
manifest 522 adj.
glass
cup 194 n.
covering 226 n.
smoothness 258 n.
draught 301 n.
brittleness 330 n.
weather 340 n.
transparency 422 n.
mirror 442 n.
optical device 442 n.
materials 631 n.
finery 844 n.
glassblower
artisan 686 n.
glasses
eyeglass 442 n.
glass eye
blindness 439 n.
glass front
window 263 n.
glasshouse
arbour 194 n.
brittleness 330 n.
gaol 748 n.
glassware
receptacle 194 n.
glassy
smooth 258 adj.adj.
tranquil 266 adj.
hard 326 adj.
undimmed 417 adj.
dim 419 adj.
transparent 422 adj.
colourless 426 adj.
glaucoma
dim sight 440 n.
tropical disease 651 n.
glaucous
green 434 adj.
glaze
facing 226 n.
coat 226 vb.
smoothness 258 n.
viscidity 354 n.
screen 421 vb.
glazed ware
pottery 381 n.
gleam
small quantity 33 n.
flash 417 n.
shine 417 vb.
glean
cultivate 370 vb.
abstract 592 vb.
select 605 vb.
store 632 vb.
acquire 771 vb.
— information
learn 536 vb.
gleaner
accumulator 74 n.
gleanings
anthology 592 n.
choice 605 n.
earnings 771 n.
glebe
soil 344 n.
benefice 985 n.
glee
vocal music 412 n.
enjoyment 824 n.
merriment 833 n.
glee club
choir 413 n.
gleeful
jubilant 833 adj.
glen
valley 255 n.
glengarry
headgear 228 n.
glib
deceiving 542 adj.
loquacious 581 adj.
glib tongue
slyboots 698 n.
glide
elapse 111 vb.
go smoothly 258 vb.
be in motion 265 vb.
fly 271 vb.
be light 323 vb.
flow 350 vb.
speech sound 398 n.
be stealthy 525 vb.
— along
move slowly 278 vb.
glider
aeronaut 271 n.
aircraft 276 n.
gliding
aeronautics 271 n.
sport 837 n.
glimmer
shine 417 vb.
glimmer 419 n.
be dim 419 vb.
hint 524 n.
glimmering
sciolism 491 n.
glimpse
look 438 n.
see 438 vb.
knowledge 490 n.
hint 524 n.
glint
flash 417 n.
shine 417 vb.
look 438 n.
glissade
descent 309 n.
ballet 594 n.
glissando
adagio 412 adv.
glisten
shine 417 vb.
glitter
flash 417 n.
shine 417 vb.
bad taste 847 n.
ostentation 875 n.
glittering
rich 800 adj.
ornamented 844 adj.
showy 875 adj.
glittering prizes
trophy 729 n.
gloaming
evening 129 n.
half-light 419 n.
gloat
be pleased 824 vb.
rejoice 835 vb.
boast 877 vb.
be malevolent 898 vb.
avenge 910 vb.
— over
enjoy 376 vb.
gaze 438 vb.
global
inclusive 78 adj.
universal 79 adj.
spacious 183 adj.
telluric 321 adj.
sharing 775 adj.
global commons
joint possession 775 n.
globalize, globalise
generalize 79 vb.

global village
region 184 n.
globe
sphere 252 n.
world 321 n.
map 551 n.
globe-trotter
traveller 268 n.
spectator 441 n.
inquisitive person 453 n.
globular
rotund 252 adj.
globule
sphere 252 n.
globulin
organism 358 n.
glockenspiel
gong 414 n.
gloom
darkness 418 n.
dimness 419 n.
adversity 731 n.
sorrow 825 n.
dejection 834 n.
be sullen 893 vb.
gloomy
black 428 adj.
Gloria
praise 923 n.
hymn 981 n.
glorified
ostentatious 875 adj.
angelic 968 adj.
paradisiac 971 adj.
glorify
augment 36 vb.
make important 638 vb.
be auspicious 730 vb.
dignify 866 vb.
honour 866 vb.
praise 923 vb.
worship 981 vb.
gloriole
light 417 n.
glorious
great 32 adj.
excellent 644 adj.
super 644 adj.
palmy 730 adj.
splendid 841 adj.
noteworthy 866 adj.
renowned 866 adj.
gloriously drunk
drunk 949 adj.
glory
light 417 n.
manifestation 522 n.
success 727 n.
prosperity 730 n.
famousness 866 n.
prestige 866 n.
divine attribute 965 n.
glory hole
chamber 194 n.
glory in
feel pride 871 vb.
boast 877 vb.
gloss
smoothness 258 n.
light 417 n.
commentary 520 n.
interpret 520 vb.
sham 542 n.
untruth 543 n.
pretext 614 n.
beauty 841 n.
ostentation 875 n.
extenuate 927 vb.
— over
neglect 458 vb.
sophisticate 477 vb.
conceal 525 vb.
cant 541 vb.
glossarist
interpreter 520 n.
glossary
word list 87 n.
commentary 520 n.
dictionary 559 n.
glossolalia
eloquence 579 n.
piety 979 n.
glossy
luminous 417 adj.
personable 841 adj.
splendid 841 adj.
glossy magazine
journal 528 n.
glottal stop
speech sound 398 n.
pronunciation 577 n.
glove
glove 228 n.
glow
heat 379 n.
be hot 379 vb.
glow 417 n.
shine 417 vb.
hue 425 n.
redness 431 n.
vigour 571 n.
warm feeling 818 n.
show feeling 818 vb.
be beautiful 841 vb.
glower
gaze 438 vb.
be angry 891 vb.
be sullen 893 vb.
glowing
red 431 adj.
(See **glow** *)*
glowing terms
praise 923 n.
glow-worm
glimmer 419 n.
glow-worm 420 n.
gloze over
mislead 495 vb.
cant 541 vb.
glucose
food content 301 n.
sweet thing 392 n.
glue
adhesive 47 n.
agglutinate 48 vb.
glued
firm 45 adj.
glue-sniffing
drug-taking 949 n.
gluey
cohesive 48 adj.
viscid 354 adj.
glum
melancholic 834 adj.
glut
productiveness 171 n.
superfluity 637 n.
cheapness 812 n.
satiety 863 n.
glutinous
viscid 354 adj.
glut oneself
gluttonize 947 vb.
glutted
sated 863 adj.
glutton
desirer 859 n.
sensualist 944 n.
glutton 947 n.
glutton for, be a
be unsatisfied 636 vb.
glutton for work
busy person 678 n.
gluttonous
greedy 859 adj.
gluttony
gastronomy 301 n.
vice 934 n.
intemperance 943 n.
sensualism 944 n.
gluttony 947 n.
glycerine
lubricant 334 n.
fat 357 n.
glyph
furrow 262 n.
sculpture 554 n.
glyptic
formative 243 adj.
glyptic 554 adj.
glyptography
engraving 555 n.
G-man
detective 459 n.
G.M.T.
clock time 117 n.
gnarled
amorphous 244 adj.
distorted 246 adj.
rough 259 adj.
gnash one's teeth
be impotent 161 vb.
gesticulate 547 vb.
regret 830 vb.
be angry 891 vb.
gnat
small animal 33 n.
insect 365 n.
gnaw
abate 37 vb.
rend 46 vb.
chew 301 vb.
rub 333 vb.
give pain 377 vb.
impair 655 vb.
hurt 827 vb.
enrage 891 vb.
gnome
elf 970 n.
gnomic
aphoristic 496 adj.
gnomon
timekeeper 117 n.
Gnostic
religionist 973 n.
heretic 977 n.
sectarian 978 n.
Gnosticism
philosophy 449 n.
deism 973 n.
heresy 977 n.
GNP
product 164 n.
gnu
mammal 365 n.
go
separate 46 vb.
operate 173 vb.
vigorousness 174 n.
be in motion 265 vb.
travel 267 vb.
walk 267 vb.
recede 290 vb.
disappear 446 vb.
function 622 vb.
restlessness 678 n.
courage 855 n.
— about
undertake 672 vb.
— across
pass 305 vb.
— adrift
stray 282 vb.
— after
aim at 617 vb.
— against
counteract 182 vb.
oppose 704 vb.
— against the grain
be difficult 700 vb.
displease 827 vb.
cause dislike 861 vb.
— all out
move fast 277 vb.
attempt 671 vb.
exert oneself 682 vb.
— all out for
aim at 617 vb.
— along with
concur 181 vb.
assent 488 vb.
— at it hammer and tongs
bicker 709 vb.
— away
separate 46 vb.
go away 190 vb.

depart 296 vb.
— back
repeat oneself 106 vb.
be old 127 vb.
revert 148 vb.
turn round 282 vb.
turn back 286 vb.
— back on
negate 533 vb.
recant 603 vb.
not observe 769 vb.
be dishonest 930 vb.
— back to the beginning
begin 68 vb.
revert 148 vb.
— bad
be unclean 649 vb.
deteriorate 655 vb.
— before
be before 119 vb.
precede 283 vb.
— begging
be superfluous 637 vb.
be useless 641 vb.
offer oneself 759 vb.
— beyond
be superior 34 vb.
overstep 306 vb.
— by
elapse 111 vb.
— by instinct
not think 450 vb.
intuit 476 vb.
— by road
ride 267 vb.
— by sea
voyage 269 vb.
— by Shanks's pony
walk 267 vb.
— by the board
be impotent 161 vb.
miscarry 728 vb.
— by the book
be cautious 858 vb.
— by train
ride 267 vb.
— cap in hand to
request 761 vb.
— down
be destroyed 165 vb.
descend 309 vb.
founder 313 vb.
— downhill
deteriorate 655 vb.
be defeated 728 vb.
have trouble 731 vb.
— down the drain
waste 634 vb.
be lost 772 vb.
— down well
be believed 485 vb.
content 828 vb.
— down with
be ill 651 vb.
— Dutch
participate 775 vb.
be sociable 882 vb.
— easy (on)
be moderate 177 vb.
be lenient 736 vb.
show mercy 905 vb.
— far
prosper 730 vb.
— farther and fare worse
deteriorate 655 vb.
— for
aim at 617 vb.
attack 712 vb.
cost 809 vb.
reprobate 924 vb.
— from bad to worse
deteriorate 655 vb.
aggravate 832 vb.
— halfway
average out 30 vb.
be halfway 625 vb.
consent 758 vb.
compromise 770 vb.
— halves
participate 775 vb.
— hand in hand with
accompany 89 vb.
concur 181 vb.
— hard with
be difficult 700 vb.
have trouble 731 vb.
— home
turn back 286 vb.
depart 296 vb.
— in
be included 78 vb.
enter 297 vb.
— in for
be resolute 599 vb.
choose 605 vb.
be wont 610 vb.
aim at 617 vb.
busy oneself 622 vb.
undertake 672 vb.
— in front
precede 283 vb.
— in one ear and out of the other
escape notice 456 vb.
forget 506 vb.
— into
enquire 459 vb.
dissertate 591 vb.
— it alone
be free 744 vb.
be unsociable 883 vb.
— off
happen 154 vb.
be violent 176 vb.
be loud 400 vb.
deteriorate 655 vb.
— off at half-cock
be unprepared 670 vb.
— off one's rocker
be foolish 499 vb.
go mad 503 vb.
— off the deep end
be great 32 vb.
— on
last 113 vb.
stay 144 vb.
go on 146 vb.
happen 154 vb.
be in motion 265 vb.
progress 285 vb.
persevere 600 vb.
be active 678 vb.
— on a fool's errand
be foolish 499 vb.
act foolishly 695 vb.
— on and on
repeat oneself 106 vb.
be tedious 838 vb.
— one better
be superior 34 vb.
outdo 306 vb.
be cunning 698 vb.
— one's own way
diverge 294 vb.
dissent 489 vb.
will 595 vb.
be obstinate 602 vb.
be free 744 vb.
— one's separate ways
quarrel 709 vb.
divorce 896 vb.
— on record
proclaim 528 vb.
— on the rampage
be violent 176 vb.
— on the rocks
be destroyed 165 vb.
fail 728 vb.
— on the warpath
wage war 718 vb.
be angry 891 vb.
— on the water-waggon
be sober 948 vb.
— on tiptoe
be stealthy 525 vb.
— out
recede 290 vb.
emerge 298 vb.
extinguish 382 vb.
be sociable 882 vb.
— out of business
cease 145 vb.
— out of one's mind
go mad 503 vb.
go out of one's way (to)
deviate 282 vb.
be willing 597 vb.
— out on a limb
be rash 857 vb.
— over
number 86 vb.
repeat 106 vb.
be inverted 221 vb.
search 459 vb.
know 490 vb.
study 536 vb.
be irresolute 601 vb.
relinquish 621 vb.
become pious 979 vb.
— over big
succeed 727 vb.
— over the top
superabound 637 vb.
charge 712 vb.
be courageous 855 vb.
— past
pass 305 vb.
— places
travel 267 vb.
— right through one
shrill 407 vb.
— round
go round 250 vb.
circle 314 vb.
circuit 626 vb.
— round in circles
be irresolute 601 vb.
— shares
be equal 28 vb.
participate 775 vb.
be sociable 882 vb.
— slow
move slowly 278 vb.
be unwilling 598 vb.
be cautious 858 vb.
— steady
court 889 vb.
— straight
be straight 249 vb.
steer for 281 vb.
be midstream 625 vb.
get better 654 vb.
be honourable 929 vb.
— the rounds
traverse 267 vb.
be published 528 vb.
change hands 780 vb.
— the whole hog
be resolute 599 vb.
carry out 725 vb.
— the wrong way about it
be unskilful 695 vb.
— through
meet with 154 vb.
infiltrate 297 vb.
pass 305 vb.
search 459 vb.
deal with 688 vb.
suffer 825 vb.
— through it
feel pain 377 vb.
have trouble 731 vb.
suffer 825 vb.
— through the motions
dissemble 541 vb.
be affected 850 vb.
— to any lengths
be resolute 599 vb.

exert oneself 682 vb.
be intemperate 943 vb.
— **to bed**
sleep 679 vb.
repose 683 vb.
— **to church/chapel**
be pious 979 vb.
offer worship 981 vb.
— **to earth**
be unseen 444 vb.
be stealthy 525 vb.
— **to extremes**
exaggerate 546 vb.
be malevolent 898 vb.
— **together**
accompany 89 vb.
— **to hell**
be destroyed 165 vb.
— **to it**
begin 68 vb.
be resolute 599 vb.
— **to law**
quarrel 709 vb.
litigate 959 vb.
— **too far**
overstep 306 vb.
exaggerate 546 vb.
do wrong 914 vb.
— **to one's head**
invigorate 174 vb.
make mad 503 vb.
make conceited 873 vb.
inebriate 949 vb.
— **to pieces**
decompose 51 vb.
be destroyed 165 vb.
deteriorate 655 vb.
— **to school**
learn 536 vb.
— **to sea**
go to sea 269 vb.
— **to the bad**
deteriorate 655 vb.
be wicked 934 vb.
— **to the country**
vote 605 vb.
— **to the wall**
be destroyed 165 vb.
perish 361 vb.
be defeated 728 vb.
— **under**
be destroyed 165 vb.
— **underground**
descend 309 vb.
be stealthy 525 vb.
— **up**
ascend 308 vb.
be dear 811 vb.
— **up in smoke**
miscarry 728 vb.
— **west**
be destroyed 165 vb.
die 361 vb.
— **with**
accord 24 vb.
accompany 89 vb.
concur 181 vb.
belong 773 vb.
— **without**
refuse 760 vb.
— **without saying**
be plain 522 vb.
— **with the stream**
acquiesce 488 vb.
— **wrong**
err 495 vb.
miscarry 728 vb.
be wrong 914 vb.
goad
stimulant 174 n.
sharp point 256 n.
impel 279 vb.
incentive 612 n.
animate 821 vb.
enrage 891 vb.
go-ahead
vigorous 174 adj.
assent 488 n.
enterprising 672 adj.
permit 756 n.
goal
extremity 69 n.
focus 76 n.
stopping place 145 n.
limit 236 n.
resting place 266 n.
direction 281 n.
goal 295 n.
objective 617 n.
desired object 859 n.
goalkeeper
player 837 n.
goal-oriented
induced 612 adj.
go-as-you-please
free 744 adj.
goat
jumper 312 n.
cattle 365 n.
goatee
hair 259 n.
goatherd
herdsman 369 n.
goatish
animal 365 adj.
lecherous 951 adj.
goat-keeping
animal husbandry 369 n.
gob
orifice 263 n.
eruct 300 vb.
naval man 722 n.
gobbet
small thing 33 n.
part 53 n.
mouthful 301 n.
gobble
absorb 299 vb.
ululate 409 vb.
gluttonize 947 vb.
— **up**
consume 165 vb.
waste 634 vb.
gluttonize 947 vb.
gobbledygook
lack of meaning 515 n.
slang 560 n.
gobbler
table bird 365 n.
gobe-mouche
dupe 544 n.
go-between
intermediary 231 n.
messenger 529 n.
mediator 720 n.
matchmaker 894 n.
goblet
cup 194 n.
goblin
intimidation 854 n.
elf 970 n.
go-cart
pushcart 274 n.
god
deity 966 n.
idol 982 n.
God
cause 156 n.
the Deity 965 n.
godchild
family 11 n.
goddess
woman 373 n.
loved one 887 n.
deity 966 n.
God-fearing
pious 979 adj.
God forbid!
489 int.
godforsaken
empty 190 adj.
distant 199 adj.
secluded 883 adj.
wicked 934 adj.
godhead
divineness 965 n.
godless
irreligious 974 adj.
impious 980 adj.
godlike
beautiful 841 adj.
godlike 965 adj.
godliness
sanctity 979 n.
godly
pious 979 adj.
god/goddess of the underworld
mythic deity 966 n.
Chthonian deity 967 n.
god/goddess of love
love god 887 n.
mythic deity 966 n.
godown
storage 632 n.
godparent
parentage 169 n.
gods
onlookers 441 n.
theatre 594 n.
gods, the
deity 966 n.
God's Acre
cemetery 364 n.
holy place 990 n.
gods and goddesses of Greece and Rome
classical deities 967 n.
God save!
981 int.
godsend
benefit 615 n.
prosperity 730 n.
God's gift to women
vain person 873 n.
godship
divineness 965 n.
God's house
church 990 n.
God's own
chosen 605 adj.
excellent 644 adj.
God's own country
home 192 n.
Godspeed
success 727 n.
God's ways
divineness 965 n.
theocracy 965 n.
God's will
fate 596 n.
God's word
revelation 975 n.
God willing
possibly 469 adv.
goer
thoroughbred 273 n.
goffer
groove 262 vb.
go-getter
planner 623 n.
busy person 678 n.
egotist 932 n.
go-getting
vigorous 174 adj.
progressive 285 adj.
goggle
gaze 438 vb.
not expect 508 vb.
wonder 864 vb.
goggle-eyed
projecting 254 adj.
dim-sighted 440 adj.
goggler
spectator 441 n.
goggles
eyeglass 442 n.
shelter 662 n.
gogo dancer
entertainer 594 n.
dance 837 n.
going
motion 265 n.
relinquishment 621 n.
way 624 n.
active 678 adj.

going away
departure 296 n.
going back
retrospective 125 adj.
reversion 148 n.
return 286 n.
going begging
superfluous 637 adj.
free 744 adj.
unpossessed 774 adj.
going on
unfinished 55 adj.
going places
successful 727 adj.
going rate
price 809 n.
going too far
exorbitant 32 adj.
vulgar 847 adj.
going up
ascent 308 n.
goitre
swelling 253 n.
gold
orange 432 n.
yellowness 433 n.
incentive 612 n.
exceller 644 n.
bullion 797 n.
money 797 n.
gold-digger
enquirer 459 n.
lover 887 n.
egotist 932 n.
gold dust, like
infrequent 140 adj.
of price 811 adj.
golden
yellow 433 adj.
valuable 644 adj.
palmy 730 adj.
promising 852 adj.
Golden Age
era 110 n.
literature 557 n.
palmy days 730 n.
happiness 824 n.
innocence 935 n.
golden calf
idol 982 n.
golden girl/boy
favourite 890 n.
golden handshake
extra 40 n.
resignation 753 n.
reward 962 n.
golden mean
average 30 n.
moderation 177 n.
middle way 625 n.
golden rule
maxim 496 n.
precept 693 n.
philanthropy 901 n.
golden touch
prosperity 730 n.
wealth 800 n.
golden wedding
anniversary 141 n.
special day 876 n.
goldfish
animal 365 n.
gold leaf
ornamental art 844 n.
gold-medallist
proficient person 696 n.
goldmine
store 632 n.
wealth 800 n.
goldsmith
artisan 686 n.
gold standard
finance 797 n.
golf
ball game 837 n.
golf course
pleasure ground 837 n.
Goliath
athlete 162 n.
giant 195 n.
gondola
rowing boat 275 n.
airship 276 n.
gondolier
boatman 270 n.
gone
past 125 adj.
absent 190 adj.
dead 361 adj.
disappearing 446 adj.
forgotten 506 adj.
lost 772 adj.
dead drunk 949 adj.
gone for a burton
dead 361 adj.
gone on
enamoured 887 adj.
goner
corpse 363 n.
gong
timekeeper 117 n.
megaphone 400 n.
resound 404 vb.
gong 414 n.
badge 547 n.
signal 547 n.
decoration 729 n.
gongorism
ornament 574 n.
goniometer
angular measure 247 n.
meter 465 n.
gonorrhoea
venereal disease 651 n.
goo
viscidity 354 n.
good
savoury 390 adj.
elegant 575 adj.
good 615 n.adj.
utility 640 n.
useful 640 adj.
excellent 644 adj.
skilful 694 adj.
prosperity 730 n.
obedient 739 adj.
pleasurable 826 adj.
amiable 884 adj.
benevolent 897 adj.
right 913 adj.
honourable 929 adj.
virtuous 933 adj.
pure 950 adj.
pious 979 adj.
good at
skilful 694 adj.
good behaviour
conduct 688 n.
courtesy 884 n.
virtue 933 n.
good books
approbation 923 n.
good breeding
etiquette 848 n.
courtesy 884 n.
goodbye!
296 int.
good cause
philanthropy 901 n.
good chance
fair chance 159 n.
possibility 469 n.
probability 471 n.
good chap
favourite 890 n.
good character
repute 866 n.
probity 929 n.
good cheer
food 301 n.
enjoyment 824 n.
merriment 833 n.
amusement 837 n.
sociability 882 n.
good citizen
person of repute 866 n.
good citizenship
patriotism 901 n.
good company
sociability 882 n.
sociable person 882 n.
good condition
health 650 n.
good conscience
virtue 933 n.
good deal
great quantity 32 n.
good deed
kind act 897 n.
good ear
hearing 415 n.
good enough to eat
beautiful 841 adj.
good example
relevance 9 n.
analogue 18 n.
fitness 24 n.
good excuse
vindication 927 n.
good fairy
fairy 970 n.
good faith
loyalty 739 n.
observance 768 n.
probity 929 n.
good fellowship
sociability 882 n.
good few, a
many 104 adj.
good fit
adaptation 24 n.
good for
useful 640 adj.
salubrious 652 adj.
good form
practice 610 n.
etiquette 848 n.
formality 875 n.
good-for-nothing
powerless 161 adj.
profitless 641 adj.
idler 679 n.
vicious 934 adj.
bad person 938 n.
good fortune
chance 159 n.
good 615 n.
success 727 n.
prosperity 730 n.
happiness 824 n.
Good Friday
fast 946 n.
holy day 988 n.
good graces
approbation 923 n.
good grounds
vindication 927 n.
good head for
aptitude 694 n.
good health
health 650 n.
good housekeeping
economy 814 n.
good humour
cheerfulness 833 n.
courtesy 884 n.
good-humoured
benevolent 897 adj.
good influence
improvement 654 n.
good in parts
imperfect 647 adj.
good law
justice 913 n.
legality 953 n.
good likeness
similarity 18 n.
good living
gastronomy 301 n.
gluttony 947 n.
good looks
beauty 841 n.
good luck
chance 159 n.
good 615 n.
nondesign 618 n.
prosperity 730 n.

goodly
great 32 adj.
good 615 adj.
beautiful 841 adj.
good manners
conduct 688 n.
etiquette 848 n.
sociability 882 n.
courtesy 884 n.

good name
repute 866 n.

good-natured
irresolute 601 adj.
benevolent 897 adj.
good neighbour
aider 703 n.
friend 880 n.
sociable person 882 n.
kind person 897 n.
benefactor 903 n.
good person 937 n.
goodness
utility 640 n.
goodness 644 n.
health 650 n.
obedience 739 n.
good taste 846 n.
benevolence 897 n.
probity 929 n.
virtue 933 n.
divine attribute 965 n.
sanctity 979 n.
good offices
aid 703 n.
pacification 719 n.
mediation 720 n.
kind act 897 n.
good of one
lifelike 18 adj.
benevolent 897 adj.
good old days
past time 125 n.
good one
witticism 839 n.
good opinion
repute 866 n.
approbation 923 n.
good opinion of oneself
vanity 873 n.
good person
exceller 644 n.
benefactor 903 n.
honourable person 929 n.
good person 937 n.
pietist 979 n.
good points
goodness 644 n.
good policy
fitness 24 n.
occasion 137 n.
sagacity 498 n.
good 615 n.
utility 640 n.
good policy 642 n.
good reason
probability 471 n.
good reception
hearing 415 n.
good reputation
repute 866 n.
good resolution
tergiversation 603 n.
good riddance
rubbish 641 n.
escape 667 n.
liberation 746 n.
relief 831 n.
hateful object 888 n.
goods
product 164 n.
thing transferred 272 n.
property 777 n.
merchandise 795 n.
goods, the
information 524 n.
exceller 644 n.
good Samaritan
aider 703 n.
kind person 897 n.
benefactor 903 n.
good person 937 n.
goods and chattels
property 777 n.
good sense
intelligence 498 n.
Good Shepherd, the
God the Son 965 n.
good shot
hunter 619 n.
success 727 n.
good sort
good person 937 n.
good sport
merriment 833 n.
favourite 890 n.
honourable person 929 n.
goods train
carrier 273 n.
train 274 n.
goods yard
railway 624 n.
good taste
discrimination 463 n.
elegance 575 n.
good taste 846 n.
etiquette 848 n.
purity 950 n.
good-tempered
inexcitable 823 adj.
amiable 884 adj.
good time
festivity 837 n.
good time coming
future state 124 n.
fantasy 513 n.
good-time girl
reveller 837 n.
good to eat
savoury 390 adj.
good turn
benefit 615 n.
kind act 897 n.
good value
cheapness 812 n.
goodwill
willingness 597 n.
concord 710 n.
friendliness 880 n.
benevolence 897 n.
good wishes
congratulation 886 n.
good works
philanthropy 901 n.
sociology 901 n.
goody-goody
foolish 499 adj.
hypocritical 541 adj.
affecter 850 n.
pietistic 979 adj.
gooey
viscid 354 adj.
retentive 778 adj.
goof
ignoramus 493 n.
mistake 495 n.
ninny 501 n.
goofy
foolish 499 adj.
googly
deviation 282 n.
sleight 542 n.
goose
table bird 365 n.
sibilation 406 n.
ignoramus 493 n.
fool 501 n.
gooseberry
three 93 n.
fruit 301 n.
gooseberry bush
obstetrics 167 n.
gooseflesh/goose pimples
roughness 259 n.
formication 378 n.
coldness 380 n.
nervousness 854 n.
goosestep
gait 265 n.
walk 267 vb.
goose that lays the golden eggs
wealth 800 n.
Gordian knot
ligature 47 n.
complexity 61 n.
difficulty 700 n.
gore
garment 228 n.
pierce 263 vb.
blood 335 n.
redness 431 n.
wound 655 vb.
gorge
be complete 54 vb.
gap 201 n.
valley 255 n.
superabound 637 vb.
sate 863 vb.
gluttonize 947 vb.
gorge-de-pigeon
variegation 437 n.
iridescent 437 adj.
gorgeous
florid 425 adj.
super 644 adj.
splendid 841 adj.
ornamented 844 adj.
showy 875 adj.
Gorgon
rara avis 84 n.
eye 438 n.
eyesore 842 n.
intimidation 854 n.
demon 970 n.
gorilla
mammal 365 n.
monster 938 n.
gormandize, gormandise
eat 301 vb.
gluttonize 947 vb.
gormandizer, gormandiser
glutton 947 n.
(See **gourmand** *)*
gormless
foolish 499 adj.
gorse
plant 366 n.
gory
sanguineous 335 adj.
murderous 362 adj.
bloodstained 431 adj.
gosling
young creature 132 n.
bird 365 n.
gospel
certainty 473 n.
truth 494 n.
news 529 n.
revelation 975 n.
Gospels
scripture 975 n.
gospel truth
truth 494 n.
orthodoxy 976 n.
gossamer
insubstantial 4 adj.
flimsy 163 adj.
filament 208 n.
lightness 323 n.
transparency 422 n.
trifle 639 n.
gossip
insubstantial thing 4 n.
topic 452 n.
inquisitive person 453 n.
informer 524 n.
news reporter 529 n.
rumour 529 n.
fable 543 n.

speak 579 vb.
chatterer 581 n.
be loquacious 581 vb.
chat 584 n.
defame 926 vb.
gossip writer
inquisitive person 453 n.
informant 524 n.
chronicler 549 n.
author 589 n.
Goth
vulgarian 847 n.
low fellow 869 n.
Gotham
city 184 n.
Gothic
olden 127 adj.
architectural 192 adj.
literal 558 adj.
print-type 587 n.
churchlike 990 adj.
Götterdämmerung
finality 69 n.
got up
dressed 228 adj.
bedecked 844 adj.
gouache
art equipment 553 n.
gouge out
make concave 255 vb.
extract 304 vb.
goulash
dish 301 n.
gourd
vessel 194 n.
gourmand
eater 301 n.
sensualist 944 n.
glutton 947 n.
gourmandise
gastronomy 301 n.
gourmet
eater 301 n.
gastronomy 301 n.
people of taste 846 n.
perfectionist 862 n.
sensualist 944 n.
glutton 947 n.
gout
rheumatism 651 n.
gouty
crippled 163 adj.
govern
order 60 vb.
moderate 177 vb.
manage 689 vb.
rule 733 vb.
governance
power 160 n.
influence 178 n.
governance 733 n.
governess
teacher 537 n.
retainer 742 n.
keeper 749 n.
governessy
authoritarian 735 adj.
governing body
director 690 n.
government
management 689 n.
government 733 n.
Government, the
authority 733 n.
master 741 n.
governmental
businesslike 622 adj.
directing 689 adj.
governmental 733 adj.
Government in Exile
malcontent 829 n.
government post
position of authority 733 n.
government servant
official 690 n.
government service
vocation 622 n.
service 745 n.
governor
teacher 537 n.
director 690 n.
leader 690 n.
governor 741 n.
governorship
position of authority 733 n.
gowk
ninny 501 n.
gown
dress 228 n.
robe 228 n.
canonicals 989 n.
GP
doctor 658 n.
GPO
postal communications 531 n.
grab
retain 778 vb.
take 786 vb.
grabber
taker 786 n.
grabble
touch 378 vb.
grace
style 566 n.
ornament 574 vb.
elegance 575 n.
skill 694 n.
permission 756 n.
gift 781 n.
beauty 841 n.
beautify 841 vb.
decorate 844 vb.
good taste 846 n.
mercy 905 n.
thanks 907 n.
forgiveness 909 n.
approbation 923 n.
divine function 965 n.
prayers 981 n.
— the occasion
be present 189 vb.
— with
honour 866 vb.
Grace
a beauty 841 n.
title 870 n.
grace and favour
permission 756 n.
no charge 812 n.
grace and favour house
retreat 192 n.
graceful
elegant 575 adj.
shapely 841 adj.
tasteful 846 adj.
lovable 887 adj.
graceless
inelegant 576 adj.
clumsy 695 adj.
dull 840 adj.
graceless 842 adj.
vicious 934 adj.
wicked 934 adj.
grace note
musical note 410 n.
Graces, the
three 93 n.
a beauty 841 n.
gracile
narrow 206 adj.
gracious
willing 597 adj.
beautiful 841 adj.
tasteful 846 adj.
courteous 884 adj.
benevolent 897 adj.
gracious living
euphoria 376 n.
good taste 846 n.
gradation
degree 27 n.
order 60 n.
arrangement 62 n.
series 71 n.
serial place 73 n.
grade
make uniform 16 vb.
degree 27 n.
graduate 27 vb.
arrange 62 vb.
class 62 vb.
serial place 73 n.
grade 73 vb.
sort 77 n.
gauge 465 vb.
class 538 n.
gradient
incline 220 n.
ascent 308 n.
gradual
gradational 27 adj.
continuous 71 adj.
slow 278 adj.
gradualism
continuity 71 n.
slowness 278 n.
reformism 654 n.
gradualist
reformer 654 n.
gradually
by degrees 27 adv.
gradatim 278 adv.
graduand
student 538 n.
graduate
graduate 27 vb.
grade 73 vb.
scholar 492 n.
student 538 n.
get better 654 vb.
proficient person 696 n.
succeed 727 vb.
gradus
word list 87 n.
dictionary 559 n.
textbook 589 n.
graffiti
record 548 n.
script 586 n.
blemish 845 n.
graft
generate 167 vb.
implant 303 vb.
cultivate 370 vb.
inducement 612 n.
booty 790 n.
improbity 930 n.
grafting
joining together 45 n.
grail
ritual object 988 n.
grain
temperament 5 n.
small thing 33 n.
tendency 179 n.
minuteness 196 n.
provender 301 n.
cereals 301 n.
weighing 322 n.
texture 331 n.
powder 332 n.
grass 366 n.
affections 817 n.
decorate 844 vb.
grained
textural 331 adj.
gram
small quantity 33 n.
weighing 322 n.
gramarye
sorcery 983 n.
grammar
curriculum 534 n.
linguistics 557 n.
grammar 564 n.
textbook 589 n.
grammarian
linguist 557 n.
grammatical
linguistic 557 adj.

grammatical 564 adj.
gramophone
gramophone 414 n.
hearing aid 415 n.
gramophone record
repetition 106 n.
gramophone 414 n.
granary
storage 632 n.
grand
great 32 adj.
whole 52 adj.
over one hundred 99 n.
architectural 192 adj.
forceful 571 adj.
important 638 adj.
super 644 adj.
funds 797 n.
impressive 821 adj.
splendid 841 adj.
worshipful 866 adj.
noble 868 adj.
proud 871 adj.
formal 875 adj.
ostentatious 875 adj.
grandad, granddad
old man 133 n.
paternity 169 n.
grand airs
affectation 850 n.
grandchildren
posterity 170 n.
grand duke
person of rank 868 n.
grande dame
proud person 871 n.
grandee
bigwig 638 n.
aristocrat 868 n.
grandeur
greatness 32 n.
vigour 571 n.
beauty 841 n.
prestige 866 n.
ostentation 875 n.
grandfather
old man 133 n.
paternity 169 n.
grand fellow
exceller 644 n.
grandiloquence
exaggeration 546 n.
vigour 571 n.
magniloquence 574 n.
eloquence 579 n.
affectation 850 n.
boasting 877 n.
grandiose
huge 195 adj.
rhetorical 574 adj.
proud 871 adj.
ostentatious 875 adj.
grand mal
nervous disorders 651 n.
grand manner
art style 553 n.
grandmother
old woman 133 n.
maternity 169 n.
woman 373 n.
grand old man
sage 500 n.
person of repute 866 n.
favourite 890 n.
grand opera
stage play 594 n.
grandparents
kinsman 11 n.
Grandsire
campanology 412 n.
grand slam
victory 727 n.
grandstand
view 438 n.
onlookers 441 n.
arena 724 n.
grand tour
land travel 267 n.
grange
house 192 n.
farm 370 n.
granite
hardness 326 n.
rock 344 n.
granny
old woman 133 n.
maternity 169 n.
granny flat
flat 192 n.
granny knot
ligature 47 n.
grant
attribute 158 vb.
qualify 468 vb.
be reasonable 475 vb.
believe 485 vb.
assent 488 vb.
confess 526 vb.
subvention 703 n.
permission 756 n.
permit 756 vb.
consent 758 n.vb.
assign 780 vb.
gift 781 n.
give 781 vb.
pay 804 n.
— asylum
admit 299 vb.
safeguard 660 vb.
granted
demonstrated 478 adj.
assented 488 adj.
supposed 512 adj.
Granth
non-Biblical scripture 975 n.
grant-in-aid
pay 804 n.
granting
if 8 adv.
provided 468 adv.
grantor
giver 781 n.
granular
minute 196 adj.
textural 331 adj.
powdery 332 adj.
granulation
texture 331 n.
powderiness 332 n.
granule
small thing 33 n.
grape
fruit 301 n.
grape, the
wine 301 n.
grapeshot
missile 287 n.
ammunition 723 n.
grapevine
informant 524 n.
rumour 529 n.
graphic
lifelike 18 adj.
expressive 516 adj.
representing 551 adj.
painted 553 adj.
forceful 571 adj.
descriptive 590 adj.
graphic art
painting 553 n.
graphics
representation 551 n.
graphite
lubricant 334 n.
graphologist
detective 459 n.
calligrapher 586 n.
graphology
hermeneutics 520 n.
writing 586 n.
graphs
mathematics 86 n.
grapnel
safeguard 662 n.
grapple
join 45 vb.
unite with 45 vb.
be resolute 599 vb.
attack 712 vb.
wrestling 716 n.
fight 716 vb.
retain 778 vb.
— with
withstand 704 vb.
contend 716 vb.
grappling iron
coupling 47 n.
safeguard 662 n.
grasp
ability 160 n.
range 183 n.
distance 199 n.
knowledge 490 n.
be wise 498 vb.
understand 516 vb.
protection 660 n.
possession 773 n.
retention 778 n.
taking 786 n.
— at
take 786 vb.
desire 859 vb.
— at shadows
attempt the impossible 470 vb.
— the nettle
undertake 672 vb.
grasping
oppressive 735 adj.
avaricious 816 adj.
greedy 859 adj.
grass
provender 301 n.
grass 366 n.
garden 370 n.
greenness 434 n.
informer 524 n.
inform 524 vb.
accuser 928 n.
knave 938 n.
drug-taking 949 n.
— over
cultivate 370 vb.
grasshopper
jumper 312 n.
insect 365 n.
grasshopper mind
changeable thing 152 n.
inattention 456 n.
grassland(s)
grassland 348 n.
plain 348 n.
farm 370 n.
grassless
dry 342 adj.
grass roots
commonalty 869 n.
grass widow/widower
widowhood 896 n.
grassy
soft 327 adj.
vegetal 366 adj.
green 434 adj.
grate
cook 301 vb.
pulverize 332 vb.
rub 333 vb.
give pain 377 vb.
furnace 383 n.
rasp 407 vb.
ululate 409 vb.
discord 411 vb.
cause dislike 861 vb.
excite hate 888 vb.
— on
displease 827 vb.
grateful
pleasant 376 adj.
pleasurable 826 adj.
content 828 adj.
grateful 907 adj.

gratefulness
gratitude 907 n.
grater
roughness 259 n.
pulverizer 332 n.
gratification
pleasure 376 n.
enjoyment 824 n.
gratify
be lenient 736 vb.
give 781 vb.
please 826 vb.
content 828 vb.
grating
disagreeing 25 adj.
network 222 n.
strident 407 adj.
(See **grate** *)*
gratis
free 744 adj.
given 781 adj.
uncharged 812 adj.
gratitude
gratitude 907 n.
reward 962 n.
gratuitous
suppositional 512 adj.
voluntary 597 adj.
given 781 adj.
uncharged 812 adj.
undue 916 adj.
gratuity
extra 40 n.
incentive 612 n.
offer 759 n.
acquisition 771 n.
gift 781 n.
undueness 916 n.
reward 962 n.
grave
great 32 adj.
excavation 255 n.
resting place 266 n.
tomb 364 n.
record 548 vb.
engrave 555 vb.
forceful 571 adj.
important 638 adj.
inactivity 679 n.
inexcitable 823 adj.
serious 834 adj.
dull 840 adj.
heinous 934 adj.
— on the mind
memorize 505 vb.
grave, the
death 361 n.
grave accent
punctuation 547 n.
grave clothes
grave clothes 364 n.
grave-digger
excavator 255 n.
interment 364 n.
church officer 986 n.
gravel
paving 226 n.
powder 332 n.
soil 344 n.
confute 479 vb.
building material 631 n.
defeat 727 vb.
gravel-blind
blind 439 adj.
graven image
image 551 n.
idol 982 n.
gravestone
covering 226 n.
obsequies 364 n.
graveyard
cemetery 364 n.
defeat 728 n.
holy place 990 n.
gravid
fertilized 167 adj.
gravitate
descend 309 vb.
weigh 322 vb.
— towards
tend 179 vb.
gravity
attraction 291 n.
materiality 319 n.
gravity 322 n.
vigour 571 n.
importance 638 n.
inexcitability 823 n.
seriousness 834 n.
prudery 950 n.
gravy
sauce 389 n.
good 615 n.
acquisition 771 n.
shekels 797 n.
Gray's Inn
bar 958 n.
graze
be near 200 vb.
be contiguous 202 vb.
shallowness 212 n.
collide 279 vb.
graze 301 vb.
rub 333 vb.
touch 378 n.vb.
wound 655 vb.
grazing
grassland 348 n.
stock farm 369 n.
grease
adhesive 47 n.
coat 226 vb.
smoother 258 n.
smooth 258 vb.
soften 327 vb.
lubricant 334 n.
fat 357 n.
grease 357 vb.
silencer 401 n.
make unclean 649 vb.
facilitate 701 vb.
hairwash 843 n.
— the palm
bribe 612 vb.
pay 804 vb.
greased lightning
velocity 277 n.
grease gun
smoother 258 n.
lubricant 334 n.
greasepaint
stage set 594 n.
cosmetic 843 n.
greaseproof
dry 342 adj.
greasy
smooth 258 adj.
unctuous 357 adj.
dirty 649 adj.
great
great 32 adj.
superior 34 adj.
powerful 160 adj.
strong 162 adj.
influential 178 adj.
large 195 adj.
plenteous 635 adj.
important 638 adj.
excellent 644 adj.
super 644 adj.
renowned 866 adj.
worshipful 866 adj.
noble 868 adj.
proud 871 adj.
great, the
aristocracy 868 n.
great circle
circle 250 n.
navigation 269 n.
uranometry 321 n.
greatcoat
overcoat 228 n.
great day
important matter 638 n.
special day 876 n.
great deal
great quantity 32 n.
great divide, the
death 361 n.
great doings
important matter 638 n.
activity 678 n.
greater
increasing 36 adj.
greatest
great 32 adj.
supreme 34 adj.
greatest, the
bigwig 638 n.
exceller 644 n.
greatest happiness of the greatest number, the
good 615 n.
philanthropy 901 n.
great expectations
looking ahead 124 n.
Greatheart
brave person 855 n.
great-hearted
disinterested 931 adj.
Great Khan
sovereign 741 n.
great majority
greater number 104 n.
great man/woman
bigwig 638 n.
person of repute 866 n.
Great Mother
mythic deity 966 n.
Semitic deities 967 n.
great name
repute 866 n.
greatness
greatness 32 n.
(See **great** *)*
great quantity
great quantity 32 n.
multitude 104 n.
plenty 635 n.
Greats
exam 459 n.
curriculum 534 n.
Great Spirit
the Deity 965 n.
great thing
chief thing 638 n.
great unwashed
commonalty 869 n.
Great Wall of China
exclusion 57 n.
partition 231 n.
defences 713 n.
great wen, the
city 184 n.
Great Year
era 110 n.
greaves
legwear 228 n.
armour 713 n.
grebe
bird 365 n.
greed
rapacity 786 n.
avarice 816 n.
desire 859 n.
selfishness 932 n.
gluttony 947 n.
greediness
overstepping 306 n.
greedy
feeding 301 adj.
unprovided 636 adj.
greedy 859 adj.
envious 912 adj.
greedy-guts
glutton 947 n.
Greek
unknown thing 491 n.
lack of meaning 515 n.
unintelligibility 517 n.
language 557 n.

Greek Calends
neverness 109 n.
Greek fire
fire 379 n.
bomb 723 n.
Greek meeting Greek
equal 28 adj.
Greek Orthodox
Catholic 976 n.
green
new 126 adj.
young 130 adj.
pleasance 192 n.
vomiting 300 adj.
grassland 348 n.
vegetal 366 adj.
sour 393 adj.
green 434 adj.
credulous 487 adj.
ignorant 491 adj.
remembered 505 adj.
gullible 544 adj.
unhabituated 611 adj.
immature 670 adj.
unskilled 695 adj.
pleasure ground 837 n.
innocent 935 adj.
green belt
space 183 n.
district 184 n.
surroundings 230 n.
plain 348 n.
Green Cross Code
traffic control 305 n.
greenery
foliage 366 n.
greenness 434 n.
green-eyed
jealous 911 adj.
green fingers
agriculture 370 n.
feeler 378 n.
aptitude 694 n.
greenfly
insect 365 n.
greengage
fruit 301 n.
greenness 434 n.
greengrocer
provider 633 n.
greenhorn
ignoramus 493 n.
ninny 501 n.
beginner 538 n.
dupe 544 n.
bungler 697 n.
ingenue 699 n.
greenhouse
arbour 194 n.
garden 370 n.
greenhouse effect
atmosphere 340 n.
green lane
path 624 n.
green light
signal light 420 n.
assent 488 n.
signal 547 n.
permit 756 n.
Green Man
mythical being 970 n.
Green Paper
report 524 n.
green pound
finance 797 n.
Green Revolution
productiveness 171 n.
greenroom
theatre 594 n.
greens
vegetable 301 n.
Greens
political party 708 n.
greensward
grassland 348 n.
garden 370 n.
green with envy
resentful 891 adj.
envious 912 adj.
greenwood
wood 366 n.
greenness 434 n.
greet
meet 295 vb.
cry 408 vb.
notice 455 vb.
gesticulate 547 vb.
speak to 583 vb.
weep 836 vb.
be friendly 880 vb.
be hospitable 882 vb.
greet 884 vb.
greetings
respects 920 n.
greetings card
correspondence 588 n.
gregarious
sociable 882 adj.
Gregorian calendar
chronology 117 n.
Gregorian chant
vocal music 412 n.
hymn 981 n.
gremlin
hinderer 702 n.
elf 970 n.
grenade
bang 402 n.
bomb 723 n.
grenadier
tall creature 209 n.
soldiery 722 n.
Gresham's law
deterioration 655 n.
grey
uniform 16 adj.
median 30 adj.
horse 273 n.
dim 419 adj.
colourless 426 adj.
whitish 427 adj.
greyness 429 n.
grey 429 adj.
neutral 625 adj.
middling 732 adj.
cheerless 834 adj.
greybeard
old man 133 n.
Grey Eminence
influence 178 n.
grey hairs
old age 131 n.
greyhound
speeder 277 n.
dog 365 n.
grey mare
spouse 894 n.
grey matter
head 213 n.
intellect 447 n.
intelligence 498 n.
grid
correlation 12 n.
electronics 160 n.
network 222 n.
griddle
cook 301 vb.
gridiron
horizontality 216 n.
network 222 n.
bicycle 274 n.
heater 383 n.
grid reference
coordinate 465 n.
grief
evil 616 n.
sorrow 825 n.
discontent 829 n.
grief-stricken
unhappy 825 adj.
grievance
evil 616 n.
annoyance 827 n.
discontent 829 n.
wrong 914 n.
grieve
suffer 825 vb.
hurt 827 vb.
be dejected 834 vb.
sadden 834 vb.
lament 836 vb.
pity 905 vb.
— for
lament 836 vb.
grievous
bad 645 adj.
distressing 827 adj.
grievous bodily harm
attack 712 n.
griffin
rara avis 84 n.
animal 365 n.
heraldry 547 n.
grill
cook 301 vb.
be hot 379 vb.
heat 381 vb.
heater 383 n.
interrogate 459 vb.
grille
network 222 n.
window 263 n.
grill room
café 192 n.
grim
resolute 599 adj.
obstinate 602 adj.
not nice 645 adj.
distressing 827 adj.
serious 834 adj.
ugly 842 adj.
frightening 854 adj.
ungracious 885 adj.
sullen 893 adj.
cruel 898 adj.
grimace
distortion 246 n.
agitation 318 n.
look 438 n.
gesture 547 n.
gesticulate 547 vb.
be unwilling 598 vb.
discontent 829 n.
smile 835 vb.
make ugly 842 vb.
affectation 850 n.
frighten 854 vb.
dislike 861 vb.
be sullen 893 vb.
grimalkin
cat 365 n.
grime
dirt 649 n.
Grimm's law
linguistics 557 n.
grimy
dim 419 adj.
dirty 649 adj.
grin
laughter 835 n.
smile 835 vb.
ridicule 851 n.
— and bear it
stand firm 599 vb.
be patient 823 vb.
be cheerful 833 vb.
be courageous 855 vb.
grind
abate 37 vb.
rend 46 vb.
demolish 165 vb.
make smaller 198 vb.
sharpen 256 vb.
chew 301 vb.
pulverize 332 vb.
rub 333 vb.
give pain 377 vb.
rasp 407 vb.
study 536 n.vb.
wound 655 vb.
labour 682 n.
oppress 735 vb.
— one's teeth
be angry 891 vb.
grinder
tooth 256 n.
pulverizer 332 n.

grindstone
sharpener 256 n.
pulverizer 332 n.
labour 682 n.
bore 838 n.
gringo
foreigner 59 n.
grip
join 45 vb.
tie 45 vb.
unite with 45 vb.
fastening 47 n.
cohere 48 vb.
vitality 162 n.
vigorousness 174 n.
influence 178 n.
bag 194 n.
handle 218 n.
gesture 547 n.
tool 630 n.
skill 694 n.
governance 733 n.
restrain 747 vb.
possession 773 n.
retention 778 n.
retain 778 vb.
impress 821 vb.
gripe
give pain 377 vb.
retain 778 vb.
discontent 829 n.
gripes
pang 377 n.
digestive disorders 651 n.
griping
oppressive 735 adj.
avaricious 816 adj.
gripping
influential 178 adj.
exciting 821 adj.
grisaille
greyness 429 n.
painting 553 n.
grisette
woman 373 n.
grisly
unsightly 842 adj.
frightening 854 adj.
gristle
solid body 324 n.
hardness 326 n.
toughness 329 n.
grist (to the mill)
powder 332 n.
materials 631 n.
provision 633 n.
grit
strength 162 n.
vigorousness 174 n.
hardness 326 n.
texture 331 n.
powder 332 n.
resolution 599 n.
stamina 600 n.
courage 855 n.
grizzle
lamentation 836 n.
weep 836 vb.
grizzled
whitish 427 adj.
grey 429 adj.
pied 437 adj.
groan
feel pain 377 vb.
cry 408 vb.
deprecate 762 vb.
discontent 829 n.
be discontented 829 vb.
be dejected 834 vb.
lamentation 836 n.
groat
small coin 33 n.
grocer
provider 633 n.
tradespeople 794 n.
groceries
provisions 301 n.
grog
alcoholic drink 301 n.
grog-blossom
alcoholism 949 n.
groggy
weakly 163 adj.
oscillating 317 adj.
sick 651 adj.
sleepy 679 adj.
groin
angularity 247 n.
groom
animal husbandry 369 n.
groom 369 vb.
clean 648 vb.
make ready 669 vb.
domestic 742 n.
— one for
train 534 vb.
grooming
beautification 843 n.
groomsman
bridal party 894 n.
groove
cut 46 vb.
regularity 81 n.
place 185 n.
receptacle 194 n.
gap 201 n.
cavity 255 n.
furrow 262 n.
groove 262 vb.
habit 610 n.
groovy
super 644 adj.
fashionable 848 adj.
grope
move slowly 278 vb.
touch 378 vb.
be dim-sighted 440 vb.
be tentative 461 vb.
be uncertain 474 vb.
not know 491 vb.
be clumsy 695 vb.
rape 951 n.
— for
search 459 vb.
grosgrain
textile 222 n.
gros point
needlework 844 n.
gross
consummate 32 adj.
whole 52 adj.
unintelligent 499 adj.
manifest 522 adj.
bad 645 adj.
not nice 645 adj.
receive 782 vb.
graceless 842 adj.
vulgar 847 adj.
heinous 934 adj.
sensual 944 adj.
impure 951 adj.
gross, a
over one hundred 99 n.
gross national product
product 164 n.
gross return
earnings 771 n.
grotesque
unusual 84 adj.
distorted 246 adj.
absurd 497 adj.
imaginative 513 adj.
inelegant 576 adj.
eyesore 842 n.
unsightly 842 adj.
ridiculous 849 adj.
grotto
pavilion 192 n.
arbour 194 n.
cavity 255 n.
grotty
trivial 639 adj.
bad 645 adj.
unclean 649 adj.
sick 651 adj.
grouch
malcontent 829 n.
be sullen 893 vb.
grouchy
discontented 829 adj.
sullen 893 adj.
ground
reason why 156 n.
territory 184 n.
situation 186 n.
base 214 n.
flatten 216 vb.
basis 218 n.
be quiescent 266 vb.
navigate 269 vb.
land 295 vb.
powdery 332 adj.
land 344 n.
educate 534 vb.
arena 724 n.
fail 728 vb.
ground and consequent
causation 156 n.
ground crew
aeronaut 271 n.
grounded
real 1 adj.
fixed 153 adj.
impotent 161 adj.
evidential 466 adj.
in difficulties 700 adj.
grounded 728 adj.
ground floor
base 214 n.
ground gained
progression 285 n.
ground glass
semitransparency 424 n.
grounding
education 534 n.
groundless
unreal 2 adj.
insubstantial 4 adj.
causeless 159 adj.
illogical 477 adj.
groundling
playgoer 594 n.
commoner 869 n.
ground plan
map 551 n.
plan 623 n.
grounds
leavings 41 n.
pleasance 192 n.
grassland 348 n.
evidence 466 n.
reasons 475 n.
motive 612 n.
lands 777 n.
ground swell
commotion 318 n.
wave 350 n.
groundwork
prelude 66 n.
source 156 n.
base 214 n.
basis 218 n.
preparation 669 n.
group
combine 50 vb.
subdivision 53 n.
class 62 vb.
group 74 n.
bring together 74 vb.
classification 77 n.
certain quantity 104 n.
party 708 n.
formation 722 n.
sect 978 n.
group captain
air officer 741 n.
groupie
youngster 132 n.
follower 284 n.
group therapy
therapy 658 n.

grouse
table bird 365 n.
be discontented 829 vb.
lament 836 vb.
be sullen 893 vb.
grouser
dissentient 489 n.
petitioner 763 n.
malcontent 829 n.
weeper 836 n.
rude person 885 n.
disapprover 924 n.
grout
adhesive 47 n.
coat 226 vb.
grouts
dirt 649 n.
grove
wood 366 n.
grovel
be low 210 vb.
knuckle under 721 vb.
obey 739 vb.
be servile 879 vb.
groveller
toady 879 n.
groves of academe
academy 539 n.
grow
become 1 vb.
grow 36 vb.
come of age 134 vb.
be turned to 147 vb.
produce 164 vb.
reproduce itself 167 vb.
expand 197 vb.
breed stock 369 vb.
cultivate 370 vb.
mature 669 vb.
— from
result 157 vb.
— into
evolve 316 vb.
— less
decrease 37 vb.
become small 198 vb.
— moss
stay 144 vb.
deteriorate 655 vb.
— nasty
threaten 900 vb.
— old
grow old 131 vb.
— on one
be wont 610 vb.
— together
cohere 48 vb.
combine 50 vb.
— up
grow 36 vb.
come of age 134 vb.
grower
producer 164 n.
growing
young 130 adj.
growing boy/girl
youth 130 n.
growing pains
beginning 68 n.
youth 130 n.
growl
ululate 409 vb.
be rude 885 vb.
anger 891 n.
be angry 891 vb.
sullenness 893 n.
be sullen 893 vb.
threaten 900 vb.
growling
hoarse 407 adj.
grown
produced 164 adj.
matured 669 adj.
grown-up
adult 134 n.
grown-up 134 adj.
matured 669 adj.
growth
increase 36 n.
conversion 147 n.
growth 157 n.
product 164 n.
production 164 n.
propagation 167 n.
expansion 197 n.
swelling 253 n.
agriculture 370 n.
cancer 651 n.
growth area
increase 36 n.
groyne
projection 254 n.
safeguard 662 n.
obstacle 702 n.
grub
young creature 132 n.
food 301 n.
creepy-crawly 365 n.
grubby
unclean 649 adj.
Grub Street
writing 586 n.
Grub Street hack
author 589 n.
grub up
extract 304 vb.
grudge
be unwilling 598 vb.
make insufficient 636 vb.
refuse 760 vb.
be parsimonious 816 vb.
discontent 829 n.
enmity 881 n.
hatred 888 n.
resentment 891 n.
gruel
cereals 301 n.
semiliquidity 354 n.
gruelling
laborious 682 adj.
fatiguing 684 adj.
paining 827 adj.
gruesome
not nice 645 adj.
unsightly 842 adj.
frightening 854 adj.
gruff
hoarse 407 adj.
taciturn 582 adj.
ungracious 885 adj.
irascible 892 adj.
sullen 893 adj.
unkind 898 adj.
grumble
roll 403 vb.
cry 408 vb.
be discontented 829 vb.
be sullen 893 vb.
grumbler
malcontent 829 n.
grumbling
ungracious 885 adj.
threatening 900 adj.
(See **grumble** *)*
grume
blood 335 n.
semiliquidity 354 n.
grummet
orifice 263 n.
grumpy
irascible 892 adj.
sullen 893 adj.
Grundyism
prudery 950 n.
grunt
rasp 407 vb.
cry 408 n.vb.
ululate 409 vb.
grunting
ungracious 885 adj.
G-string
loincloth 228 n.
G-suit
suit 228 n.
guano
fertilizer 171 n.
excrement 302 n.
guarantee
make certain 473 vb.
affirm 532 vb.
safeguard 660 vb.
patronize 703 vb.
promise 764 n.vb.
security 767 n.
guarantor
patron 707 n.
guard
doorkeeper 264 n.
driver 268 n.
attention 455 n.
surveillance 457 n.
protection 660 n.
protector 660 n.
safeguard 660 vb.
defender 713 n.
keeper 749 n.
— against
prepare 669 vb.
guard dog
protector 660 n.
guarded
taciturn 582 adj.
conditional 766 adj.
cautious 858 adj.
guardhouse
lockup 748 n.
guardian
parentage 169 n.
protector 660 n.
defender 713 n.
keeper 749 n.
guardian angel
protector 660 n.
patron 707 n.
benefactor 903 n.
angel 968 n.
guard of honour
respects 920 n.
guardrail
safeguard 662 n.
guardroom
lockup 748 n.
guards
armed force 722 n.
guard ship
warship 722 n.
guard's van
train 274 n.
guava
fruit 301 n.
gubernatorial
directing 689 adj.
governmental 733 adj.
gudgeon
pivot 218 n.
fish 365 n.
dupe 544 n.
guerdon
reward 962 n.
guernsey
jersey 228 n.
Guernsey
cattle 365 n.
guerrilla, guerilla
killer 362 n.
attacker 712 n.
soldier 722 n.
revolter 738 n.
guerrilla warfare
warfare 718 n.
guess
assume 471 vb.
intuit 476 vb.
estimate 480 vb.
opinion 485 n.
not know 491 vb.
conjecture 512 n.
suppose 512 vb.
hint 524 n.
guesswork
empiricism 461 n.
uncertainty 474 n.
intuition 476 n.
conjecture 512 n.
guest
resident 191 n.

arrival 295 n.
friend 880 n.
sociable person 882 n.
guesthouse
quarters 192 n.
guestimate
uncertainty 474 n.
guest of Her Majesty
prisoner 750 n.
guest-rope
cable 47 n.
guest worker
foreigner 59 n.
guff
empty talk 515 n.
fable 543 n.
chatter 581 n.
guffaw
laughter 835 n.
guidance
teaching 534 n.
directorship 689 n.
advice 691 n.
guide
prototype 23 n.
superior 34 n.
come before 64 vb.
precursor 66 n.
rule 81 n.
accompany 89 vb.
influence 178 vb.
itinerary 267 n.
sage 500 n.
guide 520 n.
informant 524 n.
educate 534 vb.
teacher 537 n.
indication 547 n.
indicate 547 vb.
reference book 589 n.
direct 689 vb.
director 690 n.
adviser 691 n.
guidebook
directory 87 n.
guidebook 524 n.
guided missile
rocket 276 n.
missile weapon 723 n.
guide dog
dog 365 n.
blindness 439 n.
guidelines
precept 693 n.
guidepost
signpost 547 n.
guiding star
guide 520 n.
signpost 547 n.
motive 612 n.
guidon
flag 547 n.
guild
group 74 n.
business 622 n.
community 708 n.
corporation 708 n.
merchant 794 n.
guilder
coinage 797 n.
guile
duplicity 541 n.
deception 542 n.
cunning 698 n.
guileful
deceiving 542 adj.
perfidious 930 adj.
guileless
artless 699 adj.
honourable 929 adj.
innocent 935 adj.
guillotine
end 69 n.
stop 145 n.
shorten 204 vb.
killer 362 n.
execute 963 vb.
means of execution 964 n.
guilt
badness 645 n.
wrong 914 n.
wickedness 934 n.
guilt 936 n.
lawbreaking 954 n.
guilt complex
guilt 936 n.
guilt-feeling
penitence 939 n.
guiltless
ignorant 491 adj.
perfect 646 adj.
virtuous 933 adj.
guiltless 935 adj.
acquitted 960 adj.
guilt-offering
substitute 150 n.
guilty
guilty 936 adj.
(See **guilt** *)*
guilty conscience
guilt 936 n.
guilty person
offender 904 n.
guinea
coinage 797 n.
guinea fowl
table bird 365 n.
guinea pig
animal 365 n.
testee 461 n.
guipure
textile 222 n.
guise
modality 7 n.
appearance 445 n.
pretext 614 n.
way 624 n.
conduct 688 n.
guitar
harp 414 n.
guitarist
instrumentalist 413 n.
Gulag
prison camp 748 n.
gulch
gap 201 n.
gules
red 431 adj.
heraldic 547 adj.
gulf
gap 201 n.
cavity 255 n.
gulf 345 n.
access 624 n.
gulfweed
plant 366 n.
gull
weakling 163 n.
bird 365 n.
befool 542 vb.
dupe 544 n.
defraud 788 vb.
gullet
maw 194 n.
orifice 263 n.
eater 301 n.
conduit 351 n.
gullible
misjudging 481 adj.
credulous 487 adj.
foolish 499 adj.
gullible 544 adj.
gullied
furrowed 262 adj.
Gulliver
traveller 268 n.
gully
gap 201 n.
narrowness 206 n.
valley 255 n.
conduit 351 n.
gulp
absorb 299 vb.
draught 301 n.
respiration 352 n.
breathe 352 vb.
— down
eat 301 vb.
gluttonize 947 vb.
gum
adhesive 47 n.
agglutinate 48 vb.
elasticity 328 n.
viscidity 354 n.
resin 357 n.
— up the works
be obstructive 702 vb.
gumboots
footwear 228 n.
gummy
retentive 778 adj.
(See **gum** *)*
gumption
intelligence 498 n.
gun
bang 402 n.
hunter 619 n.
gun 723 n.
gunboat
warship 722 n.
gunboat diplomacy
war 718 n.
brute force 735 n.
gun carriage
war chariot 274 n.
gun 723 n.
gun cotton
explosive 723 n.
gunfire
loudness 400 n.
bombardment 712 n.
gunman
shooter 287 n.
murderer 362 n.
combatant 722 n.
robber 789 n.
desperado 857 n.
ruffian 904 n.
gunmetal
greyness 429 n.
gunner
shooter 287 n.
soldiery 722 n.
gunnery
propulsion 287 n.
bombardment 712 n.
art of war 718 n.
arms 723 n.
gunning for, be
pursue 619 vb.
gunny
textile 222 n.
gunpowder
destroyer 168 n.
propellant 287 n.
explosive 723 n.
gunroom
chamber 194 n.
storage 632 n.
arsenal 723 n.
gunrunner
thief 789 n.
gunshot
short distance 200 n.
propulsion 287 n.
gunsmith
artisan 686 n.
gunwale, gunnel
edge 234 n.
gup
empty talk 515 n.
rumour 529 n.
fable 543 n.
gurgle
flow 350 vb.
bubble 355 vb.
sound faint 401 vb.
laughter 835 n.
rejoice 835 vb.
gurk
eruct 300 vb.
Gurkha
soldier 722 n.
guru
sage 500 n.
teacher 537 n.
religious teacher 973 n.

gush
outbreak 176 n.
outflow 298 n.
flow out 298 vb.
emit 300 vb.
ascend 308 vb.
stream 350 n.
flow 350 vb.
overestimation 482 n.
mean nothing 515 vb.
diffuseness 570 n.
be diffuse 570 vb.
chatter 581 n.
be loquacious 581 vb.
gusher
outflow 298 n.
climber 308 n.
store 632 n.
gushing
hypocritical 541 adj.
affected 850 adj.
gusset
adjunct 40 n.
garment 228 n.
gust
breeze 352 n.
gale 352 n.
excitable state 822 n.
gustation
taste 386 n.
gusto
vigorousness 174 n.
pleasure 376 n.
taste 386 n.
enjoyment 824 n.
gusty
unstable 152 adj.
windy 352 adj.
gut
destroy 165 vb.
tube 263 n.
empty 300 vb.
cook 301 vb.
extract 304 vb.
gulf 345 n.
burn 381 vb.
rob 788 vb.
gutless
weak 163 adj.
irresolute 601 adj.
gutlessness
inertness 175 n.
gut reaction
absence of thought 450 n.
intuition 476 n.
gutrot
digestive disorders 651 n.
guts
vitality 162 n.
vigorousness 174 n.
insides 224 n.
vigour 571 n.
resolution 599 n.
courage 855 n.
guttapercha
elasticity 328 n.
gutter
vary 152 vb.
furrow 262 n.
be agitated 318 vb.
drain 351 n.
be dim 419 vb.
edition 589 n.
waste 634 vb.
sink 649 n.
vulgar 847 adj.
gutter press
the press 528 n.
bad taste 847 n.
defamer 926 n.
guttersnipe
low fellow 869 n.
guttural
speech sound 398 n.
hoarse 407 adj.
dialectal 560 adj.
vocal 577 adj.
guv, guvnor
male 372 n.
master 741 n.
guy
cable 47 n.
tackling 47 n.
male 372 n.
be absurd 497 vb.
misinterpret 521 vb.
image 551 n.
misrepresent 552 vb.
laughingstock 851 n.
satirize 851 vb.
not respect 921 vb.
detract 926 vb.
guzzle
eat 301 vb.
gluttonize 947 vb.
get drunk 949 vb.
guzzler
glutton 947 n.
gybe, jibe
navigate 269 vb.
gymkhana
contest 716 n.
amusement 837 n.
gymnasium
meeting place 192 n.
academy 539 n.
classroom 539 n.
arena 724 n.
gymnast
athlete 162 n.
proficient person 696 n.
gymnastics
athletics 162 n.
education 534 n.
exercise 682 n.
contest 716 n.
sport 837 n.
gymnosophist
ascetic 945 n.
religionist 973 n.
gynaecology
obstetrics 167 n.
female 373 n.
medical art 658 n.
gynocracy
female 373 n.
government 733 n.
gypsum
materials 631 n.
gypsy
(See **gipsy** *)*
gyrate
rotate 315 vb.
gyrocompass
sailing aid 269 n.
gyropilot
directorship 689 n.
gyroscope
rotator 315 n.
gyves
fetter 748 n.

H

habeas corpus
warrant 737 n.
legal process 959 n.
haberdasher
clothier 228 n.
tradespeople 794 n.
habergeon
armour 713 n.
habit
temperament 5 n.
state 7 n.
uniformity 16 n.
composition 56 n.
continuity 71 n.
regularity 81 n.
recurrence 106 n.
tradition 127 n.
regular return 141 n.
permanence 144 n.
habit 610 n.
vocation 622 n.
use 673 n.
conduct 688 n.
fashion 848 n.
drug-taking 949 n.
habitat
place 185 n.
situation 186 n.
locality 187 n.
abode 192 n.
habitation
edifice 164 n.
abode 192 n.
habit-forming
influential 178 adj.
habitual 610 adj.
inducing 612 adj.
intoxicating 949 adj.
habit of mind
affections 817 n.
habitual
general 79 adj.
typical 83 adj.
repeated 106 adj.
immemorial 127 adj.
frequent 139 adj.
habitual 610 adj.
habituate
make conform 83 vb.
break in 369 vb.
train 534 vb.
habituate 610 vb.
make ready 669 vb.
habituated
unastonished 865 adj.
habitué
habitué 610 n.
sociable person 882 n.
hachures
indication 547 n.
hacienda
house 192 n.
farm 370 n.
lands 777 n.
hack
cut 46 vb.
ride 267 vb.
saddle horse 273 n.
author 589 n.
wound 655 vb.
worker 686 n.
servant 742 n.
hackle
plumage 259 n.
livery 547 n.
hackney carriage
cab 274 n.
hackneyed
imitative 20 adj.
known 490 adj.
aphoristic 496 adj.
feeble 572 adj.
usual 610 adj.
used 673 adj.
hackneyed saying
maxim 496 n.
phrase 563 n.
hacksaw
notch 260 n.
hackwork
writing 586 n.
labour 682 n.
had, be
be duped 544 vb.
pay too much 811 vb.
haddock
fish food 301 n.
Hades
death 361 n.
Chthonian deity 967 n.
mythic hell 972 n.
had it
destroyed 165 adj.
dying 361 adj.

had it up to here
bored 838 adj.
Hadith
tradition 127 n.
non-Biblical scripture 975 n.
haematology
blood 335 n.
haemoglobin
blood 335 n.
haemophilia
haemorrhage 302 n.
fluidity 335 n.
blood disease 651 n.
haemophiliac
sick person 651 n.
haemorrhage
outflow 298 n.
haemorrhage 302 n.
blood disease 651 n.
haemorrhoids
swelling 253 n.
digestive disorders 651 n.
haemostatic
solidifying 324 adj.
haft
handle 218 n.
tool 630 n.
hag
old woman 133 n.
sorceress 983 n.
haggard
lean 206 adj.
deformed 246 adj.
frenzied 503 adj.
fatigued 684 adj.
suffering 825 adj.
melancholic 834 adj.
lamenting 836 adj.
haggard look
ugliness 842 n.
haggis
meat 301 n.
haggle
make terms 766 vb.
bargain 791 vb.
be parsimonious 816 vb.
Hagiographa
scripture 975 n.
hagiography
biography 590 n.
praise 923 n.
theology 973 n.
hagiology
biography 590 n.
theology 973 n.
hagioscope
window 263 n.
view 438 n.
church interior 990 n.
hagridden
spooky 970 adj.
bewitched 983 adj.
ha-ha
gap 201 n.
fence 235 n.
haiku
conciseness 569 n.
verse form 593 n.
hail
crowd 74 n.
rain 350 n.
wintriness 380 n.
cry 408 n.vb.
assent 488 vb.
call 547 n.
speak to 583 vb.
greet 884 vb.
applaud 923 vb.
hail-fellow-well-met
friendly 880 adj.
sociable 882 adj.
Hail Mary
prayers 981 n.
hailstone
ice 380 n.
hailstorm
storm 176 n.
wintriness 380 n.
hair
small thing 33 n.
fibre 208 n.
filament 208 n.
hair 259 n.
hairdressing 843 n.
hairbrush
smoother 258 n.
cleaning utensil 648 n.
haircut, hairdo
hairdressing 843 n.
hairdresser
cleaner 648 n.
beautician 843 n.
hairless
hairless 229 adj.
smooth 258 adj.
hair of the dog that bit one
drunkenness 949 n.
hair on end
danger signal 665 n.
fear 854 n.
hairpiece
wig 228 n.
hair 259 n.
hairdressing 843 n.
hairpin
fastening 47 n.
hairdressing 843 n.
hairpin bend
curve 248 n.
hair-raising
exciting 821 adj.
frightening 854 adj.
hair-restorer
hairwash 843 n.
hair's breadth
short distance 200 n.
narrowness 206 n.
hair shirt
asceticism 945 n.
hairspace
interval 201 n.
print-type 587 n.
hair-splitting
discrimination 463 n.
argument 475 n.
sophistry 477 n.
fastidiousness 862 n.
hair spray
adhesive 47 n.
hairwash 843 n.
hairspring
machine 630 n.
hair style
hairdressing 843 n.
hairy
fibrous 208 adj.
hairy 259 adj.
textural 331 adj.
frightening 854 adj.
hajj, hadj
land travel 267 n.
act of worship 981 n.
hajji
traveller 268 n.
pietist 979 n.
worshipper 981 n.
hake
fish food 301 n.
hakim
doctor 658 n.
officer 741 n.
halberd
axe 723 n.
spear 723 n.
halcyon
tranquil 266 adj.
peaceful 717 adj.
palmy 730 adj.
halcyon days
palmy days 730 n.
joy 824 n.
hale
draw 288 vb.
healthy 650 adj.
half
part 53 n.
incompleteness 55 n.
bisection 92 n.
half-a-dozen
over five 99 n.
fewness 105 n.
half a loaf
compromise 770 n.
half-and-half
equal 28 adj.
mixed 43 adj.
neutral 625 adj.
half-asleep
inattentive 456 adj.
sleepy 679 adj.
half-baked
dabbling 491 adj.
immature 670 adj.
bungled 695 adj.
uncompleted 726 adj.
half-breed
hybrid 43 n.
nonconformist 84 n.
half-caste
hybrid 43 n.
mixed 43 adj.
half cock, at
immature 670 adj.
half crown
coinage 797 n.
half-cut
tipsy 949 adj.
half-dead
dying 361 adj.
half-done
incomplete 55 adj.
deficient 307 adj.
neglected 458 adj.
uncompleted 726 adj.
half-face
laterality 239 n.
sideways 239 adv.
half-frozen
semiliquid 354 adj.
half glimpse
not know 491 vb.
half-grown
infantine 132 adj.
immature 670 adj.
half-hardy
vegetal 366 adj.
half-hearted
weak 163 adj.
unwilling 598 adj.
irresolute 601 adj.
apathetic 820 adj.
indifferent 860 adj.
half-hidden
shadowy 419 adj.
half hitch
ligature 47 n.
half-inch
steal 788 vb.
half-knowledge
sciolism 491 n.
half-life
radiation 417 n.
half-light
evening 129 n.
half-light 419 n.
halfling
dwarf 196 n.
half-mast
lower 311 vb.
signal 547 vb.
half mast, at
lamenting 836 adj.
half measures
incompleteness 55 n.
shortfall 307 n.
irresolution 601 n.
middle way 625 n.
insufficiency 636 n.
lost labour 641 n.
bungling 695 n.
half-melted
semiliquid 354 adj.
half-moon
curve 248 n.
arc 250 n.
moon 321 n.

half-nelson
retention 778 n.
halfpenny
small coin 33 n.
coinage 797 n.
half-price
cheap 812 adj.
half-ripe
immature 670 adj.
half-seas over
drunk 949 adj.
half-seen
shadowy 419 adj.
indistinct 444 adj.
half-smile
content 828 n.
laughter 835 n.
half sovereign
coinage 797 n.
half-spoken
tacit 523 adj.
half-starved
underfed 636 adj.
hungry 859 adj.
fasting 946 adj.
half the battle
chief thing 638 n.
half-timbered
architectural 192 adj.
half-title
edition 589 n.
half-tone
light contrast 417 n.
hue 425 n.
picture 553 n.
edition 589 n.
half-truth
mental dishonesty 543 n.
halfway
midway 70 adv.
undeviating 625 adj.
compromise 770 n.
halfway house
middle 70 n.
retreat 192 n.
intermediary 231 n.
middle way 625 n.
shelter 662 n.
half-wit
fool 501 n.
half-witted
unintelligent 499 adj.
halibut
fish food 301 n.
halitosis
stench 397 n.
hall
edifice 164 n.
house 192 n.
chamber 194 n.
lobby 194 n.
access 624 n.
halleluja, hallelujah
rejoicing 835 n.
celebration 876 n.
hymn 981 n.
halliard
tackling 47 n.
hallmark
label 547 n.
hallmarked
genuine 494 adj.
hall of residence
quarters 192 n.
halloo
cry 408 n.
pursue 619 vb.
hallow
sanctify 979 vb.
hallowed
divine 965 adj.
hallowed by custom
usual 610 adj.
Hallowe'en
sorcery 983 n.
hallucination(s)
insubstantiality 4 n.
appearance 445 n.
error 495 n.
psychopathy 503 n.
fantasy 513 n.
deception 542 n.
hallucinatory
intoxicating 949 adj.
hallucinogen
drug-taking 949 n.
hallux
foot 214 n.
finger 378 n.
hallway
access 624 n.
halma
board game 837 n.
halo
loop 250 n.
light 417 n.
honours 866 n.
haloed
sanctified 979 adj.
halt
end 69 n.
be discontinuous 72 vb.
stop 145 n.
stopping place 145 n.
halt 145 vb.
quiescence 266 n.
come to rest 266 vb.
goal 295 n.
railway 624 n.
be obstructive 702 vb.
failure 728 n.
restrain 747 vb.
halter
halter 47 n.
fetter 748 n.
means of execution 964 n.
halter neck
neckline 228 n.
halting
fitful 142 adj.
slow 278 adj.
inelegant 576 adj.
halve
sunder 46 vb.
bisect 92 vb.
apportion 783 vb.
ham
leg 267 n.
meat 301 n.
actor 594 n.
act 594 vb.
unskilled 695 adj.
be affected 850 vb.
— up
be witty 839 vb.
hamadryad
reptile 365 n.
nymph 967 n.
hamburger
meal 301 n.
meat 301 n.
ham-handed
clumsy 695 adj.
hamlet
district 184 n.
housing 192 n.
Hamlet without the Prince, like
incomplete 55 adj.
hammam
ablutions 648 n.
hammer
be vigorous 174 vb.
hammer 279 n.
strike 279 vb.
missile 287 n.
pulverizer 332 n.
be loud 400 vb.
tool 630 n.
strike at 712 vb.
club 723 n.
— at
repeat oneself 106 vb.
exert oneself 682 vb.
— away at
persevere 600 vb.
— in/into
affix 45 vb.
pierce 263 vb.
insert 303 vb.
— into one's head
memorize 505 vb.
— out
form 243 vb.
think 449 vb.
carry through 725 vb.
hammer and sickle
heraldry 547 n.
hammer and tongs
violently 176 adv.
hammerbeam roof
roof 226 n.
hammer-toed
footed 214 adj.
blemished 845 adj.
hammock
hanging object 217 n.
bed 218 n.
hamper
basket 194 n.
impair 655 vb.
be difficult 700 vb.
hinder 702 vb.
restrain 747 vb.
hams
buttocks 238 n.
hamster
animal 365 n.
hamstring
disable 161 vb.
hinder 702 vb.
hamstrings
leg 267 n.
hand
limb 53 n.
bunch 74 n.
group 74 n.
timekeeper 117 n.
long measure 203 n.
laterality 239 n.
pass 305 vb.
person 371 n.
feeler 378 n.
finger 378 n.
indicator 547 n.
lettering 586 n.
instrument 628 n.
doer 676 n.
worker 686 n.
servant 742 n.
nippers 778 n.
portion 783 n.
— back
restore 656 vb.
— down
transfer 272 vb.
— it to
be inferior 35 vb.
be just 913 vb.
grant claims 915 vb.
praise 923 vb.
— on
transfer 272 vb.
— out
provide 633 vb.
— over
transfer 272 vb.
pass 305 vb.
relinquish 621 vb.
resign 753 vb.
transfer 780 n.
give 781 vb.
handbag
bag 194 n.
handball
ball game 837 n.
handbill
advertisement 528 n.
the press 528 n.
handbook
guidebook 524 n.
textbook 589 n.
handcart
pushcart 274 n.
hand-clapping
gesture 547 n.

handclasp
friendliness 880 n.
sociability 882 n.
courteous act 884 n.
handcuff
tie 45 vb.
arrest 747 vb.
fetter 747 vb.
handcuffs
fastening 47 n.
fetter 748 n.
handful
small quantity 33 n.
bunch 74 n.
nonconformist 84 n.
fewness 105 n.
contents 193 n.
difficulty 700 n.
hard task 700 n.
revolter 738 n.
hand grenade
bomb 723 n.
handhold
support 218 n.
retention 778 n.
hand-holder
aider 703 n.
handicap
equalize 28 vb.
advantage 34 n.
inferiority 35 n.
retard 278 vb.
inexpedience 643 n.
illness 651 n.
encumbrance 702 n.
hinder 702 vb.
contest 716 n.
handicraft
business 622 n.
ornamental art 844 n.
handiness
instrumentality 628 n.
utility 640 n.
skill 694 n.
hand in glove
concurrently 181 adv.
in league 708 adv.
friendly 880 adj.
hand in hand
joined 45 adj.
with 89 adv.
cooperatively 706 adv.
sociably 882 adv.
handiwork
effect 157 n.
product 164 n.
deed 676 n.
ornamental art 844 n.
handkerchief
cleaning cloth 648 n.
handle
opportunity 137 n.
operate 173 vb.
handle 218 n.
opener 263 n.
touch 378 vb.
name 561 n.
dissertate 591 vb.
tool 630 n.
use 673 vb.
deal with 688 vb.
manage 689 vb.
trade 791 vb.
honours 866 n.
title 870 n.
handling
action 676 n.
conduct 688 n.
management 689 n.
hand lotion
cleanser 648 n.
cosmetic 843 n.
hand-made
nonuniform 17 adj.
produced 164 adj.
handmaid
instrument 628 n.
auxiliary 707 n.
domestic 742 n.
hand of friendship
peace offering 719 n.
hand-operated
instrumental 628 adj.
handout
report 524 n.
advertisement 528 n.
news 529 n.
incentive 612 n.
subvention 703 n.
gift 781 n.
hand over fist
swiftly 277 adv.
hand over hand
continuously 71 adv.
hand-picked
chosen 605 adj.
excellent 644 adj.
handrail
handle 218 n.
prop 218 n.
hands
personnel 686 n.
handsel
initiate 68 vb.
security 767 n.
gift 781 n.
payment 804 n.
handshake
arrival 295 n.
gesture 547 n.
friendliness 880 n.
sociability 882 n.
courteous act 884 n.
hand-signal
gesture 547 n.
hands in one's pockets
without action 677 adv.
hands off!
hands off 620 int.
handsome
liberal 813 adj.
beautiful 841 adj.
handspring
overturning 221 n.
hand's turn
labour 682 n.
hand that rocks the cradle
influence 178 n.
hand-to-hand
contending 716 adj.
hand-to-mouth existence
poverty 801 n.
handwoven
crossed 222 adj.
handwriting
lettering 586 n.
writing 586 n.
handwriting expert
detective 459 n.
calligrapher 586 n.
handy
little 196 adj.
near 200 adj.
light 323 adj.
instrumental 628 adj.
useful 640 adj.
advisable 642 adj.
skilful 694 adj.
tractable 701 adj.
handyman
mender 656 n.
proficient person 696 n.
servant 742 n.
hang
come unstuck 49 vb.
pendency 217 n.
hang 217 vb.
descend 309 vb.
oscillate 317 vb.
kill 362 vb.
appearance 445 n.
show 522 vb.
execute 963 vb.vb.
— about/around
be late 136 vb.
be near 200 vb.
expect 507 vb.
be inactive 679 vb.
— back
be unwilling 598 vb.
avoid 620 vb.
refuse 760 vb.
be modest 874 vb.
— by a thread
be uncertain 474 vb.
be in danger 661 vb.
— fire
be pending 136 vb.
pause 145 vb.
be inert 175 vb.
move slowly 278 vb.
be unwilling 598 vb.
not act 677 vb.
miscarry 728 vb.
— in the balance
be pending 136 vb.
— on
affix 45 vb.
wait 136 vb.
go on 146 vb.
hang 217 vb.
persevere 600 vb.
be subject 745 vb.
— one's head
be dejected 834 vb.
be humbled 872 vb.
— on the lips of
hear 415 vb.
be attentive 455 vb.
— on to
store 632 vb.
retain 778 vb.
be selfish 932 vb.
— out the flags
celebrate 876 vb.
— over
impend 155 vb.
be high 209 vb.
jut 254 vb.
fly 271 vb.
— round
court 889 vb.
— together
accord 24 vb.
unite with 45 vb.
cohere 48 vb.
concur 181 vb.
be reasonable 475 vb.
cooperate 706 vb.
— up
terminate 69 vb.
cease 145 vb.
hang 217 vb.
be mute 578 vb.
stop using 674 vb.
— upon
depend 157 vb.
hangar
stable 192 n.
air travel 271 n.
hangdog
guilty 936 adj.
hangdog expression
humiliation 872 n.
hanger
hanger 217 n.
prop 218 n.
hanger-on
concomitant 89 n.
follower 284 n.
auxiliary 707 n.
dependant 742 n.
toady 879 n.
flatterer 925 n.
hang gliding
aeronautics 271 n.
sport 837 n.
hanging judge
tyrant 735 n.
judge 957 n.

hangings
hanging object 217 n.
covering 226 n.
hangman
killer 362 n.
punisher 963 n.
hangout
abode 192 n.
hangover
sequel 67 n.
pain 377 n.
intemperance 943 n.
crapulence 949 n.
hangup
prejudgment 481 n.
eccentricity 503 n.
hindrance 702 n.
worry 825 n.
hank
bunch 74 n.
hanker after
regret 830 vb.
desire 859 vb.
hanky-panky
deception 542 n.
foul play 930 n.
Hansard
record 548 n.
hansom
cab 274 n.
Hanukkah
holy day 988 n.
Hanuman
Hindu deities 967 n.
hap
chance 159 n.vb.
haphazard
casual 159 adj.
indiscriminate 464 adj.
designless 618 adj.
hapless
unfortunate 731 adj.
happen
be 1 vb.
happen 154 vb.
result 157 vb.
chance 159 vb.
appear 445 vb.
be true 494 vb.
— again
reoccur 106 vb.
— on
discover 484 vb.
happening
event 154 n.
happening 154 adj.
amusement 837 n.
happiness
euphoria 376 n.
good 615 n.
palmy days 730 n.
happiness 824 n.
cheerfulness 833 n.
happy
apt 24 adj.
opportune 137 adj.
comfortable 376 adj.
elegant 575 adj.
willing 597 adj.
good 615 adj.
well-made 694 adj.
concordant 710 adj.
pacificatory 719 adj.
successful 727 adj.
prosperous 730 adj.
happy 824 adj.
pleased 824 adj.
pleasurable 826 adj.
content 828 adj.
cheerful 833 adj.
drunk 949 adj.
paradisiac 971 adj.
happy either way
choiceless 606 adj.
happy ending
good 615 n.
success 727 n.
happy event
propagation 167 n.
Happy Families
card game 837 n.
happy-go-lucky
negligent 458 adj.
designless 618 adj.
unprepared 670 adj.
unskilful 695 adj.
lax 734 adj.
cheerful 833 adj.
happy hunting grounds
the dead 361 n.
mythic heaven 971 n.
happy medium
average 30 n.
middle way 625 n.
happy release
decease 361 n.
happy returns
congratulation 886 n.
happy thought
idea 451 n.
contrivance 623 n.
hara-kiri
suicide 362 n.
punishment 963 n.
harangue
teach 534 vb.
be diffuse 570 vb.
oration 579 n.
orate 579 vb.
dissertation 591 n.
harass
fatigue 684 vb.
oppress 735 vb.
torment 827 vb.
harassed
in difficulties 700 adj.
suffering 825 adj.
harbinger
precursor 66 n.
omen 511 n.
informant 524 n.
messenger 529 n.
harbour
stopping place 145 n.
goal 295 n.
shelter 662 n.
harbourmaster
nautical personnel 270 n.
hard
painfully 32 adv.
strong 162 adj.
vigorously 174 adv.
hard 326 adj.
unsavoury 391 adj.
puzzling 517 adj.
unclear 568 adj.
resolute 599 adj.
laborious 682 adj.
difficult 700 adj.
adverse 731 adj.
severe 735 adj.
thick-skinned 820 adj.
paining 827 adj.
unkind 898 adj.
pitiless 906 adj.
unjust 914 adj.
impenitent 940 adj.
intoxicating 949 adj.
impious 980 adj.
hard at it
busy 678 adj.
labouring 682 adj.
hardback
book 589 n.
hard-bitten
thick-skinned 820 adj.
unkind 898 adj.
hardboard
paper 631 n.
hardboiled
tough 329 adj.
unbelieving 486 adj.
severe 735 adj.
thick-skinned 820 adj.
unkind 898 adj.
hard breathing
fatigue 684 n.
hard by
near 200 adj.adv.
hard case
misfortune 731 n.
hard cash
money 797 n.
hard copy
data processing 86 n.
hard core
solid body 324 n.
hardness 326 n.
stamina 600 n.
obstinate person 602 n.
building material 631 n.
impurity 951 n.
hard drinker
sensualist 944 n.
drunkard 949 n.
hard drug
drug-taking 949 n.
harden
strengthen 162 vb.
be dense 324 vb.
harden 326 vb.
habituate 610 vb.
mature 669 vb.
be dear 811 vb.
make insensitive 820 vb.
— one's heart
be severe 735 vb.
refuse 760 vb.
be insensitive 820 vb.
be inimical 881 vb.
be pitiless 906 vb.
be impenitent 940 vb.
be impious 980 vb.
hardened
unfeeling 375 adj.
obstinate 602 adj.
habituated 610 adj.
(See **hard** *)*
hardened arteries
cardiovascular disease 651 n.
hard-featured
ugly 842 adj.
hard feelings
enmity 881 n.
resentment 891 n.
hard-fisted
parsimonious 816 adj.
hard-fought
laborious 682 adj.
hard going
difficulty 700 n.
hard hat
headgear 228 n.
hard-headed
intelligent 498 adj.
severe 735 adj.
hard-hearted
cruel 898 adj.
pitiless 906 adj.
hard-hitting
disapproving 924 adj.
hard knocks
fight 716 n.
hard labour
labour 682 n.
penalty 963 n.
hard life
adversity 731 n.
hard line
obstinacy 602 n.
hard-liner
obstinate person 602 n.
tyrant 735 n.
hard luck
nondesign 618 n.
misfortune 731 n.

hard-luck story
lament 836 n.
hardly
slightly 33 adv.
seldom 140 adv.
with difficulty 700 adv.
hardly any
few 105 adj.
hard-mouthed
obstinate 602 adj.
hardness
stability 153 n.
strength 162 n.
density 324 n.
hardness 326 n.
toughness 329 n.
resolution 599 n.
obstinacy 602 n.
difficulty 700 n.
severity 735 n.
moral insensibility 820 n.
inhumanity 898 n.
hardness of heart
inhumanity 898 n.
pitilessness 906 n.
wickedness 934 n.
impenitence 940 n.
hard-nosed
obstinate 602 adj.
hard nut to crack
enigma 530 n.
difficulty 700 n.
hard of hearing
deaf 416 adj.
hard on
nearly 200 adv.
oppressive 735 adj.
unjust 914 adj.
hard pad
animal disease 651 n.
hardpan
base 214 n.
solid body 324 n.
hard-pressed
hasty 680 adj.
in difficulties 700 adj.
hindered 702 adj.
poor 801 adj.
hard row to hoe
hard task 700 n.
hards
fibre 208 n.
hard sell
advertisement 528 n.
inducement 612 n.
sale 793 n.
hardship
adversity 731 n.
annoyance 827 n.
hard shoulder
road 624 n.
hard standing
base 214 n.
hard stuff
alcoholic drink 301 n.
hard task
impossibility 470 n.
undertaking 672 n.
hard task 700 n.
hard taskmaster
tyrant 735 n.
malcontent 829 n.
perfectionist 862 n.
hard times
adversity 731 n.
hard to believe
improbable 472 adj.
unbelieved 486 adj.
hard to come by
scarce 636 adj.
hard-top
automobile 274 n.
hard to place
unconformable 84 adj.
hard to please
discontented 829 adj.
fastidious 862 adj.
hard to understand
puzzling 517 adj.
hard up
unprovided 636 adj.
poor 801 adj.
hardware
data processing 86 n.
product 164 n.
hard way, the
laboriously 682 adv.
with difficulty 700 adv.
hardwood
wood 366 n.
hard words
imperspicuity 568 n.
reproach 924 n.
hard work
perseverance 600 n.
labour 682 n.
hard task 700 n.
hard worker
busy person 678 n.
hardy
stalwart 162 adj.
vegetal 366 adj.
healthy 650 adj.
courageous 855 adj.
insolent 878 adj.
hardy annual
repetition 106 n.
hare
speeder 277 n.
move fast 277 vb.
mammal 365 n.
harebrained
light-minded 456 adj.
absurd 497 adj.
foolish 499 adj.
rash 857 adj.
Hare Krishna sect
non-Christian sect 978 n.
harelip
blemish 845 n.
harem
womankind 373 n.
seclusion 883 n.
love-nest 887 n.
hares and hounds
children's games 837 n.
harijan
commoner 869 n.
outcast 883 n.
hark
pursue 619 vb.
— back
look back 125 vb.
revert 148 vb.
turn back 286 vb.
notice 455 vb.
retrospect 505 vb.
regret 830 vb.
harl
filament 208 n.
harlequin
variegation 437 n.
fool 501 n.
harlequinade
stage play 594 n.
Harley Street
doctor 658 n.
harlot
prostitute 952 n.
harlotry
social evil 951 n.
unchastity 951 n.
harm
evil 616 n.
be inexpedient 643 vb.
badness 645 n.
harm 645 vb.
impair 655 vb.
hurt 827 vb.
harmful
destructive 165 adj.
evil 616 adj.
inexpedient 643 adj.
harmful 645 adj.
insalubrious 653 adj.
baneful 659 adj.
dangerous 661 adj.
adverse 731 adj.
paining 827 adj.
malevolent 898 adj.
wrong 914 adj.
harmless
defenceless 161 adj.
weak 163 adj.
moderate 177 adj.
beneficial 644 adj.
salubrious 652 adj.
safe 660 adj.
peaceful 717 adj.
humble 872 adj.
amiable 884 adj.
innocent 935 adj.
harmonic
musical note 410 n.
harmonica
gong 414 n.
organ 414 n.
harmonic motion
oscillation 317 n.
harmonic progression
ratio 85 n.
harmonious
harmonious 410 adj.
musical 412 adj.
soft-hued 425 adj.
pleasurable 826 adj.
beautiful 841 adj.
friendly 880 adj.
(See **harmony** *)*
harmonist
musician 413 n.
harmonium
organ 414 n.
harmonize, harmonise
adjust 24 vb.
combine 50 vb.
order 60 vb.
synchronize 123 vb.
concur 181 vb.
harmonize 410 vb.
compose music 413 vb.
sing 413 vb.
pacify 719 vb.
harmony
agreement 24 n.
completeness 54 n.
order 60 n.
concurrence 181 n.
symmetry 245 n.
melody 410 n.
music 412 n.
consensus 488 n.
elegance 575 n.
concord 710 n.
peace 717 n.
pleasurableness 826 n.
harness
affix 45 vb.
tackling 47 n.
dressing 228 n.
start out 296 vb.
break in 369 vb.
equipment 630 n.
use 673 vb.
armour 713 n.
harp
harp 414 n.
harpist
instrumentalist 413 n.
harp on
repeat oneself 106 vb.
sustain 146 vb.
be tedious 838 vb.
harpoon
sharp point 256 n.
spear 723 n.

harpsichord
piano 414 n.
harpy
tyrant 735 n.
taker 786 n.
hellhag 904 n.
demon 970 n.
harridan
eyesore 842 n.
shrew 892 n.
harrier
speeder 277 n.
bird 365 n.
harrow
smoother 258 n.
draw 288 vb.
farm tool 370 n.
cultivate 370 vb.
torment 827 vb.
frighten 854 vb.
harrowing
painful 377 adj.
distressing 827 adj.
harry
pursue 619 vb.
attack 712 vb.
torment 827 vb.
be malevolent 898 vb.
harsh
exorbitant 32 adj.
vigorous 174 adj.
pungent 388 adj.
strident 407 adj.
discordant 411 adj.
florid 425 adj.
unclear 568 adj.
inelegant 576 adj.
harmful 645 adj.
oppressive 735 adj.
paining 827 adj.
insolent 878 adj.
ungracious 885 adj.
unkind 898 adj.
pitiless 906 adj.
harshness
roughness 259 n.
hart
mammal 365 n.
male animal 372 n.
hartal
strike 145 n.
hartshorn
tonic 658 n.
harum-scarum
disorderly 61 adj.
confusedly 61 adv.
light-minded 456 adj.
desperado 857 n.
rash 857 adj.
haruspex
diviner 511 n.
harvest
great quantity 32 n.
increment 36 n.
assemblage 74 n.
autumn 129 n.
growth 157 n.
product 164 n.
abundance 171 n.
agriculture 370 n.
cultivate 370 vb.
benefit 615 n.
store 632 n.vb.
plenty 635 n.
acquire 771 vb.
take 786 vb.
harvester
accumulator 74 n.
farmer 370 n.
harvest home
assemblage 74 n.
celebration 876 n.
harvest supper
feasting 301 n.
festivity 837 n.
has-been
past 125 adj.
archaism 127 n.
loser 728 n.
hash
a mixture 43 n.
medley 43 n.
confusion 61 n.
drug-taking 949 n.
Hasidim
non-Christian sect 978 n.
hasp
joint 45 n.
fastening 47 n.
hassle
quarrel 709 n.
hassock
cushion 218 n.
church utensil 990 n.
haste
vigorousness 174 n.
speeding 277 n.
commotion 318 n.
nonpreparation 670 n.
activity 678 n.
haste 680 n.
excitability 822 n.
rashness 857 n.
hasten
be early 135 vb.
cause 156 vb.
accelerate 277 vb.
move fast 277 vb.
incite 612 vb.
be busy 678 vb.
hasten 680 vb.
be rash 857 vb.
hasty
brief 114 adj.
furious 176 adj.
speedy 277 adj.
negligent 458 adj.
unwise 499 adj.
unprepared 670 adj.
hasty 680 adj.
excitable 822 adj.
rash 857 adj.
irascible 892 adj.
hat
headgear 228 n.
hat box
box 194 n.
cylinder 252 n.
hatch
group 74 n.
produce 164 vb.
generate 167 vb.
reproduce itself 167 vb.
covering 226 n.
doorway 263 n.
breed stock 369 vb.
darken 418 vb.
imagine 513 vb.
fake 541 vb.
plan 623 vb.
mature 669 vb.
— a plot
plot 623 vb.
hatchback
automobile 274 n.
hatched
born 360 adj.
hatchery
nest 192 n.
stock farm 369 n.
hatchet
sharp edge 256 n.
axe 723 n.
hatchet face
thinness 206 n.
hatchet job
destruction 165 n.
detraction 926 n.
hatchet man
destroyer 168 n.
murderer 362 n.
ruffian 904 n.
defamer 926 n.
hatchment
obsequies 364 n.
heraldry 547 n.
monument 548 n.
hatchway
doorway 263 n.
hate
dislike 861 vb.
hatred 888 n.
hate 888 vb.
resentment 891 n.
malevolence 898 n.
jealousy 911 n.
(See **hatred***)*
hateful
not nice 645 adj.
unpleasant 827 adj.
disliked 861 adj.
disreputable 867 adj.
hateful 888 adj.
hatefulness
painfulness 827 n.
odium 888 n.
hateful object
enemy 881 n.
hateful object 888 n.
hater of the human race
misanthrope 902 n.
hat in the ring
defiance 711 n.
hatless
uncovered 229 adj.
hatpin
fastening 47 n.
hatred
prejudice 481 n.
dissension 709 n.
phobia 854 n.
dislike 861 n.
enmity 881 n.
hatred 888 n.
resentment 891 n.
malevolence 898 n.
jealousy 911 n.
hatred of mankind
misanthropy 902 n.
hatted
dressed 228 adj.
hatter
clothier 228 n.
hat trick
triplication 94 n.
masterpiece 694 n.
success 727 n.
hat-waving
gesture 547 n.
hauberk
armour 713 n.
haughty
authoritarian 735 adj.
noble 868 adj.
proud 871 adj.
insolent 878 adj.
unsociable 883 adj.
despising 922 adj.
haul
navigate 269 vb.
draw 288 vb.
work 682 vb.
taking 786 n.
booty 790 n.
— down
lower 311 vb.
— down the flag
submit 721 vb.
— in
arrest 747 vb.
— over the coals
reprove 924 vb.
— up
elevate 310 vb.
indict 928 vb.
haulage
transport 272 n.
traction 288 n.
hauled up
accused 928 adj.
haulier
transferrer 272 n.
carrier 273 n.
traction 288 n.

haunches
buttocks 238 n.
haunt
focus 76 n.
reoccur 106 vb.
recur 139 vb.
go on 146 vb.
district 184 n.
locality 187 n.
be present 189 vb.
abode 192 n.
home 192 n.
dwell 192 vb.
appear 445 vb.
engross 449 vb.
attract notice 455 vb.
bias 481 vb.
be remembered 505 vb.
be wont 610 vb.
torment 827 vb.
frighten 854 vb.
haunt 970 vb.
haunted
spooky 970 adj.
bewitched 983 adj.
haunted by
obsessed 455 adj.
haunter
ghost 970 n.
haute couture
dressing 228 n.
fashion 848 n.
haute cuisine
cookery 301 n.
haute école
equitation 267 n.
hauteur
pride 871 n.
haute vulgarisation
intelligibility 516 n.
Havana
tobacco 388 n.
have
unite with 45 vb.
contain 56 vb.
comprise 78 vb.
confute 479 vb.
know 490 vb.
understand 516 vb.
befool 542 vb.
possess 773 vb.
— a baby
reproduce itself 167 vb.
— a ball
amuse oneself 837 vb.
— a bone to pick
make quarrels 709 vb.
— a case
be reasonable 475 vb.
— a down on
be biased 481 vb.
be severe 735 vb.
dislike 861 vb.
hate 888 vb.
do wrong 914 vb.
— a finger in the pie
interfere 231 vb.
meddle 678 vb.
— a funny feeling
intuit 476 vb.
— a go
attempt 671 vb.
— a good mind to
be willing 597 vb.
desire 859 vb.
— a good time
prosper 730 vb.
be cheerful 833 vb.
rejoice 835 vb.
revel 837 vb.
— a hand in
cause 156 vb.
be instrumental 628 vb.
do 676 vb.
participate 775 vb.
— a hold on
influence 178 vb.
— a hunch
intuit 476 vb.
opine 485 vb.
suppose 512 vb.
— and hold
possess 773 vb.
— an eye to
be mindful 455 vb.
foresee 510 vb.
intend 617 vb.
— at
attack 712 vb.
strike at 712 vb.
— at one's command
dispose of 673 vb.
possess 773 vb.
— a way with
manage 689 vb.
— dealings with
trade 791 vb.
be friendly 880 vb.
— designs (on)
aim at 617 vb.
plot 623 vb.
desire 859 vb.
— done with
cease 145 vb.
stop using 674 vb.
— everything
be complete 54 vb.
comprise 78 vb.
— had enough
have enough 635 vb.
submit 721 vb.
— had it
be destroyed 165 vb.
die 361 vb.
— had its day
be past 125 vb.
be old 127 vb.
— in mind
be mindful 455 vb.
expect 507 vb.
mean 514 vb.
intend 617 vb.
— it all one's own way
will 595 vb.
do easily 701 vb.
win 727 vb.
be free 744 vb.
dominate 733 vb.
— it coming to one
deserve 915 vb.
be punished 963 vb.
— it in for
be biased 481 vb.
hate 888 vb.
be malevolent 898 vb.
— it in one
be able 160 vb.
— it made
prosper 730 vb.
— no answer
be uncertain 474 vb.
be confuted 479 vb.
be unintelligible 517 vb.
— no axe to grind
be disinterested 931 vb.
— no bearing on
be unrelated 10 vb.
— no business there
be unconformable 84 vb.
— no end
be eternal 115 vb.
— no excuse
be guilty 936 vb.
— no hand in
avoid 620 vb.
— no heart
be pitiless 906 vb.
— no heart/stomach for
be cowardly 856 vb.
dislike 861 vb.
— no idea
not know 491 vb.
— no objection
consent 758 vb.
— no secrets
be visible 443 vb.
be intelligible 516 vb.
be plain 522 vb.
— no sense
be foolish 499 vb.
— no sense of pride
demean oneself 867 vb.
be humble 872 vb.
— nothing to do with
be unrelated 10 vb.
disagree 25 vb.
avoid 620 vb.
refuse 760 vb.
make unwelcome 883 vb.
— nothing to gain
be disinterested 931 vb.
— no time for
be inattentive 456 vb.
disregard 458 vb.
dislike 861 vb.
make unwelcome 883 vb.
be rude 885 vb.
— no use for
not use 674 vb.
not respect 921 vb.
despise 922 vb.
— no will of one's own
conform 83 vb.
be subject 745 vb.
— occasion for
require 627 vb.
— on
wear 228 vb.
— one by the short hairs
overmaster 727 vb.
— one covered
aim 281 vb.
threaten 900 vb.
— one know
inform 524 vb.
— one on
befool 542 vb.
be witty 839 vb.
ridicule 851 vb.
— one's cake and eat it
attempt the impossible 470 vb.
— one's day
pass time 108 vb.
triumph 727 vb.
prosper 730 vb.
— one's fling
be active 678 vb.
be free 744 vb.
be intemperate 943 vb.
— one's hands full
busy oneself 622 vb.
be busy 678 vb.
be in difficulty 700 vb.
— one's head
be free 744 vb.
— one's head turned
be vain 873 vb.
— one's measure
know 490 vb.
— one's say
affirm 532 vb.
speak 579 vb.
be loquacious 581 vb.
— one's turn
come after 65 vb.
— one's way
will 595 vb.
be free 744 vb.

— one's wits about one
have feeling 374 vb.
be careful 457 vb.
be wise 498 vb.
be skilful 694 vb.
— one's work cut out
be in difficulty 700 vb.
— only oneself to please
be selfish 932 vb.
— only oneself to thank
deserve 915 vb.
— on one's plate
busy oneself 622 vb.
deal with 688 vb.
— other fish to fry
be engaged 138 vb.
relinquish 621 vb.
be busy 678 vb.
— over a barrel
dominate 733 vb.
— recourse to
avail oneself of 673 vb.
— reservations
doubt 486 vb.
dissent 489 vb.
— second thoughts
be irresolute 601 vb.
rectify 654 vb.
be nervous 854 vb.
— seen better days
grow old 131 vb.
deteriorate 655 vb.
have trouble 731 vb.
— shot one's bolt
fail 728 vb.
— (one) taped
appraise 465 vb.
know 490 vb.
manage 689 vb.
— the advantage
be unequal 29 vb.
predominate 34 vb.
overmaster 727 vb.
— the ball at one's feet
be successful 727 vb.
have luck 730 vb.
— the best of it
confute 479 vb.
succeed 727 vb.
— the desired effect
conduce 156 vb.
be expedient 642 vb.
— the ear of
influence 178 vb.
convince 485 vb.
— the edge on
predominate 34 vb.
— the last word
argue 475 vb.
affirm 532 vb.
— the law on
litigate 959 vb.
— the law on one's side
have a right 915 vb.
— the makings of
evidence 466 vb.
be likely 471 vb.
give hope 852 vb.
— the means
find means 629 vb.
have enough 635 vb.
afford 800 vb.
— the measure of
appraise 465 vb.
manage 689 vb.
— the whip hand
predominate 34 vb.
dominate 733 vb.
— time for
notice 455 vb.
give 781 vb.
be pleased 824 vb.
be courteous 884 vb.
— time to spare
be superfluous 637 vb.
have leisure 681 vb.
— to do with
be related 9 vb.
do 676 vb.
deal with 688 vb.
— too many irons in the fire
undertake 672 vb.
act foolishly 695 vb.
— to run for it
be in danger 661 vb.
— what it takes
be strong 162 vb.
stand firm 599 vb.
persevere 600 vb.
be courageous 855 vb.
— words
argue 475 vb.
bicker 709 vb.
haven
resting place 266 n.
goal 295 n.
protection 660 n.
shelter 662 n.
have-nots, the
poor person 801 n.
lower classes 869 n.
haver
be loquacious 581 vb.
haversack
bag 194 n.
haves, the
rich person 800 n.
upper class 868 n.
havoc
disorder 61 n.
havoc 165 n.
impairment 655 n.
terror tactics 712 n.
spoliation 788 n.
haw-haw
speech defect 580 n.
hawk
eruct 300 vb.
bird 365 n.
rasp 407 vb.
hunter 619 n.
hunt 619 vb.
attacker 712 n.
militarist 722 n.
sell 793 vb.
— about
publish 528 vb.
offer 759 vb.
hawker
traveller 268 n.
pedlar 794 n.
hawk-eyed
seeing 438 adj.
hawkish
warlike 718 adj.
hawser
cable 47 n.
hay
provender 301 n.
grass 366 n.
dance 837 n.
hay box
provisions 301 n.
haycock
store 632 n.
hay fever
excretion 302 n.
ill health 651 n.
hayfork
farm tool 370 n.
hayloft
attic 194 n.
farm tool 370 n.
haymaker
knock 279 n.
hayseed
country-dweller 869 n.
haystack
farm tool 370 n.
store 632 n.
haywain
cart 274 n.
farm tool 370 n.
haywire
orderless 61 adj.
hazard
chance 159 n.
gamble 618 vb.
danger 661 n.
endanger 661 vb.
pitfall 663 n.
obstacle 702 n.
— a guess
suppose 512 vb.
hazardous
speculative 618 adj.
dangerous 661 adj.
frightening 854 adj.
haze
cloud 355 n.
uncertainty 474 n.
hazel
tree 366 n.
brown 430 adj.
hazel nut
fruit 301 n.
hazy
cloudy 355 adj.
dim 419 adj.
opaque 423 adj.
indistinct 444 adj.
uncertain 474 adj.
puzzling 517 adj.
hazy recollection
oblivion 506 n.
he
male 372 n.
children's games 837 n.
head
come first 34 vb.
come before 64 vb.
beginning 68 n.
extremity 69 n.
classification 77 n.
energy 160 n.
interval 201 n.
long measure 203 n.
head 213 n.
vertex 213 n.
central 225 adj.
face 237 n.n.
be in front 237 vb.
dome 253 n.
strike 279 vb.
precede 283 vb.
repel 292 vb.
bubble 355 n.
flower 366 n.
person 371 n.
topic 452 n.
intelligence 498 n.
teacher 537 n.
image 551 n.
picture 553 n.
sculpture 554 n.
bigwig 638 n.
direct 689 vb.
director 690 n.
trophy 729 n.
master 741 n.
drug-taking 949 n.
— for
steer for 281 vb.
— off
repel 292 vb.
converge 293 vb.
dissuade 613 vb.
hinder 702 vb.
headache
pang 377 n.
question 459 n.
illness 651 n.
difficulty 700 n.
worry 825 n.
head and shoulders above
superior 34 adj.
elevated 310 adj.
headband
headgear 228 n.
bookbinding 589 n.

head boy/girl
superior 34 n.
head-count
numeration 86 n.
headdress
headgear 228 n.
header
descent 309 n.
plunge 313 n.
head first
violently 176 adv.
in front 237 adv.
headgear
headgear 228 n.
head-hunter
killer 362 n.
hunter 619 n.
ruffian 904 n.
heading
prelude 66 n.
beginning 68 n.
classification 77 n.
label 547 n.
record 548 n.
name 561 n.
head in the sand
avoider 620 n.
inaction 677 n.
headland
high land 209 n.
projection 254 n.
headless
subtracted 39 adj.
short 204 adj.
headlight, headlamp
lamp 420 n.
headline
beginning 68 n.
advertisement 528 n.
edition 589 n.
make important 638 vb.
excitant 821 n.
headlong
violently 176 adv.
swiftly 277 adv.
hasty 680 adj.
rashly 857 adv.
headman
director 690 n.
officer 741 n.
potentate 741 n.
headmaster, headmistress
teacher 537 n.
director 690 n.
head-on
frontal 237 adj.
head over heels
completely 54 adv.
inverted 221 adj.
round and round 315 adv.
head over heels in love
enamoured 887 adj.
headphones, headset
hearing aid 415 n.
telecommunication 531 n.
headpiece
head 213 n.
intelligence 498 n.
headquarters
focus 76 n.
abode 192 n.
plan 623 n.
headrest
prop 218 n.
headroom
room 183 n.
headship
position of authority 733 n.
headshrinker
psychologist 447 n.
'heads I win tails you lose'
injustice 914 n.
foul play 930 n.
selfishness 932 n.
headsman
punisher 963 n.
heads or tails
equal chance 159 n.
heads rolling
punishment 963 n.
headstall
fetter 748 n.
head start
advantage 34 n.
heads together
advice 691 n.
headstone
prop 218 n.
obsequies 364 n.
headstrong
furious 176 adj.
wilful 602 adj.
rash 857 adj.
head to foot
longwise 203 adv.
head to tail
longwise 203 adv.
head-up
vertical 215 adj.
head waiter
servant 742 n.
headwaters
source 156 n.
stream 350 n.
headway
room 183 n.
motion 265 n.
water travel 269 n.
progression 285 n.
headwind
contrariety 14 n.
contraposition 240 n.
wind 352 n.
obstacle 702 n.
opposition 704 n.
headwork
thought 449 n.
heady
strong 162 adj.
vigorous 174 adj.
pungent 388 adj.
odorous 394 adj.
exciting 821 adj.
intoxicating 949 adj.
heal
cure 656 vb.
remedy 658 vb.
pacify 719 vb.
heal-all
remedy 658 n.
healer
mender 656 n.
doctor 658 n.
healing quality
remedy 658 n.
healing touch
medical art 658 n.
health
vitality 162 n.
draught 301 n.
euphoria 376 n.
goodness 644 n.
health 650 n.
salubrity 652 n.
celebration 876 n.
health and wealth
prosperity 730 n.
health farm
beauty parlour 843 n.
health food
food 301 n.
salubrity 652 n.
health-giving
salubrious 652 adj.
health resort
salubrity 652 n.
health salts
purgative 658 n.
health visitor
nurse 658 n.
healthy
strong 162 adj.
vigorous 174 adj.
beneficial 644 adj.
undamaged 646 adj.
healthy 650 adj.
salubrious 652 adj.
restored 656 adj.
heap
great quantity 32 n.
chief part 52 n.
accumulation 74 n.
bunch 74 n.
bring together 74 vb.
bulk 195 n.
small hill 209 n.
store 632 n.vb.
acquire 771 vb.
— on
add 38 vb.
— together
not discriminate 464 vb.
heaps
great quantity 32 n.
multitude 104 n.
hear
have feeling 374 vb.
hear 415 vb.
be attentive 455 vb.
enquire 459 vb.
be informed 524 vb.
consent 758 vb.
— a cause
judge 480 vb.
try a case 959 vb.
— nothing
be deaf 416 vb.
be incurious 454 vb.
be inattentive 456 vb.
— the call
be induced 612 vb.
hear! hear!
488 int.
923 int.
heard
sounding 398 adj.
loud 400 adj.
auditory 415 adj.
evidential 466 adj.
known 490 adj.
hearer(s)
listener 415 n.
allocution 583 n.
hearing
sense 374 n.
sound 398 n.
hearing 415 n.
listening 415 n.
auditory 415 adj.
exam 459 n.
council 692 n.
legal trial 959 n.
hearing aid
megaphone 400 n.
hearing aid 415 n.
hearken
hear 415 vb.
be willing 597 vb.
obey 739 vb.
consent 758 vb.
hearsay
evidence 466 n.
information 524 n.
rumour 529 n.
hearse
vehicle 274 n.
funeral 364 n.
heart
essence 1 n.
essential part 5 n.
middle 70 n.
focus 76 n.
interiority 224 n.
centre 225 n.
life 360 n.
spirit 447 n.
chief thing 638 n.
affections 817 n.
courage 855 n.
love token 889 n.
darling 890 n.
heartache
pain 377 n.
suffering 825 n.
dejection 834 n.

heart and soul
completely 54 adv.
willingly 597 adv.
laboriously 682 adv.
feelingly 818 adv.
heart attack
cardiovascular disease 651 n.
heartbreaking
distressing 827 adj.
heartbroken
disappointed 509 adj.
unhappy 825 adj.
heartburn
digestive disorders 651 n.
heart-burning
regret 830 n.
resentment 891 n.
jealousy 911 n.
heart condition
cardiovascular disease 651 n.
hearten
invigorate 174 vb.
aid 703 vb.
animate 821 vb.
relieve 831 vb.
cheer 833 vb.
give courage 855 vb.
heartfelt
felt 818 adj.
hearth
home 192 n.
furnace 383 n.
refuge 662 n.
hearth and home
family 11 n.
hearties
mariner 270 n.
chum 880 n.
heartily
greatly 32 adv.
willingly 597 adv.
laboriously 682 adv.
feelingly 818 adv.
amicably 880 adv.
heartland
district 184 n.
interiority 224 n.
land 344 n.
heartless
impassive 820 adj.
cruel 898 adj.
pitiless 906 adj.
impenitent 940 adj.
heart-lung machine
hospital 658 n.
heart of gold
benevolence 897 n.
good person 937 n.
heart of hearts
affections 817 n.
heart of oak
strength 162 n.
hardness 326 n.
resolution 599 n.
courage 855 n.
heart of stone
moral insensibility 820 n.
inhumanity 898 n.
heart of the matter
topic 452 n.
chief thing 638 n.
heart-rending
distressing 827 adj.
pitiable 905 adj.
heart's blood
essential part 5 n.
interiority 224 n.
life 360 n.
heart's desire
objective 617 n.
aspiration 852 n.
loved one 887 n.
heart's ease
content 828 n.
heart-shaped
curved 248 adj.
rotund 252 adj.
heart-sick
melancholic 834 adj.
heartstrings
affections 817 n.
heart surgery
surgery 658 n.
heartthrob
a beauty 841 n.
loved one 887 n.
heart-to-heart
undisguised 522 adj.
chat 584 n.
heart trouble
cardiovascular disease 651 n.
heart-warming
pleasant 376 adj.
felt 818 adj.
pleasurable 826 adj.
cheering 833 adj.
heart-whole
free 744 adj.
impassive 820 adj.
indifferent 860 adj.
unwedded 895 adj.
heartwood
interiority 224 n.
hardness 326 n.
wood 366 n.
hearty
vigorous 174 adj.
healthy 650 adj.
feeling 818 adj.
felt 818 adj.
cheerful 833 adj.
ill-bred 847 adj.
friendly 880 adj.
sociable 882 adj.
heat
summer 128 n.
dryness 342 n.
heat 379 n.
heat 381 vb.
contest 716 n.
excite 821 vb.
excitable state 822 n.
libido 859 n.
excite love 887 vb.
anger 891 n.
heated
violent 176 adj.
heater
cauldron 194 n.
heater 383 n.
heat exchanger
sources of energy 160 n.
heath
desert 172 n.
plain 348 n.
heathen
unbelieving 486 adj.
heathen 974 n.
idolater 982 n.
heathenism
ignorance 491 n.
antichristianity 974 n.
irreligion 974 n.
impiety 980 n.
idolatry 982 n.
heather
purpleness 436 n.
Heath Robinson
imaginative 513 adj.
heat measurement
thermometry 379 n.
heat retention
preservation 666 n.
heatstroke
frenzy 503 n.
heat treatment
therapy 658 n.
heat wave
weather 340 n.
heat 379 n.
heave
be periodic 141 vb.
carry 273 vb.
impel 279 vb.
propel 287 vb.
draw 288 vb.
vomit 300 vb.
oscillate 317 vb.
breathe 352 vb.
exertion 682 n.
show feeling 818 vb.
— the lead
be deep 211 vb.
navigate 269 vb.
plunge 313 vb.
measure 465 vb.
— to
bring to rest 266 vb.
navigate 269 vb.
— up
elevate 310 vb.
heaven
future state 124 n.
summit 213 n.
heaven 971 n.
heaven-born
worshipful 866 adj.
heavenly
celestial 321 adj.
super 644 adj.
pleasurable 826 adj.
splendid 841 adj.
divine 965 adj.
paradisiac 971 adj.
heavenly host
angel 968 n.
heavenly kingdom
heaven 971 n.
heavens
influence 178 n.
heavens 321 n.
heaven-sent
opportune 137 adj.
good 615 adj.
heavenward
aloft 209 adv.
heavier-than-air
aviational 276 adj.
heaviness
bulk 195 n.
sleepiness 679 n.
(See **heavy** *)*
heaving stomach
illness 651 n.
dislike 861 n.
Heaviside layer
atmosphere 340 n.
heavy
substantial 3 adj.
great 32 adj.
strong 162 adj.
inert 175 adj.
weighty 322 adj.
dense 324 adj.
odorous 394 adj.
fetid 397 adj.
nonresonant 405 adj.
unintelligent 499 adj.
the press 528 n.
forceful 571 adj.
inelegant 576 adj.
bad 645 adj.
inactive 679 adj.
laborious 682 adj.
severe 735 adj.
inexcitable 823 adj.
melancholic 834 adj.
serious 834 adj.
tedious 838 adj.
dull 840 adj.
heinous 934 adj.
heavy-armed
defended 713 adj.
heavy-eyed
sleepy 679 adj.
fatigued 684 adj.
heavy father
acting 594 n.
tyrant 735 n.
heavy-footed
clumsy 695 adj.
heavy-handed
violent 176 adj.
tactual 378 adj.
clumsy 695 adj.

oppressive 735 adj.
heavy-hearted
unhappy 825 adj.
melancholic 834 adj.
heavy-laden
full 54 adj.
hindered 702 adj.
suffering 825 adj.
heavy metal
music 412 n.
gun 723 n.
heavy sea
commotion 318 n.
wave 350 n.
heavy stuff
seriousness 834 n.
heavy traffic
activity 678 n.
heavy type
punctuation 547 n.
heavyweight
athlete 162 n.
bigwig 638 n.
pugilist 722 n.
heavy with
impending 155 adj.
fertilized 167 adj.
prolific 171 adj.
hebdomadal
seasonal 141 adj.
hebetude
unintelligence 499 n.
Hebraist
antiquarian 125 n.
Hebrew alphabet
letter 558 n.
Hecate
moon 321 n.
sorceress 983 n.
hecatomb
havoc 165 n.
oblation 981 n.
heckle
be obstructive 702 vb.
torment 827 vb.
heckler
dissentient 489 n.
hinderer 702 n.
hectare
measure 183 n.
hectic
heat 379 n.
fervent 818 adj.
excited 821 adj.
hector
boast 877 vb.
be insolent 878 vb.
threaten 900 vb.
hedge
set off 31 vb.
separation 46 n.
partition 231 n.
fence 235 n.
wood 366 n.
screen 421 n.
gamble 618 vb.
avoid 620 vb.
shelter 662 n.
obstacle 702 n.
defend 713 vb.
be cautious 858 vb.
— in
circumscribe 232 vb.
obstruct 702 vb.
hedgehog
prickle 256 n.
hedge-hop
be near 200 vb.
fly 271 vb.
hedgepriest
cleric 986 n.
hedonism
pleasure 376 n.
philosophy 449 n.
enjoyment 824 n.
sensualism 944 n.
hedonist
sensualist 944 n.
heebie-jeebies
nervousness 854 n.
heed
attention 455 n.
carefulness 457 n.
obey 739 vb.
observe 768 vb.
caution 858 n.
heedless
inattentive 456 adj.
negligent 458 adj.
forgetful 506 adj.
rash 857 adj.
heedlessness
indifference 860 n.
hee-haw
ululation 409 n.
heel
foot 214 n.
be oblique 220 vb.
rear 238 n.
kick 279 vb.
repair 656 vb.
cad 938 n.
— over
be inverted 221 vb.
navigate 269 vb.
tumble 309 vb.
heelball
art equipment 553 n.
hefty
whopping 32 adj.
stalwart 162 adj.
Hegelianism
philosophy 449 n.
hegemonic
directing 689 adj.
authoritative 733 adj.
hegemony
superiority 34 n.
precedence 64 n.
influence 178 n.
authority 733 n.
prestige 866 n.
Hegira, Hejira
departure 296 n.
heifer
young creature 132 n.
cattle 365 n.
female animal 373 n.
height
degree 27 n.
greatness 32 n.
superiority 34 n.
measure 183 n.
size 195 n.
height 209 n.
high land 209 n.
verticality 215 n.
elevation 310 n.
metrology 465 n.
heighten
augment 36 vb.
enlarge 197 vb.
make higher 209 vb.
elevate 310 vb.
exaggerate 546 vb.
aggravate 832 vb.
heights
high land 209 n.
land 344 n.
heinous
bad 645 adj.
accusable 928 adj.
heinous 934 adj.
guilty 936 adj.
heir
survivor 41 n.
successor 67 n.
descendant 170 n.
deputy 755 n.
beneficiary 776 n.
recipient 782 n.
dueness 915 n.
heirdom
possession 773 n.
heiress
descendant 170 n.
rich person 800 n.
heirloom
archaism 127 n.
dower 777 n.
heir of, be the
inherit 771 vb.
heirs
futurity 124 n.
posterity 170 n.
heirship
sonship 170 n.
acquisition 771 n.
possession 773 n.
held
credible 485 adj.
retained 778 adj.
held up
late 136 adj.
hindered 702 adj.
heliacal
celestial 321 adj.
helical
coiled 251 adj.
Helicon
poetry 593 n.
helicopter
aircraft 276 n.
heliocentric
central 225 adj.
celestial 321 adj.
heliograph
signal 547 n.vb.
Helios
sun 321 n.
classical deities 967 n.
helioscope
optical device 442 n.
heliotrope
purple 436 adj.
gem 844 n.
heliotype
photography 551 n.
printing 555 n.
heliport
air travel 271 n.
goal 295 n.
helium
lifter 310 n.
lightness 323 n.
helix
coil 251 n.
circuition 314 n.
hell
future state 124 n.
depth 211 n.
pain 377 n.
gaming-house 618 n.
bane 659 n.
suffering 825 n.
hell 972 n.
hell-bent
intending 617 adj.
rash 857 adj.
hell-born
diabolic 969 adj.
hellcat
violent creature 176 n.
hellhag 904 n.
sorceress 983 n.
hellebore
poisonous plant 659 n.
Hellenic
olden 127 adj.
Hellenist
linguist 557 n.
hellfire
fire 379 n.
hell 972 n.
hell for leather
swiftly 277 adv.
hellhag
hellhag 904 n.
monster 938 n.
hellish
damnable 645 adj.
cruel 898 adj.
heinous 934 adj.
wicked 934 adj.
diabolic 969 adj.
infernal 972 adj.

Hell's Angel
ruffian 904 n.
helm
sailing aid 269 n.
directorship 689 n.
helmet
headgear 228 n.
heraldry 547 n.
armour 713 n.
helminthology
zoology 367 n.
helmsman
navigator 270 n.
director 690 n.
helot
slave 742 n.
helotry
servitude 745 n.
help
concur 181 vb.
benefit 615 vb.
instrumentality 628 n.
be instrumental 628 vb.
utility 640 n.
be expedient 642 vb.
do good 644 vb.
cleaner 648 n.
remedy 658 n.vb.
facilitate 701 vb.
aid 703 n., vb.
aider 703 n.
servant 742 n.
give 781 vb.
— oneself
take 786 vb.
steal 788 vb.
helper
prop 218 n.
aider 703 n.
auxiliary 707 n.
servant 742 n.
friend 880 n.
benefactor 903 n.
helpful
willing 597 adj.
cooperative 706 adj.
benevolent 897 adj.
helping
meal 301 n.
provision 633 n.
portion 783 n.
helpless
defenceless 161 adj.
impotent 161 adj.
weak 163 adj.
vulnerable 661 adj.
helplessly
uselessly 641 adv.
helpmate
auxiliary 707 n.
colleague 707 n.
spouse 894 n.
helter-skelter
confusedly 61 adv.
descent 309 n.
hastily 680 adv.
pleasure ground 837 n.
hem
edging 234 n.
hem 234 vb.
limit 236 vb.
flank 239 vb.
fold 261 n.vb.
decorate 844 vb.
— in
surround 230 vb.
circumscribe 232 vb.
restrain 747 vb.
he-man
athlete 162 n.
violent creature 176 n.
male 372 n.
hemi-
fragmentary 53 adj.
bisected 92 adj.
hemiplegia
helplessness 161 n.
nervous disorders 651 n.
hemisphere
part 53 n.
bisection 92 n.
region 184 n.
sphere 252 n.
dome 253 n.
hemistich
verse form 593 n.
hemline
garment 228 n.
edging 234 n.
hemlock
poisonous plant 659 n.
means of execution 964 n.
hemp
fibre 208 n.
pungency 388 n.
drug-taking 949 n.
hen
poultry 365 n.
female animal 373 n.
hence
hence 158 adv.
henceforth
henceforth 124 adv.
henchman
aider 703 n.
auxiliary 707 n.
retainer 742 n.
hencoop, henhouse
stable 192 n.
cattle pen 369 n.
hendecasyllabic
poetic 593 adj.
henna
orange 432 n.
hairwash 843 n.
henotheism
deism 973 n.
hen party
womankind 373 n.
social gathering 882 n.
henpecked
subjected 745 adj.
hen run
stock farm 369 n.
hepatitis
digestive disorders 651 n.
heptad
over five 99 n.
heptameter
prosody 593 n.
her
female 373 n.
Hera
marriage 894 n.
Olympian deity 967 n.
herald
precursor 66 n.
precede 283 vb.
omen 511 n.
predict 511 vb.
informant 524 n.
proclaim 528 vb.
messenger 529 n.
heraldry 547 n.
deputy 755 n.
heraldic
heraldic 547 adj.
heraldry
heraldry 547 n.
herb
potherb 301 n.
plant 366 n.
medicine 658 n.
herbaceous
vegetal 366 adj.
herbaceous border
garden 370 n.
herbage
foliage 366 n.
grass 366 n.
farm 370 n.
herbal
vegetal 366 adj.
botany 368 n.
herbalist
botany 368 n.
doctor 658 n.
herbivore
eater 301 n.
animal 365 n.
herbivorous
feeding 301 adj.
herb tea
soft drink 301 n.
tonic 658 n.
Herculean
great 32 adj.
stalwart 162 adj.
huge 195 adj.
laborious 682 adj.
Herculean task
hard task 700 n.
Hercules
athlete 162 n.
demigod 967 n.
herd
group 74 n.
bring together 74 vb.
certain quantity 104 n.
animal 365 n.
groom 369 vb.
imprison 747 vb.
herd instinct
crowd 74 n.
herdsman
herdsman 369 n.
here
in place 186 adv.
here 189 adv.
hereabouts
nearly 200 adv.
hereafter
sequel 67 n.
future state 124 n.
prospectively 124 adv.
destiny 155 n.
here and there
sporadically 75 adv.
here and there 105 adv.
somewhere 185 adv.
hereditament
estate 777 n.
hereditary
genetic 5 adj.
inherited 157 adj.
filial 170 adj.
proprietary 777 adj.
heredity
heredity 5 n.
recurrence 106 n.
reversion 148 n.
reproduction 166 n.
sonship 170 n.
influence 178 n.
organism 358 n.
affections 817 n.
here goes!
599 int.
671 int.
hereof
concerning 9 adv.
heresy
unbelief 486 n.
heresy 977 n.
here, there and everywhere
nonuniformly 17 adv.
widely 183 adv.
heretic
nonconformist 84 n.
unbeliever 486 n.
heretic 977 n.
schismatic 978 n.
heretical
erroneous 495 adj.
heretical 977 adj.
impious 980 adj.
hereto
concerning 9 adv.

here today and gone tomorrow
transiently 114 adv.
heritable
genetic 5 adj.
inherited 157 adj.
proprietary 777 adj.
not retained 779 adj.
transferred 780 adj.
due 915 adj.
heritage
futurity 124 n.
posterity 170 n.
possession 773 n.
dower 777 n.
hermaphrodite
nonconformist 84 n.
double 91 adj.
eunuch 161 n.
hermeneutics
hermeneutics 520 n.
Hermes
courier 529 n.
Olympian deity 967 n.
hermetic, hermetical
cabbalistic 984 adj.
hermetically sealed
sealed off 264 adj.
hermit
nonconformist 84 n.
solitary 883 n.
celibate 895 n.
ascetic 945 n.
pietist 979 n.
monk 986 n.
hermitage
retreat 192 n.
refuge 662 n.
seclusion 883 n.
monastery 986 n.
hernia
wound 655 n.
hero
acting 594 n.
doer 676 n.
brave person 855 n.
prodigy 864 n.
person of repute 866 n.
loved one 887 n.
favourite 890 n.
good person 937 n.
Herod
violent creature 176 n.
heroes
soldiery 722 n.
heroic
olden 127 adj.
descriptive 590 adj.
poetic 593 adj.
resolute 599 adj.
laborious 682 adj.
courageous 855 adj.
worshipful 866 adj.
disinterested 931 adj.
heroic couplet
prosody 593 n.
heroics
prowess 855 n.
ostentation 875 n.
boasting 877 n.
heroin
poison 659 n.
drug-taking 949 n.
heroine
acting 594 n.
brave person 855 n.
prodigy 864 n.
person of repute 866 n.
favourite 890 n.
good person 937 n.
heroism
courage 855 n.
prowess 855 n.
disinterestedness 931 n.
heron
bird 365 n.
hero's welcome
celebration 876 n.
congratulation 866 n.
hero worship
wonder 864 n.
love 887 n.
praise 923 n.
deification 982 n.
herpes
skin disease 651 n.
herpetology
zoology 367 n.
Herr
male 372 n.
title 870 n.
herring
fish food 301 n.
herringbone
oblique 220 adj.
crossed 222 adj.
pattern 844 n.
herself
self 80 n.
hesitant
doubting 474 adj.
unwilling 598 adj.
hesitate
pause 145 vb.
be uncertain 474 vb.
be inactive 679 vb.
hesitation
changeableness 152 n.
slowness 278 n.
doubt 486 n.
speech defect 580 n.
unwillingness 598 n.
irresolution 601 n.
nervousness 854 n.
caution 858 n.
Hesperides
happiness 824 n.
Hesperus
evening 129 n.
planet 321 n.
luminary 420 n.
hessian
textile 222 n.
hetaera
kept woman 952 n.
heteroclite
abnormal 84 adj.
grammatical 564 adj.
heterodox
unconformable 84 adj.
erroneous 495 adj.
heterodox 977 adj.
heterogeneous
unrelated 10 adj.
different 15 adj.
nonuniform 17 adj.
mixed 43 adj.
multiform 82 adj.
heteronomy
governance 733 n.
heterosexual
typical 83 adj.
het up
angry 891 adj.
heuristic
enquiring 459 adj.
demonstrating 478 adj.
hew
cut 46 vb.
form 243 vb.
— down
fell 311 vb.
hex
spell 983 n.
hexad
over five 99 n.
hexagon
angular figure 247 n.
hexameter
prosody 593 n.
Hexateuch
scripture 975 n.
heyday
salad days 130 n.
palmy days 730 n.
hiatus
discontinuity 72 n.
interval 201 n.
opening 263 n.
hibernation
winter 129 n.
sleep 679 n.
Hibernian
native 191 n.
Hibernicism
dialect 560 n.
hiccup, hiccough
eruct 300 vb.
respiration 352 n.
drunkenness 949 n.
hic jacet
in memoriam 364 adv.
hick
bungler 697 n.
country-dweller 869 n.
hidalgo
aristocrat 868 n.
hidden
dark 418 adj.
invisible 444 adj.
unknown 491 adj.
unintelligible 517 adj.
concealed 525 adj.
secluded 883 adj.
cabbalistic 984 adj.
hidden depths
latency 523 n.
hidden hand
cause 156 n.
influence 178 n.
latency 523 n.
troublemaker 663 n.
director 690 n.
hidden meaning
connotation 514 n.
latency 523 n.
hidden persuader
publicizer 528 n.
hide
contain 56 vb.
measure 183 n.
skin 226 n.
screen 421 vb.
be unseen 444 vb.
disappear 446 vb.
lurk 523 vb.
conceal 525 vb.
hiding-place 527 n.
avoid 620 vb.
materials 631 n.
safeguard 660 vb.
be cowardly 856 vb.
be cautious 858 vb.
— one's light under a bushel
be modest 874 vb.
hideaway, hideout
hiding-place 527 n.
seclusion 883 n.
hidebound
narrow-minded 481 adj.
obstinate 602 adj.
restraining 747 adj.
hideous
unpleasant 827 adj.
ugly 842 adj.
frightening 854 adj.
hiding
knock 279 n.
defeat 728 n.
corporal punishment 963 n.
hiding-place
retreat 192 n.
concealment 525 n.
hiding-place 527 n.
store 632 n.
refuge 662 n.
seclusion 883 n.

hierarchy
degree 27 n.
order 60 n.
series 71 n.
the church 985 n.
clergy 986 n.
hieratic
written 586 adj.
scriptural 975 adj.
priestly 985 adj.
hierocracy
government 733 n.
the church 985 n.
hierodule
slave 742 n.
hieroglyph
lettering 586 n.
hieroglyphics
enigma 530 n.
symbology 547 n.
representation 551 n.
writing 586 n.
hierophant
religious teacher 973 n.
priest 986 n.
hi-fi
sound 398 n.
gramophone 414 n.
higgledy-piggledy
confusedly 61 adv.
high
great 32 adj.
superiority 34 n.
decomposed 51 adj.
high 209 adj.
topmost 213 adj.
elevated 310 adj.
pungent 388 adj.
unsavoury 391 adj.
fetid 397 adj.
strident 407 adj.
important 638 adj.
unclean 649 adj.
excitable state 822 n.
worshipful 866 adj.
noble 868 adj.
proud 871 adj.
drugged 949 adj.
drunk 949 adj.
Anglican 976 adj.
high and dry
fixed 153 adj.
dry 342 adj.
high and low
throughout 54 adv.
widely 183 adv.
high and mighty
worshipful 866 adj.
prideful 871 adj.
insolent 878 adj.
highball
alcoholic drink 301 n.
high birthrate
productiveness 171 n.
high-born
noble 868 adj.
highbrow
instructed 490 adj.
intellectual 492 n.
wise 498 adj.
sage 500 n.
high-caste
worshipful 866 adj.
nobility 868 n.
High Church
Catholicism 976 n.
Anglican 976 adj.
sectarian 978 adj.
high-class
genteel 868 adj.
high colour
redness 431 n.
high-coloured
florid 425 adj.
High Command
army officer 741 n.
master 741 n.
High Commission
envoy 754 n.
High Commissioner
governor 741 n.
envoy 754 n.
High Court
lawcourt 956 n.
high day
festivity 837 n.
holy day 988 n.
high-density
assembled 74 adj.
multitudinous 104 adj.
high-density housing
housing 192 n.
higher criticism
theology 973 n.
higher education
education 534 n.
higher rank
superiority 34 n.
precedence 64 n.
seniority 131 n.
higher self
subjectivity 320 n.
highest
supreme 34 adj.
high 209 adj.
topmost 213 adj.
highfalutin
rhetorical 574 adj.
ostentatious 875 adj.
high fidelity
sound 398 n.
accuracy 494 n.
high-fidelity system
gramophone 414 n.
high flier
learner 538 n.
high-flown
imaginative 513 adj.
exaggerated 546 adj.
rhetorical 574 adj.
ostentatious 875 adj.
high frequency
radiation 417 n.
high-geared
strong 162 adj.
speedy 277 adj.
high hand
violence 176 n.
high-handed
oppressive 735 adj.
proud 871 adj.
insolent 878 adj.
high-hat
prideful 871 adj.
insolent 878 adj.
high heels
footwear 228 n.
high jinks
revel 837 n.
high jump
leap 312 n.
high kicks
dance 837 n.
highland
high land 209 n.
alpine 209 adj.
prominence 254 n.
elevation 310 n.
land 344 n.
highlander
dweller 191 n.
high-level
superior 34 adj.
important 638 adj.
directing 689 adj.
high-life
festivity 837 n.
upper class 868 n.
highlight
manifest 522 vb.
publish 528 vb.
emphasize 532 vb.
indicate 547 vb.
painting 553 n.
make important 638 vb.
primp 843 vb.
high living
gastronomy 301 n.
intemperance 943 n.
sensualism 944 n.
gluttony 947 n.
highly coloured
expressive 516 adj.
splendid 841 adj.
highly-strung, high-strung
lively 819 adj.
excitable 822 adj.
nervous 854 adj.
high mass
Holy Communion 988 n.
high-minded
honourable 929 adj.
disinterested 931 adj.
high muck-a-muck
bigwig 638 n.
proud person 871 n.
Highness
sovereign 741 n.
high noon
noon 128 n.
summit 213 n.
high note
stridor 407 n.
musical note 410 n.
high octane petrol
fuel 385 n.
high-pitched
strident 407 adj.
rhetorical 574 adj.
high-potential
dynamic 160 adj.
high-powered
superior 34 adj.
strong 162 adj.
high pressure
vigorousness 174 n.
weather 340 n.
compelling 740 adj.
excitation 821 n.
high priest
leader 690 n.
priest 986 n.
high-principled
honourable 929 adj.
high-priority
important 638 adj.
high rank
prestige 866 n.
nobility 868 n.
high relief
relievo 254 n.
high-rise
architectural 192 adj.
highroad
road 624 n.
instrument 628 n.
high seas
ocean 343 n.
scope 744 n.
high society
beau monde 848 n.
upper class 868 n.
high-sounding
loud 400 adj.
affected 850 adj.
ostentatious 875 adj.
high-speed
vehicular 274 adj.
speedy 277 adj.
high-spirited
lively 819 adj.
courageous 855 adj.
proud 871 adj.
high spirits
cheerfulness 833 n.
merriment 833 n.
high-stepping
fashionable 848 adj.
proud 871 adj.
high street
road 624 n.
activity 678 n.
high tea
meal 301 n.

high temperature
heat 379 n.
high-tension
dynamic 160 adj.
strong 162 adj.
high tide
high water 209 n.
water 339 n.
high time
lateness 136 n.
occasion 137 n.
good policy 642 n.
high tone
magniloquence 574 n.
high treason
sedition 738 n.
perfidy 930 n.
high turnout
multitude 104 n.
high-ups
superior 34 n.
upper class 868 n.
high voice
stridor 407 n.
high water mark
summit 213 n.
limit 236 n.
gauge 465 n.
highway
road 624 n.
instrument 628 n.
facility 701 n.
highway code
traffic control 305 n.
highwayman
robber 789 n.
high words
quarrel 709 n.
anger 891 n.
hijack
compel 740 vb.
steal 788 vb.
threaten 900 vb.
hijacker
robber 789 n.
hike
pedestrianism 267 n.
walk 267 vb.
amuse oneself 837 vb.
hiker
pedestrian 268 n.
hilarious
merry 833 adj.
funny 849 adj.
hilarity
merriment 833 n.
hill
high land 209 n.
incline 220 n.
ascent 308 n.
hillbilly
country-dweller 869 n.
hill fort
earthwork 253 n.
hillock
small hill 209 n.
dome 253 n.
hillside
incline 220 n.
hill station
abode 192 n.
hilltop
high land 209 n.
vertex 213 n.
hilly
alpine 209 adj.
hilt
handle 218 n.
him
male 372 n.
himself
self 80 n.
Hinayana
religious faith 973 n.
hind
back 238 adj.
female animal 373 n.
country-dweller 869 n.
hinder
disable 161 vb.
counteract 182 vb.
interfere 231 vb.
back 238 adj.
retard 278 vb.
be useless 641 vb.
impair 655 vb.
hinder 702 vb.
resist 715 vb.
restrain 747 vb.
prohibit 757 vb.
(See **hindrance** *)*
hinderer
hinderer 702 n.
opponent 705 n.
hindfoot
foot 214 n.
hindleg
leg 267 n.
hind limb
limb 53 n.
hindmost
ending 69 adj.
back 238 adj.
hindquarters
buttocks 238 n.
hindrance
derangement 63 n.
delay 136 n.
stop 145 n.
dissuasion 613 n.
difficulty 700 n.
hindrance 702 n.
obstacle 702 n.
restraint 747 n.
hindsight
thought 449 n.
remembrance 505 n.
Hindu
religionist 973 n.
Hindu deities
Hindu deities 967 n.
Hinduism
philosophy 449 n.
religious faith 973 n.
hinge
joint 45 n.
fastening 47 n.
causal means 156 n.
pivot 218 n.
rotator 315 n.
hinge on
depend 157 vb.
be uncertain 474 vb.
hinny
hybrid 43 n.
woman 373 n.
hint
similarity 18 n.
tincture 43 n.
reminder 505 n.
latency 523 n.
hint 524 n.vb.
disclosure 526 n.
gesture 547 n.
indication 547 n.
speak low 578 vb.
incite 612 vb.
warning 664 n.
advice 691 n.
command 737 vb.
hinterland
district 184 n.
interiority 224 n.
rear 238 n.
land 344 n.
hip, hep
fashionable 848 adj.
hip flask
vessel 194 n.
hippie, hippy
nonconformist 84 n.
hippocras
alcoholic drink 301 n.
Hippocratic
medical 658 adj.
Hippocratic oath
code of duty 917 n.
hippodrome
theatre 594 n.
arena 724 n.
place of amusement 837 n.
hippogriff
rara avis 84 n.
hippopotamus
giant 195 n.
mammal 365 n.
hips
buttocks 238 n.
hipster
beau monde 848 n.
hipsters
trousers 228 n.
hircine
fetid 397 adj.
hire
employ 622 vb.
commission 751 vb.
assign 780 vb.
lease 784 vb.
hire 785 vb.
price 809 n.
hireling
inferior 35 n.
servant 742 n.
venal 930 adj.
hire purchase
borrowing 785 n.
purchase 792 n.
nonpayment 805 n.
hirer
possessor 776 n.
lender 784 n.
hirsute
hairy 259 adj.
his/her nibs
bigwig 638 n.
hispid
hairy 259 adj.
hiss
sibilation 406 n.
hiss 406 vb.
vociferate 408 vb.
ululate 409 vb.
gesture 547 n.
ridicule 851 n.
indignity 921 n.
disapprobation 924 n.
histogram
statistics 86 n.
histology
structure 331 n.
biology 358 n.
historian
antiquarian 125 n.
chronicler 549 n.
author 589 n.
narrator 590 n.
historic
renowned 866 adj.
historical
real 1 adj.
past 125 adj.
olden 127 adj.
certain 473 adj.
true 494 adj.
descriptive 590 adj.
historicity
reality 1 n.
truth 494 n.
historiographer
chronicler 549 n.
narrator 590 n.
history
past time 125 n.
remembrance 505 n.
record 548 n.
reading matter 589 n.
narrative 590 n.
conduct 688 n.
history of
illness 651 n.
histrionics
exaggeration 546 n.
acting 594 n.
dramaturgy 594 n.
affectation 850 n.
ostentation 875 n.

hit
place 187 vb.
knock 279 n.
strike 279 vb.
meet 295 vb.
touch 378 vb.
be visible 443 vb.
discover 484 vb.
dramaturgy 594 n.
exceller 644 n.
success 727 n.
reproach 924 n.
— back
recoil 280 vb.
retaliate 714 vb.
— below the belt
do wrong 914 vb.
— for six
defeat 727 vb.
— it off
befriend 880 vb.
— off
represent 551 vb.
— on/upon
chance 159 vb.
discover 484 vb.
plan 623 vb.
— the bottle
get drunk 949 vb.
— the hay
sleep 679 vb.
— the headlines
be published 528 vb.
— the jackpot
succeed 727 vb.
get rich 800 vb.
— the mark
place 187 vb.
aim 281 vb.
— the nail on the head
detect 484 vb.
be true 494 vb.
be successful 727 vb.
hitch
tie 45 vb.
ligature 47 n.
stop 145 n.
hang 217 vb.
break in 369 vb.
disappointment 509 n.
difficulty 700 n.
hitch 702 n.
failure 728 n.
marry 894 vb.
hitchhike
ride 267 vb.
beg 761 vb.
hither
towards 281 adv.
hitherto
retrospectively 125 adv.
hit or/and miss
negligent 458 adj.
inexact 495 adj.
hive
place oneself 187 vb.
dwell 192 vb.
stock farm 369 n.
storage 632 n.
activity 678 n.
— off
separate 46 vb.
be dispersed 75 vb.
take away 786 vb.
schismatize 978 vb.
hive of industry
activity 678 n.
workshop 687 n.
hives
formication 378 n.
skin disease 651 n.
hoar
white 427 adj.
grey 429 adj.
hoard
store 632 n.vb.
safeguard 660 vb.
acquire 771 vb.
economize 814 vb.
be parsimonious 816 vb.
hoarder
accumulator 74 n.
niggard 816 n.
hoarding
exhibit 522 n.
advertisement 528 n.
hoarfrost
wintriness 380 n.
white thing 427 n.
hoarse
muted 401 adj.
nonresonant 405 adj.
hoarse 407 adj.
vocal 577 adj.adj.
voiceless 578 adj.
hoary
ageing 131 adj.
whitish 427 adj.
grey 429 adj.
hoax
rumour 529 n.
trickery 542 n.
fable 543 n.
false alarm 665 n.
hoaxer
trickster 545 n.
hob
stand 218 n.
furnace 383 n.
Hob
elf 970 n.
hobbit
dwarf 196 n.
hobble
tie 45 vb.
disable 161 vb.
move slowly 278 vb.
hinder 702 vb.
fetter 747 vb.
fetter 748 n.
hobbledehoy
youngster 132 n.
hobby
bird 365 n.
business 622 n.
amusement 837 n.
liking 859 n.
hobbyhorse
bicycle 274 n.
eccentricity 503 n.
plaything 837 n.
hobgoblin
intimidation 854 n.
elf 970 n.
hobnob
be friendly 880 vb.
be sociable 882 vb.
hobo
wanderer 268 n.
idler 679 n.
Hobson's choice
necessity 596 n.
no choice 606 n.
compulsion 740 n.
hock
wine 301 n.
give security 767 vb.
borrow 785 vb.
hockey
ball game 837 n.
hocus-pocus
lack of meaning 515 n.
sleight 542 n.
spell 983 n.
hod
vessel 194 n.
conveyor 274 n.
Hodge
country-dweller 869 n.
hodgepodge
(See **hotchpotch**)
Hodgkin's disease
blood disease 651 n.
hoe
farm tool 370 n.
cleaning utensil 648 n.
hoe-down
dancing 837 n.
hog
pig 365 n.
male animal 372 n.
appropriate 786 vb.
be selfish 932 vb.
sensualist 944 n.
glutton 947 n.
hoggish
unclean 649 adj.
selfish 932 adj.
sensual 944 adj.
hog's back
high land 209 n.
dome 253 n.
hogshead
vat 194 n.
metrology 465 n.
hogwash
falsehood 541 n.
swill 649 n.
hoi polloi
commonalty 869 n.
hoist
verticality 215 n.
edge 234 n.
lifter 310 n.
elevate 310 vb.
flag 547 n.
— one with his own petard
retaliate 714 vb.
— sail
navigate 269 vb.
hoity-toity
prideful 871 adj.
hokum
empty talk 515 n.
hold
be 1 vb.
fastening 47 n.
cohere 48 vb.
contain 56 vb.
comprise 78 vb.
stay 144 vb.
cease 145 vb.
go on 146 vb.
be stable 153 vb.
influence 178 n.
cellar 194 n.
receptacle 194 n.
base 214 n.
handle 218 n.
support 218 n.vb.
hold within 224 vb.
opine 485 vb.
be true 494 vb.
affirm 532 vb.
storage 632 n.
store 632 vb.
preserve 666 vb.
wrestling 716 n.
governance 733 n.
imprison 747 vb.
restrain 747 vb.
possession 773 n.
retention 778 n.
retain 778 vb.
impress 821 vb.
— a brief for
deputize 755 vb.
— against
be biased 481 vb.
accuse 928 vb.
— all the aces
predominate 34 vb.
be successful 727 vb.
dominate 733 vb.
— back
pause 145 vb.
be unwilling 598 vb.
avoid 620 vb.
hinder 702 vb.
restrain 747 vb.
— by
observe 768 vb.
— cheap
underestimate 483 vb.
hold cheap 922 vb.
— court
judge 480 vb.

hold court 955 vb.
— dear
love 887 vb.
— down
lower 311 vb.
dominate 733 vb.
oppress 735 vb.
subjugate 745 vb.
restrain 747 vb.
— down a job
busy oneself 622 vb.
function 622 vb.
— fast
cohere 48 vb.
stand firm 599 vb.
retain 778 vb.
— forth
teach 534 vb.
orate 579 vb.
— good
be 1 vb.
stay 144 vb.
be proved 478 vb.
be true 494 vb.
be wont 610 vb.
— hands
caress 889 vb.
— in
restrain 747 vb.
— in abeyance
put off 136 vb.
not use 674 vb.
— in common
communalize 775 vb.
— in view
see 438 vb.
expect 507 vb.
— off
be distant 199 vb.
avoid 620 vb.
not use 674 vb.
parry 713 vb.
resist 715 vb.
— office
function 622 vb.
direct 689 vb.
rule 733 vb.
— on
wait 136 vb.
stay 144 vb.
go on 146 vb.
progress 285 vb.
retain 778 vb.
— one back
dissuade 613 vb.
— one's breath
await 507 vb.
wonder 864 vb.
— one's ground
stay 144 vb.
wage war 718 vb.
— one's horses
wait 136 vb.
pause 145 vb.
— one's nose in the air
be proud 871 vb.
be insolent 878 vb.
— one's own
be equal 28 vb.
withstand 704 vb.
parry 713 vb.
be successful 727 vb.
— one's tongue
be silent 399 vb.
keep secret 525 vb.
be mute 578 vb.
be taciturn 582 vb.
— out
affirm 532 vb.
stand firm 599 vb.
oppose 704 vb.
resist 715 vb.
offer 759 vb.
promise 764 vb.
— out for
give terms 766 vb.
bargain 791 vb.
— responsible
blame 924 vb.
accuse 928 vb.
— sway
rule 733 vb.
— the fort
substitute 150 vb.
— the lead
predominate 34 vb.
— the line
wait 136 vb.
steer for 281 vb.
— the reins
manage 689 vb.
rule 733 vb.
— the road
stabilize 153 vb.
— the scales
judge 480 vb.
— the stage
be plain 522 vb.
— tight
unite with 45 vb.
retain 778 vb.
— together
accord 24 vb.
be true 494 vb.
cooperate 706 vb.
— to ransom
compel 740 vb.
overcharge 811 vb.
threaten 900 vb.
— under
lower 311 vb.
dominate 733 vb.
— up
put off 136 vb.
halt 145 vb.
support 218 vb.
elevate 310 vb.
hinder 702 vb.
rob 788 vb.
— water
be reasonable 475 vb.
be proved 478 vb.
be true 494 vb.
holdall
bag 194 n.
storage 632 n.
holder
receptacle 194 n.
handle 218 n.
storage 632 n.
possessor 776 n.
holding
territory 184 n.
farm 370 n.
lands 777 n.
holding company
corporation 708 n.
holdup
delay 136 n.
hitch 702 n.
hole
place 185 n.
dwelling 192 n.
small house 192 n.
receptacle 194 n.
gap 201 n.
cavity 255 n.
orifice 263 n.
pierce 263 vb.
insert 303 vb.
hiding-place 527 n.
refuge 662 n.
predicament 700 n.
hole-and-corner
stealthy 525 adj.
hole in the heart
cardiovascular disease 651 n.
holey
perforated 263 adj.
dilapidated 655 adj.
holiday
lull 145 n.
leisure 681 n.
repose 683 n.
permit 756 n.
amusement 837 n.
holiday camp
meeting place 192 n.
pleasure ground 837 n.
holiday home
abode 192 n.
holidaymaker
traveller 268 n.
reveller 837 n.
holier than thou
affected 850 adj.
prideful 871 adj.
despising 922 adj.
disapproving 924 adj.
pietistic 979 adj.
holiness
virtue 933 n.
divine attribute 965 n.
sanctity 979 n.
holism
whole 52 n.
philosophy 449 n.
holland
textile 222 n.
holler
vociferate 408 vb.
hollow
insubstantial 4 adj.
completely 54 adv.
empty 190 adj.
lowness 210 n.
depth 211 n.
cavity 255 n.
concave 255 adj.
furrow 262 n.
opening 263 n.
lower 311 vb.
rare 325 adj.
resonant 404 adj.
hoarse 407 adj.
sophistical 477 adj.
hypocritical 541 adj.
voiceless 578 adj.
affected 850 adj.
ostentatious 875 adj.
boastful 877 adj.
— out
make concave 255 vb.
hollow-eyed
fatigued 684 adj.
holly
tree 366 n.
Hollywood
cinema 445 n.
drama 594 n.
holm
island 349 n.
holocaust
havoc 165 n.
slaughter 362 n.
burning 381 n.
oblation 981 n.
Holocene
secular 110 adj.
hologram
reflection 417 n.
image 551 n.
photography 551 n.
holograph
no imitation 21 n.
script 586 n.
holophrastic
linguistic 557 adj.
holster
case 194 n.
arsenal 723 n.
holt
wood 366 n.
holy
worshipful 866 adj.
virtuous 933 adj.
prudish 950 adj.
divine 965 adj.
godlike 965 adj.
religious 973 adj.
scriptural 975 adj.
sanctified 979 adj.
devotional 981 adj.
Holy Bible
scripture 975 n.
Holy City
heaven 971 n.

holy place 990 n.
Holy Communion
Christian rite 988 n.
Holy Communion 988 n.
holy day
holy day 988 n.
Holy Father
church title 986 n.
Holy Ghost
Holy Ghost 965 n.
Holy Grail
ritual object 988 n.
Holy Joe
cleric 986 n.
Holy Office
ecclesiastical court 956 n.
orthodoxism 976 n.
ecclesiasticism 985 n.
Holy of Holies
holy place 990 n.
holy orders
holy orders 985 n.
holy relic
talisman 983 n.
Holy Sacrament, the
the sacrament 988 n.
Holy See
church office 985 n.
Holy Spirit
Holy Ghost 965 n.
holystone
cleanser 648 n.
holy terror
violent creature 176 n.
bane 659 n.
evildoer 904 n.
bad person 938 n.
Holy Trinity
Trinity 965 n.
Holy Unction
Christian rite 988 n.
holy war
war 718 n.
philanthropy 901 n.
holy water
ritual object 988 n.
Holy Week
holy day 988 n.
homage
submission 721 n.
loyalty 739 n.
respects 920 n.
Homburg
headgear 228 n.
home
focus 76 n.
source 156 n.
place 185 n.
native 191 adj.
home 192 n.
house 192 n.
retreat 192 n.
near 200 adj.
interior 224 adj.
resting place 266 n.
arrive 295 vb.
refuge 662 n.
home and dry
successful 727 adj.
home-body
solitary 883 n.
home circle
family 11 n.
sociality 882 n.
homecoming
return 286 n.
arrival 295 n.
Home Counties
district 184 n.
home economics
cookery 301 n.
home from home
abode 192 n.
sociability 882 n.
home ground
focus 76 n.
home 192 n.
Home Guard
defender 713 n.
soldier 722 n.
home help
cleaner 648 n.
homeknit
jersey 228 n.
homeland
territory 184 n.
home 192 n.
homeless
unrelated 10 adj.
alone 88 adj.
unstable 152 adj.
displaced 188 adj.
travelling 267 adj.
poor 801 adj.
homeless person
wanderer 268 n.
outcast 883 n.
home life
seclusion 883 n.
home-loving
quiescent 266 adj.
homely
comfortable 376 adj.
dialectal 560 adj.
plain 573 adj.
pleasurable 826 adj.
ugly 842 adj.
plebeian 869 adj.
homemade
produced 164 adj.
native 191 adj.
artless 699 adj.
Home Office
jurisdiction 955 n.
Homeric
poetic 593 adj.
Homeric deities
classical deities 967 n.
home rule
government 733 n.
independence 744 n.
homesickness
suffering 825 n.
regret 830 n.
melancholy 834 n.
desire 859 n.
homespun
simple 44 adj.
produced 164 adj.
textile 222 n.
roughness 259 n.
textural 331 adj.
plain 573 adj.
artless 699 adj.
plebeian 869 adj.
homestead
home 192 n.
home stretch
end 69 n.
arrival 295 n.
home-sweet-home
home 192 n.
happiness 824 n.
home-thrust
lunge 712 n.
home town
home 192 n.
home truth
truth 494 n.
veracity 540 n.
plainness 573 n.
censure 924 n.
accusation 928 n.
homeward bound
regressive 286 adj.
arriving 295 adj.
homework
curriculum 534 n.
study 536 n.
preparation 669 n.
labour 682 n.
homey, homy
plain 573 adj.
homicidal maniac
violent creature 176 n.
killer 362 n.
ruffian 904 n.
homicide
homicide 362 n.
murderer 362 n.
homiletics
teaching 534 n.
church ministry 985 n.
homily
lecture 534 n.
oration 579 n.
dissertation 591 n.
ministration 988 n.
homing
regressive 286 adj.
arriving 295 adj.
incoming 297 adj.
hominid
humankind 371 n.
hominoid
human 371 adj.
homoeopath, homeopath
doctor 658 n.
homoeopathic, homeopathic
small 33 adj.
exiguous 196 adj.
medical 658 adj.
homoeopathy, homeopathy
medical art 658 n.
homoeostasis, homeostasis
equilibrium 28 n.
stability 153 n.
homogeneous
identical 13 adj.
uniform 16 adj.
similar 18 adj.
simple 44 adj.
homogenize, homogenise
make uniform 16 vb.
homograph
word 559 n.
Homoiousians
church party 978 n.
homologate
endorse 488 vb.
homologous
relative 9 adj.
equal 28 adj.
homomorphism
similarity 18 n.
homonym
identity 13 n.
equivocalness 518 n.
word 559 n.
Homoousians
church party 978 n.
homophone
identity 13 n.
equivocalness 518 n.
word 559 n.
homophonic
harmonious 410 adj.
homo sapiens
humankind 371 n.
homosexual
nonconformist 84 n.
male 372 n.
homosexuality
abnormality 84 n.
illicit love 951 n.
homunculus
small animal 33 n.
dwarf 196 n.
hone
sharpen 256 vb.
honest
genuine 494 adj.
true 494 adj.
veracious 540 adj.
plain 573 adj.
artless 699 adj.
ethical 917 adj.
honourable 929 adj.
disinterested 931 adj.

virtuous 933 adj.
honest to God
undisguised 522 adj.
veracious 540 adj.
honey
viscidity 354 n.
woman 373 n.
sweet thing 392 n.
yellowness 433 n.
a beauty 841 n.
darling 890 n.
honeycomb
network 222 n.
cavity 255 n.
porosity 263 n.
pierce 263 vb.
sweet thing 392 n.
storage 632 n.
impair 655 vb.
honeycombed
cellular 194 adj.
honeydew
fruit 301 n.
sweet thing 392 n.
honeyed words
inducement 612 n.
flattery 925 n.
honeymoon
start 68 n.
joy 824 n.
pleasurableness 826 n.
friendliness 880 n.
be in love 887 vb.
wedding 894 n.
honeymoon period
concord 710 n.
honeypot
focus 76 n.
sweet thing 392 n.
favourite 890 n.
honeysuckle
plant 366 n.
scent 396 n.
honey-tongued
courteous 884 adj.
flattering 925 adj.
honk
vomit 300 vb.
loudness 400 n.
ululate 409 vb.
danger signal 665 n.
honorarium
gift 781 n.
reward 962 n.
honorary
insubstantial 4 adj.
voluntary 597 adj.
uncharged 812 adj.
honorary degree
honours 866 n.
honorific
worshipful 866 adj.
title 870 n.
celebratory 876 adj.
honoris causa
deserving 915 adj.
honour
make important 638 vb.
decoration 729 n.
promise 764 n.
pay 804 vb.
honours 866 n.
prestige 866 n.
dignify 866 vb.
honour 866 vb.
title 870 n.
celebrate 876 vb.
pay one's respects 884 vb.
right 913 n.
grant claims 915 vb.
morals 917 n.
do one 917 vb.
respect 920 n.vb.
probity 929 n.
virtue 933 n.
purity 950 n.
reward 962 n.vb.
piety 979 n.
sanctify 979 vb.
worship 981 n.vb.
— one's obligations
keep faith 768 vb.
honourable
honourable 929 adj.
Honourable, the
title 870 n.
honourable intentions
wooing 889 n.
honourable mention
praise 923 n.
honours
decoration 729 n.
honours 866 n.
title 870 n.
reward 962 n.
hooch
alcoholic drink 301 n.
booty 790 n.
hood
covering 226 n.
headgear 228 n.
screen 421 n.vb.
low fellow 869 n.
canonicals 989 n.
hooded
covered 226 adj.
concealed 525 adj.
hoodlum
insolent person 878 n.
ruffian 904 n.
hoodoo
badness 645 n.
sorcery 983 n.
hoodwink
deceive 542 vb.
hooey
empty talk 515 n.
falsehood 541 n.
hoof
foot 214 n.
hoofer
entertainer 594 n.
hoof it
walk 267 vb.
dance 837 vb.
hoofmark
trace 548 n.
hook
coupling 47 n.
hanger 217 n.
angularity 247 n.
sharp edge 256 n.
knock 279 n.
deflect 282 vb.
propel 287 vb.
trap 542 n.
nippers 778 n.
take 786 vb.
— on
affix 45 vb.
— up
hang 217 vb.
— up with
connect 45 vb.
hookah
tobacco 388 n.
hook and eye
fastening 47 n.
hooked on
obsessed 455 adj.
enamoured 887 adj.
hooked on drugs
drugged 949 adj.
hooker
fishing boat 275 n.
prostitute 952 n.
hook, line and sinker
all 52 n.
completely 54 adv.
hookup
union 45 n.
association 706 n.
hookworm
tropical disease 651 n.
hooligan
violent creature 176 n.
ruffian 904 n.
hooliganism
lawlessness 954 n.
hoop
bond 47 n.
skirt 228 n.
circle 250 n.
plaything 837 n.
hoop-la
ball game 837 n.
hoot
cry 408 n.vb.
ululate 409 vb.
laugh 835 vb.
ridicule 851 n.
indignity 921 n.
disapprove 924 vb.
hooter
timekeeper 117 n.
megaphone 400 n.
signal 547 n.
hop
gait 265 n.
land travel 267 n.
departure 296 n.
leap 312 n.
leap 312 vb.
be agitated 318 vb.
dancing 837 n.
social gathering 882 n.
— it
decamp 296 vb.
hope
looking ahead 124 n.
expect 507 vb.
motive 612 n.
cheerfulness 833 n.
hope 852 n.vb.
desire 859 n.vb.
— on
persevere 600 vb.
hope 852 vb.
hope chest
store 632 n.
hopeful
probable 471 adj.
expectant 507 adj.
cheerful 833 adj.
hoper 852 n.
hoping 852 adj.
promising 852 adj.
hopeless
impossible 470 adj.
inexpectant 508 adj.
useless 641 adj.
unhappy 825 adj.
dejected 834 adj.
hopeless 853 adj.
unpromising 853 adj.
impenitent 940 adj.
hopelessness
impossibility 470 n.
hopelessness 853 n.
hoplite
soldier 722 n.
hopper
vat 194 n.
ship 275 n.
jumper 312 n.
hopper waggon
train 274 n.
hop picker
farmer 370 n.
hopping mad
angry 891 adj.
hoppy
tasty 386 adj.
hops
potherb 301 n.
hopsack
textile 222 n.
hopscotch
children's games 837 n.
horary
periodic 110 adj.

horde
multitude 104 n.
party 708 n.
army 722 n.
rabble 869 n.
horizon
distance 199 n.
horizontality 216 n.
edge 234 n.
limit 236 n.
view 438 n.
visibility 443 n.
horizontal
flat 216 adj.
horizontality
lowness 210 n.
horizontality 216 n.
smoothness 258 n.
plain 348 n.
hormone
drug 658 n.
hormone cream
cosmetic 843 n.
hormone therapy
therapy 658 n.
horn
cup 194 n.
cone 252 n.
protuberance 254 n.
sharp point 256 n.
hardness 326 n.
structure 331 n.
megaphone 400 n.
horn 414 n.
semitransparency 424 n.
hornbook
textbook 589 n.
horned
curved 248 adj.
tapering 256 adj.
hornet
insect 365 n.
shrew 892 n.
noxious animal 904 n.
hornet's nest
bane 659 n.
pitfall 663 n.
painfulness 827 n.
horn in
intrude 297 vb.
encroach 306 vb.
horn of plenty
abundance 171 n.
plenty 635 n.
hornpipe
dance 837 n.
horns of a dilemma
argumentation 475 n.
hornswoggle
deceive 542 vb.
horny
hard 326 adj.
horny-handed
labouring 682 adj.
horology
chronometry 117 n.
horoscope
looking ahead 124 n.
destiny 155 n.
astronomy 321 n.
prediction 511 n.
horrible
not nice 645 adj.
unpleasant 827 adj.
frightening 854 adj.
horribly
extremely 32 Adv. adv.
horrid
not nice 645 adj.
hateful 888 adj.
horrific
distressing 827 adj.
frightening 854 adj.
horrify
displease 827 vb.
frighten 854 vb.
excite hate 888 vb.
horripilation
roughness 259 n.
fear 854 n.
horror
eyesore 842 n.
fear 854 n.
dislike 861 n.
monster 938 n.
horrors, the
melancholy 834 n.
alcoholism 949 n.
horror-struck
fearing 854 adj.
hors de combat
impotent 161 adj.
useless 641 adj.
hors-d'oeuvres
hors-d'oeuvres 301 n.
savouriness 390 n.
horse
horse 273 n.
animal 365 n.
male animal 372 n.
busy person 678 n.
cavalry 722 n.
horse about
be absurd 497 vb.
horse-and-buggy
antiquated 127 adj.
horseback
conveyance 267 n.
horse-box
cart 274 n.
horse-breeding
animal husbandry 369 n.
horsecloth
coverlet 226 n.
horse doctor
animal husbandry 369 n.
doctor 658 n.
horse-drawn
vehicular 274 adj.
drawing 288 adj.
horseflesh
horse 273 n.
horsehair
hair 259 n.
horseman, horsewoman
rider 268 n.
cavalry 722 n.
horsemanship
equitation 267 n.
skill 694 n.
horse marine
bungler 697 n.
horse of another colour
variant 15 n.
horse opera
film 445 n.
horseplay
fight 716 n.
revel 837 n.
horsepower
energy 160 n.
vehicle 274 n.
horse racing
equitation 267 n.
gambling 618 n.
racing 716 n.
horseradish
potherb 301 n.
sauce 389 n.
horse sense
intelligence 498 n.
horseshoe
curve 248 n.
talisman 983 n.
horse-trading
conditions 766 n.
barter 791 n.
horsewhip
flog 963 vb.
scourge 964 n.
horsy
equine 273 adj.
amused 837 adj.
hortative, hortatory
educational 534 adj.
inducing 612 adj.
advising 691 adj.
horticulture
flower 366 n.
agriculture 370 n.
horticulturist
gardener 370 n.
hosanna
rejoicing 835 n.
celebration 876 n.
praise 923 n.
hymn 981 n.
hose
legwear 228 n.
tube 263 n.
irrigator 341 n.
extinguisher 382 n.
hosepipe
conduit 351 n.
hosier
clothier 228 n.
hosiery
legwear 228 n.
hospice
inn 192 n.
retreat 192 n.
hospital 658 n.
shelter 662 n.
hospitable
(See **hospitality** *)*
hospital
hygiene 652 n.
hospital 658 n.
hospital case
sick person 651 n.
hospitality
liberality 813 n.
friendliness 880 n.
sociability 882 n.
benevolence 897 n.
hospitalize, hospitalise
doctor 658 vb.
host
band 74 n.
multitude 104 n.
infection 651 n.
army 722 n.
friend 880 n.
sociable person 882 n.
the sacrament 988 n.
hostage
thing transferred 272 n.
prisoner 750 n.
security 767 n.
hostel
station 187 n.
quarters 192 n.
hostelry
inn 192 n.
hostess
sociable person 882 n.
hostile
contrary 14 adj.
disagreeing 25 adj.
counteracting 182 adj.
opposing 704 adj.
attacking 712 adj.
adverse 731 adj.
prohibiting 757 adj.
discontented 829 adj.
disliking 861 adj.
inimical 881 adj.
unsociable 883 adj.
hating 888 adj.
malevolent 898 adj.
disapproving 924 adj.
hostile critic
detractor 926 n.
hostile witness
counterevidence 467 n.
accuser 928 n.

hostilities
fight 716 n.
belligerency 718 n.
hostility
hindrance 702 n.
dissension 709 n.
(See **hostile** *)*
host in oneself, a
influence 178 n.
hosts
great quantity 32 n.
hot
violent 176 adj.
dry 342 adj.
hot 379 adj.
pungent 388 adj.
musical 412 adj.
radiating 417 adj.
red 431 adj.
fervent 818 adj.
excited 821 adj.
angry 891 adj.
impure 951 adj.
lecherous 951 adj.
illegal 954 adj.
hot air
insubstantial thing 4 n.
overestimation 482 n.
empty talk 515 n.
boast 877 n.
hot-air balloon
airship 276 n.
hot-air duct
heater 383 n.
hotbed
seedbed 156 n.
abundance 171 n.
heater 383 n.
badness 645 n.
infection 651 n.
pitfall 663 n.
hot blood
excitability 822 n.
hot-blooded
violent 176 adj.
rash 857 adj.
irascible 892 adj.
hotchpotch, hodgepodge
medley 43 n.
confusion 61 n.
hot composition
print 587 n.
hot dog
meal 301 n.
hotel
inn 192 n.
hotelier
caterer 633 n.
hotfoot
hastily 680 adv.
hot from the press
new 126 adj.
hot gospeller
preacher 537 n.
zealot 979 n.
pastor 986 n.
hothead
desperado 857 n.
hot-headed
hasty 680 adj.
fervent 818 adj.
excitable 822 adj.
rash 857 adj.
hothouse
extraneous 59 adj.
seedbed 156 n.
garden 370 n.
heater 383 n.
hot line
telecommunication 531 n.
hot-metal
printed 587 adj.
hot money
funds 797 n.
hot on the trail
pursuant to 619 adv.
hotplate
heater 383 n.
hotpot
dish 301 n.
hot potato
difficulty 700 n.
hot rod
automobile 274 n.
hot seat
predicament 700 n.
means of execution 964 n.
hot springs
stream 350 n.
heat 379 n.
hospital 658 n.
hotspur
violent creature 176 n.
desperado 857 n.
hot stuff
loose woman 952 n.
hot-tempered
excitable 822 adj.
irascible 892 adj.
hot under the collar
excited 821 adj.
angry 891 adj.
hot up
heat 381 vb.
endanger 661 vb.
hot water
cleanser 648 n.
predicament 700 n.
painfulness 827 n.
hot-water bottle
cauldron 194 n.
heater 383 n.
Houdini
escaper 667 n.
hound
dog 365 n.
hunter 619 n.
be malevolent 898 vb.
defame 926 vb.
cad 938 n.
knave 938 n.
hounding
pursuit 619 n.
hound's-tooth
chequer 437 n.
pattern 844 n.
hour
juncture 8 n.
period 110 n.
clock time 117 n.
hourglass
timekeeper 117 n.
contraction 198 n.
narrowing 206 n.
hour hand
indicator 547 n.
houri
a beauty 841 n.
mythical being 970 n.
hourly
while 108 adv.
periodic 110 adj.
frequent 139 adj.
often 139 adv.
seasonal 141 adj.
periodically 141 adv.
house
race 11 n.
edifice 164 n.
genealogy 169 n.
place 187 vb.
abode 192 n.
house 192 n.
zodiac 321 n.
onlookers 441 n.
class 538 n.
playgoer 594 n.
safeguard 660 vb.
corporation 708 n.
sovereign 741 n.
shop 796 n.
house arrest
detention 747 n.
houseboat
small house 192 n.
boat 275 n.
housebound
quiescent 266 adj.
house-breaker
thief 789 n.
offender 904 n.
housecarl
soldier 722 n.
retainer 742 n.
housecoat
informal dress 228 n.
house divided against itself
dissension 709 n.
houseful
crowd 74 n.
inhabitants 191 n.
household
family 11 n.
group 74 n.
inhabitants 191 n.
home 192 n.
known 490 adj.
usual 610 adj.
householder
resident 191 n.
possessor 776 n.
household gods
home 192 n.
mythic deity 966 n.
household name
famousness 866 n.
household pet
animal 365 n.
household staff
retainer 742 n.
household troops
armed force 722 n.
household words
plainness 573 n.
househusband
male 372 n.
housekeeper
resident 191 n.
caterer 633 n.
manager 690 n.
domestic 742 n.
keeper 749 n.
housekeeping
management 689 n.
houselights
lighting 420 n.
theatre 594 n.
housemaid
domestic 742 n.
housemaid's knee
rheumatism 651 n.
houseman
doctor 658 n.
housemaster, housemistress
teacher 537 n.
manager 690 n.
house of cards
weak thing 163 n.
brittleness 330 n.
House of Commons
parliament 692 n.
house of God
church 990 n.
temple 990 n.
House of Lords
parliament 692 n.
aristocracy 868 n.
lawcourt 956 n.
House of Representatives
parliament 692 n.
house party
social gathering 882 n.
house-proud
prideful 871 adj.
house style
edition 589 n.
housetop
vertex 213 n.
roof 226 n.
house-trained
well-bred 848 adj.
house-warming
start 68 n.

social gathering 882 n.
housewife
resident 191 n.
woman 373 n.
caterer 633 n.
busy person 678 n.
manager 690 n.
housework
labour 682 n.
housing
housing 192 n.
frame 218 n.
surroundings 230 n.
housing association
association 706 n.
participator 775 n.
housing estate
housing 192 n.
housings
coverlet 226 n.
Houyhnhnm
horse 273 n.
hovel
small house 192 n.
hover
vary 152 vb.
impend 155 vb.
be high 209 vb.
hang 217 vb.
be in motion 265 vb.
wander 267 vb.
fly 271 vb.
move slowly 278 vb.
approach 289 vb.
be uncertain 474 vb.
be irresolute 601 vb.
hovercraft
ship 275 n.
aircraft 276 n.
hoverfly
insect 365 n.
how
why 158 adv.
453 int.
how 624 adv.
howdah
seat 218 n.
howitzer
gun 723 n.
howl
blow 352 vb.
feel pain 377 vb.
be loud 400 vb.
cry 408 n.vb.
ululate 409 vb.
weep 836 vb.
howler
mistake 495 n.
absurdity 497 n.
how the land lies
circumstance 8 n.
hoyden
youngster 132 n.
hoydenish
artless 699 adj.
ill-bred 847 adj.
hub
middle 70 n.
focus 76 n.
centre 225 n.
wheel 250 n.
chief thing 638 n.
hubble-bubble
tobacco 388 n.
hubbub
turmoil 61 n.
commotion 318 n.
loudness 400 n.
quarrel 709 n.
hubris
pride 871 n.
insolence 878 n.
huckaback
textile 222 n.
huckster
pedlar 794 n.
huddle
crowd 74 n.
congregate 74 vb.
make smaller 198 vb.
be near 200 vb.
conference 584 n.
Hudibrastic
derisive 851 adj.
hue
character 5 n.
tincture 43 n.
hue 425 n.
hue and cry
cry 408 n.
publication 528 n.
call 547 n.
chase 619 n.
huff
breathe 352 vb.
resentment 891 n.
huff 891 vb.
huff and puff
boast 877 vb.
huffy
irascible 892 adj.
hug
cohere 48 vb.
make smaller 198 vb.
be near 200 vb.
surround 230 vb.
enclose 235 vb.
gesture 547 n.
retain 778 vb.
friendliness 880 n.
be hospitable 882 vb.
courteous act 884 n.
greet 884 vb.
endearment 889 n.
caress 889 vb.
— oneself
be pleased 824 vb.
be content 828 vb.
rejoice 835 vb.
feel pride 871 vb.
be vain 873 vb.
boast 877 vb.
— the shore
be near 200 vb.
approach 289 vb.
huge
enormous 32 adj.
stalwart 162 adj.
huge 195 adj.
tall 209 adj.
hugger-mugger
confusion 61 n.
stealthy 525 adj.
Huguenot
Protestant 976 n.
hula-hula
dance 837 n.
hulk
bulk 195 n.
ship 275 n.
bungler 697 n.
hulking
whopping 32 adj.
unwieldy 195 adj.
clumsy 695 adj.
graceless 842 adj.
hull
chief part 52 n.
uncover 229 vb.
ship 275 n.
hullabaloo
turmoil 61 n.
loudness 400 n.
cry 408 n.
hull down
beyond 199 adv.
hum
stink 397 vb.
faintness 401 n.
roll 403 n.vb.
resound 404 vb.
ululate 409 vb.
sing 413 vb.
voice 577 vb.
activity 678 n.
— and haw
stammer 580 vb.
be irresolute 601 vb.
— with
be many 104 vb.
human
animal 365 adj.
human 371 adj.
benevolent 897 adj.
philanthropic 901 adj.
frail 934 adj.
human being
humankind 371 n.
person 371 n.
humane
educational 534 adj.
benevolent 897 adj.
philanthropic 901 adj.
pitying 905 adj.
human error
vulnerability 661 n.
human interest
biography 590 n.
excitation 821 n.
humanism
philosophy 449 n.
philanthropy 901 n.
humanist
scholar 492 n.
philanthropist 901 n.
humanistic
human 371 adj.
literary 557 adj.
philanthropic 901 adj.
ethical 917 adj.
humanitarian
benevolent 897 adj.
philanthropist 901 n.
humanities
culture 490 n.
literature 557 n.
humanity
humankind 371 n.
leniency 736 n.
benevolence 897 n.
philanthropy 901 n.
pity 905 n.
humanize, humanise
be lenient 736 vb.
be benevolent 897 vb.
humankind
precursor 66 n.
humankind 371 n.
human nature
humankind 371 n.
human race
humankind 371 n.
human rights
dueness 915 n.
human sacrifice
oblation 981 n.
idolatry 982 n.
humble
inconsiderable 33 adj.
inferior 35 adj.
abase 311 vb.
unknown 491 adj.
disappoint 509 vb.
submitting 721 adj.
impress 821 vb.
plebeian 869 adj.
humble 872 adj.
humiliate 872 vb.
modest 874 adj.
respectful 920 adj.
— oneself
be humble 872 vb.
show respect 920 vb.
be pious 979 vb.
worship 981 vb.
humbug
empty talk 515 n.
falsehood 541 n.
deceive 542 vb.
fable 543 n.
impostor 545 n.
affecter 850 n.
pretension 850 n.
humdinger
whopper 195 n.
exceller 644 n.
humdrum
plain 573 adj.

tedious 838 adj.
humid
watery 339 adj.
humid 341 adj.
rainy 350 adj.
humidifier
air 340 n.
humidity
moisture 341 n.
humiliate
abate 37 vb.
abase 311 vb.
disappoint 509 vb.
cause discontent 829 vb.
shame 867 vb.
humiliate 872 vb.
not respect 921 vb.
hold cheap 922 vb.
humiliation
humiliation 872 n.
disrepute 867 n.
humility
underestimation 483 n.
submission 721 n.
humility 872 n.
modesty 874 n.
servility 879 n.
respect 920 n.
disinterestedness 931 n.
penitence 939 n.
piety 979 n.
worship 981 n.
hummock
small hill 209 n.
dome 253 n.
humoresque
musical piece 412 n.
humorist
entertainer 594 n.
humorist 839 n.
humorous
laughing 835 adj.
witty 839 adj.
funny 849 adj.
humour
temperament 5 n.
tendency 179 n.
fluid 335 n.
whim 604 n.
minister to 703 vb.
be lenient 736 vb.
permit 756 vb.
affections 817 n.
laughter 835 n.
amuse 837 vb.
wit 839 n.
flatter 925 vb.
humourless
serious 834 adj.
dull 840 adj.
humoursome
capricious 604 adj.
sullen 893 adj.
hump
small hill 209 n.
sphere 252 n.
camber 253 n.
carry 273 vb.
work 682 vb.
humpbacked
deformed 246 adj.
humpy
convex 253 adj.
humus
soil 344 n.
Hun
destroyer 168 n.
evildoer 904 n.
hunch
intuition 476 n.
supposition 512 n.
spontaneity 609 n.
hunchback
camber 253 n.
hunchbacked
deformed 246 adj.
blemished 845 adj.
hunch one's back
stoop 311 vb.
hundred
hundred 99 n.
district 184 n.
hundred percent, one
wholly 52 adv.
perfect 646 adj.
hundredweight
weighing 322 n.
hung
appearing 445 adj.
hunger
eating 301 n.
rapacity 786 n.
desire 859 n.
hunger 859 n.
be hungry 859 vb.
hunger march
deprecation 762 n.
hunger strike
fast 946 n.
hung jury
legal trial 959 n.
hungry
hungry 859 adj.
fasting 946 adj.
gluttonous 947 adj.
hungry for
inquisitive 453 adj.
desiring 859 adj.
hunk
piece 53 n.
bulk 195 n.
hunkers
buttocks 238 n.
hunks
niggard 816 n.
hunt
rider 268 n.
oscillate 317 vb.
campanology 412 n.
search 459 n.
detect 484 vb.
chase 619 n.
hunt 619 vb.
attack 712 vb.
be inimical 881 vb.
defame 926 vb.
— down
be severe 735 vb.
— for
enquire 459 vb.
search 459 vb.
pursue 619 vb.
— in pairs
cooperate 706 vb.
— out
eject 300 vb.
— with the hounds
do likewise 20 vb.
hunter
timekeeper 117 n.
rider 268 n.
thoroughbred 273 n.
killer 362 n.
hunter 619 n.
hunting
pursuit 619 n.
sport 837 n.
huntress
hunter 619 n.
huntsman
hunter 619 n.
hurdle
fence 235 n.
leap 312 vb.
obstacle 702 n.
hurdler
thoroughbred 273 n.
jumper 312 n.
hurdles
racing 716 n.
hurdy-gurdy
organ 414 n.
hurl
propel 287 vb.
— at
lapidate 712 vb.
— oneself
be violent 176 vb.
hurly-burly
turmoil 61 n.
commotion 318 n.
hurrah, hurray, hooray
cry 408 n.vb.
rejoicing 835 n.
835 int.
hurricane
turmoil 61 n.
storm 176 n.
velocity 277 n.
gale 352 n.
hurried
brief 114 adj.
negligent 458 adj.
hasty 680 adj.
hurry
move fast 277 vb.
activity 678 n.
haste 680 n.
hasten 680 vb.
— up
incite 612 vb.
680 int.
hurst
wood 366 n.
hurt
weaken 163 vb.
pain 377 n.
give pain 377 vb.
evil 616 n.
be inexpedient 643 vb.
harm 645 vb.
deteriorated 655 adj.
impair 655 vb.
hurt 827 vb.
resentful 891 Adj. adj.
huff 891 vb.
— oneself
suffer 825 vb.
hurtful
harmful 645 adj.
paining 827 adj.
maleficent 898 adj.
hurtle
be violent 176 vb.
move fast 277 vb.
husband
male 372 n.
store 632 vb.
spouse 894 n.
— one's resources
economize 814 vb.
husbandless
unwedded 895 adj.
widowed 896 adj.
husbandman
farmer 370 n.
husbandry
agriculture 370 n.
management 689 n.
economy 814 n.
hush
assuage 177 vb.
quietude 266 n.
silence 399 n.vb.
make mute 578 vb.
582 int.
— up
keep secret 525 vb.
hushed
inactive 679 adj.
hush-hush
occult 523 adj.
concealed 525 adj.
hush money
offset 31 n.
incentive 612 n.
reward 962 n.
husk
remainder 41 n.
skin 226 n.
grass 366 n.
rubbish 641 n.
huskiness
voicelessness 578 n.
husky
stalwart 162 adj.
beast of burden 273 n.

dog 365 n.
hoarse 407 adj.
beautiful 841 adj.
hussar
cavalry 722 n.
hussy
insolent person 878 n.
loose woman 952 n.
hustings
publicity 528 n.
rostrum 539 n.
vote 605 n.
arena 724 n.
lawcourt 956 n.
hustle
move 265 vb.
impel 279 vb.
propel 287 vb.
activity 678 n.
hasten 680 vb.
— out
eject 300 vb.
hustler
speeder 277 n.
busy person 678 n.
prostitute 952 n.
hustling
speedy 277 adj.
busy 678 adj.
hut
dwelling 192 n.
small house 192 n.
hutch
stable 192 n.
cattle pen 369 n.
hutments
housing 192 n.
huzza
cry 408 n.
(See **hurrah** *)*
hyaline
transparent 422 adj.
hybrid
hybrid 43 n.
nonconformist 84 n.
neology 560 n.
hybridization, hybridisation
mixture 43 n.
hybridize, hybridise
mix 43 vb.
hydra
rara avis 84 n.
hydra-headed
multiform 82 adj.
reproduced 166 adj.
hydrant
water 339 n.
current 350 n.
conduit 351 n.
extinguisher 382 n.
hydrate
combine 50 vb.
add water 339 vb.
hydraulics
fluidity 335 n.
hydro-
watery 339 adj.
hydrocele
fluid 335 n.
disease 651 n.
hydrocephalus
unintelligence 499 n.
hydrodynamics
science of forces 162 n.
fluidity 335 n.
hydroelectricity
sources of energy 160 n.
hydrofoil
ship 275 n.
hydrogen
lifter 310 n.
hydrogenate
gasify 336 vb.
hydrographer
surveyor 465 n.
hydrography
earth sciences 321 n.
hygrometry 341 n.
oceanography 343 n.
hydrology
earth sciences 321 n.
fluidity 335 n.
hygrometry 341 n.
hydrolysis
decomposition 51 n.
hydromel
soft drink 301 n.
sweet thing 392 n.
hydrometer
density 324 n.
hydrometry
fluidity 335 n.
water 339 n.
hydrophobia
infection 651 n.
hydroplane
aircraft 276 n.
hydroponics
agriculture 370 n.
hydrostatics
science of forces 162 n.
fluidity 335 n.
hydrotherapy
therapy 658 n.
hydrous
watery 339 adj.
hyena
eater 301 n.
noxious animal 904 n.
hygiene
ablutions 648 n.
cleansing 648 n.
health 650 n.
hygiene 652 n.
prophylactic 658 n.
preservation 666 n.
hygienic
safe 660 adj.
hygrometer
weather 340 n.
meter 465 n.
recording instrument 549 n.
hygrometry
hygrometry 341 n.
hygroscopic
admitting 299 adj.
hylic
material 319 adj.
Hymen
marriage 894 n.
lesser deity 967 n.
hymn
vocal music 412 n.
poem 593 n.
praise 923 n.
hymn 981 n.
worship 981 vb.
hymn book
hymnal 988 n.
hymnology
vocal music 412 n.
hymn 981 n.
hymnwriter
musician 413 n.
theologian 973 n.
worshipper 981 n.
hype (up)
advertisement 528 n.
boast 877 n.
praise 923 vb.
hyped up
overrated 482 adj.
excited 821 adj.
hyperactive
insane 503 adj.
active 678 adj.
hyperbaton
inversion 221 n.
ornament 574 n.
hyperbola
curve 248 n.
hyperbole
trope 519 n.
exaggeration 546 n.
magniloquence 574 n.
hyperborean
distant 199 adj.
hypercritical
narrow-minded 481 adj.
severe 735 adj.
discontented 829 adj.
fastidious 862 adj.
disapproving 924 adj.
hyperdulia
cult 981 n.
Hyperion
a beauty 841 n.
mythic deity 966 n.
Hyperion to a satyr
polarity 14 n.
hypermarket
shop 796 n.
hyperphysical
paranormal 984 adj.
hypersensitive
sentient 374 adj.
sensitive 819 adj.
hypersonic
speedy 277 adj.
hypersonic flight
aeronautics 271 n.
hypertension
cardiovascular disease 651 n.
hyperthermia
illness 651 n.
hyperthyroidism
overactivity 678 n.
hypertrophied
expanded 197 adj.
hyphen
bond 47 n.
hyphenation
punctuation 547 n.
hypnosis
insensibility 375 n.
sleep 679 n.
occultism 984 n.
hypnotherapy
therapy 658 n.
hypnotic
lenitive 177 adj.
influential 178 adj.
insensible 375 adj.
inducing 612 adj.
remedial 658 adj.
soporific 679 adj.
psychical 984 adj.
hypnotism
influence 178 n.
insensibility 375 n.
occultism 984 n.
hypnotist
motivator 612 n.
psychic 984 n.
hypnotize, hypnotise
influence 178 vb.
render insensible 375 vb.
convince 485 vb.
motivate 612 vb.
bewitch 983 vb.
practise occultism 984 vb.
hypocaust
heater 383 n.
hypochondria
psychopathy 503 n.
ill health 651 n.
melancholy 834 n.
hypochondriac
weakling 163 n.
madman 504 n.
sick person 651 n.
moper 834 n.
hypocrisy
duplicity 541 n.
deception 542 n.
flattery 925 n.
false piety 980 n.
hypocrite
imitator 20 n.
deceiver 545 n.
slyboots 698 n.
affecter 850 n.

toady 879 n.
flatterer 925 n.
hypocritical
hypocritical 541 adj.
hypodermic needle
perforator 263 n.
hypogeal
deep 211 adj.
hypostasis
essence 1 n.
substance 3 n.
hypostatic
substantial 3 adj.
material 319 adj.
Hypostatic Union
Trinity 965 n.
hypotension
cardiovascular disease 651 n.
hypothecate
give security 767 vb.
borrow 785 vb.
hypothermia
coldness 380 n.
illness 651 n.
hypothesis
attribution 158 n.
premise 475 n.
opinion 485 n.
supposition 512 n.
hypothetical
possible 469 adj.
uncertain 474 adj.
credible 485 adj.
suppositional 512 adj.
imaginary 513 adj.
hypsometer
altimetry 209 n.
hyssop
ritual object 988 n.
hysteria
psychopathy 503 n.
hysteric
madman 504 n.
hysterical
furious 176 adj.
insane 503 adj.
capricious 604 adj.
fervent 818 adj.
excited 821 adj.
excitable 822 adj.
hysterics
violence 176 n.
excitable state 822 n.
lamentation 836 n.
hysteron proteron
inversion 221 n.

I

I
self 80 n.
I AM
the Deity 965 n.
iambic
poetic 593 adj.
iatrogenic
diseased 651 adj.
IBA
broadcasting 531 n.
ibex
cattle 365 n.
ibidem
identically 13 adv.
Icarus
aeronaut 271 n.
ICBM
missile weapon 723 n.
ice
desert 172 n.
cover 226 vb.
smoothness 258 n.
dessert 301 n.
ice 380 n.
refrigeration 382 n.
refrigerator 384 n.
sweeten 392 vb.
transparency 422 n.
preserver 666 n.
gem 844 n.
Ice Age
era 110 n.
coldness 380 n.
iceberg
island 349 n.
ice 380 n.
unfeeling person 820 n.
solitary 883 n.
ice blink
reflection 417 n.
icebox
refrigerator 384 n.
icebreaker
ship 275 n.
ice 380 n.
ice bucket
refrigerator 384 n.
ice cap
ice 380 n.
ice cream
dessert 301 n.
sweet thing 392 n.
ice cube
ice 380 n.
iced drink
soft drink 301 n.
icefall
ice 380 n.
ice field
plain 348 n.
ice 380 n.
ice floe
plain 348 n.
ice 380 n.
ice hockey
sport 837 n.
icehouse
refrigerator 384 n.
ice pick
perforator 263 n.
ice rink
smoothness 258 n.
arena 724 n.
pleasure ground 837 n.
ice sheet
ice 380 n.
ice skate
sledge 274 n.
ice skating
sport 837 n.
ice yacht
sledge 274 n.
ice 380 n.
ichnography
map 551 n.
ichor
blood 335 n.
fluid 335 n.
ichthyology
zoology 367 n.
icicle
hanging object 217 n.
ice 380 n.
unfeeling person 820 n.
icing
covering 226 n.
sweet thing 392 n.
icon
copy 22 n.
image 551 n.
picture 553 n.
ritual object 988 n.
iconoclasm
destruction 165 n.
iconoclast
destroyer 168 n.
violent creature 176 n.
evildoer 904 n.
zealot 979 n.
iconoclastic
impious 980 adj.
iconography
representation 551 n.
art style 553 n.
iconolatry
cult 981 n.
idolatry 982 n.
iconology
theology 973 n.
icosahedron
angular figure 247 n.
ictus
pronunciation 577 n.
prosody 593 n.
icy
hard 326 adj.
cold 380 adj.
impassive 820 adj.
inimical 881 adj.
unsociable 883 adj.
id
self 80 n.
subjectivity 320 n.
spirit 447 n.
idea
reason why 156 n.
form 243 n.
thought 449 n.
idea 451 n.
opinion 485 n.
intelligence 498 n.
supposition 512 n.
ideality 513 n.
meaning 514 n.
contrivance 623 n.
idea'd
imaginative 513 adj.
ideal
insubstantial 4 adj.
prototype 23 n.
ideational 451 adj.
imaginary 513 adj.
motive 612 n.
perfect 646 adj.
perfection 646 n.
desired object 859 n.
idealess
unthinking 450 adj.
idealism
immateriality 320 n.
philosophy 449 n.
fantasy 513 n.
literature 557 n.
reformism 654 n.
fastidiousness 862 n.
philanthropy 901 n.
morals 917 n.
disinterestedness 931 n.
virtues 933 n.
idealist
revolutionist 149 n.
visionary 513 n.
reformer 654 n.
trier 671 n.
perfectionist 862 n.
kind person 897 n.
philanthropist 901 n.
good person 937 n.
idealistic
impossible 470 adj.
(See **idealism** *)*
ideality
thought 449 n.
supposition 512 n.
ideality 513 n.
idealize, idealise
overrate 482 vb.
imagine 513 vb.
idolatrize 982 vb.
ideals
conduct 688 n.
philanthropy 901 n.
morals 917 n.
disinterestedness 931 n.
virtues 933 n.
ideate
cognize 447 vb.
think 449 vb.
imagine 513 vb.
idée fixe
positiveness 473 n.

prejudgment 481 n.
opinionatedness 602 n.
identical
identical 13 adj.
one 88 adj.
identical twin
kinsman 11 n.
duality 90 n.
identifiable
manifest 522 adj.
identification
identity 13 n.
assimilation 18 n.
comparison 462 n.
identification 547 n.
identification papers
label 547 n.
identify
discover 484 vb.
(See **identification** *)*
identikit
representation 551 n.
identity
identity 13 n.
equivalence 28 n.
self 80 n.
unity 88 n.
authenticity 494 n.
identity card
label 547 n.
identity crisis
psychopathy 503 n.
ideogram, ideograph
letter 558 n.
lettering 586 n.
ideological
philosophic 449 adj.
ideologist
philanthropist 901 n.
ideology
philosophy 449 n.
creed 485 n.
ides
date 108 n.
idiocy
folly 499 n.
unintelligence 499 n.
insanity 503 n.
idiolect
speciality 80 n.
identification 547 n.
language 557 n.
idiom
speciality 80 n.
connotation 514 n.
language 557 n.
dialect 560 n.
phrase 563 n.
style 566 n.
idiomatic
apt 24 adj.
special 80 adj.
semantic 514 adj.
linguistic 557 adj.
phraseological 563 adj.
stylistic 566 adj.
forceful 571 adj.
elegant 575 adj.
idiosyncrasy
temperament 5 n.
speciality 80 n.
nonconformity 84 n.
tendency 179 n.
style 566 n.
habit 610 n.
idiot
fool 501 n.
madman 504 n.
idiotic
foolish 499 adj.
crazy 503 adj.
idle
operate 173 vb.
move slowly 278 vb.
be inattentive 456 vb.
profitless 641 adj.
unused 674 adj.
nonactive 677 adj.
lazy 679 adj.
idle gossip
chatter 581 n.
idleness
unproductiveness 172 n.
inaction 677 n.
inactivity 679 n.
leisure 681 n.
undutifulness 918 n.
idler
slowcoach 278 n.
negligence 458 n.
slacker 598 n.
avoider 620 n.
idler 679 n.
idol
image 551 n.
exceller 644 n.
desired object 859 n.
person of repute 866 n.
loved one 887 n.
favourite 890 n.
deity 966 n.n.
idol 982 n.
idolater, idolatress
worshipper 981 n.
idolater 982 n.
idolatrous
ignorant 491 adj.
approving 923 adj.
idolatrous 982 adj.
idolatry
love 887 n.
praise 923 n.
religion 973 n.
cult 981 n.
idolatry 982 n.
idolization, idolisation
deification 982 n.
idolize, idolise
love 887 vb.
respect 920 vb.
praise 923 vb.
idolatrize 982 vb.
idol-maker
sculptor 556 n.
idolater 982 n.
idol worship
idolatry 982 n.
idyll
description 590 n.
poem 593 n.
idyllic
pleasurable 826 adj.
i.e.
namely 80 adv.
in plain words 520 adv.
if
if 8 adv.
provided 468 adv.
igloo
dwelling 192 n.
igneous
fiery 379 adj.
igneous rock
rock 344 n.
ignis fatuus
glow 417 n.
glow-worm 420 n.
visual fallacy 440 n.
ignite
kindle 381 vb.
make bright 417 vb.
igniter
lighter 385 n.
ignition
burning 381 n.
ignoble
discreditable 867 adj.
plebeian 869 adj.
dishonest 930 adj.
ignominious
degrading 867 adj.
dishonest 930 adj.
ignominy
disrepute 867 n.
ignoramus
ignoramus 493 n.
dunce 501 n.
ignorance
blindness 439 n.
ignorance 491 n.
error 495 n.
unskilfulness 695 n.
artlessness 699 n.
innocence 935 n.
ignorant
ignorant 491 adj.
foolish 499 adj.
inexpectant 508 adj.
ill-bred 847 adj.
ignore
be blind 439 vb.
be inattentive 456 vb.
disregard 458 vb.
disbelieve 486 vb.
not know 491 vb.
reject 607 vb.
not observe 769 vb.
be insensitive 820 vb.
make unwelcome 883 vb.
be rude 885 vb.
not respect 921 vb.
ilk
sort 77 n.
ill
evil 616 n.
badness 645 n.
badly 645 adv.
sick 651 adj.
suffering 825 adj.
ill-advised
ill-timed 138 adj.
unwise 499 adj.
inexpedient 643 adj.
bungled 695 adj.
rash 857 adj.
ill-assorted
disagreeing 25 adj.
ill at ease
suffering 825 adj.
ill-behaved
difficult 700 adj.
ill-bred
ill-bred 847 adj.
discourteous 885 adj.
ill-considered
unwise 499 adj.
(See **ill-advised** *)*
ill-defined
amorphous 244 adj.
indistinct 444 adj.
ill-disposed
harmful 645 adj.
discontented 829 adj.
malevolent 898 adj.
illegal
anarchic 734 adj.
prohibited 757 adj.
unjust 914 adj.
unwarranted 916 adj.
dishonest 930 adj.
illegal 954 adj.
illegality
guilty act 936 n.
illegality 954 n.
illegible
unintelligible 517 adj.
illegible writing
lettering 586 n.
illegitimacy
sonship 170 n.
wrong 914 n.
undueness 916 n.
bastardy 954 n.
illegality 954 n.
ill fame
disrepute 867 n.
ill-fated
unfortunate 731 adj.
ill-favoured
ugly 842 adj.
ill feeling
dislike 861 n.

enmity 881 n.
hatred 888 n.
ill-gotten
acquired 771 adj.
ill health
ill health 651 n.
ill humour
resentment 891 n.
sullenness 893 n.
ill-humoured
irascible 892 adj.
illiberal
biased 481 adj.
parsimonious 816 adj.
selfish 932 adj.
illiberality
opinionatedness 602 n.
illicit
illegal 954 adj.
illicit gains
booty 790 n.
illicit love
love affair 887 n.
illicit love 951 n.
illimitable
infinite 107 adj.
ill-informed
uninstructed 491 adj.
mistaken 495 adj.
illiterate
uninstructed 491 adj.
ignoramus 493 n.
ill-judged
ill-timed 138 adj.
indiscriminating 464 adj.
unwise 499 adj.
bungled 695 adj.
ill-kept
neglected 458 adj.
ill-mannered
ill-bred 847 adj.
impertinent 878 adj.
discourteous 885 adj.
ill-matched
disagreeing 25 adj.
married 894 adj.
ill-natured
malevolent 898 adj.
unkind 898 adj.
illness
illness 651 n.
illogical
irrelevant 10 adj.
discontinuous 72 adj.
unthinking 450 adj.
intuitive 476 adj.
illogical 477 adj.
erroneous 495 adj.
absurd 497 adj.
unwise 499 adj.
illogicality
lack of meaning 515 n.
ill-omened
inopportune 138 adj.
cautionary 664 adj.
unpromising 853 adj.
ill-prepared
bungled 695 adj.
ill-provided
unequipped 670 adj.
ill-spent
wasted 634 adj.
profitless 641 adj.
ill-starred
inopportune 138 adj.
unfortunate 731 adj.
ill-tempered
sullen 893 adj.
ill-timed
ill-timed 138 adj.
inexpedient 643 adj.
ill-treat
force 176 vb.
ill-treat 645 vb.
misuse 675 vb.
be severe 735 vb.
ill turn
cruel act 898 n.
illuminant
lighter 385 n.
luminary 420 n.
illuminate
make bright 417 vb.
illuminate 420 vb.
colour 425 vb.
interpret 520 vb.
manifest 522 vb.
paint 553 vb.
decorate 844 vb.
illuminati
intellectual 492 n.
illumination
progression 285 n.
light 417 n.
lighting 420 n.
discovery 484 n.
knowledge 490 n.
ornamental art 844 n.
revelation 975 n.
illuminations
fireworks 420 n.
spectacle 445 n.
celebration 876 n.
illuminator
artist 556 n.
illumine
educate 534 vb.
ill-use
ill-treat 645 vb.
illusion
visual fallacy 440 n.
appearance 445 n.
error 495 n.
deception 542 n.
sleight 542 n.
illusionism
mimicry 20 n.
sorcery 983 n.
illusionist
imitator 20 n.
conjuror 545 n.
sorcerer 983 n.
illusory
immaterial 320 adj.
sophistical 477 adj.
erroneous 495 adj.
imaginary 513 adj.
deceiving 542 adj.
illustrate
exemplify 83 vb.
interpret 520 vb.
represent 551 vb.
decorate 844 vb.
illustration
example 83 n.
interpretation 520 n.
representation 551 n.
picture 553 n.
edition 589 n.
ornamental art 844 n.
illustrative
typical 83 adj.
expressive 516 adj.
illustrator
artist 556 n.
illustrious
renowned 866 adj.
ill will
discontent 829 n.
enmity 881 n.
hatred 888 n.
malevolence 898 n.
envy 912 n.
ill wind
badness 645 n.
adversity 731 n.
ill-wisher
troublemaker 663 n.
enemy 881 n.
ill wishes
malediction 899 n.
image
analogue 18 n.
copy 22 n.
reflection 417 n.
appearance 445 n.
idea 451 n.
ideality 513 n.
trope 519 n.
figure 519 vb.
exhibit 522 n.
monument 548 n.
image 551 n.
sculpture 554 n.
idol 982 n.
imagery
imagination 513 n.
metaphor 519 n.
image-worship
cult 981 n.
idolatry 982 n.
imaginable
possible 469 adj.
supposed 512 adj.
imaginary
unreal 2 adj.
insubstantial 4 adj.
ideational 451 adj.
erroneous 495 adj.
supposed 512 adj.
imaginary 513 adj.
descriptive 590 adj.
fairylike 970 adj.
imagination
vision 438 n.
thought 449 n.
idea 451 n.
imagination 513 n.
falsehood 541 n.
imaginative
original 21 adj.
imaginative 513 adj.
descriptive 590 adj.
imagine
be inattentive 456 vb.
suppose 512 vb.
imagine 513 vb.
describe 590 vb.
plan 623 vb.
hope 852 vb.
(See **imagination** *)*
imagined
imaginary 513 adj.
untrue 543 adj.
imago
insect 365 n.
'I'm all right Jack'
selfishness 932 n.
imam
governor 741 n.
priest 986 n.
imbalance
inequality 29 n.
distortion 246 n.
imbecile
weak 163 adj.
foolish 499 adj.
unintelligent 499 adj.
fool 501 n.
insane 503 adj.
imbecility
helplessness 161 n.
imbibe
absorb 299 vb.
drink 301 vb.
learn 536 vb.
imbrication
covering 226 n.
imbroglio
medley 43 n.
complexity 61 n.
confusion 61 n.
predicament 700 n.
imbrue
infuse 303 vb.
drench 341 vb.
colour 425 vb.
imbue
mix 43 vb.
pervade 189 vb.
infuse 303 vb.

drench 341 vb.
colour 425 vb.
educate 534 vb.
habituate 610 vb.
imbued with
believing 485 adj.
with affections 817 adj.
impressed 818 adj.
imitable
imitative 20 adj.
imitate
liken 18 vb.
resemble 18 vb.
imitate 20 vb.
conform 83 vb.
fake 541 vb.
represent 551 vb.
act 594 vb.
satirize 851 vb.
imitation
imitation 20 n.
copy 22 n.
substituted 150 adj.
sham 542 n.
spurious 542 adj.
representation 551 n.
bad taste 847 n.
imitative
simulating 18 adj.
imitative 20 adj.
conformable 83 adj.
repeated 106 adj.
mindless 448 adj.
unthinking 450 adj.
imitator
imitator 20 n.
actor 594 n.
humorist 839 n.
immaculate
perfect 646 adj.
clean 648 adj.
honourable 929 adj.
innocent 935 adj.
pure 950 adj.
immanent
intrinsic 5 adj.
godlike 965 adj.
immaterial
insubstantial 4 adj.
irrelevant 10 adj.
immaterial 320 adj.
psychic 447 adj.
spiritualism 984 n.
spooky 970 adj.
immateriality
immateriality 320 n.
rarity 325 n.
spiritualism 984 n.
immature
incomplete 55 adj.
beginning 68 adj.
new 126 adj.
young 130 adj.
unintelligent 499 adj.
unhabituated 611 adj.
imperfect 647 adj.
immature 670 adj.
unskilled 695 adj.
uncompleted 726 adj.
immaturity
nonage 130 n.
immeasurable
infinite 107 adj.
immediate
continuous 71 adj.
instantaneous 116 adj.
early 135 adj.
impending 155 adj.
speedy 277 adj.
hasty 680 adj.
immemorial
perpetual 115 adj.
former 125 adj.
immemorial 127 adj.
permanent 144 adj.
worshipful 866 adj.
immense
enormous 32 adj.
infinite 107 adj.
huge 195 adj.
immensity
space 183 n.
immerse
immerse 303 vb.
plunge 313 vb.
drench 341 vb.
immersed
deep 211 adj.
immersion
ingress 297 n.
immersion 303 n.
plunge 313 n.
moistening 341 n.
Christian rite 988 n.
immersion heater
heater 383 n.
immigrant
foreigner 59 n.
settler 191 n.
incomer 297 n.
immigrate
travel 267 vb.
enter 297 vb.
imminent
future 124 adj.
early 135 adj.
impending 155 adj.
approaching 289 adj.
immiscible
separate 46 adj.
nonadhesive 49 adj.
immitigable
unpromising 853 adj.
immixture
mixture 43 n.
immobile
permanent 144 adj.
fixed 153 adj.
still 266 adj.
nonactive 677 adj.
immobility
permanence 144 n.
stability 153 n.
inertness 175 n.
quiescence 266 n.
inaction 677 n.
immobilize, immobilise
bring to rest 266 vb.
make inactive 679 vb.
immoderate
violent 176 adj.
exaggerated 546 adj.
inelegant 576 adj.
redundant 637 adj.
intemperate 943 adj.
immoderately
extremely 32 adv.
immodest
undisguised 522 adj.
vain 873 adj.
unchaste 951 adj.
immolate
kill 362 vb.
give 781 vb.
immoral
dishonest 930 adj.
wicked 934 adj.
immorality
wrong 914 n.
wickedness 934 n.
unchastity 951 n.
impiety 980 n.
immortal
existing 1 adj.
perpetual 115 adj.
renowned 866 adj.
godlike 965 adj.
Immortal(s)
intellectual 492 n.
armed force 722 n.
deity 966 n.
immortality
perpetuity 115 n.
famousness 866 n.
immortalize, immortalise
perpetuate 115 vb.
honour 866 vb.
immovable, immoveable
firm 45 adj.
fixed 153 adj.
still 266 adj.
resolute 599 adj.
obstinate 602 adj.
immovables, immoveables
property 777 n.
immune
salubrious 652 adj.
invulnerable 660 adj.
nonliable 919 adj.
immunity
freedom 744 n.
nonliability 919 n.
immunization, immunisation
hygiene 652 n.
prophylactic 658 n.
protection 660 n.
immunology
medical art 658 n.
immunotherapy
therapy 658 n.
immure
circumscribe 232 vb.
enclose 235 vb.
imprison 747 vb.
— oneself
be unsociable 883 vb.
immutable
perpetual 115 adj.
permanent 144 adj.
unchangeable 153 adj.
godlike 965 adj.
imp
child 132 n.
devil 969 n.
demon 970 n.
elf 970 n.
sorcerer 983 n.
impact
affix 45 vb.
tighten 45 vb.
influence 178 n.
collision 279 n.
implant 303 vb.
excitation 821 n.
impair
derange 63 vb.
disable 161 vb.
weaken 163 vb.
deform 244 vb.
waste 634 vb.
make useless 641 vb.
harm 645 vb.
impair 655 vb.
misuse 675 vb.
hinder 702 vb.
blemish 845 vb.
impairment
incompleteness 55 n.
impairment 655 n.
impale
pierce 263 vb.
mark 547 vb.
execute 963 vb.
impalpable
minute 196 adj.
imparity
inequality 29 n.
impart
inform 524 vb.
give 781 vb.
impartial
equal 28 adj.
wise 498 adj.
choiceless 606 adj.
neutral 625 adj.
indifferent 860 adj.
just 913 adj.
honourable 929 adj.

disinterested 931 adj.
impartiality
moderation 177 n.
impartible
indivisible 52 adj.
impassable
closed 264 adj.
impracticable 470 adj.
difficult 700 adj.
impasse
closure 264 n.
impossibility 470 n.
difficulty 700 n.
obstacle 702 n.
impassible
unfeeling 375 adj.
impassive 820 adj.
inexcitable 823 adj.
impassioned
forceful 571 adj.
fervent 818 adj.
lively 819 adj.
excited 821 adj.
impassive
inert 175 adj.
still 266 adj.
unfeeling 375 adj.
incurious 454 adj.
inattentive 456 adj.
indiscriminating 464 adj.
nonactive 677 adj.
inactive 679 adj.
impassive 820 adj.
inexcitable 823 adj.
indifferent 860 adj.
unastonished 865 adj.
pitiless 906 adj.
impasto
art style 553 n.
impatience
willingness 597 n.
haste 680 n.
warm feeling 818 n.
excitability 822 n.
rashness 857 n.
desire 859 n.
rudeness 885 n.
resentment 891 n.
irascibility 892 n.
impatient
unwise 499 adj.
lively 819 adj.
impeach
blame 924 vb.
indict 928 vb.
litigate 959 vb.
impeachment
accusation 928 n.
impeccable
perfect 646 adj.
virtuous 933 adj.
innocent 935 adj.
impecunious
poor 801 adj.
impede
hinder 702 vb.
impediment
difficulty 700 n.
hindrance 702 n.
obstacle 702 n.
impedimenta
box 194 n.
thing transferred 272 n.
equipment 630 n.
encumbrance 702 n.
property 777 n.
impel
be vigorous 174 vb.
move 265 vb.
impel 279 vb.
propel 287 vb.
insert 303 vb.
motivate 612 vb.
impelling
causal 156 adj.
dynamic 160 adj.
impend
be to come 124 vb.
impend 155 vb.
frighten 854 vb.
threaten 900 vb.
impending
early 135 adj.
impending 155 adj.
approaching 289 adj.
arriving 295 adj.
expected 507 adj.
impenetrable
closed 264 adj.
dense 324 adj.
unintelligent 499 adj.
unintelligible 517 adj.
latent 523 adj.
difficult 700 adj.
thick-skinned 820 adj.
impenitence
obstinacy 602 n.
impenitence 940 n.
impiety 980 n.
imperative
necessary 596 adj.
demanding 627 adj.
important 638 adj.
authoritarian 735 adj.
commanding 737 adj.
compelling 740 adj.
imperative duty
duty 917 n.
imperator
army officer 741 n.
sovereign 741 n.
imperceptible
minute 196 adj.
slow 278 adj.
invisible 444 adj.
imperceptibly
slightly 33 adv.
imperceptive
insensible 375 adj.
indiscriminating 464 adj.
impercipient
unintelligent 499 adj.
imperfect
inferior 35 adj.
fragmentary 53 adj.
incomplete 55 adj.
preterite 125 adj.
crippled 163 adj.
deformed 246 adj.
deficient 307 adj.
inelegant 576 adj.
bad 645 adj.
imperfect 647 adj.
immature 670 adj.
bungled 695 adj.
uncompleted 726 adj.
unsightly 842 adj.
blemished 845 adj.
frail 934 adj.
imperfection
insufficiency 636 n.
imperfection 647 n.
nonpreparation 670 n.
blemish 845 n.
imperial
great 32 adj.
hair 259 n.
metrical 465 adj.
ruling 733 adj.
imperialism
nation 371 n.
governance 733 n.
imperil
endanger 661 vb.
imperious
authoritative 733 adj.
proud 871 adj.
insolent 878 adj.
imperishable
perpetual 115 adj.
unchangeable 153 adj.
renowned 866 adj.
imperium
superiority 34 n.
government 733 n.
impermanence
transience 114 n.
changeableness 152 n.
impermeable
unyielding 162 adj.
closed 264 adj.
dense 324 adj.
screened 421 adj.
impermissible
illegal 954 adj.
impersonal
general 79 adj.
impassive 820 adj.
indifferent 860 adj.
unsociable 883 adj.
just 913 adj.
impersonate
represent 551 vb.
act 594 vb.
impersonator
imitator 20 n.
entertainer 594 n.
imperspicuity
unintelligibility 517 n.
imperspicuity 568 n.
impertinence
sauciness 878 n.
rudeness 885 n.
impertinent
irrelevant 10 adj.
insolent person 878 n.
disrespectful 921 adj.
imperturbability
inexcitability 823 n.
lack of wonder 865 n.
imperturbable
impassive 820 adj.
impervious
closed 264 adj.
dense 324 adj.
screened 421 adj.
unbelieving 486 adj.
unintelligent 499 adj.
obstinate 602 adj.
thick-skinned 820 adj.
impetigo
skin disease 651 n.
impetrate
entreat 761 vb.
impetuosity
vigorousness 174 n.
rashness 857 n.
desire 859 n.
impetuous
furious 176 adj.
hasty 680 adj.
fervent 818 adj.
excitable 822 adj.
impetus
vigorousness 174 n.
spurt 277 n.
impulse 279 n.
motive 612 n.
impiety
undueness 916 n.
disrespect 921 n.
impiety 980 n.
impinge
collide 279 vb.
encroach 306 vb.
touch 378 vb.
impious
wicked 934 adj.
irreligious 974 adj.
impious 980 adj.
impish
harmful 645 adj.
fairylike 970 adj.
implacable
resolute 599 adj.

obstinate 602 adj.
severe 735 adj.
hating 888 adj.
malevolent 898 adj.
pitiless 906 adj.
revengeful 910 adj.
implant
affix 45 vb.
implant 303 vb.
cultivate 370 vb.
educate 534 vb.
habituate 610 vb.
implausible
improbable 472 adj.
erroneous 495 adj.
implement
produce 164 vb.
instrument 628 n.
tool 630 n.
do 676 vb.
carry out 725 vb.
implicate
inform 524 vb.
accuse 928 vb.
implicated
component 58 adj.
implication
relation 9 n.
complexity 61 n.
meaning 514 n.
latency 523 n.
implicative
tacit 523 adj.
indicating 547 adj.
implicit
intrinsic 5 adj.
meaningful 514 adj.
tacit 523 adj.
implied
semantic 514 adj.
tacit 523 adj.
implore
entreat 761 vb.
imply
be intrinsic 5 vb.
contain 56 vb.
accompany 89 vb.
conduce 156 vb.
evidence 466 vb.
make likely 471 vb.
mean 514 vb.
imply 523 vb.
hint 524 vb.
indicate 547 vb.
impolite
inelegant 576 adj.
ill-bred 847 adj.
impertinent 878 adj.
discourteous 885 adj.
disrespectful 921 adj.
impolitic
inexpedient 643 adj.
unskilful 695 adj.
imponderable
immaterial 320 adj.
light 323 adj.
import
relation 9 n.
transference 272 n.
ingress 297 n.
reception 299 n.
admit 299 vb.
meaning 514 n.
provide 633 vb.
importance 638 n.
importance
greatness 32 n.
superiority 34 n.
precedence 64 n.
influence 178 n.
importance 638 n.
prestige 866 n.
important
crucial 137 adj.
fundamental 156 adj.
important 638 adj.
important part
essential part 5 n.
importation
transference 272 n.
imported
extraneous 59 adj.
incoming 297 adj.
neological 560 adj.
importer
transferrer 272 n.
merchant 794 n.
importunate
requesting 761 adj.
annoying 827 adj.
importune
request 761 vb.
torment 827 vb.
impose
print 587 vb.
necessitate 596 vb.
command 737 vb.
compel 740 vb.
command respect 920 vb.
punish 963 vb.
— on/upon
deceive 542 vb.
avail oneself of 673 vb.
imposing
notable 638 adj.
impressive 821 adj.
worshipful 866 adj.
imposition
bane 659 n.
demand 737 n.
tax 809 n.
injustice 914 n.
undueness 916 n.
penalty 963 n.
impossibility
impossibility 470 n.
impossible
excluded 57 adj.
unthought 450 adj.
impossible 470 adj.
unbelieved 486 adj.
difficult 700 adj.
refused 760 adj.
intolerable 827 adj.
unpromising 853 adj.
wonderful 864 adj.
impost
taking 786 n.
tax 809 n.
impostor
imitator 20 n.
sham 542 n.
impostor 545 n.
bungler 697 n.
affecter 850 n.
boaster 877 n.
usurper 916 n.
imposture
duplicity 541 n.
deception 542 n.
cunning 698 n.
impotence
impotence 161 n.
unproductiveness 172 n.
impotent
impotent 161 adj.
crippled 163 adj.
unproductive 172 adj.
unimportant 639 adj.
useless 641 adj.
nonactive 677 adj.
unskilful 695 adj.
impound
imprison 747 vb.
impounding
expropriation 786 n.
impoverish
waste 634 vb.
make insufficient 636 vb.
fleece 786 vb.
impoverish 801 vb.
impoverishment
decrease 37 n.
deterioration 655 n.
poverty 801 n.
impracticable
impracticable 470 adj.
useless 641 adj.
difficult 700 adj.
unpromising 853 adj.
impractical
irrelevant 10 adj.
misjudging 481 adj.
imaginative 513 adj.
imprecation
entreaty 761 n.
malediction 899 n.
imprecise
inexact 495 adj.
unclear 568 adj.
imprecision
generality 79 n.
impregnable
unyielding 162 adj.
invulnerable 660 adj.
pure 950 adj.
impregnate
mix 43 vb.
combine 50 vb.
generate 167 vb.
make fruitful 171 vb.
pervade 189 vb.
infuse 303 vb.
educate 534 vb.
impresario
exhibitor 522 n.
stage manager 594 n.
imprescriptible
due 915 adj.
impress
effect 157 n.
be vigorous 174 vb.
influence 178 vb.
attract 291 vb.
cause thought 449 vb.
attract notice 455 vb.
label 547 n.
mark 547 vb.
engrave 555 vb.
motivate 612 vb.
impress 821 vb.
be wonderful 864 vb.
command respect 920 vb.
— on
emphasize 532 vb.
— on one's memory
memorize 505 vb.
educate 534 vb.
impressed
impressed 818 adj.
impressible 819 adj.
wondering 864 adj.
impressible
liable 180 adj.
impressible 819 adj.
excitable 822 adj.
impression
copy 22 n.
influence 178 n.
concavity 255 n.
sense 374 n.
appearance 445 n.
idea 451 n.
intuition 476 n.
opinion 485 n.
knowledge 490 n.
indication 547 n.
label 547 n.
representation 551 n.
printing 555 n.
letterpress 587 n.
edition 589 n.
acting 594 n.
feeling 818 n.
excitation 821 n.
impressionable
converted 147 adj.
unstable 152 adj.
sentient 374 adj.

receiving 782 adj.
impressible 819 adj.
excitable 822 adj.
Impressionism
school of painting 553 n.
impressionistic
intuitive 476 adj.
representing 551 adj.
descriptive 590 adj.
impressive
prodigious 32 adj.
influential 178 adj.
striking 374 adj.
appearing 445 adj.
credible 485 adj.
forceful 571 adj.
notable 638 adj.
felt 818 adj.
impressive 821 adj.
frightening 854 adj.
wonderful 864 adj.
worshipful 866 adj.
proud 871 adj.
respected 920 adj.
impressiveness
spectacle 445 n.
prestige 866 n.
ostentation 875 n.
imprest
lending 784 n.
imprimatur
assent 488 n.
permit 756 n.
orthodoxism 976 n.
imprint
copy 22 n.
make conform 83 vb.
concavity 255 n.
identification 547 n.
label 547 n.
mark 547 vb.
letterpress 587 n.
imprison
circumscribe 232 vb.
enclose 235 vb.
close 264 vb.
imprison 747 vb.
retain 778 vb.
punish 963 vb.
imprisoned
imprisoned 747 adj.
captive 750 adj.
imprisonment
detention 747 n.
penalty 963 n.
improbability
improbability 472 n.
unbelief 486 n.
improbable
unusual 84 adj.
improbable 472 adj.
erroneous 495 adj.
unexpected 508 adj.
wonderful 864 adj.
improbity
thievishness 788 n.
wrong 914 n.
improbity 930 n.
wickedness 934 n.
impromptu
instantaneously 116 adv.
musical piece 412 n.
spontaneous 609 adj.
unprepared 670 adj.
improper
unapt 25 adj.
unwise 499 adj.
ungrammatical 565 adj.
inexpedient 643 adj.
not nice 645 adj.
vulgar 847 adj.
discreditable 867 adj.
disreputable 867 adj.
wrong 914 adj.
undue 916 adj.
vicious 934 adj.
improper fraction
numerical element 85 n.
impropriation
transfer 780 n.
impropriety
inaptitude 25 n.
solecism 565 n.
inelegance 576 n.
inexpedience 643 n.
bad taste 847 n.
wrong 914 n.
undueness 916 n.
vice 934 n.
guilty act 936 n.
improve
flourish 615 vb.
get better 654 vb.
make better 654 vb.
beautify 841 vb.
philanthropize 897 vb.
— on/upon
be superior 34 vb.
find useful 640 vb.
make better 654 vb.
— the occasion
profit by 137 vb.
improvement
increase 36 n.
conversion 147 n.
progression 285 n.
benefit 615 n.
improvement 654 n.
improver
alterer 143 n.
reformer 654 n.
improvidence
waste 634 n.
improvident
negligent 458 adj.
unprepared 670 adj.
prodigal 815 adj.
rash 857 adj.
improvisation
spontaneity 609 n.
contrivance 623 n.
nonpreparation 670 n.
improvise
compose music 413 vb.
imagine 513 vb.
improvise 609 vb.
be unprepared 670 vb.
imprudence
folly 499 n.
imprudent
inexpedient 643 adj.
rash 857 adj.
impudent
impertinent 878 adj.
discourteous 885 adj.
impugn
cause doubt 486 vb.
negate 533 vb.
impulse
energy 160 n.
influence 178 n.
impulse 279 n.
propulsion 287 n.
intuition 476 n.
necessity 596 n.
whim 604 n.
spontaneity 609 n.
motive 612 n.
feeling 818 n.
desire 859 n.
impulsive
intuitive 476 adj.
involuntary 596 adj.
spontaneous 609 adj.
hasty 680 adj.
excitable 822 adj.
rash 857 adj.
impunity
escape 667 n.
nonliability 919 n.
acquittal 960 n.
impure
not nice 645 adj.
unclean 649 adj.
vulgar 847 adj.
disreputable 867 adj.
erotic 887 adj.
sensual 944 adj.
impure 951 adj.
impurity
wickedness 934 n.
impurity 951 n.
imputation
attribution 158 n.
slur 867 n.
detraction 926 n.
accusation 928 n.
impute
attribute 158 vb.
blame 924 vb.
in
in place 186 adv.
inside 224 adv.
fashionable 848 adj.
in a bad way
sick 651 adj.
deteriorated 655 adj.
endangered 661 adj.
unprosperous 731 adj.
in abeyance
inert 175 adj.
latent 523 adj.
unused 674 adj.
nonactive 677 adj.
in a big way
greatly 32 adv.
inability
impotence 161 n.
inutility 641 n.
unskilfulness 695 n.
in a body
together 74 adv.
with 89 adv.
in absentia
not here 190 adv.
inaccessible
removed 199 adj.
impracticable 470 adj.
in accordance (with)
agreeing 24 adv.
conformably 83 adj.
inaccuracy
negligence 458 n.
indiscrimination 464 n.
inexactness 495 n.
imperspicuity 568 n.
in a class by itself
excellent 644 adj.
in a cleft stick
in difficulties 700 adj.
in a cold sweat
fearing 854 adj.
in a coma
sick 651 adj.
inaction
inertness 175 n.
avoidance 620 n.
nonuse 674 n.
inaction 677 n.
inactivity 679 n.
in action, be
operate 173 vb.
do 676 vb.
inactive
inert 175 adj.
latent 523 adj.
inactive 679 adj.
unskilful 695 adj.
apathetic 820 adj.
dejected 834 adj.
inactivity
delay 136 n.
strike 145 n.
weakness 163 n.
unproductiveness 172 n.
quiescence 266 n.
negligence 458 n.
irresolution 601 n.
avoidance 620 n.
nonuse 674 n.
inaction 677 n.

inactivity 679 n.
leisure 681 n.
nonobservance 769 n.
tedium 838 n.
indifference 860 n.
in addition
in addition 38 adv.
with 89 adv.
inadequacy
inequality 29 n.
weakness 163 n.
inutility 641 n.
inadequate
incomplete 55 adj.
deficient 307 adj.
insufficient 636 adj.
imperfect 647 adj.
unskilful 695 adj.
in a different class
different 15 adj.
superior 34 adj.
in a dilemma
in difficulties 700 adj.
inadjustable
unconformable 84 adj.
inadmissible
unapt 25 adj.
excluded 57 adj.
extraneous 59 adj.
inexpedient 643 adj.
refused 760 adj.
wrong 914 adj.
in advance (of)
beyond 34 adv.
before 64 adv.
early 135 adj.
beforehand 135 adv.
in front 237 adv.
ahead 283 adv.
inadvertence, inadvertency
inattention 456 n.
mistake 495 n.
inadvertent
unintentional 618 adj.
inadvisable
inexpedient 643 adj.
in a fair way (to)
almost 33 adv.
tending 179 adj.
probable 471 adj.
in a fix
in difficulties 700 adj.
in a flap
agitated 318 adj.
fearing 854 adj.
in a flash
swiftly 277 adv.
in a flat spin
fearing 854 adj.
in a groove
uniformly 16 adv.
in a huff
angry 891 adj.
in a hurry
brief 114 adj.
hasty 680 adj.
in aid of
relative 9 adj.
in aid of 703 adv.
in a jam
in difficulties 700 adj.
inalienable
retained 778 adj.
due 915 adj.
in a lifetime
man and boy 110 adv.
in a line
longwise 203 adv.
straight 249 adj.
in a line with
towards 281 adv.
in all
completely 54 adv.
in all conscience
positively 32 adv.
affirmatively 532 adv.
in all directions
towards 281 adv.
in all probability
probably 471 adv.
in all quarters
sporadically 75 adv.
widely 183 adv.
in all respects
completely 54 adv.
truly 494 adv.
inalterable
unchangeable 153 adj.
in a manner of speaking
partially 33 adv.
metaphorically 519 abv.
in a mess
orderless 61 adj.
in a minority
few 105 adj.
in a moment
instantaneously 116 adv.
inamorata
loved one 887 n.
in an aside
voicelessly 578 adv.
in and out
in and out 251 adv.
to and fro 317 adv.
inane
insubstantial 4 adj.
empty 190 adj.
foolish 499 adj.
meaningless 515 adj.
feeble 572 adj.
in an evil hour
inopportunely 138 adv.
inanimate
inorganic 359 adj.
dead 361 adj.
insensible 375 adj.
mindless 448 adj.
unthinking 450 adj.
inactive 679 adj.
inanimate object
object 319 n.
inanition
weakness 163 n.
fasting 946 n.
in anticipation
before 119 adv.
beforehand 135 adv.
in preparation 669 adv.
in an undertone
faintly 401 adv.
voicelessly 578 adv.
in a nutshell
in small compass 196 adv.
proverbially 496 adv.
concisely 569 adv.
in any event
by chance 159 adv.
in a phrase
in terms 563 adv.
in a position to, be
find means 629 vb.
inappeasable
greedy 859 adj.
inapplicable
irrelevant 10 adj.
unapt 25 adj.
useless 641 adj.
inapposite
irrelevant 10 adj.
inappreciable
inconsiderable 33 adj.
minute 196 adj.
unimportant 639 adj.
inappreciation
ignorance 491 n.
inapprehensible
unintelligible 517 adj.
inappropriate
unrelated 10 adj.
unapt 25 adj.
misplaced 188 adj.
inexpedient 643 adj.
ridiculous 849 adj.
undue 916 adj.
inaptitude
inaptitude 25 n.
inexpedience 643 n.
in a quandary
in difficulties 700 adj.
in arrears
incomplete 55 adj.
behindhand 307 adv.
owed 803 adj.
nonpaying 805 adj.
in articles
studiously 536 adv.
inarticulate
voiceless 578 adj.
stammering 580 adj.
taciturn 582 adj.
artless 699 adj.
wondering 864 adj.
modest 874 adj.
inartistic
bungled 695 adj.
artless 699 adj.
graceless 842 adj.
in a rut
uniformly 16 adv.
in a sense
partly 53 adv.
significantly 514 adv.
inasmuch
concerning 9 adv.
in a spot
in difficulties 700 adj.
in a state of
such 7 adj.
in a straight line
towards 281 adv.
in a trance
insensible 375 adj.
imaginative 513 adj.
drugged 949 adj.
in a trice
instantaneously 116 adv.
in a trickle
here and there 105 adv.
inattention
inattention 456 n.
restlessness 678 n.
nonobservance 769 n.
moral insensibility 820 n.
indifference 860 n.
inattentive
deaf 416 adj.
blind 439 adj.
unthinking 450 adj.
inattentive 456 adj.
negligent 458 adj.
inexpectant 508 adj.
unskilful 695 adj.
rash 857 adj.
discourteous 885 adj.
in at the death, be
persevere 600 vb.
carry out 725 vb.
inaudible
silent 399 adj.
muted 401 adj.
deaf 416 adj.
unintelligible 517 adj.
voiceless 578 adj.
inaugural
precursory 66 adj.
beginning 68 adj.
inaugurate
auspicate 68 vb.

cause 156 vb.
celebrate 876 vb.
inauguration
debut 68 n.
fitting out 669 n.
mandate 751 n.
celebration 876 n.
inauspicious
inopportune 138 adj.
presageful 511 adj.
evil 616 adj.
adverse 731 adj.
unpromising 853 adj.
in a way
similarly 18 adv.
metaphorically 519 adv.
in a word
concisely 569 adv.
in being
on the spot 189 adj.
in between, be
be halfway 625 vb.
in bits
separately 46 adv.
fragmentary 53 adj.
in black and white
recorded 548 adj.
written 586 adj.
inboard
interior 224 adj.
inborn
genetic 5 adj.
with affections 817 adj.
inbred
genetic 5 adj.
extrinsic 6 adj.
ethnic 11 adj.
combined 50 adj.
with affections 817 adj.
inbreeding
race 11 n.
in brief
concisely 569 adv.
in sum 592 adv.
in broad daylight
manifestly 522 adv.
in bulk
collectively 52 adv.
Inca
sovereign 741 n.
in cahoots with
in league 708 adv.
incalculable
multitudinous 104 adj.
infinite 107 adj.
casual 159 adj.
in camera
secretly 525 adv.
incandescent
fiery 379 adj.
luminous 417 adj.
luminescent 420 adj.
incantation
entreaty 761 n.
spell 983 n.
incapable
unapt 25 adj.
powerless 161 adj.
unskilful 695 adj.
incapacitate
disable 161 vb.
incapacity
inaptitude 25 n.
impotence 161 n.
ignorance 491 n.
unintelligence 499 n.
unskilfulness 695 n.
incarcerate
imprison 747 vb.
incarnadine
redden 431 vb.
incarnate
material 319 adj.
alive 360 adj.
manifest 522 vb.
incarnation
essential part 5 n.
materiality 319 n.
representation 551 n.
theophany 965 n.
revelation 975 n.
in case
if 8 adv.
eventually 154 adv.
incautious
unwise 499 adj.
spontaneous 609 adj.
rash 857 adj.
incendiary
destructive 165 adj.
violent creature 176 n.
incendiarism 381 n.
evildoer 904 n.
incendiary bomb
lighter 385 n.
bomb 723 n.
incense
fumigator 385 n.
smell 394 vb.
inodorousness 395 n.
scent 396 n.
honours 866 n.
excite hate 888 vb.
enrage 891 vb.
flattery 925 n.
oblation 981 n.
ritual object 988 n.
incentive
stimulant 174 n.
impulse 279 n.
incentive 612 n.
excitant 821 n.
reward 962 n.
inception
beginning 68 n.
incertitude
uncertainty 474 n.
incessant
continuous 71 adj.
repeated 106 adj.
perpetual 115 adj.
frequent 139 adj.
unceasing 146 adj.
active 678 adj.
incest
illicit love 951 n.
inch
small quantity 33 n.
short distance 200 n.
long measure 203 n.
shortness 204 n.
move slowly 278 vb.
in chains
subjected 745 adj.
captive 750 adj.
in character
usual 610 adj.
in charge
in control 689 adv.
inch by inch
by degrees 27 adv.
piecemeal 53 adv.
gradatim 278 adv.
inchoate
beginning 68 adj.
amorphous 244 adj.
uncompleted 726 adj.
in chorus
agreeing 24 adj.
synchronously 123 adv.
harmonious 410 adj.
unanimously 488 adv.
inchworm
creepy-crawly 365 n.
incidence
event 154 n.
incident
event 154 n.
incidental
extrinsic 6 adj.
circumstantial 8 adj.
irrelevant 10 adj.
accompanying 89 adj.
happening 154 adj.
casual 159 adj.
liable 180 adj.
incidentally
incidentally 137 adv.
at random 618 adv.
incidental music
musical piece 412 n.
incinerate
destroy 165 vb.
inter 364 vb.
burn 381 vb.
incinerator
furnace 383 n.
incipient
beginning 68 adj.
in circles
round and round 315 adv.
in circulation
published 528 adj.
rumoured 529 adj.
incise
cut 46 vb.
groove 262 vb.
record 548 vb.
engrave 555 vb.
incision
wound 655 n.
incisive
keen 174 adj.
assertive 532 adj.
concise 569 adj.
forceful 571 adj.
incisor
tooth 256 n.
incite
cause 156 vb.
make violent 176 vb.
influence 178 vb.
impel 279 vb.
incite 612 vb.
advise 691 vb.
make quarrels 709 vb.
excite 821 vb.
incitement
inducement 612 n.
excitation 821 n.
incivility
ill-breeding 847 n.
sauciness 878 n.
discourtesy 885 n.
disrespect 921 n.
inclemency
storm 176 n.
wintriness 380 n.
severity 735 n.
pitilessness 906 n.
inclination
tendency 179 n.
obliquity 220 n.
will 595 n.
willingness 597 n.
choice 605 n.
liking 859 n.
love 887 n.
inclinations
affections 817 n.
incline
tend 179 vb.
incline 220 n.
make oblique 220 vb.
make curved 248 vb.
motivate 612 vb.
cause desire 859 vb.
in clover
in comfort 376 adv.
prosperous 730 adj.
include
add 38 vb.
join 45 vb.
contain 56 vb.
comprise 78 vb.
possess 773 vb.
included
intrinsic 5 adj.
included 78 adj.
accompanying 89 adj.
inclusion
inclusion 78 n.

generality 79 n.
reception 299 n.
association 706 n.
participation 775 n.
inclusive
comprehensive 52 adj.
complete 54 adj.
inclusive 78 adj.
incognito
disguised 525 adj.
anonymous 562 adj.
incognizant
ignorant 491 adj.
incoherence
disunion 46 n.
unintelligibility 517 n.
incoherent
nonadhesive 49 adj.
orderless 61 adj.
discontinuous 72 adj.
frenzied 503 adj.
meaningless 515 adj.
prolix 570 adj.
in cold blood
purposely 617 adv.
in cold blood 820 adv.
incombustible
incombustible 382 adj.
income
means 629 n.
earnings 771 n.
estate 777 n.
receipt 807 n.
reward 962 n.
incomer
intruder 59 n.
successor 67 n.
upstart 126 n.
incomer 297 n.
income tax
tax 809 n.
incoming
sequential 65 adj.
incoming 297 adj.
incommensurable
unrelated 10 adj.
disagreeing 25 adj.
numerical 85 adj.
numerable 86 adj.
incommode
be inexpedient 643 vb.
trouble 827 vb.
in common
relative 9 adj.
in common 775 adv.
incommunicable
inexpressible 517 adj.
retained 778 adj.
incommunicado
concealed 525 adj.
imprisoned 747 adj.
incommunicative
taciturn 582 adj.
cautious 858 adj.
incommutable
unchangeable 153 adj.
incomparable
inimitable 21 adj.
supreme 34 adj.
in comparison
relatively 9 adv.
comparatively 462 adv.
incompatible
contrary 14 adj.
disagreeing 25 adj.
inimical 881 adj.
incompetence, incompetency
inaptitude 25 n.
impotence 161 n.
unintelligence 499 n.
insufficiency 636 n.
inutility 641 n.
unskilfulness 695 n.
illegality 954 n.
incompetent
fool 501 n.
bungler 697 n.
unentitled 916 adj.
incomplete
incomplete 55 adj.
deficient 307 adj.
insufficient 636 adj.
imperfect 647 adj.
uncompleted 726 adj.
incompletely
partly 53 adv.
incomprehensible
infinite 107 adj.
unintelligible 517 adj.
incomprehension
ignorance 491 n.
incompressible
dense 324 adj.
rigid 326 adj.
inconceivable
unthought 450 adj.
impossible 470 adj.
unbelieved 486 adj.
unintelligible 517 adj.
wonderful 864 adj.
inconcinnity
inaptitude 25 n.
inelegance 576 n.
inconclusive
poorly reasoned 477 adj.
in condition
such 7 adj.
athletic 162 adj.
fleshy 195 adj.
healthy 650 adj.
incongruity
difference 15 n.
misfit 25 n.
incongruous
different 15 adj.
disagreeing 25 adj.
unconformable 84 adj.
illogical 477 adj.
ungrammatical 565 adj.
in connection with
concerning 9 adv.
inconsequence
absurdity 497 n.
inconsequential
irrelevant 10 adj.
illogical 477 adj.
unimportant 639 adj.
inconsiderable
inconsiderable 33 adj.
lesser 35 adj.
little 196 adj.
unimportant 639 adj.
inconsiderate
unthinking 450 adj.
inattentive 456 adj.
rash 857 adj.
discourteous 885 adj.
inconsideration
spontaneity 609 n.
rashness 857 n.
inconsistency
nonconformity 84 n.
changeableness 152 n.
inconsistent
contrary 14 adj.
nonuniform 17 adj.
disagreeing 25 adj.
illogical 477 adj.
absurd 497 adj.
capricious 604 adj.
inconsolable
regretting 830 adj.
hopeless 853 adj.
inconsonant
disagreeing 25 adj.
inconspicuous
indistinct 444 adj.
inconstancy
changeableness 152 n.
inconstant
nonuniform 17 adj.
fitful 142 adj.
light-minded 456 adj.
irresolute 601 adj.
capricious 604 adj.
perfidious 930 adj.
in contact
contiguous 202 adj.
by letter 588 adv.
incontestable
undisputed 473 adj.
manifest 522 adj.
in context
relevant 9 adj.
incontinence
helplessness 161 n.
excretion 302 n.
desire 859 n.
intemperance 943 n.
unchastity 951 n.
incontinent
impotent 161 adj.
intemperate 943 adj.
in contrast
contrarily 14 adv.
incontrovertible
established 153 adj.
undisputed 473 adj.
demonstrated 478 adj.
inconvenience
pain 377 n.
inutility 641 n.
obstacle 702 n.
suffering 825 n.
inconvenient
ill-timed 138 adj.
inexpedient 643 adj.
difficult 700 adj.
hindering 702 adj.
inconvertible
unchangeable 153 adj.
in convoy
with 89 adv.
incoordination
disorder 61 n.
incorporate
join 45 vb.
combine 50 vb.
comprise 78 vb.
absorb 299 vb.
immaterial 320 adj.
manifest 522 vb.
corporate 708 adj.
incorporation
inclusion 78 n.
incorporeal
insubstantial 4 adj.
immaterial 320 adj.
incorrect
illogical 477 adj.
inexact 495 adj.
incorrectness
solecism 565 n.
inelegance 576 n.
ill-breeding 847 n.
incorrigible
obstinate 602 adj.
wilful 602 adj.
unpromising 853 adj.
wicked 934 adj.
impenitent 940 adj.
incorruptible
perpetual 115 adj.
honourable 929 adj.
disinterested 931 adj.
pure 950 adj.
increase
increase 36 n.
grow 36 vb.
addition 38 n.
growth 157 n.
product 164 n.

propagation 167 n.
expand 197 vb.
improvement 654 n.
gain 771 n.
aggravate 832 vb.
incredible
prodigious 32 adj.
unusual 84 adj.
impossible 470 adj.
unbelieved 486 adj.
wonderful 864 adj.
incredulous
unbelieving 486 adj.
increment
increment 36 n.
addition 38 n.
extra 40 n.
expansion 197 n.
benefit 615 n.
gain 771 n.
reward 962 n.
incriminate
blame 924 vb.
accuse 928 vb.
in-crowd
party 708 n.
incrustation
facing 226 n.
incubate
generate 167 vb.
breed stock 369 vb.
mature 669 vb.
incubator
seedbed 156 n.
hospital 658 n.
preserver 666 n.
incubus
encumbrance 702 n.
suffering 825 n.
demon 970 n.
inculcate
educate 534 vb.
inculpate
blame 924 vb.
accuse 928 vb.
incumbency
job 622 n.
benefice 985 n.
incumbent
resident 191 n.
overhanging 209 adj.
weighty 322 adj.
beneficiary 776 n.
obligatory 917 adj.
cleric 986 n.
incunabula
beginning 68 n.
edition 589 n.
incur
meet with 154 vb.
be liable 180 vb.
acquire 771 vb.
incurable
characteristic 5 adj.
deadly 362 adj.
impracticable 470 adj.
obstinate 602 adj.
bad 645 adj.
sick 651 adj.
unpromising 853 adj.
incuriosity
incuriosity 454 n.
lack of expectation 508 n.
incurious
incurious 454 adj.
inattentive 456 adj.
ignorant 491 adj.
inexpectant 508 adj.
apathetic 820 adj.
indifferent 860 adj.
incursion
ingress 297 n.
attack 712 n.
incurvation
curvature 248 n.
concavity 255 n.
in custody
safe 660 adj.
imprisoned 747 adj.
captive 750 adj.
indaba
conference 584 n.
in danger of
liable 180 adj.
probable 471 adj.
vulnerable 661 adj.
indebted
indebted 803 adj.
nonpaying 805 adj.
grateful 907 adj.
indebtedness
debt 803 n.
dueness 915 n.
indecent
not nice 645 adj.
vulgar 847 adj.
disreputable 867 adj.
vicious 934 adj.
impure 951 adj.
indecent assault
rape 951 n.
indecent exposure
social evil 951 n.
indecently dressed
uncovered 229 adj.
indecision
dubiety 474 n.
irresolution 601 n.
no choice 606 n.
indecisive
uncertain 474 adj.
irresolute 601 adj.
in decline
diminuendo 37 adv.
deteriorated 655 adj.
indecorum
ill-breeding 847 n.
vice 934 n.
indeed
positively 32 adv.
truly 494 adv.
in deep water
in difficulties 700 adj.
indefatigable
persevering 600 adj.
industrious 678 adj.
in default of
instead 150 adv.
without 190 adv.
indefeasible
established 153 adj.
undisputed 473 adj.
indefectible
perfect 646 adj.
indefensible
defenceless 161 adj.
accusable 928 adj.
heinous 934 adj.
in defiance of
in defiance of 25 adv.
in opposition 704 adv.
defiantly 711 adv.
indefinable
unspeakable 32 adj.
inexpressible 517 adj.
indefinite
general 79 adj.
infinite 107 adj.
indistinct 444 adj.
unclear 568 adj.
indefiniteness
uncertainty 474 n.
equivocalness 518 n.
indelible
fixed 153 adj.
remembered 505 adj.
marked 547 adj.
indelicate
graceless 842 adj.
vulgar 847 adj.
impure 951 adj.
in demand
required 627 adj.
salable 793 adj.
desired 859 adj.
indemnification
compensation 31 n.
restitution 787 n.
atonement 941 n.
reward 962 n.
indemnify
give security 767 vb.
— oneself
recoup 31 vb.
indemnity
offset 31 n.
security 767 n.
restitution 787 n.
pay 804 n.
payment 804 n.
forgiveness 909 n.
atonement 941 n.
indent
crinkle 251 vb.
make concave 255 vb.
notch 260 n.vb.
requirement 627 n.
demand 737 vb.
contract 765 vb.
indentation
gap 201 n.
angularity 247 n.
notch 260 n.
indenture
compact 765 n.
title deed 767 n.
independence
unrelatedness 10 n.
originality 21 n.
nonconformity 84 n.
opportunity 137 n.
will 595 n.
government 733 n.
independence 744 n.
wealth 800 n.
celibacy 895 n.
nonliability 919 n.
sectarianism 978 n.
independent
revolter 738 n.
free person 744 n.
Independent
sectarian 978 n.adj.
indescribable
unspeakable 32 adj.
unusual 84 adj.
wonderful 864 adj.
indestructible
existing 1 adj.
unchangeable 153 adj.
unyielding 162 adj.
in detail
piecemeal 53 adv.
severally 80 adv.
indeterminate
causeless 159 adj.
uncertain 474 adj.
indetermination
nondesign 618 n.
index
relate 9 vb.
class 62 vb.
numerical element 85 n.
list 87 n.vb.
finger 378 n.
gauge 465 n.
indicator 547 n.
record 548 n.vb.
dictionary 559 n.
edition 589 n.
Index
prohibition 757 n.
orthodoxism 976 n.
index card
record 548 n.
Indian file
procession 71 n.
Indian ink
black pigment 428 n.
Indian mode
key 410 n.
Indian summer
summer 128 n.

autumn 129 n.
revival 656 n.
palmy days 730 n.
india rubber
elasticity 328 n.
indicate
specify 80 vb.
point to 281 vb.
mean 514 vb.
show 522 vb.
indicate 547 vb.
indication
list 87 n.
evidence 466 n.
omen 511 n.
manifestation 522 n.
hint 524 n.
indication 547 n.
trace 548 n.
warning 664 n.
indicative
evidential 466 adj.
meaningful 514 adj.
disclosing 526 adj.
indicating 547 adj.
indict
indict 928 vb.
litigate 959 vb.
indictable
punishable 963 adj.
indictment
accusation 928 n.
indifference
indifference 860 n.
indifferent
unrelated 10 adj.
moderate 177 adj.
incurious 454 adj.
inattentive 456 adj.
negligent 458 adj.
inexpectant 508 adj.
choiceless 606 adj.
neutral 625 adj.
not bad 644 adj.
nonactive 677 adj.
lax 734 adj.
nonobservant 769 adj.
apathetic 820 adj.
impassive 820 adj.
inexcitable 823 adj.
bored 838 adj.
indifferent 860 adj.
unastonished 865 adj.
in difficulties
in difficulties 700 adj.
grounded 728 adj.
unprosperous 731 adj.
poor 801 adj.
indigenous
intrinsic 5 adj.
native 191 adj.
indigent
poor 801 adj.
indigestible
cohesive 48 adj.
tough 329 adj.
insalubrious 653 adj.
uncooked 670 adj.
indigestion
digestive disorders 651 n.
indignant
angry 891 adj.
resentful 891 adj.
indignation meeting
deprecation 762 n.
malcontent 829 n.
indignity
slur 867 n.
humiliation 872 n.
rudeness 885 n.
scurrility 899 n.
indignity 921 n.
calumny 926 n.
indigo
blue 435 adj.
indirect
oblique 220 adj.
deviating 282 adj.
evidential 466 adj.
occult 523 adj.
unclear 568 adj.
prolix 570 adj.
roundabout 626 adj.
dishonest 930 adj.
in dire straits
in difficulties 700 adj.
unprosperous 731 adj.
in disarray
orderless 61 adj.
unsightly 842 adj.
indiscernible
invisible 444 adj.
indiscerptible
indivisible 52 adj.
dense 324 adj.
indiscipline
anarchy 734 n.
disobedience 738 n.
freedom 744 n.
undutifulness 918 n.
intemperance 943 n.
indiscreet
indiscriminating 464 adj.
unwise 499 adj.
informative 524 adj.
disclosing 526 adj.
rash 857 adj.
indiscretion
bungling 695 n.
guilty act 936 n.
indiscriminate
extensive 32 adj.
mixed 43 adj.
multiform 82 adj.
indiscriminate 464 adj.
designless 618 adj.
indiscrimination
generality 79 n.
indiscrimination 464 n.
misjudgment 481 n.
unintelligence 499 n.
no choice 606 n.
indifference 860 n.
indispensable
intrinsic 5 adj.
necessary 596 adj.
required 627 adj.
important 638 adj.
indispose
dissuade 613 vb.
indisposed
unwilling 598 adj.
sick 651 adj.
indisposition
unwillingness 598 n.
ill health 651 n.
indisputability
certainty 473 n.
indissoluble
indivisible 52 adj.
one 88 adj.
unchangeable 153 adj.
indissoluble 324 adj.
retentive 778 adj.
indistinct
amorphous 244 adj.
shadowy 419 adj.
indistinct 444 Adj. adj.
indistinctness
faintness 401 n.
dimness 419 n.
invisibility 444 n.
speech defect 580 n.
indistinguishable
identical 13 adj.
equivalent 28 adj.
invisible 444 adj.
in distress
in difficulties 700 adj.
poor 801 adj.
indite
compose 56 vb.
write 586 vb.
individual
unrelated 10 adj.
nonuniform 17 adj.
original 21 adj.
self 80 n.
special 80 adj.
unit 88 n.
one 88 adj.
person 371 n.
individualism
particularism 80 n.
independence 744 n.
selfishness 932 n.
individualist
free person 744 n.
egotist 932 n.
individuality
speciality 80 n.
nonconformity 84 n.
(See **individual** *)*
individualize, individualise
specify 80 vb.
indivisible
simple 44 adj.
cohesive 48 adj.
indivisible 52 adj.
one 88 adj.
dense 324 adj.
indocility
unwillingness 598 n.
obstinacy 602 n.
indoctrinate
convince 485 vb.
educate 534 vb.
teach 534 vb.
indoctrination
teaching 534 n.
Indo-European
language type 557 n.
indolence
inaction 677 n.
sluggishness 679 n.
indomitable
unyielding 162 adj.
resolute 599 adj.
persevering 600 adj.
resisting 715 adj.
courageous 855 adj.
indoor
interior 224 adj.
indoor game
indoor game 837 n.
in double harness
cooperative 706 adj.
married 894 adj.
Indra
Hindu deities 967 n.
in draft
planned 623 adj.
in drag
imitatively 20 adv.
indraught
ingress 297 n.
reception 299 n.
in dribs and drabs
piecemeal 53 adv.
here and there 105 adv.
indubitable
undisputed 473 adj.
induce
cause 156 vb.vb.
influence 178 vb.
induce 612 vb.
induced
induced 612 adj.
impressible 819 adj.
inducement
attraction 291 n.
incentive 612 n.
inducement 612 n.
offer 759 n.
induct
auspicate 68 vb.
reason 475 vb.
commission 751 vb.
celebrate 876 vb.

induction
electricity 160 n.
reasoning 475 n.
teaching 534 n.
mandate 751 n.
holy orders 985 n.
inductive
rational 475 adj.
in due course
prospectively 124 adv.
opportunely 137 adv.
in due season
in time 111 adv.
opportunely 137 adv.
indulge
smoke 388 vb.
please 826 vb.
(See **indulgence** *)*
— in
do 676 vb.
behave 688 vb.
— oneself
please oneself 734 vb.
be selfish 932 vb.
indulgence
laxity 734 n.
leniency 736 n.
permission 756 n.
enjoyment 824 n.
forgiveness 909 n.
intemperance 943 n.
sensualism 944 n.
gluttony 947 n.
indulgent
benevolent 897 adj.
induna
potentate 741 n.
indurate
be insensible 375 vb.
induration
hardening 326 n.
impenitence 940 n.
industrial
productive 164 adj.
businesslike 622 adj.
industrial archaeology
palaeology 125 n.
industrialism
business 622 n.
industrialist
producer 164 n.
agent 686 n.
industrialization, industrialisation
production 164 n.
business 622 n.
industrious
vigorous 174 adj.
attentive 455 adj.
studious 536 adj.
persevering 600 adj.
businesslike 622 adj.
industrious 678 adj.
labouring 682 adj.
industry
production 164 n.
business 622 n.
assiduity 678 n.
labour 682 n.
in duty bound
obliged 917 adj.
indwell
be intrinsic 5 vb.
inebriate
invigorate 174 vb.
drunkard 949 n.
inebriate 949 vb.
inebriation
drunkenness 949 n.
inedible
tough 329 adj.
unsavoury 391 adj.
insalubrious 653 adj.
uncooked 670 adj.
ineffable
unspeakable 32 adj.
inexpressible 517 adj.
wonderful 864 adj.
divine 965 adj.
ineffaceable
remembered 505 adj.
with affections 817 adj.
in effect
intrinsically 5 adv.
on the whole 52 adv.
ineffective
powerless 161 adj.
unproductive 172 adj.
feeble 572 adj.
useless 641 adj.
unsuccessful 728 adj.
ineffectual
powerless 161 adj.
unimportant 639 adj.
useless 641 adj.
unskilful 695 adj.
inefficient
powerless 161 adj.
useless 641 adj.
bad 645 adj.
unskilful 695 adj.
inelastic
unyielding 162 adj.
rigid 326 adj.
tough 329 adj.
brittle 330 adj.
obstinate 602 adj.
inelegant
unapt 25 adj.
inelegant 576 adj.
clumsy 695 adj.
graceless 842 adj.
vulgar 847 adj.
ineligible
unapt 25 adj.
rejected 607 adj.
inexpedient 643 adj.
ineluctable
certain 473 adj.
in embryo
unfinished 55 adj.
initially 68 adv.
future 124 adj.
impending 155 adj.
preparatory 669 adj.
inept
irrelevant 10 adj.
unapt 25 adj.
powerless 161 adj.
absurd 497 adj.
unwise 499 adj.
inexpedient 643 adj.
unskilful 695 adj.
inequality
difference 15 n.
dissimilarity 19 n.
disagreement 25 n.
inequality 29 n.
superiority 34 n.
distortion 246 n.
bias 481 n.
injustice 914 n.
in equilibrium
equal 28 adj.
inequitable
unjust 914 adj.
ineradicable
characteristic 5 adj.
fixed 153 adj.
inerrant
certain 473 adj.
inert
inert 175 adj.
quiescent 266 adj.
insensible 375 adj.
nonactive 677 adj.
inactive 679 adj.
inexcitable 823 adj.
inertia
energy 160 n.
inertness 175 n.
counteraction 182 n.
slowness 278 n.
inaction 677 n.
inactivity 679 n.
laxity 734 n.
moral insensibility 820 n.
indifference 860 n.
inescapable
impending 155 adj.
necessary 596 adj.
obligatory 917 adj.
in esse
existing 1 adj.
in essence
actually 1 adv.
on the whole 52 adv.
inessential
insubstantial 4 adj.
extrinsic 6 adj.
irrelevant 10 adj.
trifle 639 n.
inestimable
valuable 644 adj.
of price 811 adj.
in every quarter
widely 183 adv.
in every way
completely 54 adv.
inevitable
impending 155 adj.
certain 473 adj.
necessary 596 adj.
compelling 740 adj.
unpromising 853 adj.
inexact
general 79 adj.
negligent 458 adj.
indiscriminating 464 adj.
inexact 495 adj.
inexactness
imperspicuity 568 n.
in exchange
in exchange 151 adv.
inexcitable
inert 175 adj.
moderate 177 adj.
tranquil 266 adj.
inexcitable 823 adj.
inexcusable
wrong 914 adj.
accusable 928 adj.
heinous 934 adj.
inexhaustible
full 54 adj.
multitudinous 104 adj.
infinite 107 adj.
unceasing 146 adj.
plenteous 635 adj.
inexorable
certain 473 adj.
necessary 596 adj.
resolute 599 adj.
obstinate 602 adj.
severe 735 adj.
pitiless 906 adj.
inexpectant
inexpectant 508 adj.
unprepared 670 adj.
inexpedient
unapt 25 adj.
ill-timed 138 adj.
unwise 499 adj.
useless 641 adj.
inexpedient 643 adj.
hindering 702 adj.
discreditable 867 adj.
undue 916 adj.
inexpensive
cheap 812 adj.
inexperience
ignorance 491 n.
desuetude 611 n.
unskilfulness 695 n.
artlessness 699 n.
innocence 935 n.
inexperienced
foolish 499 adj.
inexpert
ignorant 491 adj.
unskilled 695 adj.

inexpiable
heinous 934 adj.
guilty 936 adj.
inexplicable
unusual 84 adj.
causeless 159 adj.
unintelligible 517 adj.
inexpressible
unspeakable 32 adj.
inexpressible 517 adj.
wonderful 864 adj.
inexpugnable
invulnerable 660 adj.
in extenso
diffusely 570 adv.
inextinguishable
unchangeable 153 adj.
unyielding 162 adj.
violent 176 adj.
inextricable
firm 45 adj.
tied 45 adj.
cohesive 48 adj.
complex 61 adj.
impracticable 470 adj.
difficult 700 adj.
in fact
actually 1 adv.
positively 32 adv.
infallibility
perfection 646 n.
infallible
certain 473 adj.
accurate 494 adj.
veracious 540 adj.
successful 727 adj.
ecclesiastical 985 adj.
infamous
discreditable 867 adj.
disreputable 867 adj.
dishonest 930 adj.
heinous 934 adj.
infamy
disrepute 867 n.
wickedness 934 n.
infancy
beginning 68 n.
nonage 130 n.
youth 130 n.
helplessness 161 n.
infant
beginning 68 adj.
young 130 adj.
child 132 n.
weakling 163 n.
descendant 170 n.
Infanta, Infante
sovereign 741 n.
infanticide
homicide 362 n.
infantile
infantine 132 adj.
foolish 499 adj.
infantile paralysis
nervous disorders 651 n.
infant prodigy
prodigy 864 n.
infantry
pedestrian 268 n.
infantry 722 n.
infarction
closure 264 n.
cardiovascular disease 651 n.
infatuated
misjudging 481 adj.
credulous 487 adj.
crazy 503 adj.
enamoured 887 adj.
infatuation
folly 499 n.
eccentricity 503 n.
deception 542 n.
liking 859 n.
love 887 n.
infect
be mixed 43 vb.
influence 178 vb.
transfer 272 vb.
infiltrate 297 vb.
make unclean 649 vb.
impair 655 vb.
excite 821 vb.
infection
badness 645 n.
infection 651 n.
insalubrity 653 n.
poison 659 n.
infectious
transferable 272 adj.
harmful 645 adj.
infectious 653 adj.
dangerous 661 adj.
infelicitous
inexpedient 643 adj.
bungled 695 adj.
unhappy 825 adj.
infer
assume 471 vb.
reason 475 vb.
demonstrate 478 vb.
judge 480 vb.
mean 514 vb.
interpret 520 vb.
imply 523 vb.
be informed 524 vb.
inferable
attributed 158 adj.
inference
sequence 65 n.
reasoning 475 n.
inferential
tacit 523 adj.
inferior
unequal 29 adj.
inconsiderable 33 adj.
inferior 35 n.adj.
low 210 adj.
back 238 adj.
insufficient 636 adj.
nonentity 639 n.
unimportant 639 adj.
bad 645 adj.
imperfect 647 adj.
loser 728 n.
unlucky person 731 n.
middling 732 adj.
dependant 742 n.
subject 745 adj.
commoner 869 n.
inferiority
inferiority 35 n.
substitute 150 n.
inferiority complex
eccentricity 503 n.
jealousy 911 n.
infernal
deep 211 adj.
damnable 645 adj.
cruel 898 adj.
heinous 934 adj.
diabolic 969 adj.
infernal 972 adj.
infernal machine
bomb 723 n.
inferno
turmoil 61 n.
hell 972 n.
inferred
attributed 158 adj.
tacit 523 adj.
infertile
impotent 161 adj.
unproductive 172 adj.
infest
congregate 74 vb.
be many 104 vb.
encroach 306 vb.
attack 712 vb.
trouble 827 vb.
infestation
bane 659 n.
infibulation
joining together 45 n.
infidel
unbeliever 486 n.
heathen 974 n.
impious person 980 n.
infidelity
unbelief 486 n.
perfidy 930 n.
illicit love 951 n.
irreligion 974 n.
in-fighting
pugilism 716 n.
dissension 709 n.
infiltrate
pervade 189 vb.
introduce 231 vb.
infiltrate 297 vb.
admit 299 vb.
infuse 303 vb.
pass 305 vb.
infiltration
mixture 43 n.
sedition 738 n.
infinite
absolute 32 adj.
multitudinous 104 adj.
infinite 107 adj.
Infinite, the
the Deity 965 n.
infinitesimal
small 33 adj.
minute 196 adj.
infinitesimal calculus
mathematics 86 n.
infinity
infinity 107 n.
perpetuity 115 n.
space 183 n.
divine attribute 965 n.
infirm
weakly 163 adj.
irresolute 601 adj.
unhealthy 651 adj.
cowardly 856 adj.
frail 934 adj.
infirmary
hospital 658 n.
infirmity
old age 131 n.
weakness 163 n.
ill health 651 n.
vice 934 n.
infirmity of purpose
weakness 163 n.
irresolution 601 n.
in fits and starts
discontinuously 72 adv.
jerkily 318 adv.
infix
add 38 vb.
implant 303 vb.
educate 534 vb.
part of speech 564 n.
in flagrante delicto
in the act 676 adv.
inflame
invigorate 174 vb.
make violent 176 vb.
itch 378 vb.
heat 381 vb.
excite 821 vb.
aggravate 832 vb.
excite love 887 vb.
inflammable
combustible 385 adj.
dangerous 661 adj.
excitable 822 adj.
irascible 892 adj.
inflammation
heat 379 n.
burning 381 n.
ulcer 651 n.
painfulness 827 n.
inflammatory
violent 176 adj.

inflatable
bladder 194 n.
inflate
enlarge 197 vb.
blow up 352 vb.
overrate 482 vb.
demonetize 797 vb.
make conceited 873 vb.
praise 923 vb.
inflated
airy 340 adj.
exaggerated 546 adj.
rhetorical 574 adj.
ridiculous 849 adj.
prideful 871 adj.
ostentatious 875 adj.
inflation
increase 36 n.
dilation 197 n.
superfluity 637 n.
finance 797 n.
inflationary
monetary 797 adj.
dear 811 adj.
inflect
make curved 248 vb.
parse 564 vb.
voice 577 vb.
inflected
linguistic 557 adj.
inflection, inflexion
curvature 248 n.
grammar 564 n.
pronunciation 577 n.
inflexible
unchangeable 153 adj.
straight 249 adj.
rigid 326 adj.
resolute 599 adj.
obstinate 602 adj.
severe 735 adj.
indifferent 860 adj.
pitiless 906 adj.
inflict
be severe 735 vb.
compel 740 vb.
punish 963 vb.
infliction
adversity 731 n.
severity 735 n.
suffering 825 n.
punishment 963 n.
in-flight
flying 271 adj.
inflorescence
flower 366 n.
inflow
ingress 297 n.
current 350 n.
influence
component 58 n.
modify 143 vb.
convert 147 vb.
causation 156 n.
cause 156 n.vb.
effect 157 n.
power 160 n.
agency 173 n.
influence 178 n.vb.
tend 179 vb.
bias 481 vb.
convince 485 vb.
teach 534 vb.
inducement 612 n.
motivate 612 vb.
instrumentality 628 n.
be important 638 vb.
make better 654 vb.
troublemaker 663 n.
action 676 n.
authority 733 n.
impress 821 vb.
prestige 866 n.
sorcery 983 n.
influential
great 32 adj.
influential 178 adj.
influenza
infection 651 n.
influx
ingress 297 n.
in force
operative 173 adj.
in for it, be
have trouble 731 vb.
inform
inform 524 vb.
divulge 526 vb.
publish 528 vb.
educate 534 vb.
warn 664 vb.
— against
inform 524 vb.
indicate 547 vb.
accuse 928 vb.
informal
unconformable 84 adj.
lax 734 adj.
unconfined 744 adj.
nonobservant 769 adj.
informal dress
informal dress 228 n.
uncovering 229 n.
informant
witness 466 n.
interpreter 520 n.
informant 524 n.
news reporter 529 n.
correspondent 588 n.
informatics
information 524 n.
information
enquiry 459 n.
testimony 466 n.
knowledge 490 n.
information 524 n.
message 529 n.
news 529 n.
broadcasting 531 n.
indication 547 n.
warning 664 n.
advice 691 n.
accusation 928 n.
informative
informative 524 adj.
disclosing 526 adj.
educational 534 adj.
loquacious 581 adj.
conversing 584 adj.
informed
instructed 490 adj.
knowing 490 adj.
informed 524 adj.
prepared 669 adj.
informed circles
informant 524 n.
informer
secret service 459 n.
witness 466 n.
informer 524 n.
tergiversator 603 n.
accuser 928 n.
knave 938 n.
litigant 959 n.
infra
after 65 adv.
infraction
nonconformity 84 n.
overstepping 306 n.
disobedience 738 n.
undueness 916 n.
infra dig
inexpedient 643 adj.
degrading 867 adj.
infrangible
cohesive 48 adj.
unyielding 162 adj.
dense 324 adj.
tough 329 adj.
infrared radiation
radiation 417 n.
infrastructure
base 214 n.
infrequency
fewness 105 n.
infrequency 140 n.
infrequent
discontinuous 72 adj.
unusual 84 adj.
infrequent 140 adj.
fitful 142 adj.
scarce 636 adj.
infringe
encroach 306 vb.
disobey 738 vb.
do wrong 914 vb.
be undue 916 vb.
infringement
nonconformity 84 n.
nonobservance 769 n.
lawbreaking 954 n.
in front
before 64 adv.
in front 237 adv.
ahead 283 adv.
in full
completely 54 adv.
in full cry
loudly 400 adv.
pursuing 619 adj.
in full feather
prepared 669 adj.
bedecked 844 adj.
in full swing
strong 162 adj.
busy 678 adj.
in fun
in jest 839 adv.
infundibular
concave 255 adj.
tubular 263 adj.
infuriate
make violent 176 vb.
make mad 503 vb.
enrage 891 vb.
infuriating
annoying 827 adj.
infuse
combine 50 vb.
infuse 303 vb.
moisten 341 vb.
educate 534 vb.
— into
motivate 612 vb.
infusible
indissoluble 324 adj.
infusion
tincture 43 n.
draught 301 n.
insertion 303 n.
solution 337 n.
tonic 658 n.
ingathering
assemblage 74 n.
ingeminate
repeat 106 vb.
ingenious
imaginative 513 adj.
planning 623 adj.
skilful 694 adj.
cunning 698 adj.
ingenue
acting 594 n.
ingenue 699 n.
innocent 935 n.
ingenuity
imagination 513 n.
skill 694 n.
cunning 698 n.
ingenuous
veracious 540 adj.
artless 699 adj.
honourable 929 adj.
trustworthy 929 adj.
ingest
absorb 299 vb.
eat 301 vb.
inglenook
home 192 n.
furnace 383 n.
inglorious
unsuccessful 728 adj.
unprosperous 731 adj.
middling 732 adj.
inglorious 867 adj.
plebeian 869 adj.
humbled 872 adj.

in good shape
healthy 650 adj.
in good spirits
cheerful 833 adj.
in good time
early 135 adj.
betimes 135 adv.
ingot
materials 631 n.
bullion 797 n.
ingraft
habituate 610 vb.
ingrained
intrinsic 5 adj.
fixed 153 adj.
habitual 610 adj.
ingratiate oneself
be servile 879 vb.
excite love 887 vb.
ingratiating
servile 879 adj.
courteous 884 adj.
flattering 925 adj.
ingratitude
oblivion 506 n.
ingratitude 908 n.
undueness 916 n.
ingredient(s)
adjunct 40 n.
part 53 n.
component 58 n.
contents 193 n.
element 319 n.
ingress
ingress 297 n.
passage 305 n.
in-group
group 74 n.
self 80 n.
ingrown
firm 45 adj.
interior 224 adj.
ingurgitation
reception 299 n.
eating 301 n.
inhabit
be present 189 vb.
dwell 192 vb.
possess 773 vb.
inhabitant
dweller 191 n.
inhabited
occupied 191 adj.
inhale
absorb 299 vb.
breathe 352 vb.
smoke 388 vb.
smell 394 vb.
inhaler
medicine 658 n.
in hand
unfinished 55 adj.
businesslike 622 adj.
stored 632 adj.
in preparation 669 adv.
unused 674 adj.
inharmonious
disagreeing 25 adj.
strident 407 adj.
discordant 411 adj.
in harmony
combined 50 adj.
concurrently 181 adv.
in harness
doing 676 adj.
busy 678 adj.
inhere
be intrinsic 5 vb.
constitute 56 vb.
be one of 58 vb.
be included 78 vb.
belong 773 vb.
inherent
intrinsic 5 adj.
component 58 adj.
included 78 adj.
possessed 773 adj.
inherit
be intrinsic 5 vb.
come after 65 vb.
ensue 120 vb.
reproduce 166 vb.
inherit 771 vb.
possess 773 vb.
receive 782 vb.
get rich 800 vb.
inheritable
not retained 779 adj.
due 915 adj.
inheritance
posterity 170 n.
acquisition 771 n.
possession 773 n.
dower 777 n.
transfer 780 n.
receipt 807 n.
inherited
genetic 5 adj.
inherited 157 adj.
filial 170 adj.
acquired 771 adj.
inheritor
survivor 41 n.
successor 67 n.
beneficiary 776 n.
recipient 782 n.
inhibit
counteract 182 vb.
inhibition
eccentricity 503 n.
hindrance 702 n.
restraint 747 n.
prohibition 757 n.
in hock
pledged 767 adj.
indebted 803 adj.
in holes
dilapidated 655 adj.
inhospitable
unsociable 883 adj.
unkind 898 adj.
inhuman
harmful 645 adj.
inhumanity
violence 176 n.
severity 735 n.
moral insensibility 820 n.
inhumanity 898 n.
misanthropy 902 n.
pitilessness 906 n.
wickedness 934 n.
diabolism 969 n.
inimical
contrary 14 adj.
disagreeing 25 adj.
opposing 704 adj.
quarrelling 709 adj.
disliking 861 adj.
inimical 881 adj.
hating 888 adj.
inimitable
inimitable 21 adj.
supreme 34 adj.
special 80 adj.
iniquitous
unjust 914 adj.
wicked 934 adj.
iniquity
wickedness 934 n.
initial
first 68 adj.
sign 547 vb.
initials 558 n.
literal 558 adj.
spell 558 vb.
initiate
initiate 68 vb.
cause 156 vb.
produce 164 vb.
admit 299 vb.
train 534 vb.
learner 538 n.
undertake 672 vb.
initiation
debut 68 n.
learning 536 n.
rite 988 n.
initiative
beginning 68 n.
vigorousness 174 n.
willingness 597 n.
restlessness 678 n.
freedom 744 n.
initiator
teacher 537 n.
inject
pierce 263 vb.
infuse 303 vb.
— with
motivate 612 vb.
injecting
drug-taking 949 n.
injection
medicine 658 n.
injudicious
unwise 499 adj.
inexpedient 643 adj.
rash 857 adj.
injunction
requirement 627 n.
precept 693 n.
command 737 n.
prohibition 757 n.
legal process 959 n.
injure
weaken 163 vb.
harm 645 vb.
impair 655 vb.
oppress 735 vb.
hurt 827 vb.
blemish 845 vb.
be malevolent 898 vb.
do wrong 914 vb.
injurious
evil 616 adj.
harmful 645 adj.
insalubrious 653 adj.
insolent 878 adj.
ungracious 885 adj.
cursing 899 adj.
wrong 914 adj.
disrespectful 921 adj.
detracting 926 adj.
injury
evil 616 n.n.
wound 655 n.
misuse 675 n.
guilty act 936 n.
injustice
misjudgment 481 n.
misrepresentation 552 n.
evil 616 n.
injustice 914 n.
improbity 930 n.
guilty act 936 n.
illegality 954 n.
ink
black thing 428 n.
art equipment 553 n.
in keeping
agreeing 24 adj.
conformably 83 adv.
in kind
correlatively 12 adv.
in exchange 151 adv.
inkling
knowledge 490 n.
supposition 512 n.
hint 524 n.
ink-slinger
author 589 n.
inkstand
stationery 586 n.
inky
dark 418 adj.
black 428 adj.
inlaid
ornamented 844 adj.
inlaid work
chequer 437 n.
inland
interior 224 adj.
land 344 n.
inland 344 adj.
inland navigation
water travel 269 n.
inland waterway
conduit 351 n.
route 624 n.

in-laws
family 11 n.
inlay
line 227 vb.
insert 303 vb.
variegate 437 vb.
ornamental art 844 n.
in league
conjointly 45 adv.
in league 708 adv.
inlet
entrance 68 n.
gap 201 n.
cavity 255 n.
orifice 263 n.
way in 297 n.
gulf 345 n.
in lieu
in return 31 adv.
instead 150 adv.
in limbo
neglected 458 adj.
forgotten 506 adj.
disused 674 adj.
in line (with)
uniform 16 adj.
conformably 83 adv.
in loco parentis
instead 150 adv.
in love
enamoured 887 adj.
inmate
resident 191 n.
interiority 224 n.
in medias res
midway 70 adv.
in memoriam
in memoriam 364 adv.
in memory 505 adv.
in honour of 876 adv.
inmost, innermost
interior 224 adj.
inmost being
interiority 224 n.
inmost soul
affections 817 n.
in mothballs
disused 674 adj.
in mourning
lamenting 836 adj.
in mufti
nonuniform 17 adj.
inn
inn 192 n.
innards
insides 224 n.
innate
genetic 5 adj.
innate ability
aptitude 694 n.
inner
included 78 adj.
interior 224 adj.
inner being
essence 1 n.
inner circle
party 708 n.
inner-city
urban 192 adj.
inner-city mission
church ministry 985 n.
inner-directed
independent 744 adj.
inner man, inner woman
essential part 5 n.
insides 224 n.
spirit 447 n.
affections 817 n.
Inner Temple
bar 958 n.
inner tube
bladder 194 n.
wheel 250 n.
inner voice
conscience 917 n.
innings
period 110 n.
innkeeper
caterer 633 n.
innocence
innocence 935 n.
acquittal 960 n.
innocent
defenceless 161 adj.
ignorant 491 adj.
ignoramus 493 n.
foolish 499 adj.
ninny 501 n.
dupe 544 n.
gullible 544 adj.
beneficial 644 adj.
perfect 646 adj.
ingenue 699 n.
artless 699 adj.
vindicable 927 adj.
honourable 929 adj.
virtuous 933 adj.
innocent 935 n.adj.
good person 937 n.
pure 950 adj.
innocuous
moderate 177 adj.
beneficial 644 adj.
salubrious 652 adj.
innocent 935 adj.
innovation
originality 21 n.
newness 126 n.
change 143 n.
innovator
precursor 66 n.
in no way
in no way 33 adv.
nay 533 adv.
innoxious
salubrious 652 adj.
Inns of Chancery
bar 958 n.
Inns of Court
bar 958 n.
innuendo
latency 523 n.
hint 524 n.
censure 924 n.
detraction 926 n.
innumerable
multitudinous 104 adj.
infinite 107 adj.
innumerate
uninstructed 491 adj.
inobservance
nonobservance 769 n.
inoculate
implant 303 vb.
teach 534 vb.
safeguard 660 vb.
inoculation
hygiene 652 n.
prophylactic 658 n.
inodorous
odourless 395 adj.
inoffensive
beneficial 644 adj.
humble 872 adj.
amiable 884 adj.
innocent 935 adj.
in on
knowing 490 adj.
informed 524 adj.
sharing 775 adj.
in one piece
whole 52 adj.
in one's bad books
disreputable 867 adj.
hated 888 adj.
disapproved 924 adj.
in one's best interests
well 615 adv.
in one's element
apt 24 adj.
facilitated 701 adj.
in one's sleeve
secretly 525 adv.
in one's stride
habitually 610 adv.
skilfully 694 adv.
in one's teeth
defiantly 711 adv.
in on the ground floor, be
auspicate 68 vb.
in open court
publicly 528 adv.
in open order
unassembled 75 adj.
inoperable
deadly 362 adj.
impracticable 470 adj.
sick 651 adj.
unpromising 853 adj.
inoperative
powerless 161 adj.
unproductive 172 adj.
useless 641 adj.
nonactive 677 adj.
inopportune
unapt 25 adj.
inopportune 138 adj.
inexpedient 643 adj.
in opposition
although 182 adv.
in opposition 704 adv.
in orbit
in flight 271 adv.
in orders
clerical 986 adj.
in order to
purposely 617 adv.
inordinate
exorbitant 32 adj.
exaggerated 546 adj.
inorganic
inorganic 359 adj.
inorganic chemistry
physics 319 n.
inorganic matter
mineral 359 n.
inosculate
connect 45 vb.
cross 222 vb.
in other words
in plain words 520 adv.
in outline
outlined 233 adj.
uncompleted 726 adj.
in particular
specially 80 adv.
in passing
transiently 114 adv.
in-patient
resident 191 n.
sick person 651 n.
in person
substantially 3 adv.
here 189 adv.
in petto
secretly 525 adv.
in phase
identically 13 adv.
agreeing 24 adj.
in pickle
impending 155 adj.
in pieces
disunited 46 adj.
separately 46 adv.
fragmentary 53 adj.
in place
apt 24 adj.
instead 150 adv.
in place 186 adv.
here 189 adv.
in plain words
significantly 514 adv.
in plain words 520 adv.
plainly 573 adv.
in play
unceasing 146 adj.
operative 173 adj.
in jest 839 adv.

in point
apt 24 adj.
typical 83 adj.
in point of fact
actually 1 adv.
in posse
unreal 2 adj.
possibly 469 adv.
in possession of one's faculties
sane 502 adj.
in possession of the facts, be
be informed 524 vb.
inpouring
ingress 297 n.
in preparation
unfinished 55 adj.
in preparation 669 adv.
in process of
continuing 108 adj.
on the stocks 726 adv.
in propria persona
here 189 adv.
input
data processing 86 n.
requirement 627 n.
in quarantine
imprisoned 747 adj.
in Queer Street
indebted 803 adj.
inquest
inquest 364 n.
enquiry 459 n.
legal trial 959 n.
in question
in question 452 adv.
moot 459 adj.
uncertain 474 adj.
dangerous 661 adj.
in quest of
pursuing 619 adj.
inquietude
changeableness 152 n.
worry 825 n.
inquiline
resident 191 n.
inquire, inquiry
(See **enquire, enquiry** *)*
inquisition
enquiry 459 n.
interrogation 459 n.
severity 735 n.
legal trial 959 n.
Inquisition
ecclesiastical court 956 n.
inquisitive
inquisitive 453 adj.
enquiring 459 adj.
inquisitive person
listener 415 n.
inquisitive person 453 n.
questioner 459 n.
meddler 678 n.
inquisitor
inquisitive person 453 n.
questioner 459 n.
tyrant 735 n.
punisher 963 n.
in re
concerning 9 adv.
in reserve
impending 155 adj.
inactively 175 adv.
stored 632 adj.
prepared 669 adj.
in return
in return 31 adv.
inroad(s)
ingress 297 n.
waste 634 n.
arrogation 916 n.
in rotation
by turns 141 adv.
inrush
ingress 297 n.
insalubrious
sealed off 264 adj.
deadly 362 adj.
harmful 645 adj.
unclean 649 adj.
insalubrious 653 adj.
dangerous 661 adj.
insalubrity
infection 651 n.
insalubrity 653 n.
ins and outs
particulars 80 n.
place 185 n.
insane
insane 503 adj.
insanitary
unclean 649 adj.
insalubrious 653 adj.
insanity
absence of intellect 448 n.
error 495 n.
unintelligence 499 n.
insanity 503 n.
excitable state 822 n.
insatiability
rapacity 786 n.
insatiable
unprovided 636 adj.
greedy 859 adj.
gluttonous 947 adj.
inscape
essential part 5 n.
form 243 n.
inscribe
list 87 vb.
record 548 vb.
write 586 vb.
— to
honour 866 vb.
inscriber
calligrapher 586 n.
commender 923 n.
inscription
obsequies 364 n.
commentary 520 n.
indication 547 n.
monument 548 n.
phrase 563 n.
script 586 n.
description 590 n.
inscrutable
unintelligible 517 adj.
impassive 820 adj.
inexcitable 823 adj.
serious 834 adj.
insect
insect 365 n.
noxious animal 904 n.
cad 938 n.
insecticide
killer 362 n.
prophylactic 658 n.
poison 659 n.
insectivorous
feeding 301 adj.
insecurity
unreliability 474 n.
vulnerability 661 n.
inseminate
generate 167 vb.
make fruitful 171 vb.
insensate
insensible 375 adj.
unwise 499 adj.
thick-skinned 820 adj.
insensibility
insensibility 375 n.
moral insensibility 820 n.
insensible
impotent 161 adj.
inert 175 adj.
still 266 adj.
insensible 375 adj.
ignorant 491 adj.
forgetful 506 adj.
sick 651 adj.
nonactive 677 adj.
inactive 679 adj.
apathetic 820 adj.
impassive 820 adj.
unkind 898 adj.
drugged 949 adj.
insensible to
indifferent 860 adj.
insensibly
slightly 33 adv.
insensitive
insensible 375 adj.
indiscriminating 464 adj.
inexact 495 adj.
inelegant 576 adj.
impassive 820 adj.
thick-skinned 820 adj.
ill-bred 847 adj.
inseparable
intrinsic 5 adj.
firm 45 adj.
cohesive 48 adj.
indivisible 52 adj.
accompanying 89 adj.
near 200 adj.
friendly 880 adj.
insert
affix 45 vb.
load 193 vb.
line 227 vb.
introduce 231 vb.
enter 297 vb.
insert 303 vb.
insertion
addition 38 n.
adjunct 40 n.
mixture 43 n.
piece 53 n.
location 187 n.
interjection 231 n.
reception 299 n.
insertion 303 n.
advertisement 528 n.
repair 656 n.
inset
insertion 303 n.
edition 589 n.
ornamental art 844 n.
inshore
near 200 adj.
inside
contents 193 n.
interiority 224 n.
inside 224 adv.
imprisoned 747 adj.
inside agent
secret service 459 n.
informer 524 n.
inside and out
widely 183 adv.
inside job
plot 623 n.
inside out
inverted 221 adj.
insides
component 58 n.
contents 193 n.
insides 224 n.
inside track
advantage 34 n.
insidious
occult 523 adj.
deceiving 542 adj.
evil 616 adj.
cunning 698 adj.
perfidious 930 adj.
insight
intellect 447 n.
discrimination 463 n.
intuition 476 n.
knowledge 490 n.
imagination 513 n.
interpretation 520 n.

insignia
badge 547 n.
regalia 743 n.
insignificance
smallness 33 n.
unimportance 639 n.
contemptibility 922 n.
insignificant
inconsiderable 33 adj.
meaningless 515 adj.
insincere
sophistical 477 adj.
unmeant 515 adj.
hypocritical 541 adj.
affected 850 adj.
flattering 925 adj.
dishonest 930 adj.
insincerity
deception 542 n.
insinuate
introduce 231 vb.
imply 523 vb.
hint 524 vb.
— oneself
enter 297 vb.
excite love 887 vb.
flatter 925 vb.
insinuation
influence 178 n.
ingress 297 n.
insertion 303 n.
latency 523 n.
hint 524 n.
censure 924 n.
detraction 926 n.
insipid
weak 163 adj.
tasteless 387 adj.
feeble 572 adj.
tedious 838 adj.
dull 840 adj.
unwanted 860 adj.
insist
emphasize 532 vb.
necessitate 596 vb.
be resolute 599 vb.
be obstinate 602 vb.
incite 612 vb.
contend 716 vb.
compel 740 vb.
request 761 vb.
— on
qualify 468 vb.
give terms 766 vb.
insistence, insistency
affirmation 532 n.
importance 638 n.
insistent
forceful 571 adj.
commanding 737 adj.
in situ
in place 186 adv.
here 189 adv.
insobriety
drunkenness 949 n.
insolation
desiccation 342 n.
heating 381 n.
insolence
insolence 878 n.
insolent
defiant 711 adj.
anarchic 734 adj.
authoritarian 735 adj.
proud 871 adj.
insolent 878 adj.
discourteous 885 adj.
disrespectful 921 adj.
insoluble
indissoluble 324 adj.
impracticable 470 adj.
puzzling 517 adj.
insolvency
insufficiency 636 n.
failure 728 n.
poverty 801 n.
insolvency 805 n.
insolvent
debtor 803 n.
insomnia
restlessness 678 n.
insomniac
sick person 651 n.
insouciance
negligence 458 n.
moral insensibility 820 n.
indifference 860 n.
insouciant
light-minded 456 adj.
inspan
start out 296 vb.
inspect
scan 438 vb.
be attentive 455 vb.
inspection
inspection 438 n.
attention 455 n.
surveillance 457 n.
enquiry 459 n.
estimate 480 n.
inspector
spectator 441 n.
enquirer 459 n.
estimator 480 n.
manager 690 n.
inspectorship
position of authority 733 n.
inspiration
causation 156 n.
influence 178 n.
respiration 352 n.
intuition 476 n.
discovery 484 n.
intelligence 498 n.
imagination 513 n.
spontaneity 609 n.
inducement 612 n.
contrivance 623 n.
warm feeling 818 n.
excitation 821 n.
excitable state 822 n.
revelation 975 n.
piety 979 n.
inspire
cheer 833 vb.
give courage 855 vb.
(See **inspiration** *)*
inspired
intuitive 476 adj.
forceful 571 adj.
induced 612 adj.
impressed 818 adj.
excited 821 adj.
revelational 975 adj.
pietistic 979 adj.
inspirit
incite 612 vb.
animate 821 vb.
cheer 833 vb.
give hope 852 vb.
give courage 855 vb.
inspissate
thicken 354 vb.
in spite of
although 182 adv.
nevertheless 468 adv.
in opposition 704 adv.
instability
changeableness 152 n.
weakness 163 n.
vulnerability 661 n.
excitability 822 n.
install
auspicate 68 vb.
place 187 vb.
commission 751 vb.
dower 777 vb.
dignify 866 vb.
installation
location 187 n.
workshop 687 n.
mandate 751 n.
celebration 876 n.
holy orders 985 n.
instalment
part 53 n.
incompleteness 55 n.
reading matter 589 n.
security 767 n.
payment 804 n.
instalment plan
borrowing 785 n.
instance
example 83 n.
request 761 n.
instancy
inducement 612 n.
instant
brief span 114 n.
instant 116 n.
present 121 adj.
impending 155 adj.
demanding 627 adj.
ready-made 669 adj.
active 678 adj.
requesting 761 adj.
instantaneous
instantaneous 116 adj.
early 135 adj.
speedy 277 adj.
instate
celebrate 876 vb.
in statu pupillari
studentlike 538 adj.
subject 745 adj.
in statu quo
as before 144 adv.
instead
instead 150 adv.
instep
foot 214 n.
instigate
induce 612 vb.
aid 703 vb.
instigator
motivator 612 n.
aider 703 n.
instil
mix 43 vb.
infuse 303 vb.
educate 534 vb.
instinct
tendency 179 n.
intellect 447 n.
absence of intellect 448 n.
absence of thought 450 n.
empiricism 461 n.
intuition 476 n.
supposition 512 n.
habit 610 n.
nondesign 618 n.
instinctive
intrinsic 5 adj.
mindless 448 adj.
unthinking 450 adj.
intuitive 476 adj.
involuntary 596 adj.
spontaneous 609 adj.
instincts
affections 817 n.
institute
auspicate 68 vb.
cause 156 vb.
produce 164 vb.
academy 539 n.
corporation 708 n.
institution
academy 539 n.
practice 610 n.
law 953 n.
rite 988 n.
institutionalism
orthodoxism 976 n.
institutionalize, institutionalise
make uniform 16 vb.
in stock
stored 632 adj.

in store
impending 155 adj.
stored 632 adj.
instruct
inform 524 vb.
educate 534 vb.
command 737 vb.
instructed
instructed 490 adj.
informed 524 adj.
prepared 669 adj.
expert 694 adj.
instruction
culture 490 n.
information 524 n.
teachino 534 n.
advice 691 n.
precept 693 n.
command 737 n.
instructive
influential 178 adj.
informative 524 adj.
educational 534 adj.
cautionary 664 adj.
instructor
teacher 537 n.
trainer 537 n.
instrument
causal means 156 n.
contrivance 623 n.
instrument 628 n.
means 629 n.
tool 630 n.
agent 686 n.
auxiliary 707 n.
slave 742 n.
title deed 767 n.
toady 879 n.
instrumental
musical 412 adj.
instrumental 628 adj.
mechanical 630 adj.
useful 640 adj.
used 673 adj.
aiding 703 adj.
instrumentalist
instrumentalist 413 n.
instrumentality
agency 173 n.
instrumentality 628 n.
instrumentation
composition 56 n.
melody 410 n.
insubordinate
anarchic 734 adj.
disobedient 738 adj.
disrespectful 921 adj.
insubstantial
unreal 2 adj.
insubstantial 4 adj.
inconsiderable 33 adj.
transient 114 adj.
powerless 161 adj.
flimsy 163 adj.
weak 163 adj.
immaterial 320 adj.
brittle 330 adj.
imaginary 513 adj.
insufficient 636 adj.
trivial 639 adj.
insubstantiality
insubstantiality 4 n.
insufferable
intolerable 827 adj.
disliked 861 adj.
insufficiency
inequality 29 n.
smallness 33 n.
inferiority 35 n.
incompleteness 55 n.
shortfall 307 n.
requirement 627 n.
insufficiency 636 n.
imperfection 647 n.
noncompletion 726 n.
insufficient
insufficient 636 adj.
unskilful 695 adj.
discontenting 829 adj.
insular
separate 46 adj.
alone 88 adj.
regional 184 adj.
dweller 191 n.
insular 349 adj.
insularity
unrelatedness 10 n.
narrow mind 481 n.
insulate
set apart 46 vb.
cover 226 vb.
safeguard 660 vb.
insulation
lining 227 n.
preservation 666 n.
insulator
electricity 160 n.
insulin
drug 658 n.
insult
hurt 827 vb.
ridicule 851 n.
slur 867 n.
sauciness 878 n.
rudeness 885 n.
hate 888 vb.
scurrility 899 n.
indignity 921 n.
not respect 921 vb.
calumny 926 n.
insuperable
impracticable 470 adj.
difficult 700 adj.
insupportable
intolerable 827 adj.
insurance
calculation of chance 159 n.
protection 660 n.
promise 764 n.
security 767 n.
caution 858 n.
insurance policy
title deed 767 n.
insure
prepare 669 vb.
give security 767 vb.
insurer
consignee 754 n.
insurgent
revolter 738 n.
insurmountable
impracticable 470 adj.
insurrection
resistance 715 n.
revolt 738 n.
in suspense
inactively 175 adv.
in suspense 474 adv.
expectant 507 adj.
intact
intact 52 adj.
complete 54 adj.
perfect 646 adj.
undamaged 646 adj.
safe 660 adj.
preserved 666 adj.
intaglio
mould 23 n.
concavity 255 n.
sculpture 554 n.
ornamental art 844 n.
intake
size 195 n.
ingress 297 n.
way in 297 n.
reception 299 n.
requirement 627 n.
waste 634 n.
in tandem
longwise 203 adv.
rearward 238 adv.
cooperative 706 adj.
intangible
unreal 2 adj.
minute 196 adj.
immaterial 320 adj.
integer
whole 52 n.
number 85 n.
unit 88 n.
integral
intrinsic 5 adj.
whole 52 adj.
complete 54 adj.
numerical 85 adj.
integral calculus
mathematics 86 n.
integral part
component 58 n.
integrate
combine 50 vb.
make complete 54 vb.
integrated circuit
electronics 160 n.
microelectronics 196 n.
integration
combination 50 n.
completeness 54 n.
inclusion 78 n.
unity 88 n.
association 706 n.
integrity
whole 52 n.
probity 929 n.
virtue 933 n.
integument
layer 207 n.
skin 226 n.
intellect
intellect 447 n.
thought 449 n.
knowledge 490 n.
intelligence 498 n.
intellectual
mental 447 adj.
philosopher 449 n.
reasoner 475 n.
instructed 490 adj.
intellectual 492 n.
wise 498 adj.
sage 500 n.
proficient person 696 n.
intelligence
head 213 n.
intellect 447 n.
secret service 459 n.
intelligence 498 n.
information 524 n.
news 529 n.
wit 839 n.
intelligence test
exam 459 n.
intelligent
knowing 490 adj.
intelligent 498 adj.
skilful 694 adj.
cunning 698 adj.
intelligentsia
intellectual 492 n.
intelligibility
plainness 573 n.
facility 701 n.
intelligible
sane 502 adj.
semantic 514 adj.
intelligible 516 adj.
manifest 522 adj.
perspicuous 567 adj.
intemperance
overstepping 306 n.
festivity 837 n.
desire 859 n.
intemperance 943 n.
sensualism 944 n.
gluttony 947 n.
drug-taking 949 n.
drunkenness 949 n.
intemperate
violent 176 adj.
selfish 932 adj.
vicious 934 adj.
intend
predestine 155 vb.

be mindful 455 vb.
expect 507 vb.
mean 514 vb.
will 595 vb.
be willing 597 vb.
be resolute 599 vb.
predetermine 608 vb.
intend 617 vb.
pursue 619 vb.
plan 623 vb.
attempt 671 vb.
promise 764 vb.
hope 852 vb.
desire 859 vb.
intendant
official 690 n.
officer 741 n.
intended
veracious 540 adj.
volitional 595 adj.
loved one 887 n.
intense
great 32 adj.
vigorous 174 adj.
florid 425 adj.
fervent 818 adj.
intensification
stimulation 174 n.
aggravation 832 n.
intensify
augment 36 vb.
invigorate 174 vb.
exaggerate 546 vb.
animate 821 vb.
aggravate 832 vb.
intensity
degree 27 n.
greatness 32 n.
vigorousness 174 n.
light 417 n.
hue 425 n.
intensive
increasing 36 adj.
part of speech 564 n.
intensive care unit
hospital 658 n.
intent
attentive 455 adj.
will 595 n.
intention 617 n.
intention
relation 9 n.
expectation 507 n.
connotation 514 n.
will 595 n.
predetermination 608 n.
motive 612 n.
intention 617 n.
plan 623 n.
aspiration 852 n.
prayers 981 n.
intentional
volitional 595 adj.
intended 617 adj.
intentness
attention 455 n.
assiduity 678 n.
inter-
correlative 12 adj.
interchanged 151 adj.
interjacent 231 adj.
inter
inter 364 vb.
conceal 525 vb.
interaction
correlation 12 n.
agency 173 n.
action 676 n.
inter alia
among 43 adv.
interbred
ethnic 11 adj.
mixed 43 adj.
intercalary
intermediate 108 adj.
interjacent 231 adj.
intercede
interfere 231 vb.
patronize 703 vb.
mediate 720 vb.
worship 981 vb.
intercept
interfere 231 vb.
converge 293 vb.
hear 415 vb.
screen 421 vb.
be curious 453 vb.
hinder 702 vb.
take 786 vb.
interceptor
inquisitive person 453 n.
hinderer 702 n.
air force 722 n.
intercession
aid 703 n.
mediation 720 n.
deprecation 762 n.
divine function 965 n.
prayers 981 n.
intercessor
intermediary 231 n.
mediator 720 n.
worshipper 981 n.
interchange
correlation 12 n.
substitute 150 vb.
interchange 151 n. vb.
displacement 188 n.
inversion 221 n.
transference 272 n.
passage 305 n.
transfer 780 n.
trade 791 vb.
interchangeable
identical 13 adj.
equivalent 28 adj.
intercom
telecommunication 531 n.
intercommunicate
connect 45 vb.
be contiguous 202 vb.
intercommunication
information 524 n.
interlocution 584 n.
intercommunion
interlocution 584 n.
public worship 981 n.
intercommunity
sociality 882 n.
interconnect
correlate 12 vb.
connect 45 vb.
intercontinental ballistic missile
rocket 276 n.
missile weapon 723 n.
intercourse
union 45 n.
coition 45 n.
interdepartmental
interchanged 151 adj.
interdependence
relation 9 n.
correlation 12 n.
interdict
prohibition 757 n.
interdictor
air force 722 n.
interdigitate
enlace 222 vb.
interest
relation 9 n.
increment 36 n.
extra 40 n.
product 164 n.
influence 178 n.
topic 452 n.
curiosity 453 n.
attention 455 n.
attract notice 455 vb.
motivate 612 vb.
benefit 615 n.
importance 638 n.
activity 678 n.
aid 703 n.
gain 771 n.
estate 777 n.
interest 803 n.
receipt 807 n.
impress 821 vb.
please 826 vb.
amusement 837 n.
— oneself in
be active 678 vb.
interested
inquisitive 453 adj.
obsessed 455 adj.
interests
affairs 154 n.
business 622 n.
interface
contiguity 202 n.
partition 231 n.
interfere
derange 63 vb.
counteract 182 vb.
interfere 231 vb.
be curious 453 vb.
meddle 678 vb.
obstruct 702 vb.
prohibit 757 vb.
— with
debauch 951 vb.
interference
radiation 417 n.
instrumentality 628 n.
hindrance 702 n.
annoyance 827 n.
interferer
meddler 678 n.
hinderer 702 n.
interferon
antidote 658 n.
interfuse
mix 43 vb.
infiltrate 297 vb.
intergalactic space
universe 321 n.
interglacial
intermediate 108 adj.
interim
interim 108 n.
period 110 n.
transience 114 n.
lull 145 n.
interval 201 n.
interior
intrinsic 5 adj.
component 58 n.
included 78 adj.
interiority 224 n.
interior 224 adj.
land 344 n.
art subject 553 n.
interior decoration
ornamental art 844 n.
interior decorator
mender 656 n.
interiority
essence 1 n.
interiority 224 n.
latency 523 n.
interior monologue
soliloquy 585 n.
interjacency
interjacency 231 n.
interject
put between 231 vb.
interjection
addition 38 n.
discontinuity 72 n.
interjection 231 n.
part of speech 564 n.
speech 579 n.
interlace
mix 43 vb.
tie 45 vb.
enlace 222 vb.

interlard
mix 43 vb.
put between 231 vb.
interleave
put between 231 vb.
interline
put between 231 vb.
write 586 vb.
interlining
lining 227 n.
interlock
join 45 vb.
enlace 222 vb.
interlocking
correlative 12 adj.
complexity 61 n.
interlocutor
questioner 459 n.
speaker 579 n.
chatterer 581 n.
interlocutor 584 n.
interloper
intruder 59 n.
interjector 231 n.
hinderer 702 n.
interlude
interim 108 n.n.
lull 145 n.
intermarry
be mixed 43 vb.
wed 894 vb.
intermediary
intermediary 231 n.
informant 524 n.
messenger 529 n.
mediator 720 n.
consignee 754 n.
intermediate
median 30 adj.
middle 70 adj.
intermediate 108 adj.
interjacent 231 adj.
undeviating 625 adj.
instrumental 628 adj.
intermediate technology
smallness 33 n.
production 164 n.
middle way 625 n.
intermedium
average 30 n.
intermediary 231 n.
interment
interment 364 n.
concealment 525 n.
intermezzo
musical piece 412 n.
stage play 594 n.
interminable
infinite 107 adj.
protracted 113 adj.
perpetual 115 adj.
long 203 adj.
intermingle
mix 43 vb.
intermission
dramaturgy 594 n.
intermit
be discontinuous 72 vb.
be periodic 141 vb.
pause 145 vb.
intermittent
discontinuous 72 adj.
infrequent 140 adj.
periodical 141 adj.
fitful 142 adj.
intermix
mix 43 vb.
intermundane
cosmic 321 adj.
intern
hold within 224 vb.
doctor 658 n.
imprison 747 vb.
internal
intrinsic 5 adj.
interior 224 adj.
internal combustion engine
machine 630 n.
internalize, internalise
hold within 224 vb.
absorb 299 vb.
internal organs
insides 224 n.
internal rhyme
prosody 593 n.
international
correlative 12 adj.
comprehensive 52 adj.
universal 79 adj.
national 371 adj.
unpossessed 774 adj.
sharing 775 adj.
international date line
limit 236 n.
internationalism
generality 79 n.
philanthropy 901 n.
internationalist
philanthropist 901 n.
internationalize, internationalise
transform 147 vb.
communalize 775 vb.
International Monetary Fund
pawnshop 784 n.
International Phonetic Alphabet
letter 558 n.
International Scientific Vocabulary
language 557 n.
International Socialists
political party 708 n.
internecine
destructive 165 adj.
murderous 362 adj.
internment
war measures 718 n.
detention 747 n.
internuncio
envoy 754 n.
interparty agreement
consensus 488 n.
interpellate
interrogate 459 vb.
interpenetrate
lie between 231 vb.
infiltrate 297 vb.
interplanetary
interjacent 231 adj.
cosmic 321 adj.
interplay
correlation 12 n.
interchange 151 n.
Interpol
police enquiry 459 n.
interpolate
put between 231 vb.
interpolation
adjunct 40 n.
numerical operation 86 n.
interjection 231 n.
insertion 303 n.
interpose
discontinue 72 vb.
put between 231 vb.
insert 303 vb.
be instrumental 628 vb.
meddle 678 vb.
hinder 702 vb.
mediate 720 vb.
prohibit 757 vb.
interpret
account for 158 vb.
play music 413 vb.
interpret 520 vb.
teach 534 vb.
facilitate 701 vb.
interpretation
answer 460 n.
connotation 514 n.
intelligibility 516 n.
interpretation 520 n.
indication 547 n.
literature 557 n.
acting 594 n.
interpreter
interpreter 520 n.
teacher 537 n.
interpreter of dreams
diviner 511 n.
interracial
ethnic 11 adj.
correlative 12 adj.
interregnum
interim 108 n.
transience 114 n.
government 733 n.
anarchy 734 n.
interrelate
correlate 12 vb.
interrogate
hear 415 vb.
be curious 453 vb.
interrogate 459 vb.
interrogation mark
question 459 n.
interrogative
enquiring 459 adj.
interrogator
inquisitive person 453 n.
questioner 459 n.
interrupt
derange 63 vb.
discontinue 72 vb.
halt 145 vb.
interfere 231 vb.
intrude 297 vb.
distract 456 vb.
be obstructive 702 vb.
be rude 885 vb.
interrupted
disunited 46 adj.
incomplete 55 adj.
interrupter
dissentient 489 n.
hinderer 702 n.
interruption
inaptitude 25 n.
untimeliness 138 n.
interval 201 n.
interjection 231 n.
hindrance 702 n.
intersection
crossing 222 n.
passage 305 n.
access 624 n.
road 624 n.
interspace
interval 201 n.
interiority 224 n.
intersperse
mix 43 vb.
put between 231 vb.
interspersion
dispersion 75 n.
interstate
correlative 12 adj.
interstellar
interjacent 231 adj.
cosmic 321 adj.
interstellar matter
nebula 321 n.
interstice
gap 201 n.
interstitial
interior 224 adj.
interjacent 231 adj.
intertribal
ethnic 11 adj.
correlative 12 adj.
intertwine
mix 43 vb.
tie 45 vb.
combine 50 vb.
enlace 222 vb.
interval
degree 27 n.
disunion 46 n.
incompleteness 55 n.

discontinuity 72 n.
interim 108 n.
period 110 n.
lull 145 n.
interval 201 n.
musical note 410 n.
dramaturgy 594 n.
repose 683 n.
intervene
discontinue 72 vb.
continue 108 vb.
interfere 231 vb.
lie between 231 vb.
meddle 678 vb.
hinder 702 vb.
mediate 720 vb.
prohibit 757 vb.
intervener
hinderer 702 n.
litigant 959 n.
intervention
interjacency 231 n.
instrumentality 628 n.
hindrance 702 n.
war 718 n.
mediation 720 n.
interview
listening 415 n.
exam 459 n.
interrogate 459 vb.
conference 584 n.
interviewer
questioner 459 n.
interlocutor 584 n.
interwar
intermediate 108 adj.
antiquated 127 adj.
peaceful 717 adj.
interweave
mix 43 vb.
combine 50 vb.
compose 56 vb.
enlace 222 vb.
put between 231 vb.
interwoven
crossed 222 adj.
intestate
obliterated 550 adj.
intestine(s)
insides 224 n.
drain 351 n.
in the act
doing 676 adj.
in the act 676 adv.
in the air
reportedly 524 adv.
in the ascendant
powerful 160 adj.
influential 178 adj.
ascending 308 adj.
successful 727 adj.
in the background
rearward 238 adv.
latent 523 adj.
in the bag
certain 473 adj.
in the black
moneyed 800 adj.
in the bud
initially 68 adv.
in the buff
uncovered 229 adj.
in the can
recorded 548 adj.
completed 725 adj.
in the chair
directing 689 adj.
in control 689 adv.
in the clear
safe 660 adj.
acquitted 960 adj.
in the dark
darkling 418 adv.
ignorant 491 adj.
in the distance
afar 199 adv.
in the face of
here 189 adv.
in opposition 704 adv.
in the flesh
alive 360 adj.
in the forefront
in front 237 adv.
noteworthy 866 adj.
in the fullness of time
in time 111 adv.
prospectively 124 adv.
opportunely 137 adv.
in the lap of the gods
impending 155 adj.
in the light
hindering 702 adj.
in the long run
finally 69 adv.
generally 79 adv.
prospectively 124 adv.
in the main
on the whole 52 adv.
in the mood
willing 597 adj.
in the name of
in aid of 703 adv.
by authority 733 adv.
in the nick of time
opportunely 137 adv.
in the offing
impending 155 adj.
afar 199 adv.
preparatory 669 adj.
in the pay of
subject 745 adj.
in the picture
informed 524 adj.
in the pink
undamaged 646 adj.
healthy 650 adj.
in the pipeline
in transit 272 adv.
in the post
in transit 272 adv.
in the red
poor 801 adj.
indebted 803 adj.
in the running
contending 716 adj.
in the same boat
with 89 adv.
sharing 775 adj.
in the swim
prosperously 730 adv.
sharing 775 adj.
fashionable 848 adj.
in the teeth of
with difficulty 700 adv.
in opposition 704 adv.
in the thick of
between 231 adv.
in the act 676 adv.
sharing 775 adj.
in the way
near 200 adv.
hindering 702 adj.
in the wind
future 124 adj.
impending 155 adj.
in the wings
prospectively 124 adv.
intimacy
relation 9 n.
coition 45 n.
knowledge 490 n.
friendship 880 n.
sociality 882 n.
love 887 n.
intimate
joined 45 adj.
private 80 adj.
near 200 adj.
interior 224 adj.
knowing 490 adj.
hint 524 vb.
inform 524 vb.
indicate 547 vb.
close friend 880 n.
friendly 880 adj.
intimation
hint 524 n.
intimidate
hinder 702 vb.
frighten 854 vb.
threaten 900 vb.
intimidation
dissuasion 613 n.
false alarm 665 n.
terror tactics 712 n.
intimidation 854 n.
threat 900 n.
intinction
ritual act 988 n.
into
obsessed 455 adj.
into, be
choose 605 vb.
intolerable
exorbitant 32 adj.
bad 645 adj.
intolerable 827 adj.
disliked 861 adj.
intolerance
uniformity 16 n.
exclusion 57 n.
narrow mind 481 n.
opinionatedness 602 n.
prohibition 757 n.
orthodoxism 976 n.
intolerant
biased 481 adj.
dissenting 489 adj.
severe 735 adj.
excitable 822 adj.
inimical 881 adj.
malevolent 898 adj.
pitiless 906 adj.
orthodox 976 adj.
intonation
sound 398 n.
voice 577 n.
intone
sing 413 vb.
in toto
wholly 52 adv.
completely 54 adv.
in touch
by letter 588 adv.
in tow
behind 284 adv.
intoxicant
drug 658 n.
poison 659 n.
drug-taking 949 n.
intoxicate
invigorate 174 vb.
excite 821 vb.
delight 826 vb.
intoxicating
strong 162 adj.
cheering 833 adj.
intoxicating 949 adj.
intoxicating liquor
alcoholic drink 301 n.
intoxication
excitable state 822 n.
intemperance 943 n.
drunkenness 949 n.
intractable
rigid 326 adj.
wilful 602 adj.
difficult 700 adj.
disobedient 738 adj.
intramural
interior 224 adj.
educational 534 adj.
intransigent
resolute 599 adj.
obstinate 602 adj.
in transit
convertibly 147 adv.
on the move 265 adv.
in transit 272 adv.

intransmutable
unchangeable 153 adj.
intrauterine device, IUD
contraception 172 n.
intravenous injection
therapy 658 n.
in tray
compartment 194 n.
intrepid
unfearing 855 adj.
intricacy
crossing 222 n.
convolution 251 n.
enigma 530 n.
intricate
tied 45 adj.
complex 61 adj.
intricate 251 adj.
difficult 700 adj.
ornamental 844 adj.
intrigant(e)
deceiver 545 n.
planner 623 n.
intrigue
latency 523 n.
motivate 612 vb.
plot 623 n.vb.
overactivity 678 n.
be cunning 698 vb.
sedition 738 n.
impress 821 vb.
love affair 887 n.
— against
deceive 542 vb.
intriguer
deceiver 545 n.
planner 623 n.
meddler 678 n.
slyboots 698 n.
intrinsic
intrinsic 5 adj.
component 58 adj.
included 78 adj.
interior 224 adj.
introduce
add 38 vb.
come before 64 vb.
initiate 68 vb.
introduce 231 vb.
precede 283 vb.
admit 299 vb.
insert 303 vb.
direct 689 vb.
offer 759 vb.
befriend 880 vb.
greet 884 vb.
— oneself
be sociable 882 vb.
introduction
prelude 66 n.
beginning 68 n.
reception 299 n.
insertion 303 n.
teaching 534 n.
friendship 880 n.
courteous act 884 n.
introductory
precursory 66 adj.
beginning 68 adj.
prior 119 adj.
introit
vocal music 412 n.
Holy Communion 988 n.
introspection
meditation 449 n.
attention 455 n.
enquiry 459 n.
knowledge 490 n.
introspective
thoughtful 449 adj.
introversion
inversion 221 n.
interiority 224 n.
unsociability 883 n.
introverted
intrinsic 5 adj.
unsociable 883 adj.
intrude
mistime 138 vb.
interfere 231 vb.
intrude 297 vb.
insert 303 vb.
encroach 306 vb.
meddle 678 vb.
obstruct 702 vb.
intruder
misfit 25 n.
intruder 59 n.
interjector 231 n.
incomer 297 n.
impostor 545 n.
hinderer 702 n.n.
offender 904 n.
intrusion
unrelatedness 10 n.
intrusive
unrelated 10 adj.
extraneous 59 adj.
intuit
not think 450 vb.
intuit 476 vb.
suppose 512 vb.
intuition
intellect 447 n.
absence of thought 450 n.
intuition 476 n.
intelligence 498 n.
conjecture 512 n.
spontaneity 609 n.
feeling 818 n.
revelation 975 n.
psychics 984 n.
intuitive
intuitive 476 adj.
involuntary 596 adj.
spontaneous 609 adj.
feeling 818 adj.
in turn
in order 60 adv.
severally 80 adv.
by turns 141 adv.
in twos and threes
sporadically 75 adv.
here and there 105 adv.
inundate
overlie 226 vb.
flow out 298 vb.
drench 341 vb.
irrigate 341 vb.
flow 350 vb.
superabound 637 vb.
inundation
havoc 165 n.
waterfall 350 n.
inurbanity
ill-breeding 847 n.
discourtesy 885 n.
inure
train 534 vb.
habituate 610 vb.
make ready 669 vb.
inured
unfeeling 375 adj.
habituated 610 adj.
thick-skinned 820 adj.
inutility
ineffectuality 161 n.
unproductiveness 172 n.
superfluity 637 n.
unimportance 639 n.
inutility 641 n.
nonuse 674 n.
invade
burst in 297 vb.
encroach 306 vb.
attack 712 vb.
wage war 718 vb.
invader
intruder 59 n.
incomer 297 n.
attacker 712 n.
invaginate
invert 221 vb.
in vain
behindhand 307 adv.
wasted 634 adj.
profitless 641 adj.
unsuccessfully 728 adv.
invalid
powerless 161 adj.
weakling 163 n.
illogical 477 adj.
useless 641 adj.
sick person 651 n.
unhealthy 651 adj.
unwarranted 916 adj.
invalidate
disable 161 vb.
confute 479 vb.
negate 533 vb.
abrogate 752 vb.
disentitle 916 vb.
invalid chair
pushcart 274 n.
bicycle 274 n.
invalid out
not retain 779 vb.
invaluable
profitable 640 adj.
valuable 644 adj.
of price 811 adj.
invariable
characteristic 5 adj.
uniform 16 adj.
orderly 60 adj.
unceasing 146 adj.
unchangeable 153 adj.
usual 610 adj.
tedious 838 adj.
invasion
crowd 74 n.
ingress 297 n.
attack 712 n.
warfare 718 n.
invective
oratory 579 n.
scurrility 899 n.
reproach 924 n.
detraction 926 n.
inveigh (against)
curse 899 vb.
reprobate 924 vb.
inveigle
ensnare 542 vb.
tempt 612 vb.
invent
initiate 68 vb.
cause 156 vb.
produce 164 vb.
cognize 447 vb.
think 449 vb.
discover 484 vb.
imagine 513 vb.
manifest 522 vb.
be false 541 vb.
fake 541 vb.
plan 623 vb.
invention
originality 21 n.
idea 451 n.
discovery 484 n.
fable 543 n.
contrivance 623 n.
inventive
original 21 adj.
causal 156 adj.
productive 164 adj.
prolific 171 adj.
imaginative 513 adj.
inventor
precursor 66 n.
producer 164 n.
enquirer 459 n.
detector 484 n.
planner 623 n.
inventory
all 52 n.
class 62 vb.
list 87 n.vb.
contents 193 n.
account 808 vb.
inverse
contrary 14 adj.

inverted 221 adj.
opposite 240 adj.
inversion
inversion 221 n.
contraposition 240 n.
trope 519 n.
invert
derange 63 vb.
nonconformist 84 n.
modify 143 vb.
revert 148 vb.
revolutionize 149 vb.
demolish 165 vb.
invert 221 vb.
lower 311 vb.
invertebrate
animal 365 n.adj.
coward 856 n.
inverted commas
punctuation 547 n.
inverted snobbery
pride 871 n.
invest
place 187 vb.
surround 230 vb.
store 632 vb.
besiege 712 vb.
commission 751 vb.
lend 784 vb.
speculate 791 vb.
expend 806 vb.
— in
purchase 792 vb.
— with
assign 780 vb.
give 781 vb.
investigate
enquire 459 vb.
estimate 480 vb.
investigation
enquiry 459 n.
police enquiry 459 n.
study 536 n.
investigative journalism
publicity 528 n.
investigator
detective 459 n.
enquirer 459 n.
investiture
dressing 228 n.
mandate 751 n.
investment
estate 777 n.
expenditure 806 n.
investments
means 629 n.
investor
lender 784 n.
creditor 802 n.
inveterate
lasting 113 adj.
immemorial 127 adj.
permanent 144 adj.
established 153 adj.
habitual 610 adj.
habituated 610 adj.
impenitent 940 adj.
invidious
unpleasant 827 adj.
hateful 888 adj.
in view
impending 155 adj.
visible 443 adj.
expected 507 adj.
invigilate
invigilate 457 vb.
invigilation
surveillance 457 n.
invigilator
keeper 749 n.
invigorate
strengthen 162 vb.
invigorate 174 vb.
promote 285 vb.
vitalize 360 vb.
incite 612 vb.
refresh 685 vb.
animate 821 vb.
cheer 833 vb.
invigorating
salubrious 652 adj.
invincible
unyielding 162 adj.
unbeaten 727 adj.
inviolable
strong 162 adj.
concealed 525 adj.
due 915 adj.
inviolate
permanent 144 adj.
concealed 525 adj.
invisibility
insubstantiality 4 n.
smallness 33 n.
invisibility 444 n.
invisible
minute 196 adj.
distant 199 adj.
invisible 444 adj.
disappearing 446 adj.
unknown 491 adj.
latent 523 adj.
invisible ink
secrecy 525 n.
invisible trade
trade 791 n.
invisibly
slightly 33 adv.
invisibly 444 adv.
stealthily 525 adv.
invitation
reception 299 n.
call 547 n.
inducement 612 n.
command 737 n.
offer 759 n.
request 761 n.
excitation 821 n.
courteous act 884 n.
invite
request 761 vb.
desire 859 vb.
be hospitable 882 vb.
inviting
accessible 289 adj.
inducing 612 adj.
pleasurable 826 adj.
invocation
allocution 583 n.
entreaty 761 n.
(See **invoke** *)*
invocatory
vocative 583 adj.
supplicatory 761 adj.
devotional 981 adj.
invoice
list 87 n.
demand 737 vb.
accounts 808 n.
price 809 n.vb.
invoke
orate 579 vb.
speak to 583 vb.
entreat 761 vb.
desire 859 vb.
worship 981 vb.
practise sorcery 983 vb.
involucre
covering 226 n.
involuntary
intuitive 476 adj.
unmeant 515 adj.
involuntary 596 adj.
spontaneous 609 adj.
unintentional 618 adj.
compelling 740 adj.
involuntary movements
nervous disorders 651 n.
involute
coiled 251 adj.
involution
complexity 61 n.
numerical operation 86 n.
convolution 251 n.
involve
be intrinsic 5 vb.
contain 56 vb.
bedevil 63 vb.
comprise 78 vb.
conduce 156 vb.
evidence 466 vb.
make likely 471 vb.
mean 514 vb.
imply 523 vb.
indicate 547 vb.
accuse 928 vb.
involved
mixed 43 adj.
tied 45 adj.
component 58 adj.
complex 61 adj.
concurrent 181 adj.
intricate 251 adj.
unclear 568 adj.
active 678 adj.
sharing 775 adj.
feeling 818 adj.
involvement
relation 9 n.
union 45 n.
complexity 61 n.
affairs 154 n.
difficulty 700 n.
participation 775 n.
feeling 818 n.
liking 859 n.
guilt 936 n.
invulnerable
strong 162 adj.
invulnerable 660 adj.
defended 713 adj.
inward
intrinsic 5 adj.
interior 224 adj.
incoming 297 adj.
inward-looking
intrinsic 5 adj.
interior 224 adj.
in words of one syllable
intelligibly 516 adv.
plainly 573 adv.
in working order
prepared 669 adj.
in writing
recorded 548 adj.
written 586 adj.
inwrought
intrinsic 5 adj.
interior 224 adj.
ornamented 844 adj.
iodine
prophylactic 658 n.
ion
element 319 n.
Ionic
ornamental 844 adj.
ionosphere
atmosphere 340 n.
iota
small quantity 33 n.
IOU
title deed 767 n.
paper money 797 n.
IPA
speech sound 398 n.
letter 558 n.
ipecacuanha
purgative 658 n.
ipse dixit
certainty 473 n.
affirmation 532 n.
decree 737 n.
ipsissima verba
identity 13 n.
ipso facto
actually 1 adv.
IQ
intelligence 498 n.
IQ test
exam 459 n.
irascibility
irascibility 892 n.
irascible
violent 176 adj.
quarrelling 709 adj.
contending 716 adj.
sensitive 819 adj.

excitable 822 adj.
ungracious 885 adj.
irascible 892 adj.
sullen 893 adj.
irate
angry 891 adj.
ire
anger 891 n.
irenics
peace 717 n.
peace offering 719 n.
iridescence
light 417 n.
variegation 437 n.
iridescent
mixed 43 adj.
changeful 152 adj.
iridescent 437 adj.
iridization, iridisation
dim sight 440 n.
iris
eye 438 n.
Iris
courier 529 n.
Olympian deity 967 n.
Irish bridge
conduit 351 n.
Irish bull
mistake 495 n.
absurdity 497 n.
Irish coffee
soft drink 301 n.
Irishism
absurdity 497 n.
dialect 560 n.
irk
torment 827 vb.
irksome
fatiguing 684 adj.
difficult 700 adj.
annoying 827 adj.
tedious 838 adj.
iron
strength 162 n.
flattener 216 n.
smoother 258 n.
food content 301 n.
hardness 326 n.
hard 326 adj.
rub 333 vb.
resolution 599 n.
clean 648 vb.
— out
unravel 62 vb.
flatten 216 vb.
straighten 249 vb.
smooth 258 vb.
facilitate 701 vb.
Iron Age
era 110 n.
ironbound coast
shore 344 n.
pitfall 663 n.
ironclad
covered 226 adj.
defended 713 adj.
warship 722 n.
Iron Cross
badge 547 n.
decoration 729 n.
Iron Curtain
exclusion 57 n.
partition 231 n.
obstacle 702 n.
iron grip
vitality 162 n.
retention 778 n.
iron hand
conduct 688 n.
brute force 735 n.
iron hand in a velvet glove
latency 523 n.
iron horse
locomotive 274 n.
ironic, ironical
figurative 519 adj.
untrue 543 adj.
witty 839 adj.
funny 849 adj.
affected 850 adj.
derisive 851 adj.
ironist
humorist 839 n.
affecter 850 n.
iron lung
respiration 352 n.
hospital 658 n.
preserver 666 n.
Iron Maiden
instrument of torture 964 n.
ironmonger
tradespeople 794 n.
iron nerve
stability 153 n.
iron pill
tonic 658 n.
iron rations
small quantity 33 n.
provisions 301 n.
provision 633 n.
insufficiency 636 n.
portion 783 n.
fasting 946 n.
irons
prop 218 n.
fetter 748 n.
pillory 964 n.
Ironsides
cavalry 722 n.
irons in the fire
affairs 154 n.
business 622 n.
activity 678 n.
ironware
product 164 n.
irony
underestimation 483 n.
trope 519 n.
mental dishonesty 543 n.
wit 839 n.
affectation 850 n.
ridicule 851 n.
reproach 924 n.
irradiate
make bright 417 vb.
irradiation
light 417 n.
lighting 420 n.
irrational
unthinking 450 adj.
illogical 477 adj.
unwise 499 adj.
irrationality
intuition 476 n.
folly 499 n.
irrational number
number 85 n.
irreclaimable
lost 772 adj.
unpromising 853 adj.
wicked 934 adj.
impenitent 940 adj.
irreconcilability
contrariety 14 n.
disagreement 25 n.
revengefulness 910 n.
irreconcilable
unrelated 10 adj.
unwilling 598 adj.
opponent 705 n.
malcontent 829 n.
discontented 829 adj.
regretting 830 adj.
inimical 881 adj.
irrecoverable
past 125 adj.
lost 772 adj.
unpromising 853 adj.
irredeemable
bad 645 adj.
lost 772 adj.
wicked 934 adj.
impenitent 940 adj.
irredentist
patriot 901 n.
irreducible
simple 44 adj.
unchangeable 153 adj.
concise 569 adj.
irrefragable
undisputed 473 adj.
demonstrated 478 adj.
irrefutable
undisputed 473 adj.
demonstrated 478 adj.
irregular
nonuniform 17 adj.
unequal 29 adj.
orderless 61 adj.
discontinuous 72 adj.
multiform 82 adj.
abnormal 84 adj.
unconformable 84 adj.
fitful 142 adj.
distorted 246 adj.
neological 560 adj.
grammatical 564 adj.
unsightly 842 adj.
wrong 914 adj.
extramarital 951 adj.
illegal 954 adj.
irregularity
nonconformity 84 n.
changeableness 152 n.
solecism 565 n.
irregular troops
soldier 722 n.
irrelevance, irrelevancy
irrelevance 10 n.
lack of meaning 515 n.
hinderer 702 n.
irrelevant
irrelevant 10 adj.
unapt 25 adj.
misplaced 188 adj.
deviating 282 adj.
absurd 497 adj.
prolix 570 adj.
unimportant 639 adj.
irreligion
philosophy 449 n.
unbelief 486 n.
irreligion 974 n.
impiety 980 n.
irreligious
negligent 458 adj.
wicked 934 adj.
irreligious 974 adj.
irremediable
bad 645 adj.
unpromising 853 adj.
irremissible
heinous 934 adj.
irremovable, irremoveable
fixed 153 adj.
obstinate 602 adj.
irreparable
unpromising 853 adj.
irreplaceable
important 638 adj.
valuable 644 adj.
irrepressible
violent 176 adj.
wilful 602 adj.
independent 744 adj.
lively 819 adj.
cheerful 833 adj.
irreproachable
perfect 646 adj.
virtuous 933 adj.
guiltless 935 adj.
irresistible
powerful 160 adj.
strong 162 adj.

influential 178 adj.
demonstrated 478 adj.
necessary 596 adj.
inducing 612 adj.
compelling 740 adj.
lovable 887 adj.
irresolute
changeful 152 adj.
weak 163 adj.
doubting 474 adj.
irresolute 601 adj.
tergiversating 603 adj.
choiceless 606 adj.
neutral 625 adj.
lax 734 adj.
cowardly 856 adj.
irrespective
unrelated 10 adj.
irresponsible
changeful 152 adj.
irresolute 601 adj.
capricious 604 adj.
rash 857 adj.
undutiful 918 adj.
lawless 954 adj.
irretrievable
lost 772 adj.
irreverent
disrespectful 921 adj.
impious 980 adj.
irreversible
established 153 adj.
unchangeable 153 adj.
progressive 285 adj.
obstinate 602 adj.
unpromising 853 adj.
irrevocable
established 153 adj.
impossible 470 adj.
certain 473 adj.
unpromising 853 adj.
irrigable
dry 342 adj.
irrigate
make fruitful 171 vb.
invigorate 174 vb.
add water 339 vb.
irrigate 341 vb.
make flow 350 vb.
irrigation
moistening 341 n.
agriculture 370 n.
irrigator
extractor 304 n.
irrigator 341 n.
irritable
contending 716 adj.
sensitive 819 adj.
excitable 822 adj.
irascible 892 adj.
irritant
excitant 821 n.
aggravation 832 n.
irritate
make violent 176 vb.
give pain 377 vb.
itch 378 vb.
make quarrels 709 vb.
excite 821 vb.
torment 827 vb.
cause discontent 829 vb.
aggravate 832 vb.
make enemies 881 vb.
enrage 891 vb.
irritation
excitation 821 n.
worry 825 n.
painfulness 827 n.
discontent 829 n.
aggravation 832 n.
anger 891 n.
resentment 891 n.
irruption
ingress 297 n.
attack 712 n.
isagogics
theology 973 n.
Ishmael
outcast 883 n.
ishtar
mythic deity 966 n.
Semitic deities 967 n.
isinglass
thickening 354 n.
Isis
mythic deity 966 n.
Egyptian deities 967 n.
Islam
religious faith 973 n.
Islamic
religious 973 adj.
Islamic sect
non-Christian sect 978 n.
Islamite
religionist 973 n.
island
region 184 n.
traffic control 305 n.
island 349 n.
seclusion 883 n.
islander
dweller 191 n.
island 349 n.
Islands of the Blest
fantasy 513 n.
happiness 824 n.
mythic heaven 971 n.
island universe
star 321 n.
isle
island 349 n.
islet
island 349 n.
ism
creed 485 n.
iso-
equal 28 adj.
isobar
weather 340 n.
isochronous
chronological 117 adj.
synchronous 123 adj.
isocracy
government 733 n.
isogloss
linguistics 557 n.
isogonic line
outline 233 n.
isolate
set apart 46 vb.
be one 88 vb.
sanitate 652 vb.
seclude 883 vb.
isolated
unrelated 10 adj.
separate 46 adj.
alone 88 adj.
insular 349 adj.
vulnerable 661 adj.
secluded 883 adj.
isolated instance
speciality 80 n.
nonconformity 84 n.
isolation
unrelatedness 10 n.
disunion 46 n.
unity 88 n.
seclusion 883 n.
isolationism
disunion 46 n.
freedom 744 n.
isolation ward
hospital 658 n.
isometric drawing
representation 551 n.
isometrics
exercise 682 n.
isomorphism
form 243 n.
isosceles
symmetrical 245 adj.
isothermal
warm 379 adj.
isotope
element 319 n.
isotropic
equal 28 adj.
I-spy
indoor game 837 n.
issue
kinsman 11 n.
subdivision 53 n.
event 154 n.
effect 157 n.
posterity 170 n.
outflow 298 n.
emerge 298 vb.
flow 350 vb.
topic 452 n.
the press 528 n.
publish 528 vb.
edition 589 n.
chief thing 638 n.
completion 725 n.
mint 797 vb.
litigation 959 n.
issueless
unproductive 172 adj.
isthmian
narrow 206 adj.
isthmus
bond 47 n.
narrowing 206 n.
land 344 n.
bridge 624 n.
it
identity 13 n.
no imitation 21 n.
authenticity 494 n.
i.t.a.
letter 558 n.
ITA
broadcasting 531 n.
italic
letter 558 n.
lettering 586 n.
written 586 adj.
print-type 587 n.
italicize, italicise
emphasize 532 vb.
italics
punctuation 547 n.
itch
attraction 291 n.
agitation 318 n.
formication 378 n.
itch 378 vb.
curiosity 453 n.
skin disease 651 n.
desire 859 n.
itching
inquisitive 453 adj.
excited 821 adj.
desiring 859 adj.
itching palm
avarice 816 n.
itchy
agitated 318 adj.
sentient 374 adj.
itchy feet
wandering 267 n.
item
in addition 38 adv.
extra 40 n.
part 53 n.
component 58 n.
unit 88 n.
object 319 n.
itemize, itemise
specify 80 vb.
list 87 vb.
items
particulars 80 n.
list 87 n.
contents 193 n.
iterate
repeat 106 vb.
iteration
duplication 91 n.
vigour 571 n.
perseverance 600 n.

ithyphallic
impure 951 adj.
itinerant
travelling 267 adj.
traveller 268 n.
itinerary
itinerary 267 n.
guidebook 524 n.
way 624 n.
itself
self 80 n.
itsy-bitsy
little 196 adj.
ivories
tooth 256 n.
piano 414 n.
gambling 618 n.
ivory
hardness 326 n.
white thing 427 n.
ivory tower
refuge 662 n.
seclusion 883 n.
ivy
tree 366 n.
Ivy League
educational 534 adj.
Ixion
rotator 315 n.
izzat
prestige 866 n.

J

jab
knock 279 n.
wound 655 n.
medicine 658 n.
lunge 712 n.
jab at
attempt 671 n.
jabber
mean nothing 515 vb.
speak 579 vb.
chatter 581 n.
Jabberwocky
rara avis 84 n.
fantasy 513 n.
jabot
neckwear 228 n.
jacaranda
tree 366 n.
jacinth
gem 844 n.
jack
prop 218 n.
missile 287 n.
lifter 310 n.
rotator 315 n.
male animal 372 n.
flag 547 n.
tool 630 n.
jackal
mammal 365 n.
auxiliary 707 n.
toady 879 n.
noxious animal 904 n.
jackanapes
fop 848 n.
insolent person 878 n.
Jack and Jill
duality 90 n.
jackass
fool 501 n.
jackboot
tyrant 735 n.
lawlessness 954 n.
jackdaw
bird 365 n.
jacket
wrapping 226 n.
jacket 228 n.
bookbinding 589 n.
Jack-in-office
official 690 n.
tyrant 735 n.
autocrat 741 n.
insolent person 878 n.
Jack-in-the-box
jumper 312 n.
lack of expectation 508 n.
plaything 837 n.
jack knife
sharp edge 256 n.
Jack of all trades
proficient person 696 n.
bungler 697 n.
Jack-o'-lantern
glow-worm 420 n.
jackpot
acquisition 771 n.
reward 962 n.
jacks
plaything 837 n.
jackstaff
prop 218 n.
jack up
support 218 vb.
elevate 310 vb.
Jacobean
revolter 738 n.
olden 127 adj.
Jacobins
political party 708 n.
revolter 738 n.
Jacob's ladder
ascent 308 n.
Jacob's staff
gauge 465 n.
jacquard
textile 222 n.
jactation
boasting 877 n.
jactitation
agitation 318 n.
jade
saddle horse 273 n.
woman 373 n.
greenness 434 n.
fatigue 684 vb.
be tedious 838 vb.
gem 844 n.
sate 863 vb.
jaeger
infantry 722 n.
jag
notch 260 vb.
drunkenness 949 n.
jagged
angular 247 adj.
sharp 256 adj.
rough 259 adj.
notched 260 adj.
jaguar
cat 365 n.
jail
gaol 748 n.
jailbird
prisoner 750 n.
offender 904 n.
jailer
doorkeeper 264 n.
gaoler 749 n.
Jain
religionist 973 n.
Jainism
religious faith 973 n.
jalopy
automobile 274 n.
jalousie
shade 226 n.
curtain 421 n.
jam
circumstance 8 n.
affix 45 vb.
tighten 45 vb.
crowd 74 n.
halt 145 vb.
make smaller 198 vb.
be quiescent 266 vb.
viscidity 354 n.
pulpiness 356 n.
sweet thing 392 n.
predicament 700 n.
obstruct 702 vb.
— in/into
fill 54 vb.
introduce 231 vb.
insert 303 vb.
jamb
pillar 218 n.
jamboree
amusement 837 n.
jam jar
vessel 194 n.
jammy
viscid 354 adj.
super 644 adj.
jam-packed
firm 45 adj.
full 54 adj.
jam session
music 412 n.
jam tart
dessert 301 n.
jam tomorrow
neverness 109 n.
different time 122 n.
jangle
resound 404 vb.
rasp 407 vb.
discord 411 vb.
bicker 709 vb.
janissaries
armed force 722 n.
janitor
doorkeeper 264 n.
servant 742 n.
Janus
duality 90 n.
tergiversator 603 n.
japan
coat 226 vb.
resin 357 n.
blacken 428 vb.
decorate 844 vb.
jape
witticism 839 n.
jar
differ 15 vb.
disagree 25 vb.
vessel 194 n.
agitation 318 n.
give pain 377 vb.
rasp 407 vb.
discord 411 vb.
dissension 709 n.
bicker 709 vb.
displease 827 vb.
cause dislike 861 vb.
excite hate 888 vb.
jardinière
vessel 194 n.
garden 370 n.
jargon
speciality 80 n.
absurdity 497 n.
unintelligibility 517 n.
slang 560 n.
jasmine
yellow 433 adj.
Jason
mariner 270 n.
jasper
gem 844 n.
jaspered
mottled 437 adj.
jaundice
digestive disorders 651 n.
jaundiced
yellow 433 adj.
biased 481 adj.
unhealthy 651 adj.
melancholic 834 adj.
sullen 893 adj.
jealous 911 adj.
jaunt
land travel 267 n.
amusement 837 n.
jaunting car
carriage 274 n.
jaunty
cheerful 833 adj.
showy 875 adj.

impertinent 878 adj.
javelin
missile 287 n.
spear 723 n.
jaw
protuberance 254 n.
be loquacious 581 vb.
jawbreaker
word 559 n.
jaws
maw 194 n.
threshold 234 n.
orifice 263 n.
eater 301 n.
jaws of death
danger 661 n.
jay
bird 365 n.
chatterer 581 n.
jay walker
inattention 456 n.
jazz
music 412 n.
jazz band
orchestra 413 n.
jazzman
musician 413 n.
jazz singer
vocalist 413 n.
jazzy
musical 412 adj.
florid 425 adj.
jealous
opposing 704 adj.
resentful 891 adj.
malevolent 898 adj.
jealous 911 adj.
selfish 932 adj.
jealousy
doubt 486 n.
quarrelsomeness 709 n.
contention 716 n.
discontent 829 n.
enmity 881 n.
love 887 n.
hatred 888 n.
jealousy 911 n.
jeans
informal dress 228 n.
trousers 228 n.
jeep
automobile 274 n.
jeer
deprecate 762 vb.
ridicule 851 vb.
indignity 921 n.
not respect 921 vb.
despise 922 vb.
jeers
lifter 310 n.
Jehovah
the Deity 965 n.
Jehovah's Witness
sectarian 978 n.
Jehu
driver 268 n.
jejune
tasteless 387 adj.
feeble 572 adj.
insufficient 636 adj.
Jekyll and Hyde
multiformity 82 n.
duality 90 n.
jell
be dense 324 vb.
thicken 354 vb.
jellaba, djellaba
cloak 228 n.
jelly
dessert 301 n.
viscidity 354 n.
sweet thing 392 n.
jellyfish
weakling 163 n.
marine life 365 n.
coward 856 n.
jemmy, jimmy
force 176 vb.
tool 630 n.
jennet
saddle horse 273 n.
jeopardize, jeopardise
endanger 661 vb.
jeopardy
danger 661 n.
jerboa
jumper 312 n.
jeremiad
lament 836 n.
censure 924 n.
Jeremiah
weeper 836 n.
jerid
spear 723 n.
jerk
revolution 149 n.
be rough 259 vb.
move 265 vb.
impulse 279 n.
draw 288 vb.
agitation 318 n.
agitate 318 vb.
ninny 501 n.
jerkin
jacket 228 n.
jerky
nonuniform 17 adj.
discontinuous 72 adj.
fitful 142 adj.
jeroboam
vessel 194 n.
jerry
latrine 649 n.
jerry-built
flimsy 163 adj.
architectural 192 adj.
brittle 330 adj.
spurious 542 adj.
unsafe 661 adj.
jersey
textile 222 n.
jersey 228 n.
Jersey
cattle 365 n.
Jerusalem
holy place 990 n.
jess
halter 47 n.
jesse window
church interior 990 n.
jest
trifle 639 n.
amuse oneself 837 vb.
witticism 839 n.
jester
fool 501 n.
humorist 839 n.
Jesuits
monk 986 n.
Jesus Christ
God the Son 965 n.
religious teacher 973 n.
jet
energy 160 n.
vigorousness 174 n.
outbreak 176 n.
aircraft 276 n.
speeder 277 n.
propellant 287 n.
outflow 298 n.
emit 300 vb.
ascend 308 vb.
stream 350 n.
black thing 428 n.
gem 844 n.
jeté
leap 312 n.
ballet 594 n.
jet lag
delay 136 n.
air travel 271 n.
jet-propelled
speedy 277 adj.
jet propulsion
energy 160 n.
propulsion 287 n.
jetsam
thing transferred 272 n.
derelict 779 n.
jet set
aeronaut 271 n.
rich person 800 n.
beau monde 848 n.
jet stream
wind 352 n.
jettison
ejection 300 n.
lighten 323 vb.
stop using 674 vb.
not retain 779 vb.
jetty
stable 192 n.
projection 254 n.
shelter 662 n.
jeu d'esprit
witticism 839 n.
jeune premier
actor 594 n.
jeunesse dorée
rich person 800 n.
beau monde 848 n.
Jew
religionist 973 n.
jewel
exceller 644 n.
a beauty 841 n.
gem 844 n.
favourite 890 n.
jeweller
artisan 686 n.
jewellery
neckwear 228 n.
jewellery 844 n.
Jewish
religious 973 adj.
Jewish sect
non-Christian sect 978 n.
Jew's harp
gong 414 n.
Jezebel
loose woman 952 n.
jib
prow 237 n.
sail 275 n.
recoil 280 vb.
deviate 282 vb.
turn back 286 vb.
be unwilling 598 vb.
be irresolute 601 vb.
avoid 620 vb.
refuse 760 vb.
deprecate 762 vb.
quake 854 vb.
resent 891 vb.
jibe
(See **gibe** *)*
jiffy
instant 116 n.
jig
leap 312 n.
agitation 318 n.
musical piece 412 n.
dance 837 n.
jigger
draught 301 n.
insect 365 n.
jiggery-pokery
deception 542 n.
jiggle
derange 63 vb.
agitate 318 vb.
jigsaw
combination 50 n.
indoor game 837 n.
jihad
war 718 n.
philanthropy 901 n.
jilt
disappoint 509 vb.
deceiver 545 n.
tergiversator 603 n.
relinquish 621 vb.
jimjams
frenzy 503 n.
alcoholism 949 n.

jingle
resound 404 vb.
advertisement 528 n.
doggerel 593 n.
jingoism
nation 371 n.
bellicosity 718 n.
boasting 877 n.
jingoist
militarist 722 n.
jingoistic
biased 481 adj.
jink
be oblique 220 vb.
be in motion 265 vb.
jinn, djinn
mythical being 970 n.
jinx
badness 645 n.
spell 983 n.
jitterbug
dance 837 n.
jitters
agitation 318 n.
nervousness 854 n.
jive
music 412 n.
dance 837 n. vb.
jiver
jumper 312 n.
Joan of Arc
brave person 855 n.
job
agency 173 n.
function 622 n.
job 622 n.
undertaking 672 n.
deed 676 n.
labour 682 n.
hard task 700 n.
stealing 788 n.
foul play 930 n.
jobbery
cunning 698 n.
improbity 930 n.
jobbing
barter 791 n.
Job Centre
job 622 n.
jobless
unused 674 adj.
nonactive 677 adj.
job lot
medley 43 n.
Job's comforter
moper 834 n.
hopelessness 853 n.
Jock
native 191 n.
male 372 n.
jockey
rider 268 n.
be cunning 698 vb.
jockeying
tactics 688 n.
jockstrap
prop 218 n.
loincloth 228 n.
jocose
witty 839 adj.
jocular
merry 833 adj.
witty 839 adj.
jocund
merry 833 adj.
jodhpurs
trousers 228 n.
Jodo sect
non-Christian sect 978 n.
jog
gait 265 n.
walk 267 vb.
impel 279 vb.
agitate 318 vb.
gesture 547 n.
gesticulate 547 vb.
incite 612 vb.
— on
go on 146 vb.
progress 285 vb.
be middling 732 vb.
— one's memory
remind 505 vb.
jogger
pedestrian 268 n.
jogging
exercise 682 n.
sport 837 n.
joggle
agitate 318 vb.
jog trot
uniformity 16 n.
gait 265 n.
pedestrianism 267 n.
slowness 278 n.
john
latrine 649 n.
John Barleycorn
alcoholic drink 301 n.
drunkenness 949 n.
John Brown
agitator 738 n.
John Bull
native 191 n.
John Citizen
commoner 869 n.
johnny
male 372 n.
Johnny-come-lately
upstart 126 n.
incomer 297 n.
Johnny-head-in-air
inattention 456 n.
Johnsonese
imperspicuity 568 n.
magniloquence 574 n.
joie de vivre
cheerfulness 833 n.
join
accrue 38 vb.
join 45 vb.
agglutinate 48 vb.
combine 50 vb.
bring together 74 vb.
be included 78 vb.
gap 201 n.
be contiguous 202 vb.
close 264 vb.
approach 289 vb.
meet 295 vb.
enter 297 vb.
repair 656 vb.
patronize 703 vb.
join a party 708 vb.
marry 894 vb.
— forces
cooperate 706 vb.
— in
conform 83 vb.
be active 678 vb.
cooperate 706 vb.
participate 775 vb.
be sociable 882 vb.
— issue
argue 475 vb.
fight 716 vb.
— up
go to war 718 n.
joiner
artisan 686 n.
joinery
formation 243 n.
joint
joint 45 n.
bond 47 n.
concurrent 181 adj.
tavern 192 n.
pivot 218 n.
angularity 247 n.
fold 261 n.
meat 301 n.
tobacco 388 n.
corporate 708 adj.
sharing 775 adj.
drug-taking 949 n.
jointed
joined 45 adj.
angular 247 adj.
joint effort
concurrence 181 n.
cooperation 706 n.
jointly
with 89 adv.
cooperatively 706 adv.
in common 775 adv.
joint operations
warfare 718 n.
joint ownership
joint possession 775 n.
joint-stock company
association 706 n.
corporation 708 n.
jointure
dower 777 n.
joist
beam 218 n.
joke
absurdity 497 n.
trickery 542 n.
trifle 639 n.
witticism 839 n.
joker
misfit 25 n.
nonconformist 84 n.
humorist 839 n.
jokey
witty 839 adj.
jollification
revel 837 n.
jollity
merriment 833 n.
amusement 837 n.
sociability 882 n.
jolly
naval man 722 n.
merry 833 adj.
amused 837 adj.
sociable 882 adj.
jolly along
cheer 833 vb.
flatter 925 vb.
jolly boat
boat 275 n.
Jolly Roger
flag 547 n.
jolt
be rough 259 vb.
move slowly 278 vb.
impulse 279 n.
agitation 318 n.
lack of expectation 508 n.
incite 612 vb.
animate 821 vb.
jolty
discontinuous 72 adj.
Jonah
unlucky person 731 n.
malcontent 829 n.
moper 834 n.
jongleur
musician 413 n.
poet 593 n.
jorum
bowl 194 n.
Joseph
virgin 950 n.
Joseph's coat
variegation 437 n.
josh
ridicule 851 vb.
joss
idol 982 n.
joss house
temple 990 n.
joss stick
fumigator 385 n.
scent 396 n.
ritual object 988 n.
jostle
be near 200 vb.
be contiguous 202 vb.
impel 279 vb.
obstruct 702 vb.
fight 716 vb.
not respect 921 vb.

jot
small quantity 33 n.
trifle 639 n.
jot down
record 548 vb.
write 586 vb.
jotter
stationery 586 n.
jottings
record 548 n.
reading matter 589 n.
joule
energy 160 n.
jounce
agitate 318 vb.
jour maigre
fast 946 n.
journal
chronology 117 n.
journal 528 n.
the press 528 n.
record 548 n.
biography 590 n.
account book 808 n.
journalese
neology 560 n.
journalism
publicity 528 n.
writing 586 n.
journalist
enquirer 459 n.
publicizer 528 n.
news reporter 529 n.
chronicler 549 n.
author 589 n.
journey
travel 267 vb.
passage 305 n.
journeyman
artisan 686 n.
journey's end
resting place 266 n.
goal 295 n.
journeywork
labour 682 n.
joust
contest 716 n.
jouster
combatant 722 n.
Jove
Olympian deity 967 n.
jovial
merry 833 adj.
amused 837 adj.
sociable 882 adj.
jowl
laterality 239 n.
joy
pleasure 376 n.
excitation 821 n.
joy 824 n.
pleasurableness 826 n.
cheerfulness 833 n.
rejoicing 835 n.
joyful
happy 824 adj.
merry 833 adj.
joyless
unpleasant 827 adj.
dejected 834 adj.
melancholic 834 adj.
joyous
happy 824 adj.
merry 833 adj.
joy ride
land travel 267 n.
borrowing 785 n.
stealing 788 n.
joystick
aircraft 276 n.
directorship 689 n.
JP
judge 957 n.
jubbah
robe 228 n.
jubilant
pleased 824 adj.
jubilant 833 adj.
rejoicing 835 adj.
celebratory 876 adj.
jubilation
merriment 833 n.
rejoicing 835 n.
celebration 876 n.
jubilee
twenty and over 99 n.
period 110 n.
anniversary 141 n.
merriment 833 n.
rejoicing 835 n.
celebration 876 n.
Judaism
religious faith 973 n.
Judaize, Judaise
make pious 979 vb.
Judas
deceiver 545 n.
knave 938 n.
Judas kiss
duplicity 541 n.
perfidy 930 n.
judder
be agitated 318 vb.
judge
discriminate 463 vb.
appraise 465 vb.
estimator 480 n.
judge 480 vb.
choose 605 vb.
leader 690 n.
have taste 846 vb.
judge 957 n.
try a case 959 vb.
punisher 963 n.
— beforehand
prejudge 481 vb.
— for oneself
will 595 vb.
judge and jury
tribunal 956 n.
judgment
intellect 447 n.
discrimination 463 n.
judgment 480 n.
opinion 485 n.
sagacity 498 n.
decree 737 n.
good taste 846 n.
legality 953 n.
legal trial 959 n.
condemnation 961 n.
punishment 963 n.
divine function 965 n.
judgment seat
courtroom 956 n.
tribunal 956 n.
judicatory
judicatory 956 adj.
judicature
jurisdiction 955 n.
judicial
judicial 480 adj.
judicatory 956 adj.
judicial murder
capital punishment 963 n.
judicial separation
divorce 896 n.
judiciary
judge 957 n.
judicious
moderate 177 adj.
discriminating 463 adj.
judicial 480 adj.
wise 498 adj.
advisable 642 adj.
judo
defence 713 n.
wrestling 716 n.
judoist
combatant 722 n.
jug
vessel 194 n.
gaol 748 n.
juggernaut
destroyer 168 n.
flattener 216 n.
lorry 274 n.
Juggernaut
monster 938 n.
idol 982 n.
juggins
ninny 501 n.
juggle
modify 143 vb.
deceive 542 vb.
be cunning 698 vb.
juggler
conjuror 545 n.
entertainer 594 n.
slyboots 698 n.
sorcerer 983 n.
jugular vein
essential part 5 n.
conduit 351 n.
juice
fluid 335 n.
moisture 341 n.
semiliquidity 354 n.
fuel 385 n.
juiceless
dry 342 adj.
juicy
new 126 adj.
vernal 128 adj.
soft 327 adj.
fluid 335 adj.
humid 341 adj.
semiliquid 354 adj.
pulpy 356 adj.
savoury 390 adj.
super 644 adj.
pleasurable 826 adj.
impure 951 adj.
jujitsu
defence 713 n.
wrestling 716 n.
juju
talisman 983 n.
jujube
sweet thing 392 n.
jukebox
gramophone 414 n.
julep
soft drink 301 n.
sweet thing 392 n.
Julian calendar
chronology 117 n.
julienne
hors-d'oeuvres 301 n.
jumble
medley 43 n.
confusion 61 n.
jumble 63 vb.
deform 244 vb.
not discriminate 464 vb.
impair 655 vb.
jumbo
giant 195 n.
jumbo jet
aircraft 276 n.
jump
interval 201 n.
gait 265 n.
fly 271 vb.
spurt 277 n.
progression 285 n.
ascent 308 n.
leap 312 n.vb.
agitation 318 n.
neglect 458 vb.
not expect 508 vb.
improvement 654 n.
obstacle 702 n.
be excited 821 vb.
be excitable 822 vb.
amuse oneself 837 vb.
fear 854 vb.
— at
be willing 597 vb.
pursue 619 vb.
consent 758 vb.
desire 859 vb.
— bail
run away 620 vb.
escape 667 vb.

— down one's throat
be irascible 892 vb.
— for joy
be pleased 824 vb.
— in
enter 297 vb.
plunge 313 vb.
— on
leap 312 vb.
restrain 747 vb.
— on the bandwagon
do likewise 20 vb.
conform 83 vb.
apostatize 603 vb.
be in fashion 848 vb.
be servile 879 vb.
— out
emerge 298 vb.
— out of one's skin
not expect 508 vb.
— over
overstep 306 vb.
leap 312 vb.
— the gun
do before 119 vb.
be early 135 vb.
— the queue
come before 64 vb.
do before 119 vb.
precede 283 vb.
— to conclusions
prejudge 481 vb.
— to it
be active 678 vb.
— up
ascend 308 vb.
lift oneself 310 vb.
jumped-up
unimportant 639 adj.
jumper
jersey 228 n.
thoroughbred 273 n.
jumper 312 n.
dance 837 n.
jumping-off ground
aider 703 n.
jump jet
aircraft 276 n.
jumpsuit
suit 228 n.
jumpy
agitated 318 adj.
active 678 adj.
nervous 854 adj.
junction
joint 45 n.
bond 47 n.
focus 76 n.
access 624 n.
railway 624 n.
road 624 n.
juncture
juncture 8 n.
present time 121 n.
occasion 137 n.
event 154 n.
Jungian psychology
psychology 447 n.
jungle
confusion 61 n.
wood 366 n.
junior
inferior 35 n.adj.
subsequent 120 adj.
young 130 adj.
subject 745 adj.
junk
sailing ship 275 n.
reject 607 vb.
rubbish 641 n.
Junker
aristocrat 868 n.
junket
dairy product 301 n.
meal 301 n.
revel 837 n.vb.
junk food
provisions 301 n.
junkie, junky
madman 504 n.
drug-taking 949 n.
Juno
woman 373 n.
marriage 894 n.
Olympian deity 967 n.
Junoesque
tall 209 adj.
beautiful 841 adj.
junta
party 708 n.
Jupiter
planet 321 n.
Olympian deity 967 n.
juridical
judicial 480 adj.
jurisdictional 955 adj.
jurisconsult
jurist 958 n.
jurisdiction
authority 733 n.
law 953 n.
jurisdiction 955 n.
legal process 959 n.
jurisdictional
jurisdictional 955 adj.
judicatory 956 adj.
jurisprudence
jurisprudence 953 n.
jurisprudential
legal 953 adj.
jurisprudential 958 adj.
jurist
jurist 958 n.
juror
estimator 480 n.
jury 957 n.
jury
estimator 480 n.
jury 957 n.
jury box
courtroom 956 n.
juryman, jurywoman
jury 957 n.
jury mast
safeguard 662 n.
just
rational 475 adj.
wise 498 adj.
veracious 540 adj.
neutral 625 adj.
indifferent 860 adj.
just 913 adj.
honourable 929 adj.
disinterested 931 adj.
virtuous 933 adj.
legal 953 adj.
just as
similarly 18 adv.
synchronously 123 adv.
just cause
vindication 927 n.
just deserts
dueness 915 n.
reward 962 n.
punishment 963 n.
just do
suffice 635 vb.
justice
indifference 860 n.
justice 913 n.
probity 929 n.
disinterestedness 931 n.
virtue 933 n.
legality 953 n.
judge 957 n.
reward 962 n.
punishment 963 n.
justice of the peace
officer 741 n.
judge 957 n.
justiciable
accusable 928 adj.
legal 953 adj.
illegal 954 adj.
jurisdictional 955 adj.
litigated 959 adj.
justiciary
judge 957 n.
justifiable
just 913 adj.
deserving 915 adj.
vindicable 927 adj.
justification
counterevidence 467 n.
pretext 614 n.
dueness 915 n.
vindication 927 n.
acquittal 960 n.
divine function 965 n.
sanctity 979 n.
justifier
vindicator 927 n.
justify
demonstrate 478 vb.
print 587 vb.
plead 614 vb.
have a right 915 vb.
justify 927 vb.
acquit 960 vb.
just in case
in preparation 669 adv.
just in time
timely 137 adj.
opportunely 137 adv.
just like that
easily 701 adv.
just married
married 894 adj.
just mention
hint 524 vb.
just now
at present 121 adv.
newly 126 adv.
just right
truly 494 adv.
sufficient 635 adj.
perfect 646 adj.
just sit there
be inert 175 vb.
just so
in order 60 adv.
accurate 494 adj.
just the thing, be
be expedient 642 vb.
just the time
occasion 137 n.
just this once
singly 88 adv.
seldom 140 adv.
just what the doctor ordered
pleasurable 826 adj.
cheering 833 adj.
jut
jut 254 vb.
be visible 443 vb.
jute
fibre 208 n.
textile 222 n.
juvenile
young 130 adj.
youngster 132 n.
infantine 132 adj.
feeble 572 adj.
immature 670 adj.
juvenile court
lawcourt 956 n.
juvenile delinquent
low fellow 869 n.
offender 904 n.
juvenile lead
actor 594 n.
juveniles
reading matter 589 n.
juxtapose
connect 45 vb.
bring near 200 vb.
juxtapose 202 vb.
compare 462 vb.

K

ka
identity 13 n.
analogue 18 n.
spirit 447 n.
kaftan
(See **caftan** *)*
kagoule, cagoule
jacket 228 n.
Kaiser
sovereign 741 n.
kala-azar
tropical disease 651 n.
kale
vegetable 301 n.
kaleidoscope
medley 43 n.
multiformity 82 n.
alterer 143 n.
changeable thing 152 n.
variegation 437 n.
optical device 442 n.
spectacle 445 n.
kaleidoscopic
coloured 425 adj.
kaleyard school
plainness 573 n.
Kali
Hindu deities 967 n.
Kalpa
era 110 n.
Kama
love god 887 n.
kamikaze
murderer 362 n.
kangaroo
jumper 312 n.
mammal 365 n.
kangaroo court
lawlessness 954 n.
Kantianism
philosophy 449 n.
kaolin
soil 344 n.
kapellmeister
musician 413 n.
kapok
fibre 208 n.
lining 227 n.
kaput
powerless 161 adj.
destroyed 165 adj.
dead 361 adj.
useless 641 adj.
defeated 728 adj.
Karaites
non-Christian sect 978 n.
karate
wrestling 716 n.
karma
effect 157 n.
fate 596 n.
karmic
fated 596 adj.
kayak
rowing boat 275 n.
kazoo
organ 414 n.
K.C.
lawyer 958 n.
kebabs
dish 301 n.
kedge
navigate 269 vb.
kedgeree
fish food 301 n.
keel
stabilizer 153 n.
base 214 n.
pivot 218 n.
ship 275 n.
keelhaul
punish 963 vb.
keel over
be inverted 221 vb.
tumble 309 vb.
keen
keen 174 adj.
sharp 256 adj.
inter 364 vb.
striking 374 adj.
cold 380 adj.
willing 597 adj.
contending 716 adj.
felt 818 adj.
lament 836 n.vb.
witty 839 adj.
desiring 859 adj.
condolence 905 n.
keener
weeper 836 n.
keen-eyed
seeing 438 adj.
keen on
enamoured 887 adj.
keep
put off 136 vb.
recur 139 vb.
dwelling 192 n.
dwell 192 vb.
provisions 301 n.
look after 457 vb.
store 632 vb.
provide 633 vb.
safeguard 660 vb.
refuge 662 n.
subvention 703 n.
patronize 703 vb.
fort 713 n.
defend 713 vb.
detention 747 n.
observe 768 vb.
retain 778 vb.
celebrate 876 vb.
ritualize 988 vb.
— accounts
number 86 vb.
account 808 vb.
— alive
sustain 146 vb.
vitalize 360 vb.
preserve 666 vb.vb.
— a lookout
be careful 457 vb.
— a low profile
keep secret 525 vb.
— a mistress
be impure 951 vb.
— an eye
look after 457 vb.
safeguard 660 vb.
— at arm's length
repel 292 vb.
parry 713 vb.
resist 715 vb.
make unwelcome 883 vb.
— a tight rein on
be severe 735 vb.
restrain 747 vb.
— at it
go on 146 vb.
persevere 600 vb.
work 682 vb.
— away
be absent 190 vb.
avoid 620 vb.
— a weather eye open for
scan 438 vb.
— back
keep secret 525 vb.
dissuade 613 vb.
store 632 vb.
restrain 747 vb.
retain 778 vb.vb.
be parsimonious 816 vb.
— body and soul together
vitalize 360 vb.
be healthy 650 vb.
— calm
restrain 747 vb.
keep calm 823 vb.
be courageous 855 vb.
not wonder 865 vb.
— company with
accompany 89 vb.
be friendly 880 vb.
— down
suppress 165 vb.
lower 311 vb.
subjugate 745 vb.
— faith
obey 739 vb.
keep faith 768 vb.
be honourable 929 vb.
— fit
be healthy 650 vb.
be salubrious 652 vb.
— for oneself
be parsimonious 816 vb.
be selfish 932 vb.
— from
refuse 760 vb.
— going
go on 146 vb.
be in motion 265 vb.
persevere 600 vb.
— holy
celebrate 876 vb.
sanctify 979 vb.
ritualize 988 vb.
— in
surround 230 vb.
imprison 747 vb.
retain 778 vb.
— in hand
store 632 vb.
not use 674 vb.
— in mind
be mindful 455 vb.
remember 505 vb.
— in sight
scan 438 vb.
be mindful 455 vb.
— in step
conform 83 vb.
synchronize 123 vb.
— in the background
keep secret 525 vb.
be cautious 858 vb.
be modest 874 vb.
— in the dark
not know 491 vb.
keep secret 525 vb.
— in touch
correspond 588 vb.
visit 882 vb.
— in with
be friendly 880 vb.
be sociable 882 vb.
— it dark
keep secret 525 vb.
— it up
sustain 146 vb.
— mum
keep secret 525 vb.
be mute 578 vb.
— nothing back
be truthful 540 vb.
— off
be distant 199 vb.
screen 421 vb.
avoid 620 vb.
parry 713 vb.
— on
recur 139 vb.
stay 144 vb.
sustain 146 vb.
progress 285 vb.
persevere 600 vb.
— one guessing
puzzle 474 vb.
cause doubt 486 vb.
be unintelligible 517 vb.
— one's cool
restrain 747 vb.
keep calm 823 vb.
— one's counsel
keep secret 525 vb.
be taciturn 582 vb.

— one's distance
be distant 199 vb.
avoid 620 vb.
show respect 920 vb.
— one's ears open
hear 415 vb.
be informed 524 vb.
— oneself to oneself
be fastidious 862 vb.
be unsociable 883 vb.
— one's eyes peeled
invigilate 457 vb.
scan 438 vb.
— one's fingers crossed
be credulous 487 vb.
deprecate 762 vb.
hope 852 vb.
— one's hair on
restrain 747 vb.
keep calm 823 vb.
— one's hand in
habituate 610 vb.
— one's head
be courageous 855 vb.
not wonder 865 vb.
— one's mouth shut
keep secret 525 vb.
be taciturn 582 vb.
— one's own company
be unsociable 883 vb.
— one's pecker up
be cheerful 833 vb.
— one's place
be in order 60 vb.
— one's powder dry
prepare oneself 669 vb.
— one's promise
keep faith 768 vb.
be honourable 929 vb.
— one's spirits up
be cheerful 833 vb.
hope 852 vb.
— open house
be liberal 813 vb.
be hospitable 882 vb.
— order
order 60 vb.
safeguard 660 vb.
manage 689 vb.
rule 733 vb.
restrain 747 vb.
— out
exclude 57 vb.
screen 421 vb.
obstruct 702 vb.
restrain 747 vb.
refuse 760 vb.
be unsociable 883 vb.
— out of the way
be absent 190 vb.
avoid 620 vb.
— pace with
be equal 28 vb.
concur 181 vb.
— posted
communicate 524 vb.
— quiet
be quiescent 266 vb.
not act 677 vb.
— something back
dissemble 541 vb.
— tabs on
look after 457 vb.
mark 547 vb.
— the ball rolling
sustain 146 vb.
persevere 600 vb.
— the wolf from the door
vitalize 360 vb.
acquire 771 vb.
afford 800 vb.
— time (with)
accompany 89 vb.
time 117 vb.
synchronize 123 vb.
— together
accord 24 vb.
— to oneself
retain 778 vb.
— track of
be mindful 455 vb.
— under
subjugate 745 vb.
restrain 747 vb.
— under wraps
keep secret 525 vb.
— up
stay 144 vb.
sustain 146 vb.
celebrate 876 vb.
— up appearances
be in fashion 848 vb.
— up with
be equal 28 vb.
be friendly 880 vb.
be sociable 882 vb.
— up with the Joneses
conform 83 vb.
afford 800 vb.
be in fashion 848 vb.
— watch
scan 438 vb.
invigilate 457 vb.
— well
be healthy 650 vb.
keeper
concomitant 89 n.
doorkeeper 264 n.
animal husbandry 369 n.
surveillance 457 n.
collector 492 n.
protector 660 n.
manager 690 n.
defender 713 n.
servant 742 n.
keeper 749 n.
consignee 754 n.
keepsake
reminder 505 n.
gift 781 n.
kef
drug 658 n.
drug-taking 949 n.
keg
vat 194 n.
kelp
plant 366 n.
kelpie
demon 970 n.
mythical being 970 n.
kelvin
thermometry 379 n.
ken
view 438 n.
knowledge 490 n.
kennel
stable 192 n.
imprison 747 vb.
lockup 748 n.
kennel maid
herdsman 369 n.
kenosis
humility 872 n.
kepi
headgear 228 n.
kept
preserved 666 adj.
retained 778 adj.
kept in the dark
uninstructed 491 adj.
kept out
rejected 607 adj.
kept quiet
occult 523 adj.
kept ready
impending 155 adj.
kept woman
loved one 887 n.
kept woman 952 n.
kerb
edge 234 n.
road 624 n.
kerb-crawler
libertine 952 n.
kerb market
market 796 n.
kerchief
headgear 228 n.
kerf
notch 260 n.
kerfuffle
commotion 318 n.
kermes
red pigment 431 n.
kermess, kermis
festivity 837 n.
kern
soldier 722 n.
kernel
essential part 5 n.
middle 70 n.
focus 76 n.
centre 225 n.
chief thing 638 n.
kerosene
oil 357 n.
fuel 385 n.
kestrel
bird 365 n.
ketch
sailing ship 275 n.
ketchup
sauce 389 n.
kettle
cauldron 194 n.
heater 383 n.
key
degree 27 n.
crucial 137 adj.
reason why 156 n.
influential 178 adj.
opener 263 n.
stopper 264 n.
island 349 n.
key 410 n.
answer 460 n.
discovery 484 n.
interpretation 520 n.
translation 520 n.
indication 547 n.
instrument 628 n.
important 638 adj.
safeguard 662 n.
keyboard
data processing 86 n.
musical note 410 n.
piano 414 n.
keyed up
expectant 507 adj.
prepared 669 adj.
excited 821 adj.
keyhole
circle 250 n.
orifice 263 n.
key man/woman
bigwig 638 n.
manager 690 n.
expert 696 n.
key moment
crisis 137 n.
keynote
prototype 23 n.
rule 81 n.
musical note 410 n.
chief thing 638 n.
key of the door
adultness 134 n.
keypunch
data processing 86 n.
keys
badge of rule 743 n.
keystone
summit 213 n.
prop 218 n.
keyword
answer 460 n.
KGB
secret service 459 n.
khaki
textile 222 n.

uniform 228 n.
brown 430 adj.
khan
inn 192 n.
sovereign 741 n.
person of rank 868 n.
khedive
governor 741 n.
kibble
vessel 194 n.
pulverize 332 vb.
kibbutz
farm 370 n.
joint possession 775 n.
kibbutznik
participator 775 n.
kibe
ulcer 651 n.
kibitzer
meddler 678 n.
kick
vigorousness 174 n.
be violent 176 vb.
kick 279 vb.
recoil 280 n.
propulsion 287 n.
propel 287 vb.
leap 312 n.
be agitated 318 vb.
pungency 388 n.
hint 524 n.
gesture 547 n.
oppose 704 vb.
strike at 712 vb.
resist 715 vb.
disobey 738 vb.
refuse 760 vb.
deprecate 762 vb.
feeling 818 n.
joy 824 n.
— off
begin 68 vb.
— oneself
suffer 825 vb.
regret 830 vb.
— one's heels
be inactive 679 vb.
— out
eject 300 vb.
reject 607 vb.
not retain 779 vb.
— over the traces
disobey 738 vb.
achieve liberty 746 vb.
— the habit
disaccustom 611 vb.
— up a shindy
be loud 400 vb.
be active 678 vb.
bicker 709 vb.
revolt 738 vb.
kickback
reward 962 n.
kicked around
subjected 745 adj.
kicking
violent 176 adj.
unwilling 598 adj.
kicks
excitation 821 n.
kick upstairs
improvement 654 n.
kid
child 132 n.
young creature 132 n.
skin 226 n.
befool 542 vb.
— oneself
be credulous 487 vb.
kid gloves
cleanness 648 n.
conduct 688 n.
leniency 736 n.
kidnap
take away 786 vb.
steal 788 vb.
kidnapper
taker 786 n.
thief 789 n.
kidney
sort 77 n.
meat 301 n.
kidney donor
good giver 813 n.
kidney failure
digestive disorders 651 n.
kidney machine
hospital 658 n.
kidneys
insides 224 n.
kid's stuff
easy thing 701 n.
kilderkin
vat 194 n.
Kilkenny cats
quarreller 709 n.
kill
destroy 165 vb.
kill 362 vb.
hinder 702 vb.
victory 727 n.
prohibit 757 vb.
execute 963 vb.
— oneself
kill oneself 362 vb.
— the fatted calf
celebrate 876 vb.
be hospitable 882 vb.
forgive 909 vb.
— the goose that lays the golden eggs
act foolishly 695 vb.
be prodigal 815 vb.
— the pain
relieve 831 vb.
— time
pass time 108 vb.
be inactive 679 vb.
amuse oneself 837 vb.
— with kindness
impair 655 vb.
sate 863 vb.
pet 889 vb.
killer
killer 362 n.
hunter 619 n.
combatant 722 n.
ruffian 904 n.
killick
safeguard 662 n.
killing
deadly 362 adj.
laborious 682 adj.
killjoy
dissuasion 613 n.
hinderer 702 n.
moper 834 n.
bore 838 n.
kiln
furnace 383 n.
kilo, kilogram
weighing 322 n.
kilometre
long measure 203 n.
kiloton
weighing 322 n.
kilowatt
electronics 160 n.
kilt
shorten 204 vb.
skirt 228 n.
fold 261 vb.
kimono
robe 228 n.
kin
kinsman 11 n.
breed 77 n.
kind
sort 77 n.
form 243 n.
beneficial 644 adj.
aiding 703 adj.
amiable 884 adj.
benevolent 897 adj.
disinterested 931 adj.
kindergarten
nonage 130 n.
school 539 n.
kind-hearted
benevolent 897 adj.
kindle
group 74 n.
cause 156 vb.
invigorate 174 vb.
make violent 176 vb.
be hot 379 vb.
kindle 381 vb.
make bright 417 vb.
incite 612 vb.
feel 818 vb.
excite 821 vb.
be excitable 822 vb.
get angry 891 vb.
kindling
fuel 385 n.
kindly
affectionately 887 adv.
benevolent 897 adj.
kindness
leniency 736 n.
friendliness 880 n.
courtesy 884 n.
love 887 n.
benevolence 897 n.
kind act 897 n.
disinterestedness 931 n.
kindred
relative 9 adj.
consanguinity 11 n.
kinsman 11 n.
kindred spirit
close friend 880 n.
kind regards
courteous act 884 n.
respects 920 n.
kind word
approbation 923 n.
kinematics
motion 265 n.
kinesics
gesture 547 n.
kinetic
dynamic 160 adj.
moving 265 adj.
kinetic art
sculpture 554 n.
kinetic energy
energy 160 n.
kinetics
motion 265 n.
king
sovereign 741 n.
aristocrat 868 n.
kingdom
territory 184 n.
political organization 733 n.
kingdom come
future state 124 n.
heaven 971 n.
Kingdom of God
theocracy 965 n.
heaven 971 n.
kingfisher
bird 365 n.
King Kong
giant 195 n.
monster 938 n.
King Log
laxity 734 n.
kingly
ruling 733 adj.
impressive 821 adj.
worshipful 866 adj.
noble 868 adj.
proud 871 adj.
kingly crown
authority 733 n.
regalia 743 n.
king-maker
director 690 n.
kingpin
fastening 47 n.
bigwig 638 n.
manager 690 n.

king post
pillar 218 n.
kingship
government 733 n.
position of authority 733 n.
king size
large 195 adj.
King's/Queen's messenger
bearer 273 n.
king's ransom
wealth 800 n.
King Stork
tyrant 735 n.
King Willow
ball game 837 n.
kink
complexity 61 n.
coil 251 n.
eccentricity 503 n.
whim 604 n.
defect 647 n.
kinky
abnormal 84 adj.
undulatory 251 adj.
kinsfolk
kinsman 11 n.
kinship
relation 9 n.
consanguinity 11 n.
similarity 18 n.
parentage 169 n.
kinship group
social group 371 n.
kinsman, kinswoman
kinsman 11 n.
kiosk
pavilion 192 n.
small house 192 n.
shop 796 n.
kip
inn 192 n.
sleep 679 n.
kipper
dry 342 vb.
season 388 vb.
preserve 666 vb.
kippers
fish food 301 n.
kirk
church 990 n.
kirk session
synod 985 n.
kirkyard
church exterior 990 n.
kirtle
skirt 228 n.
kismet
fate 596 n.
kiss
be contiguous 202 vb.
touch 378 vb.
courteous act 884 n.
endearment 889 n.
caress 889 vb.
— goodbye to
fail 728 vb.
lose 772 vb.
— hands
stoop 311 vb.
pay one's respects 884 vb.
— the rod
knuckle under 721 vb.
be servile 879 vb.
kissable
personable 841 adj.
lovable 887 adj.
kiss curl
hair 259 n.
kisser
face 237 n.
kissing cousin
kinsman 11 n.
kiss of life
revival 656 n.
kiss of peace
ritual act 988 n.
kit
accumulation 74 n.
sort 77 n.
clothing 228 n.
equipment 630 n.
kitbag
bag 194 n.
kitchen
chamber 194 n.
cookery 301 n.
heater 383 n.
workshop 687 n.
kitchen cabinet
council 692 n.
party 708 n.
kitchen garden
farm 370 n.
garden 370 n.
kitchen maid
domestic 742 n.
kitchen sink
descriptive 590 adj.
sink 649 n.
kite
airship 276 n.
bird 365 n.
noxious animal 904 n.
kite-flying
empiricism 461 n.
publication 528 n.
rumour 529 n.
kith and kin
kinsman 11 n.
kit out
provide 633 vb.
make ready 669 vb.
kitsch
art 551 n.
bad taste 847 n.
kitten
young creature 132 n.
weakling 163 n.
cat 365 n.
kittenish
infantine 132 adj.
merry 833 adj.
amused 837 adj.
kittle cattle
difficulty 700 n.
kitty
store 632 n.
association 706 n.
joint possession 775 n.
Kiwi
foreigner 59 n.
klaxon
megaphone 400 n.
danger signal 665 n.
kleptomania
mania 503 n.
thievishness 788 n.
kleptomaniac
madman 504 n.
thief 789 n.
knack
habit 610 n.
contrivance 623 n.
aptitude 694 n.
knacker
killer 362 n.
knackered
fatigued 684 adj.
knap
break 46 vb.
high land 209 n.
knapsack
bag 194 n.
knave
low fellow 869 n.
ruffian 904 n.
knave 938 n.
knavish
cunning 698 adj.
rascally 930 adj.
vicious 934 adj.
knead
mix 43 vb.
form 243 vb.
soften 327 vb.
pulverize 332 vb.
rub 333 vb.
knee
joint 45 n.
angularity 247 n.
leg 267 n.
kick 279 vb.
kneecap
leg 267 n.
torture 963 vb.
knee-high
infantine 132 adj.
dwarfish 196 adj.
knee-jerk
spontaneous 609 adj.
knee-jerk response
absence of thought 450 n.
kneel
stoop 311 vb.
knuckle under 721 vb.
be servile 879 vb.
pay one's respects 884 vb.
show respect 920 vb.
be pious 979 vb.
perform ritual 988 vb.
— to
entreat 761 vb.
worship 981 vb.
kneeler
cushion 218 n.
church utensil 990 n.
knees
seat 218 n.
knees-up
revel 837 n.
knell
ruin 165 n.
death 361 n.
obsequies 364 n.
play music 413 vb.
signal 547 n.
warning 664 n.
raise the alarm 665 vb.
lament 836 n.
Knesset
parliament 692 n.
knickerbockers
trousers 228 n.
knickers
underwear 228 n.
knick-knack, nicknack
bauble 639 n.
plaything 837 n.
finery 844 n.
knife
cut 46 vb.
sharp edge 256 n.
kill 362 vb.
sidearms 723 n.
knife-edge
narrowness 206 n.
knife-grinder
sharpener 256 n.
mender 656 n.
artisan 686 n.
knight
rider 268 n.
cavalry 722 n.
combatant 722 n.
brave person 855 n.
person of repute 866 n.
dignify 866 vb.
person of rank 868 n.
philanthropist 901 n.
knight errant
rider 268 n.
crank 504 n.
visionary 513 n.
defender 713 n.
combatant 722 n.
brave person 855 n.
philanthropist 901 n.

knight-errantry
ideality 513 n.
rashness 857 n.
philanthropy 901 n.
knighthood
prowess 855 n.
honours 866 n.
title 870 n.
knight in shining armour
paragon 646 n.
knightly
warlike 718 adj.
courageous 855 adj.
noble 868 adj.
courteous 884 adj.
honourable 929 adj.
disinterested 931 adj.
knight of the road
wanderer 268 n.
robber 789 n.
seller 793 n.
knight's move
deviation 282 n.
Knights Templars
monk 986 n.
knit
tie 45 vb.
compose 56 vb.
weave 222 vb.
close 264 vb.
— together
cure 656 vb.
knit-in
assembly 74 n.
knitting
network 222 n.
formation 243 n.
needlework 844 n.
knob
hanger 217 n.
handle 218 n.
sphere 252 n.
swelling 253 n.
knobbly
rough 259 adj.
knobkerrie
club 723 n.
knock
knock 279 n.
propulsion 287 n.
touch 378 n.
bang 402 n.
gesture 547 n.
evil 616 n.
detract 926 vb.
— about
travel 267 vb.
misuse 675 vb.
— down
demolish 165 vb.
flatten 216 vb.
fell 311 vb.
— down to
sell 793 vb.
— for six
strike 279 vb.
defeat 727 vb.
— heads together
collide 279 vb.
— into
meet 295 vb.
insert 303 vb.
— into a cocked hat
be superior 34 vb.
— into shape
form 243 vb.
— into the head
educate 534 vb.
— it back
drink 301 vb.
— off
subtract 39 vb.
cease 145 vb.
take 786 vb.
steal 788 vb.
debauch 951 vb.
— one down with a feather
surprise 508 vb.
— one's head against a brick wall
act foolishly 695 vb.
— out
render insensible 375 vb.
defeat 727 vb.
— out of shape
deform 244 vb.
distort 246 vb.
— over
demolish 165 vb.
— spots off
defeat 727 vb.
— the bottom out of
confute 479 vb.
— together
collide 279 vb.
— up
fatigue 684 vb.
knockabout
dramatic 594 adj.
funny 849 adj.
knockdown argument
confutation 479 n.
knockdown price
cheapness 812 n.
knocked out
defeated 728 adj.
knocked up
fatigued 684 adj.
knocker
hammer 279 n.
signal 547 n.
detractor 926 n.
knocking
loudness 400 n.
roll 403 n.
knock-kneed
crippled 163 adj.
deformed 246 adj.
blemished 845 adj.
knock-on effect
continuity 71 n.
knockout
end 69 n.
exceller 644 n.
victory 727 n.
a beauty 841 n.
knockout blow
ruin 165 n.
knockout drops
anaesthetic 375 n.
knoll
small hill 209 n.
knot
tie 45 vb.
ligature 47 n.
complexity 61 n.
crowd 74 n.
long measure 203 n.
cross 222 vb.
distort 246 vb.
loop 250 n.
swelling 253 n.
solid body 324 n.
difficulty 700 n.
party 708 n.
knots
velocity 277 n.
knotty
dense 324 adj.
moot 459 adj.
difficult 700 adj.
knotty point
question 459 n.
unintelligibility 517 n.
enigma 530 n.
know
unite with 45 vb.
cognize 447 vb.
be certain 473 vb.
believe 485 vb.
know 490 vb.
be wise 498 vb.
memorize 505 vb.
understand 516 vb.
be informed 524 vb.
be expert 694 vb.
befriend 880 vb.
— a hawk from a handsaw
discriminate 463 vb.
— a little
not know 491 vb.
— all the answers
dogmatize 473 vb.
know 490 vb.
be skilful 694 vb.
be cunning 698 vb.
— a thing or two
be wise 498 vb.
be expert 694 vb.
— a trick worth two of that
be cunning 698 vb.
— backwards
know 490 vb.
be expert 694 vb.
— by instinct
intuit 476 vb.
— for certain
believe 485 vb.
— no better
not know 491 vb.
be artless 699 vb.
vulgarize 847 vb.
— no bounds
be great 32 vb.
superabound 637 vb.
— one's own mind
will 595 vb.
be resolute 599 vb.
— one's place
conform 83 vb.
be modest 874 vb.
show respect 920 vb.
— one's stuff
discriminate 463 vb.
know 490 vb.
be expert 694 vb.
— the right people
influence 178 vb.
— what's what
discriminate 463 vb.
know 490 vb.
be wise 498 vb.
be skilful 694 vb.
— when to stop
be cautious 858 vb.
be temperate 942 vb.
knowall
doctrinaire 473 n.
intellectual 492 n.
wiseacre 500 n.
affecter 850 n.
vain person 873 n.
know-how
knowledge 490 n.
way 624 n.
means 629 n.
skill 694 n.
knowing
knowing 490 adj.
cunning 698 adj.
knowingly
knowingly 490 adv.
purposely 617 adv.
knowledge
knowledge 490 n.
wisdom 498 n.
information 524 n.
skill 694 n.
knowledgeable
instructed 490 adj.
wise 498 adj.
cunning 698 adj.
known
known 490 adj.
remembered 505 adj.
published 528 adj.
habitual 610 adj.
usual 610 adj.
renowned 866 adj.
known as
named 561 adj.
known by
marked 547 adj.
know-nothing
ignoramus 493 n.
knuckle
joint 45 n.
angularity 247 n.

swelling 253 n.
knuckle-duster
hammer 279 n.
club 723 n.
knucklehead
dunce 501 n.
knuckle under
knuckle under 721 vb.
knurled
rough 259 adj.
KO
ruin 165 n.
victory 727 n.
kobold
elf 970 n.
kohl
cosmetic 843 n.
koine
language 557 n.
kolkhoz
farm 370 n.
joint possession 775 n.
Komsomol
society 708 n.
kopek, kopeck
coinage 797 n.
kopje
small hill 209 n.
Koran
non-Biblical scripture 975 n.
kosher
edible 301 adj.
clean 648 adj.
ritual 988 adj.
koumiss
milk 301 n.
kowtow, kotow
obeisance 311 n.
submission 721 n.
be servile 879 vb.
courteous act 884 n.
show respect 920 vb.
kraal
dwelling 192 n.
enclosure 235 n.
kraken
rara avis 84 n.
Kremlin
position of authority 733 n.
kris
sharp edge 256 n.
sidearms 723 n.
Krishna
the Deity 965 n.
theophany 965 n.
krone
coinage 797 n.
kudos
prestige 866 n.
approbation 923 n.
Ku Klux Klan
society 708 n.
rioter 738 n.
kukri
sidearms 723 n.
kulak
farmer 370 n.
possessor 776 n.
kultur
civilization 654 n.
kung fu
wrestling 716 n.
kursaal
place of amusement 837 n.
kwashiorkor
tropical disease 651 n.
kyle
gulf 345 n.
Kyrie Eleison
prayers 981 n.

L

laager
station 187 n.
fort 713 n.
lab
classroom 539 n.
labdanum
resin 357 n.
label
class 62 vb.
label 547 n.
mark 547 vb.
labial
marginal 234 adj.
speech sound 398 n.
laboratory
crucible 147 n.
testing agent 461 n.
workshop 687 n.
laborious
persevering 600 adj.
industrious 678 adj.
laborious 682 adj.
fatiguing 684 adj.
difficult 700 adj.
labour
repeat oneself 106 vb.
obstetrics 167 n.
move slowly 278 vb.
emphasize 532 vb.
job 622 n.
make important 638 vb.
action 676 n.
assiduity 678 n.
labour 682 n.
work 682 vb.
personnel 686 n.
hard task 700 n.
bore 838 n.
— in vain
fall short 307 vb.
attempt the impossible 470 vb.
waste effort 641 vb.
act foolishly 695 vb.
fail 728 vb.
— the obvious
be intelligible 516 vb.
be superfluous 637 vb.
waste effort 641 vb.
— under
be in a state of 7 vb.
be ill 651 vb.
Labour
political party 708 n.
labour camp
compulsion 740 n.
prison camp 748 n.
labour-consuming
wasteful 634 adj.
laboured
inelegant 576 adj.
matured 669 adj.
laborious 682 adj.
labourer
producer 164 n.
worker 686 n.
labour force
personnel 686 n.
labour-intensive
businesslike 622 adj.
labourite
political party 708 n.
labour of love
voluntary work 597 n.
vocation 622 n.
undertaking 672 n.
gift 781 n.
amusement 837 n.
kind act 897 n.
disinterestedness 931 n.
labour of Sisyphus
lost labour 641 n.
labour pains
obstetrics 167 n.
contraction 198 n.
labour-saving
mechanical 630 adj.
leisurely 681 adj.
refreshing 685 adj.
tractable 701 adj.
economical 814 adj.
labours of Hercules
hard task 700 n.
labyrinth
complexity 61 n.
meandering 251 n.
enigma 530 n.
labyrinthine
complex 61 adj.
labyrinthine 251 adj.
difficult 700 adj.
lac
resin 357 n.
lace
mix 43 vb.
tie 45 vb.
network 222 n.
textile 222 n.
needlework 844 n.
lacerate
rend 46 vb.
give pain 377 vb.vb.
wound 655 vb.
lace-ups
footwear 228 n.
laches
negligence 458 n.
nonobservance 769 n.
undutifulness 918 n.
guilty act 936 n.
lachrymose
melancholic 834 adj.
lamenting 836 adj.
lack
be inferior 35 vb.
deficit 55 n.
absence 190 n.
shortfall 307 n.
require 627 vb.
scarcity 636 n.
imperfection 647 n.
noncompletion 726 n.
be poor 801 vb.
be discontented 829 vb.
— nothing
be complete 54 vb.
— self-control
be intemperate 943 vb.
lackadaisical
inactive 679 adj.
apathetic 820 adj.
inexcitable 823 adj.
dejected 834 adj.
indifferent 860 adj.
lackey
instrument 628 n.
domestic 742 n.
toady 879 n.
lacking
absent 190 adj.
deficient 307 adj.
lost 772 adj.
not owning 774 adj.
(See **lack** *)*
lacklustre
weakly 163 adj.
dim 419 adj.
colourless 426 adj.
dejected 834 adj.
lack of appetite
eating 301 n.
lack of appreciation
ingratitude 908 n.
lack of astonishment
lack of wonder 865 n.
lack of confidence
nervousness 854 n.
lack of conversation
unsociability 883 n.
lack of conviction
feebleness 572 n.
lack of expectation
improbability 472 n.

discovery 484 n.
lack of expectation 508 n.
nonpreparation 670 n.
hopelessness 853 n.
lack of experience
ignorance 491 n.
lack of feeling
moral insensibility 820 n.
bad taste 847 n.
lack of interest
incuriosity 454 n.
inattention 456 n.
lack of expectation 508 n.
indifference 860 n.
lack of manners
discourtesy 885 n.
lack of meaning
lack of meaning 515 n.
unintelligibility 517 n.
lack of practice
desuetude 611 n.
unskilfulness 695 n.
lack of progress
inaction 677 n.
lack of self-respect
servility 879 n.
lack of taste
bad taste 847 n.
lack of wonder
moral insensibility 820 n.
indifference 860 n.
lack of wonder 865 n.
laconic
concise 569 adj.
taciturn 582 adj.
lacquer
coat 226 vb.
resin 357 n.
colour 425 vb.
hairwash 843 n.
decorate 844 vb.
lacquered
smooth 258 adj.
lacrimae rerum
suffering 825 n.
pity 905 n.
lacrosse
ball game 837 n.
lactescence
semitransparency 424 n.
whiteness 427 n.
lactose
food content 301 n.
sweet thing 392 n.
lacuna
gap 201 n.
opening 263 n.
lacustrine
lacustrine 346 adj.
lacy
flimsy 163 adj.
reticular 222 adj.
lad
youngster 132 n.
male 372 n.
ladder
series 71 n.
discontinuity 72 n.
ascent 308 n.
access 624 n.
means of escape 667 n.
laden
full 54 adj.
weighty 322 adj.
la-di-da
affected 850 adj.
Ladies
latrine 649 n.
ladies' man
lover 887 n.
lading
location 187 n.
contents 193 n.
gravity 322 n.
property 777 n.
ladle
ladle 194 n.
transpose 272 vb.
lady
lady 373 n.
master 741 n.
spouse 894 n.
ladybird
insect 365 n.
Lady Bountiful
giver 781 n.
good giver 813 n.
benefactor 903 n.
Lady chapel
church interior 990 n.
Lady Day
holy day 988 n.
Lady Godiva
benefactor 903 n.
lady-in-waiting
retainer 742 n.
ladykiller
fop 848 n.
lover 887 n.
libertine 952 n.
ladylike
female 373 adj.
well-bred 848 adj.
noble 868 adj.
courteous 884 adj.
lady-love
loved one 887 n.
lady of the house
master 741 n.
Lady of the Lake
mythical being 970 n.
Ladyship
title 870 n.
lady's maid
domestic 742 n.
laevorotatory
sinistral 242 adj.
lag
be inferior 35 vb.
be late 136 vb.
cover 226 vb.
be behind 238 vb.
move slowly 278 vb.
follow 284 vb.
fall short 307 vb.
be inactive 679 vb.
offender 904 n.
lager
alcoholic drink 301 n.
laggard
lateness 136 n.
slowcoach 278 n.
lazy 679 adj.
lagging
wrapping 226 n.
lining 227 n.
lagoon
gulf 345 n.
lake 346 n.
laic
lay person 987 n.
laical 987 adj.
laicize, laicise
laicize 987 vb.
laid
born 360 adj.
laid-back
reposeful 683 adj.
laid off
disused 674 adj
nonactive 677 adj.
laid to rest
buried 364 adj.
laid up
powerless 161 adj.
sick 651 adj.
disused 674 adj.
inactive 679 adj.
lair
dwelling 192 n.
hiding-place 527 n.
refuge 662 n.
laird
master 741 n.
owner 776 n.
aristocrat 868 n.
laisser aller, laissez aller
be lax 734 vb.
give scope 744 vb.
laisser faire, laissez faire
sustain 146 vb.
negligence 458 n.
not act 677 vb.
be lax 734 vb.
freedom 744 n.
trade 791 n.
laity
laity 987 n.
lake
great quantity 32 n.
lakh
over one hundred 99 n.
lakhs
funds 797 n.
Lakshmi
Hindu deities 967 n.
Lallans
dialect 560 n.
lallation
speech defect 580 n.
lam
strike 279 vb.
— into
dispraise 924 vb.
lama
priest 986 n.
Lamarckism
biology 358 n.
lamasery
monastery 986 n.
lamb
young creature 132 n.
reproduce itself 167 vb.
skin 226 n.
meat 301 n.
sheep 365 n.
ingenue 699 n.
darling 890 n.
innocent 935 n.
lambast, lambaste
strike 279 vb.
reprove 924 vb.
lambency
touch 378 n.
glow 417 n.
lamblike
inexcitable 823 adj.
innocent 935 adj.
lambrequin
heraldry 547 n.
lame
disable 161 vb.
crippled 163 adj.
feeble 572 adj.
make useless 641 vb.
imperfect 647 adj.
impair 655 vb.
hinder 702 vb.
lame duck
weakling 163 n.
unlucky person 731 n.
nonpayer 805 n.
lame excuse
pretext 614 n.
lamellate
layered 207 adj.
lament
cry 408 vb.
vocal music 412 n.
suffer 825 vb.
be discontented 829 vb.
regret 830 vb.
lament 836 n.vb.
pity 905 vb.

disapprove 924 vb.
be penitent 939 vb.
lamentable
bad 645 adj.
distressing 827 adj.
lamentation
obsequies 364 n.
lamentation 836 n.
lamented
dead 361 adj.
lame verse
doggerel 593 n.
lamia
demon 970 n.
sorceress 983 n.
lamina
piece 53 n.
lamina 207 n.
laminate
lamina 207 n.
laminate 207 vb.
Lammas
holy day 988 n.
lamp
lamp 420 n.
guide 520 n.
signal 547 n.
lampoon
poetize 593 vb.
satire 851 n.
calumny 926 n.
lampooner
humorist 839 n.
disapprover 924 n.
lamppost
high structure 209 n.
lamp 420 n.
lamprey
fish 365 n.
lampshade
screen 421 n.
lance
sharp point 256 n.
pierce 263 vb.
strike at 712 vb.
spear 723 n.
lance corporal
army officer 741 n.
lanceolate
tapering 256 adj.
lancer
cavalry 722 n.
soldiery 722 n.
lancers
dance 837 n.
lancet
sharp point 256 n.
perforator 263 n.
land
region 184 n.
voyage 269 vb.
fly 271 vb.
aim 281 vb.
approach 289 vb.
land 295 vb.
admit 299 vb.
land 344 n.
lands 777 n.
take 786 vb.
— one in trouble
harm 645 vb.
— on one's feet
be safe 660 vb.
landau
carriage 274 n.
landed
possessing 773 adj.
proprietary 777 adj.
landed interest
owner 776 n.
aristocracy 868 n.
landfall
arrival 295 n.
land flowing with milk and honey
abundance 171 n.
pleasurableness 826 n.
land girl
farmer 370 n.
landholder
owner 776 n.
landing
layer 207 n.
vertex 213 n.
stand 218 n.
arrival 295 n.
descent 309 n.
landing craft
warship 722 n.
landing field
air travel 271 n.
landing stage
stand 218 n.
goal 295 n.
landlady
caterer 633 n.
master 741 n.
owner 776 n.
land-line
telecommunication 531 n.
landlocked
circumscribed 232 adj.
lacustrine 346 adj.
landlord
caterer 633 n.
owner 776 n.
landlubber
mariner 270 n.
bungler 697 n.
landmark
limit 236 n.
projection 254 n.
visibility 443 n.
signpost 547 n.
important matter 638 n.
landmass
region 184 n.
landmine
bomb 723 n.
landowner
owner 776 n.
Land Rover
automobile 274 n.
lands
land 344 n.
farm 370 n.
lands 777 n.
landscape
transform 147 vb.
open space 263 n.
land 344 n.
spectacle 445 n.
art subject 553 n.
beauty 841 n.
landscape gardening
agriculture 370 n.
beautification 843 n.
ornamental art 844 n.
landslide
revolution 149 n.
ruin 165 n.
incline 220 n.
descent 309 n.
defeat 728 n.
landslip
incline 220 n.
landward
in front 237 adv.
towards 281 adv.
lane
path 624 n.
route 624 n.
language
language 557 n.
dialect 560 n.
speech 579 n.
language lab
classroom 539 n.
languid
weakly 163 adj.
inert 175 adj.
slow 278 adj.
feeble 572 adj.
inactive 679 adj.
fatigued 684 adj.
languish
be weak 163 vb.
be ill 651 vb.
be inactive 679 vb.
be fatigued 684 vb.
be dejected 834 vb.
be affected 850 vb.
desire 859 vb.
court 889 vb.
languor
weakness 163 n.
inertness 175 n.
slowness 278 n.
sluggishness 679 n.
fatigue 684 n.
lank
long 203 adj.
graceless 842 adj.
lanky
long 203 adj.
narrow 206 adj.
tall 209 adj.
lanolin
unguent 357 n.
balm 658 n.
cosmetic 843 n.
lantern
lamp 420 n.
lantern jaws
thinness 206 n.
lanyard
cable 47 n.
Laodicean
apathetic 820 adj.
indifferent 860 adj.
Lao-tzu
religious teacher 973 n.
lap
part 53 n.
period 110 n.
periodicity 141 n.
seat 218 n.
dress 228 vb.
surround 230 vb.
enclose 235 vb.
outstrip 277 vb.
drink 301 vb.
outdo 306 vb.
circuition 314 n.
moisten 341 vb.
flow 350 vb.
touch 378 vb.
sound faint 401 vb.
circuit 626 n.vb.
refuge 662 n.
pet 889 vb.
— up
absorb 299 vb.
drink 301 vb.
make appetizing 390 vb.
hear 415 vb.
laparotomy
surgery 658 n.
lap dog
dog 365 n.
toady 879 n.
lapel
garment 228 n.
fold 261 n.
trimming 844 n.
lapidary
funereal 364 adj.
engraver 556 n.
lapidate
lapidate 712 vb.
execute 963 vb.
lapis lazuli
blueness 435 n.
gem 844 n.
lap of luxury
euphoria 376 n.
sensualism 944 n.
lappet
adjunct 40 n.
hanging object 217 n.
lapse
time 108 n.
elapse 111 vb.
conversion 147 n.
deviation 282 n.
inattention 456 n.
disbelieve 486 vb.

be unpractised 611 vb.
deteriorate 655 vb.
relapse 657 n.vb.
loss 772 n.
be wicked 934 vb.
guilty act 936 n.
irreligion 974 n.
lapsed
past 125 adj.
negligent 458 adj.
unbelieving 486 adj.
nonobservant 769 adj.
lapse of memory
oblivion 506 n.
Laputan
imaginative 513 adj.
lapwing
bird 365 n.
larcenist
thief 789 n.
larceny
stealing 788 n.
larch
tree 366 n.
lard
cookery 301 n.
fat 357 n.
larder
provisions 301 n.
storage 632 n.
Lares and Penates
home 192 n.
lesser deity 967 n.
large
great 32 adj.
stalwart 162 adj.
spacious 183 adj.
large 195 adj.
large-hearted
liberal 813 adj.
benevolent 897 adj.
largely
substantially 3 adv.
greatly 32 adv.
importantly 638 adv.
large number
multitude 104 n.
larger
expanded 197 adj.
largesse
gift 781 n.
liberality 813 n.
largo
slowly 278 adv.
adagio 412 adv.
lariat
halter 47 n.
loop 250 n.
lark
climber 308 n.
bird 365 n.
vocalist 413 n.
enjoyment 824 n.
revel 837 n.
lark about/around
be absurd 497 vb.
amuse oneself 837 vb.
larrikin
ruffian 904 n.
larrup
spank 963 vb.
larva
young creature 132 n.
insect 365 n.
laryngitis
respiratory disease 651 n.
larynx
air pipe 353 n.
voice 577 n.
lasagne
dish 301 n.
lascivious
lecherous 951 adj.
laser
electronics 160 n.
weapon 723 n.
lash
tie 45 vb.
stimulant 174 n.
make violent 176 vb.
filament 208 n.
strike 279 vb.
incentive 612 n.
animate 821 vb.
reprobate 924 vb.
flog 963 vb.
scourge 964 n.
— out
be violent 176 vb.
be angry 891 vb.
— out at
strike at 712 vb.
lashes
eye 438 n.
lashings
great quantity 32 n.
plenty 635 n.
lass
youngster 132 n.
woman 373 n.
Lassar fever
tropical disease 651 n.
lassitude
sleepiness 679 n.
fatigue 684 n.
lasso
halter 47 n.
loop 250 n.
last
mould 23 n.
ending 69 adj.
continue 108 vb.
last 113 vb.
foregoing 125 adj.
stay 144 vb.
completive 725 adj.
last arrival
lateness 136 n.
last breath
end 69 n.
decease 361 n.
last ditcher
stamina 600 n.
obstinate person 602 n.
opponent 705 n.
malcontent 829 n.
last gasp
end 69 n.
decease 361 n.
lasting
lasting 113 adj.
perpetual 115 adj.
permanent 144 adj.
unchangeable 153 adj.
unyielding 162 adj.
last lap
end 69 n.
arrival 295 n.
last minute
lateness 136 n.
crisis 137 n.
hasty 680 adj.
last place
sequence 65 n.
rear 238 n.
following 284 n.
last post
evening 129 n.
valediction 296 n.
obsequies 364 n.
call 547 n.
last resort
necessity 596 n.
means 629 n.
refuge 662 n.
last rites
obsequies 364 n.
Christian rite 988 n.
last straw
causal means 156 n.
encumbrance 702 n.
completion 725 n.
annoyance 827 n.
resentment 891 n.
last things
finality 69 n.
last throw
gambling 618 n.
means 629 n.
attempt 671 n.
hope 852 n.
rashness 857 n.
last word
answer 460 n.
certainty 473 n.
last word in
modernism 126 n.
exceller 644 n.
fashion 848 n.
last words
sequel 67 n.
end 69 n.
valediction 296 n.
latch
join 45 vb.
fastening 47 n.
late
anachronistic 118 adj.
former 125 adj.
modern 126 adj.
vespertine 129 adj.
late 136 adj.adv.
ill-timed 138 adj.
slow 278 adj.
dead 361 adj.
negligent 458 adj.
immature 670 adj.
unprepared 670 adj.
latecomer
successor 67 n.
posteriority 120 n.
lateness 136 n.
late developer
learner 538 n.
undevelopment 670 n.
lately
formerly 125 adv.
newly 126 adv.
latency
influence 178 n.
connotation 514 n.
latency 523 n.
intention 617 n.
(See **latent** *)*
lateness
evening 129 n.
lateness 136 n.
latent
inert 175 adj.
invisible 444 adj.
latent 523 adj.
concealed 525 adj.
deceiving 542 adj.
unclear 568 adj.
later
after 65 adv.
subsequent 120 adj.
not now 122 adv.
future 124 adj.
behind 284 adv.
lateral
lateral 239 adj.
lateral thinking
meditation 449 n.
reasoning 475 n.
latest
present 121 adj.
latest, the
modernism 126 n.
fashion 848 n.
latex
fluid 335 n.
materials 631 n.
lath
lamina 207 n.
strip 208 n.
materials 631 n.
lathe
rotator 315 n.
lather
excrement 302 n.
lubricant 334 n.
bubble 355 n.

clean 648 vb.
spank 963 vb.
lathi
club 723 n.
Latin
language 557 n.
latitude
range 183 n.
region 184 n.
breadth 205 n.
scope 744 n.
latitude and longitude
bearings 186 n.
coordinate 465 n.
latitudinarian
wise 498 adj.
free 744 adj.
latitudinarianism
heterodoxy 977 n.
latria
cult 981 n.
latrine
latrine 649 n.
latten
lamina 207 n.
latter
sequential 65 adj.
foregoing 125 adj.
latter-day
present 121 adj.
modern 126 adj.
Latter-day Saints
sect 978 n.
lattice
space 201 vb.
network 222 n.
window 263 n.
laud
honours 866 n.
praise 923 n.vb.
laudable
approvable 923 adj.
laudanum
moderator 177 n.
anaesthetic 375 n.
laudatory
approving 923 adj.
laugh
be pleased 824 vb.
be cheerful 833 vb.
laughter 835 n.
laugh 835 vb.
wit 839 n.
ridicule 851 n.
— at
reject 607 vb.
ridicule 851 vb.
not respect 921 vb.
hold cheap 922 vb.
— in one's face
defy 711 vb.
— in one's sleeve
lurk 523 vb.
ridicule 851 vb.
— off
not think 450 vb.
disregard 458 vb.
— on the wrong side of one's face
be disappointed 509 vb.
be dejected 834 vb.
lose repute 867 vb.
— to scorn
defy 711 vb.
despise 922 vb.
laughable
absurd 497 adj.
foolish 499 adj.
amusing 837 adj.
ridiculous 849 adj.
laughing gas
gas 336 n.
anaesthetic 375 n.
laughingstock
misfit 25 n.
nonconformist 84 n.
fool 501 n.
crank 504 n.
dupe 544 n.
laughingstock 851 n.
laughter
merriment 833 n.
laughter 835 n.
festivity 837 n.
ridicule 851 n.
laughter-loving
merry 833 adj.
launch
initiate 68 vb.
cause 156 vb.
navigate 269 vb.
ship 275 n.
propel 287 vb.
celebrate 876 vb.
— into
undertake 672 vb.
— out
be loquacious 581 vb.
— out at
attack 712 vb.
launching
debut 68 n.
fitting out 669 n.
launching pad
space travel 271 n.
gun 723 n.
launder
smooth 258 vb.
clean 648 vb.
launderette
ablutions 648 n.
laundress
cleaner 648 n.
laundry
ablutions 648 n.
workshop 687 n.
laurel
tree 366 n.
laurels
badge 547 n.
trophy 729 n.
honours 866 n.
lava
rock 344 n.
ash 381 n.
lavatory
chamber 194 n.
latrine 649 n.
lave
drench 341 vb.
purify 648 vb.
lavender
scent 396 n.
purple 436 adj.
preserver 666 n.
lavender water
scent 396 n.
cosmetic 843 n.
laver
vegetable 301 n.
ritual object 988 n.
lavish
many 104 adj.
plenteous 635 adj.
superabound 637 vb.
give 781 vb.
liberal 813 adj.
prodigal 815 adj.
law
rule 81 n.n.
necessity 596 n.
habit 610 n.
vocation 622 n.
precept 693 n.
decree 737 n.
compulsion 740 n.
restraint 747 n.
permit 756 n.
law 953 n.
punisher 963 n.
law-abiding
peaceful 717 adj.
submitting 721 adj.
obedient 739 adj.
honourable 929 adj.
legal 953 adj.
law and order
peace 717 n.
Law and the Prophets, the
scripture 975 n.
law-breaker
offender 904 n.
law-breaking
riotous 738 adj.
nonobservant 769 adj.
improbity 930 n.
wickedness 934 n.
lawbreaking 954 n. adj.
lawcourt
lawcourt 956 n.
legal trial 959 n.
lawful
due 915 adj.
legal 953 adj.
law-giving
legislation 953 n.
lawless
disorderly 61 adj.
unconformable 84 adj.
anarchic 734 adj.
riotous 738 adj.
rascally 930 adj.
lawless 954 adj.
lawn
textile 222 n.
smoothness 258 n.
grassland 348 n.
garden 370 n.
law officer
law officer 955 n.
law of nature
rule 81 n.
necessity 596 n.
compulsion 740 n.
law of the Medes and Persians
rule 81 n.
fixture 153 n.
precept 693 n.
laws
political organization 733 n.
law student
jurist 958 n.
lawsuit
law 953 n.
litigation 959 n.
law unto oneself, a
unconformable 84 adj.
law unto oneself, be a
please oneself 734 vb.
disobey 738 vb.
lawyer
lawyer 958 n.
lax
nonadhesive 49 adj.
weak 163 adj.
inert 175 adj.
negligent 458 adj.
feeble 572 adj.
irresolute 601 adj.
lax 734 adj.
lenient 736 adj.
nonobservant 769 adj.
indifferent 860 adj.
frail 934 adj.
laxative
excretory 302 adj.
purgative 658 n.
laxity
softness 327 n.
negligence 458 n.
inexactness 495 n.
laxity 734 n.
scope 744 n.
(See **lax** *)*
lay
reproduce itself 167 vb.
place 187 vb.
laminate 207 vb.
cover 226 vb.
emit 300 vb.
vocal music 412 n.

ignorant 491 adj.
poem 593 n.
gamble 618 vb.
unskilled 695 adj.
debauch 951 vb.
laical 987 adj.
— about one
strike at 712 vb.
— aside
exclude 57 vb.
be neglectful 458 Vb. vb.
reject 607 vb.
stop using 674 vb.
— at one's door
attribute 158 vb.
accuse 928 vb.
— bare
manifest 522 vb.
disclose 526 vb.
— by
store 632 vb.
— by the heels
defeat 727 vb.
arrest 747 vb.
take 786 vb.
— down
place 187 vb.
flatten 216 vb.
let fall 311 vb.
premise 475 vb.
suppose 512 vb.
command 737 vb.
— down the law
dogmatize 473 vb.
affirm 532 vb.
rule 733 vb.
decree 737 vb.
— ghosts
practise sorcery 983 vb.
— heads together
cooperate 706 vb.
— in
store 632 vb.
— into
eat 301 vb.
dispraise 924 vb.
— it on thick
exaggerate 546 vb.
superabound 637 vb.
flatter 925 vb.
— low
fell 311 vb.
strike at 712 vb.
— off
dismiss 300 vb.
stop using 674 vb.
make inactive 679 vb.
not retain 779 vb.
— oneself open to
be liable 180 vb.
face danger 661 vb.
— one's hands on
acquire 771 vb.
— open
uncover 229 vb.
open 263 vb.
disclose 526 vb.
— out
arrange 62 vb.
flatten 216 vb.
inter 364 vb.
plan 623 vb.
expend 806 vb.
— the foundations
auspicate 68 vb.
cause 156 vb.
prepare 669 vb.
— to
bring to rest 266 vb.
navigate 269 vb.
— to rest
inter 364 vb.
— up
store 632 vb.
stop using 674 vb.
make inactive 679 vb.
— upon
command 737 vb.
— waste
lay waste 165 vb.
make sterile 172 vb.
layabout
idler 679 n.
lay brother
monk 986 n.
lay person 987 n.
lay-by
station 187 n.
traffic control 305 n.
layer
series 71 n.
compartment 194 n.
layer 207 n.
horizontality 216 n.
covering 226 n.
cultivate 370 vb.
layering
stratification 207 n.
layette
clothing 228 n.
lay figure
mould 23 n.
image 551 n.
laying on of hands
medical art 658 n.
Christian rite 988 n.
layman, laywoman
ignorance 491 n.
lay person 987 n.
layout
arrangement 62 n.
edition 589 n.
lay people
laity 987 n.
lay preacher
preacher 537 n.
church officer 986 n.
pastor 986 n.
lay reader
church officer 986 n.
lay sister
nun 986 n.
lay person 987 n.
lazaret
hospital 658 n.
Lazarus
poor person 801 n.
laze
be inactive 679 vb.
repose 683 vb.
laziness
unwillingness 598 n.
undutifulness 918 n.
lazy
slow 278 adj.
negligent 458 adj.
profitless 641 adj.
lazy 679 adj.
lazybones
idler 679 n.
L-driver
driver 268 n.
beginner 538 n.
lea
shore 344 n.
grassland 348 n.
leach
liquefy 337 vb.
drench 341 vb.
purify 648 vb.
leachy
porous 263 adj.
lead
advantage 34 n.
predominate 34 vb.
halter 47 n.
precedence 64 n.
prelude 66 n.
initiate 68 vb.
accompany 89 vb.
do before 119 vb.
electronics 160 n.
depth 211 n.
sailing aid 269 n.
precede 283 vb.
diver 313 n.
gravity 322 n.
gauge 465 n.
hint 524 n.
print-type 587 n.
actor 594 n.
motivate 612 vb.
direct 689 vb.
— astray
mislead 495 vb.
motivate 612 vb.
make wicked 934 vb.
debauch 951 vb.
— by the nose
influence 178 vb.
dominate 733 vb.
subjugate 745 vb.
— off
come before 64 vb.
initiate 68 vb.
— on
direct 689 vb.
excite love 887 vb.
— one a merry dance
mislead 495 vb.
avoid 620 vb.
circuit 626 vb.
be difficult 700 vb.
— the way
initiate 68 vb.
precede 283 vb.
— to
conduce 156 vb.
tend 179 vb.
— to the altar
excite love 887 vb.
wed 894 vb.
— up the garden path
mislead 495 vb.
deceive 542 vb.
— up to
prepare 669 vb.
leaden
weighty 322 adj.
dim 419 adj.
colourless 426 adj.
grey 429 adj.
inactive 679 adj.
tedious 838 adj.
leader
superior 34 n.
precursor 66 n.
article 591 n.
motivator 612 n.
leader 690 n.
master 741 n.
leadership
superiority 34 n.
precedence 64 n.
influence 178 n.
directorship 689 n.
authority 733 n.
prestige 866 n.
leader writer
dissertator 591 n.
leading
supreme 34 adj.
first 68 adj.
influential 178 adj.
foremost 283 adj.
important 638 adj.
directing 689 adj.
successful 727 adj.
authoritative 733 adj.
noteworthy 866 adj.
leading article
article 591 n.
leading light
sage 500 n.
bigwig 638 n.
person of repute 866 n.
leading man/lady
actor 594 n.
leading part
influence 178 n.
leading question
question 459 n.
hint 524 n.
leading strings
nonage 130 n.
teaching 534 n.
subjection 745 n.

leads
vertex 213 n.
roof 226 n.
leaf
lamina 207 n.
shelf 218 n.
foliage 366 n.
edition 589 n.
leafless
wintry 129 adj.
uncovered 229 adj.
leaflet
branch 53 n.
foliage 366 n.
the press 528 n.
leaf through
scan 438 vb.
leafy
prolific 171 adj.
vegetal 366 adj.
green 434 adj.
league
combination 50 n.
concurrence 181 n.
long measure 203 n.
association 706 n.
society 708 n.
compact 765 n.
leak
decrement 42 n.
gap 201 n.
opening 263 n.
outflow 298 n.
be wet 341 vb.
flow 350 vb.
information 524 n.
divulge 526 vb.
waste 634 vb.
defect 647 n.
escape 667 vb.
hitch 702 n.
not retain 779 vb.
— into
infiltrate 297 vb.
— out
be disclosed 526 vb.
— through
exude 298 vb.
leakage
decrease 37 n.
loss 772 n.
leaky
porous 263 adj.
imperfect 647 adj.
unsafe 661 adj.
lean
small 33 adj.
weak 163 adj.
tend 179 vb.
lean 206 adj.
be oblique 220 Vb. vb.
be biased 481 vb.
choose 605 vb.
underfed 636 adj.
— forward
stoop 311 vb.
— on
be supported 218 vb.
compel 740 vb.
be subject 745 vb.
— over backwards
compensate 31 vb.
be willing 597 vb.
leaning
unequal 29 adj.
tendency 179 n.
willingness 597 n.
choice 605 n.
habit 610 n.
liking 859 n.
injustice 914 n.
lean-to
small house 192 n.
lobby 194 n.
leap
interval 201 n.
spurt 277 n.
move fast 277 vb.
progression 285 n.
ascent 308 n.
leap 312 n.vb.
be agitated 318 vb.
flow 350 vb.
ballet 594 n.
rejoice 835 vb.
dance 837 vb.
— at
be willing 597 vb.
pursue 619 vb.
— over
overstep 306 vb.
leapfrog
leap 312 vb.
children's games 837 n.
leap in the dark
uncertainty 474 n.
gambling 618 n.
danger 661 n.
rashness 857 n.
leaps and bounds
progression 285 n.
leap year
period 110 n.
regular return 141 n.
learn
know 490 vb.
memorize 505 vb.
understand 516 vb.
be informed 524 vb.
learn 536 vb.
prepare oneself 669 vb.
— by experience
get better 654 vb.
— one's lesson
be warned 664 vb.
be penitent 939 vb.
learned
instructed 490 adj.
studious 536 adj.
literary 557 adj.
learned person
scholar 492 n.
sage 500 n.
learner
scholar 492 n.
learner 538 n.
learning
erudition 490 n.
knowledge 490 n.
learning 536 n.
preparation 669 n.
lease
estate 777 n.
transfer 780 n.
lease 784 vb.
hire 785 vb.
leasehold
proprietary 777 adj.
lease-holder
resident 191 n.
possessor 776 n.
leash
halter 47 n.
group 74 n.
least
small 33 adj.
lesser 35 adj.
least one can do
sufficiency 635 n.
dueness 915 n.
leat
conduit 351 n.
leather
skin 226 n.
strike 279 vb.
toughness 329 n.
bookbinding 589 n.
materials 631 n.
cleaning cloth 648 n.
spank 963 vb.
leathery
tough 329 adj.
unsavoury 391 adj.
leave
separate 46 vb.
cease 145 vb.
recede 290 vb.
depart 296 vb.
relinquish 621 vb.
store 632 vb.
leisure 681 n.
repose 683 n.
facility 701 n.
leniency 736 n.
permission 756 n.
bequeath 780 vb.
nonliability 919 n.
— a gap
be absent 190 vb.
not suffice 636 vb.
— alone
not act 677 vb.
— behind
be superior 34 vb.
lecve over 41 vb.
outstrip 277 vb.
progress 285 vb.
outdo 306 vb.
forget 506 vb.
— hanging
not complete 726 vb.
— hold of
relinquish 621 vb.
not retain 779 vb.
— home
come of age 134 vb.
depart 296 vb.
— it open
facilitate 701 vb.
give scope 744 vb.
— it to
commission 751 vb.
resign 753 vb.
— no option
compel 740 vb.
— no stone unturned
search 459 vb.
— nothing to be desired
perfect 646 vb.
please 826 vb.
— nothing to chance
be cautious 858 vb.
— no trace
pass away 2 vb.
disappear 446 vb.
obliterate 550 vb.
— no wiser
misteach 535 vb.
— off
cease 145 vb.
stop using 674 vb.
— one cold
be indifferent 860 vb.
— one holding the baby
befool 542 vb.
— one in the lurch
disappoint 509 vb.
deceive 542 vb.
fail in duty 918 vb.
— on one side
pass 305 vb.
— open
facilitate 701 vb.
— out
subtract 39 vb.
exclude 57 vb.
set apart 46 vb.
disregard 458 vb.
misinterpret 521 vb.
be taciturn 582 vb.
— something to be desired
be middling 732 vb.
— to their own devices
disregard 458 vb.
give scope 744 vb.
— undone
neglect 458 vb.
not complete 726 vb.
— word
communicate 524 vb.
leaven
component 58 n.
alterer 143 n.
convert 147 vb.

stimulant 174 n.
influence 178 n., vb.
enlarge 197 vb.
cookery 301 n.
lifter 310 n.
leaven 323 n.
lighten 323 vb.
qualify 468 vb.
make better 654 vb.
leave-taking
valediction 296 n.
leavings
leavings 41 n.
rubbish 641 n.
Leavisite
interpreter 520 n.
Lebensraum
room 183 n.
scope 744 n.
lech
be impure 951 vb.
lecher
libertine 952 n.
lecherous
desiring 859 adj.
lecherous 951 adj.
lectern
rostrum 539 n.
church utensil 990 n.
lection
interpretation 520 n.
lectionary
office-book 988 n.
lector
cleric 986 n.
lecture
lecture 534 n.
teach 534 vb.
oration 579 n.
allocution 583 n.
dissertation 591 n.
reprimand 924 n.
lecturer
lecture 534 n.
teacher 537 n.
speaker 579 n.
lederhosen
trousers 228 n.
ledge
horizontality 216 n.
shelf 218 n.
edge 234 n.
projection 254 n.
ledger
covering 226 n.
record 548 n.
account book 808 n.
lee
laterality 239 n.
shelter 662 n.
leech
coherence 48 n.
doctor 658 n.
bane 659 n.
taker 786 n.
toady 879 n.
leek
vegetable 301 n.
heraldry 547 n.
leer
look 438 n.
gesticulate 547 vb.
excite love 887 vb.
court 889 vb.
lees
leavings 41 n.
lee shore
pitfall 663 n.
leeward
laterality 239 n.
leeway
room 183 n.
water travel 269 n.
deviation 282 n.
shortfall 307 n.
scope 744 n.
left
remaining 41 adj.
separate 46 adj.
sinistral 242 adj.
forgotten 506 adj.
political party 708 n.
left alone
neglected 458 adj.
left behind
remaining 41 adj.
not retained 779 adj.
left-handed
sinistral 242 adj.
clumsy 695 adj.
left-handed compliment
censure 924 n.
left high and dry
hindered 702 adj.
grounded 728 adj.
left in the lurch
in difficulties 700 adj.
hindered 702 adj.
leftish
moderate 177 adj.
leftist
political party 708 n.
sectional 708 adj.
left open
moot 459 adj.
left out
absent 190 adj.
left over
remaining 41 adj.
leftovers
leavings 41 n.
dish 301 n.
left-winger
political party 708 n.
leg
limb 53 n.
part 53 n.
stand 218 n.
leg 267 n.
legacy
sequel 67 n.
effect 157 n.
thing transferred 272 n.
dower 777 n.
gift 781 n.
legal
regular 81 adj.
possible 469 adj.
preceptive 693 adj.
permitted 756 adj.
just 913 adj.
legal 953 adj.
legal adviser
adviser 691 n.
jurist 958 n.
law agent 958 n.
legal code
law 953 n.
legalist
narrow mind 481 n.
jurist 958 n.
legality
legality 953 n.
legalize, legalise
permit 756 vb.
grant claims 915 vb.
make legal 953 vb.
legal profession
vocation 622 n.
bar 958 n.
legal separation
divorce 896 n.
legal tender
money 797 n.
legate
messenger 529 n.
army officer 741 n.
envoy 754 n.
legatee
beneficiary 776 n.
recipient 782 n.
legation
commission 751 n.
envoy 754 n.
legato
adagio 412 adv.
legend
commentary 520 n.
indication 547 n.
record 548 n.
phrase 563 n.
description 590 n.
narrative 590 n.
legendary
imaginary 513 adj.
descriptive 590 adj.
renowned 866 adj.
legerdemain
sleight 542 n.
leggings
legwear 228 n.
leggy
narrow 206 adj.
legged 267 adj.
legible
intelligible 516 adj.
legion
army 722 n.
formation 722 n.
legionary
soldier 722 n.
Legion of Honour
decoration 729 n.
legislate
decree 737 vb.
rule 733 vb.
make legal 953 vb.
legislation
management 689 n.
precept 693 n.
legislation 953 n.
legislative
directing 689 adj.
legal 953 adj.
legislative assembly
parliament 692 n.
authority 733 n.
legislator
director 690 n.
councillor 692 n.
legislation 953 n.
legislature
parliament 692 n.
leg it
move fast 277 vb.
legitimacy
authority 733 n.
legality 953 n.
legitimate
genuine 494 adj.
just 913 adj.
due 915 adj.
legal 953 adj.
legitimate theatre
drama 594 n.
legitimist
auxiliary 707 n.
defender 713 n.
legitimize, legitimise
grant claims 915 vb.
make legal 953 vb.
legless
incomplete 55 adj.
crippled 163 adj.
imperfect 647 adj.
dead drunk 949 adj.
legman
news reporter 529 n.
leg-pull
trickery 542 n.
witticism 839 n.
ridicule 851 n.
legroom
room 183 n.
legs
conveyance 267 n.
leg 267 n.
leg show
stage show 594 n.
leg to stand on
support 218 n.
pretext 614 n.
leguminous
vegetal 366 adj.
leg-up
progression 285 n.
elevation 310 n.
aid 703 n.
legwork
assiduity 678 n.
labour 682 n.

leishmaniasis
tropical disease 651 n.
leisure
opportunity 137 n.
leisure 681 n.
repose 683 n.
resignation 753 n.
amusement 837 n.
leisured
inactive 679 adj.
reposeful 683 adj.
leisurely
tardily 136 adv.
tranquil 266 adj.
slow 278 adj.
inactive 679 adj.
lazy 679 adj.
leisurely 681 adj.
reposeful 683 adj.
free 744 adj.
leisure wear
clothing 228 n.
leitmotiv, leitmotif
melody 410 n.
topic 452 n.
leman
loved one 887 n.
kept woman 952 n.
lemma
argumentation 475 n.
premise 475 n.
lemmings
suicide 362 n.
lemon
fruit 301 n.
sourness 393 n.
yellowness 433 n.
loser 728 n.
lemonade
soft drink 301 n.
lend
provide 633 vb.
aid 703 vb.
assign 780 vb.
give 781 vb.
lend 784 vb.
credit 802 vb.
— a hand
aid 703 vb.
— an ear
hear 415 vb.
be mindful 455 vb.
be willing 597 vb.
— colour to
evidence 466 vb.
make likely 471 vb.
— itself to
be instrumental 628 vb.
— oneself to
cooperate 706 vb.
— one's name
patronize 703 vb.
— wings to
accelerate 277 vb.
aid 703 vb.
lender
lender 784 n.
creditor 802 n.
length
quantity 26 n.
greatness 32 n.
piece 53 n.
measure 183 n.
size 195 n.
distance 199 n.
interval 201 n.
length 203 n.
textile 222 n.
metrology 465 n.
length and breadth of, the
throughout 54 adv.
lengthen
augment 36 vb.
continue 71 vb.
spin out 113 vb.
enlarge 197 vb.
lengthen 203 vb.
be diffuse 570 vb.
length of time
period 110 n.
long duration 113 n.
lengthy
long 203 adj.
prolix 570 adj.
leniency, lenience
leniency 736 n.
lenient
moderate 177 adj.
lax 734 adj.
lenient 736 adj.
permitting 756 adj.
benevolent 897 adj.
forgiving 909 adj.
Leninism
government 733 n.
lenitive
moderator 177 n.
lenitive 177 adj.
remedial 658 adj.
pacificatory 719 adj.
relieving 831 adj.
lenity
leniency 736 n.
mercy 905 n.
lens
convexity 253 n.
transparency 422 n.
optical device 442 n.
photography 551 n.
Lent
fast 946 n.
holy day 988 n.
lenticular
convex 253 adj.
lentils
vegetable 301 n.
lento
adagio 412 adv.
Leo
zodiac 321 n.
leonine
animal 365 adj.
leopard
cat 365 n.
maculation 437 n.
leopard's spots
fixture 153 n.
leotard
suit 228 n.
leper
outcast 883 n.
lepidopterist
zoologist 367 n.
leprechaun
elf 970 n.
leprosy
skin disease 651 n.
tropical disease 651 n.
lesbian
nonconformist 84 n.
woman 373 n.
extramarital 951 adj.
lese-majesty, lèse-majesté
sedition 738 n.
lesion
ulcer 651 n.
wound 655 n.
less
less 35 adv.
lessee
resident 191 n.
possessor 776 n.
recipient 782 n.
lessen
abate 37 vb.
decrease 37 vb.
weaken 163 vb.
moderate 177 vb.
become small 198 vb.
lesser
lesser 35 adj.
lesser evil
choice 605 n.
good 615 n.
lesson
lecture 534 n.
study 536 n.
warning 664 n.
lessons
study 536 n.
lessor
lender 784 n.
let
give scope 744 vb.
permit 756 vb.
lending 784 n.
lease 784 vb.
— alone
avoid 620 vb.
not act 677 vb.
give scope 744 vb.
— bygones be bygones
forget 506 vb.
make peace 719 vb.
forgive 909 vb.
— down
lower 311 vb.
befool 542 vb.
— fall
let fall 311 vb.
hint 524 vb.
divulge 526 vb.
— fly
be violent 176 vb.
strike 279 vb.
attack 712 vb.
fire at 712 vb.
get angry 891 vb.
— go
let fall 311 vb.
relinquish 621 vb.
liberate 746 vb.
not retain 779 vb.
be indifferent 860 vb.
acquit 960 vb.
— go by
not act 677 vb.
— in
introduce 231 vb.
admit 299 vb.
— in for
befool 542 vb.
— it rip
accelerate 277 vb.
not act 677 vb.
— loose
liberate 746 vb.
— off
be violent 176 vb.
shoot 287 vb.
acquit 960 vb.
— off steam
revel 837 vb.
get angry 891 vb.
— on
divulge 526 vb.
— one down
disappoint 509 vb.
fail 728 vb.
fail in duty 918 vb.
— one down gently
show mercy 905 vb.
— one have it
strike 279 vb.
attack 712 vb.
— one know
inform 524 vb.
— one off
deliver 668 vb.
forgive 909 vb.
— oneself go
deteriorate 655 vb.
please oneself 734 vb.
be free 744 vb.
be excitable 822 vb.
revel 837 vb.
— oneself in for
undertake 672 vb.
be in difficulty 700 vb.
— one's hair down
revel 837 vb.

let out
enlarge 197 vb.
lengthen 203 vb.
emit 300 vb.
divulge 526 vb.
liberate 746 vb.
not retain 779 vb.
lease 784 vb.
— pass
disregard 458 vb.
not act 677 vb.
— sleeping dogs lie
not act 677 vb.
— slip
be inattentive 456 vb.
lose 772 vb.
not retain 779 vb.
— slip through one's fingers
lose a chance 138 vb.
let fall 311 vb.
— the cat out of the bag
disclose 526 vb.
divulge 526 vb.
— the grass grow under one's feet
be neglectful 458 vb.
be inactive 679 vb.
— the moment pass
be late 136 vb.
lose a chance 138 vb.
— the side down
apostatize 603 vb.
— things go
be neglectful 458 vb.
be inactive 679 vb.
— up
cease 145 vb.
decelerate 278 vb.
repose 683 vb.
— well alone
not act 677 vb.
be cautious 858 vb.
let alone
in addition 38 adv.
exclusive of 57 adv.
letdown
disappointment 509 n.
disappointed 509 adj.
humiliation 872 n.
humbled 872 adj.
lethal
deadly 362 adj.
toxic 653 adj.
lethargic
inactive 679 adj.
lethargy
sluggishness 679 n.
fatigue 684 n.
moral insensibility 820 n.
Lethe
oblivion 506 n.
mythic hell 972 n.
let off
forgiven 909 adj.
acquittal 960 n.
let-out
pretext 614 n.
means of escape 667 n.
letter
mark 547 vb.
letter 558 n.
script 586 n.
print-type 587 n.
correspondence 588 n.
letterbox
postal communications 531 n.
lettered
instructed 490 adj.
literary 557 adj.
literal 558 adj.
lettering
lettering 586 n.
ornamental art 844 n.
letter of credit
paper money 797 n.
credit 802 n.
letter of the law
accuracy 494 n.
severity 735 n.
pitilessness 906 n.
legality 953 n.
letterpress
letterpress 587 n.
reading matter 589 n.
letters
culture 490 n.
erudition 490 n.
literature 557 n.
correspondence 588 n.
letters a foot high
publicity 528 n.
letters of marque
brigandage 788 n.
letters patent
warrant 737 n.
permit 756 n.
letter writer
calligrapher 586 n.
correspondent 588 n.
lettre de cachet
detention 747 n.
lettuce
vegetable 301 n.
letup
lull 145 n.
repose 683 n.
leucorrhoea
haemorrhage 302 n.
leukaemia, leukemia
blood disease 651 n.
Levant
laterality 239 n.
levee
earthwork 253 n.
social gathering 882 n.
level
uniform 16 adj.
degree 27 n.
equality 28 n.
serial place 73 n.
synchronous 123 adj.
demolish 165 vb.
near 200 adj.
layer 207 n.
flat 216 adj.
angular measure 247 n.
smooth 258 adj.vb.
fell 311 vb.
fire at 712 vb.
inexcitable 823 adj.
— at
aim 281 vb.
aim at 617 vb.
— off
decrease 37 vb.
— out
be horizontal 216 vb.
— up or down
make uniform 16 vb.
level crossing
crossing 222 n.
railway 624 n.
level-headed
wise 498 adj.
inexcitable 823 adj.
cautious 858 adj.
leveller
uniformist 16 n.
destroyer 168 n.
Leveller
agitator 738 n.
level-pegging
draw 28 n.
levels
lowness 210 n.
plain 348 n.
lever
opportunity 137 n.
causal means 156 n.
influence 178 n.
handle 218 n.
pivot 218 n.
propellant 287 n.
extractor 304 n.
lifter 310 n.
instrument 628 n.
tool 630 n.
leverage
advantage 34 n.
influence 178 n.
tool 630 n.
scope 744 n.
leviable
priced 809 adj.
leviathan
rara avis 84 n.
giant 195 n.
levigate
pulverize 332 vb.
levirate
type of marriage 894 n.
levitate
ascend 308 vb.
be light 323 vb.
Levite
priest 986 n.
levity
inattention 456 n.
folly 499 n.
irresolution 601 n.
caprice 604 n.
merriment 833 n.
rashness 857 n.
levy
assemblage 74 n.
armed force 722 n.
demand 737 n.vb.
request 761 vb.
levy 786 vb.
tax 809 n.vb.
claim 915 vb.
lewd
impure 951 adj.
lecherous 951 adj.
lexical
verbal 559 adj.
lexicographer
collector 492 n.
linguist 557 n.
lexicography
linguistics 557 n.
etymology 559 n.
lexicology
linguistics 557 n.
etymology 559 n.
lexicon
word list 87 n.
commentary 520 n.
dictionary 559 n.
reference book 589 n.
lexigraphy
spelling 558 n.
writing 586 n.
liability
tendency 179 n.
liability 180 n.
bias 481 n.
vulnerability 661 n.
encumberance 702 n.
debt 803 n.
duty 917 n.
guilt 936 n.
penalty 963 n.
liable to
liable 180 adj.
subject 745 adj.
liaison
relation 9 n.
bond 47 n.
concurrence 181 n.
love affair 887 n.
illicit love 951 n.

liana, liane
plant 366 n.
liar
liar 545 n.
boaster 877 n.
knave 938 n.
libation
drinking 301 n.
oblation 981 n.
libel
calumny 926 n.
false charge 928 n.
libellous
detracting 926 adj.
liberal
plenteous 635 adj.
reformer 654 n.
leniency 736 n.
free person 744 n.
liberal 813 adj.
prodigal 815 adj.
philanthropic 901 adj.
rewarding 962 adj.
liberal education
culture 490 n.
education 534 n.
liberalism
reformism 654 n.
freedom 744 n.
liberality
giving 781 n.
liberality 813 n.
benevolence 897 n.
disinterestedness 931 n.
liberalize, liberalise
liberate 746 vb.
Liberals
political party 708 n.
liberal studies
curriculum 534 n.
liberate
disunite 46 vb.
extract 304 vb.
deliver 668 vb.
disencumber 701 vb.
give scope 744 vb.
liberate 746 vb.
permit 756 vb.
not retain 779 vb.
exempt 919 vb.
acquit 960 vb.
liberation
freedom 744 n.
liberation 746 n.
libertarian
free person 744 n.
libertine
bad person 938 n.
sensualist 944 n.
libertine 952 n.
liberty
opportunity 137 n.
freedom 744 n.
scope 744 n.
permission 756 n.
dueness 915 n.
nonliability 919 n.
Liberty Hall
scope 744 n.
sociability 882 n.
libidinous
desiring 859 adj.
lecherous 951 adj.
libido
libido 859 n.
love 887 n.
unchastity 951 n.
Liblab
political party 708 n.
Libra
zodiac 321 n.
librarian
collector 492 n.
bookperson 589 n.
manager 690 n.
library
accumulation 74 n.
erudition 490 n.
library 589 n.
collection 632 n.
workshop 687 n.
libration
oscillation 317 n.
uranometry 321 n.
librettist
author 589 n.
poet 593 n.
dramatist 594 n.
libretto
vocal music 412 n.
stage play 594 n.
licence
anarchy 734 n.
laxity 734 n.
freedom 744 n.
scope 744 n.
permit 756 n.
dueness 915 n.
nonliability 919 n.
unchastity 951 n.
license
give scope 744 vb.
liberate 746 vb.
commission 751 vb.
permit 756 vb.
exempt 919 vb.
licensed
legal 953 adj.
licensee
consignee 754 n.
recipient 782 n.
licensing laws
prohibition 757 n.
licentious
sensual 944 adj.
lecherous 951 adj.
licentiousness
intemperance 943 n.
sensualism 944 n.
unchastity 951 n.
lichen
plant 366 n.
licit
permitted 756 adj.
legal 953 adj.
lick
small quantity 33 n.
eat 301 vb.
moisten 341 vb.
touch 378 vb.
taste 386 vb.
defeat 727 vb.
caress 889 vb.
— into shape
form 243 vb.
educate 534 vb.
make ready 669 vb.
— one's lips
enjoy 376 vb.
taste 386 vb.
gluttonize 947 vb.
— one's wounds
feel pain 377 vb.
be defeated 728 vb.
— the boots of
knuckle under 721 vb.
be servile 879 vb.
lick and a promise
ablutions 648 n.
noncompletion 726 n.
lickety-split
swiftly 277 adv.
licking
knock 279 n.
defeat 728 n.
lickspittle
toady 879 n.
lid
covering 226 n.
headgear 228 n.
stopper 264 n.
lido
shore 344 n.
pleasure ground 837 n.
lid off
disclosure 526 n.
lie
be 1 vb.
be in a state of 7 vb.
be inert 175 vb.
be situated 186 vb.
be present 189 vb.
dwell 192 vb.
be horizontal 216 vb.
misteach 535 vb.
be false 541 vb.
deception 542 n.
untruth 543 n.
misrepresent 552 vb.
be inactive 679 vb.
false charge 928 n.
— down
be horizontal 216 vb.
repose 683 vb.
— down on the job
be inactive 679 vb.
— fallow
be unproductive 172 vb.
be unprepared 670 vb.
not act 677 vb.
— in wait
ambush 527 vb.
ensnare 542 vb.
— low
disappear 446 vb.
lurk 523 vb.
seek safety 660 vb.
elude 667 vb.
— to
be quiescent 266 vb.
navigate 269 vb.
— under
be liable 180 vb.
— with
unite with 45 vb.
lie, the
negation 533 n.
lie-abed
lateness 136 n.
slowcoach 278 n.
idler 679 n.
lied, lieder
vocal music 412 n.
lie detector
detector 484 n.
liege
master 741 n.
subject 742 n.
liege lord
protector 660 n.
lie of the land
circumstance 8 n.
direction 281 n.
lieutenant
nautical personnel 270 n.
auxiliary 707 n.
soldiery 722 n.
army officer 741 n.
naval officer 741 n.
deputy 755 n.
life
existence 1 n.
substance 3 n.
essential part 5 n.
time 108 n.
period 110 n.
affairs 154 n.
vitality 162 n.
vigorousness 174 n.
organism 358 n.
life 360 n.
biography 590 n.
vocation 622 n.
activity 678 n.
life and soul of the party
cheerfulness 833 n.
humorist 839 n.
sociable person 882 n.
life belt
support 218 n.
safeguard 662 n.
lifeblood
essential part 5 n.

blood 335 n.
life 360 n.
lifeboat
boat 275 n.
safeguard 662 n.
life cycle
regular return 141 n.
transition 147 n.
life-giving
productive 164 adj.
generative 167 adj.
lifeguard
protector 660 n.
defender 713 n.
Life Guards
armed force 722 n.
life jacket
safeguard 662 n.
lifeless
inert 175 adj.
dead 361 adj.
inactive 679 adj.
lifelike
lifelike 18 adj.
lifeline
bond 47 n.
safeguard 662 n.
lifelong
lasting 113 adj.
lifemanship
tactics 688 n.
skill 694 n.
life of Riley
palmy days 730 n.
life peer
councillor 692 n.
person of rank 868 n.
life-preserver
club 723 n.
(See **life-belt** *)*
lifer
prisoner 750 n.
offender 904 n.
life-saver
preserver 666 n.
life sentence
period 110 n.
long duration 113 n.
life-size
great 32 adj.
large 195 adj.
lifespan
age 131 n.
life 360 n.
life story
biography 590 n.
life-style
habit 610 n.
way 624 n.
conduct 688 n.
life-support system
hospital 658 n.
preserver 666 n.
lifetime
period 110 n.
long duration 113 n.
life 360 n.
life work
vocation 622 n.
lift
displace 188 vb.
conveyance 267 n.
land travel 267 n.
carry 273 vb.
promote 285 vb.
draw 288 vb.
ascent 308 n.
lifter 310 n.
elevate 310 vb.
improvement 654 n.
aid 703 n.
liberate 746 vb.
permit 756 vb.
not retain 779 vb.
steal 788 vb.
relieve 831 vb.
— a finger
do 676 vb.
— off
fly 271 vb.
lifter
conveyor 274 n.
lifter 310 n.
thief 789 n.
lift-off
space travel 271 n.
ligament
ligature 47 n.
retention 778 n.
ligature
ligature 47 n.
light
insubstantial 4 adj.
unequal 29 adj.
small 33 adj.
few 105 adj.
morning 128 n.
window 263 n.
descend 309 vb.
light 323 adj.
rare 325 adj.
kindle 381 vb.
lighter 385 n.
light 417 n.
luminous 417 adj.
luminary 420 n.
illuminate 420 vb.
soft-hued 425 adj.
white 427 adj.
appearance 445 n.n.
truth 494 n.
guide 520 n.
interpretation 520 n.
irresolute 601 adj.
trivial 639 adj.
easy 701 adj.
merry 833 adj.
funny 849 adj.
rash 857 adj.
unchaste 951 adj.
revelation 975 n.
— out
start out 296 vb.
— the way
precede 283 vb.
— upon
chance 159 vb.
meet 295 vb.
acquire 771 vb.
light and shade
light contrast 417 n.
lighten
abate 37 vb.
assuage 177 vb.
make smaller 198 vb.
lighten 323 vb.
make bright 417 vb.
disencumber 701 vb.
take away 786 vb.
relive 831 vb.
light entertainment
amusement 837 n.
lighter
boat 275 n.
lighter 385 n.
torch 420 n.
lighterage
price 809 n.
lighter-than-air
aviational 276 adj.
light-fingered
thieving 788 adj.
light-footed
speedy 277 adj.
active 678 adj.
light hand
leniency 736 n.
light-headed
light-minded 456 adj.
light-hearted
cheerful 833 adj.
lighthouse
sailing aid 269 n.
signal light 420 n.
signpost 547 n.
safeguard 662 n.
lighthouse keeper
nautical personnel 270 n.
warner 664 n.
keeper 749 n.
lighting
light 417 n.
lighting 420 n.
lightless
unlit 418 adj.
lightly
slightly 33 adv.
rashly 857 adv.
light meter
optical device 442 n.
light-minded
changeful 152 adj.
light-minded 456 adj.
capricious 604 adj.
rash 857 adj.
lightning
electricity 160 n.
velocity 277 n.
flash 417 n.
luminary 420 n.
lightning conductor
electricity 160 n.
safeguard 662 n.
lightning strike
strike 145 n.
hitch 702 n.
light of nature
empiricism 461 n.
intuition 476 n.
light of one's life
loved one 887 n.
light on
insufficient 636 adj.
light rein
leniency 736 n.
light relief
contrariety 14 n.
ridiculousness 849 n.
lights
knowledge 490 n.
intelligence 498 n.
lightship
sailing aid 269 n.
ship 275 n.
signal light 420 n.
signpost 547 n.
safeguard 662 n.
light-skinned
colourless 426 adj.
lightsome
light 323 adj.
active 678 adj.
shapely 841 adj.
lights out
obscuration 418 n.
call 547 n.
light touch
touch 378 n.
lightweight
insubstantial 4 adj.
inconsiderable 33 adj.
weakling 163 n.
light 323 adj.
nonentity 639 n.
trivial 639 adj.
light work
easy thing 701 n.
light year
period 110 n.
distance 199 n.
long measure 203 n.
ligneous
wooden 366 adj.
lignite
fuel 385 n.
likable, likeable
desired 859 adj.
lovable 887 adj.
like
relative 9 adj.
similar 18 adj.
equal 28 adj.
enjoy 376 vb.
make appetizing 390 vb.
be pleased 824 vb.
desire 859 vb.
be friendly 880 vb.

love 887 vb.
— best
choose 605 vb.
— well
approve 923 vb.
like clockwork
(See **clockwork** *)*
like enough
probably 471 adv.
like father like son
similarly 18 adv.
like for like
retaliation 714 n.
likelihood
liability 180 n.
possibility 469 n.
probability 471 n.
likely
probable 471 adj.
credible 485 adj.
true 494 adj.
promising 852 adj.
like-minded
agreeing 24 adj.
assenting 488 adj.
liken
relate 9 vb.
make uniform 16 vb.
liken 18 vb.
compare 462 vb.
figure 519 vb.
likeness
similarity 18 n.
copy 22 n.
equivalence 28 n.
appearance 445 n.
comparison 462 n.
metaphor 519 n.
representation 551 n.
like new
new 126 adj.
newly 126 adv.
restored 656 adj.
likes of, the
analogue 18 n.
like this
thus 8 adv.
likewise
similarly 18 adv.
in addition 38 adv.
liking
tendency 179 n.
liking 859 n.
love 887 n.
lilac
tree 366 n.
purple 436 adj.
lilliputian
little 196 adj.
lilt
sing 413 vb.
be cheerful 833 vb.
lilting
melodious 410 adj.
lily
plant 366 n.
white thing 427 n.
a beauty 841 n.
lily-livered
cowardly 856 adj.
limb
adjunct 40 n.
limb 53 n.
piece 53 n.
extremity 69 n.
leg 267 n.
foliage 366 n.
tree 366 n.
limber
flexible 327 adj.
gun 723 n.
limber up
begin 68 vb.
prepare oneself 669 vb.
limb from limb
apart 46 adv.
piecemeal 53 adv.
limbless
incomplete 55 adj.
limbo
prison 748 n.
hell 972 n.
lime
adhesive 47 n.
fertilizer 171 n.
fruit 301 n.
tree 366 n.
bleacher 426 n.
greenness 434 n.
ensnare 542 vb.
take 786 vb.
lime kiln
furnace 383 n.
limelight
lighting 420 n.
publicity 528 n.
theatre 594 n.
limerick
doggerel 593 n.
witticism 839 n.
ridiculousness 849 n.
limestone
rock 344 n.
limey
foreigner 59 n.
mariner 270 n.
limit
finite quantity 26 n.
abate 37 vb.
completeness 54 n.
extremity 69 n.
moderate 177 vb.
farness 199 n.
summit 213 n.
circumscribe 232 vb.
edge 234 n.
limit 236 n.vb.
qualify 468 vb.
hinder 702 vb.
restrain 747 vb.
apportion 783 vb.
annoyance 827 n.
limitation
circumscription 232 n.
limit 236 n.
qualification 468 n.
defect 647 n.
hindrance 702 n.
restriction 747 n.
conditions 766 n.
limited
small 33 adj.
circumscribed 232 adj.
limited 236 adj.
unintelligent 499 adj.
limited liability company
corporation 708 n.
limiting factor
limit 236 n.
restriction 747 n.
limitless
infinite 107 adj.
huge 195 adj.
limits to growth
decrease 37 n.
production 164 n.
limn
represent 551 vb.
describe 590 vb.
limousine
automobile 274 n.
limp
weak 163 adj.
inert 175 adj.
move slowly 278 vb.
soft 327 adj.
feeble 572 adj.
limpet
coherence 48 n.
marine life 365 n.
bomb 723 n.
limpid
transparent 422 adj.
intelligible 516 adj.
perspicuous 567 adj.
limpidity
transparency 422 n.
intelligibility 516 n.
perspicuity 567 n.
limp-wristed
weak 163 adj.
linage
letterpress 587 n.
linchpin
fastening 47 n.
chief thing 638 n.
linctus
medicine 658 n.
line
race 11 n.
cable 47 n.
fill 54 vb.
sequence 65 n.
continuity 71 n.
breed 77 n.
posteriority 120 n.
strengthen 162 vb.
genealogy 169 n.
sonship 170 n.
load 193 vb.
line 203 n.
narrowness 206 n.
fibre 208 n.
overlay 226 vb.
line 227 vb.
put between 231 vb.
limit 236 n.
straightness 249 n.
groove 262 vb.
sailing aid 269 n.
direction 281 n.
insert 303 vb.
stripe 437 n.
telecommunication 531 n.
indication 547 n.
painting 553 n.
lettering 586 n.
correspondence 588 n.
vocation 622 n.
policy 623 n.
railway 624 n.
route 624 n.
tactics 688 n.
battle 718 n.
formation 722 n.
merchandise 795 n.
— one's pockets
gain 771 vb.
get rich 800 vb.
— up
be in order 60 vb.
arrange 62 vb.
run on 71 vb.
lineage
consanguinity 11 n.
continuity 71 n.
source 156 n.
genealogy 169 n.
nobility 868 n.
line ahead
series 71 n.
line 203 n.
lineal
filial 170 adj.
lineament(s)
outline 233 n.
form 243 n.
feature 445 n.
identification 547 n.
linear
continuous 71 adj.
longitudinal 203 adj.
straight 249 adj.
metrical 465 adj.
painted 553 adj.
linear accelerator
nucleonics 160 n.
linear programming
mathematics 86 n.
lined
ageing 131 adj.
rough 259 adj.
furrowed 262 adj.
mottled 437 adj.
linen
fibre 208 n.
textile 222 n.
underwear 228 n.

bookbinding 589 n.
line of communication
route 624 n.
line of country
function 622 n.
line of least resistance
sluggishness 679 n.
submission 721 n.
laxity 734 n.
line of sight
direction 281 n.
view 438 n.
liner
lining 227 n.
ship 275 n.
lines
station 187 n.
abode 192 n.
outline 233 n.
form 243 n.
fold 261 n.
feature 445 n.
poem 593 n.
stage play 594 n.
railway 624 n.
defences 713 n.
penalty 963 n.
lineup
assemblage 74 n.
linga, lingam
fertilizer 171 n.
idol 982 n.
linger
drag on 113 vb.
be late 136 vb.
go on 146 vb.
move slowly 278 vb.
lingerie
underwear 228 n.
lingo
language 557 n.
dialect 560 n.
lingua franca
language 557 n.
dialect 560 n.
linguist
interpreter 520 n.
linguist 557 n.
linguistic
semantic 514 adj.
linguistic 557 adj.
linguistics
hermeneutics 520 n.
linguistics 557 n.
etymology 559 n.
grammar 564 n.
liniment
unguent 357 n.
balm 658 n.
lining
contents 193 n.
lining 227 n.
insertion 303 n.
link
relation 9 n.
connect 45 vb.
bond 47 n.
component 58 n.
cross 222 vb.
intermediary 231 n.
linkboy
torch 420 n.
linkman
broadcaster 531 n.
links
pleasure ground 837 n.
linkup
union 45 n.
linnet
bird 365 n.
linocut
engraving 555 n.
linoleum, lino
floor-cover 226 n.
linotype
print 587 n.
linseed oil
oil 357 n.
linsey-woolsey
medley 43 n.
linstock
lighter 385 n.
lint
surgical dressing 658 n.
lintel
summit 213 n.
beam 218 n.
doorway 263 n.
lion
cat 365 n.
heraldry 547 n.
bigwig 638 n.
regalia 743 n.
brave person 855 n.
person of repute 866 n.
favourite 890 n.
lion-hearted
courageous 855 adj.
lionize, lionise
make important 638 vb.
honour 866 vb.
celebrate 876 vb.
respect 920 vb.
praise 923 vb.
lion's mouth
danger 661 n.
lion's share
chief part 52 n.
undueness 916 n.
lion-tamer
breeder 369 n.
trainer 537 n.
lip
edge 234 n.
projection 254 n.
touch 378 vb.
sauciness 878 n.
rudeness 885 n.
lip gloss
cosmetic 843 n.
lip-read
be deaf 416 vb.
translate 520 vb.
lips
speech 579 n.
lip service
sham 542 n.
ostentation 875 n.
false piety 980 n.
lipstick
red pigment 431 n.
cosmetic 843 n.
liquefy
decompose 51 vb.
soften 327 vb.
liquefy 337 vb.
make flow 350 vb.
heat 381 vb.
liquescent
fluid 335 adj.
liquefied 337 adj.
liqueur
alcoholic drink 301 n.
liquid
nonadhesive 49 adj.
amorphous 244 adj.
fluid 335 n.adj.
speech sound 398 n.
transparent 422 adj.
liquid assets
funds 797 n.
liquidate
destroy 165 vb.
slaughter 362 vb.
pay 804 vb.
liquidator
receiver 782 n.
treasurer 798 n.
liquidity
fluidity 335 n.
means 629 n.
funds 797 n.
liquidize, liquidise
cook 301 vb.
liquefy 337 vb.
liquor
stimulant 174 n.
drunkenness 949 n.
liquorice, licorice
sweets 301 n.
purgative 658 n.
lira
coinage 797 n.
lisp
voice 577 vb.
speech defect 580 n.
lissom
flexible 327 adj.
shapely 841 adj.
list
specify 80 vb.
statistics 86 n.
list 87 n.vb.
obliquity 220 n.
edging 234 n.
register 548 vb.
listed
included 78 adj.
listed 87 adj.
listed building
archaism 127 n.
preservation 666 n.
listen
hear 415 vb.
be curious 453 vb.
be attentive 455 vb.
obey 739 vb.
consent 758 vb.
— in
hear 415 vb.
be curious 453 vb.
— to
consult 691 vb.
listened to
influential 178 adj.
listener
listener 415 n.
inquisitive person 453 n.
witness 466 n.
broadcasting 531 n.
allocution 583 n.
listless
weakly 163 adj.
incurious 454 adj.
inactive 679 adj.
dejected 834 adj.
indifferent 860 adj.
lists
duel 716 n.
arena 724 n.
litany
prayers 981 n.
office-book 988 n.
literacy
culture 490 n.
literal
imitative 20 adj.
narrow-minded 481 adj.
accurate 494 adj.
semantic 514 adj.
interpretive 520 adj.
literal 558 adj.
verbal 559 adj.
observant 768 adj.
orthodox 976 adj.
literal-minded
narrow-minded 481 adj.
accurate 494 adj.
literary
instructed 490 adj.
literary 557 adj.
stylistic 566 adj.
literary criticism
interpretation 520 n.
literature 557 n.
literary person
author 589 n.
bookperson 589 n.
literate
instructed 490 adj.
literati
intellectual 492 n.
literatim
imitatively 20 adv.

alphabetically 558 adv.
literature
culture 490 n.
erudition 490 n.
information 524 n.
literature 557 n.
writing 586 n.
reading matter 589 n.
lithe
flexible 327 adj.
lithic
hard 326 adj.
lithograph
representation 551 n.
engrave 555 vb.
print 587 vb.
lithography
printing 555 n.
lithology
mineralogy 359 n.
litigable
litigated 959 adj.
litigant
accuser 928 n.
litigant 959 n.
litigate
quarrel 709 vb.
litigate 959 vb.
litigious
quarrelling 709 adj.
litigating 959 adj.
litmus paper
testing agent 461 n.
identification 547 n.
litotes
underestimation 483 n.
trope 519 n.
litre
metrology 465 n.
litter
leavings 41 n.
confusion 61 n.
jumble 63 vb.
group 74 n.
be dispersed 75 vb.
young creature 132 n.
bed 218 n.
vehicle 274 n.
rubbish 641 n.
dirt 649 n.
litter bearer
bearer 273 n.
litterbin
vessel 194 n.
litterlout
slut 61 n.
dirty person 649 n.
litter-strewn
unsightly 842 adj.
little
small 33 adj.
infantine 132 adj.
seldom 140 adv.
little 196 adj.
short 204 adj.
contemptible 922 adj.
little, a
partially 33 adv.
little at a time, a
piecemeal 53 adv.
little bird
informant 524 n.
little by little
by degrees 27 adv.
gradatim 278 adv.
little enough
insufficiency 636 n.
little game
tactics 688 n.
stratagem 698 n.
little green men
foreigner 59 n.
little learning, a
sciolism 491 n.
little man
everyman 79 n.
commoner 869 n.
little Mary
maw 194 n.
little monkey
child 132 n.
revolter 738 n.
littleness
smallness 33 n.
inferiority 35 n.
littleness 196 n.
shortness 204 n.
lowness 210 n.
invisibility 444 n.
little of what one fancies, a
pleasurableness 826 n.
little ones
child 132 n.
posterity 170 n.
little people
dwarf 196 n.
fairy 970 n.
little pitcher
listener 415 n.
littoral
edge 234 n.
coastal 344 adj.
lit up
drunk 949 adj.
liturgical
ritual 988 adj.
liturgy
church service 988 n.
office-book 988 n.
ritual 988 n.
livable, liveable
contenting 828 adj.
live
be 1 vb.
pass time 108 vb.
at present 121 adv.
dynamic 160 adj.
operative 173 adj.
dwell 192 vb.
alive 360 adj.
live 360 vb.
dramatic 594 adj.
active 678 adj.
feel 818 vb.
— and let live
not act 677 vb.
give scope 744 vb.
compromise 770 vb.
— by one's wits
be skilful 694 vb.
be cunning 698 vb.
be dishonest 930 vb.
— for
love 887 vb.
be disinterested 931 vb.
— from hand to mouth
be now 121 vb.
be poor 801 vb.
— in the past
retrospect 505 vb.
— in the present
be now 121 vb.
— it up
revel 837 vb.
be sociable 882 vb.
be intemperate 943 vb.
— off/on the fat of the land
enjoy 376 vb.
prosper 730 vb.
be sensual 944 vb.
— on
eat 301 vb.
be remembered 505 vb.
— out of a suitcase
travel 267 vb.
— through
continue 108 vb.
be restored 656 vb.
feel 818 vb.
— to fight another day
outlast 113 vb.
seek safety 660 vb.
parry 713 vb.
— under
be subject 745 vb.
— well
be sensual 944 vb.
— with
unite with 45 vb.
accompany 89 vb.
wed 894 vb.
lived in
occupied 191 adj.
livelihood
vocation 622 n.
liveliness
energy 160 n.
vitality 162 n.
vigorousness 174 n.
vigour 571 n.
restlessness 678 n.
moral sensibility 819 n.
cheerfulness 833 n.
livelong
lasting 113 adj.
lively
vigorous 174 adj.
speedy 277 adj.
agitated 318 adj.
alive 360 adj.
striking 374 adj.
imaginative 513 adj.
forceful 571 adj.
active 678 adj.
feeling 818 adj.
lively 819 adj.
excitable 822 adj.
cheerful 833 adj.
sociable 882 adj.
liven up
vitalize 360 vb.
be cheerful 833 vb.
liver
insides 224 n.
meat 301 n.
sullenness 893 n.
liver-coloured
brown 430 adj.
live relay
broadcast 531 n.
liveried
uniform 16 adj.
dressed 228 adj.
liverish
irascible 892 adj.
drunken 949 adj.
liverishness
digestive disorders 651 n.
liverwort
plant 366 n.
livery
uniform 228 n.
livery 547 n.
livery company
corporation 708 n.
livestock
animal 365 n.
cattle 365 n.
live theatre
drama 594 n.
live wire
electricity 160 n.
vigorousness 174 n.
busy person 678 n.
livid
blackish 428 adj.
grey 429 adj.
blue 435 adj.
purple 436 adj.
excited 821 adj.
angry 891 adj.
living
vocation 622 n.
benefice 985 n.
living, the
life 360 n.
humankind 371 n.
living death
suffering 825 n.

living image
analogue 18 n.
duplication 91 n.
living matter
organism 358 n.
life 360 n.
living quarters
quarters 192 n.
living room
chamber 194 n.
living soul
person 371 n.
living space
room 183 n.
scope 744 n.
living wage
sufficiency 635 n.
lixiviate
purify 648 vb.
lizard
reptile 365 n.
llama
beast of burden 273 n.
llyn
lake 346 n.
load
fill 54 vb.
bunch 74 n.
stow 187 vb.
contents 193 n.
load 193 vb.
thing transferred 272 n.
gravity 322 n.
redundance 637 n.
encumbrance 702 n.
adversity 731 n.
worry 825 n.
— the dice
deceive 542 vb.
— with
add 38 vb.
hinder 702 vb.
loaded
bearing 273 adj.
weighty 322 adj.
moneyed 800 adj.
loaded table
feasting 301 n.
plenty 635 n.
load off one's mind
relief 831 n.
loads
great quantity 32 n.
multitude 104 n.
loadstar
(See **lodestar** *)*
loadstone
(See **lodestone** *)*
loaf
head 213 n.
cereals 301 n.
intelligence 498 n.
be inactive 679 vb.
loafer
wanderer 268 n.
idler 679 n.
loam
soil 344 n.
loan
subvention 703 n.
lending 784 n.
borrowing 785 n.
credit 802 n.
loan shark
lender 784 n.
loanword
neology 560 n.
loath, loth
unwilling 598 adj.
disliking 861 adj.
loathe
dislike 861 vb.
hate 888 vb.
loathing
dislike 861 n.
enmity 881 n.
hatred 888 n.
loathsome
unsavoury 391 adj.
not nice 645 adj.
unpleasant 827 adj.
ugly 842 adj.
disliked 861 adj.
hateful 888 adj.
lob
strike 279 vb.
propel 287 vb.
elevate 310 vb.
lobby
influence 178 n.vb.
lobby 194 n.
motivator 612 n.
incite 612 vb.
access 624 n.
petitioner 763 n.
— against
deprecate 762 vb.
lobe
hanging object 217 n.
ear 415 n.
lobotomy
surgery 658 n.
lobster
fish food 301 n.
marine life 365 n.
local
focus 76 n.
regional 184 adj.
situated 186 adj.
native 191 n.
tavern 192 n.
provincial 192 adj.
near 200 adj.
local authority
jurisdiction 955 n.
local colour
accuracy 494 n.
painting 553 n.
description 590 n.
locale
situation 186 n.
locality
district 184 n.
region 184 n.
place 185 n.n.
locality 187 n.
localize, localise
place 187 vb.
restrain 747 vb.
locally
somewhere 185 adv.
near 200 adv.
locate
specify 80 vb.
place 187 vb.
orientate 281 vb.
discover 484 vb.
located
remaining 41 adj.
situated 186 adj.
located 187 adj.
directed 281 adj.
location
situation 186 n.
location 187 n.
loch
lake 346 n.
lock
join 45 vb.
fastening 47 n.
filament 208 n.
stopper 264 n.
close 264 vb.
conduit 351 n.
access 624 n.
safeguard 662 n.
firearm 723 n.
retain 778 vb.
— horns with
contend 716 vb.
— oneself in
seek refuge 662 vb.
— up
conceal 525 vb.
safeguard 660 vb.
imprison 747 vb.
punish 963 vb.
locked out
inactive 679 adj.
locked up
insane 503 adj.
imprisoned 747 adj.
locker
compartment 194 n.
locket
jewellery 844 n.
lockjaw
spasm 318 n.
infection 651 n.
lock keeper
boatman 270 n.
lockout
exclusion 57 n.
strike 145 n.
hindrance 702 n.
locks
hair 259 n.
locksmith
artisan 686 n.
lock, stock and barrel
finite quantity 26 n.
all 52 n.
lockup
lockup 748 n.
loco
crazy 503 adj.
locomotion
motion 265 n.
locomotive
dynamic 160 adj.
moving 265 adj.
locomotive 274 n.
vehicular 274 adj.
loculus
compartment 194 n.
locum, locum tenens
substitute 150 n.
doctor 658 n.
deputy 755 n.
locus classicus
example 83 n.
locust
destroyer 168 n.
eater 301 n.
insect 365 n.
bane 659 n.
noxious animal 904 n.
glutton 947 n.
locution
word 559 n.
phrase 563 n.
lode
layer 207 n.
store 632 n.
lodestar, loadstar
signpost 547 n.
motive 612 n.
directorship 689 n.
lodestone, loadstone
magnet 291 n.
incentive 612 n.
lodge
place 187 vb.
small house 192 n.
dwell 192 vb.
be quiescent 266 vb.
society 708 n.
lodger
resident 191 n.
possessor 776 n.
lodgings
quarters 192 n.
loess
soil 344 n.
loft
attic 194 n.
propel 287 vb.
elevate 310 vb.
storage 632 n.
loftiness
superiority 34 n.
lofty
high 209 adj.
elevated 310 adj.
forceful 571 adj.
worshipful 866 adj.
proud 871 adj.
insolent 878 adj.
despising 922 adj.
disinterested 931 adj.

log
sailing aid 269 n.
fuel 385 n.
gauge 465 n.
record 548 n.
materials 631 n.
logarithm
numerical element 85 n.
mathematics 86 n.
logbook
chronology 117 n.
record 548 n.
log cabin
small house 192 n.
loge
theatre 594 n.
loggia
lobby 194 n.
logic
reasoning 475 n.
curriculum 534 n.
necessity 596 n.
logical
relevant 9 adj.
philosophic 449 adj.
plausible 471 adj.
rational 475 adj.
true 494 adj.
necessary 596 adj.
logical conclusion
conformance 24 n.
logical flaw
sophism 477 n.
logical positivism
philosophy 449 n.
logic-chopping
argument 475 n.
sophistry 477 n.
logician
reasoner 475 n.
logistics
transference 272 n.
provision 633 n.
fitting out 669 n.
art of war 718 n.
logjam
obstacle 702 n.
logogram
writing 586 n.
logomachy
argument 475 n.
sophistry 477 n.
logophile
etymology 559 n.
logorrhoea
loquacity 581 n.
Logos
word 559 n.
God the Son 965 n.
logotype, logo
label 547 n.
print-type 587 n.
logrolling
interchange 151 n.
cooperation 706 n.
loin
buttocks 238 n.
meat 301 n.
loincloth
loincloth 228 n.
loins
source 156 n.
genitalia 167 n.
parentage 169 n.
loiter
be late 136 vb.
be stealthy 525 vb.
be inactive 679 vb.
loiterer
pedestrian 268 n.
slowcoach 278 n.
Loki
deceiver 545 n.
Nordic deities 967 n.
Lolita
loose woman 952 n.
loll
be horizontal 216 vb.
hang 217 vb.
be inactive 679 vb.
repose 683 vb.
Lollard
heretic 977 n.
lollipop
sweets 301 n.
sweet thing 392 n.
lollipop man/lady
traffic control 305 n.
lollop
be inactive 679 vb.
lolloping
unwieldy 195 adj.
lolly
sweets 301 n.
shekels 797 n.
Lombard Street to a China orange
probably 471 adv.
Londoner
native 191 n.
lone
nonuniform 17 adj.
one 88 adj.
unsociable 883 adj.
lonely
separate 46 adj.
alone 88 adj.
empty 190 adj.
friendless 883 adj.
secluded 883 adj.
lonely hearts club
matchmaker 894 n.
lonely person
solitary 883 n.
loner
nonconformist 84 n.
solitary 883 n.
lonesome
alone 88 adj.
friendless 883 adj.
lone wolf
nonuniformity 17 n.
revolter 738 n.
free person 744 n.
solitary 883 n.
long
lasting 113 adj.
long 203 adj.
prolix 570 adj.
tedious 838 adj.
desire 859 vb.
— for
regret 830 vb.
desire 859 vb.
long about it, be
be late 136 vb.
move slowly 278 vb.
long ago
long ago 113 adv.
formerly 125 adv.
long and the short and the tall, the
everyman 79 n.
long and the short of it, the
chief part 52 n.
conciseness 569 n.
longanimity
patience 823 n.
long arm
length 203 n.
governance 733 n.
long-awaited
protracted 113 adj.
long barrow
small hill 209 n.
earthwork 253 n.
longboat
boat 275 n.
longbow
missile weapon 723 n.
long-distance
distant 199 adj.
long-drawn out
long 203 adj.
prolix 570 adj.
long drink
draught 301 n.
long duration
long duration 113 n.
longed for
expected 507 adj.
longevity
long duration 113 n.
old age 131 n.
life 360 n.
health 650 n.
long face
dejection 834 n.
longhair
nonconformist 84 n.
intellectual 492 n.
longhand
writing 586 n.
long haul
protraction 113 n.
labour 682 n.
long-headed
intelligent 498 adj.
longing
suffering 825 n.
regret 830 n.
desire 859 n.
love 887 n.
long in the tooth
ageing 131 adj.
longitude
length 203 n.
long johns
underwear 228 n.
longlasting
perpetual 115 adj.
long-legged
narrow 206 adj.
tall 209 adj.
legged 267 adj.
long-lived
lasting 113 adj.
alive 360 adj.
long measure
long measure 203 n.
measurement 465 n.
long odds
fair chance 159 n.
improbability 472 n.
long pig
meat 301 n.
corpse 363 n.
long-playing record
gramophone 414 n.
long-range
distant 199 adj.
long run
period 110 n.
durability 113 n.
futurity 124 n.
longship
galley 275 n.
longshore
seafaring 269 adj.
on land 344 adv.
longshoreman
boatman 270 n.
long shot
improbability 472 n.
long sight
vision 438 n.
dim sight 440 n.
longsightedness
sagacity 498 n.
foresight 510 n.
long sleep
death 361 n.
longstanding
lasting 113 adj.
immemorial 127 adj.
permanent 144 adj.
longsuffering
lenient 736 adj.
patient 823 adj.
suffering 825 adj.
forgiving 909 adj.
long suit
goodness 644 n.
long-term
lasting 113 adj.
long time, a
long duration 113 n.
long time ago, a
formerly 125 adv.
longueurs
tedium 838 n.

long wave
radiation 417 n.
long way
distance 199 n.
long way round
deviation 282 n.
circuit 626 n.
longways
longwise 203 adv.
longwinded
protracted 113 adj.
prolix 570 adj.
loquacious 581 adj.
tedious 838 adj.
long words
magniloquence 574 n.
loo
latrine 649 n.
card game 837 n.
loofah
cleaning utensil 648 n.
look
similarity 18 n.
form 243 n.
look 438 n.
appearance 445 n.
mien 445 n.
be curious 453 vb.
attention 455 n.
hint 524 n.
gesture 547 n.
— after
look after 457 vb.
safeguard 660 vb.
— after oneself
be healthy 650 vb.
be selfish 932 vb.
— a gift horse in the mouth
be discontented 829 vb.
be cautious 858 vb.
be fastidious 862 vb.
be ungrateful 908 vb.
— ahead
look ahead 124 vb.
foresee 510 vb.vb.
plan 623 vb.
— as if
resemble 18 vb.
— askance (at)
dissent 489 vb.
refuse 760 vb.
dislike 861 vb.
disapprove 924 vb.
— at
gaze 438 vb.
watch 441 vb.
— back
look back 125 vb.
turn back 286 vb.
retrospect 505 vb.
regret 830 vb.
— black
predict 511 vb.
show feeling 818 vb.
be sullen 893 vb.
disapprove 924 vb.
— blank
be disappointed 509 vb.
keep secret 525 vb.
— daggers
gaze 438 vb.
be angry 891 vb.
threaten 900 vb.
disapprove 924 vb.
— down on
be proud 871 vb.
be insolent 878 vb.
not respect 921 vb.
despise 922 vb.
— foolish
be foolish 499 vb.
lose repute 867 vb.
— for
be curious 453 vb.
search 459 vb.
assume 471 vb.
expect 507 vb.
pursue 619 vb.
desire 859 vb.
— for trouble
make quarrels 709 vb.
— forward (to)
look ahead 124 vb.
expect 507 vb.
hope 852 vb.
— in
enter 297 vb.
watch 441 vb.
visit 882 vb.
— in the face
be courageous 855 vb.
— into
be attentive 455 vb.
enquire 459 vb.
— like
resemble 18 vb.
— on
be impotent 161 vb.
be present 189 vb.
see 438 vb.
watch 441 vb.
acquiesce 488 vb.
not act 677 vb.
— one up
visit 882 vb.
— one up and down
scan 438 vb.
be insolent 878 vb.
— on the bright side
be cheerful 833 vb.
hope 852 vb.
— out
invigilate 457 vb.
be cautious 858 vb.
— out for
scan 438 vb.
expect 507 vb.
— out for oneself
be selfish 932 vb.
— over
scan 438 vb.
— over one's shoulder
turn back 286 vb.
be unwilling 598 vb.
regret 830 vb.
— the other way
be blind 439 vb.
be incurious 454 vb.
avoid 620 vb.
— through
scan 438 vb.
be rude 885 vb.
— to
be attentive 455 vb.
look after 457 vb.
impose a duty 917 vb.
— twice
be cautious 858 vb.
— up to
honour 866 vb.
respect 920 vb.
lookalike
analogue 18 n.
actor 594 n.
looked for
future 124 adj.
looked up to, be
have a reputation 866 vb.
looker-on
spectator 441 n.
look-in
opportunity 137 n.
looking before one leaps
caution 858 n.
looking for kicks
excitable 822 adj.
looking glass
mirror 442 n.
looking up
improved 654 adj.
look of things
circumstance 8 n.
appearance 445 n.
lookout
high structure 209 n.
view 438 n.
spectator 441 n.
surveillance 457 n.
expectation 507 n.
function 622 n.
protector 660 n.
warner 664 n.
keeper 749 n.
worry 825 n.
look out!
455 int.
664 int.
looks
mien 445 n.
look-see
inspection 438 n.
loom
be great 32 vb.
impend 155 vb.
handle 218 n.
textile 222 n.
weaving 222 n.
be dim 419 vb.
blur 440 vb.
be visible 443 vb.
endanger 661 vb.
workshop 687 n.
loony
crazy 503 adj.
madman 504 n.
loony bin
lunatic asylum 503 n.
loop
fastening 47 n.
contraception 172 n.
handle 218 n.
loop 250 n.
meander 251 vb.
circuit 626 n.
— the loop
be inverted 221 vb.
fly 271 vb.
looper
serpent 251 n.
creepy-crawly 365 n.
loophole
window 263 n.
outlet 298 n.
pretext 614 n.
contrivance 623 n.
defect 647 n.
means of escape 667 n.
loop line
railway 624 n.
loose
disunite 46 vb.
nonadhesive 49 adj.
general 79 adj.
unstable 152 adj.
hanging 217 adj.
deviating 282 adj.
soft 327 adj.
poorly reasoned 477 adj.
feeble 572 adj.
lax 734 adj.
free 744 adj.
liberate 746 vb.
unchaste 951 adj.
— off at
shoot 287 vb.
loosebox
cart 274 n.
loose ends
negligence 458 n.
noncompletion 726 n.
loose-leaf
bibliographical 589 adj.
loose-limbed
flexible 327 adj.
loose liver
sensualist 944 n.
loose morals
wickedness 934 n.

loosen
abate 37 vb.
disunite 46 vb.
unstick 49 vb.
weaken 163 vb.
liberate 746 vb.
looseness
inexactness 495 n.
(See **loose** *)*
loose thinking
sophism 477 n.
misjudgment 481 n.
inexactness 495 n.
loose woman
loose woman 952 n.
loot
rob 788 vb.
booty 790 n.
looter
taker 786 n.
lop
subtract 39 vb.
cut 46 vb.
shorten 204 vb.
lope
gait 265 n.
pedestrianism 267 n.
move fast 277 vb.
lop-eared
hanging 217 adj.
lopped
incomplete 55 adj.
lopsided
unequal 29 adj.
clumsy 695 adj.
lopsidedness
distortion 246 n.
loquacious
informative 524 adj.
diffuse 570 adj.
loquacious 581 adj.
loquacity
loquacity 581 n.
loran
telecommunication 531 n.
lord
superior 34 n.
bigwig 638 n.
master 741 n.
owner 776 n.
person of rank 868 n.
Lord
God the Son 965 n.
lord and master
master 741 n.
spouse 894 n.
lord it (over)
oppress 735 vb.
be proud 871 vb.
be insolent 878 vb.
lordly
authoritative 733 adj.
authoritarian 735 adj.
liberal 813 adj.
worshipful 866 adj.
noble 868 adj.
proud 871 adj.
insolent 878 adj.
Lord Mayor
officer 741 n.
law officer 955 n.
Lord Mayor's Show
procession 71 n.
pageant 875 n.
Lord of Misrule
anarchist 61 n.
reveller 837 n.
lord of the manor
master 741 n.
owner 776 n.
lords
aristocracy 868 n.
Lord's day
repose 683 n.
holy day 988 n.
lordship
position of authority 733 n.
lands 777 n.
aristocracy 868 n.
Lordship
title 870 n.
lords of creation
humankind 371 n.
Lord's Prayer, the
prayers 981 n.
Lords Spiritual
councillor 692 n.
ecclesiarch 986 n.
Lord's Supper, the
Holy Communion 988 n.
Lord's table
ritual object 988 n.
altar 990 n.
lore
tradition 127 n.
erudition 490 n.
knowledge 490 n.
learning 536 n.
cunning 698 n.
Lorelei
rara avis 84 n.
vocalist 413 n.
motivator 612 n.
mythical being 970 n.
lorgnette
eyeglass 442 n.
loricate
covered 226 adj.
lorn
friendless 883 adj.
lorry
lorry 274 n.
lose
decrease 37 vb.
misdate 118 vb.
be late 136 vb.
misplace 188 vb.
outstrip 277 vb.
relinquish 621 vb.
be defeated 728 vb.
lose 772 vb.
— a chance
be late 136 vb.
lose a chance 138 vb.
— colour
be dim 419 vb.
lose colour 426 vb.
— consciousness
be impotent 161 vb.
be insensible 375 vb.
— control
be lax 734 vb.
be intemperate 943 vb.
— face
be inferior 35 vb.
lose repute 867 vb.
— ground
decelerate 278 vb.
regress 286 vb.
fall short 307 vb.
be defeated 728 vb.
— heart
be dejected 834 vb.
despair 853 vb.
— no time
be early 135 vb.
hasten 680 vb.
— one's bearings
stray 282 vb.
— one's cool
be excited 821 vb.
— one's head
go mad 503 vb.
be unskilful 695 vb.
— one's heart
be in love 887 vb.
— one's nerve
be unskilful 695 vb.
be cowardly 856 vb.
— one's temper
be rude 885 vb.
get angry 891 vb.
— one's tongue
be mute 578 vb.
be taciturn 582 vb.
— out
be defeated 728 vb.
— patience
get angry 891 vb.
— repute
lose repute 867 vb.
— sight of
be blind 439 vb.
be inattentive 456 vb.
neglect 458 vb.
forget 506 vb.
— the scent
have no smell 395 vb.
be uncertain 474 vb.
— the thread
be unrelated 10 vb.
stray 282 vb.
be inattentive 456 vb.
be uncertain 474 vb.
— the way
wander 267 vb.
stray 282 vb.
— track of
misplace 188 vb.
stray 282 vb.
be inattentive 456 vb.
— weight
decrease 37 vb.
make thin 206 vb.
lighten 323 vb.
loser
bungler 697 n.
loser 728 n.
unlucky person 731 n.
laughingstock 851 n.
losing
inexact 495 adj.
profitless 641 adj.
unsuccessful 728 adj.
losing 772 adj.
losing business
unproductiveness 172 n.
losing game
defeat 728 n.
losing ground
deterioration 655 n.
losing height
flying 271 adj.
losing one's touch
clumsy 695 adj.
losing side
loser 728 n.
losing weight
dieting 301 n.
loss
decrease 37 n.
decrement 42 n.
deficit 55 n.
ruin 165 n.
unproductiveness 172 n.
absence 190 n.
outflow 298 n.
shortfall 307 n.
disappearance 446 n.
waste 634 n.
inutility 641 n.
impairment 655 n.
loss 772 n.
losses
failure 728 n.
loss leader
incentive 612 n.
discount 810 n.
loss-making
profitless 641 adj.
loss of right
loss of right 916 n.
lost
past 125 adj.
destroyed 165 adj.
misplaced 188 adj.
absent 190 adj.
deviating 282 adj.

disappearing 446 adj.
doubting 474 adj.
unknown 491 adj.
concealed 525 adj.
lost 772 adj.
impenitent 940 adj.
condemned 961 adj.
lost cause
rejection 607 n.
defeat 728 n.
lost in thought
thoughtful 449 adj.
abstracted 456 adj.
lost in wonder
wondering 864 adj.
lost labour
unproductiveness 172 n.
lost labour 641 n.
failure 728 n.
lost leader
tergiversator 603 n.
lost sheep
bad person 938 n.
lost soul
bad person 938 n.
devil 969 n.
lost to shame
vicious 934 adj.
lost to sight
distant 199 adj.
disappearing 446 adj.
lot
state 7 n.
finite quantity 26 n.
all 52 n.
bunch 74 n.
chance 159 n.
territory 184 n.
enclosure 235 n.
oracle 511 n.
fate 596 n.
nondesign 618 n.
participation 775 n.
portion 783 n.
loth
(See **loath** *)*
Lothario
lover 887 n.
libertine 952 n.
lotion
water 339 n.
cleanser 648 n.
balm 658 n.
lots
great quantity 32 n.
multitude 104 n.
plenty 635 n.
lottery
equal chance 159 n.
gambling 618 n.
lotus-eater
idler 679 n.
louche
disreputable 867 adj.
loud
loud 400 adj.
resonant 404 adj.
strident 407 adj.
crying 408 adj.
florid 425 adj.
manifest 522 adj.
ornate 574 adj.
rhetorical 574 adj.
vulgar 847 adj.
loudhailer
megaphone 400 n.
publicity 528 n.
loudmouth
boaster 877 n.
rude person 885 n.
loud pedal
piano 414 n.
loudspeaker
megaphone 400 n.
hearing aid 415 n.
publicity 528 n.
lough
lake 346 n.
lounge
chamber 194 n.
be inactive 679 vb.
repose 683 vb.
lounge lizard
fop 848 n.
lounger
seat 218 n.
idler 679 n.
loupe
eyeglass 442 n.
lour, lower
impend 155 vb.
hang 217 vb.
be dark 418 vb.
warn 664 vb.
be rude 885 vb.
be sullen 893 vb.
threaten 900 vb.
louse
insect 365 n.
cad 938 n.
lousy
not nice 645 adj.
unclean 649 adj.
lousy with
full 54 adj.
assembled 74 adj.
multitudinous 104 adj.
lout
dunce 501 n.
bungler 697 n.
rude person 885 n.
ruffian 904 n.
loutish
ill-bred 847 adj.
plebeian 869 adj.
discourteous 885 adj.
louvre
air pipe 353 n.
lovable, loveable
personable 841 adj.
amiable 884 adj.
lovable 887 adj.
love
zero 103 n.
moral sensibility 819 n.
be pleased 824 vb.
liking 859 n.
desire 859 vb.
be friendly 880 vb.
love 887 n., vb.
loved one 887 n.
lover 887 n.
caress 889 vb.
pet 889 vb.
darling 890 n.
benevolence 897 n.
jealousy 911 n.
disinterestedness 931 n.
divineness 965 n.
— to
be wont 610 vb.
love affair
love affair 887 n.
love all
draw 28 n.
love and kisses
courteous act 884 n.
love and peace
concord 710 n.
lovebirds
lovers 887 n.
love child
descendant 170 n.
bastardy 954 n.
loved one
desired object 859 n.
loved one 887 n.
darling 890 n.
love emblem
love emblem 887 n.
love token 889 n.
love feast
social gathering 882 n.
public worship 981 n.
love god
love god 887 n.
love-hate
contrary 14 adj.
love knot
badge 547 n.
loveless
indifferent 860 adj.
unwanted 860 adj.
disliked 861 adj.
disliking 861 adj.
hated 888 adj.
hating 888 adj.
love letter
love token 889 n.
wooing 889 n.
lovelock
coil 251 n.
hair 259 n.
lovelorn
loving 887 adj.
hated 888 adj.
lovely
pleasant 376 adj.
super 644 adj.
pleasurable 826 adj.
a beauty 841 n.
beautiful 841 adj.
lovable 887 adj.
love-making
love-making 887 n.
wooing 889 n.
love-match
type of marriage 894 n.
love-nest
love-nest 887 n.
love of one's country
patriotism 901 n.
love of pleasure
sensualism 944 n.
love philtre
stimulant 174 n.
lover
patron 707 n.
desirer 859 n.
lover 887 n.
libertine 952 n.
lovers
lovers 887 n.
lovesick
loving 887 adj.
love song
vocal music 412 n.
poem 593 n.
wooing 889 n.
love story
novel 590 n.
love token
love token 889 n.
lovey
darling 890 n.
lovey-dovey
caressing 889 adj.
loving care
carefulness 457 n.
loving cup
draught 301 n.
sociability 882 n.
loving it
pleased 824 adj.
loving-kindness
benevolence 897 n.
lovingly
carefully 457 adv.
affectionately 887 adv.
benevolently 897 adv.
loving words
endearment 889 n.
low
small 33 adj.
inferior 35 adj.
weak 163 adj.
low 210 adj.
muted 401 adj.
ululate 409 vb.
not nice 645 adj.
cheap 812 adj.
dejected 834 adj.
vulgar 847 adj.
disreputable 867 adj.
plebeian 869 adj.

humble 872 adj.
rascally 930 adj.
lowborn
plebeian 869 adj.
lowbrow
uninstructed 491 adj.
ignoramus 493 n.
unintelligent 499 adj.
low-budget
cheap 812 adj.
low-caste
inferior 35 adj.
plebeian 869 adj.
Low-Church
Anglican 976 adj.
sectarian 978 adj.
low-density
few 105 adj.
lowdown
information 524 n.
lower
(See **lour** *)*
lower
inferior 35 adj.
abate 37 vb.
low 210 adj.
lower 311 vb.
impair 655 vb.
pervert 655 vb.
cheapen 812 vb.
vulgarize 847 vb.
humiliate 872 vb.
not respect 921 vb.
hold cheap 922 vb.
defame 926 vb.
— oneself
descend 309 vb.
sit down 311 vb.
demean oneself 867 vb.
— one's sights
relinquish 621 vb.
lower case
print-type 587 n.
lower classes
lower classes 869 n.
lower deck
layer 207 n.
plebeian 869 adj.
Lower House
parliament 692 n.
lowermost
undermost 214 adj.
lower orders
nonentity 639 n.
lower classes 869 n.
lowest
lesser 35 adj.
low fellow
low fellow 869 n.
low gear
slowness 278 n.
low-grade
inferior 35 adj.
bad 645 adj.
low-key
moderate 177 adj.
lowlander
dweller 191 n.
lowlands
lowness 210 n.
plain 348 n.
Lowlands
district 184 n.
low-level
inferior 35 adj.
low 210 adj.
unimportant 639 adj.
low-life
descriptive 590 adj.
lower classes 869 n.
wickedness 934 n.
lowly
inferior 35 adj.
plebeian 869 adj.
humble 872 adj.
low-lying
low 210 adj.
low-minded
vulgar 847 adj.
low neck
neckline 228 n.
bareness 229 n.
low opinion
disapprobation 924 n.
lowpaid
poor 801 adj.
low-pressure
inert 175 adj.
rarity 325 n.
weather 340 n.
lenient 736 adj.
low profile
secrecy 525 n.
low quality
badness 645 n.
low-ranking
inferior 35 adj.
low rate
price 809 n.
low spirits
dejection 834 n.
low standard
badness 645 n.
imperfection 647 n.
low temperature
coldness 380 n.
low turnout
fewness 105 n.
low voice
resonance 404 n.
voicelessness 578 n.
low water
lowness 210 n.
water 339 n.
scarcity 636 n.
poverty 801 n.
loyal
conformable 83 adj.
willing 597 adj.
obedient 739 adj.
observant 768 adj.
friendly 880 adj.
loving 887 adj.
patriotic 901 adj.
trustworthy 929 adj.
disinterested 931 adj.
pious 979 adj.
loyalist
conformist 83 n.
auxiliary 707 n.
defender 713 n.
loyalty
submission 721 n.
loyalty 739 n.
service 745 n.
duty 917 n.
lozenge
angular figure 247 n.
sweet thing 392 n.
heraldry 547 n.
medicine 658 n.
LP
gramophone 414 n.
Lsd
money 797 n.
LSD
drug-taking 949 n.
lubber
bungler 697 n.
lubberly
unwieldy 195 adj.
clumsy 695 adj.
ill-bred 847 adj.
lubricant
lubricant 334 n.
lubricate
smooth 258 vb.
soften 327 vb.
lubricate 334 vb.
facilitate 701 vb.
lubricious
smooth 258 adj.
impure 951 adj.
lubricity
changeableness 152 n.
smoothness 258 n.
lubrication 334 n.
unctuousness 357 n.
unchastity 951 n.
lucent
luminous 417 adj.
transparent 422 adj.
lucerne
provender 301 n.
lucid
luminous 417 adj.
undimmed 417 adj.
transparent 422 adj.
sane 502 adj.
intelligible 516 adj.
perspicuous 567 adj.
Lucifer
planet 321 n.
luminary 420 n.
Satan 969 n.
luck
changeable thing 152 n.
chance 159 n.
good 615 n.
nondesign 618 n.
prosperity 730 n.
luck-bringer
omen 511 n.
talisman 983 n.
luckily
by chance 159 adv.
luckless
unfortunate 731 adj.
lucky
opportune 137 adj.
successful 727 adj.
prosperous 730 adj.
happy 824 adj.
lucky charm
talisman 983 n.
lucky dip
medley 43 n.
confusion 61 n.
equal chance 159 n.
lucky fellow
prosperous person 730 n.
lucky find
extra 40 n.
discovery 484 n.
lucky man/woman
loved one 887 n.
lucrative
gainful 771 adj.
lucre
acquisition 771 n.
money 797 n.
wealth 800 n.
lucubration
thought 449 n.
dissertation 591 n.
Lucullan banquet
feasting 301 n.
sensualism 944 n.
Luddite
destroyer 168 n.
rioter 738 n.
ludicrous
absurd 497 adj.
foolish 499 adj
ridiculous 849 adj.
ludo
board game 837 n.
luff
navigate 269 vb.
lug
handle 218 n.
draw 288 vb.
ear 415 n.
tool 630 n.
luge
sledge 274 n.
luggage
box 194 n.
thing transferred 272 n.
lugger
merchant ship 275 n.
lugsail
sail 275 n.
lugubrious
cheerless 834 adj.

lamenting 836 adj.
lukewarm
warm 379 adj.
unwilling 598 adj.
irresolute 601 adj.
neutral 625 adj.
apathetic 820 adj.
indifferent 860 adj.
lull
discontinuity 72 n.
delay 136 n.
lull 145 n.
assuage 177 vb.
interval 201 n.
quiescence 266 n.
silence 399 n.vb.
befool 542 vb.
inactivity 679 n.
make inactive 679 vb.
repose 683 n.
peace 717 n.
tranquillize 823 vb.
content 828 vb.
relieve 831 vb.
flatter 925 vb.
— to sleep
bring to rest 266 vb.
lullaby
vocal music 412 n.
soporific 679 n.
lumbago
pang 377 n.
rheumatism 651 n.
lumbar
back 238 adj.
lumber
leavings 41 n.
confusion 61 n.
move slowly 278 vb.
wood 366 n.
rubbish 641 n.
be clumsy 695 vb.
encumbrance 702 n.
lumbering
unwieldy 195 adj.
inexpedient 643 adj.
clumsy 695 adj.
lumberjack
forestry 366 n.
lumber room
chamber 194 n.
luminary
star 321 n.
light 417 n.
luminary 420 n.
sage 500 n.
person of repute 866 n.
luminescent
luminescent 420 adj.
luminous
luminous 417 adj.
luminescent 420 adj.
white 427 adj.
intelligible 516 adj.
lump
great quantity 32 n.
chief part 52 n.
piece 53 n.
bulk 195 n.
swelling 253 n.
solid body 324 n.
bungler 697 n.
— together
combine 50 vb.
bring together 74 vb.
not discriminate 464 vb.
lumpenproletariat
commonalty 869 n.
lump in one's throat
feeling 818 n.
lumpish
inert 175 adj.
unwieldy 195 adj.
weighty 322 adj.
inactive 679 adj.
lump sum
funds 797 n.
lumpy
nonuniform 17 adj.
rough 259 adj.
dense 324 adj.
semiliquid 354 adj.
lunacy
folly 499 n.
insanity 503 n.
lunar
curved 248 adj.
celestial 321 adj.
lunar landscape
desert 172 n.
lunar mansion
zodiac 321 n.
lunar module
spaceship 276 n.
lunatic
insane 503 adj.
madman 504 n.
rash 857 adj.
lunatic asylum
lunatic asylum 503 n.
hospital 658 n.
shelter 662 n.
lunatic fringe
crank 504 n.
lunation
period 110 n.
lunch
meal 301 n.
eat 301 vb.
lunette
arc 250 n.
defences 713 n.
lung(s)
space 183 n.
insides 224 n.
respiration 352 n.
megaphone 400 n.
voice 577 n.
lung cancer
respiratory disease 651 n.
lunge
move fast 277 vb.
impulse 279 n.
lunge 712 n.
strike at 712 vb.
lungi
loincloth 228 n.
lunula
curve 248 n.
lupine
animal 365 adj.
lupus
skin disease 651 n.
lurch
obliquity 220 n.
walk 267 vb.
move slowly 278 vb.
tumble 309 vb.
fluctuation 317 n.
oscillate 317 vb.
be drunk 949 vb.
lure
attraction 291 n.
attract 291 vb.
trap 542 n.
incentive 612 n.
tempt 612 vb.
desired object 859 n.
lurgy
digestive disorders 651 n.
lurid
luminous 417 adj.
dark 418 adj.
florid 425 adj.
colourless 426 adj.
frightening 854 adj.
showy 875 adj.
lurk
be unseen 444 vb.
escape notice 456 vb.
lurk 523 vb.
be stealthy 525 vb.
avoid 620 vb.
elude 667 vb.
be cautious 858 vb.
lurker
hider 527 n.
slyboots 698 n.
luscious
savoury 390 adj.
sweet 392 adj.
pleasurable 826 adj.
ornamented 844 adj.
lush
prolific 171 adj.
vigorous 174 adj.
vegetal 366 adj.
plenteous 635 adj.
rich 800 adj.
drunkard 949 n.
lust
desire 859 n., vb.
libido 859 n.
love 887 n.
vice 934 n.
unchastity 951 n.
— after
desire 859 vb.
envy 912 vb.
lustful
desiring 859 adj.
loving 887 adj.
lecherous 951 adj.
lustrate
purify 648 vb.
perform ritual 988 vb.
lustre
light 417 n.
lamp 420 n.
prestige 866 n.
lustreless
dim 419 adj.
colourless 426 adj.
lustrous
luminous 417 adj.
noteworthy 866 adj.
lustrum
period 110 n.
lusty
strong 162 adj.
vigorous 174 adj.
large 195 adj.
loud 400 adj.
healthy 650 adj.
personable 841 adj.
lute
adhesive 47 n.
harp 414 n.
luteous
orange 432 adj.
yellow 433 adj.
lute player
instrumentalist 413 n.
Lutheran
Protestant 976 n., adj.
Lutheranism
Protestantism 976 n.
sectarianism 978 n.
luxuriance
vegetable life 366 n.
luxuriant
prolific 171 adj.
dense 324 adj.
ornate 574 adj.
plenteous 635 adj.
ornamented 844 adj.
luxuriate
abound 635 vb.
superabound 637 vb.
— in
enjoy 376 vb.
be pleased 824 vb.
be intemperate 943 vb
luxuries
superfluity 637 n.
luxurious
comfortable 376 adj.
rich 800 adj.
pleasurable 826 adj.
ostentatious 875 adj.
sensual 944 adj.
luxury
euphoria 376 n.
plenty 635 n.

superfluity 637 n.
prosperity 730 n.
wealth 800 n.
intemperance 943 n.
sensualism 944 n.
luxury-lover
sensualist 944 n.
lycanthrope
demon 970 n.
lycée
academy 539 n.
Lyceum
philosopher 449 n.
academy 539 n.
lychgate
doorway 263 n.
church exterior 990 n.
lyddite
explosive 723 n.
Lydian mode
key 410 n.
lye
solution 337 n.
lying
erroneous 495 adj.
false 541 adj.
deceiving 542 adj.
untrue 543 adj.
lying down
supine 216 adj.
submitting 721 adj.
lying in
obstetrics 167 n.
lying-in-state
obsequies 364 n.
lymph
fluid 335 n.
lymphatic
watery 339 adj.
inactive 679 adj.
lynch
kill 362 vb.
execute 963 vb.
lynch law
anarchy 734 n.
lawlessness 954 n.
lynx
cat 365 n.
lynx-eyed
seeing 438 adj.
lyophilize
refrigerate 382 vb.
lyre
harp 414 n.
lyre player
instrumentalist 413 n.
lyric
vocal music 412 n.
musicianly 413 adj.
poetic 593 adj.
lyrical
poetic 593 adj.
impressed 818 adj.
excited 821 adj.
excitable 822 adj.
rejoicing 835 adj.
approving 923 adj.
lyricism
vocal music 412 n.
literature 557 n.
excitable state 822 n.
lyrics
reading matter 589 n.

M

MA
academic title 870 n.
ma'am
lady 373 n.
title 870 n.
mac
overcoat 228 n.
Mac
male 372 n.
macabre
frightening 854 adj.
spooky 970 adj.
macadam
road 624 n.
macaroni
dish 301 n.
fop 848 n.
macaronics
doggerel 593 n.
macaroon
pastries 301 n.
mace
hammer 279 n.
condiment 389 n.
club 723 n.
badge of rule 743 n.
mace-bearer
officer 741 n.
law officer 955 n.
macedoine
hors-d'oeuvres 301 n.
macerate
soften 327 vb.
drench 341 vb.
starve 946 vb.
machete, machet
sharp edge 256 n.
sidearms 723 n.
Machiavellian
hypocritical 541 adj.
planning 623 adj.
cunning 698 adj.
perfidious 930 adj.
machicolation
notch 260 n.
fortification 713 n.
machination
deception 542 n.
plot 623 n.
stratagem 698 n.
machine
causal means 156 n.
produce 164 vb.
print 587 vb.
fatalist 596 n.
instrument 628 n.
means 629 n.
machine 630 n.
slave 742 n.
Machine Age
era 110 n.
machine gun
gun 723 n.n.
machine gunner
soldiery 722 n.
machinelike
involuntary 596 adj.
machine-made
produced 164 adj.
machine-minded
mechanical 630 adj.
machinery
component 58 n.
complexity 61 n.
machine 630 n.
machine tool
tool 630 n.
machinist
machinist 630 n.
artisan 686 n.
machismo
male 372 n.
ostentation 875 n.
Mach number
velocity 277 n.
macho
male 372 n.adj.
courageous 855 adj.
boaster 877 n.
mack
bawd 952 n.
mackerel
fish food 301 n.
mackerel sky
cloud 355 n.
stripe 437 n.
mackintosh
overcoat 228 n.
macramé
network 222 n.
macrobiotic diet
dieting 301 n.
macrocosm
generality 79 n.
universe 321 n.
macron
punctuation 547 n.
macroscopic
large 195 adj.
visible 443 adj.
macula
maculation 437 n.
blemish 845 n.
mad
furious 176 adj.
absurd 497 adj.
insane 503 adj.
capricious 604 adj.
excited 821 adj.
angry 891 adj.
madam
lady 373 n.
master 741 n.
title 870 n.
insolent person 878 n.
bawd 952 n.
madcap
violent creature 176 n.
foolish 499 adj.
fool 501 n.
excitable 822 adj.
desperado 857 n.
rash 857 adj.
madden
make violent 176 vb.
make mad 503 vb.
enrage 891 vb.
maddening
annoying 827 adj.
madder
red pigment 431 n.
made
produced 164 adj.
Madeira
wine 301 n.
Madeira cake
pastries 301 n.
made man
prosperous person 730 n.
mademoiselle
youngster 132 n.
lady 373 n.
title 870 n.
made of
composing 56 adj.
made to measure
adjusted 24 adj.
definite 80 adj.
tailored 228 adj.
made up
produced 164 adj.
accessible 289 adj.
culinary 301 adj.
false 541 adj.
beautified 843 adj.
mad for
desiring 859 adj.
madhouse
confusion 61 n.
lunatic asylum 503 n.
Madison Avenue
advertisement 528 n.
madly
extremely 32 adv.
affectionately 887 adv.
madman, madwoman
fool 501 n.
madman 504 n.
madness
derangement 63 n.
insanity 503 n.
excitable state 822 n.
love 887 n.
Madonna
Madonna 968 n.

madrigal
vocal music 412 n.
madrigal singer
vocalist 413 n.
Maecenas
intellectual 492 n.
patron 707 n.
maelstrom
vortex 315 n.
eddy 350 n.
pitfall 663 n.
activity 678 n.
maenad
madman 504 n.
drunkard 949 n.
maestoso
adagio 412 adv.
maestro
orchestra 413 n.
proficient person 696 n.
Mae West
safeguard 662 n.
maffick
rejoice 835 vb.
celebrate 876 vb.
Mafia
revolter 738 n.
offender 904 n.
magazine
journal 528 n.
reading matter 589 n.
storage 632 n.
arsenal 723 n.
firearm 723 n.
magdalen
penitent 939 n.
magenta
red 431 adj.
purple 436 adj.
maggot
creepy-crawly 365 n.
whim 604 n.
maggoty
capricious 604 adj.
unclean 649 adj.
Magi
sage 500 n.
magian
sage 500 n.
sorcerer 983 n.
magic
influence 178 n.
sleight 542 n.
instrumentality 628 n.
thaumaturgy 864 n.
wonderful 864 adj.
prestige 866 n.
fairylike 970 adj.
sorcery 983 n.
bewitch 983 vb.
occultism 984 n.
— away
bewitch 983 vb.
magical
magical 983 adj.
magic arts
sorcery 983 n.
magic carpet
airship 276 n.
speeder 277 n.
aid 703 n.
magician
alterer 143 n.
conjuror 545 n.
proficient person 696 n.
sorcerer 983 n.
magic instrument
magic instrument 983 n.
magic lantern
lamp 420 n.
optical device 442 n.
plaything 837 n.
magic lore
sorcery 983 n.
magic rite
sorcery 983 n.
magic symbol
indication 547 n.
magic word
spell 983 n.
magic world
fairy 970 n.
Maginot Line
defences 713 n.
magisterial
skilful 694 adj.
authoritative 733 adj.
ruling 733 adj.
insolent 878 adj.
magistracy
position of authority 733 n.
magistracy 957 n.
magistrate
official 690 n.
officer 741 n.
judge 957 n.
punisher 963 n.
magistrate's court
lawcourt 956 n.
magistrature
position of authority 733 n.
magma
a mixture 43 n.
rock 344 n.
Magna Carta
dueness 915 n.
magnanimity
benevolence 897 n.
disinterestedness 931 n.
virtues 933 n.
magnanimous
forgiving 909 adj.
disinterested 931 adj.
virtuous 933 adj.
magnate
bigwig 638 n.
aristocrat 868 n.
magnet
traction 288 n.
magnet 291 n.
incentive 612 n.
desired object 859 n.
magnetic
dynamic 160 adj.
drawing 288 adj.
attracting 291 adj.
inducing 612 adj.
magnetic field
energy 160 n.
attraction 291 n.
magnetic needle
sailing aid 269 n.
indicator 547 n.
directorship 689 n.
magnetic North
compass point 281 n.
magnetic tape
data processing 86 n.
hearing aid 415 n.
record 548 n.
magnetism
energy 160 n.
influence 178 n.
traction 288 n.
attraction 291 n.
inducement 612 n.
magnetize, magnetise
empower 160 vb.
attract 291 vb.
magneto
electronics 160 n.
Magnificat
hymn 981 n.
magnification
greatness 32 n.
optics 417 n.
vision 438 n.
(See **magnify** *)*
magnificent
large 195 adj.
excellent 644 adj.
splendid 841 adj.
ostentatious 875 adj.
magnifico
aristocrat 868 n.
magnify
augment 36 vb.
enlarge 197 vb.
overrate 482 vb.
exaggerate 546 vb.
make important 638 vb.
boast 877 vb.
respect 920 vb.
praise 923 vb.
worship 981 vb.
magnifying glass
eyeglass 442 n.
magniloquence
exaggeration 546 n.
vigour 571 n.
magniloquence 574 n.
affectation 850 n.
ostentation 875 n.
magniloquent
boastful 877 adj.
magnitude
quantity 26 n.
degree 27 n.
greatness 32 n.
size 195 n.
light 417 n.
importance 638 n.
magnolia
tree 366 n.
whitish 427 adj.
Magnox reactor
nucleonics 160 n.
magnum
vessel 194 n.
size 195 n.
magnum opus
book 589 n.
masterpiece 694 n.
magpie
bird 365 n.
chatterer 581 n.
niggard 816 n.
magus
sage 500 n.
sorcerer 983 n.
maharaja, maharajah
potentate 741 n.
maharani, maharanee
potentate 741 n.
maharishi
good person 937 n.
religious teacher 973 n.
mahatma
sage 500 n.
good person 937 n.
Mahayana
religious faith 973 n.
Mahdi
leader 690 n.
religious teacher 973 n.
mah-jong
indoor game 837 n.
mahogany
smoothness 258 n.
tree 366 n.
brownness 430 n.
mahout
rider 268 n.
maid
youngster 132 n.
domestic 742 n.
spinster 895 n.
virgin 950 n.
maiden
first 68 adj.
new 126 adj.
youngster 132 n.
woman 373 n.
spinster 895 n.
virgin 950 n.
maidenhood
celibacy 895 n.
purity 950 n.
maiden name
name 561 n.

maiden speech
debut 68 n.
maid-of-all-work
busy person 678 n.
worker 686 n.
domestic 742 n.
maid/matron of honour
bridal party 894 n.
maieutic
enquiring 459 adj.
rational 475 adj.
instrumental 628 adj.
mail
covering 226 n.
send 272 vb.
postal communications 531 n.
correspondence 588 n.
safeguard 662 n.
armour 713 n.
mailbag
postal communications 531 n.
mail-clad
defended 713 adj.
mailed fist
brute force 735 n.
compulsion 740 n.
lawlessness 954 n.
mailing list
information 524 n.
correspondence 588 n.
mail order
purchase 792 n.
maim
disable 161 vb.
impair 655 vb.
maimed
incomplete 55 adj.
imperfect 647 adj.
main
great 32 adj.
supreme 34 adj.
conduit 351 n.
communicating 624 adj.
important 638 adj.
sink 649 n.
main chance
fair chance 159 n.
chief thing 638 n.
gain 771 n.
main force
strength 162 n.
compulsion 740 n.
mainframe
counting instrument 86 n.
mainland
land 344 n.
inland 344 adj.
mainline
drug oneself 949 vb.
mainly
substantially 3 adv.
greatly 32 adv.
on the whole 52 adv.
generally 79 adv.
mainmast
sail 275 n.
main part
main part 32 n.
chief thing 638 n.
main point
chief thing 638 n.
mainsail
sail 275 n.
mainspring
cause 156 n.
motive 612 n.
machine 630 n.
mainstay
prop 218 n.
chief thing 638 n.
aider 703 n.
mainstream
greater number 104 n.
tendency 179 n.
mainstream jazz
music 412 n.
Main Street
averageness 732 n.
irreligious 974 adj.
maintain
stay 144 vb.
sustain 146 vb.
operate 173 vb.
support 218 vb.
believe 485 vb.
affirm 532 vb.
persevere 600 vb.
provide 633 vb.
preserve 666 vb.
celebrate 876 vb.
vindicate 927 vb.
maintenance
subvention 703 n.
receipt 807 n.
main thing
chief thing 638 n.
maisonette
flat 192 n.
maître
proficient person 696 n.
maize
cereals 301 n.
food 301 n.
majestic
elegant 575 adj.
authoritative 733 adj.
impressive 821 adj.
beautiful 841 adj.
worshipful 866 adj.
proud 871 adj.
formal 875 adj.
godlike 965 adj.
majesty
greatness 32 n.
superiority 34 n.
authority 733 n.
sovereign 741 n.
prestige 866 n.
nobility 868 n.
Majlis
parliament 692 n.
major
great 32 adj.
superior 34 adj.
older 131 adj.
grown-up 134 adj.
harmonic 410 adj.
important 638 adj.
army officer 741 n.
majordomo
retainer 742 n.
major in
study 536 vb.
majority
main part 32 n.
chief part 52 n.
greater number 104 n.
adultness 134 n.
majority rule
government 733 n.
make
character 5 n.
composition 56 n.
compose 56 vb.
constitute 56 vb.
sort 77 n.
convert 147 vb.
cause 156 vb.
produce 164 vb.
influence 178 vb.
form 243 vb.
arrive 295 vb.
structure 331 n.
estimate 480 vb.
make better 654 vb.
compel 740 vb.
gain 771 vb.
— a clean breast of it
confess 526 vb.
be truthful 540 vb.
— a clean sweep (of)
revolutionize 149 vb.
empty 300 vb.
clean 648 vb.
— a comeback
be restored 656 vb.
— acquainted
befriend 880 vb.
— a dead set at
attack 712 vb.
desire 859 vb.
— a dent in
waste 634 vb.
— advances
offer 759 vb.
court 889 vb.
— a face
distort 246 vb.
dislike 861 vb.
be sullen 893 vb.
disapprove 924 vb.
— a fight of it
resist 715 vb.
— a fool of
befool 542 vb.
ridicule 851 vb.
humiliate 872 vb.
— a fool of oneself
be foolish 499 vb.
act foolishly 695 vb.
— a fortune
prosper 730 vb.
gain 771 vb.
get rich 800 vb.
— a go of
succeed 727 vb.
— a hash of it
be clumsy 695 vb.
— a hit
succeed 727 vb.
excite love 887 vb.
— a killing
succeed 727 vb.
gain 771 vb.
— a man of
do good 644 vb.
give courage 855 vb.
— amends
compensate 31 vb.
restitute 787 vb.
atone 941 vb.
— a mess of it
be clumsy 695 vb.
— a monkey of
ridicule 851 vb.
— an example of
punish 963 vb.
— an exhibition of oneself
be ridiculous 849 vb.
be ostentatious 875 vb.
— an impression
be vigorous 174 vb.
cause thought 449 vb.
— a pass at
court 889 vb.
— a point of
make important 638 vb.
compel 740 vb.
— a profit
flourish 615 vb.
be useful 640 vb.
gain 771 vb.
— a scene
be angry 891 vb.
— a show of
imitate 20 vb.
dissemble 541 vb.
be affected 850 vb.
— a silk purse out of a sow's ear
attempt the impossible 470 vb.
— a splash
superabound 637 vb.
be ostentatious 875 vb.

— a stand
resist 715 vb.
give battle 718 vb.
— available
offer 759 vb.
— a virtue of necessity
have no choice 606 vb.
submit 721 vb.
compromise 770 vb.
— away with
destroy 165 vb.
kill 362 vb.
steal 788 vb.
— better
transform 147 vb.
benefit 615 vb.
make better 654 vb.
— bold to
be free 744 vb.
be insolent 878 vb.
— both ends meet
afford 800 vb.
economize 814 vb.
— bright
make bright 417 vb.
illuminate 420 vb.
clean 648 vb.
beautify 841 vb.
— capital out of
plead 614 vb.
find useful 640 vb.
use 673 vb.
— certain
corroborate 466 vb.
make certain 473 vb.
demonstrate 478 vb.
give security 767 vb.
be cautious 858 vb.
— common cause with
cooperate 706 vb.
— complete
add 38 vb.
make complete 54 vb.
carry through 725 vb.
— demands
require 627 vb.
request 761 vb.
give terms 766 vb.
— do with
substitute 150 vb.
avail oneself of 673 vb.
— enemies
make enemies 881 vb.
excite hate 888 vb.
— excuses
plead 614 vb.
avoid 620 vb.
— eyes at
gaze 438 vb.
desire 859 vb.
court 889 vb.
— fast
tighten 45 vb.
stabilize 153 vb.
— for
congregate 74 vb.
steer for 281 vb.
promote 285 vb.
— free with
be free 744 vb.
appropriate 786 vb.
be insolent 878 vb.
— friends
be friendly 880 vb.
be sociable 882 vb.
— fruitful
make fruitful 171 vb.
cultivate 370 vb.
— fun of
befool 542 vb.
be witty 839 vb.
ridicule 851 vb.
— good
compensate 31 vb.
make complete 54 vb.
corroborate 466 vb.
replenish 633 vb.
succeed 727 vb.
vindicate 927 vb.
— hay while the sun shines
profit by 137 vb.
be skilful 694 vb.
— headway
progress 285 vb.
get better 654 vb.
— heavy weather of
be busy 678 vb.
be in difficulty 700 vb.
— history
be remembered 505 vb.
do 676 vb.
have a reputation 866 vb.
— important
emphasize 532 vb.
exaggerate 546 vb.
make important 638 vb.
— impossible
make impossible 470 vb.
negate 533 vb.
be difficult 700 vb.
— inactive
disable 161 vb.
bring to rest 266 vb.
render insensible 375 vb.
make useless 641 vb.
impair 655 vb.
make inactive 679 vb.
— inroads on
encroach 306 vb.
waste 634 vb.
— into
convert 147 vb.
— it
triumph 727 vb.
prosper 730 vb.
— it one's business
pursue 619 vb.
busy oneself 622 vb.
— it up
make peace 719 vb.
forgive 909 vb.
— it up to
restitute 787 vb.
atone 941 vb.
— light of
underestimate 483 vb.
do easily 701 vb.
be indifferent 860 vb.
— love
unite with 45 vb.
love 887 vb.
caress 889 vb.
— merry
rejoice 835 vb.
revel 837 vb.
— mincemeat of
cut 46 vb.
demolish 165 vb.
— money
flourish 615 vb.
prosper 730 vb.
gain 771 vb.
get rich 800 vb.
— mountains out of molehills
overrate 482 vb.
exaggerate 546 vb.
— mouths at
not respect 921 vb.
disapprove 924 vb.
— much of
advertise 528 vb.
exaggerate 546 vb.
make important 638 vb.
honour 866 vb.
celebrate 876 vb.
love 887 vb.
pet 889 vb.
respect 920 vb.
flatter 925 vb.
— neither head nor tail of
not understand 517 vb.
— no bones about
be plain 522 vb.
affirm 532 vb.
be willing 597 vb.
do easily 701 vb.
— no demands
be easy 701 vb.
be lenient 736 vb.
— no difference
be equal 28 vb.
not discriminate 464 vb.
— no secret of
be plain 522 vb.
— no sense
mean nothing 515 vb.
— off with
steal 788 vb.
— one jump
surprise 508 vb.
frighten 854 vb.
— one laugh
amuse 837 vb.
be ridiculous 849 vb.
— one look silly
befool 542 vb.
ridicule 851 vb.
humiliate 872 vb.
— one of
be included 78 vb.
be present 189 vb.
join a party 708 vb.
— one's blood run cold
displease 827 vb.
frighten 854 vb.
— one's day
content 828 vb.
— one see red
make mad 503 vb.
excite 821 vb.
enrage 891 vb.
— oneself
be unwilling 598 vb.
— oneself at home
be free 744 vb.
be sociable 882 vb.
— oneself felt
influence 178 vb.
— oneself scarce
go away 190 vb.
decamp 296 vb.
run away 620 vb.
escape 667 vb.
— oneself sick
be intemperate 943 vb.
gluttonize 947 vb.
— oneself useful
minister to 703 vb.
serve 742 vb.
— one's hair stand on end
frighten 854 vb.
— one's heart bleed
sadden 834 vb.
— one sick
displease 827 vb.
cause dislike 861 vb.
— one sit up
impress 821 vb.
— one's mark
succeed 727 vb.
have a reputation 866 vb.
— one's mind easy
tranquillize 823 vb.
— one's mouth water
await 507 vb.
tempt 612 vb.

cause desire 859 vb.
— one's own
acquire 771 vb.
appropriate 786 vb.
— one's point
affirm 532 vb.
— one's voice heard
influence 178 vb.
— one's way
be in motion 265 vb.
travel 267 vb.
— one think
cause thought 449 vb.
puzzle 474 vb.
— or mar
cause 156 vb.
influence 178 vb.
— out
see 438 vb.
demonstrate 478 vb.
understand 516 vb.
decipher 520 vb.
succeed 727 vb.
— over
transfer 272 vb.
repair 656 vb.
assign 780 vb.
— overtures
approach 289 vb.
request 761 vb.
befriend 880 vb.
— peace
make peace 719 vb.
— play with
use 673 vb.
— possible
make possible 469 vb.
facilitate 701 vb.
— progress
get better 654 vb.
— provision
foresee 510 vb.
provide 633 vb.
— public
publish 528 vb.
— room
go away 190 vb.
be in motion 265 vb.
— sense
be intelligible 516 vb.
— sense of
interpret 520 vb.
— shift to
plan 623 vb.
attempt 671 vb.
— shift with
substitute 150 vb.
avail oneself of 673 vb.
— short work of
destroy 165 vb.
eat 301 vb.
do easily 701 vb.
succeed 727 vb.
— something of it
make quarrels 709 vb.
— sterile
unman 161 vb.
lay waste 165 vb.
make sterile 172 vb.
make useless 641 vb.
— sure
stabilize 153 vb.
make certain 473 vb.
be cautious 858 vb.
— terms
do business 622 vb.
cooperate 706 vb.
make terms 766 vb.
bargain 791 vb.
— the best of
avail oneself of 673 vb.
compromise 770 vb.
be content 828 vb.
— the grade
suffice 635 vb.
succeed 727 vb.
— the most of
overrate 482 vb.
make better 654 vb.
use 673 vb.
— the running
outstrip 277 vb.
outdo 306 vb.
— things worse
deteriorate 655 vb.
aggravate 832 vb.
— to measure
adjust 24 vb.
— too much of
overrate 482 vb.
exaggerate 546 vb.
— towards
steer for 281 vb.
approach 289 vb.
— tracks
decamp 296 vb.
— trouble
make quarrels 709 vb.
cause discontent 829 vb.
— ugly
deform 244 vb.
impair 655 vb.
make ugly 842 vb.
blemish 845 vb.
— unclean
bedim 419 vb.
blacken 428 vb.
make unclean 649 vb.
impair 655 vb.
— uniform
make uniform 16 vb.
equalize 28 vb.
regularize 62 vb.
make conform 83 vb.
— unwelcome
exclude 57 vb.
repel 292 vb.
reject 607 vb.
avoid 620 vb.
be inimical 881 vb.
make unwelcome 883 vb.
be rude 885 vb.
— up
make complete 54 vb.
compose 56 vb.
constitute 56 vb.
produce 164 vb.
imagine 513 vb.
be false 541 vb.
replenish 633 vb.
primp 843 vb.
— up for
compensate 31 vb.
atone 941 vb.
— up leeway
recoup 31 vb.
progress 285 vb.
retrieve 656 vb.
— up one's mind
be resolute 599 vb.
choose 605 vb.
— up to
approach 289 vb.
be servile 879 vb.
flatter 925 vb.
— useless
disable 161 vb.
make useless 641 vb.
make inactive 679 vb.
— use of
find useful 640 vb.
use 673 vb.
— way for
deviate 282 vb.
facilitate 701 vb.
resign 753 vb.
show respect 920 vb.
— worse
aggravate 832 vb.
make-believe
imitate 20 vb.
fantasy 513 n.
imaginary 513 adj.
hypocritical 541 adj.
sham 542 n.
untrue 543 adj.
maker
cause 156 n.
producer 164 n.
the Deity 965 n.
makeshift
inferior 35 adj.
transience 114 n.
substitute 150 n.
spontaneous 609 adj.
pretext 614 n.
instrument 628 n.
means 629 n.
sufficient 635 adj.
imperfect 647 adj.
unprepared 670 adj.
make-up
character 5 n.
composition 56 n.
speciality 80 n.
structure 331 n.
print 587 n.
cosmetic 843 n.
make-up artist
stagehand 594 n.
makeweight
offset 31 n.
plenitude 54 n.
making of, be the
influence 178 vb.
do good 644 vb.
make better 654 vb.
malachite
greenness 434 n.
maladjusted
unapt 25 adj.
inexact 495 adj.
insane 503 adj.
maladjustment
discontent 829 n.
maladministration
misuse 675 n.
bungling 695 n.
maladroit
clumsy 695 adj.
malady
disease 651 n.
bane 659 n.
malaise
pain 377 n.
evil 616 n.
suffering 825 n.
malapropism
inexactness 495 n.
absurdity 497 n.
neology 560 n.
misnomer 562 n.
solecism 565 n.
ridiculousness 849 n.
malapropos
unapt 25 adj.
ill-timed 138 adj.
inexpedient 643 adj.
malaria
tropical disease 651 n.
malarkey
empty talk 515 n.
malcontent
dissentient 489 n.
revolter 738 n.
petitioner 763 n.
malcontent 829 n.
moper 834 n.
disapprover 924 n.
mal du siècle
melancholy 834 n.
male
manly 162 adj.
male 372 n.adj.
male animal
male animal 372 n.
male chauvinism
male 372 n.

malediction
discontent 829 n.
hatred 888 n.
malediction 899 n.
detraction 926 n.
condemnation 961 n.
impiety 980 n.
maledictory
maledictory 899 adj.
threatening 900 adj.
malefactor
evildoer 904 n.
offender 904 n.
maleficent
evil 616 adj.
maleficent 898 adj.
wicked 934 adj.
male member
genitalia 167 n.
malevolence
evil 616 n.
malevolence 898 n.
malevolent
harmful 645 adj.
inimical 881 adj.
hating 888 adj.
resentful 891 adj.
malevolent 898 adj.
revengeful 910 adj.
wicked 934 adj.
diabolic 969 adj.
malfeasance
lawbreaking 954 n.
malformation
deformity 246 n.
malfunction
fail 728 vb.
malice
joy 824 n.
hatred 888 n.
malevolence 898 n.
malicious
harmful 645 adj.
malicious gossip
calumny 926 n.
malign
harmful 645 adj.
adverse 731 adj.
shame 867 vb.
malevolent 898 adj.
defame 926 vb.
malignant
deadly 362 adj.
harmful 645 adj.
hating 888 adj.
malevolent 898 adj.
malignant tumour
cancer 651 n.
malignity
badness 645 n.
annoyance 827 n.
malevolence 898 n.
malinger
dissemble 541 vb.
fail in duty 918 vb.
malingerer
impostor 545 n.
mall
pleasance 192 n.
path 624 n.
mallard
bird 365 n.
malleable
conformable 83 adj.
flexible 327 adj.
tractable 701 adj.
submitting 721 adj.
impressible 819 adj.
mallet
hammer 279 n.
malnourished
unhealthy 651 adj.
malnutrition
insufficiency 636 n.
disease 651 n.
malodorous
fetid 397 adj.
unclean 649 adj.
unpleasant 827 adj.
malpractice
misuse 675 n.
guilty act 936 n.
lawbreaking 954 n.
Malthusianism
deterioration 655 n.
maltings
workshop 687 n.
maltreat
ill-treat 645 vb.
misuse 675 vb.
torment 827 vb.
be malevolent 898 vb.
malversation
peculation 788 n.
foul play 930 n.
guilty act 936 n.
mamba
reptile 365 n.
mambo
dance 837 n.
mamelon
dome 253 n.
Mameluke
militarist 722 n.
mamma
maternity 169 n.
bosom 253 n.
mammal
mammal 365 n.
mammalogy
zoology 367 n.
Mammon
money 797 n.
wealth 800 n.
devil 969 n.
Mammonism
antichristianity 974 n.
idolatry 982 n.
mammoth
fossil 125 n.
giant 195 n.
huge 195 adj.
animal 365 n.
man
adult 134 n.
operate 173 vb.
humankind 371 n.
male 372 n.
provide 633 vb.
defend 713 vb.
domestic 742 n.
brave person 855 n.
spouse 894 n.
mana
power 160 n.
influence 178 n.
divineness 965 n.
man/woman about town
expert 696 n.
beau monde 848 n.
manacle
tie 45 vb.
fetter 747 vb.
fetter 748 n.
manage
arrange 62 vb.
be able 160 vb.
look after 457 vb.
motivate 612 vb.
undertake 672 vb.
do 676 vb.
deal with 688 vb.
manage 689 vb.
be successful 727 vb.
rule 733 vb.
deputize 755 vb.
— well enough
be middling 732 vb.
manageable
tractable 701 adj.
obedient 739 adj.
management
management 689 n.
director 690 n.
manager
stage manager 594 n.
motivator 612 n.
doer 676 n.
director 690 n.
manager 690 n.
master 741 n.
consignee 754 n.
managerial
directing 689 adj.
mañana
neverness 109 n.
futurity 124 n.
delay 136 n.
inactivity 679 n.
man and wife
spouse 894 n.
man-at-arms
soldier 722 n.
Mandaeans
non-Christian sect 978 n.
mandala
indication 547 n.
mandamus
warrant 737 n.
mandarin
fruit 301 n.
bigwig 638 n.
official 690 n.
officer 741 n.
mandate
precept 693 n.
government 733 n.
command 737 n.
mandate 751 n.
permit 756 n.
conditions 766 n.
mandated territory
political organization 733 n.
mandatory
preceptive 693 adj.
authoritative 733 adj.
commanding 737 adj.
obligatory 917 adj.
mandibles
eater 301 n.
mandolin
harp 414 n.
mane
hair 259 n.
man-eater
eater 301 n.
killer 362 n.
noxious animal 904 n.
manège
equitation 267 n.
manes
ghost 970 n.
man Friday
worker 686 n.
aider 703 n.
manful
manly 162 adj.
courageous 855 adj.
manfully
resolutely 599 adv.
mange
animal disease 651 n.
skin disease 651 n.
mangle
compressor 198 n.
flattener 216 n.
distort 246 vb.
smoother 258 n.
extractor 304 n.
dryer 342 n.
wound 655 vb.
mangled
incomplete 55 adj.
inexact 495 adj.
mango
fruit 301 n.
mangrove
tree 366 n.
mangrove swamp
marsh 347 n.
mangy
hairless 229 adj.
unhealthy 651 adj.

manhandle
move 265 vb.
misuse 675 vb.
man-hater
misanthrope 902 n.
manhole
orifice 263 n.
manhood
adultness 134 n.
male 372 n.
manliness 855 n.
manhour(s)
job 622 n.
labour 682 n.
manhunt
chase 619 n.
mania
mania 503 n.
warm feeling 818 n.
excitable state 822 n.
desire 859 n.
maniac
madman 504 n.
manic
insane 503 adj.
manic depression
psychopathy 503 n.
manic-depressive
madman 504 n.
Manichaean, Manichean
heretic 977 n.
heretical 977 adj.
Manichee
heretic 977 n.
manicure
beautification 843 n.
manicured
elegant 575 adj.
manifest
list 87 n.
open 263 adj.
appearing 445 adj.
evidence 466 vb.
manifest 522 adj.vb.
well-known 528 adj.
show feeling 818 vb.
manifestation
visibility 443 n.
appearance 445 n.
manifestation 522 n.
disclosure 526 n.
indication 547 n.
representation 551 n.
manifestly
apparently 445 adv.
manifestly 522 adv.
manifesto
publication 528 n.
electorate 605 n.
manifold
multiform 82 adj.
many 104 adj.
manikin, mannikin
dwarf 196 n.
image 551 n.
manila, manilla
fibre 208 n.
man/woman in charge
manager 690 n.
man/woman in the street
common man 30 n.
everyman 79 n.
averageness 732 n.
commoner 869 n.
maniple
formation 722 n.
vestments 989 n.
manipulate
operate 173 vb.
touch 378 vb.
fake 541 vb.
befool 542 vb.
motivate 612 vb.
plot 623 vb.
doctor 658 vb.
use 673 vb.
misuse 675 vb.
do 676 vb.
deal with 688 vb.
manage 689 vb.
manipulator
influence 178 n.
trickster 545 n.
motivator 612 n.
gambler 618 n.
manitou
the Deity 965 n.
mankind
humankind 371 n.
manly
grown-up 134 adj.
manly 162 adj.
male 372 adj.
beautiful 841 adj.
courageous 855 adj.
man-made
produced 164 adj.
man-made fibre
fibre 208 n.
manna
food 301 n.
subvention 703 n.
gift 781 n.
manned
occupied 191 adj.
mannequin
living model 23 n.
exhibitor 522 n.
mannequin parade
fashion 848 n.
manner
modality 7 n.
sort 77 n.
style 566 n.
way 624 n.
conduct 688 n.
mannered
inelegant 576 adj.
affected 850 adj.
mannerism
speciality 80 n.
nonconformity 84 n.
phrase 563 n.
style 566 n.
inelegance 576 n.
habit 610 n.
affectation 850 n.
airs 873 n.
Mannerism
school of painting 553 n.
mannerless
ill-bred 847 adj.
discourteous 885 adj.
mannerly
tasteful 846 adj.
courteous 884 adj.
manners
practice 610 n.
conduct 688 n.
good taste 846 n.
etiquette 848 n.
courtesy 884 n.
mannish
male 372 adj.
manoeuvrability
scope 744 n.
manoeuvrable
tractable 701 adj.
manoeuvre
motion 265 n.
deed 676 n.
tactics 688 n.
manage 689 vb.
stratagem 698 n.
be cunning 698 vb.
manoeuvrer
influence 178 n.
motivator 612 n.
planner 623 n.
slyboots 698 n.
manoeuvres
marching 267 n.
art of war 718 n.
man/woman of action
doer 676 n.
busy person 678 n.
man/woman of business
merchant 794 n.
man/woman of genius
prodigy 864 n.
man/woman of honour
person of repute 866 n.
man/woman of letters
scholar 492 n.
author 589 n.
bookperson 589 n.
man/woman of means
rich person 800 n.
man/woman of peace
pacifist 717 n.
man/woman of property
prosperous person 730 n.
owner 776 n.
man/woman of science
intellectual 492 n.
man/woman of spirit
brave person 855 n.
man of straw
insubstantial thing 4 n.
ineffectuality 161 n.
sham 542 n.
nonentity 639 n.
man/woman of substance
prosperous person 730 n.
man/woman of the hour
person of repute 866 n.
favourite 890 n.
man of the house
master 741 n.
man/woman of the people
commoner 869 n.
man/woman of the world
expert 696 n.
beau monde 848 n.
man/woman on the spot
presence 189 n.
delegate 754 n.
manor
house 192 n.
lands 777 n.
manorial
agrarian 370 adj.
proprietary 777 adj.
man-o'-war
warship 722 n.
manpower
means 629 n.
personnel 686 n.
manqué
unsuccessful 728 adj.
mansard roof
roof 226 n.
manse
parsonage 986 n.
manservant
domestic 742 n.
man's/woman's estate
adultness 134 n.
mansion
edifice 164 n.
house 192 n.
zodiac 321 n.
man-size
great 32 adj.
large 195 adj.
manslaughter
homicide 362 n.
mantelpiece
shelf 218 n.
mantic
predicting 511 adj.
mantilla
headgear 228 n.

mantle
wrapping 226 n.
cover 226 vb.
cloak 228 n.
bubble 355 vb.
lamp 420 n.
redden 431 vb.
show feeling 818 vb.
be modest 874 vb.
mantling
heraldry 547 n.
man/woman to watch
victor 727 n.
mantra
maxim 496 n.
mantrap
trap 542 n.
manual
series 71 n.
handed 378 adj.
musical note 410 n.
organ 414 n.
piano 414 n.
guidebook 524 n.
textbook 589 n.
instrumental 628 adj.
manual labour
labour 682 n.
manual worker
worker 686 n.
manufacture
production 164 n.
produce 164 vb.
business 622 n.
action 676 n.
manufacturer
producer 164 n.
agent 686 n.
manumit
liberate 746 vb.
exempt 919 vb.
manure
fertilizer 171 n.
make fruitful 171 vb.
excrement 302 n.
cultivate 370 vb.
manuscript
prototype 23 n.
script 586 n.
book 589 n.
many
many 104 adj.
frequent 139 adj.
many, be
be many 104 vb.
be fruitful 171 vb.
abound 635 vb.
superabound 637 vb.
many-coloured
multiform 82 adj.
coloured 425 adj.
variegated 437 adj.
many-headed
multiform 82 adj.
many parts, person of
proficient person 696 n.
many-sided
multiform 82 adj.
plural 101 adj.
lateral 239 adj.
skilful 694 adj.
many times over
repeatedly 106 adv.
Maoism
government 733 n.
map
statistics 86 n.
situation 186 n.
outline 233 vb.
itinerary 267 n.
world 321 n.
gauge 465 vb.
guidebook 524 n.
map 551 n.
represent 551 vb.
plan 623 n.
maple
tree 366 n.
maple syrup
sweet thing 392 n.
mapped
measured 465 adj.
maquette
image 551 n.
sculpture 554 n.
maquis
wood 366 n.
Maquis
soldier 722 n.
revolter 738 n.
mar
derange 63 vb.
modify 143 vb.
lay waste 165 vb.
influence 178 vb.
impair 655 vb.
be clumsy 695 vb.
hinder 702 vb.
make ugly 842 vb.
blemish 845 vb.
shame 867 vb.
marabou
bird 365 n.
marabout
solitary 883 n.
monk 986 n.
holy place 990 n.
maracas
gong 414 n.
marasmus
contraction 198 n.
disease 651 n.
marathon
lasting 113 adj.
distance 199 n.
contest 716 n.
maraud
rob 788 vb.
marauder
robber 789 n.
marble
sphere 252 n.
smoothness 258 n.
hardness 326 n.
rock 344 n.
white thing 427 n.
variegate 437 vb.
sculpture 554 n.
building material 631 n.
unfeeling person 820 n.
marbled
mottled 437 adj.
bibliographical 589 adj.
marbles
ball game 837 n.
plaything 837 n.
marcasite
finery 844 n.
march
assemblage 74 n.
gait 265 n.
be in motion 265 vb.
itinerary 267 n.
marching 267 n.
walk 267 vb.
progression 285 n.
musical piece 412 n.
route 624 n.
wage war 718 vb.
deprecation 762 n.
be ostentatious 875 vb.
— against
charge 712 vb.
— with
be contiguous 202 vb.
marcher
pedestrian 268 n.
agitator 738 n.
marches
region 184 n.
near place 200 n.
limit 236 n.
marching and countermarching
marching 267 n.
tactics 688 n.
marching orders
ejection 300 n.
command 737 n.
marchioness
person of rank 868 n.
march of events
affairs 154 n.
march of time
course of time 111 n.
progression 285 n.
improvement 654 n.
march-past
pageant 875 n.
Mardi Gras
festivity 837 n.
mare
horse 273 n.
moon 321 n.
female animal 373 n.
mare's nest
fable 543 n.
mare's tail
cloud 355 n.
margarine
cookery 301 n.
fat 357 n.
margin
difference 15 n.
remainder 41 n.
room 183 n.
edge 234 n.
edition 589 n.
superfluity 637 n.
scope 744 n.
discount 810 n.
marginal
inconsiderable 33 adj.
marginal 234 adj.
economical 814 adj.
marginal constituency
electorate 605 n.
marginalia
commentary 520 n.
record 548 n.
reading matter 589 n.
margrave, margravine
potentate 741 n.
person of rank 868 n.
marigold
orange 432 n.
marijuana, marihuana
pungency 388 n.
drug-taking 949 n.
marimba
gong 414 n.
marina
stable 192 n.
shelter 662 n.
marinate, marinade
season 388 vb.
preserve 666 vb.
marine
seafaring 269 adj.
shipping 275 n.
marine 275 adj.
oceanic 343 adj.
naval man 722 n.
marine exploration
water travel 269 n.
marine life
marine life 365 n.
mariner
traveller 268 n.
mariner 270 n.
naval man 722 n.
Mariolatry
Madonna 968 n.
cult 981 n.
marionette
image 551 n.
plaything 837 n.
marital
matrimonial 894 adj.

marital infidelity
illicit love 951 n.
maritime
marine 275 adj.
oceanic 343 adj.
marjoram
potherb 301 n.
mark
essential part 5 n.
degree 27 n.
serial place 73 n.
sort 77 n.
speciality 80 n.
effect 157 n.
feature 445 n.
notice 455 vb.
identification 547 n.
label 547 n.
mark 547 vb.
trace 548 n.
select 605 vb.
objective 617 n.
importance 638 n.
wound 655 n.
impair 655 vb.
coinage 797 n.
blemish 845 n.vb.
slur 867 n.
— down
underestimate 483 vb.
select 605 vb.
cheapen 812 vb.
— down for
intend 617 vb.
— off
gauge 465 vb.
mark 547 vb.
— out
differentiate 15 vb.
set apart 46 vb.
limit 236 vb.
indicate 547 vb.
select 605 vb.
dignify 866 vb.
— the occasion
celebrate 876 vb.
— time
pass time 108 vb.
time 117 vb.
be quiescent 266 vb.
await 507 vb.
— up
register 548 vb.
overcharge 811 vb.
marked
remarkable 32 adj.
special 80 adj.
marked 547 adj.
blemished 845 adj.
marked man
accused person 928 n.
marker
indication 547 n.
market
focus 76 n.
meeting place 192 n.
trade 791 n.
purchase 792 vb.
sell 793 vb.
market 796 n.
marketable
trading 791 adj.
salable 793 adj.
market for
sale 793 n.
market garden
farm 370 n.
marketplace
focus 76 n.
activity 678 n.
arena 724 n.
market 796 n.
market research
enquiry 459 n.
sale 793 n.
market town
district 184 n.
market trader
seller 793 n.
pedlar 794 n.
markings
identification 547 n.
mark of Cain
slur 867 n.
mark of recognition
courteous act 884 n.
marksman, markswoman
shooter 287 n.
hunter 619 n.
player 837 n.
marksmanship
skill 694 n.
marl
soil 344 n.
marlin
fish 365 n.
marmalade
sweet thing 392 n.
orange 432 n.
marmoreal
glyptic 554 adj.
maroon
set apart 46 vb.
brown 430 adj.
red 431 adj.
signal 547 n.
not retain 779 vb.
solitary 883 n.
marooned
insular 349 adj.
relinquished 621 adj.
hindered 702 adj.
marquee
pavilion 192 n.
canopy 226 n.
marquetry
chequer 437 n.
ornamental art 844 n.
marquis, marquess
person of rank 868 n.
marriage
union 45 n.
combination 50 n.
marriage 894 n.
marriageable
grown-up 134 adj.
marriageable 894 adj.
marriageable age
nubility 894 n.
marriage broker
intermediary 231 n.
matchmaker 894 n.
marriage bureau
matchmaker 894 n.
marriage ceremony
wedding 894 n.
marriage guidance counsellor
mediator 720 n.
marriage lines
record 548 n.
marriage 894 n.
marriage of convenience
type of marriage 894 n.
marriage on the rocks
divorce 896 n.
marriage service
Christian rite 988 n.
marriage settlement
dower 777 n.
married
joined 45 adj.
married 894 adj.
married couple
spouse 894 n.
marrow
substance 3 n.
essential part 5 n.
interiority 224 n.
centre 225 n.
vegetable 301 n.
marry
join 45 vb.
unite with 45 vb.
marry 894 vb.
wed 894 vb.
— into
be akin 11 vb.
— off
not retain 779 vb.
assign 780 vb.
marry 894 vb.
Mars
planet 321 n.
redness 431 n.
war 718 n.
mythic deity 966 n.
Olympian deity 967 n.
Marsala
wine 301 n.
marsh
lowness 210 n.
marsh 347 n.
plain 348 n.
semiliquidity 354 n.
dirt 649 n.
marshal
arrange 62 vb.
mark 547 vb.
official 690 n.
officer 741 n.
marshalling yard
railway 624 n.
marshmallows
sweets 301 n.
marshy
soft 327 adj.
humid 341 adj.
marshy 347 adj.
semiliquid 354 adj.
pulpy 356 adj.
dirty 649 adj.
insalubrious 653 adj.
marsupial
cellular 194 adj.
mammal 365 n.
mart
market 796 n.
Martello tower
fort 713 n.
martial
warlike 718 adj.
courageous 855 adj.
martial law
government 733 n.
brute force 735 n.
Martian
foreigner 59 n.
planetary 321 adj.
martinet
tyrant 735 n.
martingale
fetter 748 n.
Martinmas
holy day 988 n.
martlet
heraldry 547 n.
martyr
kill 362 vb.
sufferer 825 n.
torment 827 vb.
pietist 979 n.
martyrdom
death 361 n.
pain 377 n.
suffering 825 n.
disinterestedness 931 n.
capital punishment 963 n.
martyrology
list 87 n.
death roll 361 n.
biography 590 n.
martyr's crown
honours 866 n.
martyr to ill health
sick person 651 n.
marvel
prodigy 864 n.
wonder 864 vb.
marvellous
prodigious 32 adj.
excellent 644 adj.
pleasurable 826 adj.

wonderful 864 adj.
Marxism
philosophy 449 n.
Marxism-Leninism
government 733 n.
Marxist
revolutionist 149 n.
revolutionary 149 adj.
reformer 654 n.
Marxists
political party 708 n.
marzipan
sweet thing 392 n.
mascara
cosmetic 843 n.
mascot
preserver 666 n.
talisman 983 n.
masculine
generic 77 adj.
manly 162 adj.
male 372 adj.
grammatical 564 adj.
masculinity
male 372 n.
mash
mix 43 vb.
soften 327 vb.
pulverize 332 vb.
thicken 354 vb.
pulpiness 356 n.
mask
covering 226 n.
screen 421 n.vb.
conceal 525 vb.
disguise 527 n.
sham 542 n.
mental dishonesty 543 n.
masochism
abnormality 84 n.
masochist
nonconformist 84 n.
sensualist 944 n.
mason
form 243 vb.
artisan 686 n.
Masonic
sectional 708 adj.
masonry
building material 631 n.
Masorah
scripture 975 n.
Masorete
theologian 973 n.
masque
stage play 594 n.
masquerade
clothing 228 n.
concealment 525 n.
disguise 527 n.
sham 542 n.
dancing 837 n.
masquerader
hider 527 n.
impostor 545 n.
mass
quantity 26 n.
great quantity 32 n.
main part 32 n.
extensive 32 adj.
chief part 52 n.
accumulation 74 n.
crowd 74 n.
congregate 74 vb.
general 79 adj.
greater number 104 n.
bulk 195 n.
size 195 n.
matter 319 n.
gravity 322 n.
solid body 324 n.
army 722 n.
public worship 981 n.
massacre
slaughter 362 n.vb.
execute 963 vb.
massage
soften 327 vb.
friction 333 n.
touch 378 n.vb.
surgery 658 n.
beautification 843 n.
massed
multitudinous 104 adj.
dense 324 adj.
masses, the
everyman 79 n.
social group 371 n.
commonalty 869 n.
masseur, masseuse
friction 333 n.
doctor 658 n.
mass grave
tomb 364 n.
mass hysteria
crowd 74 n.
massif
high land 209 n.
massive
great 32 adj.
large 195 adj.
weighty 322 adj.
dense 324 adj.
mass media
information 524 n.
mass meeting
assembly 74 n.
mass murder
destruction 165 n.
mass-produce
produce 164 vb.
reproduce 166 vb.
mass production
uniformity 16 n.
production 164 n.
productiveness 171 n.
mast
high structure 209 n.
hanger 217 n.
prop 218 n.
sail 275 n.
mastaba
tomb 364 n.
mastectomy
surgery 658 n.
master
superior 34 n.
prevail 178 vb.
mariner 270 n.
male 372 n.
know 490 vb.
sage 500 n.
understand 516 vb.
learn 536 vb.
teacher 537 n.
artisan 686 n.
director 690 n.
proficient person 696 n.
victor 727 n.
overmaster 727 vb.
master 741 n.
owner 776 n.
title 870 n.
— one's feelings
keep calm 823 vb.
master copy
duplicate 22 n.
masterful
skilful 694 adj.
authoritative 733 adj.
authoritarian 735 adj.
master key
opener 263 n.
instrument 628 n.
masterless
independent 744 adj.
unpossessed 774 adj.
masterly
perfect 646 adj.
skilful 694 adj.
successful 727 adj.
mastermind
superior 34 n.
intellectual 492 n.
planner 623 n.
direct 689 vb.
proficient person 696 n.
master of arts
academic title 870 n.
master of ceremonies
leader 690 n.
reveller 837 n.
master of hounds
manager 690 n.
master/mistress of one's profession, be
be expert 694 vb.
master/mistress of one's time, be
have leisure 681 vb.
master of science
academic title 870 n.
Master of the Rolls
recorder 549 n.
judge 957 n.
masterpiece
product 164 n.
picture 553 n.
exceller 644 n.
perfection 646 n.
masterpiece 694 n.
success 727 n.
a beauty 841 n.
master plan
prototype 23 n.
plan 623 n.
master spirit
sage 500 n.
bigwig 638 n.
person of repute 866 n.
masterstroke
contrivance 623 n.
masterpiece 694 n.
success 727 n.
masterwork
masterpiece 694 n.
mastery
knowledge 490 n.
skill 694 n.
victory 727 n.
governance 733 n.
possession 773 n.
masthead
vertex 213 n.
label 547 n.
punish 963 vb.
mastic
viscidity 354 n.
resin 357 n.
masticate
chew 301 vb.
mastiff
dog 365 n.
mastodon
animal 365 n.
mat
seat 218 n.
enlace 222 vb.
floor-cover 226 n.
cleaning cloth 648 n.
matador
killer 362 n.
combatant 722 n.
match
analogue 18 n.
resemble 18 vb.
accord 24 vb.
compeer 28 n.
join 45 vb.
pair 90 vb.
burning 381 n.
lighter 385 n.
torch 420 n.
compare 462 vb.
contest 716 n.
marriage 894 n.
— against
oppose 704 vb.
matchbox
small box 194 n.

lighter 385 n.
match for, a
sufficient 635 adj.
matching
harmonious 410 adj.
soft-hued 425 adj.
matchless
supreme 34 adj.
best 644 adj.
matchlock
firearm 723 n.
matchmaker
intermediary 231 n.
matchmaker 894 n.
match point
juncture 8 n.
matchwood
weak thing 163 n.
brittleness 330 n.
mate
analogue 18 n.
compeer 28 n.
unite with 45 vb.
combine 50 vb.
concomitant 89 n.
pair 90 vb.
mariner 270 n.
male 372 n.
personnel 686 n.
colleague 707 n.
defeat 728 n.
chum 880 n.
spouse 894 n.
marry 894 vb.
wed 894 vb.
mater
maternity 169 n.
material
real 1 adj.
substantiality 3 n.
textile 222 n.
matter 319 n.
material 319 adj.
tactual 378 adj.
information 524 n.
materials 631 n.
important 638 adj.
materialism
materiality 319 n.
philosophy 449 n.
sensualism 944 n.
antichristianity 974 n.
impiety 980 n.
materialistic
selfish 932 adj.
irreligious 974 adj.
materialization, materialisation
manifestation 522 n.
materialize, materialise
happen 154 vb.
materialize 319 vb.
be visible 443 vb.
appear 445 vb.
practise occultism 984 vb.
materially
greatly 32 adv.
importantly 638 adv.
materials
source 156 n.
object 319 n.
means 629 n.
materials 631 n.
materia medica
medicine 658 n.
matériel
means 629 n.
maternal
akin 11 adj.
parental 169 adj.
benevolent 897 adj.
maternity
propagation 167 n.
maternity 169 n.
parentage 169 n.
woman 373 n.
maternity specialist
obstetrics 167 n.
maternity wear
clothing 228 n.
matey
friendly 880 adj.
sociable 882 adj.
mathematical
statistical 86 adj.
accurate 494 adj.
mathematical probability
calculation of chance 159 n.
mathematician
enumerator 86 n.
reasoner 475 n.
mathematics
mathematics 86 n.
reasoning 475 n.
matinée
evening 129 n.
dramaturgy 594 n.
matinée coat
jacket 228 n.
mating
coition 45 n.
mating season
libido 859 n.
matins
morning 128 n.
public worship 981 n.
church service 988 n.
matriarch
maternity 169 n.
master 741 n.
matriarchal
governmental 733 adj.
matriarchy
family 11 n.
female 373 n.
matricide
homicide 362 n.
matriculation
exam 459 n.
matrilineal
akin 11 adj.
parental 169 adj.
matrimonial
matrimonial 894 adj.
matrimony
marriage 894 n.
matrix
mould 23 n.
number 85 n.
surroundings 230 n.
print-type 587 n.
matron
adult 134 n.
maternity 169 n.
woman 373 n.
nurse 658 n.
manager 690 n.
spouse 894 n.
matronly
ageing 131 adj.
grown-up 134 adj.
female 373 adj.
matt, mat
dim 419 adj.
soft-hued 425 adj.
matted
crossed 222 adj.
hairy 259 adj.
dense 324 adj.
dirty 649 adj.
matter
substantiality 3 n.
excrement 302 n.
matter 319 n.
universe 321 n.
solid body 324 n.
fluid 335 n.
topic 452 n.
meaning 514 n.
be important 638 vb.
dirt 649 n.
ulcer 651 n.
matter in hand
undertaking 672 n.
matter of course
practice 610 n.
lack of wonder 865 n.
matter of fact
reality 1 n.
event 154 n.
certainty 473 n.
narrow-minded 481 adj.
truth 494 n.
prosaic 593 adj.
artless 699 adj.
dull 840 adj.
matter of life and death
needfulness 627 n.
important matter 638 n.
matter of time
period 110 n.
course of time 111 n.
matters
affairs 154 n.
matting
floor-cover 226 n.
mattock
sharp edge 256 n.
mattress
cushion 218 n.
maturation
maturation 669 n.
mature
grow 36 vb.
be complete 54 vb.
ageing 131 adj.
grown-up 134 adj.
come of age 134 vb.
be turned to 147 vb.
plan 623 vb.
perfect 646 vb.
make better 654 vb.
matured 669 adj.
mature 669 vb.
carry through 725 vb.
matured
formed 243 adj.
matured 669 adj.
maturity
oldness 127 n.
middle age 131 n.
adultness 134 n.
preparedness 669 n.
completion 725 n.
matutinal
matinal 128 adj.
maudlin
foolish 499 adj.
feeling 818 adj.
tipsy 949 adj.
maul
be violent 176 vb.
strike 279 vb.
ill-treat 645 vb.
impair 655 vb.
wound 655 vb.
attack 712 vb.
dispraise 924 vb.
maunder
move slowly 278 vb.
be foolish 499 vb.
be diffuse 570 vb.
be loquacious 581 vb.
Maundy Thursday
holy day 988 n.
mausoleum
tomb 364 n.
monument 548 n.
mauvaise honte
affectation 850 n.
modesty 874 n.
prudery 950 n.
mauvais quart d'heure
suffering 825 n.
reprimand 924 n.
mauve
purple 436 adj.

maverick
nonconformist 84 n.
revolter 738 n.
nonobservant 769 adj.
maw
maw 194 n.
insides 224 n.
orifice 263 n.
eater 301 n.
mawkish
unsavoury 391 adj.
feeling 818 adj.
maxim
rule 81 n.
maxim 496 n.
precept 693 n.
Maxim
gun 723 n.
maximize, maximise
augment 36 vb.
overrate 482 vb.
exaggerate 546 vb.
maximum
greatness 32 n.
superiority 34 n.
crowning 34 adj.
plenitude 54 n.
size 195 n.
may
tree 366 n.
be possible 469 vb.
maya
insubstantiality 4 n.
may be
possibly 469 adv.
May Day
festivity 837 n.
Mayday
call 547 n.
Mayfair
beau monde 848 n.
mayfly
brief span 114 n.
insect 365 n.
mayhem
disorder 61 n.
maying
spring 128 n.
mayonnaise
hors-d'oeuvres 301 n.
sauce 389 n.
mayor
official 690 n.
councillor 692 n.
officer 741 n.
law officer 955 n.
mayoralty
position of authority 733 n.
jurisdiction 955 n.
mayoress
officer 741 n.
maypole
high structure 209 n.
Mazdaism
religious faith 973 n.
maze
complexity 61 n.
meandering 251 n.
puzzle 474 vb.
enigma 530 n.
difficulty 700 n.
mazurka
musical piece 412 n.
dance 837 n.
MC
leader 690 n.
reveller 837 n.
McCarthyism
enquiry 459 n.
phobia 854 n.
MCP
male 372 n.
MD
academic title 870 n.
me
subjectivity 320 n.
mead
alcoholic drink 301 n.
sweet thing 392 n.
meadow(s)
grassland 348 n.
farm 370 n.
meagre
small 33 adj.
incomplete 55 adj.
lean 206 adj.
feeble 572 adj.
economical 814 adj.
fasting 946 adj.
meagreness
insubstantiality 4 n.
scarcity 636 n.
poverty 801 n.
meal
cereals 301 n.
meal 301 n.
powder 332 n.
festivity 837 n.
mealies
cereals 301 n.
meal-time
culinary 301 adj.
mealy
powdery 332 adj.
colourless 426 adj.
mealy-mouthed
hypocritical 541 adj.
affected 850 adj.
mealy-mouthedness
prudery 950 n.
mean
average 30 n.
middle 70 n.adj.
statistics 86 n.
mean 514 vb.
imply 523 vb.
indicate 547 vb.
represent 551 vb.
unimportant 639 adj.
bad 645 adj.
beggarly 801 adj.
parsimonious 816 adj.
disreputable 867 adj.
plebeian 869 adj.
humble 872 adj.
servile 879 adj.
unkind 898 adj.
contemptible 922 adj.
rascally 930 adj.
selfish 932 adj.
heinous 934 adj.
— business
be resolute 599 vb.
— it
affirm 532 vb.
be truthful 540 vb.
— no good
threaten 900 vb.
— no harm
be at peace 717 vb.
be innocent 935 vb.
— nothing
reason badly 477 vb.
be absurd 497 vb.
mean nothing 515 vb.
be unintelligible 517 vb.
boast 877 vb.
— to
be willing 597 vb.
intend 617 vb.
— well
be friendly 880 vb.
be benevolent 897 vb.
meander
meandering 251 n.
meander 251 vb.
deviate 282 vb.
meanie
niggard 816 n.
meaning
relation 9 n.
meaning 514 n.
interpretation 520 n.
affirmative 532 adj.
indication 547 n.
willing 597 adj.
intention 617 n.
meaningful
meaningful 514 adj.
intelligible 516 adj.
indicating 547 adj.
important 638 adj.
meaningless
absurd 497 adj.
meaningless 515 adj.
unimportant 639 adj.
dull 840 adj.
mean-minded
selfish 932 adj.
meanness
smallness 33 n.
unimportance 639 n.
parsimony 816 n.
contemptibility 922 n.
selfishness 932 n.
means
opportunity 137 n.
contrivance 623 n.
instrumentality 628 n.
means 629 n.
materials 631 n.
estate 777 n.
funds 797 n.
wealth 800 n.
means of escape
outlet 298 n.
pretext 614 n.
contrivance 623 n.
means of escape 667 n.
mean-spirited
cowardly 856 adj.
servile 879 adj.
means test
enquiry 459 n.
meant
veracious 540 adj.
meantime
interim 108 n.
while 108 adv.
meanwhile
while 108 adv.
measles
infection 651 n.
measly
unimportant 639 adj.
bad 645 adj.
measurable
numerable 86 adj.
measured 465 adj.
measure
finite quantity 26 n.
graduate 27 vb.
comprise 78 vb.
do sums 86 vb.
moderation 177 n.
measure 183 n.
size 195 n.
tempo 410 n.
tune 412 n.
gauge 465 n.
metrology 465 n.
measure 465 vb.
estimate 480 vb.
prosody 593 n.
deed 676 n.
portion 783 n.
apportion 783 vb.
— one's length
be horizontal 216 vb.
tumble 309 vb.
— up to
be equal 28 vb.
be able 160 vb.
suffice 635 vb.
measured
uniform 16 adj.
periodical 141 adj.
moderate 177 adj.
measured 465 adj.
sufficient 635 adj.

temperate 942 adj.
measured against
compared 462 adj.
measured by
comparative 27 adj.
measure for measure
compensation 31 n.
retaliation 714 n.
measureless
infinite 107 adj.
measurement
size 195 n.
measurement 465 n.
(See **measure** *)*
measures
policy 623 n.
means 629 n.
action 676 n.
measuring instrument
meter 465 n.
meat
substance 3 n.
food 301 n.
meat 301 n.
materials 631 n.
meat and two veg
dish 301 n.
meat-eater
eater 301 n.
meatless day
fast 946 n.
holy day 988 n.
meaty
substantial 3 adj.
fleshy 195 adj.
meaningful 514 adj.
forceful 571 adj.
Mecca
focus 76 n.
objective 617 n.
holy place 990 n.
mechanic
machinist 630 n.
artisan 686 n.
mechanical
dynamic 160 adj.
involuntary 596 adj.
instrumental 628 adj.
mechanical 630 adj.
mechanical device
machine 630 n.
tool 630 n.
mechanical drawing
representation 551 n.
mechanical energy
energy 160 n.
mechanically
habitually 610 adv.
mechanician
machinist 630 n.
mechanics
physics 319 n.
mechanics 630 n.
mechanism
biology 358 n.
philosophy 449 n.
machine 630 n.
mechanistic
involuntary 596 adj.
mechanization, mechanisation
instrumentality 628 n.
mechanize, mechanise
produce 164 vb.
mechanized, mechanised
productive 164 adj.
mechanical 630 adj.
medal
badge 547 n.
decoration 729 n.
jewellery 844 n.
honours 866 n.
reward 962 n.
medallion
sculpture 554 n.
jewellery 844 n.
medallist
victor 727 n.
meddle
derange 63 vb.
interfere 231 vb.
be curious 453 vb.
busy oneself 622 vb.
impair 655 vb.
meddle 678 vb.
be clumsy 695 vb.
obstruct 702 vb.
mediate 720 vb.
meddler
inquisitive person 453 n.
meddler 678 n.
adviser 691 n.
hinderer 702 n.
media, the
publication 528 n.
broadcasting 531 n.
mediaeval
(See **medieval** *)*
medial
middle 70 adj.
median
average 30 n.
median 30 adj.
middle 70 adj.
interjacent 231 adj.
mediant
musical note 410 n.
media personality
broadcaster 531 n.
favourite 890 n.
mediate
be instrumental 628 vb.
pacify 719 vb.
mediate 720 vb.
mediation
mediation 720 n.
deprecation 762 n.
mediator
moderator 177 n.
intermediary 231 n.
mediator 720 n.
medic
doctor 658 n.
medicable
restored 656 adj.
medical 658 adj.
medical
enquiry 459 n.
medical 658 adj.
medical care
therapy 658 n.
medical officer
sanitarian 652 n.
doctor 658 n.
medical practitioner
doctor 658 n.
medical school
training school 539 n.
medicament
medicine 658 n.
medicate
cure 656 vb.
doctor 658 vb.
medication
medicine 658 n.
medicinal
restorative 656 adj.
remedial 658 adj.
medicine
draught 301 n.
medical art 658 n.
medicine 658 n.
medicine man
doctor 658 n.
sorcerer 983 n.
medieval, mediaeval
olden 127 adj.
medieval times
antiquity 125 n.
medievalist, mediaevalist
antiquarian 125 n.
mediocre
inferior 35 adj.
not bad 644 adj.
middling 732 adj.
mediocrity
nonentity 639 n.
meditate
meditate 449 vb.
enquire 459 vb.
intend 617 vb.
meditation
meditation 449 n.
attention 455 n.
piety 979 n.
prayers 981 n.
meditative
thoughtful 449 adj.
pious 979 adj.
mediterranean
middle 70 adj.
interjacent 231 adj.
Mediterranean
ocean 343 n.
medium
average 30 n.
middle 70 n.
surroundings 230 n.
intermediary 231 n.
oracle 511 n.
interpreter 520 n.
instrument 628 n.
instrumentality 628 n.
middling 732 adj.
psychic 984 n.
mediumistic
psychic 447 adj.
psychical 984 adj.
medium wave
radiation 417 n.
medley
nonuniformity 17 n.
medley 43 n.
confusion 61 n.
accumulation 74 n.
musical piece 412 n.
medley of colour
variegation 437 n.
medullary
soft 327 adj.
Medusa
eyesore 842 n.
intimidation 854 n.
meed
reward 962 n.
meek
submitting 721 adj.
obedient 739 adj.
inexcitable 823 adj.
patient 823 adj.
humble 872 adj.
meerschaum
tobacco 388 n.
meet
fit 24 adj.
congregate 74 vb.
synchronize 123 vb.
meet with 154 vb.
be near 200 vb.
collide 279 vb.
converge 293 vb.
meet 295 vb.
touch 378 vb.
discover 484 vb.
withstand 704 vb.
pay 804 vb.
do one's duty 917 vb.
— an obligation
grant claims 915 vb.
— a sticky end
perish 361 vb.
— halfway
be willing 597 vb.
be halfway 625 vb.
pacify 719 vb.
— one at every turn
be present 189 vb.
pervade 189 vb.
superabound 637 vb.
— one's Maker
die 361 vb.
— requirements
suffice 635 vb.
— with approval
content 828 vb.

meet and right
right 913 adj.
meeting
union 45 n.
assembly 74 n.
event 154 n.
contiguity 202 n.
collision 279 n.
approach 289 n.
convergence 293 n.
arrival 295 n.
conference 584 n.
council 692 n.
social gathering 882 n.
public worship 981 n.
meeting house
meeting place 192 n.
church 990 n.
meeting place
focus 76 n.
meeting place 192 n.
Megaera
Fury 891 n.
megalith
antiquity 125 n.
monument 548 n.
megalithic
huge 195 adj.
megalomania
overestimation 482 n.
mania 503 n.
vanity 873 n.
megalomaniac
madman 504 n.
megalopolis
city 184 n.
megaphone
megaphone 400 n.
megaton
weighing 322 n.
megawatt
electronics 160 n.
megrim
pang 377 n.
whim 604 n.
megrims
animal disease 651 n.
melancholy 834 n.
Meistersinger
poet 593 n.
melancholia
psychopathy 503 n.
melancholy 834 n.
melancholic
insane 503 adj.
madman 504 n.
melancholic 834 adj.
melancholy
psychopathy 503 n.
bad 645 adj.
suffering 825 n.
unhappy 825 adj.
discontent 829 n.
melancholy 834 n.
melancholic 834 adj.
tedium 838 n.
sullenness 893 n.
mélange
a mixture 43 n.
melanin
black pigment 428 n.
melanism
blackness 428 n.
mêlée, melee
turmoil 61 n.
fight 716 n.
melic
musical 412 adj.
meliorate
make better 654 vb.
melioration
improvement 654 n.
meliorism
reformism 654 n.
melliferous
sweet 392 adj.
mellifluous
melodious 410 adj.
elegant 575 adj.
mellow
ageing 131 adj.
be turned to 147 vb.
soften 327 vb.
tasty 386 adj.
savoury 390 adj.
soft-hued 425 adj.
get better 654 vb.
matured 669 adj.
mature 669 vb.
drunk 949 adj.
melodeon
organ 414 n.
melodic
melodious 410 adj.
musical 412 adj.
melodic scale
key 410 n.
melodious
pleasant 376 adj.
melodious 410 adj.
musical 412 adj.
vocal 577 adj.
pleasurable 826 adj.
melodist
vocalist 413 n.
melodize, melodise
harmonize 410 vb.
compose music 413 vb.
melodrama
stage play 594 n.
excitation 821 n.
melodramatic
exaggerated 546 adj.
dramatic 594 adj.
exciting 821 adj.
melody
melody 410 n.
tune 412 n.
pleasurableness 826 n.
melon
fruit 301 n.
Melpomene
drama 594 n.
lesser deity 967 n.
melt
pass away 2 vb.
come unstuck 49 vb.
decompose 51 vb.
be dispersed 75 vb.
be transient 114 vb.
deform 244 vb.
soften 327 vb.
liquefy 337 vb.
make flow 350 vb.
be hot 379 vb.
heat 381 vb.
sound faint 401 vb.
ask mercy 905 vb.
pity 905 vb.
— away
decrease 37 vb.
disappear 446 vb.
waste 634 vb.
be lost 772 vb.
— into
shade off 27 vb.
be turned to 147 vb.
— the heart
sadden 834 vb.
meltdown
ruin 165 n.
melting
unstable 152 adj.
soft 327 adj.
fluid 335 adj.
melting point
heat 379 n.
melting pot
mixture 43 n.
crucible 147 n.
member
limb 53 n.
part 53 n.
component 58 n.
society 708 n.
delegate 754 n.
participator 775 n.
Member of Parliament
councillor 692 n.
membership
inclusion 78 n.
association 706 n.
participation 775 n.
sociality 882 n.
membrane
layer 207 n.
skin 226 n.
memento
reminder 505 n.
trophy 729 n.
memento mori
corpse 363 n.
memo
reminder 505 n.
memoir(s)
rememberance 505 n.
record 548 n.
biography 590 n.
dissertation 591 n.
memoir writer
narrator 590 n.
memorabilia
remembrance 505 n.
record 548 n.
memorable
remembered 505 adj.
notable 638 adj.
memorandum
reminder 505 n.
record 548 n.
plan 623 n.
important matter 638 n.
memorial
reminder 505 n.
report 524 n.
monument 548 n.
trophy 729 n.
request 761 n.
honours 866 n.
memorialist
chronicler 549 n.
memorial service
obsequies 364 n.
memorize, memorise
know 490 vb.
memorize 505 vb.
learn 536 vb.
memory
data processing 86 n.
memory 505 n.
storage 632 n.
famousness 866 n.
memory like a sieve
oblivion 506 n.
memsahib
lady 373 n.
title 870 n.
men
mariner 270 n.
personnel 686 n.
armed force 722 n.
menace
danger 661 n.
endanger 661 vb.
warn 664 vb.
annoyance 827 n.
frighten 854 vb.
hateful object 888 n.
threat 900 n.
threaten 900 vb.
ménage
inhabitants 191 n.
management 689 n.
ménage à trois
type of marriage 894 n.
menagerie
medley 43 n.
accumulation 74 n.
zoo 369 n.
collection 632 n.
mend
join 45 vb.
get healthy 650 vb.
get better 654 vb.

make better 654 vb.
repair 656 vb.
— one's ways
tergiversate 603 vb.
get better 654 vb.
become pious 979 vb.
mendacious
false 541 adj.
untrue 543 adj.
mendacity
falsehood 541 n.
Mendelian
inherited 157 adj.
filial 170 adj.
Mendelism
heredity 5 n.
mendicant
idler 679 n.
beggar 763 n.
menfolk
male 372 n.
menial
inferior 35 adj.
servant 742 n.
serving 742 adj.
meningitis
infection 651 n.
meniscus
curve 248 n.
optical device 442 n.
Mennonite
sectarian 978 n.
menology
chronology 117 n.
menopause
middle age 131 n.
unproductiveness 172 n.
menses
regular return 141 n.
haemorrhage 302 n.
Menshevik
moderate 625 n.
political party 708 n.
mens sana in corpore sano
health 650 n.
menstrual
seasonal 141 adj.
excretory 302 adj.
mensurable
numerable 86 adj.
measured 465 adj.
mensuration
measurement 465 n.
mental
immaterial 320 adj.
mental 447 adj.
insane 503 adj.
mental and spiritual make-up
affections 817 n.
mental attitude
conduct 688 n.
mental block
oblivion 506 n.
mental capacity
intellect 447 n.
intelligence 498 n.
mental case
madman 504 n.
sick person 651 n.
mental deficiency
unintelligence 499 n.
insanity 503 n.
mental dishonesty
concealment 525 n.
mental dishonesty 543 n.
stratagem 698 n.
mental handicap
unintelligence 499 n.
mental health
sanity 502 n.
mental hospital
lunatic asylum 503 n.
hospital 658 n.
mental illness
insanity 503 n.
mental image
idea 451 n.
ideality 513 n.
image 551 n.
mentality
intellect 447 n.
affections 817 n.
mentally handicapped
unintelligent 499 adj.
mentally ill
insane 503 adj.
mental process
thought 449 n.
mental reservation
sophistry 477 n.
equivocalness 518 n.
mental dishonesty 543 n.
mental torment
suffering 825 n.
mention
referral 9 n.
specify 80 vb.
notice 455 vb.
information 524 n.
hint 524 vb.
inform 524 vb.
speak 579 vb.
mentionable
pure 950 adj.
mentioned in dispatches, be
be praised 923 vb.
mentor
sage 500 n.
teacher 537 n.
adviser 691 n.
menu
list 87 n.
meal 301 n.
Mephistophelean
wicked 934 adj.
diabolic 969 adj.
Mephistopheles
Mephisto 969 n.
mephitis
stench 397 n.
insalubrity 653 n.
poison 659 n.
mercantile
businesslike 622 adj.
trading 791 adj.
mercantile marine
shipping 275 n.
Mercator's projection
distortion 246 n.
map 551 n.
mercenary
militarist 722 n.
avaricious 816 adj.
venal 930 adj.
selfish 932 adj.
mercer
tradespeople 794 n.
mercerize, mercerise
be tough 329 vb.
merchandise
product 164 n.
equipment 630 n.
store 632 n.
sale 793 n.
merchandise 795 n.
merchandise in
trade 791 vb.
merchant
transferrer 272 n.
agent 686 n.
merchant 794 n.
merchantman
merchant ship 275 n.
merchant navy
shipping 275 n.
merchant venturer
gambler 618 n.
merchant 794 n.
merciful
lenient 736 adj.
benevolent 897 adj.
pitying 905 adj.
forgiving 909 adj.
godlike 965 adj.
merciless
destructive 165 adj.
resolute 599 adj.
obstinate 602 adj.
severe 735 adj.
cruel 898 adj.
malevolent 898 adj.
pitiless 906 adj.
mercilessness
inhumanity 898 n.
mercurial
changeful 152 adj.
unstable 152 adj.
moving 265 adj.
speedy 277 adj.
light-minded 456 adj.
irresolute 601 adj.
capricious 604 adj.
excitable 822 adj.
mercury
changeable thing 152 n.
weather 340 n.
Mercury
planet 321 n.
courier 529 n.
Olympian deity 967 n.
mercy
peace offering 719 n.
leniency 736 n.
benevolence 897 n.
mercy 905 n.
forgiveness 909 n.
divine attribute 965 n.
mercy killer
killer 362 n.
Mercy-seat
ritual object 988 n.
holy place 990 n.
mere
absolute 32 adj.
inconsiderable 33 adj.
simple 44 adj.
lake 346 n.
meretricious
appearing 445 adj.
false 541 adj.
spurious 542 adj.
ornate 574 adj.
ornamented 844 adj.
vulgar 847 adj.
unchaste 951 adj.
mere words
sophistry 477 n.
lack of meaning 515 n.
merge
be identical 13 vb.
mix 43 vb.
join 45 vb.
combine 50 vb.
cooperate 706 vb.
join a party 708 vb.
— in
be one of 58 vb.
be included 78 vb.
— into
be turned to 147 vb.
merger
mixture 43 n.
union 45 n.
combination 50 n.
association 706 n.
meridian
noon 128 n.
region 184 n.
summit 213 n.
meringue
pastries 301 n.
bubble 355 n.
merino
fibre 208 n.
sheep 365 n.
merit
importance 638 n.

utility 640 n.
goodness 644 n.
deserve 915 vb.
virtues 933 n.
meritocracy
elite 644 n.
government 733 n.
meritorious
excellent 644 adj.
reputable 866 adj.
deserving 915 adj.
approvable 923 adj.
virtuous 933 adj.
merits
right 913 n.
dueness 915 n.
Merlin
mythical being 970 n.
sorcerer 983 n.
mermaid
rara avis 84 n.
sea nymph 343 n.
mythical being 970 n.
merriment
enjoyment 824 n.
merriment 833 n.
rejoicing 835 n.
amusement 837 n.
festivity 837 n.
wit 839 n.
merry
lively 819 adj.
happy 824 adj.
merry 833 adj.
amusing 837 adj.
sociable 882 adj.
drunk 949 adj.
merry andrew
fool 501 n.
merry-go-round
rotator 315 n.
pleasure ground 837 n.
merry-maker
reveller 837 n.
merry men
band 74 n.
soldiery 722 n.
mesa
high land 209 n.
plain 348 n.
mésalliance
type of marriage 894 n.
mescal
alcoholic drink 301 n.
mescalin, mescaline
drug-taking 949 n.
mesh
accord 24 vb.
unite with 45 vb.
gap 201 n.
network 222 n.
meshes
trap 542 n.
encumbrance 702 n.
mesmerism
influence 178 n.
occultism 984 n.
mesmerize, mesmerise
influence 178 vb.
render insensible 375 vb.
convince 485 vb.
frighten 854 vb.
practise occultism 984 vb.
mesolithic
primal 127 adj.
mesomorphic
stalwart 162 adj.
meson
element 319 n.
mesosphere
atmosphere 340 n.
Mesozoic
secular 110 adj.
mess
medley 43 n.
confusion 61 n.
eat 301 vb.
predicament 700 n.
failure 728 n.
portion 783 n.
— up
jumble 63 vb.
impair 655 vb.
message
information 524 n.
message 529 n.
telecommunication 531 n.
signal 547 n.
Messalina
loose woman 952 n.
messed up
bungled 695 adj.
messenger
precursor 66 n.
traveller 268 n.
informant 524 n.
messenger 529 n.
delegate 754 n.
deputy 755 n.
messiah
leader 690 n.
religious teacher 973 n.
Messiah
God the Son 965 n.
Messianism
aspiration 852 n.
religion 973 n.
mess kit
uniform 228 n.
messmate
eater 301 n.
chum 880 n.
messroom
chamber 194 n.
feasting 301 n.
mess tin
cauldron 194 n.
messuage
house 192 n.
lands 777 n.
messy
orderless 61 adj.adj.
amorphous 244 adj.
dirty 649 adj.
met
assembled 74 adj.
metabolism
transformation 143 n.
metacentre
centre 225 n.
metal
overlay 226 vb.
hardness 326 n.
mineral 359 n.
colour 425 n.
heraldry 547 n.
materials 631 n.
metalanguage
language 557 n.
metal detector
detector 484 n.
metalled
covered 226 adj.
accessible 289 adj.
communicating 624 adj.
metallic
inorganic 359 adj.
strident 407 adj.
metallurgical
inorganic 359 adj.
metallurgy
mineralogy 359 n.
metalwork
ornamental art 844 n.
metalworker
artisan 686 n.
metalworks
workshop 687 n.
metamorphic rock
rock 344 n.
metamorphose
modify 143 vb.
transform 147 vb.
metamorphosis
multiformity 82 n.
transformation 143 n.
metaphor
analogue 18 n.
comparison 462 n.
metaphor 519 n.
ornament 574 n.
metaphorical
compared 462 adj.
semantic 514 adj.
figurative 519 adj.
rhetorical 574 adj.
metaphrase
copy 22 n.
translation 520 n.
metaphysical
insubstantial 4 adj.
philosophic 449 adj.
metaphysician
philosopher 449 n.
metaphysics
existence 1 n.
philosophy 449 n.
metapsychics
occultism 984 n.
metapsychology
psychology 447 n.
metascience
science 490 n.
metastasis
transference 272 n.
metathesis
inversion 221 n.
transference 272 n.
trope 519 n.
metazoan
animal 365 n.
metempsychosis
transformation 143 n.
materiality 319 n.
meteor
meteor 321 n.
luminary 420 n.
meteoric
brief 114 adj.
speedy 277 adj.
meteorite
meteor 321 n.
meteoroid
meteor 321 n.
meteorologist
weather 340 n.
oracle 511 n.
meteorology
weather 340 n.
mete out
mete out 465 vb.
apportion 783 vb.
meter
meter 465 n.
gauge 465 vb.
detector 484 n.
methadone
drug-taking 949 n.
methane
gas 336 n.
fuel 385 n.
metheglin
sweet thing 392 n.
method
uniformity 16 n.
order 60 n.
arrangement 62 n.
regularity 81 n.
campanology 412 n.
way 624 n.
means 629 n.
conduct 688 n.
ritual 988 n.
Method, the
acting 594 n.
methodical
orderly 60 adj.
regular 81 adj.
Methodism
Protestantism 976 n.

Methodist
Protestant 976 adj.
methodological
rational 475 adj.
methodologist
reasoner 475 n.
Methuselah
old person 133 n.
methylated spirits
fuel 385 n.
meticulous
attentive 455 adj.
careful 457 adj.
accurate 494 adj.
fastidious 862 adj.
trustworthy 929 adj.
métier
vocation 622 n.
skill 694 n.
Metonic cycle
era 110 n.
metonymy
trope 519 n.
metoposcopy
face 237 n.
metre
long measure 203 n.
prosody 593 n.
metric
metrical 465 adj.
metrical
numerable 86 adj.
metrical 465 adj.
poetic 593 adj.
metrics
measurement 465 n.
prosody 593 n.
metric system
metrology 465 n.
Metro
railway 624 n.
metrology
metrology 465 n.
metronome
timekeeper 117 n.
metropolis
city 184 n.
position of authority 733 n.
metropolitan
dweller 191 n.
urban 192 adj.
central 225 adj.
governor 741 n.
ecclesiastical 985 adj.
ecclesiarch 986 n.
metropolitan area
district 184 n.
mettle
vigorousness 174 n.
resolution 599 n.
affections 817 n.
courage 855 n.
mettlesome
vigorous 174 adj.
active 678 adj.
lively 819 adj.
excitable 822 adj.
courageous 855 adj.
mew
ululation 409 n.
ululate 409 vb.
mewl
cry 408 vb.
ululate 409 vb.
mews
flat 192 n.
stable 192 n.
mezzanine
layer 207 n.
theatre 594 n.
mezzo-forte
adagio 412 adv.
mezzo-soprano
vocalist 413 n.
mezzotint
light contrast 417 n.
hue 425 n.
engraving 555 n.
MI5
secret service 459 n.
miaow
ululation 409 n.
ululate 409 vb.
miasma
gas 336 n.
stench 397 n.
infection 651 n.
insalubrity 653 n.
poison 659 n.
miasmal
harmful 645 adj.
insalubrious 653 adj.
mica
semitransparency 424 n.
Micawber
hoper 852 n.
Michaelmas
autumn 129 n.
holy day 988 n.
micro-
minute 196 adj.
microbe
microorganism 196 n.
insalubrity 653 n.
microbiology
biology 358 n.
medical art 658 n.
microcard
record 548 n.
microchip
microelectronics 196 n.
microcircuit
microelectronics 196 n.
microclimate
weather 340 n.
microcomputer
counting instrument 86 n.
microcosm
miniature 196 n.
universe 321 n.
microdot
miniature 196 n.
microelectronics
counting instrument 86 n.
electronics 160 n.
microelectronics 196 n.
microfiche, microfilm
copy 22 n.
miniature 196 n.
record 548 n.
photography 551 n.
microlith
antiquity 125 n.
micromesh
reticular 222 adj.
micrometry
measurement 465 n.
accuracy 494 n.
microminiaturization, microminiaturisation
microelectronics 196 n.
micron
small quantity 33 n.
long measure 203 n.
microorganism
microorganism 196 n.
animal 365 n.
insalubrity 653 n.
microphone
megaphone 400 n.
hearing aid 415 n.
telecommunication 531 n.
rostrum 539 n.
microphotography
microscopy 196 n.
photography 551 n.
microphyte
microorganism 196 n.
microprocessor
counting instrument 86 n.
electronics 160 n.
microelectronics 196 n.
microscope
microscopy 196 n.
microscope 442 n.
microscopic
small 33 adj.
minute 196 adj.
indistinct 444 adj.
microtechnique
microscopy 196 n.
microwave
radiation 417 n.
microwave oven
furnace 383 n.
mid
middle 70 adj.
between 231 adv.
Midas
rich person 800 n.
Midas touch
prosperity 730 n.
wealth 800 n.
midday
noon 128 n.
heat 379 n.
midden
rubbish 641 n.
sink 649 n.
middle
median 30 adj.
middle 70 n.adj.
interim 108 n.
centre 225 n.
interjacency 231 n.
interjacent 231 adj.
middling 732 adj.
middle age
middle age 131 n.
adultness 134 n.
Middle Ages
era 110 n.
antiquity 125 n.
middlebrow
median 30 adj.
middling 732 adj.
middle classes
social group 371 n.
averageness 732 n.
middle classes 869 n.
middle course
middle way 625 n.
middle distance
middle point 30 n.
middle 70 n.
middleman
intermediary 231 n.
provider 633 n.
agent 686 n.
consignee 754 n.
merchant 794 n.
middle-of-the-road
moderate 177 adj.
neutral 625 adj.
middle-of-the-roader
moderate 625 n.
middle way
middle way 625 n.
compromise 770 n.
middleweight
pugilist 722 n.
middling
inconsiderable 33 adj.
not bad 644 adj.
middling 732 adj.
midge
insect 365 n.
midget
small animal 33 n.
dwarf 196 n.
midi skirt
skirt 228 n.
Midlands
interiority 224 n.
inland 344 adj.
midmost
middle 70 adj.

interior 224 adj.
central 225 adj.
midnight
midnight 129 n.
darkness 418 n.
midpoint
middle 70 n.
centre 225 n.
midrib
middle 70 n.
centre 225 n.
midriff
partition 231 n.
midshipman
nautical personnel 270 n.
midships
midway 70 adv.
midst
middle 70 n.
centrally 225 adv.
between 231 adv.
midstream
middle way 625 n.
midsummer
summer 128 n.
midway
midway 70 adv.
midweek
intermediate 108 adj.
midwife
obstetrics 167 n.
instrument 628 n.
doctor 658 n.
auxiliary 707 n.
midwinter
winter 129 n.
mien
mien 445 n.
gesture 547 n.
conduct 688 n.
miffed
resentful 891 adj.
might
greatness 32 n.
power 160 n.
strength 162 n.
be possible 469 vb.
might and main
exertion 682 n.
might-have-been, the
possibility 469 n.
mighty
great 32 adj.
powerful 160 adj.
strong 162 adj.
influential 178 adj.
huge 195 adj.
worshipful 866 adj.
proud 871 adj.
mignon
favourite 890 n.
migraine
pang 377 n.
illness 651 n.
migrant
foreigner 59 n.
wanderer 268 n.
incomer 297 n.
bird 365 n.
migration
wandering 267 n.
departure 296 n.
migratory
travelling 267 adj.
Mikado
sovereign 741 n.
mike
megaphone 400 n.
hearing aid 415 n.
milady
lady 373 n.
milch cow
abundance 171 n.
cattle 365 n.
store 632 n.
mild
moderate 177 adj.
alcoholic drink 301 n.
warm 379 adj.
tasteless 387 adj.
lenient 736 adj.
inexcitable 823 adj.
amiable 884 adj.
mildew
dirt 649 n.
dilapidation 655 n.
impair 655 vb.
blight 659 n.
mildewed
antiquated 127 adj.
dim 419 adj.
mild-mannered
peaceful 717 adj.
mildness
moderation 177 n.
leniency 736 n.
courtesy 884 n.
benevolence 897 n.
mile
long measure 203 n.
mileage
distance 199 n.
length 203 n.
utility 640 n.
milepost
signpost 547 n.
miles away
abstracted 456 adj.
miles gloriosus
combatant 722 n.
boaster 877 n.
miles per hour
velocity 277 n.
milestone
degree 27 n.
serial place 73 n.
event 154 n.
situation 186 n.
itinerary 267 n.
gauge 465 n.
signpost 547 n.
important matter 638 n.
milieu
circumstance 8 n.
relation 9 n.
locality 187 n.
surroundings 230 n.
militancy
action 676 n.
activity 678 n.
bellicosity 718 n.
militant
busy person 678 n.
opposing 704 adj.
political party 708 n.
defiant 711 adj.
attacking 712 adj.
warlike 718 adj.
militarist 722 n.
courageous 855 adj.
inimical 881 adj.
militarism
bellicosity 718 n.
brute force 735 n.
military
warlike 718 adj.
military base
station 187 n.
military rank
degree 27 n.
army officer 741 n.
military service
warfare 718 n.
militate against
influence 178 vb.
counteract 182 vb.
oppose 704 vb.
militia
defender 713 n.
army 722 n.
milk
empty 300 vb.
milk 301 n.
extract 304 vb.
fluid 335 n.
groom 369 vb.
white thing 427 n.
provide 633 vb.
use 673 vb.
acquire 771 vb.
take 786 vb.
— dry
waste 634 vb.
milk and honey
prosperity 730 n.
milk and water
weak thing 163 n.
moderate 177 adj.
insipidity 387 n.
milk bar
café 192 n.
milk float
cart 274 n.
milkmaid
herdsman 369 n.
servant 742 n.
milkman
seller 793 n.
milk of human kindness
benevolence 897 n.
milk of magnesia
purgative 658 n.
milk pudding
dessert 301 n.
milk shake
soft drink 301 n.
milksop
weakling 163 n.
ninny 501 n.
coward 856 n.
innocent 935 n.
milk tooth
tooth 256 n.
milky
edible 301 adj.
semiliquid 354 adj.
semitransparent 424 adj.
whitish 427 adj.
Milky Way
star 321 n.
luminary 420 n.
mill
produce 164 vb.
roughen 259 vb.
notch 260 vb.
pulverizer 332 n.
pulverize 332 vb.
workshop 687 n.
pugilism 716 n.
— around
congregate 74 vb.
be agitated 318 vb.
millboard
bookbinding 589 n.
millenarian
hoper 852 n.
philanthropist 901 n.
millenary
fifth and over 99 adj.
millennial
secular 110 adj.
future 124 adj.
promising 852 adj.
celebratory 876 adj.
paradisiac 971 adj.
millennium
over one hundred 99 n.
period 110 n.
future state 124 n.
fantasy 513 n.
aspiration 852 n.
heaven 971 n.
miller
pulverizer 332 n.
millesimal
multifid 100 adj.
millet
cereals 301 n.
grass 366 n.
milliard
over one hundred 99 n.
millibar
weather 340 n.
millicurie
radiation 417 n.
millimetre
small quantity 33 n.

short distance 200 n.
long measure 203 n.
milliner
clothier 228 n.
millinery
dressing 228 n.
headgear 228 n.
million
over one hundred 99 n.
multitude 104 n.
million, the
commonalty 869 n.
millionaire, millionairess
rich person 800 n.
millionth
fifth and over 99 adj.
millipede
creepy-crawly 365 n.
millpond
lake 346 n.
millrace
current 350 n.
conduit 351 n.
millstone
gravity 322 n.
pulverizer 332 n.
encumbrance 702 n.
milometer
meter 465 n.
milord
person of rank 868 n.
mime
mimicry 20 n.
imitate 20 vb.
gesticulate 547 vb.
represent 551 vb.
actor 594 n.
act 594 vb.
mimeograph
copy 20 vb.
mimesis
imitation 20 n.
representation 551 n.
mimetic
dramatic 594 adj.
mimic
imitator 20 n.
imitate 20 vb.
be absurd 497 vb.
represent 551 vb.
actor 594 n.
satirize 851 vb.
mimicry
mimicry 20 n.
minaret
high structure 209 n.
minatory
cautionary 664 adj.
frightening 854 adj.
threatening 900 adj.
mince
cut 46 vb.
rend 46 vb.
walk 267 vb.
move slowly 278 vb.
meat 301 n.
pulverize 332 vb.
be affected 850 vb.
— matters
cant 541 vb.
be fastidious 862 vb.
— one's words
extenuate 927 vb.
minced
fragmentary 53 adj.
mince pies
dessert 301 n.
mind
insubstantial thing 4 n.
intellect 447 n.
spirit 447 n.
be attentive 455 vb.
be careful 457 vb.
look after 457 vb.
opinion 485 n.
remember 505 vb.
will 595 n.
willingness 597 n.
intention 617 n.
suffer 825 vb.
be discontented 829 vb.
liking 859 n.
dislike 861 vb.
resent 891 vb.
— one's own business
be incurious 454 vb.
— one's P's and Q's
be careful 457 vb.
behave 688 vb.
be courteous 884 vb.
— one's step
be careful 457 vb.
mind-bending, mind-blowing
exciting 821 adj.
frightening 854 adj.
wonderful 864 adj.
intoxicating 949 adj.
mind-boggling
unusual 84 adj.
unexpected 508 adj.
exciting 821 adj.
wonderful 864 adj.
minded
volitional 595 adj.
intending 617 adj.
desiring 859 adj.
minder
machinist 630 n.
mindful
attentive 455 adj.
careful 457 adj.
remembering 505 adj.
mindless
mindless 448 adj.
unthinking 450 adj.
foolish 499 adj.
forgetful 506 adj.
mind made up
prejudgment 481 n.
resolution 599 n.
mind of one's own
obstinacy 602 n.
mind over matter
intellect 447 n.
mind reader
psychic 984 n.
mind's eye
vision 438 n.
remembrance 505 n.
imagination 513 n.
mine
great quantity 32 n.
source 156 n.
produce 164 vb.
demolish 165 vb.
lowness 210 n.
depth 211 n.
excavation 255 n.
tunnel 263 n.
extract 304 vb.
descend 309 vb.
darkness 418 n.
trap 542 n.
store 632 n.
impair 655 vb.
workshop 687 n.
besiege 712 vb.
defences 713 n.
bomb 723 n.
acquire 771 vb.
take 786 vb.
wealth 800 n.
minefield
pitfall 663 n.
defences 713 n.
mine host
caterer 633 n.
sociable person 882 n.
minelayer
warship 722 n.
mine of information
erudition 490 n.
scholar 492 n.
miner
producer 164 n.
excavator 255 n.
extractor 304 n.
descent 309 n.
artisan 686 n.
soldiery 722 n.
mineral
food content 301 n.
object 319 n.
mineral 359 n.
inorganic 359 adj.
materials 631 n.
mineralogy
rock 344 n.
mineralogy 359 n.
mineral oil
oil 357 n.
mineral water
soft drink 301 n.
water 339 n.
Minerva
Olympian deity 967 n.
minestrone
hors-d'oeuvres 301 n.
minesweeper
warship 722 n.
minethrower
gun 723 n.
minginess
insufficiency 636 n.
mingle
mix 43 vb.
mingy
parsimonious 816 adj.
mini-
little 196 adj.
miniate
paint 553 vb.
miniature
small 33 adj.
miniature 196 n.
little 196 adj.
picture 553 n.
miniaturist
artist 556 n.
minibus
automobile 274 n.
bus 274 n.
minicomputer
counting instrument 86 n.
minikin
small 33 adj.
dwarf 196 n.
minim
small quantity 33 n.
notation 410 n.
metrology 465 n.
minimal
small 33 adj.
lesser 35 adj.
exiguous 196 adj.
Minimalist
artist 556 n.
moderate 625 n.
minimize, minimise
abate 37 vb.
misjudge 481 vb.
underestimate 483 vb.
detract 926 vb.
minimum
small quantity 33 n.
lesser 35 adj.
sufficiency 635 n.
minion
dependant 742 n.
flatterer 925 n.
miniskirt
shortness 204 n.
skirt 228 n.
miniskirted
uncovered 229 adj.
minister
agent 686 n.
manage 689 vb.
official 690 n.
envoy 754 n.
offer worship 981 vb.
pastor 986 n.

perform ritual 988 vb.
— to
look after 457 vb.
be instrumental 628 vb.
minister to 703 vb.
serve 742 vb.
philanthropize 897 vb.
ministerial
governmental 733 adj.
clerical 986 adj.
ministering
instrumental 628 adj.
serving 742 adj.
priestly 985 adj.
ministering angel
aider 703 n.
angel 968 n.
ministration
aid 703 n.
church ministry 985 n.
ministration 988 n.
ministry
vocation 622 n.
management 689 n.
clergy 986 n.
minium
red pigment 431 n.
mink
skin 226 n.
minnesinger
musician 413 n.
poet 593 n.
minnow
small animal 33 n.
fish 365 n.
minor
inconsiderable 33 adj.
lesser 35 adj.
youth 130 n.
harmonic 410 adj.
unimportant 639 adj.
middling 732 adj.
minor arts, the
art 551 n.
minority
inferiority 35 n.
part 53 n.
fewness 105 n.
nonage 130 n.
helplessness 161 n.
dissentient 489 n.
minority rule
government 733 n.
minor orders
holy orders 985 n.
Minor Prophets
scripture 975 n.
minor road
road 624 n.
minor scale
key 410 n.
Minotaur
rara avis 84 n.
minster
church 990 n.
minstrel
musician 413 n.
vocalist 413 n.
poet 593 n.
entertainer 594 n.
mint
mould 23 n.
great quantity 32 n.
produce 164 vb.
form 243 vb.
potherb 301 n.
workshop 687 n.
mint 797 vb.
— money
get rich 800 vb.
mint condition
perfection 646 n.
minting
coinage 797 n.
mints
sweets 301 n.
minuend
subtraction 39 n.
numerical element 85 n.
minuet
musical piece 412 n.
dance 837 n.
minus
nonexistent 2 adj.
difference 15 n.
less 35 adv.
subtracted 39 adj.
without 190 adv.
deficient 307 adj.
losing 772 adj.
not owning 774 adj.
minuscule
letter 558 n.
minus sign
punctuation 547 n.
minute
small 33 adj.
period 110 n.
minute 196 adj.
angular measure 247 n.
indistinct 444 adj.
attentive 455 adj.
careful 457 adj.
measurement 465 n.
record 548 vb.
diffuse 570 adj.
compendium 592 n.
minute-gun
timekeeper 117 n.
signal 547 n.
minutes
record 548 n.
minutiae
small quantity 33 n.
particulars 80 n.
trifle 639 n.
minx
insolent person 878 n.
miotic
dim-sighted 440 adj.
mirabile dictu
wonderfully 864 adv.
miracle
nonconformity 84 n.
prodigy 864 n.
miracle play
stage play 594 n.
miracle-worker
prodigy 864 n.
sorcerer 983 n.
miraculous
unusual 84 adj.
impossible 470 adj.
wonderful 864 adj.
mirage
insubstantial thing 4 n.
visual fallacy 440 n.
appearance 445 n.
error 495 n.
disappointment 509 n.
fantasy 513 n.
deception 542 n.
mire
marsh 347 n.
mirror
resemble 18 vb.
imitate 20 vb.
copy 22 n.
mirror 442 n.
oracle 511 n.
show 522 vb.
mirror image
reflection 417 n.
appearance 445 n.
mirror symmetry
contrariety 14 n.
mirth
merriment 833 n.
mirthful
merry 833 adj.
MIRV
missile weapon 723 n.
miry
marshy 347 adj.
misadventure
event 154 n.
misfortune 731 n.
misalign
mismatch 25 vb.
misalliance
misfit 25 n.
type of marriage 894 n.
misanthropic
unsociable 883 adj.
misanthropic 902 adj.
misanthropist
enemy 881 n.
shrew 892 n.
misanthrope 902 n.
misanthropy
misanthropy 902 n.
misapplication
misinterpretation 521 n.
misuse 675 n.
bungling 695 n.
prodigality 815 n.
misapply
waste 634 vb.
misuse 675 vb.
be unskilful 695 vb.
misapprehend
err 495 vb.
misapprehension
misinterpretation 521 n.
misappropriation
misuse 675 n.
peculation 788 n.
arrogation 916 n.
misbegotten
contemptible 922 adj.
bastard 954 adj.
misbehave
be foolish 499 vb.
behave 688 vb.
disobey 738 vb.
be wicked 934 vb.
misbehaviour
disobedience 738 n.
ill-breeding 847 n.
discourtesy 885 n.
wickedness 934 n.
guilty act 936 n.
misbelief
unbelief 486 n.
error 495 n.
heterodoxy 977 n.
miscalculate
misjudge 481 vb.
miscalculation
misjudgment 481 n.
mistake 495 n.
lack of expectation 508 n.
disappointment 509 n.
miscall
misname 562 vb.
miscarriage
failure 728 n.
miscarriage of justice
misjudgment 481 n.
injustice 914 n.
miscarry
be unproductive 172 vb.
fall short 307 vb.
miscarry 728 vb.
miscast
mismatch 25 vb.
dramatic 594 adj.
miscegenation
mixture 43 n.
type of marriage 894 n.

miscellaneous
nonuniform 17 adj.
mixed 43 adj.
miscellany
medley 43 n.
accumulation 74 n.
anthology 592 n.
mischance
misfortune 731 n.
mischief
destruction 165 n.
evil 616 n.
badness 645 n.
impairment 655 n.
quarrelsomeness 709 n.
wrong 914 n.
mischiefmaker
troublemaker 663 n.
hinderer 702 n.
quarreller 709 n.
agitator 738 n.
evildoer 904 n.
mischievous
destructive 165 adj.
capricious 604 adj.
harmful 645 adj.
disobedient 738 adj.
malevolent 898 adj.
wrong 914 adj.
mischievousness
evil 616 n.
quarrelsomeness 709 n.
miscible
mixed 43 adj.
misconceive
misjudge 481 vb.
err 495 vb.
misinterpret 521 vb.
misconduct
conduct 688 n.
be unskilful 695 vb.
discourtesy 885 n.
guilty act 936 n.
misconjecture
misjudge 481 vb.
misconstruction
misjudgment 481 n.
error 495 n.
misconstrue
distort 246 vb.
not know 491 vb.
misinterpret 521 vb.
miscount
err 495 vb.
miscreant
vicious 934 adj.
knave 938 n.
misdate
misdate 118 vb.
misdeed
wrong 914 n.
guilty act 936 n.
misdemeanant
offender 904 n.
misdemeanour
guilty act 936 n.
lawbreaking 954 n.
misdirect
deflect 282 vb.
mislead 495 vb.
misteach 535 vb.
be unskilful 695 vb.
misdirected
irrelevant 10 adj.
mistaken 495 adj.
misdoing
wrong 914 n.
guilty act 936 n.
misdoubting
nervous 854 adj.
mise-en-scène
stage set 594 n.
miser
accumulator 74 n.
niggard 816 n.
egotist 932 n.
miserable
unimportant 639 adj.
not nice 645 adj.
unfortunate 731 adj.
unhappy 825 adj.
melancholic 834 adj.
miserably
painfully 32 adv.
slightly 33 adv.
contemptibly 922 adv.
misericord
seat 218 n.
sidearms 723 n.
church interior 990 n.
miserly
careful 457 adj.
insufficient 636 adj.
avaricious 816 adj.
parsimonious 816 adj.
misery
evil 616 n.
adversity 731 n.
sorrow 825 n.
sufferer 825 n.
dejection 834 n.
moper 834 n.
bore 838 n.
hopelessness 853 n.
disapprover 924 n.
misfeasance
wrong 914 n.
lawbreaking 954 n.
misfire
bungling 695 n.
miscarry 728 vb.
misfit
unrelatedness 10 n.
misfit 25 n.
discontinuity 72 n.
nonconformist 84 n.
displacement 188 n.
bungler 697 n.
misfortune
evil 616 n.
misfortune 731 n.
misgiving(s)
doubt 486 n.
nervousness 854 n.
misgovern
be unskilful 695 vb.
be lax 734 vb.
oppress 735 vb.
misguide
misteach 535 vb.
misguided
misjudging 481 adj.
mistaken 495 adj.
mishandle
ill-treat 645 vb.
misuse 675 vb.
be unskilful 695 vb.
be severe 735 vb.
mishap
event 154 n.
misfortune 731 n.
mishit
mistake 495 n.
be clumsy 695 vb.
mishmash
medley 43 n.
confusion 61 n.
Mishnah
scripture 975 n.
misinform
mislead 495 vb.
misteach 535 vb.
be false 541 vb.
misinformed
uninstructed 491 adj.
mistaken 495 adj.
misinterpret
transform 147 vb.
distort 246 vb.
misjudge 481 vb.
blunder 495 vb.
misinterpret 521 vb.
be false 541 vb.
misinterpreted
unmeant 515 adj.
misinterpreted 521 adj.
misjudge
mistime 138 vb.
not think 450 vb.
misjudge 481 vb.
underestimate 483 vb.
blunder 495 vb.
be foolish 499 vb.
not understand 517 vb.
misinterpret 521 vb.
misjudgment
inattention 456 n.
misjudgment 481 n.
overestimation 482 n.
credulity 487 n.
error 495 n.
mistake 495 n.
injustice 914 n.
mislaid
misplaced 188 adj.
absent 190 adj.
mislay
derange 63 vb.
lose 772 vb.
mislead
deflect 282 vb.
puzzle 474 vb.
sophisticate 477 vb.
mislead 495 vb.
misteach 535 vb.
befool 542 vb.
deceive 542 vb.
motivate 612 vb.
obstruct 702 vb.
make wicked 934 vb.
mismanage
misuse 675 vb.
be unskilful 695 vb.
be lax 734 vb.
fail in duty 918 vb.
mismatched
disagreeing 25 adj.
misname
misname 562 vb.
misnomer
name 561 n.
misnomer 562 n.
misogamy
celibacy 895 n.
misogyny
hatred 888 n.
celibacy 895 n.
misanthropy 902 n.
misplace
misplace 188 vb.
misplaced
irrelevant 10 adj.
unapt 25 adj.
orderless 61 adj.
unconformable 84 adj.
misplaced 188 adj.
lost 772 adj.
misprint
mistake 495 n.
misprize
underestimate 483 vb.
not respect 921 vb.
hold cheap 922 vb.
mispronounce
be ungrammatical 565 vb.
voice 577 vb.
misproportion
distortion 246 n.
misproportioned
deformed 246 adj.
misquote
blunder 495 vb.
misinterpret 521 vb.
be false 541 vb.
misread
blunder 495 vb.
misinterpret 521 vb.
misreckoning
misjudgment 481 n.

misremember
forget 506 vb.
misreport
inexactness 495 n.
be false 541 vb.
misreported
inexact 495 adj.
misrepresent
make unlike 19 vb.
distort 246 vb.
sophisticate 477 vb.
misinterpret 521 vb.
misteach 535 vb.
be false 541 vb.
misrepresent 552 vb.
satirize 851 vb.
detract 926 vb.
misrepresentation
inexactness 495 n.
untruth 543 n.
misrepresentation 552 n.
calumny 926 n.
misrule
bungling 695 n.
anarchy 734 n.
oppress 735 vb.
miss
be incomplete 55 vb.
youngster 132 n.
fall short 307 vb.
lady 373 n.
blunder 495 vb.
require 627 vb.
be unsatisfied 636 vb.
bungling 695 n.
fail 728 vb.
lose 772 vb.
be discontented 829 vb.
regret 830 vb.
desire 859 vb.
title 870 n.
— a beat
be agitated 318 vb.
— a chance
be late 136 vb.
— nothing
be attentive 455 vb.
— out
be incomplete 55 vb.
exclude 57 vb.
— the boat/bus
lose a chance 138 vb.
fail 728 vb.
— the mark
fall short 307 vb.
— the point
be insensitive 820 vb.
missal
office-book 988 n.
missed
remembered 505 adj.
misshape
distort 246 vb.
make ugly 842 vb.
missile
missile 287 n.
ammunition 723 n.
missile weapon
rocket 276 n.
missile weapon 723 n.
missing
nonexistent 2 adj.
incomplete 55 adj.
misplaced 188 adj.
absent 190 adj.
deficient 307 adj.
disappearing 446 adj.
unknown 491 adj.
required 627 adj.
lost 772 adj.
missing link
incompleteness 55 n.
discontinuity 72 n.
completion 725 n.
mission
job 622 n.
vocation 622 n.
mandate 751 n.
envoy 754 n.
philanthropy 901 n.
church ministry 985 n.
missionary
preacher 537 n.
philanthropist 901 n.
religious teacher 973 n.
zealot 979 n.
pastor 986 n.
missive
correspondence 588 n.
misspell
be ungrammatical 565 vb.
misspend
be prodigal 815 vb.
misstatement
inexactness 495 n.
untruth 543 n.
missus
lady 373 n.
spouse 894 n.
Miss World
a beauty 841 n.
mist
insubstantial thing 4 n.
moisture 341 n.
cloud 355 n.
bedim 419 vb.
obfuscation 421 n.
opacity 423 n.
blur 440 vb.
invisibility 444 n.
uncertainty 474 n.
mistake
mistake 495 n.
misinterpretation 521 n.
solecism 565 n.
bungling 695 n.
failure 728 n.
mistaken
misjudging 481 adj.
mistaken 495 adj.
unwise 499 adj.
misteach
mislead 495 vb.
misinterpret 521 vb.
misteach 535 vb.
misrepresent 552 vb.
mister
male 372 n.
title 870 n.
misthrow
bungling 695 n.
mistime
mistime 138 vb.
mistletoe
plant 366 n.
mistral
wind 352 n.
mistranslate
misinterpret 521 vb.
mistreatment
misuse 675 n.
mistress
lady 373 n.
teacher 537 n.
victor 727 n.
master 741 n.
owner 776 n.
title 870 n.
loved one 887 n.
kept woman 952 n.
mistress of the wardrobe
clothier 228 n.
mistrust
doubt 486 n.vb.
nervousness 854 n.
be jealous 911 vb.
misty
insubstantial 4 adj.
cloudy 355 adj.
dim 419 adj.
opaque 423 adj.
semitransparent 424 adj.
indistinct 444 adj.
uncertain 474 adj.
puzzling 517 adj.
misunderstand
not know 491 vb.
err 495 vb.
not understand 517 vb.
misinterpret 521 vb.
misunderstanding
error 495 n.
misinterpretation 521 n.
dissension 709 n.
misusage
solecism 565 n.
misuse 675 n.
misuse
force 176 vb.
waste 634 n.vb.
ill-treat 645 vb.
impairment 655 n.
misuse 675 n.vb.
be unskilful 695 vb.
be severe 735 vb.
cruel act 898 n.
misuse of funds
prodigality 815 n.
misuse of language
inexactness 495 n.
mite
small coin 33 n.
small quantity 33 n.
child 132 n.
dwarf 196 n.
insect 365 n.
insufficiency 636 n.
Mithras
mythic deity 966 n.
mithridate
antidote 658 n.
mitigate
abate 37 vb.
moderate 177 vb.
qualify 468 vb.
make better 654 vb.
relieve 831 vb.
extenuate 927 vb.
mitigating circumstance
vindication 927 n.
mitrailleuse
gun 723 n.
mitre
joint 45 n.
join 45 vb.
badge of rule 743 n.
vestments 989 n.
mitt
glove 228 n.
feeler 378 n.
mix
mix 43 vb.
combine 50 vb.
jumble 63 vb.
modify 143 vb.
agitate 318 vb.
— in
add 38 vb.
infiltrate 297 vb.
— in society
be sociable 882 vb.
— it
fight 716 vb.
— up
mix 43 vb.
jumble 63 vb.
— with
be sociable 882 vb.
mixed-ability
educational 534 adj.
mixed bag
nonuniformity 17 n.
medley 43 n.
accumulation 74 n.
mixed blessing
inexpedience 643 n.

adversity 731 n.
mixed economy
middle 70 n.
mixed grill
dish 301 n.
mixed metaphor
metaphor 519 n.
mixed number
numerical element 85 n.
mixed up in
component 58 adj.
mixer
mixture 43 n.
mixture
mixture 43 n.
combination 50 n.
composition 56 n.
confusion 61 n.
draught 301 n.
imperfection 647 n.
medicine 658 n.
mixture as before
uniformity 16 n.
recurrence 106 n.
mixture of colour
variegation 437 n.
mix-up
confusion 61 n.
mizzenmast
poop 238 n.
sail 275 n.
mizzle
rain 350 vb.
mnemonic
reminder 505 n.
mnemonics
mnemonics 505 n.
moan
blow 352 vb.
faintness 401 n.
cry 408 vb.
be discontented 829 vb.
lamentation 836 n.
weep 836 vb.
moat
fence 235 n.
cavity 255 n.
furrow 262 n.
conduit 351 n.
protection 660 n.
obstacle 702 n.
defences 713 n.
mob
rampage 61 vb.
crowd 74 n.
multitude 104 n.
be violent 176 vb.
pursue 619 vb.
charge 712 vb.
rabble 869 n.
celebrate 876 vb.
congratulate 886 vb.
caress 889 vb.
not respect 921 vb.
disapprove 924 vb.
mob cap
headgear 228 n.
mobile
changeable thing 152 n.
moving 265 adj.
sculpture 554 n.
lively 819 adj.
mobile home
small house 192 n.
mobility
changeableness 152 n.
mobilization, mobilisation
war measures 718 n.
mobilize, mobilise
bring together 74 vb.
make ready 669 vb.
Möbius strip
continuity 71 n.
mob law
anarchy 734 n.
lawlessness 954 n.
mobster
offender 904 n.
moccasins
footwear 228 n.
mocha
brown 430 adj.
mock
simulating 18 adj.
substituted 150 adj.
disbelieve 486 vb.
spurious 542 adj.
befool 542 vb.
laugh 835 vb.
ridicule 851 n.vb.
shame 867 vb.
not respect 921 vb.
despise 922 vb.
detract 926 vb.
mock epic
doggerel 593 n.
mocker
imitator 20 n.
unbeliever 486 n.
detractor 926 n.
(See **mock** *)*
mockery
insubstantial thing 4 n.
mimicry 20 n.n.
(See **mock** *)*
mock-heroic
poetic 593 adj.
funny 849 adj.
derisive 851 adj.
mockingbird
imitator 20 n.
mock modesty
underestimation 483 n.
affectation 850 n.
mock-up
prototype 23 n.
exhibit 522 n.
mod
youngster 132 n.
fop 848 n.
modal
such 7 adj.
circumstantial 8 adj.
harmonic 410 adj.
modality
extrinsicality 6 n.
modality 7 n.
mode
modality 7 n.
statistics 86 n.
key 410 n.
practice 610 n.
way 624 n.
fashion 848 n.
model
copy 22 n.
duplicate 22 n.
prototype 23 n.
be an example 23 vb.
superior 34 n.
rule 81 n.
example 83 n.
attribution 158 n.
miniature 196 n.
little 196 adj.
form 243 vb.
comparison 462 n.
supposition 512 n.
show 522 vb.
image 551 n.
represent 551 vb.
art equipment 553 n.
sculpt 554 vb.
plan 623 n.
paragon 646 n.
perfect 646 adj.
plaything 837 n.
person of repute 866 n.
model builder
theorist 512 n.
mode of address
title 870 n.
mode of behaviour
conduct 688 n.
mode of expression
style 566 n.
moderate
median 30 adj.
small 33 adj.
abate 37 vb.
moderate 177 adj. vb.
retard 278 vb.
qualify 468 vb.
moderate 625 n.
imperfect 647 adj.
reformer 654 n.
political party 708 n.
middling 732 adj.
restrain 747 vb.
cheap 812 adj.
tranquillize 823 vb.
relieve 831 vb.
indifferent 860 adj.
modest 874 adj.
temperate 942 adj.
be temperate 942 vb.
moderation
diminution 37 n.
moderation 177 n.
counteraction 182 n.
underestimation 483 n.
middle way 625 n.
pacification 719 n.
averageness 732 n.
inexcitability 823 n.
temperance 942 n.
Moderations, Mods
exam 459 n.
moderato
adagio 412 adv.
moderator
nucleonics 160 n.
moderator 177 n.
director 690 n.
mediator 720 n.
ecclesiarch 986 n.
modern
present 121 adj.
modern 126 adj.
progressive 285 adj.
fashionable 848 adj.
modernism
modernism 126 n.
heterodoxy 977 n.
modernity
modernism 126 n.
modernize, modernise
modernize 126 vb.
change 143 vb.
modify 143 vb.
revolutionize 149 vb.
progress 285 vb.
make better 654 vb.
restore 656 vb.
be in fashion 848 vb.
modern maths
mathematics 86 n.
reasoning 475 n.
modest
inconsiderable 33 adj.
depreciating 483 adj.
artless 699 adj.
middling 732 adj.
inglorious 867 adj.
humble 872 adj.
modest 874 adj.
disinterested 931 adj.
pure 950 adj.
modesty
moderation 177 n.
plainness 573 n.
nervousness 854 n.
modesty 874 n.
purity 950 n.
modicum
small quantity 33 n.
portion 783 n.
modifiability
changeableness 152 n.
modification
difference 15 n.

change 143 n.
qualification 468 n.
modifier
alterer 143 n.
modify
make unlike 19 vb.
modify 143 vb.
transform 147 vb.
modish
fashionable 848 adj.
reputable 866 adj.
modiste
clothier 228 n.
modular
metrical 465 adj.
modulate
make unlike 19 vb.
adjust 24 vb.
modulation
change 143 n.
moderation 177 n.
key 410 n.
broadcasting 531 n.
voice 577 n.
module
prototype 23 n.
component 58 n.
modulus
numerical element 85 n.
modus operandi
way 624 n.
conduct 688 n.
modus vivendi
way 624 n.
compromise 770 n.
moggie, moggy
cat 365 n.
mogul
bigwig 638 n.
Mogul
sovereign 741 n.
mohair
fibre 208 n.
textile 222 n.
hair 259 n.
Mohammed, Mahomet
religious teacher 937 n.
(See **Muhammad** *)*
moho
world 321 n.
moidered, moithered
doubting 474 adj.
crazy 503 adj.
moiety
part 53 n.
bisection 92 n.
portion 783 n.
moil
work 682 vb.
moiler
worker 686 n.
moire
textile 222 n.
moiré
variegation 437 n.
iridescent 437 adj.
moist
watery 339 adj.
humid 341 adj.
moisten
add water 339 vb.
moisten 341 vb.
moisture
moisture 341 n.
rain 350 n.
moke
beast of burden 273 n.
moksha, moksa
liberation 746 n.
molar
tooth 256 n.
pulverizer 332 n.
molasses
sweet thing 392 n.
mole
projection 254 n.
mammal 365 n.
latency 523 n.
informer 524 n.
identification 547 n.
safeguard 662 n.
defences 713 n.
blemish 845 n.
molecule
minuteness 196 n.
element 319 n.
molehill
minuteness 196 n.
small hill 209 n.
dome 253 n.
moleskin
textile 222 n.
skin 226 n.
molest
harm 645 vb.
torment 827 vb.
be malevolent 898 vb.
debauch 951 vb.
moll
woman 373 n.
kept woman 952 n.
mollify
assuage 177 vb.
pacify 719 vb.
mollusc
animal 365 n.
marine life 365 n.
mollycoddle
weakling 163 n.
ninny 501 n.
Moloch
tyrant 735 n.
monster 938 n.
Semitic deities 967 n.
idol 982 n.
Molotov cocktail
bomb 723 n.
molten
liquefied 337 adj.
fiery 379 adj.
heated 381 adj.
moment
juncture 8 n.
date 108 n.
brief span 114 n.
instant 116 n.
occasion 137 n.
cause 156 n.
importance 638 n.
momentary
brief 114 adj.
momentous
crucial 137 adj.
eventful 154 adj.
influential 178 adj.
important 638 adj.
momentum
energy 160 n.
impulse 279 n.
monad
existence 1 n.
unit 88 n.
element 319 n.
monarch
sovereign 741 n.
owner 776 n.
monarchist
revolter 738 n.
monarchy
government 733 n.
monastic 986 adj.
retreat 192 n.
monastery 986 n.
monastic
monastic 986 adj.
monasticism
seclusion 883 n.
celibacy 895 n.
monasticism 985 n.
monaural
sounding 398 adj.
mondaine
beau monde 848 n.
monetarist
restriction 747 n.
economy 814 n.
monetary
monetary 797 adj.
money
means 629 n.
money 797 n.
wealth 800 n.
moneybags
rich person 800 n.
moneybox
box 194 n.
storage 632 n.
treasury 799 n.
money-changer
merchant 794 n.
minter 797 n.
money-conscious
economical 814 adj.
parsimonious 816 adj.
moneyed
prosperous 730 adj.
moneyed 800 adj.
money for jam/old rope
easy thing 701 n.
money-grubber
niggard 816 n.
egotist 932 n.
money-grubbing
acquisition 771 n.
avarice 816 n.
money in the bank
funds 797 n.
moneylender
provider 633 n.
lender 784 n.
moneyless
poor 801 adj.
moneymaker
rich person 800 n.
money-making
gainful 771 adj.
wealth 800 n.
money market
finance 797 n.
money order
paper money 797 n.
money-saving
economical 814 adj.
money-spinner
rich person 800 n.
money-spinning
gainful 771 adj.
money's worth
price 809 n.
cheapness 812 n.
money to burn
superfluity 637 n.
monger
tradespeople 794 n.
Mongolian
ethnic 11 adj.
mongolism
unintelligence 499 n.
mongoose
mammal 365 n.
mongrel
hybrid 43 n.
nonconformist 84 n.
dog 365 n.
moniker, monicker
name 561 n.
monism
unity 88 n.
philosophy 449 n.
monition
warning 664 n.
monitor
reptile 365 n.
listener 415 n.
look after 457 vb.
enquire 459 vb.
teacher 537 n.
official 690 n.
adviser 691 n.
warship 722 n.
monitorial system
education 534 n.
monitory
predicting 511 adj.
dissuasive 613 adj.

cautionary 664 adj.
monk
celibate 895 n.
virgin 950 n.
pietist 979 n.
monk 986 n.
monkey
imitator 20 n.
ram 279 n.
mammal 365 n.
testee 461 n.
funds 797 n.
evildoer 904 n.
bad person 938 n.
monkey around
be absurd 497 vb.
— with
impair 655 vb.
monkey business
foul play 930 n.
monkey jacket
jacket 228 n.
monkey nut
fruit 301 n.
monkey tricks
foolery 497 n.
disobedience 738 n.
revel 837 n.
monkish
unwedded 895 adj.
monastic 986 adj.
mono
one 88 adj.
sound 398 n.
sounding 398 adj.
monochrome
uniform 16 adj.
achromatism 426 n.
painting 553 n.
monocle
eyeglass 442 n.
monocotyledonous
vegetal 366 adj.
monocracy
despotism 733 n.
monocular
dim-sighted 440 adj.
monoculture
agriculture 370 n.
monocycle
bicycle 274 n.
monody
soliloquy 585 n.
poem 593 n.
monogamy
type of marriage 894 n.
monogram
label 547 n.
initials 558 n.
monograph
dissertation 591 n.
monokini
beachwear 228 n.
monolith
monument 548 n.
monolithic
uniform 16 adj.
simple 44 adj.
cohesive 48 n.
indivisible 52 adj.
one 88 adj.
dense 324 adj.
monologist
speaker 579 n.
soliloquist 585 n.
entertainer 594 n.
monologue
uniformity 16 n.
oration 579 n.
soliloquy 585 n.
monomania
attention 455 n.
prejudgment 481 n.
eccentricity 503 n.
mania 503 n.
desire 859 n.
monomaniac
madman 504 n.
monomaniacal
obsessed 455 adj.
monophonic
sounding 398 adj.
harmonious 410 adj.
Monophysite
heretic 977 n.
monoplane
aircraft 276 n.
monopolist
restriction 747 n.
egotist 932 n.
monopolistic
restraining 747 adj.
avaricious 816 adj.
monopolize, monopolise
prevail 178 vb.
engross 449 vb.
attract notice 455 vb.
possess 773 vb.
appropriate 786 vb.
be selfish 932 vb.
monopoly
exclusion 57 n.
corporation 708 n.
restriction 747 n.
possession 773 n.
sale 793 n.
board game 837 n.
monorail
railway 624 n.
monosyllabic
linguistic 557 adj.
concise 569 adj.
taciturn 582 adj.
monosyllable
word 559 n.
monotheism
unity 88 n.
deism 973 n.
monotheistic
religious 973 adj.
Monothelite
heretic 977 n.
monotone
uniformity 16 n.
musical note 410 n.
monotonous
uniform 16 adj.
equal 28 adj.
continuous 71 adj.
repeated 106 adj.
rolling 403 adj.
feeble 572 adj.
monotony
uniformity 16 n.
recurrence 106 n.
tedium 838 n.
dullness 840 n.
monotype
breed 77 n.
print 587 n.
Monsieur
title 870 n.
Monsignor
church title 986 n.
monsoon
rain 350 n.
wind 352 n.
monster
violent creature 176 n.
giant 195 n.
eyesore 842 n.
intimidation 854 n.
prodigy 864 n.
monster 938 n.
demon 970 n.
monstrance
ritual object 988 n.
monstrosity
abnormality 84 n.
hugeness 195 n.
deformity 246 n.
prodigy 864 n.
monstrous
exorbitant 32 adj.
unusual 84 adj.
huge 195 adj.
not nice 645 adj.
ugly 842 adj.
ridiculous 849 adj.
wonderful 864 adj.
heinous 934 adj.
fairylike 970 adj.
montage
cinema 445 n.
picture 553 n.
Montanism
heresy 977 n.
monte
card game 837 n.
Montessori system
education 534 n.
month
period 110 n.
monthly
seasonal 141 adj.
journal 528 n.
usual 610 adj.
month of Sundays, a
long duration 113 n.
months of the year
regular return 141 n.
monticle
small hill 209 n.
monument
antiquity 125 n.
edifice 164 n.
reminder 505 n.
monument 548 n.
trophy 729 n.
honours 866 n.
monumental
enormous 32 adj.
large 195 adj.
tall 209 adj.
monumental mason
obsequies 364 n.
sculptor 556 n.
moo
ululate 409 vb.
mooch about
move slowly 278 vb.
be inactive 679 vb.
mood
temperament 5 n.
state 7 n.
tendency 179 n.
grammar 564 n.
whim 604 n.
conduct 688 n.
affections 817 n.
moody
fitful 142 adj.
capricious 604 adj.
melancholic 834 adj.
irascible 892 adj.
sullen 893 adj.
moody person
moral sensibility 819 n.
moon
period 110 n.
changeable thing 152 n.
moon 321 n.
satellite 321 n.
luminary 420 n.
be inattentive 456 vb.
— about
be inactive 679 vb.
— after
desire 859 vb.
moon, the
impossibility 470 n.
moonbeam
glimmer 419 n.
moon buggy
vehicle 274 n.
mooncalf
fool 501 n.
Moonie
sectarian 978 n.
moonless
unlit 418 adj.
moonlight
moon 321 n.
light 417 n.
glimmer 419 n.
work 682 vb.

moonlight flit
departure 296 n.
escape 667 n.
moonlit
undimmed 417 adj.
moonraker
ninny 501 n.
moonrise
evening 129 n.
moonscape
moon 321 n.
moonshine
insubstantial thing 4 n.
alcoholic drink 301 n.
moon 321 n.
light 417 n.
empty talk 515 n.
fable 543 n.
booty 790 n.
moonstone
gem 844 n.
moon-struck
insane 503 adj.
moor
tie 45 vb.
desert 172 n.
place 187 vb.
high land 209 n.
arrive 295 vb.
marsh 347 n.
plain 348 n.
moored
quiescent 266 adj.
moorhen
bird 365 n.
mooring(s)
cable 47 n.
station 187 n.
moorland
space 183 n.
high land 209 n.
(See **moor** *)*
moose
mammal 365 n.
moot
moot 459 adj.
interrogate 459 vb.
uncertain 474 adj.
argue 475 vb.
propound 512 vb.
council 692 n.
moot point
topic 452 n.
question 459 n.
mop
hair 259 n.
dry 342 vb.
cleaning utensil 648 n.
clean 648 vb.
— and mow
distort 246 vb.
haunt 970 vb.
— up
destroy 165 vb.
absorb 299 vb.
dry 342 vb.
clean 648 vb.
carry through 725 vb.
mope
be dejected 834 vb.
be sullen 893 vb.
moped
bicycle 274 n.
moper
idler 679 n.
malcontent 829 n.
moper 834 n.
hopelessness 853 n.
disapprover 924 n.
mopes
melancholy 834 n.
moppet
child 132 n.
darling 890 n.
moraine
leavings 41 n.
thing transferred 272 n.
soil 344 n.
moral
judgment 480 n.
maxim 496 n.
commentary 520 n.
phrase 563 n.
good 615 adj.
advising 691 adj.
precept 693 n.
reputable 866 adj.
ethical 917 adj.
virtuous 933 adj.
pure 950 adj.
moral certainty
positiveness 473 n.
morale
state 7 n.
obedience 739 n.
manliness 855 n.
morale-boosting
aiding 703 adj.
moral fibre
resolution 599 n.
probity 929 n.
moral insensibility
indiscrimination 464 n.
moral insensibility 820 n.
moralistic
judicial 480 adj.
ethical 917 adj.
morality
right 913 n.
morals 917 n.
virtue 933 n.
purity 950 n.
morality play
stage play 594 n.
moralize, moralise
judge 480 vb.
teach 534 vb.
moralizing, moralising
educational 534 adj.
advising 691 adj.
preceptive 693 adj.
moral philosophy
morals 917 n.
Moral Re-Armament
reformism 654 n.
sect 978 n.
morals
conduct 688 n.
right 913 n.
morals 917 n.
virtue 933 n.
purity 950 n.
moral sensibility
discrimination 463 n.
moral sensibility 819 n.
moral support
aid 703 n.
moral training
education 534 n.
moral turpitude
improbity 930 n.
wickedness 934 n.
morass
marsh 347 n.
moratorium
delay 136 n.
lull 145 n.
nonpayment 805 n.
Moravians
sect 978 n.
morbid
abnormal 84 adj.
diseased 651 adj.
morbidity
badness 645 n.
ill health 651 n.
morbific
infectious 653 adj.
mordacious
maleficent 898 adj.
mordant
keen 174 adj.
pungent 388 adj.
pigment 425 n.
forceful 571 adj.
disapproving 924 adj.
mordent
musical note 410 n.
more
beyond 34 adv.
in addition 38 adv.
plural 101 adj.
more and more
crescendo 36 adv.
more bark than bite
scurrility 899 n.
more dead than alive
fatigued 684 adj.
more easily said than done
difficult 700 adj.
more in sorrow than in anger
forgiving 909 adj.
moreish
savoury 390 adj.
more kicks than ha'pence
rejection 607 n.
ingratitude 908 n.
more often than not
often 139 adv.
more or less
quantitative 26 adj.
about 33 adv.
nearly 200 adv.
moreover
in addition 38 adv.
mores
practice 610 n.
more sinned against than sinning
guiltless 935 adj.
more so
superior 34 adj.
crescendo 36 adv.
Moresque
ornamental 844 adj.
more than enough
plenty 635 n.
redundance 637 n.
more than ever
greatly 32 adv.
more than flesh and blood can stand
intolerable 827 adj.
more than meets the eye
latency 523 n.
more than one
plural 101 adj.
morganatic
matrimonial 894 adj.
morgue
death 361 n.
interment 364 n.
inactivity 679 n.
moribund
sick 651 adj.
dying 361 adj.
Mormon
sectarian 978 n.
morn
morning 128 n.
morning
beginning 68 n.
period 110 n.n.
morning 128 n.
earliness 135 n.
morning after
sequel 67 n.
crapulence 949 n.
morning dress
formal dress 228 n.
morning star
planet 321 n.
luminary 420 n.
morocco
skin 226 n.
bookbinding 589 n.
moron
fool 501 n.
madman 504 n.

moronic
mindless 448 adj.
unintelligent 499 adj.
insane 503 adj.
morose
melancholic 834 adj.
sullen 893 adj.
moroseness
unsociability 883 n.
misanthropy 902 n.
morpheme
word 559 n.
part of speech 564 n.
Morpheus
sleep 679 n.
lesser deity 967 n.
morphine, morphia
anaesthetic 375 n.
drug 658 n.
soporific 679 n.
drug-taking 949 n.
morphological
territorial 344 adj.
linguistic 557 adj.
morphology
form 243 n.
biology 358 n.
zoology 367 n.
linguistics 557 n.
etymology 559 n.
morris dance
dance 837 n.
morris dancer
jumper 312 n.
morrow
futurity 124 n.
morse
fastening 47 n.
telecommunication 531 n.
signal 547 n.
morsel
small quantity 33 n.
piece 53 n.
mouthful 301 n.
mortal
ephemeral 114 adj.
destructive 165 adj.
deadly 362 adj.
person 371 n.
human 371 adj.
tedious 838 adj.
guilty 936 adj.
mortal illness
decease 361 n.
mortality
transience 114 n.
death 361 n.
death roll 361 n.
humankind 371 n.
mortally
extremely 32 adv.
painfully 32 adv.
mortally ill
sick 651 adj.
mortal remains
corpse 363 n.
mortar
adhesive 47 n.
gun 723 n.
mortarboard
plate 194 n.
headgear 228 n.
mortgage
encumbrance 702 n.
security 767 n.
lending 784 n.
borrowing 785 n.
debt 803 n.
mortician
interment 364 n.
mortification
decay 51 n.
sorrow 825 n.
annoyance 827 n.
discontent 829 n.
regret 830 n.
humiliation 872 n.
envy 912 n.
asceticism 945 n.
mortify
hurt 827 vb.
cause discontent 829 vb.
humiliate 872 vb.
mortise, mortice
join 45 vb.
introduce 231 vb.
cavity 255 n.
mortise lock
fastening 47 n.
mortmain
dower 777 n.
Morton's fork
dubiety 474 n.
mortuary
death 361 n.
interment 364 n.
mosaic
nonuniformity 17 n.
medley 43 n.
combination 50 n.
multiform 82 adj.
chequer 437 n.
picture 553 n.
ornamental art 844 n.
Mosaic
scriptural 975 adj.
Moselle
wine 301 n.
mosey along
wander 267 vb.
Moslem
religionist 973 n.
religious 973 adj.
mosque
temple 990 n.
mosquito
insect 365 n.
bane 659 n.
mosquito net
canopy 226 n.
moss
marsh 347 n.
plant 366 n.
greenness 434 n.
moss-grown
antiquated 127 adj.
dilapidated 655 adj.
moss-trooper
soldier 722 n.
robber 789 n.
mossy
downy 259 adj.
soft 327 adj.
vegetal 366 adj.
most
great 32 adj.
most, the
eminently 34 adv.
most favoured nation treatment
aid 703 n.
Most Reverend
title 870 n.
church title 986 n.
mot
maxim 496 n.
witticism 839 n.
mote
small thing 33 n.
dirt 649 n.
mote in the eye
prejudice 481 n.
motel
inn 192 n.
motet
hymn 981 n.
moth
destroyer 168 n.
insect 365 n.
blight 659 n.
moth and rust
dilapidation 655 n.
mothball
scent 396 n.
preserver 666 n.
mothballed
disused 674 adj.
moth-eaten
antiquated 127 adj.
dilapidated 655 adj.
mother
kinsman 11 n.
maternity 169 n.
woman 373 n.
safeguard 660 vb.
minister to 703 vb.
pet 889 vb.
philanthropize 897 vb.
church title 986 n.
nun 986 n.
Mother Carey's chickens
bird 365 n.
warning 664 n.
mother country
maternity 169 n.
mother earth
abundance 171 n.
world 321 n.
mythic deity 966 n.
mother figure
substitute 150 n.
motherhood
family 11 n.
maternity 169 n.
parentage 169 n.
life 360 n.
mother-in-law
maternity 169 n.
motherland
territory 184 n.
home 192 n.
motherly
parental 169 adj.
loving 887 adj.
benevolent 897 adj.
mother naked
uncovered 229 adj.
Mother of God
Madonna 968 n.
mother-of-pearl
variegation 437 n.
iridescent 437 adj.
gem 844 n.
mother's darling
weakling 163 n.
favourite 890 n.
Mother Superior
ecclesiarch 986 n.
nun 986 n.
mother-to-be
maternity 169 n.
mother tongue
intelligibility 516 n.
language 557 n.
mother wit
intelligence 498 n.
motif, motive
musical piece 412 n.
topic 452 n.
pattern 844 n.
motility
motion 265 n.
motion
displacement 188 n.
motion 265 n.
progression 285 n.
defecation 302 n.
topic 452 n.
gesture 547 n.
gesticulate 547 vb.
plan 623 n.
activity 678 n.
advice 691 n.
offer 759 n.
request 761 n.
motionless
still 266 adj.
nonactive 677 adj.
inactive 679 adj.
motion pictures
film 445 n.
motivate
cause 156 vb.
influence 178 vb.
motivate 612 vb.
cause desire 859 vb.
motive
reason why 156 n.

influence 178 n.
moving 265 adj.
motive 612 n.
activity 678 n.
motiveless
capricious 604 adj.
choiceless 606 adj.
designless 618 adj.
motive power
energy 160 n.
motion 265 n.
mot juste
accuracy 494 n.
motley
nonuniformity 17 n.
mixed 43 adj.
multiform 82 adj.
clothing 228 n.
variegated 437 adj.
motocross
racing 716 n.
motor
sources of energy 160 n.
moving 265 adj.
ride 267 vb.
automobile 274 n.
machine 630 n.
motorail
train 274 n.
motorbike
bicycle 274 n.
motorboat
boat 275 n.
motorcar
automobile 274 n.
motorcycle
bicycle 274 n.
motoring
land travel 267 n.
motorist
driver 268 n.
motorized
vehicular 274 adj.
mechanical 630 adj.
motorman
driver 268 n.
motor rally
racing 716 n.
motor scooter
bicycle 274 n.
motorway
road 624 n.
mottled
mottled 437 adj.
marked 547 adj.
motto
maxim 496 n.
commentary 520 n.
heraldry 547 n.
indication 547 n.
phrase 563 n.
moue
distortion 246 n.
gesture 547 n.
affectation 850 n.
mouflon
sheep 365 n.
moujik, muzhik
farmer 370 n.
possessor 776 n.
mould
modality 7 n.
uniformity 16 n.
mould 23 n.
decay 51 n.
sort 77 n.
convert 147 vb.
form 243 n.vb.
structure 331 n.
soil 344 n.
plant 366 n.
educate 534 vb.
represent 551 vb.
sculpt 554 vb.
dirt 649 n.
blight 659 n.
use 673 vb.
decorate 844 vb.
— oneself on
do likewise 20 vb.
conform 83 vb.
mouldable
flexible 327 adj.
moulder
decompose 51 vb.
be old 127 vb.
sculptor 556 n.
be unclean 649 vb.
deteriorate 655 vb.
moulding
ornamental art 844 n.
mouldy
dirty 649 adj.
moulting
uncovering 229 n.
mound
bulk 195 n.
small hill 209 n.
dome 253 n.
defences 713 n.
mount
be great 32 vb.
grow 36 vb.
unite with 45 vb.
be high 209 vb.
support 218 vb.
enclose 235 vb.
conveyance 267 n.
ride 267 vb.
saddle horse 273 n.
start out 296 vb.
insert 303 vb.
ascend 308 vb.
climb 308 vb.
elevate 310 vb.
break in 369 vb.
art equipment 553 n.
dramatize 594 vb.
be dear 811 vb.
— guard
invigilate 457 vb.
safeguard 660 vb.
— one's high horse
be proud 871 vb.
— the throne
take authority 733 vb.
mountain
great quantity 32 n.
bulk 195 n.
high land 209 n.
mountaineer
traveller 268 n.
climber 308 n.
mountaineering
ascent 308 n.
sport 837 n.
mountainous
huge 195 adj.
large 195 adj.
alpine 209 adj.
mountebank
impostor 545 n.
mounted troops
cavalry 722 n.
Mounties
rider 268 n.
mourn
inter 364 vb.
lament 836 vb.
mourner
funeral 364 n.
weeper 836 n.
mournful
distressing 827 adj.
melancholic 834 adj.
lamenting 836 adj.
mourning
formal dress 228 n.
obsequies 364 n.
black thing 428 n.
lamentation 836 n.
mouse
small animal 33 n.
mammal 365 n.
hunt 619 vb.
submission 721 n.
coward 856 n.
humility 872 n.
mouser
cat 365 n.
hunter 619 n.
mousse
dessert 301 n.
bubble 355 n.
mousseline
textile 222 n.
mousseux
bubbly 355 adj.
moustache
hair 259 n.
mousy
colourless 426 adj.
grey 429 adj.
graceless 842 adj.
mouth
entrance 68 n.
maw 194 n.
threshold 234 n.
orifice 263 n.
way in 297 n.
eater 301 n.
chew 301 vb.
gulf 345 n.
voice 577 vb.
orate 579 vb.
sauciness 878 n.
mouthful
small quantity 33 n.
mouthful 301 n.
word 559 n.
oration 579 n.
mouthorgan
organ 414 n.
mouthpiece
orifice 263 n.
air pipe 353 n.
flute 414 n.
interpreter 520 n.
informant 524 n.
speaker 579 n.
deputy 755 n.
mouthwash
cleanser 648 n.
prophylactic 658 n.
mouth-watering
tasty 386 adj.
movable, moveable
moving 265 adj.
transferable 272 adj.
movables, moveables
property 777 n.
move
derange 63 vb.
debut 68 n.
operate 173 vb.
displace 188 vb.
be in motion 265 vb.
move 265 vb.
transpose 272 vb.
move fast 277 vb.
propel 287 vb.
attract 291 vb.
be agitated 318 vb.
propound 512 vb.
gesture 547 n.
motivate 612 vb.
attempt 671 n.
action 676 n.
deed 676 n.
be active 678 vb.
tactics 688 n.
advise 691 vb.
stratagem 698 n.
offer 759 vb.
excite 821 vb.
— away
recede 290 vb.
— heaven and earth
persevere 600 vb.
exert oneself 682 vb.
— house
depart 296 vb.
— in
dwell 192 vb.
attack 712 vb.
— one's bowels
excrete 302 vb.
— out
relinquish 621 vb.
— over
go away 190 vb.

— slowly
drag on 113 vb.
walk 267 vb.
move slowly 278 vb.
— up
bring near 200 vb.
promote 285 vb.
— with the times
modernize 126 vb.
change 143 vb.
progress 285 vb.
moved
impressed 818 adj.
impressible 819 adj.
movement
transition 147 n.
motion 265 n.
melody 410 n.
musical piece 412 n.
dramaturgy 594 n.
action 676 n.
activity 678 n.
party 708 n.
mover
producer 164 n.
influence 178 n.
motivator 612 n.
doer 676 n.
adviser 691 n.
movies
film 445 n.
photography 551 n.
moving
influential 178 adj.
moving 265 adj.
descriptive 590 adj.
exciting 821 adj.
distressing 827 adj.
moving staircase
conveyor 274 n.
mow
cut 46 vb.
shorten 204 vb.
smooth 258 vb.
cultivate 370 vb.
store 632 vb.
— down
demolish 165 vb.
slaughter 362 vb.
mowing grass
grass 366 n.
MP
councillor 692 n.
Mr
male 372 n.
Mr and Mrs
spouse 894 n.
Mr Big
bigwig 638 n.
Mr/Miss Clever
vain person 873 n.
Mr/Miss Right
favourite 890 n.
Mrs
lady 373 n.
Mrs Grundy
bore 838 n.
etiquette 848 n.
prude 950 n.
Mr Universe
a beauty 841 n.
Mr/Miss X.
unknown thing 491 n.
Ms
lady 373 n.
book 589 n.
title 870 n.
MSc
academic title 870 n.
much
great quantity 32 n.
greatly 32 adv.
many 104 adj.
much ado
activity 678 n.
much ado about nothing
overestimation 482 n.
exaggeration 546 n.
much obliged
grateful 907 adj.
much of a muchness
similar 18 adj.
imperfect 647 adj.
middling 732 adj.
much the same
similar 18 adj.
equivalent 28 adj.
mucilage
semiliquidity 354 n.
muck
excrement 302 n.
rubbish 641 n.
dirt 649 n.
muck about
be absurd 497 vb.
— up
jumble 63 vb.
make unclean 649 vb.
impair 655 vb.
muckraker
news reporter 529 n.
defamer 926 n.
muckworm
niggard 816 n.
mucky
dirty 649 adj.
mucus
excrement 302 n.
fluid 335 n.
semiliquidity 354 n.
dirt 649 n.
mud
marsh 347 n.
semiliquidity 354 n.
dirt 649 n.
mud-coloured
brown 430 adj.
muddle
confusion 61 n.
disorder 61 n.
derange 63 vb.
jumble 63 vb.
distract 456 vb.
not discriminate 464 vb.
predicament 700 n.
failure 728 n.
muddled
poorly reasoned 477 adj.
unclear 568 adj.
tipsy 949 adj.
muddle-headed
poorly reasoned 477 adj.
unintelligent 499 adj.
muddy
agitate 318 vb.
humid 341 adj.
marshy 347 adj.
semiliquid 354 adj.
dim 419 adj.
bedim 419 vb.
opaque 423 adj.
dirty 649 adj.
make unclean 649 vb.
mud flat
lake 346 n.
marsh 347 n.
mudguard
shelter 662 n.
mudlark
dirty person 649 n.
low fellow 869 n.
mud pack
beautification 843 n.
mud-slinging
detraction 926 n.
muesli
cereals 301 n.
muezzin's cry
call 547 n.
prayers 981 n.
muff
glove 228 n.
warm clothes 381 n.
blunder 495 vb.
bungling 695 n.
be clumsy 695 vb.
bungler 697 n.
muffin
cereals 301 n.
muffle
cover 226 vb.
mute 401 vb.
conceal 525 vb.
make mute 578 vb.
muffled
muted 401 adj.
nonresonant 405 adj.
occult 523 adj.
voiceless 578 adj.
muffled drum
obsequies 364 n.
signal 547 n.
muffler
neckwear 228 n.
warm clothes 381 n.
mufti
informal dress 228 n.
theologian 973 n.
priest 986 n.
mug
cup 194 n.
face 237 n.
strike 279 vb.
credulity 487 n.
ninny 501 n.
study 536 vb.
dupe 544 n.
strike at 712 vb.
rob 788 vb.
mugger
violent creature 176 n.
robber 789 n.
mugging
attack 712 n.
stealing 788 n.
muggins
ninny 501 n.
muggy
sealed off 264 adj.
humid 341 adj.
warm 379 adj.
Muhammad, Muhammed
religious teacher 973 n.
Muhammadan, Muhammedan
religionist 973 n.
Muhammadanism, Muhammedanism
religious faith 973 n.
Muharram
holy day 988 n.
mulatto
hybrid 43 n.
mulberry
fruit 301 n.
purple 436 adj.
mulch
fertilizer 171 n.
covering 226 n.
cultivate 370 vb.
mulct
fleece 786 vb.
tax 809 vb.
punish 963 vb.
mule
hybrid 43 n.
footwear 228 n.
obstinate person 602 n.
muleteer
driver 268 n.
mulish
equine 273 adj.
animal 365 adj.
obstinate 602 adj.
mull
projection 254 n.
sweeten 392 vb.
— over
think 449 vb.

mullah
theologian 973 n.
mulled wine
alcoholic drink 301 n.
mullet
fish food 301 n.
mullion
pillar 218 n.
window 263 n.
mullock
rubbish 641 n.
multi-
plural 101 adj.
multicoloured
nonuniform 17 adj.
variegated 437 adj.
multidisciplinary
educational 534 adj.
multifarious
unrelated 10 adj.
different 15 adj.
nonuniform 17 adj.
multiform 82 adj.
many 104 adj.
multifid
fragmentary 53 adj.
multifid 100 adj.
multiform
different 15 adj.
mixed 43 adj.
multiform 82 adj.
changeful 152 adj.
multilateral
lateral 239 adj.
angulated 247 adj.
contractual 765 adj.
multilingual
linguistic 557 adj.
multimedia
published 528 adj.
multimillionaire
rich person 800 n.
multinational company
influence 178 n.
corporation 708 n.
multiparous
prolific 171 adj.
multipartite
disunited 46 adj.
multifid 100 adj.
multiple
quantity 26 n.
numerical element 85 n.
plural 101 adj.
many 104 adj.
multiple personality
psychopathy 503 n.
multiple sclerosis
nervous disorders 651 n.
multiple store
shop 796 n.
multiple unit
train 274 n.
multiplex
multiform 82 adj.
multiplication
increase 36 n.
numerical operation 86 n.
reproduction 166 n.
propagation 167 n.
productiveness 171 n.
multiplication table
counting instrument 86 n.
multiplicity
multiformity 82 n.
plurality 101 n.
multitude 104 n.
multiply
augment 36 vb.
grow 36 vb.
do sums 86 vb.
be many 104 vb.
repeat 106 vb.
reproduce 166 vb.
reproduce itself 167 vb.
multiprogramming
data processing 86 n.
multipurpose
general 79 adj.
useful 640 adj.
multiracial
mixed 43 adj.
multirole
plural 101 adj.
multisect
multisect 100 vb.
multistorey
architectural 192 adj.
multitude
great quantity 32 n.
crowd 74 n.
plurality 101 n.
multitude 104 n.
multitude, the
commonalty 869 n.
multitudinous
frequent 139 adj.
multum in parvo
compendium 592 n.
mum
maternity 169 n.
voiceless 578 adj.
taciturn 582 adj.
mumble
chew 301 vb.
stammer 580 vb.
mumbo jumbo
lack of meaning 515 n.
idolatry 982 n.
spell 983 n.
mummer
actor 594 n.
mummery
sham 542 n.
ostentation 875 n.
false piety 980 n.
mummify
dry 342 vb.
inter 364 vb.
preserve 666 vb.
mummy
maternity 169 n.
corpse 363 n.
mummy's boy
weakling 163 n.
mumps
infection 651 n.
munch
chew 301 vb.
mundane
tedious 838 adj.
irreligious 974 adj.
mungo
fibre 208 n.
municipal
regional 184 adj.
municipal council
council 692 n.
municipality
district 184 n.
jurisdiction 955 n.
munificent
liberal 813 adj.
muniment(s)
record 548 n.
title deeds 767 n.
munitions
means 629 n.
arms 723 n.
mural
picture 553 n.
murder
homicide 362 n.
murder 362 vb.
oppress 735 vb.
cruel act 898 n.
execute 963 vb.
— the Queen's English
be ungrammatical 565 vb.
murderer
destroyer 168 n.
violent creature 176 n.
murderer 362 n.
offender 904 n.
murderous
murderous 362 adj.
murk
darkness 418 n.
dimness 419 n.
murky
dense 324 adj.
dark 418 adj.
opaque 423 adj.
latent 523 adj.
cheerless 834 adj.
murmur
flow 350 vb.
faintness 401 n.
sound faint 401 vb.
imply 523 vb.
danger signal 665 n.
deprecate 762 vb.
be discontented 829 vb.
murmurer
malcontent 829 n.
Murphy's Law
axiom 496 n.
murrain
animal disease 651 n.
murrey
purple 436 adj.
heraldry 547 n.
muscle
ligature 47 n.
power 160 n.
vitality 162 n.
exertion 682 n.
muscle-bound
unwieldy 195 adj.
rigid 326 adj.
muscle in
intrude 297 vb.
muscle man
athlete 162 n.
bulk 195 n.
a beauty 841 n.
muscular
stalwart 162 adj.
muscular dystrophy
nervous disorders 651 n.
muse
meditate 449 vb.
be inattentive 456 vb.
motivator 612 n.
Muses, the
musician 413 n.
literature 557 n.
poetry 593 n.
lesser deity 967 n.
musette
flute 414 n.
museum
antiquity 125 n.
collection 632 n.
museum piece
archaism 127 n.
exhibit 522 n.
exceller 644 n.
laughingstock 851 n.
mush
face 237 n.
pulpiness 356 n.
mushroom
grow 36 vb.
new 126 adj.
be fruitful 171 vb.
expand 197 vb.
dome 253 n.
vegetable 301 n.
plant 366 n.
whitish 427 adj.
brown 430 adj.
mushroom cloud
high structure 209 n.
radiation 417 n.
poison 659 n.
bomb 723 n.
mushy
soft 327 adj.

semiliquid 354 adj.
pulpy 356 adj.
music
melody 410 n.
music 412 n.
pleasurableness 826 n.
musical
melodious 410 adj.
musical 412 adj.
musicianly 413 adj.
film 445 n.
stage play 594 n.
pleasurable 826 adj.
musical appreciation
musical skill 413 n.
musical box
gramophone 414 n.
musical chairs
indoor game 837 n.
musical comedy
vocal music 412 n.
stage play 594 n.
musical glasses
gong 414 n.
musical instrument
musical instrument 414 n.
musical note
musical note 410 n.
musical piece
composition 56 n.
musical piece 412 n.
musical quality
melody 410 n.
musical saw
viol 414 n.
musical skill
music 412 n.
musical skill 413 n.
music centre
gramophone 414 n.
music critic
musician 413 n.
music hall
stage show 594 n.
theatre 594 n.
place of amusement 837 n.
musician
musician 413 n.
interpreter 520 n.
proficient person 696 n.
musicianship
music 412 n.
musical skill 413 n.
music lover
musician 413 n.
music-making
music 412 n.
music of the spheres
order 60 n.
heavens 321 n.
musique concrète
music 412 n.
musk
scent 396 n.
musket
firearm 723 n.
musketeer
shooter 287 n.
soldiery 722 n.
Muslim
religionist 973 n.
religious 973 adj.
muslin
textile 222 n.
semitransparency 424 n.
mussel
fish food 301 n.
marine life 365 n.
must
desiring 859 adj.
must, a
necessity 596 n.
requirement 627 n.
mustang
saddle horse 273 n.
mustard
condiment 389 n.
yellowness 433 n.
mustard and cress
vegetable 301 n.
mustard gas
poison 659 n.
weapon 723 n.
mustard seed
minuteness 196 n.
muster
assemblage 74 n.
bring together 74 vb.
number 86 vb.
— courage
take courage 855 vb.
muster roll
list 87 n.
must have
require 627 vb.
desire 859 vb.
musty
fetid 397 adj.
dirty 649 adj.
mutable
transient 114 adj.
changeable 143 adj.
changeful 152 adj.
mutation
abnormality 84 n.
change 143 n.
conversion 147 n.
mutatis mutandis
mutatis mutandis 143 adv.
in exchange 151 adv.
mute
speech sound 398 n.
silent 399 adj.
silencer 401 n.
mute 401 vb.
mute 414 n.
voiceless 578 adj.
taciturn 582 adj.
weeper 836 n.
muted
weak 163 adj.
muted 401 adj.
nonresonant 405 adj.
melodious 410 adj.
soft-hued 425 adj.
mutilate
deform 244 vb.
impair 655 vb.
make ugly 842 vb.
torture 963 vb.
mutilated
incomplete 55 adj.
imperfect 647 adj.
mutineer
revolter 738 n.
mutinous
quarrelling 709 adj.
defiant 711 adj.
resisting 715 adj.
disobedient 738 adj.
riotous 738 adj.
undutiful 918 adj.
mutiny
strike 145 n.
resist 715 vb.
revolt 738 n.vb.
fail in duty 918 vb.
mutt
dog 365 n.
dunce 501 n.
mutter
sound faint 401 vb.
roll 403 n.
stammer 580 vb.
be discontented 829 vb.
be sullen 893 vb.
threaten 900 vb.
mutton
meat 301 n.
muttonchops
hair 259 n.
mutton dressed up as lamb
misfit 25 n.
muttonhead
dunce 501 n.
mutual
correlative 12 adj.
interchanged 151 adj.
mutual affection
love 887 n.
mutual agreement
promise 764 n.
compact 765 n.
mutual assistance
cooperation 706 n.
mutual hostility
dissension 709 n.
mutualist
participator 775 n.
mutual support
friendship 880 n.
mutual understanding
agreement 24 n.
concord 710 n.
muzak
music 412 n.
muzzle
protuberance 254 n.
orifice 263 n.
stopper 264 n.
silence 399 vb.
make mute 578 vb.
hinder 702 vb.
firearm 723 n.
restrain 747 vb.
fetter 748 n.
muzzy
tipsy 949 adj.
M-way
road 624 n.
mycology
botany 368 n.
my country right or wrong
prejudice 481 n.
patriotism 901 n.
my lady
title 870 n.
my lord
title 870 n.
my lud
judge 957 n.
myopic
dim-sighted 440 adj.
misjudging 481 adj.
myriad
over one hundred 99 n.
many 104 adj.
myrmidon
soldier 722 n.
dependant 742 n.
myrrh
resin 357 n.
interment 364 n.
scent 396 n.
myrtle
love emblem 887 n.
myself
self 80 n.
subjectivity 320 n.
mystagogue
teacher 537 n.
leader 690 n.
mysteries
religion 973 n.
act of worship 981 n.
rite 988 n.
mysterious
unusual 84 adj.
invisible 444 adj.
uncertain 474 adj.
unknown 491 adj.
puzzling 517 adj.
occult 523 adj.
concealed 525 adj.
unclear 568 adj.
wonderful 864 adj.
cabbalistic 984 adj.
mystery
unknown thing 491 n.
enigma 530 n.

secret 530 n.
rite 988 n.
mystery play
stage play 594 n.
mystic
inexpressible 517 adj.
occult 523 adj.
religious 973 adj.
revelational 975 adj.
pietist 979 n.
worshipper 981 n.
cabbalistic 984 adj.
mystical
inexpressible 517 adj.
divine 965 adj.
devotional 981 adj.
mysticism
meditation 449 n.
religion 973 n.
occultism 984 n.
mystification
sophistry 477 n.
lack of meaning 515 n.
unintelligibility 517 n.
concealment 525 n.
misteaching 535 n.
mystify
puzzle 474 vb.
sophisticate 477 vb.
not know 491 vb.
deceive 542 vb.
mystique
prestige 866 n.
cult 981 n.
myth
fantasy 513 n.
fable 543 n.
narrative 590 n.
mythical, mythic
insubstantial 4 adj.
erroneous 495 adj.
imaginary 513 adj.
mythological 966 adj.
fairylike 970 adj.
mythical beast
rara avis 84 n.
mythical being
rara avis 84 n.
nymph 967 n.
mythical being 970 n.
mythic deity
mythic deity 966 n.
mythic heaven
the dead 361 n.
mythic heaven 971 n.
mythic hell
the dead 361 n.
mythic hell 972 n.
myth-maker
visionary 513 n.
mythological
mythological 966 adj.
mythologize, mythologise
describe 590 vb.
mythology
tradition 127 n.
anthropology 371 n.
fable 543 n.
narrative 590 n.
mythomania
falsehood 541 n.
myxomatosis
animal disease 651 n.

N

n
many 104 adj.
Naafi
café 192 n.
nab
ensnare 542 vb.
arrest 747 vb.
take 786 vb.
nabob
officer 741 n.
rich person 800 n.
nacelle
airship 276 n.
nacre
variegation 437 n.
nadir
inferiority 35 n.
extremity 69 n.
serial place 73 n.
zero 103 n.
lowness 210 n.
depth 211 n.
base 214 n.
nag
saddle horse 273 n.
incite 612 vb.
bicker 709 vb.
animate 821 vb.
torment 827 vb.
enrage 891 vb.
naiad
nymph 967 n.
mythical being 970 n.
nail
affix 45 vb.
fastening 47 n.
hanger 217 n.
sharp point 256 n.
perforator 263 n.
tool 630 n.
— one's colours to the mast
be resolute 599 vb.
nailbrush
cleaning utensil 648 n.
nail file
smoother 258 n.
cosmetic 843 n.
nail polish
cosmetic 843 n.
nails
hardness 326 n.
weapon 723 n.
nippers 778 n.
nainsook
textile 222 n.
naive, naïve
credulous 487 adj.
ignorant 491 adj.
foolish 499 adj.
artless 699 adj.
innocent 935 adj.
naked
simple 44 adj.
uncovered 229 adj.
visible 443 adj.
undisguised 522 adj.
vulnerable 661 adj.
namby-pamby
weakling 163 n.
weak 163 adj.
name
class 62 vb.
auspicate 68 vb.
specify 80 vb.
inform 524 vb.
indicate 547 vb.
word 559 n.
name 561 n.vb.
commission 751 vb.
repute 866 n.
accuse 928 vb.
— names
specify 80 vb.
divulge 526 vb.
accuse 928 vb.
name and address
identification 547 n.
nameboard
label 547 n.
name day
special day 876 n.
nameless
anonymous 562 adj.
inglorious 867 adj.
namely
namely 80 adv.
by name 561 adv.
name part
acting 594 n.
nameplate
label 547 n.
namer
nomenclator 561 n.
namesake
name 561 n.
name tape
label 547 n.
name to conjure with
prestige 866 n.
nancy
nonconformist 84 n.
nankeen
textile 222 n.
nanny
protector 660 n.
domestic 742 n.
retainer 742 n.
keeper 749 n.
nanosecond
small quantity 33 n.
naos
holy place 990 n.
nap
weaving 222 n.
hair 259 n.
texture 331 n.
sleep 679 n.
card game 837 n.
napalm bomb
bomb 723 n.
nape
rear 238 n.
napkin
cleaning cloth 648 n.
napped
hairy 259 adj.
napping
abstracted 456 adj.
sleepy 679 adj.
nappy
loincloth 228 n.
narcissism
vanity 873 n.
selfishness 932 n.
Narcissus
a beauty 841 n.
vain person 873 n.
narcosis
helplessness 161 n.
insensibility 375 n.
narcotic
lenitive 177 adj.
anaesthetic 375 n.
drug 658 n.
drug-taking 949 n.
intoxicating 949 adj.
narcotize, narcotise
render insensible 375 vb.
make inactive 679 vb.
nard
unguent 357 n.
narghile
tobacco 388 n.
nark
informer 524 n.
accuser 928 n.
narrate
remind 505 vb.
communicate 524 vb.
describe 590 vb.
narrative
fable 543 n.
record 548 n.
narrative 590 n.
descriptive 590 adj.
narrator
chronicler 549 n.
speaker 579 n.
narrator 590 n.

actor 594 n.
narrow
small 33 adj.
tighten 45 vb.
contracted 198 adj.
make smaller 198 vb.
narrow 206 adj.
narrow-minded 481 adj.
restraining 747 adj.
— down
simplify 44 vb.
place 187 vb.
— the gap
approach 289 vb.
converge 293 vb.
narrow, be
be narrow 206 vb.
converge 293 vb.
narrowboat
boat 275 n.
narrow gauge
railway 624 n.
narrowly
slightly 33 adv.
narrow-minded
narrow-minded 481 adj.
unwise 499 adj.
prudish 950 adj.
narrow squeak
escape 667 n.
narthex
church exterior 990 n.
nasal
speech sound 398 n.
dialectal 560 adj.
stammering 580 adj.
nasalize, nasalise
stammer 580 vb.
nascent
beginning 68 adj.
nastiness
bad taste 847 n.
discourtesy 885 n.
nasty
unsavoury 391 adj.
fetid 397 adj.
not nice 645 adj.
unclean 649 adj.
insalubrious 653 adj.
dangerous 661 adj.
unpleasant 827 adj.
ugly 842 adj.
hateful 888 adj.
malevolent 898 adj.
unkind 898 adj.
threatening 900 adj.
impure 951 adj.
nasty bit of work
cad 938 n.
nasty shock
lack of expectation 508 n.
natal
first 68 adj.
natality
propagation 167 n.
natatory
swimming 269 adj.
nation
nation 371 n.
national
ethnic 11 adj.
universal 79 adj.
regional 184 adj.
native 191 n.adj.
national 371 adj.
subject 742 n.
National Assembly
parliament 692 n.
national dress
clothing 228 n.
livery 547 n.
national flag
flag 547 n.
talisman 983 n.
National Front
political party 708 n.
national frontier
limit 236 n.
national grid
electronics 160 n.
National Guard
army 722 n.
National Health Service
doctor 658 n.
national holiday
strike 145 n.
National Insurance
tax 809 n.
nationalism
race 11 n.
particularism 80 n.
nation 371 n.
patriotism 901 n.
nationalistic
biased 481 adj.
sectional 708 adj.
patriotic 901 adj.
Nationalists
political party 708 n.
nationality
consanguinity 11 n.
particularism 80 n.
nation 371 n.
nationalization, nationalisation
association 706 n.
nationalize, nationalise
communalize 775 vb.
assign 780 vb.
appropriate 786 vb.
national park
pleasance 192 n.
plain 348 n.
pleasure ground 837 n.
national service
war measures 718 n.
National Socialism
government 733 n.
nationhood
independence 744 n.
nation state
nation 371 n.
political organization 733 n.
nationwide
universal 79 adj.
native
genetic 5 adj.
intrinsic 5 adj.
component 58 adj.
special 80 adj.
native 191 n.adj.
artless 699 adj.
native land
home 192 n.
native state
undevelopment 670 n.
native tongue
language 557 n.
nativity
origin 68 n.
propagation 167 n.
life 360 n.
Nativity
art subject 553 n.
holy day 988 n.
natter
chat 584 n.
converse 584 vb.
natterjack
amphibian 365 n.
natty
clean 648 adj.
personable 841 adj.
natural
real 1 adj.
substantial 3 adj.
intrinsic 5 adj.
lifelike 18 adj.
agreeing 24 adj.
typical 83 adj.
material 319 adj.
musical note 410 n.
probable 471 adj.
genuine 494 adj.
true 494 adj.
fool 501 n.
madman 504 n.
plain 573 adj.
elegant 575 adj.
spontaneous 609 adj.
usual 610 adj.
artless 699 adj.
friendly 880 adj.
natural bent
aptitude 694 n.
natural child
bastardy 954 n.
natural course
probability 471 n.
natural history
physics 319 n.
biology 358 n.
naturalism
accuracy 494 n.
literature 557 n.
description 590 n.
naturalist
imitator 20 n.
biology 358 n.
naturalistic
representing 551 adj.
literary 557 adj.
descriptive 590 adj.
naturalization, naturalisation
location 187 n.
freedom 744 n.
naturalize, naturalise
make conform 83 vb.
transform 147 vb.
admit 299 vb.
naturalized, naturalised
native 191 adj.
habituated 610 adj.
naturally
consequently 157 adv.
skilfully 694 adv.
865 int.
naturalness
adaptation 24 n.
plainness 573 n.
elegance 575 n.
artlessness 699 n.
natural philosophy
physics 319 n.
science 490 n.
natural resources
means 629 n.
store 632 n.
natural science
physics 319 n.
science 490 n.
natural selection
biology 358 n.
nature
essence 1 n.
character 5 n.
composition 56 n.
sort 77 n.
tendency 179 n.
truth 494 n.
affections 817 n.
Nature
producer 164 n.
matter 319 n.
nature cure
medical art 658 n.
therapy 658 n.
nature god/goddess
mythic deity 966 n.
nature reserve
preservation 666 n.
nature study
biology 358 n.
naturist
stripper 229 n.
sanitarian 652 n.
naturopath
doctor 658 n.
naturopathy
medical art 658 n.

naught
insubstantiality 4 n.
(See **nought** *)*
naughty
difficult 700 adj.
disobedient 738 adj.
wicked 934 adj.
impure 951 adj.
naughty word
scurrility 899 n.
nausea
voidance 300 n.
digestive disorders 651 n.
dislike 861 n.
nauseate
be unpalatable 391 vb.
displease 827 vb.
cause discontent 829 vb.
be tedious 838 vb.
cause dislike 861 vb.
excite hate 888 vb.
nauseated
vomiting 300 adj.
sick 651 adj.
unhappy 825 adj.
bored 838 adj.
disliking 861 adj.
nauseous
unsavoury 391 adj.
not nice 645 adj.
unclean 649 adj.
unpleasant 827 adj.
nautch girl
entertainer 594 n.
nautical
seafaring 269 adj.
seamanlike 270 adj.
marine 275 adj.
nautical almanac
sailing aid 269 n.
guidebook 524 n.
nautical mile
long measure 203 n.
nautical personnel
nautical personnel 270 n.
naval man 722 n.
naval
seafaring 269 adj.
seamanlike 270 adj.
marine 275 adj.
warlike 718 adj.
naval man
naval man 722 n.
naval officer
naval officer 741 n.
nave
middle 70 n.
church interior 990 n.
navel
middle 70 n.
centre 225 n.
navigable
deep 211 adj.
seafaring 269 adj.
navigate
navigate 269 vb.
orientate 281 vb.
direct 689 vb.
navigation
navigation 269 n.
water travel 269 n.
navigational instrument
sailing aid 269 n.
navigator
navigator 270 n.
aeronaut 271 n.
director 690 n.
navvy
worker 686 n.
navy
shipping 275 n.
blue 435 adj.
navy 722 n.
Navy List
directory 87 n.
list 87 n.
nawab
potentate 741 n.
person of rank 868 n.
nay
negation 533 n.
refusal 760 n.
Nazarene
religionist 973 n.
Nazarites
non-Christian sect 978 n.
naze
projection 254 n.
Nazis
political party 708 n.
Nazism
government 733 n.
brute force 735 n.
NB
455 int.
NCO
army officer 741 n.
Neanderthal man
humankind 371 n.
neap
decrease 37 n.
neap tide
lowness 210 n.
current 350 n.
near
akin 11 adj.
similar 18 adj.
future 124 adj.
early 135 adj.
impending 155 adj.
near 200 adj.adv.
approach 289 vb.
parsimonious 816 adj.
nearby
near 200 adj.
accessible 289 adj.
near enough
about 33 adv.
nearly 200 adv.
nearly
almost 33 adv.
on the whole 52 adv.
nearly 200 adv.
nearness
nearness 200 n.
near relative
kinsman 11 n.
near side
laterality 239 n.
sinistrality 242 n.
near-sighted
dim-sighted 440 adj.
near the knuckle
impure 951 adj.
near the surface
shallow 212 adj.
near the truth, be
detect 484 vb.
near thing
draw 28 n.
danger 661 n.
escape 667 n.
neat
unmixed 44 adj.
orderly 60 adj.
strong 162 adj.
careful 457 adj.
concise 569 adj.
plain 573 adj.
elegant 575 adj.
clean 648 adj.
skilful 694 adj.
personable 841 adj.
intoxicating 949 adj.
neaten
arrange 62 vb.
unravel 62 vb.
make better 654 vb.
beautify 841 vb.
neatly
skilfully 694 adv.
nebula
nebula 321 n.
nebular hypothesis
universe 321 n.
nebulous
amorphous 244 adj.
celestial 321 adj.
cloudy 355 adj.
dim 419 adj.
puzzling 517 adj.
necessarily
consequently 157 adv.
necessarily 596 adv.
necessary
necessary 596 adj.
choiceless 606 adj.
required 627 adj.
important 638 adj.
compelling 740 adj.
necessary, a
necessity 596 n.
requirement 627 n.
necessitarian
fatalist 596 n.
necessitate
predestine 155 vb.
make certain 473 vb.
necessitate 596 vb.
require 627 vb.
compel 740 vb.
necessitous
poor 801 adj.
necessitude
necessity 596 n.
necessity
destiny 155 n.
cause 156 n.
certainty 473 n.
necessity 596 n.
no choice 606 n.
predetermination 608 n.
requirement 627 n.
inexpedience 643 n.
compulsion 740 n.
poverty 801 n.
necessity for
needfulness 627 n.
neck
bond 47 n.
contraction 198 n.
narrowness 206 n.
pillar 218 n.
garment 228 n.
conduit 351 n.
bridge 624 n.
sauciness 878 n.
caress 889 vb.
neck and crop
completely 54 adv.
violently 176 adv.
neck and neck
equal 28 adj.
synchronous 123 adj.
near 200 adj.
neckerchief
neckwear 228 n.
necking
endearment 889 n.
necklace
neckwear 228 n.
loop 250 n.
jewellery 844 n.
neckline
neckline 228 n.
neck of the woods
locality 187 n.
neck or nothing
resolutely 599 adv.
rash 857 adj.
neckwear
wrapping 226 n.
neckwear 228 n.
necrology
death roll 361 n.
biography 590 n.
necromancy
divination 511 n.
sorcery 983 n.
necromantic
sorcerous 983 adj.
cabbalistic 984 adj.
necrophilia
abnormality 84 n.

necropolis
cemetery 364 n.
necrosis
decay 51 n.
nectar
draught 301 n.
savouriness 390 n.
sweet thing 392 n.
nectarine
fruit 301 n.
nectary
flower 366 n.
need
be incomplete 55 vb.
shortfall 307 n.
requirement 627 n.
require 627 vb.
scarcity 636 n.
adversity 731 n.
poverty 801 n.
desire 859 n.
needful
required 627 adj.
needful, the
funds 797 n.
needle
prickle 256 n.
sharp point 256 n.
perforator 263 n.
sailing aid 269 n.
gramophone 414 n.
indicator 547 n.
engraving 555 n.
incite 612 vb.
directorship 689 n.
torment 827 vb.
enrage 891 vb.
needlecord
textile 222 n.
needle match
contest 716 n.
needless
superfluous 637 adj.
needless risk
rashness 857 n.
needlewoman
artisan 686 n.
needlework
network 222 n.
needlework 844 n.
needy
poor 801 adj.
ne'er-do-well
idler 679 n.
desperado 857 n.
bad person 938 n.
nefarious
disreputable 867 adj.
heinous 934 adj.
negate
nullify 2 vb.
be contrary 14 vb.
tell against 467 vb.
make impossible 470 vb.
confute 479 vb.
disbelieve 486 vb.
dissent 489 vb.
negate 533 vb.
recant 603 vb.
reject 607 vb.
oppose 704 vb.
abrogate 752 vb.
refuse 760 vb.
not observe 769 vb.
negation
rejoinder 460 n.
counterevidence 467 n.
negation 533 n.
negative
copy 22 n.
numerical 85 adj.
electricity 160 n.
darkness 418 n.
confute 479 vb.
dissent 489 vb.
negative 533 adj.
negate 533 vb.
photography 551 n.
imperfect 647 adj.
unsuccessful 728 adj.
refuse 760 vb.
negativeness
nonexistence 2 n.
negative request
deprecation 762 n.
negative result
failure 728 n.
neglect
disorder 61 n.
lose a chance 138 vb.
be inattentive 456 vb.
negligence 458 n.
neglect 458 vb.
be unwilling 598 vb.
avoid 620 vb.
dilapidation 655 n.
nonpreparation 670 n.
not use 674 vb.
inaction 677 n.
not act 677 vb.
not complete 726 vb.
not observe 769 vb.
rashness 857 n.
fail in duty 918 vb.
disrespect 921 n.
— one's duty
fail in duty 918 vb.
— one's vow
not observe 769 vb.
neglected
neglected 458 adj.
undervalued 483 adj.
unknown 491 adj.
forgotten 506 adj.
unwanted 860 adj.
inglorious 867 adj.
neglectful
negligent 458 adj.
apathetic 820 adj.
negligee
nightwear 228 n.
negligence
inattention 456 n.
negligence 458 n.
inexactness 495 n.
dilapidation 655 n.
nonpreparation 670 n.
inaction 677 n.
noncompletion 726 n.
laxity 734 n.
nonobservance 769 n.
rashness 857 n.
indifference 860 n.
undutifulness 918 n.
guilty act 936 n.
negligent
negligent 458 adj.
forgetful 506 adj.
lazy 679 adj.
hasty 680 adj.
clumsy 695 adj.
apathetic 820 adj.
negligible
inconsiderable 33 adj.
unimportant 639 adj.
negotiable
transferable 272 adj.
possible 469 adj.
advisable 642 adj.
transferred 780 adj.
negotiate
accord 24 vb.
pass 305 vb.
confer 584 vb.
do business 622 vb.
cooperate 706 vb.
mediate 720 vb.
deputize 755 vb.
contract 765 vb.
make terms 766 vb.
assign 780 vb.
bargain 791 vb.
negotiations
conference 584 n.
negotiator
intermediary 231 n.
mediator 720 n.
consignee 754 n.
envoy 754 n.
signatory 765 n.
Negritude
nation 371 n.
civilization 654 n.
Negro, Negress
blackness 428 n.
Negroid
ethnic 11 adj.
negus
alcoholic drink 301 n.
Negus
sovereign 741 n.
neigh
ululate 409 vb.
neighbour
be near 200 vb.
friend 880 n.
neighbourhood
locality 187 n.
near place 200 n.
surroundings 230 n.
neighbourly
aiding 703 adj.
sociable 882 adj.
neither
neither 606 adv.
neither here nor there
irrelevant 10 adj.
neither. . .nor
neither 606 adv.
neither one thing nor the other
nonconformist 84 n.
neutral 625 adj.
neither too much nor too little
averageness 732 n.
nekton
marine life 365 n.
nem. con.
unanimously 488 adv.
Nemesis
retaliation 714 n.
avenger 910 n.
justice 913 n.
punishment 963 n.
neoclassical
architectural 192 adj.
neocolonialism
governance 733 n.
neolith
antiquity 125 n.
neolithic
secular 110 adj.
primal 127 adj.
barbaric 869 adj.
neologian
modernist 126 n.
neological
modern 126 adj.
neological 560 adj.
neologism
neology 560 n.
neologize, neologise
neologize 560 vb.
neology
neology 560 n.
neon light
gas 336 n.
lamp 420 n.
neophyte
changed person 147 n.
beginner 538 n.
pietist 979 n.
neoplasm
cancer 651 n.
Neo-Platonism
philosophy 449 n.

neoteric
modern 126 adj.
nepenthe
oblivion 506 n.
drug 658 n.
nephew
kinsman 11 n.
nephology
cloud 355 n.
nephritis
digestive disorders 651 n.
ne plus ultra
superiority 34 n.
completeness 54 n.
extremity 69 n.
farness 199 n.
summit 213 n.
limit 236 n.
perfection 646 n.
completion 725 n.
fashion 848 n.
nepotism
injustice 914 n.
improbity 930 n.
Neptune
planet 321 n.
sea god 343 n.
Olympian deity 967 n.
nereid
sea nymph 343 n.
nymph 967 n.
nerve
vitality 162 n.
strengthen 162 vb.
courage 855 n.
sauciness 878 n.
— oneself
take courage 855 vb.
nerve centre
focus 76 n.
centre 225 n.
nerve gas
poison 659 n.
weapon 723 n.
nerveless
impotent 161 adj.
weak 163 adj.
feeble 572 adj.
irresolute 601 adj.
unfearing 855 adj.
nerve-racking
distressing 827 adj.
frightening 854 adj.
nerves
psychopathy 503 n.
ill health 651 n.
excitability 822 n.
nervousness 854 n.
nervous
impotent 161 adj.
agitated 318 adj.
distracted 456 adj.
expectant 507 adj.
irresolute 601 adj.
avoiding 620 adj.
lively 819 adj.
excitable 822 adj.
nervous 854 adj.
cowardly 856 adj.
cautious 858 adj.
nervous breakdown
psychopathy 503 n.
nervous disorders 651 n.
nervous system
sense 374 n.
nervous tic
spasm 318 n.
nervy
active 678 adj.
excitable 822 adj.
nervous 854 adj.
nescient
ignorant 491 adj.
ness
projection 254 n.
nest
origin 68 n.
group 74 n.
focus 76 n.
seedbed 156 n.
nest 192 n.
dwell 192 vb.
sit down 311 vb.
refuge 662 n.
nest egg
store 632 n.
preparation 669 n.
wealth 800 n.
nestle
dwell 192 vb.
seek refuge 662 vb.
caress 889 vb.
nestled
located 187 adj.
nestling
young creature 132 n.
Nestor
old man 133 n.
sage 500 n.
adviser 691 n.
net
remaining 41 adj.
bring together 74 vb.
receptacle 194 n.
network 222 n.
textile 222 n.
enclosure 235 n.
semitransparency 424 n.
trap 542 n.
hunt 619 vb.
stratagem 698 n.
acquire 771 vb.
receive 782 vb.
take 786 vb.
netball
ball game 837 n.
nether
low 210 adj.
nethermost
undermost 214 adj.
netherworld
the dead 361 n.
hell 972 n.
net profit
gain 771 n.
receipt 807 n.
netting
network 222 n.
nettle
prickle 256 n.
bane 659 n.
hurt 827 vb.
huff 891 vb.
nettlerash
formication 378 n.
skin disease 651 n.
network
correlation 12 n.
complexity 61 n.
gap 201 n.
network 222 n.
texture 331 n.
broadcasting 531 n.
cooperate 706 vb.
networking
cooperation 706 n.
neuralgia
pang 377 n.
neurasthenia
psychopathy 503 n.
melancholy 834 n.
neuritis
pang 377 n.
neurologist
doctor 658 n.
neurology
medical art 658 n.
neuropath
madman 504 n.
sick person 651 n.
neurosis
psychopathy 503 n.
melancholy 834 n.
neurotic
insane 503 adj.
madman 504 n.
neuter
generic 77 adj.
eunuch 161 n.
impotent 161 adj.
unman 161 vb.
grammatical 564 adj.
neutral
median 30 adj.
inert 175 adj.
moderate 177 adj.
colourless 426 adj.
grey 429 adj.
choiceless 606 adj.
avoiding 620 adj.
neutral 625 adj.
nonactive 677 adj.
pacifist 717 n.
middling 732 adj.
independent 744 adj.
cautious 858 adj.
indifferent 860 adj.
just 913 adj.
neutrality
middle way 625 n.
neutralize, neutralise
nullify 2 vb.
set off 31 vb.
disable 161 vb.
weaken 163 vb.
assuage 177 vb.
counteract 182 vb.
remedy 658 vb.
neutralized
weakened 163 adj.
neutron
minuteness 196 n.
element 319 n.
neutron bomb
bomb 723 n.
neutron star
star 321 n.
never
never 109 adv.
533 int.
denyingly 760 adv.
never again
finally 69 adv.
singly 88 adv.
never-ending
perpetual 115 adj.
prolix 570 adj.
uncompleted 726 adj.
never-failing
successful 727 adj.
never forgive oneself
regret 830 vb.
never go wrong
be successful 727 vb.
never hear the last of
reoccur 106 vb.
never learn
be foolish 499 vb.
never look back
progress 285 vb.
never mind!
860 int.
nevermore
finally 69 adv.
never 109 adv.
neverness
nonexistence 2 n.
neverness 109 n.
never-never, the
borrowing 785 n.
purchase 792 n.
never-resting
industrious 678 adj.
never satisfied
discontented 829 adj.
never say die
persevere 600 vb.
hope 852 vb.
courageous 855 adj.
never set the Thames on fire
be middling 732 vb.
nevertheless
in return 31 adv.
nevertheless 468 adv.
never the same
nonuniform 17 adj.
changeful 152 adj.

new
different 15 adj.
original 21 adj.
intact 52 adj.
first 68 adj.
early 135 adj.
unknown 491 adj.
unhabituated 611 adj.
new arrival
intruder 59 n.
posteriority 120 n.
incomer 297 n.
new birth
life 360 n.
revival 656 n.
sanctity 979 n.
newborn
infantine 132 adj.
newborn babe
innocent 935 n.
new boy/girl
beginner 538 n.
new broom
successor 67 n.
alterer 143 n.
busy person 678 n.
newcomer
intruder 59 n.
successor 67 n.
incomer 297 n.
new deal
apportionment 783 n.
New Dealer
reformer 654 n.
new departure
originality 21 n.
start 68 n.
new edition
variant 15 n.
reproduction 166 n.
edition 589 n.
amendment 654 n.
newelpost
pillar 218 n.
new energy
revival 656 n.
New English Bible
scripture 975 n.
new face
intruder 59 n.
incomer 297 n.
newfangled
unusual 84 adj.
modern 126 adj.
changeable 143 adj.
neological 560 adj.
fashionable 848 adj.
New Jerusalem
heaven 971 n.
new-laid
new 126 adj.
born 360 adj.
new leaf
improvement 654 n.
New Left
political party 708 n.
new look
modernism 126 n.
repair 656 n.
fashion 848 n.
newlywed
married 894 adj.
spouse 894 n.
new man/woman
changed person 147 n.
newness
originality 21 n.
beginning 68 n.
newness 126 n.
new poor
unlucky person 731 n.
poor person 801 n.
news
topic 452 n.
information 524 n.
news 529 n.
broadcast 531 n.
important matter 638 n.
news agency
informant 524 n.
news blackout
prohibition 757 n.
newscast
publication 528 n.
news 529 n.
newscaster
broadcaster 531 n.
news flash
news 529 n.
broadcast 531 n.
newsletter
publicity 528 n.
the press 528 n.
newsmonger
news reporter 529 n.
newspaper
the press 528 n.
reading matter 589 n.
newspaperman, newspaperwoman
news reporter 529 n.
newspeak
equivocalness 518 n.
neology 560 n.
newsprint
script 586 n.
paper 631 n.
newsreader
news reporter 529 n.
broadcaster 531 n.
newsreel
film 445 n.
publicity 528 n.
news 529 n.
news reporter
inquisitive person 453 n.
enquirer 459 n.
informant 524 n.
publicizer 528 n.
news reporter 529 n.
correspondent 588 n.
author 589 n.
newssheet
the press 528 n.
newsvendor
news reporter 529 n.
newsworthy
rumoured 529 adj.
notable 638 adj.
newsy
informative 524 adj.
rumoured 529 adj.
loquacious 581 adj.
conversing 584 adj.
newt
amphibian 365 n.
New Testament
scripture 975 n.
new to
unhabituated 611 adj.
newton
energy 160 n.
Newtonian mechanics
physics 319 n.
new town
district 184 n.
new version
variant 15 n.
new wave
music 412 n.
film 445 n.
New World
region 184 n.
world 321 n.
next
sequential 65 adj.
after 65 adv.
subsequent 120 adj.
contiguously 202 adv.
next door
near place 200 n.
next of kin
kinsman 11 n.
beneficiary 776 n.
next step
progression 285 n.
next to
near 200 adj.
next to nothing
small quantity 33 n.
next world
destiny 155 n.
the dead 361 n.
nexus
bond 47 n.
Niagara
waterfall 350 n.
nib
sharp point 256 n.
stationery 586 n.
nibble
mouthful 301 n.
eat 301 vb.
taste 386 vb.
be duped 544 vb.
caress 889 vb.
— at
abate 37 vb.
nice
pleasant 376 adj.
savoury 390 adj.
careful 457 adj.
discriminating 463 adj.
accurate 494 adj.
not bad 644 adj.
clean 648 adj.
pleasurable 826 adj.
beautiful 841 adj.
tasteful 846 adj.
fastidious 862 adj.
amiable 884 adj.
Nicene Creed
orthodoxy 976 n.
nicety
differentiation 15 n.
carefulness 457 n.
discrimination 463 n.
fastidiousness 862 n.
niche
place 185 n.
compartment 194 n.
shelf 218 n.
angularity 247 n.
cavity 255 n.
hiding-place 527 n.
honours 866 n.
nick
cut 46 vb.
notch 260 n.vb.
indication 547 n.
mark 547 vb.
wound 655 n.vb.
arrest 747 vb.
lockup 748 n.
steal 788 vb.
nickel
coinage 797 n.
nickname
name 561 n.vb.
misnomer 562 n.
nick of time
occasion 137 n.
nicotine
tobacco 388 n.
poison 659 n.
niece
kinsman 11 n.
niff
stink 397 vb.
nifty
speedy 277 adj.
niggard
accumulator 74 n.
niggard 816 n.
niggardly
insufficient 636 adj.
parsimoniously 816 adv.
selfish 932 adj.
nigger in the woodpile
latency 523 n.
troublemaker 663 n.

niggle
cause discontent 829 vb.
dispraise 924 vb.
niggler
detractor 926 n.
niggling
trivial 639 adj.
nigh
future 124 adj.
near 200 adv.
night
darkness 418 n.
night and day
continuously 71 adv.
perpetually 139 adv.
night blindness
blindness 439 n.
dim sight 440 n.
nightcap
valediction 296 n.
draught 301 n.
soporific 679 n.
nightclothes
nightwear 228 n.
night club
place of amusement 837 n.
nightdress
nightwear 228 n.
nightfall
evening 129 n.
darkness 418 n.
nightingale
bird 365 n.
vocalist 413 n.
night life
festivity 837 n.
nightlight
torch 420 n.
nightly
vespertine 129 adj.
seasonal 141 adj.
nightmare
fantasy 513 n.
false alarm 665 n.
suffering 825 n.
intimidation 854 n.
monster 938 n.
demon 970 n.
nightmarish
frightening 854 adj.
spooky 970 adj.
night out
revel 837 n.
night owl
evening 129 n.
night porter
servant 742 n.
night safe
storage 632 n.
night school
curriculum 534 n.
school 539 n.
nightshirt
nightwear 228 n.
night sky
heavens 321 n.
night soil
excrement 302 n.
dirt 649 n.
nighttime
evening 129 n.
nightwatch
period 110 n.
midnight 129 n.
armed force 722 n.
night watchman
protector 660 n.
keeper 749 n.
nigrescent
blackish 428 adj.
nihilism
extinction 2 n.
disorder 61 n.
philosophy 449 n.
anarchy 734 n.
sedition 738 n.
antichristianity 974 n.
nihilist
anarchist 61 n.
destroyer 168 n.
revolter 738 n.
nihilistic
violent 176 adj.
anarchic 734 adj.
irreligious 974 adj.
nihil obstat
permit 756 n.
nil
nonexistence 2 n.
zero 103 n.
nil admirari
be insensitive 820 vb.
lack of wonder 865 n.
detraction 926 n.
nil desperandum!
852 int.
nimble
speedy 277 adj.
active 678 adj.
skilful 694 adj.
nimble-witted
intelligent 498 adj.
witty 839 adj.
nimbus
cloud 355 n.
light 417 n.
honours 866 n.
niminy-piminy
affected 850 adj.
Nimrod
hunter 619 n.
nincompoop
ninny 501 n.
nine
over five 99 n.
nine days' wonder
insubstantial thing 4 n.
brief span 114 n.
prodigy 864 n.
ninepins
ball game 837 n.
nine points of the law
possession 773 n.
nineteenth hole
refreshment 685 n.
nineteen to the dozen
swiftly 277 adv.
ninety
twenty and over 99 n.
ninety-nine per cent
chief part 52 n.
ninny
ninny 501 n.
ninth
fifth and over 99 adj.
musical note 410 n.
Niobe
weeper 836 n.
nip
make smaller 198 vb.
shorten 204 vb.
make thin 206 vb.
move fast 277 vb.
draught 301 n.
pang 377 n.
give pain 377 vb.
blight 659 n.
— in the bud
be early 135 vb.
suppress 165 vb.
hinder 702 vb.
nip in the air
wintriness 380 n.
nipper
youngster 132 n.
nippers
extractor 304 n.
finger 378 n.
tool 630 n.
nippers 778 n.
nipple
bosom 253 n.
nippy
vigorous 174 adj.
cold 380 adj.
active 678 adj.
nirvana
extinction 2 n.
happiness 824 n.
divineness 965 n.
heaven 971 n.
nisi prius
legal process 959 n.
Nissen hut
small house 192 n.
nit
insect 365 n.
dirt 649 n.
nit-picker
malcontent 829 n.
detractor 926 n.
nit-picking
trivial 639 adj.
fastidiousness 862 n.
nitrates
fertilizer 171 n.
nitrogen
air 340 n.
nitroglycerine
explosive 723 n.
nitrous oxide
anaesthetic 375 n.
nitwit
dunce 501 n.
nix
zero 103 n.
mythical being 970 n.
no
no 489 adv.
nay 533 adv.
refusal 760 n.
No, Noh
stage play 594 n.
no-account
unimportant 639 adj.
no admission
exclusion 57 n.
Noah's Ark
ship 275 n.
zoo 369 n.
no alternative
necessity 596 n.
no choice 606 n.
no appeal
severity 735 n.
no appetite
indifference 860 n.
fasting 946 n.
nob
head 213 n.
fop 848 n.
aristocrat 868 n.
no ball
failure 728 n.
nobble
disable 161 vb.
take 786 vb.
steal 788 vb.
nobbly
projecting 254 adj.
no bed of roses
adversity 731 n.
suffering 825 n.
Nobel Prize
reward 962 n.
no better
equivalent 28 adj.
deteriorated 655 adj.
no bigger than
little 196 adj.
nobility
greatness 32 n.
superiority 34 n.
beau monde 848 n.
aristocracy 868 n.
nobility 868 n.
probity 929 n.
disinterestedness 931 n.
noble
great 32 adj.
important 638 adj.
coinage 797 n.

impressive 821 adj.
splendid 841 adj.
well-bred 848 adj.
renowned 866 adj.
worshipful 866 adj.
person of rank 868 n.
noble 868 adj.
title 870 n.
proud 871 adj.
honourable 929 adj.
disinterested 931 adj.
noble descent
nobility 868 n.
nobleman, noblewoman
person of rank 868 n.
noble savage
ingenue 699 n.
noblesse
aristocracy 868 n.
nobody
nonexistence 2 n.
insubstantiality 4 n.
zero 103 n.
nobody 190 n.
nonentity 639 n.
commoner 869 n.
nobody's business
unrelatedness 10 n.
nobody's fool
unbeliever 486 n.
sage 500 n.
no business of
unrelatedness 10 n.
no case to answer
certainty 473 n.
acquittal 960 n.
no chance
impossibility 470 n.
no change
identity 13 n.
permanence 144 n.
no charge
no charge 812 n.
no chicken
ageing 131 adj.
no choice
necessity 596 n.
no choice 606 n.
no competition
facility 701 n.
no concern of
unrelatedness 10 n.
no connection
unrelatedness 10 n.
disunion 46 n.
noctiluca
glimmer 419 n.
glow-worm 420 n.
nocturnal
vespertine 129 adj.
dark 418 adj.
black 428 adj.
nocturnal mammal
mammal 365 n.
nocturne
musical piece 412 n.
art subject 553 n.
nod
hang 217 vb.
obeisance 311 n.
oscillate 317 vb.
be inattentive 456 vb.
be neglectful 458 vb.
assent 488 n.vb.
hint 524 n.
gesture 547 n.
gesticulate 547 vb.
sleep 679 vb.
be fatigued 684 vb.
command 737 n.
permit 756 vb.
consent 758 vb.
greet 884 vb.
respects 920 n.
approve 923 vb.
noddle
head 213 n.
noddy
ninny 501 n.
node
joint 45 n.
swelling 253 n.
uranometry 321 n.
foliage 366 n.
no desire for
indifference 860 n.
no distance
short distance 200 n.
no doubt
certainly 473 adv.
nodule
swelling 253 n.
no earthly use
profitless 641 adj.
Noel
holy day 988 n.
no end (of)
extremely 32 adv.
many 104 adj.
infinite 107 adj.
no entry
exclusion 57 n.
no escape
necessity 596 n.
noes, the
dissentient 489 n.
noetic
mental 447 adj.
no exception
inclusion 78 n.
no expert
ignorance 491 n.
no feelings
moral insensibility 820 n.
no fixed address
wandering 267 n.
no flies on
unbelieving 486 adj.
cunning 698 adj.
no friend
enemy 881 n.
disapprover 924 n.
noggin
cup 194 n.
head 213 n.
draught 301 n.
nogging
structure 331 n.
no go
impossibility 470 n.
useless 641 adj.
failure 728 n.
no-go area
battleground 724 n.
restriction 747 n.
no good
profitless 641 adj.
bad 645 adj.
no great shakes
inconsiderable 33 adj.
trifle 639 n.
imperfect 647 adj.
no guarantee
unreliability 474 n.
no harm done
undamaged 646 adj.
no head for
unintelligence 499 n.
no heart
moral insensibility 820 n.
pitilessness 906 n.
no help for it
necessarily 596 adv.
no holds barred
wrestling 716 n.
war 718 n.
unconditional 744 adj.
no hope
lack of expectation 508 n.
hopelessness 853 n.
nohow
impossibly 470 adv.
no hurry
slowness 278 n.
leisure 681 n.
no ifs or buts
certainly 473 adv.
no illusion
authenticity 494 n.
no imitation
no imitation 21 n.
authenticity 494 n.
no interest
incuriosity 454 n.
noise
sound 398 n.
loudness 400 n.
discord 411 n.
proclaim 528 vb.
rumour 529 n.
indication 547 n.
noise abatement
faintness 401 n.
noiseless
silent 399 adj.
noises off
mimicry 20 n.
representation 551 n.
noisome
fetid 397 adj.
bad 645 adj.
unclean 649 adj.
baneful 659 adj.
noisy
loud 400 adj.
no joke
reality 1 n.
important matter 638 n.
no kidding
veracity 540 n.
no laughing matter
important matter 638 n.
seriousness 834 n.
nolens volens
necessarily 596 adv.
by force 740 adv.
no life
extinction 2 n.
death 361 n.
moral insensibility 820 n.
nolle prosequi
abrogation 752 n.
no love lost
dissension 709 n.
enmity 881 n.
hatred 888 n.
no luck
failure 728 n.
misfortune 731 n.
nomad
extraneous 59 adj.
nonconformist 84 n.
wanderer 268 n.
nomadic
travelling 267 adj.
no manners
ill-breeding 847 n.
discourtesy 885 n.
no-man's-land
territory 184 n.
emptiness 190 n.
intermediary 231 n.
battleground 724 n.
nonownership 774 n.
no matter
trifle 639 n.
nom de plume
misnomer 562 n.
no meaning
lack of meaning 515 n.
nomenclature
arrangement 62 n.
identification 547 n.
nomenclature 561 n.
nominal
insubstantial 4 adj.
powerless 161 adj.
indicating 547 adj.
verbal 559 adj.
named 561 adj.
trivial 639 adj.

nominalism
philosophy 449 n.
nominate
select 605 vb.
commission 751 vb.
nominee
consignee 754 n.
delegate 754 n.
no morals
wickedness 934 n.
unchastity 951 n.
no more
extinct 2 adj.
past 125 adj.
dead 361 adj.
nomothetic
directing 689 adj.
legal 953 adj.
nonacceptance
rejection 607 n.
refusal 760 n.
nonadherence
nonobservance 769 n.
nonadhesive
nonadhesive 49 adj.
smooth 258 adj.
nonadjustment
inexactness 495 n.
nonadmission
exclusion 57 n.
disapprobation 924 n.
nonadult
immature 670 adj.
nonage
nonage 130 n.
helplessness 161 n.
nonagenarian
old person 133 n.
nonaggression
peace 717 n.
nonaggression pact
pacification 719 n.
treaty 765 n.
nonagreement
disagreement 25 n.
nonalcoholic beverage
soft drink 301 n.
nonalignment
no choice 606 n.
freedom 744 n.
no name
concealment 525 n.
secret 530 n.
no name 562 n.
nonappearance
absence 190 n.
invisibility 444 n.
nonapproval
rejection 607 n.
disapprobation 924 n.
nonassociation
unwillingness 598 n.
opposition 704 n.
nonattachment
disunion 46 n.
inexcitability 823 n.
nonattendance
absence 190 n.
avoidance 620 n.
nonavailability
nonuse 674 n.
nonbelligerent
pacifist 717 n.
nonbiodegradable
lasting 113 adj.
unyielding 162 adj.
nonce, the
present time 121 n.
nonce word
word 559 n.
neology 560 n.
nonchalance
negligence 458 n.
moral insensibility 820 n.
inexcitability 823 n.
indifference 860 n.
nonchalant
apathetic 820 adj.
indifferent 860 adj.
non-Christian
heathen 974 n.
irreligious 974 adj.
non-Christian sect
religionist 973 n.
non-Christian sect 978 n.
noncoherence
disunion 46 n.
noncoherence 49 n.
noncombatant
pacifist 717 n.
noncommissioned officer
army officer 741 n.
noncommittal
reticent 525 adj.
avoiding 620 adj.
neutral 625 adj.
cautious 858 adj.
indifferent 860 adj.
noncompletion
incompleteness 55 n.
shortfall 307 n.
irresolution 601 n.
insufficiency 636 n.
noncompletion 726 n.
failure 728 n.
noncompliance
dissent 489 n.
disobedience 738 n.
refusal 760 n.
nonobservance 769 n.
non compos mentis
insane 503 adj.
nonconductor
electricity 160 n.
nonconformist
misfit 25 n.
nonconformist 84 n.
unconformable 84 adj
deviating 282 adj.
dissentient 489 n.
dissenting 489 adj.
crank 504 n.
free person 744 n.
nonobservant 769 adj.
heterodox 977 adj.
schismatic 978 n.
Nonconformist
sectarian 978 n.
nonconformity
nonconformity 84 n.
dissent 489 n.
opposition 704 n.
independence 744 n.
sectarianism 978 n.
noncooperation
unwillingness 598 n.
resistance 715 n.
disobedience 738 n.
undutifulness 918 n.
noncooperator
dissentient 489 n.
opponent 705 n.
nondescript
unconformable 84 adj.
trivial 639 adj.
nondesign
chance 159 n.
nondesign 618 n.
nondiscriminatory
inclusive 78 adj.
nondrinker
avoider 620 n.
none
zero 103 n.
non-ego
extrinsicality 6 n.
nonentitlement
undueness 916 n.
nonentity
nonexistence 2 n.
inferior 35 n.
weakling 163 n.
nonentity 639 n.
object of scorn 867 n.
commoner 869 n.
no nerves
moral insensibility 820 n.
nones
date 108 n.
nonessential
extrinsic 6 adj.
irrelevance 10 n.
unimportant 639 adj.
none such
supreme 34 adj.
exceller 644 n.
paragon 646 n.
none the worse
restored 656 adj.
none to spare
scarcity 636 n.
non-event
failure 728 n.
nonexistence
nonexistence 2 n.
insubstantiality 4 n.
absence 190 n.
nonfeasance
nonobservance 769 n.
nonfiction
literature 557 n.
description 590 n.
nonfigurative
representing 551 adj.
nonflowering plant
plant 366 n.
nonfulfilment
incompleteness 55 n.
shortfall 307 n.
disappointment 509 n.
insufficiency 636 n.
noncompletion 726 n.
failure 728 n.
nonobservance 769 n.
nonfunctional
useless 641 adj.
ornamental 844 adj.
nonidentical
contrary 14 adj.
nonimmunity
vulnerability 661 n.
noninclusion
exclusion 57 n.
noninfectious
salubrious 652 adj.
noninflammable
incombustible 382 adj.
noninjurious
salubrious 652 adj.
nonintervention
avoidance 620 n.
inaction 677 n.
laxity 734 n.
freedom 744 n.
noninvolvement
avoidance 620 n.
peace 717 n.
nonjuror
schismatic 978 n.
nonliable
nonliable 919 adj.
nonobservance
negligence 458 n.
avoidance 620 n.
disobedience 738 n.
nonobservance 769 n.
undutifulness 918 n.
no-nonsense
undisguised 522 adj.
artless 699 adj.
nonownership
nonownership 774 n.
nonpareil
exceller 644 n.
paragon 646 n.

nonparticipating
inactive 679 adj.
nonpartisan
independent 744 adj.
nonpayment
nonpayment 805 n.
nonplussed
doubting 474 adj.
puzzled 517 adj.
in difficulties 700 adj.
nonpractising
unconformable 84 adj.
nonobservant 769 adj.
irreligious 974 adj.
impious 980 adj.
nonpreparation
lateness 136 n.
negligence 458 n.
lack of expectation 508 n.
spontaneity 609 n.
nonpreparation 670 n.
haste 680 n.
nonprofessional
ignorant 491 adj.
unskilled 695 adj.
non-profitmaking
losing 772 adj.
disinterested 931 adj.
nonproliferation
pacification 719 n.
nonprovision
nonpreparation 670 n.
nonrecognition
prohibition 757 n.
schism 978 n.
nonrecovery
loss 772 n.
nonrecyclable
lost 772 adj.
nonrepresentational art
misrepresentation 552 n.
nonresidence
absence 190 n.
nonresistance
submission 721 n.
obedience 739 n.
nonresonance
faintness 401 n.
nonresonance 405 n.
nonretention
relinquishment 621 n.
nonretention 779 n.
nonreturnable
useless 641 adj.
unused 674 adj.
nonsatisfaction
incompleteness 55 n.
insufficiency 636 n.
nonsense
absurdity 497 n.
silly talk 515 n.
trifle 639 n.
nonsense verse
doggerel 593 n.
nonsensical
absurd 497 adj.
foolish 499 adj.
meaningless 515 adj.
non sequitur
irrelevance 10 n.
discontinuity 72 n.
sophism 477 n.
nonskid
dry 342 adj.
nonsmoker
train 274 n.
abstainer 942 n.
nonstandard
abnormal 84 adj.
dialectal 560 adj.
nonstarter
difficulty 700 n.
loser 728 n.
nonstop
continuous 71 adj.
perpetual 115 adj.
unceasing 146 adj.
vehicular 274 adj.
loquacious 581 adj.
nonstriker
nonconformist 84 n.
revolter 738 n.
nonsuit
acquittal 960 n.
nontransferable
retained 778 adj.
non-U
unwonted 611 adj.
ill-bred 847 adj.
plebeian 869 adj.
nonuniform
nonuniform 17 adj.
disagreeing 25 adj.
multiform 82 adj.
changeful 152 adj.
nonuse
rejection 607 n.
desuetude 611 n.
relinquishment 621 n.
nonuse 674 n.
nonviolence
moderation 177 n.
peace 717 n.
nonvoter
absence 190 n.
disapprover 924 n.
nonvoting
choiceless 606 adj.
nonworshipper
impious person 980 n.
noodles
dish 301 n.
nook
place 185 n.
compartment 194 n.
angularity 247 n.
hiding-place 527 n.
noon
noon 128 n.
light 417 n.
noon and night
repeatedly 106 adv.
perpetually 139 adv.
no one
nonexistence 2 n.
nobody 190 n.
no option
necessity 596 n.
noose
halter 47 n.
trap 542 n.
means of execution 964 n.
no other
identity 13 n.
no picnic
hard task 700 n.
no preference
no choice 606 n.
no pride
moral insensibility 820 n.
servility 879 n.
no progress
inactivity 679 n.
no prospects
hopelessness 853 n.
no purpose
inutility 641 n.
no quarter
pitilessness 906 n.
no quarter!
362 int.
no question
certainly 473 adv.
no quorum
fewness 105 n.
insufficiency 636 n.
Nordic deities
Nordic deities 967 n.
no recollection
oblivion 506 n.
no regrets
impenitence 940 n.
no restrictions
laxity 734 n.
no reward
ingratitude 908 n.
no right
undueness 916 n.
norm
prototype 23 n.
average 30 n.
rule 81 n.
paragon 646 n.
precept 693 n.
N or M
everyman 79 n.
no name 562 n.
normal
average 30 n.
median 30 adj.
general 79 adj.
regular 81 adj.
typical 83 adj.
sane 502 adj.
right 913 adj.
normality
regularity 81 n.
sanity 502 n.
right 913 n.
normalize, normalise
regularize 62 vb.
make conform 83 vb.
Norman
olden 127 adj.
churchlike 990 adj.
normative
regular 81 adj.
educational 534 adj.
Norns, the
fate 596 n.
mythic deity 966 n.
North
compass point 281 n.
North and South
polarity 14 n.
region 184 n.
northbound
directed 281 adj.
northern
opposite 240 adj.
directed 281 adj.
Northerner
native 191 n.
northern lights
heavens 321 n.
glow 417 n.
luminary 420 n.
northing
bearings 186 n.
north of Potters Bar
district 184 n.
North Pole
summit 213 n.
coldness 380 n.
North Sea
ocean 343 n.
north wind
wind 352 n.
nor'wester
gale 352 n.
no saint
bad person 938 n.
no score
zero 103 n.
nose
face 237 n.
prow 237 n.
angularity 247 n.
protuberance 254 n.
person 371 n.
odour 394 n.
detective 459 n.
detect 484 vb.
informer 524 n.
— around
enquire 459 vb.
— into
be curious 453 vb.
— out
discover 484 vb.
nosebag
bag 194 n.

nose cone
rocket 276 n.
no secret
known 490 adj.
nose dive
aeronautics 271 n.
descent 309 n.
plunge 313 n.
nosegay
bunch 74 n.
fragrance 396 n.
ornamentation 844 n.
nosehole
orifice 263 n.
nose-in-the-air
prideful 871 adj.
nose job
beautification 843 n.
noseless
odourless 395 adj.
nose to tail
continuously 71 adv.
nosh
food 301 n.
no signs of
latency 523 n.
no sinecure
activity 678 n.
no slouch
busy person 678 n.
nosology
pathology 651 n.
no sooner said than done
instantaneously 116 adv.
easy 701 adj.
no spring chicken
old woman 133 n.
nostalgia
remembrance 505 n.
regret 830 n.
melancholy 834 n.
desire 859 n.
nostalgic
unhappy 825 adj.
no standing
disrepute 867 n.
no stomach for
unwillingness 598 n.
dislike 861 n.
Nostradamus
oracle 511 n.
no stranger to
knowing 490 adj.
nostril
orifice 263 n.
air pipe 353 n.
odour 394 n.
no strings attached
unconditional 744 adj.
nostrum
contrivance 623 n.
remedy 658 n.
no such thing
nonexistence 2 n.
no surrender!
715 int.
nosy, nosey
inquisitive 453 adj.
enquiring 459 adj.
nosy parker
inquisitive person 453 n.
meddler 678 n.
not a bit
in no way 33 adv.
notable
remarkable 32 adj.
bigwig 638 n.
notable 638 adj.
person of repute 866 n.
noteworthy 866 adj.
not above temptation
frail 934 adj.
not a breath of air
quietude 266 n.
not absolute
relative 9 adj.
qualifying 468 adj.
not act
wait 136 vb.
be inert 175 vb.
be neglectful 458 vb.
not act 677 vb.
not a dream
reality 1 n.
not a few
great quantity 32 n.
many 104 adj.
not a hope
impossibility 470 n.
hopelessness 853 n.
not a jot
insubstantiality 4 n.
in no way 33 adv.
not allowed
prohibited 757 adj.
not all there
unintelligent 499 adj.
crazy 503 adj.
not amused
angry 891 adj.
disapproving 924 adj.
not answerable
nonliable 919 adj.
not a patch on
inferior 35 adj.
not a pin to choose
equivalence 28 n.
notary
recorder 549 n.
notary 958 n.
not a scrap
insubstantiality 4 n.
not a soul
nobody 190 n.
no taste
bad taste 847 n.
not at all
in no way 33 adv.
nay 533 adv.
not at home
absent 190 adj.
not at home, be
be engaged 138 vb.
not at home with
ignorant 491 adj.
notation
numerical operation 86 n.
notation 410 n.
not a trace of
simpleness 44 n.
not a true picture
misrepresentation 552 n.
not bad
not bad 644 adj.
not bargain for
not expect 508 vb.
not bat an eyelid
be stable 153 vb.
be insensitive 820 vb.
keep calm 823 vb.
not bear inspection
be imperfect 647 vb.
not beat about the bush
be concise 569 vb.
speak plainly 573 vb.
not before it was time
at last 113 adv.
not believe one's eyes
wonder 864 vb.
not be moved
stand firm 599 vb.
defy 711 vb.
not born yesterday
unbelieving 486 adj.
intelligent 498 adj.
cunning 698 adj.
not bother
be neglectful 458 vb.
be inactive 679 vb.
not breathe a word
keep secret 525 vb.
not brook
prohibit 757 vb.
not budge
be quiescent 266 vb.
stand firm 599 vb.
persevere 600 vb.
be obstinate 602 vb.
not by a long chalk
in no way 33 adv.
not care
be neutral 606 vb.
be rash 857 vb.
be indifferent 860 vb.
not care a rap for
hold cheap 922 vb.
not care for
dislike 861 vb.
not catch
be inattentive 456 vb.
not catch on
be unpractised 611 vb.
notch
degree 27 n.
cut 46 vb.
gap 201 n.
angularity 247 n.
make concave 255 vb.
notch 260 n.vb.
mark 547 vb.
decorate 844 vb.
— up
number 86 vb.
register 548 vb.
notched
toothed 256 adj.
not click
escape notice 456 vb.
not come off
miscarry 728 vb.
not come up to
be inferior 35 vb.
fall short 307 vb.
not come up to expectations
disappoint 509 vb.
not concern
be unrelated 10 vb.
not consider
reject 607 vb.
not contemplate
not expect 508 vb.
not count
be unimportant 639 vb.
not counting
exclusive of 57 adv.
not cricket
injustice 914 n.
not done
unconformable 84 adj.
unwonted 611 adj.
prohibited 757 adj.
note
ululation 409 n.
musical note 410 n.
cognize 447 vb.
notice 455 vb.
reminder 505 n.
indication 547 n.
record 548 vb.
write 586 vb.
correspondence 588 n.
compendium 592 n.
paper money 797 n.
famousness 866 n.
notebook
reminder 505 n.
record 548 n.
stationery 586 n.
reference book 589 n.
notecase
case 194 n.

noted
known 490 adj.
renowned 866 adj.
not enough
insufficiency 636 n.
note of hand
title deed 767 n.
paper money 797 n.
notepaper
stationery 586 n.
paper 631 n.
notes
commentary 520 n.
record 548 n.
noteworthy
remarkable 32 adj.
special 80 adj.
unusual 84 adj.
notable 638 adj.
wonderful 864 adj.
noteworthy 866 adj.
not expect
be unlikely 472 vb.
not expect 508 vb.
not far
near 200 adj.adv.
not fit in
be unconformable 84 vb.
not fit to be seen
unsightly 842 adj.
not fit to hold a candle to
inferior 35 adj.
not fit to live with
unsociable 883 adj.
not for all the tea in China
denyingly 760 adv.
not forgetting
in addition 38 adv.
not for long
transiently 114 adv.
not for one
unapt 25 adj.
not for publication
secretly 525 adv.
not for sale
retained 778 adj.
not for the world
unwillingly 598 adv.
not get it
not understand 517 vb.
not give a hoot
be indifferent 860 vb.
hold cheap 922 vb.
not give an inch
stand firm 599 vb.
not give another thought to
forget 506 vb.
forgive 909 vb.
not give a straight answer
be equivocal 518 vb.
dissemble 541 vb.
not give a thankyou for
be ungrateful 908 vb.
not good enough
bad 645 adj.
imperfect 647 adj.
blameworthy 924 adj.
not guilty
vindicable 927 adj.
guiltless 935 adj.
acquitted 960 adj.
no thanks to
undueness 916 n.
not have a leg to stand on
be impotent 161 vb.
reason badly 477 vb.
not have an inkling
not know 491 vb.
not have one's heart in it
be indifferent 860 vb.
not have the heart to
be unwilling 598 vb.
not hear a word against
be credulous 487 vb.
not hear of
refuse 760 vb.
not help
be useless 641 vb.
be inexpedient 643 vb.
not hesitate
be willing 597 vb.
not hide one's feelings
show feeling 818 vb.
nothing
nonexistence 2 n.
insubstantiality 4 n.
zero 103 n.
trifle 639 n.
nothing but
simple 44 adj.
nothing doing
inaction 677 n.
denyingly 760 adv.
nothing for it
necessarily 596 adv.
nothing in common
dissimilarity 19 n.
nothing in it
lack of wonder 865 n.
nothing like it
best 644 adj.
nothing loath
willingly 597 adv.
nothingness
nonexistence 2 n.
(See **nothing***)*
nothing sacred
irreligion 974 n.
nothing special
inferior 35 adj.
nothing to add
completeness 54 n.
nothing to boast of
trifle 639 n.
imperfect 647 adj.
middling 732 adj.
nothing to choose between
similar 18 adj.
nothing to do with
unrelated 10 adj.
nothing to go on
uncertainty 474 n.
ignorance 491 n.
nothing to it
trifle 639 n.
easy thing 701 n.
865 int.
nothing to show for
profitless 641 adj.
nothing to spare
insufficiency 636 n.
nothing to worry about
trifle 639 n.
nothing to write home about
inferior 35 adj.
nothing wrong with
perfection 646 n.
not hold it against one
forgive 909 vb.
not hold water
be untrue 543 vb.
not hold with
dissent 489 vb.
disapprove 924 vb.
no thought for others
selfishness 932 n.
no thought for self
disinterestedness 931 n.
notice
period 110 n.
see 438 vb.
cognize 447 vb.
attention 455 n.
notice 455 vb.
estimate 480 n.
detect 484 vb.
prediction 511 n.
information 524 n.
advertisement 528 n.
article 591 n.
warning 664 n.
demand 737 n.
greet 884 vb.
noticeable
remarkable 32 adj.
visible 443 adj.
manifest 522 adj.
notice board
advertisement 528 n.
not ideal
imperfect 647 adj.
notifiable disease
disease 651 n.
notification
information 524 n.
publication 528 n.
indication 547 n.
notify
predict 511 vb.
communicate 524 vb.
proclaim 528 vb.
warn 664 vb.
not imagined
real 1 adj.
no time to lose
haste 680 n.
not immune
vulnerable 661 adj.
not in one's right mind
insane 503 adj.
not in the habit of
unhabituated 611 adj.
not in the least
in no way 33 adv.
not in the mood
unwilling 598 adj.
not in the slightest
in no way 33 adv.
not in use
inactive 679 adj.
notion
idea 451 n.
supposition 512 n.
ideality 513 n.
contrivance 623 n.
notional
ideational 451 adj.
suppositional 512 adj.
imaginary 513 adj.
not know from Adam
not know 491 vb.
not know how
be unskilful 695 vb.
not know one's own mind
be irresolute 601 vb.
not know one's place
be insolent 878 vb.
not know what to make of
be uncertain 474 vb.
not know 491 vb.
not understand 517 vb.
not know what to say
wonder 864 vb.
not know when one is beaten
be successful 727 vb.
not know when one is well off
be discontented 829 vb.
not know when to stop
exaggerate 546 vb.
be intemperate 943 vb.

not know which way to turn
be uncertain 474 vb.
be busy 678 vb.
be in difficulty 700 vb.
not last
be transient 114 vb.
not let go
persevere 600 vb.
retain 778 vb.
not let one get a word in edgeways
be loquacious 581 vb.
not let the grass grow under one's feet
be active 678 vb.
not lift a finger
not act 677 vb.
not likely
denyingly 760 adv.
not likely!
472 int.
not like the look of
dislike 861 vb.
not listen
be deaf 416 vb.
be inattentive 456 vb.
be obstinate 602 vb.
disobey 738 vb.
refuse 760 vb.
not long ago
newly 126 adv.
not look
be blind 439 vb.
be clumsy 695 vb.
not look a gift horse in the mouth
be grateful 907 vb.
not look for
not expect 508 vb.
not looking
negligent 458 adj.
rash 857 adj.
not lose sight of
be mindful 455 vb.
not make an issue of
forgive 909 vb.
not make the grade
be inferior 35 vb.
be impotent 161 vb.
fall short 307 vb.
be imperfect 647 vb.
fail 728 vb.
not many
inconsiderable 33 adj.
few 105 adj.
not matter
be unimportant 639 vb.
not meant
unintentional 618 adj.
not mean what one says
mean nothing 515 vb.
not meet requirements
not suffice 636 vb.
not mention
conceal 525 vb.
not mince one's words
speak plainly 573 vb.
be artless 699 vb.
not mind
acquiesce 488 vb.
be willing 597 vb.
be indifferent 860 vb.
not much
small 33 adj.
not much to look at
ugly 842 adj.
not nice
not nice 645 adj.
unpleasant 827 adj.
disreputable 867 adj.
not now
different time 122 n.
not now 122 adv.
prospectively 124 adv.
not often
seldom 140 adv.
not of this world
extraneous 59 adj.
imaginary 513 adj.
divine 965 adj.
not one of us
intruder 59 n.
not oneself
dejected 834 adj.
not one's type
dislike 861 n.
hateful object 888 n.
not on speaking terms
inimical 881 adj.
notoriety
disrepute 867 n.
notorious
well-known 528 adj.
disreputable 867 adj.
not out
unceasing 146 adj.
not out of the wood
endangered 661 adj.
in difficulties 700 adj.
not particular
vulgar 847 adj.
dishonest 930 adj.
not play ball
be unwilling 598 vb.
be obstructive 702 vb.
not playing the game
foul play 930 n.
not pull one's punches
reprobate 924 vb.
not pull one's weight
be unwilling 598 vb.
not put a foot wrong
be skilful 694 vb.
be successful 727 vb.
not quite
almost 33 adv.
imperfectly 647 adv.
not reach
be short 204 vb.
fall short 307 vb.
not register
be inattentive 456 vb.
not understand 517 vb.
not required
unused 674 adj.
not resident
absent 190 adj.
not respect
not observe 769 vb.
satirize 851 vb.
humiliate 872 vb.
be rude 885 vb.
not respect 921 vb.
despise 922 vb.
hold cheap 922 vb.
not respectable
vulgar 847 adj.
disreputable 867 adj.
not responsible
nonliable 919 adj.
guiltless 935 adj.
not retain
dismiss 300 vb.
let fall 311 vb.
relinquish 621 vb.
stop using 674 vb.
liberate 746 vb.
not retain 779 vb.
not right
inexpedient 643 adj.
wrong 914 adj.
not right in the head
crazy 503 adj.
not ring true
be untrue 543 vb.
no trouble
easy thing 701 n.
not say a word
be silent 399 vb.
not say boo to a goose
be lax 734 vb.
not see beyond one's nose
be blind 439 vb.
misjudge 481 vb.
be foolish 499 vb.
not see the joke
be serious 834 vb.
resent 891 vb.
not see the wood for the trees
be blind 439 vb.
reason badly 477 vb.
misjudge 481 vb.
not so
differently 15 adv.
not spare one's blushes
shame 867 vb.
praise 923 vb.
flatter 925 vb.
not stand in the way
facilitate 701 vb.
not stay the course
fall short 307 vb.
not complete 726 vb.
not stir
be quiescent 266 vb.
not act 677 vb.
not straight
distorted 246 adj.
dishonest 930 adj.
not suffice
fall short 307 vb.
not suffice 636 vb.
be imperfect 647 vb.
fail 728 vb.
cause discontent 829 vb.
not surprising
expected 507 adj.
not take into account
misjudge 481 vb.
not take it lying down
be active 678 vb.
retaliate 714 vb.
resist 715 vb.
not take no for an answer
be obstinate 602 vb.
compel 740 vb.
not take seriously
neglect 458 vb.
not the answer
inexpedience 643 n.
not the end of the world
trifle 639 n.
not there
not here 190 adv.
abstracted 456 adj.
not the same
different 15 adj.
not the thing
desuetude 611 n.
undueness 916 n.
not thinking
unthinking 450 adj.
inattentive 456 adj.
not think much of
disapprove 924 vb.
not think twice about
be indifferent 860 vb.
not thought much of
disreputable 867 adj.
not to be borne
intolerable 827 adj.

not to be forgotten
remembered 505 adj.
not to be sneezed at
important 638 adj.
not to be thought of
unthought 450 adj.
impossible 470 adj.
prohibited 757 adj.
undue 916 adj.
blameworthy 924 adj.
not to be trusted
dishonest 930 adj.
not today
different time 122 n.
not to mention
in addition 38 adv.
not too late
possible 469 adj.
not too much
sufficient 635 adj.
not to one's taste
disliked 861 adj.
not touch with a bargepole
avoid 620 vb.
not trouble one's head about
disregard 458 vb.
not turn a hair
be insensitive 820 vb.
keep calm 823 vb.
not up to expectation
disappointing 509 adj.
not up to scratch
inferior 35 adj.
deficient 307 adj.
unskilful 695 adj.
not use
be unproductive 172 vb.
waste 634 vb.
not use 674 vb.
not used to
unhabituated 611 adj.
not use one's eyes
be blind 439 vb.
be inattentive 456 vb.
not wait to be asked
offer 759 vb.
not wash
be unlikely 472 vb.
not wear it
dissent 489 vb.
not well
sick 651 adj.
not well off
unprosperous 731 adj.
poor 801 adj.
not what it was
weakened 163 adj.
not what one expected
disappointment 509 n.
discontent 829 n.
not with it
antiquated 127 adj.
abstracted 456 adj.
notwithstanding
in return 31 adv.
although 182 adv.
not wonder
be insensitive 820 vb.
be indifferent 860 vb.
not wonder 865 vb.
not work
be impotent 161 vb.
be useless 641 vb.
be inactive 679 vb.
not working
orderless 61 adj.
not worry
keep calm 823 vb.
not worth a thought
trivial 639 adj.
not worthwhile
trivial 639 adj.
profitless 641 adj.
no two ways about it
certainly 473 adv.
necessarily 596 adv.
nougat
sweets 301 n.
nought
zero 103 n.
noughts and crosses
indoor game 837 n.
noumenal
insubstantial 4 adj.
intuitive 476 adj.
noumenon
idea 451 n.
noun
name 561 n.
part of speech 564 n.
nourish
feed 301 vb.
aid 703 vb.
nourishing
nourishing 301 adj.
salubrious 652 adj.
nous
intelligence 498 n.
skill 694 n.
nouveau riche
upstart 126 n.
prosperous person 730 n.
rich person 800 n.
vulgarian 847 n.
commoner 869 n.
nouvelle cuisine
dieting 301 n.
nouvelle vague
film 445 n.
nova
star 321 n.
novel
dissimilar 19 adj.
original 21 adj.
new 126 adj.
unknown 491 adj.
reading matter 589 n.
novel 590 n.
novelese
neology 560 n.
novelette
novel 590 n.
novelettish
feeble 572 adj.
vulgar 847 adj.
novelist
author 589 n.
narrator 590 n.
novelization, novelisation
novel 590 n.
novelty
bauble 639 n.
pleasurableness 826 n.
(See **novel** *)*
novena
period 110 n.
church service 988 n.
novice
ignoramus 493 n.
beginner 538 n.
bungler 697 n.
ingenue 699 n.
monk 986 n.
nun 986 n.
lay person 987 n.
novitiate
learning 536 n.
preparation 669 n.
no voice
voicelessness 578 n.
no choice 606 n.
no vote
no choice 606 n.
now
at present 121 adv.
now, be
be 1 vb.
be now 121 vb.
nowadays
present time 121 n.
now and again/then
discontinuously 72 adv.
sometimes 139 adv.
fitfully 142 adv.
at intervals 201 adv.
no way
in no way 33 adv.
no way out
hopelessness 853 n.
nowhere
nonexistent 2 adj.
not here 190 adv.
no will of one's own
irresolution 601 n.
no wiser
uninstructed 491 adj.
no wonder
865 int.
no word of
ignorance 491 n.
concealment 525 n.
no words wasted
conciseness 569 n.
no work
inaction 677 n.
leisure 681 n.
now or never
at present 121 adv.
opportunely 137 adv.
no worse
equivalent 28 adj.
healthy 650 adj.
now this now that
changeably 152 adv.
capriciously 604 adv.
noxious
fetid 397 adj.
harmful 645 adj.
insalubrious 653 adj.
noxious animal
creepy-crawly 365 n.
bane 659 n.
noxious animal 904 n.
knave 938 n.
noyade
slaughter 362 n.
nozzle
projection 254 n.
orifice 263 n.
outlet 298 n.
air pipe 353 n.
nuance
differentiation 15 n.
degree 27 n.
small quantity 33 n.
hue 425 n.
discrimination 463 n.
nub
essential part 5 n.
focus 76 n.
centre 225 n.
swelling 253 n.
chief thing 638 n.
nubbly
convex 253 adj.
rough 259 adj.
nubile
grown-up 134 adj.
marriageable 894 adj.
nuclear
dynamic 160 adj.
central 225 adj.
nuclear blast
havoc 165 n.
nuclear bomb
bomb 723 n.
nuclear deterrent
arms 723 n.

nuclear disarmament
pacification 719 n.
nuclear family
family 11 n.
nuclear fission
separation 46 n.
nuclear-free zone
pacification 719 n.
nuclear fuel
fuel 385 n.
nuclear physics
nucleonics 160 n.
physics 319 n.
nuclear power
sources of energy 160 n.
nuclear reactor
nucleonics 160 n.
nuclear submarine
warship 722 n.
nuclear war
war 718 n.
nucleate
make smaller 198 vb.
centralize 225 vb.
be dense 324 vb.
nucleic acid
organism 358 n.
nucleolus
organism 358 n.
nucleon
element 319 n.
nucleonics
separation 46 n.
decomposition 51 n.
nucleonics 160 n.
physics 319 n.
fuel 385 n.
radiation 417 n.
nucleus
essential part 5 n.
middle 70 n.
source 156 n.
minuteness 196 n.
centre 225 n.
element 319 n.
solid body 324 n.
organism 358 n.
chief thing 638 n.
nude
uncovered 229 adj.
art subject 553 n.
nudge
knock 279 n.
agitate 318 vb.
hint 524 n.vb.
gesture 547 n.
indication 547 n.
warning 664 n.
nudge-nudge wink-wink
impure 951 adj.
nudist
stripper 229 n.
sanitarian 652 n.
nudity
bareness 229 n.
nugatory
powerless 161 adj.
unimportant 639 adj.
nugget
solid body 324 n.
bullion 797 n.
nuisance
evil 616 n.
meddler 678 n.
obstacle 702 n.
annoyance 827 n.
nuisance value
hindrance 702 n.
null
nonexistent 2 adj.
insubstantial 4 adj.
meaningless 515 adj.
null and void
powerless 161 adj.
unproductive 172 adj.
abrogated 752 adj.
illegal 954 adj.
nullifidian
unbeliever 486 n.
irreligionist 974 n.
nullify
nullify 2 vb.
set off 31 vb.
destroy 165 vb.
abrogate 752 vb.
nulli secundus
supreme 34 adj.
nullity
nonexistence 2 n.
lack of meaning 515 n.
unimportance 639 n.
divorce 896 n.
numb
inert 175 adj.
still 266 adj.
insensible 375 adj.
apathetic 820 adj.
fearing 854 adj.
number
quantity 26 n.
subdivision 53 n.
specify 80 vb.
number 85 n.
number 86 vb.
list 87 vb.
plurality 101 n.
dress 228 n.
label 547 n.
grammar 564 n.
reading matter 589 n.
— with
number with 78 vb.
numbered
statistical 86 adj.
numberless
infinite 107 adj.
number one
self 80 n.
numbers
great quantity 32 n.
multitude 104 n.
numbness
helplessness 161 n.
(See **numb** *)*
numdah
floor-cover 226 n.
numen
divineness 965 n.
numerable
numerable 86 adj.
numeracy
numeration 86 n.
culture 490 n.
numeral
number 85 n.
numerical 85 adj.
numerate
instructed 490 adj.
numeration
numeration 86 n.
numerator
numerical element 85 n.
numerical
numerical 85 adj.
numerical element
numerical element 85 n.
fraction 102 n.
numerical operation
increase 36 n.
subtraction 39 n.
numerical operation 86 n.
numerous
many 104 adj.
numinous
frightening 854 adj.
divine 965 adj.
spooky 970 adj.
numismatics
coinage 797 n.
numismatist
collector 492 n.
nummary
monetary 797 adj.
numskull, numbskull
ignoramus 493 n.
dunce 501 n.
nun
nun 986 n.
nuncio
messenger 529 n.
envoy 754 n.
nunnery
monastery 986 n.
nuptial
matrimonial 894 adj.
nuptials
wedding 894 n.
nurse
feed 301 vb.
look after 457 vb.
cure 656 vb.
nurse 658 n.
doctor 658 vb.
safeguard 660 vb.
preserve 666 vb.
mature 669 vb.
manage 689 vb.
minister to 703 vb.
patronize 703 vb.
domestic 742 n.
keeper 749 n.
please 826 vb.
relieve 831 vb.
pet 889 vb.
philanthropize 897 vb.
— an ambition
aim at 617 vb.
seek repute 866 vb.
nursemaid
teacher 537 n.
protector 660 n.
servant 742 n.
keeper 749 n.
nursery
nonage 130 n.
seedbed 156 n.
chamber 194 n.
farm 370 n.
training school 539 n.
workshop 687 n.
nursery education
education 534 n.
nurseryman, nurserywoman
gardener 370 n.
nursery rhyme
doggerel 593 n.
nursery school
school 539 n.
nursing home
hospital 658 n.
nursling
child 132 n.
dependant 742 n.
nurture
food 301 n.
feed 301 vb.
educate 534 vb.
mature 669 vb.
nut
fastening 47 n.
head 213 n.
fruit 301 n.
flower 366 n.
crank 504 n.
enthusiast 504 n.
madman 504 n.
nutation
oscillation 317 n.
uranometry 321 n.
nut-brown
brown 430 adj.
nutcase
madman 504 n.
nutcrackers
cross 222 n.
nuthouse
lunatic asylum 503 n.
nutmeg
condiment 389 n.

nutriment
food 301 n.
nutrition
eating 301 n.
food 301 n.
nutritional
nourishing 301 adj.
remedial 658 adj.
nutritionist
dieting 301 n.
doctor 658 n.
nutritious
nourishing 301 adj.
salubrious 652 adj.
nuts
crazy 503 adj.
nuts and bolts
component 58 n.
means 629 n.
machine 630 n.
nutshell
small quantity 33 n.
conciseness 569 n.
nuts on, be
be in love 887 vb.
nutter
crank 504 n.
nutty
pungent 388 adj.
crazy 503 adj.
nuzzle
touch 378 vb.
caress 889 vb.
nyctalopia
dim sight 440 n.
nylon
fibre 208 n.
textile 222 n.
nylons
legwear 228 n.
nymph
young creature 132 n.
youngster 132 n.
woman 373 n.
nymph 967 n.
mythical being 970 n.
nymphet
youngster 132 n.
loose woman 952 n.
nympholepsy
frenzy 503 n.
spell 983 n.
nympholept
crank 504 n.
nymphomania
mania 503 n.
libido 859 n.
illicit love 951 n.
nymphomaniac, nympho
loose woman 952 n.
nystagmus
dim sight 440 n.

O

oaf
dunce 501 n.
bungler 697 n.
oafish
unintelligent 499 adj.
oak
strength 162 n.
hardness 326 n.
tree 366 n.
oakum
fibre 208 n.
oar
propeller 269 n.
propellant 287 n.
oarsman
boatman 270 n.
oasis
nonconformity 84 n.
land 344 n.
oasthouse
furnace 383 n.
oath
testimony 466 n.
oath 532 n.
promise 764 n.
scurrility 899 n.
oatmeal
cereals 301 n.
brown 430 adj.
oats
cereals 301 n.
provender 301 n.
grass 366 n.
obbligato
concomitant 89 n.
musical piece 412 n.
obdurate
obstinate 602 adj.
severe 735 adj.
impenitent 940 adj.
obeah, obi
sorcery 983 n.
obedience
obedience 739 n.
service 745 n.
obedient
willing 597 adj.
submitting 721 adj.
obedient 739 adj.
observant 768 adj.
servile 879 adj.
(See **obey** *)*
obeisance
obeisance 311 n.
submission 721 n.
courteous act 884 n.
respects 920 n.
obelisk
high structure 209 n.
monument 548 n.
Oberon
fairy 970 n.
obese
fleshy 195 adj.
expanded 197 adj.

obesity
eating 301 n.
disease 651 n.
obey
be inferior 35 vb.
conform 83 vb.
acquiesce 488 vb.
obey 739 vb.
serve 742 vb.
be subject 745 vb.
do one's duty 917 vb.
obeyed
influential 178 adj.
obfuscate
darken 418 vb.
make opaque 423 vb.
conceal 525 vb.
obfuscation
obfuscation 421 n.
concealment 525 n.
misteaching 535 n.
obi
(See **obeah** *)*
obiter dictum
interjection 231 n.
obituary
obsequies 364 n.
biography 590 n.
object
substance 3 n.
product 164 n.
object 319 n.
dissent 489 vb.
part of speech 564 n.
be unwilling 598 vb.
objective 617 n.
oppose 704 vb.
resist 715 vb.
deprecate 762 vb.
be discontented 829 vb.
disapprove 924 vb.
(See **objection** *)*
objectify
make extrinsic 6 vb.
materialize 319 vb.
cognize 447 vb.
imagine 513 vb.
objection
qualification 468 n.
doubt 486 n.
dissent 489 n.
unwillingness 598 n.
dissuasion 613 n.
hindrance 702 n.
resistance 715 n.
refusal 760 n.
objectionable
inexpedient 643 adj.
unpleasant 827 adj.
disreputable 867 adj.
wrong 914 adj.
objective
substantial 3 adj.
goal 295 n.
material 319 adj.
optical device 442 n.
true 494 adj.
objective 617 n.
attempt 671 n.
aspiration 852 n.
object lesson
example 83 n.
warning 664 n.
object of scorn
nonentity 639 n.
object of scorn 867 n.
contemptibility 922 n.
objector
dissentient 489 n.
opponent 705 n.
litigant 959 n.
objet d'art
masterpiece 694 n.
ornamentation 844 n.
objet trouvé
sculpture 554 n.
objurgate
dispraise 924 vb.
oblate
worshipper 981 n.
oblation
offering 781 n.
propitiation 941 n.
oblation 981 n.
obligated
obliged 917 adj.
obligation
necessity 596 n.
needfulness 627 n.
undertaking 672 n.
promise 764 n.
debt 803 n.
dueness 915 n.
duty 917 n.
obligatory
necessary 596 adj.
commanding 737 adj.
compelling 740 adj.
conditional 766 adj.
obligatory 917 adj.
oblige
necessitate 596 vb.
require 627 vb.
compel 740 vb.
be courteous 884 vb.
impose a duty 917 vb.
obliged
indebted 803 adj.
grateful 907 adj.
obliged 917 adj.
obliging
aiding 703 adj.
courteous 884 adj.
benevolent 897 adj.
oblique
oblique 220 adj.
distorted 246 adj.
angular 247 adj.
curved 248 adj.
directed 281 adj.

deviating 282 adj.
occult 523 adj.
obliquely
obliquely 220 adv.
sideways 239 adv.
obliterate
destroy 165 vb.
conceal 525 vb.
obliterate 550 vb.
clean 648 vb.
obliteration
extinction 2 n.
oblivion 506 n.
obliteration 550 n.
oblivion
extinction 2 n.
oblivion 506 n.
obliteration 550 n.
desuetude 611 n.
oblivious
insensible 375 adj.
inattentive 456 adj.
negligent 458 adj.
forgetful 506 adj.
oblong
longitudinal 203 adj.
obloquy
slur 867 n.
detraction 926 n.
obnoxious
not nice 645 adj.
unpleasant 827 adj.
hateful 888 adj.
oboe
flute 414 n.
oboist
instrumentalist 413 n.
obscene
not nice 645 adj.
vulgar 847 adj.
disreputable 867 adj.
heinous 934 adj.
impure 951 adj.
obscenity
uncleanness 649 n.
obscurantism
ignorance 491 n.
misteaching 535 n.
opinionatedness 602 n.
obscuration
obscuration 418 n.
obscure
dark 418 adj.
darken 418 vb.
shadowy 419 adj.
blind 439 vb.
unknown 491 adj.
semantic 514 adj.
puzzling 517 adj.
latent 523 adj.
conceal 525 vb.
unclear 568 adj.
unimportant 639 adj.
difficult 700 adj.
inglorious 867 adj.
plebeian 869 adj.
obscurity
darkness 418 n.
invisibility 444 n.
uncertainty 474 n.
unintelligibility 517 n.
obsecration
entreaty 761 n.
obsequies
obsequies 364 n.
obsequious
servile 879 adj.
respectful 920 adj.
flattering 925 adj.
observable
visible 443 adj.
observance
conformity 83 n.
attention 455 n.
practice 610 n.
conduct 688 n.
obedience 739 n.
observance 768 n.
celebration 876 n.
rite 988 n.
observant
attentive 455 adj.
vigilant 457 adj.
observant 768 adj.
pious 979 adj.
observation
inspection 438 n.
look 438 n.
idea 451 n.
attention 455 n.
maxim 496 n.
affirmation 532 n.
observatory
astronomy 321 n.
view 438 n.
observe
scan 438 vb.
see 438 vb.
watch 441 vb.
affirm 532 vb.
do 676 vb.
observe 768 vb.
celebrate 876 vb.
ritualize 988 vb.
observer
spectator 441 n.
estimator 480 n.
air force 722 n.
obsess
recur 139 vb.
go on 146 vb.
engross 449 vb.
attract notice 455 vb.
make mad 503 vb.
remind 505 vb.
torment 827 vb.
trouble 827 vb.
frighten 854 vb.
obsessed
obsessed 455 adj.
crazy 503 adj.
obstinate 602 adj.
obsession
bias 481 n.
belief 485 n.
folly 499 n.
eccentricity 503 n.
psychopathy 503 n.
opinionatedness 602 n.
spell 983 n.
obsessive
unceasing 146 adj.
madman 504 n.
habitual 610 adj.
obsidian
rock 344 n.
obsolescent
antiquated 127 adj.
obsolete
extinct 2 adj.
past 125 adj.
antiquated 127 adj.
powerless 161 adj.
neological 560 adj.
useless 641 adj.
disused 674 adj.
obstacle
counteraction 182 n.
barrier 235 n.
closure 264 n.
impossibility 470 n.
inexpedience 643 n.
defect 647 n.
pitfall 663 n.
difficulty 700 n.
obstacle 702 n.
opposition 704 n.
obstetrician
obstetrics 167 n.
doctor 658 n.
obstetrics
obstetrics 167 n.
medical art 658 n.
obstinacy
obstinacy 602 n.
obstinate
unconformable 84 adj.
permanent 144 adj.
unchangeable 153 adj.
unyielding 162 adj.
narrow-minded 481 adj.
volitional 595 adj.
persevering 600 adj.
obstinate 602 adj.
difficult 700 adj.
opposing 704 adj.
resisting 715 adj.
disobedient 738 adj.
impenitent 940 adj.
obstinate person
doctrinaire 473 n.
obstinate person 602 n.
obstreperous
violent 176 adj.
obstruct
halt 145 vb.
staunch 350 vb.
screen 421 vb.
hinder 702 vb.
obstruct 702 vb.
resist 715 vb.
trouble 827 vb.
obstruction
derangement 63 n.
delay 136 n.
closure 264 n.
hindrance 702 n.
undutifulness 918 n.
obstructionist
hinderer 702 n.
opponent 705 n.
obstructive
dissenting 489 adj.
hindering 702 adj.
obtain
be 1 vb.
be general 79 vb.
be wont 610 vb.
acquire 771 vb.
obtainable
accessible 289 adj.
possible 469 adj.
obtrude
interfere 231 vb.
obstruct 702 vb.
obtrusive
vulgar 847 adj.
obtund
moderate 177 vb.
render insensible 375 vb.
obturate
close 264 vb.
obtuse
unsharpened 257 adj.
insensible 375 adj.
indiscriminating 464 adj.
unintelligent 499 adj.
thick-skinned 820 adj.
obtuse angle
angle 247 n.
obverse
face 237 n.
obviate
counteract 182 vb.
avoid 620 vb.
disencumber 701 vb.
obvious
obvious 443 adj.
certain 473 adj.
intelligible 516 adj.
manifest 522 adj.
ocarina
flute 414 n.
Occam's razor
premise 475 n.
occasion
juncture 8 n.
fitness 24 n.
occasion 137 n.
event 154 n.

reason why 156 n.
cause 156 vb.
needfulness 627 n.
instrumentality 628 n.
good policy 642 n.
amusement 837 n.
celebration 876 n.
occasional
present 121 adj.
opportune 137 adj.
infrequent 140 adj.
fitful 142 adj.
happening 154 adj.
celebratory 876 adj.
occasionally
discontinuously 72 adv.
sometimes 139 adv.
Occident
laterality 239 n.
occidental
lateral 239 adj.
directed 281 adj.
occiput
head 213 n.
occlude
close 264 vb.
obstruct 702 vb.
occult
unknown 491 adj.
unintelligible 517 adj.
occult 523 adj.
concealed 525 adj.
cabbalistic 984 adj.
occultation
obscuration 418 n.
disappearance 446 n.
occultism
spirit 447 n.
latency 523 n.
occultism 984 n.
occultist
oracle 511 n.
sorcerer 983 n.
occultist 984 n.
occupant
resident 191 n.
occupation
presence 189 n.
habit 610 n.
business 622 n.
job 622 n.
undertaking 672 n.
action 676 n.
occupational
habitual 610 adj.
businesslike 622 adj.
doing 676 adj.
occupational disease
disease 651 n.
occupational therapy
therapy 658 n.
occupied
occupied 191 adj.
busy 678 adj.
occupied, be
be engaged 138 vb.
occupier
resident 191 n.
possessor 776 n.
occupy
fill 54 vb.
dwell 192 vb.
attract notice 455 vb.
employ 622 vb.
possess 773 vb.
appropriate 786 vb.
occur
be 1 vb.
happen 154 vb.
be present 189 vb.
— to
dawn upon 449 vb.
occurrence
event 154 n.
ocean
region 184 n.
depth 211 n.
water 339 n.
ocean 343 n.
ocean-going
seafaring 269 adj.
marine 275 adj.
oceanic 343 adj.
oceanic
oceanic 343 adj.
Oceanid
sea nymph 343 n.
mythical being 970 n.
oceanographer
surveyor 465 n.
oceanography
earth sciences 321 n.
oceanography 343 n.
oceans
great quantity 32 n.
Oceanus
sea god 343 n.
classical deities 967 n.
ocelot
cat 365 n.
ochlocracy
government 733 n.
ochre
brown pigment 430 n.
orange 432 n.
o'clock
o'clock 117 adv.
octad
over five 99 n.
octagon
angular figure 247 n.
octaroon
hybrid 43 n.
Octateuch
scripture 975 n.
octave
period 110 n.
musical note 410 n.
octavo
edition 589 n.
octet
over five 99 n.
duet 412 n.
octogenarian
old person 133 n.
octopus
marine life 365 n.
tyrant 735 n.
octosyllabic
poetic 593 adj.
octroi
tax 809 n.
ocular
seeing 438 adj.
optical device 442 n.
ocular proof
visibility 443 n.
oculist
doctor 658 n.
odalisque
slave 742 n.
odd
disagreeing 25 adj.
unequal 29 adj.
remaining 41 adj.
unusual 84 adj.
numerical 85 adj.
crazy 503 adj.
puzzling 517 adj.
ridiculous 849 adj.
wonderful 864 adj.
odd fish, oddball
nonconformist 84 n.
crank 504 n.
laughingstock 851 n.
oddity
misfit 25 n.
nonconformist 84 n.
nonconformity 84 n.
crank 504 n.
prodigy 864 n.
odd-job man
servant 742 n.
oddly
remarkably 32 adv.
odd man out
dissimilarity 19 n.
misfit 25 n.
nonconformist 84 n.
dissentient 489 n.
oddment(s)
extra 40 n.
medley 43 n.
odd moments
leisure 681 n.
odds
difference 15 n.
advantage 34 n.
fair chance 159 n.
dissension 709 n.
odds and ends
leavings 41 n.
medley 43 n.
rubbish 641 n.
odds on
fair chance 159 n.
approved 923 adj.
ode
poem 593 n.
odi et amo
love 887 n.
hatred 888 n.
Odin
Nordic deities 967 n.
odious
unpleasant 827 adj.
ugly 842 adj.
disreputable 867 adj.
hateful 888 adj.
odium
odium 888 n.
odium theologicum
pietism 979 n.
odorous
odorous 394 adj.
fragrant 396 adj.
odour
odour 394 n.
fragrance 396 n.
odourless
odourless 395 adj.
odour of sanctity
virtue 933 n.
sanctity 979 n.
Odysseus
traveller 268 n.
odyssey
land travel 267 n.
oedema
swelling 253 n.
oedematous
diseased 651 adj.
Oedipus complex
eccentricity 503 n.
love 887 n.
oeillade
wooing 889 n.
oesophagus
maw 194 n.
oestrogen
drug 658 n.
oestrus
libido 859 n.
oeuvre
product 164 n.
of age
grown-up 134 adj.
marriageable 894 adj.
of all sorts
different 15 adj.
nonuniform 17 adj.
multiform 82 adj.
of all things
eminently 34 adv.
of a piece
uniform 16 adj.
similar 18 adj.
agreeing 24 adj.
of course
conformably 83 adv.
consequently 157 adv.
certainly 473 adv.
of course 478 adv.
necessarily 596 adv.
habitually 610 adv.
865 int.

off
decomposed 51 adj.
ending 69 adj.
absent 190 adj.
pungent 388 adj.
unprovided 636 adj.
unpleasant 827 adj.
off, be
go away 190 vb.
292 int.
decamp 296 vb.
run away 620 vb.
offal
insides 224 n.
meat 301 n.
rubbish 641 n.
off balance
unequal 29 adj.
off-beam
deviating 282 adj.
offbeat
unconformable 84 adj.
off-chance
possibility 469 n.
improbability 472 n.
off colour
sick 651 adj.
off-course
deviating 282 adj.
off day
untimeliness 138 n.
bungling 695 n.
off duty
leisurely 681 adj.
offence
annoyance 827 n.
resentment 891 n.
wrong 914 n.
vice 934 n.
guilty act 936 n.
lawbreaking 954 n.
offend
displease 827 vb.
cause dislike 861 vb.
huff 891 vb.
offended
resentful 891 adj.
offender
offender 904 n.
knave 938 n.
offensive
fetid 397 adj.
unclean 649 adj.
attack 712 n.
unpleasant 827 adj.
impertinent 878 adj.
ungracious 885 adj.
impure 951 adj.
offensive remark
calumny 926 n.
offensive weapon
weapon 723 n.
offer
opportunity 137 n.
affirm 532 vb.
will 595 vb.
choice 605 n.
incentive 612 n.
provide 633 vb.
attempt 671 vb.
permit 756 vb.
offer 759 n.vb.
promise 764 n.vb.
make terms 766 vb.
give 781 vb.
reward 962 n.
— oneself
be willing 597 vb.
offer oneself 759 vb.
— satisfaction
atone 941 vb.
— up
kill 362 vb.
give 781 vb.
offer worship 981 vb.
offered
voluntary 597 adj.
offering
offer 759 n.
offering 781 n.
propitiation 941 n.
oblation 981 n.
offer one cannot refuse
incentive 612 n.
offertory
oblation 981 n.
off form
imperfect 647 adj.
clumsy 695 adj.
off guard
negligent 458 adj.
inexpectant 508 adj.
offhand, offhanded
inattentive 456 adj.
negligent 458 adj.
spontaneous 609 adj.
discourteous 885 adj.
disrespectful 921 adj.
office
agency 173 n.
chamber 194 n.
function 622 n.
job 622 n.
use 673 n.
workshop 687 n.
authority 733 n.
position of authority 733 n.
mandate 751 n.
duty 917 n.
jurisdiction 955 n.
church service 988 n.
office-bearer
official 690 n.
office boy
courier 529 n.
officer
official 690 n.
officer 741 n.
office routine
business 622 n.
office worker
worker 686 n.
official
certain 473 adj.
genuine 494 adj.
usual 610 adj.
businesslike 622 adj.
directing 689 adj.
official 690 n.
authoritative 733 adj.
governmental 733 adj.
officer 741 n.
servant 742 n.
formal 875 adj.
officialese
language 557 n.
neology 560 n.
official function
formality 875 n.
Official Secrets Act
restraint 747 n.
officiate
function 622 vb.
do 676 vb.
offer worship 981 vb.
perform ritual 988 vb.
officious
inquisitive 453 adj.
meddling 678 adj.
officiousness
overactivity 678 n.
offing
distance 199 n.
offish
unsociable 883 adj.
off key
discordant 411 adj.
off-line
computerized 86 adj.
off-load
displace 188 vb.
off-off-Broadway
drama 594 n.
off one's food
sick 651 adj.
fasting 946 adj.
off one's guard
inattentive 456 adj.
vulnerable 661 adj.
off one's hands
lost 772 adj.
off one's head
crazy 503 adj.
off one's own bat
voluntary 597 adj.
off one's rocker
crazy 503 adj.
off-peak rate
cheapness 812 n.
offprint
copy 22 n.
letterpress 587 n.
off-putting
repellent 292 adj.
hindering 702 adj.
offscourings
leavings 41 n.
dirt 649 n.
rabble 869 n.
off-season
ill-timed 138 adj.
cheap 812 adj.
offset
equalization 28 n.
offset 31 n.
remainder 41 n.
quid pro quo 150 n.
qualification 468 n.
print 587 vb.
offshoot
adjunct 40 n.
branch 53 n.
descendant 170 n.
sect 978 n.
off-shore
distant 199 adj.
offside
laterality 239 n.
dextral 241 adj.
wrong 914 adj.
offspring
kinsman 11 n.
effect 157 n.
product 164 n.
posterity 170 n.
offstage
on stage 594 adv.
off switch
obscuration 418 n.
off-target
irrelevant 10 adj.
deviating 282 adj.
mistaken 495 adj.
off the beaten track
secluded 883 adj.
off the bottle
sober 948 adj.
off the cuff
instantaneously 116 adv.
extempore 609 adv.
unreadily 670 adv.
off-the-peg
tailored 228 adj.
formed 243 adj.
ready-made 669 adj.
off the point
irrelevant 10 adj.
off the rails
unconformable 84 adj.
mistaken 495 adj.
off the record
private 80 adj.
undisguised 522 adj.
occult 523 adj.
off-the-shoulder
uncovered 229 adj.
off the subject
deviating 282 adj.
off the top of one's head
extempore 609 adv.
unprepared 670 adj.
off-white
whitish 427 adj.

off with the old love, be
apostatize 603 vb.
of late
newly 126 adv.
of necessity
necessarily 596 adv.
of no consequence
unimportant 639 adj.
of no fixed address
travelling 267 adj.
of old
formerly 125 adv.
of one mind
concurrent 181 adj.
concordant 710 adj.
of one's own accord
at will 595 adv.
voluntary 597 adj.
of right
established 153 adj.
due 915 adj.
of service
useful 640 adj.
aiding 703 adj.
often
repeatedly 106 adv.
often 139 adv.
of the first water
excellent 644 adj.
ogee
curve 248 n.
convolution 251 n.
pattern 844 n.
ogham alphabet
letter 558 n.
ogive
prop 218 n.
ogle
look 438 n.
watch 441 vb.
gesture 547 n.
desire 859 vb.
court 889 vb.
ogre
giant 195 n.
tyrant 735 n.
intimidation 854 n.
monster 938 n.
demon 970 n.
ogress
hellhag 904 n.
demon 970 n.
Ogygian
immemorial 127 adj.
ohm
electronics 160 n.
metrology 465 n.
oil
sources of energy 160 n.
smoother 258 n.
cookery 301 n.
soften 327 vb.
lubricant 334 n.
oil 357 n.
grease 357 vb.
fuel 385 n.
silencer 401 n.
bribe 612 vb.
materials 631 n.
balm 658 n.
facilitate 701 vb.
oilfield
store 632 n.
oil-fired
heating 381 adj.
oil on troubled waters
moderator 177 n.
remedy 658 n.
oil painting
picture 553 n.
oils
art equipment 553 n.
oilskins
overcoat 228 n.
shelter 662 n.
oil slick
semiliquidity 354 n.
oilstone
sharpener 256 n.
oil tanker
merchant ship 275 n.
oil well
store 632 n.
oily
smooth 258 adj.
unctuous 357 adj.
hypocritical 541 adj.
dirty 649 adj.
servile 879 adj.
flattering 925 adj.
ointment
lubricant 334 n.
unguent 357 n.
balm 658 n.
OK, okay
in order 60 adv.
assent 488 n.
not bad 644 adj.
middling 732 adj.
okra
vegetable 301 n.
old
antiquated 127 adj.
olden 127 adj.
ageing 131 adj.
weak 163 adj.
old age
old age 131 n.
old-age pensioner
recipient 782 n.
old as the hills
immemorial 127 adj.
Old Bailey
lawcourt 956 n.
old boy
old man 133 n.
learner 538 n.
old-boy network
latency 523 n.
Old Country, the
home 192 n.
old couple
old couple 133 n.
old crock
automobile 274 n.
sick person 651 n.
old dutch
old woman 133 n.
spouse 894 n.
olden
past 125 adj.
olden 127 adj.
architectural 192 adj.
olden days
past time 125 n.
olden times
oldness 127 n.
older
older 131 adj.
old-fashioned
anachronistic 118 adj.
antiquated 127 adj.
unwonted 611 adj.
old flame
loved one 887 n.
old fogy, old fogey
archaism 127 n.
old man 133 n.
fool 501 n.
obstinate person 602 n.
laughingstock 851 n.
old folks, the
family 11 n.
old couple 133 n.
old girl
old woman 133 n.
learner 538 n.
Old Glory
flag 547 n.
old gold
orange 432 n.
old guard
stamina 600 n.
old hand
expert 696 n.
old hat
antiquated 127 adj.
oldie
archaism 127 n.
old lag
prisoner 750 n.
offender 904 n.
old maid
card game 837 n.
spinster 895 n.
old-maidish
prudish 950 adj.
old man
old man 133 n.
paternity 169 n.
spouse 894 n.
Old Man of the Sea
encumbrance 702 n.
mythical being 970 n.
old master
picture 553 n.
artist 556 n.
Old Moore
oracle 511 n.
oldness
beginning 68 n.
time 108 n.
durability 113 n.
past time 125 n.
oldness 127 n.
permanence 144 n.
Old Nick
Mephisto 969 n.
old people's home
shelter 662 n.
old salt
mariner 270 n.
old-school
antiquated 127 adj.
opinionatedness 602 n.
habit 610 n.
old school tie
livery 547 n.
cooperative 706 n.
old-stager
old man 133 n.
expert 696 n.
old story
repetition 106 n.
news 529 n.
old style
chronology 117 n.
Old Testament
scripture 975 n.
old-time
antiquated 127 adj.
old-timer
archaism 127 n.
old man 133 n.
old wives' tales
error 495 n.
fable 543 n.
old woman
old woman 133 n.
maternity 169 n.
spouse 894 n.
old-world
antiquated 127 adj.
courteous 884 adj.
Old World
region 184 n.
world 321 n.
oleaginous
unctuous 357 adj.
O level
exam 459 n.
olfactory
odorous 394 adj.
oligarchy
government 733 n.
olive
green 434 adj.
olive branch
peace offering 719 n.
olive oil
oil 357 n.
olivine
greenness 434 n.
gem 844 n.

olla podrida
a mixture 43 n.
ologies and isms
science 490 n.
Olympiad
period 110 n.
Olympian
aristocrat 868 n.
genteel 868 adj.
Olympian deity 967 n.
paradisiac 971 adj.
Olympian deity
Olympian deity 967 n.
Olympic Games
contest 716 n.
Olympus
mythic heaven 971 n.
ombudsman
enquirer 459 n.
estimator 480 n.
mediator 720 n.
omega
extremity 69 n.
omelette
dish 301 n.
omen
precursor 66 n.
foresight 510 n.
omen 511 n.
indication 547 n.
warning 664 n.
danger signal 665 n.
prodigy 864 n.
threat 900 n.
ominous
presageful 511 adj.
indicating 547 adj.
harmful 645 adj.
dangerous 661 adj.
cautionary 664 adj.
adverse 731 adj.
unpromising 853 adj.
frightening 854 adj.
threatening 900 adj.
omission
incompleteness 55 n.
exclusion 57 n.
negligence 458 n.
failure 728 n.
nonobservance 769 n.
omission mark
punctuation 547 n.
omit
be taciturn 582 vb.
(See **omission** *)*
omitted
nonexistent 2 adj.
absent 190 adj.
omnibus
comprehensive 52 adj.
bus 274 n.
omnibus edition
edition 589 n.
omnicompetent
powerful 160 adj.
omnifarious
multiform 82 adj.
omnipotence
power 160 n.
divine attribute 965 n.
omnipotent
strong 162 adj.
compelling 740 adj.
omnipresent
ubiquitous 189 adj.
omniscient
knowing 490 adj.
omnium gatherum
medley 43 n.
omnivore
eater 301 n.
animal 365 n.
omnivorous
greedy 859 adj.
omphalos
centre 225 n.
on
concerning 9 adv.
in place 186 adv.
on the spot 189 adj.
forward 285 adv.
on 310 adv.
shown 522 adj.
on account of
hence 158 adv.
on a hiding to nothing, be
be useless 641 vb.
on all counts
completely 54 adv.
on all fours (with)
identically 13 adv.
on all sides
around 230 adv.
on an average
on an average 30 adv.
about 33 adv.
generally 79 adv.
on and off
by turns 141 adv.
changeably 152 adv.
at intervals 201 adv.
on and on
for ever 115 adv.
diffusely 570 adv.
on approval
experimentally 461 adv.
chosen 605 adj.
on a shoestring
parsimoniously 816 adv.
on behalf of
in aid of 703 adv.
on behalf 755 adv.
on bended knees
submitting 721 adj.
supplicatory 761 adj.
on board
here 189 adv.
seafaring 269 adj.
afloat 275 adv.
on call
on the spot 189 adj.
expectant 507 adj.
prepared 669 adj.
once
singly 88 adv.
not now 122 adv.
seldom 140 adv.
once bitten, twice shy
warned 664 adj.
cautious 858 adj.
once for all
finally 69 adv.
once in a blue moon
seldom 140 adv.
once in a while
sometimes 139 adv.
once more
twice 91 adv.
again 106 adv.
once-over
inspection 438 n.
oncer
funds 797 n.
once removed
akin 11 adj.
once upon a time
when 108 adv.
not now 122 adv.
formerly 125 adv.
oncology
medical art 658 n.
oncoming
frontal 237 adj.
opposite 240 adj.
approaching 289 adj.
on credit
promissory 764 adj.
on loan 784 adv.
owed 803 adj.
on crutches
slowly 278 adv.
on demand
cash down 804 adv.
on display
shown 522 adj.
on dit
rumour 529 n.
on duty
on duty 917 adv.
one
simple 44 adj.
combined 50 adj.
whole 52 adj.
unit 88 n.
one 88 adj.
infrequent 140 adj.
person 371 n.
one after another
continuously 71 adv.
behind 284 adv.
one and all
all 52 n.
everyman 79 n.
unanimously 488 adv.
one and only
dissimilar 19 adj.
inimitable 21 adj.
one 88 adj.
one and the same
identical 13 adj.
one 88 adj.
one another
correlatively 12 adv.
one-armed bandit
gambling 618 n.
on earth
under the sun 321 adv.
one at a time
singly 88 adv.
gradatim 278 adv.
one by one
separately 46 adv.
severally 80 adv.
one day
when 108 adv.
not now 122 adv.
on edge, be
be excitable 822 vb.
be nervous 854 vb.
one-eyed
dim-sighted 440 adj.
one for the road
valediction 296 n.
draught 301 n.
one-handed
clumsy 695 adj.
one-horse
lesser 35 adj.
trivial 639 adj.
one in a thousand
exceller 644 n.
one in the eye for
disappointment 509 n.
oneirocritic
interpreter 520 n.
oneiromancy
divination 511 n.
one-legged
incomplete 55 adj.
one-liner
witticism 839 n.
one man one vote
government 733 n.
on end
vertical 215 adj.
oneness
identity 13 n.
simpleness 44 n.
whole 52 n.
unity 88 n.
one-night stand
music 412 n.
dramaturgy 594 n.
one of
component 58 n.
one of, be
constitute 56 vb.
be one of 58 vb.
be included 78 vb.
one-off
one 88 adj.

one of the best
exceller 644 n.
favourite 890 n.
good person 937 n.
one of the family
kinsman 11 n.
sociable person 882 n.
one of these days
not now 122 adv.
one or two
plurality 101 n.
fewness 105 n.
one over the eight
drunkenness 949 n.
one-piece
uniform 16 adj.
tailored 228 adj.
onerous
difficult 700 adj.
hindering 702 adj.
annoying 827 adj.
one's betters
superior 34 n.
one's day
success 727 n.
one's despair
bungler 697 n.
difficulty 700 n.
oneself again
restored 656 adj.
oneself, be
accord 24 vb.
be free 744 vb.
one's fault
guilt 936 n.
one's fill
plenitude 54 n.
sufficiency 635 n.
dislike 861 n.
one's flesh and blood
kinsman 11 n.
one-sided
biased 481 adj.
unjust 914 adj.
one's level best
attempt 671 n.
one's middle name
speciality 80 n.
one's money's worth
purchase 792 n.
one's number being up
dying 361 adj.
one's own
possessed 773 adj.
loved one 887 n.
darling 890 n.
one's own boss
independent 744 adj.
one's own devices
scope 744 n.
one's own hand
no imitation 21 n.
script 586 n.
one's own man/ woman, be
will 595 vb.
be free 744 vb.
one's own side
colleague 707 n.
one's own way
scope 744 n.
one's own worst enemy, be
have trouble 731 vb.
one's people
family 11 n.
one's solemn word
promise 764 n.
one's stars
destiny 155 n.
one-step
dance 837 n.
one step at a time
caution 858 n.
one's undoing
ruin 165 n.
one's word
affirmation 532 n.
one thing after another
continuity 71 n.
onetime
prior 119 adj.
resigning 753 adj.
one-track mind
attention 455 n.
narrow mind 481 n.
one up
superior 34 adj.
successful 727 adj.
oneupmanship
sagacity 498 n.
tactics 688 n.
on every side
around 230 adv.
one-way
directed 281 adj.
one-way street
traffic control 305 n.
road 624 n.
one with, be
be identical 13 vb.
on faith
credibly 485 adv.
on foot
continuing 108 adj.
happening 154 adj.
operative 173 adj.
on foot 267 adv.
in question 452 adv.
preparatory 669 adj.
on form, be
be skilful 694 vb.
ongoing
continuous 71 adj.
unceasing 146 adj.
ongoing situation
present time 121 n.
on good terms
concordant 710 adj.
friendly 880 adj.
on guard
vigilant 457 adj.
on hand
businesslike 622 adj.
possessed 773 adj.
on hand, be
serve 742 vb.
on heat
desiring 859 adj.
lecherous 951 adj.
on high
aloft 209 adv.
elevated 310 adj.
on hire
offering 759 adj.
on holiday
at rest 683 adv.
on horseback
on foot 267 adv.
on ice
preserved 666 adj.
on impulse
capriciously 604 adv.
on information received
reportedly 524 adv.
onion
sphere 252 n.
vegetable 301 n.
condiment 389 n.
on its last legs
weakened 163 adj.
dilapidated 655 adj.
on its merits
rightly 913 adv.
on lease
pledged 767 adj.
on leave
absent 190 adj.
leisurely 681 adj.
on-line
computerized 86 adj.
on loan
on loan 784 adv.
on location
here 189 adv.
absent 190 adj.
onlooker
spectator 441 n.
only
inconsiderable 33 adj.
slightly 33 adv.
simply 44 adv.
one 88 adj.
singly 88 adv.
only human
frail 934 adj.
only just
slightly 33 adv.
only sometimes
seldom 140 adv.
only yesterday
past time 125 n.
newly 126 adv.
on no account
denyingly 760 adv.
on oath
affirmative 532 adj.
promissory 764 adj.
on-off
discontinuous 72 adj.
fitful 142 adj.
onomasiology
linguistics 557 n.
etymology 559 n.
onomastic
naming 561 adj.
onomatopoeia
mimicry 20 n.
on one's back
horizontally 216 adv.
sick 651 adj.
on one's beam ends
impotent 161 adj.
grounded 728 adj.
poor 801 adj.
on one's best behaviour, be
behave 688 vb.
be courteous 884 vb.
on one's doorstep
near 200 adv.
on one's feet
vertical 215 adj.
respectful 920 adj.
on one's guard, be
be careful 457 vb.
be cautious 858 vb.
on one's hands
superfluous 637 adj.
possessed 773 adj.
on one's high horse
prideful 871 adj.
on one side
obliquely 220 adv.
sideways 239 adv.
distorted 246 adj.
on one's knees
respectful 920 adj.
worshipping 981 adj.
on one's last legs
dying 361 adj.
deteriorated 655 adj.
fatigued 684 adj.
on one's legs
vertical 215 adj.
healthy 650 adj.
on one's legs, be
orate 579 vb.
on one's mind
in mind 449 adv.
on one's own
alone 88 adj.
friendless 883 adj.
on one's own initiative
voluntary 597 adj.
on one's toes
attentive 455 adj.
vigilant 457 adj.
active 678 adj.
lively 819 adj.
on one's uppers
poor 801 adj.
on one's way
on the move 265 adv.
forward 285 adv.
on one's way, be
start out 296 vb.

on pain of death
threateningly 900 adv.
on parole
restrained 747 adj.
promissory 764 adj.
on pins and needles, be
suffer 825 vb.
on probation
experimentally 461 adv.
on purpose
purposely 617 adv.
on record
recorded 548 adj.
on record 548 adv.
on reflection
in mind 449 adv.
on remand
imprisoned 747 adj.
onrush
outbreak 176 n.
on second thoughts
in mind 449 adv.
onset
beginning 68 n.n.
approach 289 n.
arrival 295 n.
attack 712 n.
on Shanks's pony/mare
on foot 267 adv.
onshore
coastal 344 adj.
on show
visibly 443 adv.
shown 522 adj.
onside
laterality 239 n.
sinistrality 242 n.
onslaught
attack 712 n.
malediction 899 n.
censure 924 n.
on spec
experimentally 461 adv.
at random 618 adv.
on stage
on stage 594 adv.
on stream
dynamic 160 adj.
on strike
inactive 679 adj.
on tap
on the spot 189 adj.
provisioning 633 adj.
enough 635 adj.
on tenterhooks
expectant 507 adj.
on the agenda
impending 155 adj.
in question 452 adv.
on the air
published 528 adj.
on the anvil
preparatory 669 adj.
on the stocks 726 adv.
on the ball
attentive 455 adj.
intelligent 498 adj.
on the beam
straight 249 adj.
in flight 271 adv.
on the beat
synchronous 123 adj.
on foot 267 adv.
on the best of terms
friendly 880 adj.
on the books
on record 548 adv.
on the bottle
drunken 949 adj.
on the brain
in mind 449 adv.
in question 452 adv.
on the breadline
poor 801 adj.
on the brink of
almost 33 adv.
near 200 adv.
on the cards
impending 155 adj.
probable 471 adj.
expected 507 adj.
on the carpet
disapproved 924 adj.
on the contrary
contrarily 14 adv.
no 489 adv.
on the crest
beyond 34 adv.
aloft 209 adv.
atop 213 adv.
on the cross
obliquely 220 adv.
on the danger list
sick 651 adj.
on the defensive
avoiding 620 adj.
defending 713 adj.
nervous 854 adj.
on the dole
nonactive 677 adj.
on the dot
instantaneously 116 adv.
cash down 804 adv.
on the downgrade
deteriorated 655 adj.
unprosperous 731 adj.
on the edge of one's chair
expectantly 507 adv.
on the face of it
apparently 445 adv.
probably 471 adv.
on the fiddle
deceiving 542 adj.
thieving 788 adj.
dishonest 930 adj.
on the go
busy 678 adj.
on the heels of
behind 284 adv.
on the hook
in difficulties 700 adj.
on the horizon
impending 155 adj.
afar 199 adv.
expected 507 adj.
on the horns of a dilemma
doubting 474 adj.
on the house
cheaply 812 adv.
on the level
artless 699 adj.
honourable 929 adj.
on the lookout (for)
attentive 455 adj.
expectant 507 adj.
pursuant to 619 adv.
on the make
acquiring 771 adj.
selfish 932 adj.
on the map
renowned 866 adj.
on the mat
disapproved 924 adj.
on the mend
restored 656 adj.
on the move
on the move 265 adv.
busy 678 adj.
on the nail
at present 121 adv.
cash down 804 adv.
on the nod
unanimously 488 adv.
easily 701 adv.
on the off-chance
at random 618 adv.
on the offensive
attacking 712 adj.
on the other hand
contrarily 14 adv.
in return 31 adv.
conversely 467 adv.
in rebuttal 479 adv.
on the point of
prospectively 124 adv.
on the quiet
stealthily 525 adv.
on the qui vive
vigilant 457 adj.
on the rack
expectant 507 adj.
suffering 825 adj.
on the raw
to the quick 374 adv.
on the raw 819 adv.
on the razor's edge
endangered 661 adj.
on the receiving end
suffering 825 adj.
on the record
evidential 466 adj.
on the rocks
cooled 382 adj.
endangered 661 adj.
grounded 728 adj.
on the run
on the move 265 adv.
endangered 661 adj.
on the same wavelength, be
accord 24 vb.
on the scent
discovering 484 adj.
pursuing 619 adj.
on the scrapheap
destroyed 165 adj.
on the shelf
remaining 41 adj.
unwanted 860 adj.
unwedded 895 adj.
on the side of the angels
just 913 adj.
virtuous 933 adj.
on the spot
instantaneously 116 adv.
at present 121 adv.
on the spot 189 adj.
on the spur of the moment
instantaneously 116 adv.
extempore 609 adv.
on the square
honourable 929 adj.
on the stocks
happening 154 adj.
preparatory 669 adj.
on the stocks 726 adv.
on the streets, be
be impure 951 vb.
on the strength of
credibly 485 adv.
on the tip of one's tongue
near 200 adv.
forgotten 506 adj.
on the track (of)
discovering 484 adj.
pursuant to 619 adv.
on the trot
continuously 71 adv.
busy 678 adj.
on the up and up
successful 727 adj.
prosperous 730 adj.
honourable 929 adj.
on the verge of
almost 33 adv.
near 200 adv.
hoping 852 adj.
on the waggon
sober 948 adj.
on the warpath
attacking 712 adj.

on the way
in transit 272 adv.
towards 281 adv.
forward 285 adv.
en passant 305 adv.
via 624 adv.
on the way out
deteriorated 655 adj.
on the way to
convertibly 147 adv.
nearly 200 adv.
on the whole
on an average 30 adv.
on the whole 52 adv.
on the wing
on the move 265 adv.
in flight 271 adv.
on the wrong foot
inexpectant 508 adj.
unprepared 670 adj.
on the wrong tack
mistaken 495 adj.
on thin ice
endangered 661 adj.
on time
early 135 adj.
timely 137 adj.
on tiptoe
aloft 209 adv.
stealthy 525 adj.
on to
knowing 490 adj.
on to a good thing, be
have luck 730 vb.
ontology
existence 1 n.
philosophy 449 n.
on top
supreme 34 adj.
aloft 209 adv.
atop 213 adv.
successful 727 adj.
on top of the world
pleased 824 adj.
on trial
on trial 459 adv.
litigated 959 adj.
on trust
credibly 485 adv.
onus
demonstration 478 n.
encumbrance 702 n.
duty 917 n.
on velvet
in comfort 376 adv.
prosperous 730 adj.
on view
visibly 443 adv.
appearing 445 adj.
onward
forward 285 adv.
onyx
gem 844 n.
oodles
great quantity 32 n.
oomph
vigorousness 174 n.
ooze
move slowly 278 vb.
exude 298 vb.
be wet 341 vb.
ocean 343 n.
marsh 347 n.
flow 350 vb.vb.
semiliquidity 354 n.
— out
be disclosed 526 vb.
oozing
full 54 adj.
oozy
marshy 347 adj.
flowing 350 adj.
opacity
obfuscation 421 n.
opacity 423 n.
imperspicuity 568 n.
opal
semitransparency 424 n.
variegation 437 n.
gem 844 n.
opalescent
semitransparent 424 adj.
iridescent 437 adj.
opaque
unlit 418 adj.
opaque 423 adj.
unclear 568 adj.
opaque glass
screen 421 n.
op art
art 551 n.
open
cut 46 vb.
disunite 46 vb.
come before 64 vb.
auspicate 68 vb.
begin 68 vb.
expand 197 vb.
spaced 201 adj.
broad 205 adj.
uncover 229 vb.
open 263 adj.vb.
air 340 n.
campestral 348 adj.
visible 443 adj.
uncertain 474 adj.
manifest 522 adj.
disclosed 526 adj.
veracious 540 adj.
dramatize 594 vb.
artless 699 adj.
easy 701 adj.
unconditional 744 adj.
liberate 746 vb.
trustworthy 929 adj.
— an account (with)
trade 791 vb.
credit 802 vb.
— fire
initiate 68 vb.
shoot 287 vb.
fire at 712 vb.
give battle 718 vb.
— into
connect 45 vb.
— the door to
initiate 68 vb.
conduce 156 vb.
admit 299 vb.
permit 756 vb.
— the eyes (of)
disclose 526 vb.
educate 534 vb.
— the floodgates
empty 300 vb.
permit 756 vb.
— the mind
educate 534 vb.
— up
initiate 68 vb.
cause 156 vb.
accelerate 277 vb.
manifest 522 vb.
disclose 526 vb.
make better 654 vb.
facilitate 701 vb.
open air
exteriority 223 n.
salubrity 652 n.
open and shut case
certainty 473 n.
facility 701 n.
open arms
reception 299 n.
friendliness 880 n.
opencast mining
excavation 255 n.
open country
space 183 n.
plain 348 n.
open door
way in 297 n.
open-door policy
ingress 297 n.
market 796 n.
opener
opener 263 n.
instrument 628 n.
open-eyed
attentive 455 adj.
expectant 507 adj.
open hand
liberality 813 n.
open-handed
plenteous 635 adj.
liberal 813 adj.
rewarding 962 adj.
open-hearted
trustworthy 929 adj.
open-heart surgery
surgery 658 n.
open house
liberality 813 n.
sociability 882 n.
opening
prelude 66 n.
debut 68 n.
entrance 68 n.
opportunity 137 n.
room 183 n.
opening 263 n.
open space 263 n.
way in 297 n.
job 622 n.
open letter
publicity 528 n.
correspondence 588 n.
deprecation 762 n.
openly
openly 263 adv.
manifestly 522 adv.
publicly 528 adv.
artlessly 699 adv.
open market
scope 744 n.
trade 791 n.
open marriage
type of marriage 894 n.
open-minded
doubting 474 adj.
choiceless 606 adj.
just 913 adj.
open-mouthed
expectant 507 adj.
wondering 864 adj.
open question
uncertainty 474 n.
open secret
knowledge 490 n.
publicity 528 n.
open sesame
opener 263 n.
discovery 484 n.
instrument 628 n.
spell 983 n.
open space
space 183 n.
open space 263 n.
plain 348 n.
open to
liable 180 adj.
vulnerable 661 adj.
open to, be
be possible 469 vb.
Open University
broadcasting 531 n.
academy 539 n.
open verdict
dubiety 474 n.
open vowel
voice 577 n.
openwork
needlework 844 n.
ornamental art 844 n.
opera
vocal music 412 n.

operable
possible 469 adj.
restored 656 adj.
medical 658 adj.
opera buff
enthusiast 504 n.
playgoer 594 n.
opera glasses
telescope 442 n.
operagoer
musician 413 n.
playgoer 594 n.
opera house
theatre 594 n.
opera singer
vocalist 413 n.
actor 594 n.
operate
operate 173 vb.
motivate 612 vb.
function 622 vb.
be instrumental 628 vb.
doctor 658 vb.
use 673 vb.
do 676 vb.
deal with 688 vb.
speculate 791 vb.
— to
conduce 156 vb.
operatic
musical 412 adj.
dramatic 594 adj.
operating theatre
hospital 658 n.
operation
agency 173 n.
instrumentality 628 n.
surgery 658 n.
undertaking 672 n.
deed 676 n.
labour 682 n.
operational
operative 173 adj.
prepared 669 adj.
operational research
policy 623 n.
management 689 n.
operations
warfare 718 n.
operations room
plan 623 n.
operative
powerful 160 adj.
operative 173 adj.
instrumental 628 adj.
machinist 630 n.
worker 686 n.
operator
machinist 630 n.
doer 676 n.
agent 686 n.
merchant 794 n.
operculum
covering 226 n.
operetta
vocal music 412 n.
ophidian
reptile 365 n.
animal 365 adj.
ophthalmia
dim sight 440 n.
ophthalmic
seeing 438 adj.
ophthalmology
medical art 658 n.
ophthalmoscope
optical device 442 n.
opiate
moderator 177 n.
soporific 679 n.
opine
opine 485 vb.
opinion
idea 451 n.
estimate 480 n.
bias 481 n.
opinion 485 n.
supposition 512 n.
repute 866 n.
opinionated
positive 473 adj.
narrow-minded 481 adj.
believing 485 adj.
obstinate 602 adj.
vain 873 adj.
opinion poll
vote 605 n.
opium
moderator 177 n.
anaesthetic 375 n.
drug 658 n.
poison 659 n.
soporific 679 n.
drug-taking 949 n.
opium-eater
idler 679 n.
opossum
mammal 365 n.
opponent
dissentient 489 n.
opponent 705 n.
enemy 881 n.
disapprover 924 n.
opportune
circumstantial 8 adj.
apt 24 adj.
opportune 137 adj.
advisable 642 adj.
opportunism
good policy 642 n.
improbity 930 n.
opportunist
tergiversator 603 n.
enterprising 672 adj.
dishonest 930 adj.
egotist 932 n.
opportunity
juncture 8 n.
present time 121 n.
opportunity 137 n.
fair chance 159 n.
possibility 469 n.
good policy 642 n.
facility 701 n.
scope 744 n.
oppose
dissent 489 vb.
be obstructive 702 vb.
oppose 704 vb.
resist 715 vb.
deprecate 762 vb.
be inimical 881 vb.
(See **opposition** *)*
opposite
correlative 12 adj.
contrary 14 adj.
difference 15 n.
inverted 221 adj.
frontal 237 adj.
opposite 240 adj.
directed 281 adj.
countervailing 467 adj.
opposing 704 adj.
opposite camp
opponent 705 n.
opposite number
correlation 12 n.
compeer 28 n.
opposite poles
contraposition 240 n.
opposites
polarity 14 n.
opposites 704 n.
opposition
disagreement 25 n.
counteraction 182 n.
contraposition 240 n.
doubt 486 n.
dissent 489 n.
unwillingness 598 n.
hindrance 702 n.
opposition 704 n.
dissension 709 n.
resistance 715 n.
disobedience 738 n.
deprecation 762 n.
enmity 881 n.
opposition, the
dissentient 489 n.
opponent 705 n.
malcontent 829 n.
oppress
suppress 165 vb.
ill-treat 645 vb.
oppress 735 vb.
impress 821 vb.
torment 827 vb.
oppression
severity 735 n.
subjection 745 n.
dejection 834 n.
oppressive
exorbitant 32 adj.
violent 176 adj.
warm 379 adj.
oppressive 735 adj.
frightening 854 adj.
inimical 881 adj.
cruel 898 adj.
lawless 954 adj.
oppressor
bane 659 n.
tyrant 735 n.
opprobrious
degrading 867 adj.
opprobrium
slur 867 n.
opsimath
learner 538 n.
opt (for)
choose 605 vb.
optical
luminous 417 adj.
seeing 438 adj.
optical device
convexity 253 n.
optics 417 n.
optical device 442 n.
optical illusion
insubstantial thing 4 n.
visual fallacy 440 n.
optical instrument
optical device 442 n.
optician
doctor 658 n.
optic nerve
eye 438 n.
optics
electronics 160 n.
optics 417 n.
eye 438 n.
vision 438 n.
optical device 442 n.
optimism
overestimation 482 n.
expectation 507 n.
cheerfulness 833 n.
hope 852 n.
optimist
hoper 852 n.
optimistic
optimistic 482 adj.
(See **optimism** *)*
optimum
best 644 adj.
option
will 595 n.
willingness 597 n.
choice 605 n.
optional
volitional 595 adj.
voluntary 597 adj.
choosing 605 adj.
opulence
wealth 800 n.
opulent
plenteous 635 adj.
rich 800 adj.
opus
product 164 n.
musical piece 412 n.
opuscule
book 589 n.
or
orange 432 n.
heraldry 547 n.

oracle
answer 460 n.
certainty 473 n.
doctrinaire 473 n.
sage 500 n.
oracle 511 n.
equivocalness 518 n.
latency 523 n.
adviser 691 n.
holy place 990 n.
oracular
uncertain 474 adj.
aphoristic 496 adj.
wise 498 adj.
predicting 511 adj.
puzzling 517 adj.
equivocal 518 adj.
unclear 568 adj.
godlike 965 adj.
oral
vocal 577 adj.
speaking 579 adj.
orange
fruit 301 n.
orange 432 n., adj.
orangeade
soft drink 301 n.
orangery
arbour 194 n.
garden 370 n.
orang-outang
mammal 365 n.
orate
orate 579 vb.
oration
lecture 534 n.
oration 579 n.
allocution 583 n.
orator
preacher 537 n.
phrasemonger 574 n.
speaker 579 n.
motivator 612 n.
oratorical
figurative 519 adj.
rhetorical 574 adj.
eloquent 579 adj.
oratorio
vocal music 412 n.
oratory
style 566 n.
oratory 579 n.
church 990 n.
orb
region 184 n.
circle 250 n.
eye 438 n.
badge 547 n.
regalia 743 n.
orbit
influence 178 n.
orbit 250 n.
space travel 271 n.
fly 271 vb.
passage 305 n.
circle 314 vb.
rotate 315 vb.
function 622 n.
route 624 n.
circuit 626 n.
orbiter
satellite 321 n.
orc
elf 970 n.
orchard
wood 366 n.
garden 370 n.
orchestra
orchestra 413 n.
musical instrument 414 n.
theatre 594 n.
orchestral
musical 412 adj.
musicianly 413 adj.
orchestrate
compose 56 vb.
arrange 62 vb.
harmonize 410 vb.
compose music 413 vb.
ordain
decree 737 vb.
commission 751 vb.
make legal 953 vb.
be ecclesiastical 985 vb.
perform ritual 988 vb.
ordained
fated 596 adj.
clerical 986 adj.
ordeal
experiment 461 n.
difficulty 700 n.
suffering 825 n.
painfulness 827 n.
order
uniformity 16 n.
order 60 n. vb.
serial place 73 n.
sort 77 n.
regularity 81 n.
send 272 vb.
judgment 480 n.
badge 547 n.
practice 610 n.
plan 623 vb.
require 627 vb.
precept 693 n.
community 708 n.
decoration 729 n.
command 737 n. vb.
compel 740 vb.
badge of rank 743 n.
paper money 797 n.
honours 866 n.
nobility 868 n.
title 870 n.
impose a duty 917 vb.
legislation 953 n.
sect 978 n.
monk 986 n.
ritual 988 n.
— away
dismiss 300 vb.
orderless
orderless 61 adj.
disarranged 63 adj.
unassembled 75 adj.
unconformable 84 adj.
amorphous 244 adj.
lax 734 adj.
unsightly 842 adj.
orderly
orderly 60 adj.
regular 81 adj.
careful 457 adj.
businesslike 622 adj.
planned 623 adj.
servant 742 n.
order of service
Christian rite 988 n.
order of the day
affairs 154 n.
predetermination 608 n.
practice 610 n.
policy 623 n.
command 737 n.
order paper
topic 452 n.
orders
holy orders 985 n.
ordinal
numerical 85 adj.
office-book 988 n.
ordinance
precept 693 n.
command 737 n.
legislation 953 n.
rite 988 n.
ordinand
pietist 979 n.
cleric 986 n.
ordinary
median 30 adj.
general 79 adj.
typical 83 adj.
heraldry 547 n.
usual 610 adj.
trivial 639 adj.
not bad 644 adj.
imperfect 647 adj.
middling 732 adj.
unastonishing 865 adj.
ordinate
coordinate 465 n.
ordination
mandate 751 n.
holy orders 985 n.
Christian rite 988 n.
ordnance
gun 723 n.
ordure
excrement 302 n.
dirt 649 n.
ore
source 156 n.
rock 344 n.
mineral 359 n.
materials 631 n.
oread
nymph 967 n.
organ
limb 53 n.
organ 414 n.
the press 528 n.
instrument 628 n.
church utensil 990 n.
organ-grinder
instrumentalist 413 n.
organic
intrinsic 5 adj.
such 7 adj.
structural 331 adj.
organic 358 adj.
organic chemistry
physics 319 n.
organic matter
matter 319 n.
organism 358 n.
organic remains
organism 358 n.
corpse 363 n.
organism
structure 331 n.
organism 358 n.
life 360 n.
organist
instrumentalist 413 n.
organization, organisation
arrangement 62 n.
structure 331 n.
management 689 n.
corporation 708 n.
(See **organize** *)*
organization man
conformist 83 n.
worker 686 n.
organize, organise
compose 56 vb.
order 60 vb.
regularize 62 vb.
produce 164 vb.
plan 623 vb.
organized, organised
organic 358 adj.
planned 623 adj.
organized knowledge
science 490 n.
organizer, organiser
planner 623 n.
organ loft
church interior 990 n.
orgasm
spasm 318 n.
excitation 821 n.
orgiastic
disorderly 61 adj.
sensual 944 adj.
orgy
feasting 301 n.
plenty 635 n.
festivity 837 n.
sensualism 944 n.

Orient
laterality 239 n.
oriental
lateral 239 adj.
directed 281 adj.
orientalize, orientalise
transform 147 vb.
orientate
orientate 281 vb.
orientation
situation 186 n.
laterality 239 n.
direction 281 n.
supposition 512 n.
orienteering
land travel 267 n.
direction 281 n.
sport 837 n.
orifice
entrance 68 n.
maw 194 n.
gap 201 n.
cavity 255 n.
orifice 263 n.
oriflamme
flag 547 n.
origami
sculpture 554 n.
origin
prototype 23 n.
origin 68 n.
source 156 n.
genealogy 169 n.
home 192 n.
original
intrinsic 5 adj.
unrelated 10 adj.
original 21 adj.
prototype 23 n.
first 68 adj.
nonconformist 84 n.
new 126 adj.
fundamental 156 adj.
imaginative 513 adj.
script 586 n.
originality
difference 15 n.
dissimilarity 19 n.
originality 21 n.n.
speciality 80 n.
nonconformity 84 n.
imagination 513 n.
originally
initially 68 adv.
original sin
heredity 5 n.
guilt 936 n.
originate
initiate 68 vb.
cause 156 vb.
produce 164 vb.
will 595 vb.
— from
result 157 vb.
originative
generative 167 adj.
originator
cause 156 n.
producer 164 n.
planner 623 n.
Orion
star 321 n.
orisons
prayers 981 n.
orlop (deck)
layer 207 n.
ormolu
sham 542 n.
ornamental art 844 n.
Ormuzd
the Deity 965 n.
ornament
trope 519 n.
ornament 574 n.vb.
make better 654 vb.
beauty 841 n.
ornamentation 844 n.
decorate 844 vb.
ornamental
variegated 437 adj.
painted 553 adj.
useless 641 adj.
beautiful 841 adj.
ornamental 844 adj.
ornamental art
beautification 843 n.
ornamental art 844 n.
ornamentation
adjunct 40 n.
covering 226 n.
coil 251 n.
spectacle 445 n.
ornament 574 n.
beautification 843 n.
ornamentation 844 n.
ostentation 875 n.
ornate
figurative 519 adj.
stylistic 566 adj.
ornate 574 adj.
splendid 841 adj.
ornamented 844 adj.
affected 850 adj.
ornithology
zoology 367 n.
orography
earth sciences 321 n.
orological
alpine 209 adj.
orotund
rhetorical 574 adj.
ostentatious 875 adj.
orphan
survivor 41 n.
defenceless 161 adj.
derelict 779 n.
deprive 786 vb.
orphanage
retreat 192 n.
orphaned
remaining 41 adj.
alone 88 adj.
Orpheus
musician 413 n.
poetry 593 n.
orphrey, orfray
vestments 989 n.
orrery
astronomy 321 n.
map 551 n.
orris root
scent 396 n.
orthodontist
doctor 658 n.
orthodox
conformable 83 adj.
believing 485 adj.
creedal 485 adj.
habitual 610 adj.
orthodox 976 adj.
pious 979 adj.
worshipping 981 adj.
ecclesiastical 985 adj.
Orthodox Church
Christendom 976 n.
orthodoxy
orthodoxy 976 n.
(See **orthodox** *)*
orthographic projection
map 551 n.
orthography
spelling 558 n.
orthopaedics
medical art 658 n.
therapy 658 n.
orthoptic
seeing 438 adj.
Oscar award
trophy 729 n.
oscillate
vary 152 vb.
deviate 282 vb.
oscillate 317 vb.
be agitated 318 vb.
be irresolute 601 vb.
be drunk 949 vb.
oscillation
correlation 12 n.
periodicity 141 n.
fitfulness 142 n.
reversion 148 n.
changeableness 152 n.
hanging object 217 n.
laterality 239 n.
motion 265 n.
oscillation 317 n.
oscillator
electronics 160 n.
oscitation
sleepiness 679 n.
osculation
contiguity 202 n.
endearment 889 n.
osier
ligature 47 n.
Osiris
Egyptian deities 967 n.
osmosis
ingress 297 n.
passage 305 n.
osprey
bird 365 n.
trimming 844 n.
osseous
hard 326 adj.
Ossianic
rhetorical 574 adj.
ossified
antiquated 127 adj.
hard 326 adj.
ossify
be dense 324 vb.
harden 326 vb.
ossuary
interment 364 n.
ostensible
appearing 445 adj.
plausible 471 adj.
manifest 522 adj.
ostensible 614 adj.
ostensible motive
pretext 614 n.
ostentation
spectacle 445 n.
manifestation 522 n.
publicity 528 n.
prodigality 815 n.
ornamentation 844 n.
affectation 850 n.
vanity 873 n.
ostentation 875 n.
ostentatious
ostentatious 875 adj.
osteoarthritis
rheumatism 651 n.
osteopath
doctor 658 n.
ostler
animal husbandry 369 n.
servant 742 n.
ostracism
exclusion 57 n.
penalty 963 n.
ostracize, ostracise
exclude 57 vb.
eject 300 vb.
make unwelcome 883 vb.
disapprove 924 vb.
ostrich
speeder 277 n.
bird 365 n.
avoider 620 n.
ostrich-like
nonactive 677 adj.
Othello
jealousy 911 n.
other
different 15 adj.
other, the
extrinsicality 6 n.

other extreme
contrariety 14 n.
other half
analogue 18 n.
other man/woman, the
jealousy 911 n.
otherness
extrinsicality 6 n.
difference 15 n.
other ranks
inferior 35 n.
nonentity 639 n.
soldiery 722 n.
other self
identity 13 n.
analogue 18 n.
close friend 880 n.
other side
contrariety 14 n.
exteriority 223 n.
rear 238 n.
contraposition 240 n.
opposition 704 n.
enemy 881 n.
other side of the coin, the
variant 15 n.
other times
different time 122 n.
other way round
inversely 221 adv.
otherwise
contrarily 14 adv.
differently 15 adv.
otherwise engaged
distracted 456 adj.
otherwise engaged, be
be engaged 138 vb.
other world
immateriality 320 n.
otherworldly
immaterial 320 adj.
psychic 447 adj.
imaginative 513 adj.
pious 979 adj.
otiose
unproductive 172 adj.
otology
ear 415 n.
otoscope
hearing aid 415 n.
otter
mammal 365 n.
otterhound
hunter 619 n.
ottoman
seat 218 n.
oubliette
hiding-place 527 n.
lockup 748 n.
ought
be due 915 vb.
ouija board
spiritualism 984 n.
ounce
small quantity 33 n.
weighing 322 n.
Our Father
prayers 981 n.
Our Lady
Madonna 968 n.
ourselves
self 80 n.
humankind 371 n.
oust
eject 300 vb.
depose 752 vb.
deprive 786 vb.
ouster
loss of right 916 n.
out
absent 190 adj.
expanded 197 adj.
externally 223 adv.
open 263 adj.
astray 282 adv.
eject 300 vb.
misjudging 481 adj.
inexact 495 adj.
mistaken 495 adj.
matured 669 adj.
inactive 679 adj.
sleepy 679 adj.
disapproved 924 adj.
dead drunk 949 adj.
out and out
consummate 32 adj.
completely 54 adv.
out at elbows
dilapidated 655 adj.
beggarly 801 adj.
outback
space 183 n.
district 184 n.
outbid
outdo 306 vb.
bargain 791 vb.
outboard
exterior 223 adj.
outbreak
disorder 61 n.
beginning 68 n.
outbreak 176 n.
egress 298 n.
revolt 738 n.
excitable state 822 n.
outbuilding
small house 192 n.
outburst
outbreak 176 n.
egress 298 n.
excitable state 822 n.
anger 891 n.
outcast
excluded 57 adj.
derelict 779 n.
outcast 883 n.
bad person 938 n.
outcaste
commoner 869 n.
outcast 883 n.
outclass
be superior 34 vb.
outdo 306 vb.
defeat 727 vb.
outclassed
inferior 35 adj.
defeated 728 adj.
out cold
insensible 375 adj.
outcome
event 154 n.
effect 157 n.
outcrop
layer 207 n.
projection 254 n.
outcropping
visible 443 adj.
outcry
loudness 400 n.
cry 408 n.
lament 836 n.
disapprobation 924 n.
outdare
defy 711 vb.
be courageous 855 vb.
outdated
antiquated 127 adj.
outdistance
be distant 199 vb.
outstrip 277 vb.
progress 285 vb.
outdo 306 vb.
outdo
be superior 34 vb.
outdo 306 vb.
be cunning 698 vb.
defeat 727 vb.
outdoor(s)
exterior 223 adj.
salubrity 652 n.
outdoor life
sport 837 n.
outer
exterior 223 adj.
outer darkness
exclusion 57 n.
outer edge
farness 199 n.
edge 234 n.
outermost
exterior 223 adj.
outer space
infinity 107 n.
space 183 n.
exteriority 223 n.
universe 321 n.
outface
be resolute 599 vb.
resist 715 vb.
be courageous 855 vb.
be insolent 878 vb.
outfall
outflow 298 n.
outfit
all 52 n.
component 58 n.
unit 88 n.
clothing 228 n.
suit 228 n.
equipment 630 n.
party 708 n.
outfitter
clothier 228 n.
outflank
flank 239 vb.
outdo 306 vb.
defeat 727 vb.
outflow
outflow 298 n.
waterfall 350 n.
waste 634 n.
out for
intending 617 adj.
out for the count, be
knuckle under 721 vb.
out for thrills
excitable 822 adj.
outgoing
preceding 64 adj.
former 125 adj.
outgoing 298 adj.
flowing 350 adj.
resigning 753 adj.
sociable 882 adj.
outgoings
expenditure 806 n.
out-group
group 74 n.
outgrow
disaccustom 611 vb.
stop using 674 vb.
outgrowth
growth 157 n.
out-Herod Herod
be violent 176 vb.
exaggerate 546 vb.
outhouse
adjunct 40 n.
small house 192 n.
outing
land travel 267 n.
enjoyment 824 n.
amusement 837 n.
out in the cold
displaced 188 adj.
neglected 458 adj.
outlandish
extraneous 59 adj.
unconformable 84 adj.
ridiculous 849 adj.
wonderful 864 adj.
outlast
continue 108 vb.
outlast 113 vb.
stay 144 vb.
resist 715 vb.
outlaw
exclude 57 vb.
nonconformist 84 n.
prohibit 757 vb.
robber 789 n.
outcast 883 n.
make unwelcome 883 vb.
offender 904 n.
make illegal 954 vb.

condemn 961 vb.
outlawry
brigandage 788 n.
lawlessness 954 n.
outlay
waste 634 n.
expenditure 806 n.
outlet
orifice 263 n.
outlet 298 n.
outline
prototype 23 n.
incompleteness 55 n.
beginning 68 n.
outline 233 n.vb.
limit 236 n.
form 243 n.vb.
appearance 445 n.
suppose 512 vb.
map 551 n.
representation 551 n.
picture 553 n.
be concise 569 vb.
describe 590 vb.
compendium 592 n.
plan 623 n.
prepare 669 vb.
outlive
continue 108 vb.
outlast 113 vb.
stay 144 vb.
outlook
futurity 124 n.
destiny 155 n.
view 438 n.
opinion 485 n.
expectation 507 n.
conduct 688 n.
affections 817 n.
out loud
vocal 577 adj.
outlying
distant 199 adj.
exterior 223 adj.
outmanoeuvre
be superior 34 vb.
outdo 306 vb.
deceive 542 vb.
defeat 727 vb.
outmarch
outstrip 277 vb.
outdo 306 vb.
outmatched
defeated 728 adj.
outmoded
antiquated 127 adj.
useless 641 adj.
outnumber
be many 104 vb.
superabound 637 vb.
out of
akin 11 adj.
caused 157 adj.
born 360 adj.
out of a hat
casual 159 adj.
out of all proportion
extremely 32 adv.
exaggerated 546 adj.
out of bounds
too far 199 adv.
surpassing 306 adj.
prohibited 757 adj.
illegal 954 adj.
out of breath
voiceless 578 adj.
panting 684 adj.
out of character
unapt 25 adj.
out of circulation
powerless 161 adj.
out of commission
quiescent 266 adj.
disused 674 adj.
inactive 679 adj.
out of control
riotous 738 adj.
excited 821 adj.
out of countenance
dejected 834 adj.
humbled 872 adj.
out of court
wrong 914 adj.
out of danger
safe 660 adj.
out of date
anachronistic 118 adj.
antiquated 127 adj.
out of doors
exteriority 223 n.
air 340 n.
alfresco 340 adv.
salubrity 652 n.
out of earshot
too far 199 adv.
faintly 401 adv.
deaf 416 adj.
out of fashion
antiquated 127 adj.
unwonted 611 adj.
out of favour
unfortunate 731 adj.
disliked 861 adj.
inglorious 867 adj.
disapproved 924 adj.
out of focus
indistinct 444 adj.
out of gear
orderless 61 adj.
inexact 495 adj.
out of hand
instantaneously 116 adv.
difficult 700 adj.
out of harm's way
safe 660 adj.
under shelter 660 adv.
out of hearing
too far 199 adv.
deaf 416 adj.
out of humour
sullen 893 adj.
out of joint
unapt 25 adj.
orderless 61 adj.
evil 616 adj.
out of keeping
unapt 25 adj.
unconformable 84 adj.
out of line
disorderly 61 adj.
unconformable 84 adj.
out of luck
unfortunate 731 adj.
out of mind
forgotten 506 adj.
out of one's depth
deeply 211 adv.
deficient 307 adj.
puzzled 517 adj.
in difficulties 700 adj.
unsuccessful 728 adj.
out of one's element
unconformable 84 adj.
misplaced 188 adj.
out of one's mind
insane 503 adj.
out of order
irrelevant 10 adj.
orderless 61 adj.
useless 641 adj.
unused 674 adj.
out of place
unapt 25 adj.
orderless 61 adj.
unconformable 84 adj.
misplaced 188 adj.
inexpedient 643 adj.
out of pocket
losing 772 adj.
expending 806 adj.
out of practice
clumsy 695 adj.
out of print
obliterated 550 adj.
bibliographical 589 adj.
out of proportion
unrelated 10 adj.
disagreeing 25 adj.
out of range
distant 199 adj.
too far 199 adv.
out of reach
inimitable 21 adj.
too far 199 adv.
surpassing 306 adj.
impracticable 470 adj.
out of season
anachronistic 118 adj.
scarce 636 adj.
out of shape
distorted 246 adj.
out of sight
too far 199 adv.
invisible 444 adj.
out of sorts
sick 651 adj.
dejected 834 adj.
sullen 893 adj.
out of step
nonuniform 17 adj.
unapt 25 adj.
disorderly 61 adj.
unconformable 84 adj.
out of the ark
antiquated 127 adj.
out of the frying pan into the fire
in adversity 731 adv.
aggravatedly 832 adv.
out of the habit
unhabituated 611 adj.
out of the ordinary
special 80 adj.
unusual 84 adj.
out of the picture
displaced 188 adj.
out of the question
impossible 470 adj.
unadmitted 489 adj.
rejected 607 adj.
refused 760 adj.
unpromising 853 adj.
undue 916 adj.
out of the running
impotent 161 adj.
unimportant 639 adj.
defeated 728 adj.
out of the way
unusual 84 adj.
removed 199 adj.
roundabout 626 adj.
secluded 883 adj.
out of the wood
safe 660 adj.
out of this world
prodigious 32 adj.
supreme 34 adj.
super 644 adj.
pleasurable 826 adj.
out of time
nonuniform 17 adj.
unapt 25 adj.
out of touch
displaced 188 adj.
removed 199 adj.
ignorant 491 adj.
out of true
oblique 220 adj.
out of tune
unconformable 84 adj.
discordant 411 adj.
out of turn
ill-timed 138 adj.
out of use
disused 674 adj.
out of work
unused 674 adj.

nonactive 677 adj.
out on a limb
vulnerable 661 adj.
outpace
outstrip 277 vb.
outdo 306 vb.
out-patient
sick person 651 n.
outplay
be superior 34 vb.
defeat 727 vb.
outpoint
be superior 34 vb.
defeat 727 vb.
outpost
farness 199 n.
front 237 n.
outpouring
outflow 298 n.
information 524 n.
diffuseness 570 n.
plenty 635 n.
output
data processing 86 n.
product 164 n.
production 164 n.
earnings 771 n.
outrage
violence 176 n.
evil 616 n.
ill-treat 645 vb.
misuse 675 n.
shame 867 vb.
huff 891 vb.
cruel act 898 n.
wrong 914 n.
indignity 921 n.
not respect 921 vb.
guilty act 936 n.
debauch 951 vb.
outrageous
exorbitant 32 adj.
violent 176 adj.
exaggerated 546 adj.
harmful 645 adj.
discreditable 867 adj.
cruel 898 adj.
disrespectful 921 adj.
heinous 934 adj.
outrange
be distant 199 vb.
outdo 306 vb.
outrank
be superior 34 vb.
come before 64 vb.
outré
unusual 84 adj.
exaggerated 546 adj.
ridiculous 849 adj.
wonderful 864 adj.
outreach
be superior 34 vb.
be distant 199 vb.
outride
outdo 306 vb.
outrider
precursor 66 n.
outrigger
projection 254 n.
rowing boat 275 n.
outright
completely 54 adv.
outrival
be superior 34 vb.
outdo 306 vb.
contend 716 vb.
outrun
outstrip 277 vb.
outdo 306 vb.
outset
start 68 n.
departure 296 n.
outshine
be superior 34 vb.
defeat 727 vb.
have a reputation 866 vb.
outside
extraneous 59 adj.
exteriority 223 n.
around 230 adv.
appearance 445 n.
duplicity 541 n.
outside broadcast
broadcast 531 n.
outside chance
improbability 472 n.
outside edge
limit 236 n.
outside of
exclusive of 57 adv.
outsider
misfit 25 n.
intruder 59 n.
nonconformist 84 n.
exteriority 223 n.
outcast 883 n.
outsize
unusual 84 adj.
huge 195 adj.
outskirts
entrance 68 n.
farness 199 n.
surroundings 230 n.
outsmart
deceive 542 vb.
be cunning 698 vb.
outspan
arrive 295 vb.
outspoken
undisguised 522 adj.
assertive 532 adj.
veracious 540 adj.
speaking 579 adj.
artless 699 adj.
disrespectful 921 adj.
outspread
broad 205 adj.
outstanding
remarkable 32 adj.
superior 34 adj.
remaining 41 adj.
notable 638 adj.
owed 803 adj.
outstare
humiliate 872 vb.
be insolent 878 vb.
outstay
outlast 113 vb.
— one's welcome
intrude 297 vb.
be tedious 838 vb.
outstretched
long 203 adj.
broad 205 adj.
outstrip
outstrip 277 vb.
progress 285 vb.
outdo 306 vb.
hasten 680 vb.
outtalk
be loquacious 581 vb.
out to
intending 617 adj.
out tray
compartment 194 n.
outvote
reject 607 vb.
outvoted
defeated 728 adj.
outward
extrinsic 6 adj.
exterior 223 adj.
appearing 445 adj.
outward bound
departing 296 adj.
outgoing 298 adj.
outward-looking
extrinsic 6 adj.
exterior 223 adj.
outwards
externally 223 adv.
outwear
outlast 113 vb.
outweigh
compensate 31 vb.
prevail 178 vb.
weigh 322 vb.
outwit
be superior 34 vb.
outdo 306 vb.
befool 542 vb.
be cunning 698 vb.
outwork
projection 254 n.
labour 682 n.
fortification 713 n.
outworn
antiquated 127 adj.
oval
arc 250 n.
round 250 adj.
ovary
genitalia 167 n.
flower 366 n.
ovate
round 250 adj.
ovation
trophy 729 n.
celebration 876 n.
applause 923 n.
oven
cookery 301 n.
furnace 383 n.
oven-ready
culinary 301 adj.
ready-made 669 adj.
over-
superior 34 adj.
beyond 34 adv.
remaining 41 adj.
ending 69 adj.
past 125 adj.
overact
exaggerate 546 vb.
act 594 vb.
be affected 850 vb.
overactive
active 678 adj.
overactivity
redundance 637 n.
overactivity 678 n.
exertion 682 n.
over again
twice 91 adv.
again 106 adv.
overall
inclusive 78 adj.
longwise 203 adv.
apron 228 n.
overalls
suit 228 n.
shelter 662 n.
overambitious
enterprising 672 adj.
rash 857 adj.
over and above
beyond 34 adv.
in addition 38 adv.
superfluous 637 adj.
over and done with
extinct 2 adj.
ending 69 adj.
past 125 adj.
forgotten 506 adj.
over and over
repeatedly 106 adv.
overarching
overlying 226 adj.
overattentive
servile 879 adj.
overawe
prevail 178 vb.
dominate 733 vb.
frighten 854 vb.
command respect 920 vb.
overbalance
be unequal 29 vb.
predominate 34 vb.
tumble 309 vb.
overbear
prevail 178 vb.
overbearing
oppressive 735 adj.
proud 871 adj.
insolent 878 adj.
overbid
overstep 306 vb.
bargain 791 vb.
overblown
ageing 131 adj.
expanded 197 adj.

overborne
defeated 728 adj.
subjected 745 adj.
overburden
load 193 vb.
make heavy 322 vb.
ill-treat 645 vb.
fatigue 684 vb.
overburdened
hindered 702 adj.
overbusy
meddling 678 adj.
overcall
outdo 306 vb.
overcareful
careful 457 adj.
overcast
cloudy 355 adj.
unlit 418 adj.
shadowy 419 adj.
cheerless 834 adj.
sullen 893 adj.
overcaution
irresolution 601 n.
cowardice 856 n.
overcharge
exaggerate 546 vb.
overcharge 811 vb.
overcloud
cloud 355 vb.
darken 418 vb.
overcoat
overcoat 228 n.
warm clothes 381 n.
overcoloured
exaggerated 546 adj.
overcome
prevail 178 vb.
overmaster 727 vb.
dejected 834 adj.
sadden 834 vb.
overcompensate
compensate 31 vb.
exaggerate 546 vb.
overconfidence
overestimation 482 n.
rashness 857 n.
overconscientious
observant 768 adj.
fastidious 862 adj.
overcritical
fastidious 862 adj.
disapproving 924 adj.
overcrop
waste 634 vb.
make insufficient 636 vb.
overcropping
misuse 675 n.
overcrowded
assembled 74 adj.
overcurious
inquisitive 453 adj.
obsessed 455 adj.
overdaring
rash 857 adj.
overdecorated
ornamented 844 adj.
overdelicate
prudish 950 adj.
overdevelop
enlarge 197 vb.
overdeveloped conscience
fastidiousness 862 n.
overdevout
pietistic 979 adj.
overdo
overstep 306 vb.
exaggerate 546 vb.
superabound 637 vb.
— it
be busy 678 vb.
work 682 vb.
be fatigued 684 vb.
flatter 925 vb.
overdone
tough 329 adj.
unsavoury 391 adj.
overrated 482 adj.
absurd 497 adj.
exaggerated 546 adj.
ornamented 844 adj.
affected 850 adj.
overdose
superfluity 637 n.
poison 659 n.
satiety 863 n.
overdraft
debt 803 n.
insolvency 805 n.
overdramatize, overdramatise
misrepresent 552 vb.
act 594 vb.
overdraw
exaggerate 546 vb.
misrepresent 552 vb.
be in debt 803 vb.
be prodigal 815 vb.
overdrawn
losing 722 adj.
indebted 803 adj.
overdressed
vulgar 847 adj.
overdrink
be intemperate 943 vb.
overdrive
power 160 n.
overdue
anachronistic 118 adj.
late 136 adj.
owed 803 adj.
overeager
willing 597 adj.
desiring 859 adj.
overeating
eating 301 n.
gluttony 947 n.
overegg the pudding
superabound 637 vb.
overelaborate
exaggerate 546 vb.
ornament 574 vb.
overemphasize, overemphasise
overrate 482 vb.
exaggerate 546 vb.
overenthusiastic
optimistic 482 adj.
lively 819 adj.
overestimate
misjudge 481 vb.
overrate 482 vb.
make important 638 vb.
praise 923 vb.
overestimation
overestimation 482 n.
exaggeration 546 n.
overexertion
overactivity 678 n.
fatigue 684 n.
overexposed
colourless 426 adj.
overextension
overstepping 306 n.
overactivity 678 n.
overfall
wave 350 n.
overfamiliar
impertinent 878 adj.
overfeeding
redundance 637 n.
gluttony 947 n.
overfill
fill 54 vb.
overstep 306 vb.
sate 863 vb.
overfishing
unproductiveness 172 n.
misuse 675 n.
overflow
be complete 54 vb.
be many 104 vb.
burst in 297 vb.
outflow 298 n.
flow out 298 vb.
encroach 306 vb.
moistening 341 n.
waterfall 350 n.
drain 351 n.
abound 635 vb.
redundance 637 n.
overflowing
great 32 adj.
full 54 adj.
overflowing heart
warm feeling 818 n.
overfly
fly 271 vb.
overfulfilment
plenitude 54 n.
overstepping 306 n.
superfluity 637 n.
overfull
sated 863 adj.
overgraze
make sterile 172 vb.
waste 634 vb.
overgrazing
misuse 675 n.
overgrown
whopping 32 adj.
expanded 197 adj.
vegetal 366 adj.
hindered 702 adj.
overhang
be to come 124 vb.
be high 209 vb.
hang 217 vb.
overlie 226 vb.
projection 254 n.
jut 254 vb.
overhasty
unprepared 670 adj.
hasty 680 adj.
irascible 892 adj.
overhaul
outstrip 277 vb.
outdo 306 vb.
be attentive 455 vb.
search 459 vb.
repair 656 vb.
restore 656 vb.
overhead
aloft 209 adv.
over head and ears
deeply 211 adv.
overhead projector
optical device 442 n.
overheads
cost 809 n.
overhear
hear 415 vb.
be informed 524 vb.
overheated
hot 379 adj.
insalubrious 653 adj.
excited 821 adj.
overhung
projecting 254 adj.
overinclined
desiring 859 adj.
overindulgence
eating 301 n.
overstepping 306 n.
redundance 637 n.
laxity 734 n.
intemperance 943 n.
sensualism 944 n.
overinsure
be cautious 858 vb.
overinterested
obsessed 455 adj.
overinvolved
complex 61 adj.
overjoyed
pleased 824 adj.
jubilant 833 adj.
overkill
exaggeration 546 n.
superfluity 637 n.
overland
on land 344 adv.
overlap
run on 71 vb.
be included 78 vb.

be contiguous 202 vb.
stratification 207 n.
overlie 226 vb.
encroach 306 vb.
touch 378 vb.
superfluity 637 n.
overlavish
prodigal 815 adj.
overlay
laminate 207 vb.
overlay 226 vb.
conceal 525 vb.
ornament 574 vb.
overleaf
rearward 238 adv.
against 240 adv.
overlie
overlie 226 vb.
overload
make heavy 322 vb.
exaggerate 546 vb.
ornament 574 vb.
encumbrance 702 n.
overloaded
bearing 273 adj.
redundant 637 adj.
ornamented 844 adj.
overlong
surpassing 306 adj.
tedious 838 adj.
overlook
be high 209 vb.
be inattentive 456 vb.
disregard 458 vb.
forget 506 vb.
not use 674 vb.
forgive 909 vb.
bewitch 983 vb.
overlord
superior 34 n.
master 741 n.
overlordship
governance 733 n.
position of authority 733 n.
overly
extremely 32 adv.
redundantly 637 adv.
overlying
overhanging 209 adj.
overlying 226 adj.
overmanning
superfluity 637 n.
overmaster
prevail 178 vb.
overmaster 727 vb.
dominate 733 vb.
subjugate 745 vb.
overmatch
be strong 162 vb.
overmaster 727 vb.
overmeasure
redundance 637 n.
overmerciful
lenient 736 adj.
overmighty
proud 871 adj.
lawless 954 adj.
overmodest
modest 874 adj.
prudish 950 adj.
overmuch
redundant 637 adj.
overnight
instantaneously 116 adv.
foregoing 125 adj.
newly 126 adv.
over one's dead body
never 109 adv.
obstinately 602 adv.
denyingly 760 adv.
over one's head
overhanging 209 adj.
deeply 211 adv.
puzzling 517 adj.
overoptimism
overestimation 482 n.
overpaid
rich 800 adj.
unwarranted 916 adj.
overpaint
coat 226 vb.
conceal 525 vb.
obliterate 550 vb.
overparticular
fastidious 862 adj.
overpayment
redundance 637 n.
undueness 916 n.
overpious
pietistic 979 adj.
overplay one's hand
misjudge 481 vb.
overplus
superfluity 637 n.
overpopulate
superabound 637 vb.
overpopulated
assembled 74 adj.
multitudinous 104 adj.
overpower
be strong 162 vb.
overmaster 727 vb.
overpowering
impressive 821 adj.
overpraise
overrate 482 vb.
exaggerate 546 vb.
redundance 637 n.
praise 923 n.vb.
flatter 925 vb.
overpraised
overrated 482 adj.
overpriced
dear 811 adj.
overprint
mark 547 vb.
obliterate 550 vb.
overproduce
superabound 637 vb.
overproof
intoxicating 949 adj.
overrate
overrate 482 vb.
exaggerate 546 vb.
make important 638 vb.
praise 923 vb.
overrated
overrated 482 adj.
unimportant 639 adj.
dear 811 adj.
overreach
outdo 306 vb.
deceive 542 vb.
be cunning 698 vb.
— oneself
misjudge 481 vb.
fail 728 vb.
over-refinement
fastidiousness 862 n.
override
prevail 178 vb.
overstep 306 vb.
confute 479 vb.
be resolute 599 vb.
overmaster 727 vb.
dominate 733 vb.
overriding
supreme 34 adj.
necessary 596 adj.
important 638 adj.
compelling 740 adj.
overrighteous
pietistic 979 adj.
overripe
ageing 131 adj.
soft 327 adj.
pulpy 356 adj.
imperfect 647 adj.
matured 669 adj.
overrule
dominate 733 vb.
abrogate 752 vb.
overruling
supreme 34 adj.
important 638 adj.
authoritative 733 adj.
overrun
fill 54 vb.
be many 104 vb.
pervade 189 vb.
encroach 306 vb.
overstep 306 vb.
attack 712 vb.
appropriate 786 vb.
oversanguine
optimistic 482 adj.
rash 857 adj.
overseas
abroad 59 adv.
removed 199 adj.
overseas mission
church ministry 985 n.
oversee
manage 689 vb.
overseer
manager 690 n.
oversell
exaggerate 546 vb.
oversensitive
sentient 374 adj.
sensitive 819 adj.
excitable 822 adj.
overset
demolish 165 vb.
invert 221 vb.
oversexed
desiring 859 adj.
lecherous 951 adj.
overshadow
be superior 34 vb.
be high 209 vb.
overlie 226 vb.
darken 418 vb.
bedim 419 vb.
overshoot
overstep 306 vb.
be clumsy 695 vb.
— the mark
overstep 306 vb.
exaggerate 546 vb.
oversight
inspection 438 n.
inattention 456 n.
negligence 458 n.
mistake 495 n.
management 689 n.
oversize
huge 195 adj.
oversleep
be late 136 vb.
lose a chance 138 vb.
be neglectful 458 vb.
fail in duty 918 vb.
oversoul
divineness 965 n.
overspecialization
narrow mind 481 n.
overspend
waste 634 vb.
be prodigal 815 vb.
overspill
redundance 637 n.
overspill estate
housing 192 n.
overspread
overlay 226 vb.
shadowy 419 adj.
overstaffing
expansion 197 n.
overstated
untrue 543 adj.
exaggerated 546 adj.
overstatement
overestimation 482 n.
affirmation 532 n.
untruth 543 n.
exaggeration 546 n.
magniloquence 574 n.
overstay
overstep 306 vb.

overstep
overstep 306 vb.
not observe 769 vb.
be intemperate 943 vb.
overstock
superabound 637 vb.
overstrain
fatigue 684 vb.
overstress
exaggerate 546 vb.
overstrung
lively 819 adj.
oversubscribe
superabound 637 vb.
oversubtle
sophistical 477 adj.
oversuspicious
unbelieving 486 adj.
overt
undisguised 522 adj.
overtake
be superior 34 vb.
outstrip 277 vb.
approach 289 vb.
outdo 306 vb.
endanger 661 vb.
hasten 680 vb.
overtask
misuse 675 vb.
fatigue 684 vb.
overtax
misuse 675 vb.
fatigue 684 vb.
oppress 735 vb.
levy 786 vb.
over the moon
pleased 824 adj.
overthrow
revolution 149 n.
demolish 165 vb.
fell 311 vb.
confute 479 vb.
bungling 695 n.
overmaster 727 vb.
unthrone 734 vb.
revolt 738 vb.
overtime
extra 40 n.
protraction 113 n.
exertion 682 n.
overtone
musical note 410 n.
latency 523 n.
overtop
be superior 34 vb.
be high 209 vb.
crown 213 vb.
overtrump
overmaster 727 vb.
overtrustful
credulous 487 adj.
overture(s)
prelude 66 n.
approach 289 n.
musical piece 412 n.
peace offering 719 n.
offer 759 n.
request 761 n.
friendship 880 n.
overturn
derange 63 vb.
revolutionize 149 vb.
demolish 165 vb.
invert 221 vb.
navigate 269 vb.
lowering 311 n.
overmaster 727 vb.
overuse
misuse 675 n.
overvalue
misjudge 481 vb.
overrate 482 vb.
overview
inspection 438 n.
overweening
proud 871 adj.
vain 873 adj.
insolent 878 adj.
overweight
inequality 29 n.
fleshy 195 adj.
make heavy 322 vb.
redundance 637 n.
overwhelm
fill 54 vb.
be many 104 vb.
be strong 162 vb.
destroy 165 vb.
be violent 176 vb.
confute 479 vb.
superabound 637 vb.
attack 712 vb.
defeat 727 vb.
impress 821 vb.
sadden 834 vb.
overwhelming
prodigious 32 adj.
violent 176 adj.
felt 818 adj.
impressive 821 adj.
wonderful 864 adj.
overwork
waste 634 vb.
use 673 vb.
misuse 675 vb.
be busy 678 vb.
exertion 682 n.
work 682 vb.
fatigue 684 vb.
overwrite
write 586 vb.
overwrought
fervent 818 adj.
excited 821 adj.
ovine
animal 365 adj.
oviparous
fertilized 167 adj.
ovoid
round 250 adj.
rotund 252 adj.
ovule
arc 250 n.
flower 366 n.
ovum
genitalia 167 n.
owe
be in debt 803 vb.
— everything to
result 157 vb.
— it to oneself
incur a duty 917 vb.
— nothing to
be unrelated 10 vb.
owed
owed 803 adj.
due 915 adj.
owing to
caused 157 adj.
attributed 158 adj.
owl
bird 365 n.
omen 511 n.
owlish
unintelligent 499 adj.
own
assent 488 vb.
confess 526 vb.
possess 773 vb.
— up
confess 526 vb.
owner
master 741 n.
owner 776 n.
ownerless
unpossessed 774 adj.
ownership
possession 773 n.
own goal
bungling 695 n.
owning no master
independent 744 adj.
ox
beast of burden 273 n.
cattle 365 n.
male animal 372 n.
oxblood
red 431 adj.
oxbow
curve 248 n.
lake 346 n.
Oxbridge
educational 534 adj.
academy 539 n.
Oxford accent
speech defect 580 n.
Oxford Group
sect 978 n.
Oxford Movement
Catholicism 976 n.
oxide
ash 381 n.
oxidization
dilapidation 655 n.
oxidize, oxidise
burn 381 vb.
oxtail
meat 301 n.
oxyacetylene lamp
furnace 383 n.
oxygen
air 340 n.
oxygenate
gasify 336 vb.
aerate 340 vb.
oxygen tent
respiration 352 n.
hospital 658 n.
oxymoron
misfit 25 n.
oyster
fish food 301 n.
marine life 365 n.
greyness 429 n.
taciturnity 582 n.
ozone
air 340 n.
salubrity 652 n.

P

pabulum
food 301 n.
pace
synchronize 123 vb.
long measure 203 n.
gait 265 n.
walk 267 vb.
velocity 277 n.
measure 465 vb.
pacemaker
living model 23 n.
substitute 150 n.
leader 690 n.
pachyderm
mammal 365 n.
pachydermatous
thick 205 adj.
unfeeling 375 adj.
thick-skinned 820 adj.
pacific
inert 175 adj.
moderate 177 adj.
concordant 710 adj.
peaceful 717 adj.
amiable 884 adj.
pacification
peace 717 n.
pacification 719 n.
treaty 765 n.
pacificatory
pacificatory 719 adj.
mediatory 720 adj.
pacifier
mediator 720 n.
pacifism
peace 717 n.
pacifist
pacifist 717 n.
pacify
assuage 177 vb.
concord 710 vb.
pacify 719 vb.
mediate 720 vb.
tranquillize 823 vb.
content 828 vb.

pack
great quantity 32 n.
all 52 n.
fill 54 vb.
group 74 n.
stow 187 vb.
load 193 vb.
cover 226 vb.
line 227 vb.
be dense 324 vb.
animal 365 n.
fake 541 vb.
hunter 619 n.
store 632 vb.
make ready 669 vb.
encumbrance 702 n.
plaything 837 n.

— a punch
be strong 162 vb.
— in/into
fill 54 vb.
load 193 vb.
insert 303 vb.
— the cards
deceive 542 vb.
— the jury
do wrong 914 vb.
predetermine 608 vb.
— them in
bring together 74 vb.
— tight
load 193 vb.
make smaller 198 vb.
— up
decamp 296 vb.
be fatigued 684 vb.
fail 728 vb.
package
bunch 74 n.
package deal
inclusion 78 n.
unit 88 n.
packaging
receptacle 194 n.
wrapping 226 n.
lining 227 n.
packed
firm 45 adj.
full 54 adj.
assembled 74 adj.
packed house
playgoer 594 n.
packed jury
predetermination 608 n.
injustice 914 n.
packed lunch
meal 301 n.
packer
preparer 669 n.
worker 686 n.
packet
great quantity 32 n.
bunch 74 n.
small box 194 n.
ship 275 n.
store 632 n.
wealth 800 n.
packhorse
beast of burden 273 n.
packing
location 187 n.
lining 227 n.
packing case
box 194 n.
storage 632 n.
pack of lies
untruth 543 n.
pact
agreement 24 n.
compact 765 n.
pad
strengthen 162 vb.
abode 192 n.
load 193 vb.
enlarge 197 vb.
foot 214 n.
seat 218 n.
line 227 vb.
walk 267 vb.
saddle horse 273 n.
softness 327 n.
faintness 401 n.
be diffuse 570 vb.
stationery 586 n.
shelter 662 n.
— out
augment 36 vb.
be diffuse 570 vb.
padded cell
lunatic asylum 503 n.
shelter 662 n.
padding
adjunct 40 n.
lining 227 n.
stopper 264 n.
softness 327 n.
warm clothes 381 n.
pleonasm 570 n.
superfluity 637 n.
paddle
be in motion 265 vb.
walk 267 vb.
propeller 269 n.
row 269 vb.
swim 269 vb.
propellant 287 n.
be wet 341 vb.
spank 963 vb.vb.
— one's own canoe
behave 688 vb.
be free 744 vb.
paddle steamer
ship 275 n.
paddle wheel
propeller 269 n.
paddling
aquatics 269 n.
paddock
enclosure 235 n.
paddy
anger 891 n.
Paddy
native 191 n.
paddyfield
farm 370 n.
paddy wagon
vehicle 274 n.
Padishah
sovereign 741 n.
padlock
fastening 47 n.
lockup 748 n.
padre
title 870 n.
cleric 986 n.
paean
rejoicing 835 n.
celebration 876 n.
applause 923 n.
hymn 981 n.n.
paediatrician
doctor 658 n.
paediatrics
medical art 658 n.
paella
dish 301 n.
pagan
heathen 974 n.
profane 980 adj.
idolater 982 n.
paganism
ignorance 491 n.
antichristianity 974 n.
impiety 980 n.
idolatry 982 n.
page
part 53 n.
courier 529 n.
mark 547 vb.
edition 589 n.
retainer 742 n.
bridal party 894 n.
pageant
procession 71 n.
spectacle 445 n.
pageant 875 n.
pageantry
ostentation 875 n.
page boy
servant 742 n.
pagination
numeration 86 n.
pagoda
temple 990 n.
paid
subject 745 adj.
gainful 771 adj.
receiving 782 adj.
expended 806 adj.
paid for
bought 792 adj.
pail
vessel 194 n.
pain
pain 377 n.
give pain 377 vb.
badness 645 n.
illness 651 n.
suffering 825 n.
painfulness 827 n.
hurt 827 vb.
discontent 829 n.
sadden 834 vb.
pained
resentful 891 adj.
painful
painful 377 adj.
laborious 682 adj.
punitive 963 adj.
painfully
painfully 32 adv.
carefully 457 adv.
pain in the neck
annoyance 827 n.
bore 838 n.
painkiller
anaesthetic 375 n.
antidote 658 n.
relief 831 n.
pain-killing
lenitive 177 adj.
relieving 831 adj.
painless
comfortable 376 adj.
easy 701 adj.
pleasurable 826 adj.
painlessness
euphoria 376 n.
pains
attention 455 n.
carefulness 457 n.
exertion 682 n.
painstaking
slow 278 adj.
careful 457 adj.
assiduity 678 n.
laborious 682 adj.
fastidious 862 adj.
paint
imitate 20 vb.
coat 226 vb.
pigment 425 n.
imagine 513 vb.
sham 542 n.
represent 551 vb.
paint 553 vb.
describe 590 vb.
cleanser 648 n.
preserve 666 vb.
cosmetic 843 n.
primp 843 vb.
decorate 844 vb.
— the town red
rejoice 835 vb.
revel 837 vb.
paintbox
art equipment 553 n.
painted
coloured 425 adj.
red 431 adj.
false 541 adj.
represented 551 adj.
painted 553 adj.
beautified 843 adj.
painter
cable 47 n.
artist 556 n.
mender 656 n.

artisan 686 n.
painting
representation 551 n.
painting 553 n.
picture 553 n.
painting the Forth Bridge
noncompletion 726 n.
paints
art equipment 553 n.
pair
identify 13 vb.
analogue 18 n.
unite with 45 vb.
combine 50 vb.
group 74 n.
duality 90 n.
pair 90 vb.
compare 462 vb.
— off
pair 90 vb.
wed 894 vb.
paired
accompanying 89 adj.
dual 90 adj.
married 894 adj.
pairing
coition 45 n.
paisley
textile 222 n.
pattern 844 n.
pal
colleague 707 n.
chum 880 n.
palace
house 192 n.
position of authority 733 n.
paladin
defender 713 n.
combatant 722 n.
brave person 855 n.
philanthropist 901 n.
palaeoanthropology, paleoanthropology
palaeology 125 n.
palaeography, paleography
palaeology 125 n.
hermeneutics 520 n.
lettering 586 n.
palaeolithic, paleolithic
primal 127 adj.
palaeology, paleology
palaeology 125 n.
palaeontologist, paleontologist
antiquarian 125 n.
palaeontology, paleontology
palaeology 125 n.
palaeozoic, paleozoic
secular 110 adj.
primal 127 adj.
palaestra
arena 724 n.
palais de danse
place of amusement 837 n.
palanquin
vehicle 274 n.
palatable
edible 301 adj.
pleasant 376 adj.
tasty 386 adj.
savoury 390 adj.
palatal
speech sound 398 n.
palate
taste 386 n.
good taste 846 n.
palatial
architectural 192 adj.
palatinate
political organization 733 n.
palaver
speech 579 n.
chatter 581 n.
confer 584 vb.
pale
insubstantial 4 adj.
exclusion 57 n.
weak 163 adj.
region 184 n.
barrier 235 n.
fence 235 n.
dim 419 adj.
soft-hued 425 adj.
colourless 426 adj.
lose colour 426 vb.
whitish 427 adj.
disappear 446 vb.
heraldry 547 n.
unhealthy 651 adj.
quake 854 vb.
paleface
foreigner 59 n.
whiteness 427 n.
paleo-
(See **palaeo-** *)*
palette
plate 194 n.
colour 425 n.
art equipment 553 n.
palfrey
saddle horse 273 n.
palimpsest
script 586 n.
use 673 n.
palindrome
inversion 221 n.
paling
fence 235 n.
palingenesis
reproduction 166 n.
revival 656 n.
palinode
poem 593 n.
recantation 603 n.
palisade
barrier 235 n.
protection 660 n.
defences 713 n.
pall
coverlet 226 n.
funeral 364 n.
obfuscation 421 n.
be tedious 838 vb.
cause dislike 861 vb.
sate 863 vb.
Palladian
architectural 192 adj.
pallbearer
funeral 364 n.
pallet
plate 194 n.
basis 218 n.
bed 218 n.
carrier 273 n.
palletize, palletise
load 193 vb.
palliasse
cushion 218 n.
palliate
moderate 177 vb.
qualify 468 vb.
plead 614 vb.
make better 654 vb.
remedy 658 vb.
relieve 831 vb.
extenuate 927 vb.
palliative
moderator 177 n.
remedial 658 adj.
pallid
colourless 426 adj.
pallium
robe 228 n.
vestments 989 n.
pallor
hue 425 n.
achromatism 426 n.
pally
friendly 880 adj.
sociable 882 adj.
palm
long measure 203 n.
tree 366 n.
feeler 378 n.
touch 378 vb.
oracle 511 n.
trophy 729 n.
— off
deceive 542 vb.
— off with
substitute 150 vb.
palmate
notched 260 adj.
divergent 294 adj.
palmer
traveller 268 n.
pietist 979 n.
worshipper 981 n.
palm-greasing
inducement 612 n.
palmistry
divination 511 n.
hermeneutics 520 n.
occultism 984 n.
palm wine
alcoholic drink 301 n.
palmy
palmy 730 adj.
cheering 833 adj.
palmy days
palmy days 730 n.
joy 824 n.
palomino
horse 273 n.
palp
feeler 378 n.
palpable
substantial 3 adj.
material 319 adj.
tactual 378 adj.
visible 443 adj.
manifest 522 adj.
palpate
touch 378 vb.
palpitate
be agitated 318 vb.
show feeling 818 vb.
be excited 821 vb.
palpitating
nervous 854 adj.
palpitation
oscillation 317 n.
agitation 318 n.
feeling 818 n.
nervousness 854 n.
palpitations
cardiovascular disease 651 n.
fatigue 684 n.
palsy
insensibility 375 n.
nervous disorders 651 n.
palter
be false 541 vb.
be irresolute 601 vb.
not observe 769 vb.
paltry
inconsiderable 33 adj.
unimportant 639 adj.
contemptible 922 adj.
rascally 930 adj.
paltry sum
trifle 639 n.
pampas
plain 348 n.
grass 366 n.
pamper
pet 889 vb.
pampered
comfortable 376 adj.
sensual 944 adj.
pamphlet
the press 528 n.
book 589 n.
pamphleteer
argue 475 vb.
publish 528 vb.
teach 534 vb.

preacher 537 n.
dissertator 591 n.
pan
eliminate 44 vb.
cauldron 194 n.
plate 194 n.
scales 322 n.
photography 551 n.
dispraise 924 vb.
— out
happen 154 vb.
result 157 vb.
pan-
general 79 adj.
Pan
musician 413 n.
mythic deity 966 n.
lesser deity 967 n.
panacea
remedy 658 n.
panache
plumage 259 n.
vigour 571 n.
trimming 844 n.
courage 855 n.
ostentation 875 n.
Pan-Africanism
nation 371 n.
panama
headgear 228 n.
pancake
fly 271 vb.
dish 301 n.
pandect
compendium 592 n.
law 953 n.
pandemic
universal 79 adj.
plague 651 n.
infectious 653 adj.
pandemonium
turmoil 61 n.
loudness 400 n.
discord 411 n.
hell 972 n.
pander
provider 633 n.
bawd 952 n.
pander (to)
tempt 612 vb.
be instrumental 628 vb.
minister to 703 vb.
please 826 vb.
be servile 879 vb.
flatter 925 vb.vb.
Pandora's box
evil 616 n.
pane
lamina 207 n.
transparency 422 n.
panegyric
oration 579 n.
praise 923 n.
panel
band 74 n.
list 87 n.
lamina 207 n.
partition 231 n.
council 692 n.
consignee 754 n.
tribunal 956 n.
panel game
indoor game 837 n.
panelling
lining 227 n.
ornamental art 844 n.
pang
spasm 318 n.
pang 377 n.
suffering 825 n.
panga
sharp edge 256 n.
sidearms 723 n.
pangs of conscience
regret 830 n.
penitence 939 n.
panhandle
beg 761 vb.
panic
fear 854 n.
frighten 854 vb.
be cowardly 856 vb.
panic-buy
store 632 vb.
panicky
fearing 854 adj.
panicle
flower 366 n.
panic-stricken
fearing 854 adj.
panjandrum
aristocrat 868 n.
pannier
bag 194 n.
basket 194 n.
panoply
dressing 228 n.
protection 660 n.
armour 713 n.
panopticon
prison 748 n.
panorama
whole 52 n.
generality 79 n.
open space 263 n.
view 438 n.
spectacle 445 n.
art subject 553 n.
panoramic
visible 443 adj.
pan pipes
flute 414 n.
pansy
nonconformist 84 n.
weakling 163 n.
plant 366 n.
female 373 adj.
pant
oscillate 317 vb.
be agitated 318 vb.
breathe 352 vb.
be hot 379 vb.
be fatigued 684 vb.
show feeling 818 vb.
— for
desire 859 vb.
pantalets
underwear 228 n.
pantaloons
trousers 228 n.
pantechnicon
lorry 274 n.
pantheism
deism 973 n.
pantheist
religionist 973 n.
pantheon
tomb 364 n.
deity 966 n.
temple 990 n.
panther
cat 365 n.
panties
underwear 228 n.
pantile
roof 226 n.
pantisocracy
government 733 n.
pantograph
imitator 20 n.
train 274 n.
pantomime
mimicry 20 n.
spectacle 445 n.
gesture 547 n.
gesticulate 547 vb.
acting 594 n.
stage play 594 n.
pantry
chamber 194 n.
provisions 301 n.
storage 632 n.
pants
underwear 228 n.
pap
bosom 253 n.
food 301 n.
pulpiness 356 n.
insipidity 387 n.
papa
paternity 169 n.
papacy
church office 985 n.
the church 985 n.
papadum, popadum
cerals 301 n.
papal
ecclesiastical 985 adj.
papalists
church party 978 n.
papal nuncio
envoy 754 n.
papaya, pawpaw
fruit 301 n.
paper
insubstantial 4 adj.
weak thing 163 n.
thinness 206 n.
wrapping 226 n.
overlay 226 vb.
line 227 vb.
white thing 427 n.
report 524 n.
the press 528 n.
art equipment 553 n.
oration 579 n.
stationery 586 n.
dissertation 591 n.
paper 631 n.
— over
repair 656 vb.
— over the cracks
conceal 525 vb.
not suffice 636 vb.
not complete 726 vb.
paperback
book 589 n.
novel 590 n.
paper mill
workshop 687 n.
paper modelling
sculpture 554 n.
papers
record 548 n.
reading matter 589 n.
paper tiger
sham 542 n.
paperwork
writing 586 n.
papery
brittle 330 adj.
papier-mâché
pulpiness 356 n.
sculpture 554 n.
paper 631 n.
papilla
bosom 253 n.
papist
Catholic 976 n.
papoose
child 132 n.
pappus
hair 259 n.
pappy
pulpy 356 adj.
paprika
condiment 389 n.
papula
swelling 253 n.
papyrus
grass 366 n.
stationery 586 n.
par
equivalence 28 n.
average 30 n.
finance 797 n.
parable
metaphor 519 n.
lecture 534 n.
narrative 590 n.
parabola
curve 248 n.
parabolic reflector
astronomy 321 n.
parachronism
anachronism 118 n.
different time 122 n.
parachute
fly 271 vb.
airship 276 n.

descend 309 vb.
safeguard 662 n.
parachutist
aeronaut 271 n.
Paraclete
Holy Ghost 965 n.
parade
assemblage 74 n.
pleasance 192 n.
marching 267 n.
spectacle 445 n.
show 522 vb.
path 624 n.
pageant 875 n.
be ostentatious 875 vb.
boast 877 vb.
parade ground
meeting place 192 n.
arena 724 n.
paradigm
prototype 23 n.
grammar 564 n.
paradisal
pleasurable 826 adj.
paradisiac 971 adj.
Paradise
happiness 824 n.
heaven 971 n.
parados
defences 713 n.
paradox
contrariety 14 n.
misfit 25 n.
argumentation 475 n.
absurdity 497 n.
lack of expectation 508 n.
unintelligibility 517 n.
ridiculousness 849 n.
paradoxical
uncertain 474 adj.
paraffin
oil 357 n.
fuel 385 n.
paragon
prototype 23 n.
exceller 644 n.
paragon 646 n.
prodigy 864 n.
person of repute 866 n.
good person 937 n.
paragraph
subdivision 53 n.
punctuation 547 n.
phrase 563 n.
edition 589 n.
paralipsis
ornament 574 n.
parallax
displacement 188 n.
parallel
correlative 12 adj.
analogue 18 n.
equal 28 adj.
concurrent 181 adj.
region 184 n.
parallelism 219 n.
parallel 219 adj.
compare 462 vb.
parallel lines
parallelism 219 n.
parallelogram
angular figure 247 n.
paralogism
sophism 477 n.
paralyse
disable 161 vb.
render insensible 375 vb.
make inactive 679 vb.
hinder 702 vb.
frighten 854 vb.
paralysed
still 266 adj.
diseased 651 adj.
nonactive 677 adj.
paralysis
helplessness 161 n.
inertness 175 n.
insensibility 375 n.
inaction 677 n.
paralytic
sick person 651 n.
dead drunk 949 adj.
paramedic
doctor 658 n.
parameter
numerical element 85 n.
paramilitary
warlike 718 adj.
paramilitary formation
auxiliary 707 n.
paramount
supreme 34 adj.
important 638 adj.
authoritative 733 adj.
paramountcy
prestige 866 n.
paramour
lover 887 n.
kept woman 952 n.
parang
sharp edge 256 n.
paranoia
psychopathy 503 n.
paranoiac
madman 504 n.
paranoid
insane 503 adj.
paranormal
paranormal 984 adj.
parapet
summit 213 n.
fortification 713 n.
paraph
label 547 n.
paraphernalia
medley 43 n.
equipment 630 n.
property 777 n.
paraphrase
imitation 20 n.
copy 20 vb.
copy 22 n.
intelligibility 516 n.
translation 520 n.
phrase 563 n.
paraphrastic
semantic 514 adj.
interpretive 520 adj.
paraplegia
helplessness 161 n.
nervous disorders 651 n.
paraplegic
sick person 651 n.
parapsychology
psychology 447 n.
psychics 984 n.
paraquat
poison 659 n.
paraselene
moon 321 n.
parasite
concomitant 89 n.
resident 191 n.
insect 365 n.
plant 366 n.
superfluity 637 n.
bane 659 n.
idler 679 n.
dependant 742 n.
beggar 763 n.
desirer 859 n.
toady 879 n.
sociable person 882 n.
flatterer 925 n.
parasitical
inferior 35 adj.
residing 192 adj.
lazy 679 adj.
parasitology
pathology 651 n.
parasol
shade 226 n.
screen 421 n.
parataxis
grammar 564 n.
paratrooper
aeronaut 271 n.
descent 309 n.
paratroops
armed force 722 n.
paratyphoid
infection 651 n.
parboil
cook 301 vb.
parbuckle
lifter 310 n.
parcel
piece 53 n.
bunch 74 n.
bring together 74 vb.
— out
sunder 46 vb.
apportion 783 vb.
parcel post
postal communications 531 n.
parcener
participator 775 n.
parched
dry 342 adj.
hot 379 adj.
hungry 859 adj.
parchment
stationery 586 n.
bookbinding 589 n.
pardon
amnesty 506 n.
leniency 736 n.
liberate 746 vb.
show mercy 905 vb.
forgive 909 vb.
nonliability 919 n.
acquit 960 vb.
pardonable
vindicable 927 adj.
guiltless 935 adj.
pare
shade off 27 vb.
abate 37 vb.
subtract 39 vb.
cut 46 vb.
render few 105 vb.
laminate 207 vb.
— expenses
economize 814 vb.
paregoric
remedial 658 adj.
parent
source 156 n.
parentage 169 n.
parentage
consanguinity 11 n.
precursor 66 n.
attribution 158 n.
producer 164 n.
propagation 167 n.
parentage 169 n.
parental
parental 169 adj.
parenthesis
irrelevance 10 n.
discontinuity 72 n.
interjection 231 n.
insertion 303 n.
punctuation 547 n.
parenthood
parentage 169 n.
life 360 n.
paresis
nervous disorders 651 n.
par excellence
eminently 34 adv.
importantly 638 adv.
parfumerie
beauty parlour 843 n.
pargeting
facing 226 n.
ornamental art 844 n.

parhelion
sun 321 n.
pariah
nonconformist 84 n.
dog 365 n.
derelict 779 n.
outcast 883 n.
parietal
lateral 239 adj.
pari mutuel
gaming-house 618 n.
paring
small thing 33 n.
piece 53 n.
economy 814 n.
pari passu
equally 28 adv.
synchronously 123 adv.
parish
district 184 n.
parish 985 n.
laity 987 n.
parish clerk
church officer 986 n.
parish council
council 692 n.
jurisdiction 955 n.
parishioner
native 191 n.
lay person 987 n.
parish priest
pastor 986 n.
parish pump
trifle 639 n.
parity
similarity 18 n.
equality 28 n.
finance 797 n.
park
place 187 vb.
pleasance 192 n.
enclosure 235 n.
arrive 295 vb.
grassland 348 n.
wood 366 n.
garden 370 n.
pleasure ground 837 n.
— oneself
sit down 311 vb.
parka
jacket 228 n.
warm clothes 381 n.
parking
passing along 305 n.
parking meter
traffic control 305 n.
parking place
station 187 n.
parking zone
traffic control 305 n.
Parkinson's disease
nervous disorders 651 n.
Parkinson's law
expansion 197 n.
overactivity 678 n.
parkland
pleasance 192 n.
plain 348 n.
parky
cold 380 adj.
parlance
language 557 n.
style 566 n.
speech 579 n.
parley
interlocution 584 n.
confer 584 vb.
consult 691 vb.
make terms 766 vb.
parliament
parliament 692 n.
authority 733 n.
lawcourt 956 n.
parliamentarian
councillor 692 n.
parliamentary
parliamentary 692 adj.
parliamentary government
government 733 n.
parlour
chamber 194 n.
parlour game
indoor game 837 n.
parlour maid
domestic 742 n.
parlous state
danger 661 n.
Parnassian
poetic 593 adj.
parochial
regional 184 adj.
provincial 192 adj.
narrow-minded 481 adj.
ecclesiastical 985 adj.
laical 987 adj.
parochialism
narrow mind 481 n.
patriotism 901 n.
parodist
imitator 20 n.
humorist 839 n.
parody
imitate 20 vb.
copy 22 n.
foolery 497 n.
misinterpret 521 vb.
misrepresent 552 vb.
satire 851 n.
parole
language 557 n.
liberation 746 n.
permit 756 n.
promise 764 n.
parolee
prisoner 750 n.
offender 904 n.
paronomasia
equivocalness 518 n.
trope 519 n.
paronym
word 559 n.
paroxysm
violence 176 n.
spasm 318 n.
frenzy 503 n.
anger 891 n.
parquet
paving 226 n.
variegated 437 adj.
parricide
murderer 362 n.
parrot
imitator 20 n.
repeat 106 vb.
bird 365 n.
chatterer 581 n.
parrot-cry
repetition 106 n.
parrot-fashion
imitatively 20 adv.
repeatedly 106 adv.
parrotry
conformity 83 n.
parry
repel 292 vb.
screen 421 vb.
sophisticate 477 vb.
avoid 620 vb.
obstruct 702 vb.
parry 713 vb.
resist 715 vb.
parse
decompose 51 vb.
parse 564 vb.
parsec
long measure 203 n.
Parsee
religionist 973 n.
Parsifal
honourable person 929 n.
parsimonious
careful 457 adj.
economical 814 adj.
parsimonious 816 adj.
temperate 942 adj.
parsimony
insufficiency 636 n.
selfishness 932 n.
parsley
potherb 301 n.
sauce 389 n.
parsnip
vegetable 301 n.
parson
church title 986 n.
cleric 986 n.
parsonage
house 192 n.
parsonage 986 n.
parsonical
clerical 986 adj.
parson's cat
indoor game 837 n.
part
disunite 46 vb.
part 53 n., vb.
incompleteness 55 n.
component 58 n.
open 263 vb.
diverge 294 vb.
depart 296 vb.
melody 410 n.
vocal music 412 n.
reading matter 589 n.
acting 594 n.
function 622 n.
portion 783 n.
— company
separate 46 vb.
diverge 294 vb.
depart 296 vb.
run away 620 vb.
quarrel 709 vb.
— with
not retain 779 vb.
give 781 vb.
partake
eat 301 vb.
participate 775 vb.
part and parcel of
intrinsic 5 adj.
parterre
garden 370 n.
theatre 594 n.
parthenogenesis
propagation 167 n.
Parthian shot
valediction 296 n.
answer 460 n.
stratagem 698 n.
partial
fragmentary 53 adj.
incomplete 55 adj.
fractional 102 adj.
imperfect 647 adj.
uncompleted 726 adj.
unjust 914 adj.
partiality
prejudice 481 n.
liking 859 n.
friendliness 880 n.
injustice 914 n.
improbity 930 n.
participant
(See **participator** *)*
participate
be one of 58 vb.
be active 678 vb.
cooperate 706 vb.
participate 775 vb.
feel 818 vb.
be sociable 882 vb.
participation
inclusion 78 n.
association 706 n.
cooperation 706 n.
participation 775 n.
condolence 905 n.
participator
busy person 678 n.
worker 686 n.
colleague 707 n.
participator 775 n.

beneficiary 776 n.
particle
small thing 33 n.
minuteness 196 n.
part of speech 564 n.
particle accelerator
nucleonics 160 n.
particle counter
radiation 417 n.
parti-coloured
coloured 425 adj.
variegated 437 adj.
particular
part 53 n.
special 80 adj.
attentive 455 adj.
careful 457 adj.
discriminating 463 adj.
veracious 540 adj.
capricious 604 adj.
sensitive 819 adj.
fastidious 862 adj.
particularism
disunion 46 n.
particularism 80 n.
selfishness 932 n.
sectarianism 978 n.
particularity
speciality 80 n.
particularize, particularise
differentiate 15 vb.
specify 80 vb.
be diffuse 570 vb.
describe 590 vb.
particulars
particulars 80 n.
description 590 n.
partie carrée
social gathering 882 n.
parting
separation 46 n.
dividing line 92 n.
centrality 225 n.
partition 231 n.
limit 236 n.
divergence 294 n.
departure 296 n.
parting of the ways
divergence 294 n.
dissension 709 n.
parting shot
valediction 296 n.
(See **Parthian shot** *)*
parti pris
bias 481 n.
predetermination 608 n.
partisan
biased 481 adj.
opponent 705 n.
patron 707 n.
sectional 708 adj.
soldier 722 n.
revolter 738 n.
friend 880 n.
unjust 914 adj.
sectarian 978 adj.
partition
separation 46 n.
part 53 vb.
exclusion 57 n.
dividing line 92 n.
partition 231 n.
barrier 235 n.
limit 236 n.
screen 421 n.
obstacle 702 n.
apportionment 783 n.
apportion 783 vb.
partly
partially 33 adv.
partly 53 adv.
partner
unite with 45 vb.
combine 50 vb.
concomitant 89 n.
accompany 89 vb.
personnel 686 n.
colleague 707 n.
participator 775 n.
friend 880 n.
spouse 894 n.
partnership
concurrence 181 n.
association 706 n.
corporation 708 n.
participation 775 n.
marriage 894 n.
part of
component 58 adj.
part of speech
word 559 n.
part of speech 564 n.
partridge
table bird 365 n.
parts
region 184 n.
locality 187 n.
contents 193 n.
part song
vocal music 412 n.
part-time job
job 622 n.
parturient
fertilized 167 adj.
parturition
obstetrics 167 n.
part-work
journal 528 n.
party
assembly 74 n.
band 74 n.
follower 284 n.
person 371 n.
prejudice 481 n.
assenter 488 n.
conference 584 n.
association 706 n.
party 708 n.
signatory 765 n.
festivity 837 n.
social gathering 882 n.
litigant 959 n.
sect 978 n.
party-goer
reveller 837 n.
party line
rule 81 n.
telecommunication 531 n.
policy 623 n.
tactics 688 n.
precept 693 n.
party member
political party 708 n.
party spirit
prejudice 481 n.
cooperation 706 n.
cheerfulness 833 n.
injustice 914 n.
sectarianism 978 n.
party system
government 733 n.
party to
assenting 488 adj.
party wall
dividing line 92 n.
partition 231 n.
party worker
political party 708 n.
par value
price 809 n.
parvenu
upstart 126 n.
prosperous person 730 n.
rich person 800 n.
vulgarian 847 n.
commoner 869 n.
proud person 871 n.
pas, the
precedence 64 n.
paschal
seasonal 141 adj.
ritual 988 adj.
pas de deux
ballet 594 n.
pash
love 887 n.
pasha
governor 741 n.
pasigraphy
language 557 n.
paso-doble
dance 837 n.
pasquinade
satire 851 n.
calumny 926 n.
pass
circumstance 8 n.
be superior 34 vb.
entrance 68 n.
conform 83 vb.
continue 108 vb.
elapse 111 vb.
be past 125 vb.
be turned to 147 vb.
event 154 n.
gap 201 n.
narrowness 206 n.
opener 263 n.
be in motion 265 vb.
traverse 267 vb.
ingress 297 n.
emit 300 vb.
excrete 302 vb.
pass 305 vb.
overstep 306 vb.
assent 488 n.
sleight 542 n.
select 605 vb.
access 624 n.
suffice 635 vb.
be good 644 vb.
protection 660 n.
predicament 700 n.
lunge 712 n.
succeed 727 vb.
permit 756 n.vb.
consent 758 vb.
change hands 780 vb.
be in fashion 848 vb.
endearment 889 n.
approve 923 vb.
make legal 953 vb.
spell 983 n.
— away
pass away 2 vb.
end 69 vb.
die 361 vb.
perish 361 vb.
disappear 446 vb.
— belief
cause doubt 486 vb.
— by
elapse 111 vb.
disregard 458 vb.
— current
be believed 485 vb.
be published 528 vb.
— for
resemble 18 vb.
— muster
suffice 635 vb.
be good 644 vb.
be middling 732 vb.
be praised 923 vb.
— off
happen 154 vb.
dissemble 541 vb.
— on
transfer 272 vb.
progress 285 vb.
communicate 524 vb.
relinquish 621 vb.
— out
be insensible 375 vb.
— over
exclude 57 vb.
disregard 458 vb.
be taciturn 582 vb.
reject 607 vb.
forgive 909 vb.
exempt 919 vb.
— round
be published 528 vb.
publish 528 vb.

— sentence
judge 480 vb.
— the buck
avoid 620 vb.
not act 677 vb.
fail in duty 918 vb.
be exempt 919 vb.
— the hat
beg 761 vb.
— the point of no return
overstep 306 vb.
— the time
be 1 vb.
pass time 108 vb.
amuse oneself 837 vb.
— the time of day
converse 584 vb.
— through
meet with 154 vb.
traverse 267 vb.
pass 305 vb.
feel 818 vb.
— under review
be attentive 455 vb.
estimate 480 vb.
passable
inconsiderable 33 adj.
not bad 644 adj.
middling 732 adj.
contenting 828 adj.
personable 841 adj.
passage
bond 47 n.
part 53 n.
entrance 68 n.
change 143 n.
transition 147 n.
lobby 194 n.
gap 201 n.
flank 239 vb.
doorway 263 n.
motion 265 n.
land travel 267 n.
ride 267 vb.
water travel 269 n.
transference 272 n.
deviate 282 vb.
passage 305 n.
musical piece 412 n.
tune 412 n.
edition 589 n.
access 624 n.
passage of arms
fight 716 n.
passant
heraldic 547 adj.
passbook
permit 756 n.
account book 808 n.
passé
past 125 adj.
antiquated 127 adj.
ageing 131 adj.
passed
expert 694 adj.
permitted 756 adj.
approved 923 adj.
legal 953 adj.
passementerie
trimming 844 n.
passenger
rider 268 n.
thing transferred 272 n.
idler 679 n.
passe-partout
opener 263 n.
passerby
spectator 441 n.
passerine
animal 365 adj.
passible
sentient 374 adj.
passim
sporadically 75 adv.
somewhere 185 adv.
in place 186 adv.
passing bell
obsequies 364 n.
passing fancy
whim 604 n.
passing show
fashion 848 n.
passing strange
wonderful 864 adj.
passing word
hint 524 n.
passion
vigour 571 n.
affections 817 n.
warm feeling 818 n.
excitation 821 n.
excitable state 822 n.
desire 859 n.
love 887 n.
anger 891 n.
Passion
suffering 825 n.
passionate
fervent 818 adj.
excitable 822 adj.
loving 887 adj.
irascible 892 adj.
passionless
impassive 820 adj.
indifferent 860 adj.
Passion play
stage play 594 n.
Passion Week
holy day 988 n.
passive
inert 175 adj.
latent 523 adj.
nonactive 677 adj.
peaceful 717 adj.
obedient 739 adj.
apathetic 820 adj.
inexcitable 823 adj.
passive resistance
dissent 489 n.
resistance 715 n.
disobedience 738 n.
passkey
instrument 628 n.
pass marks
sufficiency 635 n.
Passover
holy day 988 n.
passport
opener 263 n.
credential 466 n.
label 547 n.
instrument 628 n.
protection 660 n.
warrant 737 n.
permit 756 n.
password
opener 263 n.
answer 460 n.
identification 547 n.
instrument 628 n.
warfare 718 n.
permit 756 n.
past
past 125 adj.
antiquated 127 adj.
disrepute 867 n.
past, the
priority 119 n.
past time 125 n.
pasta
dish 301 n.
past, be
come before 64 vb.
be past 125 vb.
cease 145 vb.
paste
a mixture 43 n.
adhesive 47 n.
agglutinate 48 vb.
softness 327 n.
viscidity 354 n.
pulpiness 356 n.
sham 542 n.
finery 844 n.
bad taste 847 n.
pasteboard
paper 631 n.
pastel
soft-hued 425 adj.
art equipment 553 n.
picture 553 n.
pastellist
artist 556 n.
past enduring
intolerable 827 adj.
pastern
foot 214 n.
pasteurize, pastureise
make sterile 172 vb.
sanitate 652 vb.
safeguard 660 vb.
past history
precedence 64 n.
pastiche
copy 22 n.
a mixture 43 n.
art style 553 n.
picture 553 n.
pastille
sweet thing 392 n.
inodorousness 395 n.
pastime
business 622 n.
pleasurableness 826 n.
amusement 837 n.
pasting
knock 279 n.
past it
ageing 131 adj.
weak 163 adj.
useless 641 adj.
past its best
imperfect 647 adj.
deteriorated 655 adj.
past master
proficient person 696 n.
pastor
teacher 537 n.
pastor 986 n.
pastoral
agrarian 370 adj.
art subject 553 n.
pleasurable 826 adj.
priestly 985 adj.
clerical 986 adj.
pastoral care
ministration 988 n.
pastorale
musical piece 412 n.
pastoral letter
ministration 988 n.
pastoral staff
badge of rule 743 n.
vestments 989 n.
pastorate
church office 985 n.
pastry
pastries 301 n.
sweet thing 392 n.
pastrycook
caterer 633 n.
past tense
past time 125 n.
past time
past time 125 n.
pasturage
provender 301 n.
grassland 348 n.
grass 366 n.
farm 370 n.
pasture
feed 301 vb.
graze 301 vb.
grassland 348 n.
pasty
dish 301 n.
pastries 301 n.
pulpy 356 adj.
colourless 426 adj.
pat
apt 24 adj.
fixed 153 adj.
knock 279 n.
touch 378 n.vb.
gesticulate 547 vb.
please 826 vb.
relieve 831 vb.
caress 889 vb.

— down
flatten 216 vb.
— oneself on the back
feel pride 871 vb.
boast 877 vb.
— on the back
give courage 855 vb.
applaud 923 vb.
pat-ball
ball game 837 n.
patch
adjunct 40 n.
join 45 vb.
piece 53 n.
modify 143 vb.
garden 370 n.
maculation 437 n.
variegate 437 vb.
dirt 649 n.
repair 656 n.vb.
surgical dressing 658 n.
eyesore 842 n.
cosmetic 843 n.
blemish 845 n.
— up
repair 656 vb.
make peace 719 vb.
compromise 770 vb.
patcher
mender 656 n.
patchouli
scent 396 n.
patchwork
nonuniformity 17 n.
medley 43 n.
variegation 437 n.
needlework 844 n.
patchy
nonuniform 17 adj.
inferior 35 adj.
mixed 43 adj.
discontinuous 72 adj.
mottled 437 adj.
imperfect 647 adj.
pate
head 213 n.
pâté
hors-d'oeuvres 301 n.
paten
plate 194 n.
ritual object 988 n.
church utensil 990 n.
patent
open 263 adj.
manifest 522 adj.
permit 756 n.vb.
dueness 915 n.
patented
proprietary 777 adj.
patent leather
skin 226 n.
patent medicine
medicine 658 n.
remedy 658 n.
paterfamilias
paternity 169 n.
paternal
akin 11 adj.
parental 169 adj.
benevolent 897 adj.
paternalism
despotism 733 n.
governance 733 n.
paternity
propagation 167 n.
paternity 169 n.
Paternoster
prayers 981 n.
path
direction 281 n.
way in 297 n.
outlet 298 n.
passage 305 n.
trace 548 n.
path 624 n.
pathetic
unimportant 639 adj.
bad 645 adj.
felt 818 adj.
distressing 827 adj.
lamenting 836 adj.
pitiable 905 adj.
pathetic fallacy
anthropology 371 n.
affections 817 n.
pathfinder
precursor 66 n.
traveller 268 n.
pathless
spacious 183 adj.
difficult 700 adj.
pathogen
infection 651 n.
pathogenic
diseased 651 adj.
infectious 653 adj.
pathological
diseased 651 adj.
medical 658 adj.
pathologist
doctor 658 n.
pathology
pathology 651 n.
medical art 658 n.
pathos
feeling 818 n.
excitation 821 n.
painfulness 827 n.
pathway
path 624 n.
patience
perseverance 600 n.
leniency 736 n.
patience 823 n.
card game 837 n.
caution 858 n.
forgiveness 909 n.
patient
slow 278 adj.
testee 461 n.
sick person 651 n.
patient 823 adj.
sufferer 825 n.
patina
layer 207 n.
hue 425 n.
greenness 434 n.
impairment 655 n.
blemish 845 n.
patio
lobby 194 n.
patisserie
pastries 301 n.
patois
speciality 80 n.
dialect 560 n.
patrial
native 191 n.
patriality
dueness 915 n.
patriarch
precursor 66 n.
old man 133 n.
paternity 169 n.
governor 741 n.
master 741 n.
ecclesiarch 986 n.
patriarchal
olden 127 adj.
patriarchate
church office 985 n.
patriarchy
family 11 n.
male 372 n.
government 733 n.
patrician
aristocrat 868 n.
genteel 868 adj.
patricide
homicide 362 n.
patrilineal
akin 11 adj.
parental 169 adj.
patrimony
acquisition 771 n.
possession 773 n.
dower 777 n.
dueness 915 n.
patriot
defender 713 n.
patriot 901 n.
benefactor 903 n.
patriotism
love 887 n.
patriotism 901 n.
disinterestedness 931 n.
patristic
scriptural 975 adj.
patrol
land travel 267 n.
traverse 267 vb.
pass 305 vb.
circler 314 n.
spectator 441 n.
safeguard 660 vb.
defender 713 n.
armed force 722 n.
restrain 747 vb.
patrolman, patrolwoman
police 955 n.
patron, patroness
prop 218 n.
onlookers 441 n.
enthusiast 504 n.
protector 660 n.
aider 703 n.
patron 707 n.
defender 713 n.
master 741 n.
security 767 n.
participator 775 n.
purchaser 792 n.
friend 880 n.
kind person 897 n.
benefactor 903 n.
commender 923 n.
patronage
influence 178 n.
protection 660 n.
management 689 n.
aid 703 n.
authority 733 n.
security 767 n.
purchase 792 n.
approbation 923 n.
benefice 985 n.
patronize, patronise
endorse 488 vb.
choose 605 vb.
patronize 703 vb.
defend 713 vb.
be proud 871 vb.
befriend 880 vb.
be benevolent 897 vb.
patronizing
prideful 871 adj.
patron saint
saint 968 n.
patronymic
name 561 n.
patsy
dupe 544 n.
patten
footwear 228 n.
patter
be in motion 265 vb.
walk 267 vb.
strike 279 vb.
rain 350 vb.
faintness 401 n.
roll 403 vb.
empty talk 515 n.
language 557 n.
slang 560 n.
speech 579 n.
loquacity 581 n.
pattern
correlation 12 n.
uniformity 16 n.
prototype 23 n.
composition 56 n.
arrangement 62 n.
rule 81 n.
example 83 n.
form 243 n.vb.
structure 331 n.
variegate 437 vb.
comparison 462 n.

picture 553 n.
plan 623 n.
paragon 646 n.
pattern 844 n.
decorate 844 vb.
— oneself on
do likewise 20 vb.
patty
pastries 301 n.
patulous
expanded 197 adj.
paucity
smallness 33 n.
fewness 105 n.
scarcity 636 n.
Paul Jones
dance 837 n.
paunch
maw 194 n.
swelling 253 n.
eater 301 n.
paunchy
fleshy 195 adj.
pauper
poor person 801 n.
pauperize, pauperise
impoverish 801 vb.
pause
discontinuity 72 n.
interim 108 n.
period 110 n.
delay 136 n.
lull 145 n.
pause 145 vb.
interval 201 n.
quiescence 266 n.
notation 410 n.
be uncertain 474 vb.
doubt 486 vb.
not act 677 vb.
repose 683 n.
pavane
dance 837 n.
pave
overlay 226 vb.
smooth 258 vb.
— the way
prepare 669 vb.
facilitate 701 vb.
pavement
paving 226 n.
path 624 n.
road 624 n.
pavilion
pavilion 192 n.
arbour 194 n.
canopy 226 n.
paving
base 214 n.
basis 218 n.
paving 226 n.
building material 631 n.
paving stone
paving 226 n.
pavis
armour 713 n.
Pavlovian response
intuition 476 n.
pavonine
iridescent 437 adj.
paw
foot 214 n.
strike 279 vb.
feeler 378 n.
touch 378 vb.
nippers 778 n.
caress 889 vb.
— the ground
leap 312 vb.
gesticulate 547 vb.
be angry 891 vb.
pawky
cunning 698 adj.
witty 839 adj.
pawl
fastening 47 n.
pawn
inferior 35 n.
dupe 544 n.
fatalist 596 n.
instrument 628 n.
nonentity 639 n.
slave 742 n.
security 767 n.
give security 767 vb.
transfer 780 n.
borrow 785 vb.
plaything 837 n.
pawnbroker
lender 784 n.
pax
ritual object 988 n.
Pax Romana
peace 717 n.
palmy days 730 n.
pay
coat 226 vb.
incentive 612 n.
benefit 615 vb.
employ 622 vb.
be useful 640 vb.
earnings 771 n.
be profitable 771 vb.
restitute 787 vb.
pay 804 n.vb.
expend 806 vb.
receipt 807 n.
reward 962 n.vb.
— attention (to)
be attentive 455 vb.
observe 768 vb.
— back
compensate 31 vb.
— compensation
restitute 787 vb.
atone 941 vb.
— court to
be servile 879 vb.
court 889 vb.
flatter 925 vb.
— dividends
be successful 727 vb.
— for
patronize 703 vb.
purchase 792 vb.
defray 804 vb.
be punished 963 vb.
— heed
be attentive 455 vb.
— no attention
be inattentive 456 vb.
— no regard to
disregard 458 vb.
— off
be useful 640 vb.
stop using 674 vb.
make inactive 679 vb.
be successful 727 vb.
— off old scores
retaliate 714 vb.
avenge 910 vb.
— one out
retaliate 714 vb.
punish 963 vb.
— one's respects to
honour 866 vb.
pay one's respects 884 vb.
— one's way
defray 804 vb.
— out
lengthen 203 vb.
expend 806 vb.
avenge 910 vb.
— the penalty
atone 941 vb.
— the piper
patronize 703 vb.
defray 804 vb.
— through the nose
pay too much 811 vb.
— tribute to
respect 920 vb.
praise 923 vb.
reward 962 vb.
— up
keep faith 768 vb.
restitute 787 vb.
pay 804 vb.
payable
owed 803 adj.
due 915 adj.
PAYE
tax 809 n.
payee
recipient 782 n.
paying
productive 164 adj.
profitable 640 adj.
gainful 771 adj.
rewarding 962 adj.
paying guest
resident 191 n.
payload
contents 193 n.
thing transferred 272 n.
paymaster
treasurer 798 n.
pay 804 n.
payment
incentive 612 n.
payment 804 n.
expenditure 806 n.
payment in kind
barter 791 n.
payoff
end 69 n.
completion 725 n.
pay 804 n.
pay packet
earnings 771 n.
pay rise
increment 36 n.
payroll
personnel 686 n.
p.d.q.
swiftly 277 adv.
PE
exercise 682 n.
pea
sphere 252 n.
vegetable 301 n.
peace
quietude 266 n.
euphoria 376 n.
silence 399 n.
concord 710 n.
peace 717 n.
pleasurableness 826 n.
peaceable
moderate 177 adj.
amiable 884 adj.
peace and quiet
repose 683 n.
seclusion 883 n.
peace at any price
submission 721 n.
Peace Corps
philanthropist 901 n.
peaceful
inert 175 adj.
moderate 177 adj.
tranquil 266 adj.
comfortable 376 adj.
silent 399 adj.
reposeful 683 adj.
peaceful 717 adj.
submitting 721 adj.
obedient 739 adj.
inexcitable 823 adj.
pleasurable 826 adj.
content 828 adj.
peace-lover
pacifist 717 n.
peacemaker
moderator 177 n.
pacifist 717 n.
mediator 720 n.
peacemaking
concord 710 n.
pacification 719 n.
peace offering
peace offering 719 n.
propitiation 941 n.
peace of mind
inexcitability 823 n.
content 828 n.
peace treaty
pacification 719 n.
treaty 765 n.

peach
fruit 301 n.
a beauty 841 n.
peach (on)
inform 524 vb.
divulge 526 vb.
accuse 928 vb.
peach-coloured
red 431 adj.
peachy
downy 259 adj.
peacock
table bird 365 n.
variegation 437 n.
exhibitor 522 n.
a beauty 841 n.
fop 848 n.
vain person 873 n.
be ostentatious 875 vb.
peacock-blue
blue 435 adj.
peak
superiority 34 n.
completeness 54 n.
extremity 69 n.
high land 209 n.
summit 213 n.
shade 226 n.
sharp point 256 n.
perfection 646 n.
peaky
lean 206 adj.
sick 651 adj.
peal
loudness 400 n.
roll 403 n.
resonance 404 n.
campanology 412 n.
gong 414 n.
call 547 n.
pean
heraldry 547 n.
peanut
fruit 301 n.
peanuts
small quantity 33 n.
trifle 639 n.
money 797 n.
pear
fruit 301 n.
pear drops
sweets 301 n.
pearl
semitransparency 424 n.
white thing 427 n.
exceller 644 n.
a beauty 841 n.
gem 844 n.
pearlies
clothing 228 n.
pearly
semitransparent 424 adj.
soft-hued 425 adj.
whitish 427 adj.
grey 429 adj.
iridescent 437 adj.
pearly king/queen
fop 848 n.
pear-shaped
curved 248 adj.
round 250 adj.
rotund 252 adj.
peasant
dweller 191 n.
farmer 370 n.
possessor 776 n.
country-dweller 869 n.
pease pudding
vegetable 301 n.
pea-shooter
propellant 287 n.
pea-souper
cloud 355 n.
opacity 423 n.
peat
fuel 385 n.
peat bog
marsh 347 n.
peau de chagrin
magic instrument 983 n.
pebble
hardness 326 n.
soil 344 n.
pebbledash
facing 226 n.
pecan
fruit 301 n.
peccable
imperfect 647 adj.
peccadillo
trifle 639 n.
guilty act 936 n.
peccant
bad 645 adj.
diseased 651 adj.
wicked 934 adj.
guilty 936 adj.
peck
great quantity 32 n.
certain quantity 104 n.
eat 301 vb.
metrology 465 n.
peckish
hungry 859 adj.
Pecksniffian
hypocritical 541 adj.
pectin
thickening 354 n.
pectoral
cross 222 n.
vestments 989 n.
peculate
defraud 788 vb.
be dishonest 930 vb.
peculiar
different 15 adj.
special 80 adj.
unusual 84 adj.
crazy 503 adj.
peculiarity
temperament 5 n.
speciality 80 n.
nonconformity 84 n.
peculiarly
remarkably 32 adv.
pecuniary
monetary 797 adj.
pecuniary assistance
subvention 703 n.
pedagogic
educational 534 adj.
pedagogic 537 adj.
pedagogics
teaching 534 n.
pedagogue
scholar 492 n.
teacher 537 n.
pedagogy
teaching 534 n.
pedal
footed 214 adj.
propellant 287 n.
play music 413 vb.
mute 414 n.
tool 630 n.
pedal-driven
vehicular 274 adj.
pedal power
energy 160 n.
vehicle 274 n.
pedal-pushers
trousers 228 n.
pedant
conformist 83 n.
narrow mind 481 n.
scholar 492 n.
sciolist 493 n.
teacher 537 n.
obstinate person 602 n.
tyrant 735 n.
affecter 850 n.
perfectionist 862 n.
pedantic
attentive 455 adj.
careful 457 adj.
accurate 494 adj.
peddle
sell 793 vb.
pederast
libertine 952 n.
pederasty
illicit love 951 n.
pedestal
base 214 n.
stand 218 n.
pedestrian
travelling 267 adj.
pedestrian 268 n.
feeble 572 adj.
prosaic 593 adj.
dull 840 adj.
pedestrian crossing
traffic control 305 n.
access 624 n.
pedestrian precinct
path 624 n.
pedicab
cab 274 n.
pedicel, pedicle
prop 218 n.
pediculous
unclean 649 adj.
pedicure
surgery 658 n.
beautification 843 n.
pedigree
series 71 n.
list 87 n.
genealogy 169 n.
nobility 868 n.
pediment
summit 213 n.
pedlar
traveller 268 n.
seller 793 n.
pedlar 794 n.
pedometer
meter 465 n.
pee
excrete 302 vb.
peek
look 438 n.
be curious 453 vb.
enquire 459 vb.
peel
leavings 41 n.
disunite 46 vb.
layer 207 n.
skin 226 n.
uncover 229 vb.
rubbish 641 n.
— off
come unstuck 49 vb.
unstick 49 vb.
doff 229 vb.
peen
hammer 279 n.
peep
ululate 409 vb.
look 438 n.
gaze 438 vb.
scan 438 vb.
be curious 453 vb.
enquire 459 vb.
— out
emerge 298 vb.
be disclosed 526 vb.
peepers
eye 438 n.
peephole
window 263 n.
view 438 n.
peeping Tom
spectator 441 n.
inquisitive person 453 n.
peep show
spectacle 445 n.
plaything 837 n.
peer
compeer 28 n.
gaze 438 vb.
scan 438 vb.
be dim-sighted 440 vb.
enquire 459 vb.
councillor 692 n.
person of repute 866 n.

person of rank 868 n.
peerage
honours 866 n.
aristocracy 868 n.
peeress
person of rank 868 n.
peer group
contemporary 123 n.
peerless
dissimilar 19 adj.
supreme 34 adj.
best 644 adj.
noteworthy 866 adj.
peeve
torment 827 vb.
enrage 891 vb.
peevish
discontented 829 adj.
ungracious 885 adj.
irascible 892 adj.
sullen 893 adj.
peewit
bird 365 n.
peg
degree 27 n.
fastening 47 n.
hanger 217 n.
stopper 264 n.
draught 301 n.
tool 630 n.
Pegasus
aeronaut 271 n.
horse 273 n.
peg away
go on 146 vb.
persevere 600 vb.
— out
dry 342 vb.
die 361 vb.
pegs
leg 267 n.
peg to hang something on
pretext 614 n.
peignoir
informal dress 228 n.
pejorative
depreciating 483 adj.
word 559 n.
disrespectful 921 adj.
detracting 926 adj.
pekinese, pekingese
dog 365 n.
pekoe
soft drink 301 n.
pelagian
oceanic 343 adj.
Pelagian
heretical 977 adj.
pelagic
oceanic 343 adj.
pelerine
cloak 228 n.
pelf
money 797 n.
wealth 800 n.
pelican
bird 365 n.
pelican crossing
traffic control 305 n.
pelisse
cloak 228 n.
pellagra
disease 651 n.
pellet
sphere 252 n.
missile 287 n.
excrement 302 n.
ammunition 723 n.
pellicle
layer 207 n.
skin 226 n.
pell-mell
confusedly 61 adv.
hastily 680 adv.
pellucid
undimmed 417 adj.
transparent 422 adj.
intelligible 516 adj.
Pelmanism
mnemonics 505 n.
card game 837 n.
pelorus
direction 281 n.
pelota
ball game 837 n.
pelt
skin 226 n.
move fast 277 vb.
strike 279 vb.
propel 287 vb.
rain 350 vb.
lapidate 712 vb.
not respect 921 vb.
pemmican
food 301 n.
pen
enclosure 235 n.
bird 365 n.
female animal 373 n.
recording instrument 549 n.
art equipment 553 n.
stationery 586 n.
write 586 vb.
imprison 747 vb.
lockup 748 n.
PEN
literature 557 n.
penal
prohibiting 757 adj.
punitive 963 adj.
penal code
precept 693 n.
law 953 n.
penalty 963 n.
penalize, penalise
be inexpedient 643 vb.
make illegal 954 vb.
punish 963 vb.
penal servitude
penalty 963 n.
penal settlement
prison camp 748 n.
penalty
loss 772 n.
cost 809 n.
penalty 963 n.
penalty clause
qualification 468 n.
penance
offset 31 n.
penitence 939 n.
penance 941 n.
asceticism 945 n.
punishment 963 n.
Christian rite 988 n.
Penates
mythic deity 966 n.
lesser deity 967 n.
penchant
tendency 179 n.
willingness 597 n.
liking 859 n.
pencil
flash 417 n.
recording instrument 549 n.
art equipment 553 n.
paint 553 vb.
stationery 586 n.
write 586 vb.
pencil box
small box 194 n.
pendant, pendent
analogue 18 n.
adjunct 40 n.
hanging object 217 n.
flag 547 n.
jewellery 844 n.
pendent
hanging 217 adj.
pending
continuing 108 adj.
while 108 adv.
pendragon
potentate 741 n.
pendulous
nonadhesive 49 adj.
hanging 217 adj.
oscillating 317 adj.
pendulum
timekeeper 117 n.
hanging object 217 n.
oscillation 317 n.
Penelope's web
lost labour 641 n.
noncompletion 726 n.
peneplain
plain 348 n.
penetrable
intelligible 516 adj.
penetralia
interiority 224 n.
penetrate
be general 79 vb.
pierce 263 vb.
infiltrate 297 vb.
pass 305 vb.
cause thought 449 vb.
be wise 498 vb.
understand 516 vb.
impress 821 vb.
penetrating
strident 407 adj.
intelligent 498 adj.
felt 818 adj.
penetration
interjacency 231 n.
ingress 297 n.
passage 305 n.
sagacity 498 n.
penfriend
correspondent 588 n.
chum 880 n.
penguin
bird 365 n.
penicillin
drug 658 n.
penile
generative 167 adj.
peninsula
region 184 n.
projection 254 n.
land 344 n.
island 349 n.
penis
genitalia 167 n.
penitence
tergiversation 603 n.
improvement 654 n.
penitent
regretting 830 adj.
penitent 939 n.
repentant 939 adj.
ascetic 945 n.
penitential
repentant 939 adj.
atoning 941 adj.
penitentiary
prison 748 n.
penknife
sharp edge 256 n.
stationery 586 n.
penman, penwoman
calligrapher 586 n.
penmanship
lettering 586 n.
pen name
misnomer 562 n.
pennant
flag 547 n.
penniless
not owning 774 adj.
poor 801 adj.
pennon
flag 547 n.
penny
coinage 797 n.
penny-a-liner
author 589 n.
penny dreadful
novel 590 n.
penny-farthing
bicycle 274 n.

penny pincher
niggard 816 n.
pennyweight
small quantity 33 n.
weighing 322 n.
penny whistle
stridor 407 n.
flute 414 n.
penny-wise
unwise 499 adj.
parsimonious 816 adj.
penny wise and pound foolish
prodigal 815 adj.
penology
detention 747 n.
punishment 963 n.
penpusher
recorder 549 n.
calligrapher 586 n.
author 589 n.
pensées
reading matter 589 n.
pensile
hanging 217 adj.
pension
quarters 192 n.
resignation 753 n.
earnings 771 n.
pay 804 n.
receipt 807 n.
reward 962 n.
pensionable age
old age 131 n.
pensioner
old person 133 n.
student 538 n.
resignation 753 n.
recipient 782 n.
pension off
stop using 674 vb.
not retain 779 vb.
pensive
thoughtful 449 adj.
abstracted 456 adj.
melancholic 834 adj.
penstock
conduit 351 n.
pentacle
indication 547 n.
talisman 983 n.
pentad
five 99 n.
pentagon
angular figure 247 n.
Pentagon
master 741 n.
pentagram
talisman 983 n.
pentameter
prosody 593 n.
Pentateuch
scripture 975 n.
pentathlon
contest 716 n.
Pentecost
holy day 988 n.
Pentecostalist
sectarian 978 n.
penthouse
flat 192 n.
attic 194 n.
pent up
restrained 747 adj.
penultimate
ending 69 adj.
penumbra
half-light 419 n.
penurious
poor 801 adj.
parsimonious 816 adj.
penury
poverty 801 n.
peon
servant 742 n.
peonage
servitude 745 n.
people
race 11 n.
place oneself 187 vb.
inhabitants 191 n.
native 191 n.
dwell 192 vb.
nation 371 n.
social group 371 n.
subject 742 n.
commonalty 869 n.
laity 987 n.
peopled
multitudinous 104 adj.
people of the book
religionist 973 n.
peoples of the earth
humankind 371 n.
pep
vigorousness 174 n.
vigour 571 n.
restlessness 678 n.
peplum
garment 228 n.
pepper
pierce 263 vb.
shoot 287 vb.
vegetable 301 n.
pungency 388 n.
condiment 389 n.
variegate 437 vb.
wound 655 vb.
fire at 712 vb.
pepper and salt
greyness 429 n.
chequer 437 n.
peppercorn rent
cheapness 812 n.
peppered
perforated 263 adj.
pepper mill
pulverizer 332 n.
peppery
pungent 388 adj.
irascible 892 adj.
pep pill
stimulant 174 n.
excitant 821 n.
drug-taking 949 n.
peppy
forceful 571 adj.
pepsin
condensation 324 n.
pep talk
stimulant 174 n.
allocution 583 n.
inducement 612 n.
peptic
remedial 658 adj.
peptic ulcer
digestive disorders 651 n.
pep up
invigorate 174 vb.
make appetizing 390 vb.
perambulate
walk 267 vb.
perambulator
pushcart 274 n.
per annum
periodically 141 adv.
percale
textile 222 n.
per capita
pro rata 783 adv.
perceivable
visible 443 adj.
perceive
have feeling 374 vb.
see 438 vb.
cognize 447 vb.
detect 484 vb.
know 490 vb.
per cent
ratio 85 n.
percentage
increment 36 n.
extra 40 n.
part 53 n.
ratio 85 n.
discount 810 n.
percentile
statistical 86 adj.
percept
idea 451 n.
perceptible
seeing 438 adj.
visible 443 adj.
perception
vision 438 n.
intellect 447 n.
idea 451 n.
discrimination 463 n.
knowledge 490 n.
sagacity 498 n.
perceptive
sentient 374 adj.
mental 447 adj.
perch
place oneself 187 vb.
nest 192 n.
dwell 192 vb.
long measure 203 n.
basis 218 n.
land 295 vb.
descend 309 vb.
sit down 311 vb.
fish 365 n.
gauge 465 n.
sleep 679 vb.
repose 683 vb.
perchance
by chance 159 adv.
possibly 469 adv.
Percheron
draught horse 273 n.
perching
high 209 adj.
percipience
intellect 447 n.
percolate
infiltrate 297 vb.
exude 298 vb.
pass 305 vb.
irrigate 341 vb.
flow 350 vb.
purify 648 vb.
percolating
porous 263 adj.
percolator
cauldron 194 n.
per contra
conversely 467 adv.
percussion
impulse 279 n.
orchestra 413 n.
musical instrument 414 n.
percussion cap
lighter 385 n.
percussion instrument
gong 414 n.
percussionist
instrumentalist 413 n.
perdition
ruin 165 n.
defeat 728 n.
condemnation 961 n.
hell 972 n.
perdurable
lasting 113 adj.
perpetual 115 adj.
peregrination
land travel 267 n.
peregrine falcon
bird 365 n.
peremptory
assertive 532 adj.
authoritative 733 adj.
commanding 737 adj.
compelling 740 adj.
obligatory 917 adj.
perennial
lasting 113 adj.
perpetual 115 adj.
unchangeable 153 adj.
flower 366 n.

perfect
consummate 32 adj.
whole 52 adj.
complete 54 adj.
past time 125 n.
excellent 644 adj.
perfect 646 adj.vb.
mature 669 vb.
carry through 725 vb.
beautiful 841 adj.
shapely 841 adj.
approvable 923 adj.
virtuous 933 adj.
perfect fit
adaptation 24 n.
perfect gentleman
honourable person 929 n.
perfectible
improved 654 adj.
perfection
summit 213 n.
symmetry 245 n.
goodness 644 n.
perfection 646 n.
completion 725 n.
beauty 841 n.
good person 937 n.
purity 950 n.
(See **perfect** *)*
perfectionism
carefulness 457 n.
reformism 654 n.
attempt 671 n.
discontent 829 n.
fastidiousness 862 n.
perfectionist
trier 671 n.
perfectionist 862 n.
perfections
beauty 841 n.
virtues 933 n.
perfective
completive 725 adj.
perfervid
active 678 adj.
fervent 818 adj.
perfidious
false 541 adj.
deceiving 542 adj.
tergiversating 603 adj.
undutiful 918 adj.
perfidious 930 adj.
perfidy
latency 523 n.
untruth 543 n.
sedition 738 n.
nonobservance 769 n.
perfidy 930 n.
perforate
pierce 263 vb.
pass 305 vb.
perforation
perforation 263 n.
insertion 303 n.
indication 547 n.
perforator
sharp point 256 n.
perforator 263 n.
perforce
necessarily 596 adv.
perform
produce 164 vb.
operate 173 vb.
play music 413 vb.
represent 551 vb.
act 594 vb.
function 622 vb.
be instrumental 628 vb.
do 676 vb.
observe 768 vb.
be affected 850 vb.
do one's duty 917 vb.
— a function
be useful 640 vb.
performance
effect 157 n.
production 164 n.
music 412 n.
musical skill 413 n.
representation 551 n.
dramaturgy 594 n.
action 676 n.
effectuation 725 n.
celebration 876 n.
performer
musician 413 n.
interpreter 520 n.
entertainer 594 n.
doer 676 n.
agent 686 n.
perfume
emit 300 vb.
odour 394 n.
scent 396 n.
be fragrant 396 vb.
cosmetic 843 n.
perfumed
pleasant 376 adj.
perfunctory
incomplete 55 adj.
deficient 307 adj.
negligent 458 adj.
unwilling 598 adj.
imperfect 647 adj.
bungled 695 adj.
uncompleted 726 adj.
indifferent 860 adj.
perfusion
surgery 658 n.
pergola
arbour 194 n.
perhaps
by chance 159 adv.
possibly 469 adv.
per head
pro rata 783 adv.
peri
a beauty 841 n.
fairy 970 n.
periapt
talisman 983 n.
pericarditis
cardiovascular disease 651 n.
pericarp
skin 226 n.
pericope
part 53 n.
pericranium
head 213 n.
peridot
gem 844 n.
perigee
short distance 200 n.
perihelion
short distance 200 n.
peril
danger 661 n.
perilous
dangerous 661 adj.
perimeter
surroundings 230 n.
outline 233 n.
enclosure 235 n.
limit 236 n.
perinatal
fertilized 167 adj.
per incuriam
inadvertently 456 adv.
negligently 458 adv.
period
part 53 n.
composition 56 n.
end 69 n.
time 108 n.
period 110 n.
brief span 114 n.
periodicity 141 n.
regular return 141 n.
limit 236 n.
haemorrhage 302 n.
punctuation 547 n.
phrase 563 n.
periodic, periodical
discontinuous 72 adj.
regular 81 adj.
continuing 108 adj.
periodic 110 adj.
periodical 141 adj.
fitful 142 adj.
periodical
journal 528 n.
book 589 n.
periodicity
recurrence 106 n.
frequency 139 n.
periodicity 141 n.
oscillation 317 n.
peripatetic
travelling 267 adj.
circuitous 314 adj.
Peripatetics
philosopher 449 n.
peripeteia
revolution 149 n.
event 154 n.
lack of expectation 508 n.
disclosure 526 n.
peripheral
irrelevant 10 adj.
excluded 57 adj.
distant 199 adj.adj.
unimportant 639 adj.
periphery
exteriority 223 n.
surroundings 230 n.
outline 233 n.
enclosure 235 n.
limit 236 n.
periphrasis
phrase 563 n.
pleonasm 570 n.
periphrastic
prolix 570 adj.
periscope
telescope 442 n.
periscopic
visible 443 adj.
perish
pass away 2 vb.
decompose 51 vb.
be destroyed 165 vb.
perish 361 vb.
deteriorate 655 vb.
perishable
ephemeral 114 adj.
dying 361 adj.
perishable goods
merchandise 795 n.
perishing
chilly 380 adj.
peristaltic
snaky 251 adj.
peristyle
series 71 n.
pavilion 192 n.
peritonitis
digestive disorders 651 n.
perjure oneself
be false 541 vb.
perjurer
liar 545 n.
perjury
falsehood 541 n.
untruth 543 n.
perk, perquisite
extra 40 n.
incentive 612 n.
earnings 771 n.
gift 781 n.
reward 962 n.
perk up
elevate 310 vb.
be refreshed 685 vb.
be relieved 831 vb.
be cheerful 833 vb.
perky
cheerful 833 adj.
vain 873 adj.
impertinent 878 adj.
perm
hairdressing 843 n.
permafrost
coldness 380 n.

permanence
durability 113 n.
permanence 144 n.
continuance 146 n.
stability 153 n.
perseverance 600 n.
preservation 666 n.
permanency
job 622 n.
permanent
continuing 108 adj.
permanent 144 adj.
unchangeable 153 adj.
habitual 610 adj.
(See **permanence** *)*
permanent way
railway 624 n.
permeable
porous 263 adj.
permeate
be mixed 43 vb.
prevail 178 vb.
pervade 189 vb.
lie between 231 vb.
infiltrate 297 vb.
pass 305 vb.
permissible
possible 469 adj.
permitted 756 adj.
approvable 923 adj.
legal 953 adj.
permission
permission 756 n.
consent 758 n.
permissive
lax 734 adj.
permitting 756 adj.
permissive society
scope 744 n.
unchastity 951 n.
permit
opener 263 n.
credential 466 n.
make possible 469 vb.
assent 488 n.vb.
facilitate 701 vb.
be lax 734 vb.
be lenient 736 vb.
give scope 744 vb.
commission 751 vb.
permit 756 n.vb.
consent 758 vb.
exempt 919 vb.
permitted
possible 469 adj.
legal 953 adj.
permutation
numerical operation 86 n.
change 143 n.
interchange 151 n.
pernicious
destructive 165 adj.
harmful 645 adj.
pernicious anaemia
blood disease 651 n.
pernickety
fastidious 862 adj.
perorate
be diffuse 570 vb.
orate 579 vb.
peroration
end 69 n.
oration 579 n.
peroxide
bleacher 426 n.
hairwash 843 n.
perpendicular
vertical 215 adj.
straight 249 adj.
Perpendicular
churchlike 990 adj.
perpetrate
do 676 vb.
do wrong 914 vb.
perpetrator
doer 676 n.
agent 686 n.
perpetual
existing 1 adj.
continuous 71 adj.
continuing 108 adj.
lasting 113 adj.
perpetual 115 adj.
frequent 139 adj.
permanent 144 adj.
unceasing 146 adj.
perpetuate
perpetuate 115 vb.
stabilize 153 vb.
perpetuation
perpetuity 115 n.
continuance 146 n.
preservation 666 n.
perpetuity
infinity 107 n.
long duration 113 n.
perpetuity 115 n.
permanence 144 n.
continuance 146 n.
perplex
bedevil 63 vb.
distract 456 vb.
puzzle 474 vb.
be unintelligible 517 vb.
be difficult 700 vb.
trouble 827 vb.
perplexity
dubiety 474 n.
unintelligibility 517 n.
difficulty 700 n.
perquisite
(See **perk** *)*
perry
alcoholic drink 301 n.
per se
intrinsically 5 adv.
singly 88 adv.
persecute
pursue 619 vb.
ill-treat 645 vb.
be severe 735 vb.
oppress 735 vb.
torment 827 vb.
be malevolent 898 vb.
be pitiless 906 vb.
torture 963 vb.
persecution
counteraction 182 n.
prejudice 481 n.
enmity 881 n.
inhumanity 898 n.
orthodoxism 976 n.
pietism 979 n.
persecutor
obstinate person 602 n.
tyrant 735 n.
punisher 963 n.
zealot 979 n.
Persephone
Chthonian deity 967 n.
Olympian deity 967 n.
Perseus
demigod 967 n.
perseverance
perseverance 600 n.
obstinacy 602 n.
pursuit 619 n.
assiduity 678 n.
courage 855 n.
persevere
continue 71 vb.
stay 144 vb.
go on 146 vb.
stand firm 599 vb.
persevere 600 vb.
be obstinate 602 vb.
exert oneself 682 vb.
hope 852 vb.
persevering
unyielding 162 adj.
persevering 600 adj.
impenitent 940 adj.
Persian lamb
skin 226 n.
persiennes
shade 226 n.
curtain 421 n.
persiflage
witticism 839 n.
ridicule 851 n.
persifleur
humorist 839 n.
persist
stay 144 vb.
go on 146 vb.
persevere 600 vb.
be obstinate 602 vb.
pursue 619 vb.
be active 678 vb.
persistent
lasting 113 adj.
unyielding 162 adj.
remembered 505 adj.
persevering 600 adj.
obstinate 602 adj.
persistent offender
prisoner 750 n.
person
substance 3 n.
self 80 n.
unit 88 n.
object 319 n.
person 371 n.
personable
personable 841 adj.
personage
acting 594 n.
bigwig 638 n.
persona grata
friend 880 n.
favourite 890 n.
personal
substantial 3 adj.
intrinsic 5 adj.
original 21 adj.
private 80 adj.
special 80 adj.
human 371 adj.
indicating 547 adj.
possessed 773 adj.
proprietary 777 adj.
impertinent 878 adj.
selfish 932 adj.
personal account
biography 590 n.
personal advantage
selfishness 932 n.
personal allowance
receipt 807 n.
personal attendance
presence 189 n.
personal column
advertisement 528 n.
matchmaker 894 n.
personal effects
property 777 n.
personal estate
property 777 n.
personal involvement
feeling 818 n.
personalities
sauciness 878 n.
rudeness 885 n.
calumny 926 n.
personality
substantiality 3 n.
intrinsicality 5 n.
self 80 n.
speciality 80 n.n.
influence 178 n.
materiality 319 n.
spirit 447 n.
bigwig 638 n.
affections 817 n.
personality disorder
psychopathy 503 n.
personality testing
psychology 447 n.
enquiry 459 n.
personalize, personalise
specify 80 vb.
personally
substantially 3 adv.

specially 80 adv.
here 189 adv.
personal property
property 777 n.
personal reasons
motive 612 n.
personal remarks
scurrility 899 n.
calumny 926 n.
personalty
property 777 n.
persona non grata
enemy 881 n.
personate
represent 551 vb.
act 594 vb.
personification
metaphor 519 n.
personify
materialize 319 vb.
manifest 522 vb.
represent 551 vb.
act 594 vb.
personnel
band 74 n.
means 629 n.
personnel 686 n.
perspective
relativeness 9 n.
range 183 n.
length 203 n.
depth 211 n.
convergence 293 n.
view 438 n.
painting 553 n.
perspex
transparency 422 n.
perspicacious
seeing 438 adj.
intelligent 498 adj.
perspicuous
intelligible 516 adj.
perspicuous 567 adj.
perspiration
excretion 302 n.
perspire
exude 298 vb.
be wet 341 vb.
be hot 379 vb.
persuadability
credulity 487 n.
willingness 597 n.
irresolution 601 n.
persuadability 612 n.
persuade
influence 178 vb.
convince 485 vb.
induce 612 vb.
request 761 vb.
— against
dissuade 613 vb.
— oneself
suppose 512 vb.
persuader
motivator 612 n.
persuasible
credulous 487 adj.
impressible 819 adj.
persuasion
classification 77 n.
influence 178 n.
positiveness 473 n.
belief 485 n.
teaching 534 n.
inducement 612 n.
persuasive
influential 178 adj.
plausible 471 adj.
credible 485 adj.
inducing 612 adj.
pert
cheerful 833 adj.
impertinent 878 adj.
discourteous 885 adj.
pertain
be related 9 vb.
be included 78 vb.
pertinacity
perseverance 600 n.
obstinacy 602 n.
pertinent
relevant 9 adj.
apt 24 adj.
included 78 adj.
perturb
derange 63 vb.
impress 821 vb.
perturbation
stimulation 174 n.
displacement 188 n.
agitation 318 n.
excitation 821 n.
excitable state 822 n.
nervousness 854 n.
peruke
wig 228 n.
peruse
study 536 vb.
pervade
fill 54 vb.
be general 79 vb.
prevail 178 vb.
pervade 189 vb.
pervasive
universal 79 adj.
influential 178 adj.
ubiquitous 189 adj.
perverse
erroneous 495 adj.
obstinate 602 adj.
wilful 602 adj.
capricious 604 adj.
difficult 700 adj.
disobedient 738 adj.
perversion
conversion 147 n.
misinterpretation 521 n.
misteaching 535 n.
falsehood 541 n.
untruth 543 n.
deterioration 655 n.
misuse 675 n.
illicit love 951 n.
heterodoxy 977 n.
impiety 980 n.
pervert
derange 63 vb.
nonconformist 84 n.
changed person 147 n.
convert 147 vb.
distort 246 vb.
sophisticate 477 vb.
mislead 495 vb.
misinterpret 521 vb.
misteach 535 vb.
harm 645 vb.
pervert 655 vb.
misuse 675 vb.
make wicked 934 vb.
cad 938 n.
libertine 952 n.
perverted
erroneous 495 adj.
vicious 934 adj.
lecherous 951 adj.
impious 980 adj.
pervious
porous 263 adj.
peseta
coinage 797 n.
pesky
annoying 827 adj.
peso
coinage 797 n.
pessary
surgical dressing 658 n.
pessimism
underestimation 483 n.
expectation 507 n.
dejection 834 n.
hopelessness 853 n.
pessimist
underestimation 483 n.
loser 728 n.
moper 834 n.
alarmist 854 n.
pest
evil 616 n.
plague 651 n.
bane 659 n.
worry 825 n.
annoyance 827 n.
hateful object 888 n.
noxious animal 904 n.
pester
recur 139 vb.
meddle 678 vb.
torment 827 vb.
enrage 891 vb.
pesticide
killer 362 n.
poison 659 n.
pestilence
badness 645 n.
plague 651 n.
pestilent, pastilential
infectious 653 adj.
toxic 653 adj.
baneful 659 adj.
hateful 888 adj.
pestle
pulverizer 332 n.
pet
animal 365 n.
look after 457 vb.
chosen 605 adj.
be lenient 736 vb.
please 826 vb.
love 887 vb.
caress 889 vb.
pet 889 vb.
darling 890 n.
anger 891 n.
philanthropize 897 vb.
petal
flower 366 n.
pet aversion
dislike 861 n.
enemy 881 n.
hateful object 888 n.
peter out
decrease 37 vb.
end 69 vb.
cease 145 vb.
Peter Pan
youth 130 n.
Peter's pence
offering 781 n.
Peter principle
unskilfulness 695 n.
pethidene
anaesthetic 375 n.
petiole
foliage 366 n.
petite
little 196 adj.
shapely 841 adj.
petit four
mouthful 301 n.
petition
report 524 n.
ask leave 756 vb.
request 761 n.vb.
litigation 959 n.
prayers 981 n.
— against
deprecate 762 vb.
petitioner
petitioner 763 n.
malcontent 829 n.
litigant 959 n.
worshipper 981 n.
petitio principii
sophism 477 n.
petit mal
nervous disorders 651 n.
petit point
needlework 844 n.
petits pois
vegetable 301 n.
pet name
name 561 n.
misnomer 562 n.
endearment 889 n.

Petrarchan
poetic 593 adj.
petrel
bird 365 n.
petrified
still 266 adj.
fearing 854 adj.
petrified forest
fossil 125 n.
petrify
be dense 324 vb.
harden 326 vb.
frighten 854 vb.
be wonderful 864 vb.
petroglyph
sculpture 554 n.
petrography
mineralogy 359 n.
petrol
propellant 287 n.
petroleum
oil 357 n.
fuel 385 n.
petrology
mineralogy 359 n.
petrol pump
storage 632 n.
petticoat
underwear 228 n.
female 373 adj.
pettifogger
trickster 545 n.
lawyer 958 n.
pettifogging
sophistical 477 adj.
trivial 639 adj.
rascally 930 adj.
petting
endearment 889 n.
pettish
irascible 892 adj.
sullen 893 adj.
petty
inconsiderable 33 adj.
little 196 adj.
narrow-minded 481 adj.
unimportant 639 adj.
contemptible 922 adj.
selfish 932 adj.
petty cash
money 797 n.
petty officer
naval officer 741 n.
petty sessions
lawcourt 956 n.
petty tyrant
tyrant 735 n.
autocrat 741 n.
petulant
discontented 829 adj.
irascible 892 adj.
sullen 893 adj.
pew
compartment 194 n.
seat 218 n.
church interior 990 n.
pewter
a mixture 43 n.
greyness 429 n.
peyote
drug-taking 949 n.
pfennig
coinage 797 n.
Phaëthon
classical deities 967 n.
phaeton
carriage 274 n.
phalanx
coherence 48 n.
solid body 324 n.
formation 722 n.
phallic
generative 167 adj.
impure 951 adj.
phallus
fertilizer 171 n.
phantasm
visual fallacy 440 n.
appearance 445 n.
ghost 970 n.
phantasmagoria
medley 43 n.
visual fallacy 440 n.
spectacle 445 n.
phantom
insubstantial thing 4 n.
the dead 361 n.
visual fallacy 440 n.
fantasy 513 n.
ghost 970 n.
Pharaoh
sovereign 741 n.
pharisaic, pharisaical
hypocritical 541 adj.
pietistic 979 adj.
pharisaism
duplicity 541 n.
false piety 980 n.
Pharisee
non-Christian sect 978 n.
zealot 979 n.
pharmacology
medical art 658 n.
pharmacopoeia
medicine 658 n.
pharmacy
druggist 658 n.
pharyngitis
respiratory disease 651 n.
phase
modality 7 n.
be identical 13 vb.
regularize 62 vb.
time 117 vb.
synchronize 123 vb.
appearance 445 n.
plan 623 vb.
phased
synchronous 123 adj.
changeful 152 adj.
PhD
academic title 870 n.
pheasant
meat 301 n.
table bird 365 n.
phenomenal
substantial 3 adj.
unusual 84 adj.
appearing 445 adj.
wonderful 864 adj.
phenomenalism
philosophy 449 n.
phenomenon
event 154 n.
appearance 445 n.
prodigy 864 n.
phial
vessel 194 n.
philanderer
lover 887 n.
libertine 952 n.
philandering
love-making 887 n.
wooing 889 n.
philanthropic
benevolent 897 adj.
philanthropic 901 adj.
disinterested 931 adj.
virtuous 933 adj.
philanthropist
visionary 513 n.
reformer 654 n.
kind person 897 n.
philanthropist 901 n.
good person 937 n.
philanthropy
voluntary work 597 n.
benevolence 897 n.
philanthropy 901 n.
philatelist
collector 492 n.
philharmonic
musical 412 adj.
philippic
oration 579 n.
censure 924 n.
philistine
conformist 83 n.
uninstructed 491 adj.
ignoramus 493 n.
artless 699 adj.
vulgarian 847 n.
detractor 926 n.
philistinism
moral insensibility 820 n.
phillumenist
collector 492 n.
philological
semantic 514 adj.
linguistic 557 adj.
verbal 559 adj.
philologist
collector 492 n.
linguist 557 n.
philology
linguistics 557 n.
etymology 559 n.
grammar 564 n.
philomel
bird 365 n.
vocalist 413 n.
philoprogenitive
generative 167 adj.
philosopher
philosopher 449 n.
enquirer 459 n.
sage 500 n.
philosopher's stone
remedy 658 n.
wealth 800 n.
philosophical, philosophic
philosophic 449 adj.
inexcitable 823 adj.
patient 823 adj.
content 828 adj.
philosophize, philosophise
meditate 449 vb.
reason 475 vb.
philosophy
philosophy 449 n.
enquiry 459 n.
creed 485 n.
inexcitability 823 n.
morals 917 n.
religion 973 n.
philtre
stimulant 174 n.
magic instrument 983 n.
spell 983 n.
phiz, phizog
face 237 n.
phlebitis
cardiovascular disease 651 n.
phlebotomy
surgery 658 n.
phlegm
excrement 302 n.
semiliquidity 354 n.
sluggishness 679 n.
moral insensibility 820 n.
phlegmatic
slow 278 adj.
nonactive 677 adj.
impassive 820 adj.
indifferent 860 adj.
unastonished 865 adj.
phlogiston
heat 379 n.
phobia
psychopathy 503 n.
worry 825 n.
phobia 854 n.
dislike 861 n.
hatred 888 n.

Phoebus
sun 321 n.
Olympian deity 967 n.
phoenix
rara avis 84 n.
reproduction 166 n.
fire 379 n.
paragon 646 n.
mythical being 970 n.
phoenix from the ashes, like a
restored 656 adj.
phon
sound 398 n.
phone
speech sound 398 n.
hearing aid 415 n.
communicate 524 vb.
phone call
message 529 n.
phone-in
broadcast 531 n.
phoneme
spoken letter 558 n.
word 559 n.
phone-tapper
inquisitive person 453 n.
phonetic
sounding 398 adj.
literal 558 adj.
vocal 577 adj.
phonetician
acoustics 398 n.
linguist 557 n.
phonetics
acoustics 398 n.
linguistics 557 n.
phoney, phony
false 541 adj.
spurious 542 adj.
untrue 543 adj.
impostor 545 n.
affected 850 adj.
phonics
acoustics 398 n.
phonogram
letter 558 n.
writing 586 n.
phonograph
gramophone 414 n.
phonography
acoustics 398 n.
spelling 558 n.
writing 586 n.
phonology
acoustics 398 n.
etymology 559 n.
phosphates
fertilizer 171 n.
phosphorescence
glow 417 n.
phosphorescent
luminous 417 adj.
luminescent 420 adj.
photo
photography 551 n.
photocomposition
print 587 n.
photocopier
imitator 20 n.
recording instrument 549 n.
photocopy
copy 20 vb.
copy 22 n.
duplication 91 n.
photography 551 n.
photoelectric cell
electronics 160 n.
radiation 417 n.
photoelectricity
electricity 160 n.
photo finish
draw 28 n.
short distance 200 n.
contest 716 n.
photogenic
representing 551 adj.
beautiful 841 adj.
photograph
copy 22 n.
enlarge 197 vb.
record 548 n.vb.
photography 551 n.
photograph 551 vb.
photograph album
reminder 505 n.
photographer
recorder 549 n.
photography 551 n.
photographic
lifelike 18 adj.
accurate 494 adj.
representing 551 adj.
descriptive 590 adj.
photographic memory
memory 505 n.
photography
optics 417 n.
camera 442 n.
cinema 445 n.
photography 551 n.
photogravure
copy 22 n.
photography 551 n.
picture 553 n.
engraving 555 n.
photolithography
printing 555 n.
print 587 n.
photolysis
decomposition 51 n.
photometer
optical device 442 n.
photometry
optics 417 n.
photomicroscope
microscope 442 n.
photomontage
picture 553 n.
photon
element 319 n.
radiation 417 n.
photoplay
cinema 445 n.
stage play 594 n.
photosensitive
luminous 417 adj.
photosetting
print 587 n.
photosphere
sun 321 n.
phrase
subdivision 53 n.
tune 412 n.
word 559 n.
phrase 563 n.vb.
style 566 n.
phrasemonger
phrasemonger 574 n.
stylist 575 n.
phraseology
phrase 563 n.
style 566 n.
phrasing
musical skill 413 n.
style 566 n.
phratry
race 11 n.
phrenetic
(See **frenetic** *)*
phrenology
head 213 n.
hermeneutics 520 n.
Phrygian mode
key 410 n.
phthisis
respiratory disease 651 n.
phylactery
maxim 496 n.
talisman 983 n.
phyletic
parental 169 adj.
phylogeny
biology 358 n.
phylum
breed 77 n.
physic
medicine 658 n.
doctor 658 vb.
physical
real 1 adj.
substantial 3 adj.
material 319 adj.
sensuous 376 adj.
physical being
materiality 319 n.
physical chemistry
physics 319 n.
physical condition
state 7 n.
materiality 319 n.
physical education
education 534 n.
exercise 682 n.
physical features
land 344 n.
physical insensibility
insensibility 375 n.
physical jerks
education 534 n.
physical pain
pain 377 n.
physical pleasure
pleasure 376 n.
physical presence
presence 189 n.
object 319 n.
physical science
physics 319 n.
physical sensibility
sensibility 374 n.
physical well-being
euphoria 376 n.
health 650 n.
physical wreck
dilapidation 655 n.
physician
doctor 658 n.
physicist
physics 319 n.
physics
physics 319 n.
physiognomy
face 237 n.
form 243 n.
feature 445 n.
physiography
earth sciences 321 n.
physiological
biological 358 adj.
physiology
structure 331 n.
biology 358 n.
physiotherapist
doctor 658 n.
physiotherapy
therapy 658 n.
physique
vitality 162 n.
structure 331 n.
animality 365 n.
phytography
biology 358 n.
botany 368 n.
pi
ratio 85 n.
pietistic 979 adj.
piacular
atoning 941 adj.
piaffer
equitation 267 n.
pianissimo
faintly 401 adv.
adagio 412 adv.
pianist
instrumentalist 413 n.
piano
muted 401 adj.
adagio 412 adv.
piano 414 n.
dejected 834 adj.
piano accordion
organ 414 n.
pianola
piano 414 n.
piastre
coinage 797 n.

piazza
meeting place 192 n.
lobby 194 n.
pibroch
musical piece 412 n.
pica
type size 587 n.
picador
athlete 162 n.
killer 362 n.
combatant 722 n.
picaresque
descriptive 590 adj.
rascally 930 adj.
picaroon
robber 789 n.
piccalilli
sauce 389 n.
piccolo
stridor 407 n.
flute 414 n.
pick
sharp point 256 n.
perforator 263 n.
extractor 304 n.
cultivate 370 vb.
choice 605 n.
select 605 vb.
store 632 vb.
chief thing 638 n.
elite 644 n.
clean 648 vb.
acquire 771 vb.
take 786 vb.
pride 871 n.
— a fight
make quarrels 709 vb.
— and choose
be capricious 604 vb.
select 605 vb.
be fastidious 862 vb.
— clean
clean 648 vb.
take 786 vb.
— holes
dispraise 924 vb.
detract 926 vb.
— locks
steal 788 vb.
— off
kill 362 vb.
fire at 712 vb.
— on
blame 924 vb.
accuse 928 vb.
— one's brains
interrogate 459 vb.
— oneself up
lift oneself 310 vb.
be restored 656 vb.
— one's steps
be careful 457 vb.
— one's way
travel 267 vb.
be in difficulty 700 vb.
— out
set apart 46 vb.
extract 304 vb.
see 438 vb.
discriminate 463 vb.
select 605 vb.
decorate 844 vb.
— out a tune
play music 413 vb.
— over
search 459 vb.
— to pieces
demolish 165 vb.
— up
elevate 310 vb.
hear 415 vb.
detect 484 vb.
get better 654 vb.
be restored 656 vb.
arrest 747 vb.
acquire 771 vb.
take 786 vb.
— up speed
accelerate 277 vb.
— up the bill
defray 804 vb.
— up the gauntlet
contend 716 vb.
— up the pieces
repair 656 vb.
pick-a-back
astride 218 adv.
bearing 273 adj.
pickaxe
perforator 263 n.
extractor 304 n.
picked
chosen 605 adj.
excellent 644 adj.
picked out
separate 46 adj.
ornamented 844 adj.
picked troops
armed force 722 n.
brave person 855 n.
picker
accumulator 74 n.
farmer 370 n.
'pickers and stealers'
finger 378 n.
thief 789 n.
picket
tie 45 vb.
place 187 vb.
circumscribe 232 vb.
warner 664 n.
be obstructive 702 vb.
defender 713 n.
armed force 722 n.
fetter 747 vb.
picket fence
fence 235 n.
picket line
exclusion 57 n.
pickings
choice 605 n.
earnings 771 n.
booty 790 n.
pickle
state 7 n.
circumstance 8 n.
drench 341 vb.
pungency 388 n.
season 388 vb.
preserve 666 vb.
predicament 700 n.
pickled
tipsy 949 adj.
pickles
sauce 389 n.
pick-me-up
stimulant 174 n.
pungency 388 n.
tonic 658 n.
excitant 821 n.
pick of the bunch
elite 644 n.
pickpocket
thief 789 n.
pick-up
gramophone 414 n.
loose woman 952 n.
pickup truck
lorry 274 n.
Pickwickian
meaningless 515 adj.
funny 849 adj.
picnic
meal 301 n.
easy thing 701 n.
victory 727 n.
amusement 837 n.
social gathering 882 n.
picot
edging 234 n.
pictogram
letter 558 n.
lettering 586 n.
pictorial
representing 551 adj.
painted 553 adj.
picture
composition 56 n.
miniature 196 n.
spectacle 445 n.
photography 551 n.
represent 551 vb.
picture 553 n.
description 590 n.
a beauty 841 n.
— to oneself
imagine 513 vb.
picture frame
frame 218 n.
enclosure 235 n.
art equipment 553 n.
picture house
cinema 445 n.
place of amusement 837 n.
picture of, the
analogue 18 n.
picture palace
cinema 445 n.
theatre 594 n.
picture paper
the press 528 n.
picture postcard
correspondence 588 n.
beautiful 841 adj.
pictures
film 445 n.
picture show
spectacle 445 n.
picturesque
descriptive 590 adj.
impressive 821 adj.
pleasurable 826 adj.
beautiful 841 adj.
ornamental 844 adj.
picture writing
symbology 547 n.
representation 551 n.
writing 586 n.
piddle
excrete 302 vb.
piddling
trivial 639 adj.
pidgin
language 557 n.
dialect 560 n.
pie
dish 301 n.
pastries 301 n.
bird 365 n.
print-type 587 n.
piebald
horse 273 n.
pied 437 adj.
piece
small thing 33 n.
piece 53 n.
incompleteness 55 n.
component 58 n.
unit 88 n.
product 164 n.
textile 222 n.
meal 301 n.
musical piece 412 n.
reading matter 589 n.
stage play 594 n.
gun 723 n.
portion 783 n.
coinage 797 n.
loose woman 952 n.
pièce de résistance
dish 301 n.
exceller 644 n.
masterpiece 694 n.
piece goods
textile 222 n.
piecemeal
separately 46 adv.
piecemeal 53 adv.
piece of cake
easy thing 701 n.
piece of eight
coinage 797 n.
piece of one's mind
reprimand 924 n.
piece on the board
instrument 628 n.
nonentity 639 n.

piece rate
price 809 n.
piece together
join 45 vb.
make complete 54 vb.
decipher 520 vb.
repair 656 vb.
piecework
labour 682 n.
pie chart
statistics 86 n.
piecrust
pastries 301 n.
brittleness 330 n.
pied
pied 437 adj.
pied-à-terre
abode 192 n.
Pied Piper
sorcerer 983 n.
pie-eyed
tipsy 949 adj.
pie in the sky
fantasy 513 n.
pier
stable 192 n.
pillar 218 n.
prop 218 n.
projection 254 n.
theatre 594 n.
pierce
cut 46 vb.
pierce 263 vb.
insert 303 vb.
pass 305 vb.
give pain 377 vb.
wound 655 vb.
impress 821 vb.
— the heart
hurt 827 vb.
piercing
cold 380 adj.
loud 400 adj.
strident 407 adj.
felt 818 adj.
Pierian spring
poetry 593 n.
pierrot, pierrette
entertainer 594 n.
pietà
art subject 553 n.
ritual object 988 n.
pietism
sectarianism 978 n.
pietism 979 n.
false piety 980 n.
pietist
affecter 850 n.
pietist 979 n.
piety
religion 973 n.
piety 979 n.
worship 981 n.
piezoelectricity
electricity 160 n.
piffle
silly talk 515 n.
piffling
trivial 639 adj.
pig
pig 365 n.
dirty person 649 n.
cad 938 n.
sensualist 944 n.
glutton 947 n.
pigeon
bird 365 n.
dupe 544 n.
function 622 n.
pigeon-chested
deformed 246 adj.
pigeon-fancier
breeder 369 n.
pigeonhole
class 62 vb.
classification 77 n.
put off 136 vb.
place 185 n.
compartment 194 n.
pigeonholed
neglected 458 adj.
unused 674 adj.
pigeon loft
stable 192 n.
pigeon post
postal communications 531 n.
pigeon's neck
variegation 437 n.
pigeon-toed
deformed 246 adj.
blemished 845 adj.
pig farm, piggery
stock farm 369 n.
piggin
vessel 194 n.
piggishness
gluttony 947 n.
piggyback
astride 218 adv.
piggybank
treasury 799 n.
pig-headed
obstinate 602 adj.
pig in a poke
uncertainty 474 n.
gambling 618 n.
pig iron
materials 631 n.
pig it
be intemperate 943 vb.
pig-keeping
animal husbandry 369 n.
piglet
young creature 132 n.
pig 365 n.
pigment
pigment 425 n.
pigmentation
hue 425 n.
blackness 428 n.
pigment deficiency
achromatism 426 n.
pigmy
dwarf 196 n.
little 196 adj.
pig's ear
bungling 695 n.
pigskin
skin 226 n.
bookbinding 589 n.
pigsticking
chase 619 n.
pigsty
cattle pen 369 n.
sink 649 n.
pigswill
provender 301 n.
swill 649 n.
pigtail
hanging object 217 n.
rear 238 n.
hair 259 n.
pigwidgin
elf 970 n.
pike
high land 209 n.
sharp point 256 n.
fish 365 n.
spear 723 n.
pikeman
soldiery 722 n.
pilaster
pillar 218 n.
projection 254 n.
ornamental art 844 n.
pilau, pilaf
dish 301 n.
pilchard
fish food 301 n.
pile
fastening 47 n.
accumulation 74 n.
bring together 74 vb.
edifice 164 n.
high structure 209 n.
pillar 218 n.
hair 259 n.
texture 331 n.
heraldry 547 n.
store 632 vb.
acquisition 771 n.
funds 797 n.
wealth 800 n.
— in
fill 54 vb.
enter 297 vb.
— it on
exaggerate 546 vb.
— up
bring together 74 vb.
store 632 vb.
superabound 637 vb.
acquire 771 vb.
pile driver
ram 279 n.
piles
swelling 253 n.
digestive disorders 651 n.
pileup
collision 279 n.
pilfer
steal 788 vb.
pilferer
thief 789 n.
pilgrim
traveller 268 n.
pietist 979 n.
pilgrimage
land travel 267 n.
undertaking 672 n.
act of worship 981 n.
Pilgrim Fathers
settler 191 n.
pill
sphere 252 n.
mouthful 301 n.
medicine 658 n.
punishment 963 n.
pill, the
contraception 172 n.
pillage
rob 788 vb.
booty 790 n.
pillar
fixture 153 n.
high structure 209 n.
verticality 215 n.
pillar 218 n.
monument 548 n.
refuge 662 n.
person of repute 866 n.
pillarbox
postal communications 531 n.
pillar of the community
bigwig 638 n.
person of repute 866 n.
Pillars of Hercules
limit 236 n.
signpost 547 n.
pillbox
small box 194 n.
headgear 228 n.
fort 713 n.
pillion
seat 218 n.
pillion passenger
rider 268 n.
pilliwinks
instrument of torture 964 n.
pillory
lockup 748 n.
satirize 851 vb.
shame 867 vb.
dispraise 924 vb.
defame 926 vb.
accuse 928 vb.
punish 963 vb.
pillory 964 n.

pillow
cushion 218 n.
support 218 vb.
resting place 266 n.
soften 327 vb.
euphoria 376 n.
sleep 679 n.
relief 831 n.
pill-popping
unhealthy 651 adj.
drug-taking 949 n.
pilose
hairy 259 adj.
pilot
navigator 270 n.
aeronaut 271 n.
direct 689 vb.
director 690 n.
pilot light
lighter 385 n.
pilot officer
air officer 741 n.
pilot scheme
experiment 461 n.
preparation 669 n.
pilot vessel
ship 275 n.
pimp
provide 633 vb.
cad 938 n.
bawd 952 n.
pimple
lowness 210 n.
swelling 253 n.
skin disease 651 n.
blemish 845 n.
pin
join 45 vb.
fastening 47 n.
sharp point 256 n.
perforator 263 n.
trifle 639 n.
restrain 747 vb.
retain 778 vb.
jewellery 844 n.
— down
place 187 vb.
compel 740 vb.
retain 778 vb.
— on
affix 45 vb.
accuse 928 vb.
— one's hopes on
believe 485 vb.
hope 852 vb.
pinafore
apron 228 n.
pinball
ball game 837 n.
pince-nez
eyeglass 442 n.
pincer movement
convergence 293 n.
attack 712 n.
pincers
extractor 304 n.
nippers 778 n.
pinch
circumstance 8 n.
small quantity 33 n.
certain quantity 104 n.
crisis 137 n.
make smaller 198 vb.
make thin 206 vb.
notch 260 vb.
converge 293 vb.
pang 377 n.
give pain 377 vb.
touch 378 vb.
refrigerate 382 vb.
needfulness 627 n.
predicament 700 n.
adversity 731 n.
arrest 747 vb.
steal 788 vb.
poverty 801 n.
economize 814 vb.
be parsimonious 816 vb.
endearment 889 n.
pinchbeck
spurious 542 adj.
trivial 639 adj.
pinchpenny
niggard 816 n.
pin cushion
receptacle 194 n.
Pindaric
poetic 593 adj.
pine
tall creature 209 n.
tree 366 n.
be ill 651 vb.
court 889 vb.
— for
regret 830 vb.
desire 859 vb.
pineapple
fruit 301 n.
bomb 723 n.
pinetum
wood 366 n.
pinfold
enclosure 235 n.
ping
roll 403 n.
resound 404 vb.
pingpong
ball game 837 n.
pinguid
fatty 357 adj.
pinhead
minuteness 196 n.
dunce 501 n.
pin hole
perforation 263 n.
pinion
tie 45 vb.
plumage 259 n.
wing 271 n.
fetter 747 vb.
pinioned
retained 778 adj.
pink
moderate 177 adj.
notch 260 vb.
pierce 263 vb.
strike 279 vb.
red 431 adj.
wound 655 vb.
sectional 708 adj.
pink elephants
alcoholism 949 n.
pinkeye
dim sight 440 n.
pink of condition
health 650 n.
pink of perfection
perfection 646 n.
pin money
money 797 n.
pinna
ear 415 n.
pinnace
boat 275 n.
sailing ship 275 n.
pinnacle
summit 213 n.
perfection 646 n.
pinnate
vegetal 366 adj.
pinny
apron 228 n.
pinpoint
small thing 33 n.
specify 80 vb.
place 185 n.
place 187 vb.
minuteness 196 n.
orientate 281 vb.
pinprick
small thing 33 n.
shallowness 212 n.
trifle 639 n.
annoyance 827 n.
resentment 891 n.
pins
leg 267 n.
pins and needles
pang 377 n.
formication 378 n.
pinstripe
suit 228 n.
pattern 844 n.
pint
metrology 465 n.
pinta
draught 301 n.
pintable
plaything 837 n.
Pinteresque
dramatic 594 adj.
pintle
pivot 218 n.
pinto
horse 273 n.
pied 437 adj.
pint-size(d)
little 196 adj.
pin-up
picture 553 n.
a beauty 841 n.
favorite 890 n.
Pinyin
letter 558 n.
pioneer
precursor 66 n.
initiate 68 vb.
settler 191 n.
traveller 268 n.
preparer 669 n.
undertake 672 vb.
direct 689 vb.
facilitate 701 vb.
soldiery 722 n.
pious
believing 485 adj.
pious 979 adj.
worshipping 981 adj.
pious fraud
duplicity 541 n.
deception 542 n.
mental dishonesty 543 n.
pious hope
improbability 472 n.
aspiration 852 n.
pious person
pietist 979 n.
pip
timekeeper 117 n.
flower 366 n.
signal 547 n.
pipe
vat 194 n.
cylinder 252 n.
tube 263 n.
conduit 351 n.
air pipe 353 n.
tobacco 388 n.
shrill 407 vb.
ululate 409 vb.
play music 413 vb.
flute 414 n.
metrology 465 n.
store 632 n.
— down
cease 145 vb.
be quiescent 266 vb.
be silent 399 vb.
be taciturn 582 vb.
— one's eye
weep 836 vb.
— up
cry 408 vb.
speak 579 vb.
pipe band
orchestra 413 n.
pipeclay
whiting 427 n.
pipe cleaner
tobacco 388 n.
cleaning utensil 648 n.
piped music
music 412 n.
pipe dream
insubstantial thing 4 n.
fantasy 513 n.
pleasurableness 826 n.
aspiration 852 n.

pipeline
tube 263 n.
conduit 351 n.
store 632 n.
provision 633 n.
pipe of peace
peace offering 719 n.
piper
instrumentalist 413 n.
pipette
vessel 194 n.
piping
edging 234 n.
tube 263 n.
strident 407 adj.
trimming 844 n.
piping times
peace 717 n.
palmy days 730 n.
pipkin
vessel 194 n.
pippin
fruit 301 n.
darling 890 n.
pips
broadcast 531 n.
badge 547 n.
badge of rank 743 n.
pipsqueak
dwarf 196 n.
nonentity 639 n.
piquancy
nonconformity 84 n.
pungency 388 n.
vigour 571 n.
joy 824 n.
piquant
pungent 388 adj.
savoury 390 adj.
aphoristic 496 adj.
exciting 821 adj.
pique
excite 821 vb.
hurt 827 vb.
discontent 829 n.
resentment 891 n.
huff 891 vb.
— oneself
feel pride 871 vb.
piracy
taking 786 n.
brigandage 788 n.
piranha
fish 365 n.
pirate
mariner 270 n.
militarist 722 n.
appropriate 786 vb.
robber 789 n.
thief 789 n.
knave 938 n.
piratical
thieving 788 adj.
pirogue
rowing boat 275 n.
pirouette
rotate 315 vb.
ballet 594 n.
pis aller
substitute 150 n.
contrivance 623 n.
inexpedience 643 n.
compromise 770 n.
piscatorial
pursuing 619 adj.
Pisces
zodiac 321 n.
piscina
ritual object 988 n.
church utensil 990 n.
pismire
insect 365 n.
pissed
tipsy 949 adj.
pissed off
dejected 834 adj.
piste
trace 548 n.
pistil
flower 366 n.
pistol
kill 362 vb.
pistol 723 n.
pistolshot
short distance 200 n.
bang 402 n.
piston
stopper 264 n.
piston movement
periodicity 141 n.
pit
depth 211 n.
interiority 224 n.
cavity 255 n.
excavation 255 n.
tunnel 263 n.
onlookers 441 n.
trap 542 n.
playgoer 594 n.
theatre 594 n.
pitfall 663 n.
workshop 687 n.
stratagem 698 n.
blemish 845 vb.
— against
oppose 704 vb.
make quarrels 709 vb.
pit-a-pat
agitation 318 n.
faintness 401 n.
roll 403 n.
pitch
adjust 24 vb.
degree 27 n.
serial place 73 n.
territory 184 n.
place 185 n.
summit 213 n.
make vertical 215 vb.
obliquity 220 n.
coat 226 vb.
voyage 269 vb.
propel 287 vb.
tumble 309 vb.
let fall 311 vb.
oscillate 317 vb.
be agitated 318 vb.
resin 357 n.
sound 398 n.
musical note 410 n.
black thing 428 n.
voice 577 n.
arena 724 n.
sale 793 n.
— and toss
plunge 313 vb.
— in
cooperate 706 vb.
— into
attack 712 vb.
fight 716 vb.
dispraise 924 vb.
— one's tent
place oneself 187 vb.
dwell 192 vb.
— upon/on
meet 295 vb.
acquire 771 vb.
pitched battle
fight 716 n.
battle 718 n.
pitcher
vessel 194 n.
pitchfork
propel 287 vb.
farm tool 370 n.
pitch-pipe
flute 414 n.
pitchy
resinous 357 adj.
dark 418 adj.
piteous
pitiable 905 adj.
pitfall
invisibility 444 n.
latency 523 n.
ambush 527 n.
trap 542 n.
danger 661 n.
pitfall 663 n.
stratagem 698 n.
pith
substance 3 n.
essential part 5 n.
interiority 224 n.
centre 225 n.
pulpiness 356 n.
topic 452 n.
meaning 514 n.
importance 638 n.
Pithecanthropus
humankind 371 n.
pith helmet
headgear 228 n.
pithy
substantial 3 adj.
aphoristic 496 adj.
meaningful 514 adj.
concise 569 adj.
compendious 592 adj.
pitiable
unimportant 639 adj.
bad 645 adj.
unhappy 825 adj.
distressing 827 adj.
pitiable 905 adj.
contemptible 922 adj.
pitiful
unimportant 639 adj.
bad 645 adj.
distressing 827 adj.
disreputable 867 adj.
pitiable 905 adj.
pitiless
resolute 599 adj.
severe 735 adj.
cruel 898 adj.
pitiless 906 adj.
pit pony
draught horse 273 n.
pittance
small quantity 33 n.
insufficiency 636 n.
portion 783 n.
receipt 807 n.
pitted
rough 259 adj.
blemished 845 adj.
pitter-patter
oscillation 317 n.
faintness 401 n.
pity
leniency 736 n.
be sensitive 819 vb.
lamentation 836 n.
benevolence 897 n.
pity 905 n.vb.
pity of it
regret 830 n.
pivot
joint 45 n.
causal means 156 n.
influence 178 n.
pivot 218 n.
centre 225 n.
chief thing 638 n.
pivot on
depend 157 vb.
pixie, pixy
elf 970 n.
pixilated
crazy 503 adj.
tipsy 949 adj.
pizza
dish 301 n.
pizzicato
adagio 412 adv.
placable
benevolent 897 adj.
forgiving 909 adj.
placard
exhibit 522 n.
advertisement 528 n.
placate
pacify 719 vb.
beg pardon 909 vb.

placatory
pacificatory 719 adj.
place
order 60 n.
arrange 62 vb.
serial place 73 n.
specify 80 vb.
region 184 n.
place 185 n.
situation 186 n.
locality 187 n.
place 187 vb.
house 192 n.
aim 281 vb.
meal 301 n.
discover 484 vb.
authority 733 n.
apportionment 783 n.
— after
place after 65 vb.
— at one's disposal
offer 759 vb.
— high
respect 920 vb.
— side by side
bring near 200 vb.
— under
number with 78 vb.
placebo
balm 658 n.
medicine 658 n.
placed
circumstantial 8 adj.
place in the sun
palmy days 730 n.
placement
location 187 n.
placenta
sequel 67 n.
obstetrics 167 n.
place of amusement
meeting place 192 n.
place of amusement 837 n.
place of pilgrimage
focus 76 n.
objective 617 n.
holy place 990 n.
place of residence
abode 192 n.
place of worship
temple 990 n.
placet
decree 737 n.
placid
inexcitable 823 adj.
placidity
quietude 266 n.
placket
garment 228 n.
opening 263 n.
plage
shore 344 n.
plagiarism
imitation 20 n.
repetition 106 n.
stealing 788 n.
plagiarist
imitator 20 n.
plagiarize, plagiarise
copy 20 vb.
fake 541 vb.
borrow 785 vb.
steal 788 vb.
plague
recur 139 vb.
badness 645 n.
plague 651 n.
bane 659 n.
blight 659 n.
be difficult 700 vb.
adversity 731 n.
oppress 735 vb.
annoyance 827 n.
torment 827 vb.
plague spot
badness 645 n.
sink 649 n.
infection 651 n.
pitfall 663 n.
plague-stricken
diseased 651 adj.
infectious 653 adj.
plaguey, plaguy
not nice 645 adj.
annoying 827 adj.
plaice
fish food 301 n.
plaid
cloak 228 n.
variegated 437 adj.
plain
simple 44 adj.
space 183 n.
lowness 210 n.
horizontality 216 n.
open space 263 n.
land 344 n.
plain 348 n.
sounding 398 adj.
soft-hued 425 adj.
obvious 443 adj.
meaningful 514 adj.
intelligible 516 adj.
manifest 522 adj.
undisguised 522 adj.
informative 524 adj.
assertive 532 adj.
veracious 540 adj.
stylistic 566 adj.
plain 573 adj.
elegant 575 adj.
prosaic 593 adj.
artless 699 adj.
tedious 838 adj.
ugly 842 adj.
tasteful 846 adj.
plebeian 869 adj.
disrespectful 921 adj.
temperate 942 adj.
ascetic 945 adj.
plain chant
vocal music 412 n.
plain-clothes man
detective 459 n.
police 955 n.
plain cooking
unsavouriness 391 n.
plain dealing
veracity 540 n.
plain English
intelligibility 516 n.
plain Jane
eyesore 842 n.
plain living
averageness 732 n.
temperance 942 n.
plainly
in plain words 520 adv.
plain Mr or Mrs
commoner 869 n.
plain sailing
navigation 269 n.
easy thing 701 n.
plainsong
vocal music 412 n.
hymn 981 n.
plain speaking
intelligibility 516 n.
veracity 540 n.
probity 929 n.
plain-spoken
undisguised 522 adj.
free 744 adj.
plaint
cry 408 n.
lament 836 n.
accusation 928 n.
plaintiff
malcontent 829 n.
accuser 928 n.
litigant 959 n.
plaintive
lamenting 836 adj.
plait
tie 45 vb.
ligature 47 n.
crossing 222 n.
weave 222 vb.
hair 259 n.
fold 261 n.
plan
prototype 23 n.
arrangement 62 n.
predestine 155 vb.
cause 156 vb.
produce 164 vb.
itinerary 267 n.
structure 331 n.
foresight 510 n.
guidebook 524 n.
map 551 n.
representation 551 n.
predetermine 608 vb.
intention 617 n.
plan 623 n.vb.
preparation 669 n.
undertaking 672 n.
tactics 688 n.
be cunning 698 vb.
— ahead
foresee 510 vb.
— for
intend 617 vb.
desire 859 vb.
— out
plan 623 vb.
planchette
spiritualism 984 n.
plane
horizontality 216 n.
sharp edge 256 n.
smoother 258 n.
fly 271 vb.
aircraft 276 n.
tree 366 n.
plane sailing
navigation 269 n.
planet
rotator 315 n.
planet 321 n.
planetarium
astronomy 321 n.
planetary
planetary 321 adj.
planetary influence
cause 156 n.
planet earth
world 321 n.
planetesimal hypothesis
universe 321 n.
planets
fate 596 n.
plangent
loud 400 adj.
resonant 404 adj.
lamenting 836 adj.
planimetry
geometry 465 n.
planish
smooth 258 vb.
planisphere
astronomy 321 n.
map 551 n.
plank
lamina 207 n.
shelf 218 n.
policy 623 n.
materials 631 n.
plankton
microorganism 196 n.
planless
orderless 61 adj.
designless 618 adj.
planned parenthood
contraception 172 n.
planner
producer 164 n.
theorist 512 n.
motivator 612 n.
planner 623 n.
expert 696 n.
plan of campaign
tactics 688 n.
warfare 718 n.
plant
young plant 132 n.
make fruitful 171 vb.

place 187 vb.
aim 281 vb.
vegetable 301 n.
implant 303 vb.
plant 366 n.
cultivate 370 vb.
trap 542 n.
equipment 630 n.
workshop 687 n.
property 777 n.
false charge 928 n.
plantation
wood 366 n.
plant ecology
botany 368 n.
planted
firm 45 adj.
arboreal 366 adj.
agrarian 370 adj.
planter
producer 164 n.
settler 191 n.
farmer 370 n.
gardener 370 n.
preparer 669 n.
plantigrade
footed 214 adj.
plaque
lamina 207 n.
dirt 649 n.
honours 866 n.
plash
weave 222 vb.
moisten 341 vb.
flow 350 vb.
faintness 401 n.
sibilation 406 n.
plasma
matter 319 n.
blood 335 n.
fluid 335 n.
plasmic
organic 358 adj.
plaster
add 38 vb.
adhesive 47 n.
coherence 48 n.
facing 226 n.
coat 226 vb.
surgical dressing 658 n.
fire at 712 vb.
— down
flatten 216 vb.
smooth 258 vb.
— up
repair 656 vb.
plasterboard
paper 631 n.
plaster cast
wrapping 226 n.
sculpture 554 n.
plastered
tipsy 949 adj.
plasterer
artisan 686 n.
plaster of Paris
surgical dressing 658 n.
plaster saint
paragon 646 n.
plastic
substituted 150 adj.
formative 243 adj.
formed 243 adj.
flexible 327 adj.
spurious 542 adj.
glyptic 554 adj.
materials 631 n.
impressible 819 adj.
plastic arts
art 551 n.
sculpture 554 n.
plasticine
softness 327 n.
sculpture 554 n.
plasticity
changeableness 152 n.
softness 327 n.
plastics
resin 357 n.
plastic surgery
surgery 658 n.
beautification 843 n.
plastron
armour 713 n.
plat du jour
dish 301 n.
plate
mould 23 n.
plate 194 n.
lamina 207 n.
horizontality 216 n.
coat 226 vb.
circle 250 n.
tooth 256 n.
label 547 n.
photography 551 n.
picture 553 n.
print 587 n.
edition 589 n.
trophy 729 n.
plateau
high land 209 n.
vertex 213 n.
horizontality 216 n.
plain 348 n.
plated
deceiving 542 adj.
plate glass
lamina 207 n.
transparency 422 n.
platelet
blood 335 n.
plate tectonics
world 321 n.
platform
layer 207 n.
horizontality 216 n.
stand 218 n.
publicity 528 n.
rostrum 539 n.
policy 623 n.
railway 624 n.
arena 724 n.
platinum
white thing 427 n.
bullion 797 n.
platinum blond(e)
achromatism 426 n.
whitish 427 adj.
platitude
maxim 496 n.
lack of meaning 515 n.
platitudinous
aphoristic 496 adj.
feeble 572 adj.
dull 840 adj.
Platonic
pure 950 adj.
Platonic bodies
angular figure 247 n.
Platonic love
love 887 n.
Platonic year
era 110 n.
Platonism
immateriality 320 n.
philosophy 449 n.
platoon
band 74 n.
formation 722 n.
platter
plate 194 n.
gramophone 414 n.
plaudits
rejoicing 835 n.
applause 923 n.
plausible
plausible 471 adj.
sophistical 477 adj.
credible 485 adj.
hypocritical 541 adj.
ostensible 614 adj.
promising 852 adj.
flattering 925 adj.
vindicable 927 adj.
play
agency 173 n.
operate 173 vb.
range 183 n.
oscillate 317 vb.
flow 350 vb.
play music 413 vb.
flash 417 n.
variegate 437 vb.
stage play 594 n.
act 594 vb.
gamble 618 vb.
action 676 n.
contend 716 vb.
scope 744 n.
amusement 837 n.
amuse oneself 837 vb.
wooing 889 n.
— against
contend 716 vb.
— a joke on
befool 542 vb.
— another's game
cooperate 706 vb.
— a part
influence 178 vb.
dissemble 541 vb.
act 594 vb.
do 676 vb.
— at
be inattentive 456 vb.
amuse oneself 837 vb.
— a waiting game
be pending 136 vb.
be cautious 858 vb.
— ball
cooperate 706 vb.
— cards
amuse oneself 837 vb.
— cat and mouse
hunt 619 vb.
— down
moderate 177 vb.
underestimate 483 vb.
— ducks and drakes (with)
consume 165 vb.
be prodigal 815 vb.
— fair
be honourable 929 vb.
— false
be false 541 vb.
tergiversate 603 vb.
be dishonest 930 vb.
— fast and loose with
befool 542 vb.
— for a draw
parry 713 vb.
be cautious 858 vb.
— for time
be cunning 698 vb.
be obstructive 702 vb.
— gooseberry
look after 457 vb.
— havoc with
jumble 63 vb.
harm 645 vb.
impair 655 vb.
— into one's hands
blunder 495 vb.
be clumsy 695 vb.
— it by ear
intuit 476 vb.
be cautious 858 vb.
— off against
use 673 vb.
— on
use 673 vb.
— one false
disappoint 509 vb.
— one's cards well
be skilful 694 vb.
be successful 727 vb.
— oneself in
habituate 610 vb.
— one's part
function 622 vb.
behave 688 vb.

do one's duty 917 vb.
— on one's feelings
excite 821 vb.
frighten 854 vb.
— practical jokes
be absurd 497 vb.
amuse oneself 837 vb.
— safe
seek safety 660 vb.
be cautious 858 vb.
— second fiddle
be inferior 35 vb.
obey 739 vb.
have no repute 867 vb.
be modest 874 vb.
— the fool
be absurd 497 vb.
amuse oneself 837 vb.
be rash 857 vb.
— the game
behave 688 vb.
be just 913 vb.
be honourable 929 vb.
— the market
gamble 618 vb.
speculate 791 vb.
— to the gallery
act 594 vb.
be affected 850 vb.
be ostentatious 875 vb.
— tricks on
befool 542 vb.
be cunning 698 vb.
— truant
be absent 190 vb.
run away 620 vb.
fail in duty 918 vb.
— up
overrate 482 vb.
be obstructive 702 vb.
disobey 738 vb.
— upon
operate 173 vb.
motivate 612 vb.
— with
neglect 458 vb.
be expert 694 vb.
be witty 839 vb.
ridicule 851 vb.
caress 889 vb.
— with fire
be in danger 661 vb.
be rash 857 vb.
play-acting
duplicity 541 n.
acting 594 n.
affectation 850 n.
playback
repetition 106 n.
gramophone 414 n.
playbill
list 87 n.
playboy
reveller 837 n.
beau monde 848 n.
sensualist 944 n.
play construction
dramaturgy 594 n.
played out
ending 69 adj.
player
instrumentalist 413 n.
interpreter 520 n.
actor 594 n.
gambler 618 n.
doer 676 n.
agent 686 n.
player 837 n.
player piano
piano 414 n.
playful
capricious 604 adj.
merry 833 adj.
amused 837 adj.
witty 839 adj.
innocent 935 adj.
playgoer
spectator 441 n.
playgoer 594 n.
playground
arena 724 n.
pleasure ground 837 n.
playgroup
school 539 n.
playhouse
theatre 594 n.
place of amusement 837 n.
playing field
arena 724 n.
pleasure ground 837 n.
playmate
colleague 707 n.
player 837 n.
chum 880 n.
play of colour
variegation 437 n.
play of features
mien 445 n.
feeling 818 n.
play on words
absurdity 497 n.
equivocalness 518 n.
wit 839 n.
plays
literature 557 n.
plaything
bauble 639 n.
plaything 837 n.
plaything of, the
subjected 745 adj.
playwright
author 589 n.
dramatist 594 n.
play-writing
dramaturgy 594 n.
plea
testimony 466 n.
argument 475 n.
pretext 614 n.
request 761 n.
vindication 927 n.
litigation 959 n.
pleach
weave 222 vb.
plead
testify 466 vb.
argue 475 vb.
plead 614 vb.
justify 927 vb.
do law 958 vb.
litigate 959 vb.
— guilty
confess 526 vb.
be guilty 936 vb.
— not guilty
stand trial 959 vb.
pleader
intermediary 231 n.
reasoner 475 n.
speaker 579 n.
motivator 612 n.
mediator 720 n.
law agent 958 n.
pleadings
argument 475 n.
legal trial 959 n.
pleasance
pleasance 192 n.
pleasure ground 837 n.
pleasant
pleasant 376 adj.
pleasurable 826 adj.
amusing 837 adj.
pleasantry
wit 839 n.
please
please 826 vb.
content 828 vb.
cheer 833 vb.
amuse 837 vb.
— oneself
will 595 vb.
please oneself 734 vb.
disobey 738 vb.
be free 744 vb.
pleased
willing 597 adj.
— with oneself
prideful 871 adj.
vain 873 adj.
pleasurable
pleasant 376 adj.
pleasurable 826 adj.
pleasure
pleasure 376 n.
joy 824 n.
amusement 837 n.
sensualism 944 n.
pleasure-giving
pleasant 376 adj.
good 615 adj.
pleasurable 826 adj.
sensual 944 adj.
pleasure ground
pleasance 192 n.
pleasure ground 837 n.
pleasure-loving
sensuous 376 adj.
sensual 944 adj.
pleasure-seeker
reveller 837 n.
pleasure trip
land travel 267 n.
amusement 837 n.
pleat
garment 228 n.
fold 261 n.
pleb(s)
commonalty 869 n.
plebeian
inferior 35 adj.
ill-bred 847 adj.
commoner 869 n.
plebeian 869 adj.
plebiscite
judgment 480 n.
vote 605 n.
legislation 953 n.
plectrum
harp 414 n.
pledge
thing transferred 272 n.
drink 301 vb.
oath 532 n.
promise 764 n. vb.
security 767 n.
assign 780 vb.
borrow 785 vb.
toast 876 vb.
duty 917 n.
pledget
stopper 264 n.
surgical dressing 658 n.
Pleiades
star 321 n.
nymph 967 n.
Pleistocene
secular 110 adj.
plenary
complete 54 adj.
plenipotentiary
powerful 160 adj.
delegate 754 n.
envoy 754 n.
plenitude
greatness 32 n.
plenitude 54 n.
plenty 635 n.
plentiful
plenteous 635 adj.
plenty
great quantity 32 n.
productiveness 171 n.
store 632 n.
plenty 635 n.
redundance 637 n.
prosperity 730 n.
wealth 800 n.

liberality 813 n.
plenum
materiality 319 n.
pleonasm
pleonasm 570 n.
superfluity 637 n.
plesiosaur
animal 365 n.
plethora
redundance 637 n.
satiety 863 n.
pleurisy
respiratory disease 651 n.
plexus
network 222 n.
pliability
softness 327 n.
persuadability 612 n.
pliable
flexible 327 adj.
pliancy
changeableness 152 n.
willingness 597 n.
persuadability 612 n.
pliant
conformable 83 adj.
flexible 327 adj.
irresolute 601 adj.
tractable 701 adj.
submitting 721 adj.
plié
ballet 594 n.
pliers
extractor 304 n.
tool 630 n.
nippers 778 n.
plight
state 7 n.
circumstance 8 n.
adversity 731 n.
plight one's troth
promise 764 vb.
court 889 vb.
wed 894 vb.
Plimsoll line
limit 236 n.
gauge 465 n.
plimsolls
footwear 228 n.
plinth
base 214 n.n.
stand 218 n.
plod
walk 267 vb.
move slowly 278 vb.
persevere 600 vb.
work 682 vb.
plonk
wine 301 n.
crackle 402 vb.
nonresonance 405 n.
plop
descend 309 vb.
plunge 313 vb.
sound faint 401 vb.
nonresonance 405 n.
plosive
speech sound 398 n.
plot
combination 50 n.
place 185 n.
garden 370 n.
topic 452 n.
secrecy 525 n.
deceive 542 vb.
narrative 590 n.
dramaturgy 594 n.
plot 623 n.vb.
prepare 669 vb.
stratagem 698 n.
cooperate 706 vb.
compact 765 n.
plotted
measured 465 adj.
planned 623 adj.
plotter
deceiver 545 n.
planner 623 n.
slyboots 698 n.
plotting
perfidious 930 adj.
plough
cut 46 vb.
groove 262 vb.
farm tool 370 n.
cultivate 370 vb.
disapprove 924 vb.
— back
economize 814 vb.
— through
travel 267 vb.
ploughed
unsuccessful 728 adj.
ploughman
farmer 370 n.
country-dweller 869 n.
ploughman's lunch
meal 301 n.
ploughshare
sharp edge 256 n.
farm tool 370 n.
plover
bird 365 n.
ploy
contrivance 623 n.
stratagem 698 n.
pluck
insides 224 n.
uncover 229 vb.
draw 288 vb.
extract 304 vb.
agitate 318 vb.
cultivate 370 vb.
play music 413 vb.
resolution 599 n.
stamina 600 n.
fleece 786 vb.
take 786 vb.
defraud 788 vb.
courage 855 n.
— to pieces
rend 46 vb.
demolish 165 vb.
— up courage
take courage 855 vb.
plucking
hairdressing 843 n.
plucky
persevering 600 adj.
courageous 855 adj.
plug
repeat oneself 106 vb.
covering 226 n.
stopper 264 n.
staunch 350 vb.
tobacco 388 n.
advertise 528 vb.
emphasize 532 vb.
— away at
persevere 600 vb.
— in
connect 45 vb.
empower 160 vb.
plug-ugly
low fellow 869 n.
ruffian 904 n.
plum
fruit 301 n.
purpleness 436 n.
elite 644 n.
trophy 729 n.
desired object 859 n.
plumage
plumage 259 n.
plumb
positively 32 adv.
complete 54 adj.
be deep 211 vb.
vertical 215 adj.
straight on 249 adv.
measure 465 vb.
truly 494 adv.
plumbago
lubricant 334 n.
plumber
mender 656 n.
artisan 686 n.
plumbing
conduit 351 n.
cleansing 648 n.
plumbline
verticality 215 n.
plume
plumage 259 n.
trimming 844 n.
plume oneself (on)
feel pride 871 vb.
be vain 873 vb.
boast 877 vb.
plum in one's mouth
speech defect 580 n.
plummet
depth 211 n.
verticality 215 n.
sailing aid 269 n.
founder 313 vb.
gravity 322 n.
plummy
speaking 579 adj.
super 644 adj.
plumose
downy 259 adj.
plump
instantaneously 116 adv.
fleshy 195 adj.
tumble 309 vb.
plunge 313 vb.
nonresonance 405 n.
— for
choose 605 vb.
— up
enlarge 197 vb.
plunder
acquisition 771 n.
take away 786 vb.
rob 788 vb.
booty 790 n.
plunge
decrease 37 n.vb.
revolution 149 n.
be destroyed 165 vb.
be deep 211 vb.
be in motion 265 vb.
aquatics 269 n.
swim 269 vb.
move fast 277 vb.
enter 297 vb.
immersion 303 n.
immerse 303 vb.
descend 309 vb.
lower 311 vb.
leap 312 vb.
plunge 313 n.vb.
be agitated 318 vb.
drench 341 vb.
gambling 618 n.
ablutions 648 n.
be cheap 812 vb.
be rash 857 vb.
be intemperate 943 vb.
— into
enter 297 vb.
undertake 672 vb.
plunger
diver 313 n.
gambler 618 n.
desperado 857 n.
plunging neckline
bareness 229 n.
plunk
bang 402 n.
nonresonance 405 n.
pluperfect
past time 125 n.
plural
plural 101 adj.
grammatical 564 adj.
pluralism
philosophy 449 n.
government 733 n.
pluralist
cleric 986 n.
plurality
plurality 101 n.
greater number 104 n.

plus
in addition 38 adv.
plus fours
trousers 228 n.
plush
hair 259 n.
softness 327 n.
rich 800 adj.
ornamented 844 adj.
plushy
rich 800 adj.
ostentatious 875 adj.
Pluto
planet 321 n.
Chthonian deity 967 n.
mythic hell 972 n.
plutocracy
government 733 n.
wealth 800 n.
plutocrat
master 741 n.
rich person 800 n.
plutonic
fiery 379 adj.
plutonic rock
rock 344 n.
plutonium
fuel 385 n.
poison 659 n.
pluvial
humid 341 adj.
pluviometer
hygrometry 341 n.
ply
be periodic 141 vb.
layer 207 n.
fold 261 n.
voyage 269 vb.
busy oneself 622 vb.
use 673 vb.
do 676 vb.
request 761 vb.
Plymouth Brethren
ascetic 945 n.
sect 978 n.
plywood
lamina 207 n.
materials 631 n.
p.m.
o'clock 117 adv.
evening 129 n.
pneumatic
soft 327 adj.
gaseous 336 adj.
airy 340 adj.
pneumatic drill
perforator 263 n.
pneumatics
gaseousness 336 n.
pneumatics 340 n.
pneumonia
respiratory disease 651 n.
poach
cook 301 vb.
encroach 306 vb.
hunt 619 vb.
steal 788 vb.
poached
rough 259 adj.
marshy 347 adj.
poacher
hunter 619 n.
thief 789 n.
pocket
classification 77 n.
place 185 n.
stow 187 vb.
pocket 194 n.
little 196 adj.
garment 228 n.
opening 263 n.
insert 303 vb.
battleground 724 n.
receive 782 vb.
take 786 vb.
treasury 799 n.
be patient 823 vb.
be humble 872 vb.
forgive 909 vb.
pocketbook
case 194 n.
textbook 589 n.
pocket edition
miniature 196 n.
pocket-handkerchief
little 196 adj.
pocket money
receipt 807 n.
pockmark
cavity 255 n.
skin disease 651 n.
blemish 845 n.vb.
pockmarked
mottled 437 adj.
pococurante
apathetic 820 adj.
indifferent 860 adj.
pod
receptacle 194 n.
skin 226 n.
podgy
fleshy 195 adj.
soft 327 adj.
podium
stand 218 n.
rostrum 539 n.
poem
composition 56 n.
poem 593 n.
a beauty 841 n.
poet
author 589 n.
poet 593 n.
poetaster
poet 593 n.
poetic
imaginative 513 adj.
poetic 593 adj.
poetic drama
stage play 594 n.
poetic justice
retaliation 714 n.
punishment 963 n.
poetic licence
ideality 513 n.
poetry 593 n.
poetics
poetry 593 n.
poetry
ideality 513 n.
literature 557 n.
reading matter 589 n.
poetry 593 n.
po-faced
serious 834 adj.
dull 840 adj.
pogo stick
plaything 837 n.
pogrom
slaughter 362 n.
poignancy
pungency 388 n.
vigour 571 n.
poignant
striking 374 adj.
painful 377 adj.
felt 818 adj.
point
juncture 8 n.
relevance 9 n.
degree 27 n.
small thing 33 n.
extremity 69 n.
serial place 73 n.
instant 116 n.
keenness 174 n.
place 185 n.
situation 186 n.
minuteness 196 n.
projection 254 n.
sharp point 256 n.
aim 281 vb.
point to 281 vb.
topic 452 n.
reasons 475 n.
punctuation 547 n.
gesticulate 547 vb.
lettering 586 n.
use 673 n.
wit 839 n.
— a moral
teach 534 vb.
— at
aim at 617 vb.
not respect 921 vb.
accuse 928 vb.
— out
specify 80 vb.
point to 281 vb.
attract notice 455 vb.
show 522 vb.
inform 524 vb.
indicate 547 vb.
— the other way
tell against 467 vb.
— to
focus 76 vb.
attribute 158 vb.
tend 179 vb.
point to 281 vb.
make likely 471 vb.
predict 511 vb.
mean 514 vb.
indicate 547 vb.
— up
manifest 522 vb.
emphasize 532 vb.
point at issue
topic 452 n.
question 459 n.
casus belli 709 n.
point blank
towards 281 adv.
plainly 573 adv.
point duty
traffic control 305 n.
pointed
apt 24 adj.
keen 174 adj.
sharp 256 adj.
convergent 293 adj.
obvious 443 adj.
meaningful 514 adj.
assertive 532 adj.
forceful 571 adj.
witty 839 adj.
pointedly
remarkably 32 adv.
purposely 617 adv.
pointer
dog 365 n.
indicator 547 n.
Pointillism
school of painting 553 n.
pointless
insubstantial 4 adj.
irrelevant 10 adj.
unsharpened 257 adj.
prolix 570 adj.
useless 641 adj.
dull 840 adj.
point of difference
speciality 80 n.
point of honour
probity 929 n.
point of no return
juncture 8 n.
limit 236 n.
point of time
instant 116 n.
point of view
view 438 n.
appearance 445 n.
idea 451 n.
bias 481 n.
opinion 485 n.
points
advantage 34 n.
numeration 86 n.
divergence 294 n.
railway 624 n.
point-to-point
equitation 267 n.
racing 716 n.
point well taken
reasons 475 n.
poise
equilibrium 28 n.
mien 445 n.
conduct 688 n.

inexcitability 823 n.
etiquette 848 n.
poison
destroy 165 vb.
destroyer 168 n.
alcoholic drink 301 n.
murder 362 vb.
unsavouriness 391 n.
badness 645 n.
make unclean 649 vb.
infection 651 n.
impair 655 vb.
poison 659 n.
excite hate 888 vb.
be malevolent 898 vb.
poisoner
murderer 362 n.
poisoning 659 n.
offender 904 n.
poison gas
gas 336 n.
poison 659 n.
weapon 723 n.
poisonous
deadly 362 adj.
unsavoury 391 adj.
harmful 645 adj.
diseased 651 adj.
toxic 653 adj.
baneful 659 adj.
dangerous 661 adj.
paining 827 adj.
maleficent 898 adj.
intoxicating 949 adj.
poisonous plant
poisonous plant 659 n.
poison pen
defamer 926 n.
poke
pierce 263 vb.
gesticulate 547 vb.
— at
strike 279 vb.
strike at 712 vb.
— fun at
be witty 839 vb.
ridicule 851 vb.
— into
insert 303 vb.
— one's nose in
interfere 231 vb.
be curious 453 vb.
meddle 678 vb.
— out
jut 254 vb.
poke bonnet
headgear 228 n.
poker
furnace 383 n.
card game 837 n.
poker-faced
still 266 adj.
unintelligible 517 adj.
reticent 525 adj.
impassive 820 adj.
serious 834 adj.
pokerwork
ornamental art 844 n.
poky
little 196 adj.
restraining 747 adj.
graceless 842 adj.
polacre
merchant ship 275 n.
polar
ending 69 adj.
topmost 213 adj.
opposite 240 adj.
telluric 321 adj.
cold 380 adj.
polariscope
optical device 442 n.
polarity
polarity 14 n.
duality 90 n.
tendency 179 n.
counteraction 182 n.
contraposition 240 n.
polarization
reflection 417 n.
polder
land 344 n.
pole
extremity 69 n.
farness 199 n.
long measure 203 n.
high structure 209 n.
summit 213 n.
verticality 215 n.
pillar 218 n.
pivot 218 n.
limit 236 n.
impel 279 vb.
gauge 465 n.
poleaxe
slaughter 362 vb.
axe 723 n.
polecat
mammal 365 n.
stench 397 n.
polemic
argument 475 n.
reasoner 475 n.
quarrel 709 n.
polemics
argument 475 n.
conference 584 n.
contention 716 n.
polenta
cereals 301 n.
pole position
advantage 34 n.
poles asunder
contrary 14 adj.
different 15 adj.
against 240 adv.
pole star
star 321 n.
signpost 547 n.
directorship 689 n.
pole vault
ascent 308 n.
leap 312 vb.
pole-vaulter
jumper 312 n.
police
order 60 vb.
protector 660 n.
safeguard 660 vb.
manage 689 vb.
rule 733 vb.
restrain 747 vb.
police 955 n.
police court
lawcourt 956 n.
police enquiry
police enquiry 459 n.
police force
police 955 n.
policeman, policewoman
protector 660 n.
police 955 n.
police state
despotism 733 n.
police station
lockup 748 n.
police whistle
signal 547 n.
danger signal 665 n.
policy
topic 452 n.
sagacity 498 n.
policy 623 n.
action 676 n.
tactics 688 n.
management 689 n.
cunning 698 n.
title deed 767 n.
poliomyelitis, polio
infection 651 n.
nervous disorders 651 n.
polish
facing 226 n.
smoothness 258 n.
friction 333 n.
reflection 417 n.
make bright 417 vb.
elegance 575 n.
cleanser 648 n.
civilization 654 n.
make better 654 vb.
beauty 841 n.
good taste 846 n.
etiquette 848 n.
— off
be active 678 vb.
carry through 725 vb.
politburo
party 708 n.
polite
literary 557 adj.
elegant 575 adj.
well-bred 848 adj.
courteous 884 adj.
respectful 920 adj.
politic
wise 498 adj.
advisable 642 adj.
skilful 694 adj.
political
directing 689 adj.
governmental 733 adj.
political economy
management 689 n.
political favours
incentive 612 n.
political organization
territory 184 n.
nation 371 n.
political organization 733 n.
political party
association 706 n.
political party 708 n.
government 733 n.
political prisoner
prisoner 750 n.
political science
tactics 688 n.
politician
planner 623 n.
manager 690 n.
expert 696 n.
political party 708 n.
politicking
government 733 n.
politico
political party 708 n.
politics
tactics 688 n.
government 733 n.
polity
government 733 n.
polka
musical piece 412 n.
dance 837 n.
polka dot
maculation 437 n.
pattern 844 n.
poll
numeration 86 n.
statistics 86 n.
enquiry 459 n.
judgment 480 n.
vote 605 n.vb.
pollard
make smaller 198 vb.
tree 366 n.
pollen
genitalia 167 n.
powder 332 n.
flower 366 n.
pollex
finger 378 n.
pollicitation
promise 764 n.
pollination
propagation 167 n.
productiveness 171 n.
pollster
enumerator 86 n.

enquirer 459 n.
pollute
make useless 641 vb.
harm 645 vb.
make unclean 649 vb.
impair 655 vb.
misuse 675 vb.
pollution
uncleanness 649 n.
infection 651 n.
insalubrity 653 n.
impairment 655 n.
poison 659 n.
misuse 675 n.
slur 867 n.
Pollyanna
cheerfulness 833 n.
polo
ball game 837 n.
polonaise
musical piece 412 n.
dance 837 n.
polo-neck
jersey 228 n.
neckline 228 n.
poltergeist
hinderer 702 n.
elf 970 n.
ghost 970 n.
spiritualism 984 n.
poltroon
coward 856 n.
poly-
plural 101 adj.
poly
academy 539 n.
polyandry
type of marriage 894 n.
polychromatic
coloured 425 adj.
variegated 437 adj.
polychrome
multiform 82 adj.
painting 553 n.
polydactyl
handed 378 adj.
polydaemonism
diabolism 969 n.
polyester
textile 222 n.
polygamist
polygamist 894 n.
polygamy
type of marriage 894 n.
polyglot
interpreter 520 n.
linguist 557 n.
speaking 579 adj.
polygon
angular figure 247 n.
polygyny
type of marriage 894 n.
polyhedron
plurality 101 n.
polyhistor
scholar 492 n.
polymath
scholar 492 n.
expert 696 n.
polymorphic
polymorphous
multiform 82 adj.
plural 101 adj.
polyp
swelling 253 n.
polyphony
melody 410 n.
polysemy
connotation 514 n.
equivocalness 518 n.
polystyrene
wrapping 226 n.
materials 631 n.
polysyllabic
long 203 adj.
diffuse 570 adj.
polysyllable
word 559 n.
polysynthetic language
language type 557 n.
polytechnic
academy 539 n.
polytheism
deism 973 n.
polythene
wrapping 226 n.
materials 631 n.
polyunsaturates
food content 301 n.
polyurethane
resin 357 n.
pomade
unguent 357 n.
scent 396 n.
cosmetic 843 n.
pomander
scent 396 n.
pomegranate
fruit 301 n.
pommel
handle 218 n.
sphere 252 n.
pomp
pride 871 n.
ostentation 875 n.
pompom
gun 723 n.
trimming 844 n.
pompous
rhetorical 574 adj.
inelegant 576 adj.
prideful 871 adj.
vain 873 adj.
ostentatious 875 adj.
ponce
bawd 952 n.
ponce about
be affected 850 vb.
poncho
cloak 228 n.
pond
shallowness 212 n.
lake 346 n.
ponder
meditate 449 vb.
estimate 480 vb.
ponderable
material 319 adj.
weighty 322 adj.
ponderous
weighty 322 adj.
inelegant 576 adj.
clumsy 695 adj.
dull 840 adj.
pong
stench 397 n.
stink 397 vb.
pongee
textile 222 n.
pongo
soldier 722 n.
poniard
sidearms 723 n.
pons asinorum
unintelligibility 517 n.
pitfall 663 n.
pontifex
priest 986 n.
pontiff
priest 986 n.
pontifical
positive 473 adj.
assertive 532 adj.
ecclesiastical 985 adj.
pontificals
vestments 989 n.
pontificate
dogmatize 473 vb.
be biased 481 vb.
affirm 532 vb.
church office 985 n.
pontoon
raft 275 n.
card game 837 n.
pony
cup 194 n.
pony 273 n.
funds 797 n.
ponytail
sequel 67 n.
hair 259 n.
pony-trekking
sport 837 n.
pooch
dog 365 n.
poodle
dog 365 n.
toady 879 n.
poof
nonconformist 84 n.
Pooh-Bah
officer 741 n.
pooh-pooh
disregard 458 vb.
underestimate 483 vb.
hold cheap 922 vb.
pool
lake 346 n.
store 632 n.vb.
association 706 n.
acquisition 771 n.
joint possession 775 n.
communalize 775 vb.
ball game 837 n.
— one's knowledge
communicate 524 vb.
pool room
gaming-house 618 n.
place of amusement 837 n.
pools
gambling 618 n.
poop
poop 238 n.
pooped
fatigued 684 adj.
poor
weak 163 adj.
unproductive 172 adj.
feeble 572 adj.
necessitous 627 adj.
insufficient 636 adj.
unimportant 639 adj.
bad 645 adj.
imperfect 647 adj.
dilapidated 655 adj.
unfortunate 731 adj.
unprosperous 731 adj.
not owning 774 adj.
poor 801 adj.
unhappy 825 adj.
disreputable 867 adj.
poor, the
poor person 801 n.
poor hand
bungler 697 n.
poor head
unintelligence 499 n.
poor health
ill health 651 n.
poorhouse
retreat 192 n.
poverty 801 n.
poor in spirit
humble 872 adj.
poor lookout
adversity 731 n.
hopelessness 853 n.
poorly
weakly 163 adj.
sick 651 adj.
poor performance
bungling 695 n.
poor prospect
improbability 472 n.
poor quality
inferiority 35 n.
poor relation
inferior 35 n.
nonentity 639 n.
imperfection 647 n.

object of scorn 867 n.
poor relief
sociology 901 n.
poor return
unproductiveness 172 n.
poor show
bungling 695 n.
poor-spirited
cowardly 856 adj.
poor stick
ninny 501 n.
poor taste
bad taste 847 n.
poor whites
lower classes 869 n.
poor wretch
unlucky person 731 n.
sufferer 825 n.
pop
paternity 169 n.
soft drink 301 n.
sound faint 401 vb.
bang 402 n.
music 412 n.
give security 767 vb.
borrow 785 vb.
— at
fire at 712 vb.
— in
enter 297 vb.
— into
insert 303 vb.
— off
die 361 vb.
— one's clogs
die 361 vb.
— out
jut 254 vb.
emerge 298 vb.
— the question
court 889 vb.
— up
reoccur 106 vb.
happen 154 vb.
arrive 295 vb.
be visible 443 vb.
appear 445 vb.
pop art
art 551 n.
popcorn
mouthful 301 n.
pope
sovereign 741 n.
ecclesiarch 986 n.
popedom
the church 985 n.
Pope Joan
insubstantial thing 4 n.
popery
Catholicism 976 n.
pop-eyed
projecting 254 adj.
wondering 864 adj.
pop group
band 74 n.
orchestra 413 n.
popgun
propellant 287 n.
bang 402 n.
plaything 837 n.
popinjay
fop 848 n.
poplar
tall creature 209 n.
tree 366 n.
poplin
textile 222 n.
popper
fastening 47 n.
poppet
darling 890 n.
popple
crinkle 251 vb.
roughen 259 vb.
be agitated 318 vb.
flow 350 vb.
poppy
redness 431 n.
soporific 679 n.
poppycock
empty talk 515 n.
poppyhead
pattern 844 n.
popshop
pawnshop 784 n.
pop singer
vocalist 413 n.
entertainer 594 n.
person of repute 866 n.
popsy
darling 890 n.
populace
inhabitants 191 n.
social group 371 n.
commonalty 869 n.
popular
general 79 adj.
native 191 adj.
intelligible 516 adj.
governmental 733 adj.
reputable 866 adj.
welcomed 882 adj.
approved 923 adj.
popular belief
consensus 488 n.
popular front
association 706 n.
political party 708 n.
popular hero
person of repute 866 n.
popularity
repute 866 n.
sociability 882 n.
lovableness 887 n.
approbation 923 n.
popularize, popularise
be intelligible 516 vb.
interpret 520 vb.
facilitate 701 vb.
vulgarize 847 vb.
populate
be fruitful 171 vb.
place oneself 187 vb.
dwell 192 vb.
appropriate 786 vb.
population
inhabitants 191 n.
social group 371 n.
population explosion
productiveness 171 n.
populist
political party 708 n.
philanthropist 901 n.
populous
assembled 74 adj.
multitudinous 104 adj.
porcelain
brittleness 330 n.
pottery 381 n.
porch
entrance 68 n.
lobby 194 n.
threshold 234 n.
doorway 263 n.
access 624 n.
church exterior 990 n.
porcine
animal 365 adj.
porcupine
prickle 256 n.
mammal 365 n.
pore
cavity 255 n.
orifice 263 n.
outlet 298 n.
scan 438 vb.
be attentive 455 vb.
— over
study 536 vb.
pork
meat 301 n.
pork barrel
incentive 612 n.
booty 790 n.
porker
pig 365 n.
pork pie
meat 301 n.
pornographic
erotic 887 adj.
pornography
impurity 951 n.
porous
concave 255 adj.
porous 263 adj.
porpoise
mammal 365 n.
porridge
cereals 301 n.
pulpiness 356 n.
detention 747 n.
porringer
bowl 194 n.
port
stopping place 145 n.
stable 192 n.
sinistrality 242 n.
window 263 n.
gait 265 n.
goal 295 n.
wine 301 n.
redness 431 n.
shelter 662 n.
conduct 688 n.
portable
little 196 adj.
transferable 272 adj.
light 323 adj.
broadcasting 531 n.
portage
transport 272 n.
portal
threshold 234 n.
doorway 263 n.
portcullis
barrier 235 n.
obstacle 702 n.
fort 713 n.
portend
predict 511 vb.
portent
omen 511 n.
prodigy 864 n.
portentous
presageful 511 adj.
frightening 854 adj.
threatening 900 adj.
porter
doorkeeper 264 n.
bearer 273 n.
alcoholic drink 301 n.
worker 686 n.
servant 742 n.
porterage
transport 272 n.
portfire
lighter 385 n.
portfolio
list 87 n.
case 194 n.
collection 632 n.
authority 733 n.
title deed 767 n.
jurisdiction 955 n.
porthole
window 263 n.
portico
series 71 n.
lobby 194 n.
portion
part 53 n.
fraction 102 n.
meal 301 n.
fate 596 n.
provision 633 n.
participation 775 n.
dower 777 n.
portion 783 n.
portionless
poor 801 adj.
portly
fleshy 195 adj.
portmanteau
box 194 n.

storage 632 n.
portmanteau word
compound 50 n.
word 559 n.
conciseness 569 n.
port of call
stopping place 145 n.
portolano
sailing aid 269 n.
portrait
copy 22 n.
record 548 n.
picture 553 n.
description 590 n.
portrait painter
artist 556 n.
portraiture
representation 551 n.
art style 553 n.
portray
liken 18 vb.
imitate 20 vb.
represent 551 vb.
paint 553 vb.
pose
imitate 20 vb.
be an example 23 vb.
appearance 445 n.
interrogate 459 vb.
represent 551 vb.
conduct 688 n.
be affected 850 vb.
Poseidon
sea god 343 n.
Olympian deity 967 n.
poser
question 459 n.
enigma 530 n.
difficulty 700 n.
poseur, poseuse
imitator 20 n.
affecter 850 n.
posh
fashionable 848 adj.
genteel 868 adj.
ostentatious 875 adj.
posit
premise 475 vb.
suppose 512 vb.
position
state 7 n.
order 60 n.
arrange 62 vb.
serial place 73 n.
situation 186 n.
place 187 vb.
opinion 485 n.
supposition 512 n.
job 622 n.
prestige 866 n.
position of authority
position of authority 733 n.
positive
real 1 adj.
copy 22 n.
absolute 32 adj.
numerical 85 adj.
electricity 160 n.
positive 473 adj.
narrow-minded 481 adj.
believing 485 adj.
intelligible 516 adj.
affirmative 532 adj.
forceful 571 adj.
obstinate 602 adj.
positive and negative
polarity 14 n.
duality 90 n.
positive discrimination
injustice 914 n.
positively
positively 32 adv.
positivism
materiality 319 n.
philosophy 449 n.
antichristianity 974 n.
posology
measurement 465 n.
medical art 658 n.
posse
band 74 n.
police 955 n.
possess
dwell 192 vb.
know 490 vb.
make mad 503 vb.
possess 773 vb.
dower 777 vb.
excite 821 vb.
diabolize 969 vb.
possessed
obsessed 455 adj.
frenzied 503 adj.
possession
territory 184 n.
use 673 n.
possession 773 n.
property 777 n.
excitation 821 n.
spell 983 n.
possessions
property 777 n.
wealth 800 n.
possessive
possessing 773 adj.
taking 786 adj.
avaricious 816 adj.
greedy 859 adj.
loving 887 adj.
jealous 911 adj.
selfish 932 adj.
possessiveness
exclusion 57 n.
possessor
resident 191 n.
master 741 n.
participator 775 n.
possessor 776 n.
posset
alcoholic drink 301 n.
possibility
existence 1 n.
opportunity 137 n.
fair chance 159 n.
ability 160 n.
liability 180 n.
possibility 469 n.
probability 471 n.
expectation 507 n.
supposition 512 n.
possible
unreal 2 adj.
future 124 adj.
accessible 289 adj.
possible 469 adj.
credible 485 adj.
latent 523 adj.
easy 701 adj.
post
subsequent 120 adj.
situation 186 n.
place 187 vb.
pillar 218 n.
travel 267 vb.
send 272 vb.
move fast 277 vb.
communicate 524 vb.
advertise 528 vb.
postal communications 531 n.
register 548 vb.
correspondence 588 n.
job 622 n.
hasten 680 vb.
position of authority 733 n.
commission 751 vb.
account 808 vb.
impose a duty 917 vb.
— sentries
invigilate 457 vb.
postage
price 809 n.
postal
epistolary 588 adj.
postal communications
postal communications 531 n.
correspondence 588 n.
postal order
paper money 797 n.
postbag
correspondence 588 n.
postbox
postal communications 531 n.
postbus
bus 274 n.
postcard
message 529 n.
correspondence 588 n.
post chaise
stagecoach 274 n.
postcode
postal communications 531 n.
postdate
misdate 118 vb.
posted
situated 186 adj.
located 187 adj.
informed 524 adj.
posted, be
be situated 186 vb.
poster
advertisement 528 n.
picture 553 n.
posterior
sequential 65 adj.
subsequent 120 adj.
future 124 adj.
buttocks 238 n.
back 238 adj.
posterity
survivor 41 n.
sequence 65 n.
posteriority 120 n.
futurity 124 n.
posterity 170 n.
postern
rear 238 n.
doorway 263 n.
fort 713 n.
poster paint
art equipment 553 n.
postexilic
scriptural 975 adj.
post-free
uncharged 812 adj.
postgraduate
student 538 n.
posthaste
swiftly 277 adv.
hastily 680 adv.
post horn
horn 414 n.
posthumous
subsequent 120 adj.
late 136 adj.
posthumously
post-obit 361 adv.
postilion, postillion
rider 268 n.
servant 742 n.
Post-Impressionism
school of painting 553 n.
postindustrial age
future state 124 n.
posting
location 187 n.
transference 272 n.
mandate 751 n.
postman, postwoman
courier 529 n.
postal

postal communications 531 n.
postman's knock
indoor game 837 n.
postmarital
matrimonial 894 adj.
post meridiem
post meridiem 129 adv.
postmortem
inquest 364 n.
enquiry 459 n.
post-obit
post-obit 361 adv.
post office
postal communications 531 n.
post-paid
uncharged 812 adj.
postpone
put off 136 vb.
avoid 620 vb.
relinquish 621 vb.
not complete 726 vb.
postponement
unwillingness 598 n.
postposition
sequence 65 n.
postprandial
culinary 301 adj.
reposeful 683 adj.
sociable 882 adj.
postscript
adjunct 40 n.
sequel 67 n.
extremity 69 n.
postulant
petitioner 763 n.
nun 986 n.
lay person 987 n.
postulate
premise 475 n.vb.
axiom 496 n.
supposition 512 n.
request 761 n.
posture
circumstance 8 n.
situation 186 n.
form 243 n.
mien 445 n.
conduct 688 n.
behave 688 vb.
be affected 850 vb.
postwar
dated 108 adj.
peaceful 717 adj.
posy
bunch 74 n.
ornamentation 844 n.
love token 889 n.
pot
vessel 194 n.
shorten 204 vb.
propulsion 287 n.
insert 303 vb.
pottery 381 n.
abstract 592 vb.
preserve 666 vb.
trophy 729 n.
drug-taking 949 n.
reward 962 n.
— at
shoot 287 vb.
potable
edible 301 adj.
potash
fertilizer 171 n.
potation(s)
drinking 301 n.
drunkenness 949 n.
potato
vegetable 301 n.
pot-bellied
fleshy 195 adj.
expanded 197 adj.
convex 253 adj.
pot belly
maw 194 n.
potboiler
author 589 n.
novel 590 n.
pot calling the kettle black
equivalent 28 adj.
poteen
alcoholic drink 301 n.
potency
power 160 n.
strength 162 n.
utility 640 n.
potent
powerful 160 adj.
strong 162 adj.
generative 167 adj.
operative 173 adj.
vigorous 174 adj.
influential 178 adj.
heraldry 547 n.
intoxicating 949 adj.
potentate
potentate 741 n.
person of rank 868 n.
potential
unreal 2 adj.
intrinsic 5 adj.
quantity 26 n.
future 124 adj.
energy 160 n.
possible 469 adj.
latent 523 adj.
potentiality
existence 1 n.
ability 160 n.
influence 178 n.
liability 180 n.
pother
turmoil 61 n.
excitable state 822 n.
potherb
potherb 301 n.
condiment 389 n.
pothole
cavity 255 n.
orifice 263 n.
potholed
rough 259 adj.
pot-holing
depth 211 n.
descent 309 n.
search 459 n.
discovery 484 n.
pothook
lettering 586 n.
pothouse
tavern 192 n.
pot-hunter
contender 716 n.
player 837 n.
potion
draught 301 n.
medicine 658 n.
magic instrument 983 n.
potluck
chance 159 n.
meal 301 n.
gambling 618 n.
nonpreparation 670 n.
sociability 882 n.
potpourri
medley 43 n.
scent 396 n.
musical piece 412 n.
pot-roast
cook 301 vb.
pots
great quantity 32 n.
potsherd
piece 53 n.
pot shot
propulsion 287 n.
pots of money
wealth 800 n.
potted
short 204 adj.
compendious 592 adj.
preserved 666 adj.
potter
wander 267 vb.
be inactive 679 vb.
artisan 686 n.
pottering
restlessness 678 n.
potter's clay
soil 344 n.
materials 631 n.
pottery
product 164 n.
receptacle 194 n.
brittleness 330 n.
pottery 381 n.
art 551 n.
pottle
basket 194 n.
potty
crazy 503 adj.
trivial 639 adj.
unimportant 639 adj.
latrine 649 n.
pot-valiant
courageous 855 adj.
drunk 949 adj.
pouch
stow 187 vb.
pocket 194 n.
receive 782 vb.
pouchy
expanded 197 adj.
pouffe
seat 218 n.
poulterer
provider 633 n.
poultice
pulpiness 356 n.
heat 381 vb.
surgical dressing 658 n.
relieve 831 vb.
poultry
meat 301 n.
poultry 365 n.
poultry farming
animal husbandry 369 n.
pounce
move fast 277 vb.
descent 309 n.
leap 312 vb.
— on
surprise 508 vb.
attack 712 vb.
take 786 vb.
pound
enclosure 235 n.
strike 279 vb.
weighing 322 n.
pulverize 332 vb.
sound dead 405 vb.
lockup 748 n.
coinage 797 n.
poundage
discount 810 n.
poundal
energy 160 n.
pound note
paper money 797 n.
pound of flesh
severity 735 n.
interest 803 n.
pitilessness 906 n.
pour
emit 300 vb.
let fall 311 vb.
be wet 341 vb.
flow 350 vb.
rain 350 vb.
abound 635 vb.
— down the drain
waste 634 vb.
lose 772 vb.
be prodigal 815 vb.
— in
converge 293 vb.
burst in 297 vb.

— oil on troubled waters
assuage 177 vb.
pacify 719 vb.
relieve 831 vb.
— out
land 295 vb.
flow out 298 vb.
empty 300 vb.
let fall 311 vb.
make flow 350 vb.
be diffuse 570 vb.
give 781 vb.
— scorn on
ridicule 851 vb.
—(cold)water on
restrain 747 vb.
pourboire
gift 781 n.
reward 962 n.
pourparler
conference 584 n.
pout
jut 254 vb.
gesture 547 n.
be affected 850 vb.
be rude 885 vb.
be sullen 893 vb.
poverty
feebleness 572 n.
needfulness 627 n.
scarcity 636 n.
dilapidation 655 n.
adversity 731 n.
poverty 801 n.
asceticism 945 n.
poverty-stricken
beggarly 801 adj.
POW
prisoner 750 n.
powder
overlay 226 vb.
powder 332 n.
pulverize 332 vb.
variegate 437 vb.
medicine 658 n.
explosive 723 n.
cosmetic 843 n.
primp 843 vb.
powder and shot
ammunition 723 n.
powder keg
pitfall 663 n.
arsenal 723 n.
powder monkey
naval man 722 n.
powder puff
cosmetic 843 n.
powder room
latrine 649 n.
beauty parlour 843 n.
powdery
minute 196 adj.
brittle 330 adj.
powdery 332 adj.
dry 342 adj.
power
greatness 32 n.
numerical element 85 n.
power 160 n.
empower 160 vb.
strength 162 n.
operate 173 vb.
influence 178 n.
move 265 vb.
style 566 n.
vigour 571 n.
eloquence 579 n.
instrumentality 628 n.
means 629 n.
authority 733 n.
brute force 735 n.
power behind the throne
influence 178 n.
latency 523 n.
power cut
scarcity 636 n.
power-dive
fly 271 vb.
spurt 277 n.
descent 309 n.
powered
dynamic 160 adj.
mechanical 630 adj.
powerful
powerful 160 adj.
vigorous 174 adj.
loud 400 adj.
notable 638 adj.
compelling 740 adj.
(See **power** *)*
powerhouse
sources of energy 160 n.
busy person 678 n.
workshop 687 n.
powerless
powerless 161 adj.
weak 163 adj.adj.
inert 175 adj.
unimportant 639 adj.
power line
electronics 160 n.
power of attorney
mandate 751 n.
power of speech
eloquence 579 n.
power of the purse
finance 797 n.
power pack
electronics 160 n.
power politics
selfishness 932 n.
powers of darkness
devil 969 n.
power station
sources of energy 160 n.
workshop 687 n.
powers that be
influence 178 n.
authority 733 n.
master 741 n.
power vacuum
impotence 161 n.
anarchy 734 n.
powwow
conference 584 n.
advice 691 n.
pox
venereal disease 651 n.
PR
publicity 528 n.
practicable
possible 469 adj.
useful 640 adj.
advisable 642 adj.
practical
operative 173 adj.
intelligent 498 adj.
educational 534 adj.
instrumental 628 adj.
useful 640 adj.
advisable 642 adj.
used 673 adj.
practical ability
skill 694 n.
practical experience
knowledge 490 n.
practical joke
foolery 497 n.
trickery 542 n.
witticism 839 n.
ridicule 851 n.
practical joker
deceiver 545 n.
humorist 839 n.
practically
nearly 200 adv.
practical person
doer 676 n.
practice
continuity 71 n.
regularity 81 n.
conformity 83 n.
numerical operation 86 n.
repetition 106 n.
permanence 144 n.
empiricism 461 n.
practice 610 n.
vocation 622 n.
way 624 n.
medical art 658 n.
preparation 669 n.
use 673 n.
action 676 n.
exercise 682 n.
conduct 688 n.
observance 768 n.
etiquette 848 n.
foul play 930 n.
rite 988 n.
practice run
experiment 461 n.
practise
play music 413 vb.
train 534 vb.
learn 536 vb.
habituate 610 vb.
(See **practice** *)*
practised
knowing 490 adj.
expert 694 adj.
practising
religious 973 adj.
orthodox 976 adj.
pious 979 adj.
practitioner
doer 676 n.
agent 686 n.
expert 696 n.
praenomen
name 561 n.
praetor
official 690 n.
officer 741 n.
Praetorian Guard
defender 713 n.
pragmatic
useful 640 adj.
advisable 642 adj.
pragmatism
philosophy 449 n.
good policy 642 n.
prairie
space 183 n.
plain 348 n.
praise
honour 866 vb.
thank 907 vb.
respect 920 vb.
praise 923 n.vb.
flatter 925 vb.
reward 962 n.
worship 981 vb.
praiseworthy
good 615 adj.
excellent 644 adj.
approvable 923 adj.
virtuous 933 adj.
pram
pushcart 274 n.
boat 275 n.
prance
ride 267 vb.
walk 267 vb.
leap 312 vb.
be ostentatious 875 vb.
boast 877 vb.
prandial
culinary 301 adj.
prang
aeronautics 271 n.
prank
whim 604 n.
revel 837 n.
primp 843 vb.
prate
mean nothing 515 vb.
be loquacious 581 vb.
boast 877 vb.
prattle
empty talk 515 n.
prawn
fish food 301 n.

praxis
action 676 n.
pray
entreat 761 vb.
deprecate 762 vb.
desire 859 vb.
be pious 979 vb.
worship 981 vb.
— for
patronize 703 vb.
desire 859 vb.
be benevolent 897 vb.
prayer
entreaty 761 n.
prayers 981 n.
prayer book
office-book 988 n.
prayerful
supplicatory 761 adj.
pious 979 adj.
worshipping 981 adj.
prayer mat
floor-cover 226 n.
prayer meeting
public worship 981 n.
prayers
entreaty 761 n.
kind act 897 n.
prayers 981 n.
prayer wheel
ritual object 988 n.
pre-
prior 119 adj.
preach
teach 534 vb.
orate 579 vb.
— at
be pious 979 vb.
— to the converted
misteach 535 vb.
waste effort 641 vb.
preacher
preacher 537 n.
speaker 579 n.
zealot 979 n.
pastor 986 n.
preachify
orate 579 vb.
be pious 979 vb.
preaching
teaching 534 n.
church ministry 985 n.
preachy
educational 534 adj.
pietistic 979 adj.
pre-adamite
primal 127 adj.
preamble
prelude 66 n.
oration 579 n.
prearrange
predetermine 608 vb.
plan 623 vb.
prepare 669 vb.
prebend
benefice 985 n.
prebendary
ecclesiarch 986 n.
Pre-Cambrian
secular 110 adj.
territorial 344 adj.
precarious
transient 114 adj.
unreliable 474 adj.
unsafe 661 adj.
precatory
supplicatory 761 adj.
precaution
protection 660 n.
security 767 n.
caution 858 n.
precautionary
preparatory 669 adj.
precede
come before 64 vb.
be before 119 vb.
be in front 237 vb.
precede 283 vb.
precedence
superiority 34 n.
precedence 64 n.
priority 119 n.
seniority 131 n.
importance 638 n.
prestige 866 n.
precedent
originality 21 n.
prototype 23 n.
precedence 64 n.
precursor 66 n.
beginning 68 n.
rule 81 n.
example 83 n.
priority 119 n.
guide 520 n.
habit 610 n.
precept 693 n.
precentor
choir 413 n.
church officer 986 n.
precept
rule 81 n.
maxim 496 n.
advice 691 n.
precept 693 n.
decree 737 n.
preceptor
teacher 537 n.
precepts
creed 485 n.
precession
uranometry 321 n.
pre-Christian
dated 108 adj.
heathenish 974 adj.
precinct(s)
region 184 n.
place 185 n.
surroundings 230 n.
enclosure 235 n.
preciosity
ornament 574 n.
affectation 850 n.
precious
great 32 adj.
valuable 644 adj.
of price 811 adj.
darling 890 n.
precious metal
mineral 359 n.
bullion 797 n.
precious stone
gem 844 n.
precipice
high land 209 n.
verticality 215 n.
incline 220 n.
descent 309 n.
pitfall 663 n.
precipitance
rashness 857 n.
precipitant
unprepared 670 adj.
hasty 680 adj.
precipitate
leavings 41 n.
cause 156 vb.
effect 157 n.
speedy 277 adj.
propel 287 vb.
eject 300 vb.
let fall 311 vb.
solid body 324 n.
dirt 649 n.
hasty 680 adj.
rash 857 adj.
precipitateness
haste 680 n.
precipitation
velocity 277 n.
propulsion 287 n.
ejection 300 n.
condensation 324 n.
rain 350 n.
precipitous
vertical 215 adj.
sloping 220 adj.
précis
shortening 204 n.
conciseness 569 n.
compendium 592 n.
precise
definite 80 adj.
accurate 494 adj.
intelligible 516 adj.
fastidious 862 adj.
formal 875 adj.
orthodox 976 adj.
pietistic 979 adj.
precise time
instantaneity 116 n.
precisian
conformist 83 n.
tyrant 735 n.
people of taste 846 n.
affecter 850 n.
perfectionist 862 n.
zealot 979 n.
precision
touch 378 n.
accuracy 494 n.
intelligibility 516 n.
précis-writer
epitomizer 592 n.
preclude
exclude 57 vb.
precocious
early 135 adj.
immature 670 adj.
precocity
anticipation 135 n.
nonpreparation 670 n.
precognition
knowledge 490 n.
foresight 510 n.
psychics 984 n.
preconceived
biased 481 adj.
preconception
prejudgment 481 n.
precondemn
do before 119 vb.
prejudge 481 vb.
precooked
ready-made 669 adj.
precursor
precursor 66 n.
beginning 68 n.
example 83 n.
priority 119 n.
earliness 135 n.
preceding 283 n.
messenger 529 n.
preparer 669 n.
director 690 n.
precursory
preceding 64 adj.
precursory 66 adj.
predicting 511 adj.
predator
tyrant 735 n.
taker 786 n.
noxious animal 904 n.
predatory
thieving 788 adj.
predecease
die 361 vb.
predecessor
precursor 66 n.
predella
altar 990 n.
predestination
destiny 155 n.
fate 596 n.
predetermination 608 n.
predestine
predestine 155 vb.
intend 617 vb.
predetermination
necessity 596 n.
predetermination 608 n.
predetermine
predestine 155 vb.
prejudge 481 vb.
foresee 510 vb.

predetermine 608 vb.
motivate 612 vb.
intend 617 vb.
plan 623 vb.
prepare 669 vb.
predial
agrarian 370 adj.
proprietary 777 adj.
predicament
circumstance 8 n.
complexity 61 n.
crisis 137 n.
danger 661 n.
predicament 700 n.
adversity 731 n.
painfulness 827 n.
predicant
pastor 986 n.
predicate
argumentation 475 n.
affirm 532 vb.
predicative
grammatical 564 adj.
predict
look ahead 124 vb.
predestine 155 vb.
expect 507 vb.
foresee 510 vb.
predict 511 vb.
indicate 547 vb.
warn 664 vb.
predictable
future 124 adj.
unchangeable 153 adj.
prediction
probability 471 n.
prediction 511 n.
occultism 984 n.
(See **predict** *)*
predigested
edible 301 adj.
intelligible 516 adj.
ready-made 669 adj.
predilection
tendency 179 n.
prejudice 481 n.
choice 605 n.
affections 817 n.
liking 859 n.
love 887 n.
predispose
influence 178 vb.
bias 481 vb.
motivate 612 vb.
prepare 669 vb.
predisposition
tendency 179 n.
willingness 597 n.
affections 817 n.
predominance
superiority 34 n.
power 160 n.
influence 178 n.
authority 733 n.
predominate
predominate 34 vb.
prevail 178 vb.
motivate 612 vb.
be important 638 vb.
overmaster 727 vb.
preeminence
precedence 64 n.
preeminent
supreme 34 adj.
authoritative 733 adj.
noteworthy 866 adj.
preeminently
remarkably 32 adv.
eminently 34 adv.
preempt
exclude 57 vb.
do before 119 vb.
be early 135 vb.
acquire 771 vb.
possess 773 vb.
bargain 791 vb.
purchase 792 vb.
preen
primp 843 vb.
decorate 844 vb.
— oneself
feel pride 871 vb.
be vain 873 vb.
preengagement
promise 764 n.
preexist
be 1 vb.
be before 119 vb.
prefab
house 192 n.
prefabricate
do before 119 vb.
produce 164 vb.
prefabricated
ready-made 669 adj.
preface
come before 64 vb.
put in front 64 vb.
prelude 66 n.
edition 589 n.
prefatory
preceding 64 adj.
precursory 66 adj.
beginning 68 adj.
prefect
teacher 537 n.
official 690 n.
officer 741 n.
prefecture
position of authority 733 n.
prefer
promote 285 vb.
choose 605 vb.
desire 859 vb.
be ecclesiastical 985 vb.
— charges
litigate 959 vb.
preferable
superior 34 adj.
chosen 605 adj.
excellent 644 adj.
preference
precedence 64 n.
will 595 n.
choice 605 n.
love 887 n.
preferential treatment
aid 703 n.
injustice 914 n.
preferment
progression 285 n.
improvement 654 n.
holy orders 985 n.
prefigure
predict 511 vb.
figure 519 vb.
indicate 547 vb.
prefigurement
precursor 66 n.
omen 511 n.
prefix
adjunct 40 n.
affix 45 vb.
put in front 64 vb.
precursor 66 n.
front 237 n.
part of speech 564 n.
preglacial
primal 127 adj.
pregnable
defenceless 161 adj.
pregnancy
propagation 167 n.
pregnant
fertilized 167 adj.
prolific 171 adj.
meaningful 514 adj.
concise 569 adj.
important 638 adj.
pregnant with
impending 155 adj.
presageful 511 adj.
prehensile
tactual 378 adj.
retentive 778 adj.
prehistorian
antiquarian 125 n.
prehistoric
former 125 adj.
past 125 adj.
olden 127 adj.
prehistoric animal
animal 365 n.
prehistory
antiquity 125 n.
unknown thing 491 n.
prejudge
prejudge 481 vb.
prejudice
influence 178 vb.
tendency 179 n.
prejudice 481 n.
bias 481 vb.
error 495 n.
predetermination 608 n.
motivate 612 vb.
dislike 861 n.
hatred 888 n.
injustice 914 n.
prejudicial
evil 616 adj.
harmful 645 adj.
prelacy
Catholicism 976 n.
the church 985 n.
prelate
ecclesiarch 986 n.
prelature
church office 985 n.
prelection
lecture 534 n.
preliminaries
beginning 68 n.
preliminary
preceding 64 adj.
prelude 66 n.
precursory 66 adj.
prior 119 adj.
preparatory 669 adj.
prelims
exam 459 n.
edition 589 n.
prelude
come before 64 vb.
put in front 64 vb.
prelude 66 n.
musical piece 412 n.
premarital
matrimonial 894 adj.
premature
early 135 adj.
ill-timed 138 adj.
immature 670 adj.
unsuccessful 728 adj.
premeditate
intend 617 vb.
premeditation
predetermination 608 n.
preparation 669 n.
premenstrual tension
worry 825 n.
premier
director 690 n.
premiere, première
debut 68 n.
dramaturgy 594 n.
premiership
directorship 689 n.
position of authority 733 n.
premise
premise 475 n.vb.
supposition 512 n.
premises
place 185 n.
shop 796 n.
premium
interest 803 n.
receipt 807 n.
premium bond
gambling 618 n.
paper money 797 n.
premonition
precursor 66 n.

foresight 510 n.
warning 664 n.
prenatal
prior 119 adj.
preoccupation
exclusion 57 n.
attention 455 n.
abstractedness 456 n.
preoccupy
engross 449 vb.
possess 773 vb.
preordain
predestine 155 vb.
preordination
fate 596 n.
predetermination 608 n.
prep
study 536 n.
preparation
beginning 68 n.
looking ahead 124 n.
anticipation 135 n.
foresight 510 n.
study 536 n.
provision 633 n.
medicine 658 n.
preparation 669 n.
preparatory
preceding 64 adj.
preparatory 669 adj.
prepare
arrange 62 vb.
train 534 vb.
plan 623 vb.
warn 664 vb.
prepare 669 vb.
— oneself
look ahead 124 vb.
expect 507 vb.
store 632 vb.
prepare oneself 669 vb.
prepared
vigilant 457 adj.
expectant 507 adj.
willing 597 adj.
habituated 610 adj.
prepense
volitional 595 adj.
predetermined 608 adj.
preponderance
inequality 29 n.
superiority 34 n.
authority 733 n.
preposition
part of speech 564 n.
prepossessed
biased 481 adj.
prepossessing
personable 841 adj.
lovable 887 adj.
preposterous
absurd 497 adj.
imaginative 513 adj.
exaggerated 546 adj.
ridiculous 849 adj.
undue 916 adj.
prepotent
powerful 160 adj.
Pre-Raphaelite
antiquarian 125 n.
artist 556 n.
prerelease
manifestation 522 n.
prerequisite
qualification 468 n.
requirement 627 n.
prerogative
advantage 34 n.
authority 733 n.
freedom 744 n.
nobility 868 n.
dueness 915 n.
presage
predestine 155 vb.
omen 511 n.
predict 511 vb.
indicate 547 vb.
threaten 900 vb.
presageful
impending 155 adj.
presageful 511 adj.
cautionary 664 adj.
frightening 854 adj.
presbyopia
dim sight 440 n.
presbyter
ecclesiarch 986 n.
Presbyterian
Protestant 976 n.
sectarian 978 n.
presbytery
parish 985 n.
synod 985 n.
parsonage 986 n.
church exterior 990 n.
preschool
young 130 adj.
studentlike 538 adj.
prescient
foreseeing 510 adj.
godlike 965 adj.
prescribe
doctor 658 vb.
manage 689 vb.
advise 691 vb.
decree 737 vb.
prescribed procedure
ritual 988 n.
prescribed text
curriculum 534 n.
textbook 589 n.
prescript
precept 693 n.
decree 737 n.
prescription
tradition 127 n.
habit 610 n.
remedy 658 n.
advice 691 n.
precept 693 n.
possession 773 n.
dueness 915 n.
prescriptive
established 153 adj.
habitual 610 adj.
preceptive 693 adj.
due 915 adj.
presence
existence 1 n.
generality 79 n.
presence 189 n.
arrival 295 n.
appearance 445 n.
mien 445 n.
conduct 688 n.
ghost 970 n.
present
present 121 adj.
synchronous 123 adj.
modern 126 adj.
on the spot 189 adj.
near 200 adj.
show 522 vb.
represent 551 vb.
dramatize 594 vb.
offer 759 n.vb.
gift 781 n.
befriend 880 vb.
reward 962 vb.
be ecclesiastical 985 vb.
— arms
greet 884 vb.
show respect 920 vb.
— itself
happen 154 vb.
dawn upon 449 vb.
— oneself
be present 189 vb.
present, the
present time 121 n.
presentable
personable 841 adj.
presentation
debut 68 n.
spectacle 445 n.
manifestation 522 n.
report 524 n.
representation 551 n.
offer 759 n.
giving 781 n.
celebration 876 n.
courteous act 884 n.
reward 962 n.
present day
present time 121 n.
presenter
broadcaster 531 n.
speaker 579 n.
actor 594 n.
presentient
predicting 511 adj.
presentiment
intuition 476 n.
foresight 510 n.
presentment
representation 551 n.
giving 781 n.
preservation
permanence 144 n.
protection 660 n.
preservation 666 n.
preservation order
preserver 666 n.
preservative
food content 301 n.
preserving 666 adj.
preserve
set apart 46 vb.
sustain 146 vb.
dry 342 vb.
season 388 vb.
sweet thing 392 n.
store 632 vb.
safeguard 660 vb.
preserve 666 vb.
retain 778 vb.
— for posterity
record 548 vb.
preserver
protector 660 n.
preserver 666 n.
economy 814 n.
preside
direct 689 vb.
presidency
position of authority 733 n.
president
superior 34 n.
director 690 n.
master 741 n.
officer 741 n.
presidium, praesidium
council 692 n.
press
crowd 74 n.
make smaller 198 vb.
flattener 216 n.
be supported 218 vb.
smooth 258 vb.
impel 279 vb.
weigh 322 vb.
press 587 n.
be resolute 599 vb.
incite 612 vb.
activity 678 n.
advise 691 vb.
compel 740 vb.
request 761 vb.
take away 786 vb.
caress 889 vb.
— charges
litigate 959 vb.
— in
make concave 255 vb.
burst in 297 vb.
— into service
avail oneself of 673 vb.
— on
elapse 111 vb.
progress 285 vb.
pursue 619 vb.
— the button
operate 173 vb.
wage war 718 vb.

— the flesh
greet 884 vb.
flatter 925 vb.
press, the
the press 528 n.
press agent
publicizer 528 n.
stage manager 594 n.
mediator 720 n.
press conference
publication 528 n.
press cuttings
record 548 n.
pressed for time
brief 114 adj.
hasty 680 adj.
pressgang
compulsion 740 n.
taker 786 n.
pressing
strong 162 adj.
weighty 322 adj.
record 548 n.
demanding 627 adj.
compelling 740 adj.
pressman, presswoman
news reporter 529 n.
press notice
estimate 480 n.
news 529 n.
press of business
activity 678 n.
press of sail
velocity 277 n.
press photographer
chronicler 549 n.
press release
report 524 n.
publication 528 n.
press room
press 587 n.
press-stud
fastening 47 n.
pressure
crisis 137 n.
energy 160 n.
vigorousness 174 n.
influence 178 n.
compression 198 n.
impulse 279 n.
gravity 322 n.
touch 378 n.
inducement 612 n.
instrumentality 628 n.
action 676 n.
exertion 682 n.
adversity 731 n.
restriction 747 n.
request 761 n.
endearment 889 n.
pressure group
influence 178 n.
motivator 612 n.
petitioner 763 n.
pressurize, pressurise
motivate 612 vb.
Prestel
broadcasting 531 n.
prestidigitation
sleight 542 n.
prestige
influence 178 n.
importance 638 n.
authority 733 n.
prestige 866 n.
pride 871 n.
ostentatious 875 adj.
prestigious
reputable 866 adj.
presto
instantaneously 116 adv.
swiftly 277 adv.
adagio 412 adv.
presumably
probably 471 adv.
presume
assume 471 vb.
prejudge 481 vb.
opine 485 vb.
expect 507 vb.
suppose 512 vb.
hope 852 vb.
be insolent 878 vb.
be undue 916 vb.
— on
avail oneself of 673 vb.
presumption
rashness 857 n.
arrogation 916 n.
(See **presume** *)*
presumptive
evidential 466 adj.
probable 471 adj.
presumptuous
rash 857 adj.
insolent 878 adj.
unwarranted 916 adj.
presuppose
prejudge 481 vb.
suppose 512 vb.
pretence
insubstantial thing 4 n.
mimicry 20 n.
supposition 512 n.
duplicity 541 n.
sham 542 n.
mental dishonesty 543 n.
pretext 614 n.
ostentation 875 n.
pretend
suppose 512 vb.
imagine 513 vb.
dissemble 541 vb.
be affected 850 vb.
pretender
impostor 545 n.
usurper 916 n.
pretensions
pretension 850 n.
airs 873 n.
ostentation 875 n.
pretentious
absurd 497 adj.
feeble 572 adj.
ornate 574 adj.
affected 850 adj.
vain 873 adj.
ostentatious 875 adj.
boastful 877 adj.
preterite
past time 125 n.
pretermission
negligence 458 n.
preternatural
abnormal 84 adj.
unusual 84 adj.
paranormal 984 adj.
pretext
reason why 156 n.
reasons 475 n.
sophistry 477 n.
mental dishonesty 543 n.
pretext 614 n.
stratagem 698 n.
prettify
beautify 841 vb.
primp 843 vb.
decorate 844 vb.
pretty
greatly 32 adv.
beautiful 841 adj.
pretty kettle of fish
complexity 61 n.
pretty pass
predicament 700 n.
pretty penny
dearness 811 n.
pretty-pretty
beautiful 841 adj.
ornamental 844 adj.
preux chevalier
brave person 855 n.
honourable person 929 n.
prevail
be 1 vb.
predominate 34 vb.
be general 79 vb.
be able 160 vb.
prevail 178 vb.
be wont 610 vb.
motivate 612 vb.
overmaster 727 vb.
— upon
influence 178 vb.
induce 612 vb.
prevailing taste
fashion 848 n.
prevalent
extensive 32 adj.
universal 79 adj.
powerful 160 adj.
influential 178 adj.
known 490 adj.
usual 610 adj.
prevaricate
be equivocal 518 vb.
dissemble 541 vb.
be dishonest 930 vb.
prevenience
anticipation 135 n.
prevenient grace
divine function 965 n.
prevent
counteract 182 vb.
avoid 620 vb.
obstruct 702 vb.
prohibit 757 vb.
preventable
avoidable 620 adj.
prevention
avoidance 620 n.
hindrance 702 n.
restraint 747 n.
preventive
counteraction 182 n.
prophylactic 658 n.
preserving 666 adj.
preventive detention
detention 747 n.
preventive measure
protection 660 n.
preventive medicine
hygiene 652 n.
medical art 658 n.
preservation 666 n.
preview
priority 119 n.
inspection 438 n.
film 445 n.
manifestation 522 n.
previous
preceding 64 adj.
anachronistic 118 adj.
prior 119 adj.
early 135 adj.
prevision
foresight 510 n.
prewar
prior 119 adj.
antiquated 127 adj.
peaceful 717 adj.
prey
animal 365 n.
objective 617 n.
chase 619 n.
loser 728 n.
unlucky person 731 n.
booty 790 n.
sufferer 825 n.
— on/upon
eat 301 vb.
ill-treat 645 vb.
— on one's mind
engross 449 vb.
trouble 827 vb.
prey to
liable 180 adj.
priapism
libido 859 n.
price
equivalence 28 n.
quid pro quo 150 n.
appraise 465 vb.

goodness 644 n.
price 809 n.vb.
penalty 963 n.
price index
statistics 86 n.
priceless
valuable 644 adj.
of price 811 adj.
funny 849 adj.
price on one's head
condemnation 961 n.
price ring
restriction 747 n.
prick
small thing 33 n.
cut 46 vb.
stimulant 174 n.
sharp point 256 n.
pierce 263 vb.
give pain 377 vb.
itch 378 vb.
indication 547 n.
mark 547 vb.
incite 612 vb.
wound 655 n.
excitant 821 n.
— out
cultivate 370 vb.
— up
jut 254 vb.
elevate 310 vb.
— up one's ears
hear 415 vb.
be curious 453 vb.
be attentive 455 vb.
prickle
prickle 256 n.
roughness 259 n.
foliage 366 n.
itch 378 vb.
prickliness
sharpness 256 n.
quarrelsomeness 709 n.
moral sensibility 819 n.
pride 871 n.
irascibility 892 n.
prickly
unconformable 84 adj.
prickly heat
skin disease 651 n.
pricks of conscience
penitence 939 n.
pricy
dear 811 adj.
pride
group 74 n.
pride 871 n.
vanity 873 n.
ostentation 875 n.
insolence 878 n.
unsociability 883 n.
vice 934 n.
impiety 980 n.
pride and joy
pride 871 n.
favorite 890 n.
pride of place
superiority 34 n.
precedence 64 n.
pride oneself
feel pride 871 vb.
be vain 873 vb.
prie-dieu
seat 218 n.
priest, priestess
priest 986 n.
priesthole
retreat 192 n.
hiding-place 527 n.
priesthood
church office 985 n.
clergy 986 n.
priest-ridden
pietistic 979 adj.
ecclesiastical 985 adj.
prig
affecter 850 n.
prude 950 n.
priggishness
airs 873 n.
prim
serious 834 adj.
dull 840 adj.
affected 850 adj.
fastidious 862 adj.
prudish 950 adj.
prima ballerina
actor 594 n.
primacy
superiority 34 n.
importance 638 n.
prestige 866 n.
church office 985 n.
prima donna
superior 34 n.
vocalist 413 n.
actor 594 n.
bigwig 638 n.
proficient person 696 n.
proud person 871 n.
prima facie
at sight 438 adv.
evidential 466 adj.
probably 471 adv.
manifestly 522 adv.
primal
beginning 68 adj.
primal 127 adj.
fundamental 156 adj.
primary
intrinsic 5 adj.
original 21 adj.
simple 44 adj.
first 68 adj.
fundamental 156 adj.
educational 534 adj.
vote 605 n.
important 638 adj.
primary colour
colour 425 n.
primate
mammal 365 n.
ecclesiarch 986 n.
primateship
church office 985 n.
prime
numerical 85 adj.
morning 128 n.
adultness 134 n.
earliness 135 n.
educate 534 vb.
important 638 adj.
elite 644 n.
excellent 644 adj.
make ready 669 vb.
palmy days 730 n.
church service 988 n.
prime constituent
essence 1 n.
essential part 5 n.
primed
instructed 490 adj.
informed 524 adj.
prepared 669 adj.
drunk 949 adj.
prime minister
director 690 n.
officer 741 n.
prime mover
cause 156 n.
motivator 612 n.
prime number
number 85 n.
prime of life
salad days 130 n.
middle age 131 n.
adultness 134 n.
primer
beginning 68 n.
textbook 589 n.
primeval, primaeval
beginning 68 adj.
primal 127 adj.
priming
preparation 669 n.
explosive 723 n.
primitive
past 125 adj.
primal 127 adj.
earliness 135 n.
fundamental 156 adj.
violent 176 adj.
representing 551 adj.
artist 556 n.
artless 699 adj.
barbaric 869 adj.
primitive form
prototype 23 n.
Primitive Methodist
Protestant 976 n.
primo
initially 68 adv.
primogeniture
priority 119 n.
seniority 131 n.
sonship 170 n.
primordial
original 21 adj.
beginning 68 adj.
primal 127 adj.
fundamental 156 adj.
primp
beautify 841 vb.
primp 843 vb.
be vain 873 vb.
primrose
yellowness 433 n.
primrose path
deterioration 655 n.
facility 701 n.
wickedness 934 n.
primum mobile
cause 156 n.
heavens 321 n.
divineness 965 n.
primus inter pares
superior 34 n.
primus stove
furnace 383 n.
prince
potentate 741 n.
sovereign 741 n.
aristocrat 868 n.
princely
ruling 733 adj.
liberal 813 adj.
worshipful 866 adj.
noble 868 adj.
prince of
paragon 646 n.
Prince of Darkness
Satan 969 n.
Prince of Peace
God the Son 965 n.
princess
sovereign 741 n.
loved one 887 n.
princesse lointaine
desired object 859 n.
loved one 887 n.
princess-line
tailored 228 adj.
principal
supreme 34 adj.
first 68 adj.
teacher 537 n.
director 690 n.
master 741 n.
principal boy/girl
acting 594 n.
principalities and powers
angel 968 n.
principality
political organization 733 n.
principate
position of authority 733 n.
principle
essential part 5 n.
rule 81 n.
source 156 n.
element 319 n.

idea 451 n.
premise 475 n.
opinion 485 n.
axiom 496 n.
motive 612 n.
precept 693 n.
probity 929 n.
principled
honourable 929 adj.
virtuous 933 adj.
principles
creed 485 n.
probity 929 n.
prink
dress 228 vb.
beautify 841 vb.
primp 843 vb.
print
copy 20 vb.
copy 22 n.
effect 157 n.
reproduction 166 n.
publish 528 vb.
indication 547 n.
record 548 vb.
photography 551 n.
picture 553 n.
printing 555 n.
write 586 vb.
letterpress 587 n.
print 587 n.vb.
pattern 844 n.
printable
permitted 756 adj.
pure 950 adj.
printed word
reading matter 589 n.
printer
publicizer 528 n.
printer 587 n.
printer's ink
black pigment 428 n.
printing
reproduction 166 n.
printing 555 n.
lettering 586 n.
print 587 n.n.
printing press
publicity 528 n.
press 587 n.
printout
data processing 86 n.
product 164 n.
letterpress 587 n.
print-type
letter 558 n.
print-type 587 n.
prior
prior 119 adj.
former 125 adj.
older 131 adj.
early 135 adj.
ecclesiarch 986 n.
monk 986 n.
prioress
ecclesiarch 986 n.
nun 986 n.
priority
precedence 64 n.
time 108 n.
priority 119 n.
past time 125 n.
seniority 131 n.
chief thing 638 n.
importance 638 n.
priory
monastery 986 n.
prism
angular figure 247 n.
chromatics 425 n.
variegation 437 n.
optical device 442 n.
prismatic
coloured 425 adj.
variegated 437 adj.
prison
enclosure 235 n.
prison 748 n.
seclusion 883 n.
pillory 964 n.
prison-breaker
escaper 667 n.
prison camp
prison camp 748 n.
prison cell
lockup 748 n.
prisoner
prisoner 750 n.
prisoner at the bar
accused person 928 n.
litigant 959 n.
prison officer
gaoler 749 n.
privacy
invisibility 444 n.
refuge 662 n.
seclusion 883 n.
private
inferior 35 n.
private 80 adj.
unintelligible 517 adj.
occult 523 adj.
concealed 525 adj.
soldiery 722 n.
possessed 773 adj.
commoner 869 n.
private ends
selfishness 932 n.
private enterprise
trade 791 n.
privateer
militarist 722 n.
warship 722 n.
robber 789 n.
privateering
brigandage 788 n.
private eye
detective 459 n.
protector 660 n.
private income
receipt 807 n.
private parts
genitalia 167 n.
private sector
apportionment 783 n.
trade 791 n.
private understanding
compact 765 n.
privation
loss 772 n.
poverty 801 n.
privatization, privatisation
transfer 780 n.
privatize, privatise
appropriate 786 vb.
privet
fence 235 n.
tree 366 n.
privilege
advantage 34 n.
freedom 744 n.
permit 756 vb.
dueness 915 n.
nonliability 919 n.
privy
concealed 525 adj.
latrine 649 n.
Privy Council
council 692 n.
privy purse
receipt 807 n.
privy seal
badge of rule 743 n.
privy to
knowing 490 adj.
prize
benefit 615 n.
objective 617 n.
elite 644 n.
trophy 729 n.
acquisition 771 n.
gift 781 n.
taking 786 n.
booty 790 n.
receipt 807 n.
desired object 859 n.
honour 866 vb.
love 887 vb.
approve 923 vb.
reward 962 n.
— open
force 176 vb.
prizefight
pugilism 716 n.
prizefighter
contender 716 n.
prize-giving
giving 781 n.
reward 962 n.
prizeman
student 538 n.
prizewinner
superior 34 n.
exceller 644 n.
proficient person 696 n.
victor 727 n.
recipient 782 n.
prizewinning
successful 727 adj.
pro
expert 696 n.
deputizing 755 adj.
on behalf 755 adv.
prostitute 952 n.
PRO
publicizer 528 n.
probabilism
philosophy 449 n.
irreligion 974 n.
probability
fair chance 159 n.
appearance 445 n.
probability 471 n.
expectation 507 n.
probable
future 124 adj.
impending 155 adj.
tending 179 adj.
probable 471 adj.
credible 485 adj.
promising 852 adj.
probation
experiment 461 n.
attempt 671 n.
probationer
testee 461 n.
beginner 538 n.
offender 904 n.
probation officer
keeper 749 n.
probative
evidential 466 adj.
demonstrating 478 adj.
probe
depth 211 n.
perforator 263 n.
enquiry 459 n.
interrogate 459 vb.
experiment 461 n.
be tentative 461 Vb. vb.
measure 465 vb.
detector 484 n.
probity
veracity 540 n.
right 913 n.
morals 917 n.
probity 929 n.
virtue 933 n.
problem
topic 452 n.
question 459 n.
argumentation 475 n.
enigma 530 n.
difficulty 700 n.
worry 825 n.
problematic, problematical
moot 459 adj.
uncertain 474 adj.
difficult 700 adj.
pro bono publico
usefully 640 adv.
pro bono publico 901 adv.

proboscis
protuberance 254 n.
feeler 378 n.
procathedral
church 990 n.
procedure
policy 623 n.
way 624 n.
action 676 n.
conduct 688 n.
ritual 988 n.
proceed
elapse 111 vb.
go on 146 vb.
result 157 vb.
travel 267 vb.
progress 285 vb.
do 676 vb.vb.
— to
undertake 672 vb.
proceeding
event 154 n.
deed 676 n.
proceedings
legal process 959 n.
proceeds
earnings 771 n.
receiving 782 n.
receipt 807 n.
process
computerize 86 vb.
change 143 n.
convert 147 vb.
production 164 n.
agency 173 n.
operate 173 vb.
photograph 551 vb.
way 624 n.
perform ritual 988 vb.
processable
computerized 86 adj.
processed
produced 164 adj.
ready-made 669 adj.
procession
retinue 67 n.
procession 71 n.
marching 267 n.
passing along 305 n.
pageant 875 n.
ritual act 988 n.
processional
ritual 988 adj.
process of law
justice 913 n.
process of time
course of time 111 n.
processor
data processing 86 n.
process-server
law officer 955 n.
proclaim
proclaim 528 vb.
affirm 532 vb.
make important 638 vb.
raise the alarm 665 vb.
decree 737 vb.
honour 866 vb.
proclamation
manifestation 522 n.
publication 528 n.
call 547 n.
proclivity
tendency 179 n.
proconsul
official 690 n.
governor 741 n.
deputy 755 n.
procrastinate
spin out 113 vb.
put off 136 vb.
be neglectful 458 vb.
not act 677 vb.
procrastination
unwillingness 598 n.
inactivity 679 n.
procreate
generate 167 vb.
make fruitful 171 vb.
Procrustean
regulated 83 adj.
proctor
teacher 537 n.
manager 690 n.
law agent 958 n.
proctorship
management 689 n.
procumbent
supine 216 adj.
procurator
manager 690 n.
law agent 958 n.
procurator fiscal
accuser 928 n.
law officer 955 n.
procure
cause 156 vb.
induce 612 vb.
provide 633 vb.
acquire 771 vb.
be impure 951 vb.
procurement
agency 173 n.
acquisition 771 n.
procurer
provider 633 n.
bawd 952 n.
prod
stimulant 174 n.
impel 279 vb.
gesticulate 547 vb.
incite 612 vb.
prodigal
wasteful 634 adj.
plenteous 635 adj.
expending 806 adj.
liberal 813 adj.
prodigal 815 adj.
intemperate 943 adj.
prodigality
prodigality 815 n.
prodigal son
prodigal 815 n.
bad person 938 n.
penitent 939 n.
prodigious
prodigious 32 adj.
huge 195 adj.
super 644 adj.
wonderful 864 adj.
prodigy
superior 34 n.
nonconformity 84 n.
scholar 492 n.
exceller 644 n.
paragon 646 n.
proficient person 696 n.
prodigy 864 n.
prodromal
preceding 64 adj.
produce
increment 36 n.
compose 56 vb.
cause 156 vb.
growth 157 n.
result 157 vb.
product 164 n.
produce 164 vb.
make fruitful 171 vb.
lengthen 203 vb.
form 243 vb.
manifest 522 vb.
dramatize 594 vb.
provision 633 n.
provide 633 vb.
be profitable 771 vb.
— results
be expedient 642 vb.
producer
producer 164 n.
stage manager 594 n.
product
numerical result 85 n.
event 154 n.
effect 157 n.
product 164 n.
representation 551 n.
earnings 771 n.
production
increase 36 n.
composition 56 n.
causation 156 n.
product 164 n.
production 164 n.
productiveness 171 n.
manifestation 522 n.
dramaturgy 594 n.
business 622 n.
production line
production 164 n.
workshop 687 n.
productive
productive 164 adj.
generative 167 adj.
profitable 640 adj.
gainful 771 adj.
productivity
great quantity 32 n.
production 164 n.
productiveness 171 n.
plenty 635 n.
utility 640 n.
productivity bonus
earnings 771 n.
reward 962 n.
proem
prelude 66 n.
oration 579 n.
profanation
misuse 675 n.
undueness 916 n.
impiety 980 n.
profane
unclean 649 adj.
impair 655 vb.
shame 867 vb.
cursing 899 adj.
be undue 916 vb.
not respect 921 vb.
wicked 934 adj.
irreligious 974 adj.
profane 980 adj.
be impious 980 vb.
laical 987 adj.
profanity
scurrility 899 n.
impiety 980 n.
profess
believe 485 vb.
affirm 532 vb.
plead 614 vb.
professedly
as promised 764 adv.
professing Christian
pietist 979 n.
profession
creed 485 n.
assent 488 n.
affirmation 532 n.
mental dishonesty 543 n.
pretext 614 n.
vocation 622 n.
promise 764 n.
ostentation 875 n.
duty 917 n.
professional
instructed 490 adj.
usual 610 adj.
businesslike 622 adj.
expert 694 adj.
expert 696 n.
professional foul
foul play 930 n.
professionalism
skill 694 n.
professor
scholar 492 n.
teacher 537 n.
expert 696 n.
academic title 870 n.

professoriate
scholar 492 n.
teacher 537 n.
professorship
lecture 534 n.
proffer
offer 759 n.vb.
promise 764 vb.
make terms 766 vb.
proficiency
skill 694 n.
proficient
knowing 490 adj.
expert 694 adj.
proficient person
scholar 492 n.
proficient person 696 n.
profile
outline 233 n.vb.
laterality 239 n.
form 243 n.
feature 445 n.
picture 553 n.
description 590 n.
profit
increment 36 n.
growth 157 n.
incentive 612 n.
benefit 615 n.vb.
be useful 640 vb.
good policy 642 n.
be auspicious 730 vb.
gain 771 n.
be profitable 771 vb.
reward 962 n.
— by
profit by 137 vb.
find useful 640 vb.
get better 654 vb.
be warned 664 vb.
use 673 vb.
profitable
productive 164 adj.
prolific 171 adj.
profitable 640 adj.
beneficial 644 adj.
successful 727 adj.
gainful 771 adj.
profiteer
prosperous person 730 n.
speculate 791 vb.
overcharge 811 vb.
profitless
unproductive 172 adj.
wasted 634 adj.
profitless 641 adj.
unsuccessful 728 adj.
losing 772 adj.
profit-making
trade 791 n.
(See **profitable** *)*
profit-sharing
participation 775 n.
profligacy
prodigality 815 n.
wickedness 934 n.
profligate
prodigal 815 n.adj.
vicious 934 adj.
bad person 938 n.
intemperate 943 adj.
sensualist 944 n.
libertine 952 n.
profound
great 32 adj.
deep 211 adj.
wise 498 adj.
inexpressible 517 adj.
unclear 568 adj.
felt 818 adj.
profundity
thought 449 n.
profuse
many 104 adj.
diffuse 570 adj.
plenteous 635 adj.
liberal 813 adj.
prodigal 815 adj.
profusion
great quantity 32 n.
abundance 171 n.
plenty 635 n.
redundance 637 n.
progenitor, progenitrix
source 156 n.
paternity 169 n.
maternity 169 n.
progeny
posterity 170 n.
progesterone
drug 658 n.
prognosis
foresight 510 n.
prediction 511 n.
pathology 651 n.
medical art 658 n.
prognostic
foreseeing 510 adj.
omen 511 n.
cautionary 664 adj.
program
class 62 vb.
data processing 86 n.
computerize 86 vb.
programme
list 87 n.
prediction 511 n.
publication 528 n.
broadcast 531 n.
plan 623 n.
policy 623 n.
plan 623 vb.
undertaking 672 n.
tactics 688 n.
programmed learning
teaching 534 n.
programme music
music 412 n.
programmer
enumerator 86 n.
progress
increase 36 n.
elapse 111 vb.
continuance 146 n.
conversion 147 n.
motion 265 n.
travel 267 vb.
progression 285 n.
progress 285 vb.
approach 289 vb.
pass 305 vb.
way 624 n.
improvement 654 n.
be active 678 vb.
success 727 n.
progression
series 71 n.
ratio 85 n.
progressive
continuous 71 adj.
elapsing 111 adj.
vigorous 174 adj.
progressive 285 adj.
reformer 654 n.
enterprising 672 adj.
progressive jazz
music 412 n.
progressivism
reformism 654 n.
prohibit
exclude 57 vb.
counteract 182 vb.
negate 533 vb.
obstruct 702 vb.
command 737 vb.
restrain 747 vb.
prohibit 757 vb.
make illegal 954 vb.
prohibition
prohibition 757 n.
temperance 942 n.
prohibitionist
abstainer 942 n.
prohibitive
hindering 702 adj.
prohibiting 757 adj.
dear 811 adj.
project
make extrinsic 6 vb.
externalize 223 vb.
jut 254 vb.
propel 287 vb.
emerge 298 vb.
be visible 443 vb.
curriculum 534 n.
represent 551 vb.
predetermination 608 n.
intention 617 n.
intend 617 vb.
plan 623 n.vb.
undertaking 672 n.
— an image
impress 821 vb.
projectile
missile 287 n.
ammunition 723 n.
projecting
overhanging 209 adj.
projecting 254 adj.
projection
extrinsicality 6 n.
high land 209 n.
distortion 246 n.
convexity 253 n.
projection 254 n.
propulsion 287 n.
cinema 445 n.
ideality 513 n.
manifestation 522 n.
image 551 n.
map 551 n.
representation 551 n.
projector
optical device 442 n.
cinema 445 n.
prolapse
descend 309 vb.
prole
vulgarian 847 n.
commoner 869 n.
prolegomena
prelude 66 n.
dissertation 591 n.
prolepsis
anachronism 118 n.
proletarian
vulgarian 847 n.
commoner 869 n.
proletariat
personnel 686 n.
lower classes 869 n.
proliferate
grow 36 vb.
be fruitful 171 vb.
abound 635 vb.
proliferation
propagation 167 n.
prolific
increasing 36 adj.
multitudinous 104 adj.
productive 164 adj.
prolific 171 adj.
diffuse 570 adj.
plenteous 635 adj.
profitable 640 adj.
prolix
protracted 113 adj.
prolix 570 adj.
tedious 838 adj.
prologue
prelude 66 n.
oration 579 n.
speaker 579 n.
actor 594 n.
dramaturgy 594 n.
prolong
augment 36 vb.
continue 71 vb.
spin out 113 vb.
sustain 146 vb.
preserve 666 vb.
prolongation
adjunct 40 n.
sequence 65 n.
lengthening 203 n.
prolusion
prelude 66 n.

prom
music 412 n.
promenade
pleasance 192 n.
land travel 267 n.
pedestrianism 267 n.
path 624 n.
be ostentatious 875 vb.
promenader
wanderer 268 n.
Promethean
alive 360 adj.
Prometheus
classical deities 967 n.
prominence
superiority 34 n.
convexity 253 n.
prominence 254 n.
elevation 310 n.
visibility 443 n.
importance 638 n.
prestige 866 n.
prominent
overhanging 209 adj.
projecting 254 adj.
obvious 443 adj.
manifest 522 adj.
notable 638 adj.
noteworthy 866 adj.
promiscuity
indiscrimination 464 n.
unchastity 951 n.
promiscuous
indifferent 860 adj.
promise
predict 511 vb.
oath 532 n.
affirm 532 vb.
intention 617 n.
undertake 672 vb.
be auspicious 730 vb.
promise 764 n.vb.
compact 765 n.
hope 852 n.
give hope 852 vb.
incur a duty 917 vb.
— oneself
expect 507 vb.
desire 859 vb.
promised
future 124 adj.
expected 507 adj.
promised 764 adj.
promised land
fantasy 513 n.
objective 617 n.
aspiration 852 n.
promising
probable 471 adj.
presageful 511 adj.
palmy 730 adj.
promising 852 adj.
promissory
promissory 764 adj.
promissory note
title deed 767 n.
paper money 797 n.
promontory
projection 254 n.
land 344 n.
promote
augment 36 vb.
initiate 68 vb.
conduce 156 vb.
tend 179 vb.
concur 181 vb.
promote 285 vb.
make likely 471 vb.
advertise 528 vb.
be instrumental 628 vb.
find means 629 vb.
be useful 640 vb.
be expedient 642 vb.
make better 654 vb.
aid 703 vb.
trade 791 vb.
dignify 866 vb.
promoter
publicizer 528 n.
planner 623 n.
aider 703 n.
patron 707 n.
promotion
progression 285 n.
(See **promote** *)*
prompt
initiate 68 vb.
early 135 adj.
influence 178 vb.
speedy 277 adj.
remind 505 vb.
hint 524 n.vb.
willing 597 adj.
incite 612 vb.
active 678 adj.
hasty 680 adj.
advise 691 vb.
prompt book
stage play 594 n.
prompt box
stage set 594 n.
prompter
reminder 505 n.
stagehand 594 n.
motivator 612 n.
adviser 691 n.
promptly
instantaneously 116 adv.
promulgate
proclaim 528 vb.
decree 737 vb.
prone
supine 216 adj.
inverted 221 adj.
prone to
tending 179 adj.
prong
bifurcation 92 n.
sharp point 256 n.
pronoun
part of speech 564 n.
pronounce
judge 480 vb.
proclaim 528 vb.
affirm 532 vb.
voice 577 vb.
speak 579 vb.
pronounced
obvious 443 adj.
manifest 522 adj.
vocal 577 adj.
pronouncement
judgment 480 n.
publication 528 n.
pronto
instantaneously 116 adv.
swiftly 277 adv.
pronunciamento
publication 528 n.
pronunciation
dialect 560 n.
pronunciation 577 n.
speech 579 n.
speech defect 580 n.
proof
unyielding 162 adj.
sealed off 264 adj.
hard 326 adj.
dry 342 adj.
unfeeling 375 adj.
experiment 461 n.
evidence 466 n.
certainty 473 n.
demonstration 478 n.
manifestation 522 n.
letterpress 587 n.
reading matter 589 n.
resolute 599 adj.
plan 623 n.
amendment 654 n.
invulnerable 660 adj.
defended 713 adj.
resisting 715 adj.
impassive 820 adj.
proofread
print 587 vb.
rectify 654 vb.
proofreader
printer 587 n.
prop
bond 47 n.
stabilizer 153 n.
strengthen 162 vb.
prop 218 n.
support 218 vb.
elevate 310 vb.
stage set 594 n.
refuge 662 n.
aider 703 n.
— up
preserve 666 vb.
aid 703 vb.
propaedeutics
curriculum 534 n.
propaganda
argument 475 n.
publicity 528 n.
teaching 534 n.
misteaching 535 n.
inducement 612 n.
warfare 718 n.
propaganda machine
untruth 543 n.
propagandist
publicizer 528 n.
preacher 537 n.
motivator 612 n.
propagandize, propagandise
misteach 535 vb.
pervert 655 vb.
propagate
generate 167 vb.
make fruitful 171 vb.
publish 528 vb.
propagation
coition 45 n.
production 164 n.
propagation 167 n.
productiveness 171 n.
life 360 n.
propagator
seedbed 156 n.
propagation 167 n.
propane
fuel 385 n.
propel
move 265 vb.
send 272 vb.
propel 287 vb.
eject 300 vb.vb.
propellant
propeller 269 n.
propellant 287 n.
explosive 723 n.
propeller
propeller 269 n.
aircraft 276 n.
propellant 287 n.
rotator 315 n.
propelling
dynamic 160 adj.
propensity
tendency 179 n.
willingness 597 n.
liking 859 n.
proper
characteristic 5 adj.
relevant 9 adj.
fit 24 adj.
component 58 adj.
special 80 adj.
regulated 83 adj.
advisable 642 adj.
possessed 773 adj.
personable 841 adj.
tasteful 846 adj.
well-bred 848 adj.
right 913 adj.
due 915 adj.
virtuous 933 adj.
proper fraction
numerical element 85 n.

proper motion
star 321 n.
proper noun
name 561 n.
part of speech 564 n.
propertied
possessing 773 adj.
proprietary 777 adj.
moneyed 800 adj.
proper time
occasion 137 n.
good policy 642 n.
property
essential part 5 n.
ability 160 n.
stage set 594 n.
store 632 n.
possession 773 n.
property 777 n.
property man
stagehand 594 n.
prophecy
prediction 511 n.
hermeneutics 520 n.
revelation 975 n.
prophesy
foresee 510 vb.
predict 511 vb.
prophet, prophetess
sage 500 n.
oracle 511 n.
preacher 537 n.
warner 664 n.
religious teacher 973 n.
psychic 984 n.
priest 986 n.
prophetic
foreseeing 510 adj.
predicting 511 adj.
veracious 540 adj.
indicating 547 adj.
revelational 975 adj.
prophylactic
prophylactic 658 n.
prophylaxis
hygiene 652 n.
prophylactic 658 n.
protection 660 n.
hindrance 702 n.
propinquity
consanguinity 11 n.
nearness 200 n.
propitiate
pacify 719 vb.
mediate 720 vb.
content 828 vb.
ask mercy 905 vb.
beg pardon 909 vb.
atone 941 vb.
offer worship 981 vb.
propitiation
propitiation 941 n.
divine function 965 n.
propitious
opportune 137 adj.
beneficial 644 adj.
aiding 703 adj.
palmy 730 adj.
promising 852 adj.
proponent
reasoner 475 n.
proportion
relativeness 9 n.
correlation 12 n.
fitness 24 n.
degree 27 n.
part 53 n.
order 60 n.
ratio 85 n.
numerical operation 86 n.
symmetry 245 n.
elegance 575 n.
portion 783 n.
proportional
correlative 12 adj.
proportional representation
vote 605 n.
proportionate
relative 9 adj.
correlative 12 adj.
agreeing 24 adj.
proportionately
pro rata 783 adv.
proportioned
symmetrical 245 adj.
proportions
measure 183 n.
size 195 n.
proposal
intention 617 n.
plan 623 n.
advice 691 n.
offer 759 n.
request 761 n.
wooing 889 n.
propose
argue 475 vb.
propound 512 vb.
intend 617 vb.
advise 691 vb.
patronize 703 vb.
— marriage
court 889 vb.
proposer
planner 623 n.
patron 707 n.
proposition
topic 452 n.
argumentation 475 n.
supposition 512 n.
affirmation 532 n.
plan 623 n.
advice 691 n.
offer 759 n.
request 761 n.
debauch 951 vb.
propound
propound 512 vb.
offer 759 vb.
— a question
interrogate 459 vb.
proprietary
proprietary 777 adj.
proprietary drug
medicine 658 n.
proprieties
etiquette 848 n.
proprietor, proprietress
owner 776 n.
proprietorial
possessing 773 adj.
propriety
relevance 9 n.
fitness 24 n.
elegance 575 n.
good policy 642 n.
good taste 846 n.
etiquette 848 n.
right 913 n.
purity 950 n.
propulsion
energy 160 n.
impulse 279 n.
propulsion 287 n.
ejection 300 n.
pro rata
pro rata 783 adv.
prorogation
delay 136 n.
prosaic
typical 83 adj.
unintelligent 499 adj.
feeble 572 adj.
plain 573 adj.adj.
prosaic 593 adj.
artless 699 adj.
inexcitable 823 adj.
tedious 838 adj.
dull 840 adj.
pros and cons
reasons 475 n.
proscenium
front 237 n.
stage set 594 n.
proscribe
command 737 vb.
prohibit 757 vb.
condemn 961 vb.
proscribed person
outcast 883 n.
proscription
penalty 963 n.
(See **proscribe***)*
prose
plainness 573 n.
be loquacious 581 vb.
reading matter 589 n.
prose 593 n.
be dull 840 vb.
prosecute
do 676 vb.
indict 928 vb.
prosecuted
accused 928 adj.
prosecution
pursuit 619 n.
accusation 928 n.
litigation 959 n.
prosecutor
accuser 928 n.
proselyte
changed person 147 n.
learner 538 n.
tergiversator 603 n.
proselytize, proselytise
convert 147 vb.
convince 485 vb.
teach 534 vb.
make pious 979 vb.
prose writer
author 589 n.
prose 593 n.
prosing
prolix 570 adj.
loquacious 581 adj.
prosodic
poetic 593 adj.
prosody
tempo 410 n.
prosody 593 n.
prosopography
description 590 n.
prosopopeia
metaphor 519 n.
prospect
futurity 124 n.
looking ahead 124 n.
destiny 155 n.
range 183 n.
view 438 n.
search 459 vb.
be tentative 461 vb.
probability 471 n.
expectation 507 n.
prediction 511 n.
art subject 553 n.
intention 617 n.
prospective
future 124 adj.
expected 507 adj.
prospector
enquirer 459 n.
experimenter 461 n.
detector 484 n.
prospectus
list 87 n.
prediction 511 n.
compendium 592 n.
policy 623 n.
prosper
grow 36 vb.
progress 285 vb.
flourish 615 vb.
get better 654 vb.
succeed 727 vb.
be auspicious 730 vb.
be profitable 771 vb.
get rich 800 vb.
prosperity
prosperity 730 n.
wealth 800 n.
happiness 824 n.

Prospero
sorcerer 983 n.
prosperous
opportune 137 adj.
beneficial 644 adj.
successful 727 adj.
prosperous 730 adj.
rich 800 adj.
happy 824 adj.
promising 852 adj.
prostate
genitalia 167 n.
prosthesis
substitute 150 n.
surgery 658 n.
prosthetics
surgery 658 n.
prostitute
pervert 655 vb.
debauch 951 vb.
prostitute 952 n.
prostitution
deterioration 655 n.
misuse 675 n.
social evil 951 n.
prostrate
disable 161 vb.
low 210 adj.
supine 216 adj.
flatten 216 vb.
lowered 311 adj.
sick 651 adj.
fatigued 684 adj.
submitting 721 adj.
sadden 834 vb.
servile 879 adj.
respectful 920 adj.
— oneself
stoop 311 vb.
greet 884 vb.
show respect 920 vb.
worship 981 vb.
perform ritual 988 vb.
prostration
helplessness 161 n.
destruction 165 n.
sorrow 825 n.
(See **prostrate** *)*
prosy
prolix 570 adj.
feeble 572 adj.
tedious 838 adj.
protagonist
actor 594 n.
protean
multiform 82 adj.
changeful 152 adj.
protect
accompany 89 vb.
screen 421 vb.
safeguard 660 vb.
preserve 666 vb.
patronize 703 vb.
defend 713 vb.
befriend 880 vb.
protected
salubrious 652 adj.
nonliable 919 adj.
protected species
preservation 666 n.
protected tenant
resident 191 n.
possessor 776 n.
protection
barrier 235 n.
surveillance 457 n.
protection 660 n.
safeguard 662 n.
preservation 666 n.
defence 713 n.
restriction 747 n.
trade 791 n.
protectionism
restriction 747 n.
protection racket
peculation 788 n.
protective clothing
shelter 662 n.
armour 713 n.
protective colouring
mimicry 20 n.
disguise 527 n.
protective custody
detention 747 n.
protectiveness
love 887 n.
protector
protector 660 n.
patron 707 n.
defender 713 n.
master 741 n.
keeper 749 n.
friend 880 n.
benefactor 903 n.
protectorate
territory 184 n.
political organization 733 n.
protégé(e)
dependant 742 n.
friend 880 n.
protein
food content 301 n.
organism 358 n.
protein-rich
nourishing 301 adj.
protest
dissent 489 n.vb.
affirm 532 vb.
negation 533 n.
unwilling 598 vb.
warning 664 n.
be active 678 vb.
oppose 704 vb.
resistance 715 n.
revolt 738 vb.
refusal 760 n.
deprecation 762 n.
nonobservance 769 n.
nonpayment 805 n.
be discontented 829 vb.
disapprobation 924 n.
Protestant
Protestant 976 n.adj.
church party 978 n.
protestation
dissent 489 n.
protester
dissentient 489 n.
agitator 738 n.
malcontent 829 n.
Proteus
multiformity 82 n.
changeable thing 152 n.
lesser deity 967 n.
prothalamium
vocal music 412 n.
wedding 894 n.
proto-
past 125 adj.
primal 127 adj.
protocol
practice 610 n.
treaty 765 n.
etiquette 848 n.
formality 875 n.
protogalaxy
nebula 321 n.
protohistory
antiquity 125 n.
protomartyr
precursor 66 n.
proton
minuteness 196 n.
element 319 n.
protonotary
recorder 549 n.
protoplasm
prototype 23 n.
origin 68 n.
matter 319 n.
organism 358 n.
life 360 n.
protoplasmic
organic 358 adj.
alive 360 adj.
prototype
originality 21 n.
prototype 23 n.
protozoan
microorganism 196 n.
animal 365 n.
protract
spin out 113 vb.
put off 136 vb.
sustain 146 vb.
lengthen 203 vb.
be diffuse 570 vb.
be obstructive 702 vb.
protraction
increase 36 n.
protraction 113 n.
slowness 278 n.
protractor
angular measure 247 n.
protrude
jut 254 vb.
protuberance
angularity 247 n.
convexity 253 n.
protuberance 254 n.
proud
defiant 711 adj.
proud 871 adj.
vain 873 adj.
insolent 878 adj.
despising 922 adj.
proud flesh
swelling 253 n.
prove
happen 154 vb.
expand 197 vb.
experiment 461 vb.
demonstrate 478 vb.
be true 494 vb.
vindicate 927 vb.
— one's point
argue 475 vb.
demonstrate 478 vb.
— that white is black
sophisticate 477 vb.
— the contrary
confute 479 vb.
proved
veracious 540 adj.
proven
trustworthy 929 adj.
provenance
origin 68 n.
provender
food 301 n.
provender 301 n.
provision 633 n.
proven fact
demonstration 478 n.
proverb
maxim 496 n.
proverbial
known 490 adj.
aphoristic 496 adj.
proverbially
proverbially 496 adv.
provide
find means 629 vb.
store 632 vb.
provide 633 vb.
make ready 669 vb.
offer 759 vb.
give 781 vb.
be hospitable 882 vb.
— against
foresee 510 vb.
— the means
cause 156 vb.
find means 629 vb.
facilitate 701 vb.
provided (that)
if 8 adv.
provided 468 adv.
providence
foresight 510 n.
Providence
divineness 965 n.
provident
vigilant 457 adj.
intelligent 498 adj.
foreseeing 510 adj.

providential
opportune 137 adj.
divine 965 adj.
provider
provider 633 n.
province
classification 77 n.
district 184 n.
function 622 n.
political organization 733 n.
parish 985 n.
provinces
district 184 n.
provincial
regional 184 adj.
dweller 191 n.
provincial 192 adj.
narrow-minded 481 adj.
dialectal 560 adj.
ingenue 699 n.
ill-bred 847 adj.
country-dweller 869 n.
plebeian 869 adj.
ecclesiastical 985 adj.
provincialism
narrow mind 481 n.
prejudice 481 n.
dialect 560 n.
proving ground
testing agent 461 n.
provision
accumulation 74 n.
foresight 510 n.
means 629 n.
store 632 n.
provision 633 n.
fitting out 669 n.
subvention 703 n.
conditions 766 n.
funds 797 n.
provisional
circumstantial 8 adj.
inferior 35 adj.
ephemeral 114 adj.
changeable 143 adj.
substituted 150 adj.
experimental 461 adj.
qualifying 468 adj.
uncertain 474 adj.
preparatory 669 adj.
conditional 766 adj.
Provisional
revolter 738 n.
provisionally
conditionally 7 adv.
if 8 adv.
provisionally 112 adv.
transiently 114 adv.
on terms 766 adv.
provision for
facility 701 n.
provision merchant
provider 633 n.
tradespeople 794 n.
provisions
provisions 301 n.
proviso
qualification 468 n.
pretext 614 n.
conditions 766 n.
provocation
causation 156 n.
inducement 612 n.
annoyance 827 n.
resentment 891 n.
provocative
assertive 532 adj.
defiant 711 adj.
exciting 821 adj.
impertinent 878 adj.
impure 951 adj.
provoke
cause 156 vb.
incite 612 vb.
make quarrels 709 vb.
torment 827 vb.
be insolent 878 vb.
provost
master 741 n.
officer 741 n.
provost marshal
police 955 n.
prow
prow 237 n.
prowess
deed 676 n.
skill 694 n.
prowess 855 n.
prowl
wander 267 vb.
be stealthy 525 vb.
prowler
pedestrian 268 n.
proximate
sequential 65 adj.
near 200 adj.
proximity
nearness 200 n.
contiguity 202 n.
proximo
subsequently 120 adv.
proxy
substitute 150 n.
commission 751 n.
consignee 754 n.
deputy 755 n.
prude
disapprover 924 n.
prude 950 n.
prudence
thought 449 n.
carefulness 457 n.
sagacity 498 n.
foresight 510 n.
economy 814 n.
caution 858 n.
virtues 933 n.
prudent
advisable 642 adj.
cowardly 856 adj.
prudish
severe 735 adj.
affected 850 adj.
fastidious 862 adj.
modest 874 adj.
prudish 950 adj.
prune
subtract 39 vb.
cut 46 vb.
shorten 204 vb.
fruit 301 n.
extract 304 vb.
cultivate 370 vb.
prunes and prisms
pretension 850 n.
prurience
libido 859 n.
prurient
inquisitive 453 adj.
impure 951 adj.
pruritus
skin disease 651 n.
prussic acid
poison 659 n.
pry
scan 438 vb.
be curious 453 vb.
enquire 459 vb.
— open
force 176 vb.
P.S.
adjunct 40 n.
psalm
vocal music 412 n.
rejoicing 835 n.
hymn 981 n.
psalmbook
hymnal 988 n.
psalmist
musician 413 n.
theologian 973 n.
psalmody
vocal music 412 n.
public worship 981 n.
psalm-singing
pietistic 979 adj.
worshipping 981 adj.
psalter
hymnal 988 n.
psaltery
harp 414 n.
psephologist
vote 605 n.
psephology
vote 605 n.
pseud, pseudo
impostor 545 n.
pseudo-
simulating 18 adj.
imitative 20 adj.
false 541 adj.
spurious 542 adj.
pseudonym
insubstantial thing 4 n.
misnomer 562 n.
psi faculty
intuition 476 n.
psychics 984 n.
psittacosis
animal disease 651 n.
psyche
self 80 n.
subjectivity 320 n.
intellect 447 n.
spirit 447 n.
psychedelic
intoxicating 949 adj.
psyched up
prepared 669 adj.
psychiatric hospital
lunatic asylum 503 n.
psychiatrist
psychologist 447 n.
mender 656 n.
doctor 658 n.
psychiatry
psychology 447 n.
insanity 503 n.
therapy 658 n.
psychic
immaterial 320 adj.
psychic 447 adj.
intuitive 476 adj.
psychic 984 n.
psychical 984 adj.
psychical
spooky 970 adj.
psychical 984 adj.
psychical research
psychics 984 n.
spiritualism 984 n.
psychic bid
gambling 618 n.
psychicism
occultism 984 n.
psychic profile
description 590 n.
psychics
psychics 984 n.
psychist
psychist 984 n.
psycho
madman 504 n.
psychoanalysis
psychology 447 n.
therapy 658 n.
psychoanalyst
psychologist 447 n.
doctor 658 n.
psychodrama
representation 551 n.
psychogenesis
intellect 447 n.
psychograph
spiritualism 984 n.
psychokinesis
psychics 984 n.
psychological
psychic 447 adj.
behaving 688 adj.
psychologically abnormal
insane 503 adj.

psychological moment
crisis 137 n.
psychologist
psychologist 447 n.
psychology
psychology 447 n.
insanity 503 n.
affections 817 n.
psychics 984 n.
psychomancy
sorcery 983 n.
occultism 984 n.
psychometry
psychology 447 n.
psychoneurosis
psychopathy 503 n.
psychopath
madman 504 n.
psychopathic
insane 503 adj.
psychopathology
psychology 447 n.
medical art 658 n.
psychopathy
multiformity 82 n.
psychopathy 503 n.
nervous disorders 651 n.
psychophysics
psychology 447 n.
psychophysiology
psychology 447 n.
psychosis
psychopathy 503 n.
psychosomatic
psychic 447 adj.
diseased 651 adj.
psychosurgery
psychology 447 n.
psychotherapy
psychology 447 n.
therapy 658 n.
psychotic
insane 503 adj.
madman 504 n.
psychotropic
intoxicating 949 adj.
pterodactyl
animal 365 n.
Ptolemaic system
centrality 225 n.
world 321 n.
pub
focus 76 n.
tavern 192 n.
social round 882 n.
pub-crawl
drunkenness 949 n.
puberty
propagation 167 n.
preparedness 669 n.
pubescence
youth 130 n.
hair 259 n.
public
social group 371 n.
national 371 adj.
known 490 adj.
manifest 522 adj.
well-known 528 adj.
noteworthy 866 adj.
formal 875 adj.
public-address system
megaphone 400 n.
hearing aid 415 n.
publican
caterer 633 n.
receiver 782 n.
publication
hearing aid 415 n.
disclosure 526 n.
publication 528 n.
broadcast 531 n.
call 547 n.
book 589 n.
public convenience
latrine 649 n.
public enemy
enemy 881 n.
offender 904 n.
public enemy number one
monster 938 n.
public eye
publicity 528 n.
public figure
person of repute 866 n.
public footpath
path 624 n.
public good
utility 640 n.
public health inspector
sanitarian 652 n.
public house
tavern 192 n.
(See **pub** *)*
public image
affectation 850 n.
publicist
exhibitor 522 n.
publicizer 528 n.
dissertator 591 n.
publicity
generality 79 n.
knowledge 490 n.
manifestation 522 n.
information 524 n.
publicity 528 n.
rostrum 539 n.
publicity agent
publicizer 528 n.
publicize, publicise
advertise 528 vb.
(See **publish** *)*
public knowledge
knowledge 490 n.
public life
vocation 622 n.
public opinion
belief 485 n.
consensus 488 n.
tribunal 956 n.
public ownership
joint possession 775 n.
public prosecutor
accuser 928 n.
law officer 955 n.
public purse
treasury 799 n.
public relations
publicity 528 n.
public relations officer
interpreter 520 n.
publicizer 528 n.
public school
school 539 n.
public sector
apportionment 783 n.
trade 791 n.
public servant
official 690 n.
officer 741 n.
public service
vocation 622 n.
commission 751 n.
public service vehicle
vehicle 274 n.
public speaking
oratory 579 n.
public spirit
patriotism 901 n.
public-spirited
patriotic 901 adj.
public squalor
poverty 801 n.
public transport
vehicle 274 n.
public utility
utility 640 n.
publish
attract notice 455 vb.
manifest 522 vb.
communicate 524 vb.
publish 528 vb.
print 587 vb.
published work
book 589 n.
publisher
publicizer 528 n.
bookperson 589 n.
puce
brown 430 adj.
purple 436 adj.
puck
missile 287 n.
Puck
deceiver 545 n.
elf 970 n.
fairy 970 n.
pucker
become small 198 vb.
fold 261 n. vb.
puckish
harmful 645 adj.
pudding
dessert 301 n.
puddinghead
dunce 501 n.
puddle
shallowness 212 n.
agitate 318 vb.
lake 346 n.
thicken 354 vb.
puddled
opaque 423 adj.
pudency
modesty 874 n.
purity 950 n.
pudenda
genitalia 167 n.
pudgy
fleshy 195 adj.
puerile
foolish 499 adj.
trivial 639 adj.
puerperal
fertilized 167 adj.
puff
dilation 197 n.
emit 300 vb.
pastries 301 n.
breeze 352 n.
blow 352 vb.
breathe 352 vb.
smoke 388 vb.
overrate 482 vb.
advertisement 528 n.
exaggerate 546 vb.
be fatigued 684 vb.
boast 877 n. vb.
praise 923 n. vb.
— out
enlarge 197 vb.
— up
enlarge 197 vb.
make conceited 873 vb.
puffball
sphere 252 n.
plant 366 n.
puffed up
great 32 adj.
overrated 482 adj.
prideful 871 adj.
vain 873 adj.
puffin
bird 365 n.
puffing
puffing 352 adj.
panting 684 adj.
puffy
fleshy 195 adj.
expanded 197 adj.
pug
dog 365 n.
trace 548 n.
pugilist 722 n.
puggaree, puggree
headgear 228 n.
coil 251 n.
pugilism
pugilism 716 n.
sport 837 n.
pugilist
athlete 162 n.
contender 716 n.
pugilist 722 n.

pugnacious
quarrelling 709 adj.
attacking 712 adj.
contending 716 adj.
pugnacity
bellicosity 718 n.
irascibility 892 n.
pug-nosed
short 204 adj.
puissant
powerful 160 adj.
authoritative 733 adj.
puja, pooja
rite 988 n.
puke
vomit 300 vb.
pukka
genuine 494 adj.
pulchritude
beauty 841 n.
pule
cry 408 vb.
ululate 409 vb.
weep 836 vb.
pull
advantage 34 n.
force 176 vb.
influence 178 n.n.
blunt 257 vb.
move 265 vb.
row 269 vb.
deflect 282 vb.
propel 287 vb.
traction 288 n.
draw 288 vb.
attraction 291 n.
extract 304 vb.
smoke 388 vb.
letterpress 587 n.
reading matter 589 n.
motivate 612 vb.
exertion 682 n.
— a face
make ugly 842 vb.
— a fast one
deceive 542 vb.
be cunning 698 vb.
— a gun on
threaten 900 vb.
— aside
deflect 282 vb.
— back
restrain 747 vb.
— down
demolish 165 vb.
fell 311 vb.
— in
arrive 295 vb.
— into shape
form 243 vb.
— it off
succeed 727 vb.
— no punches
be severe 735 vb.
— oneself together
be relieved 831 vb.
— oneself up
lift oneself 310 vb.
— one's leg
befool 542 vb.
be witty 839 vb.
ridicule 851 vb.
— one's punches
avoid 620 vb.
be lenient 736 vb.
— out
displace 188 vb.
enlarge 197 vb.
lengthen 203 vb.
open 263 vb.
fly 271 vb.
draw 288 vb.
decamp 296 vb.
eject 300 vb.
extract 304 vb.
— out all the stops
exert oneself 682 vb.
— out of the hat
surprise 508 vb.
— strings
influence 178 vb.
plot 623 vb.
be instrumental 628 vb.
— the rug from under one's feet
hinder 702 vb.
— the wool over one's eyes
deceive 542 vb.
— through
be restored 656 vb.
— tight
tighten 45 vb.
— together
concur 181 vb.
cooperate 706 vb.
— to pieces
demolish 165 vb.
argue 475 vb.
detract 926 vb.
— up
halt 145 vb.
come to rest 266 vb.
arrive 295 vb.
extract 304 vb.
elevate 310 vb.
pulled muscle
rheumatism 651 n.
impairment 655 n.
pullet
young creature 132 n.
poultry 365 n.
pulley
wheel 250 n.
tool 630 n.
pull-in
café 192 n.
pull-on
tailored 228 adj.
pullover
jersey 228 n.
pullulate
be many 104 vb.
be fruitful 171 vb.
pulmonary
puffing 352 adj.
pulp
demolish 165 vb.
deform 244 vb.
soften 327 vb.
thicken 354 vb.
pulpiness 356 n.
paper 631 n.
pulpit
stand 218 n.
publicity 528 n.
rostrum 539 n.
church interior 990 n.
pulpit, the
clergy 986 n.
ministration 988 n.
pulpiteer
preacher 537 n.
speaker 579 n.
zealot 979 n.
pulp literature
novel 590 n.
pulsar
star 321 n.
pulsate
be periodic 141 vb.
oscillate 317 vb.
pulsation
impulse 279 n.
feeling 818 n.
pulse
be periodic 141 vb.
electricity 160 n.
impulse 279 n.
oscillate 317 vb.
be agitated 318 vb.
pulses
vegetable 301 n.
pulverize, pulverise
break 46 vb.
demolish 165 vb.
force 176 vb.
make smaller 198 vb.
deform 244 vb.
strike 279 vb.
soften 327 vb.
pulverize 332 vb.
puma
cat 365 n.
pumice stone
friction 333 n.
cleanser 648 n.
pummel
strike 279 vb.
fight 716 vb.
pump
extract 304 vb.
brandish 317 vb.
irrigator 341 n.
blowing 352 n.
interrogate 459 vb.
— in
provide 633 vb.
— out
empty 300 vb.
rarefy 325 vb.
make flow 350 vb.
blow up 352 vb.
— up
enlarge 197 vb.
blow up 352 vb.
pumped storage scheme
sources of energy 160 n.
pumpkin
vegetable 301 n.
pump rooms
meeting place 192 n.
place of amusement 837 n.
pumps
footwear 228 n.
pun
assimilation 18 n.
absurdity 497 n.
equivocalness 518 n.
be witty 839 vb.
punch
mould 23 n.
vigorousness 174 n.
perforator 263 n.
pierce 263 vb.
draught horse 273 n.
knock 279 n.
strike 279 vb.
alcoholic drink 301 n.
mark 547 vb.
printing 555 n.
vigour 571 n.
Punch and Judy
stage play 594 n.
plaything 837 n.
punch-bowl
bowl 194 n.
cavity 255 n.
punch-drunk
insensible 375 adj.
punched cards
data processing 86 n.
puncheon
vat 194 n.
pillar 218 n.
perforator 263 n.
punch hole
orifice 263 n.
punch line
witticism 839 n.
punch-up
fight 716 n.
punchy
forceful 571 adj.
punctilio
etiquette 848 n.
formality 875 n.
probity 929 n.
punctilious
attentive 455 adj.
accurate 494 adj.
observant 768 adj.
well-bred 848 adj.
fastidious 862 adj.
formal 875 adj.

trustworthy 929 adj.
punctual
instantaneous 116 adj.
synchronous 123 adj.
early 135 adj.
periodical 141 adj.
accurate 494 adj.
punctuate
discontinue 72 vb.
variegate 437 vb.
mark 547 vb.
parse 564 vb.
punctuation
punctuation 547 n.
puncture
abate 37 vb.
make smaller 198 vb.
perforation 263 n.
pierce 263 vb.
confute 479 vb.
wound 655 n.
hitch 702 n.
detract 926 vb.
pundit
sage 500 n.
dissertator 591 n.
expert 696 n.
pungency
sharpness 256 n.
pungency 388 n.
sourness 393 n.
vigour 571 n.
pungent
keen 174 adj.
tasty 386 adj.
pungent 388 adj.
savoury 390 adj.
odorous 394 adj.
forceful 571 adj.
felt 818 adj.
witty 839 adj.
Punic faith
falsehood 541 n.
perfidy 930 n.
punish
be severe 735 vb.
shame 867 vb.
reprove 924 vb.
punish 963 vb.
punisher
avenger 910 n.
vindicator 927 n.
punisher 963 n.
punishing
vigorous 174 adj.
laborious 682 adj.
fatiguing 684 adj.
paining 827 adj.
punishment
retaliation 714 n.
suffering 825 n.
revenge 910 n.
reprimand 924 n.
condemnation 961 n.
punishment 963 n.
punitive
retaliatory 714 adj.
severe 735 adj.
punitive 963 adj.
punk
nonconformist 84 n.
youngster 132 n.
music 412 n.
bad 645 adj.
vulgarian 847 n.
ruffian 904 n.
punkah
ventilation 352 n.
punnet
basket 194 n.
punning
similar 18 adj.
absurd 497 adj.
wit 839 n.
punt
row 269 vb.
rowing boat 275 n.
propel 287 vb.
gamble 618 vb.
punter
boatman 270 n.
gambler 618 n.
puny
small 33 adj.
weak 163 adj.
little 196 adj.
unimportant 639 adj.
pup
reproduce itself 167 vb.
(See **puppy** *)*
pupa
young creature 132 n.
insect 365 n.
pupil
centre 225 n.
eye 438 n.
learner 538 n.
pupillage
nonage 130 n.
helplessness 161 n.
learning 536 n.
puppet
dwarf 196 n.
dupe 544 n.
image 551 n.
instrument 628 n.
nonentity 639 n.
auxiliary 707 n.
dependant 742 n.
slave 742 n.
puppet show
stage play 594 n.
plaything 837 n.
puppy
young creature 132 n.
dog 365 n.
fop 848 n.
insolent person 878 n.
puppy fat
youth 130 n.
Purana
non-Biblical scripture 975 n.
purblind
dim-sighted 440 adj.
misjudging 481 adj.
purchasable, purchaseable
bought 792 adj.
venal 930 adj.
purchase
influence 178 n.
pivot 218 n.
requirement 627 n.
aid 703 n.
acquisition 771 n.
booty 790 n.
purchase 792 n.vb.
purchaser
owner 776 n.
recipient 782 n.
purchaser 792 n.
purchases
purchase 792 n.
purdah
womankind 373 n.
concealment 525 n.
seclusion 883 n.
pure
absolute 32 adj.
unmixed 44 adj.
whole 52 adj.
white 427 adj.
genuine 494 adj.
plain 573 adj.
elegant 575 adj.
excellent 644 adj.
perfect 646 adj.
clean 648 adj.
salubrious 652 adj.
tasteful 846 adj.
honourable 929 adj.
disinterested 931 adj.
virtuous 933 adj.
innocent 935 adj.
pure 950 adj.
pure and simple
unmixed 44 adj.
purebred
thoroughbred 273 n.
puree
hors-d'oeuvres 301 n.
pulpiness 356 n.
pure in heart
pious 979 adj.
purely
slightly 33 adv.
simply 44 adv.
pure mathematician
reasoner 475 n.
purfling
edging 234 n.
purgation
cleansing 648 n.
penance 941 n.
purgative
opener 263 n.
excretory 302 adj.
cleanser 648 n.
purgative 658 n.
purgatory
suffering 825 n.
penance 941 n.
hell 972 n.
purge
eliminate 44 vb.
slaughter 362 n.vb.
purify 648 vb.
purgative 658 n.
purification
simplification 44 n.
ritual act 988 n.
purify
exclude 57 vb.
purify 648 vb.
sanitate 652 vb.
make better 654 vb.
purist
stylist 575 n.
people of taste 846 n.
affecter 850 n.
perfectionist 862 n.
puritan
disapprover 924 n.
prudish 950 adj.
Puritan
ascetic 945 n.
sectarian 978 n.
zealot 979 n.
puritanical
severe 735 adj.
serious 834 adj.
fastidious 862 adj.
ascetic 945 adj.
purity
simpleness 44 n.
elegance 575 n.
cleanness 648 n.
good taste 846 n.
modesty 874 n.
celibacy 895 n.
probity 929 n.
virtue 933 n.
innocence 935 n.
temperance 942 n.
purity 950 n.
sanctity 979 n.
purl
edging 234 n.
flow 350 vb.
faintness 401 n.
needlework 844 n.
purler
descent 309 n.
purlieus
district 184 n.
near place 200 n.
surroundings 230 n.
purlin
beam 218 n.
purloin
defraud 788 vb.
steal 788 vb.
purple
purple 436 adj.
purple hearts
drug-taking 949 n.

purple passage
discontinuity 72 n.
ornament 574 n.
eloquence 579 n.
purport
meaning 514 n.
purpose
will 595 n.vb.
be resolute 599 vb.
intention 617 n.
use 673 n.
aspiration 852 n.
purposeful
resolute 599 adj.
intended 617 adj.
planning 623 adj.
purposeless
capricious 604 adj.
designless 618 adj.
useless 641 adj.
purpure
heraldry 547 n.
purr
faintness 401 n.
ululate 409 vb.
be pleased 824 vb.
be content 828 vb.
purse
pocket 194 n.
become small 198 vb.
fold 261 vb.
funds 797 n.
treasury 799 n.
purse of Fortunatus
wealth 800 n.
magic instrument 983 n.
purse-proud
prideful 871 adj.
purser
provider 633 n.
treasurer 798 n.
purse-seine
network 222 n.
purse-seiner
fishing boat 275 n.
purse strings
authority 733 n.
treasury 799 n.
pursuant to
purposely 617 adv.
pursuant to 619 adv.
pursue
follow 284 vb.
be mindful 455 vb.
search 459 vb.
aim at 617 vb.
pursue 619 vb.
do 676 vb.
behave 688 vb.
desire 859 vb.
court 889 vb.
pursuer
hunter 619 n.
pursuit
search 459 n.
discovery 484 n.
intention 617 n.
pursuit 619 n.
business 622 n.
pursuivant
heraldry 547 n.
pursy
fleshy 195 adj.
purulence
ulcer 651 n.
purulent
diseased 651 adj.
toxic 653 adj.
purvey
feed 301 vb.
provide 633 vb.
purveyance
provision 633 n.
purveyor
caterer 633 n.
purview
range 183 n.
view 438 n.
intention 617 n.
pus
excrement 302 n.
fluid 335 n.
dirt 649 n.
ulcer 651 n.
push
crisis 137 n.
vigorousness 174 n.
move 265 vb.
transpose 272 vb.
impulse 279 n.
impel 279 vb.
promote 285 vb.
propulsion 287 n.
propel 287 vb.
ejection 300 n.
gesture 547 n.
motivate 612 vb.
be active 678 vb.
haste 680 n.
attack 712 n.
sell 793 vb.
— around
impel 279 vb.
despise 922 vb.
— aside
deflect 282 vb.
be neglectful 458 vb.
not respect 921 vb.
— away
repel 292 vb.
— forward
progress 285 vb.
— hard
attempt 671 vb.
— in
intrude 297 vb.
— into
insert 303 vb.
induce 612 vb.
— off
navigate 269 vb.
start out 296 vb.
decamp 296 vb.
— on
progress 285 vb.
— oneself forward
be vain 873 vb.
— one's luck
gamble 618 vb.
be rash 857 vb.
— out
eject 300 vb.
— too far
enrage 891 vb.
— up
bargain 791 vb.
push bike
bicycle 274 n.
push-button
instrumental 628 adj.
push-button war
war 718 n.
pushcart
pushcart 274 n.
pushchair
pushcart 274 n.
pushed to the wall, be
be forced 596 vb.
pusher
ram 279 n.
propellant 287 n.
busy person 678 n.
drug-taking 949 n.
pushful
vigorous 174 adj.
pushing
assertive 532 adj.
active 678 adj.
hasty 680 adj.
pushover
dupe 544 n.
easy thing 701 n.
victory 727 n.
pushy
meddling 678 adj.
pusillanimous
cowardly 856 adj.
puss
youngster 132 n.
cat 365 n.
pussyfoot
be stealthy 525 vb.
avoid 620 vb.
be cautious 858 vb.
disapprover 924 n.
abstainer 942 n.
pustule
skin disease 651 n.
put
firm 45 adj.
place 187 vb.
— about
navigate 269 vb.
circle 314 vb.
publish 528 vb.
— a brave face on it
be patient 823 vb.
be cheerful 833 vb.
take courage 855 vb.
— across
convince 485 vb.
— a damper on
depress 834 vb.
— all one's eggs into one basket
be rash 857 vb.
— an end to
terminate 69 vb.
destroy 165 vb.
defeat 727 vb.
— aside
set apart 46 vb.
exclude 57 vb.
be neglectful 458 vb.
store 632 vb.
— a spoke in one's wheel
make useless 641 vb.
be obstructive 702 vb.
— a stop to
terminate 69 vb.
halt 145 vb.
be severe 735 vb.
restrain 747 vb.
— at ease
please 826 vb.
— away
destroy 165 vb.
stow 187 vb.
store 632 vb.
— back
replace 187 vb.
restore 656 vb.
— by
store 632 vb.
— down
destroy 165 vb.
suppress 165 vb.
let fall 311 vb.
kill 362 vb.
overmaster 727 vb.
pay 804 vb.
— down to
attribute 158 vb.
— forth
expand 197 vb.
propound 512 vb.
— forward
promote 285 vb.
offer 759 vb.
— heads together
consult 691 vb.
— heart into
give courage 855 vb.
— in
number with 78 vb.
interfere 231 vb.
arrive 295 vb.
insert 303 vb.
— in a bad light
shame 867 vb.
defame 926 vb.
— in a good word for
approve 923 vb.
— in for
offer oneself 759 vb.
request 761 vb.

— in mothballs
store 632 vb.
stop using 674 vb.
— in perspective
relate 9 vb.
— in the place of
substitute 150 vb.
— in the shade
abate 37 vb.
humiliate 872 vb.
— in the way of
make possible 469 vb.
facilitate 701 vb.
— into
insert 303 vb.
— into practice
use 673 vb.
do 676 vb.
deal with 688 vb.
— in touch
connect 45 vb.
— into words
phrase 563 vb.
voice 577 vb.
— new life into
vitalize 360 vb.
— off
put off 136 vb.
deflect 282 vb.
repel 292 vb.
be neglectful 458 vb.
be irresolute 601 vb.
dissuade 613 vb.
not act 677 vb.
be obstructive 702 vb.
not complete 726 vb.
displease 827 vb.
cause dislike 861 vb.
— on
imitate 20 vb.
wear 228 vb.
dissemble 541 vb.
dramatize 594 vb.
— on airs
be affected 850 vb.
be vain 873 vb.
— on a pedestal
idolatrize 982 vb.
— one in mind of
resemble 18 vb.
remind 505 vb.
warn 664 vb.
— one in the picture
inform 524 vb.
— one off his/her stroke
distract 456 vb.
— one on the spot
be difficult 700 vb.
— one out of his/her misery
kill 362 vb.
relieve 831 vb.
show mercy 905 vb.
— one's back into it
exert oneself 682 vb.
— one's back up
cause dislike 861 vb.
huff 891 vb.
— one's best foot forward
move fast 277 vb.
exert oneself 682 vb.
— one's cards on the table
divulge 526 vb.
— oneself first
be selfish 932 vb.
— oneself forward
be ostentatious 875 vb.
— oneself out
exert oneself 682 vb.
be courteous 884 vb.
— one's feet up
repose 683 vb.
— one's finger on
place 187 vb.
detect 484 vb.
— one's foot down
accelerate 277 vb.
be resolute 599 vb.
be severe 735 vb.
prohibit 757 vb.
— one's foot in it
blunder 495 vb.
be clumsy 695 vb.
— one's hand to
sign 547 vb.
— one's hand to the plough
begin 68 vb.
— one's head in the lion's mouth
face danger 661 vb.
— one's heart into
be resolute 599 vb.
exert oneself 682 vb.
— one's house in order
make ready 669 vb.
— one's money to work
speculate 791 vb.
— one's name down
join a party 708 vb.
— one's nose out of joint
be superior 34 vb.
shame 867 vb.
humiliate 872 vb.
— one's oar in
interfere 231 vb.
— one's shirt on
be certain 473 vb.
— one's shoulder to the wheel
be resolute 599 vb.
be active 678 vb.
— one's tongue out
be insolent 878 vb.
— one's trust in
hope 852 vb.
— one through his/her paces
show 522 vb.
— one under an obligation
be benevolent 897 vb.
— one wise
inform 524 vb.
— on ice
pause 145 vb.
— on side
be affected 850 vb.
be ostentatious 875 vb.
— on the map
advertise 528 vb.
make important 638 vb.
— on the right track
orientate 281 vb.
— on weight
grow 36 vb.
expand 197 vb.
get healthy 650 vb.
— out
suppress 165 vb.
eject 300 vb.
extinguish 382 vb.
publish 528 vb.
make inactive 679 vb.
— out a feeler
touch 378 vb.
be tentative 461 vb.
attempt 671 vb.
— out of commission
disable 161 vb.
make useless 641 vb.
stop using 674 vb.
make inactive 679 vb.
— out of countenance
hinder 702 vb.
cause discontent 829 vb.
shame 867 vb.
— out to grass
feed 301 vb.
stop using 674 vb.
— over
convince 485 vb.
communicate 524 vb.
— paid to
terminate 69 vb.
— pressure on
influence 178 vb.
— right
inform 524 vb.
rectify 654 vb.
remedy 658 vb.
be just 913 vb.
— teeth into
empower 160 vb.
— the boot in
kick 279 vb.
dispraise 924 vb.
— the cart before the horse
invert 221 vb.
act foolishly 695 vb.
— the cat among the pigeons
make quarrels 709 vb.
— the clock back
be unconformable 84 vb.
look back 125 vb.
— the lid on
climax 725 vb.
— the screws on
oppress 735 vb.
compel 740 vb.
— the skids under
destroy 165 vb.
— the wind up
frighten 854 vb.
— through the mill
train 534 vb.
— through to
connect 45 vb.
— to bed
print 587 vb.
doctor 658 vb.
make inactive 679 vb.
— to flight
defeat 727 vb.
— together
join 45 vb.
combine 50 vb.
bring together 74 vb.
produce 164 vb.
— to music
harmonize 410 vb.
compose music 413 vb.
— to rights
regularize 62 vb.
— to sleep
kill 362 vb.
render insensible 375 vb.
make inactive 679 vb.
— to the test
experiment 461 vb.
— two and two together
reason 475 vb.
— under
render insensible 375 vb.
— up
place oneself 187 vb.
select 605 vb.
predetermine 608 vb.
— upon
ill-treat 645 vb.
oppress 735 vb.
— up the money
aid 703 vb.
lend 784 vb.

— up to
incite 612 vb.
— up with
acquiesce 488 vb.
knuckle under 721 vb.
be patient 823 vb.
suffer 825 vb.
putative
attributed 158 adj.
credible 485 adj.
supposed 512 adj.
put off
distracted 456 adj.
put on
hypocritical 541 adj.
affected 850 adj.
put out
distracted 456 adj.
discontented 829 adj.
putrefaction
decay 51 n.
stench 397 n.
uncleanness 649 n.
dilapidation 655 n.
putrefy
decompose 51 vb.
putrescence
uncleanness 649 n.
putrid
decomposed 51 adj.
unsavoury 391 adj.
fetid 397 adj.
not nice 645 adj.
putsch
revolt 738 n.
putt
propel 287 vb.
puttees
legwear 228 n.
putting
ball game 837 n.
putting green
arena 724 n.
putto
image 551 n.
put to it, be
be in difficulty 700 vb.
putty
adhesive 47 n.
softness 327 n.
pulpiness 356 n.
put-up job
duplicity 541 n.
predetermination 608 n.
false charge 928 n.
puzzle
complexity 61 n.
distract 456 vb.
puzzle 474 vb.
be unintelligible 517 vb.
enigma 530 n.
difficulty 700 n.
trouble 827 vb.
— out
decipher 520 vb.
puzzled
doubting 474 adj.
puzzled 517 adj.
in difficulties 700 adj.
wondering 864 adj.
puzzling
causeless 159 adj.
moot 459 adj.
unexpected 508 adj.
(See **puzzle** *)*
PWR
nucleonics 160 n.
pyaemia
infection 651 n.
pyjamas
nightwear 228 n.
pyknic
thick 205 adj.
pylon
electronics 160 n.
high structure 209 n.
pyramid
series 71 n.
accumulation 74 n.
fixture 153 n.
edifice 164 n.
bulk 195 n.
high structure 209 n.
angular figure 247 n.
tomb 364 n.
pyramidal
tapering 256 adj.
pyre
interment 364 n.
fire 379 n.
pyrexia
heat 379 n.
illness 651 n.
pyrography
ornamental art 844 n.
pyrolatry
idolatry 982 n.
pyromancy
divination 511 n.
pyromania
incendiarism 381 n.
pyromaniac
destroyer 168 n.
madman 504 n.
pyrometer
thermometry 379 n.
pyrotechnics
fireworks 420 n.
spectacle 445 n.
revel 837 n.
pageant 875 n.
pyrrhic
prosody 593 n.
Pyrrhic victory
victory 727 n.
Pyrrhonism
doubt 486 n.
irreligion 974 n.
Pythagoreanism
philosophy 449 n.
python
compressor 198 n.
reptile 365 n.
Pythoness
oracle 511 n.
priest 986 n.
pyx
small box 194 n.
ritual object 988 n.

Q

Q.C.
lawyer 958 n.
QED
argumentation 475 n.
of course 478 adv.
Q-ship
warship 722 n.
quack
ululation 409 n.
sciolist 493 n.
impostor 545 n.
be loquacious 581 vb.
doctor 658 n.
unskilled 695 adj.
affecter 850 n.
quackery
deception 542 n.
quad
quaternity 96 n.
quadrangle
place 185 n.
meeting place 192 n.
angular figure 247 n.
quadrant
angular measure 247 n.
arc 250 n.
gauge 465 n.
quadraphonic sound
sound 398 n.
quadrate
four 96 adj.
quadrate with
accord 24 vb.
quadratic equations
mathematics 86 n.
quadrature
quaternity 96 n.
angular figure 247 n.
quadrennial
seasonal 141 adj.
quadri-
four 96 adj.
quadriga
carriage 274 n.
quadrilateral
quaternity 96 n.
angular figure 247 n.
quadrille
card game 837 n.
dance 837 n.
quadrireme
gallery 275 n.
quadrisection
quadrisection 98 n.
quadrivium
curriculum 534 n.
quadroon
hybrid 43 n.
quadruped
animal 365 n.
quadruple
augment 36 vb.
fourfold 97 adj.
quadruple 97 vb.
quadruplet
quaternity 96 n.
quadruplicate
fourfold 97 adj.
quaestor
official 690 n.
officer 741 n.
treasurer 798 n.
quaff
drink 301 vb.
revel 837 vb.
get drunk 949 vb.
quaggy
marshy 347 adj.
quagmire
marsh 347 n.
dirt 649 n.
pitfall 663 n.
difficulty 700 n.
quail
table bird 365 n.
quake 854 vb.
be cowardly 856 vb.
quaint
beautiful 841 adj.
ornamental 844 adj.
ridiculous 849 adj.
quake
outbreak 176 n.
be cold 380 vb.
show feeling 818 vb.
quake 854 vb.
Quaker
Protestant 976 n.
sectarian 978 n.
qualification(s)
fitness 24 n.
ability 160 n.
counterevidence 467 n.
qualification 468 n.
aptitude 694 n.
dueness 915 n.
(See **qualify** *)*
qualified
qualifying 468 adj.
prepared 669 adj.
expert 694 adj.
qualify
modify 143 vb.
moderate 177 vb.
limit 236 vb.

discriminate 463 vb.
qualify 468 vb.
doubt 486 vb.
dissent 489 vb.
train 534 vb.
suffice 635 vb.
be good 644 vb.
succeed 727 vb.
give terms 766 vb.
— for
be expedient 642 vb.
qualitative
characteristic 5 adj.
qualities
affections 817 n.
virtues 933 n.
quality
character 5 n.
superiority 34 n.
sort 77 n.
tendency 179 n.
goodness 644 n.
excellent 644 adj.
qualms
doubt 486 n.
unwillingness 598 n.
regret 830 n.
nervousness 854 n.
quandary
dubiety 474 n.
predicament 700 n.
quango
council 692 n.
consignee 754 n.
quantify
quantify 26 vb.
specify 80 vb.
measure 465 vb.
quantitative
quantitative 26 adj.
quantity
quantity 26 n.
degree 27 n.
number 85 n.
store 632 n.
quantity, a
great quantity 32 n.
multitude 104 n.
quantity surveyor
surveyor 465 n.
quantum
finite quantity 26 n.
element 319 n.
portion 783 n.
quantum mechanics
physics 319 n.
quarantine
set apart 46 vb.
exclude 57 vb.
hygiene 652 n.
prophylactic 658 n.
protection 660 n.
preservation 666 n.
detention 747 n.
seclusion 883 n.
quark
minuteness 196 n.
element 319 n.
quarrel
differ 15 vb.
disagreement 25 n.
turmoil 61 n.
argument 475 n.
dissent 489 vb.
quarrel 709 n.vb.
contention 716 n.
be discontented 829 vb.
be inimical 881 vb.
litigation 959 n.
schism 978 n.
— with one's bread and butter
act foolishly 695 vb.
be discontented 829 vb.
quarreller
quarreller 709 n.
quarrelling
irascible 892 adj.
sullen 893 adj.
quarrelsome
quarrelling 709 adj.
contending 716 adj.
sullen 893 adj.
quarrelsomeness
bellicosity 718 n.
irascibility 892 n.
quarry
source 156 n.
excavation 255 n.
extract 304 vb.
objective 617 n.
chase 619 n.
store 632 n.
workshop 687 n.
booty 790 n.
quart
metrology 465 n.
quarter
sunder 46 vb.
part 53 n.
quadrisection 98 n.
period 110 n.
district 184 n.
place 187 vb.
poop 238 n.
laterality 239 n.
compass point 281 n.
weighing 322 n.
metrology 465 n.
informant 524 n.
heraldry 547 n.
leniency 736 n.
coinage 797 n.
mercy 905 n.
— the ground
search 459 vb.
quarter day
date 108 n.
quarterdeck
layer 207 n.
vertex 213 n.
quartered
quartered 98 adj.
quarterfinal
contest 716 n.
quartering
heraldry 547 n.
quarterly
three 93 adj.
journal 528 n.
quartermaster
navigator 270 n.
provider 633 n.
army officer 741 n.
quarters
locality 187 n.
quarters 192 n.
quarter sessions
lawcourt 956 n.
quarterstaff
club 723 n.
quartet
quaternity 96 n.
duet 412 n.
orchestra 413 n.
quartile
statistical 86 adj.
quarto
edition 589 n.
quartz
hardness 326 n.
quasar
star 321 n.
quash
suppress 165 vb.
abrogate 752 vb.
acquit 960 vb.
quasi
similar 18 adj.
supposed 512 adj.
misnamed 562 adj.
quatercentenary
anniversary 141 n.
Quaternary
secular 110 adj.
quaternion
number 85 n.
quaternity 96 n.
quaternity
quaternity 96 n.
quatrain
verse form 593 n.
quatrefoil
quaternity 96 n.
quattrocento
art 551 n.
quaver
be agitated 318 vb.
roll 403 n.
notation 410 n.
stammer 580 vb.
quake 854 vb.
quay
stable 192 n.
edge 234 n.
shelter 662 n.
queasy
sick 651 adj.
disliking 861 adj.
queen
nonconformist 84 n.
sovereign 741 n.
aristocrat 868 n.
queen it
seek repute 866 vb.
be proud 871 vb.
be insolent 878 vb.
queenly
ruling 733 adj.
impressive 821 adj.
worshipful 866 adj.
noble 868 adj.
proud 871 adj.
Queen of Hearts
favourite 890 n.
Queen of the May
exceller 644 n.
Queen of the night
moon 321 n.
queen post
pillar 218 n.
Queen's Bench
lawcourt 956 n.
Queensberry rules
justice 913 n.
Queen's English
language 557 n.
Queen's evidence
testimony 466 n.
disclosure 526 n.
Queen's Messenger
courier 529 n.
queer
nonconformist 84 n.
abnormal 84 adj.
unusual 84 adj.
crazy 503 adj.
sick 651 adj.
ridiculous 849 adj.
wrong 914 adj.
queer fish
nonconformist 84 n.
laughingstock 851 n.
queerly
remarkably 32 adv.
queer one's pitch
harm 645 vb.
Queer Street
poverty 801 n.
quell
abate 37 vb.
suppress 165 vb.
moderate 177 vb.
hinder 702 vb.
overmaster 727 vb.
subjugate 745 vb.
frighten 854 vb.
quench
suppress 165 vb.
extinguish 382 vb.
snuff out 418 vb.
sate 863 vb.
quern
pulverizer 332 n.
querulous
discontented 829 adj.
lamenting 836 adj.
irascible 892 adj.
query
question 459 n.
enquire 459 vb.
uncertainty 474 n.

quest
land travel 267 n.
search 459 n.
pursuit 619 n.
job 622 n.
attempt 671 n.
undertaking 672 n.
question
topic 452 n.
be curious 453 vb.
question 459 n.
interrogate 459 vb.
uncertainty 474 n.
doubt 486 vb.
negate 533 vb.
questionable
moot 459 adj.
disreputable 867 adj.
dishonest 930 adj.
question and answer
interlocution 584 n.
questioner
listener 415 n.
inquisitive person 453 n.
questioner 459 n.
question mark
uncertainty 474 n.
punctuation 547 n.
question master
questioner 459 n.
broadcaster 531 n.
questionnaire
list 87 n.
question 459 n.
Quetzalcoatl
Aztec deities 967 n.
queue
retinue 67 n.
procession 71 n.
line 203 n.
passing along 305 n.
queue-jumping
precedence 64 n.
preceding 283 n.
queue up
run on 71 vb.
await 507 vb.
quibble
argue 475 vb.
sophisticate 477 vb.
absurdity 497 n.
equivocalness 518 n.
pretext 614 n.
quiche
dish 301 n.
quick
brief 114 adj.
speedy 277 adj.
alive 360 adj.
intelligent 498 adj.
willing 597 adj.
active 678 adj.
skilful 694 adj.
witty 839 adj.
irascible 892 adj.
quick and the dead, the
all 52 n.
quick as lightning
instantaneous 116 adj.
quick-change artist
conjuror 545 n.
entertainer 594 n.
quick ear
hearing 415 n.
quicken
strengthen 162 vb.
invigorate 174 vb.
make violent 176 vb.
accelerate 277 vb.
live 360 vb.
animate 821 vb.
quick march
gait 265 n.
marching 267 n.
speeding 277 n.
quick one
draught 301 n.
quick on the uptake
intelligent 498 adj.
quick passions
irascibility 892 n.
quicksand
marsh 347 n.
pitfall 663 n.
quickset hedge
fence 235 n.
quicksilver
changeable thing 152 n.
quickstep
dance 837 n.
quick-tempered
irascible 892 adj.
quick-witted
intelligent 498 adj.
quid
mouthful 301 n.
tobacco 388 n.
coinage 797 n.
funds 797 n.
quiddity
essence 1 n.
essential part 5 n.
quidnunc
news reporter 529 n.
quid pro quo
offset 31 n.
quid pro quo 150 n.
retaliation 714 n.
reward 962 n.
quids in
moneyed 800 adj.
quiescence
quiescence 266 n.
repose 683 n.
peace 717 n.
quiescent
inert 175 adj.
quiescent 266 adj.
silent 399 adj.
latent 523 adj.
inactive 679 adj.
inexcitable 823 adj.
quiet
inert 175 adj.
moderation 177 n.
assuage 177 vb.
smooth 258 adj.
quietude 266 n.
still 266 adj.
euphoria 376 n.
silent 399 adj.
soft-hued 425 adj.
grey 429 adj.
dissuade 613 vb.
inaction 677 n.
reposeful 683 adj.
peaceful 717 adj.
submitting 721 adj.
middling 732 adj.
inexcitable 823 adj.
pleasurable 826 adj.
modest 874 adj.
secluded 883 adj.
quieten
bring to rest 266 vb.
silence 399 vb.
quietism
quietude 266 n.
moral insensibility 820 n.
inexcitability 823 n.
content 828 n.
quietude
quietude 266 n.
(See **quiet** *)*
quietus
end 69 n.
death 361 n.
killing 362 n.
quiff
hair 259 n.
quill
prickle 256 n.
plumage 259 n.
stationery 586 n.
quill-driving
writing 586 n.
quilt
coverlet 226 n.
variegate 437 vb.
quilting
lining 227 n.
quin
five 99 n.
quincentenary
anniversary 141 n.
quincunx
five 99 n.
crossing 222 n.
quinine
antidote 658 n.
prophylactic 658 n.
quinquennial
periodic 110 adj.
seasonal 141 adj.
quinquepartite
multifid 100 adj.
quinquereme
galley 275 n.
quint
five 99 n.
quintal
weighing 322 n.
quintessence
essential part 5 n.
goodness 644 n.
perfection 646 n.
quintet
five 99 n.
duet 412 n.
orchestra 413 n.
quintuple
fifth and over 99 adj.
quintuplet
five 99 n.
quip
witticism 839 n.
indignity 921 n.
quipu
counting instrument 86 n.
quire
edition 589 n.
paper 631 n.
quirk
speciality 80 n.
nonconformity 84 n.
whim 604 n.
witticism 839 n.
quisling
tergiversator 603 n.
knave 938 n.
quit
depart 296 vb.
relinquish 621 vb.
resign 753 vb.
fail in duty 918 vb.
quite
greatly 32 adv.
slightly 33 adv.
completely 54 adv.
quite a few
great quantity 32 n.
many 104 adj.
quite another matter
variant 15 n.
quite so
865 int.
quite something
prodigy 864 n.
quite the reverse
contrariety 14 n.
quit of
losing 772 adj.
quit rent
price 809 n.
quits
equivalence 28 n.
atonement 941 n.
quits, be
retaliate 714 vb.
quittance
liberation 746 n.
payment 804 n.
quitter
tergiversator 603 n.
avoider 620 n.
submission 721 n.
resignation 753 n.
coward 856 n.

quiver
accumulation 74 n.
oscillate 317 vb.
be agitated 318 vb.
feel pain 377 vb.
be cold 380 vb.
arsenal 723 n.
show feeling 818 vb.
be excited 821 vb.
quake 854 vb.
quixotic
imaginative 513 adj.
disinterested 931 adj.
quixotry
ideality 513 n.
rashness 857 n.
disinterestedness 931 n.
quiz
be curious 453 vb.
interrogate 459 vb.
broadcast 531 n.
indoor game 837 n.
quizzer
questioner 459 n.
quizzical
enquiring 459 adj.
derisive 851 adj.
quod
gaol 748 n.
quodlibet
question 459 n.
argumentation 475 n.
quoin
angularity 247 n.
press 587 n.
quoit(s)
circle 250 n.
missile 287 n.
ball game 837 n.
quondam
former 125 adj.
quorum
finite quantity 26 n.
electorate 605 n.
sufficiency 635 n.
quota
finite quantity 26 n.
portion 783 n.
quotation
referral 9 n.
part 53 n.
repetition 106 n.
evidence 466 n.
exhibit 522 n.
price 809 n.
quotation marks
punctuation 547 n.
quote
exemplify 83 vb.
repeat 106 vb.
manifest 522 vb.
quotidian
seasonal 141 adj.
quotient
quantity 26 n.
numerical element 85 n.

R

Ra, Re
Egyptian deities 967 n.
RA
artist 556 n.
rabbet
join 45 vb.
furrow 262 n.
rabbi
theologian 973 n.
priest 986 n.
rabbinical
theological 973 adj.
rabbit
mammal 365 n.
bungler 697 n.
coward 856 n.
rabbiting
chase 619 n.
rabbit on
be loquacious 581 vb.
rabbit punch
knock 279 n.
rabbit warren
abundance 171 n.
rabble
crowd 74 n.
rabble 869 n.
rabble-rouser
motivator 612 n.
leader 690 n.
agitator 738 n.
excitant 821 n.
Rabelaisian
impure 951 adj.
rabid
furious 176 adj.
frenzied 503 adj.
excitable 822 adj.
angry 891 adj.
rabies
animal disease 651 n.
infection 651 n.
raccoon
mammal 365 n.
race
race 11 n.
breed 77 n.
genealogy 169 n.
speeding 277 n.
outdo 306 vb.
current 350 n.
humankind 371 n.
hasten 680 vb.
community 708 n.
racing 716 n.
racecourse
meeting place 192 n.
gaming-house 618 n.
racing 716 n.
arena 724 n.
race discrimination
injustice 914 n.

racehorse
thoroughbred 273 n.
speeder 277 n.
racer
bicycle 274 n.
speeder 277 n.
contender 716 n.
race relations
sociality 882 n.
race riot
lawlessness 954 n.
Rachmanism
severity 735 n.
racial
ethnic 11 adj.
parental 169 adj.
human 371 adj.
racialism
prejudice 481 n.
hatred 888 n.
racial prejudice
prejudice 481 n.
phobia 854 n.
racing
speeding 277 n.n.
racing 716 n.
sport 837 n.
racism
prejudice 481 n.
hatred 888 n.
racist
narrow mind 481 n.
rack
compartment 194 n.
shelf 218 n.
distort 246 vb.
cloud 355 n.
pain 377 n.
ill-treat 645 vb.
purify 648 vb.
oppress 735 vb.
torment 827 vb.
torture 963 vb.
instrument of torture 964 n.
— one's brains
think 449 vb.
retrospect 505 vb.
rack and pinion
railway 624 n.
racket
turmoil 61 n.
commotion 318 n.
loudness 400 n.
roll 403 n.
discord 411 n.
trickery 542 n.
plot 623 n.
foul play 930 n.
racketeer
robber 789 n.
offender 904 n.
be dishonest 930 vb.
racketing
activity 678 n.
rackets
ball game 837 n.
rackety
riotous 738 adj.

merry 833 adj.
racking
painful 377 adj.
paining 827 adj.
corporal punishment 963 n.
rack-rent
levy 786 vb.
be parsimonious 816 vb.
rack rents
dearness 811 n.
raconteur, raconteuse
narrator 590 n.
humorist 839 n.
racy
vigorous 174 adj.
tasty 386 adj.
savoury 390 adj.
stylistic 566 adj.
forceful 571 adj.
lively 819 adj.
witty 839 adj.
impure 951 adj.
radar
location 187 n.
sailing aid 269 n.
detector 484 n.
telecommunication 531 n.
indicator 547 n.
directorship 689 n.
raddle
redden 431 vb.
radial
divergent 294 adj.
radially
longwise 203 adv.
radial velocity
star 321 n.
radian
angular measure 247 n.
radiance
glow 417 n.
light 417 n.
beauty 841 n.
radiant
luminous 417 adj.
radiating 417 adj.
luminescent 420 adj.
happy 824 adj.
cheerful 833 adj.
beautiful 841 adj.
splendid 841 adj.
radiate
separate 46 vb.
be dispersed 75 vb.
diverge 294 vb.
emit 300 vb.
radiate 417 vb.
radiation
nucleonics 160 n.
oscillation 317 n.
radiation 417 n.
poison 659 n.
radiation sickness
illness 651 n.

radiator
heater 383 n.
radical
intrinsic 5 adj.
complete 54 adj.
numerical 85 adj.
revolutionist 149 n.
revolutionary 149 adj.
source 156 n.
fundamental 156 adj.
important 638 adj.
reformer 654 n.
improving 654 adj.
sectional 708 adj.
radicalism
reformism 654 n.
Radicals
political party 708 n.
radio
electronics 160 n.
sound 398 n.
publicity 528 n.
broadcasting 531 n.
amusement 837 n.
radioactive
radiating 417 adj.
harmful 645 adj.
insalubrious 653 adj.
dangerous 661 adj.
radioactive waste
nucleonics 160 n.
radioactivity
nucleonics 160 n.
radiation 417 n.
poison 659 n.
radiocarbon dating
chronology 117 n.
radiogram
gramophone 414 n.
message 529 n.
radiography
photography 551 n.
medical art 658 n.
radio ham
listener 415 n.
enthusiast 504 n.
telecommunication 531 n.
radioisotope
radiation 417 n.
radiolocation
bearings 186 n.
(See **radar** *)*
radiology
optics 417 n.
radio mast
high structure 209 n.
radiometer
optical device 442 n.
radiophonic
sounding 398 adj.
radio receiver
reception 299 n.
radioscopy
optics 417 n.
radio station
broadcasting 531 n.
radiotelegraphy
telecommunication 531 n.
radio telescope
astronomy 321 n.
radiotherapy
medical art 658 n.
therapy 658 n.
radio transmitter
ejector 300 n.
radio wave(s)
radiation 417 n.
broadcasting 531 n.
radish
vegetable 301 n.
radius
range 183 n.
line 203 n.
breadth 205 n.
RAF
air force 722 n.
raffia
ligature 47 n.
fibre 208 n.
raffish
vulgar 847 adj.
raffle
gambling 618 n.
raft
basis 218 n.
carry 273 vb.
raft 275 n.
rafter
beam 218 n.
roof 226 n.
materials 631 n.
rag
small thing 33 n.
piece 53 n.
the press 528 n.
trickery 542 n.
book 589 n.
torment 827 vb.
revel 837 n.
be witty 839 vb.
ridicule 851 vb.
raga
key 410 n.
musical piece 412 n.
ragamuffin
slut 61 n.
low fellow 869 n.
rag-and-bone man
pedlar 794 n.
ragbag
medley 43 n.
rage
violence 176 n.
prevail 178 vb.
blow 352 vb.
be active 678 vb.
excitable state 822 n.
fashion 848 n.
desire 859 n.
anger 891 n.
be angry 891 vb.
ragged
uncovered 229 adj.
undulatory 251 adj.
ragged edge
notch 260 n.
raggedness
nonuniformity 17 n.
poverty 801 n.
raging
destructive 165 adj.
violent 176 adj.
raglan
overcoat 228 n.
sleeve 228 n.
ragout
a mixture 43 n.
dish 301 n.
rag-picker
poor person 801 n.
rags
piece 53 n.
clothing 228 n.
ragtag and bobtail
commonalty 869 n.
ragtime
music 412 n.
rag trade, the
dressing 228 n.
raid
lay waste 165 vb.
burst in 297 vb.
attack 712 n.vb.
take away 786 vb.
brigandage 788 n.
raider
attacker 712 n.
soldier 722 n.
warship 722 n.
taker 786 n.
robber 789 n.
rail
handle 218 n.
transport 272 n.
carry 273 vb.
orate 579 vb.
curse 899 vb.
dispraise 924 vb.
reprobate 924 vb.
— in
circumscribe 232 vb.
railing
handle 218 n.
edge 234 n.
fence 235 n.
safeguard 662 n.
raillery
ridicule 851 n.
railroad
carry 273 vb.
railway 624 n.
compel 740 vb.
railroaded
hasty 680 adj.
rails
parallelism 219 n.
fence 235 n.
railway 624 n.
railway
railway 624 n.
raiment
clothing 228 n.
rain
storm 176 n.
weather 340 n.
be wet 341 vb.
rain 350 n.vb.
abound 635 vb.
— blows
strike 279 vb.
rainbow
series 71 n.
arc 250 n.
light 417 n.
colour 425 n.
variegation 437 n.
raincoat
overcoat 228 n.
raindrop
moisture 341 n.
rainfall
moisture 341 n.
rain 350 n.
rain gauge
weather 340 n.
hygrometry 341 n.
rain-making
rain 350 n.
rain or shine
certainly 473 adv.
rainproof
dry 342 adj.
rainy
humid 341 adj.
rainy 350 adj.
rainy day
adversity 731 n.
raise
augment 36 vb.
initiate 68 vb.
generate 167 vb.
displace 188 vb.
make higher 209 vb.
make vertical 215 vb.
move 265 vb.
promote 285 vb.
elevate 310 vb.
lighten 323 vb.
breed stock 369 vb.
incentive 612 n.
improvement 654 n.
gain 771 n.
levy 786 vb.
relieve 831 vb.
— a laugh
be witty 839 vb.
be ridiculous 849 vb.
— Cain
be loud 400 vb.
revolt 738 vb.
be angry 891 vb.
— one's eyebrows
gesticulate 547 vb.
deprecate 762 vb.
— one's glass (to)
drink 301 vb.
toast 876 vb.

— one's hackles
enrage 891 vb.
get angry 891 vb.
— one's hand
gesticulate 547 vb.
vote 605 vb.
strike at 712 vb.
— one's hat
doff 229 vb.
greet 884 vb.
— one's sights
progress 285 n.
aim at 617 vb.
— one's voice
emphasize 532 vb.
speak 579 vb.
— one's voice against
dissent 489 vb.
deprecate 762 vb.
— spirits
practise sorcery 983 vb.
— the alarm
signal 547 vb.
warn 664 vb.
raise the alarm 665 vb.
frighten 854 vb.
— the dust
be violent 176 vb.
be active 678 vb.
— the money
find means 629 vb.
— the roof
be loud 400 vb.
applaud 923 vb.
— the spirits
cheer 833 vb.
— the subject
initiate 68 vb.
— the temperature
heat 381 vb.
excite 821 vb.
— the wind
acquire 771 vb.
raised
projecting 254 adj.
raised eyebrows
deprecation 762 n.
raised voice(s)
cry 408 n.
quarrel 709 n.
raisin
fruit 301 n.
raising agent
leaven 323 n.
raison d'être
reason why 156 n.
intention 617 n.
raj
governance 733 n.
rajah, raja
potentate 741 n.
person of rank 868 n.
rajahship
position of authority 733 n.
Rajput
aristocrat 868 n.
rake
thinness 206 n.
obliquity 220 n.
projection 254 n.
smoother 258 n.
draw 288 vb.
extractor 304 n.
farm tool 370 n.
cultivate 370 vb.
cleaning utensil 648 n.
fire at 712 vb.
bad person 938 n.
sensualist 944 n.
libertine 952 n.
— in
bring together 74 vb.
— in the shekels
gain 771 vb.
get rich 800 vb.
— out
extinguish 382 vb.
clean 648 vb.
— over
search 459 vb.
— together
acquire 771 vb.
— up
bring together 74 vb.
extract 304 vb.
retrospect 505 vb.
rake-off
earnings 771 n.
discount 810 n.
reward 962 n.
rakish
oblique 220 adj.
fashionable 848 adj.
showy 875 adj.
lecherous 951 adj.
rallentando
tempo 410 n.
adagio 412 adv.
rally
arrange 62 vb.
assemblage 74 n.
congregate 74 vb.
continuance 146 n.
interchange 151 n.
be strong 162 vb.
propulsion 287 n.
call 547 n.
persevere 600 vb.
incite 612 vb.
get better 654 vb.
be restored 656 vb.
aid 703 vb.
contest 716 n.
give battle 718 vb.
ridicule 851 vb.
give courage 855 vb.
— round
cooperate 706 vb.
rallying cry
call 547 n.
inducement 612 n.
rallying point
focus 76 n.
ram
demolish 165 vb.
ram 279 n.
collide 279 vb.
sheep 365 n.
male animal 372 n.
tool 630 n.
charge 712 vb.
strike at 712 vb.
— down
fill 54 vb.
close 264 vb.
be dense 324 vb.
— down one's throat
compel 740 vb.
Ramadan
fast 946 n.
holy day 988 n.
Ramakrishna
religious teacher 973 n.
sectarian 978 adj.
Ramapithecus
humankind 371 n.
ramble
pedestrianism 267 n.
wander 267 vb.
be insane 503 vb.
be diffuse 570 vb.
amuse oneself 837 vb.
rambler
traveller 268 n.
wanderer 268 n.
rambling
irrelevant 10 adj.
orderless 61 adj.
wandering 267 n.
deviating 282 adj.
feeble 572 adj.
sport 837 n.
ramekin
bowl 194 n.
ramification
bond 47 n.
branch 53 n.
range 183 n.
filament 208 n.
divergence 294 n.
ramify
bifurcate 92 vb.
diverge 294 vb.
ramose
symmetrical 245 adj.
ramp
be vertical 215 vb.
obliquity 220 n.
ascent 308 n.
be agitated 318 vb.
trickery 542 n.
be excited 821 vb.
be angry 891 vb.
get angry 891 vb.
foul play 930 n.
rampage
rampage 61 vb.
be violent 176 vb.
be agitated 318 vb.
be loud 400 vb.
be active 678 vb.
excitable state 822 n.
anger 891 n.
rampant
universal 79 adj.
furious 176 adj.
violent 176 adj.
vertical 215 adj.
heraldic 547 adj.
plenteous 635 adj.
rampart
refuge 662 n.
fortification 713 n.
ramrod
ram 279 n.
firearm 723 n.
ramshackle
flimsy 163 adj.
dilapidated 655 adj.
unsafe 661 adj.
ranch
stock farm 369 n.
lands 777 n.
rancher
herdsman 369 n.
rancid
decomposed 51 adj.
unsavoury 391 adj.
fetid 397 adj.
rancour
enmity 881 n.
hatred 888 n.
resentment 891 n.
malevolence 898 n.
rand
coinage 797 n.
randem
bicycle 274 n.
random
orderless 61 adj.
casual 159 adj.
deviating 282 adj.
indiscriminate 464 adj.
designless 618 adj.
random sample
example 83 n.
equal chance 159 n.
empiricism 461 n.
randy
lecherous 951 adj.
range
arrange 62 vb.
series 71 n.
accumulation 74 n.
classification 77 n.
ability 160 n.
range 183 n.
distance 199 n.
breadth 205 n.
layer 207 n.
traverse 267 vb.
plain 348 n.
furnace 383 n.
hearing 415 n.
visibility 443 n.

function 622 n.
arena 724 n.
scope 744 n.
be free 744 vb.
merchandise 795 n.
— oneself with
choose 605 vb.
join a party 708 vb.
range finder
direction 281 n.
telescope 442 n.
ranger
wanderer 268 n.
keeper 749 n.
rangy
narrow 206 adj.
tall 209 adj.
rani, ranee
potentate 741 n.
rank
relativeness 9 n.
degree 27 n.
graduate 27 vb.
consummate 32 adj.
order 60 n.
class 62 vb.
serial place 73 n.
classification 77 n.
vegetal 366 adj.
unsavoury 391 adj.
fetid 397 adj.
estimate 480 vb.
plenteous 635 adj.
importance 638 n.
bad 645 adj.
formation 722 n.
prestige 866 n.
nobility 868 n.
heinous 934 adj.
impure 951 adj.
rank and file
commonalty 869 n.
ranker
commoner 869 n.
rankle
hurt 827 vb.
huff 891 vb.
rank, person of
person of repute 866 n.
person of rank 868 n.
ranks, the
soldiery 722 n.
ransack
lay waste 165 vb.
search 459 vb.
take 786 vb.
rob 788 vb.
ransom
restoration 656 n.
deliverance 668 n.
restitution 787 n.
purchase 792 n.vb.
price 809 n.
penalty 963 n.
ransomed
sanctified 979 adj.
rant
be absurd 497 vb.
empty talk 515 n.
exaggerate 546 vb.
magniloquence 574 n.
orate 579 vb.
act 594 vb.
boast 877 vb.
ranter
speaker 579 n.
chatterer 581 n.
agitator 738 n.
boaster 877 n.
rantipole
disorderly 61 adj.
light-minded 456 adj.
rap
knock 279 n.
bang 402 n.
corporal punishment 963 n.
— out
voice 577 vb.
— over the knuckles
reprove 924 vb.
spank 963 vb.
rapacious
taking 786 adj.
avaricious 816 adj.
greedy 859 adj.
rapacity
rapacity 786 n.
thievishness 788 n.
rape
force 176 vb.
taking 786 n.
rape 951 n.
debauch 951 vb.
raper
libertine 952 n.
rapid
speedy 277 adj.
rapid-fire
speedy 277 adj.
bombardment 712 n.
rapids
waterfall 350 n.
pitfall 663 n.
rapid succession
frequency 139 n.
rapier
sharp point 256 n.
sidearms 723 n.
rapine
spoliation 788 n.
rapist
libertine 952 n.
rap on the knuckles
anger 891 n.
reprimand 924 n.
rapparee
robber 789 n.
rapport
relation 9 n.
concord 710 n.
rapprochement
concord 710 n.
pacification 719 n.
friendship 880 n.
rapscallion
knave 938 n.
rapt
attentive 455 adj.
obsessed 455 adj.
abstracted 456 adj.
impressed 818 adj.
wondering 864 adj.
raptor
bird 365 n.
raptorial
taking 786 adj.
rapture(s)
excitation 821 n.
joy 824 n.
rejoicing 835 n.
love 887 n.
rapturous
felt 818 adj.
pleased 824 adj.
rara avis
rara avis 84 n.
infrequency 140 n.
paragon 646 n.
prodigy 864 n.
mythical being 970 n.
rare
superior 34 adj.
unusual 84 adj.
few 105 adj.
infrequent 140 adj.
culinary 301 adj.
rare 325 adj.
airy 340 adj.
improbable 472 adj.
scarce 636 adj.
excellent 644 adj.
valuable 644 adj.
uncooked 670 adj.
of price 811 adj.
wonderful 864 adj.
rarefy
enlarge 197 vb.
make smaller 198 vb.
make thin 206 vb.
rarefy 325 vb.
rarely
here and there 105 adv.
seldom 140 adv.
raring to go
willing 597 adj.
prepared 669 adj.
rarity
nonconformist 84 n.
nonconformity 84 n.
infrequency 140 n.
rarity 325 n.
improbability 472 n.
paragon 646 n.
(See **rare** *)*
rascal
low fellow 869 n.
knave 938 n.
rascally
cunning 698 adj.
disreputable 867 adj.
rascally 930 adj.
vicious 934 adj.
rash
formication 378 n.
inattentive 456 adj.
negligent 458 adj.
indiscriminating 464 adj.
absurd 497 adj.
unwise 499 adj.
spontaneous 609 adj.
skin disease 651 n.
unprepared 670 adj.
hasty 680 adj.
defiant 711 adj.
excitable 822 adj.
rash 857 adj.
rasher
piece 53 n.
rasp
rub 333 vb.
breathe 352 vb.
rasp 407 vb.
discord 411 vb.
raspberry
fruit 301 n.
gesture 547 n.
reprimand 924 n.
Rastafarian, Rasta
revolter 738 n.
sectarian 978 adj.
rat
mammal 365 n.
testee 461 n.
inform 524 vb.
divulge 526 vb.
deceiver 545 n.
tergiversator 603 n.
apostatize 603 vb.
relinquish 621 vb.
coward 856 n.
noxious animal 904 n.
knave 938 n.
ratable, rateable
priced 809 adj.
ratatouille
vegetable 301 n.
ratbag
dirty person 649 n.
rat catcher
killer 362 n.
hunter 619 n.
ratchet
tooth 256 n.
notch 260 n.
rate
quantify 26 vb.
degree 27 n.
class 62 vb.
grade 73 vb.
velocity 277 n.
appraise 465 vb.
estimate 480 vb.
price 809 n.vb.
reprobate 924 vb.

ratepayer
resident 191 n.
rather
slightly 33 adv.
optionally 605 adv.
ratify
corroborate 466 vb.
make certain 473 vb.
endorse 488 vb.
sign 547 vb.
contract 765 vb.
approve 923 vb.
make legal 953 vb.
rating
nautical personnel 270 n.
measurement 465 n.
naval man 722 n.
tax 809 n.
ratio
relativeness 9 n.
degree 27 n.
ratio 85 n.
portion 783 n.
ratiocinate
cognize 447 vb.
reason 475 vb.
ration
finite quantity 26 n.
make insufficient 636 vb.
restrain 747 vb.
portion 783 n.
— oneself
be modest 874 vb.
be temperate 942 vb.
rational
numerical 85 adj.
mental 447 adj.
philosophic 449 adj.
plausible 471 adj.
rational 475 adj.
wise 498 adj.
sane 502 adj.
rationale
reason why 156 n.
attribution 158 n.
motive 612 n.
rationalism
philosophy 449 n.
reasoning 475 n.
antichristianity 974 n.
rationalist
reasoner 475 n.
irreligionist 974 n.
rationality
intellect 447 n.
reasoning 475 n.
sanity 502 n.
rationalization, rationalisation
arrangement 62 n.
sophistry 477 n.
plan 623 n.
rationalize, rationalise
reason 475 vb.
plan 623 vb.
rationing
war measures 718 n.
restriction 747 n.
rations
provisions 301 n.
provision 633 n.
ratlines
tackling 47 n.
ascent 308 n.
rat race
rotation 315 n.
activity 678 n.
contention 716 n.
rat's tails
hair 259 n.
rattan
scourge 964 n.
rat-tat, rat-a-tat
bang 402 n.
roll 403 n.
rattle
come unstuck 49 vb.
derange 63 vb.
impel 279 vb.
oscillate 317 vb.
respiration 352 n.
loudness 400 n.
megaphone 400 n.
crackle 402 vb.
roll 403 n.vb.
gong 414 n.
distract 456 vb.
chatterer 581 n.
be loquacious 581 vb.
bauble 639 n.
plaything 837 n.
frighten 854 vb.
— along
move fast 277 vb.
— on
speak 579 vb.
rattle-brained
foolish 499 adj.
rattled
distracted 456 adj.
irresolute 601 adj.
angry 891 adj.
rattlesnake
reptile 365 n.
rattletrap
automobile 274 n.
rattling
whopping 32 adj.
ratty
angry 891 adj.
irascible 892 adj.
raucous
hoarse 407 adj.
discordant 411 adj.
ravage
lay waste 165 vb.
impair 655 vb.
attack 712 vb.
wage war 718 vb.
rob 788 vb.
ravaged
unsightly 842 adj.
ravager
destroyer 168 n.
robber 789 n.
ravages
havoc 165 n.
dilapidation 655 n.
rave
overrate 482 vb.
be absurd 497 vb.
be insane 503 vb.
mean nothing 515 vb.
be pleased 824 vb.
ravel
complexity 61 n.
unravel 62 vb.
bedevil 63 vb.
enlace 222 vb.
raven
eat 301 vb.
bird 365 n.
black thing 428 n.
omen 511 n.
be malevolent 898 vb.
— for
desire 859 vb.
ravening
furious 176 adj.
ravenous
hungry 859 adj.
ravenously
gluttonously 947 adv.
rave-up
revel 837 n.
ravine
gap 201 n.
narrowness 206 n.
high land 209 n.
valley 255 n.
furrow 262 n.
conduit 351 n.
raving
frenzied 503 adj.
lack of meaning 515 n.
impressed 818 adj.
excited 821 adj.
excitable 822 adj.
pleased 824 adj.
raving beauty
a beauty 841 n.
raving lunatic
madman 504 n.
ravioli
dish 301 n.
ravish
unite with 45 vb.
force 176 vb.
take away 786 vb.
delight 826 vb.
debauch 951 vb.
ravisher
libertine 952 n.
ravishing
pleasurable 826 adj.
splendid 841 adj.
raw
incomplete 55 adj.
beginning 68 adj.
new 126 adj.
young 130 adj.
uncovered 229 adj.
amorphous 244 adj.
culinary 301 adj.
sentient 374 adj.
painful 377 adj.
cold 380 adj.
unsavoury 391 adj.
florid 425 adj.
ignorant 491 adj.
unhabituated 611 adj.
imperfect 647 adj.
immature 670 adj.
uncooked 670 adj.
unskilled 695 adj.
sensitive 819 adj.
excitable 822 adj.
raw-boned
lean 206 adj.
raw deal
misfortune 731 n.
rawhide
skin 226 n.
raw material(s)
source 156 n.
amorphism 244 n.
object 319 n.
means 629 n.
materials 631 n.
undevelopment 670 n.
raw recruit
ignoramus 493 n.
beginner 538 n.
bungler 697 n.
ray
small quantity 33 n.
divergence 294 n.
flash 417 n.
ray of comfort
content 828 n.
relief 831 n.
ray of hope
hope 852 n.
rayon
fibre 208 n.
textile 222 n.
raze
demolish 165 vb.
fell 311 vb.
obliterate 550 vb.
razor
sharp edge 256 n.
cosmetic 843 n.
razor's edge
narrowness 206 n.
danger 661 n.
razzia
brigandage 788 n.
re
concerning 9 adv.
re-
again 106 adv.

reach
degree 27 n.
ability 160 n.
range 183 n.
distance 199 n.
be long 203 vb.
straightness 249 n.
arrive 295 vb.
pass 305 vb.
gulf 345 n.
hearing 415 n.
suffice 635 vb.
governance 733 n.
— out for
take 786 vb.
— to
fill 54 vb.
extend 183 vb.
be distant 199 vb.
reach-me-downs
clothing 228 n.
react
correlate 12 vb.
be active 678 vb.
— against
dislike 861 vb.
— instinctively
intuit 476 vb.
reaction
compensation 31 n.
reversion 148 n.
effect 157 n.
counteraction 182 n.
recoil 280 n.
sense 374 n.
answer 460 n.
restoration 656 n.
retaliation 714 n.
deprecation 762 n.
feeling 818 n.
reactionary
regressive 286 adj.
tergiversating 603 adj.
opponent 705 n.
revolter 738 n.
disobedient 738 adj.
reactivation
revival 656 n.
read
be attentive 455 vb.
gauge 465 vb.
decipher 520 vb.
learn 536 vb.
study 536 vb.
speak 579 vb.
— aloud
vocal 577 adj.
speak 579 vb.
— between the lines
decipher 520 vb.
— into
misinterpret 521 vb.
— off
gauge 465 vb.
— one like a book
know 490 vb.
— the future
foresee 510 vb.
divine 511 vb.
— the Riot Act
reprove 924 vb.
— through
scan 438 vb.
readable
intelligible 516 adj.
reader
scholar 492 n.
teacher 537 n.
literature 557 n.
bookperson 589 n.
textbook 589 n.
academic title 870 n.
readership
publicity 528 n.
lecture 534 n.
readily
instantaneously 116 adv.
willingly 597 Adv. adv.
easily 701 adv.
readiness
tendency 179 n.
attention 455 n.
intelligence 498 n.
foresight 510 n.
willingness 597 n.
utility 640 n.
preparedness 669 n.
completion 725 n.
obedience 739 n.
reading
measurement 465 n.
erudition 490 n.
interpretation 520 n.
lecture 534 n.
study 536 n.
oration 579 n.
reading glasses
eyeglass 442 n.
reading list
reference book 589 n.
reading matter
journal 528 n.
literature 557 n.
reading matter 589 n.
readjust
adjust 24 vb.
equalize 28 vb.
readjustment
restoration 656 n.
ready
impending 155 adj.
on the spot 189 adj.
formed 243 adj.
attentive 455 adj.
vigilant 457 adj.
intelligent 498 adj.
expectant 507 adj.
elegant 575 adj.
loquacious 581 adj.
willing 597 adj.
useful 640 adj.
prepared 669 adj.
active 678 adj.
skilful 694 adj.
obedient 739 adj.
consenting 758 adj.
ready for
hungry 859 adj.
ready for anything
skilful 694 adj.
courageous 855 adj.
ready for more
refreshed 685 adj.
ready for use
useful 640 adj.
prepared 669 adj.
ready-made
produced 164 adj.
formed 243 adj.
ready-made 669 adj.
ready money
funds 797 n.
ready reckoner
counting instrument 86 n.
ready to
future 124 adj.
tending 179 adj.
ready to drop
fatigued 684 adj.
ready to hand
prepared 669 adj.
ready-to-serve
culinary 301 adj.
ready-to-wear
tailored 228 adj.
ready-made 669 adj.
reaffirm
emphasize 532 vb.
reafforestation
restoration 656 n.
reagent
testing agent 461 n.
real
real 1 adj.
substantial 3 adj.
inimitable 21 adj.
material 319 adj.
true 494 adj.
real estate
lands 777 n.
realism
existence 1 n.
mimicry 20 n.
philosophy 449 n.
accuracy 494 n.
veracity 540 n.
representation 551 n.
description 590 n.
Realism
school of painting 553 n.
literature 557 n.
realist
materiality 319 n.
realistic
lifelike 18 adj.
true 494 adj.
wise 498 adj.
representing 551 adj.
descriptive 590 adj.
reality
reality 1 n.
substantiality 3 n.
event 154 n.
truth 494 n.
chief thing 638 n.
realizable, realisable
possible 469 adj.
realization, realisation
existence 1 n.
event 154 n.
materiality 319 n.
appearance 445 n.
discovery 484 n.
knowledge 490 n.
representation 551 n.
effectuation 725 n.
feeling 818 n.
realize, realise
make extrinsic 6 vb.
cognize 447 vb.
imagine 513 vb.
understand 516 vb.
be informed 524 vb.
acquire 771 vb.
draw money 797 vb.
real-life
descriptive 590 adj.
real-life story
biography 590 n.
really
actually 1 adv.
substantially 3 adv.
truly 494 adv.
realm
territory 184 n.
nation 371 n.
function 622 n.
political organization 733 n.
real McCoy, the
no imitation 21 n.
authenticity 494 n.
realpolitik
tactics 688 n.
cunning 698 n.
real presence
the sacrament 988 n.
real thing, the
reality 1 n.
identity 13 n.
no imitation 21 n.
authenticity 494 n.
love 887 n.
realty
lands 777 n.
real world
matter 319 n.
ream
enlarge 197 vb.
open 263 vb.
paper 631 n.
reamer
perforator 263 n.
cleaning utensil 648 n.

reams
great quantity 32 n.
reanimate
vitalize 360 vb.
revive 656 vb.
refresh 685 vb.
reanimation
strengthening 162 n.
reap
cultivate 370 vb.
store 632 vb.
acquire 771 vb.
be rewarded 962 vb.
— the benefit of
find useful 640 vb.
— the fruits
triumph 727 vb.
be rewarded 962 vb.
— the whirlwind
be rewarded 962 vb.
reaper
accumulator 74 n.
farm tool 370 n.
reappear
reoccur 106 vb.
be restored 656 vb.
rear
sequel 67 n.
extremity 69 n.
produce 164 vb.
generate 167 vb.
make vertical 215 vb.
buttocks 238 n.
rear 238 n.
back 238 adj.
leap 312 vb.
be agitated 318 vb.
breed stock 369 vb.
educate 534 vb.
— its head
be plain 522 vb.
— up
ascend 308 vb.
elevate 310 vb.
rear admiral
naval officer 741 n.
rearguard
defender 713 n.
armed force 722 n.
rearrange
arrange 62 vb.
modify 143 vb.
— the deckchairs on the Titanic
waste effort 641 vb.
rearward
rearward 238 adv.
reason
reason why 156 n.
intellect 447 n.
cognize 447 vb.
thought 449 n.
think 449 vb.
discriminate 463 vb.
reasoning 475 n.
reason 475 vb.
sanity 502 n.
— badly
reason badly 477 vb.
misjudge 481 vb.
reasonable
moderate 177 adj.
possible 469 adj.
plausible 471 adj.
rational 475 adj.
credible 485 adj.
true 494 adj.
wise 498 adj.
sane 502 adj.
cheap 812 adj.
just 913 adj.
reasoning
reasoning 475 n.
reasons
reasons 475 n.
reason why
reason why 156 n.
attribution 158 n.
motive 612 n.
intention 617 n.
reassemble
congregate 74 vb.
repair 656 vb.
reassurance
hope 852 n.
reassure
give courage 855 vb.
reawakening
revival 656 n.
rebarbative
disliked 861 adj.
rebate
decrement 42 n.
discount 810 n.
rebel
nonconformist 84 n.
dissentient 489 n.
revolter 738 n.
revolt 738 vb.
undutifulness 918 n.
schismatic 978 n.
rebellion
revolution 149 n.
revolt 738 n.
undutifulness 918 n.
lawlessness 954 n.
rebellious
quarrelling 709 adj.
defiant 711 adj.
anarchic 734 adj.
disobedient 738 adj.
riotous 738 adj.
insolent 878 adj.
undutiful 918 adj.
rebirth
recurrence 106 n.
future state 124 n.
revival 656 n.
reboant
resonant 404 adj.
ululant 409 adj.
reborn
converted 147 adj.
rebound
recoil 280 n.vb.
rebuff
recoil 280 n.
repulsion 292 n.
rejection 607 n.
hitch 702 n.
oppose 704 vb.
resistance 715 n.
defeat 727 vb.
defeat 728 n.
adversity 731 n.
refusal 760 n.
make unwelcome 883 vb.
rudeness 885 n.
contempt 922 n.
rebuild
reproduce 166 vb.
restore 656 vb.
rebuke
humiliation 872 n.
reprove 924 vb.
punish 963 vb.
rebus
enigma 530 n.
heraldry 547 n.
label 547 n.
rebut
confute 479 vb.
rebuttal
rejoinder 460 n.
counterevidence 467 n.
confutation 479 n.
negation 533 n.
vindication 927 n.
legal trial 959 n.
recalcitrance, recalcitrancy
resistance 715 n.
recalcitrant
unconformable 84 adj.
counteracting 182 adj.
unwilling 598 adj.
opposing 704 adj.
disobedient 738 adj.
recall
transference 272 n.
remember 505 vb.
retrospect 505 vb.
recant 603 vb.
restore 656 vb.
abrogation 752 n.
depose 752 vb.
recant
negate 533 vb.
recant 603 vb.
relinquish 621 vb.
be penitent 939 vb.
become pious 979 vb.
recantation
recantation 603 n.
recapitulate
repeat 106 vb.
remind 505 vb.
describe 590 vb.
recapitulation
compendium 592 n.
recapture
retrospect 505 vb.
imagine 513 vb.
retrieve 656 vb.
acquire 771 vb.
recast
modify 143 vb.
plan 623 vb.
rectify 654 vb.
recce
inspection 438 n.
enquiry 459 n.
recede
decrease 37 vb.
revert 148 vb.
regress 286 vb.
recede 290 vb.
receipt
receipt 807 n.
receipts
means 629 n.
earnings 771 n.
receiving 782 n.
receipt 807 n.
receive
meet 295 vb.
admit 299 vb.
believe 485 vb.
receive 782 vb.
take 786 vb.
be hospitable 882 vb.
greet 884 vb.
received
usual 610 adj.
receiver
hearing aid 415 n.
receiver 782 n.
recipient 782 n.
taker 786 n.
thief 789 n.
treasurer 798 n.
recension
amendment 654 n.
recent
foregoing 125 adj.
new 126 adj.
receptacle
receptacle 194 n.
reception
inclusion 78 n.
arrival 295 n.
ingress 297 n.
reception 299 n.
sound 398 n.
hearing 415 n.
conference 584 n.
receiving 782 n.
celebration 876 n.
social gathering 882 n.
courteous act 884 n.
receptionist
recorder 549 n.
reception room
chamber 194 n.
receptive
admitting 299 adj.

intelligent 498 adj.
studious 536 adj.
willing 597 adj.
induced 612 adj.
receiving 782 adj.
recess
compartment 194 n.
angularity 247 n.
cavity 255 n.
hiding-place 527 n.
repose 683 n.
refreshment 685 n.
recesses
interiority 224 n.
recession
decrease 37 n.
contraction 198 n.
regression 286 n.
recession 290 n.
departure 296 n.
deterioration 655 n.
inactivity 679 n.
adversity 731 n.
recessional
hymn 981 n.
recessive
reverted 148 adj.
recessive characteristic
speciality 80 n.
Rechabite
sober person 948 n.
recherché
unusual 84 adj.
chosen 605 adj.
excellent 644 adj.
fashionable 848 adj.
recidivism
reversion 148 n.
relapse 657 n.
recidivist
tergiversator 603 n.
deteriorated 655 adj.
offender 904 n.
recipe
cookery 301 n.
contrivance 623 n.
remedy 658 n.
precept 693 n.
recipient
recipient 194 adj.
correspondent 588 n.
beneficiary 776 n.
recipient 782 n.
reciprocal
correlative 12 adj.
equivalent 28 adj.
numerical element 85 n.
interchanged 151 adj.
retaliatory 714 adj.
reciprocate
correlate 12 vb.
be periodic 141 vb.
cooperate 706 vb.
concord 710 vb.
reciprocation
equivalence 28 n.
interchange 151 n.
fluctuation 317 n.
reciprocity
correlation 12 n.
interchange 151 n.
cooperation 706 n.
recital
repetition 106 n.
music 412 n.
oration 579 n.
recitation
oration 579 n.
recitative
vocal music 412 n.
recite
repeat 106 vb.
speak 579 vb.
describe 590 vb.
reck
be careful 457 vb.
reckless
negligent 458 adj.
unwise 499 adj.
defiant 711 adj.
prodigal 815 adj.
rash 857 adj.
reckon
do sums 86 vb.
measure 465 vb.
expect 507 vb.
— among
number with 78 vb.
— on
believe 485 vb.
intend 617 vb.
— without
misjudge 481 vb.
— without one's host
be unskilful 695 vb.
be rash 857 vb.
reckoning
numeration 86 n.
measurement 465 n.
expectation 507 n.
accounts 808 n.
price 809 n.
punishment 963 n.
reclaim
cultivate 370 vb.
make better 654 vb.
restore 656 vb.
retrieve 656 vb.
demand 737 vb.
acquire 771 vb.
appropriate 786 vb.
claim 915 vb.
atone 941 vb.
recline
be horizontal 216 vb.
be supported 218 vb.
sit down 311 vb.
repose 683 vb.
recluse
solitary 883 n.
ascetic 945 n.
recognition
vision 438 n.
assent 488 n.
knowledge 490 n.
courteous act 884 n.
thanks 907 n.
dueness 915 n.
approbation 923 n.
reward 962 n.
recognizable, recognisable
visible 443 adj.
intelligible 516 adj.
manifest 522 adj.
recognizance, recognisance
security 767 n.
legal process 959 n.
recognize, recognise
see 438 vb.
notice 455 vb.
discover 484 vb.
know 490 vb.
remember 505 vb.
understand 516 vb.
permit 756 vb.
consent 758 vb.
greet 884 vb.
grant claims 915 vb.
recognized, recognised
influential 178 adj.
usual 610 adj.
recoil
counteraction 182 n.
recoil 280 n.vb.
recede 290 vb.
repulsion 292 n.
elasticity 328 n.
be unwilling 598 vb.
avoidance 620 n.
dislike 861 vb.
recollect
remember 505 vb.
retrospect 505 vb.
recollection
remembrance 505 n.
recommencement
reversion 148 n.
recommend
select 605 vb.
incite 612 vb.
patronize 703 vb.
— oneself
be praised 923 vb.
recommendation
credential 466 n.
advice 691 n.
friendship 880 n.
approbation 923 n.
recompense
compensation 31 n.
retaliation 714 n.
reward 962 n.vb.
reconcilable
agreeing 24 adj.
reconcile
pacify 719 vb.
content 828 vb.
reconciliation
adaptation 24 n.
conformity 83 n.
concord 710 n.
friendship 880 n.
forgiveness 909 n.
propitiation 941 n.
recondite
puzzling 517 adj.
concealed 525 adj.
recondition
repair 656 vb.
reconnaissance
inspection 438 n.
enquiry 459 n.
reconnoitre
traverse 267 vb.
scan 438 vb.
enquire 459 vb.
reconsider
meditate 449 vb.
notice 455 vb.
rectify 654 vb.
reconstitute
restore 656 vb.
reconstruct
reproduce 166 vb.
restore 656 vb.
reconstruction
conjecture 512 n.
record
enormous 32 adj.
superiority 34 n.
superior 34 adj.
list 87 n.
listening 415 n.
evidence 466 n.
record 548 n.
record 548 vb.
recording instrument 549 n.
write 586 vb.
narrative 590 n.
describe 590 vb.
abstract 592 vb.
best 644 adj.
conduct 688 n.
title deed 767 n.
account book 808 n.
recordable
recording 548 adj.
record-breaking
enormous 32 adj.
crowning 34 adj.
best 644 adj.
wonderful 864 adj.
recorded
recorded 548 adj.
written 586 adj.
recorded delivery
postal communications 531 n.
recorder
chronologist 117 n.
flute 414 n.
recorder 549 n.
recording instrument 549 n.
calligrapher 586 n.
narrator 590 n.
judge 957 n.

recording
gramophone 414 n.
broadcast 531 n.
record 548 n.
registration 548 n.
recording instrument
hearing aid 415 n.
recording instrument 549 n.
record-keeping
registration 548 n.
Record Office
recorder 549 n.
record player
sound 398 n.
gramophone 414 n.
recount
numeration 86 n.
communicate 524 vb.
describe 590 vb.
recoup
recoup 31 vb.
retrieve 656 vb.
acquire 771 vb.
recourse
contrivance 623 n.
means 629 n.
use 673 n.
recover
recoup 31 vb.
revert 148 vb.
be strong 162 vb.
counteract 182 vb.
get better 654 vb.
be restored 656 vb.
retrieve 656 vb.
deliver 668 vb.
acquire 771 vb.
appropriate 786 vb.
restitute 787 vb.
recovered
restored 656 adj.
refreshed 685 adj.
recovery
improvement 654 n.
recuperation 656 n.
revival 656 n.n.
recreant
tergiversator 603 n.
cowardly 856 adj.
knave 938 n.
recreate
rectify 654 vb.
recreation
refreshment 685 n.
amusement 837 n.
recreational
amusing 837 adj.
recreation ground
arena 724 n.
pleasure ground 837 n.
recriminate
blame 924 vb.
accuse 928 vb.
recrimination(s)
dissension 709 n.
retaliation 714 n.
reproach 924 n.
vindication 927 n.
recrudescence
relapse 657 n.
recruit
augment 36 vb.
accrue 38 vb.
beginner 538 n.
employ 622 vb.
revive 656 vb.
refresh 685 vb.
auxiliary 707 n.
soldier 722 n.
recruitment
war measures 718 n.
rectangle
angular figure 247 n.
rectangular
angulated 247 adj.
rectification
compensation 31 n.
amendment 654 n.
rectifier
mender 656 n.
rectify
adjust 24 vb.
regularize 62 vb.
modify 143 vb.
perfect 646 vb.
rectify 654 vb.
repair 656 vb.
be just 913 vb.
rectilinear
continuous 71 adj.
straight 249 adj.
rectitude
right 913 n.
probity 929 n.
virtue 933 n.
recto
face 237 n.
dextrality 241 n.
rector
director 690 n.
church title 986 n.
pastor 986 n.
rectorial
clerical 986 adj.
rectorship
church office 985 n.
rectory
parsonage 986 n.
rectum
insides 224 n.
recumbent
low 210 adj.
supine 216 adj.
oblique 220 adj.
recuperate
get healthy 650 vb.
be restored 656 vb.
refresh 685 vb.
recuperative
restorative 656 adj.
recur
reoccur 106 vb.
recur 139 vb.
go on 146 vb.
be remembered 505 vb.
recurrence
heredity 5 n.
continuity 71 n.
recurrence 106 n.
periodicity 141 n.
reversion 148 n.
relapse 657 n.
recurrent
frequent 139 adj.
periodical 141 adj.
unceasing 146 adj.
recurve
be curved 248 vb.
recusant
dissenting 489 adj.
disobedient 738 adj.
refusing 760 adj.
impenitent 940 adj.
schismatic 978 n.
recyclable
decomposable 51 adj.
recycle
repeat 106 vb.
restore 656 vb.
use 673 vb.
economize 814 vb.
recycled
reverted 148 adj.
red
fiery 379 adj.
florid 425 adj.
red 431 adj.
uncooked 670 adj.
angry 891 adj.
Red
revolutionist 149 n.
reformer 654 n.
political party 708 n.
agitator 738 n.
revolter 738 n.
redact
write 586 vb.
rectify 654 vb.
redactor
bookperson 589 n.
red alert
warning 664 n.
danger signal 665 n.
redan
defences 713 n.
red-blooded
manly 162 adj.
courageous 855 adj.
redbrick
regional 184 adj.
educational 534 adj.
red carpet
formality 875 n.
respects 920 n.
redcoat
soldier 722 n.
red corpuscle
blood 335 n.
Red Cross
doctor 658 n.
redden
redden 431 vb.
show feeling 818 vb.
be humbled 872 vb.
be modest 874 vb.
get angry 891 vb.
red dwarf
star 321 n.
redeem
compensate 31 vb.
restore 656 vb.
deliver 668 vb.
acquire 771 vb.
restitute 787 vb.
purchase 792 vb.
pay 804 vb.
atone 941 vb.
redeemable
extricable 668 adj.
Redeemer
God the Son 965 n.
redeeming feature
qualification 468 n.
goodness 644 n.
redemption
liberation 746 n.
divine function 965 n.
(See **redeem** *)*
redemptive
redemptive 965 adj.
red ensign
flag 547 n.
red-eyed
lamenting 836 adj.
red flag
flag 547 n.
danger signal 665 n.
red giant
star 321 n.
red-haired
red 431 adj.
redhanded
in the act 676 adv.
guilty 936 adj.
redhead
woman 373 n.
redness 431 n.
a beauty 841 n.
shrew 892 n.
red herring
irrelevance 10 n.
trickery 542 n.
unimportance 639 n.
hinderer 702 n.
red-hot
violent 176 adj.
hot 379 adj.
fervent 818 adj.
redintegrate
restore 656 vb.
redirect
send 272 vb.
red-letter day
important matter 638 n.
amusement 837 n.
special day 876 n.

red light
signal light 420 n.
signal 547 n.
danger signal 665 n.
red-light district
brothel 951 n.
redo
restore 656 vb.
redolent
odorous 394 adj.
fragrant 396 adj.
redouble
augment 36 vb.
double 91 vb.
repeat 106 vb.
invigorate 174 vb.
enlarge 197 vb.
redoubt
defences 713 n.
redoubtable
frightening 854 adj.
redound to
tend 179 vb.
— to one's credit
honour 866 vb.
redraft
rectify 654 vb.
red rag to a bull
resentment 891 n.
redress
restoration 656 n.
remedy 658 n.
justice 913 n.
redress the balance
equalize 28 vb.
red shift
displacement 188 n.
red tape
delay 136 n.
obstacle 702 n.
governance 733 n.
reduce
abate 37 vb.
simplify 44 vb.
decompose 51 vb.
do sums 86 vb.
render few 105 vb.
convert 147 vb.
weaken 163 vb.
make smaller 198 vb.
shorten 204 vb.
make thin 206 vb.
photograph 551 vb.
abstract 592 vb.
subjugate 745 vb.
discount 810 vb.
starve 946 vb.
— to
liken 18 vb.
convert 147 vb.
— to the ranks
depose 752 vb.
shame 867 vb.
punish 963 vb.
— weight
lighten 323 vb.
reduced
lesser 35 adj.
cheap 812 adj.
reduced circumstances
poverty 801 n.
reducing
dieting 301 n.
reductio ad absurdum
argumentation 475 n.
confutation 479 n.
reduction
diminution 37 n.
contraction 198 n.
discount 810 n.
reductionism
philosophy 449 n.
redundancy, redundance
productiveness 171 n.
pleonasm 570 n.
plenty 635 n.
redundance 637 n.
overactivity 678 n.
cheapness 812 n.
prodigality 815 n.
satiety 863 n.
undueness 916 n.
intemperance 943 n.
redundant
redundant 637 adj.
useless 641 adj.
unused 674 adj.
Red under the bed
latency 523 n.
reduplicate
double 91 vb.
repeat 106 vb.
reecho
do likewise 20 vb.
repeat oneself 106 vb.
resound 404 vb.
reed
weak thing 163 n.
grass 366 n.
flute 414 n.
stationery 586 n.
reeding
ornamental art 844 n.
re-education camp
prison camp 748 n.
reedy
strident 407 adj.
reef
fold 261 vb.
rock 344 n.
island 349 n.
pitfall 663 n.
reefer
jacket 228 n.
navigator 270 n.
tobacco 388 n.
drug-taking 949 n.
reef knot
ligature 47 n.
reek
gas 336 n.
stench 397 n.
stink 397 vb.
reel
rotator 315 n.
oscillate 317 vb.
be agitated 318 vb.
photography 551 n.
show feeling 818 vb.
dance 837 n.
— off
reproduce 166 vb.
be loquacious 581 vb.
reeling
unstable 152 adj.
tipsy 949 adj.
reentry
space travel 271 n.
return 286 n.
reestablish
restore 656 vb.
reeve
manager 690 n.
reexamination
interrogation 459 n.
legal trial 959 n.
reface
repair 656 vb.
refashion
revolutionize 149 vb.
reproduce 166 vb.
rectify 654 vb.
refection
meal 301 n.
refreshment 685 n.
refectory
chamber 194 n.
feasting 301 n.
refer
inidicate 547 vb.
— to
relate 9 vb.
attribute 158 vb.
mean 514 vb.
— to arbitration
consult 691 vb.
referee
referral 9 n.
estimator 480 n.
adviser 691 n.
mediator 720 n.
reference
referral 9 n.
relation 9 n.
attribution 158 n.
credential 466 n.
connotation 514 n.
advice 691 n.
approbation 923 n.
reference book
directory 87 n.
reference book 589 n.
reference mark
punctuation 547 n.
referendum
judgment 480 n.
vote 605 n.
refill
replenish 633 vb.
refine
rarefy 325 vb.
purify 648 vb.
make better 654 vb.
refined
elegant 575 adj.
clean 648 adj.
personable 841 adj.
tasteful 846 adj.
pure 950 adj.
refined gold
exceller 644 n.
refined manners
etiquette 848 n.
refined palate
gastronomy 301 n.
refined taste
good taste 846 n.
refinement
discrimination 463 n.
fastidiousness 862 n.
(See **refined** *)*
refinery
workshop 687 n.
refit
repair 656 vb.
reflation
dilation 197 n.
finance 797 n.
reflect
correlate 12 vb.
resemble 18 vb.
imitate 20 vb.
radiate 417 vb.
shine 417 vb.
meditate 449 vb.
retrospect 505 vb.
show 522 vb.
represent 551 vb.
— upon
shame 867 vb.
defame 926 vb.
reflecting telescope
astronomy 321 n.
reflection
analogue 18 n.
copy 22 n.
resonance 404 n.
reflection 417 n.
visual fallacy 440 n.
appearance 445 n.
meditation 449 n.
idea 451 n.
image 551 n.
slur 867 n.
scurrility 899 n.
reproach 924 n.
detraction 926 n.
reflective
radiating 417 adj.
thoughtful 449 adj.
reflector
reflection 417 n.
lamp 420 n.
mirror 442 n.
telescope 442 n.

reflex
copy 22 n.
recoil 280 n.
sense 374 n.
involuntary 596 adj.
spontaneity 609 n.
habituation 610 n.
reflex action
necessity 596 n.
reflexive
reverted 148 adj.
part of speech 564 n.
refluence
return 286 n.
refluent
recoiling 280 adj.
regressive 286 adj.
reflux
decrease 37 n.
recoil 280 n.
return 286 n.
current 350 n.
eddy 350 n.
reforest
vegetate 366 vb.
restore 656 vb.
reform
modify 143 vb.
transform 147 vb.
tergiversate 603 vb.
amendment 654 n.
make better 654 vb.
restore 656 vb.
philanthropize 897 vb.
justice 913 n.
be penitent 939 vb.
become pious 979 vb.
reformation
change 143 n.
conversion 147 n.
amendment 654 n.
restoration 656 n.
Reformation, the
Protestantism 976 n.
reformatory
improving 654 adj.
prison 748 n.
reformed character
penitent 939 n.
Reformed Church
Christendom 976 n.
reformer
alterer 143 n.
revolutionist 149 n.
reformer 654 n.
philanthropist 901 n.
religious teacher 973 n.
reformism
progression 285 n.
reformism 654 n.
justice 913 n.
reformist
reformer 654 n.
mender 656 n.
philanthropist 901 n.
Reform Jews
non-Christian sect 978 n.
reform school
school 539 n.
refract
radiate 417 vb.
refracting telescope
astronomy 321 n.
telescope 442 n.
refraction
deviation 282 n.
reflection 417 n.
visual fallacy 440 n.
refractory
wilful 602 adj.
capricious 604 adj.
difficult 700 adj.
opposing 704 adj.
disobedient 738 adj.
sullen 893 adj.
refrain
repetition 106 n.
periodicity 141 n.
cease 145 vb.
tune 412 n.
verse form 593 n.
avoid 620 vb.
not act 677 vb.
be lenient 736 vb.
be temperate 942 vb.
refresh
strengthen 162 vb.
invigorate 174 vb.
make better 654 vb.
revive 656 vb.
refresh 685 vb.
aid 703 vb.
delight 826 vb.
relieve 831 vb.
— one's memory
remind 505 vb.
refreshed
comfortable 376 adj.
refreshed 685 adj.
refresher
tonic 658 n.
refreshment 685 n.
reward 962 n.
refresher course
study 536 n.
refreshing
lenitive 177 adj.
pleasant 376 adj.
beneficial 644 adj.
salubrious 652 adj.
refreshing 685 adj.
pleasurable 826 adj.
refreshment
lull 145 n.
meal 301 n.
repose 683 n.
refreshment 685 n.
relief 831 n.
amusement 837 n.
(See **refresh** *)*
refreshment room
café 192 n.
refrigerate
be cold 380 vb.
refrigerate 382 vb.
preserve 666 vb.
refrigerator
refrigerator 384 n.
storage 632 n.
preserver 666 n.
refuel
store 632 vb.
replenish 633 vb.
refuge
retreat 192 n.
resting place 266 n.
traffic control 305 n.
hiding-place 527 n.
protection 660 n.
refuge 662 n.
fort 713 n.
refugee
foreigner 59 n.
displacement 188 n.
wanderer 268 n.
ejection 300 n.
avoider 620 n.
escaper 667 n.
outcast 883 n.
refulgence
light 417 n.
refund
offset 31 n.
decrement 42 n.
restitution 787 n.
refurbish
make better 654 vb.
repair 656 vb.
refusal
repulsion 292 n.
dissent 489 n.
negation 533 n.
unwillingness 598 n.
rejection 607 n.
avoidance 620 n.
refusal 760 n.
deprecation 762 n.
nonpayment 805 n.
disapprobation 924 n.
refuse
leavings 41 n.
waste 634 n.
rubbish 641 n.
dirt 649 n.
refuse 760 vb.
refuse collector
cleaner 648 n.
refused
disappointed 509 adj.
refused 760 adj.
retained 778 adj.
refutable
confuted 479 adj.
refutation
rejoinder 460 n.
counterevidence 467 n.
confutation 479 n.
negation 533 n.
regain
retrieve 656 vb.
acquire 771 vb.
regal
ruling 733 adj.
impressive 821 adj.
worshipful 866 adj.
noble 868 adj.
regale (with)
feed 301 vb.
delight 826 vb.
amuse 837 vb.
be hospitable 882 vb.
regalia
badge 547 n.
regalia 743 n.
formality 875 n.
regard
be related 9 vb.
look 438 n.
gaze 438 vb.
attention 455 n.
observe 768 vb.
repute 866 n.
friendliness 880 n.
love 887 n.vb.
respect 920 n.vb.
approbation 923 n.
— as
substitute 150 vb.
opine 485 vb.
regardful
attentive 455 adj.
careful 457 adj.
regarding
concerning 9 adv.
regardless
inattentive 456 adj.
negligent 458 adj.
ignorant 491 adj.
apathetic 820 adj.
rash 857 adj.
regardless of
in return 31 adv.
regards
courteous act 884 n.
respects 920 n.
regatta
racing 716 n.
regency
governance 733 n.
Regency
olden 127 adj.
regenerate
converted 147 adj.
reproduce 166 vb.
make better 654 vb.
repentant 939 adj.
sanctified 979 adj.
regeneration
conversion 147 n.
revival 656 n.
regent
potentate 741 n.
reggae
music 412 n.
regicide
homicide 362 n.
revolter 738 n.

regime
circumstance 8 n.
management 689 n.
governance 733 n.
regimen
dieting 301 n.
therapy 658 n.
regiment
make uniform 16 vb.
band 74 n.
formation 722 n.
dominate 733 vb.
subjugate 745 vb.
regimentals
uniform 228 n.
regimentation
uniformity 16 n.
compulsion 740 n.
Regina
sovereign 741 n.
region
region 184 n.
regional
regional 184 adj.
provincial 192 adj.
regionalism
decomposition 51 n.
regisseur
stage manager 594 n.
register
be identical 13 vb.
degree 27 n.
class 62 vb.
list 87 n.
musical note 410 n.
notice 455 vb.
understand 516 vb.
indicate 547 vb.
record 548 n.
register 548 vb.
represent 551 vb.
print 587 vb.
account book 808 n.
registered post
postal communications 531 n.
registrar
recorder 549 n.
doctor 658 n.
registration
registration 548 n.
registry
registration 548 n.
Regius professor
teacher 537 n.
regnant
influential 178 adj.
ruling 733 adj.
regress
decrease 37 vb.
regress 286 vb.
recede 290 vb.
fall short 307 vb.
relapse 657 vb.
regression
change 143 n.
reversion 148 n.
deterioration 655 n.
regressive
regressive 286 adj.
regret
disappointment 509 n.
be unwilling 598 vb.
sorrow 825 n.
be discontented 829 vb.
regret 830 n.vb.
desire 859 n.vb.
dislike 861 vb.
disapprove 924 vb.
be penitent 939 vb.
regretful
unwilling 598 adj.
unhappy 825 adj.
regretting 830 adj.
repentant 939 adj.
regrets
remembrance 505 n.
regrettable
regretted 830 adj.
regroup
combine 50 vb.
regular
equal 28 adj.
consummate 32 adj.
orderly 60 adj.
regular 81 adj.
frequent 139 adj.
unceasing 146 adj.
unchangeable 153 adj.
symmetrical 245 adj.
accurate 494 adj.
habitué 610 n.
soldier 722 n.
shapely 841 adj.
monk 986 n.
regularity
uniformity 16 n.
regularity 81 n.
periodicity 141 n.
regularize, regularise
regularize 62 vb.
make conform 83 vb.
regularly
to rule 81 adv.
often 139 adv.
periodically 141 adv.
habitually 610 adv.
regulate
adjust 24 vb.
order 60 vb.
regularize 62 vb.
regulation
rule 81 n.
management 689 n.
precept 693 n.
legislation 953 n.
regulations
command 737 n.
regurgitation
return 286 n.
voidance 300 n.
rehabilitate
restore 656 vb.
restitute 787 vb.
vindicate 927 vb.
rehabilitation
dignification 866 n.
rehash
repetition 106 n.
dish 301 n.
translate 520 vb.
edition 589 n.
rehearsal
dramaturgy 594 n.
rehearse
repeat 106 vb.
experiment 461 vb.
describe 590 vb.
act 594 vb.
make ready 669 vb.
prepare oneself 669 vb.
reheat
burning 381 n.
reify
materialize 319 vb.
reign
date 108 n.
influence 178 n.
governance 733 n.
rule 733 vb.
reigning beauty
a beauty 841 n.
reign of terror
anarchy 734 n.
intimidation 854 n.
reimburse
compensate 31 vb.
restitute 787 vb.
pay 804 vb.
rein(s)
halter 47 n.
moderator 177 n.
management 689 n.
fetter 748 n.
reincarnation
recurrence 106 n.
future state 124 n.
transformation 143 n.
reproduction 166 n.
materiality 319 n.
reindeer
mammal 365 n.
reinfection
relapse 657 n.
reinforce
augment 36 vb.
accrue 38 vb.
strengthen 162 vb.
enlarge 197 vb.
support 218 vb.
replenish 633 vb.
restore 656 vb.
aid 703 vb.
defend 713 vb.
reinforced concrete
hardness 326 n.
building material 631 n.
reinforcement(s)
extra 40 n.
auxiliary 707 n.
armed force 722 n.
rein in
retard 278 vb.
restrain 747 vb.
reinstall
restore 656 vb.
reinstatement
reversion 148 n.
restoration 656 n.
restitution 787 n.
reinsure
make certain 473 vb.
be cautious 858 vb.
reinvest
replace 187 vb.
restitute 787 vb.
economize 814 vb.
reinvigorate
strengthen 162 vb.
refresh 685 vb.
reissue
duplicate 22 n.
repetition 106 n.
edition 589 n.
reiterate
repeat 106 vb.
reiterated
persevering 600 adj.
reiteration
affirmation 532 n.
diffuseness 570 n.
vigour 571 n.
reject
inferior 35 n.
leave over 41 vb.
reject 607 vb.
be unsatisfied 636 vb.
rubbish 641 n.
not use 674 vb.
dislike 861 vb.
object of scorn 867 n.
outcast 883 n.
despise 922 vb.
disapprove 924 vb.
condemn 961 vb.
rejection
exclusion 57 n.
repulsion 292 n.
ejection 300 n.
dissent 489 n.
negation 533 n.
unwillingness 598 n.
rejection 607 n.
avoidance 620 n.
refusal 760 n.
nonobservance 769 n.
rejoice
be pleased 824 vb.
delight 826 vb.
rejoice 835 vb.
revel 837 vb.
celebrate 876 vb.

rejoicing
joy 824 n.
rejoicing 835 n.
celebration 876 n.
rejoin
congregate 74 vb.
meet 295 vb.
answer 460 vb.
rejoinder
interchange 151 n.
rejoinder 460 n.
confutation 479 n.
retaliation 714 n.
sauciness 878 n.
vindication 927 n.
rejuvenate
revive 656 vb.
rejuvenated
modernized 126 adj.
rekindle
kindle 381 vb.
revive 656 vb.
animate 821 vb.
relapse
reversion 148 n.
return 286 n.
tergiversation 603 n.
deterioration 655 n.
relapse 657 n.vb.
relate
relate 9 vb.
connect 45 vb.
attribute 158 vb.
remind 505 vb.
describe 590 vb.
related
akin 11 adj.adj.
near 200 adj.
relater
narrator 590 n.
relating to
concerning 9 adv.
relation
circumstance 8 n.
relation 9 n.
kinsman 11 n.
correlation 12 n.
similarity 18 n.
fitness 24 n.
bond 47 n.
relationship
relation 9 n.
consanguinity 11 n.
friendship 880 n.
relative
relative 9 adj.
akin 11 adj.
correlative 12 adj.
comparative 27 adj.
compared 462 adj.
relatively
slightly 33 adv.
comparatively 462 adv.
relativism
philosophy 449 n.
relativity
relativeness 9 n.
philosophy 449 n.
relax
abate 37 vb.
disunite 46 vb.
weaken 163 vb.
come to rest 266 vb.
soften 327 vb.
qualify 468 vb.
not act 677 vb.
repose 683 vb.
be lenient 736 vb.
keep calm 823 vb.
relieve 831 vb.
be sociable 882 vb.
relaxation
moderation 177 n.
leisure 681 n.
repose 683 n.
laxity 734 n.
liberation 746 n.
amusement 837 n.
relaxed
nonadhesive 49 adj.
tranquil 266 adj.
unthinking 450 adj.
reposeful 683 adj.
relay
periodicity 141 n.
publish 528 vb.
broadcast 531 n.
cooperation 706 n.
auxiliary 707 n.
release
disunite 46 vb.
transference 272 n.
decease 361 n.
show 522 vb.
dramatize 594 vb.
deliver 668 vb.
give scope 744 vb.
liberation 746 n.
permission 756 n.
nonretention 779 n.
exempt 919 vb.
relegate
exclude 57 vb.
displace 188 vb.
transpose 272 vb.
relegation
ejection 300 n.
relent
be moderate 177 vb.
show mercy 905 vb.
forgive 909 vb.
relenting
repentant 939 adj.
relentless
resolute 599 adj.
severe 735 adj.
pitiless 906 adj.
revengeful 910 adj.
impenitent 940 adj.
relevance, relevancy
relevance 9 n.
fitness 24 n.
meaning 514 n.
relevant
relevant 9 adj.
apt 24 adj.
rational 475 adj.
demonstrating 478 adj.
important 638 adj.
reliability
credit 802 n.
reliable
unchangeable 153 adj.
evidential 466 adj.
probable 471 adj.
certain 473 adj.
credible 485 adj.
genuine 494 adj.
veracious 540 adj.
willing 597 adj.
resolute 599 adj.
safe 660 adj.
observant 768 adj.
trustworthy 929 adj.
reliance
belief 485 n.
expectation 507 n.
hope 852 n.
relic
remainder 41 n.
archaism 127 n.
reminder 505 n.
trace 548 n.
talisman 983 n.
relics
corpse 363 n.
ritual object 988 n.
relict
widowhood 896 n.
relief
contrariety 14 n.
substitute 150 n.
moderation 177 n.
displacement 188 n.
outline 233 n.
form 243 n.
relievo 254 n.
feature 445 n.
sculpture 554 n.
recuperation 656 n.
deliverance 668 n.
refreshment 685 n.
aid 703 n.
deposal 752 n.
relief 831 n.
kind act 897 n.
relief map
map 551 n.
relieve
come after 65 vb.
assuage 177 vb.
remedy 658 vb.
disencumber 701 vb.
aid 703 vb.
liberate 746 vb.
tranquillize 823 vb.
content 828 vb.
relieve 831 vb.
cheer 833 vb.
— of
take away 786 vb.
steal 788 vb.
— oneself
excrete 302 vb.
relieved
comfortable 376 adj.
relievo
relievo 254 n.
sculpture 554 n.
ornamental art 844 n.
religion
philosophy 449 n.
religion 973 n.
piety 979 n.
public worship 981 n.
religionism
pietism 979 n.
religiose
pietistic 979 adj.
religious
observant 768 adj.
trustworthy 929 adj.
divine 965 adj.
religious 973 adj.
pious 979 adj.
monk 986 n.
nun 986 n.
religious faith
belief 485 n.
religious faith 973 n.
religious hypocrisy
false piety 980 n.
religious learning
theology 973 n.
religious mania
mania 503 n.
pietism 979 n.
religious observance
practice 610 n.
religious order
sect 978 n.
monk 986 n.
religious teacher
sage 500 n.
religious teacher 973 n.
religious truth
orthodoxy 976 n.
reline
repair 656 vb.
relinquish
cease 145 vb.
be irresolute 601 vb.
tergiversate 603 vb.
relinquish 621 vb.
stop using 674 vb.
abrogate 752 vb.
resign 753 vb.
not retain 779 vb.
relinquished
empty 190 adj.
neglected 458 adj.
relinquishment
recession 290 n.
relinquishment 621 n.
submission 721 n.
loss of right 916 n.
(See **relinquish** *)*
reliquary
ritual object 988 n.

relish
vigorousness 174 n.
pleasure 376 n.
taste 386 n.
condiment 389 n.
savouriness 390 n.
enjoyment 824 n.
pleasurableness 826 n.
liking 859 n.
reload
replenish 633 vb.
reluctance
slowness 278 n.
dissent 489 n.
unwillingness 598 n.
resistance 715 n.
dislike 861 n.
reluctant
avoiding 620 adj.
reluctantly
unwillingly 598 adv.
disapprovingly 924 adv.
rely (on)
be supported 218 vb.
assume 471 vb.
be certain 473 vb.
believe 485 vb.
expect 507 vb.
hope 852 vb.
rem
radiation 417 n.
remade
restored 656 adj.
remain
be left 41 vb.
continue 108 vb.
last 113 vb.
stay 144 vb.
go on 146 vb.
dwell 192 vb.
be quiescent 266 vb.
remainder
difference 15 n.
remainder 41 n.
piece 53 n.
numerical result 85 n.
fewness 105 n.
posteriority 120 n.
effect 157 n.
book 589 n.
superfluity 637 n.
dower 777 n.
sell 793 vb.
remains
remainder 41 n.
trace 548 n.
remake
repetition 106 n.
reproduce 166 vb.
film 445 n.
remand
put off 136 vb.
detention 747 n.
remanded
captive 750 adj.
accused 928 adj.
remand home
prison 748 n.
remark
maxim 496 n.
estimate 480 n.
affirm 532 vb.
speech 579 n.
— on
notice 455 vb.
remarkable
remarkable 32 adj.
unusual 84 adj.
visible 443 adj.
notable 638 adj.
wonderful 864 adj.
noteworthy 866 adj.
remarry
wed 894 vb.
Rembrandtesque
representing 551 adj.
remedial
lenitive 177 adj.
counteracting 182 adj.
improving 654 adj.
restorative 656 adj.
remedial 658 adj.
successful 727 adj.
relieving 831 adj.
remediless
unpromising 853 adj.
remedy
moderator 177 n.
counteract 182 vb.
answer 460 n.
contrivance 623 n.
means 629 n.
recuperation 656 n.
remedy 658 n.vb.
be just 913 vb.
remember
think 449 vb.
be mindful 455 vb.
remember 505 vb.
remembered
repeated 106 adj.
known 490 adj.
remembrance
remainder 41 n.
remembrance 505 n.
biography 590 n.
famousness 866 n.
celebration 876 n.
remembrancer
reminder 505 n.
recorder 549 n.
adviser 691 n.
remembrances
courteous act 884 n.
Remembrance Sunday
special day 876 n.
remind
remind 505 vb.
hint 524 vb.
warn 664 vb.
— oneself
remember 505 vb.
reminder
reminder 505 n.
monument 548 n.
record 548 n.
reminisce
remember 505 vb.
describe 590 vb.
remiss
negligent 458 adj.
unwilling 598 adj.
lazy 679 adj.
lax 734 adj.
remission
decrement 42 n.
lull 145 n.
moderation 177 n.
forgiveness 909 n.
remit
abate 37 vb.
pause 145 vb.
be moderate 177 vb.
send 272 vb.
forgive 909 vb.
remittance
transference 272 n.
funds 797 n.
payment 804 n.
remittent
periodical 141 adj.
fitful 142 adj.
remnant
remainder 41 n.
fewness 105 n.
remodel
transform 147 vb.
revolutionize 149 vb.
rectify 654 vb.
repair 656 vb.
remonstrance
report 524 n.
remonstrate
dissuade 613 vb.
warn 664 vb.
deprecate 762 vb.
disapprove 924 vb.
remorse
sorrow 825 n.
regret 830 n.
pity 905 n.
penitence 939 n.
remorseless
pitiless 906 adj.
revengeful 910 adj.
remote
irrelevant 10 adj.
inconsiderable 33 adj.
distant 199 adj.
invisible 444 adj.
secluded 883 adj.
remote control
directorship 689 n.
remould
modify 143 vb.
rectify 654 vb.
remount
substitute 150 n.
warhorse 273 n.
removal
subtraction 39 n.
separation 46 n.
exclusion 57 n.
displacement 188 n.
farness 199 n.
transference 272 n.
departure 296 n.
extraction 304 n.
deposal 752 n.
taking 786 n.
removal man
displacement 188 n.
transferrer 272 n.
remove
degree 27 n.
exclude 57 vb.
serial place 73 n.
destroy 165 vb.
class 538 n.
take away 786 vb.
(See **removal** *)*
remunerate
pay 804 vb.
reward 962 vb.
remuneration
earnings 771 n.
receipt 807 n.
remunerative
profitable 640 adj.
renaissance
revival 656 n.
Renaissance
era 110 n.
past time 125 n.
art 551 n.
Renaissance man
proficient person 696 n.
renascent
reproduced 166 adj.
restored 656 adj.
rend
rend 46 vb.
demolish 165 vb.
chew 301 vb.
wound 655 vb.
hurt 827 vb.
render
convert 147 vb.
coat 226 vb.
liquefy 337 vb.
play music 413 vb.
translate 520 vb.
give 781 vb.
restitute 787 vb.
rendering
facing 226 n.
translation 520 n.
rendezvous
congregate 74 vb.
focus 76 n.
meet 295 vb.
social round 882 n.
renegade
tergiversator 603 n.
knave 938 n.
renege on
not observe 769 vb.

renew
reproduce 166 vb.
make better 654 vb.
(See **renewal** *)*
renewable energy sources
sources of energy 160 n.
renewal
duplication 91 n.
repetition 106 n.
newness 126 n.
repair 656 n.
revival 656 n.
refreshment 685 n.
reniform
curved 248 adj.
renitent
counteracting 182 adj.
unwilling 598 adj.
resisting 715 adj.
rennet
condensation 324 n.
renounce
negate 533 vb.
recant 603 vb.
relinquish 621 vb.
resign 753 vb.
refuse 760 vb.
not retain 779 vb.
— the world
take orders 986 vb.
renovate
repair 656 vb.
restore 656 vb.
renovation
newness 126 n.
reproduction 166 n.
amendment 654 n.
renown
famousness 866 n.
honour 866 vb.
renowned
known 490 adj.
renowned 866 adj.
renownless
inglorious 867 adj.
rent
disunion 46 n.
gap 201 n.
hire 785 vb.
receipt 807 n.
rental
transfer 780 n.
price 809 n.
rent collector
consignee 754 n.
receiver 782 n.
rent-free
uncharged 812 adj.
rentier
idler 679 n.
receiver 782 n.
rent roll
estate 777 n.
receipt 807 n.
renunciation
negation 533 n.
recantation 603 n.
relinquishment 621 n.
laxity 734 n.
resignation 753 n.
refusal 760 n.
nonretention 779 n.
seclusion 883 n.
nonliability 919 n.
temperance 942 n.
reoccupy
possess 773 vb.
reoccur
reoccur 106 vb.
recur 139 vb.
be periodic 141 vb.
reopen
begin 68 vb.
— old wounds
retrospect 505 vb.
regret 830 vb.
reorganization, reorganisation
arrangement 62 n.
reorganize, reorganise
transform 147 vb.
rectify 654 vb.
restore 656 vb.
rep
textile 222 n.
drama 594 n.
seller 793 n.
repair
adjust 24 vb.
amendment 654 n.
rectify 654 vb.
repair 656 n.vb.
— to
travel 267 vb.
reparation
compensation 31 n.
restitution 787 n.
atonement 941 n.
repartee
interchange 151 n.
answer 460 n.
interlocution 584 n.
witticism 839 n.
repast
meal 301 n.
repatriate
replace 187 vb.
eject 300 vb.
restitute 787 vb.
repay
compensate 31 vb.
benefit 615 vb.
be profitable 771 vb.
restitute 787 vb.
pay 804 vb.
thank 907 vb.
avenge 910 vb.
reward 962 vb.
repayable
owed 803 adj.
repayment
gift 781 n.
punishment 963 n.
repeal
abrogate 752 vb.
repeat
do likewise 20 vb.
duplication 91 n.
double 91 vb.
repetition 106 n.
repeat 106 vb.
reproduce 166 vb.
memorize 505 vb.
broadcast 531 n.
emphasize 532 vb.
be diffuse 570 vb.
— oneself
repeat oneself 106 vb.
be diffuse 570 vb.
be tedious 838 vb.
repeatable
pure 950 adj.
repeated
uniform 16 adj.
many 104 adj.
repeated 106 adj.
frequent 139 adj.
tedious 838 adj.
repeated efforts
perseverance 600 n.
repeater
timekeeper 117 n.
pistol 723 n.
repeat performance
duplication 91 n.
repetition 106 n.
repel
repel 292 vb.
be unpalatable 391 vb.
parry 713 vb.
resist 715 vb.
refuse 760 vb.
displease 827 vb.
cause dislike 861 vb.
make unwelcome 883 vb.
excite hate 888 vb.
repellent
repellent 292 adj.
unpleasant 827 adj.
ugly 842 adj.
repent
tergiversate 603 vb.
become pious 979 vb.
repentance
regret 830 n.
penitence 939 n.
repentant
regretting 830 adj.
repentant 939 adj.
atoning 941 adj.
repercussion
effect 157 n.
counteraction 182 n.
recoil 280 n.
repertoire
list 87 n.
acting 594 n.
collection 632 n.
store 632 n.
repertory company
actor 594 n.
repetend
numerical element 85 n.
recurrence 106 n.
répétiteur
musician 413 n.
repetition
identity 13 n.
mimicry 20 n.
continuity 71 n.
duplication 91 n.
repetition 106 n.
frequency 139 n.
continuance 146 n.
reproduction 166 n.
affirmation 532 n.
perseverance 600 n.
repetitive
uniform 16 adj.
continuous 71 adj.
repeated 106 adj.
continuing 108 adj.
pleonastic 570 adj.
tedious 838 adj.
rephrase
repeat 106 vb.
translate 520 vb.
phrase 563 vb.
repine
be discontented 829 vb.
regret 830 vb.
be dejected 834 vb.
replace
substitute 150 vb.
replace 187 vb.
eject 300 vb.
restore 656 vb.
stop using 674 vb.
depose 752 vb.
deputize 755 vb.
not retain 779 vb.
replaceable
superfluous 637 adj.
replacement
successor 67 n.
reversion 148 n.
(See **replace** *)*
replanting
restoration 656 n.
replay
repetition 106 n.
replenish
fill 54 vb.
store 632 vb.
replenish 633 vb.
suffice 635 vb.
replete
full 54 adj.
sated 863 adj.
repletion
sufficiency 635 n.
replevin
security 767 n.
restitution 787 n.

replica
copy 22 n.
reply
answer 460 n., vb.
rejoinder 460 n.
vindication 927 n.
report
loudness 400 n.
bang 402 n.
estimate 480 n.
report 524 n.
communicate 524 vb.
divulge 526 vb.
publicity 528 n.
news 529 n.
record 548 n.
speech 579 n.
correspond 588 vb.
describe 590 vb.
repute 866 n.
— on
estimate 480 vb.
reportage
description 590 n.
reported
rumoured 529 adj.
reporter
informant 524 n.
publicizer 528 n.
news reporter 529 n.
chronicler 549 n.
narrator 590 n.
repose
pause 145 vb.
quietude 266 n.
inaction 677 n.
sleep 679 n.
leisure 681 n.
repose 683 n.vb.
be refreshed 685 vb.
— on
be supported 218 vb.
reposeful
tranquil 266 adj.
comfortable 376 adj.
leisurely 681 adj.
reposeful 683 adj.
refreshing 685 adj.
pleasurable 826 adj.
repository
receptacle 194 n.
repossess
appropriate 786 vb.
repoussé
projecting 254 adj.
sculpture 554 n.
reprehend
blame 924 vb.
reprove 924 vb.
reprehensible
not nice 645 adj.
wrong 914 adj.
blameworthy 924 adj.
heinous 934 adj.
guilty 936 adj.
represent
be 1 vb.
resemble 18 vb.
imagine 513 vb.
figure 519 vb.
affirm 532 vb.
represent 551 vb.
describe 590 vb.
deputize 755 vb.
representation
imitation 20 n.
copy 22 n.
manifestation 522 n.
report 524 n.
indication 547 n.
representation 551 n.
drama 594 n.
vote 605 n.
commission 751 n.
rite 988 n.
representational
representing 551 adj.
descriptive 590 adj.
representative
general 79 adj.
typical 83 adj.
substitute 150 n.
accurate 494 adj.
interpreter 520 n.
informant 524 n.
agent 686 n.
councillor 692 n.
mediator 720 n.
consignee 754 n.
delegate 754 n.
repress
suppress 165 vb.
hinder 702 vb.
subjugate 745 vb.
restrain 747 vb.
tranquillize 823 vb.
repression
exclusion 57 n.
counteraction 182 n.
eccentricity 503 n.
avoidance 620 n.
restraint 747 n.
prohibition 757 n.
moral insensibility 820 n.
fear 854 n.
repressive
avoiding 620 adj.
restraining 747 adj.
reprieve
put off 136 vb.
escape 667 n.
deliverance 668 n.
forgiveness 909 n.
acquittal 960 n.
reprimand
warning 664 n.
reprimand 924 n.
punishment 963 n.
reprint
copy 20 vb.
duplicate 22 n.
repeat 106 vb.
reproduction 166 n.
edition 589 n.
reprisal
retaliation 714 n.
revenge 910 n.
penalty 963 n.
punishment 963 n.
reprise
repetition 106 n.
tune 412 n.
reproach
object of scorn 867 n.
slur 867 n.
reproach 924 n.
accusation 928 n.
reproachful
resentful 891 adj.
disapproving 924 adj.
reproach oneself
regret 830 vb.
be penitent 939 vb.
reprobate
blameworthy 924 adj.
reprobate 924 vb.
wicked 934 adj.
bad person 938 n.
impious person 980 n.
reprocess
repeat 106 vb.
restore 656 vb.
reproduce
copy 20 vb.
repeat 106 vb.
reproduce 166 vb.
— itself
reproduce itself 167 vb.
be fruitful 171 vb.
reproduction
analogue 18 n.
copy 22 n.
reproduction 166 n.
propagation 167 n.
representation 551 n.
picture 553 n.
reproductive
reproduced 166 adj.
generative 167 adj.
reproductive organs
genitalia 167 n.
reproof
reprimand 924 n.
reproofed
restored 656 adj.
reprove
reprove 924 vb.
reptile
serpent 251 n.
reptile 365 n.
noxious animal 904 n.
knave 938 n.
reptile house
zoo 369 n.
reptilian
animal 365 adj.
republic
territory 184 n.
nation 371 n.
political organization 733 n.
republican
governmental 733 adj.
commoner 869 n.
Republicans
political party 708 n.
republic of letters
literature 557 n.
republish
repeat 106 vb.
repudiate
dissent 489 vb.
negate 533 vb.
recant 603 vb.
reject 607 vb.
abrogate 752 vb.
refuse 760 vb.
not pay 805 vb.
repudiation
nonobservance 769 n.
repugnance
contrariety 14 n.
unwillingness 598 n.
opposition 704 n.
resistance 715 n.
dislike 861 n.
hatred 888 n.
repulse
recoil 280 n.
repulsion 292 n.
repel 292 vb.
reject 607 vb.
hitch 702 n.
parry 713 vb.
resistance 715 n.
defeat 727 vb.
defeat 728 n.
refusal 760 n.
repulsion
energy 160 n.
repulsion 292 n.
dislike 861 n.
repulsive
repellent 292 adj.
unsavoury 391 adj.
inelegant 576 adj.
ugly 842 adj.
disliked 861 adj.
hateful 888 adj.
reputable
reputable 866 adj.
respected 920 adj.
approved 923 adj.
honourable 929 adj.
reputation
repute 866 n.
repute
importance 638 n.
credit 802 n.
repute 866 n.
probity 929 n.
reputedly
supposedly 512 adv.

request
enquire 459 vb.
require 627 vb.
demand 737 n.vb.
ask leave 756 vb.
request 761 n.vb.
request programme
broadcast 531 n.
request stop
stopping place 145 n.
requiem
obsequies 364 n.
lament 836 n.
requiem mass
Christian rite 988 n.
require
be incomplete 55 vb.
fall short 307 vb.
necessitate 596 vb.
require 627 vb.
not suffice 636 vb.
demand 737 vb.
request 761 vb.
desire 859 vb.
impose a duty 917 vb.
requirement
qualification 468 n.
necessity 596 n.
requirement 627 n.
request 761 n.
conditions 766 n.
requirements
purchase 792 n.
requisite
necessary 596 adj.
required 627 adj.
requisition
requirement 627 n.
demand 737 n.
compel 740 vb.
request 761 n.vb.
appropriate 786 vb.
requital
retaliation 714 n.
thanks 907 n.
punishment 963 n.
requite
reward 962 vb.
reredos
altar 990 n.
rerun
repeat 106 vb.
rescind
recant 603 vb.
abrogate 752 vb.
rescript
answer 460 n.
precept 693 n.
decree 737 n.
rescue
restoration 656 n.
safety 660 n.
escape 667 n.
deliverance 668 n.
deliver 668 vb.
aid 703 n.
defend 713 vb.
liberation 746 n.
restitution 787 n.
rescuer
preserver 666 n.
defender 713 n.
benefactor 903 n.
research
be curious 453 vb.
enquiry 459 n.
experiment 461 vb.
study 536 n.
research laboratory
workshop 687 n.
research worker
enquirer 459 n.
experimenter 461 n.
theorist 512 n.
student 538 n.
resection
scission 46 n.
reseda
greenness 434 n.
resemblance
similarity 18 n.
copy 22 n.
resemble
resemble 18 vb.
accord 24 vb.
appear 445 vb.
resent
be discontented 829 vb.
dislike 861 vb.
be inimical 881 vb.
hate 888 vb.
resent 891 vb.
be revengeful 910 vb.
envy 912 vb.
resentful
resentful 891 adj.
resentment
resentment 891 n.
jealousy 911 n.
(See **resent** *)*
reservation
qualification 468 n.
doubt 486 n.
dissent 489 n.
registration 548 n.
preservation 666 n.
conditions 766 n.
seclusion 883 n.
reservation of the sacraments
Christian rite 988 n.
reserve
be early 135 vb.
put off 136 vb.
substitute 150 n.
enclosure 235 n.
doubt 486 n.
concealment 525 n.
register 548 vb.
taciturnity 582 n.
select 605 vb.
require 627 vb.
store 632 vb.
not use 674 vb.
restraint 747 n.
acquire 771 vb.
modesty 874 n.
seclusion 883 n.
— for
intend 617 vb.
reserved
reticent 525 adj.
restrained 747 adj.
promised 764 adj.
possessed 773 adj.
retained 778 adj.
inexcitable 823 adj.
due 915 adj.
reserves
extra 40 n.
means 629 n.
provision 633 n.
armed force 722 n.
funds 797 n.
reservist
substitute 150 n.
soldier 722 n.
reservoir
receptacle 194 n.
irrigator 341 n.
lake 346 n.
storage 632 n.
reset
modify 143 vb.
replace 187 vb.
resettle
replace 187 vb.
eject 300 vb.
reshape
modify 143 vb.
transform 147 vb.
reshuffle
begin 68 vb.
reside (in)
be 1 vb.
dwell 192 vb.
residence
presence 189 n.
abode 192 n.
house 192 n.
resident
on the spot 189 adj.
resident 191 n.
native 191 adj.
envoy 754 n.
resident alien
foreigner 59 n.
settler 191 n.
residential area
housing 192 n.
residentiary
resident 191 n.
ecclesiarch 986 n.
residual
remaining 41 adj.
numerical result 85 n.
residue
remainder 41 n.
resign
relinquish 621 vb.
stop using 674 vb.
resign 753 vb.
not retain 779 vb.
— oneself
submit 721 vb.
be patient 823 vb.
keep calm 823 vb.
resignation
lack of expectation 508 n.
relinquishment 621 n.
submission 721 n.
resignation 753 n.
patience 823 n.
content 828 n.n.
humility 872 n.
resigned
submitting 721 adj.
obedient 739 adj.
inexcitable 823 adj.
resigning
former 125 adj.
resile
recant 603 vb.
resilience
strength 162 n.
elasticity 328 n.
resilient
cheerful 833 adj.
resin
viscidity 354 n.
resin 357 n.
resinous
resinous 357 adj.
resist
be unwilling 598 vb.
resist 715 vb.
give battle 718 vb.
restrain 747 vb.
resistance
electricity 160 n.
energy 160 n.
counteraction 182 n.
hardness 326 n.
obstinacy 602 n.
hindrance 702 n.
opposition 704 n.
defence 713 n.
resistance 715 n.
revolt 738 n.
revolter 738 n.
refusal 760 n.
resistant
resisting 715 adj.
resolute
unchangeable 153 adj.
unyielding 162 adj.
resolute 599 adj.
persevering 600 adj.
courageous 855 adj.
resolution
decomposition 51 n.
conversion 147 n.
vigorousness 174 n.
melody 410 n.

topic 452 n.
will 595 n.
resolution 599 n.
obstinacy 602 n.
intention 617 n.
plan 623 n.
assiduity 678 n.
completion 725 n.
courage 855 n.

resolve
decipher 520 vb.
be resolute 599 vb.
predetermination 608 n.
intend 617 vb.
plan 623 vb.

resonance
recoil 280 n.
oscillation 317 n.
loudness 400 n.
roll 403 n.
resonance 404 n.

resonant
sounding 398 adj.
melodious 410 adj.
rhetorical 574 adj.
speaking 579 adj.

resorb
absorb 299 vb.

resort
focus 76 n.
convergence 293 n.
contrivance 623 n.
means 629 n.
stratagem 698 n.

resort to
congregate 74 vb.
be present 189 vb.
travel 267 vb.
avail oneself of 673 vb.

resound
oscillate 317 vb.
sound 398 vb.
be loud 400 vb.
resound 404 vb.

resounding
resonant 404 adj.

resource
contrivance 623 n.
stratagem 698 n.

resourceful
imaginative 513 adj.
planning 623 adj.
skilful 694 adj.
cunning 698 adj.

resources
means 629 n.
materials 631 n.
estate 777 n.
wealth 800 n.

respect
relation 9 n.
appearance 445 n.
look after 457 vb.
observe 768 vb.
fear 854 n.vb.
honour 866 vb.
courtesy 884 n.
respect 920 n.vb.
approve 923 vb.

respectability
averageness 732 n.
repute 866 n.

respectable
great 32 adj.
not bad 644 adj.
reputable 866 adj.
respected 920 adj.
honourable 929 adj.

respected
reputable 866 adj.
respected 920 adj.

respectful
obedient 739 adj.
fearing 854 adj.
courteous 884 adj.
respectful 920 adj.

respective
relative 9 adj.
special 80 adj.

respectively
severally 80 adv.
pro rata 783 adv.

respects
courteous act 884 n.
respects 920 n.

respiration
respiration 352 n.
life 360 n.

respirator
hospital 658 n.
safeguard 662 n.
preserver 666 n.

respiratory disease
respiratory disease 651 n.

respire
breathe 352 vb.

respite
interim 108 n.
delay 136 n.
lull 145 n.
deliverance 668 n.
repose 683 n.
acquit 960 vb.

resplendent
luminous 417 adj.
splendid 841 adj.

respond
answer 460 vb.
cooperate 706 vb.
concord 710 vb.
feel 818 vb.

respondent
respondent 460 n.
litigant 959 n.

response
effect 157 n.
sense 374 n.
answer 460 n.
feeling 818 n.
friendliness 880 n.
hymn 981 n.

responsibility
liability 180 n.
function 622 n.
directorship 689 n.
mandate 751 n.
duty 917 n.

responsible
grown-up 134 adj.
causal 156 adj.
liable 180 adj.
wise 498 adj.
observant 768 adj.
indebted 803 adj.
cautious 858 adj.
obliged 917 adj.
trustworthy 929 adj.
guilty 936 adj.

responsible person
manager 690 n.

responsive
sentient 374 adj.
answering 460 adj.
feeling 818 adj.
impressible 819 adj.

rest
remainder 41 n.
be discontinuous 72 vb.
stay 144 vb.
lull 145 n.
pause 145 vb.
go on 146 vb.
stability 153 n.
inertness 175 n.
prop 218 n.
quiescence 266 n.
death 361 n.
euphoria 376 n.
pleasure 376 n.
silence 399 n.
notation 410 n.
be inactive 679 vb.
leisure 681 n.
repose 683 n.vb.
relief 831 n.

— assured
believe 485 vb.
hope 852 vb.

— on
be supported 218 vb.

— on one's laurels
be quiescent 266 vb.
not act 677 vb.

— on one's oars
cease 145 vb.
repose 683 vb.

— on one's shoulders
be one's duty 917 vb.

restart
repeat 106 vb.
revert 148 vb.

restate
repeat 106 vb.

restaurant
café 192 n.
cookery 301 n.

restaurateur
caterer 633 n.

restful
tranquil 266 adj.
comfortable 376 adj.
reposeful 683 adj.

rest home
retreat 192 n.
hospital 658 n.

rest house
inn 192 n.

resting
unused 674 adj.

resting place
stopping place 145 n.
resting place 266 n.

restitution
compensation 31 n.
reversion 148 n.
restoration 656 n.
restitution 787 n.
payment 804 n.
dueness 915 n.
vindication 927 n.
atonement 941 n.

restive
unwilling 598 adj.
wilful 602 adj.
disobedient 738 adj.
excited 821 adj.
excitable 822 adj.
discontented 829 adj.

restless
unstable 152 adj.
moving 265 adj.
travelling 267 adj.
agitated 318 adj.
irresolute 601 adj.
active 678 adj.
excitable 822 adj.
discontented 829 adj.

restlessness
restlessness 678 n.
disobedience 738 n.

restock
replenish 633 vb.

restoration
equalization 28 n.
newness 126 n.
reversion 148 n.
strengthening 162 n.
improvement 654 n.
restoration 656 n.
deliverance 668 n.
restitution 787 n.
dueness 915 n.
vindication 927 n.
penalty 963 n.

Restoration comedy
stage play 594 n.

restorative
stimulant 174 n.
salubrious 652 adj.
restorative 656 adj.
tonic 658 n.
refreshing 685 adj.

restore
compensate 31 vb.
make complete 54 vb.
transform 147 vb.
reproduce 166 vb.
replace 187 vb.
restore 656 vb.
remedy 658 vb.

refresh 685 vb.
relieve 831 vb.
(See **restoration** *)*
restored
whole 52 adj.
restored 656 adj.
restorer
reformer 654 n.
mender 656 n.
restrain
moderate 177 vb.
make smaller 198 vb.
limit 236 vb.
retard 278 vb.
dissuade 613 vb.
not suffice 636 vb.
hinder 702 vb.
restrain 747 vb.
retain 778 vb.
tranquillize 823 vb.
restrained
circumscribed 232 adj.
quiescent 266 adj.
plain 573 adj.
elegant 575 adj.
restrained 747 adj.
temperate 942 adj.
restraint
helplessness 161 n.
moderation 177 n.
counteraction 182 n.
hindrance 702 n.
compulsion 740 n.
subjection 745 n.
restraint 747 n.
prohibition 757 n.
good taste 846 n.
temperance 942 n.
restrict
limit 236 vb.
qualify 468 vb.
hinder 702 vb.
prohibit 757 vb.
restricted
small 33 adj.
moderate 177 adj.
circumscribed 232 adj.
restrained 747 adj.
restriction
qualification 468 n.
hindrance 702 n.
restriction 747 n.
trade 791 n.
(See **restrict** *)*
restrictive practice
restriction 747 n.
rest room
latrine 649 n.
result
remainder 41 n.
sequel 67 n.
end 69 n.
ensue 120 vb.
happen 154 vb.
effect 157 n.
result 157 vb.
product 164 n.
answer 460 n.
instrumentality 628 n.
completion 725 n.
resultant
eventual 154 adj.
caused 157 adj.
resume
begin 68 vb.vb.
repeat 106 vb.
revert 148 vb.
be concise 569 vb.
appropriate 786 vb.
resumé
compendium 592 n.
resumption
start 68 n.
(See **resume** *)*
resurface
repair 656 vb.
resurgence
reproduction 166 n.
revival 656 n.
resurrection
newness 126 n.
reproduction 166 n.
revival 656 n.
heaven 971 n.
resurrectionist
thief 789 n.
resuscitate
revive 656 vb.
animate 821 vb.
retable
shelf 218 n.
retail
communicate 524 vb.
publish 528 vb.
trading 791 adj.
sell 793 vb.
retailer
intermediary 231 n.
provider 633 n.
seller 793 n.
tradespeople 794 n.
retain
tie 45 vb.
cohere 48 vb.
stabilize 153 vb.
remember 505 vb.
understand 516 vb.
store 632 vb.
preserve 666 vb.
restrain 747 vb.
possess 773 vb.
retain 778 vb.
be selfish 932 vb.
retainer
inferior 35 n.
concomitant 89 n.
retainer 742 n.
reward 962 n.
retaining wall
prop 218 n.
retake
retrieve 656 vb.
retaliate
retaliate 714 vb.
avenge 910 vb.
retaliation
equalization 28 n.
compensation 31 n.
interchange 151 n.
answer 460 n.
retaliation 714 n.
penalty 963 n.
retaliatory
retaliatory 714 adj.
revengeful 910 adj.
retard
put off 136 vb.
retard 278 vb.
hinder 702 vb.
restrain 747 vb.
retarded
unintelligent 499 adj.
retch
vomit 300 vb.
retching
digestive disorders 651 n.
retell
repeat 106 vb.
retention
possession 773 n.
retention 778 n.
(See **retain** *)*
retentive
tough 329 adj.
tactual 378 adj.
retentive 778 adj.
greedy 859 adj.
retentiveness
memory 505 n.
retention 778 n.
reticent
reticent 525 adj.
taciturn 582 adj.
cunning 698 adj.
cautious 858 adj.
reticulated
spaced 201 adj.
mottled 437 adj.
reticulation
network 222 n.
convolution 251 n.
reticule
bag 194 n.
retina
eye 438 n.
retinue
retinue 67 n.
procession 71 n.
band 74 n.
concomitant 89 n.
follower 284 n.
retainer 742 n.
retire
cease 145 vb.
be quiescent 266 vb.
regress 286 vb.
recede 290 vb.
depart 296 vb.
run away 620 vb.
relinquish 621 vb.
have leisure 681 vb.
resign 753 vb.
not retain 779 vb.
retired
former 125 adj.
ageing 131 adj.
disused 674 adj.
leisurely 681 adj.
free 744 adj.
resigning 753 adj.
retirement
old age 131 n.
relinquishment 621 n.
leisure 681 n.
resignation 753 n.
seclusion 883 n.
retiring
modest 874 adj.
unsociable 883 adj.
retold
repeated 106 adj.
retort
crucible 147 n.
reversion 148 n.
interchange 151 n.
vessel 194 n.
vaporizer 338 n.
heater 383 n.
answer 460 n.vb.
testing agent 461 n.
confutation 479 n.
retaliation 714 n.
witticism 839 n.
be insolent 878 vb.
retouch
paint 553 vb.
repair 656 vb.
retrace
revert 148 vb.
retrospect 505 vb.
— one's steps
repeat oneself 106 vb.
turn back 286 vb.
retract
draw 288 vb.
recant 603 vb.
abrogate 752 vb.
resign 753 vb.
retractable
drawing 288 adj.
retractation
nonobservance 769 n.
retraction
traction 288 n.
dissent 489 n.
recantation 603 n.
retread
repair 656 vb.
retreat
decrease 37 n.vb.
revert 148 vb.
go away 190 vb.
retreat 192 n.
be concave 255 vb.
marching 267 n.

regression 286 n.
regress 286 vb.
recession 290 n.
meditation 449 n.
hiding-place 527 n.
call 547 n.
run away 620 vb.
refuge 662 n.
escape 667 n.
be defeated 728 vb.
seclusion 883 n.
prayers 981 n.
monastery 986 n.

retrench
subtract 39 vb.
restrain 747 vb.
economize 814 vb.

retrenchment
diminution 37 n.
subtraction 39 n.

retrial
legal trial 959 n.

retribution
retaliation 714 n.

retribution
justice 913 n.
punishment 963 n.

retributive
retaliatory 714 adj.
rewarding 962 adj.

retrieval
data processing 86 n.
reversion 148 n.
restoration 656 n.
deliverance 668 n.
taking 786 n.

retrieve
recoup 31 vb.
counteract 182 vb.
retrieve 656 vb.
acquire 771 vb.
restitute 787 vb.

retriever
dog 365 n.

retro-
rearward 238 adv.

retroactive
retrospective 125 adj.
reverted 148 adj.
recoiling 280 adj.
regressive 286 adj.

retrocede
restore 656 vb.

retroflex
curved 248 adj.

retrograde
regressive 286 adj.
deteriorated 655 adj.

retrogression
reversion 148 n.
regression 286 n.
deterioration 655 n.
relapse 657 n.

retrospect
look back 125 vb.
retrospect 505 vb.

retrospection
thought 449 n.
remembrance 505 n.

retrospective
retrospective 125 adj.
reverted 148 adj.
exhibit 522 n.

retroussé
curved 248 adj.

retroversion
reversion 148 n.
inversion 221 n.

retsina
wine 301 n.

return
recurrence 106 n.
be periodic 141 vb.
revert 148 vb.
product 164 n.
inversion 221 n.
recoil 280 n.vb.
turn round 282 vb.
return 286 n.
turn back 286 vb.
propel 287 vb.
arrival 295 n.
circuition 314 n.
answer 460 n.
report 524 n.
tergiversation 603 n.
vote 605 n.vb.
reject 607 vb.
benefit 615 n.
relapse 657 n.vb.
retaliate 714 vb.
commission 751 vb.
earnings 771 n.
restitute 787 vb.
receipt 807 n.
thanks 907 n.
reward 962 n.

— from the grave
be restored 656 vb.

— good for evil
be benevolent 897 vb.
forgive 909 vb.

— the compliment
interchange 151 vb.
retaliate 714 vb.

— to
repeat oneself 106 vb.

— to normal
be restored 656 vb.

returnable
owed 803 adj.

returned
chosen 605 adj.
rejected 607 adj.

return match
equalization 28 n.
repetition 106 n.

returns
record 548 n.
receipt 807 n.

return ticket
reversion 148 n.

reunion
union 45 n.
assembly 74 n.
concord 710 n.
social gathering 882 n.

reusable, reuseable
useful 640 adj.

reuse
use 673 n.vb.
economize 814 vb.

revaluation
improvement 654 n.

revamp
modify 143 vb.
repair 656 vb.

revanchist
avenger 910 n.

reveal
manifest 522 vb.
inform 524 vb.
disclose 526 vb.
publish 528 vb.
indicate 547 vb.

revealed
appearing 445 adj.
revelational 975 adj.

revealing
transparent 422 adj.
unchaste 951 adj.

reveille
call 547 n.

revel
rejoicing 835 n.
revel 837 n.vb.
celebrate 876 vb.
sociability 882 n.
be intemperate 943 vb.
drunkenness 949 n.

— in
enjoy 376 vb.

revelation
appearance 445 n.
discovery 484 n.
truth 494 n.
lack of expectation 508 n.
prediction 511 n.
manifestation 522 n.
disclosure 526 n.
revelation 975 n.

Revelation
scripture 975 n.

reveller
laugher 835 n.
reveller 837 n.

revels
rejoicing 835 n.
festivity 837 n.

revenant
ghost 970 n.

revendication
demand 737 n.
acquisition 771 n.
dueness 915 n.

revenge
compensation 31 n.
retaliation 714 n.
revenge 910 n.
jealousy 911 n.
vindicate 927 vb.
punishment 963 n.

— oneself
avenge 910 vb.
punish 963 vb.

revengeful
hating 888 adj.
resentful 891 adj.
malevolent 898 adj.
pitiless 906 adj.
revengeful 910 adj.

revenue
means 629 n.
earnings 771 n.
estate 777 n.
receipt 807 n.

reverberant
rolling 403 adj.
resonant 404 adj.

reverberate
repeat oneself 106 vb.
recoil 280 vb.
be loud 400 vb.

revere
honour 866 vb.
love 887 vb.
respect 920 vb.
be pious 979 vb.
worship 981 vb.

reverence
obeisance 311 n.
respect 920 n.vb.
piety 979 n.
worship 981 n.

reverend
worshipful 866 adj.
respected 920 adj.
sanctified 979 adj.
cleric 986 n.

Reverend
title 870 n.
church title 986 n.

reverent
respectful 920 adj.
pious 979 adj.
worshipping 981 adj.

reverie
thought 449 n.
abstractedness 456 n.
fantasy 513 n.

revers
fold 261 n.

reversal
reversion 148 n.
inversion 221 n.
lack of expectation 508 n.
tergiversation 603 n.
abrogation 752 n.

reverse
contrariety 14 n.
revert 148 vb.
invert 221 vb.
back 238 adj.
contraposition 240 n.
retard 278 vb.
turn round 282 vb.
regress 286 vb.
defeat 728 n.

adversity 731 n.
abrogate 752 vb.
loss 772 n.
reversible
regressive 286 adj.
reversion
reversion 148 n.
regression 286 n.
relapse 657 n.
possession 773 n.
dower 777 n.
transfer 780 n.
restitution 787 n.
reversion to type
deterioration 655 n.
revert
reoccur 106 vb.
revert 148 vb.
— to
repeat oneself 106 vb.
notice 455 vb.
relapse 657 vb.
change hands 780 vb.
revetment
facing 226 n.
revictual
replenish 633 vb.
review
assemblage 74 n.
inspection 438 n.
meditate 449 vb.
attention 455 n.
enquiry 459 n.
estimate 480 n.vb.
remembrance 505 n.
retrospect 505 vb.
interpretation 520 n.
report 524 n.
journal 528 n.
describe 590 vb.
article 591 n.
compendium 592 n.
rectify 654 vb.
pageant 875 n.
reviewer
estimator 480 n.
interpreter 520 n.
bookperson 589 n.
dissertator 591 n.
revile
curse 899 vb.
dispraise 924 vb.
reprobate 924 vb.
revise
modify 143 vb.
be attentive 455 vb.
study 536 vb.
letterpress 587 n.
reading matter 589 n.
plan 623 n.vb.
rectify 654 vb.
revised
superior 34 adj.
modernized 126 adj.
improved 654 adj.
Revised Version
scripture 975 n.
reviser
alterer 143 n.
author 589 n.
reformer 654 n.
revision
inspection 438 n.
study 536 n.
amendment 654 n.
revitalize, revitalise
vitalize 360 vb.
revive 656 vb.
revival
newness 126 n.
strengthening 162 n.
reproduction 166 n.
dramaturgy 594 n.
revival 656 n.
relief 831 n.
(See **revive** *)*
revivalist
sectarian 978 adj.
zealot 979 n.
worshipper 981 n.
revival meeting
public worship 981 n.
revive
repeat 106 vb.
revert 148 vb.
invigorate 174 vb.
vitalize 360 vb.
get better 654 vb.
be restored 656 vb.
revive 656 vb.
doctor 658 vb.
be refreshed 685 vb.
animate 821 vb.
reviver
tonic 658 n.
refreshment 685 n.
revivify
strengthen 162 vb.
reproduce 166 vb.
revive 656 vb.
revocable
possible 469 adj.
revocation
recantation 603 n.
revoke
suppress 165 vb.
negate 533 vb.
abrogate 752 vb.
prohibit 757 vb.
not retain 779 vb.
revolt
revolution 149 n.
be violent 176 vb.
dissent 489 vb.
opposition 704 n.
resistance 715 n.
revolt 738 n.vb.
displease 827 vb.
be discontented 829 vb.
cause dislike 861 vb.
fail in duty 918 vb.
lawlessness 954 n.
revolter
revolutionist 149 n.
dissentient 489 n.
political party 708 n.
revolter 738 n.
malcontent 829 n.
schismatic 978 n.
revolting
unsavoury 391 adj.
not nice 645 adj.
unpleasant 827 adj.
frightening 854 adj.
disliked 861 adj.
hateful 888 adj.
revolution
disorder 61 n.
regular return 141 n.
change 143 n.
reversion 148 n.
revolution 149 n.
destruction 165 n.
outbreak 176 n.
rotation 315 n.
revolt 738 n.
revolutionary
modern 126 adj.
revolutionist 149 n.
revolutionary 149 adj.
destroyer 168 n.
violent creature 176 n.
dissentient 489 n.
reformer 654 n.
revolter 738 n.
revolutionize, revolutionise
transform 147 vb.
revolutionize 149 vb.
revolve
be periodic 141 vb.
circle 314 vb.
rotate 315 vb.
meditate 449 vb.
revolver
pistol 723 n.
revue
spectacle 445 n.
stage show 594 n.
revulsion
recoil 280 n.
recession 290 n.
tergiversation 603 n.
avoidance 620 n.
hatred 888 n.
rev up
roll 403 vb.
make ready 669 vb.
reward
incentive 612 n.
trophy 729 n.
acquisition 771 n.
gift 781 n.
pay 804 n.vb.
honours 866 n.
thanks 907 n.
reward 962 n.vb.
rewardless
unthanked 908 adj.
reword
repeat 106 vb.
translate 520 vb.
phrase 563 vb.
rewrite
rectify 654 vb.
Rex
sovereign 741 n.
Reynard
mammal 365 n.
slyboots 698 n.
rhabdomancy
discovery 484 n.
Rhadamanthine
judicatory 956 adj.
infernal 972 adj.
rhapsodical
imaginative 513 adj.
rhapsodist
visionary 513 n.
poet 593 n.
rhapsodize, rhapsodise
be absurd 497 vb.
imagine 513 vb.
rhapsody
musical piece 412 n.
ideality 513 n.
Rhesus factor
blood 335 n.
rhetoric
curriculum 534 n.
vigour 571 n.
ornament 574 n.
oratory 579 n.
ostentation 875 n.
rhetorical
figurative 519 adj.
exaggerated 546 adj.
stylistic 566 adj.
rhetorical 574 adj.
eloquent 579 adj.
rhetorician
phrasemonger 574 n.
speaker 579 n.
motivator 612 n.
rheumatic
crippled 163 adj.
diseased 651 adj.
rheumatic fever
rheumatism 651 n.
rheumatism
pang 377 n.
rheumatism 651 n.
rheumatoid arthritis
pang 377 n.
rheumatism 651 n.
rhinestone
finery 844 n.
rhinitis
respiratory disease 651 n.
rhino
shekels 797 n.
rhinoceros
mammal 365 n.

rhinoceros hide
moral insensibility 820 n.
rhinoplastic
medical 658 adj.
rhizome
plant 366 n.
rhododendron
tree 366 n.
rhomboid
obliquity 220 n.
angular figure 247 n.
rhombus
angular figure 247 n.
rhubarb
fruit 301 n.
rhubarb rhubarb
roll 403 n.
empty talk 515 n.
581 int.
rhumb
compass point 281 n.
rhyme
assimilation 18 n.
recurrence 106 n.
poetry 593 n.
poetize 593 vb.
rhymer
poet 593 n.
rhyme scheme
prosody 593 n.
rhyming
harmonious 410 adj.
poetic 593 adj.
rhythm
uniformity 16 n.
recurrence 106 n.
periodicity 141 n.
symmetry 245 n.
motion 265 n.
tempo 410 n.
elegance 575 n.
prosody 593 n.
rhythmic, rhythmical
continuous 71 adj.
repeated 106 adj.
periodical 141 adj.
oscillating 317 adj.
rhythm method
contraception 172 n.
rhythm 'n' blues
music 412 n.
ria
gulf 345 n.
rib
ridicule 851 vb.
spouse 894 n.
ribald
vulgar 847 adj.
derisive 851 adj.
disreputable 867 adj.
cursing 899 adj.
impure 951 adj.
ribaldry
ill-breeding 847 n.
impurity 951 n.
ribband
(See **ribbon** *)*
ribbed
crossed 222 adj.
textural 331 adj.
ribbon
ligature 47 n.
strip 208 n.
badge 547 n.
monument 548 n.
stationery 586 n.
decoration 729 n.
trimming 844 n.
honours 866 n.
ribbon development
expansion 197 n.
overstepping 306 n.
ribbons
halter 47 n.
ribs
frame 218 n.
laterality 239 n.
meat 301 n.
rib-tickling
witty 839 adj.
rice
cereals 301 n.
food 301 n.
rich
powerful 160 adj.
prolific 171 adj.
nourishing 301 adj.
fatty 357 adj.
tasty 386 adj.
savoury 390 adj.
florid 425 adj.
diffuse 570 adj.
ornate 574 adj.
plenteous 635 adj.
valuable 644 adj.
rich 800 adj.
splendid 841 adj.
ornamented 844 adj.
funny 849 adj.
Richard Roe
no name 562 n.
riches
plenty 635 n.
wealth 800 n.
richly deserved
due 915 adj.
rich uncle
patron 707 n.
giver 781 n.
good giver 813 n.
rich vein
store 632 n.
plenty 635 n.
rick
derange 63 vb.
bunch 74 n.
disable 161 vb.
rickets
deformity 246 n.
disease 651 n.
rickety
flimsy 163 adj.
weak 163 adj.
imperfect 647 adj.
diseased 651 adj.
dilapidated 655 adj.
unsafe 661 adj.
rickshaw
cab 274 n.
pushcart 274 n.
ricochet
recoil 280 n.vb.
riddance
elimination 44 n.
escape 667 n.
deliverance 668 n.
liberation 746 n.
loss 772 n.
ridden, be
carry 273 vb.
riddle
porosity 263 n.
pierce 263 vb.
confute 479 vb.
absurdity 497 n.
unintelligibility 517 n.
enigma 530 n.
cleaning utensil 648 n.
riddled
perforated 263 adj.
ride
land travel 267 n.
ride 267 vb.
break in 369 vb.
path 624 n.
amuse oneself 837 vb.
— at anchor
be quiescent 266 vb.
— down
pursue 619 vb.
charge 712 vb.
— it out
be safe 660 vb.
— roughshod over
oppress 735 vb.
be insolent 878 vb.
despise 922 vb.
— the tiger
be in danger 661 vb.
be rash 857 vb.
— to hounds
hunt 619 vb.
rider
adjunct 40 n.
rider 268 n.
thing transferred 272 n.
cavalry 722 n.
ridge
bond 47 n.
narrowness 206 n.
high land 209 n.
ridged
projecting 254 adj.
rough 259 adj.
ridicule
underestimate 483 vb.
disbelieve 486 vb.
foolery 497 n.
misinterpret 521 vb.
befool 542 vb.
misrepresentation 552 n.
laughter 835 n.
be witty 839 vb.
be ridiculous 849 vb.
ridicule 851 n.vb.
shame 867 vb.
rudeness 885 n.
not respect 921 vb.
contempt 922 n.
disapprobation 924 n.
detract 926 vb.
ridiculous
absurd 497 adj.
foolish 499 adj.
inelegant 576 adj.
amusing 837 adj.
ridiculous 849 adj.
riding
district 184 n.
equitation 267 n.
land travel 267 n.
sport 837 n.
riding habit
jacket 228 n.
riding high
prosperous 730 adj.
rid of
escaped 667 adj.
liberated 746 adj.
losing 772 adj.
rid oneself of
eject 300 vb.
deliver 668 vb.
rifacimento
repetition 106 n.
rife, be
be 1 vb.
prevail 178 vb.
riffle through
scan 438 vb.
riffraff
rabble 869 n.
bad person 938 n.
rifle
groove 262 vb.
firearm 723 n.
steal 788 vb.
— through
search 459 vb.
rifle fire
bombardment 712 n.
rifleman
shooter 287 n.
soldiery 722 n.
rifle range
arena 724 n.
rift
disunion 46 n.
gap 201 n.
dissension 709 n.
rig
tackling 47 n.
dressing 228 n.
carriage 274 n.
rig 275 n.

fake 541 vb.
— out
dress 228 vb.
make ready 669 vb.
— the jury
do wrong 914 vb.
— the market
speculate 791 vb.
rigged
marine 275 adj.
false 541 adj.
prepared 669 adj.
rigged out
dressed 228 adj.
rigging
tackling 47 n.
prop 218 n.
sail 275 n.
right
apt 24 adj.
fit 24 adj.
dextrality 241 n.
straight 249 adj.
knock 279 n.
accurate 494 adj.
true 494 adj.
usual 610 adj.
advisable 642 adj.
repair 656 vb.
political party 708 n.
estate 777 n.
right 913 n.adj.
dueness 915 n.
probity 929 n.
virtuous 933 adj.
— itself
cure 656 vb.
— oneself
equalize 28 vb.
right-about turn
reversion 148 n.
be inverted 221 vb.
right and left
widely 183 adv.
around 230 adv.
sideways 239 adv.
right angle
verticality 215 n.
angle 247 n.
right answer
good policy 642 n.
remedy 658 n.
right as rain
perfect 646 adj.
righteous
just 913 adj.
virtuous 933 adj.
righteous, the
pietist 979 n.
rightful
genuine 494 adj.
right 913 adj.
due 915 adj.
right-handed
dextral 241 adj.
handed 378 adj.
right-hand man
auxiliary 707 n.
servant 742 n.
deputy 755 n.
Right Honourable
title 870 n.
rightist
political party 708 n.
rightly
aright 644 adv.
rightly 913 adv.
rightly served
retaliatory 714 adj.
right-minded
just 913 adj.
virtuous 933 adj.
orthodox 976 adj.
right moment
fitness 24 n.
right mood
willingness 597 n.
right of way
passage 305 n.
access 624 n.
path 624 n.
Right Reverend
title 870 n.
church title 986 n.
right royal
liberal 813 adj.
rights
freedom 744 n.
dueness 915 n.
right side
face 237 n.
right thing, the
duty 917 n.
right time
occasion 137 n.
good policy 642 n.
right wing
dextrality 241 n.
sectional 708 adj.
rigid
regulated 83 adj.
unyielding 162 adj.
straight 249 adj.
still 266 adj.
rigid 326 adj.
obstinate 602 adj.
severe 735 adj.
rigidity
hardness 326 n.
rigmarole
lack of meaning 515 n.
diffuseness 570 n.
rigorist
obstinate person 602 n.
tyrant 735 n.
perfectionist 862 n.
disapprover 924 n.
rigor mortis
decease 361 n.
rigorous
severe 735 adj.
fastidious 862 adj.
pitiless 906 adj.
ascetic 945 adj.
rigour
hardness 326 n.
accuracy 494 n.
severity 735 n.
pitilessness 906 n.
rig-out
dressing 228 n.
Rigveda
non-Biblical scripture 975 n.
hymn 981 n.
rile
torment 827 vb.
enrage 891 vb.
rill
stream 350 n.
rim
outline 233 n.
edge 234 n.
rime
wintriness 380 n.
rimose
spaced 201 adj.
rind
skin 226 n.
rinderpest
animal disease 651 n.
ring
fastening 47 n.
band 74 n.
circumscription 232 n.
outline 233 n.
enclose 235 vb.
circle 250 n.
be loud 400 vb.
roll 403 vb.
resound 404 vb.
play music 413 vb.
communicate 524 vb.
message 529 n.
association 706 n.
party 708 n.
arena 724 n.
badge of rule 743 n.
restriction 747 n.
jewellery 844 n.
love token 889 n.
wedding 894 n.
— a bell
be remembered 505 vb.
— down the curtain
terminate 69 vb.
cease 145 vb.
— in
initiate 68 vb.
time 117 vb.
— off
terminate 69 vb.
cease 145 vb.
be mute 578 vb.
— the changes
repeat 106 vb.
modify 143 vb.
vary 152 vb.
— the knell
kill 362 vb.
— true
be true 494 vb.
— up
communicate 524 vb.
— up the curtain
initiate 68 vb.
dramatize 594 vb.
ring, the
pugilism 716 n.
ringed
round 250 adj.
ringer
analogue 18 n.
substitute 150 n.
impostor 545 n.
ringing
loud 400 adj.
resonant 404 adj.
melodious 410 adj.
campanology 412 n.
ringleader
motivator 612 n.
leader 690 n.
agitator 738 n.
ringlet
loop 250 n.
coil 251 n.
hair 259 n.
ringmaster
manager 690 n.
ringside seat
near place 200 n.
view 438 n.
ringworm
skin disease 651 n.
rink
arena 724 n.
pleasure ground 837 n.
rinse
drench 341 vb.
clean 648 vb.
hairwash 843 n.
riot
be disordered 61 vb.
rampage 61 vb.
abundance 171 n.
violence 176 n.
abound 635 vb.
superabound 637 vb.
quarrel 709 n.
fight 716 n.
revolt 738 n.
rejoice 835 vb.
lawlessness 954 n.
— in
enjoy 376 vb.
rioter
anarchist 61 n.
rioter 738 n.
reveller 837 n.
riot of colour
colour 425 n.
variegation 437 n.
riotous
disorderly 61 adj.
anarchic 734 adj.
riotous 738 adj.

excitable 822 adj.
jubilant 833 adj.
ill-bred 847 adj.
intemperate 943 adj.
lawless 954 adj.
riot shield
armour 713 n.
rip
rend 46 vb.
move fast 277 vb.
wave 350 n.
wound 655 vb.
libertine 952 n.
— off
deceive 542 vb.
fleece 786 vb.
defraud 788 vb.
overcharge 811 vb.
— open
open 263 vb.
— out
extract 304 vb.
RIP
in memoriam 364 adv.
riparian
marginal 234 adj.
coastal 344 adj.
ripcord
fastening 47 n.
ripe
ageing 131 adj.
pulpy 356 adj.
savoury 390 adj.
perfect 646 adj.
matured 669 adj.
ripen
impend 155 vb.
perfect 646 vb.
get better 654 vb.
mature 669 vb.
carry through 725 vb.
ripeness
occasion 137 n.
preparedness 669 n.
ripe old age
old age 131 n.
health 650 n.
riper years
middle age 131 n.
adultness 134 n.
ripieno
musician 413 n.
rip-off
expropriation 786 n.
dearness 811 n.
riposte
recoil 280 n.
answer 460 n.vb.
retaliation 714 n.
ripple
shallowness 212 n.
hang 217 vb.
convolution 251 n.
crinkle 251 vb.
furrow 262 n.
agitate 318 vb.
wave 350 n.
flow 350 vb.
sound faint 401 vb.
rip-roaring
merry 833 adj.
riptide
current 350 n.
rise
increase 36 n.
beginning 68 n.
high land 209 n.
be vertical 215 vb.
be oblique 220 vb.
fly 271 vb.
progression 285 n.
flow out 298 vb.
ascend 308 vb.
lift oneself 310 vb.
appear 445 vb.
be duped 544 vb.
flourish 615 vb.
improvement 654 n.
go to war 718 vb.
succeed 727 vb.
revolt 738 vb.
gain 771 n.
show respect 920 vb.
— above
be superior 34 vb.
be disinterested 931 vb.
— against
withstand 704 vb.
— in price
be dear 811 vb.
— in the world
flourish 615 vb.
prosper 730 vb.
— to a peak
culminate 34 vb.
— to one's feet
be vertical 215 vb.
orate 579 vb.
show respect 920 vb.
— to the bait
be credulous 487 vb.
— to the occasion
be superior 34 vb.
improvise 609 vb.
suffice 635 vb.
succeed 727 vb.
— up
revolt 738 vb.
be discontented 829 vb.
rishi
sage 500 n.
religious teacher 973 n.
risible
laughing 835 adj.
ridiculous 849 adj.
rising
future 124 adj.
ageing 131 adj.
powerful 160 adj.
influential 178 adj.
sloping 220 adj.
resistance 715 n.
successful 727 adj.
prosperous 730 adj.
revolt 738 n.
dear 811 adj.
rising generation
youth 130 n.
posterity 170 n.
rising ground
high land 209 n.
incline 220 n.
rising star
victor 727 n.
prosperous person 730 n.
person of repute 866 n.
risk
gambling 618 n.
danger 661 n.
speculate 791 vb.
— it
chance 159 vb.
face danger 661 vb.
— one's neck
be rash 857 vb.
risk of
possibility 469 n.
risk-taker
gambler 618 n.
brave person 855 n.
risk-taking
calculation of chance 159 n.
risky
uncertain 474 adj.
speculative 618 adj.
harmful 645 adj.
dangerous 661 adj.
risotto
dish 301 n.
risqué
witty 839 adj.
vulgar 847 adj.
disreputable 867 adj.
impure 951 adj.
rissoles
meat 301 n.
rite
practice 610 n.
legality 953 n.
rite 988 n.
ritornello
repetition 106 n.
ritual
practice 610 n.
formality 875 n.
celebration 876 n.
ritual 988 n.adj.
ritualism
pietism 979 n.
ritualism 988 n.
ritualistic
formal 875 adj.
pietistic 979 adj.
ritualistic 988 adj.
ritual object
cross 222 n.
ritual object 988 n.
church utensil 990 n.
ritzy
rich 800 adj.
fashionable 848 adj.
ostentatious 875 adj.
rival
compeer 28 n.
be good 644 vb.
hinderer 702 n.
opponent 705 n.
quarreller 709 n.
contender 716 n.
enemy 881 n.
rivalry
imitation 20 n.
opposition 704 n.
contention 716 n.
jealousy 911 n.
rive
cut 46 vb.
rend 46 vb.
river
stream 350 n.
river bank
shore 344 n.
river basin
plain 348 n.
riverbed
cavity 255 n.
conduit 351 n.
river blindness
tropical disease 651 n.
riverine
marginal 234 adj.
coastal 344 adj.
flowing 350 adj.
riverside
edge 234 n.
marginal 234 adj.
shore 344 n.
coastal 344 adj.
rivet
affix 45 vb.
fastening 47 n.
frighten 854 vb.
— the attention
attract notice 455 vb.
impress 821 vb.
riviera
shore 344 n.
pleasure ground 837 n.
rivulet
stream 350 n.
RNA
organism 358 n.
roach
fish 365 n.
drug-taking 949 n.
road
housing 192 n.
transport 272 n.
direction 281 n.
traffic control 305 n.
road 624 n.
road block
closure 264 n.
obstacle 702 n.

roadbook
guidebook 524 n.
roadhog
driver 268 n.
egotist 932 n.
road-holding ability
equilibrium 28 n.
roadhouse
inn 192 n.
road junction
crossing 222 n.
roadliner
lorry 274 n.
roadman
worker 686 n.
road map
itinerary 267 n.
map 551 n.
roads, roadstead
stable 192 n.
gulf 345 n.
road show
dramaturgy 594 n.
roadside
near 200 adj.
edge 234 n.
marginal 234 adj.
accessible 289 adj.
roadster
saddle horse 273 n.
automobile 274 n.
bicycle 274 n.
road to ruin
ruin 165 n.
danger 661 n.
road traffic
conveyance 267 n.
vehicle 274 n.
passing along 305 n.
roadway
road 624 n.
roadworthy
transferable 272 adj.
roam
wander 267 vb.
be free 744 vb.
roan
horse 273 n.
brown 430 adj.
pied 437 adj.
roar
be violent 176 vb.
be agitated 318 vb.
blow 352 vb.
be loud 400 vb.
roll 403 vb.
vociferate 408 vb.
ululate 409 vb.
be excitable 822 vb.
be angry 891 vb.
threaten 900 vb.
oaring
furious 176 adj.
frightening 854 adj.
roaring drunk
drunk 949 adj.
roaring trade
prosperity 730 n.
roast
cook 301 vb.
be hot 379 vb.
heat 381 vb.
ridicule 851 vb.
reprove 924 vb.
rob
weaken 163 vb.
take away 786 vb.
rob 788 vb.
impoverish 801 vb.
— Peter to pay Paul
substitute 150 vb.
robber
robber 789 n.
robbery
stealing 788 n.
loss of right 916 n.
robe
robe 228 n.
badge of rule 743 n.
canonicals 989 n.
robes
uniform 228 n.
formality 875 n.
robin
bird 365 n.
Robin Goodfellow
elf 970 n.
fairy 970 n.
Robinson Crusoe
solitary 883 n.
robot
image 551 n.
fatalist 596 n.
instrument 628 n.
machine 630 n.
slave 742 n.
robotics
mechanics 630 n.
robot-like
mechanical 630 adj.
robust
stalwart 162 adj.
healthy 650 adj.
roc
rara avis 84 n.
rock
be unequal 29 vb.
permanence 144 n.
vary 152 vb.
fixture 153 n.
assuage 177 vb.
bring to rest 266 vb.
oscillate 317 vb.
solid body 324 n.
hardness 326 n.
rock 344 n.
sweet thing 392 n.
resolution 599 n.
refuge 662 n.
pitfall 663 n.
make inactive 679 vb.
aider 703 n.
tranquillize 823 vb.
gem 844 n.
pet 889 vb.
rock bottom
inferiority 35 n.
base 214 n.
rockbottom price
cheapness 812 n.
rock-climbing
sport 837 n.
rocker
youngster 132 n.
fluctuation 317 n.
rocket
grow 36 vb.
vigorousness 174 n.
rocket 276 n.
speeder 277 n.
missile 287 n.
climber 308 n.
signal light 420 n.
signal 547 n.
missile weapon 723 n.
reprimand 924 n.
rocketry
aeronautics 271 n.
rocket 276 n.
arms 723 n.
rocking chair
seat 218 n.
fluctuation 317 n.
rocking horse
plaything 837 n.
rock music
music 412 n.
rock 'n' roll
music 412 n.
dance 837 n.
rock 'n' roller
jumper 312 n.
rocky
unstable 152 adj.
weakly 163 adj.
hard 326 adj.
territorial 344 adj.
rococo
art 551 n.
school of painting 553 n.
ornamentation 844 n.
rod
long measure 203 n.
prop 218 n.
gauge 465 n.
incentive 612 n.
pistol 723 n.
badge of rule 743 n.
scourge 964 n.
rod and line
chase 619 n.
rodent
mammal 365 n.
rodent officer
killer 362 n.
hunter 619 n.
rodeo
contest 716 n.
rod of iron
severity 735 n.
rodomontade
empty talk 515 n.
exaggeration 546 n.
magniloquence 574 n.
oration 579 n.
boasting 877 n.
roe
fish food 301 n.
mammal 365 n.
roentgen, röntgen
radiation 417 n.
rogation
prayers 981 n.
rogue
trickster 545 n.
ruffian 904 n.
knave 938 n.
rogue elephant
nonuniformity 17 n.
solitary 883 n.
noxious animal 904 n.
roguery
improbity 930 n.
wickedness 934 n.
rogues' gallery
record 548 n.
biography 590 n.
roguish
merry 833 adj.
amused 837 adj.
witty 839 adj.
roil
make unclean 649 vb.
torment 827 vb.
roister
rampage 61 vb.
revel 837 vb.
roisterer
reveller 837 n.
Roland for an Oliver, a
retaliation 714 n.
role
acting 594 n.
function 622 n.
role-playing
representation 551 n.
conduct 688 n.
roll
piece 53 n.
bunch 74 n.
list 87 n.
make smaller 198 vb.
textile 222 n.
coil 251 n.
twine 251 vb.
cylinder 252 n.
go smoothly 258 vb.
smooth 258 vb.
hair 259 n.
fold 261 vb.
be in motion 265 vb.
move 265 vb.
aeronautics 271 n.
propel 287 vb.

cereals 301 n.
tumble 309 vb.
rotation 315 n.
oscillate 317 vb.
flow 350 vb.
loudness 400 n.
roll 403 n.vb.
resound 404 vb.
call 547 n.
record 548 n.
voice 577 vb.
book 589 n.
— along
travel 267 vb.
rotate 315 vb.
— around
laugh 835 vb.
— back
evolve 316 vb.
— in
burst in 297 vb.
enjoy 376 vb.
abound 635 vb.
superabound 637 vb.
be profitable 771 vb.
be received 782 vb.
— on
continue 108 vb.
go on 146 vb.
be in motion 265 vb.
— out
flatten 216 vb.vb.
— up
congregate 74 vb.
round 252 vb.
fold 261 vb.
arrive 295 vb.
rotate 315 vb.
— up one's sleeves
begin 68 vb.
prepare oneself 669 vb.
roll call
statistics 86 n.
nomenclature 561 n.
rolled into one
joined 45 adj.
one 88 adj.
indiscriminate 464 adj.
roller
ligature 47 n.
compressor 198 n.
flattener 216 n.
wrapping 226 n.
wheel 250 n.
cylinder 252 n.
smoother 258 n.
rotator 315 n.
pulverizer 332 n.
wave 350 n.
press 587 n.
surgical dressing 658 n.
hairdressing 843 n.
roller coaster
vehicle 274 n.
roller skates
sledge 274 n.
plaything 837 n.
rollick
be cheerful 833 vb.
rejoice 835 vb.
revel 837 n.
amuse oneself 837 vb.
rolling
unstable 152 adj.
alpine 209 adj.
undulatory 251 adj.
motion 265 n.
seafaring 269 adj.
fluctuation 317 n.
campestral 348 adj.
moneyed 800 adj.
rolling country
high land 209 n.
plain 348 n.
rolling periods
eloquence 579 n.
rolling pin
flattener 216 n.
cylinder 252 n.
smoother 258 n.
rolling stock
train 274 n.
rolling stone
wanderer 268 n.
roll of honour
list 87 n.
honours 866 n.
roly-poly
fleshy 195 adj.
dessert 301 n.
roman
written 586 adj.
print-type 587 n.
Roman candle
fireworks 420 n.
Roman Catholic
Catholic 976 n.
Roman Catholic 976 adj.
romance
musical piece 412 n.
absurdity 497 n.
fantasy 513 n.
ideality 513 n.
be false 541 vb.
fable 543 n.
novel 590 n.
love affair 887 n.
Romance
language type 557 n.
romancer
visionary 513 n.
liar 545 n.
narrator 590 n.
Romanesque
olden 127 adj.
ornamental 844 adj.
churchlike 990 adj.
Roman holiday
slaughter 362 n.
Romanism
Catholicism 976 n.
Roman nose
angularity 247 n.
Roman road
straightness 249 n.
romantic
visionary 513 n.
imaginative 513 adj.
literary 557 adj.
descriptive 590 adj.
feeling 818 adj.
impressible 819 adj.
excitable 822 adj.
loving 887 adj.
romanticism
fantasy 513 n.
feeling 818 n.
Romanticism
school of painting 553 n.
literature 557 n.
romanticist
visionary 513 n.
romanticize, romanticise
imagine 513 vb.
Romany
wanderer 268 n.
slang 560 n.
Rome
focus 76 n.
Romeo and Juliet
lovers 887 n.
Romish
Roman Catholic 976 adj.
romp
rampage 61 vb.
leap 312 vb.
revel 837 n.
amuse oneself 837 vb.
caress 889 vb.
— home
outstrip 277 vb.
win 727 vb.
rompers
trousers 228 n.
rondeau
verse form 593 n.
rondo
musical piece 412 n.
rood
cross 222 n.
ritual object 988 n.
rood screen
church interior 990 n.
roof
dwelling 192 n.
home 192 n.
vertex 213 n.
roof 226 n.
overlay 226 vb.
resting place 266 n.
shelter 662 n.
roofed in
covered 226 adj.
roofless
displaced 188 adj.
rooftop
vertex 213 n.
rooftree
home 192 n.
roof 226 n.
rooineck
foreigner 59 n.
rook
bird 365 n.
deceive 542 vb.
trickster 545 n.
defraud 788 vb.
rookery
nest 192 n.
rookie
beginner 538 n.
soldier 722 n.
room
inclusion 78 n.
opportunity 137 n.
room 183 n.
emptiness 190 n.
chamber 194 n.
scope 744 n.
room for improvement
imperfection 647 n.
room-mate
participator 775 n.
chum 880 n.
rooms
quarters 192 n.
roomy
spacious 183 adj.
roost
nest 192 n.
dwell 192 vb.
sit down 311 vb.
sleep 679 vb.
rooster
poultry 365 n.
male animal 372 n.
root
numerical element 85 n.
stabilize 153 vb.
source 156 n.
place 187 vb.
base 214 n.
plant 366 n.
word 559 n.
— about
search 459 vb.
— for
vociferate 408 vb.
incite 612 vb.
patronize 703 vb.
applaud 923 vb.
— out
eject 300 vb.
— up
destroy 165 vb.
extract 304 vb.
root and branch
completely 54 adv.
revolutionary 149 adj.
destructive 165 adj.
rooted
firm 45 adj.
immemorial 127 adj.

fixed 153 adj.
located 187 adj.
still 266 adj.
habitual 610 adj.
rootless
unrelated 10 adj.
transient 114 adj.
unstable 152 adj.
unproductive 172 adj.
displaced 188 adj.
travelling 267 adj.
rootlet
filament 208 n.
roots
source 156 n.
rootstock
source 156 n.
plant 366 n.
rope
tie 45 vb.
cable 47 n.
fibre 208 n.
safeguard 662 n.
scope 744 n.
fetter 748 n.
jewellery 844 n.
means of execution 964 n.
— off
restrain 747 vb.
rope and pulley
lifter 310 n.
rope of sand
noncoherence 49 n.
weak thing 163 n.
ropes
arena 724 n.
ropewalker
entertainer 594 n.
ropeway
railway 624 n.
ropy, ropey
thick 205 adj.
fibrous 208 adj.
dense 324 adj.
semiliquid 354 adj.
bad 645 adj.
Rorschach test
enquiry 459 n.
rosary
prayers 981 n.
ritual object 988 n.
Roscian
dramatic 594 adj.
rose
irrigator 341 n.
plant 366 n.
fragrance 396 n.
redness 431 n.
heraldry 547 n.
a beauty 841 n.
roseate
red 431 adj.
promising 852 adj.
rose-coloured
red 431 adj.
cheerful 833 adj.
promising 852 adj.
rose-coloured spectacles
misinterpretation 521 n.
rosemary
potherb 301 n.
rosette
badge 547 n.
trimming 844 n.
rosewater
moderator 177 n.
scent 396 n.
flattery 925 n.
rose window
window 263 n.
pattern 844 n.
church interior 990 n.
Rosicrucian
religionist 973 n.
occultist 984 n.
rosin
rub 333 vb.
resin 357 n.
Rosinante
horse 273 n.
roster
list 87 n.
rostrate
angular 247 adj.
curved 248 adj.
rostrum
stand 218 n.
prow 237 n.
protuberance 254 n.
publicity 528 n.
rostrum 539 n.
rosy
red 431 adj.
palmy 730 adj.
promising 852 adj.
modest 874 adj.
pure 950 adj.
rosy-cheeked
healthy 650 adj.
personable 841 adj.
rot
decay 51 n.
decompose 51 vb.
be old 127 vb.
absurdity 497 n.
silly talk 515 n.
dirt 649 n.
ulcer 651 n.
deteriorate 655 vb.
blight 659 n.
rota
sequence 65 n.
list 87 n.
regular return 141 n.
rotary
rotary 315 adj.
rotate
be periodic 141 vb.
twine 251 vb.
circle 314 vb.
rotate 315 vb.
agitate 318 vb.
dance 837 vb.
— the crop
cultivate 370 vb.
rotation
continuity 71 n.
motion 265 n.
(See **rotate** *)*
rotator
pivot 218 n.
wheel 250 n.
rotator 315 n.
rotgut
alcoholic drink 301 n.
rotisserie
café 192 n.
cookery 301 n.
rotogravure
picture 553 n.
rotor
propeller 269 n.
rotator 315 n.
rotten
decomposed 51 adj.
weakened 163 adj.
unsavoury 391 adj.
not nice 645 adj.
dirty 649 adj.
diseased 651 adj.
deteriorated 655 adj.
dilapidated 655 adj.
vicious 934 adj.
rotten borough
electorate 605 n.
rotter
hateful object 888 n.
cad 938 n.
rotund
fleshy 195 adj.
rotund 252 adj.
convex 253 adj.
rotunda
pavilion 192 n.
rouble
coinage 797 n.
roué
bad person 938 n.
libertine 952 n.
rouge
red pigment 431 n.
redden 431 vb.
beautify 841 vb.
cosmetic 843 n.
rouge et noir
gambling 618 n.
gambling game 837 n.
rough
nonuniform 17 adj.
disorderly 61 adj.
violent 176 adj.
amorphous 244 adj.
rough 259 adj.
textural 331 adj.
unsavoury 391 adj.
hoarse 407 adj.
difficult 700 adj.
hindering 702 adj.
oppressive 735 adj.
graceless 842 adj.
low fellow 869 n.
cruel 898 adj.
ruffian 904 n.
roughage
food content 301 n.
rough and ready
useful 640 adj.
imperfect 647 adj.
hasty 680 adj.
bungled 695 adj.
rough and tumble
turmoil 61 n.
fight 716 n.
rough breathing
speech sound 398 n.
pronunciation 577 n.
roughcast
facing 226 n.
plan 623 n.
rough copy
undevelopment 670 n.
rough diamond
undevelopment 670 n.
ingenue 699 n.
vulgarian 847 n.
good person 937 n.
rough draft
incompleteness 55 n.
rough edge of one's tongue
scurrility 899 n.
reproach 924 n.
roughen
roughen 259 vb.
notch 260 vb.
rough ground
difficulty 700 n.
rough guess
conjecture 512 n.
rough handling
violence 176 n.
conduct 688 n.
rough-hew
form 243 vb.
sculpt 554 vb.
prepare 669 vb.
rough-hewn
incomplete 55 adj.
roughhouse
turmoil 61 n.
violence 176 n.
fight 716 n.
roughly
nearly 200 adv.
roughneck
low fellow 869 n.
roughness
inequality 29 n.
discontinuity 72 n.
violence 176 n.
roughness 259 n.
agitation 318 n.
inelegance 576 n.
rudeness 885 n.
(See **rough** *)*

roughrider
rider 268 n.
rough sketch
outline 233 n.
experiment 461 n.
rough-stuffer
rider 268 n.
rough weather
storm 176 n.
weather 340 n.
rough with the smooth
all 52 n.
rouleau
treasury 799 n.
roulette
gambling 618 n.
gambling game 837 n.
round
uniformity 16 n.
equal 28 adj.
whole 52 n.
continuity 71 n.
numerical 85 adj.
recurrence 106 n.
period 110 n.
fleshy 195 adj.
form 243 vb.
make curved 248 vb.
circle 250 n.
round 250 adj.
rotund 252 adj.
round 252 vb.
unsharpened 257 adj.
circle 314 vb.
bang 402 n.
vocal music 412 n.
assertive 532 adj.
habit 610 n.
business 622 n.
circuit 626 n.
pugilism 716 n.
ammunition 723 n.
— off
equalize 28 vb.
make complete 54 vb.
— on
attack 712 vb.
retaliate 714 vb.
blame 924 vb.
— up
bring together 74 vb.
break in 369 vb.
roundabout
exterior 223 adj.
circumjacent 230 adj.
circle 250 n.
in and out 251 adv.
deviating 282 adj.
traffic control 305 n.
circuitous 314 adj.
rotator 315 n.
prolix 570 adj.
road 624 n.
roundabout 626 adj.
pleasure ground 837 n.
round and round
by turns 141 adv.
round and round 315 adv.
round barrow
small hill 209 n.
earthwork 253 n.
round box
cylinder 252 n.
rounded
low 210 adj.
sloping 220 adj.
curved 248 adj.
round 250 adj.
arched 253 adj.
smooth 258 adj.
shapely 841 adj.
rounded period
elegance 575 n.
roundel
circle 250 n.
badge 547 n.
roundelay
vocal music 412 n.
rounders
ball game 837 n.
round-eyed
wondering 864 adj.
round game
indoor game 837 n.
roundhouse
lockup 748 n.
roundness
rotundity 252 n.
(See **round** *)*
round of pleasure
pleasure 376 n.
festivity 837 n.
social round 882 n.
round robin
report 524 n.
request 761 n.
deprecation 762 n.
round-shouldered
deformed 246 adj.
roundsman
traveller 268 n.
circler 314 n.
seller 793 n.
round table
conference 584 n.
council 692 n.
round the bend
crazy 503 adj.
round the clock
all along 113 adv.
round trip
reversion 148 n.
land travel 267 n.
circuition 314 n.
roup
sale 793 n.
rouse
invigorate 174 vb.
incite 612 vb.
excite 821 vb.
— oneself
be active 678 vb.
rousing
vigorous 174 adj.
crying 408 adj.
eloquent 579 adj.
exciting 821 adj.
rousing cheers
rejoicing 835 n.
rout
disperse 75 vb.
defeat 727 vb.
defeat 728 n.
rabble 869 n.
route
itinerary 267 n.
direction 281 n.
passage 305 n.
route 624 n.
way 624 n.
direct 689 vb.
route march
marching 267 n.
routier
driver 268 n.
routine
uniformity 16 n.
order 60 n.
regularity 81 n.
recurrence 106 n.
regular return 141 n.
practice 610 n.
habitual 610 adj.
business 622 n.
way 624 n.
action 676 n.
conduct 688 n.
formality 875 n.
roux
sauce 389 n.
rove
wander 267 vb.
stray 282 vb.
rover
wanderer 268 n.
roving
unstable 152 adj.
roving eye
unchastity 951 n.
row
turmoil 61 n.
series 71 n.
violence 176 n.
housing 192 n.
layer 207 n.
row 269 vb.
loudness 400 n.
discord 411 n.
quarrel 709 n.
bicker 709 vb.
fight 716 vb.
rowan
tree 366 n.
rowdy
violent creature 176 n.
violent 176 adj.
loud 400 adj.
riotous 738 adj.
ill-bred 847 adj.
low fellow 869 n.
ruffian 904 n.
rowel
sharp point 256 n.
rower
boatman 270 n.
rowing
aquatics 269 n.
sport 837 n.
rowing boat
rowing boat 275 n.
rowlock
pivot 218 n.
royal
supreme 34 adj.
ruling 733 adj.
liberal 813 adj.
impressive 821 adj.
worshipful 866 adj.
noble 868 adj.
proud 871 adj.
ostentatious 875 adj.
Royal Air Force
air force 722 n.
royal blood
sovereign 741 n.
Royal Commission
council 692 n.
Royal Highness
sovereign 741 n.
title 870 n.
Royal Marines
naval man 722 n.
Royal Navy
naval man 722 n.
royal road
way 624 n.
facility 701 n.
royal standard
regalia 743 n.
royalty
authority 733 n.
position of authority 733 n.
sovereign 741 n.
receipt 807 n.
nobility 868 n.
rub
be contiguous 202 vb.
friction 333 n.
rub 333 vb.
give pain 377 vb.
touch 378 vb.
clean 648 vb.
wound 655 vb.
difficulty 700 n.
hindrance 702 n.
adversity 731 n.
painfulness 827 n.
— along with
be friendly 880 vb.
— away
abate 37 vb.
— down
smooth 258 vb.
pulverize 332 vb.

groom 369 vb.
— in
emphasize 532 vb.
make important 638 vb.
aggravate 832 vb.
— off
rub 333 vb.
obliterate 550 vb.
— off on
cohere 48 vb.
— one's eyes
wonder 864 vb.
— one's hands
rejoice 835 vb.
— one's nose in the dirt
humiliate 872 vb.
— out
rub 333 vb.
murder 362 vb.
obliterate 550 vb.
— salt in the wound
hurt 827 vb.
aggravate 832 vb.
— shoulders with
be contiguous 202 vb.
— up
make bright 417 vb.
— up the wrong way
make quarrels 709 vb.
cause dislike 861 vb.
huff 891 vb.
rub-a-dub
roll 403 n.
rubato
adagio 412 adv.
rubber
elasticity 328 n.
friction 333 n.
obliteration 550 n.
contest 716 n.
card game 837 n.
rubberneck
traveller 268 n.
spectator 441 n.
inquisitive person 453 n.
rubber soles
footwear 228 n.
silencer 401 n.
rubberstamp
conform 83 vb.
assent 488 vb.
endorse 488 vb.
rubbery
elastic 328 adj.
tough 329 adj.
rubbing
duplicate 22 n.
rubbing noses
friendliness 880 n.
rubbish
leavings 41 n.
absurdity 497 n.
silly talk 515 n.
waste 634 n.
rubbish 641 n.
dirt 649 n.
derelict 779 n.
rubbish heap
rubbish 641 n.
sink 649 n.
rubbishy
meaningless 515 adj.
spurious 542 adj.
trivial 639 adj.
profitless 641 adj.
rubble
piece 53 n.
rubefy
redden 431 vb.
rubella
infection 651 n.
Rubicon
limit 236 n.
rubicund
red 431 adj.
rubric
redness 431 n.
label 547 n.
precept 693 n.
office-book 988 n.
ruby
redness 431 n.
exceller 644 n.
gem 844 n.
ruby wedding
anniversary 141 n.
special day 876 n.
ruche
fold 261 n.
ruck
average 30 n.
crowd 74 n.
generality 79 n.
fold 261 n.vb.
rucksack
bag 194 n.
ructions
turmoil 61 n.
fight 716 n.
rudder
sailing aid 269 n.
aircraft 276 n.
directorship 689 n.
rudderless
impotent 161 adj.
ruddle
red pigment 431 n.
ruddy
florid 425 adj.
red 431 adj.
healthy 650 adj.
personable 841 adj.
rude
violent 176 adj.
amorphous 244 adj.
inelegant 576 adj.
immature 670 adj.
graceless 842 adj.
ill-bred 847 adj.
impertinent 878 adj.
discourteous 885 adj.
unkind 898 adj.
disrespectful 921 adj.
rude person
rude person 885 n.
rudiment(s)
beginning 68 n.
source 156 n.
rudimentary
beginning 68 adj.
exiguous 196 adj.
studentlike 538 adj.
immature 670 adj.
rue
unsavouriness 391 n.
regret 830 vb.
be penitent 939 vb.
rueful
distressing 827 adj.
melancholic 834 adj.
ruff
neckwear 228 n.
plumage 259 n.
overmaster 727 vb.
ruffian
violent creature 176 n.
murderer 362 n.
desperado 857 n.
low fellow 869 n.
ruffian 904 n.
bad person 938 n.
ruffianly
ill-bred 847 adj.
insolent 878 adj.
ruffle
jumble 63 vb.
edging 234 n.
roughen 259 vb.
fold 261 n.vb.
agitate 318 vb.
torment 827 vb.
enrage 891 vb.
ruffled
rough 259 adj.
excitable 822 adj.
rufous
red 431 adj.
rug
coverlet 226 n.
floor-cover 226 n.
Rugby football
ball game 837 n.
rugged
stalwart 162 adj.
amorphous 244 adj.
difficult 700 adj.
graceless 842 adj.
ungracious 885 adj.
ruggedness
nonuniformity 17 n.
roughness 259 n.
rugger
ball game 837 n.
ruin
remainder 41 n.
antiquity 125 n.
ruin 165 n.
destroy 165 vb.
influence 178 n.
descent 309 n.
waste 634 vb.
dilapidation 655 n.
bane 659 n.
defeat 728 n.
adversity 731 n.
loss 772 n.
impoverish 801 vb.
shame 867 vb.
debauch 951 vb.
ruination
ruin 165 n.
ruined
destroyed 165 adj.
grounded 728 adj.
nonpaying 805 adj.
hopeless 853 adj.
ruinous
destructive 165 adj.
harmful 645 adj.
dilapidated 655 adj.
adverse 731 adj.
ruins
oldness 127 n.
ruin 165 n.
rule
prototype 23 n.
order 60 n.
rule 81 n.
prevail 178 vb.
line 203 n.
horizontality 216 n.
judge 480 vb.
creed 485 n.
maxim 496 n.
print-type 587 n.
policy 623 n.
manage 689 vb.
precept 693 n.
governance 733 n.
rule 733 vb.
command 737 vb.
conditions 766 n.
legislation 953 n.
try a case 959 vb.
— out
exclude 57 vb.
make impossible 470 vb.
exempt 919 vb.
— the roost
dominate 733 vb.
rule, be the
be general 79 vb.
be wont 610 vb.
rule of terror
despotism 733 n.
rule of three
numerical operation 86 n.
rule of thumb
empiricism 461 n.
intuition 476 n.
rule OK
win 727 vb.
ruler
gauge 465 n.
potentate 741 n.
scourge 964 n.

rulership
position of authority 733 n.
rules and regulations
practice 610 n.
right 913 n.
rules of business
conduct 688 n.
ruling
judgment 480 n.
legal trial 959 n.
ruling class
authority 733 n.
master 741 n.
upper class 868 n.
ruling passion
eccentricity 503 n.
opinionatedness 602 n.
affections 817 n.
rum
unusual 84 adj.
alcoholic drink 301 n.
ridiculous 849 adj.
rumba
dance 837 n.
rumble
roll 403 vb.
understand 516 vb.
fight 716 n.
rumbustious
disorderly 61 adj.
loud 400 adj.
riotous 738 adj.
excitable 822 adj.
ruminant
animal 365 n.adj.
ruminate
graze 301 vb.
meditate 449 vb.
ruminative
thoughtful 449 adj.
rummage
search 459 vb.
rummer
cup 194 n.
rummy
card game 837 n.
rumour
insubstantial thing 4 n.
topic 452 n.
publication 528 n.
rumour 529 n.vb.
fable 543 n.
rump
remainder 41 n.
buttocks 238 n.
rumple
jumble 63 vb.
roughen 259 vb.
fold 261 n.vb.
agitate 318 vb.
rumpus
turmoil 61 n.
violence 176 n.
quarrel 709 n.
fight 716 n.
run
separate 46 vb.
come unstuck 49 vb.
continuity 71 n.
series 71 n.
discontinuity 72 n.
generality 79 n.
recurrence 106 n.
elapse 111 vb.
continuance 146 n.
motion 265 n.
pedestrianism 267 n.
voyage 269 vb.
move fast 277 vb.
following 284 n.
flow out 298 vb.
liquefy 337 vb.
flow 350 vb.
lose colour 426 vb.
edition 589 n.
habit 610 n.
chase 619 n.
run away 620 vb.
be active 678 vb.
hasten 680 vb.
deal with 688 vb.
manage 689 vb.
steal 788 vb.
amuse oneself 837 vb.
— after
pursue 619 vb.
desire 859 vb.
court 889 vb.
— amok
be violent 176 vb.
go mad 503 vb.
be excitable 822 vb.
— at
attack 712 n.
charge 712 vb.
— a temperature
be hot 379 vb.
— away
move fast 277 vb.
decamp 296 vb.
run away 620 vb.
seek safety 660 vb.
escape 667 vb.
— away with
take away 786 vb.
— away with an idea
be credulous 487 vb.
— counter (to)
be contrary 14 vb.
counteract 182 vb.
tell against 467 vb.
— down
decrease 37 vb.
cease 145 vb.
collide 279 vb.
underestimate 483 vb.
pursue 619 vb.
make insufficient 636 vb.
charge 712 vb.
be malevolent 898 vb.
not respect 921 vb.
dispraise 924 vb.
detract 926 vb.
— for
steer for 281 vb.
offer oneself 759 vb.
— for one's life
run away 620 vb.
seek safety 660 vb.
— high
be violent 176 vb.
— in
initiate 68 vb.
arrest 747 vb.
— in one's head
engross 449 vb.
be remembered 505 vb.
— in the family
be intrinsic 5 vb.
— into
collide 279 vb.
meet 295 vb.
— low
decrease 37 vb.
waste 634 vb.
— off
empty 300 vb.
flow 350 vb.
print 587 vb.
— off with
take away 786 vb.
— on
run on 71 vb.
go on 146 vb.
progress 285 vb.
be loquacious 581 vb.
— out
end 69 vb.
cease 145 vb.
dismiss 300 vb.
waste 634 vb.
not suffice 636 vb.
— out on
relinquish 621 vb.
— over
be complete 54 vb.
collide 279 vb.
abstract 592 vb.
— riot
be violent 176 vb.
imagine 513 vb.
exaggerate 546 vb.
superabound 637 vb.
be active 678 vb.
be excitable 822 vb.
be intemperate 943 vb.
— short
fall short 307 vb.
— the gauntlet
face danger 661 vb.
defy 711 vb.
— the risk of
be liable 180 vb.
be in danger 661 vb.
— through
make uniform 16 vb.
consume 165 vb.
prevail 178 vb.
pervade 189 vb.
pierce 263 vb.
strike 279 vb.
exude 298 vb.
kill 362 vb.
waste 634 vb.
wound 655 vb.
strike at 712 vb.
expend 806 vb.
— to
avail oneself of 673 vb.
request 761 vb.
— together
combine 50 vb.
be parallel 219 vb.
— to seed
deteriorate 655 vb.
— up
produce 164 vb.vb.
elevate 310 vb.
— up an account
be in debt 803 vb.
— wild
be violent 176 vb.
— with the hare and hunt with the hounds
be false 541 vb.
tergiversate 603 vb.
be servile 879 vb.
runabout
automobile 274 n.
runaway
wanderer 268 n.
speedy 277 adj.
tergiversator 603 n.
avoider 620 n.
escaper 667 n.
coward 856 n.
runaway match
wedding 894 n.
run-down
weakly 163 adj.
compendium 592 n.
sick 651 adj.
dilapidated 655 adj.
disused 674 adj.
rune(s)
lettering 586 n.
spell 983 n.
rung
degree 27 n.
serial place 73 n.
stand 218 n.
cylinder 252 n.
ascent 308 n.
runic
literal 558 adj.
written 586 adj.
sorcerous 983 adj.
runlet
stream 350 n.

runnel
stream 350 n.
conduit 351 n.
runner
hanger 217 n.
pedestrian 268 n.
sledge 274 n.
speeder 277 n.
courier 529 n.
contender 716 n.
servant 742 n.
thief 789 n.
runner-up
inferior 35 n.
opponent 705 n.
contender 716 n.
running
continuous 71 adj.
flowing 350 adj.
sport 837 n.
running costs
cost 809 n.
running dog
auxiliary 707 n.
running headline
edition 589 n.
running over
full 54 adj.
redundant 637 adj.
running sore
evil 616 n.
wound 655 n.
bane 659 n.
painfulness 827 n.
running track
path 624 n.
arena 724 n.
running wild
frenzied 503 adj.
runny
nonadhesive 49 adj.
outgoing 298 adj.
fluid 335 adj.
liquefied 337 adj.
flowing 350 adj.
run of, the
scope 744 n.
run-off
contest 716 n.
run-of-the-mill
median 30 adj.
generality 79 n.
run on
requirement 627 n.
runt
dwarf 196 n.
runway
air travel 271 n.
path 624 n.
rupee
coinage 797 n.
rupture
disagreement 25 n.
separation 46 n.
break 46 vb.
gap 201 n.
wound 655 n.
dissension 709 n.
rural
regional 184 adj.
provincial 192 adj.
campestral 348 adj.
agrarian 370 adj.
ruralist
dweller 191 n.
solitary 883 n.
Ruritania
fantasy 513 n.
ruse
trickery 542 n.
stratagem 698 n.
rush
rampage 61 vb.
crowd 74 n.
outbreak 176 n.
spurt 277 n.
move fast 277 vb.
commotion 318 n.
flow 350 vb.
grass 366 n.
film 445 n.
unprepared 670 adj.
be active 678 vb.
haste 680 n.
hasten 680 vb.
charge 712 vb.
— about
be excitable 822 vb.
— at
pursue 619 vb.
charge 712 vb.
be rash 857 vb.
— in/into
burst in 297 vb.
be rash 857 vb.
— to conclusions
prejudge 481 vb.
rushed
hasty 680 adj.
rushed off one's feet, be
be busy 678 vb.
rush hour
crowd 74 n.
period 110 n.
rushlight
torch 420 n.
rusk
cereals 301 n.
russet
fruit 301 n.
brown 430 adj.
red 431 adj.
Russian doll
stratification 207 n.
Russian Orthodox
Catholic 976 n.
Russian roulette
gambling 618 n.
Russophile
xenophile 880 n.
rust
decay 51 n.
oldness 127 n.
destroyer 168 n.
be unproductive 172 vb.
blunt 257 vb.
pulverize 332 vb.
bedim 419 vb.
desuetude 611 n.
dirt 649 n.
dilapidation 655 n.
deteriorate 655 vb.
blight 659 n.
stop using 674 vb.
not act 677 vb.
inactivity 679 n.
blemish 845 n.
rust-coloured
brown 430 adj.
red 431 adj.
rustic
native 191 n.
provincial 192 adj.
agrarian 370 adj.
ingenue 699 n.
ill-bred 847 adj.
country-dweller 869 n.
rustication
seclusion 883 n.
penalty 963 n.
rustic flavour
plainness 573 n.
rustle
sound faint 401 vb.
sibilation 406 n.
steal 788 vb.
— up
make ready 669 vb.
rustler
thief 789 n.
rustproof
unyielding 162 adj.
rusty
antiquated 127 adj.
unsharpened 257 adj.
strident 407 adj.
dim 419 adj.
red 431 adj.
unhabituated 611 adj.
dilapidated 655 adj.
inactive 679 adj.
clumsy 695 adj.
rut
regularity 81 n.
roughness 259 n.
furrow 262 n.
habit 610 n.
libido 859 n.
ruthless
resolute 599 adj.
cruel 898 adj.
pitiless 906 adj.
rye
alcoholic drink 301 n.
cereals 301 n.
grass 366 n.

S

Sabbatarian(s)
ascetic 945 n.
sect 978 n.
ritualist 988 n.
zealot 979 n.
Sabbath
repose 683 n.
holy day 988 n.
sabbatical year
over five 99 n.
repose 683 n.
sable
skin 226 n.
blackness 428 n.
heraldic 547 adj.
sabot
footwear 228 n.
sabotage
derangement 63 n.
disable 161 vb.
destruction 165 n.
make useless 641 vb.
impairment 655 n.
hindrance 702 n.
revolt 738 n.vb.
fail in duty 918 vb.
saboteur
destroyer 168 n.
hinderer 702 n.
rioter 738 n.
sabre
kill 362 vb.
cavalry 722 n.
sidearms 723 n.
sabre-rattling
intimidation 854 n.
boasting 877 n.
threat 900 n.
sac
bladder 194 n.
saccharine
sweet 392 adj.
flattering 925 adj.
sacerdotal
priestly 985 adj.
clerical 986 adj.
sacerdotalism
ecclesiasticism 985 n.
sachet
scent 396 n.
sack
bag 194 n.
dismiss 300 vb.
wine 301 n.
deposal 752 n.
spoliation 788 n.
sackbut
horn 414 n.
sackcloth
roughness 259 n.
asceticism 945 n.
sackcloth and ashes
lamentation 836 n.
penitence 939 n.
penance 941 n.

sackful
finite quantity 26 n.
sacking
textile 222 n.
spoliation 788 n.
sack race
racing 716 n.
sacrament
rite 988 n.
the sacrament 988 n.
sacramental
religious 973 adj.
devotional 981 adj.
ritual 988 adj.
sacramentalist
ritualist 988 n.
sacrarium
holy place 990 n.
sacred
worshipful 866 adj.
divine 965 adj.
religious 973 adj.
sanctified 979 adj.
devotional 981 adj.
sacredness
sanctity 979 n.
sacred relics
ritual object 988 n.
sacred writings
scripture 975 n.
sacrifice
decrement 42 n.
kill 362 vb.
willingness 597 n.
loser 728 n.
offer 759 n.
loss 772 n.
offering 781 n.
cheapen 812 vb.
sufferer 825 n.
be disinterested 931 vb.
propitiation 941 n.
be pious 979 vb.
oblation 981 n.
offer worship 981 vb.
— oneself
be willing 597 vb.
offer oneself 759 vb.
suffer 825 vb.
be disinterested 931 vb.
sacrificer
giver 781 n.
worshipper 981 n.
sacrificial
destructive 165 adj.
losing 772 adj.
giving 781 adj.
disinterested 931 adj.
atoning 941 adj.
devotional 981 adj.
ritual 988 adj.
sacrificial price
cheapness 812 n.
sacrilege
impiety 980 n.
sacrilegious
disrespectful 921 adj.
impious 980 adj.
sacrilegious person
impious person 980 n.
sacring bell
signal 547 n.
ritual object 988 n.
sacristan
church officer 986 n.
sacristy
church interior 990 n.
sacrosanct
creedal 485 adj.
invulnerable 660 adj.
worshipful 866 adj.
due 915 adj.
sanctified 979 adj.
sad
funereal 364 adj.
soft-hued 425 adj.
bad 645 adj.
unhappy 825 adj.
distressing 827 adj.
discontented 829 adj.
dejected 834 adj.
melancholic 834 adj.
sadden
hurt 827 vb.
sadden 834 vb.
sadder and a wiser man, a
penitent 939 n.
saddle
affix 45 vb.
narrowness 206 n.
high land 209 n.
seat 218 n.
start out 296 vb.
break in 369 vb.
— the right horse
detect 484 vb.
— with
attribute 158 vb.
hinder 702 vb.
impose a duty 917 vb.
accuse 928 vb.
saddlebag
bag 194 n.
saddlecloth
coverlet 226 n.
saddled with
hindered 702 adj.
saddled with, be
carry 273 vb.
saddle horse
saddle horse 273 n.
Sadducees
non-Christian sect 978 n.
sadhu
pietist 979 n.
sadism
abnormality 84 n.
inhumanity 898 n.
sadist
nonconformist 84 n.
monster 938 n.
sensualist 944 n.
sadistic
cruel 898 adj.
pitiless 906 adj.
safari
land travel 267 n.
safari park
pleasance 192 n.
zoo 369 n.
safe
box 194 n.
certain 473 adj.
hiding-place 527 n.
storage 632 n.
safe 660 adj.
treasury 799 n.
cautious 858 adj.
safe and sound
undamaged 646 adj.
healthy 650 adj.
safe 660 adj.
safe bet
certainty 473 n.
safe-breaker
thief 789 n.
safe conduct
opener 263 n.
instrument 628 n.
protection 660 n.
preservation 666 n.
permit 756 n.
safe-deposit
hiding-place 527 n.
storage 632 n.
treasury 799 n.
safe distance
avoidance 620 n.
safeguard
look after 457 vb.
make certain 473 vb.
protection 660 n.
safeguard 660 vb.
safeguard 662 n.
preserver 666 n.
means of escape 667 n.
obstacle 702 n.
defence 713 n.
give security 767 vb.
caution 858 n.
talisman 983 n.
safe hands
protection 660 n.
safekeeping
protection 660 n.
preservation 666 n.
defence 713 n.
safe place
hiding-place 527 n.
refuge 662 n.
safety
safety 660 n.
safeguard 662 n.
security 767 n.
safety catch
fastening 47 n.
safeguard 662 n.
safety device
safeguard 662 n.
preserver 666 n.
safety first
cowardice 856 n.
caution 858 n.
safety lamp
lamp 420 n.
safety net
receptacle 194 n.
safeguard 662 n.
safety pin
fastening 47 n.
safety valve
safeguard 662 n.
means of escape 667 n.
saffron
yellowness 433 n.
sag
be weak 163 vb.
hang 217 vb.
be oblique 220 vb.
be curved 248 vb.
descend 309 vb.
knuckle under 721 vb.
be dejected 834 vb.
saga
narrative 590 n.
sagacious
intelligent 498 adj.
foreseeing 510 adj.
sagacity
sagacity 498 n.
foresight 510 n.
skill 694 n.
sage
old man 133 n.
potherb 301 n.
intellectual 492 n.
wise 498 adj.
sage 500 n.
teacher 537 n.
bigwig 638 n.
person of repute 866 n.
religious teacher 973 n.
sage-green
green 434 adj.
Sagittarius
zodiac 321 n.
Sahara
desert 172 n.
Saharan
dry 342 adj.
sahib
male 372 n.
title 870 n.
said
preceding 64 adj.
prior 119 adj.
sail
propeller 269 n.
water travel 269 n.

voyage 269 vb.
sail 275 n.
ship 275 n.
navy 722 n.
— home
do easily 701 vb.
— into
attack 712 vb.
fight 716 vb.
— too near the wind
be in danger 661 vb.
— under false colours
dissemble 541 vb.
sailcloth
textile 222 n.
sail 275 n.
sailing
aquatics 269 n.
seafaring 269 adj.
sport 837 n.
sailing master
navigator 270 n.
sailing ship
sailing ship 275 n.
sailor
mariner 270 n.
naval man 722 n.
sailplane
aircraft 276 n.
saint
paragon 646 n.
benefactor 903 n.
good person 937 n.
saint 968 n.
pietist 979 n.
sainted
dead 361 adj.
sanctified 979 adj.
sainthood
sanctity 979 n.
saintly
honourable 929 adj.
virtuous 933 adj.
angelic 968 adj.
pious 979 adj.
saints, the
the dead 361 n.
elite 644 n.
church member 976 n.
saint's day
special day 876 n.
holy day 988 n.
Saivas
non-Christian sect 978 n.
sake, saki
alcoholic drink 301 n.
salaam
295 int.
obeisance 311 n.
courteous act 884 n.
respects 920 n.
salable, saleable
not retained 779 adj.
trading 791 adj.
salable 793 adj.
salable commodity
merchandise 795 n.
salacious
impure 951 adj.
salad
dish 301 n.
hors d'oeuvres 301 n.
vegetable 301 n.
salad days
salad days 130 n.
salad dressing
sauce 389 n.
salamander
rara avis 84 n.
amphibian 365 n.
fire 379 n.
noxious animal 904 n.
salami
hors-d'oeuvres 301 n.
salaried classes
middle classes 869 n.
salary
incentive 612 n.
earnings 771 n.
pay 804 n.
receipt 807 n.
reward 962 n.
salary earner
worker 686 n.
salat
rite 988 n.
sale
transfer 780 n.
sale 793 n.
salebrosity
roughness 259 n.
sale-price
cheap 812 adj.
salesman, saleswoman
motivator 612 n.
seller 793 n.
salesmanship
publicity 528 n.
inducement 612 n.
sale 793 n.
sales patter
empty talk 515 n.
sales representative
seller 793 n.
sales talk
inducement 612 n.
salient
region 184 n.
projecting 254 adj.
obvious 443 adj.
battleground 724 n.
salientian
animal 365 adj.
salina
marsh 347 n.
saline
salty 388 adj.
saliva
excrement 302 n.
lubricant 334 n.
fluid 335 n.
moisture 341 n.
salivate
exude 298 vb.
excrete 302 vb.
be wet 341 vb.
sallow
weakly 163 adj.
tree 366 n.
colourless 426 adj.
whitish 427 adj.
yellow 433 adj.
unhealthy 651 adj.
sally
attack 712 n.
retaliation 714 n.
witticism 839 n.
sally forth
start out 296 vb.
emerge 298 vb.
sallyport
outlet 298 n.
fort 713 n.
salmagundi
a mixture 43 n.
salmon
fish food 301 n.
fish 365 n.
salmonella
poison 659 n.
salmon-pink
red 431 adj.
salon
chamber 194 n.
beau monde 848 n.
saloon
tavern 192 n.
automobile 274 n.
salt
mariner 270 n.
salty 388 adj.
condiment 389 n.
white thing 427 n.
chief thing 638 n.
preserve 666 vb.
wit 839 n.
— away
store 632 vb.
SALT
pacification 719 n.
saltatory
leaping 312 adj.
agitated 318 adj.
salt cellar
small box 194 n.
cavity 255 n.
salted
preserved 666 adj.
salt flat
desert 172 n.
marsh 347 n.
saltimbanco
impostor 545 n.
saltire
cross 222 n.
heraldry 547 n.
saltlick
provender 301 n.
salt of the earth
elite 644 n.
favourite 890 n.
benefactor 903 n.
good person 937 n.
saltpetre
explosive 723 n.
salty
seafaring 269 adj.
salty 388 adj.
forceful 571 adj.
exciting 821 adj.
witty 839 adj.
salubrious
nourishing 301 adj.
beneficial 644 adj.
clean 648 adj.
healthy 650 adj.
salubrious 652 adj.
safe 660 adj.
salutary
beneficial 644 adj.
salubrious 652 adj.
salutation
allocution 583 n.
courteous act 884 n.
respects 920 n.
salute
notice 455 vb.
signal 547 vb.
speak to 583 vb.
celebration 876 n.
courteous act 884 n.
greet 884 vb.
congratulation 886 n.
endearment 889 n.
show respect 920 vb.
approve 923 vb.
praise 923 vb.
salvage
restore 656 vb.
deliverance 668 n.
acquire 771 vb.
price 809 n.
salvation
restoration 656 n.
preservation 666 n.
deliverance 668 n.
liberation 746 n.
divine function 965 n.
Salvation Army
sect 978 n.
Salvationist
sectarian 978 n.
salve
lubricant 334 n.
unguent 357 n.
balm 658 n.
salve one's conscience
justify 927 vb.
atone 941 vb.
salver
plate 194 n.
church utensil 990 n.

salvo
bang 402 n.
qualification 468 n.
pretext 614 n.
bombardment 712 n.
celebration 876 n.
applause 923 n.
sal volatile
pungency 388 n.
tonic 658 n.
samba
dance 837 n.
same
identical 13 adj.
uniform 16 adj.
equal 28 adj.
same age
synchronism 123 n.
same for everybody
indiscriminate 464 adj.
sameness
identity 13 n.
uniformity 16 n.
equivalence 28 n.
tedium 838 n.
same old round
recurrence 106 n.
same time
synchronism 123 n.
same wavelength
consensus 488 n.
friendliness 880 n.
samovar
cauldron 194 n.
sampan
sailing ship 275 n.
sample
prototype 23 n.
part 53 n.
example 83 n.
taste 386 vb.
enquire 459 vb.
experiment 461 vb.
exhibit 522 n.
sampler
enquirer 459 n.
needlework 844 n.
samurai
militarist 722 n.
sanative
salubrious 652 adj.
restorative 656 adj.
sanatorium
hospital 658 n.
sanbenito
penance 941 n.
sanctify
dignify 866 vb.
celebrate 876 vb.
sanctify 979 vb.
offer worship 981 vb.
idolatrize 982 vb.
be ecclesiastical 985 vb.
sanctimonious
hypocritical 541 adj.
affected 850 adj.
prudish 950 adj.
pietistic 979 adj.
sanctimoniousness
false piety 980 n.
sanction
assent 488 n.vb.
endorse 488 vb.
compulsion 740 n.
permission 756 n.
consent 758 n.vb.
approve 923 vb.
sanctioned
reputable 866 adj.
due 915 adj.
sanctions
compulsion 740 n.
sanctions of society
etiquette 848 n.
sanctity
virtue 933 n.
divine attribute 965 n.
sanctity 979 n.
sanctuary
retreat 192 n.
reception 299 n.
protection 660 n.
refuge 662 n.
holy place 990 n.
sanctum
retreat 192 n.
refuge 662 n.
seclusion 883 n.
holy place 990 n.
Sanctus
Holy Communion 988 n.
sand
powder 332 n.
soil 344 n.
sandals
footwear 228 n.
sandalwood
scent 396 n.
sandbag(s)
defences 713 n.
club 723 n.
sandbank
island 349 n.
sandbar
pitfall 663 n.
sandblast
engrave 555 vb.
clean 648 vb.
sandcastle
weak thing 163 n.
brittleness 330 n.
sandglass
timekeeper 117 n.
sandhi
speech sound 398 n.
sandman
sleep 679 n.
sandpaper
smoother 258 n.
roughness 259 n.
sands
dryness 342 n.
shore 344 n.
plain 348 n.
sandwich
stratification 207 n.
put between 231 vb.
mouthful 301 n.
sandwich board
advertisement 528 n.
sandwich course
education 534 n.
sandwich man
publicizer 528 n.
sandy
powdery 332 adj.
dry 342 adj.
territorial 344 adj.
yellow 433 adj.
sand yacht
sledge 274 n.
sane
wise 498 adj.
sane 502 adj.
intelligible 516 adj.
sangfroid
moral insensibility 820 n.
inexcitability 823 n.
sanguinary
sanguineous 335 adj.
murderous 362 adj.
bloodstained 431 adj.
sanguine
bloodstained 431 adj.
red 431 adj.
optimistic 482 adj.
expectant 507 adj.
cheerful 833 adj.
hoping 852 adj.
Sanhedrin, Sanhedrim
synod 985 n.
sanies
fluid 335 n.
sanitary
cleansing 648 adj.
healthy 650 adj.
salubrious 652 adj.
sanitary engineer
cleaner 648 n.
sanitarian 652 n.
sanitary precaution
prophylactic 658 n.
protection 660 n.
sanitation
cleansing 648 n.
hygiene 652 n.
prophylactic 658 n.
hindrance 702 n.
sanity
moderation 177 n.
sagacity 498 n.
sanity 502 n.
sannyasi
ascetic 945 n.
sans
without 190 adv.
sansculotte
revolter 738 n.
low fellow 869 n.
sanserif
print-type 587 n.
Sanskrit
language 557 n.
Sanskritist
antiquarian 125 n.
linguist 557 n.
sans peur et sans reproche
honourable 929 adj.
Santa Claus
giver 781 n.
good giver 813 n.
benefactor 903 n.
santon
monk 986 n.
sap
essential part 5 n.
disable 161 vb.
weaken 163 vb.
make concave 255 vb.
fluid 335 n.
moisture 341 n.
semiliquidity 354 n.
ninny 501 n.
impair 655 vb.
besiege 712 vb.
— the foundations
demolish 165 vb.
sapid
tasty 386 adj.
sapient
wise 498 adj.
sapless
weak 163 adj.
dry 342 adj.
sapling
young plant 132 n.
tree 366 n.
saponaceous
fatty 357 adj.
sapper
excavator 255 n.
soldiery 722 n.
Sapphic
poetic 593 adj.
sapphire
blueness 435 n.
gem 844 n.
Sapphism
abnormality 84 n.
sappy
new 126 adj.
vernal 128 adj.
fluid 335 adj.
humid 341 adj.
pulpy 356 adj.
foolish 499 adj.
sapwood
interiority 224 n.
wood 366 n.
saraband, sarabande
dance 837 n.
sarcasm
wit 839 n.
ridicule 851 n.
rudeness 885 n.
indignity 921 n.

reproach 924 n.
calumny 926 n.
sarcastic
keen 174 adj.
witty 839 adj.
derisive 851 adj.
sarcoma
cancer 651 n.
sarcophagus
box 194 n.
interment 364 n.
sard
gem 844 n.
sardine
fish food 301 n.
sardonic
derisive 851 adj.
disapproving 924 adj.
sardonyx
gem 844 n.
sari
robe 228 n.
sarong
loincloth 228 n.
skirt 228 n.
sartorial
tailored 228 adj.
sash
girdle 47 n.
frame 218 n.
belt 228 n.
window 263 n.
badge 547 n.
decoration 729 n.
badge of rank 743 n.
Sassenach
foreigner 59 n.
Satan
wickedness 934 n.
Satan 969 n.
impious person 980 n.
satanic
cruel 898 adj.
wicked 934 adj.
diabolic 969 adj.
Satanism
diabolism 969 n.
antichristianity 974 n.
satchel
bag 194 n.
satchet
bag 194 n.
sate
fill 54 vb.
superabound 637 vb.
make insensitive 820 vb.
content 828 vb.
be tedious 838 vb.
sate 863 vb.
sated
filled 635 adj.
disliking 861 adj.
sated 863 adj.
sateen
textile 222 n.
satellite
concomitant 89 n.
spaceship 276 n.
follower 284 n.
circler 314 n.
satellite 321 n.
auxiliary 707 n.
dependant 742 n.
subject 745 adj.
satellite town
housing 192 n.
satiate
suffice 635 vb.
(See **sate** *)*
satiety
plenitude 54 n.
sufficiency 635 n.
superfluity 637 n.
tedium 838 n.
dislike 861 n.
satiety 863 n.
satin
textile 222 n.
smoothness 258 n.
satire
trope 519 n.
exaggeration 546 n.
description 590 n.
wit 839 n.
satire 851 n.
reproach 924 n.
calumny 926 n.
satiric
poetic 593 adj.
satirical
figurative 519 adj.
untrue 543 adj.
funny 849 adj.
derisive 851 adj.
disrespectful 921 adj.
satirist
humorist 839 n.
disapprover 924 n.
detractor 926 n.
satirize, satirise
exaggerate 546 vb.
satirize 851 vb.
satisfaction
sufficiency 635 n.
observance 768 n.
payment 804 n.
enjoyment 824 n.
content 828 n.
approbation 923 n.
atonement 941 n.
propitiation 941 n.
satisfactorily
well 615 adv.
commendably 923 adv.
satisfactory
sufficient 635 adj.
not bad 644 adj.
contenting 828 adj.
satisfy
fill 54 vb.
demonstrate 478 vb.
convince 485 vb.
suffice 635 vb.
pacify 719 vb.
observe 768 vb.
please 826 vb.
content 828 vb.
— oneself
be certain 473 vb.
satisfying
pleasant 376 adj.
sufficient 635 adj.
contenting 828 adj.
satrap
governor 741 n.
saturate
fill 54 vb.
drench 341 vb.
suffice 635 vb.
superabound 637 vb.
sate 863 vb.
saturation
hue 425 n.
saturation bombing
bombardment 712 n.
warfare 718 n.
saturation point
plenitude 54 n.
limit 236 n.
Saturn
planet 321 n.
classical deities 967 n.
saturnalia
turmoil 61 n.
festivity 837 n.
sensualism 944 n.
saturnalian
disorderly 61 adj.
Saturnia Regna
palmy days 730 n.
happiness 824 n.
saturnine
serious 834 adj.
sullen 893 adj.
satyr
libertine 952 n.
mythical being 970 n.
satyriasis
mania 503 n.
libido 859 n.
sauce
adjunct 40 n.
stimulant 174 n.
food 301 n.
season 388 vb.
sauce 389 n.
sauciness 878 n.
rudeness 885 n.
scurrility 899 n.
saucepan
cauldron 194 n.
heater 383 n.
saucer
plate 194 n.
cavity 255 n.
saucy
defiant 711 adj.
impertinent 878 adj.
discourteous 885 adj.
disrespectful 921 adj.
sauerkraut
vegetable 301 n.
sauna
heater 383 n.
ablutions 648 n.
saunter
be late 136 vb.
wander 267 vb.
move slowly 278 vb.
saurian
animal 365 adj.
sausage
meat 301 n.
sauté
cook 301 vb.
sauve qui peut
fear 854 n.
savage
violent creature 176 n.
violent 176 adj.
ignorant 491 adj.
ill-treat 645 vb.
wound 655 vb.
immature 670 adj.
ingenue 699 n.
attack 712 vb.
severe 735 adj.
excitable 822 adj.
vulgarian 847 n.
courageous 855 adj.
low fellow 869 n.
barbaric 869 adj.
rude person 885 n.
angry 891 adj.
cruel 898 adj.
ruffian 904 n.
dispraise 924 vb.
monster 938 n.
savagely
painfully 32 adv.
savagery
violence 176 n.
artlessness 699 n.
inhumanity 898 n.
savages
humankind 371 n.
savanna, savannah
plain 348 n.
savant
scholar 492 n.
expert 696 n.
save
in deduction 39 adv.
exclusive of 57 adv.
unconformably 84 adv.
store 632 vb.
preserve 666 vb.
deliver 668 vb.
not use 674 vb.
liberate 746 vb.
acquire 771 vb.
retain 778 vb.
economize 814 vb.
— labour
have leisure 681 vb.

— one's bacon
be safe 660 vb.
escape 667 vb.
— one's breath
be taciturn 582 vb.
— up
store 632 vb.
acquire 771 vb.
saved
restored 656 adj.
sanctified 979 adj.
saver
niggard 816 n.
saving
qualifying 468 adj.
(See **save** *)*
saving clause
qualification 468 n.
conditions 766 n.
saving grace
virtues 933 n.
savings
store 632 n.
gain 771 n.
economy 814 n.
savings bank
treasury 799 n.
saving your presence
respectfully 920 adv.
saviour
preserver 666 n.
benefactor 903 n.
Saviour
God the Son 965 n.
savoir faire
knowledge 490 n.
skill 694 n.
etiquette 848 n.
savoir vivre
sociability 882 n.
savour
taste 386 n.vb.
make appetizing 390 vb.
be pleased 824 vb.
— of
resemble 18 vb.
savourless
tasteless 387 adj.
savoury
dish 301 n.
edible 301 adj.
tasty 386 adj.
savoury 390 adj.
pleasurable 826 adj.
savoy
vegetable 301 n.
savvy
know 490 vb.
intelligence 498 n.
understand 516 vb.
etiquette 848 n.
saw
cut 46 vb.
tooth 256 n.
notch 260 n.
rasp 407 vb.
discord 411 vb.
play music 413 vb.
maxim 496 n.
— the air
gesticulate 547 vb.
sawbones
doctor 658 n.
sawder
flatter 925 vb.
sawdust
leavings 41 n.
powder 332 n.
saw-edged
toothed 256 adj.
sawmill
workshop 687 n.
sawn-off
short 204 adj.
sawn-off shotgun
firearm 723 n.
saw-toothed
notched 260 adj.
sawyer
artisan 686 n.
Saxon
olden 127 adj.
saxophone
flute 414 n.
saxophonist
instrumentalist 413 n.
say
about 33 adv.
affirm 532 vb.
speak 579 vb.
decree 737 vb.
— after
repeat 106 vb.
— again
repeat 106 vb.
emphasize 532 vb.
— no
dissent 489 vb.
negate 533 vb.
refuse 760 vb.
— nothing
be taciturn 582 vb.
— one's lines
act 594 vb.
— one's piece
repeat 106 vb.
— one's prayers
be pious 979 vb.
worship 981 vb.
— one thing and mean another
dissemble 541 vb.
— to oneself
soliloquize 585 vb.
— whatever comes into one's head
improvise 609 vb.
— what is in one's mind
be artless 699 vb.
— yes
assent 488 vb.
permit 756 vb.
consent 758 vb.
sayable
permitted 756 adj.
saying
maxim 496 n.
affirmation 532 n.
phrase 563 n.
say-so
affirmation 532 n.
command 737 n.
scab
nonconformist 84 n.
covering 226 n.
tergiversator 603 n.
revolter 738 n.
hateful object 888 n.
cad 938 n.
scabbard
case 194 n.
arsenal 723 n.
scabby
rough 259 adj.
unclean 649 adj.
scab over
join 45 vb.
cure 656 vb.
scabrous
rough 259 adj.
impure 951 adj.
scads
great quantity 32 n.
wealth 800 n.
scaffold
structure 331 n.
preparation 669 n.
means of execution 964 n.
scaffolding
frame 218 n.
lifter 310 n.
scald
burn 381 vb.
wound 655 n.
scalding
hot 379 adj.
paining 827 adj.
scale
relativeness 9 n.
degree 27 n.
series 71 n.
plate 194 n.
layer 207 n.
skin 226 n.
doff 229 vb.
climb 308 vb.
scales 322 n.
key 410 n.
musical note 410 n.
obfuscation 421 n.
opacity 423 n.
gauge 465 n.
— down
abate 37 vb.
render few 105 vb.
scale drawing
plan 623 n.
scalene
unequal 29 adj.
distorted 246 adj.
scales
scales 322 n.
scallop
edging 234 n.
crinkle 251 vb.
notch 260 n.vb.
fish food 301 n.
scallywag
bad person 938 n.
scalp
head 213 n.
skin 226 n.
uncover 229 vb.
trophy 729 n.
scalpel
sharp edge 256 n.
scalplock
hair 259 n.
scaly
layered 207 adj.
dermal 226 adj.
rough 259 adj.
scamp
neglect 458 vb.
be unwilling 598 vb.
not complete 726 vb.
revolter 738 n.
evildoer 904 n.
bad person 938 n.
scamped
hasty 680 adj.
scamper
move fast 277 vb.
run away 620 vb.
scampi
fish food 301 n.
scan
look along 203 vb.
scan 438 vb.
be attentive 455 vb.
enquire 459 vb.
know 490 vb.
poetize 593 vb.
scandal
rumour 529 n.
badness 645 n.
slur 867 n.
wrong 914 n.
calumny 926 n.
false charge 928 n.
wickedness 934 n.
scandalize, scandalise
displease 827 vb.
cause dislike 861 vb.
shame 867 vb.
incur blame 924 vb.
scandalized, scandalised
wondering 864 adj.
disapproving 924 adj.
scandalizing, scandalising
unusual 84 adj.
heinous 934 adj.
scandalmonger
news reporter 529 n.
defamer 926 n.
scandalous
vulgar 847 adj.
(See **scandal** *)*

scanner
hospital 658 n.
scansion
prosody 593 n.
scant
incomplete 55 adj.
few 105 adj.
exiguous 196 adj.
insufficient 636 adj.
restrained 747 adj.
scantling
size 195 n.
scanty
small 33 adj.
few 105 adj.
exiguous 196 adj.
short 204 adj.
insufficient 636 adj.
scapegoat
substitute 150 n.
unlucky person 731 n.
deputy 755 n.
sufferer 825 n.
propitiation 941 n.
oblation 981 n.
scapegrace
revolter 738 n.
desperado 857 n.
bad person 938 n.
scapular
canonicals 989 n.
scar
high land 209 n.
rock 344 n.
identification 547 n.
mark 547 vb.
trace 548 n.
wound 655 n.
blemish 845 n.vb.
scarab
talisman 983 n.
scarce
few 105 adj.
infrequent 140 adj.
unproductive 172 adj.
deficient 307 adj.
scarce 636 adj.
of price 811 adj.
scarcely
slightly 33 adv.
seldom 140 adv.
scarcity
fewness 105 n.
absence 190 n.
scarcity 636 n.
poverty 801 n.
(See **scarce** *)*
scare
false alarm 665 n.
fear 854 n.
frighten 854 vb.
scarecrow
thinness 206 n.
sham 542 n.
image 551 n.
eyesore 842 n.
intimidation 854 n.
scaremonger
false alarm 665 n.
alarmist 854 n.
scarf
wrapping 226 n.
neckwear 228 n.
scarify
cut 46 vb.
notch 260 vb.
wound 655 vb.
scarlet
redness 431 n.
heinous 934 adj.
scarlet fever
infection 651 n.
scarlet woman
loose woman 952 n.
scarp
verticality 215 n.
incline 220 n.
fortification 713 n.
scarper
fail in duty 918 vb.
scarred
marked 547 adj.
blemished 845 adj.
scathe
harm 645 vb.
impair 655 vb.
scatheless
undamaged 646 adj.
scathing
paining 827 adj.
scatological
unclean 649 adj.
impure 951 adj.
scat singing
vocal music 412 n.
scatter
disunite 46 vb.
be disordered 61 vb.
jumble 63 vb.
dispersion 75 n.
be dispersed 75 vb.
destroy 165 vb.
displace 188 vb.
diverge 294 vb.
let fall 311 vb.
disappear 446 vb.
waste 634 vb.
defeat 727 vb.
scatterbrain
inattention 456 n.
fool 501 n.
scatterbrained
disorderly 61 adj.
light-minded 456 adj.
foolish 499 adj.
scatter diagram
statistics 86 n.
scattered
few 105 adj.
scattering
noncoherence 49 n.
disorder 61 n.
dispersion 75 n.
scatty
light-minded 456 adj.
foolish 499 adj.
crazy 503 adj.
scavenger
cleaner 648 n.
dirty person 649 n.
scenario
cinema 445 n.
reading matter 589 n.
narrative 590 n.
stage play 594 n.
policy 623 n.
scenario writer
dramatist 594 n.
scene
situation 186 n.
surroundings 230 n.
view 438 n.
visibility 443 n.
spectacle 445 n.
exhibit 522 n.
art subject 553 n.
dramaturgy 594 n.
stage set 594 n.
arena 724 n.
excitable state 822 n.
pageant 875 n.
scene-painter
artist 556 n.
stagehand 594 n.
scenery
land 344 n.
beauty 841 n.
(See **scene** *)*
sceneshifter
stagehand 594 n.
scenic
painted 553 adj.
dramatic 594 adj.
impressive 821 adj.
pleasurable 826 adj.
beautiful 841 adj.
ornamental 844 adj.
showy 875 adj.
scenic railway
pleasure ground 837 n.
scent
emit 300 vb.
odour 394 n.
smell 394 vb.
scent 396 n.
be fragrant 396 vb.
detect 484 vb.
knowledge 490 n.
foresee 510 vb.
indication 547 n.
trace 548 n.
cosmetic 843 n.
— out
detect 484 vb.
pursue 619 vb.
scentless
odourless 395 adj.
sceptic
unbeliever 486 n.
irreligionist 974 n.
sceptical
doubting 474 adj.
unbelieving 486 adj.
dissenting 489 adj.
scepticism
philosophy 449 n.
doubt 486 n.
irreligion 974 n.
sceptre
badge 547 n.
regalia 743 n.
schadenfreude
joy 824 n.
malevolence 898 n.
schedule
list 87 n.vb.
plan 623 vb.
schematic
orderly 60 adj.
arranged 62 adj.
planned 623 adj.
scheme
prototype 23 n.
arrangement 62 n.
plan 623 n.
plot 623 n.vb.
preparation 669 n.
be cunning 698 vb.
schemer
planner 623 n.
slyboots 698 n.
scheming
dishonest 930 adj.
perfidious 930 adj.
scherzo
musical piece 412 n.
schism
disunion 46 n.
dissent 489 n.
dissension 709 n.
schism 978 n.
schismatic
dissentient 489 n.
quarrelling 709 adj.
revolter 738 n.
schismatic 978 n.
schismatical 978 adj.
schist
rock 344 n.
schistose
layered 207 adj.
schistosomiasis
tropical disease 651 n.
schizoid
insane 503 adj.
madman 504 n.
schizophrenia
psychopathy 503 n.
schizophrenic
multiform 82 adj.
insane 503 adj.
schmaltzy
feeble 572 adj.
feeling 818 adj.
vulgar 847 adj.

schnapps
alcoholic drink 301 n.
scholar
antiquarian 125 n.
scholar 492 n.
learner 538 n.
expert 696 n.
scholarly
instructed 490 adj.
educational 534 adj.
studious 536 adj.
studentlike 538 adj.
scholarship
erudition 490 n.
learning 536 n.
subvention 703 n.
scholastic
intellectual 492 n.
educational 534 adj.
scholastic 539 adj.
theological 973 adj.
scholasticism
philosophy 449 n.
theology 973 n.
scholiast
interpreter 520 n.
scholium
commentary 520 n.
school
group 74 n.
creed 485 n.
educate 534 vb.
school 539 n.
academy 539 n.
school-age
young 130 adj.
school book
textbook 589 n.
schoolboy, schoolgirl
youngster 132 n.
learner 538 n.
schoolboyish
studentlike 538 adj.
school days
salad days 130 n.
schooled
instructed 490 adj.
schoolfellow
learner 538 n.
chum 880 n.
schooling
teaching 534 n.
school-leaver
learner 538 n.
schoolman
reasoner 475 n.
theologian 973 n.
schoolmaster, schoolmistress
teacher 537 n.
master 741 n.
school of painting
school of painting 553 n.
artist 556 n.
school of philosophy
philosophy 449 n.
academy 539 n.
schooner
cup 194 n.
sailing ship 275 n.
schottische
dance 837 n.
sciatica
pang 377 n.
rheumatism 651 n.
science
physics 319 n.
philosophy 449 n.
science 490 n.
skill 694 n.
science fiction
ideality 513 n.
novel 590 n.
scientific
accurate 494 adj.
educational 534 adj.
scientifically
knowingly 490 adv.
skilfully 694 adv.
scientific knowledge
science 490 n.
scientific thought
philosophy 449 n.
scientist
physics 319 n.
intellectual 492 n.
scientologist
sectarian 978 n.
scientology
religious faith 973 n.
sci-fi
(See **science fiction** *)*
scimitar
sharp edge 256 n.
sidearms 723 n.
scintilla
small quantity 33 n.
luminary 420 n.
scintillate
shine 417 vb.
be wise 498 vb.
be witty 839 vb.
sciolistic
dabbling 491 adj.
scion
branch 53 n.
young plant 132 n.
descendant 170 n.
tree 366 n.
scissile
severable 46 adj.
brittle 330 adj.
scission
scission 46 n.
scissors
cross 222 n.
sharp edge 256 n.
scissors-and-paste job
edition 589 n.
sclerosis
hardening 326 n.
scoff
food 301 n.
ridicule 851 n.vb.
not respect 921 vb.
despise 922 vb.
detract 926 vb.
gluttonize 947 vb.
— at
disbelieve 486 vb.
scoffer
unbeliever 486 n.
detractor 926 n.
scold
violent creature 176 n.
quarreller 709 n.
bicker 709 vb.
shrew 892 n.
cuss 899 vb.
reprobate 924 vb.
scolding
reprimand 924 n.
scollop
(See **scallop** *)*
sconce
lamp 420 n.
scone
cereals 301 n.
scoop
ladle 194 n.
extractor 304 n.
information 524 n.
news 529 n.
acquisition 771 n.
gain 771 vb.
— out
make concave 255 vb.
scoot
move fast 277 vb.
run away 620 vb.
scooter
bicycle 274 n.
scope
opportunity 137 n.
influence 178 n.
range 183 n.
meaning 514 n.
function 622 n.
facility 701 n.
scope 744 n.
scopophilia
inspection 438 n.
impurity 951 n.
scorch
move fast 277 vb.
dry 342 vb.
be hot 379 vb.
burn 381 vb.
impair 655 vb.
wage war 718 vb.
scorched earth policy
unproductiveness 172 n.
warfare 718 n.
scorcher
speeder 277 n.
heat 379 n.
exceller 644 n.
score
degree 27 n.
cut 46 vb.
composition 56 n.
arrangement 62 n.
numerical result 85 n.
list 87 n.vb.
groove 262 vb.
notation 410 n.
music 412 n.
compose music 413 vb.
mark 547 vb.
register 548 vb.
wound 655 vb.
triumph 727 vb.
credit 802 n.
accounts 808 n.
— off
be superior 34 vb.
confute 479 vb.
humiliate 872 vb.
— through
obliterate 550 vb.
score, a
twenty and over 99 n.
scoreboard
record 548 n.
scores
multitude 104 n.
scoria
leavings 41 n.
ash 381 n.
scorify
heat 381 vb.
scorn
underestimate 483 vb.
unbelief 486 n.
reject 607 vb.
shame 867 vb.
scurrility 899 n.
disrespect 921 n.
contempt 922 n.
despise 922 vb.
detraction 926 n.
scornful
despising 922 adj.
Scorpio
zodiac 321 n.
scorpion
creepy-crawly 365 n.
noxious animal 904 n.
scotch
notch 260 vb.
wound 655 vb.
hinder 702 vb.
Scotch mist
moisture 341 n.
Scotch whisky
alcoholic drink 301 n.
scot free
escaped 667 adj.
free 744 adj.
uncharged 812 adj.
nonliable 919 adj.
Scotland Yard
police 955 n.
scotoma
dim sight 440 n.

scoundrel
cad 938 n.
knave 938 n.
scour
traverse 267 vb.
move fast 277 vb.
pass 305 vb.
rub 333 vb.
search 459 vb.
clean 648 vb.
scourer
cleaning utensil 648 n.
scourge
evil 616 n.
plague 651 n.
bane 659 n.
adversity 731 n.
oppress 735 vb.
ruffian 904 n.
dispraise 924 vb.
flog 963 vb.
scourge 964 n.
— oneself
do penance 941 vb.
scourings
leavings 41 n.
rubbish 641 n.
dirt 649 n.
scout
precursor 66 n.
traverse 267 vb.
scan 438 vb.
spectator 441 n.
watch 441 vb.
enquirer 459 n.
detector 484 n.
reject 607 vb.
warner 664 n.
domestic 742 n.
despise 922 vb.
scowl
distort 246 vb.
look 438 n.
gesture 547 n.
discontent 829 n.
be rude 885 vb.
hatred 888 n.
anger 891 n.
sullenness 893 n.
scrabble
make concave 255 vb.
touch 378 vb.
search 459 vb.
Scrabble
indoor game 837 n.
scrag end
remainder 41 n.
meat 301 n.
scraggy
exiguous 196 adj.
lean 206 adj.
scram
292 int.
decamp 296 vb.
run away 620 vb.
scramble
mix 43 vb.
confusion 61 n.
derange 63 vb.
cook 301 vb.
climb 308 vb.
activity 678 n.
haste 680 n.
fight 716 n.
scrambler
bicycle 274 n.
scrap
small quantity 33 n.
piece 53 n.
reject 607 vb.
rubbish 641 n.
stop using 674 vb.
fight 716 n.vb.
scrapbook
reminder 505 n.
record 548 n.
anthology 592 n.
scrape
abate 37 vb.
make smaller 198 vb.
be contiguous 202 vb.
make concave 255 vb.
collision 279 n.
stoop 311 vb.
pulverize 332 vb.
rub 333 vb.
touch 378 vb.
rasp 407 vb.
discord 411 vb.
play music 413 vb.
foolery 497 n.
engrave 555 vb.
clean 648 vb.
predicament 700 n.
economize 814 vb.
be parsimonious 816 vb.
be servile 879 vb.
guilty act 936 n.
— an acquaintance
befriend 880 vb.
— home
win 727 vb.
— off
uncover 229 vb.
— through
be imperfect 647 vb.
escape 667 vb.
— together
bring together 74 vb.
acquire 771 vb.
scraper
sharp edge 256 n.
scraperboard
engraving 555 n.
scrap heap
rubbish 641 n.
scrap heap, on the
disused 674 adj.
scrapings
leavings 41 n.
scrap of paper
ineffectuality 161 n.
unreliability 474 n.
perfidy 930 n.
scrapped
disused 674 adj.
scrappy
fragmentary 53 adj.
incomplete 55 adj.
scraps
leavings 41 n.
rubbish 641 n.
scratch
inferior 35 adj.
cut 46 vb.
rend 46 vb.
be violent 176 vb.
shallowness 212 n.
make concave 255 vb.
be rough 259 vb.
groove 262 vb.
strike 279 vb.
friction 333 n.
itch 378 vb.
touch 378 vb.
faintness 401 n.
rasp 407 vb.
mark 547 vb.
trace 548 n.
tergiversate 603 vb.
relinquish 621 vb.
trifle 639 n.
imperfect 647 adj.
wound 655 n.vb.
unprepared 670 adj.
unskilled 695 adj.
fight 716 vb.
resign 753 vb.
blemish 845 n.
— a living
be poor 801 vb.
— each other's back
interchange 151 vb.
flatter 925 vb.
— out
obliterate 550 vb.
scratchiness
formication 378 n.
excitability 822 n.
scratchy
agitated 318 adj.
strident 407 adj.
irascible 892 adj.
scrawl
unintelligibility 517 n.
represent 551 vb.
misrepresentation 552 n.
write 586 vb.
scrawny
lean 206 adj.
scream
feel pain 377 vb.
be loud 400 vb.
shrill 407 vb.
cry 408 n.vb.
proclaim 528 vb.
weep 836 vb.
screaming
loud 400 adj.
florid 425 adj.
vulgar 847 adj.
scree
piece 53 n.
incline 220 n.
thing transferred 272 n.
screech
stridor 407 n.
rasp 407 vb.
cry 408 vb.
ululation 409 n.
screed
oration 579 n.
script 586 n.
dissertation 591 n.
screen
separation 46 n.
exclusion 57 n.
canopy 226 n.
partition 231 n.
porosity 263 n.
stopper 264 n.
screen 421 n.vb.
opacity 423 n.
blind 439 vb.
cinema 445 n.
enquire 459 vb.
show 522 vb.
concealment 525 n.
disguise 527 n.
stage set 594 n.
pretext 614 n.
cleaning utensil 648 n.
safeguard 660 vb.
shelter 662 n.
defence 713 n.
screened
dark 418 adj.
screened 421 adj.
invisible 444 adj.
latent 523 adj.
safe 660 adj.
secluded 883 adj.
screenplay
cinema 445 n.
stage play 594 n.
screw
affix 45 vb.
fastening 47 n.
distort 246 vb.
coil 251 n.
propeller 269 n.
saddle horse 273 n.
propellant 287 n.
rotator 315 n.
gaoler 749 n.
earnings 771 n.
rob 788 vb.
niggard 816 n.
— up
tighten 45 vb.
strengthen 162 vb.
make ready 669 vb.
— up one's courage
take courage 855 vb.

screwball
madman 504 n.
screwdriver
extractor 304 n.
tool 630 n.
screw loose
eccentricity 503 n.
defect 647 n.
hitch 702 n.
screwy
crazy 503 adj.
scribble
lack of meaning 515 n.
unintelligibility 517 n.
mark 547 vb.
write 586 vb.
scribbler
calligrapher 586 n.
author 589 n.
scribe
mark 547 vb.
recorder 549 n.
calligrapher 586 n.
theologian 973 n.
scribes and Pharisees
zealot 979 n.
scrimmage
quarrel 709 n.
fight 716 n.
scrimp
niggard 816 n.
scrimshanker
avoider 620 n.
scrimshaw
sculpt 554 vb.
ornamental art 844 n.
scrip
title deed 767 n.
paper money 797 n.
script
script 586 n.
writing 586 n.
reading matter 589 n.
stage play 594 n.
scriptural
scriptural 975 adj.
scripturalist
theologian 973 n.
the orthodox 976 n.
scripture
credential 466 n.
scripture 975 n.
script writer
author 589 n.
dramatist 594 n.
scrivener
calligrapher 586 n.
notary 958 n.
scrofulous
impure 951 adj.
scroll
list 87 n.
coil 251 n.
rotate 315 vb.
lettering 586 n.
book 589 n.
scrollwork
pattern 844 n.
Scrooge
niggard 816 n.
scrotum
genitalia 167 n.
scrounge
beg 761 vb.
take 786 vb.
scrounger
idler 679 n.
beggar 763 n.
scrub
rub 333 vb.
wood 366 n.
clean 648 vb.
abrogate 752 vb.
scrubber
loose woman 952 n.
prostitute 952 n.
scrubbing brush
roughness 259 n.
cleaning utensil 648 n.
scrubby
lean 206 adj.
arboreal 366 adj.
scruff
rear 238 n.
scruffy
not nice 645 adj.
unclean 649 adj.
beggarly 801 adj.
disreputable 867 adj.
scrum
crowd 74 n.
fight 716 n.
scrumptious
savoury 390 adj.
super 644 adj.
scrumpy
alcoholic drink 301 n.
scrunch
rend 46 vb.
chew 301 vb.
pulverize 332 vb.
rasp 407 vb.
scruple
small quantity 33 n.
weighing 322 n.
doubt 486 n.
dissent 489 vb.
unwillingness 598 n.
scrupulous
careful 457 adj.
accurate 494 adj.
fastidious 862 adj.
honourable 929 adj.
scrutator
spectator 441 n.
scrutineer
enquirer 459 n.
scrutinize, scrutinise
scan 438 vb.
scrutiny
attention 455 n.
enquiry 459 n.
scuba diver
diver 313 n.
scud
navigate 269 vb.
move fast 277 vb.
cloud 355 n.
scuff
move slowly 278 vb.
rub 333 vb.
scuffle
fight 716 n.
scuffmark
trace 548 n.
scull
propeller 269 n.
row 269 vb.
sculler
boatman 270 n.
scullery
chamber 194 n.
scullion
cleaner 648 n.
domestic 742 n.
sculp
sculpt 554 vb.
sculpt
form 243 vb.
sculpt 554 vb.
sculptor, sculptress
producer 164 n.
sculptor 556 n.
sculpture
art 551 n.
sculpture 554 n.
sculpt 554 vb.
scum
leavings 41 n.
layer 207 n.
bubble 355 n.
rubbish 641 n.
dirt 649 n.
rabble 869 n.
bad person 938 n.
scumble
coat 226 vb.
make opaque 423 vb.
paint 553 vb.
scupper
suppress 165 vb.
drain 351 n.
slaughter 362 vb.
scurf
powder 332 n.
dirt 649 n.
scurrility
scurrility 899 n.
scurrilous
insolent 878 adj.
cursing 899 adj.
disrespectful 921 adj.
detracting 926 adj.
scurry
move fast 277 vb.
be busy 678 vb.
hasten 680 vb.
scurvy
disease 651 n.
rascally 930 adj.
scut
rear 238 n.
scutage
tax 809 n.
scuttle
suppress 165 vb.
vessel 194 n.
pierce 263 vb.
move fast 277 vb.
decamp 296 vb.
plunge 313 vb.
run away 620 vb.
be cowardly 856 vb.
fail in duty 918 vb.
scutum
armour 713 n.
Scylla and Charybdis
danger 661 n.
scythe
cut 46 vb.
sharp edge 256 n.
farm tool 370 n.
sea
great quantity 32 n.
ocean 343 n.
wave 350 n.
sea air
air 340 n.
salubrity 652 n.
seaboard
shore 344 n.
seaborne
seafaring 269 adj.
sea breeze
breeze 352 n.
sea dog
mariner 270 n.
expert 696 n.
seafarer
mariner 270 n.
seafaring
water travel 269 n.
seafaring 269 adj.
marine 275 adj.
seafood
fish food 301 n.
sea front
path 624 n.
sea-girt
insular 349 adj.
sea god
sea god 343 n.
mythic deity 966 n.
sea-going
seafaring 269 adj.
sea-green
green 434 adj.
sea horse
marine life 365 n.
sea king
mariner 270 n.
seal
mould 23 n.
close 264 vb.
mammal 365 n.
credential 466 n.
make certain 473 vb.
endorse 488 vb.

label 547 n.
repair 656 vb.
carry through 725 vb.
badge of rule 743 n.
compact 765 n.
give security 767 vb.
— up
join 45 vb.
conceal 525 vb.
imprison 747 vb.
sea lane
water travel 269 n.
route 624 n.
sea lawyer
reasoner 475 n.
sealed book
unknown thing 491 n.
unintelligibility 517 n.
secret 530 n.
sealed lips
latency 523 n.
sealed off
sealed off 264 adj.
sealed orders
secret 530 n.
sea legs
equilibrium 28 n.
navigation 269 n.
sea level
lowness 210 n.
horizontality 216 n.
sea line
limit 236 n.
sealing wax
adhesive 47 n.
sea lion
mammal 365 n.
sea loch
gulf 345 n.
seal of approval
approbation 923 n.
Sea Lord
naval officer 741 n.
sealskin
skin 226 n.
seam
joint 45 n.
dividing line 92 n.
gap 201 n.
layer 207 n.
store 632 n.
seaman
mariner 270 n.
seamanlike
seamanlike 270 adj.
seamanship
navigation 269 n.
skill 694 n.
art of war 718 n.
sea mark
sailing aid 269 n.
signpost 547 n.
seamless
whole 52 adj.
seamstress
clothier 228 n.
séance
manifestation 522 n.
spiritualism 984 n.
sea nymph
sea nymph 343 n.
mythical being 970 n.
sea of, a
multitude 104 n.
sea of faces
onlookers 441 n.
sea of troubles
adversity 731 n.
seaplane
aircraft 276 n.
sea power
navy 722 n.
authority 733 n.
sear
heat 381 vb.
make insensitive 820 vb.
search
be curious 453 vb.
search 459 n.vb.
pursuit 619 n.
undertaking 672 n.
searcher
inquisitive person 453 n.
enquirer 459 n.
hunter 619 n.
trier 671 n.
searching
inquisitive 453 adj.
oppressive 735 adj.
paining 827 adj.
searchlight
flash 417 n.
lamp 420 n.
search party
search 459 n.
hunter 619 n.
search warrant
warrant 737 n.
seared conscience
impenitence 940 n.
searing
hot 379 adj.
paining 827 adj.
sea rover
mariner 270 n.
robber 789 n.
seascape
spectacle 445 n.
art subject 553 n.
sea serpent
rara avis 84 n.
seashore
edge 234 n.
shore 344 n.
seasick
vomiting 300 adj.
seaside
edge 234 n.
shore 344 n.
pleasure ground 837 n.
season
time 108 n.
period 110 n.
regular return 141 n.
season 388 vb.
make appetizing 390 vb.
qualify 468 vb.
habituate 610 vb.
preserve 666 vb.
mature 669 vb.
social round 882 n.
seasonable
apt 24 adj.
timely 137 adj.
seasonal
periodic 110 adj.
seasonal 141 adj.
celebratory 876 adj.
seasoned
habituated 610 adj.
matured 669 adj.
expert 694 adj.
seasoning
tincture 43 n.
stimulant 174 n.
condiment 389 n.
seat
equilibrium 28 n.
situation 186 n.
station 187 n.
house 192 n.
seat 218 n.
buttocks 238 n.
seat belt
preserver 666 n.
seated, be
sit down 311 vb.
seating
room 183 n.
theatre 594 n.
seat of justice
tribunal 956 n.
sea urchin
marine life 365 n.
sea wall
safeguard 662 n.
obstacle 702 n.
seaway
room 183 n.
water travel 269 n.
route 624 n.
seaweed
plant 366 n.
seaworthy
seafaring 269 adj.
marine 275 adj.
oceanic 343 adj.
perfect 646 adj.
invulnerable 660 adj.
sebaceous
fatty 357 adj.
secant
ratio 85 n.
secateurs
sharp edge 256 n.
farm tool 370 n.
secco
art style 553 n.
secede
dissent 489 vb.
relinquish 621 vb.
revolt 738 vb.
fail in duty 918 vb.
schismatize 978 vb.
secession
tergiversation 603 n.
secessionist
tergiversator 603 n.
revolter 738 n.
schismatic 978 n.
seclude
set apart 46 vb.
exclude 57 vb.
imprison 747 vb.
seclude 883 vb.
seclusion
separation 46 n.
displacement 188 n.
retreat 192 n.
farness 199 n.
island 349 n.
invisibility 444 n.
relinquishment 621 n.
seclusion 883 n.
monasticism 985 n.
second
small quantity 33 n.
inferior 35 n.adj.
sequential 65 adj.
double 91 adj.vb.
period 110 n.
instant 116 n.
angular measure 247 n.
musical note 410 n.
measurement 465 n.
endorse 488 vb.
patronize 703 vb.
auxiliary 707 n.
deputy 755 n.
secondary
inferior 35 adj.
caused 157 adj.
unimportant 639 adj.
imperfect 647 adj.
Secondary school
school 539 n.
second-best
inferior 35 adj.
substitute 150 n.
imperfect 647 adj.
middling 732 adj.
second birth
revival 656 n.
second chance
mercy 905 n.
second childhood
old age 131 n.
folly 499 n.
second-class
inferior 35 adj.
seconder
assenter 488 n.

patron 707 n.
second fiddle
inferior 35 n.
nonentity 639 n.
second-hand
imitative 20 adj.
antiquated 127 adj.
used 673 adj.
second helping
repetition 106 n.
second-in-command
deputy 755 n.
secondly
twice 91 adv.
second nature
habit 610 n.
second opinion
estimate 480 n.
second part
adjunct 40 n.
second place
sequence 65 n.
near place 200 n.
second rank
inferiority 35 n.
second-rate
inferior 35 adj.
trivial 639 adj.
imperfect 647 adj.
middling 732 adj.
seconds
cheapness 812 n.
second self
colleague 707 n.
second sight
vision 438 n.
intuition 476 n.
foresight 510 n.
psychics 984 n.
second thoughts
sequel 67 n.
thought 449 n.
tergiversation 603 n.
amendment 654 n.
regret 830 n.
caution 858 n.
second to none
supreme 34 adj.
best 644 adj.
secrecy
invisibility 444 n.
secrecy 525 n.
taciturnity 582 n.
caution 858 n.
secret
private 80 adj.
dark 418 adj.
invisible 444 adj.
unknown thing 491 n.
unintelligibility 517 n.
occult 523 adj.
information 524 n.
secrecy 525 n.
concealed 525 adj.
secret 530 n.
secret, the
interpretation 520 n.
secret agent
secret service 459 n.
secretarial college
training school 539 n.
secretariat
workshop 687 n.
management 689 n.
position of authority 733 n.
jurisdiction 955 n.
secret art
occultism 984 n.
secretary
recorder 549 n.
official 690 n.
auxiliary 707 n.
servant 742 n.
deputy 755 n.
secret ballot
vote 605 n.
freedom 744 n.
secrete
emit 300 vb.
excrete 302 vb.
conceal 525 vb.
secretive
reticent 525 adj.
cautious 858 adj.
secret passage
hiding-place 527 n.
means of escape 667 n.
secret police
police enquiry 459 n.
secret service
secret service 459 n.
secret society
latency 523 n.
society 708 n.
sect
community 708 n.
party 708 n.
sect 978 n.
sectarian
nonconformist 84 n.
biased 481 adj.
dissentient 489 n.
sectional 708 adj.
sectarian 978 n.adj.
sectarianism
sectarianism 978 n.
section
scission 46 n.
subdivision 53 n.
classification 77 n.
topic 452 n.
formation 722 n.
sectional
fragmentary 53 adj.
excluding 57 adj.
classificatory 77 adj.
sectional 708 adj.
sectarian 978 adj.
sector
subdivision 53 n.
arc 250 n.
battleground 724 n.
secular
secular 110 adj.
lasting 113 adj.
seasonal 141 adj.
irreligious 974 adj.
clerical 986 adj.
laical 987 adj.
secularism
antichristianity 974 n.
secularize, secularise
appropriate 786 vb.
laicize 987 vb.
secure
firm 45 adj.
tighten 45 vb.
be early 135 vb.
fixed 153 adj.
believing 485 adj.
safe 660 adj.
safeguard 660 vb.
give security 767 vb.
— one's object
succeed 727 vb.
secured
completed 725 adj.
promised 764 adj.
secured 767 adj.
security
safety 660 n.
promise 764 n.
security 767 n.
paper money 797 n.
hope 852 n.
dueness 915 n.
security forces
protector 660 n.
security risk
vulnerability 661 n.
sedan chair
vehicle 274 n.
sedate
slow 278 adj.
inexcitable 823 adj.
serious 834 adj.
sedated
tranquil 266 adj.
sedative
moderator 177 n.
drug 658 n.
soporific 679 n.adj.
relief 831 n.
sedentary
quiescent 266 adj.
lowered 311 adj.
sedge
grass 366 n.
sedilia
church interior 990 n.
sediment
leavings 41 n.
thing transferred 272 n.
solid body 324 n.
dirt 649 n.
sedimentary
remaining 41 adj.
indissoluble 324 adj.
sedimentation
condensation 324 n.
sedition
disorder 61 n.
sedition 738 n.
perfidy 930 n.
seditionist
revolutionist 149 n.
agitator 738 n.
revolter 738 n.
malcontent 829 n.
seditious
revolutionary 149 adj.
disobedient 738 adj.
seduce
bribe 612 vb.
induce 612 vb.
delight 826 vb.
cause desire 859 vb.
excite love 887 vb.
debauch 951 vb.
seducer
deceiver 545 n.
motivator 612 n.
libertine 952 n.
seduction
attraction 291 n.
(See **seduce** *)*
seductive
attracting 291 adj.
pleasurable 826 adj.
lovable 887 adj.
seductress
motivator 612 n.
a beauty 841 n.
loose woman 952 n.
sedulous
studious 536 adj.
industrious 678 adj.
sedulous ape
imitator 20 n.
sedulousness
perseverance 600 n.
see
have feeling 374 vb.
scan 438 vb.
see 438 vb.
watch 441 vb.
cognize 447 vb.
detect 484 vb.
know 490 vb.
455 int.
imagine 513 vb.
understand 516 vb.
visit 882 vb.
church office 985 n.
— ahead
assume 471 vb.
foresee 510 vb.
— double
be dim-sighted 440 vb.
be drunk 949 vb.
— eye to eye
assent 488 vb.
concord 710 vb.
— fit
will 595 vb.

— how far one can go
be tentative 461 vb.
— how the wind blows
be tentative 461 vb.
be cautious 858 vb.
— into
enquire 459 vb.
— it all
understand 516 vb.
— it coming
look ahead 124 vb.
expect 507 vb.
foresee 510 vb.
not wonder 865 vb.
— it through
terminate 69 vb.
persevere 600 vb.
carry through 725 vb.
— no difference
not discriminate 464 vb.
— nothing
be incurious 454 vb.
be inattentive 456 vb.
— nothing remarkable
not wonder 865 vb.
— nothing wrong with
approve 923 vb.
— off
start out 296 vb.
dismiss 300 vb.
— one side only
be biased 481 vb.
— one's way to
do easily 701 vb.
— one through
aid 703 vb.
— out
carry through 725 vb.
— red
be violent 176 vb.
go mad 503 vb.
be excitable 822 vb.
get angry 891 vb.
— sense
be sane 502 vb.
— straight
judge 480 vb.
— the difference
discriminate 463 vb.
— the end of
go on 146 vb.
persevere 600 vb.
— the error of one's ways
become pious 979 vb.
— the last of
cease 145 vb.
— the light
discover 484 vb.
be penitent 939 vb.
become pious 979 vb.
— the light of day
begin 68 vb.
— the point
be witty 839 vb.
— the world
travel 267 vb.
— things
be insane 503 vb.
— through
be wise 498 vb.
understand 516 vb.
carry out 725 vb.
not wonder 865 vb.
— to
be mindful 455 vb.
look after 457 vb.
deal with 688 vb.
seeable
visible 433 adj.
seed
small thing 33 n.
class 62 vb.
origin 68 n.
source 156 n.
product 164 n.
genitalia 167 n.
reproduce itself 167 vb.
posterity 170 n.
fertilizer 171 n.
minuteness 196 n.
powder 332 n.
flower 366 n.
cultivate 370 vb.
seedbed
seedbed 156 n.
garden 370 n.
seeded
arranged 62 adj.
chosen 605 adj.
seeded player
proficient person 696 n.
seedling
young plant 132 n.
seedsman
gardener 370 n.
seedy
weakly 163 adj.
sick 651 adj.
dilapidated 655 adj.
beggarly 801 adj.
seeing
vision 438 n.
visibility 443 n.
seeing things
frenzied 503 adj.
seek
be curious 453 vb.
search 459 vb.
pursue 619 vb.
attempt 671 vb.
request 761 vb.
seeker
inquisitive person 453 n.
enquirer 459 n.
hunter 619 n.
petitioner 763 n.
seem
resemble 18 vb.
appear 445 vb.
seeming
appearing 445 adj.
hypocritical 541 adj.
ostensible 614 adj.
seemingly
apparently 445 adv.
probably 471 adv.
supposedly 512 adv.
seemliness
good taste 846 n.
right 913 n.
seemly
fit 24 adj.
advisable 642 adj.
tasteful 846 adj.
seen
evidential 466 adj.
known 490 adj.
seen, be
be visible 443 vb.
be plain 522 vb.
seen in the right places, be
be in fashion 848 vb.
seen with, be
accompany 89 vb.
seep
infiltrate 297 vb.
exude 298 vb.
be wet 341 vb.
seepage
outflow 298 n.
seer
sage 500 n.
oracle 511 n.
visionary 513 n.
preacher 537 n.
sorcerer 983 n.
psychic 984 n.
seersucker
textile 222 n.
seesaw
correlation 12 n.
fluctuation 317 n.
to and fro 317 adv.
be uncertain 474 vb.
be irresolute 601 vb.
pleasure ground 837 n.
seethe
congregate 74 vb.
cook 301 vb.
effervesce 318 vb.
be hot 379 vb.
be excited 821 vb.
see-through
transparent 422 adj.
segment
part 53 n., vb.
piece 53 n.
subdivision 53 n.
component 58 n.
segmentation
scission 46 n.
segregate
set apart 46 vb.
segregation
separation 46 n.
exclusion 57 n.
prejudice 481 n.
seclusion 883 n.
seigneur
master 741 n.
person of rank 868 n.
seigniory
position of authority 733 n.
lands 777 n.
seine
network 222 n.
seisin
possession 773 n.
seismic
revolutionary 149 adj.
violent 176 adj.
oscillating 317 adj.
notable 638 adj.
seismic disturbance
oscillation 317 n.
seismograph
oscillation 317 n.
meter 465 n.
recording instrument 549 n.
seize
halt 145 vb.
understand 516 vb.
arrest 747 vb.
take 786 vb.
— on
make important 638 vb.
— power
take authority 733 vb.
— the chance
profit by 137 vb.
be active 678 vb.
— up
halt 145 vb.
fail 728 vb.
seizure
spasm 318 n.
illness 651 n.
nervous disorders 651 n.
taking 786 n.
loss of right 916 n.
seldom
seldom 140 adv.
seldom occur
be few 105 vb.
select
set apart 46 vb.
discriminate 463 vb.
abstract 592 vb.
select 605 vb.
excellent 644 adj.

selected
chosen 605 adj.
select few
superior 34 n.
selection
accumulation 74 n.
textbook 589 n.
anthology 592 n.
choice 605 n.
selective
separate 46 adj.
discriminating 463 adj.
choosing 605 adj.
Selene
moon 321 n.
lesser deity 967 n.
selenography
astronomy 321 n.
self
intrinsicality 5 n.
identical 13 adj.
self 80 n.
subjectivity 320 n.
spirit 447 n.
self-abasement
humility 872 n.
self-abnegation
humility 872 n.
disinterestedness 931 n.
self-absorption
interiority 224 n.
selfishness 932 n.
self-accusation
penitence 939 n.
self-admiration
pride 871 n.
vanity 873 n.
selfishness 932 n.
self-advertisement
boasting 877 n.
self-aggrandizement, self-aggrandisement
selfishness 932 n.
self-appointed task
voluntary work 597 n.
self-assertion
affirmation 532 n.
insolence 878 n.
self-assurance
vanity 873 n.
self-assured
positive 473 adj.
assertive 532 adj.
self-betrayal
disclosure 526 n.
self-centred
vain 873 adj.
selfish 932 adj.
self-centred person
vain person 873 n.
egotist 932 n.
self-chastisement
asceticism 945 n.
self-command
resolution 599 n.
inexcitability 823 n.
self-communing
thoughtful 449 adj.
self-complacency
content 828 n.
vanity 873 n.
self-condemned
repentant 939 adj.
self-confidence
positiveness 473 n.
courage 855 n.
pride 871 n.
self-confident
resolute 599 adj.
self-congratulation
rejoicing 835 n.
vanity 873 n.
self-conscious
affected 850 adj.
nervous 854 adj.
self-consciousness
intellect 447 n.
self-considering
selfish 932 adj.
self-consistent
uniform 16 adj.
agreeing 24 adj.
true 494 adj.
self-contained
complete 54 adj.
independent 744 adj.
self-contradiction
error 495 n.
self-contradictory
impossible 470 adj.
illogical 477 adj.
self-control
moderation 177 n.
will 595 n.
resolution 599 n.
restraint 747 n.
inexcitability 823 n.
disinterestedness 931 n.
virtues 933 n.
temperance 942 n.
self-convicted
repentant 939 adj.
condemned 961 adj.
self-correcting
compensatory 31 adj.
self-deception
credulity 487 n.
error 495 n.
deception 542 n.
self-defence
resistance 715 n.
vindication 927 n.
self-denial
severity 735 n.
disinterestedness 931 n.
temperance 942 n.
asceticism 945 n.
self-depreciation
underestimation 483 n.
mental dishonesty 543 n.
humility 872 n.
modesty 874 n.
self-destruct
destroy 165 vb.
self-determination
will 595 n.
independence 744 n.
self-devotion
willingness 597 n.
resolution 599 n.
disinterestedness 931 n.
oblation 981 n.
self-discipline
temperance 942 n.
self-distrust
nervousness 854 n.
modesty 874 n.
self-education
culture 490 n.
learning 536 n.
self-effacing
humble 872 adj.
modest 874 adj.
disinterested 931 adj.
self-employed
businesslike 622 adj.
independent 744 adj.
self-esteem
pride 871 n.
vanity 873 n.
self-evident
certain 473 adj.
manifest 522 adj.
self-evident truth
premise 475 n.
axiom 496 n.
self-examination
enquiry 459 n.
act of worship 981 n.
self-exile
seclusion 883 n.
self-existent
existing 1 adj.
godlike 965 adj.
self-explanatory
intelligible 516 adj.
self-expression
independence 744 n.
self-forgetful
disinterested 931 adj.
self-glorification
vanity 873 n.
boasting 877 n.
self-governing
independent 744 adj.
self-government
government 733 n.
self-help
aid 703 n.
selfhood
self 80 n.
subjectivity 320 n.
self-importance
vanity 873 n.
ostentation 875 n.
self-imposed
voluntary 597 adj.
self-imposed task
vocation 622 n.
undertaking 672 n.
self-improvement
learning 536 n.
virtue 933 n.
self-indulgence
pleasure 376 n.
selfishness 932 n.
intemperance 943 n.
sensualism 944 n.
self-interest
selfishness 932 n.
selfish
greedy 859 adj.
selfish 932 adj.
irreligious 974 adj.
selfishness
selfishness 932 n.
self-knowledge
knowledge 490 n.
humility 872 n.
selfless
disinterested 931 adj.
self-love
vanity 873 n.
selfishness 932 n.
self-made man/ woman
victor 727 n.
rich person 800 n.
self-mastery
resolution 599 n.
self-mortification
asceticism 945 n.
self-motivated
independent 744 adj.
self-opinionated person
doctrinaire 473 n.
self-pity
pity 905 n.
selfishness 932 n.
self-pitying
melancholic 834 adj.
self-possession
resolution 599 n.
inexcitability 823 n.
self-praise
pride 871 n.
vanity 873 n.
praise 923 n.
self-preservation
preservation 666 n.
selfishness 932 n.
self-protection
defence 713 n.
self-raising
light 323 adj.
self-regarding
selfish 932 adj.
self-reliant
resolute 599 adj.
independent 744 adj.
unfearing 855 adj.
self-repression
inexcitability 823 n.
self-reproach
regret 830 n.
penitence 939 n.

self-respect
pride 871 n.
self-restraint
resolution 599 n.
inexcitability 823 n.
temperance 942 n.
self-righteous
affected 850 adj.
pietistic 979 adj.
self-rule
independence 744 n.
self-sacrifice
offering 781 n.
disinterestedness 931 n.
oblation 981 n.
selfsame
identical 13 adj.
self-satisfaction
content 828 n.
vanity 873 n.
self-seeking
selfish 932 adj.
self-service
meal 301 n.
provisioning 633 adj.
self-serving
selfish 932 adj.
self-starter
start 68 n.
self-styled
misnamed 562 adj.
self-sufficiency
completeness 54 n.
sufficiency 635 n.
independence 744 n.
wealth 800 n.
self-supporting
independent 744 adj.
self-surrender
disinterestedness 931 n.
piety 979 n.
self-taught
studious 536 adj.
self-willed
volitional 595 adj.
wilful 602 adj.
disobedient 738 adj.
sell
absurdity 497 n.
advertise 528 vb.
trickery 542 n.
deceive 542 vb.
provide 633 vb.
sell 793 vb.
— an idea to
convince 485 vb.
— down the river
inform 524 vb.
be dishonest 930 vb.
— for
cost 809 vb.
— like hot cakes
be sold 793 vb.
— off
not retain 779 vb.
sell 793 vb.
— one's honour
be dishonest 930 vb.
— out
be dishonest 930 vb.
— short
detract 926 vb.
seller
seller 793 n.
pedlar 794 n.
seller's market
scarcity 636 n.
prosperity 730 n.
request 761 n.
market 796 n.
dearness 811 n.
sell-out
perfidy 930 n.
selvage, selvedge
weaving 222 n.
edging 234 n.
semanteme
word 559 n.
part of speech 564 n.
semantic
semantic 514 adj.
semantics
meaning 514 n.
linguistics 557 n.
semaphore
communicate 524 vb.
telecommunication 531 n.
signal 547 n.vb.
semasiology
linguistics 557 n.
etymology 559 n.
semblance
similarity 18 n.
mimicry 20 n.
copy 22 n.
appearance 445 n.
probability 471 n.
semen
genitalia 167 n.
fertilizer 171 n.
semester
time 108 n.
period 110 n.
semi-
fragmentary 53 adj.
incomplete 55 adj.
bisected 92 adj.
semibreve
notation 410 n.
semicircle
arc 250 n.
semicircular
curved 248 adj.
round 250 adj.
semicolon
punctuation 547 n.
semiconductor
electricity 160 n.
semiconscious
insensible 375 adj.
semidarkness
half-light 419 n.
semidetached
architectural 192 adj.
semifinal
contest 716 n.
semiliquid
fluid 335 adj.
semiliquid 354 adj.
semiliterate
dabbling 491 adj.
semilunar
curved 248 adj.
seminal
causal 156 adj.
generative 167 adj.
seminar
teaching 534 n.
class 538 n.
conference 584 n.
seminary
training school 539 n.
semiology, semiotics
meaning 514 n.
hermeneutics 520 n.
symbology 547 n.
language 557 n.
semiopaque
semitransparent 424 adj.
semiprecious stone
gem 844 n.
semiquaver
notation 410 n.
semiskilled
unskilled 695 adj.
Semitic deities
Semitic deities 967 n.
semitone
interval 201 n.
musical note 410 n.
semitransparency
semitransparency 424 n.
semivowel
speech sound 398 n.
semolina
dessert 301 n.
sempstress
clothier 228 n.
SEN
nurse 658 n.
senate
seniority 131 n.
parliament 692 n.
senator
councillor 692 n.
master 741 n.
aristocrat 868 n.
senatorial government
government 733 n.
send
displace 188 vb.
move 265 vb.
send 272 vb.
emit 300 vb.
give 781 vb.
excite 821 vb.
delight 826 vb.
— after
pursue 619 vb.
— back
put off 136 vb.
reject 607 vb.
— down
abate 37 vb.
eject 300 vb.
— flying
strike 279 vb.
propel 287 vb.
— for
pursue 619 vb.
command 737 vb.
— forth
publish 528 vb.
— home
disperse 75 vb.
liberate 746 vb.
— into ecstasies
excite 821 vb.
— mad
make mad 503 vb.
— on a fool's errand
befool 542 vb.
— one away with a flea in his/her ear
repel 292 vb.
dismiss 300 vb.
humiliate 872 vb.
be rude 885 vb.
— one off his/her head
make mad 503 vb.
— one's apologies
refuse 760 vb.
— out
emit 300 vb.
commission 751 vb.
— packing
repel 292 vb.
dismiss 300 vb.
— to blazes
be insolent 878 vb.
curse 899 vb.
— to Coventry
set apart 46 vb.
exclude 57 vb.
make unwelcome 883 vb.
— to sleep
render insensible 375 vb.
fatigue 684 vb.
be tedious 838 vb.
— up
augment 36 vb.
act 594 vb.
satirize 851 vb.
— word
communicate 524 vb.
sender
transferrer 272 n.
send-off
start 68 n.
valediction 296 n.

senescent
ageing 131 adj.
seneschal
officer 741 n.
retainer 742 n.
keeper 749 n.
senile
ageing 131 adj.
impotent 161 adj.
foolish 499 adj.
deteriorated 655 adj.
senility
old age 131 n.
senior
superior 34 n.adj.
older 131 adj.
master 741 n.
senior citizen
old person 133 n.
senior common room
scholar 492 n.
teacher 537 n.
seniority
seniority 131 n.
authority 733 n.
senior service
naval man 722 n.
senna pods
purgative 658 n.
sennet
tune 412 n.
call 547 n.
señor
male 372 n.
title 870 n.
señora, señorita
lady 373 n.
sensation
sense 374 n.
news 529 n.
feeling 818 n.
prodigy 864 n.
sensational
striking 374 adj.
dramatic 594 adj.
excellent 644 adj.
exciting 821 adj.
wonderful 864 adj.
showy 875 adj.
sensationalism
publicity 528 n.
exaggeration 546 n.
ostentation 875 n.
sense
sense 374 n.
have feeling 374 vb.
intellect 447 n.
intuit 476 vb.
detect 484 vb.
intelligence 498 n.
meaning 514 n.
feeling 818 n.
feel 818 vb.
sense datum
element 319 n.
senseless
insensible 375 adj.
absurd 497 adj.
foolish 499 adj.
meaningless 515 adj.
sense of duty
duty 917 n.
sense of humour
laughter 835 n.
wit 839 n.
sense of obligation
gratitude 907 n.
sense of occasion
discrimination 463 n.
sense of responsibility
observance 768 n.
probity 929 n.
sense organ
sense 374 n.
instrument 628 n.
sense-perception
sense 374 n.
senses
intellect 447 n.
sanity 502 n.
sensibility
liability 180 n.
sensibility 374 n.
discrimination 463 n.
moral sensibility 819 n.
sensible
material 319 adj.
sentient 374 adj.
rational 475 adj.
wise 498 adj.
useful 640 adj.
feeling 818 adj.
impressible 819 adj.
sensible of
knowing 490 adj.
sensitive
sentient 374 adj.
attentive 455 adj.
discriminating 463 adj.
accurate 494 adj.
elegant 575 adj.
receiving 782 adj.
feeling 818 adj.
sensitive 819 adj.
excitable 822 adj.
tasteful 846 adj.
irascible 892 adj.
sensitiveness
sensibility 374 n.
moral sensibility 819 n.
sensitive plant
sensibility 374 n.
moral sensibility 819 n.
sensitivity
sensibility 374 n.
discrimination 463 n.
persuadability 612 n.
moral sensibility 819 n.
sensitize, sensitise
cause feeling 374 vb.
sensor
detector 484 n.
sensorium
sense 374 n.
intellect 447 n.
sensory
sentient 374 adj.
feeling 818 adj.
sensual
material 319 adj.
sensuous 376 adj.
feeling 818 adj.
intemperate 943 adj.
sensual 944 adj.
lecherous 951 adj.
sensualism
intemperance 943 n.
sensualism 944 n.
sensualist
sensualist 944 n.
sensuality
materiality 319 n.
pleasure 376 n.
sensualism 944 n.
sensuous
sentient 374 adj.
sensuous 376 adj.
feeling 818 adj.
pleasurable 826 adj.
sensuousness
sensibility 374 n.
pleasure 376 n.
sentence
period 110 n.
judgment 480 n.
phrase 563 n.
condemn 961 vb.
penalty 963 n.
sententious
judicial 480 adj.
aphoristic 496 adj.
concise 569 adj.
forceful 571 adj.
sentient
sentient 374 adj.
feeling 818 adj.
impressible 819 adj.
sentiment
opinion 485 n.
feeling 818 n.
excitation 821 n.
love 887 n.
sentimental
foolish 499 adj.
feeble 572 adj.
feeling 818 adj.
impressible 819 adj.
loving 887 adj.
sentimentalism
moral sensibility 819 n.
excitation 821 n.
sentimentality
feeling 818 n.
moral sensibility 819 n.
love 887 n.
sentry, sentinel
doorkeeper 264 n.
spectator 441 n.
surveillance 457 n.
protector 660 n.
warner 664 n.
defender 713 n.
armed force 722 n.
keeper 749 n.
sentry box
compartment 194 n.
sentry-go
surveillance 457 n.
sepal
flower 366 n.
separability
disunion 46 n.
noncoherence 49 n.
separable
severable 46 adj.
separate
unrelated 10 adj.
different 15 adj.
separate 46 adj.vb.
decompose 51 vb.
fragmentary 53 adj.
extraneous 59 adj.
discontinuous 72 adj.
unassembled 75 adj.
disperse 75 vb.
open 263 vb.
diverge 294 vb.
discriminate 463 vb.
select 605 vb.
divorce 896 vb.
(See **separation** *)*
— the sheep from the goats
discriminate 463 vb.
separates
suit 228 n.
separation
separation 46 n.
noncoherence 49 n.
unity 88 n.
farness 199 n.
gap 201 n.
partition 231 n.
dissension 709 n.
liberation 746 n.
seclusion 883 n.
schism 978 n.
(See **separate** *)*
separatist
dissentient 489 n.
schismatic 978 n.
sepia
brown pigment 430 n.
sepoy
soldier 722 n.
sepsis
infection 651 n.
sept
race 11 n.
septennium
over five 99 n.
septentrional
opposite 240 adj.

septet
over five 99 n.
duet 412 n.
septic
bad 645 adj.
unclean 649 adj.
toxic 653 adj.
septicaemia
infection 651 n.
septic tank
sink 649 n.
septuagenarian
old person 133 n.
Septuagint
scripture 975 n.
septum
partition 231 n.
septuple
fifth and over 99 adj.
sepulchral
funereal 364 adj.
resonant 404 adj.
hoarse 407 adj.
sepulchre
tomb 364 n.
holy place 990 n.
sequel
sequel 67 n.
end 69 n.
posteriority 120 n.
effect 157 n.
sequence
relativeness 9 n.
order 60 n.
sequence 65 n.
continuity 71 n.
posteriority 120 n.
following 284 n.
poem 593 n.
sequential
sequential 65 adj.
subsequent 120 adj.
caused 157 adj.
sequester
set apart 46 vb.
exclude 57 vb.
deprive 786 vb.
not pay 805 vb.
seclude 883 vb.
sequestered
tranquil 266 adj.
invisible 444 adj.
secluded 883 adj.
sequestrate
deprive 786 vb.
sequestration
expropriation 786 n.
seclusion 883 n.
penalty 963 n.
sequin
circle 250 n.
finery 844 n.
sequoia
tall creature 209 n.
seraglio
womankind 373 n.
seraph
good person 937 n.
angel 968 n.
seraphic
virtuous 933 adj.
angelic 968 adj.
pietistic 979 adj.
Serapis
Egyptian deities 967 n.
sere
continuity 71 n.
sere, sear
dry 342 adj.
deteriorated 655 adj.
serenade
musical piece 412 n.
sing 413 vb.
wooing 889 n.
serenader
vocalist 413 n.
serendipity
chance 159 n.
discovery 484 n.
serene
tranquil 266 adj.
transparent 422 adj.
inexcitable 823 adj.
Serene Highness
title 870 n.
serenity
inexcitability 823 n.
content 828 n.
lack of wonder 865 n.
serf
farmer 370 n.
slave 742 n.
possessor 776 n.
commoner 869 n.
serfdom
servitude 745 n.
serge
textile 222 n.
sergeant
soldiery 722 n.
army officer 741 n.
sergeant major
uniformist 16 n.
tyrant 735 n.
army officer 741 n.
serial
relative 9 adj.
continuous 71 adj.
recurrence 106 n.
periodical 141 adj.
reading matter 589 n.
serialization, serialisation
sequence 65 n.
continuity 71 n.
periodicity 141 n.
serialize, serialise
publish 528 vb.
serial place
degree 27 n.
serial place 73 n.
seriatim
in order 60 adv.
severally 80 adv.
sericulture
animal husbandry 369 n.
series
all 52 n.
order 60 n.
sequence 65 n.
series 71 n.
accumulation 74 n.
number 85 n.
recurrence 106 n.
continuance 146 n.
following 284 n.
edition 589 n.
serif
print-type 587 n.
serigraphy
printing 555 n.
seriocomic
funny 849 adj.
serious
great 32 adj.
attentive 455 adj.
wise 498 adj.
resolute 599 adj.
intending 617 adj.
important 638 adj.
dangerous 661 adj.
serious 834 adj.
dull 840 adj.
heinous 934 adj.
seriously
painfully 32 adv.
positively 32 adv.
affirmatively 532 adv.
resolutely 599 adv.
seriousness
vigour 571 n.
warm feeling 818 n.
seriousness 834 n.
(See **serious** *)*
serjeant-at-law
lawyer 958 n.
sermon
lecture 534 n.
diffuseness 570 n.
oration 579 n.
dissertation 591 n.
sermonize, sermonise
orate 579 vb.
be pious 979 vb.
serpent
serpent 251 n.
reptile 365 n.
sibilation 406 n.
horn 414 n.
deceiver 545 n.
bane 659 n.
slyboots 698 n.
noxious animal 904 n.
knave 938 n.
Satan 969 n.
serpentine
snaky 251 adj.
animal 365 adj.
cunning 698 adj.
serrated
angular 247 adj.
toothed 256 adj.
serration
sharpness 256 n.
roughness 259 n.
notch 260 n.
serried
cohesive 48 adj.
assembled 74 adj.
dense 324 adj.
serrulate
notched 260 adj.
serum
blood 335 n.
fluid 335 n.
servant
instrument 628 n.
worker 686 n.
auxiliary 707 n.
servant 742 n.
serve
be inferior 35 vb.
unite with 45 vb.
operate 173 vb.
follow 284 vb.
propel 287 vb.
look after 457 vb.
benefit 615 vb.
function 622 vb.
be instrumental 628 vb.
suffice 635 vb.
be useful 640 vb.
be expedient 642 vb.
work 682 vb.
minister to 703 vb.
obey 739 vb.
serve 742 vb.
be subject 745 vb.
apportion 783 vb.
— one right
be rightly served 714 vb.
be just 913 vb.
— one's turn
be useful 640 vb.
— up
provide 633 vb.
server
auxiliary 707 n.
church officer 986 n.
ritualist 988 n.
service
agency 173 n.
benefit 615 n.
job 622 n.
instrumentality 628 n.
provision 633 n.
utility 640 n.
restore 656 vb.
preserve 666 vb.
use 673 n.
aid 703 n.
loyalty 739 n.
service 745 n.
sale 793 n.
kind act 897 n.

cult 981 n.
church service 988 n.
serviceable
operative 173 adj.
instrumental 628 adj.
useful 640 adj.
service-book
office-book 988 n.
serviceman, servicewoman
soldier 722 n.
services, the
army 722 n.
servile
conformable 83 adj.
subject 745 adj.
inglorious 867 adj.
servile 879 adj.
respectful 920 adj.
flattering 925 adj.
servility
servility 879 n.
serving
meal 301 n.
serving a sentence
imprisoned 747 adj.
servitor
domestic 742 n.
servitude
submission 721 n.
servitude 745 n.
servomechanism
machine 630 n.
servomotor
machine 630 n.
sesquicentenary
fifth and over 99 adj.
special day 876 n.
sesquipedalian
long 203 adj.
diffuse 570 adj.
ornate 574 adj.
sessile
cohesive 48 adj.
session
council 692 n.
sessions
lawcourt 956 n.
sestet
verse form 593 n.
set
modality 7 n.
uniformity 16 n.
firm 45 adj.
affix 45 vb.
coherence 48 n.
all 52 n.
component 58 n.
arrange 62 vb.
series 71 n.
accumulation 74 n.
band 74 n.
group 74 n.
sort 77 n.
unit 88 n.
young plant 132 n.
stabilize 153 vb.
tendency 179 n.
situated 186 adj.
place 187 vb.
pendency 217 n.
support 218 vb.
form 243 n.
direction 281 n.
descend 309 vb.
be dense 324 vb.
current 350 n.
cultivate 370 vb.
appearance 445 n.
positive 473 adj.
class 538 n.
printed 587 adj.
stage set 594 n.
obstinate 602 adj.
usual 610 adj.
collection 632 n.
doctor 658 vb.
make ready 669 vb.
attempt 671 n.
association 706 n.
party 708 n.
contest 716 n.
beautify 841 vb.
hairdressing 843 n.
decorate 844 vb.
— a bad example
make wicked 934 vb.
— about
begin 68 vb.
work 682 vb.
— a course
navigate 269 vb.
— against
compared 462 adj.
dissuade 613 vb.
make quarrels 709 vb.
cause dislike 861 vb.
— an example
be an example 23 vb.
motivate 612 vb.
behave 688 vb.
be virtuous 933 vb.
— apart
differentiate 15 vb.
set apart 46 vb.
exclude 57 vb.
discriminate 463 vb.
select 605 vb.
— aside
displace 188 vb.
reject 607 vb.
store 632 vb.
abrogate 752 vb.
not observe 769 vb.
— at naught
underestimate 483 vb.
oppose 704 vb.
defy 711 vb.
— at odds
cause dislike 861 vb.
make enemies 881 vb.
— back
put off 136 vb.
hinder 702 vb.
— by the ears
make quarrels 709 vb.
— down
place 187 vb.
let fall 311 vb.
write 586 vb.
— down to
attribute 158 vb.
— foot in
enter 297 vb.
— forth
start out 296 vb.
— free
deliver 668 vb.
give scope 744 vb.
liberate 746 vb.
— going
initiate 68 vb.
cause 156 vb.
impel 279 vb.
undertake 672 vb.
— in
begin 68 vb.
stay 144 vb.
tend 179 vb.
rain 350 vb.
— in motion
initiate 68 vb.
dispose of 673 vb.
— in order
compose 56 vb.
arrange 62 vb.
make ready 669 vb.
— no store by
underestimate 483 vb.
doubt 486 vb.
hold cheap 922 vb.
— off
correlate 12 vb.
set off 31 vb.
initiate 68 vb.
shoot 287 vb.
show 522 vb.
beautify 841 vb.
decorate 844 vb.
— on
incite 612 vb.
attack 712 vb.
— one on his/her legs/feet
strengthen 162 vb.
aid 703 vb.
— one's cap at
pursue 619 vb.
desire 859 vb.
court 889 vb.
— one's face against
oppose 704 vb.
refuse 760 vb.
— one's heart/mind on
be resolute 599 vb.
desire 859 vb.
— one's mind at rest
tranquillize 823 vb.
— one's shoulder to the wheel
undertake 672 vb.
— one's sights
aim 281 vb.
— one's teeth on edge
be sour 393 vb.
displease 827 vb.
— on fire
burn 381 vb.
excite 821 vb.
— on foot
initiate 68 vb.
— on its feet
stabilize 153 vb.
— out
arrange 62 vb.
travel 267 vb.
start out 296 vb.
show 522 vb.
dissertate 591 vb.
— right
rectify 654 vb.
vindicate 927 vb.
— sail
navigate 269 vb.
voyage 269 vb.
start out 296 vb.
— store by
make important 638 vb.
approve 923 vb.
— the ball rolling
initiate 68 vb.
— the cat among the pigeons
surprise 508 vb.
— the fashion
influence 178 vb.
motivate 612 vb.
be in fashion 848 vb.
— the pace
motivate 612 vb.
— the Thames on fire
attempt the impossible 470 vb.
— to
begin 68 vb.
eat 301 vb.
be resolute 599 vb.
undertake 672 vb.
work 682 vb.
fight 716 vb.
— to music
compose music 413 vb.
— to rights
repair 656 vb.
— towards
tend 179 vb.
— up
compose 56 vb.
arrange 62 vb.

auspicate 68 vb.
stabilize 153 vb.
cause 156 vb.
strengthen 162 vb.
place 187 vb.
make vertical 215 vb.
elevate 310 vb.
print 587 vb.
cure 656 vb.
— watch
invigilate 457 vb.
setback
disappointment 509 n.
hitch 702 n.
adversity 731 n.
set books
curriculum 534 n.
set fair
warm 379 adj.
palmy 730 adj.
set in one's ways
obstinate 602 adj.
set in one's ways, be
be wont 610 vb.
setose
hairy 259 adj.
set piece
article 591 n.
stage show 594 n.
set square
angular measure 247 n.
gauge 465 n.
sett
paving 226 n.
settee
seat 218 n.
setter
dog 365 n.
set theory
mathematics 86 n.
reasoning 475 n.
setting
situation 186 n.
surroundings 230 n.
musical piece 412 n.
view 438 n.
spectacle 445 n.
stage set 594 n.
hairdressing 843 n.
ornamental art 844 n.
settle
arrange 62 vb.
terminate 69 vb.
be stable 153 vb.
prevail 178 vb.
place oneself 187 vb.
dwell 192 vb.
seat 218 n.
be quiescent 266 vb.
descend 309 vb.
murder 362 vb.
make certain 473 vb.
judge 480 vb.
predetermine 608 vb.
contract 765 vb.
appropriate 786 vb.
pay 804 vb.
— differences
pacify 719 vb.
— down
be stable 153 vb.
be quiescent 266 vb.
sleep 679 vb.
— for
bargain 791 vb.
— in
enter 297 vb.
— on
choose 605 vb.
settled
ending 69 adj.
established 153 adj.
situated 186 adj.
located 187 adj.
native 191 adj.
quiescent 266 adj.
positive 473 adj.
usual 610 adj.
settlement
territory 184 n.
location 187 n.
station 187 n.
inhabitants 191 n.
compact 765 n.
transfer 780 n.
payment 804 n.
settler
settler 191 n.
incomer 297 n.
set-to
quarrel 709 n.
fight 716 n.
set-up
circumstance 8 n.
composition 56 n.
structure 331 n.
set upon
resolute 599 adj.
desiring 859 adj.
seven
over five 99 n.
seven deadly sins
vice 934 n.
seven-league boots
speeder 277 n.
magic instrument 983 n.
seven seas, the
ocean 343 n.
seventh
fifth and over 99 adj.
musical note 410 n.
Seventh-day Adventist
sectarian 978 n.
seventh heaven
happiness 824 n.
heaven 971 n.
seventy
twenty and over 99 n.
seven wonders of the world
prodigy 864 n.
sever
disunite 46 vb.
severable
severable 46 adj.
brittle 330 adj.
several
special 80 adj.
plurality 101 n.
many 104 adj.
severally
separately 46 adv.
severally 80 adv.
severance
subtraction 39 n.
separation 46 n.
severe
exorbitant 32 adj.
strong 162 adj.
vigorous 174 adj.
violent 176 adj.
plain 573 adj.
severe 735 adj.
paining 827 adj.
serious 834 adj.
fastidious 862 adj.
ungracious 885 adj.
pitiless 906 adj.
ascetic 945 adj.
severity
narrow mind 481 n.
severity 735 n.
inhumanity 898 n.
Sèvres china
pottery 381 n.
sew
join 45 vb.
tie 45 vb.
produce 164 vb.
sewage
leavings 41 n.
swill 649 n.
sewer
drain 351 n.
stench 397 n.
badness 645 n.
sink 649 n.
insalubrity 653 n.
sewerage
cleansing 648 n.
sewn up
completed 725 adj.
sex
coition 45 n.
classification 77 n.
propagation 167 n.
life 360 n.
sexagenarian
old person 133 n.
sex appeal
attraction 291 n.
inducement 612 n.
pleasurableness 826 n.
beauty 841 n.
lovableness 887 n.
sex discrimination
injustice 914 n.
sexism
prejudice 481 n.
sexist
biased 481 adj.
sexless
impotent 161 adj.
sex maniac
libertine 952 n.
sexology
medical art 658 n.
sexpot
loose woman 952 n.
sextant
angular measure 247 n.
sailing aid 269 n.
gauge 465 n.
sextet
over five 99 n.
duet 412 n.
sextodecimo
edition 589 n.
sexton
interment 364 n.
church officer 986 n.
sextuple
fifth and over 99 adj.
sexual
generic 77 adj.
generative 167 adj.
sensual 944 adj.
sexual desire
libido 859 n.
sexual intercourse
coition 45 n.
sexual inversion
abnormality 84 n.
sexuality
sensualism 944 n.
unchastity 951 n.
sexy
personable 841 adj.
erotic 887 adj.
impure 951 adj.
sforzando
adagio 412 adv.
sfumato
painted 553 adj.
shabbiness
inferiority 35 n.
poverty 801 n.
improbity 930 n.
shabby
unimportant 639 adj.
dilapidated 655 adj.
beggarly 801 adj.
parsimonious 816 adj.
disreputable 867 adj.
dishonest 930 adj.
shack
small house 192 n.

shackle
tie 45 vb.
halter 47 n.
encumbrance 702 n.
fetter 747 vb.
fetter 748 n.
shackled
restrained 747 adj.
captive 750 adj.
shade
insubstantial thing 4 n.
differentiate 15 vb.
degree 27 n.
small quantity 33 n.
shade 226 n.
corpse 363 n.
refrigerate 382 vb.
darken 418 vb.
dimness 419 n.
curtain 421 n.
screen 421 n.vb.
hue 425 n.
qualify 468 vb.
conceal 525 vb.
paint 553 vb.
safeguard 660 vb.
refresh 685 vb.
relieve 831 vb.
ghost 970 n.
— off
shade off 27 vb.
shading
obscuration 418 n.
painting 553 n.
shadoof
extractor 304 n.
irrigator 341 n.
shadow
insubstantial thing 4 n.
analogue 18 n.
imitation 20 n.
copy 22 n.
compeer 28 n.
small quantity 33 n.
concomitant 89 n.
thinness 206 n.
follow 284 vb.
refrigerate 382 vb.
darkness 418 n.
dimness 419 n.
screen 421 vb.
colour 425 vb.
fantasy 513 n.
pursue 619 vb.
auxiliary 707 n.
close friend 880 n.
— forth
predict 511 vb.
represent 551 vb.
shadow boxing
ideality 513 n.
pugilism 716 n.
shadow cabinet
futurity 124 n.
preparation 669 n.
shadowgraph
photography 551 n.
shadowing
police enquiry 459 n.
shadow of death
death 361 n.
danger 661 n.
shadow of one's former self
dilapidation 655 n.
shadow play
stage play 594 n.
shadowy
insubstantial 4 adj.
inconsiderable 33 adj.
amorphous 244 adj.
immaterial 320 adj.
dark 418 adj.
shadowy 419 adj.
invisible 444 adj.
uncertain 474 adj.
imaginary 513 adj.
puzzling 517 adj.
shady
cold 380 adj.
dark 418 adj.
shadowy 419 adj.
screened 421 adj.
disreputable 867 adj.
dishonest 930 adj.
lawbreaking 954 adj.
shaft
depth 211 n.
pillar 218 n.
excavation 255 n.
sharp point 256 n.
tunnel 263 n.
flash 417 n.
tool 630 n.
missile weapon 723 n.
shag
hair 259 n.
bird 365 n.
tobacco 388 n.
shaggy
hairy 259 adj.
shaggy dog story
fable 543 n.
witticism 839 n.
shagreen
skin 226 n.
shah
sovereign 741 n.
shake
mix 43 vb.
come unstuck 49 vb.
derange 63 vb.
vary 152 vb.
weaken 163 vb.
force 176 vb.
impulse 279 n.
brandish 317 vb.
oscillate 317 vb.
be agitated 318 vb.
be cold 380 vb.
roll 403 vb.
musical note 410 n.
cause doubt 486 vb.
dissuade 613 vb.
impair 655 vb.
show feeling 818 vb.
impress 821 vb.
laugh 835 vb.
quake 854 vb.
threaten 900 vb.
— hands
make peace 719 vb.
be friendly 880 vb.
greet 884 vb.
— hands on
contract 765 vb.
bargain 791 vb.
— off
unstick 49 vb.
outstrip 277 vb.
eject 300 vb.
elude 667 vb.
— one's fist
defy 711 vb.
— one's head
dissent 489 vb.
negate 533 vb.
refuse 760 vb.
deprecate 762 vb.
disapprove 924 vb.
— up
agitate 318 vb.
animate 821 vb.
shakedown
bed 218 n.
shaken
agitated 318 adj.
irresolute 601 adj.
shaker
mixture 43 n.
shakes, the
agitation 318 n.
illness 651 n.
Shakespearean
poetic 593 adj.
shake-up
revolution 149 n.
shaking
agitated 318 adj.
nervous 854 adj.
shako
headgear 228 n.
shaky
flimsy 163 adj.
weak 163 adj.
dilapidated 655 adj.
unsafe 661 adj.
nervous 854 adj.
dishonest 930 adj.
shale
brittleness 330 n.
rock 344 n.
shallots
vegetable 301 n.
shallow
inconsiderable 33 adj.
shallow 212 adj.
dabbling 491 adj.
foolish 499 adj.
trivial 639 adj.
affected 850 adj.
shallowness
shallowness 212 n.
inattention 456 n.
sciolism 491 n.
shallows
shallowness 212 n.
pitfall 663 n.
shalom!
295 int.
shaly
layered 207 adj.
territorial 344 adj.
sham
mimicry 20 n.
imitate 20 vb.
dissemble 541 vb.
sham 542 n.
spurious 542 adj.
mental dishonesty 543 n.
stratagem 698 n.
shaman
sage 500 n.
sorcerer 983 n.
priest 986 n.
shamble
walk 267 vb.
move slowly 278 vb.
shambles
confusion 61 n.
havoc 165 n.
slaughterhouse 362 n.
bungling 695 n.
shambling
clumsy 695 adj.
shame
disrepute 867 n.
slur 867 n.
shame 867 vb.
humiliation 872 n.
wrong 914 n.
defame 926 vb.
improbity 930 n.
wickedness 934 n.
purity 950 n.
shame, a
regretted 830 adj.
shamefaced
modest 874 adj.
guilty 936 adj.
shameful
evil 616 adj.
bad 645 adj.
discreditable 867 adj.
heinous 934 adj.
shameless
undisguised 522 adj.
thick-skinned 820 adj.
vulgar 847 adj.
insolent 878 adj.
dishonest 930 adj.
wicked 934 adj.
unchaste 951 adj.
shampoo
cleanser 648 n.
clean 648 vb.

hairwash 843 n.
shamrock
three 93 n.
plant 366 n.
heraldry 547 n.
shandy
alcoholic drink 301 n.
shanghai
ensnare 542 vb.
take away 786 vb.
Shangri-La
fantasy 513 n.
shank
stand 218 n.
leg 267 n.
print-type 587 n.
Shanks's pony
pedestrianism 267 n.
shantung
textile 222 n.
shanty
small house 192 n.
vocal music 412 n.
shantytown
housing 192 n.
shape
modality 7 n.
sort 77 n.
make conform 83 vb.
convert 147 vb.
outline 233 n.
form 243 n.vb.
structure 331 n.
appearance 445 n.
feature 445 n.
educate 534 vb.
represent 551 vb.
plan 623 vb.
decorate 844 vb.
ghost 970 n.
— up well
give hope 852 vb.
shapeless
amorphous 244 adj.
unsightly 842 adj.
shapely
symmetrical 245 adj.
shapely 841 adj.
shard, sherd
piece 53 n.
share
part 53 n.
be one of 58 vb.
sharp edge 256 n.
mete out 465 vb.
title deed 767 n.
participation 775 n.
give 781 vb.
portion 783 n.
apportion 783 vb.
feel 818 vb.
— in
participate 775 vb.
— out
part 53 vb.
apportion 783 vb.
sharecropper
farmer 370 n.
shareholder
owner 776 n.
receiver 782 n.
share-out
participation 775 n.
portion 783 n.
share-pusher
merchant 794 n.
sharing
equal 28 adj.
sharing 775 adj.
shark
fish 365 n.
trickster 545 n.
defrauder 789 n.
sharkskin
textile 222 n.
sharp
keen 174 adj.
violent 176 adj.
sharp 256 adj.
sentient 374 adj.
striking 374 adj.
pungent 388 adj.
sour 393 adj.
strident 407 adj.
musical note 410 n.
discordant 411 adj.
intelligent 498 adj.
expert 696 n.
cunning 698 adj.
felt 818 adj.
paining 827 adj.
unpleasant 827 adj.
witty 839 adj.
ungracious 885 adj.
irascible 892 adj.
disapproving 924 adj.
sharp-angled
angular 247 adj.
sharp-eared
auditory 415 adj.
sharp edge
sharp edge 256 n.
tool 630 n.
sidearms 723 n.
sharpen
invigorate 174 vb.
sharpen 256 vb.
animate 821 vb.
— a distinction
differentiate 15 vb.
sharpener
sharpener 256 n.
sharper
trickster 545 n.
slyboots 698 n.
defrauder 789 n.
sharp-eyed
seeing 438 adj.
attentive 455 adj.
vigilant 457 adj.
sharpness
sharpness 256 n.
sagacity 498 n.
vigour 571 n.
skill 694 n.
(See **sharp** *)*
sharp pain
pang 377 n.
sharp point
sharp point 256 n.
perforator 263 n.
weapon 723 n.
sharp practice
trickery 542 n.
cunning 698 n.
foul play 930 n.
sharpshooter
shooter 287 n.
sharp temper
irascibility 892 n.
sharp tongue
quarrelsomeness 709 n.
sharp-witted
intelligent 498 adj.
shatter
break 46 vb.
demolish 165 vb.
be brittle 330 vb.
pulverize 332 vb.
shattered nerves
psychopathy 503 n.
shattering
notable 638 adj.
wonderful 864 adj.
shatterproof
unyielding 162 adj.
tough 329 adj.
invulnerable 660 adj.
shave
cut 46 vb.
make smaller 198 vb.
be near 200 vb.
shorten 204 vb.
laminate 207 vb.
smooth 258 vb.
touch 378 vb.
hairdressing 843 n.
— off
subtract 39 vb.
shaven
hairless 229 adj.
clean 648 adj.
shaver
cosmetic 843 n.
Shavian
dramatic 594 adj.
funny 849 adj.
shaving(s)
small thing 33 n.
leavings 41 n.
lamina 207 n.
strip 208 n.
shawl
cloak 228 n.
shawm
flute 414 n.
shay
carriage 274 n.
she
female 373 n., adj.
woman 373 n.
sheaf
bunch 74 n.
shear
subtract 39 vb.
make smaller 198 vb.
shorten 204 vb.
distortion 246 n.
groom 369 vb.
fleece 786 vb.
shears
sharp edge 256 n.
farm tool 370 n.
sheath
contraception 172 n.
case 194 n.
receptacle 194 n.
layer 207 n.
covering 226 n.
arsenal 723 n.
sheathe
replace 187 vb.
cover 226 vb.
introduce 231 vb.
insert 303 vb.
shebeen
tavern 192 n.
shed
decrease 37 vb.
unstick 49 vb.
small house 192 n.
doff 229 vb.
emit 300 vb.
let fall 311 vb.
disaccustom 611 vb.
relinquish 621 vb.
— blood
kill 362 vb.
oppress 735 vb.
she-devil
hellhag 904 n.
sheen
light 417 n.
reflection 417 n.
sheep
imitator 20 n.
sheep 365 n.
laity 987 n.
sheep farmer
producer 164 n.
breeder 369 n.
sheep farming
animal husbandry 369 n.
sheepfold
enclosure 235 n.
cattle pen 369 n.
sheepish
animal 365 adj.
modest 874 adj.
guilty 936 adj.
sheeprun
grassland 348 n.
stock farm 369 n.
sheep's eyes
look 438 n.
wooing 889 n.
sheepshank
ligature 47 n.

sheepskin
skin 226 n.
sheepwalk
grassland 348 n.
sheer
absolute 32 adj.
simple 44 adj.
vertical 215 adj.
sloping 220 adj.
transparent 422 adj.
sheer drop
descent 309 n.
sheer off
deviate 282 vb.
sheet
great quantity 32 n.
part 53 n.
lamina 207 n.
coverlet 226 n.
dress 228 vb.
lake 346 n.
rain 350 vb.
the press 528 n.
edition 589 n.
paper 631 n.
abound 635 vb.
sheet anchor
coupling 47 n.
protection 660 n.
hope 852 n.
sheets
tackling 47 n.
sheikh, sheik
potentate 741 n.
person of rank 868 n.
shekels
shekels 797 n.
Shekinah
manifestation 522 n.
theophany 965 n.
shelf
compartment 194 n.
shelf 218 n.
projection 254 n.
shelf-room
storage 632 n.
shell
mould 23 n.
remainder 41 n.
emptiness 190 n.
exteriority 223 n.
covering 226 n.
skin 226 n.
uncover 229 vb.
rowing boat 275 n.
missile 287 n.
hardness 326 n.
structure 331 n.
fire at 712 vb.
ammunition 723 n.
missile weapon 723 n.
seclusion 883 n.
— out
give 781 vb.
pay 804 vb.
shellac
resin 357 n.
shellback
mariner 270 n.
expert 696 n.
shellfish
fish food 301 n.
marine life 365 n.
shellshock
psychopathy 503 n.
shelter
dwelling 192 n.
retreat 192 n.
small house 192 n.
stable 192 n.
dwell 192 vb.
resting place 266 n.
admit 299 vb.
screen 421 n.vb.
hiding-place 527 n.
safeguard 660 vb.
shelter 662 n.
defences 713 n.
— under
plead 614 vb.
shelterless
vulnerable 661 adj.
poor 801 adj.
shelve
put off 136 vb.
be oblique 220 vb.
be neglectful 458 vb.
avoid 620 vb.
relinquish 621 vb.
shelving
compartment 194 n.
unwillingness 598 n.
shemozzle
turmoil 61 n.
shenanigan
trickery 542 n.
Sheol
the dead 361 n.
hell 972 n.
shepherd
bring together 74 vb.
herdsman 369 n.
protector 660 n.
direct 689 vb.
leader 690 n.
servant 742 n.
pastor 986 n.
shepherdess
herdsman 369 n.
shepherd's pie
meat 301 n.
sherbet
soft drink 301 n.
sherif
potentate 741 n.
sheriff
protector 660 n.
officer 741 n.
law officer 955 n.
Sherlock Holmes
detective 459 n.
sherry
wine 301 n.
shewbread
ritual object 988 n.
shibboleth
call 547 n.
identification 547 n.
shield
covering 226 n.
screen 421 n.vb.
heraldry 547 n.
safeguard 660 vb.
shelter 662 n.
armour 713 n.
defend 713 vb.
honours 866 n.
shield-bearer
retainer 742 n.
shift
period 110 n.
periodicity 141 n.
change 143 n.vb.
transition 147 n.
displacement 188 n.
dress 228 n.
move 265 vb.
transpose 272 vb.
move fast 277 vb.
deflect 282 vb.
trickery 542 n.
mental dishonesty 543 n.
contrivance 623 n.
labour 682 n.
stratagem 698 n.
change hands 780 vb.
take away 786 vb.
— for oneself
be free 744 vb.
— one's ground
tergiversate 603 vb.
— the blame
be exempt 919 vb.
accuse 928 vb.
— the scene
modify 143 vb.
shifting
transient 114 adj.
unstable 152 adj.
shiftless
unprepared 670 adj.
shifty
changeful 152 adj.
hypocritical 541 adj.
cunning 698 adj.
dishonest 930 adj.
Shi'ite
religionist 973 n.
sectarian 978 adj.
shillelagh
club 723 n.
shilling
coinage 797 n.
shillings and pence
money 797 n.
shilly-shally
be uncertain 474 vb.
be irresolute 601 vb.
shim
lining 227 n.
interjection 231 n.
shimmer
flash 417 n.
shine 417 vb.
shimmy
wriggle 251 vb.
dance 837 n.
shin
leg 267 n.
meat 301 n.
shindy, shindig
turmoil 61 n.
quarrel 709 n.
fight 716 n.
shine
be superior 34 vb.
smoothness 258 n.
light 417 n.
shine 417 vb.
illuminate 420 vb.
be visible 443 vb.
be wise 498 vb.
clean 648 vb.
be skilful 694 vb.
be beautiful 841 vb.
have a reputation 866 vb.
— on
patronize 703 vb.
be auspicious 730 vb.
shiner
wound 655 n.
blemish 845 n.
shiners
shekels 797 n.
shingle
lamina 207 n.
roof 226 n.
shore 344 n.
building material 631 n.
hairdressing 843 n.
shingles
skin disease 651 n.
shinguard
shelter 662 n.
shining example
paragon 646 n.
shining light
sage 500 n.
good person 937 n.
Shintoism, Shinto
religious faith 973 n.
shin up
climb 308 vb.
shiny
smooth 258 adj.
luminous 417 adj.
ship
load 193 vb.
prow 237 n.
poop 238 n.
transport 272 n.
carrier 273 n.
carry 273 vb.
ship 275 n.
warship 722 n.
— oars
row 269 vb.

ship ahoy!
269 int.
shipload
contents 193 n.
ship master
mariner 270 n.
shipmates
mariner 270 n.
chum 880 n.
shipment
contents 193 n.
thing transferred 272 n.
transport 272 n.
ship of the desert
beast of burden 273 n.
ship of the line
warship 722 n.
shippen
stable 192 n.
enclosure 235 n.
shipper
transferrer 272 n.
carrier 273 n.
shipping
transport 272 n.
shipping 275 n.
shipping lane
ocean 343 n.
shipshape
orderly 60 adj.
regulated 83 adj.
marine 275 adj.
well-made 694 adj.
shipwreck
ruin 165 n.
destroy 165 vb.
shipwright
artisan 686 n.
shipyard
workshop 687 n.
shire
district 184 n.
shire horse
draught horse 273 n.
shirk
disregard 458 vb.
be unwilling 598 vb.
avoid 620 vb.
fail in duty 918 vb.
shirker
negligence 458 n.
slacker 598 n.
avoider 620 n.
shirr
fold 261 vb.
shirt
shirt 228 n.
shirtfront
garment 228 n.
shirtwaister
dress 228 n.
shirty
angry 891 adj.
sullen 893 adj.
shiver
break 46 vb.
oscillate 317 vb.
be agitated 318 vb.
be brittle 330 vb.
be cold 380 vb.
quake 854 vb.
shivers
agitation 318 n.
coldness 380 n.
illness 651 n.
nervousness 854 n.
shoal
group 74 n.
shallow 212 adj.
pitfall 663 n.
shock
bunch 74 n.
electricity 160 n.
violence 176 n.
collision 279 n.
agitation 318 n.
lack of expectation 508 n.
disappointment 509 n.
illness 651 n.
attack 712 n.
feeling 818 n.
excitation 821 n.
suffering 825 n.
painfulness 827 n.
cause discontent 829 vb.
frighten 854 vb.
cause dislike 861 vb.
be wonderful 864 vb.
excite hate 888 vb.
incur blame 924 vb.
shockable
modest 874 adj.
innocent 935 adj.
prudish 950 adj.
shock absorber
moderator 177 n.
shocker
novel 590 n.
monster 938 n.
shock-headed
hairy 259 adj.
shocking
flagrant 32 adj.
unusual 84 adj.
unexpected 508 adj.
not nice 645 adj.
distressing 827 adj.
ugly 842 adj.
frightening 854 adj.
wonderful 864 adj.
discreditable 867 adj.
heinous 934 adj.
shocking language
scurrility 899 n.
shockproof
tough 329 adj.
unfeeling 375 adj.
shock tactics
attack 712 n.
shock treatment
therapy 658 n.
shock troops
attacker 712 n.
armed force 722 n.
shod
footed 214 adj.
dressed 228 adj.
shoddy
inferior 35 adj.
flimsy 163 adj.
fibre 208 n.
spurious 542 adj.
trivial 639 adj.
bad 645 adj.
bad taste 847 n.
shoe
footwear 228 n.
shoemaker
clothier 228 n.
shogun
autocrat 741 n.
shoo away
dismiss 300 vb.
shoot
branch 53 n.
young plant 132 n.
descendant 170 n.
expand 197 vb.
navigate 269 vb.
move fast 277 vb.
kick 279 vb.
shoot 287 vb.
waterfall 350 n.
kill 362 vb.
tree 366 n.
vegetate 366 vb.
give pain 377 vb.
radiate 417 vb.
photograph 551 vb.
be loquacious 581 vb.
fire at 712 vb.
amuse oneself 837 vb.
drug oneself 949 vb.
execute 963 vb.
— ahead
progress 285 vb.
outdo 306 vb.
— a line
be ostentatious 875 vb.
boast 877 vb.
— down
fell 311 vb.
hinder 702 vb.
fire at 712 vb.
— full of holes
confute 479 vb.
— oneself
kill oneself 362 vb.
— the rapids
navigate 269 vb.
pass 305 vb.
— the sun
orientate 281 vb.
— through
pass 305 vb.
— up
grow 36 vb.
jut 254 vb.
ascend 308 vb.
shooter
shooter 287 n.
hunter 619 n.
shooting
sport 837 n.
shooting gallery
place of amusement 837 n.
shooting iron
pistol 723 n.
shooting pain
pang 377 n.
shooting range
arena 724 n.
shooting star
brief span 114 n.
meteor 321 n.
luminary 420 n.
omen 511 n.
shooting stick
prop 218 n.
shoot-out
fight 716 n.
shop
topic 452 n.
inform 524 vb.
workshop 687 n.
purchase 792 vb.
shop 796 n.
— around
choose 605 vb.
shop assistant
worker 686 n.
servant 742 n.
seller 793 n.
shopfloor
workshop 687 n.
shop girl
seller 793 n.
shop goods
merchandise 795 n.
shopkeeper
provider 633 n.
seller 793 n.
tradespeople 794 n.
shoplifter
thief 789 n.
shoplifting
stealing 788 n.
shopper
purchaser 792 n.
shopping centre
meeting place 192 n.
emporium 796 n.
shopping list
requirement 627 n.
purchase 792 n.
shop-soiled
inferior 35 adj.
imperfect 647 adj.
cheap 812 adj.
blemished 845 adj.
shop steward
official 690 n.
delegate 754 n.
shop walker
seller 793 n.

shop window
exhibit 522 n.
market 796 n.
shop 796 n.
shoran
aeronautics 271 n.
shore
region 184 n.
edge 234 n.
limit 236 n.
shore 344 n.
shoreless
spacious 183 adj.
shore up
support 218 vb.
preserve 666 vb.
shorn
short 204 adj.
shorn of
losing 772 adj.
shorn of glory
inglorious 867 adj.
short
incomplete 55 adj.
brief 114 adj.
dwarfish 196 adj.
short 204 adj.
low 210 adj.
draught 301 n.
deficient 307 adj.
brittle 330 adj.
film 445 n.
concise 569 adj.
taciturn 582 adj.
compendious 592 adj.
scarce 636 adj.
lost 772 adj.
poor 801 adj.
ungracious 885 adj.
irascible 892 adj.
shortage
decrement 42 n.
shortfall 307 n.
requirement 627 n.
scarcity 636 n.
short and sweet
brief 114 adj.
concise 569 adj.
shortbread
pastries 301 n.
shortchange
deceive 542 vb.
overcharge 811 vb.
short circuit
electricity 160 n.
circuit 626 vb.
hitch 702 n.
shortcoming(s)
shortfall 307 n.
vice 934 n.
short commons
insufficiency 636 n.
fasting 946 n.
short cut
short distance 200 n.
straightness 249 n.
short drink
draught 301 n.
shorten
abate 37 vb.
cut 46 vb.
shorten 204 vb.
abstract 592 vb.
— sail
retard 278 vb.
seek safety 660 vb.
shortfall
decrement 42 n.
deficit 55 n.
shortfall 307 n.
requirement 627 n.
insufficiency 636 n.
defect 647 n.
shorthand
writing 586 n.
shorthanded
unprovided 636 adj.
shorthand typist
stenographer 586 n.
short list
list 87 n.
choice 605 n.
short-lived
ephemeral 114 adj.
short measure
shortfall 307 n.
short memory
oblivion 506 n.
short of
incomplete 55 adj.
exclusive of 57 adv.
deficient 307 adj.
short of breath
panting 684 adj.
short run
period 110 n.
brief span 114 n.
shorts
trousers 228 n.
short shrift
pitilessness 906 n.
short sight
dim sight 440 n.
short-sighted
dim-sighted 440 adj.
misjudging 481 adj.
unwise 499 adj.
short story
novel 590 n.
short supply
scarcity 636 n.
short-tempered
irascible 892 adj.
short-term
brief 114 adj.
short work
easy thing 701 n.
shot
mixed 43 adj.
stimulant 174 n.
missile 287 n.
shooter 287 n.
insertion 303 n.
bang 402 n.
iridescent 437 adj.
conjecture 512 n.
photography 551 n.
gambling 618 n.
hunter 619 n.
medicine 658 n.
ammunition 723 n.
missile weapon 723 n.
drug-taking 949 n.
dead drunk 949 adj.
shot across the bows
warning 664 n.
terror tactics 712 n.
shot at
attempt 671 n.
shotgun
propellant 287 n.
firearm 723 n.
shot in one's locker
means 629 n.
shot in the arm
stimulant 174 n.
shot in the dark
empiricism 461 n.
conjecture 512 n.
gambling 618 n.
shot through
perforated 263 adj.
iridescent 437 adj.
should be
be due 915 vb.
shoulder
prop 218 n.
camber 253 n.
carry 273 vb.
impel 279 vb.
propel 287 vb.
elevate 310 vb.
print-type 587 n.
intend 617 vb.
— arms
prepare oneself 669 vb.
wage war 718 vb.
— one's responsibility
incur a duty 917 vb.
— one's way
be in motion 265 vb.
— the blame for
substitute 150 vb.
shoulder to shoulder
cohesive 48 adj.
in league 708 adv.
shout
loudness 400 n.
vociferate 408 vb.
proclaim 528 vb.
affirm 532 vb.
call 547 n.
voice 577 vb.
rejoicing 835 n.
boast 877 vb.
be rude 885 vb.
get angry 891 vb.
— down
make mute 578 vb.
be obstructive 702 vb.
be insolent 878 vb.
disapprove 924 vb.
shove
move 265 vb.
transpose 272 vb.
impulse 279 n.
propel 287 vb.
gesture 547 n.
be active 678 vb.
— around
oppress 735 vb.
— aside
not respect 921 vb.
— off
decamp 296 vb.
— one's oar in
meddle 678 vb.
shove-ha'penny
ball game 837 n.
shovel
ladle 194 n.
transpose 272 vb.
conveyor 274 n.
extractor 304 n.
— in
eat 301 vb.
shovel hat
headgear 228 n.
canonicals 989 n.
show
open 263 vb.
be visible 443 vb.
spectacle 445 n.
appear 445 vb.
attract notice 455 vb.
evidence 466 vb.
demonstrate 478 vb.
interpret 520 vb.
exhibit 522 n.
show 522 vb.
be disclosed 526 vb.
duplicity 541 n.
deception 542 n.
indicate 547 vb.
stage play 594 n.
amusement 837 n.
pride 871 n.
ostentation 875 n.
pageant 875 n.
— a bold front
defy 711 vb.
be courageous 855 vb.
— a clean pair of heels
move fast 277 vb.
run away 620 vb.
— fight
be vigorous 174 vb.
be active 678 vb.
defy 711 vb.
attack 712 vb.
parry 713 vb.
be courageous 855 vb.
— in
admit 299 vb.

— off
beautify 841 vb.
be affected 850 vb.
seek repute 866 vb.
be proud 871 vb.
be vain 873 vb.
be ostentatious 875 vb.
boast 877 vb.vb.
— one's age
be ugly 842 vb.
— one's back
be cowardly 856 vb.
— one's face
be present 189 vb.
be plain 522 vb.
— one's hand
divulge 526 vb.
— one's ignorance
be unskilful 695 vb.
— one's true colours
be plain 522 vb.
— out
dismiss 300 vb.
— results
be successful 727 vb.
— round
interpret 520 vb.
show 522 vb.
— signs (of)
evidence 466 vb.
be likely 471 vb.
manifest 522 vb.
indicate 547 vb.
give hope 852 vb.
— the door
dismiss 300 vb.
— the flag
be plain 522 vb.
— the ropes
train 534 vb.
— the way
come before 64 vb.
orientate 281 vb.
indicate 547 vb.
prepare 669 vb.
direct 689 vb.
— the white feather
be cowardly 856 vb.
— through
be inside 224 vb.
be transparent 422 vb.
be visible 443 vb.
— up
be present 189 vb.
arrive 295 vb.
be visible 443 vb.
confute 479 vb.
detect 484 vb.
be plain 522 vb.
satirize 851 vb.
shame 867 vb.
accuse 928 vb.
— willing
be willing 597 vb.
cooperate 706 vb.
showboat
ship 275 n.
theatre 594 n.
show business
drama 594 n.
showcase
exhibit 522 n.
showdown
disclosure 526 n.
shower
great quantity 32 n.
crowd 74 n.
propel 287 vb.
descend 309 vb.
let fall 311 vb.
rain 350 n.vb.
abound 635 vb.
ablutions 648 n.
— upon
give 781 vb.
be liberal 813 vb.
showerproof
dry 342 adj.
showery
rainy 350 adj.
showgirl
entertainer 594 n.
showing
uncovered 229 adj.
visible 443 adj.
show jumping
equitation 267 n.
showman
exhibitor 522 n.
stage manager 594 n.
showmanship
publicity 528 n.
ostentation 875 n.
show of force
vigorousness 174 n.
show of hands
vote 605 n.
showpiece
exhibit 522 n.
showplace
exhibit 522 n.
showroom
exhibit 522 n.
showy
florid 425 adj.
ornate 574 adj.
splendid 841 adj.
vulgar 847 adj.
prideful 871 adj.
showy 875 adj.
shrapnel
ammunition 723 n.
shred
small thing 33 n.
cut 46 vb.
piece 53 n.
fraction 102 n.
strip 208 n.
shredded
fragmentary 53 adj.
shreds and tatters
poverty 801 n.
shrew
small animal 33 n.
violent creature 176 n.
woman 373 n.
quarreller 709 n.
shrew 892 n.
hellhag 904 n.
defamer 926 n.
shrewd
knowing 490 adj.
intelligent 498 adj.
skilful 694 adj.
cunning 698 adj.
shrewd idea
conjecture 512 n.
shrewish
irascible 892 adj.
(See **shrew** *)*
shriek
feel pain 377 vb.
stridor 407 n.
cry 408 n.
lament 836 n.
weep 836 vb.
shrieking
florid 425 adj.
shrill
blow 352 vb.
loud 400 adj.
strident 407 adj.
shrill 407 vb.
vocal 577 adj.
shrimp
small animal 33 n.
dwarf 196 n.
fish food 301 n.
marine life 365 n.
shrine
tomb 364 n.
ritual object 988 n.
temple 990 n.
shrink
decrease 37 vb.
become small 198 vb.
recoil 280 vb.
turn back 286 vb.
recede 290 vb.
psychologist 447 n.
avoid 620 vb.
deteriorate 655 vb.
be nervous 854 vb.
be modest 874 vb.
— from
dislike 861 vb.
hate 888 vb.
shrinkage
decrement 42 n.
contraction 198 n.
shrinking
unwilling 598 adj.
modest 874 adj.
shrinkproof
unchangeable 153 adj.
shrink-wrap
cover 226 vb.
shrive
forgive 909 vb.
perform ritual 988 vb.
shrivel
become small 198 vb.
dry 342 vb.
heat 381 vb.
deteriorate 655 vb.
shrivelled
ageing 131 adj.
lean 206 adj.
dry 342 adj.
shroud
wrapping 226 n.
grave clothes 364 n.
screen 421 vb.
conceal 525 vb.
shrouds
tackling 47 n.
prop 218 n.
Shrove Tuesday
holy day 988 n.
shrub
tree 366 n.
shrubbery
wood 366 n.
garden 370 n.
shrug
be impotent 161 vb.
gesture 547 n.
be indifferent 860 vb.
— off
underestimate 483 vb.
be unimportant 639 vb.
be indifferent 860 vb.
shrunk
dwarfish 196 adj.
contracted 198 adj.
shudder
agitation 318 n.
be cold 380 vb.
quake 854 vb.
— at
dislike 861 vb.
shuffle
mix 43 vb.
jumble 63 vb.
interchange 151 n. vb.
vary 152 vb.
gait 265 n.
walk 267 vb.
transpose 272 vb.
move slowly 278 vb.
sophisticate 477 vb.
dissemble 541 vb.
mental dishonesty 543 n.
gesticulate 547 vb.
be irresolute 601 vb.
tergiversate 603 vb.
dance 837 n.vb.
be dishonest 930 vb.
— the cards
modify 143 vb.

shuffled
orderless 61 adj.
shun
avoid 620 vb.
dislike 861 vb.
shunt
transpose 272 vb.
deflect 282 vb.
shunter
locomotive 274 n.
shut
close 264 vb.
— down
cease 145 vb.
close 264 vb.
— in
surround 230 vb.
close 264 vb.
imprison 747 vb.
— one's ears
be deaf 416 vb.
— oneself up
be unsociable 883 vb.
— one's eyes to
be blind 439 vb.
permit 756 vb.
— out
exclude 57 vb.
— the door in one's face
repel 292 vb.
— the door on
exclude 57 vb.
prohibit 757 vb.
make unwelcome 883 vb.
— up
cease 145 vb.
399 int.
confute 479 vb.
be mute 578 vb.
582 int.
imprison 747 vb.
seclude 883 vb.
— up shop
terminate 69 vb.
cease 145 vb.
shutdown
stop 145 n.
inactivity 679 n.
shut-eye
sleep 679 n.
shutter
covering 226 n.
shade 226 n.
curtain 421 n.
camera 442 n.
shuttered
closed 264 adj.
shuttle
weaving 222 n.
travel 267 vb.
fluctuate 317 vb.
shuttlecock
fluctuation 317 n.
waverer 601 n.
shuttle service
periodicity 141 n.
fluctuation 317 n.
shy
recoil 280 vb.
deviate 282 vb.
propel 287 vb.
unwilling 598 adj.
avoiding 620 adj.
artless 699 adj.
lapidate 712 vb.
nervous 854 adj.
disliking 861 adj.
modest 874 adj.
unsociable 883 adj.
— at
doubt 486 vb.
refuse 760 vb.
Shylock
lender 784 n.
shyster
trickster 545 n.
lawyer 958 n.
sialogogue
expulsive 300 adj.
Siamese twins
duality 90 n.
sib
kinsman 11 n.
akin 11 adj.
sibilant
speech sound 398 n.
sibilant 406 adj.
vocal 577 adj.
sibilation
sibilation 406 n.
speech defect 580 n.
sibling
kinsman 11 n.
sibyl
oracle 511 n.
sorceress 983 n.
sibylline
predicting 511 adj.
sic
truly 494 adv.
siccative
dryer 342 n.
sick
vomiting 300 adj.
insane 503 adj.
sick 651 adj.
suffering 825 adj.
vicious 934 adj.
crapulous 949 adj.
sick and tired
bored 838 adj.
sick as a parrot
dejected 834 adj.
sick bay
hospital 658 n.
sickbed
illness 651 n.
sick benefit
subvention 703 n.
sicken
be weak 163 vb.
be ill 651 vb.
deteriorate 655 vb.
displease 827 vb.
cause discontent 829 vb.
be tedious 838 vb.
cause dislike 861 vb.
sate 863 vb.
sickening
unsavoury 391 adj.
not nice 645 adj.
discontenting 829 adj.
sickle
curve 248 n.
sharp edge 256 n.
farm tool 370 n.
sick list
sick person 651 n.
sickly
weakly 163 adj.
unsavoury 391 adj.
colourless 426 adj.
unhealthy 651 adj.
sick mind
insanity 503 n.
sickness
illness 651 n.
sick of
bored 838 adj.
disliking 861 adj.
sated 863 adj.
sick person
sick person 651 n.
sufferer 825 n.
sickroom
hospital 658 n.
sic transit gloria mundi
unsubstantially 4 adv.
side
race 11 n.
part 53 n.
situation 186 n.
edge 234 n.
laterality 239 n.
appearance 445 n.
choose 605 vb.
party 708 n.
pride 871 n.
vanity 873 n.
ostentation 875 n.
— against
oppose 704 vb.
— with
assent 488 vb.
patronize 703 vb.
join a party 708 vb.
sideboard
cabinet 194 n.
stand 218 n.
sideboards
hair 259 n.
side by side
with 89 adv.
near 200 adv.
sideways 239 adv.
in league 708 adv.
sidecar
bicycle 274 n.
side effect
effect 157 n.
side elevation
laterality 239 n.
map 551 n.
sidekick
auxiliary 707 n.
chum 880 n.
sidelight
knowledge 490 n.
hint 524 n.
sideline(s)
exteriority 223 n.
edge 234 n.
business 622 n.
sidelong
obliquely 220 adv.
sideways 239 adv.
sidereal
celestial 321 adj.
siderite
meteor 321 n.
side road
road 624 n.
sidesaddle
seat 218 n.
sideshow
trifle 639 n.
sideslip
aeronautics 271 n.
deviation 282 n.
sidesman, sideswoman
church officer 986 n.
sidesplitting
funny 849 adj.
sidestep
deviate 282 vb.
avoid 620 vb.
side to side
to and fro 317 adv.
sidetrack
deflect 282 vb.
sideways
obliquely 220 adv.
sideways 239 adv.
sidewinder
serpent 251 n.
siding
railway 624 n.
sidle
be oblique 220 vb.
flank 239 vb.
deviate 282 vb.
siege
circumscription 232 n.
hindrance 702 n.
attack 712 n.
sierra
high land 209 n.
siesta
sleep 679 n.
sieve
porosity 263 n.
cleaning utensil 648 n.
sift
eliminate 44 vb.

exclude 57 vb.
class 62 vb.
enquire 459 vb.
discriminate 463 vb.
select 605 vb.
purify 648 vb.

sigh
breathe 352 vb.
sound faint 401 vb.
cry 408 n.vb.
suffer 825 vb.
be dejected 834 vb.
lamentation 836 n.
be in love 887 vb.

— after
desire 859 vb.

sight
arrive 295 vb.
sense 374 n.
vision 438 n.
see 438 vb.
telescope 442 n.
visibility 443 n.
spectacle 445 n.
detect 484 vb.
firearm 723 n.
eyesore 842 n.
prodigy 864 n.

sight for sore eyes
pleasurableness 826 n.
a beauty 841 n.

sightless
blind 439 adj.
invisible 444 adj.

sight of
great quantity 32 n.
multitude 104 n.

sight-read
be musical 413 vb.

sights
direction 281 n.

sightsee
travel 267 vb.
scan 438 vb.

sightseer
traveller 268 n.
spectator 441 n.
inquisitive person 453 n.

sigillate
marked 547 adj.

sigmoid
snaky 251 adj.

sign
number 85 n.
evidence 466 n.
endorse 488 vb.
omen 511 n.
manifestation 522 n.
badge 547 n.
gesture 547 n.
indication 547 n.
label 547 n.
gesticulate 547 vb.
sign 547 vb.
letter 558 n.
warning 664 n.
command 737 n.vb.
contract 765 vb.
give security 767 vb.
prodigy 864 n.

— off
resign 753 vb.

— on
join a party 708 vb.

— oneself
perform ritual 988 vb.

— on the dotted line
acquiesce 488 vb.
obey 739 vb.

— the pledge
be temperate 942 vb.
be sober 948 vb.

signal
remarkable 32 adj.
signal light 420 n.
communicate 524 vb.
telecommunication 531 n.
signal 547 n.vb.
railway 624 n.
notable 638 adj.
danger signal 665 n.

signal box
railway 624 n.

signalize, signalise
indicate 547 vb.
dignify 866 vb.
celebrate 876 vb.

signaller
warner 664 n.

signalling
telecommunication 531 n.

signatory
witness 466 n.
assenter 488 n.
signatory 765 n.

signature
notation 410 n.
assent 488 n.
identification 547 n.
label 547 n.
name 561 n.
script 586 n.
edition 589 n.
compact 765 n.
title deed 767 n.

signboard
label 547 n.

signet
badge of rule 743 n.

significance
greatness 32 n.
statistics 86 n.
connotation 514 n.
importance 638 n.

significant
evidential 466 adj.
presageful 511 adj.

signification
connotation 514 n.

signify
specify 80 vb.
predict 511 vb.
mean 514 vb.
inform 524 vb.
indicate 547 vb.
be important 638 vb.

sign language
mimicry 20 n.
gesture 547 n.
language 557 n.

sign of the cross
ritual act 988 n.

sign of the times
omen 11 n.
indication 547 n.
warning 664 n.

signor
male 372 n.
title 870 n.

signora, signorina
lady 373 n.
title 870 n.

sign-painter
artist 556 n.

signpost
direction 281 n.
signpost 547 n.

signs of the zodiac
zodiac 321 n.

sign-writer
calligrapher 586 n.

Sikh
religionist 973 n.

silage
provender 301 n.
agriculture 370 n.

silence
stop 145 n.
disable 161 vb.
quietude 266 n.
silence 399 n.vb.
deafness 416 n.
confute 479 vb.
make mute 578 vb.
taciturnity 582 n.

silencer
silencer 401 n.
nonresonance 405 n.
mute 414 n.

silent
lubricated 334 adj.
silent 399 adj.
nonresonant 405 adj.
reticent 525 adj.
voiceless 578 adj.
taciturn 582 adj.
wondering 864 adj.
unsociable 883 adj.
disapproving 924 adj.

Silenus
drunkard 949 n.
lesser deity 967 n.

silhouette
copy 22 n.
outline 233 n.vb.
form 243 n.vb.
darkness 418 n.
feature 445 n.
picture 553 n.

silica
hardness 326 n.

silicon chip
microelectronics 196 n.

silicosis
respiratory disease 651 n.

silk
fibre 208 n.
textile 222 n.
smoothness 258 n.
lawyer 958 n.

silks
clothing 228 n.

silk-screen printing
printing 555 n.

silky
smooth 258 adj.
soft 327 adj.
textural 331 adj.

sill
base 214 n.
shelf 218 n.
threshold 234 n.
projection 254 n.
rock 344 n.

silly
credulous 487 adj.
absurd 497 adj.
foolish 499 adj.
fool 501 n.
gullible 544 adj.
ridiculous 849 adj.

silly fool
fool 501 n.
laughingstock 851 n.

silly season
absurdity 497 n.

silly talk
silly talk 515 n.

silo
farm tool 370 n.
storage 632 n.
preserver 666 n.
gun 723 n.

silt
leavings 41 n.
solid body 324 n.
soil 344 n.

silver
coat 226 vb.
colour 425 vb.
white thing 427 n.
bullion 797 n.
money 797 n.
decorate 844 vb.

silver jubilee
anniversary 141 n.

silver lining
relief 831 n.
hope 852 n.

silverplate
coat 226 vb.

silverpoint
engraving 555 n.

silver screen
cinema 445 n.

silverside
meat 301 n.
silversmith
artisan 686 n.
silver-tongued
melodious 410 adj.
eloquent 579 adj.
silver wedding
anniversary 141 n.
special day 876 n.
silvery
melodious 410 adj.
white 427 adj.
grey 429 adj.
silviculture
forestry 366 n.
agriculture 370 n.
simian
animal 365 adj.
similar
relative 9 adj.
correlative 12 adj.
uniform 16 adj.
similar 18 adj.
equivalent 28 adj.
similarity
similarity 18 n.
copy 22 n.
appearance 445 n.
comparison 462 n.
consensus 488 n.
representation 551 n.
simile
analogue 18 n.
comparison 462 n.
metaphor 519 n.
ornament 574 n.
similitude
similarity 18 n.
simmer
cook 301 vb.
effervesce 318 vb.
resent 891 vb.
simmering
excitable 822 adj.
Simon-Pure
genuine 494 adj.
simony
improbity 930 n.
simper
smile 835 vb.
be affected 850 vb.
simple
simple 44 adj.
credulous 487 adj.
ignorant 491 adj.
foolish 499 adj.
intelligible 516 adj.
veracious 540 adj.
plain 573 adj.
elegant 575 adj.
medicine 658 n.
artless 699 adj.
easy 701 adj.
tasteful 846 adj.
plebeian 869 adj.
simple life
temperance 942 n.
asceticism 945 n.
simple-minded
artless 699 adj.
Simple Simon
ninny 501 n.
dupe 544 n.
simple soul
ingenue 699 n.
simpleton
ignoramus 493 n.
ninny 501 n.
simplicity
simpleness 44 n.
(See **simple** *)*
simplification
simplification 44 n.
simplify
simplify 44 vb.
decompose 51 vb.
be intelligible 516 vb.
interpret 520 vb.
facilitate 701 vb.
simulacrum
similarity 18 n.
mimicry 20 n.
sham 542 n.
pretext 614 n.
simulate
imitate 20 vb.
simulation
assimilation 18 n.
mimicry 20 n.
duplicity 541 n.
simulator
testing agent 461 n.
simulcast
broadcast 531 n.
simultaneous
accompanying 89 adj.
instantaneous 116 adj.
synchronous 123 adj.
sin
badness 645 n.
disobedience 738 n.
wrong 914 n.
vice 934 n.
be wicked 934 vb.
guilty act 936 n.
be impious 980 vb.
sin bin
prison 748 n.
since
subsequently 120 adv.
hence 158 adv.
sincere
simple 44 adj.
veracious 540 adj.
artless 699 adj.
felt 818 adj.
sincerity
probity 929 n.
sinciput
head 213 n.
face 237 n.
sine
ratio 85 n.
sinecure
inaction 677 n.
leisure 681 n.
easy thing 701 n.
sine die
never 109 adv.
sine qua non
essential part 5 n.
speciality 80 n.
concomitant 89 n.
requirement 627 n.
chief thing 638 n.
conditions 766 n.
sinews
vitality 162 n.
sinewy
stalwart 162 adj.
tough 329 adj.
sinfonietta
musical piece 412 n.
orchestra 413 n.
sinful
bad 645 adj.
wrong 914 adj.
wicked 934 adj.
guilty 936 adj.
sing
resound 404 vb.
ululate 409 vb.
harmonize 410 vb.
sing 413 vb.
confess 526 vb.
poetize 593 vb.
be cheerful 833 vb.
— for joy
rejoice 835 vb.
— out
vociferate 408 vb.
— small
be humble 872 vb.
— the praises
honour 866 vb.
praise 923 vb.
singable
melodious 410 adj.
musical 412 adj.
singe
burn 381 vb.
blacken 428 vb.
singer
vocalist 413 n.
single
simple 44 adj.
whole 52 adj.
one 88 adj.
infrequent 140 adj.
gramophone 414 n.
independent 744 adj.
unwedded 895 adj.
— out
differentiate 15 vb.
set apart 46 vb.
emphasize 532 vb.
select 605 vb.
single combat
duel 716 n.
single-decker
bus 274 n.
single entry
accounts 808 n.
single file
procession 71 n.
line 203 n.
single-handed
alone 88 adj.
hindered 702 adj.
single-hearted
artless 699 adj.
trustworthy 929 adj.
single-minded
obsessed 455 adj.
resolute 599 adj.
single parent
parentage 169 n.
divorce 896 n.
single-sex
educational 534 adj.
single-storey
architectural 192 adj.
low 210 adj.
singlet
underwear 228 n.
singleton
unit 88 n.
single track
narrow 206 adj.
single voice
consensus 488 n.
singly
separately 46 adv.
singly 88 adv.
singsong
uniform 16 adj.
repeated 106 adj.
discordant 411 adj.
music 412 n.
social gathering 882 n.
singular
unusual 84 adj.
one 88 adj.
grammatical 564 adj.
singularity
speciality 80 n.
singularly
remarkably 32 adv.
sinister
sinistral 242 adj.
presageful 511 adj.
heraldic 547 adj.
evil 616 adj.
bad 645 adj.
adverse 731 adj.
frightening 854 adj.
dishonest 930 adj.
sinistral
sinistral 242 adj.
handed 378 adj.
sink
decrease 37 vb.
suppress 165 vb.
receptacle 194 n.
cavity 255 n.
descend 309 vb.
founder 313 vb.

weigh 322 vb.
drain 351 n.
storage 632 n.
badness 645 n.
sink 649 n.
be ill 651 vb.
insalubrity 653 n.
deteriorate 655 vb.
be fatigued 684 vb.
defeat 727 vb.
fail 728 vb.
lose 772 vb.
— back
relapse 657 vb.
— in
infiltrate 297 vb.
cause thought 449 vb.
be intelligible 516 vb.
impress 821 vb.
— in estimation
lose repute 867 vb.
— money
expend 806 vb.
sinker
diver 313 n.
gravity 322 n.
sinking
dying 361 adj.
sinking fund
finance 797 n.
sinking heart
dejection 834 n.
sink of iniquity
wickedness 934 n.
sink or swim
persistently 600 adv.
sinless
innocent 935 adj.
pure 950 adj.
sinner
evildoer 904 n.
offender 904 n.
bad person 938 n.
impious person 980 n.
sin offering
propitiation 941 n.
Sinologist
linguist 557 n.
Sinophile
xenophile 880 n.
sinuous
convoluted 251 adj.
sinus
cavity 255 n.
sinusitis
respiratory disease 651 n.
sip
small quantity 33 n.
mouthful 301 n.
drink 301 vb.
taste 386 vb.
siphon, syphon
soft drink 301 n.
extractor 304 n.
conduit 351 n.
siphon off
transpose 272 vb.
empty 300 vb.
extract 304 vb.
sir
male 372 n.
name 561 vb.
speak to 583 vb.
master 741 n.
dignify 866 vb.
title 870 n.
sire
generate 167 vb.
title 870 n.
sired
born 360 adj.
siren
attraction 291 n.
sea nymph 343 n.
megaphone 400 n.
vocalist 413 n.
signal 547 n.
motivator 612 n.
warning 664 n.
danger signal 665 n.
a beauty 841 n.
mythical being 970 n.
siren suit
suit 228 n.
sirloin
meat 301 n.
sirocco
wind 352 n.
heat 379 n.
sisal
fibre 208 n.
sissy, cissy
weakling 163 n.
coward 856 n.
sister
kinsman 11 n.
analogue 18 n.
woman 373 n.
nurse 658 n.
friend 880 n.
nun 986 n.
sisterhood
family 11 n.
group 74 n.
community 708 n.
friendship 880 n.
sect 978 n.
nun 986 n.
sisterly
friendly 880 adj.
loving 887 adj.
benevolent 897 adj.
Sisyphean
useless 641 adj.
Sisyphean labour
hard task 700 n.
noncompletion 726 n.
sit
place oneself 187 vb.
sit down 311 vb.
— about/around
wait 136 vb.
be inactive 679 vb.
— at the feet of
learn 536 vb.
— back
not act 677 vb.
repose 683 vb.
— down
be quiescent 266 vb.
sit down 311 vb.
— for
be an example 23 vb.
represent 551 vb.
deputize 755 vb.
— in judgment
judge 480 vb.
— on
suppress 165 vb.
subjugate 745 vb.
restrain 747 vb.
— on the fence
be uncertain 474 vb.
be neutral 606 vb.
not act 677 vb.
— out
go on 146 vb.
carry through 725 vb.
— tight
be quiescent 266 vb.
not act 677 vb.
— up
be vertical 215 vb.
be attentive 455 vb.
— up with
look after 457 vb.
sitar
harp 414 n.
sitcom
broadcast 531 n.
sit-down strike
strike 145 n.
site
place 185 n.
situation 186 n.
place 187 vb.
sit-in
presence 189 n.
sitter
living model 23 n.
exam 459 n.
testee 461 n.
art equipment 553 n.
easy thing 701 n.
sitting
maturation 669 n.
council 692 n.
sitting duck
vulnerability 661 n.
easy thing 701 n.
sitting pretty
successful 727 adj.
content 828 n.
sitting tenant
resident 191 n.
situate
place 187 vb.
situation
circumstance 8 n.n.
affairs 154 n.
place 185 n.
situation 186 n.
station 187 n.
surroundings 230 n.
direction 281 n.
job 622 n.
predicament 700 n.
Siva, Shiva
Hindu deities 967 n.
six
over five 99 n.
six-footer
tall creature 209 n.
six of one and half a dozen of the other
equivalence 28 n.
no choice 606 n.
indifference 860 n.
sixpence
coinage 797 n.
six-shooter
pistol 723 n.
sixth
fifth and over 99 adj.
musical note 410 n.
sixth form
class 538 n.
sixth sense
intuition 476 n.
occultism 984 n.
sixty
twenty and over 99 n.
sixty-four-thousand-dollar question
question 459 n.
sizable, sizeable
great 32 adj.
large 195 adj.
size
make uniform 16 vb.
degree 27 n.
greatness 32 n.
adhesive 47 n.
arrange 62 vb.
measure 183 n.
size 195 n.
coat 226 vb.
viscidity 354 n.
metrology 465 n.
importance 638 n.
— up
appraise 465 vb.
estimate 480 vb.
sizzle
effervesce 318 vb.
be hot 379 vb.
crackle 402 vb.
hiss 406 vb.
be excited 821 vb.
sizzler
heat 379 n.
sjambok
scourge 964 n.
ska
music 412 n.

skald
poet 593 n.
skat
card game 837 n.
skate
go smoothly 258 vb.
be in motion 265 vb.
sledge 274 n.
fish food 301 n.
amuse oneself 837 vb.
— on thin ice
be in danger 661 vb.
— over
neglect 458 vb.
skateboard
sledge 274 n.
skater
pedestrian 268 n.
skating
sport 837 n.
skating rink
arena 724 n.
pleasure ground 837 n.
skedaddle
move fast 277 vb.
decamp 296 vb.
run away 620 vb.
skein
bunch 74 n.
group 74 n.
crossing 222 n.
skeletal
lean 206 adj.
supporting 218 adj.
structural 331 adj.
skeleton
remainder 41 n.
chief part 52 n.
thinness 206 n.
frame 218 n.
outline 233 n.
structure 331 n.
corpse 363 n.
compendium 592 n.
plan 623 n.
skeleton at the feast
moper 834 n.
skeleton in the cupboard
secret 530 n.
skeleton key
opener 263 n.
instrument 628 n.
skep
nest 192 n.
dome 253 n.
skerry
rock 344 n.
island 349 n.
sketch
copy 22 n.
incompleteness 55 n.
outline 233 n.vb.
form 243 vb.
represent 551 vb.
picture 553 n.
be concise 569 vb.
describe 590 vb.
compendium 592 n.
stage play 594 n.
plan 623 n.
sketcher
artist 556 n.
sketch map
map 551 n.
sketchy
incomplete 55 adj.
uncompleted 726 adj.
skew
statistics 86 n.
oblique 220 adj.
distort 246 vb.
skewbald
horse 273 n.
pied 437 adj.
skewer
fastening 47 n.
sharp point 256 n.
pierce 263 vb.
skew-whiff
oblique 220 adj.
ski
go smoothly 258 vb.
travel 267 vb.
sledge 274 n.
amuse oneself 837 vb.
skiagraphy
darkness 418 n.
photography 551 n.
skiamachy
ideality 513 n.
skiascope
optical device 442 n.
skibob
sledge 274 n.
skiboots
footwear 228 n.
skid
prop 218 n.
go smoothly 258 vb.
deviate 282 vb.
fetter 748 n.
skidlid
headgear 228 n.
skidmark
trace 548 n.
skidproof
dry 342 adj.
skids
sledge 274 n.
skier
pedestrian 268 n.
skiff
rowing boat 275 n.
skiing
sport 837 n.
ski-jumping
sport 837 n.
skilful
dextral 241 adj.
intelligent 498 adj.
skilful 694 adj.
ski lift
ascent 308 n.
lifter 310 n.
skill
speciality 80 n.
ability 160 n.
sagacity 498 n.
skill 694 n.
cunning 698 n.
skilled worker
artisan 686 n.
expert 696 n.
skillet
cauldron 194 n.
skim
be near 200 vb.
be contiguous 202 vb.
travel 267 vb.
fly 271 vb.
move fast 277 vb.
purify 648 vb.
impair 655 vb.
— off
select 605 vb.
— through
scan 438 vb.
neglect 458 vb.
skimmer
ladle 194 n.
skimp
neglect 458 vb.
make insufficient 636 vb.
be parsimonious 816 vb.
skimpy
small 33 adj.
short 204 adj.
skin
leavings 41 n.
disunite 46 vb.
layer 207 n.
shallowness 212 n.
exteriority 223 n.
skin 226 n.
uncover 229 vb.
hair 259 n.
fleece 786 vb.
overcharge 811 vb.
— a flint
attempt the impossible 470 vb.
be parsimonious 816 vb.
— over
overlie 226 vb.
cure 656 vb.
skin-and-bone
lean 206 adj.
underfed 636 adj.
skin-deep
inconsiderable 33 adj.
shallow 212 adj.
exterior 223 adj.
skin disease
formication 378 n.
skin disease 651 n.
blemish 845 n.
skin diving
sport 837 n.
skinflick
film 445 n.
impurity 951 n.
skinflint
niggard 816 n.
skinful
plenitude 54 n.
skin game
peculation 788 n.
skin-grafting
beautification 843 n.
skinhead
youngster 132 n.
skinny
lean 206 adj.
skint
poor 801 adj.
skintight
cohesive 48 adj.
tailored 228 adj.
skip
be absent 190 vb.
vessel 194 n.
gait 265 n.
walk 267 vb.
decamp 296 vb.
leap 312 n.vb.
neglect 458 vb.
escape 667 vb.
not complete 726 vb.
not observe 769 vb.
rejoice 835 vb.
— over
neglect 458 vb.
skipper
mariner 270 n.
direct 689 vb.
skipping
children's games 837 n.
skippingly
discontinuously 72 adv.
skipping rope
plaything 837 n.
skirl
be loud 400 vb.
stridor 407 n.
skirmish
fight 716 n.vb.
give battle 718 vb.
skirmisher
soldier 722 n.
skirr
move fast 277 vb.
skirt
be near 200 vb.
base 214 n.
hanging object 217 n.
skirt 228 n.
edge 234 n.
flank 239 vb.
pass 305 vb.
circle 314 vb.
woman 373 n.
circuit 626 vb.

— round
avoid 620 vb.
skirt-chaser
libertine 952 n.
skit
stage play 594 n.
satire 851 n.
skitter
be in motion 265 vb.
swim 269 vb.
skittish
leaping 312 adj.
capricious 604 adj.
lively 819 adj.
excitable 822 adj.
skittle
fell 311 vb.
— out
defeat 727 vb.
skittle alley
arena 724 n.
place of amusement 837 n.
skittles
ball game 837 n.
skive
laminate 207 vb.
be inactive 679 vb.
skiver
avoider 620 n.
idler 679 n.
skivvy
domestic 742 n.
skol!
301 int.
skua
bird 365 n.
skulduggery, skullduggery
trickery 542 n.
improbity 930 n.
skulk
wander 267 vb.
be stealthy 525 vb.
avoid 620 vb.
be cowardly 856 vb.
skulker
hider 527 n.
avoider 620 n.
coward 856 n.
skull
head 213 n.
dome 253 n.
corpse 363 n.
skull and crossbones
flag 547 n.
intimidation 854 n.
skull cap
headgear 228 n.
canonicals 989 n.
skunk
mammal 365 n.
stench 397 n.
cad 938 n.
sky
space 183 n.
height 209 n.
summit 213 n.
propel 287 vb.
elevate 310 vb.
heavens 321 n.
sky-blue
blue 435 adj.
sky diver
aeronaut 271 n.
skyey
airy 340 adj.
sky-high
high 209 adj.
dear 811 adj.
skylab
satellite 321 n.
skylark
climber 308 n.
amuse oneself 837 vb.
skylarking
foolery 497 n.
skylight
window 263 n.
skyline
distance 199 n.
outline 233 n.
sky pilot
cleric 986 n.
skyrocket
grow 36 vb.
climber 308 n.
fireworks 420 n.
skyscape
art subject 553 n.
skyscraper
high structure 209 n.
skyward
aloft 209 adv.
skywriting
aeronautics 271 n.
publicity 528 n.
slab
piece 53 n.
lamina 207 n.
horizontality 216 n.
shelf 218 n.
monument 548 n.
slab-sided
tall 209 adj.
slack
nonadhesive 49 adj.
weak 163 adj.
inert 175 adj.
slow 278 adj.
soft 327 adj.
coal 385 n.
negligent 458 adj.
be unwilling 598 vb.
lazy 679 adj.
be inactive 679 vb.
lax 734 adj.
— off
repose 683 vb.
slacken
decrease 37 vb.
disunite 46 vb.
weaken 163 vb.
moderate 177 vb.
be inactive 679 vb.
— off
cease 145 vb.
— speed
decelerate 278 vb.
slacker
slacker 598 n.
idler 679 n.
slack-jawed
open 263 adj.
slack market
unproductiveness 172 n.
slack period
inactivity 679 n.
slacks
informal dress 228 n.
trousers 228 n.
slack water
middle way 625 n.
slag
leavings 41 n.
ash 381 n.
rubbish 641 n.
dirt 649 n.
slake
assuage 177 vb.
add water 339 vb.
sate 863 vb.
— one's thirst
drink 301 vb.
slalom
deviation 282 n.
racing 716 n.
slam
be vigorous 174 vb.
close 264 vb.
impulse 279 n.
strike 279 vb.
propel 287 vb.
loudness 400 n.
bang 402 n.vb.
victory 727 n.
detract 926 vb.
slammerkin
dirty person 649 n.
slander
slur 867 n.
scurrility 899 n.
censure 924 n.
calumny 926 n.
false charge 928 n.
slanderer
evildoer 904 n.
defamer 926 n.
accuser 928 n.
slang
unintelligibility 517 n.
slang 560 n.
cuss 899 vb.
dispraise 924 vb.
slanging match
quarrel 709 n.
scurrility 899 n.
slangy
linguistic 557 adj.
dialectal 560 adj.
slant
obliquity 220 n.
be oblique 220 vb.
view 438 n.
idea 451 n.
bias 481 n.
slap
strike 279 vb.
bang 402 n.
endearment 889 n.
spank 963 vb.
— down
restrain 747 vb.
slap and tickle
endearment 889 n.
slap-bang
instantaneously 116 adv.
violently 176 adv.
slapdash
negligent 458 adj.
hasty 680 adj.
clumsy 695 adj.
rash 857 adj.
slaphappy
negligent 458 adj.
rash 857 adj.
slap in the face
refusal 760 n.
humiliation 872 n.
anger 891 n.
indignity 921 n.
slapstick
stage play 594 n.
wit 839 n.
ridiculousness 849 n.
slap-up
rich 800 adj.
liberal 813 adj.
slash
cut 46 vb.
rend 46 vb.
notch 260 vb.
cheapen 812 vb.
dispraise 924 vb.
detract 926 vb.
slashing
forceful 571 adj.
slat
lamina 207 n.
strip 208 n.
shade 226 n.
slate
lamina 207 n.
brittleness 330 n.
greyness 429 n.
classroom 539 n.
electorate 605 n.
policy 623 n.
building material 631 n.
dispraise 924 vb.
reprobate 924 vb.
detract 926 vb.
slates
roof 226 n.
slattern
slut 61 n.
dirty person 649 n.
slatternly
orderless 61 adj.
clumsy 695 adj.

slaughter
destruction 165 n.
slaughter 362 n.vb.
be severe 735 vb.
cruel act 898 n.
slaughterhouse
slaughterhouse 362 n.
slave
instrument 628 n.
busy person 678 n.
worker 686 n.
minister to 703 vb.
slave 742 n.
prisoner 750 n.
— away
work 682 vb.
slave-driver
tyrant 735 n.
slaver
merchant ship 275 n.
exude 298 vb.
excrement 302 n.
taker 786 n.
merchant 794 n.
slavery
labour 682 n.
servitude 745 n.
slavey
domestic 742 n.
slavish
imitative 20 adj.
obedient 739 adj.
subjected 745 adj.
servile 879 adj.
slavishness
submission 721 n.
slay
kill 362 vb.
amuse 837 vb.
slayer
killer 362 n.
sleazy
flimsy 163 adj.
dirty 649 adj.
sledge, sled
footwear 228 n.
sledge 274 n.
sledge dog
beast of burden 273 n.
sledge-hammer
hammer 279 n.
pulverizer 332 n.
compelling 740 adj.
sleek
smooth 258 adj.
prosperous 730 adj.
personable 841 adj.
sleep
be inert 175 vb.
be quiescent 266 vb.
insensibility 375 n.
be inattentive 456 vb.
sleep 679 n.vb.
repose 683 n.vb.
— around
be impure 951 vb.
— it off
be refreshed 685 vb.
be sober 948 vb.
— on it
wait 136 vb.
meditate 449 vb.
— with
unite with 45 vb.
sleeper
basis 218 n.
railway 624 n.
idler 679 n.
sleep-inducing
soporific 679 adj.
sleeping
latent 523 adj.
inactive 679 adj.
abrogated 752 adj.
sleeping bag
bag 194 n.
sleeping partner
nonentity 639 n.
sleeping pill/tablet
drug 658 n.
soporific 679 n.
relief 831 n.
sleeping policeman
traffic control 305 n.
sleeping sickness
tropical disease 651 n.
sleepless
persevering 600 adj.
active 678 adj.
sleeplessness
restlessness 678 n.
sleepwalker
pedestrian 268 n.
sleepy
sleepy 679 adj.
fatigued 684 adj.
sleepyhead
slowcoach 278 n.
idler 679 n.
sleepy sickness
infection 651 n.
sleet
rain 350 n.vb.
wintriness 380 n.
sleeve
sleeve 228 n.
sleigh
sledge 274 n.
sleight of hand
sleight 542 n.
skill 694 n.
slender
small 33 adj.
narrow 206 adj.
insufficient 636 adj.
shapely 841 adj.
slender means
poverty 801 n.
sleuth
detective 459 n.
informer 524 n.
slew
deviation 282 n.
rotate 315 vb.
slice
cut 46 vb.
piece 53 n.
laminate 207 vb.
notch 260 vb.
deflect 282 vb.
propel 287 vb.
mouthful 301 n.
be clumsy 695 vb.
portion 783 n.
slice-of-life drama
stage play 594 n.
slicer
sharp edge 256 n.
slick
smooth 258 adj.
deceiving 542 adj.
skilful 694 adj.
cunning 698 adj.
slicker
trickster 545 n.
slide
fastening 47 n.
elapse 111 vb.
lamina 207 n.
obliquity 220 n.
smoothness 258 n.
go smoothly 258 vb.
be in motion 265 vb.
deviate 282 vb.
descent 309 n.
flow 350 vb.
photography 551 n.
deteriorate 655 vb.
be in danger 661 vb.
not act 677 vb.
pleasure ground 837 n.
— back
revert 148 vb.
relapse 657 vb.
— in
introduce 231 vb.
insert 303 vb.
slide rule
counting instrument 86 n.
gauge 465 n.
slide valve
stopper 264 n.
slight
inconsiderable 33 adj.
inferior 35 adj.
exiguous 196 adj.
narrow 206 adj.
shallow 212 adj.
rare 325 adj.
disregard 458 vb.
underestimate 483 vb.
trivial 639 adj.
not observe 769 vb.
humiliate 872 vb.
indignity 921 n.
hold cheap 922 vb.
detract 926 vb.
slim
small 33 adj.
narrow 206 adj.
shapely 841 adj.
slim chance
improbability 472 n.
slime
moisture 341 n.
semiliquidity 354 n.
dirt 649 n.
slimming
dieting 301 n.
slimy
viscid 354 adj.
dirty 649 adj.
unpleasant 827 adj.
servile 879 adj.
flattering 925 adj.
sling
bag 194 n.
hang 217 vb.
propellant 287 n.
propel 287 vb.
surgical dressing 658 n.
lapidate 712 vb.
missile weapon 723 n.
— out
reject 607 vb.
slink
lurk 523 vb.
be stealthy 525 vb.
be cowardly 856 vb.
— away
lose repute 867 vb.
— off
decamp 296 vb.
run away 620 vb.
slinky
narrow 206 adj.
tailored 228 adj.
shapely 841 adj.
slip
come unstuck 49 vb.
branch 53 n.
young plant 132 n.
youngster 132 n.
thinness 206 n.
underwear 228 n.
go smoothly 258 vb.
descend 309 vb.
tumble 309 vb.
viscidity 354 n.
mistake 495 n.
solecism 565 n.
deteriorate 655 vb.
be in danger 661 vb.
— away
go away 190 vb.
decamp 296 vb.
— back
relapse 657 vb.
— by
elapse 111 vb.
— into
wear 228 vb.

— off
doff 229 vb.
— one's lead
escape 667 vb.
— one's memory
escape notice 456 vb.
be forgotten 506 vb.
— through
escape 667 vb.
— up
blunder 495 vb.

slip case
bookbinding 589 n.
slip knot
ligature 47 n.
slipped disc
rheumatism 651 n.
slipper(s)
footwear 228 n.
informal dress 228 n.
spank 963 vb.
slippered
comfortable 376 adj.
reposeful 683 adj.
slipperiness
changeableness 152 n.
unreliability 474 n.
slippery
nonadhesive 49 adj.
smooth 258 adj.
unctuous 357 adj.
deceiving 542 adj.
tergiversating 603 adj.
avoiding 620 adj.
unsafe 661 adj.
escaped 667 adj.
cunning 698 adj.
dishonest 930 adj.
slippery slope
ruin 165 n.
danger 661 n.
wickedness 934 n.
slips
workshop 687 n.
slipshod
orderless 61 adj.
negligent 458 adj.
feeble 572 adj.
lax 734 adj.
slip stream
wind 352 n.
slip-up
mistake 495 n.
slipway
smoothness 258 n.
slit
rend 46 vb.
sunder 46 vb.
gap 201 n.
furrow 262 n.
slither
be in motion 265 vb.
slithery
smooth 258 adj.
sliver
small thing 33 n.
piece 53 n.
slob
bungler 697 n.
cad 938 n.
slobber
exude 298 vb.
emit 300 vb.
excrement 302 n.
moisture 341 n.
make unclean 649 vb.
sloe
sourness 393 n.
black thing 428 n.
slog
strike 279 vb.
propel 287 vb.
be busy 678 vb.
work 682 vb.
— away
persevere 600 vb.
— on
progress 285 vb.
slogan
maxim 496 n.
advertisement 528 n.
call 547 n.
warfare 718 n.
slogger
busy person 678 n.
pugilist 722 n.
sloop
sailing ship 275 n.
slop
let fall 311 vb.
moisten 341 vb.
waste 634 vb.
be clumsy 695 vb.
— about
fluctuate 317 vb.
— over
be complete 54 vb.
flow out 298 vb.
slope
high land 209 n.
be oblique 220 vb.
ascent 308 n.
descent 309 n.
— off
travel 267 vb.
decamp 296 vb.
run away 620 vb.
sloping
sloping 220 adj.
written 586 adj.
sloppiness
inexactness 495 n.
sloppy
orderless 61 adj.
semiliquid 354 adj.
tasteless 387 adj.
negligent 458 adj.
feeble 572 adj.
feeling 818 adj.
sloppy joe
jersey 228 n.
sloppy thinking
sophism 477 n.
slops
weak thing 163 n.
clothing 228 n.
insipidity 387 n.
swill 649 n.
slosh
strike 279 vb.
drench 341 vb.
flow 350 vb.
— about
fluctuate 317 vb.
sloshed
tipsy 949 adj.
slot
sorting 62 n.
serial place 73 n.
receptacle 194 n.
gap 201 n.
furrow 262 n.
orifice 263 n.
trace 548 n.
sloth
inertness 175 n.
sluggishness 679 n.
vice 934 n.
slothful
lazy 679 adj.
slot in
place 187 vb.
slot machine
shop 796 n.
treasury 799 n.
slouch
be low 210 vb.
move slowly 278 vb.
stoop 311 vb.
be inactive 679 vb.
sloucher
slowcoach 278 n.
avoider 620 n.
idler 679 n.
slouching
graceless 842 adj.
slough
leavings 41 n.
doff 229 vb.
marsh 347 n.
disaccustom 611 vb.
Slough of Despond
adversity 731 n.
dejection 834 n.
sloven
slut 61 n.
dirty person 649 n.
slovenly
orderless 61 adj.
negligent 458 adj.
feeble 572 adj.
dirty 649 adj.
slow
protracted 113 adj.
anachronistic 118 adj.
late 136 adj.
inert 175 adj.
slow 278 adj.
inexact 495 adj.
unintelligent 499 adj.
unwilling 598 adj.
lazy 679 adj.
leisurely 681 adj.
inexcitable 823 adj.
tedious 838 adj.
dull 840 adj.
cautious 858 adj.
— down
come to rest 266 vb.
decelerate 278 vb.
be inactive 679 vb.
repose 683 vb.
hinder 702 vb.
— up
decelerate 278 vb.
slowcoach
slowcoach 278 n.
idler 679 n.
slow-down
strike 145 n.
slowness 278 n.
slow handclap
disapprobation 924 n.
slowness
slowness 278 n.
(See **slow** *)*
slow-witted
unintelligent 499 adj.
slowworm
reptile 365 n.
slub
weave 222 vb.
slubbed
rough 259 adj.
slubberdegullion
idler 679 n.
bad person 938 n.
sludge
leavings 41 n.
semiliquidity 354 n.
dirt 649 n.
slug
strike 279 vb.
draught 301 n.
creepy-crawly 365 n.
print-type 587 n.
ammunition 723 n.
sluggard
slowcoach 278 n.
idler 679 n.
sluggish
inert 175 adj.
slow 278 adj.
flowing 350 adj.
nonactive 677 adj.
inactive 679 adj.
apathetic 820 adj.
dull 840 adj.
sluice
outlet 298 n.
irrigator 341 n.
drench 341 vb.
waterfall 350 n.
conduit 351 n.
clean 648 vb.

slum
housing 192 n.
sink 649 n.
insalubrity 653 n.
dilapidation 655 n.
poverty 801 n.
slumber
be inert 175 vb.
quietude 266 n.
sleep 679 n.vb.
slummer
philanthropist 901 n.
slummy
unclean 649 adj.
dilapidated 655 adj.
beggarly 801 adj.
slump
decrease 37 n.vb.
unproductiveness 172 n.
contraction 198 n.
regression 286 n.
descend 309 vb.
deteriorate 655 vb.
inactivity 679 n.
adversity 731 n.
be cheap 812 vb.
slur
stammer 580 vb.
slur 867 n.
calumny 926 n.
— over
neglect 458 vb.
underestimate 483 vb.
conceal 525 vb.
extenuate 927 vb.
slush
semiliquidity 354 n.
pulpiness 356 n.
slush fund
incentive 612 n.
slushy
marshy 347 adj.
cold 380 adj.
feeling 818 adj.
slut
slut 61 n.
dirty person 649 n.
loose woman 952 n.
sluttish
orderless 61 adj.
negligent 458 adj.
dirty 649 adj.
sly
hypocritical 541 adj.
cunning 698 adj.
witty 839 adj.
slyboots
trickster 545 n.
slyboots 698 n.
smack
small quantity 33 n.
tincture 43 n.
sailing ship 275 n.
knock 279 n.
taste 386 n.
bang 402 n.
spank 963 vb.
— of
resemble 18 vb.
taste 386 vb.
indicate 547 vb.
— one's lips
enjoy 376 vb.
taste 386 vb.
be pleased 824 vb.
smacker
funds 797 n.
endearment 889 n.
small
small 33 adj.
fractional 102 adj.
infantine 132 adj.
little 196 adj.
insufficient 636 adj.
unimportant 639 adj.
contemptible 922 adj.
small ad
advertisement 528 n.
small arms
firearm 723 n.
small beer
alcoholic drink 301 n.
trifle 639 n.
small chance
improbability 472 n.
small change
trifle 639 n.
coinage 797 n.
smaller
lesser 35 adj.
contracted 198 adj.
small fry
inferior 35 n.
child 132 n.
nonentity 639 n.
smallholder
farmer 370 n.
small hours
morning 128 n.
lateness 136 n.
small-mindedness
narrow mind 481 n.
small of the back
buttocks 238 n.
smallpox
infection 651 n.
small print
conditions 766 n.
small risk
fair chance 159 n.
smalls
underwear 228 n.
small screen
broadcasting 531 n.
small talk
chatter 581 n.
chat 584 n.
small-time
lesser 35 adj.
trivial 639 adj.
small voice
voicelessness 578 n.
conscience 917 n.
smalt
blue pigment 435 n.
smarm
flatter 925 vb.
— down
smooth 258 vb.
smarmy
flattering 925 adj.
smart
speedy 277 adj.
feel pain 377 vb.
intelligent 498 adj.
active 678 adj.
skilful 694 adj.
cunning 698 adj.
feel 818 vb.
suffer 825 vb.
witty 839 adj.
personable 841 adj.
fashionable 848 adj.
— for it
atone 941 vb.
be punished 963 vb.
— under
feel 818 vb.
be discontented 829 vb.
resent 891 vb.
smart aleck
wiseacre 500 n.
vain person 873 n.
smarten up
beautify 841 vb.
smart set
beau monde 848 n.
smarty-pants
wiseacre 500 n.
vain person 873 n.
smash
break 46 vb.
demolish 165 vb.
force 176 vb.
collision 279 n.
strike 279 vb.
propel 287 vb.
pulverize 332 vb.
wound 655 vb.
smash and grab raid
stealing 788 n.
smasher
exceller 644 n.
a beauty 841 n.
smash hit
exceller 644 n.
success 727 n.
smashing
super 644 adj.
smash-up
ruin 165 n.
collision 279 n.
smattering
erudition 490 n.
sciolism 491 n.
dabbling 491 adj.
smear
overlay 226 vb.
bedim 419 vb.
make unclean 649 vb.
blemish 845 n.vb.
slur 867 n.
calumny 926 n.
defame 926 vb.
smell
sense 374 n.
odour 394 n.
smell 394 vb.
stink 397 vb.
be unclean 649 vb.
deteriorate 655 vb.
— a rat
detect 484 vb.
doubt 486 vb.
— good
make appetizing 390 vb.
cause desire 859 vb.
— of
smell 394 vb.
indicate 547 vb.
— out
discover 484 vb.
— sweet
be fragrant 396 vb.
smelling of the lamp
matured 669 adj.
smelling salts
pungency 388 n.
tonic 658 n.
smelly
odorous 394 adj.
fetid 397 adj.
smelt
liquefy 337 vb.
heat 381 vb.
smelter
workshop 687 n.
smile
gesture 547 n.
be pleased 824 vb.
smile 835 vb.
greet 884 vb.
— at
ridicule 851 vb.
— on
patronize 703 vb.
be auspicious 730 vb.
smiles
cheerfulness 833 n.
smiling
happy 824 adj.
content 828 adj.
cheerful 833 adj.
sociable 882 adj.
smirch
bedim 419 vb.
make unclean 649 vb.
defame 926 vb.
smirk
laughter 835 n.
be affected 850 vb.
smite
strike 279 vb.
kill 362 vb.
impress 821 vb.

smith
artisan 686 n.
smithereens
small thing 33 n.
smithy
workshop 687 n.
smitten
enamoured 887 adj.
smock
shirt 228 n.
smocking
needlework 844 n.
smog
opacity 423 n.
insalubrity 653 n.
smoke
emit 300 vb.
gas 336 n.
vaporize 338 vb.
dry 342 vb.
be hot 379 vb.
ash 381 n.
tobacco 388 n.
smoke 388 vb.
odour 394 n.
bedim 419 vb.
screen 421 vb.
make opaque 423 vb.
blur 440 vb.
lurk 523 vb.
dirt 649 n.
preserve 666 vb.
mature 669 vb.
— out
eject 300 vb.
extract 304 vb.
smoked glass
screen 421 n.
semitransparency 424 n.
smoke-filled
insalubrious 653 adj.
smokeless zone
air 340 n.
salubrity 652 n.
smoker
train 274 n.
tobacco 388 n.n.
smoke screen
obfuscation 421 n.
opacity 423 n.
invisibility 444 n.
concealment 525 n.
disguise 527 n.
pretext 614 n.
defences 713 n.
smokestack
chimney 263 n.
smoky
heated 381 adj.
fetid 397 adj.
dim 419 adj.
black 428 adj.
dirty 649 adj.
(See **smoke** *)*
smooch
caress 889 vb.
smooth
uniform 16 adj.
equalize 28 vb.
nonadhesive 49 adj.
orderly 60 adj.
continuous 71 adj.
regular 81 adj.
make conform 83 vb.
lenitive 177 adj.
flat 216 adj.
flatten 216 vb.
hairless 229 adj.
symmetrical 245 adj.
smooth 258 adj.vb.
tranquil 266 adj.
soft 327 adj.
rub 333 vb.
touch 378 vb.
deceiving 542 adj.
elegant 575 adj.
facilitate 701 vb.
relieve 831 vb.
well-bred 848 adj.
courteous 884 adj.
flattering 925 adj.
— out
not discriminate 464 vb.
smoothbore
firearm 723 n.
smoothie, smoothy
slyboots 698 n.
smooth-running
lubricated 334 adj.
tractable 701 adj.
smooth-tongued
hypocritical 541 adj.
eloquent 579 adj.
flattering 925 adj.
smorgasbord
hors-d'oeuvres 301 n.
smother
suppress 165 vb.
moderate 177 vb.
cover 226 vb.
close 264 vb.
murder 362 vb.
extinguish 382 vb.
conceal 525 vb.
pet 889 vb.
smoulder
be inert 175 vb.
be hot 379 vb.
lurk 523 vb.
be inactive 679 vb.
resent 891 vb.
smriti
tradition 127 n.
non-Biblical scripture 975 n.
smudge
blacken 428 vb.
blur 440 vb.
make unclean 649 vb.
blemish 845 n.
slur 867 n.
smug
affected 850 adj.
vain 873 adj.
smuggle
steal 788 vb.
smuggler
thief 789 n.
smuggling
trade 791 n.
smugness
content 828 n.
smut
ash 381 n.
dirt 649 n.
smutty
unclean 649 adj.
impure 951 adj.
snack
small quantity 33 n.
mouthful 301 n.
snack bar
café 192 n.
snaffle
restraint 747 n.
take 786 vb.
steal 788 vb.
snafu
orderless 61 adj.
snag
projection 254 n.
rub 333 vb.
danger 661 n.
pitfall 663 n.
difficulty 700 n.
hitch 702 n.
snail
slowcoach 278 n.
creepy-crawly 365 n.
snail's pace
slowness 278 n.
snake
meander 251 vb.
reptile 365 n.
bane 659 n.
slyboots 698 n.
finance 797 n.
noxious animal 904 n.
snake-charmer
sorcerer 983 n.
snake in one's bosom
deceiver 545 n.
snake in the grass
latency 523 n.
deceiver 545 n.
troublemaker 663 n.
evildoer 904 n.
snakes and ladders
board game 837 n.
snaky
snaky 251 adj.
dishonest 930 adj.
snap
break 46 vb.
instantaneous 116 adj.
vigorousness 174 n.
close 264 vb.
be brittle 330 vb.
crackle 402 vb.
gesticulate 547 vb.
photography 551 n.
spontaneous 609 adj.
unprepared 670 adj.
be discontented 829 vb.
card game 837 n.
be irascible 892 vb.
be sullen 893 vb.
— at
torment 827 vb.
— one's fingers at
defy 711 vb.
disobey 738 vb.
not observe 769 vb.
be courageous 855 vb.
hold cheap 922 vb.
— one's head off
be irascible 892 vb.
— out of it
be restored 656 vb.
be cheerful 833 vb.
— up
eat 301 vb.
take 786 vb.
snap fastener
fastening 47 n.
snap of the fingers
unimportance 639 n.
snappish
irascible 892 adj.
sullen 893 adj.
snappy
vigorous 174 adj.
speedy 277 adj.
aphoristic 496 adj.
witty 839 adj.
personable 841 adj.
snapshot
photography 551 n.
snare
trap 542 n.
ensnare 542 vb.
take 786 vb.
Snark
rara avis 84 n.
snarl
enlace 222 vb.
ululate 409 vb.
ugliness 842 n.
be rude 885 vb.
be sullen 893 vb.
threaten 900 vb.
snarling
threatening 900 adj.
snarl-up
complexity 61 n.
snatch
small quantity 33 n.
take 786 vb.
— at
draw 288 vb.
pursue 619 vb.
snatcher
taker 786 n.
snatchy
discontinuous 72 adj.

snazzy
fashionable 848 adj.
sneak
informer 524 n.
be stealthy 525 vb.
coward 856 n.
be servile 879 vb.
knave 938 n.
— off with
steal 788 vb.
sneakers
footwear 228 n.
sneaking
tacit 523 adj.
(See **sneak** *)*
sneak thief
thief 789 n.
sneer
insolence 878 n.
contempt 922 n.
dispraise 924 vb.
calumny 926 n.
sneeze
breathe 352 vb.
snick
cut 46 vb.
wound 655 n.
snicker
laugh 835 vb.
snide
false 541 adj.
detracting 926 adj.
sniff
breathe 352 vb.
smell 394 vb.
be insolent 878 vb.
contempt 922 n.
— at
reject 607 vb.
dislike 861 vb.
despise 922 vb.
— up
absorb 299 vb.
sniffing
drug-taking 949 n.
sniffle
breathe 352 vb.
sniffling
puffing 352 adj.
sniffly
diseased 651 adj.
sniffy
despising 922 adj.
snifter
draught 301 n.
snigger
laugh 835 vb.
ridicule 851 n.
sniggle
ensnare 542 vb.
snip
small thing 33 n.
cut 46 vb.
piece 53 n.
notch 260 vb.
cheapness 812 n.
snipe
shoot 287 vb.
table bird 365 n.
fire at 712 vb.
sniper
shooter 287 n.
attacker 712 n.
sniping
dissension 709 n.
snippet
small thing 33 n.
piece 53 n.
snitch
informer 524 n.
inform 524 vb.
steal 788 vb.
snivel
excrete 302 vb.
weep 836 vb.
snob
vulgarian 847 n.
proud person 871 n.
snobbery
etiquette 848 n.
pride 871 n.
snobbish
biased 481 adj.
ill-bred 847 adj.
affected 850 adj.
prideful 871 adj.
despising 922 adj.
snob value
prestige 866 n.
snog
caress 889 vb.
snood
headgear 228 n.
hairdressing 843 n.
snook
sauciness 878 n.
indignity 921 n.
snooker
obstruct 702 vb.
ball game 837 n.
snoop
spectator 441 n.
inquisitive person 453 n.
be curious 453 vb.
enquire 459 vb.
informer 524 n.
be stealthy 525 vb.
snooper
inquisitive person 453 n.
detective 459 n.
snooty
insolent 878 adj.
despising 922 adj.
snooze
sleep 679 n.vb.
snore
rasp 407 vb.
sleep 679 vb.
snort
draught 301 n.
breathe 352 vb.
hiss 406 vb.
rasp 407 vb.
ululate 409 vb.
be insolent 878 vb.
be irascible 892 vb.
sullenness 893 n.
contempt 922 n.
snot
excrement 302 n.
dirt 649 n.
snout
protuberance 254 n.
tobacco 388 n.
snow
softness 327 n.
snow 380 n.
white thing 427 n.
abound 635 vb.
drug-taking 949 n.
— under
be many 104 vb.
snowball
grow 36 vb.
continuity 71 n.
accumulation 74 n.
expand 197 vb.
strike 279 vb.
missile 287 n.
snow 380 n.
dance 837 n.
snowbound
wintry 129 adj.
snowdrift
accumulation 74 n.
snow 380 n.
snowfall
snow 380 n.
snowflake
softness 327 n.
powder 332 n.
snow 380 n.
snowman
insubstantial thing 4 n.
snow 380 n.
image 551 n.
snowmobile
vehicle 274 n.
snowplough
vehicle 274 n.
snowscape
beauty 841 n.
snowshoes
sledge 274 n.
snows of yesteryear
brief span 114 n.
snowstorm
storm 176 n.
wintriness 380 n.
snow-white
white 427 adj.
snowy
cold 380 adj.
white 427 adj.
pure 950 adj.
snub
short 204 adj.
unsharpened 257 adj.
repel 292 vb.
humiliate 872 vb.
be rude 885 vb.
indignity 921 n.
reprimand 924 n.
snuff
absorb 299 vb.
extinguish 382 vb.
tobacco 388 n.
smell 394 vb.
— it
die 361 vb.
— out
nullify 2 vb.
suppress 165 vb.
snuff out 418 vb.
snuffle
breathe 352 vb.
hiss 406 vb.
stammer 580 vb.
snuffy
irascible 892 adj.
despising 922 adj.
snug
adjusted 24 adj.
chamber 194 n.
little 196 adj.
dry 342 adj.
comfortable 376 adj.
warm 379 adj.
safe 660 adj.
reposeful 683 adj.
content 828 adj.
snuggery
retreat 192 n.
snuggle
approach 289 vb.
caress 889 vb.
so
thus 8 adv.
similarly 18 adv.
greatly 32 adv.
hence 158 adv.
true 494 adj.
soak
fill 54 vb.
pervade 189 vb.
immerse 303 vb.
drench 341 vb.
superabound 637 vb.
fleece 786 vb.
overcharge 811 vb.
sate 863 vb.
get drunk 949 vb.
— through
infiltrate 297 vb.
pass 305 vb.
— up
absorb 299 vb.
dry 342 vb.
soakaway
sink 649 n.
soaking
drenched 341 adj.
ablutions 648 n.
so-and-so
person 371 n.
no name 562 n.
soap
softness 327 n.
lubricant 334 n.
fat 357 n.
cleanser 648 n.

soapbox
rostrum 539 n.
oratory 579 n.
soap opera
broadcast 531 n.
soapsuds
bubble 355 n.
soapy
bubbly 355 adj.
servile 879 adj.
flattering 925 adj.
soar
be high 209 vb.
fly 271 vb.
ascend 308 vb.
be light 323 vb.
be dear 811 vb.
— above
outdo 306 vb.
soaring
great 32 adj.
hoping 852 adj.
(See **soar** *)*
sob
respiration 352 n.
rasp 407 vb.
cry 408 n.vb.
voicelessness 578 n.
stammer 580 vb.
weep 836 vb.
sober
moderate 177 adj.
soft-hued 425 adj.
wise 498 adj.
sane 502 adj.
plain 573 adj.
inexcitable 823 adj.
serious 834 adj.
depress 834 vb.
cautious 858 adj.
temperate 942 adj.
sober 948 adj.
— down
be moderate 177 vb.
tranquillize 823 vb.
— up
be sober 948 vb.
sobered
dejected 834 adj.
repentant 939 adj.
sober 948 adj.
sobersides
moper 834 n.
sobriety
moderation 177 n.
sobriety 948 n.
sobriquet
name 561 n.
sob sister
excitant 821 n.
sob-stuff
excitation 821 n.
lament 836 n.
socage
possession 773 n.
so-called
unbelieved 486 adj.
supposed 512 adj.
spurious 542 adj.
untrue 543 adj.
named 561 adj.
misnamed 562 adj.
soccer
ball game 837 n.
sociability
sociability 882 n.
sociable
friendly 880 adj.
sociable 882 adj.
amiable 884 adj.
social
national 371 adj.
corporate 708 adj.
social gathering 882 n.
sociable 882 adj.
social anthropology
anthropology 371 n.
social climber
vulgarian 847 n.
sociable person 882 n.
social conscience
philanthropy 901 n.
Social Democrats
political party 708 n.
social engineering
reformism 654 n.
sociology 901 n.
social gathering
assembly 74 n.
social gathering 882 n.
social graces
good taste 846 n.
sociability 882 n.
social group
group 74 n.
social group 371 n.
community 708 n.
socialism
reformism 654 n.
government 733 n.
joint possession 775 n.
philanthropy 901 n.
socialistic
sharing 775 adj.
philanthropic 901 adj.
Socialists
political party 708 n.
socialite
beau monde 848 n.
sociable person 882 n.
sociality
sociality 882 n.
socialize, socialise
make better 654 vb.
communalize 775 vb.
be sociable 882 vb.
social science
anthropology 371 n.
sociology 901 n.
social security
safety 660 n.
subvention 703 n.
social services
sociology 901 n.
social work
sociology 901 n.
social worker
reformer 654 n.
worker 686 n.
aider 703 n.
philanthropist 901 n.
society
accompaniment 89 n.
social group 371 n.
society 708 n.
beau monde 848 n.
sociality 882 n.
Society of Friends
sect 978 n.
Society of Jesus
monk 986 n.
Socinian
heretic 977 n.
sociologist
reformer 654 n.
sociology
anthropology 371 n.
reformism 654 n.
sociology 901 n.
sociopath
madman 504 n.
sock
legwear 228 n.
strike 279 vb.
drama 594 n.
socket
place 185 n.
receptacle 194 n.
cavity 255 n.
socking
whopping 32 adj.
socle
stand 218 n.
Socratic method
interrogation 459 n.
argumentation 475 n.
sod
piece 53 n.
soil 344 n.
grass 366 n.
soda
soft drink 301 n.
cleanser 648 n.
soda fountain
café 192 n.
sodality
association 706 n.
community 708 n.
friendship 880 n.
soda water
soft drink 301 n.
sodden
drenched 341 adj.
drunken 949 adj.
sodomy
illicit love 951 n.
sofa
seat 218 n.
so far
thus far 236 adv.
soffit
projection 254 n.
soft
unstable 152 adj.
weak 163 adj.
lenitive 177 adj.
smooth 258 adj.
soft 327 adj.
comfortable 376 adj.
silent 399 adj.
muted 401 adj.
melodious 410 adj.
luminous 417 adj.
soft-hued 425 adj.
foolish 499 adj.
lenient 736 adj.
impressible 819 adj.
cowardly 856 adj.
pitying 905 adj.
sober 948 adj.
soft answer
leniency 736 n.
courteous act 884 n.
softball
ball game 837 n.
soft drink
soft drink 301 n.
soft drug
drug-taking 949 n.
soften
soften 327 vb.
be sensitive 819 vb.
relieve 831 vb.
extenuate 927 vb.
(See **soft** *)*
— up
influence 178 vb.
induce 612 vb.
prepare 669 vb.
fire at 712 vb.
softened
repentant 939 adj.
softening of the brain
insanity 503 n.
soft focus
dimness 419 n.
soft furnishings
covering 226 n.
soft-grained
wooden 366 adj.
softhead
ninny 501 n.
soft-hearted
impressible 819 adj.
benevolent 897 adj.
pitying 905 adj.
soft landing
space travel 271 n.
softly softly
moderately 177 adv.
cautiously 858 adv.
softness
softness 327 n.
irresolution 601 n.
persuadability 612 n.
vulnerability 661 n.

leniency 736 n.
benevolence 897 n.
sensualism 944 n.
(See **soft** *)*
soft nothings
endearment 889 n.
soft on
enamoured 887 adj.
soft option
easy thing 701 n.
soft-pedal
moderate 177 vb.
mute 401 vb.
underestimate 483 vb.
extenuate 927 vb.
soft porn
impurity 951 n.
soft sawder
flattery 925 n.
soft sell
advertisement 528 n.
inducement 612 n.
sale 793 n.
soft soap
flattery 925 n.
soft-spoken
speaking 579 adj.
amiable 884 adj.
soft spot
defect 647 n.
vulnerability 661 n.
moral sensibility 819 n.
soft touch
dupe 544 n.
easy thing 701 n.
software
data processing 86 n.
softwood
wood 366 n.
softy, softie
weakling 163 n.
ninny 501 n.
soggy
soft 327 adj.
drenched 341 adj.
pulpy 356 adj.
unsavoury 391 adj.
so happen
chance 159 vb.
soi-disant
untrue 543 adj.
named 561 adj.
misnamed 562 adj.
soigné(e)
dressed 228 adj.
elegant 575 adj.
personable 841 adj.
soil
region 184 n.
soil 344 n.
make unclean 649 vb.
make ugly 842 vb.
blemish 845 vb.
soirée
evening 129 n.
social gathering 882 n.
sojourn
be present 189 vb.
dwell 192 vb.
visit 882 vb.
sojourner
dweller 191 n.
soke
district 184 n.
solace
relief 831 n.
amusement 837 n.
amuse 837 vb.
solar
celestial 321 adj.
solar battery
sources of energy 160 n.
solar constant
thermometry 379 n.
solar energy
sources of energy 160 n.
heater 383 n.
solarium
heater 383 n.
hospital 658 n.
solar panel
sources of energy 160 n.
solar plexus
insides 224 n.
solar system
sun 321 n.
solatium
reward 962 n.
sold
salable 793 adj.
sold a pup
gullible 544 adj.
solder
join 45 vb.
adhesive 47 n.
soldering iron
heater 383 n.
soldier
defender 713 n.
wage war 718 vb.
soldier 722 n.
brave person 855 n.
— on
stand firm 599 vb.
soldierly
warlike 718 adj.
courageous 855 adj.
soldier of fortune
militarist 722 n.
soldiery
soldier 722 n.
soldiery 722 n.
sold off
not retained 779 adj.
sold on
believing 485 adj.
enamoured 887 adj.
sole
one 88 adj.
foot 214 n.
fish food 301 n.
solecism
mistake 495 n.
solecism 565 n.
solemn
great 32 adj.
affirmative 532 adj.
important 638 adj.
serious 834 adj.
formal 875 adj.
sanctified 979 adj.
devotional 981 adj.
ritual 988 adj.
solemnity
formality 875 n.
rite 988 n.
solemnization, solemnisation
celebration 876 n.
ministration 988 n.
solemnly affirm
swear 532 vb.
solenoid
magnet 291 n.
sole survivor
fewness 105 n.
sol-fa
vocal music 412 n.
solfège, solfeggio
notation 410 n.
solicitation
inducement 612 n.
offer 759 n.
request 761 n.
solicitor
law agent 958 n.
Solicitor General
law officer 955 n.
solicitous
careful 457 adj.
desiring 859 adj.
solicitude
attention 455 n.
worry 825 n.
nervousness 854 n.
solid
real 1 adj.
substantial 3 adj.
uniform 16 adj.
firm 45 adj.
cohesive 48 adj.
continuous 71 adj.
one 88 adj.
unyielding 162 adj.
material 319 adj.
solid body 324 n.
dense 324 adj.
certain 473 adj.
assenting 488 adj.
printed 587 adj.
serious 834 adj.
solidarity
unity 88 n.
stability 153 n.
association 706 n.
cooperation 706 n.
concord 710 n.
friendship 880 n.
solid body
substance 3 n.
bulk 195 n.
solid body 324 n.
solid-fuel
heating 381 adj.
solidification
condensation 324 n.
refrigeration 382 n.
solidify
cohere 48 vb.
be dense 324 vb.
solidity
substantiality 3 n.
completeness 54 n.
permanence 144 n.
stability 153 n.
materiality 319 n.
density 324 n.
opacity 423 n.
solid-state
dynamic 160 adj.
soliloquy
oration 579 n.
soliloquy 585 n.
dramaturgy 594 n.
solitaire
gem 844 n.
solitary
nonconformist 84 n.
unconformable 84 adj.
alone 88 adj.
one 88 adj.
wanderer 268 n.
solitary 883 n.
friendless 883 adj.
unsociable 883 adj.
misanthrope 902 n.
ascetic 945 n.
solitude
unity 88 n.
seclusion 883 n.
solmization, solmisation
notation 410 n.
vocal music 412 n.
solo
unit 88 n.
duet 412 n.
tune 412 n.
soloist
musician 413 n.
Solomon
sage 500 n.
Solon
sage 500 n.
so long as
while 108 adv.
provided 468 adv.
solstice
uranometry 321 n.
soluble
mixed 43 adj.
fluid 335 adj.
liquefied 337 adj.
solution
a mixture 43 n.
solution 337 n.

answer 460 n.
discovery 484 n.
interpretation 520 n.
remedy 658 n.
completion 725 n.
solve
decipher 520 vb.
solvent
liquefaction 337 n.
moneyed 800 adj.
so many
quantitative 26 adj.
somatic
material 319 adj.
somatology
anthropology 371 n.
sombre
funereal 364 adj.
dark 418 adj.adj.
soft-hued 425 adj.
black 428 adj.
grey 429 adj.
cheerless 834 adj.
sombrero
headgear 228 n.
some
quantitative 26 adj.
partially 33 adv.
plurality 101 n.
anonymous 562 adj.
somebody
substance 3 n.
person 371 n.
bigwig 638 n.
person of repute 866 n.
someday
not now 122 adv.
prospectively 124 adv.
somehow
partially 33 adv.
somehow 158 adv.
somehow feel
intuit 476 vb.
someone
person 371 n.
some other time
different time 122 n.
some other way
differently 15 adv.
some place
somewhere 185 adv.
somersault
overturning 221 n.
something
substance 3 n.
object 319 n.
something between them
compact 765 n.
love affair 887 n.
something else
variant 15 n.
something for everybody
generality 79 n.
something for nothing
acquisition 771 n.
something in common
relation 9 n.
something in hand
advantage 34 n.
store 632 n.
something missing
shortfall 307 n.
something or other
uncertainty 474 n.
something over
extra 40 n.
superfluity 637 n.
something to be said for
dueness 915 n.
something to go by/on
indication 547 n.
something to one's advantage
benefit 615 n.
something wrong
hitch 702 n.
wrong 914 n.
sometime
not now 122 adv.
former 125 adj.
sometimes
sometimes 139 adv.
somewhat
partially 33 adv.
somewhere
about 33 adv.
somewhere 185 adv.
somewhere around
nearly 200 adv.
somewhere else
not here 190 adv.
so minded
volitional 595 adj.
intending 617 adj.
somnambulism
pedestrianism 267 n.
sleep 679 n.
somniferous
soporific 679 adj.
somnolent
sleepy 679 adj.
so much
quantitative 26 adj.
son
descendant 170 n.
male 372 n.
son and heir
priority 119 n.
sonant
speech sound 398 n.
vocal 577 adj.
sonar
detector 484 n.
sonata
musical piece 412 n.
sone
sound 398 n.
metrology 465 n.
son et lumière
lighting 420 n.
spectacle 445 n.
pageant 875 n.
song
vocal music 412 n.n.
poem 593 n.
hymn 981 n.
song and dance
overactivity 678 n.
excitable state 822 n.
songster
bird 365 n.
vocalist 413 n.
song writer
musician 413 n.
poet 593 n.
sonic
sounding 398 adj.
sonic boom
loudness 400 n.
bang 402 n.
sonnet
verse form 593 n.
wooing 889 n.
sonneteer
poet 593 n.
sonny
youngster 132 n.
son of a bitch
cad 938 n.
son/daughter of the soil
country-dweller 869 n.
sonometer
acoustics 398 n.
sonority
resonance 404 n.
sound 398 n.
sonorous
loud 400 adj.
resonant 404 adj.
ornate 574 adj.
rhetorical 574 adj.
sonship
sequence 65 n.
sonship 170 n.
sonsy
personable 841 adj.
soon
instantaneously 116 adv.
not now 122 adv.
prospectively 124 adv.
betimes 135 adv.
in the future 155 adv.
soon after
subsequently 120 adv.
sooner
optionally 605 adv.
sooner or later
not now 122 adv.
prospectively 124 adv.
soot
powder 332 n.
ash 381 n.
black thing 428 n.
dirt 649 n.
sooth
truth 494 n.
soothe
assuage 177 vb.
remedy 658 vb.
make inactive 679 vb.
pacify 719 vb.
please 826 vb.
relieve 831 vb.
flatter 925 vb.
soothing
deceiving 542 adj.
inexcitability 823 n.
soothing syrup
moderator 177 n.
balm 658 n.
soothsayer
oracle 511 n.
sorcerer 983 n.
sooty
dark 418 adj.
dim 419 adj.
opaque 423 adj.
black 428 adj.
dirty 649 adj.
sop
mouthful 301 n.
moisture 341 n.
incentive 612 n.
leniency 736 n.
sophism
sophism 477 n.
sophist
reasoner 475 n.
sophist 477 n.
trickster 545 n.
sophisticate
mix 43 vb.
sophisticate 477 vb.
cant 541 vb.
impair 655 vb.
expert 696 n.
people of taste 846 n.
sophisticated
complex 61 adj.
intelligent 498 adj.
spurious 542 adj.
well-made 694 adj.
cunning 698 adj.
well-bred 848 adj.
sophistication
culture 490 n.
skill 694 n.
good taste 846 n.
sophistry
sophistry 477 n.
misteaching 535 n.
deception 542 n.
sophomore
student 538 n.
Sophy
sovereign 741 n.

soporific
moderator 177 n.
anaesthetic 375 n.
drug 658 n.
soporific 679 n.adj.
relief 831 n.
sopping
drenched 341 adj.
soppy
feeling 818 adj.
impressible 819 adj.
caressing 889 adj.
soprano
stridor 407 n.
vocalist 413 n.
sorbet
dessert 301 n.
sorcerer
conjuror 545 n.
prodigy 864 n.
sorcerer 983 n.
occultist 984 n.
sorcerer's apprentice
bungler 697 n.
sorceress
a beauty 841 n.
fairy 970 n.
sorceress 983 n.
sorcery
power 160 n.
sleight 542 n.
thaumaturgy 864 n.
diabolism 969 n.
sorcery 983 n.
occultism 984 n.
sordid
not nice 645 adj.
unclean 649 adj.
avaricious 816 adj.
vulgar 847 adj.
sordino
nonresonance 405 n.
mute 414 n.
sore
painful 377 adj.
evil 616 n.
bad 645 adj.
ulcer 651 n.
diseased 651 adj.
wound 655 n.
fatigued 684 adj.
sensitive 819 adj.
painfulness 827 n.
discontented 829 adj.
resentful 891 adj.
sorely
painfully 32 adv.
sore point
moral sensibility 819 n.
painfulness 827 n.
resentment 891 n.
sorghum
cereals 301 n.
sorites
argumentation 475 n.
sorn
beg 761 vb.
sorority
community 708 n.
sorrel
horse 273 n.
vegetable 301 n.
brown 430 adj.
sorrow
bane 659 n.
adversity 731 n.
sorrow 825 n.
dejection 834 n.
lament 836 vb.
pity 905 n.vb.
sorrowful
unhappy 825 adj.
sorry
unimportant 639 adj.
unhappy 825 adj.
regretting 830 adj.
repentant 939 adj.
sorry for
pitying 905 adj.
sorry for oneself
melancholic 834 adj.
sorry sight
painfulness 827 n.
dejection 834 n.
sort
character 5 n.
class 62 vb.
sort 77 n.
discriminate 463 vb.
— one out
retaliate 714 vb.
— out
exclude 57 vb.
render few 105 vb.
discriminate 463 vb.
reject 607 vb.
sortes Biblicae
oracle 511 n.
nondesign 618 n.
sortie
outbreak 176 n.
egress 298 n.
attack 712 n.
sortilege
divination 511 n.
sorcery 983 n.
sorting office
postal communications 531 n.
sortition
nondesign 618 n.
sort of
partially 33 adv.
SOS
signal 547 n.
danger signal 665 n.
so-so
imperfect 647 adj.
middling 732 adj.
sot
fool 501 n.
drunkard 949 n.
soteriology
theology 973 n.
so to speak
metaphorically 519 adv.
sottish
unintelligent 499 adj.
drunken 949 adj.
sotto voce
faintly 401 adv.
secretly 525 adv.
voicelessly 578 adv.
sou
small coin 33 n.
soubrette
acting 594 n.
soufflé
dish 301 n.
bubble 355 n.
sough
blow 352 vb.
sound faint 401 vb.
sought after
salable 793 adj.
welcomed 882 adj.
soul
essence 1 n.
essential part 5 n.
main part 32 n.
self 80 n.
interiority 224 n.
life 360 n.
person 371 n.
spirit 447 n.
affections 817 n.
moral sensibility 819 n.
soul brother/sister
friend 880 n.
soulful
feeling 818 adj.
soulless
impassive 820 adj.
tedious 838 adj.
soul mate
close friend 880 n.
loved one 887 n.
spouse 894 n.
soul music
music 412 n.
souls
the dead 361 n.
ghost 970 n.
soul-searching
regret 830 n.
honourable 929 adj.
soul-stirring
felt 818 adj.
exciting 821 adj.
sound
consummate 32 adj.
firm 45 adj.
regulated 83 adj.
unyielding 162 adj.
plunge 313 vb.
gulf 345 n.
sound 398 n.vb.
be loud 400 vb.
play music 413 vb.
be heard 415 vb.
radiation 417 n.
enquire 459 vb.
be tentative 461 vb.
measure 465 vb.
genuine 494 adj.
wise 498 adj.
proclaim 528 vb.
voice 577 n.
not bad 644 adj.
perfect 646 adj.
healthy 650 adj.
skilful 694 adj.
moneyed 800 adj.
orthodox 976 adj.
— like
resemble 18 vb.
— off
orate 579 vb.
speak 579 vb.
— out
interrogate 459 vb.
sound barrier
limit 236 n.
sound 398 n.
sound character
honourable person 929 n.
sound effect
sound 398 n.
sound engineer
acoustics 398 n.
sounding board
musical instrument 414 n.
publicity 528 n.
soundings
depth 211 n.
enquiry 459 n.
soundless
deep 211 adj.
still 266 adj.
silent 399 adj.
sound mind
sanity 502 n.
soundproof
silent 399 adj.
nonresonant 405 adj.
soundproofing
lining 227 n.
barrier 235 n.
faintness 401 n.
sound recording
listening 415 n.
registration 548 n.
sound track
sound 398 n.
cinema 445 n.
sound wave
oscillation 317 n.
sound 398 n.
soup
a mixture 43 n.
hors-d'oeuvres 301 n.
semiliquidity 354 n.
soupçon
small quantity 33 n.
tincture 43 n.
souped-up
dynamic 160 adj.

vigorous 174 adj.
speedy 277 adj.
soup kitchen
subvention 703 n.
sour
unsavoury 391 adj.
sour 393 adj.
amiss 616 adv.
unpleasant 827 adj.
discontented 829 adj.
aggravate 832 vb.
sullen 893 adj.
source
origin 68 n.
source 156 n.
parentage 169 n.
stream 350 n.
informant 524 n.
store 632 n.
sources of energy
sources of energy 160 n.
sourdough
experimenter 461 n.
sour grapes
impossibility 470 n.
pretext 614 n.
sourpuss
moper 834 n.
rude person 885 n.
sousaphone
horn 414 n.
souse
immerse 303 vb.
plunge 313 vb.
drench 341 vb.
preserve 666 vb.
get drunk 949 vb.
soutane
canonicals 989 n.
souter
clothier 228 n.
south
compass point 281 n.
southbound
directed 281 adj.
southern
opposite 240 adj.
Southerner
foreigner 59 n.
native 191 n.
southing
bearings 186 n.
southpaw
sinistrality 242 n.
South pole
summit 213 n.
coldness 380 n.
souvenir
reminder 505 n.
sou'wester
headgear 228 n.
gale 352 n.
sovereign
superior 34 n.
supreme 34 adj.
strong 162 adj.
remedial 658 adj.
successful 727 adj.
ruling 733 adj.
sovereign 741 n.
coinage 797 n.
aristocrat 868 n.
sovereignty
superiority 34 n.
governance 733 n.
soviet
council 692 n.
sovietism
government 733 n.
sow
disperse 75 vb.
cause 156 vb.
produce 164 vb.
let fall 311 vb.
pig 365 n.
cultivate 370 vb.
female animal 373 n.
— dragon's teeth
cause discontent 829 vb.
— one's wild oats
be foolish 499 vb.
revel 837 vb.
be intemperate 943 vb.
— the seeds of
cause 156 vb.
educate 534 vb.
— the wind and reap the whirlwind
deserve 915 vb.
sower
farmer 370 n.
preparer 669 n.
soya beans
vegetable 301 n.
sozzled
tipsy 949 adj.
spa
abode 192 n.
hygiene 652 n.
hospital 658 n.
space
quantity 26 n.
grade 73 vb.
infinity 107 n.
time 108 n.
room 183 n.
space 183 n.
size 195 n.
distance 199 n.
interval 201 n.
space 201 vb.
opening 263 n.
open space 263 n.
air 340 n.
storage 632 n.
Space Age
era 110 n.
space capsule
spaceship 276 n.
spacecraft
spaceship 276 n.
spaced out
drugged 949 adj.
space flight
space travel 271 n.
spaceman, spacewoman
traveller 268 n.
aeronaut 271 n.
space opera
film 445 n.
space probe
spaceship 276 n.
detector 484 n.
spaceship
space travel 271 n.
spaceship 276 n.
satellite 321 n.
space shuttle
spaceship 276 n.
space station
satellite 321 n.
spacesuit
suit 228 n.
space-time
time 108 n.
space 183 n.
space-time continuum
universe 321 n.
space travel
space travel 271 n.
space walk
space travel 271 n.
spacious
extensive 32 adj.
spacious 183 adj.
large 195 adj.
broad 205 adj.
spade
make concave 255 vb.
farm tool 370 n.
spadework
preparation 669 n.
labour 682 n.
spaghetti
dish 301 n.
spaghnum
plant 366 n.
span
connect 45 vb.
bond 47 n.
group 74 n.
duality 90 n.
time 108 n.
period 110 n.
extend 183 vb.
distance 199 n.
long measure 203 n.
breadth 205 n.
overlie 226 vb.
measure 465 vb.
bridge 624 n.
spandrel
pattern 844 n.
church interior 990 n.
spangle
flash 417 n.
variegate 437 vb.
finery 844 n.
decorate 844 vb.
spaniel
dog 365 n.
toady 879 n.
spank
strike 279 vb.
spank 963 vb.
spanker
whopper 195 n.
sail 275 n.
spanking
whopping 32 adj.
spanking rate
speeding 277 n.
spanner
tool 630 n.
spanner in the works
hitch 702 n.
spar
hanger 217 n.
prop 218 n.
strike 279 vb.
bicker 709 vb.
pugilism 716 n.
fight 716 vb.
spare
additional 38 adj.
remaining 41 adj.
lean 206 adj.
plain 573 adj.
avoid 620 vb.
underfed 636 adj.
superfluous 637 adj.
dispose of 673 vb.
unused 674 adj.
be lenient 736 vb.
not retain 779 vb.
give 781 vb.
economize 814 vb.
relieve 831 vb.
show mercy 905 vb.
exempt 919 vb.
— no effort
exert oneself 682 vb.
— no expense
expend 806 vb.
be liberal 813 vb.
— none
slaughter 362 vb.
be pitiless 906 vb.
— one's blushes
underestimate 483 vb.
spared
absent 190 adj.
safe 660 adj.
spare diet
fasting 946 n.
spare part(s)
extra 40 n.
component 58 n.
safeguard 662 n.
spare time
opportunity 137 n.
leisure 681 n.
spare tyre
bulk 195 n.

sparge
moisten 341 vb.
sparing
economical 814 adj.
parsimonious 816 adj.
temperate 942 adj.
spark
small quantity 33 n.
causal means 156 n.
vigorousness 174 n.
fire 379 n.
flash 417 n.
shine 417 vb.
luminary 420 n.
— off
initiate 68 vb.
cause 156 vb.
sparkle
flash 417 n.
shine 417 vb.
luminary 420 n.
(See **sparkling** *)*
sparkler(s)
fireworks 420 n.
eye 438 n.
gem 844 n.
sparkling
bubbly 355 adj.
luminous 417 adj.
forceful 571 adj.
exciting 821 adj.
happy 824 adj.
merry 833 adj.
witty 839 adj.
splendid 841 adj.
sparring partner
pugilist 722 n.
sparrow
small animal 33 n.
bird 365 n.
sparse
unassembled 75 adj.
few 105 adj.
unproductive 172 adj.
scarce 636 adj.
Spartacus
agitator 738 n.
Spartan
severe 735 adj.
temperate 942 adj.
ascetic 945 adj.
fasting 946 adj.
spasm
brief span 114 n.
fitfulness 142 n.
violence 176 n.
spasm 318 n.
pang 377 n.
nervous disorders 651 n.
activity 678 n.
feeling 818 n.
excitation 821 n.
spasmodic
discontinuous 72 adj.
unstable 152 adj.
spastic
sick person 651 n.
spat
quarrel 709 n.
spatchcock
put between 231 vb.
cook 301 vb.
spate
great quantity 32 n.
waterfall 350 n.
plenty 635 n.
redundance 637 n.
spatial
spatial 183 adj.
spatiotemporal
material 319 adj.
spat on
unrespected 921 adj.
contemptible 922 adj.
spats
legwear 228 n.
spatter
disperse 75 vb.
emit 300 vb.
moisten 341 vb.
make unclean 649 vb.
defame 926 vb.
spatula
ladle 194 n.
art equipment 553 n.
spavin
animal disease 651 n.
spawn
young creature 132 n.
generate 167 vb.
posterity 170 n.
spay
unman 161 vb.
speak
communicate 524 vb.
inform 524 vb.
divulge 526 vb.
signal 547 vb.
voice 577 vb.
speak 579 vb.
— for
deputize 755 vb.
— for itself
be visible 443 vb.
evidence 466 vb.
be intelligible 516 vb.
be plain 522 vb.
— one's mind
be truthful 540 vb.
speak 579 vb.
— out
be plain 522 vb.
affirm 532 vb.
be courageous 855 vb.
— plainly
speak plainly 573 vb.
— to
testify 466 vb.
speak to 583 vb.
— up
be loud 400 vb.
emphasize 532 vb.
be courageous 855 vb.
— up for
approve 923 vb.
vindicate 927 vb.
— volumes
evidence 466 vb.
mean 514 vb.
speakeasy
tavern 192 n.
speaker
megaphone 400 n.
speaker 579 n.
director 690 n.
speaking of
concerning 9 adv.
speaking part
acting 594 n.
speaking tube
hearing aid 415 n.
spear
sharp point 256 n.
pierce 263 vb.
spear 723 n.
spearhead
front 237 n.
precede 283 vb.
chief thing 638 n.
leader 690 n.
attacker 712 n.
spear side
race 11 n.
male 372 n.
special
characteristic 5 adj.
different 15 adj.
original 21 adj.
special 80 adj.
unconformable 84 adj.
chosen 605 adj.
special case
variant 15 n.
nonuniformity 17 n.
speciality 80 n.
special constable
police 955 n.
special correspondent
informant 524 n.
author 589 n.
delegate 754 n.
special day
anniversary 141 n.
festivity 837 n.
special day 876 n.
specialism
knowledge 490 n.
skill 694 n.
specialist
scholar 492 n.
student 538 n.
doctor 658 n.
expert 696 n.
speciality
unrelatedness 10 n.
speciality 80 n.
tendency 179 n.
dish 301 n.
qualification 468 n.
(See **special** *)*
specialize, specialise
study 536 vb.
specialized, specialised
instructed 490 adj.
expert 694 adj.
specially
greatly 32 adv.
specially 80 adv.
special messenger
bearer 273 n.
delegate 754 n.
special offer
incentive 612 n.
discount 810 n.
special pleading
argument 475 n.
sophistry 477 n.
pretext 614 n.
specialty
speciality 80 n.
specie
coinage 797 n.
species
subdivision 53 n.
group 74 n.
breed 77 n.
specific
special 80 adj.
means 629 n.
remedy 658 n.
specifically
positively 32 adv.
specially 80 adv.
specification
classification 77 n.
particulars 80 n.
report 524 n.
description 590 n.
(See **specify** *)*
specific gravity
gravity 322 n.
density 324 n.
specify
class 62 vb.
specify 80 vb.
indicate 547 vb.
name 561 vb.
specimen
duplicate 22 n.
prototype 23 n.
example 83 n.
exhibit 522 n.
specious
appearing 445 adj.
plausible 471 adj.
sophistical 477 adj.
ostensible 614 adj.
splendid 841 adj.
affected 850 adj.
ostentatious 875 adj.
flattering 925 adj.

speck
small thing 33 n.
maculation 437 n.
blemish 845 n.
speckle
maculation 437 n.
variegate 437 vb.
speckled
mottled 437 adj.
speckless
clean 648 adj.
spectacle
spectacle 445 n.
exhibit 522 n.
stage show 594 n.
beauty 841 n.
prodigy 864 n.
pageant 875 n.
spectacles
eyeglass 442 n.
spectacular
obvious 443 adj.
appearing 445 adj.
showy 875 adj.
spectate
watch 441 vb.
spectator
presence 189 n.
spectator 441 n.
witness 466 n.
spectral
insubstantial 4 adj.
variegated 437 adj.
spooky 970 adj.
spectre
visual fallacy 440 n.
appearance 445 n.
intimidation 854 n.
ghost 970 n.
spectre at the feast, be the
hinder 702 vb.
spectrogram
photography 551 n.
spectroheliosocope
astronomy 321 n.
spectroscope
astronomy 321 n.
chromatics 425 n.
optical device 442 n.
spectroscopy
optics 417 n.
spectrum
series 71 n.
light 417 n.
colour 425 n.
variegation 437 n.
spectrum analysis
chromatics 425 n.
speculate
meditate 449 vb.
suppose 512 vb.
speculate 791 vb.
speculation
calculation of chance 159 n.
meditation 449 n.
empiricism 461 n.
conjecture 512 n.
gambling 618 n.
attempt 671 n.
undertaking 672 n.
trade 791 n.
card game 837 n.
speculative
uncertain 474 adj.
speculative 618 adj.
dangerous 661 adj.
rash 857 adj.
speculator
experimenter 461 n.
theorist 512 n.
gambler 618 n.
speculum
mirror 442 n.
speech
language 557 n.
diffuseness 570 n.
voice 577 n.
oration 579 n.
speech 579 n.
allocution 583 n.
speech defect
speech defect 580 n.
speechify
orate 579 vb.
speech impediment
speech defect 580 n.
speechless
silent 399 adj.
voiceless 578 adj.
wondering 864 adj.
speech sound
speech sound 398 n.
speech therapist
doctor 658 n.
speech therapy
speech defect 580 n.
speed
motion 265 n.
velocity 277 n.
move fast 277 vb.
facilitate 701 vb.
aid 703 vb.
— up
augment 36 vb.
accelerate 277 vb.
promote 285 vb.
speedboat
boat 275 n.
speeder
driver 268 n.
speeder 277 n.
contender 716 n.
speed limit
limit 236 n.
restriction 747 n.
speedometer
meter 465 n.
recording instrument 549 n.
speed rate
velocity 277 n.
speed trap
traffic control 305 n.
speedway
racing 716 n.
speedy
instantaneous 116 adj.
speedy 277 adj.
active 678 adj.
speleology
descent 309 n.
mineralogy 359 n.
search 459 n.
discovery 484 n.
sport 837 n.
spell
period 110 n.
influence 178 n.
predict 511 vb.
mean 514 vb.
interpret 520 vb.
imply 523 vb.
indicate 547 vb.
spell 558 vb.
instrument 628 n.
malediction 899 n.
spell 983 n.
— out
specify 80 vb.
decipher 520 vb.
spell 558 vb.
speak plainly 573 vb.
spellbind
motivate 612 vb.
be wonderful 864 vb.
bewitch 983 vb.
spellbinding
eloquent 579 adj.
sorcerous 983 adj.
spellbound
still 266 adj.
obsessed 455 adj.
induced 612 adj.
wondering 864 adj.
bewitched 983 adj.
spelling
spelling 558 n.
spell of duty
labour 682 n.
spencer
jacket 228 n.
spend
waste 634 vb.
expend 806 vb.
— a penny
excrete 302 vb.
— freely
be liberal 813 vb.
be prodigal 815 vb.
— time
pass time 108 vb.
elapse 111 vb.
spender
prodigal 815 n.
spending spree
expenditure 806 n.
prodigality 815 n.
spendthrift
prodigal 815 n.
intemperate 943 adj.
Spenserian
poetic 593 adj.
spent
weakened 163 adj.
outgoing 298 adj.
fatigued 684 adj.
lost 772 adj.
expended 806 adj.
sperm
source 156 n.
genitalia 167 n.
fertilizer 171 n.
spermaceti
fat 357 n.
spermatic
generative 167 adj.
sperm bank
storage 632 n.
spermicide
contraception 172 n.
spew
vomit 300 vb.
flow 350 vb.
SPG
police 955 n.
sphere
circumstance 8 n.
group 74 n.
classification 77 n.
range 183 n.
region 184 n.
sphere 252 n.
world 321 n.
function 622 n.
spherical
round 250 adj.
rotund 252 adj.
spheroid
sphere 252 n.
spherule
sphere 252 n.
sphinx
rara avis 84 n.
secret 530 n.
sphinx-like
unintelligible 517 adj.
spica
prickle 256 n.
spice
small quantity 33 n.
tincture 43 n.
mix 43 vb.
stimulant 174 n.
cook 301 vb.
pungency 388 n.
condiment 389 n.
spice 389 vb.
make appetizing 390 vb.
preserver 666 n.
pleasurableness 826 n.
spick and span
orderly 60 adj.
new 126 adj.
clean 648 adj.
spicule
prickle 256 n.

spicy
pungent 388 adj.
fragrant 396 adj.
exciting 821 adj.
impure 951 adj.
(See **spice** *)*
spider
weaving 222 n.
creepy-crawly 365 n.
planner 623 n.
spiderman
lifter 310 n.
spider's web
complexity 61 n.
ambush 527 n.
spidery
lean 206 adj.
written 586 adj.
spiel
empty talk 515 n.
loquacity 581 n.
spifflicate
destroy 165 vb.
strike 279 vb.
spigot
stopper 264 n.
spike
mix 43 vb.
growth 157 n.
vertex 213 n.
sharp point 256 n.
pierce 263 vb.
flower 366 n.
defences 713 n.
— the guns
disable 161 vb.
be obstructive 702 vb.
spikenard
unguent 357 n.
scent 396 n.
spikes
footwear 228 n.
spiky
sharp 256 adj.
Anglican 976 adj.
spill
overturning 221 n.
flow out 298 vb.
emit 300 vb.
descent 309 n.
let fall 311 vb.
moisten 341 vb.
make flow 350 vb.
lighter 385 n.
torch 420 n.
waste 634 vb.
be clumsy 695 vb.
lose 772 vb.
— over
overstep 306 vb.
— the beans
divulge 526 vb.
spillway
waterfall 350 n.
conduit 351 n.
spilt milk
loss 772 n.
spilt salt
omen 511 n.
spin
make thin 206 vb.
weave 222 vb.
land travel 267 n.
aeronautics 271 n.
rotation 315 n.
rotate 315 vb.
fake 541 vb.
— a yarn
be untrue 543 vb.
exaggerate 546 vb.
describe 590 vb.
— out
continue 71 vb.
spin out 113 vb.
lengthen 203 vb.
be diffuse 570 vb.
be loquacious 581 vb.
be obstructive 702 vb.
— the wheel
modify 143 vb.
gamble 618 vb.
— words
show style 566 vb.
spina bifida
nervous disorders 651 n.
spinach
vegetable 301 n.
spinal
supporting 218 adj.
central 225 adj.
back 238 adj.
spindle
pivot 218 n.
rotator 315 n.
tree 366 n.
spindle-shaped
tapering 256 adj.
spindly
lean 206 adj.
legged 267 adj.
spindrift
moisture 341 n.
bubble 355 n.
spin-dry
dry 342 vb.
spine
pillar 218 n.
centre 225 n.
rear 238 n.
prickle 256 n.
bookbinding 589 n.
spine-chilling
exciting 821 adj.
spineless
impotent 161 adj.
weak 163 adj.
irresolute 601 adj.
spinet
piano 414 n.
spinnaker
sail 275 n.
spinner
weaving 222 n.
planner 623 n.
spinney
wood 366 n.
spinning wheel
weaving 222 n.
rotator 315 n.
spin-off
sequel 67 n.
effect 157 n.
spin of the coin
equal chance 159 n.
spinster
woman 373 n.
spinster 895 n.
spiny
sharp 256 adj.
spiracle
orifice 263 n.
outlet 298 n.
air pipe 353 n.
spiral
increase 36 n.
coil 251 n.
twine 251 vb.
fly 271 vb.
ascend 308 vb.
tumble 309 vb.
rotation 315 n.
spiral staircase
ascent 308 n.
spirant
speech sound 398 n.
spoken letter 558 n.
spire
high structure 209 n.
vertex 213 n.
ascend 308 vb.
church exterior 990 n.
spired
tapering 256 adj.
spirit
insubstantial thing 4 n.
essential part 5 n.
temperament 5 n.
self 80 n.
vigorousness 174 n.
subjectivity 320 n.
life 360 n.
fuel 385 n.
spirit 447 n.
meaning 514 n.
vigour 571 n.
resolution 599 n.
restlessness 678 n.
affections 817 n.
moral sensibility 819 n.
courage 855 n.
ghost 970 n.
— away
steal 788 vb.
Spirit, the
Holy Ghost 965 n.
spirit duplicator
imitator 20 n.
spirited
forceful 571 adj.
active 678 adj.
lively 819 adj.
cheerful 833 adj.
courageous 855 adj.
spiritless
apathetic 820 adj.
inexcitable 823 adj.
dejected 834 adj.
cowardly 856 adj.
spirit level
horizontality 216 n.
spirit message
spiritualism 984 n.
spirit of place
locality 187 n.
spirit of the age
tendency 179 n.
spirit-rapping
spiritualism 984 n.
spirits
state 7 n.
alcoholic drink 301 n.
tonic 658 n.
cheerfulness 833 n.
spirits, the
the dead 361 n.
spiritual
immaterial 320 adj.
vocal music 412 n.
psychic 447 adj.
divine 965 adj.
religious 973 adj.
pious 979 adj.
priestly 985 adj.
spiritual adviser
pastor 986 n.
spiritualism
occultism 984 n.
spiritualism 984 n.
spiritualist
occultist 984 n.
spiritualistic
psychic 447 adj.
spooky 970 adj.
psychical 984 adj.
spirituality
immateriality 320 n.
virtue 933 n.
sanctity 979 n.
spiritualize, spiritualise
disembody 320 vb.
make pious 979 vb.
sanctify 979 vb.
spirituel(le)
lively 819 adj.
witty 839 adj.
spirituous
edible 301 adj.
intoxicating 949 adj.
spirt
(See **spurt** *)*
spiry
high 209 adj.
tapering 256 adj.
spit
projection 254 n.
sharp point 256 n.

perforator 263 n.
pierce 263 vb.
eruct 300 vb.
excrement 302 n.
rotator 315 n.
effervesce 318 vb.
rain 350 vb.
hiss 406 vb.
be angry 891 vb.
be sullen 893 vb.
threaten 900 vb.
disapprove 924 vb.
— at/on
not respect 921 vb.
— it out
divulge 526 vb.
— out
eject 300 vb.
spit and polish
cleanness 648 n.
formality 875 n.
spite
ill-treat 645 vb.
quarrelsomeness 709 n.
severity 735 n.
oppress 735 vb.
enmity 881 n.
hatred 888 n.
resentment 891 n.
malevolence 898 n.
revengefulness 910 n.
envy 912 n.
detraction 926 n.
spiteful
malevolent 898 adj.
(See **spite** *)*
spitfire
violent creature 176 n.
shrew 892 n.
spit-roast
cook 301 vb.
spitting image
analogue 18 n.
spittle
excrement 302 n.
moisture 341 n.
spittoon
sink 649 n.
spiv
idler 679 n.
spivvish
rascally 930 adj.
splash
small quantity 33 n.
disperse 75 vb.
water 339 n.
moisten 341 vb.
lake 346 n.
flow 350 vb.
sibilation 406 n.
colour 425 n.
maculation 437 n.
advertise 528 vb.
make important 638 vb.
make unclean 649 vb.
ostentation 875 n.
— about
swim 269 vb.
— out
expend 806 vb.
splashdown
space travel 271 n.
descent 309 n.
splatter
moisten 341 vb.
splay
expand 197 vb.
be broad 205 vb.
make oblique 220 vb.
diverge 294 vb.
splay-footed
deformed 246 adj.
spleen
insides 224 n.
discontent 829 n.
melancholy 834 n.
sullenness 893 n.
envy 912 n.
spleenful
discontented 829 adj.
resentful 891 adj.
irascible 892 adj.
splendid
luminous 417 adj.
excellent 644 adj.
liberal 813 adj.
pleasurable 826 adj.
splendid 841 adj.
noteworthy 866 adj.
ostentatious 875 adj.
splendidly
greatly 32 adv.
wonderfully 864 adv.
splendiferous
excellent 644 adj.
splendour
light 417 n.
beauty 841 n.
prestige 866 n.
ostentation 875 n.
splenetic
resentful 891 adj.
irascible 892 adj.
splice
tie 45 vb.
cross 222 vb.
introduce 231 vb.
repair 656 vb.
marry 894 vb.
splint
prop 218 n.
hardness 326 n.
surgical dressing 658 n.
splinter
small thing 33 n.
break 46 vb.
piece 53 n.
thinness 206 n.
strip 208 n.
be brittle 330 vb.
splinter group
dissentient 489 n.
party 708 n.
revolter 738 n.
splintery
brittle 330 adj.
split
disunion 46 n.
sunder 46 vb.
discontinuity 72 n.
bisected 92 adj.
gap 201 n.
laminate 207 vb.
opening 263 n.
be brittle 330 vb.
inform 524 vb.
divulge 526 vb.
dissension 709 n.
apportion 783 vb.
— hairs
discriminate 463 vb.
sophisticate 477 vb.
be fastidious 862 vb.
— off
separate 46 vb.
diverge 294 vb.
— on
accuse 928 vb.
— one's sides
laugh 835 vb.
— the difference
average out 30 vb.
compromise 770 vb.
— up
divorce 896 vb.
split personality
multiformity 82 n.
psychopathy 503 n.
split second
instant 116 n.
splitting head
pang 377 n.
splotch, splodge
maculation 437 n.
blemish 845 n.
splurge
prodigality 815 n.
ostentation 875 n.
splutter
emit 300 vb.
flow 350 vb.
hiss 406 vb.
stammer 580 vb.
spoil
derange 63 vb.
weaken 163 vb.
lay waste 165 vb.
tell against 467 vb.
impair 655 vb.
be clumsy 695 vb.
hinder 702 vb.
be lax 734 vb.
be lenient 736 vb.
booty 790 n.
make ugly 842 vb.
blemish 845 vb.
sate 863 vb.
pet 889 vb.
— one's chances
act foolishly 695 vb.
— oneself
be pleased 824 vb.
— one's pleasure
disappoint 509 vb.
cause discontent 829 vb.
— one's record
lose repute 867 vb.
be wicked 934 vb.
— the look of
blemish 845 vb.
— the ship for a ha'porth of tar
waste effort 641 vb.
act foolishly 695 vb.
be parsimonious 816 vb.
spoilage
decrement 42 n.
rubbish 641 n.
spoiled child
favourite 890 n.
spoiling for
willing 597 adj.
prepared 669 adj.
desiring 859 adj.
spoiling for a fight, be
make quarrels 709 vb.
attack 712 vb.
spoils
trophy 729 n.
booty 790 n.
spoilsport
dissuasion 613 n.
meddler 678 n.
hinderer 702 n.
moper 834 n.
disapprover 924 n.
spoilt
deteriorated 655 adj.
spoke(s)
line 203 n.
divergence 294 n.
spoken
linguistic 557 adj.
vocal 577 adj.
speaking 579 adj.
spokeshave
sharp edge 256 n.
smoother 258 n.
spokesman, spokeswoman
(See **spokesperson** *)*
spokesperson
interpreter 520 n.
informant 524 n.
messenger 529 n.n.
speaker 579 n.
agent 686 n.
deputy 755 n.
spoliation
spoliation 788 n.
spondee
prosody 593 n.

sponge
fossil 125 n.
porosity 263 n.
absorb 299 vb.
dryer 342 n.
pulpiness 356 n.
obliteration 550 n.
clean 648 vb.
beg 761 vb.
be servile 879 vb.
drunkard 949 n.
sponger
idler 679 n.
beggar 763 n.
toady 879 n.
spongy
porous 263 adj.
soft 327 adj.
marshy 347 adj.
pulpy 356 adj.
sponsor
witness 466 n.
patron 707 n.
sponsorship
aid 703 n.
security 767 n.
spontaneity
whim 604 n.
spontaneity 609 n.
feeling 818 n.
spontaneous
intuitive 476 adj.
volitional 595 adj.
involuntary 596 adj.
voluntary 597 adj.
spontaneous 609 adj.
unintentional 618 adj.
unprepared 670 adj.
artless 699 adj.
spoof
mimicry 20 n.
trickery 542 n.
satire 851 n.
spook
ghost 970 n.
spooky
spooky 970 adj.
cabbalistic 984 adj.
spool
rotator 315 n.
photography 551 n.
spoon
ladle 194 n.
extractor 304 n.
spoonbill
bird 365 n.
spoonerism
inversion 221 n.
absurdity 497 n.
neology 560 n.
witticism 839 n.
ridiculousness 849 n.
spoon-feed
aid 703 vb.
be lenient 736 vb.
pet 889 vb.
spoon-feeding
teaching 534 n.
spoonful
small quantity 33 n.
spooning
love-making 887 n.
spoon out
transpose 272 vb.
spoor
identification 547 n.
trace 548 n.
sporadic
unassembled 75 adj.
infrequent 140 adj.
uncertain 474 adj.
spore
source 156 n.
powder 332 n.
sporran
pocket 194 n.
sport
variant 15 n.
misfit 25 n.
nonconformist 84 n.
athletics 162 n.
wear 228 vb.
show 522 vb.
exercise 682 n.
contest 716 n.
merriment 833 n.
sport 837 n.
amuse oneself 837 vb.
laughingstock 851 n.
prodigy 864 n.
be ostentatious 875 vb.
favourite 890 n.
honourable person 929 n.
good person 937 n.
sporting chance
fair chance 159 n.
probability 471 n.
sportive
merry 833 adj.
amused 837 adj.
amusing 837 adj.
witty 839 adj.
sportsman, sportswoman
hunter 619 n.
player 837 n.
honourable person 929 n.
sportsmanlike
just 913 adj.
honourable 929 adj.
sportsmanship
sport 837 n.
probity 929 n.
sporty
showy 875 adj.
spot
small thing 33 n.
place 185 n.
variegate 437 vb.
see 438 vb.
notice 455 vb.
detect 484 vb.
understand 516 vb.
defect 647 n.
make unclean 649 vb.
impair 655 vb.
pattern 844 n.
blemish 845 n.
slur 867 n.
spot check
enquiry 459 n.
spotless
perfect 646 adj.
clean 648 adj.
innocent 935 adj.
pure 950 adj.
spotlight
lighting 420 n.
manifest 522 vb.
publicity 528 n.
theatre 594 n.
spot on
accurate 494 adj.
spotted
mottled 437 adj.
marked 547 adj.
blemished 845 adj.
spotting
rainy 350 adj.
spotty
mottled 437 adj.
diseased 651 adj.
blemished 845 adj.
spouse
spouse 894 n.
spouseless
unwedded 895 adj.
spout
projection 254 n.
orifice 263 n.
outlet 298 n.
ascend 308 vb.
flow 350 vb.
conduit 351 n.
orate 579 vb.
be loquacious 581 vb.
sprain
derange 63 vb.
disable 161 vb.
weaken 163 vb.
distort 246 vb.
pain 377 n.
impairment 655 n.
sprat
small animal 33 n.
fish food 301 n.
sprat to catch a mackerel
trap 542 n.
sprawl
dispersion 75 n.
expand 197 vb.
lengthen 203 vb.
be horizontal 216 vb.
tumble 309 vb.
repose 683 vb.
spray
branch 53 n.
bunch 74 n.
disperse 75 vb.
propellant 287 n.
emit 300 vb.
vaporizer 338 n.
irrigator 341 n.
bubble 355 n.
foliage 366 n.
spread
grow 36 vb.
disperse 75 vb.
generalize 79 vb.
prevail 178 vb.
extend 183 vb.
pervade 189 vb.
expand 197 vb.
flatten 216 vb.
overlay 226 vb.
divergence 294 n.
feasting 301 n.
advertisement 528 n.
— around
publish 528 vb.
apportion 783 vb.
— like wildfire
be dispersed 75 vb.
prevail 178 vb.
be published 528 vb.
— out
be dispersed 75 vb.
extend 183 vb.
lengthen 203 vb.
spread-eagle
lengthen 203 vb.
diverge 294 vb.
fell 311 vb.
heraldry 547 n.
spree
revel 837 n.
sprig
branch 53 n.
young plant 132 n.
foliage 366 n.
sprightly
active 678 adj.
cheerful 833 adj.
spring
period 110 n.
spring 128 n.
vernal 128 adj.
source 156 n.
energy 160 n.
strength 162 n.
distort 246 vb.
coil 251 n.
spurt 277 n.
move fast 277 vb.
recoil 280 n.
outflow 298 n.
ascend 308 vb.
lifter 310 n.
leap 312 n.vb.
elasticity 328 n.
stream 350 n.
motive 612 n.
machine 630 n.
take 786 vb.
— something on one
surprise 508 vb.

— up
become 1 vb.
grow 36 vb.
begin 68 vb.
happen 154 vb.
lift oneself 310 vb.
leap 312 vb.
be visible 443 vb.
spring balance
scales 322 n.
springboard
recoil 280 n.
lifter 310 n.
fluctuation 317 n.
aider 703 n.
springbok
jumper 312 n.
mammal 365 n.
spring-clean
clean 648 vb.
springe
trap 542 n.
springer
prop 218 n.
springlike
vernal 128 adj.
spring tide
high water 209 n.
current 350 n.
springtime
spring 128 n.
springtime of youth
salad days 130 n.
springy
soft 327 adj.
elastic 328 adj.
sprinkle
disperse 75 vb.
emit 300 vb.
let fall 311 vb.
moisten 341 vb.
rain 350 vb.
variegate 437 vb.
sprinkler
irrigator 341 n.
extinguisher 382 n.
sprinkling
small quantity 33 n.
tincture 43 n.
cleansing 648 n.
ritual act 988 n.
sprint
spurt 277 n.
racing 716 n.
sprinter
pedestrian 268 n.
thoroughbred 273 n.
speeder 277 n.
contender 716 n.
sprit
prop 218 n.
sprite
elf 970 n.
sprocket
tooth 256 n.
notch 260 n.
sprout
grow 36 vb.
young plant 132 n.
reproduce itself 167 vb.
descendant 170 n.
expand 197 vb.
vegetate 366 vb.
sprouts
vegetable 301 n.
spruce
orderly 60 adj.
tree 366 n.
clean 648 adj.vb.
personable 841 adj.
— up
make better 654 vb.
decorate 844 vb.
sprung
soft 327 adj.
elastic 328 adj.
sprung rhythm
prosody 593 n.
spry
active 678 adj.
cheerful 833 adj.
spume
effervesce 318 vb.
bubble 355 n.vb.
spunk
vigorousness 174 n.
lighter 385 n.
resolution 599 n.
courage 855 n.
spun out
protracted 113 adj.
prolix 570 adj.
spun yarn
fibre 208 n.
spur
branch 53 n.
stimulant 174 n.
high land 209 n.
projection 254 n.
sharp point 256 n.
accelerate 277 vb.
impel 279 vb.
kick 279 vb.
incentive 612 n.
hasten 680 vb.
excitant 821 n.
spurious
false 541 adj.
spurious 542 adj.
bastard 954 adj.
spurn
kick 279 vb.
reject 607 vb.
refuse 760 vb.
despise 922 vb.
spur of necessity
compulsion 740 n.
spur of the moment
spontaneity 609 n.
motive 612 n.
spurs
badge of rank 743 n.
honours 866 n.
spurt
brief span 114 n.
vigorousness 174 n.
spurt 277 n.
accelerate 277 vb.
activity 678 n.
haste 680 n.
spurt, spirt
outbreak 176 n.
flow out 298 vb.
emit 300 vb.
ascend 308 vb.
flow 350 vb.
sputnik
satellite 321 n.
sputter
emit 300 vb.
be agitated 318 vb.
sibilation 406 n.
be dim 419 vb.
stammer 580 vb.
sputum
excrement 302 n.
spy
scan 438 vb.
see 438 vb.
spectator 441 n.
watch 441 vb.
inquisitive person 453 n.
be curious 453 vb.
detective 459 n.
secret service 459 n.
informer 524 n.
warner 664 n.
spyglass
telescope 442 n.
squab
young creature 132 n.
fleshy 195 adj.
short 204 adj.
cushion 218 n.
table bird 365 n.
squabble
quarrel 709 n.
bicker 709 vb.
squad
band 74 n.
personnel 686 n.
formation 722 n.
squadron
band 74 n.
air force 722 n.
formation 722 n.
navy 722 n.
squadron leader
air officer 741 n.
squalid
unclean 649 adj.
beggarly 801 adj.
graceless 842 adj.
disreputable 867 adj.
squall
storm 176 n.
commotion 318 n.
gale 352 n.
cry 408 vb.
pitfall 663 n.
weep 836 vb.
squalor
uncleanness 649 n.
poverty 801 n.
ugliness 842 n.
squamous
layered 207 adj.
dermal 226 adj.
squander
waste 634 vb.
make insufficient 636 vb.
misuse 675 vb.
lose 772 vb.
be prodigal 815 vb.
squanderer
prodigal 815 n.
square
equal 28 adj.
compensate 31 vb.
regular 81 adj.
make conform 83 vb.
do sums 86 vb.
quaternity 96 n.
quadruple 97 vb.
archaism 127 n.
place 185 n.
housing 192 n.
fleshy 195 adj.
verticality 215 n.
form 243 vb.
angular figure 247 n.
unsharpened 257 adj.
navigate 269 vb.
be true 494 vb.
bribe 612 vb.
formation 722 n.
bad taste 847 n.
just 913 adj.
honourable 929 adj.
— accounts (with)
pay 804 vb.
account 808 vb.
avenge 910 vb.
— the circle
attempt the impossible 470 vb.
— up to
fight 716 vb.
— with
accord 24 vb.
square dance
dancing 837 n.
square deal
justice 913 n.
square peg in a round hole
misfit 25 n.
nonconformist 84 n.
displacement 188 n.
bungler 697 n.
square-rigged
marine 275 adj.
square root
numerical element 85 n.
squash
crowd 74 n.
suppress 165 vb.

make smaller 198 vb.
flatten 216 vb.
strike 279 vb.
soft drink 301 n.
vegetable 301 n.
abase 311 vb.
soften 327 vb.
confute 479 vb.
ball game 837 n.
humiliate 872 vb.
squash court
arena 724 n.
squashy
soft 327 adj.
marshy 347 adj.
semiliquid 354 adj.
pulpy 356 adj.
squat
place oneself 187 vb.
quarters 192 n.
fleshy 195 adj.
dwarfish 196 adj.
short 204 adj.
thick 205 adj.
low 210 adj.
encroach 306 vb.
sit down 311 vb.
possess 773 vb.
appropriate 786 vb.
squatter
intruder 59 n.
resident 191 n.
possessor 776 n.
usurper 916 n.
squatting
possession 773 n.
possessing 773 adj.
squaw
woman 373 n.
spouse 894 n.
squawk
shrill 407 vb.
cry 408 vb.
ululation 409 n.
squeak
faintness 401 n.
stridor 407 n.
cry 408 vb.
squeaky
strident 407 adj.
squeal
shrill 407 vb.
cry 408 n.
ululate 409 vb.
inform 524 vb.
divulge 526 vb.
deprecate 762 vb.
discontent 829 n.
squealer
informer 524 n.
tergiversator 603 n.
knave 938 n.
squeamish
unwilling 598 adj.
irresolute 601 adj.
sick 651 adj.
disliking 861 adj.
fastidious 862 adj.
prudish 950 adj.
squeegee
cleaning utensil 648 n.
squeeze
small quantity 33 n.
crowd 74 n.
make smaller 198 vb.
touch 378 n.
gesture 547 n.
obstruct 702 vb.
oppress 735 vb.
compel 740 vb.
restriction 747 n.
levy 786 vb.
endearment 889 n.
— out/from
extract 304 vb.
— in
fill 54 vb.
stow 187 vb.
— through
pass 305 vb.
squeezer
compressor 198 n.
extractor 304 n.
squelch
suppress 165 vb.
be wet 341 vb.
sibilation 406 n.
dissuade 613 vb.
squelchy
soft 327 adj.
marshy 347 adj.
semiliquid 354 adj.
squib
bang 402 n.
satire 851 n.
calumny 926 n.
squid
marine life 365 n.
squidgy
semiliquid 354 adj.
squiffy
tipsy 949 adj.
squiggle
coil 251 n.
punctuation 547 n.
lettering 586 n.
squint
obliquity 220 n.
window 263 n.
look 438 n.
be dim-sighted 440 vb.
blemish 845 n.
church interior 990 n.
squint-eyed
malevolent 898 adj.
squire
accompany 89 vb.
male 372 n.
retainer 742 n.
owner 776 n.
aristocrat 868 n.
court 889 vb.
squirearchy
government 733 n.
aristocracy 868 n.
squirm
wriggle 251 vb.
be agitated 318 vb.
feel pain 377 vb.
be excited 821 vb.
suffer 825 vb.
squirrel
accumulator 74 n.
mammal 365 n.
squirrel away
store 632 vb.
squirt
small quantity 33 n.
dwarf 196 n.
outflow 298 n.
emit 300 vb.
flow 350 vb.
nonentity 639 n.
— in
infuse 303 vb.
squishy
semiliquid 354 adj.
SRN
nurse 658 n.
sruti
non-Biblical scripture 975 n.
S-shape
curve 248 n.
S-shaped
snaky 251 adj.
stab
cut 46 vb.
pierce 263 vb.
kill 362 vb.
pang 377 n.
wound 655 n.vb.
strike at 712 vb.
suffering 825 n.
stab at
attempt 671 n.
stabile
sculpture 554 n.
stability
equilibrium 28 n.
permanence 144 n.
stability 153 n.
power 160 n.
stabilize, stabilise
stabilize 153 vb.
support 218 vb.
stab in the back
foul play 930 n.
perfidy 930 n.
stable
group 74 n.
lasting 113 adj.
fixed 153 adj.
strong 162 adj.
stable 192 n.
horse 273 n.
groom 369 vb.
inexcitable 823 adj.
(See **stability** *)*
stable companion
concomitant 89 n.
chum 880 n.
stabling
stable 192 n.
storage 632 n.
staccato
adagio 412 adv.
stack
great quantity 32 n.
bring together 74 vb.
rock 344 n.
store 632 n.vb.
— the deck
deceive 542 vb.
stacked
predetermined 608 adj.
staddle
stand 218 n.
stadium
meeting place 192 n.
racing 716 n.
arena 724 n.
staff
prop 218 n.
notation 410 n.
employ 622 vb.
personnel 686 n.
director 690 n.
club 723 n.
army officer 741 n.
domestic 742 n.
badge of rule 743 n.
vestments 989 n.
staff college
training school 539 n.
stag
mammal 365 n.
male animal 372 n.
gambler 618 n.
purchaser 792 n.
stage
juncture 8 n.
relativeness 9 n.
degree 27 n.
serial place 73 n.
situation 186 n.
layer 207 n.
stand 218 n.
stagecoach 274 n.
goal 295 n.
show 522 vb.
rostrum 539 n.
stage set 594 n.
theatre 594 n.
dramatize 594 vb.
arena 724 n.
stage, the
drama 594 n.
stagecoach
stagecoach 274 n.
stagecraft
dramaturgy 594 n.
stage directions
dramaturgy 594 n.
stage door
theatre 594 n.
stage effect
pageant 875 n.

stage fright
acting 594 n.
fear 854 n.
stagehand
stagehand 594 n.
stage-manage
cause 156 vb.
lurk 523 vb.
dramatize 594 vb.
be ostentatious 875 vb.
stage manager
stage manager 594 n.
stage name
misnomer 562 n.
stage set
spectacle 445 n.
stage set 594 n.
stage show
spectacle 445 n.
stage show 594 n.
stagestruck
dramatic 594 adj.
stage whisper
voice 577 n.
speak low 578 vb.
stagflation
finance 797 n.
stagger
grade 73 vb.
vary 152 vb.
obliquity 220 n.
walk 267 vb.
move slowly 278 vb.
tumble 309 vb.
fluctuation 317 n.
be agitated 318 vb.
surprise 508 vb.
be fatigued 684 vb.
show feeling 818 vb.
impress 821 vb.
be wonderful 864 vb.
be drunk 949 vb.
staggers
animal disease 651 n.
staging
frame 218 n.
dramaturgy 594 n.
stagnant
inert 175 adj.
quiescent 266 adj.
insalubrious 653 adj.
apathetic 820 adj.
stagnate
be unproductive 172 vb.
be inactive 679 vb.
stagnation
inertness 175 n.
quiescence 266 n.
nonuse 674 n.
inaction 677 n.
moral insensibility 820 n.
stag party
male 372 n.
social gathering 882 n.
stagy
dramatic 594 adj.
affected 850 adj.
showy 875 adj.
staid
inexcitable 823 adj.
serious 834 adj.
stain
tincture 43 n.
coat 226 vb.
pigment 425 n.
variegate 437 vb.
mark 547 vb.
trace 548 n.
obliteration 550 n.
defect 647 n.
dirt 649 n.
impair 655 vb.
blemish 845 n.vb.
slur 867 n.
stained
unsightly 842 adj.
stained glass
variegation 437 n.
ornamental art 844 n.
church interior 990 n.
stainless
clean 648 adj.
honourable 929 adj.
virtuous 933 adj.
stair
degree 27 n.
stand 218 n.
ascent 308 n.
stairs
series 71 n.
ascent 308 n.
access 624 n.
stake
fastening 47 n.
pillar 218 n.
gambling 618 n.
endanger 661 vb.
contend 716 vb.
promise 764 vb.
security 767 n.
offering 781 n.
portion 783 n.
— a claim
claim 915 vb.
— out
limit 236 vb.
stake, the
furnace 383 n.
suffering 825 n.
means of execution 964 n.
stake-boat
departure 296 n.
stakeholder
consignee 754 n.
stakes
contest 716 n.
Stakhanovite
busy person 678 n.
worker 686 n.
stalactite
hanging object 217 n.
Stalag
prison camp 748 n.
stalagmite
verticality 215 n.
stale
repeated 106 adj.
antiquated 127 adj.
tasteless 387 adj.
unsavoury 391 adj.
fetid 397 adj.
known 490 adj.
feeble 572 adj.
insalubrious 653 adj.
deteriorated 655 adj.
used 673 adj.
fatigued 684 adj.
make insensitive 820 vb.
tedious 838 adj.
dull 840 adj.
stalemate
draw 28 n.
stop 145 n.
inaction 677 n.
obstacle 702 n.
parry 713 vb.
noncompletion 726 n.
Stalinism
despotism 733 n.
brute force 735 n.
stalk
filament 208 n.
prop 218 n.
gait 265 n.
walk 267 vb.
foliage 366 n.
hunt 619 vb.
stalking horse
ambush 527 n.
pretext 614 n.
stratagem 698 n.
stall
put off 136 vb.
halt 145 vb.
stable 192 n.
compartment 194 n.
seat 218 n.
fly 271 vb.
be equivocal 518 vb.
be obstructive 702 vb.
parry 713 vb.
fail 728 vb.
shop 796 n.
church interior 990 n.
stallion
horse 273 n.
male animal 372 n.
stalls
onlookers 441 n.
playgoer 594 n.
stalwart
stalwart 162 adj.
fleshy 195 adj.
resolute 599 adj.
healthy 650 adj.
colleague 707 n.
stamen
flower 366 n.
stamina
strength 162 n.
resolution 599 n.
stamina 600 n.
courage 855 n.
stammer
speech defect 580 n.
stammer 580 vb.
be clumsy 695 vb.
show feeling 818 vb.
stamp
character 5 n.
modality 7 n.
uniformity 16 n.
mould 23 n.
sort 77 n.
make conform 83 vb.
form 243 n.vb.
make concave 255 vb.
gait 265 n.
walk 267 vb.
knock 279 n.
be loud 400 vb.
endorse 488 vb.
label 547 n.
gesticulate 547 vb.
printing 555 n.
print 587 vb.
correspondence 588 n.
title deed 767 n.
mint 797 vb.
be excited 821 vb.
be angry 891 vb.
applaud 923 vb.
— on
suppress 165 vb.
kick 279 vb.
be severe 735 vb.
— out
suppress 165 vb.
extinguish 382 vb.
subjugate 745 vb.
stamp collector
collector 492 n.
stampede
be violent 176 vb.
move fast 277 vb.
fear 854 n.vb.
frighten 854 vb.
stamping ground
focus 76 n.
home 192 n.
stance
form 243 n.
stanchion
pillar 218 n.
stand
be 1 vb.
be in a state of 7 vb.
last 113 vb.

be pending 136 vb.
cease 145 vb.
be stable 153 vb.
be situated 186 vb.
place 187 vb.
be present 189 vb.
meeting place 192 n.
be vertical 215 vb.
stand 218 n.
support 218 vb.
be quiescent 266 vb.
view 438 n.
be proved 478 vb.
opinion 485 n.
supposition 512 n.
suffice 635 vb.
opposition 704 n.
resistance 715 n.
battle 718 n.
arena 724 n.
offer oneself 759 vb.
give 781 vb.
shop 796 n.
expend 806 vb.
be patient 823 vb.
show respect 920 vb.
— about
wait 136 vb.
— a chance
be possible 469 vb.
be likely 471 vb.
— aside
recede 290 vb.
be neutral 606 vb.
resign 753 vb.
— by
be present 189 vb.
await 507 vb.
prepare oneself 669 vb.
not act 677 vb.
aid 703 vb.
defend 713 vb.
keep faith 768 vb.
— corrected
incur blame 924 vb.
— down
resign 753 vb.
— firm
stand firm 599 vb.
persevere 600 vb.
withstand 704 vb.
resist 715 vb.
be courageous 855 vb.
— for
be 1 vb.
steer for 281 vb.
mean 514 vb.
indicate 547 vb.
represent 551 vb.
be patient 823 vb.
— in for
substitute 150 vb.
function 622 vb.
— in one's light
hinder 702 vb.
— in the corner
do penance 941 vb.
— in the way
obstruct 702 vb.
— no nonsense
be severe 735 vb.
— off
be distant 199 vb.
recede 290 vb.
make inactive 679 vb.
not retain 779 vb.
— on ceremony
be ostentatious 875 vb.
show respect 920 vb.
— one in good stead
be useful 640 vb.
— one's ground
stand firm 599 vb.
resist 715 vb.
— on one's dignity
be proud 871 vb.
— on one's head
be inverted 221 vb.
— on one's own feet
be free 744 vb.
— on one's rights
claim 915 vb.
— out
be contrary 14 vb.
be unlike 19 vb.
jut 254 vb.
be visible 443 vb.
be plain 522 vb.
be obstinate 602 vb.
not observe 769 vb.
— out against
resist 715 vb.
— over
be pending 136 vb.
— pat
stay 144 vb.
be quiescent 266 vb.
— still
stay 144 vb.
be quiescent 266 vb.
— the test
be true 494 vb.
be good 644 vb.
— to
be quiescent 266 vb.
invigilate 457 vb.
— together
concur 181 vb.
— to reason
be certain 473 vb.
be reasonable 475 vb.
be proved 478 vb.
be plain 522 vb.
— trial
stand trial 959 vb.
— up
be vertical 215 vb.
lift oneself 310 vb.
— up and be counted
be courageous 855 vb.
— up for
safeguard 660 vb.
patronize 703 vb.
approve 923 vb.
vindicate 927 vb.
— up for one's rights
be free 744 vb.
claim 915 vb.
— up in law
be legal 953 vb.
— up to
support 218 vb.
suffice 635 vb.
withstand 704 vb.
defy 711 vb.
— well with
have a reputation 866 vb.
standard
uniform 16 adj.
prototype 23 n.
degree 27 n.
median 30 adj.
general 79 adj.
rule 81 n.
typical 83 adj.
high structure 209 n.
lamp 420 n.
testing agent 461 n.
gauge 465 n.
flag 547 n.
linguistic 557 adj.
paragon 646 n.
right 913 adj.
standard-bearer
soldier 722 n.
standard deviation
statistics 86 n.
standardize, standardise
make uniform 16 vb.
regularize 62 vb.
make conform 83 vb.
standards
morals 917 n.
standby
means 629 n.
aider 703 n.
colleague 707 n.
stand-in
substitute 150 n.
actor 594 n.
deputy 755 n.
standing
existing 1 adj.
state 7 n.
circumstance 8 n.
degree 27 n.
serial place 73 n.
permanent 144 adj.
unceasing 146 adj.
fixed 153 adj.
vertical 215 adj.
prestige 866 n.
standing order
rule 81 n.
practice 610 n.
payment 804 n.
legislation 953 n.
standing rigging
tackling 47 n.
standing room
room 183 n.
standing room only
full 54 adj.
standing water
lake 346 n.
standoffish
unconformable 84 adj.
prideful 871 adj.
unsociable 883 adj.
standpipe
current 350 n.
conduit 351 n.
standpoint
situation 186 n.
view 438 n.
supposition 512 n.
standstill
lull 145 n.
stop 145 n.
quiescence 266 n.
deliverance 668 n.
difficulty 700 n.
stannary
workshop 687 n.
stanza
verse form 593 n.
staple
fastening 47 n.
chief part 52 n.
fibre 208 n.
sharp point 256 n.
texture 331 n.
materials 631 n.
important 638 adj.
merchandise 795 n.
stapler
perforator 263 n.
star
supreme 34 adj.
divergence 294 n.
star 321 n.
luminary 420 n.
guide 520 n.
punctuation 547 n.
signpost 547 n.
actor 594 n.
act 594 vb.
bigwig 638 n.
exceller 644 n.
decoration 729 n.
badge of rank 743 n.
desired object 859 n.
honours 866 n.
person of repute 866 n.
favourite 890 n.
starboard
dextrality 241 n.
starch
smooth 258 vb.
food content 301 n.
harden 326 vb.
thickening 354 n.
clean 648 vb.

Star Chamber
council 692 n.
lawcourt 956 n.
starchy
rigid 326 adj.
affected 850 adj.
prideful 871 adj.
formal 875 adj.
star-crossed
unfortunate 731 adj.
stardom
famousness 866 n.
stardust
fantasy 513 n.
stare
look 438 n.
gaze 438 vb.
watch 441 vb.
be curious 453 vb.
wonder 864 vb.
be rude 885 vb.
— one in the face
be to come 124 vb.
impend 155 vb.
be plain 522 vb.
starfish
marine life 365 n.
stargazer
astronomy 321 n.
spectator 441 n.
stargazing
abstracted 456 adj.
staring
flagrant 32 adj.
obvious 443 adj.
stark
absolute 32 adj.
completely 54 adv.
wintry 129 adj.
uncovered 229 adj.
rigid 326 adj.
florid 425 adj.
plain 573 adj.
stark naked
uncovered 229 adj.
stark staring mad
insane 503 adj.
starless
unlit 418 adj.
starlet
actor 594 n.
starlight
star 321 n.
light 417 n.
glimmer 419 n.
luminary 420 n.
starry
celestial 321 adj.
undimmed 417 adj.
starry-eyed
happy 824 adj.
hoping 852 adj.
stars
influence 178 n.
fate 596 n.
Stars and Stripes
flag 547 n.
star-shaped
tapering 256 adj.
star shell
signal light 420 n.
missile weapon 723 n.
star-spangled
celestial 321 adj.
start
advantage 34 n.
start 68 n.
begin 68 vb.
move fast 277 vb.
impel 279 vb.
departure 296 n.
leap 312 vb.
agitation 318 n.
not expect 508 vb.
incite 612 vb.
hunt 619 vb.
be excitable 822 vb.
fear 854 vb.
— again
revert 148 vb.
be restored 656 vb.
— out
begin 68 vb.
start out 296 vb.
— something
make quarrels 709 vb.
— up
initiate 68 vb.
happen 154 vb.
operate 173 vb.
ascend 308 vb.
be visible 443 vb.
starter
beginning 68 n.
hors-d'oeuvres 301 n.
contender 716 n.
starting point
start 68 n.
departure 296 n.
premise 475 n.
startle
cause doubt 486 vb.
surprise 508 vb.
raise the alarm 665 vb.
excite 821 vb.
frighten 854 vb.
be wonderful 864 vb.
star turn
stage show 594 n.
starvation
scarcity 636 n.
fasting 946 n.
starve
weaken 163 vb.
make thin 206 vb.
be poor 801 vb.
be hungry 859 vb.
starve 946 vb.
— oneself
be parsimonious 816 vb.
starveling
lean 206 adj.
underfed 636 adj.
poor person 801 n.
starving
necessitous 627 adj.
(See **starve***)*
stash away
store 632 vb.
stasis
stop 145 n.
inertness 175 n.
state
state 7 n.
circumstance 8 n.
event 154 n.
territory 184 n.
situation 186 n.
nation 371 n.
inform 524 vb.
affirm 532 vb.
community 708 n.
political organization 733 n.
affections 817 n.
formality 875 n.
— one's terms
request 761 vb.
bargain 791 vb.
state control
governance 733 n.
statecraft
management 689 n.
statehood
nation 371 n.
independence 744 n.
stateless person
outcast 883 n.
stately
rhetorical 574 adj.
elegant 575 adj.
impressive 821 adj.
beautiful 841 adj.
well-bred 848 adj.
worshipful 866 adj.
proud 871 adj.
formal 875 adj.
stately home
house 192 n.
statement
list 87 n.
musical piece 412 n.
topic 452 n.
testimony 466 n.
report 524 n.
affirmation 532 n.
description 590 n.
pretext 614 n.
accounts 808 n.
state occasion
formality 875 n.
state of affairs
circumstance 8 n.
affairs 154 n.
state of grace
innocence 935 n.
sanctity 979 n.
state of mind
affections 817 n.
state of nature
bareness 229 n.
undevelopment 670 n.
state ownership
joint possession 775 n.
stateroom
chamber 194 n.
State's evidence
testimony 466 n.
disclosure 526 n.
States-General
parliament 692 n.
statesman, stateswoman
sage 500 n.
planner 623 n.
manager 690 n.
statesmanlike
intelligent 498 adj.
skilful 694 adj.
statesmanship
sagacity 498 n.
policy 623 n.
tactics 688 n.
management 689 n.
static
permanent 144 adj.
electricity 160 n.
quiescent 266 adj.
radiation 417 n.
statics
science of forces 162 n.
gravity 322 n.
station
degree 27 n.
serial place 73 n.
stopping place 145 n.
place 185 n.
situation 186 n.
station 187 n.
abode 192 n.
railway 624 n.
nobility 868 n.
duty 917 n.
stationary
quiescent 266 adj.
nonactive 677 adj.
inactive 679 adj.
stationer
bookperson 589 n.
stationery
stationery 586 n.
paper 631 n.
stations of the Cross
ritual act 988 n.
church interior 990 n.
station wagon
automobile 274 n.
statism
despotism 733 n.
governance 733 n.
government 733 n.
statistical
statistical 86 adj.
statistician
enumerator 86 n.
accountant 808 n.

statistics
average 30 n.
statistics 86 n.
statuary
image 551 n.
sculpture 554 n.
ornamental art 844 n.
statue
copy 22 n.
monument 548 n.
image 551 n.
sculpture 554 n.
honours 866 n.
idol 982 n.
statuesque
tall 209 adj.
glyptic 554 adj.
beautiful 841 adj.
statuette
image 551 n.
sculpture 554 n.
stature
height 209 n.
status
state 7 n.
circumstance 8 n.
relativeness 9 n.
degree 27 n.
serial place 73 n.
classification 77 n.
prestige 866 n.
status quo
circumstance 8 n.
equilibrium 28 n.
permanence 144 n.
statute
precept 693 n.
legislation 953 n.
statute book
law 953 n.
statute law
law 953 n.
statutory
preceptive 693 adj.
legal 953 adj.
staunch
unyielding 162 adj.
close 264 vb.
staunch 350 vb.
resolute 599 adj.
doctor 658 vb.
friendly 880 adj.
trustworthy 929 adj.
stave
strip 208 n.
notation 410 n.
verse form 593 n.
club 723 n.
stave in
make concave 255 vb.
pierce 263 vb.
lower 311 vb.
— off
obstruct 702 vb.
parry 713 vb.
stay
tackling 47 n.
continue 108 vb.
last 113 vb.
delay 136 n.
wait 136 vb.
stay 144 vb.
cease 145 vb.
go on 146 vb.
be stable 153 vb.
be present 189 vb.
dwell 192 vb.
prop 218 n.
support 218 vb.
be quiescent 266 vb.
visit 882 vb.
— at one's post
do one's duty 917 vb.
— away
be absent 190 vb.
— put
be quiescent 266 vb.
stand firm 599 vb.
be obstinate 602 vb.
— up
revel 837 vb.
stay-at-home
quiescent 266 adj.
solitary 883 n.
stayer
thoroughbred 273 n.
stamina 600 n.
staying power
durability 113 n.
strength 162 n.
stamina 600 n.
stays
compressor 198 n.
underwear 228 n.
St Christopher medal
talisman 983 n.
steadfast
fixed 153 adj.
resolute 599 adj.
obedient 739 adj.
steady
uniform 16 adj.
equal 28 adj.
orderly 60 adj.
regular 81 adj.
frequent 139 adj.
periodical 141 adj.
unceasing 146 adj.
fixed 153 adj.
unchangeable 153 adj.
support 218 vb.
still 266 adj.
resolute 599 adj.
persevering 600 adj.
impassive 820 adj.
tranquillize 823 vb.
courageous 855 adj.
steady state theory
universe 321 n.
steak
piece 53 n.
meat 301 n.
steakhouse
café 192 n.
steal
copy 20 vb.
be stealthy 525 vb.
take 786 vb.
steal 788 vb.
— a march on
do before 119 vb.
be early 135 vb.
precede 283 vb.
outdo 306 vb.
deceive 542 vb.
be cunning 698 vb.
— away
run away 620 vb.
escape 667 vb.
— one's heart
excite love 887 vb.
— the show
be superior 34 vb.
act 594 vb.
— upon
surprise 508 vb.
stealth
cunning 698 n.
stealthy
slow 278 adj.
muted 401 adj.
occult 523 adj.
stealthy 525 adj.
cunning 698 adj.
cautious 858 adj.
steam
energy 160 n.
stimulation 174 n.
be in motion 265 vb.
voyage 269 vb.
propellant 287 n.
exude 298 vb.
emit 300 vb.
cook 301 vb.
gas 336 n.
vaporize 338 vb.
be wet 341 vb.
cloud 355 n.
heat 379 n.
heater 383 n.
steam engine
locomotive 274 n.
machine 630 n.
steamer
cauldron 194 n.
ship 275 n.
steamroller
demolish 165 vb.
flattener 216 n.
smoother 258 n.
locomotive 274 n.
compel 740 vb.
steamship
ship 275 n.
steamy
vaporific 338 adj.
cloudy 355 adj.
heated 381 adj.
steed
horse 273 n.
steel
strengthen 162 vb.
sharp edge 256 n.
hardness 326 n.
resolution 599 n.
sidearms 723 n.
— oneself
be resolute 599 vb.
be insensitive 820 vb.
— one's heart
be impenitent 940 vb.
steel band
orchestra 413 n.
steel-clad
invulnerable 660 adj.
steel plate
engraving 555 n.
steelworks
workshop 687 n.
steely
strong 162 adj.
hard 326 adj.
grey 429 adj.
blue 435 adj.
resolute 599 adj.
cruel 898 adj.
steelyard
scales 322 n.
steep
high land 209 n.
high 209 adj.
deep 211 adj.
vertical 215 adj.
sloping 220 adj.
immerse 303 vb.
ascending 308 adj.
soften 327 vb.
add water 339 vb.
drench 341 vb.
exaggerated 546 adj.
difficult 700 adj.
dear 811 adj.
steeple
high structure 209 n.
sharp point 256 n.
church exterior 990 n.
steeplechase
racing 716 n.
steeplechaser
rider 268 n.
thoroughbred 273 n.
jumper 312 n.
steeplejack
climber 308 n.
steeply
aloft 209 adv.
steer
eunuch 161 n.
cattle 365 n.
male animal 372 n.
direct 689 vb.
— a middle course
be midstream 625 vb.
— clear of
deviate 282 vb.
— for
steer for 281 vb.
pursue 619 vb.

steerage
direction 281 n.
directorship 689 n.
steering committee
director 690 n.
consignee 754 n.
steersman
navigator 270 n.
director 690 n.
stela
monument 548 n.
stellar
celestial 321 adj.
stellate
tapering 256 adj.
divergent 294 adj.
St Elmo's fire
fire 379 n.
glow 417 n.
stem
race 11 n.
chief part 52 n.
halt 145 vb.
source 156 n.
genealogy 169 n.
prop 218 n.
staunch 350 vb.
foliage 366 n.
word 559 n.
withstand 704 vb.
— the tide
withstand 704 vb.
resist 715 vb.
triumph 727 vb.
stem to stern
longwise 203 adv.
stench
odour 394 n.
stench 397 n.
stencil
duplicate 22 n.
mould 23 n.
paint 553 vb.
stenographer
recorder 549 n.
stenographer 586 n.
stenography
writing 586 n.
stenotypy
writing 586 n.
stentorian
sounding 398 adj.
loud 400 adj.
step
degree 27 n.
serial place 73 n.
short distance 200 n.
long measure 203 n.
stand 218 n.
gait 265 n.
walk 267 vb.
attempt 671 n.
deed 676 n.
— in
interfere 231 vb.
mediate 720 vb.
— into the breach
aid 703 vb.
— into the shoes of
come after 65 vb.
substitute 150 vb.
inherit 771 vb.
— on it
accelerate 277 vb.
— up
augment 36 vb.
invigorate 174 vb.
accelerate 277 vb.
promote 285 vb.
stepbrother, stepsister
kinsman 11 n.
step by step
by degrees 27 adv.
gradatim 278 adv.
stepfather
paternity 169 n.
stepladder
ascent 308 n.
stepmother
maternity 169 n.
steppe
space 183 n.
lowness 210 n.
horizontality 216 n.
land 344 n.
plain 348 n.
stepped
oblique 220 adj.
stepping-stone
degree 27 n.
opportunity 137 n.
bridge 624 n.
instrument 628 n.
steps
series 71 n.
ascent 308 n.
policy 623 n.
means 629 n.
action 676 n.
stereo
sound 398 n.
sounding 398 adj.
gramaphone 414 n.
stereometry
geometry 465 n.
stereophonic
sounding 398 adj.
stereoscope
optical device 442 n.
stereoscopic
seeing 438 adj.
visible 443 adj.
stereotype
make uniform 16 vb.
copy 22 n.
printing 555 n.
print 587 vb.
stereotyped
uniform 16 adj.
unchangeable 153 adj.
habitual 610 adj.
sterile
unproductive 172 adj.
profitless 641 adj.
clean 648 adj.
salubrious 652 adj.
sterility
impotence 161 n.
sterilization, sterilisation
impotence 161 n.
contraception 172 n.
cleansing 648 n.
hygiene 652 n.
prophylactic 658 n.
preservation 666 n.
sterilize, sterilise
sanitate 652 vb.
sterling
genuine 494 adj.
valuable 644 adj.
money 797 n.
monetary 797 adj.
virtuous 933 adj.
sterling character
good person 937 n.
stern
buttocks 238 n.
poop 238 n.
resolute 599 adj.
severe 735 adj.
serious 834 adj.
angry 891 adj.
unkind 898 adj.
sternway
water travel 269 n.
regression 286 n.
steroid
drug 658 n.
stertorous
puffing 352 adj.
hoarse 407 adj.
stethoscope
hearing aid 415 n.
stetson
headgear 228 n.
stevedore
boatman 270 n.
bearer 273 n.
stew
a mixture 43 n.
dish 301 n.
cook 301 vb.
lake 346 n.
heat 381 vb.
mature 669 vb.
predicament 700 n.
excitable state 822 n.
anger 891 n.
— in one's own juice
be one 88 vb.
have trouble 731 vb.
steward, stewardess
provider 633 n.
manager 690 n.
official 690 n.
domestic 742 n.
consignee 754 n.
treasurer 798 n.
stewardship
management 689 n.
stewed
tipsy 949 adj.
stews
brothel 951 n.
stewpan
cauldron 194 n.
stichomythia
verse form 593 n.
stick
cohere 48 vb.
halt 145 vb.
be contiguous 202 vb.
prop 218 n.
pierce 263 vb.
transfer 272 vb.
rub 333 vb.
ninny 501 n.
be unwilling 598 vb.
be in difficulty 700 vb.
club 723 n.
fail 728 vb.
scourge 964 n.
— at nothing
be resolute 599 vb.
be intemperate 943 vb.
— fast
be quiescent 266 vb.
stand firm 599 vb.
— in a rut/groove
conform 83 vb.
repeat oneself 106 vb.
be wont 610 vb.
— in one's throat
displease 827 vb.
cause dislike 861 vb.
— in the mind
be remembered 505 vb.
— it out
stand firm 599 vb.
persevere 600 vb.
— on
affix 45 vb.
— one's neck out
face danger 661 vb.
be rash 857 vb.
— out
jut 254 vb.
be visible 443 vb.
— out for
contend 716 vb.
bargain 791 vb.
— out like a sore thumb
disagree 25 vb.
attract notice 455 vb.
— to
cohere 48 vb.
retain 778 vb.
— together
unite with 45 vb.
— to one's fingers
be profitable 771 vb.
be received 782 vb.

— to one's guns
persevere 600 vb.
be obstinate 602 vb.
be courageous 855 vb.
— to the facts
be truthful 540 vb.
— to the rules
conform 83 vb.
— up
be vertical 215 vb.
rob 788 vb.
— up for
patronize 703 vb.
vindicate 927 vb.
— with it
persevere 600 vb.
sticker
adhesive 47 n.
label 547 n.
sticking plaster
adhesive 47 n.
substitute 150 n.
surgical dressing 658 n.
sticking point
resolution 599 n.
stick-in-the-mud
permanence 144 n.
obstinate person 602 n.
unskilful 695 adj.
stickleback
fish 365 n.
stickler
narrow mind 481 n.
obstinate person 602 n.
tyrant 735 n.
perfectionist 862 n.
sticks, the
district 184 n.
racing 716 n.
sticky
cohesive 48 adj.
tough 329 adj.
viscid 354 adj.
difficult 700 adj.
retentive 778 adj.
sticky wicket
predicament 700 n.
stiff
crippled 163 adj.
straight 249 adj.
still 266 adj.
rigid 326 adj.
dead 361 adj.
corpse 363 n.
narrow-minded 481 adj.
unclear 568 adj.
inelegant 576 adj.
obstinate 602 adj.
inactive 679 adj.
fatigued 684 adj.
clumsy 695 adj.
severe 735 adj.
restraining 747 adj.
dear 811 adj.
affected 850 adj.
prideful 871 adj.
formal 875 adj.
unsociable 883 adj.
stiffen
strengthen 162 vb.
harden 326 vb.
make inactive 679 vb.
stiffener
prop 218 n.
stiff job
hard task 700 n.
stiff-necked
obstinate 602 adj.
defiant 711 adj.
proud 871 adj.
stiff upper lip
resolution 599 n.
manliness 855 n.
stiff with
full 54 adj.
assembled 74 adj.
stifle
disable 161 vb.
suppress 165 vb.
kill 362 vb.
be hot 379 vb.
heat 381 vb.
extinguish 382 vb.
silence 399 vb.
mute 401 vb.
conceal 525 vb.
make mute 578 vb.
hinder 702 vb.
prohibit 757 vb.
stigma
flower 366 n.
slur 867 n.
censure 924 n.
detraction 926 n.
false charge 928 n.
stigmata
indication 547 n.
stigmatize, stigmatise
mark 547 vb.
shame 867 vb.
defame 926 vb.
accuse 928 vb.
stile
ascent 308 n.
access 624 n.
obstacle 702 n.
stiletto
sharp point 256 n.
perforator 263 n.
sidearms 723 n.
stiletto heels
footwear 228 n.
still
fixed 153 adj.
assuage 177 vb.
smooth 258 adj.
quiescent 266 adj.
still 266 adj.
vaporizer 338 n.
watery 339 adj.
dead 361 adj.
heater 383 n.
silent 399 adj.
silence 399 vb.
nevertheless 468 adv.
photography 551 n.
make mute 578 vb.
inactive 679 adj.
stillbirth
propagation 167 n.
stillborn
dead 361 adj.
unsuccessful 728 adj.
still life
object 319 n.
art subject 553 n.
still more
eminently 34 adv.
stillness
quiescence 266 n.
(See **still** *)*
stillroom
provisions 301 n.
storage 632 n.
stilly
silent 399 adj.
stilted
ornate 574 adj.
inelegant 576 adj.
affected 850 adj.
Stilton
dairy product 301 n.
stilts
stand 218 n.
leg 267 n.
lifter 310 n.
plaything 837 n.
stimulant
stimulant 174 n.
impulse 279 n.
incentive 612 n.
drug 658 n.
tonic 658 n.
refreshment 685 n.
excitant 821 n.
drug-taking 949 n.
intoxicating 949 adj.
stimulate
augment 36 vb.
cause 156 vb.
operate 173 vb.
invigorate 174 vb.
make violent 176 vb.
incite 612 vb.
refresh 685 vb.
animate 821 vb.
cause desire 859 vb.
stimulation
strengthening 162 n.
stimulation 174 n.
activity 678 n.
stimulus
cause 156 n.
stimulant 174 n.
incentive 612 n.
sting
sharp point 256 n.
pang 377 n.
pungency 388 n.
wound 655 vb.
bane 659 n.
fleece 786 vb.
overcharge 811 vb.
excite 821 vb.
suffering 825 n.
torment 827 vb.
enrage 891 vb.
stingray
fish 365 n.
stingy
insufficient 636 adj.
parsimonious 816 adj.
stink
stench 397 n.
stink 397 vb.
uncleanness 649 n.
deteriorate 655 vb.
— in the nostrils
displease 827 vb.
excite hate 888 vb.
stinker
cad 938 n.
stinking
unsavoury 391 adj.
fetid 397 adj.
not nice 645 adj.
unpleasant 827 adj.
disliked 861 adj.
impure 951 adj.
stint
finite quantity 26 n.
period 110 n.
limit 236 vb.
make insufficient 636 vb.
labour 682 n.
restrain 747 vb.
portion 783 n.
be parsimonious 816 vb.
stipend
subvention 703 n.
reward 962 n.
stipendiary
gainful 771 adj.
receiving 782 adj.
stipple
variegate 437 vb.
paint 553 vb.
engrave 555 vb.
stipulate
give terms 766 vb.
stipulation
qualification 468 n.
premise 475 n.
supposition 512 n.
requirement 627 n.
conditions 766 n.
stipule
foliage 366 n.
stir
mix 43 vb.
stimulation 174 n.
make violent 176 vb.
be in motion 265 vb.
commotion 318 n.
activity 678 n.
gaol 748 n.
excite 821 vb.

— one's stumps
move fast 277 vb.
— the blood
cause feeling 374 vb.
excite 821 vb.
enrage 891 vb.
— up trouble
cause discontent 829 vb.
stirpiculture
animal husbandry 369 n.
stirps
race 11 n.
stirrer
troublemaker 663 n.
meddler 678 n.
stirring
eventful 154 adj.
felt 818 adj.
exciting 821 adj.
stirrup
prop 218 n.
stirrup cup
valediction 296 n.
draught 301 n.
stitch
tie 45 vb.
fastening 47 n.
component 58 n.
pang 377 n.
needlework 844 n.
stitch in time
anticipation 135 n.
stoa
pavilion 192 n.
academy 539 n.
stoat
mammal 365 n.
stochastic
casual 159 adj.
stock
race 11 n.
ligature 47 n.
accumulation 74 n.
typical 83 adj.
source 156 n.
genealogy 169 n.
neckwear 228 n.
animal 365 n.
tree 366 n.
sauce 389 n.
aphoristic 496 adj.
dunce 501 n.
usual 610 adj.
materials 631 n.
store 632 n.
provide 633 vb.
property 777 n.
merchandise 795 n.
unfeeling person 820 n.
— up
store 632 vb.
stockade
barrier 235 n.
enclosure 235 n.
shelter 662 n.
defences 713 n.
stock-breeding
animal husbandry 369 n.
stockbroker
consignee 754 n.
merchant 794 n.
stockbroker belt
district 184 n.
stock car
automobile 274 n.
stock company
actor 594 n.
stock exchange
bourse 618 n.
market 796 n.
stock farm
stock farm 369 n.
stockholder
participator 775 n.
owner 776 n.
stockinette
textile 222 n.
stocking(s)
legwear 228 n.
treasury 799 n.
stock-in-trade
means 629 n.
equipment 630 n.
store 632 n.
property 777 n.
merchandise 795 n.
stock-jobber
merchant 794 n.
stock list
list 87 n.
stockman
herdsman 369 n.
stockpile
store 632 n.vb.
stockroom
storage 632 n.
stocks
seat 218 n.
lockup 748 n.
pillory 964 n.
stocks and shares
means 629 n.
estate 777 n.
stocks and stones
object 319 n.
absence of intellect 448 n.
absence of thought 450 n.
stock saying
maxim 496 n.
stocky
stalwart 162 adj.
fleshy 195 adj.
short 204 adj.
stockyard
enclosure 235 n.
stodge
food 301 n.
stodgy
semiliquid 354 adj.
plain 573 adj.
tedious 838 adj.
dull 840 adj.
stoic
unfeeling person 820 n.
stoical, stoic
impassive 820 adj.
patient 823 adj.
stoicism
philosophy 449 n.
moral insensibility 820 n.
inexcitability 823 n.
patience 823 n.
disinterestedness 931 n.
temperance 942 n.
stoke
augment 36 vb.
kindle 381 vb.
fire 385 vb.
stoker
driver 268 n.
stole
neckwear 228 n.
vestments 989 n.
stolen
unwarranted 916 adj.
stolen goods
booty 790 n.
stolid
unthinking 450 adj.
unintelligent 499 adj.
inactive 679 adj.
impassive 820 adj.
serious 834 adj.
stolidity
inertness 175 n.
stolon
plant 366 n.
stomach
maw 194 n.
insides 224 n.
taste 386 n.
be willing 597 vb.
knuckle under 721 vb.
be patient 823 vb.
liking 859 n.
be humble 872 vb.
forgive 909 vb.
stomachache
pang 377 n.
digestive disorders 651 n.
stomacher
garment 228 n.
stomata
orifice 263 n.
stomp
dance 837 n.vb.
stone
uncover 229 vb.
strike 279 vb.
missile 287 n.
weighing 322 n.
solid body 324 n.
hardness 326 n.
rock 344 n.
kill 362 vb.
dunce 501 n.
sculpture 554 n.
engraving 555 n.
building material 631 n.
lapidate 712 vb.
missile weapon 723 n.
unfeeling person 820 n.
gem 844 n.
execute 963 vb.
Stone Age
era 110 n.
antiquity 125 n.
stoned
insensible 375 adj.
dead drunk 949 adj.
drugged 949 adj.
stone's throw
short distance 200 n.
stonewall
repel 292 vb.
be obstructive 702 vb.
parry 713 vb.
stonewalling
protraction 113 n.
stoneware
hardness 326 n.
pottery 381 n.
stonework
edifice 164 n.
structure 331 n.
stony
unproductive 172 adj.
rough 259 adj.
hard 326 adj.
territorial 344 adj.
unfeeling 375 adj.
impassive 820 adj.
stony-hearted
cruel 898 adj.
pitiless 906 adj.
stooge
fool 501 n.
dupe 544 n.
instrument 628 n.
nonentity 639 n.
bungler 697 n.
auxiliary 707 n.
dependant 742 n.
humorist 839 n.
laughingstock 851 n.
stooge for
be servile 879 vb.
stook
bunch 74 n.
stool
seat 218 n.
excrement 302 n.
stoolpigeon
informer 524 n.
ambush 527 n.
trickster 545 n.
stoop
be low 210 vb.

descend 309 vb.vb.
stoop 311 vb.
plunge 313 n.
obey 739 vb.
be humble 872 vb.
be servile 879 vb.
show respect 920 vb.
— to
demean oneself 867 vb.
be dishonest 930 vb.
stop
end 69 n.vb.
stop 145 n.
halt 145 vb.
come to rest 266 vb.
266 int.
arrive 295 vb.
speech sound 398 n.
silence 399 vb.
punctuation 547 n.
repair 656 vb.
doctor 658 vb.
inaction 677 n.
obstruct 702 vb.
restrain 747 vb.
prohibit 757 vb.
retention 778 n.
— a leak
staunch 350 vb.
— for breath
pause 145 vb.
— off
arrive 295 vb.
— one's ears
be deaf 416 vb.
be inattentive 456 vb.
be obstinate 602 vb.
— short
fall short 307 vb.
— up
obstruct 702 vb.
— using
reject 607 vb.
relinquish 621 vb.
stop using 674 vb.
make inactive 679 vb.
abrogate 752 vb.
not retain 779 vb.
stopcock
stopper 264 n.
tool 630 n.
stopgap
substitute 150 n.
preparatory 669 adj.
stop-go
discontinuous 72 adj.
fitful 142 adj.
stopover
itinerary 267 n.
goal 295 n.
stoppage
strike 145 n.
closure 264 n.
hitch 702 n.
nonpayment 805 n.
stopper
covering 226 n.
stopper 264 n.
retention 778 n.
stopping
discontinuous 72 adj.
vehicular 274 adj.
stopping at nothing
resolute 599 adj.
stopping place
stopping place 145 n.
stop-press news
news 529 n.
stopwatch
timekeeper 117 n.
recording instrument 549 n.
storage
assemblage 74 n.
data processing 86 n.
room 183 n.
storage 632 n.
preservation 666 n.
storage battery
electronics 160 n.
store
great quantity 32 n.
accumulation 74 n.
stow 187 vb.
store 632 n.vb.
provide 633 vb.
plenty 635 n.
preserve 666 vb.
make ready 669 vb.
not use 674 vb.
acquire 771 vb.
retain 778 vb.
shop 796 n.
treasury 799 n.
wealth 800 n.
storehouse
storage 632 n.
storekeeper
provider 633 n.
tradespeople 794 n.
storeroom
chamber 194 n.
storage 632 n.
stores
provisions 301 n.
provision 633 n.
storey
compartment 194 n.
layer 207 n.
storied
descriptive 590 adj.
stork
obstetrics 167 n.
bird 365 n.
storm
turmoil 61 n.
crowd 74 n.
havoc 165 n.
storm 176 n.
be violent 176 vb.
burst in 297 vb.
commotion 318 n.
rain 350 n.
gale 352 n.
be loud 400 vb.
attack 712 vb.
overmaster 727 vb.
take 786 vb.
be angry 891 vb.
— against
dispraise 924 vb.
storm brewing
danger 661 n.
storm in a teacup
overestimation 482 n.
exaggeration 546 n.
trifle 639 n.
quarrel 709 n.
storm signal
warning 664 n.
storm-tossed
rough 259 adj.
storm troops
attacker 712 n.
armed force 722 n.
stormy
violent 176 adj.
windy 352 adj.
excitable 822 adj.
stormy exchange
quarrel 709 n.
scurrility 899 n.
stormy petrel
bird 365 n.
warning 664 n.
story
ideality 513 n.
news 529 n.
fable 543 n.
narrative 590 n.
story-teller
liar 545 n.
narrator 590 n.
stoup
cup 194 n.
church utensil 990 n.
stout
stalwart 162 adj.
fleshy 195 adj.
thick 205 adj.
alcoholic drink 301 n.
courageous 855 adj.
stout fellow
brave person 855 n.
good person 937 n.
stout-hearted
courageous 855 adj.
stove
furnace 383 n.
stow
stow 187 vb.
load 193 vb.
store 632 vb.
— away
conceal 525 vb.
make ready 669 vb.
stowage
room 183 n.
location 187 n.
storage 632 n.
stowaway
intruder 59 n.
incomer 297 n.
hider 527 n.
strabismus
dim sight 440 n.
straddle
connect 45 vb.
be broad 205 vb.
overlie 226 vb.
diverge 294 vb.
pass 305 vb.
fire at 712 vb.
strafe
bombardment 712 n.
reprobate 924 vb.
punish 963 vb.
straggle
be dispersed 75 vb.
be few 105 vb.
wander 267 vb.
stray 282 vb.
straggling
orderless 61 adj.
straight
uniform 16 adj.
simple 44 adj.
orderly 60 adj.
continuous 71 adj.
vertical 215 adj.
straight 249 adj.
towards 281 adv.
accurate 494 adj.
undeviating 625 adj.
shapely 841 adj.
honourable 929 adj.
straight and narrow
virtue 933 n.
straight-edge
gauge 465 n.
straighten
straighten 249 vb.
rectify 654 vb.
— out
regularize 62 vb.
— up
be vertical 215 vb.
straight face
seriousness 834 n.
straightforward
intelligible 516 adj.
undisguised 522 adj.
veracious 540 adj.
plain 573 adj.
artless 699 adj.
trustworthy 929 adj.
straightforwardness
facility 701 n.
straight from the horse's mouth
reportedly 524 adv.
straight from the shoulder
vigorously 174 adv.
assertive 532 adj.
veracious 540 adj.
straight man
laughingstock 851 n.

straight on
straight on 249 adv.
straight up
aloft 209 adv.
vertical 215 adj.
strain
temperament 5 n.
race 11 n.
tincture 43 n.
derange 63 vb.
breed 77 n.
power 160 n.
weaken 163 vb.
genealogy 169 n.
force 176 vb.
tendency 179 n.
distortion 246 n.
traction 288 n.
overstep 306 vb.
pain 377 n.
sound 398 n.
be false 541 vb.
exaggerate 546 vb.
style 566 n.
purify 648 vb.
attempt 671 n.vb.
misuse 675 vb.
exertion 682 n.
exert oneself 682 vb.
fatigue 684 n.vb.
worry 825 n.
enmity 881 n.
— at a gnat and swallow a camel
reason badly 477 vb.
act foolishly 695 vb.
— off
transpose 272 vb.
empty 300 vb.
— one's authority
be severe 735 vb.
— one's credulity
be unlikely 472 vb.
— out
exude 298 vb.
strainer
sorting 62 n.
porosity 263 n.
cleaning utensil 648 n.
strains
poem 593 n.
strait(s)
narrowness 206 n.
gulf 345 n.
predicament 700 n.
straitened circumstances
poverty 801 n.
straitening
restraining 747 adj.
straitjacket
compressor 198 n.
fetter 748 n.
straitlaced
severe 735 adj.
prudish 950 adj.
strake
strip 208 n.
strand
fibre 208 n.
hair 259 n.
shore 344 n.
stranded
fixed 153 adj.
hindered 702 adj.
grounded 728 adj.
strange
unrelated 10 adj.
extraneous 59 adj.
unusual 84 adj.
unknown 491 adj.
puzzling 517 adj.
ridiculous 849 adj.
wonderful 864 adj.
strange behaviour
eccentricity 503 n.
strangely
remarkably 32 adv.
stranger
foreigner 59 n.
stranger to, a
ignorant 491 adj.
strangle
disable 161 vb.
suppress 165 vb.
make smaller 198 vb.
close 264 vb.
kill 362 vb.
retain 778 vb.
stranglehold
retention 778 n.
strangler
murderer 362 n.
strangulation
compression 198 n.
closure 264 n.
killing 362 n.
strap
tie 45 vb.
girdle 47 n.
strip 208 n.
spank 963 vb.
scourge 964 n.
straphanger
traveller 268 n.
strappado
corporal punishment 963 n.
strapper
giant 195 n.
strapping
whopping 32 adj.
stalwart 162 adj.
fleshy 195 adj.
healthy 650 adj.
strapwork
ornamental art 844 n.
stratagem
trickery 542 n.
contrivance 623 n.
tactics 688 n.
stratagem 698 n.
strategic, strategical
planned 623 adj.
cunning 698 adj.
warlike 718 adj.
strategist
motivator 612 n.
planner 623 n.
expert 696 n.
slyboots 698 n.
strategy
policy 623 n.
tactics 688 n.
art of war 718 n.
stratification
stratification 207 n.
structure 331 n.
stratified
layered 207 adj.
stratified society
social group 371 n.
stratigraphy
land 344 n.
stratocracy
government 733 n.
stratosphere
height 209 n.
atmosphere 340 n.
stratum
layer 207 n.
horizontality 216 n.
stratus
cloud 355 n.
straw
insubstantial thing 4 n.
lightness 323 n.
grass 366 n.
trifle 639 n.
strawberry
fruit 301 n.
strawberry mark
identification 547 n.
blemish 845 n.
strawboard
paper 631 n.
straw-coloured
yellow 433 adj.
straw hat
headgear 228 n.
straw in the wind
indication 547 n.
straw poll
enquiry 459 n.
empiricism 461 n.
vote 605 n.
stray
be dispersed 75 vb.
unconformable 84 adj.
casual 159 adj.
wander 267 vb.
wanderer 268 n.
stray 282 vb.
be inattentive 456 vb.
err 495 vb.
derelict 779 n.
outcast 883 n.
be wicked 934 vb.
streak
temperament 5 n.
tincture 43 n.
line 203 n.
narrowness 206 n.
strip 208 n.
move fast 277 vb.
flash 417 n.
stripe 437 n.
variegate 437 vb.
streaker
stripper 229 n.
stream
crowd 74 n.
group 74 n.
classification 77 n.
tendency 179 n.
hang 217 vb.
motion 265 n.
be wet 341 vb.
stream 350 n.
flow 350 vb.
rain 350 vb.
class 538 n.
store 632 n.
abound 635 vb.
superabound 637 vb.
— out
flow out 298 vb.
streamed
arranged 62 adj.
educational 534 adj.
streamer
advertisement 528 n.
flag 547 n.
trimming 844 n.
streaming
nonadhesive 49 adj.
unassembled 75 adj.
prolific 171 adj.
hanging 217 adj.
streamline
smooth 258 vb.
rectify 654 vb.
stream of consciousness
intellect 447 n.
soliloquy 585 n.
narrative 590 n.
street
locality 187 n.
housing 192 n.
road 624 n.
street arab
dirty person 649 n.
streetcar
tram 274 n.
street furniture
traffic control 305 n.
streets ahead
superior 34 adj.
streetwalker
prostitute 952 n.
strength
durability 113 n.
power 160 n.
strength 162 n.
vigorousness 174 n.
toughness 329 n.
vigour 571 n.
stamina 600 n.

strengthen
augment 36 vb.
accrue 38 vb.
strengthen 162 vb.
harden 326 vb.
corroborate 466 vb.
safeguard 660 vb.
strengthless
weak 163 adj.
strength of character
resolution 599 n.
strenuous
vigorous 174 adj.
persevering 600 adj.
labouring 682 adj.
streptomycin
drug 658 n.
stress
agency 173 n.
distortion 246 n.
attract notice 455 vb.
argue 475 vb.
emphasize 532 vb.
pronunciation 577 n.
prosody 593 n.
make important 638 vb.
exertion 682 n.
difficulty 700 n.
stretch
period 110 n.
range 183 n.
space 183 n.
enlarge 197 vb.
lengthen 203 vb.
overstep 306 vb.
elasticity 328 n.
exaggeration 546 n.
exaggerate 546 vb.
detention 747 n.
— a point
be lax 734 vb.
be lenient 736 vb.
not observe 769 vb.
compromise 770 vb.
exempt 919 vb.
— one's legs
be refreshed 685 vb.
— to
be distant 199 vb.
be long 203 vb.
stretchable
flexible 327 adj.
elastic 328 adj.
stretched out
supine 216 adj.
stretcher
bond 47 n.
bed 218 n.
vehicle 274 n.
hospital 658 n.
stretcher bearer
bearer 273 n.
nurse 658 n.
stretcher case
sick person 651 n.
stretching
expansion 197 n.
lengthening 203 n.
stretching the imagination
improbable 472 adj.
stretchy
elastic 328 adj.
strew
disperse 75 vb.
striation
furrow 262 n.
stripe 437 n.
stricken
unfortunate 731 adj.
suffering 825 adj.
strict
regulated 83 adj.
severe 735 adj.
restraining 747 adj.
obligatory 917 adj.
honourable 929 adj.
orthodox 976 adj.
strictly for the birds
tedious 838 adj.
stricture
narrowing 206 n.
censure 924 n.
reprimand 924 n.
accusation 928 n.
stride
gait 265 n.
walk 267 vb.
progression 285 n.
strident
loud 400 adj.
strident 407 adj.
discordant 411 adj.
vocal 577 adj.
stride piano
music 412 n.
stridulate
rasp 407 vb.
shrill 407 vb.
ululate 409 vb.
strife
quarrel 709 n.
contention 716 n.
strigil
cleaning utensil 648 n.
strike
strike 145 n.
cease 145 vb.
strike 279 vb.
propel 287 vb.
lower 311 vb.
rub 333 vb.
be visible 443 vb.
discovery 484 n.
discover 484 vb.
ill-treat 645 vb.
be inactive 679 vb.
be obstructive 702 vb.
strike at 712 vb.
resistance 715 n.
revolt 738 n.vb.
booty 790 n.
impress 821 vb.
spank 963 vb.
— a bad patch
be in difficulty 700 vb.
have trouble 731 vb.
— a balance
equalize 28 vb.
average out 30 vb.
— a bargain
contract 765 vb.
— a blow for
do 676 vb.
— a light
kindle 381 vb.
make bright 417 vb.
— a pose
be affected 850 vb.
— at
strike at 712 vb.
— dumb
make mute 578 vb.
be wonderful 864 vb.
— home
be vigorous 174 vb.
strike at 712 vb.
— it rich
prosper 730 vb.
get rich 800 vb.
— off
exclude 57 vb.
eject 300 vb.
— oil
have luck 730 vb.
— one
dawn upon 449 vb.
attract notice 455 vb.
— one's colours
submit 721 vb.
— out
destroy 165 vb.
swim 269 vb.
start out 296 vb.
obliterate 550 vb.
— root
be stable 153 vb.
place oneself 187 vb.
— tents
decamp 296 vb.
— up
begin 68 vb.
play music 413 vb.
— up an acquaintance
befriend 880 vb.
— while the iron is hot
profit by 137 vb.
strike-breaker
tergiversator 603 n.
strike force
attacker 712 n.
striker
revolter 738 n.
player 837 n.
striking
striking 374 adj.
obvious 443 adj.
expressive 516 adj.
manifest 522 adj.
descriptive 590 adj.
impressive 821 adj.
wonderful 864 adj.
striking distance
short distance 200 n.
strikingly
remarkably 32 adv.
Strine
dialect 560 n.
string
adjust 24 vb.
tie 45 vb.
cable 47 n.
series 71 n.
band 74 n.
fibre 208 n.
pass 305 vb.
harmonize 410 vb.
viol 414 n.
jewellery 844 n.
— along
befool 542 vb.
— along with
accompany 89 vb.
— out
disperse 75 vb.
lengthen 203 vb.
— together
connect 45 vb.
— up
kill 362 vb.
execute 963 vb.
string band
orchestra 413 n.
string course
layer 207 n.
stringency
severity 735 n.
stringent
exorbitant 32 adj.
vigorous 174 adj.
stringer
news reporter 529 n.
string of names
list 87 n.
strings
influence 178 n.
orchestra 413 n.
musical instrument 414 n.
latency 523 n.
conditions 766 n.
stringy
fibrous 208 adj.
tough 329 adj.
strip
subtract 39 vb.
disunite 46 vb.
piece 53 n.
line 203 n.
narrowness 206 n.
lamina 207 n.
strip 208 n.
doff 229 vb.
uncover 229 vb.
clean 648 vb.
deprive 786 vb.
fleece 786 vb.

impoverish 801 vb.
— of one's honours
shame 867 vb.
stripe
sort 77 n.
line 203 n.
narrowness 206 n.
stripe 437 n.
variegate 437 vb.
badge of rank 743 n.
pattern 844 n.
striped
crossed 222 adj.
stripes
badge 547 n.
livery 547 n.
stripling
youngster 132 n.
adult 134 n.
stripped of
losing 772 adj.
stripper
stripper 229 n.
strip show
stage show 594 n.
striptease
uncovering 229 n.
strive
attempt 671 vb.
exert oneself 682 vb.
contend 716 vb.
— after
aim at 617 vb.
strobe light
flash 417 n.
lamp 420 n.
stroboscope
optical device 442 n.
stroke
living model 23 n.
instant 116 n.
helplessness 161 n.
aquatics 269 n.
row 269 vb.
knock 279 n.
propulsion 287 n.
spasm 318 n.
rub 333 vb.
touch 378 n.vb.
punctuation 547 n.
lettering 586 n.
contrivance 623 n.
cardiovascular disease 651 n.
nervous disorders 651 n.
deed 676 n.
director 690 n.
prowess 855 n.
caress 889 vb.
corporal punishment 963 n.
stroke of genius
masterpiece 694 n.
success 727 n.
thaumaturgy 864 n.
stroll
pedestrianism 267 n.
wander 267 vb.
move slowly 278 vb.
stroller
wanderer 268 n.
strolling
travelling 267 adj.
strong
great 32 adj.
unmixed 44 adj.
powerful 160 adj.
strong 162 adj.
vigorous 174 adj.
violent 176 adj.
influential 178 adj.
tough 329 adj.
pungent 388 adj.
odorous 394 adj.
florid 425 adj.
expressive 516 adj.
assertive 532 adj.
forceful 571 adj.
healthy 650 adj.
invulnerable 660 adj.
authoritative 733 adj.
fervent 818 adj.
intoxicating 949 adj.
strong-arm tactics
violence 176 n.
compulsion 740 n.
strongbox
treasury 799 n.
strong drink
alcoholic drink 301 n.
strong feeling
belief 485 n.
stronghold
inhabitants 191 n.
refuge 662 n.
fort 713 n.
strong in
instructed 490 adj.
strong language
vigour 571 n.
scurrility 899 n.
strongly worded
expressive 516 adj.
assertive 532 adj.
forceful 571 adj.
disapproving 924 adj.
strong man
athlete 162 n.
strong-minded
resolute 599 adj.
courageous 855 adj.
strong point
skill 694 n.
strongroom
storage 632 n.
treasury 799 n.
strong-willed
resolute 599 adj.
strontium 90
poison 659 n.
strop
sharpener 256 n.
strophe
verse form 593 n.
stroppy
irascible 892 adj.
struck
impressed 818 adj.
struck down
defeated 728 adj.
struck dumb
wondering 864 adj.
struck with
enamoured 887 adj.
structural
intrinsic 5 adj.
supporting 218 adj.
structural 331 adj.
structuralism
philosophy 449 n.
interpretation 520 n.
structure
modality 7 n.
composition 56 n.
arrangement 62 n.
edifice 164 n.
frame 218 n.
form 243 n.
structure 331 n.
pattern 844 n.
struggle
be violent 176 vb.
move slowly 278 vb.
attempt 671 n.vb.
undertaking 672 n.
exert oneself 682 vb.
be in difficulty 700 vb.
contest 716 n.
— against
withstand 704 vb.
resist 715 vb.
strum
play music 413 vb.
mean nothing 515 vb.
strumpet
prostitute 952 n.
strung
adjusted 24 adj.
strung out
unassembled 75 adj.
long 203 adj.
strung up
excited 821 adj.
strut
bond 47 n.
prop 218 n.
gait 265 n.
walk 267 vb.
be proud 871 vb.
be vain 873 vb.
ostentation 875 n.
boast 877 vb.
strychnine
poison 659 n.
stub
remainder 41 n.
tobacco 388 n.
label 547 n.
stubble
leavings 41 n.
hair 259 n.
roughness 259 n.
grass 366 n.
rubbish 641 n.
stubborn
unyielding 162 adj.
rigid 326 adj.
tough 329 adj.
persevering 600 adj.
obstinate 602 adj.
difficult 700 adj.
resisting 715 adj.
impenitent 940 adj.
stubby
short 204 adj.
thick 205 adj.
unsharpened 257 adj.
stub one's toe
collide 279 vb.
— out
extinguish 382 vb.
stucco
facing 226 n.
stuck
firm 45 adj.
still 266 adj.
hindered 702 adj.
stuck fast
fixed 153 adj.
in difficulties 700 adj.
retained 778 adj.
stuck in a groove
repeated 106 adj.
stuck-up
affected 850 adj.
prideful 871 adj.
vain 873 adj.
stud
fastening 47 n.
pillar 218 n.
sharpen 256 vb.
roughen 259 vb.
horse 273 n.
stock farm 369 n.
variegate 437 vb.
jewellery 844 n.
decorate 844 vb.
studded with
multitudinous 104 adj.
student
enquirer 459 n.
scholar 492 n.
student 538 n.
student days
salad days 130 n.
studied
predetermined 608 adj.
intended 617 adj.
affected 850 adj.
studio
chamber 194 n.
art equipment 553 n.
workshop 687 n.

studio portrait
picture 553 n.
studious
thoughtful 449 adj.
attentive 455 adj.
studious 536 adj.
industrious 678 adj.
studwork
structure 331 n.
building material 631 n.
study
retreat 192 n.
chamber 194 n.
musical piece 412 n.
scan 438 vb.
meditation 449 n.
topic 452 n.
be attentive 455 vb.
enquiry 459 n.
study 536 n.vb.
classroom 539 n.
picture 553 n.
dissertation 591 n.
intend 617 vb.
prepare oneself 669 vb.
workshop 687 n.
study group
class 538 n.
stuff
substantiality 3 n.
essential part 5 n.
fill 54 vb.
strengthen 162 vb.
load 193 vb.
enlarge 197 vb.
textile 222 n.
line 227 vb.
cook 301 vb.
matter 319 n.
texture 331 n.
silly talk 515 n.
materials 631 n.
rubbish 641 n.
preserve 666 vb.
merchandise 795 n.
sate 863 vb.
— into
insert 303 vb.
— oneself
eat 301 vb.
gluttonize 947 vb.
stuff and nonsense
absurdity 497 n.
silly talk 515 n.
stuffed shirt
insubstantial thing 4 n.
vain person 873 n.
stuffing
adjunct 40 n.
contents 193 n.
lining 227 n.
stuffy
sealed off 264 adj.
dense 324 adj.
warm 379 adj.
fetid 397 adj.
insalubrious 653 adj.
tedious 838 adj.
dull 840 adj.
stumble
walk 267 vb.
tumble 309 vb.
blunder 495 vb.
be clumsy 695 vb.
be wicked 934 vb.
— on
chance 159 vb.
discover 484 vb.
stumbling block
obstacle 702 n.
stump
remainder 41 n.
extremity 69 n.
projection 254 n.
walk 267 vb.
move slowly 278 vb.
puzzle 474 vb.
be difficult 700 vb.
— up
pay 804 vb.
stumped
doubting 474 adj.
puzzled 517 adj.
stumper
question 459 n.
stumps
leg 267 n.
stumpy
short 204 adj.
deformed 246 adj.
stun
strike 279 vb.
render insensible 375 vb.
be loud 400 vb.
deafen 416 vb.
surprise 508 vb.
impress 821 vb.
frighten 854 vb.
be wonderful 864 vb.
stung
excited 821 adj.
angry 891 adj.
resentful 891 adj.
stung, be
pay too much 811 vb.
stunner
a beauty 841 n.
stunning
super 644 adj.
exciting 821 adj.
stunt
shorten 204 vb.
fly 271 vb.
contrivance 623 n.
deed 676 n.
be expert 694 vb.
pageant 875 n.
stunted
dwarfish 196 adj.
contracted 198 adj.
deformed 246 adj.
underfed 636 adj.
stunt man/woman
athlete 162 n.
doer 676 n.
stupefy
render insensible 375 vb.
impress 821 vb.
be wonderful 864 vb.
inebriate 949 vb.
stupendous
prodigious 32 adj.
huge 195 adj.
wonderful 864 adj.
stupid
unthinking 450 adj.
credulous 487 adj.
unintelligent 499 adj.
fool 501 n.
unskilful 695 adj.
dull 840 adj.
stupidity
unintelligence 499 n.
moral insensibility 820 n.
stupor
insensibility 375 n.
sluggishness 679 n.
moral insensibility 820 n.
wonder 864 n.
sturdy
stalwart 162 adj.
Sturm und Drang
literature 557 n.
stutter
repeat oneself 106 vb.
speech defect 580 n.
be clumsy 695 vb.
show feeling 818 vb.
quake 854 vb.
St Vitus's dance
spasm 318 n.
nervous disorders 651 n.
sty
stable 192 n.
enclosure 235 n.
sty, stye
swelling 253 n.
Stygian
dark 418 adj.
infernal 972 adj.
style
modality 7 n.
sort 77 n.
chronology 117 n.
form 243 n.
flower 366 n.
meaning 514 n.
engraving 555 n.
name 561 n.vb.
style 566 n.
elegance 575 n.
way 624 n.
conduct 688 n.
skill 694 n.
beauty 841 n.
fashion 848 n.
style of painting
art style 553 n.
styling
hairdressing 843 n.
stylish
elegant 575 adj.
well-made 694 adj.
personable 841 adj.
fashionable 848 adj.
stylist
phrasemonger 574 n.
stylist 575 n.
stylite
solitary 883 n.
stylized, stylised
formed 243 adj.
stylobate
stand 218 n.
stylograph
stationery 586 n.
stylus
sharp point 256 n.
gramophone 414 n.
stationery 586 n.
stymie
obstacle 702 n.
be obstructive 702 vb.
styptic
solidifying 324 adj.
Styx
mythic hell 972 n.
suasion
influence 178 n.
suave
smooth 258 adj.
courteous 884 adj.
sub-
inferior 35 adj.
sub
substitute 150 n.
publish 528 vb.
subaltern
inferior 35 adj.
army officer 741 n.
subapostolic
scriptural 975 adj.
subaqua
sport 837 n.
subaqueous
deep 211 adj.
oceanic 343 adj.
subastral
telluric 321 adj.
subaudition
interpretation 520 n.
subconscious
spirit 447 n.
psychic 447 adj.
intuitive 476 adj.
subcutaneous
interior 224 adj.
subdivide
sunder 46 vb.
subdivision
subdivision 53 n.

classification 77 n.
district 184 n.
partition 231 n.
subdominant
musical note 410 n.
subdue
moderate 177 vb.
prevail 178 vb.
overmaster 727 vb.
subjugate 745 vb.
restrain 747 vb.
subdued
muted 401 adj.
dejected 834 adj.
subedit
publish 528 vb.
subeditor
author 589 n.
subfusc
formal dress 228 n.
brown 430 adj.
subgroup
subdivision 53 n.
arrangement 62 n.
subhead
classification 77 n.
subhuman
animal 365 adj.
human 371 adj.
subjacent
low 210 adj.
subject
living model 23 n.
prototype 23 n.
inferior 35 adj.
liable 180 adj.
topic 452 n.
testee 461 n.
part of speech 564 n.
overmaster 727 vb.
subject 742 n.
subject 745 adj.
subjugate 745 vb.
subjection
helplessness 161 n.
governance 733 n.
subjection 745 n.
subjective
intrinsic 5 adj.
immaterial 320 adj.
mental 447 adj.
misjudging 481 adj.
imaginary 513 adj.
subjective idealism
philosophy 449 n.
subjectivity
self 80 n.
subjectivity 320 n.
error 495 n.
subject matter
topic 452 n.
meaning 514 n.
subject to
liable 180 adj.
provided 468 adv.
on terms 766 adv.
subjoin
add 38 vb.
place after 65 vb.
sub judice
on trial 459 adv.
sub judice 480 adv.
in litigation 959 adv.
subjugate
overmaster 727 vb.
subjugate 745 vb.
subjugation
defeat 728 n.
sublet
lease 784 vb.
sublety
discrimination 463 n.
fastidiousness 862 n.
sublieutenant
nautical personnel 270 n.
naval officer 741 n.
sublimate
vaporize 338 vb.
purify 648 vb.
make better 654 vb.
sublime
great 32 adj.
high 209 adj.
elevated 310 adj.
impressive 821 adj.
splendid 841 adj.
proud 871 adj.
divine 965 adj.
subliminal
psychic 447 adj.
subliminal advertising
advertisement 528 n.
sublimity
superiority 34 n.
vigour 571 n.
eloquence 579 n.
beauty 841 n.
prestige 866 n.
disinterestedness 931 n.
(See **sublime** *)*
sublineation
punctuation 547 n.
submachine gun
gun 723 n.
submarine
low 210 adj.
deep 211 adj.
diver 313 n.
oceanic 343 adj.
warship 722 n.
submariner
diver 313 n.
naval man 722 n.
submediant
musical note 410 n.
submerge
suppress 165 vb.
immerse 303 vb.
plunge 313 vb.
drench 341 vb.
be unseen 444 vb.
obliterate 550 vb.
submerged
deep 211 adj.
latent 523 adj.
submergence
immersion 303 n.
submersible
descending 309 adj.
lowered 311 adj.
submission
conformity 83 n.
argument 475 n.
sluggishness 679 n.
submission 721 n.
obedience 739 n.
subjection 745 n.
resignation 753 n.
entreaty 761 n.
patience 823 n.
humility 872 n.
servility 879 n.
submissive
weak 163 adj.
willing 597 adj.
tractable 701 adj.
peaceful 717 adj.
respectful 920 adj.
submit
acquiesce 488 vb.
propound 512 vb.
affirm 532 vb.
be forced 596 vb.
be induced 612 vb.
advise 691 vb.
submit 721 vb.
be defeated 728 vb.
(See **submission** *)*
— a report
communicate 524 vb.
submultiple
numerical element 85 n.
subnormal
inferior 35 adj.
abnormal 84 adj.
unintelligent 499 adj.
subordinate
inferior 35 n.adj.
dependant 742 n.
subject 745 adj.
subordinate clause
subdivision 53 n.
suborn
bribe 612 vb.
purchase 792 vb.
subplot
narrative 590 n.
dramaturgy 594 n.
subpoena
command 737 vb.
legal process 959 n.
subregion
district 184 n.
subreption
falsehood 541 n.
acquisition 771 n.
subrogation
substitution 150 n.
sub rosa
secretly 525 adv.
subscribe
sign 547 vb.
join a party 708 vb.
contract 765 vb.
give 781 vb.
— to
endorse 488 vb.
patronize 703 vb.
subscriber
assenter 488 n.
signatory 765 n.
giver 781 n.
subscription
payment 804 n.
subsection
classification 77 n.
subsequent
sequential 65 adj.
subsequent 120 adj.
future 124 adj.
late 136 adj.
following 284 adj.
subserve
concur 181 vb.
be instrumental 628 vb.
be useful 640 vb.
minister to 703 vb.
subservience
submission 721 n.
subservient
tending 179 adj.
instrumental 628 adj.
useful 640 adj.
aiding 703 adj.
subjected 745 adj.
servile 879 adj.
subset
classification 77 n.
subside
decrease 37 vb.
be quiescent 266 vb.
recede 290 vb.
sit down 311 vb.
subsidence
descent 309 n.
subsidiary
inferior 35 n.adj.
additional 38 adj.
unimportant 639 adj.
useful 640 adj.
aiding 703 adj.
subsidize, subsidise
aid 703 vb.
subsidy
subvention 703 n.
gift 781 n.
pay 804 n.
subsist
be 1 vb.
stay 144 vb.
live 360 vb.
subsistence
existence 1 n.
subsistence farming
agriculture 370 n.
sufficiency 635 n.

subsoil
base 214 n.
interiority 224 n.
soil 344 n.
subspecies
subdivision 53 n.
breed 77 n.
substance
essence 1 n.
substance 3 n.
essential part 5 n.
main part 32 n.
interiority 224 n.
form 243 n.
matter 319 n.
structure 331 n.
meaning 514 n.
materials 631 n.
chief thing 638 n.
importance 638 n.
estate 777 n.
wealth 800 n.
substandard
inferior 35 adj.
deficient 307 adj.
cheap 812 adj.
substantial
real 1 adj.
substantial 3 adj.
great 32 adj.
strong 162 adj.
architectural 192 adj.
material 319 adj.
dense 324 adj.
true 494 adj.
meaningful 514 adj.
substantially
substantially 3 adv.
on the whole 52 adv.
substantiate
demonstrate 478 vb.
be true 494 vb.
substantive
real 1 adj.
part of speech 564 n.
substitute
inferior 35 n.
substitute 150 n.vb.
displace 188 vb.
actor 594 n.
contrivance 623 n.
imperfection 647 n.
stop using 674 vb.
deputy 755 n.
not retain 779 vb.
substitution
substitution 150 n.
deposal 752 n.
transfer 780 n.
substratum
substance 3 n.
layer 207 n.
base 214 n.
interiority 224 n.
substructure
base 214 n.
structure 331 n.
subsume
contain 56 vb.
class 62 vb.
number with 78 vb.
subteenage
young 130 adj.
subtenant
possessor 776 n.
subtend
be opposite 240 vb.
subterfuge
sophistry 477 n.
concealment 525 n.
mental dishonesty 543 n.
pretext 614 n.
stratagem 698 n.
subterranean
low 210 adj.
deep 211 adj.
latent 523 adj.
concealed 525 adj.
infernal 972 adj.
subtle
rare 325 adj.
intelligent 498 adj.
cunning 698 adj.
subtle distinction
differentiation 15 n.
subtlety
sophistry 477 n.
sagacity 498 n.
cunning 698 n.
subtonic
musical note 410 n.
subtopia
district 184 n.
housing 192 n.
averageness 732 n.
subtract
subtract 39 vb.
do sums 86 vb.
take 786 vb.
discount 810 vb.
subtraction
diminution 37 n.
separation 46 n.
numerical operation 86 n.
subtrahend
decrement 42 n.
suburb(s)
district 184 n.
housing 192 n.
near place 200 n.
surroundings 230 n.
suburban
regional 184 adj.
urban 192 adj.
circumjacent 230 adj.
tedious 838 adj.
plebeian 869 adj.
suburbanite
dweller 191 n.
native 191 n.
suburbia
dispersion 75 n.
averageness 732 n.
(See **suburb** *)*
subvention
subvention 703 n.
gift 781 n.
subversion
disorder 61 n.
revolution 149 n.
destruction 165 n.
overturning 221 n.
lowering 311 n.
revolt 738 n.
sedition 738 n.
subversive
revolutionary 149 adj.
destructive 165 adj.
disobedient 738 adj.
subvert
revolutionize 149 vb.
demolish 165 vb.
tell against 467 vb.
impair 655 vb.
subway
tunnel 263 n.
railway 624 n.
succeed
come after 65 vb.
run on 71 vb.
ensue 120 vb.
substitute 150 vb.
follow 284 vb.
flourish 615 vb.
be expedient 642 vb.
succeed 727 vb.
prosper 730 vb.
inherit 771 vb.
have a reputation 866 vb.
— to
inherit 771 vb.
receive 782 vb.
— to the throne
take authority 733 vb.
succès de scandale
disrepute 867 n.
succès d'estime
prestige 866 n.
succès fou
success 727 n.
success
success 727 n.
prosperity 730 n.
famousness 866 n.
successful
completed 725 adj.
successful 727 adj.
prosperous 730 adj.
successful person
victor 727 n.
prosperous person 730 n.
succession
sequence 65 n.
continuity 71 n.
series 71 n.
recurrence 106 n.
posteriority 120 n.
sonship 170 n.
successive
sequential 65 adj.
continuous 71 adj.
periodical 141 adj.
successor
successor 67 n.
posteriority 120 n.
substitute 150 n.
beneficiary 776 n.
recipient 782 n.
succinct
concise 569 adj.
succour
remedy 658 n.vb.
aid 703 n.vb.
succubus, succuba
demon 970 n.
sorceress 983 n.
succulent
edible 301 adj.
fluid 335 adj.
pulpy 356 adj.
plant 366 n.
savoury 390 adj.
succumb
be destroyed 165 vb.
die 361 vb.
be induced 612 vb.
be fatigued 684 vb.
knuckle under 721 vb.
be defeated 728 vb.
such
such 7 adj.
circumstantial 8 adj.
anonymous 562 adj.
such a one
person 371 n.
such as
similar 18 adj.
suck
absorb 299 vb.
drink 301 vb.
extract 304 vb.
be wet 341 vb.
smoke 388 vb.
hiss 406 vb.
— dry
dry 342 vb.
interrogate 459 vb.
waste 634 vb.
fleece 786 vb.
levy 786 vb.
— in
draw 288 vb.
absorb 299 vb.
— out
empty 300 vb.
— up to
be servile 879 vb.
flatter 925 vb.
sucker
young plant 132 n.
orifice 263 n.
tree 366 n.
credulity 487 n.
ninny 501 n.
dupe 544 n.

sucker for
desirer 859 n.
suckling
child 132 n.
sucrose
food content 301 n.
sweet thing 392 n.
suction
energy 160 n.
reception 299 n.
extraction 304 n.
suction pump
extractor 304 n.
sudatorium
ablutions 648 n.
sudden
brief 114 adj.
instantaneous 116 adj.
early 135 adj.
unexpected 508 adj.
spontaneous 609 adj.
sudorific
excretory 302 adj.
watery 339 adj.
hot 379 adj.
Sudra
commoner 869 n.
suds
bubble 355 n.
sue
claim 915 vb.
indict 928 vb.
litigate 959 vb.
— for
request 761 vb.
suede
skin 226 n.
suet
meat 301 n.
fat 357 n.
suffer
meet with 154 vb.
feel pain 377 vb.
be ill 651 vb.
have trouble 731 vb.
permit 756 vb.
feel 818 vb.
be patient 823 vb.
suffer 825 vb.
sufferance
leniency 736 n.
permission 756 n.
sufferer
sick person 651 n.
unlucky person 731 n.
sufferer 825 n.
suffering
pain 377 n.
evil 616 n.
badness 645 n.
adversity 731 n.
feeling 818 n.adj.
suffering 825 n.adj.
painfulness 827 n.
suffice
be equal 28 vb.
be able 160 vb.
suffice 635 vb.
be expedient 642 vb.
be middling 732 vb.
sate 863 vb.
sufficiency
completeness 54 n.
sufficiency 635 n.
completion 725 n.
sufficient
sufficient 635 adj.
not bad 644 adj.
contenting 828 adj.
suffix
adjunct 40 n.
place after 65 vb.
part of speech 564 n.
suffocate
suppress 165 vb.
kill 362 vb.
heat 381 vb.
suffragan
ecclesiarch 986 n.
suffrage
affirmation 532 n.
vote 605 n.
suffragette
woman 373 n.
vote 605 n.
agitator 738 n.
suffusion
mixture 43 n.
feeling 818 n.
Sufi
religionist 973 n.
pietist 979 n.
monk 986 n.
Sufism
philosophy 449 n.
religion 973 n.
sugar
food content 301 n.
sweet thing 392 n.
please 826 vb.
darling 890 n.
flatter 925 vb.
— the pill
sweeten 392 vb.
deceive 542 vb.
tempt 612 vb.
sugar daddy
lover 887 n.
sugared
sweet 392 adj.
deceiving 542 adj.
sugarloaf
cone 252 n.
dome 253 n.
sugary
pleasant 376 adj.
sweet 392 adj.
pleasurable 826 adj.
flattering 925 adj.
suggest
evidence 466 vb.
remind 505 vb.
propound 512 vb.
imply 523 vb.
hint 524 vb.
indicate 547 vb.
represent 551 vb.
incite 612 vb.
advise 691 vb.
offer 759 vb.
— itself
dawn upon 449 vb.
suggestible
irresolute 601 adj.
excitable 822 adj.
frail 934 adj.
suggestio falsi
falsehood 541 n.
mental dishonesty 543 n.
suggestion
similarity 18 n.
small quantity 33 n.
influence 178 n.
plan 623 n.
(See **suggest** *)*
suggestive
evidential 466 adj.
suppositional 512 adj.
meaningful 514 adj.
tacit 523 adj.
indicating 547 adj.
descriptive 590 adj.
exciting 821 adj.
impure 951 adj.
suicidal
destructive 165 adj.
murderous 362 adj.
hopeless 853 adj.
rash 857 adj.
suicide
suicide 362 n.
sui generis
special 80 adj.
unconformable 84 adj.
suit
uniformity 16 n.
accord 24 vb.
sort 77 n.
suit 228 n.
request 761 n.
beautify 841 vb.
wooing 889 n.
litigation 959 n.
suitable
relevant 9 adj.
fit 24 adj.
advisable 642 adj.
right 913 adj.
suitcase
box 194 n.
suite
retinue 67 n.
series 71 n.
concomitant 89 n.
flat 192 n.
follower 284 n.
musical piece 412 n.
retainer 742 n.
suiting
textile 222 n.
suitor
petitioner 763 n.
lover 887 n.
litigant 959 n.
sulcate
furrowed 262 adj.
sulk
be discontented 829 vb.
be dejected 834 vb.
be rude 885 vb.
be sullen 893 vb.
sulker
rude person 885 n.
misanthrope 902 n.
sulks
discontent 829 n.
sullenness 893 n.
sulky
carriage 274 n.
unwilling 598 adj.
discontented 829 adj.
melancholic 834 adj.
sullen 893 adj.
sullage
semiliquidity 354 n.
sullen
unwilling 598 adj.
discontented 829 adj.
serious 834 adj.
ugly 842 adj.
unsociable 883 adj.
ungracious 885 adj.
angry 891 adj.
sullen 893 adj.
malevolent 898 adj.
threatening 900 adj.
sully
bedim 419 vb.
make unclean 649 vb.
blemish 845 vb.
shame 867 vb.
defame 926 vb.
sulpha drug
drug 658 n.
sulphur
fumigator 385 n.
yellowness 433 n.
sulphurous
fetid 397 adj.
Sultan, Sultana
sovereign 741 n.
sultana
fruit 301 n.
sultanate
position of authority 733 n.
sultry
warm 379 adj.
sullen 893 adj.
sum
add 38 vb.
all 52 n.
whole 52 n.
numerical result 85 n.
numeration 86 n.
meaning 514 n.
funds 797 n.

— up
estimate 480 vb.
judge 480 vb.
be concise 569 vb.
abstract 592 vb.
try a case 959 vb.
summarize, summarise
be concise 569 vb.
abstract 592 vb.
summary
brief 114 adj.
early 135 adj.
concise 569 adj.
description 590 n.
compendium 592 n.
lawless 954 adj.
summation
addition 38 n.
whole 52 n.
numeration 86 n.
summer
pass time 108 vb.
period 110 n.
summer 128 n.
beam 218 n.
heat 379 n.
palmy days 730 n.
summerhouse
arbour 194 n.
summer solstice
uranometry 321 n.
summer time
clock time 117 n.
summery
summery 128 adj.
warm 379 adj.
summing up
estimate 480 n.
legal trial 959 n.
summit
superiority 34 n.n.
completeness 54 n.
extremity 69 n.
serial place 73 n.
height 209 n.
summit 213 n.
limit 236 n.
conference 584 n.
perfection 646 n.
council 692 n.
summit meeting
conference 584 n.
summon
bring together 74 vb.
command 737 vb.
desire 859 vb.
indict 928 vb.
litigate 959 vb.
— up
retrospect 505 vb.
excite 821 vb.
summons
publication 528 n.
call 547 n.
command 737 n.
warrant 737 n.
desire 859 n.
accusation 928 n.
law 953 n.
legal process 959 n.
summum bonum
good 615 n.
happiness 824 n.
sump
receptacle 194 n.
lake 346 n.
storage 632 n.
sink 649 n.
sumptuary
monetary 797 adj.
sumptuary law
prohibition 757 n.
economy 814 n.
sumptuous
ostentatious 875 adj.
sun
sun 321 n.
dry 342 vb.
heat 379 n.
heat 381 vb.
light 417 n.
luminary 420 n.
sunbathe
be hot 379 vb.
sunbeam
light 417 n.
sunblind
canopy 226 n.
curtain 421 n.
sunburn
burning 381 n.
sunburnt
brown 430 adj.
sundae
dessert 301 n.
Sunday
holy day 988 n.
Sunday best
clothing 228 n.
finery 844 n.
sunder
sunder 46 vb.
decompose 51 vb.
disperse 75 vb.
sundew
plant 366 n.
sundial
timekeeper 117 n.
sundown
evening 129 n.
obscuration 418 n.
sundowner
wanderer 268 n.
draught 301 n.
sundries
merchandise 795 n.
sundry
multiform 82 adj.
many 104 adj.
sun-dry
dry 342 vb.
preserve 666 vb.
sun glasses
screen 421 n.
eyeglass 442 n.
shelter 662 n.
sun god
mythic deity 966 n.
sun hat
shade 226 n.
headgear 228 n.
screen 421 n.
sunk
destroyed 165 adj.
deep 211 adj.
defeated 728 adj.
sunken
low 210 adj.
concave 255 adj.
sun lamp
lamp 420 n.
beautification 843 n.
sunless
unlit 418 adj.
sunlight
sun 321 n.
heater 383 n.
light 417 n.
sun lounge
arbour 194 n.
Sunna
tradition 127 n.
non-Biblical scripture 975 n.
Sunni, Sunnite
religionist 973 n.
sectarian 978 adj.
sunny
tranquil 266 adj.
dry 342 adj.
warm 379 adj.
undimmed 417 adj.
pleasurable 826 adj.
cheerful 833 adj.
sunrise
morning 128 n.
ascent 308 n.
sunset
evening 129 n.
descent 309 n.
glow 417 n.
redness 431 n.
sunshade
shade 226 n.
screen 421 n.
sunshine
salubrity 652 n.
palmy days 730 n.
sunshine roof
window 263 n.
sun spot
sun 321 n.
sunstroke
frenzy 503 n.
sunsuit
beachwear 228 n.
suntan
brownness 430 n.
sun trap
heater 383 n.
sun-worshipper
sanitarian 652 n.
idolater 982 n.
sup
draught 301 n.
eat 301 vb.
taste 386 vb.
— with a long spoon
avoid 620 vb.
super
superior 34 adj.
topmost 213 adj.
actor 594 n.
super 644 adj.
superable
possible 469 adj.
superabound
be many 104 vb.
overstep 306 vb.
superabound 637 vb.
superabundance
great quantity 32 n.
productiveness 171 n.
plenty 635 n.
redundance 637 n.
superadd
augment 36 vb.
add 38 vb.
superadded
extrinsic 6 adj.
superannuated
antiquated 127 adj.
ageing 131 adj.
disused 674 adj.
superannuation
earnings 771 n.
superb
excellent 644 adj.
splendid 841 adj.
ostentatious 875 adj.
supercharged
dynamic 160 adj.
supercilious
prideful 871 adj.
insolent 878 adj.
disrespectful 921 adj.
despising 922 adj.
superego
subjectivity 320 n.
spirit 447 n.
supereminent
noteworthy 866 adj.
supererogation
voluntary work 597 n.
superfluity 637 n.
superfetation
propagation 167 n.
superficial
insubstantial 4 adj.
inconsiderable 33 adj.
incomplete 55 adj.
spatial 183 adj.
shallow 212 adj.
exterior 223 adj.
appearing 445 adj.
inattentive 456 adj.
negligent 458 adj.
dabbling 491 adj.
foolish 499 adj.
trivial 639 adj.
bungled 695 adj.

uncompleted 726 adj.
dull 840 adj.
superficiality
pretension 850 n.
(See **superficial** *)*
superfine
excellent 644 adj.
superfluity
great quantity 32 n.
extra 40 n.
remainder 41 n.
expansion 197 n.
superfluous
additional 38 adj.
remaining 41 adj.
superfluous 637 adj.
superfluousness
inutility 641 n.
supergiant
star 321 n.
superhuman
divine 965 adj.
godlike 965 adj.
superhuman task
hard task 700 n.
superimpose
add 38 vb.
cover 226 vb.
superintend
manage 689 vb.
superintendent
manager 690 n.
superior
superior 34 n.adj.
bigwig 638 n.
excellent 644 adj.
improved 654 adj.
director 690 n.
master 741 n.
Superior
ecclesiarch 986 n.
superior airs
contempt 922 n.
superiority
superiority 34 n.
precedence 64 n.
seniority 131 n.
power 160 n.
importance 638 n.
goodness 644 n.
perfection 646 n.
authority 733 n.
contempt 922 n.
superlative
supreme 34 adj.
grammatical 564 adj.
excellent 644 adj.
superman, superwoman
superior 34 n.
exceller 644 n.
paragon 646 n.
prodigy 864 n.
supermarket
shop 796 n.
supernal
high 209 adj.
immaterial 320 adj.
paradisiac 971 adj.
supernatural
extraneous 59 adj.
abnormal 84 adj.
divine 965 adj.
spooky 970 adj.
magical 983 adj.
paranormal 984 adj.
supernormal
abnormal 84 adj.
supernova
star 321 n.
supernumerary
extra 40 n.
actor 594 n.
superfluous 637 adj.
superpose
cover 226 vb.
superpower
influence 178 n.
bigwig 638 n.
political organization 733 n.
superscription
label 547 n.
script 586 n.
supersede
substitute 150 vb.
displace 188 vb.
eject 300 vb.
stop using 674 vb.
depose 752 vb.
not retain 779 vb.
superseded
antiquated 127 adj.
disused 674 adj.
supersonic
aviational 276 adj.
speedy 277 adj.
sounding 398 adj.
superstition
credulity 487 n.
ignorance 491 n.
error 495 n.
heterodoxy 977 n.
idolatry 982 n.
sorcery 983 n.
superstitious
misjudging 481 adj.
superstore
shop 796 n.
superstratum
exteriority 223 n.
superstructure
structure 331 n.
supertanker
merchant ship 275 n.
supertax
tax 809 n.
supertonic
musical note 410 n.
supervene
be extrinsic 6 vb.
accrue 38 vb.
ensue 120 vb.
happen 154 vb.
supervise
manage 689 vb.
supervision
inspection 438 n.
supervisor
manager 690 n.
supine
supine 216 adj.
inverted 221 adj.
quiescent 266 adj.
lowered 311 adj.
inactive 679 adj.
submitting 721 adj.
apathetic 820 adj.
indifferent 860 adj.
supper
meal 301 n.
supperless
hungry 859 adj.
fasting 946 adj.
supplant
come after 65 vb.
substitute 150 vb.
eject 300 vb.
supple
flexible 327 adj.
tergiversating 603 adj.
servile 879 adj.
dishonest 930 adj.
supplement
increment 36 n.
augment 36 vb.
adjunct 40 n.
make complete 54 vb.
sequel 67 n.
enlarge 197 vb.
the press 528 n.
edition 589 n.
price 809 n.
supplementary benefit
subvention 703 n.
suppleness
softness 327 n.
skill 694 n.
cunning 698 n.
(See **supple** *)*
suppliant
supplicatory 761 adj.
petitioner 763 n.
supplicant
petitioner 763 n.
worshipper 981 n.
supplication
entreaty 761 n.
prayers 981 n.
supplier
provider 633 n.
supplies
means 629 n.
provision 633 n.
subvention 703 n.
merchandise 795 n.
supply
make complete 54 vb.
find means 629 vb.
store 632 n.
provide 633 vb.
support
sustain 146 vb.
strengthen 162 vb.
support 218 n.vb.
carry 273 vb.
corroborate 466 vb.
endorse 488 vb.
act 594 vb.
choose 605 vb.
instrumentality 628 n.
suffice 635 vb.
safeguard 660 vb.
preservation 666 n.
aid 703 n.
aider 703 n.
be patient 823 vb.
friendship 880 n.
approve 923 vb.
vindicate 927 vb.
supporter
prop 218 n.
follower 284 n.
onlookers 441 n.
enthusiast 504 n.
patron 707 n.
benefactor 903 n.
commender 923 n.
supporting role
inferiority 35 n.
supportive
aiding 703 adj.
suppose
assume 471 vb.
premise 475 vb.
opine 485 vb.
not know 491 vb.
suppose 512 vb.
supposed
attributed 158 adj.
credible 485 adj.
supposed 512 adj.
supposing
if 8 adv.
provided 468 adv.
suppositional 512 adj.
supposition
idea 451 n.
supposition 512 n.
(See **suppose** *)*
suppositional
mental 447 adj.
ideational 451 adj.
uncertain 474 adj.
suppositional 512 adj.
imaginary 513 adj.
suppository
surgical dressing 658 n.
suppress
suppress 165 vb.
counteract 182 vb.
conceal 525 vb.
make mute 578 vb.
overmaster 727 vb.

be severe 735 vb.
restrain 747 vb.
suppression
exclusion 57 n.
destruction 165 n.
concealment 525 n.
severity 735 n.
restraint 747 n.
abrogation 752 n.
prohibition 757 n.
suppressio veri
falsehood 541 n.
mental dishonesty 543 n.
suppurate
deteriorate 655 vb.
suppuration
excretion 302 n.
infection 651 n.
supra
before 64 adv.
rearward 238 adv.
supranatural
paranormal 984 adj.
supremacy
superiority 34 n.
importance 638 n.
authority 733 n.
governance 733 n.
supreme
supreme 34 adj.
ending 69 adj.
powerful 160 adj.
topmost 213 adj.
perfect 646 adj.
Supreme Being
the Deity 965 n.
supreme control
directorship 689 n.
governance 733 n.
Supreme Court
lawcourt 956 n.
supremely
eminently 34 adv.
Supreme Pontiff
ecclesiarch 986 n.
Supreme Soviet
parliament 692 n.
surah
textile 222 n.
surcharge
price 809 n.
surcoat
jacket 228 n.
surd
number 85 n.
speech sound 398 n.
voicelessness 578 n.
sure
certain 473 adj.
positive 473 adj.
believing 485 adj.
expectant 507 adj.
safe 660 adj.
trustworthy 929 adj.
surefire
successful 727 adj.
surefooted
vigilant 457 adj.
skilful 694 adj.
successful 727 adj.
sure of oneself
unfearing 855 adj.
sure thing
certainty 473 n.
easy thing 701 n.
surety
protection 660 n.
security 767 n.
legal process 959 n.
surf
swim 269 vb.
wave 350 n.
bubble 355 n.
surface
space 183 n.
shallow 212 adj.
exteriority 223 n.
navigate 269 vb.
emerge 298 vb.
ascend 308 vb.
be light 323 vb.
texture 331 n.
be visible 443 vb.
road 624 n.
surface area
measure 183 n.
surfboard
sledge 274 n.
plaything 837 n.
surfeit
superfluity 637 n.
satiety 863 n.
surf riding
aquatics 269 n.
sport 837 n.
surge
increase 36 n.
grow 36 vb.
congregate 74 vb.
flow out 298 vb.
eddy 350 n.
flow 350 vb.
be active 678 vb.
surgeon
doctor 658 n.
surgery
scission 46 n.
surgery 658 n.
surgical
medical 658 adj.
surgical dressing
surgical dressing 658 n.
surly
ungracious 885 adj.
sullen 893 adj.
surmise
opine 485 vb.
foresee 510 vb.
conjecture 512 n.
surmount
be superior 34 vb.
be high 209 vb.
crown 213 vb.
overstep 306 vb.
climb 308 vb.
triumph 727 vb.
surmountable
possible 469 adj.
surname
name 561 n.
surpass
be superior 34 vb.
outdo 306 vb.
surplice
vestments 989 n.
surplus
extra 40 n.
remaining 41 adj.
part 53 n.
superfluity 637 n.
surprise
lack of expectation 508 n.
surprise 508 vb.
pitfall 663 n.
nonpreparation 670 n.
attack 712 vb.
be wonderful 864 vb.
surprising
unusual 84 adj.
unexpected 508 adj.
wonderful 864 adj.
Surrealism
school of painting 553 n.
literature 557 n.
surrealistic
representing 551 adj.
literary 557 adj.
surrender
relinquish 621 vb.
nonuse 674 n.
submit 721 vb.
resign 753 vb.
surreptitious
stealthy 525 adj.
surrey
carriage 274 n.
surrogate
deputy 755 n.
surrogation
substitution 150 n.
surround
surround 230 vb.
circumscribe 232 vb.
outline 233 vb.
enclose 235 vb.
close 264 vb.
circuit 626 vb.
besiege 712 vb.
surroundings
locality 187 n.
surroundings 230 n.
surtax
tax 809 n.
surtax bracket
wealth 800 n.
surveillance
surveillance 457 n.
management 689 n.
survey
inspection 438 n.
scan 438 vb.
enquiry 459 n.
measure 465 vb.
estimate 480 n.vb.
dissertation 591 n.
compendium 592 n.
surveyor
surveyor 465 n.
survival
existence 1 n.
remainder 41 n.
durability 113 n.
life 360 n.
survival of the fittest
biology 358 n.
survive
continue 108 vb.
outlast 113 vb.
stay 144 vb.
live 360 vb.
be restored 656 vb.
escape 667 vb.
win 727 vb.
survivor
survivor 41 n.
susceptibility
ability 160 n.
persuadability 612 n.
vulnerability 661 n.
moral sensibility 819 n.
love 887 n.
susceptible
liable 180 adj.
sentient 374 adj.
impressible 819 adj.
excitable 822 adj.
susceptive
impressible 819 adj.
sus out
enquire 459 vb.
suspect
be uncertain 474 vb.
opine 485 vb.
doubt 486 vb.
not know 491 vb.
be nervous 854 vb.
offender 904 n.
be jealous 911 vb.
wrong 914 adj.
accused person 928 n.
suspend
discontinue 72 vb.
put off 136 vb.
pause 145 vb.
hang 217 vb.
stop using 674 vb.
abrogate 752 vb.
depose 752 vb.
punish 963 vb.
suspended animation
insensibility 375 n.
suspended sentence
intimidation 854 n.
suspender
fastening 47 n.
hanger 217 n.
suspense
expectation 507 n.

suspenseful
exciting 821 adj.
suspension
pendency 217 n.
softness 327 n.
elasticity 328 n.
solution 337 n.
tempo 410 n.
inaction 677 n.
penalty 963 n.
(See **suspend** *)*
suspicion
small quantity 33 n.
doubt 486 n.
conjecture 512 n.
hint 524 n.
suspicious
unbelieving 486 adj.
nervous 854 adj.
cautious 858 adj.
jealous 911 adj.
dishonest 930 adj.
sustain
continue 108 vb.
sustain 146 vb.
strengthen 162 vb.
support 218 vb.
feed 301 vb.
corroborate 466 vb.
persevere 600 vb.
aid 703 vb.
sustained
frequent 139 adj.
unceasing 146 adj.
sustenance
food 301 n.
provisions 301 n.
susurration
faintness 401 n.
sutler
provider 633 n.
sutra
maxim 496 n.
non-Biblical scripture 975 n.
suttee
suicide 362 n.
burning 381 n.
oblation 981 n.
suture
joining together 45 n.
joint 45 n.
suzerain
master 741 n.
sovereign 741 n.
svelte
narrow 206 adj.
shapely 841 adj.
swab
dry 342 vb.
cleaning utensil 648 n.
surgical dressing 658 n.
swaddle
tie 45 vb.
dress 228 vb.
swag
bag 194 n.
hang 217 vb.
curve 248 n.
booty 790 n.
pattern 844 n.
swagger
gait 265 n.
be proud 871 vb.
ostentation 875 n.
boasting 877 n.
be insolent 878 vb.
swagman
wanderer 268 n.
Swahili
language 557 n.
swain
male 372 n.
country-dweller 869 n.
lover 887 n.
swallow
speeder 277 n.
absorb 299 vb.
mouthful 301 n.
eat 301 vb.
bird 365 n.
believe 485 vb.
be credulous 487 vb.
appropriate 786 vb.
be patient 823 vb.
— one's words
stammer 580 vb.
— up
consume 165 vb.
absorb 299 vb.
— whole
not discriminate 464 vb.
be credulous 487 vb.
swallowtail
bifurcation 92 n.
flag 547 n.
swami
sage 500 n.
swamp
fill 54 vb.
be many 104 vb.
destroy 165 vb.
drench 341 vb.
marsh 347 n.
defeat 727 vb.
swampy
marshy 347 adj.
swan
bird 365 n.
white thing 427 n.
a beauty 841 n.
swan around
be ostentatious 875 vb.
— off
travel 267 vb.
decamp 296 vb.
swank
be affected 850 vb.
proud person 871 n.
airs 873 n.
be vain 873 vb.
ostentation 875 n.
boaster 877 n.
boast 877 vb.
swankpot
proud person 871 n.
swanky
fashionable 848 adj.
ostentatious 875 adj.
swan neck
curve 248 n.
swannery
nest 192 n.
cattle pen 369 n.
swansdown
textile 222 n.
smoothness 258 n.
swansong
end 69 n.
decease 361 n.
lament 836 n.
swap, swop
interchange 151 n. vb.
barter 791 n.
sward
grassland 348 n.
swarm
grow 36 vb.
crowd 74 n.
congregate 74 vb.
certain quantity 104 n.
be fruitful 171 vb.
abound 635 vb.
— over
pervade 189 vb.
— up
climb 308 vb.
— with
be many 104 vb.
swarthy
dark 418 adj.
blackish 428 adj.
swash
flow 350 vb.
swashbuckler
combatant 722 n.
boaster 877 n.
insolent person 878 n.
swastika
cross 222 n.
heraldry 547 n.
talisman 983 n.
swat
knock 279 n.
strike 279 vb.
swatch
piece 53 n.
swath, swathe
bunch 74 n.
trace 548 n.
swathe
tie 45 vb.
cover 226 vb.
fold 261 vb.
sway
vary 152 vb.
power 160 n.
be weak 163 vb.
influence 178 n.vb.
hang 217 vb.
make oblique 220 vb.
oscillate 317 vb.
be uncertain 474 vb.
be irresolute 601 vb.
motivate 612 vb.
manage 689 vb.
governance 733 n.
swear
testify 466 vb.
swear 532 vb.
promise 764 vb.
take a pledge 764 vb.
be rude 885 vb.
cuss 899 vb.
be impious 980 vb.
— by
be certain 473 vb.
believe 485 vb.
praise 923 vb.
— off
negate 533 vb.
recant 603 vb.
relinquish 621 vb.
be temperate 942 vb.
— in
impose a duty 917 vb.
— to
testify 466 vb.
— true
be truthful 540 vb.
swearing
oath 532 n.
cursing 899 adj.
swearword
word 559 n.
scurrility 899 n.
sweat
exude 298 vb.
emit 300 vb.
excrete 302 vb.
be wet 341 vb.
be hot 379 vb.
labour 682 n.
— it out
persevere 600 vb.
sweatband
headgear 228 n.
sweated labour
slave 742 n.
sweater
jersey 228 n.
sweatshirt
shirt 228 n.
sweatshop
workshop 687 n.
swede
vegetable 301 n.
sweep
range 183 n.
curvature 248 n.
traverse 267 vb.
propeller 269 n.
touch 378 vb.

scan 438 vb.
clean 648 vb.
— along
move fast 277 vb.
— all before one
win 727 vb.
— aside
confute 479 vb.
— away
empty 300 vb.
— off one's feet
excite love 887 vb.
— the board
take 786 vb.
— through
traverse 267 vb.
— under the carpet
conceal 525 vb.
— up
clean 648 vb.
sweeper
cleaner 648 n.
servant 742 n.
sweeping
comprehensive 52 adj.
inclusive 78 adj.
general 79 adj.
sweepings
leavings 41 n.
rubbish 641 n.
dirt 649 n.
sweepstake
equal chance 159 n.
gambling 618 n.
gambling game 837 n.
sweet
dessert 301 n.
mouthful 301 n.
pleasant 376 adj.
savoury 390 adj.
sweet 392 adj.
melodious 410 adj.
pleasurable 826 adj.
beautiful 841 adj.
amiable 884 adj.
lovable 887 adj.
benevolent 897 adj.
sweetbreads
meat 301 n.
sweetcorn
vegetable 301 n.
sweeten
assuage 177 vb.
make appetizing 390 vb.
sweeten 392 vb.
please 826 vb.
sweetener
offset 31 n.
gift 781 n.
sweetheart
loved one 887 n.
darling 890 n.
sweetness and light
concord 710 n.
sweet nothings
empty talk 515 n.
endearment 889 n.
sweet on
enamoured 887 adj.
sweets
sweets 301 n.
sweet thing 392 n.
sweet-scented
fragrant 396 adj.
sweet smile
laughter 835 n.
sweet-talk
induce 612 vb.
be cunning 698 vb.
flatter 925 vb.
sweet-tempered
amiable 884 adj.
sweet tooth
taste 386 n.
sweetness 392 n.
liking 859 n.
sweet will
whim 604 n.
swell
grow 36 vb.
add 38 vb.
expand 197 vb.
be convex 253 vb.
wave 350 n.
flow 350 vb.
loudness 400 n.
super 644 adj.
fop 848 n.
aristocrat 868 n.
— the ranks
accrue 38 vb.
congregate 74 vb.
be included 78 vb.
join a party 708 vb.
— up
jut 254 vb.
swelled head
pride 871 n.
vanity 873 n.
swelling
dilation 197 n.
small hill 209 n.
swelling 253 n.
loud 400 adj.
exaggerated 546 adj.
wound 655 n.
blemish 845 n.
prideful 871 adj.
swelling heart
feeling 818 n.
swelter
be hot 379 vb.
swept away
powerless 161 adj.
swept-back wing
wing 271 n.
swerve
be oblique 220 vb.
be curved 248 vb.
deviate 282 vb.
swift
speedy 277 adj.
bird 365 n.
swig
draught 301 n.
swill
drink 301 vb.
swill 649 n.
— down
clean 648 vb.
swim
swim 269 vb.
be light 323 vb.
be dim-sighted 440 vb.
— with the stream
conform 83 vb.
acquiesce 488 vb.
swimming
aquatics 269 n.
sport 837 n.
swimmingly
easily 701 adv.
successfully 727 adv.
prosperously 730 adv.
swimming pool
lake 346 n.
ablutions 648 n.
swimsuit
beachwear 228 n.
swindle
trickery 542 n.
deceive 542 vb.
peculation 788 n.
be dishonest 930 vb.
swindler
trickster 545 n.
defrauder 789 n.
swine
pig 365 n.
cad 938 n.
knave 938 n.
sensualist 944 n.
swine fever
animal disease 651 n.
swing
periodicity 141 n.
reversion 148 n.
revolution 149 n.
vary 152 vb.
range 183 n.
hang 217 vb.
deviate 282 vb.
oscillate 317 vb.
music 412 n.
scope 744 n.
pleasure ground 837 n.
be punished 963 vb.
— round
rotate 315 vb.
— the lead
be false 541 vb.
swingeing
exorbitant 32 adj.
swinger
beau monde 848 n.
swinging
fashionable 848 adj.
Swinging Sixties
period 110 n.
swings and roundabouts
offset 31 n.
swing-wing
wing 271 n.
swinish
sensual 944 adj.
swipe
knock 279 n.
strike 279 vb.
propulsion 287 n.
strike at 712 vb.
steal 788 vb.
swirl
vortex 315 n.
rotate 315 vb.
eddy 350 n.
flow 350 vb.
swish
faintness 401 n.
sibilation 406 n.
fashionable 848 adj.
switch
branch 53 n.
revolution 149 n.
substitution 150 n.
interchange 151 vb.
transpose 272 vb.
deflect 282 vb.
diverge 294 vb.
apostatize 603 vb.
instrument 628 n.
tool 630 n.
club 723 n.
hairdressing 843 n.
spank 963 vb.
— off
terminate 69 vb.
cease 145 vb.
snuff out 418 vb.
— on
initiate 68 vb.
empower 160 vb.
operate 173 vb.
hear 415 vb.
make bright 417 vb.
— over
revolutionize 149 vb.
apostatize 603 vb.
switchback
obliquity 220 n.
undulatory 251 adj.
road 624 n.
pleasure ground 837 n.
switchblade
sidearms 723 n.
switchboard
focus 76 n.
telecommunication 531 n.
swivel
pivot 218 n.
rotator 315 n.
swivel-eyed
dim-sighted 440 adj.
swiz
trickery 542 n.

swollen
great 32 adj.
expanded 197 adj.
convex 253 adj.
rhetorical 574 adj.
diseased 651 adj.
prideful 871 adj.
swollen eyes
lamentation 836 n.
swollen-headed
vain 873 adj.
swoon
helplessness 161 n.
weakness 163 n.
be insensible 375 vb.
be fatigued 684 vb.
swoop
spurt 277 n.
descent 309 n.
plunge 313 n.
swoosh
spurt 277 n.
sibilation 406 n.
swop
(See **swap** *)*
sword
destroyer 168 n.
sharp edge 256 n.
sidearms 723 n.
badge of rank 743 n.
sword, the
war 718 n.
sword of Damocles
danger 661 n.
intimidation 854 n.
threat 900 n.
swordplay
duel 716 n.
swordsman
contender 716 n.
combatant 722 n.
sworn
affirmative 532 adj.
obedient 739 adj.
contractual 765 adj.
obliged 917 adj.
sworn to
evidential 466 adj.
swot
study 536 vb.
swotter
learner 538 n.
sybarite
sensualist 944 n.
sybaritic
sensual 944 adj.
sycamore
tree 366 n.
sycophant
toady 879 n.
flatterer 925 n.
sycophantic
servile 879 adj.
flattering 925 adj.
syllabary
letter 558 n.
syllabic
literal 558 adj.
syllabify
spell 558 vb.
syllable
speech sound 398 n.
spoken letter 558 n.
spell 558 vb.
word 559 n.
phrase 563 vb.
voice 577 n.vb.
syllabus
list 87 n.
compendium 592 n.
syllogism
argumentation 475 n.
syllogize, syllogise
reason 475 vb.
sylph
a beauty 841 n.
fairy 970 n.
sylph-like
narrow 206 adj.
fairylike 970 adj.
sylvan, silvan
arboreal 366 adj.
symbiosis
union 45 n.
life 360 n.
cooperation 706 n.
symbol
insubstantial thing 4 n.
number 85 n.
substitute 150 n.
metaphor 519 n.
badge 547 n.
indication 547 n.
image 551 n.
letter 558 n.
symbolic, symbolical
figurative 519 adj.
occult 523 adj.
indicating 547 adj.
representing 551 adj.
trivial 639 adj.
ritual 988 adj.
symbolic act
ritual act 988 n.
symbolic logic
argumentation 475 n.
symbolics
creed 485 n.
theology 973 n.
symbolism
metaphor 519 n.
(See **symbol, symbolic** *)*
Symbolism
school of painting 553 n.
literature 557 n.
symbolization, symbolisation
symbology 547 n.
symbolize, symbolise
mean 514 vb.
figure 519 vb.
interpret 520 vb.
manifest 522 vb.
imply 523 vb.
indicate 547 vb.
represent 551 vb.
symmetrical
correlative 12 adj.
uniform 16 adj.
equal 28 adj.
regular 81 adj.
symmetrical 245 adj.
symmetry
relativeness 9 n.
similarity 18 n.
order 60 n.
symmetry 245 n.
elegance 575 n.
beauty 841 n.
sympathetic
agreeing 24 adj.
sharing 775 adj.
feeling 818 adj.
friendly 880 adj.
pitying 905 adj.
sympathetic magic
sorcery 983 n.
sympathetic strike
participation 775 n.
sympathize, sympathise
feel 818 vb.
(See **sympathy** *)*
sympathizer, sympathiser
collaborator 707 n.
patron 707 n.
participator 775 n.
kind person 897 n.
sympathy
bond 47 n.
attraction 291 n.
imagination 513 n.
aid 703 n.
cooperation 706 n.
concord 710 n.
participation 775 n.
feeling 818 n.
liking 859 n.
friendliness 880 n.
love 887 n.
benevolence 897 n.
condolence 905 n.
pity 905 n.
symphonic
harmonious 410 adj.
musical 412 adj.
musicianly 413 adj.
symphony
musical piece 412 n.
symphysis
combination 50 n.
symposiarch
leader 690 n.
symposiast
interlocutor 584 n.
symposium
assembly 74 n.
argument 475 n.
conference 584 n.
symptom
concomitant 89 n.
evidence 466 n.
omen 511 n.
hint 524 n.
indication 547 n.
illness 651 n.
warning 664 n.
symptomatic
visible 443 adj.
evidential 466 adj.
indicating 547 adj.
cautionary 664 adj.
symptomatology
hermeneutics 520 n.
indication 547 n.
symptoms
illness 651 n.
synaesthesia
sense 374 n.
synagogue
church 990 n.
sync, synch
synchronism 123 n.
synchromesh
machine 630 n.
synchronic
synchronous 123 adj.
linguistic 557 adj.
synchronism
synchronism 123 n.
synchronization, synchronisation
arrangement 62 n.
synchronism 123 n.
synchronize, synchronise
adjust 24 vb.
combine 50 vb.
order 60 vb.
time 117 vb.
synchronize 123 vb.
synchronized
adjusted 24 adj.
agreeing 24 adj.
synchronous 123 adj.
synchroton
nucleonics 160 n.
synclinal
sloping 220 adj.
syncopation
tempo 410 n.
music 412 n.
syncope
shortening 204 n.
insensibility 375 n.
syncretism
mixture 43 n.
combination 50 n.
syndicalism
government 733 n.
syndicalist
political party 708 n.
corporate 708 adj.
syndicate
publish 528 vb.
association 706 n.
corporation 708 n.

syndrome
composition 56 n.
structure 331 n.
illness 651 n.
synecdoche
trope 519 n.
synergism, synergy
concurrence 181 n.
cooperation 706 n.
synergistic triad
disease 651 n.
syngamy
union 45 n.
synod
synod 985 n.
synodal
parliamentary 692 adj.
synonym
identity 13 n.
equivalence 28 n.
substitute 150 n.
connotation 514 n.
word 559 n.
name 561 n.
synonym for
famousness 866 n.
synonymous
identical 13 adj.
semantic 514 adj.
interpretive 520 adj.
synopsis
whole 52 n.
list 87 n.
compendium 592 n.
synoptic
general 79 adj.
compendious 592 adj.
syntactic
grammatical 564 adj.
syntax
composition 56 n.
arrangement 62 n.
linguistics 557 n.
grammar 564 n.
synthesis
union 45 n.
combination 50 n.
argumentation 475 n.
synthesize, synthesise
compose 56 vb.
produce 164 vb.
synthesizer, synthesiser
musical instrument 414 n.
synthetic
imitative 20 adj.
produced 164 adj.
rational 475 adj.
untrue 543 adj.
syphilis
venereal disease 651 n.
syphon
(See **siphon** *)*
syringe
extractor 304 n.
irrigator 341 n.
moisten 341 vb.
syrinx
flute 414 n.
voice 577 n.
syrup
soft drink 301 n.
viscidity 354 n.
sweet thing 392 n.
systaltic
contracted 198 adj.
system
whole 52 n.
order 60 n.
arrangement 62 n.
creed 485 n.
habit 610 n.
systematic
arranged 62 adj.
regular 81 adj.
philosophic 449 adj.
rational 475 adj.
businesslike 622 adj.
systematize, systematise
order 60 vb.
regularize 62 vb.
make conform 83 vb.
plan 623 vb.
systems analysis
mathematics 86 n.
systems analyst
enumerator 86 n.
planner 623 n.
systole
contraction 198 n.
systole and diastole
fluctuation 317 n.
syzygy
contiguity 202 n.

T

tab
adjunct 40 n.
label 547 n.
mark 547 vb.
badge of rank 743 n.
tabard
jacket 228 n.
tabby
cat 365 n.
mottled 437 adj.
tabernacle
ritual object 988 n.
church 990 n.
temple 990 n.
tabla
drum 414 n.
table
arrangement 62 n.
list 87 n.
put off 136 vb.
horizontality 216 n.
shelf 218 n.
stand 218 n.
eating 301 n.
meal 301 n.
register 548 vb.
tableau
spectacle 445 n.
picture 553 n.
stage show 594 n.
pageant 875 n.
tablecloth
covering 226 n.
cleaning cloth 648 n.
table d'hôte
meal 301 n.
tableland
high land 209 n.
horizontality 216 n.
plain 348 n.
table manners
eating 301 n.
practice 610 n.
tables
statistics 86 n.
tablespoon
ladle 194 n.
tablet
lamina 207 n.
mouthful 301 n.
monument 548 n.
medicine 658 n.
table talk
chat 584 n.
table tennis
ball game 837 n.
table-turning
spiritualism 984 n.
table water
soft drink 301 n.
tabloid
the press 528 n.
taboo
set apart 46 vb.
exclude 57 vb.
prohibited 757 adj.
bewitch 983 vb.
tabor
drum 414 n.
tabouret
seat 218 n.
tabular
arranged 62 adj.
layered 207 adj.
tabula rasa
revolution 149 n.
ignorance 491 n.
obliteration 550 n.
tabulate
class 62 vb.
list 87 vb.
register 548 vb.
Tachism
school of painting 553 n.
tachograph
meter 465 n.
tachometer
velocity 277 n.
tachycardia
cardiovascular disease 651 n.
tachygraphy
writing 586 n.
tacit
tacit 523 adj.
taciturn
reticent 525 adj.
voiceless 578 adj.
taciturn 582 adj.
unsociable 883 adj.
tack
tie 45 vb.
fastening 47 n.
vary 152 vb.
sharp point 256 n.
navigate 269 vb.
direction 281 n.
deviate 282 vb.
food 301 n.
tergiversate 603 vb.
route 624 n.
— on
add 38 vb.
tackle
tackling 47 n.
begin 68 vb.
equipment 630 n.
attempt 671 n.vb.
undertake 672 vb.
do 676 vb.
tacky
cohesive 48 adj.
viscid 354 adj.
bad 645 adj.
taco
dish 301 n.
tact
discrimination 463 n.
sagacity 498 n.
skill 694 n.
good taste 846 n.
tactful
well-bred 848 adj.
benevolent 897 adj.
tactfulness
courtesy 884 n.
tactical
planned 623 adj.
behaving 688 adj.
cunning 698 adj.
warlike 718 adj.
tactician
motivator 612 n.
planner 623 n.
expert 696 n.
slyboots 698 n.
tactics
policy 623 n.
way 624 n.
deed 676 n.
tactics 688 n.
skill 694 n.
cunning 698 n.
art of war 718 n.

tactile
tactual 378 adj.
tactless
inattentive 456 adj.
indiscriminating 464 adj.
foolish 499 adj.
clumsy 695 adj.
ill-bred 847 adj.
discourteous 885 adj.
tactual
tactual 378 adj.
tadpole
young creature 132 n.
amphibian 365 n.
taedium vitae
melancholy 834 n.
tedium 838 n.
taffeta
textile 222 n.
taffrail
handle 218 n.
fence 235 n.
taffy
flattery 925 n.
Taffy
native 191 n.
tag
adjunct 40 n.
ligature 47 n.
sequel 67 n.
extremity 69 n.
hanging object 217 n.
sharp point 256 n.
maxim 496 n.
label 547 n.
mark 547 vb.
children's games 837 n.
— along
follow 284 vb.
— on
add 38 vb.
taiga
wood 366 n.
tail
adjunct 40 n.
retinue 67 n.
sequel 67 n.
procession 71 n.
hanging object 217 n.
rear 238 n.
follow 284 vb.
pursue 619 vb.
— off
decrease 37 vb.
end 69 vb.
tailback
retinue 67 n.
tail end
extremity 69 n.
tailor
adjust 24 vb.
clothier 228 n.
form 243 vb.
artisan 686 n.
tailoring
formation 243 n.
tailor-made
adjusted 24 adj.
tailored 228 adj.
tailor's dummy
mould 23 n.
image 551 n.
tailpiece
sequel 67 n.
tails
formal dress 228 n.
tail wind
propellant 287 n.
wind 352 n.
aid 703 n.
taint
infiltrate 297 vb.
badness 645 n.
defect 647 n.
make unclean 649 vb.
infection 651 n.
impair 655 vb.
slur 867 n.
shame 867 vb.
take
bring together 74 vb.
comprise 78 vb.
admit 299 vb.
photograph 551 vb.
require 627 vb.
overmaster 727 vb.
subjugate 745 vb.
arrest 747 vb.
acquire 771 vb.
receive 782 vb.
take 786 vb.
steal 788 vb.
be patient 823 vb.
— aback
surprise 508 vb.
— a back seat
be inferior 35 vb.
have no repute 867 vb.
be modest 874 vb.
be disinterested 931 vb.
— account of
notice 455 vb.
— a chance
face danger 661 vb.
attempt 671 vb.
— a dim view of
disapprove 924 vb.
— advantage of
befool 542 vb.
use 673 vb.
be skilful 694 vb.
— a fancy to
be pleased 824 vb.
be in love 887 vb.
— after
resemble 18 vb.
— a hand in
busy oneself 622 vb.
cooperate 706 vb.
— a hold on
prevail 178 vb.
— a leaf out of another's book
do likewise 20 vb.
— amiss
be discontented 829 vb.
resent 891 vb.
— an interest in
be curious 453 vb.
patronize 703 vb.
love 887 vb.
— apart
sunder 46 vb.
— as
opine 485 vb.
— aside
speak to 583 vb.
— a sledgehammer to crack a nut
be superfluous 637 vb.
— as one's due
not wonder 865 vb.
be ungrateful 908 vb.
— away
abate 37 vb.
take away 786 vb.
— back
recoup 31 vb.
revert 148 vb.
recant 603 vb.
acquire 771 vb.
take 786 vb.
— by storm
attack 712 vb.
overmaster 727 vb.
— care of
be mindful 455 vb.
look after 457 vb.
— charge of
look after 457 vb.
safeguard 660 vb.
undertake 672 vb.
— cover
be stealthy 525 vb.
— down
lower 311 vb.
record 548 vb.
write 586 vb.
— down a peg
shame 867 vb.
humiliate 872 vb.
— effect
operate 173 vb.
be successful 727 vb.
— exception to
resent 891 vb.
disapprove 924 vb.
— for granted
assume 471 vb.
premise 475 vb.
believe 485 vb.
be credulous 487 vb.
suppose 512 vb.
not wonder 865 vb.
be ungrateful 908 vb.
— heart
be cheerful 833 vb.
hope 852 vb.
take courage 855 vb.
— heed
be warned 664 vb.
— hold (of)
prevail 178 vb.
be belived 485 vb.
be wont 610 vb.
take 786 vb.
— in
comprise 78 vb.
make smaller 198 vb.
admit 299 vb.
scan 438 vb.
know 490 vb.
understand 516 vb.
befool 542 vb.
be hospitable 882 vb.
— in good part
keep calm 823 vb.
be content 828 vb.
forgive 909 vb.
— in hand
train 534 vb.
undertake 672 vb.
— in one's stride
be expert 694 vb.
do easily 701 vb.
— into account
discriminate 463 vb.
qualify 468 vb.
— into consideration
meditate 449 vb.
notice 455 vb.
— in vain
misuse 675 vb.
— it
suppose 512 vb.
knuckle under 721 vb.
be patient 823 vb.
— it badly
suffer 825 vb.
lament 836 vb.
— it easy
be neglectful 458 vb.
be inactive 679 vb.
repose 683 vb.
— it into one's head
think 449 vb.
be capricious 604 vb.
— it or leave it
have no choice 606 vb.
be indifferent 860 vb.
— it out of
fatigue 684 vb.
— it out on
be malevolent 898 vb.
— its course
go on 146 vb.

happen 154 vb.
— leave of one's senses
be foolish 499 vb.
— liberties
be free 744 vb.
be rude 885 vb.
— no interest
be incurious 454 vb.
be indifferent 860 vb.
— no notice
disregard 458 vb.
— no offence
be courteous 884 vb.
forgive 909 vb.
— no part in
be absent 190 vb.
— off
imitate 20 vb.
grow 36 vb.
subtract 39 vb.
doff 229 vb.
fly 271 vb.
start out 296 vb.
ascend 308 vb.
act 594 vb.
discount 810 vb.
satirize 851 vb.
— offence
be discontented 829 vb.
resent 891 vb.
— on
load 193 vb.
admit 299 vb.
train 534 vb.
undertake 672 vb.
do 676 vb.
withstand 704 vb.
contend 716 vb.vb.
be discontented 829 vb.
lament 836 vb.
— one for a ride
deceive 542 vb
— one's breath away
surprise 508 vb.
make mute 578 vb.
impress 821 vb.
delight 826 vb.
be beautiful 841 vb.
be wonderful 864 vb.
— one's fancy
delight 826 vb.
excite love 887 vb.
— one's hat off to
respect 920 vb.
approve 923 vb.
praise 923 vb.
— one's life in one's hands
face danger 661 vb.
— one's medicine
knuckle under 721 vb.
be punished 963 vb.
— one's part
patronize 703 vb.
— one's time
be late 136 vb.
move slowly 278 vb.
have leisure 681 vb.
be cautious 858 vb.
— one up on
dissent 489 vb.
defy 711 vb.
— on oneself
intend 617 vb.
busy oneself 622 vb.
undertake 672 vb.
promise 764 vb.
incur a duty 917 vb.
— orders
take orders 986 vb.
— out
extract 304 vb.
obliterate 550 vb.
court 889 vb.
— out of oneself
amuse 837 vb.
— over
come after 65 vb.
take authority 733 vb.
appropriate 786 vb.
— pains
be attentive 455 vb.
be careful 457 vb.
— part
be present 189 vb.
cooperate 706 vb.
— place
be 1 vb.
happen 154 vb.
— pleasure in
enjoy 376 vb.
be pleased 824 vb.
— root
be stable 153 vb.
prevail 178 vb.
place oneself 187 vb.
be wont 610 vb.
— seriously
be attentive 455 vb.
make important 638 vb.
— shape
become 1 vb.
— sides
be biased 481 vb.
choose 605 vb.
join a party 708 vb.
— silk
do law 958 vb.
— steps
prepare 669 vb.
do 676 vb.
— stock
number 86 vb.
meditate 449 vb.
estimate 480 vb.
account 808 vb.
— the biscuit/cake
be superior 34 vb.
— the bit between one's teeth
will 595 vb.
be obstinate 602 vb.
disobey 738 vb.
— the bull by the horns
be resolute 599 vb.
attempt 671 vb.
be courageous 855 vb.
— the chair
direct 689 vb.
— the count
be defeated 728 vb.
— the edge off
weaken 163 vb.
moderate 177 vb.
— the floor
orate 579 vb.
— the law into one's own hands
disobey 738 vb.
avenge 910 vb.
be illegal 954 vb.
— the lead
come first 34 vb.
come before 64 vb.
initiate 68 vb.
be important 638 vb.
have a reputation 866 vb.
— the liberty
permit 756 vb.
— the lid off
uncover 229 vb.
disclose 526 vb.
— the mickey
ridicule 851 vb.
— the offensive
be vigorous 174 vb.
attack 712 vb.
— the opportunity
profit by 137 vb.
— the place of
substitute 150 vb.
— the pledge
be temperate 942 vb.
— the plunge
initiate 68 vb.
be resolute 599 vb.
choose 605 vb.
— the rap
incur blame 924 vb.
be punished 963 vb.
— the shine out of
be superior 34 vb.
— the stand
testify 466 vb.
— the sting out of
assuage 177 vb.
make useless 641 vb.
— the strain
support 218 vb.
suffice 635 vb.
— the veil
take orders 986 vb.
— the wind out of one's sails
disable 161 vb.
hinder 702 vb.
— things as they come
keep calm 823 vb.
be content 828 vb.
— time by the forelock
be early 135 vb.
profit by 137 vb.
— to
habituate 610 vb.
befriend 880 vb.
be in love 887 vb.
— to heart
feel 818 vb.
be sensitive 819 vb.
suffer 825 vb.
resent 891 vb.
— to like a duck to water
accord 24 vb.
do easily 701 vb.
— to one's heels
run away 620 vb.
— to pieces
sunder 46 vb.
decompose 51 vb.
— to task
reprove 924 vb.
— to the cleaners
fleece 786 vb.
— to the hills
seek refuge 662 vb.
— two bites at a cherry
be clumsy 695 vb.
— umbrage
resent 891 vb.
— under one's wing
safeguard 660 vb.
aid 703 vb.
— up
shorten 204 vb.
elevate 310 vb.
study 536 vb.
choose 605 vb.
be wont 610 vb.
busy oneself 622 vb.
undertake 672 vb.
avail oneself of 673 vb.
receive 782 vb.
befriend 880 vb.
— upon oneself
undertake 672 vb.
— up the challenge
contend 716 vb.
— up the cudgels (for)
patronize 703 vb.
defend 713 vb.
— wing
travel 267 vb.
depart 296 vb.
take-away
café 192 n.

taken bad
sick 651 adj.
taken for granted
certain 473 adj.
taken in
gullible 544 adj.
taken up with
obsessed 455 adj.
taken with
enamoured 887 adj.
takeoff
air travel 271 n.
satire 851 n.
takeover
transference 272 n.
expropriation 786 n.
takeover bid
offer 759 n.
purchase 792 n.
taking
taking 786 n.
personable 841 adj.
taking one thing with another
on an average 30 adv.
in return 31 adv.
takings
earnings 771 n.
receipt 807 n.
talcum powder, talc
powder 332 n.
cosmetic 843 n.
tale
fable 543 n.
narrative 590 n.
novel 590 n.
talebearer
informer 524 n.
talent
intelligence 498 n.
aptitude 694 n.
talent scout
enquirer 459 n.
detector 484 n.
talisman
preserver 666 n.
talisman 983 n.
talk
empty talk 515 n.
inform 524 vb.
rumour 529 n.
broadcast 531 n.
lecture 534 n.
language 557 n.
speech 579 n.
speak 579 vb.
be loquacious 581 vb.
allocution 583 n.
chat 584 n.
— about
publish 528 vb.
defame 926 vb.
— big
be vain 873 vb.
boast 877 vb.
threaten 900 vb.
— into
induce 612 vb.
— it over
confer 584 vb.
— out
spin out 113 vb.
be obstructive 702 vb.
— out of
dissuade 613 vb.
— out of turn
divulge 526 vb.
— over/round
induce 612 vb.
— through one's hat
be absurd 497 vb.
be foolish 499 vb.
— to
speak to 583 vb.
converse 584 vb.
— to a brick wall
waste effort 641 vb.
— to oneself
soliloquize 585 vb.
— turkey
speak plainly 573 vb.
talkative
speaking 579 adj.
loquacious 581 adj.
talkdown
aeronautics 271 n.
talker
speaker 579 n.
talkie
film 445 n.
talking head
broadcaster 531 n.
talking to
reprimand 924 n.
talk of the town
rumour 529 n.
famousness 866 n.
talks
conference 584 n.
tall
great 32 adj.
large 195 adj.
tall 209 adj.
exaggerated 546 adj.
tallboy
cabinet 194 n.
tallith
canonicals 989 n.
tall order
undertaking 672 n.
hard task 700 n.
tallow
fat 357 n.
tall ship
sailing ship 275 n.
tall story
fable 543 n.
exaggeration 546 n.
tall talk
boast 877 n.
tally
accord 24 vb.
numerical result 85 n.
numeration 86 n.
list 87 n.
label 547 n.
record 548 n.
credit 802 n.
debt 803 n.
accounts 808 n.
— with
conform 83 vb.
tally clerk
recorder 549 n.
tallyho
cry 408 n.
chase 619 n.
tallyman
lender 784 n.
tradespeople 794 n.
Talmud
scripture 975 n.
talon
foot 214 n.
sharp point 256 n.
finger 378 n.
nippers 778 n.
talus
incline 220 n.
tambourine
drum 414 n.
tame
moderate 177 adj. vb.
break in 369 vb.
train 534 vb.
feeble 572 adj.
habituate 610 vb.
subjugate 745 vb.
inexcitable 823 adj.
servile 879 adj.
tameless
furious 176 adj.
cruel 898 adj.
Tammanyism
improbity 930 n.
Tammuz
Semitic deities 967 n.
tam-o'-shanter
headgear 228 n.
tamp (down)
impel 279 vb.
close 264 vb.
tamper (with)
mix 43 vb.
derange 63 vb.
modify 143 vb.
be false 541 vb.
impair 655 vb.
meddle 678 vb.
tampon
stopper 264 n.
surgical dressing 658 n.
tan
be tough 329 vb.
burning 381 n.
brown 430 adj.
— one's hide
strike 279 vb.
spank 963 vb.
tandem
duality 90 n.
bicycle 274 n.
cooperation 706 n.
tang
projection 254 n.
taste 386 n.
pungency 388 n.
odour 394 n.
tangent
ratio 85 n.
contiguity 202 n.
tangerine
fruit 301 n.
orange 432 n.
tangible
substantial 3 adj.
material 319 adj.
tactual 378 adj.
true 494 adj.
tangle
complexity 61 n.
bedevil 63 vb.
enlace 222 vb.
hinder 702 vb.
tangled
mixed 43 adj.
tied 45 adj.
dense 324 adj.
tangled skein
complexity 61 n.
tango
dance 837 n.vb.
tangram
enigma 530 n.
tank
vat 194 n.
war chariot 274 n.
lake 346 n.
storage 632 n.
cavalry 722 n.
tanka
verse form 593 n.
tankard
cup 194 n.
tank engine
locomotive 274 n.
tanker
lorry 274 n.
merchant ship 275 n.
tank up
get drunk 949 vb.
tanned
blackish 428 adj.
brown 430 adj.
tanner
coinage 797 n.
tannoy
hearing aid 415 n.
tantalize, tantalise
fall short 307 vb.
make impossible 470 vb.
disappoint 509 vb.
tempt 612 vb.

excite 821 vb.
cause desire 859 vb.
tantamount
equivalent 28 adj.
semantic 514 adj.
tantara
stridor 407 n.
tantivy
spurt 277 n.
Tantra
non-Biblical scripture 975 n.
Tantrist
religionist 973 n.
sectarian 978 adj.
tantrum(s)
excitable state 822 n.
anger 891 n.
Taoism
religious faith 973 n.
tap
pierce 263 vb.
stopper 264 n.
knock 279 n.
outlet 298 n.
empty 300 vb.
extract 304 vb.
water 339 n.
make flow 350 vb.
conduit 351 n.
touch 378 n.vb.
bang 402 n.
play music 413 vb.
hear 415 vb.
store 632 n.
provide 633 vb.
acquire 771 vb.
take 786 vb.
— out a message
signal 547 vb.
— the line
hear 415 vb.
be curious 453 vb.
tap dance
ballet 594 n.
dance 837 n.vb.
tape
cable 47 n.
line 203 n.
strip 208 n.
gramophone 414 n.
measure 465 vb.
record 548 n.vb.
objective 617 n.
tape machine
telecommunication 531 n.
tape measure
gauge 465 n.
taper
shade off 27 vb.
make smaller 198 vb.
be narrow 206 vb.
be sharp 256 vb.
converge 293 vb.
lighter 385 n.
torch 420 n.
tape recorder
gramophone 414 n.
recording instrument 549 n.
tape recording
gramophone 414 n.
registration 548 n.
tapering
tapering 256 adj.
tapestry
hanging object 217 n.
textile 222 n.
picture 553 n.
needlework 844 n.
tapeworm
creepy-crawly 365 n.
bane 659 n.
tapioca
dessert 301 n.
tapping
impulse 279 n.
extraction 304 n.
taproom
tavern 192 n.
taproot
source 156 n.
taps
obsequies 364 n.
call 547 n.
tapster
servant 742 n.
tar
coat 226 vb.
mariner 270 n.
resin 357 n.
black thing 428 n.
tar and feather
punish 963 vb.
tarantella
musical piece 412 n.
dance 837 n.
tarantula
creepy-crawly 365 n.
tarboosh
headgear 228 n.
tardigrade
slowcoach 278 n.
tardy
late 136 adj.
slow 278 adj.
lazy 679 adj.
tare
decrement 42 n.
discount 810 n.
tares
rubbish 641 n.
target
limit 236 n.
direction 281 n.
objective 617 n.
armour 713 n.
Targum
commentary 520 n.
scripture 975 n.
tariff
list 87 n.
restriction 747 n.
tax 809 n.
tariff wall
exclusion 57 n.
tarmac
paving 226 n.
smoothness 258 n.
air travel 271 n.
road 624 n.
tarn
lake 346 n.
tarnish
decolorize 426 vb.
make unclean 649 vb.
blemish 845 n.
shame 867 vb.
defame 926 vb.
tarot cards
oracle 511 n.
tarpaulin
canopy 226 n.
tarragon
potherb 301 n.
tarred with the same brush
similar 18 adj.
tarry
drag on 113 vb.
be late 136 vb.
stay 144 vb.
be quiescent 266 vb.
move slowly 278 vb.
resinous 357 adj.
tart
pastries 301 n.
sour 393 adj.
ungracious 885 adj.
irascible 892 adj.
sullen 893 adj.
loose woman 952 n.
tartan
variegated 437 adj.
livery 547 n.
tartar
dirt 649 n.
Tartar
shrew 892 n.
Tartarean
infernal 972 adj.
tarted up
beautified 843 adj.
bedecked 844 adj.
vulgar 847 adj.
ostentatious 875 adj.
Tartuffe
deceiver 545 n.
impious person 980 n.
Tarzan
athlete 162 n.
task
finite quantity 26 n.
job 622 n.
undertaking 672 n.
deed 676 n.
labour 682 n.
fatigue 684 vb.
hard task 700 n.
oppress 735 vb.
portion 783 n.
duty 917 n.
penalty 963 n.
task force
armed force 722 n.
taskmaster
tyrant 735 n.
tassel
hanging object 217 n.
trimming 844 n.
tassie
cup 194 n.
taste
eat 301 vb.
sense 374 n.
enjoy 376 vb.
taste 386 n.vb.
discrimination 463 n.
elegance 575 n.
choice 605 n.
feel 818 vb.
good taste 846 n.
liking 859 n.
— good
make appetizing 390 vb.
tasteful
elegant 575 adj.
personable 841 adj.
tasteful 846 adj.
tasteless
tasteless 387 adj.
unsavoury 391 adj.
feeble 572 adj.
inelegant 576 adj.
vulgar 847 adj.
tastelessness
insipidity 387 n.
indiscrimination 464 n.
bad taste 847 n.
tasty
edible 301 adj.
pleasant 376 adj.
tasty 386 adj.
savoury 390 adj.
pleasurable 826 adj.
tatterdemalion
slut 61 n.
low fellow 869 n.
tattered
beggarly 801 adj.
tatters
piece 53 n.
clothing 228 n.
tatting
network 222 n.
needlework 844 n.
tattle
be loquacious 581 vb.
converse 584 vb.
tattler
informer 524 n.
news reporter 529 n.
chatterer 581 n.
interlocutor 584 n.

tattoo
pierce 263 vb.
roll 403 n.vb.
play music 413 vb.
colour 425 vb.
variegate 437 vb.
call 547 n.
mark 547 vb.
beautify 841 vb.
pageant 875 n.
celebration 876 n.
tattooing
ornamental art 844 n.
tatty
dilapidated 655 adj.
beggarly 801 adj.
taunt
be insolent 878 vb.
enrage 891 vb.
indignity 921 n.
reproach 924 n.
calumny 926 n.
accusation 928 n.
taupe
greyness 429 n.
taurine
animal 365 adj.
Taurus
zodiac 321 n.
taut
tied 45 adj.
rigid 326 adj.
tauten
tighten 45 vb.
make smaller 198 vb.
harden 326 vb.
tautological
repeated 106 adj.
pleonastic 570 adj.
tautology
repetition 106 n.
pleonasm 570 n.
superfluity 637 n.
tavern
tavern 192 n.
taw
sphere 252 n.
tawdry
trivial 639 adj.
vulgar 847 adj.
tawny
brown 430 adj.
yellow 433 adj.
tawse
scourge 964 n.
tax
fatigue 684 vb.
oppress 735 vb.
demand 737 n.vb.
levy 786 vb.
tax 809 n.vb.
impose a duty 917 vb.
— with
accuse 928 vb.
taxable
priced 809 adj.
taxation
tax 809 n.
tax avoidance
nonpayment 805 n.
tax collector
consignee 754 n.
receiver 782 n.
tax evasion
peculation 788 n.
nonpayment 805 n.
foul play 930 n.
tax-free
uncharged 812 adj.
nonliable 919 adj.
taxi
be in motion 265 vb.
conveyance 267 n.
fly 271 vb.
cab 274 n.
taxidermy
zoology 367 n.
preservation 666 n.
taxonomy
arrangement 62 n.
classification 77 n.
botany 368 n.
tea
meal 301 n.
soft drink 301 n.
tea caddy
small box 194 n.
teach
convert 147 vb.
break in 369 vb.
convince 485 vb.
show 522 vb.
inform 524 vb.
educate 534 vb.
teach 534 vb.
habituate 610 vb.
— one a lesson
retaliate 714 vb.
— one his/her place
humiliate 872 vb.
— one's grandmother to suck eggs
be superfluous 637 vb.
be insolent 878 vb.
teachable
studious 536 adj.
willing 597 adj.
teacher
scholar 492 n.
sage 500 n.
interpreter 520 n.
teacher 537 n.
adviser 691 n.
expert 696 n.
tea chest
box 194 n.
teach-in
teaching 534 n.
conference 584 n.
teaching
teaching 534 n.
preparation 669 n.
theology 973 n.
teaching hospital
training school 539 n.
teacup
cup 194 n.
tea estate
farm 370 n.
teahouse
café 192 n.
teak
hardness 326 n.
tree 366 n.
teal
bird 365 n.
tea leaves
oracle 511 n.
team
band 74 n.
group 74 n.
party 708 n.
team spirit
cooperation 706 n.
sociality 882 n.
teamster
driver 268 n.n.
leader 690 n.
team up with
combine 50 vb.
join a party 708 vb.
team work
cooperation 706 n.
tea party
social gathering 882 n.
tea planter
farmer 370 n.
teapot
cauldron 194 n.
teapoy
stand 218 n.
tear
rend 46 vb.
be violent 176 vb.
gap 201 n.
blunt 257 vb.
groove 262 vb.
move fast 277 vb.
give pain 377 vb.
ill-treat 645 vb.
wound 655 vb.
lamentation 836 n.
— down
demolish 165 vb.
fell 311 vb.
— off
uncover 229 vb.
hasten 680 vb.
— oneself away
depart 296 vb.
be unwilling 598 vb.
— one's hair
gesticulate 547 vb.
lament 836 vb.
— out
extract 304 vb.
— strips off
reprove 924 vb.
— to bits
rend 46 vb.
demolish 165 vb.
— up
destroy 165 vb.
abrogate 752 vb.
tearaway
desperado 857 n.
teardrop
moisture 341 n.
lamentation 836 n.
tearful
unhappy 825 adj.
melancholic 834 adj.
lamenting 836 adj.
tipsy 949 adj.
tear gas
poison 659 n.
tear-jerking
distressing 827 adj.
tearless
pitiless 906 adj.
tearoom
café 192 n.
tears
moisture 341 n.
lamentation 836 n.
tease
tempt 612 vb.
excite 821 vb.
delight 826 vb.
torment 827 vb.
be witty 839 vb.
ridicule 851 vb.
cause desire 859 vb.
enrage 891 vb.
be malevolent 898 vb.
teaser
enigma 530 n.
difficulty 700 n.
worry 825 n.
humorist 839 n.
tea service
cup 194 n.
teashop
café 192 n.
teaspoon
ladle 194 n.
tea strainer
porosity 263 n.
teat
bladder 194 n.
bosom 253 n.
tea towel
cleaning cloth 648 n.
tea urn
cauldron 194 n.
technical
regular 81 adj.
dialectal 560 adj.
technical college, tech
training school 539 n.
technical drawing
representation 551 n.
technicality
trifle 639 n.

precept 693 n.
technical knowledge
skill 694 n.
technical language
speciality 80 n.
neology 560 n.
technical term
name 561 n.
technical training
education 534 n.
technician
machinist 630 n.
artisan 686 n.
expert 696 n.
Technicolor
colour 425 n.
film 445 n.
technics
mechanics 630 n.
technique
painting 553 n.
way 624 n.
means 629 n.
skill 694 n.
technocracy
government 733 n.
technocratic
governmental 733 adj.
technological
educational 534 adj.
technology
production 164 n.
physics 319 n.
science 490 n.
business 622 n.
means 629 n.
mechanics 630 n.
skill 694 n.
tectonic
structural 331 adj.
tectonics
production 164 n.
structure 331 n.
Ted
youngster 132 n.
fop 848 n.
teddy bear
image 551 n.
plaything 837 n.
Te Deum
rejoicing 835 n.
thanks 907 n.
praise 923 n.
hymn 981 n.
tedious
repeated 106 adj.
prolix 570 adj.
feeble 572 adj.
fatiguing 684 adj.
annoying 827 adj.
tedious 838 adj.
dull 840 adj.
tedium
satiety 863 n.
teem
reproduce itself 167 vb.
be fruitful 171 vb.
abound 635 vb.
teeming
assembled 74 adj.
multitudinous 104 adj.
teeming rain
rain 350 n.
teeming womb
abundance 171 n.
teenage
young 130 adj.
teenager
youngster 132 n.
teens
over five 99 n.
teenybopper
youngster 132 n.
teeny-weeny
little 196 adj.
teeter
oscillate 317 vb.
be agitated 318 vb.
be uncertain 474 vb.
be irresolute 601 vb.
teeth
vigorousness 174 n.
eater 301 n.
white thing 427 n.
weapon 723 n.
nippers 778 n.
teething troubles
beginning 68 n.
learning 536 n.
difficulty 700 n.
teetotal
temperate 942 adj.
teetotaller
abstainer 942 n.
sober person 948 n.
teetotum
rotator 315 n.
plaything 837 n.
tee up
make ready 669 vb.
tegular
overlying 226 adj.
tegument
skin 226 n.
telaesthesia
psychics 984 n.
telecast
communicate 524 vb.
broadcast 531 n.
telecommunication
telecommunication 531 n.
signal 547 n.
telegony
heredity 5 n.
influence 178 n.
telegram
message 529 n.
telecommunication 531 n.
telegraph
velocity 277 n.
communicate 524 vb.
signal 547 n.
telegrapher
telecommunication 531 n.
telegraphese
neology 560 n.
conciseness 569 n.
telegraphic
speedy 277 adj.
concise 569 adj.
telegraphy
telecommunication 531 n.
telekinesis
spiritualism 984 n.
teleology
philosophy 449 n.
intention 617 n.
telepath
psychic 984 n.
telepathic
psychical 984 adj.
telepathy
thought 449 n.
intuition 476 n.
psychics 984 n.
telephone
hearing aid 415 n.
communicate 524 vb.
telecommunication 531 n.
telephone directory
guidebook 524 n.
telephonist
telecommunication 531 n.
telephotography
photography 551 n.
telephoto lens
optical device 442 n.
teleprinter
telecommunication 531 n.
recording instrument 549 n.
telerecord
record 548 vb.
telergy
psychics 984 n.
telescope
shorten 204 vb.
astronomy 321 n.
telescope 442 n.
be concise 569 vb.
telescopic
distant 199 adj.
astronomic 321 adj.
visible 443 adj.
teletext
broadcasting 531 n.
telethon
broadcast 531 n.
televiewer
spectator 441 n.
televise
show 522 vb.
communicate 524 vb.
publish 528 vb.
television
spectacle 445 n.
broadcasting 531 n.
stage play 594 n.
amusement 837 n.
telex
communicate 524 vb.
telecommunication 531 n.
tell
number 86 vb.
influence 178 vb.
earthwork 253 n.
inform 524 vb.
divulge 526 vb.
describe 590 vb.
be important 638 vb.
be successful 727 vb.
command 737 vb.
accuse 928 vb.
— against
tell against 467 vb.
— all
confess 526 vb.
— another story
tell against 467 vb.
— fortunes
divine 511 vb.
— it like it is
speak plainly 573 vb.
— its own story
evidence 466 vb.
be plain 522 vb.
— lies
be false 541 vb.
be dishonest 930 vb.
— of
evidence 466 vb.
mean 514 vb.
— off
reprove 924 vb.
— on
inform 524 vb.
— one straight
speak plainly 573 vb.
— one where to get off
refuse 760 vb.
— the truth
be truthful 540 vb.
— the world
advertise 528 vb.
— upon
influence 178 vb.
teller
enumerator 86 n.
informant 524 n.
treasurer 798 n.
teller of tales
narrator 590 n.
telling
influential 178 adj.
evidential 466 adj.
meaningful 514 adj.
expressive 516 adj.

assertive 532 adj.
instrumental 628 adj.
important 638 adj.
impressive 821 adj.
telling against
countervailing 467 adj.
telling the truth
veracious 540 adj.
telltale
informer 524 n.
disclosing 526 adj.
indicating 547 adj.
tergiversator 603 n.
tellurian
native 191 n.
humankind 371 n.
telluric
telluric 321 adj.
territorial 344 adj.
telpher line
railway 624 n.
temerity
rashness 857 n.
temper
temperament 5 n.
state 7 n.
mix 43 vb.
composition 56 n.
strength 162 n.
strengthen 162 vb.
moderate 177 vb.
hardness 326 n.
harden 326 vb.
be tough 329 vb.
qualify 468 vb.
mature 669 vb.
affections 817 n.
excitable state 822 n.
anger 891 n.
tempera
art equipment 553 n.
art style 553 n.
temperament
temperament 5 n.
state 7 n.
composition 56 n.
affections 817 n.
moral sensibility 819 n.
excitability 822 n.
irascibility 892 n.
sullenness 893 n.
temperamental
capricious 604 adj.
lively 819 adj.
excitable 822 adj.
temperance
moderation 177 n.
avoidance 620 n.
restraint 747 n.
virtues 933 n.
temperance 942 n.
asceticism 945 n.
sobriety 948 n.
temperate
moderate 177 adj.
warm 379 adj.
cold 380 adj.
restrained 747 adj.
temperate 942 adj.
temperature
illness 651 n.
tempered
strong 162 adj.
moderate 177 adj.
hard 326 adj.
tempest
storm 176 n.
commotion 318 n.
tempestuous
disorderly 61 adj.
violent 176 adj.
speedy 277 adj.
windy 352 adj.
excitable 822 adj.
Templars
monk 986 n.
template
mould 23 n.
temple
head 213 n.
temple 990 n.
temples
laterality 239 n.
tempo
tendency 179 n.
motion 265 n.
velocity 277 n.
tempo 410 n.
temporal
transient 114 adj.
chronological 117 adj.
laical 987 adj.
temporalities
property 777 n.
benefice 985 n.
temporary
ephemeral 114 adj.
substituted 150 adj.
uncertain 474 adj.
temporize, temporise
spin out 113 vb.
put off 136 vb.
be cunning 698 vb.
tempt
influence 178 vb.
attract 291 vb.
tempt 612 vb.
cause desire 859 vb.
make wicked 934 vb.
— providence
face danger 661 vb.
be rash 857 vb.
temptation
attraction 291 n.
inducement 612 n.
desired object 859 n.
tempter
motivator 612 n.
Satan 969 n.
tempting
savoury 390 adj.
(See **tempt** *)*
temptress
attraction 291 n.
motivator 612 n.
loose woman 952 n.
ten
over five 99 n.
tenable
rational 475 adj.
credible 485 adj.
invulnerable 660 adj.
tenacious
cohesive 48 adj.
tough 329 adj.
resolute 599 adj.
persevering 600 adj.
obstinate 602 adj.
retentive 778 adj.
tenacity
retention 778 n.
tenancy
possession 773 n.
tenant
resident 191 n.
possessor 776 n.
tenantry
inhabitants 191 n.
Ten Commandments
fixture 153 n.
precept 693 n.
code of duty 917 n.
law 953 n.
revelation 975 n.
tend
conduce 156 vb.
tend 179 vb.
point to 281 vb.
groom 369 vb.
look after 457 vb.
doctor 658 vb.
serve 742 vb.
— to
conduce 156 vb.
tendency
temperament 5 n.
ability 160 n.
tendency 179 n.
liability 180 n.
probability 471 n.
bias 481 n.
willingness 597 n.
habit 610 n.
aptitude 694 n.
affections 817 n.
liking 859 n.
tendentious
tending 179 adj.
intended 617 adj.
tender
locomotive 274 n.
boat 275 n.
soft 327 adj.
sentient 374 adj.
painful 377 adj.
soft-hued 425 adj.
careful 457 adj.
lenient 736 adj.
offer 759 vb.
impressible 819 adj.
paining 827 adj.
honour 866 vb.
loving 887 adj.
benevolent 897 adj.
pitying 905 adj.
tender age
youth 130 n.
tenderfoot
intruder 59 n.
beginner 538 n.
tender-hearted
impressible 819 adj.
pitying 905 adj.
tenderize, tenderise
soften 327 vb.
tenderly
carefully 457 adv.
affectionately 887 adv.
benevolently 897 adv.
tender mercies
severity 735 n.
tenderness
weakness 163 n.
sensibility 374 n.
moral sensibility 819 n.
(See **tender** *)*
tender spot
vulnerability 661 n.
moral sensibility 819 n.
tending
tending 179 adj.
liable 180 adj.
possible 469 adj.
tendon
ligature 47 n.
tendril
ligature 47 n.
filament 208 n.
coil 251 n.
foliage 366 n.
nippers 778 n.
Tenebrae
church service 988 n.
tenements
housing 192 n.
estate 777 n.
tenet
creed 485 n.
precept 693 n.
tenfold
fifth and over 99 adj.
tenné
orange 432 n.
heraldry 547 n.
tenner
funds 797 n.
tennis
ball game 837 n.
tennis court
pleasure ground 837 n.
tenon
projection 254 n.

tenor
modality 7 n.
degree 27 n.
tendency 179 n.
direction 281 n.
vocalist 413 n.
meaning 514 n.
tense
time 108 n.
rigid 326 adj.
expectant 507 adj.
grammar 564 n.
feeling 818 adj.
fervent 818 adj.
excited 821 adj.
excitable 822 adj.
nervous 854 adj.
tensile
elastic 328 adj.
tensile strength
strength 162 n.
tension
energy 160 n.
lengthening 203 n.
dissension 709 n.
excitation 821 n.
worry 825 n.
discontent 829 n.
tent
dwelling 192 n.
pavilion 192 n.
canopy 226 n.
surgical dressing 658 n.
tentacle
feeler 378 n.
nippers 778 n.
tentative
slow 278 adj.
enquiring 459 adj.
experimental 461 adj.
attempting 671 adj.
clumsy 695 adj.
cautious 858 adj.
tentativeness
empiricism 461 n.
tented
covered 226 adj.
tenth
fifth and over 99 adj.
ten to one
probably 471 adv.
tenuity
thinness 206 n.
rarity 325 n.
tenuous
insubstantial 4 adj.
inconsiderable 33 adj.
flimsy 163 adj.
tenure
time 108 n.
possession 773 n.
estate 777 n.
tepee
dwelling 192 n.
tepid
warm 379 adj.
tequila
alcoholic drink 301 n.
Teraphim
mythic deity 966 n.
teratogen
poison 659 n.
teratology
deformity 246 n.
exaggeration 546 n.
thaumaturgy 864 n.
terce
church service 988 n.
tercentenary
anniversary 141 n.
tercet
verse form 593 n.
tergiversate
vary 152 vb.
turn back 286 vb.
be false 541 vb.
tergiversate 603 vb.
relinquish 621 vb.
fail in duty 918 vb.
tergiversation
change 143 n.
reversion 148 n.
irresolution 601 n.
tergiversation 603 n.
cowardice 856 n.
perfidy 930 n.
term
end 69 n.
serial place 73 n.
date 108 n.
period 110 n.
limit 236 n.
word 559 n.
name 561 n.vb.
termagant
violent creature 176 n.
shrew 892 n.
terminal
extremity 69 n.
ending 69 adj.
stopping place 145 n.
distant 199 adj.
limit 236 n.
goal 295 n.
terminal disease
illness 651 n.
terminate
terminate 69 vb.
cease 145 vb.
termination
end 69 n.
effect 157 n.
completion 725 n.
terminology
etymology 559 n.
nomenclature 561 n.
phrase 563 n.
terminus
extremity 69 n.
stopping place 145 n.
limit 236 n.
itinerary 267 n.
goal 295 n.
completion 725 n.
termite
insect 365 n.
termless
infinite 107 adj.
terms
conditions 766 n.
terms of reference
function 622 n.
mandate 751 n.
tern
three 93 n.
bird 365 n.
ternary
treble 94 adj.
Terpsichore
dancing 837 n.
lesser deity 967 n.
terrace(s)
house 192 n.
horizontality 216 n.
onlookers 441 n.
terracotta
pottery 381 n.
terra firma
basis 218 n.
goal 295 n.
land 344 n.
terrain
space 183 n.
region 184 n.
land 344 n.
arena 724 n.
terra incognita
unknown thing 491 n.
secret 530 n.
terrapin
reptile 365 n.
terraqueous
telluric 321 adj.
terrarium
zoo 369 n.
terrestrial
native 191 n.
telluric 321 adj.
territorial 344 adj.
terrible
not nice 645 adj.
frightening 854 adj.
terribly
extremely 32 adv.
terrier
list 87 n.
dog 365 n.
terrific
prodigious 32 adj.
excellent 644 adj.
terrify
frighten 854 vb.
terrine
bowl 194 n.
hors-d'oeuvres 301 n.
territorial
regional 184 adj.
territorial 344 adj.
soldier 722 n.
territory
territory 184 n.
land 344 n.
political organization 733 n.
lands 777 n.
terror
fear 854 n.
intimidation 854 n.
ruffian 904 n.
bad person 938 n.
terrorism
violence 176 n.
sedition 738 n.
intimidation 854 n.
terrorist
violent creature 176 n.
opponent 705 n.
revolter 738 n.
alarmist 854 n.
terrorize, terrorise
dissuade 613 vb.
oppress 735 vb.
frighten 854 vb.
terror tactics
terror tactics 712 n.
terse
short 204 adj.
aphoristic 496 adj.
concise 569 adj.
tertian
seasonal 141 adj.
tertiary
treble 94 adj.
Terylene
textile 222 n.
terza rima
verse form 593 n.
tessellated
variegated 437 adj.
tessellation
chequer 437 n.
test
exam 459 n.
enquire 459 vb.
experiment 461 N. vb.
attempt 671 vb.
hard task 700 n.
testable
experimental 461 adj.
demonstrated 478 adj.
testament
testimony 466 n.
title deed 767 n.
testamentary
proprietary 777 adj.
testator
transferrer 272 n.
giver 781 n.
test bed
aircraft 276 n.
test case
prototype 23 n.
experiment 461 n.

litigation 959 n.
tested
certain 473 adj.
excellent 644 adj.
approved 923 adj.
trustworthy 929 adj.
testee
respondent 460 n.
testee 461 n.
tester
bed 218 n.
enquirer 459 n.
experimenter 461 n.
testicles
genitalia 167 n.
testify
testify 466 vb.
affirm 532 vb.
swear 532 vb.
indicate 547 vb.
testimonial
credential 466 n.
reminder 505 n.
monument 548 n.
approbation 923 n.
testimony
testimony 466 n.
affirmation 532 n.
legal trial 959 n.
testing agent
testing agent 461 n.
test match
contest 716 n.
test pilot
aeronaut 271 n.
experimenter 461 n.
test tube
crucible 147 n.
testing agent 461 n.
test-tube baby
propagation 167 n.
testudo
armour 713 n.
testy
discontented 829 adj.
ungracious 885 adj.
irascible 892 adj.
tetanus
spasm 318 n.
infection 651 n.
tetchy
irascible 892 adj.
tête-à-tête
chat 584 n.
social gathering 882 n.
tether
tie 45 vb.
halter 47 n.
place 187 vb.
obstacle 702 n.
fetter 747 vb.
fetter 748 n.
Tethys
ocean 343 n.
classical deities 967 n.
tetra-
four 96 adj.
tetrad
quaternity 96 n.
tetragon
angular figure 247 n.
Tetragrammaton
quaternity 96 n.
the Deity 965 n.
tetrahedral
four 96 adj.
tetralogy
poem 593 n.
stage play 594 n.
tetrameter
prosody 593 n.
tetrapod
quaternity 96 n.n.
tetrarch
governor 741 n.
Teutonism
dialect 560 n.
text
prototype 23 n.
topic 452 n.
maxim 496 n.
meaning 514 n.
reading matter 589 n.
precept 693 n.
textbook
classroom 539 n.
textbook 589 n.
textile
fibre 208 n.
textile 222 n.
texture 331 n.
materials 631 n.
textual
scriptural 975 adj.
textual criticism
interpretation 520 n.
textualist
theologian 973 n.
textural
textural 331 adj.
texture
weaving 222 n.
texture 331 n.
pattern 844 n.
thalassic
oceanic 343 adj.
Thalia
drama 594 n.
lesser deity 967 n.
thallophyte
plant 366 n.
thane
person of rank 868 n.
thank
thank 907 vb.
grant claims 915 vb.
praise 923 vb.
reward 962 vb.
— one's lucky stars
rejoice 835 vb.
congratulate 886 vb.
thankful
content 828 adj.
grateful 907 adj.
thankless
profitless 641 adj.
unpleasant 827 adj.
unthanked 908 adj.
thank-offering
oblation 981 n.
thanksgiving
rejoicing 835 n.
celebration 876 n.
thanks 907 n.
act of worship 981 n.
thanks to
hence 158 adv.
through 628 adv.
in aid of 703 adv.
thatch
roof 226 n.
hair 259 n.
building material 631 n.
thatched
architectural 192 adj.
thatcher
artisan 686 n.
that is
namely 80 adv.
in plain words 520 adv.
thaumatrope
optical device 442 n.
thaumaturgic
wonderful 864 adj.
sorcerous 983 adj.
thaw
come unstuck 49 vb.
soften 327 vb.
liquefy 337 vb.
semiliquidity 354 n.
heat 381 vb.
pity 905 vb.
thawing
semiliquid 354 adj.
heating 381 n.
thearchy
government 733 n.
theatre
region 184 n.
meeting place 192 n.
view 438 n.
cinema 445 n.
theatre 594 n.
drama 594 n.
arena 724 n.
place of amusement 837 n.
theatregoer
spectator 441 n.
playgoer 594 n.
theatre nuclear warfare
warfare 718 n.
theatre of the absurd
stage play 594 n.
theatre of war
battleground 724 n.
theatre sister
nurse 658 n.
theatrical
dramatic 594 adj.
affected 850 adj.
showy 875 adj.
theatricals
dramaturgy 594 n.
theft
acquisition 771 n.
stealing 788 n.
theism
deism 973 n.
piety 979 n.
theist
religionist 973 n.
'them'
master 741 n.
thematic
interjacent 231 adj.
topical 452 adj.
theme
melody 410 n.
musical piece 412 n.
topic 452 n.
dissertation 591 n.
theme song
tune 412 n.
then
not now 122 adv.
thence
hence 158 adv.
theocracy
government 733 n.
theocracy 965 n.
the church 985 n.
theodicy
theology 973 n.
theodolite
angular measure 247 n.
gauge 465 n.
theogony
deity 966 n.
theologian
theologian 973 n.
theological
theological 973 adj.
theology
theology 973 n.
theophany
appearance 445 n.
manifestation 522 n.
theophany 965 n.
revelation 975 n.
theorbo
harp 414 n.
theorem
topic 452 n.
argumentation 475 n.
axiom 496 n.
supposition 512 n.
theoretical
mental 447 adj.
ideational 451 adj.
suppositional 512 adj.
theorist
theorist 512 n.

theorize, theorise
account for 158 vb.
meditate 449 vb.
suppose 512 vb.
theory
attribution 158 n.
idea 451 n.
opinion 485 n.
supposition 512 n.
theosophist
religionist 973 n.
occultist 984 n.
theosophy
philosophy 449 n.
religious faith 973 n.
religion 973 n.
occultism 984 n.
therapeutic
remedial 658 adj.
therapeutics
medical art 658 n.
therapy 658 n.
therapist
doctor 658 n.
adviser 691 n.
therapy
psychology 447 n.
therapy 658 n.
Theravada
religious faith 973 n.
there
in place 186 adv.
here 189 adv.
thereabouts
about 33 adv.
nearly 200 adv.
thereafter
subsequently 120 adv.
there and back
reversion 148 n.
therefore
hence 158 adv.
thereof
concerning 9 adv.
there speaks . . .
be disclosed 526 vb.
thereupon
subsequently 120 adv.
theriocephalous deity
Egyptian deities 967 n.
theriomorphic
animal 365 adj.
idolatrous 982 adj.
therm
thermometry 379 n.
thermae
ablutions 648 n.
thermal
ascent 308 n.
wind 352 n.
warm 379 adj.
thermodynamics
science of forces 162 n.
physics 319 n.
thermometry 379 n.
thermoelectricity
electricity 160 n.
thermography
thermometry 379 n.
thermoluminescence
chronology 117 n.
glow 417 n.
thermometer
thermometry 379 n.
meter 465 n.
thermonuclear
dynamic 160 adj.
thermonuclear reaction
nucleonics 160 n.
thermopile
thermometry 379 n.
thermoplastic
flexible 327 adj.
thermosetting
heating 381 adj.
thermos flask
cauldron 194 n.
preserver 666 n.
thermostat
thermometry 379 n.
thesaurus
word list 87 n.
dictionary 559 n.
collection 632 n.
treasury 799 n.
thesis
topic 452 n.
argument 475 n.
supposition 512 n.
dissertation 591 n.
prosody 593 n.
Thespian
actor 594 n.
dramatic 594 adj.
Thetis
sea nymph 343 n.
theurgy
sorcery 983 n.
they
group 74 n.
authority 733 n.
thick
great 32 adj.
middle 70 n.
fleshy 195 adj.
thick 205 adj.
dense 324 adj.
semiliquid 354 adj.
cloudy 355 adj.
dim 419 adj.
opaque 423 adj.
unintelligent 499 adj.
stammering 580 adj.
friendly 880 adj.
thick and fast
often 139 adv.
thick ear
wound 655 n.
thicken
augment 36 vb.
enlarge 197 vb.
be broad 205 vb.
be dense 324 vb.
thicken 354 vb.
make opaque 423 vb.
thickener
condensation 324 n.
thickening 354 n.
thicket
wood 366 n.
thickhead
dunce 501 n.
thickness
quantity 26 n.
thickness 205 n.
layer 207 n.
density 324 n.
metrology 465 n.
(See **thick** *)*
thick of things
middle 70 n.
activity 678 n.
thick on the ground
assembled 74 adj.
multitudinous 104 adj.
frequent 139 adj.
thickset
stalwart 162 adj.
dense 324 adj.
thick-skinned
unfeeling 375 adj.
thick-skinned 820 adj.
thick speech
voicelessness 578 n.
speech defect 580 n.
drunkenness 949 n.
thick-witted
unintelligent 499 adj.
thief
thief 789 n.
offender 904 n.
thieve
steal 788 vb.
thievery
stealing 788 n.
thievishness 788 n.
thigh
leg 267 n.
thimbleful
small quantity 33 n.
thimblerig
sleight 542 n.
thin
insubstantial 4 adj.
decrease 37 vb.
incomplete 55 adj.
few 105 adj.
weaken 163 vb.
exiguous 196 adj.
make smaller 198 vb.
lean 206 adj.
shallow 212 adj.
hairless 229 adj.
rarefy 325 vb.
transparent 422 adj.
feeble 572 adj.
insufficient 636 adj.
underfed 636 adj.
fasting 946 adj.
— out
be dispersed 75 vb.
extract 304 vb.
cultivate 370 vb.
thin air
insubstantial thing 4 n.
disappearance 446 n.
thin end of the wedge
start 68 n.
stratagem 698 n.
thing
substance 3 n.
product 164 n.
object 319 n.
thing, the
chief thing 638 n.
thingamabob, thingamajig
no name 562 n.
things
property 777 n.
thingummy
no name 562 n.
tool 630 n.
thin ice
pitfall 663 n.
think
cognize 447 vb.
think 449 vb.
opine 485 vb.
suppose 512 vb.
imagine 513 vb.
— about
meditate 449 vb.
— again
tergiversate 603 vb.
be penitent 939 vb.
— ahead
plan 623 vb.
— alike
cooperate 706 vb.
— aloud
soliloquize 585 vb.
— back
retrospect 505 vb.
— best
will 595 vb.
advise 691 vb.
— better of it
tergiversate 603 vb.
rectify 654 vb.
be nervous 854 vb.
— highly of
approve 923 vb.
— little of
disapprove 924 vb.
— nothing of
be inattentive 456 vb.
hold cheap 922 vb.
— of
initiate 68 vb.
be mindful 455 vb.
aim at 617 vb.

— over
meditate 449 vb.
— the better of
approve 923 vb.
— the world of
love 887 vb.
— the worse of
disapprove 924 vb.
— twice
be careful 457 vb.
be cautious 858 vb.
— up
produce 164 vb.
imagine 513 vb.
— well of
respect 920 vb.
approve 923 vb.
thinkable
possible 469 adj.
thinker
philosopher 449 n.
enquirer 459 n.
sage 500 n.
theorist 512 n.
thinking cap
thought 449 n.
think tank
council 692 n.
thin on top
hairless 229 adj.
thin red line
defender 713 n.
armed force 722 n.
thin-skinned
sensitive 819 adj.
irascible 892 adj.
third
treble 94 adj.
trisection 95 n.
musical note 410 n.
third degree
interrogation 459 n.
police enquiry 459 n.
corporal punishment 963 n.
third estate
commonalty 869 n.
third force
moderator 177 n.
third-rate
inferior 35 adj.
trivial 639 adj.
Third World
region 184 n.
political organization 733 n.
thirst
dryness 342 n.
be hot 379 vb.
desire 859 n.
hunger 859 n.
thirst-quenching
refreshing 685 adj.
thirsty
dry 342 adj.
hot 379 adj.
hungry 859 adj.
thirsty soul
drunkard 949 n.
thirteen
over five 99 n.
Thirty-nine Articles
theology 973 n.
orthodoxy 976 n.
this or that
uncertainty 474 n.
no name 562 n.
this, that or the other
variant 15 n.
thistle
prickle 256 n.
plant 366 n.
heraldry 547 n.
thistledown
lightness 323 n.
thither
towards 281 adv.
tholepin
pivot 218 n.
Thomism
philosophy 449 n.
theology 973 n.
thong
ligature 47 n.
scourge 964 n.
Thor
Nordic deities 967 n.
thorax
bosom 253 n.
thorn
prickle 256 n.
foliage 366 n.
suffering 825 n.
thorn in the flesh
bane 659 n.
worry 825 n.
painfulness 827 n.
thorny
sharp 256 adj.
difficult 700 adj.
thorough
consummate 32 adj.
complete 54 adj.
careful 457 adj.
resolute 599 adj.
labouring 682 adj.
completive 725 adj.
thoroughbred
unmixed 44 adj.
thoroughbred 273 n.
well-bred 848 adj.
aristocrat 868 n.
thoroughfare
open space 263 n.
passing along 305 n.
road 624 n.
thoroughgoing
revolutionary 149 adj.
(See **thorough** *)*
Thoth
Egyptian deities 967 n.
though
in return 31 adv.
provided 468 adv.
thought
small quantity 33 n.
intellect 447 n.
thought 449 n.
idea 451 n.
attention 455 n.
opinion 485 n.
supposition 512 n.
ideality 513 n.
worry 825 n.
thoughtful
thoughtful 449 adj.
attentive 455 adj.
careful 457 adj.
wise 498 adj.
disinterested 931 adj.
thoughtless
unthinking 450 adj.
inattentive 456 adj.
negligent 458 adj.
unwise 499 adj.
unprepared 670 adj.
unskilful 695 adj.
rash 857 adj.
thought-provoking
topical 452 adj.
suppositional 512 adj.
thought reader
psychic 984 n.
thousand
over one hundred 99 n.
thraldom
servitude 745 n.
thrall
slave 742 n.
thrash
strike 279 vb.
defeat 727 vb.
flog 963 vb.
— out
enquire 459 vb.
thrashing
corporal punishment 963 n.
thrashing about
violent 176 adj.
thread
small thing 33 n.
ligature 47 n.
series 71 n.
continue 71 vb.
weak thing 163 n.
thinness 206 n.
fibre 208 n.
pass 305 vb.
— together
connect 45 vb.
arrange 62 vb.
threadbare
hairless 229 adj.
uncovered 229 adj.
used 673 adj.
beggarly 801 adj.
threadworm
bane 659 n.
threat
intention 617 n.
danger 661 n.
warning 664 n.
defiance 711 n.
intimidation 854 n.
insolence 878 n.
malediction 899 n.
threat 900 n.
threaten
be to come 124 vb.
impend 155 vb.
predict 511 vb.
dissuade 613 vb.
endanger 661 vb.
warn 664 vb.
frighten 854 vb.
boast 877 vb.
threaten 900 vb.
three
three 93 n.adj.
three-card trick
sleight 542 n.
three cheers
rejoicing 835 n.
applause 923 n.
three-cornered
three 93 adj.
three-dimensional
spatial 183 adj.
formed 243 adj.
metrical 465 adj.
threefold
trebly 94 adv.
three-line whip
command 737 n.
threemaster
sailing ship 275 n.
three-mile limit
territory 184 n.
limit 236 n.
three-ply
treble 94 adj.
three-point landing
air travel 271 n.
three R's, the
curriculum 534 n.
threesome
three 93 n.
three-star
fuel 385 n.
provisioning 633 adj.
three-wheeler
three 93 n.
automobile 274 n.
thremmatology
animal husbandry 369 n.
threnody
vocal music 412 n.
lament 836 n.
thresh
strike 279 vb.
cultivate 370 vb.
— about
be agitated 318 vb.
thresher
farmer 370 n.
farm tool 370 n.
threshold
entrance 68 n.
threshold 234 n.
limit 236 n.

doorway 263 n.
thrift
gain 771 n.
economy 814 n.
thriftless
prodigal 815 adj.
rash 857 adj.
thrifty
careful 457 adj.
economical 814 adj.
thrill
be agitated 318 vb.
pleasure 376 n.
pang 377 n.
itch 378 vb.
feeling 818 n.
excitation 821 n.
excite 821 vb.
excitable state 822 n.
joy 824 n.
delight 826 vb.
thriller
film 445 n.
novel 590 n.
thrilling
descriptive 590 adj.
felt 818 adj.
exciting 821 adj.
pleasurable 826 adj.
thrill-seeker
reveller 837 n.
sensualist 944 n.
thrive
grow 36 vb.
be vigorous 174 vb.
flourish 615 vb.
be healthy 650 vb.
be active 678 vb.
prosper 730 vb.
throat
orifice 263 n.
conduit 351 n.
air pipe 353 n.
throaty
hoarse 407 adj.
throb
be periodic 141 vb.
oscillation 317 n.
spasm 318 n.
be agitated 318 vb.
give pain 377 vb.
show feeling 818 vb.
throes
violence 176 n.
spasm 318 n.
pang 377 n.
thrombosis
cardiovascular disease 651 n.
throne
seat 218 n.
regalia 743 n.
tribunal 956 n.
throng
crowd 74 n.
congregate 74 vb.
multitude 104 n.
— in
burst in 297 vb.
throttle
disable 161 vb.
close 264 vb.
retain 778 vb.
— down
retard 278 vb.
through
until now 121 adv.
vehicular 274 adj.
towards 281 adv.
communicating 624 adj.
through 628 adv.
by means of 629 adv.
through and through
completely 54 adv.
throughout
throughout 54 adv.
while 108 adv.
widely 183 adv.
throughput
data processing 86 n.
production 164 n.
transference 272 n.
through road
road 624 n.
through thick and thin
completely 54 adv.
persistently 600 adv.
through with, be
climax 725 vb.
throw
form 243 vb.
move 265 vb.
impulse 279 n.
propel 287 vb.
gambling 618 n.
exertion 682 n.
— a fit
be agitated 318 vb.
be excitable 822 vb.
— a spanner in the works
disable 161 vb.
make useless 641 vb.
be obstructive 702 vb.
— away
eject 300 vb.
act 594 vb.
reject 607 vb.
waste 634 vb.
stop using 674 vb.
lose 772 vb.
be prodigal 815 vb.
— cold water on
moderate 177 vb.
dissuade 613 vb.
— down
demolish 165 vb.
fell 311 vb.
— down the gauntlet
defy 711 vb.
— dust in one's eyes
blind 439 vb.
decieve 542 vb.
— good money after bad
lose 772 vb.
be prodigal 815 vb.
— in one's hand
relinquish 621 vb.
resign 753 vb.
— in one's teeth
defy 711 vb.
accuse 928 vb.
— in the sponge/the towel
relinquish 621 vb.
submit 721 vb.
— into the shade
be superior 34 vb.
have a reputation 866 vb.
— light on
make bright 417 vb.
interpret 520 vb.
manifest 522 vb.
— mud
disapprove 924 vb.
defame 926 vb.
— off
disaccustom 611 vb.
— off the mask
disclose 526 vb.
— off the scent
distract 456 vb.
puzzle 474 vb.
elude 667 vb.
— off the yoke
revolt 738 vb.
achieve liberty 746 vb.
— one out
trouble 827 vb.
— one's hat in the ring
defy 711 vb.
— one's money around
be liberal 813 vb.
be prodigal 815 vb.
— one's weight about
be vigorous 174 vb.
be insolent 878 vb.
— open
open 263 vb.
admit 299 vb.
manifest 522 vb.
— out
eject 300 vb.
reject 607 vb.
— out the baby with the bathwater
overstep 306 vb.
act foolishly 695 vb.
— over
tergiversate 603 vb.
relinquish 621 vb.
— overboard
eject 300 vb.
stop using 674 vb.
not retain 779 vb.
— stones at
lapidate 712 vb.
be malevolent 898 vb.
disapprove 924 vb.
— the book at
dispraise 924 vb.
indict 928 vb.
punish 963 vb.
— up
eject 300 vb.
vomit 300 vb.
elevate 310 vb.
submit 721 vb.
resign 753 vb.
throwaway
ephemeral 114 adj.
wasteful 634 adj.
throwaway manner
sauciness 878 n.
throwback
recurrence 106 n.
reversion 148 n.
deterioration 655 n.
relapse 657 n.
thrower
thrower 287 n.
player 837 n.
throwing overboard
ejection 300 n.
thrown
formed 243 adj.
grounded 728 adj.
thrown, be
tumble 309 vb.
throwstick
missile weapon 723 n.
thrum
edging 234 n.
resound 404 vb.
play music 413 vb.
thrush
bird 365 n.
vocalist 413 n.
animal disease 651 n.
thrust
energy 160 n.
vigorousness 174 n.
influence 178 n.
distortion 246 n.
spurt 277 n.
impulse 279 n.
propellant 287 n.
lunge 712 n.
thruster
propellant 287 n.
busy person 678 n.
thrustful
vigorous 174 adj.
thrustful
assertive 532 adj.
active 678 adj.
thud
impulse 279 n.
sound faint 401 vb.
nonresonance 405 n.

thug
murderer 362 n.
robber 789 n.
ruffian 904 n.
bad person 938 n.
thuggery
violence 176 n.
thumb
finger 378 n.
touch 378 vb.
study 536 vb.
gesticulate 547 vb.
use 673 vb.
— a lift
ride 267 vb.
beg 761 vb.
thumb index
edition 589 n.
thumbnail
small 33 adj.
thumbnail sketch
miniature 196 n.
description 590 n.
thumbprint
label 547 n.
thumbscrew
instrument of torture 964 n.
thumbs down
refusal 760 n.
condemnation 961 n.
thumbs up
approbation 923 n.
acquittal 960 n.
thump
knock 279 n.
sound faint 401 vb.
nonresonance 405 n.
thumping
whopping 32 adj.
large 195 adj.
thunder
storm 176 n.
be loud 400 vb.
vociferate 408 vb.
proclaim 528 vb.
emphasize 532 vb.
be angry 891 vb.
malediction 899 n.
threaten 900 vb.
thunderclap
bang 402 n.
lack of expectation 508 n.
thunderer
violent creature 176 n.
thundering
whopping 32 adj.
thunderous
loud 400 adj.
approving 923 adj.
thunderstorm
rain 350 n.
gale 352 n.
thunderstruck
inexpectant 508 adj.
wondering 864 adj.
thurible
ritual object 988 n.
thus
thus 8 adv.
hence 158 adv.
thwack
knock 279 n.
strike 279 vb.
thwart
halt 145 vb.
disappoint 509 vb.
be obstructive 702 vb.
oppose 704 vb.
adverse 731 adj.
trouble 827 vb.
thwarted
impotent 161 adj.
hindered 702 adj.
defeated 728 adj.
thyme
potherb 301 n.
tiara
headgear 228 n.
regalia 743 n.
jewellery 844 n.
vestments 989 n.
tic
spasm 318 n.
nervous disorders 651 n.
tick
instant 116 n.
periodicity 141 n.
oscillate 317 vb.
insect 365 n.
sound faint 401 vb.
roll 403 vb.
mark 547 vb.
credit 802 n.
approve 923 vb.
— off
number 86 vb.
register 548 vb.
reprove 924 vb.
— over
operate 173 vb.
move slowly 278 vb.
ticker
timekeeper 117 n.
insides 224 n.
telecommunication 531 n.
ticket
list 87 n.
opener 263 n.
ingress 297 n.
credential 466 n.
label 547 n.
electorate 605 n.
policy 623 n.
permit 756 n.
ticking
textile 222 n.
tickle
itch 378 vb.
touch 378 vb.
incite 612 vb.
delight 826 vb.
amuse 837 vb.
endearment 889 n.
— the palate
taste 386 vb.
make appetizing 390 vb.
tickled pink
pleased 824 adj.
merry 833 adj.
ticklish
sentient 374 adj.
unreliable 474 adj.
unsafe 661 adj.
difficult 700 adj.
tick-tack
signal 547 n.
tidal
periodical 141 adj.
unstable 152 adj.
flowing 350 adj.
tidal barrage
sources of energy 160 n.
tidal wave
outbreak 176 n.
wave 350 n.
tiddler
dwarf 196 n.
tiddly
tipsy 949 adj.
tiddlywink(s)
plaything 837 n.
indoor game 837 n.
tide
increase 36 n.
time 108 n.
periodicity 141 n.
progression 285 n.
ocean 343 n.
current 350 n.
— over
pass time 108 vb.
put off 136 vb.
aid 703 vb.
tidemark
limit 236 n.
gauge 465 n.
signpost 547 n.
trace 548 n.
tide mill
sources of energy 160 n.
tide of events
affairs 154 n.
tide-table
chronology 117 n.
tideway
current 350 n.
conduit 351 n.
tidings
news 529 n.
tidy
orderly 60 adj.
arrange 62 vb.
careful 457 adj.
clean 648 adj.
make better 654 vb.
personable 841 adj.
tidy step
distance 199 n.
tidy sum
wealth 800 n.
tie
draw 28 n.
be equal 28 vb.
tie 45 vb.
bond 47 n.
neckwear 228 n.
obstacle 702 n.
fetter 747 vb.
duty 917 n.
— down
compel 740 vb.
give terms 766 vb.
— in with
be related 9 vb.
— one's hands
disable 161 vb.
hinder 702 vb.
— up with
relate 9 vb.
connect 45 vb.
tie beam
beam 218 n.
tied aid
trade 791 n.
tied house
tavern 192 n.
tied to one's apron strings
subject 745 adj.
tie-dyeing
ornamental art 844 n.
tiepin
fastening 47 n.
jewellery 844 n.
tier
series 71 n.
classification 77 n.
layer 207 n.
tie-up
relation 9 n.
union 45 n.
association 706 n.
tiff
quarrel 709 n.
tiffin
meal 301 n.
tiger
violent creature 176 n.
cat 365 n.
stripe 437 n.
brave person 855 n.
noxious animal 904 n.
tiger's eye
variegation 437 n.
gem 844 n.
tight
adjusted 24 adj.
firm 45 adj.
cohesive 48 adj.
full 54 adj.
assembled 74 adj.
narrow 206 adj.

sealed off 264 adj.
rigid 326 adj.
dry 342 adj.
invulnerable 660 adj.
prepared 669 adj.
restraining 747 adj.
retentive 778 adj.
parsimonious 816 adj.
tipsy 949 adj.
tight corner
predicament 700 n.
tighten
tighten 45 vb.
make smaller 198 vb.
close 264 vb.
harden 326 vb.
restrain 747 vb.
— one's belt
economize 814 vb.
starve 946 vb.
tight-fisted
parsimonious 816 adj.
tight-fitting
adjusted 24 adj.
tight-knit
concise 569 adj.
tight-lipped
reticent 525 adj.
taciturn 582 adj.
tightrope
narrowness 206 n.
tightrope walking
skill 694 n.
tights
legwear 228 n.
tight squeeze
narrowness 206 n.
tightwad
niggard 816 n.
tigress
female animal 373 n.
(See **tiger** *)*
tilde
punctuation 547 n.
tile
lamina 207 n.
overlay 226 vb.
pottery 381 n.
variegate 437 vb.
building material 631 n.
plaything 837 n.
tiled
architectural 192 adj.
tiles
floor-cover 226 n.
roof 226 n.
till
while 108 adv.
box 194 n.
cultivate 370 vb.
recording instrument 549 n.
storage 632 n.
treasury 799 n.
till all hours
late 136 adv.
till blue in the face
for a long time 113 adv.
uselessly 641 adv.
tiller
handle 218 n.
sailing aid 269 n.
directorship 689 n.
tiller of the soil
farmer 370 n.
country-dweller 869 n.
till it hurts
painfully 32 adv.
till the cows come home
for a long time 113 adv.
tilt
be unequal 29 vb.
obliquity 220 n.
canopy 226 n.
descent 309 n.
contest 716 n.
— at
pursue 619 vb.
charge 712 vb.
dispraise 924 vb.
— at windmills
waste effort 641 vb.
— over
be inverted 221 vb.
tilth
agriculture 370 n.
timber
wood 366 n.
materials 631 n.
timbered
arboreal 366 adj.
timber-framed
architectural 192 adj.
timberwork
structure 331 n.
timbre
sound 398 n.
voice 577 n.
time
finality 69 n.
time 108 n.
era 110 n.
course of time 111 n.
time 117 vb.
tempo 410 n.
detention 747 n.
— it badly
mistime 138 vb.
time after time
repeatedly 106 adv.
often 139 adv.
time and motion study
management 689 n.
time and place
situation 186 n.
time being
present time 121 n.
time bomb
pitfall 663 n.
bomb 723 n.
time-consuming
wasteful 634 adj.
timed
adjusted 24 adj.
synchronous 123 adj.
time-honoured
immemorial 127 adj.
habitual 610 adj.
worshipful 866 adj.
respected 920 adj.
time immemorial
antiquity 125 n.
timekeeper
timekeeper 117 n.
time lag
discontinuity 72 n.
interim 108 n.
delay 136 n.
interval 201 n.
time-lapse photography
photography 551 n.
timeless
perpetual 115 adj.
time limit
limit 236 n.
conditions 766 n.
timely
apt 24 adj.
early 135 adj.
timely 137 adj.
advisable 642 adj.
time machine
vehicle 274 n.
time of day
period 110 n.
clock time 117 n.
time off
lull 145 n.
leisure 681 n.
time of life
age 131 n.
time of year
period 110 n.
time on one's hands
inaction 677 n.
leisure 681 n.
time out of mind
retrospectively 125 adv.
timepiece
timekeeper 117 n.
times, the
circumstance 8 n.
present time 121 n.
time-saving
economical 814 adj.
time scale
gauge 465 n.
timeserver
tergiversator 603 n.
toady 879 n.
egotist 932 n.
timeserving
cunning 698 adj.
servility 879 n.
perfidious 930 adj.
selfish 932 adj.
time-sharing
data processing 86 n.
time signal
timekeeper 117 n.
broadcast 531 n.
signal 547 n.
time switch
timekeeper 117 n.
meter 465 n.
timetable
directory 87 n.
chronology 117 n.
itinerary 267 n.
guidebook 524 n.
time to come
futurity 124 n.
time to kill
tedium 838 n.
time to spare
slowness 278 n.
leisure 681 n.
timewarp
time 108 n.
time was
formerly 125 adv.
time-wasting
protracted 113 adj.
time-worn
olden 127 adj.
timid
irresolute 601 adj.
nervous 854 adj.
cowardly 856 adj.
cautious 858 adj.
modest 874 adj.
timing
chronometry 117 n.
periodicity 141 n.
tempo 410 n.
discrimination 463 n.
timocracy
rich person 800 n.
timorous
nervous 854 adj.
cowardly 856 adj.
timpani
drum 414 n.
timpanist
instrumentalist 413 n.
tin
small box 194 n.
preserve 666 vb.
shekels 797 n.
tincture
small quantity 33 n.
tincture 43 n.
tendency 179 n.
colour 425 n.vb.
tinder
lighter 385 n.
tine
sharp point 256 n.

ting
resound 404 vb.
tinge
small quantity 33 n.
tincture 43 n.
mix 43 vb.
hue 425 n.
colour 425 vb.
qualification 468 n.
tingle
have feeling 374 vb.
itch 378 vb.
feel 818 vb.
be excited 821 vb.
tin god
official 690 n.
autocrat 741 n.
insolent person 878 n.
tin hat
headgear 228 n.
armour 713 n.
tinker
not suffice 636 vb.
waste effort 641 vb.
mender 656 n.
meddle 678 vb.
be unskilful 695 vb.
be cunning 698 vb.
not complete 726 vb.
tinker's cuss
trifle 639 n.
tinkle
faintness 401 n.
resound 404 vb.
tinkling
melodious 410 adj.
tin mine
workshop 687 n.
tinnitus
resonance 404 n.
tinny
strident 407 adj.
Tin Pan Alley
music 412 n.
tinplate
lamina 207 n.
tinpot
unimportant 639 adj.
tinsel
flash 417 n.
spurious 542 adj.
bauble 639 n.
finery 844 n.
bad taste 847 n.
showy 875 adj.
tinsmith
artisan 686 n.
tint
hue 425 n.
colour 425 vb.
paint 553 vb.
tintack
fastening 47 n.
tintinnabulation
resonance 404 n.
gong 414 n.
tintometer
chromatics 425 n.
tin whistle
flute 414 n.
tiny
small 33 adj.
little 196 adj.
tip
extra 40 n.
put in front 64 vb.
extremity 69 n.
vertex 213 n.
make oblique 220 vb.
cover 226 vb.
edge 234 n.
lower 311 vb.
hint 524 n.
bribe 612 vb.
advice 691 n.
thanks 907 n.
reward 962 n. vb.
— over
invert 221 vb.
— the scale(s)
be unequal 29 vb.
predominate 34 vb.
— the wink
hint 524 vb.
tip-off
hint 524 n.
warning 664 n.
tipper
giver 781 n.
tippet
hanging object 217 n.
neckwear 228 n.
vestments 989 n.
tipple
alcoholic drink 301 n.
get drunk 949 vb.
tipstaff
officer 741 n.
law officer 955 n.
tipster
diviner 511 n.
informant 524 n.
gambler 618 n.
tipsy
tipsy 949 adj.
tip-tilted
curved 248 adj.
tiptoe
atop 213 adv.
walk 267 vb.
be stealthy 525 vb.
tip-top
supreme 34 adj.
best 644 adj.
tirade
exaggeration 546 n.
diffuseness 570 n.
oration 579 n.
censure 924 n.
tire
fatigue 684 vb.
trouble 827 vb.
tired
sleepy 679 adj.
tired and emotional
tipsy 949 adj.
tireless
unyielding 162 adj.
industrious 678 adj.
tirelessness
perseverance 600 n.
tiresome
fatiguing 684 adj.
annoying 827 adj.
tedious 838 adj.
tisane
soft drink 301 n.
tonic 658 n.
tissue
chief part 52 n.
thinness 206 n.
textile 222 n.
texture 331 n.
life 360 n.
cleaning cloth 648 n.
tissue paper
weak thing 163 n.
semitransparency 424 n.
paper 631 n.
tit
bird 365 n.
Titan
giant 195 n.
classical deities 967 n.
titanic
stalwart 162 adj.
huge 195 adj.
titbit
mouthful 301 n.
savouriness 390 n.
news 529 n.
elite 644 n.
pleasurableness 826 n.
tit for tat
correlation 12 n.
interchange 151 n.
retaliation 714 n.
tithe
part 53 n.
trifle 639 n.
tax 809 n.
titillate
itch 378 vb.
delight 826 vb.
amuse 837 vb.
cause desire 859 vb.
titillation
formication 378 n.
liking 859 n.
titivate
make better 654 vb.
beautify 841 vb.
primp 843 vb.
decorate 844 vb.
title
label 547 n.
name 561 n.
book 589 n.
decoration 729 n.
honours 866 n.
title 870 n.
dueness 915 n
titled
noble 868 adj.
title deed
title deed 767 n.
dueness 915 n.
title-holder
exceller 644 n.
proficient person 696 n.
Titoism
nonconformity 84 n.
government 733 n.
titter
laughter 835 n.
laugh 835 vb.
tittle
small quantity 33 n.
trifle 639 n.
tittle-tattle
rumour 529 n.
chatter 581 n.
titubation
descent 309 n.
titular
named 561 adj.
tizzy
excitation 821 n.
T-junction
road 624 n.
TM
meditation 449 n.
TNT
explosive 723 n.
to
contiguous 202 adj.
toad
amphibian 365 n.
eyesore 842 n.
toad in the hole
meat 301 n.
toadstool
plant 366 n.
toady
minister to 703 vb.
toady 879 n.
flatterer 925 n.
to a fault
extremely 32 adv.
to all intents and purposes
actally 1 adv.
on the whole 52 adv.
plausible 471 adj.
to a man
generally 79 adv.
unanimously 488 adv.
to and fro
by turns 141 adv.
in exchange 151 adv.
to and fro 317 adv.
toast
cereals 301 n.
draught 301 n.

be hot 379 vb.
heat 381 vb.
embrown 430 vb.
a beauty 841 n.
toast 876 vb.
congratulation 886 n.
show respect 920 vb.
applaud 923 vb.
toaster
heater 383 n.
toastmaster
speaker 579 n.
reveller 837 n.
toast of the town
exceller 644 n.
favourite 890 n.
to a turn
truly 494 adv.
perfectly 646 adv.
tobacco
tobacco 388 n.
to be
subsequent 120 adj.
future 124 adj.
toboggan
sledge 274 n.
amuse oneself 837 vb.
to boot
in addition 38 adv.
toby jug
vessel 194 n.
to capacity
completely 54 adv.
to cap it all
eminently 34 adv.
toccata
musical piece 412 n.
to coin a phrase
proverbially 496 adv.
to come
future 124 adj.
impending 155 adj.
tocsin
gong 414 n.
danger signal 665 n.
to date
until now 121 adv.
today
present time 121 n.
toddle
walk 267 vb.
move slowly 278 vb.
toddler
child 132 n.
pedestrian 268 n.
toddy
alcoholic drink 301 n.
to-do
turmoil 61 n.
activity 678 n.
toe
extremity 69 n.
foot 214 n.
toed
footed 214 adj.
toehold
support 218 n.
retention 778 n.
toe in
converge 293 vb.
— the line
conform 83 vb.
acquiesce 488 vb.
obey 739 vb.
toenail
foot 214 n.
toff
fop 848 n.
aristocrat 868 n.
toffee
coherence 48 n.
sweets 301 n.
brownness 430 n.
toffee-nosed
prideful 871 adj.
toft
home 192 n.
lands 777 n.
toga
robe 228 n.
together
continuously 71 adv.
together 74 adv.
togetherness
friendship 880 n.
sociality 882 n.
together with
in addition 38 adv.
with 89 adv.
toggle
fastening 47 n.
to good effect
influentially 178 adv.
successfully 727 adv.
togs
clothing 228 n.
finery 844 n.
toil
move slowly 278 vb.
labour 682 n.
work 682 vb.
toile
textile 222 n.
toiler
worker 686 n.
toilet
dressing 228 n.
latrine 649 n.
beautification 843 n.
toiletries
cosmetic 843 n.
toilette
dressing 228 n.
toilet water
scent 396 n.
cosmetic 843 n.
toils
trap 542 n.
encumbrance 702 n.
toilsome
laborious 682 adj.
difficult 700 adj.
toilworn
fatigued 684 adj.
token
insubstantial 4 adj.
manifestation 522 n.
badge 547 n.
indication 547 n.
trivial 639 adj.
security 767 n.
gift 781 n.
tokenism
sham 542 n.
tolerable
inconsiderable 33 adj.
not bad 644 adj.
imperfect 647 adj.
middling 732 adj.
contenting 828 adj.
tolerance
limit 236 n.
wisdom 498 n.
permission 756 n.
patience 823 n.
benevolence 897 n.
tolerant
lenient 736 adj.
tolerate
acquiesce 488 vb.
not act 677 vb.
consent 758 vb.
forgive 909 vb.
(See **tolerence** *)*
to let
offering 759 adj.
toll
addition 38 n.
decrement 42 n.
roll 403 vb.
play music 413 vb.
raise the alarm 665 vb.
tax 809 n.
— the knell
inter 364 vb.
lament 836 vb.
tollgate
access 624 n.
obstacle 702 n.
tom
cat 365 n.
male animal 372 n.
Tom, Dick and Harry
everyman 79 n.
commonalty 869 n.
tomahawk
axe 723 n.
tomato
vegetable 301 n.
redness 431 n.
tomato juice
soft drink 301 n.
tomb
excavation 255 n.
resting place 266 n.
tomb 364 n.
monument 548 n.
tombola
equal chance 159 n.
gambling game 837 n.
tomboy
youngster 132 n.
tomboyish
disorderly 61 adj.
tombstone
obsequies 364 n.
tome
book 589 n.
tomentose
downy 259 adj.
tomfool
absurd 497 adj.
fool 501 n.
tomfoolery
foolery 497 n.
Tommy
soldier 722 n.
tommy gun
gun 723 n.
tommyrot
silly talk 515 n.
tomography
medical art 658 n.
tomorrow
futurity 124 n.
Tom Thumb
dwarf 196 n.
Tom Tiddler's ground
territory 184 n.
nonownership 774 n.
tomtom
drum 414 n.
ton
weighing 322 n.
fashion 848 n.
tonal
harmonic 410 adj.
linguistic 557 adj.
vocal 577 adj.
tonality
light contrast 417 n.
tone
modality 7 n.
strength 162 n.
tendency 179 n.
sound 398 n.
musical note 410 n.
hue 425 n.
painting 553 n.
style 566 n.
voice 577 n.
speech 579 n.
conduct 688 n.
affections 817 n.
— down
moderate 177 vb.
darken 418 vb.
decolorize 426 vb.
misrepresent 552 vb.
— in with
accord 24 vb.
— up
strengthen 162 vb.
make better 654 vb.

tone-deaf
deaf 416 adj.
indiscriminating 464 adj.
toneless
discordant 411 adj.
colourless 426 adj.
tone poem
musical piece 412 n.
tone row
key 410 n.
discord 411 n.
tongs
nippers 778 n.
hairdressing 843 n.
tongue
projection 254 n.
prominence 254 n.
feeler 378 n.
taste 386 n.
language 557 n.
voice 577 n.
speech 579 n.
tongue in cheek
duplicity 541 n.
deception 542 n.
mental dishonesty 543 n.
affectation 850 n.
ridicule 851 n.
tongue-lashing
reprimand 924 n.
tongue-tied
voiceless 578 adj.
stammering 580 adj.
taciturn 582 adj.
tongue-wagging
loquacious 581 adj.
tonic
stimulant 174 n.
musical note 410 n.
incentive 612 n.
salubrious 652 adj.
tonic 658 n.
remedial 658 adj.
excitant 821 n.
cheering 833 adj.
tonic accent
pronunciation 577 n.
tonic effect
strengthening 162 n.
stimulation 174 n.
tonic solfa
notation 410 n.
tonic water
soft drink 301 n.
tonnage
size 195 n.
to no avail
uselessly 641 adv.
tonsillectomy
surgery 658 n.
tonsillitis
respiratory disease 651 n.
tonsured
hairless 229 adj.
monastic 986 adj.
tontine
receipt 807 n.
ton-up
speedy 277 adj.
too
in addition 38 adv.
too bad
adverse 731 adj.
annoying 827 adj.
regretted 830 adj.
discreditable 867 adj.
blameworthy 924 adj.
too big
unwieldy 195 adj.
too big for one's boots
vain 873 adj.
too busy, be
be engaged 138 vb.
too clever
intelligent 498 adj.
cunning 698 adj.
vain 873 adj.
too few
few 105 adj.
insufficiency 636 n.
too good for, be
defeat 727 vb.
despise 922 vb.
tool
handle 218 n.
fatalist 596 n.
contrivance 623 n.
instrument 628 n.
means 629 n.
tool 630 n.
agent 686 n.
toady 879 n.
tooling
bookbinding 589 n.
tool-user
machinist 630 n.
too many cooks
bungling 695 n.
too much
great quantity 32 n.
redundance 637 n.
tedious 838 adj.
intemperance 943 n.
satiety 863 n.
too much for, be
be superior 34 vb.
overmaster 727 vb.
to one's cost
amiss 616 adv.
badly 645 adv.
to oneself
secretly 525 adv.
to one's face
defiantly 711 adv.
to one's heart's content
enough 635 adv.
successfully 727 adv.
contentedly 828 adv.
to one's name
possessed 773 adj.
to one's taste
savoury 390 adj.
pleasurable 826 adj.
lovable 887 adj.
to order
specially 80 adv.
obediently 739 adv.
too soon
beforehand 135 adv.
ill-timed 138 adj.
toot
loudness 400 n.
resound 404 vb.
play music 413 vb.
danger signal 665 n.
tooth
tooth 256 n.
notch 260 n.vb.
taste 386 n.
toothache
pang 377 n.
tooth and nail
violently 176 adv.
laboriously 682 adv.
toothbrush
cleaning utensil 648 n.
toothed
toothed 256 adj.
notched 260 adj.
tooth for a tooth
interchange 151 n.
revenge 910 n.
toothless
ageing 131 adj.
unsharpened 257 adj.
toothpaste
cleanser 648 n.
prophylactic 658 n.
toothpick
extractor 304 n.
cleaning utensil 648 n.
toothsome
savoury 390 adj.
toothy
projecting 254 adj.
toothed 256 adj.
tootle
resound 404 vb.
play music 413 vb.
too-too
affected 850 adj.
top
superiority 34 n.
fill 54 vb.
put in front 64 vb.
extremity 69 n.
summit 213 n.
covering 226 n.
shirt 228 n.
limit 236 vb.
cone 252 n.
stopper 264 n.
climb 308 vb.
rotator 315 n.
completion 725 n.
plaything 837 n.
— and lop
cultivate 370 vb.
— out
crown 213 vb.
carry through 725 vb.
— up
fill 54 vb.
replenish 633 vb.
suffice 635 vb.
topaz
yellowness 433 n.
gem 844 n.
top brass
bigwig 638 n.
director 690 n.
topcoat
overcoat 228 n.
top deck
layer 207 n.
top dog
victor 727 n.
top drawer
elite 644 n.
beau monde 848 n.
upper class 868 n.
top-dress
make fruitful 171 vb.
cultivate 370 vb.
top-dressing
fertilizer 171 n.
covering 226 n.
tope
drink 301 vb.
get drunk 949 vb.
topee, topi
shade 226 n.
toper
drunkard 949 n.
top-flight
notable 638 adj.
super 644 adj.
skilful 694 adj.
top hat
headgear 228 n.
top-heavy
unequal 29 adj.
inverted 221 adj.
weighty 322 adj.
unsafe 661 adj.
clumsy 695 adj.
topiary
horticultural 370 adj.
ornamental 844 adj.
topic
topic 452 n.
supposition 512 n.
meaning 514 n.
topical
present 121 adj.
modern 126 adj.
situated 186 adj.
topical 452 adj.
topknot
hair 259 n.
topless
uncovered 229 adj.

top-level
superior 34 adj.
important 638 adj.
directing 689 adj.
topmast
high structure 209 n.
vertex 213 n.
topmost
great 32 adj.
supreme 34 adj.
high 209 adj.
topmost 213 adj.
important 638 adj.
completive 725 adj.
top-notch
supreme 34 adj.
best 644 adj.
super 644 adj.
top of the bill
dramatic 594 adj.
top of the ladder/the tree
prestige 866 n.
topographer
surveyor 465 n.
informant 524 n.
topographical
territorial 344 adj.
metrical 465 adj.
topography
situation 186 n.
guidebook 524 n.
topology
mathematics 86 n.
toponymy
nomenclature 561 n.
top people
superior 34 n.
bigwig 638 n.
elite 644 n.
topping
covering 226 n.
super 644 adj.
topple
tumble 309 vb.
fell 311 vb.
— over
be inverted 221 vb.
tops, the
exceller 644 n.
topsail
sail 275 n.
top secret
concealed 525 adj.
important 638 adj.
top seed
favourite 890 n.
topside
meat 301 n.
topsoil
soil 344 n.
topsy-turvy
contrarily 14 adv.
orderless 61 adj.
inverted 221 adj.
top to toe
longwise 203 adv.
toque
headgear 228 n.
tor
high land 209 n.
Torah
scripture 975 n.
torch
lighter 385 n.
lamp 420 n.
torch 420 n.
torch-bearer
preparer 669 n.
toreador
killer 362 n.
combatant 722 n.
toreutics
sculpture 554 n.
ornamental art 844 n.
torii
temple 990 n.
torment
pain 377 n.
give pain 377 vb.
harm 645 vb.
bane 659 n.
oppress 735 vb.
suffering 825 n.
torment 827 vb.
enrage 891 vb.
torture 963 vb.
torn
disunited 46 adj.
tornado
turmoil 61 n.
vortex 315 n.
gale 352 n.
torpedo
suppress 165 vb.
fire at 712 vb.
bomb 723 n.
torpid
inert 175 adj.
inactive 679 adj.
apathetic 820 adj.
inexcitable 823 adj.
torpor
helplessness 161 n.
weakness 163 n.
torque
loop 250 n.
jewellery 844 n.
torrefy
heat 381 vb.
torrent
velocity 277 n.
stream 350 n.
torrential
violent 176 adj.
torrid
hot 379 adj.
torsion
convolution 251 n.
torso
chief part 52 n.
piece 53 n.
incompleteness 55 n.
image 551 n.
sculpture 554 n.
tort
wrong 914 n.
guilty act 936 n.
lawbreaking 954 n.
tortilla
cereals 301 n.
tortious
wrong 914 adj.
illegal 954 adj.
tortoise
slowcoach 278 n.
reptile 365 n.
tortoiseshell
covering 226 n.
variegation 437 n.
tortuous
convoluted 251 adj.
sophistical 477 adj.
unclear 568 adj.
dishonest 930 adj.
torture
violence 176 n.
distort 246 vb.
give pain 377 vb.
interrogate 459 vb.
ill-treat 645 vb.
oppress 735 vb.
compel 740 vb.
suffering 825 n.
torment 827 vb.
make ugly 842 vb.
cruel act 898 n.
corporal punishment 963 n.
torture 963 vb.
torture chamber
instrument of torture 964 n.
tortured
figurative 519 adj.
torturer
punisher 963 n.
to rule
to rule 81 adv.
conformably 83 adv.
torus
swelling 253 n.
Tory
sectional 708 adj.
to scale
relatively 9 adv.
tosh
silly talk 515 n.
to spare
remaining 41 adj.
superfluous 637 adj.
toss
jumble 63 vb.
propel 287 vb.
oscillate 317 vb.
agitation 318 n.
— and turn
be excited 821 vb.
— aside
not respect 921 vb.
— one's head
be proud 871 vb.
despise 922 vb.
— up
gamble 618 vb.
tossing
seafaring 269 adj.
toss of a coin
gambling 618 n.
toss-up
equal chance 159 n.
uncertainty 474 n.
tot
child 132 n.
dwarf 196 n.
draught 301 n.
pungency 388 n.
total
quantity 26 n.
consummate 32 adj.
addition 38 n.
all 52 n.
complete 54 adj.
inclusive 78 adj.
numerical result 85 n.
number 86 vb.
totalitarian
authoritative 733 adj.
authoritarian 735 adj.
totalitarianism
uniformity 16 n.
despotism 733 n.
totality
whole 52 n.
completeness 54 n.
totalizator, totalisator
counting instrument 86 n.
gaming-house 618 n.
total recall
remembrance 505 n.
total situation
circumstance 8 n.
tote
carry 273 vb.
(See **totalizator** *)*
totem
badge 547 n.
idol 982 n.
totemistic
indicating 547 adj.
representing 551 adj.
to the end
completely 54 adv.
finally 69 adv.
to the eye
apparently 445 adv.
to the full
completely 54 adv.
with observance 768 adv.
to the heart
to the quick 374 adv.
on the raw 819 adv.
to the last man
completely 54 adv.
generally 79 adv.
to the letter
imitatively 20 adv.

truly 494 adv.
on terms 766 adv.
to the point
relevant 9 adj.
apt 24 adj.
concise 569 adj.
important 638 adj.
to the purpose
relevant 9 adj.
advisable 642 adj.
to the top of one's bent
completely 54 adv.
to the tune of
to the amount of 26 adv.
priced 809 adj.
totter
come unstuck 49 vb.
be weak 163 vb.
walk 267 vb.
move slowly 278 vb.
tumble 309 vb.
oscillate 317 vb.
tottering
unstable 152 adj.
deteriorated 655 adj.
unsafe 661 adj.
totting
acquisition 771 n.
booty 790 n.
tot up (to)
number 86 vb.
touch
be related 9 vb.
be equal 28 vb.
small quantity 33 n.
tincture 43 n.
derange 63 vb.
operate 173 vb.
be situated 186 vb.
be contiguous 202 vb.
limit 236 n.
texture 331 n.
sense 374 n.
touch 378 n.vb.
musical skill 413 n.
be tentative 461 vb.
gesture 547 n.
use 673 vb.
meddle 678 vb.
skill 694 n.
excite 821 vb.
children's games 837 n.
endearment 889 n.
— down
land 295 vb.
descend 309 vb.
— for
request 761 vb.
borrow 785 vb.
— off
initiate 68 vb.
cause 156 vb.
kindle 381 vb.
— on/upon
relate 9 vb.
notice 455 vb.
hint 524 vb.
— up
colour 425 vb.
paint 553 vb.
make better 654 vb.
— wood
be credulous 487 vb.
deprecate 762 vb.
touch and go
unreliable 474 adj.
unsafe 661 adj.
touchdown
air travel 271 n.
arrival 295 n.
touched
crazy 503 adj.
impressed 818 adj.
impressible 819 adj.
touching
concerning 9 adv.
distressing 827 adj.
(See **touch** *)*
touchline
limit 236 n.
touchpaper
lighter 385 n.
touchstone
testing agent 461 n.
touchy
sensitive 819 adj.
irascible 892 adj.
tough
strong 162 adj.
violent creature 176 n.
hard 326 adj.
tough 329 adj.
unsavoury 391 adj.
uncooked 670 adj.
difficult 700 adj.
resisting 715 adj.
thick-skinned 820 adj.
courageous 855 adj.
unkind 898 adj.
ruffian 904 n.
pitiless 906 adj.
toughen
be tough 329 vb.
make insensitive 820 vb.
toughness
obstinacy 602 n.
(See **tough** *)*
tough time
adversity 731 n.
toupee
wig 228 n.
hair 259 n.
tour
period 110 n.
land travel 267 n.
circuition 314 n.
tour de force
contrivance 623 n.
deed 676 n.
masterpiece 694 n.
tourer
automobile 274 n.
touring company
wanderer 268 n.
tourism
land travel 267 n.
sport 837 n.
tourist
traveller 268 n.
spectator 441 n.
tourist-class
cheap 812 adj.
tourmaline
gem 844 n.
tournament, tourney
contest 716 n.
pageant 875 n.
tourniquet
ligature 47 n.
compressor 198 n.
stopper 264 n.
surgical dressing 658 n.
tousle
jumble 63 vb.
roughen 259 vb.
tout
request 761 vb.
petitioner 763 n.
seller 793 n.
commender 923 n.
tovarich, tovarish
title 870 n.
tow
fibre 208 n.
navigate 269 vb.
draw 288 vb.
towards
straight on 249 adv.
towards 281 adv.
towel
rub 333 vb.
dryer 342 n.
cleaning cloth 648 n.
towelling
textile 222 n.
tower
be great 32 vb.
edifice 164 n.
dwelling 192 n.
be large 195 vb.
high structure 209 n.
be high 209 vb.
ascend 308 vb.
refuge 662 n.
fort 713 n.
church exterior 990 n.
— over
be superior 34 vb.
influence 178 vb.
Tower, the
prison 748 n.
tower block
flat 192 n.
towering
furious 176 adj.
high 209 adj.
tower of silence
cemetery 364 n.
tower of strength
refuge 662 n.
aider 703 n.
tow-headed
whitish 427 adj.
to wit
namely 80 adv.
in plain words 520 adv.
towline
cable 47 n.
traction 288 n.
town
district 184 n.
abode 192 n.
housing 192 n.
town centre
focus 76 n.
town crier
publicizer 528 n.
townee
native 191 n.
township
district 184 n.
townspeople
inhabitants 191 n.
commonalty 869 n.
towny
urban 192 adj.
towpath
path 624 n.
toxaemia
infection 651 n.
poisoning 659 n.
toxic
harmful 645 adj.
unclean 649 adj.
toxic 653 adj.
baneful 659 adj.
dangerous 661 adj.
toxin
poison 659 n.
toxophilite
shooter 287 n.
toy
little 196 adj.
bauble 639 n.
plaything 837 n.
caress 889 vb.
trace
copy 20 vb.
small quantity 33 n.
remainder 41 n.
effect 157 n.
outline 233 n.vb.
detect 484 vb.
identification 547 n.
trace 548 n.
decorate 844 vb.
— back
look back 125 vb.
retrospect 505 vb.
traceable
attributed 158 adj.
recorded 548 adj.
tracery
network 222 n.

curve 248 n.
ornamental art 844 n.
pattern 844 n.
traces
coupling 47 n.
fetter 748 n.
trachea
air pipe 353 n.
trachoma
tropical disease 651 n.
track
continuity 71 n.
accompany 89 vb.
water travel 269 n.
direction 281 n.
follow 284 vb.
passage 305 n.
gramophone 414 n.
identification 547 n.
trace 548 n.
pursue 619 vb.
path 624 n.
railway 624 n.
racing 716 n.
arena 724 n.
— down
detect 484 vb.
tracker
hunter 619 n.
track events
sport 837 n.
tracking station
astronomy 321 n.
trackless
spacious 183 adj.
difficult 700 adj.
track record
conduct 688 n.
tracksuit
suit 228 n.
tract
region 184 n.
land 344 n.
reading matter 589 n.
dissertation 591 n.
piety 979 n.
tractability
willingness 597 n.
persuadability 612 n.
obedience 739 n.
tractable
flexible 327 adj.
tractable 701 adj.
Tractarian
Anglican 976 adj.
church party 978 n.
traction
transport 272 n.
traction 288 n.
traction engine
locomotive 274 n.
tractor
vehicle 274 n.
farm tool 370 n.
trad
music 412 n.
trade
interchange 151 vb.
transference 272 n.
business 622 n.
vocation 622 n.n.
transfer 780 n.
assign 780 vb.
trade 791 n.vb.
sell 793 vb.
— on
use 673 vb.
trade fair
market 796 n.
trademark
speciality 80 n.
identification 547 n.
label 547 n.
trader
merchant ship 275 n.
tradesman
artisan 686 n.
tradespeople 794 n.
trade union, trades union
association 706 n.
trade unionist
worker 686 n.
participator 775 n.
trade wind
wind 352 n.
trading centre
emporium 796 n.
tradition
tradition 127 n.
permanence 144 n.
information 524 n.
narrative 590 n.
habit 610 n.
theology 973 n.
traditional
conformable 83 adj.
immemorial 127 adj.
descriptive 590 adj.
habitual 610 adj.
orthodox 976 adj.
traditionalist
conformist 83 n.
the orthodox 976 n.
traduce
misinterpret 521 vb.
defame 926 vb.
traffic
motion 265 n.
conveyance 267 n.
passing along 305 n.
trade 791 n.
trafficator
signal light 420 n.
indicator 547 n.
traffic engineering
road 624 n.
traffic in
trade 791 vb.
traffic island
refuge 662 n.
traffic jam
procession 71 n.
obstacle 702 n.
trafficking
trading 791 adj.
traffic lights
traffic control 305 n.
traffic warden
traffic control 305 n.
tragacanth
resin 357 n.
tragedian, tragedienne
actor 594 n.
tragedy
stage play 594 n.
evil 616 n.
deterioration 655 n.
tragic
dramatic 594 adj.
distressing 827 adj.
tragic flaw
defect 647 n.
tragicomedy
stage play 594 n.
tragicomic
dramatic 594 adj.
funny 849 adj.
trail
continuity 71 n.
be dispersed 75 vb.
be long 203 vb.
hang 217 vb.
be behind 238 vb.
wander 267 vb.
move slowly 278 vb.
follow 284 vb.
draw 288 vb.
odour 394 n.
identification 547 n.
trace 548 n.
pursue 619 vb.
path 624 n.
— one's coat
make quarrels 709 vb.
enrage 891 vb.
trail bike
bicycle 274 n.
trail-blazer
precursor 66 n.
preparer 669 n.
trailer
example 83 n.
small house 192 n.
cart 274 n.
follower 284 n.
traction 288 n.
plant 366 n.
film 445 n.
advertisement 528 n.
hunter 619 n.
trailing
unassembled 75 adj.
train
adjunct 40 n.
retinue 67 n.
procession 71 n.
make conform 83 vb.
hanging object 217 n.
garment 228 n.
rear 238 n.
train 274 n.
follower 284 n.
break in 369 vb.
train 534 vb.
learn 536 vb.
habituate 610 vb.
railway 624 n.
make ready 669 vb.
— one's sights (on)
aim 281 vb.
aim at 617 vb.
train-bearer
retainer 742 n.
bridal party 894 n.
trained
instructed 490 adj.
habituated 610 adj.
prepared 669 adj.
expert 694 adj.
obedient 739 adj.
trainee
beginner 538 n.
trainer
breeder 369 n.
trainer 537 n.
preparer 669 n.
director 690 n.
training
teaching 534 n.
exercise 682 n.
training college
training school 539 n.
train of thought
thought 449 n.
train spotter
spectator 441 n.
traipse
wander 267 vb.
trait
temperament 5 n.
speciality 80 n.
feature 445 n.
identification 547 n.
habit 610 n.
affections 817 n.
traitor
deceiver 545 n.
tergiversator 603 n.
revolter 738 n.
enemy 881 n.
evildoer 904 n.
undutifulness 918 n.
knave 938 n.
traitorous
disobedient 738 adj.
perfidious 930 adj.
trajectory
curve 248 n.
route 624 n.
tram
tram 274 n.
tramlines
regularity 81 n.
parallelism 219 n.
habit 610 n.
railway 624 n.

trammel
hinder 702 vb.
fetter 747 vb.
trammels
encumbrance 702 n.
fetter 748 n.
tramp
nonconformist 84 n.
gait 265 n.
walk 267 vb.
wanderer 268 n.
voyage 269 vb.
merchant ship 275 n.
move slowly 278 vb.
idler 679 n.
beggar 763 n.
poor person 801 n.
low fellow 869 n.
trample
flatten 216 vb.
kick 279 vb.
fell 311 vb.
oppress 735 vb.
— on
ill-treat 645 vb.
subjugate 745 vb.
be insolent 878 vb.
despise 922 vb.
— under foot
suppress 165 vb.
defeat 727 vb.
not observe 769 vb.
trampled
rough 259 adj.
marshy 347 adj.
trampoline
recoil 280 n.
lifter 310 n.
tramway
railway 624 n.
trance
quiescence 266 n.
insensibility 375 n.
fantasy 513 n.
sleep 679 n.
tranquil
tranquil 266 adj.
reposeful 683 adj.
peaceful 717 adj.
impassive 820 adj.
inexcitable 823 adj.
pleasurable 826 adj.
tranquillity
content 828 n.
lack of wonder 865 n.
tranquillize, tranquillise
pacify 719 vb.
tranquillize 823 vb.
tranquillizer, tranquilliser
moderator 177 n.
drug 658 n.
transact
do business 622 vb.
do 676 vb.
deal with 688 vb.
transaction(s)
event 154 n.
affairs 154 n.
record 548 n.
action 676 n.
deed 676 n.
trade 791 n.
transatlantic
extraneous 59 adj.
removed 199 adj.
transcend
be superior 34 vb.
be good 644 vb.
transcendence, transcendency
extrinsicality 6 n.
originality 21 n.
overstepping 306 n.
perfection 646 n.
divine attribute 965 n.
transcendent
inimitable 21 adj.
supreme 34 adj.
immaterial 320 adj.
divine 965 adj.
transcendental
numerical 85 adj.
inexpressible 517 adj.
cabbalistic 984 adj.
transcendentalism
philosophy 449 n.
occultism 984 n.
transcendental meditation, T M
meditation 449 n.
transcribe
copy 20 vb.
translate 520 vb.
write 586 vb.
transcriber
calligrapher 586 n.
transcript
copy 22 n.
script 586 n.
transcription
transformation 143 n.
transference 272 n.
musical piece 412 n.
writing 586 n.
transect
bisect 92 vb.
be oblique 220 vb.
transection
crossing 222 n.
transept
church interior 990 n.
transfer
duplicate 22 n.
disunite 46 vb.
transition 147 n.
substitution 150 n.
displace 188 vb.
move 265 vb.
transference 272 n.
transfer 272 vb.
carry 273 vb.
picture 553 n.
deposal 752 n.
acquisition 771 n.
nonretention 779 n.
transfer 780 n.
assign 780 vb.
giving 781 n.
transferable
transferable 272 adj.
transferable vote
vote 605 n.
transference
change 143 n.
interchange 151 n.
transference 272 n.
passage 305 n.
metaphor 519 n.
(See **transfer** *)*
Transfiguration
theophany 965 n.
transfigure
modify 143 vb.
transform 147 vb.
make better 654 vb.
beautify 841 vb.
transfix
pierce 263 vb.
transfixed
fixed 153 adj.
still 266 adj.
wondering 864 adj.
transform
modify 143 vb.
transform 147 vb.
revolutionize 149 vb.
influence 178 vb.
make better 654 vb.
pervert 655 vb.
practise occultism 984 vb.
transformation
transformation 143 n.
beautification 843 n.
transformation scene
spectacle 445 n.
stage show 594 n.
thaumaturgy 864 n.
transformer
electronics 160 n.
transfuse
infuse 303 vb.
make flow 350 vb.
transfusion
mixture 43 n.
transference 272 n.
surgery 658 n.
transgress
encroach 306 vb.
disobey 738 vb.
not observe 769 vb.
do wrong 914 vb.
transgression
wickedness 934 n.
guilty act 936 n.
lawbreaking 954 n.
tranship, transship
displace 188 vb.
transpose 272 vb.
transience
transience 114 n.
transient
elapsing 111 adj.
transient 114 adj.
unstable 152 adj.
dweller 191 n.
dying 361 adj.
disappearing 446 adj.
uncertain 474 adj.
transilluminate
make bright 417 vb.
be transparent 422 vb.
transistor
electronics 160 n.
broadcasting 531 n.
transistorize, transistorise
empower 160 vb.
transit
transition 147 n.
motion 265 n.
passage 305 n.
transit instrument
astronomy 321 n.
transition
change 143 n.
transition 147 n.
transference 272 n.
passage 305 n.
transitive verb
part of speech 564 n.
transitory
transient 114 adj.
translate
transform 147 vb.
transpose 272 vb.
translate 520 vb.
translation
imitation 20 n.
copy 22 n.
change 143 n.
transference 272 n.
translation 520 n.
translator
interpreter 520 n.
transliterate
copy 20 vb.
transpose 272 vb.
translate 520 vb.
spell 558 vb.
translocation
displacement 188 n.
transference 272 n.
translucent
undimmed 417 adj.
semitransparent 424 adj.
transmigration
wandering 267 n.
transformation 143 n.
transmission
broadcast 531 n.
transmit
send 272 vb.

transfer 272 vb.
pass 305 vb.
communicate 524 vb.
assign 780 vb.
transmitter
broadcasting 531 n.
transmute
modify 143 vb.
convert 147 vb.
transoceanic
removed 199 adj.
transom
beam 218 n.
prop 218 n.
cross 222 n.
window 263 n.
transonic
speedy 277 adj.
trans-Pacific
removed 199 adj.
transparency
transparency 422 n.
photography 551 n.
transparent
insubstantial 4 adj.
undimmed 417 adj.
transparent 422 adj.
intelligible 516 adj.
disclosing 526 adj.
perspicuous 567 adj.
artless 699 adj.
trustworthy 929 adj.
transpire
happen 154 vb.
emerge 298 vb.
exude 298 vb.
vaporize 338 vb.
be plain 522 vb.
be disclosed 526 vb.
transplant
substitute 150 n.
implant 303 vb.
cultivate 370 vb.
surgery 658 n.
transplantation
transference 272 n.
transport
displace 188 vb.
move 265 vb.
transport 272 n.
carry 273 vb.
vehicle 274 n.
ship 275 n.
aircraft 276 n.
excitable state 822 n.
delight 826 vb.
punish 963 vb.
transportation
penalty 963 n.
transporter
carrier 273 n.
transports
warm feeling 818 n.
joy 824 n.
transpose
jumble 63 vb.
interchange 151 vb.
invert 221 vb.
move 265 vb.
transpose 272 vb.
compose music 413 vb.
transposition
change 143 n.
transsexual
nonconformist 84 n.
transubstantiation
transformation 143 n.
the sacrament 988 n.
transude
exude 298 vb.
transverse
oblique 220 adj.
crossed 222 adj.
transvestite
nonconformist 84 n.
tranter
carrier 273 n.
trap
receptacle 194 n.
orifice 263 n.
close 264 vb.
carriage 274 n.
detect 484 vb.
surprise 508 vb.
ambush 527 n.
trap 542 n.
ensnare 542 vb.
stage set 594 n.
danger 661 n.
pitfall 663 n.
stratagem 698 n.
imprison 747 vb.
take 786 vb.
trapdoor
doorway 263 n.
trapeze artist
athlete 162 n.
trapezium
angular figure 247 n.
trapezoidal
angulated 247 adj.
trapper
killer 362 n.
hunter 619 n.
trappings
dressing 228 n.
equipment 630 n.
trimming 844 n.
Trappist
taciturnity 582 n.
monk 986 n.
trash
novel 590 n.
bauble 639 n.
nonentity 639 n.
rubbish 641 n.
bad person 938 n.
trashy
meaningless 515 adj.
profitless 641 adj.
trattoria
inn 192 n.
trauma
disease 651 n.
wound 655 n.
traumatic
medical 658 adj.
felt 818 adj.
distressing 827 adj.
travail
labour 682 n.
adversity 731 n.
travel
be in motion 265 vb.
land travel 267 n.
travel 267 vb.
move fast 277 vb.
traveller
traveller 268 n.
seller 793 n.
traveller's cheque
paper money 797 n.
traveller's tale
fable 543 n.
exaggeration 546 n.
travelogue
film 445 n.
guidebook 524 n.
description 590 n.
travel-stained
travelling 267 adj.
traverse
counteract 182 vb.
beam 218 n.
traverse 267 vb.
pass 305 vb.
negate 533 vb.
travesty
mimicry 20 n.
misinterpretation 521 n.
misrepresentation 552 n.
bungling 695 n.
laughingstock 851 n.
satire 851 n.
trawl
network 222 n.
enclosure 235 n.
draw 288 vb.
be tentative 461 vb.
hunt 619 vb.
trawler
fishing boat 275 n.
hunter 619 n.
tray
compartment 194 n.
plate 194 n.
treacherous
uncertain 474 adj.
occult 523 adj.
false 541 adj.
deceiving 542 adj.
tergiversating 603 adj.
unsafe 661 adj.
malevolent 898 adj.
undutiful 918 adj.
perfidious 930 adj.
treachery
perfidy 930 n.
treacle
viscidity 354 n.
sweet thing 392 n.
treacly
viscid 354 adj.
feeling 818 adj.
tread
degree 27 n.
stand 218 n.
gait 265 n.
walk 267 vb.
ascent 308 n.
trace 548 n.
use 673 vb.
— carefully
be in difficulty 700 vb.
— down
oppress 735 vb.
— in the steps of
follow 284 vb.
— on
kick 279 vb.
ill-treat 645 vb.
subjugate 745 vb.
— on one's toes
make quarrels 709 vb.
hurt 827 vb.
— on the heels of
come after 65 vb.
be near 200 vb.
— underfoot
oppress 735 vb.
shame 867 vb.
— warily
be cautious 858 vb.
— water
swim 269 vb.
treadle
propellant 287 n.
treadmill
uniformity 16 n.
labour 682 n.
bore 838 n.
instrument of torture 964 n.
treason
sedition 738 n.
perfidy 930 n.
treasonable
perfidious 930 adj.
treasure
store 632 n.vb.
exceller 644 n.
safeguard 660 vb.
preserve 666 vb.
acquisition 771 n.
funds 797 n.
a beauty 841 n.
honour 866 vb.
love 887 vb.
pet 889 vb.
darling 890 n.
treasure chest
treasury 799 n.
treasure house
storage 632 n.
treasury 799 n.

treasure hunt
search 459 n.
treasurer
provider 633 n.
consignee 754 n.
receiver 782 n.
minter 797 n.
treasurer 798 n.
accountant 808 n.
treasure trove
discovery 484 n.
benefit 615 n.
acquisition 771 n.
treasury
accumulation 74 n.
anthology 592 n.
storage 632 n.
treasurer 798 n.
treasury 799 n.
treasury note
title deed 767 n.
paper money 797 n.
treat
modify 143 vb.
pleasure 376 n.
dissertate 591 vb.
doctor 658 vb.
remedy 658 vb.
behave 688 vb.
contract 765 vb.
make terms 766 vb.
give 781 vb.
defray 804 vb.
enjoyment 824 n.
pleasurableness 826 n.
amusement 837 n.
— as
substitute 150 vb.
— as one
identify 13 vb.
— as one's own
appropriate 786 vb.
— gently
look after 457 vb.
— lightly
not respect 921 vb.
— like dirt
subjugate 745 vb.
hold cheap 922 vb.
— with
cooperate 706 vb.
make terms 766 vb.
treatise
dissertation 591 n.
treatment
change 143 n.
agency 173 n.
painting 553 n.
way 624 n.
therapy 658 n.
use 673 n.
conduct 688 n.
treaty
conference 584 n.
treaty 765 n.
treble
augment 36 vb.
treble 94 adj.vb.
stridor 407 n.
vocalist 413 n.
treble clef
notation 410 n.
tree
tall creature 209 n.
tree 366 n.
treed
hindered 702 adj.
treeless
unproductive 172 adj.
treelike
arboreal 366 adj.
treetop
vertex 213 n.
foliage 366 n.
trefoil
three 93 n.
heraldry 547 n.
pattern 844 n.
trek
land travel 267 n.
travel 267 vb.
trekker
traveller 268 n.
trellis
frame 218 n.
network 222 n.
tremble
vary 152 vb.
be weak 163 vb.
be agitated 318 vb.
be cold 380 vb.
sound faint 401 vb.
show feeling 818 vb.
be excited 821 vb.
quake 854 vb.
— in the balance
be pending 136 vb.
be uncertain 474 vb.
be in danger 661 vb.
tremendous
prodigious 32 adj.
frightening 854 adj.
tremolo
roll 403 n.
musical note 410 n.
adagio 412 adv.
tremor
outbreak 176 n.
oscillation 317 n.
agitation 318 n.
nervous disorders 651 n.
danger signal 665 n.
feeling 818 n.
nervousness 854 n.
tremulous
agitated 318 adj.
irresolute 601 adj.
nervous 854 adj.
trench
gap 201 n.
fence 235 n.
excavation 255 n.
furrow 262 n.
conduit 351 n.
refuge 662 n.
defences 713 n.
trenchant
keen 174 adj.
assertive 532 adj.
concise 569 adj.
forceful 571 adj.
disapproving 924 adj.
trench coat
overcoat 228 n.
trencher
plate 194 n.
trencherman, trencherwoman
eater 301 n.
glutton 947 n.
trenches
battleground 724 n.
trench on/upon
be near 200 vb.
encroach 306 vb.
trend
continuity 71 n.
go on 146 vb.
ability 160 n.
tendency 179 n.
direction 281 n.
point to 281 vb.
approach 289 vb.
intention 617 n.
liking 859 n.
trend-setter
precursor 66 n.
trendy
modernist 126 n.
modern 126 adj.
fashionable 848 adj.
trephine, trepan
pierce 263 vb.
doctor 658 vb.
trepidation
agitation 318 n.
excitable state 822 n.
fear 854 n.
trespass
interfere 231 vb.
intrude 297 vb.
encroach 306 vb.
disobey 738 vb.
wrong 914 n.
be undue 916 vb.
be wicked 934 vb.
guilty act 936 n.
lawbreaking 954 n.
trespasser
intruder 59 n.
tresses
hair 259 n.
trestle
frame 218 n.
trews
trousers 228 n.
tri-
three 93 adj.
triable
legal 953 adj.
illegal 954 adj.
triad
three 93 n.
musical note 410 n.
Trinity 965 n.
trial
enquiry 459 n.
experiment 461 n.
bane 659 n.
preparation 669 n.
attempt 671 n.
difficulty 700 n.
adversity 731 n.
suffering 825 n.
legal trial 959 n.
trial and error
empiricism 461 n.
trial marriage
type of marriage 894 n.
trial of strength
contest 716 n.
trial run
experiment 461 n.
preparation 669 n.
triangle
three 93 n.
angular figure 247 n.
gong 414 n.
triangle of forces
science of forces 162 n.
triangular
angulated 247 adj.
triangulate
measure 465 vb.
tribal
ethnic 11 adj.
national 371 adj.
tribalism
social group 371 n.
government 733 n.
tribe
family 11 n.
race 11 n.
group 74 n.
breed 77 n.
multitude 104 n.
genealogy 169 n.
native 191 n.
community 708 n.
tribulation
difficulty 700 n.
suffering 825 n.
painfulness 827 n.
tribunal
council 692 n.
jurisdiction 955 n.
tribunal 956 n.
tribunate
position of authority 733 n.
tribune
rostrum 539 n.
leader 690 n.
official 690 n.
tributary
stream 350 n.
subject 745 adj.

giving 781 adj.
tribute
service 745 n.
gift 781 n.
receiving 782 n.
payment 804 n.
tax 809 n.
thanks 907 n.
dueness 915 n.
praise 923 n.
reward 962 n.
trice
instant 116 n.
trice up
tighten 45 vb.
draw 288 vb.
elevate 310 vb.
trichology
hairdressing 843 n.
trichotomy
trisection 95 n.
trichroism
variegation 437 n.
trick
trickery 542 n.
befool 542 vb.
habit 610 n.
contrivance 623 n.
labour 682 n.
skill 694 n.
stratagem 698 n.
revel 837 n.
affectation 850 n.
foul play 930 n.
— out
primp 843 vb.
decorate 844 vb.
trick cyclist
psychologist 447 n.
trickery
duplicity 541 n.
trickery 542 n.
foul play 930 n.
trickle
small quantity 33 n.
fewness 105 n.
move slowly 278 vb.
flow out 298 vb.
be wet 341 vb.
flow 350 vb.
trifle 639 n.
trick of light
visual fallacy 440 n.
trick of speech
identification 547 n.
tricks of the trade
trickery 542 n.
stratagem 698 n.
trickster
trickster 545 n.
slyboots 698 n.
knave 938 n.
tricksy
cunning 698 adj.
merry 833 adj.
tricky
deceiving 542 adj.
cunning 698 adj.
difficult 700 adj.
dishonest 930 adj.
tricolour
three 93 adj.
variegated 437 adj.
flag 547 n.
tricorne
headgear 228 n.
tricot
textile 222 n.
tricycle
bicycle 274 n.
plaything 837 n.
trident
three 93 n.
authority 733 n.
Tridentine decrees
orthodoxy 976 n.
tried
certain 473 adj.
matured 669 adj.
expert 694 adj.
approved 923 adj.
trustworthy 929 adj.
triennial
seasonal 141 adj.
triennium
three 93 n.
trier
stamina 600 n.
trier 671 n.
trifle
insubstantial thing 4 n.
small quantity 33 n.
dessert 301 n.
be inattentive 456 vb.
neglect 458 vb.
trifle 639 n.
be inactive 679 vb.
— with
befool 542 vb.
not respect 921 vb.
hold cheap 922 vb.
trifling
inconsiderable 33 adj.
light-minded 456 adj.
folly 499 n.
trivial 639 adj.
contemptible 922 adj.
triforium
church interior 990 n.
trigger
handle 218 n.
tool 630 n.
firearm 723 n.
trigger-happy
murderous 362 adj.
excitable 822 adj.
rash 857 adj.
trigger off
initiate 68 vb.
cause 156 vb.
triglyph
ornamental art 844 n.
trigon
angular figure 247 n.
trigonometry
mathematics 86 n.
angular measure 247 n.
measurement 465 n.
trilby
headgear 228 n.
trill
flow 350 vb.
roll 403 n.vb.
musical note 410 n.
sing 413 vb.
pronunciation 577 n.
voice 577 vb.
trillion
over one hundred 99 n.
trilobite
fossil 125 n.
trilogy
three 93 n.
poem 593 n.
stage play 594 n.
trim
state 7 n.
adjust 24 vb.
equalize 28 vb.
cut 46 vb.
orderly 60 adj.
make conform 83 vb.
make smaller 198 vb.
shorten 204 vb.
dressing 228 n.
form 243 n.
dissemble 541 vb.
tergiversate 603 vb.
clean 648 vb.
personable 841 adj.
hairdressing 843 n.
decorate 844 vb.vb.
trimaran
raft 275 n.
trimester
period 110 n.
trimeter
prosody 593 n.
trimmer
deceiver 545 n.
tergiversator 603 n.
trimming
edging 234 n.
trimming 844 n.
trimmings
adjunct 40 n.
leavings 41 n.
Trimurti
Hindu deities 967 n.
trine
three 93 n.
treble 94 adj.
Trinitarianism
orthodoxy 976 n.
trinity
triality 93 n.
Trinity 965 n.
trinket
bauble 639 n.
plaything 837 n.
finery 844 n.
trio
three 93 n.
duet 412 n.
triolet
verse form 593 n.
trip
be in motion 265 vb.
land travel 267 n.
walk 267 vb.
collide 279 vb.
tumble 309 vb.
elevate 310 vb.
fell 311 vb.
leap 312 vb.
mistake 495 n.
blunder 495 vb.
ensnare 542 vb.
be clumsy 695 vb.
hinder 702 vb.
failure 728 n.
excitable state 822 n.
dance 837 vb.
— out
drug oneself 949 vb.
— over
collide 279 vb.
be clumsy 695 vb.
— up
ensnare 542 vb.
hinder 702 vb.
tripartite
trifid 95 adj.
tripe
insides 224 n.
meat 301 n.
silly talk 515 n.
triphibious
three 93 adj.
triphthong
speech sound 398 n.
voice 577 n.
triplane
aircraft 276 n.
triple
augment 36 vb.
treble 94 adj.vb.
triple crown
badge of rule 743 n.
triple jump
leap 312 n.
triples
campanology 412 n.
triplet
three 93 n.
verse form 593 n.
triplex
treble 94 adj.
triplicate
treble 94 adj.vb.

triplicity
triality 93 n.
triplication 94 n.
tripod
three 93 n.
stand 218 n.
tripos
exam 459 n.
tripper
traveller 268 n.
tripping
elegant 575 adj.
active 678 adj.
trippingly
swiftly 277 adv.
by leaps and bounds 312 adv.
triptych
three 93 n.
picture 553 n.
altar 990 n.
tripwire
trap 542 n.
obstacle 702 n.
defences 713 n.
trireme
galley 275 n.
trisect
trisect 95 vb.
trishaw
bicycle 274 n.
triskelion
three 93 n.
heraldry 547 n.
Tristan and Isolde
lovers 887 n.
trite
known 490 adj.
aphoristic 496 adj.
meaningless 515 adj.
usual 610 adj.
dull 840 adj.
Triton
sea god 343 n.
lesser deity 967 n.
Triton among the minnows
superior 34 n.
giant 195 n.
triturate
pulverize 332 vb.
triumph
procession 71 n.
victory 727 n.
triumph 727 vb.
trophy 729 n.
subjugate 745 vb.
rejoicing 835 n.
celebration 876 n.
boast 877 vb.
— over
humiliate 872 vb.
triumphal
celebratory 876 adj.
congratulatory 886 adj.
triumphant
successful 727 adj.
jubilant 833 adj.
celebratory 876 adj.
boastful 877 adj.
triumvirate
three 93 n.
government 733 n.
triune
three 93 adj.
trivet
prop 218 n.
stand 218 n.
furnace 383 n.
trivia
small quantity 33 n.
trifle 639 n.
trivial
inconsiderable 33 adj.
meaningless 515 adj.
trivial 639 adj.
trivium
curriculum 534 n.
trochee
prosody 593 n.
trodden
flat 216 adj.
usual 610 adj.
communicating 624 adj.
troglodyte
dweller 191 n.
humankind 371 n.
solitary 883 n.
troika
carriage 274 n.
Trojan
busy person 678 n.
Trojan horse
ambush 527 n.
trap 542 n.
stratagem 698 n.
enemy 881 n.
perfidy 930 n.
troll
demon 970 n.
elf 970 n.
trolley
stand 218 n.
pushcart 274 n.
tram 274 n.
trolleybus
bus 274 n.
trollop
loose woman 952 n.
prostitute 952 n.
trombone
horn 414 n.
trompe-l'oeil
sham 542 n.
art style 553 n.
troop
band 74 n.
congregate 74 vb.
be many 104 vb.
walk 267 vb.
formation 722 n.
troop-carrier
air force 722 n.
trooper
cavalry 722 n.
trooping the colour
pageant 875 n.
troops
armed force 722 n.
soldier 722 n.
troopship
warship 722 n.
trope
trope 519 n.
ornament 574 n.
trophy
reminder 505 n.
badge 547 n.
monument 548 n.
trophy 729 n.
gift 781 n.
booty 790 n.
honours 866 n.
reward 962 n.
tropical
hot 379 adj.
figurative 519 adj.
tropical disease
tropical disease 651 n.
tropics
heat 379 n.
troposphere
atmosphere 340 n.
trot
gait 265 n.
pedestrianism 267 n.
ride 267 vb.
move fast 277 vb.
— out
repeat 106 vb.
manifest 522 vb.
speak 579 vb.
troth
promise 764 n.
probity 929 n.
Trotskyist, Trot
political party 708 n.
revolter 738 n.
trotter
foot 214 n.
thoroughbred 273 n.
troubadour
musician 413 n.
vocalist 413 n.
poet 593 n.
entertainer 594 n.
trouble
turmoil 61 n.
derange 63 vb.
agitate 318 vb.
give pain 377 vb.
attention 455 n.
evil 616 n.
harm 645 vb.
meddle 678 vb.
exertion 682 n.
difficulty 700 n.
predicament 700 n.
hinder 702 vb.
adversity 731 n.
worry 825 n.
annoyance 827 n.
trouble 827 vb.
— one for
request 761 vb.
— oneself
be attentive 455 vb.
exert oneself 682 vb.
troubled
agitated 318 adj.
suffering 825 adj.
dejected 834 adj.
troublemaker
bane 659 n.
troublemaker 663 n.
agitator 738 n.
troubleshooter
adviser 691 n.
mediator 720 n.
troublesome
laborious 682 adj.
annoying 827 adj.
trouble-spot
pitfall 663 n.
troublous
violent 176 adj.
evil 616 adj.
trough
bowl 194 n.
cavity 255 n.
furrow 262 n.
conduit 351 n.
trounce
strike 279 vb.
defeat 727 vb.
reprove 924 vb.
spank 963 vb.
troupe
band 74 n.
actor 594 n.
party 708 n.
trouper
actor 594 n.
trousers
trousers 228 n.
trouser suit
suit 228 n.
trousseau
clothing 228 n.
store 632 n.
trout
fish food 301 n.
fish 365 n.
trout farm
stock farm 369 n.
trouvaille
discovery 484 n.
acquisition 771 n.
trover
discovery 484 n.
acquisition 771 n.
trow
think 449 vb.
opine 485 vb.
trowel
ladle 194 n.
sharp edge 256 n.
conveyor 274 n.
farm tool 370 n.
troy weight
weighing 322 n.

truancy
absence 190 n.
relinquishment 621 n.
escape 667 n.
undutifulness 918 n.
truant
avoider 620 n.
truce
delay 136 n.
lull 145 n.
interval 201 n.
quiescence 266 n.
peace 717 n.
pacification 719 n.
truck
carrier 273 n.
lorry 274 n.
pushcart 274 n.
train 274 n.
barter 791 n.
trucker
driver 268 n.
truckle (to)
be servile 879 vb.
truckle bed
bed 218 n.
truckload
great quantity 32 n.
truculent
ungracious 885 adj.
cruel 898 adj.
trudge
walk 267 vb.
move slowly 278 vb.
true
real 1 adj.
straight 249 adj.
accurate 494 adj.
true 494 adj.
veracious 540 adj.
observant 768 adj.
trustworthy 929 adj.
true bill
vindication 927 n.
true-blue
conformable 83 adj.
sectional 708 adj.
obedient 739 adj.
patriotic 901 adj.
true-born
genuine 494 adj.
true grit
stamina 600 n.
true-hearted
veracious 540 adj.
true love
loved one 887 n.
lover 887 n.
true-love knot
ligature 47 n.
love token 889 n.
true saying
maxim 496 n.
true to life
lifelike 18 adj.
representing 551 adj.
descriptive 590 adj.
true to type
typical 83 adj.
truffle
vegetable 301 n.
trug
basket 194 n.
truism
axiom 496 n.
maxim 496 n.
lack of meaning 515 n.
truly
actually 1 adv.
positively 32 adv.
truly 494 adv.
truthfully 540 adv.
as promised 764 adv.
trump(s)
be superior 34 vb.
instrument 628 n.
means 629 n.
overmaster 727 vb.
good person 937 n.
trump card
advantage 34 n.
contrivance 623 n.
chief thing 638 n.
trumped up
false 541 adj.
deceiving 542 adj.
untrue 543 adj.
trumpery
meaningless 515 adj.
bauble 639 n.
trivial 639 adj.
trumpet
megaphone 400 n.
resound 404 vb.
shrill 407 vb.
play music 413 vb.
horn 414 n.
proclaim 528 vb.
call 547 n.
boast 877 vb.
praise 923 vb.
trumpet call
inducement 612 n.
command 737 n.
trumpeter
instrumentalist 413 n.
trumpet-tongued
loud 400 adj.
eloquent 579 adj.
truncate
shorten 204 vb.
deform 244 vb.
truncated
incomplete 55 adj.
truncheon
club 723 n.
badge of rule 743 n.
trundle
move 265 vb.
propel 287 vb.
rotate 315 vb.
trunk
chief part 52 n.
piece 53 n.
incompleteness 55 n.
box 194 n.
prop 218 n.
cylinder 252 n.
tree 366 n.
communicating 624 adj.
trunk line
telecommunication 531 n.
trunk road
road 624 n.
trunks
beachwear 228 n.
legwear 228 n.
trunnion
pivot 218 n.
truss
tie 45 vb.
bunch 74 n.
beam 218 n.
prop 218 n.
trust
belief 485 n.
expectation 507 n.
association 706 n.
corporation 708 n.
mandate 751 n.
credit 802 n.
hope 852 n.vb.
piety 979 n.
— in
be certain 473 vb.
— with
commission 751 vb.
trustee
consignee 754 n.
possessor 776 n.
recipient 782 n.
treasurer 798 n.
trusteeship
commission 751 n.
trustful
believing 485 adj.
credulous 487 adj.
trustworthy
credible 485 adj.
genuine 494 adj.
veracious 540 adj.
safe 660 adj.
observant 768 adj.
reputable 866 adj.
trustworthy 929 adj.
trusty
prisoner 750 n.
truth
reality 1 n.
demonstration 478 n.
truth 494 n.
maxim 496 n.
veracity 540 n.
probity 929 n.
truthful
true 494 adj.
veracious 540 adj.
trustworthy 929 adj.
try
taste 386 vb.
enquire 459 vb.
experiment 461 vb.
judge 480 vb.
be willing 597 vb.
persevere 600 vb.
tempt 612 vb.
attempt 671 n.vb.
avail oneself of 673 vb.
exert oneself 682 vb.
torment 827 vb.
be tedious 838 vb.
— conclusions with
quarrel 709 vb.
contend 716 vb.
— for
aim at 617 vb.
— it on
deceive 542 vb.
behave 688 vb.
— on
wear 228 vb.
— one's hand at
attempt 671 vb.
— one's luck
be tentative 461 vb.
gamble 618 vb.
trying
fatiguing 684 adj.
annoying 827 adj.
try-out
experiment 461 n.
trypanosomiasis
tropical disease 651 n.
try square
gauge 465 n.
tryst
social round 882 n.
tsar, czar, tzar
sovereign 741 n.
tsardom
position of authority 733 n.
tsetse fly
insect 365 n.
T-shirt
shirt 228 n.
tsunami
wave 350 n.
tub
vat 194 n.
vessel 194 n.
bulk 195 n.
ship 275 n.
ablutions 648 n.
tuba
horn 414 n.
tubby
fleshy 195 adj.
thick 205 adj.
tube
electronics 160 n.
cylinder 252 n.
excavation 255 n.
tube 263 n.
tunnel 263 n.

conduit 351 n.
railway 624 n.
tuber
vegetable 301 n.
plant 366 n.
tubercular
diseased 651 adj.
tuberculosis
infection 651 n.
tubing
tube 263 n.
tub-thumper
speaker 579 n.
agitator 738 n.
excitant 821 n.
tub-thumping
oratory 579 n.
tubular
tubular 263 adj.
tuck
fold 261 n.vb.
food 301 n.
tuckbox
box 194 n.
tucked away
latent 523 adj.
secluded 883 adj.
tucker
food 301 n.
tuckered out
fatigued 684 adj.
tucket
resonance 404 n.
tune 412 n.
tuck in/into
eat 301 vb.
insert 303 vb.
— up
place 187 vb.
shorten 204 vb.
Tudor
olden 127 adj.
architectural 192 adj.
Tudor rose
heraldry 547 n.
tuff
rock 344 n.
ash 381 n.
tuft
bunch 74 n.
fewness 105 n.
hair 259 n.
tug
move 265 vb.
boat 275 n.
traction 288 n.
draw 288 vb.
attraction 291 n.
extraction 304 n.
exertion 682 n.
work 682 vb.
— one's forelock
greet 884 vb.
tug of war
opposition 704 n.
contest 716 n.
tuition
teaching 534 n.
tulle
textile 222 n.
tumble
jumble 63 vb.
be inverted 221 vb.
descent 309 n.
tumble 309 vb.
fell 311 vb.
oscillate 317 vb.
— to
discover 484 vb.
understand 516 vb.
tumbledown
dilapidated 655 adj.
tumble-dry
dry 342 vb.
tumbler
athlete 162 n.
cup 194 n.
tumbril
vehicle 274 n.
tumescent
expanded 197 adj.
convex 253 adj.
tumid
expanded 197 adj.
convex 253 adj.
rhetorical 574 adj.
tummy
maw 194 n.
insides 224 n.
tummy ache
digestive disorders 651 n.
tumour
dilation 197 n.
swelling 253 n.
cancer 651 n.
tumult
turmoil 61 n.
commotion 318 n.
loudness 400 n.
discord 411 n.
activity 678 n.
revolt 738 n.
tumultuous
disorderly 61 adj.
violent 176 adj.
tumulus
earthwork 253 n.
tun
vat 194 n.
tuna, tunny
fish food 301 n.
fish 365 n.
tundra
plain 348 n.
tune
adjust 24 vb.
synchronize 123 vb.
sound 398 n.
harmonize 410 vb.
tune 412 n.
play music 413 vb.
make ready 669 vb.
— in
hear 415 vb.
tuneful
pleasant 376 adj.
melodious 410 adj.
poetic 593 adj.
— up
harmonize 410 vb.
make ready 669 vb.
tuneless
discordant 411 adj.
tunic
wrapping 226 n.
jacket 228 n.
tuning fork
prototype 23 n.
gong 414 n.
tunnel
excavation 255 n.
tunnel 263 n.
pierce 263 vb.
descend 309 vb.
bridge 624 n.
railway 624 n.
tunneller
excavator 255 n.
tunnel vision
blindness 439 n.
tup
sheep 365 n.
male animal 372 n.
tuppence
trifle 639 n.
tu quoque
rejoinder 460 n.
turban
headgear 228 n.
coil 251 n.
turbid
opaque 423 adj.
dirty 649 adj.
turbine
causal means 156 n.
sources of energy 160 n.
rotator 315 n.
machine 630 n.
turbojet
aircraft 276 n.
turboprop
aircraft 276 n.
turbot
fish food 301 n.
fish 365 n.
turbulence, turbulency
storm 176 n.
roughness 259 n.
commotion 318 n.
turbulent
disorderly 61 adj.
violent 176 adj.
excitable 822 adj.
tureen
bowl 194 n.
turf
piece 53 n.
soil 344 n.
grassland 348 n.
grass 366 n.
fuel 385 n.
arena 724 n.
Turf, the
racing 716 n.
gambling 618 n.
turf accountant
gambler 618 n.
turf out
eject 300 vb.
make unwelcome 883 vb.
turgid
expanded 197 adj.
convex 253 adj.
diffuse 570 adj.
rhetorical 574 adj.
inelegant 576 adj.
ostentatious 875 adj.
turkey
table bird 365 n.
turkey cock
proud person 871 n.
Turkish bath
heater 383 n.
ablutions 648 n.
Turkish coffee
soft drink 301 n.
Turkish delight
sweets 301 n.
Turk's head
ligature 47 n.
coil 251 n.
turmeric
condiment 389 n.
turmoil
turmoil 61 n.
havoc 165 n.
violence 176 n.
commotion 318 n.
activity 678 n.
anarchy 734 n.
revolt 738 n.
turn
period 110 n.
periodicity 141 n.
change 143 n.vb.
reversion 148 n.
tendency 179 n.
form 243 vb.
curve 248 n.
make round 250 vb.
blunt 257 vb.
land travel 267 n.
deviate 282 vb.
circuition 314 n.
rotation 315 n.
rotate 315 vb.
be sour 393 vb.
lack of expectation 508 n.
interpretation 520 n.
stage show 594 n.
circuit 626 vb.
aptitude 694 n.
parry 713 vb.
feeling 818 n.
— a blind eye
diregard 458 vb.
not act 677 vb.
— about
revert 148 vb.

turn round 282 vb.
— a deaf ear
be deaf 416 vb.
disregard 458 vb.
refuse 760 vb.
be pitiless 906 vb.
— adrift
eject 300 vb.
liberate 746 vb.
— against
tergiversate 603 vb.
dissuade 613 vb.
— an honest penny
busy oneself 622 vb.
acquire 771 vb.
— a period
be elegant 575 vb.
— aside
deviate 282 vb.
dissuade 613 vb.
avoid 620 vb.
— away
repel 292 vb.
dismiss 300 vb.
disappoint 509 vb.
be unwilling 598 vb.
refuse 760 vb.
dislike 861 vb.
— back
revert 148 vb.
invert 221 vb.
turn back 286 vb.
recede 290 vb.
— colour
show feeling 818 vb.
— down
fold 261 vb.
refuse 760 vb.
— down the volume
mute 401 vb.
— in
sleep 679 vb.
— inside out
invert 221 vb.
search 459 vb.
— into
convert 147 vb.
enter 297 vb.
translate 520 vb.
— nasty
be angry 891 vb.
— on
depend 157 vb.
operate 173 vb.
excite 821 vb.
delight 826 vb.
drug oneself 949 vb.
— one's back (on)
disregard 458 vb.
reject 607 vb.
run away 620 vb.
refuse 760 vb.
make unwelcome 883 vb.
not respect 921 vb.
— one's blood to water
frighten 854 vb.
— one's brain
make mad 503 vb.
— one's coat
apostatize 603 vb.
— one's face to the wall
despair 853 vb.
— one's hand to
busy oneself 622 vb.
undertake 672 vb.
— one's head
make conceited 873 vb.
flatter 925 vb.
— one's stomach
displease 827 vb.
cause dislike 861 vb.
— on one's heel
turn back 286 vb.
circle 314 vb.
— out
become 1 vb.
happen 154 vb.
result 157 vb.
produce 164 vb.
displace 188 vb.
eject 300 vb.
search 459 vb.
— out well
benefit 615 vb.
be successful 727 vb.
be auspicious 730 vb.
— over
be inverted 221 vb.
make curved 248 vb.
fold 261 vb.
transfer 272 vb.
meditate 449 vb.
search 459 vb.
trade 791 vb.
— over a new leaf
be turned to 147 vb.
get better 654 vb.
be penitent 939 vb.
— Queen's evidence
inform 524 vb.
confess 526 vb.
accuse 928 vb.
— round
turn round 282 vb.
circle 314 vb.
— tail
run away 620 vb.
be cowardly 856 vb.
— the corner
change 143 vb.
get better 654 vb.
be restored 656 vb.
— the heat on
compel 740 vb.
— the other cheek
be patient 823 vb.
be humble 872 vb.
forgive 909 vb.
— the scale
predominate 34 vb.
modify 143 vb.
cause 156 vb.
influence 178 vb.
prevail 178 vb.
tell against 467 vb.
dominate 733 vb.
— the stomach
be unpalatable 391 vb.
— the tables (on)
be contrary 14 vb.
invert 221 vb.
tell against 467 vb.
retaliate 714 vb.
— to
be turned to 147 vb.
speak to 583 vb.
busy oneself 622 vb.
seek refuge 662 vb.
— to good account
profit by 137 vb.
find useful 640 vb.
use 673 vb.
— turtle
be inverted 221 vb.
navigate 269 vb.
— under
fold 261 vb.
— up
happen 154 vb.
chance 159 vb.
be present 189 vb.
shorten 204 vb.
fold 261 vb.
arrive 295 vb.
be visible 443 vb.
— up like a bad penny
reoccur 106 vb.
— up one's nose
be fastidious 862 vb.
despise 922 vb.
— up one's toes
die 361 vb.
— upside down
bedevil 63 vb.
modify 143 vb.
— up trumps
be successful 727 vb.
be auspicious 730 vb.
be honourable 929 vb.
turn and turn about
correlation 12 n.
by turns 141 adv.
turncoat
changed person 147 n.
deceiver 545 n.
waverer 601 n.
tergiversator 603 n.
turned
ageing 131 adj.
turned on
excited 821 adj.
drugged 949 adj.
turned out
dressed 228 adj.
turned right up
loud 400 adj.
turned to, be
become 1 vb.
be turned to 147 vb.
turned-up
curved 248 adj.
turner
artisan 686 n.
turning
unstable 152 adj.
labyrinthine 251 adj.
turning point
juncture 8 n.
degree 27 n.
crisis 137 n.
reversion 148 n.
summit 213 n.
limit 236 n.
return 286 n.
important matter 638 n.
turnip
timekeeper 117 n.
vegetable 301 n.
turnip-shaped
rotund 252 adj.
turnkey
doorkeeper 264 n.
gaoler 749 n.
turn of expression
trope 519 n.
phrase 563 n.
turn-off
road 624 n.
turn of the tide
reversion 148 n.
summit 213 n.
inversion 221 n.
return 286 n.
turnout
production 164 n.
dressing 228 n.
turnover
pastries 301 n.
earnings 771 n.
receipt 807 n.
turnpike
road 624 n.
turnspit
domestic 742 n.
turnstile
barrier 235 n.
recording instrument 549 n.
access 624 n.
obstacle 702 n.
treasury 799 n.
turntable
rotator 315 n.
gramophone 414 n.
railway 624 n.
turnup
fold 261 n.
turnup for the book
benefit 615 n.
turpitude
disrepute 867 n.
improbity 930 n.
wickedness 934 n.

turquoise
blueness 435 n.
gem 844 n.
turret
high structure 209 n.
fort 713 n.
turtle
reptile 365 n.
turtle dove
bird 365 n.
love emblem 887 n.
tusk
tooth 256 n.
tusker
pig 365 n.
mammal 365 n.
tussle
contention 716 n.
contend 716 vb.
tussock
bunch 74 n.
small hill 209 n.
tussore, tussah
fibre 208 n.
textile 222 n.
tutelage
teaching 534 n.
learning 536 n.
protection 660 n.
subjection 745 n.
tutelary
tutelary 660 adj.
defending 713 adj.
tutelary saint
benefactor 903 n.
tutor
teach 534 vb.
teacher 537 n.
protector 660 n.
manager 690 n.
domestic 742 n.
keeper 749 n.
tutorial
teaching 534 n.
tutti
loudness 400 n.
duet 412 n.
tut-tut
deprecate 762 vb.
disapprove 924 vb.
tutu
skirt 228 n.
tuxedo
jacket 228 n.
TV
broadcasting 531 n.
(See **television** *)*
TVP
meat 301 n.
twaddle
absurdity 497 n.
silly talk 515 n.
twain
duality 90 n.
twang
resonance 404 n.
play music 413 vb.
pronunciation 577 n.
speech defect 580 n.
tweak
draw 288 vb.
give pain 377 vb.
twee
affected 850 adj.
tweed
textile 222 n.
roughness 259 n.
Tweedledum and Tweedledee
identity 13 n.
duality 90 n.
tweeds
suit 228 n.
tweedy
textural 331 adj.
tweeny
domestic 742 n.
tweet
ululate 409 vb.
tweezers
extractor 304 n.
tool 630 n.
nippers 778 n.
twelfth
fifth and over 99 adj.
twelfth man
substitute 150 n.
twelve
over five 99 n.
twelvemonth
period 110 n.
twelve o'clock
noon 128 n.
twelve-tone scale
key 410 n.
discord 411 n.
twenty
twenty and over 99 n.
twice
double 91 adj.
twice 91 adv.
twice the man/ woman one was
refreshed 685 adj.
twice-told tale
repetition 106 n.
bore 838 n.
twiddle
rotate 315 vb.
touch 378 vb.
— one's thumbs
be inactive 679 vb.
twig
branch 53 n.
foliage 366 n.
know 490 vb.
understand 516 vb.
twiggy
lean 206 adj.
twilight
evening 129 n.
half-light 419 n.
deterioration 655 n.
twilight sleep
insensibility 375 n.
twill
crossed 222 adj.
twilled
textural 331 adj.
twin
kinsman 11 n.
identity 13 n.
analogue 18 n.
compeer 28 n.
join 45 vb.
concomitant 89 n.
dual 90 adj.
double 91 adj. vb.
contemporary 123 n.
twine
tie 45 vb.
fibre 208 n.
enlace 222 vb.
distort 246 vb.
make curved 248 vb.
twine 251 vb.
deviate 282 vb.
decorate 844 vb.
twiner
plant 366 n.
twinge
pang 377 n.
suffering 825 n.
twinge of conscience
guilt 936 n.
penitence 939 n.
twinkle
vary 152 vb.
agitation 318 n.
flash 417 n.
shine 417 vb.
gesticulate 547 vb.
laughter 835 n.
twinkling
instant 116 n.
twin set
jersey 228 n.
twirl
coil 251 n.
twine 251 vb.
rotate 315 vb.
twist
tie 45 vb.
complexity 61 n.
derange 63 vb.
modify 143 vb.
force 176 vb.
fibre 208 n.
obliquity 220 n.
enlace 222 vb.
deform 244 vb.
distortion 246 n.
coil 251 n.
twine 251 vb.
be in motion 265 vb.
deviate 282 vb.
circle 314 vb.
tobacco 388 n.
bias 481 vb.
eccentricity 503 n.
misinterpret 521 vb.
pervert 655 vb.
be cunning 698 vb.
dance 837 n. vb.
make ugly 842 vb.
— and turn
meander 251 vb.
— one's arm
induce 612 vb.
compel 740 vb.
— round one's little finger
befool 542 vb.
dominate 733 vb.
twisted
distorted 246 adj.
convoluted 251 adj.
biased 481 adj.
imperfect 647 adj.
unsightly 842 adj.
twister
jumper 312 n.
gale 352 n.
trickster 545 n.
knave 938 n.
twit
fool 501 n.
ridicule 851 vb.
not respect 921 vb.
dispraise 924 vb.
twitch
move 265 vb.
draw 288 vb.
spasm 318 n.
be agitated 318 vb.
feel pain 377 vb.
gesture 547 n.
twitter
agitation 318 n.
ululate 409 vb.
sing 413 vb.
be loquacious 581 vb.
two
duality 90 n.
two-a-penny
trivial 639 adj.
cheap 812 adj.
two by two
dual 90 adj.
two cheers
indifference 860 n.
detraction 926 n.
two-dimensional
spatial 183 adj.
flat 216 adj.
formed 243 adj.
two-edged
double 91 adj.
equivocal 518 adj.
two-faced
hypocritical 541 adj.
dishonest 930 adj.
twofer
substitute 150 n.
two-hander
stage play 594 n.
two-headed
double 91 adj.
two of a kind
analogue 18 n.
two or three
plurality 101 n.

fewness 105 n.
twopenny-halfpenny
trivial 639 adj.
two shakes
instant 116 n.
two-sided
double 91 adj.
twosome
duality 90 n.
two-step
dance 837 n.
two strings to one's bow
means 629 n.
two-time
deceive 542 vb.
two-way
correlative 12 adj.
interchanged 151 adj.
tycoon
bigwig 638 n.
autocrat 741 n.
rich person 800 n.
tyke
dog 365 n.
tympanum
ear 415 n.
church exterior 990 n.
type
character 5 n.
uniformity 16 n.
analogue 18 n.
copy 20 vb.
prototype 23 n.
sort 77 n.
example 83 n.
form 243 n.
person 371 n.
omen 511 n.
indication 547 n.
image 551 n.
letter 558 n.
write 586 vb.
print-type 587 n.
— out
copy 20 vb.
typecast
dramatize 594 vb.
typeface
print-type 587 n.
typefounder
printer 587 n.
typescript
script 586 n.
book 589 n.
type-setter
printer 587 n.
typewriter
stationery 586 n.
typhoid
digestive disorders 651 n.
infection 651 n.
typhoon
storm 176 n.
gale 352 n.
typhus
infection 651 n.
typical
uniform 16 adj.
similar 18 adj.
generic 77 adj.
general 79 adj.
special 80 adj.
regular 81 adj.
typical 83 adj.
indicating 547 adj.
usual 610 adj.
typify
resemble 18 vb.
predict 511 vb.
mean 514 vb.
figure 519 vb.
manifest 522 vb.
indicate 547 vb.
represent 551 vb.
typist
stenographer 586 n.
typographer
engraver 556 n.
printer 587 n.
typographic error
mistake 495 n.
typography
composition 56 n.
form 243 n.
print 587 n.
typology
theology 973 n.
tyrannical
violent 176 adj.
authoritative 733 adj.
oppressive 735 adj.
cruel 898 adj.
lawless 954 adj.
tyrannize, tyrannise
influence 178 vb.
ill-treat 645 vb.
meddle 678 vb.
rule 733 vb.
oppress 735 vb.
be malevolent 898 vb.
tyrannosaurus rex
animal 365 n.
tyranny
despotism 733 n.
brute force 735 n.
insolence 878 n.
arrogation 916 n.
tyrant
violent creature 176 n.
bane 659 n.
tyrant 735 n.
autocrat 741 n.
usurper 916 n.
monster 938 n.
tyre
wheel 250 n.
tyremark
trace 548 n.
tyro
beginner 538 n.

U

U
well-bred 848 adj.
genteel 868 adj.
ubiety
presence 189 n.
ubiquitous
general 79 adj.
universal 79 adj.
ubiquitous 189 adj.
U-boat
warship 722 n.
U-certificate
film 445 n.
udder
bladder 194 n.
bosom 253 n.
udometer
hygrometry 341 n.
UFO
spaceship 276 n.
unknown thing 491 n.
ugh!
391 int.
861 int.
uglify
impair 655 vb.
make ugly 842 vb.
ugly
deformed 246 adj.
inelegant 576 adj.
dangerous 661 adj.
unpleasant 827 adj.
ugly 842 adj.
sullen 893 adj.
ugly customer
troublemaker 663 n.
low fellow 869 n.
ruffian 904 n.
bad person 938 n.
ugly duckling
nonconformist 84 n.
good person 937 n.
ugly person
eyesore 842 n.
UHF
radiation 417 n.
Uitlander
foreigner 59 n.
ukase
publication 528 n.
decree 737 n.
ukulele
harp 414 n.
ulcer
digestive disorders 651 n.
ulcer 651 n.
bane 659 n.
painfulness 827 n.
ulcerate
impair 655 vb.
ullage
deficit 55 n.
ulster
overcoat 228 n.
ulterior
extraneous 59 adj.
future 124 adj.
distant 199 adj.
ulterior motive
concealment 525 n.
motive 612 n.
ultimate
supreme 34 adj.
ending 69 adj.
fundamental 156 adj.
distant 199 adj.
ultimately
prospectively 124 adv.
late 136 adv.
eventually 154 adv.
ultima Thule
extremity 69 n.
farness 199 n.
limit 236 n.
ultimatum
period 110 n.
limit 236 n.
intention 617 n.
requirement 627 n.
warning 664 n.
demand 737 n.
conditions 766 n.
ultimo
before 119 adv.
ultra
extremely 32 adv.
ultramarine
blue 435 adj.
ultramontanism
Catholicism 976 n.
ultramundane
removed 199 adj.
cosmic 321 adj.
ultraviolet radiation
radiation 417 n.
ultra vires
unwarranted 916 adj.
ululate
cry 408 vb.
vociferate 408 vb.
ululate 409 vb.
weep 836 vb.
umbel
flower 366 n.
umbilical
central 225 adj.
umbilical cord
bond 47 n.
obstetrics 167 n.
umbra
darkness 418 n.
umbrage
foliage 366 n.
resentment 891 n.
umbrella
shade 226 n.

protection 660 n.
shelter 662 n.
umbrella organization
association 706 n.
umlaut
speech sound 398 n.
punctuation 547 n.
umpire
estimator 480 n.
mediator 720 n.
mediate 720 vb.
magistracy 957 n.
umpteen
many 104 adj.
unabashed
unfearing 855 adj.
proud 871 adj.
insolent 878 adj.
unabated
absolute 32 adj.
unable
powerless 161 adj.
useless 641 adj.
unskilful 695 adj.
unable to believe one's eyes
wondering 864 adj.
unable to hear
deaf 416 adj.
unable to move
still 266 adj.
unable to sleep, be
be excited 821 vb.
unabridged
intact 52 adj.
long 203 adj.
unaccented
muted 401 adj.
unacceptable
unpleasant 827 adj.
unacclimatized, unacclimatised
extraneous 59 adj.
unaccommodating
hindering 702 adj.
discourteous 885 adj.
unaccompanied
alone 88 adj.
unaccomplished
unskilful 695 adj.
unaccountable
unusual 84 adj.
changeful 152 adj.
causeless 159 adj.
unexpected 508 adj.
unintelligible 517 adj.
wonderful 864 adj.
nonliable 919 adj.
lawless 954 adj.
unaccustomed
unhabituated 611 adj.
clumsy 695 adj.
unacknowledged
unadmitted 489 adj.
unthanked 908 adj.
unacquainted
ignorant 491 adj.
unadaptable
rigid 326 adj.
useless 641 adj.
unskilful 695 adj.
unadmired
unrespected 921 adj.
unadmitted
unadmitted 489 adj.
unadorned
intelligible 516 adj.
plain 573 adj.
artless 699 adj.
unadulterated
inimitable 21 adj.
unmixed 44 adj.
whole 52 adj.
genuine 494 adj.
plain 573 adj.
unadventurous
quiescent 266 adj.
cautious 858 adj.
unaffected
intact 52 adj.
permanent 144 adj.
veracious 540 adj.
plain 573 adj.
elegant 575 adj.
artless 699 adj.
impassive 820 adj.
nonliable 919 adj.
unaffiliated
independent 744 adj.
unafraid
unfearing 855 adj.
unaggressive
inert 175 adj.
peaceful 717 adj.
unagreed
disagreeing 25 adj.
unaided
weak 163 adj.
hindered 702 adj.
unaimed
indiscriminate 464 adj.
unalike
dissimilar 19 adj.
unalloyed
unmixed 44 adj.
unalluring
unwanted 860 adj.
unalterable
unchangeable 153 adj.
unaltered
identical 13 adj.
unamazed
unastonished 865 adj.
unambiguous
positive 473 adj.
intelligible 516 adj.
veracious 540 adj.
perspicuous 567 adj.
unambitious
apathetic 820 adj.
indifferent 860 adj.
inglorious 867 adj.
modest 874 adj.
unambivalent
positive 473 adj.
un-American
extraneous 59 adj.
unamiable
unkind 898 adj.
unamused
bored 838 adj.
disapproving 924 adj.
unamusing
dull 840 adj.
unanimity
consensus 488 n.
cooperation 706 n.
concord 710 n.
unanimous
agreeing 24 adj.
unannounced
unexpected 508 adj.
unanswerable
demonstrated 478 adj.
completive 725 adj.
lawless 954 adj.
unanticipated
unexpected 508 adj.
unapologizing, unapologising
impenitent 940 adj.
unappalled
unfearing 855 adj.
unappealing
unpleasant 827 adj.
unappeasable
obstinate 602 adj.
revengeful 910 adj.
unappetizing, unappetising
tasteless 387 adj.
unsavoury 391 adj.
unapplied
unused 674 adj.
unappreciated
undervalued 483 adj.
unthanked 908 adj.
unapproachability
unsociability 883 n.
unapproachable
supreme 34 adj.
infinite 107 adj.
removed 199 adj.
impracticable 470 adj.
prideful 871 adj.
unappropriated
unpossessed 774 adj.
not retained 779 adj.
unapproved
disapproved 924 adj.
unapt
unapt 25 adj.
ill-timed 138 adj.
absurd 497 adj.
inexpedient 643 adj.
unskilful 695 adj.
unarguable
undisputed 473 adj.
unaristocratic
plebeian 869 adj.
unarmed
defenceless 161 adj.
vulnerable 661 adj.
peaceful 717 adj.
unaroused
inert 175 adj.
quiescent 266 adj.
inactive 679 adj.
apathetic 820 adj.
unastonished 865 adj.
unarranged
orderless 61 adj.
unprepared 670 adj.
unashamed
impenitent 940 adj.
unasked
volitional 595 adj.
voluntary 597 adj.
unwanted 860 adj.
unaspiring
indifferent 860 adj.
inglorious 867 adj.
unassailable
strong 162 adj.
invulnerable 660 adj.
pure 950 adj.
unassembled
disunited 46 adj.
unassembled 75 adj.
unassenting
involuntary 596 adj.
unassertive
lax 734 adj.
modest 874 adj.
unassimilated
separate 46 adj.
nonadhesive 49 adj.
extraneous 59 adj.
unsociable 883 adj.
unassuming
plain 573 adj.
artless 699 adj.
humble 872 adj.
modest 874 adj.
unastonished
indifferent 860 adj.
unastonished 865 adj.
unattached
separate 46 adj.
unstable 152 adj.
neutral 625 adj.
independent 744 adj.
unpossessed 774 adj.
unattainable
impracticable 470 adj.
unattained
deficient 307 adj.
unattempted
avoidable 620 adj.
unattended
neglected 458 adj.
unattested
unattested 467 adj.
uncertified 474 adj.

unattractive
unpleasant 827 adj.
graceless 842 adj.
unwanted 860 adj.
unauthentic
uncertified 474 adj.
erroneous 495 adj.
unauthorized, unauthorised
powerless 161 adj.
anarchic 734 adj.
wrong 914 adj.
unwarranted 916 adj.
illegal 954 adj.
heterodox 977 adj.
unavailable
absent 190 adj.
impracticable 470 adj.
scarce 636 adj.
unprovided 636 adj.
unavailing
profitless 641 adj.
unavenged
forgiven 909 adj.
unavoidable
certain 473 adj.
necessary 596 adj.
compelling 740 adj.
obligatory 917 adj.
unavowed
tacit 523 adj.
unaware
insensible 375 adj.
inattentive 456 adj.
ignorant 491 adj.
inexpectant 508 adj.
unawed
unfearing 855 adj.
unastonished 865 adj.
impious 980 adj.
unbalance
derange 63 vb.
bias 481 n.
make mad 503 vb.
unbalanced
unwise 499 adj.
crazy 503 adj.
unbaptized
heathenish 974 adj.
unbar
deliver 668 vb.
liberate 746 vb.
unbarred
open 263 adj.
unbearable
exorbitant 32 adj.
intolerable 827 adj.
unbeatable
unyielding 162 adj.
unbeaten 727 adj.
unbeaten
persevering 600 adj.
unused 674 adj.
unbeaten 727 adj.
unbecoming
unapt 25 adj.
graceless 842 adj.
discreditable 867 adj.
unbefitting
undue 916 adj.
unbegotten
unborn 2 adj.
unbeknown
unknown 491 adj.
unbelief
unbelief 486 n.
irreligion 974 n.
unbelievable
prodigious 32 adj.
unbelieved 486 adj.
wonderful 864 adj.
unbeliever
unbeliever 486 n.
unbelieving
doubting 474 adj.
impious 980 adj.
unbend
straighten 249 vb.
soften 327 vb.
repose 683 vb.
be humble 872 vb.
be sociable 882 vb.
show mercy 905 vb.
forgive 909 vb.
unbending
rigid 326 adj.
narrow-minded 481 adj.
resolute 599 adj.
obstinate 602 adj.
severe 735 adj.
restraining 747 adj.
prideful 871 adj.
unsociable 883 adj.
unbiased
judicial 480 adj.
wise 498 adj.
free 744 adj.
just 913 adj.
unbiblical
erroneous 495 adj.
heterodox 977 adj.
unbiddable
disobedient 738 adj.
unbidden
voluntary 597 adj.
disobedient 738 adj.
unwanted 860 adj.
unbind
disunite 46 vb.
deliver 668 vb.
be lax 734 vb.
liberate 746 vb.
not retain 779 vb.
unbleached
whitish 427 adj.
unblemished
unmixed 44 adj.
perfect 646 adj.
beautiful 841 adj.
innocent 935 adj.
unblest
unfortunate 731 adj.
unprosperous 731 adj.
cursed 899 adj.
heathenish 974 adj.
profane 980 adj.
unblest with
not owning 774 adj.
unblinking
still 266 adj.
unblushing
thick-skinned 820 adj.
proud 871 adj.
insolent 878 adj.
wicked 934 adj.
impenitent 940 adj.
unchaste 951 adj.
unbolt
open 263 vb.
liberate 746 vb.
unborn
unborn 2 adj.
successor 67 n.
unbosom oneself
divulge 526 vb.
unbound
unconfined 744 adj.
liberated 746 adj.
unbounded
infinite 107 adj.
unbowed
vertical 215 adj.
unbeaten 727 adj.
courageous 855 adj.
unbrace
weaken 163 vb.
unbreakable
unyielding 162 adj.
dense 324 adj.
hard 326 adj.
tough 329 adj.
invulnerable 660 adj.
unbribable
honourable 929 adj.
unbridgeable
impracticable 470 adj.
unintelligible 517 adj.
unbridled
violent 176 adj.
anarchic 734 adj.
free 744 adj.
unconfined 744 adj.
un-British
extraneous 59 adj.
unbroken
uniform 16 adj.
intact 52 adj.
complete 54 adj.
continuous 71 adj.
smooth 258 adj.
tranquil 266 adj.
unhabituated 611 adj.
unbrotherly
unkind 898 adj.
unbuild
demolish 165 vb.
unburden
disencumber 701 vb.
relieve 831 vb.
— oneself
divulge 526 vb.
unburnable
incombustible 382 adj.
unburnished
dim 419 adj.
dirty 649 adj.
unbury
exhume 364 vb.
unbusinesslike
unskilful 695 adj.
unbutton
disunite 46 vb.
doff 229 vb.
unbuttoned
reposeful 683 adj.
free 744 adj.
sociable 882 adj.
uncage
liberate 746 vb.
uncalculated
spontaneous 609 adj.
uncalculating
unwise 499 adj.
rash 857 adj.
uncalled for
superfluous 637 adj.
undue 916 adj.
uncandid
false 541 adj.
dishonest 930 adj.
uncanny
spooky 970 adj.
magical 983 adj.
uncanonical
uncertified 474 adj.
nonobservant 769 adj.
uncared for
neglected 458 adj.
unwanted 860 adj.
uncaring
negligent 458 adj.
lax 734 adj.
indifferent 860 adj.
unkind 898 adj.
uncatered for
unexpected 508 adj.
unceasing
continuing 108 adj.
perpetual 115 adj.
frequent 139 adj.
permanent 144 adj.
unceasing 146 adj.
persevering 600 adj.
active 678 adj.
uncensored
intact 52 adj.
impure 951 adj.
unceremonious
discourteous 885 adj.
uncertain
fitful 142 adj.
changeful 152 adj.
casual 159 adj.

moot 459 adj.
unattested 467 adj.
improbable 472 adj.
uncertain 474 adj.
puzzled 517 adj.
irresolute 601 adj.
capricious 604 adj.
speculative 618 adj.

uncertain temper
irascibility 892 n.

uncertainty
uncertainty 474 n.
doubt 486 n.
ignorance 491 n.
equivocalness 518 n.
gambling 618 n.

uncertified
uncertified 474 adj.

unchain
disunite 46 vb.
liberate 746 vb.

unchallengeable
undisputed 473 adj.
invulnerable 660 adj.
just 913 adj.
due 915 adj.

unchangeable
lasting 113 adj.
unchangeable 153 adj.
obstinate 602 adj.

unchanging
characteristic 5 adj.
identical 13 adj.
uniform 16 adj.
perpetual 115 adj.
permanent 144 adj.
unchangeable 153 adj.
trustworthy 929 adj.
godlike 965 adj.

unchaperoned
alone 88 adj.

uncharacteristic
abnormal 84 adj.

uncharged
free 744 adj.
given 781 adj.
uncharged 812 adj.

uncharitable
parsimonious 816 adj.
unkind 898 adj.
selfish 932 adj.

uncharted
unknown 491 adj.

unchartered
unentitled 916 adj.
unwarranted 916 adj.
illegal 954 adj.

unchaste
unchaste 951 adj.

unchastened
impenitent 940 adj.

unchastity
unchastity 951 n.

unchecked
uncertified 474 adj.
unconfined 744 adj.
rash 857 adj.

unchivalrous
discourteous 885 adj.
dishonest 930 adj.

unchosen
rejected 607 adj.
unwanted 860 adj.

unchristian
unkind 898 adj.
heathenish 974 adj.

unchurch
perform ritual 988 vb.

uncial
letter 558 n.
written 586 adj.

uncinate
angular 247 adj.

uncircumcised
heathenish 974 adj.

uncircumscribed
spacious 183 adj.

uncivil
ill-bred 847 adj.
impertinent 878 adj.
discourteous 885 adj.

uncivilized, uncivilised
ignorant 491 adj.
immature 670 adj.
artless 699 adj.
ill-bred 847 adj.
barbaric 869 adj.

unclad
uncovered 229 adj.

unclaimed
free 744 adj.
unpossessed 774 adj.
not retained 779 adj.

unclarified
semiliquid 354 adj.
opaque 423 adj.

unclasp
disunite 46 vb.

unclassical
inelegant 576 adj.

unclassifiable
unrelated 10 adj.
unconformable 84 adj.

unclassified
mixed 43 adj.
orderless 61 adj.
uncertain 474 adj.
unknown 491 adj.

uncle
kinsman 11 n.
male 372 n.
lender 784 n.

unclean
unclean 649 adj.
insalubrious 653 adj.
impure 951 adj.

unclean spirit
devil 969 n.

unclear
indistinct 444 adj.
puzzling 517 adj.
unclear 568 adj.
inelegant 576 adj.

unclench
open 263 vb.
relinquish 621 vb.
not retain 779 vb.

Uncle Sam
native 191 n.

Uncle Tom
toady 879 n.

unclinch
separate 46 vb.
not retain 779 vb.

unclipped
intact 52 adj.

uncloak
uncover 229 vb.
disclose 526 vb.

unclog
disencumber 701 vb.

unclose
open 263 vb.

unclothed
uncovered 229 adj.

unclotted
fluid 335 adj.

unclouded
undimmed 417 adj.
obvious 443 adj.

unclubbable
unsociable 883 adj.

uncluttered
orderly 60 adj.

unco
remarkably 32 adv.
foreigner 59 n.
unusual 84 adj.

unco guid, the
zealot 979 n.

uncoil
unravel 62 vb.
lengthen 203 vb.
straighten 249 vb.
recoil 280 vb.
evolve 316 vb.

uncollected
disunited 46 adj.

uncolonized, uncolonised
empty 190 adj.

uncoloured
unmixed 44 adj.
colourless 426 adj.
genuine 494 adj.
plain 573 adj.

uncombed
orderless 61 adj.

uncombined
unmixed 44 adj.
nonadhesive 49 adj.
decomposed 51 adj.

uncomely
ugly 842 adj.

uncomfortable
painful 377 adj.
suffering 825 adj.
unpleasant 827 adj.

uncomforted
discontented 829 adj.

uncomforting
cheerless 834 adj.

uncommendable
inexpedient 643 adj.
blameworthy 924 adj.

uncommitted
irresolute 601 adj.
avoiding 620 adj.
neutral 625 adj.
independent 744 adj.

uncommon
remarkable 32 adj.
special 80 adj.
infrequent 140 adj.

uncommunicated
retained 778 adj.

uncommunicative
reticent 525 adj.
unsociable 883 adj.

uncompensated
unequal 29 adj.

uncompetitive
peaceful 717 adj.

uncomplaining
patient 823 adj.
content 828 adj.

uncompleted
incomplete 55 adj.
uncompleted 726 adj.

uncomplicated
simple 44 adj.
artless 699 adj.
easy 701 adj.

uncomplimentary
ungracious 885 adj.
disrespectful 921 adj.
disapproving 924 adj.

uncompounded
unmixed 44 adj.

uncomprehending
ignorant 491 adj.

uncompressed
light 323 adj.
rare 325 adj.

uncompromising
regulated 83 adj.
resolute 599 adj.
obstinate 602 adj.
severe 735 adj.

unconcealed
manifest 522 adj.

unconceived
unborn 2 adj.

unconcern
incuriosity 454 n.
inattention 456 n.
moral insensibility 820 n.
indifference 860 n.

unconditional
unconditional 744 adj.
permitted 756 adj.
obligatory 917 adj.

unconfident
doubting 474 adj.

unconfined
facilitated 701 adj.
unconfined 744 adj.
liberated 746 adj.
unconfirmed
uncertified 474 adj.
unconfirmed report
rumour 529 n.
unconformable
unrelated 10 adj.
nonuniform 17 adj.
original 21 adj.
disagreeing 25 adj.
excluded 57 adj.
unconformable 84 adj.
dissenting 489 adj.
independent 744 adj.
nonobservant 769 adj.
heterodox 977 adj.
unconformity
nonconformity 84 n.
uncongealed
fluid 335 adj.
liquefied 337 adj.
uncongenial
disagreeing 25 adj.
cheerless 834 adj.
unconnected
unrelated 10 adj.
unconquerable
unyielding 162 adj.
persevering 600 adj.
resisting 715 adj.
unbeaten 727 adj.
independent 744 adj.
unconscionable
exorbitant 32 adj.
unconscious
impotent 161 adj.
insensible 375 adj.
ignorant 491 adj.
involuntary 596 adj.
inactive 679 adj.
sleepy 679 adj.
impassive 820 adj.
unconscious, the
subjectivity 320 n.
spirit 447 n.
unconsecrated
heathenish 974 adj.
profane 980 adj.
laical 987 adj.
unconsidered
unthought 450 adj.
neglected 458 adj.
unconsoled
discontented 829 adj.
unconstitutional
unwarranted 916 adj.
illegal 954 adj.
unconstraint
scope 744 n.
unconsumed
remaining 41 adj.
unused 674 adj.
uncontaminated
perfect 646 adj.
uncontentious
peaceful 717 adj.
uncontested
undisputed 473 adj.
assented 488 adj.
uncontrived
artless 699 adj.
uncontrollable
violent 176 adj.
frenzied 503 adj.
wilful 602 adj.
fervent 818 adj.
excited 821 adj.
excitable 822 adj.
uncontrolled
hasty 680 adj.
anarchic 734 adj.
independent 744 adj.
intemperate 943 adj.
uncontroversial
undisputed 473 adj.
assented 488 adj.
unconventional
unconformable 84 adj.
unwonted 611 adj.
independent 744 adj.
unconverted
unconformable 84 adj.
dissenting 489 adj.
unused 674 adj.
impenitent 940 adj.
heathenish 974 adj.
unconvinced
dissenting 489 adj.
unconvincing
improbable 472 adj.
feeble 572 adj.
uncooked
unsavoury 391 adj.
uncooked 670 adj.
uncooperative
unwilling 598 adj.
hindering 702 adj.
quarrelling 709 adj.
undutiful 918 adj.
uncoordinated
orderless 61 adj.
uncopied
inimitable 21 adj.
uncork
open 263 vb.
liberate 746 vb.
uncorrected
inexact 495 adj.
uncorroborated
unattested 467 adj.
uncertified 474 adj.
erroneous 495 adj.
uncorrupted
disinterested 931 adj.
innocent 935 adj.
uncounted
many 104 adj.
uncertified 474 adj.
uncouple
disunite 46 vb.
uncouth
inelegant 576 adj.
clumsy 695 adj.
artless 699 adj.
graceless 842 adj.
ill-bred 847 adj.
plebeian 869 adj.
discourteous 885 adj.
uncovenanted
unexpected 508 adj.
uncover
doff 229 vb.
uncover 229 vb.
open 263 vb.
discover 484 vb.
manifest 522 vb.
disclose 526 vb.
show respect 920 vb.
uncracked
perfect 646 adj.
uncrease
unravel 62 vb.
smooth 258 vb.
uncreated
existing 1 adj.
unborn 2 adj.
uncritical
indiscriminating 464 adj.
approving 923 adj.
uncropped
intact 52 adj.
uncross
straighten 249 vb.
uncrown
unthrone 734 vb.
depose 752 vb.
disentitle 916 vb.
uncrowned king/ queen
influence 178 n.
bigwig 638 n.
uncrumpled
smooth 258 adj.
unction
lubrication 334 n.
unctuousness 357 n.
unguent 357 n.
warm feeling 818 n.
pietism 979 n.
piety 979 n.
unctuous
unctuous 357 adj.
flattering 925 adj.
uncultivated
unproductive 172 adj.
uninstructed 491 adj.
unprepared 670 adj.
ill-bred 847 adj.
uncultured
artless 699 adj.
ill-bred 847 adj.
barbaric 869 adj.
uncurbed
unconfined 744 adj.
uncurl
straighten 249 vb.
evolve 316 vb.
uncut
intact 52 adj.
immature 670 adj.
uncynical
credulous 487 adj.
undamaged
intact 52 adj.
undamaged 646 adj.
healthy 650 adj.
safe 660 adj.
undated
anachronistic 118 adj.
undaughterly
disobedient 738 adj.
unkind 898 adj.
undutiful 918 adj.
undaunted
resolute 599 adj.
persevering 600 adj.
unfearing 855 adj.
undazzled
unastonished 865 adj.
undecayed
preserved 666 adj.
undeceive
inform 524 vb.
disclose 526 vb.
undeceived
regretting 830 adj.
undecided
moot 459 adj.
uncertain 474 adj.
unbelieving 486 adj.
irresolute 601 adj.
choiceless 606 adj.
undecipherable
unintelligible 517 adj.
undeclared
tacit 523 adj.
undecorated
inglorious 867 adj.
undecorousness
inaptitude 25 n.
undedicated
profane 980 adj.
undefeated
resisting 715 adj.
unbeaten 727 adj.
undefended
vulnerable 661 adj.
accusable 928 adj.
undefiled
unmixed 44 adj.
innocent 935 adj.
pure 950 adj.
undefined
amorphous 244 adj.
shadowy 419 adj.
indistinct 444 adj.
indiscriminate 464 adj.
uncertain 474 adj.

undeflected
straight 249 adj.
just 913 adj.
undeformed
symmetrical 245 adj.
shapely 841 adj.
undemanding
easy 701 adj.
lax 734 adj.
lenient 736 adj.
inexcitable 823 adj.
undemocratic
unequal 29 adj.
authoritarian 735 adj.
prideful 871 adj.
insolent 878 adj.
undemonstrated
uncertified 474 adj.
undemonstrative
impassive 820 adj.
undeniable
undisputed 473 adj.
demonstrated 478 adj.
creedal 485 adj.
undenominational
general 79 adj.
undependable
unreliable 474 adj.
dishonest 930 adj.
under
concerning 9 adv.
inferior 35 adj.
in place 186 adv.
low 210 adj.
under 210 adv.
subject 745 adj.
underachieve
fall short 307 vb.
underachiever
learner 538 n.
loser 728 n.
under a cloud
disreputable 867 adj.
disapproved 924 adj.
accused 928 adj.
underact
act 594 vb.
be unskilful 695 vb.
under age
young 130 adj.
under an obligation
on duty 917 adv.
under arms
warring 718 adj.
under arrest
imprisoned 747 adj.
captive 750 adj.
under a spell
involuntary 596 adj.
cursed 899 adj.
bewitched 983 adj.
under ban
prohibited 757 adj.
underbelly
lowness 210 n.
insides 224 n.
vulnerability 661 n.
under canvas
covered 226 adj.
under way 269 adv.
undercapitalized, undercapitalised
unprovided 636 adj.
undercarriage
frame 218 n.
carrier 273 n.
aircraft 276 n.
undercharge
account 808 vb.
cheapen 812 vb.
underclothes
underwear 228 n.
under consideration
in mind 449 adv.
in question 452 adv.
planned 623 adj.
under construction
in preparation 669 adv.
on the stocks 726 adv.
under control
orderly 60 adj.
obedient 739 adj.
restrained 747 adj.
under cover
covered 226 adj.
concealed 525 adj.
under shelter 660 adv.
undercover agent
secret service 459 n.
under cover of
deceptively 542 adv.
epistolary 588 adj.
undercroft
church interior 990 n.
undercurrent
cause 156 n.
current 350 n.
latency 523 n.
undercut
engrave 555 vb.
sell 793 vb.
cheapen 812 vb.
underdeveloped
incomplete 55 adj.
immature 670 adj.
underdevelopment
imperfection 647 n.
under discussion
in question 452 adv.
underdog
inferior 35 n.
loser 728 n.
unlucky person 731 n.
poor person 801 n.
underdone
culinary 301 adj.
uncooked 670 adj.
underdressed
vulgar 847 adj.
underemployment
superfluity 637 n.
inaction 677 n.
under establishment
unprovided 636 adj.
underestimate
misjudge 481 vb.
underestimate 483 vb.
err 495 vb.
misinterpret 521 vb.
not respect 921 vb.
detract 926 vb.
underestimation
untruth 543 n.
underexpose
darken 418 vb.
under false pretences
falsely 541 adv.
underfed
lean 206 adj.
underfed 636 adj.
unhealthy 651 adj.
poor 801 adj.
hungry 859 adj.
under fire
endangered 661 adj.
in difficulties 700 adj.
underfoot
low 210 adj.
subjected 745 adj.
undergo
meet with 154 vb.
feel 818 vb.
suffer 825 vb.
undergraduate
student 538 n.
immature 670 adj.
underground
low 210 adj.
deep 211 adj.
buried 364 adj.
concealed 525 adj.
hiding-place 527 n.
opposition 704 n.
revolter 738 n.
underground railway
tunnel 263 n.
railway 624 n.
undergrowth
roughness 259 n.
wood 366 n.
underhand
occult 523 adj.
stealthy 525 adj.
dishonest 930 adj.
underhung
projecting 254 adj.
under investigation
on trial 459 adv.
underived
original 21 adj.
underlay
layer 207 n.
base 214 n.
under licence
by leave 756 adv.
underlie
cause 156 vb.
be low 210 vb.
lurk 523 vb.
underline
attract notice 455 vb.
emphasize 532 vb.
mark 547 vb.
make important 638 vb.
underling
inferior 35 n.
nonentity 639 n.
servant 742 n.
commoner 869 n.
under lock and key
safe 660 adj.
captive 750 adj.
underlying
undermost 214 adj.
undermanned
unprovided 636 adj.
imperfect 647 adj.
undermine
disable 161 vb.
weaken 163 vb.
demolish 165 vb.
make concave 255 vb.
descend 309 vb.
tell against 467 vb.
plot 623 vb.
impair 655 vb.
be cunning 698 vb.
hinder 702 vb.
underneath
under 210 adv.
undernourished
underfed 636 adj.
unhealthy 651 adj.
under obligation
obliged 917 adj.
under one's belt
completed 725 adj.
under one's breath
faintly 401 adv.
voicelessly 578 adv.
under one's nose
on the spot 189 adj.
near 200 adv.
visible 443 adj.
under one's thumb
subject 745 adj.
underpaid
poor 801 adj.
cheap 812 adj.
unwarranted 916 adj.
underpants
underwear 228 n.
underpass
tunnel 263 n.
passage 305 n.
bridge 624 n.
underpin
support 218 vb.
underpopulated, be
be few 105 vb.

underpowered
deficient 307 adj.
under pressure
unwillingly 598 adv.
hastily 680 adv.
in difficulties 700 adj.
by force 740 adv.
underpriced
undervalued 483 adj.
cheap 812 adj.
underprivileged
subjected 745 adj.
poor 801 adj.
unentitled 916 adj.
underprivileged, the
poor person 801 n.
lower classes 869 n.
underproduction
decrease 37 n.
underproof
weak 163 adj.
tasteless 387 adj.
underprop
support 218 vb.
under protest
no 489 adv.
unwillingly 598 adv.
disapprovingly 924 adv.
underrate
underestimate 483 vb.
cheapen 812 vb.
not respect 921 vb.
hold cheap 922 vb.
underripe
imperfect 647 adj.
immature 670 adj.
under sail
under way 269 adv.
afloat 275 adv.
underscore
mark 547 vb.
undersea
deep 211 adj.
oceanic 343 adj.
undersecretary
official 690 n.
under sedation
tranquil 266 adj.
undersell
cheapen 812 vb.
under shelter
covered 226 adj.
safe 660 adj.
under shelter 660 adv.
undershot
projecting 254 adj.
underside
lowness 210 n.
undersigned, the
signatory 765 n.
undersized
small 33 adj.
dwarfish 196 adj.
understaffed
deficient 307 adj.
unprovided 636 adj.
understand
cognize 447 vb.
be certain 473 vb.
know 490 vb.
be wise 498 vb.
understand 516 vb.
imply 523 vb.
be informed 524 vb.
be benevolent 897 vb.
— by
mean 514 vb.
interpret 520 vb.
understandable
intelligible 516 adj.
understanding
agreement 24 n.
intellect 447 n.
consensus 488 n.
knowledge 490 n.
intelligence 498 n.
imagination 513 n.
concord 710 n.
pacification 719 n.
compact 765 n.
feeling 818 n.
friendliness 880 n.
love 887 n.
pity 905 n.
understate
underestimate 483 vb.
understatement
untruth 543 n.
detraction 926 n.
under steam
under way 269 adv.
afloat 275 adv.
understood
tacit 523 adj.
usual 610 adj.
understrapper
nonentity 639 n.
servant 742 n.
understudy
substitute 150 n.
actor 594 n.
deputy 755 n.
under suspicion
accused 928 adj.
undertake
begin 68 vb.
attempt 671 vb.
undertake 672 vb.
do 676 vb.
promise 764 vb.
contract 765 vb.
undertaker
interment 364 n.
undertaking
attempt 671 n.
undertaking 672 n.
promise 764 n.
undertenant
possessor 776 n.
under the aegis of
under shelter 660 adv.
in aid of 703 adv.
under the counter
in trade 791 adv.
illegally 954 adv.
under the hammer
salable 793 adj.
under the heel of
subjected 745 adj.
under the impression, be
opine 485 vb.
under the influence
drunk 949 adj.
under the nose of
here 189 adv.
defiantly 711 adv.
under the sun
existing 1 adj.
widely 183 adv.
under the sun 321 adv.
under the table
dead drunk 949 adj.
under the weather
sick 651 adj.
under the yoke
subjected 745 adj.
undertone
faintness 401 n.
latency 523 n.
voicelessness 578 n.
undertow
contrariety 14 n.
current 350 n.
pitfall 663 n.
under trial
sub judice 480 adv.
underused
unused 674 adj.
undervaluation
diminution 37 n.
misjudgment 481 n.
underestimation 483 n.
disrespect 921 n.
undervalue
misjudge 481 vb.
underestimate 483 vb.
not respect 921 vb.
hold cheap 922 vb.
underwater
deep 211 adj.
oceanic 343 adj.
underwater swimmer
diver 313 n.
under way
under way 269 adv.
forward 285 adv.
in preparation 669 adv.
underwear
underwear 228 n.
underweight
weakly 163 adj.
light 323 adj.
spurious 542 adj.
underworld
depth 211 n.
the dead 361 n.
lower classes 869 n.
offender 904 n.
wickedness 934 n.
hell 972 n.
underwrite
promise 764 vb.
contract 765 vb.
give security 767 vb.
underwriting
calculation of chance 159 n.
security 767 n.
undeserved
unwarranted 916 adj.
undeserving
unentitled 916 adj.
wicked 934 adj.
undesigned
unintentional 618 adj.
undesirable
inexpedient 643 adj.
troublemaker 663 n.
unpleasant 827 adj.
unwanted 860 adj.
disliked 861 adj.
bad person 938 n.
undespairing
hoping 852 adj.
undestroyed
intact 52 adj.
permanent 144 adj.
undetected
latent 523 adj.
undetermined
general 79 adj.
causeless 159 adj.
moot 459 adj.
uncertain 474 adj.
irresolute 601 adj.
choiceless 606 adj.
undeveloped
latent 523 adj.
immature 670 adj.
unskilled 695 adj.
undevelopment
undevelopment 670 n.
noncompletion 726 n.
undeviating
uniform 16 adj.
unchangeable 153 adj.
straight 249 adj.
directed 281 adj.
accurate 494 adj.
undeviating 625 adj.
indifferent 860 adj.
orthodox 976 adj.
undevout
irreligious 974 adj.
impious 980 adj.

undies
underwear 228 n.
undifferentiated
uniform 16 adj.
simple 44 adj.
indiscriminate 464 adj.
undigested
extraneous 59 adj.
immature 670 adj.
undignified
vulgar 847 adj.
dishonest 930 adj.
undiluted
unmixed 44 adj.
strong 162 adj.
undiminished
absolute 32 adj.
intact 52 adj.
strong 162 adj.adj.
undamaged 646 adj.
undimmed
undimmed 417 adj.
Undine
sea nymph 343 n.
mythical being 970 n.
undiplomatic
unskilful 695 adj.
undirected
deviating 282 adj.
indiscriminate 464 adj.
designless 618 adj.
undiscerning
blind 439 adj.
inattentive 456 adj.
indiscriminating 464 adj.
unwise 499 adj.
undischarged bankrupt
nonpayer 805 n.
undisciplined
disorderly 61 adj.
capricious 604 adj.
disobedient 738 adj.
intemperate 943 adj.
undisclosed
concealed 525 adj.
undiscouraged
persevering 600 adj.
hoping 852 adj.
undiscoverable
unintelligible 517 adj.
undiscovered
unknown 491 adj.
latent 523 adj.
undiscriminating
approving 923 adj.
undisguised
obvious 443 adj.
genuine 494 adj.
undisguised 522 adj.
veracious 540 adj.
artless 699 adj.
undismayed
unfearing 855 adj.
undisposed of
unused 674 adj.
possessed 773 adj.
undisputed
undisputed 473 adj.
undissolved
intact 52 adj.
indissoluble 324 adj.
undistinguished
middling 732 adj.
undistorted
symmetrical 245 adj.
straight 249 adj.
true 494 adj.
veracious 540 adj.
undistracted
attentive 455 adj.
undisturbed
tranquil 266 adj.
undiversified
uniform 16 adj.
undivided
intact 52 adj.
complete 54 adj.
undivulged
tacit 523 adj.
undo
disunite 46 vb.
revert 148 vb.
counteract 182 vb.
doff 229 vb.
make useless 641 vb.
abrogate 752 vb.
undoing
destruction 165 n.
undomesticated
unhabituated 611 adj.
undone
neglected 458 adj.
uncompleted 726 adj.
unfortunate 731 adj.
hopeless 853 adj.
undoubted
undisputed 473 adj.
undrained
marshy 347 adj.
insalubrious 653 adj.
undramatic
feeble 572 adj.
plain 573 adj.
undreamt
unthought 450 adj.
undress
informal dress 228 n.
uniform 228 n.
uncover 229 vb.
undressed
uncovered 229 adj.
uncooked 670 adj.
undrinkable
unsavoury 391 adj.
insalubrious 653 adj.
undue
unapt 25 adj.
inexpedient 643 adj.
undue 916 adj.
undueness
overstepping 306 n.
injustice 914 n.
undulate
crinkle 251 vb.
oscillate 317 vb.
undulation
wave 350 n.
undulatory
curved 248 adj.
undulatory 251 adj.
rough 259 adj.
oscillating 317 adj.
unduly
extremely 32 adv.
unduly 916 adv.
undutiful
negligent 458 adj.
forgetful 506 adj.
tergiversating 603 adj.
disobedient 738 adj.
nonobservant 769 adj.
undutiful 918 adj.
undying
perpetual 115 adj.
unceasing 146 adj.
unchangeable 153 adj.
remembered 505 adj.
unearned
unwarranted 916 adj.
unearned increment
benefit 615 n.
unearth
extract 304 vb.
exhume 364 vb.
discover 484 vb.
manifest 522 vb.
unearthly
extraneous 59 adj.
immaterial 320 adj.
divine 965 adj.
spooky 970 adj.
uneasiness
worry 825 n.
discontent 829 n.
nervousness 854 n.
uneatable
unsavoury 391 adj.
uneconomic
wasteful 634 adj.
prodigal 815 adj.
unedifying
misteaching 535 adj.
discreditable 867 adj.
vicious 934 adj.
unedited
intact 52 adj.
tacit 523 adj.
uneducated
uninstructed 491 adj.
unelaborated
uncompleted 726 adj.
unelevated
feeble 572 adj.
unembarrassed
well-bred 848 adj.
unembellished
plain 573 adj.
unembroidered
veracious 540 adj.
unemotional
impassive 820 adj.
unemphatic
muted 401 adj.
feeble 572 adj.
plain 573 adj.
inexcitable 823 adj.
unemployable
useless 641 adj.
unused 674 adj.
unemployed
powerless 161 adj.
unused 674 adj.
unemployment
superfluity 637 n.
inaction 677 n.
inactivity 679 n.
unemployment benefit
subvention 703 n.
unempowered
powerless 161 adj.
unentitled 916 adj.
unending
perpetual 115 adj.
unendowed
unskilful 695 adj.
unendurable
bad 645 adj.
intolerable 827 adj.
unenfranchised
choiceless 606 adj.
unenjoyable
tedious 838 adj.
unenlightened
ignorant 491 adj.
unwise 499 adj.
unenterprising
cautious 858 adj.
unentertaining
tedious 838 adj.
dull 840 adj.
unenthusiastic
unwilling 598 adj.
apathetic 820 adj.
inexcitable 823 adj.
unentitled
unentitled 916 adj.
unenvied
unrespected 921 adj.
unequal
nonuniform 17 adj.
unequal 29 adj.
inferior 35 adj.
unequalled
supreme 34 adj.
best 644 adj.

unequal to
insufficient 636 adj.
unequipped
powerless 161 adj.
unequipped 670 adj.
unequivocal
absolute 32 adj.
positive 473 adj.
intelligible 516 adj.
unerring
certain 473 adj.
accurate 494 adj.
successful 727 adj.
unescorted
alone 88 adj.
vulnerable 661 adj.
unethical
dishonest 930 adj.
unevasive
intelligible 516 adj.
uneven
nonuniform 17 adj.
unequal 29 adj.
discontinuous 72 adj.
fitful 142 adj.
rough 259 adj.
imperfect 647 adj.
unjust 914 adj.
uneventful
tranquil 266 adj.
trivial 639 adj.
tedious 838 adj.
unexaggerated
genuine 494 adj.
veracious 540 adj.
unexamined
neglected 458 adj.
unexampled
unusual 84 adj.
unexpected 508 adj.
unexceptionable
not bad 644 adj.
guiltless 935 adj.
unexceptional
general 79 adj.
regular 81 adj.
unexcited
apathetic 820 adj.
bored 838 adj.
unexciting
feeble 572 adj.
tedious 838 adj.
unexempt from
liable 180 adj.
unexercised
powerless 161 adj.
unprepared 670 adj.
unused 674 adj.
unexhausted
unyielding 162 adj.
unexpected
improbable 472 adj.
unexpected 508 adj.
puzzling 517 adj.
capricious 604 adj.
wonderful 864 adj.
unexpectedly
suddenly 135 adv.
by chance 159 adv.
unexpectedly 508 adv.
unexpended
remaining 41 adj.
stored 632 adj.
unexpired
remaining 41 adj.
unexplained
uncertain 474 adj.
unknown 491 adj.
puzzling 517 adj.
latent 523 adj.
unexploited
unused 674 adj.
unexplored
new 126 adj.
neglected 458 adj.
unknown 491 adj.
latent 523 adj.
secluded 883 adj.
unexposed
latent 523 adj.
safe 660 adj.
unexpressed
tacit 523 adj.
unexpurgated
intact 52 adj.
impure 951 adj.
unextinguished
fiery 379 adj.
unextreme
moderate 177 adj.
neutral 625 adj.
unfactual
erroneous 495 adj.
unfaded
florid 425 adj.
unfading
lasting 113 adj.
perpetual 115 adj.
coloured 425 adj.
renowned 866 adj.
unfailing
permanent 144 adj.
unceasing 146 adj.
persevering 600 adj.
liberal 813 adj.
unfair
unequal 29 adj.
unjust 914 adj.
dishonest 930 adj.
unfair, be
be biased 481 vb.
unfair picture
misrepresentation 552 n.
unfaithful
changeful 152 adj.
unbelieving 486 adj.
tergiversating 603 adj.
nonobservant 769 adj.
perfidious 930 adj.
extramarital 951 adj.
unfallen
innocent 935 adj.
pure 950 adj.
unfaltering
persevering 600 adj.
unfamiliar
unusual 84 adj.
unknown 491 adj.
unhabituated 611 adj.
secluded 883 adj.
unfashionable
unconformable 84 adj.
unwonted 611 adj.
ill-bred 847 adj.
plebeian 869 adj.
unfashioned
amorphous 244 adj.
immature 670 adj.
unfasten
disunite 46 vb.
unstick 49 vb.
unfathomable
infinite 107 adj.
deep 211 adj.
unintelligible 517 adj.
unfathomed
deep 211 adj.
unknown 491 adj.
unfavourable
inopportune 138 adj.
hindering 702 adj.
opposing 704 adj.
adverse 731 adj.
disapproving 924 adj.
unfearing
resolute 599 adj.
unfearing 855 adj.
rash 857 adj.
unfeasible
impracticable 470 adj.
unfeathered
uncovered 229 adj.
unfed
underfed 636 adj.
fasting 946 adj.
unfeeling
unfeeling 375 adj.
impassive 820 adj.
unkind 898 adj.
pitiless 906 adj.
unfeeling person
unfeeling person 820 n.
unfeigned
veracious 540 adj.
unfeminine
male 372 adj.
ill-bred 847 adj.
unfermented
sober 948 adj.
unfetter
disencumber 701 vb.
liberate 746 vb.
unfettered
facilitated 701 adj.
unconfined 744 adj.
unfilial
disobedient 738 adj.
unkind 898 adj.
undutiful 918 adj.
unfilled
unprovided 636 adj.
hungry 859 adj.
unfinished
fragmentary 53 adj.
unfinished 55 adj.
imperfect 647 adj.
immature 670 adj.
uncompleted 726 adj.
unfit
powerless 161 adj.
useless 641 adj.
inexpedient 643 adj.
imperfect 647 adj.
unskilful 695 adj.
unfit for
unapt 25 adj.
unfitness
nonpreparation 670 n.
unfitting
inexpedient 643 adj.
wrong 914 adj.
undue 916 adj.
unfix
displace 188 vb.
unfixed
unstable 152 adj.
unflagging
persevering 600 adj.
industrious 678 adj.
unflappable
inexcitable 823 adj.
unflattering
true 494 adj.
graceless 842 adj.
ungracious 885 adj.
disrespectful 921 adj.
disapproving 924 adj.
detracting 926 adj.
unflavoured
unmixed 44 adj.
tasteless 387 adj.
unflawed
perfect 646 adj.
unfledged
new 126 adj.
young 130 adj.
infantine 132 adj.
uncovered 229 adj.
immature 670 adj.
unflinching
resolute 599 adj.
courageous 855 adj.
unfold
become 1 vb.
result 157 vb.
produce 164 vb.
lengthen 203 vb.
uncover 229 vb.
straighten 249 vb.
open 263 vb.
evolve 316 vb.

interpret 520 vb.
disclose 526 vb.
unforbidden
permitted 756 adj.
unforced
voluntary 597 adj.
spontaneous 609 adj.
independent 744 adj.
unforeseeable
causeless 159 adj.
improbable 472 adj.
uncertain 474 adj.
unexpected 508 adj.
unforeseeing
unwise 499 adj.
rash 857 adj.
unforeseen
unexpected 508 adj.
unforfeited
retained 778 adj.
unforgettable
remembered 505 adj.
notable 638 adj.
unforgetting
revengeful 910 adj.
unforgivable, unforgiveable
wrong 914 adj.
accusable 928 adj.
heinous 934 adj.
unforgiving
severe 735 adj.
unkind 898 adj.
pitiless 906 adj.
revengeful 910 adj.
unforgotten
remembered 505 adj.
unformed
amorphous 244 adj.
immature 670 adj.
unforthcoming
avoiding 620 adj.
impassive 820 adj.
unsociable 883 adj.
unfortified
unmixed 44 adj.
defenceless 161 adj.
weak 163 adj.
vulnerable 661 adj.
unfortunate
unapt 25 adj.
evil 616 adj.
unsuccessful 728 adj.
unfortunate 731 adj.
unhappy 825 adj.
annoying 827 adj.
unfounded
unreal 2 adj.
insubstantial 4 adj.
illogical 477 adj.
erroneous 495 adj.
untrue 543 adj.
unfranchised
serving 742 adj.
subject 745 adj.
unentitled 916 adj.
unfreeze
liquefy 337 vb.
unfrequented
dangerous 661 adj.
secluded 883 adj.
unfriended
defenceless 161 adj.
friendless 883 adj.
unfriendly
opposing 704 adj.
disliking 861 adj.
inimical 881 adj.
unsociable 883 adj.
ungracious 885 adj.
unkind 898 adj.
unfrock
depose 752 vb.
disentitle 916 vb.
punish 963 vb.
unfrozen
warm 379 adj.
unfruitful
unproductive 172 adj.
unfuddled
sober 948 adj.
unfunny
serious 834 adj.
tedious 838 adj.
dull 840 adj.
unfurl
lengthen 203 vb.
straighten 249 vb.
evolve 316 vb.
manifest 522 vb.
unfurnished
unprovided 636 adj.
unequipped 670 adj.
unfussy
plain 573 adj.
ungainly
clumsy 695 adj.adj.
graceless 842 adj.
ungallant
discourteous 885 adj.
ungarbled
veracious 540 adj.
ungarnished
uncooked 670 adj.
ungathered
unused 674 adj.
ungenerous
parsimonious 816 adj.
unkind 898 adj.
selfish 932 adj.
ungenteel
ill-bred 847 adj.
vulgar 847 adj.
ungentle
violent 176 adj.
oppressive 735 adj.
ungentlemanly
ill-bred 847 adj.
discourteous 885 adj.
dishonest 930 adj.
unget-at-able
removed 199 adj.
ungifted
unintelligent 499 adj.
unskilful 695 adj.
unglorified
inglorious 867 adj.
ungodly
wicked 934 adj.
irreligious 974 adj.
impious 980 adj.
ungovernable
violent 176 adj.
wilful 602 adj.
disobedient 738 adj.
independent 744 adj.
lawless 954 adj.
ungoverned
anarchic 734 adj.
ungraceful
inelegant 576 adj.
clumsy 695 adj.
graceless 842 adj.
ungracious
ungracious 885 adj.
unkind 898 adj.
ungraciousness
conduct 688 n.
rudeness 885 n.
ungraded
orderless 61 adj.
ungrammatical
neological 560 adj.
ungrammatical 565 adj.
ungrateful
forgetful 506 adj.
ungrateful 908 adj.
ungratified
refused 760 adj.
discontented 829 adj.
ungrounded
illogical 477 adj.
erroneous 495 adj.
ungrown
immature 670 adj.
ungrudging
willing 597 adj.
liberal 813 adj.
disinterested 931 adj.
unguaranteed
uncertified 474 adj.
unguarded
neglected 458 adj.
inexpectant 508 adj.
spontaneous 609 adj.
vulnerable 661 adj.
unprepared 670 adj.
unguent
lubricant 334 n.
unguent 357 n.
unguessed
unexpected 508 adj.
latent 523 adj.
unguided
deviating 282 adj.
designless 618 adj.
ungulate
footed 214 adj.
mammal 365 n.
unhabituated
unhabituated 611 adj.
unprepared 670 adj.
unhackneyed
inimitable 21 adj.
new 126 adj.
unwonted 611 adj.
unhallowed
unclean 649 adj.
heathenish 974 adj.
profane 980 adj.
unhand
liberate 746 vb.
not retain 779 vb.
unhandy
clumsy 695 adj.
unhappily
amiss 616 adv.
unhappy
inopportune 138 adj.
inexpedient 643 adj.
bungled 695 adj.
unfortunate 731 adj.
unhappy 825 adj.
discontented 829 adj.
dejected 834 adj.
lamenting 836 adj.
unharmed
healthy 650 adj.
safe 660 adj.
unharness
arrive 295 vb.
unharvested
unproductive 172 adj.
unhatched
immature 670 adj.
unhealed wound
sensibility 374 n.
unhealthy
weakly 163 adj.
deadly 362 adj.
inexpedient 643 adj.
harmful 645 adj.
unhealthy 651 adj.
insalubrious 653 adj.
dangerous 661 adj.
unheard
unknown 491 adj.
inglorious 867 adj.
modest 874 adj.
unheard-of
new 126 adj.
impossible 470 adj.
improbable 472 adj.
wonderful 864 adj.
unhearing
insensible 375 adj.
deaf 416 adj.
inattentive 456 adj.
impassive 820 adj.
unheated
cold 380 adj.
unheeded
neglected 458 adj.
unheeding
inattentive 456 adj.

unheld
unpossessed 774 adj.
unhelpful
unwilling 598 adj.
inexpedient 643 adj.
hindering 702 adj.
unkind 898 adj.
unheralded
unexpected 508 adj.
unheroic
irresolute 601 adj.
cowardly 856 adj.
inglorious 867 adj.
unhesitating
believing 485 adj.
unhindered
unconfined 744 adj.
unhinge
derange 63 vb.
disable 161 vb.
make mad 503 vb.
unhistorical
erroneous 495 adj.
imaginary 513 adj.
unhitch
disunite 46 vb.
arrive 295 vb.
unholy
heathenish 974 adj.
profane 980 adj.
laical 987 adj.
unholy joy
joy 824 n.
malevolence 898 n.
unhonoured
inglorious 867 adj.
unhook
disunite 46 vb.
unhoped for
unexpected 508 adj.
unhopeful
dejected 834 adj.
hopeless 853 adj.
unhorsed
grounded 728 adj.
unhouse
displace 188 vb.
eject 300 vb.
unhurried
tranquil 266 adj.
slow 278 adj.
leisurely 681 adj.
inexcitable 823 adj.
unhurt
undamaged 646 adj.
unhygienic
unclean 649 adj.
insalubrious 653 adj.
unhymned
inglorious 867 adj.
unicameral
parliamentary 692 adj.
unicellular
organic 358 adj.
unicorn
rara avis 84 n.
animal 365 n.
heraldry 547 n.
unicycle
bicycle 274 n.
unidea'd
mindless 448 adj.
unthinking 450 adj.
unideal
true 494 adj.
unidealistic
selfish 932 adj.
unidentified
unrelated 10 adj.
unknown 491 adj.
unidiomatic
unapt 25 adj.
meaningless 515 adj.
neological 560 adj.
unification
union 45 n.
combination 50 n.
unity 88 n.
association 706 n.
unified
simple 44 adj.
one 88 adj.
uniform
identical 13 adj.
uniform 16 adj.
equal 28 adj.
orderly 60 adj.
continuous 71 adj.
regular 81 adj.
uniform 228 n.
symmetrical 245 adj.
smooth 258 adj.
livery 547 n.
badge of rank 743 n.
uniformity
uniformity 16 n.
conformance 24 n.
unify
join 45 vb.
combine 50 vb.
(See **unification** *)*
unilateral
unrelated 10 adj.
one 88 adj.
independent 744 adj.
unilluminated
unlit 418 adj.
unimaginable
unusual 84 adj.
impossible 470 adj.
improbable 472 adj.
unbelieved 486 adj.
wonderful 864 adj.
unimaginative
imitative 20 adj.
unthinking 450 adj.
indiscriminating 464 adj.
narrow-minded 481 adj.
unintelligent 499 adj.
plain 573 adj.
impassive 820 adj.
thick-skinned 820 adj.
dull 840 adj.
unastonished 865 adj.
unimitated
original 21 adj.
unimpaired
intact 52 adj.
unimpassioned
feeble 572 adj.
apathetic 820 adj.
unimpeachable
undisputed 473 adj.
approvable 923 adj.
guiltless 935 adj.
unimpeded
facilitated 701 adj.
unconfined 744 adj.
unimplied
unmeant 515 adj.
unimportance
unimportance 639 n.
unimportant
irrelevant 10 adj.
inconsiderable 33 adj.
inferior 35 adj.
unimportant 639 adj.
humble 872 adj.
contemptible 922 adj.
unimposing
modest 874 adj.
unimpressed
indifferent 860 adj.
unastonished 865 adj.
disapproving 924 adj.
unimpressionable
impassive 820 adj.
unastonished 865 adj.
unimpressive
imperfect 647 adj.
unimproved
deteriorated 655 adj.
uninfectious
salubrious 652 adj.
uninflammable
incombustible 382 adj.
uninfluenced
obstinate 602 adj.
independent 744 adj.
uninfluential
unimportant 639 adj.
uninformative
reticent 525 adj.
uninformed
uninstructed 491 adj.
inexpectant 508 adj.
uninhabitable
empty 190 adj.
uninhabited
secluded 883 adj.
uninhibited
artless 699 adj.
unconfined 744 adj.
uninitiated
ignorant 491 adj.
unskilled 695 adj.
uninquisitive
incurious 454 adj.
uninspired
feeble 572 adj.
plain 573 adj.
apathetic 820 adj.
tedious 838 adj.
dull 840 adj.
uninstructed
uninstructed 491 adj.
unprepared 670 adj.
unintegrated
extraneous 59 adj.
unintellectual
unthinking 450 adj.
unintelligent 499 adj.
unintelligent
mindless 448 adj.
unthinking 450 adj.
unintelligent 499 adj.
unintelligible
unintelligible 517 adj.
unclear 568 adj.
difficult 700 adj.
unintended
causeless 159 adj.
unmeant 515 adj.
unintentional 618 adj.
unintentional
involuntary 596 adj.
spontaneous 609 adj.
unintentional 618 adj.
uninterested
incurious 454 adj.
inattentive 456 adj.
choiceless 606 adj.
apathetic 820 adj.
indifferent 860 adj.
uninteresting
tedious 838 adj.
dull 840 adj.
uninterrupted
continuous 71 adj.
perpetual 115 adj.
unceasing 146 adj.
unintoxicated
sober 948 adj.
uninventive
imitative 20 adj.
mindless 448 adj.
unthinking 450 adj.
dull 840 adj.
uninvited
disobedient 738 adj.
unwanted 860 adj.
friendless 883 adj.

uninvited guest
intruder 59 n.
uninviting
unsavoury 391 adj.
unpleasant 827 adj.
cheerless 834 adj.
uninvolved
unrelated 10 adj.
incurious 454 adj.
intelligible 516 adj.
perspicuous 567 adj.
independent 744 adj.
indifferent 860 adj.
union
union 45 n.
coherence 48 n.
combination 50 n.
unity 88 n.
concurrence 181 n.
association 706 n.
society 708 n.
marriage 894 n.
Unionists
political party 708 n.
Union Jack
flag 547 n.
unique
dissimilar 19 adj.
inimitable 21 adj.
special 80 adj.
unconformable 84 adj.
one 88 adj.
valuable 644 adj.
unirrigated
unproductive 172 adj.
dry 342 adj.
unirritating
lenitive 177 adj.
unisex
identical 13 adj.
uniform 16 adj.
tailored 228 adj.
unisexual
generative 167 adj.
unison
agreement 24 n.
melody 410 n.
consensus 488 n.
unit
all 52 n.
whole 52 n.
component 58 n.
band 74 n.
group 74 n.
unit 88 n.
cabinet 194 n.
person 371 n.
formation 722 n.
Unitarianism
heresy 977 n.
Unitarians
sect 978 n.
unitary
one 88 adj.
unite
join 45 vb.
combine 50 vb.
bring together 74 vb.
be one 88 vb.
concur 181 vb.
converge 293 vb.
cooperate 706 vb.
— with
unite with 45 vb.
wed 894 vb.
united
agreeing 24 adj.
cohesive 48 adj.
concordant 710 adj.
married 894 adj.
united front
association 706 n.
United Nations, UN
council 692 n.
United Reformed Church
Protestantism 976 n.
unity
identity 13 n.
uniformity 16 n.
simpleness 44 n.
whole 52 n.
completeness 54 n.
unity 88 n.
association 706 n.
concord 710 n.
divine attribute 965 n.
universal
existence 1 n.
extensive 32 adj.
comprehensive 52 adj.
universal 79 adj.
one 88 adj.
ubiquitous 189 adj.
cosmic 321 adj.
usual 610 adj.
orthodox 976 adj.
Universalists
church party 978 n.
universals
premise 475 n.
universal suffrage
vote 605 n.
universe
whole 52 n.
universe 321 n.
university
academy 539 n.
univocal
certain 473 adj.
semantic 514 adj.
unjust
biased 481 adj.
bad 645 adj.
oppressive 735 adj.
unjust 914 adj.
wicked 934 adj.
unjustifiable
wrong 914 adj.
unwarranted 916 adj.
blameworthy 924 adj.
accusable 928 adj.
heinous 934 adj.
guilty 936 adj.
unkempt
orderless 61 adj.
rough 259 adj.
neglected 458 adj.
dirty 649 adj.
unkennel
disclose 526 vb.
unkind
harmful 645 adj.
unkind 898 adj.
unknot
disencumber 701 vb.
unknowable
unknown 491 adj.
unintelligible 517 adj.
unknown
new 126 adj.
unknown 491 adj.
disguised 525 adj.
anonymous 562 adj.
inglorious 867 adj.
secluded 883 adj.
unknown quantity
unknown thing 491 n.
secret 530 n.
unlaboured
elegant 575 adj.
unlace
doff 229 vb.
unladylike
ill-bred 847 adj.
discourteous 885 adj.
unlamented
hated 888 adj.
disapproved 924 adj.
unlatch
disunite 46 vb.
open 263 vb.
unlawful
prohibited 757 adj.
nonobservant 769 adj.
illegal 954 adj.
unlearn
not know 491 vb.
forget 506 vb.
unlearned
uninstructed 491 adj.
artless 699 adj.
unleash
liberate 746 vb.
unleavened
ritual 988 adj.
unless
if 8 adv.
provided 468 adv.
unlettered
uninstructed 491 adj.
ill-bred 847 adj.
unlicensed
unwarranted 916 adj.
unlicked
amorphous 244 adj.
immature 670 adj.
unlicked cub
vulgarian 847 n.
rude person 885 n.
unlighted
unlit 418 adj.
unlikable, unlikeable
not nice 645 adj.
unlike
different 15 adj.
dissimilar 19 adj.
unlikely
improbable 472 adj.
unlimited
absolute 32 adj.
infinite 107 adj.
unconditional 744 adj.
unlit
unlit 418 adj.
shadowy 419 adj.
dangerous 661 adj.
unliterary
dialectal 560 adj.
unlively
serious 834 adj.
dull 840 adj.
unload
displace 188 vb.
transpose 272 vb.
empty 300 vb.
extract 304 vb.
disencumber 701 vb.
liberate 746 vb.
— on
assign 780 vb.
sell 793 vb.
unlock
open 263 vb.
liberate 746 vb.
unlooked for
unexpected 508 adj.
undue 916 adj.
unloose
disunite 46 vb.
deliver 668 vb.
liberate 746 vb.
unlovable, unloveable
disliked 861 adj.
hateful 888 adj.
unloved
hated 888 adj.
unlovely
ugly 842 adj.
disliked 861 adj.
unloving
impassive 820 adj.
unkind 898 adj.
unluckily
by chance 159 adv.
amiss 616 adv.
unlucky
inopportune 138 adj.
evil 616 adj.
unsuccessful 728 adj.
unfortunate 731 adj.
unhappy 825 adj.

annoying 827 adj.
unlucky person
loser 728 n.
unlucky person 731 n.
unmade
unborn 2 adj.
amorphous 244 adj.
unmake
revert 148 vb.
destroy 165 vb.
abrogate 752 vb.
unmalleable
unconformable 84 adj.
rigid 326 adj.
unman
unman 161 vb.
make sterile 172 vb.
frighten 854 vb.
unmanageable
wilful 602 adj.
clumsy 695 adj.
difficult 700 adj.
disobedient 738 adj.
unmanifested
latent 523 adj.
unmanly
female 373 adj.
cowardly 856 adj.
unmannerly
ill-bred 847 adj.
discourteous 885 adj.
unmarked
undamaged 646 adj.
unmarketable
cheap 812 adj.
unmarried
unsociable 883 adj.
unwedded 895 adj.
unmarry
divorce 896 vb.
unmartial
cowardly 856 adj.
unmask
disclose 526 vb.
unmasterful
lax 734 adj.
unmatched
dissimilar 19 adj.
inimitable 21 adj.
best 644 adj.
unmated
unwedded 895 adj.
unmeaning
meaningless 515 adj.
unmeant
unmeant 515 adj.
unintentional 618 adj.
unmeasured
infinite 107 adj.
indiscriminate 464 adj.
plenteous 635 adj.
intemperate 943 adj.
unmediated
simple 44 adj.
continuous 71 adj.
intuitive 476 adj.
unmeditated
spontaneous 609 adj.
unmelodious
discordant 411 adj.
unmelting
pitiless 906 adj.
unmentionable
prohibited 757 adj.
discreditable 867 adj.
impure 951 adj.
unmentioned
tacit 523 adj.
inglorious 867 adj.
unmerciful
pitiless 906 adj.
unmerited
unwarranted 916 adj.
unmethodical
orderless 61 adj.
unmilitary
peaceful 717 adj.
cowardly 856 adj.
unmindful
inattentive 456 adj.
negligent 458 adj.
forgetful 506 adj.
ungrateful 908 adj.
unmissed
neglected 458 adj.
unwanted 860 adj.
hated 888 adj.
unmistakable, unmistakeable
visible 443 adj.
certain 473 adj.
intelligible 516 adj.
manifest 522 adj.
unmitigated
consummate 32 adj.
complete 54 adj.
violent 176 adj.
aggravated 832 adj.
unmixed
absolute 32 adj.
unmixed 44 adj.
whole 52 adj.
disinterested 931 adj.
unmodified
unmixed 44 adj.
unmolested
safe 660 adj.
content 828 adj.
unmoor
separate 46 vb.
navigate 269 vb.
start out 296 vb.
unmotivated
causeless 159 adj.
spontaneous 609 adj.
unmourned
hated 888 adj.
unmoved
quiescent 266 adj.
obstinate 602 adj.
apathetic 820 adj.
indifferent 860 adj.
unastonished 865 adj.
unkind 898 adj.
pitiless 906 adj.
impenitent 940 adj.
unmoving
still 266 adj.
unmusical
discordant 411 adj.
deaf 416 adj.
artless 699 adj.
unmuzzle
liberate 746 vb.
unnamed
unknown 491 adj.
concealed 525 adj.
anonymous 562 adj.
unnatural
disagreeing 25 adj.
extraneous 59 adj.
abnormal 84 adj.
impossible 470 adj.
inelegant 576 adj.
affected 850 adj.
cruel 898 adj.
unkind 898 adj.
unnavigable
shallow 212 adj.
impracticable 470 adj.
difficult 700 adj.
unnecessary
wasteful 634 adj.
superfluous 637 adj.
unimportant 639 adj.
useless 641 adj.
unused 674 adj.
unneeded
useless 641 adj.
unneighbourly
unsociable 883 adj.
ungracious 885 adj.
selfish 932 adj.
unnerve
unman 161 vb.
weaken 163 vb.
frighten 854 vb.
unnoticeable
inconsiderable 33 adj.
slow 278 adj.
invisible 444 adj.
unnoticed
invisible 444 adj.
neglected 458 adj.
inglorious 867 adj.
unnoticing
blind 439 adj.
inattentive 456 adj.
unnourishing
insufficient 636 adj.
unnumbered
many 104 adj.
infinite 107 adj.
unobjectionable
not bad 644 adj.
middling 732 adj.
contenting 828 adj.
vindicable 927 adj.
guiltless 935 adj.
unobliged
ungrateful 908 adj.
unobservant
blind 439 adj.
inattentive 456 adj.
unobserved
neglected 458 adj.
unobstructed
open 263 adj.
facilitated 701 adj.
unconfined 744 adj.
unobtainable
impracticable 470 adj.
scarce 636 adj.
unobtrusive
modest 874 adj.
unoccupied
empty 190 adj.
unthinking 450 adj.
nonactive 677 adj.
inactive 679 adj.
leisurely 681 adj.
unpossessed 774 adj.
unoffending
humble 872 adj.
unofficial
uncertified 474 adj.
independent 744 adj.
illegal 954 adj.
unoiled
strident 407 adj.
unopened
closed 264 adj.
unused 674 adj.
unopposed
assented 488 adj.
unordained
laical 987 adj.
unorganized
orderless 61 adj.
inorganic 359 adj.
unprepared 670 adj.
lax 734 adj.
unoriginal
imitative 20 adj.
caused 157 adj.
mindless 448 adj.
usual 610 adj.
dull 840 adj.
unorthodox
unconformable 84 adj.
heterodox 977 adj.
unorthodoxy
nonconformity 84 n.
heterodoxy 977 n.
unowed
undue 916 adj.
unowned
unpossessed 774 adj.
not retained 779 adj.
unpack
uncover 229 vb.
open 263 vb.
empty 300 vb.
extract 304 vb.

disclose 526 vb.
unpacking
displacement 188 n.
transference 272 n.
unpaid
voluntary 597 adj.
free 744 adj.
owed 803 adj.
uncharged 812 adj.
unpainted
plain 573 adj.
unpaired
dissimilar 19 adj.
alone 88 adj.
unpalatable
unsavoury 391 adj.
unpleasant 827 adj.
unparalleled
supreme 34 adj.
unusual 84 adj.
best 644 adj.
unpardonable
wrong 914 adj.
accusable 928 adj.
heinous 934 adj.
guilty 936 adj.
unparliamentary language
rudeness 885 n.
scurrility 899 n.
unpartnered
unwedded 895 adj.
unpatriotic
misanthropic 902 adj.
selfish 932 adj.
unpeople
empty 300 vb.
unperceived
neglected 458 adj.
unknown 491 adj.
unperceiving
blind 439 adj.
unperformed
uncompleted 726 adj.
unperplexed
wise 498 adj.
unpersuadable
wilful 602 adj.
unphilosophical
unwise 499 adj.
unpick
disunite 46 vb.
unpigmented
colourless 426 adj.
unpin
unstick 49 vb.
unpitied
disapproved 924 adj.
unpitying
pitiless 906 adj.
unplaced
defeated 728 adj.
unplanned
causeless 159 adj.
bungled 695 adj.
unpleasant
painful 377 adj.
unsavoury 391 adj.
fetid 397 adj.
unpleasant 827 adj.
discourteous 885 adj.
threatening 900 adj.
unpleasantness
dissension 709 n.
suffering 825 n.
unploughed
unproductive 172 adj.
unplucked
hairy 259 adj.
unused 674 adj.
unplug
disunite 46 vb.
open 263 vb.
unplumbed
deep 211 adj.
unknown 491 adj.
unpoetical
plain 573 adj.
prosaic 593 adj.
artless 699 adj.
unpointed
unsharpened 257 adj.
unpolished
rough 259 adj.
dim 419 adj.
inelegant 576 adj.
dirty 649 adj.
immature 670 adj.
artless 699 adj.
ill-bred 847 adj.
vulgar 847 adj.
plebeian 869 adj.
unpolluted
unmixed 44 adj.
unpopular
unpleasant 827 adj.
disliked 861 adj.
disreputable 867 adj.
friendless 883 adj.
hated 888 adj.
unpopularity
odium 888 n.
disapprobation 924 n.
unpossessed
unpossessed 774 adj.
not retained 779 adj.
unpossessive
disinterested 931 adj.
unpractical
useless 641 adj.
unskilful 695 adj.
unpractised
unwonted 611 adj.
unprepared 670 adj.
clumsy 695 adj.
unpraised
disapproved 924 adj.
unprecedented
original 21 adj.
first 68 adj.
new 126 adj.
infrequent 140 adj.
unknown 491 adj.
unexpected 508 adj.
unwonted 611 adj.
wonderful 864 adj.
unpredictability
fitfulness 142 n.
chance 159 n.
nondesign 618 n.
unpredictable
nonuniform 17 adj.
changeful 152 adj.
unreliable 474 adj.
unknown 491 adj.
unexpected 508 adj.
capricious 604 adj.
unprejudiced
wise 498 adj.
free 744 adj.
just 913 adj.
unpremeditated
involuntary 596 adj.
spontaneous 609 adj.
unintentional 618 adj.
unprepared
negligent 458 adj.
inexpectant 508 adj.
spontaneous 609 adj.
unprepared 670 adj.
hasty 680 adj.
bungled 695 adj.
unskilled 695 adj.
artless 699 adj.
unprepossessing
ugly 842 adj.
unpresentable
ill-bred 847 adj.
unpretentious
plain 573 adj.
artless 699 adj.
humble 872 adj.
modest 874 adj.
unpriestly
laical 987 adj.
unprincipled
dishonest 930 adj.
wicked 934 adj.
unprintable
prohibited 757 adj.
impure 951 adj.
unprivileged
serving 742 adj.
subject 745 adj.
unentitled 916 adj.
unprized
undervalued 483 adj.
unprocessed
uncompleted 726 adj.
unproclaimed
tacit 523 adj.
unprocurable
absent 190 adj.
scarce 636 adj.
unproductive
impotent 161 adj.
unproductive 172 adj.
profitless 641 adj.
unproductiveness
unproductiveness 172 n.
failure 728 n.
unprofessed
tacit 523 adj.
unprofessional
nonobservant 769 adj.
unprofessional conduct
guilty act 936 n.
unprofitable
unproductive 172 adj.
profitless 641 adj.
inexpedient 643 adj.
losing 772 adj.
unprogressive
deteriorated 655 adj.
nonactive 677 adj.
unprohibited
permitted 756 adj.
unpromising
unpromising 853 adj.
unprompted
volitional 595 adj.
voluntary 597 adj.
spontaneous 609 adj.
unpronounceable
inexpressible 517 adj.
unpronounced
tacit 523 adj.
unpropitious
inopportune 138 adj.
opposing 704 adj.
unpromising 853 adj.
unprosperous
unprosperous 731 adj.
unprotected
neglected 458 adj.
vulnerable 661 adj.
unprotesting
humble 872 adj.
unproved
unattested 467 adj.
uncertified 474 adj.
poorly reasoned 477 adj.
unprovided for
unprovided 636 adj.
poor 801 adj.
unprovoked
spontaneous 609 adj.
unwanted 860 adj.
unpublished
tacit 523 adj.
unpunctual
anachronistic 118 adj.
late 136 adj.
fitful 142 adj.
unpunishable
nonliable 919 adj.

unpunished
forgiven 909 adj.
acquitted 960 adj.
unpurified
unclean 649 adj.
unqualified
unmixed 44 adj.
complete 54 adj.
positive 473 adj.
ignorant 491 adj.
useless 641 adj.
unequipped 670 adj.
unskilled 695 adj.
unentitled 916 adj.
unquenchable
unyielding 162 adj.
greedy 859 adj.
unquestionable
undisputed 473 adj.
true 494 adj.
assertive 532 adj.
unquestioned
undisputed 473 adj.
creedal 485 adj.
assented 488 adj.
unquestioning
believing 485 adj.
unquestioning belief
credulity 487 n.
unquiet
unstable 152 adj.
moving 265 adj.
agitated 318 adj.
restlessness 678 n.
excitable 822 adj.
worry 825 n.
unquotable
impure 951 adj.
unratified
uncertified 474 adj.
unravel
simplify 44 vb.
unravel 62 vb.
straighten 249 vb.
smooth 258 vb.
evolve 316 vb.
decipher 520 vb.
disencumber 701 vb.
liberate 746 vb.
unread
neglected 458 adj.
uninstructed 491 adj.
tedious 838 adj.
unreadable
unintelligible 517 adj.
tedious 838 adj.
dull 840 adj.
unready
incomplete 55 adj.
late 136 adj.
unprepared 670 adj.
unreal
unreal 2 adj.
erroneous 495 adj.
supposed 512 adj.
imaginary 513 adj.
unrealistic
dissimilar 19 adj.
impossible 470 adj.
misjudging 481 adj.
erroneous 495 adj.
unreality
insubstantiality 4 n.
immateriality 320 n.
unrealizable, unrealisable
impracticable 470 adj.
unrealized, unrealised
unreal 2 adj.
unknown 491 adj.
uncompleted 726 adj.
unreason
absence of intellect 448 n.
intuition 476 n.
folly 499 n.
lack of meaning 515 n.
unreasonable
impossible 470 adj.
illogical 477 adj.
biased 481 adj.
unwise 499 adj.
capricious 604 adj.
wrong 914 adj.
unreasoning
mindless 448 adj.
biased 481 adj.
unwise 499 adj.
unrecognizable, unrecognisable
converted 147 adj.
invisible 444 adj.
unintelligible 517 adj.
disguised 525 adj.
unrecognized, unrecognised
unknown 491 adj.
unreconciled
unwilling 598 adj.
inimical 881 adj.
impenitent 940 adj.
unrecorded
obliterated 550 adj.
unredeemed
wicked 934 adj.
unrefined
indiscriminating 464 adj.
inelegant 576 adj.
unclean 649 adj.
artless 699 adj.
ill-bred 847 adj.
vulgar 847 adj.
unreflecting
unthinking 450 adj.
incurious 454 adj.
inattentive 456 adj.
unreformed
impenitent 940 adj.
unrefreshed
fatigued 684 adj.
unrefuted
demonstrated 478 adj.
unregarded
invisible 444 adj.
neglected 458 adj.
unrespected 921 adj.
unregenerate
impenitent 940 adj.
impious 980 adj.
unregistered
obliterated 550 adj.
unregretted
hated 888 adj.
disapproved 924 adj.
unrepented 940 adj.
unregulated
unconfined 744 adj.
unrehearsed
spontaneous 609 adj.
unintentional 618 adj.
unprepared 670 adj.
unrelated
unrelated 10 adj.
dissimilar 19 adj.
disagreeing 25 adj.
casual 159 adj.
unrelenting
pitiless 906 adj.
revengeful 910 adj.
impenitent 940 adj.
unreliable
changeful 152 adj.
unreliable 474 adj.
unbelieved 486 adj.
irresolute 601 adj.
capricious 604 adj.
unsafe 661 adj.
undutiful 918 adj.
flattering 925 adj.
dishonest 930 adj.
unrelieved
uniform 16 adj.
discontented 829 adj.
aggravated 832 adj.
cheerless 834 adj.
unreligious
irreligious 974 adj.
unrelished
disliked 861 adj.
unremarked
neglected 458 adj.
inglorious 867 adj.
unremembered
forgotten 506 adj.
unremitting
continuous 71 adj.
unceasing 146 adj.
persevering 600 adj.
unrenowned
inglorious 867 adj.
unrepeated
one 88 adj.
unrepentant
impenitent 940 adj.
unrepresentative
abnormal 84 adj.
misrepresented 552 adj.
unrepresented
absent 190 adj.
unrequired
superfluous 637 adj.
unused 674 adj.
unrequited
unthanked 908 adj.
unresentful
forgetful 506 adj.
forgiving 909 adj.
unreserved
positive 473 adj.
undisguised 522 adj.
veracious 540 adj.
artless 699 adj.
free 744 adj.
unresisting
inactive 679 adj.
peaceful 717 adj.
submitting 721 adj.
obedient 739 adj.
unresolved
uncertain 474 adj.
puzzling 517 adj.
irresolute 601 adj.
choiceless 606 adj.
unrespected
unrespected 921 adj.
contemptible 922 adj.
unresponsive
impassive 820 adj.
indifferent 860 adj.
unkind 898 adj.
pitiless 906 adj.
unrest
motion 265 n.
discontent 829 n.
unrestrained
violent 176 adj.
facilitated 701 adj.
unconfined 744 adj.
intemperate 943 adj.
unrestricted
absolute 32 adj.
unconditional 744 adj.
unrevealed
concealed 525 adj.
unreversed
unceasing 146 adj.
unrevised
inexact 495 adj.
unrevoked
unceasing 146 adj.
unrewarded
profitless 641 adj.
unsuccessful 728 adj.
unthanked 908 adj.
unrhythmical
fitful 142 adj.
unriddle
decipher 520 vb.
unrighteous
wrong 914 adj.
wicked 934 adj.

unrighteousness
impiety 980 n.
unrightful
unwarranted 916 adj.
unrigorous
poorly reasoned 477 adj.
inexact 495 adj.
unrip
open 263 vb.
unripe
incomplete 55 adj.
young 130 adj.
sour 393 adj.
immature 670 adj.
unskilled 695 adj.
uncompleted 726 adj.
unrivalled
supreme 34 adj.
unrobe
uncover 229 vb.
unroll
lengthen 203 vb.
straighten 249 vb.
evolve 316 vb.
manifest 522 vb.
disclose 526 vb.
unromantic
true 494 adj.
inexcitable 823 adj.
unroof
uncover 229 vb.
unruffled
orderly 60 adj.
smooth 258 adj.
tranquil 266 adj.
impassive 820 adj.
inexcitable 823 adj.
amiable 884 adj.
unruly
disorderly 61 adj.
violent 176 adj.
wilful 602 adj.
anarchic 734 adj.
disobedient 738 adj.
riotous 738 adj.
unrumpled
orderly 60 adj.
unsafe
uncertain 474 adj.
harmful 645 adj.
unsafe 661 adj.
unsaid
unknown 491 adj.
tacit 523 adj.
unsalable, unsaleable
profitless 641 adj.
cheap 812 adj.
unsalaried
uncharged 812 adj.
unsaluted
unrespected 921 adj.
unsalvageable
lost 772 adj.
unsanctified
heathenish 974 adj.
profane 980 adj.
unsanctioned
unwarranted 916 adj.
heterodox 977 adj.
unsatisfactory
incomplete 55 adj.
disappointing 509 adj.
insufficient 636 adj.
inexpedient 643 adj.
bad 645 adj.
unpleasant 827 adj.
discontenting 829 adj.
disapproved 924 adj.
unsatisfied
unprovided 636 adj.
discontented 829 adj.
desiring 859 adj.
greedy 859 adj.
envious 912 adj.
unsavoury
tasteless 387 adj.
unsavoury 391 adj.
unpleasant 827 adj.
disliked 861 adj.
unsay
recant 603 vb.
unscalable, unscaleable
impracticable 470 adj.
unscarred
undamaged 646 adj.
unscathed
undamaged 646 adj.
unscented
odourless 395 adj.
unscholarly
uninstructed 491 adj.
unschooled
uninstructed 491 adj.
unscientific
impossible 470 adj.
illogical 477 adj.
ignorant 491 adj.
erroneous 495 adj.
unskilled 695 adj.
unscramble
simplify 44 vb.
decompose 51 vb.
unravel 62 vb.
unscratched
undamaged 646 adj.
unscriptural
erroneous 495 adj.
heterodox 977 adj.
unscrupulous
dishonest 930 adj.
wicked 934 adj.
unseal
disclose 526 vb.
unsearchable
unintelligible 517 adj.
unseasonable
unapt 25 adj.
ill-timed 138 adj.
inexpedient 643 adj.
unseasoned
unmixed 44 adj.
tasteless 387 adj.
unhabituated 611 adj.
immature 670 adj.
unseat
unstick 49 vb.
derange 63 vb.
displace 188 vb.
unthrone 734 vb.
depose 752 vb.
unseeing
insensible 375 adj.
blind 439 adj.
inattentive 456 adj.
misjudging 481 adj.
ignorant 491 adj.
unwise 499 adj.
impassive 820 adj.
unseemly
unwise 499 adj.
inexpedient 643 adj.
unsightly 842 adj.
wrong 914 adj.
undue 916 adj.
unseen
invisible 444 adj.
unknown 491 adj.
latent 523 adj.
inglorious 867 adj.
modest 874 adj.
secluded 883 adj.
unsegregated
included 78 adj.
unselective
indiscriminating 464 adj.
designless 618 adj.
unselfish
benevolent 897 adj.
disinterested 931 adj.
virtuous 933 adj.
unsensational
plain 573 adj.
unsentimental
impassive 820 adj.
inexcitable 823 adj.
unserious
witty 839 adj.
unserviceable
useless 641 adj.
unsettle
decompose 51 vb.
derange 63 vb.
impress 821 vb.
unsettled
unstable 152 adj.
displaced 188 adj.
empty 190 adj.
travelling 267 adj.
unsevered
intact 52 adj.
unsexed
impotent 161 adj.
unshackle
disencumber 701 vb.
liberate 746 vb.
unshaded
undimmed 417 adj.
unshakable, unshakeable
firm 45 adj.
fixed 153 adj.
certain 473 adj.
creedal 485 adj.
resolute 599 adj.
retentive 778 adj.
unfearing 855 adj.
unshapely
amorphous 244 adj.
unsightly 842 adj.
unshared
possessed 773 adj.
unsharpened
unsharpened 257 adj.
unshaven
hairy 259 adj.
unsheathe
uncover 229 vb.
manifest 522 vb.
unshielded
vulnerable 661 adj.
unshifting
unceasing 146 adj.
unship
displace 188 vb.
empty 300 vb.
unshockable
impassive 820 adj.
unshod
uncovered 229 adj.
unshorn
intact 52 adj.
hairy 259 adj.
unshortened
long 203 adj.
unshrinkable
unchangeable 153 adj.
unshrinking
resolute 599 adj.
courageous 855 adj.
unfearing 855 adj.
unshriven
impenitent 940 adj.
unshut
open 263 adj.
unsightly
amorphous 244 adj.
deformed 246 adj.
unsightly 842 adj.
unsigned
uncertified 474 adj.
anonymous 562 adj.
unsinkable
light 323 adj.
unskilful
ignorant 491 adj.
unhabituated 611 adj.
unskilful 695 adj.
unskilled
immature 670 adj.
unskilled 695 adj.

artless 699 adj.
unsleeping
persevering 600 adj.
industrious 678 adj.
unsleeping eye
surveillance 457 n.
unsmiling
serious 834 adj.
ungracious 885 adj.
sullen 893 adj.
unsnarl
unravel 62 vb.
unsoaped
dirty 649 adj.
unsociable
unconformable 84 adj.
alone 88 adj.
independent 744 adj.
unsociable 883 adj.
ungracious 885 adj.
sullen 893 adj.
misanthropic 902 adj.
unsoftened
impenitent 940 adj.
unsoiled
clean 648 adj.
unsold
possessed 773 adj.
unsoldierly
cowardly 856 adj.
unsolicited
voluntary 597 adj.
unsolicited mail
advertisement 528 n.
correspondence 588 n.
unsolvable
impracticable 470 adj.
puzzling 517 adj.
unsophisticated
simple 44 adj.
credulous 487 adj.
genuine 494 adj.
artless 699 adj.
ill-bred 847 adj.
unsophisticated person
ingenue 699 n.
unsorted
mixed 43 adj.
orderless 61 adj.
indiscriminate 464 adj.
unsought
voluntary 597 adj.
avoidable 620 adj.
unsound
insubstantial 4 adj.
inferior 35 adj.
unstable 152 adj.
illogical 477 adj.
erroneous 495 adj.
bad 645 adj.
imperfect 647 adj.
unhealthy 651 adj.
insalubrious 653 adj.
unsafe 661 adj.
unskilled 695 adj.
unsounded
deep 211 adj.
silent 399 adj.
unsound mind
absence of intellect 448 n.
insanity 503 n.
unsown
unproductive 172 adj.
unspanned
broad 205 adj.
unsparing
plenteous 635 adj.
oppressive 735 adj.
severe 735 adj.
liberal 813 adj.
disinterested 931 adj.
unspeakable
unspeakable 32 adj.
inexpressible 517 adj.
wonderful 864 adj.
unspeakable villain
monster 938 n.
unspecified
general 79 adj.
unspent
remaining 41 adj.
unused 674 adj.
unspiced
unmixed 44 adj.
tasteless 387 adj.
unspiritual
material 319 adj.
sensual 944 adj.
irreligious 974 adj.
unspoiled, unspoilt
intact 52 adj.
not bad 644 adj.
undamaged 646 adj.
unspoken
silent 399 adj.
unknown 491 adj.
tacit 523 adj.
unsporting
dishonest 930 adj.
unsportsmanlike
unjust 914 adj.
dishonest 930 adj.
unspotted
perfect 646 adj.
beautiful 841 adj.
innocent 935 adj.
unsprung
rigid 326 adj.
tough 329 adj.
unstable
unequal 29 adj.
unstable 152 adj.
unreliable 474 adj.
irresolute 601 adj.
capricious 604 adj.
unsafe 661 adj.
excitable 822 adj.
unstable personality
madman 504 n.
unstaffed
empty 190 adj.
unstained
perfect 646 adj.
honourable 929 adj.
unstarched
soft 327 adj.
unstatesmanlike
unskilful 695 adj.
unsteadfast
irresolute 601 adj.
unsteady
fitful 142 adj.
unstable 152 adj.
unreliable 474 adj.
irresolute 601 adj.
unsafe 661 adj.
unsteerable
clumsy 695 adj.
unsterilized, unsterilised
unclean 649 adj.
infectious 653 adj.
unstick
disunite 46 vb.
unstick 49 vb.
displace 188 vb.
unstiffened
soft 327 adj.
unstinting
liberal 813 adj.
unstirred
apathetic 820 adj.
unastonished 865 adj.
unstirring
still 266 adj.
unstitch
disunite 46 vb.
unstop
open 263 vb.
liberate 746 vb.
unstoppable
unceasing 146 adj.
unstrained
friendly 880 adj.
unstrengthened
unmixed 44 adj.
weak 163 adj.
unstressed
muted 401 adj.
unstretchable
unyielding 162 adj.
unstrict
lax 734 adj.
unstring
disunite 46 vb.
disable 161 vb.
soften 327 vb.
— one's nerves
frighten 854 vb.
unstuck
disunited 46 adj.
unstudied
neglected 458 adj.
unprepared 670 adj.
artless 699 adj.
unsubdued
resisting 715 adj.
unbeaten 727 adj.
unsubstantial
insubstantial 4 adj.
imaginary 513 adj.
unsubstantiality
insubstantiality 4 n.
unsubstantiated
erroneous 495 adj.
unsuccessful
unproductive 172 adj.
disappointing 509 adj.
profitless 641 adj.
unsuccessful 728 adj.
unprosperous 731 adj.
unsuitable
unapt 25 adj.
rejected 607 adj.
inexpedient 643 adj.
unsuited
unapt 25 adj.
ill-timed 138 adj.
unsullied
clean 648 adj.
honourable 929 adj.
unsung
tacit 523 adj.
inglorious 867 adj.
unsupplied
unprovided 636 adj.
unsupported
unattested 467 adj.
vulnerable 661 adj.
unsure
uncertain 474 adj.
unsurpassable
supreme 34 adj.
best 644 adj.
perfect 646 adj.
unsurprised
expectant 507 adj.
indifferent 860 adj.
unastonished 865 adj.
unsusceptible
impassive 820 adj.
unsuspected
latent 523 adj.
unsuspecting
believing 485 adj.
credulous 487 adj.
inexpectant 508 adj.
unsustained
poorly reasoned 477 adj.
unswayed
courageous 855 adj.
unsweetened
unsavoury 391 adj.
sour 393 adj.
unswept
dirty 649 adj.
unswerving
straight 249 adj.
directed 281 adj.
undeviating 625 adj.
just 913 adj.

unsworn
unattested 467 adj.
unsymmetrical
disagreeing 25 adj.
distorted 246 adj.
unsympathetic
opposing 704 adj.
disliking 861 adj.
inimical 881 adj.
unkind 898 adj.
pitiless 906 adj.
selfish 932 adj.
unsystematic
nonuniform 17 adj.
orderless 61 adj.
fitful 142 adj.
untainted
undamaged 646 adj.
untaken
unpossessed 774 adj.
untalented
unintelligent 499 adj.
unskilful 695 adj.
untamable, untameable
cruel 898 adj.
untamed
unhabituated 611 adj.
warlike 718 adj.
disobedient 738 adj.
cruel 898 adj.
untangle
unravel 62 vb.
untapped
unused 674 adj.
untarnished
unmixed 44 adj.
clean 648 adj.
honourable 929 adj.
untasted
tasteless 387 adj.
untaught
uninstructed 491 adj.
spontaneous 609 adj.
unprepared 670 adj.
unskilled 695 adj.
untaxed
uncharged 812 adj.
unteach
not know 491 vb.
educate 534 vb.
misteach 535 vb.
unteachable
unintelligent 499 adj.
obstinate 602 adj.
untearable
tough 329 adj.
untempered
weak 163 adj.
untempted
indifferent 860 adj.
untenable
defenceless 161 adj.
illogical 477 adj.
unbelieved 486 adj.
untenanted
empty 190 adj.
unpossessed 774 adj.
untended
neglected 458 adj.
untested
new 126 adj.
uncertified 474 adj.
unknown 491 adj.
unthanked
unthanked 908 adj.
unthankful
ungrateful 908 adj.
unthinkable
impossible 470 adj.
unthinking
mindless 448 adj.
unthinking 450 adj.
incurious 454 adj.
inattentive 456 adj.
involuntary 596 adj.
unthorough
negligent 458 adj.
unwilling 598 adj.
irresolute 601 adj.
imperfect 647 adj.
uncompleted 726 adj.
unthought of
unthought 450 adj.
neglected 458 adj.
unthreading
separation 46 n.
unthreatened
safe 660 adj.
unthrifty
unprepared 670 adj.
prodigal 815 adj.
unthrone
unthrone 734 vb.
deprive 786 vb.
unthrustful
modest 874 adj.
untidy
orderless 61 adj.
jumble 63 vb.
agitate 318 vb.
negligent 458 adj.
dirty 649 adj.
impair 655 vb.
untie
disunite 46 vb.
doff 229 vb.
deliver 668 vb.
disencumber 701 vb.
liberate 746 vb.
not retain 779 vb.
until
while 108 adv.
(See **till** *)*
untilled
unproductive 172 adj.
unprepared 670 adj.
unused 674 adj.
until now
until now 121 adv.
untimely
unrelated 10 adj.
ill-timed 138 adj.
inexpedient 643 adj.
untinged
unmixed 44 adj.
untipped
unthanked 908 adj.
untiring
persevering 600 adj.
untitled
plebeian 869 adj.
untold
many 104 adj.
infinite 107 adj.
unknown 491 adj.
concealed 525 adj.
untouchable
prohibited 757 adj.
outcast 883 n.
commoner 869 n.
untouched
intact 52 adj.
clean 648 adj.
unused 674 adj.
apathetic 820 adj.
nonliable 919 adj.
pure 950 adj.
untoward
contrary 14 adj.
ill-timed 138 adj.
inopportune 138 adj.
inexpedient 643 adj.
adverse 731 adj.
annoying 827 adj.
untraceable
lost 772 adj.
untraditional
modern 126 adj.
unwonted 611 adj.
untrained
uninstructed 491 adj.
unhabituated 611 adj.
immature 670 adj.
unprepared 670 adj.
unskilled 695 adj.
untrammelled
facilitated 701 adj.
unconfined 744 adj.
untranslatable
inexpressible 517 adj.
untravelled
quiescent 266 adj.
untrembling
unfearing 855 adj.
untried
new 126 adj.
moot 459 adj.
uncertified 474 adj.
unknown 491 adj.
unused 674 adj.
untrodden
new 126 adj.
unused 674 adj.
untroubled
moderate 177 adj.
content 828 adj.
untrue
erroneous 495 adj.
imaginary 513 adj.
false 541 adj.
deceiving 542 adj.
untrue 543 adj.
perfidious 930 adj.
untrustworthy
unreliable 474 adj.
unsafe 661 adj.
dishonest 930 adj.
untruth
falsehood 541 n.
untruth 543 n.
calumny 926 n.
untruthful
false 541 adj.
dishonest 930 adj.
untuned
discordant 411 adj.
inexact 495 adj.
untuneful
discordant 411 adj.
untutored
uninstructed 491 adj.
unprepared 670 adj.
artless 699 adj.
untwist
unravel 62 vb.
evolve 316 vb.
untypical
dissimilar 19 adj.
abnormal 84 adj.
unusable, unuseable
useless 641 adj.
unused 674 adj.
unused
new 126 adj.
neglected 458 adj.
unused 674 adj.
clumsy 695 adj.
unusual
unusual 84 adj.
infrequent 140 adj.
unexpected 508 adj.
wonderful 864 adj.
unusually
remarkably 32 adv.
unutilized, unutilised
unused 674 adj.
unutterable
unspeakable 32 adj.
inexpressible 517 adj.
wonderful 864 adj.
unvalued
unwanted 860 adj.
hated 888 adj.
unvanquished
unbeaten 727 adj.
independent 744 adj.
unvaried
unceasing 146 adj.
unvarnished
genuine 494 adj.
veracious 540 adj.
plain 573 adj.
artless 699 adj.

unvarying
uniform 16 adj.
unceasing 146 adj.
unchangeable 153 adj.
tedious 838 adj.
unveil
uncover 229 vb.
be plain 522 vb.
disclose 526 vb.
unveiling
debut 68 n.
unventilated
sealed off 264 adj.
warm 379 adj.
fetid 397 adj.
insalubrious 653 adj.
unverified
uncertified 474 adj.
suppositional 512 adj.
unversed
ignorant 491 adj.
unskilled 695 adj.
unversified
prosaic 593 adj.
unviable
impracticable 470 adj.
unvirtuous
wicked 934 adj.
unchaste 951 adj.
unvisited
secluded 883 adj.
unvoiced
tacit 523 adj.
voiceless 578 adj.
unwanted
remaining 41 adj.
rejected 607 adj.
superfluous 637 adj.
useless 641 adj.
unused 674 adj.
unpossessed 774 adj.
unwanted 860 adj.
disliked 861 adj.
unwarlike
peaceful 717 adj.
inexcitable 823 adj.
cowardly 856 adj.
unwarned
inexpectant 508 adj.
vulnerable 661 adj.
unprepared 670 adj.
unwarrantable
illegal 954 adj.
unwarranted
exorbitant 32 adj.
uncertified 474 adj.
illogical 477 adj.
wrong 914 adj.
unwarranted 916 adj.
unwary
negligent 458 adj.
rash 857 adj.
unwashed
opaque 423 adj.
dirty 649 adj.
unwatchful
negligent 458 adj.
unwatered
unproductive 172 adj.
unwavering
unchangeable 153 adj.
resolute 599 adj.
persevering 600 adj.
unwearied
persevering 600 adj.
industrious 678 adj.
unweave
unravel 62 vb.
unwedded
alone 88 adj.
unwedded 895 adj.
monastic 986 adj.
unwelcome
unpleasant 827 adj.
unwanted 860 adj.
hateful 888 adj.
unwelcome guest
incomer 297 n.
unwelcoming
inimical 881 adj.
unsociable 883 adj.
unwell
sick 651 adj.
unprosperous 731 adj.
unwept
hated 888 adj.
unwetted
dry 342 adj.
unwhetted
unsharpened 257 adj.
unwholesome
inexpedient 643 adj.
harmful 645 adj.
insalubrious 653 adj.
impure 951 adj.
unwieldy
unwieldy 195 adj.
weighty 322 adj.
clumsy 695 adj.
difficult 700 adj.
graceless 842 adj.
unwilled
involuntary 596 adj.
unwilling
dissenting 489 adj.
involuntary 596 adj.
unwilling 598 adj.
avoiding 620 adj.
resisting 715 adj.
refusing 760 adj.
unwind
evolve 316 vb.
repose 683 vb.
unwinking
still 266 adj.
unwiped
dirty 649 adj.
unwisdom
ignorance 491 n.
folly 499 n.
unwise
unwise 499 adj.
inexpedient 643 adj.
unskilful 695 adj.
rash 857 adj.
unwish
abrogate 752 vb.
regret 830 vb.
unwished for
unwanted 860 adj.
disliked 861 adj.
unwithered
unyielding 162 adj.
unwitnessed
uncertified 474 adj.
unwitting
ignorant 491 adj.
involuntary 596 adj.
unwitty
serious 834 adj.
dull 840 adj.
unwomanly
male 372 adj.
unwonted
unusual 84 adj.
unwonted 611 adj.
unwooed
unwedded 895 adj.
unworkable
powerless 161 adj.
impracticable 470 adj.
useless 641 adj.
unworked
immature 670 adj.
unprepared 670 adj.
unworldly
credulous 487 adj.
ignorant 491 adj.
artless 699 adj.
honourable 929 adj.
innocent 935 adj.
pious 979 adj.
unworn
unyielding 162 adj.
unworried
tranquil 266 adj.
inexcitable 823 adj.
content 828 adj.
unworshipped
unrespected 921 adj.
unworthy
inferior 35 adj.
bad 645 adj.
discreditable 867 adj.
unentitled 916 adj.
vicious 934 adj.
wicked 934 adj.
unwrap
uncover 229 vb.
straighten 249 vb.
open 263 vb.
extract 304 vb.
disclose 526 vb.
unwrinkled
flat 216 adj.
smooth 258 adj.
tranquil 266 adj.
unwritten
tacit 523 adj.
obliterated 550 adj.
unwritten law
practice 610 n.
precept 693 n.
law 953 n.
unwrought
immature 670 adj.
unyielding
lasting 113 adj.
unyielding 162 adj.
tough 329 adj.
resolute 599 adj.
obstinate 602 adj.
difficult 700 adj.
resisting 715 adj.
restraining 747 adj.
unyoke
liberate 746 vb.
unzip
disunite 46 vb.
up
aloft 209 adv.
vertically 215 adv.
up 308 adv.
successful 727 adj.
up against it
in difficulties 700 adj.
unprosperous 731 adj.
up anchor
voyage 269 vb.
— sticks
decamp 296 vb.
up and about
healthy 650 adj.
up and coming
prosperous 730 adj.
up and doing
operative 173 adj.
doing 676 adj.
busy 678 adj.
up and down
by turns 141 adv.
undulatory 251 adj.
to and fro 317 adv.
sullen 893 adj.
Upanishad
non-Biblical scripture 975 n.
upbeat
tempo 410 n.
optimistic 482 adj.
cheerful 833 adj.
upbraid
reprobate 924 vb.
upbringing
teaching 534 n.
up-country
regional 184 adj.
provincial 192 adj.
interior 224 adj.
update
modernize 126 vb.
updraught
ascent 308 n.
wind 352 n.

up-end
make vertical 215 vb.
invert 221 vb.
up for grabs
offering 759 adj.
unpossessed 774 adj.
up for sale
salable 793 adj.
upgrade
promote 285 vb.
make better 654 vb.
dignify 866 vb.
upgrowth
expansion 197 n.
ascent 308 n.
upheaval
disorder 61 n.
revolution 149 n.
havoc 165 n.
elevation 310 n.
uphill
sloping 220 adj.
ascending 308 adj.
laborious 682 adj.
difficult 700 adj.
uphold
sustain 146 vb.
support 218 vb.
corroborate 466 vb.
upholster
line 227 vb.
upholstery
lining 227 n.
equipment 630 n.
up in
expert 694 adj.
up in arms
active 678 adj.
opposing 704 adj.
quarrelling 709 adj.
attacking 712 adj.
riotous 738 adj.
upkeep
preservation 666 n.
subvention 703 n.
upland(s)
space 183 n.
high land 209 n.
plain 348 n.
uplift
displace 188 vb.
move 265 vb.
elevation 310 n.
elevate 310 vb.
improvement 654 n.
make better 654 vb.
delight 826 vb.
make pious 979 vb.
upmarket
dear 811 adj.
upmost
topmost 213 adj.
upon
(See **on** *)*
up on, be
predominate 34 vb.
up on end
vertically 215 adv.
up one's street
fit 24 adj.
advisable 642 adj.
upon one's honour/ word
affirmatively 532 adv.
as promised 764 adv.
up over
beyond 199 adv.
aloft 209 adv.
upper
superior 34 adj.
drug-taking 949 n.
upper case
print-type 587 n.
upper class
social group 371 n.
upper class 868 n.
upper crust
elite 644 n.
beau monde 848 n.
upper class 868 n.
uppercut
knock 279 n.
upper hand
advantage 34 n.
influence 178 n.
victory 727 n.
Upper House
parliament 692 n.
uppermost
supreme 34 adj.
topmost 213 adj.
topical 452 adj.
important 638 adj.
upper storey
head 213 n.
intelligence 498 n.
upper ten
beau monde 848 n.
upper class 868 n.
uppish
prideful 871 adj.
uppity
ill-bred 847 adj.
prideful 871 adj.
upright
vertical 215 adj.
elevated 310 adj.
just 913 adj.
honourable 929 adj.
virtuous 933 adj.
uprising
revolt 738 n.
uproar
turmoil 61 n.
violence 176 n.
loudness 400 n.
fight 716 n.
uproarious
excitable 822 adj.
merry 833 adj.
uproot
exclude 57 vb.
destroy 165 vb.
displace 188 vb.
eject 300 vb.
extract 304 vb.
uprush
increase 36 n.
spurt 277 n.
ascent 308 n.
ups and downs
affairs 154 n.
fluctuation 317 n.
adversity 731 n.
averageness 732 n.
upset
derange 63 vb.
revolution 149 n.
demolish 165 vb.
overturning 221 n.
lowering 311 n.
distract 456 vb.
hinder 702 vb.
revolt 738 vb.
impress 821 vb.
suffering 825 adj.
trouble 827 vb.
cause discontent 829 vb.
cause dislike 861 vb.
enrage 891 vb.
upshot
event 154 n.
effect 157 n.
judgment 480 n.
completion 725 n.
upside down
contrarily 14 adv.
orderless 61 adj.
inverted 221 adj.
upsides with
equal 28 adj.
upstage
stage set 594 n.
act 594 vb.
prideful 871 adj.
insolent 878 adj.
upstairs
aloft 209 adv.
up 308 adv.
upstanding
vertical 215 adj.
elevated 310 adj.
(See **upright** *)*
upstart
intruder 59 n.
upstart 126 n.
progression 285 n.
prosperous person 730 n.
commoner 869 n.
insolent person 878 n.
upstream
towards 281 adv.
upsurge
increase 36 n.
ascent 308 n.
upswing
increase 36 n.
elevation 310 n.
improvement 654 n.
upsy-daisy!
310 int.
uptight
nervous 854 adj.
irascible 892 adj.
up to
while 108 adv.
powerful 160 adj.
up-to-date
present 121 adj.
modern 126 adj.
progressive 285 adj.
up to everything
cunning 698 adj.
up to one
obligatory 917 adj.
up to one's eyes
busy 678 adj.
up to snuff
intelligent 498 adj.
up to something
planning 623 adj.
dishonest 930 adj.
up to the ears/eyes
completely 54 adv.
deeply 211 adv.
up to the mark
sufficient 635 adj.
not bad 644 adj.
expert 694 adj.
up-to-the-minute
present 121 adj.
modern 126 adj.
fashionable 848 adj.
uptown
city 184 n.
afar 199 adv.
upturn
invert 221 vb.
ascent 308 n.
improvement 654 n.
upward curve
increase 36 n.
upwards
aloft 209 adv.
up 308 adv.
upwards of
beyond 34 adv.
plural 101 adj.
upwind
towards 281 adv.
uraeus
regalia 743 n.
uranium
fuel 385 n.
poison 659 n.
uranography
astronomy 321 n.
uranometry 321 n.
uranometry
uranometry 321 n.
Uranus
planet 321 n.
classical deities 967 n.
urban
regional 184 adj.
urban 192 adj.
urban blight
housing 192 n.

urbane
well-bred 848 adj.
sociable 882 adj.
courteous 884 adj.
urbanite
native 191 n.
urbanity
good taste 846 n.
sociability 882 n.
courtesy 884 n.
urbanize, urbanise
urbanize 192 vb.
urbanized
urban 192 adj.
urban sprawl
housing 192 n.
expansion 197 n.
urchin
youngster 132 n.
urge
influence 178 vb.
impel 279 vb.
propound 512 vb.
affirm 532 vb.
emphasize 532 vb.
be resolute 599 vb.
incite 612 vb.
hasten 680 vb.
advise 691 vb.
compel 740 vb.
request 761 vb.
animate 821 vb.
desire 859 n.
— forward
accelerate 277 vb.
— on
accelerate 277 vb.
urgency
needfulness 627 n.
importance 638 n.
haste 680 n.
urgent
strong 162 adj.
demanding 627 adj.
important 638 adj.
compelling 740 adj.
requesting 761 adj.
urinal
latrine 649 n.
urinate
excrete 302 vb.
urine
excrement 302 n.
urn
vessel 194 n.
interment 364 n.
pottery 381 n.
urogenital disease
disease 651 n.
ursine
animal 365 adj.
Ursulines
nun 986 n.
urticaria
formication 378 n.
skin disease 651 n.
us
self 80 n.
usable, useable
useful 640 adj.
used 673 adj.
usage
connotation 514 n.
habit 610 n.
us and them
group 74 n.
use
profit by 137 vb.
operate 173 vb.
habit 610 n.
require 627 vb.
instrumentality 628 n.
importance 638 n.
utility 640 n.
find useful 640 vb.
use 673 n.vb.
action 676 n.
skill 694 n.
possess 773 vb.
— one's eyes
see 438 vb.
— one's head
cognize 447 vb.
be wise 498 vb.
— one's influence
be instrumental 628 vb.
— to
be wont 610 vb.
— up
abate 37 vb.
disable 161 vb.
waste 634 vb.
impair 655 vb.
dispose of 673 vb.
use 673 vb.
expend 806 vb.
— wrongly
misuse 675 vb.
used to
habituated 610 adj.
used up
impotent 161 adj.
used 673 adj.
disused 674 adj.
useful
instrumental 628 adj.
important 638 adj.
useful 640 adj.
advisable 642 adj.
beneficial 644 adj.
used 673 adj.
aiding 703 adj.
usefulness
importance 638 n.
utility 640 n.
use 673 n.
useless
incomplete 55 adj.
powerless 161 adj.
absurd 497 adj.
spurious 542 adj.
superfluous 637 adj.
trivial 639 adj.
useless 641 adj.
inexpedient 643 adj.
bad 645 adj.
deteriorated 655 adj.
unused 674 adj.
uselessness
ineffectuality 161 n.
unimportance 639 n.
inutility 641 n.
nonuse 674 n.
usher
accompany 89 vb.
teacher 537 n.
stagehand 594 n.
retainer 742 n.
greet 884 vb.
bridal party 894 n.
— in
come before 64 vb.
initiate 68 vb.
precede 283 vb.
admit 299 vb.
predict 511 vb.
usherette
stagehand 594 n.
usual
general 79 adj.
regular 81 adj.
typical 83 adj.
usual 610 adj.
trivial 639 adj.
dull 840 adj.
fashionable 848 adj.
usual channels
intermediary 231 n.
usual thing, the
expectation 507 n.
practice 610 n.
usufruct
use 673 n.
possession 773 n.
usurer
lender 784 n.
niggard 816 n.
usurp
encroach 306 vb.
take authority 733 vb.
unthrone 734 vb.
appropriate 786 vb.
be undue 916 vb.
usurper
impostor 545 n.
taker 786 n.
usurper 916 n.
usury
gain 771 n.
lending 784 n.
interest 803 n.
utensil
tool 630 n.
uterine
akin 11 adj.
uterus
genitalia 167 n.
insides 224 n.
utile
useful 640 adj.
utilitarian
useful 640 adj.
philanthropist 901 n.
utilitarianism
philosophy 449 n.
good 615 n.
utility 640 n.
good policy 642 n.
benevolence 897 n.
philanthropy 901 n.
morals 917 n.
utility
benefit 615 n.
instrumentality 628 n.
utility 640 n.
use 673 n.
utilize, utilise
find useful 640 vb.
use 673 vb.
utmost
exorbitant 32 adj.
limit 236 n.
utmost, the
completeness 54 n.
Utopia
fantasy 513 n.
aspiration 852 n.
Utopian
visionary 513 n.
reformer 654 n.
hoper 852 n.
philanthropist 901 n.
utricle
bladder 194 n.
utter
consummate 32 adj.
complete 54 adj.
divulge 526 vb.
publish 528 vb.
voice 577 vb.
speak 579 vb.
mint 797 vb.
utterance
cry 408 n.
voice 577 n.
speech 579 n.
utterly
greatly 32 adv.
completely 54 adv.
uttermost
limit 236 n.
U-turn
reversion 148 n.
return 286 n.
circuition 314 n.
tergiversation 603 n.
uxorious
loving 887 adj.

V

V-1, V-2
rocket 276 n.
bomb 723 n.
vacancy
absence of thought 450 n.

job 622 n.
vacant
empty 190 adj.adj.
unthinking 450 adj.
unintelligent 499 adj.
unprovided 636 adj.
unused 674 adj.
unpossessed 774 adj.
vacate
be absent 190 vb.
go away 190 vb.
relinquish 621 vb.
abrogate 752 vb.
resign 753 vb.
vacation
interim 108 n.
leisure 681 n.
repose 683 n.
vaccinate
implant 303 vb.
doctor 658 vb.
safeguard 660 vb.
vaccination
hygiene 652 n.
prophylactic 658 n.
vacillate
change 143 vb.
vary 152 vb.
be uncertain 474 vb.
be irresolute 601 vb.
be capricious 604 vb.
vacuity
insubstantiality 4 n.
emptiness 190 n.
absence of intellect 448 n.
absence of thought 450 n.
unintelligence 499 n.
vacuum
nonexistence 2 n.
emptiness 190 n.
rarity 325 n.
vacuum cleaner
extractor 304 n.
cleaning utensil 648 n.
vacuum flask
cauldron 194 n.
vacuum-pack
cover 226 vb.
vade mecum
guidebook 524 n.
vagabond
wanderer 268 n.
low fellow 869 n.
outcast 883 n.
knave 938 n.
vagary
foolery 497 n.
ideality 513 n.
whim 604 n.
vagina
genitalia 167 n.
vagrancy
wandering 267 n.
deviation 282 n.
vagrant
travelling 267 adj.
wanderer 268 n.
deviating 282 adj.
poor person 801 n.
vague
insubstantial 4 adj.
general 79 adj.
amorphous 244 adj.
shadowy 419 adj.
indistinct 444 adj.
uncertain 474 adj.
uninstructed 491 adj.
equivocal 518 adj.
reticent 525 adj.
unclear 568 adj.
vague suspicion
conjecture 512 n.
vain
insubstantial 4 adj.
profitless 641 adj.
useless 641 adj.
unsuccessful 728 adj.
affected 850 adj.
prideful 871 adj.
vain 873 adj.
ostentatious 875 adj.
vainglorious
prideful 871 adj.
vain 873 adj.
boastful 877 adj.
vain person
affecter 850 n.
vain person 873 n.
boaster 877 n.
egotist 932 n.
vair
skin 226 n.
heraldry 547 n.
Vaishnavas
non-Christian sect 978 n.
valance
edging 234 n.
trimming 844 n.
vale
valley 255 n.
valediction
valediction 296 n.
courteous act 884 n.
valedictory
departing 296 adj.
oration 579 n.
valentine
loved one 887 n.
love token 889 n.
vale of sorrows
adversity 731 n.
valet
clean 648 vb.
restore 656 vb.
domestic 742 n.
valeta
dance 837 n.
valetudinarian
sick person 651 n.
unhealthy 651 adj.
valgus
deformity 246 n.
Valhalla
mythic heaven 971 n.
valiant
courageous 855 adj.
valiant effort
attempt 671 n.
valid
established 153 adj.
powerful 160 adj.
strong 162 adj.
genuine 494 adj.
affirmative 532 adj.
useful 640 adj.
validate
corroborate 466 vb.
grant claims 915 vb.
make legal 953 vb.
validity
authenticity 494 n.
legality 953 n.
valise
box 194 n.
Valkyrie
mythical being 970 n.
valley
gap 201 n.
high land 209 n.
lowness 210 n.
valley 255 n.
plain 348 n.
conduit 351 n.
vallum
fence 235 n.
fortification 713 n.
valorize, valorise
tax 809 vb.
valour
courage 855 n.
valuable
great 32 adj.
good 615 adj.
important 638 adj.
profitable 640 adj.
valuable 644 adj.
of price 811 adj.
valuables
estate 777 n.
valuation
measurement 465 n.
estimate 480 n.
value
degree 27 n.
equivalence 28 n.
quid pro quo 150 n.
hue 425 n.
appraise 465 vb.
estimate 480 vb.
meaning 514 n.
importance 638 n.
make important 638 vb.
utility 640 n.
goodness 644 n.
account 808 vb.
price 809 n.vb.
dearness 811 n.
have taste 846 vb.
honour 866 vb.
love 887 vb.
respect 920 vb.
approve 923 vb.
value for money
cheapness 812 n.
value judgment
intuition 476 n.
judgment 480 n.
valueless
trivial 639 adj.
profitless 641 adj.
cheap 812 adj.
valuer
appraiser 465 n.
estimator 480 n.
valuta
finance 797 n.
valve
electronics 160 n.
stopper 264 n.
conduit 351 n.
vamoose
decamp 296 vb.
vamp
play music 413 vb.
improvise 609 vb.
motivator 612 n.
a beauty 841 n.
excite love 887 vb.
loose woman 952 n.
— up
modify 143 vb.
make better 654 vb.
vampire
taker 786 n.
hellhag 904 n.
glutton 947 n.
demon 970 n.
van
beginning 68 n.
lorry 274 n.
(See **vanguard** *)*
Van Allen belt/layer
atmosphere 340 n.
radiation 417 n.
vandal
destroyer 168 n.
violent creature 176 n.
vulgarian 847 n.
evildoer 904 n.
vandalism
destruction 165 n.
violence 176 n.
waste 634 n.
vandalize, vandalise
impair 655 vb.
make ugly 842 vb.
Van Dyke
hair 259 n.
notch 260 vb.
vane
weather 340 n.
vanguard
precursor 66 n.
front 237 n.

preceding 283 n.
armed force 722 n.
vanilla
condiment 389 n.
scent 396 n.
Vanir
Nordic deities 967 n.
vanish
pass away 2 vb.
be transient 114 vb.
go away 190 vb.
be unseen 444 vb.
disappear 446 vb.
be stealthy 525 vb.
vanished
lost 772 adj.
vanishing cream
cosmetic 843 n.
vanishing point
minuteness 196 n.
convergence 293 n.
disappearance 446 n.
vanishing trick
disappearance 446 n.
vanity
insubstantial thing 4 n.
ineffectuality 161 n.
folly 499 n.
inutility 641 n.
affectation 850 n.
pride 871 n.
vanity 873 n.
ostentation 875 n.
boasting 877 n.
vanity case
bag 194 n.
cosmetic 843 n.
Vanity Fair
fashion 848 n.
vanquish
overmaster 727 vb.
vantage
advantage 34 n.
vantage ground
advantage 34 n.
influence 178 n.
vantage point
view 438 n.
vapid
tasteless 387 adj.
feeble 572 adj.
dull 840 adj.
vaporific
gaseous 336 adj.
vaporific 338 adj.
vaporize, vaporise
gasify 336 vb.
vaporize 338 vb.
disappear 446 vb.
vaporous
insubstantial 4 adj.
gaseous 336 adj.
vaporific 338 adj.
cloudy 355 adj.
opaque 423 adj.
imaginary 513 adj.
vapour
emit 300 vb.
gas 336 n.
cloud 355 n.
fantasy 513 n.
mean nothing 515 vb.
boast 877 vb.
vapours
melancholy 834 n.
vapour trail
aeronautics 271 n.
trace 548 n.
variable
circumstantial 8 adj.
nonuniform 17 adj.
unequal 29 adj.
multiform 82 adj.
number 85 n.
fitful 142 adj.
changeable 143 adj.
changeable thing 152 n.
unreliable 474 adj.
irresolute 601 adj.
capricious 604 adj.
excitable 822 adj.
variance
disagreement 25 n.
dissension 709 n.
variant
variant 15 n.
speciality 80 n.
variation
contrariety 14 n.
difference 15 n.
dissimilarity 19 n.
numerical operation 86 n.
change 143 n.
musical piece 412 n.
varicose veins
cardiovascular disease 651 n.
variegation
nonuniformity 17 n.
medley 43 n.
discontinuity 72 n.
changeableness 152 n.
colour 425 n.
variegation 437 n.
spectacle 445 n.
ornamental art 844 n.
variety
difference 15 n.
nonuniformity 17 n.
dissimilarity 19 n.
medley 43 n.
sort 77 n.
multiformity 82 n.
variegation 437 n.
stage show 594 n.
variola
infection 651 n.
various
different 15 adj.
nonuniform 17 adj.
dissimilar 19 adj.
many 104 adj.
varlet
low fellow 869 n.
knave 938 n.
varmint
knave 938 n.
varnish
facing 226 n.
smoother 258 n.
resin 357 n.
sophisticate 477 vb.
conceal 525 vb.
cant 541 vb.
sham 542 n.
art equipment 553 n.
cleanser 648 n.
decorate 844 vb.
ostentation 875 n.
extenuate 927 vb.
varsity
academy 539 n.
Varuna
Hindu deities 967 n.
vary
differ 15 vb.
change 143 vb.
vary 152 vb.
be capricious 604 vb.
— as
be related 9 vb.
correlate 12 vb.
vascular
capsular 194 adj.
tubular 263 adj.
vase
bowl 194 n.
vessel 194 n.
vasectomy
contraception 172 n.
surgery 658 n.
vassal
dependant 742 n.
subject 742 n.
subject 745 adj.
vast
enormous 32 adj.
spacious 183 adj.
huge 195 adj.
large 195 adj.
vat
vat 194 n.
VAT
tax 809 n.
vatic
predicting 511 adj.
Vatican
church office 985 n.
the church 985 n.
vaudeville
stage show 594 n.
place of amusement 837 n.
vault
cellar 194 n.
roof 226 n.
curve 248 n.
dome 253 n.
ascend 308 vb.
leap 312 n.vb.
tomb 364 n.
hiding-place 527 n.
storage 632 n.
church interior 990 n
vaulted
covered 226 adj.
curved 248 adj.
concave 255 adj.
vaulting
superior 34 adj.
exaggerated 546 adj.
vaunt
be affected 850 vb.
boast 877 n.vb.
VC
decoration 729 n.
brave person 855 n.
VD
venereal disease 651 n
VDU
data processing 86 n
optical device 442 n.
veal
meat 301 n.
vector
quantity 26 n.
number 85 n.
transferrer 272 n.
infection 651 n.
Veda
non-Biblical scripture 975 n.
Vedanta
philosophy 449 n.
Vedantic
religious 973 adj.
Vedic
religious 973 adj.
scriptural 975 adj.
Vedic deities
Hindu deities 967 n.
veer
change 143 vb.
vary 152 vb.
navigate 269 vb.
deviate 282 vb.
blow 352 vb.
vegan
eater 301 n.
abstainer 942 n.
vegetable
inertness 175 n.
vegetable 301 n.
plant 366 n.
vegetal 366 adj.
mindless 448 adj.
unthinking 450 adj.
vegetable kingdom
vegetable life 366 n.
vegetal
vegetal 366 adj.
vegetarian
eater 301 n.
abstainer 942 n.
vegetate
be 1 vb.
pass time 108 vb.
be inert 175 vb.

be quiescent 266 vb.
vegetate 366 vb.
be inactive 679 vb.
be insensitive 820 vb.
be unsociable 883 vb.

vegetation
vegetable life 366 n.

vehement
vigorous 174 adj.
violent 176 adj.
assertive 532 adj.
forceful 571 adj.
fervent 818 adj.
excitable 822 adj.

vehicle
conveyance 267 n.
transport 272 n.
carrier 273 n.
vehicle 274 n.
stage play 594 n.
instrument 628 n.

vehicular
vehicular 274 adj.

veil
shade 226 n.
cover 226 vb.
headgear 228 n.
darken 418 vb.
bedim 419 vb.
screen 421 n.vb.
invisibility 444 n.
conceal 525 vb.
disguise 527 n.
vocation 622 n.

veiled
uncertain 474 adj.
unknown 491 adj.
occult 523 adj.
monastic 986 adj.

vein
temperament 5 n.
state 7 n.
tendency 179 n.
filament 208 n.
tube 263 n.
conduit 351 n.
variegate 437 vb.
style 566 n.
store 632 n.
affections 817 n.

velar
speech sound 398 n.

veld, veldt
space 183 n.
plain 348 n.

velleity
will 595 n.

vellum
stationery 586 n.
bookbinding 589 n.

velocipede
bicycle 274 n.

velocity
motion 265 n.
velocity 277 n.

velour, velours
textile 222 n.
smoothness 258 n.
hair 259 n.

velvet
textile 222 n.
smoothness 258 n.
hair 259 n.
softness 327 n.
euphoria 376 n.
melodious 410 adj.
palmy days 730 n.

velveteen
textile 222 n.

velvet glove
conduct 688 n.
leniency 736 n.

velvety
smooth 258 adj.
downy 259 adj.
soft 327 adj.

venal
avaricious 816 adj.
unjust 914 adj.
venal 930 adj.
selfish 932 adj.

vend
sell 793 vb.

vendetta
quarrel 709 n.
enmity 881 n.
revenge 910 n.

vendible
salable 793 adj.
merchandise 795 n.

vending machine
shop 796 n.

vendor
seller 793 n.

veneer
layer 207 n.
shallowness 212 n.
facing 226 n.
appearance 445 n.
disguise 527 n.
sham 542 n.
ostentation 875 n.

venerable
great 32 adj.
immemorial 127 adj.
olden 127 adj.
ageing 131 adj.
respected 920 adj.

venerate
respect 920 vb.
worship 981 vb.

venereal
conjunctive 45 adj.
diseased 651 adj.
sensual 944 adj.

venereal disease
venereal disease 651 n.

venery
unchastity 951 n.

venesection
surgery 658 n.

venetian blind
shade 226 n.
curtain 421 n.

vengeance
revenge 910 n.

vengeful
revengeful 910 adj.

venial
forgiven 909 adj.
vindicable 927 adj.
guiltless 935 adj.

venial sin
trifle 639 n.
vice 934 n.
guilty act 936 n.

venison
meat 301 n.
savouriness 390 n.

Venn diagram
reasoning 475 n.

venom
poison 659 n.
malevolence 898 n.

venomous
toxic 653 adj.
baneful 659 adj.
inimical 881 adj.
malevolent 898 adj.
detracting 926 adj.

vent
orifice 263 n.
outlet 298 n.
empty 300 vb.
air pipe 353 n.
divulge 526 vb.
means of escape 667 n.
liberate 746 vb.

— one's spleen
be angry 891 vb.
resent 891 vb.

ventilate
aerate 340 vb.
enquire 459 vb.
divulge 526 vb.
publish 528 vb.
dissertate 591 vb.
purify 648 vb.
sanitate 652 vb.
refresh 685 vb.

ventilation
ventilation 352 n.
refrigeration 382 n.
inodorousness 395 n.

ventilator
ventilation 352 n.
air pipe 353 n.

ventpeg
stopper 264 n.

ventral
cellular 194 adj.

ventre à terre
swiftly 277 adv.

ventricle
compartment 194 n.

ventriloquism
mimicry 20 n.
sleight 542 n.
speech 579 n.

ventriloquist
conjuror 545 n.
entertainer 594 n.

venture
be tentative 461 vb.
gambling 618 n.
business 622 n.
danger 661 n.
attempt 671 n.vb.
undertaking 672 n.
property 777 n.
trade 791 n.
speculate 791 vb.
be courageous 855 vb.

venturesome
experimental 461 adj.
speculative 618 adj.
dangerous 661 adj.
attempting 671 adj.
enterprising 672 adj.
courageous 855 adj.
rash 857 adj.

venue
focus 76 n.
locality 187 n.

Venus
planet 321 n.
woman 373 n.
luminary 420 n.
a beauty 841 n.
love god 887 n.
Olympian deity 967 n.

veracious
true 494 adj.
veracious 540 adj.
artless 699 adj.
trustworthy 929 adj.

veracity
veracity 540 n.

verandah
lobby 194 n.

verb
part of speech 564 n.

verbal
semantic 514 adj.
informative 524 adj.
verbal 559 adj.
grammatical 564 adj.
speaking 579 adj.

verbalism
lack of meaning 515 n.
phrase 563 n.

verbalize, verbalise
voice 577 vb.

verbatim
imitatively 20 adv.
verbally 559 adv.

verbiage
empty talk 515 n.
word 559 n.
imperspicuity 568 n.
diffuseness 570 n.

verbose
verbal 559 adj.
diffuse 570 adj.
loquacious 581 adj.

verboten
prohibited 757 Adj. adj.
illegal 954 adj.
verb. sap.
hint 524 n.
verdant
prolific 171 adj.
vegetal 366 adj.
green 434 adj.
verderer
forestry 366 n.
judge 957 n.
verdict
judgment 480 n.
legal trial 959 n.
verdigris
greenness 434 n.
verdure
foliage 366 n.
grass 366 n.
greenness 434 n.
verge
extremity 69 n.
tend 179 vb.
nearness 200 n.
edge 234 n.
limit 236 n.
point to 281 vb.
road 624 n.
badge of rule 743 n.
— on/upon
be near 200 vb.
verger
officer 741 n.
church officer 986 n.
veridical
veracious 540 adj.
verifiable
experimental 461 adj.
evidential 466 adj.
certain 473 adj.
verify
experiment 461 vb.
corroborate 466 vb.
make certain 473 vb.
demonstrate 478 vb.
discover 484 vb.
give security 767 vb.
verily
positively 32 adv.
truly 494 adv.
verisimilitude
probability 471 n.
accuracy 494 n.
truth 494 n.
veracity 540 n.
veritable
genuine 494 adj.
true 494 adj.
verity
truth 494 n.
verjuice
sourness 393 n.
vermicular
snaky 251 adj.
animal 365 adj.
vermifuge
antidote 658 n.
vermilion
red pigment 431 n.
red 431 adj.
vermin
insect 365 n.
dirt 649 n.
rabble 869 n.
cad 938 n.
knave 938 n.
verminous
insalubrious 653 adj.
vermouth
wine 301 n.
vernacular
native 191 adj.
language 557 n.
dialect 560 n.
plain 573 adj.
vernal
new 126 adj.
vernal 128 adj.
vernal equinox
spring 128 n.
uranometry 321 n.
vernier
microscopy 196 n.
gauge 465 n.
verruca
swelling 253 n.
skin disease 651 n.
versant
incline 220 n.
versatile
multiform 82 adj.
changeful 152 adj.
tergiversating 603 adj.
useful 640 adj.
skilful 694 adj.
verse
subdivision 53 n.
poetry 593 n.
verse form 593 n.
versed in
knowing 490 adj.
expert 694 adj.
verse drama
poem 593 n.
stage play 594 n.
versicle
verse form 593 n.
versicolour
iridescent 437 adj.
versifier
poet 593 n.
versify
poetize 593 vb.
version
sort 77 n.
speciality 80 n.
transformation 143 n.
translation 520 n.
description 590 n.
vers libres
verse form 593 n.
verso
rear 238 n.
sinistrality 242 n.
edition 589 n.
versus
towards 281 adv.
in opposition 704 adv.
vert
green 434 adj.
heraldic 547 adj.
vertebrae
pillar 218 n.
vertebral
central 225 adj.
back 238 adj.
vertebrate
animal 365 n.adj.
vertex
extremity 69 n.
vertex 213 n.
roof 226 n.
sharp point 256 n.
vertical
vertical 215 adj.
vertically
aloft 209 adv.
vertically 215 adv.
vertical takeoff
aeronautics 271 n.
aviational 276 adj.
verticil
coil 251 n.
vertiginous
high 209 adj.
rotary 315 adj.
vertigo
rotation 315 n.
frenzy 503 n.
illness 651 n.
verve
vigorousness 174 n.
vigour 571 n.
moral sensibility 819 n.
very
greatly 32 adv.
Very light
signal light 420 n.
very same, the
identity 13 n.
very thing, the
no imitation 21 n.
fitness 24 n.
authenticity 494 n.
vesicle
bladder 194 n.
sphere 252 n.
swelling 253 n.
Vesper
evening 129 n.
planet 321 n.
luminary 420 n.
vespers
evening 129 n.
church service 988 n.
vessel
vessel 194 n.
ship 275 n.
pottery 381 n.
vest
underwear 228 n.
give 781 vb.
make legal 953 vb.
Vesta
home 192 n.
lesser deity 967 n.
vestal
spinster 895 n.
virgin 950 n.
priest 986 n.
vested
established 153 adj.
due 915 adj.
vested interest
master 741 n.
dueness 915 n.
vestibule
lobby 194 n.
access 624 n.
vestige
small quantity 33 n.
remainder 41 n.
trace 548 n.
vestigial
remaining 41 adj.
vestments
vestments 989 n.
vestry
council 692 n.
church interior 990 n.
vesture
dressing 228 n.
vet
animal husbandry 369 n.
be attentive 455 vb.
estimate 480 vb.
doctor 658 n.
veteran
olden 127 adj.
old man 133 n.
matured 669 adj.
expert 694 adj.
expert 696 n.
warlike 718 adj.
soldier 722 n.
veterinary disease
animal disease 651 n.
veterinary science
animal husbandry 369 n.
veterinary surgeon
doctor 658 n.
veto
restrain 747 vb.
prohibition 757 n.
prohibit 757 vb.
vex
harm 645 vb.
torment 827 vb.
enrage 891 vb.
vexation
difficulty 700 n.
sorrow 825 n.

annoyance 827 n.
anger 891 n.
vexatious
annoying 827 adj.
vexillum
flag 547 n.
VHF
radiation 417 n.
via
towards 281 adv.
via 624 adv.
viable
alive 360 adj.
possible 469 adj.
viaduct
crossing 222 n.
bridge 624 n.
vial
vessel 194 n.
via media
middle way 625 n.
viands
food 301 n.
viaticum
Christian rite 988 n.
the sacrament 988 n.
viator
traveller 268 n.
vibes
gong 414 n.
feeling 818 n.
vibrancy
oscillation 317 n.
vibrant
vigorous 174 adj.
oscillating 317 adj.
resonant 404 adj.
feeling 818 adj.
vibraphone
gong 414 n.
vibrate
vary 152 vb.
oscillate 317 vb.
be agitated 318 vb.
roll 403 vb.
resound 404 vb.
show feeling 818 vb.
vibration(s)
agitation 318 n.
sound 398 n.
resonance 404 n.
feeling 818 n.
vibrato
adagio 412 adv.
vibratory
unstable 152 adj.
oscillating 317 adj.
vicar
deputy 755 n.
church title 986 n.
pastor 986 n.
vicarage
house 192 n.
parsonage 986 n.
vicar-general
deputy 755 n.
vicarious
substituted 150 adj.
commissioned 751 adj.
Vicar of Bray
tergiversator 603 n.
vice
badness 645 n.
bane 659 n.
nippers 778 n.
wrong 914 n.
vice 934 n.
unchastity 951 n.
vice-
deputy 755 n.
vice-chancellor
director 690 n.
officer 741 n.
deputy 755 n.
vice-like
retentive 778 adj.
vice-president
director 690 n.
deputy 755 n.
viceroy
governor 741 n.
deputy 755 n.
vice squad
social evil 951 n.
vice versa
correlatively 12 adv.
contrarily 14 adv.
in exchange 151 adv.
inversely 221 adv.
against 240 adv.
vicinity
locality 187 n.
near place 200 n.
surroundings 230 n.
vicious
furious 176 adj.
evil 616 adj.
bad 645 adj.
disobedient 738 adj.
malevolent 898 adj.
wrong 914 adj.
vicious 934 adj.
vicious circle
continuity 71 n.
obstacle 702 n.
vicissitude(s)
changeable thing 152 n.
affairs 154 n.
adversity 731 n.
vicissitudinous
changeful 152 adj.
victim
weakling 163 n.
corpse 363 n.
dupe 544 n.
chase 619 n.
loser 728 n.
unlucky person 731 n.
booty 790 n.
sufferer 825 n.
laughingstock 851 n.
oblation 981 n.
victimize, victimise
befool 542 vb.
ill-treat 645 vb.
oppress 735 vb.
rob 788 vb.
be malevolent 898 vb.
punish 963 vb.
victor
superior 34 n.
exceller 644 n.
victor 727 n.
victoria
carriage 274 n.
Victoria Cross
badge 547 n.
decoration 729 n.
Victorian
antiquated 127 adj.
olden 127 adj.
prudish 950 adj.
Victoriana
archaism 127 n.
victorious
superior 34 adj.
successful 727 adj.
victory
victory 727 n.
victual
feed 301 vb.
provide 633 vb.
victualler
provider 633 n.
victuals
food 301 n.
vicuna
fibre 208 n.
textile 222 n.
videlicet
namely 80 adv.
video
spectacle 445 n.
appearing 445 adj.
videopack
camera 442 n.
videophone
telecommunication 531 n.
videorecorder
broadcasting 531 n.
recording instrument 549 n.
videotape
broadcasting 531 n.
record 548 vb.
vie
be good 644 vb.
— with
contend 716 vb.
vi et armis
violently 176 adv.
by force 740 adv.
vieux jeu
antiquated 127 adj.
view
range 183 n.
open space 263 n.
inspection 438 n.
view 438 n.
see 438 vb.
watch 441 vb.
appearance 445 n.
spectacle 445 n.
idea 451 n.
estimate 480 n.
opinion 485 n.
manifestation 522 n.
art subject 553 n.
intention 617 n.
beauty 841 n.
viewdata
data processing 86 n.
information 524 n.
viewer
spectator 441 n.
broadcasting 531 n.
viewfinder
telescope 442 n.
view halloo
cry 408 n.
viewing
inspection 438 n.
viewpoint
view 438 n.
opinion 485 n.
vigesimal
fifth and over 99 adj.
vigil
precursor 66 n.
period 110 n.
priority 119 n.
surveillance 457 n.
church service 988 n.
vigilance
carefulness 457 n.
sagacity 498 n.
vigilant
seeing 438 adj.
attentive 455 adj.
vigilant 457 adj.
tutelary 660 adj.
prepared 669 adj.
active 678 adj.
vigilante
protector 660 n.
vigilantism
lawlessness 954 n.
vigils
prayers 981 n.
vignette
picture 553 n.
description 590 n.
acting 594 n.
vigorous
dynamic 160 adj.
operative 173 adj.
vigorous 174 adj.
forceful 571 adj.
resolute 599 adj.
healthy 650 adj.
active 678 adj.
vigorously
greatly 32 adv.
vigorously 174 adv.
forcefully 571 adv.

vigour
energy 160 n.
vitality 162 n.
vigorousness 174 n.
affirmation 532 n.
vigour 571 n.
eloquence 579 n.
resolution 599 n.
restlessness 678 n.
warm feeling 818 n.
moral sensibility 819 n.
Viking
mariner 270 n.
vile
bad 645 adj.
cowardly 856 adj.
rascally 930 adj.
heinous 934 adj.
vilification
scurrility 899 n.
vilify
shame 867 vb.
dispraise 924 vb.
defame 926 vb.
villa
house 192 n.
villadom
inhabitants 191 n.
housing 192 n.
averageness 732 n.
village
district 184 n.
inhabitants 191 n.
housing 192 n.
village green
focus 76 n.
meeting place 192 n.
pleasure ground 837 n.
village idiot
country-dweller 869 n.
villager
dweller 191 n.
native 191 n.
villain
evildoer 904 n.
offender 904 n.
bad person 938 n.
knave 938 n.
villainous
bad 645 adj.
ugly 842 adj.
rascally 930 adj.
vicious 934 adj.
villainy
improbity 930 n.
wickedness 934 n.
villein
slave 742 n.
commoner 869 n.
villeinage
servitude 745 n.
villous
hairy 259 adj.
vim
vitality 162 n.
vigorousness 174 n.
vigour 571 n.
vinaigrette
sauce 389 n.
scent 396 n.
vincible
unsuccessful 728 adj.
vinculum
bond 47 n.
vindicable
vindicable 927 adj.
vindicate
demonstrate 478 vb.
claim 915 vb.
vindicate 927 vb.
vindication
credential 466 n.
testimony 466 n.
counterevidence 467 n.
vindication 927 n.
acquittal 960 n.
vindicatory
excusing 614 adj.
vindicating 927 adj.
vindictive
hating 888 adj.
resentful 891 adj.
malevolent 898 adj.
pitiless 906 adj.
revengeful 910 adj.
punitive 963 adj.
vine
plant 366 n.
vine-dressing
agriculture 370 n.
vinegar
sourness 393 n.
painfulness 827 n.
vinegary
irascible 892 adj.
sullen 893 adj.
vineyard
farm 370 n.
vino
wine 301 n.
vinous
drunken 949 adj.
intoxicating 949 adj.
vintage
assemblage 74 n.
date 108 n.
olden 127 adj.
product 164 n.
agriculture 370 n.
tasty 386 adj.
savoury 390 adj.
store 632 n.
goodness 644 n.
excellent 644 adj.
earnings 771 n.
vintner
provider 633 n.
vinyl
floor-cover 226 n.
viol
viol 414 n.
viola
viol 414 n.
violate
force 176 vb.
ill-treat 645 vb.
disobey 738 vb.
not observe 769 vb.
be undue 916 vb.
debauch 951 vb.
be impious 980 vb.
— a law
be unconformable 84 vb.
be illegal 954 vb.
violence
destruction 165 n.
vigorousness 174 n.
violence 176 n.
misuse 675 n.
warfare 718 n.
brute force 735 n.
excitable state 822 n.
cruel act 898 n.
violent
disorderly 61 adj.
revolutionary 149 adj.
powerful 160 adj.
violent 176 adj.
windy 352 adj.
frenzied 503 adj.
assertive 532 adj.
exaggerated 546 adj.
harmful 645 adj.
hasty 680 adj.
fervent 818 adj.
excited 821 adj.
angry 891 adj.
lawless 954 adj.
violent creature
violent creature 176 n.
violently
extremely 32 adv.
violet
fragrance 396 n.
purple 436 adj.
humility 872 n.
violin
viol 414 n.
violinist
instrumentalist 413 n.
VIP
person 371 n.
bigwig 638 n.
person of repute 866 n.
viper
reptile 365 n.
bane 659 n.
noxious animal 904 n.
knave 938 n.
viper in one's bosom
troublemaker 663 n.
enemy 881 n.
evildoer 904 n.
viperish
malevolent 898 adj.
cursing 899 adj.
virago
violent creature 176 n.
woman 373 n.
shrew 892 n.
Virgilian
poetic 593 adj.
virgin
intact 52 adj.
new 126 adj.
woman 373 n.
unknown 491 adj.
unwedded 895 adj.
virgin 950 n.
virginal
young 130 adj.
virtuous 933 adj.
pure 950 adj.
virginals
piano 414 n.
virgin birth
propagation 167 n.
virginibus puerisque
pure 950 adj.
virginity
unproductiveness 172 n.
celibacy 895 n.
purity 950 n.
virgin soil
unknown thing 491 n.
undevelopment 670 n.
Virgo
zodiac 321 n.
virgule
punctuation 547 n.
viridescent
green 434 adj.
viridian
green pigment 434 n.
virile
grown-up 134 adj.
manly 162 adj.
generative 167 adj.
vigorous 174 adj.
male 372 adj.
virility
vitality 162 n.
male 372 n.
virology
medical art 658 n.
virtu
good taste 846 n.
virtual
intrinsic 5 adj.
equivalent 28 adj.
powerful 160 adj.
virtually
actually 1 adv.
intrinsically 5 adv.
almost 33 adv.
on the whole 52 adv.
virtue
essential part 5 n.
ability 160 n.

utility 640 n.
goodness 644 n.
manliness 855 n.
morals 917 n.
probity 929 n.
virtue 933 n.
purity 950 n.
virtuosity
musical skill 413 n.
skill 694 n.
good taste 846 n.
virtuoso
musician 413 n.
proficient person 696 n.
virtuous
excellent 644 adj.
reputable 866 adj.
virtuous 933 adj.
pure 950 adj.
pietistic 979 adj.
(See **virtue** *)*
virulent
keen 174 adj.
baneful 659 adj.
hating 888 adj.
resentful 891 adj.
maleficent 898 adj.
virus
microorganism 196 n.
infection 651 n.
poison 659 n.
visa
credential 466 n.
assent 488 n.
permit 756 n.
visage
face 237 n.
feature 445 n.
vis-à-vis
concerning 9 adv.
in front 237 adv.
against 240 adv.
visceral
interior 224 adj.
felt 818 adj.
viscid
cohesive 48 adj.
thick 205 adj.
viscid 354 adj.
resinous 357 adj.
viscidity
viscidity 354 n.
retention 778 n.
viscount, viscountess
person of rank 868 n.
viscountcy
aristocracy 868 n.
viscous
cohesive 48 adj.
fluid 335 adj.
viscid 354 adj.
Vishnu
Trinity 965 n.
Hindu deities 967 n.
visibility
substantiality 3 n.
visibility 443 n.
visible
visible 443 adj.
appearing 445 adj.
intelligible 516 adj.
manifest 522 adj.
shown 522 adj.
vis inertiae
energy 160 n.
counteraction 182 n.
vision
vision 438 n.
visual fallacy 440 n.
appearance 445 n.
spectacle 445 n.
foresight 510 n.
fantasy 513 n.
manifestation 522 n.
objective 617 n.
a beauty 841 n.
aspiration 852 n.
occultism 984 n.
visionary
unreal 2 adj.
insubstantial 4 adj.
spectator 441 n.
impossible 470 adj.
crank 504 n.
visionary 513 n.
imaginary 513 adj.
reformer 654 n.
hoper 852 n.
philanthropist 901 n.
worshipper 981 n.
visionless
blind 439 adj.
visit
presence 189 n.
dwell 192 vb.
travel 267 vb.
arrive 295 vb.
enter 297 vb.
social round 882 n.
visit 882 vb.
philanthropize 897 vb.
punish 963 vb.
haunt 970 vb.
visitant
incomer 297 n.
ghost 970 n.
visitation
enquiry 459 n.
bane 659 n.
adversity 731 n.
severity 735 n.
suffering 825 n.
punishment 963 n.
visiting card
label 547 n.
visiting terms
social round 882 n.
visitor
resident 191 n.
arrival 295 n.
incomer 297 n.
enquirer 459 n.
sociable person 882 n.
visor
shade 226 n.
screen 421 n.
armour 713 n.
vista
open space 263 n.
view 438 n.
visual
seeing 438 adj.
appearing 445 adj.
image 551 n.
visual aid
classroom 539 n.
visual display unit
data processing 86 n.
optical device 442 n.
visual fallacy
insubstantial thing 4 n.
visual fallacy 440 n.
fantasy 513 n.
deception 542 n.
ghost 970 n.
visualize, visualise
see 438 vb.
imagine 513 vb.
vital
alive 360 adj.
required 627 adj.
important 638 adj.
lively 819 adj.
cheerful 833 adj.
vitalism
biology 358 n.
philosophy 449 n.
vitality
vitality 162 n.
vigorousness 174 n.
life 360 n.
vigour 571 n.
health 650 n.
restlessness 678 n.
cheerfulness 833 n.
vitalize, vitalise
vitalize 360 vb.
animate 821 vb.
vitally
greatly 32 adv.
vital role
influence 178 n.
vitals
insides 224 n.
vital spark
life 360 n.
vital statistics
statistics 86 n.
beauty 841 n.
vitamin deficiency
insufficiency 636 n.
vitamins
dieting 301 n.
food content 301 n.
vitamin tablet
tonic 658 n.
vitiate
impair 655 vb.
pervert 655 vb.
viticulture
agriculture 370 n.
vitreous
hard 326 adj.
transparent 422 adj.
vitrify
harden 326 vb.
vitriol
burning 381 n.
poison 659 n.
vitriolic
paining 827 adj.
cursing 899 adj.
vituperate
curse 899 vb.
vituperation
oratory 579 n.
scurrility 899 n.
reproach 924 n.
viva
exam 459 n.
vivace
adagio 412 adv.
vivacious
forceful 571 adj.
active 678 adj.
feeling 818 adj.
lively 819 adj.
cheerful 833 adj.
vivandière
pedlar 794 n.
vivarium
zoo 369 n.
vivid
lifelike 18 adj.
vigorous 174 adj.
striking 374 adj.
luminous 417 adj.
florid 425 adj.
obvious 443 adj.
expressive 516 adj.
representing 551 adj.
forceful 571 adj.
descriptive 590 adj.
vivify
strengthen 162 vb.
vitalize 360 vb.
animate 821 vb.
viviparous
fertilized 167 adj.
viviparous animal
mammal 365 n.
vivisect
give pain 377 vb.
experiment 461 vb.
vivisection
detraction 926 n.
vixen
mammal 365 n.
female animal 373 n.
shrew 892 n.
vixenish
irascible 892 adj.
sullen 893 adj.
viz
namely 80 adv.
in plain words 520 adv.
vizier
official 690 n.

officer 741 n.
vocable
speech sound 398 n.
word 559 n.
vocabulary
word list 87 n.
dictionary 559 n.
style 566 n.
vocal
sounding 398 adj.
musical 412 adj.
vocal 577 adj.
speaking 579 adj.
desiring 859 adj.
vocal cords
voice 577 n.
vocalist
vocalist 413 n.
entertainer 594 n.
vocalize, vocalise
sound 398 vb.
sing 413 vb.
voice 577 vb.
vocation
motive 612 n.
vocation 622 n.
conduct 688 n.
duty 917 n.
church ministry 985 n.
vocational training
education 534 n.
vocative
vocative 583 adj.
vociferate
be loud 400 vb.
vociferate 408 vb.
voice 577 vb.
vociferous
crying 408 adj.
vodka
alcoholic drink 301 n.
vogue
practice 610 n.
fashion 848 n.
repute 866 n.
vogue word
word 559 n.
neology 560 n.
voice
sound 398 vb.
cry 408 n.
publish 528 vb.
affirmation 532 n.
grammar 564 n.
voice 577 n.vb.
speak 579 vb.
vote 605 n.
voiced
sounding 398 adj.
literal 558 adj.
vocal 577 adj.
voiceless
silent 399 adj.
voiceless 578 adj.
subject 745 adj.
voicelessness
helplessness 161 n.
faintness 401 n.
voicelessness 578 n.
voice-over
sound 398 n.
cinema 445 n.
void
insubstantiality 4 n.
emptiness 190 n.
gap 201 n.
empty 300 vb.
universe 321 n.
rare 325 adj.
abrogated 752 adj.
voile
textile 222 n.
volant
flying 271 adj.
speedy 277 adj.
volatile
transient 114 adj.
changeful 152 adj.
light 323 adj.
gaseous 336 adj.
vaporific 338 adj.
light-minded 456 adj.
capricious 604 adj.
excitable 822 adj.
volatilize, volatilise
rarefy 325 vb.
vaporize 338 vb.
volcanic
violent 176 adj.
fiery 379 adj.
excitable 822 adj.
volcano
outbreak 176 n.
chimney 263 n.
ejector 300 n.
fire 379 n.
furnace 383 n.
pitfall 663 n.
vole
mammal 365 n.
volition
will 595 n.
volitional
volitional 595 adj.
choosing 605 adj.
intending 617 adj.
volley
crowd 74 n.
strike 279 vb.
propulsion 287 n.
shoot 287 vb.
bang 402 n.
bombardment 712 n.
volleyball
ball game 837 n.
volplane
fly 271 vb.
volt, voltage
electronics 160 n.
volte-face
reversion 148 n.
return 286 n.
tergiversation 603 n.
volubility
speech 579 n.
loquacity 581 n.
volume
quantity 26 n.
greatness 32 n.
subdivision 53 n.
inclusion 78 n.
measure 183 n.
space 183 n.
size 195 n.
metrology 465 n.
book 589 n.
volumetric
spatial 183 adj.
metrical 465 adj.
voluminous
great 32 adj.
spacious 183 adj.
recipient 194 adj.
large 195 adj.
diffuse 570 adj.
voluntarism
philosophy 449 n.
will 595 n.
voluntary
prelude 66 n.
musical piece 412 n.
volitional 595 adj.
voluntary 597 adj.
spontaneous 609 adj.
intending 617 adj.
uncharged 812 adj.
voluntary agency
philanthropy 901 n.
voluntary work
voluntary work 597 n.
kind act 897 n.
volunteer
volunteer 597 n.
be willing 597 vb.
undertake 672 vb.
worker 686 n.
soldier 722 n.
offer oneself 759 vb.
voluptuary
sensualist 944 n.
voluptuous
sensuous 376 adj.
pleasurable 826 adj.
sensual 944 adj.
lecherous 951 adj.
volute
coil 251 n.
volution
rotation 315 n.
vomit
vomit 300 vb.
be ill 651 vb.
dislike 861 vb.
vomitory
expulsive 300 adj.
remedial 658 adj.
voodoo
sorcery 983 n.
bewitch 983 vb.
voodooist
sorcerer 983 n.
voracious
taking 786 adj.
greedy 859 adj.
gluttonous 947 adj.
voracity
eating 301 n.
desire 859 n.
gluttony 947 n.
vortex
coil 251 n.
vortex 315 n.
commotion 318 n.
eddy 350 n.
gale 352 n.
pitfall 663 n.
activity 678 n.
Vorticism
school of painting 553 n.
votary
patron 707 n.
desirer 859 n.
lover 887 n.
pietist 979 n.
worshipper 981 n.
vote
judge 480 vb.
affirmation 532 n.
vote 605 n.vb.
decree 737 n.
commission 751 vb.
credit 802 n.vb.
— against
reject 607 vb.
oppose 704 vb.
— down
oppose 704 vb.
— for
endorse 488 vb.
patronize 703 vb.
— in
vote 605 vb.
— to order
obey 739 vb.
be subject 745 vb.
vote-catcher
motivator 612 n.
vote-catching
choosing 605 adj.
flattering 925 adj.
voted
assented 488 adj.
legal 953 adj.
voteless
choiceless 606 adj.
unentitled 916 adj.
vote of confidence
vote 605 n.
loyalty 739 n.
vote of thanks
oration 579 n.
thanks 907 n.
voter
native 191 n.
estimator 480 n.
electorate 605 n.
patron 707 n.
free person 744 n.
voting list
list 87 n.
electorate 605 n.

votive
promissory 764 adj.
giving 781 adj.
devotional 981 adj.
votive candle
ritual object 988 n.
votive offering
oblation 981 n.
voucher
credential 466 n.
record 548 n.
title deed 767 n.
receipt 807 n.
vouch for
testify 466 vb.
promise 764 vb.
vouchsafe
permit 756 vb.
consent 758 vb.
give 781 vb.
vow
affirm 532 vb.
promise 764 n.vb.
offer worship 981 vb.
vowed
obliged 917 adj.
vowel
speech sound 398 n.
spoken letter 558 n.
voice 577 n.
vox populi
judgment 480 n.
consensus 488 n.
vote 605 n.
government 733 n.
tribunal 956 n.
voyage
land travel 267 n.
water travel 269 n.
voyage 269 vb.
voyager
traveller 268 n.
voyeur
spectator 441 n.
libertine 952 n.
voyeurism
inspection 438 n.
curiosity 453 n.
impurity 951 n.
V-shape
angularity 247 n.
V-sign
sauciness 878 n.
indignity 921 n.
VSO
philanthropist 901 n.
VTOL
aircraft 276 n.
VTR
recording instrument 549 n.
Vulcan
Olympian deity 967 n.
vulcanize, vulcanise
harden 326 vb.
be tough 329 vb.
heat 381 vb.
vulgar
inferior 35 adj.
general 79 adj.
indiscriminating 464 adj.
linguistic 557 adj.
feeble 572 adj.
inelegant 576 adj.
not nice 645 adj.
artless 699 adj.
graceless 842 adj.
vulgar 847 adj.
disreputable 867 adj.
plebeian 869 adj.
showy 875 adj.
cursing 899 adj.
vicious 934 adj.
impure 951 adj.
vulgarian
upstart 126 n.
ignoramus 493 n.
vulgarian 847 n.
commoner 869 n.
vulgarism
slang 560 n.
inelegance 576 n.
bad taste 847 n.
vulgarity
wit 839 n.
bad taste 847 n.
(See **vulgar** *)*
vulgarize, vulgarise
impair 655 vb.
facilitate 701 vb.
vulgarize 847 vb.
not respect 921 vb.
vulgate
interpretation 520 n.
Vulgate
scripture 975 n.
vulnerable
defenceless 161 adj.
liable 180 adj.
imperfect 647 adj.
vulnerable 661 adj.
unprepared 670 adj.
accusable 928 adj.
frail 934 adj.
vulnerable point
defect 647 n.
vulnerary
medical 658 adj.
vulpine
animal 365 adj.
cunning 698 adj.
vulture
eater 301 n.
bird 365 n.
cleaner 648 n.
tyrant 735 n.
taker 786 n.
noxious animal 904 n.
glutton 947 n.
vulva
genitalia 167 n.

W

wacky
crazy 503 adj.
wad
piece 53 n.
bunch 74 n.
line 227 vb.
stopper 264 n.
ammunition 723 n.
paper money 797 n.
wadding
contents 193 n.
lining 227 n.
softness 327 n.
waddle
gait 265 n.
walk 267 vb.
move slowly 278 vb.
oscillate 317 vb.
wade
walk 267 vb.
swim 269 vb.
be wet 341 vb.
— into
begin 68 vb.
waste 634 vb.
— through
study 536 vb.
exert oneself 682 vb.
deal with 688 vb.
wader
pedestrian 268 n.
bird 365 n.
waders
footwear 228 n.
wadi
cavity 255 n.
stream 350 n.
conduit 351 n.
wads
great quantity 32 n.
wealth 800 n.
wafer
adhesive 47 n.
lamina 207 n.
cereals 301 n.
wafer-thin
narrow 206 adj.
waffle
cereals 301 n.
mean nothing 515 vb.
be equivocal 518 vb.
diffuseness 570 n.
be diffuse 570 vb.
chatter 581 n.
waft
carry 273 vb.
be light 323 vb.
breeze 352 n.
blow 352 vb.
odour 394 n.
wag
go on 146 vb.
brandish 317 vb.
oscillate 317 vb.
agitate 318 vb.
gesticulate 547 vb.
humorist 839 n.
— on
progress 285 vb.
— one's finger
gesticulate 547 vb.
reprove 924 vb.
wage
do 676 vb.
earnings 771 n.
reward 962 n.
— war
fight 716 vb.
wage war 718 vb.
wage earner
worker 686 n.
recipient 782 n.
wager
gambling 618 n.
contest 716 n.
wages
pay 804 n.
receipt 807 n.
cost 809 n.
reward 962 n.
wage slave
worker 686 n.
waggish
merry 833 adj.
amused 837 adj.
witty 839 adj.
funny 849 adj.
waggle
brandish 317 vb.
oscillate 317 vb.
gesticulate 547 vb.
waggon
cart 274 n.
train 274 n.
waggoner
driver 268 n.
carrier 273 n.
waggonette
carriage 274 n.
wagon-lit
train 274 n.
wagtail
bird 365 n.
Wahhabis
non-Christian sect 978 n.
waif
wanderer 268 n.
derelict 779 n.
outcast 883 n.
wail
blow 352 vb.
cry 408 n.vb.
ululate 409 vb.
be discontented 829 vb.
lamentation 836 n.
weep 836 vb.
wain
cart 274 n.
wainscot
base 214 n.
lining 227 n.

wainwright
artisan 686 n.
waist
narrowing 206 n.
waistband
girdle 47 n.
belt 228 n.
waistcoat
jacket 228 n.
waistline
narrowing 206 n.
centrality 225 n.
garment 228 n.
wait
continue 108 vb.
pass time 108 vb.
protraction 113 n.
wait 136 vb.
pause 145 vb.
be quiescent 266 vb.
await 507 vb.
not act 677 vb.
be inactive 679 vb.
— and see
wait 136 vb.
be tentative 461 vb.
be uncertain 474 vb.
not act 677 vb.
— on/upon
accompany 89 vb.
result 157 vb.
follow 284 vb.
minister 703 vb.
obey 739 vb.
serve 742 vb.
visit 882 vb.
court 889 vb.
wait-and-see policy
caution 858 n.
waiter, waitress
servant 742 n.
waiter on Providence
idler 679 n.
hoper 852 n.
waiting
future 124 adj.
on the spot 189 adj.
expectant 507 adj.
waiting game
caution 858 n.
waiting list
list 87 n.
record 548 n.
hoper 852 n.
waiting room
lobby 194 n.
waits
choir 413 n.
waive
be neutral 606 vb.
relinquish 621 vb.
not use 674 vb.
resign 753 vb.
refuse 760 vb.
not retain 779 vb.
— the rules
be lax 734 vb.
waiver
loss of right 916 n.
wake
remainder 41 n.
retinue 67 n.
continuity 71 n.
effect 157 n.
rear 238 n.
furrow 262 n.
water travel 269 n.
follower 284 n.
eddy 350 n.
obsequies 364 n.
trace 548 n.
be active 678 vb.
excite 821 vb.
lament 836 n.
festivity 837 n.
condolence 905 n.
— up
have feeling 374 vb.
be active 678 vb.
wakeful
attentive 455 adj.
vigilant 457 adj.
active 678 adj.
Waldensian
heretical 977 adj.
walk
state 7 n.
pleasance 192 n.
gait 265 n.
pedestrianism 267 n.
walk 267 vb.
move slowly 278 vb.
appear 445 vb.
path 624 n.
conduct 688 n.
haunt 970 vb.
— into the trap
not expect 508 vb.
be duped 544 vb.
— off
emerge 298 vb.
— off with
win 727 vb.
steal 788 vb.
— out
relinquish 621 vb.
deprecate 762 vb.
fail in duty 918 vb.
— out on
tergiversate 603 vb.
— out with
accompany 89 vb.
court 889 vb.
— the plank
plunge 313 vb.
perish 361 vb.
walkabout
pedestrianism 267 n.
wandering 267 n.
walked off one's feet
fatigued 684 adj.
walker
pedestrian 268 n.
traveller 268 n.
walkie-talkie
hearing aid 415 n.
telecommunication 531 n.
walking encyclopaedia
scholar 492 n.
expert 696 n.
walking on air
pleased 824 adj.
walking stick
prop 218 n.
walk of life
state 7 n.
vocation 622 n.
conduct 688 n.
walk-on part
acting 594 n.
walkout
strike 145 n.
departure 296 n.
dissent 489 n.
opposition 704 n.
walkover
easy thing 701 n.
victory 727 n.
walkthrough
dramaturgy 594 n.
walkup
flat 192 n.
wall
separation 46 n.
exclusion 57 n.
prop 218 n.
surroundings 230 n.
partition 231 n.
barrier 235 n.
solid body 324 n.
screen 421 n.
fortification 713 n.
wallaby
mammal 365 n.
wallah
worker 686 n.
wallet
case 194 n.
treasury 799 n.
wall-eyed
dim-sighted 440 adj.
wallflower
rejection 607 n.
indifference 860 n.
wallop
strike 279 vb.
alcoholic drink 301 n.
spank 963 vb.
walloping
whopping 32 adj.
wallow
be low 210 vb.
voyage 269 vb.
plunge 313 vb.
be agitated 318 vb.
weigh 322 vb.
be wet 341 vb.
marsh 347 n.
swill 649 n.
be unclean 649 vb.
— in
enjoy 376 vb.
abound 635 vb.
be pleased 824 vb.
be intemperate 943 vb.
wallower
dirty person 649 n.
sensualist 944 n.
wallpaper
covering 226 n.
lining 227 n.
wall plate
beam 218 n.
Wall Street
city 184 n.
market 796 n.
wall up
obstruct 702 vb.
imprison 747 vb.
walnut
fruit 301 n.
tree 366 n.
brownness 430 n.
Walpurgisnacht
sorcery 983 n.
walrus
mammal 365 n.
Walter Mitty
inattention 456 n.
waltz
rotate 315 vb.
musical piece 412 n.
dance 837 n.vb.
— away with
win 727 vb.
wamble
oscillate 317 vb.
wampum
coinage 797 n.
wan
dim 419 adj.
colourless 426 adj.
melancholic 834 adj.
unsightly 842 adj.
wand
badge of rule 743 n.
magic instrument 983 n.
wander
be unrelated 10 vb.
be dispersed 75 vb.
wander 267 vb.
stray 282 vb.
be inattentive 456 vb.
be insane 503 vb.
be diffuse 570 vb.
be free 744 vb.
wanderer
displacement 188 n.
wanderer 268 n.
idler 679 n.
wandering
unstable 152 adj.
wandering 267 n.
designless 618 adj.
(See **wander** *)*
wanderlust
wandering 267 n.

wane
decrease 37 n.vb.
become small 198 vb.
be dim 419 vb.
deteriorate 655 vb.
wangle
trickery 542 n.
contrivance 623 n.
be cunning 698 vb.
foul play 930 n.
want
deficit 55 n.
shortfall 307 n.
require 627 vb.
scarcity 636 n.
be unsatisfied 636 vb.
imperfection 647 n.
adversity 731 n.
request 761 n.
poverty 801 n.
desire 859 n.vb.
— one's own way
be obstinate 602 vb.
— to know
be curious 453 vb.
enquire 459 vb.
wanted
absent 190 adj.
required 627 adj.
wanting
incomplete 55 adj.
absent 190 adj.
deficient 307 adj.
unintelligent 499 adj.
crazy 503 adj.
lost 772 adj.
wanton
changeful 152 adj.
capricious 604 adj.
free 744 adj.
amuse oneself 837 vb.
rash 857 adj.
unchaste 951 adj.
loose woman 952 n.
war
destroyer 168 n.
slaughter 362 n.
dissension 709 n.
war 718 n.
wage war 718 vb.
warble
ululate 409 vb.
sing 413 vb.
voice 577 vb.
warbler
bird 365 n.
vocalist 413 n.
war cloud
warning 664 n.
war cry
call 547 n.
danger signal 665 n.
defiance 711 n.
intimidation 854 n.
ward
subdivision 53 n.
youth 130 n.
district 184 n.
hospital 658 n.
protection 660 n.
refuge 662 n.
fort 713 n.
dependant 742 n.
detention 747 n.
mandate 751 n.
warden
doorkeeper 264 n.
protector 660 n.
manager 690 n.
defender 713 n.
officer 741 n.
keeper 749 n.
warder, wardress
gaoler 749 n.
ward off
avoid 620 vb.
parry 713 vb.
wardrobe
cabinet 194 n.
clothing 228 n.
wardrobe mistress
stagehand 594 n.
wardroom
chamber 194 n.
wardship
nonage 130 n.
protection 660 n.
subjection 745 n.
war effort
war measures 718 n.
warehouse
storage 632 n.
emporium 796 n.
wares
product 164 n.
property 777 n.
merchandise 795 n.
warfare
warfare 718 n.
(See **war** *)*
war fever
bellicosity 718 n.
war footing
war measures 718 n.
warhead
rocket 276 n.
explosive 723 n.
warhorse
warhorse 273 n.
expert 696 n.
cavalry 722 n.
warlike
violent 176 adj.
quarrelling 709 adj.
warlike 718 adj.
warlock
sorcerer 983 n.
warlord
army officer 741 n.
warm
summery 128 adj.
near 200 adj.
sentient 374 adj.
comfortable 376 adj.
warm 379 adj.
heat 381 vb.
red 431 adj.
discovering 484 adj.
forceful 571 adj.
laborious 682 adj.
fervent 818 adj.
pleasurable 826 adj.
cheer 833 vb.
friendly 880 adj.
sociable 882 adj.
angry 891 adj.
irascible 892 adj.
— the heart
excite 821 vb.
delight 826 vb.
cheer 833 vb.
— to
feel 818 vb.
desire 859 vb.
befriend 880 vb.
be in love 887 vb.
— up
start out 296 vb.
heat 381 vb.
endanger 661 vb.
make ready 669 vb.
warm-blooded
animal 365 adj.
warm clothes
warm clothes 381 n.
war measures
assemblage 74 n.
preparation 669 n.
war measures 718 n.
war memorial
obsequies 364 n.
trophy 729 n.
warm-hearted
impressible 819 adj.
benevolent 897 adj.
warming pan
cauldron 194 n.
heater 383 n.
warmonger
militarist 722 n.
warm reception
applause 923 n.
warmth
heat 379 n.
vigour 571 n.
excitable state 822 n.
desire 859 n.
friendliness 880 n.
anger 891 n.
(See **warm** *)*
warn
attract notice 455 vb.
predict 511 vb.
hint 524 vb.
dissuade 613 vb.
warn 664 vb.
advise 691 vb.
defy 711 vb.
threaten 900 vb.
reprove 924 vb.
— off
exclude 57 vb.
prohibit 757 vb.
warning
precursor 66 n.
period 110 n.
omen 511 n.
warning 664 n.
danger signal 665 n.
intimidation 854 n.
warning light
signal light 420 n.
signal 547 n.
warning notice
demand 737 n.
war of nerves
terror tactics 712 n.
intimidation 854 n.
threat 900 n.
war of words
argument 475 n.
quarrel 709 n.
war on
action 676 n.
warp
break 46 vb.
modify 143 vb.
force 176 vb.
obliquity 220 n.
weaving 222 n.
deform 244 vb.
distortion 246 n.
navigate 269 vb.
draw 288 vb.
bias 481 n.vb.
impair 655 vb.
warpaint
pigment 425 n.
cosmetic 843 n.
warpath
warfare 718 n.
warrant
credential 466 n.
make certain 473 vb.
affirmation 532 n.
instrument 628 n.
safeguard 660 vb.
precept 693 n.
warrant 737 n.
mandate 751 n.
permit 756 n.vb.
promise 764 n.vb.
security 767 n.
paper money 797 n.
justify 927 vb.
legal process 959 n.
warrant officer
air officer 741 n.
army officer 741 n.
warranty
credential 466 n.
promise 764 n.
security 767 n.
warren
complexity 61 n.
dwelling 192 n.
excavation 255 n.

warrior
combatant 722 n.
soldier 722 n.
brave person 855 n.
Warsaw Pact
treaty 765 n.
warship
warship 722 n.
wart
swelling 253 n.
skin disease 651 n.
blemish 845 n.
warthog
pig 365 n.
wartime
belligerency 718 n.
warts and all
accuracy 494 n.
true 494 adj.
war-weary
peaceful 717 adj.
war whoop
defiance 711 n.
threat 900 n.
wary
vigilant 457 adj.
nervous 854 adj.
cautious 858 adj.
wash
facing 226 n.
moisten 341 vb.
lake 346 n.
eddy 350 n.
wave 350 n.
pigment 425 n.
whiten 427 vb.
be true 494 vb.
trace 548 n.
paint 553 vb.
suffice 635 vb.
be expedient 642 vb.
ablutions 648 n.
clean 648 vb.
balm 658 n.
— down
drink 301 vb.
— off
obliterate 550 vb.
— one's dirty linen in public
be plain 522 vb.
— one's hands of
avoid 620 vb.
be exempt 919 vb.
disapprove 924 vb.
— out
purify 648 vb.
— up
eject 300 vb.
clean 648 vb.
wash and brush up
refreshment 685 n.
beautification 843 n.
washboard
roughness 259 n.
ablutions 648 n.
washed out
colourless 426 adj.
fatigued 684 adj.
unsightly 842 adj.
washed up
deteriorated 655 adj.
grounded 728 adj.
washer
lining 227 n.
interjection 231 n.
washerwoman
cleaner 648 n.
washing machine
ablutions 648 n.
washlands
shore 344 n.
marsh 347 n.
wash-leather
cleaning cloth 648 n.
washout
failure 728 n.
washroom
ablutions 648 n.
latrine 649 n.
washy
weak 163 adj.
colourless 426 adj.
wasp
insect 365 n.
bane 659 n.
noxious animal 904 n.
waspish
furious 176 adj.
irascible 892 adj.
wasp-waist
contraction 198 n.
narrowing 206 n.
wassail
festivity 837 n.
revel 837 vb.
get drunk 949 vb.
wastage
decrease 37 n.
decrement 42 n.
waste 634 n.
rubbish 641 n.
loss 772 n.
waste
decrease 37 n.vb.
leavings 41 n.
consume 165 vb.
destroy 165 vb.
lay waste 165 vb.
desert 172 n.
space 183 n.
emptiness 190 n.
outflow 298 n.
waste 634 n.vb.
make insufficient 636 vb.
rubbish 641 n.
impair 655 vb.
use 673 n.vb.
misuse 675 n.vb.
loss 772 n.
expend 806 vb.
be prodigal 815 vb.
intemperance 943 n.
— away
decompose 51 vb.
become small 198 vb.
be ill 651 vb.
— effort
attempt the impossible 470 vb.
be foolish 499 vb.
be superfluous 637 vb.
waste effort 641 vb.
act foolishly 695 vb.
fail 728 vb.
— no words
be concise 569 vb.
be taciturn 582 vb.
— time
pass time 108 vb.
drag on 113 vb.
lose a chance 138 vb.
be inactive 679 vb.
wasted
lean 206 adj.
wasted 634 adj.
profitless 641 adj.
unused 674 adj.
lost 772 adj.
wasteful
wasteful 634 adj.
superfluous 637 adj.
profitless 641 adj.
prodigal 815 adj.
intemperate 943 adj.
wastelands
desert 172 n.
waste matter
excrement 302 n.
waste of time
unproductiveness 172 n.
lost labour 641 n.
waste paper
rubbish 641 n.
wastepaper basket
basket 194 n.
wastepipe
drain 351 n.
cleanser 648 n.
waste product
waste 634 n.
rubbish 641 n.
waster
negligence 458 n.
prodigal 815 n.
bad person 938 n.
waste-reprocessing plant
nucleonics 160 n.
wastrel
idler 679 n.
prodigal 815 n.
bad person 938 n.
watch
period 110 n.
timekeeper 117 n.
scan 438 vb.
spectator 441 n.
watch 441 vb.
attention 455 n.
be attentive 455 vb.
invigilate 457 vb.
warner 664 n.
not act 677 vb.
defend 713 vb.
keeper 749 n.
police 955 n.
— one's step
be careful 457 vb.
be warned 664 vb.
be cautious 858 vb.
— out for
scan 438 vb.
invigilate 457 vb.
expect 507 vb.
— over
safeguard 660 vb.
watch and ward
surveillance 457 n.
protection 660 n.
watch chain
jewellery 844 n.
watchdog
dog 365 n.
protector 660 n.
warner 664 n.
keeper 749 n.
watcher
spectator 441 n.
protector 660 n.
watchful
attentive 455 adj.
vigilant 457 adj.
intelligent 498 adj.
tutelary 660 adj.
active 678 adj.
observant 768 adj.
cautious 858 adj.
watchmaker
timekeeper 117 n.
artisan 686 n.
watchnight service
church service 988 n.
watchtower
high structure 209 n.
view 438 n.
watchword
maxim 496 n.
call 547 n.
identification 547 n.
warfare 718 n.
water
mix 43 vb.
weak thing 163 n.
weaken 163 vb.
make fruitful 171 vb.
soft drink 301 n.
excrement 302 n.
element 319 n.
fluid 335 n.
water 339 n.
add water 339 vb.
irrigate 341 vb.
lake 346 n.
make flow 350 vb.
groom 369 vb.
cultivate 370 vb.

extinguisher 382 n.
insipidity 387 n.
transparency 422 n.
provide 633 vb.
cleanser 648 n.
be auspicious 730 vb.
— at the mouth
exude 298 vb.
make appetizing 390 vb.
be hungry 859 vb.
— down
weaken 163 vb.
add water 339 vb.
waterborne
seafaring 269 adj.
waterborne sanitation
cleansing 648 n.
water butt
vat 194 n.
irrigator 341 n.
water cart
cart 274 n.
irrigator 341 n.
water channel
conduit 351 n.
water closet
latrine 649 n.
watercolour(s)
pigment 425 n.
art style 553 n.
picture 553 n.
watercolourist
artist 556 n.
watercourse
stream 350 n.
conduit 351 n.
watercress
vegetable 301 n.
water diviner
enquirer 459 n.
detector 484 n.
diviner 511 n.
psychic 984 n.
water-drinker
ascetic 945 n.
sober person 948 n.
water-driven
dynamic 160 adj.
watered
iridescent 437 adj.
waterfall
outflow 298 n.
descent 309 n.
waterfall 350 n.
waterfowl
bird 365 n.
waterfront
edge 234 n.
watergate
conduit 351 n.
Watergate
disrepute 867 n.
water gipsy
dweller 191 n.
waterhole
lake 346 n.
watering at the mouth
excited 821 adj.
gluttonous 947 adj.
watering can
vessel 194 n.
irrigator 341 n.
watering place
abode 192 n.
hospital 658 n.
water jump
gap 201 n.
obstacle 702 n.
waterless
dry 342 adj.
water level
layer 207 n.
horizontality 216 n.
water lily
plant 366 n.
waterline
edge 234 n.
gauge 465 n.
waterlogged
impotent 161 adj.
drenched 341 adj.
marshy 347 adj.
semiliquid 354 adj.
unsafe 661 adj.
hindered 702 adj.
Waterloo
ruin 165 n.
defeat 728 n.
water main
conduit 351 n.
waterman
boatman 270 n.
watermark
label 547 n.
pattern 844 n.
water meadow
shore 344 n.
grassland 348 n.
water melon
fruit 301 n.
water nymph
nymph 967 n.
mythical being 970 n.
water pistol
propellant 287 n.
plaything 837 n.
water polo
ball game 837 n.
water pot
vessel 194 n.
water power
waterfall 350 n.
waterproof
unyielding 162 adj.
overcoat 228 n.
sealed off 264 adj.
dry 342 adj.
invulnerable 660 adj.
preserve 666 vb.
water rat
mammal 365 n.
water rate
tax 809 n.
waters
obstetrics 167 n.
ocean 343 n.
watershed
summit 213 n.
partition 231 n.
waterside
edge 234 n.
waters of Lethe
oblivion 506 n.
watersports
aquatics 269 n.
sport 837 n.
waterspout
vortex 315 n.
drain 351 n.
water supply
water 339 n.
provision 633 n.
water table
layer 207 n.
horizontality 216 n.
watertight
sealed off 264 adj.
dry 342 adj.
perfect 646 adj.
water tower
storage 632 n.
water travel
water travel 269 n.
water vapour
gas 336 n.
waterway
passage 305 n.
stream 350 n.
route 624 n.
waterworks
excretion 302 n.
water 339 n.
cleanser 648 n.
waterworn
smooth 258 adj.
watery
nonadhesive 49 adj.
weak 163 adj.
excretory 302 adj.
fluid 335 adj.
watery 339 adj.
humid 341 adj.
tasteless 387 adj.
watt
electronics 160 n.
metrology 465 n.
wattle
network 222 n.
enlace 222 vb.
wattle and daub
building material 631 n.
Wat Tyler
agitator 738 n.
wave
periodicity 141 n.
hang 217 vb.
make curved 248 vb.
convolution 251 n.
be in motion 265 vb.
elevate 310 vb.
brandish 317 vb.
agitate 318 vb.
ocean 343 n.
wave 350 n.
blow 352 vb.
show 522 vb.
gesture 547 n.
hairdressing 843 n.
greet 884 vb.
— a wand
practise sorcery 983 vb.
— goodbye
start out 296 vb.
— on
signal 547 vb.
— the big stick
threaten 900 vb.
— to
gesticulate 547 vb.
— to and fro
brandish 317 vb.
waveband
radiation 417 n.
wavelength
long measure 203 n.
oscillation 317 n.
radiation 417 n.
broadcasting 531 n.
wave power
sources of energy 160 n.
waver
vary 152 vb.
be uncertain 474 vb.
doubt 486 vb.
be irresolute 601 vb.
waverer
waverer 601 n.
waves
ocean 343 n.
waves of nausea
illness 651 n.
wavy
curved 248 adj.
undulatory 251 adj.
furrowed 262 adj.
wax
grow 36 vb.
be turned to 147 vb.
changeable thing 152 n.
expand 197 vb.
smooth 258 vb.
harden 326 vb.
softness 327 n.
lubricant 334 n.
viscidity 354 n.
fat 357 n.
make bright 417 vb.
sculpture 554 n.
cleanser 648 n.
— and wane
change 143 vb.
vary 152 vb.
— lyrical
praise 923 vb.
wax candle
torch 420 n.

waxen
fatty 357 adj.
whitish 427 adj.
wax figure
mould 23 n.
image 551 n.
waxing
increase 36 n.
wax modeller
sculptor 556 n.
waxwork(s)
image 551 n.
sculpture 554 n.
collection 632 n.
waxy
soft 327 adj.
fatty 357 adj.
angry 891 adj.
way
state 7 n.
degree 27 n.
room 183 n.
itinerary 267 n.
water travel 269 n.
direction 281 n.
progression 285 n.
way in 297 n.
habit 610 n.
policy 623 n.
way 624 n.
means 629 n.
conduct 688 n.
fashion 848 n.
ritual 988 n.
wayfarer
traveller 268 n.
way in
entrance 68 n.
doorway 263 n.
way in 297 n.
Wayland Smith
mythical being 970 n.
waylay
approach 289 vb.
ambush 527 vb.
ensnare 542 vb.
be cunning 698 vb.
waymark
indicate 547 vb.
waymarked
communicating 624 adj.
way of life
habit 610 n.
conduct 688 n.
way of the world
fashion 848 n.
way-out
unusual 84 adj.
super 644 adj.
way out
doorway 263 n.
outlet 298 n.
contrivance 623 n.
means of escape 667 n.
way over
bridge 624 n.
ways
habit 610 n.
ways and means
means 629 n.
wayside
near 200 adj.
edge 234 n.
marginal 234 adj.
accessible 289 adj.
Way, the Truth and the Life, the
God the Son 965 n.
way through
access 624 n.
route 624 n.
way under
bridge 624 n.
wayward
changeful 152 adj.
wilful 602 adj.
capricious 604 adj.
disobedient 738 adj.
way with
management 689 n.
way with words
eloquence 579 n.
WC
latrine 649 n.
we
self 80 n.
weak
small 33 adj.
ephemeral 114 adj.
powerless 161 adj.
weak 163 adj.
moderate 177 adj.
little 196 adj.
brittle 330 adj.
watery 339 adj.
muted 401 adj.
poorly reasoned 477 adj.
unintelligent 499 adj.
feeble 572 adj.
irresolute 601 adj.
insufficient 636 adj.
unimportant 639 adj.
unhealthy 651 adj.
unsafe 661 adj.
lax 734 adj.
cowardly 856 adj.
pitying 905 adj.
frail 934 adj.
weak constitution
ill health 651 n.
weaken
abate 37 vb.
mix 43 vb.
modify 143 vb.
disable 161 vb.
weaken 163 vb.
moderate 177 vb.
rarefy 325 vb.
add water 339 vb.
decolorize 426 vb.
tell against 467 vb.
qualify 468 vb.
impair 655 vb.
weaker brethren
vulnerability 661 n.
weaker sex
womankind 373 n.
weak-kneed
irresolute 601 adj.
submitting 721 adj.
weakling
weakling 163 n.
sick person 651 n.
unlucky person 731 n.
coward 856 n.
weak link in the chain
defect 647 n.
weak-minded
irresolute 601 adj.
cowardly 856 adj.
weakness
weakness 163 n.
tendency 179 n.
liability 180 n.
defect 647 n.
illness 651 n.
bane 659 n.
vulnerability 661 n.
sluggishness 679 n.
laxity 734 n.
liking 859 n.
vice 934 n.
(See **weak***)*
weakness of intellect
unintelligence 499 n.
weak-willed
irresolute 601 adj.
lax 734 adj.
weal
swelling 253 n.
trace 548 n.
good 615 n.
prosperity 730 n.
blemish 845 n.
wealth
abundance 171 n.
means 629 n.
plenty 635 n.
prosperity 730 n.
independence 744 n.
estate 777 n.
money 797 n.
wealth 800 n.
wealthy
rich 800 adj.
weaned
unhabituated 611 adj.
wean from
convince 485 vb.
disaccustom 611 vb.
— oneself from
disaccustom 611 vb.
relinquish 621 vb.
weapon
destroyer 168 n.
contrivance 623 n.
instrument 628 n.
tool 630 n.
protection 660 n.
defence 713 n.
weapon 723 n.
weaponless
defenceless 161 adj.
wear
decompose 51 vb.
last 113 vb.
clothing 228 n.
wear 228 vb.
show 522 vb.
use 673 n.vb.
fatigue 684 vb.
— away
decrease 37 vb.
rub 333 vb.
disappear 446 vb.
— down
pulverize 332 vb.
induce 612 vb.
— it
acquiesce 488 vb.
— off
disappear 446 vb.
be unpractised 611 vb.
— on
elapse 111 vb.
— one's heart on one's sleeve
be plain 522 vb.
be artless 699 vb.
— out
waste 634 vb.
deteriorate 655 vb.
impair 655 vb.
use 673 vb.
fatigue 684 vb.
be tedious 838 vb.
— ship
navigate 269 vb.
deflect 282 vb.
— the crown
be superior 34 vb.
win 727 vb.
rule 733 vb.
— the trousers
influence 178 vb.
direct 689 vb.
dominate 733 vb.
— the willow
lament 836 vb.
— thin
be weak 163 vb.
be brittle 330 vb.
— well
last 113 vb.
be healthy 650 vb.
wear and tear
decrease 37 n.
decay 51 n.
waste 634 n.
dilapidation 655 n.
use 673 n.
weariness
sleepiness 679 n.
fatigue 684 n.
suffering 825 n.
dejection 834 n.

tedium 838 n.
wearisome
laborious 682 adj.
fatiguing 684 adj.
annoying 827 adj.
tedious 838 adj.
weary
weakened 163 adj.
laborious 682 adj.
fatigue 684 vb.
trouble 827 vb.
discontented 829 adj.
depress 834 vb.
bored 838 adj.
be tedious 838 vb.
weasel
vehicle 274 n.
mammal 365 n.
be equivocal 518 vb.
weasel word
equivocalness 518 n.
word 559 n.
weather
storm 176 n.
navigate 269 vb.
pulverize 332 vb.
weather 340 n.
wind 352 n.
colour 425 vb.
deteriorate 655 vb.
mature 669 vb.
— the storm
be stable 153 vb.
navigate 269 vb.
be restored 656 vb.
be safe 660 vb.
escape 667 vb.
triumph 727 vb.
weather balloon
airship 276 n.
weatherbeaten
tough 329 adj.
dilapidated 655 adj.
weatherboard
lamina 207 n.
facing 226 n.
weatherbound
restrained 747 adj.
weathercock
alterer 143 n.
changeable thing 152 n.
weather 340 n.
anemometry 352 n.
indicator 547 n.
waverer 601 n.
tergiversator 603 n.
weathered
soft-hued 425 adj.
matured 669 adj.
weather eye
navigation 269 n.
surveillance 457 n.
weather forecast
prediction 511 n.
weatherly
marine 275 adj.
weatherman, weatherwoman
weather 340 n.
oracle 511 n.
weatherproof
unyielding 162 adj.
invulnerable 660 adj.
weather station
weather 340 n.
weathervane
changeable thing 152 n.
(See **weathercock** *)*
weave
tie 45 vb.
compose 56 vb.
produce 164 vb.
textile 222 n.
weave 222 vb.
pass 305 vb.
texture 331 n.
fake 541 vb.
pattern 844 n.
— spells
practise sorcery 983 vb.
weaver
weaving 222 n.
artisan 686 n.
weaving
joining together 45 n.
weaving 222 n.
formation 243 n.
texture 331 n.
art 551 n.
web
complexity 61 n.
filament 208 n.
network 222 n.
weaving 222 n.
plumage 259 n.
texture 331 n.
trap 542 n.
press 587 n.
plot 623 n.
stratagem 698 n.
web-footed
footed 214 adj.
web offset
print 587 n.
wed
unite with 45 vb.
wed 894 vb.
wedded to
believing 485 adj.
obstinate 602 adj.
habituated 610 adj.
wedding
wedding 894 n.
wedding anniversary
special day 876 n.
wedding 894 n.
wedding ring
jewellery 844 n.
love token 889 n.
wedding 894 n.
ritual object 988 n.
wedge
affix 45 vb.
piece 53 n.
prop 218 n.
interjection 231 n.
angular figure 247 n.
sharp edge 256 n.
stopper 264 n.
tool 630 n.
— apart
sunder 46 vb.
— in
introduce 231 vb.
implant 303 vb.
wedge-shaped
angulated 247 adj.
Wedgwood china
pottery 381 n.
wedlock
union 45 n.
marriage 894 n.
wee
small 33 adj.
little 196 adj.
weed
exclude 57 vb.
render few 105 vb.
weed
weakling 163 n.
weed
plant 366 n.
cultivate 370 vb.
ninny 501 n.
— out
abate 37 vb.
eliminate 44 vb.
eject 300 vb.
purify 648 vb.
weed, the
tobacco 388 n.
weed-killer
poison 659 n.
weedy
lean 206 adj.
vegetal 366 adj.
week
period 110 n.
weekend
pass time 108 vb.
visit 882 vb.
weekend cottage
abode 192 n.
weekender
native 191 n.
weekly
seasonal 141 adj.
journal 528 n.
ween
think 449 vb.
opine 485 vb.
weeny
small 33 adj.
weep
flow out 298 vb.
be wet 341 vb.
be dejected 834 vb.
weep 836 vb.
— for
be sensitive 819 vb.
pity 905 vb.
weepie
film 445 n.
weeping
hanging 217 adj.
weeping and wailing
obsequies 364 n.
lamentation 836 n.
weepy
unhappy 825 adj.
weevil
insect 365 n.
weft
weaving 222 n.
weigh
load 193 vb.
weigh 322 vb.
meditate 449 vb.
discriminate 463 vb.
measure 465 vb.
estimate 480 vb.
motivate 612 vb.
be important 638 vb.
oppress 735 vb.
— anchor
navigate 269 vb.
start out 296 vb.
— in
influence 178 vb.
— on
oppress 735 vb.
trouble 827 vb.
— one's words
be truthful 540 vb.
weighbridge
scales 322 n.
weighed against
compensatory 31 adj.
weighing machine
scales 322 n.
weight
substantiality 3 n.
quantity 26 n.
power 160 n.
influence 178 n.
bulk 195 n.
size 195 n.
materiality 319 n.
gravity 322 n.
scales 322 n.
make heavy 322 vb.
vigour 571 n.
importance 638 n.
weighted
distorted 246 adj.
unjust 914 adj.
weighting
compensation 31 n.
weightless
light 323 adj.
weight-lifter
athlete 162 n.
weight of numbers
greater number 104 n.
power 160 n.

weight of responsibility
worry 825 n.
weight on one's mind
encumbrance 702 n.
worry 825 n.
penitence 939 n.
weights and measures
metrology 465 n.
weight-watching
dieting 301 n.
weighty
substantial 3 adj.
unequal 29 adj.
great 32 adj.
strong 162 adj.
influential 178 adj.
large 195 adj.
material 319 adj.
weighty 322 adj.
dense 324 adj.
evidential 466 adj.
forceful 571 adj.
instrumental 628 adj.
important 638 adj.
hindering 702 adj.
annoying 827 adj.
weir
waterfall 350 n.
obstacle 702 n.
weird
fate 596 n.
frightening 854 adj.
wonderful 864 adj.
spooky 970 adj.
magical 983 adj.
weird idea
whim 604 n.
weirdness
eccentricity 503 n.
weirdo
nonconformist 84 n.
welch
(See **welsh** *)*
welcome
timely 137 adj.
meet 295 vb.
reception 299 n.
pleasant 376 adj.
assent 488 n.vb.
pleasurable 826 adj.
desired 859 adj.
celebration 876 n.
be friendly 880 vb.
be hospitable 882 vb.
greet 884 vb.
congratulation 886 n.
show respect 920 vb.
applaud 923 vb.
weld
join 45 vb.
agglutinate 48 vb.
heat 381 vb.
welder
artisan 686 n.
welfare
good 615 n.
prosperity 730 n.
Welfare State
shelter 662 n.
political organization 733 n.
sociology 901 n.
welkin
heavens 321 n.
air 340 n.
well
greatly 32 adv.
receptacle 194 n.
lowness 210 n.
depth 211 n.
excavation 255 n.
water 339 n.
flow 350 vb.
well 615 adv.
store 632 n.
aright 644 adv.
healthy 650 adj.
skilfully 694 adv.
— out
flow out 298 vb.
— over
flow out 298 vb.
superabound 637 vb.
well-advised
wise 498 adj.
well-aimed
apt 24 adj.
directed 281 adj.
accurate 494 adj.
well-appointed
provisioning 633 adj.
prepared 669 adj.
well-balanced
sane 502 adj.
well-behaved
orderly 60 adj.
obedient 739 adj.
amiable 884 adj.
well-being
euphoria 376 n.
good 615 n.
health 650 n.
salubrity 652 n.
prosperity 730 n.
happiness 824 n.
well-born
worshipful 866 adj.
noble 868 adj.
well-bred
well-bred 848 adj.
courteous 884 adj.
well-built
strong 162 adj.
beautiful 841 adj.
well-connected, be
influence 178 vb.
well-cooked
savoury 390 adj.
matured 669 adj.
well-couched
phraseological 563 adj.
well-covered
fleshy 195 adj.
well-cut
adjusted 24 adj.
tailored 228 adj.
well-defined
obvious 443 adj.
well-deserved
just 913 adj.
due 915 adj.
well-directed
relevant 9 adj.
directed 281 adj.
well-disposed
willing 597 adj.
aiding 703 adj.
well-documented
evidential 466 adj.
well-done
culinary 301 adj.
matured 669 adj.
completed 725 adj.
well-dressed
dressed 228 adj.
personable 841 adj.
fashionable 848 adj.
well-drilled
orderly 60 adj.
well-earned
due 915 adj.
well-educated
instructed 490 adj.
well-endowed
gifted 694 adj.
rich 800 adj.
well-established
permanent 144 adj.
established 153 adj.
well-favoured
beautiful 841 adj.
well-fed
fleshy 195 adj.
feeding 301 adj.
well-fitting
adjusted 24 adj.
well-formed
shapely 841 adj.
well-founded
fixed 153 adj.
evidential 466 adj.
plausible 471 adj.
certain 473 adj.
true 494 adj.
well-groomed
orderly 60 adj.
clean 648 adj.
fashionable 848 adj.
well-grounded
rational 475 adj.
(See **well-founded** *)*
well-grown
fleshy 195 adj.
large 195 adj.
wellhead
source 156 n.
well-heeled
moneyed 800 adj.
well-inclined
approving 923 adj.
well-informed
instructed 490 adj.
informed 524 adj.
wellingtons
footwear 228 n.
well-integrated
mixed 43 adj.
well-intentioned
aiding 703 adj.
friendly 880 adj.
benevolent 897 adj.
virtuous 933 adj.
innocent 935 adj.
well in with
friendly 880 adj.
well-judged
wise 498 adj.
well-kept
orderly 60 adj.
preserved 666 adj.
well-knit
cohesive 48 adj.
stalwart 162 adj.
well-known
known 490 adj.
well-known 528 adj.
usual 610 adj.
renowned 866 adj.
well-lined
full 54 adj.
well-lined purse
wealth 800 n.
well-lit
luminescent 420 adj.
communicating 624 adj.
well-lubricated
tipsy 949 adj.
well-made
elegant 575 adj.
well-made 694 adj.
beautiful 841 adj.
well-mannered
well-bred 848 adj.
courteous 884 adj.
well-marked
obvious 443 adj.
well-meaning
friendly 880 adj.
innocent 935 adj.
well-met
assembled 74 adj.
well-nigh
nearly 200 adv.
well-off
prosperous 730 adj.
rich 800 adj.
well-oiled
lubricated 334 adj.
tractable 701 adj.
tipsy 949 adj.
well out of
escaped 667 adj.
nonliable 919 adj.
well-paid
rich 800 adj.
well-pitched
melodious 410 adj.
accurate 494 adj.
well-placed
located 187 adj.

directed 281 adj.
well-planned
cunning 698 adj.
well-practised
expert 694 adj.
well-preserved
ageing 131 adj.
preserved 666 adj.
well-proportioned
symmetrical 245 adj.
elegant 575 adj.
shapely 841 adj.
well-provided for
rich 800 adj.
well-read
instructed 490 adj.
studious 536 adj.
well-regarded
reputable 866 adj.
well-regulated
orderly 60 adj.
well rid of
escaped 667 adj.
well-rounded
phraseological 563 adj.
shapely 841 adj.
well-satisfied
content 828 adj.
well-seasoned
tasty 386 adj.
well set-up
stalwart 162 adj.
symmetrical 245 adj.
beautiful 841 adj.
well-spent
successful 727 adj.
well-spoken
intelligible 516 adj.
speaking 579 adj.
well-bred 848 adj.
courteous 884 adj.
wellspring
source 156 n.
well-stacked
shapely 841 adj.
well thought of
reputable 866 adj.
well-timed
timely 137 adj.
advisable 642 adj.
well-to-do
prosperous 730 adj.
rich 800 adj.
well-trodden
used 673 adj.
well-turned
elegant 575 adj.
shapely 841 adj.
well-upholstered
fleshy 195 adj.
well up in
expert 694 adj.
well-used
communicating 624 adj.
used 673 adj.
well-ventilated
airy 340 adj.
published 528 adj.
salubrious 652 adj.
well-wisher
patron 707 n.
friend 880 n.
kind person 897 n.
well-worn
usual 610 adj.
dilapidated 655 adj.
used 673 adj.
well-written
intelligible 516 adj.
welsh, welch
run away 620 vb.
elude 667 vb.
be in debt 803 vb.
not pay 805 vb.
welsher, welcher
avoider 620 n.
defrauder 789 n.
nonpayer 805 n.
Welshman, Welshwoman
native 191 n.
Welsh rarebit
dish 301 n.
welt
edge 234 n.
swelling 253 n.
trace 548 n.
blemish 845 n.
spank 963 vb.
Weltanschauung
opinion 485 n.
welter
confusion 61 n.
plunge 313 vb.
welterweight
pugilist 722 n.
Weltschmerz
suffering 825 n.
melancholy 834 n.
tedium 838 n.
wen
swelling 253 n.
letter 558 n.
blemish 845 n.
wench
youngster 132 n.
woman 373 n.
be impure 951 vb.
wend
be in motion 265 vb.
travel 267 vb.
Wensleydale
dairy product 301 n.
werewolf
hellhag 904 n.
demon 970 n.
wergild
peace offering 719 n.
atonement 941 n.
Wesleyan
Protestant 976 n.adj.
west
laterality 239 n.
compass point 281 n.
Westcountryman, Westcountrywoman
native 191 n.
West End
city 184 n.
drama 594 n.
westerly
wind 352 n.
western
lateral 239 adj.
directed 281 adj.
Western
film 445 n.
novel 590 n.
westernize, westernise
transform 147 vb.
Westminster
parliament 692 n.
master 741 n.
westward
lateral 239 adj.
wet
weakling 163 n.
watery 339 adj.
moisture 341 n.
moisten 341 vb.
rainy 350 adj.
foolish 499 adj.
leniency 736 n.
impressible 819 adj.
— oneself
excrete 302 vb.
— one's whistle
drink 301 vb.
wet behind the ears
immature 670 adj.
artless 699 adj.
wet blanket
moderator 177 n.
dissuasion 613 n.
hinderer 702 n.
moper 834 n.
disapprover 924 n.
wet-eyed
unhappy 825 adj.
lamenting 836 adj.
wether
sheep 365 n.
wetlands
marsh 347 n.
wetness
moisture 341 n.
wet nurse
provider 633 n.
keeper 749 n.
wet-nurse
patronize 703 vb.
wet rot
dirt 649 n.
blight 659 n.
wetsuit
suit 228 n.
wet through
drenched 341 adj.
whack
strike 279 vb.
portion 783 n.
spank 963 vb.
whack at
attempt 671 n.
whacked
fatigued 684 adj.
defeated 728 adj.
whacking
whopping 32 adj.
large 195 adj.
whale
giant 195 n.
mammal 365 n.
whalebone
compressor 198 n.
prop 218 n.
hardness 326 n.
elasticity 328 n.
whaler
mariner 270 n.
fishing boat 275 n.
hunter 619 n.
wham
violently 176 adv.
strike 279 vb.
propel 287 vb.
bang 402 vb.
wharf
stable 192 n.
edge 234 n.
storage 632 n.
workshop 687 n.
emporium 796 n.
what?
453 int.
what d'you call it
no name 562 n.
what makes one tick
motive 612 n.
what matters
chief thing 638 n.
what may be
possibility 469 n.
what must be
necessity 596 n.
whatnot
cabinet 194 n.
what one is worth
estate 777 n.
property 777 n.
what one thinks
idea 451 n.
what's his/her name
no name 562 n.
what should be
right 913 n.
whatsit
no name 562 n.
tool 630 n.
what's new
fashion 848 n.
what's to come
destiny 155 n.
what the doctor ordered
salubrious 652 adj.
wheat
cereals 301 n.
food 301 n.
grass 366 n.

wheedle
tempt 612 vb.
request 761 vb.
be servile 879 vb.
pet 889 vb.
flatter 925 vb.
wheedler
motivator 612 n.
flatterer 925 n.
wheel
changeable thing 152 n.
wheel 250 n.
move 265 vb.
sailing aid 269 n.
bicycle 274 n.
turn round 282 vb.
propel 287 vb.
circle 314 vb.
rotator 315 n.
tool 630 n.
directorship 689 n.
instrument of torture 964 n.
— about
turn round 282 vb.
tergiversate 603 vb.
— and deal
plot 623 vb.
— round
be inverted 221 vb.
turn back 286 vb.
wheelbarrow
pushcart 274 n.
wheelchair
pushcart 274 n.
wheeled
vehicular 274 adj.
wheeled traffic
conveyance 267 n.
vehicle 274 n.
passing along 305 n.
wheeler-dealer
planner 623 n.
slyboots 698 n.
wheel of Fortune
changeable thing 152 n.
chance 159 n.
nondesign 618 n.
wheel of life
regular return 141 n.
wheels within wheels
complexity 61 n.
machine 630 n.
wheelwright
artisan 686 n.
wheeze
breathe 352 vb.
hiss 406 vb.
idea 451 n.
contrivance 623 n.
wheezy
vocal 577 adj.
whelk
fish food 301 n.
marine life 365 n.
whelp
young creature 132 n.
reproduce itself 167 vb.
dog 365 n.
bad person 938 n.
when
when 108 adv.
when all is said and done
in return 31 adv.
finally 69 adv.
when and where
situation 186 n.
whence
hence 158 adv.
where
here 189 adv.
whereabouts
in place 186 adv.
presence 189 n.
where it hurts
on the raw 819 adv.
where the shoe pinches
difficulty 700 n.
moral sensibility 819 n.
painfulness 827 n.
wherever
widely 183 adv.
somewhere 185 adv.
wherewithal
means 629 n.
funds 797 n.
wherry
sailing ship 275 n.
wherryman
boatman 270 n.
whet
sharpen 256 vb.
animate 821 vb.
— the appetite
cause desire 859 vb.
— the knife
make ready 669 vb.
whether
nevertheless 468 adv.
whetstone
sharpener 256 n.
friction 333 n.
whey
dairy product 301 n.
fluid 335 n.
wheyface
coward 856 n.
whey-faced
colourless 426 adj.
whicker
ululate 409 vb.
whiff
breeze 352 n.
odour 394 n.
indication 547 n.
whiffle
vary 152 vb.
breathe 352 vb.
whiffy
odorous 394 adj.
fetid 397 adj.
Whiggish
sectional 708 adj.
Whigs
political party 708 n.
while
interim 108 n.
while 108 adv.
synchronously 123 adv.
between 231 adv.
while, a
time 108 n.
while away the time
pass time 108 vb.
be inactive 679 vb.
have leisure 681 vb.
amuse oneself 837 vb.
whim
foolery 497 n.
eccentricity 503 n.
ideality 513 n.
whim 604 n.
liking 859 n.
whimper
cry 408 vb.
weep 836 vb.
whimsical
multiform 82 adj.
unconformable 84 adj.
changeful 152 adj.
misjudging 481 adj.
crazy 503 adj.
unexpected 508 adj.
imaginative 513 adj.
capricious 604 adj.
witty 839 adj.
ridiculous 849 adj.
whimsy
ideality 513 n.
whim 604 n.
whine
shrill 407 vb.
cry 408 n.vb.
ululate 409 vb.
be discontented 829 vb.
lamentation 836 n.
whiner
malcontent 829 n.
weeper 836 n.
whinny
ululation 409 n.
whip
accumulator 74 n.
make violent 176 vb.
driver 268 n.
strike 279 vb.
cook 301 vb.
agitate 318 vb.
break in 369 vb.
incentive 612 n.
hasten 680 vb.
manager 690 n.
defeat 727 vb.
oppress 735 vb.
command 737 n.
officer 741 n.
excitant 821 n.
flog 963 vb.
scourge 964 n.
— on
impel 279 vb.
— out
extract 304 vb.
— up
thicken 354 vb.
excite 821 vb.
whipcord
cable 47 n.
whip hand
advantage 34 n.
influence 178 n.
victory 727 n.
governance 733 n.
whipped
light 323 adj.
whipper-in
hunter 619 n.
whippersnapper
youngster 132 n.
nonentity 639 n.
insolent person 878 n.
whippet
dog 365 n.
whipping
victory 727 n.
corporal punishment 963 n.
whipping boy
substitute 150 n.
propitiation 941 n.
whipping post
pillory 964 n.
whippy
flexible 327 adj.
whip-round
gift 781 n.
whirl
rotation 315 n.
rotate 315 vb.
be agitated 318 vb.
activity 678 n.
haste 680 n.
excitable state 822 n.
dance 837 vb.
whirligig
changeable thing 152 n.
rotator 315 n.
whirling
speedy 277 adj.
whirlpool
vortex 315 n.
commotion 318 n.
eddy 350 n.
pitfall 663 n.
whirlwind
turmoil 61 n.
vortex 315 n.
commotion 318 n.
gale 352 n.

whirlybird
aircraft 276 n.
whirr
be agitated 318 vb.
faintness 401 n.
roll 403 n.vb.
resound 404 vb.
ululate 409 vb.
whisk
move fast 277 vb.
cook 301 vb.
rotator 315 n.
agitate 318 vb.
cleaning utensil 648 n.
whisker(s)
filament 208 n.
hair 259 n.
feeler 378 n.
whisky
carriage 274 n.
alcoholic drink 301 n.
whisper
small quantity 33 n.
sound faint 401 vb.
imply 523 vb.
hint 524 n.vb.
rumour 529 n.
voice 577 n.vb.
speak low 578 vb.
detraction 926 n.
whispering campaign
discontent 829 n.
detraction 926 n.
whist
card game 837 n.
whist drive
amusement 837 n.
whistle
blow 352 vb.
megaphone 400 n.
be loud 400 vb.
hiss 406 vb.
shrill 407 vb.
ululate 409 vb.
play music 413 vb.
sing 413 vb.
flute 414 n.
signal 547 n.
be cheerful 833 vb.
wonder 864 vb.
applaud 923 vb.
disapprobation 924 n.
— for
be unlikely 472 vb.
beg 761 vb.
desire 859 vb.
whistle-blowing
warning 664 n.
whistle-stop
stopping place 145 n.
railway 624 n.
whit
small quantity 33 n.
trifle 639 n.
white
colourless 426 adj.
white 427 adj.
eye 438 n.
clean 648 adj.
pure 950 adj.
white as a sheet
fearing 854 adj.
whitebait
fish food 301 n.
white-collar worker
worker 686 n.
whited sepulchre
sham 542 n.
deceiver 545 n.
white dwarf
star 321 n.
white elephant
bane 659 n.
white feather
cowardice 856 n.
white fish
fish food 301 n.
white flag
flag 547 n.
submission 721 n.
white gold
bullion 797 n.
white goods
merchandise 795 n.
white-haired
ageing 131 adj.
Whitehall
workshop 687 n.
authority 733 n.
master 741 n.
white hope
proficient person 696 n.
white horses
wave 350 n.
White House
position of authority 733 n.
white lead
whiting 427 n.
white lie
equivocalness 518 n.
concealment 525 n.
mental dishonesty 543 n.
stratagem 698 n.
white-livered
cowardly 856 adj.
white magic
sorcery 983 n.
white man/woman
whiteness 427 n.
whiten
lose colour 426 vb.
whiten 427 vb.
show feeling 818 vb.
white-out
dimness 419 n.
White Paper
report 524 n.
record 548 n.
White Russian
revolter 738 n.
white sheet
penitence 939 n.
penance 941 n.
white-skinned
white 427 adj.
white slave
prostitute 952 n.
white slave traffic
social evil 951 n.
white stick
blindness 439 n.
white supremacist
narrow mind 481 n.
white tie and tails
formal dress 228 n.
white trash
poor person 801 n.
lower classes 869 n.
whitewash
facing 226 n.
colour 425 vb.
whiting 427 n.
sophisticate 477 vb.
conceal 525 vb.
deceive 542 vb.
cleanser 648 n.
decorate 844 vb.
extenuate 927 vb.
whither
towards 281 adv.
whiting
fish food 301 n.
whiting 427 n.
cleanser 648 n.
whitish
soft-hued 425 adj.
colourless 426 adj.
whitish 427 adj.
grey 429 adj.
yellow 433 adj.
Whitsuntide
summer 128 n.
holy day 988 n.
whittle
cut 46 vb.
laminate 207 vb.
form 243 vb.
sculpt 554 vb.
— away
shade off 27 vb.
make smaller 198 vb.
whiz, whizz
move fast 277 vb.
hiss 406 vb.
whiz kid
busy person 678 n.
prodigy 864 n.
whizzbang
missile weapon 723 n.
whoa!
145 int.
266 int.
whodunit
novel 590 n.
whole
finite quantity 26 n.
quantity 26 n.
simple 44 adj.
whole 52 n.adj.
completeness 54 n.
generality 79 n.
universal 79 adj.
numerical 85 adj.
unity 88 n.
undamaged 646 adj.
preserved 666 adj.
wholefood
food 301 n.
salubrity 652 n.
whole-hearted
simple 44 adj.
resolute 599 adj.
whole hog
completeness 54 n.
actively 678 adv.
wholemeal
cereals 301 n.
whole mind
attention 455 n.
wholesale
extensive 32 adj.
comprehensive 52 adj.
complete 54 adj.
inclusive 78 adj.
indiscriminate 464 adj.
plenteous 635 adj.
trading 791 adj.
sell 793 vb.
wholesaler
seller 793 n.
merchant 794 n.
whole skin
health 650 n.
wholesome
nourishing 301 adj.
beneficial 644 adj.
healthy 650 adj.
salubrious 652 adj.
personable 841 adj.
ascetic 945 adj.
whole time, the
time 108 n.
while 108 adv.
whole truth
truth 494 n.
disclosure 526 n.
whole world over, the
widely 183 adv.
wholly
wholly 52 adv.
completely 54 adv.
whoop
loudness 400 n.
cry 408 n.vb.
be cheerful 833 vb.
rejoice 835 vb.
whoopee
revel 837 n.
whooping cough
respiration 352 n.
infection 651 n.
respiratory disease 651 n.
whopper
whopper 195 n.
untruth 543 n.

whore
prostitute 952 n.
whorehouse
brothel 951 n.
whoremonger
libertine 952 n.
whorl
weaving 222 n.
coil 251 n.
whosoever
everyman 79 n.
Who's Who
directory 87 n.
why?
why 158 adv.
453 int.
why and wherefore, the
reason why 156 n.
wick
filament 208 n.
lighter 385 n.
torch 420 n.
wicked
evil 616 adj.
bad 645 adj.
difficult 700 adj.
wrong 914 adj.
dishonest 930 adj.
wicked 934 adj.
guilty 936 adj.
impenitent 940 adj.
lawbreaking 954 adj.
irreligious 974 adj.
impious 980 adj.
wicked fairy
sorceress 983 n.
wickedness
deterioration 655 n.
disobedience 738 n.
disrepute 867 n.
inhumanity 898 n.
evildoer 904 n.
offender 904 n.
wickedness 934 n.
(See **wicked** *)*
wickerwork
basket 194 n.
network 222 n.
wicket
doorway 263 n.
wicket-keeper
player 837 n.
widdershins
towards 281 adv.
round and round 315 adv.
wide
great 32 adj.
spacious 183 adj.
distant 199 adj.
broad 205 adj.
deviating 282 adj.
mistaken 495 adj.
wide-angle lens
optical device 442 n.
wide apart
different 15 adj.
wide-awake
attentive 455 adj.
vigilant 457 adj.
wide berth
avoidance 620 n.
safety 660 n.
scope 744 n.
wide-bodied
broad 205 adj.
wide circulation
publicity 528 n.
wide-eyed
wondering 864 adj.
innocent 935 adj.
wide horizons
space 183 n.
widely
greatly 32 adv.
throughout 54 adv.
widely 183 adv.
afar 199 adv.
widely held
orthodox 976 adj.
widen
augment 36 vb.
generalize 79 vb.
enlarge 197 vb.
expand 197 vb.
be broad 205 vb.
— the breach
make quarrels 709 vb.
wide of
beyond 199 adv.
wide of the mark
deviating 282 adj.
astray 282 adv.
erroneous 495 adj.
wide open
expanded 197 adj.
open 263 adj.
vulnerable 661 adj.
unconditional 744 adj.
wide-ranging
extensive 32 adj.
broad 205 adj.
wide reading
erudition 490 n.
learning 536 n.
widespread
extensive 32 adj.
comprehensive 52 adj.
unassembled 75 adj.
universal 79 adj.
spacious 183 adj.
expanded 197 adj.
usual 610 adj.
widgeon, wigeon
bird 365 n.
widow
survivor 41 n.
deprive 786 vb.
widowhood 896 n.
widow 896 vb.
widower
survivor 41 n.
widowhood 896 n.
widow-maker
means of execution 964 n.
widow's mite
small coin 33 n.
offering 781 n.
widow's peak
hair 259 n.
widow's weeds
formal dress 228 n.
badge 547 n.
lamentation 836 n.
widowhood 896 n.
width
quantity 26 n.
size 195 n.
breadth 205 n.
wield
operate 173 vb.
touch 378 vb.
use 673 vb.
wife
woman 373 n.
spouse 894 n.
wifehood
marriage 894 n.
wifeless
unwedded 895 adj.
widowed 896 adj.
wifely
loving 887 adj.
matrimonial 894 adj.
wife-swapping
illicit love 951 n.
wig
wig 228 n.
hair 259 n.
hairdressing 843 n.
wigging
reprimand 924 n.
wiggle
oscillate 317 vb.
wigwam
dwelling 192 n.
wild
disorderly 61 adj.
desert 172 n.
furious 176 adj.
space 183 n.
arboreal 366 adj.
light-minded 456 adj.
inexact 495 adj.
absurd 497 adj.
foolish 499 adj.
frenzied 503 adj.
avoiding 620 adj.
unskilful 695 adj.
artless 699 adj.
disobedient 738 adj.
riotous 738 adj.
excited 821 adj.
merry 833 adj.
rash 857 adj.
barbaric 869 adj.
unsociable 883 adj.
angry 891 adj.
cruel 898 adj.
unchaste 951 adj.
wild about
enamoured 887 adj.
wild beast
violent creature 176 n.
animal 365 n.
noxious animal 904 n.
wildcat
cat 365 n.
independent 744 adj.
rash 857 adj.
noxious animal 904 n.
wildcat strike
strike 145 n.
wildebeest
mammal 365 n.
wilderness
confusion 61 n.
havoc 165 n.
desert 172 n.
space 183 n.
land 344 n.
seclusion 883 n.
wildest dreams
fantasy 513 n.
wild-eyed
suffering 825 adj.
lamenting 836 adj.
wildfire
fire 379 n.
wildfire, like
swiftly 277 adv.
wild-goose chase
folly 499 n.
lost labour 641 n.
bungling 695 n.
failure 728 n.
wild life
animality 365 n.
wildlife park
zoo 369 n.
Wild West
district 184 n.
wiles
trickery 542 n.
stratagem 698 n.
wilful
volitional 595 adj.
wilful 602 adj.
capricious 604 adj.
rash 857 adj.
wiliness
cunning 698 n.
will
be to come 124 vb.
will 595 n.vb.
be willing 597 vb.
resolution 599 n.
be resolute 599 vb.
obstinacy 602 n.
predetermination 608 n.
be free 744 vb.
title deed 767 n.
bequeath 780 vb.

desire 859 n.
willies
nervousness 854 n.
willing
assenting 488 adj.
volitional 595 adj.
willing 597 adj.
resolute 599 adj.
intending 617 adj.
active 678 adj.
tractable 701 adj.
obedient 739 adj.
consenting 758 adj.
cheerful 833 adj.
willing horse
volunteer 597 n.
willingness
keenness 174 n.
willingness 597 n.
persuadability 612 n.
cooperation 706 n.
(See **will, willing***)*
will of heaven
fate 596 n.
will-o'-the-wisp
glow-worm 420 n.
visual fallacy 440 n.
deception 542 n.
incentive 612 n.
willow
tree 366 n.
lamentation 836 n.
willow pattern
pottery 381 n.
willowy
narrow 206 adj.
flexible 327 adj.
shapely 841 adj.
willpower
will 595 n.
resolution 599 n.
willy-nilly
necessarily 596 adv.
wilt
be weak 163 vb.
perish 361 vb.
deteriorate 655 vb.
be dejected 834 vb.
wily
intelligent 498 adj.
deceiving 542 adj.
cunning 698 adj.
wily person
trickster 545 n.
slyboots 698 n.
wimple
headgear 228 n.
win
superiority 34 n.
victory 727 n.
win 727 vb.
acquire 771 vb.
gain 771 vb.
appropriate 786 vb.
be rewarded 962 vb.
— hands down
do easily 701 vb.
win 727 vb.
— one's spurs
succeed 727 vb.
have a reputation 866 vb.
— over
convert 147 vb.
convince 485 vb.
induce 612 vb.
— through
arrive 295 vb.
triumph 727 vb.
wince
recoil 280 vb.
feel pain 377 vb.
show feeling 818 vb.
suffer 825 vb.
quake 854 vb.
winceyette
textile 222 n.
winch
draw 288 vb.
lifter 310 n.
wind
insubstantial thing 4 n.
changeable thing 152 n.
disable 161 vb.
voidance 300 n.
circle 314 vb.
rotate 315 vb.
gas 336 n.
air 340 n.
flow 350 vb.
wind 352 n.
smell 394 vb.
play music 413 vb.
detect 484 vb.
empty talk 515 n.
digestive disorders 651 n.
fatigue 684 vb.
— down
repose 683 vb.
— in
draw 288 vb.
— round one's little finger
influence 178 vb.
— up
terminate 69 vb.
cease 145 vb.
operate 173 vb.
invigorate 174 vb.
draw 288 vb.
elevate 310 vb.
make ready 669 vb.
windage
room 183 n.
windbag
chatterer 581 n.
windblown
orderless 61 adj.
windy 352 adj.
windbreak
wood 366 n.
shelter 662 n.
windcone
anemometry 352 n.
wind-driven
dynamic 160 adj.
winded
panting 684 adj.
wind ensemble
orchestra 413 n.
winder
handle 218 n.
rotator 315 n.
windfall
lack of expectation 508 n.
benefit 615 n.
nondesign 618 n.
acquisition 771 n.
gift 781 n.
wind gauge
velocity 277 n.
anemometry 352 n.
winding
complex 61 adj.
meandering 251 n.
convoluted 251 adj.
deviating 282 adj.
flowing 350 adj.
winding sheet
wrapping 226 n.
grave clothes 364 n.
winding up
completion 725 n.
windjammer
sailing ship 275 n.
windlass
traction 288 n.
lifter 310 n.
windless
tranquil 266 adj.
windmill
sources of energy 160 n.
rotator 315 n.
window
window 263 n.
view 438 n.
window display
shop 796 n.
window dressing
publicity 528 n.
duplicity 541 n.
ostentation 875 n.
windowless
opaque 423 adj.
insalubrious 653 adj.
window shopper
spectator 441 n.
purchaser 792 n.
windowsill
shelf 218 n.
windpipe
respiration 352 n.
air pipe 353 n.
wind power
sources of energy 160 n.
wind pump
rotator 315 n.
wind rose
anemometry 352 n.
windrow
series 71 n.
windscreen, windshield
window 263 n.
shelter 662 n.
windsock
anemometry 352 n.
indicator 547 n.
wind surfing
aquatics 269 n.
sport 837 n.
windswept
orderless 61 adj.
windy 352 adj.
wind tunnel
testing agent 461 n.
windward
laterality 239 n.
windy
gaseous 336 adj.
windy 352 adj.
meaningless 515 adj.
diffuse 570 adj.
loquacious 581 adj.
nervous 854 adj.
wine
wine 301 n.
wine and dine
feed 301 vb.
wine bar
tavern 192 n.
wine-bibber
drunkard 949 n.
wine cellar
tavern 192 n.
wine-coloured
red 431 adj.
wine cooler
refrigerator 384 n.
wineglass
cup 194 n.
wine-growing
agriculture 370 n.
wine merchant
provider 633 n.
winepress
farm tool 370 n.
wineskin
vessel 194 n.
wine-tasting
drinking 301 n.
wine, women and song
sensualism 944 n.
wing
limb 53 n.
part 53 n.
group 74 n.
laterality 239 n.
plumage 259 n.
wing 271 n.
fly 271 vb.
move fast 277 vb.
fell 311 vb.
wound 655 vb.
shelter 662 n.
hinder 702 vb.
air force 722 n.

wing commander
air officer 741 n.
winged
flying 271 adj.
speedy 277 adj.
wings
livery 547 n.
stage set 594 n.
theatre 594 n.
wingspan
breadth 205 n.
wink
look 438 n.
be blind 439 vb.
be dim-sighted 440 vb.
hint 524 n.vb.
indication 547 n.
gesticulate 547 vb.
warning 664 n.
excite love 887 vb.
approve 923 vb.
— at
disregard 458 vb.
permit 756 vb.
winker
signal light 420 n.
indicator 547 n.
winkle
fish food 301 n.
marine life 365 n.
winkle out
extract 304 vb.
winner
superior 34 n.
exceller 644 n.
victor 727 n.
recipient 782 n.
winning
superior 34 adj.
successful 727 adj.
pleasurable 826 adj.
amiable 884 adj.
lovable 887 adj.
winning post
limit 236 n.
objective 617 n.
winnings
gain 771 n.
receipt 807 n.
winning ways
inducement 612 n.
lovableness 887 n.
winnow
eliminate 44 vb.
aerate 340 vb.
cultivate 370 vb.
enquire 459 vb.
select 605 vb.
wino
drunkard 949 n.
winsome
personable 841 adj.
lovable 887 adj.
winter
pass time 108 vb.
period 110 n.
winter 129 n.
wintriness 380 n.
adversity 731 n.
winter sports
snow 380 n.
sport 837 n.
wintry
wintry 129 adj.
cold 380 adj.
wipe
dry 342 vb.
touch 378 vb.
clean 648 vb.
— away one's tears
relieve 831 vb.
pity 905 vb.
— out
nullify 2 vb.
destroy 165 vb.
slaughter 362 vb.
obliterate 550 vb.
— the floor with
defeat 727 vb.
— the slate clean
forgive 909 vb.
wire
cable 47 n.
narrowness 206 n.
filament 208 n.
information 524 n.
message 529 n.
telecommunication 531 n.
wiredraw
lengthen 203 vb.
make thin 206 vb.
wireless
broadcasting 531 n.
(*See* **radio**)
wire netting
network 222 n.
wire-puller
latency 523 n.
motivator 612 n.
director 690 n.
slyboots 698 n.
wire-pulling
influence 178 n.
plot 623 n.
wire-tapping
listening 415 n.
wireworm
creepy-crawly 365 n.
wiry
stalwart 162 adj.
lean 206 adj.
fibrous 208 adj.
wisdom
thought 449 n.
erudition 490 n.
wisdom 498 n.
caution 858 n.
wise
judicial 480 adj.
knowing 490 adj.
aphoristic 496 adj.
wise 498 adj.
foreseeing 510 adj.
way 624 n.
advisable 642 adj.
skilful 694 adj.
cunning 698 adj.
cautious 858 adj.
wise after the event
ill-timed 138 adj.
wisecrack
witticism 839 n.
be witty 839 vb.
wised-up
informed 524 adj.
wise guy
sciolist 493 n.
wiseacre 500 n.
affecter 850 n.
wise man
sage 500 n.
sorcerer 983 n.
wiser
improved 654 adj.
wise to
knowing 490 adj.
wise woman
sage 500 n.
sorceress 983 n.
wish
will 595 vb.
request 761 n.
desire 859 n., vb.
desired object 859 n.
— on
desire 859 vb.
curse 899 vb.
— one joy
congratulate 886 vb.
— to sink through the floor
be humbled 872 vb.
— undone
regret 830 vb.
dislike 861 vb.
be penitent 939 vb.
— well
be benevolent 897 vb.
wishbone
magic instrument 983 n.
wish fulfilment
content 828 n.
wishful thinking
misjudgment 481 n.
credulity 487 n.
error 495 n.
fantasy 513 n.
deception 542 n.
hope 852 n.
wishing well
magic instrument 983 n.
wishy-washy
weak 163 adj.
tasteless 387 adj.
feeble 572 adj.
wisp
insubstantial thing 4 n.
small thing 33 n.
piece 53 n.
bunch 74 n.
thinness 206 n.
filament 208 n.
hair 259 n.
wispy
fragmentary 53 adj.
flimsy 163 adj.
wisteria
tree 366 n.
wistful
regretting 830 adj.
desiring 859 adj.
wit
intelligence 498 n.
humorist 839 n.
wit 839 n.
ridiculousness 849 n.
witch
old woman 133 n.
a beauty 841 n.
eyesore 842 n.
hellhag 904 n.
fairy 970 n.
sorceress 983 n.
witchcraft
diabolism 969 n.
sorcery 983 n.
witch doctor
sage 500 n.
doctor 658 n.
sorcerer 983 n.
priest 986 n.
witchery
inducement 612 n.
pleasurableness 826 n.
sorcery 983 n.
witch-hunt
enquiry 459 n.
search 459 n.
pursuit 619 n.
defame 926 vb.
witch-hunting
phobia 854 n.
orthodox 976 adj.
witching
magical 983 adj.
sorcerous 983 adj.
witenagemot
parliament 692 n.
with
in addition 38 adv.
among 43 adv.
conjointly 45 adv.
with 89 adv.
by means of 629 adv.
with a bad grace
unwillingly 598 adv.
sullenly 893 adv.
wih a good grace
willingly 597 adv.
with an eye to
purposely 617 adv.
with a pinch of salt
provided 468 adv.
doubtfully 486 adv.
with a vengeance
extremely 32 adv.
crescendo 36 adv.
in addition 38 adv.

violently 176 adv.
with a view to
purposely 617 adv.
with a will
vigorously 174 adv.
willingly 597 adv.
with both hands
liberally 813 adv.
with care
carefully 457 adv.
cautiously 858 adv.
with child
fertilized 167 adj.
withdraw
decrease 37 vb.
subtract 39 vb.
cease 145 vb.
revert 148 vb.
go away 190 vb.
regress 286 vb.
recede 290 vb.
depart 296 vb.
extract 304 vb.
dissent 489 vb.
recant 603 vb.
tergiversate 603 vb.
run away 620 vb.
relinquish 621 vb.
stop using 674 vb.
submit 721 vb.
resign 753 vb.
not retain 779 vb.
take 786 vb.
schismatize 978 vb.
— from circulation
demonetize 797 vb.
— one's objections
acquiesce 488 vb.
withdrawal
disunion 46 n.
escape 667 n.
opposition 704 n.
seclusion 883 n.
(See **withdraw** *)*
withdrawal symptoms
drug-taking 949 n.
withdrawn
reticent 525 adj.
taciturn 582 adj.
unsociable 883 adj.
wither
be old 127 vb.
become small 198 vb.
perish 361 vb.
impair 655 vb.
deteriorate 655 vb.
be ugly 842 vb.
humiliate 872 vb.
withered
weakened 163 adj.
unproductive 172 adj.
lean 206 adj.
dry 342 adj.
inglorious 867 adj.
withering
baneful 659 adj.
despising 922 adj.
disapproving 924 adj.
withers
angularity 247 n.
with flying colours
successfully 727 adv.
with hindsight
retrospective 125 adj.
withhold
put off 136 vb.
keep secret 525 vb.
restrain 747 vb.
refuse 760 vb.
retain 778 vb.
with impunity
under shelter 660 adv.
within
inside 224 adv.
within an ace of
almost 33 adv.
nearly 200 adv.
within bounds
partially 33 adv.
moderately 177 adv.
temperate 942 adj.
within call
near 200 adv.
within earshot
near 200 adv.
auditory 415 adj.
within one's grasp
possibly 469 adv.
within one's means
cheap 812 adj.
within reach
on the spot 189 adj.
near 200 adv.
accessible 289 adj.
possibly 469 adv.
easy 701 adj.
within reason
moderately 177 adv.
with interest
in addition 38 adv.
within the law
legal 953 adj.
with it
modern 126 adj.
attentive 455 adj.
intelligent 498 adj.
fashionable 848 adj.
with one accord
concurrently 181 adv.
unanimously 488 adv.
with one, be
understand 516 vb.
with one's back to the wall
endangered 661 adj.
in difficulties 700 adj.
with one's eyes open
purposely 617 adv.
with one's hackles up
angrily 891 adv.
with one's heart in one's mouth
excitedly 821 adv.
nervous 854 adj.
with one voice
synchronously 123 adv.
assenting 488 adj.
unanimously 488 adv.
without
if 8 adv.
subtracted 39 adj.
in deduction 39 adv.
incomplete 55 adj.
unconformably 84 adv.
without 190 adv.
around 230 adv.
losing 772 adj.
not owning 774 adj.
without a care in the world
cheerfully 833 adv.
without a clue
ignorant 491 adj.
without a hitch
easily 701 adv.
without a leg to stand on
powerless 161 adj.
confuted 479 adj.
without being asked
willingly 597 adv.
without ceremony
modestly 874 adv.
without delay
instantaneously 116 adv.
suddenly 135 adv.
hasty 680 adj.
without difficulty
easily 701 adv.
without distinction
identically 13 adv.
rightly 913 adv.
without end
infinite 107 adj.
perpetual 115 adj.
without enthusiasm
in cold blood 820 adv.
without exception
uniformly 16 adv.
inclusive 78 adj.
generally 79 adv.
without excuse
accusable 928 adj.
guilty 936 adj.
without fail
certainly 473 adv.
without fear of contradiction
affirmatively 532 adv.
without fear or favour
truthfully 540 adv.
rightly 913 adv.
without issue
unproductive 172 adj.
without let or hindrance
easily 701 adv.
without notice
suddenly 135 adv.
unexpectedly 508 adv.
without number
infinite 107 adj.
without prospects
poor 801 adj.
without qualifications
unentitled 916 adj.
without rank
plebeian 869 adj.
without regrets
impenitent 940 adj.
without rhyme or reason
confusedly 61 adv.
absurd 497 adj.
without rights
unentitled 916 adj.
without side
humble 872 adj.
without stint
plenteous 635 adj.
without stopping
continuously 71 adv.
without strings
unconditional 744 adj.
permitted 756 adj.
without warning
instantaneously 116 adv.
unexpectedly 508 adv.
with pleasure
willingly 597 adv.
with reference/regard to
concerning 9 adv.
with regret
unwillingly 598 adv.
with reservations
in deduction 39 adv.
on terms 766 adv.
with respect
courteously 884 adv.
with respect to
concerning 9 adv.
specially 80 adv.
withstand
counteract 182 vb.
withstand 704 vb.
parry 713 vb.
resist 715 vb.
be inimical 881 vb.
with strings attached
conditional 766 adj.
with tears in one's eyes
supplicatory 761 adj.
with thanks
gratefully 907 adv.

with the aid of
by means of 629 adv.
with the best intentions
benevolent 897 adj.
innocently 935 adv.
with the exception of
in deduction 39 adv.
exclusive of 57 adv.
with the help of
through 628 adv.
with the intention of
purposely 617 adv.
with the proviso that
provided 468 adv.
with the understanding that
provided 468 adv.
with time to spare
betimes 135 adv.
with tongue in cheek
in jest 839 adv.
withy
ligature 47 n.
witless
foolish 499 adj.
witling
wiseacre 500 n.
fool 501 n.
witness
be present 189 vb.
see 438 vb.
spectator 441 n.
watch 441 vb.
testimony 466 n.
witness 466 n.
reminder 505 n.
informant 524 n.
signatory 765 n.
— to
indicate 547 vb.
witness box
courtroom 956 n.
wits
intellect 447 n.
intelligence 498 n.
witticism
witticism 839 n.
wittingly
purposely 617 adv.
witty
aphoristic 496 adj.
forceful 571 adj.
merry 833 adj.
witty 839 adj.
funny 849 adj.
derisive 851 adj.
sociable 882 adj.
wizard
sage 500 n.
proficient person 696 n.
prodigy 864 n.
sorcerer 983 n.
wizardry
skill 694 n.
sorcery 983 n.
wizened
ageing 131 adj.
dwarfish 196 adj.
contracted 198 adj.
lean 206 adj.
woad
blue pigment 435 n.
wobble
change 143 vb.
vary 152 vb.
move slowly 278 vb.
deviate 282 vb.
oscillate 317 vb.
be agitated 318 vb.
be irresolute 601 vb.
wobbling, wobbly
fitful 142 adj.
unstable 152 adj.
flimsy 163 adj.
wodge
piece 53 n.
woe
evil 616 n.
bane 659 n.
sorrow 825 n.
woebegone
unhappy 825 adj.
woeful
bad 645 adj.
suffering 825 adj.
distressing 827 adj.
melancholic 834 adj.
lamenting 836 adj.
woefully
painfully 32 adv.
wold
high land 209 n.
plain 348 n.
wolf
violent creature 176 n.
dog 365 n.
taker 786 n.
noxious animal 904 n.
gluttonize 947 vb.
libertine 952 n.
wolf at the door
poverty 801 n.
wolf in sheep's clothing
hider 527 n.
sham 542 n.
impostor 545 n.
wolfish
animal 365 adj.
cruel 898 adj.
gluttonous 947 adj.
wolfishness
gluttony 947 n.
wolf whistle
stridor 407 n.
wonder 864 n.
woman
athlete 162 n.
person 371 n.
spouse 894 n.
(See **man/woman** *)*
woman-hater
misanthrope 902 n.
womanhood
adultness 134 n.
womanish
weak 163 adj.
female 373 adj.
womanizer, womaniser
libertine 952 n.
womankind
humankind 371 n.
womankind 373 n.
womanly
grown-up 134 adj.
female 373 n.
woman of the streets
prostitute 952 n.
womb
origin 68 n.
seedbed 156 n.
genitalia 167 n.
parentage 169 n.
insides 224 n.
wombat
mammal 365 n.
womb of time
futurity 124 n.
women
womankind 373 n.
women and children first
ahead 283 adv.
womenfolk
womankind 373 n.
Women's Lib/ Liberation
female 373 n.
freedom 744 n.
women's quarters
womankind 373 n.
women's rights
dueness 915 n.
women's suffrage
vote 605 n.
wonder
nonconformity 84 n.
be uncertain 474 vb.
not know 491 vb.
lack of expectation 508 n.
not understand 517 vb.
exceller 644 n.
prodigy 864 n.
wonder 864 n.vb.
respect 920 n.vb.
— about
meditate 449 vb.
wonderful
prodigious 32 adj.
unusual 84 adj.
impossible 470 adj.
unbelieved 486 adj.
excellent 644 adj.
pleasurable 826 adj.
wonderful 864 adj.
noteworthy 866 adj.
worshipful 866 adj.
sorcerous 983 adj.
wondering
puzzled 517 adj.
wondering 864 adj.
wonderland
fantasy 513 n.
wonder-working
thaumaturgy 864 n.
sorcery 983 n.
wondrous
wonderful 864 adj.
wonky
flimsy 163 adj.
oblique 220 adj.
wont
habit 610 n.
use 673 n.
wonted
usual 610 adj.
woo
pursue 619 vb.
desire 859 vb.
court 889 vb.
wood
missile 287 n.
hardness 326 n.
wood 366 n.
wooden 366 adj.
fuel 385 n.
materials 631 n.
wood-block
engraving 555 n.
wood carving
sculpture 554 n.
woodcock
table bird 365 n.
woodcut
picture 553 n.
engraving 555 n.
woodcutter
forestry 366 n.
wooded
arboreal 366 adj.
wooden
wooden 366 adj.
inelegant 576 adj.
obstinate 602 adj.
impassive 820 adj.
woodenhead
dunce 501 n.
wooden spoon
unskilfulness 695 n.
trophy 729 n.
wooden walls
defences 713 n.
navy 722 n.
woodland
wood 366 n.
arboreal 366 adj.
woodlouse
creepy-crawly 365 n.
woodnote
ululation 409 n.
wood nymph
vegetable life 366 n.
nymph 967 n.
woodpecker
bird 365 n.

wood pulp
pulpiness 356 n.
paper 631 n.
woodwind
orchestra 413 n.
musical instrument 414 n.
woodwork
structure 331 n.
ornamental art 844 n.
woodworker
artisan 686 n.
woodworm
destroyer 168 n.
insect 365 n.
blight 659 n.
woody
tough 329 adj.
arboreal 366 adj.
wooden 366 adj.
wooer
concomitant 89 n.
petitioner 763 n.
desirer 859 n.
lover 887 n.
woof
weaving 222 n.
ululate 409 vb.
woofer
gramophone 414 n.
wool
fibre 208 n.
textile 222 n.
hair 259 n.
materials 631 n.
woolgathering
abstractedness 456 n.
woollens
warm clothes 381 n.
woolly
fibrous 208 adj.
jersey 228 n.
smooth 258 adj.
fleecy 259 adj.
hairy 259 adj.
poorly reasoned 477 adj.
woolpack
cloud 355 n.
woolsack
badge of rule 743 n.
tribunal 956 n.
woomera
missile weapon 723 n.
woozy
tipsy 949 adj.
word
testimony 466 n.
hint 524 n.
information 524 n.
message 529 n.
news 529 n.
call 547 n.
word 559 n.
neology 560 n.
speech 579 n.
warning 664 n.
command 737 n.
promise 764 n.
duty 917 n.
Word, the
God the Son 965 n.
scripture 975 n.
wordbook
dictionary 559 n.
word fencing
sophistry 477 n.
word-formation
formation 243 n.
word for word
imitatively 20 adv.
accurate 494 adj.
interpretive 520 adj.
verbally 559 adv.
word game
indoor game 837 n.
wordiness
loquacity 581 n.
wording
phrase 563 n.
word in the ear
hint 524 n.
warning 664 n.
wordless
voiceless 578 adj.
wondering 864 adj.
word list
word list 87 n.
dictionary 559 n.
word magic
style 566 n.
word of honour
oath 532 n.
promise 764 n.
security 767 n.
word of mouth
tradition 127 n.
testimony 466 n.
message 529 n.
word-perfect
prepared 669 adj.
word-play
equivocalness 518 n.
trope 519 n.
neology 560 n.
wit 839 n.
word processor
data processing 86 n.
words
quarrel 709 n.
contention 716 n.
word-spinning
style 566 n.
eloquence 579 n.
word to the wise
hint 524 n.
warning 664 n.
advice 691 n.
wordy
verbal 559 adj.
prolix 570 adj.
work
composition 56 n.
energy 160 n.
product 164 n.
agency 173 n.
operate 173 vb.
form 243 vb.
effervesce 318 vb.
structure 331 n.
bubble 355 vb.
musical piece 412 n.
book 589 n.
stage play 594 n.
persevere 600 vb.
business 622 n.
function 622 vb.
be instrumental 628 vb.
suffice 635 vb.
be useful 640 vb.
be expedient 642 vb.
use 673 vb.
action 676 n.
be busy 678 vb.
labour 682 n.
work 682 vb.
fatigue 684 vb.
be successful 727 vb.
ornamental art 844 n.
— against
counteract 182 vb.
plot 623 vb.
be inexpedient 643 vb.
oppose 704 vb.
— at
persevere 600 vb.
busy oneself 622 vb.
deal with 688 vb.
— for
busy oneself 622 vb.
be instrumental 628 vb.
— in
introduce 231 vb.
— like magic
be successful 727 vb.
— miracles
be wonderful 864 vb.
— on/upon
influence 178 vb.
motivate 612 vb.
use 673 vb.
excite 821 vb.
— one's passage
voyage 269 vb.
— one's way into
enter 297 vb.
— one's way up
climb 308 vb.
prosper 730 vb.
— out
do sums 86 vb.
happen 154 vb.
result 157 vb.
reason 475 vb.
decipher 520 vb.
plan 623 vb.
mature 669 vb.
deal with 688 vb.
carry through 725 vb.
— together
cooperate 706 vb.
— to rule
strike 145 n.
— up
excite 821 vb.
— up into
form 243 vb.
— wonders
be active 678 vb.
workable
powerful 160 adj.
operative 173 adj.
possible 469 adj.
advisable 642 adj.
workaday
plain 573 adj.
businesslike 622 adj.
workaholic
busy person 678 n.
workbasket, workbox
basket 194 n.
workbook
classroom 539 n.
worked
variegated 437 adj.
ornamented 844 adj.
worked up
matured 669 adj.
fervent 818 adj.
suffering 825 adj.
angry 891 adj.
worker
producer 164 n.
doer 676 n.
busy person 678 n.
worker 686 n.
servant 742 n.
worker participation
cooperation 706 n.
workers' cooperative
association 706 n.
Workers' Revolutionary Party
political party 708 n.
workhorse
busy person 678 n.
workhouse
retreat 192 n.
poverty 801 n.
working arrangement
way 624 n.
compromise 770 n.
working capital
means 629 n.
working class
personnel 686 n.
lower classes 869 n.
plebeian 869 adj.
working day
period 110 n.
job 622 n.
labour 682 n.
working hypothesis
supposition 512 n.
working lunch
conference 584 n.

working man/woman
worker 686 n.
working model
image 551 n.
working party
enquiry 459 n.
consignee 754 n.
workings
structure 331 n.
workings of the mind
thought 449 n.
working towards
tending 179 adj.
workman
doer 676 n.
worker 686 n.
workmanlike
industrious 678 adj.
well-made 694 adj.
workmanship
production 164 n.
deed 676 n.
work of art
composition 56 n.
representation 551 n.
masterpiece 694 n.
a beauty 841 n.
work of fiction
ideality 513 n.
reading$matter 589 n.
work of one's hands
product 164 n.
workout
exercise 682 n.
workpeople
personnel 686 n.
workroom
chamber 194 n.
workshop 687 n.
works
component 58 n.
structure 331 n.
writing 586 n.
machine 630 n.
workshop 687 n.
works, the
all 52 n.
workshop
class 538 n.
workshop 687 n.
work-shy
lazy 679 adj.
work study
management 689 n.
world
substantiality 3 n.
great quantity 32 n.
whole 52 n.
comprehensive 52 adj.
affairs 154 n.
space 183 n.
materiality 319 n.
universe 321 n.
world 321 n.
telluric 321 adj.
humankind 371 n.
society 882 n.
World Bank
pawnshop 784 n.
world-beater
superior 34 n.
exceller 644 n.
victor 727 n.
World Council of Churches
Christendom 976 n.
worldling
egotist 932 n.
irreligionist 974 n.
impious person 980 n.
worldly
material 319 adj.
telluric 321 adj.
selfish 932 adj.
irreligious 974 adj.
worldly wisdom
sagacity 498 n.
skill 694 n.
caution 858 n.
selfishness 932 n.
world of
great quantity 32 n.
multitude 104 n.
world of nature
substantiality 3 n.
matter 319 n.
world of one's own
seclusion 883 n.
world's end
extremity 69 n.
farness 199 n.
world-shaking
revolutionary 149 adj.
world soul
divineness 965 n.
world to come
destiny 155 n.
world-view
generality 79 n.
world-weariness
discontent 829 n.
melancholy 834 n.
tedium 838 n.
world well lost
relinquishment 621 n.
worldwide
extensive 32 adj.
comprehensive 52 adj.
inclusive 78 adj.
universal 79 adj.
spacious 183 adj.
telluric 321 adj.
worm
inferior 35 n.
coil 251 n.
serpent 251 n.
wriggle 251 vb.
creepy-crawly 365 n.
infection 651 n.
cad 938 n.
— in
introduce 231 vb.
— oneself into favour
be servile 879 vb.
— one's way into
infiltrate 297 vb.
pass 305 vb.
— out
discover 484 vb.
worm-eaten
dilapidated 655 adj.
wormlike
snaky 251 adj.
wormwood
sourness 393 n.
badness 645 n.
bane 659 n.
worn
weakened 163 adj.
shown 522 adj.
dilapidated 655 adj.
used 673 adj.
fatigued 684 adj.
unsightly 842 adj.
worn out
impotent 161 adj.
useless 641 adj.
deteriorated 655 adj.
dilapidated 655 adj.
disused 674 adj.
worn to a shadow
lean 206 adj.
worried
expectant 507 adj.
in difficulties 700 adj.
(See **worry** *)*
worries
adversity 731 n.
worry 825 n.
worry
chew 301 vb.
agitate 318 vb.
think 449 vb.
carefulness 457 n.
expectation 507 n.
evil 616 n.
bane 659 n.
adversity 731 n.
impress 821 vb.
worry 825 n.
suffer 825 vb.
annoyance 827 n.
torment 827 vb.
trouble 827 vb.
dejection 834 n.
nervousness 854 n.
worse
deteriorated 655 adj.
aggravatedly 832 adv.
worse for wear, the
weakened 163 adj.
dilapidated 655 adj.
worsen
harm 645 vb.
deteriorate 655 vb.
aggravate 832 vb.
worship
honour 866 vb.
love 887 n.vb.
respect 920 n.vb.
be pious 979 vb.
worship 981 n.vb.
deification 982 n.
idolatry 982 n.
worshipful
great 32 adj.
worshipful 866 adj.
respected 920 adj.
godlike 965 adj.
sanctified 979 adj.
devotional 981 adj.
worshipper
desirer 859 n.
church member 976 n.
pietist 979 n.
worshipper 981 n.
idolater 982 n.
worst
be superior 34 vb.
defeat 727 vb.
worst, the
misfortune 731 n.
worsted
inferior 35 adj.
fibre 208 n.
textile 222 n.
defeated 728 adj.
worst intentions
malevolence 898 n.
worst of it, the
defeat 728 n.
wort
plant 366 n.
worth
equivalent 28 adj.
quid pro quo 150 n.
utility 640 n.
goodness 644 n.
price 809 n.
virtues 933 n.
worth having
desired 859 adj.
worth its weight in gold
valuable 644 adj.
of price 811 adj.
worthless
trivial 639 adj.
profitless 641 adj.
bad 645 adj.
deteriorated 655 adj.
contemptible 922 adj.
vicious 934 adj.
worth mentioning
relevant 9 adj.
worthwhile
good 615 adj.
important 638 adj.
profitable 640 adj.
advisable 642 adj.
beneficial 644 adj.
approvable 923 adj.
worthy
excellent 644 adj.

person of repute 866 n.
reputable 866 adj.
deserving 915 adj.
approvable 923 adj.
virtuous 933 adj.
wot
know 490 vb.
would-be
misnamed 562 adj.
willing 597 adj.
intending 617 adj.
hoping 852 adj.
desiring 859 adj.
ostentatious 875 adj.
unwarranted 916 adj.
wound
cut 46 vb.
weaken 163 vb.
coiled 251 adj.
pierce 263 vb.
strike 279 vb.
pain 377 n.
ill-treat 645 vb.
ulcer 651 n.
wound 655 n.vb.
hinder 702 vb.
hurt 827 vb.
blemish 845 n.
huff 891 vb.
— the feelings
hurt 827 vb.
huff 891 vb.
wounded
suffering 825 adj.
wounds
trophy 729 n.
wound up
coiled 251 adj.
excited 821 adj.
woven
correlative 12 adj.
crossed 222 adj.
textural 331 adj.
wow
discord 411 n.
exceller 644 n.
amuse 837 vb.
wowser
prude 950 n.
zealot 979 n.
WRAC
soldier 722 n.
wrack
ruin 165 n.
plant 366 n.
WRAF
soldier 722 n.
wraith
visual fallacy 440 n.
ghost 970 n.
wraith-like
lean 206 adj.
spooky 970 adj.
wrangle
disagreement 25 n.
argue 475 vb.
dissent 489 vb.
quarrel 709 n.
wrangler
enumerator 86 n.
reasoner 475 n.
quarreller 709 n.
combatant 722 n.
wrangling
disagreement 25 n.
argument 475 n.
quarrelling 709 adj.
wrap
tie 45 vb.
cover 226 vb.
dress 228 vb.
enclose 235 vb.
fold 261 vb.
warm clothes 381 n.
— up
dress 228 vb.
carry through 725 vb.
wrapped in thought
thoughtful 449 adj.
abstracted 456 adj.
wrapped up in
obsessed 455 adj.
wrapped up in oneself
selfish 932 adj.
wrapper
receptacle 194 n.
wrapping 226 n.
informal dress 228 n.
enclosure 235 n.
wrapping
receptacle 194 n.
wrapping 226 n.
lining 227 n.
bookbinding 589 n.
wrath
hatred 888 n.
anger 891 n.
wrathful
angry 891 adj.
wreak one's malice on
ill-treat 645 vb.
be malevolent 898 vb.
— vengeance
be severe 735 vb.
avenge 910 vb.
wreath
crossing 222 n.
loop 250 n.
badge 547 n.
heraldry 547 n.
objective 617 n.
trophy 729 n.
ornamentation 844 n.
honours 866 n.
wreathe
enlace 222 vb.
surround 230 vb.
twine 251 vb.
decorate 844 vb.
celebrate 876 vb.
pay one's respects 884 vb.
wreck
remainder 41 n.
ruin 165 n.
destroy 165 vb.
dilapidation 655 n.
impair 655 vb.
defeat 728 n.
debauch 951 vb.
wreckage
remainder 41 n.
ruin 165 n.
wrecked
grounded 728 adj.
wrecker
destroyer 168 n.
troublemaker 663 n.
rioter 738 n.
robber 789 n.
evildoer 904 n.
wren
small animal 33 n.
bird 365 n.
Wren
soldier 722 n.
wrench
disunite 46 vb.
disable 161 vb.
be vigorous 174 vb.
violence 176 n.
force 176 vb.
impulse 279 n.
draw 288 vb.
extraction 304 n.
extractor 304 n.
misinterpret 521 vb.
tool 630 n.
nippers 778 n.
wrest
distort 246 vb.
— the law
do wrong 914 vb.
be illegal 954 vb.
— the meaning
misinterpret 521 vb.
wrestle (with)
contend 716 vb.
withstand 704 vb.
wrestler
athlete 162 n.
combatant 722 n.
wrestling
wrestling 716 n.
sport 837 n.
wretch
unlucky person 731 n.
sufferer 825 n.
knave 938 n.
wretched
unimportant 639 adj.
bad 645 adj.
not nice 645 adj.
unfortunate 731 adj.
unhappy 825 adj.
melancholic 834 adj.
rascally 930 adj.
wretchedly
painfully 32 adv.
wretchedness
adversity 731 n.
sorrow 825 n.
wriggle
wriggle 251 vb.
be agitated 318 vb.
be cunning 698 vb.
be excited 821 vb.
suffer 825 vb.
— out of
plead 614 vb.
escape 667 vb.
fail in duty 918 vb.
wriggling
snaky 251 adj.
wright
artisan 686 n.
wring
clean 648 vb.
levy 786 vb.
— from
extract 304 vb.
compel 740 vb.
levy 786 vb.
— one's hands
be impotent 161 vb.
gesticulate 547 vb.
regret 830 vb.
lament 836 vb.
despair 853 vb.
— out
dry 342 vb.
— the neck of
kill 362 vb.
wringer
smoother 258 n.
dryer 342 n.
wrinkle
become small 198 vb.
make angular 247 vb.
convolution 251 n.
crinkle 251 vb.
roughen 259 vb.
fold 261 n.vb.
groove 262 vb.
idea 451 n.
hint 524 n.
trickery 542 n.
impair 655 vb.
stratagem 698 n.
— one's nose
be fastidious 862 vb.
despise 922 vb.
wrinkled
ageing 131 adj.
furrowed 262 adj.
unsightly 842 adj.
wrinkles
fold 261 n.
ugliness 842 n.
wrist
joint 45 n.
wristband
sleeve 228 n.

wristlet
jewellery 844 n.
writ
precept 693 n.
warrant 737 n.
mandate 751 n.
security 767 n.
law 953 n.
legal process 959 n.
write
communicate 524 vb.
mark 547 vb.
record 548 vb.
write 586 vb.
— about
describe 590 vb.
dissertate 591 vb.
— down
record 548 vb.
account 808 vb.
— in
fill 54 vb.
give terms 766 vb.
— off
relinquish 621 vb.
stop using 674 vb.
— one's name
sign 547 vb.
write 586 vb.
— to
correspond 588 vb.
— up
dissertate 591 vb.
praise 923 vb.
write-off
nonuse 674 n.
debt 803 n.
writer
recorder 549 n.
calligrapher 586 n.
author 589 n.
dissertator 591 n.
write-up
publicity 528 n.
article 591 n.
writhe
distort 246 vb.
wriggle 251 vb.
leap 312 vb.
be agitated 318 vb.
feel pain 377 vb.
be excited 821 vb.
suffer 825 vb.
writing
composition 56 n.
production 164 n.
writing 586 n.
reading matter 589 n.
writing on the wall
omen 511 n.
warning 664 n.
danger signal 665 n.
threat 900 n.
writing paper
stationery 586 n.
written
recorded 548 adj.
literary 557 adj.
written 586 adj.
written all over one
manifest 522 adj.
written character
letter 558 n.
WRNS
naval man 722 n.
wrong
unapt 25 adj.
misjudging 481 adj.
erroneous 495 adj.
evil 616 n.adj.
amiss 616 adv.
inexpedient 643 adj.
ill-treat 645 vb.
wrong 914 n.adj.
do wrong 914 vb.
unwarranted 916 adj.
foul play 930 n.
dishonest 930 adj.
wickedness 934 n.
heinous 934 adj.
lawbreaking 954 n.
wrongdoer
evildoer 904 n.
offender 904 n.
wrong 914 n.
wrongdoing
wickedness 934 n.
lawbreaking 954 n.
wrong end of the stick
misinterpretation 521 n.
wrongful
bad 645 adj.
wrong 914 adj.
illegal 954 adj.
wrong-headed
misjudging 481 adj.
erroneous 495 adj.
unintelligent 499 adj.
wrong 914 adj.
wrongheadedness
obstinacy 602 n.
wrong idea
error 495 n.
wrong impression
misjudgment 481 n.
mistake 495 n.
wrong side
contrariety 14 n.
rear 238 n.
opposition 704 n.
wrong side of the law
illegality 954 n.
wrong side out
reversibly 148 adv.
inverted 221 adj.
wrong 'un
bad person 938 n.
wrong verdict
misjudgment 481 n.
injustice 914 n.
wrought
elegant 575 adj.
matured 669 adj.
wrought iron
hardness 326 n.
ornamental art 844 n.
wrought up
excited 821 adj.
angry 891 adj.
wry
oblique 220 adj.
distorted 246 adj.
wynd
road 624 n.
wyvern
rara avis 84 n.

X

x
number 85 n.
indication 547 n.
Xanthippe
shrew 892 n.
X certificate
film 445 n.
xebec
sailing ship 275 n.
xenophile
xenophile 880 n.
xenophobe
enemy 881 n.
xenophobia
prejudice 481 n.
phobia 854 n.
dislike 861 n.
hatred 888 n.
Xerox
copy 22 n.
X-ray
radiation 417 n.
enquire 459 vb.
photography 551 n.
X-shape
crossing 222 n.
xylography
engraving 555 n.
xylophone
gong 414 n.

Y

yacht
sailing ship 275 n.
yachting
aquatics 269 n.
water travel 269 n.
sport 837 n.
yachtsman, yachtswoman
boatman 270 n.
yahoo
low fellow 869 n.
Yahweh
the Deity 965 n.
yak
cattle 365 n.
be loquacious 581 vb.
yam
vegetable 301 n.
yammer
cry 408 vb.
weep 836 vb.
yank
draw 288 vb.
Yank, Yankee
foreigner 59 n.
yap
cry 408 vb.
ululate 409 vb.
yarborough
misfortune 731 n.
yard
place 185 n.
long measure 203 n.
prop 218 n.
enclosure 235 n.
open space 263 n.
workshop 687 n.
yardarm
prop 218 n.
yardstick
counting instrument 86 n.
testing agent 461 n.
gauge 465 n.
yarn
fibre 208 n.
news 529 n.
fable 543 n.
exaggeration 546 n.
be diffuse 570 vb.
narrative 590 n.
materials 631 n.
yarn spinner
liar 545 n.
narrator 590 n.
yashmak
headgear 228 n.
yaw
vary 152 vb.
navigate 269 vb.
deviation 282 n.
yawl
sailing ship 275 n.
yawn
open 263 vb.
respiration 352 n.
sleep 679 vb.
be fatigued 684 vb.
yawning
deep 211 adj.
opening 263 n.
sleepy 679 adj.
yawning gulf
gap 201 n.
yawp
stridor 407 n.
ululation 409 n.
yaws
skin disease 651 n.
tropical disease 651 n.

yea
assent 488 n.
year
date 108 n.
period 110 n.
contemporary 123 n.
yearbook
reference book 589 n.
year in year out
repeatedly 106 adv.
all along 113 adv.
yearling
young creature 132 n.
cattle 365 n.
yearly
seasonal 141 adj.
periodically 141 adv.
yearn
be dejected 834 vb.
desire 859 vb.
— over
pity 905 vb.
yearning
desire 859 n.
years
time 108 n.
long duration 113 n.
age 131 n.
years ago
formerly 125 adv.
years of discretion
middle age 131 n.
adultness 134 n.
yeast
stimulant 174 n.
lifter 310 n.
leaven 323 n.
bubble 355 n.
yeasty
light 323 adj.
bubbly 355 adj.
yegg
thief 789 n.
yell
feel pain 377 vb.
loudness 400 n.
cry 408 n.
vociferate 408 vb.
rejoicing 835 n.
weep 836 vb.
yellow
gild 433 vb.
yellow 433 adj.
unhealthy 651 adj.
cowardly 856 adj.
yellowcake
materials 631 n.
yellow-eyed
jealous 911 adj.
yellow fever
tropical disease 651 n.
yellow flag
danger signal 665 n.
yellowhammer
bird 365 n.
yellow lines
traffic control 305 n.
yellow peril
troublemaker 663 n.
yellow press
the press 528 n.
bad taste 847 n.
yellow streak
cowardice 856 n.
yelp
shrill 407 vb.
ululation 409 n.
yen
coinage 797 n.
desire 859 n.
ye olde
antiquated 127 adj.
yeoman
farmer 370 n.
soldier 722 n.
possessor 776 n.
country-dweller 869 n.
yeomanry
inhabitants 191 n.
cavalry 722 n.
soldier 722 n.
yes
assent 488 n.
yes and no
uncertainty 474 n.
yes-man
imitator 20 n.
conformist 83 n.
assenter 488 n.
toady 879 n.
flatterer 925 n.
yesterday
priority 119 n.
past time 125 n.
formerly 125 adv.
yet
while 108 adv.
before 119 adv.
retrospectively 125 adv.
nevertheless 468 adv.
yeti
mythical being 970 n.
yet to come
unborn 2 adj.
future 124 adj.
yew
tree 366 n.
yield
be inferior 35 vb.
conform 83 vb.
be weak 163 vb.
product 164 n.
reproduce itself 167 vb.
soften 327 vb.
acquiesce 488 vb.
be irresolute 601 vb.
be induced 612 vb.
relinquish 621 vb.
provide 633 vb.
submit 721 vb.
obey 739 vb.
consent 758 vb.
be profitable 771 vb.
not retain 779 vb.
give 781 vb.
— up
restore 656 vb.
yielding
unstable 152 adj.
tractable 701 adj.
yin and yang
polarity 14 n.
duality 90 n.
yob
youngster 132 n.
vulgarian 847 n.
ruffian 904 n.
yobbish
ill-bred 847 adj.
barbaric 869 adj.
yodel
cry 408 n.
sing 413 vb.
yoga
philosophy 449 n.
exercise 682 n.
asceticism 945 n.
religion 973 n.
yoghurt, yogurt, yoghourt
dairy product 301 n.
yogi
sage 500 n.
ascetic 945 n.
yogic
ascetic 945 adj.
religious 973 adj.
yo-heave-ho!
288 int.
yoke
affix 45 vb.
coupling 47 n.
duality 90 n.
pair 90 vb.
prop 218 n.
break in 369 vb.
servitude 745 n.
subjection 745 n.
fetter 748 n.
yoked
combined 50 adj.
yoke-fellow
concomitant 89 n.
collaborator 707 n.
yokel
native 191 n.
ingenue 699 n.
country-dweller 869 n.
Yom Kippur
holy day 988 n.
yon, yonder
distant 199 adj.
afar 199 adv.
yoni
fertilizer 171 n.
idol 982 n.
yonks
long duration 113 n.
yorker
propulsion 287 n.
young
subsequent 120 adj.
new 126 adj.
vernal 128 adj.
young 130 adj.
infantine 132 adj.
strong 162 adj.
weak 163 adj.
product 164 n.
posterity 170 n.
immature 670 adj.
young blood
youth 130 n.
young creature
young creature 132 n.
younger
subsequent 120 adj.
young 130 adj.
younger generation
modernist 126 n.
youth 130 n.
young man/woman
youngster 132 n.
lover 887 n.
youngster
youngster 132 n.
male 372 n.
woman 373 n.
Young Turk
agitator 738 n.
young 'un
youngster 132 n.
your honour
title 870 n.
yourself
self 80 n.
youth
beginning 68 n.
newness 126 n.
youth 130 n.
youngster 132 n.
adult 134 n.
youthful
young 130 adj.
strong 162 adj.
youth hostel
inn 192 n.
youth hosteller
traveller 268 n.
youth movement
society 708 n.
yowl
cry 408 vb.
ululate 409 vb.
yoyo
oscillation 317 n.
plaything 837 n.
yoyo, like a
to and fro 317 adv.
Y-shape
divergence 294 n.
Yuga
era 110 n.
yuk
dirt 649 n.

yuk!
391 int.
861 int.
Yuletide
winter 129 n.
holy day 988 n.
yummy
savoury 390 adj.

Z

zany
fool 501 n.
laughingstock 851 n.
zareba
enclosure 235 n.
fort 713 n.
zeal
keenness 174 n.
willingness 597 n.
resolution 599 n.
warm feeling 818 n.
desire 859 n.
piety 979 n.
zealot
doctrinaire 473 n.
narrow mind 481 n.
enthusiast 504 n.
obstinate person 602 n.
busy person 678 n.
religionist 973 n.
zealot 979 n.
zealous
willing 597 adj.
resolute 599 adj.
active 678 adj.
fervent 818 adj.
zebra
mammal 365 n.
stripe 437 n.
zebra crossing
traffic control 305 n.
access 624 n.
zebu
cattle 365 n.
Zeitgeist
tendency 179 n.
zemstvo
council 692 n.
Zen
philosophy 449 n.
religious faith 973 n.
zenana
womankind 373 n.
Zen Buddhist
religionist 973 n.
Zend-Avesta
non-Biblical scripture 975 n.
zenith
superiority 34 n.
summit 213 n.
zenith distance
angular measure 247 n.
zephyr
breeze 352 n.
Zeppelin
airship 276 n.
zero
insubstantiality 4 n.
quantity 26 n.
smallness 33 n.
zero 103 n.
not one 103 adj.
coldness 380 n.
zero hour
start 68 n.
date 108 n.
departure 296 n.
zero-rated
uncharged 812 adj.
zest
vigorousness 174 n.
pleasure 376 n.
taste 386 n.
enjoyment 824 n.
pleasurableness 826 n.
liking 859 n.
zestful
vigorous 174 adj.
savoury 390 adj.
zesty
pungent 388 adj.
zetetic
enquiring 459 adj.
zeugma
ornament 574 n.
Zeus
Olympian deity 967 n.
ziggurat
temple 990 n.
zigzag
obliquity 220 n.
be oblique 220 vb.
angularity 247 n.
angular 247 adj.
meander 251 vb.
deviating 282 adj.
deviate 282 vb.
to and fro 317 adv.
pattern 844 n.
zilch
zero 103 n.
zillion(s)
over one hundred 99 n.
multitude 104 n.
zincography
engraving 555 n.
Zion
focus 76 n.
heaven 971 n.
holy place 990 n.
Zionist
patriot 901 n.
zip
fastening 47 n.
vigorousness 174 n.
move fast 277 vb.
— up
join 45 vb.
wear 228 vb.
close 264 vb.
zircon
gem 844 n.
zither
harp 414 n.
zloty
coinage 797 n.
zodiac
circle 250 n.
zodiac 321 n.
zodiacal
celestial 321 adj.
zodiacal light
heavens 321 n.
glow 417 n.
zombie
corpse 363 n.
fool 501 n.
ghost 970 n.
zone
disunion 46 n.
set apart 46 vb.
region 184 n.
territory 184 n.
layer 207 n.
land 344 n.
apportion 783 vb.
zonked
drugged 949 adj.
zoo
medley 43 n.
zoo 369 n.
collection 632 n.
zoological
biological 358 adj.
animal 365 adj.
zoological 367 adj.
zoologist
zoologist 367 n.
zoology
biology 358 n.
zoom
spurt 277 n.
ascent 308 n.
ascend 308 vb.
photography 551 n.
zoom lens
optical device 442 n.
zoomorphism
animality 365 n.
idolatry 982 n.
zoophyte
microorganism 196 n.
animal 365 n.
zoot suit
suit 228 n.
Zoroaster/ Zarathustra
religious teacher 973 n.
Zoroastrianism
religious faith 973 n.
Zouave
infantry 722 n.
zucchetto
canonicals 989 n.
Zwinglian
Protestant 976 n.